THE AMERICANS
A HISTORY

The most interesting U.S. history to address the concerns of the 1990s

■ Lively Writing
"History is a great, suspenseful story whose turning points and consequences are best revealed in a narrative that is analytical and comparative."
Building a History Curriculum
Bradley Commission on History in Schools

■ Geography Linked to History
"(Geography) is an essential ingredient in the total process of educating informed citizens."
Guidelines for Geographic Education

■ Global Connections
"...an effort to put our national experience in its world setting is imperative."
Charting a Course: Social Studies for the 21st Century
National Commission on Social Studies in the Schools

☐ Integration of Humanities
"Social Studies provides the obvious connection (with) the humanities.... integration of other subject matter with social studies should be encouraged...."
Charting a Course: Social Studies for the 21st Century
National Commission on Social Studies in the Schools

■ Democracy's Story
"(American history's) first purpose must be to help students understand the essence of democracy and forces that have either promoted or obstructed it in our country."
Democracy's Half Told Story
Paul Gagnon

THE AMERICANS
A HISTORY
takes issue with the 1990s!

**The Role of Women
in the American Revolution**
"They cooked for the troops and nursed the
wounded and sick. They mended and sewed
and laundered. On the marches they carried
their share of supplies and ammunition on their
backs.... Women who could write performed
clerical and copying tasks.... At night they
crept over the battlefield...stripping [the dead
bodies] of their clothes to help keep the ragged
Revolutionary soldiers warm."
– from *The Americans*

THE AMERICANS is the most interesting senior high United States history to
address the issues of the 1990s. The text
emphasizes 20th-century history
through a lively narrative, integrated
geography concepts and skills, and
sequenced critical thinking to enhance
the interest and performance of all
students – average, basic, and gifted.

■ Lively Writing
(see Chapter 5)
Combining engaging narrative with
vivid eyewitness accounts, THE
AMERICANS humanizes the events
that have shaped our nation's history.
Abundant use of primary source materials increases students' understanding
of key concepts.

■ Geography
Linked to History
(see pages 329-331)
THE AMERICANS develops the fundamental themes of location, place, environment, movement, and regions as
identified by the *Joint Committee on
Geographic Education* and the *Association of American Geographers*.

■ Global Connections
(see page 761)
Every unit emphasizes the integration
of American and world history with a
Global Time Line and a *Focus on Global
Events* feature.

■ Integration of Humanities
(see pages 656-657)
THE AMERICANS uses great literature
and fine art to represent our heritage of
diverse peoples and cultures. *Links to
American Literature* provides literary
excerpts from famous authors to highlight particular events. *Focus on American Art* demonstrates how artists mirrored their times.

Democracy's Story
(see Chapters 6 and 7)
Entire chapters on the Constitution and Democracy offer extensive coverage of American government and the continuing development of our democratic system.

Plus, by popular request, we give you more. . .
More 20th-Century Coverage
(see Chapter 33)
Now more than half of THE AMERICANS is devoted to the 20th century, including additional coverage that goes beyond the Vietnam War to the Persian Gulf Crisis. *Linking Past to Present* features in every chapter bring meaning and perspective to today's events.

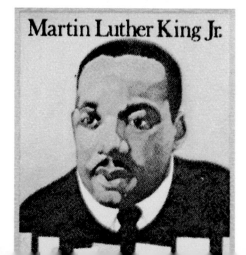

Martin Luther King Jr.

More Critical Thinking
(see pages 202-203)
THE AMERICANS encourages students to take a historical approach to decision-making through the development of critical thinking skills that link past to present. New study questions in every section, chapter, and unit reinforce understanding of important historical concepts.

More Options
(see Chapter 32)
THE AMERICANS makes the story of a diverse nation relevant to a classroom of diverse students. The text integrates the contributions of women and minorities. Teaching components accommodate the testing of students with varied abilities.

Components

Annotated Teacher's Edition provides lesson plans, teaching suggestions, and historical sidelights in wrap-around format.

Pupil's Edition has thirty-six chapters for better classroom management.

Teacher's Resource File includes:
* **Core Resources and Tests** for each unit that contain:
  — *Lesson Study Sheets* for every section
  — *Daily Activities* for every section
  — *Enrichment Activities* for every section
  — *Reteaching Activities* for every section
  — *Tests for average, basic, and advanced students* for every chapter and unit
  — *Telescoping the Times Study Sheets* providing coverage of an entire chapter's or unit's content in one practice assignment.
* **Transparency Package with Teacher's Guide** that includes:
  — Full-color global time lines
  — Full-color maps
  — Full-color artwork from the text
* **Nuclear Peacekeeping booklet with Teacher's Guide** that was written by national security experts to examine strategies for nuclear deterrence.
* **Geography Worksheets** that reinforce the connection between geography and history.
* **Primary and Literary Source Readings**
* **Specialized Worksheets for Economics, Cultural Literacy, and Skill Development**

THE AMERICANS Computer Test Generator gives you the freedom to create, edit, and store your own personalized tests and quizzes in minutes. Components include:
* Teacher's Guide
* Master Test Booklet
* Program Master Disk
* Test Bank Disks

For use with Apple II +, IIc, IIgs, and IBM PC and compatible computers.

THE AMERICANS
A HISTORY

The Americans
A History

Annotated Teacher's Edition

McDougal Littell/Houghton Mifflin

Evanston, Illinois
Boston   Dallas   Phoenix

An Annotated Teacher's Edition is not automatically included
with each shipment of a classroom set of textbooks. However, a
copy will be sent when requested by a teacher, an administrator,
or a representative of McDougal Littell/Houghton Mifflin Inc.

ISBN 0-395-74029-0

Copyright © 1996 by McDougal Littell/Houghton Mifflin Inc.
    All rights reserved.
Box 1667, Evanston, Illinois 60204
Printed in the United States of America.

  2 3 4 5 6 7 8 – WMW – 99 98 97 96

Contents

Annotated Teacher's Edition

Program Components

The Americans provides flexible teaching and testing materials with ability-level options for honors, average, and basic (at-risk) students.

Student Text

The Americans allows people from the past to tell their own stories.

- Throughout the text the words of people who lived during the time are integrated into the narrative to present an exciting and personal account of United States history. Red bars call students' attention to these primary sources.
- Diaries, songs, speeches, and historical documents make up the Focus on Primary Sources features. Using these documents, students learn to interpret and analyze primary sources.

Flexibility of *The Americans*

The Americans allows you to tailor the course to suit your district's needs. "Telescoping the Times" presents an alternative chapter and an alternative unit that compact the information from each core chapter and unit into a short, readable format. Using "Telescoping the Times" as an alternative enables you to cover the content more rapidly than teaching the usual chapter-per-week and still retain the continuity of history. Chapter 7, "Focus on Democracy," also helps you tailor the course to fit your needs. This chapter provides your students with a mini-lesson in American government. "Focus on Democracy" spans more than one hundred years of U.S. history as it relates to the Constitution and to the development of American democracy. This chapter supplements students' study of the Constitution.

Annotated Teacher's Edition

The Americans Annotated Teacher's Edition contains the pupil pages with on-page teacher's notes that provide detailed suggestions for planning and teaching each day's lesson.

- A *core lesson* provides seven steps to help you structure the lesson for students.
- Discussion questions encourage students to analyze, apply, evaluate, and synthesize information.
- Historical Sidelights add interesting facts to grab students' attention.
- Answers to all questions in the student's text appear on the page with the question in the *Annotated Teacher's Edition*.

Core Resources and Tests

The Americans Core Resources and Tests booklets—one booklet for each unit—contain study sheets, activities, and tests to meet the needs of basic (at-risk), average, and honors students. Answer keys are on the reverse side of the pages they serve. Study sheets for "Telescoping the Times" help ensure that students have read the material and are ready to go on to the next chapter or unit. Below is a description of each of the time-saving resources in *The Americans Core Resources and Tests* booklets.

Lesson Study Sheet: a two-page, fill-in-the-blank study sheet condenses the major points covered in each section of each chapter. These sheets

- encourage students to read their text
- help students learn and remember important concepts and facts about United States history
- prepare students to answer the section review questions and to pass the test that accompanies each chapter

Daily Activity: a one-page activity reinforces the information in each section of each chapter. These activities

- clarify and reinforce the lesson
- provide an opportunity for students to develop reading/study techniques such as outlining and graphically organizing information
- give students practice in integrating new material with existing knowledge
- enhance students' critical thinking skills with questions that demand more than factual recall
- serve as guided practice or independent practice in the lesson structure

Enrichment Activity: a one-page, self-contained activity enriches the information in each section of each chapter. These activities

- broaden and enrich students' knowledge of United States history
- motivate students to learn United States history through reading interesting primary-source documents
- improve students' critical thinking skills through questions that demand more than factual recall
- serve as guided practice or independent practice in the core lesson structure

Reteaching Activity: a one-page, self-contained activity reteaches the facts and concepts in each section of each chapter. These activities
- re-present the lesson for students who did not understand it the first time
- teach the lesson to students who missed the class
- reteach students who failed the test
- help students pick out main ideas and graphically organize information in a variety of ways

Chapter Review: a one-page activity reviews the chapter material in a test format. These chapter reviews
- help students synthesize the information in each chapter
- provide students with a review of the chapter to use before taking a quiz or test

Chapter and Unit Tests: three levels of tests—one each for basic (at-risk) (Level I), average (Level II), and advanced (Level III) students—test students' knowledge of each chapter and each unit in the text. Three levels of the semester test and the final examination check students' knowledge of United States history at the middle and end of the school year. These tests:
- measure students' understanding of the objectives identified for each section
- measure students' ability to deal with questions that demand more than factual recall
- measure students' ability to write a clear and concise answer to an essay question

The testing program has been designed to help students succeed. Chapter reviews in the student text incorporate information that appeared in the section reviews. Chapter tests are correlated to the chapter review. If a student can answer the questions on the chapter review, he or she will be able to obtain a passing grade on the chapter test.

Chapter and unit tests do not contain questions from Chapter 7, "Focus on Democracy." Since this chapter spans more than two hundred years in the development of our government, teachers may choose to teach it at any point in the year.

Telescoping the Times Chapter and Unit Study Sheets: a one-page, fill-in-the-blank study sheet for each chapter "Telescoping the Times" feature and a two-page fill-in-the-blank study sheet for each unit "Telescoping the Times" feature help students synthesize information. These study sheets
- provide a summary or overview of chapters and units that can be taught as alternatives to the core chapters and units
- provide a preview of chapters and units
- help students review for a quiz or test

Additional Resources

Additional resources available for use with *The Americans* include Transparencies, Literary Source Readings, Primary Source Readings, Geography Activities, Skills Activities, Thematic Activities, Economics Activities, Cultural Literacy Activities, and *Nuclear Peacekeeping* as well as a computer test generator.

CD-ROM'S and *The Americans*

There are two CD-ROM programs that have been correlated for use with *The Americans* and are available from McDougal, Littell:

The Presidents CD-ROM
1992 Time Almanac CD-ROM

The Presidents CD-Rom is an interactive multimedia resource that focuses on the life and events surrounding each of our presidents. It can be used beginning with Chapter 8 and with subsequent chapters in which a president is the primary focus. An Activity Guide, which correlates the CD-ROM disk with *The Americans* text chapters and suggests activities, is available.

The *1992 Time Almanac* CD-ROM is also an interactive media resource containing a reservoir of articles, photos, and film clips dating from the present back to *Time Magazine's* first publication in 1923. It can be used when studying Chapters 24-36. An Activity Guide that contains a CD-Rom tutorial and specific research activities related to chapter topics in *The Americans* is available.

Using the *Annotated Teacher's Edition*

The Americans Annotated Teacher's Edition was designed to help with lesson planning and with classroom management. Each chapter of the *Annotated Teacher's Edition* includes a variety of resources to help you plan and teach each day's lesson. Following is a description of the resources.

Lesson Plans

Each chapter begins with

- a list of the *Teaching Resources* contained in the *Core Resources and Tests* book followed by the *Chapter Objectives*
- two *Using the Chapter Time Line* questions, which focus students' attention on the time line and highlight relationships between two or more historical events
- *Links to American Literature*, which gives you background information to share with your students on the author of the literary excerpt that opens the chapter and on the excerpt itself
- a short paragraph, *Introducing the Chapter*, that suggests ways to motivate students to begin the study of a new time period in United States history

Core Lessons: each section contains a seven-step core lesson.

- *Anticipate the Lesson* links material in the section to earlier or current events, preparing students for the new material.
- *State the Objective* reminds students of the objective of the lesson.
- *Present the Lesson* offers suggestions for teaching the lesson.
- *Check for Understanding* enables you to see whether students have learned the material.
- *Guided Practice* provides suggestions for helping students use the material they learned.
- *Assign Independent Practice* includes activities geared to the section that give students an opportunity to work on their own.
- *Student Assignment/Homework* lists a suggested assignment for the next day.

Each chapter ends with *Concluding the Chapter*. This paragraph helps students synthesize the material in the chapter and follows the core lesson for the last section.

Core lessons also include questions to stimulate discussion. Possible student responses are given for you to use as examples and to stimulate your students to think.

Cooperative Learning: the *Annotated Teacher's Edition* contains on-page answers to all review questions and indicates with a ➤ the questions and activities that are especially suited to cooperative learning strategies.

Using the Focus Features: *The Americans* contains features that focus students' attention on geography, economics, primary sources, critical thinking skills, and global events. A three-step lesson plan—State the Objective, Present the Lesson, and Check for Understanding—accompanies each of these features.

Teaching Strategies: preceding each chapter are two pages that contain additional resources to help in planning lessons.

- Global Perspectives, a chronology of important events that occurred throughout the world, supplements the chapter time line. A discussion question accompanies the chronology to point out relationships between events. Possible student responses are also given.
- Additional Teaching Strategies contains suggestions for teaching each section to basic (at-risk) students and to honors (advanced) students.
- Further Reading for Students lists both fiction and nonfiction books of interest to students.
- Bibliography for Teachers lists books, audio-visual materials, and computer resources related to the chapter.

Research Assignment: the opening pages of each unit contain a research assignment to sharpen students' research skills and to involve students in the study of United States history.

Advantages of the Program

The Americans Program Interests and Motivates Students

- **Dramatic Chapter Openers** focus students' attention on people who dominated or exemplified the era.
- **Links to American Literature** contains exciting excerpts from well-known literary works that will involve students in the life style and events of the era.
- **Linking Past to Present,** which appears twice in each chapter, helps students relate familiar contemporary events to past events that they are studying.
- **People in the Chapter** adds anecdotes that make the people of history come alive for students.
- **Primary Sources** throughout the narrative enable people from the past to tell their own stories, giving students an up-close look at the times. Red bars call students' attention to these primary sources.

The Americans Program Develops Students' Geographical Literacy

- **Unit Openers,** illustrations of geographical settings, give students an appreciation of United States geography.
- **Narrative details** point out the physical characteristics of the land and how these features affected the history of the people who settled the land.
- **Focus on Geography** introduces students to the five geographic themes used by the National Council for Geographic Education and the Association of American Geographers. These features also highlight the interactive relationship between humans and their environment.
- **Focus on Global Events** familiarizes students with other geographical areas while relating how events outside the United States affected our history.
- **Maps,** all in color, help students see our history in its geographical context.
- **Map Skills Questions,** which follow every content map, relate the five geographic themes to the events and places illustrated by the map.
- **Atlas maps,** needed to answer some review and Map Skills questions, enable students to see the overall political and geographical features of the United States and of other nations of the world.

- **Gazetteer** helps students locate places and provides their exact location by longitude and latitude.
- **Geography Activities,** which relate to the features and to each chapter, expand students' knowledge of geographic concepts using the five geographic themes.

The Americans Program Improves Students' Skills

- **Critical Thinking Questions,** which follow each section, chapter, and unit, stimulate students to analyze, apply, synthesize, and evaluate information.
- **Focus on Critical Thinking Skills** teaches students how to better identify, analyze, and evaluate primary and secondary historical sources.
- **Schematic organizers,** such as charts and diagrams, in both the text and the activities help students see the relationships between events and help students learn to organize information.
- **Reference material** such as the Index, Gazetteer, Glossary, and Atlas help students use their research skills.
- **Skills Activities** enhance the Focus on Critical Thinking Skills features in the text, giving students practice in using these skills.
- **Primary Source Readings** are accompanied by writing assignments designed to make students think, thus linking reading, writing, and thinking.
- **Transparencies,** with two critical thinking questions for each of the sixteen transparencies, sharpen students' higher-order thinking skills.

The Americans Program Develops Students' Historical Literacy

- **Narrative** of the events of history in the text gives students a sense of the continuity of our past.
- **Time lines,** preceding each chapter and unit, along with discussion questions related to events on the time line, provide students with a historical frame of reference.
- **People in the Chapter,** anecdotal stories, makes the people of history more "real" and thus more memorable.
- **Primary Sources** quoted throughout the text give students familiarity with speeches, documents, and other writings that tell the American story. Red bars call students' attention to these primary sources.

- **Key Terms and People,** repeated in all section, chapter, and unit reviews, increases students' knowledge of historical information.
- **Linking Past to Present,** in both the narrative and the chapter and unit reviews, provides historical background for current events.
- *Nuclear Peacekeeping* gives students a historical perspective on the cold war, superpower relations, and the current nuclear-arms reduction negotiations.

The Americans Program Develops Students' Economic Literacy

- **Narrative details** explaining economic events such as the Great Depression and the stagflation of the 1970's give students an understanding of how economics influences history.
- **Focus on Economics** relates specific economic principles, such as mercantilism, taxing, and business cycles, to history.
- **Economics Activities** enrich students' knowledge of economics and give students practice in applying this knowledge.

The Americans Program Develops Students' Cultural Literacy

- **Narrative details** include the social studies terms and the historical names, dates, and events that will enable students to communicate with other educated people.
- **Art in America** helps students become familiar with artists whose names and works are well known to millions of Americans.
- **Photographs and art work,** which illustrate the text, were chosen to give students not only a sense of history but also a sense of their cultural past.
- **Links to American Literature** presents literary works of famous American authors in the context of their times.
- **Linking Past to Present** brings past events alive by integrating them with students' knowledge of present events, making history more memorable.
- **Glossary** entries include social studies terms and the names of people and places familiar to educated Americans.
- **Cultural Literacy Activities** compact information on the development of the arts, such as architecture, dance, theater, and music, into two-page activities to increase students' appreciation of our cultural heritage.

- **Literary Source Readings** give students additional fictional accounts of past events by famous American authors to supplement the factual narrative of the text.
- **Thematic Activities** follow one theme from its beginnings to the present so that students can see the development of trends such as the two-party system, our view of isolationism, and the business cycle.

Integrating the Curriculum

Writing

Writing empowers students by giving them a sense of ownership about the material. When a student restates an idea or concept, that idea then belongs to him or her and becomes a part of his or her experience. Thus internalized, concepts become more useful and less likely to be forgotten. As a teacher, you may find completed student writing assignments helpful in making informal assessments. Reading students' writing can be an excellent way of targeting weakness or misunderstanding at the concept level because confused thinking is revealed in confused writing. We have, therefore, provided opportunities for writing in both individual and group situations.

- **Research Assignments** at the beginning of each unit suggest subjects that students might research and write about in order to more fully understand material in the unit.
- **Core Lessons** provide opportunities for students to work together on writing factual, as well as creative paragraphs that they can also share with the class.
- **Essay Questions** on the tests help students learn to organize and write concise answers; answer keys enable you to quickly evaluate answers.
- **Primary Source Readings,** in blackline master form, include Reading, Writing, and Thinking exercises for each reading.

Problem Solving

Students need practice in solving problems in social studies just as they do in mathematics and science. Most students are not accustomed to using problem-solving techniques in their everyday thinking. Developing a problem-solving attitude takes time and concentration on process rather than on answers.

Core Lessons, **Discussion Questions**, and **Section**, **Chapter**, and **Unit Reviews** in *The Americans* require students to think, and they provide aids to help students develop a problem-solving attitude. For example, one of the independent practice assignments asks students to write a report on the status of Indians and to conclude with recommendations for Congress to adopt that might improve relations between Indians and other groups in American society. Developing possible solutions to the problem of how to improve rela-

tions between Indians and other groups helps students develop a problem-solving attitude. In addition, because all questions and assignments are accompanied by possible responses, teachers can give students an example to get them started.

Science and Technology

From the time of the first settlement in North America to the present, our society and culture have been shaped by technological advances. Understanding today's important issues often requires a meaningful consideration of concepts and skills from science and technology as well as the social sciences.

The Americans points up the scientific and technological revolutions that have taken place and helps students understand how advances such as mass production and computers have affected historical development. The narrative is designed to help students see the practical applications of science and technology.

A Note About Cooperative Learning

Cooperative learning is not new to schools. Recently, cooperative groups have again emerged as an effective way to organize classes for maximum learning. While group work is often done in elementary grades, recent research shows that high school students also benefit from the interaction of a small group. Some students are more willing to participate in a small group than in a large one. Often an open-ended group activity enables more students to participate in problem solving. For this reason many of the core lessons in *The Americans Annotated Teacher's Edition* suggest that students work in small groups to solve a problem or develop an outline or a paragraph. In addition, a number of the questions in chapter and unit reviews can be done by students working in small groups. A ➤ before the answers to these questions indicates that they are suitable for cooperative learning.

Improving Students' Critical Thinking Skills

As students explore world history, they need to question what they are reading rather than accept everything they read as true. In other words, they need to learn to think critically. The most important point to impress on students when teaching them critical thinking skills is the need to ask probing questions.

Experts in the field of teaching thinking skills believe that it is most helpful to teach these skills directly using the following steps:

1. Introduce and explain the skill through definition and step-by-step examples.
2. Guide students as they apply the skill.
3. Review with students the skill's definition, steps, use, and relationship to other skills.

Thinking skills should be taught with material that is already familiar to students so that they can focus on the procedures involved.

Review with students these steps in problem solving and making inferences:

- Gather and record existing information.
- Organize this information.
- Identify what is not known or what seems incorrect.
- Draw on experience and existing knowledge to identify information needed or plausible explanations.
- Formulate and state an educated guess.

Transliterating Chinese

Pinyin and Wade-Giles:
The Chinese Language in Roman Script

Since the late 1800's, a variety of systems have been used to phonetically transliterate northern Chinese (Mandarin) speech sounds into the Roman alphabet to make Chinese easier for non-Chinese people to learn and write. Today both the Wade-Giles system, begun by two British diplomats around 1900, and Pinyin, introduced by the Chinese government in 1958, are used to aid in pronouncing Chinese words. In this text we have used the Chinese-preferred Pinyin for names in the narrative and places on maps. We have made some exceptions where the names are so well known by their older spellings that the use of Pinyin would confuse students. Exceptions include Chiang Kai-shek, Tibet, Hong Kong, Mongolia, and China itself. Because Pinyin does not always use English pronunciations for the Roman letters, we have included the following pronunciation guide and list of common names and places spelled in both Wade-Giles and Pinyin.

Pinyin Pronunciation Guide

- **ai** = **ai** in **ai**sle
- **e** = **oo** in h**oo**k except before *n* or *ng*, when it's pronounced **u** as in s**u**n
- **iu** = **eo** as in L**eo**
- **o** = **aw** as in l**aw**
- **ou** = **o** as in j**o**ke
- **ui** = **ay** as in w**ay**
- **c** = **ts** as in i**ts**
- **q** = **ch** as in **ch**air
- **x** = **sh** as in **sh**e
- **z** = **ds** as in bu**ds**
- **zh** = **j** as in **j**ump

Comparative Respellings

Wade-Giles	Pinyin	Wade-Giles	Pinyin
Canton	Guangzhou	Hu Yao-pang	Hu Yaobang
Ch'ang-an	Changan (Xian)	Kuomintang	Guomindang
Chao Tzu-yang	Zhau Ziyang	Kwangtung	Guangdong
Ch'en Yi	Chen Yi	Lin Piao	Lin Biao
Ch'in Dynasty	Qin Dynasty	Mao Tse-tung	Mao Zedong
Ch'ing Dynasty	Qing Dynasty	Nanking	Nanjing
Chou Dynasty	Zhou Dynasty	Peking	Beijing
Confucius	Kong Qiu	Shih Huang Ti	Shi Huangdi
Deng Hsiao-p'ing	Deng Xiaoping	Sung Dynasty	Song Dynasty
Hsia Dynasty	Xia Dynasty	T'ang Dynasty	Tang Dynasty
Hua Kuo-fen	Hua Guofeng	Taoism	Daoism
		Ts'u Hsi	Ci Xi

Key to Audio-Visual Sources

ACI Media, Inc.
35 W. 45th St.
New York, NY 10036

American Broadcasting Company
Division of Capital Cities
825 7th Ave.
New York, NY 10019

American Heritage Publishing Co.
10 Rockefeller Plaza
New York, NY 10020

Benchmark Films, Inc.
145 Scarborough Rd.
Briarcliff Manor, NY 10510

BFA Educational Media
2211 Michigan Ave.
Santa Monica, CA 90404

Braverman Productions
Div. of Images Communication
Arts Corp.
366 N. Broadway
Jericho, NY 11753

Colonial Williamsburg
AV Distribution Center
P.O. Box C
Williamsburg, VA 23187

Columbia Broadcasting Company
2211 Michigan Blvd.
Santa Monica, CA 90406

Coronet/MTI
Film and Video
108 Wilmot Rd.
Deerfield, IL 60015

Current Affairs
P.O. Box 426
Ethan Allen Hwy.
Ridgefield, CT 06877

David L. Wolper Productions
8489 W. 3rd St.
Los Angeles, CA 90048

Department of the Army
(Address requests to Army installation serving your area.)

Encyclopaedia Britannica
Educational Corp.
425 N. Michigan Ave.
Chicago, IL 60611

Educational Audio Visual, Inc.
Pleasantville, NY 10570

Educational Enrichment Materials
of the *New York Times*
357 Adams St.
Bedford Hills, NY 10507

Films, Inc.
1144 Wilmette
Wilmette, IL 60091

Graphic Curriculum
P.O. Box 565 Lenox Hill Station
New York, NY 10021

Guidance Associates
Center for Humanities
Mount Kisko, NY 10549

Guidance Associates
Communications Park
Box 3000
Mt. Kisco, NY 10549

ICARUS Films
200 Park Ave. South
New York, NY 10003

Indiana University Audio-Visual
Center
Bloomington, IN 47401

International Business Machines
Corp.
c/o Modern Talking Picture Service
5000 Park St. North
St. Petersburg, FL 33709

International Film Bureau
332 S. Michigan Ave.
Chicago, IL 60604

Journal Films, Inc.
930 Pitner Ave.
Evanston, IL 60202

Learning Corp. of America
Div. of W. F. Hall Printing Co.
1350 Avenue of the Americas
New York, NY 10019

Liberty Mutual Insurance Co.
c/o Modern Talking Picture Service
5000 Park St. North
St. Petersburg, FL 33709

Listening Library
P.O. Box L
1 Park Ave.
Old Greenwich, CT 06870

Lucerne Films, Inc.
37 Ground Pine Rd.
Morris Plains, NJ 07950

McGraw-Hill Films
110 15th St.
Del Mar, CA 92014

Modern Talking Motion Pictures
5000 Park St. North
St. Petersburg, FL 33709

MTI Teleprograms
108 Wilmot Rd.
Deerfield, IL 60015

National Broadcasting Company
30 Rockefeller Plaza
New York, NY 10112

National Geographic Society
Washington, DC 20036

PBS Studios
475 L'Enfant Plaza
Washington, DC 20206

Pitman Publishing Corp.
6 E. 43rd St.
New York, NY 10017

Post-Newsweek Stations, Inc.
27911 Ursuline
St. Clair Shores, MI 48081

Prentice-Hall Media
150 White Plains Rd.
Tarrytown, NY 10591

Pyramid Film Productions
P.O. Box 1048
Santa Monica, CA 90406

Reaction Films
P.O. Box 2028
Austin, TX 78767

Royal Netherlands Embassy
c/o Modern Talking Picture Service
5000 Park St. North
St. Petersburg, FL 33709

Simon & Schuster Communications
108 Wilmot Rd.
Deerfield, IL 60015

Social Studies School Service
10200 Jefferson Blvd.
P.O. Box 802
Culver City, CA 90232

Society for Visual Education
1345 Diversey Pkwy.
Chicago, IL 60614

Sterling Educational Films
241 E. 34th St.
New York, NY 10016

Time-Life Video
Time-Life Building
New York, NY 10020

United Learning
6633 W. Howard St.
Niles, IL 60648

University of Illinois, Visual Aids
Service
1325 S. Oak
Champaign, IL 61820

USF&G Insurance Film Library
P.O. Box 315
Franklin Lakes, NJ 07417

Wilcom, Inc.
513 W. Taft Rd.
South Holland, IL 60473

WNET National Educational
Television
Indiana University
Bloomington, IN 47401

Yale University Audio-Visual
39 Wall St.
New Haven, CT 06511

Zenger Production Co., Inc.
Washington, DC 30026

Key to Computer Sources

Educational Activities, Inc.
P.O. Box 392
Freeport, NY 11520

Focus Media, Inc.
839 Stewart Ave.
P.O. Box 865
Garden City, NY 11530

Intellectual Software
798 North Ave.
Bridgeport, CT 06606

MECC
3490 Lexington Ave. North
St. Paul, MN 55112

MicroMedia
P.O. Box 17, Dept. G
Valley Cottage, NY 10989

Opportunities for Learning, Inc.
8950 Lurline Ave., Dept. 6
Chatsworth, CA 91311

Scholastic, Inc.
P.O. Box 7502
2931 E. McCarty St.
Jefferson City, MO 65102

Sliwa Enterprises, Inc.
P.O. Box 978
Yorktown, VA 23692

Social Studies School Service
10200 Jefferson Blvd.
P.O. Box 802
Culver City, CA 90232

Society for Visual Education
Dept. VB
1345 Diversey Pkwy.
Chicago, IL 60614

Tom Snyder Productions, Inc.
90 Sherman St.
Cambridge, MA 02140

The
Americans

The
Americans
A History

Winthrop D. Jordan
Miriam Greenblatt
John S. Bowes

 McDougal Littell/Houghton Mifflin

Evanston, Illinois
Boston   Dallas   Phoenix

Authors

Winthrop D. Jordan is a professor of history and Afro-American studies at the University of Mississippi. He holds a B.A. from Harvard, an M.A. from Clark University, and a Ph.D. from Brown University. After serving as instructor of history at Phillips Exeter Academy, Professor Jordan taught early American history for eighteen years at the University of California, Berkeley. In 1982 he began teaching at the University of Mississippi. He is the author of several books, including the highly acclaimed *White Over Black*, a study of American attitudes toward blacks from 1550 to 1812. The book won four national awards, one of which was the National Book Award.

Miriam Greenblatt is a writer, editor, and nationally recognized educational consultant. A graduate of Hunter College and the University of Chicago and an adjunct teacher at New Trier High School, she has written for or contributed to more than twenty-five elementary, junior high, and high school social studies programs. She is an officer of the American Historical Association's Committee on History in the Classroom. Greenblatt is listed in *Who's Who of American Women* for 1993–1994.

John S. Bowes holds graduate degrees in American history and in education from Boston University. He has taught United States history in junior and senior high schools in Boston and New York, and he chaired the Social Studies Department at Bayport High School. Mr. Bowes is the author of *Avenues to America's Past, Discovering Our Past: A History of the United States*, and articles in *Social Education* and *Social Studies*. He has edited and contributed to a number of social studies texts.

Consultants

Constitutional History
Francis N. Stites
Professor of History
San Diego State University
San Diego, California

Geography
Douglas C. Wilms
Professor;
   Department of Geography
   and Planning
East Carolina University
Greenville, North Carolina

ISBN 0-395-74028-2

Acknowledgments: See page 1057

Reviewers

The authors and publisher wish to thank the educators who critically reviewed this book in manuscript.

Ms. Bobbie Barnes
Lassiter High School
Marietta, Georgia

Mr. Edward Brennan
Social Studies Coordinator
Fairfield Public Schools
Fairfield, Connecticut

Sr. Anne Marie Butler
Principal
Marillac High School
Northfield, Illinois

Ms. Carol Duncan
Henry Ford High School
Detroit, Michigan

Ms. Mandy Garcia-Lopez
Teacher Specialist
Pomona Unified School District
Pomona, California

Ms. Rita Geiger
Coordinator of Social Studies
   Education
Oklahoma City, Oklahoma

Dr. Haskell Greer
Warren County Senior High
   School
McMinnville, Tennessee

Ms. Ninalea McIntosh
Evansville-Vanderburgh High
   School
Evansville, Indiana

Mr. Richard Rattan
Watkins Mill High School
Gaithersburg, Maryland

A Letter from the Authors

Dear Reader,

Why should we study American history? As Americans we are not bound together by a common religion, a common race, or a common ethnic heritage. Instead, we are bound by a tradition of ruling ourselves. In the words of Abraham Lincoln, ours is a government "of the people, by the people, for the people." To participate in such a government, it is especially important to know who we are as a people.

Because self-knowledge builds on past experience, we need to know where we have been in order to understand where we are and to know where we are going. A knowledge of our history is essential if we are to think critically, set goals, solve problems, and make decisions that will benefit ourselves, our nation, and the world.

When the stories of history are well told, they are exciting and full of adventure. They are the stories of explorers, colonists, founders, patriots, immigrants, pioneers, reformers, and Presidents— stories of extraordinary people as well as of the ordinary women, men, and children who lived in this nation. Over the years all these diverse experiences have melded together to form the continuing story that is American history. In this book we invite you to share these individual experiences as well as the national experience of our country in order to come to a deeper understanding of what it means to be an American.

Winthrop D. Jordan
Miriam Greenblatt
John Bowes

CONTENTS

UNIT 1 American Beginnings to 1783

Unit 2 A New Nation 1781-1840

Unit 3 The Nation Grows, Divides, and Reunites 1830-1876

FROM THE PLANTATION TO THE SENATE.

xi

Unit 4 The Rise of the Industrial Giant 1876 – 1915

Unit 5 Onto a World Stage 1876 – 1920

Unit 6 World War I, Causes and Consequences 1914-1940

Unit 7 World War II, Causes and Consequences 1933-1960

Unit 8 Continuity and Change 1960 – Today

Reference Section

Primary Sources and Readings

List of Maps

List of Charts and Graphs

Focus Features

GLOBAL TIME LINE

The World

1415
John Huss burned
at the stake

1452
Leonardo Da Vinci born

1453
Turks conquer
Constantinople

1494
Treaty of Tordesillas
draws first Line of
Demarcation

1498
da Gama
reaches
India

1517
Martin Luther posts 95 theses

1519-1522
Magellan's ship Victoria
sails around the world

1400   1450   1500   1550

North America

1440
Montezuma I
becomes Aztec ruler

1492
Columbus lands
at San Salvador

1521
Spain conquers Mexico

1535
Cartier explores St. Lawrence River

1565
Spain founds
St. Augustine

Research Assignment

Choose one armed conflict or war mentioned in this unit and research its causes and consequences. Prepare a three-minute talk on the conflict and how you feel it affected American history.

UNIT 1 to 1783

American Beginnings

Geographic Setting

Place/Region. "My wound is geography. It is also my anchorage, my port of call." With these words, author Pat Conroy opens his best-selling novel of the 1980's, *The Prince of Tides*. Like most good stories, Conroy's begins with a description of the physical setting in which the story takes place. This pattern is followed in *The Americans*. Each unit begins with a picture that anchors the unit in a particular place and region at a particular time. Look at the map of North America from Florida to Chesapeake Bay shown at the left. It was drawn by the English explorer and painter, John White, around 1585. It is not accurate—something that is taken for granted in modern maps but is often missing in early maps. In addition to the physical features of the land, the map depicts beasts and inhabitants that grew out of the cartographer's imagination.

Unit Overview

What does it mean to be called an American? In this unit you will begin a journey through an unknown wilderness soon to be called America. You will meet some of the remarkable people who first explored and settled this land. Also, you will understand the price the American Patriots paid to win freedom from tyranny for Americans of today. Unit 1 describes these American beginnings in five chapters.

Unit Outline

CHAPTER 1 **Migrants to a New Land to 1732**
1. The First Immigrants Arrive
2. The Europeans Reach America
3. The English Colonists Arrive

CHAPTER 2 **Colonial Life 1650–1700**
1. The South Is a Divided Agricultural Society
2. Slavery Flourishes in the South
3. The North Develops Commerce
4. Colonial Life Is Diverse

CHAPTER 3 **Conflict with Indians and England 1637–1700**
1. The Indians Fight for Their Land
2. England Creates a Colonial Empire
3. Parliament Is Supreme in the British Empire

CHAPTER 4 **Separating from Britain 1700–1775**
1. The Colonists Consider New Ideas
2. Britain Defeats France and Tightens Controls
3. The Colonies Organize Resistance to Britain

CHAPTER 5 **The War for Independence 1775–1783**
1. The Last Doubts Are Overcome
2. The Patriots Declare Independence
3. The British and American Positions Differ
4. Farmers and Shopkeepers Defeat an Empire
5. The American Revolution Changes the World

1603-1868 Tokugawa shogunate in Japan

1688 Glorious Revolution in England

1707 Aurangzeb dies in India

1725 Peter the Great dies

1756-1763 Seven Years' War

1769 Napoleon born

1776 *Wealth of Nations* published

1783 Treaty of Paris

600 — 1650 — 1700 — 1750 — 1800

1607 England founds and settles Jamestown, Virginia

1664 English take New Netherland

1732 Last English colony (Georgia) founded

1754-1763 French and Indian War

1776 Declaration of Independence

1775-1783 Revolutionary War

1

Chapter 1 Teaching Strategies

Global Perspectives

1000-1500	Africans south of the Sahara establish large kingdoms.
1368-1644	Ming Dynasty rules China.
1453	Ottoman Turks capture Constantinople.
1588	The English defeat the Spanish Armada.
1600's	Tokugawa shoguns rule Japan.
1604-1613	Civil war rages in Russia.
1632	Shah Jahan orders construction of the Taj Mahal.
1648	Peace of Westphalia ends Thirty Years' War in Europe.

For Discussion

How might the establishment of large kindgoms in Africa have affected the slave trade in the colonies? (Possible response: increased the availability of slaves as African kings could multiply their wealth by selling captured enemies.)

Additional Teaching Strategies

SECTION 1

For Basic Students: Divide students into six groups. Assign one of the migration routes on the map on page 5 to each group. Ask them to list on paper the present-day states they would travel through when migrating south. (One route might include: Washington; Oregon; California.) Have students share their lists.

For Advanced Students: Divide students into nine groups, one each representing the Aztecs, Mayas, Incas, Pueblos, Iroquois, Cherokees, Hopewells, Plains Indians, and Eskimos. Ask each group to research its tribe to find information regarding the tribe's home territory, customs, food sources, and government. Have each group select a representative to send to a council meeting called to unite all North American Indians. Council members should discuss issues they feel are important to their tribes. Have the class observe this meeting. Allow class members to make additional comments at the end of the meeting. (Topics of discussion might include: hunting grounds; protection from outside tribes; selection of council leaders.)

SECTION 2

For Basic Students: Have students construct a chart with four columns. Have them list the major European explorers discussed in this section in the first column, launch dates in the second column, countries in the third column, and accomplishments/land discovered in the fourth column. Charts might include:

Explorer	Date	Country	Land Discovered/ Accomplishments
Columbus	1492	Spain	Caribbean area
Magellan	1519	Portugal	Sailed around the world
de Soto	1539	Spain	Florida to the Mississippi River

Have students share their charts.

For Advanced Students: Have students prepare a three-paragraph report on the lasting cultural influences that Spain brought to Mexico, Portugal brought to Brazil, or France brought to Canada. (Topics might include: language; government; religion.) Have students present these reports to the class. Discuss with students examples of these influences in the U.S. today.

SECTION 3

For Basic Students: Have students list on the board the similarities and differences between Massachusetts Bay and Jamestown. (Similarities include: set up representative governments; suffered hardships, disease, and starvation in their first year. Differences include: Jamestown welcomed all newcomers; Massachusetts did not.)

For Advanced Students: Have students choose one of the following subjects: tobacco; the indenture system; free passage to the New World for women desiring marriage. They should design an advertisement for the subject suitable for publication in a 1620 London newspaper; ads should include positive information regarding subject. Display students' advertisements. Conclude by asking students to summarize the role each subject played in the growth and success of Jamestown. (Possible response: tobacco provided the colonists a cash crop to sell to England, which in turn enabled them to buy manufactured goods.)

Further Reading for Students

Bolton, Herbert Eugene, ed. *Spanish Exploration of the Southwest: 1542-1706*. New York: Barnes & Noble, 1963.

Caffrey, Kate. *The Mayflower*. New York: Stein & Day, 1975.

Driver, Harold E. *Indians of North America*. Chicago: University of Chicago Press, 1969.

Fritz, Jean. *Double Life of Pocahontas*. New York: Putnam Publishing Group, 1983.

Gill, Crispin. *Mayflower Remembered*. New York: Putnam Publishing Group, 1972.

Holbrook, Sabra. *French Founders of North America and Their Heritage*. New York: Atheneum, 1976.

Snell, Tee Loftin. *The Wild Shores: America's Beginnings*. Washington, D.C.: National Geographic Society, 1974.

Bibliography for Teachers

Books

DeVoto, Bernard A. *The Course of Empire*. Lincoln: University of Nebraska Press, 1983.

Josephy, Alvin M., Jr. *The Indian Heritage of America*. New York: Alfred A. Knopf, 1968.

Lauber, Patricia. *Who Discovered America? Settlers and Explorers of the New World Before the Time of Columbus*. New York: Random House, 1970.

Rahn, Joan Elma. *Plants That Changed History*. New York: Macmillan, 1982.

Stephenson, George M. *The Puritan Heritage*. 1952. Reprint. Westport, Conn.: Greenwood, 1978.

Tuchman, Barbara W. *The First Salute*. New York: Alfred A. Knopf, 1988.

Audio-Visuals

Exploring the New World. Coronet. Filmstrip.

How We Learn About the Past. Educational Corp. Movie.

Indian Cultures from 2000 B.C. to 1500 A.D. Journal Films. Movie.

Indians of North America. National Geographic Society. Filmstrip.

Spanish in the Southwest. BFA Educational Media. Movie.

Computer Resources

Geography Search. (Apple/TRS) MicroMedia.

Other Cultures (Apple/IBM) Intellectual Software.

Teacher's Notes:

Teaching Resources, Unit 1 Booklet

Lesson Study Sheets pp. 1-12
Daily Activities pp. 13-18
Enrichment Activities pp. 19-24
Reteaching Activities pp. 25-30
Chapter Review p. 31
Chapter Mastery Tests pp. 33-44
Telescoping the Times Study Sheet p. 45

Chapter Objectives

Students will learn:
- facts about the inhabitants of North America before the arrival of the Europeans
- the causes and consequences of European exploration and colonization of North America
- how and why the English colonies multiplied along the Atlantic coast

Using the Chapter Time Line

How many years passed between the discovery of America and the founding of the first Spanish colony? (Answer: 73) How many years passed between the founding of the Spanish colony of St. Augustine and the founding of the first English colony at Jamestown? (Answer: 42)

Picturing History One of many renditions of Christopher Columbus, the title of this portrait is *Admiral of the Ocean Sea*. It was painted shortly after the death of Columbus by the Italian artist Sebastiano del Piombo.

1450	1500	1550	1600	1650	1700	1750

1492
Columbus lands at San Salvador

1519
• Cortés begins conquest of Mexico
• Magellan begins voyage around the world

1565
Spain founds St. Augustine

1649
Toleration Act

1670
First permanent settlement in Carolina

1732
Georgia founded

1620
• Mayflower Compact signed
• Pilgrims land at Plymouth

1607
England founds and settles Jamestown, Virginia

2

CHAPTER **1** to 1732

Migrants to a New Land

Links to American Literature

The grass-plot before the jail, in Prison Lane . . . was occupied by a pretty large number of the inhabitants of Boston; . . . It might be that a sluggish bond-servant, or an undutiful child, whom his parents had given over to the civil authority, was to be corrected at the whipping-post. It might be, that an Antinomian, a Quaker, or other heterodox religionist, was to be scourged out of the town, . . . It might be, too, that a witch, like old Mistress Hibbins, the bitter-tempered widow of the magistrate, was to die upon the gallows. . . . A party of Indians—in their savage finery of curiously embroidered deer-skin robes, wampum-belts, red and yellow ochre, and feathers, and armed with the bow and arrow and stone-headed spear—stood apart, with countenances of inflexible gravity, beyond what even the Puritan aspect could attain. . . . They [sailors] were rough-looking desperadoes, with sun-blackened faces, and an immensity of beard; their wide, short trousers were confined about the waist by belts, often clasped with a rough plate of gold, and sustaining always a long knife, and, in some instances, a sword. From beneath their broad-brimmed hats of palm-leaf, gleamed eyes which, even in good nature and merriment, had a kind of animal ferocity.

— NATHANIEL HAWTHORNE, *The Scarlet Letter*

Early America was more than the well-known thanksgiving feast of Pilgrims and Indians. It was alive with the colors, sounds, and flavors of many peoples, including Puritans, Indians, Quakers, sailors, and indentured servants. It was the wonderful diversity of colonial times that set the style for what America has become today, a blending of countless cultures and peoples.

Chapter Overview

In this chapter you will learn that the earliest inhabitants of the United States came from northeast Asia and made their way south from Alaska. You will also learn about the causes and consequences of the European exploration and colonization of America. Finally, you will learn about the English colonists who settled along the Atlantic coast. This chapter relates how the struggles, accomplishments, and decisions of these early Americans affected the course of history and the lives of future generations. To discuss early America, the chapter has been divided into three sections.

Chapter Outline

1. **The First Immigrants Arrive**
2. **The Europeans Reach America**
3. **The English Colonists Arrive**

Anticipate the Lesson

Ask students to define the word *civilization*. Write all appropriate answers on the board and discuss them to arrive at a general definition. (Possible definition: a society with an advanced culture and way of life.) Ask students to name civilizations with which they are familiar. List these on the board. (Possible responses: ancient Greece or the Aztec Empire.) Tell students that although these civilizations existed at different times and in different places, they shared some common characteristics. Discuss these characteristics. (Characteristics might include: specialization of labor, organized leadership, a system of writing, common beliefs, and the existence of cities.)

State the Objective

Identify the inhabitants of North America before the arrival of the Europeans.

SECTION 1

The First Immigrants Arrive

GLOSSARY TERMS: **civilization, pueblos, League of the Iroquois**

If you look at a map of the world, you will see that a narrow stretch of water separates North America from Siberia. This stretch of water is called the **Bering Strait.** It is only fifty-six miles wide, and there are two islands in it. If you sailed across it, you would always see land.

Scientists believe that when the first Americans arrived, the strait did not exist. Instead, the two continents were connected by a land bridge called Beringia. The land bridge was formed when the glaciers of the latest **Ice Age** moved south from the North Pole. As they advanced, they drew water from the Bering Sea. When they retreated northward at the end of the Ice Age, the Bering Sea rose and once again covered Beringia.

Linking Past to Present

Evidence of the Ice Age is still visible in areas of the United States today. Montana's Glacier National Park, the Great Lakes, and moraines and rivers in the northern United States are but a few examples.

Scientists believe that the first Americans walked from Asia across Beringia to North America between thirty-five thousand and twenty-five thousand years ago. After the Ice Age ended, additional groups of people came by boat, probably around 2000 B.C.

They Come in Search of Food

Trying to understand people far back in our past is like trying to see the bottom of a well with a candle. However, judging from the evidence we now have, these early Americans were gatherers and hunters who migrated to North America in search of food. Here they found an abundance of nuts, wild rye, and such fruits as chokecherries, gooseberries, and currants. They trapped small game that was easy to kill, such as jack rabbits, coyotes, woodchucks, and raccoons. They wore hides and furs, had fire, and cooked their food.

About eleven thousand years ago, the early Americans developed the technique of big-game hunting. We know this from the so-called Clovis points that were discovered near Clovis, New Mexico, in 1932.

Picturing History
Each Clovis point in this skillfully matched pair measures about nine inches long.

People in the Chapter

Columbus was deeply moved by the generosity of the native Americans, whom he called Indians. He described them as people who were willing to share everything they possessed with "as much love as if their hearts went with it."

Jacques Marquette and **Louis Joliet** completed their twenty-five-hundred-mile, four-month exploration of the upper Mississippi River in two birch-bark canoes paddled by their five companions.

John Smith was a man of many adventures. Before leading the expedition to Jamestown, he had run off to fight the Turks, been taken prisoner and sold as a slave, killed his master to escape, and wandered through the Ukraine on his way back to England.

Pocahontas, the Indian princess who rescued John Smith, was baptized into the Church of England and renamed Rebecca when she married John Rolfe. She died of smallpox at age twenty-one while visiting London with her husband and their infant son.

Squanto was indirectly responsible for the first Thanksgiving. Had he not taught the Pilgrims how to plant Indian corn, there would have been no feast to celebrate because the Pilgrims probably would have starved to death.

Present the Lesson

Across the top of the board list the Indian groups, such as Maya/Inca, Pueblo, Eskimo, Plains Indians, Eastern Woodland, Southeastern, and Mound Builders, that are presented in this lesson. In a column on the left side of the board, list characteristics such as life style, locations, government, and food source. Ask students to come to the board and fill in facts about each group. (Facts about Eastern Woodland Indians might include: life style—tools made of stone, bone, or wood; location—east of Mississippi; government—League of tribes governed by a council of chiefs; food source—hunting, fishing, farming.)

First Migrations to the Americas

Map Skills **Movement** From what continent did the first migrants come? **Region** What kind of climate prevailed in the region of northern North America?

For Discussion
Why do people migrate? (Possible responses: food sources; job opportunities; freedom.) Compare migration of the first Americans to migration today. (Possible responses: today many migrants know their destination; in most cases travel is easier and faster; some migrants, such as migrant farm workers, still move with the food source.)

Map Skills
Asia • Cold

These are fluted spear points of stone, about five inches long, that were found sticking in the bones of mammoths, the great shaggy elephants that once roamed the American grasslands.

About ten thousand years ago, the latest Ice Age ended, and the climate of the Americas became warmer and drier. Many grasslands were replaced by desert and except on the Great Plains, large

Check for Understanding

Have students write the answers to Section 1 Review questions on paper. Go over the answers orally.

Guided Practice

Ask students what contributions early Indian groups made to our present culture. (Contributions include: foods such as corn, yams, and squash; words such as *wigwam* and *tobacco*.) Ask students to describe evidence of early American groups that is still visible today. (Possible responses: burial mounds; pueblos; ruins.) To stimulate discussion, ask students to identify some of the problems facing the descendants of the early American Indians. (Possible responses: employment; education; discrimination; preservation of Indian heritage.)

game disappeared. At the same time, small game flourished in the hardwood forests that began to cover much of the land.

About nine thousand years ago, people living in what is now central Mexico developed agriculture. At first they cultivated squash, peppers, and beans. By 5000–3500 B.C., they succeeded in domesticating maize, or corn. By 1500 B.C., corn was the most important crop throughout much of the Western Hemisphere, and the land was filled with thousands of small farming villages. Soon after, the first great **civilization,** or highly advanced way of life, in the Americas arose.

Civilizations Rise and Fall

Between 1000 B.C. and the coming of the Europeans around A.D. 1500, several civilizations developed in the valley of central Mexico, in Central America, and in Peru. In all these places, the people built cities with huge palaces and spacious squares. They erected flat-topped pyramids on which they placed stone temples to their gods. Some of their roads were better constructed and more extensive than those of the Roman Empire. Most of the civilizations had writing and calendars, and one of them invented paper.

Map Skills

Aztec and Maya • Cuzco

Several of these societies had systems of counting and writing figures up to over a billion. Their astronomers worked out a calendar of 365 days. They also could predict eclipses and chart the course of several of the planets.

The best known of these peoples are the **Aztecs** of central Mexico, the **Mayas** of Yucatán and Central America, and the **Incas** of Peru. When invaders landed on their shores, they conquered these people and their rich civilizations that were flourishing at this time. However, remnants of these great civilizations have survived.

Indian Farmers Cultivate the Southwest

The first farmers in what is now the United States were the Indians of the Southwest—Arizona, Colorado, New Mexico, and Utah. The land in which they lived was dry and sun drenched, with stony deserts in the south and steep-walled canyons farther north. To cultivate their crops of squash, beans, corn, and cotton, these people built elaborate irrigation systems that they copied from Indians in Mexico. One irrigation network stretched about 150 miles, and parts of it can still be seen.

The Southwestern farmers were a peaceful and democratic people. The dwelling places of the chiefs and of the religious leaders were rarely larger than anyone else's house. There was no division of society into classes. In each settlement four men were chosen by the inhabitants to be the ruling council. The person considered to be the best and wisest was chosen as principal leader.

At first the Southwestern farmers lived in pit houses, which were dug into the ground and covered with soil. Later, houses were built above ground and were made of adobe, or sun-dried bricks. About the year A.D. 700, the people began joining their houses together into a single building of many rooms and stories. These were often built into natural openings on the sides of canyons.

When the Spanish first saw the apartment houses of the Anasazi (ä'nə sa'zē), or ancient ones, they called them **pueblos** (pweb'lōz), the Spanish word for people or towns. The descendants of the Anasazi are known today as Pueblo Indians.

By the time the Spanish arrived in the Southwest, many of the giant apartment houses—such as Mesa Verde, Colorado, and Pueblo Bonito, New Mexico—had been abandoned. When or why is not known. It may have been because of a severe

Indian Civilizations in the Americas

NORTH AMERICA

ATLANTIC OCEAN

MEXICO

Tenochtitlán

CARIBBEAN SEA

CENTRAL AMERICA

N
W—E
S

SOUTH AMERICA

PACIFIC OCEAN

PERU

Cuzco

Aztecs

Mayas

Incas

0   700   1400 Miles
0   700   1400 2100 Kilometers

© ML & Co.

Map Skills **Location** Which Indian civilizations were located in present-day Mexico? **Location** Which city is farthest east — Tenochtitlán or Cuzco?

6

Assign Independent Practice
Have students complete Chapter 1, Section 1 Enrichment Activity.

Student Assignment/Homework
Have students read Section 2, "The Europeans Reach America," and answer on paper Section 2 Review questions.

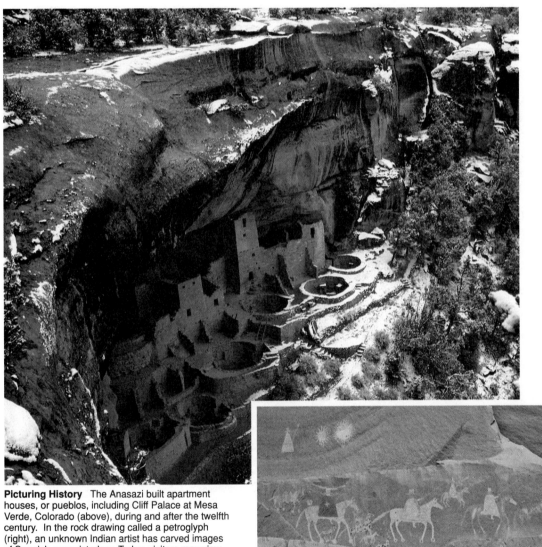

Picturing History The Anasazi built apartment houses, or pueblos, including Cliff Palace at Mesa Verde, Colorado (above), during and after the twelfth century. In the rock drawing called a petroglyph (right), an unknown Indian artist has carved images of Spanish conquistadors. Today, visitors may view the entire scene in Arizona's Canyon del Muerto.

drought that lasted for some twenty-four years. Or the Anasazi may have tried to escape from attacking nomads, such as the Navajo and the Apache Indians, who were beginning to come into the area. Some pueblos, though, were not abandoned. The pueblo of Oraibi (ō rī′bē), in Arizona, is said to be the oldest continually inhabited community in the United States. People have been living there since about 1300.

Foragers Cover California and the Northwest

California and the Northwest coast of the United States, between the Pacific Ocean and the Cascade Mountains, provided perhaps the richest environment of all for early Americans. The climate was mild and rainy. Food resources were abundant. The sea contained such animals as whales and seals, the

Indian Cultures in North America

Map Skills **Place** In which culture area is your state located? **Location** Which Indian culture was farthest north?

tidal flats furnished clams and waterfowl, and each year the rivers were filled with spawning salmon.

Another valuable resource was the thick forests of cedar that covered the land in the Northwest. The people used cedar wood for their houses, canoes, storage boxes, and ceremonial masks. They also used it for totem poles. They carved the poles with figures of people, animals, and mythological beings to show their family histories. Sometimes a totem pole recorded an outstanding experience in its owner's life.

The northernmost part of North America was home to the Eskimos, or Inuit (in′oo it), who arrived on the continent about 2000 B.C. Alaska was a difficult area in which to live. The temperature was below freezing, the snow cover lasted up to nine months a year, and fierce winds howled across the land.

The Eskimos got most of their food from sea animals, especially whales and seals. They hunted whales with harpoons from boats called umiaks (oo′mē aks′). The umiak was made of animal skin stretched over a wood frame, and it held from eight to ten people.

Focus on American Art

Picturing History   Drawing their inspiration and using materials from the bountiful earth that surrounded them, the Indians of North America designed objects to serve their social and religious needs. The beautifully crafted objects on this page reveal the high standards of workmanship that these Indian artisans set for themselves.

This beautifully carved antler comb was found in an archaeological site in Upstate New York. The three figures probably represent three tribes: the Seneca, the Onandaga, and the Mohawk.

People living in Florida around 1300 A.D. carved this wooden feline figure for ceremonial use.

The Pueblo Indians of the Southwest painted small dolls they called *kachinas* to represent powerful supernatural beings. This thirteenth century figurine, found in a cave in New Mexico, may be an early form of such a doll.

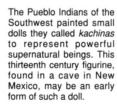

A Kwakiutl Indian from the Northwest designed this totem pole to depict his family's ancestral crests. From top to bottom the figures are: Eagle, Killer Whale, Chief, Raven, Bear.

Archaeologists found this design of a bird's claw crafted in mica in one of the Hopewell burial mounds.

This stone-carved burlwood Wampanog bowl is a rare masterpiece. Thousands of wooden utensils such as this one were burned during the smallpox epidemic of 1633-1635, when people were too weak to gather firewood.

In addition to food, sea animals provided the Eskimos with skins for clothing and with bone for harpoons, fishing hooks, knives, and needles. Seal oil was used in lamps that furnished heat and light.

In summer the Eskimos usually lived in tents made of animal skin. In winter they lived in pit houses. The passageway into the house was dug lower than the floor of the house. This kept out cold air. Some Eskimos built igloos, or domed houses made of snow blocks, with an entry passageway like the one used in pit houses.

The Eskimos traveled across the ice and snow by dog sled or toboggan. When they were not hunting, the men would gather in the village clubhouse. There they would work on their equipment, tell stories about great hunts of the past, and keep in shape by wrestling.

Plains Indians Track Buffalo

Through the middle of North America stretched the Great Plains. This flat or gently rolling land was covered mostly by short grass, with only an occasional clump of trees along the banks of a river. Its animal life included jack rabbits, prairie dogs, wolves, and coyotes. It also included millions of buffalo that provided almost everything the Plains Indians needed. As one observer noted:

> With the buffalo skins they make their houses; with the skins they clothe and shoe themselves; of the skins they make thread with which they sew their clothes and also their tents. From the bones they shape awls; the dung serves them for firewood, because there is no other fuel in that country. The stomachs serve them for pitchers, vessels from which they drink. They live on the flesh; they sometimes eat it roasted and warmed over the dung, at other times raw.

Although their numbers were sparse, the **Plains Indians** were divided into many tribes with widely differing languages. To communicate with one another, they developed an extremely effective sign language in which each gesture of the fingers and hands stood for an idea.

Hunters Roam the Eastern Woodlands

East of the Mississippi River, from the Great Lakes and the St. Lawrence River in the north to the Gulf of Mexico in the south, the land was covered with hardwood forests. The clear, spar-

Picturing History The significance of the sun is evident in this Sioux robe made of buffalo hide.

kling rivers and lakes teemed with fish, and the air was filled with flocks of birds. Wild fruits grew in abundance, and such animals as deer, bears, and panthers were common. Winters were cold in the north, while summers were warm everywhere. There was plenty of rain.

The Indians who lived in the Eastern Woodlands developed many different languages, religions, and customs. Their economies, however, were the same. They did not use metal but fashioned their tools and weapons out of stone, bone, or wood. They lived in villages set in forest clearings. During the warm weather, the men fished while the women gathered berries, roots, and nuts and cultivated gardens of squash, beans, and corn. In winter the men hunted for game on grounds that were held in common by each tribe. Since the hunting grounds were often far from the villages, the men camped there until it came time to carry home meat and hides in the spring.

Most **Eastern Woodland Indians** lived in domed houses called wigwams, which they built by covering a wood frame with either birch bark or rush mats. Smoke from the cooking fire escaped through a smoke hole in the center of the roof.

The Iroquois. One of the leading groups of Eastern Woodland Indians was the Iroquois of what is now New York State. They lived in large rectangular longhouses made of elm bark fastened on a wood frame. Each longhouse was inhabited by a dozen or more related families, and the house was partitioned so that each family had its own living space.

Iroquois society was matriarchal. Property and goods were inherited through the female line. The women owned the longhouses, the garden plots, and the garden tools. In warfare, the women decided which prisoners would live and which would die.

The Iroquois were noted for their political organization. In the 1400's they formed a league of five tribes: the Cayuga, Mohawk, Oneida, Onondaga, and Seneca. The league was governed by a council of chiefs under a constitution that was handed down orally from generation to generation. The council could not levy taxes or interfere in the affairs of individual tribes. It also lacked a police force. However, in case of a quarrel between members of different tribes, the council acted as judge. It also led the five tribes in time of war. As a result, the **League of the Iroquois** was the most powerful and feared group in the Northeast.

Picturing History This illustration of Secoton, a Tidewater Indian village in Virginia, was drawn by John White. The following description accompanied the picture when it was first published in the late 1500's:

> Their towns that are not inclosed with poles aire commonly fayer. Then suche as are inclosed, as appereth in this figure which livelye expresseth the town of Secotam. For the houses are scattered h e e r and ther, and they have gardein expressed by the letter E. wherin groweth Tobacco which the inhabitants call Uppowoc. They have also groaves wherein thei take deer, and fields wherin they sowe their

corne. In their corne fields they builde as it wear a scaffolde wher on they sett a cottage like to a rownde chaire signified by F. wherin they place one to watche, for there are suche nomber of fowles, and beasts, that unless they keep the better watche, they would soon devoure all their corne. For which cause the watcheman maketh continual cryes and noyse. They sowe their corne with a certain distance noted by H. otherwise one stalke would chocke the growthe of another and the corne would not come unto his rypeurs. G. For the leaves thereof are large, like unto the leaves of great reedes. They have also a severall broade plotte C. whear they meete with their neighbors, to celebrate their cheefe solemne feastes as the 18 picture doth declare and a place D. whear after they have ended their feaste they make merrie together. Over against this place they have a rownd plott B. wher they assemble themselves to make their solemne prayers. Not far from which place ther is a lardge buildinge A. wherin the tombs of their kings and princes, as will appere by the 22 figure. Likewise they have a garden notted by the letter I. wherin sowe pompions. Also a place marked with K. wherin they make a fyre att their solemne feasts, and hard without the towne a river L. from whence they fetche their water. This people therfore voyde of all covetousness lyve cherfullye and att their harts ease. Butt they solemnise their feasts in the night, and therefore they keepe very great fyres to avoyde darkenss, out to testifie their loye.

The Southeastern Indians. Another leading group of Eastern Woodland Indians lived in the southeastern part of the United States. This group included the Cherokees, Chickasaws, Choctaws, Creeks, and Seminoles. They adapted many ideas from Mexico and Central America. For example, they built pyramids resembling those of the Aztecs, except that they were made of mud rather than stone. One of their pyramids, which after all these centuries looks like a mound, is called Emerald Mound. Located in Mississippi, it is thirty-five feet high and covers seven acres. Inside were found pottery and drawings much like those found farther south.

The Mound Builders. Another group of Eastern Woodland hunters was the Mound Builders, whose culture developed around the Great Lakes and between the Ohio and Mississippi rivers. This culture is called Hopewell, after the man on whose farm in Ohio some of its largest remains have been found.

The Hopewell people built burial mounds of earth that often rose one hundred feet high and that were surrounded by huge walls. One such wall found in Ohio enclosed an area of four square miles. The mounds themselves were often shaped like serpents or birds.

today. (Possible response: glory is often an important motivator today.)

Anticipate the Lesson

Ask students to name the four reasons for European exploration. (Responses: spices; gold; God; glory.) Ask students which reason they feel was the most important. (Possible responses: Spaniards were most concerned with finding gold in the land that is now Mexico; Spaniards wanted to spread Christianity.) Discuss what factors might motivate explorers

Picturing History Ornate art objects have been found buried within The Great Serpent Mound in Adams County, Ohio. This mound was built about 1000 B.C.

Inside the burial mounds were objects showing what an active and far-flung trade the Hopewell people carried on. There were ornaments made of copper from the Lake Superior region. There were knives made of obsidian, or black stone, from the Rocky Mountains. There also were alligator teeth and shells from the Gulf of Mexico.

SECTION 1 REVIEW

Key Terms and People

Explain the Significance of: Bering Strait, Ice Age, civilization, Aztecs, Mayas, Incas, pueblos, Plains Indians, Eastern Woodland Indians, League of the Iroquois

Main Ideas

1. How and when did the first people arrive in North America?

2. What were the main achievements of the Aztec and Inca civilizations?
3. What is each group of the Eastern Woodland Indians known for?
4. What made the Iroquois' political organization especially powerful?
5. How did buffalo help the Plains Indians survive?

Critical Thinking

6. In general, how did Indian peoples use their environment to their advantage?

SECTION 2

The Europeans Reach America

GLOSSARY TERMS: **Renaissance, conquistadors**

Who were the first Europeans to step onto American soil? Where and when did they do so? We will probably never know entirely.

Fishermen from Ireland or from Scandinavia—Norwegians, Swedes, and Danes—may have been blown off course and later returned home to tell how they hovered off a strange coast for a day or two. They may even have spent time on shore exploring or looking for food and water. Such events, however, never entered recorded history. If they did occur, they apparently made little impression either on the voyagers or on the people who may have heard the voyagers' stories.

Early Explorers Visit America

During the 980's, Scandinavian Vikings made the first historical landings in North America. About 985, the Norwegian Viking Eric the Red crossed the Atlantic in an open boat and set up two colonies on Greenland. Some fifteen years later, his son Leif voyaged farther west to a place he called Vinland the Good because of its abundant grapes. Historians now believe that present-day Newfoundland is Leif Ericsson's Vinland. (See the map on page 15.) In 1963 a half-burned timbered house of Norse design was found there. A technique called radiocarbon analysis dated the find at about the year 1000.

According to Norwegian sagas, or tales of great deeds, Leif Ericsson was followed by another

State the Objective

Understand the causes and consequences of European exploration and colonization of America.

Present the Lesson

On the board construct a time line of European exploration from 1451 to 1588 using a different colored chalk to represent each country. Ask students to suggest the events to be included. Discuss with students the primary motivating factor for each explorer. (Time line might include: 1498, da Gama, spices; 1519, Cortés, gold.)

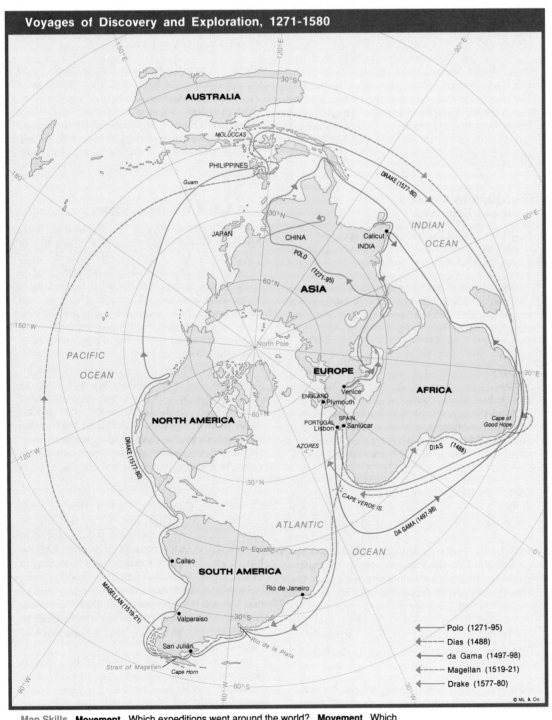

Voyages of Discovery and Exploration, 1271-1580

Polo (1271-95)
Dias (1488)
da Gama (1497-98)
Magellan (1519-21)
Drake (1577-80)

© ML & Co.

Map Skills

Magellan, Drake • England: Drake • Spain: Magellan • Portugal: Dias and da Gama • Italy: Polo

Map Skills **Movement** Which expeditions went around the world? **Movement** Which expeditions left from England? from Spain? from Portugal? from Italy?

Check for Understanding

Ask students to choose three dates from the time line that they think are most important. Have them write one or two sentences about each. (Possible response: 1498—da Gama reached India; important because his discovery of a shorter way to reach the East encouraged other explorers.)

For Discussion

What consequences resulted from European exploration and which had the most lasting effect on American development? (Possible responses: new languages and cultures; new forms of government; advanced weapons; diseases previously unknown in America. Many students will say that new languages and cultures and new forms of government had the most lasting effect.)

expedition that stayed in Newfoundland for three years. Then the colonists were driven away by Indians and did not return.

For the next four-and-three-quarter centuries, there was no known contact between Europeans and North America. Then, beginning in the late 1400's and continuing through the 1500's, a series of remarkable voyages took place. Thousands of people from Portugal, Spain, France, and England sailed across the Atlantic to explore—and eventually to colonize—the Americas. Why did they do it?

Four Reasons Motivate European Explorers

The reasons for the European voyages of exploration may be grouped under four headings. These are spices, gold, religion, and glory.

Spices. In those days European farmers slaughtered most of their pigs and cattle in late autumn and, in the absence of refrigeration, preserved the meat by packing it between layers of salt. They needed such spices as cinnamon, cloves, nutmeg, and especially pepper to disguise the meat's spoiled and salty taste. They also needed spices for making perfume, which was very popular since most Europeans never took a bath.

Spices came from eastern Asia, and the journey from there to Europe was slow, dangerous, and expensive. Many cargoes never reached the marketplace. What European merchants wanted was a faster and easier route to eastern Asia.

Gold. By the late 1400's, the feudal territories of western Europe had developed into four major nation-states: Portugal, Spain, France, and England. The monarchs of these new nation-states needed two things to maintain a strong central government. One was a bureaucracy to administer laws. The other was a standing army to replace the military services of feudal vassals. To pay the bureaucrats and the soldiers, money was needed. By the mid-1400's, however, Europe's gold and silver mines were running low. So the monarchs of Portugal, Spain, France, and England began looking overseas.

Religion. Still another reason for the European voyages of exploration was the desire to spread Christianity throughout the world. This was especially true of Spain. It had recently won its independence from the Muslim Moors after several centuries of struggle, and the religious zeal of its people was strong and fervent.

Glory. A fourth reason why Europeans set out to sea was the spirit of adventure. This attitude grew out of the **Renaissance,** the period between about 1350 and 1600 when a new way of thinking developed in Europe. The Renaissance encouraged people to regard themselves as individuals, to have confidence in what they might achieve, and to look forward to the glory their achievements might bring.

The Age of Discovery Begins

The European voyages of exploration were launched by Portugal. Under the leadership of Prince Henry the Navigator, a school for the study of geography and navigation was established in 1416. There, mapmakers pooled their knowledge of the earth's surface. There, ship captains and sailors learned how to use such navigational instruments as the astrolabe, which enabled them to tell their latitude while at sea, and the magnetic compass, which had been invented by the Chinese.

For almost forty years, Prince Henry sent his captains sailing south along the west coast of Africa. Portuguese explorations continued after Prince Henry died. Bartholomeu Dias (dē′əs) rounded the southern tip of Africa in 1488. Vasco da Gama (də gam′ə) reached India ten years later. Now the Portuguese could sail directly to eastern Asia. As a result, their costs fell and their profits rose.

Christopher Columbus. When Dias returned triumphantly to Portugal from his voyage into the Indian Ocean, one of the many people waiting to see him was an Italian named **Christopher Columbus**. It was Columbus's belief that a faster way to eastern Asia could be found by sailing west. Columbus thought the world was much smaller than it is and that he would reach land twenty-four hundred miles west of Europe. As it turned out, he was right—except that the land he reached was America and not Asia.

For some eight years, Columbus had tried to obtain financial backing for his plan. In 1492 King Ferdinand and Queen Isabella of Spain finally agreed to help, and a small fleet of three ships—the *Niña,* the *Pinta,* and the *Santa Maria*—set sail.

After about a month at sea, Columbus's sailors

To stimulate discussion on the nature of individual human effort, ask students what qualities early explorers possessed. (Possible responses: courage; foresight; imagination.) Ask students to compare these characteristics to those of heroes they admire today. (Possible responses: heroic qualities never change; heroic qualities change as society changes. Answers will depend on who students identify as contemporary heroes.) Ask students whether physical strength is as important a heroic quality as it once was. (Possible response: no, machinery and modern weapons make physical strength less important.)

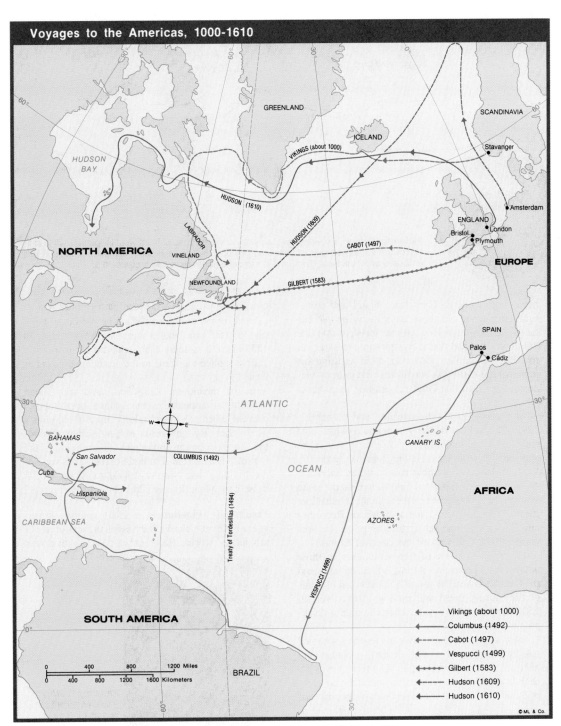

Voyages to the Americas, 1000-1610

	Vikings (about 1000)
	Columbus (1492)
	Cabot (1497)
	Vespucci (1499)
	Gilbert (1583)
	Hudson (1609)
	Hudson (1610)

© ML & Co.

Map Skills

Hudson • San Salvador or Bahamas

Map Skills **Movement** Which of the voyages shown reached present U.S. territory?
Location The territory of what modern country was reached by Columbus in 1492?

Migrants to a New Land **15**

Assign Independent Practice

Have students write three paragraphs explaining how the attitudes of Spain, France, and England toward colonization differed. (Paragraphs might include: Spain sent soldiers interested in exploiting the land's riches; Spain wanted to spread Christianity; France sent missionaries and free traders to save souls and establish trading posts; England sent settlers to farm and to colonize the land.)

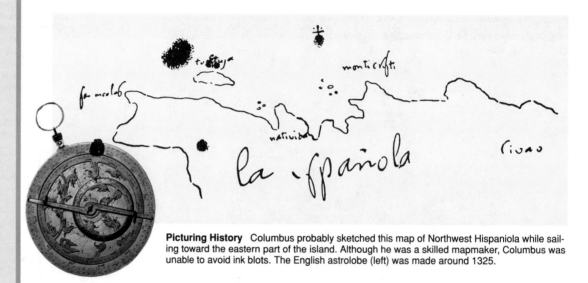

Picturing History   Columbus probably sketched this map of Northwest Hispaniola while sailing toward the eastern part of the island. Although he was a skilled mapmaker, Columbus was unable to avoid ink blots. The English astrolobe (left) was made around 1325.

began complaining. They were bored and sometimes frightened. In those days many people believed in sea monsters. Some insisted that the world was flat and that it was possible to sail over the edge. Columbus, however, kept assuring his men that the earth was round, that the journey was nearly over, and that God was guiding them accurately.

At two o'clock on the morning of October 12, 1492, the lookout of the *Pinta* saw a white cliff shining in the moonlight. "*Tierra!*" (land) he shouted. It was an island in the Bahamas, probably Watlings Island. Columbus named it San Salvador, or Holy Savior, in honor of God. Later, on the same voyage, he landed on two other islands, Hispaniola (present-day Haiti and the Dominican Republic) and Cuba, where he set up trading posts. He was convinced that he was off the coast of China.

The Spanish court backed Columbus in three additional expeditions, during which he explored the Caribbean Sea. He found no bejeweled officials of the Chinese court and little gold or silver. In 1504 he returned to Spain, where he died a disappointed man.

Surprisingly, the land Columbus reached is named not for him but for another Italian, a banker and geographer named **Amerigo Vespucci** (ves pōōt′ ōhē). In 1499 Vespucci made a voyage along the coast of Brazil, following it with a second voyage, this one along the coast of Argentina. When he returned to Europe, he voiced the opinion that what he had seen was not Asia but a new continent that "it is proper to

call a new world." A German cartographer was so excited by the phrase that when he put out a world map in 1507, he labeled the continent *America*. In 1538 Flemish cartographer Gerhardus Mercator (mər kāt′ər) applied the name to the northern continent as well.

In the meantime, King Ferdinand and Queen Isabella had appealed to the Spanish-born Pope to prevent Portugal from taking over Columbus's discoveries. By the **Treaty of Tordesillas** of 1494, the Pope drew an imaginary line dividing the world. All new-found, non-Christian lands west of the dividing line would belong to Spain, while those east of the line would belong to Portugal.

Ferdinand Magellan.   In 1519 another Portuguese navigator, Ferdinand Magellan, set out to sail around the world. He went west and south across

Picturing History a sixteenth century portrait of Ferdinand Magellan

Student Assignment/Homework
Have students read Section 3, "The English
Colonists Arrive," and complete Chapter 1,
Section 2 Enrichment Activity.

the Atlantic, around the tip of South America through a strait that still bears his name, and then north and west across the Pacific. When Europeans heard that a huge land mass lay to the west between Europe and Asia, they realized they would have to go around it, as Magellan had done, or find a way across it. Perhaps there was a water passage that ran northwest from the Atlantic to the Pacific. So began the dream of finding the Northwest Passage.

The Spanish Explore and Conquer

Columbus died before his great discoveries were recognized for what they were. However, it was not long before Spain was energetically exploring, colonizing, and plundering the Americas.

The Conquests of Mexico and Peru. In 1519 the Spanish governor of Cuba sent **Hernando Cortés** (kôr tez′) to search for gold and riches in what is now Mexico. Cortés landed with about four hundred men, sixteen horses, and fourteen cannon. He then made his way to the Aztec capital of Tenoch- titlán (tä nȯch′tē tlän′), now known as Mexico City. After sacking the city, he was forced to withdraw. He returned in 1521 with an Indian translator, la Malinche, and some one hundred thousand Indian allies who hated their Aztec rulers. Ever since then, Hispanics have used the term *malinchismo* (mal ən chĕz′mō) to mean traitor. Within a few months of the fall of the capital city, Spain was the supreme ruler of Mexico.

One reason the Spanish were so successful was that they had guns while the Aztecs had none. Another reason was that the explorers brought the diseases of smallpox and measles with them. The Indians had no resistance to the new diseases and died by the millions. Within fifty years after the Spanish invasion, the population of Mexico had dwindled from about twenty-five million to only two million.

Even so, the energy, greed, and sheer physical strength of these Spanish **conquistadors** (kän kwis′tə dôrs′), or conquerors, was astounding. By 1533 Francisco Pizarro (pi zä′rō) had invaded Peru, scaled the mighty Andes Mountains, and conquered the Inca Empire and its great gold and silver mines.

Historical Sidelight
Because of an ancient legend, the Indians of Mexico
thought that Cortés was a
god. They believed his ships
to be giant birds and they
were amazed by the half-
human, half-beast creatures
he brought with him (men on
horses). They could not believe their eyes when the
"gods" showed them sticks
which spouted smoke and
caused death (guns).

Map Skills
De Soto • Santa Fe • None

Spanish Exploration of North America, 1513–1605

→ Ponce de León (1513)
--→ Narváez (1528)
◂--- de Vaca and Estevanico (1535–36)
← Coronado (1540–42)
◄ de Soto (1539–42)
← Oñate (1596–1605)
◄◄◄ Cortés (1519–21)

Colorado R.
Missouri R.
Ohio R.
VIRGINIA
Santa Fe
CORONADO (1540–42)
DE SOTO (1539–42)
Mississippi R.
DE VACA & ESTEVANICO (1535–36)
Gulf of California
Rio Grande
TEXAS
NARVÁEZ (1528)
St. Augustine
FLORIDA
PONCE DE LEÓN (1513)
ATLANTIC OCEAN
Culiacán
OÑATE (1596–1605)
MEXICO
GULF OF MEXICO
N
W E
S
BAHAMAS
PACIFIC OCEAN
Compostela
CORTÉS (1519–21)
Havana
CUBA
Santiago
Puerto Rico
Veracruz
Tenochtitlán (Mexico City)
CARIBBEAN SEA

0 200 400 600 Miles
0 200 400 600 800 Kilometers

© ML & Co.

Map Skills **Movement** Which expedition crossed the Mississippi River? **Location** Which mod- ern U.S. city did Oñate reach? **Location** What part of present U.S. territory did Cortés reach?

Expeditions Northward. In quick succession, expeditions in search of treasure were sent north from Mexico. In 1528 Panfilo de Narváez (när *bä′*ās) led a party from Florida west along the Gulf Coast. Most of his men were lost in a storm off Texas. The survivors—Cabeza de Vaca, two other Spaniards, and an African man named Estevanico—spent about seven years wandering around New Mexico, Arizona, Texas, and possibly California, where they were the objects of great curiosity. Eventually they found their way back to Mexico, bringing wild tales about "hunchback cows" (buffalo) and people who lived in multistoried buildings. Additional expeditions in North America included those of Hernando de Soto in 1539 and Francisco Vasquez de Coronado (kôr′ə nä′dō) in 1540.

During the second half of the 1500's, the Spanish established several settlements in North America. The fort of **St. Augustine** was set up in Florida in 1565. In 1598 Juan de Oñate set up a provincial capital at Santa Fe, New Mexico.

Spanish Supremacy. By 1580 Spain was a giant that stood astride the world. **Philip II** of Spain had also become the ruler of Portugal and of all its possessions. His empire stretched from Manila in the Philippines, which were named for him, around the world to Mexico, Peru, and most of the southern and southwestern United States. Looking at a map of Spanish explorations and possessions, few would have doubted that the whole Western Hemisphere would eventually become Spanish.

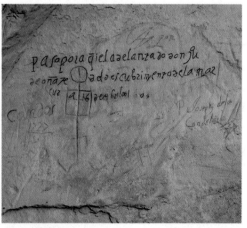

Picturing History Juan de Oñate sailed up the Rio Grande and founded the first Spanish settlement in New Mexico in the summer of 1598.

The French Preach and Trade

In the early 1600's, Spain's main competitor was France. Whereas the Spanish had come to the Americas to save souls and find treasure, the French had come to save souls and establish a fur trade. In 1524 Francis I of France sent Italian navigator Giovanni da Verrazano (ver′rä tsä′nö) along the coast of North America searching for the Northwest Passage. In 1535 **Jacques Cartier** (kår tyä′) explored the St. Lawrence River and gave the name Mount Royal to the site of present-day Montreal. The first permanent French settlement, at Quebec, was founded in 1608 by another French explorer, Samuel de Champlain (sham plān′).

After the establishment of Quebec, the French penetrated the central part of the North American continent. French priest Jacques Marquette (mär ket′) and trader Louis Joliet (jō′lē et′) explored the Great Lakes and the upper part of the Mississippi River. Sieur Robert Cavelier de La Salle (lə sal′) explored the lower Mississippi in 1682 and claimed the entire river valley, which he named Louisiana for Louis XIV. New Orleans was founded by the French, as was Biloxi on the Gulf of Mexico.

Linking Past to Present

The names of places can tell us something about the history of those places. In the midwestern United States, many cities are named for the French explorers and settlers who came to the area in the 1600's. Joliet, Illinois, is named after the French trader Louis Joliet. Marquette, Michigan, is named after the French priest Jacques Marquette. Other midwestern cities with French names include Cloquet, Minnesota; Fond du Lac, Wisconsin; Des Moines, Iowa; and Terre Haute, Indiana.

The English Search for New Lands

The northern and central parts of the North American continent had become, in effect, territories of France. The southern and southwestern parts of the continent were under the rule of Spain. Year after year, a Spanish fleet carried off vast quantities of gold and silver. Spain used these precious metals to pay for imports and for war

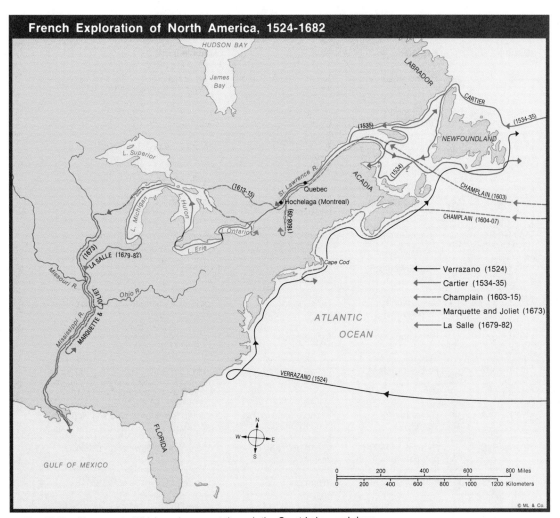

French Exploration of North America, 1524-1682

HUDSON BAY

James Bay

LABRADOR

CARTIER

(1534-35)

(1535)

NEWFOUNDLAND

(1534)

L. Superior

(1613-15)

St. Lawrence R.

Quebec

ACADIA

CHAMPLAIN (1603)

Hochelaga (Montreal)

CHAMPLAIN (1604-07)

L. Michigan

Huron

(1608-09)

L. Ontario

LA SALLE (1679-82)

(1673)

L. Erie

Cape Cod

Missouri R.

Ohio R.

MARQUETTE & JOLIET

Mississippi R.

ATLANTIC OCEAN

- **←** Verrazano (1524)
- **←** Cartier (1534-35)
- **←** Champlain (1603-15)
- **←** Marquette and Joliet (1673)
- **←** La Salle (1679-82)

VERRAZANO (1524)

FLORIDA

N W E S

GULF OF MEXICO

| 0 | 200 | 400 | 600 | 800 Miles |
| 0 | 200 | 400 | 600 | 800 | 1000 | 1200 Kilometers |

© ML & Co.

Map Skills **Movement** Which explorer went through the Great Lakes and down the Mississippi River? **Movement** Which explorer went north of Newfoundland?

Map Skills
La Salle • Cartier

debts, thus providing other European countries with capital for new manufacturing industries.

How could England compete? At first, it didn't. In 1497 Henry VII of England sent Italian explorer **John Cabot** westward into the Atlantic to seek new lands and to set up trading posts. On his first voyage, Cabot landed on an island that he named New Founde Lande. On his second voyage, he was lost at sea, as were four of his ships.

Almost one hundred years elapsed before another explorer sailed from England across the Atlantic. In 1583 Sir Humphrey Gilbert crossed the Atlantic in order to found a settlement on New-

foundland. However, on the return trip, Gilbert and his entire party were lost at sea.

A year later Elizabeth I gave Sir Walter Raleigh permission to settle anywhere north of the Spanish holdings along the Atlantic coast. The expedition Raleigh sent landed near Roanoke Island, in what is now the state of North Carolina. He named the place the fleet landed Virginia, in honor of Elizabeth, the Virgin Queen.

In 1585 Raleigh made his first attempt to establish a colony on Roanoke Island. It failed. Two years later he sent out a second group of colonists. In 1590 an expedition sent to bring new supplies to

Early Explorers	Spain	England	France	Portugal

Date	Explorer	Goal	Achievement
1488	Bartholomeu Dias	To find southern tip of Africa	Sailed around southern tip of Africa (Cape of Good Hope) into Indian Ocean
1492–1504 (four voyages)	Christopher Columbus	To find western route to Asia	Explored the West Indies and the Caribbean
1497	John Cabot	To seek and explore new lands, and set up trading posts	Explored the coast of North America
1497–98	Vasco da Gama	To sail around Africa to eastern Asia	Reached India
1499–1502 (two voyages)	Amerigo Vespucci	To explore the Americas	Explored the coast of South America and identified it as a continent
1513, 1521	Juan Ponce de León	To find gold and the Fountain of Youth	Explored Florida
1513	Vasco Núñez de Balboa	To find gold	Crossed the Isthmus of Panama and saw the Pacific Ocean
1519–1521	Hernando Cortés	To find gold	Conquered the Aztecs in Mexico and seized their gold
1519–1522	Ferdinand Magellan	To find western route to Asia	Sailed across the Atlantic, around South America, and across the Pacific; survivors were first to sail around the world
1524	Giovanni da Verrazano	To find a route to Asia through America	Explored the Atlantic Coast of North America
1528–1536	Cabeza de Vaca and Estevanico	To find gold and Seven Cities of Cibola	Explored the Southwest and Mexico
1531–1533	Francisco Pizarro	To find gold	Conquered the Incas in Peru
1534–1541 (three trips)	Jacques Cartier	To find route to Asia through America	Explored the St. Lawrence River as far as Montreal
1539–1542	Hernando de Soto	To find gold and to colonize Florida	Explored Florida and the Southeast
1540–1542	Francisco Vásquez de Coronado	To find gold and Seven Cities of Cibola	Explored the Southwest as far as Kansas; discovered the Grand Canyon
1603–1615 (seven trips)	Samuel de Champlain	To set up fur-trading posts	Explored the St. Lawrence River Valley
1609–1611 (two trips)	Henry Hudson	To find the Northwest Passage	Explored the Hudson River and the Hudson Bay area
1669–1682 (many trips)	Sieur Robert Cavelier de La Salle	To claim territory for Louis XIV	Explored the Great Lakes to the lower Mississippi River
1673	Louis Joliet and Jacques Marquette	To set up trading posts and spread Christianity	Explored the Great Lakes and the upper Mississippi River

State the Objective

Learn how and why the English colonies multiplied along the Atlantic coast.

Anticipate the Lesson

Discuss with students the idea that people must adapt to their environment. Ask students what they might have to change if they were to move to a new country. (Possible responses: language; style of clothing; foods; occupations; leisure activities; music.) Ask students how early colonists might have had to adapt to their new environment. (Possible responses: type of clothing; homes; food; work.)

Picturing History
Sir Walter Raleigh was a half brother of Sir Humphrey Gilbert. While serving in Ireland, Raleigh became a good friend and patron of the poet Edmund Spenser, author of *Faerie Queene.*

the colony found the site deserted. No one knows what became of the lost colony.

These attempts were indeed a poor beginning. Few people would have thought that England, coming so late and starting off in such a stumbling way, would end up the ruling power in North America. How did it happen?

The crucial reason why English colonies succeeded was that the English settlements were made up mostly of people who looked on North America as their home. By contrast, the Spanish and French were primarily interested in making a quick fortune. So, although Spain and France both controlled large areas of North America, it was the English who established hundreds of separate communities, brought over their families, and succeeded in building new lives for themselves and their descendents.

SECTION 2 REVIEW

Key Terms and People

Explain the significance of: Renaissance, Christopher Columbus, Amerigo Vespucci, Treaty of Tordesillas, Hernando Cortés, conquistadors, St. Augustine, Philip II, Jacques Cartier, John Cabot

Main Ideas

1. What motivated Europeans to set out on voyages of exploration?
2. How did Portugal become the leader of the European explorations?
3. How did Spain become the supreme force in the Americas?

4. What were the results of England's first efforts to explore and settle North America?

Critical Thinking

5. How did the Spanish explorers succeed in achieving their main goals and how did they fail?

SECTION 3

The English Colonists Arrive

GLOSSARY TERMS: **joint-stock companies, charter, headright system, indentured servants, burgesses, Puritans, Pilgrims, Mayflower Compact, proprietary colonies**

England's first attempts to establish colonies in North America were made by individuals. In the 1600's **joint-stock companies** provided another means of financing colonization. A joint-stock company was a group of people, each of whom put up a certain amount of capital in return for a stated number of shares. If there were one hundred shares and a person bought ten shares, that person would get 10 percent of the profits. If there were a loss, the person would be responsible for only 10 percent of it. The first successful English colonies in America were founded by joint-stock companies.

The Virginia Colony Finally Succeeds

In 1606 two groups of merchants and adventurers from the ports of London and Plymouth asked James I for permission to form a joint-stock company to found colonies in America. The King was interested. After all, the expedition would cost him nothing and might return a profit. According to custom, on such ventures the ruler got one-fifth of all gold and silver that was found. So James issued a **charter,** or official permit.

The charter was the nearest thing to a written constitution for the proposed colony. It gave the two Virginia Companies—the London Company and the Plymouth Company—permission to settle along the Atlantic coast of North America and to have a monopoly on trade. The London Company was given the right to settle the land from the Potomac south to what is now South Carolina. The Plymouth Company was given permission to settle in the region between present-day Maine and New

Answers

Main Ideas

1. The desire to acquire spices, gold, and glory and to spread Christianity.

2. Prince Henry the Navigator encouraged exploration by establishing a school for the study of geography and navigation and by sponsoring Portuguese exploration along the coast of Africa.

3. Spanish explorers captured the great wealth of the Aztecs and Incas and established settlements in North America; Philip II became ruler of Portugal and Spain and all their possessions.

4. Cabot and Gilbert were lost at sea; Raleigh's Roanoke Island colonies failed.

Critical Thinking

5. Successes—acquired spices, gold, and glory; introduced Christianity in new lands. Failures—killed many more Indians than they converted to Christianity. **(synthesis)**

Ask students to list on paper the early English colonies. Students should include information about why each colony was founded. (Lists might include: Plymouth—Puritans wished to start an independent religious colony; Rhode Island—Roger Williams left Massachusetts to start a colony that allowed freedom of worship and provided for separation of church and state.) Ask volunteers to read their papers to the class.

Check for Understanding

Call on individual students to answer Section 3 Review questions orally.

For Discussion

How did Jamestown get its start? (Response: James I issued a charter.) How did James I benefit by authorizing a joint stock company to found a colony in Virginia? (Response: the expedition would cost him nothing; but by custom, the King received one-fifth of all profits earned by any company, so he stood to gain a great deal if this one were successful.)

Map Skills

London Company •
Plymouth Company

English Land Grants, 1606

Plymouth Company
London Company
Land open to both companies

0   100   200 Miles
0 100 200 300 Kilometers

© ML & Co.

Map Skills **Place** Which land grant company had the land with the most natural harbors?
Location Which had land the farthest north?

York. The charter also declared that the colonists would have the same rights and privileges that the English people had in England. Among these rights were the right to trial by jury and the right to own land.

The Jamestown Settlement. On December 20, 1606, the Virginia Company sent out 140 men and four boys in three tiny vessels. Contrary winds slowed their progress, but finally, on April 26, 1607, they saw low on the horizon the green coast of Virginia. You can imagine their joy and excitement. As the land came into view more clearly, they must have gazed at it with the same awe and wonderment that astronauts in the 1960's felt when they looked upon the surface of the moon from a hovering spacecraft.

The English sailed slowly up a wide and beautiful river until, on a small peninsula, they located what seemed like a good spot to build a fort. They named the place Jamestown and the river the James, in honor of their King.

Jamestown was a fine choice for defense purposes. The land was flat and nearly surrounded by water. In other ways, however, it was disastrous. Much of the land was swampy, and there were swarms of mosquitoes. At that time, no one knew that mosquitoes carried deadly malaria.

Early Miseries. After about two months, on June 22, two of the ships sailed for England, leaving 105 people at Jamestown. Things went bad quickly.

People fell ill as the summer deepened. In his diary one man wrote, "There died John Asbie of a bloody flux [hemorrhage]. The ninth day died George Flower of the swelling." Some nights, three or four people died, then "in the morning, their bodies [were] trailed out of their cabins like dogs to be buried." In seven months, all but thirty-two were dead. The Indians saved those who were left. The diarist noted, "It pleased God to move the Indians to bring us corn . . . when we rather expected they would destroy us." The Indians also brought bread, fish, and meat in great quantity.

John Smith Takes Charge. In addition to their other difficulties, the men quarreled over leadership. After a year of drifting, a forceful ex-soldier named **John Smith,** twenty-seven years old, simply took charge. By sheer force of strength and personality, he got the men to clear the land and to cultivate it. The men resisted at first. Most of them were "gentlemen," and in England gentlemen did not work with their hands. Smith, however, made it clear that if they did not work, they would not eat. They worked.

Smith established a friendship with Pocahontas, the daughter of an Indian chief. According to

Picturing History Pocahontas, daughter of Indian chief Powhatan, is pictured in English clothes in the oil painting above. In the statue of Pocahontas at Jamestown, Virginia (right), the sculptor, William Ordway Patridge, has depicted the Indian princess in her traditional tribal dress.

legend, it was Pocahontas who rescued Smith when he was captured by her people. Pocahontas married a settler named John Rolfe, had a son, and later traveled to England.

The Starving Time. In 1609 Smith was injured in a gunpowder explosion, and he soon left the colony for good. By then more supplies and some four hundred additional settlers, including young women and widows, had arrived. Still, conditions in the colony went from bad to worse. During that winter, there was famine and even cannibalism. This was the so-called starving time. People lived on roots and rats, and one man even murdered his wife and salted her away like salt pork.

By spring only sixty people remained alive. They decided to abandon the colony and return to England. They were actually sailing down the James River when they met an incoming ship. Aboard was the new governor, Baron De La Warr (from whom Delaware got its name), with more settlers and supplies. Reluctantly, the colonists returned to Jamestown. The first permanent English colony in America had narrowly missed being abandoned.

Saved by Smoke. What finally got Jamestown off to economic health was something as insubstantial as smoke. At first there was no intention of growing tobacco. It was an American plant, unknown in Europe before the time of Columbus. Also, the kind of tobacco the Indians in Virginia grew and smoked tasted bitter to Europeans. Then in 1612 John Rolfe introduced a different type of tobacco from the Caribbean islands. It was much milder and suited European tastes. The plants grew well in Virginia, and cultivation did not require skilled labor. Settlers were soon busily growing the new crop.

King James opposed tobacco on the grounds that it was unhealthy. He called it a ''stinking weed.'' However, tobacco quickly became so popular in Europe that he permitted it to be brought into England, where it was handsomely taxed. The Virginia colonists had at last found a profitable crop.

The Headright System and Indentured Servants. In 1618 the Virginia Company introduced the **headright system.** Under it, any man who paid his way to Virginia would get fifty acres of land for himself and another fifty acres for every person he brought with him. Immigration increased.

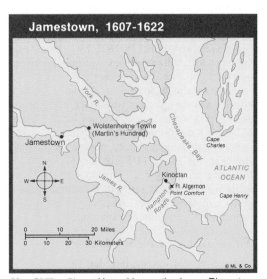

Jamestown, 1607-1622

Map Skills **Place** How wide was the James River at Jamestown? **Location** What direction from Point Comfort was Jamestown?

Most of the new immigrants, however, came as **indentured servants.** This meant that in return for their passage they agreed to work for someone for a specified number of years, usually seven, after which they were free. This practice eased unemployment in England. It also cleared English jails, for judges sent political prisoners and debtors to Virginia as indentured servants.

Two Important Events. In 1619 two things happened that had great impact on the future of the English colonies. On July 30, in the little church in Jamestown, Governor Yeardley and his council of twenty-two **burgesses,** or representatives, met to make laws for the colony. Statutes were enacted based on English common law. From this time on, Virginians jealously guarded the privilege of holding their own legislative assembly.

The second event was the arrival of a Dutch ship. In its hold were twenty "Negars" who were sold to the English settlers. They were listed as servants, and most historians believe they were treated as indentured servants who happened to be black. After a time, they received land and their freedom.

Virginia Becomes a Royal Colony. By 1624 some six thousand English people had gone to Virginia, but the total English population there was only twelve hundred. Almost five out of six had either returned home or lay under the forests of Virginia. They had died from disease, from malnutrition, or, in the case of women, in childbirth. Many were also killed in 1622 by a large-scale Indian attack. Still, the colony was growing richer as tobacco became its major crop.

Complaints of fraud against Virginia Company officials and the company's bankruptcy due to the cost of war with the Indians alarmed James I. So in 1624 the King disbanded the company and appointed a royal governor to manage the colony. However, the House of Burgesses, as Virginia's legislative assembly had come to be called, remained in existence. The settlers continued their practice of obeying laws and paying taxes only if their elected representatives authorized it.

The Puritans Arrive in Massachusetts

It was a cold, snowy day that November 15, 1620, when five Indians and a dog were out hunting along the sandy shores of Cape Cod. Suddenly, they saw in the distance an extraordinary sight: a group of sixteen bearded white men. The men wore heavy clothes and uttered strange cries, while the one who seemed to be their leader waved. This was the first known encounter between the North Americans and the Puritans.

Puritan Beliefs. The **Puritans** wanted to purify the Anglican church, England's official Protestant church. To Puritans, the rituals of this church seemed too much like those of the Roman Catholic service, which Henry VIII had abolished in the 1500's. In general, Puritans followed the teachings of John Calvin. Here are some of Calvin's and the Puritans' most important beliefs.

Puritans believed in original sin. The first book of the Bible tells about the sin of Adam and Eve, the parents of all people, who disobeyed God by eating the forbidden fruit. Puritans believed that all humans inherited the same sinful character. Since sinful people *deserved* to be damned to hell after death, it was a sign of God's mercy that He had decided to save anyone at all.

Puritans also believed in predestination, that is, that God had decided the destiny of all men and women before they were born. Each person was going either to heaven or to hell. Nothing they did could alter that fact.

Nevertheless, Puritans believed that each person was responsible for leading a moral life. Although good behavior could not earn salvation, it indicated that a person already had God's favor. As a consequence, Puritans were constantly examining their own behavior. They also examined the behavior of everyone else in their communities. They kept a sharp eye out for such sins as drunkenness, swearing, theft, and idleness. When they discovered such sins, they punished the sinners severely.

Why did the Puritans include idleness in their catalog of sins? They believed that God "called" people to their jobs. The job might be that of a minister, farmer, mother, servant, or carpenter. Whatever the job one was called to, God required men and women to work long and hard at it.

Puritans also believed in the importance of the Bible, which they regarded as the Word of God. All men and women had to know how to read so they could consult the Bible themselves. Puritan ministers were highly educated men with great reputations and influence. However, they did not rule their churches the way Anglican bishops did. Puritan ministers were hired—and could be fired—by the individual church congregations.

Student Assignment/Homework

Have students complete the Chapter 1 Review
on paper and go over their answers in class.

The Separatists. The Puritans agreed on what
was wrong with the Church of England, but they
disagreed on what should be done about it. Some
thought they should remain in the church and try to
reform it from within. Others did not think that was
possible, so they formed independent congregations with their own ministers. The **Separatists,** as
they were called, had to meet in secret because
James I was determined to punish those who did
not follow the Anglican form of worship.

In 1608 one congregation of Separatists decided
to flee from England to Holland, where the authorities were very tolerant in religious matters. After
several years, however, they became discouraged,
mostly because some of their young people were
drifting away from the Puritan faith. So they
decided to risk migrating to America, where they
felt they could live successfully as an independent
religious congregation. They obtained financial
backing and a grant of land in the northern part of
Virginia.

The Voyage of the *Mayflower*. Late in the summer of 1620, a small group of families set sail in
two ships from the English port of Plymouth.

Picturing History This painting of Edward Winslow,
governor of Plymouth, is the only known portrait of a
Mayflower passenger.

Almost immediately, one of the ships, the *Speed-
well,* began leaking so badly that the tiny expedition had to turn back. The group then crowded
aboard the sturdier *Mayflower* and once again
raised anchor.

These people called themselves **Pilgrims,** from
the story in the Bible in which Abraham and the
Hebrews are sent by God ''as strangers and Pilgrims'' into a strange land so as to better worship
the Lord. Not all Pilgrims were Separatists,
though, and some were not even Puritans. They
were adventurers eager to improve their lives by
settling in a new land.

The *Mayflower* aimed for the northern coast of
Virginia. It missed badly. Nine weeks later, when
the ship's people sighted land, they saw rolling
sand dunes with tall, waving grass. They debated
about sailing south but decided to search the coast
in front of them for a safe harbor and place for
settlement. They found a spot on the inner shore of
Cape Cod Bay and named it for the town from
which they had sailed—Plymouth.

The Mayflower Compact. The Puritans knew
that New England lay too far north for their charter
to be valid. They were also afraid that the other
passengers, who were strangers, would challenge
their authority. While still on board the *Mayflower,*
forty-one men gathered in the main cabin and
signed their names to a compact, or agreement.
They stated that the purpose of their government
would be to frame ''just and equal laws . . . for the
general good of the colony.'' Laws approved by the
majority would be binding on Puritans and non-
Puritans alike. These lines suggest that political
authority rests on the will of the people. The
Mayflower Compact was thus an important landmark in the development of the American system
of government.

The signers of the compact were the colony's
free men. They selected John Carver as their first
governor. When he died a few months later, they
chose William Bradford and they reelected him
nearly every year from 1621 until his death in
1657.

Help from the Indians. The Pilgrims' prospects
were not encouraging. The soil appeared sandy and
unpromising. Even worse, December had arrived,
and the Pilgrims felt the first bite of a New England
winter, which was far worse than any English
winter. The result was a repetition of what had

happened in Jamestown. Bradford wrote,

> In two or three months' time, half of their company died, being the depth of winter and wanting houses and other comforts . . . being infected with scurvy and other diseases.

In spring the surviving Pilgrims took advantage of some abandoned Indian cornfields and planted squash and beans. Then one day an Indian came up and dumbfounded the Pilgrims by speaking in English. He said his name was Samoset and that he had learned the language from some English fishermen. He introduced the Pilgrims to his friend Tisquantum and to the local chief, Massasoit.

Tisquantum—or Squanto, as the Pilgrims called him—had actually spent several years in England. He spoke English very well and became the Pilgrims' guide and interpreter. Indeed, the Indians' aid saved the settlers' lives in New England just as it had saved them in Virginia. Tisquantum and his friends showed the Pilgrims what corn was and how to grow and cook it. The Indians also taught the settlers how to gather and cook clams and where to catch the fattest fish.

Picturing History The title page above is from the Bible used by William Bradford. It is believed to be the same Bible he brought to Plymouth in 1620.

Thanksgiving. In November 1621, one year after their arrival, the Pilgrims gathered their first harvest. Then they invited Massasoit and some ninety of his braves to a three-day feast, which included squash, beans, corn, wild turkeys, ducks, geese, and four deer that the Indians brought. It was a time of Thanksgiving to God.

By 1642 the Pilgrims were able to repay their financial backers in London with shipments of lumber and furs. Gradually, their tiny settlement expanded. The Pilgrims then set up a governmental system whereby the men of each town elected representatives to pass laws for the entire colony. Only males who were church members could vote. Even so, a far higher proportion of men could vote in the Plymouth Colony than in England.

A New Colony on the Bay. Meanwhile, other English Puritans were turning their thoughts toward New England. They were not Separatists, but they were becoming discouraged about Anglican reform. So they began to think about establishing a holy community of their own in America.

One of these Puritans was a lawyer named **John Winthrop.** He and several friends obtained a charter for a new joint-stock enterprise, the Massachusetts Bay Company. The charter included a land grant and provisions for a government but failed to say where the company's headquarters should be. Winthrop and his friends took advantage of this omission and boldly transferred both the charter and the company's headquarters to New England. This meant that when Winthrop and other Puritans migrated, they took with them authority for an independent government.

The year 1630 saw the first really well-planned and sizable migration of English people to America. Winthrop had been named governing officer of the Massachusetts Bay Company. He and other Puritan leaders recruited between eight hundred and a thousand other Puritans for the expedition. Few of the migrants were wealthy, but they were by no means as poor as those who had gone to Virginia and to Plymouth. They had little difficulty in buying adequate supplies and a fleet of ships.

There was no starving time in the new colony. Over the next ten years, supplies kept coming. So did nearly twenty thousand people, most of whom survived. The port town of Boston became the colony's thriving capital. Settlers established other towns nearby and eventually incorporated the Plymouth Colony into the Massachusetts Bay Colony.

Picturing History John Winthrop was the first governor of the Massachusetts Bay Colony. This portrait reveals the air of authority with which he took control of affairs.

Different Settlements Begin

As you can see from the chart on page 29, eleven additional colonies were established on the eastern shore of what became the United States. Some were established under a joint-stock company charter, whereas others were **proprietary colonies.** This means that the persons receiving the charter were the proprietors, or owners, of the colony and could collect rents from settlers. Most proprietary colonies were later taken over by the crown. However, no matter what kind of charter an English colony had, it had a representative assembly. By the mid-1600's such assemblies were regarded as essential features of English colonial governments.

Other New England Colonies. Three New England colonies were set up by Puritans from Massachusetts. They were New Hampshire, Connecticut, and Rhode Island. Rhode Island, however, was unique among the colonies because of certain provisions in its charter.

Rhode Island was founded by **Roger Williams,** a Separatist minister who arrived in Massachusetts

in 1631. Most people respected him, but the colony's government felt threatened by two of his opinions. Williams declared that the English settlers had no rightful claim to the land unless they purchased it from the Indians. He also declared that government officials should devote themselves only to government business and should leave religious matters alone. To the Puritan leaders, the first idea was ridiculous, and the second was heresy, or a belief opposed to established views or doctrines. So in 1636 they banished Williams from the holy community of Massachusetts.

Williams tramped southward to the headwaters of Narragansett Bay, where he was joined by sympathizers from Massachusetts. There he established the town of Providence, which became the center of the new colony. When Rhode Island received its charter in 1644, it provided for the

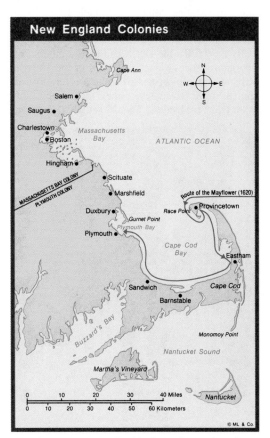

Map Skills **Location** The Mayflower first put in at the site of what town? **Location** How far was it from the site of Plymouth?

Map Skills

Provincetown • About 25 miles (40km) across the bay

separation of church and state. All Christian groups were given freedom of worship, and even men who did not belong to any church were allowed to vote.

It was in Rhode Island that **Anne Hutchinson** found refuge when she was banned from Boston for leading religious discussions in her home. In 1642 she moved to New York, where she was killed by Indians. When the Puritans learned of her death, they interpreted it as another example of God's work in the world.

The Dutch Wedge. While English Puritans were establishing colonies in New England, the Dutch were founding one to the south. As early as 1609, Henry Hudson—an Englishman employed by the Dutch—explored the Hudson River as far as present-day Albany, New York. In 1626 the Dutch bought Manhattan Island, at the mouth of the Hudson, from the Indians for trade goods worth about twenty-four dollars. They built a little town there that they named New Amsterdam, after the most important city in Holland.

By the 1630's the Dutch had built a number of enormous estates along both sides of the Hudson River. Dutch explorers also ventured as far south as the Delaware River, where they took over a tiny colony of Swedish and Finnish settlers. However,

Map Skills

Albany • Delaware River

New Netherland and New Sweden

Map Skills **Location** What modern city is on the site of Fort Orange? **Location** On what river was New Sweden?

the Dutch never migrated in large numbers to their American colony as the English did to theirs. Also, the Dutch lost a series of sea battles with the English in the middle of the century and were unable to defend their holdings in North America. In 1664 New Amsterdam was taken over by the English, who renamed it New York for the King's younger brother, the Duke of York. In fact, they named the entire Dutch area New York. The duke later gave a portion of this land to two of his friends, and it was named New Jersey for the British island of Jersey.

Maryland. When James I died, his son, Charles I, married a Roman Catholic. One of the major figures at his court, **Sir George Calvert,** was also a Catholic. Calvert had ambitions to found a

Picturing History Anne Hutchinson was banned from Boston for leading religious discussions such as this one in her home.

Types of American Colonies

Colony	Founded	Leader	Type of Charter	First Settlement
Virginia	1607	John Smith	Corporate (1607–1624) Royal (1624–1776)	Jamestown
Plymouth	1620	William Bradford	Corporate (1620–1691) Royal (1691–1776)	Plymouth
New Netherland (New York after 1663)	1626	Peter Minuit (for Dutch) Duke of York (for English)	Proprietary (1664–1685) Royal (1685–1776)	New Amsterdam (New York)
Massachusetts Bay	1630	John Winthrop	Corporate (1630–1691) Royal (1691–1776)	Boston
Maryland	1634	George Calvert	Proprietary (1632–1776)	St. Mary's
Rhode Island	1636	Roger Williams	Corporate (1644–1776)	Providence
Connecticut	1636	Thomas Hooker	Corporate (1662–1776)	Hartford
New Hampshire	1638	John Wheelwright	Proprietary (1639–1680) Royal (1680–1776)	Exeter
Delaware (Taken by Dutch from Swedish in 1655; taken by English from Dutch in 1664)	1638	Peter Minuit (who left Dutch West India Company and went into Swedish service)	Proprietary (1682–1776)	Wilmington
North Carolina: Albemarle Colony	1653	Group of eight proprietors	Proprietary (1663–1729) Royal (1729–1776)	Albemarle County
South Carolina	1663	Group of eight proprietors	Proprietary (1663–1729) Royal (1729–1776)	Charleston
New Jersey	1664	Lord Berkeley Sir Carteret	Proprietary (1664–1702) Royal (1702–1776)	East Jersey – Carteret West Jersey – Salem
Pennsylvania	1682	William Penn	Proprietary (1682–1776)	Philadelphia
Georgia	1732	James Oglethorpe	Proprietary (1732–1752) Royal (1752–1776)	Savannah

The colonies that developed on the eastern shore of what became the United States were proprietary, corporate, or royal colonies, depending on the kind of charter that was issued.

colony in America. He hoped to profit financially from such a venture, and he also wanted to establish a haven for English Catholics, who were an unhappy minority in Protestant England.

Charles I responded by giving Calvert the part of Virginia that surrounded Chesapeake Bay. Calvert gratefully named the colony Maryland in honor of Charles's Catholic Queen, Henrietta Maria. Calvert died while the charter was still being processed by royal bureaucrats. His son, **Lord Baltimore,** organized the expedition that left for Chesapeake Bay in 1633. There was no starving time because the Maryland settlers had learned from the sad experiences at Jamestown. They brought plenty of provisions with them and soon discovered that tobacco grew as well in Maryland as in Virginia.

The Calvert-Baltimore family had no desire to persecute Protestants in Maryland. As large numbers of Protestants settled in the colony, however, Lord Baltimore began to fear that the Catholics might become victims of religious persecution themselves. So in 1649 he requested that the Maryland legislature pass the **Toleration Act,** which provided for freedom of worship. After antagonism grew, the act was repealed in 1654.

The Carolinas, Pennsylvania, and Delaware.
From 1642 to 1649, England was torn apart by its great civil war between loyalists to the King and those who were loyal to Parliament, many of whom were Puritans. The armies of Parliament were victorious, and Charles I was executed in 1649. For a while, England became a commonwealth, or republic, headed first by Oliver Cromwell, a Puritan, and then by his son Richard. However, the English grew weary of the rather grim and sober Puritan rule, and in 1660 Charles II was restored to the throne of his father. Since Charles II owed political debts to his prominent supporters, he gave several of them proprietary rights to American land.

The first permanent settlement in Carolina—from the Latin for ''land of Charles''—was begun in 1670. Charles Town, which later became Charleston, was the capital and chief port of the colony. The weather proved too warm for tobacco but not for rice, which became Carolina's major crop. Later the colony split in two, and the King made both South Carolina and North Carolina royal colonies.

Pennsylvania was a gift to **William Penn,** whose late father had supported the King's return to power. Penn was a **Quaker.** The Quakers were a radical religious and social group of Protestants. They believed that a person's love of God could best be shown by brotherly love for every human being. They dressed plainly and would not raise

Map Skills

New York, New Jersey, Pennsylvania, Delaware • No

Picturing History
William Penn (above right) made peace with the Indians in 1682. Benjamin West idealized this event in this early-nineteenth-century painting.

Concluding the Chapter

Ask students to consider and comment on the interdependence between the colonies and England. (Possible responses: colonies needed manufactured goods from England; England needed raw materials from colonies.) Discuss with students the effects of interdependence between countries today. (Discussion might include: many countries are primarily self-sufficient today but still need some raw materials and fuel from other countries; countries that are dependent on each other have greater motivation to work out their difficulties than countries that do not depend on one another.)

their hats to nobles or even to the King. They used the terms "thee" and "thou" in a time when most people used the plural "you" when speaking to intimates. Lastly, the Quakers were pacifists, who disapproved of war and refused to serve in the army.

More than any other proprietor, Penn was interested in establishing a good and fair society. He did not want Pennsylvania to have a land-owning aristocracy. He wanted it to be a "holy experiment" in living. So he guaranteed every male settler fifty acres of land, which had to be purchased from the local Indians. He gave the right to vote to all adult males. Penn also helped plan the city of Philadelphia, which he called the City of Brotherly Love.

Penn's constitution also provided for a separate assembly for the three southern counties along Delaware Bay. Delaware thereby gained a somewhat separate existence. However, it continued to have the same governor as Pennsylvania.

Georgia. The last of the English colonies to be founded was Georgia, named after George II. It had a dual purpose. Its founder, a social reformer named **James Oglethorpe,** wanted to establish a refuge for people who had been imprisoned for nonpayment of debts. The English government wanted a military defense against the Spanish in Florida.

The Thirteen Colonies, 1750

Approximate area of settlement, 1750

Map Skills **Region** Which were the Middle Colonies? **Movement** Did the area of settlement reach the Ohio River in 1750?

SECTION 3 REVIEW

Key Terms and People

Explain the significance of: joint-stock company, charter, John Smith, headright system, indentured servants, burgesses, Puritans, Separatists, Pilgrims, Mayflower Compact, John Winthrop, proprietary colonies, Roger Williams, Anne Hutchinson, Sir George Calvert, Lord Baltimore, Toleration Act, William Penn, Quaker, James Oglethorpe

Main Ideas

1. How did joint-stock companies help to colonize America?
2. How did the colonists of Jamestown meet the goal of its founders?
3. What were the main Puritan religious beliefs?
4. How were the goals of the founders of the Plymouth and Massachusetts Bay Colonies similar?
5. How did the Rhode Island, Maryland, and Pennsylvania colonies attempt to promote religious tolerance?

Critical Thinking

6. In what ways did colonial rule promote governments independent of England?

State the Objective

Understand the organization of *The Americans* in order to use its features to enhance learning United States history.

Present the Lesson

Use your text, and have students use their texts, to look at each of the features described on these pages. Then call on a student to open his or her book to the first page of a unit and explain the relationship between the United States time line and the world time line. Have students turn to a chapter time line. Ask them what each chapter time line shows. (Answer: the major events they will be studying each week.) Do the time lines show all the events that took place in a given period? (Answer: no, only some important ones.)

Have another student turn to Chapter 2 "Links to Literature." Discuss possible reasons for including literature in a history book. (Possible response: literature provides another view of the past and a way to learn about the past even though all the incidents in the plot of a story may not have happened.)

Focus on Critical Thinking Skills

Using This Textbook Effectively

Understanding the Skill

Someone once described a textbook as a "fully portable, multi-purpose, readily accessed, user-friendly databank." Of course, the writer was using language that makes fun of the exaggerated claims put forward for some early computer programs. It is true, however, that a textbook can contain a wealth of information. Furthermore, once you master a few techniques, that information can be readily found. Here are some techniques to help you use this textbook most effectively.

Applying the Skill

• **Examine the Table of Contents.** *The Americans* is organized chronologically. Each chapter takes about a week to complete and each section within a chapter takes about a day to complete.

• **Scan the Links to Literature.** Each chapter begins with a short excerpt that makes a connection between American literature and American history. These selections from fiction provide insights into the culture and values of the people in each chapter.

• **Preview the unit and chapter time lines.** The unit time lines orient you to events that occurred in the United States and to events that occurred throughout the world during the time period covered in the unit. The chapter time lines

preview the major events covered in each week's work.

• **Preview the maps.** Note the Map Skills questions that accompany each map. These are designed to help you understand how geography is related to the people and events of history.

• **Study the section reviews.** These reviews will help you check your knowledge of the key terms and people and the main ideas in each section. They will also give you opportunities for critical thinking.

• **Examine the chapter and unit reviews.** The purpose of these reviews is to help you prepare for the chapter and unit tests by checking your knowledge of key terms, people, and main ideas; by providing you with the opportunity to answer critical thinking questions; and by summarizing the content of each chapter and each unit.

• **Preview the special features.** In each chapter you will find biographical features that will help you learn more about famous Americans. In addition you will find features that will help you understand, apply, and practice your skills in geography, in economics, in world history, in critical thinking, in researching and writing about history, and in interpreting primary sources.

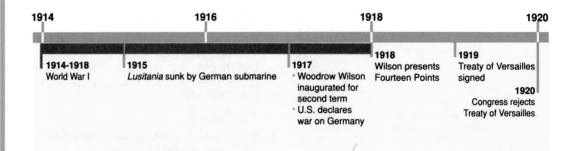

1914	1916	1918	1920

1914-1918
World War I

1915
Lusitania sunk by German submarine

1917
• Woodrow Wilson inaugurated for second term
• U.S. declares war on Germany

1918
Wilson presents Fourteen Points

1919
Treaty of Versailles signed

1920
Congress rejects Treaty of Versailles

Check for Understanding

Ask students to write answers to the questions at the end of the feature. Go over the answers. Then call on students to choose other features of the text, including the illustrations and the reference material at the end of the book, and describe the importance of this material for studying American history. (Responses should suggest the idea that the history of a country includes much more than events; history is affected by the geography, political leaders, famous people, and writings of a particular time. Responses should also point out the usefulness of reference material; for example, the table of contents provides an overview of the book, the index enables readers to quickly find specific material, and the Atlas in the back allows students to compare historical maps with present-day maps.)

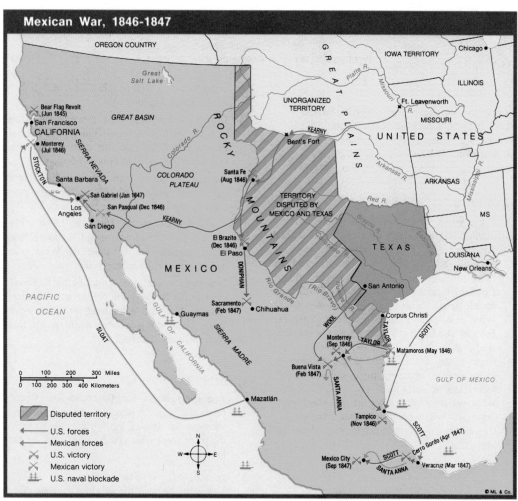

Mexican War, 1846-1847

Disputed territory
→ U.S. forces
← Mexican forces
⚔ U.S. victory
⚔ Mexican victory
⚓ U.S. naval blockade

© ML & Co.

Map Skills **Movement** From where did the American forces come to Buena Vista?
Location Where was the only Mexican victory?

FOCUS ON SKILLS

Answers

Practicing Your Skill

1. Global Time Line for Unit 1.

2. Chapter and Unit Reviews and Summaries.

3. Maps, map skill questions, and Focus on Geography features.

4. Critical thinking questions in each Section Review; nine skills features that explain critical thinking skills frequently used in history and provide exercises for applying and practicing these skills.

Map Skills

San Antonio, Corpus Christi • San Pasqual

• **Note the Chronology of American History on the end sheets of the book.** The end sheets inside the front and back covers of your book provide you with a chronological road map of American history. Refer to these for important events and milestones that will help you find the appropriate time period for the material you study in each chapter.

• **Examine the reference material at the end of the textbook.** Here you will find an atlas, a glossary, a gazetteer, special sections on the states and on the Presidents, and an index.

Practicing Your Skill

1. In what part of your book would you find out what events were going on in other parts of the world during colonial times?
2. What part of your book is designed to help you prepare for the tests on each chapter and unit?
3. What features of your book are designed to improve your knowledge of geography and to help you understand how geography is linked to history?
4. What parts of your book are designed to sharpen your skills in critical thinking?

Migrants to a New Land **33**

Answer Key

Key Terms and People

These are highlighted in the text in the order in which they appear in this list.

Main Ideas

1. Why—in search of food; when—between 35,000 and 25,000 years ago; how—walked across a land bridge in the Bering Sea; from where—Asia.

➤**2.** Central America's environment supported agriculture, especially corn cultivation. The Southwest's dry environment led the Indians to use irrigation and adobe apartment houses, or pueblos. The Northwest forests provided cedar for houses, canoes, and totem poles. The Arctic provided sea animals for boats, housing, food, tools, and light. The Great Plains buffalo provided food, houses, clothes, shoes, tools, and fuel for fires. The rich Eastern Woodlands provided materials for food, tools, weapons, and housing.

3. To find spices, gold, and glory and to spread Christianity. • The Norse may have sought adventure and a warmer climate.

4. Joint-stock company: people invested capital in a company and shared proportionately in the company's profits or losses; royal colony: a governor appointed by the king managed the colony; proprietary colony: the proprietors (owners) received the charter and collected rents from the settlers.

5. It established the ideas of majority rule and of political authority deriving from the will of the people. • Representative assemblies provided models for America's future self-government.

Critical Thinking Questions

➤**6.** Possible answers: *jail, prison, sluggish, undutiful, whipping-post, scourged, bitter-tempered, die, gallows, savage, inflexible, despera-*

does, animal ferocity. • Possible answer: Puritan life was hard. The Puritan conscience was rigid, constantly aware of evil, and full of guilt and the fear of punishment.

7. English colonists were committed to making this new land their home. Spain and France were more interested in making money.

8. Possible answer: Columbus was so committed to the search for spices, gold, and

glory and to the spread of Christianity that when he was successful at none of these, he died a bitterly disappointed man.

9. Corn (and other crops) nourished early people so that they did not need to search for food. They had time to develop a civilization.

10. Aztec influence was found in the Southwest groups' irrigation systems, in the corn, bean, and squash crops

grown almost everywhere in North America, and in the southeastern people's mud pyramids.

11. The resources of the woods made the Iroquois healthy and strong. They were well organized.

12. Vespucci first identified America as a new continent. • Columbus probably never realized that it was a new continent. • Possible other names: Columbia, Isabella,

---

CHAPTER **1** REVIEW

Write your answers on a separate sheet of paper.

Key Terms and People

Explain the significance of: Mayas, Incas, Plains Indians, League of the Iroquois, Renaissance, conquistadors, Hernándo Cortés, St. Augustine, Jacques Cartier, burgesses, Separatists, Pilgrims, Toleration Act, Quaker

Main Ideas

1. Why, when, how, and from where did the earliest migrants come to what is now called America?
2. How did the following environments mold the lives of American Indians living in them: Central America, Southwest desert, Northwest forest, Arctic, Great Plains, Eastern woodland?
3. What reasons did the Portuguese, Spanish, French, and English give for going to the new lands? Why did the Norse explore?
4. Explain the organization of the following: joint-stock companies, royal colonies, and proprietary colonies.
5. What was the importance of the Mayflower Compact? Why were the representative assemblies of the English colonies in North America important?

Critical Thinking Questions

6. **Analyzing Literature.** What words and phrases in the literary excerpt from Hawthorne's *The Scarlet Letter* give a feeling of dread? What is the author trying to tell you about life in Puritan New England?
7. **Drawing Inferences.** How did the English manage to hold North America in spite of the claims of the Spanish and French?
8. **Determining Motivations.** From Columbus's naming of the island in the Bahamas, his setting up of trading posts in the West Indies, and his dying with a broken heart, what can we deduce of his reasons for making four long ocean voyages?
9. **Formulating Hypotheses.** Why do you think the domestication of maize, or corn, was so important to early people? How did it help advance civilization?
10. **Drawing Inferences.** How do we know that the various North American Indian groups fell heir to arts and skills from the civilization in the central valley of what is now Mexico?
11. **Assessing Cause and Effect.** What factors caused the Iroquois to become the most powerful group in the Eastern Woodlands?
12. **Evaluating Decisions.** How did the new land come to be named for Amerigo Vespucci? Why did Columbus fail to name it? What other names might it have received?
13. **Drawing Conclusions.** Describe the headright system that the Virginia colony used to attract settlers. How did indentured servitude work? What social consequences might result from each of these systems?

Critical Thinking Activities

14. **Analyzing Maps for Chronological Order.** From the map on page 15, make a time line showing the date of the voyage, the explorer, the place from which each sailed, and the land he reached.
15. **Linking Past to Present.** Many English colonies were founded for religious reasons. What is the difference between the Massachusetts Puritans' idea of separation of church and state and that of Pennsylvania, Rhode Island, and Maryland? Which viewpoint has prevailed?
16. **Linking Past to Present.** As in the 1600's, many people in the modern world have chosen to leave their native land and go to a different country. What do you think would impel you to leave your home and go to a country where the language, culture, and environment were totally different from what you had been used to?
17. **Linking Past to Present.** Imagine living on a ship anchored off the shore of Cape Cod in the winter of 1620–1621. What could you do to avoid starvation, anxiety, and boredom?

and Nueva Espagne.

13. Under the headright system, the Virginia Company gave each man who paid his way to Virginia 50 acres of land and another 50 for each additional person whose passage he paid for. • An indentured servant worked for someone in the colony for a specified period of time in return for the passage to America. • The two systems made the wealthy wealthier and the poor poorer. Two social classes resulted.

14. c. 1000: Vikings—Stavanger, Scandinavia—Labrador or Vineland. 1492: Columbus—Palos, Spain—San Salvador in the Bahamas. 1497: Cabot—Bristol, England—Newfoundland or Labrador. 1499: Vespucci—Cadiz, Spain—coast of South America and West Indies. 1583: Gilbert—Plymouth, England—Newfoundland. 1609: Hudson—Amsterdam, Holland—coast of New York, New England. 1610: Hudson—London, England—Hudson Bay.

15. The Puritans allowed only Puritan leaders to be governing officials. The laws of Rhode Island, Pennsylvania, and Maryland provided for toleration of all religions and for separation of church and state.

• Separation of church and state.

16. Possible answers: curiosity, a spirit of adventure, economic need, the lure of career opportunities, avoidance of persecution.

17. Possible answers: hunt, ice fish, read, write, pray, socialize.

➤**Question suitable for co-operative learning.**

Migrants to a New Land

Many thousands of years ago, small groups of people who lived in Asia crossed a narrow strip of land that led to what is now Alaska. From that base, their descendants eventually settled in all of North and South America. These first Americans ate fruits, nuts, and small roasted animals. Later they learned how to hunt much larger animals and how to grow squash, beans, and corn.

In Mexico and Peru these people built major cities and road systems. In other places that are now parts of the United States, these people (usually called Indians) built towns, hunted, fished, farmed, and created huge mounds of earth for burying their dead. More recently, the Inuit, or Eskimo, people came from Asia and settled in parts of the Far North including what is now Alaska and Canada.

About one thousand years ago, people from northern Europe sailed across the Atlantic Ocean and landed on the northeastern shores of North America. Their discoveries, however, were nearly forgotten. Five hundred years later, people from southern Europe began to sail west, hoping to land in India, Japan, or China or on some large and important islands in the South Pacific. They did not know that they would find two large continents (North and South America) before they could ever reach those lands that they had heard about.

These Europeans wanted to find spices and gold and to convert everyone to their Christian God. They also thought that their explorations would make them famous. In this last goal they succeeded, and names such as Christopher Columbus and Ferdinand Magellan are now well known. During the early 1500's, Spanish soldiers marched into Mexico and into parts of Central and South America. French explorers did the same in the upper regions of North America.

The English found that most of the Americas had been claimed by other European nations. Therefore, they tried to settle on the Atlantic coast of North America. Several of their early colonies failed. The Virginia Colony finally succeeded, even though many people died there.

A few years later, large groups of deeply religious Puritan men and women sailed to New England. There they set up the Plymouth and Massachusetts Bay Colonies and formed other colonies as well. The Dutch settled in what later became the English colony of New York. Maryland was established as a refuge for Roman Catholics. North and South Carolina became royal colonies, but kept their representative assemblies. Quakers began the successful colony of Pennsylvania and welcomed people of all religions. The last of the thirteen English colonies to be founded was Georgia.

Chronology of Main Events

1492	Columbus lands at San Salvador
1513	Balboa discovers Pacific Ocean; de León discovers Florida
1534	Cartier explores St. Lawrence River
1565	Spain founds St. Augustine, Florida
1607	England founds and settles Jamestown, Virginia
1619	Virginia House of Burgesses first meets; first Africans brought to Virginia as indentured servants
1620	Mayflower Compact signed
1630	Puritans establish Massachusetts Bay Colony

Telescoping the Times may be used as an alternative to having students read the entire chapter, as a chapter preview, or as a chapter review.

35

Chapter 2 Teaching Strategies

Global Perspectives

1653-1658	Oliver Cromwell rules England.
1659-1661	India experiences severe drought and famine.
1665	Great Plague breaks out in London.
1685	Chinese ports open to foreign trade.
1689	William and Mary sign the English Bill of Rights.
1689-1725	Peter the Great westernizes Russia.

For Discussion

How might the opening of Chinese ports have affected European expansion in North America? (Possible response: Europeans, searching for faster and easier ways to reach China, explored much of North America in search of a Northwest Passage to Asia.)

Additional Teaching Strategies

SECTION 1

For Basic Students: Ask students in what way large Southern plantations were actually like towns. (Possible responses: plantations were almost self-sufficient; they had mills, storehouses, stables, docks, houses, and churches.) Have students write three sentences explaining why plantations became self-sufficient. (Possible responses: plantations were large and often far from a town; docks enabled farmers to ship their own crops; slaves were often trained to do work that would normally be done by artisans in town such as blacksmith, seamstress, etc.) Discuss students' answers.

For Advanced Students: Have students research and report on the rebellion led by John Culpepper in the Carolinas in the 1670's. (Reports should include: the acting governor of the Carolinas attempted to enforce the Navigation Acts, seized goods, and jailed the sea captains and a colonial leader who opposed him; Culpepper and followers seized and jailed deputy governor; rebels took over customs revenues, elected a new assembly, and elected Culpepper governor; Culpepper served for two years; was eventually tried and acquitted on charges of treason.)

SECTION 2

For Basic Students: Use the board to list the areas that served as the main sources of slaves for the colonies. (Areas include: West Africa; west coast of central Africa; West Indies; Barbados.) On a wall map, help students locate these areas. Give each student a copy of the world map in the Atlas in the back of this text and ask them to draw lines showing the routes used to bring slaves to the New World.

For Advanced Students: Ask students to prepare an imaginary diary kept by a sailor on a slave ship's voyage from Africa to the American colonies. (Diaries should include: reference to crowded, unsanitary conditions; diseases; expectations of life in America.) Have students share their diaries.

SECTION 3

For Basic Students: Ask students to review the section and to list on paper the chores done by each family member in the Northern colonies. (Lists might include: children—fetch firewood; women—spin cloth; men—clear fields, hunt.) Discuss basic jobs that family members must do today. Ask students to circle in red any jobs done in colonial times that are still done today. (Possible responses: cook, plant, build.)

For Advanced Students: Have students make posters or similar visual aids that illustrate the routes of colonial traders. (Posters should include: visual representations of the colonies, Africa, and the West Indies; the principle imports and exports of each; the trade routes.) Students should share their posters with the class. Post the projects in the classroom and encourage students to refer to them as they study Chapter 2.

SECTION 4

For Basic Students: Have students reread the text material under the heading "Seaports Prosper" and use the information to construct a street map of a typical seaport, including docks, shops, and homes. Display the finished maps and discuss how these cities differ from urban areas of today.

For Advanced Students: Ask students to assume the role of a reporter from a small Southern town and write an article describing a visit to the city of Boston. (Articles should include: information regarding housing, shopping, entertainment, crime and how these differ from life in the Southern town.) Have students share their articles with the class.

Further Reading for Students

Brooks, Geraldine. *Dames and Daughters of Colonial Days*. Salem, N.H.: Ager Publishing, 1974.

Lockridge, Kenneth A. *A New England Town: The First Hundred Years*. New York: W. W. Norton, 1985.

Madison, Arnold. *How the Colonists Lived*. New York: David McKay, 1980.

Perl, Lila. *Slumps, Grunts, and Snickerdoodles: How Colonial America Ate and Why*. Boston: Houghton Mifflin, 1975.

Tunis, Edwin. *Colonial Living*. New York: Thomas Y. Crowell, 1976.

Bibliography for Teachers
Books

Boorstin, Daniel, J. *The Americans, 1: The Colonial Experience*. New York: Random House, 1985.

Davidson, Basil. *The African Slave Trade*. Boston: Little, Brown, 1981.

Earle, Alice M. *Home Life in Colonial Days*. 1898. Reprint. Williamstown, Mass.: Corner House Publishing, 1975.

Wright, Louis. *The Atlantic Frontier: Colonial American Civilization, 1607-1763*, 1947. Reprint. Westport, Conn.: Greenwood Press, 1980.

Audio-Visuals

African Heritage. Pitman Publishing Corp. Filmstrip.

Building a Nation: The Story of Immigration. National Geographic Society. Filmstrip.

Colonial Expansion of European Nations. Coronet Films. Movie.

Pilgrim Adventure. McGraw-Hill. Movie.

Colonial America. American Heritage Publishing Co. Filmstrip.

Computer Resources

Time Liner Data Disk—Colonial Times. (Apple) Tom Snyder Productions. Educational Software.

U.S. History: Colonial Life. (Apple/Commodore 64/TRS 80) Focus Media, Inc.

Teacher's Notes:

Teaching Resources, Unit 1 Booklet

Lesson Study Sheets pp. 47-62
Daily Activities pp. 63-70
Enrichment Activities pp. 71-78
Reteaching Activities pp. 79-86
Chapter Review p. 87
Chapter Mastery Tests p. 89-100
Telescoping the Times Study Sheet p. 101

Chapter Objectives

Students will learn:
• the main class divisions in Southern colonial society
• the major reasons for the development of black slavery
• the differences between life in New England and the Middle Colonies and life in the Southern Colonies
• the diversity of colonial Americans

Using Time Lines
What important event held the attention of the British (see Unit 1 Time Line) during the decade that German immigrants were settling in Pennsylvania? (Answer: The Glorious Revolution took place in England in 1688.)

How many years passed between the founding of the colony at Jamestown, Virginia (see Chapter 1 Time Line) and Virginia's acceptance of slavery? (Answer: 83)

Picturing History Life in colonial America meant different things to different people. To the slaves, it often meant harsh treatment. To the family of the well-known artist Charles Willson Peale, painted above in 1773, it meant a relatively comfortable and prosperous life, however.

1650   1660   1670   1680   1690   1700

1676
Bacon's Rebellion

1682
Philadelphia founded

1683
German settlement begins in Pennsylvania

1689
Scotch-Irish settlement begins

1700
Slavery importation rapidly accelerates

Links to American Literature

Alex Haley: born in Ithaca, N.Y., in 1921; worked as a journalist for the Coast Guard from 1939 to 1959; traveled to the nation of Gambia in Africa to search for his heritage; was able to trace his family back seven generations to an African named Kunta Kinte who was enslaved and brought to Annapolis, Maryland, in 1767.

Writings include: *The Autobiography of Malcolm X* (1965), written anonymously and *Roots*, the story of Alex Haley's family which won a special Pulitzer Prize in 1977.

Introducing the Chapter

Ask students to skim the chapter and to make three separate lists of various religions, nationalities, and occupations common in the colonies in the second half of the seventeenth century. After independent reading, have a volunteer record the lists on the board. (Religions might include: Puritan; Mennonite; Lutheran. Nationalities might include: English; Dutch; African. Occupations might include: farmer; house slave; blacksmith; carpenter.) Ask the students to consider in which occupations the individual had the least control over his or her life. (Possible responses: African slaves; small

farmers.) Ask students to which group each would like to belong and why. (Possible response: Northern merchant because of the opportunity for wealth and power.)

CHAPTER 2 1650–1700

Colonial Life

Links to American Literature

He said that they saw stolen people chained inside long, stout, heavily guarded bamboo pens along the shore of the river. When small canoes brought important-acting toubob [white men] from the big canoes, the stolen people were dragged outside their pens onto the sand.

"Their heads had been shaved, and they had been greased until they shined all over. First they were made to squat and jump up and down," said Omoro. "And then, when the toubob had seen enough of that, they ordered the stolen people's mouths forced open for their teeth and their throats to be looked at." . . . *and stuck burning hot irons against their backs and shoulders. Then, screaming and struggling, the people were shipped toward the water, where small canoes waited to take them out to the big canoes.*

"My brothers and I watched many fall onto their bellies, clawing and eating the sand, as if to get one last hold and bite of their own home," said Omoro. "But they were dragged and beaten on." Even in the small canoes out in the water, he told Kunta and Lamin, some kept fighting against the whips and the clubs until they jumped into the water among terrible long fish with gray backs and white bellies and curved mouths full of thrashing teeth that reddened the water with their blood.

— ALEX HALEY, *Roots*

As you have seen from the previous chapter, there were many life styles in colonial America. One group of colonial Americans were slave traders who viewed their job—the acquisition, transportation, and sale of slaves—as just a business activity. Moral issues were not a consideration. Gradually, however, some people began to recognize the moral issues involved and felt strongly enough about social justice to make their voices heard.

Chapter Overview

In this chapter you will learn about the main class divisions in Southern colonial society, the major reasons for the development of black slavery, and the differences between life in New England and the Middle Colonies and life in the Southern Colonies. In addition, you will learn about the diversity of people who lived in colonial America. This chapter reveals a constant theme in American history—different regions and different social classes in our country have special interests that often conflict. Chapter 2 describes life in colonial America in four sections.

Chapter Outline

1. **The South Is a Divided Agricultural Society**
2. **Slavery Flourishes in the South**
3. **The North Develops Commerce**
4. **Colonial Life Is Diverse**

Anticipate the Lesson

Help students locate the Tidewater, Coastal Plain, Piedmont, and Appalachian Mountains on a wall map. Ask students to name the geographical differences between the Piedmont and the Tidewater areas. (Possible response: the Tidewater contains deep rivers; the Piedmont is a plateau of forests and hills.) Ask students to speculate on how life would have differed in these two areas as a result of the geographical differences. (Possible response: Tidewater would have offered more transportation and opportunities for commerce; Piedmont would have had more small, isolated farms.)

State the Objective

Describe the main class divisions of Southern colonial society.

SECTION 1

The South Is a Divided Agricultural Society

GLOSSARY TERMS: **cash crops, staple crops, Tidewater, Piedmont**

Every colony had to find products to export. In the South, food consumed on the plantation was usually grown there. In addition, **cash crops** were grown and were sold for a profit so that colonists could buy manufactured goods. Most of the Southern Colonies had one or two major agricultural products called **staple crops.** These were raw materials that had fairly large and constant markets. Virginia and Maryland had found a staple crop in tobacco. Colonists in South Carolina cultivated rice and later indigo, a blue-purple dye. North Carolina's principal exports were wood and wood by-products from its pine forests.

Large Farms Characterize the Southern Landscape

Large Farms. By 1650 Virginia had developed some of the characteristics that would mark its history. People were not settling in towns but on large plantations, or farms, scattered along the James River. Much land was needed to grow tobacco profitably. Tobacco quickly uses up the minerals in the soil, so farmers had to use new land when old fields became exhausted.

These large plantations were located next to rivers, so there was little reason for towns to develop. There was no need for city dock facilities because planters shipped their goods directly from the plantation to the Northern Colonies and to Europe. There was no need for city warehouses because goods could be stored on the plantation. Finally, because many of the goods that merchants might sell in a town were made on the plantation, there was no great need for shops, bakeries, and markets.

Cheap Labor. Tobacco farming called for lots of workers, and Virginia got them in the form of indentured servants. Hundreds of young single men and women came over from Europe to seek their fortunes in Virginia.

Perhaps as many as one-third of all white settlers in the Southern Colonies came as indentured servants. During a servant's term of indenture, he or she could be sold from one owner to another. Servants were treated miserably at first, and some were almost worked to death. Masters had the legal right to whip their servants for any kind of disobedience, and they did so often. If a servant died as the result of this "reasonable correction," the master could not be tried for murder.

As the years went by, however, the treatment of servants improved. After all, the colonial assemblies did not want to discourage the flow of servants from England. The assemblies passed laws giving servants certain rights and protections. Laws required masters to supply their servants with clothes, tools, and in some cases free land at the end of their terms.

People in the Chapter

Nathaniel Bacon was arrested for treason, but Virginia governor Berkeley accepted Bacon's admission of guilt and pardoned him. Berkeley lived to regret this decision, however, since Bacon returned to drive the governor and his forces out of Jamestown and then burned the settlement.

Sarah Kemble Knight set out on horseback for a trip from Boston to New York. In her journal she noted that the people of Connecticut were overly zealous in their punishment of "young people guilty of a harmless kiss or innocent merriment."

John Winthrop, called the Moses of New England, shared his vision with his fellow Puritans aboard ship as they sailed to Massachusetts. "[W]e shall be a city upon a hill," he said. "The eyes of all people are upon us."

William Penn was imprisoned in the Tower of London for his writing on the Quaker religion. While there he wrote a moral tract entitled *No Crosses, No Crown.*

Present the Lesson

On the board list the characteristics of large plantations and small farms in the South during colonial times. (List might include: plantations—located near rivers, usually grew tobacco or other cash crops, used many indentured servants; small farms—had less fertile soil, were subject to economic hardships resulting from low prices, had few indentured servants.) Ask students how differences between plantations and small farms contributed to social and political unrest. (Possible re- sponses: power was held by wealthy planta- tion owners; poor farmers were taxed heavily; only large landowners could vote.)

Thus a single cash crop, large farms, cheap and plentiful labor, and a mild climate began to produce a few wealthy tobacco planters who led a leisurely existence. For some of these planters, the road to riches was traveled swiftly. One colonist wrote to his friend in Holland:

> Now that your Lordship may know that we are not the veriest [worst] beggars in the world, our cow keeper here of James City on Sunday goes accoutered [dressed] all in flesh flaming silk; and a wife of one that in England [had been a miner] wears her rough beaver hat with a fair pearl hat band, and a silken suit.

Bacon's Rebellion Has Four Main Causes

The differences between the few rich and the many poor became especially important in Virginia. Some seventy years after the colony was founded, these differences contributed to a major conflict known as Bacon's Rebellion. The main causes of this conflict, which occurred in 1676, involved not only social differences but also the right to vote, the levying of taxes, and, especially, the treatment of Virginia's Indians.

Tidewater Versus Frontier Farmers. Under the headright system, any man who paid his way to Virginia got fifty acres of land and an additional fifty acres for each person he brought with him. Thus men who could afford to buy servants received more land than anyone else. More land and more servants meant that more tobacco could be raised. More tobacco brought larger profits with which the planter bought even more servants, and for each one the planter received another fifty acres. Consequently, there emerged in Virginia a powerful and wealthy aristocracy of planters. Their plantations were generally located along the James, Potomac, Rappahannock, and York rivers in an area known as the **Tidewater.**

Tidewater Virginia is the stretch of land along the Atlantic coast that extends some seventy-five miles inland. It is so named because these deep rivers are made slightly salty by the tides from the Atlantic Ocean. Beyond the Tidewater lies the **Piedmont**—a plateau of forests and rolling hills. To the west of the Piedmont are the Appalachian Mountains. (See map on this page.)

When all the good land in the Tidewater was occupied, poorer people, ex-servants, and newly arrived immigrants moved westward into the Pied-

Southern Colonies: Land Regions

Map Skills   **Region**   The Tidewater area extends from Virginia into what other state?   **Region**   How wide is the Piedmont area at the Potomac River?

mont. The younger sons of Tidewater planters also had to move on because of a system that entitled the eldest son to inherit his father's entire estate. The soil of the Piedmont hills was less fertile than that of the Tidewater. Also, Piedmont farms were often smaller. As a result of these two conditions, life in the Piedmont was much more difficult than life in the Tidewater. The small farmers on the western edge of the colonial settlements were very susceptible to economic hardships resulting from low prices. During the 1660's, the price of tobacco declined. The decline in price seriously hurt the farmers in the Piedmont.

Unfair Taxes and Voting System. At the same time, by law, taxes fell most heavily on poor people. Some wealthy members of the governing council paid very little tax. The Piedmont people bitterly resented this arrangement. Also, in Virginia only large landowners could vote. The small farmers of the backwoods areas had no vote. In fact, the colony's government was run by wealthy men largely for their own benefit. Large planters

For Discussion
What were the four main reasons for Bacon's Rebellion? (Answers: social differences; right to vote; taxes; Indian relations.) Which might still be reasons for citizens to demand change? (Answers: social differences; taxes.) How might these problems be solved? (Possible responses: letters to legislators; boycotts; demonstrations.)

 Map Skills
North Carolina • About 40 miles (60 km)

Check for Understanding

Have students write the answers to Section 1 Review questions on paper. Review their answers.

Guided Practice

One cause of Bacon's Rebellion was what many considered inequity in the tax laws. Using the graduated income tax as an example, tell students how tax laws sometimes benefit particular economic groups. (Possible example: tax deduction for mortgage interest favors homeowners.)

Assign Independent Practice

Have students complete Chapter 2, Section 1 Enrichment Activity.

made all the decisions about who could own what land. They passed tax laws that favored the rich and hurt the poor. Moreover, it seemed as if the situation would never change. In the Northern Colonies the governments were elected every year, thus giving people a chance to correct government abuses. In Virginia, though, the governor had not permitted an election in fourteen years. He kept the members of the House of Burgesses loyal to him by giving them opportunities to make money from their government positions.

Linking Past to Present

One source of Bacon's Rebellion was the inequity in Virginia's tax laws. Tax laws that favor the wealthy continue to be an issue today. President Ronald Reagan's 1986 tax reform bill—one he called "the most sweeping overhaul of our tax code in our nation's history"—actually increased the proportion of the nation's wealth owned by the top 10% of the population. (See Chapter 36, Section 1.)

Disagreement over Indians. The greatest disagreement between the planter aristocracy and the hill farmers, however, was about the Indians. Virginia's long-time governor, crusty old William Berkeley, looked upon Indians as subjects of the King. Accordingly, he believed it was his duty to protect them against attack by settlers. The governor had another reason for treating the Indians with

care: he and his wealthy friends had a profitable fur-trading arrangement with them. They did not want the trade disturbed.

The poorer people of the backwoods, though, lived much nearer to Indians and to Indian lands. They thought they did not have enough land of their own. They wanted more land from the Indians, and they preferred to fight for it rather than buy it. Bloody encounters broke out as Indians and settlers attacked each other. Many small farmers demanded that Governor Berkeley send soldiers for their protection. The governor refused to do so and warned the backwoods settlers to respect the rights of Virginia's Indians.

In 1676 some settlers attacked a group of friendly Indians and drove them farther away from the white settlements. The attack was led by **Nathaniel Bacon,** a young man of some wealth and good social connections. In fact, Bacon was a cousin of Berkeley's. However, one of Bacon's overseers had been killed by the Indians, and he sympathized with the problems of the backwoods farmers.

The Rebellion Collapses

Anger at the Virginia government now boiled over. Bacon and his armed farmers and ex-indentured servants marched on Jamestown to demand that the government protect them against the Indians and hear their other grievances. Months of chaos followed. Bacon burned Jamestown as Berkeley and his followers fled. Indentured servants ran away from their masters. Probably about one hundred colonists died in the fighting. Bacon died of a fever, and the leaderless rebellion collapsed.

Picturing History An unknown artist painted this picture of a New York farm as it appeared nestled in the valley of the Catskill Mountains in the early 1700's.

Student Assignment/Homework

Have students read Section 2, "Slavery Flourishes in the South," and answer Section 2 Review questions orally.

SECTION 2
Core Lesson

Anticipate the Lesson

Ask students to recall and share with the class times when they have not been free to make their own decisions. (Possible responses: being responsible for housework or babysitting when they would rather be with friends; having a curfew.) Ask two or three students to define the word *slave* on the board. (Possible definitions: a person who is the property of another; a person who has no freedom.)

To stimulate discussion, ask several students to explain how their experiences above differ from those of slaves in colonial America. (Possible responses: students are not owned as property; they are free to make many choices in their lives; they will eventually grow up and be on their own.)

Bacon's Rebellion was the first popular uprising in the American colonies. It was a rebellion against a government that taxed the people but did not serve their needs in the matter of protection. The rebellion did not succeed. The established wealthy planters remained in control of political affairs. They learned a lesson, though. Indentured servants were a rising political force. Furthermore, they had proven dangerous, especially because most of them owned guns. Fearing future uprisings of indentured servants, the planters turned to a different group of laborers—black slaves.

SECTION 1 REVIEW

Key Terms and People

Explain the significance of: cash crops, staple crops, Tidewater, Piedmont, Nathaniel Bacon

Main Ideas

1. How did plantation society replace the need for towns in the South?
2. What conditions in Virginia helped to create great wealth for a few tobacco planters?
3. How did the headright system contribute to the formation of class divisions in Virginia?
4. What differences between Piedmont farmers and Tidewater farmers led to Bacon's Rebellion?
5. Why did Bacon's Rebellion cause planters to turn to African slaves for their labor needs?

Critical Thinking

6. How did the cultivation of tobacco help to create class divisions in Virginia?

SECTION 2

Slavery Flourishes in the South

GLOSSARY TERMS: **middle passage, overseer, artisans**

Slavery existed in all the English colonies in America, not just in the South. The Dutch in New Netherland owned slaves, and the English continued the practice after New Netherland became New York. The first African slaves came to Massachusetts from the West Indies in 1638. South Carolina settlers brought slaves with them from Barbados. Even the Quakers of Pennsylvania had slaves.

Slavery was different from indentured servitude in four important ways. First, the master of a slave did not own just the slave's labor, as was the case with an indentured servant. The master literally owned the slave as a living piece of property, in the same way he might own a horse. Second, slavery was for life, not for a term of years. Third, the children of slaves automatically became slaves themselves. Fourth, children, fathers, mothers, and other family members were often separated and sold individually.

Slavery Develops Gradually

The English colonists did not plan to establish the institution of slavery. It developed gradually. This explains why historians do not agree on exactly when it began.

We do know that in South Carolina, Indians were enslaved from the earliest days of the colony. Occasionally, English settlers enslaved Indian prisoners of war. More often, Indians sold captives from enemy tribes to the English. However, most of the captives were difficult to control. Captive Indians had friends and relatives still living nearby. They knew the paths back to their own lands. They had far better knowledge of the fields and forests than the English did. The Indians could slip away easily, and they were hard to find. English slaveholders knew about these difficulties, so they shipped many Indian slaves to the West Indies where they were exchanged for African slaves.

From the colonial point of view, Africans made better slaves. Once in the colonies, Africans were completely cut off from their homeland. Also, they were much more used to farming than the Indians were. So eventually, slavery in the colonies became black African slavery.

SECTION 1 REVIEW
Answers

Main Ideas

1. On plantations, people produced their own goods, provided their own services, stored their own crops, and shipped their crops directly to market.

2. Conditions included a single cash crop, large farms, cheap and plentiful labor, and a mild climate.

3. Those who could afford to buy servants received more land than anyone else. More land brought greater tobacco yield and thus greater wealth.

4. Piedmont farmers were of a lower social class than Tidewater farmers, were taxed at a much higher rate, could not vote, and viewed Indians as their enemies in the fight for more land.

5. Black slaves replaced indentured servants, who had proved to be disloyal and dangerous during and after the rebellion.

Critical Thinking

6. Profitable tobacco cultivation required much land and many workers. Thus, those who could afford these resources profited enormously, whereas those who could not afford them barely survived. **(analysis)**

State the Objective

Identify the major reasons for the development of black slavery.

Present the Lesson

On the board list the characteristics of indentured servants and of slaves. (List should include: indentured servants—served a specified number of years, many volunteered to become indentured servants in return for passage to America; slaves—usually served for life, were brought by force.) Point out to students the differences between the two. Ask students why the Indians were more difficult to enslave than were the Africans. (Possible response: Indians knew the land better than the English did and had friends and relatives nearby to help them escape.)

Check for Understanding

Call on individual students to read and answer questions from Chapter 2, Section 2 Daily Activity.

Slavery did not become widespread in Virginia until after 1690. At that time there were an estimated three thousand black Africans and fifteen thousand white servants out of a total population of seventy-five thousand. Only a few black Africans were free. They had been freed by their masters, sometimes for faithful service, sometimes because they became Christians, but most often because their masters were not used to the idea of slavery.

African Slave Trade Begins

A number of African people were kidnapped in their homeland and then transported to America in 1619. They were sold as slaves to the English settlers in Virginia. At first the term of servitude was limited. However, by about 1660, other enslaved Africans were serving for life. The Maryland and Virginia assemblies began passing laws that recognized the existence of lifetime slavery.

After 1700, thousands of Africans were transported to and enslaved in the American colonies. By 1760 African people made up about 20 percent of the colonial population. (That was a higher proportion than today's figure of about 12 or 13 percent.) In the South at least 40 percent of the non-Indian population was African.

The African Homeland. African slaves came only from certain parts of Africa. In this respect they were like early European migrants to the Americas. Both groups left from the western parts of their continents. Most Africans came from West Africa and the western coast of central Africa. Although they lived near the coast, most Africans were not maritime peoples. Unlike so many of the English, they did not choose to venture far out to sea. They were basically lovers of the land. Many, however, were skilled boatmen who operated canoes on rivers and along the coastal waters.

The people of West Africa belonged to many different ethnic groups. They spoke more than one hundred distinct languages. Each language group had its own system of government and religion, and each was aware of being a distinct people. Except for a few Islamic Africans, the slaves who came to America were people of the spoken rather than the written word. Although their languages differed, they shared a common musical style—a similarity of beat and rhythm that served as an important means of communication on slave ships and in the colonies.

Lineage. There had been large empires in West Africa between the years 1000 and 1450, but they had collapsed before the Western Europeans arrived in the 1400's. Most West Africans were living in tribal units somewhat similar to those of the American Indians. They felt that lineage was their most important social unit. A lineage consisted of people who were related to one another by blood or marriage. Often the lineage was thought to include all people descended from a single, mythical ancestor. The lineage included all those relatives who had died and all those yet to be born. For most Africans, one of the worst things about slavery was separation from one's lineage.

Slavery in Africa. Slavery had existed in West Africa prior to the coming of the Europeans. In African societies, however, slavery was quite different from that in colonial America. For example, there was little plantation slavery in Africa. Slaves occupied a wide variety of positions, and most of them had legal rights. Some slaves were household workers, while others worked alongside their owners in the fields. Some were soldiers, often making up an elite unit. There were even slaves who served as governors of regions. People became slaves in Africa because they had been kidnapped, were prisoners of war, or were poor people seeking a protective master. No one in Africa ever became a slave just because he or she happened to be black.

African rulers and merchants sold slaves to European slave traders. Then, as slavery became a growing business, African chieftains began to create a larger pool of slaves. Crimes were invented as a justification for selling people into slavery. Many war prisoners from enemy African tribes were sold to the Europeans. Of course some slaves were captured directly by European sailors. However, such kidnapping was dangerous for Europeans because local African rulers were in a good position to take revenge. For the most part, European slave traders dealt with the powerful chieftains of the coast. Europeans did not go far inland and did not even settle on the African coast for long.

The Voyage. Conditions during the voyage to America were horribly brutal. Once purchased by European traders, slaves were branded by red-hot irons and herded into the holds of slave ships. Men and women were packed into separate holds. As you can see from the picture on page 44, they lay jammed side by side below deck, often without

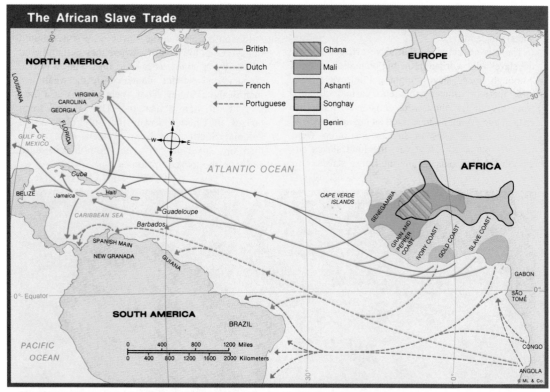

The African Slave Trade

← British	Ghana		
◄--- Dutch	Mali		
← French	Ashanti		
◄--- Portuguese	Songhay		
	Benin		

NORTH AMERICA

EUROPE

LOUISIANA
VIRGINIA
CAROLINA
GEORGIA
FLORIDA
GULF OF MEXICO

ATLANTIC OCEAN

AFRICA

Cuba
BELIZE
Jamaica · Haiti
Guadeloupe
CARIBBEAN SEA
Barbados
SPANISH MAIN
NEW GRANADA
GUIANA

CAPE VERDE ISLANDS

SENEGAMBIA
GRAIN AND PEPPER COAST
IVORY COAST
GOLD COAST
SLAVE COAST

GABON
SÃO TOMÉ

0° Equator

SOUTH AMERICA

BRAZIL

CONGO

ANGOLA

PACIFIC OCEAN

0	400	800	1200 Miles
0	400 800	1200 1600	2000 Kilometers

© ML & Co.

Map Skills   Movement At what Caribbean islands did many black Africans stop on their way to the Southern Colonies? **Movement** What country brought slaves to Louisiana?

enough space to roll over. Many died, especially when disease swept through the vessel. Some slaves spent months under such conditions. Storms during the Atlantic crossing meant closed hatches and air heavy with the smell of sweat, blood, vomit, and body wastes.

The survivors of this voyage, known as the **middle passage,** arrived in the colonies in a state of shock, grief, horror, anger, and bewilderment. Many felt relieved to escape the terrible conditions aboard ship, even though they found themselves in the hands of white men whose language and ways they could not understand.

Slaves Learn Skills in Virginia and Maryland

In Virginia and Maryland slaves were sold in small groups, often at the river landing of a wealthy planter. The slaves then walked to clearings in the woods, where rows of plants were pointed out to them and familiar-looking hoes were thrust into

their hands. Their new homes were single-room cabins standing at the end of the tobacco fields and cornfields. Usually they were many miles from their owner's house. Their work and their lives were directed by a white **overseer.** By night the overseer slept in one of the cabins, on the only mattress. By day he beat the slaves when they did not understand his orders or pretended not to. They were almost completely isolated.

Since there were few towns in Virginia, many of the jobs usually found in towns were done on the plantations instead. The slaves who did these jobs, most of whom were Virginia-born, were **artisans.** Artisans are people skilled in a trade—usually one in which they use their hands. Among the Virginia artisans were blacksmiths and carpenters. They regarded their skills with pride and usually knew more about their work than the overseers did. Unlike the field laborers, most of whom were African-born, the artisans were not under constant supervision. They had considerable independence and mobility. A carpenter, for example, might be

Assign Independent Practice

Have students write two paragraphs comparing the conditions of slaves in Virginia and Maryland to those in South Carolina. (Paragraphs may include: some slaves in Virginia and Maryland were taught trades and became skilled artisans, were mobile and somewhat independent; slaves in South Carolina were mainly unskilled, worked on rice farms, had less contact with whites and more contact with other slaves, and so they retained more of their African heritage.)

Student Assignment/Homework

Have students read Section 3, "The North Develops Commerce," and complete Chapter 2, Section 3 Enrichment Activity.

For Discussion
How did trade contribute to the successful growth of the colonies? (Possible response: gave colonies a market for raw materials and enabled them to buy manufactured goods that could not be manufactured in the colonies.)
Why is trade between countries important today? (Possible responses: everyone benefits when each country grows or produces items that best use its natural resources, trading the surplus to other countries; through trade each country then obtains products that it cannot produce or grow itself.)

sent more than twenty miles away to build a cabin or an outhouse on one of the planter's smaller parcels of land.

There is no evidence that slave artisans envied the slaves who worked in the big plantation houses. Although house slaves might get leftovers from their master's dinner table and castoff clothing from his family, they were constantly under his critical eye. What he perceived as laziness, forgetfulness, or mistakes in housework often were severely punished. However, the field slaves envied the skilled artisans and the house slaves.

Most Slaves in South Carolina Remain Unskilled

In South Carolina the slaves were concentrated in the coastal low country, where they outnumbered whites by as many as nine to one. This was rice country, and the rice planters were the wealthiest men in the colonies. They spent months at a time away from their plantations. They owned town houses in Charles Town, the only city in the colonial South. The lives of their slaves were therefore somewhat different from the lives of slaves in the tobacco colonies.

STOWAGE OF THE BRITISH SLAVE SHIP "BROOKES" UNDER THE

REGULATED SLAVE TRADE

Act of 1788.

Picturing History
A British naval officer painted this watercolor of the deck of a slave ship in 1846. It shows the conditions typical of the entire slavery era. The diagram at the left shows how it was possible to lock up over four hundred people in a single ship.

Core Lesson

Anticipate the Lesson

Ask students to relate any interesting travel experiences regarding foods, customs, and people. How were these experiences different from what the student was used to? (Possible responses: food was strange; language was not understandable.) Students should provide specific examples of how the differences made them feel. (Possible responses: out of place; scared; excited; interested.) Ask students to compare their experiences with those related by Sarah Kemble Knight. What similarities do they see? (Possible responses: different foods and customs, unusual people.)

State the Objective

Learn the differences between life in New England and the Middle Colonies and life in the Southern Colonies.

The slave artisan class in South Carolina was small because there were a number of skilled white craftsmen in Charles Town. The typical rice plantation was relatively large, requiring a minimum of thirty slaves. Rice-country slaves had less contact with whites and more with each other. The planters were wealthy enough to purchase them in large groups off the slave ships arriving in Charles Town. This meant that sizable numbers of slaves from the same ship, and even from the same African tribe, ended up living on the same plantation. As a result, they remained more African in culture than slaves elsewhere in the colonies. They began to speak a language of their own, called Gullah. It was a mixture of English and various West African languages. White overseers had to learn it.

The technique of growing rice was complicated, and the English settlers were unfamiliar with it. Fields had to be flooded and then drained at precisely the right time. They probably learned the technique from African slaves who had cultivated rice in their homeland. This need for flexibility may explain why the rice country had a unique pattern of work for slaves. Rather than being worked from dawn until dusk, slaves were simply assigned a certain amount of work that was to be done on a given day. When slaves finished their tasks, they could quit work. Many did so by mid-afternoon.

SECTION 2 REVIEW

Key Terms and People

Explain the significance of: middle passage, overseer, artisans

Main Ideas

1. How did slavery differ from indentured servitude?
2. Why did white Southerners prefer African slaves over American Indian slaves?
3. How did slavery in Africa differ from slavery in America?
4. How did artisan slaves differ from those who were field laborers?
5. How were the lives of rice-plantation slaves different from those of tobacco-plantation slaves?

Critical Thinking

6. In what ways was slavery a brutal system?

SECTION 3

The North Develops Commerce

GLOSSARY TERMS: New England Colonies, Middle Colonies, Southern Colonies

Life in the **New England Colonies** and in the **Middle Colonies** developed differently from life in the **Southern Colonies** (see the map on page 31) because the economy was different. There was no single staple crop. Settlers in New England and the Middle Colonies developed a wide variety of goods that could be sold at home and traded abroad. The story of New England's early experience shows this development.

A Triangle of Trade Develops

Many Puritan migrants brought money with them. Already-established settlers were happy to sell the Puritans corn, pigs, and other provisions to help them get established. In 1642 the great flow of migration was stopped by the outbreak of the English civil war. Immediately, New England suffered its first economic depression.

Very soon, however, a triangle of trade developed among Africa, the West Indies, and the American colonies. As John Winthrop put it, "The Lord opened up a trade with the West Indies." The great sugar boom was just getting under way in the Caribbean islands. Slaves were beginning to pour into the West Indies, where they worked the sugar cane fields. New Englanders shipped salted meat, corn, butter, and other foods to the islands. Like settlers in North Carolina, the New Englanders also sold lumber, barrels, candles, and horses to the islands. From the waters off New England and Newfoundland came fish of every variety. The scraps that could not be sold elsewhere were shipped off to West Indian planters to be fed to their slaves.

In return, New England merchants received precious cash from wealthy sugar cane planters who had earned it by shipping molasses and sugar to England. Ships from Boston and other smaller ports also returned with sugar and its less expensive by-product, molasses. West Indian molasses became the usual sweetener for New England townspeople and farmers. Molasses could also be distilled into a throat-warming liquor we now call rum.

Answers

Main Ideas

1. Slaves were owned as property, unpaid, and slaves for life; slaves' children automatically became slaves. Indentured servants labored for a specified period of time in exchange for something.

2. African slaves were familiar with farming and were easier to control, having been completely cut off from homeland, family, and friends.

3. In Africa there was little plantation slavery, slaves held a wide variety of positions, and most slaves had legal rights. In America, the opposite was true.

4. Artisans were mostly Virginia-born, were skilled workers, and had some independence. Field laborers were mostly African-born, not considered skilled, and subject to constant supervision.

5. Rice-plantation slaves had less contact with whites, retained more tribal ties and more African culture, and were allowed greater flexibility in their work patterns.

Critical Thinking

6. Possible answer: free people were enslaved on the basis of race alone; neither slaves nor their children could free themselves from the system, slaves were transported and lived under inhuman conditions, and slaves' lives were completely controlled. **(analysis)**

Check for Understanding

Ask students to answer Section 3 Review questions orally.

Guided Practice

Discuss with students the fact that a great deal of the slave trade was carried on by New England Puritans, many of whom were personally opposed to slavery. Ask students how slave traders might have reconciled these differences between their beliefs and their actions. (Possible response: traders separated

Historical Sidelight

Iron nails were very valuable during the colonial period. Some colonists, before moving, burned down their homes to retrieve the valuable iron items.

Picturing History Colonial shipwrights were skilled carpenters who not only built ships, but also repaired them.

Shipping Becomes Important

Puritan sea captains guided their vessels into the rivers and harbors of other colonies. They sold guns, tools, nails, glass bottles, and kitchen utensils. At first they obtained these articles from England. As the years went by, however, artisans of New England began to manufacture some of these goods.

New England ships became important to the British Empire's merchant marine. They carried staples from the Southern Colonies to England and southern Europe and ventured to Africa for slaves. Shipbuilding became one of the most important industries in New England. Some of these ships were sold along with their cargoes when they reached London or some other English port.

Most People Farm

Although many towns sprang up in the North, the great majority of people there were still farmers

whose lives involved long hours and hard work. Children worked at least part time from the age when they could be shown how to shell peas, shuck corn, or fetch firewood. Women performed an unending round of tasks. They cooked in metal pots that were hung over open fireplaces. They baked in hollow compartments in their chimneys, which served as ovens. They spun rough cloth and sewed it into clothing for the family. They washed clothes and bedding in wooden tubs with soap they made themselves from wood ashes called pearlash. (Pearlash was also used to bleach cloth.)

Men did most of the heavy outdoor work. They cleared fields by using horses, oxen, or mules to drag away heavy stones, logs, underbrush, and tree stumps. They sowed the seed, prayed for rain, chopped the weeds, and then prayed for clear skies at harvest time. After the harvest, they had time to build sheds, cut fence rails, mend the harnesses for the horses, trap raccoons, fix the chimneys, and help the women teach the children to behave, work, read, and pray. This heavy workload for everyone left little time for leisure.

Compensations. There were compensations, however. There was very little paperwork or, indeed, paper of any kind. There were practically no bills to pay. Goods and services were usually exchanged on the spot, between people who often knew each other very well. Often no cash was involved. Credit normally depended on one's reputation with a peddler, an owner of a tiny general store, or a neighbor.

Taxes—whether imposed by the town, county, or colonial government—were a nuisance but were tolerated even when they seemed too high. Northern farmers knew exactly what they were paying for. Taxes might be used to help support several widows and perhaps six or seven orphans in the town. They would pay the minister's salary. They would pay the travel costs of the town's two representatives to the colonial assembly. The farmers voted annually for these representatives and therefore had a sense of control over, or at least of participation in, the process of government.

Compared to farmers in Europe, American farmers were prosperous. They had a far better chance of obtaining land of their own than did farmers in England. Because land was so easy to get, American farmers did not have to cultivate it as carefully. They could abandon farms when the soil wore out and move farther west.

Assign Independent Practice

Have students write three paragraphs focusing on these questions: Why was slavery not suited to conditions in the North? Why did few cities and commercial centers develop in the South? What possible problems might have been the result of these two different life styles? (Responses might include: North did not produce tobacco or rice; many plantations were self-sufficient. Problems may include: taxes and import regulations.)

Student Assignment/Homework

Have students read Section 4, "Colonial Life Is Diverse," and answer Section 4 Review questions on paper.

City Woman Describes Country Customs

Whether people moved west, north, or south in the early 1700's, travel was difficult. In 1704 Sarah Kemble Knight took a five-month trip from Boston to New York, staying at farms and country inns along the way. She reflected on her experiences in a journal in which she described people she met. When she arrived at one inn to spend the night, the innkeeper asked her a lot of impertinent questions:

I told her she was quite rude to ask all those questions. Finally she led me to a parlor in a little shack in the back. It was almost filled with the bed. It was so high, I was forced to climb on a chair to get up to the wretched bed.

In the morning the woman brought me something to eat. It was like a twisted cable, but very white. Then she put it on a board and began to pull at it. When it began to spread, she served with it a dish of pork and cabbage. Over it she poured a purple sauce. She also gave me some Indian bread (cornbread). I was hungry but still had trouble eating this.

Next day I went to a merchant's house (store). In comes a tall country fellow. His mouth was full of tobacco. These people keep chewing and spitting as long as their eyes are open. The fellow went into the middle of the room. He nodded and spit quite a lot. These people generally stand around saying nothing when they first come into a store. I think they stand in awe of the merchant.

Picturing History Colonial fireplaces were used for warming the home and for cooking.

Picturing History A warehouse on the wharf forms the backdrop for this engraving of a colonial merchant engaged in buying and selling goods for a profit.

SECTION 3 REVIEW

Key Terms and People

Explain the significance of: New England Colonies, Middle Colonies, Southern Colonies

Main Ideas

1. How was the triangle of trade among the American colonies, the West Indies, and Africa profitable to the American colonies?
2. Why was shipping important to the colonies?
3. What hardships did Northern colonial farmers face?
4. What compensated Northern colonial farmers for their hardships?

Critical Thinking

5. How did the economic growth of the New England and Middle Colonies make life there different from life in the Southern Colonies?

Answers

Main Ideas

1. It opened up new markets for colonial goods and brought precious cash into the colonies.

2. It allowed colonial goods to reach both colonial and worldwide markets; shipbuilding became a profitable industry in New England.

3. Hard work, long hours, and little leisure time.

4. Farmers were largely debt free, were fairly taxed, and had the right to participate in government. Land was plentiful and easily obtainable and did not have to be carefully cultivated.

Critical Thinking

5. Towns, ports, merchants, cash, and shipping became more important in the Northern Colonies because of the wide variety of goods developed for trade with markets outside of North America. Thus, slavery and single cash crops became less important. **(analysis)**

Anticipate the Lesson

On the board compile a list of various ethnic groups that live in the U.S. (List may include: English; Mexican; Indian; Russian.) Explain to the students the difference between a heterogeneous and a homogeneous group. (Definitions: heterogeneous—having a different origin, a variety or diversity; homogeneous—having a common origin, all the same.) Ask students to identify some of the advantages and disadvantages of a diverse population. (Advantages might include: exposure to different foods, customs. Disadvantages might include: language barrier; isolation if the groups do not mix or share ideas.)

State the Objective

Recognize the diversity of people who lived in colonial America.

SECTION 4

Colonial Life Is Diverse

GLOSSARY TERM: **militarism**

By 1700 only about 5 percent of the colonial population lived in cities. All of these cities were seaports, because the sea was the highway to the larger world. Boston was the largest city. Philadelphia and New York were second and third in size but would soon surpass Boston. Charles Town, South Carolina, and Newport, Rhode Island, were the fourth and fifth largest cities. (See the map on page 31.)

Seaports Prosper

Many people who lived in the country never saw a city. Those who did were astounded by the crowding and the bustle. Many streets were actually paved with stones. Later, some of the streets were even lit by oil lamps.

Let us look at a colonial city on a typical day in 1700. A visiting farmer's wagon is only one of many that creak and rattle through the narrow streets. Most wagons are piled high with corn or wheat, vegetables or fruits, boards or firewood. Now and then a brightly painted gentleman's carriage slowly makes its way through the traffic. Dogs yap and nip at the horses and oxen. Pigs and an occasional goat jostle for the garbage in the streets. Small herds of sheep and cattle move along their unknowing way to slaughterhouses. Hundreds of screaming seagulls circle overhead, waiting to feed on refuse from the slaughterhouses. More gulls circle the masts of the sailing vessels that are tied up at the wharves or lying at anchor in the harbor. The gulls await more stinking garbage from the ships or the arrival of a loaded fishing vessel.

Hundreds of doorways beckon the curious visitor. One could tell a good deal about what goes on behind these doors just by peering through the windows on either side or by watching people going in and out. Gentlemen wearing wigs and accompanied by well-dressed women visit the silversmith's and the clock merchant's shops. Ship captains visit the chandler's shop to purchase clocks, telescopes, and ship fittings of all kinds. Weather-beaten mates clamber ashore from their longboats on their way to sail lofts, where sails are made, and ropewalks, where ropes are made. The buildings in which the sailmakers and rope makers work are much larger than the meetinghouses in the country villages.

There are many items to tempt a visiting farmer. Goods just off the ship from England are offered for sale in the shops of grand merchant gentlemen. There are bells, buckles, brass buttons, books, copper kettles, music boxes, iron nails, and steel knives. There are heads for axes and heads for hoes. (Farmers make their own handles.) There are hinges, pulleys, hooks, and harness fittings. There are glass bottles filled with medicines and scents. There are sweet-smelling spices, expensive oils, rolls of silks and satins, and rolls of a more humble cloth made of linen and wool or cotton and wool called linsey-woolsey.

Picturing History A sign painter's view of Philadelphia in 1720 shows a thriving city on the shore of the Delaware River. Many Scotch-Irish immigrants settled here in the early eighteenth century.

Present the Lesson

Ask students to compile lists of the various ethnic groups mentioned in this section and share their lists with the class. (Lists should include: Germans, Scotch-Irish, Swedes.) Ask students what advantages and disadvantages these groups might have faced in colonial America. (Possible responses: language barriers; prejudice; lack of education; overcrowding in cities; unemployment.)

Check for Understanding

Call on individual students to read their answers to Section 4 Review questions. Test students' understanding by having them complete Chapter 2, Section 4 Daily Activity.

Guided Practice

Have students consider why some immigrant groups are more readily accepted into a country than others. Ask them what immigrants might do to become part of their new country. (Possible responses: learn new language; adapt their clothing styles; try to learn customs.)

Picturing History Colonists twisted plant fibers called hemp to manufacture rope. Ropewalks such as the one above could be found in almost every colonial town.

Everyone seems to be busy in the city—even the rich. The merchants work long hours. They supervise their account books, write out instructions for ship captains, and correspond with their agents in other colonies, in the West Indies, and in London.

Cities Face Urban Problems

Along with the prosperity, there were problems in the cities that did not exist in the countryside. For example, by 1700 all the cities had exhausted their local supplies of firewood. This early energy crisis was met by bringing wood in from greater and greater distances. There was also the problem of crime. Cities had no regular police forces, and part-time watchmen tried to keep the peace. Much of the crime was caused by the large temporary population of sailors found in most of the seaports.

There was little sanitation at first, but generally things were better than in parts of London and Paris. In Europe, where space was a problem, people out in narrow streets had to keep alert. When they heard the warning cry of ''gardyloo!,'' they had to spring out of the way to escape garbage descending from windows of houses that loomed

up on each side. In colonial cities, pipes for drinking water and for sewers eventually were put under the ground.

Fires were a menace because the wooden houses were packed so tightly together. At one time or another, every colonial city suffered a terrible fire that wiped out entire sections. Because there were no regular firefighters, citizens organized volunteer firefighting units. So great was the fire danger that as early as 1646 the Massachusetts legislature banned smoking within five miles of any town.

Immigrants Bring Varied Abilities

All immigrants had to pass through one of the colonial ports. This influx lent additional sounds, liveliness, and interest to these cities. During the 1600's, most immigrants came from England, but soon they were outnumbered by Africans and people from other European countries. Among the latter were the Germans and the Scotch-Irish.

The Germans. The first German immigrants arrived in the 1680's from the western part of Germany. Most were attracted to Pennsylvania by William Penn's successful advertising campaign. Penn had sent paid agents into the countryside of western Germany to attract settlers to his new colony. The agents stressed Penn's policy of complete religious freedom and the availability of free land.

Not surprisingly, the first group of German settlers were members of religious groups with views similar to those of the Quakers. Soon other religious groups came, including Lutherans and **Mennonites.** The latter were hardworking, frugal, and pious people who were against **militarism** (warlike policies and attitudes) and who left Europe to escape it.

Most of the Germans were peasants and very poor. Because they could not afford to pay their way across the Atlantic, they sold themselves into

Picturing History The detail in this picture was taken from a notice about a meeting of New York City's Hand-in-Hand Fire Company held around 1750.

For Discussion

Compare and contrast the problems faced by urban areas in the 1700's with those faced by urban centers today. (Possible responses: both are crowded and have sanitation and crime problems; cities in 1700's were menaced by fires, whereas cities today are menaced by air pollution.)

Historical Sidelight

The Pennsylvania Dutch are descendants of Germans who suffered religious persecution. The term "Dutch" is a variation of the term "Deutsch," which means "German."

Assign Independent Practice

Have students complete Chapter 2, Section 4 Enrichment Activity.

Student Assignment/Homework

Have students complete the Chapter 2 Review on paper and go over their answers in class.

Concluding the Chapter

Divide the class into four groups to discuss the causes of conflict between the colonies. Assign each group one of the following areas of conflict: taxation, religion, slavery, property rights. Ask students to discuss how the conflicts might have been resolved. Ask students to determine whether the diversity of colonial life strengthened or weakened the colonies and to give reasons for their conclusions. (Possible responses: strengthened colonies because they became less dependent on England to support them; weakened colonies because each colony wanted prosperity for it-

---

SECTION 4 REVIEW

Main Ideas

1. They were busy, crowded places filled with shops, businesses, homes, and wagons.
2. A lack of firewood, inadequate fire and police protection, and substandard sanitation.
3. Germans—immigrated for religious reasons; most were indentured servants; placed greater value on their German language and culture than on learning English and the American culture. Scotch-Irish—immigrated for economic reasons; many were indentured servants; as native English speakers, adapted more readily to American culture.

Critical Thinking

4. The new immigrants made colonial culture more diverse in terms of nationality, language, religion, and customs.
(analysis)

---

indentured servitude. Ship captains bought their labor on one side of the Atlantic and sold it on the other. Actually, the ship captains sold only the survivors of each voyage, because many passengers died at sea in the holds of the overcrowded vessels. Sometimes the survivors were forced into extra years of servitude in order to pay back the cost of passage of their dead relatives.

Many of the Germans took no active interest in Pennsylvania politics. They tended to keep to themselves and often did not even bother to learn English. They set up German language schools and newspapers. Partly because of their skillful use of fertilizer, they were the most productive farmers in colonial Pennsylvania. From German farms came great quantities of wheat, barley, rye, beef, and huge hams. German cattle produced a surplus of hides, which were made into tanned leather goods or exported raw to the European market.

The Scotch-Irish. By 1700 large groups of Scotch-Irish began arriving. They came to most of the colonies south of New England. Like the Germans, though, the great majority landed in Philadelphia.

The **Scotch-Irish** were themselves the descendants of migrants. Their ancestors had been moved by Queen Elizabeth I of England and by her successor, James I, from lowland Scotland to the province of Ulster in northern Ireland. The monarchs had wanted to drive out the native Catholic Irish in Ulster and replace them with the Protestant Scots. Although their religious beliefs were much like those of the Puritans, the Protestant Scots were usually called Presbyterians. In Ulster the Scotch-Irish had prospered at the expense of the native Roman Catholic Irish. In the 1700's, however, economic depression struck northern Ireland. Tens of thousands of Scotch-Irish set off for a better life in America. Many came as indentured servants.

Linking Past to Present

Today violence still stalks Northern Ireland in the ongoing conflict between Catholics and Protestants. In 1989, scattered riots marked the twentieth anniversary of the arrival of British troops in Ulster.

In Pennsylvania most Scotch-Irish took up farming in frontier areas. There they soon got the reputation of being quick tempered, particularly with the Indians. As their numbers grew, many Scotch-Irish, as well as some Germans, moved southward from Pennsylvania into the western parts of Maryland and Virginia. Later they moved still farther south, into the backcountry of the Carolinas. The Scotch-Irish were accepted more quickly by their colonist neighbors than the Germans were, probably because they spoke English—though with a distinct accent.

A Variety of Peoples. Descendants of the Dutch in New York and northern New Jersey made up another large ethnic group. There were a number of smaller groups as well. French Calvinists fled persecution at home and settled in various American cities. A group of highland Scots as well as a few Irish Catholics settled in North Carolina. A small number of Jews, some from Portugal, settled in such cities as Newport and Philadelphia. Descendants of Swedes and Finns still lived around Wilmington, Delaware, along the banks of the Delaware River. This tiny colony of New Sweden was annexed by the Dutch in 1655.

All these different peoples, the forerunners of millions more who were to come, gave a rich and permanent character to American life. The variety of peoples and religious groups astounded European visitors to the American colonies. Only New England lacked this wide assortment of peoples.

SECTION 4 REVIEW

Key Terms and People

Explain the significance of: Mennonites, militarism, Scotch-Irish

Main Ideas

1. How did the atmosphere of seaport cities reflect their prosperity?
2. What were the main urban problems of colonial cities?
3. Compare the main characteristics of German immigrants with those of Scotch-Irish immigrants.

Critical Thinking

4. How did the influx of European immigrants in the late 1600's and early 1700's affect American colonial culture?

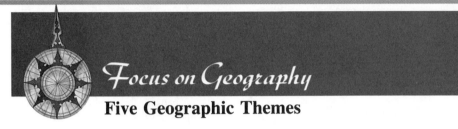

State the Objective

Understand the five geographic themes.

Present the Lesson

Across the top of the board write the five geographic themes. Divide the class into small groups of four or five students. Have each group define each of the five geographic themes. Then, using the Atlas maps of North America at the back of the book and students' current knowledge, have each group work together to find an example of each theme. Ask one student from each group to share the group's examples with the class. At the same time have another student from the group write each example on the board under the appropriate theme. (Possible responses: Location—students should give the absolute location of a place, for example, Denver, at 40° N longitude and 105° W latitude; students should also give the location of their example by telling where it is in relation to other places; for example, Denver is on the western edge of the Great Plains and the eastern edge of the Rocky Mountains. Place—students' examples should include special features that are physical, such as the humid climate of Virginia, as well as special features that relate to human characteristics, such as the Indian trails across much of the United States, many of which later became paved roads. Human-Environment Interactions—students should refer to how humans influence their environment, for example, the acid rain that results from industrial pollution and the lakes formed by damming rivers. Movement—student answers should refer to the movement of goods, ideas, and people from one location to another, such as the movement of goods due to trade or the spread

Focus on Geography

Five Geographic Themes

"I'm not so sure, in my own mind, that this country would have been involved in Vietnam to the extent that it was if our leaders had had an articulate knowledge of geography." With these words, Gilbert M. Grosvenor (grōv′ner), president and chairman of the National Geographic Society, stressed the importance of the study of geography and indicated how closely geography is linked to history.

The study of geography begins with the building blocks of location and place. *Location* can be defined as the place on the Earth where a feature such as a mountain range or a city is. Maps help us locate places precisely by providing coordinates of latitude and longitude. Knowing where places are located is just one level of geography, however. Other levels of geography include knowing why places are in particular locations and how these places influence the lives of the people who live there.

Geographers and students of geography can move from one level of geographic knowledge to another by using the five basic themes of geography. These themes are location, place, human-environment interactions, movement, and region. These themes will be developed throughout your study of American history in an effort to help you organize your knowledge about geography and about America's past.

When the first colonists landed in America, they had many questions that involved geography. Where were they? What were the physical characteristics of the land? Could they learn to live off the natural resources of the land? Could they farm and produce goods here as they did in Europe? Would it be easy to travel about the land to explore the new region? Would they be able to carry on trade with their homeland in Europe? As they found the answers to these questions, they were forming geographic concepts that centered on the five basic

Picturing History The Catskill Mountains line the western shore of the Hudson River in New York and form one of the most picturesque regions in the state.

of an idea like democracy or communism. Region—student examples should refer to an area on the earth's surface that has unifying characteristics, such as the United States or the American Southwest.) Discuss how the students chose their examples.

Ask students how conditions relating to the geographic theme of movement have changed in America over the past two hundred years. (Possible responses: the speed at which people, ideas, and goods move today; the great distances and volume that have resulted from improvements in transportation and communications.)

Map Skills

34°N, 78°W • (1) Each region shares a geographical location, such as New England, Middle Colonies, or Southern Colonies, and (2) each region shares a coastal location on the Atlantic Ocean.

geographic themes. They wrote accounts of this new knowledge and sent them to Europe. People there read the accounts and gained their first insights into the geography of America.

Location. Location answers the question *where*. Absolute and relative locations are two ways of describing *where*. For example, the Spanish colony of San Miguel de Gualdape (sän′mē gel′ də quäl′dä pä) in North Carolina dates back to 1526. The absolute, or exact, location of San Miguel de Gualdape can be determined by looking at a map and finding the colony's latitude and longitude. You will see that the location is near Wilmington, North Carolina. San Miguel de Gualdape's relative location describes where it is in relation to other places. By looking at a map of the thirteen American colonies, you can see that this Spanish colony was farther south than the English colony of Jamestown, Virginia, which was established in 1607.

Place. All places have special features that distinguish them from other places. Geographers describe places by their physical and their human characteristics. Physical characteristics include such elements as climate, soil, natural vegetation, bodies of water, and landforms. The colonists who arrived in Jamestown, for example, found luxuriant forests that were clear of undergrowth. The climate was humid and temperate. The land adjoining the James River was swampy, with no open fields. Since they could have a harbor there, they decided the site must be a safe place to establish their colony.

The human characteristics of geography include such elements as ownership and use of the land, communication and transportation networks, language and religious beliefs, and architecture. For example, about 125,000 Indians resided along the Atlantic seaboard at the beginning of the seventeenth century. The American Indians farmed, gathered wild fruits and berries, hunted, and fished. Most lived in villages varying in size from 50 to 200 inhabitants, with clearings of land all around them. The Indians had governments and social controls. They revered the earth and regarded the land as a possession of all people. Many tribes befriended the early settlers and shared the land and its bounty with them.

Human-Environment Interactions. All places have advantages and disadvantages with regard to human settlement. People interact with their environments and try to change them to their advantage. Geographers study the consequences of these changes for people and for the landscape.

The Indians changed the landscape by their farming techniques. Around their houses they had square plots of cleared ground upon which they grew tobacco, pumpkins, and squash. They burned off these fields each year after harvest, thus returning nutrients to the soil. By this means the same field could be used for up to twelve years. They also learned that they could increase important nutrients in the soil by growing beans along with corn. The Indians also practiced the "slash and burn" technique of burning forests to improve the soil's fertility. The lush grass that regrew attracted grazing animals that they could hunt.

Picturing History The sixteenth-century watercolor paintings of the explorer John White are valuable representations of the American Indians' interactions with their environment. Bodies of water provided the Indians with a source of food and a means of travel.

Check for Understanding

Call on students to answer the questions at the end of the feature. Then ask students to find questions that colonists asked about geography at the beginning of the feature and to identify the geographic theme related to each question. (Answers: (1) Where were they?—location. (2) What were the physical characteristics of the land?—place. (3) Could they learn to live off the natural resources of the land?—human-environment interaction. (4) Could they farm and produce goods here as they did in Europe?—human-environment interaction. (5) Would it be easy to travel about the land to ex-plore the new region?—movement. (6) Would they be able to carry on trade with their homeland in Europe?—movement.)

When crop yields diminished, the Indians would move to another site within the same general area and start new fields. The worn-out cleared fields that they left behind were referred to as "Indian old fields" by the colonists.

How did the Indian methods of land use affect the colonists? Their methods provided the settlers with a place to live because the land had already been cleared and abandoned. However, because forests were depleted, timber for building homes and making implements was not readily available. The colonists sometimes had to travel considerable distances to obtain their timber. Indian land use was, therefore, a disadvantage as well as an advantage to the colonists.

Movement. People living in different environments experience surpluses and shortages of different products, information, and ideas. To get what they do not have, people move and interact with each other through travel, trade, and communication. Understanding the movement of goods, people, and ideas is one of the five themes of geography.

Trade is an important motive underlying the geographic theme of movement. When the colonists first settled in America, they found that their ships could not carry enough supplies to sustain the new settlements for any length of time. The Indians supplied the colonists with food and furs in exchange for tools and trinkets. Later, the Indians would trade land for European manufactured goods.

Region. A region is an area on the Earth's surface that is defined by certain similar and unifying characteristics. These characteristics can be human or physical. By defining a region as large as Africa south of the Sahara or as small as a neighborhood, geographers can obtain information about the area and study it in greater depth.

The original thirteen colonies can be considered a political region. This region can be further divided into the New England, Middle, and Southern Colonies. As you study these three early regions, you will learn how each developed its own unique unifying characteristics.

Understanding Geography

1. What are the five basic themes of geography?
2. How can each of the five themes be used to study American history?

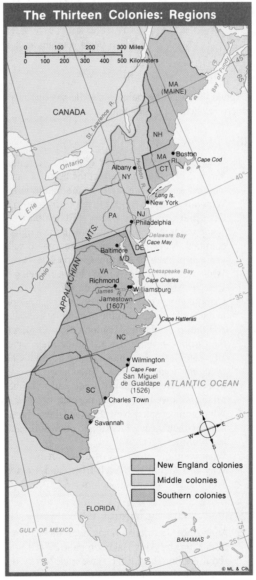

The Thirteen Colonies: Regions

New England colonies
Middle colonies
Southern colonies

© ML & Co.

Map Skills **Location** Give the absolute location of San Miguel de Gualdape. **Region** Explain two unifying characteristics of the regions.

3. Define the following terms: location, movement, region.

Critical Thinking

4. Give an example from your daily life of each of the following terms: place, human-environment interactions.

Answers

Understanding Geography

1. Location, place, human-environment interactions, movement, and region.

2. Location and place can be used to explain where things are; human-environment interactions can explain relationships within places; movement and region can explain how these places influence the lives of the people who live there.

3. Location—a position on the earth's surface that answers the question *where;* movement—understanding how goods, people, and ideas move and interact through trade, travel, and communication; region—an area of the earth that has certain similar and unifying characteristics.

Critical Thinking

4. Examples will vary but should include these elements: place—a description of the physical or human characteristics of a student's community; human-environment interactions—an example of how people in the community have changed their environment in some way. **(application)**

Answer Key

Key Terms and People

These are highlighted in the text in the order in which they appear in this list.

Main Ideas

1. Tobacco. • Needed much land and many workers to make profit. Self-sufficient plantations replaced the need for towns and city warehouses. • Indentured English servants.

2. Piedmont farmers protested (1) uneven distribution of wealth, (2) their lack of voting rights, (3) unfair taxes, and (4) lack of government help against Indian attacks.

3. Indentured servants—had chance to come to colonies despite poverty; some abused by cruel masters. Indian slaves—not separated from homeland; found escape easy. African slaves—had farming skills; were owned for life.

4. Slaves in Africa—usually war prisoners or unemployed; did many different jobs, both high and low; often had legal rights; were not separated from lineage or homeland.

5. Maps should show all thirteen colonies, Boston, New York, Newport, Charles Town, Philadelphia, and Triangle partners. Arrows should show: from Africa—slaves, gold, pepper; from Caribbean— sugar, molasses, gold, silver, fruit, wood; from New England—rum, iron, lumber, grain, fish, meat, furs, whale oil.

6. Little paperwork, little need for money because of bartering, acquaintance with their neighbors; participation in government; easy access to land ownership.

7. Lack of firewood, police and fire protection, and adequate sanitation at first.

8. Germans—for religious freedom and free land in Pennsylvania; Scotch-Irish—for economic improvement; French Calvinists—to escape persecution.

Critical Thinking Questions

➤**9.** Slaves treated with unjustifiable cruelty. • Possible answer: to show European power over Africans.

10. The preexistence of slavery in West Africa; local wars in which one group was enslaved; realization that ruler could make profit on slavery.

11. In Virginia—slaves on tobacco plantations used as farmhands, skilled workers, and house servants. In South Carolina—slaves used only for cultivating rice.

12. Puritans were intolerant of other religions.

13. Farm life: hard work but a strong community. City life: more variety but greater chance of crime and fire. Possible answers: farm life—more adventurous; city life—easier.

➤**14. Northern Colonies:** 1. people—mostly English, some pacifists; 2. farms—small; 3. products—varied; 4. slavery— not important; 5. foreign trade—necessary; 6. cities— important seaports; 7. representative assembly—yes.
Southern Colonies: 1. people—mostly English; 2. farms—huge; 3. products— one staple cash crop; 4. slavery—necessary; 5. foreign trade—necessary; 6. cities— only one, Charles Town; 7. representative government—yes. Possible answers: alike—both settled mostly by English and

---

CHAPTER 2 REVIEW

Write your answers on a separate sheet of paper.

Key Terms and People

Explain the significance of: middle passage, overseer, artisan, Mennonite, militarism

Main Ideas

1. What was the staple cash crop of Tidewater Virginia? How did this affect the need for farm workers and the life style on the plantations? Who did the farm work in early Virginia?

2. Give four reasons for Bacon's Rebellion.

3. Name the three sources of labor in the English colonies. Name one advantage and one disadvantage of each of the three sources.

4. What were some differences between being a slave in Africa and being a slave in America?

5. Using the map on page 31 and the information in the book, make a simple map of the colonies and the triangular trade among New England, the Caribbean, and Africa. On the map, label all colonies, the major cities, and the triangular-trade partners. Then draw arrows that show the direction of trade and tell what products flowed from each partner.

6. What compensated New England farm families for their heavy workload, poor soil, and harsh climate?

7. What were the problems of urban areas?

8. Why did German, Scotch-Irish, and French Protestants come to the colonies?

Critical Thinking Questions

9. **Analyzing Literature.** What does the excerpt from *Roots* by Alex Haley on page 37 tell you about the brutality of the slave trade? Why do you think the Europeans were so brutal?

10. **Analyzing Causes.** What factors in Africa caused slavery to take hold there?

11. **Comparing Life Styles.** Compare the uses of slaves in Virginia with those of slaves in South Carolina.

12. **Analyzing Cause and Effect.** Only Massachusetts lacked a diversity of people. Why was this so?

13. **Comparing Life Styles.** Compare life on colonial New England farms with life in the seaport cities. In which type of community would you prefer to have lived? Give reasons.

14. **Comparing and Contrasting.** Do you think the Southern and Northern Colonies were more alike than unlike? Base your answer on (1) the type of person who settled in each, (2) the size of farms, (3) staple crops and products, (4) the importance of slavery, (5) the importance of foreign trade, (6) the number and size of cities, and (7) whether they had representative assemblies. Make a chart of this information.

Northern Colonies	Southern Colonies

15. **Analyzing Causes.** What might have been done to prevent Bacon's Rebellion? Why were these measures not taken?

16. **Analyzing Cause and Effect.** Name several causes for the increase in the importation of African slaves in the 1700's.

17. **Making Generalizations.** What special skills were brought by these immigrants: Quakers, Germans, Scotch-Irish, Puritans, Africans?

Critical Thinking Activities

18. **Linking Past to Present.** What were the black slaves able to bring from Africa? How has this served them in the twentieth century?

19. **Linking Past to Present.** What does the map on page 43 tell you about how far-reaching the slave trade was? What does this show about how slavery was regarded at that time? What has happened in the nineteenth and twentieth centuries to change our attitude?

20. **Linking Past to Present.** The Northern colonials were divided between those living on farms and those who lived in cities. Do you think the differences between these two groups play as important a role in politics today as they did in colonial times? Explain.

had English-style representative government; unlike—had great life style differences.

15. Possible answer: could have set up fairer taxes and given Piedmont farmers voting rights, but wealthy landowners, who made such decisions, would not approve; the governing council might have helped the farmers, but it did not want to disrupt the fur trade that it conducted with the Indians' help.

16. Indentured servants—uncontrollable; Indian slaves—able to escape; African slaves—easier to manage and had more farming skills.

17. Quakers—skills in social harmony; Germans—farming skills; Scotch-Irish—self-sufficiency on the frontier; Puritans—skills in representative government and English common law; Africans—ability to survive, cultivate rice, create music and special

rhythms; all but the Puritans—tolerance.

18. Talent for music and rhythm. • Possible answer: led to the rich gospel and jazz music of today.

19. Every European nation that had a navy was engaged in the slave trade. • Many regarded it as acceptable or at least a necessary evil. • Gradually, reformers have reeducated American attitudes and demanded that civil rights be

extended to all.

➤**20.** Possible answer: each group looked after its own self-interests then as it does today. Neither group identified with the problems of the other. Today, most state legislatures are divided along urban and rural lines.

➤**Question suitable for co-operative learning.**

Colonial Life

Not long after the English colonies were established, it became apparent that two very different life styles were developing in the northern and southern colonies. A divided agricultural society developed in the South as both rich plantation owners and poorer frontier farmers sought land. Virginia and Maryland became known as the tobacco colonies. Large farms but few towns appeared there. The rivers of the area served as the main roads. In the early years, indentured servants did most of the farm work.

In 1676 Bacon's Rebellion broke out in Virginia as a result of the frontier farmers' discontent about taxes, voting, and the generous treatment of the Indians. Although the rebellion was put down by Virginia troops, it showed that Virginians were not a united people.

Slavery existed in all the colonies, but it became a vital source of labor in the South. Most slaves in South Carolina remained unskilled, working most often in the rice fields. In the tobacco colonies there was greater demand for slaves to learn skills such as carpentry. The great majority of slaves had been kidnapped from or captured in West Africa. Then they were sold to European slave traders and shipped across the Atlantic Ocean under extremely brutal conditions. Some of these victims had been slaves in West Africa, but few had known the kind of forced labor that developed on American plantations.

The New England and Middle Colonies did not rely on single staple crops such as tobacco or rice. Most people were farmers, but they grew a wide variety of crops. A smaller number of workers made all kinds of products, such as candles, iron bars, ropes, and sailing ships. The New England Colonies traded actively with the islands of the West Indies. In addition to foods, they exported all kinds of other items ranging from barrels to horses.

In return, they imported sugar and molasses. All this trade resulted in the growth of small towns and larger port cities, for the ocean was the great highway of commerce.

The port cities were busy and prosperous places. There were dozens of different kinds of shops and other buildings. Farmers brought food in from the countryside. Women worked at a variety of jobs. Sailors and fishermen seemed to be everywhere. Much more than England, America had a great diversity of peoples. Groups of immigrants often passed through the port cities. The two largest groups were the Scotch-Irish and the Germans, but there also were many other immigrants from Europe and even a few free African Americans. Yet there were problems. House fires often spread to whole sections of towns. Firewood for heating and cooking was scarce.

Chronology of Main Events

1650	Virginians have begun to settle on plantations along the James River
1655	New Sweden annexed by the Dutch
1670	Charleston founded in Carolina
1676	Bacon's Rebellion
1682	Philadelphia founded
1683	German settlement begins in Pennsylvania
1689	Scotch-Irish settlement begins
1700	African slaves begin arriving in large numbers

Telescoping the Times may be used as an alternative to having students read the entire chapter, as a chapter preview, or as a chapter review.

Global Perspectives

1637	Russian explorers cross Siberia to reach the Pacific.
1689	English Parliament passes Bill of Rights.
1695	England ends press censorship.
1697-1698	Peter the Great becomes first Russian Tsar to travel to Europe.

For Discussion

How might the colonists have viewed the passage of the Bill of Rights in England? (Possible response: as protecting their rights as well as those of Englishmen living in England.)

Additional Teaching Strategies

SECTION 1

For Basic Students: Have students look up the term *scalping* and prepare for a class discussion on the subject. Students should determine who originated the practice and why it became so important. (Discussion might include: scalping is the cutting or tearing of the skin of the scalp from an enemy, either alive or dead; it was believed to bestow the power of the victim on the victor and served as a trophy; scalping among American Indians was originally practiced mainly by tribes in small areas of eastern U. S.; it was practiced in Europe by ancient Visigoths and Franks and in Asia by the Scythians.)

For Advanced Students: Ask students to assume the role of King Philip's followers and prepare a petition to the King of England. The petition should explain the war in New England from the Indian point of view and request the King's aid against the Puritans. (Petitions might include: massacre at Mystic River; unfair seizure of Indian lands; Puritan attempts to regulate rules and customs of Indian life; continued attempts to convert Indians to Christianity.) Have students share their petitions with the class.

SECTION 2

For Basic Students: Have students prepare a chart similar to the following that lists the main products traded between Europe, North America, and Africa.

	Europe	N. Amer.	Africa
import			
export			

(Charts should include the following: colonies exported whale oil, tar, fish; imported manufactured goods, sugar. Europe exported manufactured goods; imported tobacco, masts, meat, fish. Africa exported slaves, gold; imported rum, iron.) Discuss how each benefited from trade. (Discussion might include: trade improved and balanced the economy of all; each country could obtain needed materials and profitably dispose of excess materials.)

For Advanced Students: Ask students to prepare a one-page report on colonial trade and relations with England, giving special attention to the rule of Oliver Cromwell as Lord Protector. (Reports might include: Cromwell gained control of Parliament and was given the title of Lord Protector of England in 1649; ruled in a military dictatorship from 1649 until his death in 1658; pursued a vigorous colonial policy in cooperation with the Puritans and had an aggressive commercial policy.) Have some students read their reports to the class.

SECTION 3

For Basic Students: Have students create on posterboard a two-column chart which shows the powers and limitations of a colonial governor in North America in 1696. (Chart should include: powers—call or disband assemblies, appoint councils, veto laws; limitations—colonists paid salary, assembly controlled taxes.) Discuss how these powers and limitations affected colonial government.

For Advanced Students: Divide the students into two groups and have them prepare short oral presentations on Williamsburg, Virginia, and the College of William and Mary—the two living memorials to the Glorious Revolution here in the United States. Encourage the groups to find photographs, pamphlets, or travel brochures containing information about these places. (Reports might include: Williamsburg—settled in 1632 as Middle Plantation, was made the capital in 1699, was later renamed in honor of William III; The College of William and Mary—was established by a charter granted in 1693 by William III and Mary II to the Reverend James Blair, is the second oldest college in the U. S., was closed for a short time in 1781 during the Revolutionary War and from 1861 to 1865 during the Civil War when about 90 percent of the student body enlisted in the Confederate army.)

Further Reading for Students

Averill, Esther. *King Philip, the Indian Chief*. New York: Harper & Row, 1950.

Catton, Bruce, and William B. Catton. *The Bold and the Magnificent Dream: America's Founding Years*. New York: Doubleday, 1978.

Clarke, M. P. *Parliamentary Privilege in the American Colonies*. Jersey City, N.J.: DaCapo Press, 1971.

Greene, Jack P., and J. R. Pole, ed. *Colonial British America*. Baltimore: Johns Hopkins University Press, 1984.

Hoffer, Peter C., ed. *An Empire Takes Shape: Selected Articles on the Origin of the Old English Colonial System*. New York: Garland Publishing, 1987.

Jacobs, Wilbur R. *Dispossessing the American Indian: Indians and Whites on the Colonial Frontier*. Norman: University of Oklahoma Press, 1985.

Leach, Douglas E. *Roots of Conflict: British Armed Forces and Colonial Americans*. Chapel Hill: University of North Carolina Press, 1986.

Nash, Gary B. *Red, White and Black: The Peoples of Early America*. Englewood Cliffs, N.J.: Prentice Hall, 1982.

Whipple, Chandler. *The Indian and the White Man in New England*. Stockbridge, Mass.: Berkshire Traveller, 1976.

Bibliography for Teachers

Books

Boyd, Thomas. *Shadow of the Long Knives*. 1928. Reprint. Norwood, Penn.: Norwood Editions, 1985.

Caruso, John. *The Appalachian Frontier, America's First Surge Westward*. New York: Bobbs-Merrill, 1959.

Jacobs, Wilber R. *Dispossessing the American Indian: Indians and Whites on the Colonial Frontier*. Norman, Okla.: University of Oklahoma Press, 1985.

Audio-Visuals

Penetrating the Wilderness. National Geographic Society. Filmstrip.

The Williamsburg File. Colonial Williamsburg. Movie.

Williamsburg Sampler. Colonial Williamsburg. Movie.

Teacher's Notes:

Lesson Plan

Teaching Resources, Unit 1 Booklet

Lesson Study Sheets pp. 103-114
Daily Activities pp. 115-120
Enrichment Activities pp. 121-126
Reteaching Activities pp. 127-132
Chapter Review p. 133
Chapter Mastery Tests pp. 135-146
Telescoping the Times Study Sheet p. 147

Chapter Objectives

Students will learn:
- the causes of the conflicts that developed between the colonists and the Indians
- how the economic system of mercantilism worked
- the impact of the Glorious Revolution on the colonial system

Using the Chapter Time Line

How long did King Philip's War last? (Answer: 1 year.)
How many years passed between the founding of the first English colony at Jamestown (see Chapter 1 Time Line) and the creation of the Dominion of New England? (Answer: 79)

Picturing History Lapowinsa was the chief of the Delaware tribe. He signed a treaty by which the Indians agreed to give up claims to the land between the Delaware and Lehigh rivers in the region of Bethlehem, Pennsylvania, for as far north as a person could walk in three days.

1630   1640   1650   1660   1670   1680   1690   1700

1636-1637
Pequot War

1660
Navigation Act passed
by Parliament

1675-1676
King Philip's War

1686
Dominion of New England created

1691
Massachusetts
grants religious
freedom

Links to American Literature

James Michener: born 1907; educated at Swarthmore College and the University of North Colorado; taught school from 1929 to 1940; worked as editor for a New York City publishing firm from 1941 to 1949; was naval historian in the South Pacific from 1944 to 1946.

Works include: *Tales of the South Pacific* (1947); wartime experiences provided material for Michener's first book.

Chesapeake (1978): chronicles four hundred years on Maryland's eastern shore, from late 1600's to the present; deals with many historical events and people, but focuses on the personal interactions of those who lived in and around Chesapeake Bay.

Introducing the Chapter

Ask students why good relations with the Indians were important for the colonists. (Possible responses: the Indians knew the land and animals and could help the colonists with farming and travel; colonists would not have had to constantly fear Indian attacks and could have concentrated on farming and developing the colony.) Ask students to suggest ways they might have ensured good relations if they had been the colonists. (Possible responses: make fair land treaties; invite Indians into settlement.)

CHAPTER 3 1637–1700

Conflict with Indians and England

Links to American Literature

The Nanticokes and their allies constitute a peril to this Colony and they must be disciplined. Declare war on them with every strength you have. Vanquish, destroy, plunder, kill or take prisoner. Do all these things to all or any of the said Indians you chance to meet. Put them to death or capture them alive at your pleasure. There must be no truce.

Now the hunters who clustered at Patamoke had their days of glory. They would hide behind trees that commanded well-known trails, and whenever an Indian appeared, man or woman, they would blaze away. The forests ran red with the blood of Indians, and fire consumed villages which had known no war.

The carnage was especially heavy among the confused Choptanks, who had given not a single cause for such bloodshed. In the entire history of the Choptank nation, no Indian had ever killed a white man or ever would, yet now they were hunted like squirrels.

— JAMES A. MICHENER, *Chesapeake*

At first the Indians received the colonists with great curiosity, then with warm friendliness. Time and again, entire settlements, such as Jamestown and Plymouth, were saved from starvation by the Indians. It was only after seeing the unmistakable signs that settlers intended to take over their land that the Indians became aroused to the danger. By then it was too late. The colonists' relationship with both the Indians and England deteriorated. When Charles II tried to force the colonies into the old pattern of trade, they grew angry.

Chapter Overview

In this chapter you will learn about the conflict that developed between the colonists and the Indians, about the economic system of mercantilism, and about the impact of the Glorious Revolution in England on the colonial system. The chapter explains the tragedy that resulted from a misunderstanding between the colonists and the Indians. It also foreshadows the conflict that was to be expected when the economic and political freedom of the colonists was threatened. Chapter 3 explains these issues of the colonial era in three sections.

Chapter Outline

1. **The Indians Fight for Their Land**
2. **England Creates a Colonial Empire**
3. **Parliament Is Supreme in the British Empire**

Discuss with students the types of things they own. Ask students the following questions about their belongings. How do you feel about lending these items to others? about giving them away? about sharing them? (Possible responses: most students will demonstrate pride and concern over personal property.) How would you feel if you owned a piece of property? How willing would you be to share it or give it up? (Possible responses: most students will respond favorably to owning property; most would not be willing to give it up, but might share it with someone else if given proper incentive.)

State the Objective

Understand the causes of the conflicts that developed between the colonists and the Indians.

SECTION 1

The Indians Fight for Their Land

GLOSSARY TERMS: **guerrilla warfare, pacifists**

Among the colonies along the Atlantic seaboard, the clash of interests between Indians and settlers varied in intensity. As we have already seen (Chapter 2), there was a bloody war with the Indians in Virginia as part of Bacon's Rebellion. In New Netherland, however, there was little difficulty. Few Indian tribes lived in the Hudson River Valley, and the first Dutch traders had the good sense not to anger the powerful Iroquois League of Five Nations. In Maryland the tribes were small and poorly organized. It was in New England that the greatest trouble arose.

Disputes Arise over Land and Religion

Disputes between the Puritans and the Indians arose over two issues: land and Christianity. For every acre a colonial farmer needed to support life, an Indian hunter or fisher needed twenty. The more the settlers expanded their farms, the farther away they pushed the Indians.

Moreover, the Indians did not have the same view about land that the settlers did. To the Indians, no one owned land. It was there for everyone to use. When they signed a land treaty, the Indians thought they were simply agreeing to let the white people share the land, not take it away from them. They also thought that the money, axes, kettles, or whatever they were given constituted a form of rent, which they would receive again from time to time. This misunderstanding about land, its ownership, and contracts caused a great deal of resentment between the Indians and the settlers, especially since most settlers thought it was to their advantage not to explain matters clearly before the Indians signed a treaty.

In addition, the Puritans persisted with efforts to convert the Indians to Christianity. Some Indians became sincere and dedicated Christians, but most did not. Even so, the idea of the Christian God and the rules stated in the Bible were a threat to Indian society. In Indian life the chiefs and the medicine men (the priests and healers) were the authorities. They regulated the rules and customs of Indian life. The Christian religion, with its emphasis on the Bible, undermined the authority and status of the medicine men and chiefs, and they deeply feared and resented it.

The Indians Lose the Pequot War

In 1637 the Pequot (pē′kwät) tribe decided to make a stand against the English. The colonists quickly formed an alliance with the Narragansetts, old enemies of the Pequots. The result of the **Pequot War** was the destruction of the Pequot nation. The end came at a Pequot fort on the Mystic River in Connecticut. The Puritans and their Narragansett allies surrounded the fort and set it afire. The Puritans knew that there were women and children as well as warriors in the fort. They shot

---

People in the Chapter

Metacom, the Indian chief, was given the nickname King Philip. The name reflected his proud demeanor and his habit of referring to Charles II as "my brother."

Charles II lived in exile during the government of Oliver Cromwell. Once restored to the English throne, he became known as the Merry Monarch. London was anything but merry while he reigned, however. The city was visited by the plague and the plague was followed by the Great Fire, which left London in ruins.

James II, brother of Charles II, was a stubborn and uncompromising monarch. Because of these characteristics, along with his disregard for Parliament and his attempts to restore Catholicism, he lost his kingdom to his Protestant daughter Mary and her husband William.

Increase Mather belonged to a Puritan family that included 80 clergymen among its descendants. Although he wrote 130 books and pamphlets, including one titled *Wo to Drunkards,* he was more cautious in his moral judgments than was his son, Cotton. Cotton outdid his father with 450 published works.

Present the Lesson

Have students list on the board the differences between the Puritan Indian policy in New England and the Dutch/Quaker Indian policy in the Middle Colonies. (Differences include: Puritans pushed Indians off the land, tried to convert them to Christianity, destroyed Pequot nation; Penn insisted land be purchased and treaties respected, dealt fairly with Indians.)

Check for Understanding

Call on individual students to answer Section 1 Review questions orally.

Guided Practice

Have students compare what they have read in the text with the portrayal of Indians and settlers they have seen in films and on television. (Possible responses: media often shows Indians as hostile savages and settlers as the innocent victims; media does not usually show the settlers forcing Indians off their land or attacking Indian villages.) Ask students how descendants of Indians might feel about this portrayal. (Possible response: anger at the biased portrayal of their ancestors.) Ask students how this image might be changed. (Possible responses: movies, television shows, and books could show a more accurate picture; more information in textbooks and documentaries; establishment of Indian museums; national holiday.)

the Indians as they tried to escape the flames. Only seven Pequots out of more than four hundred survived. As William Bradford described the massacre, it "was a fearful sight to see them thus frying in the fire and the streams of blood quenching the same." Bradford also noted that the Puritans praised "God, who had . . . given them so speedy a victory over so proud and insulting an enemy."

The Puritans thought that this kind of warfare was justifiable against a foreign and, in their eyes, heathen people, but their Narragansett allies were shocked by the slaughter. Like most other Indian tribes, the Narragansetts were accustomed to a different kind of warfare. They were used to taking some captives, including women and children, but not to killing large numbers of their enemies. As the Narragansetts said after the slaughter, the warfare of the English "is too furious and slays too many men."

There was no further major warfare between Puritans and Indians for almost forty years. However, great tension existed between them, and a future war was probably inevitable.

The Indians Lose King Philip's War

In 1675 the Wampanoag (wäm′pə nō′ag) Indians organized a last-ditch effort to wipe out the invaders. Two other Algonquin tribes, the Narragansetts and the Nipmucks, joined them. The alliance was led by the Wampanoag chief, **Metacom,** a son of Massasoit, the man who had welcomed the first Pilgrims. For some reason, the English called Metacom "King Philip," perhaps because of the manner he adopted when he visited Boston. There, dressed in fancy clothes, he liked to parade about town with a great deal of dignity.

Metacom's warriors began by attacking outlying Puritan towns in Massachusetts during the spring of 1675. By June, Indians were attacking towns only twenty miles west of Boston! Many tribes had obtained guns, and some Indians were crack shots. Also, some Indian chiefs now wore English armor—an iron helmet and a large rounded iron plate to protect the front of the body. Clearly, the Indians were adopting some of the settlers' practices, and to good effect. **King Philip's War** went on for months.

The English were angered and frustrated by the **guerrilla warfare,** or hit-and-run tactics, of the Indians. They responded by killing as many Indi-

Picturing History Engravings of Metacom similar to the one above appeared in London after the Indian's death.

ans as they could, even those of friendly tribes. The English burned the Indians' supply of corn as well.

Linking Past to Present

Guerrilla warfare, which was used by the Indians, was something new and particularly frustrating to the Puritans, who were familiar with a more formal style of fighting. In the 1960's and early 1970's, American soldiers in Vietnam faced a similar situation—one in which a less powerful nation was able to frustrate a more powerful one through the use of such guerrilla tactics as sabotage and ambush.

Food shortages and disease helped stop the Indians' offensive. Finally, a force of one thousand

Assign Independent Practice

Have students complete Chapter 3, Section 1 Enrichment Activity.

Student Assignment/Homework

Have students read Section 2, "England Creates a Colonial Empire," and answer Section 2 Review questions on paper.

Picturing History As the Indians watched, the Europeans cleared their forests for farmland and used the trees for timber.

men led by General John Winslow exterminated almost three thousand Indians at Narragansett Bay. Metacom was killed by an Indian friendly to the whites, and Indian power in southeastern New England was gone forever. Metacom's head was exhibited at Plymouth for twenty years, and his wife and young son were sold as slaves in the West Indies.

The Puritans, however, had paid a high price for their victories. Of some ninety-two Puritan towns, fifty-two were attacked and twelve destroyed. The frontier of English settlement had been pushed back eastward. Relative to the size of the population, more people were killed in King Philip's War than in either the American Revolution or the bloody Civil War of the 1800's.

Pennsylvania Remains a Place of Peace

Pennsylvania was a distinct exception to this dismal conflict. William Penn was determined to treat the Indians in Pennsylvania fairly. He insisted that Indian lands be purchased and that treaties with the Indians be respected. Quaker principles re-

quired that the Indians, like all other peoples, be treated with brotherly love and consideration. The Quakers had another reason for dealing openly and fairly with the Delaware, Susquehannock, and other Pennsylvania tribes. Quakers were **pacifists** and thus had to avoid the possibility of war. They were successful in doing so for many years.

With Quakers in control of the colony, relations between the settlers and the Indians were generally peaceful. For some seventy years after its founding, Pennsylvania was an exception to the violent and sorrowful pattern that prevailed in some of the other colonies.

SECTION 1 REVIEW

Key Terms and People

Explain the significance of: Pequot War, Metacom, King Philip's War, guerrilla warfare, pacifists

Main Ideas

1. What were the differences in the ways the

Anticipate the Lesson

Write the term *mercantilism* on the board and ask the students to define it on paper. Then discuss their definitions. (Possible definition: economic theory which promises a nation power through the acquisition of wealth if a favorable balance of trade is maintained, especially with that nation's own colonies.) To stimulate discussion on mercantilism, ask students the following questions. Does it seem like a fair system? (Possible response: yes, it helps a nation to grow and its people to prosper.) Who benefits in a mercantilist society? Who might be exploited? (Possible responses: the nation will benefit by increasing its wealth; colonists might benefit by having a market for raw materials and a source of finished goods; colonists might be exploited if they are allowed to trade with only one nation.)

State the Objective

Understand how the economic system of mercantilism worked.

Indians and the settlers viewed land? How did these differences affect the relationship between the two groups?
2. How did settlers' efforts to convert Indians to Christianity threaten Indian culture?
3. Why were Indians shocked by Puritan actions in the Pequot War?
4. What was Metacom's purpose in waging war against the Puritans?
5. How did Pennsylvania avoid conflict with the Indians?

Critical Thinking

6. Could the conflicts between the Indians and the settlers have been avoided? Give reasons for your answer.

SECTION 2

England Creates a Colonial Empire

GLOSSARY TERMS: **mercantilism, balance of trade, import duties**

Within just seventy-five years (1607–1682), the English colonies were established in North America. At first England paid them little attention, and the English civil war of the 1640's produced further neglect. Nevertheless, people in both England and the colonies understood that they played a part in a mutually beneficial pattern of life. This relationship was based on an economic theory that had been followed by many European nations since the 1500's—the theory of **mercantilism.**

Under mercantilism a nation becomes powerful through money that results from a favorable **balance of trade.** To maintain a favorable balance of trade, a nation has to export more than it imports. This theory received its most thorough application in the complex relationship that existed between England and its American colonies from the 1500's to the 1700's.

Mercantilism Protects British Power

The colonies in theory were to provide products, especially raw materials, that could not be found in the home country. In fact, the main reason the English government permitted colonists to go to America was to aid this development. As early as the Jamestown settlement, settlers were urged to find or grow raw materials not available in England, so that these products would not have to be purchased from another country. The raw materials were then to be sent to England and there turned into finished or manufactured goods. These goods would then be sold to the colonies and to other nations.

For the English, military power meant primarily naval power. The ships of His Majesty's navy were built in England, but trees for masts had to be imported because England had run out of suitable large trees. Northern pines were imported from Sweden and other Scandinavian countries. Such imports, though, violated mercantilist principles in two ways: they cost money, and they made England dependent on foreign powers for a vital article of defense. In wartime, such dependence could be dangerous. Thus English authorities turned to the colonies. They reserved the largest pines in New England for the use of His Majesty's navy.

At that time, there was no clear dividing line between naval warships and civilian merchant ships. Many merchant ships were armed with cannons. In wartime many of these ships were allowed to battle and seize enemy merchant vessels. For this reason, the English government encouraged the construction of ships of all sorts. According to mercantilist principles, this manufacturing should have been done in England, not in the colonies. In this case, however, the importance of defense overrode the economic principle. The English government thus encouraged one kind of manufacturing in the colonies: shipbuilding.

Picturing History In this early drawing, an unknown artist has pictured New York Harbor as it appeared in 1679.

For Discussion
What does the word *pacifism* mean? (Possible definition: policy of establishing and maintaining universal peace; opposition to war.) Describe Quaker pacifism. To what extent did it influence the Quakers' dealings with the American Indians? (Possible response: Quakers tried to be fair and settle land claims justly in order to avoid conflict.) How might pacifists be viewed today? (Possible responses: some students might think pacifists are weak and afraid to fight; others might admire their moral conviction.)

Present the Lesson

Have students outline on the board both the theory of mercantilism and the basic ideas of the Navigation Acts of the 1660's. (Outlines of mercantilism might include: nations become powerful through wealth that results from favorable balance of trade; nations need to export more than they import; nations become powerful through military strength; colonies require supervision from home government. Outlines of Navigation Acts might include: laws regulate trade and shipping; colonies could trade only with England or its colonies; some products could be exported only to England; colonial goods had to be shipped on colonial or English ships.) Encourage students to refer to this information as they study Section 2.

Check for Understanding

Have students complete Chapter 3, Section 2 Daily Activity.

Ships had to be manned by sailors. That was another reason why the government encouraged shipbuilding and a large merchant fleet. Skilled seamen on merchant vessels could be pressed into service aboard naval vessels during wartime emergencies. The government encouraged the fishing industry for the same reason. There men learned seamanship. The fishing ships, it was said, were nurseries for seamen. The government even tried to retain the old Roman Catholic tradition of not eating meat on Fridays. By eating fish instead, the English people would help support England's maritime power.

The two principles of mercantilism—wealth and naval power—usually coincided. In the 1600's and even later, these principles were in the best interests of the colonies. They did not have enough people both to farm and to engage in large-scale manufacturing. They produced raw materials that sold well in England. In return they found that English manufacturers could supply them with a broad range of manufactured goods.

Mercantilism Is Difficult to Supervise

The fit between mercantilist principles and the interests of the colonies was not perfect, however. Left to themselves, the colonists might have preferred to buy cloth from French manufacturers rather than English ones. They might have preferred to sell masts, pitch, and tar to outfitters of Dutch ships rather than English ones. To work well, the mercantilist system required supervision by the home government. The English government never doubted that it had the right to undertake such supervision, nor did the colonists. Sometimes, though, the colonists found it convenient to evade English regulations that hurt their economic interests. Obviously, the colonists had no desire to weaken English naval power or lessen England's wealth. Yet suppose the choice lay between filling colonial pockets or filling those of London merchants. The colonists would have been less than human if they had not chosen their own.

Although the need for supervision was apparent, setting up an effective system of supervision was

Colonial Trade Routes

Map Skills **Movement** What goods were shipped to the Southern Colonies from the West Indies? from Britain? **Movement** What goods were shipped from New England to the West Indies? to Britain?

Picturing History This detail from a painting of New York Harbor in the 1750's shows privately owned British warships with captured French ships.

not easy. The colonies were three thousand miles and many weeks away from London. English government officials knew what sort of activity *ought* to be going on in the colonies but often found it difficult to discover what actually *was* going on. Sometimes the colonists were less than helpful in letting them know.

London Tightens Control

Attempts to supervise the mercantilist system began in earnest after the restoration of King Charles II in 1660. Parliament passed a series of **Navigation Acts** to regulate the trade and shipping of the American colonies.

The Navigation Acts of 1660 and 1663. These acts set forth certain basic and strict regulations to safeguard the mercantilist system. They remained in force until the American Revolution. In general, the rules stated by the acts were as follows:
1. No country could trade with the colonies unless the goods were shipped in colonial or English ships.
2. All vessels had to be manned by crews that were at least three-quarters English or colonial.
3. Certain colonial products including sugar and tobacco could be exported only to England or another English colony.
4. Almost all the goods traded between the colonies and any European country had to be shipped by way of England. This meant that goods had to be unloaded at an English port before continuing on their journey. This gave jobs to dockworkers, while the **import duties,** the taxes paid on goods coming into a country, fed the English treasury.

By and large, the colonies adjusted their trade practices to follow these acts. After all, they benefited too. Shipbuilding was stimulated, and with certain goods the colonies enjoyed a monopoly in the English market. As time went on, however, the system grew more complicated. The list of goods that could be sold only to England got longer. It included such important colonial crops as rice and the wood products known as naval stores—masts, pitch, tar, and turpentine. Indigo was added to the list because it was used to color sailors' uniforms. By the early 1700's, the government limited growth in certain colonial manufacturing enterprises that had developed. Most woolen cloth, hats, and finished iron products had to be made in England.

Assign Independent Practice

Have students write three paragraphs explaining the New England colonies' resistance to England's Navigation Acts and the consequences. (Paragraphs should include: resistance—colonies continued to trade with other European nations, colonies questioned the authority of the King's commissioners; consequences—English court nullified the Massachusetts charter, James II created the Dominion of New England.)

Efforts to Enforce the Acts. Within the English government, a small group of bureaucrats, or officials, were responsible for colonial affairs. They were known as the Lords of Trade. In 1664 they sent a royal commission to the colonies to find out what was going on and to remind the colonists about their obligations under the new Navigation Acts.

The commissioners decided to look more closely at New England rather than the tobacco colonies of the South. Virginia already had a royal governor, and both Virginia and Maryland seemed to be fitting well into the mercantilist system by exporting large quantities of tobacco. New England, however, presented some problems. Except for exporting masts and rods, the New England Colonies were not contributing to the wealth of old England. Exports of furs were falling off because of overtrapping, while Boston merchants were doing nicely by trading with anyone they pleased, including the French and the Dutch.

When the commissioners arrived in Boston, Puritan leaders questioned their authority. After all, the Puritans had been used to having their own way for thirty-five years. Also, they did not take kindly to agents of a monarch who was persecuting their fellow Puritans in England. The people of Massachusetts valued the self-government that their original charter gave them.

The frustrated commissioners returned to London, where they reported that Massachusetts was a nest of arrogant "independency." They recommended that the colony be compelled to observe the Navigation Acts. Some also recommended that the Massachusetts charter be canceled.

Massachusetts Loses Its Charter. Nothing resulted from the commission's negative report. During the next twenty years, it was followed by more commissions and more reports. Massachusetts authorities and merchants went on as they had before, although they became increasingly disturbed by the visits of a young royal official named Edward Randolph. The Lords of Trade sent this able but disagreeable bureaucrat to the colonies several times. During each visit, he collected damaging information about Massachusetts violations of the Navigation Acts. Randolph also discovered that the colony had been passing laws that he said were "contrary to the laws of England." For example, Massachusetts authorities punished people who did not attend church. The punishment was more severe than that allowed by English law. The original Massachusetts charter specifically forbade this.

Over the years Randolph and other royal officials repeated the same recommendation: put an end to the Massachusetts charter. Finally Charles II was convinced. In 1684 Randolph presented his evidence to an English court, and the court nullified the Massachusetts charter. The most populous English colony in America no longer had any legal basis for existence.

Sir Edmund Andros Reigns

Charles II died in 1685 and was succeeded by his brother, the Duke of York, who became **James II.** James quickly took sweeping and drastic action to settle the Massachusetts problem. With a stroke of his pen, he created one vast colony called the Dominion of New England. This new administrative unit included all the New England Colonies, New York, and what later became New Jersey. This huge territory was to be administered from Boston by a royal governor aided by a council appointed by the crown. There were to be no representative assemblies in any part of the Dominion.

This sweeping reorganization sent a shudder throughout the colonies. What would government

Picturing History Late in his life, Sir Edmund Andros became governor of Guernsey, England.

Student Assignment/Homework

Have students read Section 3, "Parliament Is Supreme in the British Empire," and answer the Section 3 Review questions in the small groups established for the Guided Practice exercise.

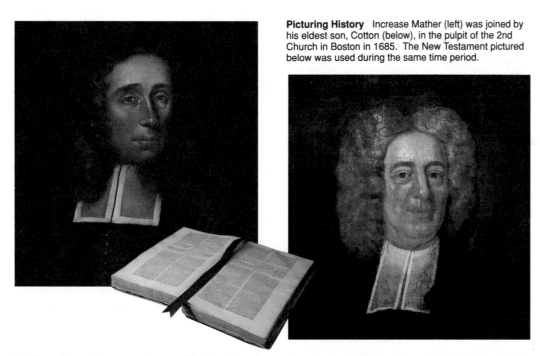

Picturing History Increase Mather (left) was joined by his eldest son, Cotton (below), in the pulpit of the 2nd Church in Boston in 1685. The New Testament pictured below was used during the same time period.

be like without the protection provided by elected colonial assemblies?

James's appointment of Sir **Edmund Andros** as governor of the Dominion of New England did nothing to calm these fears. Andros was an able administrator, but he was also arrogant and high-handed. Within a few weeks of arriving in Boston, he managed to make thousands of enemies.

Since the assemblies had been abolished, former political leaders had no roles in government. Andros and his royal councilors levied taxes simply on their own authority. This was taxation without representation in its most blatant form. Puritan leaders pointed out that such taxes violated their rights as freeborn Englishmen. Andros replied that such rights did not necessarily exist in the Dominion of New England.

Then Andros announced that the town governments established under the old Massachusetts charter were illegal. Therefore, he said, the land grants that the town had made to individuals were also illegal. Landowners would have to reconfirm their land titles with Dominion authorities and pay rent to the Dominion as well. As if this were not enough, Andros even questioned the lawfulness of the Puritan churches. The proper church for English colonists, he said, was the established Church of England. He also made it clear that the Naviga-

tion Acts would be enforced, and he brought in customs officers to do so.

The Massachusetts colonists were outraged. In 1687 they sent their most prominent minister, **Increase Mather,** to London. Mather's task was to get the old charter revived and to get Andros recalled. Just as Mather was putting his diplomatic skills to work, however, the entire political picture was changed by a bloodless revolution in England.

SECTION 2 REVIEW

Key Terms and People

Explain the significance of: mercantilism, balance of trade, Navigation Acts, import duties, James II, Edmund Andros, Increase Mather

Main Ideas

1. What did England see as the role of the colonies with regard to trade?
2. Why did England encourage shipbuilding and fishing in the colonies?
3. How did the Navigation Acts affect colonial trading patterns?
4. How did King James II attempt to settle the "Massachusetts problem"?

Conflict with Indians and England **65**

65

Anticipate the Lesson

Write the terms *revolution* and *rebellion* on the board. Ask the students to define each and explain the differences. (Possible definitions: *revolution*—a sudden, radical change or overthrow of one government and substitution of another by the governed; *rebellion*—open opposition to a person or thing in authority, defiance. The difference is that rebellion addresses a particular grievance with no thought of destroying the already existing government, whereas revolution seeks to replace the existing government.)

State the Objective

Recognize the impact of the Glorious Revolution on the colonial system.

For Discussion

What were the effects of the Glorious Revolution on the American colonies? (Possible responses: the recall of Governor Andros and abolition of the Dominion of New England; the restoration of Northern Colonies to previous status; the granting of a new charter for Massachusetts providing for a governor appointed by the crown.) In what ways was the revolution beneficial to the colonies? In what ways was it harmful? (Possible responses: beneficial—Dominion abolished, Northern Colonies restored, Massachusetts governor's council elected by the lower house of assembly; harmful—Massachusetts governor appointed by the King, colonial governors required to uphold Navigation Acts.)

5. Why was Sir Edmund Andros so unpopular in the colonies?

Critical Thinking

6. How was England's colonial trade policy at odds with the principles of the Massachusetts charter?

SECTION 3

Parliament Is Supreme in the British Empire

GLOSSARY TERMS: **Glorious Revolution, royal colonies, religious toleration, salutary neglect**

During his reign, James II managed to produce almost as much resentment in England as Andros did in Massachusetts. He was stubborn and tactless and had little idea of how much his subjects valued their Protestantism and their parliamentary rights. When James, himself a Roman Catholic, fathered a son, England was faced with the possibility of a long line of Roman Catholic monarchs.

Consequently, in 1688 a group of parliamentary leaders boldly invited William of Orange to become their new king. William, a Dutch Protestant, was married to James's Protestant daughter Mary. William and his army landed in England without opposition. James fled abroad, and **William and Mary** were installed as joint monarchs. Parliament proceeded to pass a series of laws firmly limiting the power of the Crown. An act of toleration gave religious freedom to all dissenters. These were the people who dissented from, or disagreed with, the Anglican Church of England. Ever afterward, the English called these events the **Glorious Revolution.**

When news of the revolution crossed the Atlantic, there was an immediate reaction in New York and Massachusetts. Citizens in both colonies challenged James's colonial officials directly.

Colonists in Massachusetts Revolt

Upon learning that William had landed in England, a group of armed citizens of Massachusetts marched on Andros's house in Boston. They told him that he was finished as governor. Then they declared an end to the Dominion of New England. Andros and his royal councilors fled to an island fort in Boston Harbor, and Massachusetts leaders settled back to await news of developments in England.

At first all the news was good. In London, Increase Mather succeeded in obtaining the official recall of Andros and the official abolition of the Dominion of New England. The Northern Colonies were thus returned to their previous status. However, Mather was unable to get the old Massachusetts charter restored. Instead, in 1691 a new charter was issued. In the new charter, the governor was appointed by the King. However, the governor lacked the power to appoint members of his council. In other **royal colonies,** the governor had the power to appoint council members. In Massachusetts the governor's council would be elected by the lower house of assembly—a unique arrangement. The Massachusetts charter also provided for **religious toleration.** The Puritans would no longer be able to persecute such groups as the Quakers and members of the Church of England. Puritan leaders were not altogether happy with the new charter, but they could live with it.

Colonists in New York Revolt

New York colonists also revolted. In 1689, after hearing that James II had fled England, a group of local militiamen seized control of New York City. They were led by **Jacob Leisler,** a successful German merchant who had lived in New York since the days of Dutch rule. Although he had grown rich in the fur, wine, and tobacco trades, he championed the cause of the middle class—the small merchants, artisans, and small farmers—against the large merchants and landowners. Leisler could have won widespread support. Unfortunately, he was arrogant and stubborn and soon offended even his own followers.

When the officially appointed governor arrived from England with clear instructions to take control of the colony, Leisler resisted. The new governor lost patience and accused Leisler of treason. There was a hasty trial, and Leisler and his son-in-law were hanged.

Although officials in London later reversed Leisler's sentence, the hanging and the events that preceded it created much hostility within the colony and poisoned the atmosphere of New York politics for years.

Present the Lesson

On the board list the revolution and rebellion that took place in the colonies and in England from 1688 to 1689. Ask students to state the result of each. (List should include: Glorious Revolution—took place in 1688 in England, result was that colonists in New York and Massachusetts directly challenged King James's colonial officials; Leisler's rebellion—took place in 1689 in New York, result was that Leisler was hanged for treason, and hostility over the incident poisoned the atmosphere of New York politics for years.)

Check for Understanding

Review with the class the answers to Section 3 Review questions.

The Rulers of Britain During the Colonial Period

| | Elizabeth I | William | Mary | George III |

House of Tudor	Elizabeth I	1558–1603	daughter of Henry VIII
House of Stuart	James I	1603–1625	son of Mary, Queen of Scots and Elizabeth's cousin. He was James VI of Scotland, then called himself James I of Great Britain. The phrase "Great Britain" became official when Scotland and England were joined in the Act of Union in 1707.
	Charles I	1625–1649	The English Civil War (1642–1649) abolished the monarchy. Charles I was beheaded. A new form of government called the Commonwealth was established.
The Commonwealth	Oliver Cromwell	1649–1660	The Commonwealth was headed by Oliver Cromwell and then by his son Richard. In 1660 the monarchy was restored.
House of Stuart	Charles II	1660–1685	The ruler whose agents kept close watch on the colonies.
	James II	1685–1688	James II was considered to be strongly influenced by Catholics. This brought about the Glorious Revolution (1686–1688). James II fled to France and Parliament offered the crown to Mary, daughter of James II, and her husband, William of Orange.
	William III and Mary II	1688–1702	After Mary's death, William ruled until 1702.
	Anne	1702–1714	daughter of James II
House of Hanover	George I	1714–1727	Since Anne had no surviving children, at her death her cousin George of Hanover, Germany, was made king.
	George II	1727–1760	The House of Hanover ruled until 1901.
	George III	1760–1820	

Review with students the fact that the Navigation Acts were often treated with "salutary neglect." Ask students to consider and comment on the problems that arise when laws are on the books but go virtually unenforced. (Possible responses: people might begin to break other laws they feel are unfair; people might be punished for breaking laws that they did not know existed.)

Have students complete Chapter 3, Section 3 Daily Activity.

The Navigation Acts Get New Teeth

In the early years of his reign, King William paid little attention to the colonies. His eyes were on France, with whom England was competing for control of Europe. As always when England was distracted with European problems, colonial affairs were neglected. Colonial merchants began to violate the Navigation Acts with increasing frequency, trading where they found the most profit instead of where England told them to trade. Influential people in England caught wind of these violations. Consequently, in 1696 Parliament decided to tighten up the imperial system once again.

New Rules. First, all colonial governors were required to take an oath to uphold the Navigation Acts. If they refused to do so, they were removed from office. Second, customs officers were sent to each colony to enforce the customs laws. These officials had the power to inspect vessels and warehouses and even to break into them if it was suspected that they held smuggled goods. Third, people accused of smuggling were to be tried in admiralty courts. These courts had no juries, and the judges were appointed by the Crown. The new rules gave the English government great control over colonial trade.

New Board of Trade. The king also acted in 1696 to strengthen the administration of the colonies. The old Lords of Trade were replaced by a new group of officials known as the Board of Trade and Plantations. The board could offer its advice on rules for the colonies. Thus, while the board had no official powers, it did have considerable influence.

As an example of this influence, consider the king's instructions to the royal governors. These instructions included detailed requirements about what the royal governor could and could not do in his colony. Although these instructions were issued by the king, they were actually written by the active members of the Board of Trade.

The Governors' Powers Are Limited

After 1696 the royal governors served as the most important link in the chain of imperial control. Eight of the colonies had governors appointed by the Crown. The governors of Maryland and Pennsylvania were appointed by the Baltimore and Penn family proprietors. Only Rhode Island and Connecticut elected their own governors.

The Power of Governors. Most of the governors were men of high status. Most came from England. They accepted appointment in the colonies for various reasons. One was prestige, since all governors directly represented the authority of the king. Another reason was money, since the governorships offered both a salary and the opportunity to receive various official fees.

The governors varied greatly in ability. Some had the interests of the colonists at heart, while others looked to their own interests. For example, Governor William Shirley organized the Massachusetts militia for a successful expedition against

How Britain Governed the Colonies

The Position of Colonial Governors

Student Assignment/Homework

Have students complete Chapter 3 Review on paper. Divide the class into small groups to discuss their answers.

Concluding the Chapter

Divide the class into small groups. Ask students to compare the relationships that existed between the colonists and the rulers of England from Charles II through William and Mary. Have each group prepare a chart showing the governmental changes in the colonies, when they occurred, and under what English monarch they were made. Charts might include:

Charles II: 1660–65 Parliament passed Navigation Acts; Nullified Massachusetts charter.

James II: 1685–88 Established Dominion of New England; prohibited representative assemblies; appointed Sir Edmund Andros governor.

William and Mary: 1688–1702 Parliament passed laws limiting power of crown; provided for religious freedom; abolished Dominion of New England; granted new charter to Massachusetts with governor appointed by King; returned Northern Colonies to previous status.

the French in Canada. On the other hand, Governor Benjamin Fletcher allowed pirates to operate out of New York Harbor.

The royal and proprietary governors had important legal powers. They called the meetings of the representative assemblies, and they could disband these assemblies at any time. They could also veto laws. Sometimes, however, the local pressure was so great that governors were pushed into approving laws that they disliked or that directly violated their instructions. Thus, as a safety measure, authorities in London kept the right to veto any laws passed by a colonial assembly.

In most colonies, the governor appointed the council. It consisted of wealthy, influential men who gave the governor advice. The council also served as the upper house of the colonial legislature and as the highest court of each colony.

The Weaknesses of Governors. In theory, the English government retained great power in the colonies. Yet this power was not nearly so great as it seemed on paper. Influential and wealthy colonists could dine and chat with the governor. They could tell him what a fine fellow he was, or they could describe popular resentment against him for particular actions or decisions. These subtle pressures were often very effective.

The greatest weakness of the governors was that their salaries were paid by the colonists and not by London. London might instruct a governor to raise a colonial army against the French, but the governor had to ask the colonial assembly for the necessary money. The money could be raised only by taxes passed by the assembly. Members of the assembly were, of course, patriotic men who had no more love for the French than the governor and His Majesty did. However, as some of the members hinted to the governor, before they raised taxes might the governor be willing to approve certain laws without looking too closely at his instructions? Might his own salary be reduced a trifle so that the people would not be overburdened by taxes? These questioning hints were not lost on the governors.

Imperialism Still Works Well

Throughout the 1600's and early 1700's the policy of **salutary neglect** benefited England and the colonies. This policy was an unspoken agreement to let the colonies develop without overregulation. As a result, the colonists were able to practice different forms of self-government.

Linking Past to Present

Just as the colonial governors had to ask their assemblies for money to pay their salaries, raise an army, and run the government, so the power of governors today is limited by their economic dependence on state legislatures and, ultimately, the taxpayers. Then, as now, subtle pressures from wealthy and influential individuals and groups seeking special favors proved to be effective.

As the 1700's dawned on England and the colonies, the imperial system was working fairly well. The Glorious Revolution of 1688 had permanently established the supremacy of Parliament over the monarch.

Some imperial restrictions hurt the colonies, but not seriously. The Indians had been defeated—at least for the time being. The colonies enjoyed the protection of the nation that was becoming the most powerful on earth. Even so, the colonies were changing and acquiring a distinctive way of life.

SECTION 3 REVIEW

Key Terms and People

Explain the significance of: William and Mary, Glorious Revolution, royal colonies, religious toleration, Jacob Leisler, salutary neglect

Main Ideas

1. What was the immediate reaction of the colonists to James II's ouster?
2. How did the new Massachusetts charter differ from the original?
3. What new rules, instituted after the Glorious Revolution, tightened England's control over colonial trade?
4. What powers did the royal governors in the colonies have, and how were their powers limited?

Critical Thinking

5. How did the principles of governing championed during the Glorious Revolution compare with those held by colonists? Explain.

SECTION 3 REVIEW

Answers

Main Ideas

1. New York and Massachusetts welcomed it and challenged James's colonial officials, including Andros.
2. It provided for the royal appointment of governors and for religious toleration.
3. Governors were required to swear to uphold the Navigation Acts, customs officers were appointed to enforce the laws, and accused smugglers were to be tried in admiralty courts.
4. Powers: to call and dissolve meetings of the representative assemblies; to appoint the council; to veto laws. Limitations: subject to assemblies' control of money, including their salaries; subject to pressures from influential colonists.

Critical Thinking

5. They were very similar. The revolution established the supremacy of representative assemblies over monarchs, thus reinforcing the principle that political authority rests on the will of the people. It also provided for religious toleration. **(analysis & synthesis)**

State the Objective

Understand the economic reasons behind the European desire for colonies.

Present the Lesson

On the board write "Mercantilism". Under this broad heading write "Goals" and "Means". Ask students to write these labels on a piece of paper and then, using the feature, identify and list the primary goals of mercantilism and the means European countries used to achieve these goals. Call on students to write their answers on the board. (Answers: goals — accumulating wealth (gold and silver) to increase military and economic strength. Means — using slave labor to acquire gold and silver from mines in the colonies; exporting products in exchange for gold (exports should exceed imports to create a positive balance of trade); using colonies to supply raw materials for manufactured goods; using the labor of Indians, colonists, and imported slaves to produce goods such as cotton and sugar cane for export.)

Ask students to adopt the viewpoint of an English explorer in the 1600's and to write a paragraph listing and explaining reasons why England should establish colonies in the Americas. (Paragraphs should include: England lagged behind Spain and France in attempts to colonize America; England had few natural resources; colonies could provide markets for manufactured British goods.)

Focus on Economics

The Purpose of Colonies

In 1588 Spain's monopoly of the Americas came to an end as its Invincible Armada sank into the English Channel. After this defeat of Spain, England entered the competition for American colonies. The English started slowly since the notion of making money from colonization was still a relatively new one. During the next two centuries, however, England established and managed a highly profitable string of American colonies.

Mercantilism. The primary purpose of the English colonies in America was to benefit the power and wealth of England. No one in these colonies or in England questioned this aim. After all, that was the fundamental idea of mercantilism, the economic system that was followed eagerly by most European countries and their colonies from the 1500's.

Mercantilism refers, generally, to profits from trading or other commercial activities. The theory of mercantilism held that the greater a nation's wealth, the greater its political and military power. Wealth was measured by the amount of silver and gold in a nation's treasury.

The first and most obvious way of enriching a country was simply to get hold of large stores of gold and silver. The discovery of large deposits of these precious metals in Central and South America helped to make Spain, for a time, the most powerful nation in Europe. Between 1492 and 1600, more than eight million ounces of gold were mined in South America.

There were other ways of getting gold and silver, however. A major one was through trade. Because Spain paid for imports and repaid its war debts in gold and silver, these precious metals streamed across Europe, allowing other countries to accumulate their own hoards.

The rulers of France and England believed that a ruler should control the country's commerce. After all, they reasoned, the head of a family manages the finances of the household, and the monarch is the father or mother of the nation. They took control of their economies so as to stimulate manufacturing and trade. The goods created thereby could then be sold for gold and silver.

In directing the economic affairs of their kingdoms, mercantilist rulers kept one general principle in mind. For a nation to grow economically strong, it must maintain a favorable balance of trade with competitor countries. That meant that the nation should export more to those countries than it imported from them.

Mercantilist countries soon realized that if they wanted an ever-increasing stock of gold and silver and a steady supply of raw materials for their manufacturing efforts, they could not rely solely on the resources of their own countries. Yet they did not wish to depend on other countries. The obvious solution was to acquire colonies rich with untapped resources. Governments thus financed costly expeditions for explorers and conquerors who hoped to discover and subdue rich territories in Africa, Asia, and the Americas. If a territory seemed promising, efforts were made to develop its resources and to encourage the immigration of permanent settlers. A population with roots in the land proved a more powerful defense for a colony than any army.

Colonization and the Slave Trade. Colonization and the drive to accumulate wealth contributed significantly to the development of the black slave trade in the Western Hemisphere, particularly in South and Central America, the West Indies, and the American South. Early Spanish settlers used Indian slaves to do hard labor in mines and on plantations. The Indians were not used to such exhausting work, however. They became weak and had no resistance to the diseases of the Spanish. The Indians died by the millions. Whole tribes were wiped out. Their numbers dwindled so rapidly that in 1515 a Spanish bishop, Bartolomé de Las Casas (läs kä′säs), sought to protect the few survivors by suggesting the importation of Africans into the Americas. He argued that African slaves could better withstand the heat and the drudgery of work in the colonies. As a result of this proposal (which the bishop soon regretted), millions of

Check for Understanding

Ask students to write answers to the questions at the end of the feature. Go over the answers. Then ask students what essential differences existed between Spanish and British efforts to colonize America. (Answer: Spain established colonies in South America and the southern part of the U.S.; England's colonists settled farther north along the east coast; Spain established its colonies earlier than Britain; Spanish settlers used slaves for labor while Britain relied on settlers to develop the resources of the land; the Spanish mined precious metals to increase their wealth; the British relied more on

colonists to produce raw materials as well as to serve as markets for finished goods.)

Picturing History
A South American mountain of silver, discovered in 1545, was Spain's greatest asset. This 1584 drawing shows llamas carrying ore to the mine's refinery. After England defeated the Spanish Armada in 1588, however, Spain faced a new competitor for the assets of the Americas. According to the mercantilist theory, the colonies existed for the benefit of England.

black slaves were brought in to mine the gold, pick the cotton, and cut the sugar cane—the products that would strengthen the trading positions of European colonial powers.

A Market and Raw Materials. What England wanted from its American colonies was a market for English-produced goods and a source of the raw materials that it had previously been forced to import from other countries. At first, what England wanted fitted well with what the colonies wanted. North America was a huge continent with vast natural resources and a small population. England had comparatively few raw materials and a large population. The most profitable way of life for the settlers was to provide the raw materials such as furs, iron, and lumber that the English wanted. Skilled English labor could turn the colonies' raw materials into fine furniture, clothes, and wrought iron. It was thus mutually advantageous for England to buy raw materials from the colonies and for the colonies to buy manufactured goods from England.

The British Empire in America was founded on strong commercial links between England and the colonies. Mercantilism, however, was based on the assumption that the economic dependence of the colonies would continue. It failed to take into account the growing spirit of free enterprise that existed in the colonies. The mercantilist system could not reconcile two opposite goals: the enrichment of England and the enrichment of the colonies. This gap between the economic interests of England and those of its colonies was a major factor in the American struggle for independence.

Understanding Economics

1. Why was the mercantilist system so beneficial to England and the colonies?
2. Why were settlers considered more important for colonial defense than an army?

Critical Thinking

3. How did the mercantilist idea of wealth differ from our idea of wealth today?

FOCUS ON ECONOMICS

Answers

Understanding Economics

1. The colonists profited by selling raw materials to Britain, and Britain profited by selling manufactured goods to the colonies.
2. Settlers will fight for their homes and land more fiercely than will an army brought in for a brief time from a foreign land.

Critical Thinking

3. For mercantilists, wealth was restricted to gold and silver; modern ideas of wealth extend to a nation's resources and productive capacity as well as to the population's energy and talents. **(analysis)**

Key Terms and People

These are highlighted in the text in the order in which they appear in this list.

Main Ideas

1. Puritans—followed English custom of individual ownership of land; used the land mostly for farming. Indians—believed no one owned land and that it was there for all to use; used the land mostly for hunting and gathering, much less for farming.

2. William Penn and his colonists were pacifists, who were determined to avoid war.

3. England's distance from the colonies made it hard for the English to find out what the colonists were doing. This meant that the colonists could sell their goods for more money to customers other than England without England's knowledge.

4. The royal commissions of the Lords of Trade, disturbed by the Massachusetts colony's continued evasion of the Navigation Acts, received permission from James II to reorganize the colony.

5. Unpopular Governor Andros was recalled; the Dominion of New England was abolished; a new (though not entirely well received) charter was issued.

6. They tightened control on all sides—by governors, customs officers, the court system, and the administration—so that England could more closely regulate colonial trade in true mercantilist style.

Critical Thinking Questions

7. Possible answer: The excerpt reveals the colonists' need to establish control over the Indians and the disrespect for human life typical of racist beliefs.
• Possible answer: attitudes leading to genocide motivated Hitler in Germany, Stalin in Poland, and more recently many whites in South Africa.

8. Because they dared to oppose the English.

9. He probably believed that his people could not survive the English invasion. • Possible answer: he might have been optimistic in the beginning but realized he was fighting a losing battle when he finally faced one thousand men near Narragansett Bay.

10. Puritans: tolerated no other religions; justified war against heathens; disregarded Indians' rights to the land. Quakers: practiced religious toleration; practiced pacifism; respected Indian treaties. Both—Separatists and persecuted; had similar economic status. • Possible answer: Quakers—I am against violence.

➤**11.** Puritans—had a long history of sophisticated religion and wars and of political and intellectual thought; had a comparatively complex economy. North American Indians—had a comparatively simple civilization based on respect for nature; tended to be more peaceful, making war but usually without large-scale slaughter; had no written language.

12. As England used up its scarce resources, it promoted the colonies to supply raw materials for its industry.

➤**13.** a. Use of colonial or English ships—to promote shipbuilding industry and ensure a reserve of ships in case of war; b. use of colonial or English

---

CHAPTER 3 REVIEW

Write your answers on a separate sheet of paper.

Key Terms and People

Explain the significance of: Pequot War, King Philip's War, guerrilla warfare, import duties, royal colonies, salutary neglect

Main Ideas

1. How were the uses of land different for the Puritans and for the Indians?
2. Why did William Penn and his colonists have little trouble with neighboring Indians in the 1600's?
3. What made the mercantilist system difficult to enforce?
4. Why did the Dominion of New England come into being?
5. How did the Massachusetts colony benefit by the Glorious Revolution?
6. How did the Navigation Acts of 1696 serve to enforce the mercantilist imperial system?

Critical Thinking Questions

7. **Analyzing Literature.** Imagine yourself as a citizen of colonial America in the 1600's. How would you explain the attitude toward the Indians expressed in the excerpt on page 57? Where could this attitude be seen in recent times?
8. **Analyzing a Quotation.** William Bradford called the Pequot Indians a ''proud and insulting'' foe. Why did he characterize them this way?
9. **Formulating Hypotheses.** Why did Metacom start a war against the settlers? Do you think he thought he had a chance of winning? Give reasons to support your answer.
10. **Comparing and Contrasting Ideas.** Make a chart that compares the ideas of the Puritans with those of the Quakers. To which sect would you have belonged if you had your choice? Why?

11. **Drawing Inferences.** Judging by what you know about the cultures and environments of the Puritans and the Indians, why were their life styles so different?
12. **Formulating Hypotheses.** Why were colonies an essential part of the English mercantilist system?
13. **Assessing Cause and Effect.** Consider the four rules of the Navigation Acts of 1660 and 1663 as listed on page 63. What effect was each designed to have on the economic welfare of England?
14. **Assessing Outcomes.** Why were the Massachusetts citizens and the English government doomed to come to blows?
15. **Recognizing Values.** Why do you think religious toleration was made a part of the new Massachusetts charter at the time of the Glorious Revolution?
16. **Analyzing Cause and Effect.** What was the effect of the Glorious Revolution in New York? What was the effect of the hanging of Jacob Leisler and his son-in-law?
17. **Drawing Conclusions.** Why was it so important to England to continue to keep the mercantilist theory strong by means of the Navigation Acts of 1696?

Critical Thinking Activities

18. **Analyzing Maps.** Using the book and the map on page 62, describe the famous triangular trade.
19. **Linking Past to Present.** What is the difference between the goals of mercantilism in the 1600's and the goal of keeping a worldwide balance of trade today?
20. **Linking Past to Present.** How was the power of the colonial governors limited? Is the power of the governors of the present fifty states limited in the same way? Explain.

crews—to ensure a reserve of sailors in case of war; c. export of specific products only to England—to supply all England's needs first and to directly collect a tax on products sold to countries; d. shipping most goods by way of England—to give jobs and money to the English rather than the colonies.

14. The colonists resented all the profits and jobs going to England. They also resented losing the independence they had developed while England fought the 17th-century European wars.

15. Possible answer: the Anglicans did not want to be persecuted by the Puritans, who had no tolerance of other religions.

16. The New York colonists revolted. • Relationships with England became strained.

17. English power and wealth depended on trading goods made with colonial raw materials.

Critical Thinking Activities

➤**18.** Slaves were exported from West Africa to the West Indies, where they raised sugar. Sugar and molasses were exported from the West Indies to New England, where they were made into rum. Rum was exported to West Africa to pay for the slaves.

19. Mercantilism involved the maintenance of a favorable balance of trade for one country at the expense of other countries. Today most countries try to maintain a favorable balance so that they can be buyers as well as sellers.

20. By the will of the rich and influential and by the will of the people. • Yes—today the power of the governor is limited by lobbies, by the state assembly, and by public opinion.

➤**Question suitable for cooperative learning.**

Conflict with Indians and England

As settlers sought more land, a clash of interests between Indians and colonists sometimes led to armed conflict. English and other European settlers tended to look down on the Indians because they had their own "pagan" religions. English efforts at conversion angered many Indians.

Ideas about land created even more conflict. The English thought that you could own land whether you used it or not. The English also thought that the Indians wasted land by hunting rather than by planting crops. The Indians thought no one could own the land; everyone could use it. Fighting often involved brutality on both sides. In New England the colonists defeated the Indians in two major wars. Several wars also occurred in Virginia and in the Carolinas. New York was more peaceful. However, the best relations between colonists and Indians existed in Pennsylvania, where the Quakers respected Indian rights and avoided war.

Meanwhile, using tactics that historians have now termed mercantilism, England began to establish trade relationships with its colonies. Mercantilism refers to economic practices that ensure prosperity for a country by making it as self-sufficient as possible and by building its military and naval power. In an effort to reduce its dependence on foreign suppliers for the nation's markets, England demanded that the colonies sell their raw materials only to the parent country. Such mercantilist policies helped to bring about the American Revolution.

The laws that enforced this theory were known as the Navigation Acts. They were hard to enforce. When the King learned that Massachusetts merchants were smuggling goods, he took away that colony's government charter. One of the King's officials was sent over to bring the colony into line. He arrived in Boston with powers of government that offended most of the New England colonists.

Events in England suddenly established the supremacy of Parliament over the King. A new King had meddled with the army and with Parliament and had fathered a Roman Catholic son and heir. A great many English people took alarm. Powerful men forced the King to flee the country, in what they called the Glorious Revolution. He was replaced by the Protestant William and Mary from the Netherlands.

News of these events forced out the unpopular governor of the Dominion of New England and also caused serious trouble in New York City. Yet the new King William moved to strengthen ways of governing the empire. He could not rule without consent of Parliament. However, he did get Parliament to pass new Navigation Acts. He also set up a Board of Trade to enforce them. Finally, he demanded new rules for the royal governors of the colonies.

Chronology of Main Events

1636–37	Pequot War
1660	Charles II restored to throne in England; Navigation Act passed
1675–1676	King Philip's War
1685	Death of Charles II; accession of James II
1688	William of Orange lands in England; Glorious Revolution begins
1689	Jacob Leisler leads revolt in New York City
1691	New Massachusetts charter grants religious freedom

Telescoping the Times may be used as an alternative to having students read the entire chapter, as a chapter preview, or as a chapter review.

Global Perspectives

1707	England and Scotland unite to form Great Britain.
1742	Japan codifies criminal law.
1750	Portugal and Spain sign a treaty fixing areas of rule in South America.
1762-1796	Catherine the Great reigns in Russia.
1770	Captain James Cook discovers and claims Australia for Great Britain.
1774	Regulatory Act establishes British government in India.
1774	Russian troops crush a peasant revolt.

For Discussion

How might Captain James Cook's discovery and claiming of Australia for Great Britain have affected British/colonial relationships? (Possible response: Britain might have wanted to tighten its reins on the American colonies as an example to the Australian colonists.)

Additional Teaching Strategies

SECTION 1

For Basic Students: Tell students to list on paper the natural rights identified by Locke and to give an example of each. (Lists must include: life, liberty, property. Examples might include: no person has the right to take another's life; no person has the right to take another's property unfairly.) Have student share their papers with the class.

For Advanced Students: Have students research the trial of John Peter Zenger. Choose students to act the parts of judge, jury, witnesses, and Zenger himself. Students should then present to the class a mock trial based on their research findings. (Trial should cover the following points: according to English law, a statement could be true and yet be libelous; Zenger was accused of libel for printing articles criticizing the royal governor of New York, Governor Crosby, and for printing seditious articles—those which aroused opposition to the government; Hamilton admitted Zenger published the articles but based his case on the fact that the material was true; jurors had no legal choice but to vote quietly or risk fine and imprisonment; feelings ran high amid colonists and the jury cleared Zenger; judge did not reject verdict or punish jurors.)

SECTION 2

For Basic Students: Have students construct a time line on paper showing the major events discussed in this section. (Dates might include: 1689-1763—Britain at war with France; 1747—Ohio Company formed; 1754—French and Indian War begins; Washington surrenders at Fort Necessity; Albany Congress meets; 1756—Seven Years' War begins.) Ask students to identify the effect of each event on colonial America. (Possible responses: French and Indian War causes France to lose most land in North America; Albany Congress is the first attempt to organize colonists, and many colonies begin to think of themselves as part of a single unit for the first time.)

For Advanced Students: Ask students to write a journal entry from the point of view of a delegate who attended both the Albany Congress and the Stamp Act Congress. Have students address the following questions. How had times changed? What events caused the colonists to develop more unity? (Journal entries might include: colonists were becoming more united against Britain and the government's taxation policies; colonists felt their legislatures were the only bodies that represented them; events such as enforcement of Royal Proclamation of 1763, Sugar Act of 1764, Quartering Act of 1765, and Stamp Act of 1765 caused colonists to resist Britain's control.) Discuss students' papers.

SECTION 3

For Basic Students: Have students choose one thing in their school that they would like to change. Encourage students to discuss the means of protest they might use to bring about this change as well as the advantages and disadvantages of each means. (Possible change: the addition of fresh fruit and vegetables to the cafeteria menu. Possible means of protest: letters to editor of student newspaper; advantage—calls school-wide attention to the problem; disadvantage—might not be strong enough to bring about change.) Discuss colonists' actions and compare them to the students' responses.

For Advanced Students: Have students do additional research and prepare a three-minute talk about one of these individuals or groups: Samuel Adams, Crispus Attucks, John Hancock, Sons of Liberty, The Daughters of Liberty, or John Dickinson. (Talks should include: the part each played in the colonies' decision to resist British rule; how each gained supporters for independence.)

Further Reading for Students

Chidsey, Donald Barr. *The French and Indian War*. New York: Crown Publishers, 1969.

Clapp, Patricia. *Witches' Children: A Story of Salem*. Wooster, Ohio: Norman Lathrop Enterprises, 1982.

Fisher, Dorothy C. *Paul Revere and the Minute Men*. Elgin, Ill.: Child's World, 1975.

Gipson, Lawrence H. *The Coming of the Revolution 1763-1775*. New York: Harper & Row, 1954.

May, Henry F. *The Enlightenment in America*. New York: Oxford University Press, 1976.

Morris, Richard B. *The Indian Wars*. Minneapolis: Lerner Publications, 1985.

Parkman, Francis. *Montcalm and Wolf*. New York: Atheneum Press, 1984.

Phelan, Mary K. *The Story of the Boston Massacre*. New York: Harper & Row Junior Books, 1976. (Easy)

Stein, R. Conrad. *The Story of Lexington and Concord*. Chicago: Children's Press, 1983. (Easy)

Historical Fiction

Cooper, James F. *The Last of the Mohicans*. Laguna Beach, Calif.: Buccaneer Books, 1983.

Fast, Howard. *April Morning*. New York: Bantam Books, 1962.

Forbes, Esther. *Johnny Tremain*. Laguna Beach, Calif.: Buccaneer Books, 1981.

Mason, F. Van W. *Young Titan*. Mattituck, N.Y.: Amereon, 1976.

Bibliography for Teachers

Books

Craven, Wesley F. *The Colonies in Transition, 1660-1713*. New York: Harper and Row, 1968.

De Crevecoeur, J. Hector. *Letters from an American Farmer*. 1782. Reprint. Magnolia, Mass.: Peter Smith Publisher, 1983.

Dickinson, John. *Letters from a Farmer in Pennsylvania to the Inhabitants of the British Colonies*. Reprint of 1903 ed. Irvine, Calif.: American Biography Service, 1988.

Hofstadter, Richard. *America at 1750: A Social Portrait*. New York: Alfred A. Knopf, 1971.

Peckham, Howard H. *The Colonial Wars, 1689-1762*. Chicago: University of Chicago Press, 1964.

Wahlke, J.C., ed. *Causes of the American Revolution*. 3rd ed. Lexington, Mass.: D.C. Heath, 1973.

Audio-Visuals

Colonial America: The Roots of the Revolution. Benchmark Films, Inc. Movie.

French and Indian War—Seven Years' War in America. Encyclopaedia Britannica Educational Corporation. Movie.

Great Men and Great Issues: Colonial Period. Wilcom, Inc. Audio tapes.

Last of the Mohicans. Educational Enrichment Materials of The New York Times. Movie.

Paul Revere: The Messenger of Liberty. USF & G Insurance Film Library. Movie.

Computer Resource

Colonial Merchant. Educational Activities, Inc.

Teacher's Notes:

Teaching Resources, Unit 1 Booklet

Lesson Study Sheets pp. 149-160
Daily Activities pp. 161-166
Enrichment Activities pp. 167-172
Reteaching Activities pp. 173-178
Chapter Review p.179
Chapter Mastery Tests pp. 181-192
Telescoping the Times Study Sheet p. 193

Chapter Objectives

Students will learn:
• how certain ideas of the Enlightenment influenced the English colonies
• the causes and consequences of the French and Indian War
• the events that led the colonists to separate from Great Britain

Picturing History Armed with his musket, the *Minute Man of Concord* stands ready to leave his plow behind and fight for freedom in this patriotic sculpture by Daniel Chester French. The statue has greeted visitors to the village green at Concord since 1875.

Using the Chapter Time Line

How many years passed between the Quartering Act and the first battles of the Revolutionary War at Lexington and Concord?
(Answer: 10)

| 1700 | 1715 | 1730 | 1745 | 1760 | 1775 |

1704
First colonial newspaper founded

1735
Trial of John Peter Zenger

1740
Great Awakening sweeps through the colonies

1754
Albany Congress meets

1754-1763
The French and Indian War

1765
Quartering Act

1767
Townshend Acts

1770
Boston Massacre

1775
Battles of Lexington and Concord

CHAPTER 4 1700–1775

Separating from Britain

Links to American Literature

> HAWTHORNE. *Excellency, she is condemned a witch. . . .*
>
> PARRIS. *Excellency, I would postpone these hangin's for a time. . . .*
>
> DANFORTH *(conciliatory). . . . I cannot pardon these when twelve are already hanged for the same crime. It is not just.*
>
> PARRIS *(with failing heart). Rebecca will not confess?*
>
> HALE. *The sun will rise in a few minutes. Excellency, I must have more time.*
>
> DANFORTH. *Now hear me, and beguile yourselves no more. I will not receive a single plea for pardon or postponement. Them that will not confess will hang. Twelve are already executed; the names of these seven are given out, and the village expects to see them die this morning. Postponement now speaks a floundering on my part; reprieve or pardon must cast doubt upon the guilt of them that died till now. While I speak God's law, I will not crack its voice with whimpering. If retaliation is your fear, know this—I should hang ten thousand that dared to rise against the law, and an ocean of salt tears could not melt the resolution of the statutes. Now draw yourselves up like men and help me, as you are bound by Heaven to do.*
>
> — ARTHUR MILLER, *The Crucible*

As you saw in the previous chapter, the Indians maintained their traditional beliefs and customs as they watched the palefaces betray them and claim their lands. Justice had gone seriously astray, as the famous witch trials of the late 1600's further illustrated. These trials grew out of fear of the unknown, misplaced religious fervor, and a seemingly unstoppable emotional tide. This chapter shows the importance of separating fact from opinion, particularly when issues are clouded by emotion.

Chapter Overview

As the eighteenth century dawned, it brought with it a greater sense of tolerance than had previously been known. Most of the colonists were eager to forget the past and to be open to new ideas. These new ideas developed in Europe as part of the philosophic movement known as the Enlightenment. In this chapter you will learn how certain ideas of the Enlightenment influenced the English colonies. You will also learn about the causes and consequences of the French and Indian War and about the events that led the colonists to separate from Great Britain. The chapter will tell you about these events in three sections.

Chapter Outline

1. **The Colonists Consider New Ideas**
2. **Britain Defeats France and Tightens Control**
3. **The Colonies Organize Resistance to Britain**

thinking. (Possible response: colonists might have progressed from accepting new ideas in science to accepting new ideas about religion, government.)

State the Objective

Understand how certain ideas of the Enlightenment influenced the English colonies.

Anticipate the Lesson

Ask students to comment on how discoveries in science can affect the way people think in other areas. (Possible responses: Darwin's theories caused controversy in the areas of religion and morality; the ability to harness atomic energy has changed people's ideas about military warfare and sources of electrical power.) Ask students how scientific discoveries of the times might have affected the colonists' way of

SECTION 1

The Colonists Consider New Ideas

GLOSSARY TERMS: **Enlightenment, social contract, Great Awakening**

The ideas of the **Enlightenment** developed first in the field of science. People looked beyond religious authority to explain how and why the universe worked. Instead, they relied on reason. Led by **Nicolaus Copernicus** (kō pur′ni kəs), **Galileo Galilei** (gal′ə lē′ē), **Sir Isaac Newton,** and others, people soon learned that the earth revolves around the sun and not vice versa. They also learned that the world is governed not by chance or by miracles but by fixed mathematical laws.

Once scientists began unlocking the secrets of the natural world by using reason, it was inevitable that philosophers would apply the same kind of logic to analyzing human society. If there was a law of nature—such as gravitation—there must be laws for humans, for they are also part of nature.

The Enlightenment Influences Thought

One such philosopher was the Englishman **John Locke.** In his work *Two Treatises on Government,* published in 1690, Locke declared that God had indeed provided laws of natural rights to make the human world run as smoothly as the physical world. There were three such natural rights: life, liberty, and property.

Locke believed that people originally lived without any government at all. However, the weak were often at the mercy of the strong. So in order to exercise their God-given rights without interference, people made a **social contract.** They agreed to obey a government if it would protect their natural rights. However, if the government became tyrannical, Locke maintained that people no longer needed to obey it. Indeed, they had the right to overthrow the government.

Benjamin Franklin. An outstanding example of an Enlightenment person was colonist **Benjamin Franklin.** He was born in Boston in 1706. At age twelve, he was apprenticed to his older brother as a printer's assistant. The two did not get along, however, so the younger Franklin left Boston for Philadelphia, where he set himself up as a printer. By the age of forty, he had made a small fortune. He then embarked on several careers, all of them distinguished. He was a scientist, an inventor, a writer, a statesman, and a diplomat.

Franklin invented many useful devices, including bifocal eyeglasses and a metal stove that stood in the middle of a room so that the heat could radiate from all sides. His most famous scientific experiment showed that lightning and electricity are the same thing. To give his discovery a practical application, Franklin invented the lightning rod, which ever since has protected many buildings.

Europe Versus America. In many parts of Europe, poor peasants were locked into the traditions of their ancestors. They could not read or write, and there was little opportunity for them to im-

Historical Sidelight

Franklin did not take out patents on any of his inventions, explaining, "As we enjoy great advantages from the inventions of others, we should be glad of an opportunity to serve others by any invention of ours."

People in the Chapter

Jonathan Edwards entered Yale University at the age of thirteen. A precocious child, he had already written articles in which he discussed such curious topics as the behavior of spiders as part of God's plan. Later as a pastor, he was known for his hellfire and brimstone sermons such as "Sinners in the Hands of an Angry God."

Phillis Wheatley was born in Africa and was brought to America as a slave when she was about seven. She was only thirteen when her first poem was published. George Washington was so impressed with her poetry that he invited her to visit him at his army camp.

Patrick Henry was a self-educated orator and patriot. He studied law after failing as a farmer and a shopkeeper. He urged armed resistance to the British in his famous speech in which he declared: "Give me liberty or give me death."

Samuel Adams inherited his father's business where "he did little good for lack of capacity, and little harm from lack of responsibility." After losing the business he turned to politics, organized the Boston Tea Party, and became a delegate to the Continental Congress.

Present the Lesson
Ask students to identify important leaders of the Enlightenment and the Great Awakening. Write the names of these leaders on the board. Ask students to contribute a few sentences explaining the main belief or contribution of each. (Possible responses: Locke believed in the natural rights of all people—life, liberty, and property; he believed that people made social contracts with governments; Locke believed people had the right to overthrow a tyrannical government.) Encourage students to refer to this list as they study Chapter 4. Discuss how each leader might have influenced colonial thought. (Discussion might include: Locke's ideas gave colonists further reason to resist British control.)

prove their condition. To them, the new ideas of the Enlightenment meant little or nothing. In the American colonies, however, where a new society was being created, the ideas of the Enlightenment made good sense and were received with enthusiasm.

Religious Feelings Revive

In the early 1700's, the grip of the Puritan church on the colonists began to weaken. Under the new Massachusetts charter of 1691, the Puritans were forced to allow freedom of worship. The new charter also banned the practice of permitting only Puritan church members to vote.

Furthermore, as Puritan merchants prospered, they developed a taste for fine houses, stylish clothes, and good food and wine. Their interest in maintaining the strict Puritan code declined.

Material comfort was accompanied in the early decades of the 1700's by a decline in church membership. Many people seemed to be doing so well in this world that they paid little attention to the next. Many preachers seemed to lack spiritual warmth. As a result, many people were ready for a revival of religious feelings.

Jonathan Edwards. One minister who tried to promote such a revival was **Jonathan Edwards** of the Congregational church in Northampton, Massachusetts. Edwards declared that people would not be saved for eternal life just by attending services and praying regularly. No, they had to do more. They had to *feel* their sinfulness and *feel* the need for opening themselves to God's spirit. Conver-

Focus on Biography

On May 16, 1787, Benjamin Franklin gave a dinner party for the first delegates to arrive in Philadelphia for the Constitutional Convention. All felt honored by the invitation. After all, their host was the new nation's most famous citizen. Everyone knew of Franklin's role in winning independence. Also, his popular writings and scientific papers were read in America and throughout Europe.

Since 1757 Benjamin Franklin made many trips to Britain and France as a representative of the colonies. Among his friends were the foremost writers, artists, and scientists of the day. He met with kings, ministers of state, leaders of Parliament, and court officials. All, even when they disagreed with his politics, were drawn to him.

Franklin's learning, wit, and charm astonished these sophisticated men and women. Why? What had they expected? Many, Franklin soon realized, had assumed that he would be a barely civilized backwoods savage.

This shrewd American also knew that a revolutionary idea was taking shape in the minds of European intellectuals. They had begun to believe that a great mind and spirit could unfold in a person who lacked a distinguished ancestry and an upbringing in cultured surroundings. Now they had proof of the theory! Franklin was brought up among common people. He had attended no university. Yet he had educated himself to be the equal of the most cultivated men and women of the day. At the same time, he had made a comfortable fortune by virtue of his own skill and hard work.

Franklin good-naturedly played the role of noble savage. To him, the fine theory of these Europeans was no more than common sense. In Paris when they put his image on snuff boxes and sold little dolls made in his likeness, he was amused. He wrote to his daughter, "They i-doll-ize me!"

At eighty-two, no one expected Franklin to take an active part in the Philadelphia convention. He had no reason to do so. His presence alone assured Americans that honesty and common sense would prevail.

As the convention ended, a Philadelphia woman asked Franklin "What have we got, sir, a republic or a monarchy?"

"A republic," Franklin replied, "if you can keep it." True words then, they are just as true today.

Check for Understanding

Call on individual students to answer the Section 1 Review questions orally.

Guided Practice

Divide students into small groups. Have each group choose one person who symbolizes modern times as Thomas Jefferson and Benjamin Franklin symbolize the Age of Enlightenment in America. Have each group report back to the class on what person they chose and why. (Choices might include: Mother Teresa of Calcutta, who symbolizes modern concerns for social justice; Lee Iacocca, who symbolizes modern concerns for big business, power, and money.)

Picturing History George Whitefield preached outdoors when church doors were closed to him. He also impressed skeptics. Benjamin Franklin went to hear him, determined to give no collection. Afterward, however, Franklin said: "I emptied my pocket...gold and all." A close-up of Whitefield is shown in the inset at the right.

sion, for him, was a profound emotional experience rather than an intellectual one. In his sermons Edwards described the dangers of sin and the torments that awaited sinners after death. He roused such a response in his audience that men and women alike would fall to the floor in a faint or cry aloud that they really did feel the power and love of God.

George Whitefield. Another minister stirred an even more widespread revival of religion. This movement swept through the colonies in the 1740's and became known as the **Great Awakening.** One of the men who sparked it was a young Englishman named **George Whitefield.** It was not what but how Whitefield preached that drew the crowds. In a sense, he was a great actor.

Whitefield traveled from one colony to another. His sermons were shows designed to awaken people to their religious shortcomings. First he played the part of God. Then he played the part of the Devil. Since no building in any colony could hold the thousands who flocked to hear him, he conducted his revival meetings outdoors.

New Churches Form. Many ministers saw Whitefield's preaching as the work of God and

tried to imitate his example. Other ministers were disturbed that uneducated men who knew little of the Bible or of church laws were wandering about preaching to anyone who would listen. They denounced such preachers as upstarts. In turn, they were themselves denounced as cold men of letters who totally lacked God's saving grace.

As these controversies mounted, church members began taking sides. The "Old Lights" emphasized the need for an educated ministry. The "New Lights" stressed the importance of emotional experience for both ministers and laity. As a result of such arguments, many people left their churches and founded independent churches of their own. Baptists, Methodists, and many other sects did so.

The Quaker Revival. The Quakers did not join in the Great Awakening. Instead, they had their own form of revival in the mid-1750's. They went through a process of questioning whether they were living up to their principles. In the process, a few of them concluded that slavery was wrong.

A leading antislavery Quaker was **John Woolman** of New Jersey. He spent most of his life urging his fellow Quakers to free their slaves. By the time of the American Revolution, they had done so.

Assign Independent Practice

Have students complete Chapter 4, Section 1 Enrichment Activity.

Student Assignment/Homework

Have students read Section 2, "Britain Defeats France and Tightens Control," and answer the Section 2 Review questions orally in the small groups formed for the Guided Practice exercise.

Witchcraft Comes to an End

During the Renaissance, at least 500,000 persons—most of them women—were burned or hanged in Europe as witches. Such events continued well into the mid-1700's. In the colonies, however, the belief in witchcraft faded by the turn of the century. This was due in part to the Enlightenment, which discouraged superstition. In part it was also due to the outbreak of witchcraft hysteria that swept Salem, Massachusetts, in 1692.

Two young girls jokingly accused Tituba, a half-Indian, half-black female slave, of being a witch. Her master beat her until she made a false confession and gave the names of two other women who, she said, were also witches. Excited by all the attention they were getting and at the same time terrified that they would be punished for making up such a story, the girls stuck to their claim and accused still others of being witches.

The episode snowballed. Those who were unjustly accused and afraid named other equally innocent people as witches. Hysteria gripped the town as more and more people were accused. Official trials were held. The few sensible people who tried to stop the proceedings were themselves accused of being witches. People became too terrified to speak out. Still the accusations mounted, until the most prominent people in Boston—even the governor's wife—were being accused.

Finally, Increase Mather and other leading clergymen realized that the accusations were simply unbelievable and that masses of false evidence had been given by frightened people. The court where the trial took place was closed. The witchcraft hysteria came to an end, but not before nineteen persons had been hanged and another person killed by being crushed to death. In addition, four "witches" died in jail, and about one hundred fifty spent time in prison.

A Modeſt Enquiry
Into the Nature of

Witchcraft,

AND

How Perſons Guilty of that Crime may be *Convicted* : And the means uſed for their Diſcovery Diſcuſſed, both *Negatively* and *Affirmatively*, according to *SCRIPTURE* and *EXPERIENCE*.

By John Hale,

Paſtor of the Church of Chriſt in *Beverley*, Anno Domini. 1 6 9 7.

When they ſay unto you, ſeek unto them that have Familiar Spirits and unto Wizzards that peep, &c. To the Law and to the Teſtimony ; if they ſpeak not according to this word, it is becauſe there is no light in them, Iſaiah VIII. 19, 20. That which I ſee not teach thou me, Job 34 32.

BOSTON in N. E.
Printed by B. Green, and J. Allen, for Benjamin Eliot under the Town Houſe: 1702

Picturing History Reverend John Hale's *A Modest Enquiry Into the Nature of Witchcraft* concluded that many people suffered because of the delusions of a few.

Linking Past to Present

Mass fear and hysteria over witchcraft caused people to turn on their neighbors in Salem in 1692. Fear and hysteria with a different focus gripped the nation during the McCarthy era of the early 1950's. (See Chapter 30, Section 2.) Although Senator Joseph McCarthy's sweeping, unfounded accusations of communist infiltration did not result in any hangings, they did ruin the reputations of many people for years to come. The witchcraft trials and McCarthyism are examples of what can happen when issues are clouded by intense emotion, when fact is not separated from opinion, and when accusations are not supported by evidence.

The Educational System Grows

The American public was more literate than any other in the world. The proportion of people able to read and write was highest in New England, lower in the Middle Colonies, and lowest in the South.

More than most Protestants, the Puritans insisted that members of a godly community had to know how to read the Bible. The New England pattern of

Historical Sidelights
• The Salem witchcraft hysteria may have been fueled by bad rye. A condition known as convulsive ergotism, which is caused by the ergot fungus, can produce hallucinations, convulsions, and tingling sensations in the skin. All of these symptoms were suffered by the afflicted girls at Salem. Weather records indicate that 1692 was a perfect year for the fungus to flourish in New England.
• Because of British mercantile policies, there was often little silver or gold currency in the colonies. This situation was made worse by the Currency Act of 1764. As a result, business was often conducted by means of the barter system. Harvard once allowed a young man to pay his tuition with a cow. Shortly after his admission to the school, the cow died.

For Discussion
What were some of the problems of colonial education?
(Possible responses: public support for education was not common in all the colonies; few women attended school; in places where there were few towns there were few schools.) Which of these problems still confront educators and educational systems today? (Problems include: the strength of public support for education varies.) What problems do today's educators face that colonial educators did not?
(Possible responses: drugs; social problems; size of schools; busing.)

Picturing History In 1985 Massachusetts celebrated "Phillis Wheatley Day" by unveiling a portrait of America's first black poet based on this 1773 etching of her.

orderly settlement by towns made it possible to arrange for formal schooling. From the 1640's on, Massachusetts law required all towns with more than fifty families to support a schoolmaster. In effect, all children were to be taught to read at public expense. Later, other New England colonies passed similar laws, although they were seldom observed along the frontier.

The Middle Colonies had no laws requiring the public support of schools. Various Calvinist churches, though, did require their members to learn how to read. Also, the Jewish population of these colonies had a high literacy rate.

In the South there were few towns and therefore few schools. What education most children re-

ceived was given at home. In addition, more than 40 percent of the people were slaves, and almost none of them were literate.

In all the colonies, far fewer women than men knew how to read and write. Most women were simply taught by their mothers how to be housewives. Also, no women attended college.

American Colleges. The earliest American college was Harvard in Massachusetts. It was founded in 1636 to train ministers. Students studied Latin, Greek, mathematics, some science, and the philosophy of morals. After about 1700, however, more than half the graduates went into occupations other than the ministry.

By that time two other colleges had been established: William and Mary (1693) in Virginia and Yale (1701) in Connecticut. After the Great Awakening, five more colleges were founded: Princeton, Columbia, Pennsylvania, Brown, and Rutgers. Most of these were connected to some church group, but you did not have to be a church member to attend. Most college students came from well-to-do families.

The Written Word. The printing press served almost as an educational institution. A wide assortment of books was imported from Great Britain, and books were also printed in the Northern colonies. Until about 1760, the most widely printed works were sermons. Also popular were almanacs filled with important dates and information about the stars and the weather.

Picturing History This early view of Harvard College was engraved by Paul Revere in 1767. All of these buildings shown, including the chapel (far left), were used to quarter colonial troops while Boston was under siege.

Benjamin Franklin's almanac, called *Poor Richard's Almanack,* offered bits of advice on how to get ahead in the world:

> A penny saved is a penny earned. . . . The sleeping Fox catches no Poultry. . . . Keep thy Shop, and thy Shop will keep thee. . . . The second vice is Lying, the first is running into Debt.

Poor Richard's Almanack became so popular that it was reprinted both in Britain and in France. Clergymen distributed copies to their parishioners, and landowners to their tenants.

Newspapers were the most important public tie between the colonies. Although their official circulations were tiny, they were widely read, being passed from hand to hand and being read aloud at crossroads stores to those who were illiterate.

The first continuous colonial newspaper was the Boston *News-Letter,* founded in 1704. By mid-century about twenty-five newspapers, all of them weeklies, were being published in the colonies. They contained four pages, the last two of which were mostly advertisements in small print. The only illustrations were woodcuts showing the outline of a ship or a runaway slave or an indentured servant.

Zenger's Trial Brings Freedom of the Press

It was a hot, sticky day in August 1735. An eighty-year-old Philadelphia lawyer named Andrew Hamilton was delivering a speech in New York's city hall on behalf of a client. The client was **John Peter Zenger,** a German immigrant who ran a printing press. Articles in a newspaper he printed had accused Governor William Cosby of rigging elections, accepting bribes, taking land unlawfully, making money on a treaty with the Mohawk Indians, and being overly friendly with a notorious pirate.

At that time, British law held that anyone who criticized the government in writing was guilty of criminal libel. Libel is a written statement or illustration that harms a person's reputation. Hamilton suggested a different view. The issue was not whether Zenger had printed certain critical articles. He had. The issue was whether or not the articles were true. If they were, then there was no libel.

Hamilton argued that people had a right to air grievances against their government:

> They have a right to oppose arbitrary power by speaking and writing truths. . . . It is not the cause of a poor printer, nor of New York alone, which you are trying. No! It may, in its consequences, affect every freeman that lives under a British government, on the main [mainland] of America. It is the best cause; it is the cause of liberty!

It took the jury just ten minutes to decide that the articles about Cosby were true and that Zenger was therefore not guilty of libel. As a result, colonial newspapers were encouraged to speak out more boldly and to express differing political views. An example had been set for a basic American freedom: freedom of the press.

Linking Past to Present

Although freedom of the press did not become an accepted right until the ratification of the First Amendment, Americans can trace this right back to the trial of John Peter Zenger. Today we are fortunate to live under a political system that not only allows but encourages controversy. Like all freedoms, however, this freedom has some limits. When American troops landed on Grenada in 1983 (see Chapter 36, Section 2), newspapers and major television and radio networks protested strongly when reporters were not allowed to go along. Today many debates over freedom of the press concern pornography and obscenity in magazines, movies, and television.

SECTION 1 REVIEW

Key Terms and People

Explain the significance of: Enlightenment, Nicolaus Copernicus, Galileo Galilei, Sir Isaac Newton, John Locke, social contract, Benjamin Franklin, Jonathan Edwards, Great Awakening, George Whitefield, John Woolman, John Peter Zenger

Main Ideas

1. How did ideas in the area of science change during the Enlightenment?

Anticipate the Lesson

Discuss the historic reasons for rivalry among Spain, France, and England. Review Chapter 1 at this time. Ask students what similar motives caused conflict to develop among European powers in North America. (Possible responses: the desire for land, power, and wealth were still motivating factors; France and Spain also desired a market for their manufactured goods and a source of raw materials.)

State the Objective

Identify the causes and consequences of the French and Indian War.

2. How did ideas about society change during this period?
3. What conditions paved the way for a religious revival?
4. What important idea emerged from the Quaker revival?
5. What basic concept of American freedom emerged from the trial of John Peter Zenger for libel?

Critical Thinking

6. How did the Enlightenment contribute to colonial American ideas of independence?

SECTION 2

Britain Defeats France and Tightens Control

GLOSSARY TERMS: **militiamen, Albany Congress, Treaty of Paris of 1763, Proclamation of 1763**

As the colonies grew in population and wealth, the British government became increasingly concerned about their openness to attack. To the north, west, and south, they were menaced by Britain's traditional enemies—Spain and France.

Both the colonies and the British government felt that France was a greater danger than Spain. France and Britain were fighting each other all over the world as each tried to extend its empire at the expense of the other. Between 1689 and 1763, the two countries went to war four times. Although the main battlegrounds were in Europe and India, each caused reverberations in America.

The last of the four conflicts between Great Britain and France officially broke out in Europe in 1756. (See chart on page 86.) There it was called the Seven Years' War. In America it was known as the French and Indian War, and it began in 1754.

The British Win the French and Indian War

The seeds of this last of four conflicts were sown in the settlement of the third. As a result, the French strengthened the fort of Louisbourg on Cape Breton Island, which guarded the approaches to the St. Lawrence River, and also constructed a string of forts from Lake Erie southward to the forks of the Ohio. There, where the Allegheny and Monongahela (mə nän′gə hē′lə) rivers join to form the Ohio River, they built Fort Duquesne (dü kān′). It stood on land claimed by both Pennsylvania and Virginia.

The Ohio Country.   The British side was just as busy. In 1747 a group of wealthy Virginia planters formed the Ohio Company to obtain land beyond the Appalachian Mountains for speculation purposes. They were hoping that the value of such land would rise sharply and that they would make a substantial profit. Two years later the Virginia government gave the company 200,000 acres west of the Monongahela. London authorities approved the grant in hopes of encouraging settlement in the area. In 1751 Robert Dinwiddie arrived in Virginia as the new royal governor. He promptly became a member of the Ohio Company. The interests of the British Empire and of private Virginia citizens were now locked together.

Both as a British patriot and as a land speculator, Dinwiddie took a keen interest in the Ohio Country. He wanted to find out what the French were doing there. So in 1754 he sent out a group of Virginia **militiamen,** or civilian soldiers, under the command of a twenty-two-year-old colonel named George Washington. The young man had good connections, since two of his brothers were members of the Ohio Company.

Washington led his small force toward the forks of the Ohio. He learned that a larger French force already occupied the site. Hoping for the best, Washington and his men erected a stockade some fifty miles south of the forks and aptly named it Fort Necessity. The French attacked. Outnumbered by about seven hundred to four hundred, Washington's force surrendered. Since France and Britain were not yet officially at war, the French released the Virginians. They returned to Williamsburg with word that the Ohio Country was firmly in the hands of France. The skirmish at Fort Necessity was, in fact, the opening battle of the French and Indian War.

The Albany Congress.   While George Washington was surrendering Fort Necessity, an important meeting was taking place in Albany, New York. The British government had summoned delegates from New Hampshire, Massachusetts, New York, New Jersey, Pennsylvania, Maryland, and Virginia

Present the Lesson

Tell students to study the chart, "Wars in Europe and Their Counterparts in the Colonies," on page 86. Ask students which war had the most significant effect on the colonies and why. (Answer: the French and Indian War because France lost most of its land in North America.) On the board list the four pieces of legislation described in this section and ask students to explain how each was related to the French and Indian War. (Example: The Royal Proclamation of 1763—stopped westward expansion in order to keep the colonists near the seaboard, meant to make governing easier and prevent trouble with the Indians.)

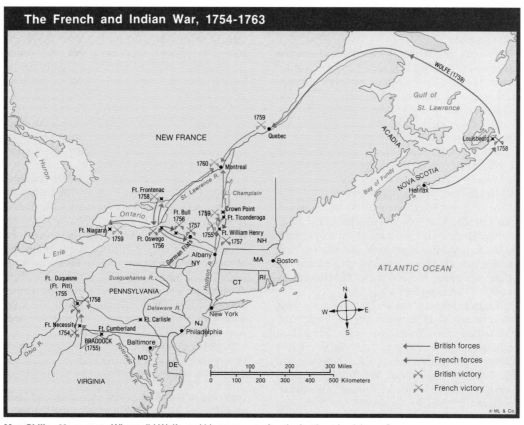

The French and Indian War, 1754-1763

Map Skills **Movement** Where did Wolfe and his troops go after the battle at Louisbourg?
Location How far was Ft. Duquesne from Ft. Carlisle?

For Discussion
Why were the colonies not interested in unity at the time of Franklin's Plan of Union? Why was London relieved? (Possible responses: each colony was still interested in its own power and wealth and was not yet ready to think as a united country; England was probably relieved to see that the colonists could not agree among themselves.)

Map Skills

To Quebec • About 160 miles (260 km)

to meet with leaders of the Iroquois Indians. All except New Jersey and Virginia responded. The British wanted the Iroquois to aid them against the French. The purpose of the **Albany Congress** was to draw up a treaty with the Indians that all the colonies would sign. Until then, each colony had made its own agreement or treaty with the Indians.

The Iroquois leaders listened politely to the customary speeches of welcome and gravely accepted the usual gifts. However, they would give no promises of support. They were well aware of growing French power in the west and had no desire to support a loser. They also felt that they had been cheated by British land speculators.

After the Indians left, the delegates discussed a plan for joint colonial action proposed by Benjamin Franklin. Franklin believed the French were confident of victory over the British settlers because the latter were divided. So he proposed the Albany Plan of the Union that would set up a colonial council to deal with the common defense. The council would also raise taxes on its own for military purposes, and it would handle relations with the Indians as well as the acquisition and settlement of western lands.

The Albany delegates sent the plan to the various colonies for their approval. In every colony it was either rejected or ignored. The assemblies did not want a council with control over western lands. Each colony wanted to press its own claims.

British Defeat Near Fort Duquesne. After the defeat of Washington's militia, Dinwiddie and other colonial governors appealed for regular troops from Great Britain. The London government obliged by sending fourteen hundred men under the

Check for Understanding

Call on the small-group leaders appointed for activities in Section 1 to present to the class their answers to Section 2 Review questions.

command of Major General Edward Braddock, who had the reputation of being one of Britain's finest generals.

Dinwiddie and Braddock then planned a major expedition to level Fort Duquesne and to drive the French from the Ohio Country. Braddock's troops were joined by more than four hundred colonial militiamen. Only eight Indian guides could be found. Nevertheless, Braddock and his men, accompanied by George Washington as a member of Braddock's staff, marched off through western Maryland and then north into Pennsylvania toward the forks of the Ohio. It was the same route Washington had taken a year before.

The long march held no problems for the Americans. Braddock, however, was used to European warfare. He could not slip through the countryside. He had to stop, hack down trees, and put logs over swamps instead of going around them. In the words of an eyewitness, he spent time "leveling every molehill" that stood in his way.

Braddock bragged that the sight of his troops would be enough to frighten away the French and their Indian allies. Washington warned Braddock of the dangers of an ambush. Sure enough, on July 9 about eight miles south of Fort Duquesne, the expedition was ambushed. The British soldiers, completely unused to frontier fighting, were bewildered and terrified by the deadly fire from men hidden in trees and bushes. They turned and fled. Braddock heroically tried to keep his men in line, but he was shot down.

With his Virginia men, Washington tried to cover the British retreat, but in vain. Two horses were shot from under him. Two bullets pierced his hat, and four pierced his coat. Later he wrote to his mother about "the dastardly behavior" of the British soldiers: "They ran as sheep pursued by dogs and it was impossible to rally them." Nearly one thousand of them were killed or wounded.

This stunning defeat of some of Britain's supposedly best soldiers raised a question in colonial minds about the ability of British troops. It also badly weakened British prestige among the Indians.

William Pitt Turns the Tide. Discouraged and angry over the French gains in North America, George II, in 1757, appointed **William Pitt** as one of his two chief government ministers. Pitt brought a new strategy to the war. He ignored the skyrocketing national debt and set about buying victory. On the European continent, he hired soldiers from his German allies and relied on them to do most of the fighting against the French. In the American colonies, he stopped begging for help from the assemblies. He instead told them that the British government would cover their wartime expenses. To get better leadership in the field, he promoted able junior officers over senior ones.

The next year, 1758, Pitt's policies began to pay off. George Washington finally had the pleasure of taking part in the capture of Fort Duquesne, which was renamed Fort Pitt and later Pittsburgh. A major British force captured Louisbourg.

In 1759 British troops sailed up the St. Lawrence River to Quebec. Quebec was a walled city built high on cliffs overlooking the river. The British general in command, James Wolfe, was young, brilliant, and daring. One night he ordered his troops up some steep goat paths that led to the top of the cliffs. The next morning the French awoke to find a British army lined up for battle on the Plains of Abraham outside the city walls. The French troops under the Marquis de Montcalm (mōn kälm′) marched out as the sun rose. In a brief but violent battle, both generals were killed.

Wolfe died knowing he had achieved a great victory. The next year British forces took Montreal, and French power in North America was at an end.

Outcome of the War. When the **Treaty of Paris of 1763** was signed, millions of square miles of land changed hands. Britain took Florida from Spain because that country had supported France during the last years of the war. From France, Britain obtained Canada and all the land east of the Mississippi River except the port of New Orleans. Britain could have gotten more, but the new king's minister was more interested in keeping a balance of power in Europe between Spain and France than he was in gaining territory. So he returned the West Indian islands of Martinique (mär′tə nēk′) and Guadeloupe (gwä′də lo͞op′) to France and persuaded that country, in a separate treaty, to give Spain New Orleans and Louisiana. In the late 1700's, Louisiana included all the land drained by the western tributaries of the Mississippi River.

Tensions Increase

The Indians in New France were alarmed by the fall of their French allies. They grew unhappier still as their old French trading partners were squeezed out by British fur traders. The British charged higher prices for their trade goods than the French

Guided Practice

Review with students the fact that the French and Indian War, though a victory for the British, had very negative effects on the British economy. Discuss with students the economic and political effects of fighting a war in a distant land. (Discussion might include: when fighting a war, a nation spends more money than it takes in; exports often decrease as men in the labor force become soldiers.) Ask students what positive effects war has on an economy. (Possible responses: industries that manufacture war supplies and other necessary goods will prosper; jobs are created.)

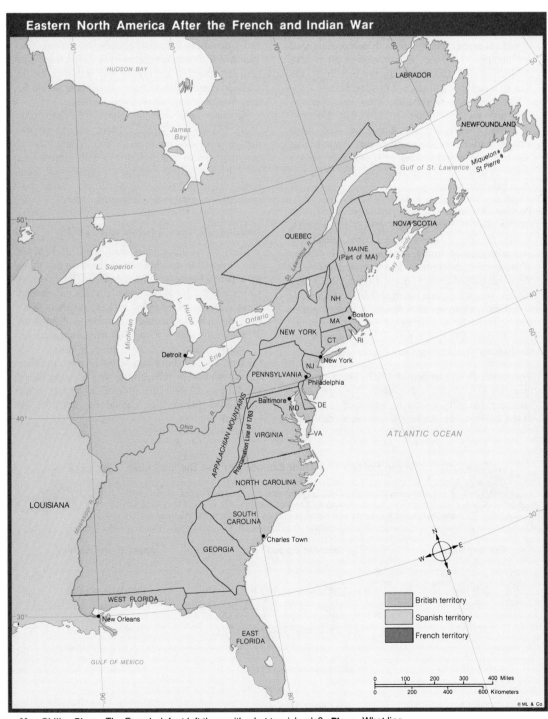

Eastern North America After the French and Indian War

HUDSON BAY

James Bay

LABRADOR

NEWFOUNDLAND

Gulf of St. Lawrence   Miquelon
St Pierre

NOVA SCOTIA

L. Superior

QUEBEC

MAINE
(Part of MA)

Bay of Fundy

St. Lawrence R.

L. Huron

L. Michigan

L. Ontario

NH

L. Erie

MA   Boston

Detroit

NEW YORK

CT   RI

New York

NJ

PENNSYLVANIA

Philadelphia

APPALACHIAN MOUNTAINS

Baltimore

MD   DE

Ohio R.

Proclamation Line of 1763

VIRGINIA   VA

ATLANTIC OCEAN

NORTH CAROLINA

LOUISIANA

SOUTH CAROLINA

Mississippi R.

GEORGIA

Charles Town

WEST FLORIDA

New Orleans

EAST FLORIDA

GULF OF MEXICO

	British territory
	Spanish territory
	French territory

0   100   200   300   400 Miles
0   200   400   600 Kilometers

© ML & Co.

Map Skills **Place** The French defeat left them with what two islands? **Place** What line separated the British colonies from the Ohio valley?

Map Skills

Miquelon and St. Pierre •
Proclamation Line of 1763

Assign Independent Practice

Ask students to study the map "Eastern North America After the French and Indian War" on page 85 to determine which present-day states were acquired by the British as a result of the French and Indian War. Ask students to list these states on paper along with a list of the lands that were retained by France. (Answer: Great Britain—Michigan, Indiana, Kentucky, Tennessee, Mississippi, Alabama, Ohio, West Virginia, Minnesota, Wisconsin, Illinois; France—the islands of Miquelon and St. Pierre.) Have students check their lists.

did, which meant that the Indians had to trap more animals. Yet at the same time, British traders would not supply the Indians with powder and lead for hunting. Then, too, British traders often gave the Indians rum. Once the Indians were drunk, the British would cheat them out of their furs.

The Indians knew little about the land speculation that was going on in the Ohio Country. However, they could see that more and more British settlers were crossing the Appalachian Mountains. The Indians feared it would be only a matter of time before their land would be filled and their game driven away.

Pontiac Attacks. In the spring of 1763, the Ottawa chief Pontiac led his warriors in an attack against the fort of Detroit. Other tribes joined in a general assault on British forts in the west. Within a few weeks, the Indians had captured seven of these outposts of British power. British troops then moved westward, and several battles followed, with heavy losses on both sides. Although peace was restored by a number of treaties, everyone knew that the differences between the colonists and the Indians would not go away.

The Royal Proclamation of 1763. In the meantime, the British colonial minister, George Grenville, decided to try to stop the westward expansion of the colonists by drawing a line on a map. The royal **Proclamation of 1763** forbade colonials from settling west of the Appalachian Mountains and ordered any colonists already west of that line "forthwith to remove themselves." The hope was that restricting colonials to the seaboard would make governing them easier. Also, there would be less chance of trouble with the Indians.

No paper fence, though, could keep out speculators, traders, and farmers. Moreover, the proclamation persuaded colonists of two things. First, it convinced them that the British government was insensitive to their interests. Second and more important, it persuaded them that the British government was unable to enforce its orders.

Britain Imposes Troops and Taxes

Even before the end of the French and Indian War, a decision had been made to leave ten thousand British troops in the colonies. The colonists suspected, but could not prove, that the presence of these troops was intended to keep them in line. Like the British themselves, colonial Americans distrusted the idea of a standing army in peacetime.

Grenville did not bother himself about such matters. He saw troops in terms of money. Since the colonies were prosperous, why shouldn't they pay for part of their own protection? In fact, there were other things they should pay for too, he believed.

Wars in Europe and Their Counterparts in the Colonies

Between 1689 and 1763 England was involved in a series of wars with France and Spain. Whenever England went to war, so did the colonies, but the wars were known by one name in Europe and by another name in the colonies.

The War Years	Name in Europe	Name in the Colonies
1689–1697	War of the League of Augsburg	King William's War
1702–1713	War of the Spanish Succession	Queen Anne's War
1744–1748	War of the Austrian Succession	King George's War
1756–1763	The Seven Years' War	The French and Indian War (began 1754)

Student Assignment/Homework

Have students read Section 3, "The Colonies Organize Resistance to Britain," and answer Section 3 Review questions on paper.

The Sugar Act of 1764. When reviewing colonial finances, Grenville had made a startling discovery. The American customs service was costing eight thousand pounds a year and bringing in only two thousand pounds. Obviously, a great deal of smuggling was going on.

Accordingly, in 1764 Grenville pushed through Parliament an act that did three things. It halved the duty on foreign-made molasses. It placed duties on certain imports that had not been taxed before. Most important of all, it provided for enforcement of the law in admiralty courts.

The **Sugar Act** alarmed many colonials. Merchants who had been smuggling cheap molasses from the French sugar islands in the Caribbean were convinced they would be ruined. Also, over the years the colonists had been very resourceful in guiding smuggling cases into local courts with local judges and juries, where acquittals were easy to obtain. Now, instead of dealing with understanding colonists, violators would have to deal with unfriendly judges from Great Britain.

The Quartering Act of 1765. The next year Grenville came up with a means of getting the colonists to help support British troops. The **Quartering Act** required any colony where troops were stationed to provide them with living quarters and certain supplies. Although the quartering of troops was a point of British law, the colonists resented the cost. New Yorkers were especially angry because most of the British troops were stationed there.

The Stamp Act of 1765. That same year, 1765, Grenville persuaded Parliament to pass the **Stamp Act.** It required that tax stamps be purchased and placed on all legal documents, liquor and other licenses, college diplomas, newspapers, almanacs, playing cards, and dice. The act also provided that violators be tried in admiralty courts.

Grenville settled back to wait for his new revenue. He never received any. Not one stamp was ever bought or used in the colonies. There was an outburst of protest and defiance the moment that word of the Stamp Act reached America.

No Taxation Without Representation. The colonial assemblies took the first steps toward confrontation. In Virginia a fiery young planter and lawyer named **Patrick Henry** took the floor of the lower house to offer seven resolutions. The house rejected two that called for outright disobedience but adopted the other five, which in general stated that Virginians could be taxed only by the Virginia assembly. Other assemblies passed similar resolutions, saying that Parliament had no right to tax the colonies since they were not represented in Parliament.

The assemblies took another important step: they decided on collective protest. In October 1765, delegates from nine colonies met in New York City for what was called the Stamp Act Congress. (Four colonies were prevented by their royal governors from selecting delegates.) The congress agreed on a Declaration of Rights and Grievances. The declaration repeated the arguments presented in Virginia's resolutions and added that Parliament had no right to expand the jurisdiction of admiralty courts. As British subjects, it argued, the colonists were entitled to trial by jury. The declaration closed by demanding repeal of both the Sugar Act and the Stamp Act.

The colonists' position was clear and consistent. The colonial assemblies were the only bodies that represented the people of the colonies. Therefore, only the colonial legislatures could tax them.

SECTION 2 REVIEW

Key Terms and People

Explain the significance of: militiamen, Albany Congress, William Pitt, Treaty of Paris of 1763, Proclamation of 1763, Sugar Act, Quartering Act, Stamp Act, Patrick Henry

Main Ideas

1. What did Benjamin Franklin hope to accomplish with the Albany Plan of the Union?
2. How did General Braddock's expedition affect the prestige of the British troops in the colonies?
3. What was William Pitt's strategy in the French and Indian War?
4. What were the effects of the royal Proclamation of 1763?
5. Why did the colonists so vigorously oppose the Stamp Act of 1765?

Critical Thinking

6. In justifying the Stamp Act, the British claimed that Americans should have to pay for the protection that the British supplied. How might a colonist reply to this?

Answers

Main Ideas

1. He hoped to set up a colonial council to deal with the common defense of the colonies.

2. The defeat weakened their prestige among colonists and Indians.

3. By ignoring the national debt, hiring mercenaries for the war in Europe, and promoting junior officers, he brought about the first British victories.

4. Colonists lost respect for the British government; westward expansion was not stopped.

5. It was one in a series of acts passed without their consent. It touched many colonists, and it violated their right as British citizens to trial by jury instead of in a military court.

Critical Thinking

6. Colonists believed that they already had paid for their own defense with taxes and militia; additionally, they claimed the right to determine how money should be raised and spent. **(synthesis)**

Anticipate the Lesson

Ask students to suggest ways that they might go about changing school policies they consider unfair. (Possible responses: petitions; picketing; Student Council intervention; speaking to school board; letters to editor of student newspaper.) Which do they think would be the most effective? Which the least effective? (Possible responses: most effective— petitions, Student Council intervention; least effective—picketing.) Ask students why compromise might be necessary. (Possible response: ideas of both sides have merit, and neither side wants to give in.)

State the Objective

Learn about events that led the colonists to separate from Great Britain.

SECTION 3

The Colonies Organize Resistance to Britain

GLOSSARY TERMS: **Sons of Liberty, nonimportation, Boston Massacre, Committees of Correspondence, Boston Tea Party, martial law, minutemen**

By the time of the Stamp Act Congress, it was apparent that some colonials were willing to go far beyond passing resolutions. That summer, citizens began to form secret organizations in most of the port cities. The Daughters of Liberty urged people not to drink British tea. Instead, they gave out recipes for tea made from birch bark, sage, and rosemary. They spun thread and made clothes for their families instead of buying British-made clothes.

The **Sons of Liberty** groups were more activist. They were composed mostly of shopkeepers, artisans, and laborers, but they were often led by gentlemen of property and standing. They aimed at defending American liberties by making sure that no stamps were distributed. If it took mob action to do so, then mob action it would be.

The Stamp Act Is Repealed

In August of 1765, a mob of men and women in Boston burned the records of the admiralty court and invaded the house of stamp distributor Andrew Oliver. The mob called for either his resignation or his head. Oliver had wisely removed himself before the mob arrived. However, the next day he read his resignation aloud to a jeering, cheering crowd. Similar mobs assembled in other cities and proved effective without killing anyone. By November 1, the day the Stamp Act was to go into effect, every stamp agent in the colonies had either resigned or promised not to issue any stamps.

Americans found another means of resistance in addition to mob action. Hundreds of merchants in the three major northern ports—Boston, New York, and Philadelphia—signed agreements not to buy British goods until the Stamp Act was repealed. This boycott of British goods was called **nonimportation.** The merchants hoped that British manufacturers and merchants would be so upset that they would force Parliament to repeal the act.

Sure enough, Parliament repealed the Stamp Act in March 1766. Yet few British leaders were willing to admit the truth of William Pitt's statement that the act had been a mistake and that Parliament had no right to tax their overseas citizens who were not represented in Parliament. Therefore, on the same day that Parliament repealed the Stamp Act, it passed the Declaratory Act. This act asserted Parliament's full right to make laws "to bind the colonies and people of America . . . in all cases whatsoever." Parliament also renewed the Quartering Act.

Linking Past to Present

The boycott has been a successful form of protest throughout American history. In 1955 Martin Luther King, Jr., organized a boycott of the city bus line in Montgomery, Alabama, to protest the arrest of Rosa Parks. (See Chapter 31, Section 3.) For more than a year, African Americans walked, rode bicycles, or carpooled until they were able to sit wherever they wanted on city buses.

When news of the repeal of the Stamp Act arrived in the colonies, there was an outburst of celebration and rejoicing. Bells rang everywhere, and the New York assembly even voted to put up statues of **George III,** who had succeeded his grandfather, George II, to the throne in 1760. Little attention was paid to the Declaratory Act and its ominous claims of parliamentary power.

The Townshend Acts Are Denounced

Four months after the repeal of the Stamp Act, a new British colonial minister was appointed. He was Charles Townshend, a man with much energy and little sense.

Townshend decided it was high time the colonies paid their fair share of taxes and learned that they must obey Parliament. A series of revenue laws were enacted that became known as the Townshend Acts. Unlike the direct internal taxes of the Stamp Act, the new duties were indirect external taxes that fell on certain manufactured goods that were imported by the colonies—glass, lead, paints, paper, and tea.

According to mercantilist theory, these duties

Present the Lesson

Ask students to build a time line on the board listing major events that affected British colonial relations between 1765 and 1770. Discuss the purpose and result of each event. (Events might include: Stamp Act (1765)—purpose was to provide additional revenue; result was colonists organized resistance so stamps were never bought or sold.)

Picturing History   Colonists pour tea down the throat of a tarred and feathered tax collector in this British view of the Boston Tea Party (left). The colonists' view of the Stamp Act is clear in the skeleton emblem that warns of the effects of the stamp tax (above). The earthenware teapot also makes a statement about the Stamp Act. It was made in England around 1765.

made no sense at all. They were bound to discourage manufacturers in Britain and to encourage manufacturers in the colonies, just the opposite of what was supposed to happen under mercantilism. Nevertheless, Townshend intended to have the new duties enforced. He provided for admiralty-court jurisdiction over customs offenders. He also created a new Board of Customs Commissioners, which would reside in Boston. To encourage the commissioners' zeal, the law provided that they would be paid from the fines imposed by the admiralty courts. The more convictions these officials obtained, the more money they would receive!

The Townshend Acts also aimed at New York's failure to comply with the Quartering Act of 1766. The New York assembly had been providing only part of the money needed to house British troops. The act shut down the assembly until the full amount was appropriated.

American Response.   American response to the Townshend Acts followed a different pattern than the response to the Stamp Act. The new duties did not affect people in general the way the stamp tax had. This time the tax burden fell mostly on merchants. They therefore revived the boycott of British imports. As with all boycotts, however, there was difficulty in gaining unanimous cooperation. If merchants in one port agreed on nonimportation, merchants in neighboring ports were tempted to continue business as usual.

The Sons of Liberty made a two-pronged attack on this problem. They visited offending merchants and spoke persuasively about the rights of the colonists. They also pointed out the dangers of not going along with the Sons of Liberty.

Letters from a Farmer.   As nonimportation gradually grew more effective, some colonists grew busy with their pens. Pennsylvania statesman **John Dickinson** published a series of correspondence called *Letters from a Farmer in Pennsylvania to the Inhabitants of the British Colonies*. In these letters, Dickinson denounced the Townshend duties as a violation of the unwritten constitution of the British Empire. Dickinson wrote:

> Let these truths be indelibly impressed on our minds, that we cannot be happy without being

Check for Understanding

Have students select three events from the time line that they feel were the most significant in provoking the break in British/colonial relations and write a paragraph explaining the reasons for their choices. (Paragraphs might include: Stamp Act was important because it helped unify colonists against the common problem of taxation without representation; it proved to Britain that the colonists could act as a united force.)

Guided Practice

Point out to students that boycotts have been frequently used as successful protests in American history. Ask students how boycotts help bring problems to national attention. (Possible response: television and newspaper coverage demonstrate to all Americans how some people feel about an issue.)

For Discussion

What qualities describe the citizens of Massachusetts? (Possible responses: citizens of Massachusetts were accustomed to a representative form of government and town meetings; many were wealthy merchants with fortunes at stake.) How did these people differ from their English rulers in their beliefs about their human rights? (Possible responses: citizens believed they had a right to participate in government; they believed they should not be taxed unless adequately represented in the government.)

free—that we cannot be free without being secure in our property—that we cannot be secure in our property if without our consent others may as by right take it away.

Dickinson also pointed out that if Parliament could shut down the New York assembly, it could shut down others. In effect, he said, New York might be merely the first victim of "unlawful tyranny."

Tension Grows in Massachusetts

Dickinson's points were restated by the Massachusetts assembly in a letter to the other colonial assemblies. The actual author of this letter, which "called upon the other colonies to unite for the common defense," was **Samuel Adams.**

Adams was a Bostonian who had graduated from Harvard with a master's degree. After failing in his father's brewery business, he turned to local politics, where he soon gained great success as a popular agitator. Adams sniffed tyranny in every breeze. He therefore pressed tirelessly for stronger measures.

The tone of the Massachusetts letter angered the British ministry, which ordered the governor of Massachusetts to dissolve the assembly if it failed to withdraw the letter. On June 30, 1768, the Massachusetts General Court voted ninety-two to seventeen against withdrawal. The next day the governor sent all the members packing.

The atmosphere in Boston was heated up further by the activities of the newly arrived customs commissioners. They would have been resented no matter what they did. As it happens, they proved to be far from saintly. They seized ships if merchants so much as filed forms in the wrong way.

One day they seized a ship belonging to a merchant named John Hancock, who thought he did not owe duty on some wine. Menacing crowds assembled outside the commissioners' houses. The commissioners thereupon removed themselves to an island in Boston Harbor and wrote to London requesting that troops be sent to protect them.

The Boston "Massacre." Rumors about the possible arrival of British troops ran through Boston during that summer of 1768. Samuel Adams and other Sons of Liberty talked up the idea of active resistance. Two British regiments did actually arrive in late September. As they marched up the wharves, the townspeople watched with appre-

hension and resentment. There was no violence, however.

The British troops lived in Boston for eighteen months before a serious incident occurred. The cause of friction was competition for jobs between local laborers and the poorly paid British soldiers who were looking for work during off-duty hours. On the afternoon of March 5, 1770, a fistfight broke out over this issue. That evening a mob gathered in front of the customshouse, which armed British soldiers were guarding.

At first the crowd taunted the soldiers with cries of "Lobster Backs," referring to their red uniforms, and "Bloody Backs," referring to the British custom of flogging soldiers for even minor offenses. Then the crowd began hurling firewood, stones, snowballs, and oyster shells. Among the colonials was a tall black man named **Crispus Attucks,** well known in the Boston dock area and probably a runaway slave.

The frustrated soldiers stood their ground until, as an eyewitness later said, Attucks grabbed a soldier's bayonet and threw the man down. The soldiers thereupon fired their muskets. Five men, including Attucks, were killed, and three were wounded.

To head off further clashes, Governor Thomas Hutchinson ordered the British troops to islands in Boston Harbor. There they remained for the next four years. Samuel Adams eagerly used what he called the **Boston Massacre** as propaganda against the British. Although the deaths of the men were tragic, to most people the affair was a brawl, not the "massacre" that Adams called it.

Lord North Calms Things Down. While anti-British feeling was being fanned in the colonies, events in Great Britain were moving in a more peaceful direction. Townshend died and was replaced as colonial minister by **Lord Frederick North.** North realized that the Townshend Acts were costing more to enforce than they would ever bring in. British merchants were complaining loudly about the colonial boycott of their goods. So North convinced Parliament to repeal all the taxes except the one on tea. He also let the Quartering Act expire.

When word of this development reached the colonies, the nonimportation movement collapsed. Business boomed, and the political atmosphere became more relaxed than at any time since word of the Sugar Act had arrived in 1764.

Assign Independent Practice
Have students complete Chapter 4 Section 3 Enrichment Activity.

Student Assignment/Homework
Have students complete Chapter 4 Test on paper. Review the answers with the class.

Picturing History Paul Revere engraved this image (above)of the Boston Massacre to win sympathy for the colonists' cause. Revere's portrait (left) is by John Singleton Copley, and the silver bowl (below) was crafted by Revere.

Events Reach the Breaking Point

From 1770 to 1773, there was a period of relative quiet. However, Samuel Adams and other agitators tried to take advantage of a few incidents. The most serious involved the *Gaspee*.

The *Gaspee* and Committees of Correspondence. For months, sailors from the British customs schooner *Gaspee* had been boarding colonial vessels in Narragansett Bay to see if they were smuggling goods. Sailors from the *Gaspee* often went ashore, where they stole pigs and chickens and cut down fruit trees for firewood. So the ship and its crew were anything but popular.

On June 9, 1772, the *Gaspee* ran aground while pursuing a local vessel. That night eight boatloads of men rowed out from Providence to the stranded schooner. They boarded it, wounded its captain, removed its crew, and burned it to the waterline.

When news of this event reached London, North's ministry correctly concluded that no convictions could be obtained in a local court. So the king named a special commission to seek out the guilty and bring them to Great Britain for trial.

Although Rhode Islanders successfully frustrated the commissioners, the plan to take colonial Americans to Britain for trial aroused widespread alarm. The assemblies of Massachusetts and Virginia set up **Committees of Correspondence** to communicate with other colonies about threats to American liberties. By 1774 most of the colonies had established such committees. They formed a network of communication.

The Boston Tea Party. Early in 1773, Lord North found a different colonial problem on his doorstep. The East India Company, which governed the British colonies in India, was corrupt, mismanaged, and on the brink of bankruptcy. However, its warehouses were bulging with seventeen million pounds of India tea. So North pushed an act through Parliament to save the company by giving it a monopoly on the sale of tea in the colonies. The new arrangement would provide colonists with cheaper tea. However, it meant that merchants would be left out of the profitable trade. Lord North thought that Americans liked tea more than they disliked monopolies. He was wrong. Mass meetings were held in most major colonial ports. Most agents of the East India Company were persuaded to resign. In most cases, either the tea ships were turned back or the tea was unloaded and placed in warehouses unsold.

In Boston, however, Governor Hutchinson refused to let the tea ships leave without discharging their cargoes. On the evening of December 16, 1773, a group of colonists disguised themselves as Indians by greasing their faces and wrapping themselves in blankets. They boarded three tea ships and threw fifteen thousand pounds of tea into the dark waters of Boston Harbor. This incident is usually referred to as the **Boston Tea Party.** Soon, people everywhere were repeating the quip: "What are the Bostonians complaining about now? They say the fish in their harbor all taste of tea."

Many colonial Americans, though, thought the Boston men had gone too far. Their minds changed rapidly when they learned of the British government's reaction to the Boston Tea Party.

The Intolerable Acts. Pressed by a furious king and indignant editorials in the British press, Parliament in 1774 passed a series of measures that came to be known in the colonies as the **Intolerable Acts.** One of these laws closed the city's harbor until the East India Company and the customs service were paid for their losses. Under a second law, royal officials charged with a capital crime while enforcing a law were to be tried in Great Britain rather than in the colonies. Another law virtually tossed the charter of 1691 out the window. The governor's council was now to be appointed by the Crown, and town meetings could be held only when called by the governor. A fourth law, a new Quartering Act, authorized military commanders to house their soldiers in private homes as well as in taverns and vacant buildings. The troops stationed on islands in Boston Harbor were reinforced and brought into the city itself.

Finally, **General Thomas Gage,** commander in chief of all British troops in the colonies, was appointed the new governor of Massachusetts. In short, Boston was now under **martial law.**

The First Continental Congress. George III and Lord North had hoped to isolate Massachusetts by singling out that unruly colony for special punishment and controls. Instead, their actions drove the colonies together.

People in other cities collected supplies to send to the suffering residents of Boston. The various Committees of Correspondence worked at keeping each other informed. Most important, all the colonies except Georgia named delegates to a meeting called the **First Continental Congress,** which was to be held in Philadelphia in September of 1774.

The Congress was to decide what steps could be taken to defend the colonies against what was considered increasing tyranny.

The first step was to endorse several resolutions known as the Suffolk Resolves. They had previously been adopted by a meeting of town delegates in Suffolk County, Massachusetts. The Suffolk Resolves denounced the Intolerable Acts and urged the colonies to form militias to resist their enforcement. The Resolves also called on the colonies to suspend trade with the rest of the empire.

The Congress then set up the Continental Association to enforce a boycott of British imports and to block exports to Britain as well. It called on every colony to set up local committees to publish the names of violators of this boycott as "enemies of American liberty." Finally, the Congress agreed to meet again in May 1775 unless American grievances were fully met.

The First Bloodshed. Encouraged by the actions of the Continental Congress, many towns in eastern New England stepped up military preparations. Special units of the colonial militia prepared to assemble at a minute's notice. These **minutemen** began stockpiling firearms and gunpowder. General Gage became increasingly aware of these activities and kept writing London for more troops. Military men in Britain, however, had a poor opinion of the colonials. One general, for example, declared that Americans could not fight and that he could march from one end of the continent to the other with five thousand men.

On April 14, 1775, Gage received a letter ordering him to attack the rebellious minutemen with the soldiers on hand. He immediately prepared to strike at Concord, Massachusetts, twenty-one miles west of Boston, where informants told him there was a large collection of arms. Gage realized he could not conceal his preparations. He had to bring in longboats from anchored warships in order to ferry his men across the Charles River.

On the night of April 18, seven hundred British soldiers set out for Concord. William Dawes, Samuel Prescott, and Paul Revere rode off to spread word of the troops' intended destination. The countryside rang with churchbells and gunshots. These were prearranged signals sent from one town to the next.

The first British troops reached Lexington, Massachusetts, five miles short of Concord, at dawn. There they found some seventy minutemen drawn

Concluding the Chapter

Divide the class into two groups—one acting as colonists in favor of breaking all ties with Britain and one acting as colonists in favor of remaining loyal to Britain. Using the chart "Revolutionary War: Advantages and Disadvantages" on p. 115, have each group prepare an editorial for a Boston newspaper declaring their opinion about separation from Britain. Have one student from each group read the group's editorial aloud and have the class decide which one is the most convincing.

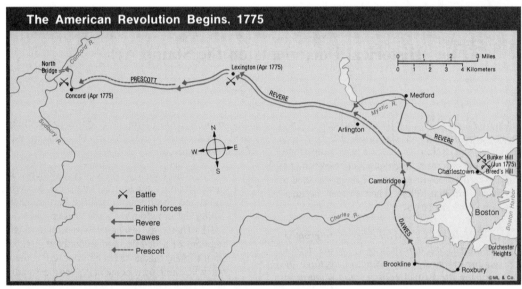

The American Revolution Begins, 1775

Map Skills Movement How far was the disastrous British march from Lexington to Concord?
Human-environment interaction What river does the North Bridge cross?

up in lines on the village green. The commanding British officer ordered them to disperse. The Americans began to do so but without laying down their arms. Someone fired—no one knows who—and the British soldiers sent a volley of shots into the dispersing militia. Eight minutemen were killed.

The British troops then pressed on to Concord. There, they drove off a small group of minutemen and searched for the store of arms. All that remained were a few gun carriages, digging tools, and some flour. After burning the flour, the British lined up for the return march to Boston.

The march turned out to be a disaster. The road seemed lined with minutemen who fired from behind trees and stone walls. Some three to four thousand New England militiamen had assembled in about twelve hours. The British fell by the dozens. Only the arrival of reinforcements from Boston saved them from complete disaster. As it was, they suffered three times as many casualties as the country farmers whom they had held in contempt.

Bloodied, exhausted, humiliated, and bewildered, the British soldiers found themselves back in Boston that night. Probably they were too tired to notice that the surrounding hills were dotted with campfires over which salt pork and johnnycake were cooking. The campfires belonged to British

colonists who had somehow become their enemies and now had Boston under seige.

SECTION 3 REVIEW

Key Terms and People

Explain the significance of: Sons of Liberty, nonimportation, George III, John Dickinson, Samuel Adams, Crispus Attucks, Boston Massacre, Lord Frederick North, Committees of Correspondence, Boston Tea Party, Intolerable Acts, General Thomas Gage, martial law, First Continental Congress, minutemen

Main Ideas

1. What did the colonists hope to accomplish by boycotting British goods?
2. What was the purpose behind the enactment of the Townshend Acts?
3. What was Adams's reason for calling a small skirmish the "Boston Massacre"?
4. Why did the colonists object to the East India Company's monopoly on tea in the colonies?

Critical Thinking

5. Why were the measures passed by Parliament in 1774 considered intolerable by the colonists?

Lesson Plan

State the Objective

Understand the important principle behind the Stamp Act.

Present the Lesson

Remind students that documents provide essential information about a historical event. Ask the class these questions: What goods did the tax affect? (Answer: any printed matter, such as newspapers and legal documents.) Who paid it? (Answer: lawyers, printers, and publishers who, as a result, opposed the tax.) Who received the tax money? (Answer: the British King.) Who enforced the tax? (Answers: British soldiers and the admiralty courts, with trial by a judge rather than a jury.) Ask students why Parliament taxed printed matter rather than taxing individuals, food, or prop- erty. (Possible response: printed matter such as newspapers and pamphlets have an enormous influence on society.) Discuss the impact of printed matter in contemporary societies.

Call on students to summarize the legal grounds on which American colonists opposed the tax. (Response: as English citizens, colonists could not be taxed without the consent of their representative legislatures and were entitled to trial by jury.) Have students look at the issue from the British point of view. Call on students to summarize the arguments in favor of Parliament taxing the colonists. (Possible responses: Parliament had the power

Focus on Primary Sources

Historical Documents on the Stamp Act

On March 22, 1765, the British Parliament voted to levy the first direct tax upon the American colonies. Opposition to this act was immediate. Read the excerpt from the Stamp Act below and the three excerpts from historical documents related to the Stamp Act that follow. Then answer the questions on these primary sources.

> WHEREAS . . . *several duties were granted, continued, and appropriated towards defraying the expences of defending, protecting, and securing the* British *colonies and plantations in* America: *and whereas it is just and necessary, that provision be made for raising a further revenue within your Majesty's dominions in* America, . . . *be it enacted . . . ,* [that] there shall be raised, levied, collected, and paid unto his Majesty, his heirs and successors, . . .
>
> For every skin or piece of vellum or parchment, or sheet or piece of paper, on which shall be ingrossed, written, or printed . . . [Here followed a schedule of payments ranging from a few pennies to several pounds for every legal paper or bill, and for each page of any pamphlet, gazette, or almanac, for any and all advertisements in the aforesaid in English or any other language. There was a charge as well for packs of playing cards, and for dice. There was a further provision.]
>
> [O]ffenses committed against any other act or acts of Parliament relating to the trade or revenues of the said colonies or plantations; shall and may be prosecuted, sued for, and recovered, in any court of record, or in any court of admiralty . . . or in any court of vice admiralty. [The significance was that such courts functioned without juries.]

Source: Reprinted in Henry Steele Commager, *Documents of American History* (New York: Appleton-Century-Crofts, 1949), 5th ed., 53–55.

In October 1765, representatives of the colonies met to protest the Stamp Act. After proclaiming their loyalty, the delegates of this Stamp Act Congress resolved,

> II. That His Majesty's liege subjects in these colonies are intitled to all the inherent rights and liberties of his natural born subjects within the kingdom of Great Britain.
>
> III. That it is inseparably essential to the freedom of a people, and undoubted right of Englishmen, that no taxes be imposed on them but with their own consent, given personally or by their representatives.
>
> IV. That the people of these colonies are not, and from their local circumstances cannot be, represented in the House of Commons in Great Britain.
>
> V. That the only representatives of the people of these colonies are persons chosen therein by themselves, and that no taxes ever have been, or can be constitutionally imposed on them, but by their respective legislatures. . . .
>
> VII. That trial by jury is the inherent and invaluable right of every British subject in these colonies.
>
> VIII. That the late Act of Parliament, entitled *An Act for granting and applying certain stamp duties,* . . . by imposing taxes on the inhabitants of these colonies; and . . . by extending the jurisdiction of the courts of Admiralty beyond its ancient limits, have a manifest tendency to subvert the rights and liberties of the colonists.

Source: Reprinted in Charles W. Eliot, ed., *American Historical Documents,* 1000–1904 (New York: Collier, 1910), 147–148.

In 1766 a bill to repeal the Stamp Act was introduced in Parliament. Lord Mansfield then laid two propositions before the House of Lords.

> First, that the British legislature [Parliament], as to the power of making laws, represents the whole British Empire, and has

to make laws for the whole British empire; Parliament had always exercised the right to enact laws in the colonies without objection.) Ask: how did the Declaratory Act aid the British plan to tax the colonists? (Answer: the Declaratory Act legalized the Mansfield propositions by stating that Parliament had the right to pass laws that are binding in the colonies.)

Check for Understanding

Have students respond orally to the questions at the end of the feature. Be sure students provide information from documents and from prior knowledge to support their opinions. To conclude the lesson, remind students of the economic aspects of the Stamp Act Congress. Point out that legal arguments found in these documents were not the driving force that repealed the Stamp Act. Rather, the hard economic reality of American colonists boycotting British goods forced the British to back down.

authority to bind every part and every subject without the least distinction, whether such subjects have a right to vote or not, or whether the law binds places within the realm or without.

Second, that the colonists, by the condition on which they migrated, settled, and now exist, are more emphatically subjects of Great Britain than those within the realm; and that the British legislature [has] in every instance exercised [its] right of legislation over them without any dispute or question till [now]. . . .

[I]t must be granted that [the colonists] migrated with leave as colonies, and therefore from the very meaning of the word were, are, and must be subjects, and owe allegiance and subjection to their mother country.

Source: Reprinted in Richard C. Wade, Louise Wade, and Howard B. Wilder, *A History of the United States with Selected Readings to 1877* (Boston: Houghton Mifflin, 1971), vol. 1, 124–125.

The Stamp Act was repealed, but to satisfy the King and others, the Declaratory Act of March 18, 1766, replaced it.

[B]e it declared. . . , That the said colonies and plantations in *America* have been, are, and of right ought to be, subordinate unto, and dependent upon the imperial crown and parliament of *Great Britain;* and that the King's majesty, by and with the advice and consent of the lords spiritual and temporal, and commons of *Great Britain,* in parliament assembled had, hath, and of right ought to have, full power and authority to make laws and statutes of sufficient force and validity to bind the colonies and people of *America,* subjects of the crown of *Great Britain* in all cases whatsoever.

And be it further declared . . . , That all resolutions, votes, orders, and proceedings in any of the said colonies or plantations, whereby the power and authority of the parliament of *Great Britain* to make laws and statutes as aforesaid, is denied or drawn into question, are, and are hereby declared to be, utterly null and void to all intents and purposes whatsoever.

Source: Reprinted in Commager, *Documents of American History,* 60–61.

Picturing History
The anger evoked by the Stamp Act can be seen on the faces of the colonists in the painting above. Colonists in Boston, who believed the purpose of the tax was to weaken the colonies, showed their opposition by staging a Stamp Act burning (right).

Analyzing Primary Sources

1. Of what two British rights did the colonists believe the Stamp Act had deprived them?
2. How did Lord Mansfield justify his opinion that the colonists were mistaken about their rights?
3. What was the purpose of the Declaratory Act? What did it accomplish?

Critical Thinking

4. Analyze the cause-effect relationships that can be found in these historical documents.

Key Terms and People

These are highlighted in the text in the order in which they appear in this list.

Main Ideas

1. Enlightenment scientists discovered that fixed natural laws govern the universe. Philosophers like Locke then reasoned that fixed natural laws must govern human behavior.
• Life, liberty, and property.

2. The Puritans insisted that their members learn to read, in order to be able to read the Bible. From the 1640's, Massachusetts law provided that all towns with more than 50 families support a schoolmaster.
• The Puritans valued their religion and took actions to preserve it.

3. The Indians believed that (1) the French would defeat the British; (2) British land speculators were cheating them out of their land; (3) the British charged higher prices than the French for trade goods, did not supply powder and lead for hunting, and gave the Indians rum and then cheated them out of money or goods due them.

4. To pay for the 10,000 troops the British left to protect the colonies and to fund the customs service, which was costing four times as much as it was bringing in.

5. Assemblies passed resolutions declaring the Stamp Act taxation without representation; colonists burned the records of the admiralty court, caused every stamp distributor to resign, and boycotted British goods.

6. 1754: Benjamin Franklin proposes Albany Plan of Union at Albany Congress. 1765: Stamp Act Congress writes Declaration of Rights and Grievances; Sons and Daughters of Liberty begin to meet secretly; merchants boycott British goods. 1774: Committees of Correspondence form.

Critical Thinking Questions

7. While the seven had not confessed, Danforth rationalized that twelve had already been executed for the same crime, these seven should be executed also.

➤**8.** In the theatrical preaching of the new ministers, people found an excitement and emotion, lacking in their old religions. • Former Puritans flocked to the more emotional preachers, and prosperity made it possible for Puritans to enjoy worldly things.

9. Indians would mostly have agreed with the natural right to property, but they believed that the land belonged to everyone, not individuals.
• Locke probably believed that the English way was the "natural" way and would not have respected the Indian point of view.

➤**10.** Possible answers: guilty of libel—Zenger should not have printed articles that damaged the governor's reputation. Libel is anything that damages a person's reputation. Not guilty of libel—the articles were true; only if they had been false and malicious would Zenger have been guilty.

11. The columns of British soldiers, trained in European-style battle, were open to surprise attack by the Indians.
• Guerrilla warfare similar to

CHAPTER 4 REVIEW

Write your answers on a separate sheet of paper.

Key Terms and People

Explain the significance of: Benjamin Franklin, John Woolman, Treaty of Paris of 1763, Proclamation of 1763, Patrick Henry, nonimportation, George III, John Dickinson, Samuel Adams, Crispus Attucks, Lord Frederick North, General Thomas Gage, martial law, minutemen

Main Ideas

1. How did the experiments and theories of Copernicus, Galileo, and Newton result in John Locke's theory of the laws of natural rights? What are these natural rights according to John Locke?

2. How and where did the American idea of free public education for all get its start? What does this show about Puritan values?

3. Why were the Indians mostly on the side of the French throughout the eighteenth century?

4. Why did Grenville impose the Sugar Act (1764), the Quartering Act (1765), and the Stamp Act (1765)?

5. How did the colonists manage to get the Stamp Act repealed?

6. Using the book, list the efforts that helped the colonists learn to act collectively at the First Continental Congress.

Critical Thinking Questions

7. **Analyzing Literature.** In the excerpt from Arthur Miller's play on page 75, why, according to Danforth, were the others bound by heaven to hang the seven?

8. **Making Deductions.** During the Enlightenment the colonies experienced a religious revival called the Great Awakening. Why were people so moved by preachers like Jonathan Edwards and George Whitefield? How did the Great Awakening and prosperity result in the decline of Puritanism?

9. **Analyzing Ideas.** What would the American Indians have thought of Locke's theory of natural right of property? What does this show about Locke?

10. **Drawing Conclusions.** Look up the word *libel* in your classroom dictionary. From the definition, would you have found Zenger not guilty if you had been on the jury in his 1735 trial?

11. **Making Deductions.** Why were the British troops defeated so easily in frontier war? What did they need to learn?

Critical Thinking Activities

12. **Analyzing Causes.** Using the book, fill in the list of British legislation and other events that drove the colonists to the First Continental Congress. Give at least one specific provision of any legislation on your list.

   a. 1764: Sugar Act: lower duty on foreign-made molasses, duties on many other commodities, and enforcement in British admiralty courts.

   b. 1765: _____

   c. 1766: _____

   d. 1768: _____

   e. 1770: _____

   f. 1773: _____

   g. 1774: Intolerable Acts: Boston harbor closed; governor's council to be appointed by the Crown; town meetings to be held only when called by governor; new Quartering Act; troops returned to city; General Gage new governor.

13. **Linking Past to Present.** The witchcraft hysteria that gripped the town of Salem, Massachusetts, in 1692 was created by lies and was continued because people were so frightened that they made false accusations. Does this remind you of anything happening in today's world? Explain.

that used by the Indians.

Critical Thinking Activities

➤**12.** 1765: Quartering Act— colony in which troops stationed must provide living quarters and certain supplies; Stamp Act—people who do not purchase stamps for all legal documents and newspapers to be tried in admiralty courts—Sons and Daughters of Liberty form; 1766: Stamp

Act repealed; Quartering Act reviewed; Declaratory Act— Parliament given right to make any laws for the colonies; Townshend Acts—people refusing to pay duty on manufactured goods to be tried in admiralty courts; fines to be used to pay customs commissioners. 1768: Massachusetts Assembly dismissed; customs officials seize John Hancock's ship; commissioners move to island in harbor. 1770: Boston

Massacre; troops move to island in harbor. 1773: East India Company gets tea monopoly, thus provoking Boston Tea Party.

➤**13.** Possible answer: the issues of AIDS, communism, and abortion have produced hysteria among some people.

➤**Question suitable for cooperative learning.**

TELESCOPING THE TIMES: 1700–1775

Separating from Britain

Americans welcomed the European ideas of the Enlightenment, which emphasized the importance of reason rather than guesswork and superstition. Benjamin Franklin became famous because he applied reason to scientific and social problems.

In 1692 a crisis arose because of alleged witchcraft in Salem, Massachusetts, but it was the last crisis to occur on this issue in the colonies. For a time religious commitment seemed to weaken, but by 1740 the Great Awakening brought a tradition of religious revivalism to America. Many new churches were established.

Both religious and Enlightenment ideas encouraged education. A few small colleges were founded. More important, many schools, especially in New England, taught boys and girls to read and write. The colonists were a people of the written word, and they welcomed the new idea of freedom of the press.

In 1754 a major war broke out between the French and the British. The first battles were fought near the site of modern Pittsburgh, and the French won victories over both colonial militia and British regular troops. The colonies tried to unite at the Albany Congress but failed. Then the tide turned, and British forces pushed up the St. Lawrence River Valley and conquered all of New France, or Canada.

At war's end, the British government began a program of tightening up control over its American empire. The Sugar Act of 1764 aimed at collecting customs duties and putting a stop to smuggling. In 1765 the Stamp Act established the first direct tax on the colonists. Proclaiming ''no taxation without representation,'' the Americans met in a general congress to protest the new British policy.

In the port cities, angry mobs blocked distribution of the hated tax stamps. Groups of men calling themselves the Sons of Liberty led the mobs and urged merchants to boycott British imports. As a result, officials in London backed down and repealed the Stamp Act.

A similar boycott forced Britain to withdraw all additional new taxes. In 1773 a group of men dressed as Indians tossed British tea into Boston Harbor. Angry British officials closed down the port and much of the government of Massachusetts. Britain sent troops to Boston, where the colonists seemed especially rebellious. Representatives of other colonies gathered in support of the rebels at the First Continental Congress. In 1775 violence broke out just outside of Boston.

Chronology of Main Events	
1701	Yale College founded
1704	First colonial newspaper, the Boston *News-Letter,* founded
1740's	Great Awakening sweeps through the colonies
1754	Albany Congress meets
1754–1763	French and Indian War
1763	Treaty of Paris signed; Proclamation of 1763 bars colonists from Indian territory
1765	Quartering Act; Stamp Act
1766	Stamp Act repealed
1770	Boston Massacre
1773	Boston Tea Party
1774	First Continental Congress meets
1775	Battles of Lexington and Concord

Telescoping the Times may be used as an alternative to having students read the entire chapter, as a chapter preview, or as a chapter review.

97

Global Perspectives

1775   Britain hires German mercenaries to fight Americans.

1776   Adam Smith publishes *Wealth of Nations*.

1777   Christianity comes to Korea.

1778   Captain James Cook discovers Sandwich Islands, later known as Hawaii.

1782   Holland recognizes American independence.

For Discussion

How might the recognition of American independence by Holland have benefited the newly formed nation? (Possible responses: it might have helped America to gain recognition from other European countries and to establish diplomatic ties.)

Additional Teaching Strategies

SECTION 1

For Basic Students: Have students prepare a time line of the events detailed in this section that contributed to separation of the colonies from Britain. (Time lines might include: May, 1775—Second Continental Congress convenes, Ethan Allen captures Fort Ticonderoga; June 17, 1775—British win Battle of Bunker Hill; March 17, 1776—British evacuate Boston.) Discuss the importance of these events to the Revolution.

For Advanced Students: Tell students to research the military background and trial of Benedict Arnold and prepare a two-minute speech to be used as a closing argument in Arnold's trial. Students may choose to argue for the defense or for the prosecution. (Speeches should include: Arnold's military achievements; reasons for his "treasonable act.")

SECTION 2

For Basic Students: Have students look up information about one of the five delegates chosen to prepare the Declaration of Independence and write a three-paragraph report highlighting his career. (Reports might include: Roger Sherman—American jurist and statesman; served in Connecticut legislature 1755-1766; appointed judge of superior court of Connecticut 1766; elected to Connecticut senate; was member of Continental Congress; served on the Committee of Five; helped write Articles of Confederation; served as mayor of New Haven; was member of Federal Constitutional Convention.) Have students share their papers.

For Advanced Students: Divide the students into two groups—one to represent the Loyalists and one to represent the Patriots. Ask each to prepare a letter to the editor of a Philadelphia newspaper expressing his or her feelings about the Declaration of Independence. (Letters should include: a statement identifying the writer as a Loyalist or a Patriot; specific reasons why the writer is for or against the Declaration of Independence.) Have students share their letters.

SECTION 3

For Basic Students: Ask students to assume the role of General George Washington. They should then write a letter to the Continental Congress describing conditions of the Continental army and requesting more financial assistance. (Letters should include: reference to lack of shoes, clothing, and blankets; reference to the need for more guns and military supplies; requests for better pay and incentives to keep soldiers in the army.) Discuss how these conditions affected the army's morale.

For Advanced Students: Have students choose one of the people discussed in this section, research that person's life and contribution to the Revolutionary War, and prepare a two-page letter to Congress asking it to award him or her a posthumous military award for outstanding service. (Letters on Molly Pitcher might include: served as a model to all young women; bravely took her husband's place in battle; showed great courage.) Have students share these letters.

SECTION 4

For Basic Students: Discuss the term alliance with the students and develop a definition. (Possible definition: a condition of mutual benefit for the parties involved.) Ask students to write a paragraph describing how the Americans and the French benefited from their alliance. (Paragraphs might include: American benefits—recognition by foreign government, increased military strength, manufactured goods, money to continue the war effort; French benefits—a chance to defeat and humiliate Britain, a new ally against Britain, a market for manufactured goods.) Discuss students' papers.

For Advanced Students: Divide the class into three groups, one each to represent the Americans, British, and French. Ask each group to draw political cartoons to express their feelings about the American-French alliance. Display these cartoons in the classroom.

SECTION 5

For Basic Students: Tell students to construct a chart showing how the Treaty of Paris affected America, Britain, France, and Spain. Have students head each of four columns with the name of one of these countries. Effects should be listed in the column under each name. (Charts might include: Britain acknowledged American independence; led to Spain receiving Florida; America agreed to let British creditors collect any debts owed them by American citizens.)

For Advanced Students: Divide students into pairs. After researching the Treaty of Paris, each pair should present to the class an interview with either John Jay, Benjamin Franklin, or John Adams to discuss each negotiator's thoughts about the treaty and the future of the new nation. (Interview with Jay might include: is pleased that his negotiations were successful; is cautiously optimistic; realizes that although France will help the colonies separate from England, it is not in France's best interest to help the colonies form a strong, independent nation.)

Further Reading for Students

Adams, Abigail, and John Adams. *The Book of Abigail and John: Letters of the Adams Family.* Cambridge: Harvard University Press, 1975.

Cunliffe, Marcus. *George Washington: Man and Monument.* New York: NAL Penguin, 1984.

Fritz, Jean. *Traitor: The Case of Benedict Arnold.* New York: Putnam Publishing Group, 1981.

Morris, Richard B. *The American Revolution Reconsidered.* Minneapolis: Lerner Publications, 1985.

Roberts, Kenneth. *The Battle of Cowpens.* Philadelphia: Eastern Acorn Press, 1981.

Rossiter, Clinton. *The First American Revolution: The American Colonies on the Eve of Independence.* San Diego, Calif.: Harcourt Brace Jovanovich, 1956.

Historical Fiction

Avi. *The Fighting Ground.* New York: Harper & Row, 1984.

Collier, James Lincoln, and Christopher Collier. *The Bloody Country.* Soquel, Calif.: Four Winds Press, 1976.

Roberts, Kenneth. *Arundel.* New York: Fawcett Book Group, 1976.

Roberts, Kenneth. *Oliver Wiswell.* New York: Fawcett Book Group, 1981.

Roberts, Kenneth. *Rabble in Arms.* New York: Fawcett Book Group, 1981.

Steele, William O. *The Man with the Silver Eyes.* San Diego, Calif.: Harcourt Brace Jovanovich, 1976.

Bibliography for Teachers

Books

Billias, George A., ed. *The American Revolution: How Revolutionary Was It?* 3rd ed. New York: Holt, Rinehart and Winston, 1980.

Catton, Bruce, and William B. Catton. *The Bold and Magnificent Dream: America's Founding Years, 1492-1815.* Doubleday, 1978.

DePauw, Linda G. *Founding Mothers: Women of America in the Revolutionary Era.* Boston: Houghton Mifflin, 1975.

Miller, John C. *Origins of the American Revolution.* Stanford: Stanford University Press, 1959.

Nelson, William H. *The American Tory.* 1961. Reprint. Westport, Conn.: Greenwood Press, 1980.

Tuchman, Barbara W. *The First Salute.* New York: Alfred A. Knopf, 1988.

Audio-Visuals

American Literature—Revolutionary Times. Coronet. Movie.

Black People in the Revolution. Encyclopaedia Britannica Educational Corp. Filmstrip.

Great Men and Great Issues: Founding the American Nation. Wilcom Corporation. Audio tapes.

John Paul Jones. Lucerne Films, Inc. Movie.

1776. Listening Library. Movie.

The World of Franklin and Jefferson. International Business Machines Corporation. Movie.

Computer Resources

Revolutions: Past, Present, and Future. (Apple/TRS 80) Opportunities for Learning.

U.S. History: American Revolution. (Apple/Commodore 64/TRS 80) Focus Media.

Washington's Decision. (Apple) Educational Activities.

The Young Republic. (Apple/Commodore 64/TRS 80) Opportunities for Learning.

Teacher's Notes:

Lesson Plan

Teaching Resources, Unit 1 Booklet

Chapter Objectives

Students will learn:
- how the colonists made their decision to separate from Britain
- the main ideas of the Declaration of Independence
- the advantages and disadvantages of the British and American positions in the Revolutionary War
- why the Americans were victorious in the Revolutionary War
- the immediate and long-term significance of the American Revolution

Using the Chapter Time Line

List four major events that occurred in the colonies during the five years from 1775 to 1780. (Answer: Revolutionary War, Assembly of Second Continental Congress, Declaration of Independence, surrender of Burgoyne) How many years did the Revolutionary War last? (Answer: 8)

Picturing History Archibald Willard's famous canvas *The Spirit of '76* was painted for the centennial celebration of the Declaration of Independence and captures the spirit that moved the Patriots.

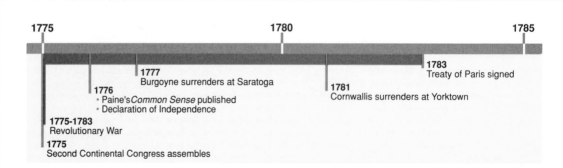

1775   1780   1785

1777
Burgoyne surrenders at Saratoga

1776
• Paine's *Common Sense* published
• Declaration of Independence

1783
Treaty of Paris signed

1781
Cornwallis surrenders at Yorktown

1775-1783
Revolutionary War

1775
Second Continental Congress assembles

Links to American Literature

Walter D. Edmonds: born on a farm near Boonville, New York, in 1903; educated at Harvard University; is best known for his historical novels about New York.

Works include: *The Matchlock Gun*, Newbery medal winner in 1942; *Bert Breen's Barn*, the 1976 National Book Award for children's literature.

Drums Along the Mohawk: a novel about the American Revolution and its effect on the Mohawk Valley farmers.

Introducing the Chapter

Review with students British actions and legislation that led the colonists toward separation from Britain. (Events might include: the royal Proclamation of 1763; the Sugar Act of 1764; the Quartering Act of 1765; the Stamp Act of 1765; the seizure of colonial merchant ships; the closing of Boston Harbor.) To stimulate discussion, ask students the following questions. What means of solving problems were still open to the colonists in 1775? (Possible responses: compromise with Britain; petitions to Parliament; acceptance of legislation; complete separation from Britain.) If you were a col-

onist, what course of action would you favor? (Possible responses: compromise—avoid war at all cost; separation—freedom is worth any price.)

CHAPTER **5**   1775–1783

The War for Independence

Links to American Literature

Then the whips began their rapid fire along the wagon train. The cartwheels screeched in starting. The still heat in the woods was overflowed with shouts, stamping hoofs, the rattle and slam of carts along the corduroy, the treading feet. The dust rose over the column. All at once it was jerking, getting started, moving. . . . A porcupine took hold of a tree and climbed it halfway, and turned his head to see the thronging, jumbled mass that heaved and started, checked, and went again along the narrow road.

The men marched in two lines, one for either rut, their rifles on their shoulders, their hats in their hands. When they came to a brook, the thirsty fell out and drank. Nobody stopped them. When they were through they wiped their mouths and looked up, startled, to see their company replaced by another. They got out of the way of other thirsty men and floundered in the bushes to catch up. There was no room left on the road to pass. . . . The heat grew. Not a breath of air in the branches anywhere, not a cloud in the bits of sky high overhead, nothing but leaves, nothing in all the woods but their own uproarious, bursting, unstemmable progress on the narrow road.

— WALTER D. EDMONDS, *Drums Along the Mohawk*

For colonial soldiers, the Revolutionary War was not a glorious one. It was a war of long, dirty marches and of hunger and thirst that were too seldom satisfied. It was a war that seemed to have no end, a war that could not be won. Yet the desire for freedom was so strong that, in spite of all odds, the Patriots did not rest until victory was theirs.

Chapter Overview

In this chapter you will learn how the colonists made their decisions about separation from Britain, and you will study the Declaration of Independence. You will also learn about the British and American positions in the Revolutionary War and why the Americans won. Finally, you will study the effects of the Revolutionary War. This chapter underscores one of the many values we have inherited as Americans—the willingness to make

heroic sacrifices for freedom from tyranny. The chapter is divided into five sections.

Chapter Outline

1. **The Last Doubts Are Overcome**
2. **The Patriots Declare Independence**
3. **The British and American Positions Differ**
4. **Farmers and Shopkeepers Defeat an Empire**
5. **The American Revolution Changes the World**

Anticipate the Lesson

Discuss ways in which countries can settle disagreements. (Discussion might include: compromise; peace treaty; mediation by a neutral country; war.) Ask students to comment on the advantages and disadvantages of each. (Possible response: a compromise would prevent bloodshed and destruction of property, but

might make both sides feel cheated.) Ask students who decides how a country will settle disputes with other nations. (Possible responses: government; military; citizens.)

State the Objective

Understand how the colonists made their decision to separate from Britain.

The Last Doubts Are Overcome

GLOSSARY TERMS: **redcoats,** *Common Sense*

The Second Continental Congress assembled in Philadelphia in May 1775 as scheduled. Among the delegates were three men who were later to have distinguished careers in the service of their country. **George Washington** of Virginia was already well-known as a military leader, based on his service during the French and Indian War. Benjamin Franklin, who had fled London to escape arrest, was someone every delegate wanted to meet. John Adams, a lawyer and an author from Massachusetts, impressed many with his patriotic vigor and sound reasoning. Somewhat later the delegates were joined by a young red-headed lawyer from Virginia, Thomas Jefferson, who was also known as an able writer on colonial rights.

Some Military Maneuvers Succeed

It was clear from the beginning that the Continental Congress would support Massachusetts, where the first battles of the Revolution had already been fought. Yet there was no formal creation of an American army. The Congress simply declared that the farmers and shopkeepers besieging Boston were the Army of the United Colonies. The same day the Congress convened, **Ethan Allen** and eighty-three volunteers called the **Green Mountain Boys** captured the British garrison at Fort Ticonderoga in New York. When news of the victory reached Philadelphia, John Adams urged that Washington be named commander in chief of the Continental army. Washington accepted the post on June 16. He did not know that he was just about to miss the bloodiest battle of the entire war.

The "Bunker Hill Victory." Cooped up in Boston, General Gage had received reinforcements from Britain. His new "top brass" included three generals: Sir **John Burgoyne,** often called Gentleman Johnny; Sir **Henry Clinton;** and Sir **William Howe.** They decided to dislodge the colonial militia from the hills around Boston. Learning of the British plan through spies in the city, the colonials beat their opponents to the punch. They dug in on Breed's Hill, on the Charlestown peninsula north of the city. (See the map on page 93.)

On the morning of June 17, some twenty-two hundred **redcoats,** or British soldiers so named because of the bright red uniforms they wore, crossed the Charles River and assembled in their customary broad lines at the bottom of the hill. They shouldered their heavy packs and began

People in the Chapter

Ethan Allen and Benedict Arnold met by chance en route to surprise the British at Fort Ticonderoga. An argument broke out over who was in charge. At last they joined forces to capture the fort. Allen later wrote about the event and failed to mention Arnold's name.

Benedict Arnold may have been motivated to commit treason because he had been slighted by his superiors and he needed money. The British, however, never fully paid him for his treason and scorned him as a traitor.

Thomas Paine was a professional activist. He donated nearly one-third of his salary to help Washington's army. After the American Revolution, he went to England and to France to fan the flames of revolution there.

Casimir Pulaski was a Polish count who had been recommended to Washington by Ben-

jamin Franklin. He lost his life while fighting with the Americans against the British.

George Rogers Clark was outnumbered by the British at Fort Vincennes. He waited until dusk to approach the enemy from behind a hilly area. Clark's men carried flags on extra long poles. As they marched around they gave the impression of being a larger force than they actually were. Intimidated by this show of strength, the British surrendered.

John Paul Jones, the courageous Revolutionary War sea captain, was forgotten for one hundred years after he died in Paris. Then his remains were returned to the United States Naval Academy to be enshrined in an elaborate tomb.

Picturing History At the Battle of Bunker Hill the British demonstrated a maneuver they used throughout the war. They massed together, were visible for miles, and failed to take advantage of ground cover. Peter Salem, a black soldier, became a hero at this battle when he killed the British commander.

marching up the slope. They stopped only to fire volleys, which fell harmlessly on Americans grouped on the hilltop behind mounds of earth and logs. The American militiamen held their fire until the last moment. When they did fire, the exposed rows of advancing redcoats went down one after the other. The survivors, including the walking wounded, retreated to the bottom of the hill. There they regrouped. A second assault produced similar results. A third assault finally succeeded when the Americans ran low on musket balls and powder. They fell back at bayonet point from the hill and then from the entire peninsula. The battle has gone down in history as the Battle of Bunker Hill, although it was actually fought on Breed's Hill. Bunker Hill was then quickly assaulted and won as the Americans retreated.

The Americans lost the battle with some four hundred casualties. The British won the battle but suffered more than one thousand casualties. As General Clinton wrote, it was "a dear bought victory, another such would have ruined us." General Gage wrote in a private letter, "The trials we have had show that the rebels are not the despicable rabble too many supposed them to be."

The British Retreat.   Some nine months after the Battle of Breed's Hill, the siege of Boston finally came to an end. The Americans, led by a former bookseller named Henry Knox, brought fifty-nine cannon from Fort Ticonderoga, New York, to Boston. The men loaded the heavy guns on wooden sleds pulled by teams of oxen and then trudged three hundred miles over snow-covered mountains to their destination. On the night of March 4, 1776, the Americans began to set the guns in place on Dorchester Heights just south of Boston, where they commanded much of the harbor. The British were waiting for reinforcements, but by March 17 General Howe realized he would not be able to defend the city. The British evacuated Boston and sailed for Nova Scotia.

The Americans were also successful in the South during that first year of fighting. On June 28, 1776, a British fleet was chased from the harbor of Charles Town (later Charleston), South Carolina. There, Patriots and black slaves had built a fort out of soft palm logs that absorbed the cannonballs from the British ships.

On November 5, 1775, the Earl of Dunmore, royal governor of Virginia, had issued a statement

Check for Understanding

Call on individual students to answer Section 1 Review questions orally.

Guided Practice

Tell students that *Common Sense* is a pamphlet that has affected history. Among other works that have had great influence are *Uncle Tom's Cabin, The Jungle, The Other America,* and *Silent Spring.* Ask students why some books have such a great impact on people. (Possible responses: they give information about a problem and show readers a different perspective; the writing can inspire people to want to change.) Ask students to name a book they have read that inspired them in some way.

saying that all slaves and indentured servants would be freed if they joined the British in suppressing the rebellion. Several hundred men answered the call, but there was no general slave uprising. On December 11 the Virginia and North Carolina militia defeated Dunmore's troops. Dunmore took refuge on a British warship anchored off Norfolk. In revenge, the British fleet bombarded Norfolk on January 1, 1776, and reduced the town's wooden houses to ashes.

The Americans Retreat. When the Second Continental Congress appointed Washington commander in chief in 1775, it also authorized **Benedict Arnold** to lead some eleven hundred Americans through Maine into Canada. The goal was to prevent the British from isolating New England by moving redcoats south through the Hudson River Valley. Arnold led his men on a grueling march of 350 miles through untracked wilderness. Half the troops died because of the bitter cold and lack of food.

After six weeks the Americans reached Quebec and laid siege to the city. Despite their lack of artillery, they remained there through the winter. With the spring thaw, though, came fresh British troops, and the Americans abandoned their hopes for a victory on the northern front. Four years later, Benedict Arnold turned traitor to the American cause. His plot to surrender West Point to the British was discovered when a British secret agent, Major John André, was caught. Arnold escaped to the British forces, but Major André was hanged.

The British Refuse a Petition for Peace

In the meantime, the Second Continental Congress was acting more and more like an independent government. It issued paper money to pay the army and named a committee for dealing with foreign powers. It established a postal department with Benjamin Franklin as postmaster general. It organized three commissions to make alliances with the frontier Indian tribes or at least to persuade them not to side with the British. In the fall of 1775, it authorized the creation of a navy.

The Olive Branch Petition. All these actions were undertaken while the Congress was still expressing its loyalty to the King. Most Americans felt such loyalty deeply. They did not blame the war on King George. They blamed it on his ministers and referred to British forces as the

"ministerial army" rather than the "King's troops." The idea of independence was so frightening that one of the delegates to the Congress said he felt "like a child being thrust violently out of his father's house." On July 8, 1775, the Congress even sent George III the so-called **Olive Branch Petition,** urging a return to "the former harmony" that had existed between Britain and the colonies.

The Petition Is Rejected. King George's response to the colonial plea for peace was clear and to the point. He refused to read it. Then he issued a proclamation stating that a general rebellion existed throughout all of North America, not just in Massachusetts, and that "utmost endeavors" were needed to "suppress such rebellion, and to bring the traitors to justice." After two months of debate, Parliament adopted a resolution to that effect by a margin of two to one. It then ordered the royal navy to blockade the American coastline.

Paine Authors *Common Sense*

Even before news of these events reached the colonies, public opinion about the King and about independence had begun to change. One of the spark plugs of the change was a poor London writer who had arrived in America two years earlier.

In an anonymous forty-seven page pamphlet called ***Common Sense*** (January 1776), **Thomas Paine** attacked King George in particular and monarchy in general. Responsibility for British tyranny, he argued, lay with "the royal brute of Britain." One honest man, in Paine's opinion, was worth "all the crowned ruffians that ever lived."

Paine declared that it was time for Americans to proclaim an independent republic and have nothing further to do with hereditary kings. Independence was the "destiny" of Americans. There were practical advantages as well. For example, an independent America could trade freely with other nations, thus obtaining money for guns and ammunition. Furthermore, if American soldiers were captured by the British, independence meant they would be treated as prisoners of war instead of as rebels. They thus would be imprisoned instead of being shot.

Also, independence would make it easier for America to obtain foreign aid. Although Spain and France, both monarchies, might not help rebels against a king, they were almost certain to help an independent country that was at war with their common enemy, Britain. Without foreign aid, it

For Discussion

Why did Paine's work *Common Sense* gain such wide acceptance? (Possible responses: the Enlightenment had caused an awakening of intellectual activity; wealthy colonial merchants were unhappy with British taxation and were looking for an excuse to rebel; Paine's arguments were logical, his thinking was sound.)

Assign Independent Practice

Have students complete Chapter 5, Section 1 Enrichment Activity.

Student Assignment/Homework

Have students read Section 2, "The Patriots Declare Independence," and complete the section review questions in small groups.

Picturing History Thomas Paine (far right) helped to overcome any last doubts about separating from Britain with his pamphlet *Common Sense,* in which he attacked George III, saying: "Ye that dare oppose not only tyranny but the tyrant, stand forth!"

was doubtful that the colonies could win.

There was yet another argument for independence, according to Paine—the chance to create a better society. He foresaw a nation where everyone would be free from tyranny and where there would be equal social and economic opportunities for all.

Common Sense was widely read (some 500,000 copies were sold) and widely applauded. It was, in fact, one of the most influential political pamphlets ever written. Encouraged by public opinion, within six months the Second Continental Congress did just what Paine had suggested.

Linking Past to Present

Throughout American history, pamphlets and books have played an important role in influencing public opinion. *Common Sense* (1776) helped to overcome doubts about the American Revolution. *The Federalist* (1788) encouraged ratification of the Constitution. *Uncle Tom's Cabin* (1852) attacked slavery and was used as propaganda for the Civil War. *The Jungle* (1906) horrified the nation into passing the first Meat Inspection Act. *Silent Spring* (1962) showed how pesticides were damaging the environment. *The Feminine Mystique* (1963) had a powerful influence on the women's movement. *Unsafe at Any Speed* (1965) ushered in a new wave of consumerism. More recently, *The Closing of the American Mind* (1987) and *Cultural Literacy* (1987) raised questions about education in the 1980's.

SECTION 1 REVIEW

Key Terms and People

Explain the significance of: George Washington, Ethan Allen, Green Mountain Boys, John Burgoyne, Henry Clinton, William Howe, redcoats, Benedict Arnold, Olive Branch Petition, *Common Sense,* Thomas Paine

Main Ideas

1. In what ways were Ethan Allen and the Green Mountain Boys typical American Revolutionary War soldiers?
2. What military experience did Washington possess that made him a good choice for commander in chief of the Continental army?
3. Why did British General Clinton write of the Battle of Bunker Hill that it was a "dear bought victory, another such would have ruined us"?
4. According to Paine's *Common Sense,* what were the practical advantages of America's declaring itself an independent republic?
5. What was King George's response to the peace overture made by the Continental Congress?

Critical Thinking

6. Why did Paine's *Common Sense* appeal to a wide audience?

SECTION 1 REVIEW

Answers

Main Ideas

1. They were relatively untrained and poorly equipped volunteers.

2. He had been a successful military leader in the French and Indian War.

3. Britain's victory cost more than 1,000 British casualties, while the Americans suffered only 400 casualties.

4. It would be able to trade freely with other nations and obtain money for munitions; captured soldiers would be treated as prisoners of war; foreign countries would be more likely to provide aid.

5. He ignored it.

Critical Thinking

6. Possible answer: it attacked King George; it reinforced the positive image many Americans had of the common man; it stated eloquently and forcefully the economic and political advantages of an independent America. **(analysis)**

Anticipate the Lesson

Ask students to define the terms *privilege* and *rights* and decide how they differ. (Possible definitions: a privilege is a special favor granted by someone else; a right is a just or proper claim to something.) To stimulate discussion, ask students the following questions. In the Declaration of Independence, are the colonists asking for rights or for privileges? Which is easier to fight for? Why? (Possible responses: colonists were asking for their rights as citizens; it is easier to fight for one's rights because one is entitled to them; rights are not given or granted by anyone else nor is there any question about whether or not they are deserved.)

State the Objective

Identify the main ideas of the Declaration of Independence.

SECTION 2

The Patriots Declare Independence

GLOSSARY TERMS: **inalienable rights, Patriots, Loyalists, Tories**

In May 1776 the Second Continental Congress advised all the colonies to form new state governments if they had not already done so. On June 7 Virginia delegate **Richard Henry Lee** made a motion that ''these United Colonies are, and of a right ought to be, free and independent States.''

While debate on the motion continued, the Continental Congress appointed a committee of five men to prepare a formal declaration that would explain to the world the reason for the colonies' actions. The five men were **John Adams** (Massachusetts), Benjamin Franklin (Pennsylvania), **Thomas Jefferson** (Virginia), Robert Livingston (New York), and Roger Sherman (Connecticut). They agreed on the main points to be covered. Then they chose Jefferson to give the declaration a ''proper dress,'' that is, to express the points suitably in writing.

In his first draft, Jefferson included an eloquent attack on the cruelty and injustice of the slave trade. However, South Carolina and Georgia, the two colonies most heavily dependent on the slave trade, objected. In order to gain the votes of those two states, Jefferson dropped the offending passage.

Abigail Adams, the wife of Massachusetts delegate John Adams, wanted something about the status of women written into law. She therefore wrote her husband the following:

> Remember the ladies and be more generous to them than your ancestors [were]. Do not put unlimited power in the hands of husbands.

Picturing History In his painting *Declaration of Independence* John Trumbull grouped the signers of the document on a canvas only thirty inches wide. Standing at the table before John Hancock are John Adams, Roger Sherman, Robert R. Livingston, Thomas Jefferson, and Benjamin Franklin. Trumbull was pleased to have played "a humble part" in this great event.

Present the Lesson

Call on a student to read aloud the first two paragraphs of the Declaration of Independence. List the following terms on the board and have students define each: natural laws, monarchy, inalienable rights, power of government, consent of the governed. (Possible definitions: natural laws—God-given laws not interfered with by people; monarchy—rule by a King or Queen; inalienable rights—just or proper claims that cannot be taken away; power of government—authority granted by the people; consent of the governed—agreement by those governed.) Have students record these concepts and refer to them as they study Section 2.

Check for Understanding

Have the students complete Chapter 5, Section 2 Daily Activity.

Remember all men would be tyrants if they could. If particular care and attention is not paid to the ladies, we are determined to foment [stir up] rebellion, and will not be bound by any laws in which we have no voice or representation.

Despite Mrs. Adams's urging, the Declaration of Independence states only that "all men are created equal."

The Patriots Defend Natural Rights

The Declaration was a masterpiece of political writing. Today the famous words of the preamble remain far better known than the long list of accusations aimed at King George. For people in 1776, however, that list summarized well the events of the preceding dozen years. The accusations were not entirely fair, though, for the King did not bear sole responsibility for many of the actions the Declaration condemned. Nevertheless, Americans were finally breaking their one remaining tie with Britain. That tie was the King, so Jefferson aimed his propaganda at that final link.

Many years later, John Adams belittled Jefferson's achievement in the preamble by claiming that it merely repeated what everyone had been saying all along. Jefferson replied that this was exactly what he had intended to do. The Declaration, he said, was "to be an expression of the American mind." He had merely expressed commonplace ideas about **inalienable rights**—those that cannot be taken away—and about the right of the people to rebel against tyranny.

Life, Liberty, Happiness. By 1776 ideas about inalienable, or natural, rights that were first stated by John Locke had become basic beliefs in the American mind. They were the way most Americans automatically thought about government. It was "self-evident" that the powers of government came from the people. The people therefore could take the powers back if a government abused its powers, and they could set up a government that would not abuse their natural rights. What were these natural rights? They were life, liberty, and property.

When Jefferson came to list these rights, he made an interesting change in one of the three. Instead of "life, liberty, and property," he substituted "life, liberty, and the pursuit of happiness." This wording has prompted some people to jest that the Declaration gives everyone the right to pursue happiness but not the right to catch up with it. However, Jefferson did not use the word *pursuit* to mean "chase." He intended the older meaning of the word, which was "to cultivate or improve by attention and care."

All Men Are Created Equal. The Declaration of Independence states flatly that "all men are created equal." When this sentence was written, it merely expressed the common assumption that free citizens were politically equal. Each had one vote of equal weight. It was not intended to mean that all men had the same ability or ought to be of equal wealth. It obviously did not apply to women, who could not vote, nor to blacks who were slaves.

Yet the Declaration's principle of equality later took on a life of its own. The phrase "all men" could very easily be regarded as meaning all human beings, not just the white men of America in 1776. Why shouldn't black men and all women be included? In later years, many people began to ponder this question.

On July 4, 1776, the Declaration of Independence was adopted by the Second Continental Congress, although the last signature did not go on it until November of that year. On July 8, 1776, the Declaration was read for the first time—to a crowd in front of the red brick Pennsylvania State House, now called Independence Hall. Everyone knew that, if any of the delegates fell into British hands, they would be hanged as traitors. A thrill of pride and anxiety ran through the crowd of **Patriots** (rebels) when they heard the delegates' vow that ends the Declaration: "We mutually pledge to each other our Lives, our Fortunes and our Sacred Honor."

The Loyalists Oppose Popular Rule

Many Americans opposed independence and the war that was being waged for it. These **Loyalists,** as they called themselves—although the Patriots called them **Tories**—varied in number from place to place and also from time to time. The best modern estimates indicate that they made up about one-fifth of the white population at the time.

Reasons for Loyalty. Numbers do not explain why some people chose to remain loyal to the British crown. For many the decision followed an agonizing crisis of conscience. Quakers and Ger-

For Discussion
What were the reasons for omitting references to women and blacks in the Declaration of Independence? (Possible responses: Southern Colonies objected to blacks being referred to as equal; most men were not willing to consider women as equals.) How might the inclusion of women and blacks have changed the course of history? (Possible responses: women may have had voting rights earlier than they did; the blacks may have been emancipated earlier, changing or eliminating the Civil War.)

Guided Practice

To stimulate discussion on the Declaration of Independence, ask students the following questions. Are there people today who, like the signers of the Declaration of Independence, are willing to die for their political convictions? (Possible responses: yes, P.L.O. soldiers, Israeli soldiers, Iranian citizens.) Are there groups of people in the U.S. today who do not enjoy the full benefits of equality as guaranteed by the Declaration of Independence? Why or why not? (Possible responses: minority groups; children; handicapped persons.

These problems are often the result of prejudice or ignorance.)

Assign Independent Practice

Have students complete Chapter 5, Section 2 Enrichment Activity.

Student Assignment/Homework

Have students read Section 3, "How the Military Positions Compare," and answer Section 3 Review questions on paper.

SECTION 2 REVIEW

Answers

Main Ideas

1. Change from colonies to free, independent states.

2. Jefferson attacked slavery, on which they were economically dependent.

3. The concept of women's equality.

4. Belief in pacifism; belief in law and order; the desire to maintain class position within British society; class opposition to "mob rule"; loyalty to other Loyalists; opposition to some ethnic groups who became Patriots; belief that Britain would win.

5. Possible answer: Those remaining were more united in their cause; those remaining were less likely to be spies for the British.

Critical Thinking

6. It justified the war. The colonists were stating their right to withdraw power from the British government since Parliament had become tyrannical, taxing the colonists and enacting repressive laws without colonial representation. **(analysis & synthesis)**

man pacifists could not become active Patriots because their beliefs did not allow them to support any war. For others it was a matter of self-interest. Those who had held posts as royal officials, for example, found it easy to retain their old loyalty. Some Loyalists were people of wealth who did not like popular rule, or mob rule as they called it. Others were staunch believers in law and order. Certain ethnic groups in certain places tended to become Loyalists because other ethnic groups in the same area were becoming Patriots.

Probably the most important factor in pushing Americans toward one side or the other was the presence of British troops in the immediate neighborhood. This presence could make Loyalists out of wavering individuals who wished to pick the winning side, or it could make Patriots out of outraged farmers who watched helplessly as redcoats made off with their corn and livestock. As the major fighting moved from one part of the country to another, more and more Americans had to make a choice. Neutrality became difficult when there was fighting in one's own backyard. This pattern placed the Loyalists at a tremendous disadvantage. British troops came and went, but their American opponents remained.

Committees of Patriots backed with bayonets drove many Loyalists from their homes and communities. The new state governments set up legal machinery for the confiscation, or seizure, of Loyalist property. Brutalities occurred on both sides, but few Loyalists lost their lives except in open battle against Patriot forces. Throughout the war, the British constantly overestimated the number of Loyalists. At the same time, they failed to take full advantage of Loyalist support. Professional British army officers often treated the Loyalists with the same contempt they had for all colonial amateur fighters.

Peaceful Departure. One basic fact about the Loyalists' opposition to the American Revolution has often been overlooked by historians. Many of the Loyalists could simply leave America without going into exile. By contrast, opponents of the French Revolution, which broke out in 1789, had to flee to foreign countries. American Loyalists, however, could return home to Britain if they had enough money for the trip or move to another part of the British Empire, especially to Canada. Many did so. When General Gage evacuated Boston, some one thousand Loyalists left with him for Nova

Scotia. The same pattern was repeated whenever the British evacuated an American port. For many Loyalists, such journeys were heart-wrenching departures from loved ones. Nevertheless, they were moving to lands where people shared the Loyalists' own language and laws and held a similar allegiance to the British crown. Many Loyalists even received money from the British government for the losses they suffered during the war. Few refugees from a major revolution have had the same opportunities.

The departure of so many Loyalists had an important effect on the future of the newly independent country. It meant that the people most vehemently against the Revolution were gone when victory was achieved and independence was finally won. Americans thus did not have to put people on trial or execute those who had opposed the war. There were no old scores to settle. There were no palaces to be invaded or hated symbols of the past government to be destroyed. The Patriots were able to start immediately on the problems of building a nation.

SECTION 2 REVIEW

Key Terms and People

Explain the significance of: Richard Henry Lee, John Adams, Thomas Jefferson, Abigail Adams, inalienable rights, Patriots, Loyalists, Tories

Main ideas

1. What important change in the status of the American colonies did Richard Henry Lee propose?
2. Why did South Carolina and Georgia object to Jefferson's first draft of the Declaration of Independence?
3. What key principle did Abigail Adams strive to have included in the Declaration of Independence?
4. Why did some colonists oppose the war for independence?
5. What effect did the departure of many Loyalists have on the American colonies?

Critical Thinking

6. In the Declaration of Independence, why was it important for the colonists to state that governments derive their just powers from the consent of the governed?

Anticipate the Lesson

Discuss with students the meaning of the term *home-court advantage* in a sporting event. (Possible definition: advantages gained by playing a game on familiar ground with a sympathetic audience.) To stimulate discussion, ask students the following questions. What benefits does a home-court advantage give a team? (Possible responses: provides confidence and crowd support; can boost team morale.) What advantages might there be to fighting a war on one's home soil? (Possible responses: soldiers know terrain; soldiers fight for their homeland; soldiers have citizen support.)

State the Objective

Compare the advantages and disadvantages of the British and American positions in the Revolutionary War.

SECTION 3

The British and American Positions Differ

GLOSSARY TERMS: **mercenaries, Hessians, privateers, Continentals**

Few people thought the rebellion would last very long. A divided colonial population of about two and a half million people, nearly one-fifth of whom were slaves, faced a nation of ten million that was backed by a worldwide empire.

Military Advantages Benefit the British

Loyalist warnings that Britain possessed enormous military advantages were well-founded. The British navy was easily the largest in the world, even though many of its ships were in poor repair. British factories were equipped to turn out large quantities of cannon, muskets, and other weapons. The British army possessed trained engineers who knew how to build fortifications and besiege cities. Its noncommissioned officers, especially its sergeants, were experienced professionals.

On the other hand, the British army was short of manpower. Although the British Empire extended worldwide, its army consisted of fewer than thirty-five thousand men, of whom seventy-five hundred were busy occupying Ireland. Army pay was so low and living conditions were so bad that few Englishmen joined up voluntarily. Most were pressed into service. Press gangs went around kidnapping able-bodied men. Sometimes the press gangs beat the men or got them drunk. When the men woke up, they found themselves in the armed forces. Desertions were common.

Accordingly, the British were forced to hire **mercenaries** (people who fight solely for money) from other nations. After being turned down by Empress Catherine the Great of Russia, Britain succeeded in obtaining some thirty thousand soldiers from six small German states. Since half of them came from the state of Hesse-Cassel, the Americans called all the mercenaries **Hessians.** As it turned out, almost five thousand Hessians deserted the British army to try their luck in America.

The British faced other important disadvantages. Chief among them was the three thousand miles of the Atlantic Ocean. In addition, they had to fight on unfamiliar, badly mapped stretches of territory. Also, the British were used to the better roads and more open countryside of their homeland.

British troops were sometimes outgunned on a one-to-one basis. Most of them carried smoothbore muskets, which were less accurate than the Pennsylvania or Kentucky rifles many Americans carried. The grooves on the barrels of the American rifles made them more accurate. On the other hand, American rifles were slow to reload and could not be equipped with bayonets.

American Assets Are Offset by Handicaps

The Americans were fighting on their own ground. However, they too faced serious difficulties despite this advantage.

Military Handicaps. A major handicap was the lack of a sizable navy. The Continental Congress could afford to pay for only a few vessels. The British navy therefore controlled the sea lanes and the American coastline except at one brief and crucial moment when Captain **John Paul Jones** refused to surrender his ship to the British. After a desperate battle, Jones declared, ''I have not yet

Picturing History The gallant Captain John Paul Jones proved himself heroic when his ship, *Bonhomme Richard,* defeated the British frigate *Serapis* in September 1779.

Present the Lesson

Have students list on the board the advantages that Britain had in the Revolutionary War and the advantages held by the colonists. (British advantages include: a large navy; factories to produce military supplies; experienced soldiers; support of the Loyalists. American advantages include: knowledge of the terrain; better weapons; the inspiring cause of independence.)

Check for Understanding

Tell the students to write two paragraphs explaining which side had the better advantage in the war and was most likely to win. Students' responses should be based only on the information listed on the board, not on the actual outcome of the war. (Paragraphs might include: the British had the most military advantages so were in the best position to win from a military standpoint; the Americans fought on home ground and were inspired by their cause for freedom, which is sometimes a stronger advantage than military strength.)

Guided Practice

Remind students that during the Revolutionary War volunteers could join a local or state militia or the Continental army. The majority of the volunteers joined a state militia rather than the Continental army. To stimulate discussion, ask students the following questions. Why did so few soldiers join the Continental army? (Possible responses: loyalty to state; low pay; rigid discipline; no pension or insurance; longer periods of service.)

begun to fight.'' His ship, *Bonhomme Richard,* went on to defeat the British forty-four gun *Serapis,* forcing its captain to surrender.

Hundreds of American warships known as **privateers** were given the right by Congress to prey on British merchant ships, and some enriched themselves considerably. Nevertheless, privateers had little effect on the course of the war.

The Americans also had great difficulty in keeping an army together. Although Americans in any given place would turn out in large numbers to fight, staying in the army and marching off through other states did not appeal to them. It meant low pay, rigid discipline, cold, hunger, and disease. There were no pensions for soldiers disabled by wounds and no insurance payments for their widows if they died. As a result, many American farmers enlisted either for a single campaign or for three months. Then they went back to their farms.

Washington's Achievement. George Washington's great achievement was managing to keep something of an army together for eight years. His command consisted of two kinds of soldiers: militia from the individual states and the men of the Continental army. It was called the Continental army because the men were paid directly by the Continental Congress rather than by the states from which they came.

The Continental soldiers, also called **Continentals,** served longer periods of enlistment and were therefore better trained and more reliable in battle than the militia. The Continentals thus took pride in themselves both as professional soldiers and as the truest of Patriots. For the most part they were intensely loyal to their tall, somewhat aloof but always devoted commander. It was the kind of loyalty possible only in a small army where the men were actually able to see the commander in chief. (It was partly for this reason that many officers rode on horseback.) For his part, Washington was a firm yet fair administrator of military discipline who spent much of his time pleading with the Continental Congress for supplies for his men.

The Role of Women. Many American women took their husbands' places on farms and at various trades when the men went off to fight. Women helped to make munitions, and supplied soldiers with food and clothing. Other women followed their husbands. As one historian noted:

Picturing History
Molly Pitcher (above) was the heroine of the Battle of Monmouth. Mercy Otis Warren (left) wrote a history of the Revolution.

They cooked for the troops and nursed the wounded and sick. They mended and sewed and laundered. On the marches they carried their share of supplies and ammunition on their backs. . . . Women who could write performed clerical and copying tasks. . . . At night they crept over the battlefield . . . stripping [the dead bodies] of their clothes to help keep the ragged Revolutionary soldiers warm.

Occasionally women took part in the actual fighting. Two who did so were Margaret Corbin and Mary Ludwig Hays. In a battle at Fort Washington, New York (1776), Corbin replaced a gunner who had been shot and was herself wounded. Congress gave her a pension and a complete set of clothes every year for life. Mary Ludwig Hays is called **Molly Pitcher** by many historians because she carried pitchers of water to wash out cannon barrels before they were reloaded. When her husband was wounded at the Battle of Monmouth, she took his place on the battlefield. For her heroism, Washington made her a sergeant.

Assign Independent Practice

Ask students to write a letter to Thomas Jefferson requesting that the Declaration of Independence be changed to include "all men and women are created equal." Use examples from among the many contributions women made to the Revolution to persuade Jefferson. (Examples might include: Margaret Corbin replaces a gunner in battle; Molly Pitcher carries water to wash out cannon barrels and replaces her husband on the battlefield; countless women nurse the wounded and feed and clothe soldiers.) Have the students share their letters with the class.

Student Assignment/Homework

Have students read Section 4, "Farmers and Shopkeepers Defeat an Empire," and answer Section 4 Review questions orally.

SECTION 4
Core Lesson

Anticipate the Lesson

Review with students the advantages held by the Americans and the British in the Revolutionary War. Ask students how the Americans might have been able to overcome the British advantages. (Possible response: Americans' fighting strategies differed from strategies the British were accustomed to, which gave the colonists an advantage over the larger British army.)

Financing the War Effort. A major problem that confronted Washington throughout the war was how to obtain supplies. With a British coastal blockade and almost no local munitions factories, arms and ammunition had to be smuggled from Europe. Most American families—except the very rich—made their own clothing at home. So it was difficult, if not impossible, for them to increase their output to equip soldiers. As Washington once wrote, "There are now in this Army . . . 4,000 men wanting blankets, near 2,000 of which have never had one, altho' some of them have been 12 months in service."

There was also the problem of how to pay the troops. The Continental Congress borrowed money by selling bonds to foreign governments, especially to France, and also to domestic investors. It printed paper money called continentals, the same name given to the Revolutionary soldiers. The value of this currency dropped so much, however, that people used the phrase "not worth a continental" to refer to anything that was worthless.

Picturing History
Continental currency.

Finally, in 1781 the Congress appointed a rich Philadelphia merchant named Robert Morris as superintendent of finance. Morris was assisted by Haym Salomon, a Jewish political refugee from Poland who had been a Son of Liberty and who had escaped from a British prison on the eve of being hanged as an American spy.

Morris and Salomon begged and borrowed on their personal credit. They obtained funds from Philadelphia's Quakers and Jews. They eventually straightened out the government's finances enough to set up an adequate supply system for the American army. On September 8, 1781, a Continental major wrote in his diary, "This day will be famous in the Annals of History for being the first on which

the Troops of the United States received one Month's Pay in Specie [coin]."

SECTION 3 REVIEW

Key Terms and People

Explain the significance of: mercenaries, Hessians, John Paul Jones, privateers, Continentals, Molly Pitcher

Main Ideas

1. What were the British advantages in the war?
2. What were the American advantages in the war?
3. How was Washington able to establish loyalty among the soldiers of the Continental army?
4. What significant contributions did American women make to the Revolutionary War?
5. How did Congress solve the problem of financing the war effort?

Critical Thinking

6. Why did John Paul Jones's declaration "I have not yet begun to fight!" become a rallying cry for the Americans?

SECTION 4

Farmers and Shopkeepers Defeat an Empire

GLOSSARY TERM: amnesty

After the British pulled out of Boston in March 1776, the theater of war shifted to the Middle States. For nineteen months American forces suffered one defeat after another. The Patriots lost control of their two largest cities, New York and Philadelphia. Then the British, having won many victories, proceeded to lose an entire army. That loss marked the turning point of the war.

The Middle States Join in the Fighting

After pulling out of Boston, the British decided to take New York. Believing that only New England was rebelling, they figured that by taking New York they could isolate New England from the other "loyal" colonies. Two brothers, General William Howe and Admiral Richard Howe, arrived in New York Harbor in the summer of 1776. The

SECTION 3 REVIEW

Answers

Main Ideas

1. Britain had the world's largest navy, well-equipped munitions factories, trained engineers, experienced officers, the wealth of a huge empire, and the support of Loyalists and some Indians.

2. Americans were fighting for an idealistic cause on their own land, often against mercenaries or uninspired British soldiers. They also had more accurate rifles.

3. Washington tried to obtain needed supplies for his army, was a firm yet fair leader, and was highly visible among his soldiers.

4. They worked to maintain agriculture and business during the war; they made munitions; they supplied soldiers with food and clothing. Women like Margaret Corbin and Molly Pitcher took part in the fighting itself.

5. It appointed Robert Morris to supervise financial affairs. They begged and borrowed money, reorganized the government's finances, and set up an army supply system.

Critical Thinking

6. Possible answer: Jones's refusal to surrender to the British and his subsequent victory were symbolic of colonial independence and the will to win against all odds.
(analysis)

State the Objective

Explain why the Americans were victorious in the Revolutionary War.

Historical Sidelight

In 1851 Emanuel Leutze created the famed painting *Washington Crossing the Delaware*. The painting, however, is filled with inaccuracies:

• The crossing took place during the night, not during the daytime.
• The stars and stripes shown on the boat did not exist in 1776.
• Washington is shown standing in the boat—a very foolish thing to do, especially in December.
• There are twelve men rowing in a fourteen-foot boat—an impossible task.

Map Skills

To Germantown • He probably would have been able to relieve Burgoyne, and the British might then have avoided the defeat at Saratoga.

The War in the Middle States, 1776-1778

American forces
British forces
American victory
British victory

© ML & Co.

Map Skills **Movement** Where did Howe go from Brandywine Creek? **Movement** How different might the situation have been if Howe had marched north?

Howes carried instructions to discuss peace terms and to make an offer of **amnesty,** or pardon, to all rebels who would lay down their arms and take an oath of allegiance to the King. They also had thirty-two thousand soldiers and ten thousand seamen to back their words.

Foreseeing the British plans, Washington rallied some eighteen thousand men to New York's defense. Not only was he outnumbered, however, but most of his troops were inexperienced farmers who lacked equipment. The Americans retreated with heavy losses. First they withdrew from the Brooklyn end of Long Island, then they headed from Manhattan northward to White Plains, and from there across the Hudson River into New Jersey.

By the late fall of 1776, Washington's army had been pushed across New Jersey into Pennsylvania. Only some eight thousand men remained under his command. The rest had gone back to their farms or had been killed or captured. Most Americans seemed to be in a state of apathy, waiting to see what would happen. As Thomas Paine wrote in his new pamphlet, *The Crisis:*

> These are the times that try men's souls. The summer soldier and the sunshine patriot will, in this crisis, shrink from the service of their country, but he that stands it now deserves the love and thanks of man and woman.

Washington was desperate for some sort of victory to revive the morale of his troops and to prove that the American cause was alive. He therefore resolved to risk everything on one bold stroke.

On the freezing Christmas night of 1776, Washington led twenty-four hundred men in boats back across the ice-choked Delaware River into New Jersey. By eight o'clock the next morning, the men had marched the nine miles to Trenton. There they surprised a group of Hessians, most of whom were sleeping off the effects of a large quantity of rum they had drunk the night before. The Americans killed thirty of the enemy and took some nine hundred captives at the cost of only five casualties.

The victory was so stunning that many of Washington's soldiers promptly reenlisted. Those who returned were further cheered by another astonishing victory at Princeton on January 5, 1777. Washington then marched his little army into winter camp near Morristown in northern New Jersey.

When spring came, General Howe decided to

Present the Lesson

Have students complete on the board a time line of major events of the Revolutionary War from 1775 to 1781. Have them use one color to indicate victories for the British and another color to indicate colonial victories. Using a wall map of North America, have students locate the sites of these events. Have students refer to this time line as they study Section 4. (Time line might include: December 26, 1776—Trenton, N.J.—American victory; January 5, 1777—Princeton, N.J.—American victory; October 17, 1777—Saratoga—American victory.)

take another major American city. His troops left New York by sea, sailed up the Delaware River, and landed near Philadelphia. Washington's troops tried to block their way at Brandywine Creek. However, the Americans lost the pitched battle, and the pleasure-loving General Howe settled back to enjoy the hospitality of the city's grateful Loyalists. A week later, Washington attempted an attack on the major British encampment outside the city at Germantown. At first, things went well for the Americans. Before long, however, patches of dense fog created so much confusion that at one point the Americans were firing on each other. Once again Howe won.

The Turning Point Comes at Saratoga

In the meantime, one of Howe's fellow British generals was marching straight into the jaws of disaster. General "Gentleman Johnny" Burgoyne had persuaded the high command in London to let him lead a major army down the route of lakes extending from Canada to Albany. In Albany he intended to link up with Howe's troops, who were heading north from New York City. When Burgoyne set out, however, he did not know that Howe had gone to Philadelphia.

Burgoyne also did not know how to lead an expedition through a forested wilderness. He had four thousand redcoats, three thousand Hessians, and one thousand Mohawk Indians under his command. He also had 138 pieces of artillery, a plentiful supply of wine and fine clothes, and his large four-poster bed. The farther south of Lake Champlain he went, the more resistance he met.

Picturing History General Horatio Gates

Felled trees and thick underbrush slowed his progress. Food supplies ran low. Militiamen and Continentals were gathering from all over New York and New England. Every time the two sides clashed—as at Bennington, Vermont—Burgoyne lost several hundred men.

Finally halted at **Saratoga** by the massed Americans, Burgoyne surrendered his battered army on October 17, 1777, to General **Horatio Gates.** The surrender at Saratoga represented the turning point of the war. From that time on, the British dared not send troops into the countryside. Instead, they kept their men along the coast, no more than fifty miles away from the big guns and supply bases of the British fleet.

Saratoga was important psychologically as well as militarily. Americans now had proof that they could defeat the British regulars. Yet American forces were still outnumbered overall. The real impact of Saratoga made itself known in Paris and London.

The French Alliance Brings a Stalemate

France's desire to humiliate Great Britain was greater than its fear of encouraging revolution. Early in 1776 the Continental Congress had sent Silas Deane as its agent to seek assistance in Paris. Soon the Americans were secretly getting about 80 percent of their gunpowder from the French. After the victory at Saratoga, the French were willing to support the Americans openly.

A formal treaty of alliance between the French and the Americans was signed in February 1778. The French agreed not to make peace with Britain unless American independence was recognized. The Americans would keep all the British-held territory they conquered. If war between France and Britain occurred, neither ally was to make peace without the consent of the other.

The American War of Independence was now transformed into still another full-scale European conflict. In 1779 Spain joined the war as France's ally. The port of New Orleans, which Spain had received from France in return for Spain's aid during the French and Indian War, thus became available for the Americans to use as a base for the war at sea. Spain later reoccupied Florida. In 1780 the Netherlands also declared war on Britain. In the long run, French seapower proved decisive. Nonetheless, the French alliance was followed by three years of discouragement for the Americans.

Check for Understanding

Review with students the answers to the Section 4 Review questions.

While American negotiators were at work in Paris, Washington's Continentals were in winter camp at **Valley Forge,** Pennsylvania. Of the ten thousand poorly fed and ragged men living on snowy ground in makeshift wood-and-clay shelters, almost twenty-five hundred died. As seventeen-year-old Joseph Martin later wrote, ''I endured hardships sufficient to kill a dozen horses.'' The time was not spent in idleness, though. The men were engaged in learning Baron von Steuben's new Prussian military drill. **Friedrich von Steuben** had joined the Americans at Valley Forge in February 1778, where he went to work ''to make regular soldiers out of country bumpkins.'' He taught the Americans how to use the bayonet and how to load

Picturing History Bernardo de Gálvez, governor of Louisiana, supplied the Americans with arms during the Revolution.

Map Skills

Charles Town • Wilmington

The War in the South, 1778-1781

Map Skills **Movement** To what city did Cornwallis go first? **Movement** To what city did the British go after the battle of Guilford Court House?

their cannons properly.

Other foreign officers also helped the Americans. **Thaddeus Kosciuszko** (käs′ē us′kō), an artillery officer, came from Poland, as did Count **Casimir Pulaski** (po͝o las′kē). Kosciuszko helped build the fortifications at West Point. Pulaski was asked by Congress to organize a United States Cavalry Corps. Pulaski died of wounds he suffered in the battle of Savannah. Today about fifteen towns and counties in the United States are named in honor of these two Poles.

In the spring of 1778, General Howe was replaced by Sir Henry Clinton. Hearing rumors about a French assault on New York City, Clinton set out from Philadelphia across New Jersey. Washing-

Picturing History
General Charles Cornwallis surrendered at Yorktown.

Picturing History
Casimir Pulaski

Picturing History
Thaddeus Kosciuszko

ton's forces pursued him but were unable to prevent his reaching New York. The Americans then camped outside the British-occupied city. There the two armies remained, facing each other, for three long years.

George Rogers Clark Wins

Although most of the important battles of the Revolutionary War took place along the Atlantic coast, the British and their Indian allies had to face the young and courageous **George Rogers Clark** on the frontier. In 1778 Clark and his band of Virginia volunteers went down the Ohio River and took the British post of Kaskaskia in the Illinois country. Later, after capturing other British forts nearby, the Patriots were in a position to lay claim to the whole Northwest.

The British Focus on the South

That same summer of 1778, the British decided to shift their main operations to the Southern states. A British expedition took Savannah at the end of that year. By the spring of 1779, a royal governor thus was once more in charge of Georgia. Hopeful that the South might turn out to be the long-sought Loyalist stronghold, Clinton, assisted by General Charles Cornwallis, embarked from New York with eighty-five hundred men and fourteen battleships. The fleet sailed to Charles Town, South Carolina, where the British won their greatest victory of the war. They captured not only the city but the entire force of American defenders, some fifty-five hundred men. Thoroughly satisfied, Clinton retired to New York, leaving Cornwallis in charge of mopping up the Carolinas.

At first Cornwallis was successful. At Camden, South Carolina, he smashed the American forces. Within three months South Carolina, like Georgia, was for all practical purposes again part of the British Empire. When Cornwallis advanced into North Carolina, however, he was hit by a series of reverses. Guerrilla bands—led by such men as Francis Marion, called the Swamp Fox, Andrew Pickens, and Thomas Sumter—constantly harassed him. In October 1780 farmers and trappers came across a Loyalist force of about eleven hundred men who were dug in atop a wooded ridge in South Carolina called Kings Mountain. It was, as one historian declared, "Bunker Hill in reverse." The frontier militia charged up the hill twice but were driven back. Finally, on the third charge, the guerrillas captured the position and the battle was won. Cornwallis retreated southward.

In the meantime, Washington sent one thousand Continentals commanded by his ablest general, **Nathanael Greene,** into the Carolinas. After a loss at Cowpens and a bloody victory at Guilford Court House, in which Cornwallis lost more than 30 percent of his troops, the British general concluded that he might do better in Virginia. Greene did not pursue him but went to capture the remaining British units farther south.

Cornwallis then made the fateful mistake of taking his army out onto the peninsula between the James and the York rivers. There his eight thousand troops set up camp at **Yorktown,** just a few miles northeast of the original English settlement of Jamestown. Cornwallis planned to fortify Yorktown, take Virginia, and then move north to join up with Clinton's forces, which subsequently would move south from New York.

The British Surrender at Yorktown

A combination of good luck and well-timed decisions now favored the American cause. In 1780 a French army of six thousand men had taken Newport, Rhode Island. In addition to the fleet stationed there, another French fleet was operating in the West Indies, attacking British ships wherever they could be found. Meanwhile, Washington's army was still encamped at White Plains, besieging the British in New York City. The idea of first combining the two armies and the two fleets and then attacking Cornwallis in Virginia was the brainstorm of the **Marquis de Lafayette** (lä′fi

yet′). Lafayette had joined the American cause even before the French alliance took place. Now he convinced Washington to try his plan.

Accordingly, the French troops left Newport and joined the Americans at White Plains. A German officer attached to the French troops described the American soldiers in the following words:

> It was really painful to see these brave men almost naked, with only some trousers and little linen jackets; most of them without stockings, but, believe it or not, very cheerful and healthy in appearance. A quarter of them were Negroes, merry, confident, and sturdy.

The all-black regiment was from Rhode Island. From White Plains, the combined armies began the long march south to Yorktown.

In the meantime, a French naval force suddenly appeared within sight of the Yorktown peninsula. Clinton desperately sent a fleet of warships south from New York. The French, however, blocked the entrance to Chesapeake Bay. After two hours of flaming combat, the British fleet was forced to turn back. Now the jaws of the trap closed on Cornwallis. British soldiers could not escape by sea as they had from Boston more than six years before, and on land they faced eight thousand French troops and nine thousand Americans. The siege of Yorktown lasted about a month. On October 19, 1781, Cornwallis, outnumbered more than two to one and cut off from reinforcements, finally agreed to have his men lay down their arms. He insisted, however, that they do so in front of the French troops rather

Picturing History The British march toward Surrender Field following their defeat at Yorktown.

Assign Independent Practice

Tell students to choose one primary source excerpt from this section and write two paragraphs that identify the author's attitude or feelings. (Possible responses: statement by the Hessian soldier—the soldier appears very impressed with the loyalty and dedication of the American army; although their clothes are ragged and their bodies injured, he believes they have fought for "Liberty and Independence.")

Picturing History Marquis de Lafayette sat for this portrait by the famous painter Charles Willson Peale in 1779.

than before the despised Patriots. The next day, as the redcoats walked forward to stack their arms in a field, the British army band played a popular marching song, "The World Turned Upside Down." It went like this:

> If ponies rode men and if grass ate the cows,
> And cats should be chased into holes by the
>   mouse. . .
> If summer were spring and the other way
>   round,
> Then all the world would be upside down.

Indeed the world *was* turned upside down. The Americans had defeated the mighty British Empire. When Lord North heard the news of the surrender, he cried out, "Oh God! It is all over." Then he resigned.

The world was amazed at what the Americans had done. One of the Hessian mercenaries serving with the British forces was filled with admiration when he saw some of the victorious Patriots lined up for inspection.

> The men looked haggard and pallid [pale] and were poorly dressed. Indeed, very many stood quite proudly under arms without shoes and stockings. What army could be maintained in this manner? None, certainly, for the whole

Revolutionary War: Advantages and Disadvantages

United States	Britain
Strengths:	**Strengths:**
1. Familiarity of home ground	1. Strong, well-trained army and navy
2. Superior weapons and marksmen	2. Strong government with available money
3. Experienced officers and soldiers trained in past colonial wars	3. Support of Loyalists
4. Leadership of George Washington	4. Indian allies
5. Inspiring cause– independence	
	Weaknesses:
Weaknesses:	1. Distance of 3,000 miles separating Britain from battlefront
1. Most soldiers untrained and undisciplined	2. Unfamiliar battlefronts
2. Shortage of food and ammunition	3. Inability to use Loyalists effectively
3. An infant navy	4. Weak military leaders
4. No central government capable of enforcing wartime policies	

Student Assignment/Homework

Have students read Section 5, "The American Revolution Changes the World," and answer Section 5 Review questions on paper.

SECTION 4 REVIEW

Answers

Main Ideas

1. Washington surprised a group of soldiers, killed 30 of them, and took 900 captives while losing only 5 of his own. It was considered a stunning victory.

2. It proved that Americans were capable of defeating British soldiers; it helped to persuade France and Spain to openly support the Americans.

3. Although 2,500 soldiers died because of harsh living conditions, the Continentals trained hard and came out of the winter a better fighting force.

4. Kosciuszko helped build the fortifications at West Point. Pulaski organized a Cavalry Corps.

5. It forced the British fleet to turn back from Chesapeake Bay, cut the British army off from its supplies, and helped force the British surrender.

Critical Thinking

6. Possible answer: the ideals gave them the conviction and drive they needed to endure the hardships of fighting a better-equipped and better-trained army. **(analysis)**

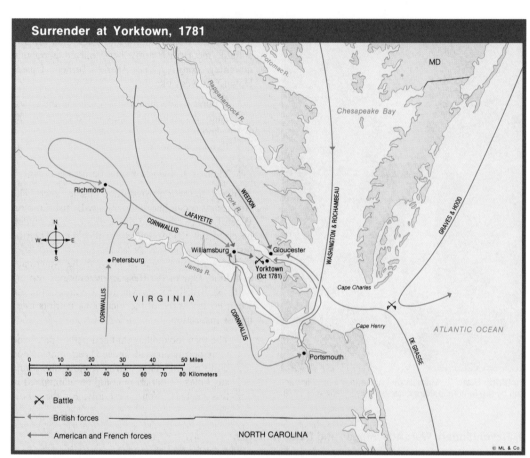

Surrender at Yorktown, 1781

Map Skills Location How far is Yorktown from Williamsburg? **Movement** How might the war have been affected if British Rear Admiral Graves had defeated French Admiral de Grasse?

army would gradually run away. This, too, is a part of that "Liberty and Independence" for which these poor fellows had to have their arms and legs smashed. But to what cannot enthusiasm lead a people!

SECTION 4 REVIEW

Key Terms and People

Explain the significance of: amnesty, Saratoga, Horatio Gates, Valley Forge, Friedrich von Steuben, Thaddeus Kosciuszko, Casimir Pulaski, George Rogers Clark, Nathanael Greene, Yorktown, Marquis de Lafayette

Main Ideas

1. What happened after Washington crossed the Delaware River that caused many soldiers to reenlist?

2. Why was Burgoyne's surrender at Saratoga an important turning point in the war?

3. What happened while Washington and the Continentals were in winter camp at Valley Forge?

4. What did Kosciuszko and Pulaski contribute to the war effort?

5. How did the French naval force help to decide the outcome of the siege of Yorktown?

Critical Thinking

6. How did the ideals of liberty and independence help the Americans to defeat the British?

Anticipate the Lesson

Ask students to suggest world events that they think have had a long-term effect on world history. (Possible responses: Columbus's voyage; development of nuclear bomb; the first moon landing; discovery of polio vaccine.) Ask students the following questions. Why did these events have such a great effect on the world? (Possible responses: they changed the way people thought; they opened up new avenues of research; they improved people's lives; they created new problems.) How do wars affect lives? (Possible responses: they might change a country's boundaries; lives are lost; land and cities are destroyed.)

State the Objective

Recognize the immediate and long-term significance of the American Revolution.

SECTION 5

The American Revolution Changes the World

GLOSSARY TERMS: **Treaty of Paris of 1783, emancipation**

Negotiating a peace treaty was a delicate and difficult business. In effect, four nations were involved—the United States, Great Britain, France, and Spain—each of which had different interests.

Spain had no formal ties with the United States. Indeed, Spain was hostile to the new nation's hopes both for independence and for a western boundary on the Mississippi River. While France was not hostile to American independence, its support was limited. One of the American negotiators, **John Jay** of New York, described France's position very accurately:

> We can depend upon the French only to see that we are separated from England, but it is not in their interest that we should become a great and formidable [powerful] people, and therefore they will not help us to become so.

Jay was quite correct. About this time, French Minister of Foreign Affairs Charles Vergennes wrote to a friend:

> We ask independence only for the thirteen states of America. . . .We do not desire that a new republic shall arise which shall become the exclusive mistress of this immense continent.

The Treaty of Paris of 1783 Has Long-Term Effects

Fortunately for the United States, the Continental Congress sent an extremely able team of negotiators to Paris: John Adams, Benjamin Franklin, and John Jay. The negotiators soon got wind of the fact that the French were secretly encouraging the British to insist on a boundary well to the east of the Mississippi River. The Americans therefore decided to ignore the French for the moment and to deal directly with the British delegation. The Brit-

Map Skills

About 10 miles (16 km)
• Graves probably would have been able to relieve Cornwallis, averting the British surrender at Yorktown and prolonging the war.

Picturing History
When Benjamin West set out to paint the signing of the Treaty of Paris of 1783, he began with the portraits (left to right) of John Jay, John Adams, Benjamin Franklin, Henry Laurens, and Franklin's grandson, William Temple Franklin. He never finished the painting because the British commissioners refused to pose.

Present the Lesson

Review the provisions of the Treaty of Paris. Write these provisions on the board. (Provisions include: Britain formally acknowledged American independence; the new boundaries of America were set at Florida, the Mississippi, and Canada; Britain recognized American fishing rights off Newfoundland; British creditors could collect debts from private American citizens; the Continental Congress would recommend that states return property seized from British Loyalists.) Ask students to explain how the treaty changed the boundaries of America. (Answer: America extended to Mississippi River.) Ask students how the U.S. boundaries have changed since then. (Answer: the U.S. now includes land to the Pacific Ocean, Alaska, Hawaii.)

Map Skills

Atlantic Ocean • Canada

ish and the Americans worked out a tentative agreement that included a western boundary at the Mississippi. By agreeing to this border, the British hoped to drive a wedge between the Americans and the French. The Americans, in turn, laid this agreement before the French as an accomplished fact, with Franklin using all of his charm to soothe them.

The **Treaty of Paris of 1783** was signed eight years after the war began. In signing the treaty, Britain formally acknowledged American independence. The boundaries of the new nation were set at Florida in the south and at the Mississippi in the west, with the border between Canada and America being much like the present one. Furthermore, the British recognized American fishing rights off the coast of Newfoundland. For their part, the Americans agreed that private British creditors could collect any debts owed them by citizens of the new nation. Finally, the Continental Congress was to "earnestly recommend" to the states that they return property seized from Loyalists. In a separate treaty, the British gave Florida back to Spain.

Afterward, George Washington went to Harlem, which was then on the outskirts of New York City, and watched for three days as the last British troops boarded their transports in New York Harbor. Meanwhile, five miles away at the lower end of

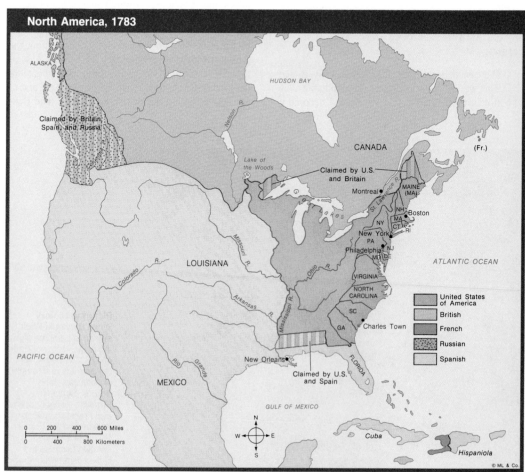

Map Skills   **Place**   The east coast of the new United States of America bordered on what large body of water?   **Region**   What was the name of the British area to the north?

Check for Understanding

Ask students to write a paragraph explaining which of the provisions of the Treaty of Paris they feel were most beneficial to the newly developed country. (Possible response: the extension of boundaries because it gave the Americans more room to explore and settle, more resources, more farmland, and the Mississippi River for navigation.)

Guided Practice

Tell the students that Revolutionary ideals have presented a challenge to the U.S. for over two hundred years. However, most of the five thousand African Americans who participated as soldiers in the Revolution found themselves slaves afterward. Ask students to define government's responsibility in equalizing opportunity. (Possible responses: government should pass and enforce laws that provide equal opportunities for all; government should not interfere in private lives.)

Picturing History   Many artists painted portraits of George Washington, and each artist saw him in a different light. This full-length portrait by John Trumbull is one of a series on the American Revolution.

Manhattan, Loyalists were busily selling off their property and goods. Finally, the nearly thirty thousand soldiers and Loyalists sailed away, and Washington entered the cheering city. He then bade farewell to his assembled officers and rode off to present his resignation as commander in chief to the Continental Congress. He told the Congress that he was leaving "all the employments of public life." He had no idea that his country would call on him again.

A New Form of Government Is Established

Historians have often asked an obvious question about the American Revolution. How much change did it produce in American society? We usually think of revolutions as being periods of great and rapid change. Certainly the French Revolution of 1789 and the more recent revolutions in China in 1912 and in Russia in 1917 produced profound changes in those societies. Was the American Revolution, in this sense, really revolutionary?

Economic Life Is Relatively Unchanged.   The American Revolution produced fewer economic changes than almost any other major modern revolution. The principal reason is that a great deal of change had already taken place during the century before the Revolution. The great majority of white men already owned some property and had good hopes of getting more through their own labors. Therefore, during the Revolution there were few demands for taking property from the wealthy. There also were no calls for changing the economic system in basic ways because it was working well. By and large, Americans were well off. Understandably, prosperous people do not like to rock the foundations of their prosperity.

Slavery Remains an Issue.   One group of Americans had no share in this prosperity—the slaves. Slavery was the conspicuous exception to the principles of the Revolution.

The war itself considerably changed the lives of some slaves. Several thousand served in the armed forces of both sides. Usually they gained their freedom by doing so. Thousands of other slaves were taken by the British when they left Georgia and South Carolina. Some went to freedom in Nova Scotia; others, to continued slavery in the West Indies. For the great majority of slaves, however, the war meant only continued toil in the fields.

Nevertheless, the ideas that sparked the Revolution threw the entire institution of slavery into question. The net result was that a number of states took steps toward abolishing it.

From Pennsylvania northward, slaves were few, so it was relatively easy to bring slavery to a gradual end there. In Massachusetts, court decisions found that slavery violated the state constitution's assertion that "all men are born free and equal." Elsewhere in the North, states passed gradual **emancipation** laws. Although these laws did not abolish slavery outright, they provided that slaves born from then on would become free at age twenty-one or twenty-eight. In many cases, July 4 was named as the date when the laws would go into effect. That date itself pointed to the force of revolutionary principles.

In the Southern states, the principles were the same, but the number of slaves was much greater. In Virginia and Maryland, where slavery was less profitable than farther south, there was considerable discussion about abolishing this institution. The difficulty was that most whites did not want free blacks around. If slavery was abolished, they argued, where would the blacks go? However, a number of slaveholders went ahead on their own and privately emancipated some or all of their slaves.

Farther south, in the Carolinas and Georgia, there was little discussion about slavery. There, slavery was highly profitable, and slaves were far more numerous in proportion to the white population.

Thus, white Americans lived up to their revolutionary principles where it was easy to do so but failed where it was difficult. Thomas Jefferson, the author of the Declaration of Independence, continued to own slaves for his entire life. Eventually, however, Americans would have to pay a terrible price for slavery.

The Revolution had one other important impact on the pattern of American slavery. The outbreak of war stopped the slave trade from Africa, and the Continental Congress prohibited the importation of new slaves from the West Indies and elsewhere. When the war was over, many people wanted to keep the ban on the slave trade.

The Churches Lose Power. The Revolution led to certain changes in the relationship between church and state. In New York and the Southern states, the established Anglican church lost its privileged position. People were no longer required to pay taxes to support it. Nevertheless, most states continued to tax their citizens for the support of the churches, but not for any particular church. The taxpayers could name the church to which the tax money would go.

Only Virginia provided for the complete separation of church and state, an arrangement that today prevails throughout the United States. Virginia's progressive position on this matter resulted largely from the influence of Thomas Jefferson and his friend James Madison.

A Political Example to the World. The ideas behind the American Revolution have echoed around the world for more than two hundred years.

As one of George III's descendants, Elizabeth II of England, said when she visited Independence Hall in 1976, "We learned a great lesson." As a result, few colonies of the British Empire had to fight a revolutionary war to obtain their freedom. Countries such as Canada, Australia, and New Zealand were given their independence gradually.

For generations, people seeking freedom from oppression have looked with admiration and longing toward the United States. It was in the realm of government that the American Revolution was truly revolutionary. A nation was born whose government and social development became the wonder of the world.

Linking Past to Present

The struggle for independence from European colonial rule has continued throughout the twentieth century. In Africa, for example, the Portuguese colonies of Mozambique and Angola did not attain independence until 1975. This was two hundred years after the first shot of the American Revolution rang out at Lexington—a shot that was said to have been heard around the world.

SECTION 5 REVIEW

Key Terms and People

Explain the significance of: John Jay, Treaty of Paris of 1783, emancipation

Main Ideas

1. What did John Jay realize about the position of the French in negotiating the peace treaty?
2. What were the borders of the new country as determined by the peace negotiations?
3. Why did the American Revolution result in little economic change?
4. What effect did the ideas of the Revolution have on the institution of slavery?

Critical Thinking

5. Why have the ideals of the American Revolution had a lasting effect on global politics?

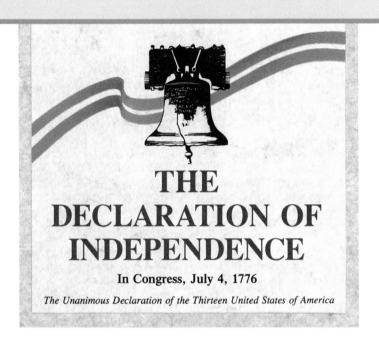

THE DECLARATION OF INDEPENDENCE

In Congress, July 4, 1776

The Unanimous Declaration of the Thirteen United States of America

For Discussion

How is the Declaration organized? (Answer: there are three parts: a preamble stating the general ideas behind the American Revolution; a list of grievances, and the formal resolution of independence.) What basic rights does the Declaration of Independence claim for all people? (Answer: the rights to life, liberty, and the pursuit of happiness.)

When, in the course of human events, it becomes necessary for one people to dissolve the political bands which have connected them with another, and to assume, among the powers of the earth, the separate and equal station to which the laws of nature and of nature's God entitle them, a decent respect to the opinions of mankind requires that they should declare the causes which impel them to the separation.

We hold these truths to be self-evident:—That all men are created equal; that they are endowed by their Creator with certain unalienable rights; that among these are life, liberty, and the pursuit of happiness. That, to secure these rights, governments are instituted among men, deriving their just powers from the consent of the governed; that, whenever any form of government becomes destructive of these ends, it is the right of the people to alter or to abolish it, and to institute new government, laying its foundation on such principles, and organizing its powers in such form, as to them shall seem most likely to affect their safety and happiness. Prudence, indeed, will dictate that governments long established should not be changed for light and transient causes; and, accordingly, all experience hath shown that mankind are more disposed to suffer, while evils are sufferable, than to right themselves by abolishing the forms to which they are accustomed. But, when a long train of abuses and usurpations, pursuing invariably the same object, evinces a design to reduce them under absolute despotism, it is their right, it is their duty, to throw off such government, and to provide new guards for their future security. Such has been the patient sufferance of these colonies; and such is now the necessity which constrains them to alter their former systems of government. The history of the present King of Great Britain is a history of repeated injuries and usurpations, all having in direct object the establishment of an absolute tyranny over these States. To prove this, let facts be submitted to a candid world.

He has refused his assent to laws the most wholesome and necessary for the public good.

He has forbidden his governors to pass laws of immediate and pressing importance, unless suspended in their operation till his assent should be obtained; and when so suspended, he has utterly neglected to attend to them.

He has refused to pass other laws for the accommodation of large districts of people, unless those people would relinquish the right of representation in the legislature—a right inestimable to them, and formidable to tyrants only.

He has called together legislative bodies at places unusual, uncomfortable, and distant from the depository of their public records, for the sole purpose of fatiguing them into compliance with his measures.

He has dissolved representative houses repeat-

For Discussion
Which of the complaints
listed by Jefferson in the
Declaration against King
George III seem to you to be
the most serious? Why?
(Possible answers: George
dissolved legislatures and invaded people's rights; he refused to hold elections; he
quartered armies against the
people's will; he imposed
taxes on people without their
consent and cut off their
trade with other nations.
• These acts violated the
very basic needs and rights
of people.)

edly, for opposing, with manly firmness, his invasions on the rights of the people.

He has refused for a long time, after such
dissolutions, to cause others to be elected; whereby
the legislative powers, incapable of annihilation,
have returned to the people at large for their
exercise; the State remaining, in the mean time,
exposed to all the dangers of invasion from without, and convulsions within.

He has endeavored to prevent the population of
these States; for that purpose obstructing the laws
for the naturalization of foreigners; refusing to pass
others to encourage their migrations hither, and
raising the conditions of new appropriations of
lands.

He has obstructed the administration of justice,
by refusing his assent to laws for establishing
judiciary powers.

He has made judges dependent on his will alone,
for the tenure of their offices, and the amount and
payment of their salaries.

He has erected a multitude of new offices, and
sent hither swarms of officers to harass our people,
and eat out their substance.

He has kept among us, in times of peace,
standing armies, without the consent of our legislatures.

He has affected to render the military independent of and superior to the civil power.

He has combined with others to subject us to a
jurisdiction foreign to our constitution, and unac-
knowledged by our laws; giving his assent to their
acts of pretended legislation:

For quartering large bodies of armed troops
among us;

For protecting them, by a mock trial, from
punishment for any murders which they should
commit on the inhabitants of these States;

For cutting off our trade with all parts of the
world;

For imposing taxes on us without our consent;

For depriving us, in many cases, of the benefits
of trial by jury;

For transporting us beyond seas to be tried for
pretended offences;

For abolishing the free system of English laws in
a neighboring province, establishing therein an
arbitrary government, and enlarging its boundaries,

so as to render it at once an example and fit
instrument for introducing the same absolute rule
into these colonies;

For taking away our charters, abolishing our
most valuable laws, and altering fundamentally the
forms of our governments;

For suspending our own legislatures, and declaring themselves invested with power to legislate for
us in all cases whatsoever.

He has abdicated government here, by declaring
us out of his protection, and waging war against us.

He has plundered our seas, ravaged our coasts,
burnt our towns, and destroyed the lives of our
people.

He is at this time transporting large armies of
foreign mercenaries to complete the works of
death, desolation, and tyranny, already begun with
circumstances of cruelty and perfidy scarcely par-
alleled in the most barbarous ages, and totally
unworthy the head of a civilized nation.

He has constrained our fellow citizens, taken
captive on the high seas, to bear arms against their
country, to become the executioners of their friends
and brethren, or to fall themselves by their hands.

He has excited domestic insurrections amongst
us, and has endeavored to bring on the inhabitants
of our frontiers, the merciless Indian savages,
whose known rule of warfare is an undistinguished
destruction of all ages, sexes, and conditions.

In every stage of these oppressions, we have
petitioned for redress, in the most humble terms:
our repeated petitions have been answered only by
repeated injury. A prince, whose character is thus
marked by every act which may define a tyrant, is
unfit to be the ruler of a free people.

Nor have we been wanting in attentions to our
British brethren. We have warned them, from time
to time, of attempts by their legislature to extend an
unwarrantable jurisdiction over us. We have reminded them of the circumstances of our emigration and settlement here. We have appealed to their
native justice and magnanimity; and we have con-
jured them, by the ties of our common kindred, to
disavow these usurpations, which would inevitably
interrupt our connections and correspondence.
They, too, have been deaf to the voice of justice
and of consanguinity. We must, therefore, acqui-

esce in the necessity, which denounces our separation, and hold them, as we hold the rest of mankind, enemies in war, in peace friends.

WE, THEREFORE, the REPRESENTATIVES of the UNITED STATES OF AMERICA, in General Congress assembled, appealing to the Supreme Judge of the world for the rectitude of our intentions, do, in the name and by the authority of the good people of these colonies, solemnly publish and declare, That these United Colonies are, and of right ought to be, FREE AND INDEPENDENT STATES; that they are absolved from all allegiance to the British crown, and that all political connection between them and the state of Great Britain, is and ought to be totally dissolved; and that, as free and independent states, they have full power to levy war, conclude peace, contract alliances, establish commerce, and to do all other acts and things which independent states may of right do. And, for the support of this declaration, with a firm reliance on the protection of Divine Providence, we mutually pledge to each other our lives, our fortunes, and our sacred honor.

John Hancock

The foregoing Declaration was, by order of Congress, engrossed and signed by the following members:—

NEW HAMPSHIRE.
Josiah Bartlett,
William Whipple,
Matthew Thornton.

MASSACHUSETTS BAY.
Samuel Adams,
John Adams,
Robert Treat Paine,
Elbridge Gerry.

RHODE ISLAND.
Stephen Hopkins,
William Ellery.

CONNECTICUT.
Roger Sherman,
Samuel Huntington,
William Williams,
Oliver Wolcott.

NEW YORK.
William Floyd,
Philip Livingston,
Francis Lewis,
Lewis Morris.

NEW JERSEY.
Richard Stockton,
John Witherspoon,
Francis Hopkinson,
John Hart,
Abraham Clark.

PENNSYLVANIA.
Robert Morris,
Benjamin Rush,
Benjamin Franklin,
John Morton,
George Clymer,
James Smith,

George Taylor,
James Wilson,
George Ross.

DELAWARE.
Caesar Rodney,
George Read,
Thomas M'Kean.

MARYLAND.
Samuel Chase,
William Paca,
Thomas Stone,
Charles Carroll
  of Carrollton.

VIRGINIA.
George Wythe,
Richard Henry Lee,
Thomas Jefferson,

Benjamin Harrison,
Thomas Nelson, Jr.,
Francis Lightfoot Lee,
Carter Braxton.

NORTH CAROLINA.
William Hooper,
Joseph Hewes,
John Penn.

SOUTH CAROLINA.
Edward Rutledge,
Thomas Heyward, Jr.,
Thomas Lynch, Jr.,
Arthur Middleton.

GEORGIA.
Button Gwinnett,
Lyman Hall,
George Walton.

Resolved, That copies of the Declaration be sent to the several assemblies, conventions, and committees, or councils of safety, and to the several commanding officers of the continental troops; that it be proclaimed in each of the United States, at the head of the army.

State the Objective

Use a five-step procedure for making decisions.

Present the Lesson

Write the five steps in the decision-making process across the top of the board. To complete the chart, have students work through the problem of revolution with England from the viewpoint of the American colonists. As they identify the problem, supply alternatives, and so forth, write each response on the board under the appropriate step. Encourage students to consider all aspects of the dilemma. (Possible responses for chart:

Identify the problem—some American colonists resent being subjects of Britain without representation in Parliament; they advocate rebellion.

List alternative solutions—live as British subjects and learn to deal with taxation and other issues as they arise or rebel and fight the British.

Recognize the values involved—those in favor of the rebellion want freedom and democracy; those opposed to the rebellion want to end the loss of life, commerce, and industry and want the protection of the British navy.

Consider the consequences—remaining a colony protected by England would bring reconciliation and peace; rebellion would bring war and loss of life but eventual independence.

Make your decision—students must make a decision and support it, based on their evaluation of the information in the first four steps.)

Ask several students to give their decision and explain how they arrived at it. Review the

Focus on Critical Thinking Skills

Making Decisions

Understanding the Skill

Suppose you are old enough to vote. In an upcoming election in your town, there are several controversial issues on the ballot. How will you decide on each? In a democracy, citizens must continually make decisions. Here are some steps to follow when faced with difficult choices.

- **Identify the problem.** What are the facts of the situation? Write the problem down to clarify your ideas and to gain objectivity. What is the cause of the problem? What will happen if nothing is done? Who is involved?
- **List alternative solutions.** What are your choices? Brainstorm about your options. What questions need consideration? Who can offer advice or expertise?
- **Recognize the values involved.** What values should you consider in making your decision? Are you bound by law or conscience to choose one course of action?
- **Consider the consequences.** What are the pros and cons of the alternatives? What are the costs and benefits of the alternatives? How will your decision affect you, your family, and your country? What conflicts can be foreseen and how can they be resolved? List the long-term effects as well as the short-term effects of your decision.
- **Make your decision.** Once your decision is made, draw up a plan of action. What commitments and responsibilities are called for? How will the results be evaluated? Once you have acted upon your decision, remember to evaluate the results from time to time. Few decisions are irrevocable.

Applying the Skill

If you had lived in the American colonies at the time of the Revolution, you would have faced hard choices. Should you remain loyal to the King, or should you take part in a rebellion against him? The consequences were long-term. Whatever you decided would affect your own life, the lives of your children and your grandchildren—even the fate of the nation. Leaders on both sides presented persuasive arguments.

Charles Inglis, a clergyman of the Church of England, argued for loyalty to the King. Of independence he said:

> The remedy is infinitely worse than the disease. It would be like cutting off a leg because the toe happened to ache. . . .
> By reconciliation with Britain, [an end] would be put to the present calamitous war by which many lives have been lost, and so many more must be lost if it continues. . . . [Then] peace . . . will be restored. In one respect peace is like health; we do not sufficiently know its value but by its absence. . . .
> Agriculture, commerce, and industry would [then] resume their customary vigor. At present they languish and droop, both here

Picturing History King George III's lack of tact and stubborn will to punish the colonies helped many colonists decide to take up arms against him.

information on the board. Then point out that it is easier to complete the steps in the decision-making process after an event has taken place. Ask students why it might have been difficult to consider all these steps as the events preceding the American Revolution were unfolding? (Possible response: Colonists on either side could not know how events would unfold; they took great personal risks with no guarantee of victory.) What decisions do people have to make today that might have consequences as far-reaching as the decisions the colonists made? (Possible responses: decisions about how tax dollars will be spent, what foreign countries to support with money and/or military personnel, what officials to elect to improve education and other aspects of life.) What seems to be the most important part of the decision-making process? (Possible response: having information about solutions and about possible consequences.)

Check for Understanding

Review the questions at the end of the feature, using the information students generated. Stress the importance of being able to accurately state the problem and of having enough information to make an educated decision.

and in Britain and must continue to do so while this unhappy contest remains unsettled. By [our] connection with Britain, our trade would have the protection of the greatest naval power in the world . . . the supreme [sea] power in the universe. . . .

[Even if we were to win,] a republican form of government would neither suit the genius of the people nor the extent of America. That form of government . . . would be utterly improper for such a continent as this. America is too unwieldy for the feeble tardy administration of democracy.

The outspoken patriot Patrick Henry addressed an illegal meeting of the Virginia House of Burgesses. (The royal governor had dismissed the House, but its members met anyway.)

Sir, we have done everything that could be done to avert the storm which is now coming on. We have petitioned; we have remonstrated; we have supplicated; we have prostrated ourselves before the throne, and have implored its interposition [intervention] to arrest the tyrannical hands of the ministry and Parliament. Our petitions have been slighted; . . . and we have been spurned with contempt. . . . There is no longer any room for hope. If we wish to be free, . . . if we mean not basely to abandon the noble struggle in which we have so long been engaged, . . . we must fight! I repeat it, sir, we must fight! An appeal to arms and to the God of hosts is all that is left to us!

They tell us, sir, that we are weak—unable to cope with so formidable an adversary. But when shall we be stronger? . . . Will it be when we are totally disarmed, and when a British guard shall be stationed in every house? . . . Shall we acquire the means of effectual resistance by lying supinely on our backs and hugging the delusive phantom of hope until our enemies have bound us hand and foot? . . . Besides, sir, we shall not fight our battles alone. There is a just God who presides over the destinies of nations and who will raise up friends to fight our battles for us. . . .

. . . Is life so dear, or peace so sweet, as to be purchased at the price of chains and slavery? Forbid it, Almighty God! I know not what course others may take; but as for me, give me liberty or give me death!

Picturing History Some colonists who chose to remain loyal to the King, sought refuge in Canada. Tories leaving for Canada are pictured above.

Practicing Your Skill

1. What decision faced the American colonists at the beginning of the Revolution? Who was involved and who would be affected by this decision?
2. What solution did Charles Inglis endorse? What arguments did Inglis give for choosing this course of action? What values were involved in these arguments?
3. What arguments did Patrick Henry present? What values were involved in his arguments? What were the alternatives as Henry saw them?
4. What were the consequences of Inglis's solution? of Henry's solution?
5. Aside from your own opinions about the outcome of the Revolutionary War, which of the two sets of arguments above do you find most convincing? Why? How did you arrive at this decision?

The War for Independence **125**

Key Terms and People

These are highlighted in the text in the order in which they appear in this list.

Main Ideas

1. How—appointed a commander in chief, raised the Continental Army, sent Benedict Arnold to Canada with another army, sent a petition for peace to King George III, issued paper money, conducted foreign and Indian relations, established a postal department, authorized creation of a navy. Why—to counter British efforts to quell colonial rebellion; to govern their own country.

2. Congress resolved that people defending Boston be called the Army of the United Colonies.

3. Ideas of inalienable rights and government created by the people, subject to abolition by them if it did not protect their rights. • Replaced "life, liberty, and property" with "life, liberty, and the pursuit of happiness."

4. Loyalists or Tories. • Royal officials; people against the "mob rule" of the Patriots; people who believed rebels had broken the law; people afraid of redcoats' power.

5. Advantages—a well-trained army and a strong navy, financial backing, munitions factories, bayonets, support of Loyalists, Indian allies; disadvantages—distance from home support, unfamiliarity with countryside, weak leadership, inability to use Loyalists effectively.

6. Advantages—knowledge of countryside, fighting at home for home, more accurate rifles, better marksmanship, George Washington, ability to use guerrilla tactics, enthusiasm; disadvantages—lack of money, no trained army or navy, need to smuggle in guns, no central government.

7. British feared fighting inland away from their sea power; French threw support to Revolution and signed treaty of alliance with Americans; Spain

later joined war as France's ally.

8. Supplied about 80 percent of gunpowder; stationed a fleet at Newport, Rhode Island; along with Washington's army and the French West Indies fleet, forced Cornwallis's surrender.

9. Spain—wanted Florida; against American independence and moving colonies' boundary to Mississippi. France—wanted to humble Britain; against all-out support

for American independence. Britain—wanted to split Americans and French; against giving Americans land. Colonies—wanted independence; against a western boundary at the Appalachians.

10. Spain—Florida, by separate treaty. France—American independence and a humbled Britain. Britain—an agreement that private British creditors could collect American debts and the recommendation that

states return Loyalists' confiscated property. Colonies—independence; boundaries set as Florida, Mississippi River, and Canada; rights to fishing off Newfoundland.

Critical Thinking Questions

11. Possible answer: shows how unnatural war is. • Army words include *whips, rapid fire, screeched, stamping*

CHAPTER **5** REVIEW

Write your answers on a separate sheet of paper.

Key Terms and People

Explain the significance of: Henry Clinton, William Howe, redcoats, Richard Henry Lee, John Adams, Abigail Adams, inalienable rights, mercenaries, Hessians, John Paul Jones, privateers, Continentals, amnesty, Horatio Gates, Valley Forge, George Rogers Clark, Nathanael Greene, Yorktown, John Jay, emancipation

Main Ideas

1. Before it declared independence, how and why did the Second Continental Congress act as an independent government?
2. How did the army of the United Colonies come into being?
3. What did Jefferson take from John Locke's philosophy for the Declaration of Independence? How did he deviate from Locke?
4. What were people opposed to independence called? Who were these people?
5. List at least four advantages the British had over the Americans in the Revolution and four disadvantages.
6. List at least four advantages the Americans had over the British in the Revolution and four disadvantages.
7. What were the effects of the American victory over General Burgoyne at Saratoga?
8. How did the French help the American war effort?
9. What did each of the four parties to the 1783 Treaty of Paris want? What did each not want?
10. What did each party get in the Treaty of Paris?

Critical Thinking Questions

11. **Analyzing Literature.** The literary excerpt on page 99 describes an army marching through a forest. What is so jarring about the juxtaposition of the cavalcade and the forest? What words describe the army? What words describe the forest? What battle might these troops be going toward?

12. **Judging Values.** What does the Olive Branch Petition, sent to King George III, show about the loyalty the American colonists felt toward the British Crown? What attitude toward the king is revealed in the Declaration of Independence? Explain.

13. **Recognizing Values.** List the battles fought before the Declaration of Independence. Who took Fort Ticonderoga? What was the risk the Patriots took in these battles? What impelled them to take such a risk?

14. **Formulating Hypotheses.** Do you think Benedict Arnold's unsuccessful foray into Canada in early 1776 had anything to do with his defection, four years later, to the British? Give reasons for your answer.

Critical Thinking Activities

15. **Making and Analyzing a Map.** Trace the map below, which covers the area from what is now New York State through Maine, Quebec, and Montreal. Label New York City, the Hudson River, the Mohawk River, Lake Champlain, Montreal, and Quebec. Imagine that you are a military strategist. Why are the points you have labeled so vital to the military strategy of the Americans and the British that they would go through forest, cold, heat, and other hostile environments to achieve control of them?

16. **Linking Past to Present.** How has the role of women in the armed forces and in industry during wartime changed since the time of Molly Pitcher?

TELESCOPING THE TIMES: 1775–1783

The War for Independence

The Second Continental Congress met in Philadelphia in May of 1775. The delegates continued to seek political solutions to their problems, but public opinion changed rapidly. Patriot forces surrounded the British army in Boston. The British won a major battle on Bunker Hill, but they lost many more men than the Americans. Later, in March 1776, British troops evacuated Boston by sea. Meanwhile, an American attempt to conquer Canada failed. In January 1776 a little pamphlet called *Common Sense* by Thomas Paine caused Americans to start talking about the startling possibility of fighting for actual independence and self-government.

Thomas Jefferson of Virginia wrote the original draft of the Declaration of Independence at the request of the Second Continental Congress. It set forth the idea of natural rights of life, liberty, and the pursuit of happiness and declared the fundamental equality of all men. The Declaration did not appear to include women and slaves. Opponents of the Revolution, called Loyalists, suffered a good deal. As a result, many of them went into exile in Great Britain or Canada.

The British and American positions differed in several respects. The British navy ruled the seas. On land its army was rigidly disciplined, but it was so short of men that the British hired mercenaries. The war had to be fought three thousand miles from home in unfamiliar territory. On the Patriot side, Commander in Chief George Washington managed to keep an army together, but it was always short of supplies. He depended on a core of Continental soldiers supplemented by state militia. Women took part in the war, sometimes even in the army. The Patriots financed the war by borrowing and by printing paper money.

After the British left Boston, the scene of warfare shifted to the Middle States. The British captured both New York City and Philadelphia.

The Patriots won several battles but lost others. In 1777 the Americans captured an entire British army at Saratoga, New York. That victory helped bring about an open alliance with France. The war then shifted to the South, where the Patriots suffered several disastrous defeats. Then, with the aid of French troops and ships, George Washington captured the major British army at Yorktown. The American Revolution was over—farmers and shopkeepers had defeated an empire.

At the signing of the Treaty of Paris in 1783, skillful American diplomats won highly favorable terms. Great Britain recognized American independence. The boundaries of the new nation were set from Spanish Florida north to Canada and all the way west to the Mississippi River. The Revolution brought few economic changes, but it meant the slow end of slavery in the Northern States and a broadening of religious freedom in several areas. The Revolution has since served as an example of self-determination for all the world.

Chronology of Main Events	
1774	First Continental Congress meets
1775–1783	Revolutionary War
1775	Second Continental Congress assembles; Battle of Bunker Hill
1776	Paine's *Common Sense* published; Declaration of Independence written; Washington takes Trenton
1779	George Rogers Clark wins Northwest
1783	Treaty of Paris signed

Telescoping the Times may be used as an alternative to having students read the entire chapter, as a chapter preview, or as a chapter review.

State the Objective

Understand the circumstances that led to the religious reformation in Europe.

Present the Lesson

Point out to students that religious reformers brought about lasting changes that affected everyone. On the board list the names of major religious reformers: John Huss, Martin Luther, John Calvin. Ask students to determine the specific reforms sought or brought about by each. As they respond, have a student fill in the information to complete the chart on the board. (Possible responses for chart: John Huss—preached against the wealth of the Catholic church and the misconduct of the clergy; Martin Luther—preached against the sale of indulgences and the belief that good works are required for salvation; John Calvin—preached the value of simple worship, strict morals, and hard work.) Ask students what consequences these religious reformers had on Europe. (Possible responses: monarchs in France, England, and Germany used the religious conflicts of the Reformation to increase their power; the fight between Protestants and Catholics for dominance in Europe grew into the Thirty Years War; in England the Puritans abolished the monarchy as they sought political power.)

Divide students into small groups of four or five. Ask each group to decide what reforms the Catholic church might have made to pre-

Focus on Global Events

Religious Conflicts in Europe

One of the primary reasons Europeans settled in the American colonies was to escape religious persecution. As a result, one of the main characteristics of United States history has been freedom of worship. In Europe, however, during the two hundred years prior to the founding of the American colonies, religion was a main cause of prejudice, discrimination, and disruption.

Religious Dissent. Toward the end of the Middle Ages, Christians in Europe began questioning the corruption they saw in the Roman Catholic Church. While many dedicated, hardworking priests and nuns did serve the people, many others abused the Church's great wealth and political power. The clergy often demanded gifts in return for religious services such as baptisms, marriages, or burials. Bishops were sometimes appointed without any regard for their merit but simply because they had powerful relatives or a great deal of money.

In Bohemia (now a part of Czechoslovakia), a priest named John Huss (1369–1415) preached against the Church's wealth and the misconduct of many of the clergy. Huss was burned at the stake as a heretic (one who disagrees with accepted belief). However, his fellow Bohemians looked upon him as a hero and did not forget his ideas.

The Reformation. By the early 1500's, many others began questioning the Church. In Germany, people resented the fact that so much church money collected from them was sent from their homeland to the Pope in Rome. This resentment needed only a spark to ignite a revolt. The spark came from Martin Luther (1483–1546), a monk who did not originally intend to divide the Church but only to restore its purity.

Beginning in 1515, Pope Leo X had authorized the sale of indulgences. Indulgences were pardons given by the Church for sinful conduct. By permitting this practice, Leo was trying to raise money to finish building St. Peter's Church in Rome. On October 31, 1517, Martin Luther nailed a series of statements, called the Ninety-Five Theses, to the

Picturing History Based on a painting by Francois Dubois, this etching shows the St. Bartholomew's Day Massacre of August 24, 1572. The massacre of French Protestant leaders began in Paris and later spread to other parts of France.

door of the church at Wittenberg. In these statements he protested that God's forgiveness could not be bought. The sale of indulgences, he said, was only a cynical effort by the Church to make money. Luther also questioned other teachings and practices of the Church. "Good works are not required for salvation," he stated; "faith alone is sufficient. God speaks to us through the Bible, not through the pope."

Pope Leo was furious; he declared Luther a

vent the Reformation. Appoint a spokesperson from each group to share their answers with the class. (Possible responses: the Catholic church could have appointed and promoted officials on merit; Pope Leo V might have rescinded his order to sell indulgences; church officials could have made certain more of the money collected in various countries stayed in those countries for good works; the Pope might have postponed the building of St. Peter's Church.)

Check for Understanding

Review the questions at the end of the feature using the information students have generated. Then ask students how the religious reformation in Europe affected the colonies. (Possible response: as various religious sects developed in Europe, they often persecuted those with different beliefs; escape from these religious persecutions was a primary reason Europeans settled in the American colonies.) How did the religious reformation affect the United States? (Possible response: after the Glorious Revolution, the principles of religious and political freedom established in England traveled to the colonies and became part of the United States Constitution.)

Picturing History Before his "sudden conversion," when he turned all of his energy to the Reformation, John Calvin studied law, the classics, and Hebrew.

heretic and excommunicated him from the Church. Luther became a hunted man. However, powerful German princes who disliked the power of the Pope gave Luther protection. He went on to found a new church.

The spirit of religious reform grew and became known in history as the Reformation. The Reformation was supported by those who sincerely wanted to improve the Church and by monarchs in France, England, and Germany who saw a way to increase their power at the expense of the Roman Catholic Church. These reformers and their followers were known as Protestants (those who protest).

The influence of the Protestants spread. In 1518 the Swiss priest Ulrich Zwingli (tsving' lē) began preaching in Zurich. He condemned monasteries, denounced fasting and confession, and urged priests to marry.

John Calvin (1509–1564) had an even greater impact throughout Europe and eventually on those who settled New England. He preached the virtues of simple worship, strict morals, and hard work. In Holland, Calvinists founded the Dutch Reformed Church, while the Calvinist Scotsman John Knox (c. 1514–1572) formed the Presbyterian Church and succeeded in making it the official church of Scotland. Calvin's followers in France called themselves Huguenots, and for nearly a century religious wars between Huguenots and Catholics tore apart that kingdom.

In Bohemia the struggle between Protestants and Catholics—each considering the other damned—started the Thirty Years' War (1618–1648). This war reduced central Europe to almost a wasteland.

Civil War in England. In England a civil war broke out in 1642 between Puritans and supporters of Charles I. After six years of strife, the king's forces were defeated, and Charles was beheaded.

The Puritan Parliament abolished the monarchy and established a republic, or commonwealth. It granted dictatorial powers to the Puritan military leader, Oliver Cromwell. After his death, the same powers were bestowed on his son Richard. Many English people grew tired of the harsh rule and moral strictness of the Puritans. They forced Richard Cromwell to resign and appealed to Prince Charles, son of Charles I, to return from exile and rule.

Charles II ruled for twenty-five years. His Catholic brother James II succeeded him. Again Protestants became alarmed. Fearing a Catholic restoration in England, they appealed to the Protestant leader of Holland, William of Orange, and his wife Mary to overturn James II and rule England. William and Mary arrived; James fled.

William and Mary became king and queen of England in 1689, agreeing to a Bill of Rights and guarantees such as trial by jury. An Act of Toleration, passed a few months later, bestowed freedom of worship on all English Protestant groups (though not on Catholics or Jews).

With the Glorious Revolution, as the reign of William and Mary was called, peace returned to a Protestant England. The principles of political and religious freedom established under the new monarchy traveled quickly to the British colonies in America. Later, these same principles were confirmed and expanded in the United States Constitution to include freedom for all religious groups.

Understanding Global Events

1. What were indulgences? Why did Luther denounce their sale?
2. To what countries did the Protestant Reformation spread from Germany?
3. Identify the major Reformation leaders and explain their significance.

Critical Thinking

4. How did the religious policies under William and Mary affect the American colonies?

Key Terms and People

These are highlighted in the text in the order in which they appear in this list.

Main Ideas

13. George Washington. • Possible answer: military leader of French and Indian War and member of Continental Congresses.

14. Benjamin Franklin. • Possible answer: inventor, publisher, writer, and diplomat.

15. Abigail Adams. • Possible answer: asked that women be mentioned in the Declaration of Independence.

16. Samuel Adams. • Possible answer: famous patriot who coined name Boston Massacre.

17. King George III. • Possible answer: he and British Parliament lost colonies.

18. Thomas Paine. • Possible answer: writer who used contemporary philosophies to inspire colonists.

19. The Marquis de Lafayette. • Possible answer: member of French aristocracy who helped win last and decisive battle of Revolution.

20. Thomas Jefferson. • Possible answer: Virginia farmer, intellectual, and Continental Congresses member.

21. Molly Pitcher. • Possible answer: she took her husband's place in battle when he was wounded.

22. Casimir Pulaski. • Possible answer: Polish officer who died of wounds from battle of Savannah.

Critical Thinking Questions

➤**23.** Possible answers: Early immigrants in Central America started farming, irrigated fields, and built pyramids and roads; the French changed the human environment of Montreal and Quebec; the Spanish caused great damage to humans with guns and germs, introduced the horse, and built forts and chapels.

24. The Indians found that the white colonists were driving them from their ancestors' land and also trying to convert them to Christianity. Such activities threatened Indian society, so the Indians fought back and were slaughtered.

25. The wealthy Virginia planters found that indentured servants could be dangerous, especially since these servants owned and could use guns, so they began to use black slaves on their plantations.

26. Under the headright system, any man who paid his own way to Virginia got 50 acres of land plus 50 more acres for each person he brought with him. Therefore a European wealthy enough to pay his and his family's and servants' ways could became even wealthier.

27. People of diverse religions who came to America to better their lot settled in colonies that practiced religious toleration.

28. Under mercantilist theory, the colony's role was to send raw materials to the mother country, which, in turn, would sell manufactured products to the colonies.

29. Massachusetts got the Dominion of New England abolished after the Glorious Revolution, but it could not get back its old charter.

UNIT **1** REVIEW

Write your answers on a separate sheet of paper.

Key Terms and People

Explain the significance of each of the following.

1. Mayas
2. League of the Iroquois
3. St. Augustine
4. Mayflower Compact
5. John Winthrop
6. Roger Williams
7. Lord Baltimore
8. William Penn
9. mercantilism
10. social contract
11. Committees of Correspondence
12. Second Continental Congress

Main Ideas

Who might have said each of the following? Give an additional fact about each person.

13. I held the Continental Army together.
14. I proposed the Albany Plan of Union.
15. I urged the creation of a legal basis for the status of women.
16. My Massachusetts assembly letter called upon the colonists to unite.
17. I refused to read the Olive Branch Petition.
18. I wrote *Common Sense* and *The Crisis*.
19. I led the French forces in America during the Revolution.
20. I wrote the Declaration of Independence.
21. I carried pitchers of water during Revolutionary War battles.
22. I organized the cavalry at Valley Forge.

Critical Thinking Questions

23. **Analyzing Effects.** Give several examples that show how immigrants and explorers from earliest times changed the environment of Central and North America.

24. **Evaluating Effects.** What happened to the relationship between the Indians and the Massachusetts colonists from the time of Squanto to the time of Metacom? Why?

Assessing Cause and Effect.

For each pair of events following, tell how the first event caused the second.

25. Bacon's Rebellion—increase in slavery
26. Headright system—wealthy planters
27. Religious toleration—diversity of people
28. Mercantilist theory—colonists send raw materials to English factories
29. Glorious Revolution—Massachusetts gets new charter
30. John Locke writes his social contract theory—Declaration of Independence
31. Indians attack Detroit—Proclamation of 1763
32. William Pitt spends money—British win French and Indian War
33. Economic prosperity—decline of Puritanism
34. British want alliance with League of Iroquois—Albany Congress

35. **Judging Values.** Judging from the description of British rule in Chapters 3, 4, and 5, would you say that British rule was on the whole a positive, negative, or neutral force? Why?

Critical Thinking Activities

36. **Evaluating Trends.** Make a time line that begins with the Treaty of Paris in 1763 and shows the events that led to the Declaration of Independence. See how many of these events you can remember without looking at the book.

1763   1776

37. **Linking Past to Present.** If you were rewriting the paragraph of the Declaration of Independence, beginning ''We hold these truths to be self-evident'' and ending with ''deriving their just powers from the consent of the governed,'' how would you change it? Why?

30. John Locke's social contract between governing and governed became the philosophical background of Declaration of Independence.

31. Indians attacked British forts west of Appalachians because the colonists, in spreading westward, were taking Indian lands. The royal proclamation tried to keep the colonists east of the Appalachians not only to preserve the profitable British fur trade with the Indians but also to control the colonists more easily.

32. British were losing the French and Indian War until William Pitt spent more money to hire soldiers and improve leadership.

33. Many people dropped the strict Puritan code as their material comforts increased.

34. Albany Congress, with delegates from most colonies, was called to make a treaty with League of the Iroquois that would be binding on all Indians and colonials in case of war with France.

35. Possible answers: positive—it provided a good economic base for colonies and sheltered them during wars with Europeans and Indians. Negative—it did not respect colonists' rights as British citizens. Neutral—both England and the colonies pursued own interests.

TELESCOPING THE TIMES TO 1783

American Beginnings

Early Americans and Explorers

The first Americans came from Asia. They arrived more than twenty-five thousand years ago. Scientists are now sure that these first Americans came on foot across a small neck of land that connected Asia and North America. During that period called the Ice Age, the level of the ocean dropped, making a land bridge. As the ice melted, water covered the bridge. Today that land lies under the ocean.

These first Americans walked thousands of miles farther and farther south. They sought a warmer climate and small animals for food. Centuries later they had developed weapons to kill mammoths in what is now the southwestern part of the United States. Thousands of years after that, they developed corn grasses into a source of food that became basic for most people in all the Americas.

In Mexico, Central America, and Peru, several groups of these immigrants established complex civilizations. Their cities had extensive road and irrigation systems. Their societies developed written languages, calendars, and rigid social classes.

Farther north in what is now the United States, Indian groups developed various ways of living. In the Southwest they built cities but had to fend off raids by nomads. In the Northwest, heavy rainfall and rivers provided abundant food. In the Far North, the Inuit, or Eskimo, people faced unique problems because of the cold. On the Great Plains, everyone depended on the millions of buffalo for food, clothing, and fuel. In the Mississippi River Valley, the original people constructed huge burial mounds.

The Eastern Woodland Indians were split into three major language groups. The Muskogean speakers lived in the Southeast; the Iroquois lived south and east of the Great Lakes; and numerous tribes who spoke Algonquin languages were scattered along the northeastern coast. With most of these groups, it was customary for women to do the farming and men the hunting, fishing, and fighting.

The first Europeans to touch American shores may have been fishermen who had no idea where they were. The first records of European contact with America came from Scandinavian sailors who pushed westward past Greenland to Newfoundland about the year A.D. 1000. Their tiny settlements on the western shores of the North Atlantic did not last, however. Nearly five hundred years later, voyagers from southwestern Europe began a more deliberate search. Their motives have been grouped under four headings: spices, gold, God, and glory.

The Portuguese took the lead in this search. They wanted to trade with Asia directly by sea rather than through the lands of the Middle East. Finally they found a sea route around the southern tip of Africa. At about the same time, Christopher Columbus persuaded the King and Queen of Spain to support his attempt to find another approach to Asia. This Italian navigator felt sure that he could reach Asia by sailing west.

A small number of Spanish conquistadors conquered much larger groups of Aztecs in Mexico and of Incas in Peru. The Spanish had guns, horses, and Indian allies. However, European diseases killed many more Indians than the Spanish soldiers did.

Spain's empire spread across America and around the world. In the sixteenth century Spain was the world's superpower. Yet France and England challenged her claims.

Settlers and Immigrants

People from England preferred to set up trading posts and towns. At first they failed, but finally in 1607 a colony succeeded at Jamestown, Virginia. A staple crop that could be shipped across the

Atlantic was needed for an economic base. In Virginia that crop turned out to be tobacco.

The example of Virginia caused other English men and women to think about settling in America. Different groups of merchants, royal officials, and religious leaders started planning colonies. The religious group known as Puritans established a small settlement at Plymouth, Massachusetts, and then a very large and prosperous one in Boston. From there, Puritans settled three new colonies: Connecticut, New Hampshire, and Rhode Island.

Colonial North America

Gradually the English gained control over much of the eastern coast of North America. Dutch traders founded New Netherland, but the English captured the area and renamed it New York. The English King simply gave individual proprietors vast territories along the Atlantic coast. These colonies included Maryland, New Jersey, North and South Carolina, the Quaker colony of Pennsylvania, and finally Georgia.

The Southern Colonies were dominated by two major staple crops, tobacco in Virginia and Maryland and rice in South Carolina and Georgia. For a while these crops were grown mainly by indentured servants, but after about 1700, large numbers of black people were forced from their homes in West Africa and shipped to America as slaves. Slavery became an important way of life in the South.

The Middle and New England Colonies grew a wider variety of crops and had fewer slaves. These northern settlements also had small cities, good harbors, and a large foreign trade. Two large non-English groups, the Scotch-Irish and the Germans, settled in Pennsylvania and spread south from there. In all the colonies, most people lived on farms.

At one time or another, warfare broke out almost everywhere between the new settlers and the Indians. The main problem was land. Unlike the English, the Indians thought the land belonged to everyone. When they signed a treaty, they thought they were agreeing to let the white people share the land. The English settlers, however, thought the land could be owned and that ownership could be transferred through a treaty. The newcomers usu-ally won these wars because the Indians were not united.

Royal officials in England began to realize that they needed to make rules for their overseas colonies. They chose a policy called mercantilism to strengthen both the economy and the defense of their nation. English officials wanted the colonies to provide England with raw materials such as iron and wood and with ships and sailors for the navy. The officials also tried to control colonial trade.

Parliament passed Navigation Acts to enforce this policy, but local governments in the colonies often ignored the laws. Massachusetts was the chief offender. The Glorious Revolution, from 1686 to 1688, was a crisis involving the English King that shook the entire empire. It ended with more efficient rule of the colonies and also with greater religious toleration. Nevertheless, the smuggling continued.

In the early years, the settlers' task was simply to stay alive. Later, the colonists began to share new ways of thinking. New ideas that came from Europe during the period called the Enlightenment asserted that human reasoning was the best way to understand the human and natural worlds.

In 1740, however, a wave of emotional religion swept the colonies. The Great Awakening began a tradition of religious revivalism. At the same time, the colonists were building new schools, publishing more books and weekly newspapers, and developing ideas about freedom of the press.

Wars and Disagreements

In 1754 a major war broke out between the French and British colonists. Both sides fought to control all of North America. Though at first colonial militia and then British regular troops met defeat, finally the British and colonial forces captured all the French forts. The peace treaty in 1763 made New France, or Canada, part of the British Empire.

Officials in Britain tightened their control. They told the colonists not to settle farther west. They demanded housing for British troops. More important, through the Sugar Act and the Stamp Act, they started to tax the colonists directly.

Mobs in the streets of colonial cities prevented

the Stamp Act of 1765 from going into effect. The representative assemblies of the colonies sent men to a general congress that demanded "no taxation without representation."

Because of this resistance, the royal government in London repealed the Stamp Act. Nevertheless, it passed new taxes called the Townshend Acts. The colonists resisted by agreeing among themselves not to import anything from Great Britain. This nonimportation policy had been effective during the Stamp Act crisis. In response, officials in London sent a new group of tax collectors to the colonies. They also sent British redcoats to occupy Boston. The presence of these troops increased tension, particularly when the soldiers fired on a mob that threatened them. A colonial agitator named Samuel Adams called the incident a "massacre."

Several years of calm followed until some colonists in Boston caused a crisis. Objecting to a new law that deprived colonial merchants of profits on British tea, they held a "tea party." Dressed as Indians, they threw the British tea into the harbor. Royal officials reacted by shutting down the port and tightening control over the Massachusetts government. Other colonies rallied to the cause of liberty and sent delegates to a Continental Congress in Philadelphia in 1774.

Revolution and Independence

In April 1775 an armed clash occurred at Lexington and at Concord, Massachusetts. The American colonists and the British government found themselves in a major war. The bloodiest battle came early, just outside Boston at Bunker Hill. The redcoats won, but they paid a terrible price in dead and wounded.

A Second Continental Congress assembled in May 1775. In January 1776, with the publication of Thomas Paine's pamphlet *Common Sense,* Americans began to think about actual independence. On July 4, 1776, the Second Continental Congress adopted the Declaration of Independence.

After nine months of fighting, British forces found themselves trapped in Boston. They finally evacuated that city in March 1776. The center of war then shifted to the Middle States. A combined British army and navy captured New York and then Philadelphia. Many Americans thought the war was lost. Then in 1777 the colonials forced the surrender of an entire British army at Saratoga, New York.

The astounding victory at Saratoga brought France into the war on the American side. The French wanted revenge against their old British enemy. They sent troops and a major naval fleet to aid the Americans. Before those forces arrived, the fighting shifted from the Middle States to the South. British forces captured Charles Town in South Carolina and five thousand American troops. As they marched north, the redcoats won several victories, but they also suffered defeats.

The war ended when a combination of French and American naval and land forces trapped the British army on the Yorktown peninsula in Virginia in 1781. The American victory that had once seemed impossible was now a reality.

In the Treaty of Paris of 1783, American diplomats won more than they had hoped for. The British agreed to independence for the thirteen colonies. In addition, the boundaries for American settlements extended from Spanish Florida to British Canada and west to the Mississippi River.

The American Revolution had two other important results. One was the gradual end of slavery in the Northern States. Even more important was victory for the idea that the common people could take matters into their own hands. This idea spread around the world.

Chronology of Main Events

1492	Columbus lands at San Salvador
1565	Spain founds St. Augustine
1607	England founds Jamestown
1754–1763	French and Indian War
1776	Declaration of Independence

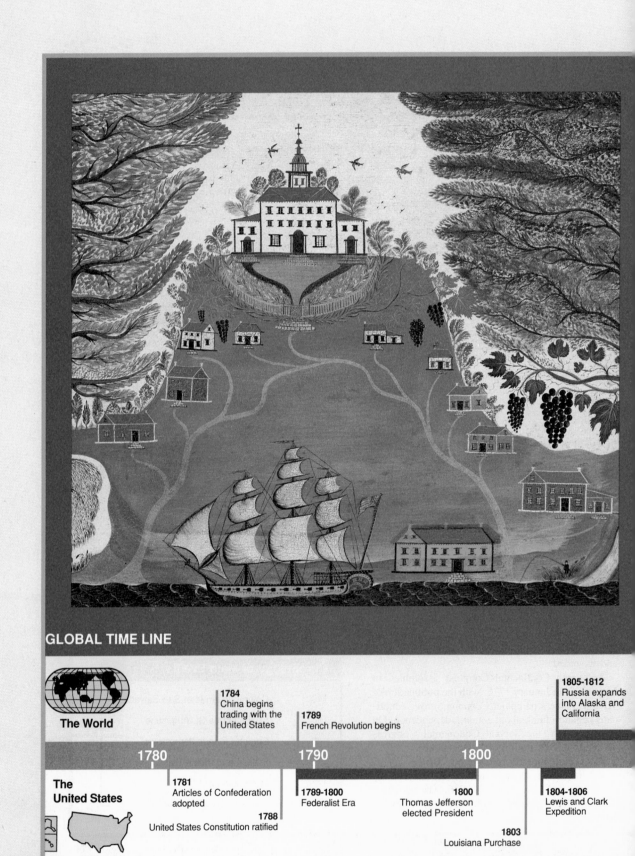

GLOBAL TIME LINE

The World

1784
China begins
trading with the
United States

1789
French Revolution begins

1805-1812
Russia expands
into Alaska and
California

1780

1790

1800

**The
United States**

1781
Articles of Confederation
adopted

1788
United States Constitution ratified

1789-1800
Federalist Era

1800
Thomas Jefferson
elected President

1803
Louisiana Purchase

1804-1806
Lewis and Clark
Expedition

Research Assignment

Have students choose a President from this unit (1781-1840) and research his positions on foreign and domestic issues as well as his major accomplishments. Tell students to use the information gathered in their research to prepare a four-minute speech encouraging citizens to vote for this President for another term.

UNIT **2** 1781–1840

A New Nation

Geographic Setting

Place/Location. Pictures can help us visualize places and locations as they appeared in earlier times. The picture at the left, for example, gives us an impression of how large plantations were set up in the post–Revolutionary War South. Such plantations often covered thousands of acres, but the buildings were grouped together much like buildings in a town. Besides the owner's large house, there were buildings for carpenters, blacksmiths, weavers, and shoemakers, plus barns, slave quarters, warehouses, and, sometimes, a schoolhouse for the owner's children. The ideal location was near a body of water with an outlet to the ocean. Docks could be built for loading the plantation's goods onto ships.

Unit Overview

The most important task facing the Americans after they gained their independence was the creation of a national government. The Articles of Confederation proved to be ineffective. By 1788, however, the Constitution of the United States had been ratified, and the new nation stood on stable ground. The Louisiana Purchase of 1803 doubled the size of the country, and more Americans moved westward. As new states were admitted to the Union, the issue of states' rights became the focus of a hot and bitter debate. Unit 2 explains in five chapters these early stages in the growth of the new nation.

Unit Outline

CHAPTER 6 **Starting a New Nation 1781–1788**
1. Delegates Draft the Articles of Confederation
2. The Nation Survives a Critical Period
3. Delegates Draft the Constitution

CHAPTER 7 **Focus on Democracy 1787 to Today**
1. The Legislative Branch Enacts Laws
2. The Executive Branch Enforces Laws
3. The Bureaucratic System Is Highly Complex
4. The Judicial Branch Interprets Laws

CHAPTER 8 **The Federalist Era 1789–1800**
1. President Washington Takes Charge
2. The First Political Parties Develop
3. Foreign Affairs Become Troublesome
4. President Adams Faces Political Strife

CHAPTER 9 **The Jefferson, Madison, and Monroe Years 1800–1830**
1. President Jefferson Leads the Nation
2. The United States Enters the War of 1812
3. Both National and Sectional Feelings Grow
4. New Inventions Change Lives

CHAPTER 10 **The Age of Jackson 1824–1840**
1. A New Two-Party System Develops
2. Jackson Shows a New Presidential Style
3. States' Rights and a Bank Cause Conflict
4. Jackson's Successors Follow His Lead

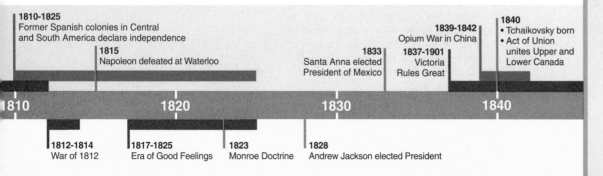

1810-1825
Former Spanish colonies in Central and South America declare independence

1815
Napoleon defeated at Waterloo

1833
Santa Anna elected President of Mexico

1839-1842
Opium War in China

1837-1901
Victoria Rules Great

1840
• Tchaikovsky born
• Act of Union unites Upper and Lower Canada

1810   1820   1830   1840

1812-1814
War of 1812

1817-1825
Era of Good Feelings

1823
Monroe Doctrine

1828
Andrew Jackson elected President

Chapter 6 Teaching Strategies

Global Perspectives

1782   Rama I begins new dynasty in Siam, with capital located at Bangkok.

1783   First successful hot-air balloon flight occurs in France.

1783   Ludwig von Beethoven publishes first works.

1785   Russia settles some of the Aleutian Islands.

1787   Rice riots occur in Edo, Japan.

1787   British acquire Sierra Leone.

Late 1700's Europeans begin to explore African interior.

For Discussion

Have students locate the Aleutian Islands on the World Political Map in the Atlas at the back of the book. How might Russia's settlement of these islands have affected later Russian-United States relations? (Possible responses: There was potential for both countries to claim the Pacific Coast area of North America as they expanded.)

Additional Resources

- Geography Activities
- Skills Activities
- Thematic Activities
- Economic Activities
- Cultural Literacy Activities
- Literary Source Readings
- Primary Source Readings
- Nuclear Peacekeeping
- Transparencies
- Computer Test Generator

Additional Teaching Strategies

SECTION 1

For Basic Students: Ask students to list the provisions of the Northwest Ordinance regarding statehood, education, slavery, and American Indians. (Response: provided for establishment of three to five territories, and when population reached sixty thousand, a territory could petition for statehood; provided one lot in every township for public schools; prohibited slavery or involuntary servitude except as a means of punishment for crimes; stated that Indian lands and property could not be taken without consent of the Indians.) Ask students to use this list to write a paragraph describing the ways in which the ordinance succeeded and the ways in which it failed. (Paragraphs may include: success—it set an orderly procedure for creation of new states; failure—provision for Indian rights was largely ignored.)

For Advanced Students: Ask students to assume the role of Thomas Jefferson and write an editorial explaining the need for passage of the Northwest Ordinance. (Letters might include: reference to the need for citizens to consider themselves primarily as Americans; the fact that western lands should belong to all Americans, not to particular states; the fact that a procedure for establishing new states would provide an orderly transition and eliminate quarreling among states.)

SECTION 2

For Basic Students: Ask students to write a letter to George Washington from the point of view of a participant in Shays's Rebellion explaining why the writer chose to rebel. The writer might have served under Washington in the Continental army. (Letters might include: writer's disillusionment with government he fought to establish; government's lack of sympathy for hard-working farmers; writer's inability to make an honest living.)

For Advanced Students: Divide the class into two groups—one to research the problems the U.S. faced in its relations with Europe and one to research the domestic problems faced by the U.S. Ask each group to present its findings to the class. Then appoint a panel of students from both groups to suggest possible solutions. (International problems include: refusal of the British to leave the Great Lakes region; the closing of British ports in Canada and the British West Indies; refusal of the Spanish to let Americans use the port at New Orleans. Domestic problems include: the plight of farmers and debtors; the refusal of citizens to adopt a national outlook.)

SECTION 3

For Basic Students: Divide students into pairs to complete Chapter 6, Section 3 Enrichment Activity.

For Advanced Students: Stage a Constitutional Convention with two or three students representing each of the original states. Have students research, discuss, and vote on issues including representation, counting slaves for representation, and the issue of slavery itself. (Students should research their state's position on the Constitution and debate and vote accordingly.)

Further Reading for Students

Commager, Henry S. *Great Constitution*. New York: Bobbs-Merrill, 1961.

Craven, Wesley F. *The Legend of the Founding Fathers*. Westport, Conn.: Greenwood Press, 1983.

Hilton, Suzanne. *We the People: The Way We Were*. Philadelphia: Westminster Press, 1981.

Tunis, Edwin. *The Young United States, 1783 to 1830*. New York: Thomas Y. Crowell, 1976.

Historical Fiction

Page, Elizabeth. *The Tree of Liberty*. New York: Holt, Rinehart & Winston, 1939.

Bibliography for Teachers

Books

Beard, Charles A. *An Economic Interpretation of the Constitution of the United States*. New York: Free Press, 1965.

Cunliffe, Marcus. *Nation Takes Shape 1789-1837*. Chicago: University of Chicago Press, 1960.

Kenyon, Cecilia M., ed. *The Antifederalists*. Boston: Northeastern University Press, 1985.

McDonald, Forrest. *A Constitutional History of the United States*. Melbourne, Fl: Krieger, 1986.

Van Doren, Carl. *The Great Rehearsal: The Story of the Making and Ratifying of the Constitution of the United States*. New York: Penguin, 1986.

Audio-Visuals

Constitution—The Compromise That Made a Nation. Learning Corporation of America. Movie

The Federal System. Prentice Hall Media. Filmstrip.

Preamble to Peace. Dept. of the Army. Movie.

Remember the Ladies. Modern Talking Picture Service. Movie.

The World of Franklin and Jefferson. International Business Machines Corporation. Movie.

Computer Resources

The Emerging Nation Period. (Apple) Focus Media.

How a Bill Becomes a Law. (Apple/IBM) Intellectual Software.

U.S. History: The Young Republic. (Apple/Commodore 64/TRS80) Focus Media.

Teacher's Notes:

Lesson Plan

Teaching Resources, Unit 2 Booklet

Lesson Study Sheets pp. 1-12
Daily Activities pp. 13-18
Enrichment Activities pp. 19-24
Reteaching Activities pp. 25-30
Chapter Review p. 31
Chapter Mastery Tests pp. 33-44
Telescoping the Times Study Sheet p. 45

Chapter Objectives

Students will learn:
- the basic structure of the first national government of the U. S.
- the serious problems faced by the new nation
- the basic principles of the Constitution of the U.S.

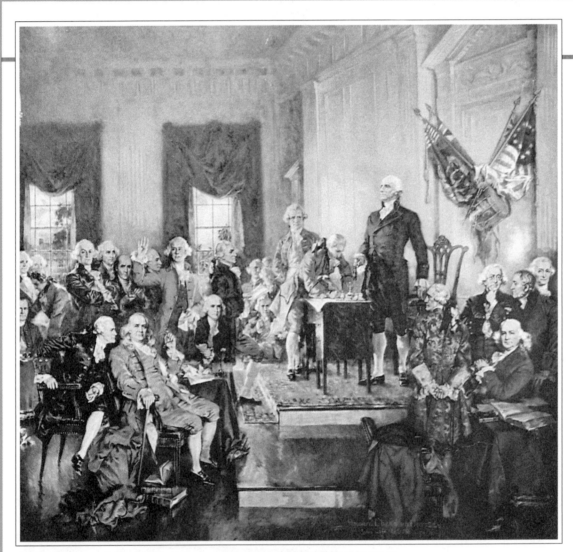

Picturing History In *The Signing of the Constitution*, illustrator Howard Chandler Christy included a portrait of every signer. Among the famous signers are George Washington, Benjamin Franklin, Alexander Hamilton, and James Madison.

Using the Chapter Time Line

For how many years were the United States governed by the Articles of Confederation? (Answer: 7) How many years passed between the drafting of the Constitution and its ratification? (Answer: 1)

1780   1782   1784   1786   1788   1790

1781
Articles of
Confederation
adopted

1785
Land Ordinance
of 1785

1786
Shays's
Rebellion
begins

1787
• Northwest Ordinance
• Constitution drafted

1788
Constitution ratified

136

Links to American Literature

Carl Sandburg: born in Galesburg, Illinois, in 1878; served in the Spanish-American War before attending Lombard College; was secretary to the mayor of Milwaukee, Wisconsin, 1910-1913; served on the staff of the *Chicago Daily News* as an editorial writer from 1918 to 1933; won Pulitzer Prize in 1940; was awarded the United States Presidential Medal of Freedom in 1964; was also widely known as singer of American folk songs.

Writings include: *Abraham Lincoln: The Prairie Years*, 1926; *Abraham Lincoln: The War Years*, 1939.

"I Am the People, the Mob": expresses a basic optimism for the future of America, as does much of Sandburg's poetry.

Introducing the Chapter

Ask students why a supreme law is important for a nation. (Possible response: It unifies the people and eliminates confusion and competition between sections.) Tell students to list some problems that might be faced by a young country as it attempts to create a government. (List might include: lack of experienced leadership; shortage of money; divided loyalties; absence of recognition by foreign governments.)

CHAPTER 6 1781–1788

Starting a New Nation

Links to American Literature

I am the people—the mob—the crowd—the mass.
Do you know that all the great work of the world is done through me?
I am the workingman, the inventor, the maker of the world's food and
*   clothes.*
I am the audience that witnesses history. The Napoleons come from me
*   and the Lincolns. They die. And then I send forth more Napoleons*
*   and Lincolns.*
I am the seed ground. I am a prairie that will stand for much plowing.
*   Terrible storms pass over me. I forget. The best of me is sucked out*
*   and wasted. I forget. Everything but Death comes to me and makes*
*   me work and give up what I have. And I forget.*
Sometimes I growl, shake myself and spatter a few red drops for history
*   to remember. Then—I forget.*
When I, the People, learn to remember, when I, the People, use the
*   lessons of yesterday and no longer forget who robbed me last year,*
*   who played me for a fool—then there will be no speaker in all the*
*   world say the name: "The People," with any fleck of a sneer in his*
*   voice or any far-off smile of derision.*
The mob—the crowd—the mass—will arrive then.

— CARL SANDBURG, *"I Am the People, the Mob"*

In 1776 the American colonists did not know they were going to form a union of states. They had simply agreed on certain rights and principles for which they were willing to fight. The world watched skeptically to see what would happen to this hodgepodge of peoples from various countries.

Chapter Overview

It took twelve years of negotiation, compromise, and extraordinary creativity to devise a system that could work successfully for years to come. This chapter illustrates how people with different interests can, by each giving up a little and working for a common end, come up with something better than any one of them could have produced alone. In this chapter you will learn about the basic structure of the first national government of the United States, about the serious problems that the new nation faced, and about the basic principles of the Constitution. To help you understand this critical period in our nation's history, Chapter 6 is divided into three sections.

Chapter Outline

1. **Delegates Draft the Articles of Confederation**
2. **The Nation Survives a Critical Period**
3. **Delegates Draft the Constitution**

Core Lesson

Anticipate the Lesson

Ask students to recall the problems faced by colonial Americans under British rule. (Possible responses: taxation without representation; quartering of soldiers; limitation of trade.) How might these problems affect the design of a new government? (Possible response: representatives would be wary of giving too much power to a central government.)

For Discussion

Divide students into six groups to discuss the problems created by the Articles of Confederation and to make recommendations for changes. Have a chairperson from each group report back to the class. Ask students to vote for the best recommendations. (Problems might include: the Articles gave the central government limited power—it could not raise an army, impose taxes, or regulate trade. Suggestions for change might include: establish a national army; regulate international trade; establish property taxes.)

State the Objective

Describe the basic structure of the first national government of the U. S.

SECTION 1

Delegates Draft the Articles of Confederation

GLOSSARY TERMS: unicameral, sovereign, confederation

When the Revolutionary War broke out, the old colonial assemblies simply transformed themselves into the governing bodies of the newly independent states. However, everyone realized that new constitutions were needed. So, despite wartime difficulties, each state adopted one.

All of the states except Pennsylvania set up a legislature with two houses. The upper house grew out of the old governor's council. Many states made an important change in the way the upper house was chosen. No longer were members appointed by the governors, whose powers had been lessened. They were elected either by the people or by the lower house, now called the House of Representatives.

Pennsylvania had never had a governor's council. It set up a **unicameral,** or one-house, legislature.

The new state constitutions lowered property requirements for suffrage. Yet they did not abandon the old idea that only men could vote and that a man ought to own some property in order to do so.

They continued the requirement that those seeking public office should have higher than usual property qualifications. In contrast to Europe, however, so many persons were able to vote that it seemed the people really ruled themselves.

The Continental Congress Debates

While the states worked on their individual constitutions, the Continental Congress tried to draft one for the states as a whole. That was much more difficult to do. There was considerable disagreement over what the role of the Congress should be. In fact, so great were the problems that it took more than a year of work before the delegates could agree on a draft. Some basic questions had to be answered.

Representation by Population or by State? The states had come together as independent political units. As such, they were equal to one another. But they were unequal in land size, wealth, and population. This posed a dilemma. Should delegates to a national congress represent people or states? Should each state elect the same number of representatives regardless of its population? Or should states with large populations have more representatives than states with small populations? For example, if Georgia with 25,000 people in 1770 could elect the same number of representatives as

People in the Chapter

Thomas Jefferson wished to be remembered as the author of the Declaration of Independence and of Virginia's statute for religious freedom and as the father of the University of Virginia. These accomplishments were more important to him than that of being President of the United States, and they were the only ones he wanted mentioned on his tombstone.

John Jay never actively sought a government office. His wisdom, moral standards, and sense of duty to his country won him appointments to a series of important national offices, including Chief Justice of the Supreme Court.

Edmund Randolph was related to Thomas Jefferson, whose mother was a Randolph. Although he proposed the Virginia Plan, he refused to sign the Constitution. In the end he

favored ratification as better than nothing.

Gouverneur Morris believed George Washington was more friendly than people made him out to be. James Madison offered to buy Morris dinner if he would slap Washington on the back and greet him informally. Madison bought the dinner, but Morris admitted Washington's reaction was so severe that he would never greet him that way again.

John Hancock inherited his uncle's fortune and at twenty-seven became the wealthiest man in New England. He expected to be chosen as commander in chief of the Continental army and resigned as president of the Continental Congress when Washington was chosen instead.

Present the Lesson

On the board construct a two-column chart. In the left column list the questions asked in "Delegates Draft the Articles of Confederation." In the right column have students fill in the proper response to each question. (Chart should include: 1. Representation by population or by state? / Each state was awarded one vote. 2. Supreme power: can it be divided? / Fundamental powers were shared between state and federal governments. 3. Western lands: who gets them? / Western lands should eventually be carved into new states.) Review Chapter 6, Section 1 Daily Activity with students.

Check for Understanding

Call on individual students to answer the Section 1 Review questions orally.

Massachusetts with 270,000 people, then a person in Georgia would have much more political power than a person in Massachusetts. On the other hand, if delegates were elected on the basis of one delegate for every 4,000 people, then large states like Virginia would have much more power in Congress than states like New Jersey with smaller populations.

For the time being, the members of Congress looked on themselves as representing independent states. Therefore, the decision was that each state would have one vote regardless of population. A state could send as many representatives as it wished, but it would still have only one vote.

Supreme Power: Can It Be Divided? Until this time most people assumed that **sovereign,** or supreme, power could not be shared. That is, either a government had supreme power or it did not. If it did not, it could not function. There could not be two supreme governments.

Yet that is exactly what the **Articles of Confederation** proposed. They proposed a new kind of government where fundamental powers were shared between two levels of government. State governments were supreme in some matters, while the national government was supreme in other matters. The delegates used an unusual word for this unusual form of government. They called it a **confederation,** or alliance.

The Articles of Confederation gave the new federal government power to declare war, make peace, and sign treaties. It could borrow money, set standards for coins and for weights and measures, establish a postal service, and deal with the Indians.

Western Lands: Who Gets Them? The framers of the Articles of Confederation expected the states to approve them quickly. Problems concerning western lands, though, created a more than three-year delay.

By their original charters, more than half the states had claims to territory in the West. Some of these claims extended beyond the Mississippi River and even to the Pacific Ocean. The claims of these "landed" states often overlapped. The landless states, such as Pennsylvania and Maryland, had western boundaries that were fixed within a few hundred miles of the Atlantic Ocean. These states refused to confederate unless the landed states turned over their western claims to the United States. They argued that the landed states would be able to pay off their war debts by selling western lands while the landless states would be forced to tax their people. The landless states feared the growth in wealth and power of the other states. They also made a less selfish argument. The war for independence, they said, was a common effort. Therefore, the whole of the western territory should be used to support it.

The deadlock was broken by patriotic sentiment and by a group of Virginians led by Thomas Jefferson. Jefferson argued that all of the land west of the original states should eventually be carved up into new states. These would be admitted into the Confederation on an equal footing with the original states. It was a bold and novel idea at the time. Yet in later years it seemed natural and inevitable. Virginia and New York gave up their western claims to the national government. Other landed states followed suit. Only then did Maryland finally approve the Articles of Confederation, which went into effect in 1781.

The Articles of Confederation Prove Weak

Adopting the Articles of Confederation was one thing. Maintaining an effective national government was another.

Most of the powers given to the Confederation Congress required the cooperation of the states, but the states feared a strong national government. As a result, although the central government did settle disputes between states and the states wanted this, the latter did not have to agree with the terms of the settlement. For example, the central government could determine how many troops each state should furnish to the nation's army, but it had no assurance that the number of troops asked for would be sent.

The national government lacked many other powers. It had no control over interstate trade. Nor did it have control over foreign trade. Worst of all, the national government had no power to collect taxes. It had to ask the states for money with which to operate, and it never received anything like the amount of money it needed to function. Finally, all the states had to agree before any changes could be made in the Articles of Confederation.

As the Revolutionary War drew to a close, the feelings of unity among the states diminished. They no longer sent able delegates to Philadelphia, and sometimes they sent none at all. Ratification of

Remind students that Americans in their formative period first had a government more powerful than they wanted and later a confederation that was less powerful than they needed. The attempt to find the proper balance is an issue even today as Americans continue to evaluate the growing power of the chief executive in relation to Congress. Ask students to think of examples of incidents in which both the President and Congress might claim supreme authority. (Possible responses: negotiations with foreign governments; Supreme Court appointments; deployment of military troops.)

Map Skills

MA, VA • NY, NC • NY, NH • VA

Western Land Claims by States, 1780

Map Skills **Location** What states claimed the areas that comprise the present states of Michigan, Tennessee, and Vermont (see U.S. Political map in the Atlas at the back of the book)? **Place** What state claimed the largest area?

Assign Independent Practice

Have students complete Chapter 6, Section 1 Enrichment Activity.

Student Assignment/Homework

Have students read Section 2, "The Nation Survives a Critical Period," and answer Section 2 Review questions on paper.

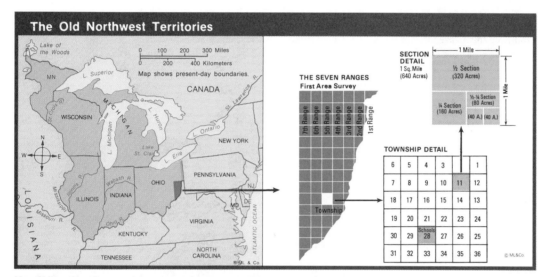

The Old Northwest Territories

Map Skills   The diagram above shows a single township in the Northwest Territory. Each township was divided into thirty-six sections.   **Location**   What present states make up the Old Northwest? **Location/Place**   Which ones touch the Ohio River? the Great Lakes?

Historical Sidelight

When viewing the U.S. from a plane, the land appears to be covered by a checkerboard pattern. This pattern did not develop by accident. The land ordinance of 1785 divided all unsettled lands into six-mile by six-mile squares called townships. This system has affected American land settling practices for nearly two hundred years.

the Treaty of Paris was delayed for months because there were not enough members to vote on it. In 1783 some Pennsylvania regiments mutinied and came to Philadelphia demanding their pay. The congressmen hastily left town.

The Confederation Congress met in a number of towns. No one seemed eager to have it in any one place, and no capital had been chosen. The turnover in membership of the Confederation Congress was high because in many ways being a member was a thankless job.

The Northwest Ordinance Provides a Guide

In one field of administration, the government was extremely successful. In 1787 the Confederation Congress passed a law for the government of part of the western lands. The law was based in large measure on a plan suggested by Jefferson. It is called the **Northwest Ordinance of 1787** because it covered "the old northwest," the land north of the Ohio River and east of the Mississippi River. (The land south of the Ohio and east of the Mississippi, known as "the old southwest," was covered by different legislation.)

The Northwest Ordinance of 1787 provided for the establishment of not less than three nor more than five territories. As soon as a territory had five thousand voting residents, it could elect its own

government. When the total population reached sixty thousand, the territory could write a constitution and become a state equal in all respects to the other states.

The Ordinance also declared:

> Religion, morality and knowledge being necessary to good government and the happiness of mankind, schools and the means of education shall be forever encouraged.

The Land Ordinance of 1785 provided the means for this. It reserved one lot in every township for the maintenance of public schools.

The Northwest Ordinance also touched on the question of slavery. It said:

> There shall be neither slavery nor involuntary servitude in the said territory otherwise than in the punishment of crimes.

Indian rights were likewise mentioned.

> The utmost good faith shall always be observed toward the Indians; their lands and property shall never be taken away from them without their consent.

The prohibition of slavery did not extend into the area south of the Ohio River, and the statement about Indian rights was simply ignored.

Although the Northwest Ordinance did not apply to all the western lands, it did establish an orderly

Anticipate the Lesson

Ask students to explain the differences between a "nationalist" and a "localist." (Possible responses: a nationalist considered himself primarily an American and favored a strong central government; a localist considered himself primarily a citizen of a particular state and favored the protection of states' rights over a strong central government.)

Main Ideas

1. Power was shared between two levels of government—state and federal.

2. They failed to give the national government the authority to control trade, enforce decisions regarding the states, or collect taxes.

3. The Articles' framers feared a strong national government.

4. It provided orderly procedures for the creation of western territories and states, encouraged education, recognized Indian rights, and prohibited slavery in most cases.

Critical Thinking

5. By prohibiting slavery, recognizing Indian rights, encouraging settlement of western lands, and extending full equality to new states and voting rights to citizens of the territories, the ordinance upheld the concept of inalienable rights and the idea that governments receive their just powers by consent of the governed.
(application & synthesis)

procedure for creating new states. The nation followed this procedure for more than a century as it expanded to the Pacific.

SECTION 1 REVIEW

Key Terms and People

Explain the significance of: unicameral, sovereign, Articles of Confederation, confederation, Northwest Ordinance of 1787

Main Ideas

1. How did the Articles of Confederation divide the powers of the government?
2. What were the most serious weaknesses of the Articles of Confederation?
3. Why did these weaknesses exist in the Articles of Confederation?
4. What were the important provisions of the Northwest Ordinance?

Critical Thinking

5. In what ways did the Northwest Ordinance carry out the principles of the Declaration of Independence?

SECTION 2

The Nation Survives a Critical Period

GLOSSARY TERM: merchant marine

Despite its limitations, the Confederation Congress tried its best to handle the problems that confronted the new nation. In some respects it succeeded, but in others it ran into a number of roadblocks. This was probably inevitable. The nation was new. Some of its leaders were inexperienced. World opinion held that the country would not last long.

Problems with Europe Cause Outrage

The most immediate problems facing the nation had to do with foreign relations. The nations involved were Great Britain and Spain, and they caused the new government a great deal of embarrassment.

Picturing History American Indians trapped animals for the fur trade, which reached its peak in North America between the 1600's and the early 1800's.

Britain Refuses to Let Go and Leave.   According to the Treaty of Paris of 1783, the British were supposed to leave their military and fur-trading posts in the west "with convenient speed." In the Great Lakes region, however, the British did not budge.

What the British really wanted was to dominate the valuable fur trade, but they said they were remaining in their forts because the United States was violating two clauses of the peace treaty. They were not entirely right. The states refused to pay debts owed to British merchants. However, they had never agreed to return property taken from the Loyalists.

Great Britain also closed ports in both Canada and the British West Indies to American ships. The first ambassador to Great Britain, John Adams, tried in vain to get this policy changed. Naturally Britain wanted to discourage the growth of a competitive **merchant marine,** or national commercial fleet.

The Confederation Congress had no power to control foreign trade, and the states acted independently of one another. If New York boycotted Canadian goods, for example, Massachusetts might be only too happy to import them.

On the board list the problems that America faced on international and national levels. (Possible responses: international problems— Britain's refusal to leave the Great Lakes region and its closing of ports in Canada and the West Indies, Spain's refusal to allow the states to use New Orleans; national problems— struggles between creditors and borrowers, rebellion of farmers, conflict between nationalists and localists.) Ask students to skim the section and identify political leaders who held nationalist views of the government and those who held localist views. (Answer: George Washington, Benjamin Franklin, Thomas Jefferson, James Madison, and Alexander Hamilton were nationalists; Samuel Adams and Patrick Henry were localists.) Discuss how these differences affected the Constitutional Convention. (Discussion might include: nationalists were concerned with developing a strong central government; localists were concerned with states' rights. Compromise was essential for survival of the national government.)

Check for Understanding

Have students complete Chapter 6, Section 2 Enrichment Activity.

Spain Closes the Mississippi. Dealing with Spain was as frustrating as dealing with Britain. Spain refused to recognize the claim of the United States to the territory west of the Appalachians and south of the Ohio River. It established forts throughout the region and made alliances with the Indians there. Further, Spain refused to allow the states to use the port of New Orleans at the mouth of the Mississippi River. This effectively prevented Americans west of the Appalachians from trading with the rest of the world. It was much too expensive to cart agricultural products over the mountains to ports on the Atlantic.

In 1785 Congress asked John Jay to try to persuade Spain to let Americans send goods down the Mississippi. Jay, however, was more interested in getting Spain to open up ports in the Spanish West Indies to New England shipping. Although these negotiations eventually fell through, westerners were outraged. They saw the negotiations as evidence that the new nation cared nothing about their interests. Many westerners began talking about setting up a separate republic west of the Appalachians. A few even held secret talks with Spain about such a possibility.

Domestic Problems Lead to Rebellion

While coping with foreign problems, the Confederation Congress also found itself confronted with problems at home. One of the most troublesome was the struggle between creditors (lenders of money) and debtors (borrowers of money).

Borrowers Versus Lenders. During the Revolutionary War, the states had piled up huge debts. Wealthy people who had lent money to the states favored high taxes so that the states would be able to pay them back. However, high taxes sent many farmers into debt. Since most creditors refused to accept repayment in farm produce, they often found themselves suing farmers in court. If a creditor won a case, the farmer's land and animals were seized and sold at auction. Even if the creditors lost, the farmer still had to pay a lawyer. This put the farmer further in debt.

Debtors and creditors argued about the usefulness of paper money. Almost everyone agreed it was essential. Debtors wanted lots of money printed. Increasing the supply of money would lessen its value and enable them to pay off their debts in cheap currency. Creditors on the other hand, wanted to keep the supply of money small so that its value would not decrease. Both groups had much to lose.

Shays's Rebellion. The conflict between debtors and creditors reached the breaking point in Massachusetts in 1786. People in the coastal towns, where merchants had sold goods to farmers on credit, pushed through a state law taxing landowners. The burden fell most heavily on poor farmers in the western part of the state. When they petitioned the assembly for relief, however, their pleas fell on deaf ears. The assembly included only a few representatives from western Massachusetts.

All through the summer and fall, farmers kept demanding that courts be closed so they would not lose their farms to creditors. That winter, their discontent boiled over into mob action. Some twelve hundred farmers closed the courts and marched through the snow toward the arsenal at Springfield. They were led by **Daniel Shays.** A veteran of Bunker Hill and Saratoga, Shays was also an angry farmer who was about to be put in debtors' prison.

Shays's Rebellion, as the farmers' protest movement came to be called, was put down at the cost of four rebels shot by the state militia. The remaining rebels, including Shays, were pardoned. Although most people in Massachusetts did not approve of the farmers' actions, they agreed that the farmers had genuine grievances.

Picturing History A rebel farmer attacks a government supporter during Shays's Rebellion of 1786.

For Discussion
(Refer students to Chapter 6, Section 2 Enrichment Activity for source readings on the rebellion.) What were the causes and results of Shays's Rebellion? How could it have been avoided? (Causes might include: the conflicts between debtors and creditors; the inability of farmers to pay their debts; the insensitivity of the government to the plight of the farmers. Results might include: the farmers' plight gained national attention; people feared a new revolution by the poor; people united and developed a strong central government to deal with such problems.)

Guided Practice

Tell students that some people have called for another Constitutional Convention. They feel that many current issues need special attention. Others are satisfied with the flexibility of the Constitution as it stands. Ask students what special issues they feel might need to be addressed by the Constitution or by amendments. (Possible responses: equal rights; abortion; atomic energy; pollution; gun control; military disarmament.)

Assign Independent Practice

Have students complete Chapter 6, Section 2 Daily Activity.

Student Assignment/Homework

Have students read Section 3, "Delegates Draft the Constitution," and answer the Section 3 Review questions on paper.

Shays's Rebellion caused dismay and panic throughout the nation. There were debt-ridden farmers in every state. Would rebellion spread from Massachusetts elsewhere? Not only was private property in danger but so was the new nation's reputation. As George Washington himself exclaimed, "What a triumph for our enemies . . . to find we are incapable of governing ourselves!"

Many Refuse to Adopt a National Outlook

Ever since the Treaty of Paris, there had been a division among American political leaders. Some took a local view, while others took a nationalist view.

Those with a local view were interested primarily in their own state and in local affairs. They felt that liberties are best defended by keeping sovereign power closely leashed to the state capital. They distrusted giving much power to a national government. Some of the people who thought this way did so partly because of their personal backgrounds. Men like **Samuel Adams** of Massachusetts and **Patrick Henry** of Virginia were highly successful politicians in their own states. However, they lacked experience at the national level, in the Congress, in the Continental army, or in diplomatic posts abroad.

The nationalists were mostly individuals with considerable experience at the national level. George Washington was obviously such a man. So were John Adams, Benjamin Franklin, Thomas Jefferson, and James Madison. Another nationally minded man was young Alexander Hamilton of New York, who had served throughout much of the war as an aide to General Washington.

These men and many others were greatly concerned about the weaknesses of the Confederation Congress. How could a government function when it was unable either to levy taxes or to enforce its decisions? As Washington wrote to a friend,

> The consequences of . . . [an] inefficient government are too obvious to be dwelt upon. Thirteen sovereignties pulling against each other, and all tugging at the federal head, will soon bring ruin upon the whole. . . . Let us have [government] by which our lives, liberty, and property will be secured or let us know the worst at once.

James Madison had Virginia call on all the states to send delegates to a general meeting at Annapolis, Maryland, in September 1786. The purpose of the meeting was to discuss problems of interstate trade. New York, for example, taxed goods coming from New Jersey. Maryland and Virginia were quarreling bitterly over which state had the right to use the Potomac River for navigation.

Only five states, however, responded to Madison's call. At the suggestion of Hamilton, the Annapolis delegates called for another general meeting to be held in Philadelphia in May 1787. The new call arrived along with the news of Shays's Rebellion. This time, every state except Rhode Island responded favorably. They sent their best political leaders to Philadelphia. State squabbles were forgotten in the greater concern over how to strengthen the central government.

The Constitutional Convention Begins

As is true of most such political meetings, the fifty-five delegates were wealthier and better edu-

Picturing History James Madison disclaimed the title "Father of the Constitution." "It ought to be regarded as the work of many heads and many hands," he said. This portrait of Madison was painted by Charles Willson Peale.

144

Anticipate the Lesson

Review with students the weaknesses of the Articles of Confederation and the reasons for the weaknesses. (Weaknesses include: federal government could not control foreign or domestic trade, collect taxes, or raise an army. Reasons: Americans still feared a strong central government.

State the Objective

Identify the basic principles of the Constitution of the U. S.

cated than the people they represented. Most were lawyers, merchants, or planters. In a day when very few people went to college, a majority were college graduates. Also, they were remarkably young by contemporary standards for such a gathering. Their average age was forty-two. The most active member of the convention, James Madison, had just passed his thirty-sixth birthday.

All the delegates were convinced that this meeting would be the final chance to put the national government on a firmer footing. They knew they had to succeed in giving the Confederation more power. Otherwise it would break up into smaller and weaker regional alliances.

On shipboard, horseback, and at overnight stops at roadside taverns, they consulted with each other and with chance companions. As they straggled into Philadelphia in the latter part of May, each of them found that his fellow delegates had been thinking along the same lines.

In Philadelphia many of them stayed in the same inns and boarding houses and so were able to meet often in small groups and talk things over. Their official meetings were held on the second floor of the Pennsylvania State House. The delegates decided to keep the proceedings secret. They were afraid that public discussion would interfere with debate. However, they deliberately announced that George Washington—the most respected man in America—would chair the meetings. They knew this would inspire public confidence.

The delegates worked all through the long hot summer of 1787. They were physically uncomfortable, especially because the windows were usually kept closed to prevent outsiders from hearing the discussions. The arguments that raged were often hotter than the weather. Yet, within seventeen weeks they succeeded in what they called their "grand experiment." They created a new form of government for the United States.

SECTION 2 REVIEW

Key Terms and People

Explain the significance of: merchant marine, Daniel Shays, Shays's Rebellion, Samuel Adams, Patrick Henry, James Madison

Main Ideas

1. How did England and Spain embarrass the new American government after the war?

2. Explain the basic economic conflict that led to Shays's Rebellion.
3. How did Shays's Rebellion endanger the entire nation?
4. In what ways did leaders who took a local view of politics differ from those who took a nationalist view?
5. In general, how did the delegates to the Constitutional Convention differ from most Americans?

Critical Thinking

6. In 1783, did the advantages to Americans of a weak central government outweigh the disadvantages? Explain.

SECTION 3

Delegates Draft the Constitution

GLOSSARY TERMS: **bicameral, checks and balances, delegated powers, reserved powers, separation of powers, veto, impeach, judicial review, electoral college, ratify**

The delegates were in general agreement about government, liberty, and the way human beings behave. This agreement was the cement that prevented the convention from coming apart.

Delegates Debate Philosophical Principles

In general, the delegates believed that humans are motivated primarily by self-interest and that society consists of many interest groups. The most important of these groups, however, were the economic groups. There were landowners, slave owners (who usually owned land as well), bankers, merchants, small farmers, and business employees. The delegates believed that each group would favor itself at the expense of the rest of society. However, they saw a way to prevent any group from becoming dominant. This was, as far as possible, to balance the interest of each group against those of the others.

On the one hand, the delegates wanted to strengthen the national government. On the other

Answers

Main Ideas

1. Both violated the Treaty of Paris by refusing to recognize American territorial rights. Britain refused to leave the Great Lakes region and closed its ports to American ships; Spain established forts in western areas and refused to allow the states to use the port of New Orleans.
2. Wealthy creditors in Massachusetts tried to collect debts by levying taxes that especially hurt poor farmers.
3. If Shays's rebellion had inspired other rebellions, they might have torn apart the weak government.
4. Local view—primarily interested in local and state affairs, believed liberty was best preserved by states' reserving sovereign power, and distrusted national government; nationalists—believed strong national government was necessary to preserve liberty.
5. They were wealthier and better educated.

Critical Thinking

6. Possible answer: a weak central government lacked the authority to collect taxes and regulate trade and therefore could not help the states preserve their own liberty. **(analysis & synthesis)**

On the board have students list the main points of the Virginia Plan, New Jersey Plan, and the Great Compromise. Discuss who would benefit from each plan. (List should include:

Virginia Plan—bicameral legislature, three branches of government, representation determined by free population—largest states would benefit;

New Jersey Plan—one-house legislature would appoint an executive branch and a high court, representation would be one vote per state, legislature would have power to tax and to regulate commerce, decisions of national government would be supreme law of land—smallest states would benefit;

Great Compromise—two-house legislature, representation in House of Representatives would be determined by population, each state would have two representatives in Senate, Congress could regulate foreign trade, powers would be divided into delegated and reserved powers—no state would have advantage over another.)

hand, they feared giving too much power to any government. The delegates believed that power belongs originally to the people. The liberties of the people would be in danger if government were too independent.

At the same time, the delegates believed that the people's power should not go unchecked. A majority could tyrannize a minority. The poor, for example, outnumbered the wealthy. Yet the rights of the minority had to be protected.

The delegates differed in just how much they trusted popular rule. At one extreme lay Alexander Hamilton, who at one point declared, "The people, sir, are a great beast." At the other extreme were those delegates who were less fearful about the masses than they were about the grasping power of the few. As one Massachusetts man put it,

> These lawyers and men of learning and moneyed men . . . expect to . . . get all the power into their own hands . . . and then they will swallow up all us little folks . . . just as the whale swallowed Jonah.

These philosophical differences came out clearly during the debates. On the whole, however, the delegates kept their eyes on the more practical matter of how the new government would work. The delegates were acutely aware that they were not writing an ideal instrument of government. They also knew that any document they drafted would have to be approved by the voters in the states.

In spite of this, the delegates quickly took a revolutionary step. The convention had been called for the purpose of revising the Articles of Confederation. The delegates soon decided, however, that the Articles were hopeless for governing a nation, so they abolished them and started from scratch to invent a new form of government.

Conflict Leads to Compromise

It took the convention only five days to elect a presiding officer, decide on secrecy, and scrap the Articles of Confederation. Then they began to consider what kind of government they wanted.

The Virginia Plan. On May 29, 1787, Virginia's Edmund Randolph proposed a plan of government. Although known as the Virginia, or Randolph, Plan, it had actually been drafted by James Madison.

The plan provided for a **bicameral,** or two-house, legislature. Instead of the previous unworkable one-state one-vote arrangement, membership in both houses would be allotted among the states according to their free population. Members of the lower house would be elected by the voters. The lower house in turn would elect members of the upper house. Both houses would then vote for a national executive and a national judiciary. Each of the three branches of government would have specific powers to check and balance the other two.

This system of **checks and balances** already existed in many states, and Madison believed it ought to exist at the national level as well. The idea quieted the fears of many delegates and made them more willing to give the proposed national government more power. As debate on the Virginia Plan went on, however, delegates from the small states

ARTICLES

OF

Confederation

AND

Perpetual Union

BETWEEN THE

STATES

OF

NEW-HAMPSHIRE, MASSACHUSETTS-BAY, RHODE-ISLAND AND PROVIDENCE PLANTATIONS, CONNECTICUT, NEW-YORK, NEW-JERSEY, PENNSYLVANIA, DELAWARE, MARYLAND, VIRGINIA, NORTH-CAROLINA, SOUTH-CAROLINA AND GEORGIA.

LANCASTER:
PRINTED BY FRANCIS BAILEY.
M,DCC,LXXVII.

Picturing History The Articles of Confederation failed to provide for a "Perpetual Union" among the states.

grew anxious. They began to realize that the small states were being asked to give up their sovereignty to the larger ones. The states with the largest populations would have the most delegates and the greatest influence in Congress.

The New Jersey Plan. Accordingly, William Paterson introduced the New Jersey Plan. It proposed to keep Congress as a single house. That house would appoint an executive branch of several men and would also appoint a high court. Voting in the legislature would be, as it had been, by state; that is, each state would have one vote. The New Jersey Plan also gave two new powers to the proposed legislature—the power to tax and to regulate commerce. The Confederation Congress had had neither.

The New Jersey Plan was intended to be a counterproposal to the Virginia Plan. It also contained a provision, the importance of which was not realized at the time. It declared that the decisions of the national government would be "the supreme law of the land." This phrase later proved to be a key one, for it meant that national law should override state law if the two conflicted.

The Great Compromise. The conflict over representation was finally settled by the **Great Compromise,** which was proposed by Roger Sherman of Connecticut. The convention agreed on a two-house legislature. Representation in the House of Representatives would be according to population, with one representative for every thirty thousand people in a state. In the upper house, the Senate, representation would be by state. Each state would have two senators regardless of its population.

Members of the House of Representatives would be elected by all the voters who were eligible to vote in elections for their own state's lower house. As Madison pointed out, this would give the people a large voice in the government and make them more loyal to it. The Senate, however, would be elected by the state legislatures. The delegates expected the Senate to be friendlier to the interests of property owners than the popularly elected House of Representatives.

The Three-fifths Compromise. This first compromise immediately raised an issue that divided Southern from Northern delegates. If representation in the House of Representatives was apportioned according to population, would slaves be counted as people? Northern delegates argued that slaves were property and therefore could not be represented. "Why should blacks . . . be in the rule of representation more than the cattle and horses of the [N]orth?" Southerners argued that "the labor of a slave in South Carolina was as productive and valuable as that of a freeman in Massachusetts . . . and that consequently an equal representation ought to be allowed for them."

Once again the convention compromised. According to the **Three-fifths Compromise,** three-fifths of a slave would be counted for purposes of representation. None of the delegates were completely comfortable with this fraction. Yet there was logic to it. Slaves were in fact treated partly as people and partly as property. Like horses, they could be bought and sold; but unlike horses, they could be tried and punished for murder. The more the delegates discussed slavery, the more uneasy

The Articles of Confederation

No chief executive or national courts
Laws need approval of 9 of the 13 states

Congress Could	Congress Could Not
Declare war and make peace	Levy taxes
Raise a defense force	Regulate trade
Make foreign treaties and alliances	Settle disputes among states
Coin and borrow money	Collect state debts owed to it
Establish a post office	Enforce any of its powers
Regulate Indian affairs	

Tell students that most of the founding fathers did not have a great deal of confidence in the ability of the common people to choose government officials, so they established the electoral college. Many people today believe that this procedure is too undemocratic for our times. Ask students to debate the issue of whether the electoral college should be eliminated. (Arguments for elimination of the electoral college may include: voters today are more educated and better aware of issues and candidates; popular vote would give more people a direct voice in the government. Arguments against elimination may include: the system has worked for two hundred years; the average citizen does not really care enough about elections and is not sufficiently knowledgeable about issues or candidates.)

they became. Almost all of them were embarrassed by its existence among a supposedly free people. They were so anxious to avoid the subject that they managed to write the Constitution without actually using the word *slaves*. They referred instead to "all other persons" or "to such persons as any of the states now existing shall think proper to admit."

The Slave Trade Compromise. At this point, economic interest came into play. The Southern economy was based on the export of staple crops produced by slave labor. When the Revolutionary War broke out, however, the slave trade had stopped. Since then, only Georgia had resumed importing slaves. Now South Carolina also wanted to resume importation. However, if Congress were given the power to regulate foreign commerce, it might decide to do away with the slave trade. South Carolina and Georgia would never agree to that.

Once again the issue was resolved by compromise. Congress was given the power to regulate foreign commerce. However, it could not do anything about the slave trade until 1808. In the meantime, importers would pay a duty of up to ten dollars for each slave brought into the country.

Powers Are Divided

There were several other areas in which the Philadelphia delegates divided the powers of government between the states and the national government. The powers that the national government received are called **delegated powers**. Those that were kept by the states are known as **reserved powers**.

For example, under the Articles, the states had had the right to keep a standing army and to wage war. Now only the federal government had this right. The states controlled education, marriage and divorce, and their own highways and other means of transportation.

The delegates adopted this division of powers in order to maintain a balance. On the one hand, they did not want the states to have too much power as compared to the national government. That had been the situation under the Articles, and it had not worked. On the other hand, they did not want the national government to have too much power, for that would mean tyranny. The important thing was that both levels of government should protect the rights of the people.

At the same time, the delegates made it clear that the new government was to be truly national, with the central government supreme over the states. As Gouverneur Morris of New York said, "We had better take a supreme government now, than a despot twenty years hence—for come he must" unless the weaknesses of the Articles were corrected. Morris did not like it that people spoke of themselves only as Georgians or Pennsylvanians and that they knew and cared almost nothing about people from other states. Yet he was hopeful. "This generation will die away and give place to a race of Americans."

Checks and Balances Are Provided

In line with their belief in balancing one interest against another, the Philadelphia delegates separated the national government's power into three parts. The Constitution defines the **separation of powers** of each branch of government.

The Executive. The delegates had briefly toyed with the idea of a monarch, for some of them believed it had good points as well as bad. However, they soon agreed that popular hatred of George III made a monarchy impossible. Besides, how could the people really control a king?

Then the question arose whether to have a single executive or several of them. The head of a government ought to be vigorous, quick-acting, and responsible. Surely it would be easier to find such qualities in three separate individuals rather than in one. In addition, each of the three executives could be "drawn from different portions of the country," thus providing each section with representation. The counterargument was that each of the thirteen states had a single executive. Having three executives would lead to conflict and chaos. So the delegates agreed that the executive branch would be headed by one person.

The President was given considerable power. He was to be commander in chief of the armed forces; he could make extensive appointments to federal offices, although Senate approval was required for the highest ones; and he could **veto** (reject) acts of Congress.

The Legislature. Yet the convention was careful to place certain checks on Presidential powers. Congress, the legislative branch consisting of the House of Representatives and the Senate, could override the President's veto by a two-thirds vote. The House of Representatives could **impeach** (bring to trial) the President for "treason, bribery,

148

Assign Independent Practice

Have students list on paper the three branches of government and briefly describe the powers granted by the Constitution to each. (Responses: executive branch—is commander in chief of the armed forces, makes appointments to federal offices with Senate approval, can veto acts of Congress; legislative branch—can override President's veto, can impeach President, makes laws, regulates trade, coins money, borrows on credit; judicial branch—is appointed by the President with consent of Congress, has final jurisdiction over cases involving the Constitution, laws of the U.S., and treaties with other countries.)

Picturing History This is a view of John Street in New York City as it appeared in 1768. A census taken of this cosmopolitan colonial city in 1773 recorded 2,737 blacks and 18,726 whites. One scholar noted that eighteen languages were spoken there in the 1770's.

For Discussion
How did the government of the U.S. change as a result of the new Constitution? (Possible responses: the Constitution united the states under a supreme law; it delineated, delegated, and reserved powers; it set up a system of checks and balances to keep any one branch of government from gaining too much power.)

or other high crimes and misdemeanors.'' If that happened, the President could be convicted by a two-thirds vote of the Senate. The chief check on executive actions was the fact that the President was an elected rather than an appointed official.

Linking Past to Present

The principle of checks and balances was found to be in good working order following the Watergate scandal that occurred during the Presidency of Richard Nixon. (See Chapter 34, Section 4.) At the time of the scandal, Watergate appeared to many to be a breakdown of our system of government, but today we can see that Watergate actually proved the workability of the system.

As a result of the economic weakness of the confederative government, the Philadelphia delegates gave Congress considerable financial powers. It received the power to regulate commerce among the states, with foreign powers, and with Indian nations. The clause permitting Congress to pay the debts of the existing United States passed unanimously. No one opposed giving the new Congress power to coin money, to set its value, and to borrow on the credit of the new government.

At the same time, the delegates restricted the powers of the states in financial matters. They prohibited states from issuing bills of credit (paper money) and provided that no state could violate ''the obligations of contracts.'' States were also banned from taxing their commerce with other states.

The Judiciary. The Articles of Confederation had made no provision for a national system of courts. The new Constitution provided for a Supreme Court to be appointed by the President with the advice and consent of the Senate. It also gave Congress the power to establish lower courts. Federal judges were to hold their offices ''during good behavior.''

The Supreme Court was given final jurisdiction over cases involving the Constitution, the laws of the United States, and treaties with other countries. The convention failed to make specific provisions for **judicial review;** that is, the Supreme Court was not explicitly given the power to strike down state or federal laws if they violated the Constitution. Article 6, Section 2, however, contained the key phrase from the New Jersey Plan—that the Constitution was to be ''the supreme law of the land.'' It was not long before the Supreme Court successfully used this phrase to review state laws.

Student Assignment/Homework

Have students complete Chapter 6 Review on paper. Go over the answers to the questions with the class.

Picturing History New York was the eleventh state to ratify the Constitution.

The Electoral College. The President and Vice-President were to be chosen by an **electoral college,** not directly by the voters. Article 2, Section 1, of the Constitution states that they are to be elected by electors appointed by the states. Each state has as many electors as it has senators and representatives in Congress. However, by the middle 1800's the electors were chosen directly by the voters. The person who received the largest number of electoral votes became President. The person receiving the next largest became the Vice-President.

Linking Past to Present

Our founders established the electoral college because they did not have a great deal of faith in the ability of the common people to choose government officials. Many people today would like to see the electoral college abolished. They believe that the election of the President should more accurately represent the popular vote.

Rules for Changing the Constitution. The convention had the foresight to provide for a way to change the Constitution. Amendments could be made through two steps:

1. Approval either by a two-thirds vote of Congress or by a new Constitutional Convention
2. Ratification either by the legislatures of, or conventions in, three-quarters of the states

Ratification Squeaks Through

On September 17, 1787, the new Constitution was signed by all but three of the delegates present. The convention then sent it to Congress, which forwarded it to the states. This was an "end run" around the state legislatures. Many of those bodies were dominated by people with a personal stake in maintaining the powers of the states. Because of this, the Constitution was to be ratified or rejected by state conventions called solely for that purpose. Nine of the thirteen states had to **ratify,** or approve, the Constitution before it could go into effect.

The debate over adoption raged for eight months. New Englanders argued in their town meetings. Supporters and opponents alike wrote numerous articles in the press. The most widely circulated of these articles appeared in the *New York Journal* over the signature of Publius. Publius was occasionally James Madison and occasionally John Jay. Most of the time, however, he was **Alexander Hamilton.** This may seem surprising because Hamilton disapproved of many of the Constitution's provisions. Yet he felt strongly that the government it set up was far better than the "anarchy and convulsion" that had existed under the Articles of Confederation. The Publius articles were published in two volumes called *The Federalist* and are now known as the **Federalist papers.**

Opponents of the Constitution offered numerous

Picturing History Alexander Hamilton began writing the essays that were first published in a newspaper and eventually collected and published in a volume called *The Federalist.* The purpose of these eighty-five political essays was to persuade New York to ratify the new Constitution. They played an important role in getting the Constitution adopted.

Picturing History
Benjamin Franklin is pictured with the "rising sun" from George Washington's chair.

arguments that showed their fears of strong, centralized governmental power. Called **Anti-Federalists** by the Federalist friends of the Constitution, the opposition smelled tyranny in nearly every clause. There was no bill of rights. State sovereignty would be destroyed. The President might become king. The territory to be set aside for the national capital would become the nesting ground for an uncontrollable standing army. Tax collectors would swarm about the countryside. Commercial treaties would sell out the South and the West. Debtors would be at the mercy of grasping, monied aristocrats. Besides which, it was not possible for a single government to manage so large a country.

Despite these and other arguments, by July 1788 eleven states had ratified the document. Both North Carolina and Rhode Island rejected the Constitution. Since the new government was now in operation, however, they were left with the choice of ratifying or going it alone. Both states held new conventions and reversed their earlier decisions.

Historians know something, although not a great deal, about who favored the Constitution and why. Many seemed to think that the new, stronger government would be favorable to commerce. In general, cities and towns and the regions of the country most touched by commercial activity tended to vote Federalist and for the Constitution. Wealthy men were inclined to vote for adoption.

In some instances, the opinion about ratification was set by local leaders. Individual local leaders like Patrick Henry and John Hancock were antifederalist and they carried a great deal of influence.

Small farmers in the West and the more rural areas tended also to be antifederalist.

Finally, if George Washington had not favored the Constitution, it might have been doomed. It was almost universally assumed that the general who had led American troops to victory would be the nation's first President. No one else inspired so much trust.

Benjamin Franklin voiced the optimistic view. At the end of the Constitutional Convention, he pointed to the chair where Washington had sat as presiding officer. On the back of the chair was the painting of a sun. Franklin said:

> I have often and often in the course of the session . . . looked at that behind the President without being able to tell whether it was rising or setting, but now at length I have the happiness to know that it is a rising, and not a setting, sun.

SECTION 3 REVIEW

Key Terms and People

Explain the significance of: bicameral, checks and balances, Great Compromise, Three-fifths Compromise, delegated powers, reserved powers, separation of powers, veto, impeach, judicial review, electoral college, ratify, Alexander Hamilton, Federalist papers, Anti-Federalists, Benjamin Franklin

Main Ideas

1. What were the basic philosophical principles on which the delegates to the Constitutional Convention agreed?
2. In what ways did the Virginia Plan and the New Jersey Plan differ?
3. What conflict did the Great Compromise settle, and how did it settle this conflict?
4. What was the purpose of the division of powers between state and federal governments?
5. Briefly explain how the delegates provided for checks and balances in the national government.

Critical Thinking

6. How did the American colonial experience with government influence the type of government created by the Constitutional Convention?

State the Objective

Learn how to analyze the strengths of a historical argument.

Present the Lesson

Remind students that our Constitution guarantees freedom of speech and that people utilize this freedom to argue for and against hundreds of issues. Write the four steps in analyzing the strength of an argument on the board. Then have students use the steps to analyze the strength of the argument presented in the feature. Write their ideas on the board. The finished chart might include:

Analyze the writer's point of view. Jensen was a history professor at the University of Wisconsin and so should be knowledgeable about the Confederation.

Analyze the main argument. Jensen argued that the nation was not falling apart at the time the Constitution was written and that the idea that it was came from partisan politics.

Separate fact from opinion. Jensen's facts come from writings of Franklin—which could be opinions—and Washington, who writes of a nation being repaired. Other facts include the information from Livingston, who lived during that time. Students might also consider the fact that the nation did not fall apart but did rebuild itself in all areas.

Focus on Critical Thinking Skills

Analyzing Historical Arguments

Understanding the Skill

The American people are justly proud of their Constitution. It is one of the most remarkable achievements in all of history. Some believe it was written and adopted just in time to save the nation from disaster. However, if the nation was in a critical period, why did many leaders of the Revolution oppose the ratification of the Constitution?

The Constitution was ratified only after a long struggle, involving debates in several states. In those debates, the losers were some of the men and women who had been most active in the Revolution. Sam Adams and Mercy Otis Warren of Massachusetts and Patrick Henry, Richard Henry Lee, and George Mason of Virginia at one time or another bitterly opposed ratification of the Constitution.

Winners of the debates were men like John Jay, James Madison, and Alexander Hamilton. They honestly feared for the future of the nation if the Articles of Confederation were not greatly strengthened. In the struggle, they sometimes exaggerated the faults and weaknesses of the Confederation government. Since their arguments prevailed, their ideas got much more attention than did the arguments of the losers.

To analyze the strength of historical arguments, or arguments based on events in history, read the argument carefully, then follow these steps.

- **Analyze the writer's point of view.** What is the background and purpose of the writer? Is this person qualified to write about the subject? Why or why not?
- **Analyze the main argument.** What is the main argument? What facts are given to support the argument? Has anything important been left out? Is the presentation of the facts objective or one-sided?
- **Separate fact from opinion.** Has the writer used opinion rather than fact to support the argument?
- **Draw a conclusion.** After following these steps, what conclusion can you draw about the strength of the arguments presented?

Applying the Skill

Merrill Jensen, a professor of history at the University of Wisconsin, was a recognized authority on the Confederation Period. He wrote a history of this time period to lay to rest the idea that it had been a critical period of American history. In his book, *The New Nation: A History of the United States During the Confederation, 1781–1789*, Jensen describes the views of some prominent Americans of the Confederation Period regarding the seriousness of the crises in government at that time:

> [Benjamin Franklin] returned to Philadelphia in September 1785, after nine years abroad. . . . He wrote many letters to his friends in Europe in which he said this new experiment in self-government would not fail. The "lying English Newspapers" came in for particular scorn. The stories of American distresses, discontents, and confusions "exist only in the wishes of our enemies. America never was in greater prosperity, her produce abundant and bearing a good price, her working people all employed and well paid, and all property in lands and houses of more than treble the value it bore before the war. . . ."
>
> [Franklin] looked on Shays's Rebellion (see page 143) as of minor importance and in no way affecting the steady growth of America. Paper money did not excite him: he thought it useful. He told Lafayette not to worry about what former enemies might think: let them think us weak and friendless so that "they may then not be jealous of our growing strength, which since the peace, does really make rapid progress. . . ."
>
> Franklin was always optimistic, but George Washington can never be accused of [that]. Yet Washington agreed with Franklin before Shays's Rebellion frightened him. . . . He wrote that despite the refusal to grant Congress the power over trade, "our internal governments are daily acquiring strength.

Draw a conclusion. Although student responses will vary, most students will state that Jensen's argument is strong.

Review the information on the board. Point out the difficulties of judging an argument without having some prior knowledge of a topic. Then ask students whether they think an argument can seem strong because of the personality of the arguer. (Possible response: yes— charismatic people are often believed because of the style of their arguments or because they have a large following.) Ask students what they think is the most difficult part of judging an argument. (Possible response: separating fact from opinion because facts and opinions are frequently mixed in the argument.)

Check for Understanding

Review the questions at the end of the feature, using the information students generated during the class discussion. Discuss whether students might have the opportunity to analyze historical arguments in real life. (Possible response: yes—many current issues are discussed in terms of what has occurred in history.)

Picturing History Charleston, South Carolina, as it appeared during the Confederation Period, which is often referred to as a critical period in American history.

The laws have their fullest energy; justice is well administered; robbery, violence or murder is not heard of from New Hampshire to Georgia. . . .

"The seeds of population are scattered over an immense tract of western country. In the old states, which were the theatres of [war] it is wonderful to see how soon the ravages of war are repaired. Houses are rebuilt, fields enclosed, stocks of cattle . . . replaced, and many a desolated territory assumes again the cheerful appearance of cultivation. In many places the vestiges of ruin are hardly to be traced.

". . . In short, the foundation of a great empire is laid, and I [believe] that providence will not leave its work [unfinished]."

. . . [Robert R. Livingston] was another man who pictured the prosperity of his country in 1787. New York's population had increased by 40,000 in the past twelve years despite the war. Few traces of the war itself were left. . . .

The next year he fought valiantly to get the Constitution ratified in New York. . . . [H]e [denied] the idle talk of American weakness and distress with which British and some American newspapers had been filled. He agreed that the governments had been weak but [claimed] that the people had been "easy and happy."

In the final chapter of his book, Merrill Jensen writes:

[T]he Confederation Period was one of great significance but not the kind that tradition has led us to believe. The "critical period" was the result of uncritical acceptance of the argument of the victorious party in a long political battle, of a failure to face the fact that partisan propaganda is not history but only historical evidence.

Practicing Your Skill

1. What is Merrill Jensen's background? Do you consider him qualified to write a history of the Confederation Period? Why or why not?
2. What was Jensen's chief argument regarding the Confederation Period?
3. How did Jensen support his argument?
4. Did Jensen use opinion rather than fact to support his argument? Explain.
5. What conclusion can you draw about the strength of Jensen's argument?

FOCUS ON SKILLS

Answers

Practicing Your Skill

1. History professor at the University of Wisconsin. • Yes—he was a recognized authority on the Confederation Period.

2. The nation was not on the brink of disaster when the Constitution was written. The tradition of viewing the Confederation Period as a critical period was the result of uncritical acceptance of the argument of the victorious party in a long political battle.

3. By quoting reputable sources such as Benjamin Franklin, George Washington, and Robert Livingston, who pictured prosperity rather than disaster in 1787.

4. Jensen supports his argument with eyewitness accounts. These accounts are, however, opinions supported with facts.

5. Possible answers: strong—because Jensen quotes reputable Americans of the time to counter the traditional view that the Confederation Period was a critical period; weak—because the sources he quotes are opinions backed by selected facts.

Key Terms and People

These are highlighted in the text in the order in which they appear in this list.

Main Ideas

1. National government was given little power.

2. Each had one vote.

3. To prevent creditors from suing for payment of debt and taking farmers' lands.

4. Representation in the legislature. • By providing for bicameral legislature made up of Senate, where each state had equal representation, and House of Representatives, where each state had representation according to population.

5. Overrides Presidential vetoes and impeaches President; also Senate approves appointments of high federal officers. • Vetoes legislation. • President appoints Supreme Court justices with advice and consent of Senate. Congress establishes lower courts.

6. Alexander Hamilton, James Madison, and John Jay. To present arguments for ratifying Constitution.

Critical Thinking Questions

7. When they remember lessons of past and refuse to be victimized again. • When they no longer forgot evils inflicted on them by King of Great Britain and declared independence.

8. Possible answers: just fought war against monarch and equated strong, central power with monarchy; frontier folk, accustomed to solving own problems; owed allegiance to states (colonies), not national government.

9. Under Articles, neither states nor federal government was in charge.

10. It established a peaceful pattern for adding new states to the Union, making them equal in every way to original states.

11. Washington, Hamilton, and Madison: Federalists, who, in

varying degrees, were motivated by their belief in strong central government. Samuel Adams and Henry: Anti-Federalists, who would not participate because they believed strongly in states' rights and feared centralized power.

12. Because their contemporaries did not have the time or money needed to pursue political and philosophical questions.

13. So document would be ratified and enacted. ....

14. Possible answer: if slavery were addressed more directly, some states might have left the convention.

15. By countering Anti-Federalist arguments against Constitution and keeping positive aspects of proposed government alive.

16. Possible answers: troops respected him; he helped win Revolutionary War; he was

completely American and a farmer; he never traveled in Europe but had traveled extensively east of the Mississippi; he stayed above politics.

Critical Thinking Activities

17. d, b, a, e, c.

➤ 18. States' rights grew as the original colonies became more independent of Britain.
• Possible answers: abortion and gun control laws.

CHAPTER 6 REVIEW

Write your answers on a separate sheet of paper.

Key Terms and People

Explain the significance of: sovereign, confederation, merchant marine, Three-fifths Compromise, delegated powers, reserved powers, judicial review, Benjamin Franklin

Main Ideas

1. What was the principal weakness of the Articles of Confederation?

2. How many votes did each state have under the Articles of Confederation?

3. Why did the farmers led by Daniel Shays want to close the courts?

4. What problem did the Great Compromise solve? How did it solve it?

5. How does Congress check the power of the President? How does the President check the power of Congress? How do the executive and legislative branches have power over the court system?

6. Who wrote the Federalist papers and why?

Critical Thinking Questions

7. **Analyzing Literature.** The "I" in the poem on page 137 is the people. According to this poem, when will the people come into power, or "arrive"? When did the colonists in America arrive?

8. **Analyzing Motives.** Why did many colonists oppose a strong central government?

9. **Inferring Results.** What was the fatal flaw in the division of powers between the states and the federal government under the Articles of Confederation?

10. **Inferring Ideas.** How did the Northwest Ordinance ensure a peaceful future for the United States?

11. **Comparing Motives.** What motivated George Washington, Alexander Hamilton, and James Madison to write the Constitution? Would Samuel Adams and Patrick Henry have been asked to participate in this project? Why or why not?

12. **Analyzing Ideas.** Why were the writers of the Constitution wealthier and better educated than most of their contemporaries?

13. **Applying Ideas.** Why was compromise so necessary in the writing of the Constitution?

14. **Synthesizing Ideas.** Why was the word *slave* not mentioned in the Constitution?

15. **Synthesizing Ideas.** How did the Federalist papers help to achieve ratification of the Constitution?

16. **Applying Ideas.** Why did people trust George Washington?

Critical Thinking Activities

17. **Organizing Chronology.** Using the appropriate letters, arrange the following events on a time line.
    a. Northwest Ordinance is adopted.
    b. Shays's Rebellion breaks out.
    c. Constitution is ratified.
    d. Articles of Confederation are adopted.
    e. The Federalist papers are first published.

1780   1785   1790

18. **Linking Past to Present.** What is the historical basis for states' rights? Cite some issues that are referred to the states today.

19. **Linking Past to Present.** Why do you think the founders chose the electoral college rather than a direct vote as a means of electing the President? Do you think this is still the way the President should be elected? Give reasons to support your answer.

20. **Linking Past to Present.** Politics has often been called the art of compromise. Give some examples of political compromise today. When is it preferable to compromise to achieve a goal?

Starting a New Nation

During the Revolutionary War, the states adopted new constitutions; most provided for weak governors, two-house legislatures, and lower property requirements for voting. The Continental Congress proposed that the states adopt the Articles of Confederation, which gave each state one vote. The new nation almost fell apart because of disagreements over western lands. Finally, the landed states gave the United States the rights to territories in the West. The federal government had to beg the states for money, since it lacked the power to tax the people directly. The major achievement of the government under the Articles of Confederation was the Northwest Ordinance. That measure provided that when new states gained a large enough population, they would be admitted to the Union on an equal basis with the original thirteen. It also banned slavery north of the Ohio River.

The new republic ran into problems during this critical period under the Articles of Confederation. British troops refused to evacuate forts east of the Mississippi River in the Old Northwest Territory. The states did not live up to some of the terms of the peace treaty. Britain closed ports in Canada and in the West Indies, but the United States Congress had no power to control foreign trade. Spain claimed control of the Mississippi River. At home, debtors and creditors came to blows. In 1786 Shays's Rebellion in western Massachusetts created great alarm. Americans were badly divided. While some people wanted more local control, nationalists worked for a stronger central government. Winning, the nationalists set up a series of meetings that led to the drafting of the United States Constitution.

Delegates to the Constitutional Convention took the revolutionary step of scrapping the Articles of Confederation. Meeting in secrecy, they worked out a compromise between the large and the small states on the issue of representation by creating a House of Representatives and a Senate. With the Three-fifths Compromise, Southern and Northern delegates agreed on how to count slaves. They also agreed to allow slave importations for twenty years. The proposed Constitution established strong executive and judicial systems. It set up checks and balances among the various branches of government. It also provided for possible amendments. When presented to special state conventions for ratification, many people opposed the Constitution.

The controversy surrounding the Constitution pitted well-known and respected figures such as Patrick Henry and John Hancock, who were opposed, against the influential George Washington and Benjamin Franklin. At the end of the Constitutional Convention the optimistic Franklin pointed to a painting of the sun on the back of Washington's chair and said:

> I have . . . looked at that behind the President without being able to tell whether it was rising or setting; but now at length I have the happiness to know that it is a rising, and not a setting sun.

Chronology of Main Events

1781 Articles of Confederation adopted

1783 Treaty of Paris signed

1785 Land Ordinance of 1785

1786 Shays's Rebellion begins

1787 Northwest Ordinance established; Constitution drafted; first Federalist papers published

1788 Constitution ratified

THE CONSTITUTION OF THE UNITED STATES OF AMERICA

"In framing a system which we wish to last for ages, we should not lose sight of the changes which ages will produce," said James Madison in 1787. Since then the Constitution of the United States, the document that established our system of government, has withstood the test of time. The fifty-five delegates who shaped the Constitution lived in a mostly rural America. For the most part they were planters, merchants, lawyers, and graduates of private colleges. Now, over two hundred years later, most Americans live in urban areas and are educated in public schools. They are pilots, computer operators, and factory workers. Still, the Constitution has managed to fulfill Madison's hope.

The Constitution is printed on parchment-colored panels. Following each panel is an explanation of that part. Each Article, or major part, is made up of Sections. Each paragraph within a section is called a Clause. Headings have been added, and the spelling and punctuation modernized for easier reading. Portions of the Constitution no longer in use have been crossed out.

156

CONTENTS OF THE CONSTITUTION

Original Articles of the Constitution

Amendments to the Constitution

THE PREAMBLE.
The Purpose of the Constitution

We the people of the United States, in order to form a more perfect Union, establish justice, insure domestic tranquility, provide for the common defense, promote the general welfare, and secure the blessings of liberty to ourselves and our posterity, do ordain and establish this Constitution for the United States of America.

Creating a new government is a momentous undertaking. The framers wanted to make their reasoning clear to other Americans and the rest of the world. The framers wanted the people to understand that their new government rested on great principles. These included freedom, equality, justice, and safety. The Preamble, or introduction, states the basic purposes of the government of the United States. When the framers of the Constitution drafted it, they stated the source of their authority to do so. They said their authority came from the people. Basic to our form of government is the idea that the people have the right and the power to determine how they should be governed. The Constitution outlines the structure of the government of the United States. The Preamble challenges every generation to reestablish the principles of the Constitution.

ARTICLE 1.   The Legislature

The First Article of the Constitution describes what the legislative branch is and what it can and cannot do. With the Second and Third Articles, this part of the Constitution assures the separation of powers of the central government into three components: the legislative, executive, and judicial branches.

SECTION 1.   Congress

All legislative powers herein granted shall be vested in a Congress of the United States, which shall consist of a Senate and House of Representatives.

Only Congress has the power to make laws. Making laws is what is meant by legislative powers. Congress is made up of two houses—the Senate and the House of Representatives. This bicameral, or two-house, legislature is the result of a "great compromise" agreed upon during the Constitutional Convention (see page 147.)

SECTION 2.   The House of Representatives

1. Elections. *The House of Representatives shall be composed of members chosen every second year by the people of the several states, and the electors in each state shall have the qualifications requisite for electors of the most numerous branch of the state legislature.*

2. Qualifications. *No person shall be a Representative who shall not have attained to the age of twenty-five years, and been seven years a citizen of the United States, and who shall not, when elected, be an inhabitant of that state in which he shall be chosen.*

The second paragraph of this section specifies the constitutional requirements for Representatives: age, citizenship, and state residence. In addition, the first paragraph, or clause, indicates that states must hold elections for their Representatives every two years. Such frequent elections, the framers of the Constitution thought, would keep Representatives responsive to the people. Voter qualifications are determined by the states. Some states used this power to limit voting to white males. Amendments 15, 19, 24, and 26 have extended voting rights to people who previously had not been allowed to vote because of state laws.

There are 435 Representatives, a number fixed by Congress in 1941. Over the years, however, each state's allotment of Representatives has varied. The number of Representatives for each state is based on that state's population.

---

3. Number of Representatives. *Representatives and direct taxes shall be apportioned among the several states which may be included within this Union according to their respective numbers, which shall be determined by adding to the whole number of free persons, including those bound to service for a term of years, and excluding Indians not taxed, three fifths of all other persons.*

The actual enumeration shall be made within three years after the first meeting of the Congress of the United States, and within every subsequent term of ten years, in such a manner as they shall by law direct. The number of Representatives shall not exceed one for every thirty thousand, but each state shall have at least one Representative; and until such enumeration shall be made, the state of New Hampshire shall be entitled to choose 3, Massachusetts, 8, Rhode Island and Providence Plantations, 1, Connecticut, 5, New York, 6, New Jersey, 4, Pennsylvania, 8, Delaware, 1, Maryland, 6, Virginia, 10, North Carolina, 5, South Carolina, 5, and Georgia, 3.

4. Vacancies. *When vacancies happen in the representation from any state, the executive authority thereof shall issue writs of election to fill such vacancies.*

5. Officers and Impeachment. *The House of Representatives shall choose their Speaker and other officers; and shall have the sole power of impeachment.*

The portions of this section no longer in use were part of the "Three-fifths Compromise," which counted three-fifths of the slave population in each state for purposes of representation and direct taxes. Here, the term direct taxes means poll and property taxes. The Thirteenth Amendment abolished slavery; the Sixteenth Amendment changed the direct taxes provision; and the Twenty-Fourth Amendment abolished poll taxes and other taxes that had been requirements for voting.

To determine the number of Representatives each state has, Congress counts Americans every ten years (five years beginning in 1985). Each member of the House now represents about 500,000 persons. When a Representative dies in office or leaves office before his or her term is over, the state governor is to call an election to fill the vacancy.

The final clause gives the House of Representatives the power to organize members into committees and the power to impeach. Impeachment is the process of accusing a public official of a crime or serious misbehavior. One President, Andrew Johnson, was impeached by the House, but the Senate found him not guilty of the charges made against him. Other federal officials have been impeached, tried in the Senate, and removed from office.

SECTION 3. The Senate

1. Numbers. *The Senate of the United States shall be composed of two Senators from each state, chosen by the legislature thereof for six years; and each Senator shall have one vote.*

2. Classifying Terms. *Immediately after they shall be assembled in consequence of the first election, they shall be divided as equally as may be into three classes. The seats of the Senator of the first class shall be vacated at the expiration of the second year, of the second class at the expiration of the fourth year, and of the third class at the expiration of the sixth year, so that one-third may be chosen every second year, and if vacancies happen by resignation or otherwise during the recess of the legislature of any state, the executive thereof may make temporary appointments until the next meeting of the legislature, which shall then fill such vacancies.*

3. Qualifications. *No person shall be a Senator who shall not have attained to the age of thirty years and been nine years a citizen of the United States, and who shall not when elected be an inhabitant of that state for which he shall be chosen.*

The Senate has two Senators from each state. Until 1913, Senators were elected by the state legislatures. The Seventeenth Amendment changed that rule by allowing the voters to choose their Senators directly. Each Senator is elected for a six-year term.

The third clause specifies the constitutional requirements for Senators. A Senator must be at least thirty, a citizen of the United States for nine years, and a resident of the state in which he is elected.

4. Role of Vice-President. *The Vice-President of the United States shall be President of the Senate, but shall have no vote unless they be equally divided.*

5. Officers. *The Senate shall choose their officers, and also a President pro tempore, in the absence of the Vice-President, or when he shall exercise the office of the President of the United States.*

6. Impeachment Trials. *The Senate shall have the sole power to try all impeachments. When sitting for that purpose, they shall be on oath or affirmation. When the President of the United States is tried, the Chief Justice shall preside; and no person shall be convicted without the concurrence of two-thirds of the members present.*

7. Punishment for Impeachment. *Judgement in cases of impeachment shall not extend further than to removal from office and disqualification to hold and enjoy any office of honor, trust, or profit under the United States; but the party convicted shall nevertheless be liable and subject to indictment, trial, judgment, and punishment, according to law.*

The Vice-President presides at Senate meetings but votes only when there is a tie.

The Senate also organizes into committees and chooses its other officers, including the president pro tempore, who presides over the Senate in the absence of the Vice-President. The Twenty-Fifth Amendment now provides for filling the vacant office of the Vice-President.

The last two clauses give the Senate the power to act as a court at impeachment trials. The Senate's power to punish a convicted official is limited, however. The Senate can remove the official from office and bar him or her from holding another United States government office. The convicted person can then be tried in the regular courts for the crime(s) that caused the loss of office and punished if found guilty.

SECTION 4. Congressional Elections

1. Regulations. *The times, places, and manner of holding elections for Senators and Representatives shall be prescribed in each* *state by the legislature thereof; but the Congress may at any time by law make or alter such regulations except as to the places of choosing Senators.*

2. Sessions. *The Congress shall assemble at least once in every year, and such meeting shall be on the first Monday in December, unless they shall by law appoint a different day.*

Federal law now requires all states to hold elections for Congress on the first Tuesday after the first Monday in November in even-numbered years. The Seventeenth Amendment provides for Senators to be elected at the same voting places as other officials.

The English kings had often kept Parliament from meeting simply by not calling it together. This is the reason for the provision that Congress must meet once a year.

The Twentieth Amendment changed Congress's meeting time to January 3, unless Congress itself rules otherwise.

SECTION 5. Rules and Procedures

1. Quorum. *Each house shall be the judge of the elections, returns, and qualifications of its own members, and a majority of each shall constitute a quorum to do business; but a smaller number may adjourn from day to day and may be authorized to compel the attendance of absent members in such manner and under such penalties as each house may provide.*

2. Rules and Conduct. *Each house may determine the rules of its proceedings, punish its members for disorderly behavior, and, with the concurrence of two-thirds, expel a member.*

3. Congressional Records. *Each house shall keep a journal of its proceedings, and from time to time publish the same, excepting such parts as may in their judgment require secrecy; and the yeas and nays of the members of either house on any question shall, at the desire of one-fifth of those present, be entered on the journal.*

4. Adjournment. *Neither house, during the sessions of Congress, shall without the consent of the other adjourn, for more than*

three days, nor to any other place than that in which the two houses shall be sitting.

Both the House and the Senate decide whether their members are legally qualified and have been fairly elected. On the basis of this section, members of Congress refused to seat members from the former Confederate states in the election following the Civil War (see page 385).

Each house disciplines its own members when the activities of those members are judged to be improper. Under this clause, Senator Joseph R. McCarthy was condemned in 1954 for his improper search for Communists. Representative Adam Clayton Powell was denied his seat in 1967 on the charge that he had misused government funds. Senator Herman Talmadge was ''denounced'' in 1979 for financial irregularities. Representative Charles Diggs was also censured in 1979 for financial misconduct. More recently, members of Congress have been disciplined for improper moral behavior.

The proceedings of both the Senate and the House of Representatives have been published together in the Congressional Record since 1873. The Record comes out daily while Congress is in session. It will omit certain matters if Congress decides that they are secret. It must show, however, how each member voted if one-fifth of the members present agree.

The last clause provides Congress with the power to decide when and where it should meet. Both houses must agree to any recess that extends beyond three days, and both must meet in the same city.

SECTION 6. Payment and Privileges

1. Salary. *The Senators and Representatives shall receive a compensation for their services, to be ascertained by law, and paid out of the Treasury of the United States. They shall in all cases, except treason, felony, and breach of the peace, be privileged from arrest during their attendance at the session of their representative houses, and in going to and returning from the same; and for any speech or debate in either house they shall not be questioned in any other place.*

2. Restrictions. *No Senator or*

Representative shall, during the time for which he was elected, be appointed to any civil office under the authority of the United States which shall have been created or the emoluments whereof shall have been increased during such time; and no person holding any office under the United States shall be a member of either house during his continuance in office.

In 1991 Representatives received a salary of $124,400 and Senators received $101,400 (and up to $23,568 in honoraria), plus office space and allowances for office costs, staff salaries, travel, and similar expenses. Congressional immunity, freedom from arrest, protects members while going to and from congressional work. Like all Americans, both Senators and Representatives may be arrested for breaking the law. A member of Congress also has immunity from prosecution for libel or slander during congressional debates or in official reports.

The second clause was included so that no member of Congress would be able to profit personally from laws that he or she helped make. This keeps Senators and Representatives from creating jobs to which they might later be appointed or from raising the salaries of jobs they someday hope to hold.

SECTION 7.   How a Bill Becomes a Law

1. Tax Bills.   *All bills for raising revenue shall originate in the House of Representa-*

tives; but the Senate may propose or concur with amendments as on other bills.

The tradition of the tax bill originating in the lower house of the legislature is a part of our legacy from England, where tax measures start in the House of Commons. However, the Senate can amend the tax bill to the extent that it rewrites the whole measure.

---

2. Law-Making Process.   *Every bill which shall have passed the House of Representatives and the Senate shall before it becomes a law be presented to the President of the United States. If he approves, he shall sign it; but if not, he shall return it with his objections to that house in which it shall have originated, who shall enter the objections at large on their journal and proceed to reconsider it. If after such reconsideration two-thirds of that house shall agree to pass the bill, it shall be sent, together with the objections, to the other house, by which it shall likewise be reconsidered; and if approved by two-thirds of that house, it shall become a law. But in all such cases the votes of both houses shall be determined by yeas and nays, and the names of the persons voting for and against the bill shall be entered on the journal of each house respectively.*

If any bill shall not be returned by the President within ten days (Sundays excepted)

The Legislative Branch

Congress

House of Representatives
Fixed membership: 435

Senate
Membership: 2 per state

Library of Congress   General Printing Office   Congressional Budget Office   General Accounting Office   Other Agencies

Source: United States Office of Personnel Management

after it shall have been presented to him, the same shall be a law in like manner as if he had signed it, unless the Congress by their adjournment prevent its return, in which case it shall not be a law.

3. Role of President. *Every order, resolution, or vote to which the concurrence of the Senate and House of Representatives may be necessary (except on a question of adjournment) shall be presented to the President of the United States; and before the same shall take effect, shall be approved by him or being disapproved by him, shall be repassed by two-thirds of the Senate and House of Representatives, according to the rules and limitations prescribed in the case of a bill.*

A bill that gains a majority vote in both the House and the Senate must be sent to the President. The President can: (1) sign it and make it a law; (2) hold it for ten days without signing it, after which time it still becomes a law; or (3) veto, or refuse to sign it, and return it to Congress with his reasons for doing so. These clauses keep Congress from making laws without the agreement of the President. They are a strong check because only 5 percent of the bills have passed over presidential vetoes.

A bill can still become a law if each house overrides the President's veto and passes the bill by a two-thirds majority. When a bill is sent to the President near the end of a congressional session, the President can hold it. If Congress adjourns within ten days, it does not become law if the President does not sign it. This is called a pocket veto. Franklin Roosevelt used 263 such vetoes. The chart on page 186 shows the process by which a bill becomes a law.

SECTION 8.   Powers Granted to Congress

1. Taxation. *The Congress shall have power to lay and collect taxes, duties, imposts, and excises, to pay the debts and provide for the common defense and general welfare of the United States; but all duties, imposts, and excises shall be uniform throughout the United States.*

2. Credit. *To borrow money on the credit of the United States.*

3. Commerce. *To regulate commerce with foreign nations, and among the several states, and with the Indian tribes.*

This section lists the powers granted to Congress. Clause 1 grants Congress the power to establish uniform taxes. Duties are taxes on goods coming into the United States. Excises are taxes on the manufacture, sale, or use of goods made within the country. Imposts are other taxes on imported goods.

Clause 2 is the basis for national banks and the Federal Reserve System. There is no limit on the amount of money the government can borrow.

Clause 3 was intended to remedy a weakness of the Articles of Confederation. Over the years, the Supreme Court has interpreted this clause so that Congress can regulate many forms of interstate commerce. As a result, Congress is concerned not only about commercial activity that crosses state boundaries but also about activity that affects commerce in more than one state. For instance, Congress can pass laws and provide funds to improve waterways, to enforce air safety measures, and to forbid interstate shipment of certain goods.

Congress can also regulate the movement of people, of stocks and bonds, and of television signals. It is a federal crime for people to flee across state lines from state or local police. This clause sees that interstate travelers receive fair treatment regardless of race or nationality.

4. Naturalization, Bankruptcy. *To establish a uniform rule of naturalization, and uniform laws on the subject of bankruptcies throughout the United States.*

5. Money. *To coin money, regulate the value thereof and foreign coin, and fix the standard of weights and measures.*

6. Counterfeiting. *To provide for the punishment of counterfeiting the securities and current coin of the United States.*

Clause 4 insures uniform rules for naturalization, the process of becoming a citizen, and rules for people who owe debts they cannot pay.

Clause 5 gives Congress the right to make currency and to regulate its value.

Clause 6 allows Congress to decide punishment for people who make imitation government bonds, stamps, or money.

----

7. Post Office. *To establish post offices and post roads.*

8. Patents, Copyrights. *To promote the progress of science and useful arts, by securing for limited times to authors and inventors the exclusive right to their respective writings and discoveries.*

9. Federal Court. *To constitute tribunals inferior to the Supreme Court.*

10. International Law. *To define and punish piracies and felonies committed on the high seas, and offenses against the law of nations.*

Congress has attempted to reform the Post Office Department, making it an independent agency. Postal workers now have the right to organize and to bargain collectively. (See chart on page 194.)

Clause 8 gives Congress the responsibility to promote science, industry, and the arts by making laws under which inventors, writers, and artists receive patents and copyrights to protect their own works. A patent is an official document that gives an inventor the exclusive right to make, use, or sell the invention for a specified number of years. A copyright is the exclusive right to publish or perform literary, artistic, or musical works for a certain number of years.

Clause 9 allows Congress to set up the federal district courts, the United States Courts of Appeals, and other special courts.

Through Clause 10, Congress has the power to make laws regarding crimes committed on the seas or oceans. It also has power to make laws to punish persons who break international laws.

----

11. War. *To declare war, ~~grant letters of marque and reprisal,~~ and make rules concerning captures on land and water.*

12. Armed Forces. *To raise and support armies, but no appropriation of money to that use shall be for a longer term than two years.*

13. Navy. *To provide and maintain a navy.*

14. Regulation for Armed Forces. *To make rules for the government and regulation of the land and naval forces.*

15. Militia. *To provide for calling forth the militia to execute the laws of the Union, suppress insurrections, and repel invasions.*

16. Regulations for Militia. *To provide for organizing, arming, and disciplining the militia, and for governing such part of them as may be employed in the service of the United States, reserving to the states, respectively, the appointment of the officers, and the authority of training the militia according to the discipline prescribed by Congress.*

According to Clause 11, only Congress can declare war. However, the President has taken military action without the consent of Congress in the case of the Korean War (1950–1953) and the Vietnam War (1955–1975). Letters of marque or reprisal are documents that authorize vessels to attack enemy ships. They are outlawed by international law today and reference to them is deleted in the clause.

The next clauses, including the two-year limit for appropriations, were intended to keep the army under the control of civilians. The navy, which was young and small, was not placed under that limitation. An air force was not even imagined then.

Clause 16 provides for a National Militia, popularly called the National Guard. Congress has given the President power to decide when a state of emergency exists. Then, the President, as its Commander in Chief, can call out the National Guard.

----

17. District of Columbia. *To exercise exclusive legislation in all cases whatsoever over such district (not exceeding ten miles square) as may, by cession of particular state and the acceptance of Congress, become the seat of government of the United States; and to exercise like authority over all places purchased by the consent of the legislature of the state in which the same shall be, for the erection of forts, magazines, arsenals, dockyards, and other needful buildings.*

18. Elastic Clause. *And to make all laws which shall be necessary and proper for carrying into execution the foregoing powers and all other powers vested by this Constitution in the government of the United States, or in any department or office thereof.*

Congress is the legislative body for the District of Columbia and for all federal property on which forts, naval bases, arsenals, and other federal works or buildings are located.

This final clause of Section 8 is called the "necessary and proper" clause, or sometimes the elastic clause. It allows Congress to deal with many matters not specifically mentioned in the Constitution.

SECTION 9.   Powers Denied Congress

1. Slave Trade. ~~*The migration or importation of such persons as any of the states now existing shall think proper to admit shall not be prohibited by the Congress prior to the year one thousand eight hundred and eight, but a tax or duty may be imposed on such importation, not exceeding ten dollars for each person.*~~

2. Habeas Corpus. *The privilege of the writ of habeas corpus shall not be suspended, unless when in cases of rebellion or invasion the public may require it.*

3. Illegal Punishment. *No bill of attainder or ex post facto law shall be passed.*

4. Direct Taxes. *No capitation or other direct tax shall be laid, unless in proportion to the census or enumeration herein before directed to be taken.*

5. Export Taxes. *No tax or duty shall be laid on articles exported from any state.*

The first clause, now obsolete, refers to foreign slave trade. Congress passed a law in 1808 stopping the importation of slaves.

A writ of habeas corpus is a legal order that protects people from being held in jail on weak evidence or none at all. During the Civil War Abraham Lincoln suspended the writ of habeas corpus in certain areas. Chief Justice Taney ruled in the Merryman case (1861) that only Congress had

the right to suspend the writ of habeas corpus. Lincoln disagreed and continued to follow his own interpretation. Several other Presidents have, too.

A bill of attainder is an act passed by a legislature to punish a person without a trial. An ex post facto law is one that provides punishment for an act that was legal when the act was committed. This clause indicates that punishment for disregarding a law is the responsibility of the courts, not Congress.

A capitation is a head tax; the word comes from the Latin designation for "head." Congress cannot levy head taxes, or poll taxes, unless all persons (men, women, and children) in the United States are taxed the same. Other direct taxes must also be based on population. The Sixteenth Amendment made it legal to have an income tax.

Clause 5 refers to export taxes, taxes on goods sent to other states or to foreign countries. Congress can regulate or prohibit shipment of certain items, but it cannot tax goods for being sent out of any state.

---

6. No Favorites. *No preference shall be given by any regulation of commerce or revenue to the ports of one state over those of another; nor shall vessels bound to or from one state be obliged to enter, clear, or pay duties to another.*

7. Public Money. *No money shall be drawn from the Treasury but in consequence of appropriations made by law; and a regular statement and account of the receipts and expenditures of all public money shall be published from time to time.*

8. Titles of Nobility. *No title of nobility shall be granted by the United States; and no person holding any office of profit or trust under them shall without the consent of the Congress accept of any present, emolument, office, or title of any kind whatever from any king, prince, or foreign state.*

Clause 6 says that Congress cannot make any laws that favor one state more than another in matters of trade and commerce. Interstate commerce was strengthened by the provision that ships from one state may enter the ports of any other state without paying charges.

Clause 7 requires that government money be

164

Federalism

Powers of the Federal Government	Powers shared by State and Federal Governments	Powers of State Governments
declare war	levy taxes	issue marriage licenses
sign treaties	build roads	pass state laws
regulate interstate commerce	finance schools	regulate intrastate commerce
coin money		

spent only after Congress passes a law for that purpose. A statement of federal income and spending must be published.

According to Clause 8, a United States official cannot have titles of nobility. A federal officer may not accept a title, position, or gift from a foreign government without the consent of Congress.

SECTION 10. Powers Denied the States

1. Restrictions. *No state shall enter into any treaty, alliance, or confederation; grant letters of marque and reprisal; coin money; emit bills of credit; make anything but gold and silver coin a tender in payment of debts; pass any bill of attainder, ex post facto law, or law impairing the obligation of contracts, or grant any title of nobility.*

Clause 1 presents certain activities that State governments cannot do. States cannot: (1) make treaties; (2) permit private citizens to make war on other nations; (3) issue money; (4) disregard federal laws dealing with money; (5) pass the kinds of laws forbidden by Section 9, Clause 3; (6) pass laws excusing people from carrying out lawful agreements; or (7) issue titles of nobility.

---

2. Import and Export Taxes. *No state shall, without the consent of the Congress, lay any imposts or duties on imports or exports, except what may be absolutely necessary for executing its inspection laws; and the net produce of all duties and imposts, laid by any state on imports or exports, shall be for the use of the Treasury of the United States; and all such shall be subject to the revision and control of the Congress.*

3. Peacetime and War Restraints. *No state shall, without the consent of Congress, lay any duty of tonnage, keep troops or ships of war in time of peace, enter into any agreement or compact with another state, or with a foreign power, or engage in war, unless actually invaded, or in such imminent danger as will not admit of delay.*

Clauses 2 and 3 specify the following things that states may do only with the consent or approval of Congress: (1) tax goods entering or leaving a state beyond what is needed to cover costs of inspection; (2) tax ships; (3) keep state troops or warships in time of peace; (4) make separate alliances with other states or foreign countries; and (5) go to war.

ARTICLE 2. The Executive Department

The President is given a number of powers in the Constitution, but the Constitution is vague about how the President is to use these powers. The primary responsibility of the President is to execute, or carry out, the laws of the United States. The President's strength lies in his or her interpretation of the Constitution and use of the powers.

The powers of the President have grown since the writing of the Constitution. Strong Presidents have expanded the powers of the chief executive and the executive department. Although the specified powers of the President have not changed, presidential customs have.

SECTION 1. The Presidency

1. Term of Office. *The executive power shall be vested in a President of the United States of America. He shall hold his office* *during the term of four years and, together with the Vice-President, chosen for the same term, be elected as follows.*

2. Electoral College. *Each state shall appoint, in such manner as the legislature thereof may direct, a number of electors, equal to the whole number of Senators and Representatives to which the state may be entitled in the Congress; but no Senator or Representative, or person holding an office of trust or profit under the United States, shall be appointed an elector.*

~~**3. Former Method of Electing President.** *The electors shall meet in their respective states and vote by ballot for two persons, of whom one at least shall not be an inhabitant of the same state with themselves. And they shall make a list of all the persons voted for, and of the number of votes for each, which list they shall sign and certify and transmit, sealed, to the seat of the government of the United States, directed to the president of the Senate. The president of the Senate shall, in the presence of the Senate and the House of Representatives, open all the certificates, and the votes shall then be counted. The person having the greatest number of votes shall be the President, if such number be a majority of the whole number of electors appointed, and if there be more than one who have such majority, and have an equal number of votes, then the House of Representatives shall immediately choose by ballot one of them for President, and if no person have a majority, then from the five highest on the list the said House shall in like manner choose the President. But in choosing the President, the vote shall be taken by states, the*~~

~~*representation from each state having one vote. A quorum for this purpose shall consist of a member or members from two-thirds of the states, and a majority of all the states shall be necessary to a choice. In every case, after the choice of President, the person having the greatest number of votes of the electors shall be the Vice-President. But if there should remain two or more who have equal votes, the Senate shall choose from them by ballot the Vice-President.*~~

4. Election Day. *The Congress may determine the time of choosing the electors, and the day on which they shall give their votes, which day shall be the same throughout the United States.*

Full executive power of the United States is vested in the President, who holds office for a four-year term. The people of the United States do not vote directly for the President. Each state chooses electors who in turn make up the electoral college. Each state has as many electors as it has members of Congress.

Clause 3 describes the original method for electing the President and Vice-President. This procedure was changed by the Twelfth Amendment after the Presidential elections of 1796 and 1800 revealed problems that were inherent to that method (see pages 221 and 225).

Clause 4 provides that the day when electors vote must be the same throughout the United States. When citizens go to the polls on the first Tuesday after the first Monday in November to vote for the President and Vice-President, they vote for the electors. The electors cast their votes on the first Monday after the second Wednesday in December. Only Congress can change these days.

The Executive Branch

President

| Vice-President | Executive Office | Cabinet | Independent Agencies |

| White House Office | Council on Economic Advisors | Domestic Policy Staff | Office of Management and Budget | National Security Council | Central Intelligence Agency | Other Agencies |

Requirements for Holding Federal Office

Position	Minimum Age	Residency	Citizenship
House of Representatives	25	state in which elected	7 years
Senate	30	state in which elected	9 years
President	35	14 years in the United States	natural-born
Supreme Court	none	none	none

5. Qualifications. *No person except a natural-born citizen* or citizen of the United States at the time of the adoption of this Constitution *shall be eligible to the office of President; neither shall any person be eligible to that office who shall not have attained the age of thirty-five years and been fourteen years a resident within the United States.*

6. Succession. *In case of the removal of the President from office, or of his death, resignation, or inability to discharge the powers and duties of the said office, the same shall devolve on the Vice-President, and the Congress may by law provide for the case of removal, death, resignation, or inability, both of the President and Vice-President, declaring what officer shall then act as President, and such officer shall act accordingly until the disability be removed or a President shall be elected.*

Clause 5 states that the President of the United States must be at least thirty-five years of age, a native citizen, and must have lived in the United States at least fourteen years.

Clause 6 has been changed by the Twenty-Fifth Amendment. This amendment clarifies the procedure for dealing with vacancies in the offices of President and Vice-President.

7. Salary. *The President shall at stated times receive for his services a compensation, which shall neither be increased nor diminished during the period for which he* *shall have been elected, and he shall not receive within that period any other emolument from the United States, or any of them.*

The President's salary includes an annual allowance for expenses and additional allowances for travel, staff support, and maintenance of the White House. After leaving office, the President is eligible for a pension, clerical assistants, office space, and free mailing privileges. Widowed wives of former Presidents also get a yearly pension. The President may not receive any other pay from the federal government or from the states.

8. Oath of Office. *Before he enter on the execution of his office, he shall take the following oath or affirmation: "I do solemnly swear (or affirm) that I will faithfully execute the office of President of the United States, and will to the best of my ability preserve, protect, and defend the Constitution of the United States."*

The Constitution does not say who shall give the oath to the newly elected President. Presidents have been sworn in by Supreme Court justices, by judges, and by ministers. Today, however, the Chief Justice usually administers the oath of office.

SECTION 2. Powers of the President

1. Military Powers. *The President shall be commander in chief of the Army and Navy of the United States, and of the militias of*

The System of Checks and Balances

Branch	Powers	Checks
Executive (President) 	**President** enforces laws; appoints officers; makes treaties; appoints Supreme Court judges; serves as commander in chief of the United States Army and Navy and of the state militia.	**Congress** shelves bills proposed by President; overrides vetoes; refuses to confirm appointments and to ratify treaties; impeaches the President. **Supreme Court** declares laws or executive acts unconstitutional.
Legislative (Congress)	**Congress** passes laws; approves treaties and appointments; provides for and maintains the navy and for calling of the militia; collects taxes; pays debts; borrows and coins money; regulates trade.	**President** vetoes laws; calls special sessions of Congress. **Supreme Court** interprets laws and treaties; reviews constitutionality of laws.
Judicial (Courts)	**Supreme Court** interprets laws and treaties; judges appointed for life; Chief Justice presides at impeachment of President.	**President** appoints judges but cannot remove them; grants pardons. **Congress** decides jurisdiction of federal courts; sets up lower courts; approves appointment of judges; impeaches judges; tries impeachments.

the several states when called into the actual service of the United States; he may require the opinion, in writing, of the principal officer in each of the executive departments, upon any subject relating to the duties of their respective offices, and he shall have power to grant reprieves and pardons for offenses against the United States except in cases of impeachment.

2. Treaties, Appointments. *He shall have power, by and with the advice and consent of the Senate, to make treaties, provided two-thirds of the Senators present concur; and he shall nominate and, by and with the advice and consent of the Senate, shall appoint ambassadors, other public ministers and consuls, judges of the Supreme Court, and all other officers of the United States whose appointments are not herein provided for and which shall be established by law; but the Congress may by law vest the appointment of such inferior offices as they think proper in the President alone, in the courts of law, or in the heads of departments.*

3. Vacancies. *The President shall have power to fill up all vacancies that may happen during the recess of the Senate by granting commissions which shall expire at the end of their next session.*

Clause 1 ensures that the military is clearly under civilian control. The executive departments mentioned have grown in number and size over the years. This clause prompted President Washington to start a cabinet, or a group of advisers.

Clause 2 is the basis of an important check on the powers of the President—the President's need for the "advice and consent" of the Senate. The President can make treaties and appoint officials only with a two-thirds approval from the Senate. Sometimes the President enters into an executive agreement with a foreign country. This has the force of a treaty and does not require Senate approval.

Clause 3 indicates that when the Senate is not in session, the President can make temporary appointments requiring no Senate confirmation.

SECTION 3. Presidential Duties

He shall from time to time give to the Congress information of the state of the Union, and recommend to their consideration such measures as he shall judge necessary and expedient; he may, on extraordinary occasions, convene both houses, or either of them, and in case of disagreement between them, with respect to the time of adjournment, he may adjourn them to such time as he shall think proper; he shall receive ambassadors and other public ministers; he shall take care that the laws be faithfully executed, and shall commission all the officers of the United States.

This section identifies four major responsibilities of the President: (1) legislative—the President must give a State of the Union message to Congress each year; (2) diplomatic—the President must receive the representatives of foreign countries; (3) executive—the President must faithfully carry out the laws of the land; (4) military—the President, as the nation's commander in chief, grants every military officer his or her commission, or rank and authority.

SECTION 4. Impeachment

The President, Vice-President, and all civil officers of the United States shall be removed from office on impeachment for, and conviction of, treason, bribery, or other high crimes and misdemeanors.

President Andrew Johnson was impeached by the House and tried by the Senate. The necessary two-thirds majority of Senators did not vote him guilty, so he remained President. President Richard Nixon resigned in 1974 before he could be impeached.

ARTICLE 3. The Judicial Department

The Constitution devotes fewer words to the judicial branch than the other two branches. Yet this branch is as powerful as the others.

SECTION 1. Federal Courts and Judges

The judicial power of the United States shall be vested in one Supreme Court, and in such inferior courts as the Congress may from time to time ordain and establish. The judges, both of the Supreme and inferior courts, shall hold their offices during good behavior, and shall at stated times receive for their services a compensation, which shall not be diminished during their continuance in office.

The Constitution keeps the courts independent from both the President and Congress. Unless judges are impeached and convicted, they can hold their jobs for life. Only two Presidents have tried to change the membership of the Supreme Court. Jefferson did so by the attempted impeachment of Samuel Chase in 1805. Years later, Franklin D. Roosevelt attempted to place additional members on the bench. Neither President was successful.

SECTION 2. The Court's Authority

1. General Authority. *The judicial power shall extend to all cases in law and equity arising under this Constitution, the laws of the United States, and treaties made or which shall be made under their authority; to all cases affecting ambassadors, other public ministers, and consuls; to all cases of admiralty and maritime jurisdiction; to controversies to which the United States shall be a party; to controversies between two or more states; between a state and citizens of another state; between citizens of different states; between citizens of the same state claiming lands under grants of different states, and between a state, or the citizens thereof, and foreign states, citizens or subjects.*

2. Supreme Court. *In all cases affecting ambassadors, other public ministers and consuls, and those in which a state shall be party, the Supreme Court shall have original jurisdiction. In all the other cases before mentioned, the Supreme Court shall have appellate jurisdiction, both as to law and fact, with such exceptions and under such regulations as the Congress shall make.*

3. Trial by Jury. *The trial of all crimes except in cases of impeachment shall be by jury; and such trial shall be held in the state where the said crimes shall have been* *committed; but when not committed within any state, the trial shall be at such place or places as the Congress may by law have directed.*

The first clause establishes the Supreme Court's right to declare laws of Congress unconstitutional. This right was established by Chief Justice Marshall's decision in *Marbury* v. *Madison* (see page 198). Judicial review is the power to review a law and decide whether it violates the Constitution.

According to the second clause, the Supreme Court has original jurisdiction, primary responsibility, in cases affecting representatives of foreign countries and in cases in which a state is one of the parties. These go directly to the Supreme Court.

The Supreme Court has appellate jurisdiction, the right to review appeals, in other kinds of cases. These cases are tried first in a lower court and then may come up to the Supreme Court for review if Congress authorizes an appeal. Congress can take away the right to appeal to the Supreme Court or fix the procedures to present an appeal.

Clause 3 guarantees trial by jury to anyone accused of a crime against the federal government, except an impeached official. The trial is held in the state where the crime was committed. If the crime occurred in a place other than a state, Congress can determine the trial site.

SECTION 3. Treason

1. Definition. *Treason against the United States shall consist only in levying war against them, or in adhering to their enemies, giving them aid and comfort. No person shall be convicted of treason unless on the testimony of two witnesses to the same overt act, or on confession in open court.*

2. Punishment. *The Congress shall have power to declare the punishment of treason, but no attainder of treason shall work corruption of blood or forfeiture except during the life of the person attainted.*

The constitutional definition of treason is limited to starting war against the United States or joining or giving aid to its enemies. Because of the strict definition, Aaron Burr was found not guilty when he was charged with treason after the killing of

Alexander Hamilton during a dual. Treason is the only crime defined in the Constitution. The phrase *no attainder of treason shall work corruption of blood* means that the family of a convicted traitor does not share the guilt of the traitor. Formerly, a traitor's family could also be punished.

ARTICLE 4. Relations Among States

Much of this article is based on the Articles of Confederation. States must honor one another's laws, records, and court rulings. Congress has the power to make laws forcing the states to respect each other's laws, records, and decisions.

SECTION 1. State Acts and Records

Full faith and credit shall be given in each state to the public acts, records, and judicial proceedings of every other state. And the Congress may by general laws prescribe the manner in which such acts, records, and proceedings shall be proved, and the effect thereof.

Section 1 demands that states respect each other's laws regarding public information about births, deaths, wills, and marriages.

SECTION 2. Rights of Citizens

1. Citizenship. *The citizens of each state shall be entitled to all privileges and immunities of citizens in the several states.*

2. Extradition. *A person charged in any state with treason, felony, or other crime, who shall flee from justice, and be found in another state, shall, on the demand of the executive authority of the state from which he fled, be delivered up, to be removed to the state having jurisdiction of the crime.*

3. Fugitive Slaves. *No person held to service or labor in one state, under the laws thereof, escaping into another, shall, in consequence of any law or regulation therein, be discharged from such service or labor, but shall be delivered up on claim of the party to whom such service or labor may be due.*

Citizens traveling from state to state enjoy all the rights and privileges of the citizens of those states. If a person is charged with a felony or other serious crime in one state and flees to another state, that person must be returned to the first state upon that governor's request. This is called extradition. Sometimes extradition is refused. The Thirteenth Amendment renders Clause 3 obsolete.

SECTION 3.   New States

> **1. Admission.** *New states may be admitted by Congress into this Union; but no new state shall be formed or erected within the jurisdiction of any other state; nor any state be formed by the junction of two or more states, or parts or states, without the consent of the legislatures of the states concerned as well as of the Congress.*
> **2. Congressional Authority.** *The Congress shall have power to dispose of and make all needful rules and regulations respecting the territory or other property belonging to the United States; and nothing in this Constitution shall be so construed as to prejudice any claims of the United States, or of any particular state.*

Congress can admit new states into the Union and control all federal property. This section also allows Congress to establish governments for land under United States guardianship, like Puerto Rico. Clause 2 also allows Congress to establish national parks.

This section once permitted Congress to deal with the question of slavery in the territories.

SECTION 4.   Guarantees to the States

> *The United States shall guarantee to every state in this Union a republican form of government, and shall protect each of them against invasion; and, on application of the legislature, or of the executive (when the legislature cannot be convened), against domestic violence.*

This section insures that each state is a republic. A republic is a form of government in which the people elect officials to represent them.

This section guarantees each state federal protection against invasion and domestic violence. President Eisenhower used this power in 1957 when he ordered the Arkansas National Guard into federal service at Central High School in Little Rock.

ARTICLE 5.   Amending the Constitution

The Fifth Article explains the process of amending, or changing, the Constitution. This article gives the Constitution its flexibility, one of its strongest features. Custom has provided that all amendments (the Twenty-First Amendment being the only exception to the custom) be proposed by two-thirds vote in Congress and ratified by state legislatures.

Amending the Constitution

Proposing Amendments	Ratifying Amendments
1. 2/3 of each house of Congress	1. 3/4 of the state legislatures
2. convention called by 2/3 of the state legislatures	2. 3/4 of special conventions held in each state

> *The Congress, whenever two-thirds of both houses shall deem it necessary, shall propose amendments to this Constitution, or on the application of the legislatures of two-thirds of the several states, shall call a convention for proposing amendments, which, in either case, shall be valid to all intents and purposes, as part of this Constitution, when ratified by the legislatures of three-fourths of the several states, or by conventions in three-fourths thereof, as the one or the other mode of ratification may be proposed by the Congress, provided that no amendment which may be made prior to the year one thousand eight hundred and eight shall in any manner affect the first and fourth clauses in the Ninth Section of the First Article; and that no state, without its consent, shall be deprived of its equal suffrage in the Senate.*

Over the years, seven thousand amendments

have been proposed in Congress, but only thirty-three have been passed and submitted to the states. To date, twenty-six have been ratified, and added to the Constitution, therefore becoming law. Since the early 1900's, most of the proposed amendments have included a clause that ratification had to be obtained within seven years.

Through the years, the Constitution has been changed by interpretation as well as by amendment. In fact, the Court has been labeled ''a continuing constitutional convention'' because of its changing opinions.

ARTICLE 6. Supremacy of the National Government

1. Valid Debts. *All debts contracted and engagements entered into before the adoption of this Constitution shall be as valid against the United States under this Constitution as under the Confederation.*

2. Supreme Law. *This Constitution and the laws of the United States which shall be made in pursuance thereof, and all treaties made or which shall be made under the authority of the United States, shall be the supreme law of the land, and the judges in every state shall be bound thereby, anything in the constitution or laws of any state to the contrary notwithstanding.*

3. Loyalty to Constitution. *The Senators and Representatives before mentioned, and the members of the several state legislatures, and all executive and judicial officers, both of the United States and of the several states, shall be bound by oath or affirmation to support this Constitution; but no religious test shall ever be required as a qualification to any office or public trust under the United States.*

This article asserts that all debts under the Articles of Confederation will be honored. Clause 2 establishes that the supreme law of the land is based on: (1) the Constitution; (2) federal laws; and (3) all treaties. According to Clause 3, all government officials must promise to support the Constitution and the clause forbids religious qualifications as a condition for holding a government job.

ARTICLE 7. Ratification

The framers set up an orderly procedure for the Constitution to be approved by the states. The Constitution did not require unanimous support to become effective.

The ratification of the conventions of nine states shall be sufficient for the establishment of this Constitution between the states so ratifying the same.

Done in convention by the unanimous consent of the states present the seventeenth day of September, in the year of our Lord one thousand seven hundred and eighty-seven and of the independence of the United States of America the twelfth. In witness whereof, we have hereunto subscribed our names. George Washington—President and deputy from Virginia.

DELAWARE
George Read
Gunning Bedford, Jr.
John Dickinson
Richard Bassett
Jacob Broom

MARYLAND
James McHenry
Dan of St. Thomas
  Jenifer
Daniel Carroll

VIRGINIA
John Blair
James Madison, Jr.

NORTH CAROLINA
William Blount
Richard Dobbs Spaight
Hugh Williamson

NEW HAMPSHIRE
John Langdon
Nicholas Gilman

MASSACHUSETTS
Nathaniel Gorham
Rufus King

CONNECTICUT
William Samuel Johnson
Roger Sherman

NEW YORK
Alexander Hamilton

NEW JERSEY
William Livingston
David Brearley
William Paterson
Jonathan Dayton

SOUTH CAROLINA
John Rutledge
Charles Cotesworth
  Pinckney
Charles Pinckney
Pierce Butler

GEORGIA
William Few
Abraham Baldwin

PENNSYLVANIA
Benjamin Franklin
Thomas Mifflin
Robert Morris
George Clymer
Thomas FitzSimons
Jared Ingersoll
James Wilson
Gouverneur Morris

Bill of Rights

The first ten amendments to the Constitution are known as the Bill of Rights. These amendments were added to the Constitution on December 15, 1791—a year and a half after the last state ratified the Constitution. James Madison drafted the Bill of Rights (see page 208). He had not forgotten that five states had approved the Constitution only after stressing the need for such an addition.

AMENDMENT 1.   Religious and Political Freedoms (1791)

Congress shall make no law respecting an establishment of religion, or prohibiting the free exercise thereof; or abridging the freedom of speech, or of the press; or the right of the people peaceably to assemble, and to petition the government for a redress of grievances.

The First Amendment protects the cornerstones of civil rights: (1) freedom of religious worship; (2) freedom of speech; (3) freedom of the press; (4) freedom to assemble; and (5) the right to voice complaints to the government. The Supreme Court has applied this amendment to a variety of situations.

AMENDMENT 2.   Right to Bear Arms (1791)

A well-regulated militia being necessary to the security of a free state, the right of the people to keep and bear arms shall not be infringed.

A citizen's right to bear arms is related to the maintenance of a militia. Various restrictions have been placed on this right, including the requirement of gun licenses and the restricted right to carry concealed weapons.

AMENDMENT 3.   Quartering Troops (1791)

No soldier shall in time of peace be quartered in any house without the consent of the owner; nor in time of war but in a manner to be prescribed by law.

Soldiers cannot be stationed in a private home during peacetime without the owner's consent. Soldiers can be stationed in homes during wartime only if Congress passes such a law.

AMENDMENT 4.   Search and Seizure (1791)

The right of the people to be secure in their persons, houses, papers, and effects, against unreasonable searches and seizures, shall not be violated; and no warrants shall issue, but upon probable cause, supported by oath or affirmation, and particularly describing the place to be searched and the persons or things to be seized.

This amendment requires authorities to obtain a specific search or arrest warrant from a judge before searches or seizure of property can take place. If evidence is obtained illegally, it is not allowed in court. Recently, this amendment has been applied to evidence secured through wiretapping. This guarantees an individual's right to privacy. A person requesting a warrant has to furnish very specific information to legal authorities.

AMENDMENT 5.   Rights of Accused Persons (1791)

No person shall be held to answer for a capital or otherwise infamous crime unless on a presentment or indictment of a grand jury, except in cases arising in the land or naval forces, or in the militia, when in actual service in time of war or public danger; nor shall any person be subject for the same offense to be twice put in jeopardy of life or limb, nor shall be compelled in any criminal case to be a witness against himself, nor be deprived of life, liberty, or property without due process of law; nor shall private property be taken for public use without just compensation.

This amendment protects the rights of those who

have been accused of some crime. A capital crime is one punishable by death. An infamous crime is punishable by death or imprisonment. A grand jury is a special group of people selected to decide whether there is enough evidence against a person to hold a trial. A person cannot be tried for the same offense by the same government twice. A person cannot be forced to say anything in a federal court that will incriminate him or her.

The federal government cannot take a person's life, freedom, or property except by due process of the law. The Fourteenth Amendment applies this law to the states, too.

The government cannot take private property for public use without fair payment. The government's right to take property for public use is called eminent domain. This land is usually used for public facilities such as parks, playgrounds, schools, highways, or government buildings.

AMENDMENT 6.   Right to a Speedy, Public Trial (1791)

In all criminal prosecutions, the accused shall enjoy the right to a speedy and public trial, by an impartial jury of the state and district wherein the crime shall have been committed, which district shall have been previously ascertained by law, and to be informed of the nature and cause of the accusation; to be confronted with the witness against him; to have compulsory process for obtaining witnesses in his favor, and to have the assistance of counsel for his defense.

A person accused of a crime is entitled to a prompt public trial before an unbiased jury chosen from the district where the crime was committed. The accused must be told what he or she is accused of and must be present when witnesses testify against him or her. The accused has the right to have the court call witnesses in his or her favor and to have an attorney. If the accused cannot afford a lawyer, one will be appointed at government expense. (See Miranda case on pages 200–201.)

AMENDMENT 7.   Trial by Jury in Civil Cases (1791)

In suits at common law where the value in

controversy shall exceed twenty dollars, the right of trial by jury shall be preserved, and no fact tried by a jury shall be otherwise reexamined in any court of the United States than according to the rules of the common law.

Common law is unwritten law based on custom and use. Statute law is written law. Although trial by jury is guaranteed in cases involving more than twenty dollars, more is usually at stake before a case is heard in federal court.

AMENDMENT 8.   Limits of Fines and Punishments (1791)

Excessive bail shall not be required, nor excessive fines imposed, nor cruel and unusual punishment inflicted.

An accused person cannot be required to pay an unnecessarily large bail. Bail is the security given by the accused to guarantee his or her appearance for trial. What constitutes "cruel and unusual punishment" is still debated. In 1972, for example, the Supreme Court ruled in *Furman* v. *Georgia* that in some cases the death penalty violated the Eighth Amendment. However, in 1976 the Court said that capital punishment was "not unconstitutionally severe."

AMENDMENT 9.   Rights of People (1791)

The enumeration in the Constitution of certain rights shall not be construed to deny or disparage others retained by the people.

The people have many rights. Some are listed in the Constitution; others are not. This amendment reaffirms that the people remain the source of power.

AMENDMENT 10.   Powers of the States and People (1791)

The powers not delegated to the United States by the Constitution, nor prohibited by

it to the states, are reserved to the states
respectively, or to the people.

The United States has only the specific powers given to it by the Constitution. All other powers, unless they are specified denial to the states, belong to the states or to the people. The source of power of the federal government rests on what the states and people give to it.

Additional Amendments

AMENDMENT 11.   Lawsuits Against States
(1798)

The judicial power of the United States
shall not be construed to extend to any suit
in law or equity commenced or prosecuted
against one of the United States by citizens of
another state, or by citizens or subjects of
any foreign state.

Citizens of one state cannot sue another state in the federal courts. An individual, however, can sue state authorities in federal court for taking away his constitutional rights. This amendment changes part of Article III, Section 2, Clause 1.

AMENDMENT 12.   Election of Executives
(1804)

The electors shall meet in their respective
states, and vote by ballot for President and
Vice-President, one of whom, at least, shall
not be an inhabitant of the same state with
themselves; they shall name in their ballots
the person voted for as President, and in
district ballots the person voted for as
Vice-President, and they shall make distinct
lists of all persons voted for as President,
and of the number of votes for each, which
lists they shall sign and certify, and transmit,
sealed, to the seat of the government of the
United States, directed to the president of the
Senate; the president of the Senate shall, in
the presence of the Senate and House of
Representatives, open all the certificates, and
the votes shall then be counted. The person
having the greatest number of votes for
President shall be the President, if such
number be a majority of the whole number of
electors appointed; and if no person have
such a majority, then from the persons
having the highest numbers, not exceeding
three, on the list of those voted for as
President, the House of Representatives shall
choose immediately, by ballot, the President.
But in choosing the President, the votes shall
be taken by the states, the representation
from each state having one vote; a quorum
for this purpose shall consist of a member or
members from two-thirds of the states, and a
majority of all the states shall be necessary to
a choice. And if the House of Representatives
shall not choose a President, whenever the
right of choice shall devolve upon them,
before the fourth day of March next
following, then the Vice-President shall act
as President, as in case of the death or other
constitutional disability of the President. The
person having the greatest number of votes
as Vice-President shall be the Vice-President,
if such number be a majority of the whole
number of electors appointed, and if no
person have a majority, then, from the two
highest numbers on the list, the Senate shall
choose the Vice-President; a quorum for the
purpose shall consist of two-thirds of the
whole number of Senators, and a majority of
the whole number shall be necessary to a
choice. But no person constitutionally
ineligible to the office of President shall be
eligible to that of Vice-President of the
United States.

The Twelfth Amendment is designed to avoid the election problems experienced in 1796 and 1800 (see pages 221 and 225). It provides that members of the Electoral College (Electors) vote for one person as President and another as Vice-President.

In the event no presidential candidate receives a majority of votes, the House of Representatives is required to choose the President from the top three candidates. Each state has a single vote. In the event no vice-presidential candidate receives a majority of votes, the Senate must elect one from the top two candidates. The House has chosen two Presidents, Thomas Jefferson (1800) and John Q. Adams (1824).

The part crossed out was changed by Amendment 20 in 1933.

AMENDMENT 13.   Slavery Abolished (1865)

Section 1. *Neither slavery nor involuntary servitude, except as a punishment for crime whereof the party shall have been duly convicted, shall exist within the United States or any place subject to their jurisdiction.*
Section 2. *Congress shall have the power to enforce this article by appropriate legislation.*

Since all slaves were not free at the end of the Civil War, this amendment was necessary to abolish slavery in the United States. This Amendment also guarantees that no one can be forced to work against his or her will except as punishment for a crime.

Congress can pass whatever laws are necessary to enforce this amendment.

AMENDMENT 14.   Civil Rights (1868)

Section 1. *All persons born or naturalized in the United States, and subject to the jurisdiction thereof, are citizens of the United States and of the state wherein they reside. No state shall make or enforce any law which shall abridge the privileges or immunities of citizens of the United States, nor shall any state deprive any person of life, liberty, or property without due process of law, nor deny to any person within its jurisdiction the equal protection of the laws.*

The first section defined citizenship, applied the definition to the former slaves, and prohibited states from limiting the immunity and rights of citizens as stated in the Constitution. Many Supreme Court rulings on civil rights have resulted from the statement that a state cannot deny anyone "equal protection of the laws." The Supreme Court outlawed segregation in public schools on the basis of this statement, saying everyone, regardless of race, must have an equal opportunity for education.

Section 2. *Representatives shall be apportioned among the several states according to their respective numbers, counting the whole number of persons in each state, excluding Indians not taxed. But when the right to vote at any election for the choice of electors for President and Vice-President of the United States, Representatives in Congress, the executive and judicial officers of a state, or the members of the legislature thereof, is denied to any of the male inhabitants of such state, being twenty-one years of age, and citizens of the United States, or in any way abridged, except for participation in rebellion, or other crime, the basis of representation therein shall be reduced in the proportion which the number of such male citizens shall bear to the whole number of male citizens twenty-one years of age in such state.*

The second section specifies how Representatives shall be distributed among the states. It cancelled the Three-Fifths Compromise of Article 1, Section 2. It was supposed to extend the right to vote to all twenty-one-year-old males, including the former slaves. The penalty for a state's refusing to comply with this section was to be reduction of that state's representation in Congress. This provision was never enforced.

Section 3. *No person shall be a Senator or Representative in Congress, or elector of President and Vice-President, or hold any office, civil or military, under the United States or under any state, who, having previously taken an oath as a member of Congress, or as an officer of the United States, or as a member of any state legislature, or as an executive or judicial officer of any state, to support the Constitution of the United States, shall have engaged in insurrection or rebellion against the same or given aid or comfort to the enemies thereof. But Congress may by a vote* of two-thirds of each house remove such disability.

Section 4. *The validity of the public debt of the United States, authorized by law, including debts incurred for payment of pensions and bounties for services in suppressing insurrection and rebellion, shall not be questioned. But neither the United States nor any state shall assume or pay any debt or obligation incurred in aid of insurrection or rebellion against the United States, or any claim for the loss of emancipation of any slave; but all such debts, obligations, and claims shall be held illegal and void.*

Section 5. *The Congress shall have power to enforce by appropriate legislation the provisions of this article.*

These sections were intended to punish Confederate leaders during the post-Civil War period. By 1898 all had been pardoned and had returned to political life.

The Union debt for the Civil War was paid, while the Confederate debt was declared void. No one was paid for loss of slaves.

AMENDMENT 15. Right to Vote (1870)

Section 1. *The right of the citizens of the United States to vote shall not be denied or abridged by the United States or by any state on account of race, color, or previous condition of servitude.*

Section 2. *The Congress shall have power to enforce this article by appropriate legislature.*

This amendment attempted to insure black males the right to vote. But blacks were often kept from the polls, and further federal action was needed.

AMENDMENT 16. Income Tax (1913)

The Congress shall have power to lay and collect taxes on incomes, from whatever source derived, without apportionment among the several states, and without regard to any census or enumeration.

Congress can pass and collect income taxes. These taxes do not have to be divided among the states according to the population. Today income taxes are the federal government's greatest source of revenue. This amendment changes Article 1, Section 9, Clause 4 of the Constitution.

AMENDMENT 17. Direct Election of Senators (1913)

Clause 1. *The Senate of the United States shall be composed of two Senators from each state, elected by the people thereof, for six years; and each Senator shall have one vote. The electors in each state shall have the qualifications requisite for electors of the most numerous branch of the state legislatures.*

Clause 2. *When vacancies happen in the representation of any state in the Senate, the executive authority of such state shall issue writs of election to fill such vacancies: Provided that the legislature of any state may empower the executive thereof to make temporary appointments until the people fill the vacancies by election as the legislature may direct.*

Clause 3. *This amendment shall not be so construed as to affect the election or term of any Senator chosen before it becomes valid as part of the Constitution.*

The Seventeenth Amendment changed Article 1, Section 3, Clause 1. By providing for their direct election, this amendment persuaded Senators to become more responsible to the voters of their state.

AMENDMENT 18. Prohibition (1919)

~~**Section 1.** *After one year from the ratification of this article the manufacture, sale, or transportation of intoxicating liquors within, the importation thereof into, or the exportation thereof into from the United States and all territory subject to the jurisdiction thereof for beverage purposes is hereby prohibited.*~~

~~**Section 2.** *The Congress and the several states shall have concurrent power to enforce*~~

this article by appropriate legislation.
    ~~Section 3. This article shall be inoperative unless it shall have been ratified as an amendment to the Constitution by the legislatures of the several states, as provided in the Constitution, within seven years from the date of the submission hereof to the states by the Congress.~~

This amendment which banned people from making, selling, or transporting liquor was later repealed by the Twenty-First Amendment.

AMENDMENT 19. Women's Suffrage (1920)

Clause 1. *The right of citizens of the United States to vote shall not be denied or abridged by the United States or by any state on account of sex.*
    Clause 2. *Congress shall have the power to enforce this article by appropriate legislation.*

For more than forty years, amendment after amendment regarding women's right to vote had been introduced in Congress. Suffrage was finally extended to women in 1920.

AMENDMENT 20. "Lame Duck" Sessions (1933)

Section 1. *The terms of the President and Vice-President shall end at noon on the twentieth day of January, and the terms of Senators and Representatives at noon on the third day of January, of the years in which terms would have ended if this article had not been ratified; and the terms of their successors shall then begin.*

This amendment provides for the efficient transfer of power among elected officials. Originally, a defeated official would continue in office for several months before the replacement was installed. This situation was compared to that of a "lame duck" whose wings were clipped. Usually very little was accomplished during these months.

The terms of President and Vice-President end on January 20 instead of March 4, and the terms of the Senators and Representatives end on January 3 of the same year they ended prior to this amendment. All successors begin their jobs at that time.

Section 2. *The Congress shall assemble at least once in every year, and such meetings shall begin at noon on the third day of January unless they shall by law appoint a different day.*

Congress must meet once every year beginning on January 3 at noon unless another date is established by law. This amendment changes Article 1, Section 4, Clause 2.

Section 3. *If, at the time fixed for the beginning of the term of the President, the President-elect shall have died, the Vice-President-elect shall become President. If a President shall not have been chosen before the time fixed for the beginning of his term, or if the President-elect shall have failed to qualify, then the Vice-President-elect shall act as President until a President shall have qualified; and the Congress may by law provide for the case wherein neither a President-elect nor a Vice-President-elect shall have qualified, declaring who shall then act as President, or the manner in which one who is to act shall be selected, and such person shall act accordingly until a President or Vice-President shall have qualified.*

This section describes the succession to the presidency if the President-elect should die before taking office on January 20. If the Vice-President-elect is unavailable, Congress must temporarily fill the office of President.

Section 4. *The Congress may by law provide for the case of the death of any of the persons from whom the House of*

Representatives may choose a President whenever the right of choice shall have devolved upon them, and for the case of the death of any of the persons from whom the Senate may choose a Vice-President whenever the right of choice shall have devolved upon them.

Section 5. *Sections 1 and 2 shall take effect on the fifteenth day of October following the ratification of this article.*

Section 6. *This article shall be inoperative unless it shall have been ratified as an amendment to the Constitution by the legislatures of three-fourths of the several states within seven years from the date of its submission.*

If a candidate dies while his or her name is on a list from which the House of Representatives or Senate must choose a President or Vice-President, Congress then decides the proper procedure for the House and Senate to follow.

Sections 1 and 2 of this amendment became law on October 15 after three-fourths of the states ratified this amendment.

AMENDMENT 21.   Repeal of Prohibition (1933)

Section 1. *The eighteenth article of amendment to the Constitution of the United States is hereby repealed.*

Section 2. *The transportation or importation into any state, territory, or possession of the United States for delivery or use therein of intoxicating liquors, in violation of the laws thereof, is hereby prohibited.*

Section 3. *This article shall be inoperative unless it shall have been ratified as an amendment to the Constitution by conversion in the several states, as provided in the Constitution, within seven years from the date of submission thereof to the states by the Congress.*

In view of widespread violations of prohibition, there was a growing fear that disrespect for this one law would breed disrespect for all laws. This amendment repealed the Eighteenth Amendment.

This is the only amendment that has ever been ratified through special state conventions.

AMENDMENT 22.   Limit on Presidential Terms (1951)

Section 1. *No person shall be elected to the office of the President more than twice, and no person who has held the office of President, or acted as President, for more than two years of a term to which some other person was elected President shall be elected to the office of President more than once. But this Article shall not apply to any person holding the office of President when this Article was proposed by the Congress, and shall not prevent any person who may be holding the office of President, or acting as President, during the term within which this Article becomes operative from holding the office of President, or acting as President during the remainder of such terms.*

Ever since George Washington served as President of the United States for two terms, a tradition limiting a President to two terms was established. The elections of Franklin Roosevelt in 1940 and 1944 broke the two-term tradition. This amendment gives that tradition the force of law. The obsolete portions were written so as not to apply to President Truman, who was in office at the time of ratification.

AMENDMENT 23.   Voting in District of Columbia (1961)

Section 1. *The District constituting the seat of Government of the United States shall appoint in such manner as the Congress may direct:*

A number of electors of President and Vice-President equal to the whole number of Senators and Representatives in Congress to which the District would be entitled if it were a state, but in no event more than the least populous state; they shall be in addition to those appointed by the states, but they shall be considered, for the purposes of the election of President and Vice-President, to be electors appointed by a state; and they shall meet in the District and perform such duties as provided by the twelfth article of amendment.

Section 2. *The Congress shall have the power to enforce this article by appropriate legislation.*

The District of Columbia has the right to participate in the election of the President and Vice-President of the United States. It has three electoral votes—the same number of votes as the state with the smallest population.

This amendment did not provide representation in Congress or a system of home rule municipal government for the district.

AMENDMENT 24. Abolition of Poll Taxes (1964)

Section 1. *The right of citizens of the United States to vote in any primary or other election for President or Vice-President, for electors for President or Vice-President, or for Senator or Representative in Congress, shall not be denied or abridged by the United States or any state by reason of failure to pay any poll or other tax.*

Section 2. *The Congress shall have power to enforce this article by appropriate legislation.*

Poll taxes in federal elections are prohibited. Previously, some southern states had used a poll tax as a way to prevent blacks from voting.

AMENDMENT 25. Presidential Disability, Succession (1967)

Section 1. *In case of the removal of the President from office or his death or resignation, the Vice-President shall become President.*

This amendment resulted from President Dwight Eisenhower's serious illness while in office. It clarifies Article 2, Section 1, Clause 6 regarding a President's disability. Its purpose was to avoid: (1) a lapse in the functioning of the presidency if the elected President was not able to perform his job; and (2) a situation in which the President's personal advisers might take over without legal authority.

In 1973, when Vice-President Spiro Agnew resigned, President Richard Nixon nominated Republican Representative Gerald R. Ford to take his place. Upon Nixon's resignation, Ford became President. President Ford then appointed Nelson Rockefeller as Vice-President. Mr. Rockefeller's appointment was confirmed by a vote of Congress.

Section 2. *Whenever there is a vacancy in the office of the Vice-President, the President shall nominate a Vice-President who shall take the office upon confirmation by a majority vote of both houses of Congress.*

Section 3. *Whenever the President transmits to the president pro tempore of the Senate and the speaker of the House of Representatives his written declaration that he is unable to discharge the powers and duties of his office, and until he transmits to them a written declaration to the contrary, such powers and duties shall be discharged by the Vice-President as Acting President.*

Section 4. *Whenever the Vice-President and a majority of either the principal officers of the executive departments, or of such other body as Congress may by law provide, transmit to the president pro tempore of the Senate and the speaker of the House of Representatives their written declaration that the President is unable to discharge the powers and duties of his office, the Vice-President shall immediately assume the powers and duties of the office as Acting President.*

Thereafter, when the President transmits to the president pro tempore of the Senate and the speaker of the House of Representatives his written declaration that no inability exists, he shall resume the powers and duties of his office unless the Vice-President and a majority of either the principal officers of the executive department, or of such other body as Congress may by law provide, transmit within four days to the president pro tempore of the Senate and the speaker of the House of Representatives their written declaration that the President is unable to discharge the powers and duties of his office. Thereupon Congress shall decide the issue, assembling within 48 hours for that purpose if not in session. If the Congress, within 21 days after receipt of the latter written declaration, or if Congress is not in session, within 21 days after Congress is required to assemble, determines by two-thirds vote of both houses that the President is unable to discharge the powers and duties of his office, the Vice-President shall continue to discharge the same as Acting President; otherwise, the President shall resume the powers and duties of his office.

This amendment further clarifies Article 2, Section 1, Clause 5, regarding the issue of presidential succession when there is a vacancy in the presidency. It also establishes a procedure for filling a vacancy in the office of Vice President. In addition, the amendment outlines a process and procedures to follow in the event that the President is incapacitated and incapable of "discharg[ing] the powers and duties" of his or her office.

AMENDMENT 26.   Eighteen-year-old Vote (1971)

Section 1.   *The right of citizens of the United States, who are eighteen years of age or older, to vote, shall not be denied or abridged by the United States or any state on account of age.*
Section 2.   *The Congress shall have the power to enforce this article by appropriate legislation.*

This amendment gives eighteen-year-olds the right to vote.

AMENDMENT 27.   Congressional Pay (1992)

No law, varying the compensation for the services of the Senators and Representatives, shall take effect, until an election of Representatives shall have intervened.

This amendment basically gives voters an opportunity to register their opinion about a congressional pay raise *before* the raise takes place.

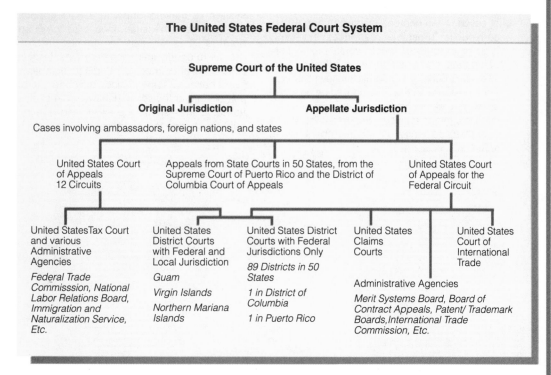

The United States Federal Court System

Supreme Court of the United States

Original Jurisdiction   **Appellate Jurisdiction**

Cases involving ambassadors, foreign nations, and states

| United States Court of Appeals 12 Circuits | Appeals from State Courts in 50 States, from the Supreme Court of Puerto Rico and the District of Columbia Court of Appeals | United States Court of Appeals for the Federal Circuit |

United StatesTax Court and various Administrative Agencies

Federal Trade Commisssion, National Labor Relations Board, Immigration and Naturalization Service, Etc.

United States District Courts with Federal and Local Jurisdiction

Guam

Virgin Islands

Northern Mariana Islands

United States District Courts with Federal Jurisdictions Only

89 Districts in 50 States

1 in District of Columbia

1 in Puerto Rico

United States Claims Courts

Administrative Agencies

Merit Systems Board, Board of Contract Appeals, Patent/ Trademark Boards,International Trade Commission, Etc.

United States Court of International Trade

Global Perspectives

1807	Britain abolishes slave trade
1833	Britain abolishes slavery in the British Empire
1848	France abolishes slavery in the West Indies
1888	Brazil abolishes slavery
1910	China abolishes slavery
1914	First World War begins
1939	Second World War begins
1940s	Germany enslaves prisoners in forced labor camps

For Discussion

Ask students to define slavery. (Answer: condition in which a person is owned by another; a slave is legally considered the property of another and deprived of rights and freedom.) Why are legal measures necessary to end slavery? (Possible response: the tendency to enslave others is a part of the human condition and so specific legal remedies are required to abolish slavery.)

Additional Resources

- Geography Activities
- Skills Activities
- Thematic Activities
- Economic Activities
- Cultural Literacy Activities
- Literary Source Readings
- Primary Source Readings
- Nuclear Peacekeeping
- Transparencies
- Computer Test Generator

Additional Teaching Strategies

SECTION 1

For Basic Students: Ask students to find the names and mailing addresses of their United States senators and their representatives in the House. (Students might find such information in the public library.) If possible, ask a representative from one of these offices to visit your class and discuss his or her job.

For Advanced Students: Have students acquire a copy of the *Congressional Record* for one day. (Copies are available through a member of your Congressional delegation. Students might check with the local public library.) Ask each group to read and prepare a brief oral presentation on the day's proceedings, the legislation debated and/or voted on, and any other important business transacted.

SECTION 2

For Basic Students: Have the students work in pairs to present a two-minute oral report on the workings of one of the units of the Executive Office (see chart on page 166.) (Reports might include: Central Intelligence Agency—created in 1947; responsible for coordinating the foreign intelligence activities of the various government departments and agencies; headed by the director of central intelligence, who is appointed by the President and confirmed by the Senate; the director is the principal advisor to the President on all matters of intelligence related to specific foreign situations affecting foreign intelligence activities.)

For Advanced Students: Organize students into two groups to research and debate the following statement: Because the President's job has now grown so complex and the pressures are so considerable, the position of President should be replaced with an executive council of seven to ten persons elected by the American public. (Possible responses: For—this type of executive branch would prove more democratic and less subject to influence from interest groups; it would also relieve the constant pressure on the President to be on top of all matters all the time. Against—too many executives might result in important decisions being stalled while all the members try to reach an agreement.)

SECTION 3

For Basic Students: Have students work together to prepare a large wall chart listing the various departments in the President's cabinet, the year each was established, the current head of each department, and some current newspaper or magazine articles about the departments. (Students might check with school libraries and the local public libraries for the information. Current articles might be found by referring to the *Readers' Guide to Periodical Literature*.)

For Advanced Students: Ask students to create a political cartoon supporting or opposing the size of the current federal bureaucracy.

SECTION 4

For Basic Students: Have each student research and report on one or more of the current Supreme Court justices. Have them use this information to prepare a chart for the class showing the makeup of the Court. (Reports might include: Warren Earl Burger—born 1907 in St. Paul, Minnesota; graduated from law school in 1931; practiced private law, both criminal and civil; taught law for twenty-two years; joined Department of Justice of the United States in 1953; was appointed to United States Court of Appeals for the District of Columbia in 1965 by President Eisenhower; was appointed to succeed Earl Warren as Chief Justice of the United States by President Nixon in 1969.)

For Advanced Students: Ask students to prepare a two-page paper discussing why justices are appointed for life. Ask them to suggest alternatives for the process of making Supreme Court appointments and to identify the advantages and disadvantages of the current system. (Essays might include: the current system of making Supreme Court appointments is good because once a justice is appointed, it is difficult for outside interest groups to unduly influence decisions; justices should be appointed for a limited number of years because some justices may begin to be complacent or too set in their ways; direct election of judges should be allowed to give the public a chance to vote on candidates.)

Further Reading for Students

Nonfiction

Ball, Howard. *Courts and Politics: The Federal Judicial System*. Englewood Cliffs, N. J.: Prentice-Hall, 1980.

Corwin, Edward S. *Presidential Power and the Constitution*. Edited by Richard Loss. Ithaca, N. Y.: Cornell University Press, 1976.

Fisher, Louise. *President and Congress*. New York: Free Press, 1972.

FitzGerald, John L. *Congress and the Separation of Powers*. New York: Praeger Publishing, 1985.

Glass, Susan, ed. *Insight and Action: Guide to the Executive Branch*. New Brunswick, N. J.: Transaction Books, 1976.

Harris, Fred R. and Paul L. Hain. *America's Legislative Processes*. Glenview, Ill.: Scott, Foresman, 1983.

Polsby, Nelson W. *Congress and the Presidency*. 4th ed. Englewood Cliffs, N. J.: Prentice-Hall, 1986.

Shane, Peter, and Harold Bruff. *The Law of Presidential Power*. Durham, N. C.: Carolina Academic Press, 1988.

Bibliography for Teachers

Books

Bailey, Harry, and Jay Shafritz. *The American Presidency: Historical and Contemporary Perspectives*. Dorsey, Chicago: 1987.

Barger, Harold M. *The Impossible Presidency: Illusions and Realities of Executive Power*. Glenview, Ill.: Scott, Foresman, 1984.

Buchanan, Bruce. *The Citizen's Presidency*. Congressional Quarterly Press Staff, ed. Washington, D.C.: Congressional Quarterly, 1987.

Corwin, Edward S. *The President: Office and Powers*. 5th ed. Edited by Randall W. Bland et al. New York: New York University Press, 1984.

Frantz, Albert T. *How Courts Decide*. Buffalo, N. Y.: William S. Hein and Co., Inc., 1968.

Goehlert, Robert U. and Fenton S. Martin. *The Presidency: A Research Guide*. Santa Barbara, Calif.: ABC-Clio, 1985.

Harris, Robert J. *The Judicial Power of the United States*. Ann Arbor: Books on Demand, Division of University Microfilm International, No. 40.

Livingston, William S., et al., eds. *The Presidency and the Congress: A Shifting Balance of Power?* Austin, Tex.: LBJ School of Public Affairs, 1979.

McDowell, Gary L. *Curbing the Courts: The Constitution and the Limits of Judicial Power*. Baton Rouge: Louisiana State University Press, 1988.

McWhinney, E.J. *Supreme Courts and Judicial Lawmaking: Constitutional Tribunals and Constitutional Review*. Norwell, Maine: Kluwer Academic Press, 1986.

Mendelson, Wallace. *American Constitution and the Judicial Process*. Dorsey, Chicago: 1980.

Rossiter, Clinton. *The Supreme Court and the Commander in Chief*. Edited by Richard P. Longaker. Ithaca, N. Y.: Cornell University Press, 1976.

Schwartz, Bernard. *The Powers of Government Volume I Federal and State Powers*. New York: Macmillan, 1968.

Schwartz, Bernard. *The Powers of Government Volume II The Powers of the President*. New York: Macmillan, 1968.

Audio-Visuals

The American Experience in Democracy. Society for Visual Education. Filmstrip.

Congress: How It Works, Doesn't Work. Opportunities for Learning. Filmstrip.

Constitutional Law in Action. Opportunities for Learning. Filmstrip.

Documents of Democracy. Society for Visual Education. Filmstrip.

The Election Process. Prentice-Hall Media. Filmstrip.

The Federal System: Checks and Balances. Prentice-Hall Media. Filmstrip.

Founding the Republic: Framing the Constitution. Encyclopaedia Britannica Educational Corp. Filmstrip.

Fundamental Freedoms. Opportunities for Learning. Filmstrip.

The House of Representatives, Voice of the People. Prentice-Hall Media. Filmstrip.

Our Constitutional Rights. Social Studies School Service. Filmstrip.

The Presidency: Powers and Personalities. Prentice-Hall Media. Filmstrip.

The Scales of Justice: Our Court System. Opportunities for Learning. Filmstrip.

The Supreme Court. The New York Times, Education Enrichment Materials. Filmstrip.

Supreme Court Cases. Educational Audio Visual. Filmstrip.

Understanding Our Government. Society for Visual Education. Filmstrip.

United States Government in Action. Opportunities for Learning. Filmstrip.

The United States Supreme Court. Prentice-Hall Media. Filmstrip.

Your Freedom & The First Amendment. Opportunities for Learning. Filmstrip.

Computer Resources

Congress. (Apple) Scholastic, Inc.

A Bill Becomes a Law. (Apple, IBM, Macintosh) Intellectual Software.

The Constitution and the Government of the United States. (Apple) Educational Activities.

U.S. Government. (Apple, IBM) Sliwa Enterprises.

Teacher's Notes:

Lesson Plan

Teaching Resources, Unit 2 Booklet

Lesson Study Sheets pp. 47-62
Daily Activities pp. 63-70
Enrichment Activities pp. 71-78
Reteaching Activities pp. 79-86
Chapter Review p. 87
Chapter Mastery Tests pp. 89-100
Telescoping the Times Study Sheet p. 101

Chapter Objectives

Students will learn:
- how our American democracy functions through the legislative branch
- how our American democracy functions through the executive branch
- why a democracy needs a bureaucracy to function effectively
- how our American democracy functions through the judicial branch

Using the Chapter Time Line

How many years passed between the passing of the Judiciary Act of 1789 and the precedent setting case of *Marbury* v. *Madison?* (Answer: 14) The Thirteenth Amendment, passed in 1865, freed the slaves. How many years passed before segregation in schools was abolished by *Brown* v. *Board of Education?* (Answer: 89)

Picturing History The Constitution provided a way in which the nation could respond to the changing needs of the American people. Congressman Claude Pepper, shown here, used the legislative process to introduce laws that would benefit older and disabled Americans.

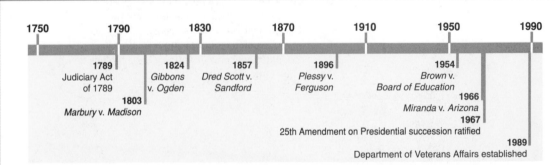

1750	1790	1830	1870	1910	1950	1990

1789
Judiciary Act
of 1789

1803
Marbury v. *Madison*

1824
Gibbons
v. *Ogden*

1857
Dred Scott v.
Sandford

1896
Plessy v.
Ferguson

1954
Brown v.
Board of Education

1966
Miranda v. *Arizona*

1967
25th Amendment on Presidential succession ratified

1989
Department of Veterans Affairs established

Links to American Literature

Harper Lee: born and raised in Alabama; attended college there; worked for a short time in New York City as an airline ticket agent; won the Pulitzer Prize in 1961 for *To Kill a Mockingbird*.

To Kill a Mockingbird: In a small southern town, a white lawyer defends a black man wrongly accused of raping a poor white woman; story is told by the lawyer's young daughter.

Introducing the Chapter

William E. Gladstone, the great English statesman of the nineteenth century, said that the United States Constitution "is the most wonderful work ever struck off by the brain and purpose of man." Remind students that this framework of government was drawn up when the population of America was approximately 4 million, mostly farmers, and yet this document still serves successfully as the fundamental framework of our government. Ask the students why this document is often called "our dynamic Constitution." (Possible responses: it has grown and expanded as the country has changed; it is simple and elastic in details and leaves room for growth.) Call students' attention to the fact that the government was designed with a number of checks and balances. Ask students why the framers of the Constitution might have been concerned about such a system. (Possible responses: they were concerned that one branch of the government might become too strong and try to take over the entire government; they feared that a President, if given too much power, would become like the monarchs of England.) As students read the chapter, ask them to keep a list of the various means of checks and balances that exist in the federal government.

CHAPTER 7 1787 to the Present

Focus on Democracy

Links to American Literature

"But there is one way in this country in which all men are created equal— there is one human institution that makes a pauper the equal of a Rockefeller, the stupid man the equal of an Einstein, and the ignorant man the equal of any college president. That institution, gentlemen, is a court. It can be the Supreme Court of the United States or the humblest J.P. court in the land, or this honorable court which you serve. Our courts have their faults, as does any human institution, but in this country our courts are the great levelers, and in our courts all men are created equal.

"I'm no idealist to believe firmly in the integrity of our courts and in the jury system—that is no ideal to me, it is a living, working reality. Gentlemen, a court is no better than each man of you sitting before me on this jury. A court is only as sound as its jury, and a jury is only as sound as the men who make it up. I am confident that you gentlemen will review without passion the evidence you have heard, come to a decision, and restore this defendant to his family. In the name of God, do your duty."

Atticus's voice had dropped, and he turned away from the jury.

— HARPER LEE, *To Kill a Mockingbird*

All people are indeed equal before the Supreme Court. Yet the Court is only one of three branches of government that the Constitution established to protect the rights of Americans. Never before in history had a government been established on a national scale consisting of a legislative, executive, and judicial branch to provide for checks and balances. Never before in history had a national government been established whose power came *from* the people. These are features that have kept the Constitution a living document that has remained central to our American democracy for over two hundred years.

Chapter Overview

Unlike other chapters, this one spans over two hundred years rather than just a few years in American history. In this chapter you will learn how our American democracy has functioned and continues to function through the legislative, executive, and judicial branches of government. More specifically, you will learn how the legislative branch enacts the laws, how the executive branch enforces the laws with the help of a complex bureaucracy, and how the judicial branch interprets the laws. To cover these objectives, Chapter 7 is divided into four sections.

Chapter Outline

1. **The Legislative Branch Enacts Laws**
2. **The Executive Branch Enforces Laws**
3. **The Bureaucracy Is Highly Complex**
4. **The Judicial Branch Interprets Laws**

Anticipate the Lesson

Ask students to define democracy. (Possible responses: a government in which all the people are allowed to have a voice, a government in which the people determine the rules and laws.) Ask students whether they believe that the United States is a true democracy. (Possible responses: it is a democracy because all people have the right to voice their opinion; it is not a true democracy because all Americans do not directly vote on laws.) Do all citizens have the right to vote? (Answer: all those over the age of eighteen whose voting right has not been revoked.) Do all citizens have the chance to voice their opinion or participate in debates before a bill becomes a law? (Answer: no.) How then do we make our views known? How do we get laws enacted: (Possible responses: we elect people at the local, state, and national levels, including members of Congress and senators; we sign and send petitions to Congress.)

State the Objective

Understand how our American democracy functions through the legislative branch.

SECTION 1

The Legislative Branch Enacts Laws

GLOSSARY TERMS: **democracy, legislative branch, expressed powers, necessary and proper clause, implied powers, nonlegislative powers**

As you know, our government is a **democracy** in which the people rule indirectly through elected representatives. The framework for our government is the United States Constitution, the supreme law of the land. The Constitution established three branches of government that provide checks and balances for one another.

Under our system of checks and balances, the **legislative branch** enacts laws. The legislative branch—usually called Congress—is composed of two bodies, the Senate and the House of Representatives.

The House of Representatives has 435 members, all of whom serve two-year terms. Each member represents a district, and each district has about the same number of constituents. Seats in the House are divided among the states such that states with small populations have fewer representatives and larger states have more. According to the Constitution, each state must have at least one representative.

The Senate has one hundred members, two from each state. Senators are elected for six-year terms. Senate seats are divided into three "classes," so that approximately a third of the senators are elected every two years.

Committees Serve as the Backbone of Congress

The chart on page 186 shows how a bill becomes a law. Though bills are introduced by individual members of Congress and ultimately voted on by individual members, their success or failure depends on **congressional committees.** The committee system has been called the backbone of Congress. Each year over five thousand bills are introduced. Congress could not possibly deal with all of these bills if the full House and Senate had to consider every one of them. The committee system enables Congress to function effectively by dividing the work.

Types of Committees.   There are twenty-two permanent standing committees in the House and another sixteen permanent standing committees in the Senate, along with a smaller number of select committees established for a limited time, usually to consider a single pressing problem. These congressional committees deal with the major operations of government, from agriculture to veterans' affairs.

People in the Chapter

Lewis Powell, Jr., served on the Supreme Court from 1972 to 1987. Although he usually took a conservative viewpoint, he did cast the decisive vote in two cases considered liberal victories. In one case he voted in favor of affirmative-action programs, and in the other case he voted in favor of a woman's right to have an abortion.

John Marshall grew up in a politically active family and it seems he set goals for himself early in life. After declining several cabinet positions, he agreed to serve as Secretary of State under John Adams. He then accepted Adams's nomination as Chief Justice of the Supreme Court, a position he held for thirty-four years.

Dred Scott had lived with his master on free soil for five years. Yet he was not allowed to sue for his freedom even though his owner initiated the case. The Supreme Court ruled that Scott was still a slave and not a citizen. Therefore, the rights of citizens did not apply to him. The decision hastened the coming of the Civil War.

Oliver Wendell Holmes, Jr., served on the Supreme Court for thirty years and retired in 1932 at the age of ninety. Known for his dissenting opinions, he argued for "free trade in ideas" and denounced wiretapping as "dirty business." His father wrote the famous poem "Old Ironsides" in protest against the destruction of the frigate Constitution.

Present the Lesson

After they read the section, ask students to work in pairs to prepare an outline of important information about the functioning of the legislative branch of the government. Outlines might include:

The legislative branch enacts laws.
I. Committees serve as the backbone of Congress.
    A. Types of committees
       1. 22 permanent committees in House
       2. 16 permanent committees in Senate
       3. Select committees formed for limited time to consider pressing problems

B. Function and organization of committees
    1. Subcommittees do initial work of scrutinizing and amending bill.
    2. After passed by the subcommittee, the bill then goes to the full committee of the Senate for approval.
    3. After passing the full committee, it continues to the Senate for a vote.
    4. After passing the Senate, it goes to the Rules Committee of the House to determine if it will get to the floor.
    5. Bill must be approved by the full Senate and the full House.

II. The Congress uses a vast support system.
    A. Congressional personnel includes employees of the Government Printing Office and Library of Congress.
    B. Office staff of senators and members of Congress
       1. Work in member's home district, taking care of concerns of constituents
       2. Help to draft bills, serve as conduit of information to and from senator or representative
    C. Staff of Congressional Committee
       1. Advise members on substance of bills

Function and Organization of Committees.

Most of the committees are divided into smaller subcommittees. Each subcommittee is composed of members particularly knowledgeable in one area. Before a subcommittee analyzes or amends a bill, it does the initial work of consolidating similar bills and deciding which bills it will or will not act on. If a subcommittee (or committee) decides that a bill deserves further attention, it will hold hearings and invite government agencies, experts, lobbyists, and the public to comment. Then the bill goes to a markup session, in which committee members pencil in, or mark up, changes they wish to make.

If the bill is passed by the subcommittee, it goes back to the full committee in the house in which it was introduced. In the Senate, if the full committee approves the bill, it will go to the Senate floor for a vote. In the House, the bill will usually go from the full committee to another committee—the Rules Committee—which will determine whether it will get to the House floor.

Finally, after each house approves its own version of the bill, the two versions will go to yet another committee, a special conference committee composed of members of each house. This committee will reach a compromise on the bill and agree on how it is to be worded. The final version is then submitted to the full House and the full Senate for approval.

Congress Uses a Vast Support System

As government has grown and problems have become more complex, the congressional support staff has mushroomed. From 1965 to 1984, the number of employees in the legislative branch grew by 50 percent, from twenty-six thousand to nearly forty thousand. Though the workers of the Government Printing Office and the Library of Congress count as legislative-branch employees, the most important (and most visible) employees of Congress are the members of the office staffs of senators and representatives and of the staffs of congressional committees.

Employees on the personal staffs of senators and representatives may serve in the congressional member's home district, taking care of the concerns of constituents caught up in government red tape. Or they may work in Washington, researching legislative issues, helping to draft laws, or providing information to the senator or representative or from him or her to the press and the public.

Picturing History Consumer advocate Ralph Nader testifies before a congressional committee.

The employees serving on congressional staffs are often experts who advise the members on the substance of bills, schedule witnesses before committees, and do research. They also develop strategies for getting legislation passed.

Congressional Powers Are Extensive

The framers of the Constitution put Congress first. In Article I, by far the longest article in the Constitution, they spelled out the powers of Congress. Congress, more than any other institution of government, was to be the people's voice.

Expressed Powers. Article I grants many powers to Congress in expressed, or explicit, terms. Some of the more important **expressed powers** are the following:
1. To collect taxes to raise revenue
2. To impose tariffs on goods shipped to the United States, and to institute excise taxes on the manufacture or sale of specific items like gasoline and liquor
3. To borrow money by selling government securities—bonds, treasury certificates, and treasury notes
4. To regulate commerce with foreign nations and among the states
5. To coin money and punish counterfeiting
6. To establish post offices
7. To establish lower federal courts and the number of justices on the Supreme Court
8. To declare war and to raise and support the armed forces (which in practice has led to sweeping powers, especially in wartime, when Congress has established a draft, set price ceilings, rationed goods, and set up special agencies like the Atomic Energy Commission)

For Discussion

Some individuals have served in Congress past the age of ninety. Should there be a mandatory retirement age? Why or why not? If so, what age would you suggest? (Possible responses: yes—there should be a mandatory retirement age of seventy so that young politicians have a chance to begin a career in politics; members of Congress beyond this age may become complacent in their position and may not be as well in tune with their constituents as they should be. No—there should be no mandatory retirement age because age has no bearing on a person's ability to serve his or her country; age brings with it a certain degree of wisdom.)

2. Schedule witnesses before committees
3. Do research
4. Develop strategies for getting legislation passed

III. Congressional powers are extensive
   A. Expressed powers
      1. Raise revenue
      2. Impose tariffs
      3. Borrow money by selling bonds, and so forth
      4. Regulate commerce
      5. Coin money
      6. Establish post offices and roads
      7. Establish and abolish federal courts
      8. Declare war and raise and support the armed forces
   B. Implied powers
      1. Authority to make legislation adequate to the needs of the nation
      2. Necessary and proper clause
   C. Nonlegislative powers
      1. Decennial census
      2. Power of impeachment

IV. Many interest groups influence lawmakers.
   A. Economic groups
   B. Human rights groups
   C. Public interest groups
   D. Single-issue groups

V. Lawmakers must keep in touch with constituents.
   A. Work with constituents
      1. Maintain offices in home district
      2. Return to home districts regularly
      3. Gauge public sentiment through calls and mail
   B. Work with districts and states
      1. Keep in mind the particular needs and interests of their district or state
      2. Work with important interest groups in area, with state and local officials, and with industries
   C. Work with political parties

Implied Powers. Even though Article I is long, it does not cover every possible role for Congress. No constitution could possibly foresee every circumstance in which a legislature would be likely to act. This is why our nation's courts have interpreted certain expressed powers of Congress—to give Congress the authority to make laws adequate to the needs of a growing nation.

Knowing that the Constitution must be flexible, the framers added an important clause granting Congress unspecified but important powers. The clause gives Congress authority ''to make all laws which shall be necessary and proper for carrying into execution . . . all . . . powers vested by this Constitution.'' The **necessary and proper clause** gives Congress broad scope. For example, the expressed power to tax and spend for the general welfare has been interpreted by the courts in such a way as to enable Congress to spend tax money for school aid, social security, and aid to foreign nations. Because none of these powers were explicitly called for in the Constitution, they are called **implied powers.**

Nonlegislative Powers. Article I also gives Congress certain powers besides the authority to pass laws. These powers are called **nonlegislative powers.** The House has the sole power of impeachment, meaning that it may bring charges against the President, the Vice-President, or any federal judge or civil official of the federal government. The Senate then tries any impeachment with the Chief Justice presiding. In all impeachments, no person can be convicted without a two-thirds vote of the senators present.

Many Interest Groups Influence Lawmakers

The Constitution says not one word about interest groups, but in practice they have come to play a very important role in how Congress does its business. These groups maintain lobbyists in Washington to represent their interests. The lobbyists are both helpful and irritating to senators and representatives. They provide a source of expertise on matters within their area of interest. They sometimes propose model legislation or persuade a member to draft legislation. They testify before congressional committees. By mobilizing support for their proposals in the member's home district, they help educate the public—and they bring pressure on the members of the Congress.

Economic Interest Groups. These groups are interested in a broad range of taxation and spending issues. The AFL-CIO represents the interests of millions of labor union members. The United

How a Bill Becomes a Law

1. Bill is Introduced	A bill can be introduced in either the House or the Senate, where it is then assigned to a committee for study.
2. Approved by Committee	Committee makes recommendation that the bill be placed on calendar.
3. Vote of House Members	Either house reads, debates, and votes on bill. If approved by majority, bill is passed and referred to the other house.
4. Passed by Other House	Committee reviews bill. Bill read, debated, and voted on by all members. Majority vote passes it.
5. Differences Worked Out	Joint Conference Committee works out differences in bill. Revised bill passes both houses.
6. Enrolled and Signed 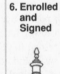	Bill is printed and verified. Vice-President signs bill and sends it to President.
7. Made a Law 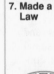	President signs bill, or holds it ten days without signing it, and it becomes a law.
8. Passed Over Veto 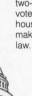	If President vetoes bill, two-thirds vote of both houses makes it a law.

Check for Understanding

Call on individual students to answer Section 1 Review questions orally.

Guided Practice

Tell students that, ideally, each individual citizen living under the government of a federal republic has an equal opportunity to affect the political process through voting. Ask students to consider whether there are any individuals or groups in our country who seem to have more power than others. (Possible responses: everyone has equal representation; powerful interest groups with a lot of money behind them seem to have greater control over the laws that are passed, so the individual is not always heard.)

Assign Independent Practice

Ask students to prepare a letter to their representative or senator stating their concerns for their district or state. They should also suggest ways to bring about improvements or ask the legislator what is currently being done at the federal level about the problems. (Letters might include: students' concerns about problems such as drugs, health care, education, or civil rights.) Ask students to go to the reference section of the public library to obtain the address for each legislator to whom the class has written and then to mail the letters.

"It's awful the way they're trying to influence Congress. Why don't they serve cocktails and make campaign contributions like we do?"

Picturing History In this cartoon, Herblock, one of America's most popular cartoonists, pokes fun at organized lobbying groups who try to buy influence in Congress through campaign contributions.

States Chamber of Commerce and the National Association of Manufacturers represent the interests of many business people. The American Association of Retired Persons, the largest membership group in the country, represents the interests of older people.

Human Rights Groups. The National Association for the Advancement of Colored People (NAACP), the Urban League, the Children's Defense Fund, La Raza, the Anti-Defamation League of B'nai B'rith, and many other groups have a particular interest in civil and human rights. Often, such groups are concerned not only with civil rights in this country but also with violations of human rights abroad.

Public Interest Groups. Groups like Common Cause and the League of Women Voters are concerned with improving political processes, eliminating corruption in government, and promoting fairness in elections. Public interest groups have broad goals that deal with a very wide spectrum of politics and government.

Single-Issue Groups. Groups like the National Rifle Association, Handgun Control, the National Abortion Rights Action League, and the National Right to Life Committee differ from public interest groups in that they are deeply concerned with one issue. On difficult, emotionally charged issues like abortion and gun control, these and other groups mobilize public support, raise funds, lobby members, and file briefs in court cases. In recent years, the number and importance of these groups has grown.

Lawmakers Must Keep in Touch with Constituents

The underlying theory of democracy is that elected officials represent the people. What does *represent* mean exactly? Should members of Congress poll their constituents on issues and vote exactly as the constituents wish? Or should they exercise independent judgment—"weigh the issues instead of the mail," in the words of former Senator Hugh Scott of Pennsylvania? In practice, they have to keep in touch with the people who sent them to Washington.

Working with Constituents. Members of Congress maintain offices in their home districts so that their staffs can help constituents who are dealing with the federal government. Congressional staffs are also useful in keeping members up to date on what people in their district are thinking.

Many members of Congress return to their districts almost weekly for meetings with constituents. They also gauge the sentiments of their constituents by paying attention to the phone calls, personal visits, and mail they receive.

Working with Districts and States. Each member of Congress represents a particular district or state. Though members' responsibilities are national in scope in that most of the laws they pass affect all Americans, they must keep in mind the particular needs and interests of their own congressional district or state. In the words of former

Anticipate the Lesson

Ask students what political figure comes to mind when they think of the executive branch of the government. (Answer: the President.) Ask students to recall times when they have seen the current President on television and explain the reason for the Presidential appearance. (Possible responses: Presidential news conference, Presidential speech, State of the Union Address, news-show clips of the Presi- dent meeting with officials from other nations, President meeting with outstanding citizens being honored at the White House.)

SECTION 1 REVIEW

Answers

Main Ideas

1. House of Representatives and Senate. • House— according to population; Senate—two senators from each state.

2. Subcommittees—conduct initial investigation of bill; de- cide whether bill should go to full committee. Standing committees—deal with major government operations; de- cide whether full Senate or House will consider bills. Se- lect committees—deal with pressing current issues; de- cide whether full Senate or House will consider bill. Rules Committee—decides whether House will vote on bill. Confer- ence committee—reaches compromise on content and language of House and Senate versions of bill.

3. Individuals who represent special interests. • Lobbyists provide expertise, propose model legislation, help draft legislation, testify before com- mittees, mobilize support and help educate public.

4. Represent constituents' in- terests; help constituents cut through federal red tape.

Critical Thinking

5. Possible responses: vote constituents' wishes— members elected to represent constituents. Vote own viewpoint—their information on issue is greater, so should vote what they believe is in constituents' best interests. **(analysis & evaluation)**

188

Speaker of the House **Thomas "Tip" O'Neill,** they can never forget that "all politics is local."

Working with Political Parties. Members of Congress also keep in close touch with their polit- ical party at home. They consult with the party chairperson, with other elected members of the party, and, usually, with large financial donors to the party.

In recent years, political parties have conducted polls, run seminars, and even distributed money to help elect members of Congress. The parties' role in campaigns remains limited, though, because candidates can and do raise funds directly from interest groups and some members of the public.

However, parties remain very important once members take their seats in Congress. The leaders of each house are elected by the parties. The majority party makes key committee appointments and controls the legislative agenda. The parties take positions on important bills, and party leaders encourage their members in Congress to vote on their side. The members vote along party lines about two-thirds of the time.

SECTION 1 REVIEW

Key Terms and People

Explain the significance of: democracy, legislative branch, congressional committees, expressed powers, necessary and proper clause, implied powers, nonlegislative powers, Thomas "Tip" O'Neill

Main Ideas

1. What two bodies make up Congress? How is their membership determined?
2. Explain the functions of subcommittees, stand- ing and select committees, the Rules Commit- tee, and the conference committee.
3. What is an interest group? How do lobbyists for interest groups aid senators and representatives?
4. What functions do lawmakers serve for their constituents?

Critical Thinking

5. When senators and representatives vote on a law, should they follow the known wishes of the majority of their constituents or, if they hold an opposing view, should their vote reflect their own viewpoint? Defend your answer.

SECTION 2

The Executive Branch Enforces Laws

GLOSSARY TERMS: **executive branch, cabinet**

Article II of the Constitution deals with the **executive branch** of government, which enforces laws and carries out policies. Article II is shorter than Article I because the framers assumed that the Presidency and the executive branch would be less central to the nation than the legislative branch. Over the years, the powers of the Presidency have grown dramatically. Now the President is consid- ered the leader of the entire nation, the head of state, and the chief of one of the nation's two major political parties.

The Constitution and Tradition Determine the President's Role

The growth in Presidential powers has not come about because of changes in the Constitution. Rather, the demands of the times—particularly with regard to welfare, national economic policy, and foreign policy—have added to the President's authority and responsibility.

Qualifications for the Presidency. The Consti- tution sets forth few qualifications for the Presi- dency. According to Article II, the President must be a natural-born citizen who has been a resident of the United States for at least fourteen years. He or she must be at least thirty-five years old. Over the years, the realities of American politics have im- posed a number of other informal qualifications— that Presidential candidates be of a certain age (generally between forty and seventy), have served in high political or military office, and have stature within one of the major political parties—but none of these qualifications is found in the Constitution.

Compensation. The Constitution provides that the President's salary shall be neither increased nor decreased during his or her term in office. While in office, the President shall not receive any other monies from the United States or any state.

Term of Office. Article II specifies that the President serve a four-year term. The first Presi- dent, **George Washington,** established the prece- dent that the President serve no more than two

State the Objective

Understand how our American democracy functions through the executive branch.

Presidential Succession*

Vice President	Party	Term of Office	Circumstances of Succession
John Tyler	Whig	1841 – 1845	death of William Harrison
Millard Fillmore	Whig	1850 – 1853	death of Zachary Taylor
Andrew Johnson	Republican	1865 – 1869	death of Abraham Lincoln
Chester A. Arthur	Republican	1881 – 1885	death of James A. Garfield
Theodore Roosevelt	Republican	1901 – 1909	death of William McKinley
Calvin Coolidge	Republican	1923 – 1929	death of Warren G. Harding
Harry S Truman	Democratic	1945 – 1953	death of Franklin Roosevelt
Lyndon B. Johnson	Democratic	1963 – 1969	death of John F. Kennedy
Gerald R. Ford	Republican	1974 – 1977	resignation of Richard Nixon

* These nine Vice-Presidents became President through the application of Article 2, Section 1 of the Constitution.

terms. This precedent was broken in the 1930's through 1940's with the election of President **Franklin D. Roosevelt** to four terms. Then in 1951, the Twenty-second Amendment made the informal two-term limit a part of the Constitution.

Succession and the Vice-President. Article II provides that Vice-Presidents shall be elected for four-year terms. The Vice-President is given only one immediate responsibility in the Constitution— to preside over the Senate and cast the deciding vote in case of ties.

The Vice-President plays an important role if the President dies, is removed from office, or becomes incapacitated, for then the Vice-President becomes President. Nine Vice-Presidents have succeeded to the Presidency. Eight became President because the President they served under died in office.

Linking Past to Present

Lyndon Johnson is a recent example of a Vice-President who succeeded to the Presidency after the assassination of a President. The most recent Vice-President to become President was Gerald Ford, who took over the nation's highest office when President Richard M. Nixon resigned in 1974.

Article II gives Congress authority to enact legislation specifying who shall become President in the event that both the President and the Vice-President are unable to serve. Over the years, Congress has passed several laws that deal with this problem. Under the current law, the Speaker of the House of Representatives is next in line after the Vice-President, followed by the president pro tempore of the Senate and then by cabinet officers beginning with the Secretary of State. None of these officials has ever succeeded to the Presidency. In the past there has always been a Vice-President in office when a President either died or resigned.

Picturing History   The order of succession through much of the 1980's: President Ronald Reagan (front); Vice-President George Bush; and Speaker of the House Thomas "Tip" O'Neill.

Present the Lesson

Prepare a chart on the board titled The Executive Branch. Divide the chart into two columns—Presidential Qualifications and Presidential Powers. Ask students to provide information from this section to complete the chart. Chart might include:

Presidential Qualifications

- Natural-born citizen
- Resident of the United States at least fourteen years
- Thirty-five years of age or older

Presidential Powers

- Is commander in chief of the armed forces
- Makes treaties (with consent of Congress), appoints ambassadors, meets with heads of state
- Appoints Supreme Court justices
- Takes care that the law is faithfully executed

Check for Understanding

Call on individual students to read their answers to Section 2 Review questions.

For Discussion

Is a President of the United States responsible for all actions of his assistants and representatives? (Possible responses: yes—a President should assume full responsibility because he approves appointments and must monitor those appointed. No—the President is not always responsible because he cannot realistically supervise all those who work for the executive branch.)

The Twenty-fifth Amendment to the Constitution, adopted in 1967, provides a method for naming a new Vice-President in the event of a vacancy in that office. It also attempts to clarify procedures in case the President becomes physically or mentally disabled.

The President Exercises Many Powers

The list of Presidential powers in Article II is notably shorter than the list of congressional powers in Article I. Yet the list provides the springboard for the growth of Presidential power over the years. Article II gives the President the following powers:

1. To be commander in chief of the armed forces
2. To make treaties (with the ''advice and consent'' of two-thirds of the Senate), appoint ambassadors to foreign nations, and receive ambassadors from other countries
3. To appoint Supreme Court justices and executive officers, and seek the opinion of the heads of executive departments
4. To affirm that the laws be faithfully executed

Executive Powers. When George Washington first took office, he supervised less than one hundred civilian federal employees. Presidents now head an executive branch employing more than two and a half million people. (See next section, The Bureaucracy.) While most federal workers are civil service employees, the President appoints about sixty-five hundred members of the executive branch, including cabinet officers and their deputies, members of regulatory boards, and other administration leaders.

Legislative and Judicial Powers. Article II gives the President several responsibilities that touch on Congress. The President is required to give Congress information on the state of the union and to recommend measures for the consideration of Congress. The President may convene Congress in special session. In addition, Article I gives the President the power to veto legislation, although Congress can override the veto by a two-thirds vote in each House.

In practice, the President is the chief legislator of the country. Over the years, as government became more complex and as Presidents became heads of their political party and achieved an informal status as leader of the entire country, the custom grew that the President would propose a complete legislative

Picturing History The Seal of the President of the United States (top) and the Seal of France (bottom) on the velvet cover of the Louisiana Purchase treaty of 1803. President Jefferson used executive power to buy land from France even though the Constitution did not give him the authority to buy land from foreign countries.

agenda to which Congress would react. Of course, Congress retains authority to pass whatever legislation it wishes (subject to the President's veto), but in fact many laws come about because of an initial proposal by the President.

Similarly, though the Senate has to approve the President's nominations for judges, the President has the more important role. The President has the power to nominate judges, which means that the Senate can only react to his nominations. The Senate may vote down a President's first choice, but the President can counter by nominating someone else of similar judicial philosophy. Over the years, most judicial nominations have received Senate confirmation.

The President cannot control judges once they are in office—they continue to hold their offices unless they are impeached and convicted (a very rare occurrence). The founders intended that judges should not be part of the partisan political life of the nation, but the power of appointment can greatly change the Court. For example, President Ronald Reagan's three appointments to the Su-

Guided Practice

Tell students that cynics of American Presidential campaigns have said that America has the "best elections money can buy." What is meant by this? (Possible responses: Presidential hopefuls spend large sums of money on television and other media advertising; therefore, the one that has the best and most extensive campaign might win, even though he or she is not necessarily the best candidate; candidates who do not have a lot of money or backing from major political parties cannot afford to buy time on television or print large ads in newspapers and magazines.) Tell students that it has been suggested that Congress appropriate a specific sum of money that would be split evenly between the two major parties to cover Presidential campaign expenses. All private contributions would then be illegal. Would this plan be a popularly accepted means of conducting a Presidential campaign? Who might favor it? Who might oppose it? (Possible responses: members of the general public who feel that the campaigns waste too much money might be in favor of the idea; candidates from small independent parties would object if money was allotted only to the two major parties; candidates from the two major parties might favor or oppose it, depending on how much money their party had to spend on the election.)

Assign Independent Practice

Ask students to complete the Chapter 7, Section 2 Enrichment Activity.

Student Assignment/Homework

Ask students to read Section 3, "The Bureaucracy Is Highly Complex," and answer the Section 3 Review questions on paper.

preme Court are thought to have shifted the balance of power on the Court and to have moved the Court significantly to the conservative side. By the time President Reagan left office, he had appointed half of the federal district court judges, thus giving a strong conservative view to the federal trial courts over which these judges presided.

Diplomatic Powers. Article II of the Constitution assumes that the President will direct the foreign policy of the country. Though Article I gives Congress the power to declare war, Congress has always followed the President's recommendations. Even though Congress attempted to assert some authority over foreign policy in the wake of the war in Vietnam, the President remains the chief American director on the diplomatic stage.

Military Powers. Forceful Presidents such as **Abraham Lincoln** have used their power as commander in chief not only to impose broad restrictions on civilians in times of war, but also to hire and fire the heads of armies and dictate battlefield strategy. Of course, the President's role as commander in chief is inseparable from the role of chief diplomat of the nation.

Spending Powers. Though Congress raises funds and authorizes their use, it is the President and the executive branch that actually collect and spend them. Congress oversees how money is spent and establishes guidelines, but normally the executive branch has flexibility in deciding exactly how programs will be implemented. As the federal budget has mushroomed, this power to implement programs has become more important. In addition to these spending powers, which are implied in the Constitution, the President has other powers related to economics.

Economic Powers. Since the New Deal of the 1930's (see Chapter 27), Americans have expected the President to develop programs to ensure prosperity. The President plans the government budget through the Office of Management and Budget. This budget is presented to Congress for its approval, but once again Congress responds to the Presidential proposals more often than it operates on its own initiative. The President makes an annual report to Congress on the state of the nation's economy, and through the Council of Economic Advisers makes recommendations on many other issues that will affect the economic life of the nation.

Party Leader. The Constitution says nothing about political parties, but parties are now vital to our political system. Presidents automatically become leaders of their party. They tend to appoint party members to office, who, in turn, actively support members of their party who run for office. Presidents also are major fund-raisers for their party. While these duties conflict somewhat with their role as head of state (in which they represent all Americans), the support of their party is essential to the success of their legislative agenda and to their effectiveness as national leaders.

The President Relies on the Cabinet

The President relies heavily on the **cabinet** and the cabinet advisors. The cabinet is composed of the heads of the fourteen major departments of government.

Selecting Cabinet Members. Generally, cabinet members are members of the President's party. Traditionally, many have had close political ties to the President. However, some cabinet members have come from outside the political sphere.

The Role of the Cabinet. When government was smaller, the cabinet often met to advise the President. Even during the Civil War, President Lincoln met frequently with cabinet members to inform them of the progress of the war and to seek their advice.

Over the years, however, meetings of the cabinet have tended to be less frequent and more formal. Even though Presidents from time to time have used the cabinet as a source of advice, in general Presidents have turned for counsel to special inter-

Picturing History First Hispanic cabinet member Lauro Cavazos, Secretary of Education (1988); first black woman cabinet member Patricia Harris, Secretary of Housing and Urban Development (1977).

Core Lesson

Anticipate the Lesson

Ask students to name some of the various people they think are necessary to run a typical high school and then to state the main responsibility of each. Write this information on the board. (List might include: principal—to see that rules are followed and school board policies are carried out; secretary—to see that day-to-day operations are handled efficiently; janitor—to see that the building and grounds are kept in good repair.) Ask students why so many people are needed. (Answer: to keep the school running smoothly.) Which ones, if any, could be eliminated without affecting the everyday operation of the school? (Students might at first think that one or all could be eliminated, but after discussion, they should see that each employee has an important function and is necessary to the operation of the school.) Compare this list to the jobs and positions students think are necessary for a smoothly functioning government. Draw on students' knowledge from the previous two sections of this chapter. (Possible responses: lawmakers—teachers; law enforcement officers—school security guards; secretaries—secretaries.)

Answers

Main Ideas

1. George Washington established the informal precedent of no more than two successive terms by any one President. After Franklin Roosevelt was elected to four successive terms, the Twenty-second Amendment was added to the Constitution (in 1951). This amendment formally limits Presidents to no more than two terms.

2. Article II.

3. Supreme Court justices are granted lifetime tenure, so the justices are no longer a part of the nation's partisan political life.

4. The cabinet and the Executive Office of the President.

Critical Thinking

5. Possible answer: advantages—a single six-year term would eliminate the need for a President to take politically expedient actions during that term in order to help ensure reelection.

Disadvantage—a single term might make a President a lame duck from the first day in office, a condition that now may exist only near the end of a President's second term of four years. **(analysis)**

---

departmental task forces or to staffs working directly under them.

The Executive Office of the President Provides Support

The days are long past since Presidents had a few private secretaries and, like Grover Cleveland and Woodrow Wilson, answered letters and wrote out state documents by hand. In 1939 the **Executive Office of the President** was created to serve the President. This office, which encompasses the White House staff, gives the President more than a thousand experts in various fields on whom the President can rely.

For example, the **National Security Council (NSC),** established in 1947, helps the President coordinate military and foreign policy. Some cabinet members and the director of the Central Intelligence Agency serve on the NSC.

The chart on page 166 shows the principal units of the Executive Office and the White House. Each unit is responsible for a specific area of policy. These units suggest the enormous range of responsibilities placed on the modern Presidency.

SECTION 2 REVIEW

Key Terms and People

Explain the significance of: executive branch, George Washington, Franklin D. Roosevelt, Abraham Lincoln, cabinet, Executive Office of the President, National Security Council (NSC)

Main Ideas

1. How has the practice of a maximum of two Presidential terms of four years each evolved over the years?
2. Which article of the Constitution outlines the powers of a President?
3. Why does a President lose the ability to control a Supreme Court justice once he or she is appointed?
4. Name two advisory bodies on which Presidents frequently rely.

Critical Thinking

5. Some people have suggested that the Constitution be amended to allow Presidents to serve for only one term of six years. List at least one advantage and one disadvantage of this change.

The Bureaucracy Is Highly Complex

GLOSSARY TERMS: **bureaucracy, public policy**

The Constitution does not explicitly provide for the **bureaucracy.** It does not even mention it, at least in so many words. Yet we currently have fourteen cabinet departments and more than fifty regulatory commissions with thousands of bureaus, divisions, and local offices. The more than two and a half million men and women who are civilian employees of the federal government do the unglamorous but essential jobs that keep our democracy working.

Complexity Requires Organization

The complex nature of a bureaucracy requires a well-defined organization. Our government is organized around a framework based on two principles: **hierarchy** and **specialization.**

Hierarchy. Our federal bureaucracy is organized as a hierarchy. This means that each member is a part of a chain of command. Thus, a bureaucrat accepts direction from above and provides direction to those below. In a well-functioning bureaucracy, direction goes from top to bottom, but information flows both ways.

Specialization. Because bureaucracies are large organizations with far too much work for any one person, the work is divided among employees according to their special skills. Specialization allows bureaucracies to develop a high degree of expertise and to handle complicated tasks.

Civil Service Includes Most Government Employees

In the early days of the republic, jobs in the federal government were part of the spoils system—they were given out by the party in power to reward the faithful. When a disappointed office-seeker assassinated President James Garfield in 1881, longstanding movements to reform the system were strengthened, resulting in the passage of the Pendleton Act in 1883. This law set up the federal civil service. (See Chapter 18.) The civil

Picturing History The federal government keeps some gold deposits at Fort Knox, Kentucky.

service is a professional career service that covers most federal workers' appointments on the basis of competitive exams and provides legal shields against political influence. It continues to the present day.

Recruitment and Classification. The key to a professional civil service is having a written description of every job, complete with the qualifications necessary to fill it. On the basis of these descriptions, competitive exams can be created to measure the skills needed to do the job. To ensure that the widest possible cross section of the public applies for federal jobs, the government actively publicizes its job openings and recruits from schools, colleges, and the general public.

Restricting Political Activity. In 1939 Congress strengthened the Pendleton Act by passing new legislation, the **Hatch Act.** This act forbade federal employees from contributing to or participating in partisan election campaigns. This controversial law was designed to insulate federal workers from political pressure. If they could not work actively for a party or contribute money, the reasoning went, then they could not be pressured by their bosses. However, the law does restrict the First Amendment right of federal employees to participate in politics (though not, of course, to vote). Nonetheless, the Hatch Act has been upheld by the Supreme Court.

Political Appointees. Not all federal workers are covered by civil service. Congress has recognized that each President must have the right to name the heads of cabinet departments and their chief dep-

uties. If these top officials are responsive to the President, the President has a better opportunity to influence each department's policies and to carry out the programs for which he campaigned.

Executive Departments Adapt to Needs

In the administration of George Washington, there were only three cabinet, or executive, departments—State, Treasury, and War (now renamed Defense). Over the years, others were added in response to the needs of the time. For example, in the late 1970's, the Department of Energy and the Department of Education were created to deal with pressing problems. In 1989 the Department of Veterans Affairs was created to replace the Veterans Administration, which had not had cabinet status. The chart on page 194 shows the dates of creation of most cabinet departments.

In theory, the departments operate separately, each in charge of its particular area. In practice, however, the work of the departments inevitably overlaps somewhat. For example, the war against drugs might be largely carried out by the Justice Department, but important contributions could be made by the Department of Defense (use of armed forces against drug traffickers), the Department of Agriculture (eradication of drug crops), the Department of State (coordination with other nations), and the Department of the Treasury (tracing drug money deposited in banks). In cases like this, interdepartmental task forces are often set up to ensure a coordinated effort.

Bureaucracy and Public Policy Interact

The bureaucracy influences and is influenced by **public policy.** Public policy is the course of action the government takes in response to a particular political problem.

The Influence of the Bureaucracy. The bureaucracy has considerable influence on public policy. One source of its influence is its expertise. Many bureaucrats are scientists, engineers, doctors, and other experts. Their job is to study a problem thoroughly and to keep abreast of new developments.

Another source of influence is the very size and complexity of the bureaucracy. Federal bureaucrats administer over a thousand federal programs and can have an impact on public policy by writing rules and regulations to implement these programs.

Ask the groups to write their lists from the previous activity on the board. After all lists have been compiled and duplicate items have been eliminated, ask students to prioritize the items in both lists from most important to least important. (Possible responses: most important positive aspect—the size allows for specialization, which facilitates the handling of complex tasks; most important negative aspect—the bureaucracy cannot always be immediately responsive to the public will.)

Tell students that qualifications for many civil service positions allow the applicant to substitute appropriate education for the experience requirements at various levels in government jobs. Should this practice be allowed? Why or why not? (Possible responses: this is a good practice because it allows qualified applicants who have just finished their education to hold appropriate jobs; it is not a good practice because it might cause experienced workers to be overlooked in favor of those with college or advanced degrees.)

Independent Agencies of the Federal Government

Postal Service	**Federal Trade Commission**
National Aeronautics and Space Administration	**Federal Communications Commission**
Environmental Protection Agency	**Other Agencies**

Members of the Presidential Cabinet and Some of the Groups They Oversee

Department of State 1789	Department of Treasury 1789	Department of Defense * 1947	Department of Interior 1849	Department of Justice 1870
United States Mission to the United Nations	Internal Revenue Service	Army	National Park Service	Federal Bureau of Investigation
Department of Agriculture 1889	**Department of Commerce** 1913	**Department of Labor** 1913	**Department of Housing and Urban Development** 1965	**Department of Transportation** 1966
Soil Conservation Service	National Bureau of Standards	Occupational Safety and Health Administration	Community Planning and Development	Federal Aviation Administration
Department of Energy 1977	**Department of Health and Human Services**** 1979	**Department of Education** *** 1979	**Veterans Administration** 1989	
Conservation and Renewable Energy	Social Security	Educational Research	Department of Veterans Affairs Medical Centers	

* *Formerly the Department of War established in 1789.*
** *Formerly the Department of Health, Education, and Welfare established in 1953.*
*** *Formerly the Department of Health, Education and Welfare established in 1953.*

Another source of bureaucratic influence on public policy stems from legal limitations designed to protect civil service employees. Since the vast majority of federal workers are protected by civil service and cannot be fired except for good cause, they are likely to remain in their positions long after their political bosses have gone. For this reason, they often have more influence on public policy than the heads of the departments in which they work.

A bureaucracy also may be influential if it is headed by a charismatic or politically savvy leader like the late **J. Edgar Hoover,** who was director of the Federal Bureau of Investigation (FBI) for decades. Part of the secret of Hoover's longevity was his exceptional rapport with Congress which enabled him to have considerable influence on public policy. Movies and radio and television shows about brave, vigilant G-men surely helped Hoover consolidate his extraordinary power.

Limitations on the Bureaucracy. Bureaucrats are often attacked by political leaders, who assert that bureaucrats are out of control and are harassing (or simply not serving) the American people, for whom they work. However, in a democracy, bureaucrats have many limits on their power. The President is the head of the entire executive branch and, as such, has an obligation to control the bureaucracy. Presidents can try to prevent bureaucracies from growing by proposing no-growth budgets. They can propose that certain agencies be pared or even eliminated. They can also carefully monitor the work of bureaucracies in politically sensitive areas to ensure that Presidential wishes are carried out.

Congress can sometimes control the bureaucracy because it has the power of the purse and the duty to see that funds are spent appropriately. In its role as overseer of the bureaucracy, Congress has uncovered major scandals, including profiteering during the Civil War and the public-land oil-leasing scheme in the 1920's known as the Teapot Dome scandal. (See Chapter 25.) In the late 1980's, congressional hearings disclosed widespread waste and mismanagement in the Department of Housing and Urban Development and in the Savings and Loan Administration.

People unhappy with a bureaucratic policy may find an ally in the courts. Many policies are overturned by the courts as a result of lawsuits asserting that the policies violate the Constitution or a particular law.

Picturing History Firefighters try to prevent a fire from spreading wildly in Yellowstone National Park, Wyoming, in 1989. When thousands of acres were lost, many Americans grew angry at the federal policy of allowing wildfires to burn out of control.

Interest groups sometimes find themselves at loggerheads with a government agency. They can attempt to influence the agency directly and/or indirectly, through Congress, through an appeal to public opinion, or through the media.

All in all, if the bureaucracy is a fourth branch of government, it is not an undemocratic one. Though it is deliberately kept out of the political process, it can be influenced at many points, by many people.

Picturing History J. Edgar Hoover is shown here on his fortieth anniversary as director of the FBI.

SECTION 3 REVIEW

Key Terms and People

Explain the significance of: bureaucracy, hierarchy, specialization, Hatch Act, public policy, J. Edgar Hoover

Main Ideas

1. How does the civil service system differ from the spoils system?
2. What are the advantages and disadvantages of the civil service system?
3. How have the executive departments changed since the administration of George Washington?
4. In what four ways does the bureaucracy influence public policy?

Critical Thinking

5. The bureaucracy is sometimes called the "fourth branch of government." Explain.

State the Objective

Understand how our American democracy functions through the judicial branch.

Anticipate the Lesson

Ask students to share any experiences they may have had in seeing the judicial branch in action. (Students may be familiar with traffic courts, divorce courts, small claims courts, or they may have seen court proceedings on television.)

For Discussion

Federal judges, appointed by the President, serve in courts throughout the fifty states. How might the President find qualified appointees living in areas where vacancies occur? (Possible responses: ask for advice from his friends; remember lawyers whose reputations have impressed him; ask senators and representatives to recommend individuals in their districts.) Tell students that the President uses all of the above ways to find qualified individuals.

SECTION 4

The Judicial Branch Interprets Laws

GLOSSARY TERMS: **lame duck, original jurisdiction, appellate jurisdiction, precedents, strict interpretation, broad interpretation, clear and present danger doctrine, separate but equal**

Decisions of federal courts affect all aspects of government. The most important powers of federal courts are to review laws to determine if they are constitutional and to interpret laws. As the authors of the Federalist papers put it, "Laws are dead letters without courts to expound and define their true meaning and operation." In performing this function, the courts rule on laws affecting everything from the free-speech rights of Americans to economic policy, civil rights, and the rights of people accused of committing a crime.

The Federal Courts Handle Specific Problems

The United States Constitution created only one court—the United States Supreme Court. Article III of the Constitution gave Congress the power to establish lower federal courts.

Constitutional Federal Courts. Constitutional federal courts are those courts that Congress has created under Article III, Section 1 of the Constitution to exercise "the judicial power of the United States." Congress has set up these federal courts in a three-tiered system of federal courts. (See chart on page 181.)

The lower trial courts, or district courts, where most cases begin, make up the first tier. As of 1986, there were 576 federal district judges serving in these courts. These judges handle both civil and criminal cases that arise under federal laws. The second tier is made up of thirteen courts of appeals, also called circuit courts. Twelve of these courts are set up geographically. A decision in one court of appeals is not binding on the others. Conflicts are resolved only by the United States Supreme Court. The third tier consists of the Supreme Court. It hears appeals from the federal appellate courts and from the state supreme courts. The Court now has nine justices, though that number can be changed by Congress. In the past, the

number ranged from six at the Court's founding to ten after the Civil War.

Appointment of Federal Judges. Most federal judges are appointed by the President and must be confirmed by the Senate. Their appointments are for life; they may be removed only through impeachment and conviction.

The people whom the President considers nominating as federal judges are invariably lower court judges or other lawyers. Often they have been politically active, usually in the same political party as the President.

Before federal judges are nominated, they are screened by the Justice Department. They must undergo FBI checks. They are also scrutinized by a fifteen-member committee of the American Bar Association. In addition to these formal mechanisms, their record is sometimes carefully examined by one or more special-interest groups.

Most district and appellate court judges are easily confirmed by the Senate. However, nominees to the Supreme Court receive a closer look. Over the years, two-thirds of these nominees have been approved in the Senate with no opposition.

A very recent nominee who failed to win approval was **Robert Bork,** a judge on one of the federal appeals courts. His story reveals the pressures at work in the confirmation process.

Before serving as an appeals judge, Bork had been a law school professor, a legal scholar, and the second highest person in the federal Justice Department. He argued many cases before the Supreme Court.

When he was nominated in July 1987, he was generally considered exceptionally well qualified to be a Supreme Court justice, and his nomination was expected to sail through the Senate. However, he was selected by a **lame duck** President, Ronald Reagan, who was serving out his final term in office. The Senate was controlled by members of the opposition party.

The President had chosen Bork to replace Justice **Lewis Powell, Jr.,** who was retiring. Justice Powell had been a moderate on the Court, and it was expected that Bork would change the Court's balance of power between liberal and conservative justices.

Bork was an outspoken man who had written many controversial articles. His nomination pleased many conservative groups. It alarmed many civil rights and women's advocates, who

Picturing History Supreme Court nominee Robert Bork (center) at his Senate Judiciary Committee confirmation hearing. Bork is flanked by former President Gerald Ford (left) and Senator Robert Dole (right).

feared how he would vote on the Court. These groups organized an unprecedented public relations campaign against him consisting of mass mailings, television commercials, and intensive lobbying of senators.

With opposition mounting, the confirmation hearings conducted by the Senate Judiciary Committee received national attention. Millions of Americans watching their television sets formed impressions of Judge Bork.

Was it his performance before the committee or the massive public relations campaign against him that led to his defeat? The answer is not clear. Whatever the case, public opinion turned against him, and ultimately he was defeated by a party-line vote of 58 to 42, the most lopsided defeat in history for a nominee to the Supreme Court.

The Court Follows Strict Procedures

Out of the hundreds of thousands of cases heard every year by American courts, only about 150 make it all the way to the United States Supreme Court. These cases follow a set of strict procedures.

A few cases get to the Court through its **original jurisdiction,** or legal authority to be the first to hear a case. These are usually cases in which one state sues another. These cases are filed directly with the Court, and no lower court hears them.

The vast majority of cases that reach the Court, however, are heard on appeal. The kinds of cases the Court may accept through its **appellate jurisdiction**—the power to review cases after other courts have heard them—are defined by laws passed by Congress. Over the years, Congress has given the justices an increasingly wide range of cases from which to choose.

Selecting a Case. In a typical year, the Court will receive five thousand or more requests to hear cases on appeal. These requests ask the Court to hear cases that have already been decided by lower courts. If the Court refuses to hear a case, the decision of the lower court stands.

The justices debate which cases to accept in private conferences held every week during the Court's term (October through June). Their deliberations are private, and their reasons for accepting or rejecting a case normally are not made public.

At least four justices have to agree that a case should be accepted before the Court will agree to hear it. The justices consider many questions in deciding whether to hear a case. Is it important? Does it raise political questions better handled by another branch of government? Is the case ripe for Supreme Court review, or does it require further lower court proceedings?

Deciding a Case. When a case is accepted, the lawyers on each side prepare written arguments, called **briefs,** detailing the reasons their side should prevail. In these briefs, the lawyers analyze the laws involved in the case and cite previous cases to support their position.

People and groups who are not parties to the case can make their views known by submitting *amicus curiae* (friend of the court) briefs. These briefs supplement the briefs of the parties by presenting additional legal arguments and pointing out how the issues raised affect various segments of society.

When the case is orally argued before the Court, each side generally has a half hour to make its points. This includes the time in which justices interrupt the lawyers' presentations with questions and requests for clarification.

After oral arguments are heard, the justices meet privately to discuss the case. After discussion, they vote on how to decide the case. If the Chief Justice is with the majority, he assigns someone in the majority to write the Court's opinion. If the Chief Justice is not in the majority, the justice with the most seniority of those voting with the majority assigns the writing of the opinion. The justices in the minority will write dissenting opinions.

Five Factors Influence Supreme Court Decisions

What factors influence the Supreme Court justices in their decision-making process? In general, these factors may be grouped into five categories.

Check for Understanding

Call on individual students to read their answers to the Section 4 Review questions.

Picturing History Justices of the United States Supreme Court: (front row, from left to right) Antonin Scalia, John Paul Stevens, Chief Justice William Rehnquist, Sandra Day O'Connor, and Anthony Kennedy; (back row, from left to right) Ruth Bader Ginsburg, David Souter, Clarence Thomas, and Stephen Breyer.

Existing Laws and Legal Precedents. The justices carefully examine **precedents,** that is, relevant laws and prior court decisions. Each of these is important, but none is beyond dispute. Constitutional provisions are often general, laws are often open to varying interpretations, and prior court decisions may not have settled important questions.

However, certain overall principles apply. If the United States Constitution is in conflict with state constitutions, state laws, or federal laws, the provisions of the Constitution will prevail. Prior decisions of higher courts have more value as precedent than prior decisions of lower courts. Prior decisions of the Supreme Court have the most weight.

Personal Legal Views of the Justices. In deciding cases, each justice will necessarily apply his or her own legal views. Some justices, for example, favor a **strict interpretation** of the Constitution. They look to the original intent of the framers of the Constitution in deciding what the Constitution means. Other justices may favor a **broad interpretation,** or a more expansive reading of the Constitution. They reason that its general language should be interpreted liberally to meet the changing needs of society.

Justices' Interactions with Each Other. The justices frequently exchange views during the process of writing opinions. The justice selected to write the majority opinion circulates a draft to all the other justices, who may make suggestions, redraft certain language, or even object vigorously to a point. Sometimes many drafts are circulated before the justices agree on their reasoning in support of a decision.

It is important for justices to agree on their reasons because a decision sets a precedent only if there is an opinion that attracts a majority of the justices voting on the case. Justices who do not agree on the reasoning can write a concurring opinion, one that agrees with the decision but disagrees with the reasoning. If a majority do not agree on the reasons for a decision, the Court is said to have decided the case by a plurality. The case is decided as far as the parties are concerned, but no precedent has been set.

Public Opinion. The justices are supposed to be insulated from public opinion. They are not elected, but are appointed for life. The Constitution guarantees that their salaries will not be reduced. Their job is to determine what the law is, not to respond to political currents.

Nonetheless, justices live in society. They read the newspapers and watch television. They cannot—and should not—be totally oblivious to what Americans think. In these ways, public opinion plays an indirect role in the Court's decisions.

Congress and the President. Similarly, the Court is indirectly influenced by the other two branches of government. The President's views are often expressed in briefs filed by the solicitor general's office of the Department of Justice. Congress sometimes makes its views known in *amicus curiae* briefs. The Court is free to ignore these opinions, but they are probably accorded some weight.

Court Decisions Affect Public Policy

As you know, the United States Supreme Court is the final authority on laws and on the Constitution. A glance at some of its major cases will indicate its broad influence on public policy.

Marbury v. *Madison* (1803). The greatest case in Supreme Court history is the case in which the Court first asserted its right to declare a law of Congress unconstitutional. The events leading to the case began the night before President John Adams left office. The President was bitter. He had just lost the election to Thomas Jefferson. As one of his last tasks in office, Adams appointed some of his Federalist supporters to be judges. The Judiciary Act of 1789 gave him the power to do this. The commissions for these offices, including one for William Marbury, were put on the Secretary of State's desk to be sealed and then delivered the next day. The Secretary of State, John Marshall, neglected to have them delivered.

When Jefferson took office, his new Secretary of State, James Madison, refused to deliver the commissions. William Marbury asked the Court to issue an order requiring Madison to hand over his commission. At this time, **John Marshall** was Chief Justice of the Supreme Court. Marshall wrote the decision in 1803.

Chief Justice Marshall was indeed justified in ordering Madison to deliver the commission to Marbury. Suppose, though, that Madison ignored the order, with President Jefferson's approval. The Supreme Court would be seriously weakened. Future Presidents might also ignore its decisions.

Marshall looked to the Constitution and to his Federalist principles for guidance. According to Article III, the Supreme Court had original jurisdiction only in "all cases affecting ambassadors, other public ministers and consuls, and those in which a state shall be party." In all other cases, the Court had only appellate jurisdiction.

Since Marbury was not an ambassador, a public minister, or a consul, and since a state was not a party to the dispute, Chief Justice Marshall concluded that the section of the Judiciary Act of 1789 that gave Marbury the right to go to the Supreme Court first to demand the delivery of his commission was unconstitutional. The Judiciary Act was adding to the original jurisdiction of the Court by giving it permission to issue orders.

Chief Justice Marshall's decision cleverly avoided making a ruling the Court could not enforce. The real issue was not whether Marbury got his job as justice of the peace but whether the Supreme Court had the power to declare a law unconstitutional. With this decision, the Supreme Court established itself as a check on the legislative and executive branches. The Court would strike down any law that contradicted the Constitution.

Marbury never got his commission. His loss was the country's gain—the new concept of judicial review.

Gibbons v. *Ogden* (1824). Thomas Gibbons and Aaron Ogden were partners in operating a steam-boat between New Jersey and New York. The partnership broke up, and each then began operating his own steamboat line. Ogden had a charter from the state of New York that gave him exclusive rights to the route. Gibbons had a charter from the federal government. Ogden took Gibbons to court for violating his exclusive charter.

With Chief Justice John Marshall writing the landmark decision, the Supreme Court ruled that in a conflict between the federal government and a state, "the law of the state must yield." The Court based its decision on the supremacy clause in Article VI of the Constitution, which clearly states that in cases where there is a conflict of laws, the national law takes precedence. Marshall gave a broad definition to the clause of the Constitution that says "Congress shall have power . . . to regulate commerce . . . among the several states." Consequently, the charter Gibbons received from the federal government was legal, and Ogden's "exclusive" right was not. Marshall's ruling was the cornerstone of later decisions giving the federal government authority to regulate almost everything that crosses state boundaries, from air travel to radio signals.

In addition, by striking down Ogden's state-granted monopoly, Marshall paved the way for competition between companies. For this reason, the case is sometimes called "The Emancipation Proclamation of American Commerce."

Dred Scott v. *Sandford* (1857). The Dred Scott case is one of the clearest examples in our history of the Court's attempting to set public policy. In this bold decision, Chief Justice Roger B. Taney and the Court attempted to settle once and for all the issue of slavery in the territories of the United States. This was an issue that threatened to tear the country apart. In this case, the Court declared that no slave or free black person could claim United States citizenship. In other words, the Constitution was made by and for white people only. (For details of the Dred Scott case, see Chapter 13.)

Among lawyers there is a saying, "Hard cases make bad law." The Dred Scott case was the hardest of cases. It involved moral and political issues as well as legal questions. The consequences were far-reaching. The Court suffered and the nation suffered. Perhaps the only one who did not suffer was Dred Scott; his owner freed him just weeks after the Court's decision. The Court's attempt to resolve the slavery issue in favor of

Assign Independent Practice

Ask students to complete the Chapter 7, Section 4 Enrichment Activity.

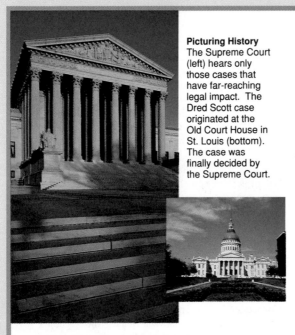

Picturing History
The Supreme Court (left) hears only those cases that have far-reaching legal impact. The Dred Scott case originated at the Old Court House in St. Louis (bottom). The case was finally decided by the Supreme Court.

Southern slave owners did not work. In effect, the Court was overruled by Lincoln's victory at the polls and by the North's victory in the Civil War. The passage of the Thirteenth and Fourteenth Amendments to the Constitution after the war ended slavery and provided citizenship for African Americans, thus reversing the Dred Scott decision.

***Schenck* v. *United States* (1919).** The First Amendment states clearly and simply, "Congress shall make no law . . . abridging the freedom of speech." That phrase, though, has been the subject of numerous court cases. Can a person say anything at any time? If not, what restrictions are constitutional?

During World War I, the Espionage Act made it illegal to disrupt recruitment efforts by the military. (See Chapter 23.) Richard Schenck was arrested for violating this act. He had distributed circulars urging men to resist the draft. His defense was that he was protected by the First Amendment.

In a unanimous Supreme Court ruling, Justice **Oliver Wendell Holmes, Jr.,** explained what the First Amendment did protect and what it did not protect. He wrote:

> We admit that in many places and in ordinary times the defendants [Schenck and others] in saying all that was said in the circular would have been within their constitutional rights. But the character of every act depends upon the circumstances in which it is done. The

most stringent [strongest] protection of free speech would not protect a man falsely shouting fire in a theater and causing a panic. The question in every case is whether the words used are used in such circumstances and are of such a nature as to create a clear and present danger that they will bring about the substantive [real] evils that Congress has a right to prevent. It is a question of proximity and degree. When a nation is at war, many things that might be said in time of peace are such a hindrance to its effort that their utterance will not be endured.

The Court ruled against Schenck. Its interpretation became known as the **clear and present danger doctrine.**

***Brown* v. *Board of Education* (1954, 1955).** Racial discrimination continued to plague the United States long after slavery was abolished. In 1896 the Supreme Court ruled in *Plessy* v. *Ferguson* that segregation was legal as long as each race was provided equal facilities. **Separate but equal** became the law of the land.

In 1954 the Court reversed the separate but equal ruling. In the case of *Brown* v. *Board of Education,* a unanimous Court said that segregation in schools was unconstitutional. According to Chief Justice Earl Warren, segregated schools led to a feeling of inferiority in black children. Such a feeling could put them at a permanent disadvantage when they grew up. Consequently, segregated schools violated the equal protection clause of the Fourteenth Amendment. (For details of *Brown* v. *Board of Education,* see Chapter 31.)

Because segregation was deeply ingrained in the culture of the United States, the Court ruled the next year that schools were to be desegregated "with all deliberate speed." In reality this meant that the elaborate legal structure of segregation would be dismantled slowly, but eventually it did come down. Thanks to the Brown decision, segregation in other public facilities was challenged and outlawed.

***Miranda* v. *Arizona* (1966).** The Fifth Amendment protects an individual from self-incrimination. The Sixth Amendment states that someone accused of a crime is entitled to have a lawyer for his defense.

The problem is, how are these rights enforced? How do people accused of a crime know that they

Student Assignment/Homework

Have students complete the Chapter 7 Test on paper. Divide the class into small groups and have students review their answers.

Concluding the Chapter

The Constitution of the United States provides for three branches of government. Why? (Possible responses: to keep one branch from gaining too much power; to avoid the possibility of a President establishing a government that resembled the monarchy of England.) Ask students to review the chapter and the list of checks and balances that they started at the beginning of the chapter.

have these rights, especially in the critical first few hours of questioning?

In a series of cases in the 1960's, the Supreme Court steadily expanded the rights of the accused. The Miranda case was the culmination of this trend.

Ernesto Miranda was arrested on charges of kidnapping and rape. Miranda did not know that he had a right to remain silent. When the police questioned him, he confessed, thus becoming a witness against himself. Miranda did not know that he had a right to have a lawyer to advise him during the questioning. Did the failure to advise Miranda of his rights mean that he had been deprived of due process of law?

The Court held that it did and that Miranda's confession could not be used as evidence. The proper way to question a suspect was explained as follows:

> Prior to any questioning, the person must be warned that he has a right to remain silent, that any statement he does make may be used as evidence against him, and that he has a right to the presence of an attorney, either retained or appointed.

The Miranda decision fundamentally changed the way police question suspects.

Linking Past to Present

Warning criminal suspects of their rights before police questioning has come to be known as "reading the Miranda rights." Ten years after the Miranda case, Ernesto Miranda was killed in a fight. Ironically, he was carrying a pile of "Miranda cards" that inform suspects of their rights. One of these cards was carefully read to the suspect at the scene as he was being arrested for Miranda's murder.

A Delicate Balance Safeguards Liberty

The framers of the Constitution created a framework for our American democracy that has functioned remarkably well for over two hundred years. The flexibility of the Constitution has permitted our government to adjust to change. In the process of

adjusting to change, however, there is always the danger that one branch of government might become too powerful and the other branches too weak. To safeguard our liberty, we must ensure that the legislative, executive, and judicial branches maintain the delicate balance outlined in the Constitution.

Safeguarding liberty is the duty not only of those who serve in the various branches of government, but of every American citizen. Alfred E. Smith, a former governor of New York and the Democratic opponent of Herbert Hoover in the 1928 Presidential election, underscored this responsibility when he said:

> Keep your eye on the Constitution. This is the guarantee, that is the safeguard, that is the night watchman of democratic representative government—freedom of speech, freedom of the press, the right of public assembly and the right to petition the government. Save all these things in the Constitution and let the Supreme Court stand behind it.

SECTION 4 REVIEW

Key Terms and People

Explain the significance of: Robert Bork, lame duck, Lewis Powell, Jr., original jurisdiction, appellate jurisdiction, briefs, *amicus curiae,* precedents, strict interpretation, broad interpretation, John Marshall, Oliver Wendell Holmes, Jr., clear and present danger doctrine, separate but equal

Main Ideas

1. What are the two most important powers of the federal courts?
2. What is meant by the term *three-tiered system of federal courts?*
3. Discuss the ways a case might reach the Supreme Court.
4. What are the five factors that influence Supreme Court decisions? Give a brief explanation of each one.
5. What power did the Court claim in *Marbury* v. *Madison?*

Critical Thinking

6. How are people's rights protected by the Miranda case and limited by the Schenck case?

SECTION 4 REVIEW

Answers

Main Ideas

1. To review laws to determine whether they are constitutional, and to interpret laws.

2. Tier 1 includes federal district trial courts and a few specialized courts; tier 2 includes 12 courts of appeals that have specific geographical jurisdictions and 1 national court of appeals; tier 3 is the Supreme Court.

3. Case goes directly to Supreme Court if it is one over which the Court has original jurisdiction; cases over which Court has appellate jurisdiction must be chosen for Review by Court on appeal from lower court.

4. Precedents—existing laws and legal precedents; personal legal views of justices—strict or broad interpretation of Constitution; exchange of justices' viewpoints—develops concurrence of opinion so precedent can be set for future cases; public opinion—influence of time in which justices live; Congress and President—present views to Court via briefs.

5. The power to declare a law unconstitutional.

Critical Thinking

6. Miranda case makes it illegal for police to fail to advise suspect of rights. Schenck case limits free speech in situations involving "clear and present danger." **(analysis)**

State the Objective

Understand how the rulings of the Supreme Court change over time.

Present the Lesson

Remind students that society continually changes. As a result, everyone learns to live and adjust to change. Ask students to give examples of how business people, educators, and artists adjust to change. (Possible responses: companies develop new products; educators introduce new issues and topics such as AIDS; architects and painters redefine space to reflect changing style.) Ask students to think about changes in their rules at home. How have the rules changed as they have grown? (Possible responses: curfews are later; more freedom in activities is allowed; more re-

sponsibility is given.) Tell students that these examples demonstrate the process of interpretation and reinterpretation of rules and ideas. In the same way, Supreme Court justices define the process of change as it relates to federal and, occasionally, state laws.

Divide the class into two groups and assign each a case from the lesson. Have the groups discuss their cases and analyze the Court's point of view. Ask the group leaders to summarize these discussions for the class. (Discussion on *Trustees of Dartmouth College* v. *Woodward* might include: Chief Justice John Marshall overturned the state decision; he said that contracts are binding, that no state could

Focus on Critical Thinking Skills

Analyzing Constitutional Interpretations

Understanding the Skill

Our Constitution has continued to work for more than two hundred years because it is able to adapt and change. Over the years, members of the Supreme Court have interpreted and reinterpreted its provisions, bringing them in line with the needs of the times.

Interpretations of the Constitution are based on the following process. A case is brought before the Court by someone claiming that a law is contrary to a provision of the Constitution. If the Court decides that the law is constitutional, it carefully explains why. In that way everyone has a clearer understanding of what the Constitution means. If the Court decides the law is unconstitutional, it also explains why. This also clarifies the meaning of the Constitution.

Because a Supreme Court decision becomes "the law of the land," it must be agreed upon by more than half the justices taking part. Justices who disagree may file dissenting opinions; those who agree may also file their own concurring opinions. Neither type of opinion has legal standing, but dissenting opinions may affect later cases. When one Supreme Court overrules a decision of an earlier Court, it bases its new opinion on an earlier dissent.

Here are some steps to follow when analyzing interpretations of the Constitution given in Supreme Court decisions:

- **Identify the main ideas of the interpretation.** What were the main ideas of the Supreme Court's decision?
- **Identify the conclusion of the interpretation.** State the Court's decision or concurring opinion.
- **Analyze the evidence.** What arguments do the justices provide to support their interpretations?
- **Analyze the author's point of view.** What circumstances might have influenced the justices?
- **Compare this interpretation with other interpretations of the same event or issue.** How do the concurring opinions differ from the dissenting opinions? How does this interpretation compare

with past interpretations?
- **Draw a conclusion about the interpretation.** Based on your analysis, do you agree or disagree with the interpretation? Explain.

Applying the Skill

In Article I, Section 10, Clause 1, the United States Constitution says, "No state shall . . . pass any . . . law impairing the obligation of contracts." In other words, states cannot pass a law that would change a legal contract. This clause has been interpreted and reinterpreted many times. Read the following interpretations carefully and answer the questions.

***Trustees of Dartmouth College* v. *Woodward* (1819).** The founders who gave money to establish Dartmouth College received a charter giving their trustees the right to control the school's affairs "forever." New Hampshire accepted this arrangement when it became an independent state in 1776. Then, in 1816, the state changed the charter so it could appoint its own trustees. (See page 245.) The state courts said that New Hampshire could make this change because the charter was not a contract according to the meaning of the word in the Constitution. No one stood to gain or lose anything of value by it. Moreover, since education was a public concern, and since schools were public, not private, institutions, the states could run them as they saw fit.

The case was appealed to the Supreme Court. In the early 1800's, the government wanted to encourage people to invest in businesses to help the country grow. Investors, however, needed to be sure that no state would change their contracts and deprive them of their profits. Chief Justice Marshall agreed. In handing down the Court's decision, he wrote:

> The founders of the college contracted . . . [that the funds they gave should be used forever for] the objects for which they were given; they contracted also, to secure that

overturn a contract, thus depriving an investor of profits.)

Ask students how they would vote if the same cases came before the Court today and why. (Possible responses: in favor of *Trustees of Dartmouth College* v. *Woodward*—contracts must be binding to protect those who enter into such agreements. In favor of *Charles River Bridge* v. *Warren Bridge*—it is the duty of the government to promote the prosperity of the community, which is of greater importance than a contract between individuals.)

Check for Understanding

Discuss students' responses to the questions at the end of the feature.

application by the constitution of the corporation. They contracted for a system, which should, as far as human foresight can provide, retain forever the government of the literary institution they had formed, in the hands of the persons approved by themselves. This system is [now] totally changed. . . . This . . . is not according to the will of the donors, and is subversive of that contract on the faith of which their property was given. . . .

It results from this opinion, that the acts of the legislature of New Hampshire, which are stated in the special verdict found in this cause, are repugnant to the [C]onstitution of the United States, and that the judgment on this special verdict ought to have been for the plaintiffs. The judgment of the state court must, therefore, be reversed.

***Charles River Bridge* v. *Warren Bridge* (1837).** In 1785 Massachusetts gave the Charles River Bridge Company a charter allowing it to collect tolls from all who used the bridge. The charter was to stand for seventy years. In 1828 the state gave a similar charter for the Warren Bridge, which was a short distance from and parallel to the earlier bridge. In six years, however, the Warren Bridge was made free to all passengers.

Owners of the Charles River Bridge sued. They claimed that their charter, like that of Dartmouth College, was a contract, and that it had been "impaired" when the state allowed a competing bridge to take their profits.

In 1837, when the case reached the Supreme Court, there was a new Chief Justice, Roger Taney. The view of contracts held by Taney and President Andrew Jackson was different from John Marshall's. They took into account a state's right to protect its people against the power of monopolies. In deciding against the Charles River Company's claim that it had a legal, unbreakable monopoly, Taney wrote:

The object and end of all government is to promote the happiness and prosperity of the community. . . . And in a country like ours . . . new channels of communication are daily found necessary, both for travel and trade; . . . And when a corporation alleges, that a state has surrendered, for seventy years, its power of improvement and public accommodation, in a great and important line of travel, along which a vast number of its citizens must daily

Picturing History Supreme Court Chief Justice Roger. Taney ruled against the Charles River Company in 1837.

pass, the community has a right to insist [that the state not surrender this line of travel to a single corporation, with the right to exact toll, and exclude competition for seventy years]. . . . The continued existence of a government would be of no great value, if by implications and presumptions it was disarmed of the powers necessary to accomplish the ends of its creation.

The new charter was legal, the Court decided. Justice Joseph Story disagreed. In his dissenting opinion he wrote:

I admit, that where the terms of a grant are to impose burdens upon the public, or to create a restraint injurious to the public interests, there is sound reason for interpreting the terms, if ambiguous, [confusing] in favour of the public. . . . [However,] no man will hazard his capital in any enterprise, in which, if there be a loss, it must be borne exclusively by himself; and if there be success, he has not the slightest security of enjoying the rewards of that success.

Practicing Your Skill

1. In both cases discussed here, what was the main issue at stake?
2. In each case, what was the Court's decision?
3. What reasons were given to support each decision?
4. What circumstances or events at the time might have influenced the Court's decision?
5. How does the dissenting opinion in the Charles River Bridge case differ from the Court's decision in that case?
6. Do you agree or disagree with the interpretations made in each decision? Explain.

FOCUS ON SKILLS

Answers

Practicing Your Skill

1. Whether a state can pass a law that alters a legal contract.

2. Dartmouth College—the state could not change the terms of the contracts. Charles River Bridge—the new charter for Warren Bridge was legal.

3. Dartmouth College—the founders contracted for a system that had been changed by the state of New Hampshire, a change that was not in the spirit of the U.S. Constitution; Charles River Bridge—the state must promote the happiness and prosperity of the community, so could not uphold a contract that eliminated competition.

4. The Chief Justice for the Dartmouth College case was Marshall, whereas Taney presided over the Charles River Bridge case.

5. Dissenting opinion—people will not risk capital if they must bear losses but cannot enjoy success. The Court's decision focused instead on the good of the community.

6. Possible answers: agree—Dartmouth—the decision of the state court violated the U.S. Constitution; Charles River Bridge—the new charter was legal because it served the public's interest. Disagree—Dartmouth—education is a public matter, so the state should be able to change the charter; Charles River Bridge—the state should not be able to interfere with a legal contract.

Key Terms and People

These are highlighted in the text in the order in which they appear.

Main Ideas

1. Enacts laws for the federal government.

2. Deals with the bills introduced in Congress that are within its area of expertise.

3. Their staffs, the Government Printing Office, and the Library of Congress.

4. The powers to raise revenue, tax, impose tariffs on imported goods and other items, borrow money, regulate commerce, coin money, manage the postal system, establish federal courts, and declare war.

5. Any natural-born citizen aged 35 years or older who has been a resident of the U.S. for at least 14 years. • Stature in a major political party or having served in high political or military office.

6. To serve as commander in chief of the armed forces, make treaties, appoint ambassadors, meet with heads of state, appoint Supreme Court justices, and execute the laws of the land.

7. Provides advice.

8. Provides experts in specialized fields.

9. *Bureaucracy:* administration of government through departments managed by appointed officials; *hierarchy:* direction from above to those below; *civil service:* jobs in government; *public policy:* government action in response to a political problem.

10. Each branch of government has checks on the bureaucracy through laws, budgets, program cutbacks, and the court system. Interest groups expose excesses of the bureaucracy.

11. Federal civil and criminal cases.

12. Confirmation by the Senate and screening by the Justice Department and the FBI.
• Yes—Supreme Court justices are investigated more closely by the Senate than are prospective federal court judges.

➤**13.** Existing laws and legal precedents, justices' personal legal views (strict versus broad interpretations of the Constitution), interaction with other justices, public opinion, the wishes of Congress and the President.

Critical Thinking Questions

➤**14.** Possible answers: they should have the courage and judgment to use one or more of these ways as the issue directs. Always voting as constituents wish may violate national interests.

15. Members of Congress must keep in mind the specific needs of the people in their districts who elected

them—or they could lose next time.

16. Assassination by a disappointed office-seeker pointed up the necessity of filling jobs by a merit system.

17. Possible answer: the Supreme Court thought that the restriction imposed by the act was less of an infringement on federal employees' freedom than was pressure on employees to back a particular party or politician.

CHAPTER **7** REVIEW

Write your answers on a separate piece of paper.

Key Terms and People

Explain the significance of: democracy, nonlegislative powers, Thomas O'Neill, executive branch, George Washington, Franklin D. Roosevelt, Abraham Lincoln, National Security Council (NSC), specialization, J. Edgar Hoover, Robert Bork, lame duck, Lewis Powell, Jr., briefs, *amicus curiae,* John Marshall, Oliver Wendell Holmes, Jr., separate but equal

Main Ideas

1. What does the legislative branch of the government do?
2. What does a congressional committee do?
3. Who helps the members of Congress in their work?
4. What powers does the Constitution give to Congress?
5. What are the constitutional qualifications for President? What are the informal qualifications that have evolved over the years?
6. What are the constitutional powers of the President?
7. What is the importance of the cabinet to the President?
8. What does the Executive Office of the President do for the President?
9. Define *bureaucracy, hierarchy, civil service,* and *public policy.*
10. How is the power of the immense federal bureaucracy kept in check?
11. What kinds of cases do the federal lower trial courts have jurisdiction over?
12. What qualifying processes must a prospective federal court judge undergo? Is the process different for prospective Supreme Court justices? If so, describe the difference.
13. List the five factors that may influence Supreme Court decisions.

Critical Thinking Questions

14. **Evaluating How Decisions Are Made.** How should members of Congress vote—as their constituents wish, by using independent judg-

ment, by voting as their political party directs, or by using a combination of these ways depending on the issue at hand? Why?

15. **Analyzing Quotations.** What did Tip O'Neill mean when he said "all politics is local"?

16. **Assessing Cause and Effect.** How did President Garfield's assassination lead to passage of the Pendleton Act, which set up the federal civil service?

17. **Forming Hypotheses.** Why do you think that the Supreme Court found the Hatch Act constitutional?

18. **Forming a Hypothesis/Making Generalizations.** Lobbyists, political parties, and the civil service were not mentioned in the Constitution. Why do you think this is so? Why are they now so important a part of our governmental system?

Critical Thinking Activities

19. **Planning for the Future.** What would you ask the member of Congress from your district?

20. **Making a Chart.** Using your textbook, set up a chart showing, in chronological order, the important Supreme Court cases listed in this chapter and, briefly, the ruling. Use these headings: Supreme Court Cases, Year, and Ruling.

21. **Analyzing a Chart.** Look at the chart on page 194. How many departments make up the cabinet? Which department regulates foreign affairs? When was it established?

22. **Analyzing Statistics.** The Defense Department has more civilian employees than does the Department of Education. Why do you think this is so? What does this show or not show about the priorities of the United States?

23. **Linking Past to Present.** What is the difference between the expressed powers and the implied powers of Congress? How do the implied powers make it possible for our Constitution to adapt to modern times?

TELESCOPING THE TIMES: 1787–Today

Focus on Democracy

The Constitution of the United States gives the national government important powers, though it reserves some powers to the states. The Constitution first provides that the Congress shall serve as the law-making, or legislative, branch of the Federal government.

Congress is made up of the Senate (two senators for each state) and the 435-member House of Representatives (number of seats per state according to size of population). Because of its size, Congress operates by dividing itself into smaller groups, or committees. Committees decide which bills they want to ask the entire Congress to approve.

The powers the Constitution grants Congress include the power to raise taxes, coin and borrow money, regulate commerce, and set up post offices. It authorizes Congress to declare war and to establish and support the armed forces. It also permits Congress to provide for federal courts below the level of the Supreme Court.

The Constitution also provides for the executive branch, which is headed by the President. The Constitution sets forth brief requirements for the Presidency concerning age, residence, pay, and term of office. It also provides for a Vice-President and deals with problems of succession.

The Constitution makes the President commander in chief of the armed forces, gives him or her power to make treaties with other nations, and authorizes him or her to nominate justices of the Supreme Court and heads of executive departments. It also gives the President veto power over bills passed by Congress, an action that can, however, be overridden by a two-thirds vote in both houses.

The executive branch, like the rest of the federal government, depends on its bureaucracy. By 1989 the number of cabinet departments had grown from three—State, the Treasury, and War—to fourteen.

The additional departments include Interior, Energy, and Education. Several million people are now employed by the executive branch of the federal government in civilian jobs.

The third branch of the federal government established by the Constitution is the judicial branch. Our federal court system has evolved, since the Constitution requires only the existence of a Supreme Court. Congress has created a three-tiered organization of the federal courts. Cases first go to the district courts. Appeals are heard in twelve regional Courts of Appeal. Final appeals are made to the Supreme Court.

The Supreme Court hears the cases that it regards as especially important. Those that the Court decides not to hear it reverts to the decision already determined in the lower courts.

Chronology of Main Events

1803	*Marbury* v. *Madison*
1824	*Gibbons* v. *Ogden*
1857	*Dred Scott* v. *Sandford*
1896	*Plessy* v. *Ferguson*
1919	*Schenck* v. *United States*
1939	Executive Office of the President created
1954	*Brown* v. *Board of Education*
1966	*Miranda* v. *Arizona*
1967	Twenty-fifth Amendment on Presidential succession ratified
1988	Department of Veterans Affairs created

205

Global Perspectives

1789-1799	French Revolution creates chaos in Europe.
1791	British Parliament passes act to organize Canadian government.
1792	Denmark becomes first European nation to ban slave trade.
1794-1804	Haitians overthrow French rule.
1796	Teheran becomes capital of Persia.
1798	Napoleon conquers Egypt.
1800	Alessandro Volta of Italy invents the electric battery.

For Discussion

How might the American Revolution have influenced Parliament to pass an act to organize the Canadian government in 1791? (Possible response: Britain might have feared another colonial revolution and therefore been willing to grant Canada concessions that otherwise would not have been considered.)

Additional Resources

- Geography Activities
- Skills Activities
- Thematic Activities
- Economic Activities
- Cultural Literacy Activities
- Literary Source Readings
- Primary Source Readings
- Nuclear Peacekeeping
- Transparencies
- Computer Test Generator

CD-ROM:
The Presidents

Begin using *The Presidents CD-ROM* with Chapter 8. See note on page T-9 and refer to *Activity Guide for Connecting The Americans and The Presidents CD-ROM.*

Additional Teaching Strategies

SECTION 1

For Basic Students: Ask each student to write two questions and answers regarding the Bill of Rights. Each question should be written on the front and the corresponding answer on the back of a 3″ × 5″ card. Collect all the questions and divide the class into two teams. Pull questions and ask alternating sides. When a student misses, he or she is out. The team with the most members left at the end of the time period is declared the winner. (Possible questions and answers: Q. Which amendment protects citizens from unlawful search and seizure? A. Fourth Amendment; Q. Which amendment might be cited by opponents to handgun control laws? A. Second Amendment.)

For Advanced Students: Have students prepare a diagram comparing the cabinet of 1789 to the present cabinet, including the name of the head of each department. Discuss why new departments have been added.

Washington's Cabinet	Today's Cabinet
• Secretary of State [Jefferson]	• Secretary of State [　　　]
• Secretary of Treasury [Hamilton]	• Secretary of Treasury [　　　]
• Secretary of War [Knox]	• Secretary of Labor [　　　]
• Attorney General [Randolph]	• Attorney General [　　　]
	• Secretary of Interior [　　　]
	• Secretary of Agriculture [　　　]
	• Secretary of Commerce [　　　]
	• Secretary of Health and Human Services [　　　]
	• Secretary of Transportation [　　　]
	• Secretary of Energy [　　　]
	• Secretary of Housing and Urban Development [　　　]
	• Secretary of Education [　　　]
	• Secretary of Defense [　　　]
	• Secretary of Veterans Affairs [　　　]

Names of Secretaries will vary depending on current cabinet. Possible reason for new departments might include: as nation grew there was a need for advisors in additional specialized areas.

SECTION 2

For Basic Students: Divide class into pairs to compose letters from Alexander Hamilton defending his policies to the editor of the *National Gazette*. (Letters might include: a balanced economy helps all Americans; farmers should not be favored as Jefferson believes; the U.S. must be able to raise money and earn the support of the nation's financial leaders.)

For Advanced Students: Have students use information from the chart "Origins of the Two-Party System" to write a three-paragraph essay explaining which political party they would have supported. Have them include any philosophies of the opposing party that they would like to see their party consider. (Pro-Republican paragraphs might include: believes in common people and does not give special privileges to rich; believes in protecting individual liberties. Other philosophies that Republicans might consider include: need for balanced economy of agriculture, trade, finance, and manufacturing; need for government aid to trade, finance, and manufacturing.)

SECTION 3

For Basic Students: Ask students to develop a "report card" for President Washington which evaluates his accomplishments in foreign policy. Each grade should be accompanied by a one- or two-sentence explanation. Areas for evaluation: relations with Spain, France, Great Britain, and Indians. (Possible response: Washington's grade for relations with Spain is excellent or A. Reasons for this grade include: Pinckney's Treaty won points with Spain; Spain gave up lands east of Mississippi River and north of Florida; Spain agreed to open Mississippi River to American traffic; Spain allowed Americans to use New Orleans port for three years.)

For Advanced Students: Have students research and present a three-minute presentation on the conflict between the Indians and the settlers between 1778 and 1800. Presentations should include a summary statement expressing how the student feels the conflicts were handled. (Presentations may include information on any of the following: General John Sullivan; General Josiah Harmar; General Arthur St. Clair; General "Mad Anthony" Wayne; the Senecas; the Treaty of Paris; Little Turtle.)

SECTION 4

For Basic Students: Ask students to write two paragraphs explaining the purpose of the Alien and Sedition Acts and Republican reaction to the acts. (Details may include: Adams's inability to deal with criticism and desire to stop Republican editors and writers; law was in effect for Adams's term of office only.)

For Advanced Students: Ask students to assume the role of retired President George Washington and compose a letter to President John Adams expressing concern over the course the government seems to be taking. (Letters may include: reference to Alien and Sedition Acts as an attempt to prohibit freedom of speech and freedom of the press; reference to the way sectionalism was replacing nationalism.)

Further Reading for Students

Baldwin, Leland D. *Whiskey Rebels: The Story of a Frontier Uprising*. Pittsburgh: University of Pittsburgh Press, 1968.

Koch, Adrienne. *Jefferson and Madison: The Great Collaboration*. New York: Oxford University Press, 1964.

Main, Jackson T. *The Anti-Federalists: Critics of the Constitution*. New York: W. W. Norton, 1974.

Miller, John C. *Crisis in Freedom: The Alien and Sedition Acts*. Boston: Little Brown, 1951.

Nock, Albert J. *Jefferson*. Lanham, Md.: University Press of America, 1985.

Historical Fiction

Johnston, Mary. *Lewis Rand*. Darby, Pa.: Arden Library, 1978.

Richter, Conrad. *The Light in the Forest*. New York: Amsco School Publications, 1970.

Stone, Irving. *Those Who Love*. New York: Doubleday, 1965.

Bibliography for Teachers

Books

Dos Passos, John. *The Men Who Made the Nation*. Garden City, N.Y.: Doubleday, 1957.

Mitchell, Broadus. *Alexander Hamilton: A Concise Biography*. New York: Oxford University Press, 1976.

Schachner, Nathan. *Founding Fathers*. New York: Putnam, 1954.

Tunis, Edwin. *The Young United States: 1783 to 1830*. New York: Crowell, 1976.

Audio-Visuals

Great Men and Great Issues: Launching A New National Government. Wilcom. Audiotapes.

Our Political System: Parties. National Geographic Society. Filmstrip.

The Spirit of John Adams in the Netherlands. Royal Netherlands Embassy. Movie.

Teacher's Notes:

Lesson Plan

Teaching Resources, Unit 2 Booklet

Lesson Study Sheets pp. 103-118
Daily Activities pp. 119-126
Enrichment Activities pp. 127-134
Reteaching Activities pp. 135-142
Chapter Review p. 143
Chapter Mastery Tests pp. 145-156
Telescoping the Times Study Sheet p. 157

Chapter Objectives

Students will learn:
- early development of our nation's federal government
- the origins of political parties in the U.S.
- major foreign policy issues during Washington's Presidency
- important political issues during Adams's Presidency

Using the Chapter Time Line

What name was given to the era that lasted from the inauguration of Washington as President to 1800 (see Unit 2 Time Line)? (Answer: Federalist Era) What important event took place in Europe (see Unit 2 Time Line) the same year Washington was inaugurated? (Answer: French Revolution began)

Picturing History The dignity George Washington conferred on the office of President can be seen in this painting. The artist, Gilbert Stuart, is best known for his portrait of Washington that appears on the dollar bill.

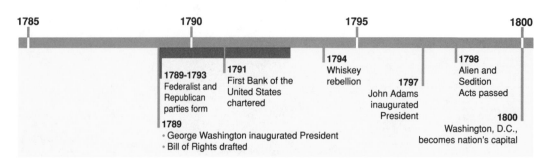

1785

1790

1795

1800

1789-1793
Federalist and Republican parties form

1791
First Bank of the United States chartered

1794
Whiskey rebellion

1797
John Adams inaugurated President

1798
Alien and Sedition Acts passed

1789
- George Washington inaugurated President
- Bill of Rights drafted

1800
Washington, D.C., becomes nation's capital

206

CHAPTER **8**   1789–1800

The Federalist Era

Links to American Literature

"We've begun to think, sir, that the uniform of a Secretary of the Treasury must be the cloak of invisibility. Not one of us has seen you for weeks."

Hamilton sighed gustily. . . .

"I've been asked to report on the public credit when Congress next meets."

"But that should be easy, sir. Not worth half a minute of invisibility. 'Honorable gentlemen, the credit of these United States is zero'—and you might add that the popular desire to right the matter is zero, too."

"You lay your finger on the crux of it, of course. Desire is zero."

Hamilton tapped his shin thoughtfully with the hat he held. "How to awaken interest—" His voice trailed off to a long pause.

James's mind reverted to the discussion of the evening before. . . .

"I could wish we were strong enough to dispense with the people. That men like you, sir, who know what should be done, must be hampered by fools!"

"They are fools certainly, most of them," Hamilton spoke slowly, "and unstable; but even fools must be coerced along a path of honor. We have leaders. We must strengthen them."

— ELIZABETH PAGE, *The Tree of Liberty*

The Constitution provided Americans with a means of settling their disputes. Still, President Washington and his cabinet faced many problems, one of which was a large national debt. Alexander Hamilton's economic proposals created such disagreement in the House of Representatives that members split into two parties. The Federalists favored Hamilton's policies, which emphasized security and prosperity. The Republicans, led by James Madison and then by Thomas Jefferson, favored policies emphasizing democracy and individual liberty.

Chapter Overview

Alexander Hamilton was not opposed to democracy, nor was Thomas Jefferson opposed to security and prosperity. They simply had different views on what should take priority. Understanding how people chose between opposing viewpoints in the past can help us decide between opposing viewpoints today. In this chapter you will learn about the early stages in the development of our federal government. You will also learn about the major foreign policy issues during George Washington's Presidency and the important political issues during John Adams's Presidency. To help you understand these issues, Chapter 8 is divided into four sections.

Chapter Outline

1. **President Washington Takes Charge**
2. **The First Political Parties Develop**
3. **Foreign Affairs Become Troublesome**
4. **President Adams Faces Political Strife**

The Federalist Era   207

State the Objective

Understand the early development of our nation's federal government.

Historical Sidelights
• George Washington remains the only President ever elected unanimously by the electoral college.
• When Washington married Martha Custis, she gave him a miniature of herself. Washington wore the miniature for the next forty years. It was removed only after the general's death in 1799.

SECTION 1

President Washington Takes Charge

GLOSSARY TERMS: **government bonds, funding, bank notes, national bank, protective tariff, excise tax**

It was shortly after noon on April 30, 1789. **George Washington,** dressed in a plain brown suit but wearing a sword, stood on the porch of Federal Hall on Wall Street in New York and said, "I do solemnly swear that I will faithfully execute the office of President of the United States and will, to the best of my ability, preserve, protect, and defend the Constitution of the United States. So help me God."

Cheers rose from the crowd as Washington said the words that made him the first President of the new nation. The cheers grew louder and bells rang as he kissed the red leather-bound Bible on which he had sworn his oath of office. Then he turned and entered the hall to talk to Congress about the "ocean of difficulties" that lay ahead.

The President and the first Congress had much work to do. First, they had to create a bureaucracy to help the President carry out laws. Second, they had to provide for a judicial system. Finally, they had to raise money for operating expenses and for paying off the country's debts. American leaders realized they were treading on fresh ground. "We are in a wilderness," James Madison wrote, "without a single footstep to guide us."

Picturing History George Washington took the oath of office on the balcony of a Wall Street building. It took him a week to reach New York City (then the nation's capital) from his home at Mount Vernon because he stopped for speeches along the way.

The Bill of Rights Is Adopted

Everyone agreed that the new government's first order of business should be the adoption of a bill of rights. These amendments to the Constitution would list the freedoms that the new federal gov-

---

People in the Chapter

George Washington objected to the use of a title when referring to the President. Benjamin Franklin thought His Mightiness would be appropriate. John Adams argued for His Most Benign Highness. The title stated in the Constitution — President of the United States — was finally chosen to settle the debate.

Alexander Hamilton grew up in the West Indies. He showed so much talent that the local merchants collected money to send him to college in America. He served as an aide to Washington during the Revolution and became secretary of the treasury at the age of thirty-four.

John Adams claimed that digging ditches played an important part in building his character. As a boy, he hated Latin grammar and asked his father for some other form of work. "Well," said his father, "you may try ditching. My meadow yonder needs a ditch." After two days of ditch digging, young Adams went back to his Latin.

Little Turtle was chief of the Miami Indians. By leading a combined force of Miami, Delaware, Shawnee, Chippewa, Potawatomi, and Ottawa Indians, he inflicted the worst defeat the United States suffered in the history of its wars with the Indians.

Present the Lesson

Ask students to skim the section to find out how President Washington and Congress attempted to solve each of the problems listed on the board. (Possible responses: Washington created executive departments to deal with the most pressing problems—foreign affairs, military matters, and financial problems; Judiciary Act of 1789 established Supreme Court.) Discuss with students which problems were the easiest to solve and which were the most complicated.

ernment could not take away from the people.

The question of a bill of rights had come up several times during the Constitutional Convention, but the delegates had voted it down. Why? Apparently they had done so because they did not think it was necessary. To them, the Constitution as a whole was a bill of rights. It listed what the new government could do, yet it did not take away any of the rights for which Americans had fought the Revolutionary War. The delegates assumed that the people retained their rights. As one of them later wrote, "It never occurred to us that personal liberty could ever be endangered in this country."

Others, however, felt differently about the matter. Thomas Jefferson had been in Paris while the convention was going on. He wrote to Madison that "a bill of rights is what the people are entitled to against every government on earth . . . and what no just government should refuse." Patrick Henry felt it was foolish to take a chance that the rulers of the new nation would turn out to be good men. To him, the only way to guarantee liberty was through a system of laws. In addition, some states had ratified the Constitution with the definite understanding that it would quickly be amended to include a bill of rights.

Accordingly, in September 1789 Congress approved twelve amendments to the Constitution and submitted them to the states. Two amendments—dealing with congressmen's salaries and congressional reapportionment—were defeated. The remaining ten were ratified and became part of the Constitution in 1791. These first ten amendments are known as the Bill of Rights.

As you can see from reading the Bill of Rights on pages 173–175, it protects people from government interference in certain areas. The Bill of Rights protects freedom of religion, freedom of speech, freedom of the press, the right to assemble peacefully with other persons, and the right to petition the federal government to correct wrongs. In addition, it requires that authorities obtain a warrant from a judge before searching or seizing any property. The Bill of Rights also provides for trial by jury in criminal cases, and it prohibits excessive bail and "cruel and unusual punishment." Furthermore, it gives individuals the right to refuse to testify against themselves in court. The Ninth and Tenth Amendments restrict the powers of the federal government to those named in the Constitution. All other powers are reserved "to the states respectively, or to the people."

Linking Past to Present

The Bill of Rights is alive and well and in the news almost daily. An ongoing debate among Americans is whether the Second Amendment gives each person the right to own a handgun. Another constitutional problem is whether prayer in a public school violates the First Amendment prohibition against the establishment of religion. Interpretations of the Constitution change with the times and with changes in the makeup of the Supreme Court. President Ronald Reagan's appointments increased the number of judges on the Court who have often taken the conservative point of view. As a result, many experts believe that conservative views will dominate Supreme Court decisions in the 1990's.

The Judicial and Executive Branches Are Organized

After approving these constitutional amendments, Congress turned its attention to the organization of the other two branches of the federal government.

Organizing the Judiciary. The Constitution had left the details of the federal court system up to Congress. Members of the first Congress faced many questions concerning the courts. How many judges should there be? How many courts should be set up? Who would prosecute the government's cases? How would court orders be enforced? What would happen if federal court decisions conflicted with state laws?

The **Judiciary Act of 1789** established a Supreme Court with a Chief Justice and five associate justices (a number since changed several times by Congress). In addition, the act established sixteen lower federal courts throughout the country (a number that likewise has been changed).

The act also provided for prosecuting attorneys and for marshals who would enforce the decisions of the federal courts. These marshals were given the job of taking the first national census in 1790. This census was required by the Constitution mostly because no one knew exactly how many

Check for Understanding

Call on individual students to answer the Section 1 Review questions orally.

For Discussion

Give examples to support the following statement: "Hamilton's economic program was designed primarily to benefit the rich and members of the upper class." (Possible responses: Hamilton's primary concern was to put the nation on a firm economic footing; wealthy speculators and businessmen gained at the expense of the average citizen; Hamilton believed that the best way for government to succeed was to have the backing of the rich; debt assumption and funding helped wealthy Northern businessmen more than small farmers.)

representatives each state should send to Congress. Finally, the Judiciary Act created the office of Attorney General.

Organizing Departments and the Cabinet. In 1789 the executive branch of the federal government consisted of two men, the President and the Vice-President. Obviously, they needed help in governing. Three executive departments were therefore created to deal with the three most pressing problem areas: the Department of State to deal with foreign affairs, the Department of War to handle military matters, and the Department of the Treasury to handle financial problems.

Washington took great care in appointing secretaries to head each department. He chose able men whom he personally knew and trusted. He also chose them from various parts of the country. He knew there were jealousies among different sections. Each section would be more interested in supporting the new government if one of its own leaders was appointed to a high executive office. Washington's most important appointments were **Thomas Jefferson** as Secretary of State, **Alexander Hamilton** as Secretary of the Treasury, Henry Knox as Secretary of War, and Edmund Randolph as Attorney General.

Originally, the President had no intention that the three secretaries and the Attorney General would form a **cabinet.** No such group is mentioned in the Constitution. Within a few years, however, the secretaries began meeting together to advise the President, and the cabinet became a lasting part of the executive branch.

Hamilton Shapes Economic Policies

As Secretary of the Treasury, Hamilton believed he had a mission: to introduce "order into our finances" and to put the new nation on a firm economic footing. He turned his attention first to the public debt, that is, the money owed by the national and state governments.

Paying Off Foreign Debts. The public debt in 1790 came to about $80 million, a huge amount for those days. About two-thirds of this debt was owed by the national government, and about one-third by various state governments.

The federal government owed money both at home and abroad. Most of the debt had been incurred during the Revolution. Patriots had lent the Continental Congress funds with which to carry on the struggle against Great Britain. Soldiers had received **government bonds** instead of hard cash as payment for their military service. (Government bonds are certificates issued by a government that promises to repay a loan with interest.) In addition, both the Continental Congress and the Confederation Congress had borrowed money from such nations as France, the Netherlands, and Spain. In contrast, states owed money only to private citizens.

There was no argument about paying off the foreign debt at face value in order to establish the new government's credit with other nations. As Hamilton said, "The debt of the United States . . . was the price of liberty." There was, however, a tremendous amount of controversy about the domestic debt. Some people objected to the method of payment that Hamilton suggested. Others opposed Hamilton's idea that the federal government should simply assume, or take over, the debts of the states.

Funding Domestic Debts. Hamilton's suggested method of payment is known as **funding.** Funding is a method of getting money by borrowing it. Hamilton proposed that the federal government issue new bonds in exchange for the old ones that had been issued by the Continental Congress and by the Confederation Congress. The new bonds would have the same value as the old ones, plus any unpaid interest.

On the surface, this seemed like a fair exchange. However, many people—including James Madison, who rapidly became the leader of the House of Representatives—strongly opposed Hamilton's plan. They felt that Hamilton was not being fair. The average person had bought the bonds to help support the government. During the hard times that followed the Revolutionary War, however, many people had sold their bonds in order to pay their bills. Moreover, since bond prices had fallen after the war, many people had sold their bonds for as little as 25 percent of the original value. Who had purchased the bonds? Wealthy speculators had, most of them merchants in Northern commercial cities. Madison and others resented the fact that these speculators would receive $100 from the government for a bond that had cost them only $25, especially since the money to buy the bonds would come from taxes. Why should speculators gain at the expense of ordinary patriotic citizens?

Guided Practice

Discuss with students the fact that the Bill of Rights is alive and well and very much a focus in current events. Debate goes on about whether the Second Amendment gives an individual the right to own a handgun. For example, the issue of whether prayer in public schools violates the First Amendment or outlawing prayer in public schools violates freedom of speech as guaranteed by the same amendment is major topic of discussion. Ask students to give their opinions on this subject and the reasons for those opinions. (Discussion might include allowing prayer in school does not force people to participate in any one religious group, so it does not violate the separation guaranteed by the First Amendment; encouraging prayer in schools is unfair to those who do not wish to participate at all.)

Far from being horrified by the situation, Hamilton had planned it. In his view, the best way to make the new federal government succeed was to get powerful, wealthy people behind it. This could be accomplished by making their interest the government's interest. People would support a government that allowed them to make money.

Assuming State Debts. Hamilton's suggestion that the federal government assume debts owed by the states also made many people in the South furious. The Southern states had already paid off most of their debts. They resented government debt assumption because it meant that they would be taxed to help pay the debts incurred by the Northern states.

Despite the opposition, Congress approved both funding and debt assumption. The congressmen felt that they had to establish a good credit reputation for the new government, and this meant paying all public debts. Also, Hamilton had made a suggestion that was particularly attractive to Southerners: rather than locate the nation's capital in New York City or Philadelphia, why not build a new city on the banks of the Potomac River? So Congress passed both parts of Hamilton's program as well as a bill establishing a new federal city on land donated by Maryland. In 1800 the federal government was moved from Philadelphia to the new capital, called Washington, D.C.

Establishing a National Bank. After Congress accepted his proposals for managing the public debt, Hamilton moved on to the second part of his economic program. He urged the establishment of a bank of the United States, with the power to issue **bank notes,** or paper money. It also would have branches in various cities.

Hamilton argued that such a **national bank** had many economic advantages. It would handle tax

Picturing History
Benjamin Banneker (left) was one of the surveyors who drew up the plan for Washington, D.C. (above).

receipts and all other government money. Since its notes would have the same value all over the nation, citizens of different states would find it easier to do business with one another. People also would have more confidence in paper money that said ''Bank of the United States'' than in paper money printed by small local or state banks.

Hamilton also believed that there were political advantages to having a national banking system. The government would own only 20 percent of the shares of stock in the bank. The remaining 80 percent would be owned by private investors. Naturally, these private investors would be the rich and wellborn people whose allegiance to the federal government Hamilton wanted to encourage. In Hamilton's view, the bank would help cement the national union.

Hamilton got his national bank, but only after arousing further suspicion about and hostility toward his entire financial program. Southerners argued, quite correctly, that the bank would make Northern merchants richer but would offer few benefits to farmers. At the same time, in the House, Madison raised a new issue. The Constitution, he said, did not give the federal government specific authority to establish a bank. Thus, in Madison's opinion, establishing a national bank was unconstitutional.

When the bill chartering the national bank for twenty years reached Washington's desk, the President was very doubtful about signing it. He asked Jefferson and Hamilton for their opinions.

Jefferson agreed with Madison's strict interpretation of the Constitution. Jefferson also was aware of a so-called elastic clause (see page 164), which said that Congress could make all the laws that were ''necessary and proper'' for carrying out its powers. However, such laws, in Jefferson's opinion, had to be really necessary, not just convenient. If Congress could carry out its powers *without* setting up a bank, for example, then it did not have the right to set up a bank.

Hamilton, on the other hand, favored a loose interpretation of the Constitution. He pointed out that Congress had the right ''to lay and collect taxes'' and ''to borrow money.'' The national bank would help with both tasks, he added. Since the Constitution did not specifically prohibit such a bank, he said, Congress had the right to set one up. President Washington took Hamilton's advice, and the First Bank of the United States was established.

Levying Taxes. ''All taxes are odious [hateful],'' said Congressman John Laurance of New York. ''It is also true some are more odious than others,'' he added. Indeed, the tax proposed by Hamilton as the

Picturing History Alexander Hamilton's Bank of the United States was a federal showplace. When it was built, marble was used in the Grecian facade but brick was chosen for the sides because of the high cost of marble. The bank still stands on South Third Street in Philadelphia.

Student Assignment/Homework

Have students read Section 2, "The First Political Parties Develop," and answer the Section 2 Review questions.

Picturing History The New York Stock Exchange was located in the Tontine Coffee House (left) at the corner of Wall and Water streets in 1794. Merchants and brokers haggled over prices for ships' cargoes scattered along the street.

third part of his economic program was so odious that it caused a tax revolt known as the **Whiskey Rebellion.**

One of the first acts of the new Congress had been the passage of a **protective tariff,** an import tax on goods manufactured in Europe. The purpose of this tariff was to protect the nation's businesses from foreign competition. By the time Hamilton took office as Secretary of the Treasury, this tax was bringing in a lot of revenue. However, more money was needed to pay off the public debt and to run the national government. So Hamilton suggested that an **excise tax** (sales tax) be levied on every gallon of whiskey that was made or sold.

Why tax whiskey? The reason was political. Most whiskey producers were small frontier farmers. Their major crop was corn. However, corn was too bulky to carry across the Appalachian Mountains and sell in the settled areas along the Atlantic. So the farmers distilled the corn into whiskey, which could be sent easily to market on the backs of mules.

Since whiskey was the main source of cash for these frontier farmers, Hamilton knew that the excise tax would make them furious. So it did. Farmers in western Pennsylvania refused to pay the tax. They beat up federal marshals in Pittsburgh, and they even threatened to secede from the Union.

Hamilton was not upset, however. He looked upon the Whiskey Rebellion as an opportunity for the federal government to show that it could enforce the law without help from the states, even

along the western frontier. Accordingly, some fifteen thousand militiamen were called up. Accompanied by Washington part of the way and Hamilton all the way, the federal troops hiked over the Alleghenies and scattered the rebels without the loss of a single life.

SECTION 1 REVIEW

Key Terms and People

Explain the significance of: George Washington, Judiciary Act of 1789, Thomas Jefferson, Alexander Hamilton, cabinet, government bonds, funding, bank notes, national bank, Whiskey Rebellion, protective tariff, excise tax

Main Ideas

1. What was the purpose of the Bill of Rights?
2. Briefly describe the federal court system established by the first Congress.
3. Explain the origin of the concept of a Presidential cabinet.
4. What were the political goals of Hamilton's economic program?
5. In general, why did many Americans oppose Hamilton's financial policies?

Critical Thinking

6. How did the Whiskey Rebellion demonstrate both the effectiveness and the shortcomings of Hamilton's policies?

Anticipate the Lesson

Ask students to list advantages and disadvantages of political parties. (Possible advantages: voters can identify issues and candidates easily; the party system eliminates excessive numbers of people running for the same office. Possible disadvantages: voters sometimes agree with some policies from each party and find it difficult to choose a candidate; candidates must sometimes compromise their philosophies in order to receive the support of a particular party.)

State the Objective

Explain the origins of political parties in the U.S.

Present the Lesson

Have students study the chart "Origins of the Two-Party System" in this section and discuss the differences in the philosophies of Jefferson and Hamilton. (Differences include: Jefferson believed in the common man while Hamilton believed the common man often acted foolishly; Jefferson favored a weak central government while Hamilton favored a strong central government; Jefferson wanted to eliminate internal taxes while Hamilton favored maintaining internal taxes.)

SECTION 2

The First Political Parties Develop

GLOSSARY TERMS: **Federalists, Republicans, two-party system**

Hamilton's view of the new nation's proper future was different from that held by Jefferson and Madison. As time went on, this difference resulted in the formation of two distinct political groups, or parties. People whose opinions were closest to those of Hamilton called themselves **Federalists.** People whose views were closer to those of Jefferson and Madison became known as **Republicans.** (Although the name is the same, this Republican party was completely different from the modern one.)

Hamilton Mistrusts the Masses

Hamilton wanted a powerful nation resting on a balanced economy of agriculture, trade, finance, and manufacturing. Agriculture, he thought, did not need any special encouragement since most people were farmers. Other, less developed parts of the economy, however, did need government help. Hamilton thought that the major weakness of the Confederation had been its inability to raise money. Therefore, he wanted to gain the support of financial leaders for the new government.

Hamilton believed that people in the mass were not to be trusted. He thought they often acted foolishly and needed a strong government to tell them what to do. The rich, the educated, and the wellborn were the only people who counted, Hamilton believed. Only they could be depended on to govern wisely because they had the most to lose from a weak or unstable government. He feared that if the common people got too much power, they might endanger private property. In other words, the have-nots might take it away from the haves.

Jefferson Believes in the Common People

Unlike Hamilton, Jefferson had a deep faith in the common people, especially the American farmer. "Those who labor in the earth," he once wrote, "are the chosen people of God." He distrusted special privilege. He also disliked the world

Picturing History The New York Chamber of Commerce commissioned this portrait of Alexander Hamilton by the well-known artist John Trumbull.

of cities, commerce, and finance. Although he later modified his views somewhat, in general he felt that city life corrupted people through ignorance and poverty. In Jefferson's view, "The mobs of great cities add just as much to the support of pure government as sores do to the strength of the human body."

Again unlike Hamilton, Jefferson favored a weak central government and strong state governments. He believed that the liberties of individuals had to be protected against all governments. That is why he fought so strongly for the Bill of Rights. He also did not favor government help for manufacturing, trade, or finance—"for the general operation of manufacture, let our workshops remain in Europe." Jefferson viewed the American nation as a land of small independent farmers and educated leaders working together in perfect harmony.

Check for Understanding

Using the chart "Origins of the Two-Party System," create a twenty-point quiz for students. Have students identify each position as belonging to either the Hamiltonian or the Jeffersonian philosophy. Sample positions follow.
1. Opposed the establishment of a national bank (Jefferson)
2. Distrusted special privilege (Jefferson)
3. Favored strong central government (Hamilton)

Guided Practice

Tell students that the terms "Jeffersonian" and "Hamiltonian" are still used by political leaders. Ronald Reagan once characterized himself as a "Jeffersonian" in his dislike of a strong central government. He also described himself as a "Hamiltonian" in regard to his concern for the welfare of business. Have students discuss whether voters today are as concerned with political parties as with individual issues. Ask students whether voters tend to vote for all Democrats or all Republicans in an election (a straight ticket) or for a mixture of candidates from both parties (a split ticket). (Possible response: voters seem to be more issue-oriented and will vote for the candidate they feel is most competent or whose philosophy is closest to theirs.)

Origins of the Two-Party System

Jefferson's Views	Hamilton's Views
On Who Should Govern	
Had deep faith in the common people, especially farmers	Believed that the common people often acted foolishly
Distrusted special privilege	Thought that the rich, educated, and wellborn were the people who should rule
Wished to lower voting qualifications	Wanted to raise voting qualifications
On the Structure of Government	
Favored a weak central government, strong state governments	Favored a strong central government
Preferred a more democratic government than that of Britain	Thought that the American government should be modeled on the British system
Wanted to reduce the number of federal employees	Wanted to increase the number of federal employees
Favored a strict interpretation of the Constitution	Supported a loose interpretation of the Constitution
Believed that individual liberties must be protected by laws	Thought that individual liberties, such as freedom of speech, should sometimes be restricted
On Economics	
Thought that agriculture should be the backbone of the nation	Wanted a balanced economy of agriculture, trade, finance, and manufacturing
Did not support giving government aid to trade, finance, and manufacturing	Favored giving government aid to trade, finance, and manufacturing
Opposed the establishment of a national bank	Established a national bank
Wanted to eliminate internal taxes	Wanted to maintain internal taxes
Wanted to pay off the national debt	Wanted to use the national debt to establish credit
On Foreign Policy	
Believed that America was obligated to help France	Supported Britain, the parent country
Jeffersonians Democratic-Republican party	**Hamiltonians** Federalist party
Made up of artisans, shopkeepers, frontier settlers, and small farmers	Consisted of bankers, manufacturers, merchants, professional people, and wealthy farmers
Was strongest in the South, in the Southwest, and on the frontier	Had the most support in New England and along the Atlantic coast

Assign Independent Practice

Have students complete Chapter 8, Section 2 Enrichment Activity.

Student Assignment/Homework

Have students read Section 3, "Foreign Affairs Become Troublesome," and answer the Section 3 Review questions on paper.

Answers

Main Ideas

1. Hamilton believed that a strong government was needed to lead the masses. Jefferson felt that a weak central government was less likely to infringe upon the rights of individuals.

2. Hamilton distrusted the masses and doubted their ability to rule sensibly; Jefferson had great faith in the common people.

3. Hamilton envisioned a strong nation built on a balanced economy of agriculture, trade, finance, and manufacturing; Jefferson envisioned a nation of small independent farmers and educated leaders working together.

4. He believed that the President should be dignified and formal and remain above the details of political conflicts.

5. Hamilton's and Jefferson's political differences led to the formation of political clubs and newspapers that supported their views.

Critical Thinking

6. The name *Federalist* showed support for a strong central, or federal, government. • The name *Republican* showed support for the idea that government should be limited, leaving supreme power with individual citizens. **(analysis)**

Linking Past to Present

The terms *Jeffersonian* and *Hamiltonian* are still used by political leaders today. For example, President Reagan characterized himself as a Jeffersonian on the basis of his dislike of a strong central government. However, he also described himself as a Hamiltonian in his regard for the welfare of business.

Washington Defines the Presidency

As hostility rose between Hamilton and Jefferson, Washington tried evenhandedly to soothe things between them. He was deeply convinced that as head of the nation he should remain above quarrels over details of public policy. He respected both men's abilities and hoped they could work together.

Washington's idea of the Presidency was to keep it formal. He held regular morning receptions as well as formal evening dances and dinners. Uniformed servants in powdered wigs stood at the doors. Some critics thought these occasions made the President seem too distant and cold. Washington, however, thought they were necessary for the dignity of the highest office in the new country.

Other critics thought all the social events were just dull. It is only necessary, one wrote, "to be clean shaved, shirted, and powdered, go make your bows with grace, and to be master of small chat on the weather . . . or newspaper anecdote of the day."

The Parties Organize

Before 1791 the *Gazette of the United States* was the only newspaper that specialized in national politics. Its editor, John Fenno, was a Hamiltonian, and his paper reflected Hamilton's views.

To offset the influence of this publication, Madison and Jefferson set out to gain popular support for their position. They toured New England and New York to explain their views to political leaders there. In New York they won over Governor George Clinton, who had long been a rival of Hamilton's wealthy father-in-law and who controlled the upstate vote. They also gained the support of Aaron Burr, who had many followers in New York City. Then in October 1791, Madison

and Jefferson established the *National Gazette,* edited by the poet Philip Freneau. The *National Gazette* aimed to criticize Hamilton's policies. Madison wrote several articles for this newspaper, referring to people who backed his own views as members of "the Republican party." Many readers responded to this call for support. They began forming Republican clubs.

Hamilton was not a man to sit idly while his opponents organized. Like the Republicans, the Federalists began setting up local clubs of supporters. In this new kind of contest, the Federalists had several advantages. They had a well-thought-out, positive program. Also, the great majority of newspaper editors and clergymen supported their ideas, as did most wealthy men. In addition, Federalists in the federal government were able to reward their party's workers with jobs.

At the time of the 1792 national election, the Republicans were not well enough organized to run a candidate for President. Besides, Washington had reluctantly agreed to serve again, and it would have been futile for the Republicans to oppose this great national hero. Washington thus was elected for a second term, with John Adams again serving as Vice-President. Nevertheless, the **two-party system** would remain a characteristic of American politics up to the present time.

SECTION 2 REVIEW

Key Terms and People

Explain the significance of: Federalists, Republicans, two-party system

Main Ideas

1. Compare Hamilton's and Jefferson's views regarding the power of the central government.
2. How did Hamilton's opinion of the masses differ from Jefferson's?
3. How did Hamilton's ideas about the way in which the new nation should develop differ from Jefferson's?
4. Briefly characterize Washington's view of the Presidency.
5. Briefly explain how the two-party system developed.

Critical Thinking

6. Why did Hamilton's supporters call themselves Federalists? Why did Jefferson's supporters call themselves Republicans?

country out of conflicts; the country's advantages in the treaties and agreements made with other nations.)

Anticipate the Lesson

Discuss the meaning of the term "foreign policy" with the students. (Possible definitions: the way a country deals with other governments; treaties and agreements between countries.) Ask students how a President's foreign policy is evaluated by the citizens. (Possible areas of evaluation: the economic health of the country; the ability of President to keep

State the Objective

Identify major foreign policy issues during Washington's Presidency.

SECTION 3

Foreign Affairs Become Troublesome

GLOSSARY TERM: **neutrality**

The new government faced old problems with the British and the Indians over land claims in the **Northwest Territory.** (See the map on page 141.) In addition, Spain still claimed the land west of the Appalachian Mountains and south of the Ohio River. The greatest difficulties, though, arose as a result of the French Revolution, which broke out only a few weeks after Washington took office in the spring of 1789.

The French Revolution Deepens Divisions

At first most Americans welcomed the French Revolution. They felt that their own principles of liberty were spreading to Europe. As a show of their support against monarchy, several American cities changed their street names. New York's Queen Street, for example, was renamed Pearl Street, while Crown Street became Liberty Street.

As the French Revolution grew bloodier, however, American public opinion began to shift. Hamilton and other Federalists expressed their fear that the Revolution's leaders were determined to destroy all authority and stability. President Washington tended to agree with Hamilton, and other Americans began to wonder if perhaps Hamilton was right when he said that the public was "a great beast."

Divided Opinions. After the beheading of Louis XVI in 1793, France declared war on Great Britain. When the news reached the United States, it immediately deepened the division between the two emerging political parties. The Republicans cheered for the cause of republicanism and against the British monarchy. Both sides traded insults. Cries of "British bootlickers" were met with such phrases as "lying dogs" and "frog-eating, man-eating, blood-drinking cannibals."

The insults masked a basic political question, namely, should the United States enter the war? Republicans argued that France had helped the United States gain its independence. We were therefore obligated to help France, especially be-

cause we had signed a treaty of alliance in 1778. Federalists, however, felt that the United States had no choice but to support Britain, our parent country.

Washington did not favor fighting for Great Britain. On the other hand, since France had started the war, he did not feel that the United States was bound by the treaty. So he issued a declaration of **neutrality,** which said that the United States would support neither side in the conflict.

Picturing History In this engraving, Louis XVI is shown on the scaffold receiving the last rites just before he was beheaded.

Genêt's Mission. In the meantime, a minister from the new French republic had arrived in the United States to persuade the Americans to join the war against Great Britain. **Edmond Genêt** (zhə nā´) was an energetic, enthusiastic young man with

---

For Discussion
What makes a two-party system work better than a multi-party system? (Possible responses: in a two-party system, one party will earn a majority of votes and therefore represent the majority of the voters; in a two-party system, the two parties tend to focus on important issues while in a multi-party system, the parties tend to get caught up in less important or primarily sectional issues.)

Have students skim the section and locate information to complete the following chart. Make three columns on the board. In the first column list Great Britain, Spain, France, and Indians. In the second column list the problems between the U.S. and these people or countries, and in the third column list the government's response to each problem. Discuss with students the degree of success of each government action. Have students complete Chapter 8, Section 3 Daily Activity.

Nation	Problem	Response
Great Britain	Land claims in Northwest Territory	Jay's Treaty
	Seizure of neutral trading vessels	
Spain	Use of Mississippi River and port on New Orleans	Pinckney's Treaty
France	French Revolution	Declaration of Neutrality
	Genet's Mission	
Indians	Land claims in Northern states	Treaty of Paris
	Indian War in the Northern states	Treaty of Greenville

a wooden leg and no sense of the appropriate. He did not bother to present himself formally to the United States government as required by the rules of international diplomacy. Instead, he organized military expeditions against the Spanish in Florida and New Orleans, and he outfitted privateers to prey on British shipping. In short, he went about undermining United States neutrality.

When Genêt finally got around to visiting the President, Washington gave him a chilly reception. Such treatment would have brought most people to their senses. However, Genêt continued to act in a way that no independent nation could tolerate from a foreign minister. Even Jefferson, who had been enthusiastic about Genêt's arrival, was put off by the latter's lack of respect for the United States. The entire cabinet backed the President's formal request for Genêt's recall. By then, however, Genêt's political backers had fallen from power in Paris. Fearing for his life, the young envoy remained in America, became an American citizen, married Governor Clinton's daughter, and retired to a country estate on the Hudson River. Alexander Hamilton called him a "burned-out comet."

The effects of Genêt's activities on the American government were less romantic. Jefferson's apparent sympathy with Genêt's early activities and his continued approval of the French Revolution aroused Washington's suspicions. The President also disapproved of the grass-roots Republican clubs Jefferson was sponsoring. Washington did not like political factions. At the end of 1793, the President accepted Jefferson's resignation as Secretary of State. Hamilton remained Washington's intimate advisor, his words no longer challenged in the cabinet by his rival.

Linking Past to Present

Neutrality has been a recurring theme in American foreign policy. The United States declared itself neutral in the early years of World War I and World War II. Whether the United States should support any particular revolution is as much an issue today as it was during the time of the French Revolution. Recent revolutions in Central America and China, for example, have placed the United States in awkward diplomatic positions.

The British Ignore American Neutrality

It proved easier to proclaim neutrality in the European contest than to maintain it. As neutrals, Americans claimed the right to carry nonmilitary goods to the ports of any warring nation. Therefore, when the French lifted their traditional mercantilist restrictions on trade with their West Indian islands in 1793, the Caribbean Sea was soon filled with the sails of American trading vessels. The British, however, took a different view of neutral rights. They claimed that no port closed in peacetime could be opened in time of war. Without warning, they began seizing American vessels in large numbers and taking over both crews and cargoes.

Republicans called for stronger measures against the British. War hysteria swept the country as Americans railed against George III, whom they referred to as that "prince of land and sea robbers." Hamilton watched United States neutrality go down the drain. Although Hamilton favored Britain, he thought the young country should stay out of war. He urged Washington to send a special envoy to London to negotiate the various points that were at issue between the two countries. Washington decided to send **John Jay,** the experienced diplomat whom he had earlier appointed as the first Chief Justice of the Supreme Court.

Jay's Treaty. Jay was in a strong negotiating position. The British did not want to fight both France and the United States again. Jay's secret instructions were to try to gain concessions from the British on neutral shipping. If he could not, then he was to get other neutral powers in Europe to agree to form an alliance to protect their rights as neutrals. While Jay was crossing the Atlantic, Washington received just such an offer from two neutrals, Sweden and Denmark. Hamilton, however, persuaded him not to accept it. He argued that such an alliance of neutrals would anger the British and make Jay's task more difficult. Then Hamilton privately told his friend the British ambassador about Washington's decision. The ambassador, in turn, sent this news to the British negotiators in London. Jay remained unaware that Hamilton had undercut his position. No matter how much he threatened that the United States would join with other neutrals to protect neutral rights, the British knew that Washington would not allow such an action.

Check for Understanding

Call on individual students to read their answers to Section 3 Review questions.

Guided Practice

Tell students that the debate over U.S. aid and support of foreign revolutions is an issue today as it was during the French Revolution. Part of the issue involves determining whether the conflict is in fact a revolution of the people or a military takeover by a minority group. Ask students to discuss what the U.S. role should be in these revolutions. Should the U.S. get involved with the problems of other countries? (Possible responses: no, the U.S. should not become involved in affairs of other governments because it has enough of its own concerns on the domestic front; yes, the U.S. should become involved when democratic governments are threatened because the U.S. has a moral duty to help other nations preserve or establish their own democracies.)

The result was that Jay was forced to make concessions that were highly favorable to the British. In the treaty the British agreed, again, to evacuate their posts in the Northwest Territory, and they soon did so. However, Jay had to give up a great deal in return. The British won the right to continue the fur trade with Indians on the American side of the Canadian-United States border. This concession angered Westerners, who had been suspicious of Jay ever since his unsuccessful talks with Spain in 1785. On the rights of neutral ships, the British budged only slightly. They would still seize neutral ships in certain waters. Both parties agreed, though, that each should have the right of free navigation of the Mississippi River through Spanish territory.

Americans Object. The public's response to Jay's Treaty was negative and loud, even greater than Washington and Hamilton had feared. Nevertheless, the Senate ratified the treaty by an exact two-thirds majority. The Republican press echoed with outraged criticisms of Jay, of the Senate, and even of the President himself. The hostile mood of the country was demonstrated by someone who chalked the following words in large letters on a Boston fence: "DAMN JOHN JAY! DAMN EVERY ONE THAT WON'T DAMN JOHN JAY! DAMN EVERY ONE THAT WON'T SIT UP ALL NIGHT DAMNING JOHN JAY!!!"

The Americans Win on the Western Frontier

Having made one of the most unpopular treaties ever ratified by the United States Senate, the Washington administration was fortunate to achieve two popular victories in the West.

Pinckney's Treaty. The first victory was a diplomatic one at the expense of Spain. John Jay's apparently minor success regarding British and American rights on the Mississippi River frightened the Spanish. The government in Madrid grew worried about possible joint British-American action against the Louisiana Territory. The American ambassador in Madrid, **Thomas Pinckney,** successfully played on these fears.

Pinckney's Treaty of 1795 won virtually every point with Spain that the Americans had been aiming for since their Revolution. Spain gave up its claims to all land east of the Mississippi River and north of Florida and recognized the thirty-first

Picturing History John Jay, painted by John Trumbull.

parallel as the northern boundary of Florida. It also agreed to open the Mississippi River to American traffic. For three years American traders would be permitted to land goods at New Orleans for reloading onto oceangoing vessels. At the end of that time, the arrangement could be renewed.

Defeating the Indians. When the Revolutionary War broke out, the Indian tribes of the League of the Iroquois were not involved at first. As the Oneidas put it, "We are unwilling to join on either side of such a contest, for we love you both—old England and new." By 1776, however, the League was no longer neutral. It was now the League of Six Nations, rather than Five Nations, since the Tuscaroras had joined the League in 1712. Four of the six nations—the Cayugas, the Mohawks, the Onondagas, and the Senecas—joined forces with the British. The two remaining tribes—the Oneidas and the Tuscaroras—threw their support to the Americans.

The Indian war in the Northern states was bloody and destructive. During 1778 and 1779, combined British and Indian troops led a series of raids on American frontier settlements. They would strike unexpectedly out of the forest, burn houses, scalp victims, and then melt away into the wilderness. In response, General John Sullivan led an American army into Seneca territory from the west. The Senecas withdrew, and the Americans burned the Indians' villages and cornfields.

A similar pattern was followed in the Southern states. The Cherokees, Choctaws, and Creeks sup-

For Discussion

What were the gains and losses of both sides in the Jay Treaty, Pinckney Treaty, and Treaty of Greenville? Why did some provisions require the use of force? (Possible responses: Jay's Treaty—highly favorable to British; British agreed to evacuate Northwest Territory but continued fur trade on American side of Canadian-U.S. border; British refused to stop seizing neutral ships in some waters; both parties agreed to free navigation on Mississippi River. Some provisions required force because the people on one side or the other were not in agreement and did not willingly follow terms of provisions.)

Ask students to write an essay either defending or criticizing Hamilton's behavior in relation to Jay and his treaty. Was Hamilton's behavior treasonous? (Essays might include: Hamilton's behavior was not treasonous because he did not actually endanger the security of the U.S. His actions were highly unethical, however, and for that reason he should have lost his job.) Students should include in their essays comments on what reactions there might be today to such behavior during negotiations with foreign powers. (Reactions might include: the press might publicize such an incident and

thus force the government official to resign; greater accountability in today's government might discourage such activity; negotiations might be called off.)

Student Assignment/Homework

Have students read Section 4, "President Adams Faces Political Strife" and complete Chapter 8, Section 4 Daily Activity.

Answers

Main Ideas

1. Whether to support the Revolution once it became violent, whether to enter the war between France and Britain, and which side to support in the war.

2. Federalists supported Britain because of the violence of the French revolutionaries and out of loyalty to the parent country. Republicans supported French republicanism against the British monarchy and believed America should honor the 1778 treaty of alliance with France.

3. Britain, refusing to recognize the right of neutral nations to conduct trade with any warring nation, seized U.S. ships.

4. Spain gave up territorial claims and opened the Mississippi to Americans; several Indian tribes were decisively defeated.

Critical Thinking

5. Possible answer: strengths—avoidance of war with France and Britain; Pinckney's Treaty, which gained territorial concessions from Spain and opened up the Mississippi; decisive victories over Indians. Weaknesses—failure to command Genet's respect for U.S. government; failure to prevent Britain from ignoring U.S. neutrality and seizing U.S. ships; Hamilton's undermining Jay's ability to negotiate a favorable treaty. **(analysis & evaluation)**

220

Picturing History
"Mad Anthony" Wayne is pictured here dictating terms of a treaty to a group of Indians.

ported the British because American settlers had pushed into Indian lands in spite of agreements to the contrary. As in the North, the Indians raided white settlements along the frontier. In return, American troops laid waste the Indian homelands.

Under the terms of the Treaty of Paris of 1783, Great Britain gave the United States title to the land between the Appalachian Mountains and the Mississippi River. However, as one negotiator pointed out, that land belonged to "free and independent nations of Indians." These Indian nations were not represented in Paris. Furthermore, they would not admit their defeat. They wanted the Americans to negotiate with them directly.

The Americans refused. Instead, they sent armies into Indian country. The first army was led by General Josiah Harmar. In 1790 Harmar's troops were defeated by a group of northern tribes under the command of a Miami warrior named **Little Turtle.** In 1791 the Miami Confederacy inflicted an even worse defeat on an army led by General Arthur St. Clair.

Finally, in 1792, Washington appointed General "Mad Anthony" Wayne. Wayne spent an entire year drilling his troops. Greatly impressed, Little Turtle told his allies.

> We have beaten the enemy twice under different commanders. . . . The Americans are now led by a chief who never sleeps. . . . We have never been able to surprise him. . . . It would be prudent to listen to his offers of peace.

The other Indian chiefs did not agree with Little Turtle's advice, and they replaced him with a far less able commander. In 1794 the Indians were decisively defeated at the Battle of Fallen Timbers, near what is now Toledo, Ohio.

The next year United States authorities negotiated the Treaty of Greenville. In exchange for an annual payment of $10,000 the Miami Confederacy gave up most of the land that eventually became Ohio. The Indians also gave up the land on which Chicago now stands.

SECTION 3 REVIEW

Key Terms and People

Explain the significance of: Northwest Territory, neutrality, Edmond Genêt, John Jay, Thomas Pinckney, Little Turtle

Main Ideas

1. What decisions did Americans have to make with regard to the French Revolution?
2. Why did the Federalist and Republican parties support different sides in the war between France and Britain?
3. How did the issue of neutral rights cause conflict between America and Britain?
4. What were the main successes on the Western frontier during this period?

Critical Thinking

5. Evaluate the overall strengths and weaknesses of American diplomacy during Washington's Presidency.

SECTION 4
Core Lesson

Anticipate the Lesson

Using the information from Chapter 8, Section 4 Daily Activity, have students begin a three-column chart on the board. In the first column list Adams's activities in government, in the second column list Adams's thoughts on government, and in the third column list the views of Adams's critics.

Adams's Activities
- Delegate to Continental Congress
- On committee to draft Declaration
- Author of Constitution of Massachusetts
- Washington's Vice-President
- Second President of U.S.

Adams's Thoughts
- Totally dedicated to country
- Believed best government brings happiness to majority
- Convinced that his ideas for governing are best
- Believed in war before injustice or dishonor

Adams's Critics
- Fell short of his goal of peace
- Not a party leader, too much an individualist
- A pure patriot
- No faith in common man

SECTION 4

President Adams Faces Political Strife

GLOSSARY TERMS: **sectionalism, sedition, nullification**

In 1796, at the close of his second four-year term, Washington made it clear that he would not serve as President again. In his **Farewell Address,** he urged the United States to "steer clear of permanent alliances" with other nations. "Temporary alliances" were acceptable in "extraordinary emergencies," he said. Americans should remember, however, that nations never give one another real favors but are concerned only with their own interests. Washington then retired to his home at Mount Vernon, where he unhappily watched the developing political parties.

Parties Divide Along Sectional Lines

To most Federalists it seemed logical that the Vice-President should succeed the retiring hero. **John Adams** was known as a friend of strong government and as an enemy of the radical experiments that were taking place in France. Whom to nominate for Vice-President, however, was a ticklish matter. Hamilton seemed the obvious choice. Yet Adams had always been suspicious of Hamilton, whom he considered sly and ambitious. Hamilton, for his part, knew that Adams was a man he could not control. Hamilton also recog-

nized that he himself did not have much of a popular following. So the Federalists selected Thomas Pinckney as their Vice-Presidential candidate.

The Republicans saw the election of 1796 as their first opportunity to gain control over national policy. They chose Jefferson as their candidate because he had wider popular appeal than Madison. They named Aaron Burr as their candidate for Vice-President.

As things turned out, Adams received seventy-one electoral votes, and Jefferson sixty-eight. However, the Constitution provided that the runner-up for President should become Vice-President. Thus, a Republican Vice-President was elected to serve under a Federalist President! What had seemed sensible when the Constitution was written seemed almost unworkable with the unexpected rise of two political parties.

Washington got no reassurance from the election. What he feared most—**sectionalism,** or placing the interests of one region ahead of the welfare of the nation as a whole—was apparent. Almost all the electors from the Southern states voted for Jefferson, while all the electors from the Northern states voted for Adams.

Adams Avoids War with France

No American politician had written more about human nature than John Adams. However, in practice he was, as Jefferson observed, "a bad calculator" of people's motives. Benjamin Franklin had once written that Adams "is always an

Picturing History After George Washington married Martha Custis, he brought her to his home at Mount Vernon.

Present the Lesson

Ask students to use information from the section to add to the chart on the board.

Adams's Activities
- XYZ Affair
- Split party by new treaty with France
- Pushed Alien and Sedition Acts through Congress
- Appointed strong Federalist judges

Adams's Thoughts
- Favored strong government
- Placed nation's interests ahead of political party's
- Regarded Republican opposition as something close to conspiracy

Adams's Critics
- "Bad calculator" of people's motives
- An honest man, but sometimes acted unsensibly
- His Alien and Sedition Acts violated First Amendment

honest man, often a wise one, but sometimes, and in some things, absolutely out of his senses.'' He was also vain, stuffy, short, and overweight, which led to the unflattering nickname of His Rotundity.

The XYZ Affair. Adam's administration began with a crisis with France. The French had been outraged by Jay's treaty with the British, which they regarded as a betrayal of the 1778 French-American alliance. Even before Adams took office in March 1797, French naval vessels had begun seizing American merchantmen bound for England. The French government refused to receive a new American ambassador. When news of this insult arrived in Philadelphia, Adams was faced with demands for war by members of his own political party.

Rather than agree to war, Adams chose to send a three-man team to Paris to negotiate about ship seizures, which were violating freedom of the seas. The French foreign minister, Talleyrand, appointed three low-level officials to meet with the Americans. The three Frenchmen explained that there could be no negotiations unless Talleyrand's palm was greased with a bribe of $240,000. Bribes were fairly common in diplomacy in those days. Yet the amount the French wanted was outrageously high.

In their indignant reports home, the American envoys referred to the three Frenchmen simply as "X, Y, and Z." When the reports became public, an uproar broke out over the so-called **XYZ Affair.** "Millions for defense, but not one cent for tribute" became the slogan of the day. Congress promptly created a navy department and authorized Ameri-

Focus on Biography

Abigail Adams (1744–1818)

Her handwriting was "unusual," her spelling "uncertain," and her punctuation "nonexistent." That's what people said about Nabby Smith. Like many girls of her time, she did not go to school, but she had the run of her father's small library. There, her quick mind absorbed all his books, as well as works in French borrowed from her brother-in-law, who taught her to read them.

When Abigail was nineteen, she married John Adams, who was twenty-nine. Her mother thought she was taking a step down in the world. In the little villages south of Boston where the couple grew up, the Smiths were much better known than the Adamses. John was a rising lawyer, but he and Abigail were able to marry only after he inherited a small house and a few acres of land across the road

from his farmer brother.

With the help of a black slave woman "borrowed" from John's mother, Abigail set up house. From the beginning, the couple got on well. Abigail's and John's views on American rights and British tyranny were never far apart. Had they not agreed, their friends said, these strong-minded people would have battled each other like tigers.

Abigail's only complaint was that John's work as a lawyer took him away from home, often for weeks at a time. These were the first of many separations— some lasting years—for the growing family. During those trying separations, Abigail was able to sharpen her business skills. By managing the farm, she kept her family afloat while John was off serving the country.

They had not been married a year when riots over the Stamp

Act rocked the colonies and public service disrupted the Adamses' lives. As the Stamp Act crisis was coming to a boil, John expressed the wish that he might return to his little farm and his family "and live on potatoes and seaweed for the rest of my life."

Abigail would have none of it. She said, "Don't fear for me! I long impatiently to have you on the stage of action."

Abigail joined John on that stage when she became the first hostess of the White House in 1800. When Abigail died in 1818, their son asked his father, "How shall I offer you consolation for your loss?"

John Adams answered, "The separation cannot be as long as [the] twenty separations before. The pangs and anguish have not been so great [since] you and I embarked for France in 1778."

Check for Understanding

Have students answer Section 4 Review questions on paper.

Guided Practice

Remind students that feelings and emotions ran high in the election of 1800, but power was transferred peacefully from one party to another. In a world where peaceful changes in government are rare, the U.S. continues to experience nonviolent changes in the state and federal governments. Ask students to suggest reasons for this peaceful shift in power. (Possible responses: change in administration does not bring about drastic, radical changes in the government; judicial branch of government stays basically intact; only a portion of the legislative branch changes at the same time as the Presidency changes; voters are not as concerned with who runs the government as with how it is run.)

Picturing History John Adams (above) sent three envoys to France. The cartoon pictures the envoys as Madame Amerique, who is being "plucked to the last feather" by French agents demanding gratuities. Americans were outraged by the incident.

can ships to seize French vessels. For the next two years, an undeclared naval war raged in the Atlantic Ocean and in the Caribbean Sea.

Ironically, while Americans were protesting paying tribute to the French, they were paying millions of dollars in tribute to the pirates of the Barbary Coast of North Africa. These Barbary pirates had been plundering and blackmailing merchant ships in the Mediterranean for years, but it was not until Jefferson became President that the United States Navy was dispatched to deal with the Barbary pirates.

Adams the Peacemaker. Extreme Federalists—or High Federalists, as they were called—continued to demand that the President ask Congress for a declaration of war. Instead, Adams acted boldly and independently. In doing so, he split his party and ruined his own political future.

Adams had received word that a new French government would now welcome an American envoy without bribe money in his pocket. So in 1799 he sent another three-man team to Paris. The two sides agreed to abandon the 1778 treaty and to work out their differences peacefully. Republicans were delighted. High Federalists were furious. Yet Adams had won the point about freedom of the seas without getting into a needless war. He rightly

remained proud of having placed the nation's interests ahead of his party's and his own. As he later wrote, "I desire no other inscription over my gravestone than: 'Here lies John Adams, who took upon himself the responsibility of peace with France in the year 1800.' "

Adams Deals with Domestic Dissent

John Adams was not a man to take criticism lightly. Like Washington—and many other Presidents since—he thought he should rise above political parties. Again like Washington, he never fully realized that his own opinions were highly political. He thought of them as being simply patriotic. As a confirmed Federalist, he regarded the Republican opposition as something close to a criminal conspiracy against the welfare of the nation. He publicly denounced "those lovers of themselves who withdraw their confidence from their own . . . Government, and place it on a foreign nation, or Domestic Faction."

The Alien Acts. In fact, Adams was heavily and unfairly criticized in the Republican press. To many Federalists this criticism seemed un-American. Some of the most vocal critics were foreign-born. They included French and British radicals as well as recent Irish immigrants who

Have students write two paragraphs evaluating the success of John Adams's administration. Encourage students to use the information from the chart on the board. (Evaluations might include: Adams successfully kept U.S. out of war; he successfully put national priorities ahead of political parties or personal ambitions; he failed as a strong party leader and succeeded only in splitting his party when he negotiated a new treaty with France.)

Map Skills

Mediterranean Sea •
Morocco, Algiers, Tunis,
Tripoli

For Discussion

Do you think that the Alien and Sedition Acts were constitutional? Which amendments might they have violated? (Possible response: no, Acts could be challenged as violation to the First, Fourth, Fifth, Sixth, Eighth Amendments; they prohibited freedom of speech and of the press and allowed for imprisonment of those suspected of crimes against the state; the powers given the President were not within the guidelines of the Constitution itself.)

The Barbary States

Map Skills **Location** Algiers is located on what large body of water? **Location** Name four nations on the northern coast of Africa.

lashed out at anyone who was even faintly pro-British. (Britain had occupied Ireland for centuries, often using force and bloodshed against its inhabitants.) In addition, the Republican party had chosen a "foreigner" as its leader in the House of Representatives. Albert Gallatin, an able Swiss immigrant, had taken over as Republican minority leader of the House when Madison retired from Congress in 1798.

So the High Federalists decided to crush this criticism. At the height of preparing for war in the early summer of 1798, they pushed four measures through Congress that have become known as the **Alien and Sedition Acts.**

The first measure raised the residence requirement for American citizenship from five to fourteen years. The second measure, the Alien Act, gave the President the power in peacetime to order any alien out of the country. The third measure, the Alien Enemies Act, permitted the President in wartime to jail aliens at his pleasure. No arrests were made under either the Alien Act or the Alien Enemies Act. Yet the laws frightened some French refugees into leaving the country.

The Sedition Act. The fourth measure, the Sedition Act, was the one most dangerous to liberty. Its key clause provided fines and jail penalties for anyone guilty of **sedition.** Sedition was defined as

speaking or writing "with intent to defame . . . or bring into contempt or disrepute" the President or other members of the government. Since the act was to remain in effect only until the next Presidential inauguration, it was clear that it was directly aimed at silencing Republican opposition to Adams's administration.

A number of Republican editors, printers, and politicians were fined and jailed under the Sedition Act. With few exceptions, the judges in these cases were Federalist party members. The trials were often unfair. Many of the juries were handpicked by court marshals who were devoted Federalists.

Republicans were alarmed, and with good reason. They had looked to the courts for protection against tyrannous acts by the other two branches of government. Now it was clear that no branch of government was free from the spirit of political persecution. Jefferson and Madison, both leaders of the Republican party, recognized the Alien and Sedition Acts for what they were—violations of the First Amendment. They were also an excellent campaign issue for the election of 1800.

The Virginia and Kentucky Resolutions. The two Republican leaders decided to organize opposition to these acts by appealing to the states. Madison drew up a set of resolutions that his friends ushered through the Virginia state legislature. Jefferson wrote some similar resolutions that were adopted by Kentucky.

The Virginia and Kentucky Resolutions denounced the offending acts as unconstitutional. Both resolutions argued that the states were the original parties to the agreement known as the Constitution. Both claimed that the states had the power to say when that agreement had been violated. Jefferson argued that each of the states had the power of **nullification,** the declaring of something as illegal and void. Jefferson's theory was that each state had the right to nullify any federal act within its borders if it thought the act was unconstitutional.

Here was a direct challenge to the supremacy of the federal government. Both resolutions asked other state legislatures to adopt similar positions. None did so. In fact, Federalists in several northern states denounced Virginia and Kentucky as having totally misinterpreted the nature of the Constitution. They argued that the Constitution was much more than an agreement among independent states. The Constitution, they said, was an agreement

Student Assignment/Homework

Have students complete Chapter 8 Review on paper. Go over their answers in class. Discuss the answers to all Critical Thinking questions. Encourage several students to contribute their ideas on these questions.

Concluding the Chapter

Ask students to discuss the Presidential terms of Washington and Adams. Ask students how they feel each man represented or failed to represent the spirit of the new Constitution. (Possible responses—Some students may feel that both Presidents represented the spirit of the new Constitution; some may feel that Adams's term was off to a bad start when his election created sectionalism, taking away from a strong national spirit.)

among all the people of the nation. They also argued that only the federal courts could decide whether the actions of the other two branches violated the Constitution.

The Virginia and Kentucky Resolutions reminded Americans that the relationship of the states to the national government was not a settled one. In fact, this question would soon arise again.

Power Is Transferred Peacefully

By 1798 everyone knew that the next Presidential election would be a contest between the President and the Vice-President. Both sides believed the future of the country was at stake.

Republicans accused Adams of being the tool of the wealthy. After all, one of the Federalist mottoes was "Those who own the country ought to govern it." Adams, they said, wanted to destroy his enemies with measures like the Alien and Sedition Acts. He was said to be intent on turning the executive branch into a monarchy based on the British model. Using the words of a popular song of the times, the Republicans urged a vote for "Jefferson and Liberty."

Federalists accused Jefferson of being a friend of France and of revolutionary disorder. He was described as a wild-eyed opponent of all property except slaves, and as an atheist (one who does not believe in God). If Jefferson were elected, warned the president of Yale College, "the Bible would be cast into a bonfire."

None of these charges against either man was accurate. Yet neither side hesitated to question the other's patriotism.

The national mood was probably inevitable. The government was new. Americans were not accustomed to the peaceful transfer of power from one political group to another. The parties regarded each other much as Protestants and Catholics had regarded one another in earlier times—as totally in error and dangerously threatening to all that was good and true. Nevertheless, both sides proved willing to fight with votes, not guns.

The electoral ballots were counted on a cold and snowy day in Washington, D.C. Adams received sixty-five votes, and Jefferson seventy-three. This constituted a victory for Jefferson. Yet there was still a problem. Burr, who was running as the Republican Vice-President, also received seventy-three votes. He realized that if he could get a majority of votes, he could become not Vice-

President but President! This meant that the House of Representatives, which was dominated by Federalists, would have to break the tie between the two Republicans.

For six feverish days, the House took one ballot after another. Finally, Hamilton intervened. Although he opposed Jefferson's policies, he feared Burr even more. He persuaded enough Federalists to cast blank ballots to give Jefferson a majority of two votes. Burr became Vice-President.

Most politicians now recognized the need to change the system of voting in the electoral college. The next Congress drafted the Twelfth Amendment. It provided that electors cast separate ballots for President and for Vice-President. This system is still in effect today.

During the few weeks remaining before Jefferson's inauguration, the outgoing Congress increased the number of judges in federal courts. Adams named strong Federalists as judges. Among them was **John Marshall,** whom Adams named Chief Justice of the Supreme Court. It turned out to be an act of lasting importance. Although the Republican party ruled for more than thirty years, Marshall kept handing down Federalist interpretations of the supreme law of the land.

SECTION 4 REVIEW

Key Terms and People

Explain the significance of: Farewell Address, John Adams, sectionalism, XYZ Affair, Alien and Sedition Acts, sedition, nullification, John Marshall

Main Ideas

1. What divisions among Americans were reflected in the 1796 election?
2. How did Adams avoid war with France?
3. Why did Congress pass the Alien and Sedition Acts?
4. What were the main provisions of the Alien and Sedition Acts?
5. In the last few weeks of his Presidency, how did Adams ensure that Federalists would continue to influence America?

Critical Thinking

6. During Adams's Presidency, how did the two-party system promote democracy? How did it discourage democracy? Explain.

SECTION 4 REVIEW

Answers

Main Ideas

1. Strong regional divisions were reflected by the Southern states' voting for the Republican Jefferson while the Northern states voted for Adams, a Federalist.

2. By resisting High Federalists' demands for war and by conducting peaceful negotiations with France.

3. To silence opposition to Adams.

4. Raised the resident requirement for citizenship to 14 years; gave the President power to deport aliens in peacetime and to jail them in wartime; provided jail terms and fines for sedition (intentionally defaming members of the government).

5. By appointing many federal judges—including John Marshall as Chief Justice of the U.S.—who would hand down Federalist interpretations of the law.

Critical Thinking

6. Possible answers: promoted democracy—fostered debate, gave voters choices, and proved that disagreements could be handled without violence; discouraged democracy—a Federalist Congress passed the Alien and Sedition Acts to crush Republican criticism; in response, Republicans in Virginia and Kentucky challenged the central government's authority. **(analysis & evaluation)**

State the Objective

Understand the kind of information historical letters provide.

Present the Lesson

Remind students that letters provide insights into the personalities of historical figures as well as facts about historical events. Friendly letters often contain information about events and people that cannot be found in encyclopedia articles.

Divide the class into small groups. Tell the groups to reread the six letters of Abigail Adams and to make a chart showing the information they could find in other sources, such as an encyclopedia, and the information that they probably could not find in another source. Have students use these headings in their charts: Facts You Could Find in an Encyclopedia and Facts You Might Not Find in an Encyclopedia. Charts might include:

Facts You Could Find in an Encyclopedia. It took five days to travel by boat from Boston to New York in 1789. President Washington was sick during June 1789. Abigail Adams had lived in Europe. As the wife of the Vice-President, Abigail Adams entertained all the senators and representatives and their families. Washington, D.C., was a wilderness in 1800 when the Adamses went to live in the new White House.

Focus on Primary Sources

Letters of Abigail Adams

In 1788, after five years in London and Paris, Abigail and John Adams returned to the United States. He was to be the nation's Vice-President; she was to join him in the capital, New York. His was a new position in the new government of a new nation. Neither could be sure what was before them. Mrs. Adams knew that to her would fall the chief social duties—and all the problems of children, furniture, trunks, and servants—not to mention responsibility for the family property in Massachusetts!

Read the following letters of Abigail Adams. The letters are reprinted exactly as she wrote them, including the spelling and punctuation. Then answer the questions at the end of the selections.

By late summer of 1789, Abigail Adams was finding the social life of the capital a heavy burden. On August 9 she wrote:

> [A]t Richmond Hill it is expected that I am at home both to Gentlemen & Ladies when ever they come out, which is almost every day since I have been here, besides, it is a sweet [pleasant] morning ride to [before] Breakfast. I propose to fix a Levey [reception] day soon. I have waited for Mrs. Washington to begin and she has fixed on every fryday 8 o'clock. I attended upon the last [reception]. . . . I found it quite a crowded Room. The form of Reception is this, the servants announce & Col. Humphries or Mr. Lear [the President's aides] receives every lady at the door & Hands her up to Mrs. Washington to whom she makes a most Respectfull courtsey and then is seated without noticeing any of the rest of the company. The Pressident then comes up and speaks to the Lady, which he does with a grace, dignity & ease that leaves Royal George [the British King] far behind him.
>
> Indeed I have been fully employed in entertaining company, in the first place all the Senators who had Ladies & families, then the remaining Senators, and this week we have begun with the House [of Representatives], and tho we have a room in which we dine 24 persons at a Time, I shall not get through them all, together with the publick ministers [officials] for a month to come.

Source: Mitchell, *Letters,* 19–20.

Some years later on May 24, 1797, Abigail wrote about her own duties as First Lady.

> At 5 I rise. From that time until 8 I have a few leisure hours. At 8 I breakfast, after which, untill eleven I attend to my Family arrangements. At that hour I dress for the day. From 12 until two I receive company, sometimes untill 3. We dine at that hour unless on company days which are tuesdays & thursdays. After dinner I usually ride out untill seven. I begin to feel a little more at Home, and less anxiety about the ceremonious part of my duty, . . . Tomorrow we are to dine the Secretaries of State & c with the whole Senate. [At least thirty-eight guests.] The Male domesticks I leave entirely to Brisler to hire and to dismiss; the female I have none but those I brought with me . . . and I am happy in not having any occasion for any others, for a very sad set of creatures they are.

Source: Mitchell, *Letters,* 91–92.

The following month, in a letter dated June 3, 1797, Abigail wrote the following to her sister.

> Today will be the 5th great dinner I have had, about 36 Gentlemen to day, as many more next week, and I shall have got through the whole of Congress, with their appendages. Then comes the 4 July which is a still more tedious day, as we must then have not only all Congress, but all the Gentlemen of the city, the Governour and officers and companies, all of whom the late [former] President [Washington] used to treat with cake, punch, and wine. What the House would not hold used to be placed at long tables in the yard. As we are here we cannot avoid the trouble and expence. I have been informed the day used to

226

Facts You Might Not Find in an Encyclopedia. Abigail Adams hated to travel by boat. She felt that the office of President was very important but that the job of entertaining was tedious, grueling, and expensive and that more money should be provided for it. Abigail felt that the White House—though new and unfinished when she moved in—would be an important building in years to come.

Provide time for students to present their ideas. Then ask why letters are an important primary source. (Possible response: letters give clues to feelings and attitudes that are not usually found in other documents.)

If time permits, discuss some of the advantages and disadvantages of being the spouse of a modern President or Vice-President. (Possible responses: advantages—opportunities for helping others; travel. Disadvantages—the loss of privacy; long hours.)

Check for Understanding

Discuss students' responses to the questions at the end of the feature. Be sure students provide information from the letters and from their experience to support their opinions.

cost the late President 500 dollors. More than 200 wt [pounds] of cake used to be expended, and 2 quarter casks of wine besides spirit. You will not wonder that I dread it, or think President Washington to blame for introducing the custom, if he could have avoided it. Congress never were present here before on the day, so that I shall have a Hundred & 50 of them in addition to the other company. . . .

The task of the President is very arduous, very perplexing and very hazardous. I do not wonder Washington wishd to retire from it, or rejoiced at seeing an old oak in his place.

Source: Mitchell, *Letters*, 98–99.

Four years later, in November 1800, the First Lady moved to Washington for the final months of the Adams Presidency.

I arrived in this city on Sunday (the 16th ult.) [of November]. Having lost my way in the woods on Saturday in going from Baltimore, we took the road to Frederick [Maryland] and got nine miles out of our road. You find nothing but a forest and woods on the way, for 16 or 18 miles not a village. Here and there a thatched cottage, without a pane of glass inhabited by Blacks. My intention was to have reached Washington Saturday. . . .

I was advised at Baltimore to make the [Snowden family's house] my stage [stop] for the night, the only Inn at which I could put up being 36 miles ride from Baltimore, . . . but I, who have never been accustomed to quarter myself and servants upon private houses, could not think of it. . . . We took a direction as we supposed right, but in the first turn went wrong, and were wandering more than two hours in the woods in different paths, holding down and breaking boughs of trees which we would not pass, until we met a solitary black fellow with a horse and cart. We inquired of him our way, and he kindly offered to conduct us, which he did two miles, then gave us such a clue as led us out to the post road and the Inn where we got some dinner. . . .

I arrived about one o'clock at this place known by the name of ''the city,'' [Washington] and the Name is all that you can call so! As I expected to find it a new country, with Houses scattered over a space of ten miles, and trees and stumps in plenty, with a castle of

a House, so I found it.

The President's House is in a beautiful situation in front of which is the Potomac with a view of Alexandria. The country round is romantic but a wild wilderness at present.

But surrounded with forests, can you believe that wood is not to be had, because people cannot be found to cut and cart it! Breisler entered into a contract with a man to supply him with wood . . . but a few cords only has he been able to get. We have had some very cold weather, and we feel it keenly. This House is twice as large as our meeting House. I believe the great Hall is as Bigg. I am sure 'tis twice as long. . . . But this House is built for ages to come. The establishment necessary is a task which cannot be borne by the present sallery. . . . Not one room or chamber is finished of the whole. It is habitable [only with] by fires in every part, thirteen of which we are obliged to keep daily, or sleep in wet and damp places. . . .

The ladies from Georgetown and in the ''city'' have many of them visited me. Yesterday I returned fifteen visits—but such a place as Georgetown! . . . It is the very dirtyest Hole I ever saw for a place of any trade or respectability of inhabitants. It is only one mile from me, but a quagmire after every rain. Here we are obliged to send daily for marketing . . . But I am determined to be satisfied and content. . . .

Source: Reprinted in Janet Whitney, *Abigail Adams* (Boston: Little Brown, 1947), 300–302.

Analyzing Primary Sources

1. Were Abigail Adams's problems greater or lesser than those faced by the wives of later Presidents and Vice-Presidents? Explain.
2. On the basis of these letters, what were Mrs. Adams's best qualities? What seemed least attractive about her?
3. Someday soon, perhaps, a woman will be President of the United States. Should she be someone like Abigail Adams? Why, or why not?

Critical Thinking

4. Why might personal letters be more reliable primary source materials than autobiographies?

FOCUS ON SOURCES

Answers

Analyzing Primary Sources

1. Possible answers: lesser—the government was smaller and far less complicated than it is today. Greater—the Washingtons and the Adamses had no precedents to guide them and got little support from Congress.

2. Possible answer: Abigail Adams was clever, resourceful, and outspoken; she also showed some signs of snobbery, provincialism, and petty resentment of the Washingtons.

3. Possible answer: Yes—in intelligence, managerial and social skills, and experience of the world, Abigail appeared adequately equipped; these would be important talents and experiences for any President—male or female.

Critical Thinking

4. Possible answer: personal letters are sometimes more intimate, candid, and accurate portrayals because they are not written for a public audience. **(evaluation)**

Answer Key

Key Terms and People

These are highlighted in the text in the order in which they appear in this list.

Main Ideas

1. To protect people from power of government.

2. Loose interpretation of Constitution (national bank was allowable since it was not specifically prohibited) versus strict interpretation (national bank was unconstitutional unless specifically allowed.)

3. Hamilton—did not trust the common people so favored strong central government run by wealthy, educated people; Jefferson—trusted the common people and favored weak central government.

4. Federalists—most had come from Britain; were appalled and frightened by the beheading of French king; were afraid of the common people. • Republicans—favored uprising of the common people; wished to return help France had given in Revolution; wished to uphold treaty with France.

5. Neither Washington nor Adams wanted war; country was about equally divided for each side; both British and French made errors in negotiations with U.S.

6. Unable to negotiate treaty to end Britain's fur trade and its seizing of neutral ships.

7. In 1796 John Adams, a Federalist, was elected President and Thomas Jefferson, a Republican, was elected Vice-President. In 1800 the candidates for President and Vice-President got the same number of votes so Vice-Presidential candidate might have become President. • Political parties developed.

8. To crush Adams's critics.

Critical Thinking Questions

9. Show desire to dispense with the will of people and to do what they think is best for the country.

10. Possible answers— organize departments of state (foreign affairs), treasury, and war; set up the courts; raise money. • To be able to deal with other nations, maintain order and justice, and pay for government services.

11. If state could nullify any federal act it thought was unconstitutional, it could disrupt national stability. • State would secede from Union and set itself above Supreme Court.

12. They stood for a strong federal government. • They favored a "state in which citizens have supreme power," the 18th-century definition of *republic.*

13. Guilty of defamation under Sedition Act.

14. Different cultures; different use of land; lack of respect by settlers of Indians (called them savages.)

15. Possible answers: Federalist—I believe that a powerful national government is able to help special interest groups; I fear the masses and believe that only the rich and well educated should run the country. Republican—I favor weak central and strong state government; I dislike special

---

CHAPTER 8 REVIEW

Write your answers on a separate sheet of paper.

Key Terms and People

Explain the significance of: Judiciary Act of 1789, cabinet, government bonds, funding, bank notes, Whiskey Rebellion, protective tariff, excise tax, Northwest Territory, Little Turtle, sectionalism, John Marshall

Main Ideas

1. Why was a bill of rights necessary?
2. What constitutional issue was raised by Hamilton's proposal for a national bank?
3. Why did Hamilton and Jefferson not trust each other?
4. What kinds of people wanted to help the British in the 1793 war between France and Britain? What kinds of people wanted to help the French? Why?
5. How did the United States manage to remain neutral during the French Revolution and the war between Britain and France?
6. How did John Jay become so unpopular?
7. What situations persuaded Congress that the electoral college system of voting for President and Vice-President must be changed? What had happened to cause these situations?
8. Why were the Alien and Sedition Acts passed?

Critical Thinking Questions

9. **Analyzing Literature.** The quotation on page 207 is an example of one technique used in historical fiction. The author has put words into the mouth of a historical character. How do Hamilton's and James's words show the Federalist political philosophy?
10. **Applying Concepts.** Imagine creating a strong central government where none had been before. What would you do first? Why?
11. **Synthesizing Ideas.** Why was Jefferson's theory of nullification, as shown in the Virginia and Kentucky Resolutions, dangerous? If taken to its logical end, where might it lead?
12. **Analyzing Categories.** Why were Alexander Hamilton and his fellow thinkers called Feder-

alists? Why were Thomas Jefferson and his party called Republicans? (Use the dictionary to help determine your answer. Do not confuse modern-day Republicans with the Republicans of the eighteenth century.)

13. **Predicting Outcomes.** If John Peter Zenger had been tried under the Sedition Act of 1798, what might have been the verdict?
14. **Evaluating Causes.** Why were the Indians and the settlers unable to keep on good terms?
15. **Applying Ideas.** If you had been alive in the late 1700's, would you have been a Federalist or a Republican? Why?
16. **Judging Values.** President Adams felt that his best deed while in office was to avoid war with France. Do you think he was correct in this judgment? Why or why not?

Critical Thinking Activities

17. **Organizing Ideas.** Using the appropriate letters, arrange these events on a time line.

   a. John Jay completes treaty with Great Britain.
   b. Maritime war waged with British.
   c. President Washington gives his first Inaugural Address.
   d. Pinckney completes treaty with Spain.
   e. France declares war on Great Britain.
   f. French Revolution begins.
   g. Washington gives Farewell Address.
   h. Washington declares neutrality.

| 1785 | 1790 | 1795 | 1800 |

18. **Linking Past and Present.** Do people get as upset over the excise taxes we have now as they did in 1789? Why or why not?
19. **Linking Past and Present.** Do you think political parties are good or bad for the United States? Could we get along without political parties? Why or why not? Why do you think Washington was so against political parties?

16. Possible answers: correct—negotiation is a better way to solve problems than war. Incorrect—British were seizing ships and crews; John Jay's negotiations with Britain did not go well; Genet and the XYZ affair worsened relations with France.

Critical Thinking Activities

➤**17.** c, f, e, h, b, a, d, g.

➤**18.** Possible answer: probably not. More people today get upset over income taxes and real estate taxes than excise taxes on liquor, tobacco, etc., which, in comparison, seem very small.

➤**19.** Possible answer: good—help organize issues; bad—powerful parties overshadow the interests of smaller groups. • No— political parties have become indispensable to democratic process, providing critiques and checks on one another. • George Washington was familiar with factions that disappeared when their cause disappeared. He had no experience with the two-party system.

➤**Questions suitable for co-operative learning.**

TELESCOPING THE TIMES: 1789–1800

The Federalist Era

Examples set by President Washington established many of the ways the new government would work. Madison pushed through a bill of rights that guaranteed fundamental freedoms of assembly, the press, religion, and trial by jury. Congress provided for executive departments and the President chose Hamilton and Jefferson to head two of these. The Judiciary Act of 1789 established the size and organization of the Supreme Court and lower federal courts. Hamilton's new financial program strengthened the nation by dealing with debts from the Revolution and by organizing a national bank for the country. New taxes stirred up a rebellion in western Pennsylvania.

Secretary of the Treasury Hamilton distrusted people as a whole. His program to aid the economy and the wealthy angered Secretary of State Jefferson, who placed his faith in the common farmer. As the formal head of state, Washington tried to remain neutral. Hamilton gave his support to a Federalist newspaper. Jefferson and Madison backed a Republican one and began setting up political clubs. The two-party system emerged, although it was neither planned nor welcomed. Washington was easily elected to a second term, with Adams as his Vice-President.

At first most Americans welcomed news of the French Revolution in 1789. Four years later, though, French radicals executed their King and went to war against Great Britain. That struggle badly divided Americans, and foreign relations continued to be troublesome. Washington tried to maintain the nation's neutrality. Instead of protecting the rights of neutrals, however, Jay's Treaty conceded so much to the British that it proved very unpopular in the United States. Pinckney's Treaty with Spain was much more successful, however. War against the Indians continued on the northwestern frontier. The settlers forced the Indians to give up huge amounts of land.

In 1796 Federalist John Adams defeated the Republican Jefferson for the Presidency. Americans fell into an undeclared naval war with France, but Adams successfully kept the nation officially at peace. He tried to stifle dissent with the Alien and Sedition Acts. The acts frightened some aliens to such an extent that they fled the country. A number of Republicans were fined and jailed by courts dominated by Federalists. Madison and Jefferson responded with the Virginia and Kentucky Resolutions. After the election of 1800, there was a peaceful transfer of power to the Republicans. Jefferson had finally become President.

Chronology of Main Events	
1789	George Washington inaugurated President; Bill of Rights drafted; French Revolution begins; Judiciary Act passed
1789–1793	Federalist and Republican parties form
1791	First Bank of the United States chartered
1793	Washington issues declaration of neutrality
1794	Whiskey Rebellion; Battle of Fallen Timbers
1795	Jay and Pinckney treaties ratified
1797	John Adams inaugurated President
1798	Alien and Sedition Acts; Kentucky and Virginia Resolutions

Telescoping the Times may be used as an alternative to having students read the entire chapter, as a chapter preview, or as a chapter review.

Global Perspectives

1807	British abolish slave trade.
1809	Ecuador gains independence from Spain.
1814	Congress of Vienna convenes.
1815	Napoleon loses Battle of Waterloo.
1818	Zulus found empire in southern Africa.
1822	Brazil declares independence from Portugal.
1822	Freed slaves establish colony of Liberia in Africa.
1830	Greeks gain independence from the Ottoman Turks.

For Discussion

What effects might the founding of Liberia have had on the slavery issue in the U.S.? (Possible response: might have helped demonstrate to the world, and to the U.S. in particular, that those held in slavery were capable of governing themselves.)

Additional Resources

- Geography Activities
- Skills Activities
- Thematic Activities
- Economic Activities
- Cultural Literacy Activities
- Literary Source Readings
- Primary Source Readings
- Nuclear Peacekeeping
- Transparencies
- Computer Test Generator

Additional Teaching Strategies

SECTION 1

For Basic Students: Using the physical map of North America in the Atlas, trace the route of the Lewis and Clark expedition. Ask students to list on paper the geographical features observed by the explorers on their journey. (Geographical features: Missouri River; Great Plains; Rocky Mountains; Columbia Plateau; Columbia River; Cascade Range; Pacific Ocean.)

For Advanced Students: After students have done further research on the topic, divide them into two teams to debate this statement: "Resolved—Aaron Burr is guilty of treason against the U.S. and should be sentenced to death." (Possible responses: agree—Burr accepted aid from Federalists who wanted to establish an independent Northern Confederacy and is therefore guilty of treason; disagree—Burr accepted the Federalists' aid but never stated that he wanted New York to leave the Union; therefore, he is guilty of an indiscretion and nothing more.)

SECTION 2

For Basic Students: Have students make a list of three important changes brought about by the War of 1812 and briefly explain why each was important. (Possible responses: northern boundary of Louisiana Territory was set at the forty-ninth parallel—no more quarrels over boundaries; Britain and U.S. agreed to a ten-year joint occupation of the Oregon Country—opened western coast to U.S.; Spain ceded Florida to U.S.—expanded U.S. territory.) Have students share their lists.

For Advanced Students: Ask students to write an editorial that either supports or condemns the Embargo Act of 1807. (Editorials against embargo might include: it was destroying American commerce; shipping centers were closing down; merchants, seamen, shipbuilders, and stevedores were out of work.)

SECTION 3

For Basic Students: Ask students to prepare a chart listing the three main themes of the American System: protective tariffs, transportation improvements, and national bank. Have students list two related details under each heading.

Protective Tariffs	Transportation	National Bank
• Stop the flow of cheap goods from Britain	• Government built roads and canals to move goods more easily	• Issued paper money that was accepted throughout country
• Protect America's infant industries	• Financed with money from protective tariff	• Paper money backed by gold or silver.
• Tariff Act of 1816		

For Advanced Students: Ask students to research and write a one-page explanation of one of the Supreme Court cases described in this section. (Reports on *Gibbons* v. *Ogden* (1824) may include: involved Gibbons and Ogden who were partners in a steamship company; when partnership broke up Ogden received a charter from state of New York and Gibbons received a charter from federal government; Supreme Court ruled that in conflict between federal and state government, state must yield; paved way for competition between companies and limited the authority of the state.)

SECTION 4

For Basic Students: Ask students to write a brief explanation of the causes and results of either the Monroe Doctrine or the Compromise of 1820. (Possible causes and results of Monroe Doctrine: causes—U.S. fear of Spain's and Portugal's attempts to re-establish colonies in the Western Hemisphere, U.S. fear of Russia pushing in from northwest; results—doctrine warned European powers not to interfere in affairs of New World, U.S. promised not to interfere with European affairs, doctrine irritated European leaders, doctrine became part of America's foreign policy for years to come.) Ask students to share their explanations.

For Advanced Students: Ask students to research the growth of the cotton industry from 1790 to 1860 and prepare a three-minute talk explaining the connection between the cotton gin, slavery, westward expansion, and development of the textile industry. Encourage students to use visual aids such as graphs, charts, and maps. (Details might include: cotton depleted nutrients in soil and new land was needed; wealthy planters bought large tracts of land and needed many workers to farm it; slaves provided cheap labor; the cotton gin made cotton more profitable to grow.) Have students share their information with the class.

Further Reading for Students

Dangerfield, George. *Defiance of the Old World: The Story Behind the Monroe Doctrine*. New York: Putnam Publishing Group, 1970.

Padover, Saul. *Jefferson*. Darby, Pa.: Arden Library, 1982.

Phelan, Mary Kay. *The Story of the Louisiana Purchase*. New York: Harper & Row, 1979.

Tunis, Edwin. *The Young United States, 1783 to 1830*. New York: Thomas Y. Crowell, 1976.

Historical Fiction

Forester, C. S. *The Captain from Connecticut*. Boston: Little Brown, 1941.

Roberts, Kenneth. *Captain Caution*. New York: Doubleday, 1934.

Roberts, Kenneth. *The Lively Lady*. New York: Doubleday, 1931.

Bibliography for Teachers

Books

Adams, Henry. *The United States in Eighteen Hundred*. Ithaca, N.Y.: Cornell University Press, 1955.

Bakeless, John, ed. *Journals of Lewis and Clark: A New Selection*. New York: New American Library, 1964.

Brodie, Fawn M. *Thomas Jefferson: An Intimate History*. New York: Norton, 1974.

Horsman, Reginald. *The Causes of the War of 1812*. New York: Octagon, 1970.

Perkins, Bradford, ed. *The Causes of the War of 1812: National Honor or National Interest?* Melbourne, Fla: Krieger, 1976.

Perkins, Dexter. *History of the Monroe Doctrine*. Boston: Little, Brown, 1955.

Audio-Visuals

Administration of Thomas Jefferson. Coronet Films. Movie.

Building Nationalism. Society for Visual Education. Filmstrip.

Great Men and Great Issues: Launching A New National Government. Wilcom. Audiotapes.

The Industrial Revolution. Liberty Fund, Inc. Videotape.

The Industrial Revolution: Beginning in the United States. Encyclopaedia Britannica Educational Corp. Movie.

John Marshall. Encyclopaedia Britannica Educational Corp. Movie.

Johnny Appleseed. Modern Talking Picture Services. Movie.

Remember the Ladies. Modern Talking Picture Services. Movie.

Computer Resources

Lewis and Clark Expedition. (Commodore 64) Society of Visual Education.

U.S. History—The Expanding American Frontier. (Apple/Tandy 1000/IBM). Scholastic.

Teacher's Notes:

Teaching Resources Unit 2 Booklet

Lesson Study Sheets pp. 159-174
Daily Activities pp. 175-182
Enrichment Activities pp. 183-190
Reteaching Activities pp. 191-198
Chapter Review p. 199
Chapter Mastery Tests pp. 201-212
Telescoping the Times Study Sheet p. 213

Chapter Objectives

Students will learn:
- the major national issues during Jefferson's Presidency
- the main causes and results of the War of 1812
- the reasons for the expansion of the national economy and government between 1815 and 1830
- how inventions and the growth of industry changed the lives of Americans

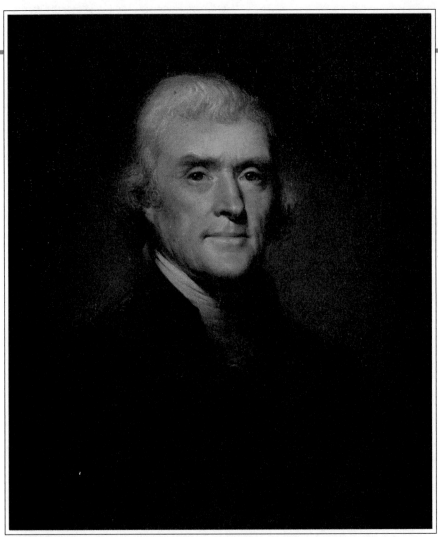

Picturing History In an age of exceptional minds, the talents and accomplishments of Thomas Jefferson were unparalleled. This portrait of Jefferson was painted in 1800 by Rembrandt Peale, son of the famous artist Charles Willson Peale.

Using the Chapter Time Line

What name was given to the years spanned by President Monroe's two terms as President (see Unit 2 Time Line)? (Answer: Era of Good Feelings) In what year did the U.S. purchase the Louisiana Territory from the French? (Answer: 1803.)

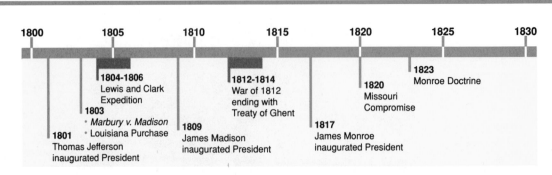

1800　　1805　　1810　　1815　　1820　　1825　　1830

1804-1806
Lewis and Clark
Expedition

1803
* *Marbury v. Madison*
* Louisiana Purchase

1801
Thomas Jefferson
inaugurated President

1812-1814
War of 1812
ending with
Treaty of Ghent

1809
James Madison
inaugurated President

1820
Missouri
Compromise

1823
Monroe Doctrine

1817
James Monroe
inaugurated President

230

CHAPTER **9** 1800–1830

The Jefferson, Madison, and Monroe Years

Links to American Literature

It was determined that we would meet across the river in New Jersey, on the heights known as Weehawk. Nathaniel Pendleton would be second to Hamilton. Van Ness would be second to me. Pistols would be our weapons. Hamilton then asked that we delay the interview until after the close of the Circuit Court. It was agreed that we meet in two weeks' time on July 11, 1804. . . . My affairs were in order. I had set out six blue boxes, containing enough material for my biography, if anyone was minded to write such a thing. Those boxes now rest at the bottom of the sea. . . . Love-letters to me were all discreetly filed, with instructions to be burned, to be returned to owners, to be read at my grave—whatever was fitting. My principal emotion that morning was relief. Everything was arranged. Everything was well-finished. . . . When I woke up on the sofa, saw dawn, I knew that I would live to see the sun set, that Hamilton would not. . . .

Hamilton fired first. I fired an instant later. Hamilton's bullet broke a branch from this tree. . . . My bullet pierced his liver and spine. . . . 'I am a dead man,' Hamilton said. I started toward him but Van Ness stopped me. Dr. Hosack was coming. So we left.

— GORE VIDAL, *Burr*

Political rivalries that began during the Federalist Era became even more heated in the early 1800's. Two well known rivals, Alexander Hamilton and Aaron Burr, fought a "gentlemen's duel." Hamilton was fatally wounded and Burr was charged with murder. This chapter is worth remembering for the examples it gives of how misunderstandings can escalate into violence.

Chapter Overview

Despite numerous setbacks and conflicts, the nation continued to grow and prosper. This was largely due to the political vision and hard work of Thomas Jefferson and his handpicked successors, James Madison and James Monroe. In this chapter, you will learn about Jefferson's Presidency, the War of 1812, the expansion of the national economy and government between 1815 and 1830, and about the important national issues during Monroe's Presidency. To help you learn about this period, Chapter 9 is divided into four sections.

Chapter Outline

1. President Jefferson Leads the Nation
2. The United States Enters the War of 1812
3. Both National and Sectional Feelings Grow
4. New Inventions Change Lives

Anticipate the Lesson

Using a wall map, review with students the boundaries of the U.S. at the time that Jefferson became President. What other countries still claimed territory in North America in 1801? (Answer: Britain; France; Spain; Mexico; Russia.) Ask students to suggest reasons for America's westward expansion. (Possible responses: more farmland; new markets for goods; ports to ship goods to China.) Ask students to list possible ways in which America might acquire additional land. (Possible responses: war; negotiations; purchase.)

State the Objective

Recognize major national issues during Jefferson's Presidency.

SECTION 1

President Jefferson Leads the Nation

GLOSSARY TERMS: **midnight judges, Louisiana Purchase**

Thomas Jefferson, in his eloquent inaugural address, extended the hand of peace to his opponents. "Every difference of opinion is not a difference of principle. . . . We are all Republicans, we are all Federalists." In a parting shot at Adams, Jefferson also announced his belief that enemies of the Republic should be left undisturbed as a sign that in the United States "error of opinion" may be tolerated. Bitter over his defeat, the former President did not attend Jefferson's inauguration. When Jefferson spoke, Adams was already in a coach rattling back to Massachusetts.

A Fresh Start Is Made

Jefferson's inauguration was the first to take place in the new federal city of Washington on the Potomac River. The ceremony itself symbolized Jefferson's feeling that a simple government was the one best suited to a republic. Washington and Adams had favored a grand, almost royal, style. Washington had driven around in a coach with six horses, just like George III. Instead of shaking hands, Adams used to bow stiffly at his receptions. Jefferson, in contrast, actually walked from his boardinghouse to his inauguration.

Jefferson continued this informality while in office. There were few servants with powdered wigs. The President often opened the White House's front door to visiting diplomats. He met senators while wearing old clothes and carpet slippers "with his toes out." The British ambassador was so shocked at such behavior that he refused to attend Jefferson's dinners. The Republicans were delighted.

Linking Past to Present

Thomas Jefferson's style as President was informal compared to that of his predecessors, Washington and Adams. This "common touch" was carried much further by Andrew Jackson. Informality has been used by some modern-day Presidents in their public appearances to give the impression that they are ordinary people despite their high office and power. President Jimmy Carter, for example, walked from the Capitol to the White House after his inauguration. The inauguration of Ronald Reagan, however, symbolized an era of more formality than that of his predecessor.

Cutting Costs and Simplifying Finances.   Jefferson's first appointments to his cabinet followed Washington's precedents. He appointed men who agreed with him, but he kept an eye on geographical balance. His most influential appointees were

Historical Sidelights

• The legendary Johnny Appleseed became popular during Jefferson's years in office. His real name was John Chapman, and he was born in New England around 1775. From 1800 until 1845 he wandered in the wilderness of the Ohio Valley, planting and pruning apple trees. • The term "White House" to refer to the President's residence probably arose because mansions of the day were commonly called "white houses."

People in the Chapter

Sacajawea proved to be a most valuable asset on the Lewis and Clark expedition. When the Indian tribes saw an Indian woman with a baby, they knew the mission was a peaceful one.

James Madison was our nation's smallest President. He was 5'6" tall and weighed one hundred pounds. After being jilted by his first fiancée, he dated no other women until he met the charming widow Dolley Payne Todd, whom he married. Before becoming First Lady, Dolley had served as White House hostess for the widower Thomas Jefferson.

Aaron Burr was charged with murder but never brought to trial for killing Alexander Hamilton in a duel. Although Hamilton accepted Burr's challenge, he was against dueling. Hamilton's only son had died in a duel at the same spot chosen for the match with Burr.

Oliver Hazard Perry provided us with a now famous quotation. Upon winning the battle of Lake Erie in the War of 1812 he exclaimed, "We have met the enemy, and they are ours."

Present the Lesson

On the board list the following topics: Presidential Style, National Administration, Judicial Changes, Westward Expansion. Ask students to skim the section and cite three to five key phrases to describe each topic under the Jefferson administration. (Possible responses: National Administration—reduced size of army; halted scheduled expansion of navy; lowered expenses for government social functions; eliminated internal taxes; reduced influence of the Bank of the United States.) Read and complete Chapter 9, Section 1 Daily Activity as a class.

Picturing History In his role as Secretary of State under President Jefferson, James Madison helped expand the nation's territory.

James Madison, who was named Secretary of State, and Albert Gallatin, who became Secretary of the Treasury.

Jefferson tried to cut the costs of government wherever possible. He reduced the size of the army, halted the scheduled expansion of the navy, and lowered expenses for government social functions. Such reductions were easier then than they would be today. The federal bureaucracy was tiny. For example, when Jefferson took office, the State Department had eight employees. Now it has over twenty-five thousand.

Jefferson also wanted to simplify the government's financial affairs and to tear down Hamilton's financial program. So all internal taxes were eliminated, and the influence of the Bank of the United States was greatly reduced.

Judicial Changes. Jefferson had been a strong opponent of the Alien and Sedition Acts. So he asked Congress to change the period of naturalization from fourteen back to five years. He pardoned the men who had been convicted under the Sedition Act and ordered their fines returned with interest.

Jefferson also began what many called a war against the judiciary. During the four months be-

tween Jefferson's election and his inauguration on March 4, 1801, the Federalists tried to increase their hold on the judiciary. They passed the **Judiciary Act of 1801,** which increased the number of federal judges. Adams promptly filled sixty-seven of the positions with members of his party. These judges were called **midnight judges** because, so the story went, Adams had signed the appointments up to midnight on the last day of his administration.

Jefferson could not dismiss the judges, who were appointed for life, but he did get the House of Representatives to impeach Supreme Court Justice Samuel Chase, who had insulted Republicans and denounced them as traitors. The Senate, however, refused to convict him. Although Chase's words and behavior had been shameful, he was not actually guilty of "high crimes and misdemeanors."

A more significant incident in Jefferson's war on the judiciary was the attempt to block William Marbury—one of Adams's last-minute appointments—from assuming his judgeship. The resulting Supreme Court case, *Marbury* v. *Madison* (1803; discussed in detail in Chapter 7, Section 4), established the principle of judicial review. This principle holds that the Supreme Court has the authority to declare acts of Congress unconstitutional. Although this principle is not directly provided for by the Constitution, it is now part of the United States government system. The Supreme Court's power to declare laws unconstitutional was expanded by later decisions to include laws passed by state legislatures as well.

The West Is Opened

Jefferson feared that the federal judiciary was gaining great power at the expense of state governments. Yet it was Jefferson himself who was responsible for a tremendous expansion of federal territory and power.

Beyond the Appalachians. For centuries the valleys of the Ohio, Cumberland, and Tennessee rivers had been the hunting grounds of the Shawnee and other Indian tribes. By 1800, however, some 250,000 white settlers had cleared homesteads in the area, and Kentucky and Tennessee had followed Vermont in becoming parts of the United States.

The main gateway to the West in those years was through the Cumberland Gap in the Appalachian

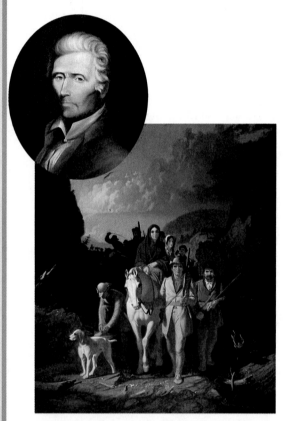

Picturing History *Daniel Boone Escorting Settlers Through the Cumberland Gap* by George Caleb Bingham depicts the celebrated scout leading a group of settlers into Kentucky. The portrait shows Boone at eighty-five. It was painted by the traveling artist Chester Harding.

Mountains. The gap is located where Kentucky, Tennessee, and Virginia come together. In 1775, under the leadership of woodsman **Daniel Boone,** a group of thirty men cleared a continuous road through the gap from eastern Tennessee to what is now Louisville, Kentucky. When it was finished, the Wilderness Road was almost three hundred miles long. At first, people journeyed over it on foot or horseback. By 1795, however, it had been graded so that it was fit for wagons.

West of Louisville, people usually went by water. If you were traveling light, you paddled a birchbark canoe. Families generally used a Kentucky ark, a roofed barge large enough to carry household goods, grain, hay, and livestock.

Pioneer Life. The lives of the pioneers who crossed the Appalachians were anything but easy.

They consisted mainly of hard work and bouts of illness. After the difficult journey, the settlers had to clear the new land and build shelters.

Illness came often. Many suffered from a fever we now know as malaria. There were few doctors, so the settlers learned to use many Indian remedies. Every family had a book full of cures for various ailments. Exchanging remedies with neighbors was as common as exchanging recipes for pies or jam.

The life of Thomas Lincoln was typical of that of a pioneer who moved west. Born in the late 1700's in western Virginia, he grew up in Kentucky. There he did some carpentry and also worked as a hired hand on farms. He never went to school, and he married Nancy Hanks, who could neither read nor write. In 1809 she gave birth to their son, Abraham. By 1816 they had settled as squatters in southern Indiana on land they did not own. "We lived the same as the Indians," one of the Hankses said later, "exceptin' we took an interest in politics and religion."

Within a year of moving to Indiana, they built a typical log cabin with a dirt floor, no windows, and a mere opening for a door. They stuffed the cracks in the roof with mud and grass to keep out the rain. They lived in this house for ten years before moving on to Illinois.

Louisiana Is Purchased

As vast as the western territories were, Jefferson dreamed of an even larger America. Soon there was an opportunity to make the dream a reality.

Napoleon Wants Louisiana. In 1800 Napoleon Bonaparte of France persuaded Spain to return the Louisiana Territory it had received in 1762. The French ruler intended to use the territory as a breadbasket for the French West Indies. When news of the secret transfer leaked out, Americans reacted with alarm. Spain was weak but Napoleon's France was not. Jefferson feared that a strong French presence in the mid-continent would force the United States into an alliance with Britain. In a letter to Robert Livingston, Jefferson wrote: "The day that France takes possession of New Orleans . . . we must marry ourselves to the British fleet and nation."

Jefferson decided to see whether he could resolve the problem by buying New Orleans and western Florida from the French. He sent James

234

Monroe to join Robert Livingston, the American ambassador, in Paris.

Napoleon Changes His Mind. Before Monroe arrived, however, Napoleon had abandoned his vision of an empire in America. Rather, his vision had been changed for him.

France's most important island colony was Haiti, then known as Saint Domingue (san də miŋ′). In the 1790's, under the leadership of **Toussaint L'Ouverture** (tōō san′ lōō ver tür′), the black slaves in Haiti revolted and won their independence. When Napoleon tried but failed to reconquer the colony, he saw no reason to keep Louisiana. Furthermore, he was expecting renewed war against Great Britain. So, in 1803, he offered to sell the entire Louisiana Territory to the United States.

With no time to consult their government, the surprised but jubilant Monroe and Livingston went ahead and closed the deal for $15 million. Fearing that Napoleon might change his mind, Jefferson pressed the treaty of purchase through the Senate. The United States had more than doubled in size.

Westerners were delighted by this enormous addition to United States territory. In general, the **Louisiana Purchase** was considered to cover the land

Picturing History
Haitian liberator Toussaint L'Ouverture became a symbol of the struggle for independence.

drained by the western tributaries of the Mississippi. However, no one knew exactly what the borders were. When the Americans in Paris asked Talleyrand, the French foreign minister, he avoided a direct answer, saying, "You must take it as we received it." This, the Americans assumed, meant they should claim as much territory as they dared at the expense of Spain and Britain.

The Lewis and Clark Expedition. Jefferson was eager to explore the newly acquired territory—and

Map Skills
St. Louis • Columbia

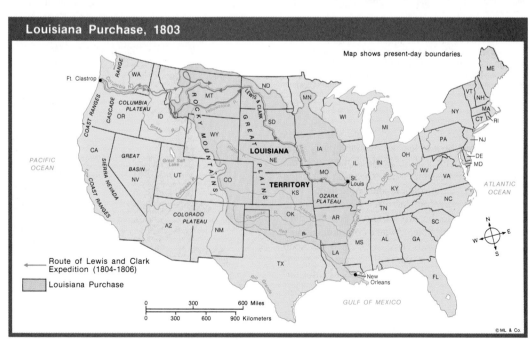

Louisiana Purchase, 1803

Map shows present-day boundaries.

→ Route of Lewis and Clark Expedition (1804-1806)

▢ Louisiana Purchase

PACIFIC OCEAN

ATLANTIC OCEAN

GULF OF MEXICO

©ML & Co.

Map Skills **Movement** From what city did Lewis and Clark leave? **Movement** Which river followed by Lewis and Clark flows into the Pacific Ocean?

Assign Independent Practice

Have students complete Chapter 9, Section 1 Enrichment Activity.

Student Assignment/Homework

Have students read Section 2, "The United States Enters the War of 1812," and answer the Section 2 Review questions on paper.

Picturing History Sacajawea (left) traveled thousands of miles with William Clark (top) and Meriwether Lewis (below). She guided the explorers through the mountain pass in Montana that later became known as Bozeman Pass. There is evidence that after the expedition Sacajawea left her young son with Clark to be educated.

beyond. In 1803 he appointed **Meriwether Lewis** and **William Clark** to lead an overland party from the French settlement of St. Louis all the way to the Pacific coast if possible. The expedition consisted of some fifty young soldiers and woodsmen.

Jefferson's scientific interests were evident in his instructions to the two leaders. Their first duty was to find, if possible, "water communication" across the continent. They were also to keep careful journals about the soil, climate, vegetation, and minerals. They were to record information about their meetings with Indian tribes, opportunities for fur trading, and possible routes for migration. They were even to take along the recently developed smallpox vaccine and show the Indians how to use it.

A Shoshone (shō shō´ nē) Indian woman, **Saca-**

jawea (säk ä gä we´ ä), served as their interpreter and guide. She helped them establish friendly relations with the Shoshone, who furnished horses for the expedition.

The Lewis and Clark expedition took two years and four months. It was a great success. It showed that overland travel in the West was possible. It opened the path for people who "would come for furs, then for gold, and then for the land itself." Finally, it strengthened American claims to the vaguely defined Oregon Territory on the northwest coast.

Hamilton Duels with Burr

In 1800, as you recall, **Aaron Burr** lost the Presidency by two votes. He was disliked by the Republicans as well as the Federalists, particularly Hamilton. Aware that he had little future in either group nationally, Burr looked around for another outlet for his energy and ambition.

In 1804 Burr ran for governor of New York State. He accepted the aid of some Federalists who, angry at the thought of national Republican rule, wanted to establish an independent northern confederacy of New York and New Jersey. Hamilton found out about the scheme and exposed it. He is supposed to have said that Burr was a "dangerous

Picturing History The political career of Aaron Burr (above) ended after his duel with Alexander Hamilton. These are the pistols used in the duel.

of 1812. (Possible responses: treaty was more favorable to British; British won the right to continue fur trade.)

Anticipate the Lesson

Review with students the problems that existed between America and Britain prior to Jay's Treaty. (See Chapter 8.) (Problems include: British refusal to leave Great Lakes area; U.S. refusal to pay war debts owed to British merchants.) Ask students how this treaty helped to set the stage for the U.S. in the War

man and ought not to be trusted with the reins of government.'' Once again Burr lost. Furious, he challenged Hamilton to a ''gentlemen's duel'' with pistols. On July 11, 1804, in Weehawken, New Jersey, Burr fatally wounded Hamilton, who had previously resolved to withhold his fire.

SECTION 1 REVIEW

Key Terms and People

Explain the significance of: Thomas Jefferson, Judiciary Act of 1801, midnight judges, Daniel Boone, Toussaint L'Ouverture, Louisiana Purchase, Meriwether Lewis, William Clark, Sacajawea, Aaron Burr

Main Ideas

1. How did Jefferson simplify the federal government during his Presidency?
2. How did Daniel Boone help to open up the West to settlement?
3. Why did Jefferson decide to purchase the Louisiana Territory?
4. What was the purpose of the Lewis and Clark expedition?

Critical Thinking

5. How did the Louisiana Purchase strengthen the federal government?

SECTION 2

The United States Enters the War of 1812

GLOSSARY TERMS: **blockade, impressment, embargo, armistice, freedom of the seas**

In 1803 the expected war between France and Great Britain broke out, and it continued for a dozen years. Before it was over, the United States was drawn into the conflict.

Americans Object to Impressment

The basic problem was one that had existed for more than a century. The American economy was based on exporting agricultural products and importing manufactured goods from Europe. Any interference with American shipping caused eco-

nomic troubles at home. Now that the colonies were an independent nation, such interference was a threat to national honor as well.

In 1806 Napoleon decided to exclude British goods from his ''fortress Europe.'' In turn, Great Britain decided that the best way of attacking the fortress was to **blockade** it, or seal it off. Neutral American ships were caught in the middle. By 1807 Britain had seized more than one thousand American ships and confiscated their cargoes, while France had seized about half that number.

The Evils of Impressment. There was one thing, however, that made Great Britain seem more offensive than France—its policy of **impressment.** For centuries, the British had manned their fleet by kidnapping British men and forcing them into naval service. Any man born in England was considered properly subject to the press.

Inevitably, this led to conflict over British-born seamen who were naturalized citizens of the United States. The conflict was made worse by incidents in which crew members from a British man-of-war would board an American merchantman and impress likely-looking sailors without paying any attention to their actual citizenship. As one British captain arrogantly declared, ''It is my duty to keep my ship manned, and I will do so wherever I find men that speak the same language with me.'' All told, about ten thousand American citizens were taken by the British.

The _Chesapeake_ Incident. In June 1807 the newly launched frigate U.S.S. _Chesapeake_ was cruising in international waters just outside the three-mile limit off Norfolk, Virginia. The British warship _Leopard_ approached and ordered the _Chesapeake_ to heave to in order to permit a search for British deserters. When the _Chesapeake's_ captain refused, the _Leopard_ opened fire. Three Americans were killed and eighteen wounded. The _Chesapeake's_ captain then permitted a British search party on board. The British took four alleged deserters—two black and two white.

An Embargo Boomerangs. To many Americans, this humiliating attack meant war. ''Never since the battle of Lexington,'' Jefferson wrote, ''have I seen this country in such a state.'' However, he preferred to try what he called ''peaceful coercion.'' He decided to keep American ships and foodstuffs off the high seas. He thought this would force European powers to respect neutral American

Answers

Main Ideas

1. By cutting government and military expenditures, eliminating internal taxes, and reducing the influence of the Bank of the United States.

2. By clearing the Wilderness Road from eastern Tennessee to what is now Louisville, Kentucky.

3. To prevent France's regaining a presence in the mid-continent through the purchase of the territory from Spain; to avoid being forced into forming an anti-French alliance with Britain.

4. To search the Louisiana Territory for a water route to the Pacific and other valuable resources; to establish trade relations with the Indians.

Critical Thinking

5. Possible answer: the expansion of federal territory brought about new sources of federal revenue and a need for federal laws and regulations to govern the new territory. **(analysis & synthesis)**

rights. The Embargo Act sailed through Congress in December 1807.

As it turned out, the **embargo** hurt the United States much more than Britain or France. Despite shipping losses, American foreign commerce had doubled between 1803 and 1807. Now it came to a standstill. Shipping centers, particularly those in New England, closed down. Merchants, shipbuilders, sailmakers, seamen, stevedores—all reacted with outrage to Jefferson's "dambargo."

Not surprisingly, the Federalists made gains at the polls in 1808. Once again, as in 1804, they selected Charles C. Pinckney and Rufus King as their candidates. However, James Madison, the Republican candidate, easily won the Presidency. Congress gradually lifted the trade restrictions. By 1810 American ships were again free to sail the Atlantic and to take their chances with seizure.

War Hawks Want War with Indians and Britain

In 1810 some bright new men in their early thirties were elected to Congress. They came mostly from the western states. Known as the **War Hawks,** these congressmen believed impressment was a major issue, not because they had maritime interests but because it was an insult to the American flag. Unlike the older generation of Republican and Federalist leaders, the War Hawks had been born under that flag. These men included John C. Calhoun of South Carolina, Felix Grundy of Tennessee, and especially Henry Clay of Kentucky, who was elected Speaker of the House of Representatives.

Indian Territory Is Invaded. Next to impressment, what bothered the War Hawks most was the "Indian problem" in the Indiana Territory. (Ohio had become a state in 1803.) The attitude of most white settlers in the area is shown in a statement made by General **William Henry Harrison,** the territorial governor.

> Is one of the fairest portions of the globe to remain in a state of nature, the haunt of a few wretched savages, when it seems destined, by the Creator, to give support to a large population, and to be the seat of civilization, of science, and of true religion?

In 1809 Harrison invited some elderly Indian chiefs to Fort Wayne, Indiana. After getting them drunk, he persuaded them to sign away three million acres of tribal land. Jefferson had told Harrison about his policy of absorbing Indians into the white man's culture by transforming them from hunters into farmers. However, he had also told Harrison that any tribe "foolhardy enough to take up the hatchet" should be driven across the Mississippi.

Tecumseh Forms a Confederacy. The Indians did in fact take up the hatchet, and eventually they *were* driven across the Mississippi. However, it was only after several years of fierce fighting and thousands of casualties on both sides.

The Indian leader in the struggle was a Shawnee chief named **Tecumseh** (ti kum´ sə). Around 1805 he began to assert that no tribe could sell land to the whites unless all the tribes east of the Mississippi gave their consent. His dream was to combine the eastern tribes into a gigantic confederacy to fight for their common homeland.

> The Great Spirit gave this great land to his red children. He placed the whites on the other side of the big water. They were not contented with their own, but came to take ours from us. They have driven us from the sea to the lakes. We can go no further.

In 1811 Tecumseh went on a six-month journey to gain support from the Creeks and other tribes in

Picturing History This painting of Tecumseh belonged to the family of explorer William Clark.

the South. His brother, disregarding Tecumseh's instructions, mounted a premature attack on a force of one thousand men assembled by Governor Harrison. A full-scale battle took place near the mouth of the Tippecanoe River. Both sides suffered high casualties, but eventually the Indians withdrew. The battle made Harrison a popular hero.

On to Canada! The War Hawks in Congress seized upon the Battle of Tippecanoe as another reason to attack Britain. Some of the firearms the Indians abandoned at Tippecanoe came from Canada. Here was another example, the War Hawks cried, of Britain insulting America. Since the quickest way to attack Britain was to head northward, the War Hawk rallying cry was "On to Canada!"

The War of 1812 Brings Mixed Results

By the middle of 1812, President Madison felt he had to give in to the war fever. Although the nation was unprepared and all the Federalists in the House of Representatives voted no, war was declared.

At the time, the war was referred to by its opponents as "Mr. Madison's War." It might as well have been called the "War for Canada," or the "Indian War Beyond the Appalachians," or the "Second War for American Independence." Probably because the reasons for it were so mixed, the conflict has become known in American history only by a date—1812.

The Canadian Front. Madison called for fifty thousand volunteers for a year's service in the regular army. Five thousand signed up. The corps of top army officers consisted largely of tired old men. Given this situation, it is not surprising that the first attempts to invade Canada were disastrous. Three separate armies tried different routes of attack. One proceeded to lose Detroit to a combined force of British soldiers plus Indian warriors led by Tecumseh. The two remaining American armies got nowhere when New York militiamen refused to cross the Canadian border.

The next year, things went better. The American fleet on Lake Erie under the command of Captain **Oliver Hazard Perry** defeated a British fleet. The Americans regained Detroit, and two American armies invaded Canada, winning battles at the Thames River, York (now Toronto), and Fort George. Tecumseh was killed at the Battle of the

Picturing History At the Battle of Tippecanoe, William Henry Harrison won the nickname "Old Tip."

Thames, and with his death his confederacy collapsed.

Overall, however, the superiority of the British fleet began to tell. By the end of 1813, most of the American navy and a good part of its merchant marine were bottled up in American ports.

The British Burn Washington, D.C. By 1814 British landing parties were burning towns all along the coast. That summer they sent a sizable force up Chesapeake Bay. The redcoats brushed aside some hastily assembled American troops and entered Washington on August 24. Madison and other federal officials had to flee from their own capital. In revenge for the American raid on York, the capital of Canada, the British burned the Capitol, the White House, and other public buildings. Although the burning of Washington had little military significance, it was a severe blow to national pride.

From Washington, the British mounted an assault on Baltimore. When it failed, they planned a three-pronged attack. One was to smash across the border at Niagara into western New York. Another was to follow the same route of lakes that Burgoyne had taken thirty-five years before. The British were stopped on both campaigns. The final prong was an attack on New Orleans.

The War of 1812

Map Skills **Movement** From where did American forces come to New Orleans? **Location** On what lake was the battle of Put-in-Bay? **Place** What was the city of Toronto called in 1813?

Map Skills

Pensacola • Erie • York

Andrew Jackson: Hero of New Orleans. For more than a year, a vigorous man from Tennessee had been running a more or less independent campaign of his own. **Andrew Jackson** was a born leader and a self-taught military genius. He led a band of Tennessee frontiersmen southward into the Mississippi Territory, fighting Indians wherever he could find them. Next, Jackson invaded Spanish territory in western Florida to head off any British attempt to take the port of Pensacola.

Jackson then turned westward to help defend New Orleans. By January 9, 1815, he had collected a force of some fifty-four hundred frontiersmen,

sailors, regular troops, and pirates. Free blacks joined the campaign as well—recruited with promises of "the same bounty in money and lands now received by white soldiers of the United States."

The Americans lay lodged behind walls of cotton bales, awaiting the eight thousand invading redcoats. The British commander ordered a frontal assault. Before he was killed, he watched his veteran soldiers go down in rows. British losses stood at more than two thousand. American casualties numbered seventy-one. Jackson instantly became known as the Hero of New Orleans.

The Battle of New Orleans provided the Amer-

Guided Practice

Tell students that, like Jefferson, modern Presidents are often under pressure to react militarily to attacks by foreign nations. President Carter was in a similar position in 1979 when terrorists surrounded the American Embassy in Teheran, Iran, and trapped many Americans inside. Carter had to weigh the risks of war against the loss of prestige and possible loss of American lives. Ask students what means other than force are available to any President. (Possible responses: negotiations; third-nation intervention; trade restrictions.)

Assign Independent Practice

Have students reread the text material under "The Treaty of Ghent" and write two paragraphs explaining the provisions and the reasons why the treaty represented a necessary compromise by both sides. (Provisions include: no exchange of territory; no mention of freedom of seas or impressment issue. Reason for compromise: each side wished to gain advantages for its country and to end war and establish peaceful relations.)

icans with their only really decisive land victory of the entire war. Ironically, the war was already over. On Christmas Eve of 1814, the American and British peace negotiators had reached an agreement. The news just had not arrived in time.

Linking Past to Present

The Battle of Tippecanoe made William Henry Harrison a popular hero. Later, the campaign slogan "Tippecanoe and Tyler too" would help to elect him President. The War of 1812 also made Andrew Jackson, the Hero of New Orleans, a popular figure and helped pave his way to the Presidency. In modern times, Dwight Eisenhower and John Kennedy became well known as military leaders and used this popularity to their advantage in their campaigns for President.

New England's Discontent. From the beginning, New Englanders felt the war would ruin their maritime interests. They also saw their section as a shrinking corner of an expanding nation. Every time a new state entered the Union, the voting weight of New England lessened in Congress and in the electoral college.

Accordingly, New Englanders did everything they could to cripple the war effort. They boycotted federal bond sales, refused to let their state militias serve beyond state borders, and blocked a military draft.

In 1814 they held a regional convention at Hartford, Connecticut. It proposed several constitutional amendments, including one that would have eliminated the three-fifths clause and thereby lessened the South's voting power in Congress. The South usually voted against New England's interests, and vice versa. However, when delegates from the Hartford Convention arrived in Washington to present these proposals, they found the capital wildly celebrating both Jackson's victory at New Orleans and a treaty of peace.

The Treaty of Ghent. Formal peace talks began at the Belgian town of Ghent in August 1814. The British negotiating team had orders to give little and demand much, including an Indian state north of the Ohio. The American negotiators were less bound by strict instructions, yet their own quarreling almost broke up the talks. Henry Clay spoke for Western interests. John Quincy Adams, the ex-President's son, had New England at heart. Each was suspicious that the other would sacrifice the interests of any section but his own. When Adams suggested that the British be allowed to navigate the Mississippi in exchange for fishing rights near Newfoundland, Clay exploded. "The navigation principle," he said, "is much too important to concede for the mere liberty of drying fish." Fortunately, Albert Gallatin of Pennsylvania managed to keep a measure of peace in the delegation.

Britain's lack of success in upstate New York forced the British negotiators to back off from their demands. The final treaty actually looked more like an **armistice** agreement. No territory changed hands, and the issues of impressment and **freedom of the seas,** the right of neutral ships to sail safely, were not mentioned. Yet Americans welcomed it. They were eager for peace, and Jackson's victory tended to block all memories of earlier military humiliations. The United States had survived a major war. The result, as Gallatin put it, was that "the people . . . feel and act more as a nation."

The Aftermath of the War. Within a few years, the United States and Great Britain were able to reach agreement on many of the issues left open at Ghent. In 1815 a commercial treaty reopened trade between the two countries. In 1817 the Rush-Bagot agreement limited the number of warships on the Great Lakes. In 1818 a British-American commission set the northern boundary of the Louisiana Territory at the forty-ninth parallel as far west as the Rocky Mountains. The two nations then agreed to a ten-year joint occupation of the Oregon Territory. No one knew it at the time, but these agreements laid the groundwork for lasting peace between the two nations.

There remained one outstanding piece of unfinished business. Most Americans assumed that Spanish Florida would eventually become part of the United States, and American settlers began to move in on their own. In 1817 there were outbreaks of violence between white settlers and Seminole Indians who were aided by fugitive slaves from Georgia. Andrew Jackson was given command of United States troops, with vague instructions to bring peace and order to the borderland region.

Jackson interpreted these instructions freely. Many times he dealt with Indians simply by de-

Have students read Section 3, "Both National and Sectional Feelings Grow" and complete Chapter 9, Section 3 Daily Activity.

SECTION 2 REVIEW

Answers

Main Ideas

1. Besides seizing cargoes, Britain impressed crew members.

2. To protest Britain's impressment policy and to force the Indians from areas well suited for white settlement.

3. The northern boundary of the Louisiana Territory was set, and Britain and the U.S. agreed to joint occupation of the Oregon Territory.

4. By boldly invading and seizing control of Florida, he helped Spain realize that if it did not give up Florida peacefully, Americans would eventually overrun it.

Critical Thinking

5. Possible answer: the war had an inconclusive outcome. On the "win" side— the collapse of Tecumseh's confederacy left Indian lands open to white settlement; agreements were reached that maintained lasting peace between Britain and the U.S.; national unity was encouraged. On the "lose" side—the heavy war casualties; the burning of Washington, D.C.; the sectional differences revealed at the Ghent peace talks.
(analysis & evaluation)

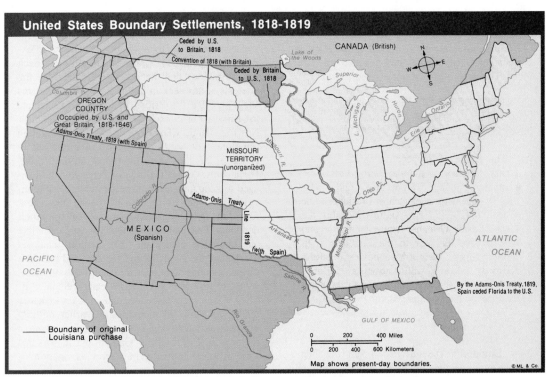

United States Boundary Settlements, 1818-1819

Ceded by U.S. to Britain, 1818
Convention of 1818 (with Britain)
Ceded by Britain to U.S., 1818
CANADA (British)
Lake of the Woods
L. Superior
OREGON COUNTRY (Occupied by U.S. and Great Britain, 1818-1846)
Adams-Onis Treaty, 1819 (with Spain)
Columbia R.
L. Michigan
L. Huron
L. Ontario
L. Erie
MISSOURI TERRITORY (unorganized)
Missouri R.
Ohio R.
Adams-Onis Treaty Line 1819 (with Spain)
MEXICO (Spanish)
Colorado R.
Arkansas R.
Mississippi R.
ATLANTIC OCEAN
PACIFIC OCEAN
Sabine R.
Red R.
By the Adams-Onis Treaty, 1819, Spain ceded Florida to the U.S.
Rio Grande
GULF OF MEXICO
Boundary of original Louisiana purchase
0 200 400 Miles
0 200 400 600 Kilometers
Map shows present-day boundaries.
© ML & Co.

Map Skills **Location** The Adams-Onis Treaty set the boundary with what Spanish colonies?
Location What river marked the western boundary of the Florida Territory?

stroying their villages. He had little respect for international law. When the Seminoles retreated into Florida, Jackson pursued them across the border and hunted them down in Spanish territory. When he reached Pensacola, he threw out the Spanish governor, set up his own garrisons, and claimed the territory for the United States.

Secretary of State John Quincy Adams was left with the problem of picking up the diplomatic pieces. He was already negotiating with Spanish minister Luis de Onis (loo ēs′ dā ōn ēs′) about the future of Florida. He convinced Onis that Spain would do well to give it up before impatient Americans simply seized it. In the **Adams-Onis Treaty** of 1819, Spain ceded the territory of Florida to the United States.

Adams was not content to let matters rest there. A skillful negotiator, he persuaded Onis to include in the treaty a firm boundary between Spanish territory and the United States all the way from Louisiana to the Pacific. Adams held a vision of continental expansion that matched Jefferson's.

The taking of all North America by the United States, he wrote, is "as much a law of nature . . . as that the Mississippi should flow to the sea."

SECTION 2 REVIEW

Key Terms and People

Explain the significance of: blockade, impressment, embargo, War Hawks, William Henry Harrison, Tecumseh, Oliver Hazard Perry, Andrew Jackson, armistice, freedom of the seas, Adams-Onis Treaty

Main Ideas

1. Why did Americans find Britain's seizure of American ships more offensive than France's seizure of American ships?

2. Why did War Hawks want the United States to declare war on Britain and the Indians?

3. What were the important results of the War of 1812?

Anticipate the Lesson

Review the information in Chapter 9, Section 3 Daily Activity with students.

State the Objective

Learn about the expansion of the national economy and government between 1815 and 1830.

4. How did Jackson's actions help to bring about the transfer of Spanish Florida to the United States?

Critical Thinking

5. Did America win or lose the War of 1812? Explain.

SECTION 3

Both National and Sectional Feelings Grow

GLOSSARY TERMS: **nationalism, Era of Good Feelings, American System, interstate commerce, Monroe Doctrine, Missouri Compromise**

A new spirit of pride and national unity, called **nationalism,** swept the country in the years following the War of 1812. A sign of this new thinking came in 1817 when President **James Monroe** arrived in Boston to a warm welcome. The idea of a Republican from Virginia being welcomed in this northern Federalist stronghold astounded the nation. As one Boston publication, the *Columbia Centinel,* declared, Americans were seeing an **Era of Good Feelings.**

The American System Brings Strength and Unity

This postwar mood also expressed itself in a theory of economic growth known as the **Ameri-** **can System.** This idea, as explained in a famous speech by Henry Clay, envisioned a United States consisting of two sections, each helping the other. An industrial North would turn out manufactured goods. An agricultural section composed of the South and West would raise grain, meat, and cotton. Factory workers in the North would form a market for agricultural products. Farmers in the South and West would buy manufactured goods.

To bring about the American System, supporters believed three things were necessary: protective tariffs, improved transportation, and a national banking system. The Republican majority in Congress set about passing the required legislation.

Protective Tariffs. To help the North, Congress set up trade barriers to protect America's infant industries from overseas competition. Immediately after the war, British merchants tried to flood the American market with iron, textiles, and other products at prices cheaper than those for the same goods produced in the United States. One member of Parliament explained that it was better to sell at a loss at first in order ''to stifle in the cradle those rising manufacturers in the United States.''

With the **Tariff Act of 1816,** Congress adopted a mild protective tariff. Then in 1828, it significantly raised the tariff rates.

Transportation Improvements. To help the West and South, the federal government authorized construction of the **National Road** from Cumberland, Maryland, to Vandalia, Illinois, and also of canals so goods could move to market more easily. The money for these **internal improvements** was obtained from the protective tariff.

Map Skills

Mexico and Florida • Mississippi

Picturing History
Pioneers traveled on the National Road, part of the transportation system that helped to build the nation. The road later became U.S. Highway 40.

Present the Lesson

Write the word *nationalism* on the board and have students recall various concepts from this section that are associated with the idea of nationalism. (Possible responses: American System of manufacturing and agriculture; protective tariffs; Second Bank of the United States; improvements in transportation.) Ask students to cite major Supreme Court cases of the Jeffersonian Era and summarize each case. (Responses: *Fletcher* v. *Peck* (1810)—first time Court declared a state law unconstitutional; *Dartmouth College* v. *Woodward* (1819)—extended principle of Fletcher deci-sion to include contracts between corpora-tions and states; *McCulloch* v. *Maryland* (1819)—extended the authority of federal law over state law; *Gibbons* v. *Ogden* (1824)—established federal government's authority over interstate commerce.) Discuss with stu-dents how these Supreme Court decisions strengthened nationalism.

Map Skills

Indianapolis • Boston Post Road • Mohawk Turnpike • Great Valley Road

For Discussion

What were the economic ad-vantages of establishing a national bank? (Possible re-sponses: the bank could issue paper money backed by gold or silver reserves; paper money from national bank could be used to buy goods throughout the coun-try; paper money had the same value all over the coun-try; paper money encour-aged trade among the states.)

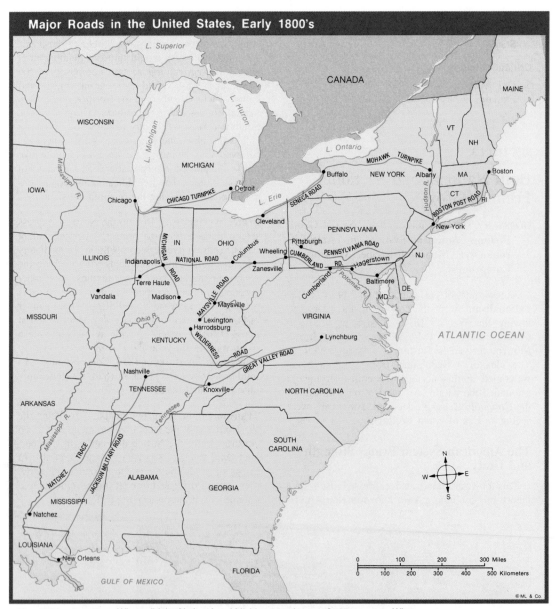

Map Skills   Location Where did the National and Michigan roads cross? **Movement** What road linked New York and Boston? Albany and Buffalo? Knoxville and Lynchburg?

The Second Bank of the United States. To help the two sections of the country do business with each other, the federal government set up a new national bank. After the charter of the first national bank expired in 1811, its business was conducted by state banks. Regulations for these banks were lax. Many of them issued a great deal more paper money than they could back up with silver or gold. Paper money, therefore, quickly lost value. In addition, money issued in one locale was often not accepted anywhere else. This made it difficult to conduct business.

Check for Understanding

Have students complete the Section 3 Review questions orally.

Guided Practice

Point out to students that booms and busts have been part of the American economy since its early days. Ask students to suggest ways the federal government tries to stimulate the economy and avoid extremes in the business cycle. (Possible responses: import quotas on foreign goods; tax credits for businesses; prohibition of monopolies; federal mediation of labor disputes.) Discuss with students the extent to which the federal government should become involved in business and industry. (Discussion might include: government should not be involved at all; government should be involved only to the extent necessary to protect the rights of its citizens; government should ensure steady business profits to generate tax money needed to support government services.)

In 1816 Congress chartered the **Second Bank of the United States** with twenty-five branches throughout the country. The national bank issued its own paper money. These notes could be used anywhere, and by increasing the money supply they fueled a two-year national business boom.

The Supreme Court Favors National Power

The Supreme Court, under the leadership of Chief Justice **John Marshall,** supported the trend toward national power. When Marshall was appointed Chief Justice in 1801, he was known as a skilled and distinguished Virginia lawyer. During his thirty-four-year tenure, however, he dominated the Court, writing more than half its opinions. Marshall's decisions enlarged the power of the Supreme Court, broadened the national government's power over the states, and established principles important to business practice. Four cases in addition to *Marbury* v. *Madison* (see pages 198–199) have had lasting significance.

In *Fletcher* v. *Peck* (1810), a new state administration had passed a law voiding a land grant made by the previous administration. When the land owners sued, Marshall ruled that the contract had to stand. Article I, Section 10 of the Constitution forbids state laws "impairing" contracts. A contract had been made between the businessmen and the state, he declared. The legislature could not legislate away its obligation. The decision also marked the first time the Supreme Court declared a state law unconstitutional.

Dartmouth College v. *Woodward* (1819; described on page 202) expanded the principle of the Fletcher decision to include contracts between corporations and states. As more business corporations were established around the country, this ruling became very important.

McCulloch v. *Maryland* (1819) extended the authority of federal law over state law. Maryland had levied a heavy tax on the local branch of the Bank of the United States, hoping to tax it out of existence. Marshall declared that if such situations were allowed, states would in effect be overturning laws passed by Congress. The Chief Justice denied the right of Maryland to tax the Bank, stating that "the power to tax is the power to destroy." He declared the Bank of the United States constitutional by virtue of Hamilton's loose interpretation of the Constitution.

Gibbons v. *Ogden* (1824; discussed in detail on page 199) was a landmark in establishing the federal government's authority over **interstate commerce.** Justice Marshall ruled that, although a state could regulate business within its borders, only Congress had the power to regulate business between the states. Federal regulation of airlines and television, for example, are based on this decision.

The Monroe Years Bring Change

On the political scene, Monroe's administration was noted for two significant developments. One defined America's role in the Western Hemisphere. The other set policy for the admission of new states to the Union.

The Monroe Doctrine. When Napoleon invaded Portugal and Spain in 1807, the two countries did

Nations in Latin America, 1804–1826

Map Skills **Region** What part of South America remained under European rule after 1826? **Place** What Caribbean islands remained under European control?

Historical Sidelight

According to legend, the Liberty Bell cracked on July 4, 1776, while pealing the news of the nation's independence. The Liberty Bell was not rung on July 4th, however. The bell cracked on July 6, 1835, while tolling for the death of Chief Justice John Marshall.

Map Skills

The Guianas • Cuba, Puerto Rico, Jamaica

Have students write a two-paragraph essay explaining why the period from 1815 to 1830 was known as the "Era of Good Feelings." (Paragraphs might include: good feelings were generated by new spirit of unity after War of 1812; the development of the American System fostered manufacturing and agriculture; national pride gradually gained momentum over state pride; the Monroe Doctrine established a strong principle of American foreign policy.)

Map Skills

Yes • Yes • Yes • IL

not have the money or the manpower to fight Napoleon and keep control of their overseas territories at the same time. Soon they began losing their colonies to national independence movements. When Napoleon was defeated in 1815, Portugal and Spain wanted to reclaim their former colonies.

Meanwhile the Russians, who had been in Alaska since 1784, were establishing trading posts in what is now California. In 1821 the Tsar of Russia claimed that Alaska's southern boundary was the 51st parallel. He forbade all foreign vessels from using the coast north of this line.

With Spain and Portugal trying to move back into their old colonial areas, and with Russia pushing in from the northwest, the United States knew it had to do something. Many Americans were interested in acquiring northern Mexico and the Spanish colony of Cuba. The Russian action posed a threat to American trade with China, which brought profits of as much as 800 percent.

Accordingly, in his 1823 message to Congress, President Monroe warned all European powers not to interfere with affairs in the Western Hemisphere. They should not attempt to create new colonies, he said, or try to overthrow the newly independent republics. The United States would consider such action ''dangerous to our peace and safety.'' At the same time, the United States would not involve itself in European affairs or interfere with existing colonies in the Western Hemisphere. These principles have since become known as the **Monroe Doctrine.**

At first Monroe's words did not attract much attention in the United States. In Europe, however, there was anger and indignation. What did the upstart new republic mean by lecturing European governments on how to behave in the Americas? Why, the United States could not even enforce the declaration without the help of the British fleet, which controlled the Atlantic. Nevertheless, the Monroe Doctrine was important because it established what was to become a major principle of American foreign policy.

Linking Past to Present

In 1904 President Theodore Roosevelt issued what became known as the Roosevelt Corollary to the Monroe Doctrine. (See Chapter 20, Section 4.) The Roosevelt Corollary expanded the Monroe Doctrine so that its purpose was not only to prevent European intervention in the Americas but also to justify intervention by the United States. Since then, the principles of these doctrines have been invoked when United States interests in the Western Hemisphere have been seriously threatened. For example, the principles of the Monroe Doctrine motivated President Kennedy to respond forcefully to the Soviet threat during the Cuban missile crisis of the 1960's. (See Chapter 32, Section 2.) Other examples include Ronald Reagan's use of military intervention in Grenada in 1983 and George Bush's use of military intervention in Panama in 1989.

The Slavery Issue. On the home front, the new spirit of nationalism was challenged by an issue that had previously confronted the framers of the Constitution. That was the issue of slavery.

In 1787 slavery had been prohibited in the Northwest Territory. The issue, however, had not been decided for the Louisiana Purchase. When the territory of Missouri applied for admission to the Union in 1819, its proposed state constitution recognized the right to hold slaves. Would admitting Missouri with slavery set a precedent for the entire Louisiana Purchase?

There was an immediate uproar in Congress. For the first time, the merits of slavery were debated long and openly. A New Hampshire representative explained the importance of the issue. ''An opportunity is now presented, if not to diminish, at least to prevent the growth of a sin which sits heavy on

Picturing History
James Monroe was the last of the so-called Virginia dynasty to be elected President.

Student Assignment/Homework

Have students read Section 4, "New Inventions Change Lives," and answer the Section 4 Review questions on paper.

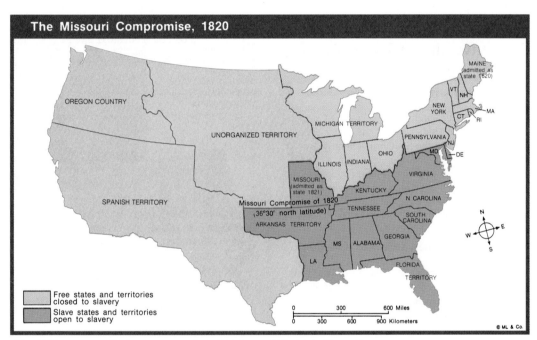

The Missouri Compromise, 1820

Free states and territories closed to slavery

Slave states and territories open to slavery

Map Skills **Region** Did the slave states include Delaware? Virginia? Missouri?
Location Which free state extended farthest south?

the soul of every one of us." Southerners took a different view. They defended the necessity of slavery and its extension westward. Many observers were alarmed by the bitterness of the controversy. "[W]e have the wolf by the ears," wrote the aging Jefferson, "and we can neither safely hold him, nor safely let him go."

Missouri's admission was stalled. Then Congress received an application from the area now known as Maine. Here was a chance to break the deadlock.

Under the leadership of Henry Clay, Congress passed a series of measures known as the **Missouri Compromise.** Maine was admitted as a free state and Missouri as a slave state, thus preserving the sectional balance in the Senate. The rest of the Louisiana Territory was split into two "spheres of interest, one . . . for the slave-holders and one for free settlers. The dividing line was set at 36° 30′ north latitude." South of the line, slavery was legal. North of the line—except for Missouri—slavery was banned.

President Monroe signed the Missouri Compromise in 1820. For a generation, the problem of slavery in federal territories seemed settled.

SECTION 3 REVIEW

Key Terms and People

Explain the significance of: nationalism, James Monroe, Era of Good Feelings, American System, Tariff Act of 1816, National Road, internal improvements, Second Bank of the United States, John Marshall, interstate commerce, Monroe Doctrine, Missouri Compromise

Main Ideas

1. What was the American System's vision of America?
2. In general, how did Marshall's Supreme Court expand and promote national power?
3. What was the main purpose of the Monroe Doctrine?
4. How did the Missouri Compromise temporarily settle the issue of the expansion of slavery?

Critical Thinking

5. How did enacting the theory of the American System broaden the powers of the federal government?

State the Objective
Determine how inventions and the growth of industry changed the lives of Americans.

SECTION 4

New Inventions Change Lives

GLOSSARY TERMS: **interchangeable parts, mass production, Industrial Revolution**

The debate surrounding the Missouri Compromise was but one indication of the importance of cotton and slaves to the Southern economy. Before the Revolution, little cotton was grown. It was unprofitable, even with slave labor, to separate the seeds from the fibers by hand. By the 1820's, however, **King Cotton** reigned as the South's most important cash crop.

The South Becomes a Cotton Kingdom

Eli Whitney's Invention.   This change was made possible by the invention of the cotton gin in 1793 by a talented young man from Massachusetts named **Eli Whitney.** Recent evidence suggests that Whitney did not invent the cotton gin without a good deal of help from Catherine Littlefield Greene, widow of General Nathanael Greene. Whitney probably had not seen a raw cotton ball until he was a guest for six months in the Greene home in Georgia. Whitney developed a machine in which rollers were implanted with wire teeth. As a handle turned the rollers, the teeth pulled the cotton seeds from the fibers. A worker using a gin could clean fifty pounds of cotton in one day, as compared to one pound by hand. Later, other inventors found ways to operate gins by horsepower and steam engine, which increased production even more.

A Land Rush.   An immediate result of the cotton gin's invention was a great land rush westward into the Old Southwest, the area between the Appalachians and the Mississippi south of the Ohio. The first pioneers were mostly poor, nonslaveholding farmers. The soil on their farms had become worn out, and they were looking for new land to cultivate. They were soon followed, however, by wealthier, slaveholding planters who could afford to buy and work large areas of land. The wealthy planters turned Louisiana, Mississippi, and Alabama into a booming Cotton Kingdom.

A Demand for Slave Labor.   The increased production of cotton created an enormous demand for slave labor. No slaves had been imported since the

Picturing History This portrait of Eli Whitney was painted by Samuel F. B. Morse in 1822. The patent model of Whitney's famous cotton gin is pictured below.

Revolution. In 1803 South Carolina legalized importation, and for the next five years Africans flooded into Charleston in unprecedented numbers. In 1808 the twenty-year period of protection of the slave trade, which had been written into the Constitution, expired. Jefferson promptly signed a law banning the importation of slaves.

More important than the international slave trade, however, was the domestic slave trade. By 1820, as one historian put it, "slaves had become a valuable cash crop." Slave owners in the eastern part of the South encouraged their slaves to have children as often as possible, and then sold the blacks they could not use to planters farther west. People called "soul-drivers" would buy slaves from a plantation, trade them at auctions, and then send them in "lots" to their new destination.

Frequently religion offered slaves comfort and hope. Ministers promised a heavenly reward to those who obeyed authority and lived a moral Christian life. In religious songs, or spirituals, slaves expressed their faith in a better life hereafter.

Running a Cotton Plantation.   Some cotton planters lived a life of luxury in white mansions with great columns supporting wide verandas and with furnishings imported from Europe. Most planters, however, were hardworking farmers whose living conditions were quite rough. A trav-

Present the Lesson

Have students list on the board events that contributed to the growth of industry in the U.S. beginning with the invention of the cotton gin. (List should include: Eli Whitney's cotton gin; Whitney's development of interchangeable parts; the development of mass production; Samuel Slater's textile factory; the Boston Associates' manufacturing plants.) Ask students how new inventions contributed to the growth of industry. (Possible response: each new invention mentioned in this section helped to speed up or eliminate a job previously done by hand; as tasks became more efficient and more specialized, industry could produce more.)

Check for Understanding

Call on individual students to read their answers to the Section 4 Review questions.

Agriculture in the South, 1839–1859

Map Skills **Region** Where were the main cotton-producing areas in 1839? in 1859?
Region Where was the main tobacco-growing area?

eler who was charged one dollar for staying overnight at a plantation house described his visit.

The house in which he stayed was indeed painted white, but there was a log cabin in the front yard that served as both kitchen and dining room. The planter and his wife slept in a bed in the parlor, while the traveler shared a straw mattress upstairs with one of the planter's sons. Everyone on this plantation walked barefoot in both summer and winter, and "nobody wore coats, except on holidays." Yet the planter was a rich man, having hundreds of acres of land, large herds of cattle and horses, and some thirty to forty slaves.

Operating a cotton plantation required considerable effort. A planter who invested several hundred dollars in a slave had to make certain that the slave remained in good health. This was especially difficult since the hot, humid months of May through November usually brought malaria. Also, many Africans resisted slavery by performing poorly. So there was a constant struggle on the part of planters to keep their work forces producing.

Financing the Cotton Kingdom. Surprisingly, perhaps, the financial capital of the Cotton Kingdom was New York City, which by 1810 had become the nation's largest city. Today New York is still the largest city in the United States.

New York merchants lent cotton planters money to buy land and slaves. They also sold to cotton planters hardware, foodstuffs, and luxury items that were not produced in the South. They sent their ships to Charleston, Mobile, New Orleans, and other Southern ports. They loaded the ships with bales of cotton and brought them back to New York for shipment to New England and Europe. Naturally, they earned a profit on every transaction. By 1830 about forty cents of every dollar that Southern planters received from the sale of cotton was going to New York.

Guided Practice

Tell students that with a factory system, great numbers of people work for someone whom they probably do not know. Ask students to suggest why a need for labor unions developed in this period. (Possible responses: to protect rights of workers; to give workers power in negotiating with their employers.) Ask students whether they think unions are still necessary today. (Possible responses: yes, unions still protect the rights of workers and ensure safe work places; no, unions have grown too strong, and their demands have driven up the prices of American-made products.)

Assign Independent Practice

Ask students to construct a time line showing the growth of the textile industry in the U.S. Time line might include:
- 1790, Samuel Slater opens cotton-spinning plant at Pawtucket, Rhode Island.
- 1791, Mrs. Slater receives patent for cotton sewing thread, the first patent issued to a woman.
- 1793, Eli Whitney invents cotton gin.
- 1807, Jefferson's embargo causes businessmen to turn from overseas trade.
- 1812, War encourages Americans to produce cloth.
- 1813, Boston Associates establish world's first integrated cotton manufacturing plant.
- 1820-1830, Boston Associates expand operations by establishing a series of plants, founding insurance companies and banks, setting up real estate firms, and organizing water power companies.
- 1828, first recorded factory strike occurs.

Picturing History America's first cotton mill drew its power from the Blackstone River. The mill's owner, Samuel Slater (inset), later established other mills.

The Industrial Revolution Spreads to America

At first the cotton grown in the Cotton Kingdom went mostly to textile mills in Great Britain. Gradually, however, a large textile industry developed in New England. In this, too, Eli Whitney played a major role.

The Use of Interchangeable Parts. After inventing the cotton gin, Whitney applied for a patent from the federal government and opened a factory to manufacture the new device. His machine was so easy to copy, though, that people simply made their own. Whitney's enterprise failed.

Whitney's inventive mind then turned to another mechanical problem. At the time, every rifle was a unique unit. If one part broke, the entire gun had to go back to the manufacturer because only he could fix it. Whitney looked at a gun as a combination of parts. He developed machines to produce each part. To make a gun, these parts could be assembled quickly. If one part broke, it could be replaced. A gun manufacturer could now turn out a great many guns in a short time. In addition, the guns could now be repaired by unskilled workers instead of master mechanics.

Whitney's system of **interchangeable parts** was applied to dozens of other products. Soon factories throughout the North were turning out goods on a mass basis, beginning the process now called **mass production.**

The Growth of Mills. As in England, America's **Industrial Revolution** started with the machinery for making textiles, specifically cotton goods. (See page 252.) The textile industry soon became the largest in the nation.

In the United States the industry began in 1789, when a twenty-one-year-old Englishman named **Samuel Slater** stepped onto a New York dock. When he left England, he had declared himself to be a farmer. Actually, he was a skilled mechanic. Because the British wanted to guard the secrets of their industrial development, they had banned the export of machine designs and even the emigration of mechanics. Slater, however, memorized the plans for a complete textile mill and then came to this country. With financial backing from Quaker merchant Moses Brown, he opened a cotton-spinning plant at Pawtucket, Rhode Island. Samuel Slater & Company became the first successful full-time factory in America and was soon widely imitated.

In 1807 Jefferson's embargo caused many busi-

Student Assignment/Homework

Have students complete Chapter 9 Review on paper. Have students review their answers in small groups.

Concluding the Chapter

Ask students to write three paragraphs comparing the approaches of Jefferson, Madison, and Monroe to issues concerning the central government, finances, and expansionism. (Paragraphs might include: Jefferson favored a weak central government, cut costs, reduced size of army, eliminated internal taxes, reduced influence of Bank of the United States, and purchased Louisiana Territory; Madison lifted trade embargoes, entered War of 1812, and established commercial treaty with Britain after war; Monroe issued Monroe Doctrine, provided protective tariffs, improved transportation, re-established power of national banking system, and obtained Florida from Spain.)

nessmen to turn from overseas trade to industry. The War of 1812 likewise encouraged Americans to produce their own cloth. In 1813 a group of wealthy Bostonians decided to band together as the Boston Associates and pool their capital resources. They established the world's first integrated cotton manufacturing plant. All operations from the un-baling of the cotton to the dyeing of the finished cloth were carried out under one roof.

During the 1820's and 1830's, the Boston Associates expanded operations by establishing a series of plants, each of which specialized in a different textile product. They also founded insurance companies and banks in order to have a steady supply of capital. They set up real-estate firms to buy the best sites for their factories. They even organized water-power companies to develop the rivers whose falling waters powered their machines.

Working Conditions. Conditions in the New England textile mills were far from pleasant. The buildings were six or seven stories high. Ceilings were low and ventilation poor. Windows were kept closed even in summer in order to maintain the humidity that was supposed to prevent the cotton thread from breaking. In winter smoky fumes from whale-oil lamps mixing with the thick cotton dust in the air made it difficult to breathe.

Work began at five o'clock in the morning. At half-past seven there was a short pause for breakfast. Workers took half an hour for lunch at noon, and the day ended at half-past seven in the evening. The workweek was six days. On Sunday workers were expected to attend church.

All the workers in Slater's first mill were children, who were paid lower wages than adults. In 1832 it was reported that two out of five textile workers were between six and seventeen years of age. The balance of the work force consisted of young women from seventeen to twenty-four, who flocked to the mill towns from the worn-out farms of New England.

The Boardinghouses. Since these women workers did not come from the mill towns and many were young enough to require permission from their families to work, mill owners developed the so-called Lowell or **Waltham system,** named after two of the leading Massachusetts mill towns. Under this system, women textile workers lived in boardinghouses. The company deducted room and board from their paychecks, and employed housemothers— usually local widows—to cook meals, check up on church attendance, and in general provide an atmosphere of respectability.

Most boardinghouses were closely regulated. Boarders were expected to enter quietly, observe good manners at all times, and take turns making beds and sweeping out the bedrooms. No lights were allowed in the bedrooms, and all the doors were locked at ten o'clock. The women were kept in line by the fact that they were paid only two or four times a year. If they did not obey the rules, they were fired without wages.

The First Factory Strike. Industrialists thought work in the mills benefited women and children. After all, they were learning the value of labor, the worth of money, and the merits of strict moral behavior. Understandably, the women and children involved sometimes took a different view.

The first recorded factory strike in American history took place in 1828. The mill owners in Paterson, New Jersey, tried to change the lunch hour from twelve to one o'clock. The children went out on strike "for fear," said one observer, "if they assented to this, the next thing would be to deprive them of eating at all." The mill owners called in the militia—and the strike was broken.

SECTION 4 REVIEW

Key Terms and People

Explain the significance of: King Cotton, Eli Whitney, interchangeable parts, mass production, Industrial Revolution, Samuel Slater, Waltham System

Main Ideas

1. How did the development of the cotton gin increase the demand for slave labor?
2. In what two ways did Southerners attempt to satisfy the need for more slaves?
3. How did some New Yorkers profit from the Cotton Kingdom?
4. What important developments brought about the Industrial Revolution in America?
5. Briefly describe the working conditions in textile mills during this period.

Critical Thinking

6. Did the Industrial Revolution benefit all Americans? Explain.

Present the Lesson

Ask students to pretend they are British textile entrepreneurs during the time of the Industrial Revolution. Then have students use the information from the feature to create a business opportunity advertisement for a newspaper. The ad should describe resources available for the development of a textile business in Great Britain in the late 1700's. Ask volunteers to read their ads to the class. (Ads might refer to the following resources: British wool and cotton from the colonies; a large pool of labor from a growing city population; new inventions such as the flying shuttle, the water-powered spin-ning machine, and the steam-powered weaving loom; expanding markets in the colonies; good ports for shipping; a powerful navy to protect commerce.)

Focus on Economics

The Industrial Revolution

The American Revolution was a dramatic event that captured the attention of the world. At the same time, another revolution was going on, totally unplanned and unnoticed, that finally transformed the lives of Americans as much as, or perhaps more than, the revolution of 1775–1783. This silent change was called the Industrial Revolution.

Basic Resources. Industrialization began in England because of certain geographical, social, and economic conditions. It was based on that country's ample supply of natural resources. Large coal and iron deposits were crucial for the construction of machinery and factories in all industries. The rapid currents of the many rivers and streams provided the water power to keep machines running. The nation's coastline furnished numerous ports from which manufactured goods could be shipped to foreign buyers. In addition, British wool as well as cotton from the colonies helped spur the expanding British textile industry.

Great Britain could also draw upon a large labor force for its industrial needs. New advances in medicine and sanitation caused the population to double. Farms became overpopulated. With fewer jobs on the farm, men and women streamed into the factories in the cities, where there was hope of work.

Capital and Support. The Industrial Revolution was further advanced by the huge amounts of capital that British merchants and landowners had accumulated. These savings could now be invested with much profit in such expanding industries as mining, ironmaking, and textiles.

Finally, the British government did its best to stimulate the growth of industry. Following the principles of laissez faire, it relaxed taxes and mercantilist regulations that hampered trade. In addition, the powerful British navy was sent out to defend Britain's commercial interests around the world.

New Inventions. The increased demand for cloth on the part of both new city dwellers and expand-ing foreign markets spurred the search for new methods of production and led to the mechanization of the textile industry. The flying shuttle that John Kay developed in 1733 cut weaving time in half. In 1769 Richard Arkwright's water-powered spinning machine made it possible to produce many strong threads at once. By 1785 Edmund Cartwright had invented the first successful steam-powered weaving loom.

To acquire these and other inventions, business owners had to invest considerable amounts of money. To make a profit, they had to run the machines twenty-four hours a day and provide them with expert maintenance and repair. The new inventions also required a steady source of power, which at first had to come from swift streams. As a result, clusters of factories soon dominated the landscape in the north of England.

Steam Engines. The invention of the steam engine, however, was the greatest aid to factory building. Factories using steam engines could be built anywhere, not just along streams.

In 1698 Thomas Savery had built the first practical steam pump. Years later James Watt and others had so perfected the engine that by 1800 steam had replaced water as the chief source of power in British factories.

Picturing History
The Savery steam engine cost fifty pounds and required one bushel of coal per day to operate.

Changing Times. Overnight Great Britain had changed from an agricultural to an urban society because factories and jobs were to be found in

Check for Understanding

Ask students to compare living conditions in British cities at the end of the 1700's to living conditions in large U.S. cities today. (Possible responses: the population of the cities grew in the late 1700's, a trend that continues today; crime and disease spread with the population, and today's cities still have high rates of crime; early British cities lacked sewers and paved streets, whereas today's U.S. cities have paved streets, running water, sewers, telephones, and other services; housing for workers was dark, overcrowded, and poorly built, and now although most American workers live in ade-

quate housing, some are homeless, and homes in some areas are in poor condition.)

Picturing History
This William Hogarth etching shows a typical British fabric factory of the eighteenth century. Hogarth was apprenticed to a silver-plate engraver at age 15 and in later life became a painter and satirist as well as an engraver.

cities. The speed of the transformation was striking. At the beginning of the Industrial Revolution, England had only four cities with populations over fifty thousand. By 1850 there were thirty-one cities over this size, and 50 percent of the English population lived in them.

In many ways, the cities were not prepared to receive their new inhabitants. Crime and disease grew along with the population. Cities lacked sewers and paved streets. Housing for workers was dark, overcrowded, and poorly built. Working conditions were no better. The workday was fifteen hours long, fifteen hours in the noise and dirt of the factory for less than a living wage.

Women and children worked in the factories and rarely saw the sun because they worked from five-thirty in the morning until eight at night. The work itself was dull and repetitive. Assembly-line workers could take little pride in their work because they contributed only a small part to the finished product. Even worse, the lack of safety devices on industrial machines resulted in frequent accidents, and a worker injured in the factory seldom received any compensation.

In its early stages, therefore, the Industrial Revolution seems actually to have lowered living standards for many working people.

Improvements. As the pace of technological change slowed and stabilized, however, conditions gradually improved. In the 1820's a powerful movement for workers' rights and for the reform of working conditions arose. By 1830 the wages of

skilled laborers had risen to a level where meat, a luxury in the 1700's, became a common item on the working family's table.

As the Industrial Revolution spread to Belgium, France, Germany, and the United States, the miseries bred by technological change were followed by efforts at reform. In 1842 Great Britain passed a law prohibiting the use of women and children in underground mines. A bill passed in 1847 made the ten-hour day standard for British workers. In later years workers gradually managed to improve their wages and working conditions. As a result, workers in industrialized countries now enjoy a standard of living and exercise a political influence unheard of in preindustrial times.

Pollution and stubborn pockets of poverty remain problems in developed countries. Nonetheless, in the long run, the Industrial Revolution resulted in longer lives and a better living standard for millions of people.

Understanding Economics

1. Why did the Industrial Revolution begin in England?
2. What were some unpleasant side effects of the Industrial Revolution?
3. Why did the growth of industry and cities occur at about the same time?

Critical Thinking

4. How might the Industrial Revolution have encouraged the growth of labor unions?

FOCUS ON ECONOMICS

Answers

Understanding Economics

1. England had large iron and coal deposits, ample water power, a large labor force, huge amounts of capital, and the support of the government.

2. Some unpleasant side effects included: a rapid growth of cities resulting in housing shortages and considerable crime; low wages; a high rate of industrial accidents; a temporary lowering of living standards.

3. The growth of industry and cities occurred at about the same time because factories needed large numbers of workers.

Critical Thinking

4. Possible answer: the Industrial Revolution brought large groups of laborers together in extremely poor working conditions. This situation forced people to band together to support one another and to fight for decent wages and working conditions. **(synthesis)**

Answer Key

Key Terms and People

These are highlighted in the text in the order in which they appear in this list.

Main Ideas

1. Judiciary Act of 1801— number of federal judges increased; Adams chose Federalist judges, the so-called midnight judges.

2. Favored limited government, government close to people; wanted federal judiciary that was less powerful than state governments.

3. Were former British citizens; spoke English; besides, most Britains refused to admit America had won the war.

4. Ended war, but decided nothing of importance.
• Avoided issues of freedom of seas and impressment.

5. Protective tariffs to protect industries from foreign competition; internal improvements such as National Road and canals; and creation of Second Bank of the U.S., which could issue a national paper money.

6. It might set precedent for other territories in Louisiana Purchase to become slave states, upsetting balance.
• The Missouri Compromise: Missouri to be a slave state, Maine a free one. After Missouri, slavery not permitted north of 36°30′ parallel.

7. Cotton gin made cotton king and slaves very valuable; interchangeable parts became first step toward mass production.

8. Brought from Britain plans for cotton-spinning factory, starting U.S. Industrial Revolution.

Critical Thinking Questions

9. That Burr's life is organized—his papers in order and love letters taken care of. • Yes—believes someone may want to write his biography. • Has no regrets about killing Hamilton.

10. Louisiana Purchase doubled country's size and, therefore, responsibilities of federal government. • Jefferson aimed to reduce size and responsibilities of federal government.

11. Jefferson—abolish the bank to simplify financial affairs. Monroe—support bank to help American System.

➤**12.** Possible answers: yes—embargoes interfere with people's lives. No—his laissez-faire philosophy said

things would work out.
• Embargo shut down shipping industry and ruined trade.

13. Britain and France seizing U.S. ships; Britain impressing U.S. sailors; Canada supplying Indians with firearms; War Hawks wished to save U.S. flag from insult.

14. Westerners wanted Indians removed and agricultural interests strengthened; New Englanders wanted industries protected. • Westerners

wanted new states; New Englanders wanted to maintain voting power against Western states and protect maritime interests. • Realized that West needed New England's products and New England needed Western market.

15. Country changed from farm economy to farm/industrial economy.

16. Maryland tried to destroy local branch of bank with heavy tax. Supreme Court

---

CHAPTER 9 REVIEW

Write your answers on a separate sheet of paper.

Key Terms and People

Explain the significance of: Daniel Boone, Meriwether Lewis, William Clark, Sacajawea, Aaron Burr, blockade, William Henry Harrison, Tecumseh, Oliver Hazard Perry, Andrew Jackson, Adams-Onis Treaty, nationalism, Tariff Act of 1816, Monroe Doctrine

Main Ideas

1. How did the Federalists increase their hold on the judiciary in 1801?
2. Why did Jefferson want to cut the costs of government, reduce taxes, and fight the judiciary?
3. Why did British ship captains think they had a right to impress citizens of the United States?
4. What did the 1814 Treaty of Ghent decide? What problems did it avoid?
5. What legislation did Congress pass in order to ensure the continued success of the American System? What was the purpose of each type of legislation?
6. Why was there such an uproar over admission of Missouri to the Union? How was the issue resolved?
7. How did Eli Whitney change the economies of both the South and the North?
8. How did Samuel Slater change the economy of the North?

Critical Thinking Questions

9. **Analyzing Historical Fiction.** This chapter begins with a selection taken from a historical novel, *Burr*, by Gore Vidal. This is Vidal's view of what Burr would think, do, and say in preparation for the duel. What do you learn about Aaron Burr in this selection? Does he think highly of himself? How does he feel about Hamilton?

10. **Assessing Cause and Effect.** How did the Jeffersonian Presidency result in a tremendous increase in the power of the United States government? What was so ironic about this?

11. **Contrasting Ideas.** Compare Jefferson's attitude toward a national bank with that of Monroe in 1816.

12. **Predicting Effects.** Could Jefferson have foreseen the effects of his 1807 embargo? What were these effects?

13. **Analyzing Causes.** Why did Madison decide that the nation had to go to war?

14. **Judging Values.** Compare the desires of Westerners and New Englanders in the early 1800's. Why were these two groups at odds during the War of 1812? How did they become reconciled during the Era of Good Feelings?

15. **Predicting Effects.** What caused the change in Republican philosophy from Jefferson's philosophy of laissez faire, in which the government intrudes as little as possible into the economy, to that of the initiators of the American System of Monroe's time, in which the government uses its power to protect and stimulate the economy?

16. **Analyzing a Quotation.** "The power to tax involves the power to destroy." How is this opinion of John Marshall illustrated in the case of *McCulloch* v. *Maryland*?

17. **Evaluating Sources.** What might you have liked or disliked about your job and your living conditions if you had been a Waltham system employee?

Critical Thinking Activities

18. **Analyzing Comparisons.** Make a chart to show the differences in political beliefs, constitutional interpretation, and personal characteristics between John Adams and Thomas Jefferson. The chart should be based on an examination of the Alien and Sedition Acts (see Chapter 8) and of Jefferson's inaugural address in 1801.

19. **Linking Past to Present.** How did the federal government intervene in the economy after the War of 1812? How does it intervene today?

254

The Jefferson, Madison, and Monroe Years

As President, Jefferson adopted a simple style. He cut the costs of running the national government. He repaired much of the damage caused by the Alien and Sedition Acts. He battled the Supreme Court but usually lost. The case of *Marbury* v. *Madison* established the Court's right of judicial review. After the success of Haiti's revolution against Napoleon, Jefferson doubled the size of the new nation by buying Louisiana from France in 1803. The Lewis and Clark expedition encouraged more and more westward settlement. Despite hardships, American pioneers like the Lincoln family moved across the Appalachian Mountains.

Diplomatic relations became difficult as American ships got entangled in the great war between Britain and Napoleon's France. Impressment of American seamen by the British navy angered the nation. Jefferson tried to solve the problem through an embargo, but the policy failed. New young congressmen known as War Hawks demanded the conquest of Canada. President Madison let the country slip into the War of 1812. Americans battled against Tecumseh's Indian confederacy and traded victories and defeats with British troops in Canada. Jackson's victory at New Orleans came two weeks after a peace agreement had been reached in Europe. The Adams-Onis Treaty gave Spanish Florida to the United States.

After the war, an Era of Good Feelings promoted national unity. Congress voted for a protective tariff, a new national bank, and internal improvements. Marshall's Supreme Court decided many cases that emphasized the superiority of the national government over the states. The Monroe Doctrine told European powers that they must not interfere with events in the Western Hemisphere. The Missouri Compromise smoothed over a controversy about slavery. Maine was admitted to the Union as a free state and Missouri as a slave state.

Slavery was banned forever from the area north of the 36°30′ line drawn west from Missouri.

The nation's economy was also changing. In 1793 Whitney invented the cotton gin, which brought major changes to people in the lower South. Cotton became the money-making crop. The demand for slaves soared. Many blacks were forced into Alabama, Mississippi, and Louisiana for labor in the cotton fields. In the North, Whitney's use of interchangeable parts also made changes in manufacturing possible. More important, new textile mills became the first real factories on the continent. Wealthy men hired women and children to labor long hours. The first protests against working conditions came from the workers themselves.

Chronology of Main Events

1801	Thomas Jefferson inaugurated President
1803	*Marbury* v. *Madison;* Louisiana Purchase
1809	James Madison inaugurated President
1812–1814	War of 1812 against Britain
1815	Battle of New Orleans
1817	James Monroe inaugurated President; Rush-Bagot agreement signed
1819	Spain cedes Florida
1820	Missouri Compromise
1823	Monroe Doctrine

Telescoping the Times may be used as an alternative to having students read the entire chapter, as a chapter preview, or as a chapter review.

255

Global Perspectives

1824-1826 First Burmese War; British take Rangoon.

1831 Michael Faraday discovers principle of electromagnetism.

1833 British occupy Falkland Islands.

1836 Charles Dickens writes first successful book, *The Pickwick Papers*.

1839-1842 First Opium War in China; British seize Hong Kong.

For Discussion

How might the First Opium War in China and the British seizure of Hong Kong have affected American trade in the Far East? (Possible responses: British might have blockaded Chinese ports to keep goods from being imported and exported; British might have seized American vessels trying to trade with China.)

Additional Resources

- Geography Activities
- Skills Activities
- Thematic Activities
- Economic Activities
- Cultural Literacy Activities
- Literary Source Readings
- Primary Source Readings
- Nuclear Peacekeeping
- Transparencies
- Computer Test Generator

Additional Teaching Strategies

SECTION 1

For Basic Students: Ask each student to prepare a checklist of five basic reasons why Jacksonian Democrats eventually gained control of the government. (Checklist might include: Jackson was a popular war hero; Jackson's supporters felt the 1824 election had been unfairly won by Adams; many people were unhappy with Adams's administration; people began to favor a two-party system; Martin Van Buren built a political machine in New York and then moved to the national scene; new campaign techniques were used; Western states had universal white male suffrage without property qualifications; people felt Jackson was one of them, a common man.)

For Advanced Students: Ask students to research and prepare a short oral report on the role of either Andrew Jackson, Martin Van Buren, John C. Calhoun, or Thomas Hart Benton in the founding of the Democratic party. (Details might include: Van Buren—was an adroit politician; became leader of a group known as the Albany Regency which controlled New York State politics through the skillful use of the patronage system; was called the Little Magician in recognition of his effective partisanship; was elected to U.S. Senate in 1821 and worked to promote the Democratic party; supported candidacy of Andrew Jackson for President in 1828.)

SECTION 2

For Basic Students: Ask students to prepare for class by reading an encyclopedia article about Andrew Jackson. Discuss Jackson's philosophy and personality. (Details might include: bitterly resented gossip about his wife, Rachel; distrusted special interest groups; was slow to forgive; believed in political patronage; opposed excessive government controls.)

For Advanced Students: Ask students to research the case of *Cherokee Nation* v. *Georgia* (1831) and reread the text material in this section entitled "Jackson 'Removes' the Indians." Discuss the events surrounding the Cherokee question, especially the failure of the Supreme Court to check President Jackson's Indian policy. (Discussion might include: in 1827 Cherokee Indians living in northwestern Georgia set up a government and declared themselves an independent nation; legislature of Georgia passed resolutions claiming ownership of Indian land and extending the laws of Georgia over all Cherokee Indians, annulling all laws and customs of the Cherokees; Indians appealed to Supreme Court, and Justice Marshall stated that the Indians constituted not foreign governments but domestic independent nations.)

SECTION 3

For Basic Students: On the board list these items: Tariff of Abominations; nullification; Webster-Hayne debate; Tariff of 1832; Compromise of 1833. Ask students to write two or three sentences on the board about each term and how it related to the dispute between Jackson and Calhoun, which in turn led to the nullification crisis. Discuss students' responses. (Possible response: "Tariff of Abomination"—helped the North by taxing manufactured imports; manufactured goods became too costly for Southerners to purchase; Calhoun declared the "Tariff of Abominations" not binding in South Carolina; Jackson believed states' rights came second to the federal government and that all states were bound by federal laws.)

For Advanced Students: Divide the class into two teams to debate the following: "Resolved—that states' rights are superior to national rights." After teams have researched and prepared material, each team should choose a captain and three members to present its views in the debate. (Each team should present logical arguments and examples from current news items and political issues to support its side.)

SECTION 4

For Basic Students: Have each student make a poster supporting William Henry Harrison or Martin Van Buren in the election of 1840. Display all posters and have the class vote for the most effective.

For Advanced Students: Have students assume the role of former President Andrew Jackson. After researching one of the three Jackson successors, each student should compose a letter stating how he or she feels the new President is doing in carrying on Jacksonian programs and policies. (Jackson's letter to President Tyler might include: Jackson's approval of Tyler's veto for internal improvements; Jackson's agreement with a higher tariff in 1842 and the continued use of state banks over a national bank; Jackson's disapproval of Tyler's repeal of Van Buren's independent Treasury and his aggressive stand on states' rights.)

Further Reading for Students

Abernethy, Thomas P. *From Frontier to Plantation in Tennessee: A Study in Frontier Democracy.* Westport, Conn.: Greenwood Press, 1979.

Brown, Dee. *Bury My Heart at Wounded Knee.* New York: Washington Square Press, 1984.

Bugg, James L., ed. *Jacksonian Democracy.* Lanham, Md.: University Press of America, 1986.

Historical Fiction

Blos, Joan W. *A Gathering of Days: A New England Girl's Journal, 1830-32.* New York: Scribner, 1979.

Bibliography for Teachers
Books

Current, Richard N. *Daniel Webster and the Rise of National Conservatism.* Boston: Little, Brown, 1962.

DeTocqueville, Alexis. *Democracy in America.* Trans. Henry Reeve and Frances Bowen; ed. Thomas Bender, et al. New York: Arden Library, 1986.

Hofstadter, Richard. *The American Political Tradition and the Men Who Made It.* New York: Knopf, 1973.

Schlesinger, Arthur M. Jr. *Age of Jackson.* Boston: Little, Brown, 1945.

Van Deusen, Glyndon G. *Jacksonian Era: 1828-48.* New York: Harper & Row, 1959.

Van Deusen, Glyndon G. *The Life of Henry Clay.* Westport, Conn.: Greenwood, 1979.

Van Every, Dale. *The Day the Sun Died.* Boston: Little, Brown, 1971.

Audio-Visuals

Great Men and Great Issues: Sectional Controversy. Wilcom. Six audiotapes.

The Jackson Years: The New Americans, Educational Audio Visual. Filmstrip.

Teacher's Notes:

Lesson Plan

Teaching Resources, Unit 2 Booklet

Chapter Objectives

Students will learn:
- the major reasons for the reemergence of the two-party system in American politics
- the changes that occurred in the federal government under the leadership of Andrew Jackson
- Andrew Jackson's use of Presidential power
- the impact of Andrew Jackson on his successors to the Presidency

Picturing History This portrait of General Andrew Jackson was painted by renowned artist Thomas Sully about a month after Jackson's death. Some critics believe that the dropped glove is a symbol of the defeat of Old Hickory by death.

Using the Chapter Time Line

Who was President when the Cherokee were removed from their ancestral lands? (Answer: Martin Van Buren)
In what years were Presidents from the Adams family inaugurated (see Chapter 8 Time Line)? (Answer: 1797 and 1825)

1824   1828   1832   1836   1840   1844

1825
John Quincy Adams inaugurated President
1829
Andrew Jackson inaugurated President

1832
Jackson vetoes bank bill

1838
Cherokees endure Trail of Tears
1837
• Martin Van Buren inaugurated President
• Panic of 1837

1841
• William Henry Harrison inaugurated President
• President Harrison dies and is succeeded by John Tyler

Links to American Literature

Irving Stone: born in San Francisco, 1903; educated at the University of California at Berkeley.

Works include: magazine articles; seventeen plays; fictionalized biographies—*Lust for Life* (1934) about the life of painter Vincent van Gogh, *Love is Eternal* (1954) about Mary Todd Lincoln, and *The Agony and the Ecstasy* (1961) about artist Michelangelo.

The President's Lady: the story of Rachel and Andrew Jackson.

Introducing the Chapter

Explain to the students that the title of this chapter offers an important insight into Jackson's administration. Few periods of time are identified by the name of the President—so the fact that 1824 to 1840 is known as the Age of Jackson shows his powerful influence. Tell students to look for evidence of Jackson's influence as they study this chapter.

CHAPTER 10   1824–1840

The Age of Jackson

Links to American Literature

"According to our best reports the vote is going to be split between Adams, Clay, Crawford and myself [Jackson]. I doubt if anyone of us will get a majority of the electoral votes. The election will therefore be thrown into the House." . . .

"What do you intend to do about the election?"

"Remain home and watch it. Maybe write a few letters. My advisers want me to attend a number of musters and barbecues to meet the people. They say it's a new form of campaigning, because this is the first time the president is going to be elected by the voters instead of the Congress. I'm not going, of course. But could we have open house on July Fourth? It comes on a Sunday this year."

Barbecues being the new vogue, she had a great pit dug down by their old cabin for the roasting of venison, beef and lamb. Four hundred of their neighbors came, spicing the roasted meats with peppered speeches and the reading of editorials. The one that aroused the greatest shout of derision was from a Louisville newspaper which reported that at a military muster in Ohio, where Andrew had drubbed Henry Clay in a test vote . . . "the rowdies, the very dregs of the community, had won the day."

— IRVING STONE, *The President's Lady*

Extensive media coverage of political candidates and week-long televised political conventions are familiar phenomena today. Campaigning for public office has not always been so streamlined and glossy, however. It was not until 1828, during Andrew Jackson's bid for the Presidency, that the political campaign was born.

Chapter Overview

In contrast to nations that experience violent changes in leadership, the United States has a two-hundred-year tradition of changing leaders peacefully. What is the secret of our nation's comparative political stability? This chapter offers an opportunity to consider answers to this question. In the chapter you will learn why Americans believe in the two-party system and what changes occurred in the federal government under the leadership of Andrew Jackson. You will also learn how Jackson used Presidential power. Chapter 10 is divided into four sections.

Chapter Outline

1. A New Two-Party System Develops
2. Jackson Shows a New Presidential Style
3. States' Rights and a Bank Cause Conflict
4. Jackson's Successors Follow His Lead

State the Objective

Identify major reasons for the reemergence of the two-party system in American politics.

Anticipate the Lesson

Ask students to name the two major political parties in the U.S. today. (Answer: Democrats and Republicans.) Ask them to name the most recent Presidential candidates from each party. (Answer will depend on current administration and election year.) Ask students to recall slogans or issues of either party. (Issues might include: education; taxes; defense spending; aid to social programs.)

SECTION 1

A New Two-Party System Develops

GLOSSARY TERMS: states' rights, Democratic party, political machine

As the Presidential election of 1824 approached, everyone assumed Monroe would not run for a third term largely because Washington had not done so. Monroe's heir apparent was **John Quincy Adams,** for by this time it was traditional for the Secretary of State to succeed to the Presidency.

Adams's candidacy was challenged by three other rising politicians. Neither they nor Adams was associated with any political party. Everyone was assumed to be a Republican because the Federalist party had died during the Era of Good Feelings. William Crawford of Georgia was a personally attractive man who claimed to be the true heir of Thomas Jefferson. Kentucky's **Henry Clay** had built a political power base as Speaker of the House of Representatives. He also had a broad popular following because of his American System, which you read about in Chapter 9. **Andrew Jackson** of Tennessee had become an overnight hero at the Battle of New Orleans and had kept himself in the public eye by his exploits in Florida. Popularity and sectional interests rather than national issues dominated the campaign.

Adams's Election Enrages Jacksonians

The war hero won at the popular polls but lost the election. Jackson received the largest number of popular votes and the largest number in the electoral college. Since he did not have an electoral majority, however, the election went into the House of Representatives. Clay, with the least number of electoral votes, was thrown out of the running under the terms of the Twelfth Amendment, which says that if no Presidential candidate receives a majority of votes, the House of Representatives chooses a President from the top three candidates. Crawford had suffered a stroke. So the contest came down to a struggle between Jackson's supporters and those who favored Adams.

Picturing History Henry Clay was a brilliant orator whose political career spanned almost fifty years. Despite several attempts, he never achieved his highest goal—the Presidency.

Because of his power in the House, Clay could swing the election either way. Jackson's supporters urged Clay to support their candidate because he had the largest popular vote. However, Clay disliked Jackson personally and mistrusted his lack of political experience. "I cannot believe," Clay commented, "that killing twenty-five hundred Englishmen at New Orleans qualifies [him] for the various difficult and complicated duties of [the Presidency]." Adams, on the other hand, agreed

---

People in the Chapter

John Quincy Adams is the first President of whom a photograph exists. On warm summer mornings, Adams liked to swim in the Potomac. One day a reporter surprised him at the river and sat on his clothes until he promised to give her an interview. She got it.

Osceola was tricked into meeting General Thomas Jesup under the flag of truce. During the meeting, Jesup captured the Seminole leader and threw him in prison, where he died after a short time.

Andrew Jackson had only ninety dollars in cash when he left the Presidency. He also was thousands of dollars in debt for his estate, The Hermitage.

John Tyler was the only President who was not an American citizen at the time of his death. After he served as President, Tyler joined the Confederacy and therefore had to give up his United States citizenship. During Jimmy Carter's administration Tyler's citizenship was restored.

Have students complete Chapter 10, Section 1 Enrichment Activity. Ask students to skim the section to find major events associated with the founding of the Jacksonian Democratic party. Discuss the importance of each. (Major events include: Jackson loses 1824 election to Adams in hotly debated contest; President Adams's policies are unpopular with people; Southern states dislike Adams's protection of Creek Indians; a two-party system enables people to band together and express their beliefs; Van Buren organizes Democratic party to support Jackson, revive Jefferson's philosophy

of government, and reduce sectional feelings.) Ask students to prepare a list on the board of campaign methods used in the 1828 Presidential election. (Possible responses: songs; slogans; parades; rallies; dinners; buttons and clothing with candidates' names; cartoons; candidate symbols.) How many are still used today? (Answer: all, to some extent.)

Check for Understanding

Call on individual students to answer Section 1 Review questions orally.

with Clay's American System. The two men held a private talk, and Adams was elected President by a majority of the states represented in the House.

Everyone knew that Adams and Clay had consulted with each other, though no one knew (or knows today) what was said. Then, a few days later, Adams announced that he planned to appoint Clay as his Secretary of State. Jackson's supporters were convinced that a deal had been made to rob the general of his victory. "Unholy coalition!" "Bargain and corruption!" they shouted. Representative John Randolph of Virginia was so outraged that he denounced Clay as a man who "shines and stinks like rotten mackerel by moonlight." No sooner had Adams begun his term than the Jacksonians started campaigning to put their man in the White House at the next election.

Adams's Policies Are Unpopular

Adams's father was still alive in Quincy, Massachusetts, busily corresponding with Thomas Jefferson about statecraft, religion, and the nature of humankind. Yet, while the younger Adams was

Picturing History John Quincy Adams was the first President to pose for a camera. According to Adams's diary, this event occurred in March 1843.

President, a remarkable thing happened. Both his father and Jefferson died on the same day. That day was July 4, 1826, the fiftieth anniversary of the signing of the Declaration of Independence. Many people felt that this was a sign that the hand of God was indeed guiding the American people.

Young Adams, however, was not the kind of man who attracted public sympathy. He was the last President to regard political parties with distaste. Also, because he was a proud, intensely patriotic, high-minded man, he never quite got over the fact that he was a minority President. With stubborn courage and conviction, he proceeded to propose a program that was political suicide. He tried to continue the strong national program the Republicans had taken over from the Federalists. Now, however, most voters wanted less power in the federal government and less influence by the East on national policy.

National Policy Defeated. In his first message, Adams reminded Congress that the Constitution gave it the power to provide for the common defense and to promote the general welfare. He then proceeded to stretch the concept of general welfare. The national government, Adams said, should establish a national university, finance scientific expeditions, reform the patent system, and promote literature and the arts. Above all, Congress should use income from the sale of public lands to finance national internal improvements. Adams's program got nowhere. People said it was foolish to spend public money on such frivolous subjects as art and literature.

Adams's program perhaps deserved more serious attention than it received. Much of it was eventually adopted years later. Adams was quite right when he claimed that "the spirit of improvement is abroad upon this earth." Yet many of his opponents thought he was stretching the Constitution too far. Many also would have opposed any proposals he offered, no matter what their merits. Jackson's friends were determined that Adams's administration should look bad. More and more people began to believe the propaganda that Adams had "stolen" the election from Jackson.

Indian and Foreign Policies Defeated. Adams also irritated Southern states when he tried to protect the rights of the Creek Indians. Under pressure from land speculators, Georgia began a survey of Creek territory in 1826 with the intention

Discuss the pros and cons of the "common man" idea. Tell students that some of our recent Presidents—Reagan, Carter, Kennedy—have made attempts to be pictured in the media as "regular" people. Ask students whether a President can ever be just like everyone else. (Possible responses: the President can never be like everyone else because of the power of the office; the President has no private life and is under enormous pressure; most Presidents come from wealthy families and have made a lot of money in business, so they are not common people when they run.)

Historical Sidelight
Andrew Jackson was the first President to be attacked by a would-be assassin. The attack, which took place in the Rotunda of the Capitol, failed when both of the attacker's pistols misfired. Both guns were later found to be in perfect working order. The odds against two such misfirings were several thousand to one.

Focus on American Art

Picturing History The artist George Caleb Bingham (inset) has been called "a visual Mark Twain." Although he was born in Virginia, Bingham was taken to the Missouri Territory as a young child. His paintings tell the stories of the common people and the American frontier. Bingham was always interested in politics, and he actively campaigned for William Henry Harrison and Henry Clay. He portrayed a typical election day in *The Verdict of the People* (above), which he completed in 1855. Other famous Bingham paintings include *Canvassing for a Vote, The County Election,* and *Daniel Boone Escorting Settlers Through the Cumberland Gap* (see page 234).

of selling land to white settlers. Adams threatened to send in federal troops to stop the survey and talked about the supremacy of the national government. The governor of Georgia defied him and talked about **states' rights.** Eventually the Creeks agreed to move west of the Mississippi River. Adams was humiliated.

Even in foreign affairs, Adams was far less successful than he had been as Secretary of State. Political enemies in Congress blocked his attempt to send delegates to a convention in Panama called by Latin American republics.

The Democratic Party Is Born

The Presidential campaign of 1828 marked a fundamental change in the national attitude toward political parties. Since 1800, people had gradually

been moving away from President Washington's view that parties were a danger to the republic. Instead, more and more people were coming to believe that a two-party system helped the nation. It enabled people of differing views to band together and express their beliefs. It also provided a means by which citizens could challenge the way their government was functioning. Finally, it enabled political power to pass from one group to another in a systematic manner without bloodshed.

Since the collapse of the Federalists in 1820, the only party in the United States had been the Republican party. Soon after the congressional elections of 1826, however, a new political party came into existence. Between 1826 and 1828, both Adams and Jackson called themselves Republicans. Yet, while Adams called himself a National Republican, Jackson called himself a Democratic Repub-

Assign Independent Practice

Ask students to write two paragraphs tracing the development of the two-party system from 1800 to 1828, explaining why the system died and then was reborn during this era. (Details might include: Federalist party collapsed in 1820 and the Republican party became the only party; soon after congressional elections of 1826, the Republican party split; Adams led the National Republicans and Jackson lead the Democratic Republicans; the two-party system provided a means of peacefully challenging the existing government.)

Student Assignment/Homework

Have students read Section 2, "Jackson Shows a New Presidential Style," and complete Chapter 10, Section 2 Daily Activity.

lican. After Jackson's election in 1828, his party became known as the **Democratic party.**

The Democratic party was organized in large part by a short, charming, extremely discreet, and extremely ambitious politician named **Martin Van Buren,** also known as the Little Magician. He started out by building a **political machine** in New York State that granted favors in exchange for votes or money. From New York he decided to move onto the national scene. Van Buren believed that Jackson would make an excellent President. He also wanted to revive Jefferson's philosophy of government, namely, states' rights and as little federal spending as possible. He believed that the best way to achieve this was to unite "the planters of the South and the plain people of the North." Besides, there was another advantage to such a move, Van Buren felt. It would reduce sectional feelings about slavery.

Accordingly, Van Buren began a national party with several prominent political figures. Chief among them were John C. Calhoun of South Carolina and Thomas Hart Benton of Missouri.

A New Campaign Style Develops

Van Buren and his fellow politicians also developed a campaign style that is still popular today. As one historian described it:

> They introduced songs and slogans into election campaigns. They inaugurated parades, barbecues, tree plantings, dinners, rallies. They provided buttons and clothes to designate one's party and candidate; and through a chain of newspapers covering the nation they turned out a mountain of party propaganda, including cartoons, songs, and funny stories. . . . One of the more effective gimmicks invented by the Democrats was the use of the hickory as a symbol of their candidate and party. Jackson had been nicknamed **"Old Hickory"** during the War of 1812 by his soldiers because hickory was the toughest wood they knew. . . . Hickory sticks, hickory canes, hickory brooms shot up across the country, at crossroads, at steeples, on steamboats, in the hands of children—everywhere. Local Democratic clubs and military companies also organized ceremonies to plant hickory trees in their village and town squares as part of their campaign to heighten public interest in the election.

Jackson Wins the White House

Heighten interest it did. There was also the fact that Western states had universal white male suffrage without property qualifications, which meant that many more individuals could vote. Also, Jackson was the first Presidential candidate from west of the Appalachians and the first to come from a poor family. People felt that he was one of them, and they elected him. The turnout of voters in 1828 was three times what it had been in 1824.

The scene at Jackson's inauguration symbolized the new political spirit. An immense crowd gathered in Washington, D.C. As eyewitness Margaret Bayard Smith, wife of a Maryland senator, wrote,

> Country men, farmers, gentlemen, mounted and dismounted, boys, women and children, black and white. Carriages, wagons, and carts all pursuing him to the President's house.

There they stood with their muddy boots on the satin-covered chairs, bawled out political slogans, tossed plates and glassware about, and got drunk. It was obvious to everyone that the American Presidency now belonged to the masses. Others said that **King Mob** now ruled the nation.

SECTION 1 REVIEW

Key Terms and People

Explain the significance of: John Quincy Adams, Henry Clay, Andrew Jackson, states' rights, Democratic party, Martin Van Buren, political machine, Old Hickory, King Mob

Main Ideas

1. Why were Jackson's supporters upset by the results of the 1824 election?
2. How did Adams's national and Indian policies conflict with the sentiments of the nation?
3. How did the philosophy of the Democratic party differ from that of the Republican party?
4. What did Van Buren add to the 1828 campaign that made it different from previous campaigns?
5. What was Jackson's appeal to the common people?

Critical Thinking

6. Contrast Jackson's inauguration to the pomp and ceremony of Washington's. What does this reveal about the changes America was undergoing during this period?

SECTION 1 REVIEW

Answers

Main Ideas

1. They felt that Adams and Clay had conspired to steal the deadlocked election from Jackson.

2. His policies aimed at increasing federal involvement, whereas the national mood suggested reducing federal powers.

3. Democrats—states' rights; reduce federal spending. Republicans—increase federal powers.

4. He introduced slogans, parades, rallies, and so on, thereby creating a new campaign style.

5. They felt he was one of them.

Critical Thinking

6. Jackson's inauguration was informal, raucous, and open to all; it reflected the rise of a powerful new electorate, the common people, who had few advantages except a "can do" spirit. Washington's was very formal, reflecting the new nation's need to gain support and respect.
(analysis & synthesis)

Core Lesson

Anticipate the Lesson

Ask students to recall and discuss a time when they were rewarded for helping a friend or family member accomplish a task. How did they feel? Have they ever rewarded someone for helping them? Ask students whether the practice of rewarding friends should become part of our government. Have students identify some of the advantages and disadvantages of an award system. (Possible responses:

advantages—people will vote for you again and be loyal to your administration; disadvantages—it excludes good workers who may not have campaigned for you.)

State the Objective

Recognize the changes that occurred in the federal government under the leadership of Andrew Jackson.

For Discussion

How did the development of the spoils system and the national political convention aid the growth of democracy during the Jacksonian era? (Possible responses: spoils system made government more representative of the people since more people held government jobs for at least a short time; political conventions allowed voters to elect delegates to the convention.)

Jackson Shows a New Presidential Style

GLOSSARY TERMS: **Kitchen Cabinet, spoils system, assimilate, caucus, nominating convention**

Jackson himself did nothing to discourage the popular mood. He thought of himself as a man of the common people. He had been born in poverty in the Carolina backcountry, the son of Scotch-Irish immigrants. He was the first President since Washington without a college education. He and his supporters made a great deal of these facts.

At the time of his election at the age of sixty-one, however, Jackson was hardly one of the common people. He had built a highly successful career in Tennessee in law, politics, land speculation, cotton planting, and soldiering. His home, the Hermitage, was a mansion, not a log cabin. Anyone who owned more than a hundred slaves, as Jackson did, was a very wealthy man.

Common People Become Leaders

Although he had been elected with the help of sectional interests, Jackson regarded himself as representing the nation as a whole. Because he had a suspicious nature, he disliked special-interest groups and men whose power came from privilege. Lurking beneath the surface of his iron will was a deep streak of anger. When crossed, he lashed back, and he found it hard to forgive. He was also the only President ever to have killed a man in a duel. Jackson seemed to symbolize the virtues of the new America—a common man who climbed the ladder of success, ready to destroy aristocratic privileges wherever he found them.

The Kitchen Cabinet. It was characteristic of Old Hickory that most of his cabinet appointments went to undistinguished men. The only exception was Secretary of State Martin Van Buren. Jackson preferred to rely on the advice of personal intimates. Several Western newspaper editors became the core of what soon was called the **Kitchen Cabinet.** The thirteen men of this group supposedly slipped into the White House through the kitchen on their way to see the President. Today they would be called White House advisors.

The Spoils System. One of Jackson's first moves was characteristic of the man and of his thinking. He fired nearly 10 percent of federal government employees, most of them holdovers from the Adams administration, and he gave their jobs to loyal Jacksonians. The practice was not new, and later Presidents followed it much more vigorously. Jackson called this practice a "rotation in office, a leading principle in the republican creed." The President believed that common people should have the right to hold office. Unless there was a regular turnover of personnel, he declared, officeholders would become inefficient and corrupt.

Jackson's action became known as the **spoils system,** from an old saying that in war "to the victor belong the spoils of the enemy." Actually, Jefferson had removed about the same percentage of officeholders as Jackson. Yet, by Jackson's time the federal bureaucracy had grown, so the number of people who were fired was much larger. Since then, Jackson's name has been associated with the system by which incoming political parties throw out former appointees and replace them with their own friends.

The spoils system did make government officials more representative of the people as a whole. However, it did not prevent corruption. In fact, one of Jackson's appointees was the first person to steal $1 million from the federal government.

A Political Alliance. The 1820's and 1830's saw the arrival of many Catholic immigrants, especially from Ireland. The National Republicans disliked the new arrivals, but the Democrats welcomed them. This alliance would continue on into the twentieth century.

Jacksonian Vetoes. Jackson's beliefs led him to veto more legislation than had all previous Presidents combined. One of his most famous vetoes concerned the proposed Maysville Road in Kentucky. As passed by Congress, the Maysville Bill required the federal government to purchase stock in a private road-building corporation. To Jackson, this smelled of privilege. He vetoed the bill on the grounds that since the road was going to be built within the boundaries of a single state, the state—not the federal government—should take the responsibility of paying for it.

Although internal improvements were very popular, Jackson had his eye on the politics of the situation. Kentucky was the home state of Henry

On the board write *kitchen cabinet, the spoils system,* and *veto power.* For each category, ask students to give examples that show Jackson's changes in government. (Possible responses: kitchen cabinet—Jackson relied on advice of personal friends and Western newspaper editors rather than the usual distinguished statesmen; the spoils system—Jackson replaced federal government employees with loyal Jacksonians; veto power—Jackson vetoed more legislation—especially those laws calling for internal improvements at the expense of the federal government—than all previous Presidents.) Ask students to describe Jackson's Indian policy. (Possible responses: Jackson felt that Indians could not be assimilated into American life style and should therefore be removed to lands west of the Mississippi River; acts of Congress replaced Indian lands in twenty-four states for land in the Indian Territory—later known as Oklahoma; some tribes such as the Creeks and Choctaws resisted the new laws.)

Picturing History Andrew Jackson's Kitchen Cabinet is satirized in this cartoon, which appeared around 1833 under the heading "Major Downing Quelling the Riot in the Kitchen Cabinet."

Clay, so the veto was a blow at one of the President's archenemies. Also, Pennsylvania and New York, which had supported Jackson's campaign, had spent a great deal of state money on their own internal improvements. They did not want the federal government to pay for such projects elsewhere.

Jackson's veto also pleased the South. Most of the money for the Maysville Road and similar projects was to come from the protective tariff, and Southerners were becoming increasingly unhappy about the tariff. Southerners had to pay high prices for Northern goods when they could have gotten such products cheaper from Europe.

In the long run, continued vetoes of internal improvements would have thoroughly angered the West. However, Jackson was easier on so-called pork-barrel legislation, that is, legislation that benefited his political friends. He signed many bills to improve facilities where Democrats were numerous. In return, he expected loyalty to the party and to himself.

Jackson "Removes" the Indians

Since the 1600's, the attitude of white settlers toward the Indians had fluctuated. Sometimes whites favored extermination. At other times they tried to convert the Indians to Christianity, turn them into farmers, and **assimilate** (absorb) them into the white culture.

Both Washington and Jefferson had favored a policy of assimilation. Yet by Jackson's time, most Americans agreed with Henry Clay that "it was impossible to civilize Indians . . . [because] they were essentially inferior to the Anglo-Saxon race." Or, to put it differently, many Americans felt that the sooner the Indians were eliminated, the better.

A New Policy. Despite his background as an Indian fighter, Jackson did not support extermination. Yet he felt that assimilation could not work. A third possibility—allowing Indians to live in their own areas—would have required too many troops to keep the areas free of white settlers who wanted Indian lands. The only solution was to move the Indians from their lands to areas farther west. As Jackson wrote:

> Say to the [Indians] where they now are, they and my white children are too near to each other to live in harmony and peace. . . . Beyond the river Mississippi . . . their father has provided a country, large enough for them all, and he advises them to remove to it. There, their white brethren will not trouble them . . . and they can live upon it, they and all their children as long as grass grows or water runs in peace and plenty.

So Congress passed the Indian Removal Act in 1830. Under this law, the federal government

Check for Understanding

Have students answer Section 2 Review questions on paper.

Guided Practice

Remind students that Jackson's Indian policies were rather painful and arbitrary. Ask students the following questions. Does the U.S. owe compensation to Indians who are the descendants of people deprived of their land under Jackson's policies? Should Jackson's actions simply be forgotten? Draw students' attention to recent legislation that will compensate Japanese-Americans who were forced into detention camps during World War II. (Possible responses: Some students may feel that America should compensate the Indians; oth-

ers may feel that the wrong is part of the past and the matter should be dropped.)

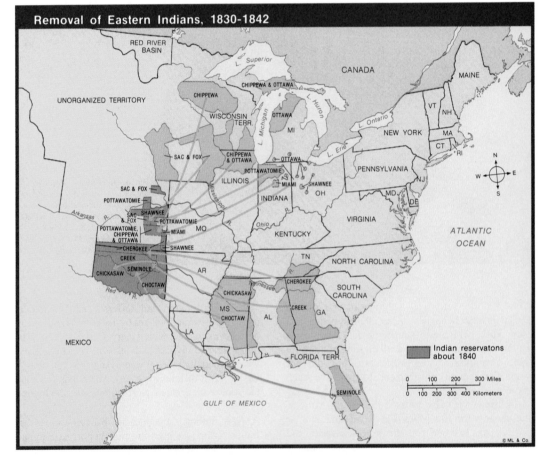

Removal of Eastern Indians, 1830-1842

Map Skills
The Seminole • OK

Map Skills **Movement** Which Indian group was removed from Florida? **Location** In what present-day state were most of the Indian reservations located in about 1840?

would provide funds to negotiate treaties that would force the Indians to move west. About ninety **Indian removal** treaties were signed. For Jackson, the removal policy was "not only liberal, but generous," because it would enable the Indians to maintain their way of life.

Black Hawk and Osceola Resist. Most tribes, however, were unwilling to leave their ancestral lands. Some removal thus was carried out with considerable brutality. The Creeks in Alabama, for example, were removed in metal chains. The Choctaws were forced out of Mississippi in the dead of winter without proper clothing and provisions. In Illinois in 1832, some hungry Sac and Fox Indians, led by Chief Black Hawk, tried to plant grain on their old farmland and were slaughtered by

local militia. This became known as the **Black Hawk War.** The Seminole Indians in Florida, aided by some escaped black slaves, put up a fierce fight under the skillful and vigorous leadership of Chief **Osceola.** It took seven years for government troops to finally wipe out the last pockets of resistance.

The Court Supports the Cherokees. One Indian tribe that tried to follow white ways fared no better. The Cherokees in Georgia had done what Jefferson had asked. They had turned from hunting to farming. They had established small manufacturing shops, built schools, and begun publishing a newspaper in their own language. In 1827 they decided to form a separate state with its own constitution. Georgia, however, refused to recog-

264

Assign Independent Practice

Have students complete Chapter 10, Section 2 Enrichment Activity.

Student Assignment/Homework

Have students read Section 3, "States' Rights and a Bank Cause Conflict," and answer the Section 3 Review questions on paper.

Picturing History The Seminole chief Osceola (left) was painted by artist George Catlin, who traveled throughout the West in the 1830's documenting the tribal life of the American Indians. Chief Black Hawk and his son, Whirling Thunder (center), were painted by John Wesley Jarvis in 1833. Sequoya (right) created an alphabet for the Cherokee people and made it possible for them to publish a newspaper, *The Cherokee Phoenix.*

nize the action of the Cherokees and opened Cherokee land to white settlement.

The legality of the matter wound up before the Supreme Court. Chief Justice Marshall's decision in *Worcester* v. *Georgia* (1832) held that the Cherokees formed a nation with clearly defined boundaries within which "the laws of Georgia can have no force." Furthermore, citizens of Georgia could not enter Cherokee territory without Cherokee consent. In effect, Marshall claimed that the Cherokee nation existed because the federal government wanted it to exist. The state of Georgia had no say in the matter.

The Trail of Tears. Georgia defied the Court decision. Jackson told the Cherokees that they "could not flourish in the midst of a civilized community" and that they had only one choice, to "remove to the west." In 1835 the Cherokees agreed to do so. Yet they suffered greatly over the next few years as Georgia militiamen brutally rounded up some seventeen thousand Indians and packed them off to Oklahoma.

The eight-hundred-mile journey was made partly by steamboat and railroad and partly on foot. Along the way, government officials stole the Cherokees' money, while outlaws made off with

Picturing History In this modern painting, Creek-Seminole artist Jerome Tiger depicts the Cherokee people carrying their heavy burdens—often a dying child—along the frozen ground of The Trail of Tears.

State the Objective

Understand Andrew Jackson's use of Presidential power.

Anticipate the Lesson

Ask students to recall a previous time in American history when the question of states' rights versus federal rights was a key issue. (Response: immediately following the Revolutionary War.) What solutions were tried? (Response: Articles of Confederation; Virginia and New Jersey Plans; the Constitution.)

Answers

Main Ideas

1. Alike—wealthy landowner; successful in many fields. Different—born to poor, immigrant parents; not a college graduate.

2. He believed that government service should be open to the common people and that turnover would discourage corruption and inefficiency.

3. He believed that he was the voice of all the people and that they wanted limited government; it was politically advantageous.

4. To remove Indians to a separate "homeland" west of the Mississippi.

5. They had become farmers, started businesses, built houses and schools, and started their own newspaper.

Critical Thinking

6. Possible answers: they showed that without the support of either Congress or the President, Supreme Court rulings could not be enforced.
• No—it is unconstitutional to ignore a branch of government and immoral of government to fail to protect certain groups of people.
(analysis & synthesis)

their livestock. The Cherokees buried more than a quarter of their people along the **Trail of Tears.** Then as usual, when the Indians reached their final destination, they ended up on land far inferior to that which they had been forced to leave.

Linking Past to Present

Today the Bureau of Indian Affairs deals with the question of providing compensation to descendants of American Indians who were deprived of their land under Andrew Jackson's policies. In 1985 the federal government acknowledged that it had a trust responsibility for 506 federally recognized Indian groups eligible for federal services. More recently, officials of United States museums have held discussions with Indian leaders regarding the return of skeletal remains and sacred objects taken from Indian burial grounds.

The First Nominating Convention Is Held

In 1828 Jackson had been nominated by **caucus,** or meeting, of the Democratic congressmen in Washington, D.C. Previous Presidential and Vice-Presidential candidates had likewise been nominated either by caucus or by state legislature.

In 1831, however, a little party called the Anti-Masonic party appeared. Before it went into oblivion in 1836, it made a major contribution to the American political system. The Anti-Masons decided to hold a **nominating convention** to choose their candidates. The people would elect delegates to the convention and tell them whom to nominate. The system was immediately adopted by other parties and has been followed ever since.

SECTION 2 REVIEW

Key Terms and People

Explain the significance of: Kitchen Cabinet, spoils system, assimilate, Indian removal, Black Hawk War, Osceola, Trail of Tears, caucus, nominating convention

Main Ideas

1. How was Jackson's background like that of previous Presidents, and how was it different?
2. Why did Jackson support the principle of "rotation in office"?
3. What two factors led Jackson to use his veto power so frequently?
4. What was Jackson's answer to the Indian problem?
5. How were the Cherokees in Georgia different from most Indian tribes?

Critical Thinking

6. What did Jackson and Congress demonstrate about the interaction between the legislative, judicial, and executive branches by ignoring the Supreme Court's decision regarding the Cherokees? Was their action legally or morally justified? Explain.

SECTION 3

States' Rights and a Bank Cause Conflict

GLOSSARY TERMS: secede, pet banks, Whig party

The two most important problems Jackson had to struggle with during his Presidency concerned states' rights and the Bank of the United States. He met the two issues straight on.

How Much Power Should the Government Have?

The issue of how much power the federal government should have and how much power state governments should have is one that has confronted the United States since the Constitution was adopted. In the 1830's the issue grew so hot that it almost led to civil war. It began with the question of land, shifted to the question of tariffs, and finally centered on whether a state could secede from the Union.

The issue arose in Congress over a proposal by Senator Thomas Hart Benton of Missouri. Benton wanted unsold federal lands to be reduced in price and finally to be given away if they remained unsold. Northerners saw this proposal as a scheme to

On the board make two columns, one titled States' Rights and one titled Bank of the United States. Explain to the students that these were the two most important issues Jackson faced during his Presidency. Ask students to review the text material and complete on the board a brief outline of each problem. (Outline for States' Rights might include: Senator Benton's proposal to reduce price of unsold federal land is opposed by Northerners and supported by Southerners in hopes of winning a reduction in 1828 tariff; Vice-President Calhoun coins "Tariff of Abomination"; Calhoun creates nullification theory; Tariff and states' rights are debated in Congress; Jackson and Calhoun split on the issue of states' rights; Jackson drops Calhoun from 1832 ticket; South Carolina threatens to secede; Congress passes the Force Bill in 1833; Henry Clay proposes a compromise.)

draw off workers from the older sections of the country and thus increase the power of western states in Congress. Southern spokesmen, however, agreed to support Benton in hopes of winning western support for something the South wanted— a reduction in the 1828 tariff, which they felt not only discriminated against them but, some said, was unconstitutional.

Tariff of Abominations.   As you recall, when the War of 1812 ended, British manufacturers wanted to destroy their United States competitors by flooding the American market with cheap goods. For that reason, in 1816 Congress passed a tariff to protect the infant United States industries. The tariff was raised in 1824 and again in 1828.

Jackson's Vice-President, John Calhoun of South Carolina, called it a **Tariff of Abominations.** As an agricultural region dependent on a single crop— cotton—the South had to compete in an unprotected world market. Yet the high tariff on manufactured goods prevented Great Britain from selling its goods in the United States. Britain had less money and therefore bought less cotton. The South, on the other hand, could not buy the cheap manufactured goods it needed from Britain but had to buy the more expensive Northern manufactured goods. The North was getting rich at the expense of the South. One observer remarked that when Southerners "see the flourishing villages of New England they cry, 'We pay for all this.' "

Calhoun's Nullification Theory.   John Calhoun was in a peculiar and dangerous position. He had long been known as a nationalist spokesman, and he had supported the protective tariff of 1816. He was on his way to a career as a national statesman and had served under both Adams and Jackson as Vice-President. The situation in his home state, however, had made him change his views. South Carolina's economy failed to recover fully from the depression of 1819. Cotton prices remained low because planters and their slaves were moving to more fertile lands in Alabama and in the lower Mississippi River Valley. Some South Carolina politicians began to wonder if Calhoun really cared about the needs of his state. Calhoun soon showed them that he did.

He devised a nullification theory much like that expressed in Jefferson's Kentucky Resolution against the Alien and Sedition Acts, which you read about in Chapter 8. To nullify, you may recall, means to declare something not legal or not in force. Calhoun's argument was that the United States Constitution was based on a compact among the sovereign states. If the Constitution was established by thirteen sovereign states, he said, then they must still be sovereign, and each had the right to determine whether an act of Congress was constitutional. If it was not, then each state had the right to declare the offending law nullified within

Picturing History   John C. Calhoun as painted by Charles B. King in 1823.

its borders. If the states did not have this right, Calhoun reasoned, a majority in the federal government might trample on the rights of a minority. In 1828 Calhoun wrote down his theory for the state legislature in a document entitled "The South Carolina Exposition," but he did not sign his name to it. Nor did he say what he privately felt: that if the federal government refused to permit a state to nullify a federal law, the state had the right to **secede,** or withdraw from the Union.

Robert Hayne Versus Daniel Webster.   The tariff question (and the underlying states' rights issue) was discussed in one of the great debates in American history. For more than a week in January 1830, visitors to the Senate listened to Senator Robert Y. Hayne of South Carolina debate Senator Daniel Webster of Massachusetts.

Hayne gave a lengthy condemnation of the tariff. He charged that Southern planters were slaves of Northern industrialists. Vice-President Calhoun, who presided over the Senate's deliberations, listened with satisfaction as Hayne borrowed liberally from Calhoun's pamphlet. "The tariff is unconstitutional and must be repealed," Calhoun had written. "The rights of the South have been destroyed, and must be restored. . . . The Union is in danger and must be saved."

Senator Daniel Webster was already the most famous orator of the age, at a time when people seemed to have an unlimited appetite for long and flowery speeches. In his reply, Webster spoke for four hours without notes.

Check for Understanding

Have students complete Chapter 10, Section 3
Daily Activity. Review the worksheet in class.

For Discussion
Reread the quotes by Jackson and Calhoun in the section Jackson Versus Calhoun and tell how these statements related to the controversy over states' rights. How does each quote reflect the personality of the speaker? (Possible responses: Calhoun's statement that liberty was more important than the Union showed that he believed the states to be more important than the federal government; Jackson's statement that the federal Union must and would be preserved showed that he considered the federal government superior to state governments.)

Picturing History   George P. A. Healy's dramatic painting shows Daniel Webster (right) in the senate chamber in 1830 replying to Senator Robert Hayne of South Carolina. At the far left is Vice-President John C. Calhoun. The inset (left) is a painting of Daniel Webster by artist Chester Harding.

The Union, Webster argued, was more than a mere compact among sovereign states. The national government was supreme in the powers given to it by the Constitution. Any disputes between the states and the federal government should be settled by the courts and the electoral process. Webster made a direct attack on the theories of states' rights and nullification: "I go for the Constitution as it is, and for the Union, as it is. It is, Sir, the people's Constitution, the people's government, made for the people, made by the people, and answerable to the people." Webster concluded, "Liberty and Union, now and forever, one and inseparable!"

Jackson Versus Calhoun. Once the **Hayne-Webster debate** was over, everyone looked to the President for a statement of his position. Jackson kept the public waiting for several months. Finally, at a public dinner, he confronted his Vice-President. As was customary, the dinner included dozens of short speeches or toasts. After listening to a number of them about the right of the states to decide constitutional questions, the President rose and raised his glass. "Our Union: it must be preserved," he said. Calhoun responded with a

toast of his own: "The Union, next to our liberty, most dear." After the dinner, the President changed his wording for the newspapers. So the public read that Jackson had said, "Our Federal Union: it must and shall be preserved." The President's attitude was now clear.

In the following months, Jackson and Calhoun came to a complete break. The grounds for the split were personal as well as political. A social scandal involving the reputation of a cabinet member's wife found Jackson on one side of the controversy and Calhoun on the other. To top matters off, Calhoun cast the deciding vote in the Senate's rejection of Martin Van Buren as ambassador to Britain. Jackson promptly told Democratic party leaders to drop Calhoun from the 1832 national ticket and to substitute Van Buren as Jackson's running mate.

South Carolina Threatens to Secede. In 1832 Congress passed a new tariff law that actually lowered duties somewhat. However, this did not satisfy most South Carolinians. Encouraged by Calhoun, states' rights supporters called a special state convention. The convention pronounced the tariffs of 1828 and 1832 "unauthorized by the

Guided Practice

Tell students that the Jackson years made it clear that sectionalism would be an important part of American history. Discuss the extent to which the North and South differ today. (Discussion might include: South is still agricultural, but many businesses are relocating there because of lower costs and/or taxes; North still is very industrial.) Point out to students that both the Republican and Democratic parties try to "balance" their tickets with candidates from different sections of the country. (Examples include: Kennedy/Johnson—Massachusetts/Texas; Reagan/Bush—California/Texas; Bush/Quayle—Texas/Indiana; Dukakis/Benson—Massachusetts/Texas.)

Constitution" and "null, void, and no law."

The convention called for an end to customs collections and warned that if any federal forces were sent to collect the duties, South Carolina would immediately secede from the Union.

Jackson was furious. He took South Carolina's action as a challenge to him personally as well as to the nation as a whole. He threatened to hang Calhoun and to lead federal troops in the field if necessary. He did more than bluster since he had just been overwhelmingly reelected. No other Southern state was willing to back nullification. So he issued a proclamation declaring that South Carolina's actions threatened "the existence of the Union" and violated "the letter of the Constitution." He warned that the laws of the United States required him to meet treason with force.

Henry Clay's Compromise. In an atmosphere of mounting crisis, Congress passed the **Force Bill** in February 1833. Known in South Carolina as the Bloody Bill, it authorized the use of the federal army and navy against South Carolina if state authorities resisted federal customs officials.

At this point Henry Clay, at Jackson's urging, once again stepped in as a compromiser. He introduced a new tariff bill that gradually lowered duties over a ten-year period. Thereupon, the South Carolina convention met once again and repealed its previous ordinance of nullification. To save face, however, the delegates passed another ordinance nullifying the Force Bill. Jackson was wise enough, though, to disregard this last challenge.

Both sides claimed victory. Yet most Americans were aware that the national government had successfully weathered a major crisis.

Jackson Declares War on the "Monster" Bank

The second great crisis of Jackson's administration concerned the Second Bank of the United States. In this case, too, Jackson's actions strengthened the Presidency and brought the nation safely through a difficult time.

Reasons for Opposing the Bank. In Jackson's eyes, the national bank symbolized Eastern wealth and power. He regarded it as an agent of the aristocracy, whose members cared nothing for ordinary people. Because of the bank's financial strength and influence on the economy, it was a threat to American democracy. It might bribe officials and even try to buy elections with the intent of controlling the government and changing its character.

State banks hated the national bank because it was a powerful competitor. Farmers hated the bank because they distrusted paper money. The only real money, they said, was "hard money"—gold and silver. They also felt that they were the ones who created real wealth in the form of cotton, corn, tobacco, hogs, and other agricultural products. Bankers, in their opinion, did not create real wealth but instead made money by playing with pieces of paper called loans and mortgages. Often this was at the expense of people's happiness, for when loans were not paid, the bank took away people's farms and homes. In addition, the national bank had a monopoly on government business: the federal government turned all its funds over to the bank for investment purposes. Yet the money these public funds earned did not go to the taxpayers. It went mostly to the wealthy stockholders of the bank.

Adding to popular dislike of the bank was its leader, **Nicholas Biddle.** A Philadelphia aristocrat, he was bright, articulate, and capable. He was also extremely arrogant and thought nothing of using bank funds for loans to friendly congressmen at rates well below those that the bank usually charged.

In 1831 Senator Benton introduced a resolution against rechartering the bank, even though recharter was not due for another five years. For several hours Benton assailed the bank for adding to the "inequality of fortunes." This privileged institution, he declared flatly, made "the rich richer and the poor poorer." No other remark could have united so many Americans of the Jacksonian Age.

An Election Issue. As the election of 1832 approached, Jackson's political opponents, Henry Clay and Daniel Webster, wanted to embarrass him. They badly underestimated public dislike of the Second Bank of the United States. So they urged Nicholas Biddle to press for a recharter before the election. They knew that Jackson would be so furious that he might veto the charter and thus make the bank a major campaign issue. Thus they gave Jackson just the sort of election issue he wanted.

First, Jackson denounced the supporters of the bank for their "grants of monopolies and special privileges." He described the bank as a "monster"

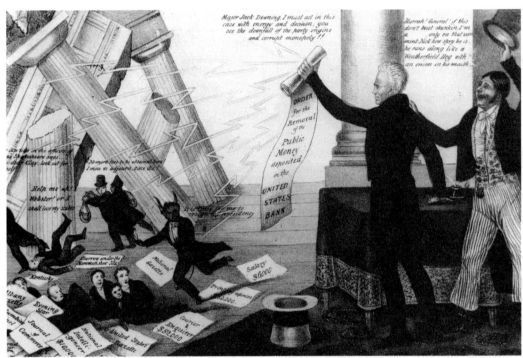

Picturing History In this newspaper cartoon, Andrew Jackson stands victorious as the Second Bank of the United States collapses. Nicholas Biddle, the bank's president, is depicted fleeing from the wreckage.

with horns, hooves, and tail that corrupted "our statesmen" and wanted "to destroy our republican institution." Then he vetoed the charter. As he told the man who would be his next Vice-President, "The Bank, Mr. Van Buren, is trying to kill me, but *I will kill it.*"

The bank became the principal issue of the 1832 election campaign. The National Republicans chose Clay as their candidate because he had a wider popular following than Webster. The national bank contributed about $100,000 to Clay's campaign. There was little doubt about the final outcome. Jackson, with Van Buren as his running mate, won easily.

The long-range significance of the veto was that Jackson took the issue to the people. By making approval of his veto a campaign issue Jackson was, in effect, telling Congress that before they passed a law, they should consider what the President thought of that law. Or, to put it another way—which is how men like Clay and Webster put it—Congress was no longer the most important of the three branches of government. The President was.

Jackson Beats the Bank. The bank war continued after the election, with results that were nearly disastrous to the American economy. Jackson was determined to weaken the bank before its charter expired in 1836. He ordered that all government deposits be withdrawn from the bank's branches and placed in certain state institutions. His opponents labeled these state banks Jackson's **pet banks.**

Biddle lashed back by calling in loans to individuals and to privately-owned businesses. He also decided not to lend money for new business. He argued that such steps were necessary since the bank was being forced to close. His motives, however, were political. He hoped to generate public pressure to force Jackson to reverse his policy.

The financial community nearly panicked for a few months in the winter of 1833–1834. Bankruptcies became widespread as merchants and manufacturers found themselves without credit. Delegations of businessmen descended on Washington, D.C., to appeal to the President. Jackson firmly told them they were talking to the wrong man. "Go," he

Assign Independent Practice

Have students use one of the outlines developed in Present the Lesson as the basis for a three-paragraph essay explaining Jackson's use of Presidential power. (Possible details: Jackson's actions strengthened the Presidency, brought nation through difficult time; Jackson regarded bank as a symbol of Eastern wealth and power and vetoed its charter; the veto became a principal issue in 1832 election; Jackson ordered withdrawal of all government funds from bank.)

Student Assignment/Homework

Have students read Section 4, "Jackson's Successors Follow His Lead," and be prepared to discuss it in class.

said, "to Nicholas Biddle." Thus, Biddle's policy of shrinking credit was hurled back in his face.

Pressure from financial leaders finally forced Biddle to adopt a more generous loan policy. However, the entire chain of events had by this time cost him much of his backing, even with the Eastern business community. In 1836 the Second Bank of the United States quietly expired.

The Bank War Has Two Results

Jackson's war on the national bank was part of a fundamental hostility to special privilege that runs deep throughout United States history. It can be seen in Bacon's Rebellion, the Boston Tea Party, and Shays's Rebellion. It continues to the present.

New York Becomes the Financial Capital. Biddle's bank became just one of many state institutions and finally went bankrupt in 1841. Other state banks and Jackson's pet banks—many of them in New York City—received the money that would have gone into the Bank of the United States. As historian Samuel Eliot Morison wrote:

> After the lapse of more than a century, it is clear that although democracy won the battle with the Bank, it lost the war. The bankers of New York City, almost splitting their sides laughing over the discomfiture of rivals . . . [in] Philadelphia, promptly picked up the pieces of the [Bank of the United States] and on Wall Street constructed a vastly bigger money power than anything ever dreamed of by Mr. Biddle. Poor farmers, mechanics, and frontiersmen gained nothing by this bank war; the net result was to move the financial capital of the United States from Philadelphia to New York.

There it has been ever since.

The Whig Party Is Formed. The bank war, especially the panic of 1833–1834, resulted in the formation of a new political party. Its core consisted of Republicans. They were joined, however, by Democrats, mostly from the industrial North, who disapproved of Jackson's policy toward the national bank and who believed that his actions in general were those of a monarch rather than a President. "King Andrew the First," they called him. Also joining the new party were believers in states' rights.

BORN TO COMMAND.

OF VETO MEMORY.

HAD I BEEN CONSULTED.

KING ANDREW THE FIRST.

Picturing History Andrew Jackson's autocratic ways are satirized in this caricature of 1832.

In 1834 this new party was named the **Whig party.** The Whigs in Britain were a group that tried to limit royal power, and the term *Whig* is generally applied to a person who opposes a chief executive having too much political power.

SECTION 3 REVIEW

Key Terms and People

Explain the significance of: Tariff of Abominations, secede, Hayne-Webster debate, Force Bill, Nicholas Biddle, pet banks, Whig party

Main Ideas

1. How did the tariff of 1816 affect the South?
2. How did Calhoun's view of the power of the federal government differ from Webster's view?
3. What was Jackson's opinion regarding the battle for power between the states and the federal government?
4. What was South Carolina's response to the new tariff law passed in 1832?

SECTION 3 REVIEW

Answers

Main Ideas

1. It forced the South to buy expensive Northern goods rather than cheap British goods; in turn, the British bought less Southern cotton.

2. Calhoun—Any state had the right to nullify federal laws it deemed unconstitutional. Webster—The federal government was supreme in any power granted to it in the Constitution, including the right to determine the constitutionality of laws.

3. The Union had to be preserved, even to the detriment of individual states.

4. It declared the tariff null and void, and threatened to secede if the federal government tried to enforce the law.

5. He felt that the bank symbolized Eastern wealth and power and threatened democracy. After Jackson vetoed the bank's charter, Clay ran for President against Jackson on a platform that favored the bank.

Critical Thinking

6. Possible answer: Jackson claimed to represent the common people and to favor a weak federal government; ironically, he had significantly increased the power of the Presidency so the Whigs referred to him as "King Andrew the First." **(synthesis)**

5. How did Jackson feel about the national bank, and how did his opinion become an issue in the 1832 campaign?

Critical Thinking

6. Why is it ironic that the Whigs felt that Jackson had become a monarch?

SECTION 4

Jackson's Successors Follow His Lead

GLOSSARY TERMS: **wildcat banks, specie, depression**

The sheer force of Andrew Jackson's personality has tended to make the Presidents who followed him—Van Buren, Harrison, and Tyler—seem weak, shadowy figures. Yet each was associated with important developments in our nation's history, and each followed policies of Old Hickory.

Picturing History President Martin Van Buren.

When Jackson announced that he would not run for a third term, the Democrats chose Vice-President **Martin Van Buren** as their Presidential candidate. The newly formed Whig party ran three regional candidates: William Henry Harrison, Daniel Webster, and Hugh T. White. With Jackson's support, Van Buren won the election of 1836.

Depression Strikes in 1837

Less than three months after Van Buren took office, the country was hit by a financial panic. Although "Martin Van Ruin" was blamed, a major cause lay in the previous administration.

You recall that after withdrawing federal funds from the national bank, Jackson deposited them in various state pet banks. Many of these pet banks were located in western states. These banks began to print bank notes, which they lent to persons who wanted to buy federally owned land. As a result, the sale of public land boomed. However, many pet banks were **wildcat banks** that printed notes far in excess of the federal funds they had on deposit. This meant that the notes were not worth much. Thus, the federal government found that while it was selling millions of acres of land, it was receiving almost worthless currency in exchange.

Jackson decided to stop the land speculation. He issued an executive order stating that the Treasury would accept payment for land only in gold and silver, called **specie,** or in bank notes that were backed by gold and silver. This order is known as the **Specie Circular.** The state banks did not have enough specie to redeem the notes, so they closed their doors. These bank closings wiped out the savings of thousands of people, and many businesses failed. Unemployment rose, and there were bread riots in New York City.

The Substitute for Banks. The new President spent much of his administration trying to deal with the vacuum left by the disappearance of the monster bank. Van Buren, like Jackson, was convinced that banks in general were a threat to working people. He pressed for what he called an independent Treasury. The government would deposit its temporary surplus funds in vaults in various cities. These vaults would not be tied in any way to state banks or to a central federal financial institution. Whig leaders were not happy with the idea, but they lacked a better alternative. In 1840, in the darkest year of the **depression** (severe decline in business activity), Congress finally went along with Van Buren's plan. It seemed to work no worse than the rest of the economy.

World Economic Forces. As the depression deepened, people looked for its cause. There was no one cause, however, nor were all the causes to be found in local conditions. What few people realized was that the American economy had become intertwined with a world economy. What happened outside the country could affect the people in the United States. It was not understood that a drought in cotton-producing Egypt could cause the price of cotton in the United States to rise.

As a result of this interdependence, a depression in one country could affect another. During the booming 1830's, for example, British investment in the United States rose from about $60 million to

Guided Practice

Tell students that even in 1837 the American economy was tied to the world economy, though that fact was not as readily apparent then as it is now. Today, more and more of the U.S. economic welfare depends on imports and exports and businesses that are multinational. Discuss with students the changes in American life necessary to adapt to this increased economic interdependence. (Discussion might include: use of metric system; extensive air travel; need to know and understand different cultures.) Ask students whether they believe economic isolation from the rest of the world is possible—or desirable—today and why. (Possible response: economic isolation is impossible because one country does not have all the natural resources it needs, nor can it produce enough of all the manufactured goods it needs; it also needs markets for its surplus manufactured items and raw materials.)

Picturing History In 1840 the Whigs used the symbols of the log cabin and hard cider to portray William Henry Harrison as a man of the common people.

$175 million. British banks made huge loans to United States banks. When hard times hit Britain, however, British banks asked that the loans be paid. Unfortunately, the United States banks did not have the money. They had lent it out to their customers, who were, in turn, asked to repay their debts. Cotton planters, for example, had to sell slaves and cotton to repay their local bank. Since they were all trying to repay their debts, the market was flooded with cotton and slaves. Therefore, the price of both plunged.

Linking Past to Present

Even in 1837, the American economy was tied to the world economy, though not to the extent that it is today. Daily news reports keep us aware that the economic welfare of the United States depends on imports and exports and on businesses that are multinational.

The Whigs Win in 1840

In 1840 Van Buren still had enough clout in his own party to run again. The Whigs, however, smelled victory. They ran an old war hero from Ohio, ex-territorial Governor and ex-General **William Henry Harrison.** The Whig nominating convention rightly concluded that this pale imitation of Old Hickory would be liked by the voting public.

Campaign Hoopla. Whig politicians had learned from the Jacksonians and turned the campaign into a circus. In fact, they outdid the Democrats by transforming Harrison into a man of the common people. Van Buren never made a great deal of money, but the Whigs insisted that he lived a life of luxury while common folk starved. The Whigs described the President as spending his time sampling French cooking from golden plates while reclining on a cushioned sofa.

A tactless editor of a Democratic newspaper played into their hands. He declared that if Harrison were given an annual pension of $2,000, the aging hero of Tippecanoe would be content to live in a log cabin with a barrel of hard cider as his sole companion. The truth was that Harrison came from a wealthy family. He was college educated and at the time lived in a sixteen-room mansion. Yet a log cabin and hard cider became campaign symbols. People in torch-lit parades rolled cider barrels through the streets to demonstrate Harrison's supposedly humble origins. Songbooks with such titles as *The Log Cabin Song Book* were published. "Tippecanoe and Tyler too" and "Van, Van is a used-up man" became campaign slogans. As one

Historical Sidelight
William H. Harrison, as a young military officer, met and fell in love with a woman he referred to as "Miss M." He loved her so much that he offered to give her up if she found someone who could give her more. Harrison eventually was married, not to Miss M. but to Anna Tuthill Symmes.

Assign Independent Practice

Ask students to prepare a two-minute speech explaining how Jackson's campaign tactics changed the style of future campaigns such as that of the 1840 election. Students might add examples from current campaigns. (Possible details: politics that appeal more to emotion than to reason; speeches that become a form of mass entertainment. Example from current campaigns would be the wide-scale coverage of both the Republican and Democratic conventions by the news media.)

Student Assignment/Homework

Have students complete Chapter 10 Review on paper. Divide the class into small groups to go over the answers.

Concluding the Chapter

The present Democratic party was born during the Presidency of Andrew Jackson. Ask students to write a brief essay on whether they believe Democrats of today would be staunch Jackson supporters had they lived in the Jacksonian Era. Students should list examples from Jackson's administration to support their stand. (Reasons for supporting Jackson: he was a common man; represented the nation as a whole; disliked special interest groups and men whose power came from privilege; rewarded supporters with jobs. Reasons for not supporting Jackson: he owned over one hundred slaves; developed Indian policy that could be considered cruel and prejudiced; continually vetoed legislation for internal improvements.)

---

historian put it, "Processions involved miles of marchers; [rallies] attracted acres of people."

A Voting Record. Despite all this hoopla, Harrison's portion of the popular vote was only 53 percent. Yet what was truly extraordinary was that 78 percent of those eligible turned out to vote. That figure is a record high in the history of American politics. The entire election, said one observer, was a "totally new phase in party politics."

Tyler Enrages His Party

Clay, Webster, and other Whig politicians expected to easily control Harrison. However, Old Tippecanoe died of pneumonia one month after his inauguration, and for the first time a Vice-President succeeded to the Presidency.

John Tyler was a strong-minded Virginia aristocrat who had broken with Jackson over nullification and the national bank. Whig leaders had chosen him in hopes of winning Southern votes for their ticket. They soon wished they hadn't.

Clay thought the time had come for putting his American System into full effect. As a states' rights man, Tyler thought otherwise. He vetoed bills for internal improvements and reluctantly agreed to a somewhat higher tariff in 1842. He also agreed to repeal Van Buren's independent Treasury. Yet, when the Whigs tried repeatedly to establish another national bank, Tyler vetoed one proposal after another. The federal government continued to use state banks. Gradual economic recovery made the issue of a national bank seem less important. The banking issue thus disappeared as a major factor in American politics for more than twenty years.

Picturing History President John Tyler.

Tyler's vetoes outraged Whig leaders, but they lacked enough votes in Congress to override them. National domestic legislation came almost to a standstill. Angry Whig congressmen issued a formal statement reading Tyler out of the party. His entire cabinet resigned except for Webster, who stayed on as Secretary of State to complete certain diplomatic negotiations.

The victory of 1840 turned out to be a nearly fruitless one for the Whigs. Party leaders began arguing among themselves. They lost their majority in the House in 1842. Clay resigned his Senate seat to try once again for the Presidency.

Jackson Leaves a Legacy

Just as in the 1790's, when people divided politically into Jeffersonian Republicans and Hamiltonian Federalists, so did people in the 1830's divide into two distinct parties, each with loyal followers. They identified themselves either as Jacksonian Democrats or as Whigs. These parties held center stage until the 1850's.

The style of politics, however, had drastically changed since the 1790's. Politicians appealed more to passion than to reason. They courted popularity in a way that John Quincy Adams and his predecessors never would have done. Political speeches became a form of mass entertainment. Thus, politicians involved far more Americans in the political process. The average citizen was more politically aware and had more political power than ever before. That is exactly what Andrew Jackson had wanted.

SECTION 4 REVIEW

Key Terms and People

Explain the significance of: Martin Van Buren, wildcat banks, specie, Specie Circular, depression, William Henry Harrison, John Tyler

Main Ideas

1. How did Jackson's actions against the national bank contribute to economic problems under Van Buren?
2. How did a new economic development, international economic interdependence, affect the United States in the 1830's?
3. What did the cider barrel represent in the election of 1840?
4. How did Tyler block the implementation of Clay's American System?

Critical Thinking

5. Which term best describes Jackson's political legacy, "Jacksonian democracy" or "the Jackson reign"? Explain.

Lesson Plan

State the Objective

Understand how the physical geography of America influenced the westward movement.

Present the Lesson

Divide the class into two groups. Ask half the students to list some of the accurate assessments the early settlers made about the physical geography of America. Ask the remaining students to list some of the inaccurate assumptions early settlers made about geography. Ask students to share their lists. (Accurate assessments include: in summer months, rainfall along the southeast coast was heavier than in areas farther north; differences in climate were partly due to latitudinal location and the direction of prevailing winds. Inaccurate assessments include: temperatures in the Ohio Territory were higher than those at similar latitudes on the Atlantic Coast.)

Ask students which reports of land and climate encouraged the movement westward. (Possible responses: "well watered" land; temperatures in the Ohio Territory that were warmer than those on the Atlantic coast; precious metals that were rumored to be located just beyond the settlements; abundant natural resources.) Ask students whether such descriptions would have motivated them to move west. (Possible responses: no—the hardships and dangers far outweighed the possible advantages. Yes—the adventure and promise of good farmland would be enough incentive to

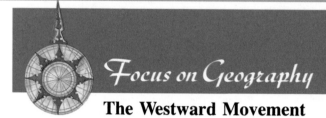

Focus on Geography

The Westward Movement

The Geographic Theme of Place

Fourteen-year-old Sallie Hester, traveling westward with her family in 1849, made the following entries in her diary:

> July 29—Passed Soda Springs. Two miles further on are the Steamboat Springs. They puff and blow and throw the water high in the air. The springs are in the midst of a grove of trees, a beautiful and romantic spot.
>
> Hot Springs, August 18—Camped on a branch of Mary's River, a very disagreeable and unpleasant place on account of the water being so hot. . . . The dust is horrible. The men wear veils tied over their hats as a protection.

The history of America's westward movement is a story of settlers traveling vast distances over many types of landscapes such as those described above. The settlers' perceptions of the geography of North America were based on maps and descriptions provided by those who had explored the new land previously. Although some of the maps turned out to be inaccurate, the information the settlers received greatly influenced their settlement patterns. Because people perceive characteristics of places according to their own experiences, geographers call these characteristics of place **human characteristics** and **observed characteristics.**

In addition to the human and observed characteristics of place, the geographic theme of place includes the **physical characteristics** of an area. When geographers describe places, they go beyond personal descriptions and include the physical characteristics of particular places. These include features such as climate; topographic features such as mountains, plains, and rivers; and natural resources. In this geography feature you will learn how the physical features of place were related to the westward movement.

Climates Describe Places. Geographers of the eighteenth century described the climate of North America more favorably than it actually was. One reason for this was the desire to entice settlers to go to certain geographic areas. Another reason was national pride. This was a spontaneous reaction to charges made by some British writers who claimed that the American climate was inferior to that of Europe.

When eighteenth-century geographers inspected their instruments and the weather records compiled by others, they pronounced the land to be "well watered." They reported that rainfall in North America was generally adequate and dependable. They correctly pointed out that in the summer months the rainfall along the southern coast was heavier than in areas farther north and that in New England the amount of moisture was about the same in summer and in winter. Nearly half the annual moisture in New England, however, fell in the solid form of snow.

Much of this early information about climate was erroneous. Even by 1810 actual weather records had not been kept long enough to tell anything important about changes of temperature or rainfall. These records were cited, however, when someone wanted to prove a point. Proving the point was often more important than stating the facts. Thomas Jefferson, for example, believed and wrote that temperatures were higher in the Ohio Territory than those in similar latitudes on the Atlantic coast. He based his belief on the evidence that certain kinds of birds and vegetation normally found in the South were also found in the northwestern parts of the country but not in the northeastern parts. This belief became popular and encouraged western settlement.

By 1810, however, geographers had reached the conclusion that differences in climate were caused by the direction of the prevailing winds and by their latitudinal location.

Topographic Features Describe Places. In addition to climate, geographers use topographic features to describe places. Topographic features are the natural features of the land surface, such as take the risks.) Ask students to pretend they are settlers moving west, and to write letters to someone in Europe describing their experiences.

Check for Understanding

Have students write the answers to the questions at the end of the feature. Call on students to read their answers.

Ask students to identify geographic features that aided settlers in their move westward. (Possible responses: ample rainfall and fertile plains aided farming; rivers expedited travel; natural resources such as coal and iron ore provided added income; timber supplied fuel and materials for homes, ships, soaps, resins, and tars.)

mountains, rivers, and plains. Topographic features were much less of a barrier to the westward movement than early cartographers assumed.

Mountains. Early maps of North America showed high mountain ranges occupying much of the interior portion of the continent. As more exploration was done, these mountains gradually disappeared from the maps and were replaced by various mountain chains.

By the 1790's, settlement had penetrated far beyond the eastern base of the Appalachian Mountains. People had settled into mountain coves and fertile valleys. Men and women constantly pressed on through river-cut gaps in successive mountain ridges. Settlement patterns and transportation routes conformed to the natural surface features of the land.

Plains. The Atlantic coastal plain that extended southward from Massachusetts to Florida between the Atlantic Ocean and the Appalachian Mountains was referred to as the Sea Sand Region. Its swamps and sandy soils were not well suited to agriculture. However, because of its coastal location, this plain was the first to be settled.

Rivers. During the period of westward expansion, rivers were dredged or cleared of snags so that riverboat traffic could flow smoothly where it

Map Skills

Cumberland and Vandalia
• Look for characteristics mentioned in the text (climate, topographic features). Depending on the route chosen, possible answers based on the map could be: variation from constantly moist areas to dry areas; variation from mild to cold winters and cool to hot summers; features such as plains (Great Plains), rivers (Arkansas, Missouri, Platte, Colorado, etc.), and mountains (Rocky Mountains, Sierra Nevada).

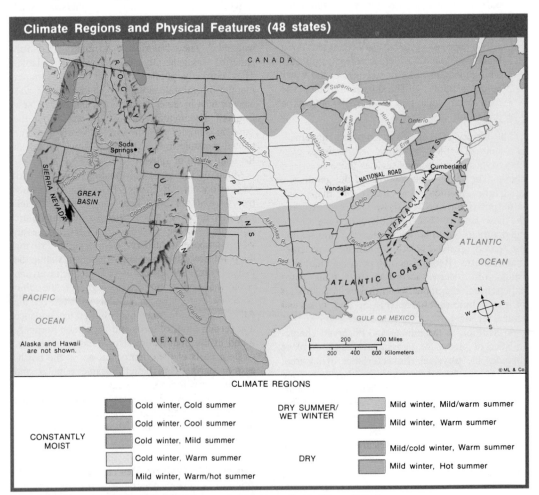

Climate Regions and Physical Features (48 states)

CLIMATE REGIONS

CONSTANTLY MOIST
- Cold winter, Cold summer
- Cold winter, Cool summer
- Cold winter, Mild summer
- Cold winter, Warm summer
- Mild winter, Warm/hot summer

DRY SUMMER/WET WINTER
- Mild winter, Mild/warm summer
- Mild winter, Warm summer

DRY
- Mild/cold winter, Warm summer
- Mild winter, Hot summer

Map Skills **Movement** The National Road connected what two cities? **Place** Describe some place characteristics a pioneer would encounter on a trip from Vandalia to the Pacific coast.

Picturing History
Bryce Canyon National Park in southern Utah ranks among the most unusual and colorful places in the Southwest. Hues of copper, cream, and gold change with the sunlight. Rocks shaped as castles, cathedrals, and various animals can be identified depending on the imagination of the observer.

formerly had been hindered by rapids. A system of canals and locks was built in the early 1800's to link separate rivers into water systems. A proposal to link rivers that flowed east and west from the Appalachian Mountains was rejected as impractical, however. Instead, a National Road was constructed across the mountains. Eventually the National Road connected the growing cities of the New West and carried settlers from the East Coast to Vandalia, Illinois.

Natural Resources Describe Places. Little was known about the underground resources of North America at the time of the westward movement. Early rumors of precious metals in places beyond the settlements of the early 1800's proved to be untrue. Resources such as iron, coal, and forests soon became evident, however. Descriptions of places where these resources were plentiful helped to lure the early settlers westward.

Iron and Coal. Settlers in Pennsylvania accidentally discovered coal as they were digging cellars and wells. Iron ore was also found this way. During the early 1800's, however, there was little market for these resources. Local farmers mined iron and coal merely to provide additional income.

Forests. The importance of forests during the early 1800's cannot be overestimated. Besides providing the material for building homes and ships, wood was the principal means of fuel. Wood

was also used for many byproducts such as resin and tar. The burning of logs to get potash for fertilizer and for soap was also prevalent. The depletion of forests around cities continually encouraged settlers to respond to descriptions of lands farther west where the supply of wood was abundant.

Descriptions of Places Westward. Travel westward in early nineteenth-century America was slow and difficult. Settlers were encouraged to undertake the journey, however, because of the descriptions of places with good climates for farming and with many natural resources. By studying places in the geography of North America, settlers were able to travel along the rivers, cross the mountain passes, and follow the early hunting trails to establish new homes for themselves and for those who would come after them.

Understanding Geography

1. How do geographers generally describe places?
2. Give an example of a topographic feature that influenced settlement patterns.
3. How did natural resources lure settlers westward?
4. How did descriptions of places encourage the westward movement?

Critical Thinking

5. Write a geographic description of a place that might be used to lure new residents today.

Answer Key

Key Terms and People

These are highlighted in the text in the order in which they appear in this list.

Main Ideas

1. Many people thought he had stolen election in House of Representatives; Jacksonians made him look bad; he supported strong national government when people wanted less government.

➤**2.** A popular candidate, Jackson; a genius at organization, Van Buren; people were ready to accept political parties.

3. Common people in the White House; Jackson's reliance on the Kitchen Cabinet and the spoils system; no legislation or policy that favored the wealthy.

4. (1) Extermination—kill all Indians. (2) Assimilation—integrate Indians into the white culture. (3) Removal—move Indians to land west of the Mississippi.

5. Jackson favored Federal Union over states' rights. • Calhoun favored nullification.

6. Bank symbolized Eastern special privilege that gave it power over legislation and elections. • Poorer banks: could not compete; farmers: resented getting no income from investment at bank; bank president viewed as crooked and arrogant.

7. Jackson's pet banks failed; America's cotton prices and sales dropped due to the depressed condition of the British economy.

8. Tyler opposed internal improvements and the national bank; Whigs supported Clay's American System.

Critical Thinking Questions

9. Jackson's July Fourth barbecue became a big campaign party.

➤**10.** Usually a major party candidate gets majority of electoral votes.

11. Caucus—private meeting of party leaders; nominating convention—party leaders and elected delegates. • Convention.

12. Similarities: intensely patriotic, distrusted Jackson, backed Clay's American System. Differences: Adams—New England aristocrat, stubborn; Clay—Western War Hawk, compromiser.

13. Possible answers: good—bank's national currency created a national economy. Bad—bank made rich richer, poor poorer.

Critical Thinking Activities

14. b, e, d, f, a, c.

15. Possible answer: vote against high tariff that keeps British sales low in U.S. so Britain cannot afford to buy my cotton. I must buy expensive New England manufactured goods.

16. Hayne—for states' rights; for nullification and right to secede, also believed tariff hurt South and was unconstitutional; "The rights of the South have been destroyed, and must be restored"; "The Union is in danger and must be saved." Webster—against states' rights; national government supreme, also believed disputes should be settled by courts and electoral process, not nullification or secession; "I

CHAPTER 10 REVIEW

Write your answers on a separate sheet of paper.

Key Terms and People

Explain the significance of: political machine, Old Hickory, King Mob, Force Bill, wildcat banks, specie, Specie Circular, depression, William Henry Harrison

Main Ideas

1. Why did John Quincy Adams become so unpopular?
2. Between 1826 and 1828, what conditions contributed to the successful formation of the Democratic party?
3. How was the Jacksonian style manifested?
4. Name and explain the three approaches to the treatment of Indians.
5. What was Jackson's position on states' rights? Why did Jackson substitute Van Buren for Calhoun as his running mate when he ran for a second term?
6. Why did Jackson oppose the national bank? Why did others oppose it?
7. What were the causes of the depression that hit just after Van Buren was elected?
8. How did Tyler's policies differ from those of the Whigs who had elected him Vice-President?

Critical Thinking Questions

9. **Analyzing Literature.** What does the literary selection on page 257 tell you about the origin of Jackson's form of campaigning?
10. **Synthesizing Ideas.** How does the two-party system help to avoid having the House of Representatives make Presidential election decisions?
11. **Drawing Inferences.** What is the difference between a caucus and a nominating convention? Which is more democratic?
12. **Classifying Information.** What did John Quincy Adams and Henry Clay have in common? How did they differ?
13. **Evaluating Decisions.** Do you think the Second National Bank was good or bad for the economy? Support your answer.

Critical Thinking Activities

14. **Organizing Chronology.** Using the appropriate letters, arrange the following events in chronological order.

   a. The Democratic party is born.
   b. Adams, Crawford, Jackson, and Clay run for the Presidency.
   c. Jackson is elected President.
   d. Adams and Clay have a private talk.
   e. Jackson wins the popular and the electoral vote but not a majority of either.
   f. House of Representatives elects Adams.

1824   1826   1828

15. **Evaluating Sources.** If you had been a South Carolina cotton planter in 1828, what would you have written Senator Hayne about the Tariff of Abominations?

16. **Contrasting Ideas.** Use your book to make a chart comparing the positions of Hayne and Webster on the issue of states' rights. Include examples and quotations from the book.

	Position on States' Rights	Explanation and Examples	Quotations
Hayne			
Webster			

17. **Analyzing Maps.** Look at the map on page 264. Do you agree with Jackson that the removal of the Eastern Indians was ''not only liberal, but generous''?

18. Linking Past to Present. What is the lasting legacy of Jackson?

TELESCOPING THE TIMES: 1824–1840

The Age of Jackson

In the four-way race for President in 1824, every candidate claimed to be a Republican. Jackson won the most popular votes, but no candidate won a majority in the electoral college. Thus, the election was decided by the House of Representatives, and the victory went to John Q. Adams. He backed a strong nationalist program and internal improvements, but he had little success. Jackson's supporters kept reminding Adams that he was a minority President. They began to organize the Democratic party. Jackson and the Democrats won the White House in 1828 with a new and wildly popular campaign style.

Jackson felt that he was the representative of the common people. With the exception of Van Buren, he appointed undistinguished men. He relied on his Kitchen Cabinet of Western editors. He defended the spoils system by saying that government jobs ought to be open to everyone. He vetoed numerous acts of Congress, especially internal improvements, such as the Maysville Road, that were backed by political enemies, most notably Clay of Kentucky. He defied the Supreme Court when he forced Indians to leave their homelands and move farther west. His second election saw the first political nominating conventions.

Conflict increased during the Jackson Era over sectional differences. Most Southerners opposed a tariff because it protected Northern industries and raised the price of manufactured goods. South Carolina claimed the right to nullify a new federal tariff. The country shook with debates when Calhoun endorsed the right of secession and Webster defended the ideal of the national union. Jackson pushed Congress to pass the Force Bill, which effectively denied South Carolina's claim. The President declared war on the national bank and managed to destroy that "monster" of wealth. His angry opponents formed the new Whig political party to oppose the President, whom they called King Andrew.

Van Buren was picked by Jackson as the next Democratic candidate. He won the election but then fell victim to the results of Jackson's financial policies. The nation's banks were hit by a major financial panic just after Van Buren took office. Inevitably the voters blamed him, and the economic depression resulted in a Whig victory in 1840. American voters loved the hoopla of the campaign, and a higher percentage of voters turned out for this election than for any other election before or since. Harrison, the new President, soon died, however, and Vice-President Tyler, whom the Whigs did not like, assumed the Presidency.

Chronology of Main Events

1825 John Quincy Adams inaugurated President

1828 Tariff of Abominations passed

1829 Andrew Jackson inaugurated President; Democratic party established

1830 Hayne-Webster debate; Indian Removal Act

1834 Whig party formed

1837 Martin Van Buren inaugurated President; Panic of 1837

1838 Cherokees are forced to leave Georgia and suffer along the Trail of Tears to Oklahoma

1841 William Henry Harrison inaugurated President; dies within a month, and John Tyler succeeds him

Telescoping the Times may be used as an alternative to having students read the entire chapter, as a chapter preview, or as a chapter review.

State the Objective

Understand the causes and results of the French Revolution.

Present the Lesson

Divide the class into small groups. Have each group develop a list of conditions that triggered the French Revolution. Ask one member of each group to share the group's list with the class. (Lists might include: the revolution in America fanned the fires of support for liberty, equality, and no taxation without representation; the tax system of Louis XVI was unjust, heavily favoring the clergy and nobility; at a meeting of the Estates General, members of the Third Estate demanded equal representation with the clergy and nobility.)

Ask students to identify the immediate ac-

tions of the National Assembly that met after the first uprising of the revolution and the long-term consequences of the assembly's actions. (Answers: actions—repealed the privileges and tax exemptions of the nobles and the clergy; issued a *Declaration of the Rights of Man and of the Citizen;* abolished the absolute rule of the King; established a constitutional monarchy. Consequences—rulers in Europe felt threatened by the actions of this assembly and tried to restore Louis XVI to his former power.) Ask students what caused the downfall of the Directory that ruled following the Reign of Terror. (Answer: members of the Directory were jealous of one another's power; mem-

Focus on Global Events

The French Revolution

France's combination of soldiers and ships helped the American colonists win their independence from Great Britain. However, this assistance helped to further the cause of revolution in France itself. The King of France, Louis XVI, had aided the colonists because he wanted to weaken Britain, the great rival of France. He did not suspect that such dangerous and revolutionary ideas as liberty, equality, and "no taxation without representation" would spread to his own people.

The French as well as the American colonists had been influenced by the ideas of the Enlightenment. By the late 1780's, the French people were calling for wide-ranging social reforms based on reason and on a respect for human rights.

In comparison to the American Revolution, however, the French struggle was longer, bloodier, and less successful. After the colonies won their independence from Britain, the revolution was over and a prosperous, stable society began to be established. The French Revolution, on the other hand, was really a series of revolutions—one causing the next—that lasted for years.

The Background. The revolution eventually toppled the monarchy by which France had been ruled for 802 years. During the 1780's, a mounting public debt (aggravated by France's aid to the American colonies) forced Louis XVI to attempt an overhaul of his country's unjust and inefficient tax system. The existing system favored the clergy and nobility over all other classes in France. To accomplish his reforms, Louis had to call a full session of the *Estates General*, a legislative body that had not met for more than 170 years. The Estates represented the three officially recognized classes of French people. These were the clergy (called the First Estate), the nobility (the Second Estate), and everybody else (the Third Estate). The most influential members of the latter group were professionals such as doctors, lawyers, and merchants.

As the meeting began in May 1789, members of the Third Estate protested voting procedures that gave one vote each to the clergy, the nobility, and

their own class. Since the Third Estate was much larger, they demanded as many representatives as the First and Second Estates combined. They also wanted to vote as individuals rather than as groups. The king granted their first demand but rejected their second.

The Beginning. In the first great act of revolution, members of the Third Estate walked out of the meeting. They declared themselves the National Assembly of France. On June 20, 1789, they met at an indoor tennis court to swear the Tennis Court Oath. They pledged not to return home until they had written a new constitution for France.

Louis XVI replied that this act was treason and called twenty thousand troops to the palace of Versailles. Parisians armed themselves against a possible attack by the king's troops. On July 14, 1789, a Parisian mob seeking weapons stormed the Bastille, a prison that had come to symbolize for them all of the monarchy's abuses of power. As news of the July 14 uprising spread through the provinces, peasants took up arms, killing many of their hated landlords.

The National Assembly immediately repealed the privileges and tax exemptions of the nobles and the clergy. On August 27, 1789, the Assembly issued a *Declaration of the Rights of Man and of the Citizen*. This document proclaimed that legitimate government must be based on liberty, equality, and natural rights.

In September 1791, the National Assembly issued the constitution it had promised. The first French Revolution was over. The middle class had abolished the king's absolute rule and had established a constitutional monarchy.

The New Revolution. Then a new and far bloodier revolution broke out. Rulers of Europe banded together and tried to restore Louis XVI to his former powers. In France this news sparked a war hysteria, accompanied by the massacre of royalists and some who had helped start the first revolution. In August 1792, a mob marched to the palace of Versailles and threatened the king and his family. A

280

Check for Understanding

Picturing History After serving as First Consul of the French republic for five years, Napoleon crowned himself emperor and his wife, Josephine, empress. Napoleon commissioned painter Louis David to portray the ceremony, which took place at the Cathedral of Notre Dame in Paris on December 2, 1804.

new constitution was drawn up abolishing the monarchy altogether. France was now a republic.

Now France found itself at war with most of Europe. As the war intensified, a wave of fear and hatred against the royalty arose. In December 1792, Louis XVI was dragged before a court and tried for treason. Convicted, he was beheaded before cheering mobs on January 21, 1793.

The Terror. Hunger, inflation, and peasant rebellion soon ravaged France at home while the nation suffered one defeat after another abroad. By summer a group of radicals established a twelve-member executive board known as the Committee of Public Safety. Under the leadership of Maximilien Robespierre, the committee began a Reign of Terror. Between August 1792 and July 1794, more than forty thousand men and women, including the queen of France, Marie Antoinette, lost their heads to the guillotine. Thousands more were sent to prison.

By summer of 1794, the French revolted again. The bloody dictatorship of the Committee of Public Safety was dissolved and Robespierre and many of his supporters were executed. As one writer noted, "The French Revolution devoured its children."

With the end of the Reign of Terror, moderate and conservative members of the middle class returned to power. However, they were jealous of their own privileges, and the founders of the new government, called the Directory, permitted even fewer citizens to vote than had been permitted in 1791.

The Empire. When those citizens finally went to the polls in 1797, they shocked the government by electing a considerable number of royalist sympathizers. In panic, members of the Directory called upon the young general Napoleon Bonaparte for a show of force. With Bonaparte's help, the Directory illegally disregarded the recent elections.

Then to satisfy his own ambitions for political power, Napoleon Bonaparte joined yet another conspiracy that overthrew the Directory. He imposed a new government on the French—the sixth in ten years. In this new republic, Napoleon served as First Consul. Five years later, First Consul Bonaparte betrayed this revolution as well by crowning himself emperor.

Kings and Republics. After Napoleon, France experienced a succession of three kings, a Second Republic lasting three years, and a Second Empire, which fell at the end of the Franco-Prussian War in 1870. From 1871 to the present, however, France has maintained some form of republican government. Today, over two hundred years after its revolution, France now lives under its Fifth Republic.

Understanding Global Events

1. How did France's aid to the cause of American independence hasten its own revolution?
2. Why was the French Revolution more violent than the American one?
3. What were the results of the French Revolution?

Critical Thinking

4. What does the observation "the revolution devoured its children" mean?

FOCUS ON GLOBAL EVENTS

Answers

Understanding Global Events

1. The cost of the aid forced Louis XVI to attempt an overhaul of his country's unjust and inefficient tax system, which led to the calling of the Estates General, which in turn led to the first act of the French Revolution. In addition, ideas and successes of the American Revolution set an example for the French.

2. Once the American Revolution was over, a prosperous, stable society was rapidly established. On the other hand, the French Revolution was really a series of bloody revolutions that went on for many years, crippling the nation.

3. Napoleon crowned himself Emperor, followed by a succession of three Kings, a Second Republic, and a Second Empire. From 1871 to the present, France has maintained some form of republican government.

Critical Thinking

4. The expression "the French Revolution devoured its children" means the leaders of the dictatorship established in France by the radical Committee of Public Safety became obsessed with the use of terror and executions as a means of governing and in the process were themselves overthrown and devoured by the revolution. **(analysis)**

Key Terms and People

These are highlighted in the text in the order in which they appear in this list.

Main Ideas

1. (3) 1794—Whiskey Rebellion: President Washington, Alexander Hamilton.

2. (5) 1798—Virginia and Kentucky Resolutions: President John Adams, Thomas Jefferson, James Madison.

3. (1) 1803—Louisiana Purchase: President Jefferson, James Monroe, Meriwether Lewis, William Clark, Sacajawea.

4. (2) 1812—War of 1812: President James Madison, Oliver Hazard Perry, Andrew Jackson.

5. (6)1820—Missouri Compromise: President Monroe; Henry Clay.

6. (7) 1828—Democratic party born: President John Quincy Adams, Martin Van Buren, Andrew Jackson.

7. (4) 1830—Nullification theory debated: President Jackson, Robert Hayne, Daniel Webster, John Calhoun.

8. (8) 1837—Depression strikes as national bank disappears: President Van Buren, Andrew Jackson.

Critical Thinking Questions

➤**9.** Possible answers: for—young or ailing industries, such as new industries in the early years of the United States and car manufacturers today, need to be protected against competition by tariffs. Against—when a country sets up a protective tariff, other countries generally retaliate by raising their own tariffs. Often the people in neither country get the products as cheaply as they did before the tariffs were placed. This situation occurred after the tariffs of the early 1800's when Southerners had to pay high New England prices for goods they used to buy cheaply from Britain.

10. Possible answers: for preservation of the Union—much U.S. strength comes from its size and the ability of its people to cooperate; a reduction in size would make the country less rich; barriers to trade, transportation, and the movement of people might be set up. The people made the federal government and the government is sovereign. For right of nullification—the states came before the Union; they should have the right to se-cede if the federal government is not meeting their needs.

11. Betrayed by a system of justice that seemed to work only for the white people.

12. Possible answers: justified—Jackson saw that the Eastern wealth and power of the bank could bribe officials and buy elections; the situation was undemocratic. Unjustified—Jackson did not understand economics, that banks are necessary to fi-nance capital, and that a solid currency is necessary for commerce. Jackson should have reformed the bank rather than destroy it. • Partly—Jackson used pet banks that were poorly run; when he tried to stop the land speculation (begun by the pet banks) with the Specie Circular, he helped to bring on the depression of 1837. The world economy was also to blame.

UNIT 2 REVIEW

Write your answers on a separate sheet of paper.

Key Terms and People

Explain the significance of each of the following:

Articles of Confederation
Northwest Ordinance
Daniel Shays
Judicial review
Daniel Boone
Monroe Doctrine
Industrial Revolution
Pet banks

Main Ideas

List the events below in chronological order. For each event, give the date and name the President in office at the time and at least one other person closely associated with the event.

1. Louisiana Purchase
2. War of 1812
3. Whiskey Rebellion
4. Nullification theory debate in the Senate
5. Virginia and Kentucky Resolutions adopted
6. Missouri Compromise
7. Democratic party born
8. Depression strikes as national bank disappears

Critical Thinking Questions

9. **Formulating Hypotheses.** There is a continuing debate as to whether free world trade or protectionism is better for the world economy. Decide which you think is better. Give both historic and current reasons to support your answer.

10. **Assessing Decisions.** Jackson came to the conclusion that "Our Federal Union: it must and shall be preserved." Would you have come to the same conclusion? Why or why not?

11. **Evaluating Sources.** When the Supreme Court declared that the Cherokee nation had a legitimate right to the land it claimed, Jackson ignored the decision. If you had been a Cherokee at the time, how would you have felt when you had to move off the land?

12. **Assessing Decisions.** Was Jackson justified in his war against the Second Bank? Was the bank's demise instrumental in causing the depression of 1837? Explain.

Critical Thinking Activities

Recognizing Cause and Effect. On the chart below, fill in the blanks for Cause and Effect. The first blank has been filled in for you.

Cause	Effect
Daniel Shays's Rebellion	Articles of Confederation scrapped
13. Whitney's interchangeable parts	_____
14. _____	Removal of Indians
15. Tariff of Abominations	_____
16. Alien and Sedition Acts	_____
17. _____	Bank war
18. Desire for protection of individual against government	_____

19. **Linking Past and Present.** Henry Clay and John Calhoun were known as War Hawks because they wanted to go to war against Britain. Name some recent leaders whom some people might call war hawks because of their military stance in certain situations. Explain.

20. **Linking Past and Present.** The Monroe Doctrine warned European nations not to involve themselves further in any lands of the Western Hemisphere. At the same time, the United States would not involve itself in European affairs. Do we still back this doctrine today? How? Give examples.

21. **Linking Past and Present.** Use *The New York Times Index* to research cases in which the Supreme Court has used its power of judicial review within your lifetime. Give examples.

TELESCOPING THE TIMES: 1781–1841

A New Nation

The Articles of Confederation

During the Revolution, all the states adopted new constitutions. Most of these documents provided for two-house legislatures, weak governors, and lower property requirements for voting and office holding.

At the same time, the Continental Congress drafted Articles of Confederation that they hoped would give the colonies formal unity. The Articles provided that voting in Congress should be by states rather than by representatives based on population. The states were slow to accept the Articles because they disagreed over the disposition of the western lands.

The Confederation had grave difficulties. The new nation faced foreign threats from the British in the Northwest and from the Spanish on the Mississippi River. The Confederation had the power to borrow money but no power to tax. It could make treaties with foreign nations and with the Indians, but it could only ask the various states for troops. Any changes in the Articles had to be approved by all thirteen states. The United States was experimenting with dividing power.

The Confederation Congress's one great success was the Northwest Ordinance of 1787. This law provided that the vast Northwest Territory should be split up from three to five smaller territories. When any of these territories had enough population, it could apply for statehood on an equal basis with the original states. In addition, the ordinance banned slavery from the whole region.

The Constitutional Convention

A small group of nationalists worked quietly to rescue the nation and to defend their own interests. They arranged for a convention in Philadelphia in May 1787. The delegates were wealthy and well-educated. They saw society as being made up of different economic, religious, and other kinds of special interest groups. They thought that the majority of people should rule but that smaller groups should be protected. They feared both the power of wealth and the power of the mob.

The first actions the fifty-five delegates took were to hold their discussions in secret and to scrap the Articles. The first crisis of the Convention came because of conflict between states with large populations and those with small ones. Everyone agreed that there should be a representative legislature, but should it represent the states or the people? The Great Compromise solved this problem by establishing a bicameral legislature that consisted of a House of Representatives and a Senate.

The second crisis that summer was caused by slavery. Southern delegates said that slaves should be counted as people and therefore should be represented in the House. Northern delegates said that slaves were pieces of property and should not be represented. At last the delegates compromised. They agreed that a slave should be counted as three-fifths of a person for representation.

The Philadelphia convention agreed that the Constitution should have checks and balances among the different branches of government. The President was to be commander in chief of the armed forces, and was able to veto acts of Congress. Yet the President's veto could be overridden by a two-thirds majority of both Houses. The chief executive could appoint members of the new Supreme Court but only with the consent of the Senate. The convention also provided for amending the Constitution.

The new document was to be ratified by a special convention in each of the states. Many people opposed it because it greatly strengthened the national government. In several key states, the Constitution barely squeaked through, but it went

Telescoping the Times may be used as an alternative to having students read the entire unit, as a unit preview, or as a unit review.

into effect in 1788.

As soon as it was empowered, Congress submitted the Bill of Rights. These ten amendments to the Constitution guaranteed fundamental freedoms to the people. Congress also organized the executive and judicial branches of the government. The latter included a Supreme Court and a system of lower federal courts.

The Federalists

Washington was elected President as everyone expected him to be. In this role, he was very much aware that all his actions would set an example for the future.

As Secretary of the Treasury, Hamilton pushed through a sweeping financial program. His plan provided funding for foreign debts as well as for state debts. To do this, he levied a sales tax on whiskey, which made the farmers who produced the whiskey furious. He also convinced Congress and the President that there were political advantages in establishing a national bank.

Two political parties began to develop, even though no one welcomed them at first. Hamilton led the Federalists. Jefferson and Madison organized the Republicans. Washington did his best to remain above party politics but in fact leaned toward Hamilton.

The Federalist John Adams succeeded Washington to the Presidency in 1797. French naval vessels attacked American merchant ships, but Adams refused to be pushed into a formal state of war. On the home front he backed the Alien and Sedition Acts to suppress dissent. Madison and Jefferson wrote the Virginia and Kentucky Resolutions in direct response to this abridgement of civil rights. Federalist judges actually fined and jailed a number of Republicans.

The Jeffersonians

When Jefferson won the Presidency in 1800, power was transferred peaceably from one political party to the other. The new President moved quickly to remedy the wrongs of the Alien and Sedition Acts. He made the Presidency less formal, and he cut government costs. In 1803 Jefferson doubled the size of the country by buying the vast territory of Louisiana from France. He sent Lewis and Clark on a long expedition to explore the area. They came back with glowing reports.

America's neutral shipping again became entangled in the war between Napoleon's France and Great Britain. Impressment of American seamen by the British navy greatly angered Americans. An incident concerning the U.S.S. *Chesapeake* caused many Americans to call for war against the British.

Madison won the Presidency in 1808. A group of new young congressmen, many elected in 1810, became known as War Hawks. They talked about conquering Canada, and they urged stronger measures against the Indians. In the Old Northwest Territory, a Shawnee chief named Tecumseh began organizing a large confederation of tribes. General Harrison defeated these Indians at the Battle of Tippecanoe.

In 1812 Madison gave in to widespread pressure for war against Great Britain. The War of 1812 had very mixed success on the field. The British navy blockaded American ports. In the Old Northwest Territory, American troops fought against the Indians. On the Canadian border, victories and defeats occurred on both sides. British forces burned several American coastal towns. In Washington, D.C., they burned the White House and other government buildings. This blow to national pride was balanced by Jackson's stunning victory against a large British army at New Orleans.

When Jackson became the hero of New Orleans, no one in America knew that the war had been over for two weeks. The Treaty of Ghent left United States boundaries intact and turned several disputes over to special diplomatic meetings that occurred later. After the war, the Adams-Onís Treaty gave Spanish Florida to the United States. It laid out the southern border of the United States all the way to the Pacific Ocean.

The end of war also brought about an end to political strife. Most politicians were calling themselves Republicans. One editor called Monroe's administration the Era of Good Feelings.

Marshall's Supreme Court contributed to the feeling of national power. In a series of vital decisions, Marshall strengthened the power of contracts. He stressed the superiority of the federal government over the states and over interstate commerce. He even declared a state law unconstitutional. In the case of *Marbury* v. *Madison,* the Supreme Court established the right of judicial review.

The Monroe Doctrine announced that the United States would not permit European nations to interfere anywhere in the Western Hemisphere. This claim was meaningless unless the British controlled the oceans.

Missouri's application for statehood produced a crisis because it was a slave state. Northerners were worried about the sectional balance of power in the Senate. The halls of Congress shook with angry debates. In 1820 Congress adopted the Missouri Compromise. Maine separated from Massachusetts and was admitted as a free state to balance the admission of Missouri. In addition, slavery was banned forever north of a line extending from the southern border of Missouri all the way west.

Because the cotton gin had made cotton more profitable, tens of thousands of settlers moved into the land between the Appalachians and the Mississippi south of the Ohio River. The Atlantic slave trade had been banned in 1808, and the demand for slave labor drove the price of slaves up and up. The great majority of Southern whites owned few slaves or, more often, none. Most slaves lived on a few large plantations. They were forced to work long hours and sometimes resisted by refusing to work efficiently. They shaped their own kind of Christian worship and re-created the music they had brought from Africa.

While the South was becoming the Cotton Kingdom, the North turned to industry. Textile mills, using technology from Great Britain, became the first real factories in America. New machinery produced cloth quickly and cheaply. To tend the machinery, the wealthy mill-owners hired women and children who worked long hours in dangerous conditions.

The nation's politics changed suddenly in 1824. Because the Federalist party had collapsed, candidates for President called themselves Republicans. The House of Representatives had to decide the election because no candidate won a majority of electoral votes. John Quincy Adams won the Presidency, even though Jackson received more popular votes. Adams disappointed people as President, and Andrew Jackson won the election of 1828.

Jacksonian Democracy

Jackson was a strong and forceful President. He regarded himself as the only real representative of all the common people. He endorsed the spoils system by saying that public offices should be open to everyone. He vetoed more laws than all previous Presidents combined. He forced thousands of Indians to move westward across the Mississippi. When the Supreme Court objected to this Indian removal, he defied its ruling. When South Carolina nullified a new federal tariff, Jackson forced the state to back down. He denounced Calhoun's claim that a state could secede from the Union.

President Van Buren inherited the problems that were caused by Jackson's financial policies. Soon after he took office, banks began to fail. The resulting economic depression cost him reelection in 1840. By that time, two new political parties had clearly emerged—the Jacksonian Democrats and the Whigs. In a campaign marked by wild hoopla, the Whig Harrison was victorious. He died a month after taking office, however, and Whig leaders found themselves having to deal with President Tyler, who disagreed with their policies.

Chronology of Main Events	
1781	Articles of Confederation adopted
1788	U.S. Constitution ratified
1800	Thomas Jefferson elected President
1803	Louisiana Purchase
1812–1814	War of 1812 ending with the Treaty of Ghent
1823	Monroe Doctrine
1828	Andrew Jackson elected President

GLOBAL TIME LINE

The World

1820-1830
George IV rules
Great Britain

1821
Napoleon dies

1825
Decembrist Revolt in Russia

1827
Beethoven dies

1833
Slavery ended in British Empire

1842
Hong Kong becomes
British colony

1848
Revolutions sweep
Europe

1820   1830   1840

**The
United States**

1825
Erie canal finished

1836
Texas declares independence from Mexico

1846-1848
Mexican War

1848
First women's rights convention

Research Assignment

Read the story of Senator Edmund G. Ross in John F. Kennedy's *Profiles in Courage* (Harper & Row, 1983, paper.) and consider the qualities that characterize a hero. Choose one person from this unit whom you consider a hero. Research that person's life and present a three-minute talk to the class on why he or she should be considered a hero.

UNIT 3   1830–1876

The Nation Grows, Divides, and Reunites

Geographic Setting

Human-Environment Interactions / Movement.
E. Sachse drew this lithograph of the capital city in 1851. Washington remained a small city until the Civil War, when newcomers streamed into the capital and its population doubled.

Unit Overview

From 1830 through 1876, the United States grew at an astonishing rate. As the nation's boundaries expanded, differences between the North and the South intensified. When attempts at compromise failed, the nation came apart. The Civil War ended slavery and settled the question of the right of states to leave the Union. The Union was preserved, but the relationship between the federal government and the states was changed. Unit 3 explains this period of growth, division, and reunion in five chapters.

Unit Outline

1853-1854 erry opens nese ports U.S. trade

1857-1858 Sepoy Rebellion in India

1858 British take over India

1859 *On Liberty* published

1859-1869 Suez Canal built

1861 Serfs freed in Russia

1870-1871 Franco-Prussian War

50   1860   1870   1880

1852 *Uncle Tom's Cabin* ▪lished

1857 Dred Scott decision

1854 Republican party formed

1861-1865 Civil War

1862 Emancipation Proclamation issued

1865 Lincoln assassinated

1865-1876 Reconstruction

1869 Ulysses S. Grant inaugurated President

1873 Economic depression begins

1877 Rutherford B. Hayes inaugurated President

Global Perspectives

1842	Britain loses First Afghan War.
1842	Boers set up Orange Free State in Africa.
1845	Potato blight causes famine in Ireland.
1848	Popular revolutions for independence sweep Europe.
1849	Britain repeals 200-year-old Navigation laws.

For Discussion

What effect might the Irish famine have on the U.S. if it were to occur today? (Possible response: increase in U.S. food exports to Ireland and in Irish immigration to U.S.)

Additional Resources

- Geography Activities
- Skills Activities
- Thematic Activities
- Economic Activities
- Cultural Literacy Activities
- Literary Source Readings
- Primary Source Readings
- Nuclear Peacekeeping
- Transparencies
- Computer Test Generator

Additional Teaching Strategies

SECTION 1

For Basic Students: Ask each student to prepare a poster advertising a major invention of the pre-Civil War era. Display the posters and discuss the effect of each invention on daily life.

For Advanced Students: Ask students to look up information on one of the following inventors: Cyrus McCormick, Charles Goodyear, Isaac Merrit Singer, or Samuel F. B. Morse. Prepare a short oral report on how he represented the spirit of American ingenuity. (Reports might include: *McCormick*—first produced reapers in Virginia, built a factory in Chicago, introduced reaper to Europe in 1851, continued to improve product, used deferred payment plans, guarantees, and testimonials to sell reapers; *Goodyear*—no formal education, failed in hardware business, experimenting with rubber, eventually developed process known as vulcanization; *Singer*—instrumental in pooling patents for various sewing machines and laying groundwork for mass production; *Morse*—educated at Yale, studied painting, became a professor, developed magnetic telegraph and Morse Code, later experimented with submarine cable telegraphy.)

SECTION 2

For Basic Students: Ask students to write on paper two reform movements of the first half of the nineteenth century that they feel are most important and the reasons for their choices. Have students share their reasons and come to a consensus on the two major movements.

For Advanced Students: Ask each student to assume the character of Dorothea Dix and compose a letter to her congressman explaining the need for aid to mental patients in the U.S. Letters may include descriptions of unsanitary and crowded conditions and inhumane treatment of patients.

SECTION 3

For Basic Students: Have students read the text under the heading "Garrison Tries to Change Public Opinion" and make a list of Garrison's basic arguments against slavery. (Lists should include: blacks were not Africans but Americans; blacks were entitled to the rights stated in the Declaration of Independence.)

For Advanced Students: Ask students to prepare background reports on the underground railroad and its effect on slavery. Have them share the information with the class. (Reports might include: flourished between 1830 and 1860; carried over 50,000 slaves to freedom; used homes of opponents of slavery as "stations"; centered in Philadelphia because of the large Quaker population; notable persons included Quaker Levi Coffin, abolitionists John Brown and Wendell Phillips.)

SECTION 4

For Basic Students: Have students design and write material for handbills to advertise the Women's Rights Convention. (Ads should include details such as: Seneca Falls, N.Y.; Frederick Douglass; Declaration of Sentiments; July, 1848.)

For Advanced Students: Divide class into groups of about six to debate the issue of women's rights. They should focus on whether the moral superiority conferred on women by society maintains women's inferior political and economic status. Have group leaders summarize the debate for the class.

Further Reading for Students

Douglass, Frederick. *The Life and Times of Frederick Douglass.* Secaucus, N. J.: Lyle Stuart, 1983.

Gurko, Miriam. *The Ladies of Seneca Falls: The Birth of the Women's Rights Movement.* New York: Macmillan, 1976. (Easy)

Howells, William Dean. *The Rise of Silas Lapham.* New York: W. W. Norton, 1982.

Historical Fiction

Styron, William. *The Confessions of Nat Turner.* New York: Bantam Books, 1981.

Bibliography for Teachers
Books

Genovese, Eugene D. *The World the Slaveholders Made: Two Essays in Interpretation.* New York: Random House, 1971.

Lutz, Alma. *Susan B. Anthony: Rebel, Crusader, Humanitarian.* Washington, D.C.: Zenger Publishing Co., 1976.

Madison, Charles A. *Critics and Crusaders: A Century of American Protest.* New York: Frederick Ungar, 1947.

Audio-Visuals

The Industrial Revolution: Beginnings in the United States. Encyclopedia Britannica. Movie.

Like Hens That Crow: The Women's Rights Movement in America. Prentice-Hall Media. Movie.

Computer Resource

U.S. History—Inventions and Technology. (Apple/Tandy 1000/IBM) Scholastic.

Teacher's Notes:

Teaching Resources, Unit 3 Booklet

Lesson Study Sheets pp 1-16
Daily Activities pp. 17-24
Enrichment Activities pp. 25-32
Reteaching Activities pp. 33-40
Chapter Review p. 41
Chapter Mastery Tests pp. 43-54
Telescoping the Times Study Sheet p. 55

Chapter Objectives

Students will learn:
- how inventions helped revolutionize American life
- the importance of reform movements in the U.S. prior to the Civil War
- how the abolitionist movement led to increased sectional controversy
- the origins of women's struggle for equality

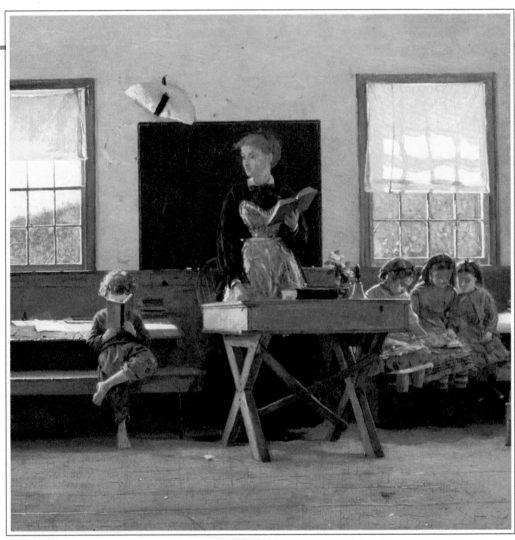

Picturing History Winslow Homer's *The Country School* depicts a classroom typical of the late nineteenth century.

Using the Chapter Time Line

Who was President (see Chapter 10 Time Line) when McCormick invented the reaper? (Answer: Andrew Jackson) How many years elapsed between the ratification of the Constitution and the Women's Rights Convention at Seneca Falls, N.Y.? (Answer: 60)

1830   1835   1840   1845   1850

1833 American Anti-slavery Society formed

1837 John Deere invents steel plow

1844 Telegraph put into use

1848 Women's rights convention at Seneca Falls, N.Y.

1842 Dorothea Dix reports on conditions of mentally ill

1831
- Cyrus McCormick invents reaper
- Nat Turner leads slave revolt in Virginia

288

CHAPTER **11**   1830–1850

An Era of Reform

Links to American Literature

I went to the woods because I wished to live deliberately, to front only the essential facts of life, and see if I could not learn what it had to teach, and not, when I came to die, discover that I had not lived. I did not wish to live what was not life, living is so dear; nor did I wish to practice resignation, unless it was quite necessary. I wanted to live deep and suck out all the marrow of life, to live so sturdily and Spartan-like as to put to rout all that was not life, to cut a broad swath and shave close, to drive life into a corner, and reduce it to its lowest terms, and if it proved to be mean, why then to get the whole and genuine meanness of it, and publish its meanness to the world; or if it were sublime, to know it by experience, and be able to give a true account of it in my next excursion.

— HENRY DAVID THOREAU, *Walden*

Social and political reform earmarked the early nineteenth century. No one represents the ideal of this reform better than Henry David Thoreau. He and many others like him, such as his mentor Ralph Waldo Emerson, scorned conventionalism. They questioned the values and ceremony of the time. They encouraged people to reevaluate what was important in life.

This nation thrived not only because it had gifted writers, leaders with vision, and inventors with genius, but also because it had ordinary people who became reformers and educators. Although not as well known as the writers and inventors, these reformers and educators cared enough about their fellow human beings to see that social injustices were attacked..

Chapter Overview

In this chapter, you will study four areas of great change and reform in our nation's history. First, new inventions helped to revolutionize American life. Second, attempts were made at social change, especially in religion and education. The third area was the rise of the abolition movement, which increased sectional controversy. Last, but certainly not least, the era saw the origin of women's struggle for equality—which continues to the present day. These areas will be discussed in four chapter sections.

Chapter Outline

1. **Inventions Improve American Life**
2. **Reformers Work for Social Changes**
3. **Americans Speak Out on Slavery**
4. **Women Struggle for Equality**

Core Lesson

Anticipate the Lesson

Have volunteers list on the board familiar household appliances. (Lists might include: dishwasher; food processor; vacuum cleaner; microwave oven.) Discuss with students how each makes life easier. Have students list on the board next to their list of household appliances the tool that Americans living between 1830 and 1850 might have used to accomplish a similar task. (Lists might include: bucket and water; knife; broom; fireplace.) Refer students to the list on the board and ask them how inventions have changed the lives of Americans.

State the Objective

Identify inventions and learn how they helped revolutionize American life between 1830 and 1850.

Inventions Improve American Life

GLOSSARY TERMS: **assembly line, telegraph**

During the first half of the 1800's, the standard of living in the United States, which had been fairly low during colonial years, took a big jump. Independence, followed by territorial expansion and the stimulus of the War of 1812, brought about changes and improvements for most white Americans. These were further reinforced by several significant inventions in agriculture, manufacturing, transportation, and communication.

Farming Becomes More Profitable

From the landing at Jamestown to the Revolutionary War, American farmers had continued to use traditional farming tools and methods. They turned the soil with wooden plows. They cut grain with hand sickles. They threshed grain by having oxen or mules trample out the seeds on a threshing floor.

In 1797 Charles Newbold patented a cast-iron plow. At first farmers were reluctant to use it because they were afraid that iron "poisoned the land." They soon found, however, that they were able to turn many more acres of soil than before.

Then settlers moved into the area we now call the Middle West. There they ran into a problem. Although they found the prairie soil to be very fertile, it was hard packed and difficult to plow.

A solution was found in 1837, when a blacksmith named **John Deere** invented the steel plow. It worked where the iron plow did not. Prairie soil does not contain stone and grit, so it sticks to

Picturing History The Deere plow became popular worldwide in the late 1800's because of its steel blades.

People in the Chapter

Samuel F. B. Morse quit painting around 1837 to devote himself to experimenting. When Ralph Waldo Emerson was told that Morse's telegraph made it possible for Maine to talk to Florida, Emerson replied, "Yes, but has Maine anything to *say* to Florida?"

Noah Webster published his *Compendious Dictionary of the English Language* only to find that many words in it were condemned by scholars as being vulgar New Englandisms. Among these "vulgar" words were *lengthy, spry, belittle,* and *caucus.*

Frederick Douglass, denied the opportunity to attend school, devised a method of learning from the white children in his neighborhood. In his autobiography he wrote: "I used to carry bread with me . . . .This bread I used to bestow on the hungry little urchins, who, in return, would give me that more valuable bread of knowledge."

Lucretia Mott was so talkative as a child that her mother called her Long Tongue. When as an adult she began to speak out against slavery, she met serious opposition. Nevertheless, she remained poised despite the hostility of her audiences. After the Fugitive Slave Law was passed, Lucretia and her husband opened their home to runaway slaves escaping on the Underground Railroad.

Emma Willard was one of seventeen children. With her father's encouragement, she managed to acquire an education "beyond that ordinarily thought proper for a girl." When she proposed a plan for improving the education of women, members of the legislature ridiculed her course of studies for girls as "contrary to God's will."

iron—but not to steel. Also, Deere's plow cut furrows at an angle instead of straight up and down. Soil offers less resistance to a slanting blade than it does to a vertical blade. Still another advantage of the steel plow was its lightness. It could be drawn by horses rather than oxen, and horses cover much more ground than slow-moving oxen. In 1847 Deere established a factory at Moline, Illinois. By the late 1850's, he was selling thirteen thousand of his plows each year.

Another invention enabled farmers to harvest more wheat than ever before. **Cyrus McCormick** patented a mowing and reaping machine in the early 1830's. McCormick's reaper became a tremendous success because it enabled farmers to do without large numbers of hired hands. The various parts of the reaper were packed and then shipped directly to the farmer, together with a handbook of directions for assembling and operating the machine. This invention, along with the steel plow and other inventions, raised wheat production in the United States so much that American farmers were soon exporting a surplus to Europe.

Picturing History An ad for the McCormick harvesting machine appears above. McCormick's reaper featured a knife that moved alternately back and forth.

Daily Life Becomes Easier

Americans also invented a variety of nonagricultural tools and processes, all of which improved the quality of American life.

Some directly affected daily life. For example, there was a special bit for cutting chunks of ice large enough to permit people to bring them into cities without melting. Having ice for refrigeration meant that city dwellers, as well as farmers, could enjoy fresh food. There was vulcanized rubber,

developed by **Charles Goodyear** in 1839. Not only did it protect boots and shoes from rain, snow, and mud, but—unlike the previously used India rubber—it did not become sticky or melt in hot weather.

Picturing History Elias Howe claimed Isaac Singer's sewing machine (left) infringed on the patent rights for his machine (above).

In 1846 **Elias Howe** patented the sewing machine. Originally, it was used in factories to make shoes. In 1851 **I. M. Singer** improved the sewing machine by inventing the foot treadle. These two inventions made life for the homemaker much easier. Now it took only half an hour, instead of four hours, to make and mend clothes. Even more important, clothing could now be mass-produced in factories. Prices tumbled by more than three-quarters, and even ordinary people could afford something that was store-bought.

Singer also made two notable contributions to marketing. He came up with the ideas of advertising his sewing machine in newspapers and magazines and of allowing customers to pay for their machines on the installment plan. His business boomed, and his ideas were soon adopted by other industries.

Among the new industries that developed during this period was the meat-packing industry. Many meat-packing plants used a method that became known as the **assembly line.** In these plants, an animal's carcass would slide down an inclined table. As it moved along, each worker would cut away a particular part. In a modern assembly line, a product moves along on a conveyor belt, and each worker performs one task in putting together the finished product.

Transportation Becomes Faster

The expansion of agriculture and industry created a demand for better transportation facilities.

For Discussion
To what extent did inventions of this period, 1800-1850, unify and nationalize the nation? (Possible responses: telegraph enabled people in all parts of the country to communicate quickly; canals and railroads connected remote areas and promoted migration and trade.)

Ask the recorder from the previous exercise to report to the class; students should feel free to contribute additional insights. (Group responses may include: telegraph is still in use but fax machines and computers now transmit data over phone lines; additional improvements have mechanized grain farms, but migrant workers continue to harvest some crops.)

Picturing History Robert Fulton was best known as the builder of the *Clermont* (above), the first steamboat to be a commercial success in America. His self-portrait appears in the inset.

Historical Sidelight
Robert Fulton built the first commercially successful steamboat in 1807. However, in 1787 John Fitch had built a boat propelled by paddles driven by a steam engine and in 1790 started the first regular steamboat service in the U.S. His boat could not carry heavy loads and was considered frivolous. Unable to make a profit, Fitch ended the service and died a disappointed man.

Farmers and manufacturers alike wanted faster, more direct ways of shipping their goods to market.

Boats Run by Steam. In 1804 Oliver Evans of Philadelphia designed a high-pressure steam engine that was less bulky and more adaptable to various uses than earlier versions. Evans claimed that he could build a steam-driven wagon that would be able ''to run on a level road against the swiftest horses.'' He could not find any financial backing, however, so he turned to other projects.

Robert Fulton of New York showed that the new steam engine could be made to propel a boat. In 1807 his *Clermont* made a 150-mile trip up the Hudson River from New York City to Albany in thirty-two hours. This successful demonstration marked the beginning of the steamboat era. The new method of transportation spread quickly to the Ohio and Mississippi rivers. Transportation on the Mississippi was particularly affected. Until this time, most travel on the river had been southward, with the current.

The steamboats were built of wood. They were propelled by a stern wheel or side wheels, and were fueled by logs from woodpiles along the riverbanks. They were an exciting sight as they moved along, their three decks riding high above the water and their smokestacks giving off both smoke and sparks. They were also dangerous; fires and boiler explosions were common.

By 1830 there were some two hundred steamboats on the western rivers flowing into the Mississippi. Both freight rates and voyage time dropped dramatically. Steamboats were put to work on some eastern rivers as well. Above all, the steamboat cemented the economic life of the North to that of the South. New Orleans became one of the nation's major ports.

Canals Speed Up Transportation. Even on the best of roads, transporting bulky products such as wheat was slow. Since waterways were more efficient, Americans set about creating them where they did not exist naturally. However, canals cost far more to build than roads. Because of the expense, most early canal projects were undertaken in the wealthier Northern states. (See the map of canals on page 293.)

In 1816 the country had one hundred miles of canals. Twenty-five years later it had more than thirty-three hundred. The granddaddy of these projects was the Erie Canal, which stretched a breathtaking 363 miles from Albany to Buffalo. It was ten times longer than any other American canal and the longest in the Western World at the time. Building it involved much more than simply digging a big ditch. Towpaths for oxen, horses, and mules had to be laid out along the canal's banks. The banks themselves had to be shored up with cement in many places to prevent the canal from

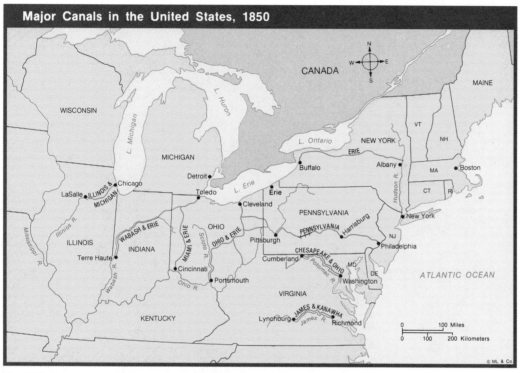

Major Canals in the United States, 1850

Map Skills **Movement** By the 1820's, many canals were being dug. Which one linked the Hudson River and Lake Erie? **Movement** How did the Illinois and Michigan Canal get its name?

Picturing History To open the Erie Canal, Governor De Witt Clinton used the keg at the left to pour water from Lake Erie into the Atlantic Ocean. The *Marriage of the Waters* (above) portrays the event.

becoming a muddy ditch. A system of locks was constructed that raised and lowered barges, since Lake Erie was slightly higher than the Hudson River at Albany.

The Erie Canal was an enormous success. Begun in 1817, it was completed in 1825. Within seven years, tolls paid off the cost of construction. Moreover, the cost of shipping goods through the canal was only one-tenth of what it was by road.

Dozens of other canal projects were less spectacularly successful, but many of them also paid off eventually. Now Ohio was no longer tied by the strings of commerce only to New Orleans. Ohio farmers could ship grain by canal and river to New York City, which became the nation's major port. Thus the canals helped bind the two sections of the North together, thereby opening the heartland of America to world markets.

In 1848 the Illinois and Michigan Canal linked Lake Michigan with the Mississippi River system. This canal led to the rise of Chicago as a great port, years before that city became an important railroad center.

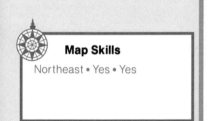

Map Skills

Northeast • Yes • Yes

Railroads in the United States, 1850

Map Skills **Region** What was the only part of the United States to have a
developed railway network in 1850? **Movement** Could a rail trip have been made
from Boston to Baltimore? to Buffalo?

Railroads Shrink the Country. During the
1830's, Americans began to experiment with the
new steam engine set on rails. They liked its speed.
By 1840 there was more than three thousand miles
of railroad track in the United States, most of it in
the Northeast. By 1850 there was almost ten
thousand miles of track, some of which was in
almost every state east of the Mississippi River. At
this time, most of the lines did not join one another,

so there was no national network. (See the map
above.)

Nevertheless, travel by rail gradually began to
replace travel by water. It was more expensive but
much faster. Freight could be hauled at an average
speed of eleven miles per hour. Passengers were
whisked along at the astonishing speed of thirty
miles per hour. European travelers objected to all
the cigar smoke and to the American habit of

Student Assignment/Homework

Have students read Section 2, "Reformers Work for Social Changes," and answer the Chapter 11, Section 2 Review questions on paper.

Picturing History For his telegraph (above), Samuel F. B. Morse (left) devised the Morse code.

spitting tobacco juice on the floors of the railroad cars. Nonetheless, the speed was thrilling.

Communication Improves

In addition to better transportation, the expanding American economy called for better means of communication. The two major inventions in this field were the **telegraph** and the rotary-cylinder printing press.

The telegraph was invented by Joseph Henry and improved by a New England painter named **Samuel F. B. Morse.** In 1844, with aid from the federal government, Morse set up a demonstration of his device. From Washington, D.C., he tapped out the words "What hath God wrought?" in code and sent them over an iron wire. Seconds later, the message was received in Baltimore and a reply was on its way.

Soon, business people everywhere were using the device to transmit orders and up-to-date information on prices and sales. Railroads used the telegraph to keep trains moving regularly and to warn engineers of safety hazards down the line. This is one reason why most telegraph poles were erected along the railroads' right of way, that is, the narrow strip of land on each side of the track that belongs to the railroad.

The telegraph also affected newspapers, by creating a demand for daily publication of the latest news. In 1847 Richard M. Hoe met that demand with a streamlined printing press that turned out eight thousand newspapers an hour.

The Nation Becomes More Interdependent

Each of these new developments contributed to the others. The growth of manufacturing stimulated

agriculture, because the industrial cities needed food. In return, American farmers stimulated industry. Farmers made fewer things of their own and bought more from the cities. Improved transportation and communication tied regions of the country more closely together.

Just as events overseas affected the American economy, so did events in one part of the nation affect the economy in other parts. For example, a rise in the price of hogs in Mississippi could raise the price of shoes (made of pigskin) in Alabama and the price of brushes (made of hog bristles) in Vermont.

Linking Past to Present

Inventions have contributed to the technological revolution of the twentieth century just as they contributed to the Industrial Revolution of the nineteenth century. Today, supersonic jets, satellites, mobile phones, personal computers, and fax machines have created a global village.

SECTION 1 REVIEW

Key Terms and People

Explain the significance of: John Deere, Cyrus McCormick, Charles Goodyear, Elias Howe, I. M. Singer, assembly line, Robert Fulton, telegraph, Samuel F. B. Morse

Main Ideas

1. How did the steel plow and the reaper make farming more profitable?
2. How did vulcanized rubber and the sewing machine improve people's daily lives?
3. How did Americans increase the speed and efficiency of transportation?
4. In general, what caused the regions of America to become more interdependent during the first half of the 1800's?

Critical Thinking

5. How did improvements in farming, transportation, and communication during the early 1800's affect life in the twentieth century?

State the Objective

Understand the importance of the reform movements in the U.S. prior to the Civil War.

Anticipate the Lesson

Ask students to suggest meanings for the word *reform*. Write all responses on the board. (Possible responses: change; improvement; replacement of old with new.) Ask why people might accept or reject various types of reform. (Possible responses: accept—economic need, unhappiness with present situation; reject—fear of unknown, economic pressure.)

SECTION 2

Reformers Work for Social Changes

GLOSSARY TERM: **utopian communities**

By 1830 several movements to reform society had sprung up in the United States. Individually or through organizations, thousands of Americans set out to fight a variety of social ills. Most of the reformers were middle-class Northerners—farmers, homemakers, business people, educators, and other professionals. Many of them became interested in reform for religious reasons. They saw social reform as a way of eliminating sin and creating a better, more moral world.

Religious Horizons Broaden

In 1831 on a visit to America, the Frenchman Alexis de Tocqueville (tōk'vil) noted that there was "no other country in the world where the Christian religion had a greater influence over the souls of men than in America."

The people of the United States had been deeply religious and mainly Protestant since the earliest settlements. There were hundreds of flourishing churches. In upstate New York, religious revivals were numerous. The fires of religious feeling burned so hot in the area that it became known as "the burned-over district." In the late 1700's and early 1800's, though, that religious feeling began to change, particularly in churches around Boston. There was a reaction against the emotional revivalism of preachers like George Whitefield and Jonathan Edwards. There also was a rejection of the stern Puritan and Calvinist view of the world. Many thought that humans were better than the Puritans believed them to be. Increasingly, ministers told people that they could be saved if they only believed in God. One of the ways they could show this belief was by trying to reform society. Groups of people formed new churches that would permit them to serve God by showing concern for human welfare.

Channing and the Unitarians. The stern Calvinist view of predestination had been questioned by many, but none objected to it more strongly than the Unitarians, a group of New England Congregationalists who eventually formed their own denomination. They also shocked other Christians by rejecting the Trinity and asserting that Jesus and God were two separate beings.

The principal spokesman of the Unitarians was William Ellery Channing. His pulpit eloquence and published writings won prominent Bostonians over to Unitarianism; his interest in social reform and his opposition to slavery extended his influence far beyond Boston. His close friends and protégés included Horace Mann, Dorothea Dix, and Ralph Waldo Emerson.

Education Expands

President James Madison once stated, "A people who mean to be their own governors must arm themselves with the power which knowledge gives." Most Americans probably agreed with him. However, the question of who should pay for educating the people was something else again.

The First Sixty Years. Before the 1850's, there was no uniform educational policy in the United States. Towns in New England maintained public schools that were open to all, although families who could afford it were expected to pay tuition. Many schools in the Middle States, such as New York and Pennsylvania, were private. They were run by church groups or independent citizens. In the South several planters would join together and hire a teacher for their children. In rural areas parents "subscribed" to a school; that is, they all chipped in, put up a building, and paid a teacher. Part of the pay often included room and board at a pupil's home.

School attendance was not compulsory, and even those who managed to attend school rarely went beyond the fourth grade. The curriculum consisted of reading, writing, and arithmetic. Schools were not divided into grades. While the younger pupils recited their lessons, the older ones were supposed to study. To make sure they did, teachers had a supply of birch rods with which to thrash anyone who misbehaved.

The most popular textbook was the *Blue-Backed Speller,* written by **Noah Webster,** who also compiled, in 1828, the famous dictionary. Webster was a strong believer in "American education for Americans." He tried to get people to talk less like the British and more like people in his native state of Connecticut. As a result of his efforts, the spelling of many words was simplified—for example, "plow" instead of "plough" and "labor" instead of "labour."

Present the Lesson

Review all the definitions of reform written on the board and decide on a general definition such as: *reform,* to improve by changing form or removing faults. Ask students to name the three major reform movements and their effects during the first half of the nineteenth century. (Responses should include: religion—work toward social justice, founding of Unitarian Church as a separate organization; education—public tax-supported schools; mental illness—more humane treatment; alcohol—American Temperance Society, prohibition in some states.)

Check for Understanding

Have students complete Chapter 11, Section 2 Daily Activity.

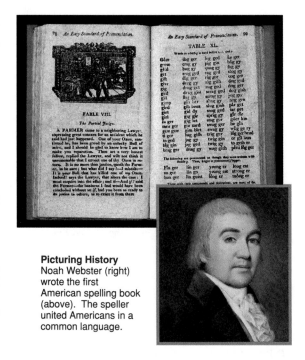

Picturing History
Noah Webster (right) wrote the first American spelling book (above). The speller united Americans in a common language.

Universal Public Education. By the 1830's, Americans had increased their demands for tax-supported public education for everyone. Pennsylvania passed the Free School Act in 1834, establishing a public school system that initially met with a storm of opposition. It came mostly from wealthy taxpayers who saw no reason to support schools that their children in private schools would not attend. Opposition also came from some German immigrants who were afraid that their children would forget the German language and culture. Within three years, however, about 42 percent of children who were of elementary-school age in Pennsylvania were attending a public school.

Massachusetts and other states were also in the vanguard of the movement for public education. By the 1850's every state had provided for a system of public elementary schools. In states farther west and in Southern states, however, it took years before schools were actually established. As a result, in 1860 only 15 percent of eligible children were attending school.

One of the leaders in the public school movement was **Horace Mann** of Massachusetts. In 1837 he became the first secretary of that state's board of education. Two years later he helped establish the first American college for training teachers.

Social Evils Are Attacked

Social reformers worked in other areas besides education. Two of these areas were the care of the mentally ill and the reforming of alcoholics.

Dorothea Dix and the Mentally Ill. The most outstanding figure in the first area was **Dorothea Dix,** who grew up in Boston and taught for a while at a fashionable girls' school. She became interested in the way insane people were treated after teaching a Sunday school class in a prison. A quiet and gentle, but very determined, person, she inspected the places where insane people were held. She found many such people in jails, where they were mixed in with criminals. She found others hidden away in closets, attics, or cellars. Almost everywhere, she found them "chained, naked, beaten with rods and lashed into obedience." In 1843 she sent a report of her findings to the Massachusetts legislature, which at first ignored her but later passed a law aimed at improving conditions.

Dix then visited other parts of the country. Between 1845 and 1852, she persuaded nine Southern states to set up public hospitals for the insane. As a result of her lobbying, the insane were housed in clean hospital rooms and were treated more humanely.

Down with "Demon Rum." During the colonial period, rum had played a major part in the triangular trade between West Africa, the West Indies, and New England. Other alcoholic drinks that were popular in the colonies included beer, wine, and

Picturing History
Dorothea Dix rescued the insane from prison chains.

An Era of Reform **297**

Guided Practice

Point out to students that political, religious, and social groups have continued to work for reform over the years. Ask students to name some current areas of reform. (Possible responses: civil rights; women's rights; tax reform.) Discuss with students the outcome of the alcohol prohibition movement of the 1920's, including gangster-controlled industry, widespread breaking of law, and the eventual repeal of prohibition laws. Ask students to compare these problems to those faced by current reformers in their attempts to control the use of drugs. (Possible responses: drug control problems—legalization versus tougher fines and penalties; breaking of laws; expense of enforcement.)

Assign Independent Practice

Ask students to reread James Madison's quote concerning education in this section and write a paragraph describing Madison's possible reaction to today's public education. (Paragraphs should include: to evaluate and vote for political leaders voters must be educated.) Ask some students to share their paragraphs with the class.

Student Assignment/Homework

Have students read Section 3, "Americans Speak Out on Slavery," and be prepared to discuss it in class.

cider. Americans found that drinking alcohol helped counterbalance the taste of the salted meat and fish that formed a basic part of their diet. Until anesthetics (substances that reduce pain) were developed in 1842, doctors would dose patients with whiskey or brandy before operating. It was also common for politicians to distribute free drinks to voters before an election.

By the 1800's, however, many people had begun to realize that drunkenness was a serious problem. The American Temperance Society, which tried to restrict the amount of liquor people consumed, was organized in 1826. Within a few years, there were about one thousand local temperance societies throughout the country. They held rallies and put out pamphlets. They organized children into clubs called "The Cold Water Armies." Lecturers went from town to town, describing through stories the dreadful results of drunkenness. One such story was about "a drunkard who fell into a pig sty. As the hogs grunted in alarm, he muttered, 'Hold your tongues; I'm as good as any of you.'"

The first state to prohibit the sale of liquor altogether was Maine. By 1857 twelve other states had done the same.

Linking Past to Present

The efforts to control the use of alcohol in the 1800's can be compared with current attempts to control the use of illegal drugs. Public service groups bought television time to warn Americans about the dangerous effects of drug and alcohol abuse. The national Drug Enforcement Administration intensified its crackdown on drug dealers. Numerous government-funded organizations helped those with drug and alcohol problems. Yet, as the slogan "Just say no!" implies, Americans have learned from the experience of the past that the individual rather than the state must take the primary responsibility in the war on substance abuse.

Utopian Communities. A number of individuals decided that the evils of society were too great to be dealt with by piecemeal reform. Small groups of men and women established their own **utopian communities,** or perfect societies, where they could live together in harmony. Sometimes all property was held in common. Sometimes children were raised in common. The two best-known communities were New Harmony, Indiana, and Brook Farm, near Boston. Although they aimed at perfection, most utopian communities got into financial difficulties and collapsed after a few years of struggle.

SECTION 2 REVIEW

Key Terms and People

Explain the significance of: Noah Webster, Horace Mann, Dorothea Dix, utopian communities

Main Ideas

1. How did religious changes in the United States lead to social reforms?
2. Describe the education policy in the United States before the 1850's.
3. Why did well-to-do taxpayers object to universal public education?
4. What changes in the care of the mentally ill resulted from Dorothea Dix's work?

Critical Thinking

5. During the first half of the 1800's, what goals did reformers have in common?

SECTION 3

Americans Speak Out on Slavery

GLOSSARY TERMS: **abolition, underground railroad**

Until about 1830, many men and women, most of them in the North but some in the South, believed that slavery would eventually disappear. However, as cotton became king and the demand for slave labor increased, these people grew uneasy. They began to call for an immediate end to slavery.

The Antislavery Movement Begins

The first antislavery society in the United States was formed in Philadelphia in 1775. By the 1820's there were about 143 societies throughout the country. Their members advocated a moderate approach to ending slavery. They favored gradual

SECTION 3
Core Lesson

Anticipate the Lesson
Conduct a general discussion on how the abolitionists affected Southern attitudes toward slavery.

State the Objective
Realize that the abolitionist movement led to increased sectional controversy.

emancipation and payment to slaveholders for the loss of property. Most of them were opposed to accepting free African Americans as equals. They believed that the solution lay in shipping all black Americans back to Africa.

There were free African Americans who also thought that their best hope was to go back to Africa. One such person was Paul Cuffee, a wealthy Massachusetts shipbuilder. He made a trip to Sierra Leone, on Africa's west coast, to investigate the possibility of founding an African American colony there. Then, in 1815 he chartered a ship at his own expense and carried thirty-eight African Americans to Africa. He quickly discovered, however, that the expense involved in founding a colony was more than one person could bear. Still, his efforts inspired others. Two years later, the American Colonization Society was organized. Among its supporters were such leading figures as Senators Henry Clay and Daniel Webster, Supreme Court Justice John Marshall, and President James Monroe. With help from the federal government, the society obtained some land in West Africa, which it named Liberia, meaning "place of freedom." Its capital was named Monrovia, after the President.

The American Colonization Society was popular and well financed. Nevertheless, by 1830 only about two hundred slaves had been freed and sent to Liberia. Some twelve thousand free African Americans, however, did eventually settle in Liberia.

Garrison Tries to Change Public Opinion

On the Fourth of July, 1829, a young man with wire-rimmed glasses stepped up to the pulpit of the Park Street Church in Boston to deliver an address. His name was **William Lloyd Garrison,** and his message was both new and revolutionary.

Garrison asserted that blacks were not Africans but Americans and that they were not subjects but citizens: "This is their country by birth, not by adoption." Accordingly, African Americans were entitled to the same rights set forth in the Declaration of Independence as other Americans were, and until African Americans obtained those rights, "the American Revolution was not yet over." Garrison did not advocate using force to get rid of slavery. He was, in fact, a pacifist. He believed the answer lay in constitutional changes brought about by public opinion. Since the population of the free

Picturing History
William Lloyd Garrison published and edited *The Liberator,* a weekly newspaper dedicated to the abolition of slavery.

states was nearly double that of the slave states, it remained only to convince Northerners that slavery was a sin and must be removed at once.

Therefore, Garrison set out to change public opinion. On New Year's Day, 1831, the first issue of his weekly newspaper, *The Liberator,* appeared in Boston. Garrison was both publisher and editor. Of its first 2,300 subscribers, some 1,725 were free African Americans. Garrison's main financial backers and salespeople also were African Americans.

In the first issue of *The Liberator*, Garrison called for the immediate and unconditional **abolition,** or ending, of slavery.

> I am aware that many object to the severity of my language; but is there not cause for severity? . . . On this subject, I do not wish to think or speak or write with moderation. No! No! Tell a man whose house is on fire to give a moderate alarm . . . tell the mother to gradually extricate [remove] her babe from the fire into which it has fallen—but urge me not to use moderation in a cause like the present. I am in earnest. . . . I will not retreat a single inch—AND I WILL BE HEARD.

And heard he was, for thirty-five years, until the last slave was free.

Nat Turner Leads a Revolt

The same year *The Liberator* began publication, the bloodiest slave rebellion in American history broke out in Virginia's Southampton County. South-

On the board briefly outline the growth of the antislavery movement from 1775 to 1850.

1775	Philadelphians organize the first anti-slavery society.
1815	African Americans migrate from the U.S. to Sierra Leone, Africa.
1817	Americans form the American Colonization Society.
1829	William Lloyd Garrison speaks out against slavery.
1831	Garrison publishes *The Liberator*.
1831	Nat Turner leads a revolt.
1833	Americans found the American Anti-slavery Society.
1841	Frederick Douglass lectures against slavery.

Check for Understanding

Discuss Section 3 Review questions with students.

erners promptly blamed it on the writings of Garrison, and a price was put on his head.

Actually, the revolt was born in the mind of a black slave named **Nat Turner.** Turner had been taught to read and write by his parents. When he was about twenty-five years old, he fled from his master's plantation after a severe flogging and spent a month in the Virginia woods. However, instead of following his father's example and fleeing north, he decided to return to slavery. Apparently, while in the woods, he experienced a vision in which God told him that his task on earth was to "lead and organize his fellow slaves in a struggle for freedom."

For six years Nat Turner preached to the slaves with whom he worked in the fields. Then, on February 12, 1831, there was a partial eclipse of the sun. Turner took this as a sign that the time was ripe. Six months later, he led some fifty or sixty slaves in attacks against a number of plantation houses. The first four attacks resulted in the death of fifty-five whites. By the time the fifth house was attacked, however, the alarm had been given. The whites were armed and ready, and the members of Turner's band were either captured or killed.

Turner himself hid out for several weeks. He was finally taken, tried, and hanged. Southern states then forbade the circulation within their borders of printed antislavery material.

Douglass Urges Nonviolence

In 1833 Garrison helped found the American Anti-slavery Society. By 1840 the organization boasted some 600 local groups and 200,000 members. Among its most effective lecturers were former slaves who had escaped to freedom. Probably the most outstanding of these was **Frederick Douglass.**

Douglass was born a slave in 1817. He was taught to read and write by the wife of one of his owners. Later he continued to study on his own, buying books with the money he earned when not working for his owners. In 1838, while employed in a Baltimore shipyard, he decided to make a break for freedom. He borrowed the identity of a friend, a free black merchant seaman. Dressed as a sailor and carrying an official "protection" paper indicating that he was not a slave, Douglass took a train to Philadelphia and stepped out a free man. As he later wrote in his autobiography, "A new world had opened upon me. . . . I lived more in one day than in a year of my slave life."

In 1841 Garrison invited Douglass to become a lecturer for the American Anti-slavery Society. Douglass, a superb speaker, thrilled his audiences with the power of his words. His hope was that abolition would come about without violence. In fact, he believed that abolition was the only way to prevent violence: "Let us not forget that justice to the Negro is safety to the nation." Douglass also started a newspaper called *The North Star*. It was named after the steady star that runaway slaves used as a guide as they fled northward to freedom.

Sojourner Truth Tells Her Story

Frequently Frederick Douglass shared the speaker's platform with Sojourner Truth, a former slave. Sojourner Truth had a deep voice and a simple

Picturing History Sojourner Truth (right) and Frederick Douglass (far right) were leading abolitionists who also distinguished themselves in other areas of reform.

Guided Practice

Have students prepare a two-column chart listing arguments for and against slavery. In class
discussion, use these charts to help students
understand the views of both sides.

For

- South needed labor force.
- Institution was both social and economic.
- Was a positive good.
- African Americans were neither social nor
  political equals.

- Slaves were property.
- There was prejudice against African Americans.
- Freed slaves might become wandering bandits.

Against

- African Americans were people with the
  same rights and responsibilties as others.
- African Americans were Americans entitled
  to the rights listed in the Declaration of Independence.
- Slavery was morally wrong.

message and at times rivaled Douglass in eloquence. William Lloyd Garrison wrote a preface to *The Narrative of Sojourner Truth* by Olive Gilbert, which won widespread support for the abolitionist cause.

Harriet Tubman Joins the Underground Railroad

Another slave who helped in the cause of freedom was **Harriet Tubman.** Like Douglass, Tubman had escaped from slavery in Maryland, but she returned there time and again to assist some three hundred other slaves in their flight to freedom.

In doing so, Tubman became a leading "conductor" on the so-called **underground railroad.** This was a network of persons—men and women, white and black—who helped fugitive slaves on their way north. They provided such things as hiding places, food, dry clothing, money, and guides. Although they risked being fined and imprisoned for breaking the law, they felt that their obligation to "the law of God" was more important.

Historians do not know for certain how many "running abolitionists" escaped from slavery before the Civil War. Thousands did, but not enough to undermine the institution of slavery.

Opposition to Abolition Grows

There was fierce opposition in the South to the abolition of slavery. The abolitionists were attacking the South's most important social and eco-

Focus on Biography

Harriet Tubman (1820–1913)

A sharp blow on the head at the age of thirteen caused Harriet Tubman to suffer dizziness and fainting spells for the rest of her life. Harriet's master had struck her because she had tried to help another slave who was being mistreated. The punishment did not stop Harriet Tubman from helping her people then or for the rest of her life.

From her birth in 1820 until she ran away in 1849, Harriet lived in the border state of Maryland. In 1849 she escaped to Philadelphia by means of the underground railroad. (See above.) As an escaped slave, Harriet could have lived quite safely in the free states. Instead, time and again she returned to the South and led others through woods and swamps to freedom.

Two of Tubman's brothers had set out with her on her first escape in 1849, but turned back before reaching freedom. Of

course, this endangered everyone in the party. Thereafter, when she was leading a party and some of her charges became tired, frightened, or discouraged and wished to turn back, Harriet Tubman used every means to drive them forward. If all else failed, she threatened to shoot the fainthearted, telling them, "You'll be free or die!"

It is estimated that, one way or another, Harriet Tubman led at least three hundred runaway slaves to freedom. Slave owners paid her the compliment of offering a reward of $40,000 for her capture. It was an enormous sum, but the "property" Tubman had deprived them of was worth ten times that amount.

Nearly all the conductors on the underground railroad in the North were white people. They ran some risk of being arrested, fined, or imprisoned if caught by federal authorities. However,

there was no comparison between the dangers they faced and those braved by conductors in the South. The Southern conductors were nearly all black, often themselves runaways. Many of them were women. A beating and a return to the conditions from which they had escaped was a certainty for any of them who might be captured in a slave state.

Tubman made only one boast about her activities. She said, "I never ran my train off the track, and I never lost a passenger."

When the Civil War began, Tubman followed the Union armies south. Along the Carolina coast, she worked as a nurse and as a Union spy. Her ability to move undetected through the countryside served her and her people well once again.

Have students choose one of the following
people and write two paragraphs on the role
he or she played in the antislavery crusade:
Nat Turner, Frederick Douglass, Harriet Tubman, William Lloyd Garrison. (Paragraphs
might include: Turner led a slave revolt in 1831;
Douglass lectured for the American Antislavery Society; Tubman helped runaway
slaves; Garrison was a Northern abolitionist
and publisher of *The Liberator*.) Students
should also read Section 4, "Women Struggle
for Equality."

For Discussion
How did the 1960's move-
ment to include positive
achievements of African
Americans in social studies
materials affect education?
(Possible responses: in-
creased African Americans'
awareness of their heritage,
developed pride; other minorities wanted their accomplishments included also.)

nomic institution. However, there was also strong
resistance to abolition in the North.

Prejudice Against Blacks. Many Northerners
viewed abolitionists as fanatics who were out to
wreck the Union. During the 1830's, mobs attacked abolitionist meetings. They burned Pennsylvania Hall in Philadelphia prior to just such a
meeting there. A mob of citizens in Boston threatened Garrison's life. Elijah P. Lovejoy, an abolitionist editor in Alton, Illinois, was murdered by a
mob that attacked him and threw his printing press
into the Mississippi River.

Why was there such hostility in the North? Apart
from the sincere belief that abolitionists were
wrecking the Union, there was a more widespread
underlying reason—prejudice against blacks. Free
blacks in the North were subject to all kinds of
discrimination. In many states they could not vote
or go to school with whites. Most blacks could get
only the lowest-paying jobs. Many white Northerners simply had no interest in a movement to give
rights to black slaves. Even some of the abolitionists did not think that blacks could ever be the
social and political equals of white people.

Slavery Is Declared a "Positive Good." Before
1830 many white people in the South thought of
slavery as a "necessary evil." They would have
liked to do away with it, but they could not do so.
Slaves, they argued, were property, and people
should not have their property taken away without
their consent. Also, they feared that freed slaves
would become wandering bandits who would endanger the lives of all white people.

After about 1830, however, white Southerners'
views on slavery changed rapidly. This was partly
in response to the increased abolitionist agitation,
which infuriated Southerners. A more important
reason, though, was that after 1830 the South
became increasingly dependent on cotton for its
economic prosperity, and cotton producers became
increasingly dependent on slaves to cultivate the
crop.

Now the South could not abolish slavery without
suffering what it considered an unbearable economic loss. About this time Southerners began
declaring that slavery, far from being a "necessary
evil," was in fact a "positive good."

Black people in the South were much better off,
said the defenders of slavery, than were black people
in the North. Virginia's George Fitzhugh wrote several books claiming that Northerners practiced "wage
slavery," which was far worse than anything that
existed in the South. Northern wage earners, he said,
were totally at the mercy of their employers. When
sick or old, they were simply thrown out of work.
Fitzhugh argued that Southern slaves were much
better off since their owners took care of them in
sickness and in old age.

It was not long thereafter that Southerners began
to describe their slaves as happy and contented.
Indeed, they described the slaves as loving people
who were devoted to their masters. Thus, in the
face of a great deal of evidence to the contrary,
white Southerners firmly decided that black people
were happy in their bondage. They thereby created
a myth that did not begin to break down until many
years later.

Picturing History The stylized
painting shows slaves dancing in a
festive mood. The photograph taken
of the whip-scarred back of a slave
presents another view of slavery.

Anticipate the Lesson

Have students list on the board the problems faced by women in the early nineteenth century. (List should include: they could not vote or sit on juries; a woman's property became her husband's when she married; there were no educational opportunities or protection from physical abuse.)

SECTION 3 REVIEW

Key Terms and People

Explain the significance of: William Lloyd Garrison, abolition, Nat Turner, Frederick Douglass, Harriet Tubman, underground railroad

Main Ideas

1. What did the American Colonization Society attempt to do in Liberia?
2. How did William Lloyd Garrison's beliefs differ from those of most early abolitionists?
3. How did Southern states react to Nat Turner's slave rebellion?
4. In what ways did Northerners discriminate against African Americans?
5. What circumstances caused white Southerners to view slavery as a positive good?

Critical Thinking

6. Briefly argue for or against the following statement: Nat Turner's rebellion was justified.

Picturing History
Sarah Grimké (above left), Angelina Grimké (above right), and Lucretia Mott (left) were abolitionists who helped launch the movement for women's rights.

SECTION 4

Women Struggle for Equality

GLOSSARY TERM: **women's rights movement**

To many people, one of the most disturbing things about the abolition movement was the active involvement of women. Female speakers sat on the same platforms with men. Some, like **Lucretia Mott** and the sisters **Sarah Grimké** and **Angelina Grimké,** became famous as eloquent spokeswomen for the antislavery movement. Hundreds and then thousands of women began attending abolitionist meetings. They raised money, distributed literature, and collected signatures on petitions to Congress.

These women met a great deal of opposition. Southern spokesmen denounced the sexually mixed meetings. Many men in the North also thought that women were getting out of hand. A group of New England clergymen announced that when a woman "assumes the place and tone of a man as a public reformer . . . her character becomes unnatural." That did not stop the women, however. Many saw the abolitionist cause as one that would help them as well. As Abby Kelley Foster, reformer and wife of composer Stephen Foster, said, "We have good

cause to be grateful to the slave. . . . In striving to strike his irons off, we found most surely, that we were manacled [chained] ourselves."

Laws Limit Women's Rights

Foster was right. Many laws limited the rights of women. They could not vote or sit on juries. When a woman married, her property became her husband's. Any money she earned had to be turned over to her husband. She was not even entitled to protection against physical abuse. A husband had the legal right to beat his wife with "a reasonable instrument," which a Massachusetts judge defined as a "stick no thicker than my thumb."

Custom as well as law limited women's rights. Probably most Americans regarded women as weak and as intellectually inferior to men. At the same time, they believed that women were morally superior to men. Accordingly, a woman's proper place was in the home, where she could guard the family's morals and give religious training to the children. Since these beliefs about women were so firmly held, it was especially shocking to hear a woman challenge them. Sarah Grimké, for one, did so as early as 1838, declaring that man "has done all he could to . . . enslave her mind" and that now he calls her "his inferior." She continued, "All I

SECTION 3 REVIEW

Answers

Main Ideas

1. Attempted to set up a colony for freed slaves.

2. He viewed African Americans not as Africans but as American citizens.

3. Printed antislavery material was banned in the Southern states; Southern hostility toward abolitionists increased.

4. Through voting restrictions; separate, inferior education; low-paying jobs.

5. Increasing economic dependence on cotton; reaction to abolitionists.

Critical Thinking

6. Possible answer: for—it was justified because African Americans suffered inhuman living and working conditions and had no legal avenues for change. **(evaluation)**

Present the Lesson

Review with students the advances made by women in education, health, and industry during the 1800's. List the advances on the board. (List might include: education—high schools, colleges, schools for black women; health—less restrictive clothing, women doctors, hospital care for women; industry—organizations for women workers, sick funds, classes.) Divide the class into small groups. Have the groups refer to the list as they discuss the changes that have lessened or eliminated the problems women faced in the early nineteenth century. (Discussion might include: right to vote; joint property laws; strict abuse laws; entrance to colleges and universities.)

Check for Understanding

Have students name four major women leaders of the early nineteenth century and explain an important contribution of each. (Possible responses: Emma Willard opened first high school for girls; Mary Lyon founded first women's college; Myrtilla Miner founded school for black women teachers; Elizabeth Smith Miller reformed women's clothing; Amelia Bloomer published women's rights paper; Elizabeth Blackwell became first woman doctor in the U.S.; Elizabeth and Emily Blackwell founded New York Infirmary for Women and Children; Lucretia Mott and Elizabeth Cady Stanton planned first women's rights convention.)

Picturing History
Colleges for women were unheard of until Mary Lyon founded Mount Holyoke, which opened in 1837.

ask of our brethren is that they will take their feet from off our necks and permit us to stand upright.''

Women Take Responsibility for Change

Women's first attempts to improve their status were directed toward certain areas of immediate concern. These included education, health, and working conditions in the industrial marketplace.

Change in Education. Until the 1820's, women who wanted a high school education were more or less out of luck. As Sarah Grimké observed, a woman was considered sufficiently learned if she knew "chemistry enough to keep the pot boiling, and geography enough to know the location of the different rooms in her house." Then in 1821 **Emma Willard** opened the nation's first high school for girls in Troy, New York. The curriculum included mathematics, history, geography, languages, art and music, and English writing and literature, as well as domestic sciences. Despite tremendous ridicule—"They will be educating the cows next," people said mockingly—Willard's school prospered.

In 1837 it became possible for women in the United States to attend college. The first women's college, Mount Holyoke Female Seminary, was founded in South Hadley, Massachusetts, by **Mary Lyon.** That same year, Oberlin College in Ohio admitted four women, thus becoming the nation's first coeducational college.

The education of black women was even more limited than that of white women. In 1831 Prudence Crandall, a white Quaker, opened a school for girls in Canterbury, Connecticut. One of her pupils, Sarah Harris, was an African American. The townspeople protested so vigorously against this mixing of the races that in 1833 Crandall decided to have black pupils only. This aroused even more opposition. The following year Crandall was forced to close her school and move away. In 1851 a white woman named Myrtilla Miner started a school in Washington, D.C., to train black women as teachers. In general, however, education for black women had to wait until after the Civil War.

Change in Health. The state of women's health was as poor as the state of their education. Bathing was uncommon and outdoor exercise rare. As for clothing: "Fashionable ladies wore tightly laced corsets lined with whalebone stays which tended to force the lungs up into the chest cavity, making breathing difficult and fainting common. They also wore several petticoats and long skirts that dragged on the floor or street."

Elizabeth Smith Miller, who liked to garden, tried to reform women's clothing with a "short dress." This was a dress or skirt that came about four inches below the knee and was worn over loose-fitting pants tied at the ankles. **Amelia Bloomer,** publisher of a women's rights paper called *The Lily,* wrote an article describing the costume and was promptly swamped with requests for sewing patterns. Gradually the costume became known as *bloomers.* Few women, however, had the courage to wear it outside the home.

Picturing History
Amelia Bloomer in her bloomers.

Elizabeth Blackwell took a different approach to women's health. In 1849 she became the first woman to receive a degree in medicine in the United States. Unable to get practical experience here, she went to Paris. When she returned, her private practice was very slow to develop. Finally, she and her sister, Emily Blackwell, opened their own medical clinic, the New York Infirmary for Women and Children.

Change in the Marketplace. The 1830's and 1840's also saw increasing numbers of women

304

Guided Practice

Tell students that some people feel the women's movement still has not achieved its economic goals. Many women's organizations point out that women earn about sixty-four cents to every dollar earned by a man for comparable work. Ask students for suggestions on correcting such economic inequalities. (Possible responses: laws; media exposure; pressure from women's groups; pressure from women in management.)

Assign Independent Practice

Have students answer Section 4 Review questions in small groups. Discuss their answers. Have students complete Chapter 11, Section 4 Daily Activity.

Student Assignment/Homework

Have students answer Chapter 11 Review questions on paper. Go over the material with the class.

Concluding the Chapter

Ask students which areas of reform mentioned in the chapter still offer cause for concern today. (Possible responses: expanding educational opportunities; mental health.) Ask students what areas of concern today differ from those of 1830 to 1850. (Possible responses: issues such as AIDS and drug abuse.)

moving into the industrial labor force. By 1850 about one-fourth of the nation's manufacturing workers were women. Most were employed in textile mills. Others sewed, made straw hats, bound shoes, or worked as compositors in printing shops. In most instances they received between one-fourth and one-half the wages that men did for the same kind of work. Their hours, however, were equally long: usually fourteen hours a day, six days a week.

Some women tried to organize in order to improve their working conditions. In Philadelphia, for example, women workers from different industries formed a citywide organization in 1835. The Female Improvement Society for the City and County of Philadelphia succeeded in gaining some wage increases but then went out of existence. In Massachusetts, women textile workers organized the Lowell Female Labor Reform Association in 1844. Its main goal was a ten-hour day, which it failed to achieve. It did, however, set up sick funds for its members, organize a library, hold classes, and publish a newspaper called *Voice of Industry*.

A Women's Rights Movement Begins

In 1840 a single incident sparked the beginning of a formal **women's rights movement.** Lucretia Mott and **Elizabeth Cady Stanton** traveled with other abolitionists to the World's Anti-slavery Convention in London. Once there, the two women were refused proper seating because of their sex, despite the protests of Garrison and some other American men.

Mott and Stanton began thinking about organizing a convention back in the United States, a convention that would be devoted solely to women's rights. Since neither wanted to abandon the cause of the slave, however, it took them several years to accomplish their aim. Finally, in 1848 the women's rights convention was held at Seneca Falls, New York. Two hundred sixty women and forty men gathered there and elected Frederick Douglass to chair the meeting.

The convention boldly issued a Declaration of Sentiments, which was carefully modeled on the Declaration of Independence. It began, "We hold these truths to be self-evident: that all men and women are created equal." Then the group passed a series of resolutions that denounced the many unfair legal restrictions on women. All but one passed unanimously. The exception was the reso-

Picturing History Elizabeth Cady Stanton is pictured with her daughter and granddaughter.

lution demanding that women be given the right to vote.

Why was there opposition to this one resolution? Some people at the convention, even though a minority, were afraid that such a demand would create too much anger and ridicule on the part of the American people.

In any event, the convention marked the start of a national campaign for women's equality. The campaign still continues.

SECTION 4 REVIEW

Key Terms and People

Explain the significance of: Lucretia Mott, Sarah Grimké, Angelina Grimké, Emma Willard, Mary Lyon, Amelia Bloomer, Elizabeth Blackwell, women's rights movement, Elizabeth Cady Stanton

Main Ideas

1. In the early 1800's, what rights of women were limited by law?
2. What obstacles did Elizabeth Blackwell face after she became the first woman to receive a medical degree in the United States?
3. What 1840 incident sparked the beginnings of a formal women's rights movement?
4. In general, what did the resolutions passed at the women's rights convention in 1848 denounce?

Critical Thinking

5. Evaluate the significance of the opening sentence of the Declaration of Sentiments for women of that time.

SECTION 4 REVIEW

Answers

Main Ideas

1. Women could not vote, sit on juries, own property if they were married, or obtain legal protection from physical abuse by their husbands.
2. Had to go abroad to get practical experience; was not accepted when she returned so opened her own clinic.
3. Refusal to seat Lucretia Mott and Elizabeth Cady Stanton at the World's Antislavery Convention because of their sex.
4. Unfair legal restrictions on women.

Critical Thinking

5. Possible answer: supported and encouraged women because it duplicated the basic wording of the Declaration of Independence but declared men *and women* equal; it also implied that women planned to struggle for their rights within the American system. (evaluation)

State the Objective

Compare ideas of nineteenth-century reformers.

Present the Lesson

Ask students to identify key social concerns in each of the documents. On the board, list their responses, horizontally, as column heads. (List should include: Mental Health; Crime; Homelessness; Women's Rights; Education.) Divide the class into groups, one for each concern listed. Have each group identify the solution suggested in the readings. Then have a member from each group write the solution under the appropriate heading on the board. (Solutions might include: Emerson stressed love and acceptance to combat criminal behavior; the Shakers took in orphans and the homeless;

legislative groups recommended free public education to lessen crime and reinforce good citizenship; women demanded economic, political, and educational equality; Dix believed that the insane should be treated humanely.)

Focus on Primary Sources

Reformers of the Early 1800's

The United States has known several periods of reform and social change. Each was ushered in by sweeping technological advances. The steam engine, the railroad, and the telegraph might appear tame when compared to atomic energy, space travel, and the computer, but the effect was much the same. Both altered American life in ways undreamed of until that time. If such wonders were possible, thoughtful people asked, was anything impossible?

Excerpts from two great American reformers are printed below. In addition, an eyewitness account that describes a religious reform movement as well as two historical documents on nineteenth-century reforms are presented as primary source materials.

Read these excerpts carefully. Be aware that reformers often present a one-sided view and that more than one viewpoint might be possible. Then answer the questions that follow.

These words of Ralph Waldo Emerson might have been written in 1969 as well as in 1841.

> In the history of the world the doctrine of reform had never such scope as at the present hour. . . .
> We are to revise the whole of our social structure, the state, the school, religion, marriage, trade, science, and explore their foundations. . . . What is a man born for but to be a reformer, a remaker of what man has made, a renouncer of lies, a restorer of truth and good?
> . . . There will dawn erelong on our politics, on our modes of living, a nobler morning . . . in the sentiment of love. This is the one remedy for all ills. . . . We make, by [our] distrust, the thief, and burglar, and incendiary, and by our court and jail we keep him so. . . . [L]ove . . . would bring the felon and outcast to our side in tears.

Source: Ralph Waldo Emerson, "Man the Reformer," *The Dial* (April, 1841), vol. 1, 523, 534–537.

In 1843, Dorothea Dix (page 297), a teacher and hospital worker, appealed to the state legislature for better treatment of the insane.

> I come to present the strong claims of suffering humanity. I come to place before the legislature of Massachusetts the condition of the miserable, the desolate, the outcast. I come as the advocate of helpless, forgotten, insane, and idiotic men and women: of beings sunk to a condition from which the most unconcerned would start with real horror; of beings wretched in our prisons, and more wretched in our almshouses. . . .
> I proceed, gentlemen, briefly to call your attention to the *present* state of insane persons confined within this Commonwealth in *cages, closets, cellars, stalls, pens! Chained, naked, beaten with rods,* and *lashed into obedience!* [Miss Dix went on to describe conditions she had found in twenty-eight Massachusetts communities.]

Source: Dorothea Dix, "Memorial to the Legislature of Massachusetts," *Old South Leaflet* Number 148 (Leaflet Committee, Boston: Old South Meetinghouse, 1843).

The Shakers were a religious group with several communities in America by the 1850's. Here is a description of a Shaker village in Ohio.

> [They were] a community of two or three hundred industrious persons, all engaged in agriculture and useful manufactures, paying no rents, having no costly vices, producing for themselves all the necessaries of life, and selling their surplus produce. Men, women, and children all work. There are no idlers, and no time is lost. As the honesty of the Shakers is proverbial, they have command of the best markets for their wooden wares, agricultural implements, brooms, garden seeds, preserved fruits and vegetables, and the surplus of their cloth, leather, etc. . . .

306

Check for Understanding

Discuss students' responses to the questions. Ask students to describe social concerns in our society today and to suggest some solutions. (Possible responses: problems—drugs; homelessness; unemployment; crime; poor education. Solutions—increased federal money for education, housing, and correctional institutions; private and governmental efforts to solve problems of crime, drugs, and education; passage of laws that support equal rights.)

As there are no marriages, all the men and women living together like brothers and sisters, their only increase is by the accession of new members from "the world," or by taking in orphan and destitute children, sometimes children from the workhouse. People with whom the world has dealt hardly, widows, or wives deserted by drunken husbands, with families of children, go to the Shakers. They are never turned away.

Source: Thomas Low Nichols, *Forty Years of American Life, 1821–1861* (London, 1871). Reprinted in Henry Steele Commager, ed., *The Heritage of America* (Boston: Little Brown, 1939), 439–440.

In 1834, a committee of the Pennsylvania legislature recommended a system of free public schools.

In a republican government, no voter should be without the rudiments of learning; for aside from political considerations, education purifies the morals, and lessens crime. Investigators who visit our jails have ascertained [found] that more than half the convicts are unable to read. It is better to avert [prevent] crime, by giving instruction to our youth, than punish them when men, as ignorant convicts.

Source: Reprinted in Richard Brown, ed., *The Human Side of American History* (Boston: Ginn, 1962), 90–91.

At the Seneca Falls, New York, Women's Rights Convention, in 1848, a Declaration of Sentiments was adopted (page 305). It carefully followed the form and language of the Declaration of Independence, including these words:

We hold these truths to be self-evident: that all men and women are created equal. . . .

The history of mankind is a history of repeated injuries and usurpations on the part of man toward woman, having in direct object the establishment of an absolute tyranny over her. . . .

He has never permitted her to exercise her inalienable right to the elective franchise [to vote].

He has compelled her to submit to laws, in the formation of which she had no voice.

Picturing History Shaker furniture and woodenware is characterized by its simple, handsome design. It is as admired today as it was in the 1800's.

He has withheld from her rights which are given to the most ignorant and degraded men—both natives and foreigners. . . .

He has made her, if married, in the eye of the law, civilly dead.

He has taken from her all right in property, even to the wages she earns. . . .

He has monopolized nearly all the profitable employments, and from those she is permitted to follow, she receives but a scanty remuneration. . . .

He has denied her the facilities for obtaining a thorough education, all colleges being closed against her.

Source: Reprinted in Irwin Glasker and Richard M. Ketchum, eds., *American Testament, Fifty Great Documents of American History* (New York: American Heritage, 1971), 110–111.

Analyzing Primary Sources

1. What reform movements do these primary sources represent? What do these movements have in common?
2. Which reformers do you find most persuasive? Why?
3. Describe at least three parallels between these reform movements and those being advocated today.

Critical Thinking

4. Might there be more than one viewpoint on any of these reform issues? Explain.

Answers

Analyzing Primary Sources

1. The sources represent reform movements for a reshaping of society along the idealistic, utopian lines; for better treatment of the insane; for better education for all; and for women's rights. • All movements attempted to better society and in some way to protect and improve human rights and the human condition.

2. Possible answers: reformers whose causes were most like those of the present time probably will have the greatest appeal to students.

3. Possible answers: some communes started in the 1960's are still in existence; the search for innovative approaches to education is ongoing; concern for homeless people has been renewed; and interest in women's rights continues to be important.

Critical Thinking

4. Possible answers: yes—in the early 1800's, many Americans believed the insane to be evil rather than sick and believed in punishment and discipline as a cure for mental illness; some people believed that education was the responsibility of the individual, not the government. **(synthesis)**

Answer Key

Key Terms and People

These are highlighted in the text in the order in which they appear in this list.

Main Ideas

1. The steel plow and reaper allowed farmers to produce a surplus of grain, which was sold outside the country; the sewing machine made possible mass production of clothing. Both inventions made life easier, created more products to buy.

2. Food grown in one part of the country was transported and traded for manufactured goods in another part; telegraph made it possible to order goods faster.

➤3. Webster wanted to Americanize pronunciation and spelling. • *Labour, labor; colour; color*

4. Using alcohol, such as rum, for trade resulted in increased alcoholism.

5. To abolish slavery without violence. • William Lloyd Garrison.

6. Southerners whose way of life was threatened, Northerners who believed abolitionists would wreck the Union, and people who were prejudiced against African Americans.

7. Vote, sit on juries, go to college, own property.

8. Women began to share leadership with men in antislavery societies. • They discovered they were enslaved too when men objected to their assertiveness. • Lucretia Mott, Sarah Grimké, Angelina Grimké learned to organize by working in the antislavery movement.

Critical Thinking Questions

➤9. Wanted to learn from living alone in the woods.
• Wanted to find out what was positive about life. • Agree—want to learn how to live on one's own to the fullest;

disagree—need people around to learn how to live fully.

10. Steel plow made plowing easier and put more land into production; reaper increased production; vulcanized rubber gave farmer protection from mud, rain, and snow; sewing machine created clothing faster. All inventions improved life for the farmer.

11. The inventions created jobs in industries making the items: steel, clothing, rubber

protective clothing, and transportation; jobs were also created in marketing and selling these items.

➤12. Steel plows made it easy to farm more Indian lands; steamboats and railroads carried settlers to Indian lands; vulcanized rubber and sewing machines had little effect.

➤13. Religion, education, and social reform.

14. Possible answer: people

must be educated so they can fulfill their responsibilities as citizens and evaluate government officials.

15. Her hatred of slavery and her desire to make escape possible for others.

Critical Thinking Activities

16. Sewing machine, steel plow, reaper, ice cutter. • By train and boat.

17. Possible answers: by road

CHAPTER 11 REVIEW

Write your answers on a separate sheet of paper.

Key Terms and People

Explain the significance of: I.M. Singer, assembly line, Samuel F.B. Morse, utopian communities, Nat Turner, Emma Willard, Mary Lyon, Amelia Bloomer, Elizabeth Blackwell

Main Ideas

1. How did the inventions of the steel plow, the reaper, and the treadle sewing machine affect the American standard of living?
2. How did steamboats, railroads, and the telegraph make the country interdependent?
3. Why do British and American spellings differ? Give some examples.
4. What problem in society caused the formation of the American Temperance Society?
5. Why was the American Anti-slavery Society formed? Who were the individuals most involved in its formation?
6. Who opposed abolition?
7. What could women not do in the early nineteenth century that they can do now?
8. What alerted women to their slavery? In what ways were women's rights limited? Why did the women's rights movement and the abolition movement grow together?

Critical Thinking Questions

9. **Analyzing Literature.** Why did Thoreau live in the woods? What was his philosophy of life? Do you agree with his way of seeking solitude in nature?
10. **Drawing Conclusions.** How did the inventions described in Section 1—John Deere's steel plow, Cyrus McCormick's reaper, Charles Goodyear's vulcanized rubber, Elias Howe's sewing machine, Robert Fulton's steamboat, and the steam trains—help the farmer?
11. **Drawing Conclusions.** How did the inventions listed in number ten above help industry?
12. **Analyzing Effects.** How did these inventions affect the Indians?
13. **Making Deductions.** Look up Ralph Waldo

Emerson in a reference book. What would he and close friends William Ellery Channing, Horace Mann, and Dorothea Dix have talked about?

14. **Interpreting a Quotation.** James Madison said, "A people who mean to be their own governors must arm themselves with the power which knowledge gives." Why do the principles upon which the United States was founded make public education necessary?
15. **Analyzing Causes.** What do you think gave Harriet Tubman the courage to do what she did?

Critical Thinking Activities

16. **Formulating Hypotheses.** Pretend you are a member of a farm family living near Chicago, Illinois, in 1848. What new inventions might you have? How do your crops get to market?
17. **Analyzing Maps.** Look at the map below. How would wheat travel from Cincinnati to New York City? How would a sewing machine have been sent from Philadelphia to Pittsburgh?

18. **Linking Past to Present.** Why do you suppose people thought the problems of slavery would be solved by sending the African Americans to Africa? Why did this idea not work?
19. **Linking Past to Present.** Universal public education is one of the unusual experiments that the United States has made. What contributions has it made to the country? How has it failed?

from Cincinnati to New York City; by the Ohio and Erie Canal to Cleveland, across Lake Erie to Buffalo, and down the Erie Canal to New York City. • The Pennsylvania Canal.

18. People thought the problems of slavery would be gone if African Americans were sent away. • By 1850, most African Americans had lived in the U.S. longer than they had lived in Africa; also colonizing was expensive.

19. Possible answers: contributions—a common culture and language; a pool of skilled workers for industry. • Failures—city schools have high dropout rates, functional illiteracy remains a problem.

▶**Question suitable for cooperative learning.**

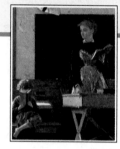

An Era of Reform

Inventions in agriculture, manufacturing, transportation, and communication helped to revolutionize American life. The steel plow and the mechanical reaper (for harvesting wheat) made farming easier and more efficient. Improvements were made in cutting ice from ponds and in making rubber. The new sewing machine meant that shoes and clothes could be made in factories. Steamboats, an enormous system of canals, and railroads made transportation much faster. Communication improved with the invention of the telegraph and steam-driven newspaper presses. The whole country was being drawn together. Economically, Americans were becoming more dependent on each other.

Many Americans were also working for social changes. Foreign visitors thought Americans were a very religious people. Old Puritan ideas such as predestination were rejected by new groups like the Unitarians. Preachers at revivals stressed that people could be saved if they wanted to be and if they truly believed. Increasingly, the states began to adopt systems of free and compulsory education. Reform was in the air. Dorothea Dix crusaded for better treatment of the mentally ill. Thousands of people joined the battle against alcohol. Small groups of reformers banded together to live in utopian communities.

Many reformers began to speak out against slavery and joined the abolitionist movement. Before about 1830, many Americans wanted to send black people back to Africa. William Lloyd Garrison successfully denounced such a program and demanded an immediate and complete end to slavery in the United States. At the same time, the Virginia slave Nat Turner alarmed white Americans by leading a revolt. Frederick Douglass, an escaped slave, became a leading abolitionist. Harriet Tubman helped lead other blacks from slavery to freedom in the North. However, many whites denounced abolitionist organizations and their activities. Increasingly, Southern whites claimed that slavery was a positive good for society rather than a necessary evil.

Many of the abolitionists were women. They aroused opposition by speaking in public not only for the rights of slaves but for their own rights as well. In fact, both custom and law drastically limited what women could do. Yet women became active in such causes as their own education and health. In factories where they worked long hours for little pay, women united to improve their conditions. Finally, several women organized a formal women's rights movement at a conference at Seneca Falls, New York, in 1848.

Chronology of Main Events

1825   Erie Canal completed

1830   Steamboats come into common use

1831   Cyrus McCormick invents reaper; *The Liberator* first published; Nat Turner leads slave revolt in Virginia

1833   American Anti-slavery Society formed

1834   Pennsylvania starts first tax-supported public schools

1837   Horace Mann begins educational reforms; John Deere invents steel plow

1843   Dorothea Dix reports to Massachusetts legislature on conditions of mentally ill

1844   Telegraph put into use

1848   Women's rights convention at Seneca Falls, N.Y.

Telescoping the Times may be used as an alternative to having students read the entire chapter, as a chapter preview, or as a chapter review.

Global Perspectives

1834   Santa Anna proclaims himself ruler of Mexico.

1837   Queen Victoria begins 64-year reign in Britain.

1847   Liberia becomes an independent republic.

1848   Karl Marx and Friedrich Engels publish the *Communist Manifesto*.

1848   Austrians abolish serfdom.

For Discussion

How might expansion of the British empire under Queen Victoria have affected relations with the U.S.? (Possible response: British interests in India and Africa so occupied the British that there was little time to devote to relations with the U.S.)

Additional Resources

- Geography Activities
- Skills Activities
- Thematic Activities
- Economic Activities
- Cultural Literacy Activities
- Literary Source Readings
- Primary Source Readings
- Nuclear Peacekeeping
- Transparencies
- Computer Test Generator

Additional Teaching Strategies

SECTION 1

For Basic Students: Have students prepare a model, map, or detailed illustration of the Alamo and display it in class.

For Advanced Students: Tell students to write a two-paragraph explanation of the social, political, or economic effects of American expansion in the Southwest and share their work with the class. (Explanations might include: exposed people to new cultures; demonstrated the importance of free state versus slave state controversy; showed the need for territorial governments; provided new markets for goods.)

SECTION 2

For Basic Students: Have students locate the two slogans in this section and explain the meaning of each. (Answers: "Who is James K. Polk?"—Polk is a political unknown so should not be elected. "Fifty-four Forty or Fight!"—desired latitude of northern boundary of Oregon.)

For Advanced Students: Tell students to prepare a report on the issues and outcome of the election of 1844 and the viewpoints of the well-known Henry Clay and the dark horse James K. Polk. (Issues might include: annexation of Texas; reoccupation of Oregon; tariffs; slavery. Viewpoints: Polk—in favor of annexing Texas and taking the entire Oregon country; Clay—undecided. Outcome: Clay lost the election.)

SECTION 3

For Basic Students: Have students list in chronological order the territories acquired by the U.S. from 1783 to 1853. (List should include: Louisiana Purchase, 1803; Texas, 1845; Oregon, 1846; Mexican Cession, 1848; Gadsden Purchase, 1853.)

For Advanced Students: Tell students that Henry David Thoreau was one of the first American protesters. He wrote the famous essay "Civil Disobedience." Discuss with students the meaning of the term *civil disobedience*. (Definitions might include: refusal to support the government without actively seeking its overthrow; breaking a law as part of an organized effort to change the law.). Ask students to name leaders who have used Thoreau's strategy. (Possible responses: Gandhi; Martin Luther King, Jr., objectors to the war in Vietnam.)

SECTION 4

For Basic Students: Have students study "Henry Clay's Compromise" in this section and rewrite the seven resolutions of Clay's plan in their own words. (Answers should include all points made by Clay.) Have each student decide which resolution was most important and share the reasons for their choices.

For Advanced Students: Have students prepare a report on President Taylor's death noting the cause of death and the state of medical treatment in 1850. (Reports might include: Taylor ate cherries with milk in summer; developed gastrointestinal upset; endured poor sanitary conditions; took calomel, opium, quinine; doctors tried to raise blisters and draw out "bad blood.") Ask students what role chance played in regard to Taylor's death and the passage of the Compromise of 1850. (Possible response: The compromise was likely to be defeated until Taylor's death because he opposed the measure.)

Further Reading for Students

Parkman, Francis. *The Oregon Trail*. New York: New American Library, 1964.

Ruiz, Ramon E., ed. *The Mexican War: Was It Manifest Destiny?* New York: Henry Holt, 1963.

Bibliography for Teachers
Books

Merk, Frederick and Lois B. Merk. *Manifest Destiny and Mission in American History: A Reinterpretation*. Westport, Conn.: Greenwood Press, 1983.

Ruiz, Ramon Eduardo, ed., *The Mexican War: Was It Manifest Destiny?* New York: Holt, Rinehart and Winston, 1963.

Stone, Irving. *Men to Match My Mountains: The Story of the Opening of the Far West, 1840-1900*. Garden City, N.Y.: Doubleday, 1956.

Turner, Frederick Jackson. *The Frontier in American History*. Melbourne, Fla.: R. E. Krieger Publishing Co., 1976.

Audio-Visuals

California, Texas, and the Mexican War. Yale University Audio-Visual Center. Filmstrip.

The Opening of the West: The Regional Writers and Mark Twain. Listening Library. Two filmstrips and cassettes.

Computer Resources

Across the Plains. (Pet/Commodore) Society for Visual Education.

American History Keyword Series—Westward Ho! (Apple) Focus Media.

Lincoln's Decisions. (Apple/TRS 80) Opportunities for Learning.

Santa Fe Trail. (Apple) Educational Activities.

Teacher's Notes:

Lesson Plan

Teaching Resources, Unit 3 Booklet

Lesson Study Sheets pp. 57-72
Daily Activities pp. 73-80
Enrichment Activities pp. 81-88
Reteaching Activities pp. 89-96
Chapter Review p. 97
Chapter Mastery Tests pp. 99-110
Telescoping the Times Study Sheet p. 111

Chapter Objectives

Students will learn:
- the reasons for American expansion in the mid-1800's
- how Americans moved westward across the continent to the Pacific
- the main causes for and results of the war with Mexico
- the significance of the Compromise of 1850

Picturing History Pioneer families traveled together across the plains, determined to reach their goal—Colorado, California, Oregon—despite the odds. The faces in this early photograph reflect the courage with which these settlers faced the hardships of the journey westward.

Using the Chapter Time Line

How many years passed between the Missouri Compromise (see Chapter 9 Time Line) and the end of the Mexican War? (Answer: 28) How many years after Texans declared their independence did the Mexican War begin? (Answer: 10)

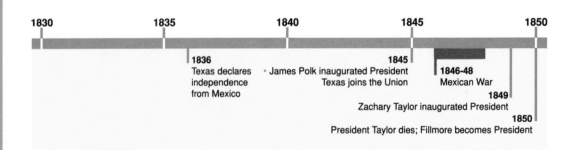

| 1830 | 1835 | 1840 | 1845 | 1850 |

1836
Texas declares
independence
from Mexico

1845
• James Polk inaugurated President
Texas joins the Union

1846-48
Mexican War

1849
Zachary Taylor inaugurated President

1850
President Taylor dies; Fillmore becomes President

CHAPTER **12**   1830–1850

Expansion and Conflict

Links to American Literature

*San Felipe de Austin,
Coahuila-y-Tejas
20 April 1829*

Dear Mr. Macnab,

    . . . I can assure you, Mr. Macnab, that the citizens of Texas are just as responsible and law-abiding as those of New Orleans or Cincinnati, and that ruffians will never be allowed in this colony. The settlers already here are greatly superior to those of any new country or frontier that I have ever seen and would lose nothing in comparison with those of any southern or western state. They are, in my judgment, the best men and women who have ever settled a frontier.

    You say you are apprehensive about living under the Government of Mexico. . . . The present ruler of Mexico is a man to be trusted, and the Constitution of 1824, under which he rules, is just and liberal, and in no way inferior to the constitutions of your various states. I can foresee no possible trouble that you might have with the Government of Mexico, . . .

    All that is required in Texas is to work hard and maintain harmony among ourselves. This is a gentle, law-abiding, Christian society and we would be most pleased to have you join us.

Stephen F. Austin

— JAMES A. MICHENER, *Texas*

The pioneers who settled the American frontier shared the qualities of strength, a willingness to work, and a desire to begin a new life. Sometimes, however, these qualities were not enough to maintain peace. In the Southwest, relations between Texans and Mexicans deteriorated. In the Northeast, people grew more afraid that slavery would spread as the pioneers moved westward.

Chapter Overview

This chapter records the prelude to the Civil War. It describes and connects the two most important political developments of the period immediately preceding the war: westward expansion and slavery. In the chapter, you will learn the main reasons for American expansion into the Southwest and westward to the Pacific in the mid-1800's. You will also learn the major causes and results of the Mexican War and the significance of the Compro-

mise of 1850. These three objectives will be developed in the following chapter sections.

Chapter Outline

1. **The Spirit of Expansion Sweeps into Texas**
2. **The Nation Expands Westward to the Pacific**
3. **War with Mexico Results in New Territory**
4. **The Compromise of 1850 Postpones a Crisis**

State the Objective
Learn the reasons for American expansion into the Southwest in the mid-1800's.

Anticipate the Lesson

Ask students how Americans in the early 1800's might have defined manifest destiny. (Possible response: inevitable, right, and proper expansion of Americans across the continent.) Discuss with students how a government might obtain land for expansion. (Discussion might include: purchase; war; claim as colony.)

Historical Sidelight
President Zachary Taylor was so short that an aide had to help him onto his horse; he never voted in a Presidential election; his son-in-law was Jefferson Davis.

SECTION 1

The Spirit of Expansion Sweeps into Texas

GLOSSARY TERM: **manifest destiny**

For some twenty-five years after the War of 1812, Americans did not seem very interested in adding to their already vast territory. They were busy exploring, settling, and developing what they had. In the 1840's, however, a feverish interest in expansion swept the country. As one person said, expansion was a way of "extending the area of freedom." The expansion fever was fed from time to time by the phrase **manifest destiny.**

Americans Dream of Manifest Destiny

The word *destiny* implied that further expansion of the United States was inevitable, that nothing could stop it. The word *manifest* meant that this destiny was obvious. Americans believed it was clearly inevitable that the United States would expand to the Pacific Ocean and into part or all of Mexico. This expansion was not only inevitable; it was right and proper.

The origin of the term *manifest destiny* was not widely known at the time. Although it has been attributed to John L. O'Sullivan, a New York magazine editor, the phrase was probably first used in Congress by Robert C. Winthrop of Massachusetts. The term rapidly became common because most Americans knew instantly what it meant. According to one editor, it meant to spread over "and to possess the whole of the continent" which God "has given us for the development of the great experiment of liberty and . . . self-government."

Six Reasons Explain the New Mood

Why did so many Americans begin talking this way? Many historians think the following reasons were involved:

1. Since the founding of Jamestown, Americans had always hungered for land. Some wanted their own farms. Others were interested in land speculation. Still others sought new and fertile soil because the older lands had been worn out.

2. Merchants and manufacturers believed that expansion would create new markets for their goods and services.

3. Millions of immigrants meant that more living space was needed.

4. Americans wanted to expand trade with China. Taking Oregon would give the United States several excellent harbors that could also serve as naval stations for a Pacific fleet.

5. The panic of 1837 led many unemployed persons to decide that it would be easier to cope with hard times "anyplace but here." Moving west would enable them to escape their creditors and to make a fresh start.

6. Americans wanted to spread what they considered were the virtues of their government.

Mexico Invites Settlers

The first area to be touched by expansionist fever was Texas, which was then the northernmost province of the Mexican state of Coahuila (kỏ´ ä wē´ lä). When Mexico gained its independence from Spain in 1821, Texas was only sparsely settled.

People in the Chapter

Sam Houston answered to the beat of a different drummer. He went to live with the Cherokee Indians when he was seventeen after refusing to pay a fine for "disorderly riotously, wantonly with an Assembly of Militia annoying the Court with the noise of a Drum."

James K. Polk had "Hail to the Chief" written for him at the insistence of his wife. Polk was so short that people did not notice when he entered a room. "Hail to the Chief" solved the problem.

Daniel Webster turned down the job of Vice-President, saying, "I do not propose to be buried until I am really dead and in my coffin."

Zachary Taylor rewarded his horse, Old Whitey, for serving him so well during the Mexican War. When Taylor became President, he let Old Whitey graze on the White House lawn where the old shaggy horse became a favorite of the tourists.

Present the Lesson

Ask students to list on paper six factors that influenced American expansion. (Answers: new farm land; new markets; influx of immigrants; port on the Pacific to facilitate trade with China; movement of unemployed to escape debt and start a new life; spread of democracy.)

Check for Understanding

Ask students which of the six factors led to settlement in the southwest lands owned by Mexico. (Possible responses: any of the previous responses except "Port on the Pacific.") Ask students how American expansion affected relations between Mexico and the U.S. (Answer: eventually led to war.)

The Mexican government wanted to develop Texas. Therefore, in 1821 and again in 1823 it offered land grants to people who would bring in settlers. The only conditions attached to the grants were that the settlers would obey Mexican laws and follow the official religion of Roman Catholicism.

In 1821 an American cotton planter named Moses Austin obtained a Texas land grant and made plans to establish a colony of settlers there from the United States. He died, however, before his plans could be realized. After his death, his son Stephen took over and in 1823 led three hundred families to a fertile area along the Brazos River. Each family received nearly two hundred free acres of farm land, more than thirteen thousand free acres for stock grazing, and a six-year exemption from paying taxes. The colony prospered, and soon thousands of other Americans, most of them Southerners, were streaming across the border into Texas.

Mexican-American Difficulties Increase

By 1830 the population of Texas included about twenty thousand Anglos, or English-speaking whites, and from one thousand to fifteen hundred slaves, who worked in the cotton and sugar cane fields. The presence of slaves was now a problem, however, for in 1829 Mexico had abolished slavery. Since then the Mexican government had made several attempts to enforce the law. It wanted the Texans to free their slaves.

The Mexican government was also becoming fearful of the continuing influx of people who spoke a different language—English—and who practiced a different religion—Protestantism. In addition, more and more Americans were talking about extending the boundaries of the United States to the Rio Grande (known in Mexico as the Río Bravo). In fact, President John Quincy Adams had previously offered to buy Texas for $1 million, while President Jackson had upped the price to $5 million.

In 1830 the Mexican government closed the border to any further immigration from the United States and slapped a heavy tax on the importation of American goods. It also sent Mexican troops north to Texas to ensure that the laws were obeyed. However, there were not enough troops to patrol the border, so Americans kept coming in.

In 1833 **Stephen Austin** went to Mexico City, that nation's capital, with a petition seeking that Texas be allowed to form a separate state within the Mexican union. His petition was rejected, however, and on his way home he was arrested for treason and imprisoned for eighteen months. Protest erupted throughout Texas, yet the Mexican government responded merely by sending in more troops.

By this time, too, new settlers were coming into Texas. They were ambitious men with forceful personalities. They included people such as **Sam Houston,** former congressman from Tennessee, and **Davy Crockett,** who had also served in Congress. These men and others like them saw no reason to live under Mexican law, for in truth it was difficult to respect a government that kept changing all the time as general succeeded general as head of the country.

Picturing History Stephen Austin (left) opened Texas to settlers. Sam Houston (right) fought for its independence.

Americans Remember the Alamo

In 1835 President Antonio López de Santa Anna abolished all state governments in Mexico. He then marched north at the head of six thousand troops and besieged a group of Texans who were holed up in the Alamo, a chapel and fort in San Antonio. The siege lasted from February 23 until March 6, 1836. It ended only after Mexican troops finally succeeded in scaling the Alamo's walls. All one hundred eighty-seven American defenders were killed, at a cost of some sixteen hundred Mexican dead. Santa Anna then ordered his men to pour oil on the bodies of the defenders and burn them. The only Americans who survived were Mrs. Dickenson, wife of one of the defenders, her infant child, and two black slaves.

Many Texans saw a clear similarity between the oppression suffered by the colonists under Britain during the time of George III and their own situation under Santa Anna. They felt that their fundamental rights were being threatened.

Use the board to construct a time line tracing the major events leading to the establishment of the Republic of Texas. Write the events as you ask students to contribute information.

1821   Mexico becomes independent from Spain.
1821   Mexican government offers land to settlers.
1821   Moses Austin obtains a land grant.
1823   Stephen Austin establishes a colony of U.S. settlers.
1833   Stephen Austin petitions for Mexican statehood for Texas.
1835   Santa Anna abolishes state governments in Mexico and lays siege to the Alamo.
1836   Texas declares independence; Texans elect Sam Houston president.

For Discussion
Defend the position of either side in the question of Texas independence. (Details supporting Mexico might include: land belonged to Mexico; grants were given to settlers; settlers agreed to follow laws of Mexico. Details supporting American settlers might include: they were invited by Mexico; they settled, farmed the land, and wanted slaves.) Could a compromise have satisfied both?

Map Skills

Rio Grande • San Jacinto

Texans Declare Independence

On March 2, 1836, the Texans declared their independence. They then drew up a constitution based on that of the United States.

Even as the Alamo battle raged, the Republic of Texas set up a temporary government. The president was David G. Burnet, and the vice-president was Lorenzo de Zavala, a Mexican American and a foe of Santa Anna. These men guided the republic during the chaotic first months until the Mexican forces were driven out and a regular election could be held.

The Alamo victory proved to be a costly one for Santa Anna, for it aroused fighting fury among Texans. Six weeks later, an army led by commander in chief Sam Houston met the Mexicans in a grove of live oaks by the San Jacinto River. Shouting war cries such as "Remember the Alamo!" the Texans soundly defeated the Mexican forces and captured Santa Anna. After the Battle of San Jacinto, when he signed a treaty pledging to recognize the independence of Texas, Santa Anna was allowed to go free. Understandably, however, the Mexican government refused to recognize the legality of a treaty Santa Anna was forced to sign.

Nevertheless, Texas had declared itself to be independent, and France and Great Britain recognized this fact. In September 1836 Sam Houston was elected president of the **Lone Star Republic,** and Mirabeau B. Lamar was named vice-president. The new nation created a flag with a lone star on it. It also established a small navy and an even larger army, and adopted a constitution based on that of the United States.

Picturing History
Lorenzo de Zavala.

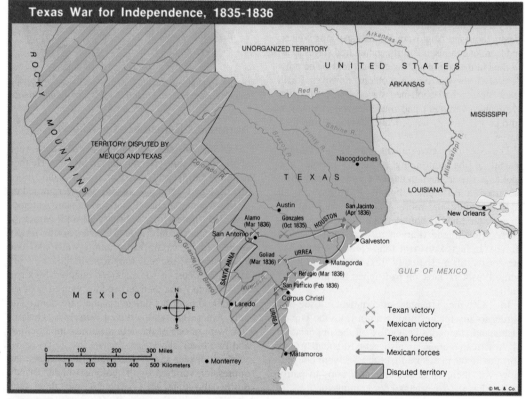

Map Skills   **Region**   What river did Texas claim as its boundary with Mexico?
Location   Which battle was farthest east?

Assign Independent Practice

Have students write the answers to the Section 1 Review questions on paper.

Student Assignment/Homework

Have students complete Chapter 12, Section 1 Daily Activity and read Section 2, "The Nation Expands Westward to the Pacific."

Texas Joins the Union

Most Texans hoped their republic would eventually be annexed by the United States, but again opinion was divided along sectional lines in the states. Many people, especially in the South and West, wanted to take over this republic that had been won by Americans. Southerners also wanted to extend slavery, which was already established in Texas. Northerners, on the other hand, were opposed to taking over more slave territory. Still others feared that annexation would cause a war with Mexico.

Meanwhile, Great Britain began to take an interest in Texas. Although the British opposed slavery, they welcomed the idea of an independent Texas. They thought it would be a counterweight to United States power. They also wanted to buy its cotton and to sell manufactured goods to Texas without paying a United States tariff. Britain even went so far as to get Mexico to finally recognize the independence of Texas.

Britain's interference alarmed many Americans. This could explain why President Tyler succeeded in gaining congressional approval of annexation just before he left office. On December 29, 1845, Texas became the twenty-eighth state. The Mexican government was furious and immediately recalled its ambassador from Washington.

Wagons Head West on the Santa Fe Trail

During the noisy dispute over Texas, a quiet but important trade continued between Americans and Mexicans. The trade route was called the **Santa Fe Trail,** and it led some eight hundred miles from Independence, Missouri, to Santa Fe, New Mexico. (See the map on page 317.) Each spring, between 1821 and 1843, American traders loaded their covered wagons with textiles, cutlery, and firearms, and then set off toward the Southwest.

The first leg of the journey—about 150 miles to Council Grove, Kansas—was covered by each trader individually. Beyond Council Grove, however, there existed a serious danger of attack from Kiowa, Comanche, and other Indian tribes. Therefore, at Council Grove the traders would organize a caravan of up to one hundred wagons. First they elected a captain, who in turn selected four lieutenants. Each lieutenant was put in charge of twenty-five wagons. The wagons moved across the plains in four parallel columns. A few scouts on horseback rode ahead of and behind the columns to keep an eye out for Indians.

At night the caravan would form a hollow square, twenty-five wagons to a side. By interlocking their wheels, the wagons formed a corral within which the horses, mules, and oxen slept. This formation prevented the possibility of a night stampede and also provided a defense against Indian attack.

The traders followed this system until Santa Fe came into view. Then it was every man for himself. The traders would whip their teams as they raced toward the town, each trying to be the first to pass through Mexican customs. After several days of trading and relaxation, the wagons would regroup into a caravan and head back to Independence laden with silver, gold, and furs and restocked with horses and mules.

The results of this trade were not only economic but also emotional. American expansionist fever rose. People learned about the Spanish Southwest and the vast stretches of land that seemed to be there for the taking. They also learned that Mexican control over the area was weak. Finally, they learned the technique of covering hundreds of dusty miles in safety. More and more pioneers began to copy the technique as they headed west to Oregon, California, and Utah.

SECTION 1 REVIEW

Key Terms and People

Explain the significance of: manifest destiny, Stephen Austin, Sam Houston, Davy Crockett, Lone Star Republic, Santa Fe Trail

Main Ideas

1. What were some of the reasons for expansion fever?
2. Why did the Mexican government open Texas to settlers from the United States?
3. Why did the Mexican government finally close Texas to further settlement?
4. Why were the arguments about statehood for Texas usually divided along sectional lines?
5. What part did the Santa Fe Trail play in westward expansion?

Critical Thinking

6. Did the United States' reasons for expansion justify the taking of Mexican territory? Explain.

SECTION 1 REVIEW

Answers

Main Ideas

1. To gain more land, new markets, living space, and seaports; to escape from creditors; to spread the American way of life.

2. To develop the sparsely populated area.

3. Unhappiness with the presence of slaves and the large numbers of English-speaking Protestants.

4. Northerners did not want to annex a slave territory; Southerners wanted to extend slavery.

5. Opened the Southwest to expansion and demonstrated practical ways of travel in the West.

Critical Thinking

6. Possible answers: yes—because the territory was sparsely populated and badly governed. No—because the violation of a country's sovereignty was not justifiable. **(evaluation)**

State the Objective

Understand how Americans moved westward across the continent to the Pacific coast.

Anticipate the Lesson

Ask students to imagine that they are traveling west on the Santa Fe or Oregon Trail in a covered wagon. Have them write and then share a paragraph of five or six sentences desciding their feelings about the events in their lives. (Paragraphs might include: boredom as the days drag by; excitement as they near a town; fear when they see Indians.)

For Discussion

Keep in mind that U.S. expansion to the Pacific brought Americans into contact with new cultures. What contributions to our culture were made by Russians, Spanish, Mexicans, Indians, Chinese, and Japanese? (Categories of responses: food; language; music; religion; clothing.)

Map Skills

Pigeon, Rainy • 10 miles (15 km)

SECTION 2

The Nation Expands Westward to the Pacific

GLOSSARY TERM: **Liberty party**

During the 1840's, the boundaries of the United States expanded westward until the nation reached the shores of the Pacific Ocean. It was a triumph of manifest destiny.

The Northern Boundary Dispute Is Settled

The War of 1812 had not fully resolved differences between the United States and Great Britain. The biggest difficulty was the American-Canadian boundary.

Part of the land disputed by the two nations, since the Treaty of Paris of 1783, was a forested area that included the Aroostook River, now part of Maine. During the winter of 1838–1839 Canadian lumberjacks began logging operations there, but they were soon chased out by Maine militiamen. Although no one was killed, the fight was known locally as the Aroostook War. Other areas where the boundary line was in dispute included the northern part of what is now Minnesota.

Fortunately, neither Great Britain nor the United States wanted to go to war over the matter. So in 1842 two skilled negotiators—Daniel Webster for the Americans and Lord Ashburton for the British—worked out a treaty that split the disputed territories roughly in half.

The **Webster-Ashburton Treaty,** however, did not settle the dispute over the boundary line in the Far West. It simply continued the "joint occupation" of the Oregon Territory that had first been agreed upon in 1818 when the two nations drew up a ten-year compact.

Oregon Fever Rises

Originally, five nations—Britain, France, Russia, Spain, and the United States—had shown an interest in Oregon. In the early 1800's, France and Spain gave up their claims, while Russia fixed the southern border of Alaska at 54°40′. That left Britain and the United States to resolve their claims.

Both nations were represented mostly by fur traders, who sold guns, tools, and liquor to the Nez Percé, Walla Walla, Yakima, and other Indian tribes in the area. In the 1830's some Methodist ministers made their way into the Oregon country and set up a number of mission schools. Their letters east spoke glowingly of the fertile soil and

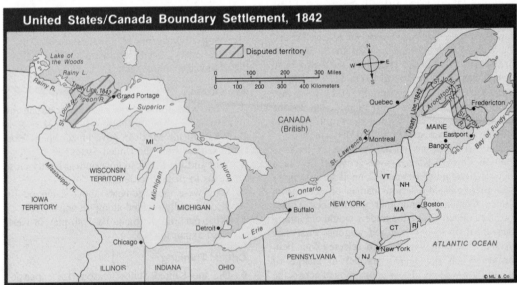

United States/Canada Boundary Settlement, 1842

Map Skills   Region   What two rivers formed the United States-Canadian border west of Lake Superior?   **Location**   About how close to the St. Lawrence River was the U.S. claim in Maine?

Discuss with students the various reasons settlers had for choosing Oregon, Utah, or California as their destination. (Discussion might include: Oregon—fur trading and, later, farming; Utah, Mormons—escape from religious persecution, desire for land no one else would want; California—climate, ports, cattle ranches, and, later, gold.)

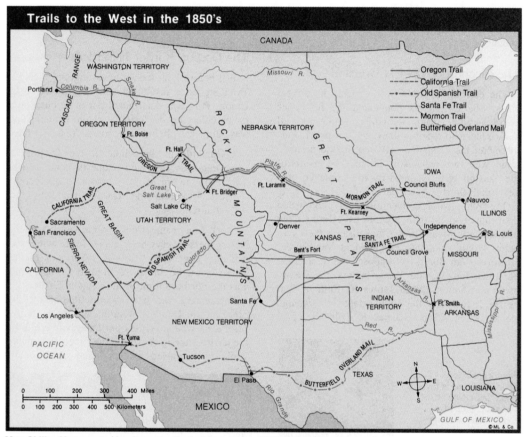

Trails to the West in the 1850's

Map Skills

1,350 to 1,450 miles (2,160 to 2,320 km) • 90 to 96 days

Map Skills **Movement** How long was the trail from Council Bluffs to Sacramento?
Movement At a wagon train speed of 15 miles a day, how long would that trip take?

abundant rainfall. Soon hundreds of Americans were off on the Oregon Trail. The route led from Independence, Missouri, to Portland, Oregon, and was similar to the one followed by Lewis and Clark. (See the map above.)

Some of the Oregon pioneers bought wagons, occasionally the heavy and awkward Conestoga wagons that were covered with sailcloth and pulled by oxen. Most of the pioneers walked, however, pushing handcarts loaded with a few precious possessions. They packed food to last throughout the journey, such as dried pork, beans, and corn. They packed one or two iron pots for cooking. They also brought leather bags to hold water for themselves and for their animals when going over the dry stretches between rivers.

The trip between Independence and Portland now takes a few days of superhighway driving. In

the 1840's, however, it took several months—if all went well. Sickness was a common problem. Babies threw up from the heat or the altitude. Wagon axles broke, and coyotes howled at night. There also was always the danger of Indian attack. The caravans provided protection and companionship. They helped combat the loneliness of traveling mile after mile without seeming to get anywhere.

What lay at the far end of the two-thousand-mile journey? The situation can be summarized by two entries in the diary of James Nesmith:

Friday, October 27—Arrived at Oregon City at the falls of the Willamette [River].
Saturday, October 28—Went to work.

By 1844 about five thousand Americans were farming in the green and fertile Willamette River

Check for Understanding

Call on individual students to answer the Section 2 Review questions orally.

Valley. Understandably, demands for the occupation of Oregon became a major issue in the Presidential campaign.

The Election of 1844 Is Unusual

The election of 1844 was unusual in several ways. The Democrats nominated the first *dark horse* candidate, that is, a candidate who is not well known but who receives unexpected support. Furthermore, the campaign revolved around a single issue: westward expansion. Finally, the results of the election were changed by the existence of a very small third political party.

The Whig party convention easily nominated their most popular man, "Glorious" **Henry Clay** of Kentucky. Meanwhile it looked as if the Democrats would nominate ex-President Van Buren. However, Van Buren had opposed the annexation of Texas. Finally, after many ballots, the Democratic convention named **James K. Polk** of Tennessee. In response, the Whigs adopted a campaign slogan asking, "Who is James K. Polk?"

Map Skills
Columbia River • 49° north

Picturing History
James Polk was in favor of the "reannexation" of Texas and argued, as Jackson had, that the United States had bought Texas as part of the Louisiana Purchase.

Polk deliberately made the annexation of Texas an issue. He was for it, make no mistake about that. Clay, on the other hand, could not seem to make up his mind—at least in public. First he announced that he was against annexation; then that he was for it; and later that maybe, possibly, and probably he was for it. By the time of the election, no one knew exactly where he stood. Polk went further. He not only wanted Texas but he declared that the United States should also take the entire Oregon Territory.

Although the main issue was territorial expansion, the election was actually decided by a completely different matter. Polk won in the electoral college, 170 to Clay's 105. The popular vote, however, was extremely close. Clay lost because he failed to carry New York State. He lost New York because a tiny abolitionist group called the

Liberty party received nearly 62,300 votes, most of which would otherwise have gone to Clay.

The Oregon Border Is Settled

Just before Polk took office, outgoing President Tyler signed a resolution admitting Texas to the Union. Polk was determined not to be outdone as far as enlarging the territory of the United States was concerned. In his inaugural address, he stated:

> Our title to the whole of the Territory of Oregon is clear and unquestionable, and already are our people preparing to perfect that title by occupying it with their wives and children.

Most Americans strongly approved his words. Newspapers everywhere came forth with such war-like slogans as "Fifty-four Forty or Fight." This slogan, of course, referred to 54°40´, which was the northern limit of the Oregon Territory.

Fortunately, the issue was settled peacefully. Since men had stopped wearing beaver hats, British fur traders were no longer particularly interested in the territory along the Columbia River. Polk meanwhile was advised that the land north of the

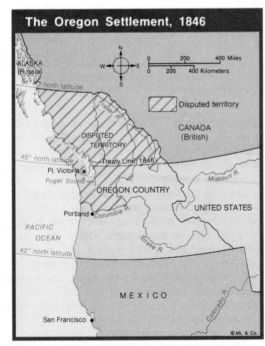

The Oregon Settlement, 1846

Disputed territory

ALASKA (Russia)

CANADA (British)

DISPUTED TERRITORY

49° north latitude — Treaty Line 1846

Ft. Victoria

Puget Sound

OREGON COUNTRY

UNITED STATES

Portland • Columbia R.

PACIFIC OCEAN

42° north latitude

Snake R.

Missouri R.

MEXICO

San Francisco

Colorado R.

© ML & Co.

Map Skills **Region** What was the southern limit of the disputed area? **Location** What latitude was the border?

Guided Practice

Review with students the various personal reasons pioneers had for moving westward, and list the reasons on the board. (Possible responses: new farm land; new markets; influx of immigrants; movement of unemployed to escape debt and start a new life; spread of democracy.) Discuss with students which of these factors they think were the most important.

forty-ninth parallel was not well suited to agriculture. So in 1846 the two nations agreed to extend the boundary along that parallel westward from the Rocky Mountains to Puget Sound. The only exception was the southern tip of Vancouver Island, which was ceded to Britain. The boundary President Polk agreed to remains today.

Americans Move into California

When the Spaniards first arrived in California, it was inhabited by some 200,000 Indians. They were hunters and food gatherers who lived in small communities of 100 to 500 persons. Each community was self-sufficient, and there was little trade or travel between them. In all there were 135 different tribes, almost none of whom spoke the same language.

In 1765 British and Russian fur traders began casting their eyes on California. To counteract the traders, the Spaniards sent in soldiers and missionaries from central Mexico. They established a series of twenty-one missions along the coast, extending from San Diego to San Francisco. These missions consisted of a central church, outlying buildings, and a fort. The missionaries converted the Indians to the Catholic faith. They also taught the Indians how to farm; how to herd horses and cattle; and how to perform such skills as blacksmithing, shoemaking, and pottery making. Unfortunately, many of the Indians died of the diseases that the newcomers brought in too.

In 1834 the missions were taken over by the Mexican government. Within a few years, about seven thousand Mexican settlers had moved into the area They set up cattle ranches and used the Indians as workers. The ranches produced hides and tallow, which the Mexicans sold to American trading vessels to be taken to Boston and other Eastern manufacturing cities of the United States.

Some of these ranches were like small kingdoms, often exceeding 50,000 acres. The ruling Mexican *rancheros* were noted for their horsemanship, style, and hospitality. Children learned to ride horses at the age of four. Women as well as men wore brightly colored jackets and silver spurs. Dancing was a passion. Weddings and parties often lasted for three days, and, as an American visitor put it, "a Californian would have paused in a dance for an earthquake, and would be pretty sure to renew it, even before the vibrations had ceased."

By the mid-1840's, there were also about seven hundred Americans living in California. Most were sailors who had deserted from whaling vessels. The rest were merchants and traders who did business in such towns as Los Angeles, Monterey, and Santa Barbara.

The annexation of California was not an issue in the 1844 Presidential campaign. Nevertheless, some Americans began to think about California's future possibilities, especially because it had two of the best harbors on the Pacific coast: San Diego and San Francisco. To Americans, California looked too empty. It also seemed to be badly governed. The Mexican government did not think so, however; and in any event, they did not think it was any business of the United States. When President Polk offered to buy California, the Mexican government indignantly refused. Would Polk sell one of the United States, they wondered?

Picturing History
Mission San Juan Capistrano was established in California by the Spanish Franciscan missionary Father Junipero Serra in 1776. This photograph of the mission probably was taken in 1897. It shows partial restoration of the chapel after the great church was destroyed by an earthquake in 1812.

Assign Independent Practice

Have students complete Chapter 12, Section 2 Daily Activity.

Student Assignment/Homework

Have students read Section 3, "War With Mexico Results in New Territory," and answer the Section 3 Review questions on paper.

Picturing History In this painting by William Henry Jackson, Mormon covered wagons line up for the ferry to take them across the Missouri River at Council Bluffs, Iowa, in 1846. The phenomenal growth of the prosperous Mormon church was due mainly to the genius and skillful organizing abilities of Brigham Young (inset).

The Mormons Settle Utah

Most Americans in the Far West hoped that their new settlements would come under the American flag. This was true in Texas, in the Oregon Territory, and in California. However, one migration to the Far West was undertaken by Americans who hoped to get away from the United States. These people were members of a religious group called the Church of Jesus Christ of Latter-day Saints. Today they are commonly known as **Mormons.**

Joseph Smith Founds a New Church. Mormon history dates back to 1823 in upstate New York, where eighteen-year-old **Joseph Smith** announced that he had received a special message from God. He said he had found a book "written upon golden plates" buried in a hillside. This *Book of Mormon* was written in an ancient language, Smith claimed, but he could translate what it said. His words attracted many followers. They came to think of themselves as an entirely separate and different people. Smith and his associates formed the Mormon church in 1830, establishing their headquarters in Kirtland, Ohio.

However, some Mormon views and beliefs alarmed and angered many other Americans. Insults and violence followed. Smith and his growing band of believers decided to move west, eventually stopping at Nauvoo, Illinois, in 1839. There they stayed for five years and grew to some fifteen thousand.

Serious conflict developed when Smith proclaimed that male members of the church could have more than one wife. This idea of polygamy shocked most Americans, especially Smith's neighbors in Nauvoo. Those who differed with Smith began publishing their disagreements. Smith was charged with destroying their printing press and was jailed. An anti-Mormon mob then broke into the jail, hauled him out, and murdered him.

Brigham Young Founds Salt Lake City. Such a disaster would have crushed many religious movements. Nevertheless, the Mormons quickly rallied behind a remarkable new leader, **Brigham Young.** He urged them to band together to again move west. The Mormons began to walk north to Nebraska, across Wyoming to the Rockies, and then south. In 1847 they found themselves in a lonely land.

They were in a desert by a salt lake in the northern part of what was then Mexico. The enormous lake lay like a giant drop of water at the bottom of a teacup. It was ringed by high mountains. The salty lake was useless for plants or animals. Dry and dusty winds swirled down the sides of the mountains and scorched the Mormons. Young realized that his people might be safe there. Who else would want such an unpleasant land? "This is the place," he said. It was there the Mormons began to build Salt Lake City.

They dug irrigation ditches leading from streams in the mountains, and they decided to give land to each settler according to his particular skill. However, water and timberland were to be held in common by the people, not by individuals. After much hardship, the Mormons made the desert fruitful, developing settlements and farms out of land that seemed extremely unpromising. They prospered in a land they called Deseret.

Anticipate the Lesson

Ask students what might lead a government to declare war. (Possible responses: defense against attack; desire for land, power, resources, or wealth; revenge.) Discuss with students, when these reasons might be ethically defensible. (Discussion might include: defensible—defense against attack; indefensible—desire for power or wealth.)

State the Objective

Understand the causes for and results of the war with Mexico.

Linking Past to Present

Despite all their troubles, the Mormons eventually gained the admiration of many Americans by their hard work, their steady faith, and their good character. The area they settled became the state of Utah in 1896. By 1990, the population of Salt Lake City's metropolitan area exceeded the one million mark.

SECTION 2 REVIEW

Key Terms and People

Explain the significance of: Webster-Ashburton Treaty, Henry Clay, James K. Polk, Liberty party, Mormons, Joseph Smith, Brigham Young

Main Ideas

1. What dispute was *not* settled by the War of 1812?
2. What was appealing about Oregon to the settlers who traveled there?
3. What issue was central to the Presidential election of 1844?
4. How did the arrival of missionaries in California change the lives of the Indians?
5. Why did Brigham Young choose to have the Mormons settle in Utah? Why were they successful there?

Critical Thinking

6. What were some of the similarities between the settlers who went to Oregon and those who went to Utah? What were some of the differences?

SECTION 3

War with Mexico Results in New Territory

GLOSSARY TERMS: **Bear Flag Republic, Gadsden Purchase**

President Polk had been eager to compromise with Britain on the division of the Oregon Territory because the United States was already at war with Mexico. That war came about for several reasons. Mexican patriots were still angry about the American annexation of Texas. Furthermore, Texas insisted that its southern border was the **Rio Grande,** while Mexico held that it was the **Nueces** (noō ā´ sās) **River.** (See the map on page 323.) Finally, control of the Mexican government changed hands quite often, and these changes interfered with negotiations between the two countries.

Polk Urges War

The most important reason for the war, however, was the attitude of "Polk the Purposeful," who was determined to take New Mexico and California. He was willing to buy these huge territories and offered $30 million for them. If necessary, he was prepared to raise his offer to $40 million. So when the Mexican government flatly refused even to consider the offer, Polk decided to use force.

Polk ordered General **Zachary Taylor** to move his troops from the Nueces to the Rio Grande and to build a fort to blockade the river. To Mexico, this was an invasion of its territory. Mexican troops therefore crossed the Rio Grande and in a small skirmish killed and wounded sixteen American soldiers. Polk sat down at once to write a war message to Congress. In it he declared:

> Mexico has passed the boundary of the United States, has invaded our territory and shed American blood upon the American soil. . . . War exists, and notwithstanding all our efforts to avoid it, exists by act of Mexico herself.

After only two hours of debate, Congress overwhelmingly voted for war.

Thoreau and Webster Oppose War

The Mexican people were more united about the war than the Americans were. Mexicans felt that they were defending their territory against invaders. In the United States, the war was popular in the South and the West, where expansionist sentiment was especially strong. In the Northeast, however, it was not popular at all. Religious groups such as the Unitarians and the Congregationalists felt it was immoral to support a struggle that would extend slavery to new territory. **Henry David Thoreau** protested by refusing to pay his poll tax and was jailed for his action. This led him to write his famous essay "The Duty of Civil Disobedience"

Answers

Main Ideas

1. The American-Canadian boundary.
2. Fertile soil and abundant rainfall.
3. Westward expansion.
4. The Indians converted to Catholicism and were taught farming, how to raise livestock, and other useful skills.
5. He thought they would be free of persecution in a place where few others wanted to live. • They worked hard, kept their faith, and tried to live productive lives.

Critical Thinking

6. Possible answers: both were willing to suffer great hardships and work hard. • Those who went to Utah were Mormons and were looking for religious freedom. **(analysis)**

Present the Lesson

Have students make a chart on paper showing in the first column the causes and in the second column the results of the Mexican War. (Charts might include: causes—Mexican resentment over annexation of Texas, border dispute, unstable Mexican government; results—Mexico loses California and New Mexico, the Rio Grande becomes the border between the U.S. and Mexico, the U.S. pays Mexico $15 million for the land.)

Check for Understanding

Review students' answers to the Section 3 Review questions. Ask students to contribute ideas from their charts. Use their responses to complete a chart on the board showing the causes and results of the war.

Picturing History Henry David Thoreau was one of several well-known New Englanders who protested the Mexican War. (See his thoughts from *Walden* in Links to Literature on page 289.)

in which he discussed what people should do when moral law conflicts with civil law.

Additional opposition came from such Whigs in Congress as Daniel Webster, who believed that Polk had usurped Congress's right to declare war. "What is the value of this Constitutional provision," asked Webster, "if the President of his own authority may make such military movements as must bring on war?"

Some Leaders Are Victorious

For the Americans, one military victory followed another. Why? Because although Mexican troops gallantly defended their own soil, American soldiers were fired up by dreams of expansion. Most were volunteers from such states as Illinois, Kentucky, and Tennessee. Many had been frontier hunters and therefore were crack shots. They also were well trained and well led by graduates from the new national military academy at West Point. In contrast, the Mexican army was top-heavy with generals—none of them very good—while the ordinary soldiers were

mostly ill-trained. In addition, the Americans were equipped with light, mobile artillery that overwhelmed the Mexican cavalry. Furthermore, the United States naval forces were used to good advantage.

Old Rough and Ready. The American invasion of Mexico lasted about a year, starting in the summer of 1846. The Americans advanced on four different fronts. The first thrust, under the leadership of General Zachary Taylor, was into northeastern Mexico. Affectionately called Old Rough and Ready by his men, Taylor became a national hero after his victory over Santa Anna in the Battle of Buena Vista.

Old Fuss and Feathers. An even more able general commanded the American thrust toward Mexico City itself. At six feet four and one-quarter inches, General **Winfield Scott** looked the way a general should—especially when wearing his full-dress blue uniform with a yellow sash around his waist. His vanity and attention to discipline won him the nickname Old Fuss and Feathers. Scott carefully supervised an amphibious landing at Veracruz, where an army of fourteen thousand men disembarked from two hundred ships within twenty-four hours. It was an extraordinary feat.

After capturing Veracruz, the army began a difficult march along a twisting route that took them thousands of feet upward from the coast to the great central plateau of Mexico. On September 14, 1847, Scott's troops finally forced their way into the Mexican capital.

Picturing History A flier announced the exhibit of this painting of General Zachary Taylor standing in front of his tent after the Battle of Buena Vista. His horse, Old Whitey, appears at the left saddled up and waiting for Old Rough and Ready. Americans flocked to buy tickets at twenty-five cents apiece to see one of the few good likenesses of their military hero.

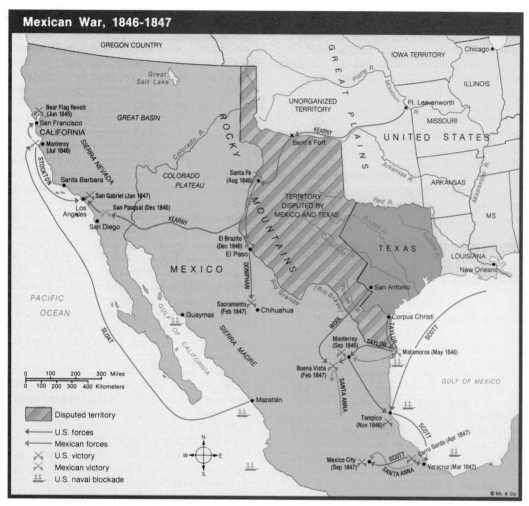

Mexican War, 1846–1847

OREGON COUNTRY

Great Salt Lake

GREAT BASIN

Bear Flag Revolt (Jun 1845)
San Francisco
CALIFORNIA
Monterey (Jul 1846)
STOCKTON
Santa Barbara
SIERRA NEVADA
San Gabriel (Jan 1847)
San Pasqual (Dec 1846)
Los Angeles
KEARNY
San Diego

ROCKY MOUNTAINS

Colorado R.

COLORADO PLATEAU

Santa Fe (Aug 1846)

KEARNY
Bent's Fort

UNORGANIZED TERRITORY

GREAT PLAINS

Platte R.
Missouri R.

IOWA TERRITORY

Chicago

ILLINOIS

Ft. Leavenworth

MISSOURI

Arkansas R.

ARKANSAS

TERRITORY DISPUTED BY MEXICO AND TEXAS

Red R.

Brazos R.

TEXAS

San Antonio

MS

LOUISIANA

New Orleans

Mississippi R.

El Brazito (Dec 1846)
El Paso

DONIPHAN

MEXICO

Rio Grande

Colorado R.

(Rio Bravo)

Nueces R.

Sabine R.

Sacramento (Feb 1847)
Chihuahua

Guaymas

SIERRA MADRE

PACIFIC OCEAN

GULF OF CALIFORNIA

SLOAT

Mazatlán

Corpus Christi
WOOL
TAYLOR
SCOTT
Monterrey (Sep 1846)
TAYLOR
Matamoros (May 1846)
Buena Vista (Feb 1847)
SANTA ANNA

GULF OF MEXICO

Tampico (Nov 1846)
SCOTT
Cerro Gordo (Apr 1847)

Mexico City (Sep 1847)
SCOTT
SANTA ANNA
Veracruz (Mar 1847)

0 100 200 300 Miles
0 100 200 300 400 Kilometers

Disputed territory
U.S. forces
Mexican forces
U.S. victory
Mexican victory
U.S. naval blockade

N W E S

© ML & Co.

Map Skills **Movement** From where did the American forces come to Buena Vista?
Location Where was the only Mexican victory?

Long Marcher. In the meantime, a small group of Americans led by General **Stephen Kearny** (the Long Marcher) went from Fort Leavenworth, Kansas, to Santa Fe, New Mexico. They captured Santa Fe without firing a shot, probably because the Mexican governor there had been bribed to disappear. Kearny then led his troops off on another long march, this time to southern California.

The Bear Flag Republic. In California, the situation was complicated by the fact that American settlers there had already proclaimed the area an independent republic called the **Bear Flag Republic.** (The grizzly bear remains on the California flag

to this day, even though there are no longer any grizzlies in the state.) The American settlers and Kearny's men eventually joined forces with an American naval expedition. Mexican forces, which were few and scattered, were soon overcome, and California fell to the United States.

A Peace Treaty Ends the War

Mexico lost its northern territories, its capital city, and thousands of young men. Santa Anna stepped down as leader, and a new Mexican government agreed to make peace. The terms of the Treaty of Guadalupe Hidalgo (1848) were fairly

Have students choose one U.S. military leader mentioned in this section and write a paragraph describing his involvement in the conflict with Mexico. (Paragraphs might include: Taylor—defeated Santa Anna in northeast Mexico; Scott—captured Vera Cruz and Mexico City; Kearny—captured Santa Fe and southern California.)

Map Skills

Louisiana Purchase • Gadsden Purchase • 1803, 1845, 1846, 1848 • Alaska and Hawaii

For Discussion
To what extent do you feel Polk was responsible for the Mexican War? (Possible response: Polk was responsible because he was more involved with Mexico than he should have been, tried to buy land from Mexico, ordered troops to the Rio Grande, wrote a war message to Congress, campaigned for annexations.)

simple. Mexico recognized the Rio Grande as its boundary with Texas, and the United States received a huge chunk of land that included New Mexico and California. In all, Mexico lost about one-third of its territory. In return, it received $15 million. Five years later, in 1853, the United States paid Mexico $10 million for a small piece of territory south of the Gila (hē´lə) River. This **Gadsden Purchase** included land that seemed especially suitable for a transcontinental railroad. (See the map on page 325.)

The United States had won an aggressive war and an enormous amount of new territory. As things turned out, however, it had also uncaged the lions of sectional conflict.

Linking Past to Present

The acquisition by the United States of about one-third of Mexico's territory in the mid-1800's has had a lasting effect on Latin American attitudes toward the United States. As one Mexican American said recently of the resident Mexicans who in 1853, as a result of the Gadsden Purchase, became American at the stroke of a pen: "They had all the disadvantages of a vanquished nation, but none of the advantages of the Marshall Plan [see Chapter 30, Section 2], or even the understanding that there are differences in cultural groups." Today *La Raza*, literally translated "the race" and connoting the historical and cultural ties uniting all Spanish-speaking peoples, has become more than a slogan. It has become a way of life for Mexican Americans who seek full equality of rights as citizens of the United States.

Does Slavery Go with the Territory?

Congressman David Wilmot raised the question of slavery in the territories almost as soon as the war began. If he had not offered his famous proviso, someone else would have, for the issue of slavery was on everyone's mind. The **Wilmot Proviso** stated that "neither slavery nor involuntary servitude shall exist in any part" of the land taken from Mexico.

Slavery did not exist in Oregon or in any of the territories taken from Mexico. Why, then, did Americans feel so strongly about the possibility that it might spread to these areas, especially when the climate and soil were unsuited to plantation crops? The reason was that two questions were haunting people's minds:

1. Could slaves be used in other occupations? Many people argued that slavery had not reached its natural limits. By this they meant that even if large plantations did not develop in the West, slaves could still be used on ranches, on small farms, and in mining and lumbering. To prove their point, they correctly noted that some slaves already worked at such activities in the South.

2. Could slavery exist in any American territory? Many people wanted the United States to expand even farther, possibly to Cuba, where plantation slavery already existed. With this possibility in mind, both sides wanted to know whether slavery could or could not exist in any territory the United States might buy or occupy in the future.

Southerners strongly supported the extension of slavery, even if it did not seem a practical possibility. They also saw themselves as being put on the defensive. As a representative from Virginia said, banning slavery in the territories was a "direct attack on the institutions" of the Southern people, an "insult and injury, outrage and wrong, on them."

As you already know, an increasing number of Northerners were beginning to view slavery as a moral issue. If in fact it was a moral wrong, then it was wrong everywhere.

Many Northerners opposed slavery, but not because it was morally wrong. They opposed it because they didn't like African Americans, and if slavery were banned, there would be fewer African Americans in the territories.

Taylor Is Elected in 1848

The entire subject of slavery was still being debated in Congress and in the country at large when the time arrived for the 1848 Presidential election. Polk refused to run again. He had said all along that he would serve only one term, and he had already accomplished everything he had set out to do. The Democrats therefore nominated colorless Lewis Cass and said nothing about the extension of slavery. A small group of antislavery Democrats were so disgusted that they nominated

324

Have students read Section 4, "The Compromise of 1850 Postpones a Crisis," and complete Chapter 12, Section 3 Daily Activity.

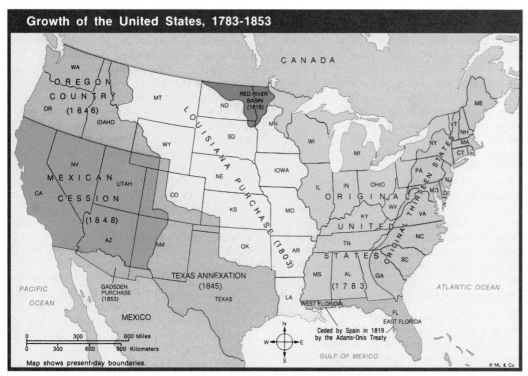

Growth of the United States, 1783-1853

Map Skills **Region** What territory was added to the United States in 1803? in 1853?
Region In what years was Wyoming added? **Location** Which two states are not shown?

Martin Van Buren to lead a new party, the **Free-Soil party.** The party stood for the abolition of slavery in the territories and supported federally financed internal improvements. It also wanted the government to give free land to settlers. The Whigs nominated General Zachary Taylor. Although Old Rough and Ready did not have many firm political beliefs, he was ready to run.

The election of 1848 demonstrated several things. First, it proved that a Presidential election could be dull and boring. Second, it showed that the two national political parties could avoid the issue of slavery. Third, it demonstrated that an antislavery party could gain 10 percent of the popular vote. Finally, it showed that Taylor could beat Cass by a narrow margin.

SECTION 3 REVIEW

Key Terms and People

Explain the significance of: Rio Grande, Nueces

River, Zachary Taylor, Henry David Thoreau, Winfield Scott, Stephen Kearny, Bear Flag Republic, Gadsden Purchase, Wilmot Proviso, Free-Soil party

Main Ideas

1. What was the main cause of the war between the United States and Mexico?
2. How did people in the United States view the war?
3. What were the effects on Mexico of losing the war?
4. Why did Southerners feel so strongly that new territories should be open to slavery?
5. What important issue was virtually ignored by the two national political parties in the Presidential election of 1848 and why?

Critical Thinking

6. How did President Polk force Congress into declaring war on Mexico?

Core Lesson

Anticipate the Lesson

Discuss the term *compromise* and develop with students a definition. (Possible definition: to settle an issue so that all parties give and take, no one gets all that is wanted.) Ask students to give examples of compromises in their lives. (Possible responses: curfew; time and type of meals; family responsibilities; allowance.)

State the Objective

Understand the significance of the Compromise of 1850.

Present the Lesson

Divide the class into at least four groups of about five students each. Assign each group one of the following names: Clay, Calhoun, Webster, Douglas. Ask them to determine the importance of each man's role in the Compromise of 1850. Assign a student in each group to record the group's responses.

For Discussion

Why were Southerners concerned when California, Minnesota, Oregon, and Kansas were admitted to the Union between 1850 and 1861?
(Possible response: Southerners were afraid either that the free state majority would end slavery and their economy would collapse or that the fugitive slave laws would not be enforced.)

The Compromise of 1850 Postpones a Crisis

GLOSSARY TERM: **secession**

Zachary Taylor was a good general, but he was not a very good President. He had plenty of common sense but no experience with national politics. Soon after he took office, the sectional crisis reached the boiling point.

When Polk left the White House in March 1849, the signs of crisis were already apparent. The New Mexico and California territories still had no civilian government. Abolitionists were demanding an end to the slave trade in the District of Columbia. Proslavery people in the South were demanding that fugitive slaves be returned from the North.

California Applies for Statehood

In the midst of all the controversy, something happened that riveted attention on California. In January 1848 a man named James Marshall discovered gold on the property of Johann Sutter. The few specks of shiny metal he found set off a frantic

Picturing History Forty-niners who were working in California and a woman who had probably brought them food posed for the photograph above. At the left, a miner pans for gold. The excitement of the gold rush has been captured in the writings of Bret Harte and Jack London.

wave of gold fever throughout the nation and indeed throughout the world.

In California itself, some men abandoned their ranches and others abandoned their businesses, but all headed for the diggings. So many sailors jumped ship that San Francisco Bay looked like a forest of masts. Everyone expected to strike it rich, and a few did. Most of the money, however, ended up in the pockets of men and women who set up stores to sell food and mining supplies.

The result of the 1849 gold rush was that California's population grew enormously almost overnight. Clearly, California was ready for statehood. In 1849 a constitutional convention met at Monterey and drew up a constitution outlawing slavery. When California's application for statehood arrived in Congress, however, the storm broke.

Three Old Senators Debate

Southerners were furious. If California were admitted as a free state, to be followed by New Mexico, what then? The Union could fall into the grasp of men who were hostile to the special interests of the South.

Many people in the North became equally angry. Slavery, they said, must never find a footing in California or in any other territory obtained from Mexico. A few wanted to go further. They called for the abolition of slavery in the District of Columbia.

Secession in the Air. The word **secession** was heard everywhere. It was whispered or shouted in the halls of Congress, in the dining rooms of Washington hotels, in the press, and in the nation at large.

At this point, **Henry Clay** moved to save the Union. It was his finest hour. Old and sick, he was still swallowing his disappointment at not winning the White House. Yet his vision of the nation's future had always been a broad one. Now he worked night and day to shape a compromise that both the North and the South could accept. He took the unusual step of consulting with **Daniel Webster,** his old Whig rival. In response, Webster offered his support.

On January 29, 1850, Clay rose unsteadily from his seat in the Senate to offer his plan of compromise. Several days later, he rose again to defend it. He spoke for two days. It was the last important speech of his life.

Check for Understanding

Have each group share its responses with the class. (Possible responses: Clay proposed resolutions; Calhoun opposed Clay; Webster argued to save the Union; Douglas separated the contents of the bill to ensure passage.) Students may contribute additional thoughts and insights.

Guided Practice

Tell students that some people regard compromise as a sellout of principles; others feel that compromise is necessary for progress and to maintain peace. Discuss with students whether issues exist within the U.S. or between the U.S. and other nations in which compromise may not be possible. (Issues might include: civil rights; disarmament; response to terrorism; human rights.)

Picturing History Henry Clay offered his compromise to the Senate in 1850. In his efforts to save the Union, Clay denounced extremists and secured for himself the nickname The Great Compromiser.

Henry Clay's Compromise. Clay proposed a series of seven resolutions that carefully balanced the interests of the North and the South. They were as follows:

1. California should be admitted as a free state.
2. Utah should be separated from New Mexico, and the two territories should be allowed to decide for themselves whether to have slavery or not.
3. The disputed land between Texas and New Mexico should be assigned to New Mexico.
4. The United States should pay the debts that Texas had incurred before annexation.
5. Slavery should not be abolished in the District of Columbia without the consent of its residents and the surrounding state of Maryland, and then only if the owners were paid for their slaves.
6. Slave trading (but not slavery) should be banned in the District of Columbia.
7. A stricter fugitive slave law should be adopted.

Clay's resolutions were followed by one of the most magnificent debates in American history. The Senate galleries were crowded with senators' wives and important government officials. Eloquent speeches went on for hours and even for days. They were widely reported in the press, where they were eagerly followed by the nation's citizens.

John Calhoun's Reply. **John Calhoun** led the attack on Clay's proposals. He was too old and weak, though, to read his own speech. Therefore, he sat in his Senate chair with a warm cloak around

him as he listened to his words being read by another Southern senator. Calhoun looked like an aging eagle, his fierce eyes peering over his nose and over the deep lines in his face. Although he wanted to preserve the Union, he was willing to tear it apart if necessary to protect the interests of the South. "If you," he said to the senators from the North, "cannot agree to settle [these issues] on the broad principle of justice and duty, say so." If that was the case, he added, then "let the States we both represent agree to separate. . . in peace. If you are unwilling [that] we should part in peace, tell us so." In the latter event, Calhoun warned, "we shall know what to do."

Daniel Webster's Speech. Three days after Calhoun delivered his grim warning, Daniel Webster raised his bulky body to deliver the last great oration of his life. In the flickering gas lights of the Senate chamber, his deep-set eyes still glowed. Sometimes he paused at strange moments, as his mind groped for words. Yet the old powerful logic and sentiment were still there. He would speak, he said, "not as a Massachusetts man, nor as a [N]orthern man, but as an American. I speak for the preservation of the Union. Hear me for my cause."

Webster denounced Calhoun's warnings about secession. However, Webster also called upon the North to make concessions, especially in support of a new, strict fugitive slave law.

The Great Compromise Is Adopted

The debate went on for months. Almost every senator had his say. Some senators remained bitter enemies of the compromise right up to the end. Senator William H. Seward of New York raised a great many eyebrows when he claimed that there was "a higher law than the Constitution." The law of God, Seward claimed, prohibited slavery from all the territories. If this was the case, many of his listeners thought, what good was the Constitution at all? Southerners denounced Seward's claim as "fanaticism."

Early in July, President Taylor suddenly developed an inflamed stomach and died. He was succeeded by Vice-President **Millard Fillmore,** who quickly indicated that he was willing to go along with the compromise. Members of Congress began to see light at the end of the tunnel. Henry Clay had become too feeble, however, to continue the fight. So in the final months, Illinois Senator

Assign Independent Practice

Have students complete Chapter 12, Section 4 Daily Activity.

Student Assignment/Homework

Have students answer Chapter 12 Review questions on paper. After students complete the review, discuss the Critical Thinking questions.

Concluding the Chapter

Ask students whether Polk led the nation toward expansion or merely reflected the mood of the people. They should support their conclusions. (Possible responses: Leader—Polk's only campaign issue was westward expansion; tried to buy California; sent troops to establish new border. Reflection—spirit of manifest destiny; American desire to obtain farm land, new markets, and Pacific ports.)

SECTION 4 REVIEW

Answers

Main Ideas

1. Gold was discovered.

2. It raised the question of slavery and slavery's future.

3. Admit California as a free state, ban slave trading in Washington, D.C., and enact a stricter fugitive slave law.

4. Douglas divided it into a series of bills to be voted on individually.

Critical Thinking

5. Possible answer: factions were too bitterly opposed. The North had its moral outrage; the South had its financial and cultural dependence on slavery. **(evaluation)**

Map Skills

New Mexico Territory and Utah Territory
• 36° 30′ north

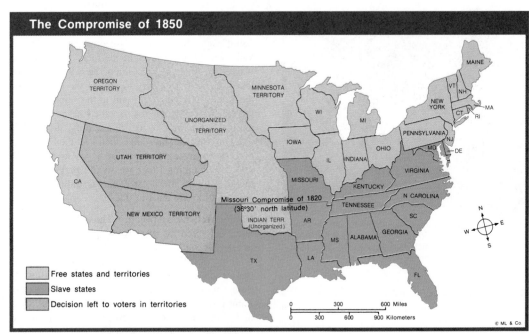

The Compromise of 1850

Map Skills   Place In which territories was the slavery question to be decided by voters?
Location What parallel marked the boundary of slavery in the Missouri Compromise?

Stephen A. Douglas took charge of the behind-the-scenes efforts to gain votes. Short and somewhat stout, the young senator from Illinois was a skilled political operator.

Clay had presented his compromise as an omnibus bill. The term *omnibus* means "covering everything." In other words, Clay had presented his resolutions as a package, to be considered on an all-or-nothing basis. Douglas realized that the compromise would fail if it was offered this way because every congressman hated at least one of its provisions. So Douglas separated the contents of the omnibus bill into a series of bills to be voted on individually. Thus any individual congressman could vote for the provisions he liked and could vote against, or abstain from voting on, the provisions he disliked.

Douglas had found the key to passing the entire compromise. Things turned out as he had hoped because so many opponents abstained.

By September 1850 the Great Compromise was adopted, much in the form originally proposed by Clay. Calhoun had died during the crisis. Within two years, Clay and Webster were both dead, too.

The country seemed to sigh with relief. News-

papers everywhere hailed the settlement. Peace and harmony reigned in Washington. When Congress met at the end of that year, the sectional conflict over slavery seemed to be over.

SECTION 4 REVIEW

Key Terms and People

Explain the significance of: secession, Henry Clay, Daniel Webster, John Calhoun, Millard Fillmore, Stephen A. Douglas

Main Ideas

1. What 1840's event brought California into the national spotlight?
2. Why did California's application for statehood cause a national uproar?
3. Summarize the main points of Henry Clay's compromise.
4. What tactical maneuver by Stephen Douglas resulted in the passage of Clay's compromise?

Critical Thinking

5. Why was it unrealistic to expect Clay's compromise to solve the slavery question?

328

Present the Lesson

List on the board vertically the following human characteristics of place: Land Use, Use of Native Plants, Housing, and Social Customs. At the top of the board, make two columns and label one Then and the other Now. Ask students to use the feature and their knowledge of present-day America to determine some of the differences in human characteristics between Indians of the 1850's and Americans today. Ask volunteers to complete the chart by writing comparisons for each characteristic. Charts should include:

	Then	**Now**
Land Use	Flood farmers grew corn, beans, peppers, squash, melons, and cotton.	Farmers grow a wider variety of crops, including wheat, alfalfa, oats, and rice.
Use of Native Plants	Cactus, vines, and trees provided fruits, seeds berries, and leaves.	Plants provide fruits and vegetables and are used in landscaping and decorative gardens.

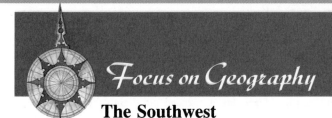

Focus on Geography
The Southwest

The Geographic Theme of Place

Places are a little bit like people. They have distinctive human cultural traits that give them meaning and shape their character. The study of place looks at these human characteristics of a region as well as at its physical characteristics. During the early 1800's, the Southwest was influenced by the human characteristics of three distinct cultural groups: the Indians, the Hispanics, and the colonial settlers. In this geography feature you will learn the characteristics of each of these groups. You will also learn how these characteristics have blended to form the unique region known today as the Southwest. The human characteristics of the Southwest include the kinds of houses, types of food, ways of farming, use of natural resources, and social practices common to the peoples who have lived in the Southwest.

Types of People. Three groups contended for the new Southwest Territory in the first half of the 1800's. The first group was the Indians, who had lived there for centuries. The second group was the Hispanics from Mexico, whose ancestors had shared the region with the Indians for almost four hundred years. The third group was the colonial settlers, who were rapidly moving into the area. The Treaty of Guadalupe Hidalgo of 1848 established the rights of Mexicans in territories ceded to the United States. Mexican Americans, however, assert that since then other American settlers have largely usurped the land grants made and protected by the treaty from the families and pueblos that held them.

Location and Place. The part of the Southwest Territory where these three cultures first met encompasses what is now Arizona and New Mexico. (See the map on page 331.) This is a land of desert earth, pine-clad hills and mountains, and swirling rivers that flow during the flood stage across broad acres of sun, dust, and cactus. Each culture adapted to this land in different ways.

Indians. There were about fifty thousand Indians

in the Southwest by 1850. About half this number were called the Pueblos by the Spanish explorers, who used this word meaning "town" to refer to both the people and their villages. The Pueblos were concentrated in about twenty-five towns in New Mexico. They irrigated and cultivated the soil and seldom strayed far from their homes.

A second group of Indians, the Navajos, migrated to the Southwest from the Northwest about A.D. 1000. They were taught to farm by the Pueblos. Later, they became farmers and sheep ranchers. Many skilled Navajo craft workers became self-sufficient by weaving wool blankets and making harnesses and turquoise jewelry, which they sold.

The Gila River tribes, who farmed the rich land at the bottom of a small wooded canyon in the Gila Wilderness of southwestern New Mexico, formed the third main group of Indians. These Indians used the water of the Gila River to irrigate their farmland.

Picturing History A Navajo family herds their sheep, August, 1891.

Housing	Pueblos—cliff dwellings; Gila—homes dug in the ground and made of reeds.	Homes are made of brick, stone, or wood.
Social Customs	Navajo and Gila were mostly peace-loving and gathered frequently to welcome visitors.	People gather for sporting events, concerts, religious services, and other social events.

Check for Understanding

Ask students to write their answers to the questions at the end of the feature. Review their answers orally.

Ask students to pretend they are Hispanics living in the Southwest in the 1850's. Have students write a diary entry describing one benefit brought by the colonial settlers and one contribution their culture made to colonial life. (Diary entries might include: colonial settlers—newspaper and books; fine furniture and clothing; new farm technology. Hispanics— mining and home-building techniques; livestock management; style of dress.)

Map Skills

New Mexico • Possible answers: mixture of Indian, Spanish, and English (American) people, languages, architecture, and food • The map shows the locations for Indian and Spanish people, includes Spanish names (pueblo, Santa Fe, Rio Grande, Colorado, San Juan, etc.) and English (American) names (Salt River), and indicates the division of the area into states, which are part of the American political system.

Use of Native Plants. The Southwest Indians made full use of the cactuses, shrubby plants, vines, and trees that yielded fruits, seeds, berries, and leaves. They used these plants for fibers for weaving cloth as well as for foods. They ate fruit and syrup from the cactuses. They used the aloe plant to make black paint and a coarse textile suitable for rope.

Land Use. Because of limited rainfall, the Indians planted fields that would be most likely to receive water during flood stages. This is called flood farming. They also built earthen dams and dug ditches to direct and divert the flow of water.

The Indians planted carefully. To disturb the soil as little as possible, they dropped a seed into a hole made with a sharp stick. In time, these seeds would produce corn, beans, peppers, squash, melons, and cotton. Corn was the staple of the Indians' food supply. They would boil the corn, grind it, use it for flour to make tortillas, and mix it with meat and peppers to make tamales.

Housing. The pueblo villages found in New Mexico were cut into the clifflike flat-topped sides

of hills called mesas. The Indians used ladders to climb to these apartmentlike homes that were three or four stories high. The Gila River Indians built rounded homes that resembled enlarged beehives. They dug a rounded pit slightly below ground, erected poles, covered the poles with reeds and mud, cut a small hole in the top to release smoke, and cut a small hole in the side for a door.

Picturing History A Navajo hunter stands outside his hogan on the reservation in 1891.

Social Customs. Although the Pueblo and Gila River tribes differed in language and in such customs as funeral rites, both were relatively peace-loving peoples. More friendly than the Navajos, these tribes gathered quickly in large crowds to welcome visitors.

Hispanics. Hispanics established missions and forts in the southwestern part of what is now the United States in the 1700's. By the time Mexican rule ended, Hispanic ranches and villages could be found in every irrigable valley around the mountains near present-day Santa Fe, New Mexico.

Land Use. Many Hispanics got land grants from the Mexican government and started ranches where they raised sheep and cattle. Others engaged in subsistence farming and grew cotton and other crops. Because of the shortage of workers and attacks from unfriendly Indians, commercial farming was not prevalent until the 1830's.

Housing. Hispanic villages were clusters of adobe and stone houses with mud or thatched roofs. Pole-and-brush corrals were used to contain farm animals. Most homes consisted of only one room, and even homes of the well-to-do with large families seldom had more than three or four rooms. The homes had little furniture. Most ranchers and farmers had little time and money. Generally, they

Picturing History A Pueblo village in Taos, N.M. For centuries, adobe houses made of clay, the only building material available, have been common.

The Southwest, Early 1800's

Location of Indian groups
Extent of Spanish control

WY
NE
NV
CO
UT
Arkansas R.
Colorado R.
San Juan
NAVAJO
Little Colorado
AZ
PUEBLO
Pecos R.
CA
GILA
Salt R.
NM
Gila R.
Rio Grande
TX
MEXICO

0   50   100   150 Miles
0 50 100 150 200 Kilometers

Map shows present-day boundaries.

© ML & Co.

Map Skills **Location** In what state did most of the Navajo live? **Place** Describe some human characteristics of the Southwest shown on this map.

did not see the need to build more than a simple dwelling.

Social Customs. The Hispanic social structure was based on wealth. Large landowners dominated the poorer workers. At times the landowners even bought captured Indians who then became the landowners' indentured servants.

Hispanic women had many rights. They could own land. They had easy access to the courts and could sue and be sued. Most Hispanic women not only maintained their households but shared farming and ranching responsibilities as well.

Colonial Settlers. The first colonial settlers migrated to the Southwest as soldiers and traders. This helped the Hispanics to expand, as the presence of each newcomer made the land a little bit safer from Indian attack.

The second surge of colonial settlers consisted

mainly of cattlemen. They established large ranches near small Hispanic villages. Some settled in the larger Hispanic towns and opened shops for trade.

The cattlemen brought with them new tools and technology. They began building roads and two-story adobe homes. By the 1830's they had brought fine furniture and fashionable clothing to the region. A colonial settler began the first Southwestern newspaper in 1823, and soon books were being printed throughout the area.

Culture Borrowing. The Indians remained a distinct culture. However, around the middle of the 1800's, United States Army troops began to push them from their land and onto reservations. (See Chapter 16.) Some Indians who intermarried with the Hispanics or worked for them became part of the new culture of the Southwest.

The colonial settlers brought new technology that improved the agricultural and ranching practices of the area. They also brought new goods to trade and to sell. The Hispanics shared their traditions, their mining and livestock-management techniques, and their law with the new settlers. Although English became the dominant language, much of the area remained bilingual.

Cultural borrowing worked both ways. The frontier became increasingly Americanized but, despite the fashionable clothing from the Northeast, the Hispanic traditions in dress and housing continued and were adopted by the colonial settlers. The region had developed unique characteristics of its own based upon the customs of three different cultural groups. These unique characteristics and traditions are still found in the Southwest today.

Understanding Geography

1. What are some examples of the types of human characteristics of place that are studied by geographers?
2. Which three cultural groups existed in the Southwest from 1800–1850?
3. Give an example of a Hispanic characteristic that was borrowed by the colonial settlers.

Critical Thinking

4. Has the blending of the three cultural groups in the Southwest had positive or negative consequences for the people involved? Give evidence to support your view.

Key Terms and People

These are highlighted in the text in the order in which they appear in this list.

Main Ideas

1. To develop Texas and exploit its resources. • Trading helped both groups— American goods were traded for Mexican silver, furs, horses, and mules.

2. Americans refused to free slaves; they also were intent on acquiring land. • Mexicans closed the border, sent troops to enforce laws, and taxed American goods.

3. Lewis and Clark. • From Independence, Missouri, up the Platte River, over the mountains to the Snake River, and to the Columbia River.

4. Young thought the land was so unpleasant no one else would want it and the Mormons would be safe. • Driven out of Kirtland, Ohio, they went to Nauvoo, Illinois, where they were also driven out. They then walked through Council Bluffs to the Platte and south to the salt lake. • Because of their beliefs, especially in polygamy.

5. Thoreau: war was immoral; Webster and other Whigs: war was unconstitutional because Polk, in forcing Mexico to warlike acts, had bypassed Congress; religious groups: immoral to extend slavery.

►**6.** Texas: war; the rest of Texas, half of New Mexico: invasion; California, Utah, Nevada, and California: war, negotiation and payment (Treaty of Guadalupe Hidalgo.)

7. California a free state; Utah and New Mexico Territories given right to vote on slavery; New Mexico gets land from Texas; U.S. pays Texas's debts; D.C. and Maryland can vote out slavery; no slave trading in D.C.; stricter fugitive slave laws.

8. Clay won over Webster. Douglas divided compromise into individual bills, each of which satisfied enough senators and congressmen for passage.

Critical Thinking Questions

9. Possible answer: Yes, Austin praised settlers in the state and reassured Mr. Macnab of the justice, liberalism, and stability of Mexican government. He presented the community as law-abiding and Christian and mentioned no problems.

10. Assumed that it was their right and duty to expand, that they were the only free people, that they had the only workable government, and that God had given the land to them.

►**11.** Possible answers: yes— U.S. government has been more stable; nation is wealthier; size and population makes U.S. more powerful. No— Mexico might have been stronger if it could have kept land; Indians might have prospered; Texas wouldn't have been a slave state.

12. Possible answer: Americans' determination and ambition to leave native lands made them independent; they wanted to govern themselves.

13. American settlers joined Kearny's men and the U.S. naval force; the Mexican forces were few and scattered.

►**14.** Possible answers: He believed that the Constitution is a compromise for political purposes and does not replace moral law.

CHAPTER **12** REVIEW

Write your answers on a separate sheet of paper.

Key Terms and People

Explain the significance of: Sam Houston, Davy Crockett, Lone Star Republic, Webster– Ashburton Treaty, Liberty party, Joseph Smith, Nueces River, Winfield Scott, Stephen Kearny, Bear Flag Republic, Wilmot Proviso, Free-Soil party, Millard Fillmore

Main Ideas

1. Why did Mexico invite settlers into its country? Why did the Mexicans invite traders to Santa Fe?
2. What happened to persuade the Mexicans that they did not want American settlers in their country? How did they try to discourage this immigration?
3. Whose early exploration did the Oregon Trail follow? Where did the trail go?
4. Why did the Mormons settle in Utah? Describe the journey they made to get there from Kirtland, Ohio. Why did they have to make so many moves?
5. For what reasons did Henry David Thoreau, Daniel Webster, and various other people in the Northeast oppose the Mexican War?
6. How—by war, sale, negotiation, or invasion— did Mexico lose possession of what is now: Texas (1836); the rest of Texas plus half of New Mexico (1846–7); California, Nevada, Utah, and Arizona (1848)?
7. List the seven provisions of Clay's Great Compromise of 1850.
8. How did Clay and Steven A. Douglas manage to get the Great Compromise adopted?

Critical Thinking Questions

9. **Analyzing Literature.** From reading the letter to Mr. Macnab, would you say that Stephen Austin was a master at public relations? Why?
10. **Making Assumptions.** Why did Americans find it so easy to believe in manifest destiny?
11. **Judging Effects.** Americans rationalized that spreading the virtues of their government was a good thing. Do you believe that Texas, New Mexico, Arizona, California, Utah, and Nevada are better off than they would have been if they had remained under the domination of Mexico? Why?
12. **Making Generalizations.** What made Americans rebel against the established rule wherever they settled?
13. **Analyzing Cause and Effect.** In California, why were the Americans able to win over the Mexicans in a relatively short time period?
14. **Analyzing Ideas.** Senator William Seward believed that there is a higher law than the Constitution. Explain.
15. **Organizing Chronology.** Use the book to put these events in their proper order. Give the year each happened.

   a. Texas declares independence.
   b. Gadsden Purchase is made.
   c. Texas joins the Union.
   d. Mexico invites settlers to Texas.
   e. Treaty of Guadalupe Hidalgo is signed.
   f. Mexicans besiege the Alamo.
   g. Mexico closes Texas border.

Critical Thinking Activities

16. **Formulating Hypotheses.** How would you, using today's public relations methods, have made the 1848 Presidential election more interesting to the electorate?
17. Linking Past to Present. Do you think the Chinese student protesters in Tiananmen Square in Beijing in May of 1989 thought that there was a higher law than that of their rulers? Explain.
18. Linking Past to Present. Identify two people or groups today who are working for the country as a whole, not for a political party or a part of the country.

15. d—1821, 1823; g—1830;
f—(February) 1836;
a—(March) 1836; c—1845;
e—1848; b—1853.

**Critical Thinking
Activities**

16. Possible answers: use
street rallies and fiery
speeches about past glories.

17. Possible answer: yes—
they thought their protest was
just and right despite the fact

that it was illegal.

18. Possible answers: environmentalists, consumer advocates, educators, Supreme
Court justices.

➤**Question suitable for cooperative learning.**

TELESCOPING THE TIMES: 1830–1853

Expansion and Conflict

Manifest Destiny was the name used to describe the enthusiasm of Americans for westward expansion. Many Americans thought it was the nation's right and duty to expand all the way to the Pacific Ocean. At first the Mexican government invited Americans to settle in the Mexican province of Texas. Tensions arose, however, and eventually fighting occurred between these American settlers and Mexican troops. In 1836 the Americans declared Texas to be an independent republic. After many complications, Texas joined the Union in 1845. American traders learned more about Mexico through contacts made along the Sante Fe Trail.

The spirit of expansion spread northwest and westward to the Pacific as well as southwest. The United States and Great Britain negotiated the position of the Canadian border peacefully. The Oregon Territory caused some trouble because it was claimed by Britain but settled largely by Americans who traveled there on the Oregon Trail. Motivated by a desire for new land, new markets, and new harbors, American settlers also began to move into California, which was a Mexican province. Seeking religious freedom, a group of Americans known as Mormons marched westward into Utah where they founded Salt Lake City.

President Polk wanted the United States to gain vast territories from Mexico, including California and the other areas west of Texas. He provoked war between the two countries. American troops invaded Mexico from several different directions. Eventually they captured the capital, Mexico City, and the Mexican government agreed to a peace treaty. Mexico gave up a third of its territory and received $15 million in return. From the beginning of the war, Americans argued among themselves about whether slavery should be allowed in these conquered lands. The election of 1848 did not suggest that a crisis over slavery was coming.

The California gold rush took place in 1849. The next year California applied to Congress for admission to the Union as a free state. Southerners were furious and began to talk about seceding from the Union if slavery was banned in the new territories. Great debates shook the Senate. Three elderly and eloquent giants, Clay, Webster, and Calhoun, gave the last great speeches of their careers. Eventually, a compromise was hammered out. California was admitted as a free state, but the status of slavery in the unorganized territories was left open.

Chronology of Main Events	
1836	Fall of the Alamo; Texas declares independence from Mexico
1842	Webster-Ashburton Treaty
1845	James K. Polk inaugurated President; Texas joins the Union
1846–1848	Mexican War
1846	Wilmot Proviso proposed
1847	Brigham Young founds Salt Lake City
1848	Treaty of Guadalupe Hidalgo; Free-Soil party organized
1849	Zachary Taylor inaugurated President; California gold rush
1850	Compromise of 1850 passed; President Taylor dies, and Millard Fillmore succeeds him
1853	Gadsden Purchase

Telescoping the Times may be used as an alternative to having students read the entire chapter, as a chapter preview, or as a chapter review.

Chapter 13 Teaching Strategies

Global Perspectives

1851-1855	Taiping Rebellion weakens China.
1854	Commodore Perry opens two Japanese ports to U.S. trade.
1854-1856	Crimean War ends Russian claims in the Ottoman Empire.
1856	Boers establish the South African Republic (Transvaal).
1859	Charles Darwin publishes *Origin of the Species*.
1861	Alexander II frees Russian serfs.

For Discussion

How might the opening of Japanese ports to U.S. trade affect Americans? (Possible answer: fuel expansionist sentiments by increasing Americans' desire for Pacific ports from which to ship goods to and from Japan.)

Additional Resources

- Geography Activities
- Skills Activities
- Thematic Activities
- Economic Activities
- Cultural Literacy Activities
- Literary Source Readings
- Primary Source Readings
- Nuclear Peacekeeping
- Transparencies
- Computer Test Generator

Additional Teaching Strategies

SECTION 1

For Basic Students: Tell students to look up the word *propaganda* in the Glossary. Have one student read the definition aloud. (Definition: doctrines, information, or ideas, often deceptive and distorted, that are spread to further one's own cause or damage that of another.) Ask students how the novel *Uncle Tom's Cabin* fits this definition. (Possible response: written by an abolitionist to further the abolitionist cause.)

For Advanced Students: Form two debate teams and have students argue the following statement: The Fugitive Slave Law of 1850 is a disgrace to the nation and must be repealed. Have the class determine the winner. (Arguments might include: pro—slavery is immoral and denies freedom in a free society; con—slaves are not citizens but an investment, property that is bought and sold and must be protected.)

SECTION 2

For Basic Students: Have students list and then discuss the causes and effects of three incidents of violence associated with the Kansas crisis of the 1850's. (Lists might include: proslavery men attack Lawrence, Kansas; rioters destroy presses of Free-Soil newspaper; John Brown attacks proslavery settlement at Pottawatomie; Northern abolitionists send crates of rifles and ammunition; Brooks attacks Senator Sumner after the senator defends Kansas as a free state.)

For Advanced Students: Have students assume the role of editor of the Free-Soil newspaper in Lawrence, Kansas and write an editorial defending John Brown's actions in Pottawatomie. (Defenses might include: Brown was defending Free Soilers and antislavery movement; he was upholding a moral principle.) Have students share their papers.

SECTION 3

For Basic Students: Have students list reasons for hostility toward immigrants. (Possible responses: fear of job competition; differences in religion, language, and customs; clannishness and unwillingness of some immigrants to accept and learn a new language and customs.) Have them discuss the problems caused by this hostility in the first half of the 1800's.

For Advanced Students: Divide the class into two groups to debate the issue of limiting immigration into America. The time is the mid-1800's. (Arguments might include: for limitation—preserve American customs, save jobs and land for Americans, strengthen U.S. patriotism, limit number of Catholics who might be controlled by foreign Pope; against limitation—increase population, help settle the West, provide cheap labor for industry, provide source for new ideas and skills.)

SECTION 4

For Basic Students: Tell students to read "Douglas's Freeport Doctrine." Ask them to explain how this doctrine helped Douglas win the senatorial election and how it led to his defeat in the Presidential election of 1860. (Possible responses: won Senate election because the doctrine convinced Illinois voters that slavery could not exist in a territory that refused to pass proslavery laws; lost Southern support in 1860 Presidential election because Southerners considered Dred Scott case a major victory for slavery, and they were angered that popular sovereignty could circumvent the Dred Scott decision.)

For Advanced Students: Have students read "Dred Scott Loses His Case" and highlight the legal issues debated. (Issues include: Does freedom go with land? Is black citizenship allowable? Could territories exclude slavery?) Ask students to assess the impact of this case on American history. (Possible responses: caused further division between North and South; caused claims of inferiority of blacks by whites; increased hostility and prejudice between blacks and whites.)

Further Reading for Students

Catton, Bruce. *The Coming Fury*. Garden City, N. Y.: Doubleday, 1961.

Lester, Julius. *To Be a Slave*. New York: Scholastic, 1986. (Easy)

Mitgang, Herbert. *Lincoln As They Saw Him*. New York: Hippocrene Books, 1980.

Stowe, Harriet Beecher. *Uncle Tom's Cabin: Or Life Among the Lowly*. New York: Penguin Books, 1981.

Bibliography for Teachers

Books

Craven, Avery O., *The Coming of the Civil War*. Chicago, Ill.: University of Chicago Press, 1966.

Higham, John. *Strangers in the Land: Patterns of American Nativism, 1860-1925*. Westport, Conn.: Greenwood Press, 1981.

Nevins, Allan. *Ordeal of the Union, Emergence of Lincoln: Douglas, Buchanan & Party Chaos*, vol. 3. New York: Charles Scribner's Sons, 1971.

Oates, Stephen. *To Purge This Land with Blood: A Biography of John Brown*. Amherst: University of Massachusetts Press, 1984.

Stampp, Kenneth M. *The Imperiled Union: Essays of the Background of the Civil War*. New York: Oxford University Press, 1981.

Audio-Visuals

The Election of 1860. Encyclopedia Britannica Educational Corp. Filmstrip.

Computer Resources

American History I. (Apple/IBM) Sliwa Enterprises, Inc.

Lincoln's Decisions. (Apple/TRS 80) Opportunities for Learning.

Teacher's Notes:

Teaching Resources, Unit 3 Booklet

Chapter Objectives

Students will learn:
- how the issue of slavery generated strong feelings in the North and South
- how the Kansas-Nebraska Act escalated tension between North and South
- what new political developments and alignments occurred during the 1850's
- why Southern states seceded from the Union

Picturing History Harriet Beecher Stowe's book *Uncle Tom's Cabin* helped to polarize Northerners and Southerners on the issue of slavery. When Mrs. Stowe visited President Lincoln in 1862, he exclaimed, "So this is the little lady who wrote the book that made the big war."

Using the Chapter Time Line
Who was President when Perry opened Japanese ports to U.S. trade (see Unit 3 Time Line)? (Answer: Franklin Pierce) How many years passed between the Compromise of 1850 and the Kansas-Nebraska Act? (Answer: 4)

1850		1854		1858		1862

1850	1853	1854	1857	1858	1860	
Fugitive Slave Law passed	Franklin Pierce inaugurated President	Kansas-Nebraska Act passed	• James Buchanan inaugurated President • Dred Scott decision	Lincoln-Douglas debates	South Carolina secedes	

1861
• Abraham Lincoln inaugurated President
• Confederacy formed

Links to American Literature

God's Angry Man by Leonard Ehrlich: published in 1932; took four years to write; shows Brown as a fanatic leader who was regarded by some as a martyr and by others as a criminal; portrays Brown as man of stature who, like heroes of Greek tragedies, fails due to a tragic flaw—in this case, blind fanaticism.

Introducing the Chapter

Have students find the reference for *secession* in the Glossary. Review with them major events leading to the secession controversy during Jackson's Presidency: the South is unhappy with tariff laws of 1832; South Carolina state convention declares law null and threatens secession; Jackson threatens harsh action; Clay acts as compromiser. Point out that one of the most troubling times in U.S. history was the 1850's. Ask students to list the economic and political sources of conflict between the North and South in 1850 and write their responses on the board. (Possible responses:

North—had industrial economy; favored high tariffs, free states, and abolition. South—had agricultural economy; favored lower tariffs, slave states, and slavery in the territories.)

CHAPTER 13 1850–1861

A Decade of Crisis

Links to American Literature

They were hunting John Brown as they hunted a wolf. They wanted him dead or living, better dead—a gray, gaunt man, almost sixty, with intense eyes, a mouth that was bitter, and seven huge sons. He walked with a long springing step and an inward air, his right shoulder thrust forward as though to meet life full on. He had a power of quickness and no fear; knew how to fade in a swamp or ride like a wind through hills; and he would stand and shoot against twenty. He could be tender with a sick lamb, and he could take men from their beds at night and kill them. "Right is everything, God is a god of wrath," he said, and took five men from their beds and killed them. It was near the Marais des Cygnes water, in the wild Osawatomie region of Kansas. There was a clear spring moon up and soft spring air and a host of warm stars, and that, the twenty-fourth of May, 1856, was the night he did it, using sabres to make silent work. Later, someone said to him, "You should have let the two Doyle boys go. They were slavers, but they were so young, only boys."

— LEONARD EHRLICH, *God's Angry Man*

From 1850 to 1860 the Great Compromise gradually fell apart like a sandcastle on a stormy beach. In Lincoln's words, the nation became "a house divided against itself." Slavery was more than a yes-or-no proposition. Even those who were proslavery disagreed about what constituted fair treatment of slaves. Abolitionists disagreed about what means were justified to gain freedom for all. Some, like John Brown, were extremists: any means, even killing, justified the end. Others actively worked with the underground railroad, and still others just waited and hoped that the law would change.

Chapter Overview

This chapter offers opportunities for critical thinking about ethical choices. Given an evil such as slavery, for which the cure may be costly or painful, what are the advantages and disadvantages of compromise on the one hand and of radical action on the other? In this chapter, you will learn how the issue of slavery generated strong feelings in the North and South and how the Kansas-Nebraska Act escalated the tension. You will also learn how new political developments and realignments occurred in the 1850's and why Southern states seceded. To help you learn about this decade of crisis, the chapter is divided into four sections.

Chapter Outline

1. **The Subject of Slavery Refuses to Die**
2. **A New Proposal Opens Old Wounds**
3. **New Arrivals Lead to New Political Parties**
4. **Crises Lead to a Showdown**

Anticipate the Lesson

Ask students why slavery became the dominant national issue in the pre-Civil War era.
(Possible responses: slaves were a necessity
for the survival of the South's way of life; North
strongly opposed slavery; new territories had
to decide slavery question; abolitionists
aroused emotional responses; underground
railroad helped slaves escape.)

State the Objective

Understand how the issue of slavery generated strong feelings in the North and South.

SECTION 1

The Subject of Slavery Refuses to Die

GLOSSARY TERM: **Fugitive Slave Law of 1850**

The decade of the 1850's began quietly enough.
When people went to vote in November 1852, they
had a very dull choice. In the South, the majority
voted for the Democratic candidate, **Franklin
Pierce** of New Hampshire. He had been nominated
as another dark horse. No one outside his native
state knew much about him or what he stood for.
Nevertheless, he was elected over the aging General Winfield Scott, whose negative feelings toward foreigners antagonized a large number of
German and Irish voters in Northern cities.

Meanwhile, the Whig party more or less came
apart. Both of its old leaders—Clay and Webster—
died during the campaign. Northern Whigs who did
not like Scott refused to vote, or they split their
votes between Whig and Free-Soil candidates, or
they switched to the Democratic party.

At first, Americans hoped the new President
would be able to keep the nation on an even keel.
Before long, however, President Pierce was seen to
be as colorless as Millard Fillmore had been.
Moreover, he was even less able to control the
events that swirled around him.

The Fugitive Slave Law Spells Trouble

The **Fugitive Slave Law of 1850,** part of the
compromise of that year, provided for the recovery
of slaves who ran away to free states. Slaveholders
or their hired agents could seize their runaway
slaves in any Northern state. To accomplish this,
they could demand assistance from federal marshals. A slaveholder could then go before a federal
judge to make a legal claim. If the judge decided in
the slaveholder's favor, the slave could be taken
south.

Unjust Practices.   Abolitionists charged that the
law made it easy to kidnap free African Americans.
Judges received ten dollars if they ruled that an
African American was a slave, but they received
only five dollars if they ruled that he or she was
legally free. In addition, an African American
accused of being a runaway was not entitled to a
trial by jury and was not even allowed to testify in
his or her own behalf. The law also imposed a fine
of $1,000 and six months in jail on anyone con-
victed of helping a fugitive slave.

The Fugitive Slave Law spread fear among
African Americans in the North, whether they were
escaped slaves or legally free. Kidnapping of freed
slaves could and did happen. Some African Americans became so alarmed that they migrated to
Canada where the law could not reach them. Black
leaders, such as Frederick Douglass, called on the
black community to resist the law with force.

Personal Liberty Laws.   Many Northern states
passed personal liberty laws in an attempt to get
around the new federal statute. Those laws forbade
state officials from cooperating with federal officials who were returning fugitive slaves to the
South. As a result, state and federal officials often

People in the Chapter

Franklin Pierce campaigned with the slogan
"We Polked 'em in '44, and we'll Pierce 'em in
52." Mrs. Pierce fainted when she heard the
news that her husband had been nominated.

Harriet Beecher Stowe refused to take credit
for writing *Uncle Tom's Cabin.* When a visitor
asked to shake hands with the author of the
successful novel, Mrs. Stowe replied that she
was not the author. "God wrote it," she said. "I
merely wrote his dictation."

Jefferson Davis received an unusual gift while
he served as secretary of war under Franklin

Pierce. The President presented Davis with a
"sleeve dog" brought from the Orient by Commodore Matthew Perry. Davis rode around
Washington with the tiny dog in his pocket.

John C. Frémont was known as the Pathfinder
because of his daring expeditions on the Oregon Trail and through the Rockies. He made
his guide, Kit Carson, a legendary hero when
he wrote about their adventures in the West.

Present the Lesson

Divide the class into groups of four to six students to discuss how the Fugitive Slave Law and personal liberty laws further divided the North and South. Have students first agree on the meaning of the Fugitive Slave Law and personal liberty laws. Appoint a student to record the important points of the discussion.

Check for Understanding

Have group leaders report to the class. (Reports might include: people followed different laws in different areas; there was no cooperation between sections.) Students should respond to each report with ideas and insights.

Picturing History
The bill for a slave included a full description keyed to a numbered identification tag (left) worn by the slave.

found themselves in conflict with one another. In Ohio, for example, a crowd of men from Oberlin College rescued a fugitive from a slave catcher. Members of the crowd were convicted by a federal jury. Later a state court ordered the arrest of the slave catcher and of all the federal officials who had cooperated with him. In this case, a compromise was worked out, but it became clear that the Fugitive Slave Law would be difficult to enforce.

Horrifying Cases. A number of dramatic incidents greatly inflamed Northern opinion about both slavery and the South. Early in 1851 a black man named Frederick Wilkins was working quietly as a waiter in a Boston coffeehouse. Suddenly he was seized by a Virginia slave catcher who knew him as Shadrach, a runaway slave. While Wilkins was being held for return to Virginia, a crowd of African Americans burst into the courthouse and led him away to safety.

In New York City James Hamlet, another escaped slave, was seized and packed off to Maryland so fast that he was not even allowed to say goodbye to his wife and children. Hamlet was lucky, however, for his black friends and a few sympathetic whites managed to raise $800 to purchase his freedom.

Several years later, federal troops lined the streets of Boston as a fugitive slave named Anthony Burns was marched from the courthouse to a ship waiting to carry him back to Virginia. A gigantic crowd of fifty thousand people hissed and shouted in protest.

About three hundred African Americans were returned to slavery under the Fugitive Slave Law. As more and more slaves were returned, however, an increasing number of Northerners became abolitionists. Previously, slavery had seemed distant and remote. Now it seemed much closer to home. A mere glimpse of Anthony Burns in chains was far more vivid than the most awful tales found in abolitionist literature.

Uncle Tom's Cabin Is a Best Seller

In 1852 a woman wrote a book that brought slavery into the living rooms of a great many Americans. Her story had more impact than any single piece of writing since Thomas Paine's *Common Sense*. It reached more people and changed more minds than any TV series has done in modern times.

The Author. **Harriet Beecher Stowe** was the daughter of one Calvinist minister and the wife of another. One of her older brothers, the minister Henry Ward Beecher, had been a supporter of

Picturing History
The cover from a children's edition of *Uncle Tom's Cabin*.

Picturing History This picture, based on a stage version of Uncle Tom's Cabin, shows Eliza fleeing across the Ohio River to escape from slavery. Stage versions of the novel often contained scenes that were not in the book.

For Discussion
The textbook states that "many people have said that *Uncle Tom's Cabin* did not deserve to be rated as a great novel." Ask the class what they think makes a novel great. (Possible responses: subject matter; writing style; social relevance.) Which of these criteria catapulted *Uncle Tom's Cabin* to fame? (Answers: subject matter; social relevance.) Suggest that students read the novel and discuss its contents.

Guided Practice

Tell students that the Fugitive Slave Law was immoral in the eyes of many people. The issue of whether a person should obey a law that he or she considers immoral arose then as it does now. Ask students to give examples of laws people might refuse to obey on moral grounds. (Possible responses: draft laws; segregation laws.) Ask whether such action is justified in a democratic country. (Possible responses: yes, it is our right to disagree, one must act according to conscience; no, it would create chaos if people were allowed to decide which laws they wished to obey.)

Assign Independent Practice

Have students answer Section 1 Review questions and complete Chapter 13, Section 1 Daily Activity.

Map Skills

Toronto and Montreal • SC, MS, LA

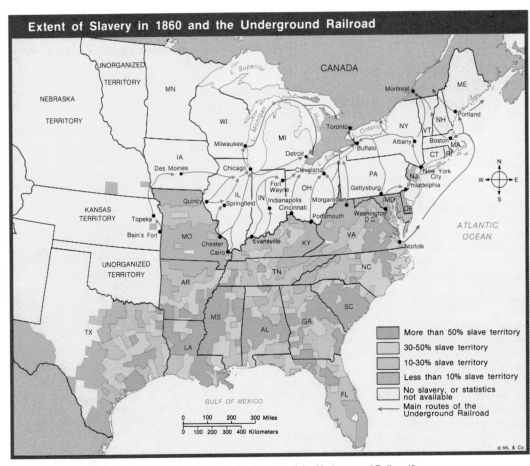

Extent of Slavery in 1860 and the Underground Railroad

- More than 50% slave territory
- 30–50% slave territory
- 10–30% slave territory
- Less than 10% slave territory
- No slavery, or statistics not available
- → Main routes of the Underground Railroad

0   100   200   300 Miles
0   100   200   300   400 Kilometers

© ML & Co.

Map Skills   Movement   What Canadian cities were destinations of the Underground Railroad?
Region   Which states had the largest areas that were more than 50 percent slave?

abolitionist Elijah Lovejoy. When Lovejoy was murdered by a proslavery mob, Stowe decided to make the cause of slavery her own. Her feelings were reinforced when her eighteen-month-old son died in a cholera epidemic. She saw the epidemic as a modern version of the biblical plagues that struck Egyptians when their pharaoh refused to let Jewish slaves go free. She then sat down and wrote *Uncle Tom's Cabin, or Life Among the Lowly.*

The novel was first published as a series of magazine articles. Then in the spring of 1852, the publisher brought Stowe's story out in book form. He printed only five thousand copies at first because he thought it would not sell well. It sold out in two days! Within a year, the publisher had sold three hundred thousand copies. No other book except the Bible had ever sold so many copies.

People everywhere talked about it. In the North it was hailed, while in the South it was condemned.

The Story.   How could one book create such a fuss? Clearly, Harriet Beecher Stowe used her story to tell many Northerners what they wanted to hear about slavery and what many Southerners did not want to hear at all.

The story deals mostly with Uncle Tom, a loyal and deeply Christian slave who grows to manhood in Kentucky. However, financial difficulties force Tom's kindly master to sell him. Thus, Tom is forced to leave his wife and his "old Kentucky home" for the long trip "down the river" to New Orleans.

On that downriver trip, Tom befriends and saves the life of a white child, Eva St. Clare, and is later

Student Assignment/Homework

Have students read Section 2, "A New Proposal Opens Old Wounds," and answer the Section 2 Review questions on paper.

SECTION 2

Core Lesson

Anticipate the Lesson

Discuss with students the term *popular sovereignty* and decide on a definition as it applies to the question of slavery. (Possible definition: Settlers decide whether or not to permit slavery in their territory.) Ask students what events might prevent popular sovereignty from working properly. (Possible responses: fixed elections; minority rejection of majority vote.)

bought by her grateful father. Tom spends some time with the St. Clare family in New Orleans but is later sold to a cruel slave owner in Arkansas named Simon Legree. In the end, Tom is lashed to death at Legree's orders. As he dies, Tom forgives the two black overseers who have killed him.

The Propaganda. Stowe's story was excellent propaganda, for it exaggerated everything. It was as sentimental as a soap opera, and its characters and situations were often totally unbelievable. Ever since its publication, many people have said that *Uncle Tom's Cabin* does not deserve to be rated as a great novel.

Even so, the book deeply touched millions of Americans. It did so primarily for three reasons. First, it told a simple story. Second, it showed that slavery was evil, even when good people were involved, because it was contrary to both Christian ethics and to the Declaration of Independence. Finally, it showed that slavery damaged families, white as well as black.

The Reaction. Northerners reacted extremely favorably to the book and increased their agitation to abolish the Fugitive Slave Law. Southerners hated the book, even if they couldn't put it down. They viewed it as an attack, not just against slavery but against the South as a whole. Southerners felt that they did not treat their slaves any worse than factory owners in the North treated their workers. At least a dozen Southern writers wrote novels that attempted to show that *Uncle Tom's Cabin* was a pack of lies. The most successful, *Aunt Eva's Cabin,* had illustrations showing lace curtains in the windows of Aunt Eva's cabin. Northerners thus were reminded that Aunt Eva was happy. Nevertheless, they could not forget that she was a slave.

SECTION 1 REVIEW

Key Terms and People

Explain the significance of: Franklin Pierce, Fugitive Slave Law of 1850, Harriet Beecher Stowe

Main Ideas

1. What conditions led to the passage of personal liberty laws in Northern states?
2. How did the publicity surrounding the return of runaway slaves promote opposition to slavery in the North?

3. Explain why *Uncle Tom's Cabin* could be considered propaganda.
4. What effect did *Uncle Tom's Cabin* have on the nation?

Critical Thinking

5. Why were Northern legislators willing to risk violating a federal law by passing personal liberty laws?

SECTION 2

A New Proposal Opens Old Wounds

GLOSSARY TERM: popular sovereignty

When Franklin Pierce took office at the age of forty-eight, he was the youngest man to become President up to that time. People liked him, for he was friendly and sociable. He named a strong cabinet, which included both Northerners and Southerners. However, he could not control them or the members of Congress. He tried to please extremists on both sides of the sectional controversy. The nation needed a steady hand to guide the ship of state, but Pierce's hand was as weak as his smile was friendly. Soon he lost all control over political events.

Stephen Douglas, the dynamic young senator from Illinois, stepped into the political vacuum. Without meaning to, this top Democratic party leader, now that Calhoun was dead, wrecked the Compromise of 1850.

Picturing History President Franklin Pierce tried to appease the South, but he was unable to reduce the tensions that finally led to war.

Tension Mounts over Kansas and Nebraska

In 1854 Douglas introduced a bill to organize the vast Nebraska Territory, which lay completely

SECTION 1 REVIEW

Answers

Main Ideas

1. The gross injustices of the Fugitive Slave Law.

2. It brought the issue of slavery closer to home for Northerners.

3. It exaggerated characters and situations to gain the reader's sympathy.

4. It solidified the North against slavery and put the South on the defensive.

Critical Thinking

5. They found the Fugitive Slave Law so unfair and immoral that they wanted to circumvent it. **(analysis)**

State the Objective

Understand the role of the Kansas-Nebraska Act in escalating tension between North and South.

Present the Lesson

Ask students to list on the board the provisions of the Kansas-Nebraska Act. (Answer: divided Nebraska into Nebraska and Kansas; repealed Missouri Compromise; decided slavery question by popular sovereignty.) How did people react to the bill? (Possible responses: both North and South protested; each feared the other would gain control of the Senate.) Have students refer to the list of provisions as they study this section.

Check for Understanding

Ask students to state Douglas's reasons for wanting Chicago to be the railroad center of the U.S. How was this desire related to the Kansas-Nebraska Act. (Answer: Douglas owned land in Chicago and wanted to gain support for his Presidential hopes. Douglas felt routing the railroad through the Nebraska Territory would be possible only if the territory was organized.)

Map Skills

Fifteen (plus Indian Territory) • Sixteen (plus three territories)

For Discussion

What were some acts of violence and lawlessness that occurred in the Kansas Territory? (Possible responses: vote fraud; formation of two governments; burning of hotel in Lawrence by proslavery men; John Brown raid of proslavery settlement.) Does this crisis demonstrate the failure of our political system to deal with the slavery question and growing violence? (Possible responses: yes, the federal government could have sent troops and taken a firm stand on slavery issue; no, the federal government was trying not to alienate any group and to let the majority rule.)

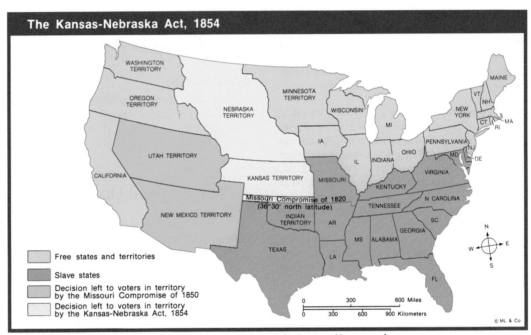

The Kansas-Nebraska Act, 1854

Free states and territories
Slave states
Decision left to voters in territory by the Missouri Compromise of 1850
Decision left to voters in territory by the Kansas-Nebraska Act, 1854

Map Skills **Region** How many slave states were there in 1854? **Region** How many free states were there in 1854?

north of 36°30´. The bill, which became known as the **Kansas-Nebraska Act,** divided the Nebraska Territory, setting off the southern portion as the territory of Kansas and the northern portion as the territory of Nebraska. It also repealed the Missouri Compromise, which specified that there would be no slaves north of 36°30´ in the territory that was part of the Louisiana Purchase. Under the new act, both territories would have **popular sovereignty—** that is, the settlers themselves would decide whether or not they wanted slavery in their territory.

The bill caused an immediate howl of protest in the North. Douglas had seriously underestimated Northern hostility toward slavery in the territories. At his home base in Chicago, he was hooted off the platform by members of his own Democratic party.

Why did Douglas take this fateful step? Historians are still not certain. What they do know is that Douglas wanted a transcontinental railroad. On this subject he stated, "No man can keep up with the spirit of this age who travels on anything slower than the locomotive. . . . We must therefore have Rail Roads . . . from the Atlantic to the Pacific." He wanted the railroad to start at Chicago, where he owned considerable real estate, and to run west through the Nebraska Territory. Southerners, how-

ever, wanted the railroad to begin at New Orleans or Memphis and to follow a southern route through El Paso to San Diego.

Douglas did not favor slavery in Kansas and Nebraska. He believed it could not exist on the open prairies, since none of the crops requiring slave labor could be grown there. However, in order to win Southern support for his railroad route and for his own Presidential hopes, he agreed to support repeal of the Missouri Compromise. He thought this action would have no practical effect on the territories themselves, but he proved to be dead wrong.

Popular Sovereignty Fails in Kansas

The Kansas-Nebraska Act inflamed opinions in both the North and South. Although popular sovereignty seemed a logical way of deciding the fundamental issue of slavery in the territories, events showed that it did not work. One crucial question remained: When should settlers decide about slavery? Should they do so before the territory had an official government, after, or when the territory became a state? The question was never really settled. Instead, a minor war broke out in Kansas.

Guided Practice

Review with students the fact that John Brown was a man willing to take extreme actions for a cause he felt was morally right. Have the class discuss other situations in which people assume a moral responsibility that might be labeled extremist. (Possible examples: PLO terrorists; communist guerillas; conscientious objectors; political activists; freedom fighters.)

Assign Independent Practice

Have students complete Chapter 13, Section 2 Daily Activity.

Government Against Government. Proslavery settlers began moving into Kansas from Missouri. In March 1855 the first territorial election took place. Although only fourteen hundred residents were eligible to vote, some six thousand votes were cast. Most of the voters were from Missouri. They crossed the border just long enough to mark their ballots and then returned home. The new territorial legislature promptly passed laws in support of slavery, including one that imposed the death penalty for aiding a fugitive slave.

Antislavery residents of Kansas refused to recognize this new government. Instead, they organized one of their own. Kansas now had two governments, one based on fraud and the other lacking any legal basis.

Settler Against Settler. In the mid-1800's, Kansas was very much a frontier society. Violence and lawlessness were common. Also, most of the settlers were young, single men. The absence of women and families made them quick to draw their knives and pistols.

Soon, major incidents of violence broke out. In one instance, a large group of tough proslavery men rode into Lawrence, Kansas, in search of several leading Free-Soilers. The proslavery legislature had indicted those Free-Soilers for treason, so the raiders of Lawrence felt that they had legal backing. They burned down the tiny town's only hotel, destroyed several homes, and smashed the presses of a new Free-Soil newspaper. When Northern newspapers learned about the raid, they called it the "Sack of Lawrence" and exaggerated every detail.

Elsewhere in Kansas a single-minded abolitionist decided on revenge. John Brown gathered four of his sons and two other followers. In May 1856 they rode into the small proslavery settlement at Pottawatomie Creek, dragged five men out of their homes, and killed them. Brown claimed that he had God's support for this murderous action.

Soon all of Kansas was an armed camp. More settlers moved in from Missouri and from other slave states. In the North, abolitionists organized the New England Emigrant Aid Company to assist Free-Soilers who would migrate to Kansas. Tension between the Northern and Southern settlers increased when one of Harriet Beecher Stowe's brothers, who was a popular preacher, said that guns would be more useful against slavery than Bibles. In response, crates of "Beecher's Bibles" began arriving in free-soil Kansas settlements—crates packed with rifles and ammunition. **Bleeding Kansas** turned into a battleground on which more than two hundred people eventually died in a miniature civil war.

Congressman Against Congressman. The spirit of violence spread to the heart of the nation. Late one day in 1856, while the Senate was not in session, Senator **Charles Sumner** of Massachu-

Picturing History In this cartoon, Representative Preston S. Brooks is shown beating Senator Charles Sumner while he is down—an act generally considered the mark of a bully.

SECTION 3

Core Lesson

Anticipate the Lesson

Ask students to list possible reasons for moving from one country to another. (Possible reasons: opportunity for land, wealth, or education; to escape oppression.) Discuss what problems immigrants might face in a new land. (Problems might include: language difficulties; differences in food, customs, and jobs; prejudice.)

State the Objective

Understand new political developments and alignments that occurred during the 1850's.

SECTION 2 REVIEW

Answers

Main Ideas

1. It divided the Nebraska Territory into two new territories and repealed the Missouri Compromise by providing for popular sovereignty in both territories.

2. Proslavery voters fraudulently won and set up a government; Free-Soilers set up their own government.

3. Tension between proslavery and antislavery forces, a frontier mentality, and lack of an accepted government to enforce laws.

4. Guns and ammunition meant to support the antislavery cause in Kansas.

Critical Thinking

5. Possible answer: the brutal beating reflected the fact that the nation was past the point of debate over slavery. **(application)**

---

setts was writing at his desk on the Senate floor. He hated slavery and used vulgar language to defend his high principles. Two days earlier he had finished a speech that later became known by the title "The Crime Against Kansas." He had demanded the immediate admission of Kansas as a free state. He lashed into Senator Douglas of Illinois and Senator Andrew Butler of South Carolina, using language sometimes heard in the streets but not on the floor of the Senate. Many people were deeply shocked. Sumner continued his speech with a cruel remark about Butler's speech difficulties, which were caused by a heart condition. While he was speaking, someone overheard Douglas grumble, "That damn fool will get himself killed by some other damn fool."

As Sumner sat writing, a young kinsman of Butler approached him. Preston S. Brooks was a representative from South Carolina, and he had been driven to fury by Sumner's remarks. He held in his hand a heavy cane with a gold head. Sumner did not even notice the approaching man. Brooks waited for a minute while a woman left the back of the hall. Then he rushed forward and began pounding Sumner over the head. Sumner struggled to rise, but his knees were caught under his desk. Soon he was lying on the floor with blood pouring from his head.

In the South, Brooks was cheered for having supported the honor of both his family and the South. In the North, Brooks was denounced as a bully. His action was described as typical of a violent, slaveholding society. The entire incident confirmed each section's suspicions about the other. Sumner lived, although it took him three years to recover from his injuries. In the meantime, his empty desk stood like a silent accusation.

SECTION 2 REVIEW

Key Terms and People

Explain the significance of: Kansas-Nebraska Act, popular sovereignty, Bleeding Kansas, Charles Sumner

Main Ideas

1. What were the main provisions of the Kansas-Nebraska Act?
2. What was the immediate result of the first territorial election in Kansas?
3. What conditions led to a minor war in Kansas?
4. What were "Beecher's Bibles"?

Critical Thinking

5. How did Preston Brooks's actions toward Senator Sumner reflect the atmosphere created by the Kansas-Nebraska Act?

SECTION 3

New Arrivals Lead to New Political Parties

GLOSSARY TERMS: **nativism, Know-Nothings, Republican party**

During this violent and dramatic time, other equally significant but less startling events were taking place. From 1845 to 1860, a great flood of immigrants came to the United States from Europe. Many were from Scandinavia and Germany, but the majority came from Ireland. Although New York City was the great immigrant port, Boston, Philadelphia, Baltimore, and New Orleans also received large numbers.

Most of these immigrants settled in the free states. More jobs were available there in factories and construction work, and the newcomers would not have to compete with slave labor. Most of the Germans and Scandinavians bought farms and settled in the Midwest. The Irish were usually too poor to buy even cheap farmland; therefore, many of them remained in Eastern cities. Soon, however, many Irish followed the railroad and canal lines that were spreading through the North.

Immigrants Face Opposition

In the long run, the immigrants prospered. The nation's economy was vigorous and was expanding very rapidly. In 1850 the United States had only one-tenth the number of people it has today. Thus, there seemed to be room for everyone who wanted to come here. However, these new immigrants faced opposition.

Nativism. The policy of favoring native-born people over immigrants is called **nativism.** The Native American Association was organized in Washington, D.C., in 1837. The nativists held their first national convention in Philadelphia in 1845 and adopted the name Native American party. Nativist sentiment grew rapidly in the 1840's and 1850's. In the cities, the main reason was fear of job competition. Immigrants had to have work, and they were

Present the Lesson

On the board write the terms *Know Nothing* and *Republican*. Have students write the basic platforms of each political movement. Platforms might include:

Know Nothing

- Include nativist Americans
- "Protect" America
- Restrict immigration
- Require twenty-one-year wait for citizenship
- Nominate only white native-born Protestants

Republican

- Raise wages
- Establish transcontinental railroad
- Raise tariffs
- Bar slavery from all territories

Check for Understanding

Ask students to describe briefly the three Presidential candidates in the 1856 election. (Possible responses: Buchanan—Democrat, "Kansasless"; Fremont—Republican, military hero; Fillmore—American/Know Nothing, former President.) Ask students to explain the outcome of the election. (Possible responses: Buchanan wins; Republicans show growing power in North; Know-Nothings realize they won't win a Presidential election unless they unite with Republicans.)

desperate. Therefore, they were willing to work for much less pay than native-born Americans, who were, at the same time, trying to get higher wages. There were other causes of hostility as well.

Linking Past to Present

The 1965 Immigration Act reopened the door for a new wave of immigrants to the United States. By the late 1980's, one out of every two of these immigrants had come from Asia. While the immigrants of European ancestry have overcome nativist hostility and have adopted new identities by changing their names, the Asian immigrants could not blend into the mainstream simply by a change of name. Although they are no longer victims of exclusionist laws, many Asian Americans still experience hostility and discrimination and describe themselves as "strangers from a different shore."

Anti-Catholicism. Nativists objected to so many immigrants being Roman Catholics. They resented the increasing numbers of priests and nuns, parochial schools, and Catholic colleges. Many Americans had grown up in an anti-Catholic tradition that was as old as the Reformation in England. They believed that the Pope headed an organization that wanted to wipe out Protestantism and take over the world. They also were convinced that Catholics could not understand democracy because they were used to following orders from the Pope.

As a result, anti-Catholic books and magazines circulated widely. Shops and factories carried NINA signs, indicating that No Irish Need Apply. On some occasions, mobs turned to violence against Catholics. In Massachusetts one mob burned a convent to the ground. In view of these incidents, clearly these opponents of Catholicism never would have believed that the United States would one day have a Catholic President (John F. Kennedy) or that in 1979 and again in 1987 Pope John Paul II would make a tour of the United States and be warmly welcomed by millions of American Protestants as well as Catholics.

German immigrants encountered much less hostility, at least on religious grounds. However, these immigrants were often referred to in derogatory terms. Nativists made fun of their strange-sounding language and their habit of group singing in social halls. Nativists were also suspicious of what they regarded as German clannishness, or unwillingness to Americanize. They resented Germans forming their own clubs, organizing German-language schools and churches, and publishing German-language newspapers.

New Parties Develop

During the 1840's, nativist Americans organized a number of secret societies with such names as the Sons of America and the Sons of '76. They aimed at "protecting" Americans from the threat of Catholic immigration. In the early 1850's, many of these societies united as a single national organization called the Supreme Order of the Star-Spangled Banner. Its members were pledged to secrecy about the organization's structure and leaders. When questioned about the organization, a member was supposed to say, "I know nothing." Soon, members of the organization were being called **Know-Nothings.**

The Know-Nothings. The Know-Nothings decided they could best achieve their aims by entering politics. They especially wanted to restrict the flow of immigration. They therefore called for changes in the naturalization laws that would require aliens to wait twenty-one years before they could apply for citizenship. They also pledged to support only white, native-born Protestants for public office.

The Know-Nothings were extremely successful at the polls. In 1854 they obtained 25 percent of the vote in New York State and 40 percent of the vote in Pennsylvania. They elected numerous state legislators and governors, and at least seventy-five members of Congress. In 1856 they became known as the American party and nominated ex-President Millard Fillmore for President on the slogan "Americans Must Rule America."

Why were the Know-Nothings such a success? Two reasons seem especially important. First, nativist sentiment was strong and widespread. Second, the American party was stepping into the political vacuum caused by the collapse of the Whigs. It remained to be seen whether the American party would replace the Whigs as one of the national political parties.

A New Republican Party. While the American party was gaining ground, another new party was doing the same. However, unlike the Know-Nothings, this party was based entirely in the North.

For Discussion

What are some contributions made by immigrants to the culture of the U.S.? (Contributions might include: Albert Einstein, science; Irving Berlin, music; Samuel Gompers, workers' rights; Mother Jones, workers' rights; John L. Lewis, workers' rights; Wernher Von Braun, space program; Dr. Edward Teller, science.)

Discuss the hostility some Americans felt toward immigrants. Ask students what kinds of programs might help reduce hostility toward immigrants. (Possible responses: ESL classes; citizenship classes; foreign exchange programs.)

Assign Independent Practice

Have students write two paragraphs comparing the immigrants from Germany and Scandinavia to those from Ireland. Paragraphs should answer these questions: How were they treated? Why? Paragraphs might include:

Germans/Scandinavians

- Worked farms—Midwest
- Were mostly Protestant
- Were ridiculed for language
- Were considered clannish
- Had own language, newspaper, organizations

Irish

- Worked in factories—East
- Built railroads and canals
- Were mostly Catholic
- Worked for less
- Triggered fear of Pope's intervention

Historical Sidelights

• James Buchanan was America's only bachelor President. As a young man he had fallen in love with a wealthy young lady. However, she died under mysterious circumstances shortly after a disagreement with Buchanan. Stricken with grief, the future President never again showed an interest in marriage. • Millard Fillmore was the first President to introduce books into the White House. When he took office in 1850, there was not even one book in the White House. The Fillmores persuaded Congress to allocate money for books: the amount? $250.

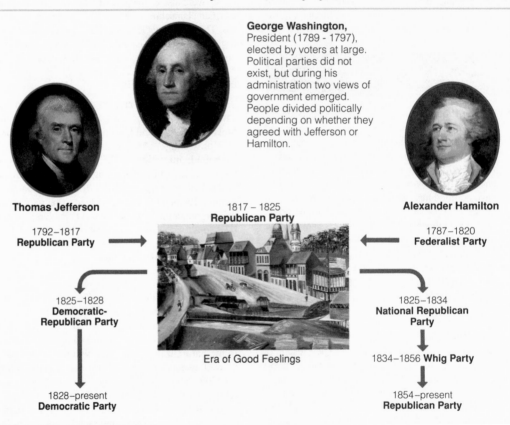

The History of the Two-Party System

George Washington, President (1789 - 1797), elected by voters at large. Political parties did not exist, but during his administration two views of government emerged. People divided politically depending on whether they agreed with Jefferson or Hamilton.

Thomas Jefferson

1792–1817
Republican Party

1817 – 1825
Republican Party

Alexander Hamilton

1787–1820
Federalist Party

1825–1828
Democratic-Republican Party

Era of Good Feelings

1825–1834
National Republican Party

1834–1856 **Whig Party**

1828–present
Democratic Party

1854–present
Republican Party

In the summer of 1854, a group of people representing Whigs, Free-Soilers, and antislavery Democrats met in Jackson, Michigan, and formed the present-day **Republican party.** (It had no connection, however, with Jefferson and Madison's old Republican party.) Unlike the American party, it was not organized around a single issue. Instead, it favored certain economic policies, such as higher wages for labor and the construction of a transcontinental railroad. It also supported a high protective tariff on the basis that if business flourished, so would the worker. Nonetheless, what unified the party and made it grow was the belief that slavery must be barred from all territories.

Buchanan Is Elected in 1856

In 1856 the Democrats nominated **James Buchanan** of Pennsylvania for President. Although

the Democratic platform advocated popular sovereignty in all the territories, Buchanan himself was "Kansasless." He had been out of the country during the Kansas-Nebraska uproar, and so he had not offended anyone on the subject. The Republicans turned to Colonel **John C. Frémont,** an explorer and a hero of the Mexican War. Millard Fillmore headed the American party ticket.

Although the Democrats won the three-way race, the Republicans demonstrated that they were the party of the future. Buchanan, the only President never to marry, received 45 percent of the popular vote; Frémont, 33 percent; and Fillmore, 22 percent. Almost all of Frémont's votes came from Northern states. Most observers realized that the Know-Nothings would never capture the Presidency. However, if the Know-Nothings voted Republican in the next election, the Republicans

Have students complete Chapter 13, Section 3
Enrichment Activity and read Section 4, "Crises Lead to a Showdown."

SECTION 4

Core Lesson

Anticipate the Lesson

Have students review Article 3 of the Constitution. Then ask them the purpose of the Supreme Court. (Answers: to hear original cases affecting ambassadors and states; to hear appellate cases from other courts; to decide legality of laws.) Have students suggest areas in which the Supreme Court has ruled on national issues. (Possible responses: slavery; discrimination; equal rights.)

Picturing History James Buchanan won the Presidency by appeasing the North and the South. Later, however, his inability to make hard decisions delayed the onset of war and led to Lincoln's election as President.

might win—and quite possibly without a single vote from the less populous South.

SECTION 3 REVIEW

Key Terms and People

Explain the significance of: nativism, Know-Nothings, Republican party, James Buchanan, John C. Frémont

Main Ideas

1. Why did most of the immigrants to the United States between 1845 and 1860 settle in free states?
2. Why did nativism spread so rapidly?
3. Why were the Know-Nothings so successful?
4. How did the new Republican party differ from the American party?

Critical Thinking

5. Why did the political beliefs of the American party doom it to eventual failure?

SECTION 4

Crises Lead to a Showdown

GLOSSARY TERM: **Confederacy**

From the time sixty-six-year-old "Old Buck" Buchanan became President, with John C. Breckinridge serving as Vice-President, a series of events took place that led like a trail of powder to a final explosion. The first was a decision of the Supreme Court in the case known as *Scott* v. *Sandford.*

Dred Scott Loses His Case

The case concerned Dred Scott, a black man who was born a slave in Virginia and raised in Missouri. In 1834 Scott's master took him to the free state of Illinois, then to the free Wisconsin Territory, and then back to Missouri. In 1846 Scott sued for his freedom on the grounds that freedom went with the land. Since he had lived in a free state and in a free territory, Scott argued, he was therefore a free man.

The nine justices of the Supreme Court faced two basic legal questions. First, was Scott a citizen of the United States? If not, he could not sue in federal court, and the case would have to be thrown out. Second, did Scott's residence in a free territory

Picturing History Dred Scott's taste of freedom was tragically brief. Although he was freed by his owner after the 1857 Supreme Court decision that held he was a slave and not a citizen, he died the following year.

SECTION 3 REVIEW

Answers

Main Ideas

1. More jobs; no competition from slave labor.

2. Native-born Americans feared losing their jobs to low-paid immigrants.

3. Growing nativist sentiments and the collapse of the Whig party helped them elect congressmen who supported their cause.

4. Republicans supported many issues—was based entirely in the North. Americans: a single-issue party; based nationwide.

Critical Thinking

5. The party's beliefs severely limited its constituency; immigration was changing the ethnic makeup of the country; native-born white Protestants were a shrinking power base. **(analysis)**

make him a free man, even though he had returned to a slave state?

The **Dred Scott decision** was handed down on March 6, 1857. The opinion of Chief Justice Roger B. Taney carried the most weight. Taney declared that blacks had never been regarded as citizens, either before or after the adoption of the Constitution. They had been treated, Taney said, as "beings of an inferior order," with "no rights which any white man was bound to respect." Thus, in this view, national citizenship was for whites only. Two justices disagreed strongly, pointing out that several colonies and states had allowed blacks to vote. A majority of the Court, however, agreed that Scott lacked the legal standing to sue in federal court.

The Court also ruled that being on free territory did not make a slave free. For territories to exclude slavery, Taney said, would be to take away an owner's property "without due process of law." This was a violation of the Fifth Amendment. In effect, the Supreme Court declared the Missouri Compromise unconstitutional. This was the first time since *Marbury* v. *Madison* (1803) that the Court struck down an act of Congress.

The decision in *Scott* v. *Sanford* was one of the most important the Court had ever made. All blacks were declared noncitizens of the United States. Moreover, slavery could exist in any territory of the United States. The decision infuriated the North and delighted the South. What particularly irritated Northerners was the realization that the majority of Supreme Court justices were Southerners. Chief Justice Taney came from a Maryland slaveholding family, although he had freed his own slaves long before. In short, many people believed that the Court had not made an impartial or a fair judgment.

The Economy Fails

In 1857 the national economy suffered a depression. Banks and businesses folded, and tens of thousands of people were out of work. The effects of the depression were greater in the North than in the South because the Southern economy depended on agriculture rather than on business and finance. Southern writers and politicians were quick to point this fact out. They said that the cynical and greedy attitude of Northern merchants and manufacturers was largely responsible for the depression. Northerners snapped back that the Southern economy was more stable only because it rested on the unspeakable evil of slavery.

Linking Past to Present

When banks failed in 1857 and again in 1929, there was no federal insurance program to guarantee deposits. Fortunately, such a program is in place today. However, American taxpayers must pay for this federal insurance. As a result of the failure of more than five hundred savings and loan associations in the late 1980's, it could cost Americans $500 billion over the next three decades to fund the bailout plan. According to some financial experts, that cost will erode economic recovery and growth during the 1990's.

The dispute illustrated the enormous economic differences that existed between the North and the South. The latter may have believed its way of life was superior, but at the same time it feared that it was being overwhelmed by Northern economic power. Hinton Rowan Helper, a Southerner, wrote a book about this matter, called *The Impending Crisis of the South: How to Meet It*. In this book Helper claimed that slavery was actually holding back the economic development of the South. Other Southerners were outraged over Helper's view, but they agreed that he did present some facts of Southern life:

> In one way or another we are slaves to the North. As babies, we are wrapped in Northern muslin. In childhood, we have toys made in the North. In maturity, we serve as a market for all sorts of Northern industries. In old age, we wear glasses made in the North. When we die, our bodies are draped in Northern sheets. We are taken to the grave in a Northern carriage, buried with a Northern spade. Over us rests a Northern gravestone.

In other words, Helper felt that the South should abandon slavery and become industrialized.

Lincoln and Douglas Debate

In 1858 **Stephen A. Douglas,** a leading Democrat, ran for reelection to the United States Senate. Everyone thought that if he was elected, Douglas would run for President in 1860. Therefore, the

Present the Lesson

Ask students how each of the four main events in this section contributed to sectional fears and conflict. (Possible responses: the Dred Scott Decision made the Missouri Compromise unconstitutional and angered Northerners; the failure of the economy showed Southerners the advantages of their agricultural economy as the industrial North was especially hard hit; John Brown's attack on Harpers Ferry and subsequent death sentence aroused intense feelings on both sides; Lincoln's victory in 1860 increased the South's fears for its economy and way of life.)

Republican party hoped it could stop him now. Republicans in Illinois chose **Abraham Lincoln** to oppose Douglas. Lincoln challenged him to a series of seven open-air debates to be held in various parts of the state. These debates drew wide attention. They concerned the most important issue of the day—slavery's expansion in the territories. The speakers were stimulating because of the dramatic contrast in their words and manner. Public interest was stirred also because the speeches were taken down in shorthand by newspaper correspondents who accompanied the candidates. Thus, peo-

Picturing History Photographs of Stephen A. Douglas and Abraham Lincoln are shown at the left. A caricature of long-legged Abe is used in the cartoon below to show Lincoln as "The Fittest of All Candidates" in the 1860 Presidential race.

Check for Understanding

Ask students to prepare a chart showing the four Presidential candidates in 1860 in the first column, their parties in the second column, and main policies in the third column. Chart should include:

Candidate	Party	Policies
Breckinridge	Southern Democrats	Government obliged to protect slavery in territories
Douglas	Northern Democrats	Defended popular sovereignty
Bell	Constitutional Union	Supported the Constitution, the Union, and laws
Lincoln	Republican	Opposed slavery in territories

Presidential Election, 1860

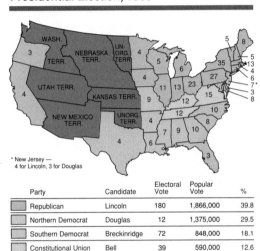

* New Jersey —
4 for Lincoln, 3 for Douglas

Party	Candidate	Electoral Vote	Popular Vote	%
Republican	Lincoln	180	1,866,000	39.8
Northern Democrat	Douglas	12	1,375,000	29.5
Southern Democrat	Breckinridge	72	848,000	18.1
Constitutional Union	Bell	39	590,000	12.6

303 Total Electoral Vote

ple everywhere were kept abreast of what the two men said.

How They Looked. Although short and stocky, Douglas was called the Little Giant by his admirers. He dressed in the latest fashion, including a colorful vest. He traveled from place to place with a large group of followers in a private railroad car. When he arrived for a debate, he rode at the head of a large parade, complete with blaring band. When he spoke, he was all energy and self-confidence. He paced back and forth and used his hands to pound home his points. If one wanted a man who seemed to know everybody and everything, one would choose the Little Giant.

By contrast, Abraham Lincoln was extremely tall and thin. He seemed even taller because of his stove-pipe hat, in which he kept his notes and other odd pieces of paper. He appeared plain and even awkward as he stood solemnly addressing crowds. His clothes were far from fashionable and were usually rumpled. He often slept in them because he traveled in a regular railway car. When speaking, Lincoln talked in direct and plain language.

Lincoln was born in Kentucky but moved to Indiana and then later to Illinois. By age twenty he had reached his full height of six feet four inches. He enjoyed wrestling and other feats of strength. However, he also had qualities that were not common to most frontier youths. Despite having had little formal education, Lincoln was very well

read. All his life, his language reflected the elegant style of the Bible and Shakespeare. He was also a great storyteller. Most of his stories were frontier tales and jokes that probably would not seem funny today. At that time, however, they appealed to people in frontier Illinois.

Lincoln had a successful career as a lawyer and a state politician. He took all kinds of cases and argued both for and against the return of fugitive slaves. He also did legal work for a large railroad corporation. As a state legislator and a one-term congressman, he voted, like other Whigs, in favor of internal improvements. As a young and middle-aged man, however, Lincoln went through long periods of depression. He was, in the term of the day, a "melancholy" man. Nevertheless, there was something attractive about him. He always spoke straight out, without beating around the bush. He was clearly a man one could trust. It thus was no accident that he earned the nickname Honest Abe.

What They Said. In their speeches, Lincoln and Douglas kept their arguments consistent. Douglas believed deeply in popular sovereignty. Lincoln believed just as strongly that Congress could and should keep slavery out of the territories. This was the main issue of the **Lincoln-Douglas debates.** While neither man wanted slavery in the territories, they disagreed as to how to keep it out.

In the course of the debates, each candidate tried to distort the views of the other. Lincoln tried to make Douglas look like a defender of slavery and of the Dred Scott decision. Neither charge was true. In turn, Douglas tried to show that Lincoln was an abolitionist. That charge also was not true. Lincoln said, "I am not, nor ever have been, in favor of bringing about in any way the social and political equality of the white and black races." At the same time, he insisted that slavery was a moral, social, and political wrong and hoped it would eventually disappear where it existed in the South. He confessed that he had no idea how or when this would happen. However, he stressed again and again that the moral wrong of slavery should not be allowed to spread.

Douglas had a difficult time defending popular sovereignty. At first he thought the concept would prove popular in Illinois and throughout the nation. After all, his motto was "Let the people decide." What position could be more acceptable to American voters?

Guided Practice

Tell students that Abraham Lincoln was not an abolitionist. He did not promise to free the slaves if elected. Debate continues among historians about whether Lincoln should be considered a hero of the antislavery movement. One group suggests that Lincoln did not believe in equality of the races, while another suggests that he was far from being a racist compared to other influential whites of his time. Ask students to reread the section "What They Said" and discuss in small groups their feelings about the question of Lincoln's heroism. (Discussions might include: hero—

declared slavery to be morally wrong; not hero—was not in favor of social and political equality of whites and blacks.) Have one person from each group report to the class on that group's consensus.

Lincoln, however, discovered a major weakness in Douglas's argument. In Freeport, Illinois, Lincoln asked his opponent a crucial question: Could the settlers of a territory vote to exclude slavery before the territory became a state? Everyone knew that the Dred Scott decision said no.

Douglas's Freeport Doctrine.   Douglas immediately retorted with an answer that became known as the **Freeport Doctrine.** He acknowledged that slavery could not exist without laws to support it—laws dealing with runaways, the sale of slaves, and the like. If the people of a territory refused to pass such laws, Douglas said, slavery could not exist in practice, no matter what the Supreme Court said about the theory of the matter.

Douglas convinced many Illinois voters who simply wanted to keep slavery out of the territories.

As a result, he won the senatorial election. His Freeport Doctrine cost him most of his support in the South, however. Many Southerners had considered the Dred Scott decision a major victory. Now they heard Douglas saying that settlers could easily get around it.

Although Lincoln lost the election, he was now more than just another ambitious state politician. Suddenly, many Republicans saw him as a possible candidate for the Presidency. Lincoln knew this and was not displeased.

John Brown Strikes Again

While politicians debated the slavery issue, others took a more active approach. **John Brown** had disappeared for several years after his murders at Pottawatomie Creek in Kansas. When he surfaced

Picturing History
Horace Pippin, an African-American artist, painted this scene of John Brown on his way to be hanged. The daguerreotype (above) shows a true likeness of Brown, who wrote the letter at the right.

Assign Independent Practice

Have students answer Section 4 Review questions on paper and complete Chapter 13, Section 4 Daily Activity.

again in 1859, his name became a household word overnight.

Brown had studied the slave uprisings in ancient Rome and on the French island of Haiti. He decided the time had come for something similar to take place in the United States. He obtained secret financial backing from several prominent Boston abolitionists. On October 16, 1859, assisted by only eighteen free blacks and white men, Brown attacked the federal arsenal at Harpers Ferry on the Virginia side of the Potomac River. He and his followers hoped that such an act would encourage the blacks of Virginia to revolt. Brown captured some arms and took several slaveholders hostage, together with several slaves. Then he and his men dug in and waited for news of a general slave rebellion.

No revolt took place, however. Instead, Virginia militiamen and federal troops from Washington, D.C., under the command of Colonel Robert E. Lee, raced to Harpers Ferry and surrounded the arsenal. The raiders found themselves pinned down by rifle fire. Brown held out for two days. With more than half his men dead, however, he surrendered.

The episode shocked the nation. What followed did nothing to heal the new sectional wound. Brown was placed on trial for his life and was found guilty of treason to Virginia. Throughout the trial he insisted calmly that his cause had been just. The wife of the governor of Massachusetts wrote to the wife of Virginia's governor asking if she could come south and nurse Brown's wounds while he was in jail. She got back a stinging letter of refusal. Some men began to call him a martyr for the sacred cause of freedom. Nevertheless, on December 2, 1859, Brown was hanged in the presence of federal troops and a crowd of curious observers. As he walked straight and proudly to the gallows, Brown predicted, "I . . . am now quite certain that the crimes of this guilty land will never be purged away but with blood."

The entire episode aroused fierce emotions in both sections of the country. For months, little incidents continued to inflame both sides. In the South, outraged mobs assaulted whites who were suspected of being antislavery. A North Carolina man, who said he was a long-time supporter of the Union, wrote angrily, "I am willing to take the chances of . . . disunion, sooner than submit any longer to Northern insolence and Northern outrage."

Lincoln Is Elected President

The Presidential election of 1860 was a four-way race. The parties, their platforms, and their candidates were as follows:

1. Southern Democrats took the position set forth in the Dred Scott decision; namely, that the federal government was obligated to protect slavery in the territories. They nominated Vice-President John C. Breckinridge of Kentucky.
2. Northern Democrats lined up behind Stephen A. Douglas, declaring that the best way to decide the slavery question in the territories was by popular sovereignty.
3. The remnants of the Whig and American parties formed the Constitutional Union party, which did not say much except that it supported "the Constitution, the Union, and the laws." Its candidate was John Bell of Tennessee.
4. The Republican party ran Abraham Lincoln on a platform that opposed extending slavery into the territories.

Lincoln won with only 40 percent of the popular vote, but he received 59 percent of the electoral vote—all from the Northern states. Lincoln's election was a clear signal to the South that their economy and their way of life was in grave danger.

Six weeks later, South Carolina seceded from the Union. It was soon followed by six other states in the Lower South: Mississippi, Florida, Alabama, Georgia, Louisiana, and Texas. These were the states where slavery was well established and very profitable. White people in the Cotton Belt knew that slavery was essential to their way of life. They thus were ready to leave the Union in order to defend it.

Forming the Confederacy. In February 1861 representatives of the secessionist states met in Montgomery, Alabama. There they formed a new confederation of states called the Confederate States of America. The new government's constitution resembled that of the United States except for two clauses. Each state in the **Confederacy** was to be "sovereign and independent," and people were guaranteed the right to own slaves. Ex-Senator **Jefferson Davis** of Mississippi was chosen President of the Confederacy. Shortly thereafter, Confederate soldiers began occupying federal post offices, courthouses, customshouses, arsenals, and forts throughout the Lower South.

350

Student Assignment/Homework

Have students answer Chapter 13 Review questions. Go over the answers with students in class.

Concluding the Chapter

Refer students to the map and chart titled "Presidential Election of 1860." Ask them to write a paragraph on the conclusions that can be drawn from the election results regarding the economic and political conflicts of the 1850's. (Conclusions might include: industrial North opposed slavery and supported Lincoln; Southerners, in order to maintain their slavery-based economy, voted for Breckinridge.)

Picturing History   Jefferson Davis, President of the Confederacy, faced a dilemma when his need for a strong centralized rule conflicted with his states' rights policy.

What Happens Now?   During the early months of 1861, the weather was milder than usual in much of the nation. However, a dark thundercloud hung over the American people and their elected officials. Seven slave states had seceded and formed a new nation. Eight slave states remained within the Union. Would they secede also? What was to be done?

People were more confused than angry. In the White House, President Buchanan tried his best to keep the Union together until Lincoln's inauguration on March 4. When one of his cabinet ministers resigned to return to Georgia, the President replaced him with a supporter of the Union. However, Buchanan's lack of firmness was obvious. He announced that secession was illegal but that it would also be illegal for him to do anything about it. In effect, he tied his own hands. Even if he hadn't been so timid, though, there was not much he could have done.

One problem was that Washington was really a Southern city. There were secessionists in Congress and in all the departments of the federal government, as well as in the President's cabinet. Consequently, mass resignations took place. To some people it seemed as if the federal government were melting away.

Furthermore, there was no great groundswell of opinion to indicate what the public was thinking. The North had heard threats of secession so often that when it finally happened, the news was received calmly. **Horace Greeley,** founder of the *New York Tribune,* may have expressed the feelings of many people when he wrote to the Southern states: "Wayward sisters, depart in peace."

Meanwhile, the President-elect sat quietly in Springfield, Illinois. He could do nothing until he was inaugurated in March. He said little publicly. However, he wrote privately that he would not agree to any "compromise in regard to the extension of slavery."

SECTION 4 REVIEW

Key Terms and People

Explain the significance of: Dred Scott decision, Stephen A. Douglas, Abraham Lincoln, Lincoln-Douglas debates, Freeport Doctrine, John Brown, Confederacy, Jefferson Davis, Horace Greeley

Main Ideas

1. What was the significance of the Dred Scott decision?
2. How did the economies of the North and South differ?
3. How did Lincoln's and Douglas's opinions on the question of the expansion of slavery to new territories differ?
4. How did Lincoln's election affect the South?
5. How did the geographical location and political realities of Washington, D.C., make it a Southern city?

Critical Thinking

6. Lincoln stated that he was against social and political equality of the races, but he also said that slavery was "a moral, social, and political wrong." What kind of a social-political system was Lincoln advocating? How does this compare to today's system?

State the Objective

Understand bias in written accounts of events.

Present the Lesson

Suggest to students that although writers usually try to be unbiased, it is almost impossible to approach a topic with absolutely no bias. Discuss ways in which experience, education, nationality, and religious beliefs shape a person and become part of the way that individual views life.

Have a volunteer read aloud the passages by Macrae. Point out to students that the reading was meant to be humorous. Point out also that Macrae completely ignored the African Americans in the United States. This oversight highlights Macrae's bias. To stimulate discus-

sion on bias, ask students the following questions: Would you consider this excerpt a historical document? Why or why not? (Possible responses: yes—it describes events that really happened. No—the facts are interpreted according to Macrae's experience, so they show some bias; Macrae is speaking about only one segment of American society at this time, a segment that was not representative of all America.)

Tell students that bias is a form of persuasion and that, if accepted as truth, can have devastating results. Ask students to suggest when bias might have negative effects. (Possible response: bias can foster racial, religious,

Focus on Critical Thinking Skills

Detecting Bias

Understanding the Skill

Imagine that you have just finished reading a book on the Civil War. You found the book interesting and informative but are unsure how to judge its accuracy. Determining accuracy requires the ability to recognize bias. The word *bias* comes from the French word *biais*, meaning "sloped or slanted."

We might suspect a referee's bias when a call that we believe to be unfair is made against our team. Of course, it is also possible that because we are biased in favor of our team, our own judgment might be somewhat influenced. Authors, like the rest of us, have biases, and those biases appear in their writing to one degree or another. While some authors do try to be open-minded and cite opinions that differ from their own, others ignore dissenting opinions. The burden is on the reader to sort out fact from opinion and to identify other, more subtle forms of bias.

Bias is usually the result of an author's experience, education, nationality, and religious beliefs. For example, two nineteenth-century historians, one from the North, and one from the South, might write very different accounts of the Battle of Gettysburg. Even though both attempt to present an objective report on the event, biases can and do creep in. The critical reader looks for economic, political, social, sexual, or religious bias when evaluating the accuracy of a source. In the account of the Battle of Gettysburg, for example, the reader must recognize that the historians might have been influenced by political ties or strong feelings of loyalty to the Union or the Confederacy.

Here are some techniques for recognizing an author's bias.

• **Analyze the author's point of view.** Who is the author? How well does he or she know the subject? Can the author be considered an expert on this topic? Was the author an eyewitness to what is described? Does the author belong to a special-interest group, religious organization, political party, or social movement that might

promote a one-sided or slanted viewpoint on the subject?

• **Search for clues.** Are there words, phrases, statements, or images that might convey a positive or negative slant? What might these clues reveal about the author's bias?

• **Examine the evidence.** How reliable is the evidence presented? Is what the author relates consistent with other accounts? Is the behavior described consistent with human nature as you have observed it?

Applying the Skill

The following excerpt is taken from a book called *The Americans at Home*. Author David Macrae, a minister from Scotland, wrote his impressions of American women after visiting the United States in the 1860's.

As you read, look for clues that point to possible bias. Keep in mind that although we most often recognize negative bias, positive bias can also be hidden in a humorous or light-hearted piece. As you think about this excerpt, be careful not to confuse the accuracy of the writer's statements with his bias.

> I found many women discharging public functions which have in Britain been monopolized by men. In New Jersey I found a lady "Doctoress" Fowler, acting as a public physician, with the reputation of being the most skillful, and having the largest and most lucrative practice in the district. . . . In different parts of the country I heard ladies delivering public lectures—one of them, Miss Anna Dickinson, amongst the most popular in the States. In Massachusetts I heard of a female . . . clergy*woman*, . . . the Rev. Olympia Brown, who has a good congregation. . . . I heard of "another of the same," the Rev. Miss Chapin, pastor of the Milwaukee Society. . . .
>
> American women, as a rule, are just as gentle, as kind, as agreeable, as affectionate,

or social prejudice, which can have results ranging from unfair treatment of an individual to serious physical and emotional abuse.) Ask students how having the facts can help a reader to detect bias. (Possible response: by knowing the facts about an issue, an individual can make a judgment about how the facts are presented.)

Check for Understanding

Review the answers to the questions at the end of the feature. Ask students to bring in newspaper and magazine articles and editorials that show bias. Have students share their articles.

GODEY'S FASHIONS FOR DECEMBER 1870.

Picturing History "American girls, however, are generally *too* pale and thin," said Scottish minister David Macrae.

and as lovely as our own. . . .

. . . American girls, however, . . . are generally *too* pale and thin. . . . This paleness in the American girls, though often beautiful, is too universal; an eye from the old country begins to long for a rosy cheek. . . . My private impression is . . . the peculiar paleness of the . . . girls connects itself with too much . . . pie. I have strong convictions on this subject of pie. Not to speak of mere paleness, I don't see how the Americans can . . . live to the age they do, considering the amount of pie they eat, and the rapidity with which they generally eat it. I rarely sat down to dinner in America . . . without finding pie, . . . often of several kinds, on the table. . . . Everybody partook of it, down to the . . . baby. Pie seems indispensable. . . . I believe the prohibition of pie would precipitate a revolution. . . .

Paleness and pie notwithstanding, the American girls are very delightful. And in one point they fairly surpass the majority of English girls—they are all educated and well informed. . . . The admirable educational system . . . covering the whole area of soci-

ety, has given them education whether they are rich or poor, has furnished them with a great deal of general information, and has quickened their desire for more. An American girl will talk with you about anything, and . . . seem to feel interest in it. Their tendency is perhaps to talk too much, and . . . it seemed to me sometimes to make no perceptible difference whether they knew anything of the subject they talked about or not. But they usually know a little of everything; and their general intelligence and vivacity make them very delightful companions.

Practicing Your Skill

1. What is bias? What are some types of bias?
2. What words, phrases, statements, or images in the excerpt from *The Americans at Home* point to a possible bias?
3. What in David Macrae's background might help the reader identify and understand his bias?
4. Based on his observations, Macrae has come to certain faulty conclusions. What are these conclusions? What bias has led Macrae to these conclusions?

FOCUS ON SKILLS

Answers

Practicing Your Skill

1. Bias is an author's slant on the facts. • Economic, political, social, sexual, and religious bias.

2. Possible answers: "Doctoress" Fowler; clergy*woman*; "*too* pale and thin"; "paleness…is too universal"; "an eye from the old country begins to long for a rosy cheek"; "an American girl will talk with you about anything, and…seem to feel interest in it. Their tendency is perhaps to talk too much, and…it seemed to me sometimes to make no perceptible difference whether they knew anything of the subject they talked about or not."

3. As a Scottish minister, Macrae is perhaps more conservative than most Americans of the time.

4. Faulty conclusions include: the paleness of American girls is due to the amount of pie they eat; the prohibition of pie would cause a revolution. • Macrae has a national bias. Apparently people in his country, especially women, do not eat such a quantity of pie.

Answer Key

Key Terms and People

These are highlighted in the text in the order in which they appear in this list.

Main Ideas

1. Slaveholders or agents could seize slaves in Northern states, with help from federal marshalls if necessary; judges were paid a higher fee for ruling against slaves; people who aided fugitive slaves were fined and jailed. • Because other fugitive slave laws weren't strict enough.

2. Cruelty to fugitive slaves brought evil of slavery close to home.

3. Divided Nebraska Territory into Kansas and Nebraska territories; gave each popular sovereignty. • Stephen A. Douglas. • Repealed Missouri Compromise and caused violence in Kansas.

4. Proslavery settlers set up fraudulent government; antislavery settlers set up another government; a civil war resulted.

5. Fear of job competition and Catholic religion. • Know-Nothings and Americans. • Know-Nothings formed secret societies about which they would tell nothing. Americans felt they were more American than anyone else.

6. Higher wages, transcontinental railroad, high protective tariff, no slavery in territories.

7. Missouri Compromise was ruled unconstitutional: slavery could exist in any territory; African Americans were declared noncitizens.

8. Encourage a slave revolt and obtain weapons for it.

Critical Thinking Questions

9. Gray, gaunt, intense eyes, bitter mouth; had no fear, was clever, was sure he was right. • Angry at slavery because he knew it was wrong.

10. Freed slaves could be kidnapped, could not have a jury trial, and could not speak in court to prove they were free;

judges were paid double for declaring black people slaves; people aiding fugitives were fined and jailed. • To placate the South when California became a free state in the Great Compromise.

➤**11.** That Supreme Court, composed of seven Southerners, would never have found it unconstitutional. Chief Justice Taney declared that African Americans were not citizens. Also, the Court said that tak-

ing away property—slaves—violated the Fifth Amendment.

➤**12.** If tested against the supremacy clause in Article 6, they might well have been found unconstitutional. These state laws were trying to nullify a federal law.

13. The idea of "letting the people decide" was popular with Americans.

➤**14.** South was dependent on manufactured goods of the North. • Possible answers:

yes—South would have wanted to manufacture its own goods. No—South wanted to defend its way of life and would never agree to change.

Critical Thinking Activities

15. Possible answers: Southern reaction—book is propaganda; slave owners take care of slaves and need them to maintain economy. Northern

---

CHAPTER **13** REVIEW

Write your answers on a separate sheet of paper.

Key Terms and People

Explain the significance of: Franklin Pierce, Charles Sumner, James Buchanan, John C. Frémont, Confederacy, Jefferson Davis, Horace Greeley

Main Ideas

1. What were the provisions of the Fugitive Slave Law of 1850? Why was this law passed?
2. How did the Fugitive Slave Law result in increasing the ranks of Northern abolitionists?
3. What were the provisions of the Kansas-Nebraska Act? Who was the primary author of this act? What was the effect of the act?
4. Why was Kansas known as Bleeding Kansas during the 1850's?
5. Why did nativism develop? What were two popular names for the political party the nativists formed? Why were these names attached to them?
6. What was the platform of the new Republican party?
7. What were the effects of the Dred Scott decision?
8. What did John Brown expect to achieve by attacking the federal arsenal at Harpers Ferry?

Critical Thinking Questions

9. **Analyzing Literature.** List the characteristics and physical qualities of John Brown as shown in the excerpt from *God's Angry Man*. Why was he so angry?
10. **Drawing Conclusions.** What was so unjust about the Fugitive Slave Law? Why was it written the way it was?
11. **Making Deductions.** Do you think the Fugitive Slave Law would have been declared unconstitutional by the same Supreme Court that ruled in the Dred Scott decision? Why or why not?
12. **Synthesizing Ideas.** Review the *McCulloch* v. *Maryland* decision in Chapter 9, page 245. Do you think the personal liberty laws that were passed by several Northern states might have

been found unconstitutional by the Supreme Court? Why or why not?
13. **Evaluating Decisions.** Why do you think Douglas continued the idea of popular sovereignty in the Democratic platform in 1860 after it had proved so devastating in Kansas?
14. **Predicting Outcomes.** In *The Impending Crisis of the South* Hinton R. Helper wrote, ''In one way or another we [Southerners] are slaves to the North.'' What did he mean by this? Do you think that if war had not occurred, the Southern economy would have gradually become industrialized, leading ultimately to the phasing out of slavery? Why or why not?

Critical Thinking Activities

15. **Evaluating Sources.** If you were the owner of a cotton plantation in Arkansas, how would you review *Uncle Tom's Cabin* for your local paper? What would you say if you were a shoe manufacturer in New England? Write a three paragraph review showing either the Northern or the Southern reaction.
16. **Comparing People and Ideas.** Compare Lincoln and Douglas in the areas listed below.

	Lincoln	Douglas
a. Physical features		
b. Beliefs on slavery		
c. Stand on popular sovereignty		

17. **Analyzing Maps.** Look at the map on page 348, ''Presidential Election of 1860.'' How many states comprised the United States in 1860? How many were slave states? Why do you think the border states—Virginia, Kentucky, and Tennessee—voted for Bell? Why did Missouri vote for Douglas?
18. **Linking Past to Present.** Name a few issues that have led to conflict in recent history. What violence did they cause?

reaction—book shows a race of people being degraded.
16. Lincoln: tall, thin, plain, awkward, thoughtful; slavery was a moral wrong, against slavery in territories; explored weaknesses in Douglas's doctrine. • Douglas: short, stocky, fashionable, energetic; against expansion of slavery in territories; defended popular sovereignty with Freeport Doctrine.
17. Thirty-three • Fifteen. • Border states didn't support secession, yet were against Douglas and Lincoln, who were against extension of slavery. • Missouri voted for Douglas because it felt more like a Northern state but couldn't support Lincoln's stand on slavery as a moral wrong.
➤**18.** Possible answers: civil rights marches have ended in death for some; integrated education has resulted in backlash reaction—harrassment of black children; antiwar demonstrations have ended in destruction of property and injury and death.

➤**Question suitable for cooperative learning.**

TELESCOPING THE TIMES: 1850–1861

A Decade of Crisis

The new Fugitive Slave Law made it easier for slave catchers to return runaways to slavery. Freed slaves in the North knew that they too were in danger. Many Northern states passed personal liberty laws that conflicted with the federal act. Horrifying incidents of captures and rescues brought slavery home to many Northerners. So did a novel, *Uncle Tom's Cabin*. It condemned the system of slavery in highly dramatic terms. Northerners praised the novel, and Southerners called it a pack of lies. Harriet Beecher Stowe's book became one of the most influential books ever written in this country.

In 1854 Senator Stephen A. Douglas of Illinois introduced the Kansas-Nebraska Act. The act repealed the Missouri Compromise of 1820 and left the question of slavery in those territories for their residents to decide. This provision became known as "popular sovereignty." The act made both Northerners and Southerners furious. Soon Kansas had two rival governments. A civil war broke out among the frontier settlers. Violence flared even on the floor of Congress when a representative from South Carolina seriously beat a senator from Massachusetts with a cane. The Kansas-Nebraska Act had opened old wounds.

From 1845 to 1860 huge numbers of European immigrants came to the United States from Scandinavia, Germany, and Ireland. Many Americans felt hostile toward the newcomers, partly because they were foreign and even more because most of the Irish were Roman Catholics. Nativist sentiment became so strong that it formed the basis for a new political party, the Know-Nothings. For a short time that party was very successful. Then a new Republican party won support in the Northern states because it opposed the further extension of slavery.

In the Dred Scott case of 1857, the Supreme Court declared that no United States territory could keep out slavery. The Court also said that no black could be a citizen of the United States. The economic depression of 1857 hit the North much harder than the South. The next year saw dramatic political debates about slavery between Senator Douglas and Abraham Lincoln, both candidates for senator. John Brown, a white abolitionist, led a raid on a federal arsenal in Virginia, hoping to stir the slaves to revolt. In 1860 Lincoln was elected President entirely by Northern votes. Seven states in the deep South seceded and formed the Confederacy.

The new Southern government was formed in 1861. Ex-Senator Jefferson Davis of Mississippi was chosen as President of the Confederacy. The constitution of the Confederacy was similar to that of the United States except that each state was to be independent and slavery was to be legal.

Chronology of Main Events

1850	Fugitive Slave Law passed
1852	*Uncle Tom's Cabin* appears
1853	Franklin Pierce inaugurated President
1854	Republican party founded; Kansas-Nebraska Act passed
1856	Violence erupts in Bleeding Kansas
1857	James Buchanan inaugurated President; Dred Scott decision
1858	Lincoln-Douglas debates
1859	John Brown raids Harpers Ferry
1860	South Carolina secedes
1861	Abraham Lincoln inaugurated President; Confederacy formed

Telescoping the Times may be used as an alternative to having students read the entire chapter, as a chapter preview, or as a chapter review.

Global Perspectives

1862   Bismarck becomes Prime Minister of Prussia.

1863   Dutch West Indies abolish slavery.

1863   French establish protectorate over Cambodia.

1864   First Communist International organized.

1865   Joseph Lister introduces antiseptic surgery.

For Discussion

How many years passed from the publication of the *Communist Manifesto* to the organization of the First Communist International? (Answer: 16 years—see Global Perspectives, Chapter 12.)

Additional Resources

- Geography Activities
- Skills Activities
- Thematic Activities
- Economic Activities
- Cultural Literacy Activities
- Literary Source Readings
- Primary Source Readings
- Nuclear Peacekeeping
- Transparencies
- Computer Test Generator

Additional Teaching Strategies

SECTION 1

For Basic Students: Give students a copy of the outline map of the U.S., and have them outline and label the Confederate states in gray (South Carolina, Mississippi, Florida, Alabama, Georgia, Louisiana, Texas, Virginia, Arkansas, Tennessee, North Carolina), the Union states in blue (Maine, Vermont, New Hampshire, Massachusetts, New York, Rhode Island, Connecticut, Pennsylvania, New Jersey, West Virginia, Ohio, Indiana, Illinois, Michigan, Wisconsin, Iowa, Minnesota, Kansas, Oregon, California), and the border states in red (Maryland, Missouri, Kentucky, Delaware). List these states on the board, and encourage students to refer to the list frequently as they work.

For Advanced Students: Have students write a report on the Copperheads and explain why even they began to favor the war effort after the battle at Fort Sumter. (Reports might include: Copperheads had sympathized with South and saw no reason to fight; the Copperheads felt that they must defend the Union after the Confederate attack on Fort Sumter.)

SECTION 2

For Basic Students: Ask students to look up the terms *Gatling gun, submarine,* and *ironclad* in an encyclopedia and report on the role each of these weapons played in the Civil War. (Reports might include: they made wars less human; enabled soldiers to fight enemy from greater distances; enabled navies to better wage war in water and enforce naval blockades.)

For Advanced Students: Ask students to assume the role of newspaper reporters and write articles on the Battle of Shiloh. Students should decide if they are writing for a Confederate or Union paper and write from the appropriate point of view. (Articles might include: Union General Grant leads Union troops to victory; cost in lives is 13,000 Union and 10,000 Confederate soldiers. Union does not accept surrender; both sides use scouts, divisional commanders, and fortifications.)

SECTION 3

For Basic Students: Ask each student to list and discuss the reasons for at least three sources of friction between the U.S. and Great Britain during the Civil War. (Possible sources: British were divided on whether to recognize the Confederacy; British needed cotton from South; many British were happy to see their former colonies fighting among themselves.)

For Advanced Students: Have the students stage a mock congressional debate to decide whether to pass the Emancipation Proclamation. Ask one team to present the views of those favoring the bill and the other team to present the views of congressmen opposed to the bill. Allow each team a ten-minute preparation period, a three-minute presentation, a two-minute rebuttal by the opposing team, and a one-minute summary statement. (Reasons for support might include: unification of Northern population; good way to punish South. Reasons for opposition might include: it frees no slaves in Union states; it cannot be enforced in the Confederacy.)

SECTION 4

For Basic Students: Ask each student to assume the role of a teenager living during the Civil War. Students should decide whether they live in the North or South. Ask each student to compose a letter to a European friend or relative describing their lives and the shortages experienced during the war. (Shortages might include: meat; shoes; candles or oil for lamps; warm clothing.)

For Advanced Students: Ask each student to write a letter to the editor of a Northern Civil War era newspaper declaring outrage at the reported conditions in prisoner-of-war camps. Students should appeal to the public to help change these conditions. (Details might include: unsanitary conditions; lack of food and clothing; inadequate medical care.)

SECTION 5

For Basic Students: Ask students to prepare a chart listing five important battles of the Civil War in the first column, where each was fought in the second column, when each was fought in the third column, and which side won in the fourth column. When students have finished, compare information and determine by consensus which five military actions were most important to the Union victory. Charts might include:

Battle	State	Year	Victory
Bull Run	Virginia	1861	Confederate
Shiloh	Tennessee	1862	Union
Manassas Junction	Virginia	1862	Confederate
New Orleans	Louisiana	1862	Union
Antietam	Virginia	1862	Union
Gettysburg	Pennsylvania	1863	Union

Note: This is a cumulative exercise; it includes information from all of Chapter 14.

For Advanced Students: Ask each student to assume the role of a Lincoln delegate at the 1864 Republican Convention. Have each student compose a two-minute speech focusing on reasons to re-elect Lincoln for President. (Speeches might include: experienced with war concerns; freed slaves; held nation together; honest and compassionate.)

Further Reading for Students

Higginson, Thomas W. *Army Life in a Black Regiment*. New York: W. W. Norton, 1984.

Kantor, MacKinlay. *Andersonville*. Bergenfield, N. J.: New American Library, 1971.

Reid, Mitchell. *Civil War Soldiers*. New York: Viking Penguin, 1988.

Sandburg, Carl. *Abraham Lincoln: The Prairie Years and The War Years*. San Diego, Calif.: Harcourt Brace Jovanovich, 1974.

Time-Life Books. *Sherman's March*. Civil War Series. Alexandria, Va.: Time-Life Books, 1986.

White, Henry. *Robert E. Lee and the Southern Confederacy*. Brooklyn, N.Y.: Haskell Booksellers, 1969.

Bibliography for Teachers

Books

Commager, Henry Steele, ed. *Fifty Basic Civil War Documents*. Melbourne, Fla.: R.E. Krieger Publishing Company, 1982. Paper.

Jordan, Robert Paul. *The Civil War*. Washington, D.C.: National Geographic Special Publications, 1969.

Meredith, Roy. *Mathew Brady's Portrait of an Era*. New York: W.W. Norton, 1982.

Audio-Visuals

The Civil War. Educational Enrichment Materials of the New York Times. Filmstrip.

The Red Badge of Courage and Other Stories. Listening Library. Audio cassettes.

Walt Whitman: A Poet of the Civil War. Coronet. Filmstrip and cassette.

Computer Resources

American History Keyword Series-Civil War Keyword. (Apple) Focus Media.

American History II. (Apple) Sliwa Enterprises.

Electoral College. (Apple/TRS 80) Opportunities for Learning.

Lincoln's Decisions. (Apple/TRS 80) Opportunities for Learning.

Teacher's Notes:

Teaching Resources, Unit 3 Booklet

Lesson Study Sheets pp. 169-188
Daily Activities pp. 189-198
Enrichment Activities pp. 199-208
Reteaching Activities pp. 209-218
Chapter Review p. 219
Chapter Mastery Tests pp.. 221-232
Telescoping the Times Study Sheet p. 233

Chapter Objectives

Students will learn:
- how the Civil War began
- the results of Northern and Southern military strategies
- how the impact of military events affected the political conduct of the war
- how the war changed domestic life in the North and South
- how and why the North won

Using the Chapter Time Line

How many years did the Civil War last? (Answer: 4) Who was President during the entire Civil War? (Answer: Abraham Lincoln)

Picturing History Two young men, a Union soldier (left) and a Confederate soldier (right), posed for these Civil War photographs. This was the first war in which the camera was used extensively, and families at home were eager to receive snapshots.

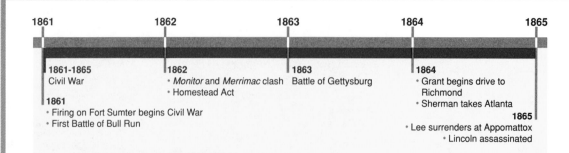

1861   1862   1863   1864   1865

1861-1865
Civil War

• *Monitor* and *Merrimac* clash **1863** Battle of Gettysburg
• Homestead Act

1864
• Grant begins drive to Richmond
• Sherman takes Atlanta

1861
• Firing on Fort Sumter begins Civil War
• First Battle of Bull Run

1865
• Lee surrenders at Appomattox
• Lincoln assassinated

Links to American Literature

Stephen Crane: born 1871 in Newark, New Jersey; educated at Lafayette College and Syracuse University; first worked as free-lance reporter in the slums of New York; worked as an American and foreign newspaper correspondent during the Greco-Turkish War (1897) and the Spanish-American War (1898).

Works include: *Maggie, a Girl in the Streets*; published under the pen name Johnston Smith, *Maggie* was commercially unsuccessful.

The Red Badge of Courage: published in 1895, earned Crane international recognition; was viewed as a penetrating, realistic, psychological study of a young soldier in the Civil War.

Introducing the Chapter

Ask students to look at the maps and pictures in the chapter and volunteer facts they already know about the Civil War. (Possible responses: Lincoln was President; it was a war between North and South.) Discuss reminders of the war still evident today. (Reminders include: Confederate flags; North-South rivalries; popular novels; made-for-TV movies.)

CHAPTER 14 1861–1865

The Civil War

Links to American Literature

To the youth it was an onslaught of redoubtable dragons. He became like the man who lost his legs at the approach of the red and green monster. He waited in a sort of horrified, listening attitude. He seemed to shut his eyes and wait to be gobbled. . . .

He yelled then with fright and swung about.

Directly he began to speed toward the rear in great leaps. His rifle and cap were gone. His unbuttoned coat bulged in the wind. The flap of his cartridge box bobbed wildly and his canteen, by its slender cord, swung out behind. On his face was all the horror of those things which he imagined. . . .

The moment the regiment ceased its advance the protesting sputter of musketry became a steady roar. Long and accurate fringes of smoke spread out. From the top of a small hill came level belchings of yellow flame that caused an inhuman whistling in the air. . . .

The youth ran like a madman to reach the woods before a bullet could discover him. He ducked his head low like a football player. In his haste his eyes almost closed and the scene was a wild blur.

— STEPHEN CRANE, *The Red Badge of Courage*

The Civil War was perhaps the most wrenching war to be fought by Americans. It took more American lives than any other war in which Americans have fought. In the struggle between North and South, friend fought against friend, brother against brother. Each side believed it was right. Neither understood the deep conviction of the other. Families were destroyed. Frightened sixteen- and seventeen-year-olds died on the battlefields. The South was wrecked and impoverished.

Chapter Overview

The word *trauma* describes a past shock so severe that it affects the way a person later thinks or behaves. For the entire nation, the Civil War was a trauma. The more we learn about this war, the better we will understand our nation and ourselves. In this chapter, you will learn about the events and military strategies of the war's first two years. Next, you will study the war's impact on politics and on daily life. Finally, you will learn how and why the North won. To achieve these objectives, the chapter is divided into five sections.

Chapter Outline

1. **The Union Divides**
2. **The Real War Begins**
3. **The Goals of War Change**
4. **Life Goes on Behind the Lines**
5. **The Road to Peace Is Rugged**

SECTION 1

The Union Divides

GLOSSARY TERMS: **Copperheads, border states**

When Lincoln took his oath of office on March 4, 1861, seven of the southernmost states had already seceded. Nevertheless, many Americans thought that actual war could be avoided. Indeed, probably a majority of Americans opposed the idea of war. Within six weeks, however, fighting broke out between the North and the South. By May 20, four more states had left the Union. Another four looked as if they might secede, too.

Events at Fort Sumter Lead to War

As you know from the previous chapter, soon after the Confederacy was formed, it began taking over federal offices and forts. By the time Lincoln was inaugurated, only two forts in Confederate States remained in Union hands. The more important of these stood at the mouth of the harbor in Charleston, South Carolina. **Fort Sumter** was built of heavy brick, but it was within easy range of cannon positioned on the nearby shore. The Confederates wanted to take control of this fort because it symbolized Union power. Over it flew the Stars and Stripes rather than the Stars and Bars, the Confederate flag. Lincoln was equally determined to keep the fort. However, he did not want to shed the first blood.

The commander of Fort Sumter, Major Robert Anderson, sent Lincoln word that he could not hold the fort for more than six weeks unless he received reinforcements and supplies. Lincoln responded that he would not send fresh troops to Fort Sumter since such an action would look like an attack on the Confederacy. He did, however, order that supplies be sent to the troops already stationed there.

Now the burden of responsibility lay with the Confederates. If the fort remained in Union hands, the new Confederate government would appear weak. On the other hand, if they attacked peaceful ships carrying food and medical supplies, they would be guilty of firing the first shot.

In the early morning dark of April 12, 1861, Confederate commander General **P. G. T. Beauregard** gave the order for the cannon to begin firing. The Union supply fleet stood off at a distance, helpless against the shore-based cannon. The walls of the fort began to crumble. After thirty-four hours, Major Anderson surrendered. He and his men were allowed to sail back north on one of the supply ships. The Stars and Bars now flew over Fort Sumter. Miraculously, no one was killed in the heavy shelling.

The incident electrified the North. Until then, there had been a considerable difference of opinion as to whether the federal government should oppose secession. Many Northerners felt that because the Southern states had entered the Union peacefully, they therefore had the right to withdraw peacefully. Abolitionists such as William Lloyd Garrison were actually pleased by secession because they did not want slave states in the Union.

People in the Chapter

Robert Anderson, Union commander at Fort Sumter, surrendered to Confederate General P. G. T. Beauregard, his former instructor at West Point. Jefferson Davis, another West Point graduate, telegraphed Beauregard to "tender my friendly remembrance to Major Anderson."

Thomas Jackson received his nickname Stonewall after holding off the Union at the First Battle of Bull Run. A fellow officer said, "There is Jackson standing like a stone wall." The remark was intended for the whole unit, but the name Stonewall stuck to Jackson.

George Meade won the great battle at Gettysburg but failed to pursue Lee's retreating army across the Potomac. President Lincoln wrote Meade, "He was within your grasp, and to have closed upon him would . . . have ended the war." Lincoln, however, reconsidered and tore up the letter the following day.

William Tecumseh Sherman was named after a Shawnee prince. His friends called him Cump and observed that he was as lively as an Indian war party. A colleague wrote that he "talked incessantly and more rapidly than any man I ever knew." Perhaps his most quoted remark is "Hold the fort! I am coming!"

358

Present the Lesson

Have students prepare a time line that traces events of the Civil War from the 1860 election through the First Battle of Bull Run. Time lines should include:

November 1860   Lincoln elected.
December 1860   South Carolina secedes.
March 1861   Lincoln inaugurated.
April 1861   Confederates capture Fort Sumter.
May 1861   Seceded Southern states total eleven.
July 1861   Confederates win at First Battle of Bull Run.

Check for Understanding

Ask a student to write his or her time line on the board. Ask the class what cause and effect relationships exist among the events on the time line. (Answers: Lincoln's election prompted seven states to secede; the Confederate capture of Fort Sumter encouraged four more Southern states to secede.)

Picturing History   This Currier and Ives print dramatizes the attack by Confederate forces on Fort Sumter in Charleston Harbor on April 12, 1861.

They figured that in a South cut off from the industrial North, slavery would wither away. So-called **Copperheads,** or Northern Democrats, sympathized with the South and asked "Why fight?" To them, a war was a needless sacrifice. Instead they felt that Northerners should concentrate on turning the United States into a worldwide industrial power.

Nevertheless, the news from Fort Sumter united most Northerners. As Senator Stephen A. Douglas himself said, "Every man must be for the United States or against it. There can be no neutrals in this war—only patriots and traitors."

Other Southern States Secede.   On April 15 President Lincoln issued a proclamation calling for volunteers to fight in the Union army. Two days later Virginia seceded on the ground that the call for volunteers was an act of war. Virginia was followed by Arkansas, Tennessee, and North Carolina. However, the western part of Virginia, which had few slaves, had little sympathy with the Confederacy. With some military help from the federal government, the area seceded from Virginia and applied for admission to the Union. West Virginia thus became a separate state—the thirty-fifth—on June 20, 1863.

The Border States.   The big question at this time was, what would the **border states** do? These states were Maryland, Missouri, Kentucky, and Delaware. All were slave states.

Delaware had few slaves and remained loyal to the Union. Maryland had many more. In fact, on the way to his inauguration in Washington, Lincoln

had to go through Baltimore in disguise because he thought he might be killed by Southern sympathizers. During this time, a Massachusetts regiment on its way to the capital was mobbed in Baltimore. Troops and civilians were killed. Despite all this pro-Southern opinion, however, Maryland remained within the Union. Kentucky was also divided in opinion. However, although Kentuckians fought on both sides during the Civil War, the state government remained under the control of Unionists.

In Missouri, the fourth border state, fighting between the Confederate and Union forces went on for nearly two years. In the end, however, Missouri remained within the Union, too.

Advantages and Disadvantages Are Assessed

Now that war had broken out, what advantages and disadvantages did each side have? At first glance it seemed that the North had all the advantages. A closer look, however, proved this view misleading.

The Northern Position.   The North had a great advantage in terms of sheer numbers. Its overall population was 22 million, compared with the South's 9 million. More important, in 1861 the North had almost three times as many men of fighting age as the South did, about 4 million to the South's 1.5 million. The Confederacy could have had more soldiers, but it refused to arm any of its 3.5 million blacks. Blacks were used, however, to build fortifications.

Have students study "Advantages and Disad-vantages Are Assessed" (pages 359-360) and prepare a chart that lists the advantages of the North and South at the start of the war. Chart might include:

North
- Has greater population
- Has more industry
- Produces more food
- Controls most railroads
- Has strong civilian leadership

South
- Defends home soil
- Has strong military leadership
- Exports cotton to Europe

Assign Independent Practice

Have students answer the Section 1 Review questions orally.

Map Skills

TX, LA, MS, AL, GA, FL, SC, AR, TN, NC, VA • Northern part

For Discussion

What were some of the weaknesses of the Confederate government? (Possible responses: poor civilian leadership; disagreement over states' rights; little industry or food-based agriculture.) Which were the most serious immediate problems? (Possible responses: lack of civilian leadership; discord over states' rights.) Which were the most serious long-range problems? (Possible response: lack of industry and agriculture to provide supplies and food for the troops.) What were some possible solutions for short and long-range weaknesses? (Possible responses: hold new elections; revise Constitution; develop foreign trade to get products they could not produce; change from cotton to food crops; ration civilian supplies.)

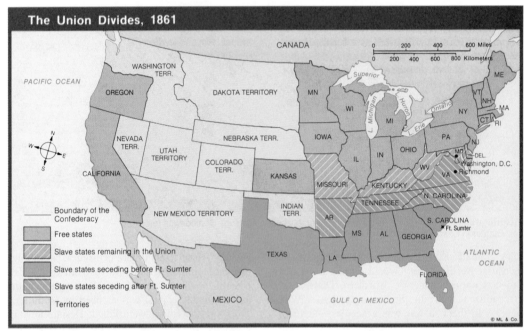

Map Skills **Region** Which states seceded from the Union? **Location** Where in the Confederacy were the states that seceded after the battle at Ft. Sumter?

The North had an even greater advantage in manufacturing and food production. The free states produced four-fifths of the nation's industrial goods. They also produced two-thirds of the nation's food. The North produced far more grain than the South. Indeed, after a while the plantations and farms of the South were forced to switch from growing cotton to growing food, just to feed their people. In addition, the North contained two-thirds of the country's railroad mileage. It could transport men and supplies much faster and in greater numbers than could the South.

Civilian leadership in the North also proved to be very effective. Lincoln himself was a patient yet decisive administrator. He appointed to his cabinet the most capable Republicans he could find. Lincoln also removed known secessionists from the bureaucracy and replaced them with Northern sympathizers.

The Southern Position. The South also had certain advantages, especially in the early years of the struggle. First, in order to exist as a new nation, the Confederacy had merely to defend its own soil. In contrast, Northern armies had to attack, capture, and occupy territory far from their home bases.

Second, on the whole, Confederate troops had better leadership in the field than Northern troops did. Finally, Southerners were more accustomed than Northerners to handling guns and horses.

The South also had "King Cotton," on which the British textile industry relied. Southern leaders therefore were convinced that Britain would be forced to recognize and assist the new Confederate nation.

One of the South's weaknesses was its civilian leadership. **Jefferson Davis** was President of the Confederacy throughout the war. Davis looked and acted like a Southern aristocrat. Although he had gone to West Point and served in the Mexican War, most historians consider him a poor military strategist.

The South Stands Strong at Bull Run

When Virginia seceded from the Union, the capital of the Confederacy was transferred from Montgomery, Alabama, to Richmond, Virginia. Thus the capitals of the two nations were only one hundred miles apart. Richmond became the symbol of the Southern rebellion. If Richmond fell, the Confederacy would fail.

Student Assignment/Homework

Have students complete Chapter 14, Section 1 Enrichment Activity and read Section 2 "The Real War Begins."

SECTION 2
Core Lesson

Anticipate the Lesson

Ask students how the Battle of Antietam differed from other early battles of the war. (Answer: It was fought in the North.) Remind students that most of the fighting of the Civil War took place on Southern soil. Ask how this might have affected Southern soldiers. (Possible response: Southerners were fighting to save their homeland, their families and property, so had more at stake than Northerners.)

State the Objective

Understand the results of Northern and Southern military strategies from Bull Run to Antietam (1861-1862).

Like most people, Lincoln expected a short war. His first call for volunteers had provided for terms of enlistment lasting only three months. By July 1861, however, those terms were nearly up. Meanwhile, the newspapers and politicians of Washington were calling "On to Richmond." Lincoln therefore sent some thirty thousand inexperienced young soldiers on the road south toward the Confederate capital.

Shortly after crossing the Potomac into Virginia, they were stopped at the little creek of Bull Run. Here the Northern soldiers confronted an equally inexperienced Confederate army. At this **First Battle of Bull Run** the civilian population was similarly unacquainted with the realities of war. In Washington, for instance, ladies and gentlemen put on their best clothes and mounted their carriages and horses. Carrying picnic baskets and iced champagne, they rode out to observe the battle!

At first, the Union forces had the upper hand. In the middle of the day, however, more Virginia troops arrived under the command of Thomas J. Jackson. Their strong stand turned the tide and gave their leader a permanent nickname, **Stonewall Jackson.**

As often happens with untrained and inexperienced soldiers, the Northern army's retreat became a rout. The men streamed back to Washington, jamming the roads along with the carriages of the civilian "observers." For days the city of Washington, D.C., expected invasion. However, the Southern troops were also disorganized and exhausted, and they failed to seize this opportunity to pursue the Northern army and capture the capital.

SECTION 1 REVIEW

Key Terms and People

Explain the significance of: Fort Sumter, P. G. T. Beauregard, Copperheads, border states, Jefferson Davis, First Battle of Bull Run, Stonewall Jackson

Main Ideas

1. To the South, what did the Union occupation of Fort Sumter symbolize?
2. What was the effect in the North of the South's taking Fort Sumter?
3. What advantages did the North have over the South?
4. What advantages did the South have over the North?
5. What happened at the First Battle of Bull Run?

Critical Thinking

6. How did Lincoln attempt to discourage war during the first weeks of his Presidency?

SECTION 2

The Real War Begins

GLOSSARY TERM: **ironclads**

The First Battle of Bull Run shocked people on both sides of the Potomac River. For the first time they began to realize what was happening. They were at war in earnest. This was not a skirmish, and it was not going to be over by Christmas. Time was needed for training and equipping real armies. While the victory at Bull Run gave the people of the Confederacy a great boost in morale, it made Northerners grow grim and determined.

Tactics Are Paramount in Modern Warfare

At first, both sides in the great conflict relied on volunteers for their armies. When the two governments first called for volunteers, however, more men signed up than could be used effectively. Furthermore, each of the states raised its own regiments, resulting in regiments that did not wear the same colors. It was only in the later years of the war that Confederate soldiers wore gray and that Union forces wore blue.

New Guns. At the beginning of the war, troops on both sides were armed with old-fashioned muskets. These were not much more efficient than the ones used in the American Revolution. They had smooth bores, or interior cylinders, and their gunfire hardly reached more than 100 yards. This meant that until troops came within a hundred yards of the enemy, nothing much happened. Once they were within range, however, victory usually depended on numbers, especially if the attackers used fixed bayonets.

Within a year, soldiers on both sides were using breech-loading rifles. *Breech-loaded* means that the powder and ball went into the gun at the near end

SECTION 1 REVIEW

Main Ideas

1. Federal power.

2. Northerners united against the South and for the war.

3. Northern advantages—greater population, more men of fighting age, more manufacturing, plentiful food production, more railroad mileage, and strong civilian leadership.

4. Southern advantages—defense of its own soil, better military leadership, and the wealth provided by "King Cotton."

5. Two inexperienced armies met; the South routed the North.

Critical Thinking

6. Possible answer: he refused to reinforce Fort Sumter with new troops, and he refused to fire the first shot. He allowed border states to remain in the Union despite their sympathy with the Confederacy.
(synthesis)

Present the Lesson

Have students skim the section and on the board make a chart showing the effects of military tactics and new weapons employed by Civil War military leaders. Make two columns: in the first column list the weapon or tactic; in the second column list its effects.

Weapon/Tactic	Effect
Breech-loading rifle	Fighting impersonal, cavalry less important, frontal infantry charges no longer effective
Iron-clad, steam-propelled warships	All-wood, wind-propelled ships no longer effective
Naval blockade	Harmed civilians as well as military and lowered morale

For Discussion
What were some advances in military machinery and weapons during the Civil War? (Possible responses: breech-loaded rifles; steam-driven and ironclad warships.) How did these weapons and machinery change the way wars were fought? (Possible response: War became less human because soldiers no longer fought face to face with the enemy.) What are some military advances of the 1900's and what effect do they have on warfare? (Possible responses: Machine guns, grenades, bombs, airplanes, and poisonous gas have made wars more dangerous; nuclear bombs make world destruction a possibility.)

of the barrel, not the muzzle at the far end. These guns also had rifled bores in place of smooth ones. This means that the guns had spiral grooves that made the bullet turn around on itself. In the same way that a spiral football pass is more accurate than a wobbly one, a rifled or spiraled bullet was much more accurate and went farther than a nonrifled one.

Using the new type of gun had several effects. First, it made fighting much more impersonal. In the past, soldiers saw their opponents as recognizable human beings. Now, as historian Bruce Catton put it, the enemy "was simply a line of snaketail fence or a grove of trees or a raw length of heaped-up earth, from which came clouds of powder smoke and a storm of bullets."

Second, cavalry lost its importance. Cavalry could no longer be used successfully to attack infantry or artillery. Instead, it was used mostly to scout and to screen an army's movements.

Third, frontal infantry charges were no longer effective. They resulted only in extremely heavy casualties. This made tactics more important than ever before.

Better Warships. Other technological changes took place on naval vessels. Most warships now were driven by steam rather than by wind and sail. The newer steamboats had screw propellers rather than paddle wheels, and they were much faster. Furthermore, in the early years of the war, both sides began to build **ironclads,** wooden ships with ironplate armor.

One such ironclad was the Union ship *Monitor.* This ship was the first to have a revolving gun turret. The South had previously captured another Union ironclad called the *Merrimac* but had changed its name to the *Virginia.* In 1862 the two ships engaged in battle in the channel off southeast Virginia known as Hampton Roads. (See the map on page 363.) It was the first naval battle in American history between ironclads. Although the battle ended in a draw, the *Virginia* had to return to Norfolk for repairs. The new ironclads made it clear that the days of all-wood naval ships were over.

Union Strategy Is Three-pronged

After Bull Run, President Lincoln decided that he needed a new commander for the **Army of the Potomac.** He chose thirty-four-year-old **George McClellan,** who, like most generals on both sides, was a veteran of the Mexican War. McClellan, however, refused to move until he had organized his army and drilled his troops for months on end.

As the fall of 1861 turned into the winter of 1862, Northerners grew increasingly impatient with Tardy George McClellan. Finally, even Lincoln remarked that he would "borrow McClellan's army if the general himself was not going to use it."

The Battle of Shiloh. In addition to the eastern campaign to take Richmond, there were two other parts in the three-pronged Union strategy. The second part was a western campaign to drive Confederate troops from the Tennessee River Valley and then from the Mississippi River Valley so as to split the Confederacy in two. So, while McClellan polished and repolished his army, the western front was where full-scale fighting began.

In February 1862 a Union army invaded western Tennessee. It was led by a veteran United States Army officer named **Ulysses S. Grant.** Grant had a rough look—he wore wrinkled uniforms and smoked cigars that stained his beard. These char-

Picturing History
The close-range battle between the *Monitor* and the *Merrimac* (renamed the *Virginia* by the Confederacy) is recreated in this Currier and Ives lithograph. The Confederates later destroyed the *Merrimac* after Union forces took Norfolk, Virginia. The *Monitor* eventually sank after its crew had to abandon it in a storm.

Check for Understanding

Call on students to answer the Section 2 Review questions.

Guided Practice

As they refer to the chart on the board, ask students to comment on the overall effect the tactics and new weapons had on the Civil War combatants. (Possible responses: death toll very high due to new breech-loading rifle; civilians in South suffered many hardships because of blockades.) In relation to the Union's naval blockade, ask students the importance of open supply lines in wartime. (Possible response: necessary to move food, ammunition, and other supplies to front.) Ask students to identify any international supply lines that the U.S. would try to keep open in the event of a

limited war today. (Possible responses: Persian Gulf; Panama Canal; Suez Canal.)

acteristics proved minor, however, for while McClellan sat, Grant moved. With the help of gunboats, Grant captured two major Confederate forts—Fort Henry on the Tennessee River and Fort Donelson on the Cumberland River. The latter exploit gained him a nickname. When the Confederate commander asked for surrender terms, Grant replied, ''No terms except unconditional and immediate surrender can be accepted.'' From then on, Grant was known as Unconditional Surrender Grant.

As Grant's army drove south toward Mississippi, it paused for the night near a crossroads called Shiloh. Early the next morning, the Union troops were surprised by an all-out Confederate assault. Many Union troops were shot while making coffee; some died while they were still lying in

their blankets. The charges and countercharges continued all day. Woods and meadows became filled with corpses and with the bodies of thousands of wounded men. By nightfall, Union forces were on the edge of disaster. Then more Union troops arrived. Grant reorganized his men and artillery, and the next day he drove the Confederates from the field.

The **Battle of Shiloh** taught both sides several lessons. First, generals began thinking more about sending out scouts, communicating with divisional commanders, digging trenches, and building fortifications. In short, they began to think more defensively. Second, people gave up any hope of an easy victory. More than thirteen thousand Union soldiers were dead or wounded, while the Confederates suffered more than ten thousand casualties.

The Civil War, 1861–1862

	Union states
	Confederate states
	Area under Union control
	Area under Confederate control
⚔	Battle
←	Union forces
◄	Confederate forces
★	United States capital
☆	Confederate capital

Map Skills

VA, TN, MS, AR, AL • New Orleans, Baton Rouge • Memphis

Map Skills **Region** What Confederate states were partly under Union control? **Movement** What cities did Farragut capture in 1862? **Movement** What city on the Mississippi did Grant capture?

The appalling slaughter made people realize that war was not all bravery and glory. It could kill men in numbers that no one had imagined.

Although the Battle of Shiloh seemed to be a draw, it was actually decisive. The Confederates needed to win in order to maintain their Ohio-Kentucky frontier. Their failure to win meant that they would not be able to hold onto the Mississippi River Valley and that one part of the three-way Union strategy would succeed.

A Naval Blockade. Along with an eastern campaign and a western campaign, the third part of the Union's strategy called for a blockade of the Confederate coast in order to cut off its commercial lifeline with Europe. Union ships took up positions outside each major Southern seaport. They succeeded in keeping regular ocean-going vessels from entering or leaving the harbors. Nevertheless, they were unable to prevent blockade running. Small, low boats would dash in under cover of darkness with a cargo of weapons or luxury goods, and then they would dash out again with a load of cotton. As the war progressed, however, fewer and fewer blockade runners were able to get through. In any event, they could not carry enough cargo to make up for the regular trade that the blockade had cut off.

Union strategy combined the blockade with direct attacks on Southern ports. The most significant

Focus on Biography

David Farragut (1801–1870)

In 1810 David Farragut applied for appointment as a navy midshipman. He was told to come back after his next birthday. By then the young recruit would be ten—the minimum age for a commission! At that time, midshipmen were sent off aboard the nation's warships to get on-the-job training.

The sea was in young David's blood. His father, Captain Jorge Farragut, had been an officer in the Spanish navy and merchant service. He had come to South America before the American Revolution and had enthusiastically joined the colonists in their war against Britain. Later he settled in New Orleans.

As a teenager, Midshipman Farragut saw action in the War of 1812. After the war, there were pirates to be chased in the Caribbean. During the Mexican War, there were blockades to be enforced. Farragut did both while climbing slowly up the career ladder.

Through all those years, Farragut was a careful observer and a long-term planner. He never sailed into a port anywhere on the earth without memorizing its depth, entrance channels, and defenses.

When the Civil War began, Captain Farragut's career could have ended. He was sixty years old and although a Northerner in spirit, he was a Southerner by birth. His country was in no hurry to call on him.

When the order finally came in 1862, it was to command the Union blockade in the Gulf of Mexico and to capture the port of New Orleans. Farragut did just that by passing the New Orleans forts under cover of darkness, smashing through the boom (an underwater barrier), and then engaging and defeating the Confederate fleet. Using similar tactics at Port Hudson, Farragut helped General Grant capture Vicksburg.

Farragut's greatest victory was at Mobile, Alabama, on August 5, 1864. Mobile was the Confederacy's last port on the Gulf, and it was fiercely defended. As usual, Farragut had planned well. With his mine sweeper disabled, he moved his flagship into the lead and then twisted and veered his way past the blazing forts in Mobile Bay to destroy what remained of the Confederate navy.

Farragut's order ''Damn the torpedoes! Full speed ahead!'' in the face of enemy mines looked like half-witted recklessness. It was not. The great naval commander's confidence came from long hours of careful planning. Few were surprised when in 1866 Congress created the rank of full admiral for this heroic Hispanic American.

took place in the spring of 1862. A Union naval force steamed forty miles up the Mississippi from the Gulf of Mexico and captured New Orleans. This naval expedition was commanded by **David Farragut,** who as a young boy had participated with his Spanish father in the War of 1812. His father was also one of the many Hispanics who fought in the American Revolution. By May, Farragut's gunboats had advanced upriver and taken Baton Rouge, Louisiana. With Grant moving south, the Confederate States were now dangerously close to being split in two. Southern forces controlled only one section of the Mississippi River—between Vicksburg, Mississippi, in the north and Port Hudson, Louisiana, in the south. If Union troops and sailors could close this gap, they would cut off Texas, Louisiana, and Arkansas from the rest of the Confederacy. However, it took them another year to do so.

The Peninsula Campaign. McClellan's army finally got under way a few days before the Battle of Shiloh. After successfully occupying Yorktown, Virginia, his troops advanced at a snail's pace up the peninsula between the York and James rivers toward Richmond. McClellan was terribly cautious and kept asking for reinforcements. Lincoln, however, refused to send them because of a brilliant maneuver by the Confederate officer General Stonewall Jackson. The Confederates swept through the Shenandoah Valley and threatened a direct attack on Washington, D.C. Instead, Jackson's troops pulled away to help defend Richmond, Virginia, against McClellan's slow-moving army.

During the month of June 1862, one battle followed another outside of Richmond. Although the two armies were fairly evenly matched in numbers, McClellan was clearly outgeneraled by a new Confederate commander named **Robert E. Lee.**

In many ways, Lee was the opposite of McClellan. He was bold and imaginative, and he directed many of the most brilliant military movements of the war. Lee was greatly loved by his fellow officers and soldiers. He had freed his slaves some years earlier. A quiet, modest, but forceful man, Lee won more respect from Northerners than did any other Confederate leader. He had graduated second in his class at West Point, served in the Mexican War, and happened to be in charge of the federal troops that put down John Brown's raid at Harpers Ferry. Later, he had been informally of-

Picturing History Alexander Gardner's photograph of President Lincoln, taken on the battlefield of Antietam in October 1862, was first published in 1866.

fered command of the Union armies by Lincoln. He decided instead to remain loyal to his home state, Virginia.

At the beginning of July, after a series of defeats and one draw, Lincoln pulled the Army of the Potomac out of the peninsula and back to Washington, D.C. While he did not officially remove McClellan, he gave effective command of the army to General John Pope. Lee, however, went on the attack. On the last two days of August, Lee's troops won a clear victory at Manassas Junction, also called the **Second Battle of Bull Run.** (For some reason, Northerners usually identified battles by rivers and streams; Southerners named them after nearby towns.) Union forces were now no closer to Richmond than they had been at the beginning of the war. A desperate President therefore called on McClellan to head the Army of the Potomac once again.

Antietam. Following the victory at Manassas Junction, the South shifted from a defensive strategy to an offensive one. Lee boldly decided to push his forces into enemy territory. McClellan at first pursued him northwest of Washington, D.C., with his usual caution. Then he had a stroke of luck. Some Union soldiers found a copy of Lee's secret army orders being used as a wrapping for a bunch of cigars. Months earlier, Lincoln had complained that McClellan had "the slows." Now, however, McClellan grew bolder because he knew something of Lee's plans. McClellan caught up with Lee just after Lee crossed the Potomac River into Maryland.

Student Assignment/Homework

Have students read Section 3 "The Goals of War Change" and answer Section 3 Review questions orally in small groups.

Core Lesson

Anticipate the Lesson

Discuss with students the Emancipation Proclamation. Ask students these questions. What events influenced Lincoln's decision to issue the proclamation? (Possible responses: war was dragging on; Northerners were pressuring Lincoln to free slaves; Union wanted support of Great Britain.) How might the freeing of slaves have weakened the Confederacy? (Possible responses: Union earned Britain's support; Union earned support of blacks and abolitionists.)

SECTION 2 REVIEW
Answers

Main Ideas

1. It made them realize that the war would not end quickly.

2. Guns could shoot farther and with greater accuracy, so soldiers no longer saw their opponents close up.

3. He refused to move his army until it was well drilled.

4. Lee was a bold and brilliant military strategist who was greatly respected by both sides.

5. McClellan had allowed Lee's army to retreat from Antietam, thus losing a chance for a really decisive victory.

Critical Thinking

6. New guns, ironclads, and faster steamboats plus military inexperience caused unexpected heavy casualties. The stunned people no longer expected a short, glorious war. **(synthesis)**

Picturing History The Battle of Antietam, the bloodiest battle of the Civil War.

A major and crucial battle took place near the village of Sharpsburg, Maryland, at **Antietam** Creek. Union forces outnumbered Lee's army, seventy thousand to forty thousand. When night fell on September 17, more than twenty-two thousand men lay dead or wounded on that bloody ground. The casualties were about even on both sides, but McClellan had far more fresh troops at his command. A bolder general would have ordered an all-out attack at dawn. Instead, McClellan did nothing. Lee's troops watched and waited for the entire day. That evening, his battered army began limping back toward Virginia. Many dead and wounded had to be left behind. McClellan had "won" the Battle of Antietam, but he had let a truly decisive victory slip through his fingers. This time Lincoln fired him permanently.

SECTION 2 REVIEW

Key Terms and People

Explain the significance of: ironclads, *Monitor, Merrimac,* Army of the Potomac, George McClellan, Ulysses S. Grant, Battle of Shiloh, David Farragut, Robert E. Lee, Second Battle of Bull Run, Antietam

Main Ideas

1. How did the First Battle of Bull Run change ordinary people's thinking about the war?
2. How did technological changes in guns make the Civil War more impersonal than previous wars?
3. How did George McClellan earn the nickname Tardy George?
4. In what ways did Lee differ from McClellan?
5. Why did Lincoln permanently fire McClellan?

Critical Thinking

6. How did technological and military realities as reflected in the first Civil War battles affect people's ideas about the war?

SECTION 3

The Goals of War Change

GLOSSARY TERMS: Radical Republicans, conscription, bounties, bounty jumpers

Although Antietam's military effect was limited, its political effect was tremendous. After Antietam, Britain and France decided to postpone recognizing the Confederacy. Also, Antietam persuaded Lincoln to issue his Emancipation Proclamation. He told his cabinet that he had made a promise to God. If the rebels were driven out of Maryland, he would free the slaves. Antietam had cleared the rebels from Maryland.

Britain Remains Neutral

In the fall of 1861, Britain had almost slipped into war against the North. The captain of a United States warship had stopped a British merchantman, named the *Trent,* on its way home from Havana, Cuba. He had seized two Confederate diplomats, James M. Mason and John Slidell, who were traveling to Europe. This was a clear violation of neutral rights. The British cabinet drafted an angry letter of protest and sent eight thousand troops to Canada. Not wanting to fight two foes at the same time, the United States finally released the diplomats. It also sent Great Britain a note congratulating it on accepting the principle of freedom of the seas over which the War of 1812 had been fought.

Another grave problem arose between the United States and Britain over Confederate warships built in Britain. The United States warned Britain that such construction was an act of war. Britain thereupon ceased building ships for the South.

After the war, the United States presented Britain with a bill, called the *Alabama* claims, for $419 million. This was to pay for the damage the *Alabama* and similar ships had caused the Union during

State the Objective

Understand the impact of military events on the political conduct of the Civil War.

Present the Lesson

Have students list on the board the main points of the Emancipation Proclamation. (List might include: freed slaves in areas behind Confederate military lines only; broadened base of the war; encouraged recruitment of black soldiers in the Union army.) Ask students why Lincoln decided to broaden the focus of the war to include a crusade against slavery. (Possible responses: to appease Radical Republicans; to punish the South; to attract black soldiers; to gain British support.)

the Civil War. Britain and the United States agreed to submit the bill to arbitration. (In 1871 both sides presented their case to an international jury in Geneva, Switzerland. The tribunal awarded $15 million to the United States. This was the first time such a delicate matter of national honor was settled by the majority vote of an international jury.)

Although Britain ceased building warships for the South, its neutrality was still in doubt. British public opinion was divided on the question of whether or not to recognize the Confederate States. Many British leaders were pleased that their former colonies had been unable to maintain their unity. On the other hand, most British people disliked slavery.

In addition, cotton did not turn out to be nearly as important to Britain as the South had hoped. When the war began, British mills already had a good supply on hand. They also found alternate sources of cotton in Egypt and India. Furthermore, an industrialized Britain depended heavily on imports of grain to feed its workers. Much of this grain came from Northern farms. To Britain, the fear of losing its breadbasket was stronger than the fear of losing one of its sources of cotton. Therefore, there was no economic reason to aid the Confederacy. Quite soon an event occurred that ensured British neutrality.

Linking Past to Present

During the Civil War, Great Britain faced the issue of whether to support the section that was most important economically (the South) or the section that opposed slavery (the North). Today the United States faces a similar predicament in its relations with its ally South Africa. South Africa is economically important to the United States, but its racial segregation policy of apartheid offends most Americans. In 1986, Congress passed a bill imposing economic sanctions against South Africa. By 1990, South Africa began to dismantle its apartheid system. However, U.S. sanctions remained firm in light of continued racial discrimination and black disenfranchisement.

Slavery Becomes the Main Issue

At the beginning of the Civil War, neither side declared slavery to be the central issue. It was, but neither side was willing to admit this fact. Lincoln and most other Republicans instead insisted that the federal government had no power over slavery in the states where it already existed. Southerners agreed.

As the war dragged on into its second year, however, this opinion began to change, especially in the North. Some Republicans became known as Radicals. *Radical* means one who favors great or extreme changes. **Radical Republicans** believed

For Discussion
Consider the following hypothetical situation. Suppose that Great Britain had reacted to the Trent affair by declaring war on the U.S. and had formed an alliance with the Confederacy. What effect might this alliance have had on the course of history? (Possible responses: Union might have had to divide its army and send part to Canada; Confederacy might have been able to break blockade; Confederacy might have become part of British Empire.)

Picturing History The soldiers of Company E, Fourth United States Colored Infantry (right), fought bravely, but they were paid less than the white soldiers. The recruiting poster (above) appealed to black patriotism.

Check for Understanding

Have students complete Chapter 14, Section 4 Daily Activity.

Guided Practice

Have students review in class the answers to the Section 3 Review questions.

Assign Independent Practice

Have students write two paragraphs comparing the conscription acts of the North and the South. (Paragraphs might include: Confederacy—called up able-bodied white males between ages eighteen and thirty-five, exempted men in certain industries, allowed soldiers to hire substitutes; Union—called up men between ages twenty and forty-five; offered bounties to volunteers; allowed soldiers to hire substitutes.)

Picturing History Black field hands are shown planting sweet potatoes in the photograph above, believed to have been taken in 1862. Abraham Lincoln said that if his name ever went down in history, it would be for signing the Emancipation Proclamation.

that abolition was in fact the main reason for the war. These Radicals insisted that Lincoln should free the slaves, and they passed several laws in Congress to this effect. Lincoln, however, did not think the laws were constitutional. Therefore, he did not enforce them. He believed that the purpose of the war was to save the Union—and nothing else. He doubted that most Northerners would fight for the freedom of blacks.

Three developments caused Lincoln to change his mind. First, the bloody fighting made many Northerners want to hurt the South as much as possible. Abolishing slavery would help do that. Second, slavery helped the Southern war effort. Slaves helped to build military fortifications, and they produced food. Third, slavery was a crucial issue on the Union's diplomatic front with Britain. Britain's leaders would not support a war whose aim was to keep the United States together. However, British public opinion would back a war against slavery.

Lincoln realized that he could use emancipation as a weapon of war. He could also satisfy his own personal hope that everyone everywhere would eventually be free.

Emancipation Is Proclaimed

In June 1862 Congress passed a law prohibiting slavery in the territories. On January 1, 1863, Lincoln issued the final form of his **Emancipation Proclamation.** No slaves became free immediately

because the proclamation applied only to areas behind Confederate military lines. It did not apply to the slave states that had remained loyal to the Union, nor did it apply to Confederate territories already occupied by Union forces. Critics commented that it applied only in areas where Lincoln did not have the power to enforce it.

Nevertheless, the proclamation had a powerful symbolic effect. It broadened the base of the war by turning it into a fight for freedom as well as for unity. It thereby gave the Northern cause the weight of a moral crusade.

White Southerners were deeply angered, of course. They realized that if they lost the war they would lose their entire way of life. Meanwhile, in Britain, the Emancipation Proclamation had just the effect that Lincoln had hoped for. Now that the Union was clearly fighting against slavery, British public opinion supported the Union's cause.

The Emancipation Proclamation also encouraged the recruitment of black soldiers into the Union army. Two of the first and most famous units were the Fifty-fourth and Fifty-fifth Regiments of Massachusetts Volunteers. All told, nearly 300,000 blacks served in the Union army. They were not

Student Assignment/Homework

Have students read Section 4 "Life Goes On Behind the Lines" and answer Section 4 Review questions orally.

State the Objective

Understand how domestic life in the North and South changed during the Civil War.

Anticipate the Lesson

Discuss with students the products and services they might have to do without if the U.S. engaged in a limited war. (Responses might include: designer clothing; unlimited gasoline; recreational activities.) Ask students to compare this list with that both the Confederacy and Union had to do without. (Possible responses: food; clothing; homes; men to run the farms and plantations; doctors.)

always well treated, and until 1864 they were paid only half as much as white soldiers. Nonetheless, they proved their bravery and skill in numerous battles.

The Draft Begins

At first, both sides relied on volunteers for their armies. By 1863, however, both the North and the South were forced to pass **conscription,** or draft, acts. Although individual states had used the draft in the past, this was the first time it was applied by a central government.

In 1862 the Confederacy led off the draft with a law that called up all able-bodied white men between the ages of eighteen and thirty-five (later extended to seventeen and fifty). Few Southerners were actually drafted, however. They considered the draft shameful and preferred to volunteer instead.

Several provisions of the draft created considerable resentment. Men in certain industries were exempt, and many persons could not see why teachers and mailmen did not have to serve. Furthermore, a man could hire a substitute to go in his place, but the price was $10,000 in Confederate money, which most Southern whites could not afford. Still another provision aroused even more bad feeling. It said that for every twenty slaves on a plantation, one white man—the planter, his sons, or his overseer—would be exempt from the draft. The provision was included because of fears of slave uprisings. However, it led to widespread grumbling about "a rich man's war and a poor man's fight."

The Union adopted the draft in 1863, calling up men between the ages of twenty and forty-five. Here, too, draftees were allowed to hire substitutes to go in their place. In addition, many Northern states offered **bounties,** or cash payments, to volunteers. This practice led to considerable abuse, for a man could enlist, take his bounty, desert his regiment, and do the same thing all over again. Patriotic Northerners resented these **bounty jumpers.**

SECTION 3 REVIEW

Key Terms and People

Explain the significance of: Radical Republicans, Emancipation Proclamation, conscription, bounties, bounty jumpers

Main Ideas

1. What factors affected Britain's decision not to recognize the Confederacy?
2. How did the Radical Republicans' view about the main reason for the war differ from Lincoln's original view?
3. What caused Lincoln to change his mind about the reason for the war?
4. Why were the slaves not freed immediately after the Emancipation Proclamation was issued?

Critical Thinking

5. Why did Lincoln choose not to free slaves in the Union states?

SECTION 4

Life Goes on Behind the Lines

GLOSSARY TERMS: greenbacks,
         transcontinental railroad, Homestead Act

The Civil War changed the lives of Americans in both the South and the North. On both sides, the war brought grief to hundreds of thousands of families. Grief arrived in many ways. It came with the news that sons and fathers were dead, either on the battlefield or in camp from disease. It came with a man limping up the steps on crutches, one leg of his trousers empty. It also came with no news at all. Sometimes the soldier just did not come back—ever.

The South Suffers from Food Shortages

During the war, the Confederate government seemed more harmful than helpful. Early on, it passed a tax on farm products. Then it began to print paper money to finance the war. It printed so many Confederate dollars that they began to fall in value.

Even those who could afford the high prices found it impossible to get many goods. There were no linens, shoes, or clothing. People wrote letters on the back of wallpaper because there was no stationery. Meat was served once a week at the most. In 1863 the food shortage in Richmond, Virginia, became so severe that a huge mob of men and women staged a bread riot in front of the government buildings. The mob broke up only

SECTION 3 REVIEW

Answers

Main Ideas

1. Cotton's economic importance fell, while the importance of Northern grains rose; Antietam foreshadowed the North's victory; and most British favored the North's anti-slavery stand.

2. Radicals wanted to abolish slavery; Lincoln sought to save the Union.

3. Freeing slaves would reduce slave help in the South's war effort and gain British support.

4. It applied only to Confederate areas—where Lincoln could not enforce it.

Critical Thinking

5. To avoid dissension in loyal border states and to avoid costly enforcement. **(analysis)**

Present the Lesson

Divide the class into five groups and assign one of the following laws to each group: Morrill Tariff, transcontinental railway legislation, National Banking Act, Homestead Act, Morrill Land Grant Act. Ask groups to discuss how these bills reflected government policy and what impact the laws had on the U.S. economy.

Check for Understanding

Ask group leaders from the previous activity to summarize their discussions for the class. (Summaries might include: government was willing to become actively involved in nation's economy; government would aid agriculture and business.) Ask students to construct charts that list each law in one column and its main provision in a second column.

Law	Main Provision
Morrill Tariff	Raised import duties to twenty-five percent
Legislation to build a trans- continental railway	Provided land and money for railroads
National Banking Act	Did away with state banks and set up national banks
Homestead Act	Gave free land to settlers
Morrill Land Grant Act	Gave land to states and territories to support agricultural and technical colleges.

For Discussion

Divide the class into two groups to debate the issue of whether women should or should not have worked outside the home during the Civil War. Each side should present reasons for its stand.

(Possible responses: for working—provided additional workers in the factories, freed men for fighting; against working—should have been home with the children, could not handle pressure, were untrained for work outside home.)

when President Davis climbed up on an overturned wagon and promised the rioters that he would distribute food from government warehouses to those in need.

At the same time, a small group of people— mostly blockade runners, gunmakers, and contractors who provided food and supplies to the army— grew rich. As one historian described this group, they "dined on caviar, lobsters, oysters, roast beef, sugar, ham, roast fowl, and thick steaks, while the children of soldiers went to bed whimpering with hunger."

For blacks in the South, the first few years of the war made little difference in their lives. The only significant change was that many of the men were pulled out of the cotton fields and put to work building fortifications and repairing roads. As Union troops conquered more and more Southern territory, however, thousands of blacks ran away from their masters and joined the Yankees. Since there was no official policy about escaped slaves, each military officer did what he thought best. A few returned the runaways. Most, however, protected them, and the blacks reciprocated by working for the Union forces as teamsters, cooks, laundresses, and guides.

The North Prospers from Its Industry

In the North eventually there was a wartime boom. After 1863 immigration increased significantly because wartime industries created a large demand for workers. Agriculture also flourished. Meanwhile, the government was buying all kinds of equipment for the armed forces. Some businessmen profited so much that they laid the groundwork for famous millionaire fortunes.

To help pay for the war, Congress passed the first income tax in United States history. It levied a 5 percent tax on incomes between $600 and $5,000 and a 10 percent tax on incomes above $5,000. The government also issued some $450 million worth of **greenbacks,** or paper money. However, the government refused to redeem the greenbacks with gold, so the value of the currency went up and down depending on the latest news from the war front.

Congress also passed several important laws to aid both business and agriculture. Before the war, Southern representatives had opposed a high tariff. Now Congress passed the **Morrill Tariff** of 1861, which raised the average import duty on manufactured goods to 25 percent. By 1864 the rates reached an all-time high of 47 percent. This tariff protected American manufacturers from European competition. Congress next voted to build a **transcontinental railroad** that would connect the Atlantic coast with the Pacific coast in a week's journey. A north-central route was chosen, and Congress supported the proposal with vast grants of public lands and large government loans. In 1862 Congress passed the **Homestead Act.** This act gave 160 acres of public land free to any citizen (which, until the Fourteenth Amendment was ratified in 1868, excluded blacks). All a citizen had to do was occupy and cultivate the land and pay registration fees ranging from twenty-six dollars to thirty-four dollars. In addition, the **Morrill Land-Grant Act** of 1862 gave land to states and territories for the support of colleges that would teach agricultural and mechanical skills. Finally, in 1863 Congress also adopted the **National Banking Act.** This act did away with state banks and set up a system of national banks. This system gave the United States a new, uniform currency: the national bank note.

Taken together, these laws showed an important new trend. It now was clear that the national government could and would give aid to agriculture and business. These acts also showed that the government was becoming much more actively involved in the nation's economy than ever before.

Women Support the War Effort

The Civil War also brought great changes in the lives of millions of American women. On both sides, women were left to run plantations and farms on their own. Furthermore, some American women were doing completely new jobs, ones they had never dealt with before.

Factory and Office Work. Women found work in wartime factories, especially in the North. Since sewing was a traditional task for women at home, many women took sewing jobs in factories that made uniforms for the army. They were paid very low wages—from seventeen to twenty-four cents for a fifteen-hour day—and they were always supervised by men. The long hours and low pay were so clearly unfair that some women organized to protest these conditions. Although their organizing met with little success, they won a good deal of sympathy. In New York, middle-class women organized a Protective Union to serve as an employment agency and also to provide women workers with free legal services for settling grievances.

Guided Practice

Have students relate the war crimes carried out in Civil War camps to similar situations in recent wars. (Possible responses: German concentration camps; Korean and North Vietnamese prisoner-of-war camps; inhumane treatment, physical and psychological torture, starvation, and unsanitary conditions in any prison camp.) Ask students whether there is such a thing as a crime against someone with whom one's nation is at war. (Possible response: Students may answer this from a political, religious, economic, or humanitarian standpoint.)

Assign Independent Practice

Have each student write a brief summary statement that explains the effect of the Civil War on American women. (Summaries may include: Women worked in factories, on farms, and for the government.)

Picturing History A Union doctor attends wounded Confederate soldiers lying in makeshift shelters after the Battle of Antietam (above). Clara Barton (left) was one of the brave women who cared for soldiers on the front lines. A Civil War surgeon might have used the medical kit shown at the right.

For the first time, women also found jobs working for the government. Both the Union and the Confederate governments grew during the war and thus needed many new workers. Most of the "government girls" worked as clerks and copyists. (In those days, all letters and documents had to be copied by hand, for there were no typewriters or copying machines.) Indeed, the Civil War period was the first time that large numbers of women did office work of any kind.

Dorothea Dix and Nursing. The Civil War opened one other major area of work for women. Fighting on the battlefields resulted in a great need for nurses to care for the wounded. Many women on both sides volunteered their services. The Union government appointed **Dorothea Dix** as superintendent of nurses. Dix was well aware that many Americans had doubts about women working in army hospitals. Would they distract the men? Did a proper woman belong in a tent filled with men, even if many of the men were groaning and screaming? Finally, could women themselves stand the awful smells of sweat, blood, and gangrene? Dix met some of these doubts by requiring that government nurses be over age thirty and "plain in appearance." In fact, the women fulfilled their duties with great skill and efficiency.

Linking Past to Present

During the Civil War, women passed through the battle lines to deliver supplies, search for the missing, and nurse the wounded. One of these women was Clara Barton, who later founded the American Red Cross. Today the Red Cross is known throughout the world for the relief it provides in times of natural disasters as well as in wartime.

Prisons Are Brutal Pestholes

The men involved in the Civil War had more to fear than being counted among the high casualty figures. There was also the possibility that they might be included among the large numbers of prisoners that were taken by both sides and kept under miserable conditions.

Probably the worst prisoner-of-war camp was the Confederate military prison near Andersonville, Georgia. One historian described it as

a pesthole of a place, a ghastly, stinking sore which blighted the ground on which it stood. . . . Union prisoners were . . . reduced to living like animals. They ate scraps of food, wore rags, and were surrounded by filth, vermin, disease and death.

Student Assignment/Homework

Have students read Section 5 "The Road to Peace Is Rugged" and complete Chapter 14, Section 4 Daily Activity.

SECTION 5
Core Lesson

Anticipate the Lesson

Ask students to discuss what advantages the North had that enabled it to defeat the South. (Possible responses: more industry; more soldiers; stronger navy; sufficient food supplies.) Was the defeat of the South inevitable? (Possible responses: yes, the North had far more advantages; no, if the South had been able to develop supply lines and hold out longer, it might have survived as a country.)

State the Objective

Understand how and why the North won the Civil War.

SECTION 4 REVIEW
Answers

Main Ideas

1. Food and clothing scarce, high prices, and loss of lives.

2. Agriculture, industry, and business prospered.

3. They worked in wartime factories, government offices, and army hospitals.

4. Miserable. There were disease, food shortages, and in many cases ill-treatment.

Critical Thinking

5. The need to encourage and regulate agriculture, industry, and business because they contributed to the war effort. **(analysis)**

Map Skills

Shenandoah and Potomac
• The South would have had a strong bargaining position for independence.

More than twelve thousand of them died. Part of the problem was the fact that the South was short of food and thus was unable to feed its captives much. Another part of the problem was the brutality of Captain Henry Wirz, the camp's commander. After Andersonville was captured by Union forces in 1865, the Yankees hanged him as a war criminal.

Northern prisoner-of-war camps—such as those at Elmira, New York, and at Camp Douglas, Illinois—were not much better. There was more food than in Southern camps but little or no heat. Unused to cold winters, hundreds of Confederate soldiers contracted pneumonia and failed to recover. Hundreds of others died from dysentery and malnutrition.

SECTION 4 REVIEW

Key Terms and People

Explain the significance of: greenbacks, Morrill Tariff, transcontinental railroad, Homestead Act, Morrill Land-Grant Act, National Banking Act, Dorothea Dix

Main Ideas

1. As the war progressed, what hardships did civilians face in the South?
2. What effect did the war have on the North's economy?
3. How did women support the war effort?
4. What were the conditions like in prison camps in both the North and the South?

Critical Thinking

5. What led the federal government to become more involved in the economy during the war?

SECTION 5

The Road to Peace Is Rugged

GLOSSARY TERM: **Gettysburg Address**

The year 1863 saw the tide turn toward a clear-cut Union victory. The superior power of the North gradually wore the South down. The cost in human life, however, was terrible. As a result, Northern newspapers began calling the Union's most successful general "Grant the butcher."

The Tide Turns at Gettysburg

In the first battles after Antietam, Confederate forces came off very well. Lincoln, still searching for a general who would bring him victories, chose Ambrose E. Burnside to command the Army of the Potomac. Burnside had a good military record. He also had bushy side whiskers that were called "burn sides" and that since have become known as "sideburns." However, he had doubts about his own abilities and accepted the command reluctantly. Unfortunately, his doubts were justified. On December 13, 1862, at Fredericksburg, Virginia, he ordered an all-out attack on Confederate troops, who were dug well in on several hills. The result was a bloody defeat for the Union forces, which suffered some thirteen thousand casualties to the Confederacy's fifty-three hundred. Lincoln replaced Burnside with General Joseph "Fighting Joe" Hooker.

The Road to Gettysburg, 1862-1863

Map Skills **Place** Harpers Ferry is located at the junction of what two rivers? **Movement** How might the war have been affected if Union forces had lost at Gettysburg?

Present the Lesson

Ask students to list on the board the major events in the Civil War from the Battle of Fredericksburg to Lincoln's assassination and, in the case of battles, to explain their outcome. (Details may include: Fredericksburg—Confederate victory; Chancellorsville—limited Confederate victory; Confederate military leader Stonewall Jackson dies; Gettysburg—Union victory; Vicksburg—Union victory; Gettysburg Address; Union victories at Wilderness, Spotsylvania, Cold Harbor, Yellow Tavern, and Petersburg; Sherman captures Atlanta and Savannah; Lincoln's re-election; Lincoln's assassination.) Ask students to use the events to draw some conclusions about the course of the war. (Possible responses: tide turned in Union's favor with the Battle of Gettysburg; the loss of Jackson hurt the South; Union gained momentum with each victory.)

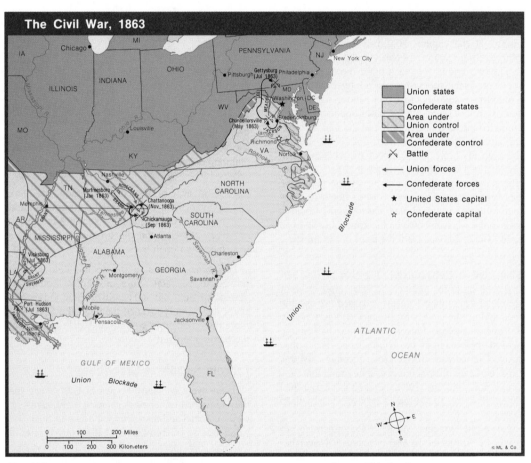

The Civil War, 1863

Map Skills **Movement** The capture of Vicksburg gave Union forces control over which river?
Location Which battle was fought in Pennsylvania?

Map Skills
Mississippi • Gettysburg

Victory at Chancellorsville. Hooker almost lost the Army of the Potomac when Lee pulled a daring maneuver at Chancellorsville. Lee split his army and sent General Stonewall Jackson with thirty thousand men to attack Hooker from the side. Hooker was totally surprised. The battle began at six o'clock in the evening. If it had started earlier in the day, Lee might have captured the entire Union army. As it was, the next dawn found the Union forces better organized. Since they outnumbered the Confederates two to one, they were able to avoid complete defeat and to withdraw northward.

The Confederate victory at Chancellorsville was a costly one. Lee lost twelve thousand troops. Jackson was hit by a bullet from one of his own men when he returned in the darkness from patrol.

A surgeon amputated his left arm in an effort to save his life, and Lee sent him a message: "You have lost only your left arm while I have lost my right." Eight days later, Jackson was dead.

A saddened Lee decided to press his advantage. If he could invade the free states, perhaps the Union would come to terms. He also had another reason for wanting to invade the North. To the west, Grant's army was threatening to take Vicksburg in order to finally cut the Confederacy in two. Perhaps invading the North would cause Grant to pull back.

On June 15, 1863, Lee's army marched off. Meanwhile, an even larger force of Union troops moved directly north so as to keep themselves positioned between Lee and the city of Washington, D.C. A discouraged President Lincoln re-

Check for Understanding
Have students complete Section 5 Review
questions on paper.

placed Hooker with General George Meade. It
soon became clear, however, that Lee was not
aiming at the capital. His army instead crossed
Maryland into southern Pennsylvania.

The two armies met each other more or less by
accident. Near the village of Gettysburg, some
Confederate soldiers, many of whom were barefoot, were out searching for shoes and boots. They
stumbled into a Union patrol, and the minor shooting attracted more troops from both sides. Meade
drew up his army just south of the village. Each
end of the Union line was anchored on a hilltop.
The center of the line ran along a ridge that since
has been named Cemetery Ridge. Lee's infantry
and artillery occupied Seminary Ridge, about a
mile to the west. In between the armies lay an open
field. The stage was set for a fight to the finish.

Slaughter at Gettysburg. The two armies battled each other for three days. Wave after wave of
Confederate soldiers bravely charged across the
field and up the slope of Cemetery Ridge. On July
3 General George Pickett led a massive charge
against the center of the Union lines. For a moment, Confederate troops broke through. By this
time, however, they had lost so many men that they
could not hold the ridge. Pickett's charge had
failed. For the first time, Lee had clearly been
defeated.

Lincoln telegraphed Meade, "Call no council of
war. . . . Do not let the enemy escape." Nevertheless, Meade hesitated. Instead he called his officers
together, and the guns were silent throughout the
Fourth of July. The next day Lee's battered army
moved south in the pouring rain. No Union troops
followed them. The Union had won a decisive
victory at Gettysburg, and yet, as Lincoln said
later, "Our army held the war in the hollow of its
hand and would not close it."

That same Fourth of July, Grant's army finally
captured **Vicksburg,** Mississippi. Port Hudson,
Louisiana, fell to Union forces shortly afterward.
(See the map on page 373.) The strategy of cutting
the Confederacy in two had finally worked.

The field at Gettysburg remained carpeted with
bodies. Even veterans of other battles were shocked
by the slaughter. One experienced Union officer
described those awful days as follows:

> We see the poor fellows hobbling back from
> the crest, or unable to do so, pale and weak,
> lying on the ground with the mangled stump

Picturing History
General Ulysses S. Grant.

Picturing History
General Robert E. Lee.

> of an arm or leg, dripping their life-blood
> away; or with a cheek torn open, or a shoulder
> mashed. And many, alas! hear not the roar as
> they stretch upon the ground with upturned
> faces and open eyes.

For some soldiers, a trip to the field hospital
proved to be fatal. Surgeons knew nothing of
germs, so they did not sterilize their knives and
saws; they simply cleaned them. In the Civil War,
more men died from wounds and sickness than on
the battlefield itself.

Lincoln Speaks at Gettysburg

There were so many bodies at Gettysburg that
they remained unburied for months. Buzzards circled overhead and then dropped down to feed. The
smell was so overpowering that no one wanted to
go near the place. When Northern newspapers
raised a cry about this scandal, the Union government decided to erect a national cemetery on the
site. At the dedication ceremonies in autumn,
Edward Everett of Massachusetts gave the main
speech. He was famous as a public speaker, nearly
as eloquent as Daniel Webster had been. Everett
spoke for two hours. The President spoke also—for
about two minutes. Today no one remembers what
Everett said, yet many people are familiar with the
eloquent words of Lincoln's **Gettysburg Address:**

> Four score and seven years ago our fathers
> brought forth on this continent a new nation,
> conceived in liberty, and dedicated to the
> proposition that all men are created equal.
> Now we are engaged in a great civil war,
> testing whether that nation, or any nation so
> conceived and so dedicated, can long endure.
> We are met on a great battlefield of that war.
> We have come to dedicate a portion of that

In relation to Sherman's march to the sea, discuss with students why a military target may not always be easily distinguishable from a nonmilitary target. (Possible response: difficulty arises if they are in close proximity or government camouflages military buildings in civilian areas; Sherman's army destroyed food supplies, harming both the Southern army and the civilians.) Discuss with students the problems involved in determining whether a farm supplying food to soldiers should be considered a military target. What problems do students think modern pilots might have in distinguishing military from nonmilitary targets? (Possible responses: pilots do not determine targets; planes fly too far above their targets to see them; pilots rely on radar to detect targets.)

field as a final resting place for those who here gave their lives that that nation might live. It is altogether fitting and proper that we should do this.

But, in a larger sense, we cannot dedicate—we cannot consecrate—we cannot hallow—this ground. The brave men, living and dead, who struggled here, have consecrated it far above our poor power to add or detract. The world will little note nor long remember what we say here, but it can never forget what they did here. It is for us, the living, rather, to be dedicated here to the unfinished work which they who fought here have thus far so nobly advanced. It is rather for us to be here dedicated to the great task remaining before us—that from these honored dead we take increased devotion to that cause for which they gave the last full measure of devotion; that we here highly resolve that these dead shall not have died in vain; that this nation, under God, shall have a new birth of freedom; and that government of the people, by the people, for the people, shall not perish from the earth.

Grant Heads the Union Army

Lincoln finally found a general who would fight. In March 1864 he named Ulysses S. Grant, the hero of Vicksburg, as supreme commander of all the Union armies. Grant adopted a simple yet costly strategy. He appointed **William T. Sherman** to command the Union army in Tennessee. Sher-

The Civil War, 1864-1865

Map Skills
Atlanta • Savannah, GA; Columbia, SC; Raleigh, NC • Richmond

Map Skills Movement Where did Sherman go from Chattanooga? Then where did he go?
Movement From what city did Lee go to Appomattox Court House?

man's army was to fight its way from Tennessee through Georgia to the Atlantic coast and then move north through the Carolinas. In the meantime, Grant's Army of the Potomac would keep Lee's forces pinned down in Virginia.

Wearing Them Down. Grant believed in pushing ahead at all costs, following his own advice of "When in doubt, fight." His main purpose was not necessarily to take Richmond but rather to grind up the South's forces. To this end, the Union armies drove south through Tennessee toward Georgia. In January 1863 Murfreesboro, Tennessee, fell. Despite a Southern victory at Chickamauga, Georgia, in September, Chattanooga, Tennessee, was in Union hands by the end of the year.

In 1864 Grant ordered his men into one battle after another in central Virginia—the Wilderness, Spotsylvania, Cold Harbor, Yellow Tavern, and Petersburg. In one month alone, his army suffered sixty thousand casualties, and Lee's army suffered half that number. As expected, the Union forces were able to replace their losses, while the Confederates were not. Grant was slowly but steadily wearing Lee down, not by superior tactics or better fighting but by brute strength.

Sherman's March to the Sea. Sherman had lived in the South for several years, so when war broke out, the Confederacy offered him a high military post. Just the opposite of Lee, Sherman decided to support the Union. He believed the best way to end the horrors of war was to defeat the other side as quickly as possible.

Picturing History
Gen. William T. Sherman.

In September his troops captured Atlanta, Georgia. Then they set off on a famous march to the sea, which he reached at Savannah. Sherman was not a cruel man, but he wanted to crush Confederate morale. Announcing that "war is hell," he deliberately led his troops on a path of destruction. He aimed to destroy the countryside and to strike at the civilian population. His troops burned houses and barns. They destroyed food and killed livestock. They terrorized the people, even though there was not much actual killing of civilians. "To realize what war is," Sherman said, "one should follow in our tracks."

Sherman's invasion marked a turning point in the history of modern warfare. His march illustrated a shift in the belief that only military targets should be destroyed. Now civilian population centers were fair game, too.

Lincoln Is Reelected

The mounting death toll deepened Lincoln's natural sadness. He had not been back to Springfield, Illinois, since becoming President. Even then, in 1861, he wondered whether he would ever see home again. The tragedies of the war had deeply lined his face. He began to dream about his own death.

In the fall 1864 election campaign, Lincoln faced a great deal of opposition. Many Northerners were unhappy with the way the war was going and especially with the high casualty figures. So the Democrats, who had made gains in the congressional elections of 1862, nominated George McClellan on a platform of a negotiated peace. On the other side, Radical Republicans opposed Lincoln's renomination because of how he planned to handle the rebel states when they were finally defeated. Lincoln favored readmitting them into the Union as soon as 10 percent of the voters in each state took an oath of loyalty to the United States. Radical Republicans, on the other hand, wanted a majority of the voters in each state to take the oath. The Radical Republicans also wanted the Southern states to free their slaves before being readmitted.

Lincoln's backers decided to drop the name *Republican* in order to win some Democratic votes. They called themselves the National Union party in order to emphasize their major purpose of saving the Union. Also, they chose a Unionist Democrat from Tennessee as Lincoln's running mate. His name was Andrew Johnson.

Lincoln was reelected because of Union victories. First, Admiral Farragut captured Mobile, Alabama. Then General Sherman telegraphed Lincoln with the message "Atlanta is ours." Finally, General **Philip Sheridan** swept the Confederates out of the Shenandoah Valley. Public opinion in the North shifted in Lincoln's favor, and he won the election with 55 percent of the popular vote.

Lee Surrenders

On April 2, 1865, as the Virginia countryside burst into bloom, the smoking city of Richmond finally fell to Union troops. The badly outnum-

Picturing History John Wilkes Booth (left) opened the unguarded door of the Presidential box at Ford's Theater and crept close to the President. He aimed a small pistol and fired, hitting the back of Lincoln's head.

bered Confederate army retreated west. On April 7 Lee sent a message to Grant. Two days later, the generals met at a farmhouse near **Appomattox Court House.** Lee was dressed in his best uniform, with a silk sash tied around his waist, and wearing a sword. Grant, whose baggage had been lost, wore his usual rumpled and mud-spattered uniform. He had no sword. Soldiers of both armies stood close by. They were so tired that they stood in uneven lines. Grant was not a man of words, so he relied on orders from the President that read: "Let them have their horses to plow with, and, if you like, their guns to shoot crows with. I want no one punished." Lee himself hinted that the horses would be welcome, but he was too proud to ask

directly. The two generals looked each other in the eye and shook hands. For these two men, the great war ended in mutual respect.

Lincoln Is Assassinated

Five days later, Abraham Lincoln did something unusual. He went to the theater to see a play called *Our American Cousin.* He had not relaxed for a long time. He sat with Mrs. Lincoln in a special box that nearly hung over the stage. No one saw a strange man creep up behind him. When the pistol shot rang out, Lincoln fell forward with a bullet in his head. However, he was not dead. The assassin, **John Wilkes Booth,** an actor and a Southern sympathizer, jumped down onto the stage, breaking his leg. Nevertheless he managed to escape. (Federal troops later recovered a body, believed to be that of Booth, from a burned-down barn in Virginia. Several others were convicted of a conspiracy to assassinate the President and were hanged.)

There was difficulty in moving the tall, unconscious President to a house across the street. Finally he lay stretched out on a bed in a small room, surrounded by a dozen worried people. The sun rose over the Potomac and the capital city. The President still breathed a little. The sun turned from red to yellow. He still breathed. Then suddenly he stopped.

SECTION 5 REVIEW

Key Terms and People

Explain the significance of: Vicksburg, Gettysburg Address, William T. Sherman, Philip Sheridan, Appomattox Court House, John Wilkes Booth

Main Ideas

1. Why was the Battle of Gettysburg so important?
2. In the Gettysburg Address, to what cause did Lincoln say the living should be dedicated?
3. How did Sherman's march to the sea mark a turning point in the history of modern warfare?
4. What was the most important factor in Lincoln's successful reelection in 1864?

Critical Thinking

5. What did William T. Sherman mean when he said, "To realize what war is, one should follow in our tracks"?

State the Objective

Recognize the various purposes of period songs.

Present the Lesson

Divide the class into small groups and assign one song from this feature to each group. Ask each group to answer the following questions about their song: What purpose did the writer have in mind? Who is the intended audience? Have a leader from each group summarize the information for the class. (Possible responses: "The Bonnie Blue Flag"—purpose was to glorify the Southern cause; likely audience was all Southern states, including those that had not yet joined the fight. "The Old Union Wagon"—purpose was to show everyone that the Union was still strong with thirty-four states; audience was Northern states and perhaps Southern states as well. "Marching Song of the First Arkansas Regiment"—purpose was to show that black men were brave soldiers who fought hard for freedom; audience was Northerners and Southerners whom they wished to warn of their intent. "The War Song of Dixie"—purpose was to call new recruits; audience was Southern men. "Tenting on the Old Camp Ground"—purpose was to cheer the soldiers; audience was soldiers and their families.)

Tell students that war songs sometimes reflect the everyday hardships of battle or tell of the bravery of soldiers in battle. Thus, the

Focus on Primary Sources

Songs of the Civil War

"Dixie" composed by Dan Emmett and "The Battle Hymn of the Republic" composed by Julia Ward Howe are the two best remembered songs of the Civil War. Many more songs, however, were written during this period. Some were patriotic ballads that often moved the folks back home more than those in the front lines. Others were recruiting songs. Tunes with sentimental lyrics of loneliness and homesickness and those expressing jealousy and frustration were also popular.

Carefully read through the following songs of the Civil War. Be alert to words or phrases that express certain views or emotions. Then answer the questions that follow.

The Bonnie Blue Flag

Harry McCarty, of Arkansas, wrote this song to an old tune, "The Irish Jaunting Cart." As various states joined the Confederacy, verses were added. Only the first two are given here.

We are a band of brothers,
  And native to the soil,
Fighting for the property
  We gained by honest toil;
And when our rights were threatened,
  The cry rose near and far—
"Hurrah for the Bonnie Blue Flag
  That bears the single star!"

CHORUS

Hurrah! Hurrah!
For Southern rights, hurrah!
Hurrah for the Bonnie Blue Flag
That bears the single star!

As long as the Union
  Was faithful to her trust,
Like friends and like brothers
  Both kind were we and just;
But now, when Northern treachery
  Attempts our rights to mar,
We hoist on high the Bonnie Blue Flag
  That bears the single star!

Source: Mortimer Adler, ed., *The Annals of America, 1493–1986* (Chicago: Encyclopaedia Britannica, 1986), vol. 9, 304–305.

The Old Union Wagon

One Northern answer to "The Bonnie Blue Flag" was written by Robert M. Hart to the music of "Wait for the Wagon," a popular tune of the day.

The eagle of Columbia, in majesty and
  pride,
Still soars aloft in glory, though the
  traitors have defied
The flag we dearly cherish, the emblem
  of our will,
Baptized in blood of heroes, 'way down
  on Bunker Hill.

CHORUS

Sam built the wagon,
The old Union wagon,
The star-crested wagon,
To give the boys a ride.

There's none can smash the wagon, 'tis
  patented and strong,
And built of pure devotion, by those
  who hate the wrong;
Its wheels are made of freedom, which
  patriots adore,
The spokes when rightly counted, just
  number thirty-four.

CHORUS

Keep to the wagon,
The old Union wagon,
The oft-tested wagon,
While millions take a ride.

Source: Willard A. Heaps and Porter W. Heaps, *The Singing Sixties: The Spirit of Civil War Days* (Norman: University of Oklahoma Press, 1960), 67.

378

songs can provide later generations with a more personal view of the war than is contained in a historical narrative.

Marching Song of the First Arkansas (Black) Regiment

Oh, we're the bully soldiers of the "First of Arkansas,"
We are fighting for the Union, we are fighting for the law,
We can hit a Rebel further than a white man ever saw,
As we go marching on.

> *Glory, glory hallelujah,*
> *Glory, glory hallelujah,*
> *Glory, glory hallelujah,*
> *As we go marching on.*

See, there above the center, where the flag is waving bright,
We are going out of slavery; we're bound for freedom's light;
We mean to show Jeff Davis how the Africans can fight,
As we go marching on!

CHORUS

Source: Adler, *Annals of America,* vol. 9, 303–304.

The War Song of Dixie

Before the war, "Dixie" was an immensely popular minstrel tune. Its Northern abolitionist composer was mortified when it was used as a Confederate anthem. The wonderfully catchy tune was borrowed by dozens of writers on both sides. Every state, North and South, seemed to have at least one "Dixie" song. Confederate Albert Pike fitted the tune to these words.

Southrons, hear your country call you!
Up! lest worse than death befall you!
    To arms! to arms! to arms! in Dixie!
Lo, all the beacon-fires are lighted,
Let all hearts be now united!
    To arms! to arms! to arms! in Dixie!

CHORUS

Advance the flag of Dixie! Hurrah! Hurrah!
For Dixie's land we'll take our stand,
To live or die for Dixie.
To arms! to arms! and conquer peace for Dixie!
To arms! to arms! and conquer peace for Dixie!

CHORUS

Strong as lions, swift as eagles,
Back to their kennels hunt those beagles!

To arms! to arms! to arms! in Dixie!
Cut the unequal swords asunder,
Let them each other plunder!
    To arms! to arms! to arms! in Dixie!

CHORUS

Source: Heaps and Heaps, *Singing Sixties,* 67.

Tenting on the Old Camp Ground

Walter Kittredge wrote this sad refrain. As the war dragged on, it was sung by soldiers on both sides and became a favorite at both Union and Confederate veterans' reunions. Two verses follow.

We're tenting tonight on the old camp ground,
    Give us a song to cheer
Our weary hearts, a song of home
    And friends we love so dear.

CHORUS

Many are the hearts that are weary tonight,
Wishing for the war to cease;
Many are the hearts that are looking for the right
To see the dawn of peace.
Tenting tonight, tenting tonight,
Tenting on the old camp ground.

We are tired of war on the old camp ground,
    Many are dead and gone
Of the brave and true who've left their homes,
    Others been wounded long.

CHORUS

Source: Heaps and Heaps, *Singing Sixties,* 160.

Analyzing Primary Sources

1. Why were so many Civil War songs written to the same popular tunes?
2. Which song appears to have been written by soldiers? Does it differ in any way from the rest? How?
3. Does it surprise you that "Tenting on the Old Camp Ground" was popular with both armies? Explain.

Critical Thinking

4. List these songs under the purpose for which you believe they were written.

Answer Key

Key Terms and People

These are highlighted in the text in the order in which they appear in this list.

Main Ideas

1. Control of Fort Sumter; but by firing first shot, Confederates helped unite Northern public opinion in favor of war.

2. Possible answers: North—large population; produced four-fifths of nation's industrial goods and food; twice the railroad mileage; good civilian leaders. South—defend own soil; better military leaders; soldiers skilled with guns and horses; hope for British aid.

3. Better and more accurate guns made fighting more impersonal; long-range bullets made cavalry obsolete;tactics became important because infantry charges no longer effective.

4. He did not follow up at Antietam and so lost a chance to end war sooner.

5. Britain was unsure about recognizing Confederacy; they did not like slavery; they were not as dependent on Southern cotton as they had thought; they needed Northern grain more.

6. It prohibited slavery behind military lines of Confederacy upon issue: January 1,1863.
• The war became freedom war and South fought to save its way of life; kept Britain from joining Confederate cause; brought black soldiers into Union army. • Many people did not want numbers of jobless ex-slaves put into society; to Lincoln saving the Union was more important than ending slavery.

7. Morrill Tariff: protected U.S. manufacturers from foreign competition; Homestead Act: gave 160 acres of public land to any citizen who would cultivate it; Morrill Land-Grant Act: gave land for agricultural and engineer colleges; National Banking Act: set up national banks. • Involved the federal government in the economy at many levels.

8. South—took care of businesses and plantations; North—worked in industry, government, nursing.

9. Gettysburg—the first defeat of Lee; he was never able to mount invasion of North. Vicksburg—effectively cut South in half.

10. Grant wore down Southern forces by constant fighting.
• He lost more men than Lee but was always able to replace his losses.

Critical Thinking Questions

11. Possible answers: run away or stayed and fought.
• Soldiers needed moral conviction and discipline to stay.
• Ashamed and cowardly.

➤**12.** Possible answers: their ties to the Union were stronger than those to slavery; none were in the cotton belt; many citizens had freed their slaves.

➤**13.** Possible answers: most students will identify with views of the North because of slavery issue. Cooperheads might attract some because war and its aftermath were so terrible. Geography would have much to do with decision since soldiers supported views of their families.

14. Lincoln thought the North could win easily; Washington society thought it was entertainment since they had not experienced horrors of war,

---

CHAPTER **14** REVIEW

Write your answers on a separate sheet of paper.

Key Terms and People

Explain the significance of: P. G. T. Beauregard, Jefferson Davis, Stonewall Jackson, ironclads, *Monitor, Merrimac,* Army of the Potomac, Battle of Shiloh, David Farragut, Second Battle of Bull Run, Radical Republicans, bounties, bounty jumpers, greenbacks, Philip Sheridan, John Wilkes Booth

Main Ideas

1. What did the Confederates accomplish by firing upon and capturing Fort Sumter?
2. List at least three advantages the North had and at least three the South had at the onset of the war.
3. What were the effects of the new, breech-loading rifle? Why?
4. What led Lincoln to fire General McClellan after Antietam even though McClellan had won the battle?
5. Why did the British refuse to recognize the Confederacy?
6. What were the terms of the Emancipation Proclamation? What were its effects? Why did Lincoln not free all the slaves?
7. Explain the importance of each of these acts of Congress: the Morrill Tariff, 1861; the Homestead Act, 1862; the Morrill Land-Grant Act, 1862; the National Banking Act, 1863. Explain their importance as a group.
8. How were women able to help in the war effort, both in the South and in the North?
9. Why were the Union victories at Gettysburg and Vicksburg so important?
10. How did General Grant win the war? How was he helped by one of the advantages of the North listed in your answer to Question 2?

Critical Thinking Questions

11. **Analyzing Literature.** How would you have reacted if you had been faced with the environment described in the excerpt from Stephen Crane's *The Red Badge of Courage?* What kind of discipline must be required to keep everyone from running away? How do you suppose the youth felt when he realized what he had done?
12. **Making Inferences.** Why do you think the border states of Maryland, Delaware, Kentucky, and Missouri remained in the Union instead of seceding with the Confederacy, even though they were slave states?
13. **Making Decisions.** If you had been the age you are now when the secession occurred, would you have been sympathetic with the Southern cause? the Northern cause? the Copperheads? Would geography have had anything to do with your choice?
14. **Identifying Assumptions.** In the beginning, what did Lincoln and Washington society assume about war that made them think the war would not last long and that they could take picnics to battle?
15. **Making Comparisons.** Compare life behind the lines in the Southern agricultural society with that in the Northern industrial society during the war.
16. **Analyzing Quotations.** What do you learn about Lincoln from the Gettysburg Address and the message he sent Grant at Appomattox?

Critical Thinking Activities

17. **Analyzing Geography in History.** Refer to a map of the United States to answer the following questions. Pretend you are a Northern general working on war tactics. What Southern city should you try to take first? Why? Where would you first try to divide the South? Why did Grant go down the Mississippi? Why would you march from Chattanooga through Atlanta to Savannah? What seaports would you blockade? Why did Lee drive into Pennsylvania at Gettysburg?
18. **Linking Past to Present.** The Civil War has been called the first modern war. What likenesses can you think of between the Civil War and what you know of World War II? What are some differences? Does it bear any resemblance to what World War III might be like?

only reports of the Mexican War, which was more a farce than a war.

15. Southern—shortage of workers for farms and plantations; cotton crop shifted to food crops; no industry; boycott of goods from Europe made getting supplies difficult. Northern—industry thrived; expanded into territories; began construction of transcontinental railroad.

16. Lincoln had compassion for all; didn't want to make South pay for its defeat; was aware that life had to go on after the war.

➤**17.** See completed map at the back of the book. • Possible answers: take Richmond first because it is close and capital of Confederacy. You could then divide South along eastern Appalachians through Chattanooga. • Grant went down Mississippi because Richmond hadn't been taken.

• Going through Georgia would divide South on east-west line. • Blockade Charleston, Savannah, Mobile, New Orleans. • Divide the North.

➤**18.** Possible answers: in both wars the use of modern weapons meant soldiers did not always see the enemy; tactics became more important; conscription was important; income taxes were needed to pay for war; civilian targets were used. • Used airplanes in WW II; fought on foreign soil. • Nuclear weapons will bring about greater destruction.

➤**Question suitable for cooperative learning.**

The Civil War

When Lincoln actually took office, not all the slave states had seceded. Yet when South Carolina forces bombarded and took the Union's Fort Sumter, other Southern states had to decide whether to leave the Union. Four including Virginia seceded, but four border slave states remained in the Union. The North had many more people and more industry than the South, but when the real fighting came, Confederates had an edge because they were defending their homeland. They won the First Battle of Bull Run, southwest of Washington, D.C.

The Union strategy was three-pronged: to capture Richmond, to gain control of the Mississippi and Tennessee river valleys and split the Confederacy, and to blockade the South. At first Lincoln had trouble finding competent generals. Then General Grant won the bloody Battle of Shiloh. Both sides lost so many men that they became more cautious. By now people realized that the war would not be short. Lincoln fired McClellan because he did not pursue a decisive victory at the Battle of Antietam, or Sharpsburg. That battle killed or wounded twenty-two thousand men.

The Union government used skillful diplomacy to persuade Great Britain not to aid the Confederacy. At first Lincoln said the North was fighting only to save the Union. Later he issued the Emancipation Proclamation as a war measure. At first it had no real practical effect on slavery, but symbolically it changed the atmosphere of the war. Abolishing slavery was popular with Northerners and with the British, and it hurt the South. The use of conscription by the North and the South led to abusive practices that caused resentment.

Nearly every American knew at least one man who had died or been maimed in the war. In the South both black and white people suffered from food shortages, uncontrolled inflation, and invading armies. In the North, some businessmen actually profited from the war, and women got jobs in factories. In both sections women found completely new opportunities working in government offices as well as in hospitals. Conditions were terrible in the prisoner-of-war camps in which so many men died.

After another Confederate victory in Virginia, Lee's army was defeated at the enormous Battle of Gettysburg. Union forces finally captured the last Confederate forts on the Mississippi River, and Grant was transferred to Virginia, where he used his huge army to wear down his opponents. General Sherman led a Union army through Georgia, the heart of the South. Lincoln was reelected. Lee surrendered to Grant at Appomattox. The war was over, but Lincoln was assassinated.

Chronology of Main Events

1861 Firing on Fort Sumter begins Civil War; First Battle of Bull Run; Morrill Tariff adopted

1862 *Monitor* and *Merrimac* clash in the first naval battle in American history between ironclads; Grant takes Shiloh; Homestead Act; greenbacks issued; Morrill Act sets up land-grant colleges; Second Battle of Bull Run

1863 Emancipation Proclamation; national banking system adopted; Battle of Gettysburg; surrender of Vicksburg

1864 Grant opens drive to Richmond; Sherman takes Atlanta and Savannah

1865 Lincoln inaugurated for second term; Lee surrenders at Appomattox; Lincoln assassinated

Telescoping the Times may be used as an alternative to having students read the entire chapter, as a chapter preview, or as a chapter review.

Global Perspectives

1867	Alfred Nobel patents dynamite.
1867	Austrians and Hungarians create a dual monarchy.
1868	Britain stops transporting convicts to Australia.
1869	Egyptians open the Suez Canal.
1870	Italy completes unification.
1873	Japan begins compulsory military service.

For Discussion

What effect might the opening of the Suez Canal have had on the U.S. in 1869? (Possible responses: provided a faster and cheaper route to the East which affected the prices of some foreign trade items; could be used to move military forces and materials more quickly between Europe and Asia.)

Additional Resources

- Geography Activities
- Skills Activities
- Thematic Activities
- Economic Activities
- Cultural Literacy Activities
- Literary Source Readings
- Primary Source Readings
- Nuclear Peacekeeping
- Transparencies
- Computer Test Generator

Additional Teaching Strategies

SECTION 1

For Basic Students: Divide the class into two groups. Have one group list on the board the rights given freedmen by the Black Codes. Ask the other group to list on the board the restrictions imposed by the Black Codes. (Possible responses: rights—legally marry, own property, sue in court, go to school; restrictions—not serve on juries, not carry weapons, not testify against whites, not marry whites.) Discuss with students how they might feel about these codes if they were newly freed blacks.

For Advanced Students: To discuss checks and balances, ask students the following questions. What is the purpose of the system of checks and balances as defined in the Constitution? (Possible responses: prevents any of the branches of government from abusing authority; assures that no one faction or party controls all power.) What decisions did the President and the Congress each want to make after the Civil War? (Possible responses: Reconstruction of the South; readmittance of Confederate states; amnesty.) What are some recent examples of the application of the system of checks and balances? (Possible response: Congress blocked the President's nominee for the Supreme Court.)

SECTION 2

For Basic Students: Ask the class to outline on the board: **I** the Thirteenth, **II** Fourteenth, and **III** Fifteenth Amendments. Give **A** the year each went into effect and **B** the main provision of each.

I. Thirteenth Amendment
  A. 1865
  B. Banned slavery and involuntary servitude in U.S.
II. Fourteenth Amendment
  A. 1868
  B. Protected rights of citizens
III. Fifteenth Amendment
  A. 1870
  B. Declared right to vote could not be denied because of race, color, or previous condition of servitude

For Advanced Students: Have students research President Johnson's impeachment case and hold a mock trial at which the issues are argued. Let students act as prosecution and defense attorneys, judge, jurors, and President Johnson. (Issues might include: Johnson's veto of the Reconstruction Act; his dismissal of Secretary of War Stanton.) Remind students that they must argue as would the group they represent (Radical Republicans, freedmen, etc.)

SECTION 3

For Basic Students: Review with students the systems of sharecropping and tenant farming that developed in the South during Reconstruction. (Details might include: landowners divided their land among sharecroppers; each grower gave a share of crops to the owner; theoretically sharecroppers could move up on economic ladder and become tenant farmers as they gradually earned profits.) Ask students to explain why these practices might be regarded as slavery in another form. (Possible responses: sharecroppers rarely had any money left after paying landowner and other debts; sharecroppers were at the mercy of the market due to fluctuation in price of cash crops.)

For Advanced Students: Ask students to choose one of the following Reconstruction figures and write two paragraphs on that figure's view of Reconstruction. Students should state whether that person viewed Reconstruction as a success or failure: Abraham Lincoln, Andrew Johnson, Thaddeus Stevens, Hiram Revels, Booker T. Washington, Nathaniel Bedford Forest, W.E.B. DuBois, or Charlotte Forten. (Paragraphs might include: Lincoln—Reconstruction was a limited success because it preserved the Union and gave citizenship to blacks, but it was too harsh on the Southern whites; Revels—Reconstruction was a success because blacks were given the opportunity to participate in government.)

SECTION 4

For Basic Students: Divide the class into three groups, one to represent Northern whites, one for Southern whites, and one for freed blacks. Have each group prepare a list of successes and failures of Reconstruction. (Possible responses: Northern whites favored rights for blacks and many felt South should have been punished; Southern whites felt unfairly treated because of occupation by federal troops; freed blacks were glad for freedom but needed jobs, education, and protection from terrorist societies.) Have the groups share their lists with the class.

For Advanced Students: Ask students to research and report on the Supreme Court decisions in *Smith* v. *Allwright* (1944) and *Sweatt* v. *Painter* (1950). Students might share the details of these cases with the class. In 1944 Lonnie Smith, a black, was barred from participation in the Texas Democratic primary. The Court ruled that any exclusion of blacks from voting in primaries is the type of state action that is forbidden by the Fifteenth Amendment and the Equal Protection Clause of the Fourteenth Amendment. In 1950 all nine justices ruled that the University of Texas Law School could not bar a qualified black applicant from a school by placing him or her into a newly created black school that would be inferior.

Further Reading for Students

Lomask, Milton. *Andy Johnson: President on Trial*. New York: Octagon Books, 1973.

Woodward, C. Vann. *The Strange Career of Jim Crow*. New York: Oxford University Press, 1974.

Bibliography for Teachers

Books

DuBois, W.E.B. *Black Reconstruction in America, 1860-1880*. New York: Atheneum, 1969. Paper.

Franklin, John Hope. *Reconstruction: After the Civil War*. Chicago: University of Chicago Press, 1962. Paper.

Sefton, James E. *Andrew Johnson and the Uses of Constitutional Power*. Boston: Little, Brown, 1980. Paper.

Trefousse, Hans L. *Andrew Johnson*. New York: Norton, 1989.

Audio-Visuals

Reconstruction: A Changing Nation— 1865-1880. Graphic Curriculum. Movie.

Computer Resource

American History II. (Apple) Sliwa Enterprises, Inc.

Teacher's Notes:

Lesson Plan

Teaching Resources, Unit 3 Booklet

Chapter Objectives

Students will learn:
- that U.S. leaders lacked a political consensus concerning Reconstruction policies
- the effect of the Civil War on the growth of congressional power
- the impact of Radical Reconstruction on the Southern states
- the successes and failures of Reconstruction

Picturing History In *Upland Cotton* (above), Winslow Homer painted the ex-slaves with the compassion he showed toward all those who faced adversity in life. Homer, one of the giants of American art, was an artist-journalist for *Harper's Weekly* during the Civil War.

Using the Chapter Time Line

What three events took place in 1865 (see Chapter 14 Time Line)? (Answer: Lee surrendered, Lincoln assassinated, Johnson succeeded Lincoln as President) Who was President when the Suez Canal opened (see Unit 3 Time Line)? (Answer: Grant)

1865	1870	1875	1880

1867 Reconstruction Act

1865 Andrew Johnson succeeds to Presidency

1868 President Johnson impeached

1869 Ulysses S. Grant inaugurated President

1873 Grant inaugurated for second term

1876 Presidential election returns disputed; Rutherford B. Hayes wins

Links to American Literature

Margaret Mitchell: born 1900 in Atlanta, Georgia; educated at the Washington Seminary and Smith College; worked as a reporter and feature writer for the Atlanta *Journal* from 1922 to 1926.

Gone With the Wind: completed in 1936; was an instant success; sold over 1,500,000 copies in its first year; translated into thirty languages; awarded the Pulitzer Prize in 1937; made into a movie in 1939 and continues to be one of the most popular films of all times.

Introducing the Chapter

Write the term *bias* on the board and discuss its meaning. (Possible definitions: partiality; prejudice; lack of objectivity in dealing with a situation; distorted judgment.) Discuss with students the concept and consequences of bias. Ask students to respond to the following questions. What are some examples of bias from your experience or reading? (Possible response: unfair treatment because of age, religion, color, size.) How might bias be overcome? (Possible responses: positive personal experiences; education.) How might bias have affected plans for Reconstruction? (Possible responses: Southern whites were biased against blacks; Radical Republicans were biased against Southern whites; because of bias the plans for Reconstruction were controversial and difficult to carry out.)

CHAPTER 15 1865–1876

Reconstruction and Its Effects

Links to American Literature

When she arose at last and saw again the black ruins of Twelve Oaks, her head was raised high and something that was youth and beauty and potential tenderness had gone out of her face forever. What was past was past. Those who were dead were dead. The lazy luxury of the old days was gone, never to return. And, as Scarlett settled the heavy basket across her arm, she had settled her own mind and her own life.

There was no going back and she was going forward.

Throughout the South for fifty years there would be bitter-eyed women who looked backward, to dead times, to dead men, evoking memories that hurt and were futile, bearing poverty with bitter pride because they had those memories. But Scarlett was never to look back. . . .

Hunger gnawed at her empty stomach again and she said aloud: "As God is my witness, as God is my witness, the Yankees aren't going to lick me. I'm going to live through this, and when it's over, I'm never going to be hungry again. No, nor any of my folks. If I have to steal or kill—as God is my witness, I'm never going to be hungry again."

— MARGARET MITCHELL, *Gone with the Wind*

Like Scarlett O'Hara, many Southerners threw all their efforts into rebuilding their lives in the years following the Civil War. Other Southerners despaired over their losses. Yet others saw great opportunity and worked to build a new South. Reconstruction of the South was not without problems. Northern soldiers occupied the South as conquerors. Graft and corruption became a way of life. Slavery came to an end, but the freed slaves were not truly free; the war did little to improve their daily lives. Feelings of anger and futility were common among Northerners and Southerners. Traces of these feelings still remain today.

Chapter Overview

This chapter serves as a reminder that history is more than facts and dates to be memorized. To study history is to search for truth in a story that includes villains as well as heroes and problems that seem to have no solutions. In this chapter, you will study the period after the Civil War known as Reconstruction. You will learn about two plans for putting the Union back together, and you will study how the power of Congress grew during this time.

You will also analyze the impact and assess the outcome of Reconstruction policies. Chapter 15 explains this period in four sections.

Chapter Outline

1. **Reconstruction Plans Differ**
2. **The Radicals Gain Control**
3. **Radical Reconstruction Is Enforced**
4. **Reconstruction Efforts Come to an End**

Reconstruction and Its Effects **383**

Anticipate the Lesson

On the board write the heading *Pre-War*. Have students take turns listing the problems that confronted the nation in 1861. (List might include: extension of slavery into territories; dissension over states' rights.) Head another column *Post-War*. In this column have students list solutions to the pre-war problems. (List might include: Emancipation Proclamation abolished slavery; Civil War prevented seces-

sion.) Discuss with students the new problems these solutions might have created. (Problems might incude: freed slaves needed jobs, homes, education.)

State the Objective

Realize that U.S. leaders lacked a political consensus concerning Reconstruction policies.

SECTION 1

Reconstruction Plans Differ

GLOSSARY TERMS: **pocket veto, black codes**

At war's end, the country faced three main problems. The first was a human one. What were the four million newly freed black people in the South to do? They had no land, no jobs, and few skills outside of farming. How would they feed and clothe themselves? How would they live?

The second problem was political. What was to happen with the Southern states? Were they to be received back into the Union as Lincoln wished, "with malice toward none"? Or were they to be treated as conquered territories that would be occupied and punished, as some Northerners wished?

The third problem was a constitutional one. Who had the right to determine how the Confederate States would be readmitted to the Union? Was it the President, as head of the executive branch of government, or Congress, the legislative branch?

Lincoln Hopes to Heal Wounds

Even in the midst of war, Lincoln had wondered how to treat the Confederate States if the Union should win. In general, he believed they had never legally seceded. In fact, an important purpose of the war was to prove that secession was not constitutionally possible. Lincoln believed that it was individuals who had rebelled and knew that the Constitution gave the President the power to pardon individuals.

Lincoln was eager to restore the Union as quickly as possible, so he wanted a Reconstruction that would be mild and forgiving. He wanted the South's return to be as easy and painless as possible. In December 1863 he announced his Proclamation of Amnesty and Reconstruction. Amnesty means a pardon for crimes against the government. The proclamation granted pardons to all Confederates who would swear allegiance to the Union and promise to obey its laws. However, this pardon did not include high officials of the Confederacy and those accused of crimes against prisoners of war.

Under the proclamation, a Confederate state could form a state government as soon as 10 percent of those on the 1860 voting lists took an oath to uphold the United States Constitution. That state could then send its representatives and senators to Congress.

Lincoln's Reconstruction plan by no means satisfied Congress. Many Northerners, particularly the Radicals, wanted the political power of the slave-owning class destroyed. They also wanted the Southern black people to be given full citizenship—meaning all civil rights, including the right to vote. This demand does not seem radical or extreme now, but it did at the time.

The Radicals Propose Their Plan

In July 1864 the Radicals in Congress adopted their own blueprint for Reconstruction—the **Wade-Davis Bill.** This bill proposed that Congress, not the President, be responsible for Reconstruction. It

---

People in the Chapter

Andrew Johnson never went to school. He was a tailor's apprentice in North Carolina until he ran away to Tennessee and married a schoolteacher, who taught him to write. He was the only Southern senator to support the Union during the Civil War.

Josephine Griffing made her home a station on the Underground Railroad. After the Civil War, she moved to Washington, D.C., to help deal with the problems of the landless and the jobless in the South.

Booker T. Washington was born a slave. He wanted to go to school after emancipation

came, but his impoverished family needed him to work. Washington worked in a salt furnace from 4 A.M. until 9 A.M., went to school, and then returned to work to pack salt for another two hours.

Edwin Stanton, secretary of war, wanted to prevent Lincoln's assassin from becoming a Civil War hero, so he arranged for John Wilkes Booth's body to be buried at sea while crowds watched. This was a fake burial, however, and the actual body was buried elsewhere.

Picturing History Stunned survivors wander aimlessly through the rubble and ruins of Richmond, Virginia, in this haunting photograph taken in April 1865. Much of the city was torched by proud Confederate soldiers who did not want to see it occupied by Union troops. The aftermath of the war was almost as hard as the war itself for families who had lost their loved ones, their homes, and their livelihood.

also declared that for a state government to be acceptable, a majority—not just 10 percent—of those eligible to vote in 1860 would have to take an ironclad oath to support the Constitution. In addition, they would have to swear that they had never supported the Confederacy in any way. Clearly, if more than half a state's voters had been loyal to the Union, the state would not have seceded in the first place!

Lincoln did not condemn the Radical plan. Instead, he waited until Congress adjourned, and then he killed the bill with a **pocket veto.** According to the Constitution, the President may, within ten days of the end of a congressional session, use a pocket veto. He simply ignores a bill (puts it in his pocket) and, if Congress adjourns within ten days, it automatically fails to become law.

The Radical Republicans responded by issuing a manifesto, or proclamation, in which they called Lincoln's pocket veto a "stupid outrage" and declared the authority of Congress to be supreme. They warned Lincoln to confine himself to his executive duties and to leave Reconstruction up to Congress. The Radicals took the position that the Confederate States actually had seceded. Thus, they now were territories seeking admission to the Union. Furthermore, it was Congress, not the

President, that controlled territorial matters. A serious quarrel was shaping up.

After the fall elections of 1864, Arkansas and Louisiana, acting under Lincoln's plan, sent representatives to Washington. However, the Radicals barred them from taking their seats. That was early in March 1865. Within a month, the war was over and Abraham Lincoln was dead.

Many historians believe that had Lincoln lived, he might have been able to deal with this difficult situation. However, his successor, Vice-President **Andrew Johnson,** a man with many good qualities, lacked the quiet dignity and diplomatic skill of Lincoln.

Johnson Continues Lincoln's Policy

Andrew Johnson was always aware that he had not been elected but had become President as a result of Lincoln's assassination. This bothered him a bit at first, but not for long. What he could not forget, however, was that he had been a poor boy who had to work his way to the top. He scorned people who had had an easier time. He was a man of strong conviction and great energy. His political ideas were a mixture of Jefferson's and those of an earlier Tennessean, Andrew Jackson.

Guided Practice

Remind students that Lincoln was willing to pardon the average Confederate soldier for taking part in war activities that some considered treasonous. Discuss with students whether the U.S. should pardon people considered traitors. (Responses should include students' reasons for their beliefs.) Ask students whether the U.S. should pardon those who fled to Canada to evade the draft during the 1960's and 1970's. (Possible responses: yes, they were not people who actively worked for the overthrow of the government; no, they refused to obey the law and to fight for their country.)

Like them, he disliked cities and manufacturing, distrusted banks and bondholders, and feared wealth that was not based on land.

White Southerners did not know what to make of this man. They considered him a traitor to his region. The Radicals, on the other hand, thought he was one of them. Both were wrong.

Almost at once, Johnson surprised everybody by announcing that he would continue Lincoln's plan of Reconstruction. He declared that any state could be readmitted to the Union if it would declare its secession illegal, swear allegiance to the Union, promise not to pay any Confederate debts, and ratify the **Thirteenth Amendment,** which abolished slavery.

The Southern states quickly took advantage of these easy terms. Within a few months, these states—except for Texas—held constitutional conventions, set up state governments, and elected representatives to Congress. In December 1865, the newly elected Southerners arrived in Washington to take their seats. Fifty-eight of them had previously sat in the Congress of the Confederacy, six had served in its cabinet, and four had fought against the United States as rebel generals. Johnson gave them all pardons, a gesture that shook the Radicals deeply.

Picturing History Andrew Johnson was described by his attorney as "a man of few ideas, but they are right and true, and he could suffer death sooner than yield up or violate one of them."

Johnson's Vetoes Enrage Republicans

In the last month of the war, President Lincoln had established a special bureau to assist former slaves and poor whites in the South. He had taken this step at the urging of Josephine Griffing, a prominent abolitionist.

The **Freedmen's Bureau** gave food and clothing to former slaves and needy whites. In all, it set up over forty hospitals, four thousand primary schools, sixty-one industrial institutes, and seventy-four teacher-training establishments. The backbone of the bureau's schools was its women teachers, both black and white. They came from all over the country and worked almost around the clock to meet the former slaves' demand for schooling.

Charlotte Forten, a black teacher from Philadelphia, was one of the seventy Northern teachers who went to Georgia to teach. She wrote:

> I never before saw children so eager to learn. . . . The older ones, during the summer, work in the fields from early morning until eleven or twelve o'clock and then come to school, after their hard toil in the hot sun, as bright and as anxious to learn as ever.

Former slave and educator Booker T. Washington recalled those times as follows:

> It was a whole race trying to go to school. Few were too young and none were too old.

By 1869 about 600,000 African Americans of all ages were in elementary schools.

Life was not always pleasant for the students or for the teachers, however. Sometimes the teachers could not find places to live. Other times they could not get credit at local stores. In addition, whites threw stones at the students as they went to and from school. Nevertheless, neither teachers nor students would give up.

In February 1866 Congress voted to continue and to enlarge the Freedmen's Bureau by backing it with more money. One month later, Congress passed the Civil Rights Bill of 1866. This act gave blacks citizenship and forbade states from passing discriminatory laws.

President Johnson stunned everyone when he vetoed both measures. It was the opening shot in his battle with Congress over Reconstruction of the South. Johnson said that Congress had gone far beyond "anything contemplated by the authors of

386

Focus on American Art

Picturing History By the late 1800's, people began to realize that photography could play a significant role in documenting history. Two early documentary photographers were Matthew Brady and Frances Benjamin Johnston. Brady's pictures documented the Civil War, and Johnston's, the rural South in the 1890's. Other documentary photographers left us their work, but their names are lost in time.

In 1899 Frances Johnston traveled through rural Virginia taking photographs of the everyday life of black families including this charming one of children on a fence. She also took pictures of the famous Hampton Institute and its students.

An unknown photographer captured the hand and torch of the Statue of Liberty while it was on display at Madison Square in 1877 before the complete statue was assembled.

This Matthew Brady image of the first Japanese delegation to visit the United States clearly portrays the vast cultural differences between the two societies. Taken in Washington, D.C., in May 1860, the photograph predates the Civil War pictures for which Brady is most famous.

Assign Independent Practice

Have students complete Chapter 15, Section 1 Daily Activity.

Student Assignment/Homework

Have students read Section 2 "The Radicals Gain Control" and write answers to Section 2 Review questions on paper.

SECTION 1 REVIEW

Answers

Main Ideas

1. Mild and forgiving, it reflected his feeling that the South should not suffer more hardships.

2. It sought revenge on and pain for the South.

3. Both expected his support for Radical Reconstruction; he supported Lincoln's plan instead.

4. Supplied food and clothing; set up schools, hospitals, and teacher-training and industrial institutes to aid former slaves and needy whites.

5. Limited their rights and mobility.

Critical Thinking

6. Possible answer: although they were no longer slaves, they were homeless and jobless; they were allowed to own land but had no money to buy it; and they were unable to prevent the loss of their new rights. **(analysis)**

Picturing History
Booker T. Washington was able to take advantage of the opportunities for education offered by Reconstruction. He attended night school until he was sixteen and then walked and hitchhiked five hundred miles to enroll in the Hampton (Virginia) Normal and Agricultural Institute. "I felt that I had reached the promised land," he said.

the Constitution." The Radicals, on the other hand, believed that Johnson was protecting Southerners who had no intention of giving blacks their full rights. Indeed, there was good reason for the Radicals to think so because the Southern states had passed some repressive laws.

The Black Codes Keep Freed Slaves Down

Black codes were laws aimed at regulating the economic and social lives of freed slaves. Immediately after the war, many blacks, while delighted to be free, nevertheless did not know what to do. There were no jobs, and the old way of plantation life was gone. Therefore, many of them drifted from place to place around the South seeking work. Others traveled about in the hope of finding relatives from whom they had been separated during slavery days. Seeing this great mass of free black men and women wandering around infuriated Southern whites. They thus passed black codes, which put blacks in an inferior position. As one historian said, they were in a "kind of twilight zone between slavery and freedom."

The black codes varied. Generally, they all stated that blacks could legally marry, own property, sue in court, and go to school. Thus, the codes recognized that blacks had certain rights they did not have before. At the same time, however, blacks could not serve on juries, carry weapons, testify against whites, or marry whites. Blacks also

had to obey a curfew, and they needed permits in order to travel. Furthermore, they were not allowed to start their own businesses. In some states, blacks could not rent or lease farm land. In South Carolina, blacks needed special licenses to work other than as servants or farm laborers.

The codes confirmed the Radicals' darkest suspicions about the South. Northern voters now began asking themselves if they had won the war after all.

Linking Past to Present

The black codes were part of a historical pattern to keep African Americans from gaining economic and political power. It was not until the Twenty-fourth Amendment was ratified in 1964 that the use of poll taxes to prevent African Americans from voting was abolished. In the 1980's, African American leaders such as Jesse Jackson made the registration of black voters an important goal in their political strategy.

SECTION 1 REVIEW

Key Terms and People

Explain the significance of: Wade-Davis Bill, pocket veto, Andrew Johnson, Thirteenth Amendment, Freedmen's Bureau, black codes

Main Ideas

1. How did Lincoln's plan for Reconstruction reflect his personal feelings?
2. In general, how did the Radicals' initial plan for Reconstruction differ from Lincoln's?
3. Why was Johnson's approach to Reconstruction a surprise both to white Southerners and to the Radicals?
4. What were the main accomplishments of the Freedmen's Bureau?
5. How did black codes affect the lives of freed slaves?

Critical Thinking

6. In what ways was the period of Reconstruction frustrating for the recently freed slaves?

Anticipate the Lesson

Ask students to give contemporary examples of how a President uses his executive powers. (Possible responses: arms negotiations with Soviet Union; decision to invade Grenada.) Ask students to contrast the role of the executive branch in political life in this century to the growth of congressional influence immediately after the Civil War. (Possible responses: After the Civil War, Congress attempted to make it-

self the most powerful branch of the government. For example, Congress set severe readmittance restrictions on Southern states, tried to impeach the President, and attempted to assume the authority of the executive branch. The balance of power is generally considered to be satisfactory today.)

State the Objective

Understand the effect of the Civil War on the growth of congressional power.

SECTION 2

The Radicals Gain Control

GLOSSARY TERMS: **equal protection of the law, due process of law**

Andrew Johnson had not been President a year when his "easy" Reconstruction program reached a dead end. Congress refused to recognize the state governments that he had encouraged to be set up. When the Radicals gained a two-thirds majority in Congress, they were able to override Johnson's vetoes. That meant that power passed from the executive branch into the hands of the Radical Republicans in Congress and their leader, **Thaddeus Stevens.**

Picturing History Thaddeus Stevens hated slavery and was determined to teach white Southerners a hard lesson.

The Battle Gets Hotter

Stevens had piercing eyes, a thin-lipped mouth, and a tall, thin body. In spite of a crippled foot, he was a famous horseman and swimmer. Before being elected to Congress, he had practiced law in Pennsylvania. There he had used his considerable talents to defend runaway slaves. Stevens hated slavery, and in time he came to hate white Southerners as well. He was determined to teach them a hard lesson they would never forget. As he said, "I look upon every man who would permit slavery . . . as a traitor to liberty and disloyal to God." When he died, Stevens asked to be buried in a cemetery for black people. He said that he wanted to show in death "the principles which I advocated

throughout a long life: equality of man before his Creator."

The Fourteenth Amendment Is Adopted. In mid-1866 the moderate Republicans, who felt that Johnson was stepping on Congress's toes, joined with the Radicals to override the President's veto of the bill extending the Freedmen's Bureau. The leaders in Congress then finished drafting the **Fourteenth Amendment.** This amendment was to take the place of the Civil Rights Act that Johnson had vetoed.

The first clause of the Fourteenth Amendment made "all persons born or naturalized in the United States" citizens of the country. All were entitled to **equal protection of the law,** and no state could deprive any person of life, liberty, or property without **due process of law.** The amendment did not grant black citizens the right to vote because that was still viewed as a matter to be decided by the states. However, if a state barred black people from taking part in elections, that state would lose some of its seats in Congress.

Another provision of the Fourteenth Amendment barred most Southern leaders from holding federal or state offices. The ban could be lifted only by a two-thirds majority of Congress.

The South Rejects the Amendment. Congress adopted the Fourteenth Amendment and sent it to the states for their approval. If the Southern states had ratified it, most Northerners would have been satisfied. Johnson, however, believed that the amendment was too harsh and that the Southern states should be guided gently back to partnership in the Union. More importantly, he believed that Congress did not have the constitutional power to treat states in this way. Therefore, he advised the states to reject the amendment. All of them except Tennessee did. The amendment was not ratified. Congress was now convinced that stronger measures were called for.

The Radicals Control Congress

In 1866 the congressional elections focused partly on the question of who should control Reconstruction: the President or the Radicals. Johnson went on a long speaking tour, urging voters to elect to Congress those men who agreed with his policy of an easy Reconstruction. His trip was a disaster, however, because he was his own worst enemy. He had a hot temper, and he embar-

For Discussion
Remind students that black codes did not permit blacks to serve on juries. In the past, all-white juries in the South have rendered verdicts in cases involving civil rights. Discuss with students whether a segregated jury can be impartial. (Discussion may include: yes, lawyers have power to remove biased jurors; no, it would be impossible to identify all prejudices in the process of interviewing prospective jurors.) Ask students whether black defendants should be tried by all-black juries and white defendants by all-white juries. (Possible responses: yes, it would be more fair to be judged by one's peers; no, the jury might be biased in favor of the defendant.)

Ask students to skim the section to find examples of constitutional issues during Reconstruction. (Possible examples: Congress refused to recognize states set up in the South under Johnson's Reconstruction plan and refused to seat congressmen from these states; Congress passed the Fourteenth Amendment and the First Reconstruction Act.) Have students discuss whether the conflict between Congress and the President represented a failure of the constitutional system. (Discussion might include: it was a time of trial and error because the country had no experience with such problems; the problems tested the strength of the system of governmental checks and balances.)

For Discussion
Discuss with students the basic details of the movement to impeach Richard Nixon in 1974. (Possible details you might present: Nixon's impeachment proceedings centered around three specific articles, obstruction of justice, abuse of power, and failure to comply with congressional subpoenas; Nixon resigned before impeachment proceedings began.) Ask students to compare these details with similar elements of Johnson's impeachment. (Possible responses: Johnson's impeachment centered around vague accusations and alleged violations of the Tenure in Office Act; Johnson's case came to trial and he was not convicted.)

rassed many people with his rough language and undignified behavior.

In addition, vicious race riots erupted in the South, particularly in Memphis, Tennessee, and in New Orleans, Louisiana. This strengthened many people's belief that the federal government had to take action to protect freed slaves against their former masters.

The voters gave the Radicals a two-thirds majority in Congress, which meant that Radicals could now override Presidential vetoes. Now they felt strong enough to move forward, and in the spring of 1867 they began putting their policy into effect.

The First Reconstruction Act. This act, which was followed by two others, divided all of the seceded states except Tennessee into five military districts. The civilian courts in these districts were replaced by military tribunals. Each district was placed under a major general who was to oversee the drawing up of new constitutions in the states that were under his control. The constitutions were required to give black males the right to vote. In addition, before states could be readmitted to the Union, their legislatures had to ratify the Fourteenth Amendment.

Not surprisingly, Johnson vetoed the First Reconstruction Act, saying that it was "without precedent and without authority, in clear conflict with the plainest provisions of the Constitution." Congress promptly overrode the veto.

The First Reconstruction Act stunned Southern whites. Had they not surrendered their armies? Had they not admitted that secession was impossible? Had they not freed their slaves? What more could be expected of them? The fact was, of course, that white Southerners could not bring themselves to regard black people as equals. They did not want to give blacks more civil rights than were absolutely necessary. Moreover, they had passed harsh, unjust laws against their ex-slaves. The First Reconstruction Act was therefore the price they had to pay. Some twenty thousand federal troops were sent to the South during the spring and summer of 1867 to keep law and order.

Tenure of Office Act. Radical leaders next turned their energies to getting rid of the hated President Johnson. The Radicals felt that Johnson was not carrying out his constitutional obligation to enforce the First Reconstruction Act. For instance, he removed military officers who were helping black people. Also, members of his cabinet ignored the required oaths and appointed many Confederates to positions in their departments.

Accordingly, the Radicals decided to lay the groundwork for impeachment, that is, to charge a public official—in this case the President—with misconduct in office. In fact, they made a bold attempt to seize control of the Presidency by passing the **Tenure of Office Act.** This law stated that Presidents could not remove cabinet officers they had themselves appointed without first obtaining a two-thirds vote of the Senate. So that no one would misunderstand the real purpose of the act, one clause flatly stated that breaking the act would be a "high misdemeanor." The phrase "high crimes and misdemeanors" is used in the Constitution (Article 2, Section 4) to define an impeachable offense.

Johnson, as well as many others, was sure that Congress had overreached itself and that the act was unconstitutional. Still it had to be tested in court. Johnson therefore fired Secretary of War Edwin M. Stanton, a Radical sympathizer.

Johnson Is Impeached

On February 24, 1868, the House voted to impeach the President. His trial before the Senate lasted from mid-March to May 26, 1868.

There were two questions to be decided at Johnson's trial. One involved a narrow constitutional case, which was easily knocked down by the President's lawyers. The Tenure of Office Act, they pointed out, did not even apply to Stanton. He had been appointed by Lincoln, not Johnson. Therefore, no criminal act as defined by the Constitution was committed.

The second question had to do with Johnson's conduct in office. He was accused of "intemperate language" and of having brought "disgrace, ridicule, contempt, and reproach" on Congress. To press criminal charges against a man because Congress did not like the way he talked or behaved seemed ridiculous to those not caught up in the passion of the moment. Nevertheless, there was an underlying issue. Senator Charles Sumner of Massachusetts stated that Johnson personally stood for the "tyrannical slave power." Keeping him in the Presidency, Sumner went on, would mean leaving loyal Unionists of the South—both black and white—at the mercy of their enemies. The question thus was political, not legal. Impeachment, said

Check for Understanding

Ask each student to prepare a newspaper story and headline explaining one of the constitutional issues discussed in class. Students should keep in mind the five W's of good reporting (who, what, when, where, why). (Possible headlines: First Reconstruction Act Vetoed; Johnson Impeachment Inevitable.)

Guided Practice

Have students complete Chapter 15, Section 2 Enrichment Activity.

Assign Independent Practice

Ask students to construct a chronological time line of events leading to the impeachment of Andrew Johnson. (Events might include: Johnson vetoes Civil Rights Act; Johnson advises states to reject Fourteenth Amendment; Johnson vetoes First Reconstruction Act.)

Sumner, is "as broad as the Constitution itself." It applied, he said, to "any act of evil example or influence."

The Massachusetts senator had raised a serious issue. There is no doubt that the Radicals were trying to change the way the Constitution worked. They were trying to destroy the federal government's system of checks and balances, and to make the executive branch answerable to the legislature (as it is in the British system).

On the day when the final vote at the trial was to be taken, the streets leading to the Senate were packed with people. The atmosphere was tense in the crowded Senate galleries. Would the Radicals get the two-thirds vote needed for conviction? Johnson was silent and maintained his dignity. Finally the moment of decision came. People in the Senate chamber leaned forward and held their breaths as the senators were asked one by one to give their verdict. As each one said "Guilty" or "Not guilty," they heaved a great sigh: some a sigh of hope, others of despair.

When the last senator was asked his verdict and he declared "Not guilty," the vote was thirty-five to nineteen, one vote less than the two-thirds needed to convict the President. Johnson thus was saved by one vote. Roars, shouts, and jeers rang down from the gallery. Some people were delighted; others were furious. Thaddeus Stevens was seen leaving the chamber, his face red with rage. Waving his arms, he cried, "The country is going to the devil."

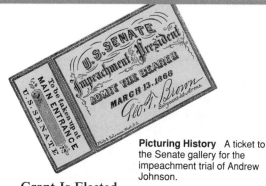

Picturing History A ticket to the Senate gallery for the impeachment trial of Andrew Johnson.

Grant Is Elected

The Democrats knew they could not win the 1868 election with Johnson. Instead, they nominated the wartime governor of New York, Horatio Seymour. The Republicans put up **Ulysses S. Grant,** the hero of the Civil War. In November Grant was elected President with an impressive majority vote of 214 to 80 in the electoral college. The popular vote, however, was something else. With almost 6 million ballots cast, Grant led by only 310,000. About 500,000 Southern blacks had voted (only 1 percent of the nation's black population lived in the North at that time), most of them for Grant. The importance of the black vote to the Republican party was obvious.

The Radicals feared that Southern whites might try to limit black suffrage in the future. Therefore, the Radicals introduced the **Fifteenth Amend-**

Linking Past to Present

Andrew Johnson was the only President of the United States to be impeached. His impeachment, however, did not bring his political career to an end—he was elected to the Senate after leaving the White House. This was not the case with Richard Nixon, however. In July 1974, the House Judiciary Committee concluded that the conduct of President Nixon deserved "impeachment and trial and removal from office." Although Nixon was never impeached, his resignation from the Presidency on August 9, 1974 marked the end of his official political career. (See Chapter 34, Section 4.)

Picturing History Ulysses S. Grant was nominated on the first roll call by the Republicans. The fact that he was not a politician increased his popularity.

Student Assignment/Homework

Have students read Section 3 "Radical Reconstruction Is Enforced" and answer Section 3 Review questions on paper.

SECTION 3
Core Lesson

Anticipate the Lesson

Ask students to make inferences about the impact of the Civil War on white Southerners. (Possible responses: Southern whites lost slaves and plantations; many families were separated; South was ravaged.) Ask students to make inferences about the impact of the war on freedmen. (Possible responses: freedmen were no longer slaves; could attempt to reunite their families; had no way to earn a living.) Conclude by asking the class to summarize the similar experiences of the Southern whites and freedmen during Northern occupation. (Possible responses: both experienced changes in voting laws, in state governments, in life styles.)

SECTION 2 REVIEW

Answers

Main Ideas

1. Unlike the Civil Rights Act, a Constitutional amendment could not be vetoed.

2. It used military administrators and federal troops.

3. He vetoed important legislation, refused to enforce the Reconstruction Act, and publicly attacked Congress.

4. Congress tried to make the President directly answerable to it rather than independent and separate in powers and duties.

5. In both the North and the South, it guaranteed the right to vote to all males, including blacks formerly barred from voting.

Critical Thinking

6. Possible answer: yes—because of the emotional nature of the issues, black codes, desire for revenge by Northerners whose relatives died in the war, the South's rejection of the Fourteenth Amendment, and Johnson's vetoes of Reconstruction laws. **(analysis & evaluation)**

Presidential Election, 1868

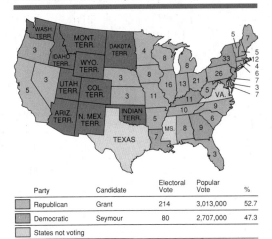

Party	Candidate	Electoral Vote	Popular Vote	%
Republican	Grant	214	3,013,000	52.7
Democratic	Seymour	80	2,707,000	47.3
States not voting				

294 Total Electoral Vote

© ML & Co.

ment. It states that no one can be kept from voting because of race or color or for having once been a slave. Most Northern states at this time barred blacks from voting, so these states also were affected by the Fifteenth Amendment. It was ratified in 1870.

SECTION 2 REVIEW

Key Terms and People

Explain the significance of: Thaddeus Stevens, Fourteenth Amendment, equal protection of the law, due process of law, Tenure of Office Act, Ulysses S. Grant, Fifteenth Amendment

Main Ideas

1. Why did Congress feel that there was a need for the Fourteenth Amendment?
2. How did Congress enforce the First Reconstruction Act?
3. What events led to President Johnson's impeachment?
4. How was the impeachment of Johnson a threat to the American system of checks and balances?
5. How did the Fifteenth Amendment affect the North as well as the South?

Critical Thinking

6. Evaluate the conduct of the Radical Republicans. Were their actions toward the South and toward President Johnson justified? Support your answer.

SECTION 3

Radical Reconstruction Is Enforced

GLOSSARY TERMS: sharecropping, tenant farming, scalawags, carpetbaggers, segregated, graft

The period of Radical Reconstruction lasted from 1867, when the First Reconstruction Act was passed, to 1877, when the last federal troops were withdrawn from the South. However, Reconstruction was not uniform. For example, in only three states—Florida, Louisiana, and South Carolina—did it last the full ten years. In the other former Confederate States, Reconstruction governments were soon replaced—sometimes within one year—by governments that represented traditional white rule.

Plantations Are Divided

Thaddeus Stevens and other Radicals had promised every freedman "forty acres and a mule." They intended to take the plantations belonging to the seventy thousand or so "chief rebels," as Stevens called them, and to redistribute the land. They never did. The reason was that moderate Republicans considered private property a basic American right. It could not be taken away from its owners without due process of law. Congress therefore made no land provisions for the freed people.

Consequently, two land arrangements developed in the South: **sharecropping** and **tenant farming.** Plantation owners had land, but they had no workers and no cash to hire them. Blacks and poor whites, on the other hand, were able to work, but they had no land, no tools, and sometimes no place to live. Here were grounds for an economic bargain. Landowners divided their land and gave each worker a few acres, seed, tools, and food to live on. When the crops were harvested, the grower gave a share—usually two-thirds—to the landowner. This arrangement paid the owner back, and it was over until the next year.

As sharecroppers, ex-slaves had some independence. At least they could now keep part of what they produced. Also, the system had some flexibility. In theory, "croppers" who saved a little and bought their own tools could drive a better bargain

State the Objective

Analyze the impact of Radical Reconstruction on the Southern states.

Present the Lesson

Ask students to list and explain changes in the social and political structure of the South caused by Radical Reconstruction. (Possible responses: sharecropping and tenant farming developed; blacks voted and held government offices.) Discuss with students ways in which white Southerners expressed their feelings about Radical Reconstruction and Southern blacks. (Possible responses: some white Southerners accepted the changes brought about by Reconstruction; some refused to register to vote; some turned to violence and terrorism.)

with landowners. Those who got their own horses or mules might even become tenants and rent the land for cash. Eventually they might move up the economic ladder to become outright owners of their farms.

It seldom worked that way, however. By the time sharecroppers had shared their crops and paid their debts, they rarely had any money left. Also, most sharecroppers grew only cash crops such as cotton or tobacco. This put them at the mercy of the market. Sometimes the demand was high and the prices were good; sometimes they were not. Furthermore, because the croppers' plots of land were small, they did not have enough space to increase the crop yield when prices were high. Finally, intense production of the same crop, year after year, eventually exhausted the soil.

The war had devastated Southern agriculture. Sharecropping and tenant farming were means of coping with this situation. They may not have been the most desirable means, but they worked. The problem was that they kept Southern farmers dependent on one or two crops. The farmers would have been better off either growing food for themselves or diversifying into growing such commercial crops as fruits and vegetables, and raising livestock.

African Americans Serve in Government

One legend of Reconstruction is that it was a time of black rule in the South, a time when whites were not permitted to use the ballot. The fact is that under Radical Reconstruction, some 704,000 blacks and 660,000 whites were registered to vote. In 1860, the last year before the Civil War, 721,000 voters were registered—all of them white. In other words, there was a drop of at most 10 percent in the number of registered white voters. Most of those included in this percentage were not allowed to register because they were former Confederate leaders. Some could have registered if they had wanted to; they refused, however, in order to show their opposition to black suffrage.

Although there were more black than white voters in the South, out of one hundred twenty-five Southerners elected to Congress during Reconstruction, only sixteen were black. South Carolina was the only state where blacks were a majority in the state legislature. Moreover, no state elected a black governor, although some elected black lieutenant governors.

Many of the blacks elected to office were min-

isters or teachers who had gone to school in the North. Some had educated themselves. One had learned to read by watching through the window of a white schoolroom that stood across an alley from the shop where he worked.

The sixteen black people elected to Congress during Reconstruction—two senators and fourteen representatives—were at least as well prepared as the whites with whom they sat. For instance, Senator **Hiram Revels** of Mississippi had graduated from Knox College in Illinois and had become a minister. During the war he had served as a chaplain with the Union army. In the Senate he held

the seat that had once belonged to Jefferson Davis, President of the Confederacy. Senator Blanche K. Bruce, also from Mississippi, had been a slave in Virginia but had escaped to freedom before the war. Bruce attended Oberlin College in Ohio before settling in Mississippi, where he became a planter and entered politics.

Picturing History Hiram Revels was the first African American to serve in the U.S. Senate.

Another charge made against the Radicals is that they gave the vote to large numbers of black people who could neither read nor write. This is true. However, the drive to extend voting rights to all adult males had gone on since before Andrew Jackson's time. Besides, nowhere had the ability to read and write been made a voting requirement.

In Eastern cities at the time of Reconstruction and afterward, even citizenship was not always necessary in order to vote. Immigrants fresh off the boat, who could neither speak English nor write in any language, were regularly lined up at the polls. There, a party worker—usually a Democrat—told them how they should mark their ballots. Whatever its effects at the time, this policy came to be regarded as useful. It gave the immigrants a crude but helpful introduction to politics. The same reasoning could be applied to black citizens as well.

Scalawags and Carpetbaggers Profit

In addition to black people, the Radical Reconstruction governments in Southern states were sup-

Check for Understanding

Have students review their answers to Section 3 Review questions in small groups.

Guided Practice

Discuss with students the economic conditions of freedmen after the Civil War and the government's responsibility for economic conditions then and now. Ask students the following questions. What economic problems did freedmen encounter after the Civil War? (Possible responses: freedmen had no skills or jobs; they could not afford to buy land.) What role, if any, could government have played in insuring economic opportunity for freedmen? (Responses will vary: some may feel the government should have provided educational

opportunities and job training; others may feel the government should not interfere.)

ported by scalawags and carpetbaggers.

Scalawags were white Southerners who joined the Republican party. Some had been Whigs before the Civil War. They wanted the South to industrialize as quickly as possible and believed this could best be done under the Republicans. Other scalawags had opposed slavery and secession, and they did not want the former planter aristocracy to return to power. Finally, some scalawags were selfish individuals who hoped to get themselves into office with the help of black voters and then steal as much as they could. These scalawags would parade blacks to the polls, pad voting lists, and stuff ballot boxes. Whatever their motives, scalawags were considered traitors by most white Southerners. (The word *scalawag* means scoundrel.)

Carpetbaggers were Northerners who moved to the South after the war. (The nickname came from the belief that they carried all their belongings in a bag made of carpeting material.) Like the scalawags, carpetbaggers had mixed motives for supporting Radical Reconstruction. Some were teachers and members of the clergy who felt a moral duty to help former slaves. Some were Union soldiers who preferred to live in the warm climate of the South. Some were business people who hoped to start new industries. The iron works in Birmingham, Alabama, and in Chattanooga, Tennessee, for example, were founded by Ohioans John T. Wilder and Willard Ware. In addition, some carpetbaggers were dishonest, irresponsible adventurers. Horace Greeley, editor of the *New York Tribune*, described them as having "both arms

Picturing History
Reconstruction cartoons similar to this British one were widely circulated throughout the nation to win sympathy for the South. Here the South is shown as a woman in chains struggling under the burden of a huge carpetbag upon which is perched the dissipated Napoleonic figure of Ulysses S. Grant.

around the Negroes, and their hands in their (Negroes') rear pockets, seeing if they can't pick a . . . dollar out of them.''

State Governments Bring Mixed Results

The results of Reconstruction were as mixed as the motives of the people who supported it. On the one hand, many political and social conditions were improved. On the other hand, there was widespread corruption.

On the positive side, the new constitutions drafted by the Southern states under Reconstruction not only set up black suffrage. They also eliminated property qualifications for voting and for holding office. This gave poor whites their first chance to take part in politics. In addition, the new constitutions abolished imprisonment for debt. Reconstruction governments also wrote the region's first laws establishing a system of public schools. On the negative side, however, New Orleans had a **segregated** system, with separate schools for whites and blacks.

Reconstruction governments faced the immense problem of rebuilding a land that had been devastated by war. Roads, bridges, railroads, and factories had to be repaired or replaced. This cost money, as did the public schools, orphanages, hospitals, and other social welfare institutions that were now open to blacks as well as to whites. Since little capital was available in the South, the state governments borrowed funds by selling bonds in the North. Southern credit was so poor, however, that for every $100 bond sold, the Reconstruction government often received only $25 while the Northern investor received $75! Added to this, taxes on real estate kept going higher and higher, which made it harder than ever for planters to get out of debt. The situation became even worse after the 1873 depression, which led to a sharp drop in prices for the South's agricultural products.

Another factor that pushed government costs up was **graft.** Some officials took bribes from companies in return for construction and printing contracts. Some officials spent public funds for carriages, liquor, furniture, and other personal items. One carpetbagger governor managed to earn $100,000 during his first year in office even though his official salary was only $8,000.

Secret Societies Oppose Reconstruction

Most white Southerners had been taught from infancy that black people were inferior. They

Assign Independent Practice

Ask students to write two paragraphs explaining who scalawags and carpetbaggers were and what their motives and methods were during Radical Reconstruction. (Details might include: scalawags were white Southerners who joined the Republican party and wanted to industrialize the South; some hoped to help blacks, others to get rich. Carpetbaggers were Northerners who moved South to help with Reconstruction; some were teachers and clergy, others were opportunists who hoped to become wealthy.)

Student Assignment/Homework

Have students complete Chapter 15, Section 3 Daily Activity, read Section 4 "Reconstruction Efforts Come to an End" and be prepared to discuss Section 4 in class.

therefore found it very difficult to accept the idea of African Americans voting and taking part in government. They blamed black people for the high taxes. In addition, they resented the presence of federal troops in the South, although there were never more than twenty thousand and they were usually confined to army camps.

Most white Southerners swallowed their resentment. Some expressed their feelings by refusing to register to vote. A few white Southerners, however, turned to terrorism and violence. They did so through secret societies, of which the most notorious was the **Ku Klux Klan.**

The Ku Klux Klan began in Tennessee in 1866, even before Radical Reconstruction. Supposedly as a joke, a group of Confederate veterans covered themselves and their horses with bedsheets and hid their faces behind white masks. Costumed in this way, they rode to a nearby meeting of freedmen, pretending to be the ghosts of Confederate soldiers killed in battle. The meeting broke up at once.

Soon such costumes were no longer a joking matter, though. They were worn by whites who were determined to bring down Reconstruction governments and drive blacks from the polling booths back to the fields "where they belonged." At first the Ku Klux Klan, as well as other secret groups, such as the **Knights of the White Camelia,** simply warned blacks not to vote. They also tried to persuade white Freedmen's Bureau workers to quit their jobs.

After a while, however, the secret societies began burning black-owned cabins and churches. Eventually they turned to murder. Between 1868 and 1871, the Klan and other secret groups are reported to have killed several thousand men, women, and children, most of them blacks. The Klan's activities became so violent, in fact, that its

The South Rejoins the Union

Year	State	Year	State
1866	Tennessee	1868	North Carolina
1868	Alabama	1868	South Carolina
1868	Arkansas	1870	Georgia
1868	Florida	1870	Mississippi
1868	Georgia*	1870	Texas
1868	Lousiana	1870	Virginia

*Georgia was readmitted to the Union in 1868 but was returned to military rule until 1870 for not complying with the Reconstruction Acts.

leader, Grand Wizard Nathaniel Bedford Forrest, a former general in the Confederate army, tried to get the organization to disband.

To curtail Klan violence, Congress passed several acts in 1870 and 1871. These are commonly called the **Force Acts.** One act provided for the federal supervision of elections in Southern states. Another act gave the President the power to declare martial law in areas where the Klan was active. In October 1871 President Grant did so in nine counties in South Carolina.

In May 1872 Congress passed the Amnesty Act. It returned to about 160,000 former Confederates the right to vote and to hold federal and state offices. Only about 500 of the highest Confederate leaders did not receive their political rights back under this act. That same year, Congress allowed the Freedmen's Bureau to expire.

By this time, there was considerable opposition to the Klan's activities on the part of many white Southerners. Therefore, the Klan temporarily died out. Meanwhile, in one Southern state after another, Reconstruction governments were replaced by governments that represented traditional white rule. This process was called "redemption."

SECTION 3 REVIEW

Key Terms and People

Explain the significance of: sharecropping, tenant farming, Hiram Revels, scalawags, carpetbaggers, segregated, graft, Ku Klux Klan, Knights of the White Camelia, Force Acts

Main Ideas

1. Why did sharecropping and tenant farming prove to be unsatisfactory land arrangements?
2. What was the reality behind the charges that Reconstruction excluded Southern whites from voting and that it allowed illiterate blacks to vote?
3. What were the motives of the people from the North and the South who supported Reconstruction?
4. What were some of Reconstruction's positive effects on poor whites?
5. How did Congress attempt to protect black people from racist secret societies?

Critical Thinking

6. How did the goals of Reconstruction disappear as "redemption" became a reality?

SECTION 3 REVIEW

Answers

Main Ideas

1. After paying off the landowners, blacks seldom could save enough money to buy land.

2. During Reconstruction, white voter registration was almost as before the Civil War. Illiterate blacks were allowed to vote, but literacy had never been a requirement for voting.

3. Some scalawags and carpetbaggers were selfish, greedy, and scheming; others in both groups wanted to help the South and blacks.

4. They could vote for the first time, attend newly established public schools, and not be imprisoned for debt.

5. With laws for the federal supervision of elections and the use of federal troops to protect blacks.

Critical Thinking

6. Reconstruction was intended to build a "new" South and a new life for freed slaves. "Redemption" gradually wiped out any progress, as traditional white rule returned to the South. **(synthesis)**

Anticipate the Lesson

Review the definitions of the following terms with students: Jim Crow laws, laws that legitimized separation of races in the South; grandfather clause, a clause added to state constitutions that allowed people who could not pass a literacy test or pay a poll tax to vote if their fathers or grandfathers had voted. Ask two students to write these definitions on the board. Encourage students to refer to the definitions as they discuss this section. Ask students how these laws were outgrowths of Radical Reconstruction. (Possible response: they were a way for white Southerners to legally oppose Radical Reconstruction and maintain some aspects of their former way of life.)

State the Objective

Identify the successes and failures of Reconstruction.

Historical Sidelight

After leaving the White House in 1877, Ulysses S. Grant was bankrupted by a business partner. Desperate for money to support his family, Grant decided to write his memoirs. Grant then found that he had throat cancer. Despite the pain, he continued to dictate his life story. He finished one week before his death. The book earned more than $450,000 for his needy family.

SECTION 4

Reconstruction Efforts Come to an End

GLOSSARY TERMS: **discrimination, literacy tests, poll taxes, grandfather clause, Jim Crow laws**

The Radical plan of Reconstruction for the South ended in 1877. It ended partly because giving blacks voting rights was not combined with giving them help in achieving economic independence. It also ended in part because of white resistance, violent and otherwise. It ended for other reasons, too. One was growing Northern indifference. Another was that the Republican party was torn by scandal and corruption.

The North Is Indifferent

Outside the South, the idea grew that having achieved freedom, blacks should now take care of themselves. Northerners were weary of the seemingly endless trouble in the South. Both Thaddeus Stevens and Charles Sumner were dead, and the Radicals were losing their influence within the Republican party. Also, pressing for full civil rights in the South would have raised embarrassing questions about segregation in the North. In addition, Northern business interests wanted stability in the South. That usually meant having traditional white leadership in control. Finally, the dominant Republican party no longer needed the black vote, and perhaps it did not even need the South.

Grant's Administration Is Corrupt

As you have learned, there was considerable graft in the Reconstruction governments of the South. However, it was more than matched by the corruption that existed at the national level.

Although President Grant, who was elected for a second term in 1872, was an honest man, he had had no political experience before becoming President. He thus found it hard to believe that his friends might use him for their own advantage. As some historians explained it, the main trouble with Grant was that he could not tell the difference between an honest person and a crook. In fact, he surrounded himself with crooked individuals.

Beginning in 1873 a series of long-simmering scandals erupted. First came the Treasury Department scandal involving kickbacks on a tax-collection contract. It led to the resignation of the secretary of the treasury.

Then came the so-called Whiskey Ring, which involved internal revenue collectors who had helped defraud the federal government of millions of dollars of revenue taxes on whiskey. The scandal reached up to Grant's private secretary, General Orville E. Babcock, who was one of 238 persons indicted.

Next it was discovered that Secretary of War **William W. Belknap** had accepted bribes from merchants in Indian territory who wanted to keep their profitable trading concessions. The House of Representatives impeached Belknap, who promptly resigned. Similarly, the secretary of the navy had taken bribes from shipbuilders, and the secretary of the interior had had dealings with land speculators. On it went, with bribe money being used both for personal enrichment and to build up the Republican political machine.

A Depression Strikes the Nation

As if political scandals were not enough, the nation was hit by a depression in 1873. The economy had been expanding since the end of the Civil War. People in railroads and manufacturing thus thought that business would always be good and that profits would always go up. They therefore borrowed enormous amounts of money and built new facilities as quickly as possible. Unfortunately, many bankers and businessmen became overextended—that is, they assumed more debts than they could pay. In September 1873 Jay Cooke and Company, a major banking firm, went bankrupt, setting off a series of financial failures. Within a year, eighty-nine railroads went broke, and hundreds of companies folded. In the five-year depression that followed, three million workers lost their jobs. Dislike of the Grant administration grew as a result, and white interest in black welfare declined.

The 1876 Election Is Disputed

In 1876 the Republicans decided, understandably, not to run Grant for a third term. Instead, they chose the stodgy governor of Ohio, **Rutherford B. Hayes.** Smelling victory, the Democrats put up one of their ablest leaders, Governor **Samuel J. Tilden** of New York. Tilden had helped clean up the graft

Present the Lesson

Ask students to list on paper and then discuss the positive and negative effects of Reconstruction. (List might include: positive effects—blacks vote, blacks hold government offices, Union is preserved; negative effects—South passes Jim Crow laws, whites form terrorist societies, insufficient education and job preparation available for freedmen.)

Picturing History
Rutherford B. Hayes was nominated by the scandal-ridden Republican party as an upright political leader. Hayes had a distinguished record as a general in the Union army and made it to the White House by a single electoral vote.

that had flourished in New York City under the Tweed Ring. (You will read about the Tweed Ring in Chapter 19.)

As most people expected, Tilden carried the popular vote—by a margin of 250,000. He also received 184 electoral votes to Hayes's 165. However, Tilden needed 185 electoral votes to win, and 20 electoral votes were in dispute. One was from Oregon. The rest were from Florida, Louisiana, and South Carolina. In those three Southern states, Radical Republicans were still in control. Local Democrats, however, had frightened away enough blacks and Radical voters to win. Each state's Radical leaders had then thrown out a quantity of Democratic ballots and made up returns to show

that Republicans had carried the state. Since no one knew which set of returns was the accurate one, Florida, Louisiana, and South Carolina sent both sets to Washington.

Historians are now quite sure that the Democrats would have carried Florida even if the election had been run honestly. In other words, Tilden deserved that state's four electoral votes—and the Presidency. However, he did not get them.

An electoral commission, made up of eight Republicans and seven Democrats, was appointed to deal with the problem. The commission voted along straight party lines. All the disputed votes thus were given to Hayes, who became President with a minority of the popular vote.

Why did the nation stand for this boldfaced robbery? The answer is that, in the oldest tradition of politics, a deal was made. Southern Democrats were willing to accept Hayes if they could get something in return. The price they demanded was, first of all, assurance that federal troops would be withdrawn from Florida, Louisiana, and South Carolina. This action would enable local Democrats to overthrow the last Radical regimes. Second, they wanted federal money for building a railroad extending from Texas to the West Coast, and for improving their rivers, harbors, and bridges. Their third demand was for a conservative Southerner in the cabinet. The Republican leaders agreed to these demands, and Hayes was peacefully inaugurated.

White Supremacy Is Restored

For at least ten years or so after the end of Radical Reconstruction, blacks in the South continued to vote and were occasionally elected to office. The last Southern black elected to Congress served until 1900. There were black policemen in some Southern cities, too. Gradually, however, the Southern states adopted a policy of rigid legal separation of whites and blacks. By 1890 they had also adopted various techniques to keep blacks away from the polling booths.

Emergence of Poor Whites. Because of the long history of slavery, many whites—especially poor ones—found it hard to form new attitudes about blacks. Middle-class whites did not have to compete with blacks for jobs. Poor whites did. In the 1880's and 1890's, agricultural conditions were so bad that many poor farmers were forced to leave

Presidential Election, 1876

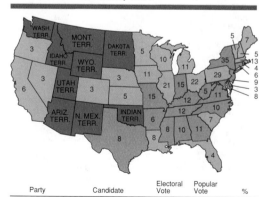

Party	Candidate	Electoral Vote	Popular Vote	%
Democratic	Tilden	184	4,284,000	51.0
Republican	Hayes	185	4,037,000	48.0
Greenback	Cooper		82,000	1.0

369 Total Electoral Vote

Check for Understanding

Have students use lists developed for the exercise on p. 397 as the basis for a two-paragraph essay expressing their opinion on the success or failure of Reconstruction. Ask students to share these essays with the class. Students should use concrete details to support their opinions. (Paragraphs might include: Reconstruction was a success because the Union was preserved; Reconstruction failed because it did not provide the job preparation and education freedmen needed to become contributing members of society.)

Guided Practice

Tell students that many people feel that interest in social justice declines during a period of economic hard times, as it did in 1873. Ask students to consider reasons for this decline. (Possible responses: widespread unemployment leaves few taxpayers to carry the burden of government-funded programs; people are so involved with their own problems and survival that they have little time or energy to devote to the needs of others.) Ask students what types of programs are usually eliminated during times of recession. (Possible responses: aid to the arts and other "non-essential" programs; later, programs to aid the unemployed, children, and education, as well as community service programs.) Discuss with students how the government budget might be reduced without cutting aid to social programs.

For Discussion

Highlight the circumstances, the issue, and the meaning of the ruling in *Plessy* v. *Ferguson*. (Responses might include: Plessy, a black man, sued because he was not allowed to sit with white passengers; the railroad contended it had separate but equal cars for blacks and whites; Supreme Court sided with railroad; ruling provided a legal precedent to separate blacks and whites in all public facilities.) Do you agree or disagree with the Court's decision? Give reasons for your opinions. (Possible responses: agree—if conditions are the same, blacks are not injured; disagree—separate cannot be equal because separation assumes inequality.)

their farms. They came to Southern cities to work in coal mines, in the growing iron and steel foundries, and in the cotton mills. Their pay varied from forty to fifty cents a day, which meant that women and children had to work too if the family were to survive. These people did not want competition from free blacks. Furthermore, because their economic position was so low, the only things that gave these poor whites a sense of pride were the fact that they were white and the belief that the white race was superior.

The poor white farmers who did not leave their farms also had problems. They needed backcountry roads so they could bring their crops to market. They needed credit facilities so they could borrow money to carry them over until harvest time. They also needed schools and hospitals.

As you will read in Chapter 18, these farmers became active in the Populist movement. In many cases, they courted the black vote. Then, under the leadership of Governor "Pitchfork Ben" Tillman of South Carolina, the elected representatives of the poor whites made a deal with the Democratic party. If the Democrats would work to improve the economic conditions of poor whites, the Populists would join the Democratic party and help end black participation in politics. This is precisely what happened.

Political Restrictions.　By the end of the century, new voting regulations were adopted in all Southern states. These were carefully drawn to stay within the bounds of the Fourteenth and Fifteenth Amendments, but they contained subtle **discrimination.** For example, a requirement for voting might be the ability to "read and understand" the law. Tests of understanding were administered orally. Blacks and others who might vote Republican were given hard questions and were told they had failed. Democratic party members, on the other hand, received easy questions.

In addition to **literacy tests,** there were laws calling for the payment of **poll taxes.** An individual had to pay a poll tax before being allowed to vote. The tax was small, usually a few dollars, but it had to be paid long before election day. Blacks might not get reminders of the due date, but whites would. Those blacks who remembered on their own were often unable to find an official to accept their money.

The literacy test and the poll tax kept many poor whites as well as blacks away from the polls. There-fore, beginning in 1898 several Southern states added a **grandfather clause** to their constitutions. The clause stated that even if a man failed the literacy test or could not afford the poll tax, he was still entitled to vote provided that he had been eligible to do so on January 1, 1867—before Radical Reconstruction—or provided that his father or grandfather had been eligible to do so. The grandfather clause enabled many poor whites to vote. However, it did not apply to blacks, because blacks did not have suffrage before Radical Reconstruction. (In 1915 the grandfather clause was declared unconstitutional in *Guinn* v. *U.S.*)

As a result of these tactics, most Southern blacks stopped voting. In Louisiana, for example, 130,334 blacks voted in 1896. Eight years later, only 1,342 cast ballots.

"Separate but Equal."　At the same time that blacks were losing their voting rights in state after state, a pattern of segregation in all public facilities was being put into effect. The laws establishing this pattern were called **Jim Crow laws.** The term comes from the name of a character in a minstrel show who sang a song that ended with the words

Picturing History Using symbols to represent his concepts, the famous political cartoonist Thomas Nast made this commentary on Southern white supremacy. Nast's cartoons had a strong influence on public opinion.

Assign Independent Practice
Have students complete Chapter 15, Section 4 Enrichment Activity.

Student Assignment/Homework
Have students write answers to Chapter 15 Review questions on paper. Go over the answers with the class.

Concluding the Chapter
Refer students to the statements of Frederick Douglass and Kenneth Stampp in this chapter. Ask them to select the viewpoint that more closely reflects their own; then have them prepare a brief essay supporting their position. (Essays should cite specific facts on which they have based their conclusions such as: blacks were given the right to vote; Jim Crow laws flourished throughout the South.)

"Jump, Jim Crow." How the name became attached to the laws enforcing segregation is uncertain.

Prior to Jim Crow, there was a period of fifteen or twenty years during which black and white Southerners mingled to some degree. At least in cities, places such as railroad lunch counters, ice cream parlors, and theaters were often unsegregated.

The first Jim Crow law was passed in 1881 in Tennessee. It provided that whites and blacks had to ride in separate railway cars. Other states adopted similar laws. By the 1890's Jim Crow was being applied to schools, hospitals, restaurants, railroad stations, parks, playgrounds, water fountains—every imaginable place where whites and blacks might come together. There also were Jim Crow entrances to factories and theaters. Furthermore, black taxicab drivers were not even allowed to pick up white passengers.

In 1896, in the case of **Plessy v. Ferguson,** the Supreme Court ruled that such separation of the races was legal. Plessy, a black man living in Louisiana, had sued because he was denied a seat in a railroad car reserved for white passengers. The railroad replied that the separate facilities for black people were just as good as the ones for whites. The Supreme Court sided with the railroad. Thus, the Fourteenth Amendment was not violated. Facilities might be **separate but equal,** the Court said. (The only dissent came from Justice John Marshall Harlan, a Southerner. Harlan argued that "our Constitution is colorblind, and neither knows nor tolerates classes among citizens. In respect of civil rights, all citizens are equal before the law.")

After the *Plessy* v. *Ferguson* decision was handed down, public facilities in the South were separate but far from equal. As one historian said, what blacks got was "the old battered schools and beat-up railroad cars, the rundown tenements and the muddy parks." Thus, Jim Crow continued as the legal way of life in the South for another fifty-eight years, until the Supreme Court case of *Brown* v. *Board of Education.* You will read about this case in Chapter 31.

Reconstruction Fails to Achieve Equality

The expressed purpose of Radical Reconstruction was to give black Americans equality. That goal was not achieved, however, in the years after the Civil War. Radical Republicans sincerely wanted to help the former slaves, but they made two serious mistakes. First, they assumed that giving Southern black people the vote would enable them to protect themselves politically. Second, although they were willing to give millions of acres of land to railroad companies, Radical Republicans were unwilling to give land to the freed slaves so that they could become economically independent. Black abolitionist Frederick Douglass summed up this last failure when he said:

> You gave us no acres. You turned us loose to the sky, to the storm, to the whirlwind, and worst of all, you turned us loose to the wrath of our infuriated masters.

Nevertheless, Radical Reconstruction should not be written off as a failure. Historian Kenneth Stampp has said that the Fourteenth and Fifteenth Amendments were the greatest achievements of Reconstruction and could have been passed only at that time. These amendments were extremely important because they were the springboards from which black people, after a very long struggle, could at last achieve full political and civil rights.

SECTION 4 REVIEW

Key Terms and People

Explain the significance of: William W. Belknap, Rutherford B. Hayes, Samuel J. Tilden, discrimination, literacy tests, poll taxes, grandfather clause, Jim Crow laws, *Plessy* v. *Ferguson,* separate but equal

Main Ideas

1. What were the main reasons why Northern support for Radical Reconstruction lessened in the late 1870's?
2. What were the main problems that plagued Grant's second term?
3. What were the main elements of the deal that gave the 1876 Presidential election to Hayes?
4. How was voting by black people restricted?
5. How was legal segregation of public facilities accomplished?

Critical Thinking

6. Why were constitutional amendments that guaranteed civil rights for blacks valuable despite the fact that laws could be, and were, passed to get around the provisions of these amendments?

SECTION 4 REVIEW

Answers

Main Ideas

1. Northerners tired of the problems it caused; its leaders had died; business interests wanted stability in the South; and the Republican party no longer needed the black vote.
2. Widespread corruption and economic depression.
3. Removal of federal troops from the South, more federal money for the South's transportation facilities, and the appointment of a Southern cabinet member.
4. By laws with restrictions—such as poll taxes and literacy tests—that seemed to apply to everyone but actually excluded only blacks from voting.
5. Southern legislatures passed laws allowing separate facilities. The Supreme Court confirmed them as long as the facilities were "equal."

Critical Thinking

6. Possible answer: amendments are more powerful than laws because, unlike laws, they cannot be struck down by a Supreme Court decision. Despite many pressures, the Fourteenth and Fifteenth Amendments upheld the ideals of the whole country and became the basis of all major civil rights legislation in the 20th century.
(application & synthesis)

State the Objective

Understand how the business cycle operates in the American economy.

Present the Lesson

Ask students to identify the link between income/employment and business cycle upswings and downswings. (Answer: when income and employment are high, individuals and businesses have money to spend which in turn fuels an upswing; conversely, when income and employment are down, spending drops and economic activity declines.)

Ask students to describe the similarities between the Great Depression of the 1930's and the panic of 1837. (Answer: in both cases employment declined, banks failed, and people suffered great economic hardships.)

Focus on Economics

Business Cycles

Seasons of the year . . . stages of life . . . waves on the ocean. Almost everything has a pattern, a familiar rhythm. Historians identify patterns when they refer to certain periods as the Gilded Age, the Federalist Era, or the Roaring Twenties. Labeling these historical periods gives a sense of order to history.

Boom and bust . . . inflation and depression . . . good times and hard times. These phrases describe patterns in business activity. The nation's economy expands and contracts, with periods of prosperity alternating with economic slowdowns. Look at the graph below. Over the years, this expansion and contraction process seems like a roller coaster. Economists call these patterns in a free-enterprise system business cycles.

Phases of Each Cycle. Four phases make up every business cycle. First there is a period of prosperity, the peak of productivity. In this phase, production, prices, and profits are high; unemployment is low; and most people can buy the goods and services they need. The second phase is a period of decline. Here, business activity slows down, fewer goods and services are produced, fewer people have jobs, and investment profits begin to decrease. The third phase is the low period, also called the trough. In this phase, everything is low: production, employment, income, and morale. The fourth phase is the upswing, or expansion, in which business gradually

improves. This phase leads to a period of prosperity—and so the cycle continues.

Because of free enterprise, business activity always experiences the ups and downs of the economic roller coaster. Before the Industrial Revolution, these ups and downs depended on external forces such as the weather. Times were good when crops were plentiful, and times were hard when food was scarce. When the American Revolution ended the restraints of British trade policies, a free-market economy based on the forces of supply and demand developed in the United States. More Americans began to produce goods for sale instead of for themselves, and they were able to buy goods for their own use.

Encouraged by a growing network of roads, canals, and turnpikes, by new inventions, and by the demands of Western and foreign markets, the American economy gradually took on the features of capitalism. Entrepreneurs, individuals willing to take risks in the hope of making a profit, began to invest their profits in new and even larger enterprises.

All Kinds of Theories. What caused the recurrent cycles that characterized this new system? Some early observers actually explained business cycles in terms of sunspots! Even today economists do not agree on the causes of business cycles. Some hold to the theory that business cycles depend on psychology, on people's moods of

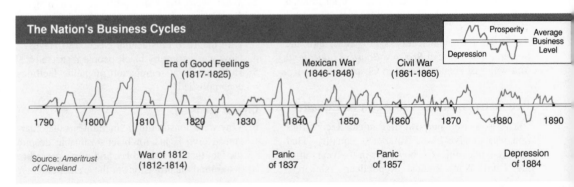

The Nation's Business Cycles

Prosperity / Average Business Level / Depression

Era of Good Feelings (1817-1825)

Mexican War (1846-1848)

Civil War (1861-1865)

1790   1800   1810   1820   1830   1840   1850   1860   1870   1880   1890

Source: *Ameritrust of Cleveland*

War of 1812 (1812-1814)

Panic of 1837

Panic of 1857

Depression of 1884

400

Check for Understanding

Ask students to write out their answers to the questions at the end of the feature. Review the answers with the class.

Ask students to imagine that the President of the U.S. has been told by his board of economic advisors that a severe recession is inevitable. Ask students whether this information should be broadcast to the nation. Students should give reasons for their answers. (Possible responses: yes—people have a right to know, so they can adjust their spending and saving accordingly. No—the release of this information might result in pessimism and cut-

backs in spending and investment, which would actually intensify the effects of a recession.)

optimism or pessimism. They claim that if most people are optimistic about the future, business will be good, but that if most people foresee doom and gloom, then business will be bad.

Another theory holds that business cycles are brought about by changes in the money supply. Economists who support this line of reasoning claim that if government and banks make money available through easy credit, business investments will rise, people will spend, and the economy will grow. If governments and banks tighten the money supply and reduce lending, business in general will tend to decline.

Still another theory deals with levels of saving and consumption. According to this explanation, saving and investing too much money creates more productive capacity than society needs. Then farmers and manufacturers cannot sell what they produce, goods pile up in warehouses, and people lose their jobs and businesses.

Probably no single factor explains business cycles. The panic of 1837 (page 272), for example, was brought about by easy credit and overspeculation in Western lands coupled with crop failures, a drop in cotton prices, and President Jackson's new specie requirements. On the other hand, the panic of 1873 was caused by a shortage of gold, which in turn led to bank failures and slowdowns in railroad building that gradually affected the entire economy.

The Great Depression. Business cycles vary in length and in intensity. Generally, the four phases occur over a period of about eight to ten years from peak to valley and back to peak. Usually the recessions (slumps) bottom out without causing drastic hardship to large numbers of Americans. During the 1930's, many Americans did suffer, however. Despite measures aimed at recovery, the Great Depression was long and severe. Unemploy-

ment went as high as 25 percent. The nation's output of goods and services fell by one-half. Before it was over, eleven thousand banks had closed. Not until the 1940's and the boom of World War II did full production resume.

The Great Depression was so devastating that the federal government has tried since then to prevent another. Since World War II, the government has assumed responsibility for managing business cycles. It encourages the economy when business contracts, and it applies the brakes when business expands. Gradually, over the past fifty years, the federal government, in trying to provide citizens with a more stable economic environment, has assumed increasing responsibility for production, jobs, and national wealth.

Most citizens now expect this kind of control from their government. After all, roller coasters may be great fun at an amusement park, but most people do not want them in their economic life. People would much rather move along smoothly toward an ever-higher standard of living.

Understanding Economics

1. Describe the four phases of a business cycle. Why do business cycles exist?
2. What reasons explained the business downturn in 1837? In 1873?
3. How can government policies influence business cycles?

Critical Thinking

4. What events might explain the phases of the business cycle that have occurred since 1985? See Chapter 36 and do outside research, if necessary, to answer this question.

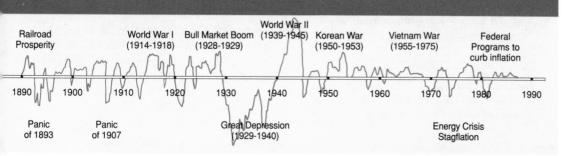

Answer Key

Key Terms and People

These are highlighted in the text in the order in which they appear in the list.

Main Ideas

1. Granted pardons to all Confederates who would swear allegiance to the Union, except high officials; state government could be formed when 10 percent of 1860 voting population took oath. • Congress responsible for Reconstruction; majority of 1860 voters needed to take oath. • Lincoln wanted to restore the Union; Radical Republicans wanted revenge.

2. Abolitionists wanted it. • Set up hospitals, schools, vocational and teacher training. • Went beyond Constitution. • Protect white Southerners who did not want to give black Southerners their rights.

3. Take the place of the Civil Rights Act vetoed by Johnson; to punish Confederate leaders. • It was too harsh; Congress didn't have power to treat states this way.

4. Take the place of the then unratified Fourteenth Amendment. • Confederacy divided into five military districts in which military tribunals replaced civilian courts; black males could vote; states readmitted to Union only after ratifying Fourteenth Amendment.

5. Positive—elected a few African Americans to political positions; black males got to vote. • Negative—could not educate all African Americans nor make them economically independent.

6. Scalawags—Southerners who joined the Republican party because it seemed the best route for personal gain; some helped African Americans register and vote. • Carpetbaggers—Northerners who moved south during Reconstruction for personal profit, though a few were helpful.

7. Disputed elections in Florida, Louisiana, Oregon, and South Carolina were decided by

electoral commission in the House composed of eight Republicans and seven Democrats, who voted along party lines. • Deal was struck— federal troops were withdrawn from the three states; federal money was granted for transportation improvements in South; conservative Southerner was appointed to cabinet.

8. The government was corrupt and lacked power; also

Southern states eventually were able to control voting with discriminatory laws and secret societies.

Critical Thinking Questions

9. Endured hunger, poverty; most lost hope. • She was hardened by war.

➤ **10.** Johnson believed Congress didn't have power to control states. Once in power,

Radical Republicans limited authority of Presidency. • Decision would have been based on makeup of the Court.

11. States could not secede under the Constitution.

12. Possible answers: war ended with either the Thirteenth or Fourteenth Amendments, decision on Brown case, or civil rights struggles in the 1960's. All Americans won when a measure of political and economic equality was

---

CHAPTER **15** REVIEW

Write your answers on a separate sheet of paper.

Key Terms and People

Explain the significance of: pocket veto, black codes, Tenure of Office Act, Ulysses S. Grant, sharecropping, tenant farming, Hiram Revels, segregated, graft, Ku Klux Klan, Knights of the White Camelia, Force Acts, William W. Belknap, discrimination, literacy tests, poll taxes, grandfather clause, Jim Crow laws

Main Ideas

1. What were the terms of Lincoln's 1863 Proclamation of Amnesty and Reconstruction? What were the terms of the Wade-Davis Bill? What was the difference in reasoning behind each?
2. What group urged Lincoln to establish the Freedmen's Bureau? What did the bureau do? Why did President Johnson say he vetoed the bill that would have enlarged it? Why did people think he vetoed the bill?
3. Why was the Fourteenth Amendment adopted by Congress? Why did President Johnson ask the states that had been part of the Confederacy not to ratify it?
4. Why did Congress pass the First Reconstruction Act? What were its terms?
5. From the Radical Republicans' viewpoint, what were the positive results of Reconstruction? What were the negative results?
6. What was the difference between the scalawags and the carpetbaggers? What did they do?
7. How did Rutherford B. Hayes win the 1876 election even though he received fewer popular votes and fewer electoral votes than Tilden? Why was the election never disputed?
8. Why did Radical Reconstruction fail to give African Americans equality?

Critical Thinking Questions

9. **Analyzing Literature.** In the excerpt from *Gone with the Wind*, what do we learn about the horrors suffered in the South by those who

were not in battle? Why had "something that was youth and beauty and potential tenderness" left Scarlett's face?
10. **Assessing Outcomes.** Explain the constitutional question involved in the conflict between President Johnson and the Radical Republicans in Congress. How do you think this question might have been resolved if it had gone to the Supreme Court?
11. **Analyzing Point of View.** Explain why Lincoln thought that the Confederate states had never legally seceded.
12. **Analyzing Cause and Effect.** If the Civil War was a fight for freedom and equality as the Radical Republicans believed, when in your opinion was the Civil War won, who won it, and what was achieved?
13. **Assessing Motivation.** Why was Johnson, a Southern Unionist Democrat, picked to be Lincoln's running mate in the 1864 election?

Critical Thinking Activities

14. **Classifying Information.** Make a chart using the categories below.

	Lincoln	Johnson	Stevens
Highest Title in Life			
State of Legal Residence, 1865			
Political and Related Affiliation and Experience			
Purpose of Civil War			
Attitude Toward Amnesty			

15. **Linking Past to Present.** Why do you think Lincoln has been so revered over the years?
16. **Linking Past to Present.** Would you have voted to impeach President Johnson if you had been in the House of Representatives at the time? Why or why not?

TELESCOPING THE TIMES: 1865–1876

Reconstruction and Its Effects

Lincoln had wanted to adopt a mild and forgiving policy toward the defeated rebels. The Radicals in Congress, however, thought the South ought to be punished. They also felt that Congress and not the President should make Reconstruction policy. The new President, Andrew Johnson, wished to continue Lincoln's proposals. He enraged the Radicals by vetoing some of their measures. In the South a federal Freedmen's Bureau attempted to provide hospitals, teachers, and schools for the former slaves. However, the states of the former Confederacy passed black codes that legally restricted the rights of the newly freed African Americans.

At first President Johnson was successful in the struggle over Reconstruction policy. He encouraged the Southern states to reject Congress's proposed Fourteenth Amendment. After the elections of 1866, however, the Radicals gained control of Congress and overrode several of Johnson's vetoes. Then the House impeached the President. At his trial in the Senate, Johnson was acquitted by a razor-thin margin. Grant won election in 1868, and Congress became free to follow its Radical Reconstruction policies. It successfully proposed the Fifteenth Amendment, which gave black men the right to vote.

Although black people had acquired freedom, they had no land or jobs. Most became sharecroppers or tenant farmers. A few black men won election to Congress, and many more sat in Southern state legislatures. They received support from both scalawags and carpetbaggers. These legislatures faced huge postwar problems of replacing roads, bridges, and railroads and building schools and hospitals for blacks. It was expensive to borrow money for these purposes. Many white and black lawmakers were involved in financial corruption. A few white Southerners formed secret organizations, such as the Ku Klux Klan, that used violence to keep blacks from becoming too independent.

Many Northerners began to grow tired of the turmoil in and about the South. Their attention was attracted to scandals and corruption in Grant's administration. They were also distracted by the major economic depression that began in 1873. Then in 1876 there was a disputed Presidential election. Politicians and businessmen worked out a deal, and the Republican Hayes was declared the winner. Whites now fully controlled the South, and gradually took the vote away from blacks and introduced a policy of racial segregation. The Supreme Court gave its blessing to that policy in 1896.

Chronology of Main Events	
1865	Vice-President Andrew Johnson succeeds Lincoln as President; Thirteenth Amendment ratified
1866	Civil Rights Bill passed by Congress; Ku Klux Klan founded
1867	Reconstruction Act
1868	President Johnson impeached; Fourteenth Amendment adopted
1869	Ulysses S. Grant inaugurated President
1870	Fifteenth Amendment ratified
1870–1871	Force Acts
1873	Grant inaugurated for second term; Panic of 1873
1876–1877	Presidential election returns disputed; Rutherford B. Hayes declared winner.

Present the Lesson

On the board write the terms *peninsulares, Creoles, mestizos,* and *Indians*. Have volunteers identify each group and write their definitions under the appropriate terms. Then ask students to identify the positions and interests of each group just before Mexico gained independence. (Answers: peninsulares—Mexicans born in Spain who held the wealth and ran the government; they were interested in independence from Spain but also wanted to keep the old ways that allowed them to retain their position as masters. Creoles—Mexicans who had Spanish parents but were themselves born in Mexico; they played minor roles in government, owned haciendas, and were interested in keeping their social position. Mestizos—Mexicans of mixed Spanish and Indian parentage; they were among Mexico's poorer classes; they wanted equality so they could share in the country's wealth. Indians—original inhabitants of Mexico who lived in poverty with little freedom; they wanted to share in Mexico's wealth.)

Ask students to identify problems of the movement for Mexican independence. (Possible responses: many Creoles fled to Spain after the revolution; Mexico did not have experience in statecraft; the country was poor and

Focus on Global Events

Mexico—The New Nation to the South

For about two hundred years, the people of Spanish Mexico and the people of the English colonies along the Atlantic seaboard lived in relative peace. Once they both won their independence, however, trouble began. Although the United States congratulated Mexico when Mexico gained independence from Spain in 1821, over the next twenty-five years, relations between the two deteriorated into war.

Spanish Rule. As you remember, Hernando Cortés conquered Mexico for Spain in 1521. The Aztec Emperor Montezuma was killed, and the great capital of Tenochtitlan (tä nóch′tē tlän′), present-day Mexico City, was occupied. Communication was so slow between Spain and its colony that Spanish rulers were not able to make decisions when they were needed. So viceroys, or men who could act for the ruler, were sent to Mexico from Madrid. For nearly three hundred years, New Spain was ruled by a series of sixty-two viceroys.

Don Antonio de Mendoza (men dō′zə), the first viceroy, arrived in 1535 and organized the colonial government and the courts. The Spaniards took most of the profitable farmlands for themselves, forming large plantations known as *haciendas* (hä′sē en′dəz). The Indians, who once occupied the land, were reduced simply to working on it. The silver and gold mines of Mexico belonged to the Spanish monarch, but the nobles could work the mines as long as they paid their ruler part of the profits. Although slavery was generally abolished in Mexico by 1600, the Indians lived in poverty and had little freedom. They rebelled from time to time but were always put down with cruelty and bloodshed.

Strict Class System. Society under Spanish rule in New Spain, just as in Old Spain, was characterized by a rigid class structure. There was a small, rich upper class and a huge, poor lower class. The Spanish, unlike the English and the French, had a small middle class, a result of their view that commercial activity was not dignified.

In New Spain a small group of Spanish people who had been born in Spain had the riches and ran the government. They were called *peninsulares* (pə nin′syσo la′räs) because they came from the Iberian peninsula, which Spain shares with Portugal. Next came the *Creoles* (krē′ōlz), who had Spanish parents but who were born in New Spain. They were allowed to hold lower positions in government, and many of them owned large haciendas. Then came the *mestizos* (mes tē′zōz), or those with mixed Spanish and Indian parentage, and the Indians.

Today Mexico has become a republic, and the mestizos and the Indians are the pride of the country. They are a majority and reflect the blend of Indian and Spanish cultures that characterizes modern Mexico.

This earlier rigid class structure worked smoothly as long as Spain was in power. When Mexico began moving toward independence, however, a struggle broke out. On one side were the conservative peninsulares and the Creoles, who, although they wanted an independent Mexico, also wanted to keep the old ways that kept them the masters. On the other side were the liberal mestizos and the Indians, who wanted equality so they could share their country's wealth.

Cry of Dolores. The American and French revolutions encouraged the Mexicans. The first strong Mexican independence movement was headed by a Creole priest, Father Miguel Hidalgo (hi dal′gō). In the pre-dawn hours of September 16, 1810, in the town of Dolores, he called the townspeople to church and cried, "Mexicans, long live Mexico!" This is called the *Grito de Dolores* (the Declaration of Dolores). Every year on this date the President of Mexico rings a bell and repeats the *Grito de Dolores*. Mexicans celebrate September 16 as Independence Day.

Hidalgo wanted freedom from Spain and equality for mestizos and Indians. He also demanded that haciendas be broken up and the land distributed. Hidalgo's followers swept across the counwas eventually taken over by army officers; government officials borrowed heavily from foreign countries at high interest rates; little money was left to invest in economic growth and education.)

Check for Understanding

Ask students to write answers to the questions at the end of the feature. Review their answers in class.

Ask students which leader they think did the most for the cause of Mexican independence, Father Miguel Hidalgo or General Santa Anna. Students should give reasons to support their opinions. (Possible responses: Father Hidalgo—he first took up the cause of independence; he fought for freedom from Spain and equality for mestizos and Indians. General Santa Anna—he led a revolt against a conservative regime; he helped Mexico become a re-

public and adopt a constitution based on that of the U.S.)

Picturing History
Father Miguel Hidalgo (above) and General Santa Anna.

tryside, gathering people as they went. This huge but untrained army of farmers soon controlled almost all of Mexico. However, Spanish troops captured Hidalgo in 1811 and executed him.

Struggle for Independence. The struggle was taken up by another priest, Father José Morelos (mỏ *re'lỏs*). He also declared Mexico independent and set up a government. By now, however, the Creoles and peninsulares were becoming alarmed. They did not want the mestizos and Indians to come to power. So they abandoned Morelos, who was captured and shot by Spanish troops. The conservatives, in turn, backed a military leader, Agustín de Iturbide (ē′toͦr′bē′thā). With his help Mexico became independent in August of 1821. Iturbide was crowned Emperor Agustín I. However, his rule and

that of the empire was brief. In 1823 a revolt organized by a former officer in Iturbide's army drove the emperor from his new throne. The leader of this revolt, backed by liberals, was General Antonio López de Santa Anna. In 1824 Mexico became a republic with a constitution based on that of the United States. The first President was Guadelupe Victoria, a friend of Hidalgo and Morelos.

Victoria held office for a full four-year term, however, it was a very troubled period. Conservatives and liberals fought endlessly. In 1833 Santa Anna, who switched between the conservative and liberal sides quite often, was elected President. The following year he became dictator.

Problems of Independence. Mexico had no background of self-government like that of the American colonies. Mexicans who were accustomed to ruling and those with money were usually the peninsulares and the Creoles. When Mexico became a republic, most of them fled to Spain. Inexperienced in statecraft, Mexico was a poor country as well. When there was not enough money in the public treasury to pay the army, the officers revolted. They took over the government and then borrowed money from foreign countries. Interest rates on these loans were extremely high. There was little money from the loans to go into education and other economic and social improvements. When people grew dissatisfied, other army groups seized power. Throughout the history of Mexico, democracy has played second fiddle to military and other dictatorships. In the end, however, the government that provides the fairest opportunities for its people to have adequate food, clothing, and shelter will be the one most likely to survive.

Understanding Global Events

1. What was the difference in Mexico between the peninsulares and the mestizos?
2. Why do Mexicans celebrate their Independence Day on September 16?
3. Why did the government change so often in the early years of the Mexican Republic?

Critical Thinking

4. Compare and contrast Spanish society with French and British society.

FOCUS ON GLOBAL EVENTS

Answers

Understanding Global Events

1. Peninsulares were Spanish-born people who were wealthy and ran the government, while mestizos were Mexican-born people of mixed Spanish and Indian parentage who were usually poor and were not allowed to take part in the government.

2. The first strong Mexican independence movement was headed by a Creole priest, Father Miguel Hidalgo. On September 16, 1810, he first called the people together in the struggle for independence. The Mexicans now celebrate their independence on September 16.

3. The government changed so often in the early years because the people had no background of self-government and because the army revolted whenever there was not enough money to pay soldiers' salaries. The latter happened frequently because the country was so poor and the economy was mismanaged.

Critical Thinking

4. The Spanish, unlike the French and the British, had a small middle class, a result of their view that commercial activity was not dignified. **(analysis)**

Key Terms and People

These are highlighted in the text in the order in which they appear in this list.

Main Ideas

1. New England factories made goods that were needed in the West and South. New inventions in farming machines were needed all over the country. Factory orders were telegraphed all over and shipped by railroads and steamboats. All parts of the country became interdependent.

➤**2.** a—1845; Tyler; Britain began to take interest in Texas, Congress annexed Texas even though it would be a slave state. b—1846; Polk; British lost interest in the fur trade, Canada-U.S. boundary settled peacefully along 49° parallel. c—1848; Polk; war with Mexico resulted in U.S. acquisition of land north of the Rio Grande, including all of what is now California, Nevada, Arizona, and Utah, and parts of New Mexico, Colorado, and Wyoming. d—1850; Fillmore; came in as free state when the Compromise of 1850 was adopted by Congress.

3. Possible answers: Fugitive Slave Law brought horrors of slavery to North; *Uncle Tom's Cabin* was published; Kansas became a battleground over slavery; Supreme Court declared African Americans were not citizens; Lincoln-Douglas debates over slavery in the territories; John Brown's raid.

4. Southern Democrat—slavery protected in territories; Breckinridge of Kentucky; won in Maryland, Delaware, and all Southern states that seceded except Tennessee and Virginia. • Northern Democrat—popular sovereignty; Stephen Douglas; won Missouri. • Constitutional Union—supported "the Constitution, the Union, and the laws"; John Bell of Tennessee; won Tennessee, Kentucky, Virginia. • Republican—opposed extension of slavery into territories; Lincoln; won all Northern states, including California and Oregon.

Critical Thinking Questions

5. Wanted to save the Union; thought freeing the slaves where they existed was unconstitutional; was against extending slavery into territories.
• Turned into a war for freedom because in 1862 Northerners wanted to defeat the South because slaves were helping Southern war effort, because British didn't like slavery, be- cause Lincoln issued the Emancipation Proclamation in 1863.

6. Possible answers: had fewer soldiers; didn't have a strong civilian leader; had no industry; cotton economy had to shift to food.

7. Lincoln's view was to bring the states back into the Union as soon as possible; didn't think the states could secede because that was unconstitutional; thought as President he could pardon individuals in- volved. Radical Republicans wanted revenge; thought Congress was the branch of government that should handle Reconstruction; wanted to destroy power of slave owners; wanted to give African Americans citizenship. • Johnson espoused Lincoln's plan; Radical Republicans thought he was on the side of the South; he vetoed legislation and did not enforce laws Congress passed; Radicals were trying

---

UNIT **3** REVIEW

Write your answers on a separate sheet of paper.

Key Terms and People

Explain the significance of: John Deere, abolition, women's rights movement, manifest destiny, Henry Clay, Daniel Webster, Fugitive Slave Law, Know-Nothings, Jefferson Davis, Ulysses S. Grant, Emancipation Proclamation, Thaddeus Stevens, Fourteenth Amendment, separate but equal

Main Ideas

1. How did the advances in industry, farming, transportation, and communication contribute to the interdependence of all parts of the country?
2. When did each of the following states or territories first fly the United States flag? Who was President at the time? Under what circumstances did the annexation occur?
   a. State of Texas
   b. Oregon Territory
   c. California and New Mexican territories
   d. State of California
3. Name at least five events that kept the problem of slavery alive after the Great Compromise.
4. What political parties were involved in the election of 1860? What was the position of each on slavery? Who was the standard bearer of each? Which states did each win?

Critical Thinking Questions

5. **Recognizing Point of View.** What was Lincoln's justification for fighting the Civil War? How did this reason change toward the middle of the war? Why?
6. **Assessing Cause and Effect.** Why did the South lose the war?
7. **Contrasting Ideas.** What were the two opposing views on Reconstruction? Why was President Johnson impeached?
8. **Evaluating Effects.** How did the Reconstruction period end? What did it accomplish?

Critical Thinking Activities

Organizing Chronology. Put the following events into the proper order.

9. a. Frederick Douglass speaks for nonviolence; publishes *The North Star*.
   b. Harriet Tubman walks to freedom; becomes a conductor on the Underground Railroad.
   c. Nat Turner revolts; South forbids circulation of antislavery material.
   d. William Lloyd Garrison publishes first issue of *The Liberator*.
10. a. Wilmot Proviso decrees "neither slavery nor involuntary servitude" in any part of land taken from Mexico.
    b. Texas applies for statehood as a slave state.
    c. California applies for statehood.
    d. Henry Clay designs a compromise.
    e. Treaty of Guadalupe Hidalgo gives huge territory to the United States.
11. a. Sumner is attacked by Preston Brooks on the Senate floor.
    b. *Uncle Tom's Cabin* is published.
    c. Fugitive Slave Law is passed.
    d. Kansas-Nebraska Bill provokes civil war in Kansas.
12. a. Supreme Court decides against Dred Scott.
    b. Lincoln is elected President.
    c. Confederacy is formed.
    d. Lincoln and Douglas debate.

13. **Linking Past to Present.** Henry David Thoreau protested the Mexican War by refusing to pay his poll tax of $1. This led him to be jailed for a night and, ultimately, to write an essay, "The Duty of Civil Disobedience." Define *civil disobedience* and cite at least two times when it has been used in recent history.
14. **Linking Past to Present.** Look up the present immigration regulations in a reference book such as the *World Almanac*. Compare immigration laws of the 1850's to those of today.

TELESCOPING THE TIMES: 1824–1876

The Nation Grows, Divides, and Reunites

Inventors and Reformers

The period from 1824 through 1877 brought more changes in the lives of many Americans than had occurred during the previous two hundred years. Some of these changes resulted from new inventions. Improvements in technology made most white Americans more productive and more prosperous. These improvements also meant that Americans became much more mobile. Transportation on wagon roads, canals, rivers, and railroads greatly heightened the mobility of goods and people. The steamboat, for example, could move rapidly upstream.

Other inventions aided agricultural productivity. The steel plow and the reaper helped open up the Middle West. Other mechanical improvements permitted the use of ice for refrigeration and the rapid stitching of shoes and clothing with the sewing machine. The idea of the assembly line quickened the process of meat packing.

New inventions also speeded the spread of information. The telegraph helped feed information to daily newspapers that were printed by fast-rolling, steam-powered presses. The speed and ease of production pushed down the price of newspapers so everyone could buy one.

While Americans were boasting that they lived in an age of improvements, many of them began to see serious evils in their society and to demand an end to them. After 1830 the cause that drew the most attention was the movement to abolish slavery. William Lloyd Garrison and others began demanding immediate abolition and calling slaveholders sinners. Some free blacks became famous in the abolitionist cause.

The great majority of white Northerners detested abolitionists. They disliked blacks, and they feared sectional division. Mobs attacked abolitionists in the streets. Yet some of the strongest abolitionists were white women. These women soon realized that women in general also lacked many rights such as the right to vote, to an education, and to own property. Thus, a women's rights movement got under way. Virtually all of its leaders had started out in the abolitionist movement, but rights for women became a separate issue. The cause of women's rights was most vividly symbolized by the convention at Seneca Falls, New York, in 1848.

Destined for Expansion

The age of reform was also the age of expansion. Using the phrase *manifest destiny,* Americans began talking about taking over the entire West to the Pacific. Some people even spoke about seizing the whole continent, but diplomats worked out peaceful solutions to the border disputes with Canada.

The Southwest was another matter. Mexico looked like a weak nation, and few Mexicans had settled in the Southwest north of the Rio Grande or in California. Texas was a province of Mexico. White Americans and some of their slaves began moving there peacefully by invitation of the Mexican government, but by the mid-1830's they were battling Mexican troops. The Americans won independence and proclaimed Texas the Lone Star Republic. They began working for annexation by the United States. After complicated negotiations, Texas was admitted to the Union in 1845.

That same year President Polk began to negotiate with Great Britain about the Oregon Territory. The two nations agreed to split the territory at the forty-ninth parallel, the line that still remains the border between the United States and Canada.

Polk himself strongly favored expansion, and he was determined to gain California and other territory at the expense of Mexico. Between California and Texas lay a vast but very dry land inhabited largely by Indians, who had lived there for centu-

Telescoping the Times may be used as an alternative to having students read the entire unit, as a unit preview, or as a unit review.

407

ries. However, one particular group of Americans was about to settle in the region. The religious group known as the Mormons established a flourishing settlement at Salt Lake City in Utah.

Polk remained convinced that the United States had a right to take all this land. He deliberately provoked a war with Mexico by ordering American troops onto Mexican soil. Inevitably they were fired upon, so Polk was able to claim that Mexico had started the conflict. The resulting war saw American armies invading Mexico from several different directions. American soldiers captured Mexico City. The peace treaty provided that the United States pay Mexico $15 million in return for one-third of its national territory. It included California and what is now the southwestern part of the United States. A few years later, the United States acquired a small additional portion of land through the Gadsden Purchase.

From the beginning, many Americans had opposed the war because they feared an increase in land that would be open to slavery. The Wilmot Proviso, a resolution to prohibit slavery in any territory that might be acquired from Mexico, met defeat in the Senate. The question came to a head after the war.

In 1849 there was a gold rush in California, and the next year that territory applied to Congress for admission as a state, free of slavery. California was admitted as a free state, the status of slavery in the other territories was left uncertain, and a tough new Fugitive Slave Act was put into effect.

Compromise and Crises

This Compromise of 1850 seemed a triumph of good statesmanship. It postponed a confrontation over the issue of secession. The election of 1852 marked the beginning of the end for the Whig party. There was little talk about states seceding from the Union.

In the North the Fugitive Slave Act caused great resentment among whites and fear among free blacks. The law favored slave catchers over fugitive slaves. People saw and heard about dramatic incidents of runaways being dragged back to the South or, sometimes, being violently rescued. Some free blacks fled to Canada. To all Northerners, slavery no longer seemed a distant problem.

Beginning in 1854, the nation underwent a series of crises concerning slavery. Senator Stephen A. Douglas caused an uproar by pushing his Kansas-Nebraska Act through Congress. The act provided for "popular sovereignty" concerning slavery in those two territories. In effect, the settlers themselves would decide whether or not to permit slavery. Slaveholders and Northerners rushed into Kansas. Soon a small civil war broke out there.

In 1854 a new nativist political party was formed. This so-called Know-Nothing party was remarkably successful in state elections. At the same time, another new party—the Republican—appeared. Republicans based their 1856 Presidential campaign on opposition to slavery in the territories. They failed to win, but gained enough votes to effectively destroy the Know-Nothings and become the chief rivals of the Democrats.

Events thereafter moved toward a crisis. In its Dred Scott decision, the Supreme Court ruled that Congress could not keep slavery out of the territories and that no blacks could be citizens of the United States. Senator Douglas and a Republican politician named Abraham Lincoln held a widely publicized series of debates on the expansion of slavery into the territories. A radical abolitionist named John Brown led a raid on a federal arsenal in hopes of leading slaves to freedom.

Civil War

The election of 1860 brought things to a climax. The nation split along sectional lines. Among the four candidates, Lincoln won with only 40 percent of the votes, all from the North. As they had threatened, first South Carolina and then six more states in the lower South seceded. They established a new nation, the Confederate States of America.

After Lincoln took office, South Carolinians fired on the American flag at Fort Sumter. Lincoln called for troops. The slave states of the upper South now had to decide which way to go. Virginia and three other slave states joined the Confederacy, but the four slave states bordering on the North remained in the Union.

When the Civil War began, most people thought it would not last long. However, it lasted four long years, with far more death and destruction than anyone could believe. Union armies fought battle after battle in an attempt to take the Confederate capital of Richmond, Virginia. In the West, Union forces were finally able to slice through the Confederacy by taking control of the entire Mississippi River. Toward the end of the war, a Union army made a devastating march through the heart of the South, burning Atlanta in the process.

On the home front, wartime needs caused Northern business to boom. Southerners suffered as their land was invaded. Both governments had to resort to a much-resented military draft. Lincoln's Emancipation Proclamation changed the war into a battle over the existence of slavery. Real freedom for slaves, however, came with the arrival of Union armies and by the efforts of the slaves themselves.

In 1865 General Lee surrendered to General Grant at Appomattox. The far more populous and industrial North had defeated the attempt of most of the slave states to leave the Union.

Reconstruction Years

The assassination of Lincoln at the end of the war was followed by a struggle for power within the federal government. President Johnson tried to continue Lincoln's forgiving policy toward the rebels. Radicals in Congress, on the other hand, wanted punishment and continued federal control over the Confederate states. The struggle between the President and Congress very nearly resulted in Johnson being thrown out of office.

This period of Radical Reconstruction did not bring much change in the South. Although blacks began to participate in political life, they met tremendous hostility. Some Southern whites adopted a policy of terror to keep the freedmen from becoming too independent. Because blacks had no jobs or land, they became sharecroppers in a kind of economic slavery.

In the North the early years of Reconstruction were characterized by economic expansion. However, a major depression occurred in 1873. In addition, public attention was diverted by the graft and corruption in President Grant's cabinet. After about ten years of Reconstruction, Northerners grew tired of dealing with the conflicts of the South. Federal troops were withdrawn. Following a

disputed Presidential election in 1876, white Southerners assumed full control. During the next twenty years, they took steps to stop blacks from voting. They also introduced a policy of complete segregation of the races.

The most important legacy of Reconstruction has proved to be three amendments to the Constitution. The Thirteenth abolished slavery, the Fourteenth guaranteed the rights of citizens, and the Fifteenth gave black men the constitutional right to vote. The interpretation of these amendments by the Supreme Court has caused important changes in American life.

As we look back now, we can see certain threads that ran throughout the period from 1824 to Reconstruction. The American people experienced astonishing economic growth. The nation's boundaries expanded dramatically. Despite some changes, Americans remained devoted to a two-party political system. Despite successes, they were able to see evils in their society. Above all, the condition of black people dominated the entire era. The nation came apart over that issue. The slaughter of the war accomplished something, for it brought an end to slavery and to the supposed right of states to leave the Union.

Chronology of Main Events

1836	Texas declares independence from Mexico
1846–1848	Mexican War
1848	First women's rights convention
1861–1865	Civil War
1865–1877	Reconstruction
1869	Ulysses S. Grant inaugurated President
1877	Rutherford B. Hayes inaugurated President

OSWEGO STARCH FACTORY.

RPORATED 1848   OSWEGO NY.   T. KINGSFORD & SON M

GLOBAL TIME LINE

The World

1868-1912
Meiji era
in Japan

1882
Italy, Germany, and Austria form Triple Alliance

1880
Britain defeats Zulu kingdom in Africa

1889
Brazil becomes an
independent republic

1887
First National
Congress in India

1865   1875   1885

The United States

1876
Sioux Indians defeat Custer's troops

1879
Edison invents incandescent light bulb

1885
Grover Cleveland
inaugurated President

1886
American Federation of Labor formed

1890
Sherman
Antitrust Act

1891
Populist Party
organized

UNIT **4** 1876–1915

The Rise of the Industrial Giant

Geographic Setting

Human-Environment Interactions. Watercolors like the one of the Oswego Starch Factory at the left, were often commissioned by nineteenth-century industrialists to document their success. This painting is a colorful example of how people chose a geographic setting and adapted it to meet their economic needs. The location of the factory along a river and the roads that were built for horses, buggies, and wagons ensured an efficient transportation system for incoming supplies, for the distribution of the factory's starch products, and for employees and business clients.

Unit Overview

Following the Civil War, the old frontier began to disappear. New and improved transportation and communication systems and the harnessing of electrical power led to a new industrial age. As powerful businesses emerged and mass production increased, workers grew more and more dissatisfied and turned to labor unions to help them in their uphill battle against the giants of industry. Unit 4 explains the rise of the industrial giant in three chapters.

Unit Outline

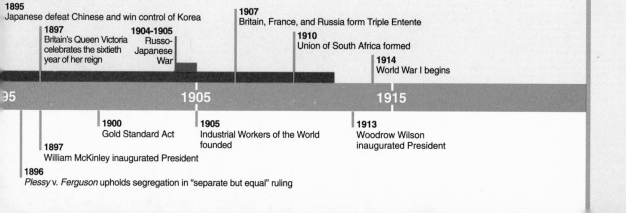

1895
Japanese defeat Chinese and win control of Korea

1897
Britain's Queen Victoria celebrates the sixtieth year of her reign

1904-1905
Russo-Japanese War

1907
Britain, France, and Russia form Triple Entente

1910
Union of South Africa formed

1914
World War I begins

95   **1905**   **1915**

1900
Gold Standard Act

1905
Industrial Workers of the World founded

1913
Woodrow Wilson inaugurated President

1897
William McKinley inaugurated President

1896
Plessy v. *Ferguson* upholds segregation in "separate but equal" ruling

411

Global Perspectives

For Discussion

What effect might the enforcement of the three-mile limit for territorial waters have had on the U.S.? (Possible response: it kept the ships of other countries at least three miles from the U.S. coast.)

Additional Resources

- Geography Activities
- Skills Activities
- Thematic Activities
- Economic Activities
- Cultural Literacy Activities
- Literary Source Readings
- Primary Source Readings
- Nuclear Peacekeeping
- Transparencies
- Computer Test Generator

Additional Teaching Strategies

SECTION 1

For Basic Students: Ask students to list on the board the reasons for the mass slaughter of the buffalo by the white settlers. Discuss the validity of each. (Reasons include: railroads hired hunters to kill buffalo so herds would not stampede into trains; European visitors enjoyed shooting buffalo from the trains as recreation; a Pennsylvania tannery discovered that buffalo hide was useful and profitable; Army leaders encouraged the slaughter of buffalo as a military tactic against the Indians. Some students may feel that none of the reasons are valid; others may feel that killing the animals was acceptable only to the extent that it did not put them in danger of extinction.)

For Advanced Students: Divide the class into five groups and have each group research and prepare a group report on one of the following topics: Chief Gall of the Sioux Indians, Chivington Massacre, Sand Creek Reserve, the Sioux and Cheyenne Indian tribes, Generals S.R. Curtis and Philip Sheridan. (Report should include: locations, dates, and outcomes of battles; history and customs of Indians; background and military history of generals.)

SECTION 2

For Basic Students: Tell students to research and write a two-page report on one of the following people: George Armstrong Custer, Tatanka Yotanka, Tashunka Witko, or Helen Hunt Jackson. (Reports should include: information about birthdate, birthplace, early life, career, importance in history.)

For Advanced Students: Have each student work with a partner to research the key terms and people in this section and then use the information they find to construct a crossword puzzle. When puzzles are completed, have students exchange and work the puzzles.

SECTION 3

For Basic Students: Have each student assume the role of a cowboy on a cattle drive in 1870. Using information from this section, have each compose a letter home describing the drive and telling whether it is what was expected. (Details should include: number of men in crew; number of cattle; descriptions of the trail boss, horse wrangler, cook; length of workday; dangers encountered; ending the drive.)

For Advanced Students: Have students research one of the following and prepare a newspaper article or short story featuring one of his or her exploits: Buffalo Bill, Wild Bill Hickock, Billy the Kid, Nat Love, or Calamity Jane. Remind students of the five W's of good reporting—who, what, when, where, why. (Article on Buffalo Bill might include: description of an outstanding rodeo performance of shooting, roping, and riding tricks.)

SECTION 4

For Basic Students: Ask students to draw or construct a model of a sod house or a dugout, labeling each part and describing the materials used.

For Advanced Students: Ask students to choose one of the four inventions discussed in this section and, after doing additional research, prepare an ad campaign for the product. The campaign should include ideas for posters, billboards, slogans, testimonials from satisfied customers, and guarantees.

Further Reading for Students

Brown, Dee. *Bury My Heart at Wounded Knee*. New York: Holt, Rinehart and Winston, 1981.

Garland, Hamlin. *Boy Life on the Prairie*. Lincoln: University of Nebraska Press, 1961.

Garland, Hamlin. *Main-Travelled Roads*. New York: New American Library, 1962.

Holbrook, Stewart H. *Wyatt Earp: U.S. Marshall*. New York: Random House, 1956.

Sandoz, Mari. *The Battle of the Little Bighorn*. Lincoln: University of Nebraska Press, 1978.

Sandoz, Mari. *Cheyenne Autumn*. New York: Avon, 1964.

Historical Fiction

Cather, Willa. *My Antonia*. Boston: Houghton Mifflin, 1946.

Cather, Willa. *O Pioneers!* Boston, Houghton Mifflin, 1941.

Ferber, Edna. *Cimarron*. New York: Doubleday, 1951.

Lasky, Kathryn. *Beyond the Divide*. New York: Macmillan, 1983.

Talbot, Charlene Joy. *The Sodbuster Venture*. New York: Atheneum, 1982.

Bibliography for Teachers

Books

Brown, Dee. *The Gentle Tamers: Women of the Old Wild West*. Lincoln: University of Nebraska Press, 1981.

Custer, George. *My Life on the Plains*. Secaucus, N.J.: Citadel Press, 1974.

Dick, Everett N. *The Sod-House Frontier: 1854-1890:* a Social History of the Public Lands of the Northern Plains from the Creation of Kansas and Nebraska to the Admission of the Dakotas, Lincoln: University of Nebraska Press, 1979.

Durham, Philip, and Everett L. Jones. *The Negro Cowboys*. Lincoln: University of Nebraska Press, 1983.

Lowie, Robert H. *Indians of the Plains*. Lincoln: University of Nebraska Press, 1982.

Stratton, Joanna. *Pioneer Women: Voices from the Kansas Frontier*. New York: Simon & Schuster, 1982.

Turner, Frederick Jackson. *The Frontier in American History*. Melbourne, Fla.: R.E. Krieger, 1976.

Utley, Robert M. *Cavalier in Buckskin: George Armstrong Custer and the Western Military Frontier*. Norman: University of Oklahoma Press. 1988.

Webb, Walter Prescott. *The Great Plains*. Lincoln: University of Nebraska Press, 1981.

Audio-Visuals

Great American Indian Speeches. Listening Library. Audio cassette.

Computer Resource

The Time Tunnel—American History 1860-1920. (Apple) Focus Media, Inc.

Teacher's Notes:

Teaching Resources, Unit 4 Booklet

Lesson Study Sheets pp. 1-16
Daily Activities pp. 17-24
Enrichment Activities pp. 25-32
Reteaching Activities pp. 33-40
Chapter Review p. 41
Chapter Mastery Tests pp. 43-54
Telescoping the Times Study Sheet p. 55

Chapter Objectives

Students will learn:
- how Indian lands were continually invaded by other Americans
- what events led to the end of Indian independence
- how the cattle industry developed on the Great Plains
- what major factors affected the settlement of the West

Picturing History In *Stampeded by Lightning,* Frederic Remington—an artist and a reporter—portrays the drama and excitement of life in the West. Here a cowboy heads off a stampede of longhorn cattle and also runs for his life.

Using the Chapter Time Line

Who was President (see Chapter 15 Time Line) when Custer and his troops were massacred at Little Bighorn? (Answer: Grant) What three events occurred from 1887 to 1890? (Answer: Dawes Act assigns land to Indians, Oklahoma land rush, Battle of Wounded Knee)

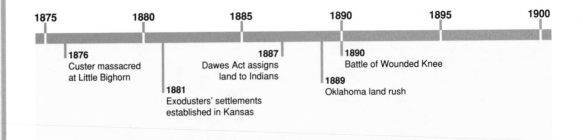

1875	1880	1885	1890	1895	1900

1876
Custer massacred at Little Bighorn

1881
Exodusters' settlements established in Kansas

1887
Dawes Act assigns land to Indians

1890
Battle of Wounded Knee

1889
Oklahoma land rush

CHAPTER **16** 1876–1900

The Passing of the Old Frontier

Links to American Literature

They came from Texas, and Arkansas and Colorado and Missouri. They came on foot, by God, all the way from Iowa and Nebraska! They came in buggies and wagons and on horseback and muleback. In prairie schooners and ox carts and carriages. . . .

"There we stood, by the thousands, all night. Morning, and we began to line up at the Border, as near as they'd let us go. Militia all along to keep us back. They had burned the prairie ahead for miles into the Nation, so as to keep the grass down and make the way clearer. To smoke out the Sooners, too, who had sneaked in and were hiding in the scrub oaks, in the draws, wherever they could. Most of the killing was due to them. They had crawled in and staked the land and stood ready to shoot those of us who came in, fair and square, in the Run. . . .

"Twelve o'clock. . . .The thousands surged over the Line. It was like water going over a broken dam."

— EDNA FERBER, *Cimarron*

After the Civil War, the wilderness west of the Mississippi River began to disappear. To the nineteenth-century pioneers who settled this area, land was everything. It was wealth, freedom, and the opportunity for a new start in life. As the federal government opened new land for settlement, people came from all over. In the process, however, the first inhabitants of the land, the American Indians, were simply pushed aside by trickery or by force. Many were killed. All were eventually made to change their way of life.

Chapter Overview

An enormous gulf separated the values of the Indians from those of the settlers. Could the Indians have done anything to preserve some of their homelands? Could the settlers have overcome some of their greed? This chapter offers us an opportunity to understand ourselves by examining human behavior in the past. In the chapter, you will learn how Indian independence came to an end. You will also learn how the cattle industry developed and how the Great Plains were settled by American farmers. To help you understand life on the frontier, Chapter 16 is divided into four sections.

Chapter Outline

1. **Indian Homelands Are Invaded**
2. **Treaties Are Broken for Gold**
3. **Cowboys Become Folk Heroes**
4. **Farmers Tame the Frontier**

413

Anticipate the Lesson

Review with students the treatment the Indians received under President Jackson (Chapter 10, Section 2). Have students write the various choices for an Indian policy on the board and discuss the advantages and disadvantages of each.

State the Objective

Understand how Indian lands were continually invaded by other Americans.

Present the Lesson

Ask students to skim the section to find the Indian policy that the federal government put into effect after the Civil War. (Answer: removal of Indians to reservations.) On the board make a three-column chart. In the first column have students list reasons for the government's choice of Indian policy. (List should include: white settlers wanted farmland; railroad companies wanted to lay transcontinental tracks;

settlers discovered gold.) In the next column have students list reasons why the policy was inappropriate for the Indians and their way of life. (List should include: Indians were nomads; they followed the buffalo so needed much land; they were not farmers.) In the third column have students list the reasons for failure of the government's Indian policy. (List should include: treaties were often made with malcontents rather than tribal leaders; many government officials cheated the Indians; Indians did not want to give up their culture.) Have students read and discuss Chapter 16, Section 1 Daily Activity and Enrichment Activity.

SECTION 1

Indian Homelands Are Invaded

GLOSSARY TERMS: **Great Plains, Forty-Niners, Cape Horn, reservation**

Horses Change the Indian Culture

Before the arrival of the Spaniards, there were only a few thousand Indians on the **Great Plains.** (See the map of the United States in the Atlas.) The Indians were primarily farmers who grew maize, beans, and squash. By the Civil War, the Indian population of the region had climbed to about 225,000. The reason for the population explosion was the introduction of the horse.

Horses had been brought to the New World as early as 1598 by the Spanish, but until the 1700's Plains Indians still hunted buffalo on foot. Since it was difficult to creep close enough to shoot without scaring the herd, the Indians had to make do with young or weak animals that fell behind the main body.

The use of the horse enabled the Indians to become more efficient hunters, which meant that the region could support more people. By the 1700's, the Great Plains were filled with some thirty different tribes that had moved there from all directions. At the same time, the horse extended an individual tribe's hunting range—and sometimes brought it into conflict with another tribe. After the early 1700's, almost all the Indian tribes on the Great Plains gave up farming. They became no-

madic warriors, used to fighting and resentful of anyone who interfered with the buffalo hunt.

On the other hand, the warfare the Plains Indians practiced—although frequent—was not particularly bloody. The main object was either to steal horses or to avenge a defeat. Casualties were few. A warrior who "counted coup"—that is, touched a live enemy with his hand and got away unharmed—received much more honor and praise than did a warrior who killed an enemy. Skill and individual courage were considered more important than force.

The Indians Fight Removal

Until the middle of the 1800's, there was little conflict between Plains Indians and other Americans. This was primarily because other Americans tried to avoid the region as much as possible. Early explorers, who came from wooded areas with abundant rainfall, considered the Great Plains unsuitable for farming. It was shown on maps as the Great American Desert. Even most of the **Forty-Niners,** who rushed to California seeking gold in 1849, preferred to reach the West coast by sailing clipper ships around dangerous **Cape Horn** at the southern tip of South America or by portaging through the jungle at the Isthmus of Panama.

Indians Are Restricted. As people began to move across the area to the Pacific, railroad companies began sending out survey parties to determine the best place to lay transcontinental tracks. The United States Army, responding to appeals

---

People in the Chapter

George Armstrong Custer was the youngest general in the Civil War and received the Confederate flag when Lee surrendered. At the Battle of Little Bighorn, however, Custer disobeyed written orders, which resulted in the great defeat known as Custer's Last Stand.

Tatanka Yotanka ("Sitting Bull") performed the Sun Dance, in which he submitted to ritual torture. After the dance, he reported that in a vision he had seen soldiers falling into his camp like grasshoppers from the sky. His prophecy was fulfilled at the Battle of Little Bighorn.

William Cody ("Buffalo Bill") led a royal buffalo hunt to entertain Grand Duke Alexis, the son of Tsar Alexander I of Russia, on his visit to the United States. The grand duke emptied two pistols but failed to kill a buffalo. Then Cody gave him "my old reliable 'Lucretia'" — a pistol that brought Alexis success and was then given to him as a souvenir to take home.

Wild Bill Hickok earned 150 dollars a month as marshal of Abilene, Kansas. In addition, he was paid 25 percent of all the money he collected in fines.

Check for Understanding

Call on individual students to answer Section 1 Review questions orally.

Guided Practice

Discuss with students the Indians' view of the relationship of people to nature. (Discussion should include: Indians felt that nature was for all to enjoy and cherish and not to be mistreated or abused; land and water belonged to all people and could not be owned by a few.) Discuss steps that can be or are being taken to preserve our environment. Are these steps adequate, or are they too little and too late? (Steps for preservation include: environmental groups such as Greenpeace; stricter laws on pollution; more community awareness of such helpful habits as recycling. Some students

may feel that these steps will halt the destruction of the environment; others may feel that too much permanent damage has been done, such as the creation of holes in the ozone layer.)

Picturing History
In *Buffalo Hunt Under White Wolf Skins* the artist George Catlin portrays two Indians using a common method of approaching a buffalo herd.

from settlers on their way to Oregon, built a series of forts on the Great Plains. Gradually, however, reports began coming eastward that many parts of the Great Plains were very good for farming. Finally, in 1858 the discovery of gold in Colorado drew tens of thousands of miners into the region.

The United States government had first planned to keep the entire Great Plains as one big **reservation** for the Indians. As pressure from pioneers built up, however, the government changed its mind. It began signing treaties with Indian tribes. Under the treaties, the Indians were to remain within certain boundaries. The remainder of the land was to be opened to white settlement. Also, the federal government was allowed to build roads and railroads across Indian territory. In exchange for limiting themselves to reservations, the Indians were to be helped to become farmers. The federal government promised to give them supplies including food, blankets, and seed corn.

Indians Are Cheated. The policy did not work. It was the same old story of trickery and greed. The treaties usually were made not with real tribal leaders but with Indians who for one reason or another opposed their chiefs. Most Indians never agreed to the treaties. Also, many of the government officials in charge of supplying the reservations were dishonest. The agents for the Indian Bureau looked upon their government jobs as a chance to make money. For example, the annual salary of an Indian Bureau agent was $1,500. Yet many agents racked up as much as $15,000 a year by such methods as mixing flour with sawdust or

stealing goods and selling them instead of distributing them to the Indians.

Another reason the reservations policy did not work is that the Indians did not want to give up their culture. As Chief Gall of the Sioux said:

> [We] have been taught to hunt and live on the game. You tell us that we must learn to farm, live in one house, and take on your ways. Suppose the people living beyond the great sea should come and tell you that you must stop farming, and kill your cattle, and take your houses and lands, what would you do? Would you not fight them?

Indians Fight Back. The Indians fought on and off from 1862 to 1890. Leaders in the struggle against the encroaching Americans were the Sioux and the Cheyenne.

The struggle began in 1862 when a small band of young Sioux, while searching for food, killed five whites near a reservation in Minnesota. The white farmers in the area promptly fled for their lives. Equally frightened, the Sioux split into two groups. One fled the vicinity, but the other, afraid of retaliation, decided to attack first. Hundreds of settlers were killed and their farmhouses burned before the state militia succeeded in defeating the Sioux. Most of the Indians who were taken prisoner were later pardoned by President Lincoln, but thirty-eight were hanged "at a great hanging-bee" the day after Christmas, 1862. In 1863 the remaining Minnesota Sioux, defeated, were forced to yield their land and leave the state.

For Discussion
Reread the quotation by Chief Gall of the Sioux. To what foreign customs does Chief Gall object? (Response: change in the way the Indians live and make a living.) How might you have reacted if such changes were demanded of you and your family? (Possible responses: anger; frustration; violence.)

Ask students to imagine that they are honest government agents assigned to write a report for the Indian Bureau detailing the effects of the reservation policy on the nomadic hunting tribes of the Great Plains. Conclude the report with recommendations for Congress to adopt in reforming Indian-white relations. (Possible details: Indians have few tools and little knowledge about farming; Indians' main source of food and materials is the buffalo; buffalo migrate and Indians need to follow them. Possible recommendations: return some hunting land to Indians; protect buffalo population; offer Indians a choice of where to live.)

Have students read Section 2, "Treaties Are Broken for Gold," and answer the Section 2 Review questions on paper.

The Sioux were more successful in Montana and Wyoming. There they were able to prevent the construction of a wagon road along the Bozeman Trail that would have cut through their best hunting grounds. In fact, under the terms of the peace treaty signed in 1868, the United States government abandoned several forts it had built on Indian land. This was one of the few Indian-American peace treaties in which the United States government retreated.

Chivington Massacres the Cheyenne

Farther south, in the Colorado Territory, the situation was quite different. There, miners had forced the Cheyenne into a barren area known as the Sand Creek Reserve. Short of food, bands of Indians began raiding nearby trails and settlements. Colorado Governor John Evans immediately called out the militia. At the same time, he urged those Indians who did not want to fight to report to Fort Lyon where they would be safe from harm.

In the fall of 1864, some five hundred Cheyenne were encamped on Sand Creek. Two flags fluttered above the camp: the Stars and Stripes, and a white flag—both symbols of the Indians' desire for peace. In the meantime, General S. R. Curtis, United States army commander in the West, had sent a telegram to the head of the Colorado militia, Colonel J. M. Chivington: "I want no peace till the Indians suffer more." So at daybreak of November 29, Chivington and his troops fell upon the sleeping Indians and killed about four hundred fifty of them.

The **Chivington massacre** led to four more years of savage fighting between the United States and various Indian tribes. Finally in 1868, most of the Plains Indians agreed to withdraw to two reservations, one in the Black Hills of the Dakota Territory, the other in what is now Oklahoma.

The Buffalo Are Destroyed

One reason American troops were victorious was that they had the Winchester repeating rifle. The new weapon enabled the American militiamen to fire bullets faster than the Indians could shoot arrows. Another reason was the construction of a railroad network across the Great Plains. The railroad lines split up the buffalo herds, thus making it harder for Indians to hunt. They also brought in millions of settlers.

Picturing History At the left, taxidermist C. W. Hawkins displays his stuffed buffalo heads outside the Kansas Pacific General Freight Office. *A Herd of Buffaloes on the Bed of the River Missouri* (below) was painted by William Jacob Hays around 1860.

Anticipate the Lesson

Ask students to read silently and then discuss questions 1 through 4 of Chapter 16, Section 2 Daily Activity. Discuss how the basic traditions of the Indians as expressed in the quotations differ from the ideas of the white Americans.

The main reason for the American victory, however, was simply the slaughter of the buffalo. Out of fifteen million animals in 1865, only six hundred remained in 1886. Some were killed by hunters hired by the railroads, who did not want to contend with stampeding herds. Some were killed by rich European visitors enjoying a new form of recreation.

In 1871 a Pennsylvania tannery discovered that buffalo hides could be tanned into leather for harnesses, furniture, floor covering, and other products. With railroad lines available to take the hides to market, as many as three million buffalo were killed each year for the next three years. With the disappearance of the buffalo went the economic basis for the Plains Indians' way of life.

United States Army leaders encouraged the killing of buffalo as part of their military tactics. Buffalo hunters, said General Philip Sheridan,

> have done more in the last two years, and will do more in the next year, to settle the vexed Indian question, than the entire regular army has done in the last thirty years. . . . For the sake of peace let them kill, skin, and sell until the buffalo are destroyed.

SECTION 1 REVIEW

Key Terms and People

Explain the significance of: Great Plains, Forty-Niners, Cape Horn, reservation, Chivington massacre

Main Ideas

1. How did the introduction of horses affect the lives of the Plains Indians?
2. What did the federal government want from the Plains Indians in exchange for supplies and help with farming?
3. Give the three main reasons why the agreements between the federal government and the Plains Indians did not work.
4. What happened at the Chivington massacre, and how did it affect later relations between Indians and settlers?

Critical Thinking

5. Why did many Plains Indians aggressively resist removal to reservations? Was this resistance justified? Explain.

SECTION 2

Treaties Are Broken for Gold

GLOSSARY TERMS: **Dawes Act, Americanization**

The treaty of 1868 had promised the Sioux that they could live forever in *Paha Sapa,* the Black Hills area of what is now South Dakota and Wyoming. To the Sioux the area was sacred. It was the center of their land, the place where warriors went to await visions from their guardian spirits. It was also the only good hunting ground remaining to them.

Unfortunately for the Sioux, the Black Hills contained large deposits of gold. As soon as white Americans learned that gold had been discovered, they poured into the Indians' territory and began staking claims.

The Indian Wars Have Skillful Leaders

The Indians appealed to Washington to enforce the treaty terms and remove the miners. The government responded by sending out a commission to either lease mineral rights or buy *Paha Sapa* outright. The Indians refused the commission's offer, whereupon the government sent in the Seventh Cavalry to remove not the miners but the Indians.

The Seventh Cavalry was under the command of a tall, handsome man with blue eyes and long, curly blond hair. He was Lieutenant-Colonel **George Armstrong Custer.** He had gained an enviable military reputation during the Civil War. In fact, he became a general when he was only twenty-three. When the war ended, his regiment was transferred to the frontier and he resumed his prewar rank. A Democrat who opposed Radical Reconstruction, Custer was rumored to have Presidential ambitions.

Tatanka Yotanka ("Sitting Bull") was a medicine man whose visions often showed him what actions to take. He was also a remarkable politician. Plains Indians usually took orders only from the leader of their clans. When different clans or different tribes held joint conferences, every chief was considered equal to every other chief. Tatanka Yotanka, however, was acknowledged as being "above all the others." In 1876 he succeeded in forming an alliance among the Arapaho, the Cheyenne, and the Sioux.

SECTION 1 REVIEW

Answers

Main Ideas

1. The Indians gave up farming and became efficient hunters, fighting anyone who interfered with the buffalo hunt.

2. They wanted permission to build on Indian territory and to confine the Indians on reservations.

3. Treaties were not signed by the real Indian leaders; crooked government agents administered the treaties; the Indians did not want to give up their culture.

4. The Colorado militia killed 450 Cheyenne. This led to four more years of fighting between the Plains Indians and the federal government.

Critical Thinking

5. Possible answer: the Plains Indians had the basic human desire and right to preserve their culture and way of life. They also had negative experiences with the dishonesty and greed of many whites who dealt with Indians.
(analysis & evaluation)

Ask students to skim the section for information and construct a time line on the board tracing major Indian conflicts from 1868 to 1890. Discuss the importance of each in bringing about an end to Indian independence.

1868	Treaty promises Sioux they can live in Paha Sapa (Black Hills). It limits Indian land. Gold is discovered in Black Hills. White settlers flood Indian territory. Indians appeal to government. They attempt a peaceful solution. Government sends Seventh Cavalry to remove Indians. They lose the only lands remaining, thus their way of life.
1876	Tatanka Yotanka unites Arapaho, Cheyenne, and Sioux. The Indians struggle to retain independence. June 25, Custer's Last Stand. Indians claim their greatest victory.
1877	Crazy Horse surrenders and is murdered at Fort Robinson. Indian hopes for independence grow weak.
1881	Sitting Bull surrenders. All hope for independence vanishes.
1887	Dawes Act abolishes the tribal system. Act is a formal denial of the Indian way of life.
1889	Wovoka presents himself as Messiah. Indians search for an answer to their problems.
1890	December 29, Battle of Wounded Knee; Indians are needlessly slaughtered. It becomes apparent that there will be no return to the old way of life.

Historical Sidelight
George Custer graduated at the bottom of his class at West Point. He then became the youngest army general in American history at age twenty-three.

Tashunka Witko (''Crazy Horse'') was the Indians' field commander. He was always coming up with new ways of moving his troops around and attacking the enemy where it was least expected. He was especially skilled at making charges and fake retreats that would draw off part of the opposing forces. Heroic young Crazy Horse and Sitting Bull were the leaders in the Battle of the Little Bighorn.

Custer Makes His Last Stand

The battle known as **Custer's Last Stand** took place on June 25, 1876, along the banks of the Little Bighorn River in Montana. When it was over, Custer and all 264 of the officers and men with him were dead. It was the greatest victory the Plains Indians scored against United States forces. It was also the last.

The death of Custer and his men shook the United States. Buildings in major cities were draped in black cloth. Newspapers wrote editorials about a group of ''savages'' humiliating a nation of fifty million. Calls for vengeance were common. Congress promptly voted money to enlarge the army and to send thousands of additional troops to the frontier.

In 1877 Crazy Horse chose to surrender. He was murdered at Fort Robinson, Nebraska, later that year. Sitting Bull escaped across the border into Canada, where he and other Indian refugees succeeded in holding out for four years. Finally, in 1881, Sitting Bull also surrendered. For the next nine years, he spent part of his time on a reservation and part touring with Buffalo Bill's Wild West Show. Ironically, Buffalo Bill, whose real name was **William F. Cody,** had earned his nickname by killing more than four thousand buffalo for the Kansas Pacific Railroad.

''Bury My Heart at Wounded Knee''

In 1889 the Sioux made one more attempt to keep their way of life. A Paiute (pī´ yo͞ot) Indian named Wovoka presented himself as the Messiah, or savior. He said:

> In the beginning, God made the earth, and then sent the Christ to earth to teach the people, but white men had treated him badly, leaving scars on his body, and so he had gone back to heaven. Now he had returned to earth as an Indian, and he was to renew everything as it used to be and make it better.

Then, as historian Dee Brown wrote in *Bury My Heart at Wounded Knee: An Indian History of the American West:*

Picturing History Amos Bad Heart Bull, an Oglala Sioux from the Pine Ridge Reservation, portrayed the Battle of Little Bighorn on this pictograph. Custer is identified on the left. Crazy Horse stands before him, and Sitting Bull appears in the lower right corner.

Check for Understanding
Have students complete Chapter 16, Section 2 Daily Activity.

Guided Practice
Discuss with students the concept of assimilation. (Discussion should include the definition: to make alike or similar; to become absorbed or a part of.) Discuss what is lost and what is gained when a person from one culture is assimilated into another. (Possible losses: heritage; traditions; language; identity. Possible gains: acceptance into new culture; business success.) Ask students whether the Indians lost or gained more as a result of attempted assimilation. (Possible response: they lost more; a comfortable way of life that was replaced by unfamiliar customs, poverty, and illness.)

Assign Independent Practice
Ask students to write three paragraphs that outline the provisions of the Dawes Act of 1887 and explain why it was a failure. (Provisions include: all Indian tribes were abolished; each male head of an Indian family could claim 160 acres of reservation land. Reasons for failure include: Indians were not given any tools or taught how to farm; dishonest speculators bought two-thirds of reservation land; Indian schools were poorly equipped.)

In the next springtime, when the grass was knee high, the earth would be covered with new soil which would bury all the white men, and the new land would be covered with sweet grass and running water and trees. Great herds of buffalo and wild horses would come back. The Indians who danced the Ghost Dance would be taken up in the air and suspended there while a wave of new earth was passing, and then they would be set down among the ghosts of their ancestors on the new earth, where only Indians would live.

The Sioux began to dance. They danced on all the reservations. They danced instead of farming or trading or going to school. The reservation agents, terrified that the dancing would lead to an armed uprising, sent for the Seventh Cavalry.

On December 29, 1890, the cavalry rounded up a group of about three hundred fifty Sioux—mostly old men, women, and children—and searched them for weapons. Two rifles were found. There was a scuffle, and a shot rang out. At once, soldiers on a nearby hill opened up with Hotchkiss machine guns. When the smoke cleared from the so-called **Battle of Wounded Knee,** about two hundred Indians and twenty-five whites lay dead. Most of the whites had been killed by bullets from their own side.

The Americanization Policy Fails

Though some military officials wanted to eliminate all Indians, many Americans had different opinions. Anthropologist Lewis Morgan, for example, argued that the Indians were only acting in self-defense. **Helen Hunt Jackson,** a well-known writer, published two books—*A Century of Dishonor* and the novel *Ramona*—in which she called attention to the government's broken promises to the Indians. Even President Grant in his farewell speech in 1876 acknowledged that white miners should not have been allowed to enter the Black Hills.

Gradually, the mood in Congress shifted. Realizing that the Indians had been treated shamefully, congressmen now asked, "Why not 'Americanize' them?" The idea was to make them give up the tribal system and become individual farmers. This was what Thomas Jefferson had hoped for.

Linking Past to Present

In 1876 President Grant acknowledged the mistake our government had made in allowing white miners to enter the Black Hills. In the 1970's, a group of Hopi Indians who objected to the stripping of coal from their land wrote to President Nixon: "The white man's desire for material possessions and power has blinded him to the pain he has caused Mother Earth by his quest for what he calls natural resources. And the path of the Great Spirit has become difficult to see by almost all men, even by many Indians who have chosen instead to follow the path of the white man."

The Dawes Act. In 1887 Congress passed the **Dawes Act.** Under the act, Indian tribes were officially abolished. Each male head of an Indian family could claim 160 acres of reservation land as a farm. Bachelors and women could claim a smaller acreage. The federal government would hold the land in trust for twenty-five years while the Indians supposedly learned how to handle their own affairs. Then the Indians would receive legal title to the land. In the meantime, however, they would become American citizens. In 1906 the Burke Act postponed citizenship until the twenty-five-year period was over.

Failure of the Dawes Act. The **Americanization** policy was a dismal failure. The Indians were not given any farm equipment or even taught how

Picturing History
Helen Hunt Jackson's books aroused a public outcry over the plight of the American Indian.

For Discussion
Compare the events at the Battle of the Little Bighorn with those at the Battle of Wounded Knee. (Possible response: Battle of the Little Bighorn—Cavalry was sent to remove Indians from their land; Custer and all his men were killed; Congress sponsored more money to expand army and send more troops. Battle of Wounded Knee—Cavalry, looking for guns, rounded up old men, women, and children of Sioux tribe; two hundred Indians were killed; most of the few whites killed were struck by bullets from their own men; Congress appointed committees to look into the killings.)

Student Assignment/Homework

Have students read Section 3, "Cowboys Become Folk Heroes," and complete Chapter 16, Section 3 Enrichment Activity.

SECTION 2 REVIEW

Answers

Main Ideas

1. The discovery of gold on the Indian territory of *Paha Sapa*.

2. He was regarded by Indians as being "above all the others" and thus was able to form an alliance among several tribes.

3. The public cried for vengeance, and Congress voted money for troops to fight Indians.

4. It abolished the tribal system, provided Indians with farm lands, and granted them citizenship.

5. U.S. Cavalry soldiers opened fire with machine guns on a group of 350 virtually unarmed Sioux civilians.

Critical Thinking

6. Possible answer: the plan was most likely doomed to failure because of (a) the futility of providing land but no training to people who did not know how to farm, (b) the lack of opportunity for input by the Indians, (c) the likelihood that whites would have bought up the land even if it had been successfully farmed by the Indians, and (d) the disease-ridden, discouraging life of the Indians. **(analysis, evaluation, & synthesis)**

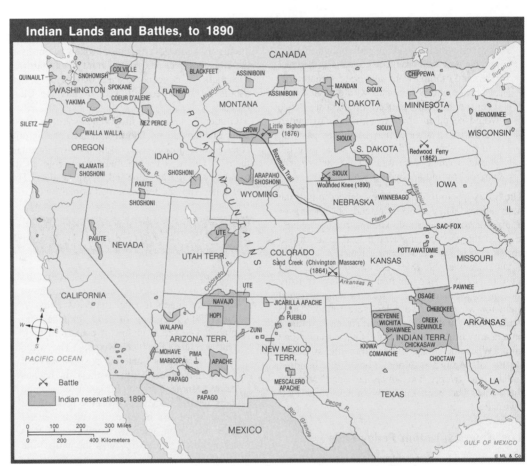

Indian Lands and Battles, to 1890

Map Skills   Place   Which present-day state was mostly Indian territory in 1890?   **Location**   In which state were the Zuni?   **Location**   In what state was the Battle of Wounded Knee fought?

to farm. Speculators managed to buy up more than two-thirds of the reservation land through loopholes in the law. The Office of Indian Affairs did not provide the Indians with proper health services. Disease and malnutrition were common on the reservations, and the death rate was high.

In addition, although the government set up schools for Indian children, most of the teachers were poorly trained. Worse still, many teachers taught the children that Indians were "skulking savages" and that the Indian way of life consisted of "idleness, superstition, and barbarism." When the children left the schools, they found themselves between two cultures. They felt uncomfortable on the reservations. Yet if they left the reservations to work in the cities, they were discriminated against by the whites.

SECTION 2 REVIEW

Key Terms and People

Explain the significance of: George Armstrong Custer, Tatanka Yotanka, Tashunka Witko, Custer's Last Stand, William F. Cody, Battle of Wounded Knee, Helen Hunt Jackson, Dawes Act, Americanization

Main Ideas

1. What prompted the federal government to break the peace treaty of 1868 with the Plains Indians?
2. What distinguished Tatanka Yotanka from other Indian chiefs?
3. What was the national reaction to the Indians' victory at Custer's Last Stand?

the chapter and determine which concepts are factually accurate and which are not.

State the Objective

Describe the development of the cattle industry on the Great Plains.

Anticipate the Lesson

Discuss Western stereotypes students might have encountered in books, on television, or in the movies. (Discussion might include: the cowboys were always the good guys; cowboy life was glamorous and exciting.) Have students associate words and ideas they connect with the West and cattle drives and write these on the board. Refer to this list when discussing

4. How was the Dawes Act of 1887 supposed to "Americanize" the Indians?
5. Why is what happened at Wounded Knee referred to as a so-called battle?

Critical Thinking

6. Could the Americanization policy have been changed to make it successful, or was it by nature doomed to failure?

SECTION 3

Cowboys Become Folk Heroes

GLOSSARY TERMS: **longhorns, vaqueros, long drive**

Probably the greatest American folk hero is the cowboy. Young, slim, wearing jeans and a ten-gallon hat, he slouches in his saddle, his eyes gazing into the distance. Then off he gallops after the herd of cattle he is driving north to grazing land and railroad towns.

Cattle Ranching Becomes Big Business

The American cattle industry that thrived on the Great Plains from 1866 to about 1890 was born in Mexico. This includes the cattle that were driven along the trails; the horses that cowboys rode; and the cowboys' clothes, equipment, and techniques.

The cattle were a sturdy breed called Texas **longhorns,** a cross of Spanish and British stock. They had long legs and needle-pointed horns that measured five to six feet across. They stood heat well, could travel many miles without water, and were able to forage for food on their own. Their only drawback was nervousness. Any sudden noise or movement was liable to panic them and start them running in all directions.

The Mexican Background. The Spaniards introduced cattle and horses to the Americas. By the mid-1600's, a flourishing cattle industry in Mexico was centered in the province of Texas. In 1823 Stephen F. Austin led a group of people from the United States into Mexico where they settled in the valley of the Brazos River. (See Chapter 12.) The climate was mild, and there was plenty of water, grass, and shade trees—perfect cattle country. The Anglo-Americans proceeded to learn about ranch-

ing from the Mexican **vaqueros** (vä ker´ ōz), "people who work with cows."

The Anglo-Americans also adopted many Mexican words. *Corral, bronco, loco,* and *sombrero* were taken straight from Spanish. Other Spanish words became corrupted because of the English-speaking immigrants' inability to pronounce them clearly. Examples are *ranch* from the Spanish *rancho, rodeo* from *rodear,* and *stampede* from *estampida.*

Expanding the Cattle Industry. Following their war for independence in 1836, the Texans expanded the ranching industry. They sent longhorns to New Orleans by steamboat, or they drove them overland to Sedalia, Missouri.

When the Civil War broke out, Texas men joined the Confederate army and left their cattle to fend for themselves. The animals managed so well that by 1865 they had increased from several hundred thousand head to at least three-and-a-half million.

Texans returning from the war thus found themselves with a prime asset. They faced a problem, though. How could they get all that beef to the industrial workers and European immigrants who were flooding Northern cities? No railroads came into the Texas cattle country, and Mississippi River steamboats could carry only a few animals at a time.

The person who solved the problem was an Illinois cattle dealer named Joseph G. McCoy. In 1867 he built a shipping yard at Abilene, Kansas. The village was situated on the Kansas Pacific Railroad. McCoy's venture paid off. That first season, some thirty-five thousand longhorns moved along the Chisholm Trail. From Abilene, a thousand cattle cars shipped the animals to packing plants in Chicago. The next year, seventy-five thousand longhorns plodded northward. By 1871, more than six hundred thousand head of cattle were making the **long drive.**

Cowboys Risk the Long Drive

The typical herd on the long drive consisted of one thousand to three thousand cattle. The trail crew consisted of eight to eighteen cowboys, depending on the size of the herd. There was a trail boss, who was in command of the drive. There was also a horse wrangler, who was in charge of the extra horses. Each cowboy used five or six horses in the course of a drive. Finally, there was a cook, usually Mexican, who drove the mule-drawn chuck

Map Skills

OK • NM • SD

Have the class develop a list on the board of events that led from the cattle industry in Mexico to the U.S. meat-packing industry of the 1890's. (List should include: cattle industry of Great Plains began in Mexico, including cattle drivers, horses, clothing, equipment, and techniques; Anglo-Americans led by Stephen F. Austin settled near the Brazos River and adopted Mexican ranching techniques including Spanish terms; Texas expanded its ranching industry after it became independent in 1836 and sent cattle to market over land and by steamboat; Texans left cattle to fend for themselves during the Civil War; after the war cattle were a prime asset in Texas, but a way was needed to get them to Northern cities; Joseph McCoy built the first shipping yard at Abilene, Kansas, in 1867; animals were moved over the trails, then shipped by railroads to packing houses; cattle trails shifted west as farmers moved into Kansas.)

Historical Sidelight

More Americans die in car accidents every year than in all the gun fights that occurred in the Wild West.

---

wagon carrying food, bedding, and other camp equipment.

Life on the Drive. The cowboys worked from sunrise to sunset, with an additional two hours of night duty. Their morning alarm clock was the cook's call for breakfast, "Wake up Jacob, day's abreakin', beans in the pan and sourdough's a-bakin'." The cowboys would put on their trousers, boots, and hats; roll up their bedding and place it in the chuck wagon; gulp down their food; and saddle and mount their horses.

The cowboys kept the herd moving until about an hour before noon. Then they would camp for several hours. The cattle would be watered and allowed to graze. The men would take turns eating lunch. In late afternoon, the herd would be started up again and kept on the move until sundown, when the animals would sink to their knees and bed down for sleep. A herd could cover ten to twenty miles a day. So a long drive lasted about three to four months.

Dangers of the Drive. There were four things cowboys dreaded on the long drives: stampedes, thunder and lightning, rivers, and drought. Stampedes were probably the worst. It took hours to round up the scattered animals, and many were so badly injured they had to be shot. The cowboys were sometimes hurt, too. They might be thrown from their horses over a bluff or crushed to death by the cattle in their headlong flight. Stampedes are one reason there are so many cowboy songs. Cowboys used to sing lullabies to calm the cattle as they rode around the herd at night.

Although thunder and lightning were the most common cause of a stampede, lightning was equally dangerous to the cowboys. They took their chances while riding. In camp, however, they would always remove their six-shooters, spurs, belt buckles, and other metal objects, and pile them on the ground away from the campfire.

Rivers were a problem because they were difficult to cross. If something frightened the herd, the lead animals would try to turn back. The result was that the herd would mill around in the water, unable to either advance or retreat. After a time, the animals would become so tired that they would lose their footing and be swept downstream.

To save the animals, the cowboys rode their horses into the tangle of horns and kicking hooves. They hit the steers, shouting and trying to make them head for the bank. Many a man was swept off by the current and his body never found.

The rivers caused other problems, especially in spring when snow melting in the Rocky Mountains caused them to rise in their banks. In summer the problem was just the opposite—no rain in a land without trees. Then the animals' tongues would swell up and turn black, the cowboys' lips would crack in the heat, and an alkali dust would settle on men and cattle alike.

Ending the Drive. As you may imagine, by the time the herd reached a cow town and the longhorns were sold, the cowboys were raring to go. With their pay in their pockets, they would drop in on a saloon, a gambling parlor, or a dance hall. After several days of blowing off steam, they would head back home to Texas. They would spend the winter on the ranch, telling yarns about their experiences up north. Then in the spring they would start all over again.

What Is the Truth About Cowboys?

Your parents and grandparents would probably not recognize the description of the cowboy's life you just read. What they learned was very different. Their cowboys were always having knock-down, drag-out fistfights in saloons. Their villains wore black hats and scowled. Their heroes were six feet tall, wore white hats, and held shootouts with the villains on dust-covered streets at high noon. Wild Bill Hickok was handsome and dashing, while Calamity Jane was a petite, spunky blonde.

The myth portrayed in old Westerns began in the late 1800's with dime novels. Buffalo Bill's Wild West Show and Owen Wister's best seller *The Virginian* helped spread the myth throughout the United States. Then came the movies.

The first big cowboy film was *The Great Train Robbery,* made in 1903. Although a silent movie with subtitles, it was full of excitement. The high point of the film was the chase in which a cowboy fired his six-shooter directly at the audience! *The Great Train Robbery* earned so much money that other filmmakers began turning out Westerns by the dozen. Later, radio and television carried on the legends.

What was the truth? Well, for one thing, a cowboy didn't like to fight with his fists. He needed strong, healthy hands in his work and could not afford to take the chance of injuring them in a fight. The typical cowboy was only five and a half feet

Check for Understanding

Have students write the answers to Section 3 Review questions on paper.

Guided Practice

Examine the image of the cowboy as he exists in people's minds and as he is portrayed in films. Discuss his qualities and whether or not his approach to life is appropriate to today. (Discussion should include: length of time away from home and family; job security; benefits; time for personal life.) Discuss with students why they think blacks were rarely among the cowboy characters in Western films and stories, even though there were a number of black cowboys. (Possible responses: stories and films were mostly written by whites from a white person's point of view; the general population viewed blacks as unskilled laborers and farm hands, not as skilled cowboys.)

Picturing History The rare early photograph above shows cowboys rounding up cattle, preparing to continue a drive across the barren plains. The cowboy at the left was born a slave and headed west in 1869 at the age of fifteen. Later, he published his autobiography, entitled *The Life and Adventures of Nat Love*.

tall. Shootings were rare. One out of every seven cowboys was black. One of the best-known black cowboys was Nat Love; his nickname was **Deadwood Dick.**

Wild Bill Hickok was a drifter, unable to hold down a job for more than a few months. He was a crack shot, though, and served as a United States marshal in Abilene during the summer of 1871. In 1876 Hickok was shot in the back of the head while playing poker in a Deadwood, South Dakota, saloon.

Calamity Jane, born Martha Jane Cannary, was rough and burly and passed as a man for most of her life. Two of her jobs were that of a mule skinner and a scout in Custer's command. Luckily for her, she was hospitalized during June 1876. Otherwise, she might have been killed at the Battle of the Little Bighorn. Instead, she lived until 1903 and was buried beside Wild Bill Hickok in Mt. Moriah Cemetery in Deadwood.

The Cowboys' Frontier Disappears

By 1872, the prairie around Abilene had filled up with farmers. They did not like longhorns trampling their crops. The cattle trails shifted to western Kansas, ending up at such cow towns as Dodge City, Ellsworth, and Wichita.

In the meantime, the buffalo herds were killed off, and the Plains Indians were pushed onto reservations. This left millions of square miles of publicly owned grasslands that were unfenced and unused. Cattle could be fed on this pasturage free of charge. The Northern cattlemen no longer needed to bring grown steers to market from Texas. Instead, they took to buying young animals and then fattening them for two or three years on the open range of Colorado, Montana, Wyoming, and the Dakotas. Since the pasturage was free, they stood to make a great deal of money.

The early 1880's were a boom period for the cattle industry. Demand was high, as Americans shifted from eating mostly pork to eating mostly beef. The invention of refrigerator cars and canning machinery helped get Western beef to all parts of the United States and even to Europe. Prices kept rising. Hundreds of investors, many of them British, flocked to the region to make their fortunes.

Then came disaster. From December 31, 1885, through January 2, 1886, the worst blizzard in the history of the West hit the Great Plains. More than three hundred persons, mostly cowboys attempting

Assign Independent Practice

Have students complete Chapter 16, Section 3 Daily Activity.

Student Assignment/Homework

Have students read Section 4, "Farmers Tame the Frontier," and prepare to discuss it in class.

For Discussion

Why was the development of a national transportation system crucial to the success of the livestock industry? (Possible responses: to move cattle to market efficiently; to cut costs; to eliminate long overland drives.)

Focus on American Art

Picturing History Without the works of certain painters, we might not have the information we do about life in the Old West. In some cases, these painters recorded a life style that was disappearing before their eyes. Their works of art document the lives and actions of American Indians and cowboys of the Old West. They range from paintings by George Catlin (1796-1872) that show the character of the Indian to the scientific paintings of Carl Bodmer (1809-1893). Easterner Frederic Remington (1861-1909) captured the high drama in the life of the cowboy, while Western-born Charles M. Russell (1864-1926) simply put his own experiences as hunter, rider, and wrangler onto the canvas. Today these works of art appeal to art lovers and historians alike, just as they did when they were first introduced.

The Outlaw, Frederic Remington (1906).

Indians Hunting Buffalo, Charles M. Russell (1894).

MEW-HEW-SHE-KAW, The White Cloud Chief of the Ioways, George Catlin.

Interior of a Hut of a Mandan Chief, Carl Bodmer (1836).

Coming and Going on the Pony Express, Frederic Remington (1900).

Anticipate the Lesson

Do Chapter 16, Section 4 Daily Activity with the class. Focus especially on questions 4 and 5. Review with students the reasons for settlement of the Great Plains. (Possible responses: farmland; gold; land for transcontinental railroad.)

to bring cattle to safety, froze to death. Many ranchers lost up to three-fourths of their stock, and hundreds of cattlemen were ruined.

That summer there was a drought. Streams and rivers dried up, while temperatures of 120 degrees in the shade were common. Prairie fires raged continuously, filling the air with ash and smoke. With little grass left, tens of thousands of cattle starved to death.

The final blow came that winter. Once again, blizzards hit the Great Plains. When the spring thaw finally came, it revealed the frozen carcasses of 1.5 million animals!

The blizzards and drought resulted in wholesale bankruptcy and a basic change in the cattle industry. If the cattle were to survive, it was obvious that they could no longer be left to fend for themselves. They had to be protected. Instead of using public lands for grazing, cattlemen would have to buy their own grazing land and fence it in. They would also have to raise hay for winter feed.

Soon the cattle industry changed even more. Ranchers began to limit themselves to breeding and raising cattle. Then they would ship the animals by rail to farmers farther east who would fatten them for market. By 1890 the open range was fenced in, the cattle industry was a part of the meat-packing industry, and the cowboys' frontier had disappeared.

SECTION 3 REVIEW

Key Terms and People

Explain the significance of: longhorns, vaqueros, long drive, Deadwood Dick, Wild Bill Hickok, Calamity Jane

Main Ideas

1. Why were Mexican vaqueros important to the American cattle industry?
2. How did Joseph G. McCoy solve the problem of transporting Texas cattle to northern cities?
3. What were the main dangers that cowboys faced on the long drive northward?
4. Briefly describe the stereotype of the cowboy that was perpetuated by dime novels and Hollywood movies.

Critical Thinking

5. Why was fencing cattle-grazing land a benefit to both farmers and ranchers?

SECTION 4

Farmers Tame the Frontier

GLOSSARY TERM: sod house

It took 263 years—from the first settlement at Jamestown until 1870—to turn 400 million acres of forests and prairies into flourishing farms. Changing the second 400 million acres took only 30 years, from 1870 to 1900. This rapid settlement of the West was due to federal land policy and the transcontinental railroads.

Farmers Settle the Great Plains

In 1862 Congress passed the Homestead Act, giving 160 acres to anyone who would live on the land for five years. (See Chapter 14.) About 400,000 families took advantage of the government's offer. Some were from the South. Some were New Englanders eager to exchange their worn-out fields for more fertile land farther west. Some were German and Scandinavian farmers unable to earn a living in their native lands. Several thousand were "exodusters"—blacks who moved from the post-Reconstruction South to Kansas in a great exodus.

Free land, however, was not enough to lure farmers onto the Great Plains. What was needed was good transportation, both to bring people in and to take crops out. During the 1870's and 1880's, four transcontinental railroads were built. As the tracks moved westward toward the Rocky Mountains, they were followed by streams of settlers.

To encourage construction, the federal government had given the railroads huge tracts of land. In fact, the railroads were given about twice as much land as had been set aside under the Homestead Act. Both the Union Pacific and the Central Pacific, for example, received ten square miles of public land for every mile of track laid in a state, and twenty square miles of public land for every mile laid in a territory. Because of its location along the railroad tracks, such land was very desirable to farmers. So they bought it from the railroads for two to ten dollars an acre.

To further encourage land sales, the railroads took to advertising up and down the frontier, calling their lands "better than a homestead." Some railroads opened offices in London and sent agents all over Europe urging people to come to the

Main Ideas

1. They taught Americans how to run cattle ranches.

2. He built a shipping yard near the Kansas Pacific Railroad, making it possible to transport cattle to northern markets by rail.

3. Dangers resulted from lightning, rounding up stampeding cattle, driving cattle across rivers, and droughts.

4. They were handsome, dashing, exciting men who fought villains in fistfights and shoot-outs.

Critical Thinking

5. Fences protected farmers' crops from damage by wandering cattle and allowed ranchers to eliminate most of the risks, such as wild animals and rustlers, found on the open plains.
(analysis & synthesis)

Present the Lesson

Divide the class into three groups. Have each group skim the section and develop a brief summary of the government land policy regarding free land and land grants to the railroads. Identify how these government policies affected the settlement of the Great Plains.

Free Land

- Homestead Act enacted, 1862.
- 160 acres given free to each Homesteader.
- Southerners and New Englanders needed fertile land.
- Immigrants wanted farm land.
- 400,000 families took advantage of offer for free land.

Land Grants to Railroads

- Railroads were given ten square miles of land for every mile of track laid.
- Settlers needed transportation and moved west with the railroad.

Map Skills

Southern • Goodnight-Loving • Missouri Pacific

Map Skills **Movement** In what part of Texas did the cattle trails begin? **Movement** Which trail went to Cheyenne? **Movement** To what railroad did the Sedalia Trail go?

Great Plains. They were very successful in their campaign. The 1880 census showed that the percentage of foreign-born settlers in the West ranged from 44 percent in Nebraska to more than 70 percent in Minnesota and Wisconsin.

Although most plains farmers bought their land either from the government or from railroads, there was a distribution of free homesteads that took place in 1889 in what is now Oklahoma. The American writer Edna Ferber described what happened in her novel *Cimarron*. (See page 413.) In less than twenty-four hours, the land-hungry settlers claimed two million acres. Ironically, Okla-

homa is known as the Sooner State after the settlers who jumped the gun.

Prairie Life Is Hard

The hinges are of leather and the windows have no glass,
While the roof, it lets the howling blizzard in,
And I hear the hungry coyote, as he sneaks up through the grass,
'Round my little old sod shanty on the claim.

The **sod house** described in this folk ballad was the typical prairie house of the period. Why sod?

Check for Understanding

Have a student representative from each group present the group's summary to the class and list key ideas on the board.

Guided Practice

Have students compare the effect of railroad transportation costs on the early American farmer to the present effect of transportation costs on the American economy. (Response: both suffer from the ripple effect; when fuel costs or transportation costs in general rise drastically, the cost of manufactured goods and produce will also rise.)

Picturing History
The Sylvester Rawding family pose outside their sod house, part of which was dug into a Nebraska hillside. This photograph was taken around 1889.

Because trees were scarce on the plains, and there was neither stone nor clay for bricks.

Life in Sod Houses. In making a "soddy," farmers would plow a strip of sod about a foot wide and five inches thick. Then they would chop the strip into blocks and place the blocks on the ground, grass side down, to start the wall of the house. The typical wall was thirty inches thick. After leveling the first layer of sod, farmers would put on the second layer, mismatching the two layers so as not to leave any cracks for mice and snakes. Window and door frames were made out of packing boxes; the door, of planks nailed together; and the windows, of heavy oiled paper.

The biggest problem was the roof. Usually it consisted of thin wooden planking nailed to rafters and topped with a layer of sod, grass side up. Such roofs were very pretty in the springtime, when wild-flowers bloomed on them. Unfortunately, if there was a heavy rain, they also leaked like sieves. However, the sod did provide insulation against the winter cold.

Dugout Homes. After the Civil War, the governor of Kansas, John P. St. John, invited as many black people as could come to settle in Kansas. Many joined with the exodusters. Thousands of blacks settled there in one year. By 1881 they had built ten settlements. One of the settlements was in the Solomon River Valley of western Kansas. The town was named Nicodemus in honor of a former slave. Because of the lack of wood, this settlement began as a collection of dugouts. They were even more primitive than sod houses. At least most sod houses were on the surface of the ground. For these Kansas dwellings, however, settlers dug out a space on a bank or into a hill. Then they covered the opening with a roof of sod. People were living under the ground, but it was a protection against

snow and rain. One of the early settlers was Mrs. William Hickman, who arrived in Kansas on a cold and wet March evening. Years later she recalled that night.

> The men shouted, "There is Nicodemus."
> . . . I said, "Where is Nicodemus? I don't see anything."
> My husband pointed out some smoke coming out of the ground in several places. . . .
> Then I could see that people really were living in dugouts really in holes in the ground.

What Mrs. Hickman had seen was her first prairie home.

Physical Strain. Rain and cold were not the only natural hazards that homesteaders faced on the plains. Dry summers with blazing hot sun often brought raging prairie fires in their wake. Hailstorms pounded people and animals with stones the size of marbles. In the early 1870's, the region suffered a series of grasshopper plagues in which hundreds of millions of insects destroyed all the wheat and corn. They lay from four to six inches deep on the ground and even prevented the Union Pacific trains from moving along the tracks.

Emotional Strain. Another problem that plains farmers faced was not physical but emotional. It was loneliness. The land stretched for miles on end without even a tree to break its flat monotony. There was no place to go for recreation; there were no neighbors to drop by in the morning for coffee and conversation. Winter snows kept homesteaders indoors for weeks and sometimes months at a time—and with no telephone, radio, or television! People became cranky and restless. They would strike out, verbally or physically, at other members of the family. Once in a while they would break under the strain.

Assign Independent Practice

Call on individual students to answer Section 4 Review questions on paper.

Student Assignment/Homework

Have students complete Chapter 16 Review on paper. Go over the answers to all Critical Thinking questions with the class.

Concluding the Chapter

Have students prepare a brief essay explaining how their ideas on the West, cowboys, or Indians have changed since they studied this chapter. Students should list specific examples. (Essays might include: change in view from the belief that Indians were always the aggressors, to view that Indians often acted in defense of their homes and families only.)

About four out of five families that tried homesteading on the plains between 1865 and 1890 never made it. After a while, they moved back east to easier surroundings. The ones who lasted had to be tough.

Four Inventions Bring Relief

Fortunately for plains farmers, the technological boom that took place in the United States before and after the Civil War included agriculture. Thanks to four major inventions—barbed wire, the steel windmill, the steel plow, and the reaper—the plains in the 1880's became America's breadbasket.

Historians usually credit the invention of barbed wire to **Joseph F. Glidden,** who received his patent in 1874. Farmers needed barbed wire for two reasons: to prevent their own cattle from wandering off and to keep stray animals from trampling their crops. Longhorns could walk through a fence of ordinary wire without much trouble. Barbed wire, however, was an effective barrier even to a stampeding herd.

The steel windmill enabled plains farmers to cope with the water shortage. Since rainfall was inadequate, subsurface water was the only alternative. However, farmers had to sink wells as much as four hundred or five hundred feet under the ground in order to tap a water supply. Hand-operated pumps and old oaken buckets obviously could not do the job of bringing the water to the surface.

The steel windmill was developed in the 1860's. The huge fan on top, powered by the constant prairie wind, powered the machinery that pumped water up to the surface. Factories in Illinois and Wisconsin began manufacturing windmills near the end of the decade, and by the 1870's they were a fairly common sight.

You will recall that the steel plow had been invented in 1837 by John Deere. (See Chapter 11.) This enabled the plains farmers to grow large quantities of wheat. Yet, because of hailstorms and sudden frosts, farmers needed a faster means of harvesting their crops. Soon manufacturers improved upon the McCormick reaper. They designed reapers that not only cut the wheat but threshed it as well. Before the Civil War, the average plains farmer sowed about eight acres for each worker on the farm. By 1890 the figure was one hundred thirty-five acres per worker.

Farmers Depend on Banks and Railroads

In these ways, improved technology helped plains farmers increase their productivity. Yet it made them increasingly vulnerable to forces over which they had little control. All that labor-saving machinery was expensive, which meant that most farmers had to buy it on credit. So long as wheat prices were high, farmers had no trouble paying their debts. When wheat prices fell, however, the only way out other than bankruptcy was to grow more wheat. This in turn meant farmers had to mortgage the land they already owned in order to buy more land.

In addition to being dependent on banks, plains farmers were dependent on railroads. Without railroads, they could not get their crops to eastern and overseas markets. The railroads naturally charged whatever the traffic would bear. Farmers resented being gouged. Railroad officials looked at it this way: "What would it cost for a man to carry a ton of wheat one mile? What would it cost for a horse to do the same? The railroad does it at a cost of less than a cent."

By the 1890's, the farmers' frontier was rapidly disappearing from the Great Plains. Farming itself had changed. Farms were larger and required investments of tens of thousands of dollars. Plains farmers were as concerned about railroad rates and the cost of credit as they were about the weather or the opposition of Indians and cattlemen.

SECTION 4 REVIEW

Key Terms and People

Explain the significance of: sod house, Joseph F. Glidden

Main Ideas

1. How did the Homestead Act help to turn the Great Plains into settled farmland?
2. What problems contributed to the high failure rate of plains farmers?
3. How did technological advances affect wheat farming on the plains?
4. Why were plains farmers dependent on banks and railroads?

Critical Thinking

5. How did both the sod house and the windmill illustrate the ingenuity of plains settlers?

State the Objective

Understand the physical and human characteristics of the Great Plains.

Present the Lesson

Tell students that Congress passed the Homestead Act in 1862 to encourage settlement of the Great Plains region. On the board write Homestead Act and underneath this heading make two columns labeled For and Against. Divide the class into two groups. Ask one group to give reasons for taking advantage of the Homestead Act, and ask the other group to give reasons against taking advantage of the act. Students should base their answers on the feature and on the description of the act on page 370. Ask a leader from each group to write the group's responses on the board. (Re-

sponses might include: for—to benefit from the discovery of gold in the Black Hills; to get a free homestead from the government; to raise livestock on the grassy plains. Against—the harsh climate; the lack of trees and sources of fuel; drought; high winds; unpredictability of rainfall.)

Focus on Geography
The Great Plains

The Geographic Theme of Region

A region of the United States that was once known as the Great American Desert has been transformed into the Great Plains, one of the great wheat-growing regions of the world. In light of the drought of 1988, however, there are those who predict that the long-term history of this region is not favorable. In this geography feature you will learn how to use a region as a tool to define, describe, explain, and analyze the physical and human characteristics of its environment.

A geographic region is an area that displays unity in terms of its physical and human characteristics. In terms of physical characteristics, the Great Plains are characterized by dry climate, flat landscape, and rich grassland soils. Because of the

scarcity of wood and water, American settlers had to learn how to use this land in order to make it productive.

Location. The Great Plains region lies between the Rocky Mountains and the ninety-eighth meridian. It covers more than 600,000 square miles and extends from Canada to Mexico in a strip that averages about 400 miles wide. These plains cross ten states including the western parts of North Dakota, South Dakota, Nebraska, Kansas, Oklahoma, and Texas, and the eastern parts of Montana, Wyoming, Colorado, and New Mexico.

Physical Characteristics. The climate of the Great Plains is marked by extreme temperature changes. Winters are bitterly cold in the far north,

Map Skills

East/southeast • Missouri, Arkansas, and Red rivers empty into the Mississippi River; Platte River empties into the Missouri River; Rio Grande River empties into the Gulf of Mexico.

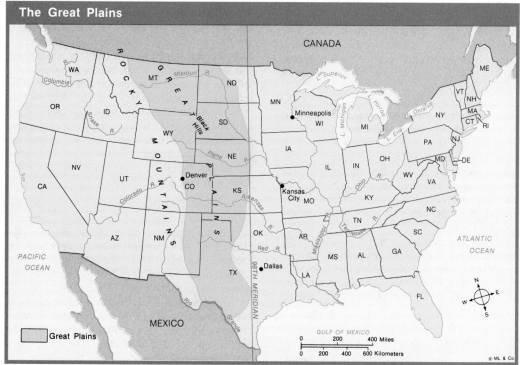

The Great Plains

Map Skills   **Region**   The map shows several major rivers flowing through the Great Plains. In which directions do these rivers flow?   **Movement**   Into what bodies of water do they empty?

Ask students to write their answers to the questions at the end of the feature. Review the answers with students.

Tell students to imagine that they are senators from Montana who have been asked to give a rousing Fourth of July speech in Billings. Their topic is "American Characteristics and Innovations That Transformed the Great Desert into the Great Plains Region." Have students prepare a one-minute speech. Then ask several students to present their speeches to the class. (Speeches might include: the Great Plains were settled by people with resilience and the capacity to adapt to the harshness of the land; early settlers developed dry farming and ranching techniques; ranching was spurred on by the completion of the transcontinental railroad in 1869; Great Plains farmers continue to develop new drought-resistant crops and better irrigation techniques.)

Picturing History Some of the nation's most fertile soil is found in the eastern half of North Dakota. In the 1880's, the flat land of this part of the Great Plains was transformed into rich wheat country.

where meteorologists have recorded the lowest temperatures experienced in any of the fifty states, excluding Alaska. Summer temperatures throughout the area, however, soar well over one hundred degrees Fahrenheit.

The unpredictable weather hazards that accompany the climatic conditions can be just as devastating for agriculture on the Great Plains. The frost-free season, for example, can vary as much as one hundred days from one year to the next. As a result farmers face great difficulty deciding when to plant their crops. After the crops are planted, they run the risk of being ruined by hailstorms or destroyed by locusts.

With few hills or forests to block them, strong winds sweep freely over the northern Great Plains in winter. Although this region receives relatively little snowfall, the "grizzlies of the Plains," as winter blizzards are called, cause extremely cold temperatures and high drifts that can prevent cattle from getting to their food supplies. On the other hand, hot, drying winds in summer often wither the growing crops and can blow away loose, plowed topsoil.

Drought is a constant problem because of the unpredictability of rainfall. The area depends upon the moist air from the Gulf of Mexico for much of its precipitation. Records show, however, that rainfall may be above or below average for as long as a decade at a time.

Human Characteristics. In terms of human characteristics, the Great Plains have always created problems for the people who live there. These plains were populated mainly by nomadic Indians until well into the nineteenth century. Geography teachers and policymakers of the early 1800's considered the Great Plains to be a desert because of the climate and the lack of farming techniques then available to cultivate the land. For these people there were three main problems.

Environmental Problems. The first problem was that the area was almost treeless. People from the East believed that land that would not grow trees was not good land. In addition, since there was no substitute for wood, there was no means of building fences or frame houses and no source for fuel. The second problem was the dryness that made the Great Plains unsuited for the crops of the East that were grown in the short, wet seasons. The third problem for those who considered settling the plains, was the limited, undependable water supply. Rivers often flowed only seasonally, and water holes were few and far between.

Historical Changes. In 1862, however, the United States Congress passed a law that radically altered the character of the Great Plains. This Homestead Act brought in many thousands of settlers. (See page 370.) The completion of the transcontinental railroad in 1869 also boosted settlement on the Great Plains. The discovery of gold in the Black Hills lured thousands more to South Dakota in the 1870's. Wetter-than-normal decades created a false impression of humidity and fertility and caused increased settlement. The dry decades that followed, however, robbed farmers of any possibility of being able to tide themselves over.

Land Use. This region had advantages as well as disadvantages, however. One advantage the Great Plains had was plentiful grasslands that were excellent for livestock grazing. After the railroads made the long drive of Texas cattle to Eastern markets unnecessary, cattle ranching spread throughout the region.

Another advantage was the practice of dry crop farming that frontier farmers began to develop in the 1880's. Dry farming consists of raising a crop of grain, usually wheat, every second year and cultivating the uncropped field during alternate years when no crops are grown. The purpose of dry farming is to prevent weed growth and to conserve moisture.

The gradual development and improvement of these two land-use systems—ranching and dry farming—made the permanent settlement of this problem area known as the Great Desert possible. This region also became more attractive to settlers because it was now known as the Great Plains.

Present Conditions. In recent years the Great Plains, while still largely rural, have become increasingly industrialized and urban. Many smaller communities have lost services or ceased to exist as railroad lines have been discontinued and services consolidated. Large cities such as Denver, Kansas City, Dallas, and Minneapolis, which are located on the edges of the Great Plains, now serve as distribution centers for the whole area.

The primary economic activity on the plains is still agriculture, although mining activities are expanding. Those who farm the Great Plains today are in a somewhat better position to cope with the unpredictability of the climate than those who settled there in the nineteenth century. Today's farmers have improved varieties of drought-resistant crops and better irrigation techniques. They have access to crop insurance and disaster relief as well as aid from soil-conservation and federal credit programs. In addition, new insecticides are available for insect control. On the other hand, newer farming techniques have also meant that fewer people are needed to work on the farms.

During the drought of 1988, however, there were those who still predicted doom and gloom for those who have made the Great Plains their home. In July 1988 Frank Popper, a Rutgers University political scientist and urban planner, told an audience in North Dakota that the 1990's look ''as ominous as any time in American history'' for the region.

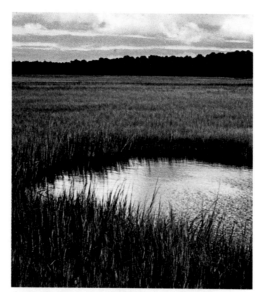

Picturing History The Great Plains, once called the Great American Desert, has few trees, except along river banks, where the land is always fertile.

Popper's comments stirred controversy at North Dakota State University's Center for Rural Revitalization. Arlen Leholm, an agricultural economist at the center, disagreed with Popper. ''He assumes we have no entrepreneurial spirit at all. His theory assumes that we will lie down and die, and we're not going to do that,'' Leholm said.

The regional study of the Great Plains is a study of people struggling to overcome a harsh environment and to make the land productive as well as liveable. That was the challenge of the past. It is still the challenge of the present. It will remain the challenge of the future.

Understanding Geography

1. What are the major physical and human characteristics of the Great Plains?
2. What were the three main environmental problems encountered by the early settlers on the Great Plains?
3. How have farmers on the Great Plains learned to cope with adverse weather conditions today?

Critical Thinking

4. Do you agree with Frank Popper's theory that the future of the Great Plains is not favorable? Give arguments to support your position.

Key Terms and People

These are highlighted in the text in the order in which they appear in this list.

Main Ideas

1. Realized that the plains would make good farmland. • Treaties were poorly devised and took advantage of the Indians; greedy, dishonest agents administered the treaties and gave the Indians little help, so the treaties eventually were broken by both sides.

2. They didn't want to give up their way of life.

3. To drive the Indians out of the Black Hills.

4. Give land to the Indians to farm; make them citizens. • Indians were not given tools or instructions in farming; land was stolen from them.

5. Drive herds from Texas to Kansas.

6. Truths: they didn't like fistfights; some were short; they rarely used guns; one in seven was black; they endured many hardships in cattle drives. • Wanted to sell books and movies and thought people would like adventures rather than the truth.

7. Free land through Homestead Act; four transcontinental railroads built; could buy railroad land.

8. Life was hard with few comforts; weather was extreme; insects ruined crops; emotional strain caused by loneliness.

Critical Thinking Questions

➤9. Possible answers: no—it was unfair because the only qualification was to get there first; it also promoted violence. • Because the people who were hardy enough to reach the land first might be hardy enough to live there.

10. Horses allowed Indians to hunt efficiently. • Indians were not given the proper training or tools to make them want to give up their way of life.

➤11. Possible answer: yes—I would fight for my way of life if a foreign people tried to make me give up my way of life.

➤12. Both Chief Justice Taney and Curtis expressed a racist point of view; Taney believed that black people were basically inferior. Curtis held the same view of Indians.

13. At first Indians farmed, but after horses were introduced, they gave up farming and began to hunt buffalo. Cowboys used the land to graze cattle and to drive the cattle to the railroads. White farmers fenced their land and raised crops, horses, and cattle. • Indians gave up farming to hunt. Later the Indians' hunting lifestyle ended when they were restricted to the reservations. The climate destroyed the cowboy-managed cattle industry.

Critical Thinking Activities

14. North and south. • East and west. • To link the cattle with the railroads and the Western states with Eastern markets.

15. A steamboat up the Missouri River. • A steamboat up the Mississippi River.

➤16. The buffalo are nearly extinct; Indians had to find an-

CHAPTER 16 REVIEW

Write your answers on a separate piece of paper.

Key Terms and People

Explain the significance of: Forty-Niners, Cape Horn, Chivington massacre, Tatanka Yotanka, Tashunka Witko, Custer's Last Stand, William F. Cody, Battle of Wounded Knee, Helen Hunt Jackson, longhorns, vaqueros, sod house, Joseph F. Glidden

Main Ideas

1. Why did the United States government change its mind about keeping the whole of the Great Plains as a reservation for Indians? What happened to the treaties with the Indians?
2. Why did the Indians fight for their land?
3. Why were Custer and the Seventh Cavalry sent to South Dakota?
4. Give the terms of the Dawes Act. Why was it unsuccessful?
5. What did the cowboys have to do in order to sell the cattle?
6. What is the truth about cowboy life? Why did the creators of dime novels and movies invent the myth about Westerners like Wild Bill Hickok and Calamity Jane?
7. List three incentives that caused settlers to go to the Great Plains in droves.
8. Why did many of the farmer-settlers on the Great Plains give up and return to the East?

Critical Thinking Questions

9. **Analyzing Literature.** Reread the selection from Edna Ferber's *Cimarron*. Then reread the paragraph about the distribution of Oklahoma land in the textbook on page 426. Do you think this method is a good way to distribute land? Why or why not? Why do you think this method was used?
10. **Assessing Cause and Effect.** Why had the use of the horse caused the Plains Indians to give up farming for hunting in the 1700's? Why was the Dawes Act not able to reverse this shift in the late 1800's?
11. **Analyzing a Quotation.** Read the quotation on page 415 in which Chief Gall tries to explain to whites why the Indians are fighting. How would you answer Chief Gall's question?
12. **Identifying Assumptions.** In 1857 Supreme Court Chief Justice Taney said that blacks as defined by the Constitution were ''beings of an inferior order'' with ''no rights which any white man was bound to respect.'' Compare his viewpoint about African Americans with that of General Curtis about Indians when he said, ''I want no peace till the Indians suffer more.''
13. **Comparing Cultures.** Four groups of people—Indian farmers, Indian hunters, cowboys, and white farmers—are described in this chapter. Compare the way the land was used by each group. What caused the demise of the first three ways of life?

Critical Thinking Activities

14. **Analyzing Maps.** Use the map on page 426 to answer the following questions. In general, in what direction do the cattle trails go? In what direction do the railroad lines go? Why?
15. **Analyzing Maps.** How would people travel from Omaha, Nebraska, to Bismarck, North Dakota? from New Orleans, Louisiana, to Vicksburg, Mississippi?
16. **Linking Past to Present.** What were the human and environmental results of the massacre of the buffalo? Why are we now trying so hard to increase the number of buffalo?
17. **Linking Past to Present.** Americans are still moving West in large numbers. Compare the reasons for today's migration with the reasons for the migration after the Civil War.
18. **Linking Past to Present.** Do you think the space frontier will have as much influence on Americans of the future as the Western frontier had on Americans after the Civil War? Why or why not?

other way to live; killing of the buffalo made it possible to defeat the Indians. • Because they nearly became extinct.

17. People migrated after Civil War for free land, gold, and other minerals. Today people move for better climate and jobs.

➤**18.** Possible answers: yes—we can use space environment for laboratories, colonies, and some kinds of

manufacturing. No—it is too hard to conquer these areas.

➤**Question suitable for co-operative learning.**

TELESCOPING THE TIMES: 1876–1900

The Passing of the Old Frontier

Originally, Indians of the Great Plains were farmers and hunted buffalo on foot. Later, horses from Spain enabled them to hunt more efficiently, so the region could support more people. After the Civil War, white Americans moved westward onto these lands. They were interested in mining, constructing railroads, and farming. The United States forced the Indians onto small portions of the land. Members of about thirty Indian tribes were cheated by government agents. Almost inevitably there was armed conflict. At the Chivington massacre, United States troops killed hundreds of peaceful Indians. The newcomers also shot enormous numbers of buffalo, which ruined the Indians' economy.

The Sioux Indians had been promised eternal rights to their sacred lands in the Black Hills of South Dakota. White Americans began to come in, however, when gold was found there. Custer's Seventh United States Cavalry was sent to protect the miners. Under the leadership of Tatanka Yotanka and Tashunka Witko, the Sioux wiped out Custer's force at Little Bighorn in 1876. Later, at the so-called Battle of Wounded Knee, United States troops massacred two hundred Sioux and, mostly by accident, twenty-five whites as well. The Dawes Act of 1887 tried to Americanize the Indians by abolishing tribes and putting them on reservations, but the program was a complete failure.

The Spanish had brought cattle as well as horses with them to America. Cowboys from the United States learned from the Mexicans how to handle cattle. In doing so, they borrowed Mexican words such as *corral, ranch,* and *rodeo.* Cowboys and their Texas longhorns flourished for twenty years after the Civil War. The tough work of herding the nervous animals northward to railroad junctions made cowboys folk heroes. Their lives were not nearly as romantic, however, as they later were

made out to be in books and motion pictures. In the mid-1880's, blizzards and a drought ended the great era of the open range. To protect their cattle from the elements, ranchers had to buy their own grazing land, fence it in, and raise hay for winter feed.

Farmers could get free land on the plains through the Homestead Act, or they could buy land from the railroads. Eventually, the Indian territory of Oklahoma also was opened to settlement. Farmers from the East and from Europe rushed toward this opportunity to own land. They built houses out of sod or, in the case of blacks in Kansas, lived in houses dug in the ground. Many of the people who tried to earn a living in this tough country retreated east in the face of droughts, grasshoppers, and sheer loneliness. Several inventions helped turn the plains into productive farmland. These were barbed wire, the steel windmill, the steel plow, and an improved reaper. Farmers depended more and more on railroads and banks.

Chronology of Main Events

1864	Chivington massacre
1868	Treaty with Sioux
1874	Glidden patents barbed wire
1876	Custer massacred at Little Bighorn
1887	Dawes Act assigns land to Indians
1889	Oklahoma land rush
1890	Battle of Wounded Knee

Telescoping the Times may be used as an alternative to having students read the entire chapter, as a chapter preview, or as a chapter review.

Global Perspectives

1879   First telephone exchange operates in London.

1881   Transvaal gains independence under the Boers.

1882   Italy, Germany, and Austria form the Triple Alliance.

1884   Great Britain grants suffrage to all adult males.

1889   Japan adopts a Constitution.

1896   First modern Olympic games take place in Athens.

For Discussion

Why do you think the U.S. failed to enforce the Monroe Doctrine when European nations began to claim parts of Africa? (Possible responses: U.S. was not interested in a continent so far away; Monroe Doctrine referred only to the Americas; U.S. felt that if Europeans were busy in Africa, they would not interfere in North and South America.)

Additional Resources

- Geography Activities
- Skills Activities
- Thematic Activities
- Economic Activities
- Cultural Literary Activities
- Literary Source Readings
- Primary Source Readings
- Nuclear Peacekeeping
- Transparencies
- Computer Test Generator

Additional Teaching Strategies

SECTION 1

For Basic Students: Ask students to list on the board all the inventions mentioned in this section. Ask them to choose three inventions and, on paper, write the name of the invention and the inventor, a resource needed to produce the invention, and a sentence describing the importance of the invention. Have students discuss the completed assignment and rank the inventions in order of their importance. (Possible responses: telegraph—Samuel F.B. Morse; electric power; speed up communications for military, newspapers; electric light bulb—Thomas Alva Edison; electric power; more efficient than previous arc lights.)

For Advanced Students: Divide the class into six groups. Have each group research and report on the most significant changes brought about by nineteenth century inventions in one of the following areas: recreation, home life, transportation, communication, industry, or agriculture. Inventions might include: communication—telegraph, fountain pen, linotype machine; industry—refrigeration; vulcanized rubber; sewing machine. Changes might include: communication—became more efficient, faster; industry—food could be stored for longer periods; factory production of clothing became possible.)

SECTION 2

For Basic Students: Ask students to imagine that in 1890 they are taking a trip west on the railroad line of their choice. Have them write three diary entries describing states, towns, geographical sights, and wildlife encountered during the trip. Students should use the map on page 442 to choose a route. (Diary entries might include: name of railroad line such as Northern Union Pacific; states such as Minnesota, North Dakota, Montana, Idaho, Washington; cities such as Duluth, Fargo, Billings, Spokane, Seattle; the look of the Great Plains and Rocky Mountains; animals such as buffalo, bear, wolf, coyote.)

For Advanced Students: Divide the class into four groups. Assign each group to represent one of the following: workers on the Union Pacific, workers on the Central Pacific, the Grangers, and passenger-consumers. Have students prepare letters to Congress listing their grievances against the railroads and asking Congress for assistance. (Letters might include: workers—reference to wages and working conditions; Grangers—reference to diminishing grazing and farming land and high costs of shipping by railroad; passengers—reference to cost, comfort, and time spent on railroad travel.)

SECTION 3

For Basic Students: Review with students the various types of corporate combinations. Have students choose two corporate organizations and illustrate their structures in a diagram. Diagram of interlocking directorate might include:

Directors

company   company

For Advanced Students: Tell students to research and prepare a three-minute talk on one of the following entrepreneurs: Andrew Carnegie, John D. Rockefeller, Cornelius Vanderbilt, J.P. Morgan, Henry Clay Frick, Gustavus Swift, Gail Borden, Charles A. Pillsbury. (Talks should include: birthdate and birthplace; education; occupations; reasons for business successes.)

Further Reading for Students

Shippen, Katherine B. *Alexander Graham Bell Invents the Telephone*. New York: Random House, 1982.

Historical Fiction

Alger, Horatio, Jr. *Making His Way: Frank Courtney's Struggle Upward*. Salem, N.H.: Ayer Company, 1975.

Howells, William Dean. *The Rise of Silas Lapham*. New York: W.W. Norton, 1982.

Norris, Frank. *The Pit; a Story of Chicago*. Cambridge, Mass.: Robert Bentley, Inc., 1971.

Bibliography for Teachers

Books

Burlingame, Roger. *Machines that Built America*. New York: Harcourt, Brace, Jovanovich, 1953.

Carnegie, Andrew. *The Gospel of Wealth*. Cambridge, Massachusetts: Harvard University Press, 1962.

Hacker, Louis M. *World of Andrew Carnegie, 1865-1901*. Philadelphia: Lippincott, 1968.

Hofstadter, Richard. *The American Political Tradition and the Men Who Made It*. New York: Knopf, 1973.

Hofstadter, Richard. *Social Darwinism in American Thought*. Boston: Beacon Press, 1955. Paper.

Holbrook, Stewart H. *The Story of American Railroads*. New York: Crown Publishing, 1981.

Josephson, Matthew. *The Robber Barons: The Great American Capitalists, 1861-1901*. New York: Harcourt, Brace, Jovanovich, 1962.

Shippen, Katherine. *Andrew Carnegie and the Age of Steel*. New York: Random House, 1964.

Audio-Visuals

Mark Twain Gives an Interview. Coronet. Movie.

The Rise of Big Business, 1865-1918. Indiana University Audio-Visual Center. Movie.

Computer Resource

The Tunnel-American History 1860-1920. (Apple) Focus Media, Inc.

Teacher's Notes:

Teaching Resources, Unit 4 Booklet

Lesson Study Sheets pp. 57-68
Daily Activities pp. 69-74
Enrichment Activities pp. 75-80
Reteaching Activities pp. 81-86
Chapter Review p. 87
Chapter Mastery Tests pp. 89-100
Telescoping the Times Study Sheet p. 101

Chapter Objectives

Students will learn:
- the impact of new inventions on the expansion of American industry
- the important role railroads played in the development of the U.S. during the late nineteenth century
- how and why large, complex business organizations developed in the U.S.

Picturing History Andrew Carnegie (center) was one of the more generous American industrialists. In his book *The Gospel of Wealth*, he expressed his view that the rich had a responsibility toward society. Carnegie gave millions to build libraries throughout the United States.

Using the Chapter Time Line

What two events took place in 1876 (see Chapter 16 Time Line)? (Answer: Custer massacred at Little Big Horn, Bell invents the telephone) How many years passed between the founding of the Standard Oil Trust and the passage of the Sherman Antitrust Act? (Answer: 8 years)

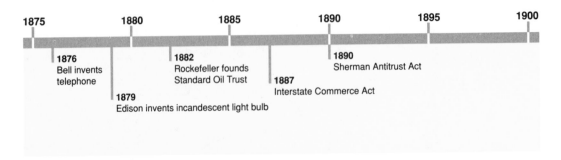

1875   1880   1885   1890   1895   1900

1876
Bell invents telephone

1879
Edison invents incandescent light bulb

1882
Rockefeller founds Standard Oil Trust

1887
Interstate Commerce Act

1890
Sherman Antitrust Act

434

Links to American Literature

Mark Twain (Samuel Langhorne Clemens): born in Florida, Missouri, on November 30, 1835; had many jobs including river boat pilot and gold miner; wrote humorous accounts of gold mining in Nevada which earned him a job with the *Territorial Enterprise*, a newspaper in Virginia City, Nevada; most likely took his pen name, Mark Twain, from the riverboating term *mark twain* meaning a water depth of two fathoms or twelve feet.

Works include: *The Celebrated Jumping Frog of Calaveras County, The Adventures of Huckleberry Finn, The Adventures of Tom Sawyer, The Prince and the Pauper, A Connecticut Yankee in King Arthur's Court, The Tragedy of Pudd'nhead Wilson,* and *The Innocents Abroad.*

Introducing the Chapter

Tell students that the last twenty-five years of the nineteenth century constituted a time of rapid industrial expansion in the U.S. Many changes came about in the way Americans conducted business. Refer students to the map on page 440 and discuss reasons why Pittsburgh and Chicago became steel manufacturing centers. (Discussion should include: were near resources; had well-developed transportation systems; were already industrial cities.) Then have students study the map on page 442 and suggest reasons why railroads played such a key role in industrial expansion. (Possible responses: connected major cities of the nation; provided a means of moving resources, agricultural products, and manufactured goods.)

CHAPTER **17** 1876–1900

The New Industrial Age

Links to American Literature

"If I am going to travel by rail, I shan't need it [accident insurance]. Lying at home in bed is the thing I am afraid of." . . .

I may say I have travelled sixty thousand miles during the three years I have mentioned. And never an accident. . . .

I hunted up statistics, and was amazed to find that after all the glaring newspaper headings concerning railroad disasters, less than three hundred people had really lost their lives by those disasters in the preceding twelve months. . . .

Well, the Erie kills from thirteen to twenty-three persons out of its *millon* in six months; and in the same time 13,000 of New York's million die in their beds! My flesh crept, my hair stood on end. "This is appalling!" I said. "The danger isn't in travelling by rail, but in trusting to those deadly beds. I will never sleep in a bed again." . . .

When we consider that every day and night of the year full fourteen thousand railway trains of various kinds, freighted with life and armed with death, go thundering over the land, the marvel is, not that they kill three hundred human beings in a twelvemonth, but that they do not kill three hundred times three hundred!

— MARK TWAIN, *"The Danger of Lying in Bed"*

Between the end of the Civil War and 1900, the United States underwent striking changes. Railroads crossing the countryside were but one sign of the development of an industrial society. Although the railroads were most important for their contribution to industry, they also became the safest and most efficient means of passenger travel. In addition to moving goods across the nation, they brought people in the far corners of the United States closer together.

Chapter Overview

By 1900 the United States had surpassed Britain to become the mightiest industrial power on earth. This chapter tells the story of America as many saw it then: a land of golden opportunity where poor people with vision and determination could rise from rags to riches. At the same time, the chapter raises questions about the value and meaning of work and the price of success. In this chapter, you will learn how new inventions and the railroads encouraged the expansion of American industry. You will also learn how and why large, complex business corporations developed. To help you understand this new industrial age, the chapter has been organized around three sections.

Chapter Outline

1. **Industries Expand**
2. **Railroads Connect the Nation**
3. **Businesses Become More Complex**

Anticipate the Lesson

Ask students to name appliances used in their homes or school. (Possible responses: refrigerator; stove; microwave; telephone.) List these items in a column on the board. Continue by asking students to list in a second column industries that are needed for the production or use of each of these appliances. (Possible response: microwave—plastic, glass, frozen foods, power/utilities, cleaning products.)

Have students name additional industries that are needed by those industries in the second column. (Possible response: frozen foods—farming, trucking, utilities, packaging.) Remind students that all industries rely on other industries to supply materials or to use what they produce. In this way all new industries help create or support other industries.

State the Objective

Understand the impact of the new inventions on the expansion of American industry.

SECTION 1

Industries Expand

GLOSSARY TERM: **technology**

Like the Industrial Revolution, the new industrial age grew out of new **technology,** the application of scientific discoveries to industry. However, the Industrial Revolution had been based on the steam engine. The new industrial age was sparked by electricity.

Electricity Is a Silent Servant

Electric power is more portable than steam power. Once you had portable power, you no longer had to build a factory near a waterfall. Instead, you could build it near your raw materials or market or labor supply or in an area of cheap land and low taxes. The use of electric power helped spread factories to all parts of the nation.

Electric motors, moreover, were much more flexible than steam engines. Steam engines had to be large because they used large quantities of fuel and water. Electric motors could be made in whatever size best suited your needs.

Electric motors became important in transportation as well as manufacturing. Many cities followed the example of Richmond, Virginia, and replaced horse-drawn cars with public trolley systems. As trolley-car lines spread outward from the center of town, so did new construction. Cities grew larger, and their populations became more dispersed.

The Electric Telegraph. People also applied electric power to communication. The American version of the electric telegraph had been developed in the 1830's and 1840's by **Samuel F. B. Morse.** During the Civil War, President Lincoln received military news via telegraph directly from the field; he sent instructions to his generals the same way. The South did not have this direct communication. Thus the North was able to respond to changing battle conditions more rapidly.

Gradually, too, newspaper columns headed "By telegraph from . . . " became common. People grew accustomed to learning about events within twenty-four hours after they happened. Newspaper sales increased and so did the influence of the press. Papers began carrying detailed national as well as local news. Americans began to get more of a sense of what they were like as a nation.

When the Civil War ended, the United States had about seventy-six thousand miles of telegraph lines. By 1900 the telegraph network was about a million miles long, and Americans were sending some sixty-three million business and personal messages a year.

The Electric Light Bulb. Another area to which people applied electric power was illumination. Here the great name is **Thomas Alva Edison.** He is often called the Wizard of Menlo Park because in

---

People in the Chapter

Thomas Alva Edison was caught napping on the job. As a teenager, Edison was a telegraph operator on the Grand Trunk Railway from 7 P.M. to 7 A.M. Throughout the night he took catnaps so that he could work on his chemistry experiments during the day. The young inventor set up a system that tapped out messages while he slept. His supervisor became suspicious when he was unable to reach Edison and soon had him transferred to another position.

Alexander Graham Bell offered his patent for the telephone to William Orton, president of Western Union Telegraph Company, for $100,000. "What use could this company make of a toy?" was Orton's response. Bell's patent became one of the most valuable ones ever

issued. Orton's decision became one of the worst in American business history.

George Pullman built a sleeping car that provided luxury accommodations on trains. At first it seemed like a white elephant. It was too big to pass under bridges or through railway stations. When it was to become part of Abraham Lincoln's funeral train, however, bridges were raised and stations torn down to make room for it.

Andrew Carnegie, like many other wealthy men of the times, hired a substitute to fight for him in the Civil War. The cost was three hundred dollars. He did, however, help the war cause as a superintendent of telegraph lines.

Present the Lesson

Write the following topics on the board: Electricity, Communication, Steel, and Natural Resources. Divide the class into four groups, and assign one topic to each group. Ask each group to review the section and to develop and outline events that highlight one of the titles. Outlines might include:

Communication

I. Telegraph
   A. Invented in 1830's and 1840's by Samuel F. B. Morse
   B. Instrumental in communication of Union armies in Civil War
   C. Provided news to the newspapers and public within twenty-four hours of occurrence

II. Telephone
   A. Invented in 1876 by Alexander Graham Bell
   B. Speeded communication and helped tie nation together
   C. Used mainly women employees, who worked for less pay than men

III. Typewriter
   A. Invented in 1867 by Christopher Sholes
   B. Revolutionized offices and businesses throughout the nation
   C. Used mainly by women employees aged fifteen to twenty-four.

Ask the leader of each group to write their outlines on the board. Encourage students to refer to these outlines as they study this section.

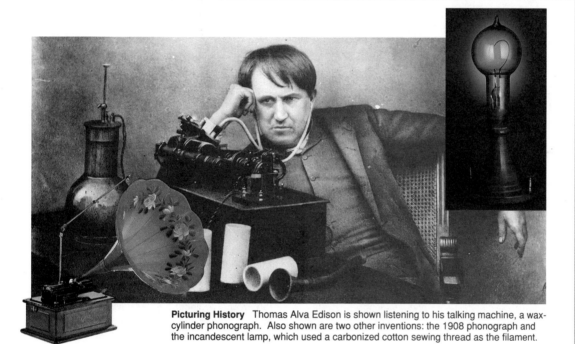

Picturing History Thomas Alva Edison is shown listening to his talking machine, a wax-cylinder phonograph. Also shown are two other inventions: the 1908 phonograph and the incandescent lamp, which used a carbonized cotton sewing thread as the filament.

later life he worked in his own laboratory at Menlo Park, New Jersey. Actually, it was more of an invention factory than a laboratory, for Edison knew little about basic science. He was essentially a tinkerer, a person who tries to solve specific problems and who likes to experiment.

Edison was born in 1847. He started school at the age of seven. After only three months, when the headmaster called him addled (confused), his mother decided to teach him at home. The child took to reading and exploring the world around him. He was immensely curious. He built a fire in his father's barn just to see what would happen. What happened was that he got a spanking. To find out why geese squatted on eggs, he got as close as he could to a nest and watched for hours. He also experimented with chemicals and built his own telegraph set.

Later he worked as a telegraph operator. Not having electric lights to read by at night, he chose the night shift so he could spend his days reading. The most important book he read was *Experimental Researches in Electricity* by British scientist Michael Faraday, inventor of the dynamo, or generator.

Edison soon began turning out inventions of his own. They included the phonograph, the motion picture camera, and the microphone. All told, he took out more than a thousand patents with the United States Patent Office—an average of one every two weeks!

In 1879 Edison produced what was perhaps his most revolutionary invention—the incandescent light bulb. Electric lamps were already being made during the 1870's. They were called arc lamps because an arc of light was created by jumping an electric current between two sticks of carbon. In 1878 merchant John Wanamaker of Philadelphia got ahead of his competitors by putting arc lights in his department store and doing business at night. By 1880 several cities had installed arc lights on their major streets.

Arc lights, however, were not an efficient way to use electricity. What needed to be done was to replace the carbon sticks with a filament that would glow for a long time without melting or exploding. Edison tried thousands of possible filaments, including hairs from his assistants' beards. Fortunately for the assistants, the best substance turned out to be carbonized bamboo from Japan. Later the bamboo was replaced by the metallic chemical element tungsten.

Communication Takes New Forms

Two other inventions that helped change American life between 1865 and 1900 were the telephone and the typewriter.

Check for Understanding
Call on individual students to answer Section 1
Review questions orally.

The Telephone. The telephone first appeared in public at the 1876 Philadelphia Centennial Exposition, a year after it had been invented for practical use by **Alexander Graham Bell.** The machine did not make much of an impression at first. Then Dom Pedro II, the visiting emperor of Brazil, walked by. He had met Bell during an earlier visit to Boston because he had been interested in the way Bell was teaching deaf-mutes how to speak. When Dom Pedro saw Bell sitting with his machine, he insisted on being shown how it worked. "My God, it talks!" he exclaimed. The emperor's excited shouts immediately drew a large crowd. More important, the exposition's judges, who had passed by the exhibit just a few minutes before, turned back to see what the fuss was about.

The telephone soon became extremely popular. The first switchboard, in New Haven, Connecticut, began operating in 1878 with 21 subscribers. Two years later there were 54,000 telephones in service. By 1900 there were 1.5 million. Forests of telephone poles sprouted in all major cities and then began to move cross-country. By 1887 New Yorkers were talking long-distance to Philadelphia. The New York-Chicago line began operating in 1892. The transcontinental line was in service in 1915.

Bell's invention not only speeded up communication but helped to tie the different parts of the nation together. It also had a profound effect on the role of women in the economy. The first telephone switchboard operators were men. Then employers discovered that women would do the work just as well for less pay. By 1900 there were some seventy-seven thousand female telephone operators, about 96 percent of the total.

The Typewriter. Even more significant in its consequences for women workers was the typewriter. It was invented by Christopher Sholes in 1867. Sholes, who had worked as an editor and a postmaster, looked on his invention as a toy. The Remington Arms Company took a different view. In 1874 the firm bought Sholes's patent rights to the machine and proceeded to revolutionize offices throughout the nation.

In 1870 women made up less than 5 percent of office workers. By 1900 they made up more than 75 percent, or about 500,000. Most of them were between fifteen and twenty-four years old, single, and living at home. Most of them were also white and native-born. If a woman were black, Jewish, or an immigrant, she was out of luck. White-collar work was reserved for "real Americans." It was cleaner and easier than factory or domestic work, and it was usually steady so one was less likely to be laid off. With such an economic base, women began to press more strongly for suffrage.

Sholes received only $12,000 from the Remington Arms Company (later Remington Rand) for his invention. His financial backer, who took royalties from Remington rather than cash, ended up with $1.5 million. Sholes was philosophical. "All my life I have been trying to escape being a millionaire," he said, "and now I think I have succeeded."

Rivers of Fire Produce Steel

The new industrial age would not have been possible without steel. Both wood and cast iron, which people used in earlier machines, are weaker materials than steel and wear out easily. Also, it is difficult to mold them to exact specifications. Steel, on the other hand, is strong, long-lasting, and easily shaped.

Before the Civil War, only a few thousand tons of steel were produced in the United States. Consequently, it was very expensive and was used only for such special items as swords and high-grade tools. Then at about the same time, the American William Kelly and the Englishman Henry Besse-

Picturing History Scottish-born Alexander Graham Bell is shown in October 1892 making the first New York-to-Chicago telephone call.

Guided Practice

Ask students whether opportunities still exist for imaginative inventors in the U.S. today. (Possible response: room still exists for imaginative individuals to develop inventions, but the process is often involved, costly, and plagued by legal complications. Usually, only research firms have the money and work force to deal with these problems.)

Picturing History The telephone and the typewriter brought thousands of women into the workplace. Shown here are women engaged in two new occupations—switchboard operator and typist. The typist is Lillian Sholes, daughter of the inventor of the typewriter.

mer came up with a new manufacturing technique that made steel production more efficient and much less expensive. Some years later another technique known as the open-hearth process made it possible to control the quality of steel. By the 1890's, millions of tons of liquid steel, like rivers of fire, were pouring out of open-hearth furnaces.

Most of the nation's steel mills were concentrated in Pennsylvania, and most of the steelworkers were Slavs. They created a folk hero named Joe Magarac. Arriving one Sunday at a local contest of strength, so the legend goes, this seven-foot giant

> with a back as broad as a door, easily lifted in one hand an 800-pound bar. . . . All he needed was five good meals a day. His home was the mill where he worked night and day, feeding the open-hearth furnace, stirring the molten steel with his fingers and shaping rails with his bare hands.

The rails Joe Magarac reputedly shaped with his hands were but one of dozens of steel products that came from American factories. Among the most significant were barbed wire and tin-plated steel cans. Barbed wire, as you know, changed both the cattle industry and farming on the Great Plains. The canning of food made marketing easier and meals more varied.

Resources Come from the Earth

The major resources needed in the new industrial age were iron and coal for making steel and oil for

lamps. Fortunately, the United States had ample supplies of all three.

Iron. At first iron ore came mostly from Eastern deposits. Around the middle of the century, prospectors discovered new ore fields in the Lake Superior region. In 1855 the Soo Canal was built between Lake Superior and Lake Huron. It enabled iron ore to be shipped by water most of the way to the Pennsylvania steel mills. In 1887 the iron-ore deposits in the Mesabi Range of Minnesota were discovered. The Mesabi fields have yielded more iron ore than any other deposit in the world. In addition, Mesabi ore lies near the surface, so expensive underground mining is not necessary.

Coal. Most United States coal comes from an area that lies in a strip just west of the Appalachian Mountains from Pennsylvania to Alabama. People had used coal since colonial times for heating and cooking. In the early 1800's, locomotives used coal as a fuel. As the United States became more industrialized, coal production jumped from 33 million tons in 1870 to more than 250 million tons in 1900.

Oil. Before the Civil War, Americans did not drill for oil. They simply skimmed it from creeks or other places where it had seeped to the earth's surface. They used it mostly to grease their wagons and as a rub for rheumatism.

In the 1850's, people began thinking of kerosene as a substitute for whale oil in lamps. The whale population was declining, and the price of whale

Assign Independent Practice

Have students complete Chapter 17, Section 1 Daily Activity and Enrichment Activity.

Student Assignment/Homework

Have students read Section 2, "Railroads Connect the Nation," and answer the Section 2 Review questions on paper.

SECTION 1 REVIEW

Answers

Main Ideas

1. More portable: factories no longer had to be built near water-power sources; more flexible: electric motors could be built to meet different size specifications.

2. Newspapers became more common and influential; Americans developed a better sense of their common identity.

3. Edison invented the incandescent light bulb, the phonograph, the microphone, and the motion picture camera.

4. Iron, coal, and oil were available in the U.S.

Critical Thinking

5. The inventions provided new sources of employment for many women (as office workers and telephone operators) because they were willing to work for less money than were men. However, these inventions had little economic effect on women who could not get white-collar jobs—African Americans, Jews, and immigrants.
(synthesis & evaluation)

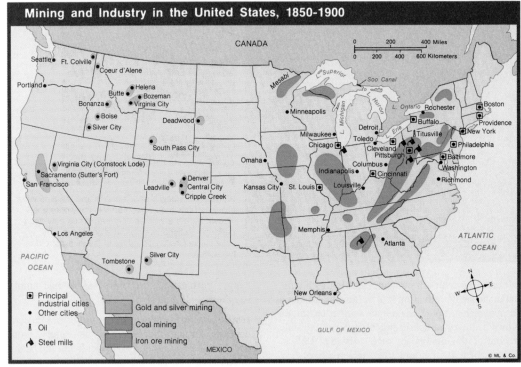

Mining and Industry in the United States, 1850-1900

Legend
▣ Principal industrial cities
• Other cities
⚱ Oil
⚒ Steel mills
▨ Gold and silver mining
▨ Coal mining
▨ Iron ore mining

© ML & Co.

Map Skills **Location** What principal industrial cities are shown? **Place** Around what city were several steel mills located? **Place** What products were mined in the Butte-Helena area?

oil was going up. So in 1858 **Edwin L. Drake** started drilling for oil in Titusville, Pennsylvania. In 1859 "Drake's folly" gushed in, and the petroleum industry was on its way.

At first the oil was refined primarily into kerosene for lamps. Gasoline, an oil by-product, was thrown away because people had no use for it. In the 1890's, the internal-combustion engine was put into a car. It operated not on steam but on gasoline. Today gasoline is the most valuable product that oil refineries turn out.

Linking Past to Present

Many areas of the country that once prospered from iron mining, steel production, and coal mining are depressed today. Foreign competition, ecological problems, and the end of abundant mineral deposits have all had an effect on these industries.

SECTION 1 REVIEW

Key Terms and People

Explain the significance of: technology, Samuel F. B. Morse, Thomas Alva Edison, Alexander Graham Bell, Edwin L. Drake

Main Ideas

1. What were the two main advantages that electric power offered over the steam engine?
2. How did the invention of the electric telegraph affect national communication?
3. What were the main accomplishments of the "Wizard of Menlo Park"?
4. What natural resources were needed to produce the essential materials of the new industrial age, and where could they be found?

Critical Thinking

5. Did the inventions of the telephone and the typewriter have a positive or a negative effect on the economic status of most women? Explain.

SECTION 2

Railroads Connect the Nation

GLOSSARY TERMS: transcontinental railroad, Crédit Mobilier, Grange, public utility, bloc

Of all the industries that developed between 1865 and 1900, perhaps the one that most affected people's lives was the railroad.

The Iron Horse Wields Immense Influence

Statistics bear out the immense importance of railroads in the new industrial age. In 1870 the railroads employed 163,000 persons. By 1900 they employed more than a million and were the largest industry in the nation.

Railroads influenced popular culture as well as the economy. People hung pictures of famous trains on the walls of their living rooms. They used railroad phrases in their conversation, like "working up a full head of steam" or "getting side-tracked." They sang songs about the men who built the railroads, songs like "John Henry" and "I Been Working on the Railroad" and "The Gandy Dancers' Ball." Most important of all, railroads influenced time.

Originally, each railroad followed its own time. If there were five different railroad lines using the same station, there would be five different clocks on the wall, no two of them alike. There were also different times within a state. If you were traveling from coast to coast, you had to change your watch at least twenty times along the way.

In 1870 Professor C. F. Dowd of Saratoga Springs, New York, started a campaign for uniform time. He suggested that the earth's surface be divided into twenty-four time zones, beginning at Greenwich, England (which is at zero degrees longitude). Each zone would represent one hour. The continental United States would have four such zones, which Dowd named Eastern, Central, Mountain, and Pacific. Thus, when it was noon in New York City, it would be eleven o'clock in Chicago, ten in Denver, and nine in San Francisco.

In 1883 Dowd's plan finally went into effect. No sooner did the railroads adopt standard time zones than the rest of the nation did the same. As one newspaper declared, "The sun is no longer boss of the job. People, 55 million of them, must eat, sleep and work, as well as travel, by railroad time." In 1918 Congress passed an act making the four time zones official. In 1966 Congress set up eight time zones, thus including Alaska, Hawaii, and all United States possessions. Congress also adopted daylight-saving time in summer as a fuel-saving measure. To date, the only exceptions are Arizona, Hawaii, Puerto Rico, American Samoa, the Virgin Islands, and part of Indiana.

The Golden Spike Opens the West

The first railroad locomotive arrived in the United States from England in 1829. By 1854 the railroad reached the Mississippi. A few years later, work began on the first **transcontinental railroad.**

The idea of a railroad that would run from the Atlantic to the Pacific was first raised in 1832. No one gave the idea much attention, however, until gold was discovered in California. Then people became very interested indeed.

In 1862 President Lincoln signed the Pacific Railroad Act. A second railroad act was passed in 1864. Under these acts, the Union Pacific and Central Pacific Railroad companies received about 20 million acres of federal land, as well as federal loans of $60 million. Additional money was invested by individuals hoping to make a profit and by towns that wanted to make certain that the railroad would not pass them by. The Union Pacific was to build westward from Omaha, Nebraska. The Central Pacific was to build eastward from Sacramento, California.

The Tracks Begin. Construction of the two lines moved slowly at first, for the nation's attention was focused on the Civil War. In 1865, however, thousands of young veterans found themselves at loose ends. They were strong, used to danger, and trained to do what they were told. They were as eager to work as the railroad was eager to hire them. The majority of those who laid tracks for the Union Pacific were Irish immigrants.

The Union Pacific work gangs were headed by former Union General Jack S. Casement and his brother Dan. Jack Casement stood five feet four inches; his brother was "five feet nothing." However, as they organized men and equipment and moved out across hundreds of miles of almost uninhabited land, it soon became obvious that they were "the biggest little men you ever saw."

The difficulties were truly tremendous. Lines had to be surveyed despite the danger of attacks by

Map Skills

Chicago, St. Louis, Cincinnati, Cleveland, Pittsburgh, Buffalo, Baltimore, Philadelphia, New York, Providence, and Boston • Pittsburgh • Gold, silver

Historical Sidelight

On his way to the ceremonies marking the completion of the transcontinental railroad, the private railroad car of Thomas Durant, general manager of the Union Pacific Railroad, was commandeered by an angry group of unpaid workers. Because Durant was trapped, the railroad quickly paid the workers.

Present the Lesson

Ask students to review the section and construct a time line on the board showing the growth of the railroad industry from 1829 to 1900.

1829	First locomotives arrive from England.
1854	Railroad reaches Mississippi River.
1862	President Lincoln signs Pacific Railroad Act.
1864	Congress passes second railroad act.
1865	Railroads begin to hire war veterans and immigrants.
1869	Rail lines meet at Promontory Point, Utah, completing the first transcontinental railroad.
1870	Railroads employ 163,000 persons. The Grange fights railroad price fixing.
1877	*Munn* v. *Illinois*, Granger laws regulating prices remain in effect.
1886	*Wabash Case*, only the federal government can regulate interstate commerce.
1887	Interstate Commerce Act establishes Interstate Commerce Commission to enforce laws.
1900	Railroads become the largest industry in the nation, employing more than one million persons.

Have students refer to the time line as they study this section.

Map Skills

Texas & Pacific • Kansas Pacific • Central

For Discussion

Why and how did railroads bring about the creation of time zones? What other changes can you think of that were caused by railroad development? (Response: railroads caused creation of time zones to standardize schedules for arrivals and departures. Changes include: a faster way to travel; a fast, efficient means of shipping goods; wider distribution of fresh produce and meat in refrigerated cars.)

Railroad Land Grants and Time Zones, 1850-1900

Map Skills **Movement** What railroad linked Dallas and El Paso? Kansas City and Denver?
Place In what time zone was Cleveland in 1883?

the Sioux and Cheyenne. Iron nails, hardware, and timber for ties and trestles had to be transported from five hundred to fifteen hundred miles, as did food and water for the workers. Accidents were common, many men were killed in drunken brawls, and pneumonia and other diseases took a heavy toll.

The Chinese Workers. The Central Pacific had its problems, too. The main difficulty was a shortage of labor, for there were few Civil War veterans in California. Then Charlie Crocker, the railroad's general superintendent, decided to hire Chinese. About twenty-five thousand had come from Canton in 1850 to take part in the gold rush.

Crocker's decision was greeted with skepticism. How could men who weighed only 110 pounds move earth and stone? "Did they not build the Chinese Wall," Crocker asked, "the biggest piece of masonry in the world?"

The Chinese, soon known as Crocker's pets, turned out to be excellent workers—steady, patient, and brave. Some of the tasks they performed were astounding. In 1866, for example, it was necessary to drive a tunnel through a mountain. The granite was so hard that it took twelve hours to chip away eight inches. (Dynamite had just been invented but was not in general use.) The tunnel took a full year to dig—and for five months the work was done with work camps buried under forty feet of snow. Chimneys and air shafts had to be dug to the surface, lanterns burned twenty-four hours a day, and the Chinese lived and worked "like moles, in dim passages far below the earth's surface." Avalanches made life even more difficult. Hundreds of Chinese were swept away and their bodies not recovered until the spring thaw. Some were found "with shovels or picks still clutched in their frozen hands."

Yet the Chinese received less than white workers

Check for Understanding

Call on individual students to read their answers to Section 2 Review questions orally.

Guided Practice

Discuss with students the phenomenal growth of the American railroad system in the nineteenth century and identify its present problems. (Problems include: ridership down; costs up; need to update equipment.) Ask students whether they think American railroads should be restored at government expense. (Possible responses: yes, the railroad is part of our heritage; no, competition should determine the most efficient means of transportation.)

for their efforts. The Chinese worked from sunrise to sunset; white workers, eight hours a day. The Chinese earned thirty-five dollars a month; white workers, from forty to sixty dollars. The Chinese had to buy their own dried fish, rice, and tea; white workers were fed by the railroad free of charge.

A Workers Duel. The last few months of construction were sparked by a duel between the workers of the Union Pacific and those of the Central Pacific to see which group could lay the most track in a single day. Both sides kept increasing production until finally Casement's men laid 7.5 miles of track in twelve hours. Crocker thereupon promised that his men would lay 10 miles in one day. When the vice-president of the Union Pacific heard about the promise, he bet Crocker $10,000 that it couldn't be done. To everyone's amazement, it was—a record that has never been broken.

Finally, on May 10, 1869, the greatest engineering and construction effort undertaken since the arrival of the first Europeans in America was over. The two rail lines were joined with a golden spike at Promontory Point, Utah, and the United States was joined from coast to coast with rails of steel.

Transcontinental Travel Becomes a Great Adventure

The greatest adventure Americans could experience during the 1870's and 1880's was to travel the continent by rail. Just think of all the wonderful things you could see on the eight- to ten-day trip! The Missouri River bridge, which framed the seemingly endless prairies beyond; the snow-topped ranges of the Rockies; the strange shapes and colors of canyon rocks; the streamlined streets of Salt Lake City; prairie-dog villages and antelope that raced the train (the antelope usually won); and, especially, herds of buffalo and real Indians. The vast size and variety of the West created a feeling of awe among travelers, as well as an intense sense of patriotism.

Picturing History Railroaders celebrate the joining of the Central Pacific and the Union Pacific railroad track, which linked the United States coast to coast with rails of steel. A golden spike bearing a prayer for national unity was used to link the two railroad lines.

Tell students to write three paragraphs identifying the abuses of the railroad companies and explaining how these actions led the government to assume a regulatory role. (Details should include: Credit Mobilier and Union Pacific were run by same individuals; officials awarded themselves construction contracts at double or triple the actual cost; officials gave shares of stock to congressmen to guarantee continued grants and subsidies; Credit Mobilier gave state officials free rail passes. The Grange believed the railroads were public utilities and elected legislators who supported the Grange push for government regulation of railroads. This led to government involvement: 1877—*Munn* v. *Illinois;* 1886—*Wabash Case;* 1887—Interstate Commerce Act.)

Sleeping accommodations depended on whether you rode a Pullman car, a day coach, or a Zulu car. A Pullman car, first introduced in 1859 by **George M. Pullman,** was the best. For one hundred dollars plus four dollars a day, travelers could ride on a comfortable sofa that converted into a bed with warm blankets and a certain amount of privacy. For day-coach passengers, who paid seventy-five dollars, the seat back was lowered at night and the footrest extended. Zulu cars cost forty dollars and usually contained rows of backless benches. Passengers—mostly European immigrants to whom the railroads had sold land—took turns sleeping under the benches or in the aisles.

Then there were the private cars of wealthy business people and politicians. They contained such items as marble baths, plate-glass mirrors, wood-burning fireplaces . . . and solid-gold light fixtures. They cost as much as $50,000 to build.

Scandals Lie Beneath the Tracks

One reason many business people and politicians were able to afford private railroad cars was the **Crédit Mobilier** (crā dē′mō bil′ē ā). This was the construction company that built the Union Pacific Railroad, and it operated in the following way. Crédit Mobilier and Union Pacific were both run by the same individuals. These men realized that it was not the owners or operators who made the most money out of building railroads. It was the construction contractors. So, in their capacity as officials of the Union Pacific, these men formed a construction company called the Crédit Mobilier. Then, in their capacity as officials of the Union Pacific, they gave their own construction company a contract to lay track at two to three times the actual cost! They divided the excess profits among themselves. These profits were later estimated as ranging from $33 to $50 million. Similar tactics were followed by the Central Pacific Railroad, which was paid $120 million to build a line that actually cost about $58 million.

Nor was this all. The railroad officials wanted to be sure that Congress would continue giving the railroads land grants and construction subsidies. They also wanted to prevent a congressional investigation of their financial dealings. So they gave shares of stock in Crédit Mobilier to twenty or so congressmen, including James Garfield of Ohio, who later became President of the United States. The stock paid dividends of several hundred percent.

In 1872 a crusading newspaper, the *New York Sun,* exposed the bribery. The next year a congressional committee investigated the matter. Two congressmen were censured, but otherwise the result was a complete whitewash. As one congressman said, when asked what his constituents would think about his having accepted stock in Crédit Mobilier, "They would ask why I didn't take more!"

There was corruption at lower levels of government, too. For example, railroads commonly gave state officials passes entitling them and their families to travel by rail at any time, anywhere, free of charge. Naturally, such officials were reluctant to tax railroads or to pass safety laws or other legislation that would increase costs.

The Grange Fights for Regulations

In 1867 a farmer named **Oliver Kelley** organized the Patrons of Husbandry, popularly known as the **Grange.** Its original purpose was to provide a way for isolated farm families to get together socially

Picturing History Private railroad cars offered the comforts of home and more, but only for the wealthy.

and also learn more about scientific methods of farming. By the 1870's, however, farmers in the Grange lodges were spending most of their time and energy fighting the railroads. Since there were more than twenty thousand lodges with a membership of more than 1.5 million—women as well as men—they put up an extremely effective fight.

What angered the Grangers were the rate policies the railroads followed. Since most communities were served by only one line, there was no price competition. Furthermore, there were no alternative means of transportation. If farmers wanted to send their crops to market, they had to pay whatever shipping rate the railroad set. All too often, the railroad charged all that the traffic would bear.

Railroads Are a Public Utility. The Granger idea was that railroads were a **public utility,** that is, they were public in nature even though they were privately owned and managed. Since they were public utilities, the public had the right to regulate them through their government.

Accordingly, the Grangers, by voting as a **bloc,** or unified group, elected enough state legislators to get so-called Granger legislation passed in fourteen states, including the breadbasket states of Illinois, Iowa, Minnesota, and Wisconsin. In general, these laws established state railroad commissions with the power to set freight rates according to distance.

The railroads fought back in every way they could. They spent huge sums of money to defeat state legislators who had voted in favor of the Granger laws. They refused to let trains stop in towns that had Granger lodges. They kept filing lawsuits against the Grangers.

Railroad attorneys argued that Granger legislation took away private property without due process of law. In 1877, however, in the case of *Munn* v. *Illinois,* the Supreme Court ruled that state Granger laws were constitutional. Owners of property "in which the public has an interest . . . must submit to be controlled by the public for the common good."

The Interstate Commerce Act. In 1886 the Supreme Court took most of the teeth out of *Munn* v. *Illinois* by a new ruling. In the *Wabash* case, the Court held that even within its own borders, a state could not set rates on railroad traffic that either came from another state or was headed for another state. Only the federal government, the Court said, had the power to regulate interstate commerce.

So in 1887, responding to public pressure, Congress passed the **Interstate Commerce Act.** It required railroad rates to be "reasonable and just" and established a five-member Interstate Commerce Commission (ICC). All the ICC could do, however, was prohibit railroads from charging more for short hauls than for long hauls. It had no power to set maximum rates. Also, the only way it could enforce a decision was by suing the railroad—and such cases dragged on for years. The ICC did not really become effective until after Theodore Roosevelt became President in 1901. (See Chapter 21.) As for the Granger movement, it lost its drive and again became a social and educational organization.

Nevertheless, the Granger movement marked a turning point in American history. It helped establish the principle that the federal government has the right to regulate private business if it is in the public interest and if the states are not able to do so.

Linking Past to Present

Before 1978, a few major airlines carried most passengers. Competition was regulated by the Civil Aeronautics Board, an agency of the federal government. Critics of this regulation insisted that greater competition would bring down airfares and improve service. In 1978, Congress voted to deregulate the airlines. As a result, competition increased sharply, and within five years, twenty new airlines had been started. However, by the early 1990's, because of increasingly severe competitiveness and rising fuel and labor costs, a number of airlines were forced to merge. Some had even declared bankruptcy.

SECTION 2 REVIEW

Key Terms and People

Explain the significance of: transcontinental railroad, George M. Pullman, Crédit Mobilier, Oliver Kelley, Grange, public utility, bloc, *Munn* v. *Illinois,* Interstate Commerce Act

Main Ideas

1. In general, how did the expansion of railroads affect the United States?

SECTION 2 REVIEW

Answers

Main Ideas

1. It influenced the economy, the nation's popular culture, and the acceptance of uniform time zones.

2. Racism, low wages, long working hours, dangerous working conditions, strenuous labor, and difficult weather conditions.

3. It marked the joining of the western and eastern ends and, thus, the completion of the transcontinental railroad.

4. The Grangers objected to price gouging and promoted the idea that the railroad was a public utility and should be regulated by the government.

5. The Granger laws applied only to rail traffic within state borders; legislation was needed for traffic coming from or going to other states.

Critical Thinking

6. Government incentives— free land and federal loans— gave railroad companies enormous sources of revenue and a great deal of power, especially over thousands of employees, government officials, and farmers. **(analysis)**

State the Objective

Understand how and why large, complex business organizations developed in the U.S.

profits; larger markets; more resources; cheaper labor. Possible disadvantages: foreign government intervention; language barriers; differences in customs and business practices.)

Anticipate the Lesson

Ask students to name businesses in their community or in nearby communities. Write these on the board. Ask students to circle ones that represent nationwide or worldwide businesses. (Businesses might include: McDonald's; Sears; General Electric; Xerox.) Ask students to suggest possible advantages and disadvantages of nationwide and worldwide businesses. (Possible advantages: higher

---

2. What hardships were faced by the Chinese railroad laborers?
3. What was the significance of the golden spike?
4. What railroad activity angered the Grangers, and how did they try to alleviate the problem?
5. Why was it necessary for Congress to pass the Interstate Commerce Act even though the Granger laws had been ruled constitutional?

Critical Thinking

6. How did the government's encouragement of railroad expansion affect the power of the railroad companies?

Historical Sidelight
Andrew Carnegie gave away more than 300 million dollars during his lifetime. He contributed money to the creation of more than 2,500 of the nation's community libraries.

SECTION 3

Businesses Become More Complex

GLOSSARY TERMS: **holding company, merger, trust, interlocking directorate, rebates, robber barons, Social Darwinism**

Industrial development requires more than energy, technology, and resources. It also requires individuals who can organize business. Between 1865 and 1900, hundreds of such individuals helped change both the shape and the size of American industry.

Carnegie Is the Steel Captain

Andrew Carnegie was a Scottish immigrant who came to this country and got his first job in 1848 when he was thirteen years old. He worked as a bobbin boy, changing spools of thread in a cotton mill twelve hours a day, six days a week. His wages were $1.20 per week, plus another 80 cents for firing the furnace. Fifty-three years later, he sold his own steel company for almost $500 million. About two-fifths of that sum went to his associates. The balance, invested, gave Carnegie a monthly income of more than $1 million—at a time when there was no income tax!

Preparing for Advancement. Carnegie started his climb from rags to riches by leaving the cotton mill and becoming a telegraph messenger. He immediately began enlarging the possibilities of his new job. He learned the faces and names of

---

Pittsburgh's leading business people and was able to deliver telegrams to them in a club or office without delay. While waiting to be sent out on deliveries, he studied Morse code so that he could become a telegraph operator instead of just a messenger. He spent his free time reading to make up for his limited formal education.

Seizing Opportunities. At seventeen Carnegie became a telegraph operator with the Pennsylvania Railroad and proceeded to learn all he could about the railroad business. One day there was an accident on the line. The division superintendent, Thomas A. Scott, was not available. So Carnegie took it on himself to send several telegrams signed with Scott's name, giving orders to untangle the traffic snarl and get the trains moving again. When Scott learned about Carnegie's actions, he made Carnegie his private secretary. Seven years later, Carnegie had Scott's job.

In 1865 Carnegie left the Pennsylvania Railroad and devoted himself full time to looking after his investments. After a while, he decided to concentrate on the steel industry, and in 1873 he launched what later became the Carnegie Steel Corporation.

Balancing Quality and Cost. Carnegie stressed certain business practices that are now widespread. For example, he was always trying to turn out a better product at a lower cost. He spent large sums of money to install new technology in his steel plants. He hired chemists and metallurgists to improve the steel's quality. He installed detailed accounting systems so that he knew precisely what each process cost. He hired top-notch assistants, offered them stock in the firm, and then set them competing against one another to increase production and to cut costs.

Carnegie was also interested in controlling as much of the steel industry as possible. He bought out rival plants whenever he had the chance. He lowered his prices—which he could afford to do—and undersold his competitors, many of whom went out of business. He developed an operation that included not only steel plants but also coal and iron mines, ore freighters, and railroad lines. This is called an integrated operation because it controls every step in the manufacturing process from mining the raw materials to delivering the finished product to the consumer. Carnegie was producing 25 percent of the nation's steel when he sold his property in 1901. He then devoted himself to

Present the Lesson

Have students construct on the board a three-column chart showing the types of abuses that led to the passage of the Sherman Anti-Trust Act, the purpose and provisions of the Act, and a comparison between the Sherman Anti-Trust Act and the Interstate Commerce Act. (See Section 2.) Have students refer to this chart as they study Section 3.

Abuses	Purposes and Provisions	Comparison
Formation of trusts	break-up of monopolies	both difficult to enforce
controlling price	trusts, conspiracies, and other restraints of trade declared illegal	both produced many court cases
forcing small businesses to close		both were ineffective and no longer enforced

Picturing History Andrew Carnegie holding the results of his philanthropy. He thought it a disgrace to die wealthy and sought to divest himself of his wealth.

philanthropy and endowed libraries throughout the world.

Corporations Combine

Carnegie Steel became the core of the United States Steel Corporation, which was the largest business organization in the world at that time. United States Steel was a **holding company.** It did not actually make steel. Rather, it sold stock in itself and then used the money to buy control of companies that *were* making steel.

There were other ways by which companies combined to form bigger and stronger businesses. The easiest way was the **merger.** In a merger, two or more corporations united to form a single corporation. Usually, one corporation would buy the stock of the others.

Yet another way of forming a larger business unit

was a **trust** agreement. The stockholders of several competing companies would turn their stock over to a group of trustees. In return, the stockholders received trust certificates that entitled them to receive dividends from the trust's profits. In the meantime, the trustees ran the various companies in the trust as if they were one.

Then there was the **interlocking directorate** that existed whenever directors of one firm also served as directors of another firm. The two firms might have completely separate ownership. Yet because they had the same directors, their operating policies and practices were the same.

Although large business units were formed in different ways, all were popularly known as trusts. In addition to steel, there were trusts in oil refining, sugar refining, whiskey distilling, meat packing, and tobacco processing, as well as in the production of wire and nails, bicycles, agricultural machinery, salt, matches, crackers, lead, copper, electrical supplies, and many other items. By 1900 trusts dominated about four-fifths of the industries in the United States. Not only that—about 2 percent of the firms were making 50 percent of the products.

What made trusts so popular? In many instances, large-scale businesses are more efficient than small businesses. They can reduce waste by getting rid of duplication. They can afford to install new and more productive equipment. Since they buy supplies in large quantities, they pay lower prices and can therefore sell their products for less. Also, they can afford to introduce new products and wait several years for the products to return a profit.

Linking Past to Present

The combining of companies to form bigger and stronger businesses was a significant feature of the late 1800's. This activity occurred on a larger scale during the 1980's, a decade of numerous mergers and acquisitions. Buyout mania tore through the stock market like a roller coaster as one company after another became the target of a takeover. The daily dealings of investors such as Donald Trump became media events in which the classic negotiating position was "You need me more than I need you."

Check for Understanding

Have students write the answers to the Section 3 Review questions on paper.

Guided Practice

Explain to students that the process of business consolidation continues today with the advent of multinational companies. Ask students whether they think these companies are a danger with their great power or a hope for international cooperation. (Possible responses: danger—development of monopolies; hope—to insure profits large businesses may pressure governments to seek peaceful means of settling disputes.)

For Discussion

Define the word *monopoly*. How did business monopolies operate? (Possible definition: exclusive control of a commodity, service, or means of production in a particular market; business monopolies drove out competitors, then controlled market and prices.) How did the appearance of business monopolies in the American economy change the competitiveness of the free enterprise system? (Possible response: small businesses were forced to close because their prices were no longer competitive.)

Were the Captains Also Robber Barons?

Why, then, did antitrust feelings develop in the United States during the 1880's and 1890's? Primarily because some trusts behaved in a destructive way. Instead of lowering prices, they raised prices. Since they dominated an industry, there was nothing that other companies or customers could do.

John D. Rockefeller, who founded the Standard Oil Trust in 1882, carried this further. He would sell products below cost until he had driven all of his competitors out of business. Then he would jack up his prices to several times their previous level. He also forced railroads to give him **rebates,** or refunds, of part of his payments for shipping his products. This was against the law. Yet the railroads felt they had no choice, because they could not operate if they lost Standard Oil's business. After all, the trust controlled at least 90 percent of the nation's oil refining and marketing.

Rockefeller and other business people who operated in a similar manner were dubbed **robber barons** by critics who considered them ruthless, unjust, and interested only in power and money. The robber barons acted not to improve their own business, these critics argued, but to destroy others. Economic giants like Standard Oil had too much power—especially in a democracy.

As more and more people came to feel that way,

Congress in 1890 passed the **Sherman Antitrust Act.** The act stated that "every contract, combination in the form of trust or otherwise, or conspiracy, in restraint of trade . . . is hereby declared to be illegal."

Enforcing the act, however, proved almost impossible. It was vaguely worded and did not define such terms as *trust* and *conspiracy*. Many trusts simply reorganized as single corporations, thus avoiding prosecution. In addition, seven of the first eight cases the federal government brought against trusts were thrown out of court. The government soon stopped trying to break up trusts, and big business kept on getting bigger.

A New Definition of Success Arises

The philosophy that people used to help explain why Carnegie, Rockefeller, and other industrialists succeeded is called **Social Darwinism.** This philosophy grew out of the theory of biological evolution developed by the English biologist Charles Darwin. Darwin observed that no two creatures are exactly the same and that children are not exactly the same as their parents. Also, in any generation, some survive while others do not. Darwin concluded that some individuals in a species are better able to adapt to their environment than others. To put it another way, Darwin said, there is a process

Picturing History
"The Bosses of the Senate," a cartoon from January 1889, draws attention to the control big business had over Congress.

Assign Independent Practice

Have students complete Chapter 17, Section 3 Daily Activity.

Student Assignment/Homework

Have students complete Chapter 17 Review on paper. Divide the class into small groups and have students review their answers.

Concluding the Chapter

Refer students to "Horatio Alger and Success." Ask students to prepare an essay on the principles of Horatio Alger's American Dream as it applies today. (Essays might include: education and tax laws today try to equalize wealth and opportunity; to get to the top requires working your way up through the ranks.)

of natural selection at work. Those individuals who are best fitted to survive, do. The weaker ones drop by the wayside.

Herbert Spencer's *First Principles*. Darwin's ideas were transferred from biology to business by the English philosopher Herbert Spencer. In his book *First Principles,* published in 1862, Spencer argued that free competition was a natural law and that it was dangerous to interfere with it. If the government would just leave business and business people alone, the fittest would naturally survive. The more productive the business, the larger it would grow. The more competent the individual, the richer he or she would become. Whatever survived must be good, and the more effectively it survived, the better it was. Is it any wonder that Social Darwinism appealed to people like Carnegie and Rockefeller?

Horatio Alger and Success. Social Darwinism did not appeal just to the four thousand millionaires who had made their money in business since the Civil War. The idea had mass appeal as well.

Again, it was the written word that spread the message. The writer was **Horatio Alger, Jr.** The word was a series of more than a hundred books that sold between 125 and 250 million copies. (Spencer's *First Principles* sold about 300,000 copies.) Some of the Alger titles were *Bound to Rise, Luck and Pluck, Making His Way, Brave and Bold, In Search of Treasure, Strive and Succeed,* and *Risen from the Ranks.* Each book had a similar plot. One historian described it as being about

> the rise to riches of a street urchin. Alger heroes . . . demonstrated beyond any doubt that the poor boy who worked hard and cheerfully, who was kind, decent, took baths, was respectful to his betters and elders, and was always more or less honest in his dealings, why, this boy was sure to become rich and honored.

Not only that—he was practically certain to marry the boss's daughter.

Many a young American must have had satisfying dreams when reading such scenes as this from *Herbert Carter's Legacy:*

> "Is that the latest style?" inquired James Leech, with a sneer, pointing to a patch on Herbert Carter's pants.
>
> Herbert's face flushed. He was not ashamed

of the patch, for he knew that his mother's poverty made it a necessity. But he felt it was mean and dishonorable in James Leech, whose father was one of the rich men of Wrayburn, to taunt him with what he could not help. Some boys might have slunk away abashed, but Herbert had pluck and stood his ground.

> "It is my style," he answered firmly, looking James boldly in the face.

Horatio Alger's books inspired thousands of Americans to take advantage of the opportunities that opened up during the new industrial age. The books had a political effect as well. Although there was widespread poverty in the United States during this period, as will be seen later, the majority of Americans tended to revert to old Puritan ideas and lay the blame entirely on individuals. There was nothing wrong with the economic system. Riches were a sign of God's favor. If people were poor, they must be either lazy or inferior. There was no need to pass social legislation or to change the way businesses and other institutions operated. As a consequence, as you will learn in Chapter 18, movements for economic reform had a difficult time.

SECTION 3 REVIEW

Key Terms and People

Explain the significance of: Andrew Carnegie, holding company, merger, trust, interlocking directorate, John D. Rockefeller, rebates, robber barons, Sherman Antitrust Act, Social Darwinism, Horatio Alger, Jr.

Main Ideas

1. What business practices were used by Carnegie to produce better steel at a lower cost?
2. How did Carnegie achieve his goal of controlling a large percentage of the steel industry?
3. Name the main ways in which companies were combined into large-scale businesses, and explain why combining was popular.
4. Why was the Sherman Antitrust Act practically impossible to enforce?

Critical Thinking

5. What did the heroes of the novels of Horatio Alger, Jr., have in common with Andrew Carnegie and John D. Rockefeller?

SECTION 3 REVIEW

Answers

Main Ideas

1. He used new technology, experts, detailed accounting systems, and management incentives to raise productivity while cutting costs.

2. He developed an integrated operation, undersold his competitors, and bought out rivals.

3. They were combined through holding companies, mergers, trust agreements, and interlocking directorates; large units were able to reduce costs, eliminate competition, and make greater profits.

4. The act's terms were vague, and trusts could avoid prosecution by reorganizing as individual corporations. Also, the courts threw out many federal government suits.

Critical Thinking

5. All exemplified the theory of Social Darwinism, valued individual success, and took advantage of the opportunities available to them in the new industrial age. **(analysis)**

State the Objective

Understand views and biases in visual representations

Present the Lesson

Discuss with students the control a photojournalist or cartoonist has over the presentation of a subject. To stimulate discussion, ask students the following questions: Is a cartoonist obliged to give background information or a balanced viewpoint? (Possible response: no—a cartoonist usually approaches a subject from one point of view; the purpose of the political cartoon is to present a very definite viewpoint and to persuade others to see the subject from the same viewpoint.) Does a photojournalist have similar control over his or her subject? (Possible response: yes—a photo-journalist may choose to show a person in a positive or negative light, thus convincing the audience to think likewise.)

Have students bring to class a cartoon or photograph of the President. Divide the class into small groups to discuss and analyze the visuals according to the steps presented in the feature. Students should answer the following questions about each visual: Is the President portrayed in a positive or a negative light? Which symbols and details are complimentary? Which are critical?

Focus on Critical Thinking Skills

Analyzing Visual Sources

Understanding the Skill

During the second part of the nineteenth century, newspaper circulation greatly increased in the United States. Because photographs could not be reproduced at first, newspapers started printing drawings and cartoons. Cartoons held up public figures for admiration or ridicule. Today both photographs and cartoons are important features of newspapers. In fact, certain photojournalists and political cartoonists have large reader followings.

A political cartoon is an interpretive picture that presents a positive or negative point of view of an event, person, or group. Because a cartoon gets its message across in a simple and humorous manner, it can be a powerful communicator. Cartoons make use of caricature—drawings that exaggerate and distort characters to convey a message. Cartoons also use symbols. For example, the Republican party is portrayed as an elephant, the Democratic party is portrayed as a donkey, and the United States is represented by Uncle Sam. Captions or labels present the central theme of the cartoon.

Since cartoons are artists' interpretations of events and photos show actual events, are photos more historically reliable than cartoons? Not always. Recall photos you have seen of public demonstrations, for example. A close-up view of someone being clubbed by a police officer can give a different impression than a view of the entire crowd. Publishing the close-up rather than the larger view affects what people think of the event. Through such choices, photojournalists reveal their opinions and biases.

Both cartoons and photos are visual sources that provide information and opinions about issues or events. However, since both can be misleading, careful readers must learn to interpret them. You can follow certain steps to help you understand and interpret cartoons and photos.

- **Identify the main idea.** Who or what is shown in the cartoon or photo? Try to name each figure or object shown.
- **Analyze the point of view.** Are figures presented in a positive or negative light? You can often get clues by looking at how the figures are shown or drawn. Does the photo or cartoon show all or part of an event? Does the choice of photo express any bias?
- **Identify important details and symbols.** Determine what each symbol means. Is there a symbol for a political party? for an ideal such as love or peace? What do details in the photo communicate?
- **Interpret the message of the visual.** Read the labels or caption. Try to put the message of the cartoon or photo in your own words.

Picturing History John D. Rockefeller, American industrialist and philanthropist, is caught doing one of his good deeds.

Applying the Skill

One of the nineteenth century's notorious personalities was John D. Rockefeller. As a powerful

Check for Understanding

Discuss the questions at the end of the feature.

Have students bring to class two photos or political cartoons that portray a single event from different viewpoints. Have students share their samples and discuss the biases these photos and cartoons represent.

Picturing History This cartoon appeared in 1905 with the following quote from a speech by John D. Rockefeller: "The American beauty rose can be produced in all its splendor only by sacrificing the early buds that grow up around it."

businessman, he was called a captain of industry. He was also called a robber baron because he wielded more power, behaved more ruthlessly, and made and gave away more money than any man in his time.

In 1863, four years after oil was discovered in Pennsylvania, Rockefeller established a refinery in Cleveland, Ohio. By 1865 it was the largest in the Ohio town. Rockefeller was able to expand his company because he sold high quality oil at low cost and received rebates from railroads. By 1904 Rockefeller's company was refining 84 percent of all crude oil in the United States. With his enormous profits, Rockefeller branched out into the banking, steel, and coal industries.

Americans had long feared the power Rockefeller wielded and the methods he used. Newspapers attacked him through editorials, stories, and cartoons. The cartoon on page 448 shows Rockefeller's Standard Oil Trust as one of several giant trusts. Each is shown as a larger-than-life-sized businessman who appears confident and smart. They keep their eyes focused on the legislators, who are portrayed as small, unimportant, and incompetent.

Rockefeller never replied to the criticisms against him. Throughout his life, however, he gave over $500 million to many charitable organizations. Often, he gave secretly. Toward the end of his life, the public became aware of his generosity. By the time he died at age ninety-eight, Americans considered him a kindly gentleman. Perhaps the photographer who took the photo of Rockefeller was trying to capture the man who was criticized so harshly during his life for his business success yet donated so much of his profits to help others.

Rockefeller is shown in a cartoon and a photo here. Compare the visuals and answer the following questions.

Practicing Your Skill

1. What is the main idea of the cartoon? the photograph?
2. Compare the points of view expressed in the visuals. What details in the cartoon reinforce the negative view many people had of Rockefeller?
3. What is the message of each visual?
4. Why do you think certain photojournalists and political cartoonists have large reader followings? Do you follow any particular ones? If so, why?

Answers

Analyzing Visual Sources

1. Rockefeller is portrayed as a gardener who ruthlessly prunes his rose bush to produce one perfect flower.
• Rockefeller is portrayed as a kindly old man.

2. The photographer has caught Rockefeller in a caring act, stooping to give a child a coin. The cartoonist shows Rockefeller using huge shears to cut off rosebuds, which are represented as human skulls. He does not seem to mind that he is standing next to hundreds of skulls. The cartoonist reinforces Rockefeller's negative image as a robber baron who acquired great wealth by exploiting others.

3. The photo shows Rockefeller as a grandfatherly man reaching out in generosity towards a child. The cartoon shows Rockefeller as a miserly man willing to destroy anything or anyone who impedes his progress.

4. Possible answer: certain photojournalists and political cartoonists have the ability to capture the essence of a complex story or issue in a simple drawing or photo. • Students may find certain artists appealing because of their artistic style or because of their subject material.

Answer Key

Key Terms and People

These are highlighted in the text in the order in which they appear in this list.

Main Ideas

1. Introduced new products and allowed factories to locate in many new places. • Electric motors, trolley cars, telegraph, telephone, electric lights. • Light bulb, phonograph, motion pictures, microphone.

2. Coal, iron ore, oil. • Steel, railroad, and petroleum industries.

3. More workers were needed than were available. • Irish and Chinese workers. • Union Pacific—Indian attacks, drunken fights, disease, accidents; Central Pacific—mountainous terrain, cutting tunnels through solid rock, extreme weather, avalanches.

4. To allow farm families to socialize and learn more about scientific methods of farming. • To oppose railroad rate policy. • Company that supplies an essential public service and ought to be regulated by the government.

5. Holding company could buy other companies; two companies could merge into single company; several companies could form a trust; directors of one firm could act as directors of another so both were run in the same way. • Big companies could run more economically; they could buy in quantities and reduce duplication; had more capital to buy equipment.

6. Because people thought big corporations had too much power—they were able to drive small companies out of business, to charge any price, and they ignored the welfare of the workers. • Because the law was vaguely worded, the trusts could avoid prosecution simply by changing their corporate form; also government cases did not hold up in court.

Critical Thinking Questions

7. He is supposedly "proving" that riding the railroads is safer than staying in bed. The fault is in assuming a faulty cause-effect relationship. People who are sick and dying usually are in bed and so die in bed; beds, of course, are not the cause of death.

8. Provided mobility, adventure, comfortable travel. • Carried resources and finished goods to consumers. • Popular songs and illustrations, language.

➤ **9.** Read and do needlework and art work more easily.

10. Gave women jobs.

11. In *Munn v. Illinois*, railroads were considered public utilities. The *Wabash* case said only the federal government could control interstate commerce. Both cases led to the Interstate Commerce Commission controlling interstate commerce.

12. Realized importance to industry and agriculture. • Everyone wanted to make money in this new industry.

13. They believed some were more fit than others, whatever survived was good and competent, survival and competence meant riches. Therefore an impoverished person must be unfit for survival. • Possible

---

CHAPTER 17 REVIEW

Write your answers on a separate sheet of paper.

Key Terms and People

Explain the significance of: technology, Samuel F. B. Morse, Alexander Graham Bell, Edwin L. Drake, George M. Pullman, Oliver Kelley, bloc, rebates

Main Ideas

1. How did the development of electric power cause industry to expand? What inventions did electricity make possible in the fields of transportation, communication, and illumination? What inventions was Edison responsible for?

2. What natural resources were made more accessible to people in the last half of the nineteenth century? What new industries did they make possible?

3. Why did the builders of the transcontinental railroad turn to immigrant labor? Who were the immigrants? What dangers did workers on the Union Pacific and the Central Pacific meet?

4. Why was the Grange organized? Why did the Grange fight the railroads? What did Grangers mean when they called a railroad a public utility?

5. Describe four ways that businesses could combine to become bigger. Why were big companies supposed to be better than small companies?

6. Why was the Sherman Antitrust Act passed? Why was it a failure?

Critical Thinking Questions

7. **Analyzing Literature.** Mark Twain was a noted humorist. What is the fallacy—the error in reasoning—that he uses on page 435 to create humor?

8. **Analyzing Effects.** What did railroads do that made them so valuable for people? Why were they so valuable to agriculture and industry? Name several areas of popular culture the railroads affected.

9. **Predicting Effects.** Imagine living in the 1890's and getting electricity in your home for the first time. You have been accustomed to flickering natural gas lights in one or two spots in each room. List several things that you might do now that you have electricity that you could not do before.

10. **Assessing Cause and Effect.** How did the typewriter and the telephone boost the women's movement?

11. **Assessing Outcomes.** Review the Supreme Court rulings in *Munn* v. *Illinois* and in the *Wabash* case. How, under these rulings, could the Interstate Commerce Act be constitutional?

12. **Evaluating Decisions.** Why did the federal government give so many advantages to the railroad builders? Why were scandals like that of Crédit Mobilier allowed to develop?

13. **Contrasting Ideas.** Social Darwinists thought poverty was an indication of some defect in the individual who was impoverished. Why did they think this? Do you think this is true? Why or why not?

Critical Thinking Activities

14. **Writing a Story.** Write a Horatio Alger type of story as though you were writing for your school newspaper. Choose an entrepreneur from your schoolmates or fantasize about a successful industrial or computer tycoon.

15. **Linking Past to Present.** Explain the concept of a public utility as developed by the Grange movement. How are we indebted to the Grangers' thinking today?

16. **Linking Past to Present.** In the last half of the nineteenth century, there were holding companies, mergers, trusts, and interlocking directorates. We now have takeovers. What is the difference, if any, between the nineteenth-century ways of building large companies and today's methods? Why are many takeovers not contested today? Are they good for the workers or bad?

452

answers: yes—anyone should be able to succeed. No—many do not have means to take advantage of opportunities.

Critical Thinking Activities

➤**14.** Stories will probably include people who are good students, kind, and determined to leave poverty and seize an opportunity.

15. A privately owned industry—especially a monopoly—that provides a service to the public must submit to control by the public, through the government, for the common good. • Granger legislation set legal basis for commissions that regulate telephone and electric companies.

➤**16.** They are very similar with the exception of the way money is borrowed to finance

deals. • To counter a large takeover requires enormous resources, which are unavailable to most people. • Possible answers: good—because they make companies more efficient in production; bad—people lose jobs in takeovers.

➤**Question suitable for cooperative learning.**

The New Industrial Age

Electricity became the key to many important economic developments that helped industry to expand. Electric trolley cars helped cities to grow. The electric telegraph linked the entire nation. Edison's electric light bulb caused a revolution in lighting. Bell's telephone speeded up communication and, along with the typewriter, brought many women into the labor force. New methods of making steel brought its price down and improved its quality, making it suitable for dozens of uses. The United States was becoming the world's greatest industrial power. It had the three major natural resources of iron ore, coal, and oil. At first oil was used for lamps, but in the 1890's the by-product called gasoline was used to fuel the new internal combustion engine.

Railroads grew to be the largest industry in the nation. Their expansion westward led to the adoption of the official time zones we have today. Two railroad companies got government grants to construct a transcontinental line. The company working east to west hired war veterans, many of whom were Irish immigrants. The one working east from California employed Chinese at lower pay. The two lines met in Utah in 1869. Political corruption and overcharging, especially the Crédit Mobilier scandal, marred their triumph. Farmers organized the Grange to fight the railroads' unfair pricing practices. Congress passed the Interstate Commerce Act, which gave the federal government some power to regulate railroad rates. However, this act did not become effective until after 1901. Although the Grange eventually became soley a social organization, it established the principle that the federal government had the right to regulate private industry under certain conditions.

Many industrialists became millionaires as businesses became more complex. Andrew Carnegie is a good example of how a poor boy could rise to

wealth by hard work and keen observation. He became a multimillionaire by making his efficient steel business an integrated operation. Companies could combine in various ways, through holding companies, mergers, trusts, and interlocking directorates. Huge trusts came to dominate American businesses. Shrewd and even illegal practices earned some businessmen the name of "robber barons." The Sherman Antitrust Act of 1890 proved ineffective. Spencer's writing spread the ideas of Social Darwinism. Similar ideas were set forth in the Horatio Alger stories. These widely popular books described how young people could rise from rags to riches by honesty and hard work. Many people accepted the idea that poverty was the fault of the individual.

Chronology of Main Events

1867	Beginning of the Grange; Sholes invents typewriter
1869	First transcontinental railroad completed
1872	Crédit Mobilier scandal
1873	Carnegie founds Carnegie Steel Corporation
1876	Bell patents telephone
1877	Granger laws ruled unconstitutional
1879	Edison invents incandescent light bulb
1882	Rockefeller founds Standard Oil Trust
1887	Interstate Commerce Act
1890	Sherman Antitrust Act

Telescoping the Times may be used as an alternative to having students read the entire chapter, as a chapter preview, or as a chapter review.

Chapter 18 Teaching Strategies

Global Perspectives

1879	Britain occupies the Khyber Pass.
1887	France organizes Union of Indo-China.
1905	Japan defeats Russia in Russo-Japanese War.
1907	Britain, France, and Russia form the Triple Entente.
1909	First airplane flight is completed across English channel.
1910	Sun Zat-sen founds Nationalists Peoples Party in China.
1914	Panama Canal opens.
1914	Europeans control most of Africa.

For Discussion

How might the opening of the Panama Canal affect U.S. policy toward Asia? (Possible response: as an emerging world power the U.S. navy now had a short route between the Atlantic and Pacific and a greater ability to extend its influence in Asia.)

Additional Resources

- Geography Activities
- Skills Activities
- Thematic Activities
- Economic Activities
- Cultural Literacy Activities
- Literary Source Readings
- Primary Source Readings
- Nuclear Peacekeeping
- Transparencies
- Computer Test Generator

Additional Teaching Strategies

SECTION 1

For Basic Students: Have students research and write one paragraph explaining the meaning and origin of Labor Day as a national holiday. (Paragraphs should include: holiday set aside to honor all American workers; first celebrated in 1882.)

For Advanced Students: Ask students to research and write a newspaper editorial on the causes of and possible solutions for the problem of labor unrest during the late nineteenth and early twentieth centuries. Have students share their editorials and then discuss why the public perceived unions as a radical force trying to overthrow capitalism. (Editorials should include: a strong statement in support of unions or in support of management; suggestions for solving labor problems.)

SECTION 2

For Basic Students: Divide students into pairs and have them construct three-column charts showing the efforts in the states, in the courts, and in Congress to gain woman suffrage.

States	Courts	Congress
Wyoming gives women vote, 1869.	*Minor* v. *Happensatt.* Supreme Court rules that citizenship does not automatically include right to vote.	1878, Anthony Amendment introduced.
Congress resists Wyoming's application for statehood, but eventually admits it as state.		Committee does not recommend passage.
Utah, Colorado, Idaho pass woman suffrage bills.		Supporters reintroduce bill every year for eight years.
Fourteen states defeat woman suffrage bills.		1886, bill is called for debate and voted down.
		Bill is reintroduced again for nine years without success.

For Advanced Students: Divide the students into groups of four to research and report on the history of women's voting rights in their own state. Have students give their reports orally.

SECTION 3

For Basic Students: Ask students to write definitions for the following terms: *initiative, referendum, recall*. Have students explain in a paragraph why Populists supported these reforms. (Possible definitions: initiative—process of petitioning a legislature to introduce a bill; referendum—process in which voters can approve or reject bills already passed by a legislature; recall—procedure whereby voters can remove elected officials from office before their term ends. Populists supported these reforms because they wanted more of a say in the government and more control over the legislature so that the average man, and not special interest groups, would benefit.)

For Advanced Students: Have students research and prepare an oral presentation on Marcus Hanna, William McKinley, and William Jennings Bryan and their part in the election of 1896. (Presentation might include: Hanna was a wealthy Ohio businessman who supported and raised money for McKinley's campaign; McKinley stayed at home and addressed the crowds from his front porch during his campaign; McKinley ran on the Republican ticket, stressing high tariffs and maintenance of the gold standard; Bryan ran on the Democratic-Populist ticket, in direct opposition to McKinley.)

Further Reading for Students

Historical Fiction

Bellamy, Edward. *Looking Backward*. New York: Penguin, 1982. Paper.

Hale, Edward Everett. *The Man Without a Country*. Cutchogue, N.Y.: Buccaneer Books, 1988.

Harte, Bret. *The Luck of Roaring Camp*. Providence, R.I.: Jamestown Publishing, 1976.

London, Jack. *The Iron Heel*. Little Neck, N.Y.: Lawrence Hill, 1980.

Norris, Frank. *The Octopus*. New York: Penguin, 1986. Paper.

Sinclair, Upton. *The Jungle*. New York: Bantam, 1981.

Bibliography for Teachers

Books

Burnett, Constance B. *Five for Freedom: Lucretia Mott, Elizabeth Cady Stanton, Lucy Stone, Susan B. Anthony, Carrie Chapman Catt*. Westport, Conn.: Greenwood Press, 1968.

Gompers, Samuel, *Labor and the Common Welfare*. Salem, N.H.: Ayer Co. Publishing, 1969.

Hicks, John D. *The Populist Revolt: A History of the Farmers' Alliance and the People's Party*. Westport, Conn.: Greenwood Press, 1981.

Hofstadter, Richard, ed. *The Progressive Movement 1900-1915*. New York: Simon and Schuster, 1986.

Lindsey, Almont. *The Pullman Strike*. Chicago: University of Chicago Press, 1964.

Nevins, Allan, ed. *Letters of Grover Cleveland, 1850-1908*. New Jersey City, N.J.: DaCapo, 1970.

Peterson, Florence. *Strikes in the United States 1880-1936*. St. Clair Shores, Mich.: Scholarly, 1972.

Takaki, Ronald. *Strangers from a Different Shore: A History of Asian Americans*. Boston: Little, Brown, 1989.

Audio-Visuals

The Blue Collar Trap. Indiana University Audio-Visual Center. Movie.

The Gilded Age. Prentice-Hall Media. Filmstrip.

Great Men and Great Issues: Industrial Growth Transforms the Nation. Wilcom, Inc. Four audio tapes.

Money on the Land. Time-Life Video. Movie.

The Progressive Era. Encyclopaedia Britannica Educational Corporation. Movie.

Progressives, Populists and Reform in America (1890-1917). Guidance Associates. Movie.

Computer Resources

American History II. (Apple) Silwa Enterprises, Inc.

Social Studies Volume I. (Apple No. 710) MECC.

The Time Tunnel—American History 1860-1920. (Apple) Focus Media, Inc.

Teacher's Notes:

Lesson Plan

Teaching Resources, Unit 4 Booklet
Lesson Study Sheets pp. 103-114
Daily Activities pp. 115-120
Enrichment Activities pp. 121-126
Reteaching Activities pp. 127-132
Chapter Review p. 133
Chapter Mastery Tests pp. 135-146
Telescoping the Times Study Sheet p. 147
Unit Mastery Tests pp. 149-160
Telescoping the Times Unit 4 Study Sheet
  p. 161

Chapter Objectives
Students will learn:
- how labor attempted to organize unions and why most of them failed
- the successes and failures of both government and private efforts at political reform
- the cause and effects of the third party reform movement known as Populism

Picturing History A suffragette marches down Fifth Avenue in New York City to call attention to women's rights. Women earned the right to vote in 1920, but only after a long struggle.

Using the Chapter Time Line
What two events during this period indicate the growing importance of labor? (Answer: American Federation of Labor founded, Pullman rail strike) Which President served during the Haymarket Riot? (Answer: Grover Cleveland)

1875	1885	1895	1905	1915

1881
- James A. Garfield inaugurated President
- Chester A. Arthur succeeds to Presidency

1885
Grover Cleveland inaugurated President

1886
- Haymarket riot
- American Federation of Labor founded

1889
Benjamin Harrison inaugurated President

1894
Pullman strike

1897
William McKinley inaugurated President

1911
Triangle Shirtwaist Company fire

454

Links to American Literature

Gore Vidal: was known as a political activist; was co-chairman of the People's party from 1970 to 1972; ran as a Democratic candidate for Congress from New York City.

Works include: plays; short stories; essays; *Williwaw; Burr.*

1876: written in 1976; focuses on the ambitions of Charlie Schuyler who, with his daughter, finds himself at the center of American social and political power when the country is turning from the ideals of a young republic to the excitement of an empire.

Introducing the Chapter

Ask students to recall the expansion of the railroad system and the growth of business as described in Chapter 17 and consider how this growth might have affected the common worker. Have students list on the board some possible problems workers might have encountered. (Problems might include: low wages for long hours; high prices resulting from monopolies.) Have students refer to this list as they study Chapter 18. Ask students to look at the illustrations in this chapter to find clues about the life style of the American worker.

CHAPTER **18** 1876-1915

Unionism, Political Reforms, and Populism

Links to American Literature

The Republican nominee for president of the United States is one Rutherford Birchard Hayes, three times governor of Ohio, a general of no distinction in the late war, and a man entirely unknown to most of the convention that has just nominated him. . . . Rutherford B. Hayes, who is, this morning's paper informs us, fifty-three years old, five feet eight inches tall, and weighs one hundred and seventy pounds—which is plainly wishful thinking on the part of the Governor, who must weigh, according to his photograph, about two hundred pounds; he has a long grizzled beard, an aquiline nose, and a fierce gaze. . . .

In silence the votes of each state were read and tallied. Hayes was elected president by a single vote. Nor was the silence broken as Ferry intoned, "Wherefore, I do declare: that Rutherford B. Hayes, of Ohio, having received a majority of the whole number of electoral votes, is duly elected president. . . ."

There was no applause. Only a long weary sigh from the embattled Congress. . . .

Today, for the first time since Lincoln's murder, the front page of the New York Sun *appeared with a band of mourning.*

— GORE VIDAL, *1876*

The growth of industry caused widespread discontent among workers. This discontent was mirrored by unrest on the political stage. The Presidential election of Rutherford B. Hayes is an example of this unrest. Hayes set about his self-appointed task of social reform by issuing executive orders. Although he failed to bring about lasting reform, he was able to restore the American people's faith in government simply because he was a man of integrity.

Chapter Overview

The stories of people in this chapter caution us to avoid stereotypes of politicians and reformers. As the drama of American history unfolds, we need to remember that good and evil can be found on both sides of many issues. In this chapter, you will learn about labor's attempts to organize unions. You will also learn about civil service reform and why woman suffrage did not become a reality until

1920. Finally, you will learn about the third-party movement known as Populism and its consequences. Chapter 18 tells the story of all these movements in three sections.

Chapter Outline

1. **Workers Organize**
2. **Demands for Political Reforms Grow**
3. **Farmers Begin the Populist Movement**

Anticipate the Lesson

Tell students that as business and industry grew so did discontent on the part of the workers. Ask students to list reasons one might be unhappy with a job. (Possible responses: boring work; low pay; unsatisfactory work conditions; inconvenient hours.) What recourse do unhappy workers have? (Possible responses: put up with job; quit; talk to management.)

State the Objective

Understand labor's attempts to organize unions and the reasons why most of them failed.

SECTION 1

Workers Organize

GLOSSARY TERMS: **strike, yellow-dog contracts, scabs, arbitration, American Federation of Labor, craft unions, collective bargaining, industrial unionism, injunction**

When the Civil War broke out, there were about 1.3 million factory workers in the United States. By 1900 the figure had risen to 5.3 million, with an additional 4 million people employed in construction and transportation.

A growing work force was not the only effect of industrialization. More important were the basic changes in the working conditions of labor and the development of a new spirit of unity on the part of many workers.

Workers Have Cause for Complaints

Perhaps the biggest change for workers in the new industrial age was the fact that they were now machine operators, not artisans. Before, a shoemaker, for example, made an entire shoe. Now a worker using a machine made only a small part of the shoe, such as the sole. Since no particular ability was needed to run the machine, the worker could take little satisfaction in doing the job. Also, since anyone could run the machine, the worker could easily be replaced.

Loss of Freedom. In addition to losing skills, workers lost a sense of comradeship and personal freedom. A cigar maker described conditions in earlier times this way:

> The craftsmanship of the cigar maker was shown in his ability to utilize wrappers to the best advantage, to shave off the unusable to a hairbreadth, to roll so as to cover holes in the leaf and to use both hands so as to make a perfectly shaped and rolled product. These things a good cigar maker learned to do more or less mechanically, which left us free to think, talk, listen, or sing. . . . Often we chose someone to read to us who was a particularly good reader, and in payment the rest of us gave him sufficient of our cigars so he was not the loser.

With the introduction of machines, there was no longer any talking or singing or listening. The machines made too much noise, and there were usually factory rules prohibiting these activities. The emphasis was on increasing production.

Loss of Identity. Still another result of industrialization was a growing gap between workers and employers. In the past a boss knew all those who worked in the shop, saw them as distinct human beings, and often took a personal interest in their welfare. To Andrew Carnegie, on the other hand, the thousands of workers in his steel mills could only be abstract numbers.

Long Hours, Low Wages. Factory workers were expected to put in long hours at their jobs. A typical workweek was twelve hours a day, six days a week. For some industries the seven-day week

---

People in the Chapter

Chester Arthur refused to move into the White House after Garfield's assassination. He described the White House as "a badly kept barracks" and had twenty-four wagonloads of furniture removed before having it redecorated.

Benjamin Harrison moved into the White House with his extended family of eleven persons. At the time, the Executive Mansion had only one bathroom.

Elizabeth Cady Stanton delivered her address on women's rights to the New York State Legislature. Afterwards a woman in the audience asked, "What have you done with your children?" Mrs. Stanton replied, "It takes me no longer to speak than you to listen, what have you done with your children the two hours you have been sitting here?"

Julia Ward Howe wrote "The Battle Hymn of the Republic" while visiting an army camp. She sold it to the *Atlantic Monthly* for four dollars. It was then set to an old folk tune also used for "John Brown's Body."

was the rule. There were no vacations or days off for sickness. Nor was there any unemployment compensation.

For these long hours, workers averaged between $3 and $12 a week. By contrast, the weekly cost of living for a family of six in 1864 was $18.50 a week, and this excluded entertainment and clothing.

Dangerous Working Conditions. In addition to long hours and low pay, working conditions in many industries were extremely hazardous. There was no payment for injuries suffered on the job. In the railroad industry, for example, some 230,000 workers were killed and more than 2 million were injured between 1890 and 1917.

The dangers of working in the coal mines were described by a reporter in 1906:

> Crouched over the chutes, the boys sit hour after hour picking out the pieces of slate and other refuse from the coal as it rushes past to the washers. . . . The coal is hard, and accidents to the hands, such as cut, broken or crushed fingers, are common. . . . Sometimes there is a worse accident: a terrified shriek is heard, and a boy is mangled and torn in the machinery, or disappears in the chutes to be picked out later smothered and dead.

Child Labor. "The most beautiful sight that we see is the child at labor." This statement was typical of what many Americans in the new industrial age believed: namely, that idleness for children was bad and that factories were a godsend that would keep children from wasting their lives. A second argument in favor of child labor was economic necessity. Many families could not have survived unless everyone worked. As a result, by 1910 one out of every five children under the age of fifteen was earning wages. Many child workers were as young as five.

In 1903 reporter Maria Van Vorst described children coming home from the textile mills at eight o'clock in the evening:

> They are usually beyond speech. They fall asleep at the table, on the stairs; they are carried to bed and there laid down as they are, unwashed, undressed; and the . . . bundles of rags so lie until the mill summons them with its . . . cry before sunrise.

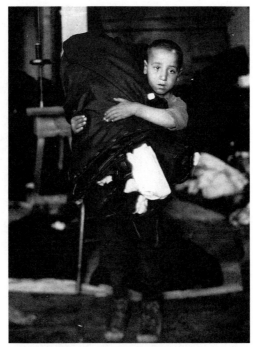

Picturing History A child carries home piecework. Long hours and little pay meant a life of little hope.

Child workers suffered in still another way. Going to work meant giving up school and thus any possibility of a better life as adults.

The Sweatshop System. The growth in manufacturing also gave rise to the sweatshop system in which certain products were made in people's homes. For example, a wholesale clothing manufacturer would parcel work out to a subcontractor known as a "sweater." The sweater usually set up shop in two rooms of a tenement flat. In one room, anywhere from six to twenty employees worked, ate, and slept. The sweater lived in the other room.

The manufacturer provided the supplies, but the workers were required to furnish the tools, such as sewing machines, needles, scissors, and the like. Payment was on a piecework basis. The more goods the worker turned out, the more money the worker received. In 1910 the average weekly earnings were five dollars for about one hundred hours of work.

Mr. Pullman's Town. "We are born in a Pullman house, fed from the Pullman shop, taught in

Tell students that in the late 1800's workers tried to improve their working conditions by forming unions. On the board construct a five-column chart headed by the names of the national labor unions discussed in this section: NLU, Knights of Labor, AFL, ARU, and ILGWU. Ask students to review the section and list under each heading information such as start-up date, type of union, leader, membership, goals and tactics, accomplishments, and reasons for decline. Charts should include:

NLU

- Started in 1866
- Was a federation of unions
- Led by William H. Sylvis
- Consisted of 300 local unions
- Organized political party
- Persuaded Congress to pass eight-hour work day for federal employees
- Ran candidate for President in 1872
- Declined due to depression of 1873

Picturing History
"Breaker boys" work in a coal mine. By 1914 most states prohibited child labor under a specified age, usually fourteen.

For Discussion

What workers' grievances mentioned in this section are still considered problems today? (Possible response: low wages and dangerous conditions in some industries like mining and meatpacking.) What new grievances might workers have today? (Possible responses: insufficient benefits; layoffs; lack of maternity/paternity leave; insufficient sick leave or retirement benefits.)

the Pullman school, catechized in the Pullman church, and when we die we shall be buried in the Pullman cemetery and go to the Pullman hell.'' So said one of the five thousand workers at the Pullman Palace Car Company, then the largest manufacturer of passenger railway cars. The worker was referring to the town of Pullman that George M. Pullman had built on the outskirts of Chicago in 1880.

Like hundreds of other factory communities, Pullman was a company town. Only company workers and their families lived in the town, and the company owned everything in it. Pullman determined the wages his workers received. He also fixed the rents they paid and the prices of goods in the company store. Pullman even appointed the town's government, including policemen and school teachers. Spies reported anyone who criticized the company. As the *New York Sun* stated in 1885, ''The people of Pullman are not happy. . . . They want to run the municipal government themselves, according to the ordinary American fashion.''

The Labor Movement Takes Shape

As the new industrial age developed, many workers began to feel that they had to do something to improve their lot. Skilled workers had formed local unions in the early 1800's. However, it was not until 1866 that the first national federation came into being. Manufacturers were now conducting

business on a national basis. It seemed reasonable for workers to do the same.

The National Labor Union. The new organization was called the National Labor Union (NLU). It consisted of about three hundred local unions from thirteen states, led by an iron molder named William H. Sylvis. Its main demand was for an eight-hour workday. How would labor get the eight-hour day? Sylvis's answer was political action. He urged labor to organize its own national party, the way workers in Europe were doing.

Sylvis also argued in favor of including women and blacks in the NLU. Kate Mullaney, head of the Laundry Workers Union in Troy, New York, became assistant secretary of the national federation. The carpenters and joiners agreed to open their locals to black members. Other unions, however, refused to follow suit.

The NLU grew to 650,000 members. In 1868 it persuaded Congress to pass an eight-hour law for government workers. In 1872 it ran a candidate for President on the Labor Reform party ticket.

Then came the depression of 1873. The National Labor Union did not survive.

The Great Strike. CITY IN POSSESSION OF COMMUNISTS, the newspaper headline screamed. It was announcing the first nationwide **strike** in United States history.

The strike began in July 1877, organized by workers for the Baltimore and Ohio Railroad in

Check for Understanding

Call on individual students to answer Section 1
Review questions orally.

West Virginia. Ever since the 1873 depression, the railroad industry had been in trouble. In an effort to lower costs and still pay the 8 to 10 percent annual dividend that stockholders expected, railroad management had cut wage rates 35 percent, lengthened the workday from fifteen to eighteen hours, and doubled the train size.

Then, on July 11, the railroad announced yet another pay cut. On July 16, when the new pay scale went into effect, forty firemen and brakemen quit their jobs in protest. They were replaced at once, and the freight trains started down the line. When they reached Martinsburg, West Virginia, sympathetic trainmen surrounded the railroad depot. No trains would leave, they said, until wages were restored to their original level. The wives and mothers of the trainmen, who joined the demonstration, agreed. "Better to starve outright," said one of them, "than to die by slow starvation."

Meanwhile, a sympathy strike broke out in Pittsburgh. Federal troops were summoned to break up the demonstration. They killed twenty-six strikers and wounded hundreds. Enraged by this bloodshed, some twenty thousand persons, including thousands of workers from Pittsburgh's steel mills and coal mines, attacked the federal troops and drove them out of the city. Then they began to destroy railroad property.

Similar strikes flared up all along the nation's railroad lines. Everywhere, federal troops were used against peaceful strikers and rioters alike.

By August 2 order had been restored and trains began running again. Most workers who had gone out on strike lost their jobs. However, the workers had made their point. Most railroads decided either to restore wage cuts or at least not to lower wages any further.

After the strike, railroads and many other corporations began to organize against unions. Companies required new employees to sign **yellow-dog contracts,** that is, pledges not to join a union. They also hired private detectives to spy on union members and to serve as **scabs,** or strikebreakers. These outsiders were called **Pinkertons** after the Pinkerton Detective Agency, which had become famous for this type of work. Nevertheless, the American union movement continued to develop as a new national organization rose to prominence.

The Knights of Labor. The Noble Order of the Knights of Labor was organized in 1869 by **Uriah Stephens,** a garment cutter from Philadelphia. It started out as a secret society, with a password and a distinctive hand grip that members used when greeting one another. Its motto was "An injury to one is the concern of all."

Unlike the NLU, the **Knights of Labor** was an organization of individuals rather than unions. Membership was open to all workers regardless of race, sex, or degree of skill. The only occupations that were excluded were lawyers, bankers, professional gamblers, and liquor dealers.

Like the NLU, the Knights supported the eight-hour day. They were opposed to child and convict labor. They championed health and safety laws. They advocated "equal pay for equal work" for men and women. These ideas were considered quite radical at the time.

The Knights believed that the road to labor success lay in political activity and in the education of the public. They did not favor the use of strikes except as a last resort. They preferred **arbitration,** that is, the settlement of disagreements between employers and workers by an impartial third party.

At first the Knights grew slowly. Then in 1879 a mechanic named **Terence V. Powderly** of Scranton, Pennsylvania, became the order's Grand Master Workman. Under his leadership, the Knights expanded from 28,000 members in 1880 to about 700,000 in 1886.

One reason for the Knights' success was that Powderly was an excellent leader. An energetic

Picturing History Striking workers pull the crew off a train in West Virginia. Federal troops were called in when the local militia refused to fire on the strikers.

Guided Practice

Ask students the following questions to stimulate a discussion on the rights and responsibilities of workers and employers. Do you feel that
laborers have a right to join unions and make
demands? Is it an employer's right to hire and
fire whomever he or she wants? (Possible responses: laborers have the right, and even the
duty, to join unions; if they do not work for their
own rights, they cannot expect respect from
their employers; an employer can hire and fire
whomever he or she wishes; it is an employer's
responsibility to do what is best for the company.)

organizer and a superb orator, he electrified people
wherever he spoke. Also, Powderly dropped the
Knights' veil of secrecy and made the organization
public.

A second reason for the Knights' success was,
ironically, a series of successful strikes. The most
important were those against Jay Gould's railroads.
The Knights struck several of Gould's lines to
cancel pay cuts, and they won. When Gould's
Wabash line fired several hundred men for being
union members, the Knights ordered its members
to refuse to handle Wabash railroad cars and
locomotives. Although Gould had once boasted, "I
can hire one-half the working class to kill the other
half," he could not afford to have all work stop on
twenty thousand miles of railroad track. He rehired
the fired workers and membership in the Knights
grew by leaps and bounds.

Yet the Knights' days of glory were numbered.
By the mid-1890's, the organization was practically extinct. Its downfall can be laid to two main
factors: the **Haymarket affair** and the rise of the
American Federation of Labor.

The Haymarket Affair.   The evening of May 4,
1886, was windy and chilly, with a hint of rain in
the air. Haymarket Square, in Chicago, was filled
with some twelve hundred people. They were listening to three so-called radicals—Albert Parsons, August Spies, and Samuel Fielden—who were arguing
in favor of the eight-hour day and were condemning
a police action that had taken place on May 3. There
had been a fight between pickets and strikebreakers
at the McCormick Harvester plant. The police had
killed four workers and wounded several others.

Shortly after ten o'clock, rain began to fall. As
the crowd broke up, about one hundred eighty
policemen appeared in the square. Suddenly, there
was a terrific explosion. Someone had thrown a
dynamite bomb! It hit the ground near the police
column, killing seven officers and wounding sixty-
seven others. The police immediately opened fire
and then charged on horseback. When the shooting
and clubbing were over, ten workers lay dead and
another fifty wounded.

No one knows, even today, who threw the bomb.
However, the police arrested Parsons, Spies, and
Fielden. They also arrested five other radicals who
in the past had advocated violence. Although only
three of the accused men were actually in Haymarket Square and although there was no proof that
any of them had either planted or thrown a bomb,

Picturing History   Samuel Gompers favored organizing
workers by crafts. He headed the AFL for some
thirty-seven years.

all eight men were convicted. Four of them, including Parsons and Spies, were hanged.

Like those convicted of the crime, the Knights of
Labor had no known connection to the Haymarket
violence. Yet, because they were the leading labor
organization involved in the strike at the McCormick Harvester plant, they paid for it. Throughout
the press they were pictured as a gang of radicals
with bombs in their pockets. Public opinion swung
sharply against them.

The American Federation of Labor.   The
Knights of Labor had been organized on the basis
that all workers had the same interests. Therefore,
there was no need for specialized unions. Now a
different kind of unionism was developing. Known
as bread-and-butter unionism, its interest was less
in political reform and more in shorter hours,
higher wages, and better working conditions for
skilled, specialized workers. The ideas came
mainly from a man named **Samuel Gompers.**

Gompers was born in London of Dutch-Jewish
parents. His father, a cigar maker, was active in the
British cigar makers' union. Young Gompers absorbed both his father's skill and his views on

unions. At the age of thirteen, he came to the United States and went to work in a cigar-making shop.

In 1881 Gompers helped found the Federation of Organized Trade and Labor Unions of the United States of America and Canada. The name was shortened in 1886 to the **American Federation of Labor** (AFL). Gompers was elected president in 1886, and except for one year, he continued to lead the organization until his death in 1924.

Like the NLU, the AFL was a federation of unions. However, the unions were national rather than local, and they included skilled workers only. Unskilled workers were not permitted to join. Women and blacks, for the most part, were also excluded. Unions that include only skilled workers in a particular craft are known as **craft unions.**

The AFL was, in Gomper's words, "the business organization of the workers." It avoided third-party political activity. Instead, it supported whichever candidate or party agreed with its demands. It used **collective bargaining,** or group negotiations between workers and their employers, whenever possible, and strikes whenever necessary. It succeeded in its basic goals. Between 1890 and 1915, the average weekly wages in unionized industries rose from $17.57 to $23.98, while the average workweek fell from 54.4 to 48.9 hours.

In spite of these successes, craft unionism was limited. The problem was that skilled workers made up less than 30 percent of the labor force. Most workers were unskilled or semiskilled. Moreover, their numbers kept growing as big business broke production down into increasingly simpler tasks.

Some labor leaders began to feel that craft unionism was not the answer. In their opinion, the future of labor lay in **industrial unionism,** that is, in organizing workers—whether skilled or unskilled—who worked in the same industry.

The American Railway Union. The man who made the first major attempt at industrial unionism was **Eugene V. Debs.** Debs went to work in the railroad yards when he was fourteen years old. Later he became an officer of the Brotherhood of Locomotive Firemen and Enginemen, to which only skilled workers belonged.

In 1893 the Switchmen's Union went on strike. Debs's brotherhood and three others refused to support the strike. Disgusted, Debs resigned his union position and organized the American Rail-

Picturing History Eugene Debs, shown here on the campaign trail, ran for the Presidency in 1900, 1904, 1908, 1912, and 1920.

way Union to include all railroad workers. Most of its members were unskilled and semiskilled workers who were not eligible for the brotherhoods. However, many skilled engineers and firemen joined, too. Despite Debs's efforts, blacks were not admitted.

The next year the American Railway Union won a strike for higher wages. Within two months its membership climbed to 150,000 compared with 90,000 in the four brotherhoods. Debs's idea that workers had to "march together, vote together, and fight together" seemed to be on its way.

The Industrial Workers of the World Unite

In 1905 a group of radical unionists and socialists made a second attempt at industrial unionism. The new organization was called the Industrial Workers of the World (IWW), and its members became known as Wobblies.

The head of the IWW was William "Big Bill" Haywood, a former hard-rock miner. Haywood used to explain the difference between craft unionism and industrial unionism in the following way:

Student Assignment/Homework

Have students read Section 2, "Demands for Political Reforms Grow."

"The A. F. of L. organizes like this!" [he would say], separating his fingers, as far apart as they would go, and naming them—weavers, loom-fixers, dyers, spinners. Then he would say, "The I.W.W. organizes like this!"—tightly clenching his big fist, shaking it at the bosses.

Most of the IWW's organizing took place in the West, and most of its members were miners, lumbermen, and cannery and dock workers. Unlike the AFL, the IWW included both women and blacks. But the IWW never attracted more than 150,000 workers at its peak. Its only major strike victory took place in the textile town of Lawrence, Massachusetts, in 1912. Then during World War I, IWW membership dwindled. Yet the IWW influenced the American labor movement. It proved that unskilled workers *could* be organized. It gave unskilled workers a sense of dignity and self-worth.

Women Become Labor Organizers

There had always been women who worked for wages in the United States. As the new industrial age developed, their numbers increased until, by 1910, they made up about 21 percent of the labor force. Most were concentrated in certain industries, such as textiles, the garment trade, tobacco, and retail sales, as well as nursing and teaching. In general, they held so-called women's jobs. These were usually unskilled and offered very little opportunity for moving up the job or pay ladder. Wages were a far cry from equal pay for equal work. Women earned about one-third to one-half as much money as men, even for the same kind of work.

As the union movement developed in the United States, several women organizers became prominent. Among them were Mary Harris Jones and Pauline Newman.

Mother Jones of the Mines and Mills. During the 1880's and 1890's, almost every mining town had a "mother." Her job was to mobilize the miners' wives when their husbands went out on strike. The women would bang on tin pans to frighten the mine mules and would throw garbage on the scabs whom the mining companies hired. If the women were imprisoned for disturbing the

Picturing History Mary Harris ("Mother") Jones was strongly identified with the mine labor movement, but she organized strikes and demonstrations in several other industries, too.

peace, they would take their babies to jail with them. The more their babies cried at night, the less time the women usually had to spend behind bars.

The most famous mining town mother was Mary Harris Jones. **Mother Jones** took part in her first labor action during the great railroad strike of 1887. From then on, she devoted her life to the labor movement.

Although Mother Jones concentrated her organizing efforts on the mining industry, she did not stop there. In the spring of 1903, she was in Kensington, Pennsylvania, where some seventy-five thousand textile workers were on strike. About ten thousand were children. Mother Jones was horrified by how many were stooped and old at the age of ten, or were missing fingers and even hands that had been cut off by mill machinery. She decided she must do something to arouse public opinion against child labor.

The idea that Mother Jones came up with was a children's march to see President Theodore Roosevelt at his home in Oyster Bay, Long Island. She received permission from Kensington mothers to take about eighty children on a week's march. The children carried signs that read "We want more schools and less hospitals," "We want time to play," and "Prosperity is here. Where is ours?"

In New York, Mother Jones addressed a crowd of some twenty thousand sympathetic people. She said:

> Fifty years ago, there was a cry against slavery and men gave up their lives to stop the selling of black children on the block. Today the white child is sold for two dollars a week to the manufacturers. Fifty years ago the black babies were sold C.O.D. Today the white baby is sold on the installment plan.

Mother Jones and the children never managed to see President Roosevelt. Yet the march was a success in the long run. It drew a tremendous amount of publicity, and a year later Pennsylvania passed a law prohibiting child labor under the age of fourteen.

Pauline Newman of the Garment Trade. Pauline Newman went to work for the Triangle Shirtwaist Company in 1901 when she was eight years old. In 1909, at the age of sixteen, she became the first woman organizer for the International Ladies Garment Workers Union (ILGWU). Her first task was to raise money to support the "Uprising of the

Picturing History The 1911 fire at the Triangle Shirtwaist Company factory in New York City killed 146 workers in the Triangle factory district and aroused the sympathy and anger of people all over the nation.

20,000." This was a general strike that broke out against New York City's garment industry. About three-fourths of the strikers were young women between the ages of sixteen and twenty-five, and almost all were either Jewish or Italian. The strike lasted thirteen weeks and achieved many of its goals, including a fifty-two-hour, instead of a fifty-nine hour, workweek.

The Triangle Shirtwaist Company, however, refused to agree to all the union's demands. Eventually, its employees returned to work under what they considered dangerous working conditions.

On March 25, 1911, a fire broke out at the Triangle factory. Since there was no sprinkler system, the flames spread swiftly through the oil-soaked machines and piles of cloth. It quickly engulfed the seventh, eighth, and ninth floors. The workers tried desperately to escape. All the factory doors were locked except one, and it opened inward instead of outward. The one fire escape went down only to the second floor. Some workers leaped from the windows, only to crash through the

Answers

Main Ideas

1. They became machine operators rather than artisans; their jobs often were more dangerous and provided less social contact; they were more anonymous to their employers.

2. Groups of workers subcontracted to make products in homes. They were paid on a piecework basis.

3. Unlike the Knights of Labor and NLU, Gompers avoided politics, working instead for shorter hours, better working conditions, and higher wages, through a national union composed only of white male skilled workers.

4. Unskilled industrial workers could organize and win strikes if they were united at all times.

5. Courts issued injunctions prohibiting strike activity on the grounds that strikes were "a conspiracy in restraint of trade."

Critical Thinking

6. Mother Jones's March and the Triangle Shirtwaist Company fire. • Possible answer: as more women entered the work force and became labor leaders, the rights of women laborers received more attention by government. **(analysis)**

---

fire department's safety nets to the street below. In all, 146 workers died.

On April 5 about 120,000 men, women, and children marched in silence in the pouring rain to honor the Triangle dead. The two owners of the Triangle Shirtwaist Company were tried on manslaughter charges but were acquitted. The jurors regarded the accident as an act of God.

The general public, however, took a different view. A task force was set up to look into factory working conditions throughout the state. Its members included Alfred E. Smith, later the 1928 Democratic candidate for President, and **Frances Perkins,** later the nation's first woman cabinet member, Secretary of Labor under President Franklin D. Roosevelt.

As a result of the investigation, the New York legislature passed several laws to improve working conditions. They provided for, among other things, strict fire safety codes in factories, a fifty-four-hour workweek for women and minors, the prohibition of Sunday work, and the abolition of child labor under the age of fourteen years.

Government Supports Management

Despite these victories, both craft and industrial unions found it difficult to make much progress. This occurred primarily because government used its powers to support management against labor.

One example of this took place in 1894. A dispute over wage cuts at the Pullman Company had escalated into a strike by 125,000 members of the American Railway Union (ARU). Within four days, rail traffic between Chicago and the West Coast was just about at a standstill. At this point, the General Managers Association, an organization of twenty-four of the nation's biggest railroads, decided to step in.

First the managers brought in scabs. Then they asked United States Attorney General Richard Olney, a former railroad lawyer, for help. Olney convinced President Cleveland to send in federal troops to guarantee the delivery of mail. In truth, however, the ARU strike was not interfering with mail trains at all.

Olney then appointed a special federal attorney, who promptly sought an **injunction,** or court order, prohibiting all strike activity against the railroads. He argued that railroads were not a private business but "a public highway." If workers quit as a group, they were interfering with interstate commerce.

The court agreed and issued the injunction.

The combination of federal troops and the injunction was too much for the union. Soon after, the strike ended, and the American Railway Union fell apart.

The use of the injunction gave business a strong edge over unions. All a company had to do was say that a strike, a picket line, or a boycott would hurt its sales. A federal or state court would then issue an injunction on the grounds that such activity by a union was "a conspiracy in restraint of trade" and violated the Sherman Antitrust Act of 1890.

Some judges went even further. They prohibited unions from supporting strikes "by letters, printed or other circulars, telegrams or telephones, word of mouth, oral persuasion, or suggestion, or through interviews to be published in newspapers."

Under these conditions, unions found it difficult to organize workers. In 1910 only 8.3 percent of industrial workers were in unions.

SECTION 1 REVIEW

Key Terms and People

Explain the significance of: strike, yellow-dog contracts, scabs, Pinkertons, Uriah Stephens, Knights of Labor, arbitration, Terence V. Powderly, Haymarket affair, Samuel Gompers, American Federation of Labor, craft unions, collective bargaining, industrial unionism, Eugene V. Debs, Mother Jones, Frances Perkins, injunction

Main Ideas

1. What changes did workers face during the industrialization of the late nineteenth century?
2. What was the sweatshop system?
3. How did the methods of the Knights of Labor and the NLU differ from the bread-and-butter unionism of Samuel Gompers?
4. What idea did Eugene Debs contribute to unionism?
5. How was the Sherman Antitrust Act of 1890 used in the context of labor-management disputes?

Critical Thinking

6. Which two dramatic events led to improved working conditions in the garment industry? Analyze the relationship between these events and the increase of women in the work force.

SECTION 2

Demands for Political Reforms Grow

GLOSSARY TERMS: **patronage, merit system, civil service, laissez faire**

Making money was the American dream in the new industrial age, and politicians were as eager to do so as business people. In fact, the level of corruption that existed in national politics from 1870 to 1896 led writer Mark Twain to call the period "the Gilded Age." In a novel of that name (written in collaboration with Charles Dudley Warner), Twain had a United States senator declare, "I think I can say, and say with pride, that we have some legislatures that bring higher prices than any in the world." Thus, the term **Gilded Age** came to be used to describe the outwardly showy but inwardly corrupt culture of the era of industrialization.

At the same time, the Gilded Age saw the beginnings of several movements to bring about political reforms. These movements represented a growing belief that as society changed, government should change as well.

Civil Service Replaces Patronage

From James K. Polk on, every President complained about the amount of time he spent on problems of **patronage.** Patronage is the practice of giving jobs to those who help a candidate get elected. If the candidate wins, to him or her belong the spoils—hence the phrase "spoils system."

Not only cabinet positions were involved in Presidential patronage. Even people who scrubbed the steps of federal buildings got their jobs through the referral of a political boss. Consequently, with each change of administration there were always thousands of positions to fill. It was up to the President to make the final decision.

Gradually, many people began to press for a federal **merit system** to replace the spoils system. (See Chapter 10.) Under the merit system, jobs in **civil service,** or government administration, would go to the most qualified persons, no matter what political views they held or who recommended them.

Hayes Versus the Stalwarts. About one month after being declared winner of the 1876 election, Republican President **Rutherford B. Hayes** wrote in his diary, "Now for Civil Service Reform." Unfortunately, Hayes was unable to get legislative support for his ideas, even from members of his own party. So he did what he could through executive orders and appointments.

Hayes began by naming able independents to his cabinet. One appointee set up a merit system in his department. Another took the unheard-of step of

Picturing History Three Presidents who served during the Gilded Age: Rutherford B. Hayes, 1877-1881; James A. Garfield, 1881; and Chester A. Arthur, 1881-1885. Although the period during which they presided was a time of corruption, it was also a time of movement toward political reform.

Present the Lesson

Divide the class into three groups. Have each group review the section and prepare a list of events that led to changes in one of the following areas: Civil Service, Tariffs, or Women's Suffrage. Have each group leader write his or her outline on the board. Encourage the class to refer to the outlines as they study this section. Outlines might include the following information:

Civil Service

- Jobs were traditionally given out according to spoils system.
- People began to press for federal merit system.
- President Hayes used executive orders and appointments to reform civil service jobs.
- President Garfield continued reforms.
- President Arthur continued reforms and urged passage of civil service law.
- Pendleton Act of 1883 provided for open competitive exams.

firing clerks who did not have enough work to do.

Hayes's next act was to appoint a commission to investigate the nation's customshouses. These customshouses were a source of great corruption. The New York Customs House, for example, had more than one thousand employees, all of whom spent most of their time working for the Republican party.

When the commission turned in its report, Hayes fired the two top officials at the New York Customs House. Senator Roscoe Conkling, the New York Republican boss, was outraged. Conkling and his supporters, who were called **Stalwarts,** waged political war on the President for the rest of his term.

Garfield Continues Reform. Hayes decided not to run for reelection in 1880. So there was a free-for-all at the Republican convention between Conkling's Stalwarts and reform Republicans. Since neither side could obtain a majority, the convention finally settled on an independent candidate, Congressman **James A. Garfield** of Ohio. Garfield, however, was a close personal friend of the reform candidate. Therefore, the Republicans decided to balance the ticket by nominating a lieutenant of Conkling's for Vice-President. He was **Chester A. Arthur,** one of the two officials of the New York Customs House whom Hayes had fired.

Once elected, Garfield gave anti-Conkling Republicans most of the patronage positions at his disposal. He even appointed one as head of the New York Customs House. The Stalwarts were furious.

On July 2, 1881, the President went to the Washington, D.C., railroad station to travel to his twenty-fifth college reunion. As he strolled through the station, two shots rang out. They were fired by a mentally unbalanced lawyer named Charles Guiteau, whom Garfield had turned down for a job. As police officials seized the assassin, he shouted, "I did it and will go to jail for it. I am a Stalwart and Arthur will be President." Garfield lingered throughout the summer but finally died from the gunshot wounds on September 19. Guiteau was convicted of murder and hanged.

Arthur and the Pendleton Act. To everyone's amazement, once he became President, Arthur turned reformer. In his first message to Congress, he urged the legislators to pass a civil service law.

Under the **Pendleton Act** of 1883, sponsored by Senator George H. Pendleton, the President was authorized to appoint a three-member, bipartisan civil service commission. The commission was to give "open competitive examinations" to all applicants for "classified" jobs. These constituted about 10 percent of all federal jobs and included almost all the workers at the New York Customs House.

The act also gave the President the power to add to the "classified list." Today the merit system covers about 85 percent of all federal jobs. In addition, the Pendleton Act said that federal employees could no longer be forced to kick back part of their salaries as contributions to a political party.

The Pendleton Act had mixed consequences. On the one hand, an ever-growing proportion of federal jobs came to be held by people with qualifications other than just political ones. Public administration became more honest and more efficient as a result.

On the other hand, as politicians lost patronage, they had to find other sources of campaign funds. The most obvious source was wealthy business people. So the alliance between the federal government and big business became stronger than ever.

Efforts to Regulate Tariffs Fail

Most Americans agreed that tariffs were necessary to protect domestic industries from foreign competition. Without tariffs, the reasoning went, American firms could be forced out of business and American workers would lose their jobs. The chief question was how high the tariffs should be.

During the Civil War, tariffs were very high. When the war ended, a general tariff reduction seemed reasonable. Yet every suggestion for lowering the duty on a particular item was opposed by those members of Congress who came from districts where many voters worked for the industry that produced the item. Economists might argue that high tariffs raised domestic prices and encouraged monopolies to develop. Nevertheless, members of Congress were more concerned with getting reelected.

In 1884 the Democratic party captured the Presidency for the first time in twenty-eight years. Their successful candidate was **Grover Cleveland,** a former mayor of Buffalo and governor of New York. He believed in **laissez faire** (les' ā fer'), or the limitation of government interference in busi-

Check for Understanding
Have students write the answers to Section 2
Review questions on paper.

Picturing History
Members of the
executive committee
of the First Interna-
tional Council for
Women included
Susan B. Anthony
(seated second from
left) and Elizabeth
Cady Stanton (seat-
ed fourth from left).

For Discussion
What characteristics might
groups in society that favor
reform share? (Possible response: low incomes, little influence or power, and the
feeling of being abused, neglected, or cheated by the
existing system.)

ness activity. In 1887 President Cleveland tried to
lower tariff rates. He felt that high tariffs were "a
burden upon those with moderate means and the
poor." Congress, however, did not agree.

When Cleveland ran for reelection in 1888, it
was on a party platform of lower tariffs. His
Republican opponent was **Benjamin Harrison,** the
grandson of President William Henry Harrison.
Harrison's campaign was financed by large contributions from companies that wanted even higher
tariffs. The Republican campaign was the most
expensive in United States history up to that time.
Although Cleveland polled about 100,000 more
popular votes than Harrison, it was Harrison who
received a majority of the electoral votes.

The new Congress accordingly set to work on a
high protective tariff bill. The **McKinley Tariff
Act** of 1890 raised duties on manufactured goods to
the highest level ever.

In 1892 Cleveland was returned to the White
House for a second term, becoming the only
President to serve two terms that were not consecutive. He initially supported a bill for lowering the
McKinley Tariff. On its way through Congress,
however, the bill was altered. Although it lowered
duties overall, it was still too high by Cleveland's
standards. He refused to sign it. The **Wilson-
Gorman Tariff** became law in 1894 without his
signature. In 1897 William McKinley was inaugurated President, and the **Dingley Tariff Act** raised
duties once again. Thus, the attempt at tariff reform
ended in failure.

Women Struggle for Suffrage

Another area in which reformers attempted to
bring about political change was woman suffrage.
The struggle had gotten off to a rocky start.

Woman Suffrage Delayed. Ironically, the en-
franchisement of black men proved a major setback
to woman suffrage. The Fourteenth Amendment
(1868) had added the word "male" to the United
States Constitution for the first time. The amendment said that any state denying *male* citizens the
right to vote could lose some of its representation in
Congress. This seemed to imply that women were
not citizens. The Fifteenth Amendment (1870)
declared that the right to vote could not be denied
because of race or color. Discrimination on the
basis of sex was not mentioned.

The women objected bitterly. Yet even their
former co-workers in the abolitionist cause—
people such as Wendell Phillips, William Lloyd
Garrison, and Frederick Douglass—felt that
women should remain silent for the time being. As
one of them said, "This is the Negro's hour. . . .
The Negro once safe, the woman comes next."

The Fourteenth and Fifteenth Amendments split
the women's movement, with some women supporting the amendments and others opposing them.
By 1890, however, most suffragists were united in
the National American Woman Suffrage Association. Among its leaders were **Susan B. Anthony,
Elizabeth Cady Stanton, Lucy Stone,** and **Julia
Ward Howe.**

Picturing History Called "the Napoleon of the woman's rights movement," Susan B. Anthony devoted her life to attaining equality for men and women under the law. She was the first woman to be pictured on United States currency.

The women used three main approaches. First, they tried to convince state legislatures to change voting laws. Second, they tried to test the Fourteenth Amendment in the courts. Third, they pushed for a national constitutional amendment.

Efforts in the States. The strategy to secure women's voting rights at the state level faced its first test in Wyoming. In 1869 the territory of Wyoming gave women the right to vote. In 1889 the territory applied for statehood. However, because its constitution contained a woman suffrage provision, there was considerable resistance in Congress.

The Wyoming delegate wired home for instructions. The Wyoming legislature promptly wired back, "We will remain out of the Union a hundred years rather than come in without the women." Congress conceded, and Wyoming was admitted as a state the following year.

Similarly, Utah, Colorado, and Idaho passed woman suffrage bills. Efforts in fourteen other states, however, ended in defeat.

Efforts in the Courts. In 1871 and 1872 there were some 150 attempts by women to vote in ten

states and in the District of Columbia. The most famous attempt was that of Susan B. Anthony in Rochester, New York.

Anthony felt that women were entitled to vote under the first article of the Fourteenth Amendment. The article stated that "all persons born or naturalized in the United States . . . are citizens . . . [and] no State shall make or enforce any law which shall abridge the privileges . . . of citizens." In other words, since the article did not forbid women to vote, they were entitled to do so if they were born or naturalized in this country.

Accordingly, on November 1, 1872, Anthony and fifteen "sturdy, determined, and respectable housewives" appeared at the registration desk in Rochester's Eighth Ward and asked to be listed as voters. The inspectors agreed. On November 5 the sixteen women went to the polls and voted. That night, Anthony wrote to Stanton, "Well, I have been and gone and done it! Positively voted the Republican ticket, straight, this A.M. at 7 o'clock."

Three weeks later Anthony and her followers were arrested and convicted for voting illegally. Anthony refused to pay the $100 fine. She had hoped her case would go to the Supreme Court, but this did not happen.

The following year, however, the Supreme Court *did* rule on the relationship between the Fourteenth Amendment and woman suffrage. In the case of *Minor* v. *Happersett,* the Court agreed unanimously that women were citizens. However, the justices said, citizenship did not automatically include the right to vote. If the states could withhold suffrage from certain men such as criminals, the mentally unfit, and those under twenty-one, then the states could withhold it from all women.

Efforts in Congress. In 1878 Senator A. A. Sargent of California introduced an amendment to the United States Constitution. Known as the Anthony amendment, it read:

> The right of citizens of the United States to vote shall not be denied or abridged by the United States or by any state on account of sex.

The measure was sent to the Senate Committee on Privileges and Elections. The committee held hearings at which representatives of the women's organizations testified. Elizabeth Cady Stanton described her experience:

Assign Independent Practice

Ask students to list five major reasons given for opposition to the woman suffrage movement. (List should include: voting was not a woman's place; giving women the right to vote would increase the divorce rate; factory owners feared women voters would press for shorter hours and safer working conditions; liquor industry feared women voters would press prohibition of alcohol; Southern whites feared it would reopen the entire black suffrage question.)

Student Assignment/Homework

Have students read Section 3, "Farmers Begin the Populist Movement," and answer Section 3 Review questions on paper.

I have never felt more exasperated than on this occasion. . . . The peculiar aggravating feature . . . was the studied inattention and contempt of the chairman, Senator Wadleigh of New Hampshire. . . . He alternately looked over some manuscripts and newspapers before him, and jumped up to open or close a door or a window. He stretched, yawned, gazed at the ceiling, cut his nails, sharpened his pencil, changing his occupation and position every two minutes. . . . It was with difficulty that I restrained the impulse more than once to hurl my manuscript at his head.

Senator Wadleigh's committee did not recommend passage of the bill. Even so, supporters of woman suffrage reintroduced it every year for the next eight years. In 1886 the bill was finally called up for debate, but it was voted down in January 1887. It was reintroduced again for the next nine years without success.

Antisuffrage Opinions. Many groups opposed woman suffrage. Their reasons were as diverse as their memberships.

Both men and women argued that voting was not a woman's place. For generations, the idea had been firmly fixed in people's minds that women were better suited to homemaking and child rearing than to participation in public affairs. Less kindly but more directly, the New York *Tribune* snapped that all the suffragists needed was a "cradle and a dimple-cheeked baby." Another popular argument was that voting would increase "the already alarming prevalence of divorce."

Many factory owners opposed woman suffrage because they feared that women voters would support legislation for shorter work hours and safer working conditions. Such legislation would cost employers money.

Members of the liquor industry were nervous about suffragists because many of the women were also active in the temperance movement. Distillers spent hundreds of thousands of dollars opposing woman suffrage.

White Southern politicians fought woman suffrage because they were afraid that the issue of woman suffrage would reopen the entire black suffrage question. As these white Southern politicians said, it would lead to "another period of Reconstruction horrors, which will introduce a set of female carpetbaggers as bad as their male prototypes [original examples] of the sixties."

After Reconstruction, one Southern state after another had passed Jim Crow laws, which deprived black males of their right to vote. As a result of all this opposition, the campaign for woman suffrage made little headway during the Gilded Age. Nevertheless, in 1910 the movement began again, as you will see, and finally achieved success.

Linking Past to Present

Questions regarding the merit system, tariff protection, and women's rights are as important today as they were a century ago. For example, in the 1980's and 1990's the growth of Japan's economic power led to calls in Congress for protection against imports of Japanese products in several industries.

SECTION 2 REVIEW

Key Terms and People

Explain the significance of: Gilded Age, patronage, merit system, civil service, Rutherford B. Hayes, Stalwarts, James A. Garfield, Chester A. Arthur, Pendleton Act, Grover Cleveland, laissez faire, Benjamin Harrison, McKinley Tariff Act, Wilson-Gorman Tariff, Dingley Tariff Act, Susan B. Anthony, Elizabeth Cady Stanton, Lucy Stone, Julia Ward Howe

Main Ideas

1. What views held by President Garfield provoked his assassin?
2. Why did members of Congress repeatedly oppose the idea of lowering tariffs on imported goods?
3. What did the Fourteenth Amendment imply about women's right to vote?
4. What three approaches did the leaders of the National American Woman Suffrage Association take to gain voting rights for women?

Critical Thinking

5. Were male abolitionists justified in not supporting woman suffrage during efforts to pass the Fourteenth and Fifteenth Amendments? Explain.

SECTION 2 REVIEW

Answers

Main Ideas

1. Garfield favored a merit system for government employment over the patronage system of the past.
2. They were afraid of angering constituents whose businesses might suffer from increased competition.
3. That women were not entitled to vote because only males were citizens.
4. They tried to convince state legislatures to change the laws; they tried to test the Fourteenth Amendment in the courts; they pushed for a new constitutional amendment.

Critical Thinking

5. Possible answers: yes—supporting woman suffrage might have kept the vote from black males. No—their support for the amendments made it even more difficult for women to have their rights recognized.
(analysis & evaluation)

Anticipate the Lesson

Review in Chapter 17 the farmers' position against railroads. (Details should include: farmers believed railroads were taking advantage of their monopoly and charging unfair prices.) Ask students why farmers were unable to bring about change at this time. (Possible responses: they were not organized; they did not have strong backing or sufficient money to back candidates who supported their ideas.)

State the Objective

Explain how the third party reform movement known as Populism began and what changes it brought about.

SECTION 3

Farmers Begin the Populist Movement

GLOSSARY TERMS: **Populism, deflation, inflation, cheap money, alliances, graduated federal income tax, initiative, recall, referendum, subsidies, bimetallism, gold standard**

Labor unrest and government reform were not the only political issues in the Gilded Age. The period also saw the rise of a movement that threatened to realign the Democratic and Republican parties. This movement, begun by farmers, was called **Populism.** Its name comes from the Latin word *populus,* meaning "the people." The widening gap between the farmer and other economic interests can be felt in this song of the time:

When the banker says he's broke
And the merchant's up in smoke,
They forget that it's the farmer feeds them all.
It would put them to the test
If the farmer took a rest;
Then they'd know that it's the farmer feeds them all.

Farmers Demand Cheaper Money

The period after the Civil War was one of **deflation** as the prices for goods and services fell. This was good news for consumers because every dollar they had now bought more goods. However, it was bad news for farmers. Those who had taken out loans now had to repay them with dollars that were worth more than those they had borrowed. In addition, deflation meant that the prices farmers received for their products were lower than before.

Mint More Money. The farmers thought the

Picturing History This cartoon from 1891 pokes fun at the Alliance's demands to increase the money supply. Many farmers' organizations sought cheaper money to offset the disastrous deflation after the Civil War.

Present the Lesson

Ask students to skim the section and complete a chart on the board showing the reasons for the development of the Populist Movement, reasons for its growth, and reasons for its decline.

Development

- Deflation caused farm prices to fall; farmers could not pay their debts.
- Farmers wanted the following: currency inflation to be counteracted by printing or coining of additional money; establishment of postal savings banks; establishment of federal loan program.
- Farmers formed alliances.
- Alliances founded Populist, or People's, party in 1891.

Growth

- Party leaders were talented orators.
- Party demanded reforms in money, transportation, and government.
- Widespread unemployment and farm foreclosures caused many voters to support party.

Decline

- Populist candidates for President defeated in 1892, 1896, 1900, 1904, and 1908.
- A number of Populist reforms were enacted and conditions requiring reforms later improved.

only solution to their problem was to force prices up by increasing the money supply. This is known as **inflation.** During a period of inflation, the purchasing power of money declines, resulting in what is commonly called **cheap money.**

When the Civil War ended, the farmers attempted to persuade the government to print more greenbacks. (Greenbacks were the paper currency issued by the federal government during the war.) Instead, the government decided to retire the number in circulation. This made greenbacks even more expensive.

Next, the farmers sought the unlimited coinage of silver. This tactic failed as well. In 1878 the Bland-Allison Act provided for the limited rather than unlimited coinage of silver. Although the act added between $2 and $4 million a month to the money supply, this amount was not enough to produce the cheaper money the farmers wanted.

The Populist Party Is Organized

When the Granger movement died out as a political force for farmers, its role was taken over by three groups known as **alliances.** One was the Northern Alliance. Its main strength lay in the wheat-growing states of Kansas, Nebraska, Minnesota, and the Dakotas. The Southern Alliance, the largest of the three groups, had more than a million white members throughout the Southern states. Black farmers in the South belonged to a separate group, the Colored Farmers' Alliance.

The alliances started by supporting state laws to limit the foreclosing of mortgages and to restrict unfair railroad practices. Gradually, however, farmers began to feel that the only way to get results was to organize a third party. In May 1891 they founded the Populist, or People's, party. In June 1892 the party slated its first candidates.

Populist Leaders. Although most Populists were farmers, the Populist party's leaders were mainly lawyers and other professionals. On the whole, they were poor politicians. However, they were remarkably talented orators who roused listeners wherever they spoke.

One of the most important Populist leaders was Thomas E. Watson of Georgia. He was the first Populist leader to favor cooperation between Southern white and black farmers. In later years, however, Watson became disillusioned and embittered over his failed attempts to bring about inter-racial unity. He changed his views, joined the Democratic party, and wrote violent books against African Americans and against Jews and Catholics as well. **Mary Elizabeth Lease** of Kansas was a Populist leader with a grand style and resonant speaking voice. She all but hypnotized her audiences as she declared:

> What you farmers need to do is to raise less corn and more *Hell!* We want the accursed foreclosure system wiped out. . . . We will stand by our homes and stay by our firesides by force if necessary, and we will not pay our debts to the loan-shark companies until the Government pays its debts to us.

The Populists Present Their Platform

The main demands of the Populists fell into three categories. These had to do with money, transportation, and government.

The proposed financial reforms were as follows:

1. Currency inflation to be accomplished by either printing paper money or coining silver
2. A **graduated federal income tax** that would take a higher proportion of large incomes than of small incomes
3. The establishment of postal savings banks
4. The establishment of a federal loan program under which farmers could store nonperishable products in government warehouses and then borrow up to 80 percent of their value from the United States Treasury

In the field of transportation, the Populists called for government ownership and operation of the

Picturing History
Mary Elizabeth Lease, a leader in the Populist party.

Check for Understanding

Call on individual students to read their answers to Section 3 Review questions. Discuss the answers with the class.

Guided Practice

Point out to students that some Populist ideas were successful even though the party itself never won the Presidency. Ask students which Populist ideas are now common practice. (Possible responses: Populist ideas now common practice—graduated income tax; postal savings banks; government loans to farmers; direct election of U.S. senators; secret ballot; recall; initiative; referendum; shorter work day.)

railroads. They also wanted the government to take over the telegraph and telephone systems.

Among the governmental reforms the Populists proposed were the following:

1. The election of United States senators by direct popular vote instead of by state legislatures
2. A single term for the President and the Vice-President
3. A secret ballot to end vote fraud
4. The **initiative,** which would enable the people to introduce bills in Congress and in state legislatures by petition
5. The **recall,** which would enable voters to remove officials from elected positions before their terms were completed
6. The **referendum,** which would allow the people to vote on bills after they had been passed by a legislature

The Populists hoped to represent labor as well as farming interests. Accordingly, they called for the eight-hour workday in factories and for restrictions on immigration. They also opposed any **subsidies,** or grants, to private corporations.

Depression Aids the Populist Cause

In the 1892 Presidential election, the Populists polled more than a million votes against a combined eleven million votes for the Democratic and Republican parties. They also elected five senators, ten representatives, three governors, and some fifteen hundred state legislators. It was the best first-year showing of any third party.

The Populists did even better in the 1894 campaign because of widespread unemployment and farm foreclosures caused by the panic of 1893. It was the worst depression the United States had suffered up to that time. Some five hundred banks and fifteen thousand businesses failed, and some three million people lost their jobs. As one Populist said, it seemed that the nation would be "brought to the verge of ruin." Farmers and cheap-money advocates were more frightened and angry than ever. Then came the election of 1896.

"Free Silverites" Battle the "Goldbugs"

The central issue of the 1896 campaign was what metal would be the basis of the nation's monetary system. On one side were the "free silverites," who favored **bimetallism.** Under bimetallism, the government would give people either gold or silver in exchange for other forms of money such as paper currency and checks. Bimetallists wanted the dollar to be defined as equal to both one ounce of gold and sixteen ounces of silver.

On the other side were the "goldbugs," who favored the **gold standard.** That is, they wanted the dollar to be defined in terms of gold. Under this plan, the government would exchange only gold for other forms of currency.

The backing of the currency was a hotly contested campaign issue because people at the time regarded paper money as worthless if it could not be turned in for silver or gold. Whether paper money was backed with one metal or two would affect the supply of money available and thus its price. In other words, the goldbugs wanted a stable currency, while the free silverites preferred cheap money.

The 1896 campaign was basically a struggle between different regions and different economic interests. In the Republican camp were the financial and business interests of the nation. Their strength lay in the industrialized Northeast. In the Democratic camp were the farmers and laborers of the United States. They were based in the agrarian South and West.

The Republican party came out firmly in favor of the gold standard. It nominated Governor **William McKinley** of Ohio.

The Democratic party, after a bitter struggle, came down on the side of bimetallism and unlimited coinage. It nominated **William Jennings Bryan,** a

Presidential Election, 1896

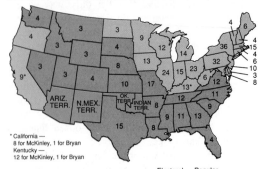

* California —
8 for McKinley, 1 for Bryan
Kentucky —
12 for McKinley, 1 for Bryan

Party	Candidate	Electoral Vote	Popular Vote	%
Republican	McKinley	271	7,102,000	51.1
Democratic	Bryan	176	6,493,000	46.7
Minor parties			315,000	2.2

447 Total Electoral Vote

Picturing History In this cartoon, the cross is a symbol of one of William Jennings Bryan's most famous speeches.

them: You shall not press down upon the brow of labor this crown of thorns, you shall not crucify mankind upon a cross of gold.

For a moment, the thousands of delegates stood silent. Then bedlam broke loose, like "a great sea thundering against the dikes." For a full hour, according to an observer, the delegates were "shouting, weeping, rejoicing. They lifted Bryan, who was known as 'the Boy Orator of the Platte,' upon their shoulders and carried him as if he had been a god. At last a man!"

Bryan's campaign broke new ground. For the first time, a Presidential candidate stumped, or traveled about the country making political speeches. Traveling some eighteen thousand miles by train, Bryan visited twenty-seven states and delivered approximately six hundred speeches to audiences totaling five million people.

McKinley, "The Front Porch Campaigner." McKinley won his party's nomination for two main reasons. First, his appearance was solid, stable, and reassuring. Second, he was backed by **Marcus Alonzo Hanna,** who was an extremely successful

former member of Congress from Nebraska and the editor of the Omaha *World-Herald*. The Populists also nominated Bryan but, unable to accept his running mate—a wealthy shipbuilder and banker from Maine—put up their own Thomas E. Watson instead.

Bryan's "Cross of Gold" Speech. The thirty-six-year-old Bryan had not been the immediate choice of the Democratic convention. However, he was famed as a speaker. At the convention he had gotten up to speak on a motion. He delivered what historians now refer to as the "Cross of Gold" speech.

> You come to us and tell us that the great cities are in favor of the gold standard; we reply that the great cities rest upon our broad and fertile prairies. Burn down your cities and leave our farms, and your cities will spring up again as if by magic; but destroy our farms and the grass will grow in the streets of every city in the country. . . .
>
> Having behind us the producing masses of this nation and the world, supported by the commercial interests, the laboring interests, and the toilers everywhere, we will answer their demand for a gold standard by saying to

Picturing History William McKinley, the twenty-fifth President, defeated William Jennings Bryan twice.

Student Assignment/Homework

Have students complete Chapter 18 Review on paper. Go over the answers to the Critical Thinking questions with students.

Concluding the Chapter

Ask students to consider the effects of unions, third party (Populist) movements, and women's movements as presented in this chapter. In a three-paragraph essay have them explain how the three movements were interrelated and what changes each brought about. (Essays might include: all groups represented minority viewpoints; all brought problems to national attention; unions brought about better working conditions and wages; third party movement brought new ideas and fresh life into the political system; women's movement brought about safer working conditions for women and children by organizing women workers.)

SECTION 3 REVIEW

Answers

Main Ideas

1. Farmers were suffering economically as a result of the post-Civil War deflation. They felt a need to organize politically and did so by forming their own party.

2. Money, transportation, and government.

3. "Free silverites" favored backing paper money with gold and silver (cheap money). "Goldbugs" favored backing only with gold (stable currency).

4. Although they were diminished as a party, many of their reforms were incorporated in state and federal laws.

Critical Thinking

5. Possible answer: third parties such as the Populists can bring minority viewpoints to public notice for future consideration; such viewpoints are often overlooked by the major parties. **(analysis, application, & synthesis)**

businessman, the Republican boss of Cleveland, and one of the best political organizers the United States has ever known. Hanna realized that McKinley was a poor orator but an impressive-looking individual. So he arranged for McKinley to conduct a front porch campaign. McKinley stayed in his hometown of Canton, Ohio, where he received delegation after delegation of supporters brought there with the help of free tickets and cheap excursion rates. Dressed in a frock coat, he would come out on the porch, deliver a set speech, and shake several thousand hands. In all, some 750,000 people from thirty states came to see the Republican candidate.

Hanna did not stop there. He raised some $3.5 million in campaign contributions from oil companies, meat-packing firms, railroads, and other big businesses. (Bryan, in comparison, was able to raise only one-tenth that amount.) Then he organized a "campaign of education" to persuade city workers that "any threat to the gold standard was a threat to their jobs." He sent thousands of speakers—from Civil War generals to Terence V. Powderly, former grandmaster of the Knights of Labor—to all parts of the country. He had two hundred million pieces of literature, an average of fourteen per voter, printed in twelve languages besides English. It was an effective political advertising campaign.

Almost every newspaper in the United States came out in support of McKinley. Preachers thundered that issuing cheap money was the same as stealing. Employers had their shop supervisors lecture workers on the best way to cast their ballots. As one Democratic senator said, "Boys, I'm afraid it beats us. If I were a working man and had nothing but my job, I am afraid when I came to vote I would think of Molly and the babies."

The Middle Class Elects McKinley

When the returns were in, McKinley had approximately 7 million votes; Bryan, about 6.5 million. As expected, McKinley carried the East, while Bryan swept the South. The West split; higher prices for agricultural products had lessened farmer discontent. However, it was the voters of the industrial Middle West—Ohio, Illinois, Wisconsin, and Michigan—who brought McKinley into office. It was also the rising middle class, who were afraid that currency inflation would lower the values of their savings accounts, insurance, and stocks. "God's in his Heaven, all's right with the world!" Hanna telegraphed happily to his victorious candidate.

Bryan ran against McKinley again in 1900 and was again defeated. That same year, the Gold Standard Act made gold the legal basis for United States currency.

Linking Past to Present

Although the Populists faded away, many of their ideas were eventually adopted, some during the Progressive movement of the early 1900's, others during the New Deal of the 1930's. The graduated income tax, postal savings banks, government loans to farmers, the direct popular election of United States senators, the secret ballot, the recall, the initiative, the referendum, and a shorter workday—all eventually became part of our system of government. Third parties seldom get their candidates elected, but they often present ideas that the major parties later adopt.

SECTION 3 REVIEW

Key Terms and People

Explain the significance of: Populism, deflation, inflation, cheap money, alliances, Mary Elizabeth Lease, graduated federal income tax, initiative, recall, referendum, subsidies, bimetallism, gold standard, William McKinley, William Jennings Bryan, Marcus Alonzo Hanna

Main Ideas

1. What conditions led to the founding of the National People's party in 1891?
2. In what three areas did the Populists demand to see reforms?
3. How did "free silverites" differ from "goldbugs" on national monetary issues?
4. What became of the Populists and their reforms after they were defeated by McKinley a second time, in 1900?

Critical Thinking

5. Using the Populists as an example, explain how third parties can help to improve democracy in the United States.

Focus on Geography

Urban Growth

The Geographic Theme of Place

Atlanta, Dallas, Los Angeles, Chicago, Boston, New York. What caused these and other major cities in the United States to grow into the giant urban areas they are today? Nowhere is the ability of human beings to change their physical environment more evident than the development of cities. That is why the human characteristics of the geographic theme of place can be used to study urban growth. In this geography feature you will learn about the human characteristics, or factors, that have contributed to urban growth and that help to explain why certain cities grew where they did.

Picturing History Telephone cables streak the skies over New York. Later, these wires would be relaid underground.

Form Follows Function. Louis Sullivan, who ranks as one of the great American architects of the 1800's, popularized the phrase "form follows function." Geographers use these same concepts—function and form—when studying urban growth. The function of a city explains its purpose or the economic activity that caused it to come into existence. For instance, Washington, D.C., and many state capitals have a political function. New York City serves a financial function as a center for banking and trading activities. Pittsburgh and Detroit developed as manufacturing cities. Other urban areas sprang up as mining towns, resort towns, and university towns.

The form of a city follows a city's function and explains how urban land is used within a city. Some areas of a manufacturing city might contain warehouses, while others might have a high concentration of industrial parks. Major transportation depots and stations might be centralized in another area. The central business districts of older cities such as New York and Chicago contain financial institutions, major retail stores, and government offices. These central business districts usually have high land values and are characterized by tall buildings, pedestrian traffic, and retail shops with large windows for viewing the merchandise available for sale. Residential areas tend to grow around the fringes of these business districts.

Early Factors Contributing to Urban Growth. America's earliest cities grew on sites that offered certain physical advantages. Early settlers chose these sites because of such factors as sheltered bays, protected islands, or high ground. These factors, however, were to become less important as time went on.

Cities grew quite rapidly after the 1840's. This growth may be attributed to two major causes. The first cause was the development of technology, which created new industries as well as a demand for workers. The Industrial Revolution, and the many factories it brought into existence, required a large supply of workers who could live close to the workplace. While urbanization can occur without industrialization, industrialization cannot occur without urban growth.

The second cause of urban growth was large-scale foreign immigration. Between 1860 and 1900, the urban population of the United States

475

Present the Lesson

On the board write the heading Growth of Cities. Underneath, list the following factors as subheadings: Industrial Revolution, Agricultural Productivity, Transportation Networks, Invention of Steam. Ask students how each of these factors influenced the development of cities. Have volunteers write the responses under the appropriate factors. (Possible responses: Industrial Revolution—required a large supply of workers in a central workplace. Agricultural Productivity—improvements freed workers for industry and provided surplus food for these workers. Transportation

Networks—moved people, agricultural goods, and raw materials to the cities. Invention of Steam—led to larger scale production, which required more workers.)

Tell students that even more factors contribute to the growth of cities today. Ask students how the following factors can influence such growth: job opportunities; positive image; expanding transportation networks; cultural, shopping, and entertainment opportunities. (Possible responses: job opportunities—cities attract new workers and grow when unemployment is low. Positive image—cities viewed as desirable places to live attract new residents; an example is Seattle, which has a reputation

for open space, natural beauty, and lack of congestion. Expanding transportation networks—air and ground transportation must be accessible and efficient; highway systems must expand with a city to encourage continued growth. Cultural, shopping, and entertainment opportunities—these elements encourage urban growth when they are strong; some people prefer to live in a city that offers a broad range of cultural activity rather than in a suburb, where such opportunities may be more limited.)

Map Skills

San Francisco-Oakland, Los Angeles-Long Beach, Houston, and Dallas-Fort Worth • Most are located near major bodies of water (Atlantic and Pacific oceans, Lake Michigan, Lake Erie). Such places develop into transportation and communication centers and entry/exit points for people and products. These advantages create jobs and attract people.

Picturing History Horse-drawn cars and carriages were among the sights and sounds of New York and other major cities at the turn of the century.

more than doubled until it represented 40 percent of the nation's total population. By 1900 the pattern of urban centers was firmly established. The major industrial cities of the northeastern manufacturing belt had become the most populous urban centers in the nation.

Urbanization was accompanied by changes in population distribution. By 1900, for example, the central business districts in older cities occupied areas that were equal to the size of entire settlements at the beginning of the 1800's. The separation of home from work had also been established by this time as improved transportation permitted people to move to the suburbs.

Other Factors Contributing to Urban Growth. By 1920 urban areas contained more than half of the population of the United States. This increase in urbanization reflected the many changes that occurred in the economic and social organization of the country during this time. Although initially these changes were caused by the Industrial Revolution, other factors also contributed to this growth.

An Efficient Agricultural System. A fundamental prerequisite for the growth of cities is an efficient agricultural system. There must be enough food readily available to support the increased population. Fortunately, the United States had extensive areas of agricultural land that could be brought into use to produce surplus food throughout most of the 1800's. After 1860, improvements in farming technology permitted a reduction in the

number of people needed to produce food for the growing population. As a result, many rural dwellers moved to the cities to take urban jobs.

Scientific Discoveries and Inventions. A second major factor contributing to urban growth was the growing number of scientific discoveries and inventions that made power-driven machinery possible. Most important was the introduction of steam as a source of power. This discovery moved manufacturing from one system made up of many small-scale units of production into another system composed of bigger factories requiring large numbers of workers. As the scale of industry increased, division of labor became necessary, and the production and distribution of products became concentrated in cities.

New Methods of Transportation. A third important factor for urban growth was the development of new and improved methods of transportation. The introduction of railroads, intercity streetcars, and, finally, automobiles and trucks led to better and faster ways to move raw materials and finished products to their markets. Some cities served as points of collection and distribution of goods for the areas surrounding them. Service industries became increasingly important. These new transportation systems provided ways for people to move efficiently between their homes and their jobs. The new methods also caused urban functions to become decentralized as the boundaries of cities continued to expand.

Check for Understanding

Ask students to write answers to the questions at the end of the feature. Review the answers in class.

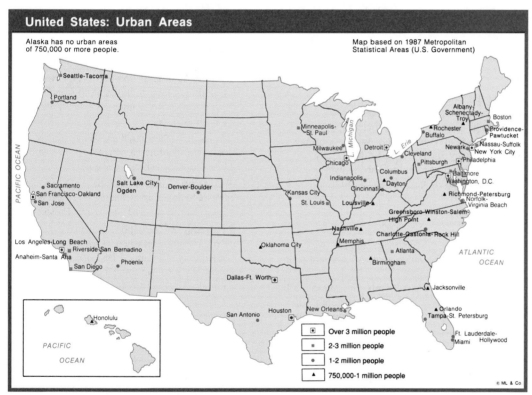

United States: Urban Areas

Alaska has no urban areas of 750,000 or more people.

Map based on 1987 Metropolitan Statistical Areas (U.S. Government)

Over 3 million people
2-3 million people
1-2 million people
750,000-1 million people

© ML & Co

Map Skills **Location** Which urban areas of over 3 million people are west of the Mississippi River? **Place** Use the map to explain why the largest urban areas are located where they are.

New Demographic and Social Trends. A fourth factor influencing urban growth could be seen in the new demographic and social trends. Demographics is the study of population changes. Until late in the 1800's, large cities experienced a natural decrease in population because the number of deaths exceeded the number of births. After the turn of the century, improvements in medicine and in sanitary conditions resulted in a natural increase in city population. Births began to exceed deaths, and urban areas tended to generate their own growth.

Although the economic opportunities of the city exerted the greatest pull on migrants, this pull was reinforced by the social advantages of life in the city. To many, the excitement of city life was most influential in causing them to move there.

Cities Today. In recent years, the growth of cities has slowed, and some cities have even lost population. Industries have moved out to take advantage

of suburbia's lower taxes and larger expanses of land. People have left the city to follow their jobs and send their children to less crowded and better equipped suburban schools. Nevertheless, cities continue to play a significant role in shaping the human characteristics of our American landscape.

Understanding Geography

1. How can the human characteristics of place be used to study urban growth?
2. What were the early factors that contributed to urban growth in the United States?
3. What four major factors have influenced urban growth in the last century?

Critical Thinking

4. Trace the pattern of urban growth for a major city in your state.

FOCUS ON GEOGRAPHY
Answers

Understanding Geography

1. Geographers use the concepts of form and function when studying urban growth. The function of a city explains its purpose, and the form follows the function and explains how the land is used.

2. The early factors that contributed to urban growth in the United States were physical advantages related to site, such as sheltered bays, protected islands, and high ground.

3. Four major factors that have influenced urban growth in the last century are an efficient agricultural system, scientific discoveries and inventions, new methods of transportation, and new demographic and social trends.

Critical Thinking

4. Students' answers should include reference to some of the factors influencing urban growth as explained in this geography feature, including demographic and social trends. **(analysis)**

Unionism, Political Reforms, and Populism **477**

477

Key Terms and People

These are highlighted in the text in the order in which they appear in this list.

Main Ideas

1. Work was broken up into jobs done by machine requiring little skill; became noisy; rules prohibited socializing; low wages, long hours, and dangerous conditions were common.

2. NLU—1866; by William Sylvis; 300 local unions; eight-hour day. Knights of Labor—1869; by Uriah Stephens and Terence Powderly; individual workers; eight-hour day, no child or convict labor, health and safety laws, equal pay for equal work. AFL—1881; by Samuel Gompers; a federation of national unions, skilled workers only; shorter hours, higher wages, better working conditions. ARU—1893; Eugene Debs; all railroad workers; higher wages.

3. President was empowered to appoint civil service commission to give open competition exams for federal jobs. • The civil service was established and now covers most federal jobs. Patronage at the federal level decreased.

4. Attention was focused on rights of African Americans. • Attained suffrage in four states.

5. Possible answers: currency inflation; graduated income tax; postal savings banks; federal loan program for farmers; government ownership of railroad, telephone, and telegraph; election of senators by direct popular vote.

6. "Free silverites"—government gives gold or silver in exchange for paper or checks; William Jennings Bryan. "Goldbugs"—gold only; William McKinley. • McKinley won election.

Critical Thinking Questions

7. His acid comments show his negative feelings.

8. Workers were not artisans anymore; lost individuality. • Unions addressed these issues.

▶9. Possible answers: no—living in company town one has little freedom, can't criticize the company. Yes—provided housing, job security.

10. Both appalled by conditions in textile workplace; both took action to improve conditions. • Mother Jones got support with children's march to the President, which resulted in legislation prohibiting child labor. Pauline Newman worked for legislation to better conditions in the garment industry.

11. The Stalwarts expected Arthur to support patronage rather than civil service reform as Garfield had, but Arthur supported reform.

▶12. He was being sarcastic about the amount of graft politicians can extract from lobbyists and others interested in pushing certain bills in Congress. • National politics were corrupt and gilded with money: money could get bills passed, people elected.

CHAPTER **18** REVIEW

Write your answers on a separate piece of paper.

Key Terms and People

Explain the significance of: strike, yellow-dog contracts, scabs, Pinkertons, collective bargaining, Frances Perkins, patronage, merit system, McKinley Tariff Act, Wilson-Gorman Tariff, Dingley Tariff Act, Elizabeth Cady Stanton, Lucy Stone, Julia Ward Howe, deflation, cheap money, alliances, Marcus Alonzo Hanna

Main Ideas

1. What changes were made in the workplace when industrialization and the assembly line became the norm?

2. Complete the chart comparing these early national labor unions—National Labor Union (NLU), Knights of Labor, American Federation of Labor (AFL), American Railway Union (ARU).

Union	When organized?	By whom?	For whom?	Goals

3. What were the provisions of the Pendleton Act of 1883? What were the results of the act?

4. What kept the women's rights movement from making progress? Where did it succeed?

5. List at least five items in the political platform of the Populists.

6. Define "free silverites" and "goldbugs." In the 1896 Presidential campaign, which political leader advocated each? Which one won?

Critical Thinking Questions

7. **Analyzing Literature.** What do you think Gore Vidal thinks of Rutherford B. Hayes? Give reasons to support your answer.

8. **Recognizing Values.** What did the workers lose when changes were made in the workplace because of industrialization and the assembly line? Why did these losses help bring about the rise of labor unions?

9. **Judging Values.** If you had been a worker in the Pullman factory in the 1880's and 1890's, would you have wanted to live in Pullman? Why or why not?

10. **Comparing Personalities.** What do Mother Jones and Pauline Newman have in common? How did each achieve her goals?

11. **Assessing Outcomes.** What was so ironic about a Stalwart assassinating President Garfield in order to make Chester Arthur President?

12. **Analyzing a Quotation.** What did humorist Mark Twain mean when he had a United States senator say, ''I think I can say, and say with pride, that we have some legislatures that bring higher prices than any in the world''? What did Twain mean by the Gilded Age?

13. **Making Deductions.** Why was Benjamin Harrison on the side of higher tariffs and Grover Cleveland on the side of lower tariffs in the election of 1888? Why did Harrison win?

14. **Recognizing Point of View.** What prompted Susan B. Anthony and her followers to vote in 1872? What was the Supreme Court ruling on the subject?

15. **Identifying Assumptions.** Why did farmers favor bimetallism and industrialists back the gold standard? What assumption was made by both?

Critical Thinking Activities

16. **Linking Past to Present.** Using the book, review the terms of the Populist platform. Which of their ideas have been adopted? Which have been discarded? Which are still being fought for?

17. **Linking Past to Present.** In the 1880's the labor movement wanted an eight-hour day, equal pay for equal work, health and safety laws, and the elimination of child labor. Are these goals still the same? What do you think the goals of labor unions should be today?

13. Harrison's campaign was financed by contributions from companies wanting high tariffs. Cleveland felt high tariffs were unfair to the poor. • Industrial capitalists supporting Harrison convinced people that what was good for industry was good for the country.

➤**14.** Her interpretation of the 14th Amendment and the fact that she had been born in the U.S. • Court agreed

women were citizens but ruled that citizenship did not include the right to vote.

15. Farmers wanted to increase money supply to pay loans and get more money, since prices of farm products were dropping. Industrialists wanted a stable currency backed by gold. • Both assumed paper had to be backed by valuable metal.

Critical Thinking Activities

➤**16.** Possible answers: adopted graduated income tax, government ownership and operation of railroads, senate election reform, secret ballot. • Discarded postal savings banks, government ownership of telegraph and telephone, single terms for President and Vice-President. • Some still fighting for national use of initi-

ative, recall, and referendum and for restrictions on immigration.

➤**17.** Still working for equal pay for equal work; still working on health and safety issues; however, child labor in factories seems not to exist. Possible answer: unions should keep working toward safe and fair working conditions.

➤**Question suitable for cooperative learning.**

Unionism, Political Reforms, and Populism

New industries meant a hard life for more and more workers. Large factories demanded long hours for low pay. Industrial expansion brought dangerous working conditions, child labor, sweatshops, and company towns. The railroad strike of 1877 was nationwide and resulted in corporations organizing against unions. The Knights of Labor ran a successful series of strikes under Powderly's leadership but collapsed because of the Haymarket bombing. It also had competition from Gompers's craft union, which was called the American Federation of Labor. Debs organized all levels of railroad workers into one industrial union, the American Railway Union. Mother Jones led women in support of coal miners. Newman organized other women into the International Ladies Garment Workers Union. The tragic fire at the Triangle Shirtwaist Company factory helped their cause. The police and the courts opposed these early unions. Business owners controlled the powers of government, which in turn tried to prevent workers from organizing.

Demands for political reforms grew, however, as political corruption became a major issue. Congressmen and other officeholders gave out government jobs in return for support. Presidents Hayes and Garfield pushed for reform. When Garfield was assassinated, President Arthur surprised everyone by also urging change. The Pendleton Act of 1883 established the civil service system. This system resulted from the belief that government jobs should be based on merit and not on politics. Woman suffrage became a major issue. At first women had to struggle for suffrage state by state. Wyoming and several other Western states led the way. Anthony and Stanton fought for women's right to vote. They faced much opposition. Their opponents were public opinion, factory and liquor-store owners, and Southern politicians.

American farmers backed the Populist movement. They wanted to put more money in circulation because the whole economic system was hurting them badly. They also demanded reforms in government. The Populists became a political party. In the South the Populist Watson used hatred of blacks as a political weapon. McKinley's front porch campaign of 1896 was crucial. The Democrat Bryan called for a system that would make silver and gold the base of the nation's money. Farmers backed this policy of inflation. The Republican McKinley called for a gold standard. Gold was much more scarce and would therefore bring deflation. McKinley won. Yet many of his opponent's ideas were later adopted.

Chronology of Main Events

1881 James A. Garfield inaugurated President; Garfield assassinated; Chester A. Arthur succeeds to Presidency

1883 Pendleton Act

1885 Grover Cleveland inaugurated President

1886 Haymarket riot; A.F. of L. founded

1889 Benjamin Harrison inaugurated President

1891 Populist party organized

1893 Cleveland inaugurated President

1897 William McKinley inaugurated President

Telescoping the Times may be used as an alternative to having students read the entire chapter, as a chapter preview, or as a chapter review.

State the Objective
Understand the rise and fall of the British Empire.

Present the Lesson
Ask students to give reasons why the British Empire was able to survive for as long as it did. (Possible responses: the British had a strong navy; many other large ruling forces in the world, such as the Moghul dynasty in India, the Manchu dynasty in China, and the Ottoman Empire, were in decline, making room for the British; Britain brought benefits such as trade and education to its protectorates.)

Ask students to describe some of the policies adopted by Britain toward its Asian and African colonies. (Possible responses: trade between Britain's colonies was free; taxes were lowered or abolished; Britain brought schools, its language, and its ideals of political freedom to colonies in Africa and Asia.) Ask students why they think Britain's policy changed from what it had been when America was a colony. (Possible response: British trade had expanded, and it was in Britain's economic interest to encourage independence and active trade.)

Focus on Global Events

The Rise and Fall of the British Empire

During the French and Indian War (1754–1763), when France and England were struggling for supremacy in North America, these same two countries were also competing for territory a world away. The prize was even more valuable: the subcontinent of India. India and other distant countries held out prospects of huge markets for the products of any country that could control them.

India. Both the English and French gained their first foothold on the Indian subcontinent during the 1600's through the British East India Company and the French East India Company. These were mercantilist trading companies similar to the Virginia Company in the Americas.

The British and French arrived at a time when the Moghul dynasty of India was at the height of its power. The Moghul emperors allowed the British East India Company to establish small settlements at the city of Surat on the west coast and at Calcutta and Madras on the east coast. Later, the Moghuls also granted the English control over Bombay.

About fifty years after the English, the French East India Company founded settlements along the east coast. The rivalry between the two groups of European merchants intensified as the Indian government grew weaker.

Gradually, the British government was drawn into Indian affairs in order to protect the personnel and interests of the East India Company. In 1756 the ruler of Bengal attacked Calcutta, throwing sixty-four Englishmen into a narrow, airless dungeon. By morning, most of the prisoners had suffocated in what the English came to call the "Black Hole of Calcutta."

Under the leadership of Robert Clive, a brilliant officer of the English East India Company, a fleet of English ships sailed north to Calcutta from Madras. Clive easily routed the Bengal ruler at the battle of Plassey in 1757. In 1761 the French settlement at Pondichéry also fell to British attacks. With superior naval forces, Robert Clive eliminated French influence from India and established English rule in Bengal.

In 1858 Parliament officially abolished the English East India Company and handed over its property and authority to the British crown. It also appointed a viceroy to govern the country. In 1876 Queen Victoria was proclaimed Empress of India.

China and Southeast Asia. A similar combination of business interests and a declining dynasty allowed the British to gain a foothold in China. In 1839 a war broke out between Great Britain and China, which was ruled by the once great but now failing Manchu dynasty. The conflict was called the Opium War because the British were trying to sell opium in China. The treaty of 1842 ending that war granted the English possession of Hong Kong.

Capitalizing on Chinese weakness, the British moved into Burma, long considered a Chinese satellite. English forces also took control of Singapore, the northern part of Borneo, and Ceylon.

Australia. Before the Revolutionary War in North America, Britain had shipped many of its convicts to the colonies, particularly to Georgia. After the American colonies gained their independence, Britain had to find a new dumping ground. In 1770 Captain James Cook had explored the southeast coast of Australia and claimed it for Great Britain. In 1788 the first boatload of convicts arrived at Botany Bay near the present city of Sydney. These people were soon followed by free settlers, particularly after 1851, when gold was discovered. Australia soon became an established British colony, and in 1841 New Zealand also joined the British Empire.

As the empire expanded, the English government abandoned mercantilism and adopted a laissez-faire policy. Tariffs were lowered or abolished. Colonies were allowed to trade with one another and with other countries.

Africa. A weak and crumbling dynasty facilitated British entry into the interior of Africa. Since the early 1500's, Egypt had been a province of the Ottoman Empire of Turkey, a world power that was in decline by the 1800's. In 1875 Ismail Pasha, the governor of Egypt, was having difficulty repaying debts to European banks that had helped to mod-

Ask students to write out answers to the questions at the end of the feature. Then ask students to play the role of a travel guide for British royalty in the 1850's. Have students write a plan for a trip throughout the British Empire, detailing places to see and their importance to the empire. Ask several students to read their travel guides to the class. (Travel guides might include: in the 1850's, a trip for royalty might have started in India and continued through places such as Calcutta, Surat, and Madras—trading centers of the British East India Company; the trip might have continued to Hong Kong, Borneo, and Singapore, where the British had trading privileges as a result of the weakness of the Manchu dynasty and the British victory in the Opium War; the trip might have continued to Botany Bay (near Sydney) in Australia, where prisoners had been sent in the late 1700's; Australia might be mentioned in the travel guide as a place where people settled to look for gold.)

Map Skills

Five • The Suez Canal provides a direct route for Great Britain to its interests in Africa, Asia, and Australia.

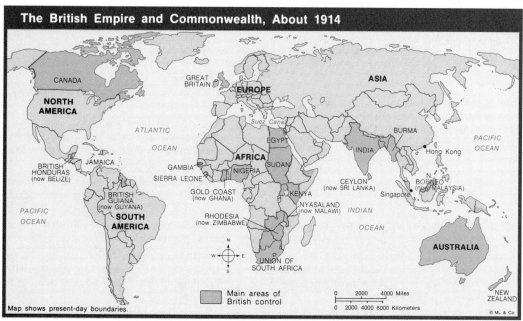

The British Empire and Commonwealth, About 1914

Map shows present-day boundaries.

Main areas of British control

0   2000   4000 Miles
0   2000 4000 6000 Kilometers

© ML & Co.

Map Skills **Location** On how many continents, not including Europe, were there British- controlled areas in 1914?
Movement What can you tell about the importance of the Suez Canal to Great Britain?

ernize his territory. Desperate for money, he sold the British government his shares in the Suez Canal Company, making Great Britain the largest single stockholder. The British thus acquired effective control of the Suez Canal as well as an open door to the African continent. Riots in Egypt in 1882 provided Britain with an excuse to proclaim the country a British protectorate. The Sudan fell next to the British in 1898.

The arrival of British explorers often preceded the actual colonization of an African territory. One of the most original personalities among British colonialists in Africa was the entrepreneur and adventurer, Cecil Rhodes. This millionaire owner of South African diamond and gold mines dreamed of building a British railway between Cairo and Cape Town. Through commercial agreements, bribes, propaganda, and military adventurism, Rhodes secured huge areas in southern Africa for Great Britain.

By 1914 Britain had carved out for itself an African empire second in size only to that of the French. Wherever British colonists settled, they brought with them their language, educational system, and ideals of political freedom.

The Commonwealth. By the end of the 1800's, demands for self-government were voiced in numerous British colonies. After World War I, a weakened Great Britain could no longer ignore these demands. As a result, in 1931, the British Parliament established a system by which Canada and colonies like India, Nigeria, Kenya, and Jamaica could attain the status of independent nations while maintaining close ties with Great Britain.

Colonies achieving independence could thus pursue their own development with the support of a worldwide community of friendly nations. With this new policy, the British Empire began to evolve into the Commonwealth of today.

Understanding Global Events

1. How was the French and British conquest of India a reflection of mercantile policies?
2. How was Britain's relationship with its Asian and African colonies different from that with its American colonies?
3. How did events in Georgia affect developments in Botany Bay, Australia?

Critical Thinking

4. How does the Commonwealth differ from the British Empire?

Answers

Understanding Global Events

1. The first European settlements in India were made by private, French, and British trading companies. The respective governments were drawn into Indian affairs in order to protect the personnel and policies of the trading companies.

2. Britain's occupation of its Asian and African colonies involved only a small number of British settlers, most of whom were active in government. Britain's occupation of its American colonies involved large numbers of British settlers, who built new homes and a permanent way of life for themselves. In Asia and Africa, Britain had to deal with existing governments, whereas in the American colonies it did not.

3. After Georgia—as one of the thirteen colonies—gained its independence, Great Britain had to find a new place to send its convicts. It chose Australia, and the first boatload of British convicts landed at Botany Bay in 1788.

Critical Thinking

4. The British Empire consisted of the mother country and its colonies. Under the Commonwealth of Nations, former colonies are now independent nations, although they maintain close economic and cultural ties with Great Britain. **(analysis & synthesis)**

Key Terms and People

These are highlighted in the text in the order in which they appear in this list.

Main Ideas

1. Railroads built across Indian land; Indians confined to particular areas; treaties were broken; buffalo were killed. • Ranching.

2. Lands became available and accessible to farmers. • Barbed wire, windmills, steel plows, and reapers made farming possible. Railroads took farmers' products to market.

3. Railroads, steel, oil. Possible answers (choose at least six): electricity, telegraph, telephone, typewriter, light bulb, oil well, Bessemer furnace.

4. They used every possible means to extract riches from other industries and individuals. • Social Darwinism saw competition as natural; it justified ruthlessness and opposed government intervention.

5. Because unions worked to improve the terrible working conditions of workers in industrial age. • Because businesses were national, unions became national. • National Labor Union—William H. Sylvis; Knights of Labor—Uriah Stephens and Terence V. Powderly; American Federation of Labor—Samuel Gompers; American Railway Union—Eugene Debs.

6. To bring attention to their plight. • Reforms, including graduated income tax, postal savings banks, government loans to farmers.

Critical Thinking Questions

7. Myth was more exciting than reality. Answers will favor desire for either fantasy or reality.

8. b, e, a, d, c. • Discovery of gold led people to want a quick route. As railroads moved across plains, people

decided land could be farmed. Indians fought for access to their land. Congress became contrite and decided to Americanize the Indians and divide up reservation land among the farmer-Indians.

9. Congress wrongly assumed Indians would be glad to give up their culture in exchange for the white American way of life; Indians were not taught to farm; speculators bought their land; health services were

poor. • Act showed no respect for Indian culture or way of life.

10. Yellow-dog contracts were pledges made by new employees promising not to join a union; Pinkertons were outsiders hired to cross picket lines and spy on union workers; injunctions were court orders to forbid a strike. • Police did not interfere because both state and federal governments supported industry.

➤**11.** Possible answers: they could not afford to quit their jobs; they could not afford to live elsewhere.

12. Passed Sherman Antitrust Act. • Act was worded so loosely that courts could not convict under it; trusts reorganized as single corporations; enforcement was nearly impossible.

13. Possible answers: legislators still believed in Social Dar-

---

UNIT **4** REVIEW

Write your answers on a separate sheet of paper.

Key Terms and People

Explain the significance of: Forty-Niners, George Armstrong Custer, Battle of Wounded Knee, longhorns, Joseph F. Glidden, technology, public utility, Andrew Carnegie, Susan B. Anthony, bimetallism, William Jennings Bryan

Main Ideas

1. Why did Indian life and culture on the Great Plains disappear in the late 1800's? What activities replaced the Indians' way of life?
2. How and why did the Great Plains ultimately get settled by farmers? What inventions helped the farmers succeed?
3. Name three huge industries that developed in the late nineteenth century. Name at least six inventions and new technologies that made these industries possible.
4. Why were industrialists like John D. Rockefeller called robber barons? Why did they believe in Social Darwinism?
5. Why did labor unions become so important during the late nineteenth century? Why did national unions spring up? Name four national labor unions of the time and the leaders who organized them.
6. Why did the farmers enter politics? What did Populism accomplish?

Critical Thinking Questions

7. **Recognizing Point of View.** Why do you think the United States media made up a myth about the cowboy? Do you like the myth or would you rather have the reality portrayed in novels, movies, and television shows? Why?
8. **Organizing Chronology.** Arrange the following events in order of occurrence. Then tell how each event affected the next event.

   a. Indians fight for their land.
   b. Gold is found in California.
   c. Indians are finally limited to reservations.
   d. Dawes Act provides for Americanization of

the Indians.
   e. Transcontinental railroad lines are surveyed and planned.

9. **Identifying Assumptions.** What went wrong with the United States Indian policy established in 1887 by the Dawes Act? Why was the Dawes Act unsuccessful?
10. **Drawing Conclusions.** Explain how corporations used each of the following against labor: yellow-dog contracts, Pinkertons, court injunctions. Why was it possible to do these things legally?
11. **Forming Hypotheses.** If the employees of the Pullman Company were unhappy about living in a company town, why did they continue to live there?
12. **Predicting Effects.** What did Congress do in 1890 to try to regulate industry? Why should the legislators have known it would not work?
13. **Analyzing Relationships.** Why did the federal and state governments in the 1880's and 1890's support management against labor?
14. **Analyzing Trends.** Make a chart listing the Presidents in office from 1877 through 1901 (Hayes through McKinley). List dates in office, party affiliation, and one or more significant events that occurred during each term.
15. **Making Generalizations.** Which group—Indians, labor, farmers, women, Chinese railroad workers—do you think was the most discriminated against in the late 1800's?

Critical Thinking Activities

16. **Linking Past to Present.** Farmers still suffer from drought, blizzard, and other natural hazards. How do they deal with these hazards? What do government and private companies do to help?
17. **Linking Past to Present.** If you were organizing a union of students to negotiate with the school board in the 1990's, how would you go about it? Why might you want to go about it?

The Rise of the Industrial Giant

Life on the Frontier

At first the Great Plains was the land of the buffalo. There were no horses in the Americas until the Spanish brought them. These animals thrived in the wild. The Indians used them for hunting buffalo and for war.

The United States government first planned to reserve the Great Plains for Indians. As more white Americans moved west, however, the government tried to put Indians on reservations. Misunderstandings and disagreements led to war. The Chivington massacre took place at Sand Creek in the Colorado Territory.

In addition, the Indians suffered from the destruction of the buffalo. The new railroads brought more and more people from the East. Shooting buffalo became a kind of sport.

General Custer led United States cavalry into an area that the Sioux regarded as sacred. The Indian troops under the command of Tashunka Witko destroyed the entire regiment at Little Bighorn. In 1889 United States soldiers massacred more than two hundred Sioux at Wounded Knee.

In 1887 Congress passed the Dawes Act. It was based on the hope that the Indians would give up their tribal groups and become farmers. The policy failed badly. The United States government did not provide training, farm equipment, or adequate schools and health services.

After the Civil War, cowboys became heroes of the American culture. They mastered the tough breed of cattle known as Texas longhorns. The Americans borrowed Mexican ways of handling the animals and they also borrowed Mexican words such as *corral* and *ranch*. Life on the cattle trails was hard. The long drives to the railroad towns sometimes lasted two or three months. Later on, when cowboy stories were filmed, most movies did not show that some of these cowboys were black.

The cowboys' frontier went through major changes. As farmers moved in, the cattle were pushed farther west. Then a terrible blizzard struck in the winter of 1885–1886. It was followed by a drought that summer and then another blizzard. About two million cattle died. Cattlemen had to change. They began fencing in the land and raising hay for wintertime feeding.

In 1862 Congress passed the Homestead Act, which gave 160 acres to anyone willing to live on it. Hundreds of thousands of families took up the offer. They included Americans from the East, who were new immigrants from Europe, and they included former slaves, who became known as "exodusters" when they moved to Kansas.

Even more important than the Homestead Act in settling the West was the federal government's policy toward the four transcontinental railroads. The railroad companies received huge grants of land and sold it in small parcels. The railroads provided crucial transportation for getting farm products to market. People from the East and from Europe came in response to their advertisements. In 1889 the government also opened the Indian territory of Oklahoma to settlement.

There were several physical hardships on the prairies. Both hailstorms and the sun beat down on people and on animals. Dry summers meant prairie fires. The early 1870's were marked by a series of grasshopper plagues. In addition, many families suffered from emotional strains.

Four Inventions

Four inventions helped farmers on the Great Plains, though. One was barbed wire. It kept cattle from wandering off and also kept them from trampling crops. A second important invention was the steel windmill. The steady prairie winds drove the pumps needed to bring the water from the deep wells

Telescoping the Times may be used as an alternative to having students read the entire unit, as a unit preview, or as a unit review.

to the surface. A third and earlier invention was Deere's steel plow, which made it possible to break the tough prairie sod. Finally, an improved reaper not only cut wheat but also threshed it. Inventions like these made the Great Plains highly productive.

All this machinery cost money, and farmers had to borrow from banks. They also found themselves at the mercy of the railroads. Normally there was only one railroad in a given area, and the companies were able to charge very high rates.

The Industrial Age

The new industrial age rested on changes in technology. The most important was electricity. It provided the energy for the telegraph. By 1900 Americans were sending sixty-three million telegrams a year. Edison applied for more than one thousand patents, but his most important invention was the light bulb. Bell's popular telephone also depended on electricity. The need for telephone operators opened up a whole new field of jobs for women.

Sholes's invention of the typewriter did even more for the employment of women outside the home. The typewriter provided steady work that seemed better than work in a factory. By 1900 three-quarters of office workers were women. The jobs were usually restricted to white women born in the United States.

The new industrial age depended on steel, which was much stronger and easier to work with than iron. A new process brought down the price of steel, and soon the open hearths of Pittsburgh and other cities were pouring forth enormous quantities of this metal. People found hundreds of uses for steel. The new canning industry used steel cans coated with tin. Railroads and construction companies bought huge quantities of steel for rails and skyscrapers.

The nation was blessed with the natural resources needed for this revolution. Three of them—iron, coal, and oil—proved to be especially important.

Railroads and Corruption

By 1900 the railroad industry was the largest business in the United States. The speed of trains over long distances pushed the country into adopting time zones. Today there are twenty-four time zones around the earth. Many people urged the development of a transcontinental railroad. Two companies received government land to support their efforts. The Union Pacific laid track west from Nebraska. It employed veterans of the Civil War and immigrants from Ireland. The Central Pacific laid track east from California. It hired thousands of Chinese workers. Both groups of workers had to face many dangers, especially while tunneling through the high mountains of the Far West. When the tracks came together in Utah in 1869, the nation was joined from coast to coast.

The amount of money that went into this project was enormous, as was the amount of corruption. The Crédit Mobilier construction company skimmed off a great deal. The owners of this company were railroad officials who both overcharged and overpaid out of government funds. They also bribed members of Congress.

Farmers began to fight back against the railroads. A new organization called the Grange demanded lower rates and laws to regulate the big companies. Railroad lawyers tried to stop the Grangers by suing them. In 1887 Congress passed the Interstate Commerce Act, which set up the Interstate Commerce Commission. It did not work well at first. The courts gave farmers little sympathy. However, the act established the idea that the government could regulate private business for the public good.

Big Business

New methods of agriculture and industry needed new methods of doing business. Carnegie was one of the most successful organizers of industry. As a young boy he started out in a factory and ended up the owner of the largest steel company in the world. His business integrated steel production by controlling all steps of the process.

Various businesses found ways of controlling large parts of the American economy. They combined businesses through holding companies, mergers, interlocking directorates, and trusts. These methods gave people such as Rockefeller a grip on huge industries. The Sherman Antitrust Act failed to break up these trusts. Social Darwinism and Horatio Alger stories justified wealth for self-fulfillment and success.

Workers and Reformers

All this new industry brought misery for many workers. Factories were noisy and impersonal. A typical workweek lasted seventy-two hours. Accidents with machinery killed and injured thousands of people. Child labor, sweatshops, and company towns became ways of life for many Americans.

The National Labor Union aimed for an eight-hour workday. It achieved that goal for government workers. The organization did not survive the depression of 1873 because so many people were unemployed. Another depression in 1877 led to a bloody strike on the nation's railroad lines when the companies cut wages and lengthened the workday. A local strike spread from one railroad to another and then to coal miners and steelworkers in Pittsburgh. The government called out troops to keep the railroads open. American workers were killed by American soldiers.

The Knights of Labor succeeded for a while under the leadership of Powderly. By the mid-1800's, it boasted 700,000 members. Two developments led to its downfall. The Haymarket bombing in Chicago gave unions a bad name, and other unions competed with the Knights of Labor.

Two new concepts about labor unions took change in another direction. Gompers organized the American Federation of Labor. The AFL pulled together unions of various skilled crafts into one national organization. Debs tried a different approach. Usually called industrial unionism, his idea was to organize all workers in a single industry no matter what their job. His American Railway Union included all railroad workers.

Women also began to organize. Employed in certain industries, such as textiles and clothing, they received far less pay than men. Newman organized a union for the young immigrant workers of the garment industry. A fire at the Triangle Shirtwaist Company factory actually helped change public opinion by revealing deadly working conditions. Mother Jones also appealed to public opinion in her crusade against child labor. Usually, though, the government and the courts supported management rather than labor unions.

Gradually, people began to urge reform of the government itself. They demanded that the spoils system be changed into a merit system for government workers. Presidents Hayes, Garfield, and Arthur all pressed for a less corrupt way of appointing government workers. The 1883 Pendleton Act set up a civil service based on the merit system.

Women called for reform of the suffrage. They won the vote in several Western states. Yet Anthony and other women met strong opposition at the national level. For a long time, suffrage for women seemed to get nowhere.

Farmers in debt demanded a national policy of currency inflation. They called for more greenbacks and more silver. Eventually, three groups of farmers came together to form the Populist party—one group came from the plains, one was composed of white farmers in the South, and one was made up of black farmers in the South. In 1892 Populists offered a platform of reform for the American economy and political system. The election of 1896 was a major battle. The voters had to choose between Bryan's policy of inflation through bimetallism and McKinley's deflationary policy of a gold standard. McKinley won. The Populists faded away because of the nation's new prosperity, but many of their demands have since been met.

Chronology of Main Events

1876 Sioux Indians defeat Custer's troops

1885 Grover Cleveland inaugurated President

1890 Sherman Antitrust Act

1891 Populist Party organized

1896 *Plessy* v. *Ferguson*

1897 William McKinley inaugurated President

1900 Gold Standard Act

GLOBAL TIME LINE

The World

1882
British troops occupy Egypt

1886
Gold discovered
in South Africa

1889
First Pan American Conference

1894
France and Russia
sign military alliance

1880

1890

**The
United States**

1881
President Garfield
assassinated

1890
Sherman Antitrust Act

1891
Populist party formed

1896
Plessy v. *Ferguson*
upholds segregation in
"separate but equal" ruling

1898
Spanish-American War

UNIT 5 1876–1920

Onto a World Stage

Geographic Setting

Movement. People from all over the world flocked to Chicago in 1893 for the Columbian Exposition. Before the fair, Chicago had been looked upon as an unsophisticated Midwestern city. After the fair, it rose in stature to become a center of science, industry, and culture. The fair provided a world tour and an opportunity to learn about new scientific and technological advances. A visitor could view (from the left) the Egyptian obelisk, the Spanish Renaissance spires of Machinery Hall, the Administration Building, and the neoclassic palace, which exhibited the wonders of electricity. In this spectacular setting, spectators could study new designs and inventions.

Unit Overview

The expansion of industry stimulated the development of new cities and brought rapid growth to older ones. Industrialization increased the demand for unskilled labor and attracted waves of immigrants to the land of opportunity. Increased productivity led to the need for new markets, and Americans began to build an empire to enhance their position in world trade. The turn of the century saw the rise of the Progressive movement as many Americans pressed for social and political reforms. Unit 5 explains in four chapters how the nation moved into the twentieth century.

Unit Outline

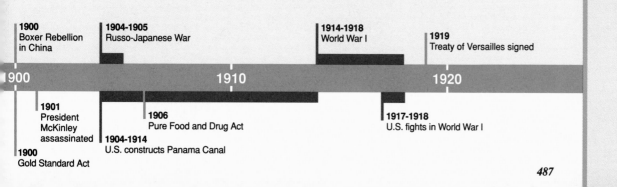

1900 Boxer Rebellion in China

1904-1905 Russo-Japanese War

1914-1918 World War I

1919 Treaty of Versailles signed

1900   1910   1920

1901 President McKinley assassinated

1906 Pure Food and Drug Act

1904-1914 U.S. constructs Panama Canal

1917-1918 U.S. fights in World War I

1900 Gold Standard Act

Global Perspectives

1877	Queen Victoria becomes Empress of India.
1886	Gold is discovered in South Africa.
1894	Japan and Korea declare war on China.
1899	Sigmund Freud publishes *The Interpretation of Dreams*.
1901	Australia declares its independence.
1912	China establishes a Republic.

For Discussion

How might the discovery of gold in South Africa have affected Africa's relations with Europe and the U.S.? (Possible response: European nations as well as the U.S. might have been anxious to develop a sphere of influence over the area containing the gold.)

Additional Resources

- Geography Activities
- Skills Activities
- Thematic Activities
- Economic Activities
- Cultural Literacy Activities
- Literary Source Readings
- Primary Source Readings
- Nuclear Peacekeeping
- Transparencies
- Computer Test Generator

Additional Teaching Strategies

SECTION 1

For Basic Students: Ask students to write the names of the jobs of one or both parents, a sibling, or themselves. Collect the papers, read the job titles, and discuss with students which of these jobs must be performed in an urban area. Ask students what problems are created by the heavy concentration of jobs in urban areas. (Possible responses: crowded housing conditions; transportation problems; lack of efficient sanitation system; corrupt city governments; maintenance of law and order.)

For Advanced Students: Ask each student to assume the role of an 1890's city planner in a newly developing industrial city. Students should design a city that would eliminate or substantially reduce at least one of the urban problems described in this section. Students may use sketches, maps, or models to explain their innovations. Display students' work.

SECTION 2

For Basic Students: Have students reread aloud the primary source readings on pages 495 and 496. Ask students to write a paragraph answering the following questions: What did a precinct captain for a political machine do? What kept voters loyal to the machine? What did the machine do to subvert free elections? (Paragraph should include: precinct captains helped people in need, secured jobs for voters, provided recreation; voters remained loyal because the machine helped them with jobs, housing, etc.; the machine paid voters to vote more than once, listed dead people and animals on polling lists.) Have students share their paragraphs.

For Advanced Students: Ask students to locate newspaper editorials or editorial cartoons critical of some aspect of local or federal government. Then discuss the role of a free press in maintaining democratic institutions. (Discussion might include: free press holds government officials accountable for their actions and promises; it may expose problems to the public that would otherwise go unnoticed.)

SECTION 3

For Basic Students: Ask students to write two paragraphs explaining why immigrants settled in ethnic ghettos and listing the advantages and disadvantages of such areas. (Reasons for settling in ethnic ghettos might include: family or friends already lived there; people understood language and might get help in finding housing and employment; immigrants felt more secure. Advantages of ethnic ghettos include: security; no language problems; no discrimination. Disadvantages of ethnic ghettos include: immigrants did not learn new language, customs, foods; they became victims of prejudice; school was difficult for children.)

For Advanced Students: Ask students to imagine they are newly arrived immigrants. Ask them to keep a journal of their first two weeks in America, focusing on the problems they face, how they adapt, and what they are feeling. (Problems might include: new language; inability to find way around city; strange food; no job or income; cramped living quarters. Feelings might include: happiness at finally being in America; fear; anxiety; loneliness; homesickness.) Have students share their journals.

SECTION 4

For Basic Students: Ask students to prepare a quiz of questions to match the Key Terms and People from this section. Then have students exchange papers and complete the quizzes.

For Advanced Students: Have students complete additional research on anti-Asian legislation. Students should then give a two-minute presentation arguing for or against passage of the acts. (Presentations should include: the purpose of the legislation; the proposed results; reasons for or against passage.)

Further Reading for Students

Antin, Mary. *The Promised Land*. Salem, N.H.: Ayer Publishing, 1980.

Beard, Annie E. *Our Foreign Born Citizens*. New York: Crowell Jr. Books, 1968.

Coppa, Frank J., and Thomas J. Curran. *The Immigrant Experience in America*. Boston: Twayne, 1976.

Neidle, Cecyle S. *America's Immigrant Women*. New York: Hippocrene Books, 1976. Paper.

Strasser, Susan. *Never Done: A History of American Housework*. New York: Pantheon Books, 1982.

Historical Fiction

Crane, Stephen. *Bowery Tales*. Charlottesville: University Press of Virginia, 1969.

Crane, Stephen. *Maggie, A Girl of the Streets and Other Short Fiction*. New York: Bantam, 1986. Paper.

Ferber, Edna. *Saratoga Trunk*. New York: Fawcett Book Group, 1980. Paper.

Flavin, Martin. *Journey in the Dark*. Westport, Conn.: Greenwood Press, 1970.

Bibliography for Teachers

Books

Asimov, Isaac. *The Golden Door: The United States from 1865 to 1918*. Boston: Houghton Mifflin, 1977.

Brownstone, David M., and Irene M. Franck, ed. *Island of Hope, Island of Tears*. New York: Penguin, 1986.

Katz, William Loren, and Jacqueline Hunt Katz. *Making Our Way: America at the Turn of the Century in the Wards of the Poor and Powerless*. New York: Deal, 1975.

Kraut, Alan M. *The Huddled Masses: The Immigrant in American Society, 1880-1921*. Arlington Heights, Ill.: Harlan Davidson, 1982.

Riis, Jacob. *The Making of an American*. Philadelphia: Century Bookbindery, 1983.

Schlesinger, Arthur M. Jr., and D.R. Fox, eds. *Rise of the City 1878-1898*. History of American Life Series, vol. 10. New York: Macmillan, 1933.

Steiner, Stan. *Fusang: The Chinese Who Built America*. New York: Harper & Row, 1980.

Audio-Visuals

America, the Melting Pot: Myth or Reality? Current Affairs. Filmstrip.

The Immigrant Experience: The Long, Long Journey. Omaha-Orange Films. Movie.

Immigration in America's History. Coronet. Movie.

Urban Bosses and Immigrants. Encyclopaedia Britannica Learning Corporation. Filmstrip.

Computer Resources

Ethnic Groups. (Apple/IBM) Intellectual Software.

Social Studies Vol. I. (Apple) MECC.

Teacher's Notes:

Teaching Resources, Unit 5 Booklet

Lesson Study Sheets pp. 1-16
Daily Activities pp. 17-24
Enrichment Activities pp. 25-32
Reteaching Activities pp. 33-40
Chapter Review p. 41
Chapter Mastery Tests pp. 43-54
Telescoping the Times Study Sheet p. 55

Chapter Objectives

Students will learn:
- the problems faced by urban Americans in the late nineteenth and early twentieth centuries
- why political machines were an important part of nineteenth-century urban America
- the patterns of immigration and the problems faced by the new immigrants in the late nineteenth century
- the origins of immigration restrictions in the U.S.

Using the Chapter Time Line
How many years passed between the opening of Japanese ports to U.S. trade (see Unit 3 Time Line) and the signing of the Gentlemen's Agreement? (Answer: 54) What was happening in Europe (see Unit 5 Time Line) when the Immigration Restriction League was forming in the U.S.? (Answer: France and Russia were entering into a military alliance)

Picturing History In this photograph, a family registers some of the emotions—curiosity, homesickness, fear, fatigue, and excitement—felt by immigrants coming to the United States through Ellis Island.

1875   1885   1895   1905   1915

1882
Chinese immigration restricted

1889
Benjamin Harrison inaugurated president

1894
Immigration Restriction League founded

1907
Gentlemen's Agreement reached with Japan

1913
Alien Land Law passed in California

Links to American Literature

Howard Melvin Fast: born in 1914; won a Stalin International Peace Prize; wrote propagandistic works for the Communist party; was blacklisted from the Hollywood film studios; writes historical fiction.

Works include: *Conceived in Liberty* (1939); *Citizen Tom Paine* (1943); *April Morning* (1961); *The Immigrants, Second Generation, The Establishment*, and *The Legacy* set in San Francisco; children's books, short stories, plays, biographies, and detective and mystery novels.

The Immigrants: introduces immigrants from all over the world; deals with problems common to all immigrants as well as problems particular to those who arrived on the West Coast.

Introducing the Chapter

Have students skim the chapter and look at photographs, cartoons, and pictures. Ask students what information these visuals provide about life in the late nineteenth century. (Possible responses: life was difficult; there were few conveniences; many immigrants were coming to America.) Survey the class to find out how many students have relatives or friends who have migrated from other countries. List these countries on the board and have students locate them on a large wall map. Ask students to suggest reasons people might leave their homeland. (Possible responses: famine; unemployment; oppressive government.)

CHAPTER **19** 1876–1915

Cities and Immigrants

Links to American Literature

During the two hours he had been there, on the busy wharf crowded with buyers and sellers and fishermen and commission men and market owners, he had spoken to no one and asked no questions. That was only common sense and reasonable caution. This was 1910 and San Francisco, and he was Chinese. He lived and breathed and walked and talked by sufferance, and there was no moment in his life when he was not alert and wary. . . .

He went to the door of the shanty, took off his hat, and knocked. . . .

"Well?" . . .

"Please, sir, with all humility, may I announce that my name is Feng Wo. I am thirty-four years old and in good health, and I am a bookkeeper."

"What the . . .—"

"Please, sir, please do not send me away without hearing my argument. Here in the News"—he held out the paper—"here I read your advertisement."

"The ad says four P.M."

"And I am Chinese."

"You sure . . . are," Lavette agreed.

'And if I appeared at four, as the advertisement says, there would be ten Caucasians here. Then who would hire a Chinese bookkeeper?"

— HOWARD FAST, *The Immigrants*

As industry grew, so did America's cities. Between 1870 and 1900, the urban population tripled. Crowding, poverty, and unemployment became pressing problems, especially for the immigrants who faced a difficult road as they tried to cope with a new language, new customs, and prejudice. Understanding our nation's immigrants is an important key to understanding ourselves.

Chapter Overview

In this chapter you will learn about the problems of urban Americans at the turn of the century and about the political machines that developed during that time. You will also learn about the new immigrants who came to our shores and about the reasons for the rise of a movement to shut America's "golden door." To help you understand the problems of cities and immigrants, this chapter is divided into four sections.

Chapter Outline

1. **Problems Arise as Cities Grow**
2. **Political Machines Acquire More Power**
3. **The New Immigrants Arrive**
4. **Demands Grow for Restrictions on Immigration**

489

Core Lesson

Anticipate the Lesson

Discuss with students the phrase "quality of life" and develop a general definition. (Possible definition: the degree to which basic needs and luxuries of life are met.) Have students list on the board things that can affect the quality of life. (Possible responses: money; friendships; job; family; status in the community.) Ask students to circle those that might have been important to people in the late nineteenth

and early twentieth centuries. (Possible response: students will likely circle all responses that are not of a material nature, since items such as friendship and family reflect values that have changed very little.)

State the Objective

Understand the problems faced by urban Americans in the late nineteenth and early twentieth centuries.

SECTION 1

Problems Arise as Cities Grow

GLOSSARY TERMS: **urbanization, dumbbell tenements, de facto segregation, ghettos**

Urbanization, or the movement of people from the country to the city, was concentrated in the northeastern part of the United States. That was natural because the Northeast was where most of the nation's industry was located.

The cities grew because the factories, mines, mills, and transportation systems needed millions of workers to turn out the goods that were making the nation rich. Additional millions were needed in trade and service occupations—to sell goods; to clean houses; and to work in laundries, real estate offices, restaurants, and banks.

People flocked to the cities for the same reason they had flocked to the western frontier—they were seeking the opportunity to work, to escape poverty, and to carve out a better life for themselves and their children. The majority of newcomers came from American farms. The rest came from overseas, mostly from Europe. Like their American counterparts, most of them left a rural environment to enter an urban one.

As a result of this tremendous growth, American cities in the new industrial age faced a variety of problems. The most fundamental was housing.

Newcomers Need Housing

For wealthy people, housing in cities was no problem. They lived in large private homes with a staff of servants that took care of the cooking, cleaning, and children. When they wanted to go somewhere, their horse-drawn carriages took them. The only inconvenience was the absence of zoning laws. An elegant mansion might be situated near a slaughterhouse or a gasworks. Wealth was no protection against polluted city air.

Middle-Class Options. The situation for middle-class families was different. When the new industrial age began, they had a simple choice. They could buy a house on the outskirts of town where land was cheap and commute into the central business district when necessary. Or they could live in a centrally located boardinghouse where they shared the kitchen and the dining room with several other families.

As the industrial age developed, builders began to offer two additional possibilities: the apartment house and the row house. The first apartment house was built in 1870 on East 18th Street in New York City. Each apartment contained six rooms and a bath. Rents ranged from $1,000 to $1,500 a year. The idea caught on quickly. By the 1880's there were numerous six- and eight-story apartment buildings throughout the city. They had such modern conveniences as elevator service, a built-in kitchen range, and a hot-water heater.

It was the **row house,** however, that really captured the fancy of middle-class urban dwellers. With row housing, each family could own a home. At the same time, construction costs were low because a row house shared its side walls with its neighbors and took up comparatively little land. By the 1880's New York contained hundreds of

People in the Chapter

William Tweed ("Boss Tweed") was the only member of the Tweed Ring tried and convicted of embezzlement. After a sensational escape from prison, he turned up in Spain and was sent back to the United States. He died in prison.

Grover Cleveland was a portly bachelor who created quite a stir when he married his pretty young ward, Frances Folsom. The name of their baby, Ruth, was borrowed for a candy bar. Their second child, Esther, was the first child ever born in the White House.

Henry Cabot Lodge, Sr., was an outspoken Massachusetts senator with distinguished lineage that dated back to colonial times. His son, Henry Cabot Lodge, Jr., became a key political figure during the Vietnam era.

Theodore Roosevelt was the youngest man to become President. He was forty-two when he took the office following the assassination of William McKinley.

490

Present the Lesson

On the board write the following headings: Housing; Transportation; Water and Sanitation; Law and Order; Fire Protection. Ask students to review the section to find information and to complete an outline that shows why each was a problem in urban areas and how cities tried to solve each one. Outlines might include:

Housing

- Multi-family dwellings were called tenements; some contained no windows or plumbing.
- Rents were high.
- Building codes were not enforced.
- Tenements were overcrowded, filthy.
- New York passed a law (1879) to improve living conditions by creating "dumbbell" tenements which also soon became overcrowded and filthy.

Discuss with students the extent to which the cities were successful in solving their problems. (Possible responses for housing: successes—row houses and apartment buildings; failures—dumbbell tenements.)

brownstone blocks whose row houses, looking very much alike, were built of reddish-brown sandstone and had cast-iron fences in the front.

Row-House Living. Living in a row house was comfortable. Each room had brass fixtures for gas jets or, by the early 1900's, electric bulbs. The furnace fire glowed all night, so you did not wake up shivering with cold. A gas flame heated the water in the water tank and fueled the stove. Every house had a bathroom with tiled walls, an indoor water closet (toilet), running water, and porcelain or enameled fixtures.

Middle-class families who could afford row houses usually could take advantage of several other changes in life style. The invention of the refrigerator meant you had to shop for food only twice a week. If you owned a telephone, you did not even have to make the trip to the store because grocery stores delivered to homes. In addition, you no longer had to bake your own bread but could have it delivered fresh each morning. You could buy vegetables in season and milk from the wagons of the grocer and the milkman as they made their daily rounds. Likewise, cleaning was easier. The newly invented carpet sweeper was much more efficient than the broom. There was an abundance of hot water for doing dishes. Commercial laundries took care of most of the family wash. New soaps, oils, and waxes that could be used on a regular basis meant you no longer had to go through the ordeal of a thorough spring cleaning.

The Development of Tenements. Poor people, who made up the majority of a city's population, lived in multifamily dwellings called tenements. Originally tenements had developed as industrial areas expanded. When this happened, middle-class families moved away from the factories to more desirable areas. After they left, their residences were converted into housing for several families rather than one. Because each family was on a different floor, some had no water or plumbing. After a while, rooms as well as floors were divided, so most tenants found themselves without windows. Outhouses and stables were likewise converted into dwellings. Rents were high, and because building codes were not enforced, landlords seldom maintained the property even though their profits ranged from 30 to 100 percent a year.

These tenements soon became overcrowded, airless, and filthy. Jacob Riis, a Danish-born news-

Picturing History The back porches of tenements were places for meeting and exchanging gossip, particularly on wash days. These tenements were on Roosevelt Street in New York City's Lower East Side.

paper reporter, described the relationship between tenements and disease in his book *How the Other Half Lives.*

> Suppose we look into one? . . . Be a little careful, please! The hall is dark and you might stumble over the children pitching pennies back there. . . . Close? Yes! What would you have? All the fresh air that ever enters these stairs comes from the hall-door that is forever slamming. . . .
>
> Here is a door. Listen! That short hacking cough, that tiny helpless wail—what do they mean? . . . Oh! a sadly familiar story. . . . The child is dying with measles. With half a chance it might have lived; but it had none. That dark bedroom killed it.

For Discussion

What are some urban problems in your community or nearby city? (Possible responses: crime; garbage collection; streets and sidewalks in need of repair; decaying or abandoned buildings.) Compare these with the problems described in this section. Which problems exist now as they did then? (Possible responses: crime control; overcrowding.) Which problems did not exist in the late nineteenth century? (Possible responses: drug control; traffic control.)

Check for Understanding

Call on individual students to answer Section 1
Review questions orally.

Picturing History Many of the urban
poor lived in overcrowded, unsanitary,
and unhealthy conditions such as these.

Attempt at Reform. As the largest city in the
nation, New York had the largest slum areas with
the worst tenements. In 1879 it passed a law
designed to improve slum conditions. The law
called for construction of **dumbbell tenements.**
These were long, narrow buildings, five- or six-
stories high, that covered the entire lot of twenty-
five by one hundred feet except for a tiny yard at
one end. The central part was indented on either
side to allow for an air shaft and, thus, an outside
window for each room.

Dumbbell tenements, however, quickly became
overcrowded. People dumped their wastes into the
air shafts. Since there was no way to clean the
bottom of the shafts, they became breeding places
for rats and vermin. The stench was so bad that
people nailed the air-shaft windows shut. These
problems made the dumbbell tenements even worse
places to live than the converted row houses.

Workers Need Transportation

Housing was not the only problem confronting
American cities. Transportation was another.

Before the new industrial age, people moved
around town on foot or by horsecar. Horsecars,
however, were small and went only six miles an
hour. New means of transportation were needed to
move large numbers of workers to and from their
jobs.

In 1867 New York became the first city to build
an elevated railway, or el, that ran on a track above
the street. The el was driven by a coalburning
steam locomotive. Although the el carried hundreds of passengers at a time, it had several
disadvantages. The track structure cut off light and
air from buildings along the way, and the trains
dropped soot and hot ashes on pedestrians below.

Gradually other mass-transit innovations were
introduced. In 1873 San Francisco, a city of steep
hills, installed a cable car driven by a moving
underground chain. The electric trolley car, or
street car, began running in Richmond in 1888. In
1897 the electric subway was introduced in Boston.

Water and Sanitation Systems
Need Attention

At the start of the new industrial age, urban
Americans bought their drinking water in bottles
that were sold from horse-drawn carts. By the turn
of the century, most cities had installed water mains
and piped water directly to homes.

Sanitation was more difficult to handle. True,
scavenger pigs no longer roamed about, and some
cities employed workers to sweep the streets and

Guided Practice

Explain to students that many of the housing patterns that existed in the 1900's persist in some cities today. A common pattern of movement in many American cities in the 50's, 60's, and 70's was "white flight" to the suburbs. Ask students to suggest ways that cities have made progress in changing this pattern. (Possible responses: tax breaks to businesses who move back to the cities; revitalization of major downtown areas; restoration of old areas; low interest loans for those buying and restoring homes in these areas.) Ask students to identify the advantages of a culturally diverse city.

(Possible responses: exchange of ideas; exposure to new cultures, languages, foods, integration.)

Assign Independent Practice

Ask students to reread the section on middle-class housing and list all the late nineteenth and early twentieth century innovations that are standard equipment for domestic households today. Students should then identify any innovation that has since become obsolete.

Standard Equipment
- Indoor bathroom
- Elevator service
- Built-in kitchen range
- Furnace
- Refrigerator
- Hot water heater
- Electric lights

Obsolete Equipment
- Carpet sweeper

dampen down the dust. The typical situation, however, was described by writer H. L. Mencken:

> All the sewers of Baltimore, whether private or public, emptied into the Back Basin in those days, just as all those of Manhattan empty into the North and East rivers. . . . But I should add that there is a difference, for the North and East rivers have swift tidal currents, whereas the Back Basin . . . had only the most lethargic. As a result it began to acquire a powerful aroma every Spring, and by August smelled like a billion polecats.

Law and Order Is Difficult to Maintain

Another problem that confronted American cities was how to maintain law and order. Full-time, salaried police forces with special uniforms were not organized until the 1850's—and then only in such large cities as Boston, New York, and Philadelphia. These forces were usually small. Certainly they were too small to handle the increased crime that went along with the increased population of the cities. Pickpockets and shoplifters flourished in urban crowds, while confidence men found it easy to sell counterfeit money to country folk and non-English-speaking immigrants.

Violent crimes were likewise commonplace. Tour guides in 1876, for example, warned tourists to "Reach the city in the daytime" and "Take the car or stage which passes nearest your stopping place." Areas of certain cities were known as Robbers' Roost and Murderers' Alley. Gangs of young toughs controlled such areas, and it was dangerous for police to enter them.

Linking Past to Present

In 1900 three American cities—New York, Chicago, and Philadelphia—had populations of over one million. By 1990, there were 39 metropolitan areas with populations over one million. As such areas grew, crime and other urban problems increased significantly. According to a 1987 Census Bureau study, the average city spends $85.71 annually per resident for police protection. This cost has been the largest single expenditure in city budgets for many years.

New Firefighting Methods Are Sought

On October 8, 1871, a wagon driver named Daniel "Peg Leg" Sullivan was drinking whiskey in his neighbor's barn as he often did. The reason he drank there and not at home was that his mother disapproved of the habit. That night, so the story goes, Sullivan took one drink too many and dropped a kerosene lamp into a hay pile. Mrs. Catherine O'Leary's barn caught fire, and what was called the most destructive accidental blaze in history swept through Chicago. When it was over, about 500 persons were dead; 18,000 buildings were destroyed; and more than 100,000 persons, almost one-third of the city's population, were left homeless.

Almost every American city suffered a major fire during the 1870's and 1880's. One reason was that most houses were still built of wood. Another reason was the existence of volunteer rather than salaried fire departments. Although volunteers were skilled firefighters, they were also very competitive. Instead of cooperating to put out a blaze, they would fight over which company's hose would get attached to the fire hydrant.

Gradually, however, the situation improved. The city of Cleveland had set an example by establishing the nation's first salaried fire department in 1853. By 1900 the only volunteer fire departments left were in suburbs or small towns. Another aid to fighting fires was the automatic fire sprinkler, which was invented in 1877. Most important, however, was the fact that numerous wooden buildings were replaced by buildings made of brick, stone, and concrete.

African Americans Are Segregated in Urban Ghettos

When the Civil War ended, most of the nation's African Americans lived in rural areas. Fewer than 5 percent of the black population lived in cities. By 1890 the proportion had increased to 12 percent, and by 1910 it had reached 25 percent. About three out of four urban African Americans lived in Washington and in such Southern cities as Atlanta, Baltimore, Memphis, New Orleans, Savannah, and Shreveport. The rest were concentrated in such Northern communities as Chicago, New York, Philadelphia, and St. Louis.

Until about 1890 urban blacks and whites often shared the same neighborhood. After 1890 Jim Crow legislation brought about strict racial segre-

Student Assignment/Homework

Have students read Section 2, "Political Machines Acquire More Power," and write the answers to Section 2 Review questions on paper.

Anticipate the Lesson

Review the major areas of urban problems: housing, transportation, water and sanitation, law and order, fire protection. Then ask students how local political machines might have contributed to these problems. (Possible responses: poor political leadership; patronage; excesses; corruption; vote fraud.)

SECTION 1 REVIEW

Answers

Main Ideas

1. Housing shortages, substandard housing, inadequate transportation, poor sanitation, crime, inadequate fire protection, and racial segregation.

2. Apartment houses and row houses. Both came with fixtures, furnaces, hot water, and private bathrooms.

3. To improve slum conditions of tenements.

4. African Americans were forced to live in the worst tenements in the worst sections of cities, and a large proportion of their earnings went to pay rent.

Critical Thinking

5. Possible answer: yes—despite urban problems, most people could use the work opportunities and modern conveniences that cities offered to improve their lives. **(evaluation)**

gation of housing in the South. The rest of the country did not adopt Jim Crow laws. However, increasing racial prejudice, spurred by competition for industrial jobs, brought about **de facto segregation,** that is, a pattern of segregation supported by custom rather than law. (Segregation supported by law is known as de jure segregation.)

What were the results of de facto segregation? As the New York *Freeman,* a black newspaper, said in 1885:

> [African Americans] are not only forced to colonize in the worst sections of the city, and into the very worst tenements, but they are charged fabulous prices for the luxury of having a place to sleep and eat.

Picturing History De facto segregation kept poor urban blacks at a disadvantage: they made less than whites at their jobs, but they paid more for goods and services than did whites.

It was estimated that urban blacks had to spend between one-third and one-half of their earnings on rent. Urban whites usually spent only one-fifth of their earnings on rent.

At the same time, however, the concentration of African Americans in a particular area encouraged them to set up their own commercial institutions. Some were in businesses that provided personal services to blacks such as hairdressing and undertaking. Others entered areas of finance that whites considered too risky, such as insuring blacks' lives and property or arranging credit for them. Thousands of such enterprises were established in New York's Harlem and other black **ghettos.** (A ghetto is a section of a city in which members of a

minority group live or to which they are restricted because of economic pressure or social discrimination.) Most black businesses were small, and many failed. Nevertheless, a black middle class gradually developed in the nation's cities.

SECTION 1 REVIEW

Key Terms and People

Explain the significance of: urbanization, row house, dumbbell tenements, de facto segregation, ghettos

Main Ideas

1. In general, what were the main urban problems during the new industrial age?
2. What two new housing options became available to the urban middle class in the new industrial age, and what modern conveniences did they provide?
3. What was the purpose of the New York City law that called for the construction of dumbbell tenements?
4. What were the negative effects of de facto segregation on the urban black population during this period?

Critical Thinking

5. For most people, did the advantages of city living outweigh the disadvantages during this period? Explain.

SECTION 2

Political Machines Acquire More Power

GLOSSARY TERMS: **political machine, Tweed Ring**

Many of the problems you have just read about are now handled by local government. In the new industrial age, local government itself was a problem. As scholar James Bryce wrote in 1888, "There is no denying that the government of cities is the one conspicuous failure of the United States." Two years later, another scholar called American cities "the worst [governed] in Christiandom—the most expensive, the most inefficient, and the most corrupt."

494

State the Objective

Understand how political machines played an important part in nineteenth-century urban America.

Present the Lesson

Ask students to skim the section for information and to prepare a chart showing the positive and negative activities of political machines. Remind students to look at political machines from various viewpoints.

Positive
- Dealt with problems in the areas of housing, fire, money, employment, immigration, police and legal matters
- Provided for social needs

Negative
- Bought votes with favors
- Accepted payment for favorable treatment
- Padded lists of eligible voters
- Padded bills at taxpayers' expense

Encourage students to refer to these lists as they study this section.

Perhaps local government was so inept because cities mushroomed almost overnight. Their leaders did not have a chance to learn how to handle a few problems gradually. Instead, they found themselves facing a tremendous number of problems within a short period.

Consider New York, for example. Its population doubled five times in less than a generation as millions of immigrants from here and abroad moved in. Yet the city's government was divided among a mayor, a city council, and various boards, none of which had clear responsibility for anything. In addition, the old-line leadership tended to look down on the newcomers and ignore their needs.

The absence of responsible government, combined with the sheer size of urban problems, opened the way for a new power structure. This was the **political machine.** Dominated by a political boss, the political machine was a well-organized group that controlled all the activities of a political party in a large area.

Voters Support Political Machines

The typical party machine worked on two levels. It provided services to the general population in exchange for votes. It provided favorable treatment from government officials for businesses in exchange for money.

Working a District. George Washington Plunkitt, a precinct captain for **Tammany Hall,** the Democratic political machine in New York City, explained why the people in his district voted the way he wanted.

If there's a fire in Ninth, Tenth, or Eleventh Avenue, for example, any hour of the day or night, I'm usually there . . . as soon as the fire engines. If a family is burned out, I don't ask them whether they are Republicans or Democrats, and I don't refer them to the Charity Organization Society, which would investigate their case in a month or two and decide they were worthy of help about the time they are dead from starvation. I just get quarters for them, buy clothes for them if their clothes were burned up, and fix them up till they get things runnin' again. It's philanthropy, but it's politics, too, mighty good politics. . . . The poor are the most grateful people in the world, and, let me tell you, they have more friends in their neighborhoods than the rich have in theirs. . . .

Another thing, I can always get a job for a deservin' man. I make it a point to keep on the track of jobs, and it seldom happens that I don't have a few up my sleeve ready for use.

Nor did Plunkitt stop with helping people who were hit by fire or unemployment. He helped immigrants with their naturalization proceedings. He put in a good word for youngsters who got into trouble with the police. He paid court fines for constituents who were picked up for being drunk. He paid attention to people's needs for social outlets.

I hear of a young feller that's proud of his voice. . . . I ask him to come around . . . and join our Glee Club. He comes and sings, and he's a follower of Plunkitt for life. Another young feller gains a reputation as a base-ball

Picturing History
Immigrants kept many of the traditions they had enjoyed in their homeland. Here, a German band poses in front of the Cincinnati Music Hall.

Check for Understanding

Have students write two paragraphs explaining a political machine and its connections with city government and newly-arrived immigrants. (Possible details: political machine helped find housing and employment and eased the naturalization process; it ran the city and padded contracts to make money.)

Guided Practice

Discuss with students the steps cities might take in order to put the management of cities in more professional hands. (Possible responses: voter awareness campaigns; political party support of highly qualified candidates.)

Assign Independent Practice

Have students complete Chapter 19, Section 2 Enrichment Activity.

player in a vacant lot. I bring him into our base-ball club. That fixes him. You'll find him workin' for my ticket at the polls next election day . . . I rope them all in by givin' them opportunities to show themselves off. I don't trouble them with political arguments.

Sometimes, however, even the loyalty of the poor was not enough to carry an election. Under those circumstances, political machines turned to fraud. They padded the lists of those eligible to vote with the names of dead dogs, children, and nonexistent persons. Then they cast as many votes as were needed to win.

Municipal Graft. Once a political machine got its candidates into office, there were numerous opportunities for making money. The basic technique was the same that businessmen involved in the Crédit Mobilier scandal had used: namely, padding bills. (See page 444.) If you worked for the city, you simply turned in a bill that was a fixed percentage higher than the actual cost of the materials or service. Then you paid the difference to the machine.

Perhaps the most extravagant example of graft was that involved in the construction of the New York County Courthouse, which was built while Tammany Hall was under the control of the **Tweed Ring,** a group of unscrupulous politicians led by William Marcy "Boss" Tweed. The building cost about $11 million, or 1.5 times as much as it cost to buy Alaska. (Secretary of State William H. Seward had engineered the purchase of Alaska from Russia in 1867 for $7.2 million.) Expenditures included $179,729.60 for three tables and forty chairs, and $41,190.95 for brooms. Although the entire building was made of marble and iron, the plastering bill came to $2,870,464.06, of which almost half was for repair work that had to be done before the building was even finished! All in all, it was a grand boondoggle that provided unnecessary government jobs for everyone involved. The only people who suffered were the taxpayers.

Boss Tweed Takes a Tumble

The wholesale graft practiced in Tammany Hall under Tweed's leadership gradually aroused public anger. The *New York Times* printed one scathing editorial after another. Cartoons by **Thomas Nast** appearing in the *Times* and in *Harper's Weekly* were even more devastating. As Tweed himself

Picturing History
Thomas Nast's cartoon shows Boss Tweed as the power behind the throne of New York Governor John Hoffman. Tweed (right) was finally brought down, partly because of Nast's cartoons, which even people unable to read English could interpret.

said, "I don't care what people write, for my people can't read. But they have eyes and they can see as well as other folk."

The Tweed Ring was finally broken in 1871 when a disgruntled member of the machine provided the *New York Times* with direct proof of corruption. That year, reformers were elected to every municipal office in New York. Tweed himself was indicted on 120 counts. His first trial ended without a verdict, his second with a twelve-year sentence. He escaped from jail but was recaptured in Spain. Spanish officials recognized him from a drawing by Nast. In 1878 Tweed died in prison.

Similar situations existed in other cities. Why did voters tolerate this? Because, as *The Nation* magazine pointed out in its farewell to Tweed,

Let us remember that he fell without loss of reputation among the bulk of his supporters.

For Discussion
Think about Boss Tweed and how he got along with the press. Why do you think the press and politicians often are natural antagonists? (Possible responses: in looking for a good story, the press may publish stories that give more information than politicians want revealed; some stories may be slanted, leaving out important facts.)

Student Assignment/Homework

Have students read Section 3, "The New Immigrants Arrive," and be prepared to discuss it in class. Have students complete Chapter 19, Section 2 Daily Activity.

SECTION 3
Core Lesson

Anticipate the Lesson

Use the completed Chapter 19, Section 3 Daily Activity to stimulate a discussion on the changing patterns of immigration.

State the Objective

Understand the patterns of immigration and the problems faced by the new immigrants in the late nineteenth century.

The bulk of the poorer voters of this city today revere his memory, and look on him as the victim of rich men's malice; as, in short, a friend of the needy who applied the public funds to the purposes to which they ought to be applied—and that is to the making of work for the working man.

So long as municipal governments did not address themselves to certain social needs, the majority of voters supported the political machines that gave at least some help to the poor.

SECTION 2 REVIEW

Key Terms and People

Explain the significance of: political machine, Tammany Hall, Tweed Ring, Thomas Nast

Main Ideas

1. What conditions led to the development of political machines in the cities?
2. What did political machines receive in return for the services they provided to citizens and businesses?
3. Why did voters tolerate political machines?

Critical Thinking

4. How did political machines affect the ability of municipal governments to govern cities in beneficial ways?

SECTION 3

The New Immigrants Arrive

GLOSSARY TERMS: immigration, melting pot

Between 1880 and 1914 **immigration** patterns changed. A massive wave of immigrants arrived in the United States and caused tremendous controversy. It was not the numbers of people entering the country to take up residence that bothered Americans, because the proportion of immigrants to native-born Americans remained at about 12 percent. What caused controversy were two conditions. First, there were considerable cultural differences between this group of immigrants and those who preceded them. Second, most of the new immigrants were concentrated in certain geographical areas, which made for political and economic friction.

Cultural Differences Become More Apparent

Many people today disagree with the idea that a nation's citizens must resemble one another. Most Americans of the new industrial age, however, felt very threatened by immigrants from different cultures. Instead of coming from northern Europe, these new immigrants were coming from southern and eastern Europe and Asia. How would it be possible for such strange people to become Americanized?

SECTION 2 REVIEW

Answers

Main Ideas

1. The absence of responsible government and the overwhelming problems faced by rapidly growing cities.

2. Machines received money from businesses and votes from the people they helped.

3. The machines were perceived as allies of the poor, while municipal governments were not.

Critical Thinking

4. Possible answer: political corruption negatively affected governments' leadership, finances, and ability to affect change. **(analysis)**

Changing Patterns of Immigration

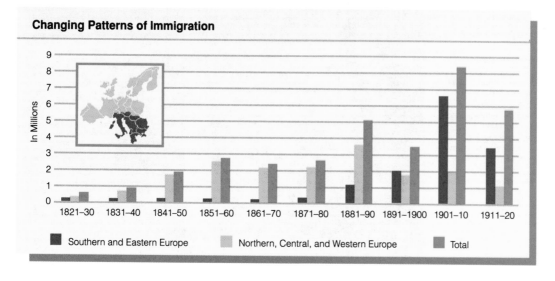

In Millions

■ Southern and Eastern Europe   Northern, Central, and Western Europe   Total

Cities and Immigrants **497**

Present the Lesson

Divide the class into four groups. Ask each group to prepare an outline on one of the following problems faced by immigrants in America: culture, language, religion, race. Outlines might include:

Language
- Did not speak English.
- Retained native language and used it in daily conversation.
- Shopped at stores where native language was spoken.
- Read newspapers in native language.
- Could not hold a job where reading or understanding English was required.
- Tended to form "ethnic islands."

Have the leader of each group write the outline on the board. Have students refer to the outlines as they study this section.

Language. One major cultural difference was language. Until the 1880's, except for Germans and African Americans, most immigrants spoke English. The newer immigrants, on the other hand, spoke one of a variety of languages.

Furthermore, they tended to retain their native language in the United States. They used it in daily conversation. They shopped only at stores that carried signs in their native tongue. They read newspapers in their native language rather than those in English.

Religion. Another cultural difference was religion. A majority of the new immigrants were Roman Catholic. Catholics had been coming to the United States since the 1500's. However, many of the newcomers, especially those from Italy and what is now Poland, did not care for the predominantly Irish clergy they found in the United States. They preferred national parishes in which priests of their own nationality conducted services.

Then there were the Eastern Orthodox Catholics from eastern Europe and the Balkans. Their bearded clergy and their church buildings with onion-shaped roofs were very different from anything previously seen in the United States.

Also very different were the Jews. Most earlier Jewish immigrants had come from Portugal and Germany. The great majority of Jews who arrived after 1880 came from Russia and what is now Poland, where they had been forced to live in areas apart from the rest of the population. They spoke and read Yiddish, a language derived from medieval High German and spoken by East European Jews. They observed religious dietary laws that included the prohibition of pork and shellfish, and sent their children to Hebrew school after public school was over for the day. Most of the men were bearded, while most of the women either wore wigs or covered their hair with kerchiefs.

Race. The third cultural difference was race. The great majority of Americans were white. To many of them, Chinese and Japanese immigrants did not look like real Americans.

The Melting Pot Theory Is Challenged

In 1782 **Jean de Crèvecoeur,** a French writer living in New York, asked and then answered the question,

> What then is the American, this new man? He is . . . a strange mixture of blood, which you will find in no other country. I could point out to you a family whose grandfather was an Englishman, whose wife was Dutch, whose son married a French woman, and whose present four sons have now four wives of different nations. . . . Here individuals of all nations are melted into a new race . . . whose labors and posterity will one day cause great changes in the world.

Picturing History In this Thomas Nast cartoon, people of all nations have been invited to Uncle Sam's Thanksgiving dinner. Nast depicted many of the reasons people came to the United States to live: the ideals of Washington and Lincoln, the right to self-government, and universal suffrage.

UNCLE SAM'S THANKSGIVING DINNER.

Check for Understanding

Have students write the answers to Section 3
Review questions on paper.

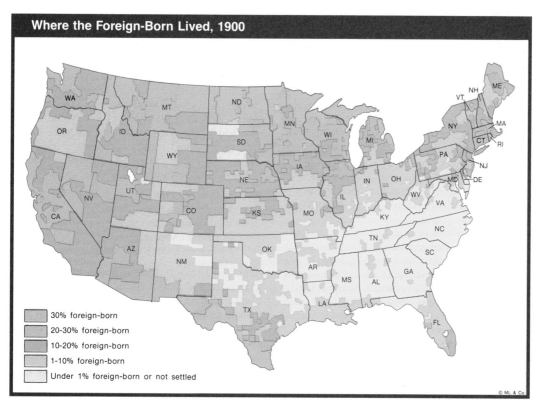

Where the Foreign-Born Lived, 1900

- 30% foreign-born
- 20-30% foreign-born
- 10-20% foreign-born
- 1-10% foreign-born
- Under 1% foreign-born or not settled

© ML & Co.

Map Skills Region Which region had the smallest proportion of foreign-born population?
Region What was the largest area with the largest proportion of foreign-born?

Map Skills
Southeast • Upper Midwest
(northern MI, MN, ND, WI)

For Discussion
Compare the melting pot
theory and the salad bowl
theory. Which one do you
think is a more realistic description of American society
today? (Possible response:
the salad bowl theory is
more realistic because many
immigrants continue to hold
on to and to be proud of their
traditions, language, native
cooking, and customs.)

In other words, Americans were becoming a new people, blended from many nations.

In 1909 British playwright Israel Zangwill wrote a play called *The Melting Pot,* which glorified this concept and gave it a name. At the end of the play, Vera and David are looking at New York City.

> **David:** . . . There she lies, the great Melting Pot. . . . Ah, what a stirring and a seething! Celt and Latin, Slav and Teuton, Greek and Syrian—black and yellow—
> **Vera:** Jew and Gentile—
> **David:** Yes . . . the palm and the pine, the pole and the equator, the crescent and the cross—how the great Alchemist melts and fuses them with his purging flame! Here shall they all unite to build the Republic of Man and the Kingdom of God. Ah, Vera, what is the glory of Rome . . . compared with the glory of America, where all races and nations come to labor and look forward!
>
> (An instant's solemn pause. The sunset is swiftly fading. . . . Far back, like a lonely guiding star, twinkles over the darkening water the torch of the Statue of Liberty. From below comes up the softened sound of voices and instruments joining in ''My Country 'tis of thee.'' The curtain falls.)

The concept of the **melting pot** was very ideal-istic. Yet it had a price. It called for immigrants to throw away their past, to give up their entire history and culture in order to become Americans.

Later, many of the new immigrants declared that they thought of America not as a melting pot but as a mixed salad in which each immigrant group contributed to the whole but still kept its individual flavor. Others regarded new immigrant groups as additions to the great mosaic of American society.

Urban Immigrants Face Resentment

In addition to challenging the melting pot theory, the new immigrants created controversy for other reasons. One of these was that they settled mostly

Tell students that a current debate centers on the question of whether a large population of immigrants helps or hurts the economy. Use this information to stimulate a discussion on immigration. Ask students whether they think immigrants actually take jobs from others or whether the increase in population helps the economy expand. (Possible responses: immigrants take low paying unskilled jobs that need to be done and then use their wages to buy food, clothing, and housing, thus putting the money back into the economy; immigrants often cannot find work and must be supported by taxpayers.)

in the Northeast and the Middle West. Half of them were concentrated in just four states: Massachusetts, New York, Pennsylvania, and Illinois. All of them were concentrated in cities, where they were highly visible. In 1880 in Boston, for example, almost two-thirds of the population either were born abroad or had parents who were foreign-born. By 1890 there were twice as many Irish in New York as in Dublin, while the largest Polish city in the world was not the Polish capital of Warsaw but Chicago.

As you have read, immigrants tended to become strong supporters of city machines. So people who opposed the machines began to regard the newcomers as corrupt.

There was also economic friction. The tremendous supply of immigrant labor meant that for a long time employers were able to keep wages down. If workers struck for a raise in pay, it was easy for an employer to replace the strikers with immigrants. Since most immigrants did not read or speak English, they could not understand the arguments of the labor unions. As a result, many native-born workers began to resent the newcomers. They regarded the new immigrants as cheap scabs who took their jobs.

Difficulties Confront the New Immigrants

While many native-born Americans looked on the new immigrants mainly as a threat and a source of problems, the immigrants viewed their own situation from a very different point of view. Not only had they suffered physical discomforts on their journey across the Atlantic, but they also experienced the mental anguish caused by separation, loss, and fear of the unknown.

The Journey. Before the Civil War, immigrants came to the United States mostly by sailing ship. By the 1870's almost all immigrants were arriving by steamship. This cut the Atlantic crossing from about two months to a mere ten days. The Pacific crossing fell from three months to about twenty days. Yet, despite the shorter time, crossing the ocean was uncomfortable and scary.

Most immigrants traveled in steerage, that is, in the cargo holds below the ship's waterline. There were no portholes, so the only ventilation came from open doors and the only light, from a few scattered lanterns. There were perhaps six toilets for every hundred passengers. Although food was adequate, passengers were seldom allowed on deck. They spent most of the time crowded together in the gloom, unable to stretch their legs or to catch a breath of fresh air.

Coupled with physical discomforts were psychological ones. Unlike most early colonists who came in organized groups, most new immigrants came as individuals. How do you think you would feel if you had to leave your parents and the home where you grew up and journey thousands of miles by yourself to a strange land? As a Japanese woman immigrant wrote in later years:

> In spite of aging,
> Still the homesick child in me
> Who sailed so far out
> From Yokohama harbor. . .
> I still long for my hometown.

Passing Through Ellis Island. In addition to loneliness and homesickness, the new immigrants faced the anxiety of not knowing whether they would be admitted to the United States when they arrived. First they had to pass inspection. If they had tuberculosis or head lice, back they went. If they were fifteen years and eight months old instead of sixteen and were not accompanied by a parent, back they went. If they were ex-convicts or believed in the forcible overthrow of government, back they went. If they did not have twenty-five dollars with them, that too was grounds for return. Sometimes a family would be split, with one member accepted and another rejected. In a few instances, it took as long as eleven years before a family was reunited.

Another hazard of inspection involved a change of name. Immigration inspectors often could not pronounce or spell the new immigrants' names. In this case they simply wrote down an Anglicized version. Jeivute became Eva. Czernovitsky turned into Charnow, and Iorizzo ended up as Rice.

From 1892 to 1924 the chief immigration station of the United States was **Ellis Island** in New York Harbor. Historians estimate that more than 16 million people passed through its facilities. During the peak immigration years from 1905 to 1907, ten thousand immigrants a day smelling of Ellis Island disinfectant would walk down the long staircase to take the ferry to Manhattan. If you visit the main building today, you can still see the "kissing balcony" in the great hall from which friends and relatives used to search for newcomers in the crowds below.

Assign Independent Practice

Have students complete Chapter 19, Section 3
Enrichment Activity. Divide the class into small
groups to discuss their answers.

Picturing History   Having passed the test and survived the waiting, some new arrivals
head for New York City—America at last! Many immigrants were convinced that America
had enough and more for all who wished to come. It was merely a question of being
worthy of being admitted.

Culture and Language Barriers.   Once the new
immigrant stepped on shore, there was an immediate **culture shock,** a sudden awareness of new
things. Edward Corsi, who arrived in the United
States from Italy in 1907, observed:

> I was first struck by the fact that American
> men did not wear beards. In contrast to my
> own fellow countrymen, I thought they looked
> almost like women. Also on this boat [the
> ferry that ran from Ellis Island to Manhattan]
> I saw my first Negro. But these wonders
> melted into insignificance when we arrived at
> the Battery [a park at the southern tip of
> Manhattan] and our first elevated trains ap-
> peared on the scene. There could be nothing in
> America superior to these!

Many of the problems confronting the new
immigrants were the same problems that confronted all Americans: finding a place to live,
earning a living, establishing a family. There were
also special difficulties, however. Carl Christian
Jensen, who arrived from Denmark in 1906, described the situation this way.

> I was a man and stronger than most men. Yet
> my second childhood began the day I entered
> my new country. . . . I had to learn life over in

a brand new world. And I could not talk. My
first desire was for chocolate drops, and I
pointed my finger at them. My second was for
fishing tackle, and I pointed my finger at a
wrapping cord and heaved up an imaginary
fish.

Ethnic Islands.   Another difficulty was of special
concern to youngsters. As the new immigrants
crowded into the cities, they formed **ethnic islands,** or national districts, with each language
group living in its own section of town. People
from one section were not welcome in another. The
late comedian Harpo Marx described his experiences in New York in the early 1900's.

> The upper East Side was subdivided into Jew-
> ish blocks (the smallest area), Irish blocks, and
> German blocks, with a couple of independent
> Italian states thrown in for good measure. That
> is, the cross streets were subdivided. The
> north-and-south Avenues—First, Second,
> Third, and Lexington—belonged more to the
> city than the neighborhood. They were neutral
> zones. But there was open season on strangers
> in the cross streets.
>
>   If you were caught trying to sneak through
> a foreign block, the first thing the Irishers or

Student Assignment/Homework

Have students read Section 4, "Demands Grow for Restrictions on Immigration," and answer the Section 4 Review questions on paper.

Picturing History Italian grocery store in New York City.

Germans would ask was, "Hey, kid! What Streeter?" I learned it saved time and trouble to tell the truth. I was a 93rd Streeter, I would confess.

"Yeah? What block 93rd Streeter?"

"Ninety-third between Third and Lex." That pinned me down. I was a Jew.

The worst thing you could do was run from other Streeters. But if you didn't have anything to fork over for ransom, you were just as dead. I learned never to leave my block without some kind of boodle in my pocket—a dead tennis ball, an empty thread spool, a penny, anything. It didn't cost much to buy your freedom; the gesture was the important thing.

It was all part of the endless fight for recognition of foreigners in the process of becoming Americans. Every Irish kid who made a Jewish kid knuckle under was made to say "Uncle" by an Italian, who got his lumps from a German kid, who got his insides kicked out by his old man for street fighting and then went out and beat up an Irish kid to heal his wounds. "I'll teach *you*!" was the threat they passed along, Irisher to Jew to Italian to German. Everyone was trying to teach everybody else, all down the line.

Generation Gap. Even when the new immigrants had learned English and no longer fought with one another, there often remained a cultural gap between generations.

The immigrants themselves seldom sounded like the teachers in school or looked like the people whose pictures appeared in the newspapers. As author Mario Puzo wrote:

> They wore lumpy work clothes and handlebar mustaches . . . and they were so short that their high-school children towered over them. They spoke a laughable broken English and the furthest limit to their horizon was their daily bread.

The immigrants' children, eager to move into the mainstream of American life, were sometimes embarrassed by their parents. The children no longer recited the traditional prayers. They no longer spoke their parents' native tongue or knew anything about their parents' native land. "Why did we come to America," many immigrants wondered, "if our own children are strangers in our house?"

If immigrants were anxious to adopt American standards as quickly as possible, that too created difficulties. In most instances, parents often learned about American ways from their children. Instead of parents teaching children, the situation was reversed. This disrupted the traditional structure of family life.

After a time, the generations grew to understand one another better. Members of the first generation born in America began to respect their parents'

Picturing History Immigrants encouraged their children to learn English.

Ask students to consider what the Statue of Liberty might symbolize to immigrants arriving in America. (Possible response: America is a haven for those looking for a better way of life.) To stimulate discussion on immigration, ask students the following questions. Has the U.S. always welcomed all people? (Response: no.) What types or groups of people have been excluded? (Possible responses: revolutionaries; people with contagious diseases; criminals; those nationalities considered undesirable for some reason.) Who has the right to decide which groups are allowed to enter the country and which are not? (Possible response: the government.)

State the Objective

Understand the origins of immigration restrictions in the U.S.

---

courage in immigrating. The next generation began to take greater pride in its cultural heritage. In turn, the immigrants came to realize that new ways were not necessarily evil. For example, when their children spent money for pleasure—which European peasants did not do because they had no extra money—it did not mean that the children lacked character. It only meant that their circumstances and values were different.

Helping Each Other. The new immigrants tried in many ways to ease the difficulties of adjusting to a new life. People from the same village in Italy or Poland or Russia would pool their money to build their own church or synagogue. They formed social clubs where people could meet to talk and read letters from home. The clubs also provided places where their sons and daughters could meet young people of similar background. Groups of immigrants set up mutual-benefit societies that furnished medical treatment for members and helped with medical costs. They founded orphanages and old people's homes. They established cemeteries so that they would not have to be buried among strangers.

SECTION 3 REVIEW

Key Terms and People

Explain the significance of: immigration, Jean de Crèvecoeur, melting pot, Ellis Island, culture shock, ethnic islands

Main Ideas

1. What important cultural differences existed between native-born Americans and new immigrants?
2. How did the "melting pot" concept differ from the "mixed salad" concept?
3. From an economic standpoint, why did many native-born workers resent the influx of new immigrants?
4. What made adjusting to life in the United States difficult for the new immigrants?

Critical Thinking

5. In describing his childhood, Harpo Marx said that fighting between ethnic groups was "all part of the endless fight for recognition of foreigners in the process of becoming Americans." Explain how this could be true.

SECTION 4

Demands Grow for Restrictions on Immigration

GLOSSARY TERMS: **radicals, naturalized citizen**

Beginning in the late 1870's, demands for restricting immigration to the United States grew increasingly strong. There were several reasons for this development.

Nativism Is Reborn

As you have read, the Know-Nothing movement was undercut in the 1856 election by the issue of slavery. During the Civil War and Reconstruction, there were few signs of nativism. Then the old frontiers disappeared, to be replaced by an increasingly urban and industrial society that presented all sorts of new challenges. Just as sectionalism in the 1850's led to feelings of "us against them" on the part of both North and South, so did conditions in the 1880's lead to similar feelings about immigrants.

The Status Quo Is Threatened. The Haymarket affair (see page 460) convinced many Americans that the government was being undermined by wild-eyed foreign **radicals,** or extremists. Along with the fear of foreign radicals, there developed a fear of growing Catholic political influence. This was partly due to the large number of Irish politicians in the governments of such cities as Boston, Chicago, New York, and San Francisco.

Then there was the demand of Catholic parochial schools for a share of public-school funds. Catholics had argued for many years that they were paying twice for education, once by being taxed for public schools and again by paying tuition for parochial schools. Many Protestants regarded the Catholic position as a foreign attack on the traditional American classroom. As a result, a number of secret anti-Catholic societies sprang up that pledged to defend the public school system and to oppose Catholic influence in politics.

Anglo-Saxonism. Another element of nativism was racial prejudice. As sociologist Robert Hunter wrote in 1904:

> The direct descendants of the people who fought for and founded the Republic, and who

Answers

Main Ideas

1. Language, religion, and race.
2. Melting pot—new immigrants blended with old immigrants to create a new people. Mixed salad—new immigrants contributed to the nation while retaining their individual differences.
3. Immigrants were willing to work for lower wages and therefore made labor unions less effective.
4. Loneliness, homesickness, loss of identity, cultural shock, language barriers, and cultural generation gaps.

Critical Thinking

5. Possible answer: most new immigrants struggled to retain their cultural identity while trying to gain acceptance as Americans. **(application)**

Ask students to review the section and give examples of the following: antiradicalism, anti-Catholicism, and Anglo-Saxonism. Have students explain how each contributed to immigration restrictions. (Possible responses: antiradicalism—a desire to protect the country from disruptive political influences resulted in restrictions on immigration and prohibition of aliens from owning land; anti-Catholicism—nativists' fear of influence of Catholic Church on government, resulted in a number of anti-Catholic societies and restrictions on the number of immigrants from predominantly Catholic countries; Anglo-Saxonism—strong feelings that "true" Americans were of Anglo-Saxon origin—created negative attitudes toward those immigrants who came from areas other than western Europe, eventually limiting immigration from these other countries.) Write the following terms on the board and ask students to supply information about how each was designed to restrict immigration: Literacy Test, Chinese Exclusion Act, Gentlemen's Agreement, Alien Land Act. (Possible responses: Literacy Test required immigrants to read or write forty words before being admitted to U.S.; Chinese Exclusion Act prohibited Chinese workers from entering U.S., those here could not even send for wives; Gentlemen's Agreement prohibited Japan from issuing passports to workers unless they had relatives in U.S. or had lived here before; Alien Land Act prohibited Asians from owning agricultural land.) Ask students to identify the results of these acts. (Response: the golden door was slammed shut and those Asians already in the U.S. faced severe discrimination.)

Check for Understanding

Call on individual students to read their answers to Section 4 Review questions.

What conditions in the 1880's led to anti-immigrant feelings? (Possible responses: depression; loss of American jobs to immigrants, who worked for less; increased numbers of immigrants who began to exert some control over the government through the political machine.)

gave us a rich heritage of democratic institutions, are being displaced by the Slavic, Balkan, and Mediterranean peoples. . . . This is . . . race suicide.

As Prescott F. Hall explained further, the question was whether Americans wanted their nation

to be peopled by British, German, and Scandinavian stock, historically free, energetic, progressive, or by Slav, Latin, and Asiatic races, historically down-trodden . . . and stagnant.

This attitude was especially strong in New England. There the traditional Yankee leadership was being successfully challenged by the Irish. That was bad enough, many Yankees felt. In addition, they were afraid that American civilization would not be able to assimilate the increasing number of new immigrants and would fall apart. So in 1894 a group of "Boston blue bloods" set up the Immigration Restriction League. The organization began a campaign to keep out the "undesirable classes" from southern and eastern Europe.

Cleveland Vetoes the Literacy Test. The Immigration Restriction League was reluctant to exclude immigrants for the stated reason of race. So they came up with the idea of a literacy test. Only immigrants who could read and write forty words, either in their own language or in some other language, would be admitted. In 1896 Senator Henry Cabot Lodge of Massachusetts introduced a bill to this effect.

The bill passed Congress but was vetoed by President Cleveland. Cleveland argued that the test measured opportunity, not ability. Just because people had never had a chance to learn how to read and write, he said, did not mean that they were incapable of learning. However, a literacy test was passed and enacted in 1917.

Congress Passes Anti-Asian Acts

Another area in which nativists triumphed was that of Asian exclusion. Starting in 1882 Chinese and then Japanese immigrants were subjected to restrictive legislation.

Keeping Out the Chinese. As you know, Chinese people first came to California during gold-rush days. (See Chapter 17.) Later they helped build the nation's first transcontinental railroad, as

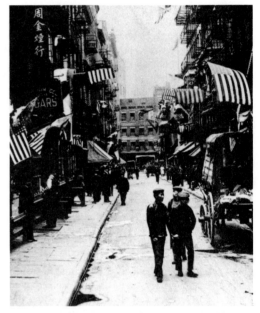

Picturing History A scene in Chinatown in New York City around 1912.

well as other western roads. When the railroads were completed, the Chinese turned to farming, mining, and domestic service. Nevertheless, they labored under a cloud.

Most Chinese immigrants were men. They did not bring their wives with them because they expected to return to China someday so that they could be buried near their ancestors. Not having a family in the United States, they lived in bachelor quarters, several men to a room, in certain areas of towns. These areas of shops, temples, restaurants, and homes were called Chinatowns.

Not only did Chinese immigrants live differently from most Americans, they looked different. It was not just a matter of skin color or the shape of the eyelid. At that time, a Chinese man wore his hair in a queue, a long braid, down his back. Men also wore quilted cotton jackets, cotton pants, and conical hats. Their hairstyle and dress looked odd to most other Americans.

Then came the depression of 1873. As economic conditions worsened, anti-Chinese feeling in California grew more intense. The Chinese were disliked because they would work for less than white men. Dennis Kearney, himself an immigrant from Ireland and a recently **naturalized citizen,** spearheaded the anti-Chinese movement. He founded

Guided Practice

Tell students that lawmakers have worked very hard to eliminate bias against race, religion, and nation of origin. Ask students what reasons a country might have for monitoring individuals who want to immigrate. (Possible response: to prevent certain dangerous individuals—convicted criminals, those who have contagious diseases, those who want to overthrow the existing government—from entering the country.)

Assign Independent Practice

Divide students into small groups and have them complete Chapter 19, Section 4 Enrichment Activity.

Student Assignment/Homework

Have students complete Chapter 19 Review on paper. Go over the Critical Thinking questions with the class.

Concluding the Chapter

Ask students to write a brief essay explaining the relationship between the growth of cities and the expanding industrialization and immigration in the nineteenth century. (Essays might include: as industries grew they needed workers; cities continued to develop as workers moved close to their jobs; immigrants seeking better lives came to American cities to look for jobs, which caused the cities to grow even larger; industries supported immigrants who worked in factories for low pay.)

the Workingman's party and made hundreds of speeches throughout the state, each speech ending with the words "The Chinese must go!"

Finally, in 1882 Congress passed the **Chinese Exclusion Act.** This prohibited Chinese workers from entering the United States for the next ten years. In 1892 the law was extended for another ten years. In 1902 all Chinese immigration was indefinitely suspended. In addition, the Chinese men already living in the United States were prohibited from sending for their wives.

Resisting the "Yellow Peril." In 1886 Japan allowed its people to emigrate for the first time in almost three hundred years. In the beginning, several hundred Japanese men, women, and children arrived in the United States each year. After the turn of the century, the number rose to several thousand a year. By 1910 there were about 130,000 Japanese, mostly men, in the country.

At first the Japanese settlers were welcomed for they were hard-working and well-behaved. Gradually, however, the same fears about economic competition that had led to anti-Chinese agitation resulted in anti-Japanese agitation. Newspapers began carrying articles with such headlines as: JAPANESE INVASION THE PROBLEM OF THE HOUR, MORE THAN 100,000 OF THE LITTLE BROWN MEN ARE NOW IN THE UNITED STATES, and CRIME AND POVERTY GO HAND IN HAND WITH ASIATIC LABOR.

In addition, Japan's victories in the 1895 war with China and again in the Russo-Japanese War of 1905 frightened many Californians. Suppose Japan were to wage war against the United States? Why, the whole country might be inundated with the "Yellow Peril"!

The issue came to a head in 1906. A scandal about municipal graft in San Francisco was about to explode. In an attempt to distract people's attention, the city's political leaders apparently decided to exploit the racial issue. The local board of education ordered all Chinese, Japanese, and Korean children removed from neighborhood schools and segregated in special Oriental schools.

Anti-American demonstrations broke out immediately in Japan. Alarmed, President Theodore Roosevelt persuaded the San Francisco authorities to withdraw the segregation order. In exchange, he urged the Japanese government to limit emigration on its own. Under the **Gentlemen's Agreement** of 1907–1908, Japan agreed not to issue passports to

workers unless they had already been to America or had relatives in this country. Some thirty thousand Japanese had come in 1907. By 1909 the figure had dropped to three thousand.

In addition, in 1913 the California state legislature passed an **Alien Land Law.** Since the Japanese and other Asians were "aliens ineligible for citizenship," they were prohibited from owning agricultural land. Not only had the golden door slammed shut, but even those who had successfully gotten through found stiff discrimination against them.

Linking Past to Present

Recent efforts to control immigration have not been aimed at any one ethnic group. The 1986 Immigration Reform and Control Act attempted to reduce the number of aliens illegally entering the United States. The act increased border patrols, mandated action against employers who knowingly hire illegal aliens, and provided amnesty for those who have lived in the United States continuously since 1982.

SECTION 4 REVIEW

Key Terms and People

Explain the significance of: radicals, naturalized citizen, Chinese Exclusion Act, Gentlemen's Agreement, Alien Land Law

Main Ideas

1. What groups were represented in the "us against them" mentality of nativism in the 1880's?
2. In the 1880's, what helped to cause feelings of anti-Catholicism?
3. Why did President Cleveland veto a bill that would have imposed a literacy test on immigrants?
4. What were the terms of the Chinese Exclusion Act of 1882?

Critical Thinking

5. Were nativists' fears of the new immigrants justified? Were the nativists' actions that were based on these fears justified? Explain.

SECTION 4 REVIEW

Answers

Main Ideas

1. "Us"—native-born, or old immigrant, Americans; "them"— new immigrants.

2. The growth of Catholic political influence in urban areas; the demand of Catholic parochial schools for public aid.

3. He thought that it discriminated against those who had never had educational opportunities and that illiteracy should not be equated with the inability to learn.

4. It prohibited Chinese workers from entering the U.S. for a period of 10 years.

Critical Thinking

5. Possible answers: no—the already precarious economic, social, and political position of many native-born Americans during the new industrial age was unintentionally threatened by the influx of new immigrants; • No—the new immigrants were just an easy target for the nativist. **(evaluation)**

505

State the Objective

Understand the government's role in taxation.

Present the Lesson

On the board write the heading British and Colonial Attitudes Toward Taxation. Underneath write the subheadings Similarities and Differences. Ask students to identify the similarities and differences in attitudes toward taxation of the British Parliament and the Colonial legislators at the time of the Revolutionary War. Have volunteers write their responses on the board under the appropriate headings. (Possible responses: similarities—British believed Parliament had the right to tax, and colonists believed the colonial legislatures had the right to tax; British Parliament curbed the taxing powers of the King, and colonial legislatures curbed the taxing powers of the royal governors. Differences—British Parliament believed they should be able to tax the colonies, but colonial legislators thought the British did not have the right to tax the colonists.)

Ask students to identify the three periods when the U.S. Congress tried to impose an income tax. Ask students to state whether each law was implemented. (Answer: Civil War—Congress levied an income tax; the law was implemented but dropped by 1881, when the Supreme Court decided it was a violation of the Constitution. 1894—Congress passed the Wilson-Gorman Act, which levied a 2 percent

Focus on Economics

Taxes

"In this world," wrote Benjamin Franklin, "nothing is certain but death and taxes." If you have a job, you probably know what Franklin meant. When you get your paycheck, some of your earnings have already been deducted for taxes. One figure represents the amount of income tax withheld; a second figure shows the deduction made for social security taxes. In some cases, another amount may be taken out for city or state taxes. After all taxes have been subtracted, the remainder —your take-home pay—is usually much less than your total earnings.

Public debate over taxes is part of our nation's British heritage. Throughout the 1600's, England's Parliament struggled with the monarch over control of the public purse strings. During the time after the Glorious Revolution in 1688, Parliament finally won the power to tax. After this event, the Crown could no longer take a person's property without consent. According to John Locke, when Parliament won the authority to tax, it also established a basic right of free people everywhere.

Battling for Power.   During the 1700's the thirteen colonial legislatures were also trying to assert control over taxation. Colonists had always been concerned with the question of who had the authority to levy taxes. In Virginia the House of Burgesses claimed the power to tax for itself alone; one of its earliest laws prohibited the royal governor from imposing taxes without the representatives' consent. The same spirit pervaded the other colonies. Partly because of British neglect, colonial assemblies asserted the right to levy their own taxes rather than be taxed by Parliament.

These centers of power—one in Great Britain and one in America—functioned relatively well until the French and Indian War. Then, after 1763, changes in British tax policies helped bring about the American Revolution. Faced with huge war debts and the high cost of protecting the colonies, Parliament tried taxing the colonists. After 1763 many colonists felt that Parliament was seizing

powers that belonged to colonial legislatures by tradition and right.

Thus, the Revolutionary War was not fought over paying taxes. Instead, the Revolution concerned the debate over the authority to impose taxes. In failing to understand the colonial opposition to British taxation, Parliament could not hope to understand the colonial struggle for responsible independence.

Protests Are Nothing New.   Since Revolutionary times, tax protests have characterized our nation. In 1846, for example, Henry David Thoreau spent a night in jail because he failed to pay his taxes. Thoreau objected to paying taxes to fund the war against Mexico. If the United States were to win the war, slavery—a practice Thoreau abhorred— would be extended into the Southwest. He chose to go to jail rather than compromise his personal principles.

Thoreau's protest struck at the heart of the relationship between government and the individual. Collecting taxes is a basic right of the legislature. Paying taxes is a citizen's responsibility to a government dedicated to promoting the general welfare, since without tax payments, a government cannot carry out its programs. For those who oppose the government's programs, refusing to pay taxes is a potent way of challenging the authority of those who govern.

Levying an Income Tax.   Although local taxes have existed since colonial times, the federal tax on personal income began only in the early 1900's. An income tax levied during the Civil War was challenged in the courts. The Supreme Court finally upheld the constitutionality of the Civil War measure in the case *Springer* v. *United States* (1881), though the personal income tax by then had been dropped.

In 1893 severe circumstances in the form of a depression once again strained the federal treasury. To remedy this money shortage, Congress passed

506

tax on income; in 1895 the Supreme Court found the tax unconstitutional, and it was dropped. 1913—Congress passed an income tax law and guaranteed its legality by adding to the Constitution the Sixteenth Amendment, which empowered Congress to tax income.)

ETTA HULME ©1985 FORT WORTH STAR-TELEGRAM
ETTA HULME
Courtesy Ft. Worth Star-Telegram

Picturing History
Waiting for tax reform can be a taxing experience! In 1985 Ronald Reagan promised taxpayers that a revision of the tax laws would be his top priority for his second term of office. Although it faced stiff opposition in Congress, the new tax law was finally passed in 1986.

the Wilson-Gorman Act in 1894. It levied a 2 percent tax on all kinds of income—rents, interest, dividends, salaries, and profits. Soon a case challenging the constitutionality of this federal income tax reached the Supreme Court.

This time, in the case *Pollock* v. *The Farmers' Loan and Trust Company* (1895), the Court decided that sections of the law dealing with an income tax were unconstitutional. The Court denied Congress the right to levy personal income taxes. Not until the ratification of the Sixteenth Amendment in 1913 was Congress finally authorized to tax personal incomes. That year the first modern federal income tax began. It is still in effect, though it has changed a great deal over the years.

Future Trends. Americans today pay much more in taxes than their ancestors ever would have imagined—or allowed. Anyone who has paid any type of taxes during the past several decades has felt the sharp increases. In 1902, for example, the revenues for all federal, state, and local taxes collected in the United States totaled about $1.4 billion—representing an average tax payment that year of $17.34 per person. For 1980, all tax revenues in the nation totaled about $574.2 billion—an average payment of $2,535.24 per person. Despite some scattered tax decreases, the

overall trend is to increased taxation of property, income, and consumer goods.

In the fall of 1986, President Reagan signed into law what he called "the most sweeping overhaul of our tax code in our nation's history." By the end of 1987, the national debt had reached a staggering $2.4 trillion. Its continuing growth represents one of the country's most pressing concerns. For a nation accustomed to abundance, the notion of living within limits—specifically within the limits of tax revenues—has been difficult to accept.

Understanding Economics

1. What basic conflict over taxes existed between the colonists and the British Parliament? What objections did Thoreau have to paying his taxes?
2. What issues regarding taxation concern many people today? What is being done to remedy these problems?
3. How do the concerns people today have about taxes differ from the concerns of colonists? How are they similar?

Critical Thinking

4. Which taxes may increase or decrease during your lifetime? How might different groups of people react to these changes? Why?

Key Terms and People

These are highlighted in the text in the order in which they appear in this list.

Main Ideas

1. Housing, transportation, water and sanitation, law and order, fire, local government.

2. Improve slum conditions. • Became unsanitary and overcrowded.

3. Machine acted as welfare and employment agency; helped with naturalization; helped those in trouble with police; set up social outlets.

4. Ring was broken in 1871 when a disgruntled member of the machine provided the *New York Times* with direct proof of corruption.

➤**5. New**—southern and eastern Europe and Asia; native language; Roman Catholic; some of mongoloid race; segregated themselves to keep national identity; half in Massachusetts, New York, Pennsylvania, and Illinois. • **Old**—northern Europe; English and German; Protestant; white; integrated with the rest of society; east coast and Midwest.

6. Settled in cities and were highly visible; supported political machines and so seemed corrupt; worked for low pay; acted as scabs during strikes.

7. New England leaders were being displaced by Irish and were afraid American civilization would fall apart; Protestants believed Catholics' request for tax dollars for parochial schools threatened traditional schools.

8. He thought the test measured opportunity and not ability and that people should not be excluded because they could not read and write.

Critical Thinking Questions

9. Possible answers: yes—he showed enterprise by coming early; confronted prejudice against Chinese; had common sense; was alert and wary. No—employer was too prejudiced to hire a Chinese no matter how good and loyal he might be.

➤**10.** Possible answers: helpful—helped immigrants with jobs and services; harmful—were corrupt.

11. Possible answer: no—other groups that might have helped such as churches, ethnic organizations, or schools.

12. Possible answers: yes—for freedom of speech and of worship; desire to join friends and relatives. No—fear of ocean voyage; fear of new conditions.

13. Because they looked different.

➤**14.** No—Congress has such power. • All people, citizens or not, are protected under U.S. law while they are in the U.S.

Critical Thinking Activities

15. Plans might include more space, provisions for sewage, recreation, energy-efficient heating and cooling.

16. Local government was expensive, inefficient, corrupt, and unorganized. • Possible answers: still applies—cities have problems of crime, homeless people, pollution, garbage, poor public transportation, and education. Does not apply—cities provide jobs, housing, cultural activities.

17. Possible answer: unwilling

CHAPTER **19** REVIEW

Write your answers on a separate sheet of paper.

Key Terms and People

Explain the significance of: row house, de facto segregation, ghettos, Tammany Hall, Thomas Nast, Jean de Crèvecoeur, melting pot, Ellis Island, ethnic islands, radicals, naturalized citizen, Chinese Exclusion Act, Gentlemen's Agreement, Alien Land Law

Main Ideas

1. What were the main problems of urbanization in the 1880's?
2. What problem were the dumbbell tenements meant to address? Why did they not solve the problem?
3. Why did low-income voters support urban political machines?
4. How did the Boss Tweed scandal become exposed?
5. Fill in this chart to compare the new and the old immigrants. Use the map on page 499.

	New	Old
Place of origin		
Language		
Religion		
Race		
Integration		
Where they settled		

6. Why did the general population, including the old immigrants, resent the newcomers?
7. Why were the Anglo-Saxons of the Northeast, especially New England, so determined to keep their way of life?
8. Why did President Cleveland veto the bill that required an immigrant to pass a literacy test in order to enter the country?

Critical Thinking Questions

9. **Analyzing Literature.** Read the excerpt from *The Immigrants* by Howard Fast. Do you think Feng Wo got the job? Why or why not?
10. **Drawing Conclusions.** Were the urban political machines of the late 1800's helpful or harmful? Give reasons for your answer.
11. **Analyzing Choices.** Were political machines the only means by which lower-income voters could relate to their government? What other groups might have taken the place of these machines?
12. **Predicting Outcomes.** If you were thinking of immigrating to the United States and knew from relatives and friends who had gone before what awaited you in the new country, would you have made the journey? Why or why not?
13. **Making Generalizations.** Why were Asians more discriminated against than other immigrants?
14. **Applying Principles.** Are Congressional laws that restrict immigration unconstitutional? Why does the Bill of Rights protect legal immigrants? Explain your answers.

Critical Thinking Activities

15. **Applying Concepts.** Imagine that you are an architect in the 1880's. What improvements would you include on plans for low-income housing to replace the dumbbell apartments?
16. **Linking Past to Present.** Scholar James Bryce wrote, "There is no denying that the government of cities is the one conspicuous failure of the United States." Why did he make this statement? Does it apply to cities in the United States today? Explain your answer.
17. **Linking Past to Present.** What attitude is shown by Americans' desire to limit immigration? What is so ironic about this attitude?
18. **Linking Past to Present.** Do we still have political machines in urban areas today? Why or why not?

Cities and Immigrants

Wealthy people had an easy life in the growing cities. Middle-class families lived in the new apartment houses and in row houses. Poor people were confined to dark and overcrowded tenements. As cities grew, elevated railways and electric trolleys met transportation needs. Water and sanitation problems still had to be solved. Crime was common. Large cities like Chicago suffered major fires because most buildings were still made of wood. More and more African Americans migrated to the cities. After 1890, customs and prejudices forced these black people to live in segregated areas.

Local governments proved inept at handling city problems. Incredibly rapid growth put great strains on outdated ways of governing. Politicians gave favors to people in exchange for votes. Political machines took over in many cities, especially in New York. The nation's largest city came under the rule of a political machine called Tammany Hall. Its Boss Tweed ran corrupt schemes for the construction of public buildings. The Tweed Ring pocketed enormous amounts of money at the expense of the taxpayers. Eventually the *New York Times* exposed Tweed, and he went to prison.

Huge numbers of immigrants came to the United States between 1880 and 1914. They met hostility from native-born Americans because they seemed so different. Many of the new immigrants did not speak English. Many believed in a different kind of Christianity, namely Catholicism. Many were Jews. A few came from Asia. Most of the new immigrants settled in cities in the Northeast and lived together in ethnic neighborhoods. Their trip across the Atlantic and their inspection at Ellis Island often involved great suffering. For many immigrants, however, the most difficult experience was seeing their children grow up differently from the way they did.

The immigration of political radicals, Catholics, and Asians led to demands for a new immigration policy. This hostility was especially strong in New England. In California many white Americans demanded that immigration of Chinese be stopped. Beginning in 1882, Congress passed several acts to prevent more Chinese people from entering the country. Both the California government and the federal government took steps to limit the number of Japanese immigrants as well. This resistance to the "yellow peril" caused great hostility in Japan. President Theodore Roosevelt tried to restore peace with the Gentlemen's Agreement.

Chronology of Main Events

1871 Great Chicago Fire; Tweed Ring exposed

1872 Crédit Mobilier scandal

1873 Panic of 1873

1882 Chinese immigration restricted

1885 Grover Cleveland inaugurated President

1894 Immigration Restriction League founded

1897 Boston opens first electric subway

1901 William McKinley assassinated; Theodore Roosevelt succeeds to Presidency

1905 Treaty of Portsmouth ends Russo-Japanese War

1908 Gentlemen's Agreement reached with Japan

1913 Alien Land Law passed in California

Telescoping the Times may be used as an alternative to having students read the entire chapter, as a chapter preview, or as a chapter review.

Global Perspectives

1885	The Congo becomes the personal possession of Leopold II.
1885	First All-India National Congress meets.
1888	Brazil abolishes slavery.
1910	Union of South Africa is established.
1910	Japan annexes Korea.
1911	Amundsen reaches the South Pole.
1912-1913	Balkan Wars take place.

For Discussion

How might Japan's annexation of Korea have influenced America's expansionist feelings? (Possible response: U.S. expansionist desires would have been fueled by Japanese interest in Korea which pointed out the availability of new markets and territory.)

Additional Resources

- Geography Activities
- Skills Activities
- Thematic Activities
- Economic Activities
- Cultural Literacy Activities
- Literary Source Readings
- Primary Source Readings
- Nuclear Peacekeeping
- Transparencies
- Computer Test Generator

Additional Teaching Strategies

SECTION 1

For Basic Students: Have students work in small groups to review the section and to list in chronological order the major events in Cuban-American relations from the early 1800's to the time of the Spanish-American War. At the end of this list, students should write one sentence that tells how Cuba fit into the scheme of American imperialism. (Events might include: Jefferson considers annexing Cuba; Polk offers to buy Cuba from Spain; Democratic party, prior to Civil War, calls for annexing Cuba as a slave state; after first war of independence, American businessmen invest in sugar cane plantations; U.S. abolishes tariff on Cuban sugar in 1884, and sugar production increases; Wilson-Gorman Tariff restores duty and ruins Cuba's economy; Second War of Independence in 1895 results in destruction of U.S. mills and plantations; yellow journalists sensationalize Spanish atrocities in Cuba. Cuba was very much a part of American imperialism; it supplied a popular product not then produced in the U.S.—sugar.)

For Advanced Students: Ask students to draw a political cartoon about the Cuban crisis of 1898 that might be the type published in either Hearst's or Pulitzer's newspaper. Have students bring to class and display examples of current political cartoons to use as models.

SECTION 2

For Basic Students: Have students research the Rough Riders in biographies and encyclopedias and write several journal entries centered around the preparations for and the attack on San Juan Hill. (Journal entries might include: information on types of men who enlisted with the Rough Riders; details about Roosevelt; details of the battle.)

For Advanced Students: Divide class into groups of two or three. Have them research and prepare oral reports on one of the following men and his involvement in the Spanish-American War: Enrique Dupuy de Lome, Theodore Roosevelt, Admiral George Dewey, General Emilio Aguinaldo. (Reports should include: details about their backgrounds; information on their military careers; the effect they had on the outcome of the war.)

SECTION 3

For Basic Students: Have students research in an encyclopedia and then give a two-minute oral report on the work of Dr. Walter Reed or yellow fever. (Reports should include: the effect of the disease on U.S. expansion.)

For Advanced Students: Ask students to assume the role of a member of a Hawaiian, Filipino, Puerto Rican, or Cuban delegation to the U.S. Senate and present a three-minute speech on the status of their country and their delegation's desires for its future. (Speeches should include: the current status of the country; reasons why the country desires a new status or new laws.)

SECTION 4

For Basic Students: Give students copies of the outline map of the world at the back of the book and ask them to locate and label with the name and year all U.S. overseas acquisitions up to 1917.

For Advanced Students: Ask the students to research the differences between the isolationism of the Monroe Doctrine and the internationalism of the Open Door Policy. Divide the class into two groups and assign one to the Monroe Doctrine and the other to the Open Door policy, each to present arguments in favor of one or the other foreign policy plan. (Possible responses: Monroe Doctrine—warned European powers against interference in Western Hemisphere; pledged that U.S. would not involve itself in European affairs; was a good foreign policy plan because it freed the U.S. from responsibilities abroad, allowing it to concentrate on solving problems at home. Open Door policy—allowed all nations to do business in China; regulated railroad, harbor, and tariff rates in Asia; allowed nations to compete on equal terms in Asia; was a good foreign policy plan because it fostered growth through trade and competition.)

Further Reading for Students

Conroy, Robert. *The Battle of Manila Bay*. New York: Macmillan, 1968.

Marks, Frederick W. III. *Velvet on Iron: The Diplomacy of Theodore Roosevelt*. Lincoln: University of Nebraska Press, 1979.

McCullough, David. *Mornings on Horseback*. New York: Simon and Schuster, 1982.

McCullough, David. *The Path Between the Seas: The Creation of the Panama Canal, 1870-1914*. New York: Simon and Schuster, 1978.

Morris, Edmund. *The Rise of Theodore Roosevelt*. New York: Ballantine Books, 1980. Paper.

Roosevelt, Theodore. *Autobiography of Theodore Roosevelt*. Jersey City, N.J.: Da Capo Press, 1958. Paper.

Stanley, Pat. *A Nation in the Making: The Philippines and the United States, 1899-1921*. Cambridge: Harvard University Press, 1974.

Werstein, Irving. *Eighteen Ninety-Eight: The Spanish-American War and the Philippine Insurrection Told with Pictures*. Totowa, N.J.: Cooper Square Publishers, 1966. (Easy)

Historical Fiction

Thane, Elswyth. *Ever After*. Mattituck, N.Y.: Amereon Ltd., 1976.

Bibliography for Teachers
Books

Beisner, Robert L. *From the Old Diplomacy to the New, 1865-1900*. Arlington Heights, Ill.: Harlan Davidson, 1986. Paper.

Boardman, Tom W. Jr. *America and the Progressive Era: 1900-1917*. New York: Walcik, 1970.

Cooper, John M. *The Warrior and the Priest: Woodrow Wilson and Theodore Roosevelt*. Cambridge: Harvard University Press, 1983.

Gould, Lewis L. *The Spanish-American War and President McKinley*. Lawrence: University Press of Kansas, 1982. Paper.

Graebner, Norman A. *Empire on the Pacific: A Study in American Continental Expansion*. Claremont, Calif.: Regina Books, 1983.

Lawson, Don. *The United States in the Spanish American War*. New York: Crowell Junior Books, 1976.

Herbert, Wally. *The Noose of Laurels: Robert E. Peary and the Rail to the North Pole*. New York: Atheneum, 1989.

Perkins, Whitney T. *Constraint of Empire: The United States and Caribbean Interventions*. Westport, Conn.: Greenwood Press, 1981.

Ruiz, Ramon. *Cuba: The Making of a Revolution*. New York: W.W. Norton, 1970.

Trask, David F. *The War with Spain in Eighteen Ninety-Eight*. New York: Macmillan, 1981.

Unger, Irwin, and Debi Unger. *The Vulnerable Years: The United States, 1896-1917*. New York: New York University Press, 1978.

Wiebe, Robert H. *The Search for Order, 1877-1920*. New York: Hill and Wang, 1966. Paper.

Audio-Visuals

History of the U.S. Navy: Naval Decline, the New Navy, and the War with Spain. Creative Arts Studio. Movie.

The Queen's Destiny. WNET-TV. Movie.

Theodore Roosevelt. David L. Wolper Productions. Movie.

The United States Becomes a World Power. Sandler/Ward Documentary Associates. Movie.

United States Expansion: Overseas. Coronet. Movie.

Teacher's Notes:

Lesson Plan

Teaching Resources, Unit 5 Booklet

Lesson Study Sheets pp. 57-72
Daily Activities pp. 73-80
Enrichment Activities pp. 81-88
Reteaching Activities pp. 89-96
Chapter Review p. 97
Chapter Mastery Tests pp. 99-110
Telescoping the Times Study Sheet p. 111

Chapter Objectives

Students will learn:
- why the U.S. adopted a policy of imperialism in the late 1800's
- the causes and results of the Spanish American War
- how the U.S. expanded beyond its continental borders in the early 1900's
- how the U.S. became a world leader around the turn of the century

Using the Chapter Time Line

The construction of the Panama Canal (see Unit 5 Time Line) coincided with the announcement of what U.S. foreign policy? (Answer: Roosevelt Corollary)

Roosevelt's Corollary related to the Monroe Doctrine. How many years had passed since Monroe issued his warning (see Chapter 9 Time Line)? (Answer: 81)

Picturing History Queen Liliuokalani, a skillful leader. was the last monarch to rule Hawaii before it was annexed by the United States in 1898. She is still remembered for "Aloha Oe," the traditional farewell song of Hawaii.

1880   1885   1890   1895   1900   1905   1910   1915

1898
• Spanish-American War
• Treaty of Paris ends war

1900
Open Door policy proclaimed

1901
Platt Amendment authorizes
U.S. intervention in Cuba

1905
Treaty of Portsmouth
ends Russo-Japanese War

1904
Roosevelt Corollary announced

1914
Panama Canal opened

510

CHAPTER **20**   1880–1914

The Nation Claims an Empire

Links to American Literature

. . . on January 29, 1891, royalty of a far different sort ascended the throne and trouble was inescapable. Queen Liliuokalani was a short, moderately stout woman of regal bearing. . . . It was her custom to deliver important messages seated in front of a golden-yellow cape of feathers, both because this was an antique royal custom which set off her dignity and because she was slightly crippled and did not move with grace. For many years she had been plain Lydia Dominis, strong-minded wife of a slim haole [a non-Polynesian] of Italian descent, . . . Upon the death of her brother, the king, she ascended the throne, bringing with her a desire to reverse the trend toward haole domination. . . . She was a highly intelligent woman and had traveled to the courts of Europe, where the role played by Queen Victoria impressed her, and she had a love of political power. Had she acquired the throne immediately after the passing of the Kamehameha, she might have made Hawaii a strong and secure monarchy, for she had a lively imagination and much skill in manipulating people; but she attained ultimate power too late; republicanism had infected her people; sugar had captured her islands.

— JAMES A. MICHENER, *Hawaii*

During the 1840's, the notion of "manifest destiny" was invoked to justify the expansion of the United States to the shores of the Pacific Ocean. In the 1890's, the nation's spirit was again imperialistic. With United States intervention in Hawaii and other island nations, the American belief in self-determination stated in the Declaration of Independence was put to a severe test. As Americans today make decisions regarding United States foreign policy, they still must struggle to balance their desire for economic power against the democratic principles upon which this nation was founded.

Chapter Overview

In this chapter you will learn why and how the United States expanded beyond its continental borders in the late nineteenth century. In addition, you will learn why the United States went to war with Spain and why it was necessary for the nation to assume a new role as a world leader by the turn of the century. To help you follow the steps by which the United States claimed an empire, Chapter 20 describes these events in four sections.

Chapter Outline

1. **America Is Ready to Expand**
2. **The United States Goes to War with Spain**
3. **New Lands Come Under the American Flag**
4. **The United States Becomes a World Power**

Anticipate the Lesson

Review with students the factors that led such European countries as England, France, and Portugal to establish empires overseas in the 1500's and 1600's. List these factors on the board. (Factors might include: desire for wealth, land, power, glory, and to spread Christianity; route to Asia; market for manufactured goods; new sources of raw materials.)

State the Objective

Understand why the U.S. adopted a policy of imperialism in the late 1800's.

For Discussion

How do the terms *manifest destiny* and *imperialism* apply both to the Mexican War, 1846-1848 (Ch. 12) and the Spanish-American War, 1898? (Possible responses: at both times Americans believed it was their right and destiny to expand and take over new territories.)

SECTION 1

America Is Ready to Expand

GLOSSARY TERMS: imperialism, lobby

In the years immediately following the Civil War, the American people focused their attention on domestic matters. Even the purchase of Alaska from Russia in 1867 was of little interest. If Secretary of State William H. Seward wanted to waste $7,200,000 on a frozen wasteland, that was **Seward's Folly.** Reconstructing the South, conquering the West, and developing industry seemed far more important.

Several Needs Support Imperialism

As the 1880's progressed, however, Americans began to give more attention to the idea that the United States should obtain colonies overseas. There were several reasons for this belief.

The Need for Markets and Materials. American farmers and workers, backed by machines, were extremely productive. As Senator Albert J. Beveridge of Indiana argued,

Today we are raising more than we can consume. Today we are making more than we can use. . . . Therefore we must find new markets for our produce, new occupation for our capital, new work for our labor.

Also, American factories needed certain raw materials such as rubber and tin that could be obtained only from abroad. **Imperialism,** or the policy of conquering other countries to build an empire, seemed to offer a solution to both these problems.

Anglo-Saxon "Superiority." Economic factors, however, were not the only reasons for the change in public opinion. Equally significant was the concept that combined the ideas of **Charles Darwin** about the survival of the fittest with a belief in the racial superiority of Anglo-Saxons.

As **Josiah Strong,** a Congregational minister and writer, put it in 1885:

It seems to me that God, with infinite wisdom and skill, is training the Anglo-Saxon race for an hour sure to come in the world's future. . . . The . . . lands of the earth are limited, and will soon be taken. . . . Then will the world enter upon a new stage of its history—the final competition of races. . . . Then this [Anglo-Saxon] race of unequaled energy, with all the majesty of numbers and the might of wealth behind it—the representative . . . of the largest liberty, the purest Christianity, the highest civilization . . . will spread itself over the earth.

People in the Chapter

William McKinley first learned about Dewey's victory in Manila from the *Chicago Tribune.* After defeating the Spanish, Dewey cabled the news to President McKinley from Hong Kong. A reporter sent his story, which did not have to be decoded, at the express rate. In this case the newspaper outwitted the navy.

Frederic Remington was admired by all who loved the Old West. Teddy Roosevelt said, "He [Remington] is, of course, one of the most typical artists we have ever had. . . the soldier, the cowboy and rancher, the Indian, the horse and the cattle of the plains, will live in his pictures and bronzes. . . for all times." Owen Wister, author of *The Virginian*, wrote "Remington is not merely an artist, he is a national treasure." In the words of art historian Vincent Price,

"Remington's paintings are as American as the buffalo and as glamorous as an Indian war bonnet."

Queen Liliuokalani firmly believed native Hawaiians should rule Hawaii. The United States minister in Honolulu disagreed. "The Hawaiian pear is now fully ripe," he wrote, "and this is the golden hour for the United States to pluck it."

Emilio Aguinaldo was part Chinese, well educated, and a charismatic Filipino leader. Dewey brought him out of exile in Asia to weaken the Spanish resistance in the Philippines. The Admiral later regretted this decision when Aguinaldo led an insurrection against the United States.

Present the Lesson

Have students list on the board the major reasons why America desired colonies overseas. (Answers: need for markets and materials; belief in Anglo-Saxon superiority.) Have students compare these reasons to the factors that led to European imperialism. (Possible response: the need for markets and materials was a factor for Americans and Europeans.) To generate discussion on Admiral Mahan's sea power theory, first have students write the main points of the theory on the board. (Responses: sea power was essential if the nation wanted to be rich in peace time and unbeatable in war time;

Navy needed to defend U.S. shipping lanes; strategically located bases were needed for fueling; U.S. should acquire a modern fleet, naval bases in the Caribbean, a canal across the Isthmus of Panama, Hawaii and other islands in the Pacific.) Then ask students how this policy would have encouraged imperialism. (Possible response: Mahan made U.S. expansion appear to be essential for survival as a nation.)

Check for Understanding

Call on individual students to answer Section 1 Review questions orally.

Already, Anglo-Saxons and other Europeans were dividing Africa into colonies, and they seemed ready to do the same with China. Surely the United States could not afford to fall behind.

Admiral Mahan Calls for Sea Power. Among the leading exponents of American expansion overseas was Captain, later Admiral, **Alfred Thayer Mahan.** In 1886 he became president of the newly established Naval War College in Newport, Rhode Island. There he gave a series of lectures that were later published under the title *The Influence of Sea Power upon History 1660–1783.*

Mahan argued that sea power was essential if a nation wanted to be rich in peacetime and unbeatable in wartime. A nation needed a navy to defend its shipping lanes. It also needed strategically located bases where its fleets could refuel. Specifically, according to Mahan, the United States should acquire four things: a modern fleet, naval bases in the Caribbean Sea, a canal across the Isthmus of Panama, and Hawaii and other islands in the Pacific.

Mahan's book had a tremendous influence. Gradually the United States acquired all the things Mahan said it needed.

First came a modern fleet. Prodded by Secretary of State James Blaine, one of Mahan's staunchest supporters, Congress set about building up the American navy. Between 1883 and 1890, nine steel cruisers were completed, and construction was started on the nation's first modern battleship, the *Maine.* By 1898 the United States was the third largest naval power in the world. Only Great Britain and France ranked higher.

After the modern fleet came naval bases in the Caribbean. The United States obtained these, as well as a number of Pacific islands, as a result of the Spanish-American War. The war was fought in 1898. It was a brief conflict, lasting only three months and twenty-two days. It was almost bloodless. Out of two hundred thousand American troops, fewer than four hundred were killed in battle, while about four thousand died from yellow fever and dysentery. In the opinion of many historians, the war was unjustified. It all began over Cuba.

Americans Disagree over Cuba

American interest in Cuba dated back to the early 1800's. President Thomas Jefferson had considered the possibility of annexing the island.

Picturing History Alfred T. Mahan. His book on the effects of sea power on history was studied worldwide by students of war and politics.

President James Polk had tried to buy it from Spain. The Democratic party's national platform prior to the Civil War contained a plank calling for Cuba's admission as a slave state.

First War for Independence. In 1868 the first war for independence broke out in Cuba. It lasted for ten years and resulted in some 250,000 casualties. Although the rebels lost, Spain agreed to abolish slavery and to allow a certain amount of self-government. The latter promise, however, was not kept.

After the emancipation of Cuba's slaves in 1886, American capitalists began investing tens of millions of dollars in Cuba. In particular, they bought large tracts of land and set up sugar cane plantations. Sugar was the basis of the Cuban economy, and now the United States became the island's main market. In 1884 the United States abolished its tariff on Cuban sugar. This sent sugar production skyrocketing even higher than before. Ten years later, however, as a result of the efforts of the American Sugar Refining Company **lobby** (a pressure group formed to influence lawmakers), the Wilson-Gorman Tariff restored a 40 percent duty on imports of Cuban sugar. The Cuban economy was ruined.

Second War for Independence. The second war for independence broke out in 1895. It was led by **José Martí** (mär tē´), a poet and journalist who had spent much of his life in exile in New York City.

Picturing History *José Julian Martí* by Herman Norman, 1891.

To stimulate a discussion on the extent to which American journalists either heighten or weaken a potentially dangerous national movement such as imperialism, ask the following questions. If the purpose of a newspaper is to report the news, how can that paper influence its readers in a positive or negative way? (Possible response: through editorials or biased stories.) What effect did the yellow press have on imperialism? (Possible response: it heightened interest in Cuba and perhaps drew out the war by printing sensational and untrue stories.)

Have students complete Chapter 20, Section 1 Daily Activity.

Have students read Section 2, "The United States Goes to War with Spain," and answer the Section 2 Review questions on paper.

For Discussion
What do the terms *yellow journalism* and *imperialism* mean? What was their relationship in the late 1800's?
(Possible definitions: yellow journalism—sensationalizing news and even writing lies for the purpose of creating a "great newspaper" and outselling the competitor; imperialism—a policy that dictates acquisition of an empire by controlling the economic and political affairs of weaker nations. Journalists used incidents such as the Cuban fight for independence to justify American involvement.)

Picturing History This cartoon from 1898 shows Uncle Sam—the United States—about to swallow Cuba.

Picturing History Spanish General Valeriano Weyler's harsh action against Cuban rebels was attacked by the United States press. Newspapers referred to him as the Butcher.

There he organized Cuban resistance against Spain. Unable to defeat the Spanish troops in battle, the rebels took to the hills and began an active guerrilla campaign. Their strategy included destroying property, especially American-owned sugar mills and plantations. The rebels did this deliberately, for they hoped the United States would intervene. Apparently they were willing to have their rebellion put down if, in exchange, Cuba would become free from Spain.

Public opinion in the United States was split. Many business people wanted the government to support Spain in order to protect their investments. Other Americans, however, were enthusiastic about the rebel cause. Wasn't the cry of *"Cuba Libre!"* ("A Free Cuba!") a bit like Patrick Henry's cry of "Give me liberty or give me death"?

The Threat of War Escalates

In 1896 the Spanish government sent to Cuba a new general, Valeriano Weyler (wā´ lər), with orders to put down the revolt. Weyler decided that regular military methods would not work against the rebels' guerrilla tactics. He moved the entire rural population of central and western Cuba, areas in which the rebels were particularly active, into reconcentration camps.

Unfortunately for the people in the camps, sanitation facilities were miserable and food was in short supply. Disease and famine took a high toll. Of the 1.6 million people whom Weyler reconcentrated, about 200,000 died within two years.

The Yellow Press. While Weyler was attempting to put down the Cuban revolt, supporters of the rebel cause were active in the United States. Large quantities of money and arms were collected and smuggled onto the island.

More important, newspaper tycoons William Randolph Hearst and Joseph Pulitzer were carrying on a circulation war. Each was determined that his paper would outsell the other's. Both began to play up Spanish "atrocities." General Weyler was nicknamed the Butcher. Legitimate accounts of suffering in the reconcentration camps were mixed with fake stories of wells being poisoned and little children being thrown to the sharks. American

Anticipate the Lesson

Ask students to consider what aspects of the Spanish-American War could classify it as an imperialist venture. Have students list these on the board. The list might include:

Imperialist Venture

- Spain was already improving conditions in Cuba and the U.S. did not need to interfere.
- Roosevelt sent Dewey to Manila before war was declared.
- Americans wanted to annex Philippines.
- McKinley believed that the U.S. had no honorable choice but to take control of the Philippines.

State the Objective

Understand the causes and results of the Spanish-American War.

correspondents, who were not allowed to enter areas where fighting was going on, would sit around the bars in Havana and make up reports about battles that never took place. Artist **Frederic Remington,** who had been illustrating reporters' dispatches, cabled Hearst saying that a war between the United States and Spain seemed very unlikely. Back came Hearst's reply: "You furnish the pictures and I'll furnish the war."

SECTION 1 REVIEW

Key Terms and People

Explain the significance of: Seward's Folly, imperialism, Charles Darwin, Josiah Strong, Alfred Thayer Mahan, lobby, José Martí, Frederic Remington

Main Ideas

1. What were the main reasons that Americans supported imperialism in the late nineteenth century?
2. According to Admiral Mahan, what did America need in order to achieve superiority over other nations?
3. How did American public opinion split over Cuba's second war for independence?
4. How did American press coverage of Cuba's second war for independence attempt to influence Americans' views of the war?

Critical Thinking

5. Was nineteenth-century American imperialism a logical extension of the American belief in manifest destiny? Explain.

SECTION 2

The United States Goes to War with Spain

GLOSSARY TERM: Rough Riders

Both the Democratic and the Republican platforms of 1896 had proclaimed sympathy for the Cuban rebels. President McKinley, however, did not want the United States to fight against Spain. He had been through the Civil War, and as he told a friend, "I have seen the dead piled up, and I do not want to see another [war]." With regard to Weyler's actions, McKinley observed that "there

were some outrages on both sides if the truth were known."

Toward the end of 1897, it seemed as if McKinley's hope might turn into reality. A new government took power in Madrid. It recalled Weyler, closed down the reconcentration camps, and offered Cuba self-government in all matters except defense, foreign relations, and the court system. The rebels, however, rejected the offer. They would settle only for complete independence. Nevertheless, in his first annual message to Congress, McKinley urged American firebrands to give Spain "a reasonable chance to realize . . . the new order of things." Two incidents, however, provoked Americans to demand war.

The de Lôme Letter Incites Americans

The first incident had to do with a private letter written by Enrique Dupuy de Lôme, the Spanish minister to the United States. A Cuban rebel stole the letter from a Havana post office and leaked it to Hearst's *Journal.* In the letter, de Lôme called McKinley a weak President and a common politician who took both sides of an issue and always sought the admiration of the crowd.

This was much milder than some of Theodore Roosevelt's comments. Roosevelt, assistant secretary of the navy, considered McKinley "a white-livered cur" with "no more backbone than a chocolate eclair!" Nevertheless, foreign ministers are supposed to be discreet and are not supposed to put critical statements down on paper. Before an indignant State Department could demand his recall, de Lôme resigned. Six days later came the second incident.

The U.S.S. *Maine* Explodes

Early in 1898 President McKinley had ordered the U.S.S. *Maine* to Havana. Officially, it was a courtesy call. Actually, the battleship had responded to a telegram from the American consul general in Havana. He was afraid that American citizens there might be in danger from local rioters.

When the *Maine* arrived in the city's harbor, all seemed calm. The ship's officers went sightseeing ashore and even took in a bullfight. The evening of February 15, Captain Charles D. Sigsbee was sitting in his cabin writing a letter to his wife. Suddenly there was a terrible explosion, and the ship's ammunition went up in flames. Some 260 of the 350 officers and men on board lost their lives.

SECTION 1 REVIEW

Answers

Main Ideas

1. To expand U.S. export markets, to import more raw materials, and because they believed in the racial superiority of Anglo-Saxons.

2. A modern fleet, Caribbean naval bases, a canal across Panama, and some Pacific islands.

3. Many business people wanted the government to support Spain in order to protect their investments in Cuba, while other Americans supported the Cuban rebels' causes of liberty and freedom.

4. By printing stories that exaggerated war atrocities and intentionally gave both true and fabricated accounts of events, newspaper tycoons attempted to promote American involvement in the war.

Critical Thinking

5. Possible answer: no—although both manifest destiny and imperialism had elements of expansionism and a belief in American superiority, manifest destiny applied only to the North American continent, whereas imperialism could be applied anywhere.
(analysis & synthesis)

Present the Lesson

Ask students to chart on the board the causes and results of the Spanish-American War.

Causes

• Sympathy for Cuban rebels
• Spanish atrocities in Cuba
• De Lome letter criticizing McKinley
• Explosion of U.S.S. *Maine* in Havana Harbor

Results

• Cuba became independent
• U.S. took possession of Puerto Rico, Guam, and Philippines
• U.S. paid Spain $20 million

Have students complete Chapter 20, Section 2 Daily Activity in class.

Check for Understanding

Call on individual students to read their answers to Section 2 Review questions.

Historical Sidelight

Who or what caused the explosion of the *Maine*? Most evidence points to an accidental internal explosion caused by spontaneous combustion or bad wiring. The truth will probably never be known for in 1911-12 the *Maine* was hauled into deep water and given a full military burial at sea.

Even today no one really knows what caused the *Maine* to explode. A naval court of inquiry decided that the ship had hit a submarine mine. Other investigators believed there was an internal explosion in the coal bunkers. William Randolph Hearst, however, had no doubt about the matter at all. His *Journal's* headline read: THE WARSHIP MAINE WAS SPLIT IN TWO BY AN ENEMY'S SECRET INFERNAL MACHINE. The paper offered a reward of $50,000 for the capture of the evil Spaniards who had committed the outrage.

Now there was no holding back the forces that wanted war. Everyone seemed to be crying, "Remember the *Maine*!" As the *New York Times* put it, "It would have been as easy to end the war of the Revolution at Bunker Hill or the Civil War at Bull Run as to turn back now." It made no difference that the Spanish government agreed on April 9 to almost everything the United States demanded, including a six-month cease-fire.

On April 11 McKinley sent a message to Congress asking for the right "to use the military and naval forces of the United States" to bring peace to Cuba. On April 19 Congress agreed. On April 20 the United States went to war with Spain.

Dewey Takes Manila

The Spanish-American War was fought on both sides of the globe in the Caribbean and in the Philippines. Engagements included both sea and land forces. Some of them inspired songs:

> O Dewey was the morning
> Upon the first of May,
> And Dewey was the Admiral
> Down in Manila Bay;
> And Dewey were the Regent's eyes,
> Them orbs of royal blue!
> And Dewey feel discouraged?
> I Dew not think we Dew.

On February 25 John Long, Secretary of the Navy, left his office for some badly needed rest. No sooner had he gone than the assistant secretary, Theodore Roosevelt, sent a cable to Commodore (later Admiral) **George Dewey,** head of the Pacific fleet. The cable told him to sail for the Philippine Islands in case war with Spain broke out.

On May 1 Dewey steamed into the harbor of Manila, the capital of the Spanish-owned Philippine Islands. Thanks to Secretary of State Blaine's preparedness campaign, the squadron included four heavily armed cruisers. The Spanish fleet, although larger, carried only a few obsolete guns.

As one historian wrote, it "was more a practice shoot than a battle." Dewey brought his ships within three miles of the Spanish fleet and then remarked to an officer, "You may fire when ready, Gridley." Then back and forth went the American squadron, firing gunpowder for several hours, until

Picturing History "Remember the *Maine*" became a rallying cry of those favoring war with Spain after the United States battleship mysteriously exploded in Havana Harbor. At right are the charred remains of the ship.

Picturing History Admiral George Dewey (second from right) served on the United States-Philippine Commission.

the entire enemy fleet was destroyed. Spanish casualties numbered three hundred eighty-one. American casualties numbered one: an overweight engineer who died of heat prostration.

Over the next two months, some eleven thousand American troops landed in the Philippines. There they joined forces with Filipino rebels led by General **Emilio Aguinaldo** (ä'gē näl'dô). The rebels had been fighting for freedom since 1896. In August the Spanish troops in Manila surrendered. However, they surrendered only to the Americans. Aguinaldo's troops were not allowed into the city.

The United States Invades Cuba

Back in the Caribbean, hostilities began with a naval blockade. After searching for the main Spanish fleet for almost a week, Rear Admiral William T. Sampson located it in the harbor of Santiago, Cuba. He immediately bottled it up.

American Troops Organize. While Admiral Sampson staged his blockade, American troops organized to invade the island. Unfortunately, unlike the navy, the army was ill-prepared. About 125,000 Americans had volunteered to fight, including a large number of African Americans who hoped the war would help achieve "justice at home as well as abroad." However, there were not enough up-to-date guns to go around. Nor was there any khaki cloth for lightweight uniforms. This meant the soldiers had to wear heavy blue wool in the tropical climate. Furthermore, most of the officers were Civil War veterans who spent a great deal of time reminiscing about old battles and almost no time training the volunteers.

Nevertheless, in mid-June about seventeen thousand men managed to sail from Tampa, Florida, and land in Cuba. They included all four black regiments of the regular army, as well as the First Volunteer Cavalry Regiment. The latter had been organized in part by **Theodore Roosevelt,** who had resigned as assistant secretary of the navy in order to fight. Roosevelt's **Rough Riders** were a mixture of cowboys, Indians, and former sheriffs from the Western territories of Arizona, New Mexico, and Oklahoma. There were also "polo players and gentlemen riders from New York's Harvard, Yale, and Princeton clubs."

Map Skills

Hong Kong • Luzon

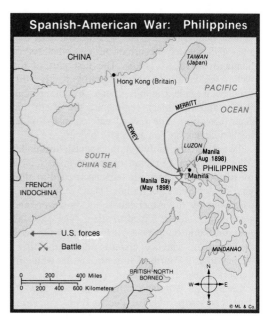

Spanish-American War: Philippines

CHINA

TAIWAN (Japan)

Hong Kong (Britain)

PACIFIC

MERRITT

OCEAN

DEWEY

SOUTH CHINA SEA

LUZON

Manila (Aug 1898)

PHILIPPINES

Manila

Manila Bay (May 1898)

FRENCH INDOCHINA

→ U.S. forces

⚔ Battle

MINDANAO

0 200 400 Miles
0 200 400 600 Kilometers

BRITISH NORTH BORNEO

N W E S

© ML & Co.

Map Skills **Movement** Dewey sailed to Manila from what British colony? **Location** On what island is Manila located?

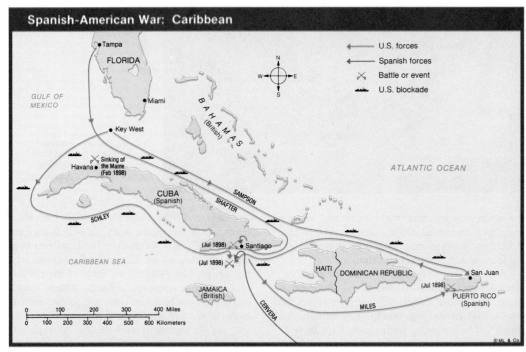

Spanish-American War: Caribbean

Map Skills   **Movement**   Shafter sailed from what U.S. city?   **Location**   In what direction is Puerto Rico from Florida?   **Location**   How far is Havana from Key West?

Map Skills

Tampa • Southeast • 110 to 120 miles (180 or 190 km)

The Rough Riders Take Santiago. The most famous land battle in Cuba was the Battle of San Juan Hill, which occurred on the outskirts of Santiago on July 1, 1898. The first part of the battle, which took place on nearby Kettle Hill, featured a gallant uphill charge by the Rough Riders and two black regiments, the Ninth and Tenth Cavalries. The second part consisted of an infantry attack on San Juan Hill proper.

Two days later, on July 3, the Spanish fleet under Admiral Pascual Cervera (ser ver´ ə) made a dash for freedom. The Spanish ships succeeded in slipping out of Santiago Harbor. They were quickly overtaken by the American ships, however, and were either sunk or forced to shore. The next day Admiral Sampson cabled Washington, D.C., with the message, ''The fleet under my command offers the nation as a Fourth of July present the whole of Cervera's fleet.''

On July 17 Santiago surrendered. On July 26 American troops invaded Puerto Rico. An armistice was declared on August 12. Finally, on December 10 the United States and Spain signed the **Treaty of Paris of 1898.**

The United States Annexes the Philippines

The American and Spanish commissioners in Paris agreed on most issues. Cuba was to become independent. The United States would take over Puerto Rico and the Spanish-owned island of Guam in the Pacific. The sticking point was what to do with the Philippines.

When the war broke out, the idea of annexing a group of islands six thousand miles west of California was probably the last thing in most Americans' minds. President McKinley admitted that he did not even know where these islands were. Mahan, Roosevelt, and their followers, though, believed that the islands had strategic and commercial importance.

As the war progressed, more Americans began to feel that annexation of the Philippines was a good idea after all. McKinley waffled at first. Then in late October, he came to a decision. Here is how he explained it to a group of Methodist ministers:

I walked the floor of the White House night after night until midnight, and I am not

Student Assignment/Homework

Have students read Section 3, "New Lands Come Under the American Flag," and answer the Section 3 Review questions on paper.

Picturing History The Rough Riders, a motley group of volunteers that included Western frontiersmen and Eastern gentlemen, pose with their leader, Theodore Roosevelt (center), at the top of San Juan Hill.

ashamed to tell you gentlemen, that I went down on my knees and prayed to Almighty God for light and guidance more than one night. And one night later it came to me this way—I don't know how it was, but it came: (1) That we could not give them [the Philippine Islands] back to Spain—that would be cowardly and dishonorable; (2) that we could not turn them over to France or Germany—our commercial rivals in the Orient—that would be bad business and discreditable; (3) that we could not leave them to themselves—they were unfit for self-government; . . . and (4) that there was nothing left for us to do but to take them all, and to educate the Filipinos, and uplift and Christianize them, and by God's grace do the very best we could by them, as our fellow-men for whom Christ also died.

McKinley apparently did not remember that most Filipinos had been Christians for several hundred years. In any event, under the Treaty of Paris the United States took over Spain's role as ruler of the Philippines. In exchange, the United States promised to pay Spain $20 million.

The struggle for ratification was touch and go. Although a majority of Americans favored ratification, many vocal people opposed it. These included former Presidents Benjamin Harrison and Grover Cleveland as well as Jane Addams, Andrew Carnegie, and Mark Twain. They believed that imperialistic expansion by the United States to gain colonies went against American tradition. One

said, "A republic can have no subjects." Speaker of the House Thomas B. Reed felt so strongly about the matter that he later resigned his congressional seat in protest. In addition, labor leaders such as Samuel Gompers were afraid that Filipino workers would compete against Americans for jobs, while racists like "Pitchfork Ben" Tillman did not want any more dark-skinned Americans. Still, the treaty passed the Senate with one vote to spare—and the United States had an empire.

SECTION 2 REVIEW

Key Terms and People

Explain the significance of: George Dewey, Emilio Aguinaldo, Theodore Roosevelt, Rough Riders, Treaty of Paris of 1898

Main Ideas

1. What two incidents led to the start of the Spanish-American War?
2. How was Manila captured by the Americans?
3. What resulted from the Battle of San Juan Hill and the naval battle between Sampson's and Cervera's fleets?
4. What were the main terms of the Treaty of Paris of 1898?
5. Why did many Americans oppose ratification of the Treaty of Paris?

Critical Thinking

6. Was the United States justified in declaring war on Spain? Explain.

State the Objective

Understand how the U.S. expanded beyond its continental borders in the early 1900's.

Anticipate the Lesson

Review reasons for U.S. expansion in the late 1800's. (Reasons: need for markets and materials; feeling of superiority.)

For Discussion

What were the provisions and results of the Platt Amendment? (Provisions: Cuba could not make treaties that would limit its independence; Cuba could not permit any foreign power to control any part of its territory; U.S. had the right to intervene in Cuba's internal affairs; Cuba could not go into debt; U.S. could buy or lease land for naval stations. Results: Cuba became a protectorate of U.S.; U.S. naval base was established at Guantanamo Bay; U.S. exerted great influence in Cuba's economy.)

SECTION 3

New Lands Come Under the American Flag

GLOSSARY TERMS: **protectorate, Platt Amendment, commonwealth**

As of 1898 the United States found itself for the first time with possessions overseas: Puerto Rico and the Philippines. It also had military control over Cuba. Furthermore, in that year, the United States acquired Hawaii, as you will soon read. How did the people in these overseas possessions fare under American rule?

Cuba Becomes a Protectorate

A **protectorate** is a country whose affairs are controlled by a stronger power. A few months before he died fighting in Cuba, José Martí warned his compatriots against depending too much on the United States. Martí was fearful that the United States would try to take Spain's place in controlling the island.

For the first three years of Cuban independence, it seemed as if Martí had been right. American occupation forces appointed the same local officials who had served the Spaniards. Cubans who protested such actions were either put in prison or exiled.

At the same time, the American military government did its best to improve the people's well-being. It gave food and clothing to thousands of families. It built roads, railroads, and dock facilities. It helped farmers put land back into cultivation. It reopened the University of Havana and organized a large number of elementary schools.

Conquering Yellow Fever. Perhaps the most spectacular accomplishment of the military government was the elimination of yellow fever almost completely. Each year, about eight hundred persons died from the disease in Havana alone. In 1900 an epidemic swept the island. A team of four army surgeons under Dr. Walter Reed was appointed to try to find out what caused the disease.

The team decided to work on a theory that had been proposed by a Cuban, Dr. Carlos Finlay. Dr. Finlay believed that yellow fever is carried from person to person by a species of mosquito. Within a year the theory was proved correct. The doctors identified the guilty species of mosquito and

Picturing History
Carlos Finlay. His theory about yellow fever led to a cure for the disease.

cleared out its breeding places. By 1901 Havana was free of yellow fever.

The United States Writes Cuba's Constitution. That same year, Cuba adopted a constitution. Many of its provisions, however, were not written by the Cuban constitutional assembly. Instead, they were drafted in Washington, D.C., and were presented to the assembly merely for its approval. Collectively these provisions are known as the **Platt Amendment** because they took the form of an amendment to a military appropriations bill.

The Platt Amendment provided the following: (1) Cuba was not to make any treaties that might limit its independence; (2) Cuba was not to permit any foreign power to control any part of its territory; (3) the United States was to have the right to intervene in Cuba's internal affairs "for the protection of life, property, and individual liberty"; (4) Cuba was not to go into debt; and (5) the United States could buy or lease land on the island for coaling or naval stations.

The result of the Platt Amendment was to make Cuba a protectorate of the United States. As the stronger of the two nations, the United States protected Cuba by partially controlling its affairs. A major American naval base was set up at Guantánamo Bay. Although American troops were removed from the island in 1902, they were sent back three times between 1906 and 1920 to support a particular political group. In addition, it was common practice for the American ambassador in Havana to present his government's views to the Cuban President about the policies the latter was following.

United States Economic Domination. There was economic influence on Cuba as well. The United States made large loans to the Cuban government. American corporations invested heavily in the island's sugar plantations and refineries, its public utilities (especially telephone and electricity), and its railroads. The bulk of Cuba's foreign trade was with the United States, which bought about 90 percent of the island's sugar.

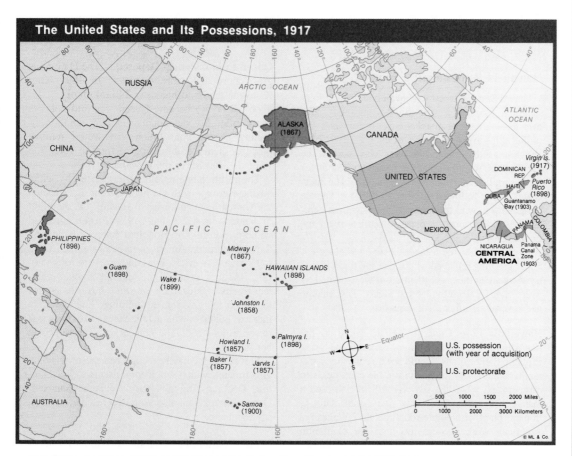

The United States and Its Possessions, 1917

Map Skills

Cuba • About 6000 miles (10,000 km) • Nicaragua, Panama

Map Skills **Location** Where is Guantanamo Bay? **Location** How far are the Philippines from the U.S.? **Place** What Central American countries have been U.S. protectorates?

The United States was concerned about conditions in Cuba because of the island's location. Only ninety-two miles off the coast of Florida, Cuba offers a good base for any nation that wants to threaten the United States. From the Cuban viewpoint, however, the United States was treating it like a child. Also, American businesses in Cuba paid low wages and low taxes, while the high profits they earned went back to the United States.

The Platt Amendment was finally abrogated, or abolished, in 1934, although the United States retained a naval base in Cuba. American economic influence on the island, however, continued until the early 1960's, as you will read in Chapter 32.

Puerto Rico Becomes a Commonwealth

The changeover from military to civilian rule was far smoother in Puerto Rico than in Cuba. The Foraker Act of 1900 provided for a governor to be appointed by the President of the United States. The President also received the power to appoint members of the legislature's upper house. Members of the lower house were popularly elected.

In 1917 Puerto Ricans were given the right to elect members of both legislative houses. They also became citizens of the United States. In 1950 Puerto Ricans drafted their own constitution. Two years later the island became a **commonwealth.** That means Puerto Rico makes its own laws and handles its own finances, while the United States takes care of defense and tariffs. Residents of Puerto Rico may move freely between the island and the United States.

Several elections have taken place in Puerto Rico on the issue of whether to remain a commonwealth, become a state of the Union, or become an inde-

Check for Understanding

Work with the students to complete Chapter 20, Section 3 Daily Activity.

Guided Practice

Discuss with students the current commonwealth status of Puerto Rico and the advantages and disadvantages of that status. (Possible responses: advantages—a commonwealth enjoys citizenship and U.S. protection but handles its own finances and makes its own laws; disadvantages—a commonwealth limits the control the people have over their activities.)

pendent nation. Thus far, the Puerto Ricans have voted to continue their commonwealth status.

Hawaii Is Permanently Changed

United States interest in Hawaii had been of long standing. No sooner was the Revolutionary War over than American merchants set out in their tall sailing ships to obtain a share of the lucrative China and East India trade. On their way across the Pacific, they would stop at the Hawaiian Islands for fresh supplies of fruits and vegetables. The merchants were followed in the 1820's by Yankee missionaries, who transformed the Hawaiian capital of Honolulu into "a pleasant replica of a New England town."

In the 1850's the islands' economy changed. Sugar growing replaced whaling as the main industry. Almost all the sugar plantations were owned by white planters from the United States. This change had several significant consequences.

Hawaiians Lose Control. First, it led to the importing of contract laborers. As one historian explained, Hawaiians "could see no sense in working hard all day in the hot sun in the cane fields to earn money, when the sea was full of fish, and a man could eat well off his own small taro [a tropical plant with edible roots] patch." Wages for American workers were too high for plantation owners to make a profit. So young male Chinese, then Portuguese, and finally Japanese were brought into Hawaii by the tens of thousands to work in the cane fields. By 1872 the Hawaiians were a minority in their own nation. They were outnumbered almost two to one by foreigners and immigrant laborers.

A second result of the economic change was a desire on the part of plantation owners for closer ties with the United States. In 1875 a treaty between the two nations removed American tariffs on Hawaiian sugar, as well as Hawaiian tariffs on American goods. The treaty was renewed in 1887, at which time the United States acquired Pearl Harbor as a coaling station for its Pacific fleet.

That same year, Hawaiian-born white businessmen forced King Kalakaua (kä′ lä′ kä ᴏᴏ ä) to change the constitution. Under the change, only men who owned land or had a certain income were allowed to vote. Since most Hawaiians either were poor or did not own land and since immigrant laborers were not citizens, control of the govern-

ment passed into the hands of businessmen of American descent.

Queen Liliuokalani Is Deposed. The Hawaiians grew more and more resentful. In 1891 King Kalakaua died and his sister **Liliuokalani** (li lē′ ᴏᴏ ō′ kä lä′ nē) became Queen. She did not like white rule. So she announced her intention of issuing a new constitution that would remove property qualifications from the right to vote. She wanted "Hawaii for the Hawaiians."

The result was a revolution organized by white business groups with the help of John L. Stevens, the United States minister to Hawaii. On the night of January 16, 1893, the U.S.S. *Boston* appeared without warning in Honolulu harbor. Following Stevens's orders, American marines moved ashore to "protect American lives and property in case of riot." As they marched through the streets, volunteer troops organized by the white business groups took over the government building. The Hawaiian flag was pulled down, and the Stars and Stripes was raised in its stead. The Queen was imprisoned in her palace.

Stevens immediately recognized the provisional government, which sent a commission to Washington, D.C., asking that the islands be annexed. Queen Liliuokalani also sent a representative, asking for justice.

From Kingdom to Republic to State. President Cleveland ordered a special investigator to Hawaii to learn what was going on. The investigator reported that "in my judgment, Minister Stevens had been responsible for the revolution." Cleveland then demanded that the provisional government restore Queen Liliuokalani to the throne. Instead, the provisional government formed the Republic of Hawaii, wrote a constitution, and elected pineapple grower Sanford B. Dole as president.

By this time it was clear to the United States that only force could put the Queen back on her throne, yet Congress did not want to use force. Instead, in 1894 it adopted a resolution saying that the United States should not interfere further in Hawaii.

Then came the Spanish-American War. Public opinion in the United States changed. When the Republic of Hawaii again petitioned for annexation, Congress agreed. On August 12, 1898, the Hawaiian Islands became a territory of the United States. In 1959 Hawaii became the fiftieth state in the Union.

Assign Independent Practice

Have students each write a paragraph of four or more sentences explaining the various political and military problems a nation might face when it gains control of overseas possessions. (Problems might include: maintaining control of government; keeping local officials honest; maintaining military supply lines over great distances; preventing dissatisfied factions from overthrowing the government; deciding how much self-rule is best.)

Picturing History Filipino rebels eventually turned to guerrilla tactics in fighting for independence. The Philippines finally became an independent republic on July 4, 1946.

Americans Fight Rebels in the Philippines

The Filipino rebels led by Emilio Aguinaldo had proclaimed their independence from Spain in June 1898. Two months later, as you know, the Spanish troops in Manila agreed to surrender only to the Americans. Then in December the Treaty of Paris gave the United States ownership of the Philippine Islands. In the meantime, a Filipino constitutional assembly had drafted a document similar to the Constitution of the United States. In January 1899 the first Philippine Republic was inaugurated. General Aguinaldo was sworn in as its first President. He was not President of an independent country, however, but of a country that was about to become a United States possession. The Filipinos were furious over what they considered betrayal on the part of the United States.

Conflict Erupts. Throughout the month of January, 1899, tension between American and Filipino soldiers kept rising. The Americans were demoralized by the heat, the humidity, the torrential rains, and the lack of anything to do.

On the night of February 4, as the annexation debate in the United States Senate was nearing a climax, a Filipino soldier began to walk across a bridge on the outskirts of Manila. Seeing the shadowy figure in the dark, an American enlisted man fired at it—and the Philippine-American War was on.

The war to conquer the Philippines lasted for three years. At first the United States was confident that it would be over in a few weeks. As Filipino resistance continued, however, more and more American troops were sent in. Unable to defeat them in regular battle, Aguinaldo turned to guerrilla tactics.

Gradually, the fighting became bloodier and more brutal on both sides. Wounded soldiers were killed instead of becoming prisoners. Villages were burned to the ground in an attempt to flush out guerrillas. Even torture was sometimes used.

Some African Americans Condemn the War. Complicating matters was the fact that many of the seventy thousand American troops were black. Once an area was conquered, ties of friendship soon developed between the Filipinos and the African Americans. White Americans, on the other hand, tended to look down on the Filipinos because of their skin color.

A number of black newspapers in the United States wondered why black soldiers were "fighting to curse the country [the Philippines] with colorphobia, [Jim Crow] cars, disfranchisement, lynchers, and everything that prejudice can do to blight the manhood of the darker races." Many African Americans deserted to the Filipino side.

From Commonwealth to Independence. The war began to wind down in 1901 when Aguinaldo was captured. Except for an outbreak of fighting on the island of Mindanao, peace was more or less in effect by mid-1902.

From 1901 until 1904, William Howard Taft served as civilian governor of the Philippines.

Historical Sidelight
Blacks experienced prejudice, not just in the U.S. but also in U.S. territories and commonwealths. For example, in the Philippines, blacks were segregated in Jim Crow cars on trains.

Student Assignment/Homework

Have students read Section 4, "The United States Becomes a World Power," and answer the Section 4 Review questions on paper.

SECTION 3 REVIEW

Answers

Main Ideas

1. Cuba could not make treaties that compromised its independence, could not allow foreign powers to control any of its territory, and was not to go into debt. The U.S. claimed the right to intervene in Cuba's land for coaling or naval stations.

2. The U.S. maintained control over Cuba's government, military, internal affairs, economy, and foreign relations. Puerto Rico basically ruled itself, with the U.S. controlling its tariffs and military only.

3. Importing sugar plantation workers made Hawaiians a minority in Hawaii-U.S. ties; this desire led to new voting laws, the overthrow of the Hawaiian monarchy, and, eventually, the Hawaiian Islands' becoming a U.S. territory.

4. Many Filipinos believed that the U.S. had betrayed them by refusing them complete independence after the Spanish-American War.

Critical Thinking

5. Possible answers: Cuba—gained independence from Spain; yellow fever conquered. Puerto Rico— achieved greater independence; established democracy. Hawaiian Islands— few, if any, benefits during this period, but eventually achieved statehood. Philippines— eventually achieved independence; literacy improved greatly. **(evaluation)**

524

Picturing History William Howard Taft, civilian governor of the Philippines, at a baseball game in Manila.

Legislative functions were placed in the hands of an appointed commission and an elected assembly. In 1916 the **Jones Act** replaced the appointed commission with an elected senate. In 1934 the Tydings-McDuffie Act offered the Philippines complete independence after a ten-year trial period as a commonwealth. The Filipinos accepted the offer in 1936. Ten years later, on July 4, 1946, the islands became an independent republic.

Linking Past to Present

Since gaining independence, the people of the Philippines have had to contend with periodic political upheaval. Following a bitter election campaign in 1986, President Ferdinand Marcos was accused of winning the election dishonestly. Marcos, who had served twenty years as President, resigned and fled the country. Presidential candidate Corazon Aquino, widow of slain opposition leader Benigno Aquino, was immediately recognized as President of the Philippines by the United States and other nations. She promised land reforms and a democratic government.

The Insular Cases. Whether or not the United States would grant full constitutional privileges to the people of new possessions was decided in 1901 by the Supreme Court in the so-called **Insular Cases**. The Court ruled that the Constitution did not automatically apply to newly acquired possessions of the United States. It left up to Congress the decision whether or not to extend constitutional provisions and privileges.

United States Youths Lend a Hand. During the years between annexation and independence, Americans brought about several changes in the Philippines. Perhaps the most significant was in public education. Within six weeks after President Taft's administration began, the U.S.S. *Thomas* docked in Manila harbor. Aboard were 540 young American college graduates who soon became known as the Thomasites. Settling in various communities throughout the islands, they taught day and evening classes for children and adults, and they trained Filipino teachers. During the first year and a half, twenty-seven of the Thomasites died from cholera or were killed by bandits. Yet the work continued.

It continued so well that the literacy rate more than doubled between 1902 and 1935. In 1898 only five thousand Filipino students were attending elementary school. By 1920 there were over a million and by 1946 over two million. As Filipino diplomat Carlos Rómulo said,

> Public education transformed a nation ready to be transformed. . . . The American school teachers joined with us in creating the literacy, the knowledge, the self-confidence, and devotion to democracy on which it was possible to establish our Republic.

SECTION 3 REVIEW

Key Terms and People

Explain the significance of: protectorate, Platt Amendment, commonwealth, Liliuokalani, Jones Act, Insular Cases

Main Ideas

1. What were the terms of the Platt Amendment?
2. How did Cuba's protectorate status differ from Puerto Rico's commonwealth status?
3. What economic and political changes in Hawaii were brought about by American sugar plantation owners?
4. What was the main cause of the Philippine-American War?

Critical Thinking

5. Which territory benefited most from its relations with the United States during this period— Cuba, Puerto Rico, the Hawaiian Islands, or the Philippines? Explain.

Anticipate the Lesson

Write the terms *isolationism* and *internationalism* on the board. Ask students to define both and explain the advantages and disadvantages of each. (Responses: isolationism is the belief that a nation should remain free of international alliances and should not intervene in the affairs of other nations; advantages—no entanglements, little threat of war because of treaties or alliances with other nations; disadvantages—limited trade opportunities, no allies in time of war. Internationalism is the belief that cooperation among nations will advance the common welfare; advantages—more trade opportunities, shared knowledge in areas such as science and medicine; disadvantages—commitments that could lead to war, inability to remain neutral.)

SECTION 4

The United States Becomes a World Power

GLOSSARY TERMS: **spheres of influence, extraterritoriality, Open Door policy, Roosevelt Corollary, dollar diplomacy**

An overseas empire meant that the United States had to develop policies for defending its possessions and also for dealing with other imperialist nations. The two areas of greatest concern were Asia and Latin America.

China's Door Is Opened

When the United States set up a colonial government in the Philippines it became interested in the mainland of Asia. The vast but weak nation of China was in danger of being carved up by France, Germany, Great Britain, Japan, and Russia. Each nation had its **spheres of influence,** areas where it had special trading privileges and where numbers of its merchants, missionaries, and other nationals lived. In these areas the people who might be charged with criminal behavior were tried according to their own laws and by their own courts, not by Chinese laws and courts. This right of **extraterritoriality** had been forced on China by the stronger powers.

The United States was not interested in acquiring

Spheres of Influence in China, 1900

Map Skills **Place** Which foreign enclaves in China were British? **Location** Along what bodies of water were main treaty ports located?

colonies on the Asian mainland. Nor did it want to risk a war. On the other hand, it *did* want a larger share of the rich China market.

A solution to the difficulty was proposed by Secretary of State **John Hay.** He sent notes with the same message to Britain, Germany, and Russia and, later, to France, Italy, and Japan. Hay asked the powers to promise two things with regard to their spheres of influence:

1. They would not prevent other nations from doing business there.
2. They would not charge other nations higher railroad, harbor, and tariff rates than they charged their own merchants.

In other words, there would really be no advantage in having a sphere of influence because every other nation would be allowed to compete there on equal terms.

The nations involved more or less said no to Hay's note. Nevertheless, on March 20, 1900, Hay announced that the **Open Door policy** had been accepted and was in effect.

The Boxer Rebellion. At this point, a Chinese secret society, known to Westerners as the Boxers,

Picturing History During the Boxer Rebellion, anxious foreigners took refuge in the various embassies in Beijing. This illustration shows a happy group being rescued from the British Embassy.

State the Objective

Understand how the U.S. became a world
leader around the turn of the century.

began an armed movement to "expel the barbarians." The Boxers objected to what they saw as a
foreign takeover of their country. After they killed
several thousand Chinese Christians in northern
China and laid siege to foreign legations in two
Chinese cities, an international military force was
sent in. These troops, which included Americans,
British, French, Germans, and Japanese, put down
the rebellion within two months.

Although the colonial powers now had an excellent excuse to take over more territory from China,
Hay moved to prevent this. He announced that it
was United States policy to "preserve the Chinese
territorial and administrative entity" and to "safeguard for the world the principle of equal and
impartial trade with all parts of the Chinese Empire."

As a result of Hay's statement, the colonial
powers agreed not to occupy additional parts of
China after all. Even more important, the policy
paved the way for greater American influence in
Asia. Within a few years, that influence showed
itself in the settlement of the Russo-Japanese War
of 1904–1905.

Roosevelt Mediates for Russia and Japan

Japan and Russia came to blows over Korea.
Japan had received Korea from China in 1895 and
had set it up as a partly independent state within the
Japanese sphere of influence. After the Boxer
Rebellion, the Russians set up Manchuria, the
northernmost region of China, within their sphere
of influence and began to cast their eyes at Korea.
Japan suggested that these two imperialist nations
agree to respect each other's sphere and stay off
each other's turf. Russia refused. Japan thereupon
gave Russia "a last and earnest warning" and in
February 1904 launched a surprise attack.

Japan the Victor. To everyone's amazement,
Japan destroyed the Russian Pacific fleet. Then it
also destroyed Russia's European fleet, which had
been ordered to Asia after the Pacific fleet was
defeated. Through a series of land battles in China,
Japan obtained firm control over Korea and a
foothold in Manchuria as well.

Japan's victories, however, cost a great deal of
money. So the Japanese asked the United States to
mediate the conflict. President Theodore Roosevelt
agreed. In the summer of 1905, he invited Russia
and Japan to send delegates to a conference in
Portsmouth, New Hampshire.

Roosevelt the Peacemaker. The first meeting
took place at lunch on the Presidential yacht, the
Mayflower. The meeting was prickly at first.
Roosevelt, however, had a way of grasping a
person's hand and saying in his special way,
"*Dee*-light-ed." His smile was so broad and so
genuine that few people were not charmed by him.
The Russians and the Japanese began to enjoy
themselves. After an excellent lunch, they shook
hands cordially with one another.

Japan wanted Sakhalin Island, off the coast of
Siberia, and a large sum of money from Russia.
Russia refused. Finally, Roosevelt persuaded Japan
to accept half of the island and to forget about the
cash indemnity. In exchange, Russia agreed to let
Japan take over its interests in Manchuria and
Korea. As a result of the **Treaty of Portsmouth,**
Roosevelt was awarded the Nobel Peace Prize in
1906.

A Path Between the Seas Is Needed

By 1900 the United States had acquired three of
the four things Mahan said it needed to become a
world power. It had a modern fleet, naval bases in
the Caribbean, and Hawaii. What it did not have
was a canal across the Isthmus of Panama.

Preparing the Way. Interest in a water passage
between the Atlantic and the Pacific dated back to

Picturing History On the yacht *Mayflower*, President
Theodore Roosevelt greets diplomats from Russia and
Japan during the negotiations he successfully mediated
between the two nations.

Divide the class into three groups to skim the section for information and then to discuss and prepare on the board an outline on one of the following and its connection with the emergence of the U.S. as a world leader: Boxer Rebellion, Russo-Japanese War, Panama Revolution. (Outlines on the Boxer Rebellion might include: Boxers began armed movement to expel foreigners; an international force including Americans arrived to protect foreigners in China and put down rebellion; colonial powers contemplated taking more territory from China, but America announced its policy to preserve Chinese government and safeguard free trade; colonial powers agreed not to occupy additional parts of China; America accepted its share of war indemnity, returning half to China; Hay's Open Door Policy in China prevented further division of China and paved the way for greater American influence in Asia.) Review these outlines with the students, and encourage them to refer to the outline as they study this section.

the time of the Spanish Empire. A relative of Cortés had hoped to "open the land of Castilla del Oro . . . from sea to sea." In 1552 a priest named Francisco Lopez de Gomara wrote, "There are mountains, but there are also hands, and for a king of [Spain], few things are impossible." However, not until the mid-1800's did the steam engine and improvements in hydraulic engineering actually make a canal possible.

In the Clayton-Bulwer Treaty of 1850 the United States and Great Britain agreed that they would have equal rights to any canal that might be built between the Atlantic and the Pacific oceans. In 1901, however, the two nations made a new agreement. Under the Hay-Pauncefote Treaty, the United States received exclusive rights to build, control, and presumably fortify a canal across the narrow part of Central America. In return, the United States promised that all nations would be allowed to send their commercial and fighting ships through such a canal without discrimination.

Choosing a Route. Now the question arose of where to build the canal. The two possibilities were Nicaragua and the province of Panama in Colombia. Nicaragua was several hundred miles closer to the United States. It contained lakes and rivers that could form part of the route and thus reduce construction costs. Although the government of Nicaragua was cooperative, the final decision was in favor of the Panama route.

The man largely responsible for this choice was **Philippe Bunau-Varilla** (boo̅ nō′ và rē′yà). Born in France, he graduated from college with a degree in engineering. In 1878 a French company headed by Ferdinand de Lesseps, who had directed the construction of the Suez Canal, began digging in Panama. Bunau-Varilla joined the company in 1884 and soon became its chief engineer.

In 1889 the French abandoned the project and sold the concession and the rusted machinery to the New Panama Canal Company. This company consisted of a group of speculators, one of whom was Bunau-Varilla. After negotiating first with Russia and then with Great Britain, the company approached the United States. President Roosevelt and Congress were receptive to the idea of America building the canal. An investigating committee recommended Nicaragua as the site of the canal, and the House of Representatives agreed.

At this point, Bunau-Varilla, who was acting as the company's agent in the United States, pulled a

WHICH WAY WILL IT TIP NEXT THURSDAY?

Picturing History The cartoon shows the Senate on a seesaw over the issue of where to build the canal. The stamp sent to senators is shown at the right.

brilliant public relations coup. He sent each of the ninety-two senators in the United States Senate a Nicaraguan stamp with a picture of an erupting volcano. The Senate voted to build the canal in Panama instead.

Trouble with Colombia. In March 1903 the Senate ratified the Hay-Herrán Treaty between the United States and Colombia. The treaty stated that the United States would give Colombia $10 million, plus an annual rent of $250,000, for a six-mile-wide strip across the Isthmus of Panama. However, a new government had just come to power in Colombia, and it turned the treaty down.

On October 10, 1903, Bunau-Varilla met with President Roosevelt at the White House. Bunau-Varilla predicted that there might soon be a revolution in Panama. The canal would have meant an economic boom for the area, and the Panamanians were very disappointed.

Roosevelt did not say flat out that the United States would prevent the landing of Colombian troops on the isthmus. However, as he observed some time later,

> He [Bunau-Varilla] is a very able fellow, and it was his business to find out what he thought our Government would do. I have no doubt that he was able to make a very accurate

Check for Understanding

Call on individual students to read their answers to the Section 4 Review questions.

Map Skills

Mexico • Managua, Nicaragua

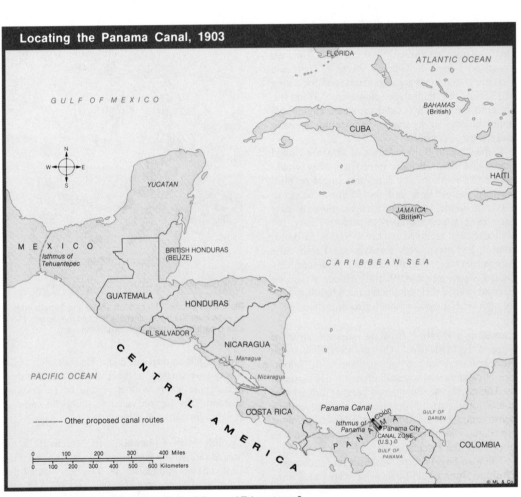

Locating the Panama Canal, 1903

Map Skills **Location** In what country is the Isthmus of Tehuantepec?
Location The proposed canal route in Nicaragua went through what two lakes?

guess, and to advise his people accordingly. In fact, he would have been a very dull man had he been unable to make such a guess.

On October 30, 1903, the commander of the U.S.S. *Nashville* received instructions from Washington, D.C., to head for the harbor of Colón in Panama. If a rebellion broke out there, he was to take over the Panama Railroad. He was also to "prevent the landing of any armed forces with hostile intent" within fifty miles of the city. Thus, the only way the Colombian government could send troops to Colón was by sea.

Panama Becomes Independent. The *Nashville*

entered Colón harbor on November 2. The next day a rebellion against Colombia broke out. On November 4 ten American warships appeared in Panamanian waters, and Panama declared its independence. On November 6 the United States recognized the new republic. Bunau-Varilla became the first Panamanian minister to the United States. Finally, on November 18 the **Hay-Bunau-Varilla Treaty** was signed. It gave the United States a ten-mile-wide canal zone in perpetuity, or forever. It gave Panama $10 million plus $250,000 a year after nine years. The treaty also guaranteed Panama's independence but added that the principles of the Platt Amendment—including the right of American intervention—would apply.

Guided Practice

Explain to the class that the Carter administration negotiated a treaty to relinquish control of the Panama Canal on December 31, 1999. Ask students whether they consider this action appropriate. Ask them to identify some advantages and disadvantages of Panamanian control of the canal. (Possible responses: advantage—we will no longer pay for, maintain, or defend the canal; disadvantages—Panamanians might decide to exclude certain nations from using the canal; in time of war, the canal may fall into hands of an unfriendly nation, and U.S. would lose user's right.)

In 1911, commenting on his actions, President Roosevelt said the following:

> The Panama Canal I naturally take special interest in because I started it.
>
> There are plenty of other things I started merely because the time had come that whoever was in power would have started them.
>
> But the Panama Canal would not have been started if I had not taken hold of it, because if I had followed the traditional or conservative method, I would have submitted an admirable paper occupying a couple of hundred pages detailing all of the facts to Congress and asking Congress' consideration of it.
>
> In that case there would have been a number of excellent speeches made on the subject in Congress; the debate would be proceeding at this moment with great spirit and the beginning of work on the canal would be fifty years in the future.
>
> Fortunately the crisis came at a period when I could act unhampered. Accordingly I took the Isthmus, started the canal, and then left Congress not to debate the canal, but to debate me.

Picturing History After visiting the site for the canal, Roosevelt wrote to his son, "They are eating steadily into the mountain."

The Panama Canal greatly strengthened the position of the United States as a world power. Nevertheless, it severely damaged relations with Latin America. As the American minister to Colombia explained in 1912:

> By refusing to allow Colombia to uphold her sovereign rights over a territory where she had held dominion for eighty years, the friendship of nearly a century disappeared; the indignation of every Colombian, and millions of other Latin Americans, was aroused. . . . The confidence and trust in the justice and fairness of the United States, so long manifested, has completely vanished.

The Panama Canal Is Completed

The canal opened after ten years of monumental effort under the competent supervision of **George Goethals** (gō thəlz). Mud slides, rock slides, and premature dynamite explosions were only some of the engineering problems. The amount of earth to be removed was staggering: enough to fill a train of empty cars four times around the equator. About fifty-six hundred workers, forty-five hundred of whom were African Americans, lost their lives from disease and accidents. Costs ran higher than for anything the United States government had built up to that time. In fact, buying the Panama Canal cost more than five times as much as buying the Louisiana Territory, Florida, California, and Alaska put together.

On August 15, 1914, the waterway was finally opened for business. In 1921 Congress paid Colombia $25 million for its loss of Panama. An apology for Roosevelt's actions, however, was dropped from the treaty that authorized payment.

Linking Past to Present

In 1978, after a heated debate, the United States Senate approved a new treaty with Panama, agreeing to withdraw all United States troops from the Canal Zone and to turn over the canal to Panama by December 31, 1999. In a second treaty, Panama agreed to guarantee the permanent neutrality of the canal.

Assign Independent Practice

Have students complete Chapter 20, Section 4 Enrichment Activity.

Student Assignment/Homework

Have students complete Chapter 20 Review on paper. Divide the class into small groups to discuss and review their answers.

Map Skills

7,000 mi (10,500 km)
• Central America

For Discussion

What were *big stick diplomacy* and *dollar diplomacy*? (Possible responses: big stick diplomacy—the U.S. acted as an international police force; dollar diplomacy—the U.S. government guaranteed loans made to foreign countries by U.S. businessmen.) What were the basic differences between Theodore Roosevelt's policies and those of William Howard Taft? (Possible responses: Roosevelt believed in obtaining cooperation through strength or force if necessary; Taft believed in influencing a country's economy to obtain cooperation.)

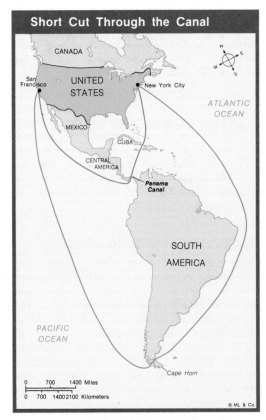

Short Cut Through the Canal

Map Skills **Movement** What was the distance from New York to San Francisco via the Panama Canal? **Place** Through what land was the canal dug?

The Monroe Doctrine Is Expanded

Latin America was now the United States's major sphere of influence. Like all imperialist nations, the United States wanted to keep its sphere of influence as free as possible from foreign competition or control.

The main problem had to do with the financial condition of the smaller nations, especially those in the Caribbean. Most of them had borrowed heavily from European banks to build railroads and other public works and to develop their mines, farms, and industries. However, they were not always able to pay the interest on their loans. This made a very tempting situation for European imperialist nations. If Haiti, for example, owed money to France but could not pay it back, why shouldn't France move into Haiti in order to protect the investments of its citizens? Once in, there was always the possibility of remaining.

France had actually done just that in Mexico in 1863. When Mexico's President, **Benito Juárez** (hwä´ res), stopped payment on European loans, Napoleon III sent troops to Mexico and overthrew the government. He also set up Maximilian of Austria as his puppet Emperor of Mexico. The United States, at that time in the midst of a civil war, could do little but protest. However, after Appomattox Secretary of State Seward warned Napoleon III to remove his troops. He did so, and the foolish but brave Maximilian died before a Mexican firing squad.

The Roosevelt Corollary. President Roosevelt was well aware of the danger of foreign interference in the Western Hemisphere. After becoming President in 1901, he told Minnesota state fairgoers:

> There is a homely adage which runs, "Speak softly and carry a big stick; you will go far." If the American nation will speak softly and yet build and keep at a pitch of the highest training a thoroughly efficient navy, the Monroe Doctrine will go far.

Adopting this West African proverb as his own, Roosevelt soon put his words into action in Latin America. In 1904, in a message to Congress, he expressed what historians call the **Roosevelt Cor-**

Picturing History Benito Juarez (left) and Maximilian and Carlota of Austria. In Mexican history, Juarez is hailed as a great political leader, while Maximilian and Carlota are remembered as tragic figures.

Concluding the Chapter

Have students write three paragraphs explaining what the U.S. gained as a result of the Spanish-American War and why many South and Central American nations came to dislike the U.S. during this period. (Possible responses: U.S. gained control of Philippines, Cuba, and Puerto Rico; U.S. established itself as a world power. The U.S. came to be disliked because it assumed a superior role over many countries; it assumed it was U.S. duty to "protect weaker nations"; it took control of nations' industries; it exploited natural resources of the nation.)

Picturing History In this cartoon, Roosevelt is drawn as a policeman—the preserver of law and order in a world of anarchy. A paper in his belt gives the message, "Tell yer troubles to the Policeman."

ollary (extension) to the Monroe Doctrine. In sum, if any foreign nation was to interfere in the affairs of a Latin American country, it would be the United States that would do the interfering. "The adherence of the United States to the Monroe Doctrine may force the United States, however reluctantly . . . to the exercise of an international police power," he said.

Dollar Diplomacy. During the next decade or so, the United States did intervene in Latin America on several occasions. American bankers took over the foreign debt of the Dominican Republic in 1905. In 1911 there was a revolution in Nicaragua, and the nation was on the verge of bankruptcy. Roosevelt's successor, William Howard Taft, quickly arranged for United States bankers to loan Nicaragua enough money to pay its debts. In return, the bankers were given the right to recover their money by collecting Nicaragua's customs duties. The United States bankers also received control of Nicaragua's state-owned railroad system and the nation's national bank.

When the Nicaraguan citizens heard about this deal, they revolted against President Adolfo Díaz (dē' äs). To prop up Díaz's government and to protect United States economic interests, some two thousand marines were sent to Nicaragua. The revolt was put down, but some marine detachments remained in the country until 1933 to ensure that United States business interests did not suffer.

The policy of using the United States government to guarantee loans made to foreign countries

by United States business people was called **dollar diplomacy** by those who opposed it. The policy was followed again in Haiti in 1916. It was justified as a method of keeping Europeans out of the Caribbean area.

SECTION 4 REVIEW

Key Terms and People

Explain the significance of: spheres of influence, extraterritoriality, John Hay, Open Door policy, Treaty of Portsmouth, Philippe Bunau-Varilla, Hay-Bunau-Varilla Treaty, George Goethals, Benito Juárez, Roosevelt Corollary, dollar diplomacy

Main Ideas

1. What was the purpose of the Open Door policy?
2. In general, what resulted from the Open Door policy?
3. What conflict brought about the war between Japan and Russia, and how was it settled?
4. How did the United States get around Colombia's unwillingness to allow the building of a canal in Panama?
5. What was the purpose of the Roosevelt Corollary to the Monroe Doctrine?

Critical Thinking

6. Who benefited more from United States actions in Latin America during this period—the United States or Latin America? Explain.

SECTION 4 REVIEW

Answers

Main Ideas

1. To encourage free trade in China, thereby gaining a larger share of China's market for the U.S.

2. It prevented the further division of China after the Boxer Rebellion and brought about greater American influence in China.

3. The conflict was over which nation's sphere of influence included Korea. President Roosevelt mediated an agreement by which Japan gained Korea, parts of Manchuria, and half of Sakhalin Island.

4. The U.S. took the matter out of Colombia's control by covertly encouraging and providing military support for the revolution that led to Panama's independence and thus to Panama's ability to authorize the building of the canal.

5. To recognize Latin America as being within the U.S. sphere of influence and to prevent other nations from interfering in that sphere.

Critical Thinking

6. Possible answer: the U.S. benefited more in terms of improvements in its economy and international standing; Latin America benefited less because it was not politically or economically equal in the relationship. **(evaluation)**

Present the Lesson

Remind students that although primary sources such as letters, newspaper reports, and other written materials give invaluable information about historical events, each one must be evaluated to determine the reliability of the source. Divide the class into small groups. Have the groups analyze and compare the reliability of Bryson's and Scovel's newspaper stories. Suggest that students use the four steps for evaluating source reliability presented in this feature. Have the group leaders summarize the information for the class. (Summaries might include: (1) Analyze the author's background—although the reporters were assigned to Havana at the time of the explosion, they were not on board the *Maine* when it sank. (2) Analyze the authors' purpose—both reporters were motivated by their newspaper owners' rivalry. (3) Compare this account with others—Bryson's report is short and draws a conclusion without much evidence. Scovel acknowledges the uncertainty surrounding the event and presents facts that might help a reader form an opinion. (4) Determine the reliability of the source—most students will state that Scovel is more reliable, since his report uses known facts and acknowledges the uncertainty of the case.)

Focus on Critical Thinking Skills

Evaluating Source Reliability

Understanding the Skill

Experience tells us that each person's version of specific events in the past is somewhat different. How can we know what really happened? Historians draw conclusions about events in the past by analyzing primary sources. You will recall that a primary source is direct or firsthand information about an event or a period of history. Primary sources include letters, memoirs, diaries, autobiographies, legal documents, newspapers, cartoons, poetry, songs, advertisements, and other types of written and oral materials. If a primary source is an account of an event written by someone who was an eyewitness to the event, a casual reader might assume that the account is more reliable than one found in a secondary source, such as a textbook, which gives the information secondhand. This assumption is not always valid. A person might write an autobiography many years after the events have taken place. Since no one's memory is foolproof, the author may introduce errors into the account. Here are some steps to follow when trying to evaluate the reliability of a source.

- **Analyze the author's background.** Who is the author? Did the author witness the event firsthand?
- **Analyze the author's purpose.** What motivated the author to write about this event? How will the author's purpose affect his or her point of view?
- **Compare this account with others.** Is this account consistent with other accounts? If not, how does it differ?
- **Determine the reliability of the source.** Is this a reliable source? Why or why not?

Applying the Skill

Today United States citizens can be reasonably sure that the media are not directly controlled by their government. This assurance is no ironclad guarantee of accuracy, however. Information embarrassing to the government is sometimes held back. Government officials may influence the way the news is presented. Furthermore, the media are in fierce competition with one another. While correspondents make great efforts to get a story right, they also experience powerful pressure to get the story first.

Competition for news is not a recent development. At the end of the last century, a new type of daily newspaper appeared. Based on greater advertising revenue, it was aimed at a wider, less educated public. One such paper, *The* (New York) *World,* carried a cartoon called "The Yellow Kid." *The World* and its rival the *New York Journal* were soon tagged "the yellow press" because they frequently distorted or exaggerated the news in sensational ways. (See page 514.) These newspapers are believed to have had a lot to do with starting the Spanish-American War.

Picturing History
So determined was William Randolph Hearst to be first with the news of the Spanish American War, that he even chartered the steamer *Sylvia* and set out for the war himself.

The battleship *Maine* exploded on the night of February 15, 1898. (See page 515.) Joseph Pulitzer's *The World* boasted of being the first to print the story of the sinking of the *Maine* in its morning edition on February 16. The story, which was cabled from Havana correspondent Sylvester Scovel, hinted that the explosion may not have been an accident:

Not to be outdone by a competitor, William Randolph Hearst's *Evening* (New York) *Journal* reported a story from Havana carrying George Eugene Bryson's byline:

Check for Understanding

Review the questions at the end of the feature. Discuss how often students might have the opportunity to determine the reliability of a source in real life. Have students bring to class examples of printed materials that might be slanted due to the writer's background and purpose. Encourage students to share their examples and ideas on this topic.

Picturing History Hungarian-born newpaper publisher Joseph Pulitzer (above) bought *The World* in 1883 when its circulation was fifteen thousand. By 1900 the newspaper was selling a million copies a day. As the cartoon at the right indicates, Pulitzer used every means available to sell his paper.

FOCUS ON SKILLS

Answers

Practicing Your Skills

1. This skill is important because authors' interpretations of past events differ depending on their background and their purpose for writing.

2. These correspondents were assigned to Havana at the time the *Maine* exploded. They worked for rival newspapers that featured sensational headlines and stories.

3. The eagerness to be first with the story was based on the intense rivalry between the publishers. • It appears that in their haste, the correspondents neglected to get all the information necessary for a reliable account of the explosion of the *Maine*.

4. Scovel's first account merely hints that the explosion may not have been an accident. Bryson's account assigns blame for the explosion to "Spanish treachery." Scovel's second account, which was published two days after the explosion, cites the cause as "undetermined." The accounts varied due to the goals of the reporters. Both reporters were eager for a quick sensational story, but Scovel waited until more details were available before attempting to assign blame.

5. Scovel's account published two days after the explosion appears to be the most reliable. This report acknowledges the conjecture, uncertainty, and excitement that the explosion caused and the need for further investigation.

The discovery of the hole in the bottom of the *Maine,* giving undoubted proof of Spanish treachery and hostility, shows that the great battleship and her crew of American sailors were deliberately sacrificed.

One day later, *The World,* ran the following story cabled from Scovel:

The cause of the disaster to the United States battleship *Maine* is undetermined.

It is not known whether it resulted from a bomb or a torpedo, an explosion in the magazine, [a place where explosives are stored] or the carelessness of officers.

All is conjecture, uncertainty, excitement. . . .

The cause of the blowing up of the ship will not be known until divers go down and examine the wreck. If their investigation shows that the indention in the hull is inward, the conclusion that the magazine was exploded by a bomb or torpedo placed beneath the vessel is inevitable.

If the indention is outward, it will be indicated that the first explosion was in the magazine. This will be determined within twenty-four hours. [This was too optimistic. The investigation was long delayed, and its results were inconclusive.]

Practicing Your Skill

1. Why is it important to determine the reliability of our sources of information about past events?
2. What was the background for the newspaper reports of Sylvester Scovel and George Bryson?
3. Why were these correspondents so eager to get their accounts to their publishers? How might this eagerness have affected their reports?
4. What are the differences between the three accounts of the sinking of the *Maine?*
5. Which of these accounts appears to be the most reliable? Why?

Answer Key

Key Terms and People

These are highlighted in the text in the order in which they appear in this list.

Main Ideas

1. Modern fleet—by 1898 the U.S. was the world's third largest naval power; naval bases in Caribbean—Treaty of Paris after Spanish-American War, 1898; canal across Isthmus of Panama—1914; Hawaii and islands in the Pacific—Hawaii annexed by Hawaii's request in August 1898, others in Treaty of Paris, 1898.

2. Americans thought Cuban cause was much like their own American Revolution; reports of atrocities in Spanish reconcentration camps angered Americans. • To sell papers.

3. He had lived through the Civil War and did not want to see another war; he realized that both Cuban rebels and Spanish had committed outrages. • Publication of the de Lome letter; explosion of the *Maine*.

4. Filipino rebels were fighting Spain for their freedom. • Dewey was sent by assistant secretary of the navy Theodore Roosevelt without the knowledge of Roosevelt's superior.

➤5. A country whose affairs are controlled by a stronger power. • A country that makes its own laws and handles its own finances, but whose defense and tariffs are handled by a stronger power. • 1901. • The Philippines became a commonwealth in 1936, Puerto Rico in 1952.

6. American businessmen had poured money into Hawaiian agriculture; soon imported workers outnumbered Hawaiians. Stevens staged a revolution and the Americans took over the government. After the Spanish-American war, American interests in Hawaii applied for annexation.

7. China—Open Door Policy; the Boxer Rebellion. • Japan and Russia—Treaty of Portsmouth.

8. Philippe Bunau-Varilla sent senators stamps showing volcanoes on Nicaragua. When Colombia refused to sell land to U.S., Panama declared independence and U.S. and Panama signed a treaty for the land.

Critical Thinking Questions

9. Americans invested heavily in sugar plantations and passed laws keeping poor Hawaiians and landless laborers from voting. In effect, American sugar controlled the islands.

10. Need for new markets; need for raw materials; desire to keep up with European countries who were dividing up Africa and China.

11. Possible answers: yes—they were unfit for self-government. No—imperialistic expansion was against American tradition.

12. Gave the U.S. control over shipping lanes in both the Atlantic and Pacific oceans and gave the U.S. naval control over both U.S. coasts.

➤13. The events listed show that Roosevelt believed in action at any cost; this attitude made him a brave, decisive leader.

CHAPTER 20 REVIEW

Write your answers on a separate sheet of paper.

Key Terms and People

Explain the significance of: Seward's Folly, Charles Darwin, Josiah Strong, Frederic Remington, Emilio Aguinaldo, Jones Act, Insular Cases, spheres of influence, extraterritoriality, John Hay, Open Door policy, Hay-Bunau-Varilla Treaty, George Goethals, Benito Juárez, dollar diplomacy

Main Ideas

1. List the four essentials that Admiral Mahan said would give the United States superiority in sea power. When was each obtained?
2. Why did some Americans want to help the Cuban rebels led by José Martí? Why did Hearst want a war?
3. Why did President McKinley not want to go to war? What events finally caused the country to demand war?
4. Why was there fighting in the Philippines? Why did Commodore Dewey go to the Philippines?
5. What is a protectorate? a commonwealth? When did Cuba gain protectorate status? When did the Philippines and Puerto Rico achieve commonwealth status?
6. Why did the United States annex Hawaii?
7. How did the United States influence affairs in China, Japan, and Russia between the years 1880 and 1914?
8. Why did the United States choose Panama instead of Nicaragua for its canal? How did the United States get the land from Colombia?

Critical Thinking Questions

9. **Analyzing Literature.** What does James Michener mean when he says that Liliuokalani "attained ultimate power too late; . . . sugar had captured her islands"?
10. **Analyzing Causes.** Why was the country ready to expand in the late 1800's? List at least three causes that influenced public thinking at that time.

11. **Making Decisions.** If you had been a United States senator in 1898, would you have voted to annex the Philippines? Give reasons.
12. **Assessing Cause and Effect.** What did the Panama Canal contribute toward the United States becoming a world power?
13. **Judging Character.** Use this list of Theodore Roosevelt's actions to assess what kind of leader he was.

   1898: Sends Dewey to the Philippines; resigns as assistant secretary of navy; helps to organize Rough Riders and take Santiago
   1903: Takes Panama from Colombia
   1904: Extends Monroe Doctrine with corollary
   1905: Negotiates Treaty of Portsmouth

Critical Thinking Activities

14. **Analyzing Maps.** Look at the map on page 518 of the islands in the Caribbean Sea. Why has the United States always been concerned about events in Cuba? What is the relationship between Cuba and the United States today?
15. **Linking Past to Present.** What is the present governmental status of each of the following: Cuba, Puerto Rico, the Philippines, and Hawaii?
16. **Linking Past to Present.** Discuss how the Thomasites were similar to the Peace Corps. (See Chapter 32.)
17. **Linking Past to Present.** From what you have learned about China when it was under the control of foreign spheres of influence, what might be one reason that it is so fearful of European and American influences today?
18. **Linking Past to Present.** What problems does the United States still have in its diplomatic relations with Latin America? From your study of history, why might this be so?

TELESCOPING THE TIMES: 1880–1914

The Nation Claims an Empire

Toward the end of the 1800's it became clear that the United States was ready to expand. Four factors caused the nation's expansion overseas—a need for markets and raw materials, a sense of Anglo-Saxon superiority, competition from Europe, and Admiral Mahan's call for naval power. The latter caused the United States to begin building a modern naval fleet. American interest in Cuba increased as the United States imported more and more sugar from that island. In 1895 Cubans began a second war for independence from Spain. General Weyler's brutal policy of reconcentration gave the American yellow press an excuse to call for war with Spain.

President McKinley did not want war with Spain. The de Lôme letter and the sinking of the *Maine*, however, forced him to ask Congress for war. Admiral Dewey defeated the Spanish naval fleet at Manila Bay in the Philippine Islands. United States troops then took over the Philippines from Spain. United States soldiers also invaded Cuba, where Theodore Roosevelt's Rough Riders won a battle at San Juan Hill. American ships destroyed the Spanish fleet outside the Santiago (Cuba) harbor. The peace treaty gave possession of the Philippines to the United States. Many Americans opposed an overseas empire, but the Senate ratified the treaty.

In addition to the Philippines, other new lands soon came under the American flag. Although Cubans had fought for independence, the United States made Cuba a protectorate. The American government drafted the Platt Amendment in order to control Cuban affairs. Americans also dominated the Cuban economy. Puerto Rico was made a United States commonwealth. Previously, the Hawaiian Islands had come under the control of American businessmen and missionaries. Foreign workers outnumbered the native Hawaiians. In 1898 Hawaii became a United States territory. In the Philippines, Aguinaldo led a war against the United States. Much later, in 1946, the Philippines became an independent republic.

As the United States entered the twentieth century, signs that the nation was becoming a world power increased. Hay's Open Door policy helped stop European countries from turning China into a colony. President Roosevelt helped bring peace between Japan and Russia. For many years Americans had searched for a way that ships could go through Central America. A French company tried and failed to build a canal. The United States succeeded. In doing so, however, the United States interfered with Colombia's sovereign rights, severely damaged relations with Latin America, spent huge amounts of money, and risked and spent thousands of human lives. The United States began to use dollar diplomacy and troops in Latin America.

Chronology of Main Events

1898 Spanish-American War; Hawaii annexed; Puerto Rico, Guam, and Philippines acquired

1900 Open Door policy; Boxer Rebellion

1901 Platt Amendment authorizes U.S. intervention in Cuba

1904 Roosevelt Corollary announced

1905 Treaty of Portsmouth

1912 Marines land in Nicaragua

1914 Panama Canal opened

Telescoping the Times may be used as an alternative to having students read the entire chapter, as a chapter preview, or as a chapter review.

535

Global Perspectives

1899	First Hague peace conference takes place.
1900	Britain annexes Transvaal and Orange Free State.
1895	Roentgen discovers X-rays.
1905	Church and state are separated in France.
1907	Rudyard Kipling receives Nobel Prize in literature.

For Discussion

How might the annexation of Transvaal and the Orange Free State have affected the U.S.? (Possible response: U.S. felt threatened by Britain's growing empire and thought it was important to annex additional territory.)

Additional Resources

- Geography Activities
- Skills Activities
- Thematic Activities
- Economic Activities
- Cultural Literacy Activities
- Literary Source Readings
- Primary Source Readings
- Nuclear Peacekeeping
- Transparencies
- Computer Test Generator

Additional Teaching Strategies

SECTION 1

For Basic Students: Have students write a paragraph explaining the origins of the city-manager form of government. (Paragraph should include: voters elect council members to make laws; council appoints a manager with experience and training in public administration to run the city.) Have students share their papers.

For Advanced Students: Have students read an article by one of the following muckrakers: Lincoln Steffens, Samuel Sidney McClure, Ida M. Tarbell, Ray Stannard Baker, Edward Bok, Edwin Markham, or Upton Sinclair. Ask students to share their articles with the class. Discuss the emotional impact each article might have had on its audience.

SECTION 2

For Basic Students: Divide the class into small groups of two or three. Have each group write two specific examples of Roosevelt's policies in each of the following areas: labor, business, transportation, health, and conservation. (Examples might include: labor—mediated strikes, set precedence for government intervention in a strike if the public welfare was involved; business—filed forty-four antitrust suits, attacked Northern Securities Company; transportation—Elkins Act of 1903, Hepburn Act of 1906; health—Meat Inspection Act, Pure Food and Drug Act; conservation—withdrew acreage from public sale, called conservation conference.) Have the groups share their information.

For Advanced Students: Divide the class into two groups to debate the following statement: Progressivism was a proper response to the abuses of capitalism and an attempt to halt the growing threat of socialism. (Arguments in agreement might include: corruption was so prevalent that society had no choice but to respond; socialism was one response, but not one the Progressives liked. Arguments in disagreement might include: the government interfered too much; businesses and workers should be left to work out their problems on their own.)

SECTION 3

For Basic Students: Have each student choose a partner and have each pair prepare a chart that lists the political parties, Presidential candidates, and the eventual winner of the 1912 election. Students should be able to explain how the President-elect was able to win.

Candidate	Party	Winner
Taft	Republican	
Roosevelt	Bull Moose	
Wilson	Democrat	X

(Reasons for Wilson's victory include: the liberal and Progressive elements of the Republican party shifted to the Bull Moose party and split the Republican vote, enabling the Democrats to win.) Students should share their information.

For Advanced Students: Divide the class into three groups, one each to represent the Democratic, Republican, and Bull Moose parties. After they research the election of 1912, ask students to design posters, buttons, and other campaign materials for their candidate. One representative from each group should present a nomination speech for its candidate to the class, stressing his achievements and qualifications. Display students' work.

SECTION 4

For Basic Students: Divide the class into three groups to report on major legislation of the Wilson administration that attacked the triple wall of privilege. Have the groups share their findings. (Reports should include: tariff—Underwood Tariff (1913); high finance—Federal Reserve Act (1913), Federal Farm Loan Act (1916); trusts—Federal Trade Commission Act of 1914, Clayton Act of 1914.)

For Advanced Students: Have students research and discuss the similarities and differences between Roosevelt's "Square Deal" and Wilson's "New Freedom." (Similarities include: both men believed in a strong executive branch; both had been chosen by their parties for governorships; both split from their parties and worked to reform government. Differences include: Roosevelt was personable and well-liked while Wilson seemed cold and distant; Roosevelt favored regulating trusts while Wilson favored breaking them up; Roosevelt filed antitrust suits while Wilson filed suits and passed new antitrust regulations.) Have students present their findings to the class.

Further Reading for Students

Fleming, Alice. *Ida Tarbell*. New York: Thomas Y. Crowell Co., 1971. (Easy)

Goldman, Eric F. *Rendezvous With Destiny: A History of Modern American Reform*. New York: Random House, 1978.

Link, Arthur S., and Richard L. McCormick. *Progressivism*. Arlington Heights, Ill.: Harlan Davidson, 1983. Paper.

Bibliography for Teachers
Books

Blum, John Morton. *The Pressive Presidents: Theodore Roosevelt, Woodrow Wilson, Franklin Roosevelt, Lyndon Johnson*. New York: W.W. Norton, 1982. Paper.

Chambers, John W. *The Tyranny of Change: America in the Progressive Era, 1900-1917*. New York: St. Martin's Press, 1980.

Colburn, David R., and George E. Pozzella, eds. *Reform and Reformers in the Progressive Era*. Westport, Conn.: Greenwood Press, 1983.

Ekirch, Arthur A., Jr. *Progressivism in America: A Study of the Era from Theodore Roosevelt to Woodrow Wilson*. New York: Franklin Watts, 1974.

Filler, Louis. *The Muckrakers*. University Park: Pennsylvania State University Press, 1975. Paper.

Grunden, Robert M. *Ministers of Reform: The Progressives' Achievement in American Civilization, 1889-1920*. New York: Basic Books, 1982.

Hofstadter, Richard, ed. *The Progressive Movement, 1900-1915*. Englewood Cliffs, N.J.: Prentice Hall, 1964. Paper.

La Follette, Robert M. *La Follette's Autobiography: A Personal Narrative of Political Experiences*. Madison: University of Wisconsin Press, 1960.

Mowry, George E. *The Progressive Era, 1900-20: The Reform Persuasion*. Washington, D.C.: American Historical Association, 1972. Paper.

Pinchot, Gifford. *Breaking New Ground*. Tucson: University of Arizona Press, 1985. Paper.

Steffens, Lincoln. *The Autobiography of Lincoln Steffens*. New York: Harcourt Brace Jovanovich, 1968. Paper.

Thelen, David. *Robert M. La Follette and the Insurgent Spirit*. Madison: University of Wisconsin Press, 1986. Paper.

Audio-Visuals

The Progressive Era. Encyclopaedia Britannica Educational Corporation. Movie.

The Progressives. McGraw-Hill Book Company. Movie.

Trust and Trust Busters. Sandler/Wald Documentary Associates. Movie.

Computer Resource

Social Studies, Volume 1. (Apple) MECC.

Teacher's Notes:

Lesson Plan

Teaching Resources, Unit 5 Booklet

Lesson Study Sheets pp. 113-128
Daily Activities pp. 129-136
Enrichment Activities pp. 137-144
Reteaching Activities pp. 145-152
Chapter Review p. 153
Chapter Mastery Tests pp. 155-166
Telescoping the Times Study Sheet p. 167

Chapter Objectives

Students will learn:
- the origins of the Progressive movement
- how Theodore Roosevelt implemented Progressivism at the national level
- characteristics of Progressivism during Taft's Presidency
- what role Woodrow Wilson played in the Progressive movement

Picturing History Theodore Roosevelt reluctantly accepted the Vice-Presidency in 1900 and became President when McKinley was assassinated in 1901. His experience for the job included work as a scholar, rancher, colonel, police commissioner, and governor.

Using the Chapter Time Line

Who succeeded McKinley as President in 1901? (Answer: Theodore Roosevelt) How many Presidents were in office during the period 1900 - 1916? (Answer: 4)

1900	1905	1910	1915	1920

1901
- William McKinley inaugurated President for second term
- McKinley assassinated; Theodore Roosevelt succeeds to Presidency

1905
Roosevelt inaugurated for first full term

1906
Meat Inspection Act

1909
William Howard Taft inaugurated President

1914
Clayton Antitrust Act

1913
- Woodrow Wilson inaugurated President
- Federal Reserve Act

536

CHAPTER **21** 1900–1916

The Progressive Era

Links to American Literature

There was never the least attention paid to what was cut up for sausage; there would come all the way back from Europe old sausage that had been rejected, and that was moldy and white—it would be dosed with borax and glycerine, and dumped into the hoppers, and made over again for home consumption. There would be meat that had tumbled out on the floor, in the dirt and sawdust, where the workers had tramped and spit uncounted billions of consumption germs. There would be meat stored in great piles in rooms; and the water from leaky roofs would drip over it, and thousands of rats would race about on it. It was too dark in these storage places to see well, but a man could run his hand over these piles of meat and sweep off handfuls of the dried dung of rats. These rats were nuisances, and the packers would put poisoned bread out for them, they would die, and then rats, bread, and meat would go into the hoppers together. This is no fairy story and no joke; the meat would be shovelled into carts, and the man who did the shoveling would not trouble to lift out a rat even when he saw one—there were things that went into the sausage in comparison with which a poisoned rat was a tidbit.

— UPTON SINCLAIR, *The Jungle*

The period from the turn of the century to World War I was yet another era of reform, commonly called the Progressive Era. During this time, the United States was adjusting to its new image as a great industrial nation. As cities and industries grew, the need for social reform and government regulation became overwhelming. Certain factories, such as the meat-packing plants, had become horrors both for the workers and for consumers of their products. Since these industries did not regulate themselves, it was time for the federal government to intervene. The pressure for reform is a recurring theme throughout American history.

Chapter Overview

In this chapter you will learn about the origins of the Progressive movement and the role Theodore Roosevelt played in implementing Progressive reforms. You will also learn how William Howard Taft disappointed the Progressives and how Woodrow Wilson continued their reforms. Chapter 21 presents the Progressive Era in four sections.

Chapter Outline

1. **The Progressive Movement Begins**
2. **Roosevelt Becomes a Progressive Leader**
3. **Progressivism Continues Under Taft**
4. **Woodrow Wilson Declares a "New Freedom"**

537

Briefly review the Populist movement with students. (Refer to Chapter 18.) Ask students to list several Populist ideals. (Possible responses: graduated income tax; postal savings bank; federal loan program for farmers; direct election of senators; single term for President; secret ballot; initiative, recall, and referendum.) Ask students to recall reasons for the failure of the Populist movement. (Possible responses: Populists were mostly farmers; Populist leaders were inexperienced politicians; they failed to elect a Populist President.)

State the Objective
Understand the origins of the Progressive movement.

For Discussion
What were the reasons for the success of the Progressive movement? (Possible responses: stimulus came from three powerful sources—religious leaders, the press, and radical political groups; corruption became so widespread that issues were easy to support and difficult to argue against.)

Historical Sidelight
William H. Taft was America's heaviest President. When he entered the White House he weighed more than 325 pounds. The special bathtub that was installed for him could hold four ordinary-size men.

The Progressive Movement Begins

GLOSSARY TERMS: **Progressive movement, muckrakers, Socialist party, socialism, commission form of government, council-manager form of government, direct primary**

The immediate stimulus to the **Progressive movement** came from three main sources: religion, the press, and a number of radical political groups that called for extreme measures to bring about change. Progressives could be found among Democrats as well as Republicans. Many Progressives were white-collar workers who were finally joining the farmers in their demands for reform. The farmers' crusade for change could be traced back to Populism. (See Chapter 18.)

Religious Groups Seek Reform

A basic strand in the reform movement was religion. Baptist minister Walter Rauschenbusch was an early exponent of what was called the "social gospel." He put it this way: "It is true that any regeneration [reform] of society can come only through the act of God and the Presence of Christ, but God is now acting, and Christ is now here." In other words, the churches should work to improve conditions for workers and for the poor.

After the Civil War several religious associations were transplanted to the United States from Great Britain. They included the Young Men's Christian Association (YMCA), the Young Women's Christian Association (YWCA), and the Salvation Army. All three concentrated their efforts on helping newcomers adjust to life in the big cities. They encouraged the establishment of settlement houses, investigated slum conditions, and provided food and clothing to people in need.

Gradually, many religious leaders and organizations began to shift their efforts from private charity to public reform. In 1905 twenty-seven Protestant churches formed the Federal Council of the Churches of Christ in America. The council called for legislation on several issues including the abolition of child labor and of the sweatshop system, one day of rest in seven, a living wage, and safety rules in factories and shops.

Muckrakers Expose Social Evils

A second strand in the reform movement came from a group of journalists known as **muckrakers.** They were given the name by Theodore Roosevelt. He compared them to a character in John Bunyan's novel *Pilgrim's Progress,* a character who is so busy raking the muck, or dirt, on the floor that he does not see the good things that are above his head. Roosevelt felt that the muckrakers were making people discontented by pointing out what was wrong with society. The muckrakers felt that unless people got angry about social wrongs, they would not fight for change.

People in the Chapter

Ida Tarbell spent five years researching her exposé of the Standard Oil Company. Nevertheless, *McClure's* was so worried about lawsuits that the magazine paid as much as three thousand dollars to verify each article she wrote. No lawsuit was ever filed.

William Howard Taft and his wife, Helen, visited Tokyo while he was Governor General of the Philippines. Mrs. Taft fell in love with the cherry trees and was instrumental in having three thousand Japanese cherry trees sent to Washington. These trees still delight visitors to the city every spring.

Joseph "Uncle Joe" Cannon wielded almost dictatorial power as Speaker of the House. Representatives usually had to secure permission to speak before Uncle Joe would recognize them on the floor. Apparently he was no threat to President Taft, who once went to sleep while Cannon was talking to him.

Woodrow Wilson was the only President to have earned a doctorate. He had a unique definition for conservatism. He called it the policy of "make no change and consult your grandmother when in doubt."

Picturing History Three muckrakers who tried to bring about reform in business, labor, and politics: Upton Sinclair (left), whose book *The Jungle* turned some readers into vegetarians; Lincoln Steffens (center), who once suggested that a railroad executive whose trains were plagued by rear-end collisions solve the problem by cutting off the last car; and Ida Tarbell (right), who exposed the business practices of Standard Oil in nineteen installments in *McClure's Magazine.*

Actually, journalists had been writing muckraking articles for years. What made the difference in the early 1900's was the rise of mass-circulation magazines. These appealed to a nationwide audience through their romantic fiction, their advertisements, and their low price of ten cents an issue. Chief among them was *McClure's,* founded by Irish immigrant Samuel Sidney McClure. *McClure's* and other magazines such as *Hampton's, Cosmopolitan,* the *American, The Ladies' Home Journal,* and *Everybody's* not only published muckraking articles but also paid the journalists while they did their research and reinforced the articles with vivid illustrations. Readers reveled in one sensational disclosure after another.

The exposés covered many topics. **Lincoln Steffens** wrote about the links between big business and crooked politicians in "The Shame of the Cities." **Ida M. Tarbell,** in her "History of the Standard Oil Company," described that firm's cut-throat methods of eliminating competition. Ray Stannard Baker raked over the railroads and their stock swindles.

Then there was **Upton Sinclair.** In 1906 his novel *The Jungle* appeared. It described in graphic detail the lives of stockyard workers and the operations of the meat-packing industry. (See page 537.)

Radical Groups Criticize Capitalism

In addition to being a muckraker, Sinclair was an on-and-off member of the **Socialist party.** This was one of the radical groups that formed the third strand of the Progressive movement. The party had been organized in 1901 by, among others, labor leader **Eugene V. Debs.** Debs had become a socialist while sitting in jail after the Pullman strike. Later he was the Socialist party's Presidential candidate in several elections and received almost a million votes in 1912 and again in 1920. Commenting on the relationship between big business, government, and the people, Debs said:

> As long as a relatively few men own the railroads, the telegraph, the telephone, own the oilfields and the gasfields and the steel mills and the sugar refineries and the leather tanneries—own, in short, the sources and means of life—they will corrupt our politics, they will enslave the working class, they will impoverish and debase society, they will do all things that are needful to perpetuate their power as the economic masters and the political rulers of the people.
>
> Competition was natural enough at one time, but do you think you are competing today? Many of you think you are competing. Against whom? Against Rockefeller? About as I would if I had a wheelbarrow and competed with the Santa Fe [railroad] from here to Kansas City.

The Progressives did not agree with Debs's proposed solution of **socialism,** which would eliminate private ownership of the means of production. (See page 608.) They wanted to keep the capitalist system. There was no denying, however, that many of Debs's criticisms were true. Big business was

Check for Understanding

Call on individual students to answer Section 1 Review questions orally.

Guided Practice

Ask students to identify the various levels on which Progressive reforms were made. (Answer: city; state; local.) Ask students whether they think it is necessary for a party to elect a President in order for its policies to be carried out. Remind students to base their answers on what they have read in this section. (Possible response: no, a party can effect changes on the city and state level and pass laws on the national level.)

Picturing History Workers march in a May Day parade sponsored by Socialists in 1903 (top). At the turn of the century, African Americans made up most of the labor force in the tobacco industry. The lower picture shows women and children—the lowest paid of all workers—stripping stems from tobacco leaves.

ruthless. It did enjoy special privileges from government. Women and children did have difficulty protecting themselves in the urban industrial marketplace. Wages and working conditions in most mines, shops, and factories were shocking.

The Progressives tried to steal socialism's thunder without adopting socialism. They concentrated on improving capitalism by making government more responsive to social problems.

The Local Level Listens

The nation's large cities contained the most obvious problems of the new industrial age. Accordingly, the Progressives began by trying to improve municipal government. This reform took two forms: (1) "throwing the rascals out" and (2) making institutional changes.

Reform Mayors. The best examples of reform city mayors were Hazen Pingree of Detroit, Thomas L. Johnson of Cleveland, and Samuel M. "Golden Rule" Jones of Toledo.

Pingree, who served from 1889 to 1896, concentrated on economic issues. He built schools, parks, and a municipal lighting plant. He lowered streetcar and gas rates. He also set up a system of work relief for unemployed persons.

Johnson governed from 1901 to 1909. He appointed competent, honest men to city jobs. He reassessed property values for tax purposes, which had not been done for more than thirty years. Finally, because he believed people should take an active part in government, he held meetings in a large circus tent and invited citizens to ask officials any questions they wished about the way the city was being run.

Jones, who held office from 1899 to 1904, believed in applying the teachings of Christ to government. The story is told that one evening a tramp came up to him and asked for money for a night's lodging. Not having any coins, Jones gave the tramp a five-dollar bill and asked him to bring back the change. When the tramp returned, Jones put the money in his pocket without counting it. "Ain't you goin' to count it?" asked the tramp. "Did you count it?" asked Jones. Yes he had, and it was all there. "Well, then, there's no need for me to count it, is there?" Then Jones gave the tramp a half-dollar.

In addition to the Progressive mayors, there were eighteen Socialist mayors. In general, they practiced "gas and water socialism." That is, they threw out the crooked private owners of gasworks, waterworks, and transit lines and substituted municipal ownership of utilities.

New Forms of Government. In 1900 a hurricane and tidal wave swept out of the Gulf of Mexico and almost demolished Galveston, Texas. The job of relief and rebuilding was a huge one, and the politicians on the city council botched it. They were so incompetent, in fact, that the Texas legislature appointed a five-member commission of experts to take over. Each expert was put in charge of a different city department. The commission soon got Galveston back on its feet, and the city decided to adopt the **commission form of govern-**

Assign Independent Practice

Have students construct a chart identifying the following people and their contributions to Progressive reform: Walter Rauschenbusch, Upton Sinclair, Eugene V. Debs, Hazen Pingree, Thomas Johnson, Samuel Jones, Robert La Follette, and Louis Brandeis. Responses should include:

- Rauschenbusch—Baptist minister; was exponent of "social gospel."
- Sinclair—writer; exposed details of working conditions in the stockyards and meat-packing plants.

- Debs—Socialist party leader; called for government ownership and operation of utilities, better conditions for working class.
- Pingree—mayor of Detroit; built schools, parks, and set up work relief system for unemployed.
- Johnson—mayor of Cleveland; reassessed property taxes, held city meetings, appointed honest men.
- Jones—mayor of Toledo; applied teachings of Christ to government.

- La Follette—governor of Wisconsin; wanted business out of politics, attacked railroads.
- Brandeis—lawyer; argued for freedom of women to sign or refuse to sign contracts.

ment. By 1914 some four hundred cities had followed Galveston's example.

In 1913 another natural disaster—this time a flood in Dayton, Ohio—led to the widespread adoption of the **council-manager form of government.** This system was already being used in Staunton, Virginia. People elect a city council to make laws. In turn, the council appoints a manager—usually someone with training and experience in public administration—to run the city's departments. By 1923 about three hundred cities were being governed by managers.

In both instances, the Progressives were transferring sound management principles from business to public life. If specialists could improve business, they believed, specialists would improve government as well.

The States Respond

From reforms at the local level, the Progressives moved on to reforms at the state level. In a way they had to. Cities are created by state legislatures. So municipal reforms could be maintained only if state governments were also reformed.

Reform Governors. The outstanding reform governor of the period was **Robert M. La Follette** of Wisconsin. First elected in 1900, he served three terms before entering the United States Senate in 1906. He remained in the Senate until his death in 1925.

"Fighting Bob" La Follette's goal, as he explained it, "was not to *smash* corporations, but to drive them out of politics, and then to treat them exactly the same as other people are treated." A major target was the railroad industry. La Follette taxed railroad property at the same rate as other business property. He set up a railroad commission to regulate rates, and he forbade railroads from issuing free passes to state officials, as they had been doing. Some of his reforms helped the industry as well as the public. Lower rates, for example,

Picturing History
Robert M. La Follette, campaigning in Wisconsin.

created enough new traffic to increase the railroads' income.

Other governors who attacked "the interests" included Charles B. Aycock of North Carolina, Albert B. Cummins of Iowa, John A. Johnson of Minnesota, and Joseph W. Folk of Missouri.

"The Oregon System" and Other Reforms. In some cases, state reforms came about through the efforts of ordinary citizens rather than governors. Among the most effective individuals was William S. U'Ren (ơor en´) of Oregon. As a result of his leadership, Oregon adopted the secret ballot, the initiative, the referendum, and the recall. (See page 472.) By 1920 another twenty states had adopted at least one of these techniques.

Even more significant was the adoption of the **direct primary.** By using this means, instead of being chosen by political machines, candidates for public office are chosen through a special popular election. The direct primary was first adopted by Wisconsin in 1903. By 1916 every state except three had done the same.

Adopting the direct primary led to the Seventeenth Amendment to the Constitution. Before 1913 United States senators were chosen by state legislatures. As a result, most senators were either party bosses or directors of their state's leading corporations. Progressives agreed that the level of intelligence in the Senate was high. Nevertheless, they believed that the Senate represented special business interests rather than the public. The Senate at first refused to go along with the idea of popular election. Gradually, however, more and more states began choosing senators by means of the direct primary. As a result, the Seventeenth Amendment was approved in 1912 and became part of the Constitution in 1913. (See page 177.)

Social Legislation. The Progressives pushed for social reforms as well as political ones. Some were members of the National Child Labor Committee; others belonged to the National Consumers' League. Most of them agreed that a woman's place was in the home but that her interests should also include public affairs. Women's groups did research on social problems and hired lobbyists to present their views in state capitals. They succeeded in bringing about a number of changes.

By 1914, for instance, almost every state had passed a law either prohibiting the employment of children under fourteen or requiring them to attend

Student Assignment/Homework

Have students read Section 2, "Roosevelt Becomes a Progressive Leader," and complete Chapter 21, Section 2 Daily Activity.

school until age fourteen. Unfortunately, most of these laws did not cover farm work or domestic service. Also, the opposition of Southern textile mill owners kept the laws from being enforced in some areas.

In 1908 the Supreme Court in the case of *Muller* v. *Oregon* reversed itself on the issue of whether a state could limit the working hours of women. In the past the Court had held that such limits interfered with freedom of contract. This time, however, lawyer **Louis D. Brandeis,** assisted by Josephine Goldmark and Florence Kelley, submitted a 112-page legal brief. Brandeis, reminding the

Court that freedom of contract meant that women were as free as corporations to sign or not to sign a contract, argued that a woman was much more economically insecure than a giant corporation and thus needed protection. The "Brandeis Brief" convinced the Court, which said that Oregon's law limiting women to a ten-hour day was constitutional. In 1917 a similar brief in *Bunting* v. *Oregon* persuaded the Court to uphold a ten-hour workday law for men. As a result of these two decisions, many states passed laws limiting working hours.

Another area in which Progressive reforms succeeded was workers' compensation. Every year

HELEN KELLER
ANNE SULLIVAN

Focus on Biography

Helen Keller (1880–1968)

When President Woodrow Wilson asked Helen Keller why she chose to attend Radcliffe College and not one of the other fine colleges, she replied, "Because they didn't want me at Radcliffe, and, being stubborn, I chose to override their objections."

Keller had met Presidents since Grover Cleveland invited her to the White House when she was ten years old and already world famous. Queen Victoria had questioned a distinguished American visitor about her. Prominent writers and scientists boasted of having met her. She was the miracle child.

Until she was seven, Helen was locked in a world of permanent darkness and silence. An illness at eighteen months had left her blind and deaf. Inside this awful prison was a first-class mind and an indomitable spirit. At six, strong and unmanageable, Helen kicked, screamed, threw dinner plates, and hurled

herself down stairs. Her family feared she would have to be locked away.

Then came a ray of hope. Helen's father decided to take her to Alexander Graham Bell for a consultation. Bell advised the Kellers to write to the Perkins Institution for the Blind in Boston, which his son-in-law directed. It was there that a blind and deaf girl had been taught to communicate through a "manual" alphabet and to read and write in Braille.

Off went a letter to the Perkins Institution. Could they send a teacher to work with little Helen? Twenty-one-year-old Anne Sullivan was sent down to Tuscumbia, Alabama, where Helen lived.

At their first encounter, Helen attacked Sullivan, almost knocking her down. Frustrating weeks followed. Helen learned the codes for several words as Sullivan pressed them into her hand.

Then came the miracle at the well.

Sullivan held one of Helen's hands under flowing water and spelled the word *water* slowly, then rapidly, in her other hand. Keller later wrote, "The mystery of language was revealed to me. I knew then that *w-a-t-e-r* meant the wonderful cool something that was flowing over my hand. That living word awakened my soul, gave me light, hope, joy, set it free!"

The experience also released the keen memory and phenomenal powers of concentration that mark a true genius. By the time she reached her twenties, Helen had mastered a dozen ancient and modern languages. She swam, skated, danced, traveled widely, and even spoke in public. A true child of the Progressive Era, Helen Keller devoted her talents to improving conditions for the blind and the deaf throughout the world.

542

State the Objective

Recognize how Theodore Roosevelt implemented Progressivism at the national level.

Anticipate the Lesson

Call on individual students to read their answers to Chapter 21, Section 2 Daily Activity. Focus especially on the insights this reading gives about Theodore Roosevelt.

Picturing History Louis D. Brandeis and Florence Kelley worked for passage of laws limiting work hours for women.

about 35,000 workers were killed on the job and another 700,000 injured. Beginning with Maryland in 1902, one state after another passed legislation requiring employers in dangerous occupations to pay benefits to injured employees.

SECTION 1 REVIEW

Key Terms and People

Explain the significance of: Progressive movement, muckrakers, Lincoln Steffens, Ida M. Tarbell, Upton Sinclair, Socialist party, Eugene V. Debs, socialism, commission form of government, council-manager form of government, Robert M. La Follette, direct primary, Louis D. Brandeis

Main Ideas

1. What were the main groups in the Progressive movement?
2. How did the Progressive view of the way to bring about social change differ from the Socialist view?
3. What was the general theory underlying the two new forms of local government that were inspired by the Progressive movement?
4. What political reforms on the state level did the Progressive movement help to bring about?
5. What effect did the Progressive movement have on state labor laws?

Critical Thinking

6. Why did political machines, which had controlled many municipal and state governments in the latter half of the 1800's, lose power during the early 1900's?

SECTION 2

Roosevelt Becomes a Progressive Leader

GLOSSARY TERMS: **conservation, natural resources, square deal, closed shop**

It was at the national level that the Progressive movement really made its mark. Moreover, if you were to ask which President personified Progressivism, most historians would answer, **Theodore Roosevelt.**

A Rough Rider Enters the White House

Theodore Roosevelt was born in 1858 into an old Dutch merchant and banking family in New York State. Asthmatic and nearsighted as a child, he overcame his physical weaknesses by hard exercise and sheer force of will. After graduating from Harvard, he became a cattle rancher in the Dakotas. He fell in love with the out-of-doors and developed a deep and lifelong interest in the **conservation** (preservation) of **natural resources**—forms of wealth supplied by nature, such as air, land, water power, forests, oil, and coal. He wrote two historical works: one on the War of 1812, the other on the winning of the West. He entered politics and moved from assemblyman and police commissioner in New York City to civil service commissioner and assistant secretary of the navy in Washington, D.C.

Roosevelt's spectacular charge up San Juan Hill during the Spanish-American War brought him to the attention of Senator Thomas C. Platt, the Republican boss of New York State. Platt needed a Republican governor to help him in his business affairs. Although he had misgivings about Roosevelt's interest in Progressive legislation, he decided to run the former Rough Rider for office anyway.

No sooner was Roosevelt elected, however, than he began attacking the ties between business and government. He refused to appoint Platt's choice for state insurance commissioner. He also forced through a law requiring streetcar companies to pay taxes on the value of their franchises. Platt was furious. If such actions continued, New York's Republican machine would lose its financial support from big business. It was unthinkable to renominate Roosevelt for governor. The only solu-

Answers

Main Ideas

1. Religious groups, radical political groups, and muckraking journalists.

2. Progressives believed that change could be achieved by making government more responsive to social needs. Socialists believed that real change could occur only by eliminating private ownership of the means of production.

3. Sound business-management practices could be applied to the running of municipal governments.

4. Equal taxation and treatment of big business, railroads, and ordinary citizens; the direct primary, which eventually led to the adoption of the Seventeenth Amendment, providing for the popular election of U.S. senators; the secret ballot; the initiative; the referendum; and the recall.

5. Most states passed laws limiting work hours, prohibiting most child labor, and providing for workers' compensation.

Critical Thinking

6. Possible answers: political machines not only failed to solve urban problems but actually added to them; most Progressive groups did not support political machines; the Progressive reforms destroyed those things that once made the machines powerful. **(analysis)**

Have students list on the board examples of Roosevelt's support of Progressivism at the national level. (List should include: mediated coal strike; wanted to curb trusts if their actions were oppressive to the public but did not want to destroy large corporations; filed forty-four antitrust suits; supported Elkins Act of 1903, Hepburn Act of 1906, Meat Inspection Act of 1906, Pure Food and Drug Act of 1906, all regulating big business; called for new conservation measures; appointed Gifford Pinchot supervisor of national forests, pushed for Passage of Newlands Reclamation Act, and called White House conservation conference in 1908.)

Check for Understanding

Have students answer Section 2 Review questions on paper.

Historical Sidelight
On October 14, 1912, a saloonkeeper, John N. Schrank, tried to assassinate Theodore Roosevelt. An eyeglass case in Roosevelt's pocket deflected the bullet and saved his life.

tion was to nominate him for Vice-President on the national ticket headed by **William McKinley.** The Vice-Presidency was considered a political graveyard.

Mark Hanna, Republican political organizer, objected. Didn't Platt realize "that damned cowboy" would be only one heartbeat away from the White House? Nevertheless, Platt's scheme worked, and "Mack and Teddy" were swept into office in 1900. Then in September 1901, Hanna's worst fears came true. McKinley was shot by an assassin and Theodore Roosevelt became President of the United States. (In 1904 Roosevelt was elected to his first full term, defeating Judge Alton B. Parker by the largest margin of victory ever recorded to that time.)

Picturing History On September 6, 1901, a young anarchist named Leon Czolgosz shot President McKinley in the chest and abdomen. The assassination occurred while McKinley was standing in a reception line at the Pan-American Exposition in Buffalo, New York. McKinley died eight days later.

Six Achievements Equal a Square Deal

The new President represented a great change from his predecessor. For one thing, he crackled with energy. While in the White House, he boxed with professionals, one of whom blinded him in the left eye. He played strenuous tennis. He galloped a hundred miles on horseback in one day (using several horses) to prove that it could be done. Moreover, he energetically shot bears on what he called a restful vacation. His red-blooded advice to young people was, "Don't flinch, don't foul, and hit the line hard."

In politics, as in sports, Roosevelt believed in action. The federal government was responsible for the national welfare. He believed it should step in whenever the states proved incapable of handling problems. He also believed that because the President represented all the people, he should play a major role in shaping legislative policy. If big business was squeezing farmers, workers, and small business people, then he, Roosevelt, would see to it that they received a **"square deal."** He said, "I believe in a strong executive," and he proceeded to put his beliefs into practice.

Increasing Federal Power. There was another aspect to Roosevelt's political behavior. It was based on a knowledge of American history and a vision of national unity. Americans had filled out a continent and built an industrial empire. However, they had not, in Roosevelt's opinion, developed the political tools for managing what they had created. "A simple and poor society can exist as a democracy on the basis of sheer individualism. But a rich and complex society cannot so exist," he said. In the 1900's, according to Roosevelt, the federal government needed to manage certain areas of society so that the nation could develop in an orderly manner.

Mediating a Coal Strike. One example of Roosevelt's approach was his handling of a coal strike in 1902. Coal miners in Pennsylvania struck for higher wages, an eight-hour day, and the right to organize a union. The mine operators refused to bargain or even to meet with the labor leaders at the White House. George Baer, a mine owner and the president of the Reading Railroad, said that it was his religious duty to defeat the strikers. He added, "The rights and interests of the laboring men will be protected and cared for—not by labor agitators, but by Christian men to whom God in his infinite

Remind students that President Theodore Roosevelt did much to begin the movement to preserve wilderness areas in the U.S. In contrast, the Reagan administration came under sharp criticism for opening up public lands to private use. To stimulate discussion on conservation issues, ask students the following questions. How much wilderness is enough? Why? Should the government be responsible for protecting it? (Possible responses: some students will say that enough land has been set aside for national preserves, that the rest is needed by the people for homes and agriculture; others will say that the government should continue to buy, preserve, and protect wilderness land, because once the land is gone, it is gone forever.)

Picturing History
Miners parade silently during the coal strike of 1902. Mine operators accepted Roosevelt's arbitration proposal, but not enthusiastically. However, many agreed that settling a strike without resorting to violence was progress.

wisdom has given control of the property interests of the country.''

To counter the company, Roosevelt threatened to seize the mines and have the army run them. However, he decided to appoint a commission to make recommendations for settling the strike.

The mine operators finally agreed to arbitration. The settlement was a compromise. The workers received a 10 percent pay hike and a nine-hour day. They did not obtain a **closed shop,** that is, an agreement under which operators will not hire anyone who does not belong to the union. In addition, the workers agreed not to strike again for three years.

More important than the actual settlement, however, was the establishment of a new principle. In the past, Presidents had sent in federal troops only to protect private property or to keep such services as the United States mail going. Now, Roosevelt was saying that the federal government could intervene in a strike if the public welfare was involved. In addition, Roosevelt was emphasizing the Progressive belief that disputes should be settled in an orderly way with the help of experts.

Regulating Trusts. Roosevelt also used his skills as a mediator in dealing with the question of trusts. In the public mind, trusts were bad and should be smashed. (See pages 447-448.) Roosevelt, however, believed that how a trust acted was more significant than how big it was. He wanted to curb trusts if their actions became oppressive to the public, but he did not want to destroy large corporations.

The President thus concentrated his efforts on filing suits under the Sherman Antitrust Act of 1890. He attacked the Northern Securities Company, which had established a monopoly over Western railroads. He also sued the beef trust, the oil trust, the steel trust, the sugar trust, and the tobacco trust. All in all, his administration filed forty-four antitrust suits. Nevertheless, although the government won a number of cases and broke up a number of trusts, it did not stop the merger movement in business.

Regulating Transportation. Roosevelt was more successful in railroad regulation. Under his urging, Congress put some teeth in the Interstate Commerce Act of 1887.

The **Elkins Act** of 1903 made it illegal for railroad officials and shippers either to give or to receive rebates. It also said that once a railroad had set rates, it could not change them without notifying the public.

The **Hepburn Act** of 1906 went several steps further. It gave the Interstate Commerce Commission power to set maximum railroad rates, subject to court approval, whenever shippers complained. Within two years, the commission received more than nine thousand complaints and lowered a great many rates. In addition, the railroads were told to use uniform methods of accounting and to stop giving out free passes.

Protecting Health. President Roosevelt—like millions of Americans who stopped eating canned meat—was horrified when he read *The Jungle*. He

Map Skills

AK • Acadia

For Discussion

What was the impact of writings such as *The Jungle* on the reform movement? (Possible responses: writings describe the details of the lives of the stockyard workers and the unsafe and unclean conditions in the industry; writings led to a federal investigation and passage of stricter controls on foods and on the food industry.)

promptly appointed a commission to investigate Upton Sinclair's charges. The commission found the charges to be true, so in 1906 Congress passed the first federal Meat Inspection Act.

That same year, Congress passed a **Pure Food and Drug Act.** Credit for this legislation belongs mostly to Dr. Harvey Washington Wiley, chief chemist in the Department of Agriculture. For years, Wiley had lectured across the country, criticizing the harmful preservatives that were added to food. There was coal-tar dye and borax in sausage, formaldehyde in canned pork and beans, and so on. Wiley wanted such information printed on the labels of cans and other food packages. The 1906 act also placed some restrictions on the manufacturers of prepared foods and patent medicines. An amendment in 1911 prohibited the use of misleading labels. As one historian commented, ''American stomachs and insides generally have been better than they would have been had Wiley not lived and labored.''

Linking Past to Present

Although United States laws have banned the use of food additives that can cause cancer, the use of potentially cancer-causing pesticides has more than doubled since the early 1960's. In 1989 many school boards temporarily removed apples from their school lunch programs after tests conducted by Consumer Union showed that several brands of apple juice contained high levels of the chemical known by the trade name Alar. Apple growers reassured the public that they had stopped using Alar years ago. Apples were tested, found to be safe, and returned to school lunches. Nevertheless, public concern continues over the presence of dangerous chemical residues in our food.

Conserving Natural Resources. The federal government had paid almost no attention to the nation's natural resources. The Forest Bureau had been established in 1887. Presidents Harrison, Cleveland, and McKinley had withdrawn several million acres of timberlands from public sale and put them into a national forest reserve. Other than

this, nothing had been done.

This was not surprising. From the time the first Europeans landed in America, the resources of the continent seemed limitless. Forests stretched as far as the eye could see. Clear rivers tumbled down to the sea. No matter how far west people moved, there was always more land beyond the horizon.

In fact, Americans regarded the environment as something to be exploited rather than conserved. Pioneer farmers leveled forests by cutting and burning. They plowed up the prairies. Ranchers allowed their cattle to overgraze the Great Plains. Coal companies mined only ore that was easily reached. Lumber companies ignored the effect of their logging operations on flood control and did not replant what they cut down. Cities dumped untreated sewage and industrial wastes into rivers, creating health hazards and destroying fish.

By the end of the 1800's, however, people began to realize that the nation's natural resources were not limitless after all. Millions of acres of farmland were either unusable or unproductive without large amounts of fertilizer. Many of the nation's forests had disappeared. There were tens of thousands of abandoned mines.

When Roosevelt became President, he called the forest and water problems ''perhaps the most vital internal problems of the United States.'' Then he proceeded to attack the problems with his usual gusto. He withdrew over 148 million acres of forest land from public sale. (This was an area larger than Germany.) He also withdrew 1.5 million acres of land containing some 2,500 water-power sites. Finally, he withdrew another 84 million acres of land that he asked the United States Geological Survey to explore for mineral and water resources.

To help people enjoy the wonders of nature, Roosevelt established over fifty wildlife sanctuaries, five national parks, and eighteen sites as national monuments. He put **Gifford Pinchot,** (pin´ shō) a professional conservationist, in charge

Picturing History
Gifford Pinchot was one of the original proponents of the conservation movement. Roosevelt chose him to supervise the national Division of Forestry.

Student Assignment/Homework

Have students read Section 3, "Progressivism Continues Under Taft," and answer Section 3 Review questions on paper.

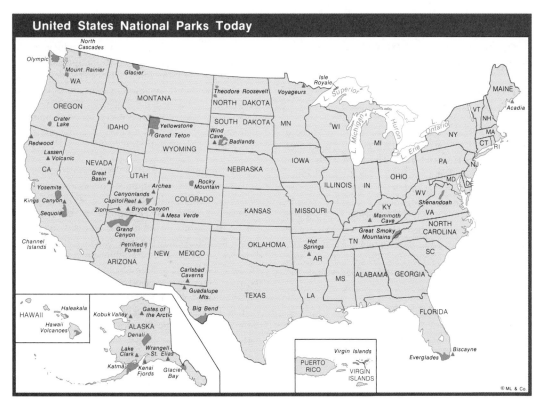

United States National Parks Today

Map Skills **Location** Which state has the most national parks? **Location** Which national park in the continental United States is farthest east?

of supervising the national forests. He also pushed for passage of the Newlands Reclamation Act. Under it, money from the sale of public lands in the West was set aside to build irrigation projects that would enable farmers to cultivate the desert. Both the Roosevelt Dam in Arizona and the Shoshone Dam in Wyoming were built under this act.

In 1908 Roosevelt called a White House conservation conference. As a result, forty-one of the forty-six states that were part of the union at that time set up conservation agencies. A national commission began a study to find out what the nation's resources were. Perhaps most important, people began to realize how important conservation was.

SECTION 2 REVIEW

Key Terms and People

Explain the significance of: Theodore Roosevelt, conservation, natural resources, William McKinley, square deal, closed shop, Elkins Act, Hepburn Act, Pure Food and Drug Act, Gifford Pinchot

Main Ideas

1. Why did Senator Platt come to regret supporting Theodore Roosevelt's political career?
2. To whom did President Roosevelt promise a "square deal"?
3. What was Roosevelt's attitude toward trusts?
4. What efforts were made during Roosevelt's Presidency to protect American health?
5. In general, what efforts were made during Roosevelt's Presidency to conserve America's natural resources?

Critical Thinking

6. How did Roosevelt's square deal exemplify the Progressive cause?

Answers

Main Ideas

1. As a Progressive leader, Roosevelt opposed the ties between big business and New York's Republican machine, led by Platt.

2. To farmers, workers, and small business people.

3. He wanted to curb trusts whose actions became oppressive to the public; he did not want to destroy corporations only because they were big.

4. Congress passed the first federal Meat Inspection Act and a Pure Food and Drug Act, thus helping to ensure safer foods and medicines for the public.

5. He withdrew millions of acres of land from public sale, established wildlife sanctuaries and national parks, and inspired the set up of state conservation agencies.

Critical Thinking

6. Possible answer: the square deal actively tried to improve public health and welfare, fought against oppressive business practices, and sought to make the democratic system more responsive to the average citizen. **(analysis)**

Anticipate the Lesson

Review with students the reasons for the rise of third parties in American politics. (Chapter 18) (Reasons include: voters' unhappiness with current government or political parties; voters' desire for change; national crisis or concern that requires a new way of looking at the issues.)

SECTION 3

Progressivism Continues Under Taft

GLOSSARY TERMS: conservatives,
    Progressive party

In 1908 Roosevelt wanted his successor to be a man who would carry out his policies. His choice was **William Howard Taft.** The Democrats nominated William Jennings Bryan for the third time. (See pages 472-474.) Instead of free silver, Bryan campaigned on the slogan of "Let the people rule." He called for a federal income tax, a lower tariff, and new antitrust laws. Nevertheless, he polled even fewer votes than he had in 1896. As the Republicans said, "Vote for Taft this time—you can vote for Bryan any time." The voters did exactly that.

Taft Enters the White House

Taft's background and personality were excellent for the Supreme Court justice that he later became. They were not really suited for a President, however, especially a President following such a hard act as Roosevelt's. Taft was cautious and legalistic, a "horse-drawn carriage" in comparison with Roosevelt's "automobile." He hesitated to bring problems to public attention or to organize opinion around an issue. He did not even know how to handle members of his own party. As one congressman remarked, Taft was "a well-meaning man who was born with two left feet."

Stumbling over a Tariff.   Taft soon found himself in hot water on a number of issues. The first was the tariff. Taft had run on a platform of lowering tariffs. The House did in fact pass the Payne Bill, which lowered rates on many manufactured goods. When the bill reached the Senate, however, conservative Republicans restored most of the cuts. Under pressure from big business, they boosted other rates as well. Taft signed the Payne-Aldrich Tariff Act amid cries of betrayal.

The President then went out on the stump to defend the new tariff. In Winona, Minnesota, before a hostile audience of grain growers, he asserted that the new law was "the best [tariff] bill

Picturing History   Taft tries to figure out what to do, while Roosevelt turns a disapproving eye.

Present the Lesson

Have each student choose a partner; then have partners review the section and briefly outline Taft and his Presidency. Outlines should include: was cautious and legalistic; believed in compromise; could not handle members of his own party; signed Payne-Aldrich Tariff Act amid public outcry; returned government land to public sale; fired Pinchot; supported Joseph Cannon in House; contributed to split in Republican party. Have students share information. Ask students to contrast Taft's operation of the Presidency to that of Theodore Roosevelt. (Possible responses: Roosevelt—brought

problems out into the open; believed in strong leadership; placed major emphasis on conservation. Taft—hesitated to bring problems to public attention; believed in compromise; sold public lands.)

Check for Understanding

Call on individual students to read their answers to Section 3 Review questions.

the Republican party ever passed.'' Farmers everywhere groaned because the tariff would make the manufactured articles they needed more expensive. Taft made matters even worse by saying he dictated the speech hurriedly between two railroad stations and had not bothered to reread it for meaning.

Carelessness over Resources. The next area in which Taft ran into difficulty was conservation. He removed Roosevelt's secretary of the interior and appointed his own man, Richard A. Ballinger. Ballinger returned to public sale many water-power sites plus extensive coal fields and timberlands that Roosevelt had previously withdrawn. When Pinchot, Roosevelt's appointee as head of the forestry service, protested, Taft restored some of the lands to the forest reserve. However, he fired Pinchot.

Linking Past to Present

Since the beginning of the twentieth century, Presidents have walked a fine line between trying to please conservationists and bowing to the demands of industrialists. The great fires in Yellowstone in 1988 and the Alaskan oil spill in 1989 reminded Americans once again how vulnerable our natural resources are to sudden destruction. Today, as in the past, difficult choices must be made if we are to preserve our natural resources not only for the present but for generations to come.

Supporting Unpopular Officials. Still another of Taft's mistakes was his support of **Joseph Cannon,** Speaker of the House of Representatives. Cannon was a heavy-swearing, cigar-chomping man who referred to himself as a ''hard-boiled hayseed.'' At that time, the Speaker had the power to choose the members of all House committees. ''Uncle Joe'' Cannon, who hated what he called ''this babble for reform,'' appointed only **conservatives,** or those who tended toward established tradition and resisted change. He ignored congressmen whose seniority, or length of service, entitled them to committee posts. In addition, Cannon appointed himself head of the Committee on Rules, which decided what bills Congress would or would

not consider. He rarely decided on progressive bills. He was a virtual dictator of the House.

Blocked in their efforts to pass Progressive legislation, a group of reform-minded Republicans decided that the only thing to do was to strip Cannon of his power. In March 1910, with the help of the Democrats, they succeeded. One of them, Representative George W. Norris of Nebraska, introduced a resolution calling for the entire House to elect the Committee on Rules. After thirty-six hours of violent debate, the resolution was adopted. As *The Wall Street Journal* observed, ''The clock has struck for Uncle Joe. He has stood between the people and too many things that they wanted and ought to have.'' The next Congress changed the rules even further: the entire House would elect all committees, not just the Rules Committee.

Picturing History Joseph (''Uncle Joe'') Cannon, the ultra-conservative Speaker of the House, was challenged by the Progressives, who thought he wielded too much power.

Losing Power. By 1910 the Grand Old Party (GOP), as the Republican party was known, was splitting at the seams. The Progressives were on one side, and the ''old guard'' was on the other. People were unhappy about the rising cost of living, which they blamed on the Payne-Aldrich Tariff. They also were upset with Taft's stand on conservation. As a result, the Republicans lost the 1910 election. For the first time in sixteen years, Democrats controlled the House of Representatives.

Progressives Form the Bull Moose Party

Following Taft's election, Roosevelt had gone to Africa to shoot lions and other big game. In 1910 he came home to a hero's welcome. People sang such songs as ''When Rough and Ready Teddy Dashes Home,'' ''Ho, Ho! For Teddy!'' and ''Mr.

Ask students to reread the material on the Bull Moose (Progressive) platform and discuss which of its proposals were later adopted. (Responses: direct election of Senators; adoption of initiative and referendum; recall; woman suffrage; worker's compensation; eight-hour work day; minimum wage for women; regulation of child labor; establishment of a federal trade commission.) Ask students whether they think the party succeeded. (Possible response: yes, although they never elected a candidate to the White House, it succeeded in bringing many issues to national attention and those issues were eventually addressed by the two main political parties.)

Assign Independent Practice

Have students complete Chapter 21, Section 2 Enrichment Activity.

Student Assignment/Homework

Have students read Section 4, "Woodrow Wilson Declares a 'New Freedom,'" and complete Chapter 21, Section 3 Enrichment Activity.

SECTION 3 REVIEW

Answers

Main Ideas

1. Taft was more cautious, more willing to compromise, and less willing to lead or persuade others.

2. He supported tariffs even though he had run on an antitariff platform; his appointees were careless about conservation efforts; he supported Joe Cannon's bid to defeat Progressive legislation in the House of Representatives.

3. The exit of liberal and Progressive elements of the Republican party changed the nature of the party; the Democrats were given a chance to win back the Presidency.

Critical Thinking

4. Possible answer: no—the national mood called for progress and reform. Taft supported conservative rather than Progressive causes and exhibited poor leadership in matters of reform. **(evaluation)**

Roosevelt Our Country Calls for You." Roosevelt responded by delivering a speech at Osawatomie, Kansas (where John Brown had spoken out against slavery). "Property shall be the servant and not the master," he said. He went on to say that the country needed a **"New Nationalism"** under which the federal government would extend its power and use it for "the welfare of the people."

Roosevelt—Again!   Taft felt that Roosevelt was attacking him unfairly. Roosevelt felt that Taft had fallen down on the job. "Taft means well," he said, "but he means well feebly." By 1911 Roosevelt was regretting his pledge of no third term. In February 1912 he decided to throw his hat into the Presidential ring after all. As he explained, just because a man says he does not want a third cup of coffee at breakfast does not mean he is never going to take another cup of coffee.

The Republican Party Splits.   An incumbent President, however, has certain advantages. In Chicago in June 1912, Taft's supporters seized control of the Republican convention. They refused to seat delegates who were backing Roosevelt. Then they renominated Taft on the first ballot. Roosevelt's supporters—screaming "Fraud!"—stormed out and held their own convention in Chicago in August. They formed a new third party, the **Progressive party.** It was commonly called the Bull Moose party after a statement Roosevelt made to Mark Hanna in 1900: "I am as strong as a bull moose and you can use me to the limit." Then, in an atmosphere of near-hysteria, the new party nominated Roosevelt as its candidate for President. After hearing Roosevelt, newspaper editor William A. White wrote, "Roosevelt bit me and I went mad."

The Bull Moose platform called for various Progressive reforms including the direct election of senators and the adoption in all states of the initiative, referendum, and recall. It also advocated woman suffrage, national workers' compensation, an eight-hour work day, a minimum wage for women, a federal law against child labor, and a federal trade commission to regulate business.

The split in Republican ranks had two main results. In the long run, it changed the nature of the Republican party. Since the Civil War, the GOP had been known as "the party of new ideas and positive leadership." Now, liberal and Progressive elements had shifted to the Bull Moose party. In the

Picturing History   Roosevelt, the Bull Moose candidate, campaigning for President in Morrisville, Vermont. The split in Republican votes gave the victory to Wilson.

short run, the Republican split provided the Democrats with their first real chance at the Presidency since Grover Cleveland was elected. In the 1912 Presidential election, they put forward as their candidate a reform governor of New Jersey named Woodrow Wilson.

SECTION 3 REVIEW

Key Terms and People

Explain the significance of: William Howard Taft, Joseph Cannon, conservatives, New Nationalism, Progressive party

Main Ideas

1. In general, how did Taft's personality and leadership style differ from Roosevelt's?
2. What actions by President Taft led many to criticize his ability to govern?
3. What were the main consequences of the Republican party's split in 1912?

Critical Thinking

4. Did Taft's policies and actions accurately reflect the national mood during his Presidency? Explain.

Anticipate the Lesson

Call on individual students to read their answers to Chapter 21, Section 3 Enrichment Activity. Ask students to develop a sentence or two that characterizes President Wilson. (Characteristics might include: calm; logical; just; humanitarian.)

SECTION 4

Woodrow Wilson Declares a "New Freedom"

GLOSSARY TERMS: **liberals, elastic currency**

Woodrow Wilson was born in Staunton, Virginia. His father was a Presbyterian minister, and his mother was the daughter of a Presbyterian minister. Wilson received a strict moral upbringing. After graduation, he became a lawyer but soon shifted into teaching political science at the college level. In 1902 he became president of Princeton University. In 1910, like Roosevelt, he was picked by the state's political boss to run for governor. Again like Roosevelt, once he was elected, he declared his independence of the party machine and proceeded to reform the state government.

A critic of Wilson once wrote that he was "born halfway between the Bible and the dictionary and never got away from either." Wilson was a calm, cool, highly logical thinker. He had a strong sense of justice and a conviction that he knew what was right and what was wrong. He was a humanitarian who cared deeply about people as a whole. Nevertheless, he found it difficult to relate to individuals. So he often seemed cold-blooded and an intellectual snob. He believed that social problems could and should be solved. He failed to realize, however, that people are often moved by emotion rather than reason.

Again like Roosevelt, Wilson believed in a strong executive. However, he favored a role for the federal government different from that favored by Roosevelt. Wilson did not think that trusts should be regulated. He thought they should be broken up. He did not think government should get bigger; he thought business should be made smaller.

Picturing History During the campaign, Wilson ignored the Taft-Roosevelt feud, saying, "Don't interfere when your enemy is destroying himself."

When the votes were counted, Wilson was the winner, and the Democrats controlled the House and the Senate. Wilson received only 42 percent of the popular vote, the lowest figure of any President since Abraham Lincoln. However, the combined vote for Wilson, Roosevelt, and Debs, all of whom supported Progressive ideas, came to 75 percent. The nation was obviously in favor of more political and social reforms.

Wilson's campaign theme had been a **"New**

Presidential Election, 1912

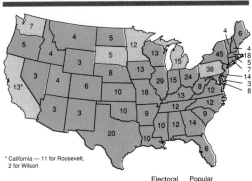

* California — 11 for Roosevelt, 2 for Wilson

	Party	Candidate	Electoral Vote	Popular Vote	%
	Democratic	Wilson	435	6,297,000	41.9
	Progressive	Roosevelt	88	4,119,000	27.4
	Republican	Taft	8	3,487,000	23.2
	Minor parties			1,136,000	7.5

531 Total Electoral Vote

For Discussion
What were some reasons for the split in the Republican party? (Possible responses: many Republicans were unhappy with the Taft administration; people blamed the rising cost of living on Taft's tariff bill; Roosevelt was denied the nomination at the Republican convention.)
What was the effect of the split on the election of 1912? (Response: the Republican party split enabled the Democrat Wilson to win the election.)

Ask students to construct a time line on the board showing major legislation passed during the Wilson "Progressive Revolution." Students should be able to state the dictate of each law.

1913   Underwood Tariff provides for the first real lowering of tariff since Civil War, from 41 percent to 29 percent.

1913   Sixteenth Amendment provides for federal income tax.

1913   Federal Reserve Act divides nation into twelve regions headed by a Federal Reserve Bank.

1914   Clayton Act strengthens the Sherman Antitrust Act.

1914   Federal Trade Act sets up Federal Trade Commission to investigate unfair business practices.

1916   Federal Farm Loan Act authorizes banks to lend money to cooperative farm-loan associations.

Check for Understanding

Call on individual students to answer Section 4 Review questions orally.

For Discussion

Do you think that the federal government has the right, or even the responsibility, to intervene in business? Should some vital services such as telephone, railroads, or airlines be owned by the government? (Possible responses: some students will favor government control; others will say that the government has no place intervening in business in a capitalistic society.)

Freedom," and it involved an attack on the "triple wall of privilege": the tariff, high finance, and the trusts.

Income Tax Replaces a High Tariff

Wilson began by reviving an old tradition. In 1801 Thomas Jefferson had sent his message to Congress to be read by a clerk. Since then, no President had appeared on Capitol Hill. When the new Congress met in 1913, however, Wilson, an excellent public speaker, strode onto the rostrum and delivered a stirring appeal for tariff reform. He also appealed to the people through the press. He asked them for help against the "Third House of Congress." This, he said, was composed of the lobbyists who tried to get tariffs for certain industries raised. Wilson's appeal to public opinion was a technique that he had used as governor, and one he was to use many times as President.

The **Underwood Tariff** of 1913 marked the first real lowering of the tariff since the Civil War. Overall, tariff rates were reduced from about 41 percent to about 29 percent.

The new tariff changed the entire revenue basis of the federal government. Before 1913 most federal income came from tariffs. The lower rates of the Underwood Tariff obviously meant a loss of revenue. However, the Sixteenth Amendment, which provided for a federal income tax, had just been ratified before Wilson was inaugurated. A graduated tax ranging from 2 to 6 percent was imposed on incomes over $20,000. At the time, few congressmen realized the possibilities of the income tax. Today, income tax on corporations as well as on individuals is the federal government's main source of revenue.

The Banking System Is Improved

After tackling tariff reform, Wilson turned his attention to financial reform. Both **liberals,** who favored reform, and conservatives, who did not, agreed that the nation needed some way to move credit out of such financial centers as New York and Boston and to make it easily available everywhere. The nation also needed an **elastic currency;** that is, the amount of money in circulation should change depending on the needs of the economy.

The Federal Reserve System.   Wilson's solution was a decentralized private banking system under federal control. Under the Federal Reserve Act of 1913, the nation was divided into twelve regions, or districts. Each district had a Federal Reserve

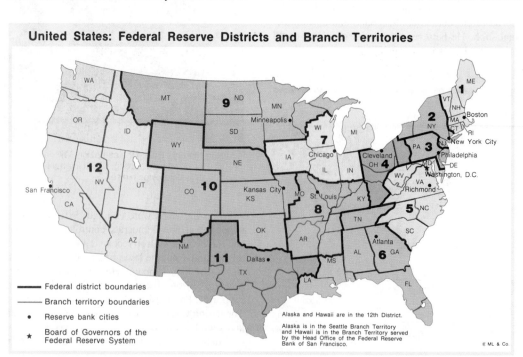

United States: Federal Reserve Districts and Branch Territories

Minneapolis
Boston
New York City
Philadelphia
Cleveland
Washington, D.C.
Chicago
San Francisco
Kansas City
St. Louis
Richmond
Dallas
Atlanta

— Federal district boundaries
— Branch territory boundaries
• Reserve bank cities
★ Board of Governors of the Federal Reserve System

Alaska and Hawaii are in the 12th District.

Alaska is in the Seattle Branch Territory and Hawaii is in the Branch Territory served by the Head Office of the Federal Reserve Bank of San Francisco.

© ML & Co.

Guided Practice

To stimulate discussion on current federal income tax problems, ask students the following questions. Is federal income tax excessive and unequal in its application? Would a flat percentage rate for all individuals and businesses be more equitable? (Possible responses: some students may say the income tax laws are fair since everyone pays a percentage of income; others may say they are unfair because there are so many loopholes for higher income brackets.)

Assign Independent Practice

Ask each student to construct a diagram that shows the structure of the Federal Reserve System. Display the finished products.

Federal Reserve Bank (12)

national banks   state banks

Student Assignment/Homework

Have students complete Chapter 21 Test on paper. Divide the class into small groups to review the answers.

Concluding the Chapter

Using their lists of Progressive reforms, students should write three paragraphs explaining whether or not the period from 1900 to 1916 actually deserves the title "Progressive Era." (Paragraphs might include: yes, because so many reforms were made, especially by Roosevelt and Wilson, in the areas of conservation, antitrust regulation, and working conditions.)

bank to which all the national banks within the district belonged. State banks within the district could join if they met certain requirements.

The Federal Reserve banks had the power to issue a new paper currency in emergency situations. The member banks could then use the new currency to make loans to their customers. The **Federal Reserve System** could regulate the amount of notes it issued by raising or lowering the interest it charged to member banks. If it raised the interest rate, it reduced the amount of money in circulation. If it lowered the interest rate, more money became available for loans. In addition, Federal Reserve banks could transfer funds to member banks that ran into trouble, thus keeping them from closing, and protecting the savings of their customers. Once the Federal Reserve System was put in place, it could control the nation's money supply by expanding or contracting it as the needs of the economy required.

The Federal Reserve Board. The Federal Reserve System was put under a Federal Reserve Board. This body consisted of the Secretary of the Treasury plus seven other persons appointed by the President. By 1923 about 70 percent of the nation's banking resources belonged to member banks of the Federal Reserve System. In 1935 Congress removed the Secretary of the Treasury from the Federal Reserve Board in order to protect the board from political control.

Farm Loan Banks. In 1916 a similar system was set up especially for farmers. Under the **Federal Farm Loan Act,** twelve regional farm loan banks were authorized to lend money to cooperative farm loan associations. Interest was limited to 6 percent, and profits were distributed to association members.

Trusts Are Brought into Line

Two main antitrust measures were passed during Wilson's administration. One was the Federal Trade Commission Act of 1914. The other was the Clayton Act of 1914.

The Federal Trade Act. This act set up a five-member **Federal Trade Commission** (FTC). The commission had the power to investigate unfair business practices, such as inaccurate labeling. If the commission found that a corporation was doing something it should not be doing, the commission could tell the corporation to cease and desist, or

stop, such practices. Both the commission and the corporation could then turn to the courts for a final decision.

The Clayton Act. This legislation was designed to strengthen the Sherman Antitrust Act. It declared certain business practices illegal. For example, a corporation could not acquire the stock of another corporation if that would create a monopoly. In addition, if a company violated the law, the company officers could be prosecuted.

The **Clayton Antitrust Act** further said that labor unions and farm organizations were not subject to antitrust laws. In other words, they had a legal right to exist. Also declared legal were strikes, peaceful picketing, boycotts, and the collection of strike benefits. Injunctions were prohibited unless there was "irreparable [unable to be remedied] injury to property."

The FTC handed down almost four hundred cease-and-desist orders during Wilson's administration. Samuel Gompers called the Clayton Act labor's "Magna Carta." The outbreak of World War I, however, slowed down the Progressive movement, and—as you will read later on—the effects of both acts gradually lessened.

SECTION 4 REVIEW

Key Terms and People

Explain the significance of: Woodrow Wilson, New Freedom, Underwood Tariff, liberals, elastic currency, Federal Reserve System, Federal Farm Loan Act, Federal Trade Commission, Clayton Antitrust Act

Main Ideas

1. How did Wilson's views of trusts differ from Roosevelt's?
2. What was the intent of Wilson's New Freedom campaign?
3. Why didn't the loss of revenue resulting from the Underwood Tariff bring about federal financial problems?
4. How was financial reform instituted during Wilson's Presidency?
5. How did the Clayton Antitrust Act benefit labor?

Critical Thinking

6. Was Wilson's New Freedom campaign successful? Explain.

SECTION 4 REVIEW

Answers

Main Ideas

1. Wilson favored destroying trusts; Roosevelt favored regulating them.

2. To attack the "triple wall of privilege": the tariff, high finance, and trusts.

3. The Sixteenth Amendment, providing for a federal income tax and thus a new source of revenue, was ratified prior to the passage of the tariff.

4. By establishment of the Federal Reserve System, the Federal Reserve Board, and Farm Loan Banks.

5. By recognizing the legality of unions, strikes, peaceful picketing, boycotts, and strike benefits and by limiting the use of injunctions in labor disputes.

Critical Thinking

6. Possible answer: yes—he lowered the tariff substantially, decentralized high finance, and helped pass antitrust laws that benefited labor and limited big business. **(evaluation)**

Lesson Plan

State the Objective

Use primary sources to understand the Progressive Era.

Present the Lesson

Remind students that most progressives believed they could change the ills of society by instituting various social reforms. To stimulate discussion on the progressive attitudes of Steffens and Roosevelt, ask students the following questions. What impression does Steffens give of Cox? (Possible responses: he was a shrewd, big man who ran Cincinnati from a saloon; he was a man who enjoyed controlling others.) What was Steffens implying about Cox's power? (Possible response: he controlled all political activity in Cincinnati.) Is Steffens objective about the way he presents Cox?

(Possible response: no—Steffens has already condemned him.) What did Roosevelt believe about muckrakers who uncovered evil and social injustice? (Answer: he thought wrongdoers should go to jail, but that sensationalizing evil caused more damage to the "public mind than the crime itself.")

Do you think either Roosevelt or Steffens would have objected to the type of investigatory writing done by Ralph Nader? (Possible response: both would have agreed that some cars and other products were unsafe.)

Focus on Primary Sources

Progressives Speak Out

The Progressive Era began in the 1890's and lasted until World War I. There were many problems, and many reformers who knew what the problems were. Sometimes it seemed they talked and wrote of little else. Those in the Progressive movement also knew, or thought they knew, exactly how each problem could be solved. Honest elections, efficient government, control of the trusts, equality for women, strong child labor laws, better education for all—these were some of the answers to the social problems of that time.

Lincoln Steffens, a leading muckraker, exposed political corruption in American cities.

> When I went to Cincinnati . . . I sought out Boss Cox. His office was over his "Mecca" saloon, in a mean little front hall room one flight up. The door was open. I saw a great hulk of a man, sitting there alone, his back to the door, his feet up on the window sill; he was reading a newspaper. I knocked; no response. I walked in; he did not look up.
>
> "Mr. Cox?" I said.
>
> An affirmative grunt.
>
> "Mr. Cox, I understand that you are the boss of Cincinnati."
>
> Slowly his feet came down, one by one. They slowly walked his chair around, and a stolid face turned to let two dark, sharp eyes study me. While they measured, I gave my name and explained that I was "a student of politics, corrupt politics, and bosses." I repeated that I had heard he was the boss of Cincinnati. "Are you?" I asked.
>
> "I am," he grumbled in his hoarse, throaty voice.
>
> "Of course you have a mayor, and a council, and judges?"
>
> "I have," he admitted, "but"—he pointed with his thumb back over his shoulder to the desk—"I have a telephone, too."
>
> "And you have citizens, too, in your city? American men and women?"
>
> He stared a long moment, silent, then

turned heavily around back to his paper. That short interview was a summary of the truth about Cincinnati.

Steffens, Lincoln, *The Autobiography of Lincoln Steffens* (New York: Harcourt, Brace, 1931), 183–184.

President Theodore Roosevelt was much admired among the progressives, but he thought they sometimes went too far, especially the muckrakers. Roosevelt's views on muckrakers are stated in the following excerpt.

> In Bunyan's *Pilgrim's Progress* the Man with the Muckrake is set forth as the example of him whose vision is fixed on carnal instead of on spiritual things. . . .
>
> There are in the body politic, economic and social, many and grave evils, and there is urgent necessity for the sternest war upon them. There should be relentless exposure of and attack upon every evil man, whether politician or businessman, every evil practice, whether in politics, in business, or in social life. . . .
>
> Expose the crime and hunt down the criminal; but remember that even in the case of crime, if it is attacked in sensational, lurid, and untruthful fashion, the attack may do more damage to the public mind than the crime itself. It is because I feel that there should be no rest in the endless war against the forces of evil, that I ask that the war be conducted with sanity as well as with resolution. The men with the muckrakes are often indispensable to the well-being of society, but only if they know when to stop raking the muck, and to look upward to the celestial crown above them, to the crown of worthy endeavor. There are beautiful things above and round about them; and if they gradually grow to feel that the whole world is nothing but muck, their power of usefulness is gone.

New York Tribune, April 15, 1906.

554

Mary Anderson came to America from Sweden and went to work in a Chicago shoe factory. There she joined the union movement, in time rising to head the Women's Bureau of the United States Department of Labor.

The seven years I spent at Schwab's marked my entrance into the trade union movement. Although I did not know it at the time, this was to be the real beginning of life for me in America. . . .

I did not know anything about the union when I first joined. A business agent for the Boot and Shoe Workers Union came to the factory and asked some of the girls if they would join. The girls asked me. I wanted to go along with them just to be friendly but I said I would like to know something about it first. We all went to a meeting, heard that a union would mean better wages and shorter hours, and then we joined. After a few weeks I became the shop collector for the union and in about a year I was elected president of the Stitchers Local 94 of the International Boot and Shoe Workers Union. . . .

. . . We worked a ten-hour day, from seven thirty in the morning until six in the afternoon. I would have to start to work very early because it was a long walk from my home on the North Side of the city to the factory on the West Side. After work was over I would go home for supper and then I was usually off to meetings that sometimes lasted very late. Fortunately, I was strong and well and enjoyed the work I was doing, so it was not too hard on me physically. . . .

[In 1910 Miss Anderson took part in a garment workers' strike.] In order to keep in touch with the picketers and find out when they were arrested, I was waiting about two blocks away from the picket line when one of the picketers came rushing up to me with the news that several of them were being arrested . . . suddenly I felt a hand on my shoulder and heard a gruff voice say, "You are under arrest."

It was a policeman who had followed the girl bringing me the message. When I asked why I was arrested and said I had done nothing and had not been in the picket line, the answer was just "Shut up! You are under arrest." He refused to let me telephone to the

LOOK BEFORE YOU EAT—
AND SEE IF YOU CAN DISCOVER ANY UNADULTERATED FOOD.

Picturing History The cartoonist's warning reinforced the theme of muckraker Upton Sinclair's novel *The Jungle*. In this book, Sinclair exposed the corruption in the meatpacking industry. The investigation that resulted brought about the passage of both the Pure Food and Drug Act and the Meat Inspection Act in 1906.

office of the [Women's Trade Union] league to tell them what had happened and made us walk with him to the Des Plaines Street police station. About six of the girls who had been picketing were there too. . . .

I was alone in a filthy cell with nothing in it except a dirty old cot and a wooden chair. The cell had an open sewer running through it and the smell was disgusting. . . .

Anderson, Mary, as told to Mary N. Winslow, *Woman at Work* (Minneapolis: University of Minnesota Press, 1951), 20–22, 53–54.

Analyzing Primary Sources

1. Why did Boss Cox point to the telephone to explain his power over the city?
2. What social problems does Mary Anderson's account address?
3. What crime had Mary Anderson and her fellow strikers committed that led to their arrest?

Critical Thinking

4. Would Theodore Roosevelt have regarded Steffens and Anderson as good or bad muckrakers? Explain your answer.

Key Terms and People

These are highlighted in the text in the order in which they appear in this list.

Main Ideas

1. Possible answers (choice of five or more): child labor, substandard wages, sweatshops, dangerous work conditions, links between big business and crooked politicians, unhealthy meatpacking, special privileges to big business from government.

2. Possible answers: taxation of railroads at same rate as other business property—La Follette in Wisconsin; secret ballot, initiative, referendum, recall—U'Ren in Oregon; direct primary—Wisconsin.

3. Assemblyman and police commissioner in New York City, civil service commissioner and assistant secretary of the navy, governor of New York state, Vice-President.

4. Possible answer: increased federal power; mediated a coal strike; regulated trusts; regulated transportation; protected health; conserved natural resources.

5. Signed a bill for higher tariffs, reversing his stand in his campaign platform; returned to public sale many lands Roosevelt had withdrawn; fired Pinchot; supported Cannon.

6. Republicans refused to seat convention delegates backing Roosevelt. Roosevelt's backers left the convention and formed their own party.

7. Presbyterian upbringing; studied law and political science; president of Princeton; governor of New Jersey; Democrat; reformer.

8. Attacked high tariffs, high finance, and trusts. • Underwood Tariff lowered tariff rates; Federal Reserve Act gave government power over banking and amount of money in the economy; Federal Trade Act gave power to investigate unfair business practices; Clayton Act strengthened Sherman Antitrust Act.

Critical Thinking Questions

9. Possible answer: no—Sinclair was exposing legitimate problem; even Roosevelt stopped eating canned meat.

10. Possible answers: growth of the social gospel; evils of the city, corrupt politics, excesses of big business, increase in mass circulation magazines, rise of socialism.

➤**11.** Possible answer: socialism was a European idea not needed in this country because there were more opportunities for good life here; Americans have sought conservative solutions to problems.

12. In the 1894 strike, management brought in scabs, persuaded the federal government to send troops, had the courts issue an injunction. In the 1902 coal strike, Roosevelt threatened to have government seize the mines, and mine operators agreed to arbitration. Difference was idea that government could intervene and help solve disputes in an orderly way with expert help.

➤**13.** Possible answer: Experience, bravery, was a problem-solver, had a sense of history, believed federal government should address important problems. • Wilson had similar qualities but was not as suc-

---

CHAPTER 21 REVIEW

Write your answers on a separate sheet of paper.

Key Terms and People

Explain the significance of: Lincoln Steffens, Ida M. Tarbell, Socialist party, commission form of government, council-manager form of government, Robert M. La Follette, direct primary, Louis D. Brandeis, closed shop, Elkins Act, Hepburn Act, Gifford Pinchot, New Nationalism, liberals, elastic currency, Federal Farm Loan Act

Main Ideas

1. Name at least five specific evils in society that the Progressives wished to correct.
2. Name several reforms the Progressives made on the state level. Who helped institute some of these reforms? In what state did the reform first appear?
3. What political experience had Theodore Roosevelt had before he became President?
4. Name six of Theodore Roosevelt's achievements under the square deal.
5. What actions of William Howard Taft made him unpopular with Progressives?
6. Why did Roosevelt's supporters form a third party?
7. What was Woodrow Wilson's family and political background?
8. What did Wilson's New Freedom attack? What legislation accomplished his purposes?

Critical Thinking Questions

9. **Analyzing Literature.** Do you think that Roosevelt's definition of a muckraker—one who is so busy raking the muck that the good things are not seen—was justified in Upton Sinclair's case? Why or why not?
10. **Identifying Trends.** What trends in American life had to come together to cause the period of reform known as the Progressive Era?
11. **Identifying Assumptions.** Review the history of this country as far as you have read it this year. Why do you think socialism has never been a major force in United States politics?
12. **Comparing Actions.** Compare Theodore Roosevelt's handling of the coal strike in 1902 with the industry's and the government's handling of the Pullman strike in 1894.
13. **Evaluating Performances.** What qualities in Teddy Roosevelt made him a strong President? What qualities in Woodrow Wilson made him a strong President? What qualities do you think a candidate for the Presidency should have?
14. **Analyzing a Quotation.** Theodore Roosevelt said, ''A simple and poor society can exist as a democracy on the basis of sheer individualism. But a rich and complex society cannot so exist.'' What did he mean by this?

Critical Thinking Activities

15. **Judging Actions.** Read more about William Howard Taft in a reference book. Then fill in the following chart. Do you think Taft should be called a Progressive? Why or why not?

Progressive Actions	Antiprogressive Actions

16. **Linking Past to Present.** Read the following quotation from Eugene Debs: ''As long as a relatively few men own the railroads, the telegraph, the telephone, . . . they will corrupt our politics, they will enslave the working class. . . .'' Might this be true today?
17. **Linking Past to Present.** Are cities better places to live today than they were one hundred years ago? Explain your answer.
18. **Linking Past to Present.** Look at the map of the national parks on page 547. There is a continuing national debate as to whether national parkland should be used for cattle grazing, timber cutting, and other commercial uses. Do you stand with the conservationists on this issue or with the people who think too much land has been set aside? Give reasons to support your answer.

The Progressive Era

The Progressive movement had several sources of support. One was religious. Another came from muckraking writers in the new popular magazines. The Progressives rejected socialism. They also demanded an end to corruption in city and state governments. In state after state, they won reforms. Today we take these laws for granted, but at the time these reforms seemed revolutionary. They included the secret ballot, the initiative, the recall, the direct primary, and the direct election of senators. Progressives also won court decisions that limited working hours and that compensated workers injured on the job.

Theodore Roosevelt made his reputation as a war hero and as the Progressive governor of New York State. As Vice-President he succeeded the assassinated McKinley. A man of great energy, he stepped into the middle of a coal strike and forced a settlement by arbitration. Although he tried to move against some of the trusts, he was more successful in regulating interstate commerce. One of Roosevelt's great interests was the American West. He adopted a policy of conservation, and he established millions of acres of national parks.

Roosevelt handpicked William Howard Taft as his successor. The new President, however, proved to be far less energetic and skillful than Roosevelt. Taft stumbled badly over the issue of a higher tariff. His appointees reversed some of Roosevelt's conservation policies. He supported the unpopular Joe Cannon, who was Speaker of the House of Representatives. Members of the House revolted against Cannon's dictatorial ways and greatly reduced his powers. Democrats won control of the House in the election of 1910. Roosevelt started the Progressive party, which split the old Republican party.

The split in the Republican party resulted in the election of the Democrat Woodrow Wilson. He was both deeply religious and highly educated. His first years in the Presidency saw major reforms in the relationship between the American government and the economy. Wilson spoke to Congress in person and appealed to public opinion. He pushed through a lower tariff and the first income tax since the Civil War. His establishment of the Federal Reserve System made the nation's currency much more flexible. Other laws put more teeth into the regulation of trade and of the trusts. At the time, leaders of labor unions rejoiced.

Chronology of Main Events

1901 William McKinley inaugurated President for second term; McKinley assassinated; Theodore Roosevelt succeeds to Presidency

1903 Elkins Act strengthens ICC; direct primary adopted in Wisconsin

1905 Roosevelt inaugurated for first full term

1906 Meat Inspection Act; Pure Food and Drug Act; Hepburn Act

1909 William Howard Taft inaugurated President; Payne-Aldrich Tariff

1912 Progressive party nominates Theodore Roosevelt

1913 Sixteenth Amendment authorizes income tax; Woodrow Wilson inaugurated President; Seventeenth Amendment provides for popular election of senators; Underwood Tariff lowers rates; Federal Reserve Act

1914 Federal Trade Commission set up; Clayton Antitrust Act passed

Telescoping the Times may be used as an alternative to having students read the entire chapter, as a chapter preview, or as a chapter review.

Global Perspectives

1885	Daimler develops the internal combustion engine.
1895	Marconi invents the wireless telegraph.
1896	Modern day Olympic Games begin.
1904	Tibet opens to Western trade.
1906	Egypt forces Turkey to cede the Sinai.

For Discussion

How might Marconi's invention have affected communication in the U.S.? (Possible responses: made communication faster and easier; turned formerly inaccessible areas into part of the mainstream.)

Additional Resources

- Geography Activities
- Skills Activities
- Thematic Activities
- Economic Activities
- Cultural Literacy Activities
- Literary Source Readings
- Primary Source Readings
- Nuclear Peacekeeping
- Transparencies
- Computer Test Generator

Additional Teaching Strategies

SECTION 1

For Basic Students: Have students research and write a two-page report on Henry Ford or Orville and Wilbur Wright that will include their educational background and their contributions to the transportation revolution. (Report on the Wright brothers might include: details about their initial experiments; their educational background; the transition from experimental plane to the first viable airplanes.)

For Advanced Students: Organize students into groups of three. Ask each group to choose a simple item that they might like to manufacture in a factory they own and to draw a diagram with explanations showing how the assembly line procedure would work in the construction of their product. Have students share their diagrams with the class.

SECTION 2

For Basic Students: Ask students to find and bring to class examples of newspaper advertisements for department stores, chain stores, a shopping center, and a mail order house. Display the ads, and discuss with students the advantages associated with each type of shopping. (Possible responses: department stores offer a wide selection of items; chain stores usually have lower prices because of volume buying power; shopping centers offer many specialty stores in a small area; mail order houses allow shoppers the convenience of shopping at home.)

For Advanced Students: Have students research and report on the contributions to urban development made by Louis Sullivan, Frederick Law Olmsted, or Daniel H. Burnham. Students may include photographs, sketches, or models to show examples of each man's work.

SECTION 3

For Basic Students: Ask students to write two paragraphs explaining how industrialization eventually produced the leisure time necessary for athletic competition, theater-going, and other recreational activities. (Paragraphs might include: better manufacturing methods meant workers did not have to work such long hours; they had more money and time for leisure activities.) Have students share their papers with the class.

For Advanced Students: Have each student choose a partner, and ask each pair to find and bring to class three newspaper headlines and the accompanying articles. Have each pair rewrite the headlines as they might appear in the *New York World*. Have students read the headlines out loud to see if the class can predict what the story might be about. Have students display the original headline and article and the new headline.

SECTION 4

For Basic Students: After they research the history of Mexico in encyclopedias or nonfiction books, ask students to work together to construct a time line showing Mexican-American relations from the time of the Mexican-American War to the withdrawal of American troops in 1917. Dates might include:

1845	Texas is annexed.
1846-1848	Mexican War begins and ends.
1848	Treaty of Guadalupe Hidalgo is signed and Rio Grande becomes southern U.S. border. U.S. pays Mexico $15 million and agrees to settle all claims of American citizens against Mexico.
1853	Gadsden Purchase takes place. U.S. buys land south of the Gila River.
1910	Mexicans revolt against Porfirio Díaz.
1911	Francisco Madero is elected President.
1913	U.S. investments in Mexico total $1 billion. Victoriano Huerta seizes government. U.S. refuses to recognize Huerta's regime. Wilson institutes a "watchful waiting policy." Mexicans wage guerrilla warfare against Huerta.
1914	Tampico incident occurs. Wilson orders blockade of Veracruz. Marinea seizes Veracruz. Huerta resigns. Carranza assumes Presidency and American troops withdraw.
1915	Carranza promises to protect foreigners and investments. Wilson recognizes Carranza's government.

Have students share their time lines with the class.

For Advanced Students: Ask each student to prepare a newspaper editorial supporting or opposing the U.S. government's refusal to recognize a foreign government that has come to power as a result of violence and force. (Editorials might include: support—the government is forcing a nondemocratic regime on a population that wants democracy; oppose—the country must be allowed to work out its own problems.)

Further Reading for Students

Constant, Alberta Wilson. *Does Anybody Care About Lou Emma Miller?* New York: Scholastic, 1988. Paper.

Holt, Rackham. *George Washington Carver: An American Biography.* Garden City, N.Y.: Doubleday, 1963.

Schwartz, Alvin, ed. *When I Grew Up Long Ago.* New York: Harper & Row Junior Books, 1978.

Bibliography for Teachers

Books

Davis, Allen F. *American Heroine: The Life and Legend of Jane Addams.* New York: Oxford University Press, 1973. Paper.

DeSantis, Vincent, compiler. *Gilded Age, Eighteen Seventy-Seven to Eighteen Ninety-Six.* Arlington Heights, Ill.: Harlan Davidson, Inc. 1973. Paper.

Educational Research Council of America. *Into the Twentieth Century (1880-1939).* Needham Heights, Mass.: Allyn and Bacon, 1977.

Franklin, John H., ed. *Three Negro Classics.* New York: Avon, 1965. Paper.

Hawkins, Hugh. *Booker T. Washington and His Critics.* Lexington, Mass.: D.C. Heath, 1974.

Magnuson, Norris. *Salvation in the Slums: Evangelical Social Welfare Work, 1865-1920.* Metuchen, N. J.: Scarecrow Press, 1977.

May, Henry F. *The End of American Innocence: A Study of the First Years of Our Own Time, 1912-1917.* New York: Oxford University Press, 1979.

Meller, H. E. *Leisure and the Changing City, 1870-1914.* Boston, Mass.: Routledge and Kegan Paul of Americ, 1976.

Twain, Mark, and Charles D. Warner. *The Gilded Age: A Tale of Today.* New York: New American Library, 1985. Paper.

Vandiver, Frank E. *Black Jack: The Life and Times of John J. Pershing.* College Station: Texas A & M University Press, 1977.

Walker, Robert H. *Life in the Age of Enterprise.* Melbourne, Fla.: Robert E. Krieger, 1988.

Audio-Visuals

The Gilded Age. Prentice-Hall Media. Filmstrip.

Great Men and Great Issues: The Progressive Reformers. Wilcom. Four audiotapes.

Great Men and Great Issues: U.S. Becomes a Great World Power. Wilcom. Four audiotapes.

Mark Twain Gives an Interview. Coronet. Movie.

Mark Twain's America. National Broadcasting Company. Movie.

Toward a Gilded Age. National Broadcasting Company. Movie.

The United States in the Twentieth Century, 1912-1920. Simon and Shuster. Movie.

Visions of Stephen Crane. Guidance Associates. Filmstrip.

Teacher's Notes:

Lesson Plan

Teaching Resources, Unit 5 Booklet

Lesson Study Sheets pp. 169-184
Daily Activities pp. 185-192
Enrichment Activities pp. 193-200
Reteaching Activities pp. 201-208
Chapter Review p. 209
Chapter Mastery Tests pp. 211-222
Telescoping the Times Study Sheet p. 223
Unit Mastery Tests pp. 225-236
Telescoping the Times Unit 5 Study Sheet
   p. 237

Chapter Objectives

Students will learn:
- how life was improved by early twentieth century advancements in transportation
- how changes improved urban life
- how changes came about in public education
- why the U.S. adopted a new foreign policy and refused to recognize a government that had come to power by force

Using the Chapter Time Line

How many years after the Dred Scott decision (see Unit 3 Time Line) did Booker T. Washington found Tuskegee Institute? (Answer: 24) Name two important milestones in U.S. transportation history that occurred between 1903 and 1908. (Answer: Wright Brothers' first flight and Ford's introduction of the Model T)

Picturing History Mark Twain aboard a riverboat. The Civil War ended his happy years on the Mississippi. In his new career as reporter, author, and lecturer, he gave us a clear picture of life in the United States during the late 1800's.

1880	1890	1900	1910	1920

1889
Jane Addams founds Hull House

1888
George Eastman invents Kodak camera

1908
Henry Ford introduces Model T

1916
Border campaign waged against "Pancho" Villa

1881
Booker T. Washington founds Tuskegee Institute

1903
Wright brothers make first heavier-than-air flight

Links to American Literature

Joel Gross: born in 1951; attended Columbia University; completed his first novel at age nineteen.

Works include: articles for *The New Yorker* and *Seventeen* magazines; numerous scripts for television and the stage; novels such as *The Books of Rachel*, *Maura's Dream*, and *Spirit in the Flesh*.

Sarah: pays scrupulous attention to historical detail of the life and career of Sarah Bernhardt, an actress who performed even after the amputation of a leg, and who hunted alligators, drank champagne while ballooning over Paris, and performed the title role in Hamlet at age fifty-five.

Introducing the Chapter

To stimulate discussion on recreation in our society today, ask students the following questions. What is the connection between increased technology and increased leisure time? (Answer: increased technology makes people's work easier and faster, which results in more leisure time.) What is the connection between increased leisure time and increased interest in recreational activities? (Answer: people want to fill leisure time with fun and interesting activities, and they have the time and money to spend on these activities.)

CHAPTER **22**   1880–1920

The Nation Comes of Age

Links to American Literature

This was Sarah's scene, not her partner's, chosen so that she would have center stage, the large speech, the long minute under the full glare of the lamps. She watched her scene partner move stage left, near the exit; he faded into the background as Sarah held the stage. Suddenly there was absolute silence. Sarah let a thin smile raise the corners of her mouth, knowing that her carmined lips would be visible to everyone in the house. She touched a finger to her left eye, she allowed a sigh to rise from her belly out of her throat and into the glow of the stagelight. Everyone listened, everyone watched. Then words came to her lips, syllable by golden syllable, so beautifully spoken that many in the audience were afraid to laugh at all. Sarah took no notice of the laughter or the lack of it. She was an instrument, playing a song; a spirit romped through her body like a divine wind, and nothing was more effortless, more joyful. There was no fear, only jubilation. She could have stayed there under the lights forever, but the scene was short, and the curtain was suddenly lowered, and muffled applause reached her almost at once through the heavy fabric wall.

— JOEL GROSS, *Sarah*

In addition to political reforms, the Gilded Age and the Progressive Era witnessed fundamental changes in people's everyday lives. This was a time of renewed interest in the arts and in foreign culture. The awe inspired by French actress Sarah Bernhardt in her American audiences is just one example of this new cultural passion. For students of history, becoming familiar with our nation's cultural and social past not only is enjoyable but is also necessary. Only by weaving together the different strands of history can we accurately represent the story of the Americans.

Chapter Overview

In this chapter you will learn about improvements in transportation and in city life and about the tremendous interest in education and culture that characterized these times. You will learn why the United States adopted a new policy toward countries in the Western Hemisphere that was to have far-reaching consequences. To describe these developments, Chapter 22 is divided into four sections.

Chapter Outline

1. **A Transportation Revolution Begins**
2. **Americans Improve Cities and Services**
3. **Americans Seek Other Improvements**
4. **The United States Intervenes in Mexico**

559

Anticipate the Lesson

Ask students to name occupations that rely on automobiles or aviation. (Possible responses: taxi driver; toll collector; pilot; air traffic controller.) Ask students to recall a time when they or their families have been without cars or public transportation for an extended period of time due to break-down, strikes, or snowstorms. Ask students what problems this caused. (Possible answers: was late for work or school; couldn't go out on a date; had to depend on someone else to drive.) Ask students to list on the board some ways that the invention of the automobile and the airplane changed life for the average American. (List might include: travel was faster and easier; goods could be more easily transported; mail got through faster; people could live further away from work.) Have students add to this list as they study this section.

For Discussion
What are some ways that Henry Ford revolutionized the American way of life?
(Possible responses: Ford made cars affordable and easy to repair; new jobs and services were created due to the availability of cars; Ford used the nation's first true assembly line for manufacturing automobiles; Ford paid workers better than average wages to keep a constant workforce; Ford proved that profits would increase if sales and production increased.)

SECTION 1

A Transportation Revolution Begins

GLOSSARY TERMS: **urban sprawl, free enterprise**

Beginning in the 1880's, the internal combustion engine was used in two major ways. The first was moving people on the ground. The second was getting people off the ground and into the air.

Americans Are Put on Wheels

The automobile was not invented by any one person. Rather, it was a combination of devices produced by American, English, French, and German inventors.

Commonly called the horseless carriage, the automobile started out as a plaything for the very rich. Early autos were as elaborate as the private railroad cars of business tycoons. One wealthy man, for example, had the lamps of his car plated with gold. The cars of society women contained sealskin lap robes for day and ermine lap robes for evening. Woodrow Wilson, then president of Princeton, anxiously observed in 1906 that ''nothing has spread socialistic feeling in this country more than the use of the automobile. To the countryman, they are a picture of the arrogance of wealth.''

All sorts of restrictions were placed on the use of early cars. In one California town, motorists were required to stop dead within three hundred feet of every approaching horse. Tennessee residents could take an automobile trip only if they posted a notice to that effect a week in advance.

Yet even then, some people found automobiles a good means of transportation. City doctors made their rounds in quiet electrics. Country doctors used gasoline cars during the summer and reverted to the horse and buggy when winter snows fell. Rural clergymen who served several parishes also found gasoline cars useful in their work.

The Model T. The person most responsible for putting America on wheels was **Henry Ford.** Born in 1863, Ford spent most of his youth tinkering with machinery. Later, he became an engineer. In 1903 he organized the Ford Motor Company. Five years later, he introduced his famous Model T. It came in one color—black— and its shape remained unchanged from year to year. As one historian observed, it ''looked like a creation only a father could love.'' However, it was a very efficient piece of machinery. It was tough enough to travel on rugged dirt roads. It also was easy to fix and was priced under $300. This price was easily within reach of the average wage earner.

Americans told jokes about the homely car. ''Can I sell you a speedometer?'' ''I don't use one. When my Ford is running five miles an hour, the fender rattles; twelve miles an hour, my teeth rattle;

People in the Chapter

Orville and Wilbur Wright never went to college. However, they were children of a minister who was interested in science and a mother who inspired them to think critically about mechanical things. They took their knowledge of bicycle mechanics and went on to build the first successful flying machine.

George Washington Carver today is acclaimed internationally as an agricultural scientist. He had many obstacles to overcome, however, on his road to success. After paying his college tuition, he had ten cents left. To get through school he lived in a shack and took in laundry, which he washed in two tubs that he bought on credit.

Nellie Bly was the pen name of successful journalist Elizabeth Cochrane Seaman. (The name came from a popular Stephen Foster song.) One of her early tasks as a journalist was to get herself committed to a New York insane asylum by pretending insanity. Her exposé of conditions there brought about some improvements in patient care.

Emiliano Zapata is recognized as a champion of agrarian reform. According to legend, he was motivated to seek land reform by reflecting on the difference between the dirt-floored hovel that was his Mexican home and the clean, tiled stables provided for his master's horses.

State the Objective

Understand how life was improved by early twentieth century advancements in transportation.

Present the Lesson

Divide the class into two groups to discuss and develop outlines detailing the development of the automobile industry and the airline industry. Outline of automobile industry might include:

I.   The automobile was developed by English, French, and German inventors.

II. Henry Ford was most responsible for putting Americans on wheels.
     A. Organized Ford Motor Co. in 1903
     B. Introduced the Model T in 1908

III. The automobile triggered many changes.
     A. Stimulated construction of roads
     B. Changed architecture—houses now had driveways and garages
     C. Created new jobs
     D. Enabled workers to live greater distances from job
     E. Provided new recreation

IV. First assembly lines operated in 1914.

and fifteen miles an hour the transmission drops out.'' Yet while Americans laughed at the Model T, they also loved it—and millions of them were soon driving the ''Tin Lizzie.''

Changing the Nation. Gradually, the automobile helped to change both the American landscape and American society. It stimulated the construction of paved roads suitable for year-round driving in all weather. It changed architecture; some houses were now built with a garage and a driveway. It created filling stations, repair shops, public garages, and tourist camps. It enabled workers to live miles from their job. It led to **urban sprawl**—the spread of cities in all directions. It broke down the isolation of rural families and substituted ''joy riding'' for sitting on the front porch. It spawned a variety of new industries and provided an economic underpinning for such cities as Akron, Dearborn, Detroit, Flint, and Pontiac. It attracted people to such oil-producing states as California and Texas. Instead of spreading socialism as Wilson feared, it became a symbol of the success of American **free enterprise,** which allowed private industry to compete freely with a minimum of government control. In no other country did middle- and lower-class people move about as freely as members of the upper class.

The Assembly Line. By 1914 the Model T was being built on the nation's first true assembly line. Until then, the car's different parts were built in separate areas. Then they were brought to a specified place where one or two mechanics put them together. Ford found, however, that this method did not produce cars fast enough to keep up with demand. So he hired Walter Flanders, a student of Frederick Winslow Taylor. Taylor was an advocate of **scientific management;** that is, he believed that you could increase efficiency by reorganizing and standardizing the way work was done.

Flanders put Taylor's theory of line production into practice. Instead of grouping all machines of one kind together, Flanders arranged them in sequence according to what was being done to the car. He also assigned the final assembly to a group of mechanics, each of whom handled only one part of the job. Soon, all the work was being broken up into increasingly smaller and simpler tasks.

Next, an electronic conveyor belt was installed to carry the gradually assembled car from one worker to another. Production soared. Before line production, it had taken twelve hours and twenty-

Picturing History Henry Ford drives naturalist John Burroughs (left) and Thomas Edison in a Model T. An engineer, racer, inventor and businessman, Ford put the nation on wheels.

eight minutes to put a Model T together. After the conveyor belt went into operation in 1914, it took only ninety-three minutes. The assembly-line technique has since been applied to most industries here and abroad.

The Five-Dollar Day. Ford announced another idea in 1914. His company would pay workers five dollars for an eight-hour day. This was more than twice the going rate.

The idea, which actually came from Ford's associate James Couzens, was designed to counteract the high rate of labor turnover at the Ford plant. The plant employed fourteen thousand workers but had to hire fifty-three thousand workers every year to maintain a constant work force. Ford workers quit in such huge numbers mostly because of poor working conditions. Workers were treated as if they were parts of machines. They had to repeat the same motions for four hours at a time without a break, and the pace of work kept increasing as the conveyor belt was moved faster and faster. Also, although workers were crowded very close together, conversation was not allowed.

Despite the poor working conditions, Ford's new wage rate stabilized employment at his plant. It also cost the company $12 million in 1914, leading to dire predictions by bankers that ''Ford's follies'' would bankrupt him. Instead, the company's profits rose from $25 million to $30 million. The next year they doubled, reaching $60 million.

Check for Understanding

Ask a student from each group to put the group's outline on the board and review its main points with the class. Call on individual students to answer the Section 1 Review questions orally.

Guided Practice

To stimulate discussion on the many effects of the automobile on American society, have students speculate on what life would be like today without the automobile. They should also consider car-related products, services, and entertainment such as drive-in restaurants, garages, drive-in movies. (Discussion might include: life would be slower paced; people would need to live closer to jobs; people would eat only fresh food native to their areas.)

Assign Independent Practice

Have students complete Chapter 22, Section 1 Enrichment Activity.

Student Assignment/Homework

Have students read Section 2, "Americans Improve Cities and Services," and complete Chapter 22, Section 2 Daily Activity.

SECTION 1 REVIEW

Answers

Main Ideas

1. It increased mobility, broke down rural isolation, led to urban sprawl, and spawned a variety of new jobs.

2. The assembly line, the electric conveyor belt, and the idea that the higher wages could lead to increased production.

3. For military purposes.

Critical Thinking

4. Possible answers: Ford—his profits increased tremendously, and although workers' pay increased, they had to accept monotonous working conditions. **(evaluation)**

Picturing History Orville (left) and Wilbur Wright with the *Flyer*, their heavier-than-air flying machine. The Wrights made four flights on December 17, 1903. They asked an assistant to snap a picture if their invention flew.

What Ford showed was that profits can increase if production and sales increase. When that happens, even though individual wages go up, the labor cost per unit of production goes down. In 1913 the Ford plant produced 30,000 cars. In 1915 the figure stood at 300,000. So the company was making much more money per automobile. Also, since workers were earning more, they themselves were now able to afford a Model T.

Americans Take to the Air

Apart from the ancient Greek legend of Icarus and Leonardo da Vinci's plans for a flying machine, the idea of heavier-than-air flight is usually traced to Englishman George Cayley. In 1799 Cayley said that the solution was not to imitate the flapping wings of a bird but to use rigid wings. He also described the kind of engine that would be needed for such an effort.

That engine became available in the late 1800's. Among those who experimented with it were two bicycle manufacturers from Dayton, Ohio, named **Orville Wright** and **Wilbur Wright.** The Wright brothers began by building a glider. Next they developed a wind tunnel to test how differently shaped wings behaved. Then they built their own four-cylinder internal combustion engine, figured out the best design for a propeller, designed a biplane with a forty-foot wingspan—and went aloft on December 17, 1903. The flight at Kitty Hawk, North Carolina, lasted fifty-nine seconds and covered 852 feet.

Public response was almost nil. Only two newspapers in the country even bothered to print the story. There seemed to be a "national suspicion that the sky was a place only for birds, angels and fools." Within two years, however, the Wrights were flying distances of twenty-five miles or more. By 1908 the United States government began to take an interest in the new machine. After America entered World War I, the armed forces used airplanes for scouting and in combat. The first transcontinental airmail service in the country started operating in 1920.

SECTION 1 REVIEW

Key Terms and People

Explain the significance of : Henry Ford, urban sprawl, free enterprise, scientific management, Orville Wright, Wilbur Wright

Main Ideas

1. In general, how did widespread use of the automobile change American society?
2. What industrial and labor changes were introduced at the Ford Motor Company?
3. How was the airplane first used by the United States government?

Critical Thinking

4. Who benefited more from the five-dollar day, Henry Ford or his workers? Explain.

562

State the Objective

Understand how changes improved urban life.

Anticipate the Lesson

Call on individual students to read their answers to Chapter 22, Section 2 Daily Activity. Discuss reasons why someone might move to a large city. (Reasons might include: to be near jobs, family, recreation, and shopping.) Review some of the problems associated with cities. (Problems might include: pollution; overcrowding; insufficient fire and police protection; water and sanitation inefficiencies.)

SECTION 2

Americans Improve Cities and Services

GLOSSARY TERM: settlement houses

Although the American city of the new industrial age was unquestionably filled with problems, it was also filled with wonders. There were skyscrapers that soared twenty stories high; electric lights that turned the streets from night into day; trolleys that moved at the incredible speed of twenty miles an hour; and giant bridges, like the Brooklyn Bridge, that leaped across rivers almost one-third of a mile wide.

Coupled with these wonders were attempts to make the city more livable. Some of these attempts had to do with the physical environment. Others had to do with the mind and the spirit.

Skyscrapers Solve Space Problems

Until the Civil War, most large buildings in the United States were three or four stories tall and resembled the temples of ancient Greece. After the invention of the elevator in the 1850's, the skyscraper became popular. At first its floors were supported by thick stone walls. Then, in 1890, the great architectural pioneer **Louis Sullivan** designed the Wainwright Building in St. Louis. It was the first building that clearly emphasized the fact that its framework of steel supported both floors and walls. Sullivan popularized the phrase "form follows function," meaning that the design of a building should express its purpose.

Many experts consider the skyscraper America's greatest contribution to architecture. It solved the practical problem of how to make the best use of limited and expensive real estate. It was also the towering symbol of a rich and optimistic society.

Urban Planners Create City Parks

As cities grew larger and more crowded, open space for recreation became increasingly important. The movement for planned urban parks began with **Frederick Law Olmsted.** In the 1850's he designed Manhattan's Central Park with boating and tennis facilities, a zoo, and bicycle paths in a natural setting. In the 1870's he planned the landscaping for Washington, D.C. Olmsted was also responsible for the initial design of the Fenway, the park system in Boston.

Another well-known urban planner was **Daniel H. Burnham.** He helped design the general plan for the Columbian Exposition, a world's fair that was held in Chicago in 1893 and drew more than 27 million visitors. Burnham also developed an overall park plan for the city. As a result, most of Chicago's lake front is a curving bank of green grass instead of a mass of piers and warehouses.

Although only a few other cities established park systems, most did manage to scatter small playgrounds and playing fields here and there. Many cities also boasted amusement parks on their outskirts. These were usually built by trolley-car companies that wanted more people to use their lines. These parks contained picnic grounds, bathing beaches, and a variety of rides. The first roller coaster began operation at Coney Island in Brooklyn, New York, in 1884. The first Ferris wheel turned in Chicago in 1893. Some amusement parks offered outdoor spectaculars. Twenty thousand people would jam the amphitheater at Brooklyn's Manhattan Beach, for example, to watch a recreation of the London Fire complete with rockets.

Picturing History *The Columbian Fountain,* built for the Columbian Exposition of 1893. The fair opened on the twenty-second anniversary of the Great Chicago Fire. Ironically, most of the exposition's buildings burned down shortly after the fair closed.

Present the Lesson

Prepare a chart on the board and head the columns with the following items: Architecture, City Planning, Stores, Settlement Houses. Ask the students to review the section to find at least two changes that occurred in each of these areas during this time and the names of people who made important contributions to each field. Have students add this information to the chart. Chart might include:

Architecture 1850's—elevator
1890—first skyscraper
• Louis Sullivan

City Planning Central Park
Washington, D.C.
• Frederick Law Olmsted
Columbian Exposition
• Daniel H. Burnham

Stores Department stores
• Marshall Field
Chain stores
• Frank W. Woolworth
1890—first shopping center

Settlement Houses Hull House, Chicago
• Jane Addams and Ellen Gates Starr
Locust Street Social Settlement
• Jamie Porter Barrett

Check for Understanding

Have students answer Section 2 Review questions on paper.

"Give the Lady What She Wants"

With concentrated urban markets on the one hand and vast quantities of reasonably priced manufactured goods on the other hand, it was inevitable that city merchants would change their sales methods. Among the major retailing innovations of the period were the department store, the chain store, and the shopping center.

The Department Store. **Marshall Field** of Chicago led the way in department-store operations. He began his career as a sales clerk in a dry goods store. He soon discovered that by paying close attention to each woman customer he could increase sales considerably. In 1865 he decided to open his own store and practice the motto, "Give the lady what she wants."

Field's store allowed women to take merchandise home on approval and return it if they were not satisfied. Field's aimed its advertising directly at women in such specialized publications as the *Chicago Magazine of Fashion*. In 1885 Field's pioneered the bargain basement, which carried goods that were "less expensive but reliable." In 1890 Field's opened a restaurant where women shoppers might lunch at their leisure.

Linking Past to Present

By the mid-1900's, the story of the department store closely mirrored the story of many American cities. When families started moving to the suburbs, department stores followed. Later, however, as sales in suburban stores slowed down, many department store chains renovated their downtown stores to draw customers back to the city. During the 1980's, department stores were prime players in the architectural rebirth of cities like Boston, San Francisco, and Chicago.

The Chain Store. In 1879 a retail clerk named **Frank W. Woolworth** found himself with a group of miscellaneous items. On an impulse, he placed them on a tray and priced them at five or ten cents apiece. By the end of the day, the tray was almost empty. Woolworth was soon in business for himself. Within six years, he had a chain of twenty-five

stores. By 1911 there were more than one thousand F.W. Woolworths throughout the United States.

The five-and-ten-cent store chain was followed by the establishment of chain grocery stores and chain drugstores. They did not carry as many items as the shoppers of today expect. Nevertheless, they used such modern sales methods as brand names, standard packaging, high volume, and low-cost sales.

The Shopping Center. The nation's first shopping center opened in Cleveland, Ohio, in 1890. A glass-topped arcade contained four levels of jewelry, leather goods, and stationery shops. The arcade also provided band music on Sundays, and it was a popular pastime for Cleveland residents to spend Sunday afternoons strolling through the arcade and looking at the window displays.

Americans Dine Out

City dwellers changed their eating habits as well as their shopping methods. Having meals away from home became common.

Business executives impressed potential customers at such elegant and expensive restaurants as Delmonico's in New York. White-gloved waiters,

Picturing History Members of New York City's high society, dining at Delmonico's in 1899. The Delmonico menu included such entrees as "Vol au vent of chicken and mushrooms," "Sweet-bread in paper," and "Mignons fillet of beef, Vernon"—priced at one dollar and fifty cents each!

Review with students the fact that one of the advantages of a city is that it brings together large numbers of consumers and enables a great variety of products to be sold at a relatively low cost. This trend continues as an ever-increasing number of choices is offered to the American consumer. Discuss how these advantages, in addition to the possibilities for cultural, recreational, and social experiences, might counterbalance the disadvantages of increased crime, pollution, and other problems. (Discussion might include: depending on the specific area in which they live, some students will say that the advantages outweigh the disadvantages; other students may experience very few of the advantages, and tend to disagree.) Poll the class to see how many favor urban, suburban, or rural living. (Possible responses: students who are happy with their current living situation will tend to support that area; dissatisfied students may see another life style as more desirable.)

Have students complete Chapter 22, Section 3 Daily Activity.

Have students read Section 3, "Americans Seek Other Improvements," and answer Section 3 Review questions on paper.

Picturing History Jane Addams reads to children at Hull House. Addams described the location of the house as follows: "Streets...inexpressibly dirty,...sanitary legislation unenforced,...paving miserable...stables foul beyond description."

imported wines, flowers, and music provided the proper background for the sumptuous meals.

Lower on the scale were short-order houses. These were designed to serve as many people as possible in the shortest period of time. A British visitor in 1876 estimated that the average urban American needed only six minutes and forty-five seconds to bolt down a full meal of pudding, pastry, vegetables, and meat. As for the noise, "There was as much din in the order of dishes and the clash of plates and knives and forks, as if a brass band had been in full blast." The meal was a financial bargain, though—only ten cents.

If all you could afford was five cents, you went to a saloon and bought a nickel beer. Then you walked over to the buffet counter and helped yourself to cold meats, hard-boiled eggs, sausages, and pickles.

Settlement Houses Offer Social Services

Along with places in which to play, shop, and eat, a few American cities provided places where people could obtain help and friendship. These places were known as **settlement houses,** and they were set up in slum neighborhoods by private reformers.

Settlement houses provided classes in such subjects as English, health, crafts, drama, music, and painting. There were college extension classes "for ambitious young people," and reading circles in which books were read aloud to illiterates. Settlement houses also emphasized social services. They tried to get "support for deserted women, insurance for bewildered widows, damages for injured operators, furniture from the clutches of the installment store." They also sent visiting nurses into the homes of the sick.

The leading settlement houses in the United States were Hull House, founded in Chicago in 1889 by **Jane Addams** and Ellen Gates Starr, and the Henry Street Settlement House, established in New York in 1893 by Lillian D. Wald. Jamie Porter Barrett founded the first settlement house for African Americans—the Locust Street Social Settlement in Hampton, Virginia—in 1890.

SECTION 2 REVIEW

Key Terms and People

Explain the significance of: Louis Sullivan, Frederick Law Olmsted, Daniel H. Burnham, Marshall Field, Frank W. Woolworth, settlement houses, Jane Addams

Main Ideas

1. What physical changes in urban environments were made during the late 1800's?
2. What circumstances allowed for the development of both department and chain stores?
3. How did city dwellers change their eating habits during this period?
4. What services did settlement houses provide to the urban poor?

Critical Thinking

5. What roles did women play in the improvement of urban areas and services during the late 1800's?

SECTION 2 REVIEW

Answers

Main Ideas

1. Skyscrapers and park systems.
2. Concentrated urban markets and the availability of great quantities of inexpensive manufactured goods.
3. They ate their meals away from home more often.
4. They provided a place to meet people and form friendships, they offered classes, and also social services that aided the sick, battered, injured, destitute, and bereaved.

Critical Thinking

5. Possible answer: women founded and ran settlement houses providing services to the urban poor; women also became major customers of the successful new retail stores and could demand more services for their money. (analysis)

Anticipate the Lesson

Write the term *public education* on the board. Have the students list some of its advantages in one column and disadvantages in a second column. (Advantages might include: is affordable; is available to all; has trained teachers. Disadvantages include: money for supplies varies from one district to another; classes are sometimes too large; politics sometimes greatly influences the operation of a district.)

For Discussion

How did public education serve the following groups: white males, white females, black males? (Possible responses: by 1910 the majority of urban white teenagers, especially boys, were enrolled in public high school; they studied history, literature, and vocational courses; high school graduates were admitted to colleges without entrance exams; by 1900 about four out of five colleges were co-educational but less than 10 percent of the student body was female; Tuskegee Institute was created to teach agriculture, domestic, and mechanical work to blacks.)

SECTION 3

Americans Seek Other Improvements

GLOSSARY TERM: **yellow journalism**

Changes in urban life were matched by changes in education, the spread of information, and leisure activities. At no time in our history was there more interest in such matters.

Educational Opportunities Increase

Between 1865 and 1895, thirty-one states passed laws making elementary school attendance for children between the ages of eight and fourteen compulsory for from twelve to sixteen weeks a year. By 1900 about 72 percent of all school-age children were in school, most of them in the cities. The curriculum was straightforward: reading, writing, arithmetic, physical education, cooking and sewing, and manual training (woodworking).

Almost every pupil used the same basic text: one of the six *Eclectic Readers* put together by William H. McGuffey. Like the works of Horatio Alger, the **McGuffey *Readers*** sold about 125 million copies. They not only helped students to read better, but they also stressed moral behavior and the importance of work. Here is an example:

1. Henry Bond was about ten years old when his father died. His mother found it difficult to provide for the support of a large family. . . . By good management, however, she contrived to do so. . . .

2. At one time . . . Henry wanted a grammar, in order to join a class in that study, and his mother could not furnish him with the money to buy it. He was very much troubled about it, and went to bed with a heavy heart, thinking what could be done . . . .

3. On waking in the morning he found that deep snow had fallen.

4. He rose, ran to the house of a neighbor, and offered his services to clear a path around his premises . . . . Having completed this work and received his pay, he went to another place for the same purpose, and then to another, until he had earned enough to buy a grammar . . . .

6. From that time, Henry was always the first in all his classes. He knew no such word as fail, but always succeeded in all he attempted. Having the will, he always found the way.

The Growth of High Schools. High-school attendance, unlike that of elementary school, was not compulsory. However, as the new industrial age developed, it became clear that the economy needed certain technical and managerial skills. Also, as Andrew Carnegie (and other business leaders) pointed out, one way to keep workers loyal to capitalism was to "provide ladders upon which the aspiring can rise."

The number of "ladders," or public high schools, jumped from one hundred before the Civil War to six thousand in 1900. The curriculum expanded to include history, literature, and vocational courses designed to help graduates find jobs. By 1910 the majority of urban white teenagers, especially boys, took going to high school for granted. Often, however, they did not remain in high school long enough to graduate.

Picturing History Laws requiring school attendance increased opportunities for immigrant children. The *Eclectic Readers* taught literature and morality.

566

Linking Past to Present

Today school attendance is compulsory in every state. Most states require attendance through age fifteen, although many states make exceptions to the age requirement. The nation's dropout rate, however, is still a major concern. In the late 1980's, approximately one out of every four students dropped out of high school. In the past, high school dropouts could find work in factories. Now that we are moving from an industrial to a technological age, this is no longer possible. In many urban areas, manufacturing has declined and factory work is no longer easy to find. In 1988, only 40 percent of the 1987–88 high school dropouts found full-time employment.

Higher Education. Going to college was another matter. Although the number of colleges doubled from five hundred at the time of the Civil War to one thousand in 1900, only a small percentage of the population were college graduates. Nevertheless, here too there were changes in both curriculum and admission policies.

Before the Civil War, colleges emphasized theology, mathematics, and the classics. After the war, the curriculum included courses in agriculture, engineering, economics, foreign languages, and the physical sciences.

At the same time, colleges opened their doors wider. State universities in the Midwest and California admitted high-school graduates without a test and charged only token tuition. More important was the admission of women. By 1900 about four out of five colleges were coeducational. The proportion of coeds, however, averaged less than 10 percent of the student body.

The Education of African Americans. In the fall of 1872, a sixteen-year-old former slave wearing the only suit he owned began a five-hundred mile journey, most of it on foot, from West Virginia to Hampton, Virginia. His name was **Booker T. Washington.** He had left his job as a coal miner to seek an education at the all-black Hampton Normal and Agricultural Institute. (A normal school taught students to be teachers.) Hampton emphasized vocational education, mostly farming and handi-crafts, plus some geography, history, grammar, and science.

In 1881 Washington opened his own normal school in the Alabama town of Tuskegee. It was called the Tuskegee Normal and Industrial Institute. Like Hampton, Tuskegee stressed courses that would enable its graduates to teach and to do agricultural, domestic, or mechanical work. Other areas were ignored. Washington did not urge blacks to compete economically with whites. Nor did he believe at that time that they should seek social equality.

Most white people in both the North and the South accepted Washington's ideas with interest and some relief. They were tired of racial and regional conflicts and thought that Washington pointed a way for whites and blacks to live productively and peacefully side by side. In fact, it seemed to many that Washington's ideas would keep black people in a position of permanent inferiority.

As the years passed, many black people began to disagree with Washington's philosophy. They wanted a more energetic push toward equal rights. Nevertheless, Washington's ideas were generally accepted until the early 1900's.

One of Tuskegee Institute's best-known instructors was **George Washington Carver.** Through his position as professor of botany he spread a knowledge of scientific farming throughout the South. Carver, in fact, revolutionized Southern agriculture by developing hundreds of new uses for the sweet potato and the peanut. He helped end the dependence of Southern farmers on cotton.

Picturing History George Washington Carver in his laboratory at Booker T. Washington's Tuskegee Institute.

Present the Lesson

On the board, write the terms *compulsory elementary education, public high schools*, and *state universities*. Ask students to determine how each was an example of the growth that characterized public education in the U.S. in the late nineteenth century. Write student responses on the board and discuss each item. Responses might include:

Compulsory elementary education
- By 1895 thirty-one states had passed compulsory elementary education laws.
- By 1900 72 percent of all school-age children were in school.

- The curriculum included 3R's, physical education, domestic science, and manual training.
- Education stressed moral behavior and importance of work.

Public high schools
- High school was not compulsory.
- New industries required new training.
- By 1900 there were six thousand high schools in the U.S.
- The curriculum included history, literature, and vocational courses.

Universities
- By 1900 there were about a thousand colleges.
- The curriculum included agriculture, engineering, economics, foreign languages, and physical sciences.
- Most schools abolished entrance exams.
- They charged token tuition.
- Four out of five colleges were coeducational.

Ask students how these changes encouraged the growth of public education. (Possible response: increased availability, low cost, and a new emphasis on the merits of education.)

Sources of Information Multiply

Education did not stop with public schools and colleges. By 1900 there was at least one good art gallery in every large city. The galleries were established by the country's new millionaires, who wanted to do more than just install art treasures in their palatial houses.

Also, by 1900 most American cities boasted a public library. Beginning in 1881, Andrew Carnegie donated about $45 million to build some twenty-eight hundred public libraries. The municipalities in which they were built provided the land and levied taxes to buy books and to pay librarians.

Technological Changes.   As the literacy rate rose from 70 to almost 90 percent, the United States became a reading nation. Newspapers, books, and magazines appeared in ever-increasing numbers. The technology that changed printing during this period covered four main areas: paper, presses, typesetting, and photography.

Prior to the Civil War, paper was made mostly from wastepaper and rags. In the 1860's, several German chemists discovered that paper could be made from wood pulp. By the 1880's, American paper mills were turning out huge quantities of paper that was strong enough to be used in high-speed presses and, at the same time, cheap enough so that newspapers could be sold for a penny a copy. This development put newspapers within the economic reach of many more Americans than before. Magazines likewise dropped in price, from the typical twenty-five cents to a nickel.

Printing was speeded up tremendously by William Bullock's invention of the web-perfecting press. Instead of printing on paper sheets, Bullock's press, which was electrically powered, printed on both sides of a continuous paper roll. It also cut the roll into pages, folded the pages, and counted the papers as they came down the line.

With strong, cheap paper and fast presses, the next problem was how to set type more quickly. Ottmar Mergenthaler invented a Linotype machine that was first used by a newspaper in 1886. The operator used a typewriter-like keyboard to cast an entire line of metal type at one time instead of going through the old laborious process of hand-assembling separate bits of metal, one for each letter.

At about the same time, changes occurred in photography. Before, photography had been a profession rather than a hobby. Because of the time needed to make a shot and the weight of the equipment, it was almost impossible to shoot a moving object. The first change came about in the 1870's, when new techniques eliminated the need for photographers to develop pictures right away. Instead of carrying the dark room around with them, they could send the film to a factory for processing.

Then, in 1888, came the major change. **George Eastman** invented the Kodak camera. It was light enough to be held easily, and it was simple to operate. It turned millions of Americans into amateur photographers. The Kodak camera also created photojournalism, for now reporters could photograph events as they occurred. In addition, the halftone process of chemical engraving, invented in 1880, made it possible to reproduce photographs and paintings accurately. Soon illustrations became common in newspapers, magazines, and books.

The Growth of Advertising.   Improvements in printing pictures reinforced the rapid growth of newspaper and magazine advertising. Expenditures for advertising rose from $20 million in 1870 to more than $70 million in 1890 and kept climbing.

Patent medicines received the largest number of advertising lines. Next came soaps, followed by baking powders. Royal Baking Powder, in fact, had the largest advertising budget of any product in the world. Next in order were cereals such as Cream of Wheat and Quaker Oats, the Eastman Kodak Company, and manufacturers of shoes, trousers, shirts, collars, and undergarments.

Picturing History
Famous advertising trademarks: a Quaker scattering oats on the Capitol (left) and Nipper, the fox terrier (below), listening to His Master's Voice.

Check for Understanding

Call on individual students to read their answers to Section 3 Review questions.

Pulitzer, Hearst, and the Yellow Press. JERKED TO JESUS and THE VALLEY OF DEATH are two of the typical headlines that newspapers of the new industrial age splashed in thick black type across their front pages. The first, from the *Chicago Times,* had to do with the 1875 hanging of four murderers who repented on the gallows. The second, from the *New York World* of June 3, 1889, referred to the horrors of a flood in Johnstown, Pennsylvania, in which at least six thousand died. These headlines were quite a change from such previous staid headlines as POLITICS IN ALBANY and CHARMING DOG SHOW. Then again, newspapers were no longer written primarily for the upper class. They were designed to attract the urban masses.

The use of huge, black, screaming headlines was only one of the techniques that newspapers followed in their drive for higher circulation. Equally popular were numerous promotional stunts and crusades. For example, in 1871 the *New York Herald* sent reporter Henry M. Stanley to Africa to look for explorer David Livingstone, who had not been heard from for several years. Stanley found Livingstone and became so interested in his work that he also became an African explorer. In 1881 the *New York Tribune* started a fresh-air fund to send children from the slums to the countryside for a week in summer. In 1890 the *New York World* sent reporter Nellie Bly around the world in imitation of a fictional character in Jules Verne's novel *Around the World in Eighty Days.* Bly made it in just over seventy-two days. Her reports, filed from places with exotic names, kept the *World*'s readers in a constant tizzy wondering what would happen next.

In 1894 that same paper printed a full page of comic strips in color. Several years later, H. C. Fisher's "Mutt and Jeff" became the first comic strip to appear every day. Other innovations included a large Sunday edition, a daily sports section, and a daily women's section.

The individuals most responsible for these changes were Joseph Pulitzer and William Randolph Hearst. **Joseph Pulitzer,** a Hungarian immigrant, began his career as a reporter on a German-language newspaper in St. Louis. He then bought two bankrupt local papers and combined them into the *St. Louis Post-Dispatch.* It soon became a flourishing enterprise. From there Pulitzer moved to New York, where he bought the *World* in 1883. With a circulation of 15,000 and an annual loss of $40,000, the *World* did not seem much of a bargain. By 1889, however, its

Picturing History An 1897 cartoon showing Pulitzer and Hearst riding over the falls of public protest.

circulation had jumped to 300,000, and Pulitzer was earning a million dollars a year.

How did Pulitzer do it? He hired talented writers and editors and set them competing against one another. He tried to arouse his readers to the evils of slum life and the need for tax and election reforms. Above all, he emphasized "sin, sex, and sensation." Since the *World* used yellow ink in its cartoons, the latter tactics became known as **yellow journalism.** Papers that used such tactics were referred to as the "yellow press."

In 1895 Pulitzer's newspaper leadership in New York was challenged by **William Randolph Hearst,** whose father had made a fortune in mining. Hearst already owned the *San Francisco Examiner.* His next step in building a chain of papers was to buy the *New York Morning Journal.* Hearst decided that the only way to compete against Pulitzer was to outdo him in yellow journalism. He proceeded to fill the *Journal* with exaggerated stories about personal scandals, animal cruelty, hypnotism, the imaginary conquest of Mars, and the like.

As the circulation war escalated, both papers became more and more sensational. The climax

Remind students that today, with the impact of television, many Americans do less and less reading. Ask students how the nation might be affected if the decline in reading, especially reading for news information, continues. (Possible responses: people may not fully understand issues or problems; voters may be influenced by how candidates present themselves on television.) Ask students what responsibilities citizens have to be informed about current issues. (Possible response: citizens need to understand the issues in order to make informed decisions when they vote.)

came in 1898 when the *Journal* and the *World* actually helped to prod the United States into a shooting war with Spain. (See Chapter 20.) By that time, each paper was selling 1.5 million copies a day.

When the Spanish-American War was over, Pulitzer apologized for the role the *World* had played.

> The great mistakes which have been made . . . have been caused by an excess of zeal. Be just as clever as you can. Be more energetic and enterprising than any other man if you can, but above all, be right.

Since then, yellow journalism has more or less faded from the scene.

Literature.   The outstanding literary figure of the period was **Mark Twain.** Born Samuel Langhorne Clemens, he grew up in Hannibal, Missouri, on the Mississippi River. He worked as a printer, a Mississippi River steamboat pilot, a newspaperman, and a gold miner before becoming a novelist and humorous lecturer. His pseudonym comes from his experience on the Mississippi. ''Mark Twain'' is the pilot's call for a water depth of two fathoms, or twelve feet.

Twain's most famous books deal with his boyhood in Hannibal. *The Adventures of Tom Sawyer* contains one of the great scenes in American literature, the one in which Tom gets his chums to pay him for the privilege of whitewashing Aunt Polly's fence. His most important book, *The Adventures of Huckleberry Finn,* describes how Huck helps the runaway slave Jim escape from his pursuers. Twain's work combines humor with social criticism. His main target was the hypocrisy of people. One of his major targets was religious hypocrisy. From a literary viewpoint, his books are significant because they employ humorous satire and an informal style.

Other authors of the period wrote about characters from various walks of life. They used vivid language and occasionally introduced violence into their plots. For example, William Dean Howells dealt with the triumphs and tragedies of a self-made man in his book *The Rise of Silas Lapham.* Stephen Crane in *The Red Badge of Courage* portrayed the feelings of a young soldier in battle for the first time. Jack London described the struggle for survival in the Yukon in *The Call of the Wild.* Theodore Dreiser in *Sister Carrie* told about a girl from the slums who ends up with a career. Willa Cather captured the experiences of the pioneers who settled the Nebraska prairies in *My Antonia.*

Americans Enjoy Leisure

> Oh, somewhere in this favored land the sun is shining bright,
> The band is playing somewhere, and somewhere hearts are light,
> And somewhere men are laughing, and somewhere children shout,
> But there is no joy in Mudville—mighty Casey has struck out.

These lines from the famous poem ''Casey at the Bat'' by Ernest L. Thayer first appeared in the *San Francisco Examiner* in 1888. In the 1880's people believed that any city that aspired to greatness needed three things: trolley lines, an opera house, and a baseball team.

Baseball.   Legend has it that the game of baseball was invented in Cooperstown, New York, by Abner Doubleday in 1839. It seems more likely, however, that baseball began as a children's game in the late 1700's and evolved into its present form.

At any rate, the first professional baseball team, the Cincinnati Red Stockings, took to the field in

Picturing History   This watercolor by the realist painter Thomas Eakins shows baseball players without gloves or a catcher's mitt.

1869. In 1876 the first professional league, the National League, was organized with teams from eight cities. In 1899 the Western League was formed; it was renamed the American League in 1901. Intercity rivalry was fierce. Even fiercer was the "world championship" competition between the champions of each league.

Other Sports. Another flourishing spectator sport was boxing. By the 1800's, it had become sufficiently respectable that women could attend.

The first great heavyweight boxer was **John L. Sullivan,** who won his title in 1882. The Great John L. fought most of his bouts with bare knuckles. He was a flamboyant personality and was extremely popular with the crowds. People were shocked when he was knocked out in the twenty-first round of a fight in 1892 by James J. "Gentleman Jim" Corbett.

What defeated Sullivan was the fact that boxing was becoming more scientific because of the adoption of the Marquess of Queensbury rules. Corbett had practiced using the new five-ounce gloves. He also took full advantage of several new punches, as well as feints and quick footwork that confused his opponent.

A third great urban sport of the period was cycling. In 1876 Colonel Albert A. Pope began to mass-produce bicycles. By 1890 indoor ovals in Chicago, New York, and Philadelphia were drawing even more spectators than the local major league baseball clubs. The first cycling championship race was held in 1893. Five years later, Charles Murphy gained the nickname of Mile-a-Minute Murphy by cycling one mile in less than sixty seconds.

Drama and Spectacle. During this period, dozens of acting troupes toured the country. Among the most popular performers were Sarah Bernhardt, the great French actress who spoke hardly a word of English; Lily Langtry of Great Britain; and singer Jenny Lind, "the Swedish Nightingale."

Like sports, the theater was highly organized. Bostonians B. F. Keith and E. F. Albee, for example, controlled a nationwide chain of more than four hundred theaters into which they booked talent. Other managers specialized in productions featuring a particular star. Charles Frohman, for example, created the first matinee idol in 1892 when he starred John Drew in *The Masked Ball.* Audiences, mainly women, came to afternoon performances and watched the handsome Drew with worshipful attention.

There were three main kinds of theatrical entertainment at this time. The first was serious drama. To most Americans, serious drama meant intrigue, discovery, swordplay, gasping death, and exalted language. In other words, audiences preferred Shakespeare's tragedies, especially when starring Edwin Booth. Booth had temporarily retired from the stage after his brother assassinated President Lincoln. However, the public welcomed him with open arms on his return, apparently feeling that family tragedy had increased his already great talent.

American actors were also popular abroad. Ira Aldridge was a Shakespearean actor of the time. This black American artist took Europe by storm and received both public and critical success as he performed in European capitals.

The second main kind of theatrical entertainment was melodrama. Melodrama had two forms. The most popular form was the so-called Tom Show, or dramatization of *Uncle Tom's Cabin.* Such shows emphasized complicated staging. People sat at the edge of their seats as real bloodhounds chased Eliza over ice floes that moved on a rotary belt.

The second form of melodrama was symbolized by such plays as *Under the Gaslight.* The heroine was tied to the railroad tracks and rescued by the hero just as the mail express came pounding down the line. Sometimes the roles were reversed. The hero was tied to a sawmill log and rescued by the heroine as the chain saw moved ever closer.

The revue and vaudeville comprised the third, and most popular, kind of theater. Both included songs, dances, comedy skits, and such specialty acts as ventriloquists and magicians. Revues often featured a chorus line of scantily clad females. Minstrel shows were performed in blackface, although one minstrel show, *Primrose & West,* had forty white and thirty black performers on stage together, each of whom received equal billing.

It was also in this era that one of the most spectacular events began touring the country. When **P. T. Barnum** joined forces with his rival James Anthony Bailey in 1881, they gathered together ringmasters and acrobats, elephants and stallions. With these they presented dazzling fetes and pageants, which delighted audiences under the circus tent. The annual arrival of "The Greatest Show on Earth"—the Barnum & Bailey Circus—thrilled children and adults alike.

Student Assignment/Homework

Have students read Section 4, "The United States Intervenes in Mexico," and answer Section 4 Review questions on paper.

SECTION 3 REVIEW

Answer

Main Ideas

1. Elementary school attendance became compulsory in many states; the number of elementary schools, high schools, and colleges increased; many colleges became less expensive and were open to women; and Tuskegee Institute was founded to educate a few fortunate African Americans.

2. Art galleries, libraries, newspapers, books, and magazines.

3. Spectator sports such as baseball, boxing, and cycling; the theater, including serious drama, melodrama, and revues; and the movies.

Critical Thinking

4. Possible answers: the McGuffey *Readers* blamed poverty on the individual, stressing that those who were moral and hardworking "always found the way." • At Tuskegee Institute, African Americans were taught the skills necessary for employment in a limited number of areas in society. • Harm—educators popularized and perpetuated stereotypes and harmful beliefs that have not yet disappeared. **(evaluation)**

Picturing History Entertainment and stars in the early 1900's: P. T. Barnum's circus; Charlie Chaplin; *The Perils of Pauline* serials; and *Birth of a Nation* (bottom), which, because of D. W. Griffith's film techniques, is considered the first real movie.

Going to the Movies. Live entertainment was supplemented by motion pictures. The first films were one-reel, ten-minute sequences consisting mostly of vaudeville skits or faked newsreels. In 1903 *The Great Train Robbery* introduced both

Westerns and a plot to the silver screen. By 1914 films consisted of two-hour features with such stars as Mary Pickford, Lillian and Dorothy Gish, Fatty Arbuckle, Charlie Chaplin, John Barrymore, William S. Hart, Harold Lloyd, and Douglas Fairbanks. There were also serials such as *The Perils of Pauline* starring Pearl White. As Pauline Marvin, a headstrong heiress seeking adventure, she fought off Indians, fell off cliffs, disappeared through trap doors in haunted houses, and was tied to a railroad track in front of an oncoming train. To the relief of her enraptured audience, though, she was always saved in the nick of time by her courageous boyfriend.

Probably the most significant motion picture of the decade was **D. W. Griffith's** *Birth of a Nation*, which opened in 1915. Three hours long, it told the story of the Civil War and Reconstruction from the viewpoint of the Confederacy. Audiences thrilled to its blockbuster scenes filled with hundreds of extras. In the North, audiences also rioted in protest against scenes that presented a realistic picture of the Ku Klux Klan and the lynching of black people.

SECTION 3 REVIEW

Key Terms and People

Explain the significance of: McGuffey *Readers*, Booker T. Washington, George Washington Carver, George Eastman, Joseph Pulitzer, yellow journalism, William Randolph Hearst, Mark Twain, John L. Sullivan, P. T. Barnum, D. W. Griffith

Main Ideas

1. How did educational opportunities increase during the late 1800's?
2. What sources of information, other than schools, became more available to urban dwellers during the late 1800's?
3. List the leisure activities that were available to city dwellers in the late 1800's.

Critical Thinking

4. What view of the source of poverty was advanced by the McGuffey *Readers*? What view of the position of African Americans was advanced by Tuskegee Institute? Did these views of educators benefit or harm the groups to which they directly applied?

SECTION 4

The United States Intervenes in Mexico

GLOSSARY TERM: watchful waiting policy

While Americans were viewing scenes of violence in movie theaters, wars and revolutions were raging around the world. In addition to the outbreak of World War I (which you will read about in the following chapter), an uprising even closer to home was threatening the nation. In 1823 the United States issued the Monroe Doctrine warning other nations against expanding their influence in Latin America. Under the Roosevelt Corollary of 1904, the United States asserted that it had the right to exercise an international police power in the Western Hemisphere. In 1913 President Wilson took the Monroe Doctrine a step further. He announced what historians call a "missionary policy." According to this policy, it was not enough for Latin American countries to protect American economic interests. Nations in the Western Hemisphere were also pressured to establish democratic governments of which the United States approved.

Mexicans Revolt Against Dictatorship

In 1910 the Mexicans had revolted against **Porfirio Díaz,** who had ruled as a dictator since 1877. During Díaz's regime, the Mexican government had offered tax benefits and other privileges to foreign investors so they would develop the nation's mineral and industrial resources. One result was that by 1913 United States investments in Mexican oil wells, mines, railroads, and ranches stood at almost $1 billion.

In 1911 **Francisco Madero** (mä de´ rô) was elected President. A well-meaning but politically timid person, Madero could not handle the conflicting demands of different Mexican groups. Poor peasants wanted land of their own to farm. Rich landowners, on the other hand, did not want any limitations on the amount of land they owned. Many factory workers wanted the government to nationalize industries, including those owned by foreigners. The urban middle class, however, wanted continued foreign investment.

After two years, the government was taken over by **Victoriano Huerta** (wer´ tä), a hard-drinking general, who ordered Madero shot. The American

ambassador urged the United States to recognize Huerta at once.

Wilson Adopts a Watchful Waiting Policy

Ever since the time of Jefferson, it had been the policy of the United States to recognize any government that controlled a nation. It did not matter how that government had come to power. Nor did it matter whether the government was democratic or dictatorial.

President Wilson, however, felt strongly that only a democratic government supported by the people deserved recognition. So he changed United States policy. Instead of recognizing Huerta, he placed an arms embargo on Mexico and urged other nations to do likewise. Wilson hoped this would cause the Huerta government to collapse.

Wilson's policy did not work. Moreover, American business people with investments in Mexico grew increasingly unhappy over the possibility that their property would be either damaged or confiscated. Wilson then reversed himself and lifted the arms embargo. Soon bands of Mexicans led by **Venustiano Carranza** (kär rän´ sa), **Emiliano Zapata** (sä pä´ tä), and **Francisco "Pancho" Villa** (vē yä), were waging guerrilla warfare against Huerta.

Picturing History Rebels in the Mexican Revolution, a bloody ten-year-long conflict resulting in the establishment of the modern nation of Mexico.

Present the Lesson

Ask students to construct a time line on the board showing the Mexican Revolution and America's involvement in it. Time line might include:

1910   Mexicans revolt against Porfirio Díaz.

1911   Francisco Madero became President, but could not handle conflicting demands of different Mexican groups.

1913   Victoriano Huerta took over and ordered Madero shot. President Wilson placed an arms embargo on Mexico. Unhappy American business people forced Wilson to reverse his stand. Bands of Mexican guerrillas attacked Huerta.

1914   Tampico incident; Huerta regime collapsed. Carranza assumed Presidency. Wilson recognized the Carranza regime.

Check for Understanding

Ask the students to write two paragraphs contrasting Wilson's "missionary policy" with the Monroe Doctrine and the Roosevelt Corollary. (Possible responses: Monroe Doctrine warned other nations against expanding their influence in Latin America; Roosevelt Corollary asserted U.S. right to exercise international police power in Western Hemisphere; missionary policy stated it was not enough for Latin American countries to protect American economic interests; they were also pressured to establish U.S. approved democratic governments.)

Focus on American Art

Picturing History   By the 1890's, it became clear that photography could be used to bring about reform as well as to document history. Jacob Riis, Edward S. Curtis, and William H. Jackson were three photographers whose visual representations made a significant contribution to bringing about reforms.

This photograph of Black Eagle of the Assiniboin tribe is one of a series of photographs by Edward S. Curtis that documents almost every American Indian tribe.

Jacob Riis's *How the Other Half Lives* became a landmark in the struggle for reform. In "Street Arabs—Night Boys in Sleeping Quarters," Riis captured the plight of homeless boys in New York City.

The photographs of William H. Jackson, such as this one of the Lower Basin of Mammoth Hot Springs, Yellowstone, were important in helping to establish the National Park System.

574

Tell students that since the issuance of the Monroe Doctrine in 1823, the U.S. has assumed a Big Brother role in the affairs of Western Hemisphere nations. To stimulate discussion on America's self-appointed role as protector, ask the following questions. Is this position justified today? Can we afford to safeguard all of the Western Hemisphere? (Possible responses: some students may believe that the U.S. is justified and even has a duty to protect the Western Hemisphere, that the U.S. is not imposing its democratic views but is supporting those countries in which the people want a democratic government; others may say that the U.S. has enough problems and should stay out of the affairs of other countries.)

Assign Independent Practice

Have students answer Section 4 Review questions on paper.

Student Assignment/Homework

Have students complete Chapter 22 Review on paper. Go over the Critical Thinking questions with the class.

Concluding the Chapter

Have students write a three-paragraph essay explaining the connections among increased public education, increased technology, increased sources of information, and the increased popularity of sports and the arts. (Essays might include: increased education and sources of information helped speed up technological progress; technological progress gave people more leisure time to enjoy sports and the arts; as people learned to enjoy the arts they became more interested in education and in ways of obtaining information.)

Picturing History
Caricature of Woodrow Wilson. His first venture in foreign relations was the Mexican Revolution. His watchful waiting policy satisfied few observers.

In April 1914 two incidents occurred. A group of American marines were arrested near Tampico, Mexico, for supposedly violating martial law. Although they were quickly released, Huerta refused to apologize. The refusal gave Wilson an excuse to order American ships to blockade the port of Veracruz, toward which a German ship carrying weapons for Huerta was heading. When the German government protested, Wilson ordered the marines to seize Veracruz in order to keep the munitions cargo from being unloaded. Some 126 Mexicans were killed in the operation.

For a few weeks, it seemed as if war might again break out between the United States and Mexico. A conference suggested by Argentina, Brazil, and Chile was held at Niagara Falls, Ontario (Canada) to try to resolve matters. Wilson stood firm. Under no circumstances would the United States recognize a government that had come to power as a result of force and violence. As it turned out, the Huerta regime soon collapsed. Huerta was unable to obtain arms from European nations. In July 1914 he resigned and went into exile in Spain.

After some maneuvering, Carranza assumed the Presidency in August 1914. Soon after, American troops were withdrawn from Veracruz. In 1915 Carranza promised that his government would not confiscate foreign-owned property and would protect the lives of foreigners. Wilson thereupon ended his **watchful waiting policy** and recognized the Carranza regime as the official government of Mexico.

Pershing Pursues Pancho Villa

In the meantime, both Villa and Zapata had revolted against Carranza. They feared that he would not reform the nation's land-owning system enough to help the great mass of peasants. Villa in particular was infuriated by Wilson's recognition of Carranza and made threats against the United States.

Then, in January 1916 about fifteen American mining engineers working in northern Mexico were taken off a train by Mexican bandits and shot. Two months later, some of Villa's guerrillas raided the border town of Columbus, New Mexico, and killed a number of Americans. Although there was no direct evidence that Villa had had a hand in either action, it was generally agreed that he was to blame.

After this incident, Wilson sent five thousand American troops under General **John J. Pershing** across the border with orders to capture Villa "dead or alive." For eleven months the Americans pursued the elusive guerrilla without success. In the meantime, the Mexicans got angrier and angrier over the American invasion of their territory. In June 1916 there was even an armed clash between the Americans and Carranza's army. Finally, in January 1917, shortly before the United States entered World War I, Wilson withdrew Pershing's soldiers, and relations between the two nations became normal once again. The Mexican people, though, had developed a deep distrust of "Yanqui imperialism."

SECTION 4 REVIEW

Key Terms and People

Explain the significance of: Porfirio Díaz, Francisco Madero, Victoriano Huerta, Venustiano Carranza, Emiliano Zapata, Francisco "Pancho" Villa, watchful waiting policy, John J. Pershing

Main Ideas

1. What was President Wilson's "missionary policy"?
2. How did Wilson apply his missionary policy to Mexico?
3. What American interests were directly threatened by revolution in Mexico?
4. Why did Wilson order General Pershing to invade Mexican territory?

Critical Thinking

5. Was Wilson's missionary policy democratic? Explain.

Lesson Plan

State the Objective

Understand the role of the multinational corporation in the global economy.

Present the Lesson

On the board write the heading Multinational Companies: Benefits to Parent Companies. Ask students to list reasons why companies might benefit from having multinational branches. Ask several students to write their lists on the board. (Lists might include: to use natural resources such as copper and oil that are found in other countries; to grow commodities such as tropical fruit, carnations, strawberries, and asparagus in the most favorable climates; to produce goods more economically in places such as Taiwan, Singapore, and Hong Kong where wages are lower than they are in the U.S.; to expand markets and to avoid tariff barriers that prevent importation of goods manufactured in other countries.)

Remind students that many economists predict that multinationals will dominate the world markets by the twenty-first century. The resulting global economic interdependence among nations could serve as a unifying force for the world. Ask students how the growth of internationals might result in unity. (Possible responses: if a corporation's interests are spread out among many nations, it will work toward peaceful relations among these countries in order to protect its interests; if a nation knows that it needs essential commodities from other

Focus on Economics

Multinational Corporations

Map Skills

Europe • Yes

By the end of the 1800's, a new type of company was beginning to emerge. It was called a multinational corporation. Economists predict that by the end of the 1900's, more than half of the business in the world will be conducted by multinational corporations. There are now several multinationals whose annual gross sales are larger than the gross national product of most nations. For example, if General Motors were a country, it would be among the richest nations in the world.

Economists usually define a multinational as a corporation that produces and sells its goods and services in at least two nations. Some economists specify that to be multinational, a corporation must operate in at least six nations and earn at least $100 million in gross sales each year. According to that standard, the Japanese dominate the multinational field with a strong presence in such key industries as automobiles, communications, and electronics. Multinationals are also known as global corporations. Some of the largest are Ford Motor, Exxon Oil, Royal Dutch/Shell, Mitsubishi, Xerox, and IBM.

Beginnings. The first firms to become multinationals were in mining and plantation agriculture. A company that mined for copper, drilled for oil, or raised tropical fruit obviously had to invest wherever it could find the necessary natural resources. Thus, the nineteenth century saw the rise of such early multinationals as Anaconda Copper, British Petroleum, and United Fruit.

After World War I, many nations put up tariff barriers against the importation of manufactured products. These barriers did not apply to products made domestically by foreign-owned companies, however. As a result, many firms got around the tariff barriers by investing directly in other nations' businesses.

Growth. The Great Depression and World War II slowed world economic growth. It picked up after 1945, though, when American firms realized that a profitable market existed in helping war-torn coun-

tries rebuild their economy. Another reason for direct overseas investment was the fact that goods could be produced more cheaply abroad. Wage rates in such places as Taiwan, Hong Kong, and Singapore were much lower than those in the United States. It therefore cost less to send a product's components abroad for assembly and then to reship the finished product home than it did to manufacture the same product in the United States.

Most foreign subsidiaries of American firms were industries that produced such goods as autos, cameras, chemicals, clothing, computers, electronics, and television sets. Sales of all of these items increased during the 1950's and 1960's.

Adjustments. During that same period, however, feelings against multinationals were becoming stronger. This was especially true in areas that had formerly been European colonies. One result was that some nations expropriated, or took over, foreign-owned companies within their borders. This led multinationals to begin working out more flexible arrangements with such nations. Instead of 100 percent ownership of foreign subsidiaries, multinationals often agreed to an ownership ratio of less than 50 percent. Instead of investing directly, they agreed to provide technology, managerial skills, and capital in exchange for a fee plus a share of the profits. As a consequence, multinational corporations have continued to grow, with annual profits reaching billions of dollars.

One of the most significant aspects of the expansion of multinationals in recent years has been the strength of Japanese corporations. In the late 1980's, Japanese profits doubled and tripled. However, four of the five most profitable multinationals today are American-owned: IBM, Exxon, Ford Motor, and General Motors.

Benefits. The impact of American multinationals on Europe since World War II has been considerable. American sales methods have successfully encouraged the mass consumption of goods. For nations, it might be deterred from war with those nations.)

Check for Understanding

Ask students to write out their answers to questions at the end of the feature. Discuss their answers. Ask students to imagine they are government officials in a less developed country and have been asked to give a report to the President explaining the benefits and disadvantages of business investment by foreigners. Divide the class into small groups to discuss these advantages and disadvantages. (Discussions might include: benefits—the possibility of learning new technology from foreign countries; the potential for more jobs and income, leading to better life styles; the potential for increasing the country's economic growth. Disadvantages—foreign corporations might use up local resources and take income and profits out of the country; they might cause pollution, disrupt local social customs, and drive local competition out of business.)

instance, the United States has increased the number of agricultural products sold abroad and the number of fast food restaurants there.

Less-developed countries—where many multinationals have established subsidiaries—also benefit. Multinationals bring in modern technology and modern methods of organizing business. They often increase local income in a dramatic way. For example, when an American engine manufacturer first opened a plant in India, the company needed three buses to bring its workers to the plant. After a few years, the plant's biggest problem was not the need for buses but the lack of parking space for the workers' bicycles and cars.

Drawbacks. In the long run, global companies often raise living standards. In the short run, however, they often disrupt the way people live. One example is what happened in Mexico when Sears, Roebuck brought in mass merchandising. The stores offered a greater selection of goods than most Mexicans had ever seen. However, the stores also did away with the social life offered by the old-fashioned local markets. Fewer social contacts meant a loss of neighborliness.

Such drawbacks may turn out to be relatively insignificant, however, when one looks at the best possible long-term benefit of multinational corporations. Many economists predict that multinationals will dominate world markets by the twenty-first century. If they do, the global economic interdependence among nations that is created by these giant corporations could serve as a key unifying force, and the world may edge a little closer toward peace and cooperation.

Understanding Economics

1. What are the characteristics of a multinational corporation?
2. In what ways can multinational corporations change a society's way of life?
3. What generalizations can be drawn from the map on this page?

Critical Thinking

4. Do the benefits of multinational corporations outweigh the drawbacks? Give reasons to support your answer.

FOCUS ON ECONOMICS

Answers

Understanding Economics

1. Some economists define a multinational corporation as one that obtains its raw materials and capital, and produces and sells its goods and services, in at least two nations. Others say that the corporation must operate in at least six nations and do at least $100 million worth of business a year.

2. Multinational corporations can help a society by bringing in modern technology and modern methods of doing business and by increasing local income. Multinational corporations can disturb a society by changing social patterns and by encouraging the production of luxury items rather than basic foodstuffs.

3. Multinational corporations must be truly multilingual in order to conduct business efficiently. Regional sales offices are located in major population centers of the continents.

Critical Thinking

4. Answers will vary. For examples of advantages and disadvantages, see information above in Check for Understanding. **(analysis)**

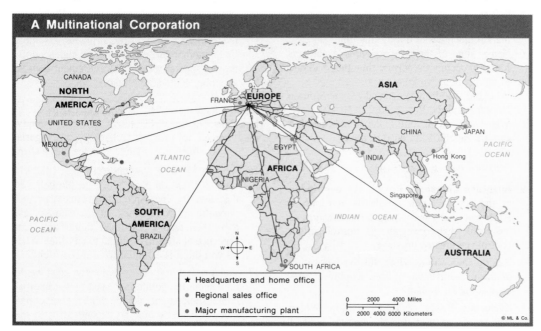

A Multinational Corporation

★ Headquarters and home office
● Regional sales office
● Major manufacturing plant

0   2000   4000 Miles
0 2000 4000 6000 Kilometers

© ML & Co.

Map Skills **Location** On which continent is the home office? **Region** Is there a regional sales office on every continent shown, not including Europe?

Answer Key

Key Terms and People

These are highlighted in the text in the order in which they appear in this list.

Main Ideas

1. Brought suburbs and urban sprawl; added garages and driveways to houses; created jobs to service cars.

2. Assembly line made jobs more specialized; created new jobs; made it possible to produce more.

3. Cities were the site of improvements: skyscrapers, department stores, amusement parks, theaters, sports, cheap transportation, settlement houses. • Olmsted created parks in cities; Burnham created plans for growing cities.

4. Innovations—bargain basement, restaurants in stores, chain stores, volume buying.

5. Manufacture of paper from wood pulp; presses that printed continuously; new cameras and methods of processing film; methods of typesetting.

➤**6.** Leisure reading, sports events, theater, movies, amusement parks, shopping, evening education.

7. Added the "missionary policy" under which U.S. actively sought to establish democratic governments in Latin American countries.

8. Because Villa was thought to be responsible for terrorist acts, Wilson felt justified in pursuing him in his own country.

Critical Thinking Questions

9. Sarah held the stage: everyone listened; everyone watched; words…so beautifully spoken; she was an instrument; playing a song; nothing was more effortless, more joyful.

10. Workers were more willing to withstand bad working conditions for higher pay.

➤**11.** Possible answers: railroads made the move west

easier; automobiles give individual control over transportation; airplanes decrease travel time and allow people to visit faraway places.

12. Education could give a worker skills to move out of a boring assembly line job into a responsible managerial job. • McGuffey *Readers* stressed ambition and good behavior; students learned to read and were given a model for success in life at the same time.

13. During the competitive publishing race with Hearst, Pulitzer printed lies; later, he had the courage to apologize for lying.

14. That a one-hundred-year old tradition of recognizing any government that took control of a nation would continue under Wilson. • That the government would not be democratic.

Critical Thinking Activities

15. Possible answer: electric lights made possible activities after dark; assembly line made more products possible; settlement houses gave aid to poor and needy in cities, automobiles gave people independence, high schools provided more educational opportunities.

CHAPTER 22 REVIEW

Write your answers on a separate piece of paper.

Key Terms and People

Explain the significance of : free enterprise, Booker T. Washington, George Washington Carver, George Eastman, yellow journalism, Mark Twain, John L. Sullivan, D. W. Griffith, Porfirio Díaz, Francisco Madero, Venustiano Carranza, Emiliano Zapata

Main Ideas

1. How did the automobile change the face of the nation?
2. How did scientific management as used in the manufacture of the automobile change the working habits of the nation?
3. How did cities grow more liveable between 1880 and 1920? Name one or two of the people whose talents helped in this transformation.
4. How did the retail world led by Marshall Field and Frank W. Woolworth change during this period?
5. What new technologies made access to information much easier during this time?
6. Name some of the new activities Americans found to occupy the leisure time they had due to the ten-hour workday laws.
7. What did Woodrow Wilson add to the Monroe Doctrine and the Roosevelt Corollary?
8. Why was General John J. Pershing ordered to capture Pancho Villa dead or alive?

Critical Thinking Questions

9. **Analyzing Literature.** Review the description of the actress Sarah Bernhardt in Links to American Literature on page 559. List some of the details that convey the illusion of perfect control she created on stage.
10. **Making Deductions.** How did the innovation of the five-dollar day reduce employee turnover at the Ford plant?
11. **Evaluating Means of Transportation.** Which method of transportation changed the lives of Americans most: the railroad, the automobile, or the airplane? Give reasons for your answer.

12. **Making Deductions.** Why was education so important in preparing young people for a place in industry? How did the McGuffey *Readers* help motivate students?
13. **Judging Values.** Why did Joseph Pulitzer apologize to the country for the role his newspaper played in the Spanish-American War?
14. **Identifying Assumptions.** When Victoriano Huerta took over the Mexican government in 1913, what did the American ambassador assume by urging President Wilson to recognize Huerta's government at once? What assumption did Woodrow Wilson make when instead he adopted his policy of watchful waiting?

Critical Thinking Activities

15. **Making Judgments.** The items listed below came into being between 1880 and 1920. Choose five you think are most important and complete the chart. Put your five choices in order from most important to least important. Be ready to defend your order. Choose from the following: advertising, airplanes, assembly line, automobiles, electric lights, high schools, movies, parks, restaurants, settlement houses, shopping centers, skyscrapers.

Item	Why Important?

16. **Linking Past to Present.** "In the 1880's," states the text on page 570, "people believed that any city that aspired to greatness needed three things: trolley lines, an opera house, and a baseball team." Do these things represent aspects that are still essential to city life? What do you think is essential for a modern city?
17. **Linking Past to Present.** Knowing what we do now about the pollution caused by the internal combustion engine, do you think it good or bad that we have become so dependent upon the automobile? If we did not have the automobile, what might have taken its place?

TELESCOPING THE TIMES: 1880–1920

The Nation Comes of Age

In the early 1900's, a transportation revolution occurred. Automobiles helped to change American society. Henry Ford made the Model T at a low price and kept the same black paint and style year after year. Automobiles scattered Americans across long distances, but the new machines also brought them together. Today, we take for granted many of the changes brought about by the automobile. They include paved roads, filling stations, and public garages. Ford's assembly lines and five-dollar workday revolutionized the nation's factories. The Wright brothers' airplane also offered new possibilities. This incredible invention was used in World War I.

Other inventions soon transformed cities and services. The combination of steel and the electric elevator changed American cities. The new buildings were so tall that they were called skyscrapers. As cities became more crowded, Olmsted and others designed urban parks. Businessmen saw new challenges in the growing cities. Marshall Field's department store and F. W. Woolworth's chain store paved the way to new methods of merchandising. The first shopping center appeared in the 1890's. Short-order restaurants became popular. At the same time, poor people were suffering from bad housing and ill health. A few reformers organized settlement houses to help meet the needs of the poverty-stricken.

Education was a high priority for most Americans. After the Civil War, many states passed laws that required every child to go to school through the eighth grade. High school came into fashion. Many colleges were established. Some even admitted women. Separate colleges gave African Americans a chance at higher education. Public libraries multiplied. New inventions in printing and communications expanded newspaper coverage. The Pulitzer-Hearst newspaper battle showed the power of yellow journalism. The camera brought new ways of looking at the world. Americans began to enjoy baseball, boxing, and other sports. They also loved the theater and, later, the movies.

On the southern border, Anglo-Americans and Mexicans came very close to war after Mexico's 1910 revolution. For several years the Mexican government was shaken by political difficulties. Wilson thought that Mexican officials such as Madero and Huerta were corrupt and refused to recognize the new government. He adopted a foreign policy toward Mexico that did not work. In 1916 fighting broke out. Wilson ordered United States troops under General Pershing into Mexican territory. The President withdrew Pershing's soldiers early in 1917, however, because the United States was about to enter World War I.

Chronology of Main Events

1881 Booker T. Washington founds Tuskegee Institute

1888 George Eastman invents Kodak camera

1889 Jane Addams founds Hull House

1890 Nation's first shopping center opened, in Cleveland

1903 Wright brothers make first heavier-than-air flight

1908 Henry Ford introduces Model T

1914 Wilson orders seizure of Veracruz

1915 U.S. recognizes Carranza regime

1916 Border campaign waged against Francisco "Pancho" Villa

Telescoping the Times may be used as an alternative to having students read the entire chapter, as a chapter preview, or as a chapter review.

State the Objective

Understand patterns of colonization and the fight for independence in Africa.

Present the Lesson

Ask students why Europeans and Americans took an interest in Africa in the last half of the nineteenth century. (Possible responses: Western missionaries viewed Africa as an opportunity to spread Christianity; explorers were curious and intrigued by Africa's mysteries, jungles, wildlife, and vegetation; *New York Herald* reporter Henry Stanley's trip to find the lost Dr. Livingstone in Africa heightened interest in that country; European interest in Africa was spurred by the Industrial Revolution and the possibility of finding raw materials and markets in that country.)

Ask students to describe events and conditions that led African nations to independence between 1945 and 1980. (Possible responses: the colonizing powers took much of the land's raw materials and the people of the area did not get a fair share; WWII fueled the desire for independence in Africa; Portugal and France gave up their colonies after bloody wars; many Europeans were weary of war and peacefully relinquished control of their colonies after World War II.)

Focus on Global Events

The Rush to Colonize Africa

Map Skills

France, Great Britain
• Belgium

The end of the slave trade conducted by Americans and Europeans did not mean the end of European interest in Africa. During the late 1800's, the seven European nations of Great Britain, France, Germany, Portugal, Italy, Belgium, and Spain divided almost the entire African continent among themselves.

Begun by Missionaries and Explorers. In the early 1800's, Christian missionaries and explorers made journeys to Africa. Their reports on the African interior, the exotic vegetation, and the animal life stimulated the imagination of the world.

In 1871 the *New York Herald* backed reporter Henry Morton Stanley's trip to find Dr. David Livingstone, a Scottish missionary who had disappeared in the heart of Africa. Millions of newspaper readers followed Stanley's trip with high excitement. After an eight-month march from the east coast of Africa into the interior, Stanley did find Dr. Livingstone on the shores of Lake Tanganyika. The rejoicing was worldwide, and interest in Africa increased. Explorers pushed into the African interior, searching for the sources of the Nile and the Congo rivers. The explorers were soon followed by traders, who hoped to find new buyers among the African people for their goods.

Fueled by Greed. At first the Europeans were interested only in developing trade and introducing the Africans to Christianity. However, Europe was now in the midst of the Industrial Revolution. Africa, which had previously been neglected except as a source of slaves, loomed as a source of raw materials. Furthermore, as scientists developed drugs to combat tropical diseases and as technologists produced superior weapons, the Europeans became more interested in taking control of the continent.

The change came quickly. In 1850 the only two European powers with influence in Africa were the British, who had replaced the Dutch in the Cape Colony of South Africa, and the French, who had occupied Algeria. About sixty years later, however, the only two independent countries remaining in

Africa were Liberia—founded by ex-slaves from the United States—and Ethiopia. The rest of Africa had been divided into colonies by European powers.

To avoid fighting with each other, the nations carved up Africa by diplomatic (and often secret) agreements. Nevertheless, the competition for African land led to increasingly serious confrontations and finally became a major cause of World War I.

Carved by Agreement. While the partition of Africa was in progress, an International Congress met in Berlin in 1885 to discuss the issue. The vast basin of the Congo River was given to King Leopold of Belgium and became known as the Belgian Congo. The powers in Berlin then agreed that they would not disturb claims already staked out in Africa. The French had claimed all of the Sahara and part of Equatorial Africa in 1880, and Tunisia in 1881. Later, in 1912, the French also laid claim to Morocco, but recognized three areas of Spanish influence.

Britain, which had taken control of Egypt in 1881, extended its power southward. The Anglo-Egyptian Sudan was taken between 1883 and 1898, Uganda in 1890, and what came to be called British East Africa in 1886. From the Cape Colony, the British extended their power north to take control of Rhodesia (known today as Zimbabwe) in 1890 and the Orange Free State and the Transvaal by 1902. (In 1910, the Orange Free State and the Transvaal became part of the Union of South Africa.) In general, French colonies were in West Africa and the English colonies, except for Nigeria, Ghana (known then as the Gold Coast), and Sierra Leone, were in East Africa. Even today the second language in most West African countries is French and in most East African countries is English.

Germany was a latecomer to this African feast and, as a result, got only the leavings. The territory now consisting chiefly of Tanzania, Rwanda, and Burundi became known as German East Africa. The nation that is known today as

Ask students to write out answers to the questions at the end of the feature. Review the answers with the class. Have students play the role of American newspaper reporters sent to Europe to cover the 1885 International Congress in Berlin. Ask students to write news articles describing the purpose of the conference and some of the major decisions made at the conference. Have several students read their articles to the class. (Stories might include: the Congress met to discuss the partition of Africa; the claims already staked out in Africa would not be disturbed; King Leopold of Bel-

gium was given the vast basin of the Congo River which became the Belgian Congo; the French claimed the Sahara, part of Equatorial Africa, and Tunisia.)

Namibia became German Southwest Africa. The Germans also took the Cameroons and tropical Togoland, which is now partly Togo and partly Ghana. (Germany was forced to give up its colonies after its defeat in World War I.)

Portugal revived numerous land claims that dated from the Portuguese exploration of the 1400's. Most people had forgotten them. The Portuguese claimed Cabinda, Angola, and Portuguese Guinea (the former name of Guinea-Bissau) in the west and Portuguese East Africa (known today as Mozambique). Spain contented itself with Rio de Oro (the former name of Western Sahara) and three zones of Morocco, which they called Spanish Morocco.

Colonial Conditions. Some colonies did not accept their fate quietly, and riots and revolts ensued. By 1920, however, the colonizing powers were in full control. Life in the colonies varied. In general, Africans received more education than they had before. Highways, railroads, and airfields were built. New cities and new jobs developed.

In the south an industrial society was established, but the Africans did not benefit much from it. They got the lowest paying jobs and, in most areas, had to live strictly segregated from the Europeans.

In more tropical areas, Europeans ruled with the help of the African population. In Nigeria the British ruled through Nigerian officials. This practice was called indirect rule.

In many colonies there was more prosperity than ever before. However, the colonizing power often took much of the land's raw materials and did not give the people of the area a fair share. No matter how well off Africans were, they could not forget that they were not really independent.

Independence Explosions. After World War II, the desire for independence swept through Africa like a forest fire. The European colonial powers, exhausted by the war, had to make a decision. Did they have the energy and power to engage in more wars to keep their colonies? Or would they give them up? Portugal fought a series of wars with its colonies. France underwent a bloody eight-year war to keep control of Algeria. Both countries failed. Their colonies became independent.

The other European nations gave up their colonies more or less gracefully. Most nations of Africa became independent even faster than they had become colonies. Between 1951 and 1977,

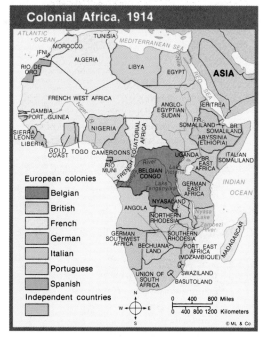

Colonial Africa, 1914

European colonies
- Belgian
- British
- French
- German
- Italian
- Portuguese
- Spanish
- Independent countries

Map Skills **Region** Which two European countries had the largest African empires? **Location** Which controlled the smallest coastal area?

forty-two nations in Africa became independent. In 1989 U.N. peacekeeping troops moved into Namibia, the only remaining non-independent territory in Africa, and in 1990 it became independent. Namibia, a German colony until 1919, had since then been governed by South Africa. Today, South Africa is governed by Afrikaners, descendants of the early Dutch settlers. This white majority's policy of apartheid, or strict racial segregation and discrimination against nonwhites, is one of the most serious problems on the continent.

Understanding Global Events

1. What two African countries remained independent throughout the nineteenth century?
2. Explain the South African racial policy known as apartheid.

Critical Thinking

3. What part did the Industrial Revolution play in the colonizing of Africa by the European countries during the nineteenth century?

Answers

Understanding Global Events

1. Liberia and Ethiopia remained independent throughout the 19th century.

2. Apartheid is the practice of strict racial segregation and discrimination against nonwhites.

Critical Thinking

3. European countries could so easily dominate African countries during the 19th century because they were modern, industrial powers with strong armed forces. European countries were also motivated to find more and more natural resources to fuel growing industries. **(analysis)**

Answer Key

Key Terms and People

These are highlighted in the text in the order in which they appear in this list.

Main Ideas

1. a-VIII; b-IV; c-X; d-VI; e-III; f-II; g-VII; h-V; i-I; j-IX

Critical Thinking Questions

2. Possible answers: **for**—if allowed to immigrate, the Chinese laborer will take our jobs; people should be able to understand the language so they can vote. **Against**—this is the land of opportunity and we should not deny entry to anyone; people who have had no chance at education should not be punished for the deficiency.

▶ **3.** Both reconciled the two approaches by rationalizing that colonies governed by the United States were much better off than if governed by another country or if permitted self-government.

▶ **4.** Chart: **Advantages**—mobility, faster travel, wider access to jobs and recreational facilities, shelter in bad weather; **disadvantages**—pollution, dangerous speed, traffic in cities, expense.

5. Possible answer: that Americans value their workers and the skills they have, value literacy, value equality, and value a society with the knowledge to govern itself.

Critical Thinking Activities

6. Possible answers: 1898—McKinley; explosion of the *Maine;* Spanish-American War. 1904—Roosevelt; start of Panama Canal; *The Jungle* published. 1909—Taft; Payne-Aldrich Tariff passed; Pinchot fired. 1913—Wilson; Underwood Tariff passed; Federal Reserve System created.

7. Newspapers exist that rely on sensationalism to sell copies. • It puts stories of sensational nature on front page with large photographs. • Editorials try to influence policy.

8. The U.S. government gave military aid to the *contra* rebels fighting the Sandinista government until 1989; invaded the island of Grenada after the collapse of its government; invaded Panama to capture Gen. Manuel Noreiga and bring him to the U.S. to face drug-trafficking charges; gave military aid to the government of El Salvador to fight rebels.

▶ **Question suitable for cooperative learning.**

UNIT 5 REVIEW

Write your answers on a separate sheet of paper.

Key Terms and People

Explain the significance of: Thomas Nast, Ellis Island, naturalized citizen, Seward's Folly, Charles Darwin, spheres of influence, dollar diplomacy, Progressive movement, Robert M. La Follette, closed shop, Mark Twain, John L. Sullivan, Porfirio Díaz, Emiliano Zapata

Main Ideas

1. Match each of these people with his or her achievement.

   a. Jane Addams
   b. Philippe Bunau-Varilla
   c. George Washington Carver
   d. Eugene V. Debs
   e. Liliuokalani
   f. Alfred Thayer Mahan
   g. Gifford Pinchot
   h. Upton Sinclair
   i. William Marcy Tweed
   j. Booker T. Washington

   I. led a political machine, Tammany Hall, in New York City
   II. wrote a book called *The Influence of Sea Power upon History, 1660–1783*
   III. wanted Hawaii for the Hawaiians
   IV. speculator who was instrumental in locating the Atlantic-Pacific canal in Panama
   V. wrote the novel *The Jungle*
   VI. a Socialist labor leader
   VII. the professional conservationist who supervised the national forests under Theodore Roosevelt
   VIII. founded Hull House, a settlement house in Chicago
   IX. founded the Tuskegee Normal and Industrial Institute in 1881
   X. revolutionized Southern agriculture

Critical Thinking Questions

2. **Recognizing Values.** If you had been alive in the 1880's, would you have been for or against the Chinese Exclusion Act and the literacy test for immigrants? Give reasons for your answer.

3. **Forming Hypotheses.** How could Presidents McKinley and Theodore Roosevelt embrace Progressive ideals and imperialism at the same time? Discuss the philosophies of both leaders.

4. **Assessing Effects.** Make a chart to assess the effects the automobile has had on this country. List several effects that seem beneficial and several effects that do not.

Advantages	Disadvantages

5. **Judging Values.** Public education supported by the taxes of all the people was one of the reasons immigrants were attracted to this country. What does our system of public education indicate about American values?

Critical Thinking Activities

6. **Organizing Chronology.** For each date listed on the time line below, name the President in office and one or two events that happened around that date.

| 1898 | 1904 | 1909 | 1913 |

7. **Linking Past to Present.** What evidence can you give to support the claim that we still have a yellow press in this country? What do tabloids do to attract buyers? Do you think magazines and newspapers today try to influence foreign policy?

8. **Linking Past to Present.** Review the Monroe Doctrine on pages 245–246, the Roosevelt Corollary on pages 530–531, and Wilson's missionary policy on page 573. What actions has the United States government taken in the last ten years that might be explained by these policies?

Onto a World Stage

Cities and Immigrants

After the Civil War, American cities grew at an astounding rate. This growth resulted in huge problems that no one knew how to deal with. New York had become the nation's largest city and the place of arrival for immigrants from Europe. In New York and other large cities, wealthy people lived in luxury. People in the middle class were able to choose either the new apartments or the new row houses. The poor greatly outnumbered those who had money. They lived in tenements that were small, dirty, and often windowless.

Several problems about health came to the surface. How could cities get clean water? How could they handle human and animal wastes? As cities grew in size, transportation difficulties arose. People no longer lived where they worked. How would they get from their homes to their factories or offices? The answer turned out to be what today we would call mass transit.

Just before the Civil War, several cities had organized full-time police forces. As cities grew in size, crime increased. Fighting fires was another problem. The great Chicago fire of 1871 alerted many people to the need for full-time professional firefighters.

During this time, many black people from the South settled in Northern cities. They were driven out of the South partly by laws that enforced segregation. In Northern cities, many of these migrants were disappointed by poor housing, de facto segregation, and the lack of jobs.

Political machines under the control of bosses began to usurp power in the cities. In return for favors, the bosses helped people who had trouble with their trash or with their immigration papers. Obviously, such a system led to graft. The most conspicuous graft was in New York City.

Between 1880 and 1914 huge numbers of immigrants from southern and eastern Europe came to the cities of the United States. Their language and cultural differences upset native-born Americans. They were not Protestant, they seemed at odds with the familiar Irish Catholic Church, and they lived and spoke among themselves instead of joining mainstream America. Jews from Poland and Russia and Russian Orthodox Catholics were even more different than Italy's Roman Catholics. Yet, to the native-born Americans, most different of all were the Asians.

The immigrants themselves had no easy time of it. They suffered on the voyage across the Atlantic, they lived in slums, and they worried about keeping their cultural tradition and their language intact. Worst of all, their children were losing their cultural heritage. Sometimes, their only help in this new land came from the political machines.

Many Americans grew angry about the newcomers. Some thought that all these "foreigners" were radicals. Others became even more hostile to the Catholic Church. Wealthy New Englanders called for a halt to this new immigration. Californians wanted to stop the Chinese and Japanese from entering the country. Nativist public opinion pushed Congress to pass laws against uncontrolled immigration.

Expansion and Power

Although many Americans were interested in expanding the nation's borders, Seward's purchase of Alaska in 1867 drew little attention. Later, in the 1880's, four reasons made Americans become eager to expand overseas. One reason was a need to acquire new markets and raw materials. A second reason was the notion of Anglo-Saxon superiority. A third reason was competition from Europe. A

Telescoping the Times may be used as an alternative to having students read the entire unit, as a unit preview, or as a unit review.

fourth reason was that Admiral Mahan successfully convinced the country of the importance of sea power and of a powerful navy.

New battles broke out in Cuba. Public opinion in the United States was split. The island was still a Spanish colony, but the Spanish General Weyler's brutal policies convinced most Americans that the island ought to be independent. The yellow press did a great deal to bring about war between Spain and the United States. President McKinley was reluctant, but the publication of the de Lôme letter and the explosion on the *Maine* pushed the nation into war.

On the other side of the world, Admiral Dewey's ships easily took Manila in the Philippines. However, Aguinaldo's troops fought off the invasion from the United States. American soldiers invaded the former Spanish colony of Cuba. Teddy Roosevelt led a successful assault on San Juan Hill. The United States navy defeated the Spanish fleet in the Caribbean Sea, and the United States conquered the Spanish-owned island of Puerto Rico. The peace treaty provided that Cuba would remain independent and that the United States would take over the Philippines, Guam, and Puerto Rico. Though many Americans objected, the United States acquired an overseas empire.

As things turned out, Cuba became an American protectorate. The Platt Amendment made that island subject to political domination by the United States. This domination resulted in the conquest of yellow fever in Cuba, but it also meant economic rule by American business interests.

The former Spanish colony of Puerto Rico had a very different history. Puerto Rico was a much smaller island than Cuba and was not scarred by battle in the Spanish-American War. Eventually Puerto Rico achieved a unique position not as a state but as a commonwealth of the United States.

In their thrust overseas, Americans also seized the Hawaiian Islands. The growth of sugar plantations had attracted more planters from the United States. Laborers from Japan, China, and Portugal began to take the places of native Hawaiians and soon outnumbered them. Marines from the United States forced Queen Liliuokalani from her throne. Again many Americans protested, but the Hawaiian monarchy was changed to a republic dominated by the United States.

Expansion into the Pacific region increased American interest in China. The United States was worried by the policy of extraterritoriality that European nations and Japan were forcing on China. Secretary of State Hay pushed through the Open Door policy and enforced it after the Boxer Rebellion.

Russia and Japan went to war over spheres of influence in northeast Asia. The Japanese surprised the world by destroying the Russian naval fleet. President Theodore Roosevelt helped those two nations make peace.

The United States had long been interested in a canal for shipping across Central America. Roosevelt encouraged a revolution by Panama against the government of Colombia. In doing so he made the canal possible, but his actions angered many people in Latin America. Yet it made the United States still more impressive as a world power.

The United States began to intervene in many Latin American countries. It practiced dollar diplomacy with such nations as Nicaragua.

The Progressive Movement and Reforms

In the early 1900's, the Progressive movement began when muckrakers started exposing social evils. These writers in new, mass-circulation magazines uncovered political corruption, industrial greed, and unsafe foods. Debs spoke for socialism, but most Americans disagreed.

The whole notion of improvement seemed to dominate this era. Reform mayors fought for better schools and improved city services. Some cities adopted a new form of government that included a city manager. State governments adopted such reforms as the secret ballot, the initiative, and the recall. Progressive politicians succeeded in passing an amendment to the Constitution to the effect that senators would be elected directly by the people and no longer by state legislatures. Many states passed laws that gave new rights to women and children. Courts provided for workers' compensation.

Theodore Roosevelt was a Progressive and also a Republican. He became truly well known as the

Progressive governor of New York State. When he became President, he brought great energy to the White House. He settled the coal strike through arbitration rather than violence. He regulated trusts and urged Congress to pass laws to regulate interstate transportation. He supported laws that helped clean up the nation's supply of food and drugs. As a result of his great passion for conservation, he set aside millions of acres for public parks.

His chosen successor was Taft. Yet Taft soon disappointed Roosevelt by backing a new high tariff and by paying little attention to the country's natural resources. Taft also made the mistake of backing Joe Cannon, the increasingly unpopular Speaker of the House of Representatives.

Roosevelt became so angry about Taft's policies that for the election of 1912 he established a third party. His Progressive, or Bull Moose, party split the Republicans down the middle, which enabled the Democrat Woodrow Wilson to win.

President Wilson took bold steps. He lowered the tariff and pushed through a new income tax. He successfully urged Congress to adopt a new financial system, the Federal Reserve System, that is still with us. Wilson also established farm loan banks and made major attacks on the trusts.

Inventions, Improvements, and an Intervention

At the same time, other significant changes in American society were taking place. The automobile brought the biggest change of all. Ford put his Model T on the road at a price that many Americans could afford. Ford's five-dollar workday astonished everyone and made it possible for Ford's workers to buy the cars they worked on. The Model T brought new jobs to Detroit and other cities. It brought the assembly line and scientific management to American industry. Eventually, the new machine brought urban sprawl.

The Wright brothers' invention at first had less effect than the automobile. However, the airplane's importance became evident during World War I.

The rapid growth of cities brought many problems. City parks were needed to make urban life more liveable. Many cities built amusement parks that offered picnic grounds and moving electric rides. Marshall Field's new department store in Chicago set a model for the nation. Soon Americans could go to shopping centers. They could eat at elegant restaurants or at short-order houses. Yet the poor in the growing cities were neglected. Jane Addams and others organized settlement houses to meet some of their needs.

After the Civil War, many states had adopted laws that required all young people to go to school. This compulsory education introduced many American children to the McGuffey *Readers*. The new high schools also became standard for the nation's urban boys. Now more than before, Americans began going to college. Booker T. Washington and George Washington Carver offered educational opportunities to blacks.

Technological developments changed the way people communicated with each other. Typesetting and new kinds of paper meant that newspapers could be produced fast and cheaply. Hearst and Pulitzer struggled for domination of the newspaper business. With his Kodak camera, Eastman brought about a revolution in photography.

Mark Twain became the outstanding literary figure of this period he named the "Gilded Age." Professional sports, especially baseball, became a major topic of conversation. At the same time, the theater and dramatic movies such as Griffith's *Birth of a Nation* attracted large audiences.

In 1910 the Mexican government underwent a revolution that greatly disturbed the United States. American troops invaded Mexico, but they were withdrawn before the United States entered World War I in 1917.

Chronology of Main Events	
1881	President Garfield assassinated
1898	Spanish-American War
1901	President McKinley assassinated
1904–1914	U.S. constructs Panama Canal
1906	Pure Food and Drug Act
1917	U.S. enters World War I

GLOBAL TIME LINE

The World

1914-1918
World War I

1917
Bolshevik Revolution
in Russia

1920
Gandhi becomes leader
of National Congress in India

1922
Mussolini comes
to power in Italy

1910　　　　　1915　　　　　1920

**The
United States**

1912
Woodrow Wilson elected President

1917
U.S. enters World War I

1920
Nineteenth
Amendment passes

1923
Calvin Coolidge
succeeds to
Presidency

UNIT 6 1914–1940

World War I, Causes and Consequences

Geographic Setting

Human-Environment Interactions. The invention of the airplane had a tremendous effect on society and the way wars were fought. When it was used for reconnaissance missions, to transport people and supplies, and to destroy enemy targets, the airplane brought human-environment interactions to a new level.

Unit Overview

World War I was a watershed in both world history and American history. The war swept away many of the old governments and nations in Europe, and it changed the United States view of itself. The war also led to great economic and social changes. At the same time, this period brought economic decay, which culminated in the Great Depression. In Unit 6 you will learn about the causes and consequences of the Great War in five chapters.

Unit Outline

1931
Japan invades Manchuria

1933
Hitler comes to power in Germany

1936-1939
Spanish Civil War

925   1930   1935   1940

1927
First sound film produced

1929
Stock Market crashes

1933
Franklin D. Roosevelt inaugurated President

1933-1939
New Deal aids economic recovery

1935
Social Security Act

1940
President Roosevelt elected for third term

587

Chapter 23 Teaching Strategies

Global Perspectives

1915	Germans introduce the use of poison gas.
1917	Bolsheviks seize power in Russia.
1919	Ignace Paderewski becomes Premier of Poland.
1919	Lady Astor becomes the first female member of British Parliament.
1920	Jewish state of Palestine is created.

For Discussion

How might the Bolshevik Revolution in Russia have affected the U.S. role in World War I? (Possible response: the revolution might have led to a reduction in military power for the Allies, making the U.S. feel a need to step in.)

Additional Resources

- Geography Activities
- Skills Activities
- Thematic Activities
- Economic Activities
- Cultural Literacy Activities
- Literary Source Readings
- Primary Source Readings
- Nuclear Peacekeeping
- Transparencies
- Computer Test Generator

Additional Teaching Strategies

SECTION 1

For Basic Students: Ask students to research World War I in an encyclopedia and prepare a wall-chart showing countries of the Central Powers including countries that sided with them, Allied Powers and countries that sided with them, and those countries that remained neutral during World War I. Charts may include:

Central Powers	Allied Powers	Neutral Powers
Germany	Britain	Norway
Austria-Hungary	Australia	Sweden
	Montenegro	Denmark
Bulgaria	Belgium	Netherlands
Ottoman Empire	France	Switzerland
	Libya	Spain
	Portugal	Luxembourg
	Egypt	Albania
	Cyprus	Persia
	Algeria	
	Japan	
	U.S.	
	Greece	
	Italy	
	Russia	
	Romania	
	Serbia	
	Tunisia	

(Note: Charts may vary since the status of some countries changed during the war.)

Have students display the chart in the classroom and refer to it as they study the chapter.

For Advanced Students: Ask students to research and find additional information concerning the assassination of Archduke Ferdinand and the role of the Serbian nationals. (Reports might include: Serbian nationalists wanted to liberate the South Slavs of Austria-Hungary; believed that their cause would be furthered by the death of Archduke Ferdinand, heir presumptive to the Austrian emperor; assassination was carried out by a Bosnian Serb, Gavrilo Princip.) Have students present their findings to the class.

SECTION 2

For Basic Students: Have students use an encyclopedia or other reference book to research and write a two-paragraph report on one of the new weapons or technologies developed during World War I. (Report on fighting aircraft might include: Sopwith Camel fighters are equipped with machine guns; fighter-bombers are developed; twin-tailboom Capronis carry rear-gunners; Germany develops the Gotha biplane.) Have students share their reports.

For Advanced Students: Organize students into three groups, one each to represent Progressives (antiwar), Democrats (loyal to President Wilson), and Republicans (prowar). Have students research their positions and debate the U.S. declaration of war on Germany. (Progressives might argue: war is wrong; what happens in Europe does not affect U.S. Democrats might argue: take care of America first, Europe second; wait for overt aggressive activity. Republicans might argue: economic ties with Europe must be protected; America must fight to protect democracy.)

SECTION 3

For Basic Students: Ask the students to use information in this section to construct a time line of events during World War I.

April 2, 1917	Wilson delivers his war message.
April 6, 1917	U.S. officially declares war against Germany.
May 18, 1917	Congress passes Selective Service Act.
June, 1917	Congress passes Espionage Act.
1917	War Industries Board is established.
1918	War Labor Board is created.
March 3, 1918	Russia signs treaty with Germany.
May, 1918	Congress passes Sedition Act.
November 9, 1918	Kaiser Wilhelm abdicates.
November 11, 1918	Germany signs armistice with Allies.

Encourage students to refer to their lists as they study this section.

For Advanced Students: Ask students to write two paragraphs describing how the war might have ended if the U.S. had not entered on the side of the Allies. (Paragraphs might include: the Allies might have eventually defeated Germany if the U.S. had remained neutral; Germany might have succeeded and have begun a new German empire.)

SECTION 4

For Basic Students: Organize students into groups of three and ask them to research and present to the class a report on the structure and functions of the League of Nations using charts, graphs, diagrams, or pictures. (Information on structure should include: Secretariat; Council; Assembly; World Court.)

For Advanced Students: Organize students into three groups, one each representing the pro-treaty senators, reservationists, and anti-treaty senators. After researching their position and individuals who held that position, students should hold a mock senatorial debate on the question of ratification of the Treaty of Versailles.

Pro-Treaty Senators
- Were Democratic minority
- Favored ratification without changes
- Included Senator Gilbert Hitchcock

Reservationists
- Were large block of Republicans
- Wanted amendments to protect U.S.
- Included Henry Cabot Lodge

Anti-Treaty Senators
- Were a small group
- Opposed treaty and defended isolationism
- Included Hiram Johnson, Robert La Follette

Further Reading for Students

Albrecht-Carrie, Rene. *The Meaning of the First World War*. Englewood Cliffs, N.J.: Prentice Hall, 1965.

Hemingway, Ernest. *A Farewell to Arms*. New York: Scribner, 1987.

Hoehling, Adolph A. *The Great War at Sea: A History of Naval Action, 1914-18*. Reprint of 1965 ed. Westport, Conn.: Greenwood Press, 1978.

Jacobs, David. *An American Conscience: Woodrow Wilson's Search for World Peace*. New York: Harper & Row, 1973. (Easy)

Jantzen, Steven. *Hooray for Peace, Hurrah for War*. New York: Alfred A. Knopf, 1972. (Easy)

Remarque, Erich Maria. *All Quiet on the Western Front*. New York: Fawcett, 1987.

Stein, R. Conrad. *The Story of the Lafayette Escadrille*. Chicago: Children's Press, 1983. (Easy)

Tuchman, Barbara W. *The Zimmermann Telegram*. New York: Macmillan, 1966.

Bibliography for Teachers
Books

Barbeau, Arthur E., and Florette Henri. *The Unknown Soldiers: Black American Troops in World War I*. Philadelphia: Temple University Press, 1974.

Garraty, John A. *Woodrow Wilson: A Great Life in Brief*. Reprint of 1956 ed. Westport, Conn.: Greenwood Press, 1977.

Ginger, Ray. *Eugene V. Debs: A Biography*. New York: Macmillan, 1962.

Greenwald, Maurine W. *Women, War, and Work: The Impact of World War I on Women Workers in the U. S.*. Westport, Conn.: Greenwood Press Inc., 1980.

Kennan, George F. *American Diplomacy, 1900-1950*. Chicago: University of Chicago Press, 1985.

Kennedy, David M. *Over Here: The First World War and American Society*. New York: Oxford University Press, 1980.

Link, Arthur S., ed. *Woodrow Wilson and a Revolutionary World, 1913-1921*. Chapel Hill: University of North Carolina Press, 1982.

Smith, Gene. *When the Cheering Stopped: The Last Years of Woodrow Wilson*. New York: William Morrow, 1964.

Tuchman, Barbara. *The Guns of August*. New York: McMillan, 1962.

Vaughn, Edwin Campion. *Some Desperate Glory: The World War I Diary of a British Officer, 1917*. New York: Holt, 1988.

Audio-Visuals

The Black Soldier. Columbia Broadcasting Company. Movie.

Goodbye Billy: America Goes to War, 1917-1918. Cadre Films. Movie.

Great Men and Great Issues. Wilcom. Audiotapes.

Home Front, 1917-1919: War Transforms American Life. Columbia Broadcasting Company. Movie.

The U. S. and the Twentieth Century, 1912-1920. Simon & Shuster Communications. Movie.

The Winds of Change. Department of the Army. Movie.

World War I—A Documentary on the Role of the U.S.A. Encyclopaedia Britannica Educational Corporation. Movie.

The Yanks Are Coming. David L. Wolper Productions. Movie.

Teacher's Notes:

Teaching Resources, Unit 6 Booklet

Lesson Study Sheets pp. 1-16
Daily Activities pp. 17-24
Enrichment Activities pp. 25-32
Reteaching Activities pp. 33-40
Chapter Review p. 41
Mastery Tests pp. 43-54
Telescoping the Times Study Sheet p. 55

Chapter Objectives

Students will learn:
- the causes of World War I
- why the U. S. was unable to remain neutral in World War I
- how the U. S. mobilized for and participated in the war effort
- the major terms of the Treaty of Versailles

Picturing History In the best-known World War I recruiting poster, by James Montgomery Flagg, a stern Uncle Sam calls out to Americans to volunteer for the struggle ahead.

Using the Chapter Time Line

In what year did World War I begin; in what year did it end? (Answer: 1914, 1918) What major event occurred in Russia (see Unit 6 Time Line) the same year Wilson was inaugurated to his second term? (Answer: Bolshevik Revolution)

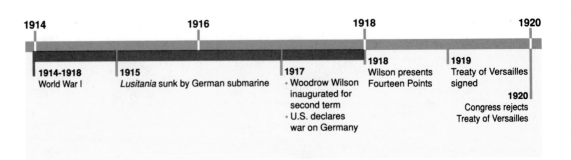

1914	1916	1918	1920

1914-1918 World War I

1915 Lusitania sunk by German submarine

1917
• Woodrow Wilson inaugurated for second term
• U.S. declares war on Germany

1918 Wilson presents Fourteen Points

1919 Treaty of Versailles signed

1920 Congress rejects Treaty of Versailles

CHAPTER **23** 1914–1920

The First World War

Links to American Literature

Dearest Mama and Papa, Alessandro wrote.

I have been writing infrequently because although we don't do much here, it takes up all the time we have. . . . I stare out into the hills and mountains for twelve hours, and then I'm free. Presumably, with all the time in the world to reflect, I could write brilliant essays and letters that you might read more than once, but I can't. It's too tense here, and everyone is too unhappy. . . .

Today I saw something miraculous. I was looking southward through a firing port, with a telescope. It was evening and the light was coming from the northwest. Over the trenches a black cloud appeared, changing direction and moving as rapidly as an airplane, but it was the size of a palace. It writhed, dropped, rose, and fell again, catching the light like chain mail or dulled sequins. It was a cloud of starlings or swallows that feed upon the corpses in the no-man's-lands between the lines. Guariglia, who has served farther down, says that they come out every evening and dance over the dead. I don't know what to make of it, as it is at once so beautiful and so grotesque.

— MARK HELPRIN, *A Soldier of the Great War*

In the early 1900's, Mexico was not the only trouble spot in the world. Europe was divided into opposing camps, waging World War I. The United States itself could not remain neutral in the war. However, American young people questioned the motives that could result in the kind of death and destruction that were being reported daily. They questioned why technology was so efficient at creating new ways to kill but could not create peace. These are questions that face us today, in the nuclear age. After the war, tales and pictures of horror that surfaced helped to fuel the isolationist movement. The American people were determined to oppose any further involvement in European affairs.

Chapter Overview

In this chapter you will learn about the causes of World War I and the reasons why the United States was unable to remain neutral. In addition, you will learn how the United States mobilized for war, how Americans participated in the war effort, and how the terms of the Treaty of Versailles planted the seeds of future conflict. To help you understand these causes and consequences of the First World War, Chapter 23 is divided into four sections.

Chapter Outline

1. **World War I Begins**
2. **The United States Tries to Remain Neutral**
3. **The Nation Goes to War**
4. **Wilson Fights for Peace**

589

Core Lesson

Anticipate the Lesson

Discuss with students some reasons that countries go to war. Ask students to give specific examples for each reason. (Possible responses: to break away from an oppressive government—Revolutionary War, French Revolution; to gain land—Mexican War, Spanish-American War, French and Indian War.) List the reasons and examples on the board. Ask students to suggest ways in which countries can

avoid wars. (Possible responses: peace treaty; negotiation; compromise.)

State the Objective

Understand the causes of World War I.

Present the Lesson

Divide the class into four groups. Ask each group to review the section and to prepare and present to the class a brief report explaining one of these causes of World War I: Nationalism, Imperialism, Alliance system, Militarism. Reports might include:
- Nationalism: was characterized by a desire for freedom and self-determination within various ethnic groups.
- Imperialism: was characterized by competition for colonies and overseas markets.
- Alliance system: was characterized by the fear and jealousy that led European nations

SECTION 1

World War I Begins

GLOSSARY TERMS: **Triple Entente, Allies, Triple Alliance, Central Powers**

World War I lasted four years, from 1914 to 1918, and involved more than thirty nations from six continents. It was the bloodiest war in history up to that time. About 15 million persons were killed. Millions of these were civilians, 80 percent of whom died as a result of disease, starvation, and exposure. Economic costs also ran high, totaling over $350 billion. The Great War, as it came to be called, left the world a legacy of hatred, extreme nationalism, and economic depression.

Complex Causes Lead to War

For decades before the outbreak of war, the countries of Europe became increasingly suspicious of and competitive with one another. The complex, underlying causes of World War I were the rise of intense nationalism, the growth of imperialism, the formation of a system of military alliances, and increased militarism.

Nationalism. As ethnic groups that spoke the same languages banded together, they became increasingly nationalistic. The Poles, for example, had been divided among Germany, Austria-

Hungary, and Russia. Now they wanted to reunite as a self-governing Polish state. The Slavic-speaking peoples of central and southern Europe also sought independence from foreign control. The French were still smarting over their 1871 loss to Germany of the French-speaking provinces of Alsace and Lorraine. This spirit of nationalism went beyond a patriotic feeling for one's own nation. For many, the desire for freedom and self-determination was so strong that they were willing to risk war to attain their goals.

Imperialism. While many nations were fueling the fires of nationalism, the major powers of the world were competing for colonies to add to their empires. Great Britain and Germany were carving out colonies in Africa and the Middle East and looking for markets throughout the world. France and Germany were clashing over Morocco. Even though France's overseas empire was second only to that of Great Britain, the French feared that their old enemy Germany was growing too rapidly for comfort.

Then there was Russia. In 1905, as you know, it had been decisively defeated by Japan. Hoping to gain more territory as well as regain its lost stature, Russia shifted its attention from Asia to Europe. Russia considered itself to be the leader of the continent's Slavic peoples. Among these were the Serbs. At that time, Serbia was an independent nation, but millions of other Serbs were under the

People in the Chapter

Colonel Edward M. House advised a number of Texas governors, one of whom gave him the honorary title of colonel. Colonel House became a close friend and advisor of President Wilson in 1912. The President referred to Colonel House as "my second personality. . . my independent self."

George M. Cohan wrote the most popular patriotic song of World War I, "Over There." His other hits include such titles as "I'm a Yankee Doodle Dandy," "Give My Regards to Broadway," and "You're a Grand Old Flag."

Bernard "Barney" Baruch headed the War Industries Board, which sought to support the

war by reducing waste and increasing production. Among the means chosen to accomplish these goals were the following: eight thousand tons of steel were cut yearly from women's corsets, women were encouraged to become "farmerettes," and an old saying was changed to: "A Woman's Place Is in the War."

John J. Pershing won a reputation for bravery in the Spanish-American War. He suffered a great tragedy when his wife and three daughters died in an army post fire. Later, Pershing became the nation's most famous World War I general. He is often called the architect of the modern American army.

590

to form alliances. Triple Entente (the Allies) included France, Great Britain, and Russia; Triple Alliance—Germany, Austria-Hungary, and Italy (the Central Powers).
- Militarism: was characterized by the stockpiling of arms by European nations. Competition for international trade led to a naval arms race.

Ask students to construct on the board a time line of the events surrounding the assassination of the Archduke and the outbreak of war.

June 28, 1914   Archduke Ferdinand is assassinated.

July 28, 1914   Austria-Hungary declares war on Serbia.

July 30, 1914   Russia mobilizes troops to aid Serbia.

August 1, 1914   Germany declares war on Russia.

August 3, 1914   Germany declares war on France.

August 4, 1914   Great Britain declares war on Germany.

Have students refer to the time line as they study this section.

Check for Understanding

Call on individual students to answer Section 1 Review questions orally.

rule of Austria-Hungary. As a result, Russia and Austria-Hungary were rivals in the Balkans.

A System of Alliances. All of these mutual hostilities, jealousies, fears, and desires led the nations of Europe to sign treaties of assistance with one another. By 1914 there were two major alliances. The **Triple Entente**, later known as the **Allies**, consisted of France, Great Britain, and Russia. (Russia also had a separate treaty with Serbia.) The **Triple Alliance** consisted of Germany, Austria-Hungary, and Italy. Germany and Austria-Hungary, together with Turkey, were later known as the **Central Powers**. The members of each alliance vowed to support one another against attack.

Linking Past to Present

The system of alliances that existed before World War I bears some similarity to the alliance systems established by the North Atlantic Treaty Organization (NATO) and the Warsaw Pact during the Cold War. These ties weakened in the late 1980's as democratic and free market reforms erupted in East Germany, Hungary, Czechoslovakia, Poland, and Romania. The Warsaw Pact eventually dissolved in 1991 with the collapse of the U.S.S.R.

Militarism. In addition to forming alliances, the major powers of Europe were stockpiling military arms. Each nation wanted to keep its armed forces stronger than those of any potential enemy.

Competition for international trade led to a naval arms race. The major European countries, as well as the United States and Japan, strengthened their navies to protect their shipping routes. Britain and Germany started a massive buildup of giant battleships. Soon the United States, Austria-Hungary, Italy, and Japan began adding more battleships to their war fleets.

An Assassination Provides an Excuse for War

On June 28, 1914, the streets of the little town

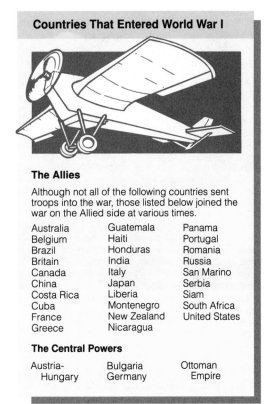

Countries That Entered World War I

The Allies

Although not all of the following countries sent troops into the war, those listed below joined the war on the Allied side at various times.

Australia	Guatemala	Panama
Belgium	Haiti	Portugal
Brazil	Honduras	Romania
Britain	India	Russia
Canada	Italy	San Marino
China	Japan	Serbia
Costa Rica	Liberia	Siam
Cuba	Montenegro	South Africa
France	New Zealand	United States
Greece	Nicaragua	

The Central Powers

Austria-Hungary	Bulgaria	Ottoman Empire
	Germany	

of Sarajevo (sar′ ə yä′ vō), capital of Austria-Hungary's province of Bosnia (now Yugoslavia), were jammed with people. They had gathered to see the **Archduke Franz Ferdinand**, nephew and heir of the Austrian Emperor, and his wife, Sophie. The royal couple waved gaily to the crowd as their open carriage moved along. Suddenly a young man leaped from the curb toward them. Before the guards could react, he fired a series of shots. The archduke and his wife were killed.

As luck would have it, the teen-aged assassin, Gavrilo Princip, turned out to be a member of a secret society known as the Black Hand. The society's aim was to unite all Serbs under one government. This incident was the excuse Austria-Hungary needed to make an example of Serbia and to prevent a nationalist uprising within Austria-Hungary. Accordingly, on July 28 it declared war against Serbia.

At once the system of alliances went into effect. On July 30 Russia ordered full mobilization of its

Guided Practice

Ask students to consider whether alliances make the world more or less secure. Ask them whether they think today's alliances are likely to lead to World War III. (Possible responses: no, even countries that are part of an alliance tend to be more cautious and to work out differences, perhaps because they fear nuclear war; yes, countries with similar ideals tend to band together, creating inevitable conflict.)

Assign Independent Practice

Have students complete Chapter 23, Section 1 Daily Activity.

Student Assignment/Homework

Have students read Section 2, "The United States Tries to Remain Neutral," and answer Section 2 Review questions on paper.

SECTION 2
Core Lesson

Anticipate the Lesson

Review with students their lists of the causes of World War I. (Review should include: nationalism; imperialism; alliance system; militarism; assassination of Archduke Ferdinand.)

SECTION 1 REVIEW

Answers

Main Ideas

1. More money, countries, and people were involved; more deaths occurred; and the long-term political and economic effects were substantially greater than in previous wars.

2. The rise of nationalism, the growth of imperialism, the formation of military alliances, and increased militarism.

3. Triple Entente: France, Great Britain, and Russia; Triple Alliance: Germany, Austria-Hungary, and Italy. Their purposes were to deter attack by hostile powers and to provide aid in the event of war.

Critical Thinking

4. Possible answer: the alliance system and the military buildup virtually guaranteed that widespread war would break out in Europe. Almost any controversial event or action could have precipitated war. **(synthesis)**

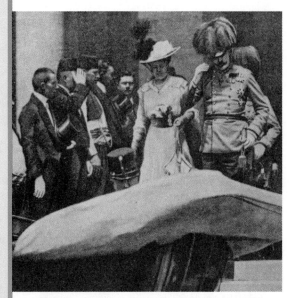

Picturing History Archduke Franz Ferdinand and his wife enter their car in Sarajevo. Shortly afterward, Gavrilo Princip, a Serbian extremist, assassinated both of them.

armed forces in order to help Serbia. Two days later Germany declared war on Russia. On August 3 Germany declared war on France. The following day Great Britain declared war on Germany. The First World War had begun.

SECTION 1 REVIEW

Key Terms and People

Explain the significance of: Triple Entente, Allies, Triple Alliance, Central Powers, Archduke Franz Ferdinand

Main Ideas

1. What made World War I different from previous wars?
2. What four conditions led to World War I?
3. What countries were in the Triple Entente? What countries were in the Triple Alliance? What were the purposes of these alliances?

Critical Thinking

4. Would World War I have occurred if Archduke Franz Ferdinand had not been assassinated? Explain.

SECTION 2

The United States Tries to Remain Neutral

GLOSSARY TERMS: **trench warfare, stalemate, contraband, U-boat,** *Sussex* **pledge, Zimmermann note**

The United States did not enter World War I until three years after hostilities began. Until almost the last minute, there was considerable doubt as to whether or not America would take part. **Woodrow Wilson** even won a second term in 1916 on the campaign slogan "He Kept Us Out of War." What, then, made the United States change its mind?

Americans Favor Neutrality

Millions of naturalized United States citizens favored the nations from which they had emigrated. For example, many Americans of German descent sympathized with Germany. Many Americans of Irish descent remembered the centuries of British oppression in Ireland and saw the war as a chance for Ireland to gain its independence.

Of course, some Americans believed the war was evil. Pacifists such as William Jennings Bryan argued that it was the obligation of the United States, "the greatest of the Christian nations," to set an example of peace for the world. Socialists such as Eugene V. Debs criticized the war as an imperialist struggle between Germany and British businessmen. Since both groups wanted to control raw materials and markets in China, Africa, and the Middle East, Socialists said it was "a plague on both . . . houses."

Overall, there was a general feeling of sympathy for Great Britain and France. Many Americans felt close to Britain as a consequence of sharing a common ancestry, language, and literature, as well as similar democratic institutions and legal systems. Ties with France, although much weaker, went back to 1778 when France had helped the thirteen colonies in their fight for independence. As a New York editor put it:

> Forget us, God, if we forget
> The sacred sword of Lafayette.

Most Americans in 1914 saw no reason for being drawn into a struggle that was three thousand miles away. No American lives or properties were threat-

State the Objective

Understand why the U. S. was unable to remain neutral in World War I.

ened. Whether the Allies beat the Central Powers
or the other way around did not seem a matter of
direct national concern. This does not mean that
individual Americans were indifferent to who
would win the war—quite the contrary.

The majority of Americans, however, undoubtedly favored victory for the Allies rather than for
the Central Powers. Yet they did not feel strongly
enough to want to help the Allies. As President
Wilson said, "Our whole duty for the present, at
any rate, is summed up in the motto 'America First:
Let us think of America before we think of Europe.' "

Germany Invades Belgium

Americans were appalled with the German inva-
sion of Belgium on August 3, 1914. Although
Belgium was a neutral nation, it was the gateway to
France.

Since Germany was fighting on two fronts—
Russia on the east and France on the west—it
decided to follow a plan that had been drawn up in
1905 by Count Alfred von Schlieffen, chief of the
German general staff. The **Schlieffen Plan** called
for a holding action against Russia, which was
always slow to mobilize because of its vast size and
its shortage of railroads. This holding action was to
be combined with a quick drive in strength through
the Belgian lowlands to Paris. Then, after France
had fallen, the two German armies would unite to
defeat Russia.

After the German invasion of neutral Belgium,
American correspondents sent frightening accounts
of a military juggernaut (a terrible irresistible force)

on the move. War correspondent Richard Harding
Davis, for example, described the German army
that entered Brussels as an unbroken "river of
steel" that flowed "gray and ghostlike" with all
"the mystery and menace of fog rolling toward you
across the sea." For twenty-six hours the German
army rumbled by, Davis wrote, with "no halt, no
breathing time, no open spaces in the ranks." It
was inhuman.

The Allies Stop Germany.   Unable to save Belgium, the French and the British retreated to the
Marne River, where they stopped the German
advance in September 1914. By the spring of 1915,
two lines of trenches ran across northern and
eastern France. They were dug deep enough into
the ground for soldiers to stand up to shoot their
machine guns and still be protected. Although vast
numbers died as a result of this **trench warfare**,
the western front reached a three and one-half year
stalemate, or deadlock, with neither side able to
conquer the other. In 1916 the Germans tried to
break through the Allied defenses but were thrown
back at Verdun and the Somme, where both sides
suffered hundreds of thousands of casualties.

Both Sides Design New Weapons.   In 1914 the
Germans first used a new weapon nicknamed Big
Bertha against Belgium. This cannon could hurl an
eighteen-hundred-pound shell a distance of nine
miles.

In 1915 the chemical industries of both sides
added poison gas to the horrors of war. This gas
came in tubes containing either chlorine, which
suffocated, or mustard gas, which burned skin and

For Discussion
Is it possible for a nation to
maintain its neutrality and its
right to trade during wartime
when a blockade is in effect?
(Possible response: neutrality may be impossible.) Did
American-European trading
interdependence make U.S.
entry into World War I inevitable? (Possible response: yes,
because Americans de-
pended on European mar-
kets, the U.S. had to go to
war to protect its economic
interests.)

Picturing History
A crude but complex
network of tunnels linked
thousands of miles of
trenches on the Allied
lines.

Divide the class into two groups. Have one group prepare a list of reasons for U.S. neutrality and have the other prepare a list of reasons for U.S. entry into the war. Ask a representative from each group to put the group list on the board.

Reasons for neutrality

- No American lives or property were threatened.
- Some citizens believed war was wrong.
- Some citizens criticized the war as an imperialist struggle.

Reasons for declaring war

- Naturalized citizens favored U.S. aid for their homelands.
- Germany invaded Belgium.
- Germany unleashed U-boats.
- Germany sank *Lusitania*.
- Zimmermann note was sent to Mexico.
- Germany sank unarmed U.S. ships.
- American economic ties with Allies were strong.

Picturing History
Propaganda posters depicted both the destructive nature of the enemy and the need to support the war effort by buying war bonds.

blinded. The Germans used poison gas first, at the Second Battle of Ypres early in 1915.

In September 1916 the British introduced tanks. At first the Germans were petrified by these steel monsters. Soon, however, they discovered that flame throwers, weapons that could shoot a stream of flaming gasoline, could be used effectively against them.

Modern technology had produced these devastating weapons, and the brutality they inflicted sickened the imagination. For three years the European railway system delivered shipments of arms and masses of men to the battlefront. By 1917 neither victory nor defeat was in sight. There was only exhaustion, frightful human suffering, and death.

When the Germans leveled the entire town of Louvain because a Belgian sniper killed a German soldier, American newspapers began warning their readers about the menace of the "Huns." They were comparing the Germans with the Hunni, an Asiatic people who had invaded Europe in the fifth century A.D.

German Submarines Threaten Neutrality

As Great Britain controlled the seas, it made good use of its naval strength. During 1914, it set up a blockade along the German coast to prevent **contraband**—that is, weapons and other military goods—from getting through. The British, however, enlarged the definition of contraband to include such items as cotton and foodstuffs. They also extended the blockade to neutral ports in the Netherlands, Denmark, Norway, and Sweden. Furthermore, instead of searching neutral merchant ships at sea—which was the customary practice—Britain insisted that neutral vessels go to British ports for examination.

All of these actions were contrary to the international law of freedom of the seas. Many Americans reacted as angrily as their ancestors had in 1812. President Wilson protested sharply, calling the blockade "ineffective, illegal, and indefensible." The feelings against Great Britain, however, did not last long. For Germany began waging submarine warfare.

Germany Unleashes the U-Boats. By 1915 the British blockade had almost eliminated the flow of military supplies to Germany from neutral nations. So **Kaiser Wilhelm**, the German ruler, announced a counterblockade by **U-boat** (from *Unterseeboot*, the German word for submarine). All cargoes moving toward Britain—food as well as munitions—would be considered contraband, he said. Any ship found in the waters around Britain would be sunk. He added that it would not always be possible to warn crews and passengers. Since U-boats had no room to take aboard people from a ship before sinking it, the Kaiser's declaration meant that many more neutral lives would be lost.

Unleashing the U-boats turned out to be a colossal blunder on Germany's part. Britain declared a counterblockade of its own, one result of which was that the importation of chemical fertilizers into Germany fell off. Since Germany was using all its available nitrates for munitions, it could not produce fertilizers of its own. Without fertilizers, German farmers could not grow enough food.

By 1917 famine stalked the country. It is estimated that 750,000 Germans starved to death as a result of the British blockade. This is one hundred times the number of persons who lost their lives from submarine warfare.

Most people, however, were unaware of the German famine. The British blockade worked slowly, and its effect was not visible except inside Germany. U-boat attacks, on the other hand, were spectacular events. News services flashed accounts of sinking ships and drowning persons around the world within a matter of minutes. As a result, neutrals who had been angry at Britain because of damage to their property were soon outraged with Germany because of the loss of life.

The *Lusitania* Is Sunk. By May 1, 1915, German attacks on shipping had led to the loss of four American lives. Then on May 7 a German submarine sank the British liner ***Lusitania*** off the south-

Check for Understanding

Call on individual students to read their answers to Section 2 Review questions.

ern coast of Ireland. Of the 1,198 persons who lost their lives, 128 were Americans. The Germans defended their action on the grounds that the liner was carrying arms and, possibly, heavy explosives. The *Lusitania* was carrying munitions, but it was a rule of international law that a passenger ship must be warned before being sunk. Most Americans, therefore, agreed with the New York minister who said:

> This sinking . . . is not war; it is murder! . . . This is organized murder and no language is too strong for it. . . . If I see a ruffian in the street beating a boy I may want to be neutral. But God help me, I am less than a man if I don't thrust in my hand. So it is getting to be too much to ask America to keep out when Americans are drowned as part of a European war.

The *Sussex* Pledge. The United States protested sharply against the sinking of the *Lusitania*. Three months later a U-boat sank another British liner, the *Arabic*. Although only two Americans were drowned, anti-German sentiment in the United States was so intense that Germany agreed not to sink any more liners without warning "provided that the liners do not try to escape or offer resistance."

In March 1916 Germany broke its promise and torpedoed an unarmed French passenger steamer, the *Sussex*. The *Sussex* did not sink, but about eighty passengers, including Americans, were killed or injured. Once again the United States warned that it would break off diplomatic relations unless Germany changed its tactics. Again Germany agreed, in the so-called *Sussex* **pledge**. There was a string attached, though. If the United States could not persuade Britain to lift the "hunger blockade," Germany said, it would consider itself free to renew **unrestricted submarine warfare**.

Wilson Wins Again in 1916

Although many Americans now believed that war was inevitable, President Wilson made several attempts to mediate the conflict. He sent his personal advisor, Colonel Edward M. House, to Europe. Only after House's peace missions came to nothing did Wilson decide to take Theodore Roosevelt's advice and push for a program of preparedness. This program involved increasing the size of the regular army, establishing officers' training camps, and expanding the navy. In addition, the Council of National Defense was created to make plans for mobilizing national resources in the event of war. Also, the United States Shipping Board was set up to build and buy merchant ships.

In November came the Presidential election. The Democrats had renominated Wilson. The Progressives had renominated Theodore Roosevelt. Roosevelt, however, realized that the only way to defeat Wilson, whom he called "that damned Presbyterian hypocrite," was for the Progressives to rejoin the GOP. So he threw his support to the Republican candidate, Supreme Court Justice **Charles Evans Hughes**.

Picturing History Americans were stunned by the sinking of the *Lusitania*. Germany published ads (above) warning of possible attack.

Tell students that one of the largest American industries is munitions manufacturing. To stimulate discussion, ask students the following questions. Should the U.S. produce and distribute munitions to nations at war? Is it realistic to believe that nations would not obtain certain weapons if the U. S. did not sell them? (Possible responses: yes, the U.S. should manufacture and sell munitions because if we don't some other country will; no, it is immoral to facilitate war.)

Have students complete Chapter 23, Section 2 Daily Activity.

Picturing History Woodrow Wilson married Edith Bolling Galt (right) after his first wife died. Edith handled all communication for Wilson after his stroke.

Map Skills

Belgium, Britain, France, Greece, Italy, Montenegro, Portugal, Romania, Russia, Serbia • Austria-Hungary, Bulgaria, Germany, Ottoman Empire • Britain

The election revolved around two issues: peace and progressivism. Wilson campaigned on the slogan "He Kept Us Out of War" but also pointed to the preparedness campaign and to the *Sussex* pledge. In domestic matters he won the support of labor by pushing an eight-hour-day law through Congress.

Hughes pledged to uphold America's right to freedom of the seas but also promised not to be too severe on Germany. However, his vague speeches and lack of forcefulness led many to call him "Charles Evasive Hughes." In addition, Roosevelt antagonized thousands of potential Hughes supporters by comparing Wilson to Pontius Pilate, "with apologies to the latter."

The election in 1916 proved to be extremely close. It was well into the day after the election before the actual victor was known—Wilson.

Last Efforts at Peacemaking Fail

Following the election, Wilson made an attempt to end the war by calling upon both sides to state their war aims. Wilson hoped that peace could then be negotiated. This attempt failed. Then on January 22, 1917, Wilson appealed to world public opinion through a speech before the Senate. He called for "a peace without victory . . . a peace among equals" in which neither side would impose harsh terms on the other. Instead, all the nations would join a League for Peace. The league would work to extend democracy, maintain freedom of the

seas, and reduce armaments.

Nine days later came the German response. The fortunes of war had swung in Germany's favor, and its leaders felt that they had a good chance to knock out Britain by resuming unrestricted submarine warfare. So on January 31 the Kaiser announced that all ships in the waters around Britain, France, and Italy would be sunk on sight. Italy had joined the Allies because of competition with Austria-Hungary for control of the Adriatic Sea.

Wilson was stunned. In view of his earlier statements, the German announcement meant that the United States would have to go to war. Still, the President held back, saying that he would wait for "actual overt acts" before breaking diplomatic relations.

The overt acts came. First was the **Zimmermann note**, sent by the German foreign secretary to the German ambassador in Mexico and intercepted by British agents. The telegram suggested an alliance between Mexico and Germany and promised that if war with the United States broke out, Germany would support Mexico in recovering "the lost territory in Texas, New Mexico, and Arizona." Next came the sinking of four unarmed American merchant ships with a loss of thirty-six lives.

In addition, there were several indirect factors. In March 1917 the repressive tsarist regime in Russia was overthrown and replaced by a provisional, or temporary, government that promised democratic elections. Now one could say that the

Presidential Election, 1916

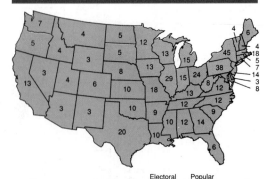

Party	Candidate	Electoral Vote	Popular Vote	%
Democratic	Wilson	277	9,128,000	49.4
Republican	Hughes	254	8,534,000	46.2
Minor parties			819,000	4.4

531 Total Electoral Vote

596

Student Assignment/Homework

Have students read Section 3, "The Nation Goes to War," and be prepared to discuss it in class.

Europe During World War I, 1914-1918

Allies
Central Powers
Neutral countries
Limit of advance by Central Powers
British blockade
German U-boat counter blockade

Map Skills   Region   Which countries comprised the Allied Powers? the Central Powers?
Location   Around what country was the German naval blockade?

war against Germany, Austria-Hungary, and the Ottoman Empire was a war of democracies against brutal monarchies. Also, American trade with the Allies had risen from $825 million in 1914 to $3.2 billion in 1916, and American bankers had lent the Allies about $2 billion. Business leaders did not press for war. However, America's economic ties with the Allies were certainly stronger than their economic ties with the Central Powers.

SECTION 2 REVIEW

Key Terms and People

Explain the significance of: Woodrow Wilson, Schlieffen Plan, trench warfare, stalemate, contraband, Kaiser Wilhelm, U-boat, *Lusitania*, *Sussex* pledge, unrestricted submarine warfare, Charles Evans Hughes, Zimmermann note

Main Ideas

1. Why did the United States not enter World War I immediately?
2. What are some examples of new technology used in the war and what was the effect of their use?
3. Why did Americans find the British blockade less offensive than the German blockade?
4. What were the main issues in the 1916 Presidential election, and which one seemed to be most important?
5. What overt acts by Germany finally convinced Wilson that the United States had to enter the war?

Critical Thinking

6. Was the entry of the United States into the war inevitable? Explain.

Answers

Main Ideas

1. Many Americans opposed going to war because of conflicting loyalties or strong anti-war ideals. Others simply did not believe that Europe's struggles directly affected them, and they adopted an attitude of "America First."

2. The use of powerful cannons, poison gas, and tanks resulted in frightful human suffering, including millions of casualties.

3. Britain only searched ships and seized cargos, whereas German U-boats sank ships, killing most of the people on board.

4. Peace and progressivism. Peace.

5. The Zimmermann note and the sinking of four unarmed American merchant ships.

Critical Thinking

6. Possible answer: America might not have entered the war if Germany had not directly threatened U.S. interests by sinking U.S. ships, killing U.S. citizens, and suggesting that Mexico seize U.S. territory. Also Germany proved itself untrustworthy by breaking several agreements it had made with the U.S. **(synthesis)**

State the Objective

Understand how the U. S. mobilized for and participated in the war effort.

Anticipate the Lesson

Review with students the events that prompted the U.S. to declare war on Germany. (Response: German invasion of Belgium; German U-boat activity; Zimmermann note; sinking of unarmed merchant ships and *Lusitania;* American economic ties with Allies.) Have students speculate about what a country or government might do to prepare for war.

SECTION 3

The Nation Goes to War

GLOSSARY TERMS: **Espionage and Sedition Acts, convoy system**

A light drizzle fell on Washington, D.C., on April 2, 1917. Members of Congress, Supreme Court justices, ambassadors, and other guests crowded into the Capitol to hear President Wilson deliver his war message.

Wilson began by stating: "Property can be paid for; the lives of peaceful and innocent people cannot be." German submarine warfare was "nothing less than war against the government and people of the United States." Therefore, he said, the United States had no choice but to enter the war that had been thrust upon it.

Wilson then moved on to speak of larger goals. "We are glad . . . to fight thus for the ultimate peace of the world and for the liberation of its peoples, the German peoples included; for the rights of nations great and small and the privilege of men everywhere to choose their way of life. . . . The world must be made safe for democracy. . . . We have no selfish ends to serve. We desire no conquest, no dominion. We seek no indemnities."

The President closed by saying: "It is a fearful thing to lead this great peaceful people into war. . . . But the right is more precious than peace, and we shall fight for the things which we have always carried nearest our hearts."

Congress officially declared war on April 6, 1917. The vote was 82 to 6 in the Senate, and 373 to 50 in the House.

The Military Mobilizes

> Over there, over there.
> Send the word, send the word over there,
> That the Yanks are coming, the Yanks are coming,
> The drums rum-tumming ev'rywhere.
>   —from the song "Over There"
> by George M. Cohan

America's entry into World War I assured the Allies' final victory in 1918. Without troops, ships, food, and military supplies from the United States, the war could have gone the other way—and the whole history of the world since 1918 would have been very different indeed.

Picturing History   Sporting a revolutionary tricorn, Nora Bayes symbolized American enthusiasm for the war as she introduced George M. Cohan's song "Over There."

The first task that confronted the United States was that of raising an army. When war was declared, there were only about 200,000 men in the service. Almost all the army's weapons were obsolete, while the air force consisted of fifty-five rickety planes and 130 pilots.

The lack of manpower was soon solved by a draft. Congress passed the Selective Service Act, which required all men between the ages of twenty-one and thirty to register for the draft. Almost 10 million men were registered by June 5, and—unlike the Civil War experience—not a single riot took place. Two additional registrations were held in 1918, raising the total pool of men to 24 million. About 4.2 million were inducted into the service. Of this number, about 2 million reached Europe before the armistice was signed, with three-fourths seeing actual combat. The ages of the inductees ranged from eighteen to forty-five. However, since married men and those with dependents were generally excused, the overseas army consisted mostly of young men. Training lasted for nine months: six months in the United States, two months in Europe before going to the front, and a final month on the battle line in a quiet sector. Then the men were moved to wherever the fighting was hottest.

The proportion of black Americans in the service was double their proportion to the general population. As in earlier wars, black soldiers were segregated in separate units and had separate living quarters and recreational facilities. Although most of their officers were white, for the first time the

List on the board the following groups: War Industries Board, Railway Administration, Fuel Administration, Emergency Fleet Corporation, National War Labor Board, and Food Administration. Discuss with students the accomplishments of each group and/or its importance to the war effort. Have volunteers write the appropriate information under the name of each group.
- War Industries Board: organized in 1917 and reorganized by Bernard Baruch in 1918; through the use of mass production improved output of manufactured goods.

- Railway Administration: operated nation's railways as a single system, thereby conserving resources.
- Fuel Administration: regulated supplies of coal and oil; encouraged conservation.
- Emergency Fleet Corporation: built ships.
- National War Labor Board: dealt with disputes between labor and management.
- Food Administration: headed by Herbert Hoover; relied on voluntary cooperation to conserve food.

Have students list on the board the highlights of American involvement in World War I and the events that marked the end of the war. (Possible responses: On April 2, 1917, Wilson delivers his war message; America institutes convoy system; American troops help repel German attacks in France; on November 9, 1918, Kaiser Wilhelm abdicates; on November 11, 1918, Germany signs an armistice with the Allies.)

United States Army trained some black officers and placed them in command of black troops. Although most black troops were assigned to noncombat duties, the all-black 369th Infantry Regiment saw more continuous duty on the front lines than any other American regiment. Two soldiers of the 369th, Henry Johnson and Needham Roberts, were the first Americans to receive the French military honor of the *Croix de Guerre* (krwä də ger').

Productivity Increases

The second task facing the United States was to transport millions of soldiers overseas and to equip and feed not only its own troops but those of the Allies as well. It was an immense task that was ultimately accomplished by increasing the powers of the federal government.

Industry. Congress gave President Wilson the power to fix prices. He could also regulate, and even nationalize, certain war-related industries.

The main regulatory body was the **War Industries Board**. It was established in 1917 and was reorganized in 1918 under the leadership of **Bernard Baruch**. The board did a great deal to improve production by encouraging the use of mass-production techniques. The board also did psychological testing to help find the right person for the right job. Civilians were urged to use substitutes for products containing steel or tin. Price controls, however, were applied only at the wholesale level. As a result, retail prices soared. Corporate profits soared as well, especially in such industries as chemicals, copper, lumber, meatpacking, oil, and steel.

Other federal agencies included the Railway Administration, which operated the nation's railroads as a single system, and the Fuel Administration, which regulated supplies of coal and oil. In addition, many people adopted gasless Sundays and lightless nights to help conserve fuel. The Emergency Fleet Corporation built some ten million tons of shipping. Most of the ships, however, were finished too late to be of much use. The majority of American troops moved across the Atlantic either in British vessels or in German ships that had been seized in American ports when war was declared.

Labor. Wages in certain industries—especially the metal trades, shipbuilding, and meatpacking—rose during the war years by as much as 20 percent. White-collar workers, on the other hand, lost about 35 percent of their purchasing power because of inflation. As a result, union membership increased by more than 70 percent, and in 1917 there was a wave of strikes protesting the high cost of living.

In 1918 President Wilson set up the National War Labor Board to deal with disputes between management and labor. In general, labor agreed not to strike in exchange for the right to organize and bargain collectively and the right to keep the eight-hour workday wherever it already existed. Workers who were reluctant to go along with board decisions were warned that they would lose their draft exemption. "Work or fight," they were told.

The wartime need for labor brought more than a million more women into the labor force. As one writer observed:

> Suddenly a male-dominated America was confronted with the spectacle of women auto mechanics, telegraph messengers, elevator operators, and streetcar conductors—and that was not all. They toiled on factory assembly lines, carried ice for iceboxes, plowed fields, and became traffic cops. Women invaded even the sanctuary of the armed forces, about eleven thousand female yeomen enlisting in the navy as clerks and stenographers.

Picturing History The all-black 369th Infantry Regiment returns after fighting extensively "over there."

For Discussion
How was the U.S. able to become the richest and most powerful nation in the world during World War I? What was the long-term effect of the war on the U.S.? (Possible responses: U.S. supplied natural resources, manufactured goods, munitions, and food to the Allies, stimulating economic growth. Long-term effects include: U.S. built a large foreign market; U.S. established diplomatic ties and became directly involved with the welfare of many European countries.)

Check for Understanding

Call on individual students to read their answers to Section 3 Review questions.

Picturing History American women took an active part in the war effort. These women move bombs for shipment to France.

However, although President Wilson called for equal pay for equal work, women doing war work received less pay than men. Moreover, almost all of them were fired when the war ended.

Food. Yet another task that confronted the United States was that of producing and conserving food. As one joke went:

> My Tuesdays are meatless,
> My Wednesdays are wheatless,
> I'm getting more eatless each day.

The person in charge of the **Food Administration** was **Herbert Hoover**. A former mining engineer, he had successfully headed the Commission for Relief in Belgium from 1914 through 1917.

Hoover relied heavily on voluntary cooperation. His entire staff except for clerks consisted of volunteers. Instead of rationing food, he organized a tremendous publicity campaign that called on people to follow the gospel of the clean plate. Since Europeans were used to eating wheat, Americans were urged to eat corn so they could send their wheat abroad. Homeowners planted "victory gar-

dens" in their yards. Schoolchildren spent their after-school hours raising vegetables in public parks.

Hoover also set a high government price on wheat and other staples. Farmers responded by putting an additional forty million acres of land into production. In the process, they increased their income by almost 30 percent.

Americans Buy War Bonds

The war cost the United States about $33 billion in direct expenses. About one-third of this amount was raised through taxes, mostly through an excess profits tax on corporate earnings. The bulk of the war costs, however, was raised through public borrowing.

As Treasury Secretary William G. McAdoo explained, "We capitalized the profound impulse called patriotism." Instead of selling government bonds through banks, McAdoo went directly to the people. No one received a commission or made a profit on bond sales. Instead, tens of thousands of volunteers, sparked by such movie stars as Douglas Fairbanks and Mary Pickford, spoke at rallies in factories, in schools, and on street corners. Newspapers and billboards carried advertisements for the bonds free of charge. There were sales talks between theater acts and war-bond parades in the center of almost every town. All told, four great Liberty Loan drives and one Victory Loan drive were held. On the average, every adult American lent the government $400.

The Great Witch Hunt Unfolds

Early in 1917 President Wilson observed: "Once lead this people into war, and they'll forget there was ever such a thing as tolerance." The President's prediction turned out to be correct. As soon as war was declared, conformity became the order of the day. Civil liberties were attacked both unofficially and officially.

Super-Americanism. The main targets of the drive for conformity were so-called hyphenated Americans, that is, Americans who had emigrated from other nations. The most bitter attacks were directed against the 2 million Americans who had been born in Germany.

Many Americans with German-sounding names were fired from their jobs. Symphony orchestras no longer played the music of Mozart and Beethoven. Pretzels were banned from lunch counters. Books

600

Guided Practice

Tell students that President Wilson attempted to maintain neutrality in World War I. Ask students whether a nation with the power and resources of the U.S. can easily maintain neutrality today. (Possible response: because we live in a global community with many foreign ties, it is difficult to remain neutral.)

by German authors were removed from libraries. Americans changed the name of German measles to "liberty measles." Hamburger became "liberty steak," and sauerkraut was renamed "liberty cabbage."

The Espionage and Sedition Acts. In June 1917 Congress passed the Espionage Act. In May 1918 it passed the Sedition Act. Under these laws a person could be fined up to $10,000 and/or sentenced to twenty years in jail for interfering with the draft, obstructing the sale of government bonds, or saying anything disloyal, profane, or abusive about the government or the war effort.

Like the Alien and Sedition Acts of 1798, these laws clearly violated the First Amendment. Their passage led to some six thousand arrests and fifteen hundred convictions. A man named Walter Mathey was imprisoned for attending an antiwar meeting and contributing twenty-five cents. The Reverend Clarence Waldron received fifteen years in the penitentiary for telling a Bible class that "a Christian can take no part in the war." Farmer John White was sentenced to twenty-one months in jail for complaining about conditions in the army.

Socialists and labor leaders were major targets of the **Espionage and Sedition Acts**. Eugene V. Debs was sentenced to ten years in prison because he opposed the war. (He was pardoned by President Warren G. Harding after serving three years.) Anarchist "Red Emma" Goldman received a two-year sentence and a $10,000 fine for lobbying against the draft. (When she came out of jail, she was deported.) Big Bill Haywood and other leaders of the Industrial Workers of the World were convicted of sabotaging the war effort because they urged workers to strike for better conditions and higher pay. Haywood received thirty years; most of the others received five to ten.

Additional results of the Espionage and Sedition Acts included the loss of mailing privileges for newspapers and magazines that opposed the war or even criticized the British Empire. Victor Berger, a Socialist congressman from Wisconsin, was denied his seat in the House of Representatives because of his antiwar views.

The Allies Defeat Germany

American military might showed itself first at sea. The United States Navy helped tighten the British blockade around Germany. It also played a

major role in laying down a 230-mile (370-kilometer) barrier of mines from Scotland to Norway. Stretching across the North Sea, these mines were designed to bottle up the U-boats and keep them out of the Atlantic Ocean.

American Rear Admiral William S. Sims persuaded the British that the best way to defeat the U-boats was through the **convoy system**. It had been the practice for merchant ships to cross the Atlantic either singly or in small groups. While this practice lessened the chance of being spotted by a submarine, it also made defense difficult. Sims suggested instead that merchant vessels travel in a large group with a guard of circling destroyers and cruisers. The British agreed, and by midsummer of 1917 shipping losses had been cut in half. Eventually the United States put one hundred submarine chasers and five hundred airplanes into the anti-U-boat campaign.

Fighting in Europe. General **John J. Pershing** commanded the American land forces. At first they were used mostly as replacements for European casualties. (These American infantrymen were nicknamed "doughboys" because of the white

Picturing History American doughboys, commanded by General John J. Pershing (right), participated in the Allied offensives during the summer and fall of 1918.

Assign Independent Practice

Have students write a paragraph explaining and giving examples of the term *Super-Americanism*. (Possible explanation: Super-Americanism was a drive for conformity and for rejection of any foreign influence. Examples might include: firing of workers with German-sounding names; refusal of orchestras to play Mozart or Beethoven; banning of pretzels; renaming of German measles, hamburger, and sauerkraut.)

Student Assignment/Homework

Have students read Section 4, "Wilson Fights for Peace," and complete Chapter 23, Section 4 Daily Activity.

Map Skills

20 to 25 miles (35 to 40 km) • Marne • Germany

Historical Sidelight

Sergeant Alvin York was perhaps one of the most famous soldiers to emerge from WWI. York was a religious young man from the mountains of Tennessee. In October of 1918 he captured 132 Germans—by himself. The movie *Sergeant York* is based on his heroic story.

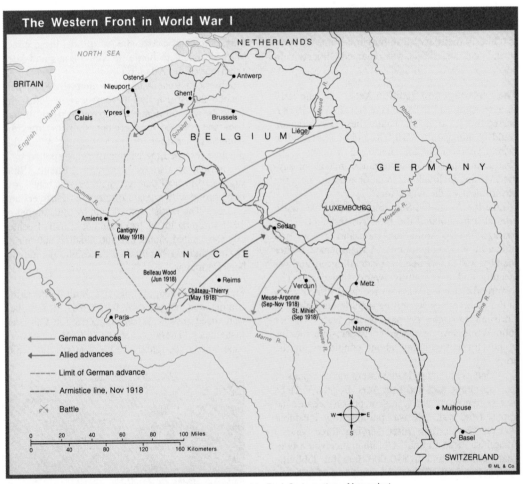

Map Skills **Movement** How close did German forces get to Paris? **Location** Near what river was the battle of Chateau-Thierry? **Location** In what country is the Rhine River?

belts they wore, which they cleaned with pipe clay or "dough.") By April 1918, however, Black Jack Pershing had convinced the Allies that the Americans should fight as a separate army, under the overall direction of French **Marshal Ferdinand Foch**, commander of all Allied armies in Europe. American troops played a major role in throwing back German attacks at Château-Thierry, Belleau Wood, and Reims, near Paris. They sparked offensives against the Germans at Saint-Mihiel and in the Meuse-Argonne area. All told, the United States lost forty-eight thousand men in battle, with an additional fifty-six thousand dying of disease.

Also active on the western front were American fighter pilots. Even before the United States en-

tered the war, Americans had flown in a special unit of the French Flying Corps called the Lafayette Escadrille. After the United States entered the war, the Lafayette Escadrille was disbanded and its pilots joined one of the American units. Fighter pilots involved in dogfights, or air combat at close quarters, were probably the most glamorous of America's war heroes. This was especially true if they were "aces" who had shot down five enemy planes. America's leading ace was Captain Edward V. Rickenbacker. He shot down twenty-two enemy planes and four balloons. Germany's leading ace, Manfred Richthofen, was nicknamed the Red Baron. He was personally credited with shooting down eighty allied aircraft.

Anticipate the Lesson

Call on individual students to read their answers to Chapter 23, Section 4 Daily Activity. Ask students to list arguments for each senatorial position on the Treaty of Versailles. (Possible responses: pro-treaty senators argued for ratification without reservations; moderate senators argued that provisions must be made to protect U.S. interests; anti-treaty senators argued in favor of isolationism.)

Another Revolution in Russia. In November 1917 the democratic government that had been formed after the overthrow of the Tsar was itself overthrown by the Bolsheviks, a small group led by Vladimir Lenin. (See page 608.) The new government realized that the country was exhausted by the war. As a result, Russia withdrew from fighting and signed a separate peace treaty with Germany on March 3, 1918, which became known as the Treaty of Brest-Litovsk.

The End. By September 1918 the superior power of the Allies was evident. On November 3 a mutiny broke out at the German naval base of Kiel. On November 9 Kaiser Wilhelm abdicated his throne and took refuge in the Netherlands. Two days later Germany signed an armistice, or truce, with the Allies. It was in the eleventh month, on the eleventh day, at the eleventh hour that the guns fell silent.

SECTION 3 REVIEW

Key Terms and People

Explain the significance of: War Industries Board, Bernard Baruch, Food Administration, Herbert Hoover, Espionage and Sedition Acts, convoy system, John J. Pershing, Marshal Ferdinand Foch

Main Ideas

1. After entering World War I, how did the United States resolve the personnel shortage in the American armed forces?
2. In general, what was the purpose of the War Industries Board and the railway, fuel, and food administrations?
3. How did the United States finance the cost of fighting the war?
4. What was the main purpose of the Espionage and Sedition Acts? How did the acts violate the First Amendment?
5. How did American military forces contribute to the Allied victory?

Critical Thinking

6. President Wilson said that once Americans went to war, they would "forget there was ever such a thing as tolerance." Does intolerance reflect true American patriotism? Explain.

SECTION 4

Wilson Fights for Peace

GLOSSARY TERMS: Fourteen Points, self-determination, League of Nations, mandates, reparations, isolationists

When the United States entered World War I, it was almost like embarking on a crusade. What could be more idealistic than ending war forever and making the world safe for democracy? Yet after the war, the Senate twice rejected the Versailles treaty, refused to join the League of Nations, and, in the words of one historian, "broke the heart of the world." Let us see how it happened.

Wilson's Plan Includes Fourteen Points

On January 8, 1918, President Wilson went before Congress and delivered his famous **Fourteen Points** speech. The fourteen points, Wilson's suggested ground rules for peace, were divided into three groups. First were five points designed to remove what Wilson believed were the causes of war:

1. Open covenants openly arrived at, that is, open diplomacy and no secret treaties
2. Freedom of the seas
3. The removal of tariffs and other economic barriers between nations
4. Arms reduction "to the lowest point consistent with domestic safety"
5. Colonial policies that would take into account the interests of the colonial people as well as the interests of the imperialist powers

Next were eight points dealing with boundary changes. These were based on the principle of **self-determination** "along historically established lines of allegiance and nationality." In other words, national groups were to decide for themselves what nation they wanted to be part of.

The fourteenth point called for the formation of a **League of Nations** to keep world peace. The members of the league would be bound to protect any nation that was attacked by another.

Versailles Brings Victory But Not Peace

The peace conference was held at the palace of Versailles, near Paris. President Wilson himself headed the United States delegation. Accompanying him were personal aide Colonel House, Secre-

Answers

Main Ideas

1. By passing the Selective Service Act calling for a military draft.

2. To regulate and mobilize the economy, industry, and the everyday lives of citizens for the war effort.

3. Through taxes, especially corporate taxes, and the sale of war bonds to American citizens.

4. To aid in the war effort by silencing the opposition. By infringing of people's rights of freedom of speech and freedom of the press.

5. The navy helped strengthen the blockade around Germany and developed the convoy system that cut shipping losses substantially. Land and air forces played major roles in several important battles.

Critical Thinking

6. Possible answers: no—most American freedoms guaranteed by the Constitution require tolerance. People who uphold the Constitution, and therefore practice tolerance, are American patriots. Yes—toleration of what is morally wrong or unconstitutional would not be patriotic. **(evaluation)**

tary of State Robert Lansing, General Tasker H. Bliss, and diplomat Henry White. Only one of the four, White, was a Republican, although the 1918 congressional campaign had given the GOP a majority in both houses. None was a senator, although the Senate would have to ratify the peace treaty.

Before going to Versailles, Wilson visited Great Britain and Italy. Everywhere he went, cheering crowds waited hours to see him pass. Italians displayed his picture in their windows. Parisians strewed the road with flowers. Representatives of one minority group after another—Armenians, Jews, Ukrainians, and Poles—approached him with appeals for help in setting themselves up as independent nations.

Practical Politics. Once the peace conference began, however, Wilson's idealism ran into practical politics. Premier Georges Clemenceau (klem′ ən sō′) of France had lived through two invasions of his country by Germany, and he was determined to prevent this from happening again. British Prime Minister David Lloyd George had just won reelection on the basis of the slogan of "Make Germany Pay." Prime Minister Vittorio Orlando of Italy wanted Austrian territory.

Contrary to custom, the peace conference did not include the defeated Central Powers. Nor did it include Russia or the smaller Allied nations. Instead, the **Big Four**—Wilson, Clemenceau, Lloyd George, and Orlando—worked out the treaty's details among themselves. In general, Wilson gave in on most of his fourteen points in return for the establishment of the League of Nations.

Results of the Treaty. The **Treaty of Versailles** was signed on June 28, 1919. As you can see by the map on page 605, nine new nations emerged, and the boundaries of other nations were shifted. Some areas were carved out of Turkish territory and given to France and Britain as **mandates**. A mandate, or temporary colony, was to be administered by the victorious Allied country until the area was ready for self-rule and then independence. The mandates included Iraq, Syria, Lebanon, and Palestine (now Israel and Jordan). Former German colonies in Africa and on the Pacific islands were likewise turned over to one or another of the Allied nations as mandates. In addition, Germany's armed forces were drastically reduced, and the country was required to pay **reparations**, or war damages. A commission later set the reparations at $56 billion.

Weaknesses of the Treaty. Contrary to Wilson's hopes, the Treaty of Versailles failed to establish any sort of lasting peace. In fact, there were at least three areas in which the treaty laid the groundwork for postwar international problems and the Second World War.

The first area was Germany. The treaty contained a war-guilt clause under which Germany acknowledged that it alone was responsible for World War I. Most historians now consider this unfair. Although German aggression had certainly played a major role in starting the conflict, other European nations had been just as anxious to fight. The result of the war-guilt clause and the loss of the Saar was that Germans of all political viewpoints hated the treaty. As you will read in Chapter 32, opposition

Picturing History
Wilson (with paper) in the Hall of Mirrors at Versailles during the peace negotiations in 1919. To his left are Georges Clemenceau and David Lloyd George.

Present the Lesson

Divide the class into small groups. Have students review the section and make group lists of President Wilson's Fourteen Points and the terms of the Treaty of Versailles.

Wilson's Fourteen Points: open diplomacy, no secret treaties, freedom of seas, removal of tariffs and trade barriers, arms reduction, just colonial practices, boundary changes based on principle of self-determination and nationality, formation of League of Nations

Treaty of Versailles: nine new nations emerged, boundaries of other nations were shifted, areas of Turkey given to France and Britain as mandates, former German colonies turned over to Allied nations, Germany forced to reduce armed forces, Germany eventually assessed $56 billion in reparations, war-guilt clause created for Germany.

Have volunteers put their lists on the board. Discuss the lists and encourage students to refer to them as they study this section.

Check for Understanding

Have students answer Section 4 Review questions on paper.

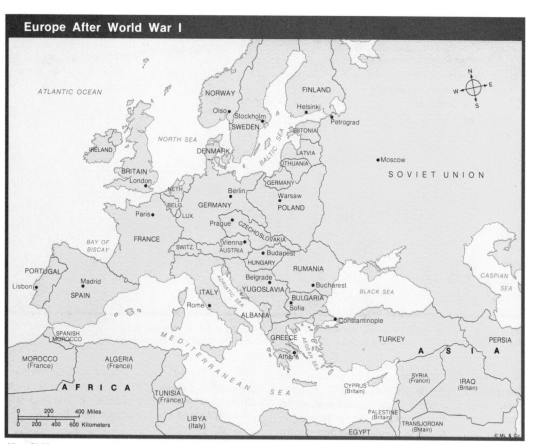

Europe After World War I

Map Skills
Poland • Soviet Union

Map Skills **Location** Compare this map with the map on page 597. What new country lies between Germany and the Soviet Union? **Place** What country lost the most territory as a result of the war?

to the treaty was one reason for the 1933 rise to power of Nazi dictator Adolf Hitler.

Germany's national pride was also insulted because, when Austria-Hungary was split up, three million German-speaking people were placed in an area of northern Czechoslovakia known as the **Sudetenland**. These Germans would much rather have remained part of Austria. (One of the steps leading to World War II was Germany's occupation of the Sudetenland in 1938.)

The second area in which the Treaty of Versailles created problems was Russia. For three years that country had fought on the side of the Allies. Its battle casualties numbered two million, more than those of any other nation. Yet not only was Russia excluded from the peace conference, but it lost much more territory than Germany did—some to Poland, some to Romania, and some to the four new Baltic nations of Finland, Estonia, Latvia, and Lithuania. These Baltic nations were created to serve as a buffer zone against the spread of communism. The result was that the Union of Soviet Socialist Republics (U.S.S.R.), as Russia was officially called after 1922, became determined to regain as much of its former territory as possible.

The third area in which the Treaty of Versailles created problems was Southeast Asia. Here the fault did not lie with anything in the treaty itself but rather in what the treaty left out. In the early 1900's most of Southeast Asia was ruled by France. Ever since the 1890's, a nationalist movement for independence had been developing in what is now Vietnam. At Versailles, a young Vietnamese man who was later known as **Ho Chi Minh** appealed to President Wilson for help. Ho Chi Minh wanted a constitutional government for his country that

Guided Practice

Ask students to compare President Wilson's ideas on maintaining world peace to the current idea that maintaining a balance of power is sufficient to preserve peace. (Possible response: Wilson's ideas depend on trust, openness, and unselfish behavior by all nations; today's theory is very different—to balance power, not relinquish it.) Ask students whether unilateral disarmament is a realistic deterrent to world war in today's unstable world. (Possible response: unrealistic—some countries might feel the need to secretly stockpile weapons; others might try to take advantage of weaker, disarmed nations.)

Assign Independent Practice

On the board write the term *Big Four*. Then write the names Wilson, Clemenceau, Lloyd George, and Orlando. Have students write a paragraph explaining the role of each at the Versailles Conference. (Possible details: Clemenceau of France was determined to crush the Germans and prevent them from attacking France again; Lloyd George of Great Britain won reelection on a promise to "make Germany pay"; Orlando of Italy wanted Austrian territory; Wilson of America worked for a fair and lasting world peace.) Have one or two students read their paragraphs to the class.

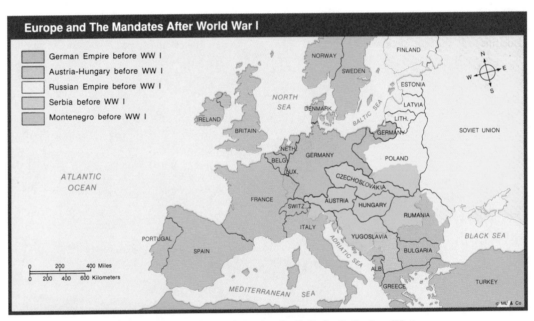

Europe and The Mandates After World War I

German Empire before WW I
Austria-Hungary before WW I
Russian Empire before WW I
Serbia before WW I
Montenegro before WW I

Map Skills **Region** What three new countries are located on the Baltic Sea? **Region** What two countries on the Balkan Peninsula ceased to exist as a result of the creation of Yugoslavia?

Map Skills

Latvia, Lithuania, Estonia • Serbia, Montenegro

would give the Vietnamese people the same civil and political rights as the French. Wilson, however, apparently believed that self-determination applied only to Europeans. Instead of listening to Ho Chi Minh's proposal, Wilson had him thrown out into the hall. As you will read in Chapter 33, Ho Chi Minh later founded the Indochina Communist party and led the fight against American forces in the Vietnam War.

The Senate Rejects the Treaty

When Wilson returned to the United States to get Senate approval for the peace treaty, he found several groups opposed to it. Some people, like Herbert Hoover, believed that the peace terms were too harsh. It did not seem possible for Germany, which had lost much of its coal resources as well as its colonies, to pay reparations, and failure to do so could only lead to trouble.

Others objected to the treaty because Europe's new national boundaries did not satisfy every group's demand for self-determination. For example, before the war, the Poles under German rule did not have self-determination. Now, it was the Germans in Poland who did not have self-determination. Italian Americans were unhappy that Italy did not receive all of the Austrian territory containing a majority of Italian inhabitants. Irish Americans were bitter because Wilson had not secured Ireland's independence from Britain.

Isolationist Fears. The main opposition, however, centered on the issue of the League of Nations. The convenant providing for the league's establishment formed the first section of the Versailles treaty. If the Senate ratified the treaty, the league would automatically be approved. To Wilson, the league presented the "only hope for mankind." He felt the covenant could not be eliminated or even changed without destroying the entire treaty.

The Senate was divided into three groups. The Democratic supporters of Wilson favored immediate ratification. The moderates, headed by **Henry Cabot Lodge**, favored participation in the league with reservations to protect American interests. The "irreconcilables," such as William Borah and Hiram Johnson, advocated total rejection of the covenant.

Many senators believed that the United States should isolate itself from Europe's problems. Even though the league could not make its members go to the aid of any country that was attacked, these

Student Assignment/Homework

Have students complete the Chapter 23 Review on paper. Discuss the Critical Thinking questions with students.

Concluding the Chapter

Have students write an essay to support or refute the claim that World War I was an inevitability even if Archduke Ferdinand had not been assassinated. Students should use facts from this chapter to support their opinion. Ask several students to share their essays with the class.

isolationists were suspicious. They pointed out that the covenant (1) did not recognize the Monroe Doctrine, (2) did not acknowledge that member nations had authority over their own internal affairs, (3) did not indicate that a member nation had the right to withdraw from the league if it wished, and (4) did not recognize that Congress had to approve any action the United States might take in the league.

If Wilson had been either more tactful or more willing to accept a compromise on the league, it is possible that the Senate might have approved both the treaty and the League of Nations. Wilson, however, was exhausted from his efforts at Versailles. As a result, he was cold, aloof, and even dictatorial. Things had to go exactly as he wished or they would not go at all.

A Last-Ditch Fight. Realizing that the Senate might not approve the treaty and the league, Wilson decided to go directly to the people. Despite warnings from friends and doctors that his health was fragile, he set out in September 1919 on an eight-thousand-mile tour. He made thirty-five speeches in twenty-two days, explaining the need for the United States to join the league. Senators Borah and Johnson followed in his footsteps, speaking in the same towns against the league.

The effort was finally too much for the President. He collapsed and was rushed back to the White House. On October 2 he suffered a stroke (a blood clot in the brain) and lay partially paralyzed for more than two months. He could not even meet with his cabinet, while his once-powerful voice was no more than a thick whisper.

The treaty came up for a vote in the Senate in November 1919. Senator Lodge introduced a number of amendments, called "reservations." Wilson appealed from his sick bed to "all true friends of the treaty" to defeat the **Lodge reservations**. The Senate did so by a majority vote. When the Senate voted on the treaty itself, however, Wilson's supporters could not obtain the necessary two-thirds vote.

Failure. The treaty came up again in March 1920. Again Wilson urged the Democrats to reject it if the Lodge reservations were included. Democratic Senator Henry Ashurst explained the outcome:

As a friend of the President, as one who has loyally followed him, I solemnly declared to him this morning, 'If you want to kill your own child because the Senate straightens out its crooked limbs, you must take the responsibility and accept the verdict of history.'

The Senate again rejected the Lodge reservations—and again failed to muster enough votes to ratify the treaty.

The United States finally signed a separate peace treaty with Germany in 1921, after Wilson was no longer President. The country never joined the League of Nations. Could World War II have been avoided if the United States had become a member of the League? This remains an open question. At any rate, the nation instead turned its attention inward to domestic issues.

Linking Past to Present

World War I lasted four years. World War II lasted six years. Advances in nuclear warfare are such that World War III might last only the time it takes to exchange nuclear weapons: less than thirty minutes.

SECTION 4 REVIEW

Key Terms and People

Explain the significance of: Fourteen Points, self-determination, League of Nations, Big Four, Treaty of Versailles, mandates, reparations, Sudetenland, Ho Chi Minh, Henry Cabot Lodge, isolationists, Lodge reservations

Main Ideas

1. What were Wilson's Fourteen Points designed to accomplish?
2. In what three areas of the world did the Treaty of Versailles produce the greatest postwar international problems, and what were these problems?
3. What were Americans' main objections to the Treaty of Versailles?

Critical Thinking

4. Based on your knowledge of the shortcomings of the Treaty of Versailles, how do you think it might have been improved?

SECTION 4 REVIEW

Answers

Main Ideas

1. To remove the causes of war, to establish fair territorial boundaries, and to establish a League of Nations that would encourage world peace.

2. Germany—war guilt and loss of territory; Soviet Union—loss of territory; Southeast Asia—maintenance of European imperialism.

3. Some believed that the peace terms were too harsh; others said that it did not satisfy every group's demands for self-determination; and isolationists objected to the provision for American membership in the League of Nations.

Critical Thinking

4. Possible answers: ensuring representation among the treaty writers of all parties affected by the treaty, including the Central Powers, the Soviet Union, and Southeast Asia; modifying the excessively harsh terms for Germany; and taking adequate care in drawing borders and forming new countries. **(synthesis)**

FOCUS ON ECONOMICS

Lesson Plan

State the Objective

Understand the three types of economic systems: capitalism, socialism, and communism.

Present the Lesson

Ask students to identify the basic ideals behind capitalism, socialism, and communism. Write these ideals on the board and have students refer to them during this lesson. (Possible responses: capitalism—to promote free enterprise; socialism—to ensure fair distribution of wealth; communism—to guarantee the rights of all workers.)

Ask students to describe two basic characteristics of capitalism as we know it today and to identify two ways in which each of these characteristics contributes to individual freedom. (Possible responses: one characteristic of capitalism is private ownership of the means of production; private ownership gives individuals the freedom to own and operate businesses and to receive compensation for their roles as entrepreneurs, investors, and risk takers. A second characteristic of capitalism is government regulation for balanced growth; this characteristic gives individuals freedom from exploitation by unfair monopolies and from unfair business practices; it also gives workers freedom to bargain for better wages and working conditions and guarantees consumers certain rights and protection.)

Tell students that in the Soviet communist system, government had the role of centrally

Focus on Economics

Comparing Economic Systems

As Americans, we have come to understand and appreciate the workings of our economic system called capitalism. Basically, capitalism is a free market system in which private individuals and businesses own most of the resources. These entrepreneurs seek a profit on their investments, which include the means of production (machines, factories, land, and so on). Over the years, the United States had become the world's leading capitalist society.

However, there are other ways to organize an economy. Socialism and communism are two systems that operate in large areas of the world today. Both are fundamentally different from capitalism.

Socialism.   Socialism is an economic system in which the government owns the means of production. Decisions concerning how much to produce, what prices to charge, what wages to pay, and so on are made by government officials.

As with capitalism, the principles of socialism originated in Europe. Because early socialists believed that people could be persuaded to work without a profit, they were considered idealistic. Some were called utopians, or believers in a perfect world. These early idealists thought it was possible to reform the economic system to distribute wealth more fairly. In the United States, however, experiments in socialism—such as the community in New Harmony, Indiana—ended in failure.

Marx's Philosophy.   Karl Marx (1818–1883), the most influential socialist thinker of the nineteenth century, eventually went beyond socialism. With Friedrich Engels, Marx wrote a pamphlet in 1848 entitled the *Communist Manifesto.* The word *communism* comes from the Latin word *communis,* meaning "belonging to all in common." Marx used this word in his title because he believed that the world's goods should belong to everyone in common, not to private individuals. He also wanted to distinguish his ideas from those of other socialists.

Marx's pamphlet presented its readers with an economic interpretation of history. In it, Marx argued that the group controlling economic power also has political and social power. He believed that history is a conflict between opposing economic forces—a class struggle. According to this view, these classes, the "haves and have-nots," have struggled for control throughout history. With the coming of the Industrial Revolution, many people saw the class struggle developing between the bourgeoisie and the proletariat—that is, between the owners of the means of production and the laborers in factories and mines, who owned nothing but their ability to work.

In Marx's view, workers did not receive the entire value of their labor. Instead, capitalists took most labor value as profit. As a result, the bourgeoisie got richer and richer while the proletariat became poorer and poorer.

Marx was encouraged, however, by the lessons he saw in history. He believed that class struggle was a law of society that would continue to operate whenever economic inequality existed. Eventually, Marx predicted, economic conditions would become so bad that the proletariats would rise up and seize power from their capitalist oppressors.

Picturing History   Karl Marx (left) and Lenin.

Communism.   Although the ideas of Marx have had worldwide influence, they had their greatest impact in Russia. There, radical socialists favored quick, drastic action to achieve their goals. Headed by V. I. Lenin, these revolutionaries called themselves Communists and declared that socialism was only a temporary stage through which a nation

Picturing History A housing complex and a metro entrance in modern-day Moscow. Despite some improvements in life during more than seventy years of Communist rule, widespread discontent and political-economic reform led to the dissolution of the U.S.S.R. in 1991.

passed on the way to a truly Communist state. After the start of the Russian Revolution in 1917, the Soviet Communists broke completely with other socialist groups. Eventually, the Communists under Lenin's direction won a bloody civil war and then established a Communist government called the Union of Soviet Socialist Republics (U.S.S.R.). In setting up their economic system, Communist leaders also set up a political system that left no room for individual rights or personal freedom.

The Communist leaders demanded complete government ownership of factories, machines, land, and other basic means of production. Private enterprise was outlawed. They held that the government should be run by the Communist party, which would plan all of the nation's economic activity. The Soviets encouraged other Communists around the world to unite in overthrowing capitalism—if necessary, by using force and violence.

United States Rejects Other Systems. Although the Communist takeover in Russia caused concern in the United States, the economic ideas included in that system did not have a strong impact on American society. Similarly, socialists never received more than a small percentage of votes in any American presidential election.

Why did socialism fail to attract a significant following in the United States? One important reason is that capitalism can be regulated. Over the years, Americans and their elected representatives have successfully modified the less desirable features of capitalism. Without regulations, capitalism can lead to unfair monopolies that restrict competition. When that happens, workers can be denied just wages for their labor.

The federal government responded to the problems involved in the growth of capitalism during the late 1800's. To check the problems of unrestricted capitalism, the government eventually encouraged the growth of labor unions and became involved in the regulation of business. Thus, our current economic system is actually a modified capitalist system. However, the additional rules and regulations have created more overall equity and justice. They have also made systems such as socialism and communism unattractive to most Americans.

The goals of many socialists have changed over the years, and today socialist democracies are common in European nations. Communism, however, usually has a strong appeal in poor, undeveloped nations. Although communist systems in the U.S.S.R. and Eastern Europe have recently been overturned in favor of free market reforms, the struggle between capitalism and communism continues.

Understanding Economics

1. How does capitalism differ from communism?
2. Explain Marx's view of history. Have his predictions proven to be correct?
3. Why did the economic system of the U.S.S.R. not have a strong impact on the United States?

Critical Thinking

4. Why does communism appeal to many people living in poorer, more underdeveloped nations? What can the United States do to counteract this appeal?

Key Terms and People

These are highlighted in the text in the order in which they appear in this list.

Main Ideas

1. Nationalism created demands for more freedom and led to the assassination of Archduke Franz Ferdinand. Imperialism led to clashes between nations wanting colonies. System of alliances created treaties calling for member nations to go to the aid of other members. Militarism caused stockpiling of arms and an arms race, bringing nations to the brink of war.
2. Austria declared war on Serbia. Since Serbia was an ally of Russia, Russia then declared war on Austria; the allies of both nations then joined the war.
3. Some were pacifists; some felt the war was a matter between imperialists; some felt the war did not involve American interests.
4. German U-boats sank three passenger ships on which Americans were traveling—
• *Lusitania, Arabic, Sussex*; did not respect neutral flags; sank ships that were not from combatant nations.
5. Businesses and factories were forced to hire more women; military drafted African Americans; labor unions began striking for better working conditions.
6. U.S. supplied troops, ships, food, and military supplies to the Allies; helped tighten the blockade around Germany; supplied ships, sub chasers, and airplanes to protect convoys; fielded an army in France; provided fighter plane unit. • Pershing.
➤**7.** Open covenants openly arrived at; freedom of the seas; removal of tariffs and other economic barriers; arms reduction; colonial policies to respect interests of colonial peoples. • Boundary changes. • Wilson felt League of Nations was the only way to keep the peace.

8. Defeated Axis powers were not represented at the peace conference; Germany was assigned blame for the war and lost the Saar, so all Germans were against the treaty; Russia was not represented and lost more territory than Germany did. The interests of colonial nations in Southeast Asia were not respected. • Wilson, Clemenceau, Lloyd George, Orlando.

Critical Thinking Questions

9. Possible answer: It was miraculous to see something so wondrous and beautiful in such horrible circumstances.
10. To be ready in case of war.
11. Because of the system of alliances. • U.S. policy of neutrality.
12. Possible answer: was a powerful, invincible force.

➤**13.** Possible answers: the Zimmerman note; German declaration of unrestricted submarine warfare; a major financial interest in the Allied powers; Wilson's goal to make the world safe for democracy gave Americans justification for war.
14. Prevent espionage and damage to war effort by penalizing anyone who interfered with the draft, obstructed the

---

CHAPTER 23 REVIEW

Write your answers on a separate sheet of paper.

Key Terms and People

Explain the significance of: Triple Entente, Triple Alliance, Schlieffen Plan, trench warfare, stalemate, contraband, Kaiser Wilhelm, Charles Evans Hughes, Zimmermann note, War Industries Board, Bernard Baruch, Food Administration, Herbert Hoover, Marshal Ferdinand Foch, mandates, Sudetenland, Ho Chi Minh

Main Ideas

1. Name the four factors that led to the outbreak of war between the Central Powers and the Allies. Explain how these factors caused the First World War.
2. Why was the assassination of Archduke Franz Ferdinand the immediate cause of the war?
3. Why did most Americans feel that the war in Europe was not their concern?
4. How did the activities of the German U-boats draw the United States into the war? Give specific examples.
5. How did America's war effort change American society?
6. In what specific ways did the Americans help the Allies win the war? Who was chief of the American forces?
7. List the first five of Wilson's Fourteen Points. What were the next eight points about? Discuss Wilson's reasons for proposing the League of Nations.
8. Why did the Treaty of Versailles fail to establish a lasting peace? Who were the Big Four who wrote it?

Critical Thinking Questions

9. **Analyzing Literature.** The selection on page 589 presents the thoughts of a young Italian soldier during World War I. Why do you think he calls the black cloud "something miraculous"?
10. **Analyzing Motives.** Why did the European nations stockpile arms in the early 1900's?
11. **Comparing Motives.** Why did the nations of

Europe mobilize so quickly after the assassination of Archduke Franz Ferdinand? Why did the United States resist getting involved in war?
12. **Analyzing Quotations.** What do you learn about the German army from reading Richard Harding Davis's description of it on page 593?
13. **Making Inferences.** Why do you think President Wilson finally decided to declare war on Germany?
14. **Synthesizing Ideas.** What was the original purpose of the Espionage and Sedition Acts? How did they become a means of crushing dissent?
15. **Analyzing Ideas.** What part did Henry Cabot Lodge and isolationists play in defeating ratification of the Treaty of Versailles?

Critical Thinking Activities

16. **Organizing Ideas.** Complete a chart listing reasons Americans had for and against entering the war.

World War I Involvement

Reasons For	Reasons Against

17. **Analyzing Maps.** Compare the maps on pages 597 and 605. What happened to the Austrian-Hungarian Empire after World War I? What happened to Serbia and Montenegro?
18. **Linking Past to Present.** World War I was called "the war to end all wars." Can you think of another war that was intended to end all aggression on earth? Did it succeed? Why or why not?
19. **Linking Past to Present.** The First World War introduced the use of new, more deadly weapons in warfare. Are today's weapons as deadly or are they more destructive than those used in World War I? Which of the earlier war's weapons are still in use?

TELESCOPING THE TIMES: 1914–1920

The First World War

The First World War brought death to millions of people, especially in Europe. As we look back now, we can identify several long-range causes of the war, such as nationalism, imperialism, increased militarism, and military alliances. Each of several ethnic groups wanted to form its own nation. Russia saw itself as champion of all Slavic peoples, even those in Austria-Hungary. In addition, industrialization and nationalism led to imperialism overseas, where Great Britain, France, and Germany were competing for colonies. Competing nations built up their military and naval forces. A system of alliances created a dangerous situation. The assassination of Archduke Franz Ferdinand, however, was the immediate cause of World War I.

Before America's entry into World War I, most Americans agreed with President Wilson's policy of neutrality toward the war in Europe, even though a majority favored Britain and France. The American people regarded with horror the German invasion of France and the ensuing years of bloody trench warfare, with terrible new weapons adding to the millions of deaths. British warships blockaded Germany, and German submarines began to take American lives at sea. In 1916, Wilson won reelection by promising to keep the United States out of the war. However, renewed attacks on American ships by German submarines pushed him to the brink of war. The Zimmermann note and the revolution in Russia added to the pressure.

Gradually, the nation edged closer to active participation in the war. Finally, on April 6, 1917, Congress declared war on Germany. By means of a draft, Americans mobilized a huge army, which included black troops in segregated units. To mobilize the economy, Congress gave the executive branch new wartime powers. Federal boards regulated key industries, labor unions, and food pro-

duction. The government borrowed billions of dollars by selling United States savings bonds. Among the people, conformity became the order of the day. The Espionage and Sedition Acts were used against radicals, pacifists, and others who spoke against the war. Americans were also suspicious of everything German. After Russia withdrew from the war because of the Bolshevik Revolution, the arrival of American troops in Europe led eventually to victory for the Allies.

At the Versailles Peace Conference, Wilson fought for his Fourteen Points. These included the establishment of a League of Nations. The 1919 peace treaty carved out new nations from territories previously held by Germany, Austria-Hungary, Turkey, and Russia. By the treaty's terms, Germany had to give up its overseas colonies, admit guilt for the war, reduce its armed forces, and pay reparations. After the peace conference, isolationist fears mounted in the United States Senate. Wilson stubbornly refused to compromise with his critics in the Senate, and the Senate refused to ratify the treaty. By now ill and broken, Wilson failed to bring the United States into the League of Nations.

Chronology of Main Events	
1914	World War I begins in Europe
1917	Wilson inaugurated for second term; Germany resumes unrestricted submarine warfare; U.S. declares war on Germany
1918	Wilson presents Fourteen Points; armistice ends war
1919	Treaty of Versailles signed

Telescoping the Times may be used as an alternative to having students read the entire chapter, as a chapter preview, or as a chapter review.

Global Perspectives

For Discussion

How might Gandhi's civil disobedience campaign have influenced future protests in the U.S.? (Possible response: civil rights leaders such as Dr. Martin Luther King, Jr., influenced by Gandhi's practice of nonviolent protest, applied his philosophy to civil rights problems in U.S.)

Additional Resources

- Geography Activities
- Skills Activities
- Thematic Activities
- Economic Activities
- Cultural Literacy Activities
- Literary Source Readings
- Primary Source Readings
- Nuclear Peacekeeping
- Transparencies
- Computer Test Generator

CD-ROM:
1992 Time Almanac

Begin using the *1992 Time Almanac* with Chapter 24. See note on page T-9. For specific activity suggestions, refer to *Activity Guide for Using 1992 Time Almanac CD-ROM* with The Americans.

Additional Teaching Strategies

SECTION 1

For Basic Students: Have students use encyclopedias or other reference books to research and write a three-paragraph essay about the history and current status of the Women's Christian Temperance Union in the United States. (Essay might include: was founded in Cleveland, in 1874; spread to other countries; is headquartered in Evanston, IL; is much diminished in influence today.)

For Advanced Students: After they do additional research on the Scopes trial, choose students to present closing arguments for Clarence Darrow and William Jennings Bryan. The rest of the class should act as jurors and judge the case on the facts and on the closing arguments presented by the student lawyers. (Closing arguments might include: Darrow—church and state should be separate; Darwin's theory is a legitimate scientific subject and should be taught. Bryan—Christian teachings should guide curriculum; Darwin's theory is not proven; the Bible should be the only guide.)

SECTION 2

For Basic Students: Have students research to find pictures, sketches, or photos of the styles of the 1920's and prepare a display of these. Ask students to find examples of current styles that may be similar. Have students present their displays to the class.

For Advanced Students: Have each student choose a partner and write a chapter that might have appeared in Dorothy Canfield Fisher's 1924 novel *The Homemaker*, paying particular attention to the language, customs and roles of the 1920's. Have students share their chapters with the class.

SECTION 3

For Basic Students: Have each student choose a partner. Ask each pair to prepare a list of five major figures associated with the Harlem Renaissance and note at least one factor about each person's contribution to black culture. (Lists might include: Langston Hughes—poetry; Countee Cullen—poetry; Paul Robeson—acting and singing; Roland Hayes—singing; Louis Armstrong—jazz musician; W. C. Handy—composer; Josephine Baker—singer/dancer.) Have students share their lists.

For Advanced Students: Have students research and prepare a two-page report on the Chicago race riot of 1919, emphasizing its causes and the effects it had on the city. Have students discuss their findings. (Causes include: black migration to the North; competition for jobs; housing shortages. Effects include: tension between the races; repression; creation of black ghetto; new restrictive laws.)

SECTION 4

For Basic Students: Ask students to choose and research one of the popular national figures from the 1920's mentioned in this chapter and to prepare a short article on that person for *People* magazine, identifying his or her field and major accomplishments. (Article on Jack Dempsey might include: born in Manassa, CO; had eighth-grade education; won heavyweight championship in 1919; held crown for seven years; lost crown to Gene Tunney in 1926.)

For Advanced Students: Have students research one major work by F. Scott Fitzgerald or T. S. Eliot and write a short summary of the work explaining how it criticized society at that time. (Summary of Eliot's *The Waste Land* might include: describes the problems of post-World War I society and the poet's sense of futility; contains many criticisms of the social strata, the dull world of workers, and the monotony of 1920's society.)

Further Reading for Students

Nonfiction

Allen, Frederick Lewis. *Only Yesterday: An Informal History of the Nineteen-Twenties*. New York: Harper & Row, 1964.

Carter, Paul A. *The Twenties in America*, 2nd ed. Arlington Heights, Ill.: Harlan Davidson, 1975.

Du Bois, W.E.B. *The Souls of Black Folk*. Bergenfield, N. J.: New American Library, 1969.

Ross, Walter S. *The Last Hero: Charles A. Lindbergh*. New York: Woodhill, 1979.

Williams, Martin. *The Jazz Tradition*, rev. ed. New York: Oxford University Press, 1983.

Fiction

Fitzgerald, F. Scott. *The Great Gatsby*. New York: Charles Scribner's Sons, 1981.

Fitzgerald, F. Scott. *This Side of Paradise*. New York: Charles Scribner's Sons, 1987.

Lewis, Sinclair. *Main Street*. New York: New American Library, 1974.

Bibliography for Teachers

Books

Baritz, Loren, ed. *The Culture of the Twenties: 1920-1929*. New York: Macmillan, 1970.

Boardman, Tom W. *America and the Jazz Age: A History of the Twenties*. New York: Henry Z. Walck, 1968.

Breckinridge, Sophonisba P. *Women in the Twentieth Century: A Study of Their Political, Social, and Economic Activities*. Reprint of 1933 ed. Salem, N. H.: Ayer Company, 1972.

Leuchtenburg, William. *The Perils of Prosperity: Nineteen Fourteen to Nineteen Thirty Two*. Chicago: University of Chicago Press, 1958.

Lewis, David L. *When Harlem Was in Vogue*. New York: Alfred A. Knopf, 1981.

Sinclair, Andrew. *Era of Excess: A Social History of the Prohibition Movement*. New York: Harper & Row, 1964.

This Fabulous Century, Volume III, 1920-1930. New York: Time-Life Books, 1969.

Audio-Visuals

Harlem in the Twenties. Encyclopaedia Britannica Educational Corp. Movie.

Jazz Age. McGraw-Hill Films. Movie.

Men in Crisis: Lindbergh vs. The Atlantic (Ordeal by Air). University of Illinois Film Center. Movie.

The Reckless Years: 1919-1927. Guidance Associates. Movie.

The United States in the Twentieth Century, 1920-1932. Simon & Shuster Communications. Movie.

Will Rogers' 1920's: A Cowboy's Guide to the Times. Churchill Films. Movie.

Teacher's Notes:

Teaching Resources, Unit 6 Booklet

Chapter Objectives

Students will learn:
- why a conflict in value systems developed during the 1920's
- how the status of women changed during the 1920's
- the major events and accomplishments of the Harlem Renaissance
- what prompted changes in education and popular culture in the 1920's

Using the Chapter Time Line

How many years passed between the first women's rights convention (see Unit 3 Time Line) and the passage of the Nineteenth Amendment? (Answer: 72) How many years passed between the Wright Brothers' first flight (see Chapter 22 Time Line) and Lindbergh's solo flight to Paris? (Answer: 24)

Picturing History   Charles Lindbergh, known as the Lone Eagle, helped design the Spirit of St. Louis for the purpose of flying nonstop from New York to Paris. He was determined to win the $25,000 prize that was promised to the first person to accomplish this feat.

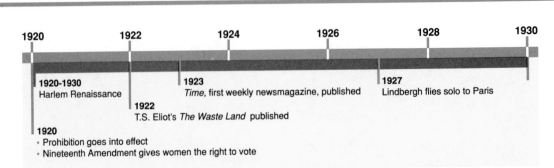

1920   1922   1924   1926   1928   1930

1920-1930
Harlem Renaissance

1923
Time, first weekly newsmagazine, published

1927
Lindbergh flies solo to Paris

1922
T.S. Eliot's *The Waste Land* published

1920
• Prohibition goes into effect
• Nineteenth Amendment gives women the right to vote

Links to American Literature

F. Scott Fitzgerald: born in St. Paul, Minnesota, 1896; educated at Princeton University; served in U.S. Army from 1917 to 1919; lived in Europe from 1924 to 1931; moved to Hollywood in 1937 to write for motion pictures; focused later writings on the corruption of individuals by the crassness of modern society; lived a dramatic life marked by the mental illness of his wife, Zelda, and an early death from alcoholism.

Works include: *Flappers and Philosophers* (1920); *Tales of the Jazz Age* (1922); *The Beautiful and the Damned* (1922); *The Great Gatsby*

(1925); *The Last Tycoon* (published posthumously in 1941).

This Side of Paradise: a keen and sensitive insight into the falseness of the jazz era in America.

Introducing the Chapter

Discuss with students the idea that change is a constant and on-going process. The 1920's, however, were marked by great changes in many areas. Ask students how society as a whole responds to change. (Possible responses: usually reacts very slowly; often overreacts to changes; enforces new rules to maintain status quo.) As they read this chapter, have students watch for and note the changes that occurred in the 1920's and the conflicts the changes created.

CHAPTER **24** 1920–1930

The 1920's Bring Social Change

Links to American Literature

"A slicker."

"What the devil's that?"

"Well, it's something that—that—there's a lot of them. You're not one, and neither am I, though I am more than you are."

"Who is one? What makes you one?" . . . They spent two evenings getting an exact definition. The slicker was good-looking or clean-looking; he had brains, social brains, that is, and he used all means on the broad path of honesty to get ahead, be popular, admired, and never in trouble. He dressed well, was particularly neat in appearance, and derived his name from the fact that his hair was inevitably worn short, soaked in water or tonic, parted in the middle, and slicked back as the current of fashion dictated. The slickers of that year had adopted tortoise-shell spectacles as badges of their slickerhood, and this made them so easy to recognize that Amory and Rahill never missed one. The slicker seemed distributed through school, always a little wiser and shrewder than his contemporaries, managing some team or other, and keeping his cleverness carefully concealed. . . . The slicker was a definite element of success, differing intrinsically from the prep school "big man."

— F. SCOTT FITZGERALD, *This Side of Paradise*

The 1920's were a time of great social change characterized by apparent prosperity, new ideas, and personal freedom. The economic boom of the era was short-lived, but most of the social changes were lasting.

Chapter Overview

In this chapter you will learn about the conflict of values that came about during the 1920's as a result of changing manners and morals. In addition, you will learn about the changes in the status of women, about the accomplishments of the Harlem Renaissance, and about the changes in education and popular culture that occurred at that time. To help you understand the period that is often called

the Roaring Twenties, Chapter 24 is divided into four sections.

Chapter Outline

1. **Manners and Morals Change**
2. **Women Enjoy New Careers and Life Styles**
3. **A Black Renaissance Emerges**
4. **Education and Popular Culture Change**

Anticipate the Lesson

Ask students what causes differences in values to develop between groups of people. (Possible responses: advancing technology; changing attitudes; education; fluctuations in the economy.)

State the Objective

Understand why a conflict in value systems developed during the 1920's.

Present the Lesson

Ask students to review the section and to discuss the highly publicized clash over religious issues. (Discussion might include: Scopes taught Darwin's theory of evolution in public school; fundamentalists objected; Darrow defended Scopes, who was open about his action; Bryan appeared as prosecutor in a trial that was turned into a media circus; Scopes was found guilty and fined; Tennessee Supreme Court later set aside verdict on a technicality.)

Ask students to list on the board the highlights of the conflict over alcohol consumption. (List should include: on January 16, 1920, the Eighteenth Amendment establishing Prohibition goes into effect; speakeasies open and sell liquor illegally; bootlegging flourishes; in 1933, Prohibition is repealed by the Twenty-first Amendment.)

SECTION 1

Manners and Morals Change

GLOSSARY TERMS: **Prohibition, speakeasies**

The 1920 census was the first to show that a majority of the United States population was urban. A little more than half of the nation's 106 million people now lived in cities and towns. Ten years later the population had increased by 17 million, with an increase of 15 million in urban areas.

Two Ways of Life Exist in America

Living in cities, especially for people who moved there from rural areas, often meant a change in behavior. Standards of conduct were more relaxed in the city. City dwellers tended to be more tolerant of such activities as drinking and gambling. Social relations between men and women were less carefully regulated. Many small-town people were shocked by this. They felt that city life must inevitably lead to moral decay. City dwellers, on the other hand, felt that behavior was a matter of personal choice rather than public decision.

At the same time, life in urban communities was unquestionably lively and stimulating. There were many things to see—museums, art exhibits, plays, athletic events, trade expositions, and the like. New ideas in science were examined and often accepted. People tended to be judged on their accomplishments rather than on their social background. As a result, the city held great appeal for thousands of young men and women who had returned from the war in Europe. That experience had broadened their horizons, and as a popular song of the time wondered, "How ya gonna keep 'em down on the farm, after they've seen Paree?"

Clashes Occur over Religious Matters

The most vigorous clash between modern and more traditional Americans took place over religion. An example was the so-called monkey trial held in Dayton, Tennessee, in 1925. John T. Scopes, in teaching his high-school biology class, used a textbook outlining Darwin's theory of evolution. This theory was accepted by a majority of scientists. Many fundamentalists, however, were shocked by the idea that humans had evolved over millions of years from lower life forms. (Fundamentalists believe in a literal interpretation of the Bible.) They pointed to the Bible's clear statement that the universe and humanity had been created in six days. To deny that, fundamentalists said, was to deny the Scriptures and to blaspheme against God. They did not want the theory of evolution taught to their children.

Earlier in March 1925 Tennessee passed a law that forbade the teaching of evolution. Scopes went on trial for violating the state law in July. The American Civil Liberties Union (ACLU) engaged **Clarence Darrow**, the most famous trial lawyer of

People in the Chapter

Carrie Chapman Catt and her husband signed a contract before their marriage that guaranteed Ms. Catt two months each spring and two months each fall to do her suffrage work. When the wealthy magazine editor Miriam Leslie died, she left almost one million dollars to Ms. Catt for the cause of woman suffrage.

Claude McKay was a black drama critic. When he tried to get seated on the main floor for a Broadway performance of "He Who Gets Slapped," the usher took his tickets and replaced them with balcony seats. "The important fact, with which I was suddenly slapped in the face," recalled McKay, "was my color."

Louis Armstrong captivated audiences around the world. His gravelly voice, which was once described as sounding like a fish-horn, became his trademark. He was nicknamed Satchelmouth by a London editor. The name was shortened to Satchmo, but his fans loved to call him Pops.

Charles Lindbergh was greeted in New York by four million people after his historic nonstop flight. The ticker-tape parade up Broadway produced a blizzard of eighteen thousand tons of paper. It was the most enthusiastic welcome in the city's history.

614

Check for Understanding

Call on individual students to answer Section 1 Review questions orally.

Guided Practice

Tell students that the controversy over teaching evolution in public schools is not over. There is still a movement to ensure that the "creationist" version of evolution is included in school curricula. Ask students whether they think both the theory of evolution and creationism should be presented as two theories of the origin of man, thereby enabling students to make their own judgments. (Possible re-

sponses: some students may argue in favor of presenting both theories as being most equitable; others may see the creationist theory as a religious teaching and feel that it violates separation of church and state.)

Assign Independent Practice

Ask students to write a two-paragraph essay describing the differences between city and rural life styles in the 1920's and explaining why these differences led to conflict between the two groups. (Differences might include: standards of conduct were more relaxed in the city; city dwellers were more tolerant of drinking and gambling; relations between men and women were less carefully regulated in the city; small town people believed life in the city might lead to moral decay.) Have one or two students read their paragraphs to the class.

the day, for the defense. William Jennings Bryan, three-time Democratic candidate for President, appeared as a special prosecutor. There was no question of guilt or innocence; Scopes was open about his action. The trial was supposed to hinge on a teacher's freedom to teach. Actually it became a battle of wits between Darrow—who did not believe in organized religion—and Bryan—a fundamentalist Christian—over the meaning of the Scriptures.

Reporters and photographers from big-city dailies, who had come to make fun of rural values, gave the **Scopes trial** a circus air. The jury found Scopes guilty and he was fined, but the Tennessee Supreme Court set the verdict aside on a technicality.

Picturing History Clarence Darrow (in suspenders) and William Jennings Bryan defended opposite sides at the Scopes trial.

Americans Try the Noble Experiment

Some of the abuse heaped on traditionalist America in the 1920's resulted directly from its greatest victory. On January 16, 1920, the Eighteenth Amendment—prohibiting the manufacture, sale, or transportation of alcoholic beverages—went into effect. Progressive reformers saw in the liquor trade a prime source of corruption. They felt that drunkenness led to crime, child abuse, accidents on the job, and similar problems. They had pushed the measure, but it took the church-affiliated Anti-Saloon League and the Women's Christian Temperance Union—which regarded drinking as a sin—to put the amendment across. As with woman suffrage, large areas of the country had adopted **Prohibition** by state law even before the constitutional amendment was ratified.

Use of Alcohol Declines. The persistent myth that drinking increased under Prohibition is not true. Drunkenness and alcoholism declined significantly in spite of **speakeasies** (places where liquor was illegally sold) that operated almost openly in working-class neighborhoods. For some people, however, liquor's illegality added to its attractiveness, and such persons may have increased their alcoholic consumption. At least in sophisticated circles, serving illegal liquor was a sign of being modern. Many films, plays, and novels helped reinforce that attitude.

Bootlegging Flourishes. Providers of illegal drink were known as bootleggers. They smuggled beer and whiskey in from Canada or stole it from government warehouses. Often they mixed the liquor with other substances including embalming fluid. Like large-scale gambling, bootlegging was controlled by hoodlums like **Al Capone**. Again like large-scale gambling, bootlegging could exist only because bribes were paid to police and judges. As a result, many people grew skeptical about the honesty of public officials, and disrespect for the law increased.

Picturing History During Prohibition in the 1920's, bootleggers wore oversized overcoats to hide tins of beer and whiskey strapped to their legs. The bootleggers usually smuggled the liquor to cutting plants, where it was watered down and bottled.

Prohibition Repealed. Before the 1920's were far advanced, many Americans decided that Prohibition's social benefits were not worth the costs. Organized crime had increased to a fantastic extent, and taxes (to pay for law enforcement) had gone up. In addition, many Americans felt that Prohibition invaded their individual rights. Why should society control how they behaved in private? Yet the supporters of Prohibition—especially religious fundamentalists and rural dwellers—

Student Assignment/Homework

Have students read Section 2, "Women Enjoy New Careers and Life Styles," and answer Section 2 Review questions on paper.

SECTION 2

Core Lesson

Anticipate the Lesson

Discuss with students the woman suffrage activities of Alice Paul, Lucy Burns, and the National Women's party between January 10, 1917, and January 9, 1918. (Discussion should include: members of the party carried banners outside the White House urging passage of the Anthony amendment; they were subjected to abuse from hostile crowds; they were eventually jailed as public nuisances; they were force-fed when they attempted a hunger strike; their tactics and the public's reactions forced Congress to deal with the issue of woman suffrage.)

SECTION 1 REVIEW

Answers

Main Ideas

1. Small-town: behavior is a public issue and should be regulated by communities. Urban: behavior is a matter of personal choice, and society should be tolerant.

2. Evolutionists, who represented modern views, clashed with fundamentalists, who represented traditional views, over opposing views of creation.

3. While public drunkenness and alcoholism declined, so did general respect for the law; both organized crime and taxes to pay for law enforcement increased.

Critical Thinking

4. Possible answer: the Constitution, as the law of the land and as a historical document, symbolizes the principles and the continuity of American democracy. Amendments, therefore, should be considered carefully, have lasting value, and apply to the nation as a whole. **(evaluation)**

Picturing History The more liquor federal agents destroyed, the more there seemed to be to replace it.

would not yield. Alfred E. Smith's open opposition to Prohibition counted heavily against him in two national elections. Other politicians, such as Robert La Follette, Herbert Hoover, and Franklin D. Roosevelt, skirted the issue. Hoover, for example, called Prohibition "a noble experiment," that is, something that may or may not work. Nevertheless, the Eighteenth Amendment was finally repealed in 1933 by the Twenty-first Amendment.

SECTION 1 REVIEW

Key Terms and People

Explain the significance of: Clarence Darrow, Scopes Trial, Prohibition, speakeasies, Al Capone

Main Ideas

1. In general, how did the views of small-town Americans about morality and personal conduct differ from those of city dwellers during the 1920's?
2. How did the Scopes trial demonstrate religious differences between modern and more traditional Americans?
3. What were the important results of Prohibition?

Critical Thinking

4. Prohibition involved two amendments to the Constitution, one to establish the measure and one to abolish it. Did these amendments constitute an abuse of the Constitution? Explain.

SECTION 2

Women Enjoy New Careers and Life Styles

GLOSSARY TERM: **flappers**

President Wilson's New Freedom program became a reality on another level. After a long and difficult struggle (see page 467), women began the decade with a new freedom: the right to vote.

During World War I, women served their country in almost every possible capacity. They took jobs in steel foundries, chemical plants, and munitions factories. Many went overseas as nurses in the newly created Army Corps of Nurses. Their experiences away from home and traditional women's work gave them a strong moral argument for the right to vote. As the war progressed, an increasing number of men joined women in seeing the absurdity of fighting for freedom in Europe but denying full freedom to women at home.

Although women were urged not to disrupt the war effort and to put aside their struggle for the vote until later, some women refused to be put off. They had been told to wait after the Civil War and were reluctant to do so again. In 1914 **Alice Paul** and **Lucy Burns** formed the National Woman's party and began a campaign of parades and picketing patterned after the English suffrage movement to draw attention to the issue. Beginning on January 10, 1917, they took a stand outside the White House and for almost a year—in sunshine, rain, sleet, and snow—they carried purple, white, and gold banners urging passage of the constitutional amendment that would give them the right to vote. This became known as the Anthony amendment. President Wilson invited them into the White House for hot coffee but otherwise did nothing to help. The women were subjected to jeers and even physical abuse by onlookers. Finally, they were carried off to jail as public nuisances. When they went on a hunger strike to protest their treatment, they were force-fed.

Woman's Suffrage Finally Succeeds

The tactics of the women and the shameful way they were treated finally forced Congress to deal with the issue. On January 9, 1918, President Wilson declared himself in favor of woman suffrage, and on January 10 the Anthony amendment

State the Objective

Understand how the status of women changed during the 1920's.

Present the Lesson

On the board write the following categories: political status, fashion, interests, goals, jobs, roles. Ask students to identify at least one specific example of changes women of the 1920's experienced in these areas. (Possible responses: political status—passage of the Nineteenth Amendment gave women the right to vote; fashion—shorter skirts, shorter hair, make-up, drinking and smoking in public; interests—social, economic, and political problems; goals—public office, child labor laws, equal rights amendment; jobs—increase in number of women doctors, bankers, lawyers, police; roles—women as part of work force, the sharing of household responsibilities with husbands.)

Picturing History Victory at last! When the Nineteenth Amendment was ratified on August 26, 1920, members of the National Woman's party celebrated their hard-won right to vote. These women continued to work for women's rights in general.

passed the House with the bare two-thirds majority. The crowd in the gallery clapped and shouted approval. Women broke into the hymn "Praise God from Whom All Blessings Flow." Still, it took another year and a half as well as the election of a new Congress to get the amendment through the Senate. Finally, on August 26, 1920, the last of the necessary thirty-seven states ratified the **Nineteenth Amendment** and it became law.

In 1923 **Carrie Chapman Catt**, former president of the National American Woman Suffrage Association, described the effort it had taken to secure adoption of the Anthony amendment, which was named after reformer Susan B. Anthony:

> To get the word "male" in effect out of the Constitution cost the women of the country 52 years of pauseless campaign. . . .During that time they were forced to conduct . . . 480 campaigns to get legislatures to submit suffrage amendments to voters; 47 campaigns to get state constitutional conventions to write woman suffrage into state constitutions; 277 campaigns to get state party conventions to include woman suffrage planks; . . . and 19 campaigns with 19 successive Congresses.

For some people, concern over the changing status of women did not center on participation in politics. Instead, it centered on such matters as wearing short skirts, cutting hair, painting faces, and smoking and drinking in public. Many women and men were deeply shocked by such behavior. They believed it was a symptom of moral decay. Others, in contrast, regarded it as a symbol of freedom and progress.

After 1910 women's skirts rose above their traditional street length. That length had been difficult to walk in and had collected street dirt as well. Since fashion is changeable, people predicted skirts would soon go down again. Nevertheless, wartime shortages of fabric and more active occupations kept them nine inches above the ground. Then in the twenties they climbed even higher, finally going just above the knee. During the twenties, too, the whalebone-reinforced corset, which constricted the waist and sometimes damaged the body's internal organs, was thrown into the trash can along with layers of petticoats.

Women's hairstyles were next to undergo drastic changes. The short haircut that swept the nation in the 1920's was called a bob, or a boyish bob if very short. Like the new clothing styles, it was sensible, healthy, and neat—and the subject of loud public outcry.

Linking Past to Present

Because fads and fashions reflect specific attitudes about life, they can reveal a great deal about a particular period of time. The hippies of the 1960's expressed their alienation from society by their choice of clothing in much the same way that women of the 1920's showed their rebellion with short skirts and bobbed hair.

For Discussion

Why do you think the struggle for woman suffrage was able to make progress during the 1920's when for so long it had been stalled? (Possible responses: after assuming greater responsibilities during World War I, women were more determined than ever to secure the right to vote; many returning soldiers felt that they had fought for all Americans and that women deserved the same rights as men.)

The 1920's Bring Social Change **617**

Check for Understanding

Call on individual students to read their answers to Section 3 Review questions.

Guided Practice

Discuss the correlation between fashion and social attitudes. Ask students whether their clothing, hairstyles, and make-up represent their specific attitudes about life in the same way that short skirts and bobbed hair represented rebellion in the 1920's. (Possible responses: clothing and hairstyles reflect their rejection of parents' and elders' view of society; clothing and hairstyles reflect students as they see themselves.)

Assign Independent Practice

Ask students to write two paragraphs explaining how World War I contributed to women's new careers and life styles. (Possible details: women served their country in the military, in steel foundries, in chemical plants, and in munitions factories; women took on the responsibilities of providing for a family and making decisions that were left to men before the war; women who served in the military saw new life styles and had experiences that prepared them to assume new roles and jobs.)

Picturing History Flappers were in vogue in the 1920's. The distinguished photographer Edward Steichen photographed them, and magazines portrayed them kicking up their heels doing the Charleston.

Women's Interests and Goals Change

Young women who adopted all or most of the new styles were called **flappers**. However, the truly emancipated or "new" women of the twenties were something more. They had received upbringings and educations similar to those of men. Progressive Era reforms had sharpened their interest in social, economic, and political problems. Victorious in the suffrage struggle, they had gained self-assurance and were beginning to be able to deal with men on equal terms.

One of the most active and controversial women of the period was Margaret Sanger. As an obstetrical nurse in some of the worst slums of New York City, she saw firsthand the burden placed on poor women who had many children in rapid succession. That led her to open the nation's first birth-control clinic in 1916. She was arrested and

imprisoned eight times for violating the Comstock Law, the national law that prohibited the distribution of birth-control information. Nevertheless, the courts of New York State eventually recognized the right of women to obtain such information. The subject of birth control continues to be extremely controversial.

In addition to voting, some women attempted to enter politics. However, the highest elective offices were still closed to them. Most women got their offices because they were chosen as successors to their husbands, such as two women governors, Nellie Ross of Wyoming and Miriam "Ma" Ferguson of Texas. In 1933 Nellie Ross became the first woman director of the United States mint. In 1916 Jeannette Rankin of Montana was elected to the House of Representatives on her own, but her opposition to America's role in World War I brought defeat in 1918. (She would, however, be back in the House in 1941 to vote against the United States entry into World War II.)

Other political goals of women during the decade ended in disappointment. Florence Kelley led the movement for a constitutional amendment barring child labor, but it was never ratified. An equal rights amendment fared worse; it could not even win the approval of Congress. For most of the public, both measures had become associated with radicalism—a fatal drawback in the 1920's.

Women Assume New Jobs and New Roles

Between 1910 and 1930 the proportion of women in the labor force remained at about 20 percent. However, there was a notable change in the kinds of work some women did. The number of female cooks, dressmakers, household servants, and farmhands dropped. The number of women doctors, bankers, lawyers, police and probation officers, social workers, and hairdressers rose.

Nevertheless, most women remained in the lowest-paying occupations. Unfortunately, in any occupation women were often preferred only because they would work for lower wages than men. As veteran suffragist Anna Howard Shaw explained: "You younger women have a harder task than ours. You will want equality in business, and it will be even harder to get than the vote."

For all the changes in status during the twenties, it was still generally accepted—even by most women—that "woman's place is in the home."

Student Assignment/Homework

Have students read Section 3, "A Black Renaissance Emerges," and prepare a three-column chart showing the goals, ideals, and accomplishments of Booker T. Washington, W.E.B. Du Bois, and Marcus Garvey.

SECTION 3

Core Lesson

Anticipate the Lesson

Draw the outline for a chart on the board heading the columns with Booker T. Washington, W.E.B. Du Bois, and Marcus Garvey. Have students use the charts they constructed for the previous homework assignment to fill in information on each man's ideals, goals, and accomplishments.

Washington: advised blacks to learn vocational skills, live a quiet life, and avoid strife and competition with whites.

Du Bois: was a professor of history and economics, helped found Niagara Movement and NAACP, editor of *The Crisis*, wanted blacks to strive toward higher education.

Garvey: began Universal Negro Improvement Association, believed blacks should go to Africa and build a country of their own, believed blacks should *not* seek integration with whites.

Picturing History In the 1920's, publishing houses employed women who were skilled at operating Linotype keyboards.

Men should earn more than women, it was thought, because usually they supported wives and children. Women workers generally were single. In some states, women teachers who married lost their jobs.

SECTION 2 REVIEW

Key Terms and People

Explain the significance of: Alice Paul, Lucy Burns, Nineteenth Amendment, Carrie Chapman Catt, flappers

Main Ideas

1. How did women succeed in getting the federal government to recognize their right to vote?
2. How did Americans view the new fashions and hairstyles for women in the 1920's?
3. How did flappers differ from more emancipated women of the 1920's?
4. In the 1920's, what important change took place in the female labor force?

Critical Thinking

5. How did women's suffrage improve American democracy? Explain.

SECTION 3

A Black Renaissance Emerges

GLOSSARY TERMS: **National Association for the Advancement of Colored People (NAACP), Harlem Renaissance, Mason-Dixon line**

Until about 1900 most black people in the United States generally accepted Booker T. Washington's advice, which you read about in Chapter 22. He advised blacks to learn vocational skills, live a quiet life (preferably in the country), and avoid strife and competition with whites. Gradually, however, many blacks grew dissatisfied with a life that seemed to promise little future for them economically or intellectually. Consequently, new movements arose in the black community.

African Americans Migrate Northward

Beginning in 1910 the black population of the United States became more urban than the white population. It also began to shift from the South to the North.

In 1914 Henry Ford opened his assembly line to black workers. The outbreak of World War I and the drop in European immigration increased job opportunities in steel mills, munitions plants, and stockyards. In addition, many cotton fields, where African Americans traditionally had been employed in large numbers, were ruined by the boll weevil, an insect that had come to the United States from Mexico. Floods and drought added to the economic difficulties of black sharecroppers and field hands.

So Southern African Americans boarded railroad trains and headed for the top of the world. Between 1910 and 1920 about 1 million African Americans migrated to such Northern cities as Chicago, New York, and Philadelphia. Another 800,000 migrated during the 1920's. This movement is known as the great migration.

Black migrants faced considerable prejudice in their new surroundings. Part of the prejudice was economic. Blacks not only competed with unskilled whites for jobs but also were used as strikebreakers in many Northern industries. Part of the prejudice was racial. Some whites believed they were better than blacks and tried to assert the superiority of the Caucasian race.

SECTION 2 REVIEW

Answers

Main Ideas

1. By picketing, campaigning, agitating, and refusing to give in to the opposition.

2. To some, the new styles were a sign of moral decay; to others, they represented freedom and progress.

3. Flappers adopted the new fashions and styles, but did not adopt the emancipated women's new, confident attitude and political, social, and economic interests.

4. Women began entering traditionally male professions, such as politics, medicine, banking, and law enforcement.

Critical Thinking

5. Possible answer: women's suffrage extended an important democratic right to a large sector of the population. Other minorities could take comfort in the fact that the guaranteed right of protest existed in fact and that government was responsive to it. **(synthesis)**

619

State the Objective

Understand the major events and accomplishments of the Harlem Renaissance.

Present the Lesson

Divide the class into three groups. Have each group prepare a list of notable figures in the Harlem Renaissance and their accomplishments in one of the following areas: literature, theater, music.
Literature: James Weldon Johnson—poet; Langston Hughes—poet; Countee Cullen—poet.
Theater: Roland Hayes—concert singer; Paul Robeson—actor and singer.
Music: King Oliver—jazz; Louis Armstrong—jazz; Cab Calloway—jazz; Duke Ellington—jazz; Ethel Waters—jazz; Bessie Smith—jazz; Josephine Baker—singer and dancer.

Sometimes the prejudice took violent form. The worst race riot in United States history occurred in 1919 in Chicago. Before it ended, some 10,000 persons were involved; 38 were killed (23 blacks and 15 whites), 520 were injured (342 blacks and 178 whites), and 1,000 were left homeless. The riot was sparked on July 27 when a seventeen-year-old black youth swimming in Lake Michigan swam from the water off the so-called black beach to the white beach. There, white bathers threw rocks at him until he drowned. Blacks who were bathing in the area attacked whites in retaliation, and within a few hours mobs were fighting throughout the city. State troops finally restored order after three days.

"We Return Fighting"

Events such as these increased the appeal of more militant black leaders. One was the Massachusetts-born writer and teacher **W. E. B. Du Bois**. The holder of four academic degrees, he was a professor of history and economics at the University of Atlanta from 1897 to 1919. In 1905 he helped found the **Niagara Movement.** According to one historian, this was the "first organized attempt to protest the shameful treatment [African Americans] had suffered since the end of Reconstruction." In 1909 he helped found the **National Association for the Advancement of Colored People (NAACP)** and in 1910 he became a director of that association, a position he held for twenty-four years. He was also editor of its official magazine, *The Crisis.*

Du Bois disagreed with Booker T. Washington regarding goals and tactics. He accused Washington of educating African Americans only to be farmers and artisans. Du Bois wanted black people to strive toward higher education and the industrial mainstream of America. He also was more militant than Washington. In the May 1919 issue of *The Crisis*, he spoke for many returning black soldiers when he wrote: "We *return.* We *return from fighting.* We *return fighting.* Make way for Democracy! We saved it in France—and by the Great Jehovah we will save it in the U.S.A. or know the reason why!"

"Black Is Beautiful"

Another important figure was **Marcus Garvey,** who began the Universal Negro Improvement Association (UNIA) in his native Jamaica in 1914. Two years later, he moved the UNIA to New York City, and by the mid-1920's, he had enrolled more than 500,000 African Americans in its ranks.

Garvey's organization was based on two ideas. First, black people should go back to their African homeland and build a country of their own. This was an idea as old as Paul Cuffe's effort in Sierra Leone in 1815 and the founding of Liberia. (See Chapter 11.) Garvey wanted African Americans to found "a free, redeemed and mighty nation. Let Africa be a bright star among the constellation of nations." The second idea was the slogan "black is beautiful." Blacks should not envy or imitate whites or seek integration. "You are better than white people," Garvey told his followers. He reminded them of their African heritage and urged them to be proud of it.

Picturing History
In *The Souls of Black Folk*, W. E. B. Du Bois proclaimed, "The problem of the twentieth century is the problem of the color line." He vowed to fight against it.

Linking Past to Present

The slogan "black is beautiful," which first appeared in the 1920's, was revived during the 1960's and 1970's. Then in the 1980's, many black Americans stated that they would rather use the term *African American* than the word *black* to identify themselves, preferring to be known in terms of their origins rather than in terms of their skin color. Today, *African American* is widely used in the United States. Marcus Garvey would have strongly supported its usage.

To finance his colonization scheme, Garvey collected money from his followers and started a successful newspaper, *The Negro World.* However,

Picturing History
Marcus Garvey designed this uniform of purple and gold complete with feathered hat for his role as "Provisional President of Africa."

Picturing History
When Ida B. Wells-Barnett began her crusade against lynching, she was a writer and an editor. Later she became a lecturer and community organizer.

his plan for a steamship company, the Black Star Line, failed and led to his being sent to prison for mail fraud. Upon release, he was deported to England.

Many African Americans, especially from the working class, were swept along by Garvey's oratory and developed a strong pride in being black. His scheme for resettlement in Africa, however, held no appeal. Black people were, after all, Americans and had been for generations. Instead of trying to redeem Africa, they felt they should redeem their own country by fighting for equal rights.

African Americans Turn to Congress and the Courts

The NAACP attempted to do just that, mostly through legislation and court cases. In 1919 its secretary, poet and lawyer **James Weldon Johnson,** managed to have an antilynching law introduced in Congress. (Between 1889 and 1919, 3,224 black men and women had been shot, burned, or hanged without trial. Between 1919 and 1927, another 400 blacks were lynched, 10 while wearing their World War I uniforms.) The bill passed the House but was filibustered to death in the Senate. (To filibuster means to hold the floor by talking at length, sometimes for days, in an attempt to postpone or avoid a vote being taken on a subject.) However, the NAACP kept up its campaign through numerous antilynching organizations that had been established earlier by **Ida B. Wells-Barnett.** Gradually the number of lynchings diminished.

The NAACP had little success in its legal battle to do away with white primaries. In most parts of the South, there was virtually no Republican party after Reconstruction. November elections, therefore, were no more than empty formalities. The real decisions were made in Democratic primary elections. Because primaries were open only to party members, it was easy to keep blacks from voting since only whites could join the Democratic party. Although a court victory to bar this practice was obtained in 1927, it proved to be a hollow one. Over time, state officials were able to get around the ruling and find other ways to keep black voters away from the polls.

The Harlem Renaissance Begins

Living conditions in the black ghettos of Northern cities were appalling. Like European immigrants before them, African Americans moved into run-down buildings in slum neighborhoods where they paid high rents for cramped and unsanitary quarters. They were likely to be victimized by landlords and criminal elements, and their children often died of diseases that, in other circumstances, were preventable.

Nevertheless, the move north, especially to New York City's Harlem, released a great burst of creative energy. Harlem was the center of the nation's black intellectual and cultural life, and out of it flooded achievements in literature, music, drama, dance, and painting. These achievements are known collectively as the **Harlem Renaissance,** though some of the best work was done elsewhere.

Guided Practice

Discuss the term *Renaissance* with the class. (Response: a French word meaning a new birth, resurrection.) Ask students why this term is applied to this particular period in black history. (Possible response: black Americans were beginning to demonstrate pride in their own culture and heritage, and from that pride came a wealth of cultural advancements in music, literature, and the performing arts)

Picturing History Many talented African Americans won recognition during the Harlem Renaissance. Pictured from left to right are poet Langston Hughes; editor and sociologist Charles Johnson, who became the first black president of Fisk University; sociologist E. Franklin Frazer; physician and writer Rudolph Fisher; and lawyer and judge Hubert Delany.

Writers. The most lasting contribution of the Harlem Renaissance may have been in poetry. James Weldon Johnson was already well established in 1920, but **Claude McKay, Langston Hughes,** and **Countee Cullen** made their reputations during the decade. Here is part of Cullen's poem "Saturday's Child."

> Some are teethed on a silver spoon,
> With the stars strung for a rattle;
> I cut my teeth as the black raccoon—
> For implements of battle . . . .
> Some are swaddled in silk and down,
> And heralded by a star;
> They swathed my limbs in a sackcloth gown
> On a night that was black as tar . . . .
> For I was born on Saturday—
> "Bad time for planting a seed,"
> Was all my father had to say,
> And, "One mouth more to feed."

Actors and Musicians. It was in the performing arts that African Americans gained their widest audiences. Tenor Roland Hayes won renown as a concert singer, as did Paul Robeson, the son of a runaway slave. Robeson, after making a brilliant record as a student and athlete at Rutgers, went on to Columbia University Law School. His magnificent bass voice and commanding presence brought him early fame as an actor. In 1924 he was the original *Emperor Jones* in Eugene O'Neill's play of the same name. His performance in Shakespeare's *Othello*, first in London and later in New York, made stage history. Nevertheless, the slights and indignities he experienced turned him away from the United States. He spent most of his later years in England and the Soviet Union.

Jazz is generally considered America's outstanding musical achievement. It originated in the latter part of the nineteenth century and was based mostly on black work songs and spirituals, or deeply emotional religious songs. In 1915 New Orleans, or Dixieland, jazz found its way to Chicago. There, King Oliver and a small group, including trumpeter **Louis Armstrong,** played

622

Assign Independent Practice

Have students complete Chapter 23, Section 3
Daily Activity and Enrichment Activity.

Student Assignment/Homework

Have students read Section 4, "Education and
Popular Culture Change," and answer Section
4 Review questions on paper.

what was probably the first jazz heard north of the
Mason-Dixon line, the boundary line between
Pennsylvania and Maryland, which had become a
symbol of division between North and South. The
music quickly spread from Chicago to Kansas City,
Los Angeles, and New York. Black composers and
performers such as Cab Calloway, Duke Ellington,
Ethel Waters, and Bessie Smith helped create the
jazz sound in the 1920's and over time planted it
firmly in American culture.

Many black musical artists achieved great fame
in Europe. Perhaps the most popular was Josephine
Baker, who lived and worked in Paris. She was a
star dancer and singer for forty years. After World
War II, the French government awarded her the
Legion of Honor for her devotion to her adopted
land.

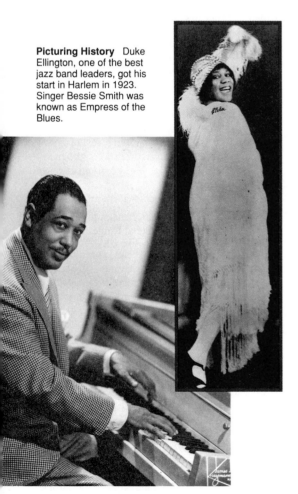

Picturing History Duke
Ellington, one of the best
jazz band leaders, got his
start in Harlem in 1923.
Singer Bessie Smith was
known as Empress of the
Blues.

Picturing History The brilliant jazz recorded by Louis
Armstrong in the 1920's lives on and on.

SECTION 3 REVIEW

Key Terms and People

Explain the significance of: W. E. B. Du Bois,
Niagara Movement, National Association for the
Advancement of Colored People (NAACP),
Marcus Garvey, James Weldon Johnson, Ida B.
Wells-Barnett, Harlem Renaissance, Claude
McKay, Langston Hughes, Countee Cullen,
Louis Armstrong, Mason-Dixon line

Main Ideas

1. What was the great migration, and why did it
   occur?
2. How did W. E. B. Du Bois's views on improving the position of African Americans in America differ from Booker T. Washington's views?
3. On what ideas was Marcus Garvey's Universal
   Negro Improvement Association based?
4. During the 1920's, what resulted from the
   NAACP's attempts to bring about change
   through court cases and legislation?
5. What were the main areas of achievement
   during the Harlem Renaissance?

Critical Thinking

6. The word *renaissance* means "revival, or rebirth." What was revived or reborn during the
   Harlem Renaissance? Explain.

Answers

Main Ideas

1. It was the migration of a
large number of African Americans from the rural South to
the urban North during the
early twentieth century. Reasons were primarily economic.

2. Du Bois, more militant than
Washington, believed blacks
should strive for immediate
change by gaining an aca-
demic education, not just
trade and technical training.
He also wanted them to compete directly with whites in the
economic arena. Washington
favored working for long-term
change in limited areas that
would not seem threatening to
whites.

3. That American blacks
should establish a country of
their own in Africa and that,
because "black is beautiful,"
blacks should not imitate
whites or seek integration.

4. Although Congress failed to
pass a federal antilynching
law, the NAACP's efforts did
help reduce the incidence of
lynchings. The NAACP did win
the legal battle to abolish
white primaries in the South,
but state officials found ways
around the ruling.

5. African Americans made
contributions in poetry, theater, and music both in America
and abroad.

Critical Thinking

6. Possible answer: the accomplishments of black artists
revived black culture and
black pride. **(analysis)**

education; new textbooks and methods of teaching might be evident.)

State the Objective

Understand what prompted changes in education and popular culture in the 1920's.

Anticipate the Lesson

Have students recall the changes in manners and morals, the changes in women's life styles, and the changes in black society that took place in the 1920's. Ask students what changes might come about in education as a result of so many changes occurring in other parts of society. (Possible response: as society advances, education makes changes to keep up; moral liberal attitudes might be reflected in

For Discussion

What were the major factors that reshaped American secondary education in the 1920's? How has high-school education changed since then? (Factors include: increased prosperity of Americans; higher educational standards required for jobs in industries. Changes might include: courses focusing on new technology; increased emphasis on math and sciences; courses on various foreign languages.)

SECTION 4

Education and Popular Culture Change

GLOSSARY TERMS: **tabloids, materialism**

Education, communication, and recreation were other areas in which changes took place during the twenties. The decade also provided the setting for some of our major American novels.

Education Becomes a Growth Industry

American education became a growth industry during the twenties. Its chief area of expansion was in the high school. Until that time, the eighth grade had been the end of formal education for most children. High school—even though it was free—meant financial sacrifice, because most children were counted on to work and to provide a share of the family income until they married and established families of their own.

Increasing Enrollment. In 1914 only half a million Americans were in high school preparing for college or for better jobs in industry. By 1926 the number had jumped to four million. Yet this eightfold increase still accounted for only half the population of high-school age. The remarkable increase was due to prosperous times and to higher educational standards for jobs in mass-production industries. If a person wanted a good job, he or she needed a high-school education.

Increasing Taxes. The greater numbers of high-school students meant a steep increase in taxes. School costs doubled from 1913 to 1920, and they doubled again by 1926. The first jump was a result of inflation, but it was a staggering sum nevertheless. In fact, the total cost of American education in the mid-1920's—2.7 billion dollars a year—was half the amount spent on education by all other countries combined!

The modern high school appeared during this time. Before this, high school had been designed primarily for those going on to college. Now it had courses for the entire community. Larger student bodies meant wider offerings of courses, including vocational training and home economics.

Educating Immigrants. A special challenge schools faced in the 1920's was educating the children of immigrants. Although schools had been doing that for over fifty years, the period just before World War I saw the largest immigration in the nation's history—close to a million newcomers a year. Unlike the earlier English and Irish immigrants, many did not speak the language of the country. By the 1920's their children were filling city classrooms. It is a measure of the schools' accomplishment and the students' determination that a higher proportion of such children learned to read and write than that of the children of native-born whites.

News Coverage Expands

One result of increased education was a higher readership of newspapers and magazines. During the war, interest in the news had risen. To meet the demand, *Time,* the first weekly newsmagazine, appeared in 1923 and soon became extremely popular. Newspapers also expanded their coverage, and some brought out huge, magazine-type Sunday supplements. Others bought or opened radio stations. Some of the money for this expansion came from high circulation, for city papers cost only two cents on weekdays and ten on Sunday. However, most of the expanded coverage was paid for out of the great increases in advertising revenues, of which newspapers got a large portion. Never before had Americans been able to get so much news from so many places.

To catch an even wider readership, **tabloids** were introduced. These were half the regular page size and made liberal use of pictures. They were something like the sensationalist yellow press of the late nineteenth century. They specialized in news of murders, kidnappings, and activities of gangsters and show people. Pictures were large and often violent, and bold headlines screamed the news. The *Daily News* and the *Daily Mirror,* both in New York, were the most widely imitated.

Ballyhoo. Largely because of tabloids, the twenties produced its version of what is now called media hype. That is, insignificant events were blown way out of proportion to their real importance. In those days it was called "ballyhoo," but the result was the same.

Lindbergh, the Hero. Even when the ballyhoo specialists had a genuine hero, they misrepresented him. On May 20, 1927, **Charles A. Lindbergh** began his solo flight across the Atlantic Ocean. He

Present the Lesson

Write the words *education* and *popular culture* on the board. Ask students to skim the section to find changes that occurred in these areas during the 1920's. Write these on the board.
Education: it grew during the 1920's; in 1926 there were 4 million high school students; the increase in the number of students was due to prosperous times and to higher educational standards for jobs; the cost of education rose; the modern high school evolved, offering vocational training; improvement in the education of immigrants took place.

Popular Culture: news coverage was expanded; national heroes included Lindbergh, Ruth, Grange, and Dempsey; movies and Yiddish Theater became popular; writers such as F. Scott Fitzgerald, Sinclair Lewis, Ernest Hemingway, and T.S. Eliot opposed the materialism of the 1920's.

Check for Understanding

Call on individual students to read their answers to Section 4 Review questions.

Picturing History   In 1924 halfback Red Grange made four touchdowns in twelve minutes in the opening quarter of a game against Michigan. Later he scored a fifth touchdown and passed eighteen yards for a sixth.

flew nonstop from New York to Paris in thirty-three and a half hours. It was a startling feat, and the papers played it up to the hilt. They did it using such terms as Lucky Lindy and the Flying Fool. Lindbergh was no fool, and luck had nothing to do with his achievement. He succeeded by working out every possible detail of his flight in advance. Nevertheless, the press felt it had to present him in the most startling way possible.

Ruth, the Babe.   Interest in what one historian called "children's games played by grown men for money," that is, professional athletics, reached a new peak in the twenties. Each sport had a single figure of legendary accomplishment.

In baseball the figure was George Herman Ruth, commonly known as **Babe Ruth.** He was a hard-drinking, salty-talking character whom the fans took to their hearts as they would a good-natured, unruly younger brother. Ruth's record of sixty home runs hit in one season for the New York Yankees in 1927 has been surpassed, but many claim that only a longer playing season and a livelier ball made that possible. In any event, Ruth

led the Yankees to seven world-series between 1921 and 1932. Yankee Stadium, which opened in 1923, was called the house that Ruth built. Ruth was noted for paying visits to youngsters in hospitals, and shortly before his death in 1948, he set up a foundation to help underprivileged children.

Grange, the Galloping Ghost.   College football had its hero in Harold Edward "Red" Grange, otherwise known as the Galloping Ghost for his feats at the University of Illinois. Why a college sport caught the attention of so many people who never finished high school is hard to determine—perhaps it was because in those years its dominance passed from Eastern Ivy League schools to the huge Midwestern universities. Loyal citizens of Michigan or Ohio could pile into new stadiums seating seventy or eighty thousand people on Saturday afternoons and scream themselves hoarse for "their" team. The Fighting Irish of Notre Dame appealed to Americans of Irish descent. This was despite the school's legendary coach having the Norwegian name of **Knute Rockne,** as well as many of its players being the sons of Slavic coal miners from Pennsylvania.

Picturing History   Babe Ruth's plaque in the Baseball Hall of Fame reads: "Greatest drawing card in history of baseball. Holder of many home run and other batting records. Gathered 714 home runs in addition to 15 in World Series."

Using the careers of Big Bill Tilden, Babe Ruth, Red Grange, and Jack Dempsey as examples, discuss the rise of popular sports heroes as national idols. To stimulate discussion, ask students the following questions. Are there any such national idols today? What values are reflected by the American tendency to create such national heroes? Compare heroes of the 1920's with those of today. (Possible responses: Americans value winners and those with athletic prowess. Values reflected include physical strength and athletic ability. Heroes of today are often fleeting and soon forgotten.)

Assign Independent Practice

Have students construct charts with three columns. They should label the columns Movies, Sports, and Newspapers, and record several examples of advancements made during the 1920's and notable figures for each.

Movies: became the nation's fourth largest industry; even small communities built movie theaters; D. W. Griffith—director; Charlie Chaplin—popular comedian; Al Jolson—in first talkie.

Sports: professional sports reached its peak; sports stars became national idols; tennis, golf, and racing became popular; Babe Ruth—baseball player; Knute Rockne—football coach; Jack Dempsey—boxer.

Newspapers: weekly news magazines appeared; newspapers expanded coverage because of reader demands; ballyhoo was common.

Picturing History An authority on heavyweight boxers described Jack Dempsey as having "a neck like a bull, a granite jaw and fists like iron."

Dempsey, the Manassa Mauler. Heavyweight boxing was particularly open to ballyhoo treatment. It was easy to work up popular frenzy over the periodic world-championship bouts. Here, a million-dollar gate in paid admissions was the goal. One of the most popular figures was **Jack Dempsey** of Manassa, Colorado. Thousands watched the career of this champion fighter. In 1927, when ex-champion Dempsey met Gene Tunney for their second bout and Dempsey's second defeat, the promoters raked in $2,650,000.

Other Sports Idols. Men's tennis had its hero in Big Bill Tilden, and the women's game was dominated by Helen Wills. Their games and lives were followed by millions of people through radio, the press, and newsreels. Atlanta's Bobby Jones was the only golfer in history to make a "grand slam" by winning all major British and American open and amateur matches in a single year (1930), after which he retired. Even racing had its wonder horse, Man-of-War, whose descendants are still prized animals.

Movies and the Theater Become Popular

By 1925 making and exhibiting films had grown to be the nation's fourth largest industry. More than 20,500 movie houses were operating throughout the United States. The smallest community had at least one cranking away for seven or eight hours a day and showing six pictures a week in three "double bills" (two movies for the price of one). Larger communities had one or more first-run houses downtown, where new films played before being shown in neighborhood theaters. The downtown "palaces" featured a mighty Wurlitzer organ or even a small symphony orchestra to accompany the films. Neighborhood theaters made do with tiny pianos.

Hollywood, a small town near Los Angeles, became the film capital of the country and, later, of the world. There, director D. W. Griffith introduced the close-up and the moving camera. In Hollywood, actor **Charlie Chaplin** invented his world-famous character of the Little Tramp, a funny-looking little man, pretentious and impish, but warmhearted under it all. There, in 1927, the first major film with sound was produced. It was *The Jazz Singer,* starring **Al Jolson,** and it marked the start of a new age in motion pictures.

Picturing History Rumpled but elegant, Charlie Chaplin delighted audiences around the world as the Little Tramp. His awkward walk in oversized shoes added to his childlike charm.

Yiddish Theater. The theater also bloomed during the 1920's, especially the Yiddish theater in New York City. (Yiddish is the language that developed from a combination of languages spoken by Eastern European Jews.) Many of the developments that took place on the Yiddish stage showed up a few years later in the English-speaking theater on Broadway. Yiddish theater continued the tradi-

626

Student Assignment/Homework

Have students complete Chapter 24 Review on paper. Go over the answers with the class.

Concluding the Chapter

During the decade of the 1920's, individual rights often came into conflict with generally accepted customs. Ask students to write a two-paragraph essay describing the effect of one of the following on individual rights: the Scopes trial, Prohibition, the woman suffrage movement, or the Harlem Renaissance. (Responses should include: Scopes—should cover freedom to teach controversial subjects; Prohibition—should describe effects of the attempt to regulate morals; suffrage—should describe the achievements as well as aims of women's rights movement; Harlem Renaissance—should cover notable achievements of blacks in this period.)

Picturing History   Sinclair Lewis (left), Ernest Hemingway (center), and F. Scott Fitzgerald (right) spoke for the social discontent of their generation.

tions of the Gilded Age—broad melodramas, comedies, and Shakespeare. Later it performed works by Henrik Ibsen, Maxim Gorky, and others.

Writers Speak for the Twenties

A common theme of most novels of the period was opposition to **materialism.** Materialism is usually defined as the single-minded pursuit of money and possessions. Most writers were against the modern business culture. **F. Scott Fitzgerald,** fresh from Princeton and the army and as handsome as a film star, published *This Side of Paradise* in 1920. He won instant acclaim as the spokesman for the twenties generation. In this novel and others, he described the confusion and tragedy caused by a frantic search for material success.

Sinclair Lewis, author of *Babbitt* and *Main Street,* was the sharpest critic of materialism and of the narrowness of small-town life. He also attacked American medicine in *Arrowsmith* and religion in *Elmer Gantry.* The harsh views of Lewis had little effect. Nevertheless, he won the Nobel Prize for literature in 1930.

In *The Sun Also Rises* and *A Farewell to Arms,* **Ernest Hemingway** expressed disgust with prewar codes of behavior and the glorification of war. He also developed a clear, straightforward prose that set a new, tough, "hard-boiled" literary style.

Poet **T. S. Eliot's** *The Waste Land* was perhaps the most agonizing view of the dehumanizing effects of the machine age. It is considered by some critics to be the great poem of the twentieth century.

Many American writers and artists felt stifled in what they called the "vulgar, money-grubbing" society of the 1920's. They fled to Europe where they felt they could live a richer cultural and intellectual life. From there they watched with dismayed fascination the fast-paced business life of the United States, which you will read about in the next chapter.

SECTION 4 REVIEW

Key Terms and People

Explain the significance of: tabloids, Charles A. Lindbergh, Babe Ruth, Knute Rockne, Jack Dempsey, Charlie Chaplin, Al Jolson, materialism, F. Scott Fitzgerald, Sinclair Lewis, Ernest Hemingway, T. S. Eliot

Main Ideas

1. What changes in education took place during the 1920's?
2. During the 1920's, how did news coverage expand?
3. What special kind of theater bloomed in New York City in the 1920's? Where did the developments in this kind of theater show up later?
4. What was a common theme of many novels of the 1920's?

Critical Thinking

5. Why are the years from 1920 to 1929 often referred to as the Roaring Twenties?

SECTION 4 REVIEW

Answers

Main Ideas

1. High school enrollment greatly increased.

2. *Time,* the first weekly newsmagazine, appeared, newspapers expanded their coverage of the news, and tabloids were introduced.

3. The Yiddish theater. In the English-speaking theater on Broadway.

4. Opposition to materialism.

Critical Thinking

5. Possible answers: the wild restless lifestyle and the skyrocketing prosperity and production seemed to roar. The changing moral values, the availability of cars and radios, and the burgeoning entertainment industry also roared. There were real roars of the crowds at the sporting events, at the wild, faddish activities at universities, and in the ever-growing cities. **(synthesis)**

State the Objective

Recognize stereotypes in primary sources.

Present the Lesson

Write the following statements on the board:
- All teen-agers fight with their parents.
- Corporations never care about their employees.

Discuss with students whether they agree or disagree with the statements. (Discussion might include: teen-agers, parents, and corporations vary, so making gross generalizations like these is unfair.) Direct students to the definition of stereotype in the feature. Ask students to think of other stereotypical statements about teen-agers, parents, and corporations. Add these to the statements on the board. (Possible responses: teens are lazy; parents always nag; corporations are interested only in making money.)

Ask students what they think are good ways to overcome stereotyping. (Possible responses: to judge each person as an individual, not as a member of a group, race, or religion; to accept and respect differences in others.)

Focus on Critical Thinking Skills

Recognizing Stereotypes

Understanding the Skill

The 1920's has been called an era of intolerance. World War I is blamed for much of the ill feeling of the time. President Wilson had predicted that war would have a divisive effect on the American people. Indeed, during the war, German Americans and other Americans—notably those who opposed the war—were persecuted. Moreover, the bad feelings did not cease when the shooting stopped. Instead, the targets shifted from German Americans and pacifists to other groups in society. People intolerant of change began attributing certain negative characteristics to members of groups whom they thought threatened the status quo: farmers, urban dwellers, African Americans, women, Catholics, Jews, and so on.

Such a practice is called stereotyping. A stereotype is a general fixed notion about an individual, a group, or an idea. When people stereotype others, they assume that all members of a group are alike. In ignoring the characteristics of individuals, stereotypes dehumanize people. Stereotypes are formed about nationalities, ethnic backgrounds, ages, beliefs, occupations, and so on. The image of a Mexican American taking a siesta with a sombrero over his face is an example of a stereotype.

Stereotyping compromises critical thinking because it causes people to accept statements that they might otherwise reject as unlikely. Even stereotypes that are flattering can, because they fail to address people as individuals, lead to misunderstandings and mistakes in reasoning.

To better identify stereotypes in a written account, you can do the following:

- **Examine characteristics attributed to an individual, group, or idea.** Is a whole group being judged by what a few members do or say?
- **Look for clue words that often signal stereotyping.** Are words such as *all, never, always,* and *none* used to generalize or exaggerate? Is the language manipulated in other ways to demean and dehumanize people?
- **Evaluate the source of the material.** Is the source reliable? Are statements based on observed facts and reliable evidence, or are they based on physical appearance, ethnic background, religious preference, or some other characteristic that often serves as a basis for stereotyping?
- **Use your knowledge of people and history to interpret the statement.**

Applying the Skill

During the 1920's great social changes took place, accompanied by much intolerance toward new ideas and whole groups of people. Foreigners, especially those from eastern and southern Europe and from Asia, were discriminated against for many reasons.

The intolerance of the period is reflected in the growth of the Ku Klux Klan. Unlike the Klan of the post-Civil War period, the group in the twenties was not just antiblack. The Klansmen of the 1920's believed that a threat to American culture came from southern and eastern Europeans and from Catholics and Jews. By 1924 the Ku Klux Klan had gained control of the legislatures in Texas, Oklahoma, Oregon, and Indiana.

The following is a statement of the time by a leader of the Ku Klux Klan.

> The Klan aims to protect the American electorate from further dilution by alien elements . . . by restricting the franchise to men and women who are able through birth and education to understand Americanism. This means . . . to native-born children. . . .
> . . . the Klan aims to protect the Nation from any further evils of unassimilated and unassimilable elements through an immediate complete stopping of immigration.

In the statement, notice the words that dehumanize immigrants: *alien, evils of unassimilated elements.* Such words serve to treat people as if they were dangerous objects. Reviewing your own knowledge of the Ku Klux Klan also helps you recognize this statement as directed toward an entire group rather than toward its few undesirable members.

628

Check for Understanding

Discuss students' responses to the questions at the end of the feature. Point out that many people are still victims of stereotyping. Have students bring newspaper articles to share with the class that focus on incidents resulting from stereotyping.

Picturing History This 1893 cartoon makes fun of those immigrants who, once they were established in the United States, stereotyped other immigrants.

The following statements are by two more people of the period. Read and analyze them to identify possible stereotypes.

Madison Grant, a leader in the anti-immigrant movement of the 1920's, spoke out against southern and eastern European immigrants and Asian immigrants.

It is evident that in large sections of the country the native American [that is, the white Anglo-Saxon Protestant] will entirely disappear. He will not intermarry with inferior races and he cannot compete in the sweat shop and in the street trench with the newcomers. Large cities . . . have always been gathering points of diverse races, but New York is becoming a [sewer of nationalities] which will produce many amazing racial hybrids and some ethnic horrors.

In the early twenties, any immigrant from Russia, Poland, or southern Europe was thought to be a possible revolutionary. One such individual reported that he had been arrested, beaten, and held in prison without charge or trial for several months. Here is part of his statement.

In the autumn of 1919 I was a member of the Union of Russian Workers. I am not an anarchist, Socialist or Bolshevik and do not take much interest in political theories. I joined the Russian Workers because I was a workman speaking Russian and wanted to associate with other Russians and have the benefit of the . . . instruction in mechanics which the society gave. . . . I was arrested with all the other men at the meeting, 63 in number.

Practicing the Skill

1. How do these quotations show stereotypes?
2. What words indicate negative stereotyping in Grant's quotation? Explain why they are harmful.
3. Compare the sources of the last two quotations. How do they differ?
4. What is the underlying message in each of the last two quotations?
5. How can knowledge of history aid in identifying stereotypes?

FOCUS ON SKILLS

Answers

Practicing Your Skill

1. The first quotation uses phrases such as *alien elements* and *evils of unassimilated elements,* which dehumanize immigrants. The second quotation uses such phrases as *inferior races* and *ethnic horrors.* The third quote describes discriminatory action that resulted from stereotyping all Russian immigrants as subversive.

2. *Inferior races; street trench; sewer of nationalities; racial hybrids.* • These terms are harmful because they are negative in tone and they judge an entire group of people—they do not allow for individual differences.

3. Grant was a native-born American, and the other writer was a Russian immigrant.

4. Grant—immigrants are dangerous to American society and will destroy the perfection of the nation. Russian immigrant—immigrants are subjected to insensitive and unfair treatment because of their heritage.

5. Possible answer: knowledge of history helps one to analyze the reliability of sources and to trace trends of behavior.

Answer Key

Key Terms and People

These are highlighted in the text in the order in which they appear in this list.

Main Ideas

1. Fundamentalist Christian belief in the literal interpretation of the Bible challenged accepted scientific thought regarding evolution.

2. People broke the law in order to obtain liquor; public officials often accepted bribes from bootleggers to overlook illegal activities.

3. Formed National Woman's party to promote suffrage; led demonstrations and picketed White House to persuade lawmakers to pass Nineteenth Amendment.

4. Women made new choices in styles and attitudes; their choices expanded to include interests in social, economic, and political problems.

5. Helped found Niagara Movement and NAACP; edited *The Crisis*; encouraged African Americans to enter mainstream of American life.

6. Many black writers, artists, and musicians voiced the experiences of African Americans.

7. Began educating students for better jobs; became training grounds for future leaders in business.

8. Many believed that Americans were too concerned with search for success and money and should be more concerned with self-awareness and cultural issues.

Critical Thinking Questions

9. Represents excessive interest in trendiness, which the author satirizes.

➤**10.** No one knew whether it would work. • Impossible to make people good by enacting laws.

➤**11.** They seemed to symbolize the new freedom achieved by women, who had made gains in industry during World War I and who were finally able to vote.

12. Du Bois was not satisfied with Washington's belief that African Americans should be content with becoming farmers or artisans; he believed they should reach higher. • Du Bois's.

➤**13.** Jazz, based on work songs and spirituals, originated with blacks; later refined by other black musicians, including Louis Armstrong and Duke Ellington.

14. Prosperous times brought greater high-school enrollment; higher taxes paid for more schools; new job requirements encouraged attendance. • Possible answers: economic—people felt a better education would get them better jobs; social—people who graduated from high school were respected for this achievement.

15. I-b, II-c, III-a, IV-d, V-e

Critical Thinking Activities

➤**16.** • More legislation today applying to women's rights; more women in positions of power and authority; and more women making contributions in diverse fields.

➤**17.** Possible answer: black artists are still voicing experiences of African Americans in significant new works.

CHAPTER 24 REVIEW

Write your answers on a separate sheet of paper.

Key Terms and People

Explain the significance of: Clarence Darrow, speakeasies, Al Capone, Carrie Chapman Catt, Niagara Movement, Ida B. Wells-Barnett, Langston Hughes, Countee Cullen, Mason-Dixon line, tabloids, Knute Rockne, Charlie Chaplin, Al Jolson, Sinclair Lewis, Ernest Hemingway, T. S. Eliot

Main Ideas

1. How did the Scopes trial reveal the clash between science and traditional religious beliefs?
2. How did Prohibition lead to illegal activity and to the corruption of public officials?
3. In what ways did Alice Paul and Lucy Burns influence the passage of the Nineteenth Amendment?
4. Describe how the flappers of the 1920's represented new choices for American women.
5. How was W. E. B. Du Bois instrumental in helping African Americans achieve more civil rights?
6. How was the Harlem Renaissance an expression of the new cultural awareness of African Americans?
7. What new role did high schools play as a result of the changes in the American economy?
8. Why did many writers make materialism a main theme of their work?

Critical Thinking Questions

9. **Analyzing Literature.** Explain how the selection by Fitzgerald on page 613 portrays the social attitude of Americans in the 1920's.
10. **Analyzing Ideas.** Explain why Prohibition was called ''a noble experiment.'' What did this experiment show about legislating morals?
11. **Evaluating Causes.** In what way was the appearance of flappers a result of the passage of the Nineteenth Amendment?
12. **Evaluating Sources.** How was W. E. B. Du Bois's stand on black progress in direct contrast to that taken by Booker T. Washington (as shown in Chapter 22)? Whose position became the one followed by most African Americans?
13. **Making Deductions.** What was the role of black musicians in the development of jazz as a national musical art form?
14. **Evaluating Ideas.** Describe how the modern high school developed following the end of World War I. Were economic or social factors more important in its development?
15. **Organizing Events.** Match the events listed below with the Roman numerals on the time line.

a. Scopes trial is held.
b. Eighteenth Amendment goes into effect.
c. *Time* magazine is founded.
d. Lindbergh flies across the Atlantic to Paris.
e. Prohibition is repealed.

Critical Thinking Activities

16. **Linking Past to Present.** The improvement in the status of women in the 1920's was a major social change. Compare it with the changes in women's status today. Describe specific advances that have taken place.
17. **Linking Past to Present.** The Harlem Renaissance was a flowering of black culture. How does today's black culture represent a continuation of the Harlem Renaissance?
18. **Linking Past to Present.** How do you think the press ballyhoo over such sports figures as Babe Ruth and Jack Dempsey compares with the modern media's promotion of certain sports stars? Is today's press coverage of celebrities more exaggerated or not? Explain.

The 1920's Bring Social Change

In the aftermath of World War I, it became increasingly clear that the United States was becoming an urban nation. Meanwhile, people in rural areas were horrified by urban standards of conduct. They and other holders of traditional religious values were represented by the fundamentalists who challenged the theory of evolution in the Scopes trial. The fundamentalists, who forbade the teaching of evolution in the schools, won the case. Traditional values won another apparent victory with the passage of the Eighteenth Amendment, which banned alcohol. However, though alcoholism decreased somewhat, this ban inadvertently encouraged crime and political corruption. As a result, many Americans came to feel that Prohibition would never work. The amendment was repealed in 1933, but Americans remained divided on the matter.

The 1920's were a watershed for American women. Prior to 1920 several states had given women the right to vote. Then in 1920, after a long struggle, woman suffrage was adopted on a national basis. Women expressed their new freedom with new clothing styles and hairstyles. Margaret Sanger promoted the cause of birth control. A handful of women took on political careers, but more entered such fields as law and medicine that were newly open to women and required higher education. Still, most women remained in the home or worked at jobs for far less pay than men received.

It was also during the 1920's that a black renaissance took place. After 1910 so many African Americans migrated to Northern cities that their movement became known as the great migration. They took jobs in industry but met prejudice and discrimination almost everywhere. Race riots rocked Northern cities. Marcus Garvey led a back-to-Africa movement. W. E. B. Du Bois helped found the National Association for the Advancement of Colored People. The NAACP demanded an end to the lynching of blacks and to primaries for whites only. Despite poverty and slum conditions, black people forged a literary and artistic movement known as the Harlem Renaissance. Jazz music, poetry, literature, and art flourished as never before in the black community.

Education and popular culture also changed during the twenties. Prior to the 1920's, most Americans went no further in school than the eighth grade. Then in that decade high schools began to expand their student bodies and curricula. Millions of children of recent immigrants required education. Taxes were increased for the purpose, and schools rose heroically to the challenge. Meanwhile, cheap city newspapers ballyhooed heroes like Charles Lindbergh. Professional and college sports, with heroes like baseball's Babe Ruth and football's Red Grange, began to attract attention. Boxing, golf, and tennis had their fans. The Yiddish theater blossomed in New York, and a parade of talented writers attacked American materialism.

Chronology of Main Events

1920	Prohibition goes into effect; Nineteenth Amendment gives women the right to vote
1920–1930	Harlem Renaissance
1923	*Time,* first weekly newsmagazine, published
1925	Scopes trial
1927	Lindbergh flies solo to Paris; first sound film produced

Global Perspectives

1921	Albert Einstein wins Nobel Prize in physics.
1926	Hirohito becomes Emperor of Japan.
1922	Mussolini forms fascist government in Italy.
1924	Ibn Saud takes control of most of Arabia.
1924	Lenin's death starts power struggle in USSR.
1928	Nationalists unite China under one government.

For Discussion

How might Lenin's death have lessened worries about communism in the U.S.? (Possible responses: Lenin's death might have made people less apprehensive about communism in the U.S. because the USSR was divided by a power struggle; his death might have led people to hope that the next Communist leader would be less interested in world domination than was Lenin.)

Additional Resources

- Geography Activities
- Skills Activities
- Thematic Activities
- Economic Activities
- Cultural Literacy Activities
- Literary Source Readings
- Primary Source Readings
- Nuclear Peacekeeping
- Transparencies
- Computer Test Generator

Additional Teaching Strategies

SECTION 1

For Basic Students: Have students work in small groups to prepare charts listing the following people: Calvin Coolidge, Samuel Gompers, A. Mitchell Palmer, Hiram Evans, William Z. Foster, John L. Lewis, and Nicola Sacco and Bartolomeo Vanzetti. Students should identify each individual and his occupation and summarize the role he played in the 1920's.

Coolidge	Massachusetts governor; called out National Guard during Boston police strike.
Gompers	President of AFL; appealed to Governor Coolidge to rehire fired policemen after strike ended.
Palmer	U.S. Attorney General; led raids against Communist and Socialist organizations; ignored civil rights.
Evans	Grand Wizard of Ku Klux Klan; opposed blacks, Catholics, Jews, and foreigners; opposed unions; supported Prohibition.
Foster	Radical organizer of steel workers; joined Communist party and ran for President in 1924, 1928, 1932.
Lewis	President of United Mine Workers; organized a successful strike in 1919.
Sacco/ Vanzetti	Italian immigrants and anarchists; evaded draft in World War I; were arrested for robbery during Red scare; were executed in 1927.

Have students share their charts with the class.

For Advanced Students: Have students do additional research on the Sacco-Vanzetti case and present to the class two-minute arguments for the guilt or innocence of these men. (Details of the arguments might include: the controversial murder trial was held in Massachusetts in 1921; both defendents were Italian immigrants; both were carrying pistols when arrested; Sacco's gun was the same caliber as the gun used in the murder of two custodians of a shoe company; both defendants were known anarchists; both were convicted and sentenced to die; Judge Webster Shayer indicated that he felt their guilt was assumed because they were anarchists.)

SECTION 2

For Basic Students: Ask students to reread the section entitled "Nativists Want Limited Immigration" and list the provisions of each immigration act.

- Emergency Quota Act of 1921—introduced quota system based on national origins.
- Immigration Act of 1924—European nations were given a quota of 2 percent of the number of its nationals who were living in the U.S. in 1890; classified Japanese as "aliens ineligible for citizenship."
- National Origins Act of 1929—changed base year of 1924 Immigration Act to 1920; reduced to 150,000 the total number of persons to be admitted to U.S. each year; did not apply to immigrants from the Western Hemisphere.

Discuss the fairness of each act. (Discussion might include: Emergency Quota Act of 1921 ignored orientals; Immigration Act of 1924 discriminated against people from eastern and southern Europe; National Origins Act of 1929 created pitifully small quotas for some countries.)

For Advanced Students: Have each student research one of the following major figures of the Harding administration: Charles Evans Hughes, Herbert Hoover, Andrew Mellon, Henry C. Wallace, Harry M. Daugherty, and Albert B. Fall. Students should then present a two-minute talk to the class on their subjects. (Possible responses: Hughes—respected public servant, became Chief Justice of Supreme Court; Hoover—popular Secretary of Commerce, good administrator; Mellon—multimillionaire, served three Presidents as Secretary of Treasury; Wallace—Secretary of Agriculture, pioneer in agriculture; Daugherty—corrupt Attorney General, member of "Ohio gang"; Fall—Interior Secretary, member of "Ohio gang.")

SECTION 3

For Basic Students: Ask students to use encyclopedias or other reference materials to prepare a two-paragraph report on Woolworth's five-and-tens, the A & P, United Drug, Thom McAnn, J.C. Penny, United Cigar, Sears and Roebuck, or Piggly-Wiggly during the 1920's and how the store contributed to the prosperity of that time. (Paragraphs might include: Woolworth created a new method of retailing; A & P was a grocery chain that used Woolworth's technique; United Drug was a pharmacy chain, also used this technique; Thom McAnn was a shoe store chain, also used this technique; J.C. Penny was a department store in rural areas, used this technique; United Cigar was a tobacco store chain, used new technique; Sears, Roebuck opened retail stores when catalog sales declined; Piggly-Wiggly was a self-service grocery chain.) Have students share their paragraphs.

For Advanced Students: Have students research and prepare background reports on one of the unsuccessful candidates in the 1924 election: Al Smith, John W. Davis, or Robert La Follette. Reports should include reasons for the candidate's unsuccessful Presidential bid. (Reports might include: Al Smith—governor of New York, Democrat, lost nomination due to Ku Klux Klan influence; John W. Davis—Democrat, wealthy corporate lawyer, could not beat Coolidge in popular appeal; Robert La Follette—Progressive, also failed to overcome the appeal of Coolidge.) Have students share their reports with the class.

SECTION 4

For Basic Students: Ask students to assume the roles of farmers in the 1920's and to draft letters to Congress urging passage of the McNary-Haugen bills. (Letters might include: reference to the high cost of farm machinery, land, and electricity; information on the drop in demand for such products as cotton, beef, pork, and flour.) Have students share their letters.

For Advanced Students: Ask each student to draw a political cartoon that portrays the uneven distribution of wealth in the U.S. in the 1920's. Display the projects in the classroom.

SECTION 5

For Basic Students: Ask students to list the similarities of Herbert Hoover and Alfred Smith. (List might include: born poor; succeeded on their own with brains, guts, and hard work; were superior administrators; admired Woodrow Wilson; believed in American capitalism but knew it needed reform.) Have students share their lists. Point out that even people with different styles and personalities can work for common good.

For Advanced Students: After they review the concepts of the Monroe Doctrine (Ch. 9) and the Roosevelt Corollary (Ch. 20), have students write three paragraphs explaining how President Hoover worked to change the "big stick" image of American foreign policy to a "good neighbor" image. (Paragraphs might include: avoided overreacting to nationalistic economic changes in Latin America; made goodwill tour of eleven Latin American nations; repudiated Roosevelt Corollary; denounced dollar diplomacy; withdrew troops from Nicaragua and Haiti; attempted to treat Latin American nations as equals; first used the term "good neighbor.") Have two or three volunteers read their paragraphs to the class.

Further Reading for Students
Nonfiction

Adams, Samuel Hopkins. *Incredible Era: The Life and Times of Warren Gamaliel Harding*. Reprint of 1939 ed. New York: Hippocrene Books, 1979.

Galbraith, John K. *The Great Crash, Nineteen Twenty-Nine*. Boston, Mass.: Houghton Mifflin, 1988.

Lathem, Edward Connery, ed. *Your Son, Calvin Coolidge*. Rutland, Vermont: Academy Books, 1968.

Bibliography for Teachers
Books

Allen, Frederick Lewis. *Only Yesterday: An Informal History of the 1920's*. New York: Harper & Row, 1964.

Bernstein, Irving. *The Lean Years. A History of the American Worker, 1920-1933*. New York: Da Capo, 1983.

Chalmers, David M. *Hooded Americanism: The History of the Ku Klux Klan*, 3rd ed. Durham, N.C.: Duke University Press, 1987.

Handlin, Oscar. *Al Smith and His America*. Boston, Mass.: Northeastern University Press, 1958.

Lavine, Sigmund A. *Famous Merchants*. New York: Dodd, Mead, 1965.

Mee, Charles L., Jr. *The Ohio Gang: The World of Warren G. Harding*. New York: M. Evans, 1981.

Murray, Robert K. *Red Scare: A Study in National Hysteria, 1919-1920*. Reprint of 1955 ed. Westport, Conn.: Greenwood Press, 1980.

O'Connor, Richard. *The First Hurrah: A Biography of Alfred E. Smith*. New York: Putnam, 1970.

Sobel, Robert. *The Great Bull Market: Wall Street in the 1920's*. New York: W. W. Norton, 1968.

Audio-Visuals

The Conservative Revival: 1920's. Prentice-Hall Media. Filmstrip.

Herbert Hoover: Portrait of Power. Social Studies School Service. Filmstrip.

The Reckless Years: 1919-1929. Guidance Associates. Movie.

The United States in the Twentieth Century, 1920-1932. Simon and Shuster Communications. Movie.

Teacher's Notes:

Lesson Plan

Teaching Resources, Unit 6 Booklet

Lesson Study Sheets pp. 113-132
Daily Activities pp. 133-142
Enrichment Activities pp. 143-152
Reteaching Activities pp. 153-162
Chapter Review p. 163
Chapter Mastery Tests pp. 165-176
Telescoping the Times Study Sheet p. 177

Chapter Objectives

Students will learn:
- what major domestic problems faced the U.S. after World War I
- the successes and failures of the Harding administration
- how American businesses and corporations were mainly responsible for the partial prosperity during the Coolidge administration
- the exceptions to the general level of prosperity of the 1920's
- the major economic events and trends of the late 1920's

Picturing History *American Gothic* by Grant Wood, 1930. Wood is known for his illustrations of the rural Midwest, especially Iowa, his birthplace and home for most of his life.

Using the Chapter Time Line

How many years passed between the end of World War I (see Chapter 23 time line) and the adoption of the Dawes Plan to help Germany pay its war reparations? (Answer: 6) Who was President when the Stock Market crashed? (Answer: Herbert Hoover)

1920

1922

1924

1926

1928

1930

1921
Warren G. Harding inaugurated President

1923
Harding dies;
Calvin Coolidge succeeds to Presidency

1924
Dawes Plan for Germany adopted

1925
Calvin Coolidge inaugurated for first full term

1929
• Herbert Hoover inaugurated President
• Stock market crashes

Links to American Literature

Melvin B. Tolson: born in Moberly, MO, February 6, 1898; graduated from Lincoln University in Oxford, PA, where he won awards in speech, debate, dramatics, and classical literature; taught at Wiley College in Marshall, TX, from 1924 to 1947; helped organize sharecroppers during the 1930's; was appointed poet laureate of Liberia in 1947; died of cancer August 29, 1966.

Works include: a weekly column in the *Washington Tribune* from 1937 to 1943 that commented on a wide variety of topics concerning black life; a collection of poetry including *Ren-* *dezvous with America* (1944), *Libretto for the Republic of Liberia* (1953), *Harlem Gallery, Book I: The Curator* (1965).

A Gallery of Harlem Portraits: a collection of poems depicting the lives of black individuals in Harlem.

CHAPTER **25** 1920–1929

Politics and a Thin Prosperity

Links to American Literature

The scar Fritz Rickman received
The night Ku Klux riders
Drove all the Negroes out of Salem, Missouri,
Still shows on the back of his head.
He remembers the hooded figures in his bedroom,
The curses and threats and vulgarities,
The cold muzzle of a forty-four jammed against his temple.
He remembers harassed fugitives
Hurrying along rutty streets
With sacks and baskets and bundles. . . .
The cries and whimpers of little children . . .
The collapse from heart failure of Uncle Jake,
Who loved his good white folk.
He remembers the honking cars and galloping horses
And the brutal curses to move on.
He remembers the daggers of pain ripping through his brain
And his mind becoming blacker than Salem.

— MELVIN B. TOLSON, *"Fritz Rickman"*

The Republican administrations of the 1920's made a sharp break with the reforms of the Progressive Era. While certain businesses boomed, minorities did not share in the prosperity. This unequal distribution of income was one of the signs that foreshadowed economic troubles. The social climate had already begun to change, as evidenced by the growth of organizations such as the Ku Klux Klan. Such cycles of boom and bust have been constant in our nation's history, prompting George Santayana to note, "Those who cannot remember the past are condemned to repeat it."

Chapter Overview

In this chapter you will learn about the major domestic problems that faced the United States at the end of World War I. You will also learn about the successes and failures of the Harding administration and about the prosperity that existed during the Coolidge administration. Finally, you will learn about the major economic trends during the last part of the 1920's. To help you understand the course of events that brought an end to an era of prosperity, Chapter 25 is divided into five sections.

Chapter Outline

1. **Americans Confront Postwar Controversy**
2. **The Nation Returns to Normalcy and Isolation**
3. **Coolidge Conducts the Nation's Business**
4. **Problems Threaten Economic Prosperity**
5. **A Slipping Economy Signals the End of an Era**

Display examples of the financial section from the daily newspaper, and ask students how many are familiar with the basic workings of the stock market. Ask students how the stock market represents the free enterprise system. (Possible responses: people in all economic groups can become involved; owning stock allows people to participate in the running of a company, as well as to receive profits.)

Historical Sidelights
Presidential Quotes:
• Harding—"I am not fit for this office and never should have been here."
• Coolidge—"If you don't say anything, you won't be called on to repeat it."
• Hoover—"We are nearer today to the ideal of the abolition of poverty and fear from the lives of men and women than ever before in any land."

634

Anticipate the Lesson

Ask students to consider what problems a country might face following a large-scale war such as World War I. (Possible responses: many returning soldiers need jobs; factories that had supplied goods for the military close, and workers are let go; fear of another war hampers recovery; towns and cities that were damaged in the war must be rebuilt.) What groups in a society might be fearful of a communist takeover? Why? (Possible responses: businessmen; government officials; the wealthy; the middle classes. Communism calls for sharing the wealth, and these people would have to give up some or all of their position and possessions.)

SECTION 1

Americans Confront Postwar Controversy

GLOSSARY TERMS: **communism, Comintern, Ku Klux Klan (KKK), Sacco-Vanzetti case**

The police of Boston were angry. They had not had a raise since the beginning of World War I, and by 1919 the cost of living had doubled. They sent a group of representatives to the police commissioner to ask for what they considered might be a living wage. The commissioner promptly fired everyone in the group, and the remaining police responded by going out on strike. In the absence of police protection, some looting took place in downtown Boston, a number of windows were smashed, and people openly rolled dice on Boston Common. After an appeal from the mayor, Governor Calvin Coolidge called out the National Guard. Peace was restored, and the police called off the strike.

The police commissioner, however, refused to allow the men to return to their jobs. Instead he hired a new police force, which, ironically, received everything the strikers had asked for. Months later, when Coolidge received an appeal on behalf of the fired men from AFL president Samuel Gompers, he replied, "There is no right to strike against the public safety by anyone, anywhere, anytime." His statement made headlines throughout the country, and he was praised for saving Boston, if not the nation, from anarchy.

Communism Frightens Americans

If the public seemed to be overreacting to events in Boston, there were reasons for such behavior. What frightened many Americans was the threat of **communism,** an economic and social system in which there is one political party, the needs of the state are emphasized over those of the individual, and all property is, eventually, owned by all persons in common. (See pages 608–609.)

In 1919 there were Communist attempts to overthrow the governments of Germany and Hungary. Also, in March 1919 the Third Communist International—consisting mostly of delegates from the Russian Communist party—convened in Moscow for the stated purpose of encouraging worldwide revolutions. The Communist International, called the **Comintern** for short, advocated the overthrow of the capitalist system and the abolition of free enterprise and private property.

Many radicals in the United States were Communists, but many more were not. The public, however, found it difficult to distinguish between the two. Many Americans feared that radical support of unions was really an attack on the free enterprise system. Their fears were fed by the numerous strikes of 1919.

During World War I, strikes were few because nothing was allowed to interfere with the war effort. However, 1919 saw more than three thousand strikes, during which some four million workers walked off the job at one time or another. Wages had not kept up with prices, but employers did not want

---

People in the Chapter

Warren Harding was the first President to ride to his inauguration in an automobile. He also made the first radio broadcast to honor the author of "The Star-Spangled Banner." The occasion was the dedication of the Francis Scott Key Memorial at Fort McHenry, Baltimore, Maryland.

Albert Fall had been a political opponent of Woodrow Wilson. He visited Wilson after the President had suffered a stroke. "We have all been praying for you, Mr. President," said Fall. "Which way, Senator?" asked Wilson. Later, as a member of Harding's Ohio gang, Fall became the first cabinet member to be sent to jail for accepting bribes.

Calvin Coolidge was awakened in the middle of the night by his father, who called up the stairs, "Calvin, wake up. You're President of the United States." Coolidge had been visiting his family when the news came that President Harding had died.

Herbert Hoover took an optimistic view in a speech he delivered the year before the stock market crash ushered in the Great Depression. "We in America today are nearer to the final triumph over poverty than ever before in the history of any land," he said. "The poorhouse is vanishing among us."

State the Objective

Understand what major domestic problems faced the U.S. after World War I.

Present the Lesson

Write the following topics on the board: Labor Unrest; Red Scare; Ku Klux Klan. Have students read the section to find at least two important facts about each of these major issues that faced the U.S. at the end of World War I. Write the facts on the board. Have students evaluate the importance of each issue.

Labor Unrest: police strike in Boston; Governor Coolidge calls out the National Guard; steel workers' strike (1919) is broken after eighteen workers are killed; 1923—Committee publishes report on working conditions in mills; John L. Lewis, president of United Mine Work-

ers, pushes for arbitration in coal miners' strike.

Red Scare: 1919—Communists attempt to overthrow governments in Germany and Hungary; the Third Communist International (Comintern) convenes in Moscow; Americans fear labor unrest is caused by Communists; Attorney General Palmer raids offices of suspected Socialists and Communists.

Ku Klux Klan: renewed in 1915; seeks to keep blacks "in their place" and to drive out Catholics, Jews, and other "foreigners"; Grand Wizard—Hiram Evans; expresses fears and frustrations through racial violence.

Picturing History The Ku Klux Klan marches down Pennsylvania Avenue in 1925. The Klan's membership rose after World War I, when the organization opposed Catholics, Jews, and "foreigners" as well as African Americans.

to give their employees raises. Nor did they want their employees to join unions. Some employers, either out of sincere belief or because they saw a way to keep wages down, attempted to show that union members were planning revolution. Newspaper headlines screamed: CRIMES AGAINST SOCIETY, CONSPIRACIES AGAINST THE GOVERNMENT, and PLOTS TO ESTABLISH COMMUNISM.

In April 1919 bombs began turning up in the United States mail. They were hidden in packages addressed to various government and business leaders. Random explosions and outbreaks of violence in a number of cities caused something close to panic to grip the nation. On May 1, or May Day—the international worker's holiday—the violence was intense. It was followed throughout the summer by heavy labor unrest. In the fall, two major strikes closed down the nation's steel mills and coal mines.

That same fall, agents of United States Attorney General **A. Mitchell Palmer** raided the offices of anarchists (who oppose all forms of government) as well as Socialist and Communist organizations. Most Americans were unaware that the three were different kinds of radical movements and that not all believed in violent revolution. It scarcely mattered. Many of the members of these groups were recent immigrants or people with foreign-sounding names, and that was enough to prove that they were un-American and undesirable.

In his earnestness, Palmer ran roughshod over people's civil rights. The Palmer raids were often conducted without search warrants. People were kept locked up for long periods without being

allowed to see a lawyer. Many were arrested not because of their actions or affiliations but because they were friends of persons Palmer considered suspicious. Many of those arrested were not American citizens. In December 1919 some 249 of these aliens were deported.

Palmer was a great hero for a time. However, he kept predicting riots that never came. Finally, he said there would be serious trouble on May Day, 1920. After a calm May 1, people began to lose interest in Palmer and his anti-Red crusade.

The Klan Becomes More Powerful

Meanwhile, another group, the **Ku Klux Klan (KKK),** was growing swiftly. The Klan of Reconstruction days had more or less died out in the 1870's. Revived in 1915, it reached a peak membership of 4.5 million in 1924, a membership it described as white males who were native-born gentile citizens. The old practices of wearing hoods and of burning crosses were still used, but the KKK widened its interests and its appeal. As well as keeping black people "in their place," it sought to drive Catholics, Jews, and other "foreigners" from the land. It opposed union organizers and helped enforce Prohibition.

Klan members, as Grand Wizard Hiram Evans explained, were "plain people . . . the everyday, not highly cultured, not overly intellectualized, but entirely unspoiled and not de-Americanized, average citizens of the old stock." In other words, they were people who felt threatened by the changes taking place in American society. Klan members

For Discussion

Why do problems such as racism and labor unrest develop? How might they be minimized or eliminated? (Possible responses: feelings of nativism or prejudice produce racism; racism is difficult to eliminate but might be minimized through education and increased awareness of different cultures; labor unrest is caused by conflicts between workers and management and can be minimized by arbitration and compromise.)

Check for Understanding

Call on individual students to answer Section 1 Review questions orally.

Guided Practice

Tell students that the Red Scare of the 1920's is related to the practice of nativism—that is, the favoring of native-born Americans and the placing of restrictions on immigrants. Ask students what other groups have been victims of this false sense of patriotism. (Possible responses: blacks, American Indians, Chinese, Japanese, Mexicans.) Why is nativism a contradiction in a country founded by immigrants? (Possible response: it is an attitude hostile to foreigners, and foreigners settled the U.S.)

resented the small advances made by African Americans during the war. They felt that their moral values were being attacked by urban intellectuals. They feared job competition from immigrants. They were convinced that foreigners were going to overthrow the American way of life.

Klan members expressed some of their frustrations through racial violence. They also tried to influence national and state politics. Klan leaders in Indiana, however—the only state to fall under its control—committed such outrages that the law finally moved against them. After a while, most of the Klan's members drifted away.

The Steelworkers Strike

The public had been outraged by the Boston police strike. It was equally opposed to the steel strike that began in September 1919.

Most steelworkers put in seven twelve-hour days every week in hot and noisy foundries. Since steel furnaces must operate around the clock, there were two shifts. Once every two weeks, a steelworker "swung" from the day shift to the night shift. This "swing shift" meant that the worker had to put in an incredible twenty-four hours of labor! Furthermore, that was labor as hard, uncomfortable, and dangerous as any in American industry.

The steel industry was not unionized although more than twenty unions belonging to the American Federation of Labor wanted to represent various occupations in the mills. This unwieldy group formed an organizing committee under William Z. Foster, but its efforts were badly coordinated. The AFL unions were jealous of one another, and Foster offended and frightened many with his radicalism. He later joined the Communist party and was its Presidential candidate in 1924, 1928, and 1932.

The steel strike was broken in January 1920, after eighteen workers were killed by a combination of United States Steel security police, state militia, and federal troops. At first, people in general were relieved that another threat by "un-American elements" had been turned back. Then, in 1923, a Protestant interfaith committee published a report on working conditions in the mills. The report shocked the public, and the steel companies agreed to establish an eight-hour workday. Nevertheless, steelworkers remained unorganized.

Lewis Leads the Coal Miners

Unionism was more successful in America's coal fields. In 1919 the United Mine Workers, organized since 1840, got a new president. He was a burly young man who was equally ready to throw an insult or a punch at anyone who got in his way. His family came from Wales, and they had been mining coal and organizing miners for generations.

John L. Lewis called his union's members out on November 1, 1919. On November 9 Attorney General Palmer got a court order sending the miners back to work. Lewis declared the strike over. "We cannot fight the government," he said with uncharacteristic meekness. However, he quietly gave the word for the strike to continue.

The mines stayed closed for another month. Finally, President Wilson promised to have an arbitrator decide the issues between the miners and

Picturing History Labor leader John L. Lewis shown in a 1925 photograph and in a watercolor by William Auerbach-Levy. Lewis's rallying cry for union workers was "No contract, no work." One cartoonist commented that Lewis was "one of God's greatest gifts to cartoonists in the twentieth century."

Assign Independent Practice

Have students complete Chapter 25, Section 1 Daily Activity.

Student Assignment/Homework

Have students read Section 2, "The Nation Returns to Normalcy and Isolation," and complete Chapter 25, Section 2 Daily Activity.

Picturing History   A photograph shows Bartolomeo Vanzetti (center) and Nicola Sacco (right) chained to their jailer. A panel from Ben Shahn's painting shows the pair in their coffins.

the mine owners. In due course the miners received a 27 percent wage increase, and John L. Lewis became a national figure. He fought often and hard and with great success to get better wages and working conditions for the miners. As a result, he was both one of the most admired and one of the most hated men of his time.

Sacco and Vanzetti Go on Trial

Other figures in the 1920's were even more controversial than Lewis. Two of them, Italian immigrants Nicola Sacco and Bartolomeo Vanzetti, described themselves as "a good shoemaker and a poor fish peddler." They were also anarchists who had evaded the draft during World War I.

On May 5, 1920, they were arrested for a payroll robbery in South Braintree, Massachusetts, in which the paymaster and his guard were shot and killed. Although anarchists sometimes committed such crimes to get money for their cause, the evidence in the **Sacco-Vanzetti case** was circumstantial, or indirect. Nevertheless, they were found guilty and sentenced to death. The state supreme court refused to grant a new trial, and the governor refused to pardon them or to change the sentence. He did postpone execution while a committee of three distinguished citizens examined the case. Although the committee strongly criticized the behavior of the judge, who had not remained impartial during the proceedings, it upheld the conviction. In spite of protests and demonstrations in the United States, Europe, and Latin America, Sacco and Vanzetti were electrocuted on August 23, 1927.

In 1961, ballistics tests were done on the pistol that had been found on Sacco. Some authorities believe this new evidence proves that this was the gun used in the murder. Other experts claim that the evidence against each man remains inconclusive. Researchers continue to look for new facts and to reinterpret existing information.

SECTION 1 REVIEW

Key Terms and People

Explain the significance of: communism, Comintern, A. Mitchell Palmer, Ku Klux Klan (KKK), John L. Lewis, Sacco-Vanzetti case

Main Ideas

1. During the postwar years, what were the causes of the fear many Americans felt about radical groups?
2. What fears, resentments, and prejudices led some people to support the Ku Klux Klan after the war?
3. What conditions led to the steelworkers' strike in September 1919?
4. What resulted from the United Mine Workers' strike in 1919?
5. What was the outcome of the Sacco–Vanzetti trial?

Critical Thinking

6. Why was the Sacco–Vanzetti trial so controversial?

State the Objective

Understand the successes and failures of the Harding administration.

Anticipate the Lesson

Discuss Chapter 25, Section 2 Daily Activity with the class. Ask students how scandals such as the Teapot Dome scandal affect the people's view of the Presidency. (Possible responses: some might lose faith in the President; others might believe that the illegal activity took place without the President's knowledge, therefore the President is not to blame.) How might a President minimize the

SECTION 2

The Nation Returns to Normalcy and Isolation

GLOSSARY TERMS: **Ohio gang, naval holiday, arms race, quota system, Teapot Dome scandal**

Sometimes when a political party has been out of office for a while and sees a chance for victory, it searches for its best possible candidate. The Republicans in 1920 did not do so. They instead nominated Senator **Warren G. Harding,** whom the *New York Times* called "a respectable Ohio politician of the second class." Some people believed that the *Times* had been too generous; they felt that Harding was not respectable. However, he was handsome, good-natured, and, as one of his followers said, he "looked like a President ought to look." Governor Coolidge of Massachusetts, the hero of the Boston police strike, was nominated as his Vice-President.

Picturing History Warren G. Harding (left) and his cabinet. Vice-President Calvin Coolidge is at far right.

Presidential Election, 1920

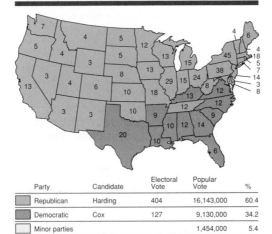

Party	Candidate	Electoral Vote	Popular Vote	%
Republican	Harding	404	16,143,000	60.4
Democratic	Cox	127	9,130,000	34.2
Minor parties			1,454,000	5.4

531 Total Electoral Vote

In November 1920 Harding and Coolidge swamped Democratic candidates James M. Cox and Franklin D. Roosevelt by 16 million to 9 million votes. The electoral count was even more of a landslide: 404 to 127.

Harding Maintains the Status Quo

The new President favored a two-part policy. On the domestic front, it involved a "return to normalcy." By this Harding apparently meant the simpler days before the Progressive Era. He was opposed to the federal government's taking a role in business affairs, and he disapproved of most social reforms. On the foreign front, Harding disagreed with Wilson's ideas about the League of Nations. "We seek no part in directing the destinies of the Old World," he said.

Harding made some excellent cabinet appointments. **Charles Evans Hughes,** Secretary of State, was an able and dedicated public servant who went on to become Chief Justice of the Supreme Court. Herbert Hoover, Secretary of Commerce, was a popular figure because of his masterly handling of food supplies and refugee problems during the war. **Andrew Mellon,** Pittsburgh banker and financier, served twelve years as a cabinet member and was considered by many to be the greatest Secretary of the Treasury since Alexander Hamilton. Henry C. Wallace, Secretary of Agriculture, was a pioneer in advanced farming methods.

Unhappily, the cabinet also included the so-called **Ohio gang,** the President's poker-playing cronies from back home. There was Attorney General Harry M. Daugherty, a lobbyist for tobacco and meatpacking companies who had been the first to push Harding for the Presidency. Finally, there was Interior Secretary **Albert B. Fall,** a close friend of various oil executives, about whose behavior you will read more.

Nations Agree on Arms Control and Peace

During the Presidential campaign, the Republicans had talked of having some form of interna-

Present the Lesson

Prepare a two-column chart on the board, heading one column Successes and one column Failures. Have students write in the appropriate columns the successes and failures of the Harding administration.

Successes: cabinet appointments of Charles Evan Hughes, Herbert Hoover, Andrew Mellon, and Henry C. Wallace; the Dawes Plan.

Failures: cabinet appointments of Ohio gang; increased isolationism; uneven and unfair immigration quotas; scandals involving Jessie Smith, Charles Cramer, Charles R. Forbes, Colonel Miller; Teapot Dome scandal.

Check for Understanding

Have students write the answers to Section 2 Review questions on paper.

tional cooperation as a substitute for the League of Nations. In August 1921 Harding invited all the major powers except the Soviet Union to a conference in Washington, D.C., to discuss reducing naval armaments and preserving the peace in Asia.

Naval-Force Reductions. When representatives of the major nations gathered in Washington that November, they were expecting a routine speech of welcome from Secretary of State Hughes. Instead, they were startled to hear a series of concrete proposals about arms control.

First, Hughes suggested a ten-year **naval holiday,** during which time the nations would not build any warships. Second, he suggested that the five major powers—the United States, Great Britain, Japan, France, and Italy—adjust the size of their fleets. The United States, Hughes said, would scrap 845,000 tons of capital ships, that is, battleships and cruisers. Britain would do the same with 583,000 tons and Japan with 480,000 tons. That would leave the United States and Britain with 500,000 tons of capital ships each and the Japanese with 300,000 tons—a ratio of 5:5:3. France and Italy were to restrict themselves to 175,000 tons each.

In the end the conference agreed to accept this proposal. The agreement was called the Five-Power Treaty.

Preserving Peace in Asia. The American capital was the setting for the **Washington Naval Conference,** which also attempted to keep things calm in Asia. The United States, Britain, Japan, and France signed the Four-Power Treaty, in which they agreed to respect one another's interests in the

Picturing History The Four-Power Treaty protected American, Japanese, British, and French interests.

Pacific. The same nations joined with China, Italy, Belgium, the Netherlands, and Portugal to sign the Nine-Power Treaty. In this treaty they promised to uphold the Open Door policy and to keep China from being carved up further.

The Five-Power Treaty probably headed off a costly **arms race,** or competition among nations to build more military weapons. The other agreements may also have eased tensions between the United States and the rising power of Japan. In all, the conference was an admirable first step toward world peace. A second step was never taken, however. Efforts to limit the number of submarines and other small vessels met with no success, nor did efforts to reduce land armaments.

The United States Demands Reparations

Behind the international glow of the Washington Naval Conference, the Harding administration was actually turning its face away from Europe. The United States was trying to defuse trouble spots in Asia and to cut down on the cost of armaments. At the same time, it was not retreating from its stand on war debts.

Through American bankers, Allied nations had borrowed over $10 billion to finance their war efforts. When the fighting ended, Britain and France expected that some part of that debt would be written off as a contribution to the common struggle. The American government nevertheless insisted on payment in full. The bankrupt Allies could raise the money in only two ways. One was through reparations that Germany had promised to give the Allies. The other was by exporting more goods to the United States.

Higher Tariffs. United States policy in the 1920's was firmly against either solution. From the first moment of peace, America had urged Britain and France not to press their demands on Germany. Then, in 1922, the United States raised its tax on imported goods to the highest level to date. The **Fordney-McCumber Tariff Act** openly aimed at keeping foreign goods out of American markets. It succeeded. European exports to the United States fell from $5 billion in 1920 to $2.5 billion in 1922. Since Great Britain and France could not sell their products in the States, they were even less able to pay their debts.

The Dawes Plan. A series of international conferences tried to cope with the tangle of wartime debts and reparations. Charles G. Dawes, an American banker, and Owen D. Young, chairman of General Electric, were responsible for the system that emerged. Between 1923 and 1930, American investors loaned about $2.5 billion to the German government and to German corporations. During those same years, Germany paid $2 billion in reparations to Britain and France, who in turn paid $2.6 billion on their war debts to the United States.

While this was going on, the United States still officially held that there was no connection between German reparations and Allied war debts. American business at the time was outraged that Britain and France would not pay their debts unless they could get the money from Germany. However, the war had exhausted and bankrupted the two Allied nations who had borne much of the war burden. America's unwillingness to lower or cancel their debts led to great bitterness between them and the United States.

Nativists Want Limited Immigration

Another sign of isolationism that appeared after World War I had to do with immigration. As you know, nativist sentiment had been growing ever since the 1880's, when new immigrants from southern and eastern Europe began coming to the United States in large numbers. (See page 497.) Nativist feelings were strengthened by the fact that many of the people involved in postwar labor disputes were immigrant anarchists and socialists. In addition, demand for unskilled labor decreased after the war. The railroads had been built, and basic industries such as coal mining, steel, and textiles were well developed.

In 1921 the immigration rate—a modest 141,000 in 1919—shot up to 805,000, and Congress decided that the time had come to limit immigration from Europe. (Immigration from China had already been suspended in 1902.) The Emergency Quota Act of 1921 introduced a **quota system** based on national origins. Congress pushed through a series of additional measures, ending with the Immigration Act of 1924.

According to the 1924 law, each European nation was given a quota of 2 percent of the number of its nationals who were living in the United States in 1890. This law discriminated against people from eastern and southern Europe, who did not start coming to America in large numbers until after 1890. The Immigration Act of 1924 also excluded Japanese immigrants as "aliens ineligible to citizenship." This was an insult to Japan, whose gentlemen's agreement with Theodore Roosevelt had been faithfully kept. (See page 505.) By ignoring that agreement, the United States wiped out much of the goodwill that had resulted from the Four-Power Treaty.

Under the National Origins Act of 1929, the base year was shifted to 1920. This change was offset by reducing to 150,000 the total number of persons to be admitted in any one year. As a result, some national quotas were pitifully small. The national origins system was not applied to immigrants from the Western Hemisphere, however. During the 1920's, about a million Canadians—many of them Catholics—and at least 500,000 Mexicans crossed the nation's borders.

Scandals Plague Harding's Cabinet

Before the Harding administration was well into its third year, it began to come apart. The reason was the same as that which had plagued Grant's administration nearly fifty years before—graft among the President's friends.

In the spring of 1923, Jesse Smith, an assistant to Attorney General Daugherty, was exposed as a "bagman." A bagman carries a bribe from the person giving it to the person getting it. The money is often carried in a black bag, hence the name. Banished from Washington, D.C., Smith committed suicide in May. Shortly thereafter, Charles F. Cramer, principal legal advisor of the Veterans Bureau, took his life for similar reasons.

Next, it turned out that Charles R. Forbes, the head of the Veterans Bureau, had swindled the country of at least $250 million through kickbacks from contractors building veterans' hospitals. In 1925 Forbes was sentenced to prison for fraud and bribery. Colonel Thomas W. Miller, head of the Office of Alien Property, was also convicted for fraud. In exchange for bribes, he had taken valuable German chemical patents that the government had seized during the war and had sold them to American firms for far less than their worth.

The most daring wrongdoing, however, concerned naval oil reserves and became known as the **Teapot Dome scandal.** As a result of the conservation movement of the Progressive Era, oil-rich public lands at Teapot Dome, Wyoming, and Elk Hill, California, had been set aside for use by the United States Navy. Secretary of the Interior Fall managed to get the reserves transferred from the

Ask each student to prepare a chart or poster that "exposes" the scandals of the Harding administration. They should note at least three specific incidents of corruption, list the people involved, and summarize the details of the scandal.

- Bribery: Jessie Smith was the bagman for Attorney General Daugherty, who received bribes; Charles Cramer, legal advisor of Veterans' Bureau, also took bribes; Albert Fall, Secretary of the Interior, transferred oil reserves from the navy to the Department of the Interior, then leased land to private oil companies, in exchange for bribes.
- Swindling: Charles R. Forbes, head of the Veterans' Bureau, received $250 million in kickbacks.
- Fraud: Colonel Thomas W. Miller, head of the Office of Alien Property, sold German patents for less than their worth.

Display the charts and posters in the classroom.

Student Assignment/Homework

Have students read Section 3, "Coolidge Conducts the Nation's Business," and complete Chapter 25, Section 3 Daily Activity.

---

navy to the Interior Department. He then secretly leased the land to two private oil companies. Soon after, Fall, who had been having financial troubles, became the owner of $325,000 in bonds and cash, as well as a large herd of cattle. Eventually, Fall was charged with bribery, convicted, fined $100,000, and sentenced to a year in prison.

By the summer of 1923, Harding realized what had been going on. He knew that a day of reckoning was coming. A hurt and confused man, he declared, ''I have no trouble with my enemies. . . . But my damned friends, . . . they're the ones that keep me walking the floor nights!'' At that point he left on a goodwill trip to Alaska. Everyone noticed how tired and distracted he was. Returning from Alaska to San Francisco, he became critically ill. On August 2, 1923, Warren G. Harding died.

The American people sincerely mourned their good-natured President. Few of them realized at the time the extent to which his friends had betrayed him and the country. Fortunately, Harding's successor, Calvin Coolidge, was respected as a man of integrity. He helped to restore the people's faith in the Republican party.

Linking Past to Present

No government is without its share of scandals. One of the reasons the Teapot Dome scandal has gone down in American history is that it involved a member of President Harding's cabinet, Secretary of the Interior Albert B. Fall. In 1989, the HUD scandal came to light when a House subcommittee began investigating charges that under President Reagan's Secretary of Housing and Urban Development, Samuel Pierce, HUD had allowed well-connected Republicans to amass huge fees for helping developers land multimillion-dollar federal housing contracts. It was estimated that losses due to the HUD scandal were somewhere around $6 billion.

Picturing History The Teapot Dome scandal, portrayed in a 1924 cartoon, involved Secretary of the Interior Albert Fall (left) and oilman Harry F. Sinclair (right). Charles R. Forbes (bottom), head of the Veterans Bureau, cheated the U.S. government out of millions.

SECTION 2 REVIEW

Key Terms and People

Explain the significance of: Warren G. Harding, Charles Evans Hughes, Andrew Mellon, Ohio gang, Albert B. Fall, naval holiday, Washington Naval Conference, arms race, Fordney-McCumber Tariff Act, quota system, Teapot Dome scandal

Main Ideas

1. How did President Harding's foreign and domestic policies attempt to return America to ''normalcy''?
2. What were the main results of the Washington Naval Conference?
3. What plan made it possible for Britain and France to pay the majority of their wartime debts to the United States and how did this plan work?
4. What was the main purpose of both the Emergency Quota Act of 1921 and the Immigration Act of 1924?
5. What caused the American public to lose faith in the Harding administration's ability to govern?

Critical Thinking

6. How did the United States, Germany, Britain, and France all benefit from the Dawes Plan?

Answers

Main Ideas

1. His domestic policy opposed progressive reforms, and his foreign policy returned America to its prewar position of isolation from European problems.

2. The number of battleships and cruisers was reduced, peace was preserved in Asia, and an arms race was avoided.

3. Through the Dawes Plan, an agreement was reached whereby U.S. investors loaned money to Germany, Germany paid reparations to Britain and France, who in turn repaid a large portion of their wartime debts to the United States.

4. Both acts were designed to restrict European immigration.

5. The exposure of widespread corruption among high-placed government officials who were also Harding's friends.

Critical Thinking

6. The Dawes Plan enabled the United States to maintain isolationism and high tariffs as well as collect its wartime loans; it enabled Britain and France to pay their wartime debts to the U.S.; and it allowed Germany to meet its reparations agreements with Britain and France. **(analysis)**

Anticipate the Lesson

Discuss Chapter 25, Section 3 Daily Activity. Ask students to list probable reasons for Coolidge's victory in the 1924 election. (Possible responses: Coolidge was the incumbent President; Democrats were divided over Prohibition and religion; voters believed Coolidge was a simple, honest man; business leaders liked Coolidge because he wanted to keep taxes down and profits up.)

State the Objective

Understand how American businesses and corporations were mainly responsible for the partial prosperity during the Coolidge administration.

SECTION 3

Coolidge Conducts the Nation's Business

GLOSSARY TERMS: **installment plan, planned obsolescence**

The new President, **Calvin Coolidge,** was sworn into office by his father, a notary public, between two and three o'clock in the morning in the family farmhouse in Plymouth, Vermont. It was a moving scene, lighted by a kerosene lamp. Coolidge took his vow on the family Bible. Americans who had grown up on the farm were deeply touched. In the following months, as one scandal after another came out concerning Harding's administration, the new chief executive looked even more reassuring. He seemed, and was, a simple, honest man who obviously would not steal a nickel.

Business leaders also liked Coolidge because he wanted to keep taxes down and profits up. "The chief business of the American people is business," he intoned. "The man who builds a factory, builds a temple," he declared. Such sentiments seemed to foretell a golden age for business.

To many people, the solemn Coolidge seemed to be an unusual President for the rapidly changing United States. Careful about what he said, he never said much. "I have never been hurt by what I haven't said," he quipped. Many persons called him Silent Cal. Still, America was ready to take it easy for a while and let the good times roll. As one

Picturing History Calvin Coolidge being sworn into office by his father at the family farmhouse in Vermont.

campaign poster put it, "Keep Cool with Coolidge."

The Republicans Win in 1924

Coolidge easily won the Republican nomination in 1924. The Democrats, on the other hand, were divided. Their Southern and rural members favored Prohibition, while their Northern, big-city members wanted it repealed. Those same factions were at odds over the religion of one prominent contender for the nomination. He was Governor Alfred E. Smith of New York, a Catholic. The Ku Klux Klan threw its considerable weight against Smith, and the Democratic convention dragged on for an incredible 102 ballots.

The compromise candidate, wealthy corporation lawyer John W. Davis, had no chance against Coolidge. Even the presence on the ballot of Progressive candidate Robert La Follette of Wisconsin did not make a difference. Coolidge got almost 16 million of the 29 million votes cast.

Presidential Election, 1924

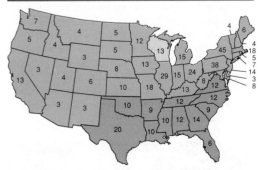

Party	Candidate	Electoral Vote	Popular Vote	%
Republican	Coolidge	382	15,718,000	54.0
Democratic	Davis	136	8,385,000	28.8
Progressive	LaFollette	13	4,831,000	16.6
Minor parties			154,000	0.5

531 Total Electoral Vote

Americans Experience Prosperous Times

Coolidge kept most of those members of the Harding cabinet who had not been involved in its scandals. The kingpin of the group was Andrew Mellon, the only Secretary of the Treasury, as one wit later said, "under whom three Presidents had served." Mellon was a multimillionaire, the head of the aluminum trust, and the owner of several steel mills, oil companies, banks, and utilities. His policies were everything the business community

Present the Lesson

Have students use the headings in this section to outline the section. Write the beginning of the outline on the board.

I. The Republicans Win in 1924.
  A. Coolidge wins Republican nomination.
  B. Democrats are divided on issues.
    1. Prohibition.
    2. Religion of Al Smith—Catholic.
    3. Compromise candidate—John W. Davis.
  C. Progressive candidate is Robert La Follette.
  D. Coolidge receives 16 million of 29 million votes.
II. Americans Experience Prosperous Times.
  A. Treasury Secretary is Mellon.
    1. Favored cutting excess profit tax.
    2. Favored reducing public debt.
    3. Wanted to keep government spending down.
  B. Businesses thrive.
  C. Low interest rates make borrowing easier.
  D. Construction booms.
  E. Technological developments add to nation's well-being.

Have students refer to their outlines as they study the section.

Focus on Biography

George Gershwin (1898–1937)

At age six, George Gershwin walked past an amusement arcade. Inside, a mechanical piano was grinding out Anton Rubinstein's "Melody in F." Whatever an adult music lover might have thought, little George was captivated. "The peculiar jumps of the melody," he said later, "held me transfixed."

The spell was to last for the rest of George's life. It was deepened in his youth by the sounds he heard coming from a neighborhood jazz club one night. He returned there again and again to sit on the sidewalk, listening as wonderful, complex rhythms floated through the club's open door.

Meanwhile, on pianos in the houses of friends, George picked out popular tunes of the day and made up others of his own. He was twelve before his parents, who were Jewish immigrants from Russia, became aware of his talents. Then they bought him a piano and found a teacher to give him lessons.

Although he studied serious music, George Gershwin's chief ambition was to write popular songs. At fifteen, he left high school and went to work for a music publisher for fifteen dollars a week. He was soon working for a different house which had offered him thirty-five dollars a week and a chance to work as he pleased.

In 1919, when he was barely twenty-one, George produced his first hit song, "Swanee." Al Jolson, a popular performer of the day, introduced the number in a Broadway show. Eight years later, Jolson repeated it in Hollywood's first talking picture, *The Jazz Singer.*

"Swanee" established George's reputation and brought him countless offers and opportunities. He persuaded his brother, Ira, to join him as a lyricist. Ira already had some songs to his credit (written under another name so people would not think he was trading on George's reputation). From then on the two were an inseparable team.

In 1922 the young composer tried his hand at a one-act opera first called *Blue Monday* and later *135th Street.* The opera failed both commercially and artistically. It was too somber for Broadway tastes, but it got the attention of Paul Whiteman. Whiteman, called the King of Jazz, was the most popular band leader of the 1920's.

Whiteman asked George to compose a symphonic piece based on jazz rhythms. The band leader wished to feature the piece at a concert. In 1924, George produced *Rhapsody in Blue,* scored for jazz band and piano. The concert, with the composer as soloist, startled the music world. A number of Europeans had tried, with little success, to do what the twenty-six-year-old composer had now accomplished.

Rhapsody in Blue is probably the most popular twentieth-century American orchestral piece. In addition to being successful in concert halls around the world, it also earned a great deal of money for its composer.

On top of that triumph, George achieved tremendous success on Broadway. His career as a popular composer peaked in 1931 with the musical play *Of Thee I Sing.* The work, a satire on American politics, featured music and lyrics by George and Ira Gershwin. *Of Thee I Sing* was the first musical comedy ever to win a Pulitzer Prize.

Then, in 1935, George wrote *Porgy and Bess,* considered by many to be the best American opera. It is a tale of life among poor black people in Charleston, South Carolina. *Porgy* has been given countless productions in the United States and around the world, including a tour in the Soviet Union.

In the 1930's, as film became the chief American entertainment medium, the Gershwins were drawn to Hollywood. There, in 1937, George became ill and died during an unsuccessful operation.

It is hard to imagine what George Gershwin might have done for American music had he lived a normal lifetime. Surely there would have been other operas and symphonic scores, as well as dozens more popular songs. As it is, his contributions to American popular and classical music are immeasurable.

Check for Understanding

Have students write the answers to Section 3 Review questions on paper.

Guided Practice

Tell students that advertising in the U.S. has become a multi-billion dollar business. Ask students to consider whether advertising helps to make Americans a consumption-oriented people and, consequently, a more wasteful people. Ask students whether we want more because we see more or we need more because our high-tech society requires more. (Possible response: Americans tend to want many more things than they actually need; advertising plays a key role in this process by showing us glamorous, wealthy, and happy people enjoying the products being sold.)

wanted. He favored cutting the excess profits tax and reducing the public debt left over from the war, which meant keeping government spending down. He also wanted to lower taxes on incomes over $66,000 a year while raising taxes for poorer citizens. "Let the rich keep their wealth," Mellon said. "They will invest it and so create jobs." He also favored raising postal rates.

The economy responded well to Mellon's policies. Business had never been so good. No less than 40 percent of the world's wealth belonged to Americans. The number of millionaires rose from forty-five hundred in 1914 to eleven thousand in 1926. Low interest rates set by the Federal Reserve Board made borrowing easy. Construction of industrial plants, homes, office buildings, and hotels boomed. The soaring 102-story Empire State Building in New York City, the world's tallest building at that time, was the era's architectural triumph.

Household Electricity. Technological developments added to the nation's well-being. The use of alternating electric current made it possible to step up electric power by means of a transformer. Now electricity was no longer restricted to central cities but could be transmitted over great distances to outlying suburbs and even to farms. Between 1913 and 1927, there was a 465 percent increase in the number of electrified households. Such labor-saving devices as vacuum cleaners, washing machines, refrigerators, toasters, and electric irons and stoves became widely used. By the end of the decade, household current made it possible for a radio to look like living-room furniture rather than a piece of laboratory equipment.

Competition for Ford. By the mid-1920's, the Model T began to lose ground. Essentially, it had not changed since 1908. General Motors' Chevrolet had appeared, costing little more than a fully equipped Ford sedan and providing much more comfort. To meet the challenge, Ford shut down his enormous operation for several months to retool. Then he unveiled his 1928 Model A, a well-designed four-cylinder automobile with a standard stick gearshift. A popular song of the day said that "Henry made a lady out of Lizzie." The lady was not lucky, however, for the Model A never captured people's imaginations as had the Model T.

Retailers Try New Sales Techniques

Ever since the Gilded Age, Americans had been familiar with the chain store. Frank W. Woolworth's five-and-tens had set the pattern of buying goods in large quantities, storing them in warehouses, and then selling them in several stores—all

Picturing History The chains acquire more links: by 1929 F. W. Woolworth had 1,825 five-and-tens; Standard Oil of New Jersey had 1,000 filling stations; and the A & P had 15,418 food stores.

Assign Independent Practice

On the board write the following quotes from Calvin Coolidge: "The business of America is business" and "The man who builds a factory, builds a temple." Ask students to write two paragraphs explaining Coolidge's economic philosophy based on these quotes. (Paragraphs might include: Coolidge believed in free enterprise; he believed that business was the foundation of American society; he believed that businesses kept the government running.)

Student Assignment/Homework

Have students read Section 4, "Problems Threaten Economic Prosperity," and answer Section 4 Review questions on paper.

of which looked more or less alike and all of which carried the same merchandise. The technique eliminated wholesalers. During the twenties, the technique was adopted by A & P, United Drug, Thom McAnn, J. C. Penney, and United Cigar, among others.

At the same time, Sears, Roebuck and Company opened retail stores as its customers—mostly farmers—began throwing away their mail-order catalogs and driving to town in their Model T's. Also, Clarence Saunders of Memphis, Tennessee, introduced his Piggly-Wiggly stores. Called grocery-cafeterias, these self-service stores were forerunners of the modern supermarket.

In addition to these methods of distribution, industry came up with several solutions to the problem of finding consumers for the mountain of goods it turned out each year. One solution was easy credit, then called the **installment plan,** or "a dollar down and a dollar forever." It enabled people to buy goods without having to put up much money at the time of purchase. Banks provided the money at low interest rates. Other techniques for moving goods included annual model changes. Automobiles, for instance, were built with **planned obsolescence,** that is, a policy of making goods that last only a few months or years before they must be replaced.

Advertisers Create Desire

Still another technique was the use of advertising. In the 1920's, businesses advertised almost entirely in print. Of $1.5 billion spent in 1927 to sell various products, two-thirds went to newspapers and magazines. Another $300 million was spent on direct mail, and $200 million went to outdoor advertising, such as signs and billboards.

Advertising people no longer just sold space. They hired psychologists to study the best ways of appealing to the buyer. What colors will be best for what packages? What are the best words to use in an advertisement? The new field of motivational research tried to answer these and similar questions as it studied the reasons why people buy. No executive could fail to be impressed with the results. The slogan "Say It with Flowers," for instance, doubled the florist business between 1921 and 1924. "Even Your Best Friend Won't Tell You" helped to sell a great many deodorants, as well as cures for bad breath and athlete's foot.

While Calvin Coolidge occupied the White House, most Americans believed that good times

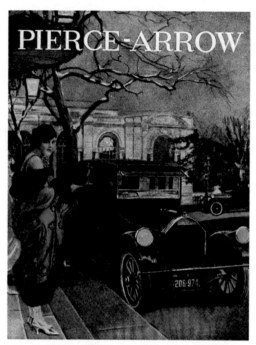

Picturing History Ads for the Pierce-Arrow sold glamour, youth, and prosperity. They said little about the product itself.

would last forever. There were gaps in the twenties' booming prosperity, however, and by the decade's end they had begun to worry some careful observers.

SECTION 3 REVIEW

Key Terms and People

Explain the significance of: Calvin Coolidge, installment plan, planned obsolescence

Main Ideas

1. What factors contributed to the Republican landslide in the election of 1924?
2. In what ways was the 1920's a time of prosperity?
3. In general, what was the purpose behind both the introduction of the installment plan and the idea of planned obsolescence?

Critical Thinking

4. Who benefited most from the prosperity of the 1920's, producers or consumers? Explain.

SECTION 3 REVIEW

Answers

Main Ideas

1. Divisiveness within the Democratic party and Coolidge's popularity among the American people.

2. Business and the construction of new buildings, plants, and so on, boomed, the wealthy became wealthier, and technological advancements made everyday life easier.

3. To create a large market for the incredible number of goods that industry turned out each year.

Critical Thinking

4. Possible answers: producers—business boom made many people wealthy; consumers—easy credit increased many people's standard of living. **(evaluation)**

Anticipate the Lesson

Review with students the examples of prosperous times discussed in Section 3.

State the Objective

Understand exceptions to the general level of prosperity of the 1920's.

Present the Lesson

Write the following topics on the board: Railroads, Textiles, Coal Mining, Agriculture. Ask students to reread the section to find information that explains the reasons why each of these industries was in trouble in the 1920's. List these reasons on the board.

Railroads: Esch-Cummins Act of 1920 placed railroad rates and service under government control but left ownership in private hands; railroads were unable to earn a modest 6 percent return; government would not let railroads abandon lines that were losing money; growing

---

SECTION 4

Problems Threaten Economic Prosperity

GLOSSARY TERMS: **bloc, price supports, buying on margin**

Tremendous wealth was being created in the 1920's, but it was not evenly distributed. Many corporations made fortunes but did little for their workers. About half the population lived at or below the Department of Labor's estimated cost of a decent standard of living. As one song proclaimed: "The rich get richer and the poor get poorer." Yet no one seemed to question the economic ideas of Andrew Mellon.

Old Industries Face New Competition

Certain industries were in deep trouble. High on the list of those not enjoying good times were some that had helped build the nation. These included railroads, textiles, and coal mining.

Railroads. America's experience during World War I had shown that railroads could be more efficiently run as a unified system. William G. McAdoo, who had administered the system from 1917 through 1919, proposed a five-year peacetime trial. Glenn E. Plumb, a lawyer for the railroad brotherhoods, drew up a detailed plan.

Continued government ownership of a basic industry, however, smacked of socialism. So the Plumb plan got nowhere. Instead, Congress passed the Esch-Cummins Act of 1920, which placed railroads under government control as to rates and service but left ownership in private hands. However, the railroads were never able to earn the modest 6 percent return on investment that the new act allowed. Part of the reason was that the government was unwilling to allow the railroads to abandon lines that were losing money. A more important reason was the growing competition from trucks, buses, and private automobiles.

Textiles. Even before World War I, the textile industry had begun to shift from New England to the South. It made economic sense to manufacture cotton cloth nearer the source of raw material. A stronger motive was the desire for cheap labor. There were many labor unions in the mills of the

North but few in the South. Also, Southern wage rates were considerably lower than Northern ones.

There was no escape, though, from two other developments. One was foreign competition from Japan, India, China, and Latin America, all of whom produced cheap goods for the world textile market. The second development was the radical change in women's clothing, which eliminated yards of skirt and petticoat material and thus lowered the demand for cloth.

Linking Past to Present

American automobile, steel, and electronic manufacturers faced some of the same changes in the 1970's and 1980's that the Northern textile industry faced in the 1920's. The desire for cheaper labor and overhead moved manufacturing south and west. Foreign competition, chiefly from Japan, caused many industries to restructure operations, lay off workers, and, in some cases, shut down entirely.

Coal Mining. Another industry that felt an economic pinch was coal mining. It had expanded to meet wartime needs. During the twenties, however, the increased demand vanished. In addition, oil, natural gas, and hydroelectric power became widely available. By the early 1930's these sources were filling more than half the energy needs that had once depended on coal. The price of soft coal thus fell to a point at which high-cost mines were forced to close. Since some of the high costs came from paying union wages, it was the nonunion mines that remained open.

Farmers Suffer from Overproduction

Serious though they were, none of these problems threatened the nation's economic welfare as basically as the problems of agriculture. Chief among these was the problem of overproduction.

Overproduction. During the war, farmers had expanded their operations. They had cultivated lands in the West that did not regularly get enough rainfall for planting. They had replaced scarce human labor with new kinds of farm machinery. As competition from trucks, buses, and automobiles developed.

Textiles: the processing of cotton shifted from New England to Southern states; cheap foreign-made textiles flooded the market; changes in women's clothing styles eliminated yards of cloth per garment, reducing textile production.

Coal Mining: mining had expanded to meet wartime demand; oil, natural gas, and hydroelectric power had become widely available; price of soft coal fell; high-cost mines were forced to close.

Agriculture: farmers had expanded production during the war; new machinery increased productivity; farmers paid for expansion with borrowed money; world competition caused prices to fall; demand for cotton, beef, pork, and flour dropped; farmers tried to improve through electricity; farm bloc tried to help farmers in Congress; McNary-Haugen bills proposed price supports; President Coolidge vetoed these bills.

Picturing History In the 1920's, falling prices for farm goods forced many farmers to sell out. Coolidge's response: "Well, farmers never have made money."

a result, they had astonished the world with their productivity.

At the same time, farmers had paid for expansion with borrowed money. Then, in 1920, mostly as a result of world competition, prices of staple crops such as wheat, corn, and cotton tumbled almost 50 percent. To make matters worse, overproduction was coupled with a drop in demand as clothing manufacturers turned from cotton to rayon fabrics and as families began eating less beef, pork, and flour and more fruits and vegetables.

Farmers tried to improve matters through further investments, such as electrifying their farms. This only piled up more debts. By 1930 farmers who raised staple crops owned three times as many tractors as in 1920—and also owed three times as much on mortgages as they did in 1912. Better seeds and fertilizers and still more tractors continued to expand American output. Yet there was no comparable rise in demand.

Price Supports. In 1921 a group of congressmen from the farm states became a unified group of voters known as the **farm bloc.** It included members of both political parties who aimed at improving the economic well-being of their constituents.

In 1924 Senator Charles L. McNary of Oregon and Representative Gilbert N. Haugen of Iowa

introduced several pieces of legislation. The McNary-Haugen bills proposed that the federal government buy surplus wheat, corn, cotton, and tobacco at a reasonable price. In that way the government would set a floor, or minimum price, for each crop, since no farmer would be likely to sell it for less. As a result of these **price supports,** government could then unload the surplus abroad for whatever price it would bring. Since the world price would be lower than the domestic price, the difference was to be made up by a special tax on all farm crops. The theory was that while farmers would lose something by paying the tax, on balance they would be better off.

The McNary-Haugen bills were introduced repeatedly from 1924 to 1928. Each time Congress passed them, President Coolidge vetoed them. He believed that they represented an unconstitutional use of federal power. In any event, as he observed, "Farmers have never made money. I don't believe we can do much about it."

The Rich Get Richer, the Poor Get Poorer

In 1929 a national study of family income showed that three-fifths of the nation's wealth was owned by 2 percent of its people: "The 27,500

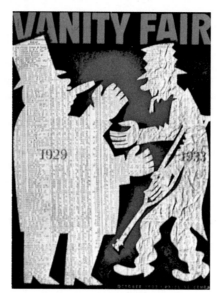

Picturing History The cover of a 1933 magazine used cutouts from stock-market quotations to compare the fat cat of the 1929 market with his crippled counterpart of 1933.

Tell students that overproduction is still a problem for American farmers, but foreign markets offer great opportunities for export. Farm exports, however, can become involved in international politics; for example, when the Soviets invaded Afghanistan in 1980, the U.S. placed an embargo on grain shipments to the Soviet Union. Ask students whether the U.S. government should use food embargoes to pressure other nations. (Possible response: no, because an embargo causes the general public rather than the military or government to suffer.)

Have students complete Chapter 25, Section 4 Daily Activity.

Have students read Section 5, "A Slipping Economy Signals the End of an Era," and write the answers to Section 5 Review questions on paper.

SECTION 4 REVIEW

Answers

Main Ideas

1. Railroads, textiles, coal mining, and farming.

2. Three-fifths of the wealth was owned by 2 percent of the people.

3. By buying on margin, paying only a percentage of the stock's cost and borrowing the rest from the stockbroker.

Critical Thinking

4. Possible answer: similarity—farmers, like most other Americans, were in debt and getting poorer. Differences—farmers had acquired their debt by overproducing and buying expensive equipment during the war; they also were not trying to get rich or buying stocks on margin. **(analysis)**

648

Picturing History A farm family's simple dining room and William Randolph Hearst's baronial dining room illustrate the uneven distribution of income during the 1920's.

wealthiest families in America had as much money as the twelve million poorest families." Miners and lumbermen, for example, earned $10 a week. Andrew Mellon paid an income tax of almost $2 million, and Henry Ford's income tax was $2.6 million.

This uneven distribution of income might not have been serious if the lowest-income families had been living at a decent level. Nearly half the nation's families, however, earned less than $1,500 a year, then considered the minimum amount needed for a decent life. Even families earning twice that sum could not afford most of the products that manufacturers were turning out in great numbers and at great speed. It is estimated that the average man or woman bought a new outfit of clothes only once a year. Scarcely half the homes in many cities had electric lights or furnace heat. Only one city home in ten had electric refrigeration.

Low consumer demand was not the only consequence of the uneven distribution of income. Wealthy people can spend only so much, because they can eat just so much food, wear just so many clothes, and the like. So the wealthy people of America invested their surplus funds in the stock market. Less wealthy people did the same, hoping to get rich quickly. Some bought stocks on margin. **Buying on margin** meant that they paid only a

percentage of the stock's cost and borrowed the rest from the stockbroker, intending to pay him back when they sold the stock at a higher price. As more speculators entered the stock market, the prices of stocks rose above their real value.

President Coolidge might say, as he did in a rare public statement: "Everything is fundamentally sound." However, some of the foundations on which prosperity rested were shaky indeed.

SECTION 4 REVIEW

Key Terms and People

Explain the significance of: farm bloc, price supports, buying on margin

Main Ideas

1. Name three industries that suffered during the post-World War I years.
2. How was wealth distributed in the United States at the end of the 1920's?
3. How were Americans who were not wealthy able to invest in the stock market?

Critical Thinking

4. Compare and contrast the plight of the typical American farmer with that of most other Americans after World War I. Use specific examples.

Anticipate the Lesson

Review with students the information from Sections 3 and 4 on the economy. Make a two-column chart on the board showing the prosperity and economic difficulties of the time. Have students add details to the chart. Chart might include:

Prosperity: low interest rates were common; construction boomed; technology advanced;

new retailing techniques evolved; installment plans made credit easy.
Difficulties: railroads were unable to make a profit; textiles suffered because of foreign imports and decreased demand for cloth; coal mining suffered as use of oil, natural gas, and hydroelectric power increased; agriculture suffered because of over-production and excessive borrowing by farmers.

State the Objective

Understand the major economic events and trends of the late 1920's.

SECTION 5

A Slipping Economy Signals the End of an Era

GLOSSARY TERMS: **Solid South, Good Neighbor Policy, stocks, Black Tuesday**

The decade's last political drama was the election of 1928, which pitted two remarkable men against each other. Personally they were as different as night and day. **Herbert Hoover,** secretary of commerce for eight years, was stiff, serious and reserved, and had never run for office. **Alfred E. Smith,** governor of New York, was a witty, outgoing politician who could get along with anyone.

In some ways, however, the two Presidential candidates were alike. Both had been born poor, Hoover on an Iowa farm, and Al Smith in a slum of New York City known as the Lower East Side. Both had succeeded on their own with brains, guts, and hard work. Each was a superb administrator. Hoover had proved it by making a fortune in the mining engineering business before he was forty. He had also organized efforts to feed and house thousands of refugees during World War I. Smith had given New York the most efficient and up-to-date government of any state in the nation. Both had admired Woodrow Wilson. Both believed in American capitalism but knew it needed reform.

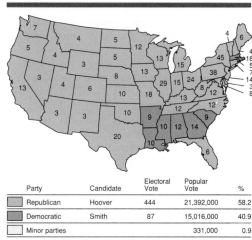

Presidential Election, 1928

Party	Candidate	Electoral Vote	Popular Vote	%
Republican	Hoover	444	21,392,000	58.2
Democratic	Smith	87	15,016,000	40.9
Minor parties			331,000	0.9

531 Total Electoral Vote

Hoover Wins in 1928

Ordinarily, one would have expected the Republican candidate to be Coolidge. However, in 1927 he announced, without warning or explanation, that he did not choose to run. So party leaders turned to Hoover, "the Great Engineer," who was the favorite choice of forward-looking business leaders.

Picturing History Herbert Hoover's Presidential campaign, Iowa, 1928. Most Americans identified with the rugged individualism of Hoover.

Politics and a Thin Prosperity **649**

Have students list on the board and then discuss the major factors influencing the 1928 elections. (Possible responses: Ku Klux Klan attacked Smith because he was Catholic; Smith called for repeal of Prohibition; radio campaign emphasized Smith's New York accent and alienated many small-town people; prosperity was at its peak; Republicans were in the majority and people were basically satisfied with the way things were.)

Have students skim the section to find indicators of the false base of prosperity of the 1920's. List these on the board. (Possible responses: 1926–1929—housing starts and construction were declining, creating a downward spiral in other industries; 1929—business inventories were three times higher than in 1928, indicating lowered consumption and causing industrial production and wholesale prices to fall.)

Check for Understanding

Call on individual students to read their answers to Section 5 Review questions.

On the Democratic side, Smith could not again be denied a chance to run. Too many loyal party members had been angered when he lost to Davis in 1924. This time Smith got the nomination on the first ballot.

The weakened Ku Klux Klan roused itself to attack Smith once more because he was a Catholic. Yet, Smith's call for repeal of Prohibition may have cost him as many votes as his religion. In addition, radio was widely used in the campaign. It carried Smith's rasping voice and exaggerated New York City accent straight to the people of rural America. It was a big-city accent they suspected and disliked.

More than anything else, though, Smith lost because the Republicans were in the majority and there was no reason to oust them. The Coolidge prosperity was at its peak. Smith's defeat by 21 million votes to 15 million was all the more stinging because the **Solid South** broke ranks. Five Southern states ignored their one-party tradition and voted Republican for the first time since Reconstruction.

The Nation Tries to Be a Good Neighbor

One of Hoover's solid accomplishments was to continue improving relations with Latin America. In doing so, he was following in the steps of his predecessor.

Coolidge had made a start in that direction. Mexico's 1917 constitution had sharply curbed the activities of foreign oil companies. In 1927 the Mexican government further limited the rights of outsiders in Mexican oil fields. This action led war hawks to call for an invasion of Mexico. Instead, Coolidge appointed Dwight W. Morrow as ambassador and told him to try conciliation. Within a year, economic restrictions on American oil companies were lifted.

Morrow's efforts began a more moderate United States foreign policy that guarded against overreaction to nationalist economic changes in Latin America. Hoover continued the policy and expanded it. Before assuming office, he made a goodwill tour of eleven Latin American nations. In 1930 he repudiated the Roosevelt Corollary to the Monroe Doctrine, which had stated that the United States would act as a policeman in the Western Hemisphere. (See page 530.) Hoover also denounced dollar diplomacy. He withdrew American marines from Nicaragua and started withdrawing those stationed in Haiti. He attempted to treat Latin American nations as equals. It was he who first used the term "good neighbor," though it is part of his political ill-luck that most people associate the **Good Neighbor Policy** with his archrival Franklin D. Roosevelt.

The Economy Turns Downward

Hoover's worst luck, though, was having the Great Depression begin during his first year in office. It is generally agreed today that the Great Depression was not brought about solely by the stock-market crash of October 1929. All through the year there had been signs that the boom was over. A number of the indicators that economists and business leaders carefully watch were pointing to a downturn. (See pages 788–789.)

Beginning in 1926 and continuing through 1929, housing starts and other forms of construction were declining. Construction then, as now, is an important multiplier industry. Not only does it use enormous resources, but it stimulates other businesses. New construction means new furnishings, new equipment, and new appliances. Insurance and other services are needed. Jobs are created. On the other hand, a decline in construction creates a downward spiral in other industries.

In 1929, too, business inventories were three times higher than they had been during the previous year. In other words, people were not buying. Orders were likely to be cut back until products had moved. As predicted, freight shipments fell, indicating that orders were shrinking. Industrial production and wholesale prices soon followed the downward trend. The demand for staple crops had also declined throughout the 1920's, leaving farmers with huge surpluses.

The Stock Market Crashes

Given these signs, shrewd stock-market speculators began to unload their **stocks,** or certificates that guarantee partial ownership in a corporation, and to take their profits. Bernard Baruch, the wartime production head, was one who did so. Joseph P. Kennedy, father of future President John F. Kennedy, was another. Thousands of little and not so little investors went on buying, however, so prices continued to rise. The days of reckoning came in the fall.

After Labor Day the market did not bounce back as had been expected. Instead, it faltered. On October 21 it took a big drop. On October 24 there

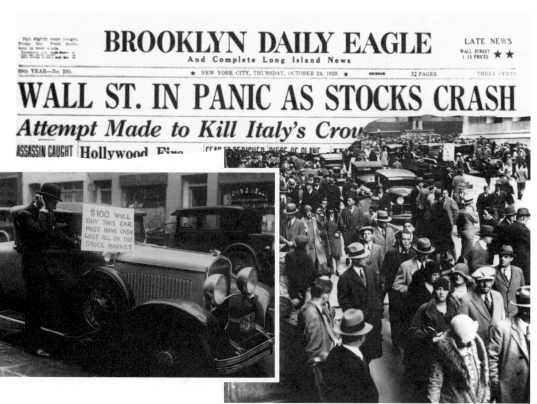

Picturing History Three images of the stock-market crash: huge headlines announcing Wall Street panic, a seemingly well-to-do investor trying to raise cash, and crowds of bewildered faces lining both sides of Wall Street.

was a wave of selling orders as people who had bought on margin were forced to sell in order to cover their loans. Almost 13 million shares changed hands. Several banks and insurance companies bought stocks in order to stabilize prices.

Then, on October 29—**Black Tuesday**—the bottom fell out. People and corporations alike frantically tried to sell their stocks before prices went lower still. The number of shares dumped that day was a record sixteen million. Additional millions of shares could not even find buyers. The panic continued for two more weeks. By mid-November, as one historian described it, "$30 billion had blown away—the same amount of money America had spent on World War I."

A depression had begun, but no one realized it until the stock market crashed. Economist John Kenneth Galbraith summed up conditions that led to the crash in a single sentence. "The end had arrived," he wrote, "but it was not yet in sight."

SECTION 5 REVIEW

Key Terms and People

Explain the significance of: Herbert Hoover, Alfred E. Smith, Solid South, Good Neighbor Policy, stocks, Black Tuesday

Main Ideas

1. What disadvantages did Albert E. Smith have in the 1928 Presidential race?
2. What actions did Hoover take to show he was a "good neighbor" to Latin America?
3. What signs indicated that the economy was on a downward turn toward the end of the 1920's?

Critical Thinking

4. John Kenneth Galbraith wrote of the predepression period: "The end had arrived, but it was not yet in sight." What had ended and why was it invisible?

State the Objective

Use primary sources to understand aspects of daily life in the 1920's.

Present the Lesson

Have students volunteer to list on the board some of the techniques used in ads today. (List might include: testimonies by famous people; claims that the product will change a person's life; appeals to vanity.) Discuss the ad for the Playboy car in light of the ad techniques listed on the board. To stimulate discussion, ask students the following questions: Whom do you think the ad is directed toward? (Possible response: young people who are interested in adventure, power, and fun.) To what is the car compared? (Answer: a horse that is powerful, graceful, and fast.) Do you think most women today would approve of this kind of ad? Why or why not? (Possible responses: yes— because the girl is adventurous and independent. No— because she is pictured as rebellious rather than as serious or hard-working.)

Discuss the Stout Airlines ad's emphasis on pilot performance and airplane maintenance. To stimulate discussion, ask students the following questions: To what degree was ballyhoo used in this ad? (Possible responses: ballyhoo was used to create the illusion that flying was perfectly safe and comfortable when it was not; however, claims were tempered by the disclaimer.) What kinds of information do you see in airline ads today? (Possible responses: infor-

Focus on Primary Sources

Life in the Roaring Twenties

The nineteen twenties have been called everything from the Jazz Age to the Era of Wonderful Nonsense and the Ballyhoo Years. *Ballyhoo* is an obscure word associated with sideshow promoters and others skilled at creating artificial enthusiasm for worthless products and spectacles. Nowhere was the art of ballyhoo practiced to better effect than in advertising.

In the twenties, advertising took on methods it continues to use over half a century later. According to the editors of *Life* magazine, ''The decade's dominant . . . trend was the increasing use of psychology, the deepening appeal to the secret emotions that motivated people to buy. If any single ad epitomized the trend . . . it was Ned Jordan's 173-word classic, 'Somewhere West of Laramie' ''

> Somewhere west of Laramie there's a broncho-busting, steer-roping girl who knows what I'm talking about.
>
> She can tell what a sassy pony, that's a cross between greased lightning and the place where it hits, can do with eleven hundred pounds of steel and action when he's going high, wide and handsome.
>
> The truth is—the Playboy was built for her.
>
> Built for the lass whose face is brown with the sun when the day is done of revel and romp and race.
>
> She loves the cross of the wild and the tame.
>
> There's a savor of links about the car—of laughter and lilt and light—a hint of old loves—and saddle and quirt. It's a brawny thing—yet a graceful thing for the sweep o' the Avenue.
>
> Step into the Playboy when the hour grows dull with things gone dead and stale.
>
> Then start for the land of real living with the spirit of the lass who rides, lean and rangy, into the red horizon of a Wyoming twilight.

This Fabulous Century, Vol. 3, 1920–1930 (New York: Time-Life Books), 118.

Note that the ad tells readers nothing they should know about a car they might buy—performance, handling, safety features, cost. Have you seen car ads like Ned Jordan's lately?

The art of ballyhoo was also applied to people who had accomplished some unusual feat such as swimming the English Channel, seeing which couple could outdance the others in the dancing marathons, or—believe it or not—flagpole sitting.

Publicity surrounding Lindbergh's Paris flight (see page 624) increased people's interest in flying, but few were able to try it and not all those who might have tried it would. Under the best conditions flying was expensive, uncomfortable, bumpy, and dangerous. However, fledgling airlines hired advertising writers to assure people that flying was smooth, relaxing, and—above all—safe.

Picturing History A copy of the ad for the Jordan motor car.

mation about pilot expertise and experience; information about airplane maintenance; claims of safety and in-flight comfort.) What information is missing from ads today? (Possible response: disclaimers for responsibility for injury or loss of baggage.)

Check for Understanding

Discuss with students the questions at the end of the feature. During the discussion, emphasize how advertising reflects society.

Ask students what historians of the future will learn about our society by looking at ads of today. (Possible response: many ads today emphasize the importance of social standing, of individuality, of sex appeal.)

Stout Airlines' advertising department put out this reassuring information.

> Don't worry. Relax, settle back and enjoy life. If there's any worrying to be done, let the pilot do it; that's what he's hired for. Be patient while the plane taxis to the corner of the field before taking off. The luxury of flying doesn't appear until you begin to use the third dimension.
>
> The pilot always banks the plane when turning in the air. Take the turns naturally with the plane. Don't try to hold the lower wing up with the muscles of the abdomen—it's unfair to yourself and an unjust criticism of your pilot.
>
> The atmosphere supports the plane just as firmly as the ocean supports a ship. At the speed you are traveling, the air has a density practically equivalent to water; to satisfy yourself, put your hand out the window and feel the tremendous pressure—your guarantee of absolute safety. . . .
>
> Our motto is: Safety—First, Last and Always. In addition to employing only the safest plane, we maintain a daily inspection far more rigorous than any ever given to any other form of vehicle. Your pilot is one of the best in the country. An expert motor and plane mechanic flies every trip and is also trained as an alternate pilot. Nothing is omitted that we believe may add to your safety and comfort. Hence we repeat—settle back, or move around as you wish, enjoy the trip, and—Get the Maximum Enjoyment out of your Flight!
>
> The Company is not liable for any damages by reason of damage or injury to any passenger or to his goods or baggage.

This Fabulous Century, Vol. 3, 73.

If airlines had little effect on the everyday lives of most Americans, the same could not be said of the automobile. Nothing so changed the way they lived, worked, shopped, traveled, and socialized as the arrival in the 1920's of affordable automobiles. The Jordan car mentioned in this chapter was not affordable and very few of them were sold, but thousands of others—some costing only a few hundred dollars—filled the landscape. Sociologists Robert S. Lynde and Helen Merrell Lynde measured the effect of autos on family life. What follows was part of the Lyndes' study of a place

they called "Middletown"—actually Muncie, Indiana.

> [The automobile upset such time-honored habits and attitudes as] "Rain or shine, I never miss a Sunday morning at church"; "A high-school boy does not need much spending money"; "I don't need exercise, walking to the office keeps me fit"; "I wouldn't think of moving out of town and being so far from my friends"; "Parents ought always to know where their children are." . . .
>
> "We'd rather do without clothes than give up the car," said one mother of nine children. "We used to go to his sister's to visit, but by the time we'd get the children shoed and dressed there wasn't any money left for carfare. Now no matter how they look, we just poke 'em in the car and take 'em along."
>
> Many families feel that an automobile is justified as an agency holding the family group together. "I never feel as close to my family as when we are all together in the car," said one business class mother.
>
> . . . [Cars could also be a source of trouble in families.] The fact that 348 boys and 382 girls in the three upper years of the high school placed "use of the automobile" fifth and fourth respectively in a list of twelve possible sources of disagreement between them and their parents suggests that this may [become a greater source of conflict].

Lynde, Robert S., and Helen Merrell Lynde, *Middletown: A Study in Contemporary American Culture* (New York: Harcourt, Brace, 1929), 253–258.

Analyzing Primary Sources

1. What impulse of car buyers did the Jordan advertisement appeal to? Explain your answer.
2. Who are some recent media heroes? What did they accomplish? Is their fame justified?
3. As a nervous, first-time flyer, would you have been reassured by the airline statement you read here? What really *does* keep an airplane's tons of weight in the air?

Critical Thinking

4. Do you agree that automobiles help keep families together, or are they more likely to divide them? Explain.

Answers

Analyzing Primary Sources

1. Possible answer: the Jordan ad appealed to car buyers' desire for power, independence, and adventure. There is also an appeal to the romance of the Old West. Jordan knew that people are drawn to experiences outside what they consider to be their mundane lives.

2. Possible answer: Arsenio Hall—he worked on *Saturday Night Live*, starred in movies, and now hosts his own late-night show; his fame is justified because he worked his way up through the ranks of the entertainment business and proved himself at each level.

3. Possible answers: yes; no.
• Airplanes are supported by the difference in air density above and below the wing. The difference is a function of speed and wing configuration.

Critical Thinking

4. Possible answers: keep families together—family outings; family vacations; visits to family who live far away. Divide families—money problems created by car payments; fights between teens and parents over the use of the family car. **(evaluation)**

Key Terms and People

These are highlighted in the text in the order in which they appear in this list.

Main Ideas

1. Thought communism would destroy private property and democracy.

2. The two men were foreign-born anarchists who had evaded the draft; many people believed that labor unrest was a danger to the country and the result of the work of such radicals.

3. Tried to limit the building of warships and the size of war fleets.

4. Scandals involved top officials he had appointed, so he was responsible for their presence in government; Harding was hurt, distracted, and very tired. In 1923 Harding became ill and died while in office.

5. Quantity buying for chain stores, installment plan, planned obsolescence, advertising.

6. Content to let things take their course.

7. Caused a drop in prices of agricultural products; put farmers deeper in debt.

8. He believed supports represented an unconstitutional use of federal power; that farmers had never made money and there was no way they ever could.

9. Al Smith was attacked because he was Catholic and wanted to repeal Prohibition; was suspect because he was from New York City; prosperity was at its peak and there was no way to oust incumbant Republicans.

10. Investors believed trends were a bad sign and began unloading their stocks; this action caused others to sell too.

Critical Thinking Questions

11. In the light of attacks on African Americans by whites. • As victims of racial violence. • African Americans.

➤**12.** Raids aimed at members of socialist and commu-

nist organizations, many of whom were aliens and foreign-born immigrants; raids were not legal because they were conducted without search warrants; people were held in jail without legal representation.

13. Lewis used nonviolent tactics: he seemed to obey court order to return to work while quietly encouraging strike to continue; avoided arousing public anger. Steelworkers

were not well organized; they frightened people with their seeming radicalism.

14. Appointed old cronies and political pals to high office; did not realize they betrayed him by accepting bribes and favors.

➤**15.** The prosperity during Coolidge's term was mostly a result of Mellon's policies. Mellon cut excess profits tax and reduced government war debt

and spending; he cut income taxes on the wealthy and encouraged reduced interest rates to make borrowing easy. Prosperity was also a result of the general optimistic mood of the time.

16. To continue improving relations with Latin America. • Denounced dollar diplomacy; withdrew marines from Nicaragua and Haiti; tried to treat Latin Americans as equals. • Yes—he succeeded in deal-

---

CHAPTER **25** REVIEW

Write your answers on a separate sheet of paper.

Key Terms and People

Explain the significance of: Comintern, Ku Klux Klan (KKK), Charles Evans Hughes, Andrew Mellon, Albert B. Fall, Washington Naval Conference, Fordney–McCumber Tariff Act, Teapot Dome scandal, Solid South, stocks

Main Ideas

1. Why did many Americans in 1919 see communism as a threat to their way of life?
2. In what way did the Sacco-Vanzetti trial and the general labor unrest seem to be examples of foreign interference in American affairs?
3. How did the naval holiday represent an American effort to reduce arms in Europe?
4. How did the bribery, kickback, and fraud scandals in the Harding administration damage President Harding's reputation and his health?
5. What methods did businesses use to increase customer spending in the 1920's?
6. Explain Calvin Coolidge's approach to the Presidency.
7. How did overproduction by farmers present a serious threat to the economy?
8. Why was Coolidge against price supports for farmers?
9. Why did Herbert Hoover win the Presidency in 1928 instead of Al Smith?
10. How did the downward trend in industrial production and wholesale prices lead to Black Tuesday?

Critical Thinking Questions

11. **Evaluating Literature.** How does the selection by Melvin B. Tolson on page 633 portray race relations in the postwar years? How does this poem portray African Americans? With whom does the poet sympathize?
12. **Evaluating Policies.** How did the raids by A. Mitchell Palmer present a threat to civil liberties?
13. **Evaluating Tactics.** Why was John L. Lewis successful in the miners' strike, while the steelworkers' strike failed?

14. **Analyzing Policies.** What errors did President Harding make that led to the Harding scandals?
15. **Analyzing Ideas.** Was the prosperity that followed Coolidge's election a matter of sheer luck or was it due to governmental wisdom and commercial enterprise? Explain.
16. **Evaluating Decisions.** Why did Hoover repudiate the Roosevelt Corollary? In what ways did he try to be a good neighbor to Latin America? Do you think he succeeded?

Critical Thinking Activities

17. **Organizing Events.** Match the events listed below with the letters on the time line.

1919 1920 1921 1923 1927 1928 1929

I II III IV V VI VII VIII IX

a. Sacco and Vanzetti are electrocuted.
b. Harding is elected.
c. Boston police strike occurs.
d. Black Tuesday—stock market collapses.
e. Emergency Quota Act is passed.
f. Hoover is elected.
g. United Mine Workers strike.
h. Steelworkers strike.
i. Coolidge succeeds Harding.

18. **Linking Past to Present.** In 1919 communism was seen as a major threat to American society. Is it still seen that way? Why or why not?
19. **Linking Past to Present.** In the post-World War I era, nations were concerned with the revival of the arms race. In what way have worries of this kind decreased in recent years?
20. **Linking Past to Present.** During the late 1920's, many people worried that the economy was weakening. Is this concern still present today? Research today's economic health and write a brief report for the class on whether you think the future looks bright or dismal.

TELESCOPING THE TIMES: 1920–1929

Politics and a Thin Prosperity

After World War I, the world remained troubled. Americans confronted postwar controversy on the home front. Calvin Coolidge, then governor of Massachusetts, denounced and crushed the Boston police strike. Communism and other forms of radicalism generated fear among Americans who applauded Attorney General A. Mitchell Palmer's anti-Red crusade. A newly awakened Ku Klux Klan achieved political power. Steelworkers struck against long hours, but it would be several years before they won the eight-hour day.

In 1920 President Harding won a landslide Republican victory, and the nation returned to "normalcy" and isolation. Harding's Secretary of State, Charles Evans Hughes, won the international control and reduction of naval warships and also helped to preserve peace in Asia. The United States demanded that France and Britain pay their war debts, but tariffs were set so high that they could not do so. Congress began to close the door to immigrants from southern and eastern Europe and Japan. In contrast to Hughes and other successful cabinet appointments, a group of high officials in Harding's administration engaged in fraud and bribery. Harding felt betrayed by these friends and, while still in office, died.

Vice-President Calvin Coolidge succeeded Harding and brought back confidence in government. He easily won the 1924 election over a Democratic and a Progressive candidate. Under Coolidge business boomed, encouraged by Secretary of the Treasury Andrew Mellon's policies and low interest rates. Among private citizens, many households finally gained access to electricity. Consumers saw the spread of chain stores, which encouraged buying on the installment plan. Manufacturers chose planned obsolescence, and advertisers became skillful at creating widespread consumer demand.

As the twenties advanced, it became increasingly clear that serious problems threatened economic prosperity. Though some Americans were becoming wealthy, many more could not earn a decent living. Important industries were in trouble. For example, railroads were losing in the competition with trucks and automobiles, textile production suffered from foreign competition and changes in dress styles, and coal mining faced a challenge from the petroleum industry. Farmers produced far more food than they could sell at a profit, but Coolidge vetoed price supports. In hopes of finding wealth, Americans turned to the stock market, and many bought stocks on margin.

As the decade drew to a close, the slipping economy signaled the end of an era. The election of 1928 pitted two self-made men against each other. Herbert Hoover, a man from a Protestant and rural background, soundly defeated Al Smith, a Roman Catholic from New York City. Hoover inherited a troubled home economy. As early as 1926, housing starts had begun to decrease. Business inventories were high. In 1929 the stock market began a steady decline and finally crashed. The Great Depression had begun.

Chronology of Main Events

1921 Warren G. Harding inaugurated

1923 Administration scandals break; Harding dies; Calvin Coolidge succeeds to Presidency

1924 Teapot Dome scandal; immigration drastically curtailed

1925 Calvin Coolidge inaugurated President

1929 Herbert Hoover inaugurated President; stock market crash

Telescoping the Times may be used as an alternative to having students read the entire chapter, as a chapter preview, or as a chapter review.

Global Perspectives

1929	First major conflict occurs between Jews and Arabs in Palestine.
1930	Haile Selassie becomes Emperor of Ethiopia.
1931	Spain becomes a republic.
1931	Japan occupies Manchuria.
1932	Iraq becomes independent.
1933	Germany withdraws from League of Nations.

For Discussion

What are some possible reasons for Germany's withdrawal from the League of Nations in 1933? (Possible responses: Germany might have felt it had been unfairly treated after World War I; Germany might have wanted to rebuild its military and regain power; Germany might have felt that the League of Nations was powerless to control world affairs.)

Additional Resources

- Geography Activities
- Skills Activities
- Thematic Activities
- Economic Activities
- Cultural Literacy Activities
- Literary Source Readings
- Primary Source Readings
- Nuclear Peacekeeping
- Transparencies
- Computer Test Generator

Additional Teaching Strategies

SECTION 1

For Basic Students: Ask students to reread "One Family's Story" and briefly summarize the long quote from the Cleveland woman. (Possible response: father loses his job; family moves to a garage; they tolerate poor living conditions.) Discuss with students their impressions of the selection.

For Advanced Students: Have students interview someone who lived through the Great Depression and remembers the experience. Have them report the results of their interviews to the class. (Interviews should include: what life was like; how the individual dealt with problems particular to the depression; living conditions when the depression ended.)

SECTION 2

For Basic Students: Ask each student to design a campaign poster supporting Franklin D. Roosevelt for President in 1932. The poster might incorporate one of the three anti-Hoover images: "Hoovervilles," "Hoover Blankets," or "Hoover Flags." Display the posters in the classroom.

For Advanced Students: Assign each student to one of three groups. Have each group research and prepare an oral presentation on one of the Democratic "hopefuls" at the 1932 Democratic National Convention: Franklin Delano Roosevelt, Alfred E. Smith, and John Nance Garner. After the presentations, ask the other students to vote on their choice for Democratic nominee and to explain the reasons for their choices. (Possible responses: Roosevelt—is confident and experienced, is governor of New York, is well-organized; Smith—is a good campaigner, has an urban background, is supported by the New York City political machine; Garner—is a Texas lawyer and legislator, has thirty years in Congress, was Speaker of the House.)

SECTION 3

For Basic Students: Have students use an encyclopedia or other reference materials to research and write a short report on the life of Franklin D. Roosevelt before 1932. (Reports might include: born in Hyde Park, N.Y.; came from a wealthy background; was assistant secretary of the Navy; ran for Vice-President in 1920; was twice governor of New York.) Have one or two volunteers read their reports to the class.

For Advanced Students: Have students read a copy of President Roosevelt's first inaugural address and imagine that they are hearing the speech for the first time on March 4, 1933. Ask them to write a short essay explaining which of the President's statements impressed them most and why. (Possible response: "the only thing we have to fear is fear itself"; this statement encouraged Americans; it instilled confidence; Roosevelt warned Americans to avoid being paralyzed by fear and not acting.) Ask two or three students to read their essays to the class.

Further Reading for Students

Nonfiction

Hearn, Charles R. *The American Dream in the Great Depression*. Westport, Conn.: Greenwood Press, 1977.

McElvaine, Robert S., ed. *Down and Out in the Great Depression: Letters from the Forgotten Man*. Chapel Hill: University of North Carolina Press, 1983.

Olsen, Violet. *The Growing Season*. New York: Macmillan, 1982. (Easy)

Terkel, Studs. *Hard Times: An Oral History of the Great Depression in America*. New York: Partheon Books, 1986.

Bibliography for Teachers

Books

Burner, David. *Herbert Hoover: The Public Life*. New York: Alfred A. Knopf, 1978.

Kennedy, David. *The American People in the Depression*. West Haven, Conn.: Pendulum Press, 1973.

Olson, James S. *Herbert Hoover and the Reconstruction Finance Corporation, 1931-1933*. Ames: Iowa State University Press, 1977.

Schlesinger, Arthur M., and Fox, Dixon R., eds. *The Age of the Great Depression, 1929-1941*. New York: Macmillan, 1950.

Schlesinger, Arthur M. Jr. *Age of Roosevelt: The Crisis of the Old Order*, Vol. 1. Boston, Mass.: Houghton Mifflin, 1957.

Smith, Gene. *The Shattered Dream: Herbert Hoover and the Great Depression*. New York: McGraw-Hill, 1984.

Stevens, Irving L. *Fishbones: Hoboing in the 1930's*. Corinna, Maine: Moosehead Products, 1982.

Warren, Harris G. *Herbert Hoover and the Great Depression*. Reprint of 1970 ed. Westport, Conn.: Greenwood Press, 1980.

Winslow, Susan. *Brother, Can You Spare a Dime?* New York: Paddington Press, 1976.

Audio-Visuals

The Depression: 1929-1932. Prentice-Hall Media. Filmstrip.

The Election of 1932 (The Roosevelt Years). American Broadcasting Company. Movie.

The Great Depression. Social Studies School Service. Filmstrip.

Herbert Hoover: Portrait of Power. Social Studies School Service. Filmstrip.

The Okies—Uprooted Farmers (The American Challenge). Twentieth Century-Fox. Movie.

The United States in the Twentieth Century, 1920-1932. Simon and Shuster Communications. Movie.

The United States in the Twentieth Century, 1932-1940. Simon and Shuster Communications. Movie.

Computer Resource

American History III. (Apple/IBM) Sliwa Enterprises, Inc.

Teacher's Notes:

Lesson Plan

Teaching Resources, Unit 6 Booklet

Chapter Objectives

Students will learn:
- the causes of the Great Depression
- why Americans rejected the policies of the Hoover administration in the election of 1932
- what tone was established during the early days of the Roosevelt administration

Picturing History *Migrant Mother,* 1936. The years of the Great Depression produced some of the most poignant pictures of the twentieth century. This photo, by world-famous photographer Dorothea Lange, shows the gaunt, haunting face of an exhausted California mother.

Using the Chapter Time Line

How many years passed between the depression in 1873 and the beginning of the Great Depression? (Answer: 56) Who came to power in Germany (see Unit 6 Time Line) in the same year that Franklin Roosevelt was being inaugurated in the U.S.? (Answer: Adolph Hitler)

1929	1930	1931	1932	1933
1929 • Herbert Hoover inaugurated President • Stock market crash • Great Depression begins	1930 Hawley-Smoot Tariff Act		1932 • Bonus Army marches to Washington, D.C. • Reconstruction Finance Corporation set up	1933 • Franklin D. Roosevelt inaugurated President • Emergency Banking Relief Act

656

CHAPTER **26** 1929–1933

The Great Depression Begins

Links to American Literature

Carloads of oranges dumped on the ground. The people came for miles to take the fruit, but this could not be. How would they buy oranges at twenty cents a dozen if they could drive out and pick them up? And men with hoses squirt kerosene on the oranges, and they are angry at the crime, angry at the people who have come to take the fruit. A million people hungry, needing the fruit—and kerosene sprayed over the golden mountains.

And the smell of rot fills the country.

Burn coffee for fuel in the ships. Burn corn to keep warm, it makes a hot fire. Dump potatoes in the rivers and place guards along the banks to keep the hungry people from fishing them out. Slaughter the pigs and bury them, and let the putrescence drip down into the earth.

There is a crime here that goes beyond denunciation. There is a sorrow here that weeping cannot symbolize. There is a failure here that topples all our success. The fertile earth, straight tree rows, the sturdy trunks, and the ripe fruit. And children dying of pellagra must die because a profit cannot be taken from an orange.

— JOHN STEINBECK, *The Grapes of Wrath*

As the boom of the 1920's collapsed, the aftermath of World War I entered its second phase: the Great Depression. It was a time of harsh contrasts. As drought and dust storms consumed countless acres of farmland, farmers migrated to their promised land, California. There, in a land of abundance, thousands starved. Everywhere, food was destroyed because it did not bring a good price. Families could not earn enough to feed themselves. There appeared to be no end to the deprivation. As Steinbeck wrote, "In the souls of the people the grapes of wrath are filling and growing heavy."

Chapter Overview

In this chapter you will learn about the causes of the Great Depression, why Americans rejected Hoover's policies, and how Franklin Roosevelt inspired confidence during the early days of his administration. This chapter is important because it points out the dramatically different effects of differing political philosophies. The depression produced some of the greatest problems this nation ever faced. It challenged our whole system of democracy and greatly increased the role of the federal government in American society. To tell this dramatic story Chapter 26 is divided into three sections.

Chapter Outline

1. **The Nation's Economy Crashes**
2. **Hoover's Policies Have Little Effect**
3. **Roosevelt Faces a Difficult Challenge**

657

Anticipating the Lesson

Review with students the events that led to the crash (Chapter 25).

State the Objective

Understand the causes of the Great Depression.

SECTION 1

The Nation's Economy Crashes

GLOSSARY TERMS: **national income, direct relief, Bonus Army**

At first people found it hard to believe that economic disaster had struck the country. On October 25, 1929, for example, President Hoover told Americans that "business is on a sound and prosperous basis." Several days later Henry Ford declared that "things are better today than they were yesterday." The following month Hoover again reassured the people: "Any lack of confidence in the economic future . . . is foolish."

Yet despite the comforting words, the most severe depression in American history was well on its way. What had brought it about?

Several Factors Caused the Depression

Historians and economists believe the Great Depression was the result of several factors rather than one. Although there is considerable disagreement, the factors usually cited are the uneven distribution of income, the availability of easy credit, the imbalance in foreign trade, and the mechanization of American industry.

Uneven Distribution of Income. As discussed in Chapter 25, about half the nation's families lived at or below a minimum level of income. They could not afford to buy most goods. Profits from production generally went to stockholders and business owners or were put back into the business in order to increase production. If, instead, businesses had paid workers higher wages, they would

have been able to sell more goods. Similarly, if farmers could have received higher prices for their crops, they too would have been able to buy what factories were turning out.

Another way to explain the matter is that there was a lack of balance between production and consumption. American industry was extremely productive, as were American farms. Many American consumers, however, lacked purchasing power, and little was done during the twenties to increase it.

Easy Credit. Individuals had piled up huge debts during the twenties. People had bought goods on the installment plan and then were unable to buy more goods or even to keep up payments on those they had already purchased. Others had borrowed money to speculate on the stock market.

Federal banks were forbidden to lend money for stock-market speculation. Private banks, however, could—and did. Then, when the stock market turned down and people could not repay their loans, many banks were forced to close their doors. Sometimes there was a chain reaction of bank failures. One bank would call in its loans from other banks, which in turn would press a third set of banks. People had their lifetime savings swept away in a single day.

Unbalanced Foreign Trade. All through the twenties, the United States had followed a high-tariff policy designed to keep out foreign products so that Americans would buy American-made goods. In 1930 Congress passed the **Hawley-Smoot Tariff Act**, creating the highest protective tariff in United States history. This was, one can see now, a mistake. Nations unable to sell their

---

People in the Chapter

Franklin Delano Roosevelt claimed to have ancestors who came to Massachusetts on the *Mayflower*. Genealogists believe Roosevelt was also related by blood or by marriage to eleven different previous Presidents of the United States.

Harry Hopkins was known as "the world's greatest spender" because he distributed over $10 billion in both monetary relief and work relief during the depression.

Harold Ickes was known for his verbal attacks that enlivened the newspapers of the day. He once described Huey Long as having "halitosis of the intellect."

Frances Perkins worked briefly with Jane Addams at Hull House and later for New York politician Al Smith before becoming the first woman to serve on a President's cabinet.

goods in the American market were also unable to buy American products. In addition, some nations took the high-tariff policy as a declaration of economic warfare and retaliated by cutting back their purchases of American goods. United States exports kept dropping.

The problem was complicated by the aftereffects of World War I. Not only had vast amounts of property in Europe been destroyed, but European nations were faced with heavy debts. This made them reduce their purchases of American goods even more.

Mechanization. During the postwar boom, new plants had been built, many with the latest technological improvements. Yet, while the plants turned out increasing quantities of goods, they employed fewer workers because the new machines required fewer people to operate them. Machines, however, do not buy goods. Fewer workers meant less money paid out in wages, which in turn meant less money to buy the goods rolling off the assembly lines.

Human Suffering Multiplies

Between 1929 and 1932, economic conditions grew steadily worse. The **national income**, or total payments to producers of the nation's goods and services, fell almost in half, from $81 billion to $41 billion. During the same three-year span, 85,000 businesses shut their doors; about 400,000 farms were lost through foreclosure (whereby the mortgage holder takes over mortgaged property because payments have not been made) and bankruptcy sales; and 6,000 banks, one-fourth of the country's total number, failed, wiping out 9 million savings accounts. Each week, 100,000 more workers lost their jobs, until 12 million persons, about one-fourth of the labor force, found themselves unemployed.

Hunger and Suffering. In human terms, all this spelled hunger and suffering. There was no federal system of **direct relief** by which foods, money, or jobs could be given by the government to those in need. There was no public welfare, and there were no social security benefits for older or disabled Americans. In most states and cities, facilities for the poor were swamped within a few months. Although every other industrialized country in the world had some form of unemployment insurance, the United States, except for the state of Wisconsin, did not.

Desperate poverty led to scenes never witnessed in this nation before. It became common to see men, women, and children digging through piles of rotting garbage for food. More than a million men, and some women, became hobos. They stole rides on freight trains and rode back and forth across the country looking for work, any kind of work. Thousands were reduced to panhandling, or begging.

Picturing History As the depression grew worse, some private groups distributed free food to the needy. So-called bread lines and unemployment lines were seen across the country as more and more people lost their jobs.

Check for Understanding

Have students write the answers to Section 1
Review questions on paper.

For people who had believed in the American dream, sure that hard work would bring rewards, the mental suffering caused by the depression was as bad as the physical. As one social commentator observed:

> Men who have been sturdy and self-respecting workers can take unemployment without flinching for a few weeks, a few months, even if they have to see their families suffer: but it is different after a year . . . two years . . . three years.

It is hardly surprising that admissions to state hospitals for the insane tripled. The suicide rate also climbed as the depression worsened.

The Position of Women. During the first months of the depression, female workers generally did better than males, possibly because they worked for less. As the depression wore on, however, unemployed women often had a harder time finding jobs than men, particularly if they were no longer young. Although government surveys showed that 13 percent of all working women were the sole supporters of two or more persons, it was assumed that men needed work more than women did.

Some people even believed that the depression would end as soon as all married women left the job market and were replaced by men. In 1931 this belief led three-fourths of the nation's cities to bar married women from teaching jobs. If single female teachers got married, they were fired. The practice continued into the 1940's.

One reason it was assumed that women had it easier than men was that few women were seen begging or standing in bread lines. As one social worker pointed out, however, women were reluctant to do so because their shame was too great. As a matter of fact, many were starving to death in cold garrets and rooming houses.

The Position of Children. The weight of the depression fell on children as well as adults. At one New York City health center, for example, cases of malnutrition rose from 18 percent in 1928 to 60 percent in 1931. State after state reported big drops in milk consumption. Child welfare was one of the first services to go when cities and states cut budgets.

Many children were not in school. Instead, they were forced to look for work, and many found it in sweatshops. By 1933 some twenty-six hundred schools across the nation had shut their doors for

lack of funds. Other schools were open perhaps sixty days during the year.

The Plight of Farmers. Farmers had been in trouble all during the twenties as the demand for staple crops declined. Then in 1930 they were struck by a terrible drought. From Virginia westward to Arkansas, ponds, streams, and wells dried up. Even the mighty Mississippi River sank to the lowest level ever recorded until 1988.

Foreclosures and bankruptcy sales increased, and many farm owners were forced to become tenants. Landowners were often in almost as bad a shape as their tenants. They owed money for supplies, they owed the mortgage company, and they owed the tax collector.

By 1932 the situation in farm states had grown so desperate that farmers began destroying their crops. What was the point in spending thirty dollars to fatten a hog for market when the selling price was only twenty-one dollars? Much better to slit its throat. Apples spoiled in the orchards and cotton rotted in the fields because low prices did not cover the cost of harvesting them.

Some farmers tried to solve their problems by force. When a farm was put on the auction block, neighbors of the farmer whose land was up for sale would keep potential buyers away. They would

Picturing History
Hoping to boost prices by lowering the supply, some Illinois farmers milked their cows and then poured the milk on the ground. These farmers also hoped to heighten national awareness of their desperate economic plight.

Point out to students that there is a current trend favoring the restriction of importation of foreign goods and encouraging consumers to "buy American." Ask students to evaluate this policy in light of the Great Depression. (Possible response: restriction of foreign imports may reduce the capital those countries can use to purchase American goods; if American goods are not sold to foreign markets, the U.S. economy suffers.) Ask students whether import restrictions can be justified under a free enterprise system. (Possible response: import restrictions might be justified in order to save the jobs of American workers.)

Picturing History
Anacostia Flats was the main camp of the Bonus Army, the place where the World War I veterans and their families assembled to lobby Congress.

puncture the tires of the buyers' automobiles and cut telephone lines to prevent anyone from calling the sheriff. Then they would stand quietly but grimly around the auctioneer until he sold the land back to its original owner for next to nothing.

One Family's Story. Some families managed to keep fairly cheerful despite the hard times. One woman remembers how the depression affected her family in Cleveland.

> I remember all of a sudden we had to move. My father lost his job and we moved into a double garage. The landlord didn't charge us rent for seven years. It was awfully cold when you opened those garage doors. We would sleep with rugs and blankets over the top of us and we would dress under the sheets.
>
> In the morning we'd get out and get some snow and put it on the stove and melt it and wash around our faces. Never the neck or anything. Put on our two pairs of socks on each hand and two pairs of socks on our feet, and long underwear and lace it up with Goodwill shoes. Off we'd walk, three, four miles to school.
>
> My father owned three or four houses. His father left them to him. But he lost these one by one. One family couldn't pay the rent. But they owned a bakery and for a while they paid

him half in money, half in cookies. We lived on crumbled cookies and those little bread things. So my father was pretty sharp in a way. He always had something for us to eat. We lived about three months on candy cods, they're little chocolate squares. We had these melted in milk. And he had a part-time job in a Chinese restaurant. We lived on those fried noodles for weeks. I can't stand them today.

> My mother used to bake bread, put it under a blanket to raise. Oh, that was tasty. I have never tasted such good bread since.

The Bonus Army. On July 28, 1932, American soldiers wearing gas masks, holding fixed bayonets, and backed by cavalry and tanks marched from Washington, D.C., to Anacostia Flats, an open field at the outskirts of the capital. The troops were led by Army Chief of Staff Douglas MacArthur and his aide, Major Dwight D. Eisenhower. Firing tear gas canisters and wielding their bayonets and cavalry sabers, the soldiers soon cleared out those camping on the flats and set fire to their shacks. In the course of the operation, more than one thousand persons were gassed, including an eleven-month-old baby who died and an eight-year-old boy who was partially blinded.

It was a sad end for a group of World War I veterans who called themselves the Bonus Expedi-

Have students read Section 2, "Hoover's Policies Have Little Effect," and complete Chapter 26, Section 2 Enrichment Activity.

Anticipate the Lesson

Discuss Chapter 26, Section 2 Enrichment Activity with students. Ask students what Hoover revealed about his philosophy in this speech. (Possible responses: Hoover believed in decentralized government, ordered liberty, equal opportunity, and freedom of individuals; Hoover did not believe in handouts; Hoover felt that businesses and state governments could administer programs with federal guidance.)

SECTION 1 REVIEW

Answers

Main Ideas

1. Uneven distribution of income, overextended personal debts, unbalanced foreign trade, and industrial mechanization.

2. Large numbers of businesses and banks failed; farms were lost through foreclosure; unemployment rose to record numbers.

3. Many suffered from malnutrition, were forced to get jobs, and were unable to go to school.

4. They did not have enough money to pay for mortgages, taxes, and supplies.

Critical Thinking

5. Answers should note that the United States was the only industrialized nation without some form of government protection for the unemployed, elderly, or handicapped. Wisconsin was the only state with unemployment insurance. On the other hand, many believed in a hands-off policy for government. **(evaluation)**

tionary Force. The name was a reminder that fifteen years earlier they had served in the American Expeditionary Force that had sailed to France. In 1924 Congress had voted veterans a cash bonus to be paid in 1945. The bonus was to make up for the wages the men had missed by serving in the army at only $30 a month while others back home had worked at higher-paying wartime jobs. In 1931 veterans were allowed to borrow money against the bonus. The next year, in desperate financial straits, the veterans asked for full payment of what was due, an average of $500 to each man. Representative Wright Patman introduced a bill to this effect.

Led by William Waters, an unemployed cannery worker, the first marchers of the **Bonus Army** left Oregon and started across the country to lobby for passage of the Patman Bill. Others joined along the way. By June about seventeen thousand veterans, some with wives and children, had arrived in the nation's capital and were camped on Anacostia Flats. On June 17 the Senate voted down the Patman Bill. The government then offered the veterans money for transportation home. The money was to be deducted from their bonuses when paid. Although most of the veterans agreed to leave, about two thousand without jobs or homes refused to go. They were driven away on July 28.

SECTION 1 REVIEW

Key Terms and People

Explain the significance of: Hawley-Smoot Tariff Act, national income, direct relief, Bonus Army

Main Ideas

1. What four factors are generally considered in part responsible for the Great Depression?
2. What were the main results of the worsening economic conditions between 1929 and 1932?
3. In general, how did the depression affect children?
4. What problems did farmers face because of the reduced demand for crops and the drought of the early 1930's?

Critical Thinking

5. Were the state and federal governments at fault for not being prepared for the Great Depression? Explain.

SECTION 2

Hoover's Policies Have Little Effect

GLOSSARY TERMS: **humanitarian, rugged individualism, Hoovervilles, moratorium, New Deal, brain trust**

Treasury Secretary Andrew Mellon favored a hands-off policy on the part of the federal government in dealing with the depression. He believed that depressions were a normal part of the business cycle. (See pages 400-401.) Business bankruptcies and human suffering were a way for the economy to correct the lack of balance between production and consumption. In his opinion, the federal government should stand back and let the capitalist system recover on its own.

President Hoover believed that the twentieth-century industrial economy was too complicated for Mellon's do-nothing policies. By taking an active role in bolstering business, Hoover went far beyond what any previous President had done during a depression.

Solutions Come Too Late

First, Hoover set about trying to restore confidence. He convinced business leaders not to cut payrolls and labor leaders not to ask for higher wages or shorter hours. Then he put through a tax cut and had the Federal Reserve Board make it easier to borrow money. He set aside almost $800 million for public works so that people would have jobs; among the projects begun under this program was **Boulder Dam** (now known as Hoover Dam) on the Colorado River. Hoover asked farmers to limit their production voluntarily so that prices would not fall further. Finally, he persuaded Congress to set up the Federal Farm Marketing Board to help farmers market their crops.

Conditions, however, failed to improve, so Hoover recommended some additional measures. Most important, he established the **Reconstruction Finance Corporation** (RFC) to make loans to banks, railroads, and other industries so that they could get back on their feet. An agency designed to prevent foreclosures on homes and farms was created under the **Home Loan Bank Act**.

In the meantime, other things in the President's program got bogged down in politics. As a result of

State the Objective

Understand why Americans rejected the policies of the Hoover administration in the election of 1932.

Present the Lesson

Have students list on the board President Hoover's attempts to solve the economic crisis in the U.S. List might include:

Hoover's solutions
- Convinced business leaders not to cut payrolls.
- Convinced labor leaders not to ask for higher wages or shorter hours.
- Pushed through tax cuts.
- Ordered Federal Reserve Board to make borrowing money easier.
- Set aside $800 million for public works.
- Persuaded Congress to set up Federal Farm Marketing Board.
- Established Reconstruction Finance Corporation.
- Passed Home Loan Bank Act.

Ask students why Hoover's policies did not end the depression. (Possible responses: policies were too little too late; Democratic Congress opposed Hoover; Hoover feared direct federal handouts; he was not flexible.)

the 1930 election, the Republicans had lost control of the House, while their majority in the Senate had been reduced to one vote. By 1932 relations between the President and Congress were cool. Congressmen believed that Hoover's programs were too little and too late. For instance, the RFC had made loans of about $2 billion, whereas Congress wished to spend $40 billion over the next five years.

Hoover dismissed Congress's spending plans as an attempt to "squander our way to prosperity." He also accused the legislators of dragging their feet on his program. He said, probably correctly, that Democrats hoped the depression would continue until the Presidential election. People would then blame Hoover and vote Democratic.

Hoover Believes in Rugged Individualism

Of course Hoover was not responsible for the depression. At the same time, his actions puzzled and angered many people. Hoover was a great **humanitarian**, one who wanted to help others. In one of his first speeches after becoming President, he said:

> Our first objective must be to provide security from poverty and want. We want security in living for every home. We want to see a nation built of home owners and farm owners. We want to see their savings protected. We want to see them in steady jobs. We want to see more and more of them insured against death and accident, unemployment and old age. We want them all secure.

Hoover, however, believed in **rugged individualism**. This meant that individuals and local government agencies were the ones to care for children and the sick, old, and disabled. The federal government should direct and guide relief measures, Hoover believed, but not through a vast federal bureaucracy. His reasons were philosophical.

> You cannot extend the mastery of government over the daily working life of the people without, at the same time, making it the master of the people's souls and thought.

Hoover also feared that direct federal handouts would weaken people's self-respect. In short, he thought the depression could best be cured by individual initiative and private charity. Hoover lent money to the states for relief. He also lent millions to corporations to help them resume production and employ workers. He refused, however, to permit federal payments to the poor and hungry.

The unemployed and homeless were not comforted by Hoover's philosophy. Nor did they understand why money was going to support failing corporations while people starved. The Democratic National Committee hired a public relations expert to further damage the President's image. Hoover's name was linked to the depression's worst features. The groups of shacks filled with homeless men and women that grew up outside many cities were called **Hoovervilles**. Old newspapers worn under clothing for greater warmth were called Hoover blankets. Empty pockets turned inside out were Hoover flags. These were cruel comments on a great humanitarian.

The Great Engineer Cannot Adapt

President Hoover was often called the Great Engineer because he had indeed been a very good one before entering government. Engineers are known for the efficient and precise way they deal with blueprints and figures. Politicians, however, deal with people. They should be flexible and adaptable. Hoover lacked those political qualities. For example, instead of simply denouncing Congress's $40 billion spending plans, he might have said what was good about the program and then challenged Congress to act.

Another example of Hoover's rigidity occurred in the summer of 1932 during the Bonus Army march. The veterans had repeatedly invited the President to address them. A number of people urged Hoover to do it: "Explain why the country

Picturing History Hooverville, Central Park, New York City, 1932. Homeless and unemployed men and women built shacks such as these in city parks throughout the U.S.

Check for Understanding

Call on individual students to answer Section 2 Review questions orally.

Guided Practice

To stimulate discussion, ask students the following questions. What aspects of economic depression cause the spiral to continue downward? What events seem to have negative effects on the business world? Which have positive results? (Possible responses: a "run" on banks can produce a downward spiral resulting in additional panic-triggered activities; a "sell" psychology can take over the stock market and cause people to sell out of fear. Events that negatively affect business might be: government legislation; cheap foreign imports; droughts; floods; civil unrest. Events that positively affect the business world might be: favorable tax laws; peace treaties; few labor problems; high crop production.)

can't meet their demands, but give them something to hope for. Remind them that you're their commander in chief, speak to them from the heart.'' Hoover refused. James Watson of Indiana, Republican leader of the Senate, advised the President to invite Bonus Army leader Waters and a few others to the White House for dinner, talk to them frankly, and ask them to leave the city peacefully. There would be no need to use troops. Instead, Hoover wanted the marchers rounded up and fingerprinted.

Hoover also showed his unbending quality in certain of his dealings with other countries. By 1931 Europe was feeling the effects of the depression. American investors withdrew their money, and the United States government stopped all loans. In May, Austria's largest bank collapsed, and financial panic swept central Europe. A month later Hoover proposed a **moratorium**, or postponement of payments, on Allied war debts and German reparations. Before anyone could agree to this plan, however, Britain and other European countries went off the gold standard. That is, their paper money could no longer be exchanged for gold. This made gold drop in value, which meant that Europeans would be buying American goods and repaying American loans in cheap currency.

Hoover was furious over the abandonment of the gold standard. His administration was committed to paper money backed by gold. The President became more upset when the former Allies agreed to reduce Germany's war reparations by 90 percent. All Hoover wanted was a postponement. Although his own Secretary of State, Henry L. Stimson, had been trying for over a year to persuade him that canceling war debts would aid world recovery, Hoover insisted the obligations be paid.

Linking Past to Present

The repayment of debt remains a major issue in world relations today. In the 1970's many American banks loaned large sums of money to developing nations worldwide. In the 1980's, however, many of these nations found themselves unable to meet the loan repayment plans. In 1989–1990, debt restructuring plans were adopted. However, none of these plans has been entirely successful and the problem continues.

Roosevelt Pledges a New Deal

By mid-1932 the situation was grim indeed. One historian described it this way:

> Travelers crossing America that summer saw a land of harsh contrasts. Surplus food was being spilled into the ocean or piled high in grain elevators while men were breaking store windows to steal a loaf of bread. Shoe factories were shut down in New England while children stayed home from school because they had nothing to put on their feet. . . . Families went in ragged clothing while farmers could not market millions of bales of cotton. All this in the richest country on earth, with the fattest acres, the tallest buildings, the mightiest machinery, the biggest factories.

Something had to be done.

With the election of 1932 approaching, it was clear that the American people were unhappy with Hoover. However, he had tried to deal with the depression. The Republicans knew that if they did not nominate him, they would be blaming him publicly for the nation's economic woes. So Hoover again became the Republican standard-bearer, although many observers thought the party's convention in Chicago was about as joyful as a funeral.

A Dramatic Entrance. By contrast, Democrats came to Chicago a few weeks later certain of victory in November. A majority of delegates were

Presidential Election, 1932

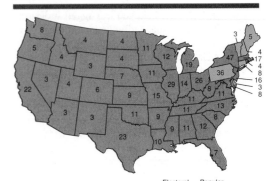

Party	Candidate	Electoral Vote	Popular Vote	%
Democratic	Roosevelt	472	22,810,000	57.4
Republican	Hoover	59	15,759,000	39.7
Minor parties			1,153,000	2.9

531 Total Electoral Vote

Picturing History Raymond Moley and Rexford Tugwell (third and fourth from left), members of the brain trust, helped Roosevelt develop the economic and social programs of the New Deal.

pledged to Governor **Franklin Delano Roosevelt** of New York. At that time, however, the nomination required a two-thirds majority. Roosevelt's main opponents, former candidate Alfred E. Smith of New York and Speaker of the House John Nance Garner of Texas, hoped for a deadlock and a compromise candidate. After three ballots, however, Garner, the favorite of Southern and Western delegates, threw his votes to Roosevelt and accepted the Vice-Presidential slot.

Roosevelt flew to Chicago to give his acceptance speech. This tradition-breaking move added a touch of urgency and drama to the convention. Then, in a rousing speech, the candidate pledged "a new deal" for the American people. No one knew exactly what the **New Deal** program was, but it brought to mind the successful square deal of the candidate's favorite cousin, former President Theodore Roosevelt.

The Brain Trust. It is possible that Roosevelt himself was not sure at the time about the details of the New Deal. Meanwhile, a group of his close advisors labored in Albany, New York, outlining various economic and social programs. At the center of the group were three Columbia University professors: Adolf A. Berle, Jr., Raymond Moley, and Rexford Guy Tugwell. Newspapers were soon referring to them as the **brain trust**. Their ideas formed a background for Roosevelt's campaign speeches. The candidate, however, was careful to avoid making definite promises. He did not want to say anything that might anger large groups of voters.

A Democratic Landslide. Actually, neither party platform gave voters much guidance. The most visible difference was over Prohibition. Democrats called for outright repeal, while Republicans favored revision.

If the campaign lacked a focus on issues, however, it clearly showed the deep contrast between the candidates. The tired, gloomy, worn-out President was no match for his handsome, optimistic challenger. Even the upward tilt of Roosevelt's head bespoke confidence, a quality the nation sorely needed in 1932.

In the November election, the popular vote for Roosevelt was 23 million and for Hoover 16 million. Democrats carried the South, the West, and all but six states in the Northeast. In the Senate they claimed nearly a two-thirds majority. In the

Student Assignment/Homework

Have students read Section 3, "Roosevelt Faces a Difficult Challenge," and answer Section 3 Review questions on paper.

SECTION 3

Core Lesson

Anticipate the Lesson

Review with students the reasons for Roosevelt's victory in the 1932 Presidential election. (Possible responses: Hoover's policies did not end the depression; Hoover refused federal payments to the poor and hungry; people did not understand why government funds supported failing corporations while people starved; Franklin Roosevelt offered a fresh, confident outlook.)

SECTION 2 REVIEW

Answers

Main Ideas

1. Persuaded business leaders not to cut payrolls, labor leaders not to make demands, and farmers to limit production; cut taxes; made borrowing money easier; earmarked money for public works; set up a board to help farmers market their crops; and established the RFC.

2. He talked about protecting people from poverty, yet he refused to give federal aid to the needy.

3. Local government agencies and individuals.

4. He was neither adaptable nor flexible.

5. Roosevelt was handsome, energetic, and optimistic, while Hoover was tired, gloomy, and worn out.

Critical Thinking

6. Possible answer: it was extremely unlikely that anyone, except perhaps Washington or Lincoln, could have been reelected in 1932. Hoover was blamed by many for the depression, and people wanted a change. **(evaluation)**

House they won almost three-fourths of the seats, their greatest victory since before the Civil War.

Americans Endure a Period of Waiting

Although Americans were anxious to know what sort of President they had elected and what he planned to do about the depression, they had a long wait. Still in effect was a four-month period between the November election and the March inauguration. (The **Twentieth Amendment**, which moved Presidential inaugurations back to January, was not ratified until February 1933.)

The economy, however, did not wait. It steadily declined. More businesses went bankrupt, more people lost their jobs, more homes and farms were foreclosed, and the production of goods and services dropped further than ever.

The banking situation was even worse. People panicked and withdrew their money. When the banks ran out of money, they were forced to close. By Inauguration Day, scarcely a bank was open.

SECTION 2 REVIEW

Key Terms and People

Explain the significance of: Boulder Dam, Reconstruction Finance Corporation (RFC), Home Loan Bank Act, humanitarian, rugged individualism, Hoovervilles, moratorium, Franklin Delano Roosevelt, New Deal, brain trust, Twentieth Amendment

Main Ideas

1. How did Hoover attempt to restore confidence and end the country's depression?
2. Why were many people confused and angered by Hoover's approach to ending the depression?
3. Whom did Hoover believe was responsible for caring for needy children and the sick, old, and disabled?
4. How was Hoover's personality ill-suited for dealing with the complex political and economic problems posed by the depression?
5. What physical traits and personality characteristics gave Roosevelt an advantage over Hoover in the 1931 Presidential campaign?

Critical Thinking

6. Given the state of the economy in 1932, could anyone have been reelected President at that time? Explain.

SECTION 3

Roosevelt Faces a Difficult Challenge

GLOSSARY TERMS: pragmatist, bank holiday, nationalize, fireside chats

Outgoing President Hoover blamed worsening conditions on people's fear of Roosevelt and what his administration might do. Hoover called on the President-elect to continue the policies of the past four years. However, FDR, as the headline writers were beginning to call him, rejected Hoover's suggestions. He also refused, until he was President in his own right, to take part in international talks to stabilize the world's money supply.

FDR Instills Confidence

Saturday, March 4, 1933, dawned cold and raw across much of the nation. At noon millions of

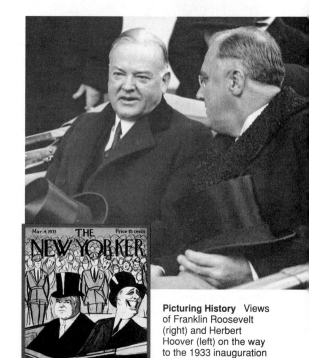

Picturing History Views of Franklin Roosevelt (right) and Herbert Hoover (left) on the way to the 1933 inauguration of FDR.

State the Objective

Understand what tone was established during the early days of the Roosevelt administration.

Americans gathered by their radios as Franklin Delano Roosevelt swore to uphold and defend the Constitution. Then the thirty-second President turned to the microphones and to the 100,000 persons gathered before the east front of the Capitol. His firm, clear voice rang out,

> This great nation will endure as it has endured, will revive and will prosper. . . . Let me assert my firm belief that the only thing we have to fear is fear itself—unreasoning, unjustified terror, which paralyzes needed efforts to convert retreat into advance.

Roosevelt continued with reassurances. He would provide the action that the people wanted. He would call Congress into session and ask for executive power to wage war against poverty and pessimism. He wanted, he said, a power "as great as the power that would be given me if we were in fact invaded by a foreign foe."

Outgoing Secretary of State Stimson was frightened by the President's words. One writer saw them as "grim," and others saw in them the threat of dictatorship. It is probable, however, that comedian Will Rogers spoke for most frustrated Americans when he said, "If he burned down the Capitol, we would cheer and say, 'Well, we at least got a fire started somehow.' "

A Determined President Takes Charge

Who was this man to whom Americans were entrusting their future? What did he stand for?

Franklin Roosevelt was born into a branch of the same well-to-do old New York family that had produced President Theodore Roosevelt. Though a loyal Democrat, young Franklin admired his famous cousin and followed in his footsteps by winning election to the New York Senate, becoming assistant secretary of the navy (in the Wilson administration), and running for Vice-President (with James M. Cox in 1920).

Overcoming a Physical Handicap. In 1921 Roosevelt was severely stricken with polio, which left his legs almost totally paralyzed. Everyone thought his political career was finished. Yet, calling on inner resources no one dreamed he had, he fought and worked to walk again. Month after month, he clamped heavy iron braces on his legs, pulled himself upright, more often than not crashed painfully to the floor, and began the entire process again. Through it all he was supported, literally and psychologically, by his wife, Eleanor, and his aide Louis M. Howe.

By the time of the 1924 Democratic convention, Roosevelt was ready to appear in public without crutches. Wearing fifty-pound braces and supporting himself by holding the speaker's stand, he nominated Al Smith for President and took up public life once more. In 1928 he succeeded Smith as governor of New York. He was reelected in 1930.

Linking Past to Present

Medical science finally won the battle against polio in 1955 as a result of Jonas Salk's research and development of a polio vaccine. However, disabled people did not enjoy the same opportunities for education that others enjoyed until 1975 when Congress passed the Education for All Handicapped Children Act. As a result of this law, disabled children between the ages of three and twenty-one are entitled to "a free and appropriate education in the least restrictive environment." This provision means that disabled children are to be taught in regular classrooms and are to receive special instruction according to their individual abilities.

Political Beliefs. Roosevelt, like Abraham Lincoln, was an extremely complex person. He had always liked people, and his physical problems, coming in his forties, made him deeply compassionate toward others who suffered. He was interested in new ideas, but those around him were often confused as to what he was thinking. Sometimes his dislike of hurting people made it seem he was agreeing with them when in fact he was not.

Roosevelt was more interested in reforming capitalist institutions than in changing them. He believed in capitalism, and he was a sincerely religious man. Like many of his generation, Roosevelt was a product of the Progressive Era. He clung to its values. Philosophically he was a **pragmatist**, that is, one who believes that the value of an idea is whether or not it works. He was also creative and adventurous. He once said, "It is common sense to take a method and try it. If it fails, admit it frankly and try another. But above all, try something."

Present the Lesson

Read and discuss Chapter 26, Section 3 Daily Activity, which describes Roosevelt's bipartisan cabinet. Have students skim the section and list on the board the key events of the first few weeks of FDR's New Deal. List should include:

New Deal

- Appointment of knowledgeable advisors.
- Appointment of bipartisan cabinet.
- Passage of Emergency Banking Relief Bill.
- Radio talk the day before the first bank reopened.

Check for Understanding

Call on individual students to read their answers to Section 3 Review questions.

The Roosevelt Team Works Effectively

The New Deal attracted to Washington the brightest group of people since the Progressive Era. Dozens of young lawyers, economists, political scientists, and social workers flooded the nation's capital. Some became junior members of the brain trust, while others worked in the White House or in the new federal agencies. Many went on to start Washington law firms or, in later administrations, to serve as cabinet officers or sit on the Supreme Court.

Aides and Advisors. One of the most influential of the new people was **Harry Hopkins**. A young social worker, he had supervised relief activities in New York State while Roosevelt was governor. Apart from his administrative ability, his main contribution to the New Deal was his strong preference for work relief rather than monetary relief. Money helped people buy food, Hopkins acknowledged. Work, however, not only enabled them to eat but also gave them confidence and self-respect. Other nonofficial cabinet members included Thomas C. "Tommy the Cork" Corcoran, whose quick wit enlivened many a serious discussion, and Benjamin Cohen, who provided a scholarly base for much New Deal legislation.

A Bipartisan Cabinet. Roosevelt's official cabinet represented a balance. It combined the states-man's realization that people in key positions should be able as well as loyal and the politician's realization that various special-interest groups should be satisfied. It included Republicans as well as Democrats.

Roosevelt named Senator **Cordell Hull**, a courtly gentleman from Tennessee, as Secretary of State. Hull had no particular experience in foreign affairs, but he was highly regarded by his fellow legislators, with whom he had served for thirty years. He supported the South's traditional stand in favor of lower tariffs. William H. Woodin, a conservative Republican businessman, became FDR's first Secretary of the Treasury. Because of poor health, however, Woodin remained in the cabinet for less than a year. He was succeeded by Henry Morgenthau, Jr.

Reform members of the cabinet included Henry Wallace and **Harold Ickes**. Wallace's father had been Secretary of Agriculture in the Harding and Coolidge cabinets, and Roosevelt appointed the son to the same position. Ickes, a Chicago attorney and a strong conservationist, was put in charge of the Interior Department. Described as "elderly, peppery, persnickety," he soon became known as the Old Curmudgeon (an ill-tempered person).

In some ways, FDR's most interesting appointment was that of **Frances Perkins** as Secretary of Labor. The position had usually gone to a labor-union official. "Madam Perkins," as she was

Picturing History FDR's first cabinet was a diverse group, comprising Democrats, Republicans, progressives, and isolationists. It also included the first female cabinet member, Secretary of Labor Frances Perkins. All members were extremely loyal to the President.

Guided Practice

Point out to students that Eleanor Roosevelt established a standard of high visibility and activity for subsequent First Ladies. Discuss the role of the First Lady and the manner in which this "unofficial official" role has been filled by the wives of recent Presidents. (Discussion might include: acted as "goodwill ambassadors" for their husbands; initiated anti-drug, anti-poverty, and literacy programs.)

Assign Independent Practice

Have students write two paragraphs explaining how Roosevelt's actions in the early days of his Presidency set the tone for his entire term of office. (Paragraphs might include: Roosevelt called for a power "as great as the power that would be given me if we were in fact invaded by a foreign foe"; he brought together some of the most intelligent minds in the country; he chose a bipartisan cabinet; he was successful in pushing legislation through Congress; he kept the nation aware of his plans and ideas through "fireside chats.") Have two or three students read their paragraphs to the class.

called, had no such connection. She was, however, a nationally recognized expert on industrial safety. The first woman to sit in a President's cabinet, she was somewhat resented in the beginning. Nevertheless, her quiet manner and administrative ability soon won widespread respect.

An Energetic Wife. A key member of Roosevelt's team had no official standing in the administration and drew no salary. **Eleanor Roosevelt** was the niece of Theodore Roosevelt, who gave her away at her wedding. The bride should have been the center of attention, but because President Theodore Roosevelt was there, she was hardly noticed. Being put in the background was the story of her young life. Her parents died while she was still a child, leaving her to be brought up by a bullying grandmother. Her childhood was bleak and friendless, and she grew into a tall, awkward girl. She had inherited a lot of her famous uncle's driving energy, most of which she devoted to social work.

Eleanor Roosevelt's work among the poor brought her into contact with her cousin Franklin. As their friendship turned to romance, his mother, Sara Delano Roosevelt, did her best to stop it. After the marriage, she bullied her daughter-in-law much as Eleanor's grandmother had.

While raising five children in New York and Washington, Eleanor Roosevelt kept her interest in helping the less fortunate. Her husband's illness was as much a turning point in her life as it was in his. Whereas Sara Roosevelt wanted her son to be a permanent invalid who would depend on her, Eleanor Roosevelt fought for his right to lead a useful life. Later, she represented him at public meetings and private conferences and campaigned for him when he ran for governor. She handled these duties with considerable political skill.

Many of the things Eleanor Roosevelt did are now expected from the wives of political leaders. In the thirties they were not. After FDR became President, she traveled widely and reported her findings to him. The President often introduced an idea to his cabinet by beginning, "My missus says . . . ." She took a particular interest in young people and often spoke to them about possibilities for the future. She also helped to make policy, especially in matters concerning women, African Americans, and other minorities. Rexford Tugwell said that no one could ever doubt her influence when they heard her say, as she looked the President firmly

Picturing History Eleanor Roosevelt became a familiar figure to most Americans through her sincere commitment to ending the depression.

in the eye, "Franklin, I think you should . . ." or "Franklin, surely you will not . . . ."

A Tough Banking Act Brings Relief

On Monday, March 6, two days after his inauguration, FDR ordered a **bank holiday**. This meant that every bank in the nation closed to help stop the panic caused by people withdrawing their money. On March 9, Congress met in special session. It listened to the terms of Roosevelt's Emergency Banking Relief Bill and passed it in four hours. Before the day was over, the bill had been signed into law. It authorized the Treasury Department to inspect the country's banks. Those that were sound could reopen at once, those that needed help could receive loans, and the insolvent ones were to stay closed. About one out of ten banks fell into the last category. Although the measure was drastic, it ended the banking crisis. Now people would not have to wonder whether or not a bank was sound. If its doors were open, its deposits were safe. The federal government said so.

The Emergency Banking Relief Act also forbade the hoarding or exporting of gold. In effect, it took the United States off the gold standard. Conservatives were outraged. Radicals were likewise out-

For Discussion
Remind students that Franklin Roosevelt was the first President to use radio regularly as a means of keeping the public informed and maintaining a sort of personal relationship with Americans. How have recent Presidents made use of radio, television, and newspapers to communicate with voters? Do they project the same personal warmth and concern as FDR? (Possible response: many Presidents have tried to show the warm, personal side of their personalities; not many have been able to duplicate FDR's appeal.)

Student Assignment/Homework

Have students complete Chapter 26 Review on paper. Divide the class into small groups to discuss their answers.

Concluding the Chapter

Divide the class into small groups. Have students compare the personalities and political beliefs of Herbert Hoover and Franklin D. Roosevelt, noting similarities and differences. (Responses might include: Hoover was inflexible and did not adapt well, whereas Roosevelt was flexible and willing to try anything to help the economy; both were efficient and precise leaders; Hoover was aloof and did not meet with the people, whereas Roosevelt instituted fireside chats to inform the public of his plans and ideas; Hoover believed that individuals and state governments should handle the welfare issue, whereas Roosevelt believed the federal government must step in and provide welfare relief.) Have the group leaders summarize the discussions for the class.

SECTION 3 REVIEW

Answers

Main Ideas

1. Fear itself.

2. Intelligence, determination, creativity, pragmatism, courage, compassion, and a sense of adventure.

3. By being much more active and outspoken and by openly advising the President.

4. To reassure people that any bank that was open was financially sound.

5. The restoration of public confidence in the American banking system.

Critical Thinking

6. Intelligence, energy, talent, and well-developed but differing political philosophies. **(synthesis)**

raged, for they had wanted the federal government to **nationalize**, or to take control of, the banking system. FDR chose a middle road combining private ownership with government regulation. It was a road down which most Americans would be likely to follow the President.

Americans Listen to Straight Talk

Some of the renewed confidence in the banking system resulted from a radio talk Roosevelt delivered to the nation Sunday evening, March 12, the day before the first banks were to reopen. In his broadcast, he explained in clear, simple language how the banking system worked:

> When you deposit money in a bank, the bank does not put the money into a safe deposit vault. It invests your money in many different forms of credit: bonds, commercial paper (business loans), mortgages, and many other kinds of loans. In other words, the bank puts your money to work to keep the wheels of industry and agriculture turning around. A comparatively small part of the money you put into the bank is kept in currency—an amount which in normal times is wholly sufficient to cover the cash needs of the ordinary citizen. In other words, the total amount of currency in the country is only a small fraction of the total deposits in all of the banks.

Roosevelt then went on to explain that when too many people demanded their deposits in cash, banks would fail, not because they were weak, but because even the soundest banks could not meet such heavy demands.

FDR thanked the people for their patience during the crisis and praised their patriotism. Finally, he asked them to return, as soon as their bank reopened, any money or gold they might have drawn out. After assuring them it would be safe to do so, the President finished with these words:

> After all, there is an element in the readjustment of our financial system more important than currency, more important than gold, and that is the confidence of the people. Confidence and courage are the essentials of success in carrying out our plan. You people must have faith; you must not be stampeded by rumors or guesses. Let us unite in banishing fear. We have provided the machinery to

> restore our financial system; it is up to you to support and make it work.
>
> It is your problem no less than mine. Together we cannot fail.

This radio talk was the first of what came to be called **fireside chats**. They were the best means FDR discovered for explaining New Deal measures to the voters. They also represented the most creative use of radio by any political leader up to that time. Roosevelt never overlooked the fact that though his audience numbered millions, it was made up of individuals and families, each seated in a room. He spoke directly to them in a friendly, intimate tone.

On this optimistic note, the Roosevelt administration got under way. Over the next few weeks, a billion dollars in gold and currency was dug up from backyards or removed from mattresses and deposited in banks. Listening to people talk, anyone might have thought the depression was already over. Even responsible leaders in the government expected a rapid end to the nation's economic ills. However, the problems were too basic and too deep for quick, easy solutions. The depression had at last reached bottom, but the road to recovery was long and steep.

SECTION 3 REVIEW

Key Terms and People

Explain the significance of: pragmatist, Harry Hopkins, Cordell Hull, Harold Ickes, Frances Perkins, Eleanor Roosevelt, bank holiday, nationalize, fireside chats

Main Ideas

1. What did Roosevelt say was the only thing America had to fear?
2. What personality traits did Roosevelt have that made him well-suited for dealing with the problems of the depression?
3. How did Eleanor Roosevelt change the traditional role of the First Lady?
4. What was the purpose of the Emergency Banking Relief Bill?
5. What did Roosevelt hope to accomplish with his radio message on the banking system?

Critical Thinking

6. What qualities did Roosevelt look for in his advisors and aides?

State the Objective

Understand the problems of farmers in the Dust Bowl region of the Great Plains.

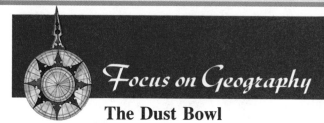

Focus on Geography

The Dust Bowl

The Geographic Theme of Human-Environment Interactions

During and after the drought of 1988, geographers, economists, and others analyzed its effects. A similar drought had occurred in 1932. East of the Mississippi, the 1932 drought dried up streams and ponds. West of the Mississippi, it dried up crops and turned land to dust. Beginning in fall 1933 and continuing through spring 1935, winds blew the dust eastward in a "black blizzard." As one historian described it:

> The skies were darkened. . . . The dry soil drifted like snow; automobiles had to use their headlights at noon; families stuffed door and window cracks to keep from being choked; livestock died of thirst; and the dust blew farther east and fell into the Atlantic Ocean. Millions of acres of farm land lost their topsoil and thousands of families fled their homes. Most of them headed for California in battered trucks and limping passenger cars, with such furniture and other possessions as they could stuff inside or fasten to the sides and roof. Although they came from a dozen states, they were known mostly as "Okies" since Oklahoma was especially hard hit.

On April 14, 1935, a dust storm struck Dodge City, Kansas, and quickly traveled through Oklahoma and the northen part of Texas. A reporter covering the storm used the term "Dust Bowl" to describe the region. Almost immediatley, the public adopted this term. (See map.)

Human-Environment Interactions. The phenomenon of drought and dust was not a new one. People in the Great Plains had been living with drought and dust storms for years. A Baptist missionary who first surveyed the area in 1830 wrote, "The dust and sand were so dense that one appeared in danger of suffocation." A homemaker who cleaned her house after one of these storms in the 1880's claimed that she swept eleven pounds of dust from her kitchen. A farmer who recalled a dust storm in 1910 noted, "We had to wear rags over our faces to keep the sand from cutting the skin off our bodies."

Why did settlers continue to endure the hardships of this unpredictable climate and struggle to farm this difficult land? To answer this question, we need to examine the relationship between the people and their environment. To understand the human side of the equation, we will analyze the soil-cultivation

Picturing History The devastation caused by the dust storms of the 1930's was beyond belief. In April 1935, one of these storms damaged almost twenty million dollars worth of wheat in the Texas Panhandle alone.

On the board write the heading Dust Bowl. Underneath make two columns labeled Misuses of Land and Consequences of Misuse. Ask students to describe (1) some of the inappropriate practices that led to land erosion and the Dust Bowl and (2) the consequences of these practices. Ask volunteers to write their responses on the board under the appropriate columns. (Possible responses: Misuses—cultivating land and sandy soil unsuitable for agriculture; allowing cattle to overgraze. Consequences—in dry periods, winds carried off loose topsoil; in wet periods, torrential rains

caused rivers to flood and carry off rich topsoil.)

Ask students to describe the impact of the two world wars on farming in the Great Plains. (Possible responses: during both wars, European demand for wheat increased; demand coincided with wet periods in the Great Plains, making it possible for farmers to supply the wheat and prosper. In both cases the land was overcultivated, leading to soil erosion in dry periods. The dry period following World War II, however, was not as severe as the one following World War I because farmers had been aided by government soil-conservation programs.)

Ask students whether they would have stayed on the land after the drought if they were Great Plains farmers in the 1930's. Students should give reasons for their answers. (Possible responses: yes—the soil was rich in nutrients such as potassium, phosphorous, and nitrogen, and the land yielded bountiful wheat crops in wet periods; work might have been difficult to find in the city. No—the drought, dust, and soil erosion would have been too much to deal with.)

Map Skills

Wind erosion • Caused people to migrate from the Dust Bowl to other parts of the U.S.

techniques that people have used to reap bountiful harvests from this frequently hostile environment. To understand the environment side of the equation, we will look for trends in the wet and dry cycles that offer both advantages and disadvantages to settlers. Finally, we will learn about some of the steps the federal government has taken since 1935 to help farmers practice soil conservation as well as get through difficult times.

Soil Cultivation. The purpose of agriculture is to convert the nutrients of the soil into food and other crops. Farmers cultivate by plowing the soil, which breaks it up into small chunks. This makes it easier to plant seeds and ensures that the seedlings will receive water, air, and fertilizer. Since natural vegetation competes with the seeds for these elements, farmers must also remove any existing ground cover. These basic methods of soil cultivation are used today. They are the same methods that were used by the first wave of settlers that moved into the Great Plains.

These first settlers found the grassland soil on the plains extremely fertile and resistant to erosion. Rich in potassium, phosphorous, and nitrogen, this soil contributed to high crop yields. Not all the soil was suited for agriculture, however. Its composition ranged from rich clay to shallow sand. All of the land had a natural cover of short sod-forming grass. Obviously, the cycle of droughts and the burrowing of animals had done little lasting damage. The settlers' task was to conserve the rich soil for continual use.

Drought Cycles and Settlement Patterns. When the first settlers came to the Great Plains in the 1880's, they experienced a period of heavy rainfall. They found the natural vegetation green and luxuriant and set about using their new steel plows and reapers to produce an abundance of crops. In 1890 a severe drought hit the plains and lasted for about ten years. Many of the early settlers moved on. By 1900 the rains had returned, and a new wave of settlers came to plow the fields and plant wheat in the soil that was again productive.

In 1910 another dry spell began to seriously damage the soil. The original soil structure had been broken down by cultivation. Some farmers had even cultivated the sandy soil that was unsuitable for agriculture. Where bare soil had been exposed to the drying effect of the sun, dust began to blow. The winds removed much of the topsoil. Many farmers gave up and moved to areas where

YEARS OF DUST

RESETTLEMENT ADMINISTRATION
Rescues Victims
Restores Land to Proper Use

Picturing History
Ben Shahn's lithograph was intended to reassure discouraged farmers, victimized by dust storms, and to inform them that help was available from government agencies.

the rainfall was more predictable.

When World War I began in 1914, there was an increased demand for wheat from European nations. High wheat yields and returning rains led farmers back to the plains. All land that was suitable for agriculture, and much that was not suitable for agriculture, was cultivated. Fortunately, the wet cycle continued for nearly fifteen years, and the farmers prospered.

In the early 1930's a double catastrophe took place. The United States plunged into a severe economic depression and drought returned to the plains. This new drought was the most severe to date. To compound the problem, continuous cultivation had damaged the soil during the previous decade. The series of dust storms that began in the fall of 1933 buried roads, fences, and even houses. As much as twelve inches of topsoil was lost in some places. Food was in short supply. Farmers who went to the city could not find work because of the depression. The double catastrophe made the nation aware of the need for soil conservation.

Soil Conservation Since 1935. In 1935 the Soil Conservation Service was created to help farmers implement sound land-use practices. Grass was replanted in areas where the plow should never have been used, areas severely affected by erosion.

Rains came again in the 1940's and with them came World War II, resulting in an increased demand for wheat. Farms were restored to productivity, and millions of acres of newly planted grasslands were again plowed for cultivation.

When drought returned in the 1950's, dust storms arose from the eroded farmland and the overgrazed ranges. This time, however, the impact was not so severe. Federal aid was given to the

Check for Understanding

Ask students to write out answers to the questions at the end of the feature. Review the answers with the class. Then ask students to pretend they are government officials from the Department of Agriculture at the time of the depression. They have been assigned to prepare a report for the President of the U.S. describing a program that would conserve soil and help farmers in the Dust Bowl region. Ask several students to read their reports to the class. (Reports might include: grass should be replanted on land not suitable for agriculture; displaced farmers should be assisted in relo- cation; federal aid should be given to needy farmers; farmers should be encouraged to irrigate, plant drought-resistant crops, and store grain for dry spells.)

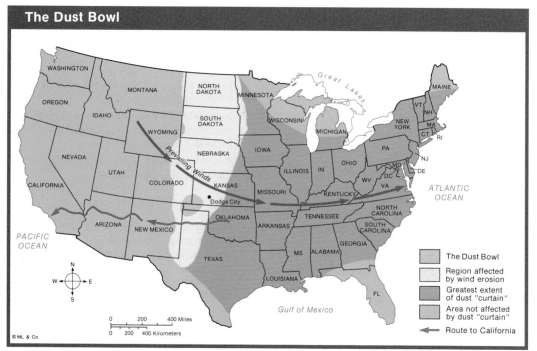

The Dust Bowl

Legend:
- The Dust Bowl
- Region affected by wind erosion
- Greatest extent of dust "curtain"
- Area not affected by dust "curtain"
- → Route to California

Map Skills **Region** What was the main environmental condition that created the Dust Bowl?
Human-Environment Interactions How did the Dust Bowl affect people of that region?

needy farmers in the region. Displaced farmers could find jobs in nearby cities. Farms were larger in the fifties, and had fewer people.

When the next wet period came, in 1957, another consequence of the misuse of the land occurred. These were not gentle rains; they were torrential downpours. They fell on the dust-blown, eroded lands of the Great Plains. Rivers flooded and carried off soil from the once-fertile farms. At that time the Soil Conservation Service estimated that at least 55 million cultivated acres should be returned to grass.

The soil still blows in this region and will continue to do so when drought, wind, and inadequate vegetation provide the necessary ingredients for a dust storm. Dust Bowl farmers will always have to make major adjustments in the farming operation as weather conditions in this region change. They must irrigate when necessary, plant drought-resistant crops, and reduce animal grazing on pasture lands during dry periods. In the drought of 1988, for example, the farmers' pain was not spread evenly. Those who had irrigated their crops, stored their grain from a previous season, and prac- ticed other conservation measures reaped profits.

Given the right circumstances, another dust bowl could occur. If so, those who suffer the least will be those who have learned how to interact with their environment by practicing conservation techniques.

Understanding Geography

1. Why is the history of the region known as the Dust Bowl an example of the geographic theme of human-environment interactions?
2. What were the human and environmental causes of the Dust Bowl conditions?
3. What soil-conservation techniques can be used to prevent a recurrence of the conditions that cause a major dust bowl?

Critical Thinking

4. Drought is a necessary ingredient for a dust storm. The drought of 1988 touched American lives in many different ways. Write an essay on the effects of drought using Longfellow's famous line for a title: "Into Each Life Some Rain Must Fall."

Key Terms and People

These are highlighted in the text in the order in which they appear in this list.

Main Ideas

1. Uneven distribution of income—poor people could not buy goods to keep manufacturers in business; easy credit—people who overextended their incomes buying installment plan purchases could afford no more; unbalanced foreign trade—caused by high American tariffs that prevented foreign countries from selling their goods here; mechanization—put many people out of work.

2. Women—finding work with good pay because of fewer jobs. Children—malnutrition because of poverty; need to leave school to work. Farmers—less income and heavy debt.

3. Programs were too late. • Possible answers (choice of three): construction programs, Reconstruction Finance Corporation (RFC), Home Loan Bank Act, tax cuts to ease borrowing of money, Federal Farm Marketing Board.

4. Unhappiness over Hoover's failure to halt the depression; welcomed Roosevelt's promise of new ideas and swift action.

5. Ordered a bank holiday; passed Emergency Banking Relief Act.

6. Was intended to stop people from withdrawing money from banks, thus causing banks to fail; kept money in circulation.

Critical Thinking Questions

7. Surplus crops were to be destroyed in order to keep the prices up to give a living wage for farmers. • Those who needed food.

➤ 8. Both led to belief that the poor had only themselves to blame.

9. Symbolized the discontent because the veterans had been promised bonuses after the war but had never received them.

➤ 10. Hoover lacked an understanding of the world economy. When the European nations went off the gold standard, he was furious and refused to cancel German war debts to ease Germany's economic problems.

11. Roosevelt was more flexible and dynamic than Hoover. • Roosevelt tried to encourage a feeling of optimism in Americans and restore confidence.

12. To get the best advice from all branches of business and education. • Acted as the President's representative at many events; campaigned for him; advised him on important issues; actively supported minorities and women.

13. Roosevelt spoke personally to listeners through his radio talks and gave a sense of bringing them together to understand the nation's problems.

Critical Thinking Activities

14. Hoover: Bonus Army— driven out by Hoover; Boulder Dam—started by Hoover to give jobs to people; gold standard—Britain went off and started printing paper money not backed by gold;

CHAPTER 26 REVIEW

Write your answers on a separate sheet of paper.

Key Terms and People

Explain the significance of: national income, direct relief, humanitarian, Hoovervilles, moratorium, brain trust, pragmatist, Harold Ickes, nationalize

Main Ideas

1. What were the factors that caused the depression? Explain their role in the collapse of the economy.
2. What problems did the following groups face during the depression: women? children? farmers?
3. Why did Hoover's attempts to halt the depression fail? List three of his actions that should have helped.
4. Why did Americans choose Franklin Roosevelt over Herbert Hoover in 1932?
5. What were the first steps that President Roosevelt took to halt the depression?
6. What was the purpose of the bank holiday, and how did it help the economy?

Critical Thinking Questions

7. **Analyzing Literature.** In the selection by John Steinbeck on page 657, why were the hungry people not allowed to eat the oranges? With whom does Steinbeck sympathize?
8. **Analyzing Causes.** How did Social Darwinism and the ideas of Horatio Alger, Jr., contribute to the fact that the United States was the only industrialized country without any form of unemployment insurance in 1929?
9. **Analyzing Motives.** Why was the Bonus Army an expression of national restlessness and lack of faith in the government?
10. **Analyzing Consequences.** Explain why President Hoover's inability to adapt to conditions caused a crisis in Europe's economy as well as that of the United States.
11. **Comparing Policies.** Compare President Roosevelt's approaches to the nation's problems to Hoover's. In what way did Roosevelt use psychology in his approach?
12. **Synthesizing Ideas.** Why do you think Roosevelt selected a bipartisan cabinet? How did Eleanor Roosevelt aid Roosevelt?
13. **Analyzing Effects.** How did Roosevelt's fireside chats affect the nation?

Critical Thinking Activities

14. **Organizing Ideas.** Place the following events in the correct administration. Give one fact or detail about each event in your chart.

    Bank holiday is decreed.
    Bonus Army is routed.
    Boulder Dam construction begins.
    Britain goes off gold standard.
    Emergency Banking Relief Act is passed.
    Federal Farm Marketing Board is created.
    First woman cabinet member appointed.
    Hawley-Smoot Tariff Act is passed.
    Home Loan Bank Act becomes law.
    New Deal is created.
    Reconstruction Finance Corporation is established.
    Twentieth Amendment is ratified.

Hoover's Administration		Roosevelt's Administration	
Event	Fact	Event	Fact

15. **Linking Past to Present.** Hoover's belief was that government should interfere as little as possible in people's lives. How does this belief compare with what you know of government's role in society today? Do you think that Hoover was right? Explain.

16. **Linking Past to Present.** If Franklin Roosevelt had been a candidate in the last Presidential election, do you think he would have won? Do you think he would have the same appeal today as he did in the past? Explain your answers.

Federal Farm Marketing Board—created to help farmers market their crops; Hawley-Smoot Tariff—highest tariff in history; Home Loan Bank Act—created to prevent foreclosures on homes and farms; Reconstruction Finance Corporation—lent money to banks and large corporations; Twentieth Amendment—moved up inauguration of new President to January 20.
• **Roosevelt:** bank holiday—

kept people from withdrawing money; Emergency Banking Relief Act—helped banks reopen if sound; first woman cabinet member—Secretary of Labor; New Deal—name of course of action.
➤**15.** Possible answers: government is very active in shaping people's lives and providing for them. • Hoover's belief would be hard to defend today in view of the services that people expect from gov-

ernment.
➤**16.** Possible answers: yes—his plans to help people had timeless appeal; he was vigorous and practical. • Yes—pollsters have proved that image is much more powerful than the issues and FDR's charisma was one of his most powerful assets.

➤**Question suitable for co-operative learning.**

TELESCOPING THE TIMES: 1929–1933

The Great Depression Begins

The stock-market crash of 1929 signaled the end of the prosperous twenties and the beginning of the longest and most devastating depression in American experience. The Great Depression resulted from such factors as the uneven distribution of income, easy credit, an imbalance in foreign trade, and the mechanization of industries. The economy lacked a solid base of consumers. In the three years following the 1929 stock-market crash, the national income fell by half. Farms were sold, businesses folded, banks failed, and unemployment skyrocketed. Worse, there were no public or governmental agencies that could deal with the crisis. Millions of Americans, especially women and children, suffered unprecedented poverty and mental anguish. Farmers had to stop producing food they could not sell. Then in 1930 a major drought hit some of the farm states. In 1932 the Bonus Army, composed of war veterans, marched on Washington. There people of different political persuasions presented different solutions to the enormous problems of the depression.

Herbert Hoover did more about economic depression than had any previous President. He tried to restore confidence. He backed some public works projects as well as government agencies to support loans to businesses and prevent more foreclosures on homes and farms. Yet he got bogged down in political arguments. He hated human suffering, but he also believed in rugged individualism. He refused to give in to the demands of the Bonus Army and those of foreign countries.

Democrats blamed Hoover for the depression. Their Presidential candidate, Franklin Delano Roosevelt, promised Americans "a new deal." He formed a brain trust of advisors. The Democrats won both the Presidential and the congressional elections of 1932. By the time FDR took office in March 1933, even more businesses had failed, and many banks had closed their doors.

Because FDR faced a difficult challenge, he particularly wanted his inaugural address to instill confidence. In it, he reassured the nation in a clear, strong tone. As a pragmatist, Roosevelt sought to reform his country's economic system rather than to change it completely. He brought a talented, bipartisan group of aides and advisors to Washington to help him. His wife, Eleanor, though she held no official position, nevertheless had great influence, which she used to promote the needs of the poor and the cause of racial justice.

FDR's first major task was to push through Congress the Emergency Banking Relief Act, which immediately helped restore some public confidence in the nation's banking system. Frantic over the country's critical economic situation, Congress rubber-stamped this and other bills drafted by FDR and his advisors. During the first Hundred Days of FDR's administration, Congress would pass New Deal legislation aimed at bringing the nation relief, recovery, and reform.

Chronology of Main Events

1929 Herbert Hoover inaugurated President; stock market crash; Great Depression begins

1932 Bonus Army march; Reconstruction Finance Corporation set up

1933 Franklin D. Roosevelt inaugurated President; Twentieth Amendment moves Presidential inaugurations back to January; Roosevelt declares bank holiday; Emergency Banking Relief Bill passed

Telescoping the Times may be used as an alternative to having students read the entire chapter, as a chapter preview, or as a chapter review.

Global Perspectives

Mid-1930's	Millions die during Stalin's Great Purge.
1934-1935	Chinese Communists conduct the Long March.
1935	Italy invades Ethiopia.
1935-1940	Italy, Germany, and Russia launch invasions in Europe and Africa.
1936-1939	Spanish civil war is fought.
1939	Germany annexes Czechoslovakia; Italy invades Albania.
1940	USSR invades Baltic republics.

For Discussion

What are some possible reasons why the U.S. did not intervene in the invasions of Europe and Africa between 1935 and 1940? (Possible responses: U.S. was deeply involved in recovering from the Great Depression; U.S. felt that the conflict was not its concern because invasions were not occurring in the Western Hemisphere; U.S. was attempting to maintain a policy of isolationism as it dealt with its own problems.)

Additional Resources

- Geography Activities
- Skills Activities
- Thematic Activities
- Economic Activities
- Cultural Literacy Activities
- Literary Source Readings
- Primary Source Readings
- Nuclear Peacekeeping
- Transparencies
- Computer Test Generator

Additional Teaching Strategies

SECTION 1

For Basic Students: Ask students to do research in an encyclopedia and write a one-page report on the Tennessee Valley Authority (TVA). (Report should include: created in 1933; built dams and power plants; operates the National Fertilizer Development Center at Muscle Shoals, Alabama, where scientists seek to develop fertilizers and improve methods of producing them.) Have students share their reports.

For Advanced Students: Ask the students to assume the role of a conservative Republican newspaper editor and prepare an editorial pointing out the shortcomings of FDR's first Hundred Days, or to assume the role of a liberal Democratic editor and prepare an editorial praising the accomplishments of FDR's first Hundred Days. (Democratic editorial on FDR's accomplishments may include: employed many people; gave loans to homeowners; helped farmers and minorities; ensured that people would not lose money by putting it into banks.) Have two or three students read their editorials to the class.

For Present the Lesson: Charts for this activity should include the following information:

Civilian Conservation Corps
Provisions: Built roads, planted trees, created soil-erosion and flood-control projects.
Purpose: To employ male youths aged seventeen to twenty-eight.

Federal Emergency Relief Act
Provisions: Provided $250 million in direct grants-in-aid to states to feed and clothe the unemployed, the aged, and the ill. • Provided for distribution of additional $250 million on basis of one federal dollar for every three state dollars.
Purpose: To provide more general help for the unemployed.

Civil Works Administration
Provisions: Created federal jobs for over 4 million people. • Established minimum pay.
Purpose: To give aid directly through local authorities.

Agriculture Adjustment Administration
Provisions: Provided for farmers who did not plant. • Paid farmers to destroy surplus crops and livestock.
Purpose: To provide relief for farmers. • To raise farm prices.

Tennessee Valley Authority
Provisions: Created factories and jobs; improved agriculture, health, and education in Tennessee River Valley.
Purpose: To develop regional natural resources.

Emergency Banking Relief Act
Provisions: Allowed sound banks in Federal Reserve System to reopen. • Forbade hoarding or exporting of gold.
Purpose: To stop run on banks. • To achieve federal control of banks.

Economy Act
Provisions: Lowered salaries of government workers. • Reduced payments to veterans.
Purpose: To appease those worried about excess government spending.

Home Owners Loan Corporation
Provisions: Provided government loans to homeowners.
Purpose: To save homeowners from foreclosure.

Securities Act
Provisions: Gave Federal Trade Commission power to supervise new securities. • Required companies wanting to sell stock to disclose full information.
Purpose: To control sale of new securities.

Glass-Steagall Act
Provisions: Set up Federal Deposit Insurance Corp. • Protected bank deposits up to $5,000.
Purpose: To protect bank deposits.

National Industrial Recovery Act
Provisions: Limited production in industry so prices would go up. • Set up fair trade codes. • Gave laborers right to organize. • Set up National Labor Board. • Established Public Works Administration.
Purpose: To boost industry.

SECTION 2

For Basic Students: Have students write two paragraphs summarizing the purposes and provisions of the Social Security Act. (Paragraphs should include: provided pensions for retired workers and their spouses; provided death benefits and support for surviving children; established a joint federal-state unemployment insurance system; provided aid to handicapped persons, the needy, elderly, and neglected children.) Have students share their paragraphs.

For Advanced Students: Organize students into groups of three and have them research and prepare oral presentations on the social security system, the Security and Exchange Commission, or the Federal Reserve System. (Presentations on the social security system should include: social security provides cash payments to help replace income lost as a result of retirement, unemployment disability, or death; people become eligible to receive benefits by working a certain period at a job covered by social security.)

For Present the Lesson: Charts for this activity should include the following information:

Works Progress Administration

Provisions: Created a budget of $5 billion and employed 8 million people. • Built airports, libraries, hospitals, schools; repaired roads. • Supported cultural arts and artists.

Purpose: To combine relief programs. • To create jobs quickly.

Social Security Act

Provisions: Provided pension system for retired workers and their spouses. Provided death benefits and support for surviving children. • Established joint federal-state unemployment insurance system. • Provided for handicapped, needy, elderly, neglected children.

Purpose: To create a pension system for retired people and to provide for those unable to care for themselves.

Securities and Exchange Commission

Provisions: Prevented insider trading.

Purpose: To protect investors.

Public Utility Holding Company Act

Provisions: Regulated holding companies that provided electric light and power.

Purpose: To promote efficiency and savings in utilities.

Revenue Act of 1935

Provisions: Increased gift and estate taxes. Increased tax rate for those with high incomes. • Provided graduated corporate income tax.

Purpose: To break up large accumulations of wealth.

Banking Act of 1935

Provisions: Gave power to raise or lower nation's money supply and to raise or lower interest rates.

Purpose: Control nation's money supply.

SECTION 3

For Basic Students: Have each student choose a partner. Each pair should then do research in an encyclopedia or other source book and present to the class a three-minute oral report on Huey Long, Father Coughlin, Upton Sinclair, or Dr. Francis E. Townsend. (Reports on Father Coughlin might include: born 1891; died 1979; was an American Roman Catholic priest; became known before World War II for his political activities, radio shows, and paper, *Social Justice*; favored inflation and isolationism.)

For Advanced Students: After they do additional research on *Schechter Poultry Corporation* v. *United States* and *United States* v. *Butler*, have students discuss the Supreme Court's decisions. (Discussion might include: in *Schechter* v. *United States* the Supreme Court ruled that NIRA was unconstitutional; NIRA empowered the President to set up codes of fair competition for businesses and industries; in 1935 NIRA was ruled unconstitutional because it delegated excessive legislative power to the President and it gave the federal government power to regulate intrastate trade.)

SECTION 4

For Basic Students: Ask students to list ten influential women of the 1930's and their areas of achievement. (Lists might include: Literature—Margaret Mitchell, Pearl Buck, Edna Ferber, Lillian Hellman, Dorothy Parker; Sports—"Babe" Didrikson; Anthropology—Ruth Benedict, Margaret Mead; Medical research—Maude Slyde, Florence Sabin; Education—Mary McLeod Bethune; Music—Marian Anderson.) Have students share their lists.

For Advanced Students: Have students research and prepare a two-page biographical sketch of one of the outstanding women of the 1930's mentioned in this section. (Biographical sketches on Florence Sabin might include: born in Central City, Colorado, in 1871; studied and taught at Johns Hopkins University School of Medicine; worked at Rockefeller Institute for Medical Research 1925-1938; became involved in public health work after retirement; died 1953.) Have several students present their reports to the class.

Further Reading for Students

Nonfiction

Hiebert, Roslyn, and Ray E. Hiebart. *Franklin Delano Roosevelt, President for the People.* New York: Franklin Watts, 1968. (Easy)

Lawson, Don. *FDR's New Deal.* New York: Harper & Row, 1979.

Roosevelt, Eleanor. *Autobiography of Eleanor Roosevelt.* New York: Harper & Row, 1961.

Fiction

Warren, Robert Penn. *All the King's Men.* New York: Random House, 1960.

Bibliography for Teachers

Books

Banks, Ann. *First-Person America.* New York: Alfred A. Knopf, 1980.

Brinkley, Alan. *Voices of Protest: Huey Long, Father Coughlin, and the Great Depression.* New York: Alfred A. Knopf, 1982.

Burns, James M. *Roosevelt: The Lion and the Fox.* New York: Harcourt Brace Jovanovich, 1963.

Latham, Frank B. *FDR and the Supreme Court Fight, 1937.* New York: Watts, 1972.

Louchheim, Katie, ed. *The Making of the New Deal: The Insiders Speak.* Cambridge, Mass.: Harvard University Press, 1983.

Sitkoff, Harvard. *A New Deal for Blacks: The Emergence of Civil Rights As a National Issue: the Depression Decade.* New York: Oxford University Press, 1978.

Whitney, Sharon. *Eleanor Roosevelt.* New York: Franklin Watts, 1982.

Audio-Visuals

Agriculture and the New Deal. Encyclopaedia Britannica Educational Corp. Movie.

Demagogues and Do-Gooders: Noisy Voices of the Depression. Time-Life Films. Movie.

Franklin D. Roosevelt: The New Deal. (The History Makers Series). Hearst Corporation. Movie.

The Helping Hand. P.B.S. Studios. Movie.

Mary McLeod Bethune. Eye Gate. Movie.

The New Deal. (American History Series) McGraw-Hill Book Company. Movie.

Roosevelt and U.S. History (1930-1945). Coronet Film and Video. Movie.

TVA. Tennessee Valley Authority. Movie.

Computer Resource

Scholastic PFS: World Geography, Cultures, and Economic Databases. (Apple) Scholastic Software.

Lesson Plan

Teaching Resources

Lesson Study Sheets pp. 225-240
Daily Activities pp. 241-248
Enrichment Activities pp. 249-256
Reteaching Activities pp. 257-264
Chapter Review p. 265
Chapter Mastery Tests pp. 267-278
Telescoping the Times Study Sheet p. 279
Unit Mastery Tests pp. 281-292
Telescoping the Times Unit 6 Study Sheet
   p. 293

Chapter Objectives

Students will learn:

- signs of recovery that characterized the first hundred days of the Roosevelt administration
- why some important New Deal measures have endured
- why the New Deal was criticized by people from both ends of the political spectrum
- what major social changes occurred in the U.S. during the 1930's as a result of the New Deal

Picturing History Franklin Delano Roosevelt salutes the American flag at a parade in Warm Springs, Georgia. His confident expression shows his determination to bring the United States out of the depression.

Using the Chapter Time Line

What European country was engaged in a civil war (see Unit 6 Time Line) during Roosevelt's second term as President? (Answer: Spain)

How many years passed between the beginning of the New Deal and the Beginning of the Second New Deal? (Answer: 2)

1932	1934	1936	1938	1940

1933
- Franklin D. Roosevelt inaugurated President
- New Deal Begins

1934
Securities and Exchange Commission established

1935
- Second New Deal begins
- Committee for Industrial Organization founded
- Social Security Act

1937
Roosevelt inaugurated for second term

1938
Fair Labor Standards Act

676

Links to American Literature

Archie Hobson: a native New Yorker; is an inveterate traveler; associate editor of the *Concise Columbia Encyclopedia*.

Works include: numerous articles for journals, newspapers, and organizations.

Remembering America, A Sampler of the WPA American Guide Series: a collection of more than five hundred passages from state and city guides written from 1935 to 1943 under the Federal Writers' Project, a branch of the New Deal Works Progress Administration; includes folklore, local history, and social commentary as well as nearly one thousand illustrations; is a celebration of America's diversity and its triumph over the depression; includes now well-known writers such as John Cheever, Studs Terkel, Saul Bellow, and Ralph Ellison.

Introducing the Chapter

Have students study the chart on page 683. Ask students what acts or agencies they recognize as being still important today. (Possible responses: Tennessee Valley Authority; Federal Deposit Insurance Corp.; Securities and Exchange Commission; Food, Drug and Cosmetic Act; Federal Housing Administration; Social Security.) Tell students that most of these programs were considered daring and controversial at the time. Ask students to name agencies or acts that are controversial today. (Possible responses: AIDS legislation; Equal Rights Amendment; abortion legislation; Drug Enforcement Agency; national health care legislation.)

CHAPTER **27**   1933–1940

The New Deal and Reform

Links to American Literature

SAUNA. The Finns are a clannish people who cling to their Old World manners and customs, and to a stranger may sometimes seem unfriendly. At one time a suspicious farmer accused them of practicing magic and of worshipping pagan deities. Entire families, he claimed, wrapped themselves in white sheets and retreated to a small square building set apart from the dwellings and worshipped their gods, calling upon them to bring rain and good harvests to Finns, and wrath upon their neighbors. On investigation, however, it was discovered that although they did wrap themselves in sheets and visit these "shrines" almost daily, it was not in the zeal of religion but for the purpose of taking baths. The Finns here are almost fanatical advocates of cleanliness, and each has his own "sauna" or steam bathhouse.

Minnesota

— ARCHIE HOBSON, ed. *Remembering America: A Sampler of the WPA American Guide Series*

    Once inaugurated, Franklin D. Roosevelt called a special session of Congress to bring economic relief to a depressed nation. Later he shifted the emphasis from relief and recovery to reform. Roosevelt addressed the nation's problems with conviction and determination, creating programs such as the Works Progress Administration (WPA) and providing the energetic leadership that was needed to mobilize the country. Thousands of writers were put to work for the Federal Writers' Project, a branch of the WPA, to create a detailed picture of life in "real America." At a time when democracies in Europe were being replaced by dictatorships, Roosevelt was able to bring about reform without revolution. Nevertheless, his opponents were widespread. He did not go far enough for left-wing radicals, and he went too far for right-wing conservatives.

Chapter Overview

    In this chapter you will learn about FDR's first hundred days. You will also learn about the New Deal reforms that have endured and about those that came under attack from people on both ends of the political spectrum. Finally, you will learn about the major social changes that occurred during the 1930's because of the New Deal. To help you learn about this period of relief, recovery, and reform, Chapter 27 is divided into four sections.

Chapter Outline

1. **The First Hundred Days Set the Tone**
2. **Roosevelt Seeks to Reform the System**
3. **The New Deal Comes Under Attack**
4. **Many Changes Occur During the New Deal**

SECTION 1

The First Hundred Days Set the Tone

GLOSSARY TERMS: **Hundred Days, Glass-Steagall Act, price controls, pump priming**

In his inaugural address, President Roosevelt declared, ''Our greatest primary task is to put people to work. This is no unsolvable problem if we face it wisely and courageously.''

Then he called Congress into a special session. It sat from March 9 to June 16, 1933. In the first **Hundred Days,** it passed more significant legislation than Congress usually manages in two years. This haste was considered necessary because of the country's urgent problems.

Many People Need Jobs

Congress's task was to increase consumers' purchasing power and to restore prices to a level that would allow producers sufficient profit to make it worthwhile for them to produce goods. To increase purchasing power, people needed money—not through handouts, but through productive jobs.

The Civilian Conservation Corps. In the first month of the new administration, the **Civilian Conservation Corps (CCC)** was established. Unemployed single males aged seventeen to twenty-eight were put to work building roads, planting trees, and helping in soil-erosion and flood-control projects. The young men lived in camps run by army officers. The work was directed by experienced foresters and construction foremen. Members of the CCC got thirty dollars a month, twenty-two of which was sent to their dependent families. They also received free food and uniforms.

Many of the camps were located on the Great Plains. There, within a period of eight years, the men of the CCC planted more than 200 million trees. This tremendous reforestation program was aimed at preventing another dust bowl. (See page 671.) By the time the program ended in 1941, almost 3 million young men had passed through the CCC.

Emergency Relief. Congress's second action was to pass the Federal Emergency Relief Act (FERA), which gave more general help to the unemployed. It provided $250 million in direct grants-in-aid to the states to be used to furnish food and clothing to the unemployed, the aged, and the ill. An additional $250 million was distributed on the basis of one federal dollar for every three state dollars contributed. **Harry Hopkins** was placed in charge of the program.

These measures were not enough, however, so Hopkins set up the Civil Works Administration (CWA). Instead of channeling aid through the states, it gave aid to people in need through local authorities. Within two months, more than 4 million persons were working for the federal government at jobs that did not compete with existing

People in the Chapter

Joseph Kennedy was the father of a future President, John F. Kennedy. On John's twenty-first birthday his father was most generous. He gave John a one-million-dollar trust fund.

Amelia Earhart became the object of rumors after her strange disappearance over the Pacific. Some believed she was part of a secret espionage mission that was shot down. Others speculated that she had been stranded on a Pacific atoll, was captured by the Japanese, and lived under an assumed name after her release. No trace of her or her plane was ever found.

Mildred "Babe" Didrikson Zaharias was one of the finest American athletes. Her achievements are almost too many to recount. As the nation's leading golfer, "Babe" won seventeen consecutive victories in one year.

Mary McLeod Bethune was the daughter of former slaves. She raised the money to build the schoolhouse that eventually became part of Bethune-Cookman College in Florida. She became president of the college after serving as a director in Roosevelt's National Youth Administration.

State the Objective

Recognize the signs of recovery that characterized the first Hundred Days of the Roosevelt administration.

Present the Lesson

Have students read the Section to find information regarding the acts and agencies established under the New Deal. Use this information to prepare a chart on the board listing each act or agency, its provisions, and its purpose. (See answers on page 675a.) Discuss with students their views of the relative success of each act or agency.

Picturing History Young men in 1933, lined up to enlist in the Civilian Conservation Corps. At its height, the CCC put to work 500,000 men aged eighteen to twenty-five.

For Discussion
How do you feel about the deliberate destruction of food under the Agriculture Adjustment Act (AAA) when many Americans were going hungry? Do you feel that the destruction of food was justified? Give reasons for your answer. (Possible response: the food should have been purchased by the government and distributed to the needy throughout the country rather than being destroyed.)

jobs. The pay was minimal, and some of the jobs were so unnecessary that the word *boondoggle* came to be used to describe them. Still, as a Michigan county administrator reported, men left her office ''weeping for sheer happiness'' at the idea of working again after years of being unemployed.

Farmers Agree to Limit Production

The nation's farmers were caught between huge surpluses and low prices. President Hoover had tried to persuade farmers to limit production, but the voluntary program had not worked. Now Roosevelt decided to follow the same approach, but with a twist. Instead of using words, the federal government would pay farmers cash for reducing production. The money for the ''benefit payments'' would come from a tax on processors, that is, the people who milled flour, packed meat, manufactured cloth, and so on. By limiting production, farmers would also get more money for the crops and livestock they did raise.

The Agricultural Adjustment Act was launched in May 1933 at the urging of Henry A. Wallace, Secretary of Agriculture. The act established the

Agricultural Adjustment Administration (AAA). Under the act the federal government agreed to pay farmers a certain amount for every acre of land left unseeded. Some crops, however, were too far advanced for the acreage reduction to take effect. So the government paid cotton growers $200 million to plow under 10 million acres of their crop. It also paid hog farmers to slaughter 6 million swine.

These crop-control measures aroused a great deal of criticism. A few newspapers wrote sentimental articles about the ''slaughter of baby pigs.'' A more serious objection came from people who were upset by the deliberate destruction of food at a time when many Americans were hungry. In addition, the tax on processors was passed along to consumers in the form of higher prices for food and clothing.

Still, the AAA program succeeded in its goals. Prices of farm commodities rose, and farmers received more income.

The TVA Develops Natural Resources

Among the longest-lasting New Deal projects was the **Tennessee Valley Authority (TVA).** Ever since World War I, Congress had been arguing

Guided Practice

Tell students that the Civilian Conservation Corps (CCC) employed millions of youths before 1941. Ask students whether such a program would be advisable today. For example, our nation's roads and bridges are in great need of repair. With unemployment a continuing problem, would the nation benefit from hiring the unemployed to do the necessary repairs? (Possible responses: yes, public works jobs are a means of curbing inflation and helping the unemployed; no, a CCC today would mean higher taxes and more bureaucracy.)

about what to do with some hydroelectric plants the government had built on the Tennessee River at Muscle Shoals, Alabama, to produce nitrates for explosives. When the war ended, private utility companies wanted to buy or lease the plants. However, a group of congressmen led by Senator George W. Norris of Nebraska insisted that the federal government should continue the Progressive policy of conserving and developing the country's natural resources.

In May 1933 the TVA was established. (For a detailed explanation of the TVA, see page 697.) It was the first example of regional planning by the federal government. The Tennessee River Valley was transformed. There were new factories, new energy, and new jobs. Today farms are more productive, farmhouses are electrified, health and education are improved, and the region is filled with lakes for recreation. Most people would agree that the TVA was one of the most successful accomplishments of the New Deal.

Congress Regulates Finance

FDR's first action had been to declare a bank holiday (see page 669), and the first law passed during the first Hundred Days was the Emergency Banking Relief Act. Inspectors from the Department of the Treasury permitted sound banks in the Federal Reserve System to reopen under carefully controlled conditions. The hoarding and export of gold were forbidden. This act, which gave the President broad powers over the financial affairs of banks, renewed many people's faith in the banking system. A series of other acts dealing with financial matters further increased public confidence.

The Economy Act lowered the salaries of government workers and reduced payments to veterans. FDR hoped this act would appease people who were worried about excessive federal spending and its possible long-lasting effects.

The **Home Owners Loan Corporation (HOLC)** provided government loans to home owners who were facing foreclosure because they could not meet their mortgage payments. By 1936 when the act expired, it had saved the homes of almost a million families.

The Securities Act gave the Federal Trade Commission the power to supervise new securities. Now companies that wanted to sell stock had to give the public full information. The **Glass-Steagall Act** set up the Federal Deposit Insurance

Corporation to protect bank deposits up to $5,000. (The current amount insured by the FDIC is $100,000.) As a result, depositors no longer had to worry about losing their life savings if a bank failed.

The NIRA Promises to Help Industry

The **National Industrial Recovery Act (NIRA)** was one of the most controversial acts of the New Deal. At first, however, it was so popular with some people that a number of babies born at the time were named "Nira."

The act created the National Recovery Administration (NRA). Beginning in June 1933 and

Picturing History By displaying the National Recovery Administration's symbol of the blue eagle, companies showed that they followed the new wage and hour labor codes.

continuing through May 1935, almost every store, factory, and office building in the United States displayed in its windows posters with an enormous blue eagle, under which were the words "We Do Our Part." The brainchild of General Hugh Johnson, the blue bird was the symbol of the NRA.

The two main parts of the act had to do with public works projects and with codes detailing fair practices for industry. The codes were designed to limit production so that prices would go up and producers would make a profit. Many small business people pointed out that these codes favored big business.

Write the terms *Relief, Recovery,* and *Reform* on the board. Ask the students to define each term as it was used in the Roosevelt administration and prepare a chart that shows into which category each act or agency discussed in this Section falls. (Some may fall into more than one category.)

Relief (direct payments to individuals): Civilian Conservation Corps; Federal Emergency Relief Act; Agriculture Adjustment Act; Emergency Banking Relief Act; Civil Works Administration

Recovery (Help to "prime the pump": Tennessee Valley Authority; Economy Act; Home Owners Loan Corporation; National Industrial Recovery Act; Public Works Administration

Reform (improve existing practices): Securities Act; Glass-Steagall Act

Student Assignment/Homework

Have students read Section 2, "Roosevelt Seeks to Reform the System," and answer the Section 2 Review questions on paper.

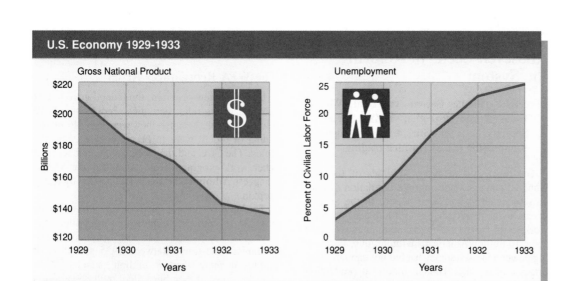

U.S. Economy 1929-1933

Answers

Main Ideas

1. FDR believed it would increase purchasing power and restore profitability to producing goods.

2. Huge farm surpluses and low prices.

3. By establishing the first regional planning authority, the Tennessee Valley Authority.

4. The NRA tried to eliminate cutthroat competition with price controls, and the WPA tried to give people buying power by employing them in federally funded jobs.

Critical Thinking

5. The CCC, CWA and PWA were all New Deal programs set up to create new jobs. **(synthesis)**

Setting Up Fair Trade Codes. The NRA helped about five hundred industries set up codes of "fair competition." Even such industries as shoulder pad manufacturers and the dog food industry took part. Each code fixed the prices to be charged for that industry's products. These **price controls** were designed to end cutthroat competition in which goods were sold for less than it cost to make them. The workweek was limited to forty hours; the minimum wage was set at thirty to forty cents an hour; and child labor was abolished. The right of workers to unionize was recognized, and a National Labor Board was set up to settle disputes.

Priming the Pump. The second part of the act set up the Public Works Administration (PWA). The PWA was to undertake **pump priming.** That is, the government would spend money to create jobs. It undertook projects that required many workers and much material in order to provide wages that would give workers buying power, thus stimulating the economy. The PWA was placed under Harold Ickes, who was also Secretary of the Interior. Honest Ickes lived up to his nickname. He moved carefully to make sure that each public works project was worthwhile and a good buy for taxpayers. Eventually, more than $4 billion was spent on some 34,000 projects including the Triborough Bridge in New York; the causeway connecting the Florida mainland and Key West; the port of Brownsville, Texas; hospitals with beds

totaling 120,000; fifty military airports; and two aircraft carriers.

SECTION 1 REVIEW

Key Terms and People

Explain the significance of: Hundred Days, Civilian Conservation Corps (CCC), Harry Hopkins, Agricultural Adjustment Administration (AAA), Tennessee Valley Authority (TVA), Home Owners Loan Corporation (HOLC), Glass-Steagall Act, National Industrial Recovery Act (NIRA), price controls, pump priming

Main Ideas

1. Why did Roosevelt consider putting people to work as the solution to the country's major problem?
2. What conditions brought about the need for the Agriculture Adjustment Act?
3. How did Congress respond to the needs to conserve and to develop the country's natural resources?
4. How did the agencies created by the National Industrial Recovery Act attempt to regulate the economy?

Critical Thinking

5. What did the Civilian Conservation Corps, the Civil Works Administration, and the Public Works Administration have in common?

Anticipate the Lesson

Ask students to evaluate the success of FDR's first Hundred Days. (Possible response: the first Hundred Days were a success because Congress passed more significant legislation during those days than it usually does in two years; legislation included job programs, emergency relief to the unemployed, aid to farmers, lower pay for government workers, and loans to homeowners.) Using the first Hundred Days as

an indicator, ask students to predict the success of Roosevelt's remaining time in office. (Possible response: Roosevelt's administration will continue to be successful in eliminating many of the causes of the depression in the U.S.)

For Discussion

Recall that the federal government began supporting cultural activities in the 1930's. Do you think that government support of the arts should continue in good times, too? Why or why not? (Possible responses: government should support the arts so that Americans can have enjoyable and productive leisure-time activities; the arts reflect the culture and education of a nation and represent its creativity, which should be encouraged.)

SECTION 2

Roosevelt Seeks to Reform the System

GLOSSARY TERMS: **Second New Deal, Works Progress Administration (WPA), Social Security Act, Securities and Exchange Commission (SEC), insider trading**

The relief and recovery activities of the first Hundred Days did not improve the nation's economy as much as had been hoped. In the area of unemployment, although 4 million persons were working for the federal government, there were still some 10 million Americans without jobs. Purchasing power had risen somewhat but not enough to lift prices a great deal. Though industrial production had increased somewhat, business people lacked the confidence to invest their surplus funds.

The congressional elections of 1934 gave the Democrats even more of a landslide than they had received in 1932. In the House they had 319 members to the Republicans' 103. In the Senate the balance was 69 to 25.

In January 1935 President Roosevelt announced a somewhat different approach to the nation's problems:

> When a man is getting over an illness, wisdom dictates not only cure of the symptoms but removal of their cause.

He recommended that the federal government shift its emphasis from relief and recovery to reform. ''I want to save our system, the capitalistic system,''

he said. The body of legislation that began in 1935 is usually called the **Second New Deal.**

The WPA Reorganizes Relief

Under the new program, the federal government reorganized its relief activities. People who were not employable because they were too old or too young or too ill were to be taken care of by the states. The CCC and the PWA were continued. All other work programs were put under the **Works Progress Administration (WPA)** headed by Harry Hopkins.

The WPA set out to create as many jobs as fast as possible. It received a budget of $5 billion, the largest sum any nation had ever spent for public welfare at one time. Between 1935 and 1943, it employed more than 8 million persons. WPA workers, most of them unskilled, built 850 airports throughout the country. They built or repaired 651,000 miles of roads and streets. They put up 110,000 libraries, schools, and hospitals. Sewing groups, in which most women workers were employed, made 300 million garments for the needy.

The WPA also found work for unemployed writers, artists, musicians, and actors. Soon post offices and other public buildings were decorated with murals. Newly formed symphony orchestras gave free public concerts and helped to make known the music of **Aaron Copland, Virgil Thomson,** and other American composers. People who had never seen a play were able to attend productions such as *Waiting for Lefty* by **Clifford Odets,** which dealt with a taxi drivers' strike, and *The Hot Mikado,* a black version of a Gilbert and Sullivan operetta. Authors who became well

Picturing History Under the Works Progress Administration, workers built and repaired thousands of miles of roads.

State the Objective

Understand why some important New Deal measures have endured.

Present the Lesson

Ask students to reread the Section for information to use in developing a chart of Roosevelt's Second New Deal programs. (See answers on page 675a.) Discuss with students their ideas on the relative success of each measure.

New Deal Legislation

The Act or Agency	The Purpose
Farm Relief and Rural Development	
Agricultural Adjustment Administration AAA (1933)	To aid farmers and to regulate crop production.
The Tennessee Valley Authority TVA (1933)	To develop the resources of the Tennessee Valley.
Rural Electrification Administration REA (1935)	To provide cheap electricity for isolated rural areas.
Business Assistance and Reform	
Emergency Banking Relief Act EBRA (1933)	To regulate bank transactions in credit, currency, foreign exchange, gold and silver.
Banking Act of 1933 (Glass-Steagall Act)	To set up the Federal Deposit Insurance Corporation.
Federal Deposit Insurance Corporation FDIC (1933)	To protect bank deposits up to $5,000. The amount now protected by the FDIC is $100,000.
National Recovery Administration NRA (1933)	To provide "codes" of fair competition and to give labor the right of collective bargaining.
Securities and Exchange Commission SEC (1934)	To supervise the stock exchanges and eliminate dishonest practices.
Public Utilities Holding Company Act (1935)	To eliminate holding companies of utilities that did not operate efficiently and economically.
Banking Act of 1935	To create a seven-member board of public officials to regulate the nation's money supply and the interest rates on loans.
Food, Drug and Cosmetic Act (1938)	To require manufacturers to list ingredients in food, drugs, and cosmetics.
Employment Projects	
Civilian Conservation Corps CCC (1933)	To provide jobs for young single males on conservation projects.
Federal Emergency Relief Act FERA (1933)	To help states provide aid for the unemployed.
Civil Works Administration CWA (1933)	To provide work even if it means "making work" in federal jobs.
Public Works Administration PWA (1933)	To create jobs in public works which would increase worker buying power and stimulate the economy.
Works Progress Administration WPA (1935)	To create as many jobs as possible as quickly as possible, from jobs in the construction industry to jobs in symphony orchestras.
National Youth Administration NYA (1935)	To provide job training for unemployed youths and part-time jobs for students in need.
Housing and Social Security	
Home Owners Loan Corporation HOLC (1933)	To give loans at low interest to home owners who could not meet mortgage payments.
Federal Housing Administration FHA (1934)	To insure loans for the building and repair of houses.
Social Security Act (1935)	To provide a pension for retired workers and their spouses and to aid the handicapped.
United States Housing Authority USHA (1937)	To provide federal loans for a nation-wide home improvement program.
Labor Relations	
National Labor Relations Act (Wagner-Connery Act of 1935)	To define "unfair labor practices" and to establish a National Labor Relations Board to settle differences between employers and employees.
Fair Labor Standards Act (1938)	To set up a national minimum hourly wage, a maximum work week and to prohibit children under sixteen from working in factories.

List the following groups on the board: elderly, banking institutions, stock market, wealthy businessmen, utility consumers. Ask students to write one or two sentences describing how each group was affected by the New Deal measures described in this Section. (Possible responses: elderly—received social security pensions and aid for the needy; banking institutions—deferred economic decisions concerning nation's money supply and interest rates to public officials; stock market—was controlled by SEC prohibition of insider trading; wealthy businessmen—paid increased rates on gifts and estates, increased tax rates, and graduated income tax for corporations; utility consumers—were protected from unfair holding companies.)

Tell students that the social security system is facing serious funding problems as fewer workers support a growing number of social security recipients. Ask students to suggest changes that might be enacted to maintain the system for future generations. (Possible response: each individual might pay into his or her own account with the stipulation that the funds not be distributed to anyone else. The government could invest the money so that the accounts earn interest.)

---

known later, such as **Nelson Algren** and **Richard Wright,** received training and help.

The WPA was efficiently and honestly run on the whole. However, it was criticized for encouraging people to vote Democratic in return for handouts. Actually, some WPA officials were guilty of shady election practices. Furthermore, many Americans did not believe the federal government should support cultural activities. They resented the fact that about 20 percent of WPA funds went into the arts instead of into construction.

Congress Begins Social Security

In 1935 the United States followed the example of other industrial nations and established a system of social insurance. The centerpiece of the **Social Security Act** was a pension system for retired workers and their spouses. Also included were death benefits and support for surviving children up to the age of eighteen. None of these provisions were tied to need. Anyone could collect. The benefits were to come out of a payroll tax paid half by workers and half by employers. The Social Security Act also established a joint federal-state unemployment insurance system and provided for aid to crippled and blind persons, the needy elderly, neglected children, and others.

Not all groups of workers were covered at that time. Farm workers and domestics, for example, were exempt. In the long run, however, the Social Security Act has probably affected the lives of more people in the United States than any other legislation passed under the New Deal.

Linking Past to Present

The effect of the Social Security program has been impressive. Thirty years ago, 35 percent of the nation's elderly had an income below the official poverty line. By 1987, as a result of Social Security benefits and supplements, that figure had dropped to just over 12 percent. Some demographers predict, however, that by the year 2020 the number of elderly people will be so large and the number of wage earners contributing to Social Security will be so small that the trust fund may become quickly depleted if provisions are not made to compensate for the changes.

The New Deal Reforms Business

Under the NIRA, the federal government had favored big business. Under the Second New Deal, more attention was given to small business.

Overseeing the Stock Market. The **Securities and Exchange Commission (SEC),** which had been established in 1934, was given the power to prevent **insider trading.** This occurred when people with inside information about companies "rigged" the stock market, that is, made prices go up or down for their own profit regardless of the real value of the stock. Placed in charge of the new SEC was Joseph P. Kennedy. The business community at first objected to government interference. However, when Richard Whitney, president of the New York Stock Exchange, was sent to prison for dishonest financial practices, insiders saw the need for a change.

Picturing History
Joseph P. Kennedy, father of John Fitzgerald Kennedy, built an investment and real estate empire using profits gained from the stock market.

Reforming Utility Companies. In 1935 about 75 percent of electric light and power companies were controlled by a dozen holding companies. Supposedly the purpose of holding companies is to provide economies in management. (See page 447.) To encourage this result rather than promote monopolies, the Public Utility Holding Company Act said that holding companies that failed to promote efficiency and savings over the next five years would be dissolved. Lobbyists for the holding companies immediately launched a million-dollar attack against this "death sentence" clause.

684

Focus on American Art

Picturing History One of the programs set up by the Works Progress Administration (WPA) was the Federal Art Project. Its purpose was to help the nation's struggling actors, artists, musicians, and writers survive the Great Depression. Between 1935 and 1943, the project employed about 5,000 artists who produced over 100,000 paintings, 18,000 pieces of sculpture, over 11,000 original prints, and 2,500 murals. Among the artists who took advantage of this opportunity were Arshile Gorky, William Gropper, Chaim Gross, Doris Lee, Jackson Pollock, and Ben Shahn. The project restored the confidence of many artists, helped American art survive a critical period in the nation's history, and brought about a new relationship between the artist and the community.

The dynamic quality of WPA murals can be seen in this panel from William Gropper's *Construction of a Dam.*

Arshile Gorky, an Armenian immigrant who brought European modernism to American painting, stands beside one of his murals.

Chaim Gross created this mahogany wood carving.

Doris Lee drew this sketch, entitled *General Store and Post Office,* for a mural in the headquarters of the Post Office Department in Washington, D.C.

Student Assignment/Homework

Have students read Section 3, "The New Deal Comes Under Attack," and complete Chapter 27, Section 3 Daily Activity.

SECTION 3
Core Lesson

Anticipate the Lesson

Discuss with students Chapter 27, Section 3 Daily Activity. Ask students why FDR was willing to risk massive opposition, even from his own party, in order to pass his "court-packing bill." (Possible response: because he thought it was the only way that he could get the Supreme Court to act in his favor.)

SECTION 2 REVIEW

Answers

Main Ideas

1. The goal of the Second New Deal was to reform capitalism. The goal of the New Deal was to provide recovery and relief.

2. To create as many jobs as fast as possible.

3. That it encouraged people to vote Democratic in exchange for handouts and that it spent too much money on the arts.

4. By establishing that the rich should carry a heavier tax burden than the poor.

5. By giving the power to make major economic decisions to public officials instead of to private bankers.

Critical Thinking

6. The act established at least partial government responsibility for the welfare of the elderly, the poor, and the handicapped. **(application)**

They did not succeed, but enforcing the act proved difficult.

Taxing the Wealthy. The Revenue Act of 1935 was an attempt to break up large accumulations of wealth. It increased the rates of gift and estate taxes. It increased the tax rates for people with large incomes. In addition, it provided for a graduated corporate income tax that favored small businesses over large ones. Some described the act as "soaking the rich," although most rich people found ways to avoid paying the highest rates. For a time the act established the idea that the well-to-do should carry a distinctly heavier tax burden than the poor.

Controlling Banks. The Banking Act of 1935 replaced the old Federal Reserve Board with a seven-member board of governors to be appointed by the President for fourteen-year terms. The board was given the power to decide whether to raise or to lower the nation's money supply by printing more or less paper money. It was also given the power to raise or to lower interest rates, or the cost of borrowing money. As a result, economic decisions that until then had been made by private bankers were now made by public officials.

SECTION 2 REVIEW

Key Terms and People

Explain the significance of: Second New Deal, Works Progress Administration (WPA), Aaron Copland, Virgil Thomson, Clifford Odets, Nelson Algren, Richard Wright, Social Security Act, Securities and Exchange Commission (SEC), insider trading

Main Ideas

1. How did the goal of the Second New Deal differ from that of the First New Deal?
2. What was the purpose of the Works Progress Administration (WPA)?
3. What were the main criticisms of the WPA?
4. How did the Revenue Act of 1935 change the structure of the American income tax system?
5. How did the Banking Act of 1935 change banking practices in the United States?

Critical Thinking

6. What present-day American principle was firmly established by the Social Security Act?

SECTION 3

The New Deal Comes Under Attack

GLOSSARY TERMS: **Wagner Act, National Labor Relations Board (NLRB), Fair Labor Standards Act, parity, court-packing bill**

As the New Deal struggled with the nation's economic problems, criticisms of its activities grew stronger and stronger. Some came from liberals on the left who believed that the New Deal was not doing enough to correct the evils of capitalism. Criticism also came from conservatives on the right who believed that FDR was antibusiness and was leading the nation into socialism or even into communism. (See page 608.) Roosevelt's opponents complained to their congressmen. Some brought suit against the government.

The Court Declares NIRA Unconstitutional

In 1935 and 1936 the Supreme Court handed down decisions that eliminated certain New Deal agencies. The first decision came in the case of *Schechter Poultry Corporation* v. *United States,* otherwise known as the "sick chicken" case. It involved a Brooklyn poultry corporation that supposedly sold an unfit chicken to a butcher. The Court declared that Congressional regulation of interstate commerce did not apply to a New York poultry business. In deciding this case the Court ruled that the National Industrial Recovery Act was unconstitutional for two reasons: (1) it gave legislative powers to the executive branch of government, and (2) some of the industry codes covered business that took place entirely within a state, whereas the federal government has power to regulate commerce between states only.

As a result of the Court's decision, the labor provisions of the NIRA likewise were no longer in effect. Congress then passed the National Labor Relations Act, more commonly known as the **Wagner Act** after its sponsor, Senator Robert F. Wagner of New York. The act reversed the attitude of the federal government toward collective bargaining. Instead of supporting employers, the federal government was now on the side of unions.

The Wagner Act said that employers had to

State the Objective

Understand why the New Deal was criticized
by people from both ends of the political spectrum.

Picturing History Senator Robert F. Wagner sponsored
the National Labor Relations Act, which stimulated the
growth of labor unions and controlled the power of corporations. Wagner was noted for his investigations of
conditions in factories.

bargain with their workers. It listed unfair labor
practices that companies could not follow. Among
these were threatening workers, firing union members, and interfering with union organizing efforts.
The act also set up the **National Labor Relations
Board (NLRB)** to hear testimony about unfair
practices and to hold elections among workers to
find out if they wished to be represented by a
union.

To replace that part of the NIRA that dealt with
wages and hours, Congress in 1938 passed the **Fair
Labor Standards Act.** For the first time, there was
a national minimum hourly rate for wages: twenty-
five cents an hour at first, forty cents an hour in two
years. There was also a national maximum workweek: forty-four hours to begin with, forty hours in
two years. Those under age sixteen were banned
from factory work (age eighteen if the work was
hazardous).

The Court Declares AAA Unconstitutional

In the 1936 case of *United States* v. *Butler,* the
Supreme Court struck down the Agricultural Adjustment Act. It ruled that the processing tax out of
which farmers were paid to restrict production was
not a tax at all. It was a way of regulating agriculture—
and that went beyond the proper powers of Congress.

Congress responded at first by passing a law
based on conservation. The law provided for government payments to farmers who planted crops
and grasses that enriched the soil instead of commercial crops that took nutrients out of the soil.
Then in 1938 Congress passed a new Agricultural
Adjustment Act, which the Supreme Court later
declared constitutional.

The new act worked like this: If two-thirds of the
farmers in a district agreed, each was given a
certain quota of acres to plant in staple crops. If a
farmer produced a surplus, it was no longer destroyed. However, it could not be put on the market
because that would cause prices to drop. So the
AAA kept the surplus in storage. Meanwhile, it
lent the farmer money for living expenses.

Under the act, farmers were supposed to receive
a fair price for their crops. What was considered a
fair price? It was one that gave farmers the same
purchasing power they had between 1910 and
1914. That period was considered to be the last one
during which farmers got a fair price for their
goods. Another name for this fair price was **parity.**
(The word *parity* means equal to or equivalent to.)
When prices reached parity, farmers sold their
stored crops and repaid their loans to the government. If the market price remained below parity,
farmers did not pay back the loans, and the
government kept the crops in storage.

The Liberty League Attacks the New Deal

By the mid-1930's, the air was filled with
charges that the New Deal was endangering the
Constitution and slowly establishing a dictatorship.
The charges were made by an organization called
the **Liberty League.** Although it invited all classes
of people to join, many of its members were rich
industrialists, bankers, and corporation lawyers.
Ironically, Alfred E. Smith, the 1928 Democratic
Presidential candidate, belonged, but former President Hoover refused to join.

The kindest thing the Liberty League called FDR

Have students read and discuss Chapter 27, Section 1 Enrichment Activity. Divide the class into small groups to discuss and list the criticisms of FDR and his New Deal. Have group leaders produce a class list on the board.

Criticisms of FDR

- Supreme Court declared National Industrial Recovery Act and Agricultural Adjustment Act unconstitutional.
- Liberty League called FDR a "traitor to his class"; members were mostly well-to-do and had little political influence.
- Upton Sinclair, author, called for higher income and inheritance taxes and fifty-dollar pensions for elderly; he ran for governor of California.
- Dr. Francis E. Townsend, physician and California health officer, called for $200 a month income for elderly.
- Father Coughlin, Catholic priest, originally supported FDR, but later attacked "international bankers"; he formed the National Union for Social Justice.
- Senator Huey P. Long, governor of Louisiana, championed the poor against corporate giants; he introduced "Share Our Wealth."

Have students refer to the list as they study this Section.

---

was a "traitor to his class," that is, to the well-born and the well-to-do. The League was no real threat politically, however. As one observer said, its slogans had appeal only "to anyone with an income of a hundred thousand dollars a year."

Extremists Voice Their Opposition

Another challenge to the New Deal came from those who said it was not doing enough for the country. Extremists such as Upton Sinclair, Dr. Francis Townsend, Father Charles Coughlin, and Senator Huey Long were quick to voice their opposition.

Upton Sinclair. A leading muckraker of the Progressive Era, **Upton Sinclair** helped bring about passage of the first Federal Meat Inspection Act with his novel *The Jungle.* (See Chapter 21.) In the 1930's he wrote a book called *I, Governor of California, and How I Ended Poverty.* This novel helped him win the Democratic nomination for governor of that state in 1934. In his campaign, Sinclair called for higher income and inheritance taxes, fifty-dollar-a-month pensions for the elderly, and consumer cooperatives. Sinclair lost. The real significance of the election, however, was that the Republicans used a professional public relations firm for the first time. Since then, the practice has become common.

Dr. Francis Townsend. When Sinclair lost his election bid, many of his followers turned to Dr. **Francis Townsend.** Townsend was a South Dakota physician who had become an assistant health officer in Long Beach, California. Many of the town's residents were retired farmers and small business people, impoverished by the depression. Dr. Townsend devised a plan that would pay everyone over sixty years of age $200 a month. The only requirement was that the entire amount be spent within thirty days. This was to keep money circulating, which in turn would keep business healthy. The pensions were to be paid for by a 2 percent tax on business transactions. A bill to set up the plan was defeated in Congress. However, Townsend's movement helped to push through the Social Security Act.

Father Coughlin. A more startling voice than Townsend's was that of the Reverend **Charles Coughlin,** a Catholic priest from the Detroit suburb of Royal Oak. Even before the depression

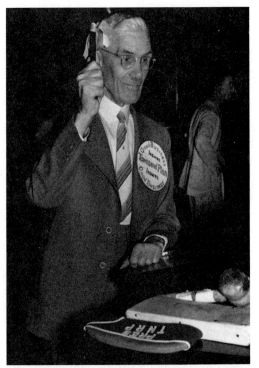

Picturing History Dr. Francis E. Townsend addresses a convention in Indianapolis, Indiana, to secure support of his pension plan. Congress voted against a version of the plan in 1939.

began, Father Coughlin was delivering Sunday afternoon sermons over a local radio station. As his audience grew, the talks moved from religious to social and political topics. Other stations picked up the broadcasts, and soon they were being carried nationwide. By 1934 some ten million persons were listening to Father Coughlin each week and were sending him half a million dollars a year.

Father Coughlin had originally supported FDR, telling his listeners that it was "Roosevelt or ruin." Before long, however, he was attacking "international bankers." In late 1934 he formed the National Union for Social Justice, which came out for nationalizing banks, public utilities, and natural resources. As time went on, it became clear that Father Coughlin was strongly anti-Semitic, or prejudiced against Jews. Eventually, his superiors in the Roman Catholic Church made him stop broadcasting.

Senator Huey Long. The most able, and therefore potentially the most dangerous, of the New

688

Picturing History Huey P. Long, known as the Kingfish, headed a powerful political organization in Louisiana. As senator, Long called for economic relief, including a guaranteed income for every American family.

Deal's extremist foes was Senator **Huey Long** of Louisiana. Starting as a dirt-poor salesman of patent medicines, Long studied law and was soon skillfully fighting cases against the oil and utility companies that controlled the state. He was an extremely effective speaker, although his loud clothes—orchid shirts, pink ties, and brown and white shoes—startled some people. His championship of the poor against corporate giants made him a hero to many people, and in 1928 he was elected governor. He gave the state badly needed schools, roads, bridges, and hospitals. He provided free textbooks for public school students and spent lavishly on the state university, providing it with the Sugar Bowl football stadium and "the best team that money could buy." In 1930 the people of Louisiana sent him to the United States Senate.

The Kingfish, as Long was called, spent the next few years building a personal political machine in his home state and eyeing the Presidency. In 1934 he introduced a nationwide social program called Share the Wealth. Its motto was Every Man a King,

and its key provision was a $5,000 guaranteed annual income for every family in the United States. The money for this program was to be raised by taking over the wealth of the millionaires and by dividing up some of the nation's land and mineral treasures. According to the Kingfish, every American family was entitled to own a house, an automobile, and a radio.

At the height of his popularity, Long was shot to death in the statehouse at Baton Rouge. The lone killer was gunned down on the spot by the senator's bodyguards, and Long's family continued to dominate Louisiana politics for many years.

Until his death, Long was Roosevelt's greatest political threat. Though unquestionably dictatorial, he was intelligent, colorful, and lively. He was also unique among Southern politicians of his time and type—he appeared to be without racial prejudice. He said he wanted black people to share the wealth and be kings, too.

In 1936 Roosevelt Wins Again

"America is in peril. We invite all Americans, [regardless] of party, to join us in defense of American institutions." So began the 1936 Republican platform. To lead the campaign, the Republicans nominated Alfred M. Landon, the able governor of Kansas, and Frank Knox, a Chicago newspaper publisher. During the campaign, Landon was called a Kansas Coolidge because he had balanced his state's budget. Actually, both he and Knox were Progressives who had supported Theodore Roosevelt's Bull Moose campaign.

Picturing History Republican Alfred Landon, governor of Kansas, won only Maine and Vermont in the 1936 Presidential election.

Guided Practice

Tell students that in many ways criticism of the New Deal is similar to recent criticism of the strength and spending of the federal government. Ask students to suggest ways in which government spending might be cut. What agencies or programs do they think should not be cut? (Ways to cut spending might include: waste in all areas of government could be greatly reduced. Programs that should not be cut might include: those that serve the needy, children, and elderly.)

Picturing History Roosevelt's Supreme Court portrayed as Nine Old Men. From left to right are Justices Roberts, Butler, Brandeis, and Van Devanter; Chief Justice Hughes; Justices McReynolds, Sutherland, Stone, and Cardozo.

For Discussion
What effect did FDR's attempted "court-packing" have on his image? How might it have altered your opinion of him? (Possible responses: even some of FDR's own party members opposed him; some might believe the "court-packing" to be unethical; others might admire and support FDR for doing what was necessary to carry out programs he felt would benefit those in need.)

Landon probably would have continued many New Deal programs.

Roosevelt and Garner were renominated by the Democrats. In his acceptance speech, Roosevelt told his listeners that "to some generations much is given. Of other generations much is expected. This generation of Americans has a rendezvous with destiny." On that note, he kicked off a campaign directed not against his Republican opponent but

Presidential Election, 1936

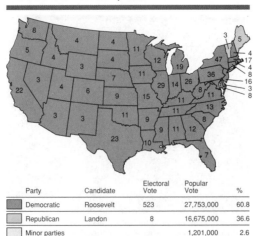

Party	Candidate	Electoral Vote	Popular Vote	%
Democratic	Roosevelt	523	27,753,000	60.8
Republican	Landon	8	16,675,000	36.6
Minor parties			1,201,000	2.6

531 Total Electoral Vote

against the Liberty League. The strongest issue raised against Roosevelt was that 9 million people were still unemployed. He countered by asking campaign crowds, "Are you better off than you were four years ago?" The crowds roared back, "Yes."

On election day, FDR carried every state except Maine and Vermont. The popular vote was 27.7 million to 16.6 million, while the electoral vote was 523 to 8. The Democratic congressional majority stood at 331 to 89 in the House and 76 to 16 in the Senate. This landslide victory represented the first time that most African Americans voted Democratic rather than Republican. Finally, it represented the first time that labor unions gave their united support to a single candidate—Roosevelt—instead of dividing their votes between the major parties.

FDR Attempts to Pack the Supreme Court

In his second inaugural address, Roosevelt spoke about the need for more reform. He pointed out that "one-third of a nation [was still] ill-housed, ill-clad, ill-nourished." He promised to do something about it. Instead of proposing new economic legislation, however, Roosevelt asked Congress to reorganize the federal judiciary.

690

Assign Independent Practice

Divide the class into small groups. Have each group create a poster-sized political cartoon showing the successes or failures of the New Deal. Display the posters in the classroom.

Student Assignment/Homework

Have students read Section 4, "Many Changes Occur During the New Deal," and answer Section 4 Review questions on paper.

Roosevelt's message to Congress claimed that federal courts could not keep up with their case loads, that more judges were needed, and that part of the problem was that too many judges were "aged or infirm." He proposed that federal judges retire within six months after reaching the age of seventy. If they did not, then the President should have the power to appoint additional judges.

This measure was obviously aimed at the Supreme Court. Since six of its justices were seventy years old or older, Roosevelt would be able to enlarge it to fifteen members. He had not yet had the opportunity to appoint a single Supreme Court justice. Undoubtedly, he believed that the Court had been too conservative in knocking down the NIRA, the AAA, and other New Deal measures. What if it declared the Social Security Act and the National Labor Relations Act unconstitutional as well?

The President's bill set off a storm of protest in Congress and in the newspapers. Cries about "separation of powers" and "independence of the judiciary" were heard from all sides. People began calling the measures a **"court-packing bill"** that would fill the Supreme Court with justices who would agree with FDR's personal economic ideas. FDR replied that the Nine Old Men were already deciding cases on the basis of their personal economic ideas.

The bill Roosevelt wanted never got through Congress. In the meantime, however, several changes took place. Two Supreme Court justices shifted their votes in favor of giving the federal government power to regulate the economy. In a series of five-to-four decisions, the Court declared both the Social Security Act and the National Labor Relations Act constitutional. Then one of the older, more conservative justices retired. That opened the way for the President to appoint New Dealer Hugo L. Black of Alabama to the Court.

In the end, Roosevelt got the kind of Supreme Court he wanted. He appointed seven justices in the next four years. However, the attempt to pack the Court turned out to be a serious political mistake. It antagonized many congressmen and others who believed that the President had been dictatorial. It also strengthened opposition to the New Deal. As a result, the 1938 congressional elections brought into office a number of conservative southern Democrats as well as many more Republicans. After the second Agricultural Adjustment Act and the Fair Labor Standards Act—both already described—no more major New Deal legislation was passed. By 1939 the New Deal, for all practical purposes, was over.

SECTION 3 REVIEW

Key Terms and People

Explain the significance of: *Schechter Poultry Corporation* v. *United States,* Wagner Act, National Labor Relations Board (NLRB), Fair Labor Standards Act, *United States* v. *Butler,* parity, Liberty League, Upton Sinclair, Francis Townsend, Charles Coughlin, Huey Long, court-packing bill

Main Ideas

1. How did Supreme Court rulings in 1935 and 1936 affect New Deal legislation?
2. How did Congress respond to these court rulings?
3. What was the basis for the political right's criticism of the New Deal?
4. In what ways was the New Deal considered a failure by people like Sinclair, Townsend, and Long?
5. What was Roosevelt's main purpose in trying to reorganize the federal judiciary?

Critical Thinking

6. Why was it remarkable that Roosevelt could not get Congress to pass his judicial reorganization bill?

Picturing History
Senator Hugo L. Black, after his confirmation as Supreme Court justice.

spend our money; the media greatly influences
the way people look at the world.)

Anticipate the Lesson

Ask students to state reasons for the great
number of changes that took place in the way
Americans lived in the 1930's. (Possible responses: the Great Depression; New Deal legislation; developments in the radio and film
industries.) Ask students to consider whether
government legislation, the economy, and the
media still influence our way of life. (Possible
responses: they influence how we make and
spend our money; the media greatly influences
the way people look at the world.)

SECTION 4

Many Changes Occur During the New Deal

GLOSSARY TERMS: **Committee for Industrial Organization (CIO), sit-down strike, Indian Reorganization Act**

The 1930's saw a number of changes in the way Americans lived. Some were direct results of New Deal legislation. Others were brought on by the depression. Still others were outgrowths of developments in radio and film that had begun in earlier decades.

Labor Unions Grow

Until the 1930's, organized labor mostly meant the craft unions that made up the American Federation of Labor. However, a number of labor leaders considered the AFL's attitude old-fashioned. They wanted to organize industrial unions, particularly in such mass-production industries as automobiles, steel, textiles, and rubber.

After the Wagner Act was passed in 1935, John L. Lewis of the United Mine Workers Union, along with David Dubinsky of the International Ladies Garment Workers Union, Sidney Hillman of the Amalgamated Clothing Workers, Philip Murray of the United Steelworkers, and Walter P. Reuther of the United Automobile Workers, among others,

formed the **Committee for Industrial Organization (CIO).** The CIO began signing up unskilled and semiskilled workers as fast as it could, and within two years it had succeeded in gaining union recognition in the steel and automobile industries. Among the techniques the CIO used was the **sit-down strike.** Instead of walking off their jobs, workers remained inside the plant but did not work. This prevented the plant owners from carrying on production with strikebreakers.

The sit-down strike was declared unconstitutional in 1939. By that time the CIO was no longer part of the AFL. Its organizational success had caused jealousy among the older, more traditional unions. Also, John L. Lewis did not like AFL president William Green, claiming that he was only a figurehead and did not actively work for the union. In 1937 the AFL expelled the CIO unions. Nevertheless, the CIO went ahead with their organizing drives and by 1938 claimed 4 million members. That same year the CIO changed its name (but not its initials) to the Congress of Industrial Organizations. The split in the labor movement lasted until the AFL and the CIO combined again in 1955.

Minorities Receive More Attention

Of course, minority groups in the United States suffered greatly from the depression. During the 1930's, however, the position of minorities improved somewhat.

Picturing History Some United Auto Workers stage the first successful sit-down strike against General Motors in Flint, Michigan, in 1937.

Picturing History
Marian Anderson gives a concert on the steps of the Lincoln Memorial, Washington, D.C., April 9, 1939.

Historical Sidelights
• Black track star Jesse Owens won three gold medals in the 1936 Olympics in Nazi Germany. • Wiley Post made the first solo flight around the world from July 15 to July 22, 1933, completing a distance of 15,596 miles in seven days, eighteen hours, and forty-nine minutes, breaking the world record.

African Americans. African Americans benefited from New Deal relief measures. Officially, these measures were color blind, that is, they applied equally to whites and to blacks. The CCC and WPA, for instance, gave help to blacks. There also were a number of black administrators in New Deal agencies. For example, Secretary of the Interior Ickes, who had been president of the Chicago NAACP, hired William Hastie, later the governor of the Virgin Islands and an appeals court judge. He also hired Robert Weaver, who went on to become the first Secretary of Housing and Urban Development when he was appointed to that position by President Johnson in 1965. FDR often sought the opinions of highly placed black government workers, who were sometimes referred to as the **Black Cabinet.**

The new CIO unions included black members, although most AFL unions did not. The Supreme Court, too—in 1932 and 1934 cases—upheld the right of accused African Americans to have competent legal advice and to be tried by juries that included African Americans.

In those years, Washington, D.C., was still a Jim Crow town. (See page 398.) President and Mrs. Roosevelt often trampled on the feelings of its white inhabitants by entertaining distinguished black people at the White House. Eleanor Roosevelt's most spectacular step in recognizing black achievement involved the singer **Marian Anderson.** In 1939 the Daughters of the American Revolution refused Anderson the use of Constitution Hall in Washington, D.C., for a concert because of her color. Eleanor Roosevelt publicly resigned from the organization and arranged for the concert to be given at the Lincoln Memorial.

American Indians. The year 1924 had been a turning point for American Indians. They won full citizenship in acknowledgment of their services to the nation during World War I. In 1933 President Roosevelt appointed **John Collier,** a former officer of the American Indian Defense Organization, to be Commissioner of Indian Affairs. Collier made several suggestions that became part of the **Indian Reorganization Act** of 1934.

The act strengthened the Pueblo Indians' claims to their ancient lands. It ended the allotment policy that had been established by the Dawes Act of 1887 under which parts of reservations were granted to individual Indians. It also tried to restore reservation land to tribal authority. Indians were now allowed to enter court. The act provided for practical education for Indians, including farming, animal husbandry, soil conservation, and marketing.

Indians who wanted to return to traditional tribal life were pleased with the act. Those who had become more "Americanized," however, felt that

Picturing History Comedians George Burns and Gracie Allen (right) satirized domestic life of the 1930's in their radio shows. By 1931, most Americans owned a radio.

the act would make it harder for Indians to improve themselves economically.

Mexican Americans. Like African Americans and other minorities, Mexican Americans suffered more from the depression than did the general population. Since 1920 they had been moving in great numbers to Texas, California, and other parts of the Southwest, increasing the Hispanic population in the region. Mexican Americans worked most often as farm laborers, an occupation less well protected by federal and state laws than other kinds of work. When the dust bowl sent thousands of ruined farmers to California, Mexican Americans found it harder than ever to make a living there. Competition among workers drove some farm wages as low as nine cents an hour. Efforts to unionize were often met with legal action and guns. The CCC and WPA were helpful to some Mexican Americans, but migrant workers who had no permanent address could not qualify for these programs.

Family Life Includes Entertainment

The typical middle-class family of 1936 was not on relief. The family consisted of two adults and their two children. The husband worked outside the home, and the wife was a homemaker. The family lived in a six-room house or in a four-room apartment. Fewer people were getting married. The rate fell from 10.14 marriages per thousand people in 1929 to 7.8 per thousand in 1932. The birthrate fell from nineteen births per thousand couples in 1929 to 16.5 per thousand in 1933. Babies were expensive. As a result of the depression, young families were distinctly smaller than ever before.

The main source of amusement was the radio. By 1931, 29 million families, or 85 percent of the population, owned radios. In the early afternoon, there were serials portraying romantic adventure and small-town life such as "The Romance of Helen Trent," "The Guiding Light," and "Ma Perkins." The main characters in these stories were women. Later in the afternoon, there were adven-

694

Check for Understanding
Call on individual students to read their answers to Section 4 Review questions.

Guided Practice
Remind students that the New Deal influenced the voting patterns, winning over many black and middle class white voters to the Democratic party. Thus, the New Deal changed a pattern that had existed since the Civil War. Ask students to suggest reasons why the Democrats were successful at winning over so many voters. (Possible response: the New Deal administration addressed the special needs of certain groups.)

ture stories for children, including "Little Orphan Annie," "The Green Hornet," and "The Lone Ranger." The evening had excellent dramas and variety programs featuring such stars as Bob Hope, Orson Welles, Eddie Cantor, Jack Benny, and George Burns and Gracie Allen.

For outside entertainment, the family usually went to a movie. Stars such as Greta Garbo, Clark Gable, Fred Astaire and Ginger Rogers, Marlene Dietrich, and Loretta Young played in dramas and musicals that reflected a life of sophistication and luxury. This was done deliberately, because people in pinched economic circumstances got vicarious, or second-hand, pleasure in watching the make-believe frolics on the silver screen.

Big bands were big business in the 1930's. By 1935 Benny Goodman was known as the King of Swing, and by 1939 Glenn Miller had achieved world fame as a big band leader.

Linking Past to Present

Some—but not all—aspects of family life have changed since the depression. The most significant change in the past fifty years is the increase in single-parent families. A higher divorce rate and an increase in births to unwed teenage mothers are the driving forces behind this shift. According to the National Center for Health Statistics, 25.7 percent of all births in the United States in 1988 were to unmarried women. In urban areas in the 1980's, one in four American children was being raised by a single parent. Families still find babies are expensive, however. The period from 1960 to 1987 showed a drop in the United States birth rate from 23.7 per thousand to 15.7 per thousand.

Women Make Their Mark

In the 1930's women were the most popular movie stars. Names like Janet Gaynor, Joan Crawford, and Bette Davis attracted moviegoers nationwide. (That was the reverse of the 1960's and early 1970's, when the most popular stars were men.) In the thirties, women were competing successfully with men in the literary field. Margaret Mitchell wrote *Gone with the Wind*, which sold over 12

million copies and won the Pulitzer Prize for literature in 1937. (See page 383.) Other novelists were Pearl Buck and Edna Ferber. (See page 413.) Famous short story writers included Dorothy Parker and Katherine Anne Porter. Dorothy Thompson was a celebrated journalist. Playwright Lillian Hellman wrote some of the most memorable plays to appear on Broadway, and she also wrote movies.

Male-dominated fields were also opening up for women. Amelia Earhart became the first female passenger on a transatlantic flight in 1928. In 1932 she flew alone across the Atlantic. In 1937, while attempting an around-the-world flight, she was lost in the Pacific. In the 1932 Olympics, Mildred "Babe" Didrikson won two gold medals and one silver medal in track and field events. In the field of anthropology, Ruth Benedict became internationally known for her work. Margaret Mead, a student of Benedict, won international acclaim with her first work, *Coming of Age in Samoa*. Maud Slye did cancer research at the Rockefeller Foundation, while Florence Sabin made valuable discoveries concerning blood and bone marrow. Ruth Bryan Owen, a former member of Congress, served as

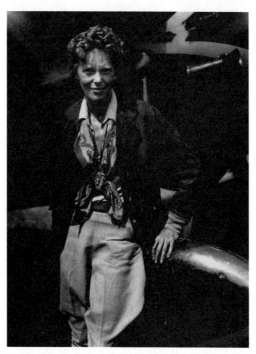

Picturing History Amelia Earhart was the first woman to receive a pilot's license. Although her fate is still a mystery, her courage is unquestionable.

For Discussion
To what extent did the New Deal alter the free enterprise system? Do you think this legislation was positive or negative? (Possible response: positive—provided for insurance on savings; it raised minimum wage; gave workers the right to unionize.)

Ask students to list in order of importance first the successes and then the failures of the New Deal. (The order may vary somewhat.)

Successes: raised income of farmers and workers; helped preserve natural resources; provided a cushion for sick and aged; enabled unions to organize; added to material wealth of nation; eliminated business excesses; guaranteed the safety of bank deposits; reduced unemployment.

Failures: raised national debt; doubled federal bureaucracy; failed to increase private business activity; failed to reduce unemployment below 7.5 million.

Student Assignment/Homework

Have students complete Chapter 27 Test on paper. Divide the class into small groups to review the answers.

Concluding the Chapter

After they complete the chapter, have students write an essay specifying what they consider to be the three most significant pieces of New Deal legislation. Students should defend their choices with facts. (Essays might include: establishment of Federal Deposit Insurance Corporation to protect bank deposits; establishment of Securities and Exchange Commission to regulate stock market.) Have several students read their essays to the class.

SECTION 4 REVIEW

Answers

Main Ideas

1. CIO members were unskilled and semiskilled industrial laborers. AFL members were skilled craft laborers.

2. New Deal relief measures were intended to be color blind; CIO unions admitted blacks; FDR appointed black administrators and sought prominent blacks' advice; court rulings recognized rights of blacks.

3. In most depression-era families, the father was employed outside the home while the mother was a homemaker with two children; the family was not on relief, and typically spent leisure time listening to the radio, attending movies, and dancing to big-band music.

4. Women became more active in literature and the arts; they also made significant contributions in fields formerly dominated by males.

Critical Thinking

5. Students who believe the effects of the New Deal were primarily positive should argue in support of principles such as government responsibility for those who cannot care for themselves. Students arguing against the legacy of the New Deal should point out the burdens such as enormous government debt and bureaucracy. **(evaluation)**

696

ambassador to Denmark. Mary McLeod Bethune, founder of Bethune-Cookman College in Florida, gave the Roosevelts advice on the needs and interests of African Americans. Margaret Bourke-White and Dorothea Lange earned recognition in the new art form of photography.

Picturing History Mary McLeod Bethune was appointed to various government posts by Presidents Coolidge, Hoover, Roosevelt, and Truman. She was the first African American woman to head a federal agency.

Historians Disagree About the New Deal

The New Deal was a daring experiment about which historians are still divided. On the one hand, it raised the incomes of farmers and workers, helped preserve natural resources, provided a cushion for the sick and aged, enabled unions to organize, and added to the material wealth of the nation. It eliminated business excesses, guaranteed the safety of bank deposits, and reduced unemployment. On the other hand, it raised the national debt, doubled the federal bureaucracy, and failed to increase private business activity. Despite the CCC and the WPA, in 1940 there were still 7.5 million people without jobs. Economically, the New Deal was a mixed success. The real end of the Great Depression was brought about by World War II.

Politically, however, the New Deal is generally considered a rousing success. In the 1930's, many Americans believed that government participation in the economic life of a nation inevitably led to socialism, communism, or some form of dictatorship. They believed that there was no middle ground between a more-or-less unregulated capitalism and a strictly regimented society. They saw, with fear and loathing, such regimented societies developing on the European continent and already established in the Soviet Union. The New Deal showed Americans that it was possible to provide a certain amount of economic security without destroying fundamental political freedoms. By helping those who needed aid, while at the same time turning back demands for more radical measures, the New Deal probably saved both democracy and the free enterprise system.

The New Deal also marked a shift in the relationship between the federal government and the American people. In the Progressive Era, the role of the federal government had been that of an economic regulator. As a result of the New Deal, the federal government began to play a more active part in the economy. For better or for worse, most Americans now believe that a government is responsible for the economic welfare of its people.

SECTION 4 REVIEW

Key Terms and People

Explain the significance of: Committee for Industrial Organization (CIO), sit-down strike, Black Cabinet, Marian Anderson, John Collier, Indian Reorganization Act

Main Ideas

1. In what way did the members of the Committee for Industrial Organization (CIO) differ from those of the American Federation of Labor (AFL)?
2. How did the position of African Americans improve under the Roosevelt administration?
3. What was the status of the average middle-class family during the depression?
4. How did the role of women change during the depression?

Critical Thinking

5. Did the good things that the New Deal accomplished offset the bad things that it caused? Explain.

State the Objective

Understand how the Tennessee Valley Authority shaped the environment of the Tennessee River Valley.

Focus on Geography

The Tennessee Valley Authority

The Geographic Theme of Human-Environment Interactions

Throughout the history of the United States, people have changed their environments for a variety of reasons. Economic, aesthetic, and cultural factors have all played a part in shaping the American landscape. Many of these changes have improved the natural setting, while others have destroyed it. The story of the Tennessee Valley Authority (TVA) is a story of people improving their environment. A great American river, the Tennessee, provides the setting, and the people who have lived in its valley play the major roles.

The River's Location. As you can see from the map on the next page, the Tennessee River is formed by a number of rivers that begin in the Great Smoky Mountains and the Blue Ridge Mountains. These smaller rivers flow into a valley, where they merge to form the powerful Tennessee. The main river follows the valley to Chattanooga, where it turns west and cuts through the southern end of the Appalachian Plateau in a deep gorge. Then it flows northwest and joins the Ohio River. The river basin covers parts of seven states and extends for about forty thousand square miles.

The River Controls the People. For years the people living in "the Valley"—as they call it—accepted annual floods as a way of life. Until the 1930's the river was wandering and unpredictable. Farm fields in the valley had grown old and no longer produced good crops. Heavy rains on steep slopes had caused soil erosion, and the excess water frequently choked the river, causing it to

Picturing History Norris Dam, located on a branch of the Tennessee River in eastern Tennessee, is one of many dams that were constructed by the Tennessee Valley Authority (TVA).

Present the Lesson

On the board write the heading Tennessee Valley Authority. Underneath make two columns—Purpose and Consequences. Ask students to identify the purpose of the TVA and some of the social and economic consequences that resulted from the implementation of the TVA program. Ask several students to write their responses on the board in the appropriate columns. (Possible responses: Purpose—to control flooding; to improve navigation; to generate power; to reforest the valley. Consequences—millions of acres were returned to cultivation; a 625 mile waterway was created for shipping; new water power attracted plants, which produce food, paper, aluminum, and chemicals, and thus create employment opportunities in the area; the amount of timber in the area doubled after 1933; the threat of malaria declined; the urban areas in the valley grew.)

Ask students whether they think the Tennessee Valley would be as prosperous as it is today without the TVA. Students should give reasons for their responses. (Possible responses: yes—industry or state and local governments or some combination of these groups might have achieved much the same thing. No—the area was so depressed socially and economically that it required a broad-based federal program for recovery; the U.S could achieve what individual states and governments could not have done.)

Map Skills

Seven • People built dams to control their environment in this case to control rivers and eliminate severe flooding.

flood. At other times, lack of water kept the river too low for navigation.

Adding to the problems caused by the forces of nature were the problems caused by people's misuse of natural resources. Uncoordinated and short-sighted timber harvesting had depleted the surrounding forests, and the barren lands promoted soil erosion. Also, poor farm management and farming practices further damaged the soil.

By 1933 the Tennessee Valley had become synonymous with poverty. The average income and farm production per person was only two-fifths of the national average. Only three of every one hundred farms had electricity. The incidence of malaria and vitamin deficiency was high. Farmers in the region were generally in debt, and their families were undernourished. There was little manufacturing and, consequently, few related types of employment opportunities. In spite of a population of over two million, the urban centers were few. Those that did exist were relatively small and economically depressed. The people of the Tennessee Valley had become victims of a river that controlled their lives.

The People Control the River. For more than a hundred years, engineers had discussed possible solutions to the problems created by the Tennessee River. Economists and geographers had struggled with questions such as how to harvest the vast energy of the river, how to correct the damage that had been done to the landscape, and how to make the river work for the people instead of against them. In the end, however, it was the politicians who made the final decision to control the river by creating the Tennessee Valley Authority.

The Tennessee Valley Act of 1933 assigned six important tasks to the TVA: to control flooding, to improve navigation, to improve the use of land, to develop electric power facilities, to reforest the valley where necessary, and to improve the socioeconomic conditions of the people. This project was a massive attempt on the part of one segment of the American people to control their environment.

The Tennessee Valley Today. The TVA consists of nine major dams on the Tennessee River and eighteen smaller dams on its tributaries. The nine major dams are multipurpose. In addition to storing

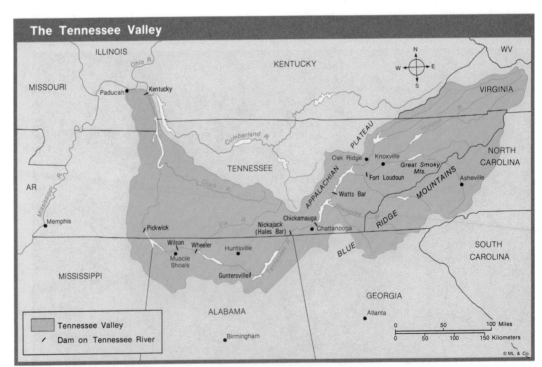

The Tennessee Valley

Tennessee Valley
/ Dam on Tennessee River

Map Skills **Location** How many states are part of the Tennessee Valley region?
Human-Environment Interactions What evidence of human-environment interaction do you see on the map?

Picturing History This photograph shows the construction of Wilson Dam, built across Muscle Shoals of the Tennessee River. At the time this dam was built, it was the largest power navigation effort ever attempted.

water, they create a 625-mile inland waterway that is used today for shipping products from Knoxville, Tennessee, to the Ohio River. A few years after TVA was established, these dams served yet another purpose. They made it possible for millions of acres once ruined by floods to be returned to cultivation.

It was obvious from the beginning, however, that if the Tennessee River was to be controlled, it would take more than the building of dams. The Soil Conservation Service initiated a campaign to check erosion. More than a million acres of trees were planted so that today the region has twice as much timber as it did in 1933. At the same time, the newly formed shorelines were engineered to avoid the creation of breeding places for mosquitoes. The threat of malaria declined greatly as a result.

New industries were attracted to the area because the available water power could be used to produce electricity inexpensively. Employment opportunities multiplied in paper mills, food processing plants, and factories producing aluminum and chemicals. Large projects such as the Oak Ridge atomic energy complex and the NASA rocket center were also located nearby.

Major urban centers now dot the landscape. Significant growth has taken place in Chattanooga and Knoxville as well as in Asheville, North Carolina, and Huntsville, Alabama. Suburbs are also developing around these areas, and tourists are enjoying these urban centers as well as the river and the many artificial lakes created by the TVA.

The Tennessee Valley Authority is a positive example of human-environment interactions. Since it was established, there has not been a major flood in the region. Working together, the people of the Tennessee Valley have succeeded in controlling the river, improving individual lives, and beautifying the landscape.

Understanding Geography

1. Identify three environmental problems that existed in the Tennessee Valley before the establishment of the TVA.
2. What tasks were assigned to the TVA?
3. Why is the TVA a positive example of human-environment interactions?

Critical Thinking

4. Evaluate the accomplishments of the TVA.

Key Terms and People

These are highlighted in the text in the order in which they appear in this list.

Main Ideas

1. Congress passed more significant legislation than it usually passes in a two-year session; most was initiated by the President.

2. Possible answer: the CCC hired unemployed for projects; FERA provided more money directly to unemployed; TVA organized efforts to improve the Tennessee Valley.

3. Employment, social insurance, business.

4. Creating many jobs in construction, in clothing manufacturing, and in fine arts.

5. NIRA was accused of giving legislative powers to executive branch; some codes covered commerce within a state. Court ruled AAA procedures to restrict production were not taxes but a regulation of agriculture, which was beyond powers of Congress.

6. Possible answer: Upton Sinclair—high income and inheritance taxes, monthly fifty-dollar pensions for elderly, consumer cooperatives; Francis Townsend—monthly $200 for elderly; Father Coughlin—nationalize banks, public utilities, natural resources. • Had the most political power.

7. NLRB began investigating unfair labor practices; CIO was recognized by the steel and automobile industries; federal government recognized the right of collective bargaining.

8. New Deal legislation helped everyone regardless of color; Ickes hired African Americans, and woman was appointed to cabinet; the CIO unions had black members; FDR sought advice from his Black Cabinet; Court upheld civil rights; Indian Reorganization Act of 1934 strengthened Indian civil rights.

Critical Thinking Questions

9. Describes a Finnish custom practiced in U.S. • Some

thought it was a cult ritual.

10. All received government money to create jobs. • Possible answers: yes—programs resulted in construction of many government buildings, dams, national parks. No—7.5 million people were still jobless in 1940.

11. Hoover asked farmers to voluntarily limit production; Roosevelt paid them to limit production. • Yes—prices rose and farmers were paid more.

• Seemed wrong to waste crops.

➤**12.** Supreme Court thought some programs, such as NIRA and AAA, were unconstitutional. Also the Court had a conservative majority. Congress feared FDR was overstepping his powers, especially the independence of the judiciary.

13. Possible answers: yes—Roosevelt should have gone further. No—Roosevelt went

as far as he could; Americans were not ready for more drastic measures.

➤**14.** Some historians feel it kept people alive; opponents thought it showed the way for government to manipulate the economy. • Possible answer: New Deal was a success because it helped many people.

Critical Thinking Activities

15. Possible answers: WPA—

CHAPTER 27 REVIEW

Write your answers on a separate sheet of paper.

Key Terms and People

Explain the significance of: Tennessee Valley Authority (TVA), Home Owners Loan Corporation (HOLC), Glass-Steagall Act, price controls, pump priming, Aaron Copeland, Virgil Thomson, Clifford Odets, Nelson Algren, Richard Wright, Securities and Exchange Commission (SEC), insider trading, parity, sit-down strike, Black Cabinet, Marian Anderson, John Collier, Indian Reorganization Act

Main Ideas

1. Why were the first Hundred Days a significant period for the first Roosevelt administration?
2. Describe at least three of the programs that were set in motion during the Hundred Days. How did each try to help the nation's economy?
3. What areas vital to the economy did the Second New Deal seek to reform?
4. What did the Works Progress Administration (WPA) under Harry Hopkins succeed in doing?
5. Why did the Supreme Court rule the National Industrial Recovery Act (NIRA) in *Schechter Poultry Corporation* v. *United States* and the Agricultural Adjustment Administration (AAA) in *United States* v. *Butler* unconstitutional?
6. List at least three extremists other than Huey Long and their proposals for new programs for the 1930's. Why was Huey Long considered the foremost threat to Roosevelt's policies?
7. In what ways were labor unions and workers' rights strengthened during the 1930's?
8. In what areas did minorities and women make progress during the 1930's?

Critical Thinking Questions

9. **Evaluating Literature.** How does the selection by Archie Hobson on page 677 reflect the variety of ethnic life in the United States? How does it reflect the suspicion with which the foreign-born were regarded?
10. **Evaluating Effects.** One of Roosevelt's chief

goals was to give people jobs. How were the Civilian Conservation Corps, the Civil Works Administration, the Works Progress Administration, and the Public Works Administration alike in their methods to achieve this goal? Do you think they succeeded? Why or why not?

11. **Evaluating Policies.** Explain how Roosevelt's agricultural policies were radically different from those of Herbert Hoover. Were they more effective? For what were they criticized?
12. **Evaluating Reactions.** The reactions of the Supreme Court and Congress to some New Deal programs were negative. Discuss the reasons for these negative reactions.
13. **Analyzing Sources.** In your opinion were the charges made against the New Deal by Father Coughlin and Huey Long justified?
14. **Evaluating Ideas.** How do historians disagree about the role of the New Deal in history? How do you evaluate the New Deal? Explain your judgment.

Critical Thinking Activities

15. **Evaluating Programs.** Grade each of the following New Deal programs on a scale of A to E, considering A as the highest grade: WPA, CCC, Social Security, NLRB, and Minimum Wage. Be prepared to defend your grading.

16. **Linking Past to Present.** How did President Roosevelt try to instill in the American people confidence in the future? What techniques did he use? How would these techniques work today? What other techniques might we use today?

17. **Linking Past to Present.** In this period of joblessness, the first task was to sponsor projects to put people to work. What help is available today for people out of work?

18. **Linking Past to Present.** Roosevelt's programs in the New Deal helped many minorities and women. Compare his programs with today's efforts to help the same groups.

The New Deal and Reform

President Franklin Delano Roosevelt launched his New Deal by prodding his first special session of Congress—which lasted one hundred days—into passing dozens of laws. Some created public works agencies like the Civilian Conservation Corps, which put young men to work planting trees. Other laws provided federal aid to the poor and help for the states to deal with unemployment. The Agricultural Adjustment Administration paid farmers to cut back production in order to raise farm prices. The Tennessee Valley Authority proved to be an enduring conservation project. Other acts regulated stocks and insured bank deposits. Still another act created the National Recovery Administration to pour money into construction projects that Congress and the President hoped would get the economy moving again.

The legislation of the first Hundred Days did not seem to solve many problems. After Democratic victories in the Congressional elections of 1934, FDR pushed for more basic reforms. The Works Project Administration gave employment to millions of laborers, artists, and writers. The Social Security Act laid the foundation of a pension system. Other laws tried to regulate utility companies. New tax laws raised rates for wealthy corporations and individuals and strengthened the graduated income tax. One of several banking acts increased the Federal Reserve System's power.

Many critics challenged the reforms of the New Deal. Some thought FDR's program was too conservative; others thought it was too radical. Roosevelt ran into trouble with the Supreme Court, which declared several New Deal laws unconstitutional. In angry response to the rulings, Congress passed acts that strengthened the power of unions, set up a minimum wage, and guaranteed parity prices for farmers. Groups like the Liberty League attacked the President in print. These critics immediately accused FDR of trying to pack the Supreme

Court when, after reelection in 1936, he attempted to change its structure.

Despite the controversy, change continued throughout the 1930's in several areas. For example, before the Great Depression most labor unions were organized on a craft basis. Then in the 1930's the industrial unions enlisted all the workers in a single industry, regardless of individual skills. Union innovations extended to the CIO's new technique, the sit-down strike. Federal domestic policies paid more attention to African Americans, American Indians, and Mexican Americans than had the policies of previous administrations. In the American public, the depression resulted in families' having fewer children. Radio and the movies provided new forms of entertainment. More women entered formerly off-limits fields such as drama, journalism, aviation, athletics, and research. Most historians think that the New Deal rescued the nation over the long term even if it did not do so in the short term.

Chronology of Main Events

1933 Franklin D. Roosevelt inaugurated President; CCC, AAA, NRA established; TVA created

1934 Securities and Exchange Commission established; Indian Reorganization Act

1935 WPA established; Wagner Act; CIO founded; Social Security Act

1937 Roosevelt inaugurated for second term; President's court-packing bill rebuffed

1938 Fair Labor Standards Act

State the Objective

Understand the history of the Russian Revolution.

Present the Lesson

Ask students to identify forces at work in the early 1900's that contributed to the success of the Russian Revolution. (Possible responses: the rule of the tsars was cruelly oppressive, which led to popular unrest; the Bolsheviks were led by Lenin, who was an excellent propagandist; the tsar's regime was fatally weakened by huge losses in World War I; the tsar abdicated.)

Divide the class into small groups. Have the groups discuss the role of Lenin in the Russian Revolution. (Discussions might include: Lenin was a leader of the Bolsheviks; he lived and wrote outside of Russia to avoid arrest by the tsarist regime; Lenin made promises of peace to the Germans if they helped him gain power; after an unsuccessful attempt to overthrow the government in July 1917, Lenin was forced to flee Russia for Finland; Lenin urged the Bolsheviks to seize power; the resulting October Revolution of 1917 was successful.)

Ask students what the Mensheviks of the early 1900's might have thought about the collapse of the Communist regime and recent democratic reforms in the former Soviet Union. (Possible response: since Mensheviks favored a parliamentary government, it is likely they would have welcomed this change.)

Focus on Global Events

The Russian Revolution

During the 1920's, many people in the United States and throughout the world watched the events in Russia with mixed interest and alarm. The country was officially known as the Union of Soviet Socialist Republics (the U.S.S.R. or Soviet Union for short) after 1922. Soviet revolutionaries had established a new government there. Over time they would alter the economy of the country and eventually make the U.S.S.R. one of the major powers in international politics.

The Background. Actually the revolutionary upheavals of 1917 were the culmination of a long revolutionary tradition in Russia. The cruelly oppressive rule of the Tsars provoked numerous violent reactions, and there had been several attempts during the 1800's to overthrow the monarchy. In 1905 a full-scale revolution broke out. It was put down but proved to be a dress rehearsal for the 1917 rebellions.

By the early 1900's, several revolutionary groups were competing for power in Russia. One group favored a parliamentary system of government. These people wanted to overthrow the Tsar entirely or reduce him to a mere figurehead. Another group was made up of Marxists, followers of the teachings of Karl Marx. They looked to the small urban industrial class, or proletariat (prō'lə ter'ē ət), to overthrow the Tsar and set up a socialist system. It was this last group that eventually succeeded in establishing a new government in Russia.

The Revolutionaries. Members of the Marxist party (officially called the Russian Social Democratic Labor party) held opposing viewpoints regarding membership in the party. The *Bolsheviks* (bōl'shə viks'), or majority, favored limiting party membership to a small group of highly disciplined revolutionaries who would work full time in promoting revolution. The *Mensheviks* (men'shə viks'), or minority, wanted a more democratic organization that would be open to wide membership.

The major leader of the Bolsheviks was Vladimir I. Ulyanov (ōōl yän'ôf), who adopted the name Lenin. Lenin's personal magnetism, energy, organizing ability, and sheer ruthlessness gained him the eventual command of the Bolsheviks. He was also an excellent propagandist and pamphleteer. To avoid arrest by the tsarist regime, he spent many years living abroad. When war between Germany and Russia broke out in 1914, he went to Switzerland, a neutral country. From Switzerland, Lenin maintained contact with other Bolsheviks and bided his time for a return to Russia.

The Tsar Falls. By 1917 conditions in Russia had become desperate. Tsar Nicholas II seemed unable to cope with the crises at home and abroad. His regime had been fatally weakened by the huge loss of life and resources in World War I. People from all classes were clamoring for change and for an end to the war. There were food riots in many cities. Soldiers mutinied, deserted, or ignored orders. Faced with massive opposition, the Tsar abdicated his throne on March 15, 1917.

A provisional government was established. By July a moderate named Alexander Kerensky (kə ren'skē) had become the head of it. Despite terrible problems with the war effort, Kerensky decided to continue the fight. In this he was strongly encouraged by Britain and the United States, who feared that a Russian peace with Germany would free up German troops to be moved farther west to face British and American forces.

As conditions inside Russia worsened, angry peasants began to seize land while urban workers grew militant. Lenin realized he had a great opportunity. He convinced Germany to help him get back into Russia. The Germans hoped that once Lenin was in the country, his actions would weaken Russia even more. Sent through Germany in a sealed railway boxcar, Lenin reached Petrograd, the Russian capital, in April. (Petrograd's prewar name of St. Petersburg had been changed because it sounded German. In 1991 citizens voted to change the name back to St. Petersburg.)

702

Picturing History
Nicholas II was the last Tsar of Russia. He is shown here with his wife, Alexandra, and their children shortly before the family was assassinated by revolutionaries in 1918.

The October Revolution. Once there, Lenin urged the Bolsheviks to try to seize power. Under the command of Leon Trotsky—Lenin's most able lieutenant—armed workers seized important points throughout the city. On November 6, 1917, the cruiser *Aurora* and its mutinous crew sailed into the Neva River and aimed its guns at the Winter Palace, headquarters of the provisional government, demanding surrender. The provisional government collapsed. By November 15 the Bolsheviks controlled Moscow as well.

The Civil War. Lenin, who was now the most powerful man in Russia, decided to sue for peace. Germany's terms were humiliating, but Lenin accepted them, signing the Treaty of Brest-Litovsk in March 1918. At this point anti-Communist Russians, called White Russians, decided to organize an attack on the new government. White Russian armies were formed, aided by troops from France, Great Britain, Japan, Czechoslovakia, the United States, and other countries that opposed the Bolshevik government. The Allied effort was not an all-out one, however. Weary from World War I, the Allies were unwilling to fight another prolonged war. President Wilson, moreover, did not think that the Soviet government would succeed. Despite only half-hearted outside support, the Whites con-

tinued fighting. The civil war between the White Russians and the Reds (as the Communists called themselves) lasted into the 1920's.

The Bolsheviks Win. Invasion, revolution, and civil war left Russia totally exhausted. The Bolsheviks emerged victorious, but at a terrible cost—13 million people perished in the war and the famine that followed. The economy was totally shattered. The Communists exerted dictatorial power in all but name.

The architect of the revolution, Lenin, died in 1924, and a struggle for succession between Leon Trotsky and Josef Stalin ensued. Stalin succeeded in gaining power and remained an absolute dictator until his death in 1953.

Understanding Global Events

1. How did the Bolsheviks differ from the Mensheviks?
2. Why were the Germans eager to help Lenin return to Russia?

Critical Thinking

3. In what ways were the Russian Revolution and the French Revolution similar? In what ways were they different?

Answer Key

Key Terms and People

These are highlighted in the text in the order in which they appear in this list.

Main Ideas

1. Nations were engaged in an arms race; feelings of nationalism and imperialism; system of alliances existed that called for allies to come to the aid of members of the alliance.

2. Failed to gain cooperation of Congress; many felt his plan involved U.S. too much in European affairs. • Treaty humiliated Germany; took land away from Russia; ignored Southeast Asia and other colonial peoples.

3. People did not like Prohibition so they broke the law to get liquor; speakeasies were against the law so the owners openly bribed officials; gangsters ran liquor business. Open disregard for law made people cynical of all laws.

4. Women felt liberated from long hair and constrictive clothing; gained confidence in workplace and politics.

5. Many Americans believed communists were responsible for labor unrest and union activism, and the situation incited people to violence.

6. Overproduction and low prices in agriculture sector; increased poverty; too much easy credit; housing starts down; business inventories up.

7. Loss of jobs, loss of investments, and bank failures meant people lost savings and homes; working people had pay cuts.

8. Voters would have reelected Hoover if his actions had worked.

9. Possible answer: CCC paid young men to build roads and plant trees; FERA gave grants-in-aid to states, who gave food and clothing to needy; through local authorities CWA gave people jobs that did not compete with existing ones; AAA paid farmers for not planting; TVA built dams to provide electricity.

10. Status of women improved; African Americans

were able to find better jobs; workers gained protection; people began to look to government for help.

Critical Thinking Questions

➤**11.** Possible answers: right—problems of Europe did not involve U.S. politically. Wrong—U.S. did have friends in Europe; unrestricted warfare gave U.S. little choice.

➤**12.** Scopes trial—clash between traditional and new beliefs and between rural and urban Americans; Prohibition—conflict between those who did and did not believe that morals could be legislated.

13. Boom based on confidence in the market and that buying on margin was sound.

14. c, e, a, f, d, b.

15. f, d, c, a, e, b.

16. a, f, b, e, d, c.

Critical Thinking Activities

17. The U.S. President is very influential in world politics; U.S. has allies in Western Europe through NATO; U.S. supplies money, food, and arms to many countries of the world.

➤**18.** Jazz; dances; authors. • F. Scott Fitzgerald, Sinclair Lewis, Louis Armstrong, Bessie Smith, Duke Ellington.

➤**19.** Provides money for retirement.

UNIT 6 REVIEW

Write your answers on a separate sheet of paper.

Key Terms and People

Explain the significance of: Triple Alliance, Charles Evans Hughes, Herbert Hoover, Ho Chi Minh, Clarence Darrow, Carrie Chapman Catt, Marcus Garvey, Charlie Chaplin, Andrew Mellon, Teapot Dome scandal, Solid South, direct relief, humanitarian, brain trust, pragmatist, Tennessee Valley Authority (TVA), Richard Wright, parity, sit-down strike, Marian Anderson

Main Ideas

1. Explain how the conditions in Europe before 1914 were ripe for a major conflict.
2. Why was Woodrow Wilson's plan for a lasting peace a failure at home? In what areas was the Treaty of Versailles flawed?
3. How did Prohibition affect the way Americans regarded the laws of their country and the way some public officials used their offices?
4. In what ways did the social changes of the 1920's benefit women?
5. How did the conflict over communism and union activism create an atmosphere of violence?
6. What signals warned that all was not well in the nation's economy?
7. In what ways did the depression affect the lives of most citizens?
8. Why was the election of Franklin Roosevelt in 1932 a rejection of Hoover's policies?
9. List five programs that the Roosevelt administration created in the first Hundred Days. Give at least one fact about each one.
10. What social changes came about as a result of the New Deal programs?

Critical Thinking Questions

11. **Evaluating Ideas.** In what way were some Americans right in saying that the United States should not get involved with troubles in Europe in 1914? In what ways were they wrong?
12. **Analyzing Changes.** In the 1920's, many social changes were expressed in the form of clashes between traditional beliefs and new ways of thinking. Name two of these clashes and how they represented social changes.
13. **Evaluating Events.** The economic crash of 1929 revealed the serious weaknesses of the American economy. Explain why the boom period in the stock market prior to the crash was one of the major signs of weakness.

Organizing Ideas. Arrange each of the following groups of events in chronological order. In some cases your answers will show cause and effect relationships.

14. a. Treaty of Versailles
     b. isolationism
     c. alliances
     d. Lodge reservations
     e World War I
     f. League of Nations

15. a. Franklin Roosevelt elected
     b. Emergency Banking Relief Bill
     c. Bonus Army
     d. Hawley-Smoot tariff
     e. Twentieth Amendment ratified
     f. Black Tuesday

16. a. NAACP
     b. Dixieland came to Chicago
     c. Black Cabinet
     d. Harlem Renaissance
     e. antilynching law introduced in Congress
     f. UNIA moved to New York City

Critical Thinking Activities

17. **Linking Past to Present.** By the end of World War I, the United States was regarded as a world power. Explain in a few sentences why the United States is still a world power today.
18. **Linking Past to Present.** What aspects of the 1920's culture still are popular today? What artists and writers are still remembered?
19. **Linking Past to Present.** The legacy of the New Deal is still present in today's legislation. For example, the Social Security Act is still in effect. Explain how it is vital to citizens' lives.

World War I, Causes and Consequences

The First World War

Complex causes led to a massive war in Europe. A growing spirit of nationalism, rivalries for overseas empires, and an arms buildup combined to make Europe a powder keg. In 1914 the assassination of Archduke Franz Ferdinand set off an explosion that rocked Europe for the next four years. Britain, France, and Russia—the Allies—battled Germany, Austria-Hungary, and Turkey—the Central Powers.

Soon after the outbreak of war, German troops invaded neutral Belgium on their way to France. Later, British and French armies prevented the Germans from capturing Paris. The resulting trench warfare employed a retinue of new deadly weapons, including enormous artillery shells, machine guns, poison gas, tanks, and flamethrowers. Another new weapon, the submarine, would be responsible for eventually bringing the United States into the war in 1917. It was introduced by 1915, when the Germans unleashed their so-called U-boats in response to the British naval blockade of Germany. The same year, American lives were lost when a U-boat torpedoed the British liner *Lusitania*.

President Wilson won reelection in 1916. He redoubled his efforts at peacemaking, but then the German government announced that *all* ships in Allied waters were to be sunk on sight. The Zimmermann note, suggesting a Mexican alliance with Germany, helped push Wilson over the line. In April 1917 he asked Congress to declare war.

The federal government assumed broad wartime powers over the economy through the War Industries Board. Wilson also established a National War Labor Board to control strikes. To meet wartime production quotas, more and more women entered the labor force. The government encouraged farmers to increase their production of food and urged all citizens to buy Liberty Bonds. Super-

Americanism became a prevailing mood, and the government jailed several people under the Espionage and Sedition Acts.

The United States mobilized millions of men by means of a military draft. In Europe the arrival of American troops turned the tide. By September 1918 the superior power of the Allies was evident. The fighting finally ended when Germany signed an armistice on November 11, 1918.

The Terms of Peace

In hammering out the terms of the peace treaty as one of the Big Four at Versailles, Wilson struggled to make peace permanent by means of his Fourteen Points. Britain and France, however, were intent on revenge against Germany, and they demanded huge financial reparations. In the end, Germany was stripped of its overseas colonies and forced to admit guilt for the war. The treaty also divided territory so that millions of German-speaking people lived in new countries like Czechoslovakia. Further, it stripped Russia of a great deal of territory and failed to deal with colonial problems in Southeast Asia.

Wilson struggled to get the Senate to ratify the Treaty of Versailles, including the covenant for the League of Nations. However, his valiant efforts failed in the face of mounting isolationist sentiment. The United States never joined the League of Nations. Instead, Americans turned their attention to affairs at home.

The 1920's and Social Change

The 1920's proved to be an era of social change. For the first time, more than half of the American people lived in cities and towns. Rural and urban values tended to differ.

The national ban on alcohol went into effect in 1920. While the use of alcohol declined, bootlegging flourished. Prohibition played into the hands of criminals and corrupt public officials. This "noble experiment" was repealed in 1933.

Another amendment that passed in 1920, after forty long years of struggle, gave women the right to vote. The Nineteenth Amendment provided encouragement for the small number of women who entered politics in the 1920's and the many more who took professional jobs outside the home.

Another dramatic social change resulted from the great migration. Between 1910 and 1930 nearly 2 million African Americans migrated from the South to Northern cities to fill the many factory jobs created as a result of World War I. They met prejudice and discrimination. After the war, race riots broke out in several cities.

Black leaders were becoming more vocal and protested publicly against racial injustice. White Southerners found ways to keep black people from voting. In effect, they nullified the Fifteenth Amendment to the Constitution, which had given black men the right to vote.

In New York City, the Harlem Renaissance was an extraordinary flowering of black achievement in literature, drama, music, dance, and art. Major black writers appeared. Black jazz artists became even better known than before. Indeed, the 1920's have often been called the Jazz Age.

The twenties also saw a dramatic rise in high-school enrollment. High schools broadened the range of their courses and by 1926 were attracting about half the people of high-school age.

Postwar Controversy

The Bolshevik Revolution in Russia caused a Red scare in the United States. A. Mitchell Palmer's raids were popular for a time, even though they violated civil liberties. The Ku Klux Klan revived with a new agenda of hate directed at Roman Catholics, Jews, and foreigners in general. The Boston police strike and the steel strike were unpopular with the general public. John L. Lewis's coal miners' strike, while it may have been generally unpopular, did result in a wage increase.

Soon after these events, Warren G. Harding became President. He seemed at first like a fine choice, because he was a good friend to business.

Most of the nation's attention, however, focused on itself. The government tried to collect war debts from the bankrupt Allies but, by enacting extremely high tariff rates at the same time, threatened the Allies' ability to raise money. Financial corruption in the President's cabinet came to light, and Harding died in office knowing that his friends had betrayed him.

Politics and a Thin Prosperity

President Coolidge and Secretary of the Treasury Andrew Mellon presided over prosperous times. New technological developments contributed to this prosperity. The most notable was the automobile, which was beginning to transform America in dozens of ways. Yet there were signs of trouble, especially in the railroad, textile, and coal mining industries. Perhaps most ominous of all, beneath the country's veneer of wealth lay millions and millions of Americans who lived in real poverty.

Herbert Hoover defeated Al Smith in 1928, and the Republicans remained in power. Though there had been signs of an economic slowdown before Hoover took office, he had been President for just over six months before the Wall Street market crashed.

The Great Depression

The Great Depression had several interrelated causes. They included uneven distribution of wealth, excessive use of credit, rising tariffs in international trade, and the increasing mechanization of American industry. The depression brought hunger and suffering to millions of Americans.

The veterans' Bonus Army and other popular efforts in response to the depression got nowhere. Hoover tried to create jobs by encouraging public works and enabling federal loans to industries, but the depression only deepened. He may have been discouraged from an all-out relief program by his belief in rugged individualism and in a limited role for the federal government. Nevertheless, as national crises are always blamed on the acting President, so Hoover was blamed for the depression. In the landslide election of 1932, he was trounced by the Democratic candidate, Franklin Delano Roosevelt.

FDR and the New Deal

FDR possessed a fresh spirit of optimism and showed deep empathy with the poor. Having battled paralysis in his own body, he urged Americans not to give up in despair. His instincts were pragmatic, which means that he was optimistic, insisted on taking action, and would try anything. He was determined to restore prosperity by reforming the system until it worked again. Toward that end, he formed a brain trust of able advisors. He appointed an able and bipartisan cabinet that included a woman.

FDR's first action as President was to close the nation's banks. He then got Congress to pass an Emergency Banking Relief Bill, which helped solve the banking crisis. He talked to the nation on the radio, using clear and forceful words to explain how the banking system operated. In the first of Roosevelt's broadcasts, or fireside chats, he proved himself a master at inspiring public confidence through creative use of the radio, a recent invention.

During the first Hundred Days of his administration, FDR persuaded Congress to churn out laws to deal with the depression. The laws created a wide variety of government agencies and projects to provide jobs, pay farmers to cut back production, lend money to homeowners, insure bank deposits, ensure fair trade, and supervise public works projects.

Yet the depression continued. In 1935 Roosevelt shifted his emphasis from relief to reform. He put Harry Hopkins in charge of the Works Progress Administration (WPA). This new agency's goal was to create jobs. The WPA employed millions of people in a wide variety of public projects. The year 1935 also saw the establishment of the social security system. Other New Deal reform measures expanded the government's power to oversee the stock market, to investigate unfair practices in utility companies, and to regulate the nation's money supply.

Many critics challenged the New Deal. Radicals attacked it for not destroying capitalism. Conservatives attacked it for undermining capitalism. The Supreme Court attacked the New Deal by declaring some of its measures unconstitutional. In angry response, Congress passed the Wagner Act, the Fair Labor Standards Act, and legislation that established parity prices for farmers.

After Roosevelt's stunning reelection sweep in 1936, he decided to take on the Supreme Court. However, Congress refused to adopt his proposal to add six justices. Eventually Roosevelt was able to appoint the kind of justices he wanted. Nevertheless, his hold on Congress weakened after the congressional elections of 1938. By 1939 the New Deal was essentially at an end.

Other domestic developments during the 1930's include the formation of the CIO and the rapid growth of other labor unions. In addition, African Americans and American Indians received favorable attention from the federal government. Another minority, Mexican Americans, was especially hard hit by the depression. In fact, all American families were affected by the depression.

The Great Depression was finally ended by World War II. Some New Deal policies had been effective, others less so, but by giving the government a more active role in the economy, the New Deal marked a watershed in the relationship between the federal government and the American people.

Chronology of Main Events
1917 U.S. enters World War I
1923 President Harding dies; Calvin Coolidge succeeds to Presidency
1929 Herbert Hoover inaugurated President; stock market crashes; Great Depression begins
1933 Franklin D. Roosevelt inaugurated President
1939 World War II begins in Europe
1940 President Roosevelt elected for third term

GLOBAL TIME LINE

The World

1933-1945
Hitler leads Germany

1937
Japan attacks
China

1939-1945
World War II

1940
France surrenders to German

194
D-Day invasi

1930

1935

1940

**The
United States**

1934
Nye Committee investigates war profits

1935-1937
Congress approves Neutrality Acts

1941
Japan attacks
Pearl Harbor

Research Assignment

Choose one person, other than a politician, whom you studied in this unit. Research his or her life and prepare for the class a two-minute talk explaining why this person was significant in U.S. history.

UNIT **7** 1933–1960

World War II, Causes and Consequences

Geographic Setting

Human-Environment Interactions. When we see a mushroom cloud rising from an atomic-bomb testing site, we are reminded of how powerful and deadly human beings' interactions with the environment can be. Over seventy thousand people died from the atomic attack on Hiroshima in World War II. Another 36,000 died when the atomic bomb was dropped on Nagasaki. This awesome new power demanded new decisions about our lives and about the life of every other living being on earth.

Unit Overview

As the aftermath of World War I and the Great Depression fostered the rise of dictators in Europe, the seeds of World War II were planted. When war finally broke out, the United States officially remained neutral—until Japan attacked Pearl Harbor. The use of the atomic bomb finally brought the war to an end. Although the nation tried to plan for a more peaceful world, that world became characterized by a cold war between the United States and the Soviet Union. The cold war turned hot when North Korea invaded South Korea in 1950. Otherwise, the 1950's were a relatively quiet decade in the United States.

Unit Outline

CHAPTER 28 **The Road to War 1933–1940**

1. Storm Clouds Gather
2. America Struggles to Remain Neutral
3. The Crisis Deepens
4. Early Events Warn Americans

CHAPTER 29 **The Second World War 1939–1945**

1. The United States Prepares for War
2. The Nation Performs a Production Miracle
3. War Rages Across North Africa and Europe
4. Allied Troops Advance on the Pacific Front
5. The Allies Plan for the Postwar World

CHAPTER 30 **Postwar Period, Cold War, Korean War 1945–1956**

1. A New Leader Faces a Difficult Period
2. A Former Ally Becomes an Enemy
3. The Cold War Turns Hot

CHAPTER 31 **Adjustments of the 1950's 1950–1960**

1. New Patterns of Living Develop
2. Americans Enjoy New Forms of Entertainment
3. Minorities Make Some Progress
4. Crises Threaten International Peace

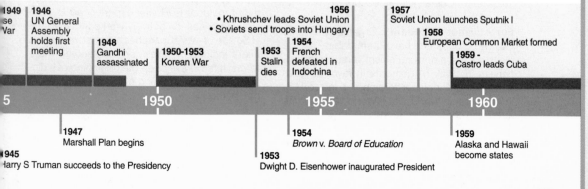

1949 se Var

1946 UN General Assembly holds first meeting

1948 Gandhi assassinated

1950-1953 Korean War

1953 Stalin dies

1954 French defeated in Indochina

1956 • Khrushchev leads Soviet Union • Soviets send troops into Hungary

1957 Soviet Union launches Sputnik I

1958 European Common Market formed

1959 - Castro leads Cuba

5 1950 1955 1960

1947 Marshall Plan begins

1954 Brown v. Board of Education

1959 Alaska and Hawaii become states

1945 Harry S Truman succeeds to the Presidency

1953 Dwight D. Eisenhower inaugurated President

Chapter 28 Teaching Activities

Global Perspectives

1934	Hitler and Mussolini first meet.
1936	Edward VIII of England abdicates.
1936	Italy annexes Ethiopia.
1940	Churchill becomes the British Prime Minister.
1940	Leon Trotsky, exiled Russian leader, is assassinated in Mexico.

For Discussion

What subjects might Hitler and Mussolini have discussed at their first meeting? (Possible responses: a German-Italian alliance; spheres of influence; political philosophies.)

Additional Resources

- Geography Activities
- Skills Activities
- Thematic Activities
- Economic Activities
- Cultural Literacy Activities
- Literary Source Readings
- Primary Source Readings
- Nuclear Peacekeeping
- Transparencies
- Computer Test Generator

Additional Teaching Strategies

SECTION 1

For Basic Students: Have students make a chart with a heading for each of the three sites of aggression discussed in this section: Manchuria, Ethiopia, and the Rhineland. Under each heading they should list the location of the site, the parties or countries involved, and the outcome. Charts should include:

Manchuria
- Location—Chinese mainland
- Countries—Japan and China
- Outcome—Japan takes over Manchuria in September 1931; U.S. issues Stimson Doctrine; Japan sets up puppet state of Manchukuo in 1932.

Ethiopia
- Location—Africa
- Countries—Italy and Ethiopia
- Outcome—Italy takes over Ethiopia in June 1936; League of Nations unsuccessfully tries to apply sanctions on Italy.

Rhineland
- Location—Germany
- Party—Nazi
- Outcome—Germany remilitarizes the Rhineland; Britain and France fail to act decisively to stop German moves.

For Advanced Students: Ask students to research and prepare a report on the early life of Adolf Hitler or Benito Mussolini, his family, educational background, and early political activities. (Report on Mussolini might include: born in central Italy; graduated from teacher training school; taught elementary school for a short time; moved to Switzerland, where he was in trouble with police for vagrancy and fighting; worked for a Socialist newspaper in Austria.) Have students share their reports.

SECTION 2

For Basic Students: Have students construct a time line of the years 1931 to 1937 showing incidents that threatened world peace. Students may refer to Section 1 for additional information. Time line should include:

1931	Japan invades Chinese province of Manchuria.
1935	Italy attacks Ethiopia.
1936	Spanish Civil War begins; Mussolini and Hitler aid Franco.
1937	China incident occurs. *Panay* incident occurs.

For Advanced Students: Organize students into two groups and have them debate for the class the issue of isolationism versus interventionism in 1937. (Arguments in favor of isolationism might include: foreign ties led to U.S. involvement in World War I; World War I and its aftermath contributed to the severity of the depression. Arguments in favor of interventionism might include: U.S. needed foreign markets for its goods to prevent another depression; U.S. had a moral obligation to help the cause of democracy throughout the world; conflict in Europe could have spread to America.)

SECTION 3

For Basic Students: Have students use an encyclopedia or other reference book to research and write a one-page report on a famous immigrant who fled German persecution and on his or her contributions to America. (Report on Albert Einstein might include: born March 14, 1879, in Ulm, Württemberg, Germany; was father of the atomic age; wrote to FDR explaining the possibility of building an atomic bomb; worked on the quantum theory of light; was instrumental in the development of the photoelectric cell, or "electric eye," making possible such inventions as sound motion pictures, television, and automatic doors.) Have several volunteers read their reports to the class.

For Advanced Students: To stimulate discussion on whether World War II was inevitable, have students answer the following questions. Could the behavior of Great Britain, France, and the Soviet Union have facilitated Hitler's rise to power? (Possible response: yes—by not sending troops to defend Austria and Czechoslovakia, they allowed Hitler to gain a stronghold.) At what point might action against Germany have been effective, if ever? (Possible response: Great Britain, France, and the Soviet Union should have stepped in as soon as Hitler began aggressive activities.)

SECTION 4

For Basic Students: Have students refer to the chart on page 728 and identify events that indicated that the U.S. was likely to become involved in the war. (Events might include: Germany and the Soviet Union sign a nonaggression pact; France and Britain declare war on Germany; France surrenders; Canada and U.S. set up joint Board of Defense; U.S. begins military draft; Lend-Lease Act is enacted; U.S. sends forces to Iceland.)

For Advanced Students: Ask students to present to the class a two-minute speech in favor of or against FDR's election to a third term. (Speeches in favor of FDR's reelection might include: FDR was experienced in dealing with crises; he actively worked to keep the U.S. out of war. Speeches against reelection might include: no President had served three terms; it may have been the beginning of a dictatorship or the granting of too much power to one person.)

Further Reading for Students

Nonfiction

Frank, Anne. *Anne Frank: The Diary of a Young Girl*. Garden City, N. Y.: Doubleday, 1967.

Kimball, Warren F. *Franklin D. Roosevelt and the World Crisis, 1937-1945*. Lexington, Mass.: D. C. Heath, 1974.

Lash, Joseph P. *Roosevelt and Churchill, 1939-1941: The Partnership that Saved the West*. New York: W. W. Norton, 1976.

Remak, Joachim. *Origins of the Second World War*. Englewood Cliffs, N. J.: Prentice-Hall, 1976.

Bibliography for Teachers

Books

Dawidowicz, Lucy S. *The War Against the Jews, 1933-1945*. New York: Free Press, 1986.

Divine, Robert A. *The Illusion of Neutrality*. Chicago: University of Chicago Press, 1962.

Rossiter, Clinton. *Conservatism in America* ed. Cambridge: Harvard University Press, 1982.

Audio-Visuals

Failure of American Neutrality. American Broadcasting Company. Movie.

The Outbreak of World War II. Society for Visual Education. Filmstrip.

The Road to World War II. McGraw-Hill. Movie.

The United States in a Troubled World, 1920-1945. Eye Gate House. Filmstrip.

The United States in the Twentieth Century, 1932-1940. Simon and Schuster Communications. Movie.

World War II Prologue, U.S.A. Encyclopaedia Britannica Educational Corporation. Movie.

Computer Resources

American History III. (Apple/IBM) Silwa Enterprises.

American History Keyword Series—World War II Keywords. (Apple) Focus Media.

Teacher's Notes:

CHAPTER 30

Lesson Plan

Teaching Resources, Unit 7 Booklet

Lesson Study Sheets pp. 1-16
Daily Activities pp. 17-24
Enrichment Activities pp. 25-32
Reteaching Activities pp. 33-40
Chapter Review p. 41
Chapter Mastery Test pp. 43-54
Telescoping the Times Study Sheet p. 55

Chapter Objectives

Students will learn:
- the important events of the 1930's that eventually led to World War II
- how world events challenged the U.S. policy of neutrality
- how Germany's political actions of 1939 became the immediate causes of World War II
- the early events of World War II both in Europe and in the U.S.

Picturing History In the 1930's, the United States offered refuge to many victims of fascism and Nazism. The remarkably gifted scientist, writer, and professor Albert Einstein, a Jewish immigrant from Nazi Germany, is shown here (center) taking the oath of citizenship in 1940.

Using the Chapter Time Line

How many years after Hitler became chancellor did he annex Austria? (Answer: 5.) Name three countries that invaded other nations between 1935 and 1939. (Answer: Italy, Japan, and Germany.)

1932	1934	1936	1938	1940
1933 Hitler becomes German chancellor	**1935** • Mussolini conquers Ethiopia • First Neutrality Act	**1937** Japan invades China	**1938** • Hitler annexes Austria • Munich Pact signed	**1939** Germany invades Poland; World War II begins in Europe	**1940** Nazi blitzkrieg begins

Links to American Literature

Bernard Malamud: born in Brooklyn, N.Y., in 1914; studied at CCNY and Columbia University; worked as a clerk with the Census Bureau in 1940, as he recounted, "conscientiously checking estimates of drainage ditch statistics"; taught English and literature in New York City high schools and at Oregon State University and Bennington College; received two National Book Awards, the Rosenthal Award, the Golden Medal for fiction, and the Pulitzer Prize.

Works include: *The Natural* (1952), *The Assistant* (1957), *The Magic Barrel* (1958), *The Fixer* (1966), *Dubin's Lives* (1979), *God's Grace* (1982), and *The People* (1989).

"The Armistice": In this short story, originally written in 1940 but published posthumously in 1989, Malamud's Morris Lieberman recalls the haunting persecution of a Russian pogrom as he listens to radio accounts of Nazi persecutions of the Jews in Germany. The story takes place in Brooklyn, before the U.S. has entered the war. Both the issue of neutrality and Nazi sympathizers weigh heavily upon many Americans and serve as the backdrop for this story.

Introducing the Chapter

Review with students isolationism and U.S. desire to maintain neutrality during European conflicts. Ask students to recall times when the U.S. attempted to maintain neutrality. (Possible responses: the early 1800's; the years prior to World War I.) To what extent was the U.S. able to maintain neutrality in those times? (Answer: not at all—the U.S. was drawn into conflict and found it impossible to maintain neutrality.) As students study this chapter, have them look for similarities in the ways in which the U.S. became involved in the two world wars.

CHAPTER **28** 1933–1940

The Road to War

Links to American Literature

> When he was a boy, Morris Lieberman saw a burly Russian peasant seize a wagon wheel that was lying against the side of a blacksmith's shop, swing it around, and hurl it at a fleeing Jewish sexton. The wheel caught the Jew in the back, crushing his spine. In speechless terror, he lay on the ground before his burning house, waiting to die.
>
> Thirty years later Morris, a widower who owned a small grocery and delicatessen store in a Scandinavian neighborhood in Brooklyn, could recall the scene of the pogrom with a twisting fright that he had felt at fifteen. He often experienced the same fear since the Nazis had come to power.
>
> The reports of their persecution of the Jews that he heard over the radio filled him with dread, but he never stopped listening to them. . . . because in listening he shared the woes inflicted upon his race.
>
> When the war began, Morris placed his hope for the salvation of the Jews in his trust of the French army. He lived close to his radio, listening to the bulletins and praying for a French victory in the conflict which he called "this righteous war."
>
> — BERNARD MALAMUD, *"Armistice"*

While the world tried to cope with the Great Depression, war clouds gathered over Europe, Africa, and Asia. As Roosevelt led the nation out of economic depression, the European dictators Adolf Hitler and Benito Mussolini were mustering their Nazi and Fascist forces. That such men could garner almost unlimited followers and resources frightened Americans, who came to realize that democracy could no longer be taken for granted. This chapter is important because it explains what was at stake in World War II. We can easily imagine the evil that would have infected the world had Hitler won the war.

Chapter Overview

In this chapter you will learn about the important world events that took place during the 1930's, in the years leading up to World War II. You will learn how these events challenged the American policy of neutrality and led to the start of a global war in 1939. Finally, you will learn about the military and political tactics used both in Europe and in the United States during the early stages of the war. To help you understand the beginnings of World War II, Chapter 28 is divided into four sections.

Chapter Outline

1. **Storm Clouds Gather**
2. **America Struggles to Remain Neutral**
3. **The Crisis Deepens**
4. **Early Events Warn Americans**

Core Lesson

Anticipate the Lesson

To stimulate discussion of the Kellogg-Briand Pact, ask students the following questions. What was the Kellogg-Briand Pact? (Possible response: the pact was signed by sixty-two nations who pledged never to make war again and to settle all future disputes by peaceful means.) Why was it ineffective? (Possible response: it made no provisions for the use of economic or military force against any nation

that broke the agreement.) How could the pact have been strengthened? (Possible response: by providing for economic sanctions against any nation that broke the agreement.)

State the Objective

Understand the important events of the 1930's that eventually led to World War II.

For Discussion

Why did World War I fail to "make the world safe for democracy"? (Possible responses: the Treaty of Versailles was too harsh on the losing nations; war debts were enormous, forcing nations to seek foreign markets through conquest; Japan, Germany, and Italy held to the idea that war would be the solution to their problems; people suffering from economic depression were prime targets for fanatical rulers such as Hitler and Mussolini.)

SECTION 1

Storm Clouds Gather

GLOSSARY TERMS: **Nazi party, fascism, totalitarian, sanctions**

On January 15, 1929, the United States Senate ratified the Kellogg-Briand Pact. Named for United States Secretary of State **Frank B. Kellogg** and French Foreign Minister Aristide Briand, the pact was eventually signed by sixty-two nations. They promised never to make war again and to settle all future disputes by peaceful means. The pact was misleading, however, because it still permitted defensive war. Furthermore, the only way of enforcing the pact was through public opinion. The treaty had no provisions for the use of economic or military force against any nation that broke the agreement.

Some writers and historians believe that the Kellogg-Briand Pact is an example of what was wrong with American diplomacy during the 1930's. One historian has characterized the pact as being an attempt to create peace through incantation, that is, through the mumbling of magic words. It might have worked, he said, in a world that longed for peace. Unfortunately, it could not work in a world where three nations—Japan, Germany, and Italy—wanted war. As the depression deepened worldwide throughout the thirties, each of these three nations saw war as a possible solution to its problems.

Japan Attacks Manchuria

The island kingdom of Japan depended on world trade for the food and raw materials its 70 million people required. Even before the depression, its economic position had been shaky. Now, faced with the loss of overseas markets for its manufactured goods, the Japanese government became increasingly imperialistic. Ignoring the objections of more moderate officials, military leaders invaded the Chinese province of Manchuria in September 1931 and took over its rich coal and iron deposits.

When news of the Japanese attack reached Washington, D.C., Secretary of State Henry L. Stimson proposed an international boycott of Japanese goods. This would damage Japan's economy and presumably force the Japanese to withdraw from China. President Hoover, however, rejected Stimson's suggestion. He wanted only a statement of disapproval. So the United States declared, in the **Stimson Doctrine**, that it would not recognize any territorial gains made by force.

The Stimson Doctrine had no effect on Japan, which proceeded to conquer Manchuria and set up the **puppet state** of Manchukuo in 1932. (A puppet state is one that is independent in theory but whose officials and actions are actually controlled by another nation.) When the League of Nations criticized Japan for its actions, Japan simply quit the league. Then, in violation of the Five-Power Treaty that had been signed in Washington, D.C., in 1922, it began to build up its navy.

People in the Chapter

Adolf Hitler resorted to arson to assure his election as chancellor of Germany. Just before the crucial election, the German Parliament building was gutted by fire. The Nazis blamed the disaster on a Communist plot. Later evidence showed the Nazis had started the fire themselves.

Benito Mussolini had his son-in-law executed as a rebel. Some believe this was done to show Hitler what a tough dictator he was. Afterwards Mussolini's daughter Edda made the following comment on her father: "There are only 2 solutions that will rehabilitate him in my eyes, to run away or to kill himself."

Francisco Franco set himself up as a dictator in Spain with the help of an abundant supply of arms and troops from his fellow dictators, Hitler and Mussolini. Meanwhile, Americans adopted a peace-at-any-price stance.

Albert Einstein was so slow to speak as a child that his parents were afraid he was retarded. When they asked a teacher what courses the boy should take, the teacher replied that it did not matter since the boy would never be a success at anything. In later life he developed the theory of relativity, which helped to revolutionize physics.

Present the Lesson

Divide the class into three groups, one each to discuss and prepare a list of events occurring in the 1930's in Japan, Germany, and Italy. Have the group leaders write their lists on the board. Lists might include:

Japan
- Suffered economically because of world-wide depression.
- Lost overseas markets during depression.
- Invaded Manchuria in September 1931 and took over coal and iron deposits.
- Set up a puppet state.
- Was criticized by League of Nations.
- Withdrew from League of Nations.
- Began to build up its navy.

Germany
- Had suffered economically since World War I.
- Endured business failures and unemployment.
- Called on Hitler and the Nazi party to form a new government.
- Withdrew from League of Nations in 1933.
- Began secret military buildup.
- Sent troops into the Rhineland in March 1936.

Italy
- Wanted to revive the glory of ancient Rome.
- Annexed Ethiopia in June 1936.

Ask students how the U.S. reacted to the activities of each nation. (Possible responses: Japan—issued Stimson Doctrine, declaring that it would not recognize any territorial gains made by force; Germany—African Americans, Jews, and labor unions denounced Hitler's actions; Italy—African Americans collected food, money, and supplies for Ethiopians.)

Japanese Aggression, Early 1930's

Map Skills **Region** What region of mainland China did Japan control? **Location** What three countries border Manchuria?

Dictators Come to Power

Meanwhile, **Adolf Hitler** was threatening the democratic government of Germany. The German economy had been shaky since the end of World War I. During the twenties, it had suffered a disastrous inflation. Also, it depended on heavy borrowing from United States banks and investors.

Picturing History This photo of Germans carrying worthless German marks to a bank in wicker laundry baskets illustrates the extent to which inflation had destroyed the German economy.

When those sources of funds dried up in 1930 and 1931, business failures and unemployment spread throughout the country. None of the political parties was able to win a majority of votes. Paul von Hindenburg, the aged and ailing President, called on the largest party in the country to form a government. This was Hitler's National Socialist German Workers' party, commonly called the **Nazi party**. This was how, on January 30, 1933, the Nazis came into power.

The word *Socialist* in the Nazi party's title is misleading. The Nazis were not democratic socialists. They were Fascists. **Fascism** is a political movement characterized by the belief that the state is more important than the individual and that a nation should have a strong centralized government headed by a dictator with absolute power. Both fascist and Nazi governments are **totalitarian** dictatorships that maintain complete control over the people of a nation. Individuals have no rights, and all opposition to the government is suppressed by force. Fascism was given its name by **Benito Mussolini,** who seized power in Italy in 1922. Hitler, however, added racism to Mussolini's fascist doctrine. In his book *Mein Kampf* (*My Struggle*), Hitler proclaimed his belief that Germans, especially those who were blond and blue-eyed, made up a "master race" that was destined to rule the world. Other "races," such as Jews, Slavs, and certain nonwhites, were inferior "races" that contaminated society and were fit only to serve the Germans or to be exterminated.

The Nazi party, like Mussolini's Fascist party, was strongly anticommunist. As a result, it was supported by many conservative business leaders who gave it funds during the twenties when it was trying to come to power. The Nazi party was also intensely militaristic. War veterans made up much of its membership. Many belonged to one of Hitler's two private armies: the brown-shirted storm troopers (the *Sturmabteilung,* or SA) and the black-shirted SS (*Schutzstaffel,* which means "protective group"). Their armbands showed the party symbol, a hooked black cross called the swastika. During the ten years before Hitler took office and suspended the German constitution, these storm troopers paraded about, shouted slogans, and beat up anyone who opposed them. Their particular targets were union leaders, Communists, and Jews. Hitler blamed the Jews, who made up less than one percent of the population, for Germany's defeat in World War I. A chief goal of the Nazis was to undo

Map Skills
Manchuria • Soviet Union, Mongolia, China

Historical Sidelight
In 1936 Hitler and Mussolini signed an agreement known as the Axis Pact. The term *Axis* originated from a statement made by Mussolini that the world would soon turn on a new axis running from Rome to Berlin.

Check for Understanding

Call on individual students to answer the Section 1 Review questions orally.

Guided Practice

Tell students that an American Nazi party continues to make public demonstrations. Ask whether an organization with attitudes hostile to a democratic system should be allowed to exist within that system. (Possible responses: yes—freedom of speech is guaranteed in the Bill of Rights; therefore, all groups have the right to express their beliefs. No—such freedoms do not pertain to groups that violate the rights of others; therefore, such groups should be banned.)

Picturing History Both Hitler (left) and Mussolini (right) had a flair for the dramatic and could manipulate their audiences and hold them spellbound during speeches. They built massive public buildings and huge rooms as symbols of their power. Having to approach Mussolini in his immense marble-lined private office would have been an awesome experience.

the results of that war symbolized by the Treaty of Versailles and to make Germany once more the dominant power in Europe. "One state! One people! One leader!" was their motto.

European Aggression Begins

For all his talk, Hitler at first moved cautiously on the international scene. In October 1933 he pulled Germany out of the League of Nations. Then he began a secret buildup of the nation's armed forces. Publicly, however, nothing else happened until 1936.

Mussolini Attacks Ethiopia. It was Mussolini who next threatened world stability. For years he had been boasting about his plans to turn the Mediterranean Sea into an Italian lake and to revive the glories of the ancient Roman Empire. In 1934 Italian and Ethiopian troops clashed along the

border of Ethiopia and Italian Somaliland in Africa. That event was followed by a ten-month drumfire of charges by Italy, manufactured incidents, and propaganda. In the next few years, the world was to see this scenario replayed often. It meant that a stronger country was getting ready to attack a weaker one. By May 1936 it was all over. In June Ethiopia was annexed to Italy.

The League Does Not Act. Four days after the invasion began, the League of Nations branded Italy the aggressor and tried to apply **sanctions** (penalties), including an arms embargo as well as a boycott of Italian goods. Other nations, however, would not agree to deny Mussolini oil for his highly mechanized army. Nor would Great Britain and France agree to keep Italian troops and munitions from passing through the Suez Canal. By this time it was clear that the League of Nations was more or less useless as a means of preventing war.

Student Assignment/Homework

Have students read Section 2, "America Struggles to Remain Neutral," and prepare for discussion.

Anticipate the Lesson

Review with students the reasons nations come into conflict with each other. (Reasons might include: wealth; land; power.) Ask students how these reasons motivated Hitler and Mussolini. (Possible responses: each leader wanted his country to become powerful; both saw the need to conquer other nations in order to enlarge their territories and increase their wealth.)

Aggression Condemned. Many groups and individuals bitterly protested Italy's actions. Black communities in the United States were particularly outraged by Italy's aggression. They responded by raising money and collecting medical supplies for the Ethiopians. Years later, Ethiopian Emperor Haile Selassie said,

> We can never forget the help Ethiopia received from Negro Americans during the terrible crisis. . . . It moved me to know that Americans of African descent did not abandon their embattled brothers, but stood by us.

Hitler Arms the Rhineland. Taking advantage of the international distraction over Ethiopia, Hitler made his first aggressive moves. In 1935 he announced that Germany would rearm despite the Versailles treaty. (See Chapter 23.) In March 1936 he sent troops into the Rhineland, an area in western Germany that was supposed to remain free of soldiers and fortifications. Hitler's remilitarization of the Rhineland was a threat to France and Britain. If at that time the two democracies had moved their own troops into the Rhineland, it is quite likely that Hitler would have backed down, for the German army was still weak. The two democracies could not agree on joint action, however, so Hitler was not stopped.

SECTION 1 REVIEW

Key Terms and People

Explain the significance of: Frank B. Kellogg, Stimson Doctrine, puppet state, Adolf Hitler, Nazi party, fascism, totalitarian, Benito Mussolini, sanctions

Main Ideas

1. What conditions led to Japan's decision to invade Manchuria?
2. What post-World War I conditions in Germany led to the rise of the Nazi party?
3. What was the major goal of the Nazi party?
4. How did many African Americans respond to Italy's invasion of Ethiopia?

Critical Thinking

5. What message did Japan send to the rest of the world when it invaded Manchuria, quit the League of Nations, and started rebuilding its navy?

SECTION 2

America Struggles to Remain Neutral

GLOSSARY TERMS: **reciprocal trade agreements, quarantine,** *Panay* **incident**

The United States Acts Cautiously

It is possible that President Roosevelt could have eased European tensions somewhat during this period by wiping out Allied war debts. Yet Congress would not have gone along with such an action. Most Americans agreed with Calvin Coolidge. "They hired the money, didn't they?" that stern Yankee had said. However, the United States did take several important steps in the area of foreign affairs.

Recognizing the Soviet Union. Ever since the Russian Revolution of 1917, the United States had refused to recognize that country's government. This was partly because the Soviet government had taken over American property and refused to repay the loans that the United States had made to the Russian monarchy. In November 1933, however, President Roosevelt agreed to exchange ambassadors with Moscow. The Soviet Union did not attempt to alter its often-stated policy of overthrowing the capitalist system of government wherever and whenever it could. Nor did the Soviets repay the debt. Still, the fact that American diplomats could now be stationed in Moscow where they could study the Soviets was useful. It was useful to know more about what was going on inside the Soviet Union. Even more useful, the Soviet Union now became a possible market for American exports. It was also a possible counterweight to Japanese aggression in Asia.

Reciprocal Trade Agreements. As you know from Chapter 26, the Hawley-Smoot Tariff of 1930, which raised American tariffs to their highest point ever, had resulted in a sharp decline in American trade. To correct this trend, in 1934 Congress passed a Reciprocal Trade Agreement Act giving the President the power to make agreements with other countries that would reduce tariffs by as much as 50 percent. Under the leadership of Secretary of State Cordell Hull, a strong supporter

Main Ideas

1. Japan was dependent on world trade for food and raw materials. Because the depression had dried up the market for its manufactured goods, Japan decided simply to take, rather than trade for, Manchuria's coal and iron.

2. Poor economic conditions, including high rates of inflation and unemployment, and an unstable political situation.

3. To make Germany the dominant power in Europe.

4. By expressing outrage, denouncing Italy's actions, and sending money and medical supplies to the Ethiopians.

Critical Thinking

5. Japan demonstrated its determination to do whatever it thought was in its own interest, without regard for world opinion. **(analysis)**

State the Objective

Understand how world events challenged the U.S. policy of neutrality.

Present the Lesson

Have students review the section and summarize on paper the provisions of the Neutrality Acts passed by Congress between 1935 and 1937. Summaries should include:

- Neutrality Act of 1935—once the President declared that a state of war existed, it would be unlawful to ship or sell arms to those countries involved; the President could warn Americans traveling on ships of warring nations that they were doing so at their own risk.
- Neutrality Act of 1936—prohibited loans and credits to warring nations.

- Neutrality Act of 1937—made the 1935 and 1936 acts permanent but more flexible; the President could permit the sale of goods other than weapons on a "cash-and-carry" basis.

To review, have volunteers read their papers to the class. Encourage students to refer to their papers as they study this section.

For Discussion

How did the findings of the Nye committee contribute to the isolationist movement in the U.S.? (Possible responses: the committee suggested that certain American corporations had urged Wilson to go to war to make a profit; people believed that to avoid this situation in the future the U.S. should avoid all foreign financial entanglements, keep its citizens at home, and refrain from exercising its neutral rights.)

of low tariffs, the United States signed more than twenty **reciprocal trade agreements** over the next five years. America's foreign trade increased, and other nations, especially in Latin America, became more friendly toward the United States.

The Good Neighbor Policy. Roosevelt continued the Good Neighbor Policy begun by Presidents Coolidge and Hoover. In 1933 a Pan-American conference at Montevideo, Uruguay, heard the United States representative promise to end all armed intervention in Latin American nations. The words were soon matched by action. In 1934 the United States signed a treaty with Cuba that abrogated, or abolished, the Platt Amendment (see Chapter 20) but retained the naval base at Guantanamo Bay. That same year, the last United States marines were withdrawn from Haiti, where they had been stationed since 1915. American supervision of Haitian finances, however, was maintained until 1942.

Roosevelt then traveled seven thousand miles to Buenos Aires—a long way for Presidents to travel in those days—to attend the 1936 Inter-American Conference for Peace. There the President declared that he was a "traveling salesman for peace" and again stated the new United States policy of nonintervention in Latin American affairs.

Campaigns Promote Isolationism

During the 1930's the Girl Scouts of America changed the color of their uniforms from khaki to green to make them appear less militaristic. The same antiwar spirit was behind other campaigns. One sought to end the sale of toy soldiers lest their owners develop a taste for battle. Another campaign tried to abolish Memorial Day on the ground that decorating soldiers' graves glorified past wars. Such campaigns reflected a widespread feeling in the United States that the country should isolate itself from the possibility of war.

The Nye Committee. Gerald P. Nye was a senator from North Dakota. Beginning in April 1934, he headed a committee to investigate the reasons for United States entry into World War I. Specifically, Nye's committee wanted to know what made Woodrow Wilson change from the candidate who "kept us out of war" in 1916 to the President who led us into war in 1917. The committee conducted hearings for three years and then published its findings.

The main point of the Nye committee's report

was that certain American corporations, particularly those in munitions and banking, had made lots of money during World War I. There was also a suggestion, but without evidence to back it up, that some large corporations had urged Wilson to go to war so they could make a profit.

These findings were published as sensational exposés by newspapers and magazines. The public was horrified. The term "merchants of death" was applied to the corporations, and the number of isolationists in the nation skyrocketed.

The isolationists' belief was that the United States could remain at peace in a future war. All it had to do was avoid financial entanglements, keep its ships and its citizens at home, and refrain from exercising its neutral rights. Accordingly, Nye and other isolationists in Congress passed a series of neutrality acts designed to keep the United States out of another world war.

The Neutrality Acts. The first Neutrality Act was passed in 1935 after the invasion of Ethiopia. According to this act, once the President declared that a state of war existed, it would be unlawful for the United States to ship or sell arms to those countries that were fighting. The President could also warn American citizens traveling on ships of warring countries that they were doing so at their own risk. This measure was designed to prevent another *Lusitania* incident.

Picturing History Isolationists deodorize the skunk —Nazi Germany—while Charles Lindbergh stoops to feed him.

Walt Disney (1901–1966)

While war clouds gathered abroad, Americans facing economic depression at home turned to the movies to help them forget their troubles. They were fortunate to have a true showman in their midst. He was Walt Disney, one of the great entertainers of recent times.

After working as a commercial artist's assistant as a young man in Kansas City, Missouri, Disney took a partner and began making two-minute advertisements. The partners' ads were crude animated cartoons, drawn by Disney and photographed with a second-hand movie camera. They were shown during motion picture shows, much as commercials are shown on television today.

The two young businessmen turned next to seven-minute animated children's stories. However, this enterprise failed, mostly because the partners were cheated by a New York distributor.

Disney moved to Los Angeles in 1923 and formed a new partnership, this time with his brother Roy. Both moves proved excellent. The Disneys hoped to make animated cartoons, and Hollywood was already the center of the motion picture business. Roy Disney, it turned out, was a shrewd and able business manager.

After a few false starts, Walt Disney hit upon the right cartoon formula—an animal who would think and act like a human being. Oswald the Rabbit did not work out, but then

Mickey Mouse was born.

The young company had two cartoon shorts in production in 1927 when talking movies came out. Both shorts were scrapped, and a new feature was developed, one in which Mickey talked—in a suitably squeaky voice, supplied by Walt Disney.

The film short was called *Steamboat Willie,* and the public—old and young alike—loved it. The Disney brothers added other characters: Mickey's girlfriend, Minnie Mouse; the bad-tempered Donald Duck; a not very bright dog called Pluto; and an even stupider hound named Goofy.

In 1933, the very worst year of the Great Depression, Walt Disney released another adaptation of his early idea of making children's stories. It was *The Three Little Pigs,* featuring a villainous, scheming wolf. Contributing to the success of this venture was a cheerful, lilting tune, "Who's Afraid of the Big Bad Wolf?" "A wolf at the door" was the very personification of hard times. This wolf was defied, overcome, and destroyed by the shrewd, cheerful little pigs. It was just the medicine a frightened, discouraged nation needed. As a morale builder, the song was almost as effective as Franklin D. Roosevelt's motto, "The only thing we have to fear is fear itself."

Disney's next breakthrough was a full-length animated film, *Snow White and the Seven*

Dwarfs. It mixed humans (Snow White, the Prince, and the Wicked Witch) with assorted caricatures and little forest creatures. It took three years to make and was followed by *Pinocchio, Dumbo,* and *Fantasia.*

Fantasia had no story line; instead it was a series of musical pieces accompanied by performing animated creatures. The music was conducted by the renowned Leopold Stokowski, who also appeared in the film—shaking hands with Mickey Mouse! This event marked another first.

Following World War II, Disney began turning out "True-Life Adventures." These were features about nature, such as *Seal Island* and *Beaver Valley.* Music critics had disliked *Fantasia,* and scientists were just as unhappy with the nature films, which were cleverly edited more for "cuteness" than for a true depiction of animal life. The public, nevertheless, loved them.

By the 1950's, Disney Productions was a full-fledged Hollywood operation, turning out shorts, full-length features, and television series. As the movie business changed, the corporation changed as well. Still trading on the early cartoon characters, it began to operate its very successful theme parks.

Walt Disney died in 1966, denying to the end that what he had created was art. "It's show business," he said, "and I'm a showman." He was.

Check for Understanding

Have students answer the Section 2 Review questions on paper.

Guided Practice

Tell students that many people who lived through the era when the U.S., Great Britain, and France "appeased" the Nazis warn against the same attitudes toward aggressive nations today. Ask students to consider the consequences of the U.S. ignoring or appeasing such aggressions today. (Possible response: appeasement could upset the balance of power in a region as well as cause widespread suffering. When Iraq invaded Kuwait in August 1990, there was also the danger of massive oil reserves falling into the wrong hands.)

Assign Independent Practice

Have students write a paragraph explaining how the U.S. circumvented the Neutrality Acts with regard to the July 1937 China incident. Students should recognize that the incident moved Americans further from their isolationist position. (Paragraphs might include: Japanese and Chinese troops clashed near Beijing; Americans favored China; Roosevelt did not invoke Neutrality Act because Japan referred to the conflict as an "incident"; Americans continued to supply arms and other goods to China and helped build the Burma Road, a supply highway.)

The second Neutrality Act was passed in February 1936. It expanded the terms of the first act to prohibit extending loans and credit, as well as selling arms, to warring nations.

Five months later, an army revolt in Spain set off a civil war. Hitler and Mussolini made common cause with fascist-minded General **Francisco Franco,** who had attacked the Spanish republican government. Both dictators gave Franco all-out aid, including armed forces. It was an opportunity to try out their soldiers and weapons in a sort of dress rehearsal for bigger battles. The Soviet Union gave similar, but considerably less, assistance to the Loyalists, as the Spanish republican government forces were called. (This made the Loyalists look like communists, although most of them were not.) Also, about three thousand volunteers from the United States formed the Abraham Lincoln Brigade to fight against Franco. The civil war ended in March 1939 with the fall of Madrid to Franco. Thus, another fascist state was established in Europe. In the meantime, Italy and Germany cemented their friendship with a formal alliance called the Rome-Berlin Axis.

When the Spanish civil war broke out, Roosevelt asked Congress to apply the provisions of the neutrality acts to civil wars as well as to international ones. This was done in January 1937. In May 1937 the third Neutrality Act was passed. It made the first and second ones permanent. It also made them more flexible. The President could now permit the sale of goods other than weapons on a "cash-and-carry" basis. These goods had to be paid for on delivery, and they had to be taken from a United States port by the buyer.

Picturing History Spanish refugees escape to France at the end of the Spanish civil war.

Roosevelt Challenges Isolationism

President Roosevelt was not an isolationist. He was aware of the dangers of fascism and Nazism, and he felt it was important to take a firm stand against them. At the same time, however, he did not want to be considered a warmonger.

Neutrality and the "China Incident." In July 1937 Japanese militarists struck again in China. Chinese and Japanese troops clashed at the Marco Polo Bridge near Beijing. Using the clash as an excuse, Japanese forces moved swiftly and were soon in control of most of China's seacoast.

Most Americans favored China rather than Japan, so Roosevelt did not invoke the Neutrality Act. His excuse was that Japan itself referred to the conflict as an incident, not a war. Americans continued sending arms and other supplies to China. In addition, American engineers helped the Chinese build the 700-mile-long Burma Road, a supply highway that led from the town of Lashio in Burma across rough mountain country into China's interior.

The Quarantine Speech. On October 5, 1937, Roosevelt delivered a speech in Chicago. The President expressed his fears about the international situation and the behavior of Germany, Italy, and Japan. What was needed, he said, was collective security on the part of the peace-loving nations of the world. They should behave the way a community behaves when faced by an epidemic. He added: "[It] joins in a **quarantine** of the patients in order to protect the health of the community against the spread of the disease." In other words, instead of the United States isolating itself from the rest of the world, Roosevelt was suggesting that democratic nations get together and isolate the aggressor nations.

The President was deluged with mail. Some was favorable. Most of the letters, however, accused him of trying to lead the country into war. Two months later, Americans got a real war scare.

The *Panay* Incident. On December 12, 1937, on the Yangtze River in China, a navy gunboat, the U.S.S. *Panay,* and the three oil tankers it was escorting were attacked without warning by Japanese planes. Two servicemen were killed and several others wounded. The *Panay* had been clearly marked and had a legal right to be where it

Student Assignment/Homework

Have students read Section 3, "The Crisis Deepens," and answer the Section 3 Review questions on paper.

Anticipate the Lesson

Review the response of Great Britain and France to Germany. (Possible response: when Germany sent troops into the Rhineland, Great Britain and France could not agree on joint action, so they did nothing; both promised to protect Czechoslovakia; both signed the Munich Pact with Germany, which allowed Hitler to take the Sudetenland.)

was. The attack obviously was no accident. Japanese authorities apologized at once, offering to pay for damages and promising to punish those responsible. The United States accepted Japan's offer, and most Americans heaved a sigh of relief. A public opinion poll taken one month after the *Panay* **incident** showed that 70 percent of the public felt it would be better to pull out completely from China—withdrawing ships, marines, missionaries, and business people—rather than to run the risk of getting into war. It was difficult to find any vital United States interest in China.

Linking Past to Present

Fifty years after the *Panay* incident, a similar kind of tragedy occurred in the Persian Gulf. In May 1987, during the Iran-Iraq War, an Iraqi warplane fired on and hit the U.S.S. *Stark,* a frigate sent by the United States to protect oil tankers in the gulf. Thirty-seven Americans were killed. Iraq pleaded mistaken identity and apologized.

SECTION 2 REVIEW

Key Terms and People

Explain the significance of: reciprocal trade agreements, Francisco Franco, quarantine, *Panay* incident

Main Ideas

1. Why did the United States open relations with the Soviet Union in 1933?
2. How did the Reciprocal Trade Agreement Act help to offset the effects of the Hawley-Smoot Tariff?
3. How did isolationists in Congress attempt to ensure the United States' neutrality in the 1930's?
4. What was President Roosevelt's attitude toward the increasing international conflicts during the 1930's? What role did he expect the United States to play in these conflicts?

Critical Thinking

5. Why were the revelations of the Nye committee's report particularly horrifying to the American public at the time the report was released?

SECTION 3

The Crisis Deepens

GLOSSARY TERMS: Munich Pact, appeasement, nonaggression pact

In Europe the smell of gunpowder grew stronger. For months the German propaganda machine had trumpeted the charge that Germans living in Austria were being treated as a despised minority. Hitler declared that Germany would have to do something to help them.

Hitler Begins to March

In February 1938 Austrian Chancellor Kurt von Schuschnigg was summoned to meet Hitler at the dictator's villa at Berchtesgaden, high in the Bavarian Alps. When Schuschnigg arrived, diplomatic niceties were thrown out the window. After being verbally abused by Hitler, Schuschnigg was told that unless Austria signed an agreement dismissing members of its present government and installing Austrian Nazis in their place, Germany would attack.

Schuschnigg was appalled. He protested that he had no power to sign such an agreement. He would have to refer the matter to his cabinet in Vienna. He was allowed to return to the Austrian capital, but immediately after, the German propaganda machine again began denouncing the "wrongs" suffered by Germans in Austria. The charges were false. However, as Hitler once remarked, no matter how big the lie, if it is repeated often enough, eventually people will believe it.

Hitler Annexes Austria. A month later Hitler declared that he had to help his "fellow Germans." On March 11, 1938, German forces marched into Austria without opposition and two days later annexed it to Germany. By this *Anschluss* (union), one of Europe's oldest states vanished.

The shock of events in Europe was felt in the United States. That spring the United States set about building a two-ocean navy. Until then, the country had concentrated its naval forces in the Pacific, believing that the Atlantic sea frontier was reasonably secure in British hands. Now Congress voted to spend a billion dollars over a ten-year period to expand the American fleet so it could protect both the Atlantic and Pacific coasts by itself.

SECTION 2 REVIEW

Answers

Main Ideas

1. To learn more about the Soviet system; to develop the Soviet Union as a market for American goods and as a potential counterweight to Japanese aggression.

2. Reciprocal trade agreements fostered international trade by reducing U.S. tariffs on the goods of many foreign nations.

3. By passing a series of neutrality acts to penalize countries that engaged in warfare.

4. FDR feared the growth of the fascist and Nazi movements. • He suggested that the U.S. join other democratic nations to isolate and stop the aggressors.

Critical Thinking

5. The report implied that the deaths of American soldiers during World War I might have been avoided if large corporations had not persuaded Wilson to enter the war, and that these "merchants of death" might take advantage of the increasing tensions overseas to force the U.S. into another war. **(analysis)**

State the Objective

Understand how Germany's political actions of 1939 became the immediate causes of World War II.

Picturing History As the war grew more intense in Europe, American industry stepped up wartime production. In 1942 Henry J. Kaiser's Portland, Oregon, shipyards were building a new freighter every eighty days. By 1944 the time needed to build a freighter was reduced to twenty-two days. The freighter shown here, half completed, was launched by the shipyard workers and finished afloat.

Hitler Takes Czechoslovakia. Once Hitler had annexed Austria, he began threatening another neighbor. In the western part of Czechoslovakia, along its border with Germany, is a mountainous region called the Sudetenland. A large German minority lived there. Hitler charged that the Sudeten Germans were being persecuted by the Czechoslovakian government. By then, this was such a familiar story that everyone knew what it really meant. Hitler wanted to annex Czechoslovakia!

The spring and early summer of 1938 saw a buildup of German military strength along the Czech border. Then, in late summer, Hitler summoned Czechoslovakia's aged President, Emil Hácha (hä′kà), to Berlin. After the long train ride, the elderly man was not allowed to rest but was taken immediately before the German dictator. Hitler promptly went into his carefully calculated fit of rage. He screamed that Hácha had to submit to German military occupation of the Sudetenland or else the entire country would face complete destruction. Hácha sat as if turned to stone as Hitler declared that the President had to sign such an agreement immediately. Hitler warned him that German troops were massed at the borders and that bomber planes were already loaded and warming up their engines at airfields throughout Germany.

Hitler indicated a table where the papers and pens were lying. He left the room, and his aides practically thrust a pen into the old man's hand. The shock was too great, and Hácha fainted. But Hitler's doctor brought him around, however, with an injection of vitamins. Hácha signed the agreement and returned home a brokenhearted man.

Munich Means Appeasement

Both France and Great Britain had promised Czechoslovakia that they would protect it from a German takeover. Now British Prime Minister **Neville Chamberlain** asked for a meeting with Hitler. President Roosevelt sent messages expressing his fear of war to all the nations involved. Chamberlain flew to Berlin three times to talk with the German dictator.

Finally, at the end of September 1938, Hitler, Mussolini, Chamberlain, and the French premier, Edouard Daladier (dà làd′yā), met in Munich. Neither Czechoslovakia, which was the subject of discussion, nor the Soviet Union, which had a friendship treaty with Czechoslovakia, was included. At Munich, Hitler told the assembled diplomats that the Sudeten area would be his "last territorial demand." The British and French leaders

Picturing History British Prime Minister Neville Chamberlain proclaiming "peace for our time."

Present the Lesson

Ask students to skim the section and volunteer details for a time line showing Hitler's rise to power and the deepening of the crisis in Europe. Write the time line on the board. The time line should include:

1933	Hitler sets an economic boycott against German Jews.
1935	Nuremberg Laws take away Jews' political rights.
March 11-13, 1938	German forces march into Austria and annex it.
Summer 1938	Hitler takes control of the Sudetenland.
September 30, 1938	Hitler signs Munich Pact with Great Britain, France, and Italy.
November 7, 1938	Nazi gangs wage Crystal Night.
August 23, 1939	Hitler signs a nonaggression pact with the Soviet Union.
September 1, 1939	Hitler attacks Poland.
September 3, 1939	Great Britain and France declare war on Germany.

Have students refer to the time line as they study this section.

feared war so much and wanted to believe Hitler so desperately that they agreed to let him have the Sudetenland. They did so simply because their hopes triumphed over their experience. They should have known what would happen. However, they also believed that their people would not fight, as Chamberlain put it, "over a far-off country of which we know little." The **Munich Pact** was signed on September 30, and German troops immediately crossed the border into Czechoslovakia.

Chamberlain declared that the Munich Pact had brought about "peace in our time," and he was wildly cheered on his return to London. His rival in Parliament, and also his successor, was **Winston Churchill.** Churchill and a small but growing segment of the British people took a different view. They felt that Britain and France had failed to act in the face of German aggression in Austria. The two powers had also broken their promise to protect Czechoslovakia and had adopted a policy of **appeasement** by giving in to Hitler's demands. As Churchill put it, "Britain and France had to choose between war and dishonor. They chose dishonor. They will have war."

Within six months of the Munich Pact, Hitler broke his promise not to seek additional territory. In March 1939 Germany took over the rest of Czechoslovakia. Not to be outdone, Mussolini

Axis Conquests in Europe, 1936-1939

Axis powers
Areas of Axis conquest
← Axis thrusts
(1937 boundaries)

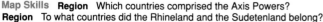

Map Skills **Region** Which countries comprised the Axis Powers?
Region To what countries did the Rhineland and the Sudetenland belong?

Map Skills

Germany, Italy • Rhineland—Germany; Sudetenland—Czechoslovakia

Check for Understanding

Have students write two paragraphs explaining how the invasion of Poland served as the straw that broke the camel's back and triggered a global war. (Paragraphs might include: it was the final act in a long series of aggressive acts by Hitler; France and Great Britain began to realize the strength and terror of the Nazi army and worried about their own safety; Hitler broke the Munich Pact.)

invaded the tiny kingdom of Albania the following month and soon added it to the Italian empire.

Germany's Jews Suffer Persecution

While Hitler was on the march outside of Germany, the plight of Germany's Jews was becoming more desperate. On coming to power in 1933, Hitler had announced a national economic boycott against them. They were forbidden to enter or remain in the medical or legal professions or to obtain business licenses. All Jewish teachers and other civil service employees were fired, as were Jews who worked in firms owned by non-Jews. It became increasingly difficult for German Jews to earn a living.

The Nuremberg Laws. Two years later, in 1935, the Nuremberg Laws took away the Jews' political rights. They lost their citizenship. They were expelled from German schools and denied medical care. They were segregated on trains and other means of transportation. They could not have telephones in their homes. They could go shopping only during special hours, and they had to be off the streets after 8:00 P.M. To make identification easier, all Jews over the age of six were required to wear a Jewish star—black on a yellow background—over the left breast of their clothing.

The new laws also forbade Aryans, by which Hitler meant non-Jews of "pure" German blood, from marrying Jews. Jews who left Germany were not allowed to take any of their property or money with them. To prevent the smuggling of valuables out of the country, later laws forced Jews to register everything they owned. This measure was applied to Austrian Jews after Germany and Austria were united in 1938.

Crystal Night. Worse was to come. On November 7, 1938, a seventeen-year-old Jewish refugee assassinated a German diplomat in Paris. Two nights later came *Kristallnacht,* the night of broken glass. Throughout Germany, Nazi gangs entered and burned most of the nation's synagogues. They broke into Jewish homes and places of business, looted them, and beat up the occupants. Shattered glass littered the streets. Several hundred Jews committed suicide, more than one thousand were murdered, and twenty-six thousand were thrown into concentration camps. In addition, a fine of one billion marks—about 20 percent of what they owned—was levied on the entire German-Jewish community.

Picturing History Germans stand on sidewalks littered with broken glass to view a Jewish business that was vandalized by Nazi gangs on *Kristallnacht.*

Plight of the Refugees. Many German Jews still loved their homeland and decided to remain in Germany in hope that the Nazi storm would soon blow over. Others, however, were extremely anxious to get out. They had begun to think the unthinkable—that Hitler actually meant to get rid of the entire Jewish population one way or another.

The League of Nations set up the High Commission for Refugees from Germany, but it had only limited success. Great Britain agreed to accept some 80,000 refugees. About 60,000 fled to the United States, and many more wanted to come. However, the Roosevelt administration did little to help them. This was partly because the United States was suffering from widespread unemployment. It did not want to take in additional people who might add to unemployment or take away jobs that Americans could have. Still, some 400,000 openings in the nation's immigration quotas that were available for people from countries under Hitler's rule were not filled.

Illustrious Names. Many of those who succeeded in gaining entry to the United States were artists, scientists, and business people. In other words, they were the kind of newcomers who were more likely to create jobs than to take them away. The list—headed by mathematician **Albert Einstein,** conductor **Arturo Toscanini,** author **Thomas Mann,** physicist **Enrico Fermi,** and architect **Walter Gropius**—is impressive. They and others who

722

Tell students that the U.S. has been criticized for its failure to do enough to help Jewish refugees during World War II. Ask students what responsibility they think the U.S. should assume today in offering relief and refuge to those seeking political asylum. (Possible responses: the U.S. has a moral obligation to offer sanctuary to those who are persecuted because our country was founded by people in similar situations; although aiding political refugees is a moral and responsible thing to do, it is not practical because the number of refugees could be too large for the U.S. to handle;

we would be faced with additional problems in the areas of housing, employment, and overcrowding.)

Have students complete Chapter 28, Section 3 Enrichment Activity.

---

came here from Germany and Italy had much to do with America's leap to the forefront in science and in the arts immediately after World War II. Many also went to Canada, where they eventually rose to top positions in government and in private industry.

The Soviet Union and Germany Conspire

Great Britain and France became increasingly nervous during the summer of 1939. Hitler was once again giving his usual signs of wanting more territory. This time his target was the Polish Corridor and the free city of Danzig. (See map on page 721.) The Versailles treaty had given the corridor to Poland so that it would have an outlet to the Baltic Sea; Danzig was the seaport at the corridor's end. The population of both was mostly German, and in addition the corridor separated East Prussia from the rest of Germany.

Accordingly, Hitler went into his usual routine. He declared that Germans in both places were being brutalized by unfeeling Poles and that he must rescue them. There were some who thought the Nazi leader was bluffing this time. After all, an invasion of Poland would bring Germany into contact with its avowed enemy, the Soviet Union, Poland's eastern neighbor. Furthermore, an attack on Poland would probably mean a two-front war for Germany against the Soviet Union in the east and against France and Great Britain in the west. (Chamberlain had announced in March that Britain would help Poland if it were attacked.) Fighting on two fronts had helped bring about Germany's defeat in World War I. Surely, some people thought, Hitler would not be so stupid as to repeat that mistake!

In April the Soviet dictator **Joseph Stalin** suggested to Britain that his nation and France follow the principle of collective security and back Britain's guarantee to Poland. Chamberlain turned down the idea. It would have given the Soviets the right to send their armies into Poland to fight the Germans—and the Poles refused to have Soviet troops on their soil. Soviets and Poles were enemies of long standing, and the eastern part of Poland had been Soviet territory before World War I. Poland suspected—correctly, as it turned out—that the Soviet Union wanted that territory back.

Stalin realized that Britain and France had no love for the Soviet Union. Nor was he sure how much help he would get from them in case Germany attacked his country. So he changed his policy. On August 23, 1939, he signed a **non-aggression pact** with Nazi Germany. The two nations agreed not to fight one another. They also signed a secret agreement in which Hitler promised that German troops would take only part of Poland and would let Soviet troops take over the eastern section.

Hitler had outwitted the democratic countries. He had removed the threat of a two-front war. His way was now clear to attack Poland.

Picturing History Soviet dictator Joseph Stalin (right) and German Foreign Minister Joachim von Ribbentrop (left) stand behind Soviet Foreign Minister V. M. Molotov as he signs the German-Soviet nonaggression pact in August 1939. The pact guaranteed Soviet neutrality if Germany went to war against Great Britain and France.

World War II Begins in Europe

The next day, August 24, President Roosevelt asked Germany and Poland to settle their differences peacefully. Would they, he asked, accept the decision of an outside third party? Poland agreed. Hitler refused.

At dawn on September 1, Germany attacked Poland with planes, tanks, ships, and almost 2 million troops. This time, however, Hitler misjudged the Western powers. There was a limit beyond which they could not be pushed. Britain and France declared war on Germany on September 3. World War II had begun.

That same evening, President Roosevelt discussed the war in a fireside chat. He said,

> This nation will remain a neutral nation, but I cannot ask that every American remain neutral in thought as well. Even a neutral has a right to take account of the facts. Even a neutral cannot be asked to close his mind or his conscience.

Roosevelt made no secret of his pro-British sympathies.

What message did FDR give the American people in his fireside chat of September 3, 1939? (Possible responses: he said that the U.S. would remain neutral but that he would not ask for every American to remain neutral in thought; he said that individuals could not always remain neutral after taking the facts into account; he revealed his pro-British sympathies.)

Have students read Section 4, "Early Events Warn Americans," and answer the Section 4 Review questions on paper.

Anticipate the Lesson

Review with students the maps showing the Axis nations and Axis conquests. Ask students how they think Americans may have reacted to the declaration of war by Great Britain and France. (Possible responses: some favored the French and British and called for a change in the Neutrality Acts; some called for a greater degree of isolationism; some hoped to make a profit by manufacturing war supplies.)

SECTION 3 REVIEW
Answers

Main Ideas

1. Hitler's frequent propaganda statements claimed that Germans living in Austria and Czechoslovakia were being persecuted and were in need of Germany's aid.

2. To avoid another world war.

3. German Jews lost their citizenship and were stripped of their economic power as well as their political, civil, and basic human rights.

4. Germany's invasion of Poland.

Critical Thinking

5. Possible answers: yes—the U.S. government needed to balance its social and economic responsibilities to its own citizens with its moral responsibilities to the oppressed people of foreign nations. No—the U.S. should have opened its doors to all oppressed people. **(evaluation)**

Linking Past to Present

Geography has always played a key role in Poland's political history. Situated between Germany and the Soviet Union, Poland has waged a continual struggle to free itself from foreign domination. In 1945, as a result of World War II, the Soviet Union took over Poland. Then in 1981 martial law was declared and less than a year later the Polish trade union, Solidarity, was outlawed. By 1989, however, times had changed. As the worsening economic crisis in the Communist bloc countries put increasing pressure on the Soviet government, Mikhail Gorbachev developed his policies of openness and restructuring. One important result was that the Soviets allowed Poland to experiment with democracy—with dramatic consequences. Tadeusz Mazowiecki, who had been jailed in 1982 as editor of Solidarity's newspaper, took office in 1989 as Poland's Prime Minister. Then in December, 1990, Poland elected a new president—Lech Walesa, leader of the once-outlawed Solidarity labor movement.

SECTION 3 REVIEW

Key Terms and People

Explain the significance of: Neville Chamberlain, Munich Pact, Winston Churchill, appeasement, Albert Einstein, Arturo Toscanini, Thomas Mann, Enrico Fermi, Walter Gropius, Joseph Stalin, nonaggression pact

Main Ideas

1. How did Hitler use propaganda to gain acceptance for his aggression against Austria and Czechoslovakia?
2. Why did the British and French appease Hitler at Munich?
3. In general, how did the Nuremberg Laws affect German Jews?
4. What event finally convinced Britain and France to declare war on Germany?

Critical Thinking

5. Was the United States right in not accepting more refugees from Germany? Explain.

SECTION 4

Early Events Warn Americans

GLOSSARY TERMS: blitzkrieg, genocide, Holocaust, Axis powers

As soon as war broke out in Europe, the United States declared itself neutral. Three weeks later, however, President Roosevelt called Congress into special session and asked for passage of a fourth Neutrality Act. The act, approved in November, repealed the arms embargo. Great Britain, France, and their allies could now purchase American weapons and ammunition on a cash-and-carry basis. American ships were forbidden to enter the war zone. The United States and the Latin American countries agreed to establish a ''safety belt'' ranging from three hundred to one thousand miles around the coasts of North and South America. They warned others not to engage in naval action in those waters.

New Horrors Are Unleashed

While the United States and other nations tried to protect themselves, the Germans proceeded to put new military and political tactics into effect. Not since the Mongol invasions of the thirteenth and fourteenth centuries had there been such rapid conquests or such open contempt for human life and dignity.

Blitzkrieg. The German army raced through Poland. The world had never seen anything like it and learned a new word: *blitzkrieg,* or lightning war. It began with dive-bomber attacks that destroyed Polish airfields and then smashed the large cities, disrupting communications and creating general confusion. The bombers were followed by mechanized panzer (armored) divisions that moved swiftly over roads that had been strafed, or machine-gunned, by low-flying planes to clear them of defense forces and refugees. Except for guerrillas, who fought in the forests to the end of the war, Polish resistance was over in less than a month. In the third week of fighting, Stalin's armies attacked from the east. The Soviet Union got slightly more than half of Poland's territory, while Germany took almost two-thirds of its population.

Slave Labor. With the victory in Poland, the Nazis gave full play to their racist ideas. According

State the Objective

Understand the early events of World War II both in Europe and in the U.S.

to these fantasies, Slavic people like the Poles were inferior to Germans. Hundreds of thousands of able-bodied Polish soldiers and civilians, regardless of education or past accomplishments, were shipped to Germany as slave labor for German factories and farms. Towns were emptied of their Polish inhabitants and refilled with German settlers. Poles were removed from the best farmlands to make way for German farmers.

The Nazis were also determined to wipe out Poland's culture. They burned Polish libraries. They also murdered or imprisoned a quarter of a million clergymen, intellectuals, and other leaders.

Genocide. Another horrifying word that became known to many people for the first time was *genocide,* the deliberate and systematic killing of a group of people. In 1939 the Nazis proceeded toward a "final solution of the Jewish question." The plan was to exterminate all the Jews of Europe, beginning with the 2 million in German-occupied Poland.

Special mobile killing units were assigned to round up Jewish men, women, and children; strip them of their clothing; and then shoot them in cold blood. Other Jews were herded into special areas of Polish cities called ghettos. There they were left to starve or die of disease.

In time these methods proved inefficient. They did not kill fast enough. Late in 1941 the Germans set up six death camps in Poland: Auschwitz, Belzec, Chelmno, Majdanek, Sobibor, and Treblinka. Each camp contained several huge gas chambers in which as many as six thousand persons could be suffocated by cyanide gas each day. The corpses were then taken to a room where their gold dental fillings were removed and their hair was shaved off to be used for stuffing mattresses and pillows.

At first the bodies were buried in mass graves. However, as one historian explained:

> The decaying corpses left odors that spread for miles, and when the rate of killing increased, the space needed for graves was enormous. Worse, mass graves were evidence of mass killings. . . . [So the Germans] turned to burning the bodies in open pits. This proved to be the cheapest and most efficient method.

For Discussion

German behavior went far beyond that of other wartime aggressors throughout history. Do you think that there is any kind of behavior that is not appropriate or justified once two nations have declared total war? (Possible responses: no— war is an irrational and inhumane activity, and abnormal behavior is sometimes excused in the chaos of war; yes—the destruction of cities and farms and the killing of innocent civilians is not justifiable.)

Picturing History The horror of the Nazi atrocities that occurred during the Holocaust is well documented in photographs such as the ones shown here. Above, a Jewish family is arrested by Nazi troops in Warsaw, Poland, in 1939. At the left, open doors reveal the ashes of women burned in the human disposal ovens in Weimar, Germany. Gold teeth and clothing were removed before cremation.

Have students skim the section to find examples of countries that suffered German aggression, examples of German military tactics, and examples of German persecution of the Jews. Have volunteers write their examples on the board. (Examples might include: countries that suffered German aggression—Denmark, Norway, the Netherlands, Belgium, Luxembourg, France, Great Britain; German military tactics—blitzkrieg, slave labor; German persecution of Jews—genocide, death camps, Holocaust.)

Ask students how the U.S. began to prepare for possible entry into the war in reaction to German aggression. (Responses: the U.S. passed the fourth Neutrality Act, which repealed the arms embargo and enabled Great Britain, France, and their allies to buy American weapons; the U.S. and Latin American countries agreed to establish a "safety belt" around the coasts of North and South America and warned against naval action in those waters; FDR appointed a bipartisan cabinet; the Selective Training and Service Act created the first peacetime draft; FDR was reelected.)

All told, by the time World War II ended in 1945, about 6 million Jews, as well as several thousand gypsies and others who spoke against the Nazis, were slaughtered in these death camps. The systematic murder of these people is known as the **Holocaust.**

Correspondents Broadcast Live Reports.   One reason why people were able to follow events in Europe with such horrified attention was the presence there of a group of extremely talented newspeople. Journalists like Dorothy Thompson, Anne O'Hare McCormick, and William L. Shirer were tireless in covering the news for their papers and magazines. Also, for the first time correspondents made firsthand reports by radio directly to the people back home. Americans were able to hear history unfold in their living rooms. It was a stunning new experience in communication.

Both the Columbia Broadcasting System (CBS) and the National Broadcasting Corporation (NBC) signed up correspondents. CBS employed as its European director a young man under thirty named **Edward R. Murrow,** who became one of the most famous broadcasters in history.

Picturing History   Americans learned about the war from correspondents. Dorothy Thompson reported from Germany, while Edward R. Murrow broadcast from London.

France Falls and Britain Stands Alone

While Poland was being overrun by the Germans, what was happening on the western front? Nothing—for seven months! The French and the British sat in the Maginot (mazh′ a nō′) line, a system of fortifications along France's eastern border, and stared at the Germans, who sat in the Siegfried (sēg′ frēd) line a few miles away and stared back. Soldiers ate, dozed, played cards, and

wrote letters home. There was no fighting. Planes flew over enemy territory but only to observe and to drop leaflets. People called this period the phony war, or "sitzkrieg." Later it became known as the winter of illusion.

Illusion let the Allies believe they could win the war by blockading Germany and starving Hitler out. Beginning in April 1940, they learned otherwise. Early that month and without warning, the German blitzkrieg struck at the neutral nations of Denmark and Norway. Denmark was overrun in a few hours, but Norway resisted for several weeks. The Norwegians even managed to sink several German ships. By month's end, however, the King and his ministers had fled to Britain, where they joined the Poles as a government-in-exile.

The following month, the German blitzkrieg struck at the neutral nations of the Netherlands, Belgium, and Luxembourg, also known as the Low Countries. Before the end of May, all three had been overrun by Hitler's war machine.

The Fall of France.   Hitler's strike into the Low Countries soon led to even greater disaster for the Allies. The Maginot line did not extend as far as the English Channel but stopped at the border of France and Belgium. The invading German armies simply swung around to the north of it. In four weeks they had pinned the British against the English Channel, cut the French army to pieces, and taken Paris. Hitler had accomplished in four weeks what Kaiser Wilhelm's armies had failed to do in four years. That was truly a blitzkrieg!

A third of a million British troops were miraculously rescued from the beaches of Dunkirk by a makeshift flotilla of tugboats, power launches, fishing craft, and private yachts that shuttled back and forth across the Channel for almost a week. It was a remarkable achievement, but heavy arms and equipment had to be left behind.

A few days later, Italy declared war on the side of Germany and invaded France from the south. On June 22, 1940, France surrendered—in the same railway coach in the forest of Compiègne (kōn pyen′ y′) where, twenty-two years earlier, Germany had signed the armistice that ended World War I. The Germans occupied the northern part of the country. A puppet government for France's southern region was set up at Vichy (vish′ ē) under aged Marshal **Henri Pétain** (pā tan′). This meant that yet another government-in-exile was organized in London. The Free French were headed by a very

Check for Understanding

Call on individual students to read their answers to the Section 4 Review questions.

Guided Practice

To stimulate discussion on the Holocaust and on how it could have happened in a modern, technologically sophisticated country with a high rate of literacy, ask students the following questions. How could the German people have let the Holocaust happen? Do you think such an event could happen somewhere in the world again? (Possible responses: the German people were anxious to accept Hitler because he pulled them out of their financial depression; they were looking for someone to blame for their problems; they were victims of a brilliant propaganda machine. Such an event is unlikely to occur today because of the availability of news through television, radio, and the press; knowing what happened in Germany, many groups in the U.S. and other countries would exert pressure on their governments to deal with an aggressor nation that attempted similar activities.)

tall general who for years had been advocating the theory of mobile warfare, the kind of warfare that had just crushed his nation. His name was **Charles de Gaulle** (də gôl′).

Nazi occupation of western Europe was not as savage as it was in the east. However, hostages, including women and children, were shot in reprisal for sabotage and other guerrilla activities against the Germans. In time the occupied countries had to pass laws against their Jewish citizens and round them up for shipment to the death camps. Other people of the occupied countries were sent to work in war industries in Germany.

Some of them were made to work as servants, and others were picked as farm workers.

The Battle of Britain. After the fall of France, Nazi officials declared: "We have just one more battle to win." Who could doubt that Hitler had a master plan prepared for the invasion of Britain? In fact, he had none. He did, however, have the illusion that Britain would recognize how hopeless its position was and would ask for terms. He completely misjudged the British. Even before France's fall, Winston Churchill, who had replaced Chamberlain as Prime Minister, had told Parlia-

World War II in Europe, 1940

- Axis powers
- Areas of Axis conquest, 1936–1939
- Areas of Axis conquest, 1940
- Vichy France and areas it controlled
- ✕ Battle
- ← Axis thrusts

(1937 boundaries)

Map Skills

About 550 miles (900 km)
• France • Northern Africa
(Morocco, Algeria, Tunisia)

Map Skills **Location** How far is Paris from Berlin? **Location** In what country is Dunkirk located? **Region** What area besides southern France did the Vichy government control?

Assign Independent Practice
Have students complete Chapter 28, Section 4
Daily Activity.

Student Assignment/Homework
Have students complete Chapter 28 Test on
paper. Review all Critical Thinking questions
with the class.

ment, "We shall defend our island, whatever the cost may be. We shall fight on the beaches, we shall fight on the landing-grounds, we shall fight in the fields and in the streets, we shall fight in the hills. We shall never surrender."

The Germans began to assemble barges and landing craft along the French coast of the English Channel. First, however, they had to establish air supremacy. They had to destroy the Royal Air Force (RAF).

The Battle of Britain was fought through the summer and autumn of 1940. Hitler had twenty-six hundred bombers at his disposal. On a single day—August 15—one thousand of Hitler's planes ranged over Britain. Every night for two solid months, two hundred bombers pounded London.

Picturing History The will and determination to stop Hitler is reflected in Winston Churchill's stern gaze. Buildings in London crumbled during the Battle of Britain.

When the attacks concentrated on airfields and aircraft factories, they were a severe threat to the RAF. When the Germans switched to cities and land transportation, however, the RAF won a breather. Its resistance was deadly. Alerted by the new device of radar, which British scientists had perfected, British pilots soared aloft day after day, and sometimes night after night as well, to destroy the German planes. Eventually, German losses became so great that Hitler decided to postpone his

attempt to invade Britain. In fact, the idea was never considered again.

Terrible night raids against British cities continued throughout the winter of 1940–1941 in an effort to crack the people's morale. That, too, failed. The lights of freedom had gone out on the European continent, but they continued to burn on the British Isles.

In the meantime, Japan joined into a three-power agreement with Germany and Italy. Each was to help the others against any future enemies. The Rome-Berlin-Tokyo Axis was now official. The three became known as the **Axis powers.**

America Prepares for War

In June 1940 Roosevelt responded to an appeal from Churchill. Using a 1917 law, he sent Britain 500,000 rifles, 80,000 machine guns, 900 field

Chronology of Events before Pearl Harbor		
1931	Sept.	Japan invades Manchuria
1933	Jan.	Hitler becomes Chancellor of Germany
1934	March	Germany begins to rearm
1935	Oct.	Italy invades Ethiopia
1936	March	Germany reoccupies the Rhineland
	Oct.	Germany and Italy form the Axis
1938	March	Germany occupies Austria
	Sept.	Germany takes the Sudetenland
1939	March	Germany takes Czechoslovakia
	April	Italy invades Albania
	Aug.	Germany and the Soviet Union sign nonaggression pact
	Sept.	Germany invades Poland; France and Britain declare war on Germany
	Nov.	Soviet Union attacks Finland
1940	June	Italy declares war on Britain and France; three-fifths of France is occupied by Germany
	Sept.	The U.S. begins a military draft
1941	March	Lend-Lease Act passes
	June	Germany invades the Soviet Union
	Dec.	Japan attacks Pearl Harbor; U.S. declares war on Japan, Germany, and Italy

guns, and 130 million rounds of ammunition to help replace what had been lost at Dunkirk. On September 3 Britain received fifty destroyers for use against German submarines in the North Atlantic. They were World War I ships with four smokestacks but were still useful. In return, the United States obtained ninety-nine-year leases on eight naval and air bases in Newfoundland, Bermuda, the West Indies, and British Guiana (now Guyana).

A Bipartisan Cabinet. That same summer of 1940, FDR brought two distinguished Republicans into his cabinet. Henry L. Stimson, who had been Hoover's Secretary of State, became Secretary of War. Frank Knox, the 1936 Republican candidate for Vice-President, was made Secretary of the Navy. Having two such able Republicans in key positions strengthened the administration for the coming struggle and broadened its popular base.

Selective Service. A further defense measure was the adoption of the nation's first peacetime draft. Under the Selective Training and Service Act, 16 million men between the ages of twenty-one and thirty-five were registered. Of this number, a million were selected for training the first year, and 800,000 reserves were called up.

FDR Wins a Third Term

Meanwhile, in 1940 the nation was in the midst of a historic election campaign. If he won, Roosevelt would break a two-term tradition that went back to George Washington's time. Many believed that by seeking a third term, Roosevelt was setting himself above Washington. They also feared he would become a dictator. The third term was a major issue in the campaign, but the war was not. The Republican candidate, a public utilities executive named Wendell Willkie who had never before run for political office, supported FDR's program of aid to Britain.

Isolationists organized the America First Committee and urged the country to abandon Britain and to concentrate on building its own strength. Some well-known Republicans were on the America First Committee, but the committee lost its bid to control the Republican convention. They could not make the war an election issue.

In the end, a majority of Americans decided in favor of Roosevelt. With so little difference in the views of the two candidates, it seemed safer not to

Presidential Election, 1940

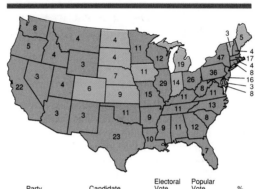

Party	Candidate	Electoral Vote	Popular Vote	%
Democratic	Roosevelt	449	27,244,160	54.8
Republican	Wilkie	82	22,305,198	44.8
Minor parties			221,516	0.4

531 Total Electoral Vote

change horses in midstream. FDR's 27 million votes were about 54 percent of the total; the electoral vote was 449 to 82. That was firm backing for the President's policy of giving Britain "all aid short of war."

SECTION 4 REVIEW

Key Terms and People

Explain the significance of: blitzkrieg, genocide, Holocaust, Edward R. Murrow, Henri Pétain, Charles de Gaulle, Axis powers

Main Ideas

1. Briefly describe the military action Germany took against Poland and the effects of that action on Poland.
2. What was the Nazis' "final solution of the Jewish question"?
3. After the fall of France, Nazi officials announced that Germany had "just one more battle to win." What battle was that, and what were its results?
4. How did Roosevelt prepare the United States for eventual entry into World War II?

Critical Thinking

5. What changed the isolationist sentiments that Americans held in the 1930's enough so that in 1940, they were willing to elect a President who was selling arms to European allies and who appeared to be preparing the nation for war?

State the Objective

Use primary sources to understand views of isolationism.

Present the Lesson

Review with students American attitudes about foreign involvement after World War I. Point out that the U.S. did not join the League of Nations and that many Americans believed the arms industry was the only group that profited from the war. Stress the great difference in political philosophy between the expansionist and totalitarian nature of Italian Fascism and German Nazism and the democratic ideals of the U.S.

Divide the class into four groups and have each group examine one document. Ask students to evaluate their document by determining whether the stated policy was in the best interest of the U.S. Have group leaders summarize their discussions for the class. (Summaries might include: Nye—only bankers and industrialists benefit from war; staying out of the war would protect American lives and resources. Roosevelt—America hates war and hopes for peace so must actively engage in winning peace; becoming involved would ensure continued peace and safety for Americans. Hull—information available to the President proves the urgent need to become involved in Europe; failing to become involved could risk the security of the U.S.; Lindbergh—Europe must be allowed to work out its own

Focus on Primary Sources

Views on Isolationism

Senator Gerald P. Nye of North Dakota was a leader among those in Congress who feared America would be dragged into a second European war. Strict neutrality laws, they believed, would keep America out of any future conflict (page 716). In May 1935 Nye addressed a meeting of peace groups on the topic "How to Keep America Out of War." After repeating the belief that World War I had been a fruitless waste of lives and resources, he made the following plea.

> The hour for action is now. Why not make the most of it?
>
> Today we think of public enemies as those who threaten and kill for profit. With a war looming on the European horizon, let us broaden our definition. Public enemies should be those among us who do the things which result in having other people killed for their own profit.
>
> Public enemy no. 1 should be the munitions maker, who wants to sell his powder and poison gas, and sends it in American ships, wrapped up in the American flag, manned with American seamen, to be sunk by submarines and bombing planes. The result of his act will inevitably drag us into war.
>
> Public enemy no. 2 is the banker who raises money to pay for the munitions and who speculates in the stocks of the war babies [industries] steel, gas, and chemicals, and who lures the people into believing there is both profit and honor in this blood money— until that time when he can no longer tell the difference between profit and honor.
>
> Public enemy no. 3 is the industrialist who knows that the only way to get fascism established in America is to get the country into a war with all the military dictatorship that involves.
>
> Public enemy no. 4 is the American who goes into the war zones to make money, recklessly indifferent of the consequences to his nation and to hundreds of thousands of men better than himself.

> In conclusion, we ought to be ready to face facts. We should be seeking profit from experience. If we will but do this we will fight with determination for legislation such as will greatly simplify our task of trying to stay out of another war.

Garraty, John A., and Robert A. Divine, *Twentieth Century America: Contemporary Documents and Opinions* (Boston: Little, Brown, 1968), 445.

Two years later, the situation in Europe and Asia had become more serious. President Roosevelt wanted to escape the neutrality straight jacket so that the United States could aid democratic countries when they were attacked by aggressive dictators. In October 1937 in Chicago, he spoke out against the isolationists.

> The present reign of terror and international lawlessness began a few years ago. It began through unjustified interference in the internal affairs of other nations or the invasion of alien territory in violation of treaties, and has now reached a stage where the very foundations of civilization are seriously threatened. . . .
>
> Without a declaration of war and without warning or justification of any kind, civilians, including women and children, are being ruthlessly murdered with bombs from the air.
>
> In times of so-called peace, ships are being attacked and sunk by submarines without cause or notice. Nations are fomenting and taking sides in civil warfare in nations that have never done them any harm. Nations claiming freedom for themselves deny it to others. . . .
>
> . . . The peace, the freedom, and the security of 90 percent of the population of the world is being jeopardized by the remaining 10 percent who are threatening a breakdown of all international order and law.
>
> Surely the 90 percent who want to live in peace under law and in accordance with moral

destiny, as must the U.S.; America would not be affected by what evolves in Europe.)

Check for Understanding

Discuss the students' responses to the questions. Then divide the class into two groups. Have one group take the side of the isolationists and the other group the side of Roosevelt and those who favored U.S. involvement, in Europe. Have the groups debate the issue of U.S. involvement, using facts from the feature and the chapter to support their views.

standards that have received almost universal acceptance through the centuries, can and must find some way to make their will prevail. . . .

When an epidemic of physical disease starts to spread, the community approves and joins in a quarantine of the patients in order to protect the health of the community against the spread of the disease. . . .

War is a contagion, whether it be declared or undeclared. It can engulf states and peoples remote from the original scene of hostilities. We are determined to keep out of war, yet we cannot insure ourselves against the disastrous effects of war and the dangers of involvement. We are adopting such measures as will minimize our risk of involvement, but we cannot have complete protection in a world of disorder in which confidence and security have broken down. . . .

America hates war. America hopes for peace. Therefore, America actively engages in the search for peace.

Hofstadter, Richard, and Beatrice K. Hofstadter, eds., *Great Issues in American History,* vol. 3, *From Reconstruction to the Present Day, 1864–1981* (New York: Random House, 1982) 379–384.

In the face of an unfavorable response from the public, FDR dropped the matter (page 718). Then in July 1939, a few weeks before war broke out in Europe, the Senate Foreign Relations Committee voted to postpone any action on neutrality until January 1940. Secretary of State Cordell Hull arranged a meeting of the Senate Committee members with Roosevelt. Hull described the session.

As the meeting came to order in the President's upstairs study, a reasonable cordiality was apparent on the surface, but the feeling underneath was tense. . . .

The President opened the discussion by referring to Senator Nye's extreme isolationist views which were blocking the passage of our measure in the Senate [repeal of the arms embargo]. [Senator] Borah [of Idaho] rather quickly interrupted and, with a sweeping gesture, said, "There are others, Mr. President." . . . A dialogue followed between the President and Borah, during which Borah emphasized his opposition to repeal of the arms

embargo and stated emphatically his view that no war would occur at least in the near future.

The President thereupon turned to me and said, "Cordell, what do you think about the possibility of danger ahead?"

I replied earnestly, restraining myself as much as I could: "If Senator Borah could only see some of the cables coming to the State Department about the extremely dangerous outlook in the international situation, I feel satisfied he would modify his views."

Thereupon Borah, in a tone of emphasis and absolute finality, said he had access to information from abroad which satisfied him in his judgment. This information was that there would be no war in Europe in the near future. He implied that it was more reliable information than that received at the State Department. . . .

Never in my experience had I found it nearly so difficult to restrain myself and refrain from a spontaneous explosion. . . .

Only five weeks later we had to exert [our] influence in a final effort to prevent a European war. Our influence, so far as Hitler was concerned, was undoubtedly weakened by his realization that Congress had refused to follow the lead of the administration, and by his belief that Britain and France could not obtain arms, ammunition, or airplanes in the United States.

Hull, Cordell, *The Memoirs of Cordell Hull,* Vol. 1 (New York: Macmillan, 1948), 648–651.

Analyzing Primary Sources

1. According to Senator Gerald Nye, what would draw the United States into a foreign war?
2. If you were Senator Nye and a reporter had asked you for a brief comment on President Roosevelt's Chicago speech, how would you have answered?
3. Could Hitler have been influenced by America's refusal to lift the arms embargo? Explain.

Critical Thinking

4. It would have made little difference to the United States, Charles Lindbergh said, if the nation confronted a Europe dominated by Nazi Germany. Do you agree or disagree? Explain.

FOCUS ON SOURCES

Answers

Analyzing Primary Sources

1. Nye believed that the greed of American industrialists and financiers would draw us into war, as he said they had in World War I.

2. Possible answer: becoming involved in the European conflict would only serve the public enemies that Nye had warned about; the rest of America would suffer from such involvement.

3. Possible answers: no—Hitler depended on winning so quickly that the U.S. would not have a chance to play a significant role. Yes—the arms embargo did not diminish U.S. influence early in the war.

Critical Thinking

4. Possible answers: no—foreign relations would have been radically changed had the tyranny and racism of the Third Reich succeeded in dominating Europe; the U.S. may have eventually been forced to fight a war at home if Hitler then decided to expand his empire to North America. **(synthesis)**

Key Terms and People

These are highlighted in the text in the order in which they appear in this list.

Main Ideas

1. All were ruled by military dictators who wanted to expand their territory.

2. The league rules would not allow strong actions against aggressors; when the league issued a reprimand, the countries simply quit the league.

3. Political leaders stayed clear of foreign affairs in Europe and the Far East, passed Neutrality Acts.

4. He wanted to join with other nations in isolating dictators, but Congress was not prepared to back him.

5. Scientists and artists who came to U.S. to escape fascism. • Einstein—physicist and mathematician; Toscanini—conductor; Mann-author; Fermi—physicist; Gropius—architect.

6. Jews were denied civil rights and were often killed. • Belief that Germans composed the master race and that other "races" such as Jews, Slavs, and some non-whites were inferior and contaminated society.

7. Blitzkrieg and surprise.

8. Sent Britain arms, ammunition, and warships; started the Selective Service System; created a bipartisan cabinet.

Critical Thinking Questions

9. Many felt that the war was righteous because it was fought against Nazis who engaged in genocide.

10. Could only be enforced through public opinion. • Pact had little effect. It assumed all nations wanted peace, but Germany, Italy, and Japan wanted war.

11. African Americans felt empathy with Ethiopians.

▶12. U.S. refusal to cancel war debts caused financial problems in Europe; isolationism encouraged Germany and Italy to think the U.S. would

not interfere in European affairs. • Possible answer: no—a world power can sometimes cause harm by doing nothing.

13. Chamberlain believed he could avert war by agreeing to appease Hitler by separating the Sudetenland from Czechoslovakia. • Churchill realized that Hitler would take more and more territory.

14. Hitler did not want to wage war on two fronts; Stalin

wanted to regain land he had lost. • Yes—until 1941, when Hitler attacked the Soviet Union.

15. The mood of the country was isolationist, supporting our withdrawal from China. • The *Maine* exploded 90 miles from Florida, while the *Panay* incident occurred 5,000 miles from the U.S.

▶16. Possible answer: dictators of the world would have destroyed personal liberty of

many people, but eventually people would have rebelled against them.

▶17. Roosevelt would not blame people if they took sides in the war even if the nation remained neutral.

Critical Thinking Activities

▶18. Possible answers: withdraw ambassadors, impose economic sanctions, refuse to sell arms.

C H A P T E R **28** R E V I E W

Write your answers on a separate sheet of paper.

Key Terms and People

Explain the significance of: Frank B. Kellogg, Nazi party, fascism, sanctions, reciprocal trade agreements, Francisco Franco, quarantine, Holocaust, Edward R. Murrow, Henri Pétain, Charles de Gaulle

Main Ideas

1. What did Japan, Germany, and Italy have in common?
2. What role did the League of Nations play in encouraging the expansion of Japan, Italy, and Germany?
3. How did isolationism play a vital role in United States foreign policy?
4. In what way was President Roosevelt's approach to the aggressions of the dictators different from that of Congress?
5. What did Albert Einstein, Arturo Toscanini, Thomas Mann, Enrico Fermi, and Walter Gropius have in common? What field of endeavor did each belong to?
6. What was the Nazis' policy toward the Jews? What was their rationale for this?
7. What methods did the Germans use to overrun western Europe in 1940?
8. How did President Roosevelt react to the fall of France and western Europe?

Critical Thinking Questions

9. **Analyzing Literature.** In the selection on page 711, Morris refers to the war as "this righteous war." What do you think he means? Did it become a "righteous war"?
10. **Analyzing Policies.** What was the basic flaw in the Kellogg-Briand Pact of 1929? What effect did the pact have?
11. **Analyzing Responses.** Reaction to Mussolini's invasion of Ethiopia was strong in the United States. Why do you think African Americans were so supportive of the Ethiopians?
12. **Evaluating Foreign Policy.** Even though the United States remained isolationist in the mid-

1930's, how did its foreign policy affect the events in Europe? Is it possible for a world power to be truly neutral?
13. **Analyzing Ideas.** What reasoning did Neville Chamberlain use to defend his deal with Hitler at Munich? Why did Churchill say appeasement would result in both dishonor and war?
14. **Synthesizing Ideas.** What did Hitler and Stalin hope to achieve by signing their nonaggression pact in 1939? Did it work? Explain.
15. **Comparing Reactions.** How was the public reaction to the *Panay* incident different from the reactions to the explosion of the *Maine* thirty-nine years earlier? What do you think was the reason for this difference?
16. **Predicting Effects.** What might our world be like today if the Axis powers had won World War II?
17. **Analyzing a Quotation.** On the evening of the day Britain and France declared war on Germany, Roosevelt discussed the war in a fireside chat: "I cannot ask that every American remain neutral in thought. . . . Even a neutral cannot be asked to close his mind or his conscience." What was Roosevelt telling the American public?

Critical Thinking Activities

18. **Linking Past to Present.** Further attempts at genocide have been made since World War II. What is the best way for one country to act in order to influence another country to halt attempts at genocide?
19. **Linking Past to Present.** If you had been a senator in 1940, would you have supported President Roosevelt in his effort to prepare this country for war? Explain.
20. **Linking Past to Present.** It is not always easy to know when to make peace and when to take a stand. Take an event of recent years in which either course was possible. Make your choice and defend it in class.

19. Possible answers: yes—
Hitler could not have been
stopped except by force. No—
the U.S. had no reason to get
involved in a European war because it was too far away and
did not affect us.

➤**20.** Possible answer: the invasion of Panama in 1989 was
necessary because Manuel
Noriega's drug deals were affecting the U.S.

➤**Question suitable for cooperative learning.**

TELESCOPING THE TIMES: 1933–1940

The Road to War

While the world tried to cope with the Great Depression, war clouds gathered over Asia, Europe, and Africa. The Kellogg-Briand Pact tried futilely to outlaw war. The Stimson Doctrine was likewise unsuccessful in stopping Japan's aggression in Manchuria. In Germany, Hitler and his Nazi party came to power, vowing to avenge Germany's defeat in World War I. Italy's dictator, Mussolini, attacked and annexed Ethiopia. When Hitler armed the Rhineland in violation of the Versailles Treaty, Britain and France, though threatened, did not make him back down. Meanwhile, Roosevelt moved cautiously to recognize the Communist government of the Soviet Union, to lower tariffs through reciprocal trade agreements, and to expand the Good Neighbor Policy toward Latin America.

While keeping a careful watch on foreign affairs, the United States struggled to remain neutral. Congress promoted isolationism through the investigations of the Nye committee and with a series of neutrality acts. Meanwhile, Americans watched as Spain was taken over by a fascist dictator. The United States began to take the side of China in its struggle against Japanese invasion. Roosevelt advocated a quarantine of European dictatorships, while the *Panay* incident reaffirmed that Americans were determined to stay out of war. Hitler explained the annexation of Austria by saying he wished to protect his fellow Germans. With the same excuse he threatened to invade Czechoslovakia. British and French appeasement at Munich permitted him to do so.

The European crisis deepened as Hitler mounted a campaign of hate against Jews. His Nuremberg Laws deprived German Jews of their civil rights. Then, on Crystal Night in 1938, Nazi gangs killed many Jews. Thousands more fled abroad, but the United States did not fully open its doors to them. Hitler and Stalin made a pact to carve up Poland.

When Nazi forces invaded that country, Britain and France finally declared war. The Second World War began in Europe in September 1939.

Nazi forces, waging a blitzkrieg, rapidly captured Poland, then Denmark and Norway, then the Low Countries, and finally France. British troops barely escaped at Dunkirk. German forces enslaved many of the conquered people. They rounded up Jews, gypsies, and others and methodically killed them in concentration camps. At the front, Hitler failed to win the air war known as the Battle of Britain. The United States openly aided the British in this battle with supplies and ships. At home, Roosevelt brought Republicans into his cabinet. In 1940 Congress passed the first peacetime military draft, and FDR won an unprecedented third term.

Chronology of Main Events

1933　Hitler becomes German chancellor

1935　Mussolini seizes Ethiopia; first
　　　Neutrality Act passed; Nuremberg
　　　Laws passed in Germany

1936　Germany occupies the Rhineland

1937　Japan invades China; Roosevelt gives
　　　quarantine speech

1938　Hitler annexes Austria; Munich Pact
　　　signed

1939　Germany occupies all of
　　　Czechoslovakia; Soviets sign
　　　nonaggression pact with Germany;
　　　Germany invades Poland; World War
　　　II begins in Europe

1940　Roosevelt elected for third term

Telescoping the Times may be used as an alternative to having students read the entire chapter, as a chapter preview, or as a chapter review.

Global Perspectives

1941	Penicillin is first used on humans.
1941-1944	The Tojo government rules in Japan.
1942-1943	The Soviet Union wins Battle of Stalingrad, a turning point in World War II.
1944	The International Red Cross wins Nobel Peace Prize.
1945	The Arab League is formed.

For Discussion

How might the development of penicillin have helped the U.S. during World War II? (Possible response: it could be used to prevent infection and disease among soldiers, significantly lowering the number of war-related deaths.)

Additional Resources

- Geography Activities
- Skills Activities
- Thematic Activities
- Economic Activities
- Cultural Literacy Activities
- Literary Source Readings
- Primary Source Readings
- Nuclear Peacekeeping
- Transparencies
- Computer Test Generator

Additional Teaching Strategies

SECTION 1

For Basic Students: Ask students to list on paper the major provisions of the Atlantic Charter, choose the one they feel is most important, and explain their choice. (Provisions of the Atlantic Charter include: no territorial expansion; no territorial changes without the consent of the inhabitants; self-determination for all people; freer trade; cooperation for the improvement of other nations; the disarming of all aggressors.) Have students share their papers.

For Advanced Students: Have students write an essay in which they compare the Atlantic Charter with Wilson's Fourteen Points (Chapter 23). (Similarities might include: freer trade; arms reduction; self-determination for all people. Differences might include: Fourteen Points called for formation of League of Nations and the continuance of colonial empires.)

SECTION 2

For Basic Students: Have students work together to develop a wall-sized chart showing the steps the government took in each of the following areas when converting from a peacetime economy to a wartime economy: manufacturing, farming, consumer prices, taxes.

Manufacturing
- Federal government built new plants for war production.
- War Production Board allocated raw materials, assigned production, rationed gasoline, and organized recycling.
- Harry S Truman headed a committee to supervise government buying.

Farming
- Work force declined.
- Improved equipment, greater use of fertilizers, and good weather increased output.
- Farm output and prices doubled.

Consumer Prices
- Office of Price Administration fixed rents, set maximum prices on goods, and set up rationing systems.
- Inflation remained below 30 percent.

Taxes
- The government raised income tax rates and extended the tax to millions who had never before paid.
- The 1943 payroll deduction law was passed.

Have students display their chart in the classroom.

For Advanced Students: Organize students into pairs and have them research and prepare an oral report on one of the scientists mentioned in this section and his contribution to the war effort. (Reports on Oppenheimer might include: born 1904, New York City; educated at Harvard, Cambridge, and Gottingen; was a physicist; served as director of the atomic bomb project at Los Alamos, New Mexico, from 1943 to 1945.)

SECTION 3

For Basic Students: Ask students to compare the maps on pages 721 and 747 and identify three formerly independent countries that came under German control after 1939. (Responses might include: France, Norway, Denmark, Belgium, the Netherlands, Hungary, Yugoslavia, Greece, Rumania, and Bulgaria were among the countries controlled by Germany.)

For Advanced Students: Have students research and present to the class three-minute oral reports on one of the Big Three—Stalin, Roosevelt, and Churchill—examining each man's background, style of leadership, and motivation. After the presentations, discuss with students the similarities and differences between these three world leaders. (Reports on Stalin might include: was expelled from university for failing to attend exams; was an active member of the Social-Democratic revolutionary movement; was arrested in 1902 and exiled to Siberia; was the editor of the Bolshevik newspaper *Pravda;* believed in spreading communism through revolution; had political opponents arrested and deported; instituted five-year plans for economic improvement; transformed corrective labor camps into slave camps; established terroristic state police. Similarities among the three world leaders include: all exercised their power throughout the war; all cooperated in defeating the Axis powers. Differences include: Roosevelt and Churchill were freely elected, whereas Stalin was a dictator; Roosevelt and Churchill came from wealthy families, whereas Stalin came from a humble background.)

SECTION 4

For Basic Students: In small-group discussion, have students identify sites of major Allied military offensives in the Pacific. Have students use maps in this chapter as they work on this project. Students should include the date and victor of each offensive. (Offensives might include: Japan, bombing raid in Tokyo, April 1942, Allied victory; Australia, Battle of Coral Sea, May 1942, Allied victory; Battle of Midway, June 1942, Allied victory; Battle of Guadalcanal, August 1942-spring 1943, Allied victory; capture of Solomon, Gilbert, Marshall islands, February 1944, Allied victory; Mariana Islands, June 1944, Allied victory; Battle of Leyte Gulf, October 1944, Allied victory; capture of Iwo Jima, Okinawa, spring 1945, Allied victory.)

For Advanced Students: Ask students to research and report to the class the history of the Japanese kamikaze. After hearing the reports, ask students whether there is any difference between the Japanese kamikaze attitude and that of a U.S. soldier who is prepared to give his life for his country. (Possible responses: *kamikaze* means "divine wind," after the typhoon that saved Japan from Chinese invasion in 1281; kamikaze pilots crashed their bomb-laden planes into American ships, sacrificing their lives for their country. Students might feel that the kamikaze, like Arab terrorists of today, were far more fanatical than American soldiers, who may be willing to die for their country, but who also have some hope for survival.)

SECTION 5

For Basic Students: Organize students into pairs to research and prepare a chart or diagram of the United Nations' structure, showing the function of each section. (Information might include: General Assembly—all member nations; discusses and makes recommendations, Security Council—15 members, of which 5 are permanent and 10 elected to two-year terms; has powers of enforcement, Economic and Social Council—twenty-seven members, elected to three-year terms; responsible for economic and social activities, Trusteeship Council—responsible for supervision of territories that are not independent, International Court of Justice—principal judicial organ, Secretariat for Administration—Secretary-General and staff.)
Display the diagrams in the classroom.

For Advanced Students: Ask each student to assume the role of a senator who favors U.S. membership in the United Nations. Each student should prepare and present to the class a two-minute speech urging Congress to vote in favor of membership. (Speeches might include: the need for world peace; the need for the U.S. to move away from isolationist attitudes; the need to control the spread of communism.)

Further Reading for Students
Nonfiction

Blum, John Morton. *V Was for Victory: Politics and American Culture During World War II*. New York: Harcourt Brace Jovanovich, 1976.

Hersey, John. *Hiroshima*. New York: Random House, 1989. (Easy)

Irons, Peter. *Justice at War: The Inside Story of the Japanese American Internment*. New York: Oxford University Press, 1983.

Purcell, John. *Best-Kept Secret: The Story of the Atomic Bomb*. New York: Vanguard Press, 1963.

Stokesbury, James L. *A Short History of World War Two*. New York: William Morrow, 1980.

Bibliography for Teachers
Books

Davis, Daniel S. *Behind Barbed Wire: The Imprisonment of Japanese Americans During World War II*. New York: E. P. Dutton, 1982.

Eisenhower, Dwight D. *Crusade in Europe*. Jersey City: Da Capo Press, 1977.

Gilbert, Martin. *The Holocaust*. New York: Hill & Wang, 1979.

Hastings, Max. *Overlord: D-Day, June 6, 1944*. New York: Simon & Schuster, 1984.

Neu, Charles E. *The Troubled Encounter: The United States and Japan*. Huntington, N.Y.: Robert E. Krieger., 1979.

Reynolds, David. *The Creation of the Anglo-American Alliance, 1937-41: A Study in Competitive Cooperation*. Chapel Hill: University of North Carolina Press, 1988.

Sherwin, Martin J. *A World Destroyed: Hiroshima and the Origins of the Arms Race*. New York: Random House, 1977.

Terkel, Studs. *The Good War: An Oral History of World War Two*. New York: Pantheon Books, 1984.

Wohlstetter, Roberta. *Pearl Harbor: Warning and Decision*. Palo Alto, Calif.: Stanford University Press, 1962.

Audio-Visuals

Aftermath of World War II: Prologue to the Cold War. McGraw-Hill. Movie.

D-Day: A Turning Point of World War II. Encyclopaedia Britannica Educational Corp. Filmstrip.

F.D.R.: Third Term to Pearl Harbor. McGraw-Hill. Movie.

Failure of American Neutrality, 1933-1939 (The Roosevelt Years). American Broadcasting Company. Movie.

Parallels: The President and the Dictator. Reaction Films. Movie.

The Outbreak of World War II. Society for Visual Education. Filmstrip.

Truman and the Atomic Bomb. Learning Corporation of America. Movie.

U.S. Industrial Conversion to World War II. Social Studies School Service. Movie.

Wartime Relocation of Japanese Americans. Social Studies School Service. Movie.

World War II: The American Home Front. Encyclopaedia Britannica Educational Corp. Filmstrip.

World War II Prologue, U.S.A. Encyclopaedia Britannica Educational Corp. Movie.

The Yalta Conference. Social Studies School Service. Movie.

Computer Resource

American History Keyword Series—World War II Keywords. (Apple) Focus Media.

CHAPTER 29
Lesson Plan

Teaching Resources, Unit 7 Booklet

Lesson Study Sheets pp. 57-76
Daily Activities pp. 77-86
Enrichment Activities pp. 87-96
Reteaching Activities pp. 97-106
Chapter Review p. 107
Chapter Mastery Tests pp. 109-120
Telescoping the Times Study Sheet p. 121

Chapter Objectives

Students will learn:
- how the U.S. was drawn into World War II
- how the nation's economy was organized for the war effort
- the major battles and campaigns of the European and North African theaters
- the major events of the Pacific theater
- the major results of the Allied victory in World War II

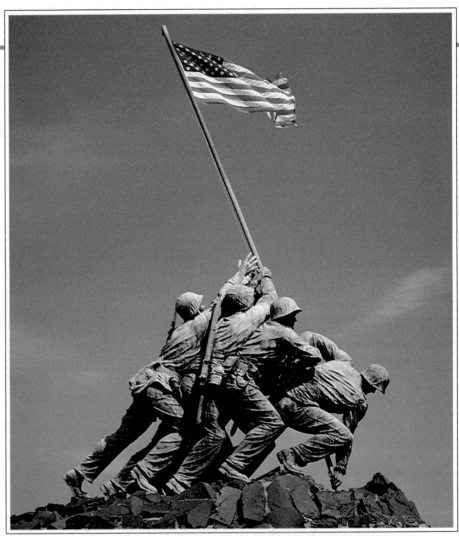

Picturing History This sculpture of U.S. Marines raising the flag on Iwo Jima is based on a famous photograph from the Second World War. On Iwo Jima, six thousand Americans died in the effort to bring U.S. forces within striking distance of Japanese cities.

Using the Chapter Time Line

How many years passed between the passage of the first Neutrality Act (see Chapter 28 Time Line) and U.S. entrance into World War II? (Answer: 6) In what year did World War II begin (see Chapter 28 Time Line); in what year did it end? (Answer: 1939, 1945)

1939	1940	1941	1942	1943	1944	1945

1941
- Japan attacks Pearl Harbor
- U.S. enters World War II

1942
Allies invade North Africa

1943
- Germans surrender at Stalingrad
- Allies invade Italy

1944
Allies land in France

1945
- Roosevelt dies; Harry S Truman succeeds to Presidency
- Germany surrenders
- Atomic bombs dropped on Japan
- Japan surrenders

734

Links to American Literature

William Styron: born in Newport News, Virginia in 1925; graduated from Duke University; served almost three years in U.S. Marine Corps during World War II.

Works include: *Lie Down in Darkness* (1951), winner of the Prix de Rome of the American Academy of Arts and Letters; *The Long March* (1953); *Set This House on Fire* (1960); *The Confessions of Nat Turner* (1967), winner of the 1968 Pulitzer Prize; *In the Clap Shack* (1973), a play.

Sophie's Choice: tells the story of Sophie, a Polish Catholic woman who has survived the terrors of a Nazi concentration camp but who continues to suffer both physical and emotional agonies long after she has been freed.

Introducing the Chapter

Have students skim the chapter, noting especially maps, pictures, and heads. Based on their observations about the maps, discuss with students one way in which this war was different from World War I. (Possible response: it involved more nations and was fought on more continents.) Ask students how this war was similar to World War I. (Possible responses: In each war, U.S. tried at first to remain neutral. U.S. supported Great Britain in each war; both times, U.S. was forced to enter the war after suffering hostilities.)

CHAPTER **29** 1939–1945

The Second World War

Links to American Literature

In this war everyone suffers—Jews, Poles, Gypsies, Russians, Czechs, Yugoslavs, all the others. Everyone's a victim. The Jews are also the victims of victims, that's the main difference. . . .

At first I couldn't make out what it was, just a jumble of sticks—a great mass of sticks like small tree limbs. Then I saw what it was—this unbearable sight, a boxcar full of dead children, scores of them, maybe a hundred, all of them in these stiff and jumbled positions that could only come from being frozen to death. The other photographs were the same—other boxcars with scores of children, all stiff and frozen.'

" 'These are not Jewish children,' Wanda said, 'these are little Polish children, none of them over twelve years old. . . . In due time the train, like a lot of others, was diverted onto sidings where the children were allowed to die in the condition you see here. Others starved to death, still more suffocated in hermetically sealed cars. Thirty thousand Polish children have disappeared from the Zamość region alone. Thousands and thousands of these have died.

— WILLIAM STYRON, *Sophie's Choice*

The atrocities committed during World War II were so horrible that for a long time the free world could not believe that they were really happening. Never in history had such wholesale slaughter taken place. By the time the United States officially addressed the problem, more than six million Jews and other Europeans had been exterminated. This chapter not only presents the suffering of World War II but also introduces a suffering that has continued to the present day. World War II produced a totally new element that changed the nature of warfare—nuclear weapons. The result has been an age of anxiety in which international relations have been dominated by fear, suspicion, and rivalry.

Chapter Overview

The United States entered World War II in December 1941. In this chapter you will learn about the events that drew the United States into the war. You will also learn about the ways in which the nation's economy was reorganized for the war effort. Then you will trace the major battles and campaigns of the European and Pacific theaters of war. Finally, you will analyze the results of the Allied victory. To help you understand these events and the effects of the Second World War, Chapter 29 is divided into five sections.

Chapter Outline

1. **The United States Prepares for War**
2. **The Nation Performs a Production Miracle**
3. **War Rages Across North Africa and Europe**
4. **Allied Troops Advance on the Pacific Front**
5. **The Allies Plan for the Postwar World**

735

State the Objective
Understand how the U.S. was drawn into World War II.

Anticipate the Lesson
Review with students some ways in which America prepared for war. (Possible responses: Roosevelt appointed a bipartisan cabinet; first peacetime draft was adopted.) Ask students to identify one way in which the U.S. was already involved in the war in Europe. (Response: the U.S. was supplying military equipment and destroyers to Great Britain in

SECTION 1

The United States Prepares for War

GLOSSARY TERMS: **lend-lease, scorched-earth policy, Atlantic Charter**

President Roosevelt's measures "short of war" were just barely short of it. In fact, one might say that the United States was waging an undeclared war against the Axis during most of 1941. Early that year, American military leaders held secret talks with British officials in Washington and, later, with the British and the Dutch in Singapore. The conferences laid plans for joint military operations to be conducted after the United States entered the war.

FDR Proposes Lend-Lease

As 1940 drew to a close, FDR gave a fireside chat to the American people. In it he declared his belief that the United States must become "the great arsenal of democracy." By this time, however, Britain was almost bankrupt. Cash-and-carry was no longer of use. Therefore, on January 6, 1941, in his first State of the Union address after his unprecedented election to a third term, Roosevelt proposed a different means by which Britain could obtain military equipment and supplies. He called it **lend-lease;** in other words, the President would lend or lease arms and other goods to "any country whose defense was vital to the United States."

For Discussion
Did the U.S. policy of lend-lease make U.S. involvement in World War II inevitable? (Possible responses: yes—it gave Americans a large economic and moral stake in the outcome of the war. No—America probably would not have entered the war if Japan had not attacked Pearl Harbor.)

FDR compared lend-lease to letting a neighbor use a hose when his or her house was on fire, to keep the blaze from spreading. Once the emergency was over, the hose might be returned, replaced, or paid for. Senator Robert A. Taft of Ohio, an isolationist, compared the process to lending someone chewing gum; he said you would not want it back. Nevertheless, in March Congress passed the measure by sizable majorities in both houses and appropriated $7 billion for it. In all, $50 billion was spent under the Lend-Lease Act.

Britain was not the only nation to benefit from lend-lease. On June 22 Hitler ignored his peace treaty with the Soviet Union and sent 3 million soldiers across the Soviet-German border. At first people everywhere were convinced that the Soviet Union would collapse within a month or two. The Soviets, however, fought grimly in defense of their country. They adopted a **scorched-earth policy,** destroying everything—even their first hydroelectric project, the Dnieper Dam—that could be of use to the advancing Germans. Some tied bombs to their belts and threw themselves at German tanks. Hitler's troops managed to reach the outskirts of Moscow and Leningrad (St. Petersburg). Then the terrible Soviet winter set in, and the invading army came to a halt. In November the Soviets got a billion dollars in lend-lease credits.

Germans Sink American Ships

Keeping the supply lines from the Americas open was vital to Britain and, later, to the Soviet Union. Hitler was just as determined to close the

People in the Chapter

George Marshall was the only career soldier ever to win the Nobel Peace Prize. Churchill claimed Marshall was "the true organizer of victory" in World War II.

Thomas Dewey was only forty-two when he ran against President Roosevelt in 1944. Harold Ickes turned Dewey's youth into a liability when he said the candidate had cast his diaper into the ring.

Douglas MacArthur watched his former aide, Dwight Eisenhower, rise to the rank of five-star

general in World War II. Eisenhower said of MacArthur, "I studied dramatics under him for five years."

James "Jimmy" Doolittle figured out a way to strike back at the Japanese after Pearl Habor. Everyone thought this would be impossible since there was no safe place to launch planes to attack Japan. Jimmy suggested using an aircraft carrier to launch the longer-range land-based B-25 bombers. The Japanese were not as safe as they had once thought.

Present the Lesson

Ask students to skim the section for information to use in constructing a time line of the major events from the beginning of the lend-lease program to the attack on Pearl Harbor. Write the time line on the board.

March 1941	Congress approves the lend-lease program.
April-May 1941	Germans sink 2.3 million tons' worth of British ships.
May 1941	U.S. merchant ship *Robin Moor* is sunk by Germans.

June 22, 1941	Hitler invades the Soviet Union.
August 1941	Congress votes to continue the draft. Roosevelt and Churchill meet secretly and agree on the Atlantic Charter.
September 1941	U.S. destroyer *Greer* is attacked in the North Atlantic.
October 1941	U.S. destroyer *Kearny* is torpedoed off the coast of Iceland. U.S. destroyer *Reuben James* is sunk off the coast of Iceland. General Hideki

	Tojo becomes premier of Japan.
November 1941	Secretary of State Hull begins meetings with Japanese ambassador and special envoy.
December 7, 1941	Japanese attack Pearl Harbor.

lines, and he had the means to do it. Hundreds of submarines, traveling in groups of fifteen to twenty known as wolf packs, and a few of Germany's new pocket battleships, which were the size of cruisers but had the firepower of battleships, roved the Atlantic. During five weeks in April and May 1941, they sank 2.3 million tons of British shipping. This was more than three times the losses of the previous six months. Also, it was done despite the fact that American naval forces were trailing German U-boats and radioing their locations to the British.

German submarines paid no attention to the so-called safety zones off the coasts of North and South America. In May the *Robin Moor,* an American merchantman, was sunk off the coast of Brazil. In September the American destroyer *Greer* was attacked in the North Atlantic. FDR responded by ordering the navy to shoot on sight any Axis ships they might run into. In October the American destroyer *Kearny* was torpedoed near Iceland, and eleven of its crew were killed. A few weeks later, in the same waters, the destroyer *Reuben James* was sunk, with the loss of almost a hundred American lives. As a result of these events, the United States began arming its merchant ships.

In the meantime, Congress, in August, agreed to an eighteen-month extension of the draft that had been legislated in 1940. The vote was very close, with only a one-vote margin in the House. The reluctance stemmed partly from the fact that the enlistment periods of men who had been drafted the previous October would now be extended for eighteen months. There was fear of mass desertions, and, indeed, the letters *OHIO* (standing for Over the Hill in October) began appearing on the walls of barracks. However, no one actually tried to leave an army camp. Uncle Sam's draftees did not like the extension, but they accepted it.

The Atlantic Charter States War Aims

The same month in which the draft was extended, Roosevelt and Churchill met secretly aboard a warship off the coast of Newfoundland. Churchill had come hoping for a military commitment from the United States, but he had to settle for a general statement of war aims somewhat similar to Wilson's Fourteen Points. Called the **Atlantic Charter,** it contained the following principles: (1) no territorial expansion, (2) no territorial changes without the consent of the inhabitants, (3) self-

determination for all people, (4) freer trade, (5) cooperation for the improvement of other nations, and (6) the disarming of all aggressors.

Churchill indicated that the principle of self-determination could not be applied to the British Empire. As he later said, "We mean to hold our own. I have not become the King's First Minister in order to preside over the liquidation of the British Empire." In any event, the Atlantic Charter was endorsed within a month by fifteen countries including the Soviet Union. It later became the basis for the United Nations.

Japan Attacks Pearl Harbor

The German attack on the Soviet Union had effects half a world away. It encouraged Japan to act. The most pressing need of the Japanese war machine was oil. The Dutch East Indies (now Indonesia) was the most convenient source, but invasion there would mean war with the United States and Britain. With Japan's old enemy—the Soviet Union—fighting for its life, however, the gamble looked more attractive.

Setting the Stage. In July 1941 Japan forced the French puppet government of Vichy to give it military bases in southern Indochina (now Vietnam and Cambodia). FDR promptly froze all Japanese assets in the United States; that is, Japanese companies and individuals could no longer use any money or investments they had in this country. Japan immediately did the same with American assets in Japan, and trade between the two nations came to a halt.

In October 1941 General Hideki Tojo (hī də ki tō′ jō), a strong militarist, became the Premier of Japan. A month later, Secretary of State Hull began a series of talks with the Japanese ambassador and a special envoy. The Japanese wanted the United States to unfreeze their assets, supply them with oil, and stop sending lend-lease aid to China. Instead of yielding, the United States demanded that Japan withdraw from China and from Southeast Asia.

As it happened, that previous December the United States had broken Japan's secret diplomatic code. Hull knew that Japan was preparing a military attack. However, he expected it to come either on the Malay Peninsula or in the Dutch East Indies. In the meantime, the United States was strengthening its defense of the Philippines. No one in

Check for Understanding

Have students answer the Section 1 Review questions on paper.

Guided Practice

Remind students that the Soviet Union suffered terrible losses during World War II. Ask students how these losses might explain the longtime Soviet-European border of puppet states. (Possible response: the border might have represented the Soviets' attempt to protect themselves from another invasion.) Ask students whether such a border could still protect the Soviet Union from attack. (Possible response: no—it would not help them in the event of a nuclear missile attack.)

Map Skills

Attu, Kiska • Manila

Historical Sidelight

The Japanese attacked Pearl Harbor on December 7, 1941. However, many of the personnel caught in the attack did not die immediately. For several days the pounding and scratching of men trapped inside the sunken vessels could be heard. They eventually suffocated.

Washington, D.C., knew that on November 25 six aircraft carriers, two battleships, three cruisers, and eleven destroyers had sailed east from Japan's Kuril Islands. Aboard the carriers was a strike force of over four hundred planes. Their destination: the United States Pacific Fleet in Hawaii. The Japanese warlords had taken the gamble.

The Attack. At 7:55 on the sleepy Sunday morning of December 7, 1941, the Japanese bombers struck the American naval base at **Pearl Harbor.** Of the eight United States battleships docked side by side, three were sunk, one was run aground, and another was capsized. The remaining three were badly damaged. Eleven smaller ships were also sunk or disabled, some one hundred seventy planes were destroyed on the ground, and almost twenty-four hundred people, including sixty-eight civilians, were killed. In a single hour on the day Roosevelt called ''a date which will live in in-

famy,'' the United States Navy suffered more damage than it received during all of World War I. In carefully coordinated operations, Japan also struck at the Philippines, Guam, Midway, Hong Kong, and Malaya. (See map on page 739.)

Far away in Washington, D.C., it was 12:55 in the afternoon when the first bombs fell on Pearl Harbor. The Japanese envoys had been sent coded orders to give Secretary Hull their government's final rejection of American terms at precisely one o'clock Washington time. Because of a delay in the decoding, the envoys reached Hull's office an hour late—just as he was getting the first incredible reports from Hawaii. For a few minutes, the courtly statesman lost his self-control. He dressed down the two diplomats in the colorful language of his native Tennessee hills.

The following day the United States declared war on Japan. Hitler, who had not been told about his ally's Pearl Harbor scheme, at first thought it

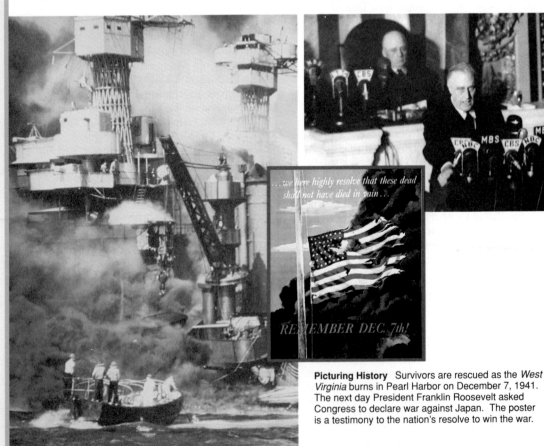

Picturing History Survivors are rescued as the *West Virginia* burns in Pearl Harbor on December 7, 1941. The next day President Franklin Roosevelt asked Congress to declare war against Japan. The poster is a testimony to the nation's resolve to win the war.

Assign Independent Practice

Ask students to write two paragraphs explaining the Soviet Union's scorched earth policy and how it slowed the advance of Hitler's army against the Soviet Union. (Possible response: Soviets destroyed any utility, factory, or crop that could be used by the advancing German troops; when winter came the Germans were stopped because of the harsh weather and lack of provisions.)

Student Assignment/Homework

Have students read Section 2, "The Nation Performs a Production Miracle," and answer the Section 2 Review questions on paper.

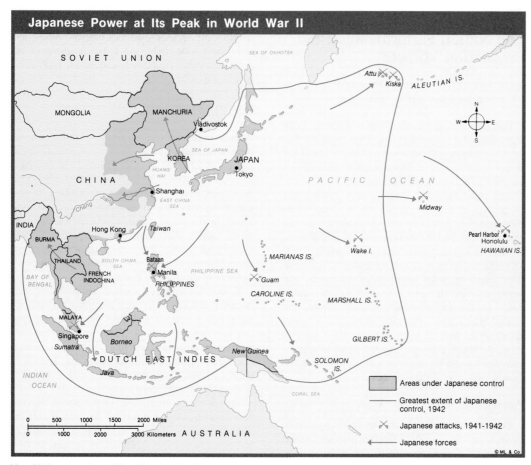

Japanese Power at Its Peak in World War II

Areas under Japanese control

Greatest extent of Japanese control, 1942

Japanese attacks, 1941-1942

Japanese forces

© ML & Co.

Map Skills   Location   What islands in the Aleutians were occupied by the Japanese?
Location   What city was near the battle of Bataan?

was a propaganda trick. When the news was verified, however, he and Mussolini declared war on the United States.

The attack on Pearl Harbor was one of the most successful military actions in history. Even Hitler never managed anything like it. With one swift blow, the Japanese high command had apparently removed the only real obstacle to their country's domination of a third of the world's surface.

SECTION 1 REVIEW

Key Terms and People

Explain the significance of: lend-lease, scorched-earth policy, Atlantic Charter, Pearl Harbor

Main Ideas

1. What advantage for America's allies did the lend-lease program have over the cash-and-carry system?
2. Why was the Atlantic Charter drafted?
3. Why was Japan willing to risk war with the United States and Britain over oil?
4. What did Roosevelt refer to as "a date which will live in infamy"?

Critical Thinking

5. Why was the Soviet Union's scorched-earth policy an effective tactic against Germany? Would this tactic have been as effective in the hands of other nations under German attack, such as France or Denmark? Explain.

State the Objective

Trace the ways in which the nation's economy was organized for the war effort.

Anticipate the Lesson

Ask students to suggest ways in which a country prepares for war. List the responses on the board. (Possible responses: enlarges army and navy; stockpiles munitions; builds airplanes, tanks, and other military equipment; stores food for military; begins rationing gas and other vital resources.) Ask students which of these measures the U.S. took before the attack on Pearl Harbor. (Response: buildup of military strength through the draft.)

SECTION 2

The Nation Performs a Production Miracle

GLOSSARY TERMS: Nisei, Office of Price Administration (OPA), rationing

The Japanese had counted on one thing when they attacked the United States. They believed that the American people were soft and incapable of the discipline, courage, and hard work required for a long war. That was a serious mistake. By 1944 the United States industrial machine was grinding out as much war material as all the Axis countries combined. The figures for the whole war are almost unimaginable: 76,000 tanks, over 300,000 planes, 2.5 million machine guns, and 64,000 landing craft for tanks and infantry. There were also 6,500 naval ships, ranging from small mine sweepers and destroyers—or tin cans, as the sailors called them—all the way to mighty aircraft carriers and battleships. There were also some 5,874 cargo ships, about half of them a type called Liberty ships. Although slow-moving and squat in appearance, they could be turned out by shipyards in the then record time of fifty-six days.

Americans Mobilize for War

People, not machines, are the chief ingredients of the armed forces. The **Selective Service System** provided 16.5 million men to the armed forces. Eventually, all males between the ages of eighteen and sixty-five were registered, but early in the war the system stopped drafting men over age thirty-eight. Most of the draftees were single men under the age of thirty.

Military Strength. Training camps were scattered throughout the nation to prepare and to equip the young men who had been notified by their draft boards to report for duty. Military leaders were faced with the impossible task of turning these young recruits into expert soldiers in three months of basic training and, possibly, three to six months of specialized unit training. The training of officers took place in the nation's colleges. At peak strength, the army numbered over 8 million men, the navy numbered over 3 million, and the marines numbered over half a million.

Life for the average soldier—now called a GI, which stood for "government issue"—brought regimentation, boredom, danger, and fear of horrible wounds or death. This was a mechanized war, fought with airplanes, aircraft carriers, ships, and tanks over vast areas. As a result, most of the casualties came from shell and bomb fragments. Americans were proud of their fighting men and hailed the bravery of their heroes—especially those awarded Congressional Medals of Honor.

Women in the Service. For the first time, women were permitted to volunteer for the armed forces, and about 216,000 of them enlisted. Most joined the Women's Army Corps (WAC), headed by Texas newspaper executive **Oveta Culp Hobby.** Others joined the navy, the Coast Guard, or the marines. Those in the navy and in the Coast Guard were given names that translated, respectively, into Waves and Spars. The female component of the United States Marines was, simply, the Women's Reserve of the Marine Corps.

To become a Wac, a woman had to be between twenty and forty-nine years old, have no children under age fourteen, and have completed at least two years of high school. Wacs served in separate noncombat units as accountants, bakers, bookkeepers, clerk-typists, and radio operators. Nurses in the Navy Nurse Corps received sea duty so that they could train hospital corpsmen.

The Women's Auxiliary Ferry Service (WAFS) first piloted planes across the Atlantic. Later the Wafs flew planes that towed targets for antiaircraft and gunnery practice. Despite the hazards of their duty, Wafs were considered civilian employees without military status or veterans' benefits.

African Americans. About one million African Americans entered the armed forces, and about half of them served overseas. Like women, African Americans were segregated in the service except at army officer-candidate schools and briefly, as an emergency measure, during the Battle of the Bulge. (See page 750.) The navy and the Coast Guard restricted African Americans to such noncombat service jobs as cooks, messengers, and mess-hall attendants until almost the end of the war. Nevertheless, some black navy personnel won combat decorations. The merchant marine was more liberal: four of its ship captains were black. One of the army's black units, the 761st Tank Battalion, saw 183 days of combat in Europe. The 332nd Fighter Group, commanded by Colonel Benjamin O. Davis, Jr., son of the army's first

Focus on American Art

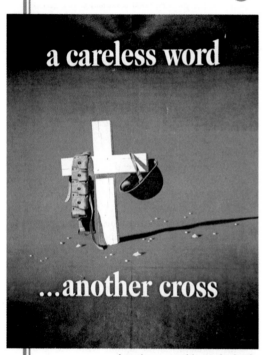

a careless word

...another cross

Americans could not doubt the consequence of careless talk after seeing this poster, which appeared around 1943.

Picturing History Propaganda is the promotion of ideas that further one's own cause or that damage an opponent's cause. Throughout history, propaganda has been a powerful weapon in the arsenal of war. During World War II, each warring nation had its own propaganda strategy. American propagandists urged people on the home front to keep their lips sealed, to conserve resources, and to buy government bonds. Nazi propagandists idealized the Aryan superhero. Each side created a savage stereotype of its enemy.

When you ride ALONE you ride with Hitler !

Join a Car-Sharing Club TODAY !

American civilians were strongly encouraged to conserve oil and other natural resources in support of the war effort.

DER DEUTSCHE STUDENT

KÄMPFT FÜR FÜHRER UND VOLK

IN DER MANNSCHAFT DES NSD-STUDENTENBUNDE

The translation of this Nazi poster of the 1930's reads: "The German Student Fights for the Führer and the People."

KEEP THESE HANDS OFF !

BUY *the New* VICTORY BONDS

Few could resist the emotional appeal of this threatened mother and child.

On the board, write the headings African Americans, Japanese Americans, and Women. Under each heading students should describe the involvement of that group in World War II and the effects of the war on that group.

African Americans
- About 1 million entered armed forces.
- Were segregated from whites except in army officer-candidate schools and during Battle of Bulge.
- Were restricted to noncombat jobs in navy and Coast Guard until near end of war.
- Won some combat decorations in navy.
- Captained four Merchant Marine ships.
- 761st Tank Battalion was African American and saw 183 days of combat in Europe.
- Benjamin O. Davis, Jr., was first African American major general.
- Industrial employment was opened to African Americans.
- Families migrated to northern and western cities.

Japanese Americans
- About seventeen thousand enlisted in military.
- Were segregated from whites.
- Some served in U.S. intelligence service.
- 442nd Regiment received more decorations than any other unit.
- Those living in western U.S. were sent to internment camps, which were surrounded by barbed wire and guarded by soldiers.
- Japanese Americans living in Hawaii were not interned.

Women
- Were permitted to volunteer for armed forces for first time.
- Most joined Women's Army Corps (WACS).
- Oveta Culp Hobby was made head of WACS.

black general, flew escort sorties into central Europe with the Fifteenth Air Force. (An escort sortie is a plane that accompanies a bombing squadron.)

Japanese Americans. Yet another group of Americans who were segregated in the service were **Nisei** (nē′sā), or Americans of Japanese descent. About seventeen thousand of them enlisted in the armed forces. Some served in the United States intelligence service. Others fought in Italy, France, and Germany. The 442nd Regiment, popularly known as Go for Broke, received more decorations than any other American combat unit.

The Nation Relocates Japanese Americans

The performance of the Nisei was especially impressive considering how people of Japanese descent in California, Oregon, Washington, and Arizona were treated during the war. Some 120,000, two-thirds of them citizens, were rounded up by the army and by the FBI on the grounds that they posed a threat to the nation's security. Forced to abandon their homes and property, they were shipped to ten hastily built internment camps. The camps were located in the desert regions of California, Arizona, and other western states and in the swamplands of Arkansas. Except for the men who enlisted in the armed forces, most Japanese Americans remained in the camps, surrounded by barbed wire and guarded by soldiers, until almost the end of the war.

In 1944 the Supreme Court upheld the exclusion order in the case of *Korematsu* v. *United States*. Speaking for the majority, Justice Hugo Black argued that the government's action was caused by "military necessity." (Strangely enough, most Japanese Americans living in Hawaii, which contained many military installations, were left alone.) Speaking for the minority, Justice Frank Murphy said that the treatment of Japanese Americans reminded him of the Nazi treatment of the Jews.

Linking Past to Present

Historians today agree that the exclusion order grew out of more than military necessity. The order also reflected anti-Japanese racism. Not a single Japanese American was charged with committing a disloyal act, such as spying or sabotage, during the war. Furthermore, no relocation orders were even considered against people of German or Italian descent. After the war, the federal government paid Japanese Americans $35 million to compensate them for their lost property. The actual value of the property, however, has been put at $400 million.

In August 1988 the nation acknowledged the harm it had caused these Japanese Americans and made apologies. Congress passed a reparations bill giving $20,000 tax-free payments to those who were shipped to relocation camps during the Second World War.

Picturing History A Japanese-American grandfather and his grandchildren await a bus to take them to the internment camps. The sign on a Japanese-American grocery store proclaims the owner's patriotism.

- WACS served in noncombat positions.
- Many joined navy (WAVES), Coast Guard (SPARS), marines (Women's Reserve of the Marine Corps).
- Navy Nurse Corps trained hospital corpsmen.
- Women's Air Ferry Service piloted planes across Atlantic and towed targets for artillery practice.
- Joined or replaced men in nation's munitions factories.
- Received 60 percent lower pay than men.

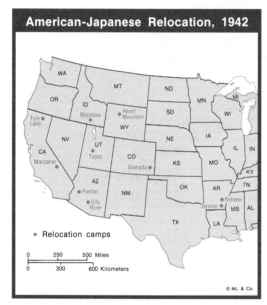

American-Japanese Relocation, 1942

● Relocation camps

Map Skills **Location** Which camps were farthest east? **Region** Which states had more than one camp?

The Work Force Expands

The need for people in the armed forces and in war industries wiped out the depression's unemployment figure of 7 million. The work force increased from 46.5 million to 53 million. In addition, by 1944 the average workweek was 45.2 hours. Since union representatives were able to maintain the standard 40-hour week with time-and-a-half pay for overtime, average weekly wages rose 70 percent during the war years. Union membership grew from 10.5 million in 1942 to almost 15 million in 1945.

Limiting Strikes. Immediately after the attack on Pearl Harbor, both the AFL and the CIO pledged not to strike while the war lasted. In return, the federal government set up the National War Labor Board to enforce settlements on wages, hours, and working conditions. To enforce the board's rulings, the government could seize a business and operate it.

In general, most unions kept their promise. Only a fraction of working time was lost during the war because of strikes. However, in 1943 the United Mine Workers went out on strike. Although wages had been frozen the previous year, the miners felt that rising prices and business profits justified a wage increase. FDR promptly seized the coal

mines. Congress then passed the Smith-Connally Anti-Strike Act, overriding the President's veto. The act said that unions had to give thirty days' notice before striking. It also said that a strike in an industry being run by the government was a federal crime.

Employing Women in War Plants. About 2 million women joined or replaced men in the nation's war plants. In all, there were 4 to 5 million women workers by 1945. However, they had two disadvantages: they received 60 percent less pay than men, and they had little job security. A wartime equal-pay-for-equal-work drive got nowhere. This was partly because of FDR's desire to hold down inflation and partly because the view was still widely held that married women should not work outside the home. Even women supporting families knew that they would be laid off as soon as the war was over and servicemen returned to reclaim their old jobs.

Nevertheless, the efforts of women on the assembly line were widely recognized and applauded. One of the most popular songs of the time was "Rosie the Riveter."

Banning Discrimination. Other additions to the industrial work force included more than 1 million African Americans, American Indians who left their reservations to take part in the war effort, and Mexican Americans. In June 1941 President

Map Skills

Jerome, Rohwer ● CA, AZ, AR

Picturing History American women answered the call to keep U.S. industries producing.

Check for Understanding

Call on individual students to read their answers to the Section 2 Review questions.

Guided Practice

Tell students that many people believe racism was never more apparent in American government policy than in the internment of Japanese Americans who were, in fact, American citizens. In August, 1988, Congress passed a reparations bill allotting tax-free payments of $20,000 to those who had been relocated. Ask students whether they think attempts should be made to amend mistakes of many decades ago. (Possible responses: yes—the government should be held accountable for disrupting the lives of innocent people and should make amends. No—it is too costly to pay such reparations and to set up agencies to administer them; it is too difficult to establish a fair dollar amount for reparations.)

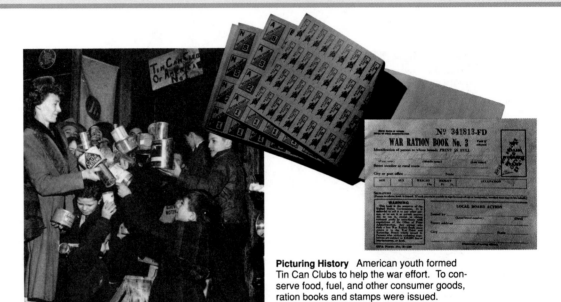

Picturing History American youth formed Tin Can Clubs to help the war effort. To conserve food, fuel, and other consumer goods, ration books and stamps were issued.

For Discussion

To what extent do you think government should be allowed to control the economy during wartime?
(Possible response: government should control the economy to ensure that wartime needs are met and to keep profiteers from taking unfair advantage of the war.)

Roosevelt issued an executive order barring racial discrimination in the hiring and firing of workers in plants that held government contracts. The order was to be enforced by the Fair Employment Practices Committee (FEPC). However, the order was issued only after **A. Philip Randolph,** president of the Brotherhood of Sleeping Car Porters, threatened to arouse the nation's conscience and pressure the government by leading a march of 10,000 African Americans on Washington, D.C.

Opening up industrial employment to African Americans and other minorities had several effects. The movement of black families from the South into northern and western cities continued the change in the nation's racial map that had started during World War I. It also led to a series of lynchings and race riots. The worst outbreak took place in Detroit in June 1943. Twenty-five blacks and nine whites were killed, and countless others were injured. Despite the violence, the economic standing of African Americans improved considerably during the war.

Production Increases

Lend-lease and war production ended the depression in American industry. There was much confusion, especially in the first years of war, as to who would produce the needed war material. Some companies were wary of again being branded merchants of death. (See page 716.) Others feared that after the war they would be caught with more production capacity than they could use. As a result, about 85 percent of the plants needed for war production were built by the federal government. The government then leased the plants to private firms who operated them.

Allocating Materials. The government also set up a **War Production Board (WPB).** Its first chief was Donald M. Nelson, a former executive of Sears, Roebuck and Company. The WPB decided which firms would receive raw materials. It told certain companies to convert from peacetime to wartime production. It limited the amount of gasoline people could buy, in order to conserve oil and rubber. It also organized nationwide drives to collect scrap iron, tin cans, and fats. The scrap iron and tin cans were melted down and used for weapons and ammunition. The fats were used to make soap and as lubricants for weapons and machinery. The WPB was controlled by the policy-making **Office of War Mobilization (OWM)** headed by James F. Byrnes. This agency was set up to oversee the nation's industrial production.

Supervising Contracts. To supervise government buying, the Senate set up a committee headed by Senator **Harry S Truman** of Missouri. The committee uncovered a great deal of inefficiency and bungling on war contracts, but although more than $300 billion were spent, there was very little wrongdoing. As a result of Senator Truman's vigorous work, he became a national figure.

Increasing Farm Production. Like manufacturers, American farmers outdid themselves in producing for the war. Although the farming work force declined, improved equipment and the greater use of fertilizers combined with good weather resulted in a doubling of output per worker. Farm prices likewise doubled.

Congress Acts to Curb Inflation

Larger incomes plus fewer civilian goods meant higher prices. To prevent inflation from skyrocketing the way it had during World War I, Congress set up the **Office of Price Administration (OPA).**

The OPA. The OPA was given the power to fix rents and to set maximum prices on goods. It also had the power to set up a system of **rationing.** Under this system, people could buy meat, shoes, butter, sugar, coffee, and other items needed by the armed forces only if they had stamps from ration books. Some people cheated by shopping at black markets, where they bought goods without stamps at prices above those set by the OPA. Overall, however, the combination of price controls and rationing kept inflation below 30 percent for the entire war period. This was about half the increase

that had taken place in the First World War. It should be noted, however, that prices did not rise equally. Clothing, for example, went up 40 percent, while food shot up 50 percent. Rents, on the other hand, were generally stable, increasing by only 4 percent.

Taxes. The government adopted several other techniques to curb inflation. It raised income tax rates and extended the tax to millions of Americans who had never paid it before. In addition, in 1943 Congress passed a payroll deduction law. Since then, employers have withheld income taxes from workers' paychecks each month and have had the responsibility of sending the money to the federal government.

Bonds. As in World War I, people bought government bonds to the tune of $100 billion. In all, Americans came out of the war with $129 billion in savings that they could not wait to spend on homes, cars, and other things they had gone without during sixteen years of depression and war.

Scientists Play a Key Role

Scientists played a key role in the Second World War. During the Battle of Britain, you recall, radar gave the Royal Air Force a great advantage in its fight with Hitler's bombers. The **Allies** (see chart below) also had antibiotics such as penicillin and the powerful insecticide DDT. The Allied armies in World War II were probably the first in history to be

Allies, Axis, and Neutral Nations in World War II

Allies

Argentina (1945) *	Dominican Republic (1941)	Iraq (1943)	Peru (1945)
Australia (1939)	Ecuador (1945)	Lebanon (1945)	Poland (1939)
Belgium (1940)	Egypt (1945)	Liberia (1944)	San Marino (1944)
Bolivia (1943)	El Salvador (1941)	Luxembourg (1940)	Saudi Arabia (1945)
Brazil (1942)	Ethiopia (1942)	Mexico (1942)	South Africa (1939)
Canada (1939)	France (1939)	Mongolian People's	Syria (1941)
Chile (1945)	Great Britain (1939)	Republic (1945)	U.S.S.R. (1941)
China (1941)	Greece (1940)	Netherlands (1940)	United States (1941)
Colombia (1943)	Guatemala (1941)	New Zealand (1939)	Uruguay (1945)
Costa Rica (1941)	Haiti (1941)	Nicaragua (1941)	Venezuela (1945)
Cuba (1941)	Honduras (1941)	Norway (1940)	Yugoslavia (1941)
Czechoslovakia (1941)	India (1939)	Panama (1941)	
Denmark (1940)	Iran (1941)	Paraguay (1945)	

Neutral Nations

Eire (Ireland)	Spain	Switzerland
Portugal	Sweden	Turkey

Axis Powers

Bulgaria (1941)	Hungary (1940)	Romania (1940)
Finland (1941)	Italy (1940)	Thailand (1942)
Germany (1939)	Japan (1940)	

* Date indicates year each country entered World War II

Anticipate the Lesson

Review with students the answers to the questions in Chapter 29, Section 3 Daily Activity and Enrichment Activity. Emphasize the importance of strategy in addition to strength of troops and equipment, in achieving a military victory.

SECTION 2 REVIEW

Answers

Main Ideas

1. Women were permitted to enlist.

2. World War II reduced unemployment. • Unions agreed not to strike during the war.

3. Private companies were afraid of being labeled "merchants of death," and some were also afraid that expanding production capacity during the war years would lead to financial disaster later.

4. By establishing the Office of Price Administration to set price controls and ration scarce goods, and by raising taxes and extending the tax to many more people. Payroll deduction took people's money before they could spend it and drive prices up. War bonds encouraged savings.

5. To organize a program to develop the atomic bomb as quickly as possible.

Critical Thinking

6. Possible answer: No—the government had no evidence to suggest the guilt of any Japanese person who was interned; the internment was based on economic, emotional, and racist reasons, not national security. **(evaluation)**

relatively free of body lice. Germany, on the other hand, developed the first jet aircraft engines, and its rockets were superior to anything the Allies developed. When the war ended, some German scientists went to the Soviet Union to help in rocket research and in the development of intercontinental missiles. Other German scientists came to the United States to do the same kind of work.

The greatest scientific achievement of the war, however, resulted from the splitting of the atom, which, by 1939, German scientists had shown could be done. The energy thus released opened up the possibility of making an atomic bomb. Albert Einstein, a Jewish refugee from Hitler's Germany, wrote a letter to FDR warning him that such a bomb was possible and that the Germans might well develop it first. In 1941 Roosevelt set up the Office of Scientific Research and Development to organize a crash program to develop the atomic bomb as quickly as possible.

SECTION 2 REVIEW

Key Terms and People

Explain the significance of: Selective Service System, Oveta Culp Hobby, Nisei, A. Philip Randolph, War Production Board (WPB), Office of War Mobilization (OWM), Harry S Truman, Office of Price Administration (OPA), rationing, Allies

Main Ideas

1. How did the composition of the United States armed forces change during World War II?
2. What effect did the war have on the labor force in the United States? How did labor unions cooperate in the war effort?
3. Why were so many of the plants that produced war-related goods built by the federal government?
4. How did Congress manage to keep inflation down when goods were scarce and incomes were high?
5. What was the main purpose of the Office of Scientific Research and Development?

Critical Thinking

6. Was the United States justified in detaining 120,000 civilians of Japanese descent in the name of national security? Explain.

SECTION 3

War Rages Across North Africa and Europe

GLOSSARY TERMS: convoys, *Afrika Korps*, partisans

The Allies and the Axis waged their struggle everywhere: on land and in the air, on the sea and beneath the sea. Although China and the Soviet Union ran their own operations, the United States and Great Britain worked closely together.

The Anglo-American Command Strategizes

Decisions concerning the two English-speaking nations were made by their combined Chiefs of Staff, headquartered in Washington, D.C., after consultation with Roosevelt and Churchill. These two men were unlike in many ways, but they came from a similar aristocratic tradition. They had the same kind of education and experience, and many of the same ideas about honor, discipline, and gentlemanly conduct. Churchill also had an American mother. As a result of all this, there was an easy friendship between the two leaders that added greatly to Anglo-American cooperation.

The Commanders. Both nations had strong military and civilian teams. In particular General **George Marshall,** United States Army Chief of Staff, was a forceful yet sensitive man who thought nothing of working seventy hours a week. Marshall was regarded by subordinates and equals alike with much the same mixture of respect and awe that George Washington had received.

General **Dwight D. Eisenhower,** commander of the European theater of operations, had the military and political skills needed to run a two-nation command. Bright, energetic, and outgoing, he did all he could to encourage Anglo-American teamwork. Ike, as Eisenhower was popularly called, had pamphlets about British life and customs given out to American troops before they left the United States for Britain. He once sent an American officer home for cursing a British officer. "If you had called him a so-and-so, I wouldn't have minded," Ike told the American. "But you called him a British so-and-so."

The First Decisions. Far-reaching decisions

State the Objective

Understand the major battles and campaigns
of the European and North African theaters.

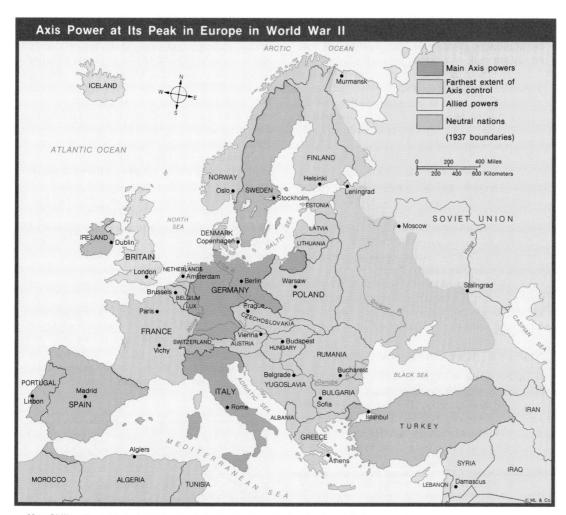

Axis Power at Its Peak in Europe in World War II

Main Axis powers
Farthest extent of
Axis control
Allied powers
Neutral nations
(1937 boundaries)

Map Skills **Region** What did Ireland, Spain, Sweden, Switzerland, and Turkey have in common as of 1937? **Region** Did the Axis Powers control Britain? France? the Soviet Union?

Map Skills

Neutrality • No • Yes • A large part of it

were arrived at early in the war. The first was to give priority to defeating Hitler and to let the all-out effort against Japan wait. There were several reasons for this strategy. One was the possibility that Germany might be able to crush the Soviet Union and cut Britain off from America, something Japan would never be able to do. Another was that once Germany was defeated, the Allies could join forces to take Japan.

The second major decision—like that made by Grant in the Civil War—was to accept only the unconditional surrender of the enemy. Some historians believe that this second decision was a mistake. They feel that it led Germany and Japan to fight longer and more desperately than they might otherwise have.

Convoys Risk the Atlantic

With **convoys,** or groups, of merchant ships, troop carriers, and protective escort ships sailing across the North Atlantic, the waters off the eastern coast of the United States were left weakly defended. The Germans were quick to take advantage of this situation. By January 1942, submarine packs were striking from Newfoundland to New

Have students use a large wall map or the map on page 751 to identify the areas of Allied offensives from the east, south, and west that led to the defeat of Germany. Have students then identify the nations involved in each offensive and highlight the important events.

East: Stalingrad
- Germans besieged the city for two months.
- Soviets launched a counteroffensive.
- Stalingrad was considered the turning point of the war on the Eastern Front.

South: North Africa
- Allies launched an invasion called Operation Torch, in November 1942.
- Landings occurred at Casablanca, Oran, and Algiers.
- U.S. and British forces drove toward the Germans in Tunisia.
- Rommel and his Afrika Korps were defeated by the British in Egypt at the Battle of El Alamein.
- Allied forces crossed the sea to Sicily and secured the island.

South: Italian Front
- Italy and eastern Europe including Yugoslavia were involved.
- king of Italy arrested Mussolini and prepared to surrender.
- Germany took over Italy and freed Mussolini.
- Allies landed at Salerno in September 1943.

For Discussion
What advantage did the British gain from the Anglo-American Alliance? What advantage did the Americans gain? (Possible responses: Britain was financially exhausted and needed U.S. money; Britain was able to easily obtain military equipment from the U.S. once the U.S. had entered the war; Americans were able to fortify British positions and join in defeating Hitler; Great Britain also strengthened the U.S. in the fight against Japan.)

Orleans. In three months, 200 ships were sunk; in the next two months, 182. Silhouetted against the bright glow of shore lights, merchant vessels and oil tankers made easy targets for enemy torpedoes.

By the end of the year, however, several tactics succeeded in lowering American losses. The tactics included tighter air and sea patrols (some making use of private boats) and a strict brownout of coastal cities, which cut the use of electricity and thus reduced sky glow.

Meanwhile the North Atlantic battle went on. The "polar bear route," which went from Iceland around the north cape of Norway above the Arctic Circle to the Soviet port of Murmansk, was the only route by which large amounts of American supplies could reach the Soviet Union. (See map on page 747.) It was a dangerous route, for German planes and submarines based in Norway sank one merchant ship after another. Seamen who were not blown up or drowned suffered from exposure to the Arctic weather. Yet the convoys kept sailing, bringing the Soviets badly needed supplies, which they were soon using to good advantage.

Stalingrad Marks the Turning Point

By the spring of 1942, the initial German push into the Soviet Union had stalled in front of Leningrad and Moscow. The Soviets' scorched-earth policy prevented the Nazis from living off the land. Hitler decided to try a different tactic. His war machine was beginning to run low on oil, and

there were large oil fields in the Caucasus Mountains. In addition, Hitler wanted to cut the movement of military supplies along the Volga River to Moscow. So he decided to kill two birds with one stone. In the summer of 1942, he flung his troops at the city of Stalingrad (now Volgograd) on the river's west bank. (See map on page 747.)

For three months the Germans besieged the city, conquering it house by house and street by street. Then, in November, the Soviets launched a counteroffensive, moving in one army from the north and another from the south. All through the bitter winter the fighting went on. It was so cold—about 44° below zero—that tanks would not start, rifles misfired, and food turned hard as stone. By December the German army was surrounded. On the second day of February 1943, according to one historian's description, some 91,000 "dazed and frost-bitten [German] scarecrows hobbled into captivity." They were all that remained of the original force of 330,000.

Soviet losses—both military and civilian—totaled about 1,250,000, more than the total American casualties for World War II. Despite this staggering death toll, the battle at Stalingrad was the turning point of the war on the eastern front. From there, the Soviets began to move steadily west.

Picturing History Only the chimneys are left standing after the battle at Stalingrad. Soviet soldiers held their position during a brutal winter campaign.

West: Europe
- Allied troops pushed north through Italy as Soviets pushed west into Poland.
- Normandy invasion, D-Day, took place on June 6, 1944.
- By September 1944, France, Belgium, Luxembourg, and part of the Netherlands were liberated.
- Battle of the Bulge took place.
- American and Soviet troops met at the Elbe River in April 1945.

Check for Understanding

Have students write a brief essay explaining the roles played by the U.S., Great Britain, France, and the Soviet Union in the defeat of Hitler. (Essays might include: U.S. spearheaded invasions of North Africa, Sicily, Italy, France; Great Britain defeated Rommel, assisted in invasion of France, applied radar in Battle of Britain; France aided Allies in the conquest of France and Germany; Soviet Union launched counteroffensive against Germans at Stalingrad, pushed west into German-held Poland.)

The Allies Turn to the Mediterranean

While the battle at Stalingrad was raging, Stalin, who alone in Europe was fighting Hitler, kept urging the United States and Britain to open a "second front"—an attack on Hitler's western European frontier. The Americans were anxious to try it, but the British held back. Going in too soon, they said, would result in disaster. They wanted neither another Dunkirk nor a repetition of the trench warfare of World War I. They compromised.

Invading North Africa. The compromise was **Operation Torch,** an invasion of western North Africa, which was held by the German-dominated Vichy French government. On November 7–8, 1942, Allied landings were made at Casablanca, Oran, and Algiers. (See map on page 751.) The Vichy French offered only token resistance. The center of North Africa was occupied by the remnants of Mussolini's troops, who were strengthened by the German General **Erwin Rommel** and his *Afrika Korps.* The previous month, General Rommel's forces had been defeated by the British in Egypt at the Battle of El Alamein. The Allied strategy was to trap Rommel as he retreated from El Alamein to Tunisia and thus secure the Mediterranean for shipments of supplies to the Soviet Union. Rommel had the area fortified by the time the Allies reached it in early 1943. After three months of heavy fighting, however, with General Eisenhower's troops closing

Picturing History General Eisenhower (left) advises General Patton, whom he put in charge of the troops in Tunisia.

in on them from the west, and British General Bernard L. Montgomery's forces closing in on them from the east, the remnants of the *Afrika Korps* surrendered on May 13, 1943. With this defeat the Axis lost control of Africa and of the Mediterranean as well. The triumphant Allied forces then crossed the narrow sea between Tunisia and Sicily, securing that island in a month.

The Italian Campaign. The Allied forces were now ready to attack what Churchill called "the soft underbelly of the Axis"—Italy, Yugoslavia, and eastern Europe. At that point, the King of Italy arrested Mussolini and prepared to surrender unconditionally.

Unfortunately, the Germans moved faster than the Allies. They took over Italy and dug themselves in. They even rescued Mussolini by dropping one hundred parachutists at his mountain prison and then flying him off to Munich. The Allied landings at Salerno, Italy, in September 1943 and at "Bloody Anzio" the following January gave American troops some of the hardest fighting they encountered in Europe. At Salerno, only the timely drop of two paratroop battalions saved the Allies from being pushed back into the sea. In all, it took eighteen months of mud and mountain warfare before the Allies were able to drive the Germans from the Italian peninsula.

Mussolini was recaptured on April 28, 1945, by Italian **partisans.** Partisans were members of the underground resistance movement that existed in the Nazi-held countries. They derailed trains, sabotaged factory machinery, hid Allied flyers who had been shot down, smuggled Jews to neutral countries, and did everything else they could to help defeat the Nazis. The partisans shot Mussolini and hung his body in a Milan square.

Allied Forces Invade France

As Anglo-American troops pushed north through Italy, and the Soviets pushed west into Poland, plans for invading Hitler's Fortress Europe moved ahead. Before the Allies could mount their cross-channel invasion of France, however, they had to control the air. From October 1943 through May 1944, the Americans bombed Germany by day, while the British bombed it by night. By June 1944, the Allies had a thirty-to-one superiority over the German air force, which had been decimated by the Allied bombings.

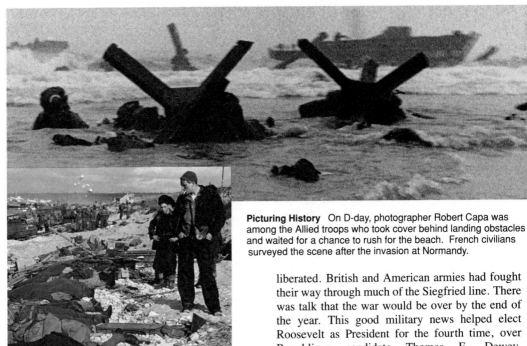

Picturing History On D-day, photographer Robert Capa was among the Allied troops who took cover behind landing obstacles and waited for a chance to rush for the beach. French civilians surveyed the scene after the invasion at Normandy.

The Beaches of Normandy. The invasion of France on **D-day,** June 6, 1944, carried the code name **Operation Overlord.** It was the largest amphibious, or combined land and sea, operation in history. In all, there were 176,000 troops involved, as well as 4,000 landing craft, 600 warships, and 11,000 planes. It had taken two years of planning and work to set into motion.

German defenses were enormous. They included about 250,000 troops protected by every conceivable type of underwater mine, tank trap, and guns mounted in concrete forts. By clever deception, however, the Allies kept the enemy off balance for twenty-four hours after the landing. They bombed in an area east of the actual landing place so heavily that the Germans, certain it was the real invasion point, shifted men and equipment there. Even so, German fire at one of the five real landing places, Omaha Beach, was so intense that the invaders were almost wiped out. Nevertheless, all the beachheads were held. Within a month, the Allies had landed a million troops, 567,000 tons of supplies, and 170,000 vehicles.

By September 1944, France, Belgium, Luxembourg, and part of the Netherlands had been liberated. British and American armies had fought their way through much of the Siegfried line. There was talk that the war would be over by the end of the year. This good military news helped elect Roosevelt as President for the fourth time, over Republican candidate Thomas E. Dewey. Roosevelt's Vice-President was Senator Truman. Then a snag developed.

The Battle of the Bulge. Three things upset the Allied timetable. First, the Nazis in the port of Antwerp, Belgium, held out longer than expected. As a result, American tanks under the command of General **George Patton** ran out of gas. Second, an airborne landing at Arnhem in the Netherlands fizzled badly. Third, when least expected, the enemy counterattacked.

On December 16, under cover of fog, German troops hit an eighty-mile front along the Belgian border of the Ardennes Forest. The area was thinly defended by inexperienced American troops. Nevertheless, they put up a heroic defense of Bastogne, an important transportation center in southeast Belgium, holding out until Christmas. At one point the Germans broke through the Allied lines, creating a bulge. Then relief arrived for what became known as the **Battle of the Bulge.** The weather cleared, American planes took to the air once more, and the German threat was over.

The idea for the attack had been Hitler's. After it failed, his forces were never able to make another, although there continued to be sharp battles as the Germans retreated.

Ask students to write a paragraph explaining *unconditional surrender* and tell why the Allies' demand for it might have prolonged the war. (Paragraphs might include: a country that agrees to unconditional surrender puts itself at the mercy of the victorious nation and takes no part in negotiating a peace treaty; both Japan and Germany feared complete surrender to the Allies and so were willing to risk fighting longer to avoid it; perhaps either or both hoped for a negotiated peace.) Ask several students to read their paragraphs to the class.

A Meeting at the Elbe.   At the end of March 1945, the western Allies crossed the Rhine River, the last major obstacle between them and the heart of Germany. In April the Soviets entered the outskirts of Berlin after having pushed the Germans back for more than a thousand miles. As one eyewitness remembered that time:

> Throughout those April days you could see a nation collapse. Tens of thousands of people fled westward toward the approaching American and allied troops. German soldiers, civilian men and women, and children—some in their mothers' arms—scurried along the ru-

ined roads and across shell-pocked fields. They were eager to reach the western armies because they did not wish to be captured by the Russians. . . .

At the broad, swift-flowing Elbe River, the masses hardly halted. Across the water they came in boats and rafts. Some plunged into the river and swam. Others held onto whatever floating driftwood they could find. Many were carried away by the current.

Gratefully the survivors surrendered to American and British soldiers and disappeared behind their lines.

The Crushing of Nazi Germany, 1944-1945

→ Allied forces
— Battlefronts (Dec 1944)
✕ Battle
(1937 boundaries)

Map Skills
North • North • Belgium • Soviet Union • Egypt

Map Skills   **Movement** From what direction did the Allies come to Normandy? to Casablanca?
Location In what country was the Battle of the Bulge fought? the siege of Leningrad? the battle of El Alamein?

Student Assignment/Homework

Have students read Section 4, "Allied Troops Advance on the Pacific Front," and answer Section 4 Review questions on paper.

Anticipate the Lesson

Review with students the Anglo-American strategies for dealing with Germany and Japan. (Strategies might include: the Allies agreed to defeat Hitler before waging an all-out campaign against Japan; once Hitler was defeated, the Allies could concentrate all their efforts on the Pacific.) Ask students whether they think the strategies were the best in light of the circumstances. (Possible response: yes—Germany was closer to the U.S.; Germany was developing an atomic bomb; Germany could have succeeded in cutting Britain off from the U.S. so had to be dealt with immediately.)

SECTION 3 REVIEW

Answers

Main Ideas

1. To give priority to defeating Germany rather than Japan and to accept only unconditional surrender.

2. By sending them along the "polar bear route," above the Arctic Circle. • Enemy attacks and brutal weather.

3. After the battle, Hitler's armies were never able to regain their strength, so an Allied victory in Europe was assured.

4. Hitler committed suicide.

Critical Thinking

5. Possible answers: Victory— the battle was the turning point on the eastern front that saved the Soviet Union from Germany. Defeat—it came at a heavy price—the loss of 1,250,000 Soviet lives. **(evaluation)**

On April 25 American and Soviet infantrymen stood looking at each other from opposite banks of the broad Elbe River, which runs through eastern Germany. (See map on page 751.) Some Americans, against orders, rowed quietly across the river. The Soviets met them with hearty hugs and handclasps, although for most, it was the first time they had seen an American.

The End of Hitler. In his underground headquarters in Berlin, Hitler, his longtime friend Eva Braun, whom he hastily married, and a few faithful followers waited for the end. Deep as they were, they could feel the shudder as bombs hit the ground above their heads. Hitler, determined to avoid capture by the Soviets, decided to go out in flames like a warrior of old. On April 30 he shot himself, while his wife took poison. Then, following instructions, their bodies were taken up to the garden, doused with gasoline, and burned. Two days later, Berlin fell to the Soviets.

On May 7 General Eisenhower accepted the unconditional surrender of Nazi Germany. The next day, **V-E day** (Victory in Europe), marked the official end of one part of the war.

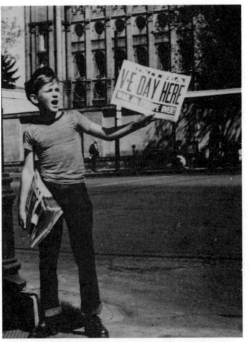

Picturing History A newsboy announces V-E Day.

SECTION 3 REVIEW

Key Terms and People

Explain the significance of: George Marshall, Dwight D. Eisenhower, convoys, Operation Torch, Erwin Rommel, *Afrika Korps*, partisans, D-day, Operation Overlord, George Patton, Battle of the Bulge, V-E Day

Main Ideas

1. What were the first important decisions made by the American-British alliance?
2. How did the Americans manage to get badly needed supplies to the Soviets? What were the dangers associated with the method used?
3. What significance did the Battle of the Bulge hold for the Allied forces?
4. How did Hitler avoid capture by the Soviets as they entered Berlin?

Critical Thinking

5. Was the Battle of Stalingrad a victory or a defeat for the Soviets? Explain.

SECTION 4

Allied Troops Advance on the Pacific Front

GLOSSARY TERMS: kamikaze, Manhattan Project, Hiroshima

Although Roosevelt and Churchill had agreed that victory over Germany came first, the Americans did not wait until V-E Day to move against Japan. On the contrary, as soon as possible, the United States began to wage an aggressive military campaign in the Pacific.

The Japanese Win Early Victories

During the first five months after the attack on Pearl Harbor, the Japanese made tremendous advances in all directions. They overran Hong Kong, French Indochina (now Laos, Cambodia, and Vietnam), Malaya (including the naval base at Singapore), Burma, Thailand, and the Dutch East Indies (now Indonesia), reaching as far south as New Guinea and the Solomon Islands. To the east, they captured Guam and Wake Island, as well as two islands in the Aleutian chain in Alaska.

Picturing History
As Supreme Allied Commander of forces in the Southwest Pacific, Douglas MacArthur ordered the invasion of the Japanese islands.

Picturing History
Congress awarded Colonel James "Jimmy" Doolittle a Medal of Honor for his courageous bombing raid on Tokyo.

In the Philippines, some 36,000 American and Filipino troops under General **Douglas MacArthur** succeeded in holding off a Japanese army of 200,000 for four months in the Bataan peninsula and then for another month on the fortress island of Corregidor, at the entrance to Manila Bay. When it became clear that the situation was hopeless, Army Chief of Staff George Marshall ordered MacArthur to escape to Australia. MacArthur did so, saying as he left, "I shall return."

As a result of Japan's conquests, the prestige of white people in Southeast Asia, which had been based on their hitherto unquestioned military power, was destroyed. Even after the Japanese were gone, people in the area were never again willing to live under white rule.

The Allies Stem the Japanese Tide

By the spring of 1942, Japanese armies were at the gates of India, the Japanese fleet was menacing Australia, and even the Pacific coast of the United States was threatened. In April, however, the gloom lightened. Sixteen B-25 bombers, commanded by Colonel James H. Doolittle, took off from the aircraft carrier *Hornet* and dropped a few bombs on Tokyo. The daring daylight raid had no strategic value, and all the planes went down in China, where the crews were forced to bail out. Nevertheless, the raid made the Japanese realize that their islands were vulnerable to bombs. It also made Americans feel a lot better.

Then early in May, a combined American and Australian fleet intercepted a Japanese fleet in the Coral Sea. In the battle that followed, there was no ship-to-ship contact. All fighting was done by carrier-based planes. Although the Americans and Australians lost more ships than the enemy, they halted Japan's attempt to invade Australia.

A month later Japan met a worse defeat at the Battle of Midway. Four aircraft carriers it could never replace were sunk, other ships were badly damaged and two hundred fifty-three planes were destroyed. American losses were one carrier, one destroyer, and one hundred fifty planes. In this battle also, carrier aircraft rather than ships were the decisive element. The Japanese, who had been heading for Hawaii, turned back to their base. They no longer held unchallenged control over the Pacific.

Allied Troops Leapfrog to Japan

The Pacific theater of war, or area where the fighting took place, posed several serious problems for the United States and its allies. Japan was protected by some three thousand miles of water in which were literally hundreds of fortified islands. Even small coral atolls (an *atoll* is a ring-shaped island surrounding a central lagoon) contained an airstrip, guns, and determined Japanese. To storm every island would probably have taken a generation. Instead, MacArthur came up with a different tactic that he called leapfrogging. That is, the Americans would mount attacks only on selected islands. The Australians and New Zealanders would then bomb and mop up the Japanese garrisons that had been bypassed.

The Battle of Guadalcanal. The American offensive began in August 1942. United States ma-

Present the Lesson

For geographical reference, have students use a large classroom map as well as information in this chapter to develop a time line of major military offensives in the Pacific. Write the time line on the board. Ask students to locate the sites of the offensives on a map and to state the victor of each.

April 1942	U.S. bombs Tokyo; action has no real strategic value but makes Japanese realize their vulnerability.
May 1942	U.S. and Australian fleets stop attempted invasion of Australia in the Battle of the Coral Sea.
June 1942	U.S. forces are victorious at the Battle of Midway.
August 1942	U.S. begins battle for Guadalcanal.
1943	Japanese withdraw from Guadalcanal.
February 1944	U.S. captures Solomon, Gilbert, and Marshall islands.
June 1944	U.S. attacks Mariana Islands—Battle of the Philippine Sea.
October 1944	U.S. forces converge on Leyte Island in Philippines.
Spring 1945	Battle of Iwo Jima and Battle of Okinawa take place.
August 6, 1945	U.S. drops atomic bomb on Hiroshima.
August 9, 1945	U.S. drops atomic bomb on Nagasaki.

rines landed on Guadalcanal in the Solomon Islands, which form a thousand-mile-long barrier east of New Guinea and Australia. (See map on page 755.) Two days after American troops had established a beachhead, Japanese cruisers sank almost all the American transport ships.

For the next six months the marines, who were short of food and equipment, clung to the island's airstrip while Japanese and American ships and planes fought one engagement after another. The tropical sun and rain created a steaming hell by day, while the strange bird and animal sounds made the jungle nights a time of uneasy rest. The American fleet under Admiral William F. Halsey routed a massive Japanese fleet in November. Finally, early in 1943, the Japanese withdrew from Guadalcanal, leaving the Americans with a valuable base from which to launch their offensive.

Return to the Philippines. The American return to the Philippines was actually made from two directions. MacArthur's troops moved toward the islands from the south, while a fleet under Admiral **Chester W. Nimitz** moved toward the islands from the east. By February 1944 Japan's outer defenses had been cracked with the capture of the Solomon, Gilbert, and Marshall islands. By June 1944 the Americans were attacking Japan's inner defenses in the Mariana Islands. The Japanese fought a tremendous naval engagement—the Battle of the Philippine Sea—in an effort to prevent the landings in the Marianas. However, the battle dealt a crippling blow to Japan's carrier planes, 345 to a loss of only 17 for the Americans. It also placed Japan's home islands within reach of American land-based bombers for the first time.

In October the MacArthur and Nimitz forces—consisting of 174,000 soldiers in 738 ships—converged on Leyte Island in the Philippines. (See map on page 755.) MacArthur himself and a few officers, most of whom had fled the Philippines two years earlier, headed for land in a small barge. Fifty yards from shore, MacArthur stepped off into the knee-deep water, waded to the beach, and announced, "I have returned."

The Japanese threw their entire fleet into the Battle of Leyte Gulf. **Kamikaze** (kä′mi kä′zē) suicide pilots crashed their bomb-laden planes into American ships, killing themselves and large numbers of the ships' crews. (The word *kamikaze* means "divine wind" after a typhoon that in 1281 destroyed Kublai Khan's fleet when it attempted to

invade Japan from China.) After three days of fighting, however, it was the Japanese fleet that was crushed. Three battleships, four aircraft carriers, thirteen cruisers, and almost four hundred planes disappeared beneath the sea.

A New President Takes the Reins

Roosevelt did not live to see the final victory of the Allies. On the morning of April 12, 1945, the President was posing for an artist who was painting his portrait. He sat in an armchair in the living room of the Little White House in Warm Springs, Georgia. Suddenly he put his hand to his forehead and said, "I have a terrific headache." Then he slumped over. He was put to bed, and doctors were called. He had suffered a stroke. Within hours he was dead.

He was mourned throughout the world. There were people in the armed services who could not remember a time when FDR had not been President. Harry Truman, uneasy and inexperienced, took over the reins of office.

Picturing History The face of Navy serviceman Graham Jackson expresses the sorrow of all those who lined the streets as FDR's body was carried to the train at Warm Springs on the day after his death.

The Atom Bomb Ends the War

After the capture of the Philippines, only two major battles remained. However, they were

Check for Understanding

Call on individual students to read their answers to Section 4 Review questions.

Guided Practice

Remind students that the advent of nuclear weapons has totally transformed warfare. Ask students to consider whether it is possible for a nation to think today of war as a means to achieve a particular end, as nations might have in the past. (Possible response: no—nuclear weapons make warfare a global concern; nuclear weapons have the capacity to devastate large areas and cause further destruction through nuclear fallout; nations must now weigh the ends they seek and try to achieve them through means other than armed conflict.)

Assign Independent Practice

Ask students to write a newspaper editorial supporting or opposing the nuclear bombing of Hiroshima. (Possible responses: supporting—it hastened an end to the war and thus saved countless Allied lives. Opposing—hundreds of thousands of innocent people died; the aftereffects of the bomb have still not been fully realized.)

among the worst of the war—Iwo Jima (ē′wō jē′ mə) and Okinawa (ō′ ka nä′ wə). The Japanese forces on each island held out for many weeks in the spring of 1945. Furthermore, each was so savagely defended that it gave Americans a chilling foretaste of what the invasion of Japan's home islands would be like. Churchill thought that the cost would be "a million American lives and half that number of British."

As matters turned out, no invasion of Japan was necessary. In 1942 a controlled nuclear reaction had been achieved in a small laboratory under the concrete football stands at Stagg Field at the University of Chicago. Colonel, later General, Leslie Groves of the Army Corps of Engineers had then been given the task of producing the uranium

235 and the plutonium 239 needed for an explosive device. Under the code name of the **Manhattan Project,** two plants for this purpose had been built at Oak Ridge, Tennessee, where they could make use of the vast water and electric power resources of the TVA. A third plant was located at Hanford, Washington.

Creating the A-Bomb. At the same time, a group of American, British, and European-refugee scientists headed by Dr. **J. Robert Oppenheimer** had put together the first atomic bomb at Los Alamos, New Mexico. At 5:30 on the morning of July 16, 1945, it was exploded in the desert near Alamogordo air base. There was a burst of blinding light, visible 180 miles away, a deep-growling

Map Skills

Midway • Hiroshima, Nagasaki • India • Soviet Union

Map Skills **Location** Which battle was farthest east? **Location** Which Japanese cities were hit by A-bombs?
Movement From what country did Allied forces go into Burma? Manchuria?

Student Assignment/Homework

Have students complete Chapter 29, Section 4 Daily Activity and Enrichment Activity and read Section 5, "The Allies Plan for the Postwar World."

Picturing History The shell of the Hiroshima Museum of Science and Industry (left) stands as a memorial of the atomic blast. General Douglas MacArthur (above) signs the Japanese surrender aboard the USS *Missouri.* A watch (right) found in the ruins of Hiroshima marks the blast.

blast, scalding wind, and then a gray mushroom cloud that rose slowly toward the sky. Words from the *Song of God,* a sacred Hindu text, came into Dr. Oppenheimer's mind as he watched: "I am become Death, the shatterer of worlds, waiting that hour that ripens to their doom." In truth, the world has not been the same since.

On July 26, 1945, a warning was sent to Japan that it faced "prompt and utter destruction" unless it surrendered. This warning was issued by the participants at the Potsdam Conference held in Berlin. (See page 758.) On August 6 a 9,000-pound atomic bomb was put aboard a B-29 bomber named the *Enola Gay,* after the mother of pilot Colonel Paul W. Tibbets, Jr. At 8:15:30 A.M. the bomb was dropped on the city of **Hiroshima,** an important military center. It killed about 71,000 people, horribly injured another 68,000, and flattened four square miles of the city. Three days later a second bomb hit Nagasaki, killing 36,000 persons, injuring 40,000, and leveling almost half the city. Together, though, the two atomic bombs took fewer lives than the regular air raids on Tokyo had.

On August 14 Emperor Hirohito, despite opposition from some of his military leaders, made the decision to surrender unconditionally. Dozens of American and British ships sailed into Tokyo Bay.

There, on September 2, 1945, the formal surrender was signed on the deck of the battleship *Missouri.* History's first total and global war was over.

SECTION 4 REVIEW

Key Terms and People

Explain the significance of: Douglas MacArthur, Chester W. Nimitz, kamikaze, Manhattan Project, J. Robert Oppenheimer, Hiroshima

Main Ideas

1. What effect did Japan's victories in Southeast Asia have on Asian attitudes toward white rule?
2. What did the Battle of the Coral Sea and the Battle of Midway show about the Pacific?
3. What military significance did its victory at Guadalcanal hold for the United States?
4. What was the mission of the *Enola Gay?*

Critical Thinking

5. Discuss some possible reasons for the choice of the name *kamikaze* for the Japanese suicide pilots. How might the name have inspired the young pilots?

Anticipate the Lesson

Review with students the Treaty of Versailles and the creation of the League of Nations following World War I. (See Chapter 23.) Ask students to list the weaknesses of the treaty and of the League of Nations. (Possible responses: the Treaty of Versailles was never ratified by the U.S.; the treaty demanded high reparations from ruined nations; it sought revenge. League of Nations was rejected by Congress;

State the Objective

Examine the major results of the Allied victory in World War II.

SECTION 5

The Allies Plan for the Postwar World

GLOSSARY TERMS: **Yalta Conference, United Nations (UN), General Assembly, Security Council**

The World War II Allies had learned some lessons from 1919. One was to prepare for peace even as they were making war and not to put off questions about the postwar world until the fighting ended.

Wartime Conferences Prepare for Peace

Beginning with the August 1941 meeting at which Roosevelt and Churchill signed the Atlantic Charter, the United States took part in fifteen major international conferences. Most were between Roosevelt and Churchill; three included Soviet dictator Joseph Stalin; and one, establishing the United Nations, was attended by representatives of fifty nations.

Cairo. The early conferences between Roosevelt and Churchill dealt with military matters, such as the decision to invade North Africa and the setting of a target date for the Normandy invasion. Later conferences concerned political questions about the postwar world.

In November of 1943, FDR, Churchill, and **Chiang Kai-shek** (chan′ kī shek′) of China met in Cairo, Egypt. They agreed on two issues: (1) Korea, then under Japanese domination, would become independent; and (2) Formosa, now Taiwan, would be returned by Japan to China.

Teheran. In late November, Roosevelt and Churchill proceeded from Cairo to Teheran, Iran. There they promised Stalin that a second front would soon be opened. Stalin in turn promised to attack Japan after Germany was defeated.

The Teheran meeting was FDR's first encounter with Stalin. The American President had looked forward to it. He was sure that he would be able to establish the same kind of relationship with the Soviet leader that he had with Churchill. Out of this relationship he hoped would come a lasting postwar alliance. Roosevelt apparently regarded Stalin in the same way he regarded a tough Democratic political boss, that is, as someone whom he could handle through a combination of charm and polit-

ical favors. FDR was wrong. Stalin's methods in his climb to power involved murder and treachery. It was a measure of Stalin's skill that Roosevelt came away from Teheran pleased at his success. He assured Congress and the American people that future relations with the Soviet Union would be easy sailing.

Yalta. In his next meeting with Stalin, at the **Yalta Conference** on the Black Sea, FDR may have had doubts. It was now February 1945, and the European war was drawing to a close. The Soviet armies were deep in central Europe. Many people doubted that these troops would draw back to the Soviet Union.

The **Big Three** reached some tentative decisions about what to do with Germany after the war. The three leaders also agreed that German and Japanese leaders would be tried as criminals for the atrocities they had committed. The three decided to set up the United Nations later in the year. Stalin, in exchange for Japan's Kuril and Sakhalin islands, again promised to enter the war against Japan two or three months after Germany surrendered. The atomic bomb had not yet been developed. The United States felt that it would need Soviet help for the invasion of Japan.

While these issues were fairly easily resolved, the question of Poland proved sticky. The Soviet Union supported a Communist regime for that nation. Great Britain and the United States, on the other hand, favored the Polish government-in-exile that had been in London since 1939. From Stalin's point of view, the Soviet Union had to have friendly governments on its western borders. It had suffered over 25 million casualties during the war, as well as tremendous property damage. It had neither oceans nor mountains to protect it against invasion. Finally, Britain and the United States agreed to support the Polish Communist government provided that it was expanded to include a few representatives from the government-in-exile in London. Stalin then promised that after the war, there would be "free and unfettered elections" in Poland and other Eastern European countries occupied by Soviet troops. Unfortunately, he never kept this promise.

San Francisco. In April 1945, representatives of fifty nations met in San Francisco to establish an international peace-keeping body. By then the Soviet Union was displaying considerable suspiciousness and stubbornness. The country was made up

---

For Discussion

To what extent did the dropping of the atomic bomb change the world permanently? (Possible response: the world entered the nuclear age, making possible a future world war that could destroy the entire earth; it gave countries that had nuclear warfare capability a powerful means of counteracting aggression by other nations.)

Construct a four-column chart on the board with the headings Cairo, Teheran, Yalta, and Potsdam. Ask the students to skim the section to find information about the events that took place at each. Ask students to make a generalization about each conference.
Chart should include:

Cairo
November 1943—FDR, Churchill, Chiang Kai-shek agreed that: 1. Korea would become independent of Japan. 2. Formosa would be returned by Japan to China. Possible generalization: Conference established postwar geography in the Far East.

Teheran
November 1943—FDR, Churchill, Stalin agreed that: 1. Allies would open a second front against Hitler. 2. Soviet Union would attack Japan after Germany was defeated. Possible generalization: Conference dealt with tactics in Europe and Far East.

Yalta
February 1945—FDR, Churchill, Stalin agreed that: 1. German and Japanese leaders would be tried as criminals. 2. The United Nations would be established. 3. Soviet Union would receive Japan's Kuril and Sakhalin islands for promising to declare war on Japan after Germany surrendered. 4. Britain and the U.S. would support the Polish Communist government provided that it included representatives from the government-in-exile. 5. Free elections would be held in Poland and other Eastern European countries after the war. Possible generalization: Conference decided the fate of Germany and Japan, postwar geography, occupation of conquered territories, and world government.

Picturing History President Truman (center) met at Potsdam with Winston Churchill (left) and Joseph Stalin (right) to clarify and implement agreements reached previously at Yalta.

For Discussion
What might the world have been like if the Allies had lost World War II? (Possible responses: Germans might have dominated the world; all Jewish people might have been exterminated; Germany and Japan might eventually have fought for control of the Pacific; the Soviet Union might have become part of Germany, and communism would likely have faded.)

of fifteen separate Soviet republics and wanted all fifteen to be represented in the United Nations. (As defined in the Soviet Union, a republic is a state in which the supreme power rests in all the citizens who are entitled to vote.) The other countries refused. It would have been much like having all the states of the United States represented. However, a compromise was reached. Two Soviet republics—the Ukraine and Byelorussia (White Russia)—as well as the Soviet Union as a whole, were given a seat.

Potsdam. In July 1945 President Truman went to Potsdam, Germany, for the final wartime conference. Although final decisions were reached about the postwar treatment of Germany, it seemed to many observers that the wartime alliance was definitely breaking up. Stalin made it clear that he had no intention of allowing free elections in Eastern Europe. Nor could the Big Three decide on Poland's western boundary. They did, however, decide to move 6.5 million Germans out of Czechoslovakia, Hungary, and Poland and into Germany.

The United Nations Replaces the League

The charter establishing the **United Nations (UN)** was signed in June 1945. Like the League of Nations, the UN had a large deliberative body and a smaller executive body. Its charter provided for a **General Assembly** of all member nations. Real power, however, was placed in the hands of the **Security Council.** On this council, the United States, Great Britain, France, the Union of Soviet Socialist Republics, and China were to have permanent seats, with six other nations elected on a rotating basis. Voting in the Security Council would be by majority, but the majority would have to include all five permanent members. Thus, each of the **Big Five** nations would have veto power over any council action. The Economic and Social Council, the Trusteeship Council (for former colonies), the International Court of Justice, and the Secretariat for Administration completed the UN's main structure.

In 1919 and 1920, the United States Congress had spent eight months debating whether or not to join the League of Nations and had finally decided against doing so. In 1945, however, it took the Senate only six days to approve the country's membership in the United Nations. In fact, the United States was the first nation in the world to accept the UN charter. After building its headquarters in New York City, the organization began its work on a great wave of goodwill and optimism.

Potsdam

July 1945—Churchill, Stalin, Truman agreed that 6.5 million Germans would be moved from Czechoslovakia, Hungary, and Poland back to Germany. They could not agree on: 1. Free elections in eastern Europe. 2. Poland's western boundary. Possible generalization: Allies began to break up, agreeing only on the removal of German nationals from the East.

Focus on Biography

Eleanor Roosevelt (1884–1962)

Happiness and fulfillment came late in life to Eleanor Roosevelt. For all the comfort and privilege her well-to-do family could provide, Eleanor's childhood was a lonely one. She was raised by a grandmother who appeared to dislike her and who sent her off to school in England.

Even at her wedding in 1905 to her distant cousin Franklin Roosevelt, Eleanor was not the center of attention. Guests were more interested in her dynamic uncle Theodore, President of the United States. Her marriage was not entirely happy, and her husband's mother showed Eleanor as little affection as her grandmother had.

Raising a daughter and four sons kept young Eleanor Roosevelt from sharing her husband's life as a rising politician. Then, in 1921, an attack of polio appeared to cut off Franklin's career. Never again would he stand or walk without the aid of braces and crutches.

In the early 1920's, Eleanor Roosevelt allied herself with her husband's political friends and against his formidable mother. Eleanor and Governor Alfred E. Smith encouraged Franklin's efforts to regain some use of his legs and to remain active in New York state politics. In 1928, they persuaded him to run for governor of New York. He did and was elected.

Eleanor now had more time for politics, and her husband's affliction made it necessary for her to travel and to speak on his behalf. Although extremely timid as a child, she taught herself to face huge and sometimes hostile audiences.

After her husband became President in 1933, Eleanor Roosevelt continued to serve as his "eyes and ears." Now, however, she did it on a national scale. Inspection trips, speaking engagements, and goodwill tours took her to every corner of the nation, especially to places where social problems needed attention.

People often approached Eleanor Roosevelt with ideas and plans they hoped she would pass on to "the Boss." Whether these people were sincere or self-serving, she turned down all but one. She did convince her husband to establish the National Youth Administration, a popular and useful program.

The First Lady's greatest satisfaction, however, was that people at last stopped thinking of her as a mouthpiece for her husband. They "realized that I had ideas of my own with which he might not agree," she wrote. "Then I felt freer to state my views."

During World War II, Eleanor became the assistant director of the Office for Civil Defense. She visited American troops in Europe and the Pacific. In a single year she flew more than thirteen thousand miles. She took the same interest in the welfare of service personnel as she had in coal miners and migrant workers. On top of that, from 1936 until her death, she wrote a daily newspaper column called "My Day."

When Franklin Roosevelt died in April 1945, the former First Lady did not fade back into private life. President Truman appointed her as a delegate to the newly established United Nations. There she was elected to chair the Human Rights Commission and played a major role in drafting the Universal Declaration of Human Rights.

At the United Nations, too, Eleanor was able to assist the thousands of refugees whom the war had scattered over Europe and Asia. That achievement brought her to a face-to-face confrontation with Andrei Vishinsky, the leading Soviet legal advisor. She won the debate.

Eleanor Roosevelt was First Lady for twelve years—longer than anyone else. During that time, and in her years of public service afterward, she became an international figure in her own right. No other First Lady before or since has achieved that stature. Perhaps she summed up her key to success in her last book when she wrote,

"We do not have to become heroes overnight, just a step at a time, meeting each thing that comes up, seeing it is not as dreadful as it appeared, discovering we have the strength to stare it down."

Guided Practice

Tell students that the U.S. continues to face hostility from many nations in the United Nations and a number of Americans would like to see the U.S. pull out of the organization—or at least reduce its substantial funding. Ask students to discuss the positive and negative effects such a move might create. (Possible responses: Positive—the U.S. would be spending less money on U.N. affairs and could use the money to fund domestic programs. Negative—the U.S. would be leaving an important forum for leadership at the very time the Soviet Union has lost its status as a world power.)

longer be able to promote democracy through a multinational political organization.)

Major Events and Military Leaders in World War II

September 1, 1939	Germany invades Poland	May 8, 1945	V-E Day
June 22, 1940	France falls	August 6, 1945	Atomic bomb dropped on Hiroshima
June 22, 1941	Germany invades Soviet Union		
December 7, 1941	Japanese bomb Pearl Harbor	August 8, 1945	Soviet Union declares war on Japan
November 8, 1942	Allies invade North Africa		
September 8, 1943	Italy surrenders	August 9, 1945	Atomic bomb dropped on Nagasaki
June 6, 1944	D-Day	August 10, 1945	Japan surrenders
May 7, 1945	Germany surrenders	August 15, 1945	V-J Day
		September 2, 1945	Japan signs formal surrender

Allied Leaders

American
General Dwight D. Eisenhower
  Commander in Chief Allied Forces
General Omar Bradley
General Mark Clark
General Douglas MacArthur
General George S. Patton, Jr.
Admiral Chester Nimitz
Admiral William Halsey

British
General Bernard L. Montgomery

Free French
General Charles de Gaulle

Soviet
General Georgi Zhukov
  Commander in Chief
Marshal Ivan Konev

Axis Leaders

German
Marshal Hermann Goering
General Alfred Jodl
General Erwin Rommel
Admiral Karl Doenitz

Japanese
General Hideki Tojo
Admiral Isoroku Yamamoto

World Leaders Deal with the Enemy

As suggested at Yalta and confirmed at Potsdam, Germany was divided into four zones, or sections. The United States, Britain, France, and the Soviet Union were to occupy and administer one zone each. Germany's capital of Berlin, although within the Soviet zone, was also divided into four separately administered sectors.

The Occupation of Japan. Japan was handled differently. Technically there was an eleven-nation Far Eastern Commission that met in Washington, D.C., and made recommendations to a four-power Allied Council for Japan in Tokyo. This council, in turn, sent instructions to the Supreme Commander for the Allied Powers (SCAP). In practice, however, control lay in the hands of the Supreme Commander, General Douglas MacArthur.

The United States occupation of Japan lasted for six years. During that time, MacArthur brought in many aspects of democracy. They included freedom of the press, no secret police, woman suffrage, and recognition of labor's right to form unions. MacArthur also brought about extensive

land reforms that freed farmers from paying rents to absentee landlords. He helped break up the large business organizations that had previously controlled about 80 percent of Japan's economy. By retaining the Emperor and working through officials of the former Japanese government, MacArthur was able to accomplish these and other changes with fewer than forty thousand troops.

In September 1951 the United Nations and Japan agreed to a peace treaty calling for an end to the occupation the following year. The Soviet Union, however, refused to sign because no restrictions were put on the Japanese economy.

The War Crimes Trials. During 1945 and 1946, Nazi leaders went on trial at Nuremberg, Germany, before an international tribunal representing twenty-three nations. Some thirty American judges took part in the proceedings. Supreme Court Justice Robert H. Jackson was a chief counsel for the prosecution. Defendants in the **Nuremberg trials** included industrialists and government officials, as well as generals and admirals. The charges were (1) waging aggressive war and (2) violating gener-

Assign Independent Practice
Have students complete Chapter 29, Section 5 Enrichment Activity.

Student Assignment/Homework
Have students complete Chapter 29 Test on paper. Divide the class into small groups and have students discuss their answers.

Concluding the Chapter
Ask students to write a brief essay on why they think the Senate ratified U.N. membership but refused to ratify the Treaty of Versailles. (Possible responses: the Senate saw a need to have a world peace-keeping organization; isolationism was obsolete; the UN did not interfere with U.S. sovereignty.) Have several students read their essays to the class.

Picturing History Some half-dead survivors of Buchenwald concentration camp await their Allied rescuers in this famous photo taken by Margaret Bourke-White at the war's end. Many of these people died soon after their release because of the deprivations they suffered while imprisoned.

*"When they came for the Communists, I did not speak,
because I was not a Communist.
When they came for the Jews, I did not speak,
because I was not a Jew.
When they came for the Union Leaders, I did not speak,
because I was not a Union Leader.
When they came for the Catholics, I did not speak,
because I was not a Catholic.
When they came for me, there was no one left to speak."*

Martin Neimoeller
German clergyman, after
his release from Dachau

ally accepted rules about how to treat prisoners of war and how to behave toward civilians in occupied territory. Twelve of the defendants received death sentences, seven received prison terms, and three were acquitted. Later, trials of lesser leaders were held. In all, thousands of Nazis were found guilty of war crimes.

Similar trials were held in Tokyo. Top officials were charged with war crimes and atrocities. Former Premier Hideki Tojo and several other Japanese leaders were executed, while about four thousand Japanese were convicted and received prison terms of varying lengths.

Linking Past to Present

By the end of the 1980's, Soviet power was in retreat in East Germany and thousands of East Germans were fleeing to West Germany. On October 3, 1990, a black, red, and gold flag was raised in front of the Reichstag in Berlin. That ceremony symbolized the reunification of East and West Germany after 41 years of forced separation.

SECTION 5 REVIEW

Key Terms and People

Explain the significance of: Chiang Kai-shek, Yalta Conference, Big Three, United Nations (UN), General Assembly, Security Council, Big Five, Nuremberg trials

Main Ideas

1. Why did the question of Poland's form of government prove difficult to resolve at the Yalta Conference?
2. What important decisions were reached at the Yalta Conference?
3. How did the United States' response to the establishment of the United Nations differ from its response to the founding of the League of Nations?
4. What democratic changes were introduced in Japan as a result of American occupation after the war?

Critical Thinking

5. Why was it particularly appropriate that the Nuremberg trials were held in the same city where the Nuremberg Laws were passed?

State the Objective

Use primary sources to understand the sequence of events that led to the surrender of Japan.

Present the Lesson

Use a time line to review the events that led up to the surrender of Japan. Write these 1945 dates on the board: July 16, July 26, August 6, August 9, August 14, September 2. Then discuss with students each date as it relates to Japan's surrender. As students discuss the material, have volunteers complete the time line on the board. (Answers: July 16—first atomic bomb was successfully tested at Los Alamos, New Mexico; July 26—Potsdam Proclamation was issued calling on Japan to surrender or face "prompt and utter destruction"; August 6—atomic bomb was dropped on Hiroshima; August 9—atomic bomb was dropped on Nagasaki; August 14—Japanese Emperor Hirohito decides to surrender; September 2—the formal surrender of Japan is signed aboard the battleship USS *Missouri*.)

After the time line is completed, ask the following questions to stimulate discussion. As stated in the Potsdam Proclamation, what did the Allies plan to do with Japan? (Answer: to occupy Japan and destroy its warmaking power; to establish a new society based on peace, security, and justice.) What would happen if Japan didn't agree to the ultimatum? (Answer: Japan would be destroyed.)

Focus on Primary Sources

Eyewitness Accounts from World War II

The Surrender of Japan

Nuclear power has been used as a weapon of war only twice—both times by the Americans in August 1945 on the Japanese cities of Hiroshima and Nagasaki.

On July 26, 1945, the heads of government issued the Potsdam Proclamation calling upon Japan to surrender unconditionally at once. In part, the Proclamation stated the following.

> The time has come for Japan to decide whether she will continue to be controlled by those self-willed militaristic advisers whose unintelligent calculations have brought the Empire of Japan to the threshold of annihilation, or whether she will follow the path of reason.
>
> Following are our terms. We will not deviate from them. There are no alternatives. We shall brook no delay.
>
> There must be eliminated for all time the authority and influence of those who have deceived and misled the people of Japan into embarking on world conquest, for we insist that a new order of peace, security and justice will be impossible until irresponsible militarism is driven from the world.
>
> Until such a new order is established *and* until there is convincing proof that Japan's war-making power is destroyed, points in Japanese territory to be designated by the Allies shall be occupied. . . .
>
> . . . The alternative for Japan is prompt and utter destruction.

Butow, Robert J.C., *Japan's Decision to Surrender* (Stanford, Calif: Stanford University Press), 243–244.

In the summer of 1945, many Japanese leaders realized that the war was lost. However, the Supreme War Council was not yet ready to defy the army, so it delayed answering the Potsdam Declaration. The Japanese response was careless and President Truman took it for a contemptuous refusal. On August 6, he addressed the nation.

> Sixteen hours ago an American airplane dropped one bomb on Hiroshima, an important Japanese Army base. That bomb had more power than 20,000 tons of TNT. It had more than 2,000 times the blast power of the British "Grand Slam," which is the largest bomb ever yet used in the history of warfare.
>
> The Japanese began the war from the air at Pearl Harbor. They have been repaid manyfold. And the end is not yet. With this bomb we have now added a new and revolutionary increase in destruction to supplement the growing power of our armed forces. In their present form these bombs are now in production, and even more powerful forms are in development.
>
> It is an atomic bomb. It is a harnessing of the basic power of the universe. The force from which the sun draws its power has been loosed against those who brought war to the Far East. . . .
>
> We are now prepared to obliterate more rapidly and completely every productive enterprise the Japanese have above ground in any city. We shall destroy their docks, their factories, and their communications. Let there be no mistake; we shall completely destroy Japan's power to make war.
>
> It was to spare the Japanese people from utter destruction that the ultimatum of July 26 was issued at Potsdam. Their leaders promptly rejected that ultimatum. If they do not now accept our terms they may expect a rain of ruin from the air, the like of which has never been seen on this earth. Behind this air attack will follow sea and land forces in such numbers and power as they have not yet seen and with the fighting skill of which they are already well aware.

Public Papers of the Presidents of the United States: Harry S Truman, Containing the

What was the purpose of Truman's speech? (Answer: to announce the dropping of the atomic bomb on Hiroshima; to threaten the use of additional bombs and an invading army if Japan didn't surrender.)

Have students summarize the eyewitness account of the Nagasaki bombing. What details demonstrate the power of the atomic bomb? (Possible answers: Even three miles from the bombsite, the resulting wind was so violent it tore the leaves off trees; the mushroom cloud loomed over Mount Kawabira and glowed with a blinding glare.) How would you describe Makoto's reaction to the bombing?

(Possible answers: He was primarily worried about the safety of his sister and mother; He was permanently saddened by the horrible sight of the victims of radiation, who "looked like a parade of roast chickens.") Remind students that primary sources provide invaluable information. Eyewitness accounts recorded at the time of an event tend to be more reliable than accounts recalled many years later.

Check for Understanding

Review with students the answers to the questions at the end of the feature.

Public Messages, Speeches, and Statements of the President, April 12 to December 31, 1945 (Washington, 1961), 197–200.

There being no response from the Japanese, three days later, a second bomb was dropped, this one on Nagasaki. Makoto was an eyewitness to that bombing. His mother was killed at Nagasaki. Twenty-five teachers in his school and twelve hundred pupils had died. Others had radiation sickness and would succumb later. Only four of the sixty in his class came to school after the bombing.

I was ten. We were staying at the cottage in Koba [three miles from town, on the other side of a mountain] and I was down at the river swimming.

All of a sudden there was an airplane. It came from down the river. I looked up at the sky. I was at the bottom of the valley so I could see only a narrow strip of sky between the hillsides. . . . Suddenly there was awful light in the sky, toward Urakami. I just dived head-first into the water. . . . From down the river came noise like thunder. It was a terrific rush of wind. The leaves were torn off all the trees and came racing along. My pants that I had left on a rock were blown along with the leaves.

It was getting dark and cold very fast. I thought an airplane must have crashed into the sun. Without anything on I started running up the hill toward the cottage. Somebody I couldn't see shouted at me from behind some bushes:

"What the devil are you doing? Hide! Quick! They'll spot you!" I ran and got under a taro [a plant]. The big leaves hid me completely. But I was worried about my little sister Kayano. I picked a taro leaf and held it over my head and ran to the house that way.

Everything was smashed. The pots had been blown off the stove. Kayano was all right but she was very excited. She was watching something over Mount Kawabira.

"Brother!" she yelled, "Look! Look! Over there!" I looked toward the mountain, where she was pointing.

What a sight! The biggest thing I ever saw, the biggest that ever was, was sticking up into the sky from the other side of the mountain. It was like a cloud but it was like a pillar of fire

too. It looked hard and soft and alive and dead all at the same time, and beautiful and ugly, too, all at once. The light it sent out was like all the colors of the rainbow. It almost blinded me with the glare. It kept getting taller and taller all the time, and wider and wider, twisting and rolling around just like smoke from a chimney. It was growing from the top, I mean the top was getting pushed up from inside. Then the top began to spread out, so that it looked like an umbrella opening up. . . .

I began to be worried about my mother because the thing was in the direction of Urakami. [His mother was killed by the bomb.] I was just burning up inside I was so worried. I couldn't stand it. I ran back down the river and jumped right into the water to cool off. . . .

After a few minutes I saw something coming up the road along the river that looked like a parade of roast chickens. Some of them kept asking for "Water! Water!"

I wasn't burning up any more. I shivered. I ran back to the cottage.

I would rather blind myself than ever have to see such a sight again!

Nagai, Takrashi, *We of Nagasaki: The Story of Survivors in an Atomic Wasteland* (New York: Duell, Sloan and Pearce, 1951), 22–28.

Analyzing Primary Sources

1. Did the Potsdam Proclamation give Japan fair warning that the Allies were about to use a nuclear device? Should it have revealed this? Explain.
2. What would you have found most startling in President Truman's announcement that a nuclear device had been dropped on Japan? Why?
3. What circumstances probably saved Makoto from immediate death or radiation sickness?

Critical Thinking

4. In *The Good War* by Studs Terkel, Akira Miura, a Japanese survivor, asks why the Japanese went to war against the Americans when they had no chance of winning. How do you think most other Japanese would have answered Miura's question? Explain.

Key Terms and People

These are highlighted in the text in the order in which they appear in this list.

Main Ideas

1. Roosevelt proposed, and Congress passed, the Lend-Lease Act to supply arms and equipment to Britain, Russia, and China.

2. U.S. refused to unfreeze Japanese assets, to supply Japan with oil, and to stop lend-lease aid to China.

3. With the Selective Service System. • 16.5 million draftees.

4. Built factories for lease to industries; set up the War Production Board to allocate raw materials; supervised war contracts; set up the Office of Price Administration to control inflation.

5. Defeat Hitler first; accept only unconditional surrender.

6. Possible answer: Soviet defeat of Germans at Stalingrad in 1943; invasion of France in 1944.

7. Had Americans attack selected islands and later used Australians and New Zealanders to mop up the islands that had been bypassed.

8. Used the atom bomb on Hiroshima and Nagasaki.

9. Divide Germany and Berlin into four Allied zones; establish the United Nations; govern Japan by a four-power Allied Council; try Axis leaders for war crimes. • Stalin did not hold free elections in eastern Europe.

10. Instituted freedom of the press, suffrage for women, and land reform; abolished secret police; broke up large business organizations; retained the emperor, but not as a god.

Critical Thinking Questions

11. Victims of Nazi extermination. • Nazis wished to exterminate "races" that were not Aryan.

12. FDR believed a concerted effort with Britain, Russia, and China would be most success-

ful against Germany and Japan.

➤13. Belief that Japanese Americans might try to help Japan. • Possible answer: no—Japanese Americans were unjustly discriminated against.

14. Women took jobs formerly only held by men; African Americans, American Indians, and Mexican Americans also found new opportunities. • No—these new workers were the first to be laid off.

➤15. People who have never before lived under a democratic system are not used to the freedoms they are entitled to or the responsibilities of the governing body to maintain those freedoms.

16. 1940—Atlantic Charter; 1941—*Reuben James;* 1942—Midway; 1943—Stalingrad; 1945—Yalta; 1945—United Nations

17. Possible answers: yes—the bomb brought the war to

an end and saved Allied lives. No—using the bomb was a cruel act.

Critical Thinking Activities

18. A limited war or a serious threat of war.

19. Possible answers: colleges and high schools graduated classes early; families lived in trailer camps at army bases; families doubled up because of housing shortages.

764

CHAPTER 29 REVIEW

Write your answers on a separate sheet of paper.

Key Terms and People

Explain the significance of: scorched-earth policy. Oveta Culp Hobby, Nisei, Office of War Mobilization, convoys, partisans, D-day, George Patton, Battle of the Bulge, V-E Day, kamikaze, Manhattan Project, General Assembly, Security Council, Big Five, Nuremberg trials

Main Ideas

1. In 1941 what policy did President Roosevelt propose to help those nations threatened by Axis aggression?
2. What events led to the Japanese decision to attack the American fleet at Pearl Harbor?
3. How did the United States increase the number of soldiers in the armed forces after Pearl Harbor? How many people were provided?
4. List the ways the federal government increased and supervised war production.
5. What major military goals were set by the Allied leaders early in the war?
6. Name two major turning points in the war against Hitler. In what year did each happen?
7. What tactic did the Allies under MacArthur use to fight the Japanese in the South Pacific?
8. What step did President Truman take that effectively ended the war with Japan?
9. What decisions were made by the Big Three at the end of war? Which promise did the Soviets break?
10. How did the United States go about changing Japan into a democratic nation?

Critical Thinking Questions

11. **Evaluating Literature.** In the selection by William Styron on page 735, what is Wanda describing? What does it have to do with Nazi racial policies?
12. **Analyzing Policies.** What motives might have moved President Roosevelt to help the nations fighting Germany and Japan?

13. **Evaluating Ideas.** What idea lay behind the government policy of relocating West Coast Japanese Americans during the war? Do you think this was a fair policy?
14. **Analyzing Results.** As a result of adapting to the number of men fighting in the war, how did war production change American society? Were these changes permanent? Explain.
15. **Synthesizing Ideas.** Why is democracy a hard system for many people to follow?
16. **Organizing Ideas.** Copy the time line, and place the following events on it.

1940 1941 1942 1943 1944 1945 1946 1947

Soviets defeat Germany at Stalingrad.
Atlantic Charter is signed.
United Nations is founded.
United States defeats Japan at the Battle of Midway.
Reuben James is sunk.
Yalta Conference convenes.

17. **Evaluating a Decision.** President Harry Truman made an important decision regarding the atomic bomb. Do you think he was right to use the bomb? Why or why not?

Critical Thinking Activities

18. Linking Past to Present. The Selective Service System still exists today, but only as a matter of preparedness, in case of emergency. What kind of an emergency might bring the selective service back into action?
19. Linking Past to Present. Interview at least three people who were growing up or adults during World War II. Ask them to recall social changes that took place during the war. Write a paragraph about the conclusions you draw from these interviews.

The Second World War

The early events of World War II warned the American people that it was time to prepare for the possibility of their involvement in the war. The United States began with the lend-lease program, providing massive amounts of supplies to Britain and the Soviet Union. Nazi submarines began sinking American ships. Roosevelt went so far as to meet with Churchill to set forth peace aims in the Atlantic Charter. On December 7, 1941, Japanese naval and air forces launched a successful surprise attack on the main United States naval base in the Pacific, at Pearl Harbor. They also attacked in many other places in the western Pacific. The following day the United States declared war on Japan. Germany and Italy then declared war on the United States.

American industry, agriculture, and technology proved equal to the task of mobilizing for war. Women and minorities entered the industrial labor market in large numbers. The work force expanded greatly, and production increased. Many unions agreed to a wartime moratorium on strikes. American scientists produced experimental nuclear reactions.

Overseas, the Anglo-American military command's first priority was the defeat of Germany. Its second priority was the unconditional surrender of the Axis powers. To achieve these aims, it was essential that the Allies win control of the Atlantic. A turning point of the war took place when the Soviets stopped the Nazi advance at Stalingrad. However, there were several other theaters of war. After victory in North Africa and then in Italy, Allied forces crossed the English Channel and invaded France. Despite several Allied setbacks, Berlin finally fell to the Soviets, and Hitler took his own life. On May 7, 1945, General Eisenhower accepted the unconditional surrender of Nazi Germany.

Meanwhile, the tide had turned in the western Pacific, where the Japanese advance had at first been highly successful. Japanese forces came within range of American bombers, and General MacArthur's policy of leapfrogging selected Pacific islands was successful. Much of the Japanese navy was destroyed. Finally, Japan was forced to surrender after the United States dropped atomic bombs on two Japanese cities.

Even before the victory in Japan, however, the Allies began planning for the postwar world. Roosevelt and Churchill guided the Anglo-American alliance. They began to have difficulty with Stalin when they met him at Yalta in February 1945. Stalin was determined to control eastern Europe. Two months later Roosevelt died, leaving the final decisions of the war to his successor, Harry S Truman. An international conference established the United Nations. MacArthur took charge of the United States occupation of Japan without a large occupying army. The Allies divided Germany and its capital, Berlin, into four different occupied zones and set up courts to try Nazi and Japanese leaders for war crimes.

Chronology of Main Events

1941 Japan attacks Pearl Harbor; U.S. enters World War II

1943 Germans surrender at Stalingrad

1944 Rome liberated; Allies land in France; Paris liberated; Battle of the Bulge

1945 Yalta Conference; Roosevelt dies; Harry S Truman succeeds to Presidency; Germany surrenders; Japan surrenders

Telescoping the Times may be used as an alternative to having students read the entire chapter, as a chapter preview, or as a chapter review.

Global Perspectives

1947	India becomes independent; Pakistan is created.
1947-1949	India and Pakistan fight over Kashmir.
1948	Israel becomes an independent nation.
1948-1949	First Arab-Israeli war is fought.
1949	Indonesia gains independence.
1952	Allied occupation of Japan ends.
1953	Egypt becomes a republic.
1953	Sir Edmund Hillary scales Mt. Everest.
1954	Vietnam is divided into North and South Vietnam.
1955	Peron dictatorship in Argentina is overthrown.

For Discussion

What problems might the U.S. have faced as a result of the first Arab-Israeli War? (Possible responses: keeping the conflict from escalating into a world war; supporting Israel, since the U.S. had supported the creation of the state of Israel; protecting its interests in Arab oil.)

Additional Resources

- Geography Activities
- Skills Activities
- Thematic Activities
- Economic Activities
- Cultural Literacy Activities
- Literary Source Readings
- Primary Source Readings
- Nuclear Peacekeeping
- Transparencies
- Computer Test Generator

Additional Teaching Strategies

SECTION 1

For Basic Students: Ask students each to draw a poster advertising the GI Bill of Rights to returning soldiers. Encourage students to cover more than one aspect of the GI Bill on their posters and to suggest that the benefits provided by this bill were a well-deserved reward for service to the nation.

For Advanced Students: Have students choose one of the four Presidential candidates in the 1948 election—Democrat Harry Truman, Dixiecrat Strom Thurmond, Republican Thomas E. Dewey, or Progressive Henry A. Wallace—research the candidate, and present a two- to three-minute speech endorsing him. (Speeches might include: Thomas Dewey—served as U.S. attorney for southern district of New York; served as special assistant to U.S. Attorney General Homer Stille Cummings from 1934 to 1935; was appointed special prosecutor for a New York grand jury investigating vice and racketeering; served as governor of New York; ran against FDR in 1944. Henry A. Wallace—served as thirty-third Vice-President; served as FDR's Secretary of Agriculture and formulated reforms incorporated into Agricultural Adjustment Act; opposed Truman's stand against the Soviet Union.)

SECTION 2

For Basic Students: Have students work together to prepare a wall chart showing the NATO nations and the Warsaw Pact nations. Chart should include:

NATO	Warsaw Pact
U.S.	Soviet Union
Belgium	Albania
Canada	Bulgaria
Denmark	Czechoslovakia
France	East Germany
Great Britain	Hungary
Iceland	Poland
Italy	Rumania
Luxembourg	
the Netherlands	
Norway	
Portugal	
Greece	
Turkey	
West Germany	

Have students display their chart in the classroom.

For Advanced Students: Have students each draw a political cartoon that is either supportive or critical of Senator Joseph McCarthy and his campaign against communists. Ask students to share their cartoons with the class.

SECTION 3

For Basic Students: Have students work together to complete a three-column chart on poster board. In the first column, they should list the following people: Chiang Kai-shek, Mao Zedong, Albert Wedemeyer, Syngman Rhee, Kim Il Sung, Harry Truman, Robert Taft, and Douglas MacArthur. In the second column have students identify the position each person held, and in the third column have them write a significant fact about each. Chart should include:

Name	Position	Fact
Chiang Kai-shek	President of Nationalist China	Was backed by U.S. Headed Chinese government that was dictatorial, inefficient, and corrupt.
Mao Zedong	Chinese Communist leader	Drove Nationalists from mainland China.
Albert Wedemeyer	U.S. general sent to China by Truman	Recommended that U.S. continue to support Nationalists in China.
Syngman Rhee	Head of South Korean government	Spent many years in U.S. working for Korean independence.
Kim Il Sung	Head of North Korean government	Had fought as a guerrilla against Japanese since the 1930's. Claimed right to rule all of Korea.
Harry Truman	U.S. President	Ordered naval and air support for South Korea. Removed MacArthur from command in Asia.
Robert Taft	Republican senator from Ohio	Opposed sending troops to South Korea.
Douglas MacArthur	U.S. general	Commanded UN troops in South Korea. Wanted to extend the Korean War into China by blockading Chinese coast and dropping atomic bombs.

Have students display their chart in the classroom.

For Advanced Students: Have students research and present two-minute nominating speeches for Dwight Eisenhower or Adlai Stevenson. Each speech should emphasize the candidate's qualifications, experience, and positions. (Speeches might include: Stevenson—educated at Princeton, Harvard, and Northwestern; served in federal government as special counsel to Agricultural Adjustment Administration and Federal Alcohol Control Administration; served as special assistant and counsel in Department of Navy; served in Department of State; attended UN conference in 1945 as advisor and press secretary to U.S. delegation; served as governor of Illinois, where he initiated reforms in health and education, crime control, highway construction, and civil service.)

Further Reading for Students

Nonfiction

Acheson, Dean. *Present at the Creation: My Years in the State Department*. New York: W. W. Norton, 1987.

Fencher, E.B. *The War in Korea*. New York: Franklin Watts, 1981.

Luard, Evan. *A History of the United Nations, 1945-1955: The Cold War Years*. New York: St. Martin's Press, 1982.

Rovere, Richard. *Senator Joe McCarthy*. New York: Harper & Row, 1973.

Truman, Harry S. *The Autobiography of Harry S Truman*. Edited by Robert H. Ferrell. Boulder: Colorado Associated University Press, 1980.

Historical Fiction

Shute, Nevil. *On the Beach*. New York: Ballantine Books, 1978.

Bibliography for Teachers

Books

Bundy, McGeorge. *Danger and Survival: The Political History of the Nuclear Weapon*. New York: Random House, 1989.

Chafe, William H. and Harvard Sitkoff, eds. *A History of Our Time: Readings on Postwar America*. New York: Oxford University Press, 1982.

Gaddis, John. *The United States and the Origins of the Cold War, 1941–1947*. New York: Columbia University Press, 1972.

McKeever, Porter. *Adlai Stevenson: His Life and Legacy*. New York: Morrow, 1989.

Robbins, Jhan. *Bess and Harry: An American Love Story*. New York: G. P. Putnam's Sons, 1980.

Audio-Visuals

American Foreign Policy Series. Films Incorporated. Movie.

The Berlin Airlift: Turning Points in History. Social Studies School Service. Filmstrip.

The Cold War: The Early Period (1947–1953). Richard Kaplan Productions. Movie.

Joseph McCarthy. McGraw-Hill. Movie.

Men in Crisis: MacArthur vs. Truman. David L. Wolper Productions. Movie.

Postwar Hopes, Cold War Fears. P.B.S. Studios. Movie.

That War in Korea. Encyclopaedia Britannica Educational Corp. Movie.

The Truman Years. Teaching Film Custodians. Movie.

Computer Resources

From World War to Cold War. (Apple) Focus Media.

Super Powers in the Nuclear Age. (Apple) Focus Media.

Teacher's Notes:

Lesson Plan

Teaching Resources, Unit 7 Booklet

Chapter Objectives

Students will learn:
- the major domestic problems that faced the Truman administration
- the origins of the cold war that developed between the U.S. and the Soviet Union and how the cold war affected the American people
- why events in Asia in the early 1950's threatened U.S. interests and led the U.S. to fight in the Korean War

Picturing History The faces of American GI's manning a bunker during the Korean War register the uncertainty and tension felt whenever there was a break in the fighting. Communist aggression against South Korea was finally halted after three years of fighting.

Using the Chapter Time Line

How many years passed between the United Nations' first meeting (see Unit 7 Time Line) and its intervention in Korea? (Answer: 4) For how many years were UN troops in Korea before a truce was signed? (Answer: 3)

1944	1948	1952	1956
1947 Truman Doctrine and Marshall Plan announced	**1948** Berlin airlift	**1949** Truman inaugurated for first full term	**1950** UN intervenes in Korea
			1953 • Dwight Eisenhower inaugurated President • Armistice ends Korean War
			1956 Eisenhower wins second term

Links to American Literature

Edward Franklin: born in Santa Rosa, California, in 1930; joined Marine Corps in 1951 and was wounded in Korea in 1952; graduated from San Francisco State College in 1955; worked as an executive for Standard Oil Company of California.

It's Cold in Pongo-Ni: received the Phelan Award; tells the story of the day-to-day heroism of the fighting men in Korea; depicts eight Marines on a mission into Communist-held territory; reveals the thoughts, the strengths and weaknesses, and the loyalties of a group of men bound together by war.

Introducing the Chapter

Explain to the students that even though this chapter covers a relatively short time span, that period was extremely important in setting the stage for organizations and situations that still exist today, such as NATO. Read orally President Truman's remarks on page 781. Ask students whether they agree with Truman's position. (Possible response: yes—Hitler, Mussolini, and Japan were successful in their offensives because no strong nations stood up to them; Truman was justified in his belief that opposing North Korea was right and might reduce the probability of a third world war.)

CHAPTER **30**   1945–1956

Postwar Period, Cold War, Korean War

Links to American Literature

They creep along the base of the ridge, sheltered now from the worst of the wind but moving through a deeper darkness. The leader stops frequently, sniffing, listening. It seems colder to him here at the bottom of the slope and odors come stinging in the dark, causing his nose to ache way in the back. There's the smell of the dirt road. It isn't cold enough to be frozen, yet the dust that rises like ghostly dogs around his legs smells of icy soil. And from the streambed, the stink of water-soaked roots. And in the quiet, crouched moments comes the odor of his hands, blood together with gun oil.

The leader is cautious, tiptoeing along, stopping often with one foot in midair, a monument to trepidation.

Halt.

Why, what was that?

It was, it was the cat.

Or Ashcraft's heavy nose-breathing or Howard Trask stumbling again or one of the 3rd Platoon men on the outpost coughing.

— EDWARD FRANKLIN, *It's Cold in Pongo-ni*

Harry S Truman led the United States out of World War II and into the first years of an uneasy peace. During these years, the United States found itself involved in a new kind of war, a so-called cold war. In 1950 President Truman sent General MacArthur to aid the Republic of Korea in repelling the attacks of North Korea, which was militarily superior to its southern neighbor. Thus began American involvement in the Korean War.

Chapter Overview

In this chapter you will learn about the major domestic problems that the Truman administration faced, about the cold war that developed between the United States and the Soviet Union, and about its effects. United States relations with the Soviet Union and Korea today can best be understood against the historical background of this chapter. The Korean War was a key issue when Dwight D. Eisenhower campaigned for the election of 1952.

In the final part of this chapter, you will learn about the changes that took place under Eisenhower's administration. To help you study this period, Chapter 30 is divided into three sections.

Chapter Outline

1. **A New Leader Faces a Difficult Period**
2. **A Former Ally Becomes an Enemy**
3. **The Cold War Turns Hot**

767

Anticipate the Lesson

List the following categories on the board: Postwar Economy, Returning Military Personnel, and Labor Relations. For each category, ask students to project the problems that they think might confront a nation after a war. Write students' responses on the board and have students refer to them as they study this section. (Possible responses: postwar economy—a rise in prices after government lifts restrictions; returning military personnel—job shortage; labor relations—insufficient raise in wages to match the cost of living.)

State the Objective

Understand the major domestic problems that faced the Truman administration.

Historical Sidelights

• Harry Truman's middle name was "S". Truman's parents could not decide whether he should be named Shippe (for his father's father) or Soloman (for his mother's father). The middle name of S was a compromise that pleased both families. Truman did not use a period after the S.

• Quotes from President Eisenhower:
"Always take the job, but never yourself, seriously."
"I hate war as only a soldier who has lived it can, only as one who has seen its brutality, its futility, its stupidity."

SECTION 1

A New Leader Faces a Difficult Period

GLOSSARY TERMS: Dixiecrats, Fair Deal

Harry S Truman learned from his predecessor's widow that he had become the thirty-third President of the United States. When he asked Eleanor Roosevelt if there was anything he could do for her, she replied, "Is there anything *we* can do for *you*? You are the one in trouble now."

Truman Assumes Postwar Leadership

In many ways Truman *was* unprepared for the responsibilities of national and world leadership. He had not been briefed on military matters or on the continuing peace negotiations. He was unaware that the atomic bomb existed.

He was also very different personally from Roosevelt, which made it difficult for some people to accept him. He was neither tall nor handsome, and he spoke not with an upper-class accent cultivated at Harvard but with the flat twang of Missouri. Except for Cleveland, Truman was the only President since Lincoln who had not attended college. Before entering politics, he had tried to run a men's clothing store. The business failed. However, instead of declaring bankruptcy, he spent the next fifteen years paying off his debts.

Truman had many positive qualities in addition to being honorable. He was direct, down-to-earth, and self-confident. His mind was quick, and his memory retentive; he never had to be told the same thing twice. Perhaps most important of all, he had the ability to make difficult decisions and to accept full responsibility for them. As the plaque on his White House desk read, "The Buck Stops Here."

Returning to Civilian Life. The United States had put together a mighty military machine in a very short time. Now the country's objective was to "bring the boys home" just as fast as it could. By the summer of 1946, about 10 million men and women had been released from the armed forces. The army was down to 1.5 million, and the navy to 980,000. That left just enough soldiers to perform occupation duties in Germany and Japan and to meet the minimum requirements of defense.

To ease the return to civilian life for those whose schooling or careers had been interrupted, Congress, in 1944, passed the Servicemen's Readjustment Act, commonly called the GI Bill of Rights. Under the **GI Bill,** veterans attending college or technical school had their tuition paid and received a small monthly income. Between 1944 and 1956, more than 7.8 million veterans took advantage of these educational benefits. The GI Bill also provided federal guarantees of loans to veterans for buying homes and farms and for establishing businesses. Thus, home, or farm, and business ownership became possible for millions of young families who might otherwise never have been able to afford it.

Reorganizing the Military. In 1947 Congress passed the **National Security Act,** which reorganized the military. The three services—army, navy and air force—were brought under a new executive department, the Department of Defense. The National Security Council was established to coordinate the country's defense policies and to advise the President on matters involving national security. Under the council the Central Intelligence Agency (CIA) was set up to gather intelligence, or

---

People in the Chapter

Harry S Truman has become more respected in recent years than he was during his Presidency. Martha Taft, wife of Senator Robert Taft, expressed the view of many Republicans at that time when she said, "To err is Truman."

Winston Churchill praised President Truman for the Marshall Plan saying, "You, more than any other man, have saved Western civilization."

Joseph McCarthy was called low-blow Joe by those who saw him destroying the reputations of honorable people by his smear-and-slander tactics.

Dwight Eisenhower changed the name of FDR's Maryland retreat from Shangri-la to Camp David. Eisenhower thought Shangri-la was "just a little too fancy for a Kansas farm boy."

information, from abroad. The CIA later received power to carry out covert actions, or secret political warfare in support of American foreign policy. As you will learn later, covert actions have included the actual or attempted overthrow of several governments.

A Wartime Economy Converts to Peace

Most economists foresaw a postwar depression. After all, war industries would close down. What would such companies do with their plants and equipment? Also, millions of veterans and war workers would be seeking jobs. Where would they find them?

Boom Times. The economists were wrong. They failed to consider the backlog of consumer needs and wants. They also failed to listen to financier and wartime production head Bernard Baruch. He had predicted that there would be more work after the war than there would be people to do it. People had done without during the depression and during the years of wartime shortages. Now, with more than $135 billion in savings from defense work, service pay, and investments in war bonds, people could and would pay for consumer goods.

Americans began buying. Automobiles and appliances were snapped up as fast as they appeared. Houses and apartment buildings could not be constructed fast enough. Spot shortages occurred in such items as men's suits, beef, and nylon stockings.

The results of the shopping spree showed up quickly in employment and production, both of which rose. Unfortunately, prices rose as well. Wartime price controls ended on June 30, 1946. In the next two weeks, prices soared 25 percent, or double the increase of the previous three years. They continued to rise for the next two years until the supply of goods caught up with the demand.

In the late 1940's, another boom occurred—this one in entertainment. Sports became the main attraction as athletes and their fans returned from the war. Although still in its infancy, television was the new medium with which the theater had to compete for audiences. Tennessee Williams had two smashing successes, however, with *The Glass Menagerie* and *A Streetcar Named Desire*. Box-office lines were also forming for tickets to Arthur Miller's *Death of a Salesman*. Finally, success came to Richard Rodgers and Oscar Hammerstein as they produced one masterful musical after another: *Oklahoma!, Carousel,* and *South Pacific.*

Millions of Americans continued to follow the screen careers of their movie idols in between visits to their local movie houses. Twelve-year-old Elizabeth Taylor became an overnight success in 1944

Picturing History Musicals such as *South Pacific* with Mary Martin and *Oklahoma!* reflected the mentality of Americans in the late 1940's.

Check for Understanding

Call on individual students to answer the Section 1 Review questions.

Guided Practice

Tell students that President Truman's term *Fair Deal* was coined by political leaders, beginning with Theodore Roosevelt, to highlight their programs. Ask students what they think is the function of terms such as *New Freedom, New Deal, New Frontier*. (Possible response: they are catch phrases that are readily associated with the President.) Ask students to suggest similar phrases that describe past or current administrations. (Possible responses: Dwight Eisenhower—the New Peace; George Washington—the New Nation; Lyndon Johnson—the Great Society.)

with her hit film *National Velvet*. Frank Sinatra crooned his way into Hollywood and, in 1946, won an Academy Award for a short film on racial prejudice called *The House I Live In*. The most popular movie in 1946 was *The Best Years of Our Lives,* which was the story of a disabled veteran whose hands had been blown off on D-day. Drive-in movies became popular in the late 1940's, and busy carhops scurried around attaching trays of refreshments to the car windows of drive-in movie-goers.

Labor Unrest. In spite of the boom times, many workers found themselves earning less. Prices were climbing, but gone were the high-paying war jobs. Gone too was the weekly overtime. So workers began striking for higher wages.

A strike involving 750,000 steelworkers began in January 1946 and lasted eighty days. No sooner had these workers returned to their jobs than 400,000 coal miners left their pits. Eighteen days later, on April 19, two railroad brotherhoods announced that *they* would go out on strike in thirty days.

Truman was generally a strong supporter of organized labor. However, the walkout by the railroad unions threatened to stop rail traffic throughout the nation. So on May 17 the President threatened to seize the railroads. Two days later he appeared before a special session of Congress and began to deliver a speech asking for authority to draft the striking workers into the army. Before he could finish his speech, the brotherhoods gave in.

A few days earlier, Truman had seized the coal mines. Federal authorities had then worked out a contract, which the mine owners refused to accept. So the government continued to operate the mines. In October, following unofficial word from **John L. Lewis** that the workers should observe the policy of "no contract, no work," the miners struck against the government. The following month, Lewis and the United Mine Workers were fined $3.5 million, the largest fine in labor history. Truman then announced that he would broadcast a direct appeal to the striking miners to save their country by returning to work. Lewis ordered his workers back to the mines.

The Taft-Hartley Act. The 4.6 million workers who went out on strike in 1946 set a record. The public became frightened. It felt that the booming economy would be seriously hurt unless organized labor was curbed.

In the 1946 election, the Republican party gained control of both the Senate and the House of Representatives for the first time since 1930. The following year the Eightieth Congress passed a new labor law, the **Taft-Hartley Act,** over Truman's veto. The law prohibited the closed shop, an arrangement requiring that a person be a union member in order to be hired. It abolished the checkoff system by which employers collected union dues. In addition, union officials had to take a loyalty oath, swearing that they were not Communists. Union funds could not be used in political campaigns. (This provision was later declared unconstitutional.) Finally, if a strike threatened the nation's health or safety, the President could obtain an injunction delaying the strike for an eighty-day cooling-off period.

Labor leaders were furious. They felt that the loyalty oath was an insult, and they called the act a "slave-labor law." Yet despite Taft-Hartley, union membership climbed from 14.3 million in 1945 to 17 million in 1952.

Other Legislation. Earlier, Congress had passed two other important laws. One was the Employment Act of 1946. For the first time, the federal government committed itself to promoting "maximum employment, production, and purchasing power." Americans could now expect the government to act vigorously to counter a depression. The act also established the Council of Economic Advisers, whose job was to analyze economic trends and recommend programs to the President.

The second law, also passed in 1946, created the Atomic Energy Commission (AEC). The AEC was

Picturing History A porter and a trainman aboard a train at Boston's North Station read about Truman's threat to seize the railroads.

authorized to promote research into the peaceful uses of atomic energy and to develop facilities for producing it. After considerable controversy, Congress put atomic energy under the control of civilians rather than the military.

Truman Fights for Civil Rights

As early as 1945, President Truman asked black leaders what they considered their top priorities. The first, they said, was a federal antilynching law that would make prosecution of lynching a federal rather than a state concern. Authorities in certain states sometimes looked the other way when mobs took violent action against African Americans accused of serious crimes. The second priority was the abolition of the poll tax as a voting requirement. It was not the amount of the poll tax that concerned African Americans, but the selective manner in which it was collected. The third priority was the establishment of a permanent commission to replace the wartime Fair Employment Practice Committee that was due to expire in 1946.

"To Secure These Rights." Congress would not pass any of these measures. So in 1946 Truman appointed a biracial Committee on Civil Rights to investigate the situation and to report its findings to the nation. The report, issued in 1947, was called "To Secure These Rights." In addition to the antilynching, poll-tax, and FEPC measures, it recommended that a permanent civil rights commission be established and that federal legislation be passed to eliminate discrimination in voting. In February 1948 Truman sent these recommendations to Congress. Again, Congress did nothing.

Accordingly, Truman turned to executive action. In July 1948 he issued an executive order calling for "equality of treatment and opportunity" for members of the armed forces "without regard to race, color, religion, or national origin." The order was issued despite the opposition of almost every general and admiral. As it turned out, the shift to full integration of the services went more smoothly than anyone had hoped. Truman also set up a Fair Employment Board within the Civil Service Commission.

Jackie Robinson. Another step forward in easing discrimination occurred in major league baseball. The color line was broken in 1947 when **Jackie Robinson** signed a contract to play for Branch Rickey's Brooklyn (later, Los Angeles) Dodgers. Until then, African-American baseball players, no matter how talented, had been allowed to play only in

Picturing History A Jackie Robinson baseball card. Robinson, who was named Rookie of the Year in 1947, is remembered for being the first African American to break into major league baseball.

all-black leagues. Rickey, however, believed that the time for change had come. After much searching, he chose Robinson to be the pioneer.

At first there was considerable resistance to Robinson. Unhappy baseball fans shouted insults from the stands, and some threw bottles and other objects onto the playing field. Several of Robinson's teammates refused to eat or to socialize with him. However, his skill and personality gradually impressed colleagues and public alike, and in 1949 he was voted the Most Valuable Player in the National League.

Other teams soon followed the example of the Dodgers and began signing black players. Robinson remained with the Dodgers for his entire career, until 1956. In 1962 he became the first black person to be inducted into the Baseball Hall of Fame.

The 1948 Election Is a Great Upset

Although Truman was blamed for the nation's inflation and labor unrest, he was nominated by the Democrats in 1948. However, he insisted that a strong civil rights plank be incorporated in the party platform. This caused Southern delegates to the national convention, the so-called **Dixiecrats,** to withdraw. They formed the States' Rights Democratic party and ran their own candidate, Governor **J. Strom Thurmond** of South Carolina. At the other extreme, former Vice-President **Henry A. Wallace** led supporters into a new Progressive party. Wallace disapproved of Truman's "get tough with Russia" policy, which you will read about later in this chapter.

The Republican candidate, Governor **Thomas**

For Discussion
What changes took place, or what events occurred, to make civil rights advances more likely during Truman's administration? (Possible response: African Americans and other minorities were fully integrated into the armed services; they were needed to work in industries during World War II; many had moved to Northern cities during the war.)

Student Assignment/Homework

Have students read Section 2, "A Former Ally Becomes an Enemy," and answer the Section 2 Review questions on paper.

E. Dewey of New York, was an able administrator. Opinion polls gave him a comfortable lead, and newspaper and magazine articles pointed to his victory. Republicans, pollsters, and writers overlooked one thing, however—Truman's fighting spirit. He had filled out Roosevelt's fourth term. Now he was determined to be elected on his own.

Truman developed a winning strategy. First he called the Republican-dominated Congress back into session. He asked it to pass laws supporting such planks in the Republican party platform as more housing, aid to education, a higher minimum wage, and extended social security coverage. Not one law was passed.

Presidential Election, 1948

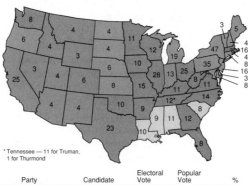

*Tennessee — 11 for Truman, 1 for Thurmond

Party	Candidate	Electoral Vote	Popular Vote	%
Democratic	Truman	303	24,106,000	49.6
Republican	Dewey	189	21,970,000	45.1
States' Rights	Thurmond	39	1,169,000	2.3
Minor parties			1,444,000	3.0

531 Total Electoral Vote

Truman then took his campaign to the people. He traveled from one end of the country to the other by train, speaking from the rear platform. Day after day, to crowds that ranged from 10 to 250,000, the President denounced the "do-nothing, good-for-nothing Eightieth Congress." As he later commented, "I met the people face to face, and I convinced them, and they voted for me."

It was the greatest upset in the nation's political history. The morning after the election, the early edition of the *Chicago Tribune,* for example, was out on the streets. Its headline screamed DEWEY DEFEATS TRUMAN. In actuality, the Democrats won by 24 million votes to 22 million for the Republicans. Wallace and Thurmond each got a million votes. In the electoral college Truman had 303 votes; Dewey, 189; and Thurmond, 39. The Democrats won without the Solid South, which they had carried since Reconstruction days. The Republicans even lost control of Congress.

Why, apart from Truman's "give 'em hell" campaign, did the Republicans lose? In part it was the result of overconfidence. Dewey's belief in victory added a touch of arrogance to his manner, which many felt was already cold and distant. Also, his speeches were thin. He talked in generalities—"for unity, cleanliness, better water, and faith," as one historian described it. Truman, on the other hand, dealt with what he believed were the specific economic and social issues of concern to the people. Finally, labor preferred Truman to Dewey, while farmers, who usually vote Republican when times are good, saw the bad crop figures for the 1948 growing season and went Democratic.

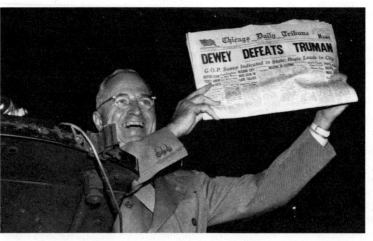

Picturing History Truman's face beams as he holds the now-famous *Chicago Tribune* headline proclaiming his defeat. In a race to be first with the news, the paper based its story on early election returns favoring Dewey. Truman surprised the experts.

SECTION 2

Core Lesson

Anticipate the Lesson

Review with students actions taken by the Soviet Union in World War II. (See Chapter 29.) (Actions include: signed nonaggression pact with Hitler; tried to defend against attack by Germany; initiated scorched-earth policy; fearing future attacks, tried to establish puppet states around its borders.)

State the Objective

Understand the origins of the cold war that developed between the U.S. and the Soviet Union and how the cold war affected the American people.

A Fair Deal Replaces the New Deal

Theodore Roosevelt offered a square deal, and FDR gave the nation the New Deal. Following his victory, Truman began pushing for what he called a **Fair Deal** for the American people. It was an extension of the New Deal—only stronger.

Truman proposed a nationwide system of compulsory health insurance and a steady income for farmers to replace price supports. Southern and some Northern Democrats combined with Republicans in Congress to defeat both measures.

Truman's other proposals, however, did win congressional approval. They included (1) an increase in the minimum wage from forty to seventy-five cents an hour, (2) extension of social security coverage to about 10 million more people, (3) more flood control and irrigation projects, and (4) financial help to cities for slum clearance and for the construction of 810,000 housing units for low-income families.

Domestically, then, Truman realized some of his goals. He continued many of FDR's social programs and achieved advances in civil rights. In foreign affairs, however, the record was less than satisfactory.

SECTION 1 REVIEW

Key Terms and People

Explain the significance of: Harry S Truman, GI Bill, National Security Act, John L. Lewis, Taft-Hartley Act, Jackie Robinson, Dixiecrats, J. Strom Thurmond, Henry A. Wallace, Thomas E. Dewey, Fair Deal

Main Ideas

1. How did the GI Bill help the United States demobilize after its war effort?
2. What postwar conditions led to labor strife, and how did the federal government respond to this strife?
3. What were the main postwar priorities of black leaders?
4. What factors led to Truman's landslide victory in the 1948 Presidential election?
5. In general, how did Truman's Fair Deal extend Roosevelt's New Deal?

Critical Thinking

6. How does the Jackie Robinson story illustrate Truman's concept of "equality of treatment and opportunity"?

SECTION 2

A Former Ally Becomes an Enemy

GLOSSARY TERMS: cold war, Truman Doctrine, Marshall Plan, Berlin blockade, North Atlantic Treaty Organization (NATO), satellite nations, subversion, containment, McCarthyism, Red scare

When W. Averell Harriman, United States ambassador to Moscow, learned of Roosevelt's death, he rushed home to warn the new President about Stalin. A few minutes of conversation with the new chief executive reassured Harriman. Truman, like the ambassador, considered Stalin a slippery character and believed that the best way to handle the Soviet Union was to take a blunt, hard line.

The Soviet Union Dominates Eastern Europe

It had been FDR's hope that the Big Three would continue their wartime alliance in the United Nations and in the postwar world. Difficulties arose almost immediately, however.

In the eyes of the West, the Soviet Union was a state dedicated to world revolution and to the overthrow of capitalism everywhere. For its part, the Soviet Union had a historic distrust of the West. Moreover, the U.S.S.R. had suffered over 25 million casualties during World War II, as well as extensive damage. Without oceans or mountains to protect them from invasion and with vast open borderlands to their west, Soviet leaders felt that they must have friendly countries as neighbors. To the Soviets, that meant Communist countries whose governments they controlled.

At Yalta, you will recall, the United States and Great Britain had insisted on free, open elections in Poland and in other Eastern European nations after the war. Stalin had agreed. By the time the Potsdam conference took place, however, it was clear that Stalin would not keep his promise. With the Red Army occupying the area, nothing could be done.

In March of 1946 Winston Churchill, who was no longer Britain's Prime Minister but simply a member of Parliament, delivered a speech at Fulton, Missouri, that graphically described the situation in Europe:

SECTION 1 REVIEW

Answers

Main Ideas

1. It provided financial aid to veterans for schooling, buying homes and farms, and starting up businesses.

2. High consumer prices and the scarcity of high-paying jobs led many to strike for higher wages. The government responded by temporarily seizing the industries affected and by issuing Truman's personal pleas. It also passed the Taft-Hartley Act to regulate the labor movement.

3. A federal antilynching law, the abolition of the poll tax as a voting requirement, and a permanent Fair Employment Practice Commission.

4. The Republican Congress's failure to accept Truman's challenge to pass laws supporting its party's platform; Truman's taking his campaign message directly to the people; Dewey's overconfidence and lack of a specific program; and the support of organized labor and farmers.

5. By calling for government programs to assist needy people and by establishing public works projects.

Critical Thinking

6. Possible answer: Truman hoped to apply the concept societywide, not just in the armed services. Robinson exemplified Truman's hope by overcoming great prejudices and hardships, eventually being named the National League's Most Valuable Player. **(application)**

Present the Lesson

On the board list the following terms under the heading *Response:* Marshall Plan, NATO, Truman Doctrine, and Berlin blockade. Ask students to skim the section to identify the major problem to which each of these was a response. In each case, they should also evaluate the success of the response. Write the problems and evaluations under separate headings on the board. Have students refer to the board as they study this section.

Response	Problem	Evaluation	Response	Problem	Evaluation
Marshall Plan	Western Europe suffered from economic chaos, cold winter, unemployment.	Plan was successful both politically and economically. Malnutrition disappeared; industry improved; Western Europe flourished; Communist parties in Europe weakened.	NATO	Soviets invaded Czechoslovakia. There was threat of more Communist aggression.	NATO was successful in providing protection for member nations. In response to NATO, Soviets formed Warsaw Pact.

Picturing History Winston Churchill delivers his "iron curtain" speech warning Americans of the expansive tendencies of the Soviet Union under Stalin.

> A shadow has fallen upon the scene so lately lighted by the Allied victory. . . . An iron curtain [a barrier of secrecy and censorship] has descended across the Continent. Behind that line lie all the capitals of the ancient states of Central and Eastern Europe.

A Cold War Develops in Europe

The dispute over the holding of elections in Eastern Europe was the start of what historians call the **cold war.** The term, the title of a book by political theorist Walter Lippmann, refers to a state of hostility between nations without actual fighting. After 1945, both the United States and the Soviet Union tried to spread their political and economic influence wherever they could. They formed military alliances, carried on an arms race, and supported opposing sides in several civil wars.

The Truman Doctrine. One of the first places in which the cold war expressed itself was in the eastern Mediterranean. For several hundred years, one of Russia's goals had been to acquire an ice-free seaport on the Mediterranean. During World War II, Stalin asked for postwar control of the Dardanelles, the Turkish straits that lead out from the Black Sea. He was turned down by the

United States and Britain. When the Soviet Union persisted in pressuring Turkey for bases in the area, Truman sent a naval task force into the eastern Mediterranean.

Soon afterward, Britain told the United States that it could no longer afford to give economic aid to Turkey. Britain also said that it could no longer help the Greek monarchy, which was trying to put down a revolt by communist-led guerrillas.

On January 12, 1947, Truman went before Congress and asked for $400 million in economic and military aid for the two Eastern European nations. In his speech the President also said that the United States should prevent communist governments from being set up anywhere in the world where they did not already exist. This statement later became known as the **Truman Doctrine.**

The doctrine aroused considerable controversy. Some people felt that it meant interfering in the internal affairs of other nations. Other people argued that America's power would be spread too thin if the country tried to carry on a global crusade against communism. Still others were opposed to helping dictatorial governments even if they *were* anticommunist. A few people favored trying to improve American-Soviet relations.

Congress, however, decided that the doctrine was essential to keeping Soviet influence from spreading in Europe. So between 1947 and 1950, about $660 million in aid was sent to Turkey and Greece. As a result, the danger of communist governments being established in those nations was greatly reduced.

The Marshall Plan. In the meantime, an even more serious situation had developed in Western Europe. The nations there were in economic chaos as a result of the war. Most of their factories had been looted by the Germans or bombed to the ground by the Allies. There were no raw materials, nor was there any power. As a result, millions of Europeans could not find work, and many turned to the black market and theft in order to survive. Additional millions of people who had been uprooted by the Nazis or who had fled before the advancing Soviets were living in refugee camps while European governments tried to figure out where they could go.

To make matters worse, the winter of 1947 was the bitterest in several centuries. Temperatures remained below zero, and snow piled up in record-breaking amounts. Crops were severely damaged,

774

Response	Problem	Evaluation	Response	Problem	Evaluation	Check for Understanding
Truman Doctrine	Communist aggression escalated in Turkey and Greece.	Doctrine aroused controversy. Congress approved aid to Turkey and Greece.	Berlin blockade	U.S., Great Britain, and France favored reunification of Germany. In 1948 three western zones were united. Soviets cut surface traffic into West Berlin.	U.S. and British airlift into West Berlin was successful in forcing Soviets to lift blockade.	Call on individual students to read their answers to the Section 2 Review questions.

Europe After World War II: NATO and the Warsaw Pact

Member of North Atlantic Treaty Organization (NATO)

Member of Warsaw Treaty Organization (Warsaw Pact)

Nonaligned

Map Skills

Norway, Iceland, Britain, France, Belgium, Netherlands, Denmark, West Germany, Italy, Portugal, Greece, Turkey • Soviet Union, East Germany, Poland, Czechoslovakia, Hungary, Rumania, Bulgaria, Albania • Germany

Map Skills **Region** Which nations belong to NATO? to the Warsaw Pact? **Place** What nation was divided into two separate nations, one east and one west?

and a fuel shortage developed when all the rivers froze, cutting off water transportation. In Britain, the use of electricity was limited to a few hours each morning, and food rations were lower than they had been during the war. Former President Herbert Hoover, whom Truman sent to visit twenty-two countries and to report on conditions there, said that many people, especially children, were on the brink of starvation.

In June 1947 General George Marshall, who was now Secretary of State, delivered a historic speech at the Harvard College commencement exercises.

He offered United States aid to all European nations that needed it, saying that this move was directed "not against any country or doctrine but against hunger, poverty, desperation, and chaos." However, the nations receiving aid had to agree to remove trade barriers and to cooperate economically with one another.

Sixteen Western European nations applied for aid. The Soviet Union, which had been included in Marshall's offer, refused. It denounced the plan as an "imperialist plot" by the United States to dominate Europe.

Guided Practice

Tell students that the McCarthy era raised the issue of whether or not a person should be restricted from certain jobs because of past or present political beliefs. Today, candidates can run for office on the Communist Party ticket. Ask students whether the Communist Party should be allowed to function in a democracy. (Possible response: a democracy makes it possible for all people to run for office and express their views; people have the right to vote for or against a communist candidate.)

Congress debated the **Marshall Plan** for several months. It was expensive—about $12.5 billion—and was opposed by people who felt that the country could not afford it. They referred to the provision of further aid to Europe as "Operation Rathole." Then in February 1948, Soviet tanks rumbled into Czechoslovakia and took over the country, which had a sizable Communist minority. The takeover was followed by a purge in which many democrats disappeared or died, including Foreign Minister Jan Masaryk, son of the nation's founder, who reportedly fell to his death from his office window. In response to these events, Congress approved the Marshall Plan.

The plan was a great success both economically and politically. Malnutrition disappeared. Industry improved. By 1952 Western Europe was flourishing, and Communist parties were weakened.

Picturing History For nearly one year the United States, Britain, and France airlifted tons of food, fuel, and medicine to West Berlin, keeping the city alive.

Picturing History The first shipment of industrial goods to be made under the Marshall Plan arrives in Istanbul, Turkey.

The Question of Germany. Another major issue between East and West was the question of German reunification. The Soviet Union, whose land had been invaded and devastated by German armies twice in thirty years, wanted Germany to remain weak and divided. The United States, Great Britain, and France disagreed. They believed that Europe would be more stable if German industry were producing and the German people were not

agitating for unity. In 1948 they decided to combine the three western zones within Germany. The Soviets responded by cutting off all surface traffic into West Berlin in an attempt to force the Western nations to reconsider.

West Berlin's 2.1 million inhabitants had food for only 36 days and coal for 45. American and British officials gambled on an airlift. For 327 days, planes took off and landed every few minutes around the clock. In 277,000 flights they brought in 2.5 million tons of supplies—everything from food, fuel, and medicine to Christmas presents that the planes' crew members bought with their own money. By May 1949 the Soviets realized they were beaten and lifted the **Berlin blockade.**

That same month voters in the three western zones approved a constitution. By fall the Federal Republic of Germany, commonly called West Germany, was established, with its capital in Bonn. The Soviet Union thereupon turned *its* zone into the German Democratic Republic, commonly called East Germany, with its capital in East Berlin.

The Formation of NATO. The Soviet advance into Czechoslovakia led not only to American approval of the Marshall Plan but also to the formation of a defensive military alliance called the **North Atlantic Treaty Organization (NATO).** At first members included Belgium, Canada, Denmark, France, Great Britain, Iceland, Italy, Luxembourg, the Netherlands, Norway, Portugal, and the United States. In 1952 Greece and Turkey joined, and in 1955 West Germany, which had been allowed to rearm, was admitted. All fifteen countries promised that an attack on one would be regarded as an attack on all. They also promised to resist such an attack with armed force if they thought it necessary.

When West Germany became a member of NATO, the Soviet Union formed its own defensive military alliance, the Warsaw Pact. It included Eastern European **satellite nations**—Albania, Bulgaria, Czechoslovakia, East Germany, Hungary, Poland, and Romania—that were dominated by the Soviet Union. Albania later withdrew.

On September 23, 1949, Americans learned that the Soviet Union had exploded an atomic bomb. The forties were ending, and with them, the security the United States had enjoyed first with its ocean frontiers and then with its nuclear weapons. The shock that resulted from this knowledge drove many Americans into behavior they had not exhibited since the end of World War I.

The Nation Seeks Internal Security

Most Americans have always disliked communism. During World War II, anticommunist feelings took a back seat to admiration for the Soviet Union's fight against Hitler. Then the war ended, and it again became clear that the two superpowers held very different views about what the world should be like. As the Soviet Union expanded into Eastern Europe, Americans became increasingly concerned about possible communist **subversion,** or plots to overthrow the government, within their own country. George F. Kennan, one of the State Department's experts on the Soviet Union, believed that the answer to Soviet challenges was **containment.** By this he did not mean a military response. Rather, he called for steady pressure to contain the Soviets, or to keep them from expanding their power.

Loyalty Checks. In September 1945 a Soviet clerk at the Soviet embassy in Ottawa, Canada, defected to the West and sought political asylum. Several of the documents he brought with him revealed that a few Canadian government workers had been giving secret information about the atomic bomb to the Soviet Union.

President Truman immediately issued an executive order setting up the Loyalty Review Board. Its purpose was to make sure that a similar situation did not exist within the United States government.

The Attorney General drew up a list of ninety "subversive" organizations, membership in which was grounds for suspicion. From 1947 to 1951, 3.2 million government employees were investigated. Of these, 212 were dismissed as security risks. Another 2,900 resigned, some because they did not want to be investigated, others because they felt that the investigation violated their constitutional rights. Individuals being investigated were not allowed to see the evidence against them or even to know who had accused them of disloyalty.

Congress, however, thought that Truman's action did not go far enough. In 1950 it passed the McCarran Internal Security Act. This measure made it unlawful to plan any action that might lead to the establishment of a totalitarian dictatorship (a government that exercises complete control and suppresses individual freedom) in the United States. Truman vetoed the act, saying, "In a free country, we punish men for crimes they commit, but never for the opinions they hold." Congress passed the measure over Truman's veto.

Spy Cases. One reason for the repressive attitude of Congress can be found in two spy cases that were going on at the time. One case involved a former member of the State Department named **Alger Hiss,** who was accused of passing classified, or secret, government documents to the Communist party. Hiss was eventually convicted of perjury and sent to jail.

The second case involved Julius and Ethel Rosenberg, who were minor activists in the Communist party. In 1950 they were arrested shortly after British physicist Klaus Fuchs admitted giving the Soviet Union information about America's atomic bomb. The information probably enabled Soviet scientists to develop their own atomic bomb eighteen months sooner than they would have otherwise. Fuchs implicated the Rosenbergs, who were convicted of espionage. The Rosenbergs died in the electric chair in 1953. Fuchs was sentenced to fourteen years in a British prison.

McCarthyism. The individual who received the most publicity for anticommunist activity in the late 1940's and early 1950's was Senator **Joseph McCarthy** of Wisconsin. A former small-town lawyer, he had won the Republican senatorial nomination and election on the strength of an exaggerated war record. In 1950, facing reelection, McCarthy looked about for an issue and hit on anticommunism.

777

Student Assignment/Homework

Have students complete Chapter 30, Section 2 Daily Activity and read Section 3, "The Cold War Turns Hot."

SECTION 2 REVIEW

Answers

Main Ideas

1. The U.S.S.R., which has no natural barriers to deter attacks, wanted some other way to secure itself against aggressors.

2. The U.S.S.R. invaded Czechoslovakia, blockaded Berlin, and formed the Warsaw Pact.

3. The U.S. announced the Truman Doctrine, gave aid to Turkey and Greece in order to avoid Communist takeovers in those countries, helped form West Germany, set up the Marshall Plan, and founded NATO.

4. Truman set up the Loyalty Review Board to investigate 3.2 million government employees for evidence of association with subversive organizations.

Critical Thinking

5. Possible answer: McCarthy flagrantly violated the civil liberties of many Americans; caused thousands of people to lose their jobs and others to be regarded with fear and suspicion. **(analysis & evaluation)**

Picturing History Senator Joseph McCarthy uses a map to demonstrate the extent of Communist party infiltration.

Soon McCarthy was making one reckless accusation after another. At various times he claimed to have in his hands the names of 57, 81, or 205 Communists in the State Department. (He never actually produced a single name.) McCarthy charged that the Democratic party was guilty of "twenty years of treason" and that Secretary of Defense General George Marshall was "serving the world policy of the Kremlin."

McCarthy's technique, which became known as **McCarthyism,** was never to explain a charge he made or offer evidence to support it. When he was questioned, he would respond by making another accusation. He gave the impression of being so overwhelmed by the monstrous conspiracy he had supposedly uncovered that he had no time to waste on petty details. However, he was always careful to do his name-calling only when inside the Senate, where he had legal immunity. Thus, he could not be sued for slander.

The Republicans hoped for a victory in the 1952 election and did nothing to stop McCarthy's attacks. After General Dwight D. Eisenhower was elected, however, McCarthy turned on the new President and on other Republicans. Finally, in 1954 he accused the United States Army of coddling Communists and of mistreating an assistant of his who had been drafted. The result was a televised Senate investigation. Some 20 million persons watched for thirty-six days as McCarthy bullied witnesses, refused to reveal where he had obtained information, interrupted proceedings, and made one empty charge after another. He soon lost his supporters and his power. The Senate condemned him for improper conduct that tended "to bring the Senate into disrepute." McCarthy died a broken man three years later.

Eisenhower, in his memoirs, said that "McCarthyism took its toll on many individuals and on the nation. No one was safe from charges recklessly made from inside the walls of congressional immunity. . . . The cost was often tragic." Indeed it was. Thousands of people lost their jobs as a result of "guilt by association," that is, for knowing someone who had once attended a Communist meeting, for reading a foreign language magazine, or for being listed in a privately printed publication such as *Red Channels*. Like the Palmer raids of 1919, this new **Red scare** called McCarthyism undoubtedly reflected popular fears about the growing menace of communism throughout the world. However, most historians consider the McCarthy hearings one of the worst violations of constitutional rights in our nation's history.

Linking Past to Present

Although the Soviet-led Communist system began to crumble in Eastern Europe in 1989, the cold war and the distrust of Communists that in the past had led to McCarthyism caused some Americans to remain skeptical and cautious regarding relations with the Soviets today.

SECTION 2 REVIEW

Key Terms and People

Explain the significance of: cold war, Truman Doctrine, Marshall Plan, Berlin blockade, North Atlantic Treaty Organization (NATO), satellite nations, subversion, containment, Alger Hiss, Joseph McCarthy, McCarthyism, Red scare

Main Ideas

1. Why did the Soviet Union consider its domination of Eastern Europe to be of vital importance?
2. What were the Soviet actions that contributed most to the beginning of the cold war?
3. What were the American actions that contributed most to the beginning of the cold war?
4. How did Truman attempt to make sure that there were no subversives in the United States government?

Critical Thinking

5. Eisenhower said that McCarthyism took its toll on the nation. What might that toll have been?

SECTION 3

The Cold War Turns Hot

GLOSSARY TERM: **cease-fire agreement**

No sooner had the United States adopted a policy of containment toward communism in Europe than trouble broke out in Asia. By 1950 America was fighting a limited war on the mainland of Asia. A limited war is one that is fought not to defeat an enemy completely but to achieve a certain aim. In Korea that aim was, as President Truman said, "to stop aggression and to prevent a big war." Specifically, it was to turn back the North Koreans who had invaded South Korea, but to do so without having the war spread to China.

The Communists Win China

In 1931, you will recall, Japanese armies had seized China's northeast province of Manchuria. (See Chapter 28.) In 1937 Japan launched a massive invasion of the rest of China. For the next eight years, the Chinese people resisted as best they could. The Nationalists under China's president, **Chiang Kai-shek,** led the struggle in the south. The Communists under **Mao Zedong** (mou′zə′ duŋ′) led the struggle in the north.

Two Views of Chiang Kai-shek. For many Americans, Chiang Kai-shek was one of the most admired of world leaders. In 1938 he had moved his government fourteen hundred miles inland in order to continue fighting against Japan. Millions of Chinese had followed him westward, carrying factory equipment, schoolbooks, and household goods on their backs. Americans were impressed by the courage and determination the Chinese showed. Chiang's popularity was increased by his conversion to Christianity and by the fact that his wife had been educated in the United States.

United States military and State Department officials who dealt with Chiang held a different view of him. They found his government dictatorial, inefficient, and hopelessly corrupt. For example, during World War II, the United States sent the Nationalist regime approximately $3.5 billion in aid. It is estimated that $3 billion of this aid ended up in the pockets of Chiang's relatives and friends.

Furthermore, the political and economic policies that Chiang's government followed were in sharp contrast to those practiced by the Communists. For

Communist Victory in China, 1949

Communist advances
Nationalist retreat

Map Skills **Movement** To what island did the Nationalists retreat? **Location** How far was it from the mainland of China?

example, the Nationalists collected a grain tax from farmers even during the famine of 1944. When city dwellers demonstrated against a 10,000 percent increase in the price of rice that had occurred over a three-year period, Chiang's secret police opened fire on them. In contrast, after the Communists took over an area, they redistributed the land and reduced rents. They also organized health services and set up schools to teach farmers how to read and write. As a result, Chinese popular support for the Communists increased.

Civil War. During World War II, differences between the Nationalists and the Communists were played down. As soon as Japanese soldiers left the mainland, however, civil war broke out between the two groups.

The United States tried several times to act as peacemaker. From September 1944 to November

State the Objective

Understand why events in Asia in the early 1950's threatened U.S. interests and led the U.S. to fight in the Korean War.

1945, United States Ambassador Patrick J. Hurley tried to reconcile the Nationalists and Communists. He did not succeed. In 1946 President Truman sent General George Marshall to China with a plan for setting up a coalition government that would include both sides. The plan failed.

In 1947 Truman sent yet another general, Albert Wedemeyer, to China on a fact-finding mission. Wedemeyer recommended that the United States continue helping the Nationalists. However, he felt that the only way the Nationalists could win the civil war was if Chiang changed his economic policies and if the United States sent in several hundred thousand troops. Truman was unwilling to commit American soldiers. He did, however, send $2 billion in military equipment and supplies to Chiang over the next two years.

Unfortunately for the Nationalists, their military leadership was poor. Nationalist troops outnumbered Communist troops three to one. However, instead of attacking the center of Communist strength in northern China, Nationalist forces holed up in the cities. The Communists were thus able to cut Nationalist supply lines. Gradually, one isolated city after another surrendered to Mao's troops. The last Nationalist stronghold, Shanghai, fell in May 1949. Chiang and what remained of his government and army fled to the island of **Taiwan** (formerly Formosa).

The Search for a Scapegoat. The American public was astounded at the turn of events. A debate on the nation's China policy promptly broke out.

In Congress a group of conservative Republicans and Democrats attacked the Truman administration for supplying only limited aid to Chiang. If containing communism was important in Europe, they asked, why was it not equally important in Asia?

The State Department replied by saying that what had happened in China was a result of internal forces. The United States had tried to influence these forces, unfortunately without success. Trying to do more would only have meant a new war, which most people did not want. However, the United States would continue to recognize the Nationalist regime as China's legal government and would oppose the admission of Red China, as it was called, to the United Nations.

Most Americans accepted the State Department's arguments, but some did not. They could not believe that Chiang and his regime were re-

sponsible for the Nationalist defeat. They were convinced that somehow the United States had "lost" China, probably because the American government was riddled with Communist agents. They spoke out bitterly on the matter.

Linking Past to Present

In 1972 President Nixon visited China at the invitation of Premier Zhou Enlai. In 1978 the United States formally recognized the People's Republic of China as the sole government of China. Diplomatic relations between the two nations were established on January 1, 1979. Between April and June 1989, hundreds of thousands of students and other Chinese took to the streets of Beijing to demonstrate for democracy. Their demonstrations culminated in the Tiananmen Square massacre of June 4, when Chinese troops shot unarmed citizens at random. The government subsequently established martial law and demanded that student leaders surrender. Later China announced that it had put to death several dozen "counterrevolutionaries."

Koreans Go to War

The peninsula of Korea (the name means Land of the Morning Calm) juts out from the mainland of Asia toward Japan. In 1910 Japan took over Korea and ruled it until August 1945. As World War II ended, Japanese troops there surrendered to the Allies. Troops north of the **38th parallel** surrendered to the Soviets. Troops south of the parallel surrendered to the Americans.

Two Koreas. The 38th parallel was not supposed to be a permanent boundary. As was the case in Germany, however, two nations developed, one in each zone of occupation.

In 1948 the Republic of Korea, usually called South Korea, was established in the American zone. The government was headed by the elderly **Syngman Rhee,** who had spent many years in the United States working for his country's independence. South Korea included Seoul, the country's traditional capital, as well as two-thirds of the peninsula's people and most of its farmland. In

Present the Lesson

Ask students to review the section for information to use in constructing a time line on the board showing the development of conflicts in China and Korea from 1931 through 1953. Discuss how the U.S. responded to these conflicts. Time line might include:

China

1931	Japan seizes Manchuria.
1937	Japan launches attack on the rest of China.
1938	Chiang Kai-shek moves Nationalists to inland China.

1945	Civil war erupts in China; U.S. ambassador tries to mediate.
1946	General George Marshall tries to set up coalition government.
1947	Truman sends General Wedemeyer on fact-finding mission to China; U.S. supports Nationalists against Communists.
1949	Last Nationalist stronghold falls to Communists; Chiang and Nationalists flee to Taiwan.

(U.S. responses include: Some Americans blamed Truman for allowing communists to gain power in China; State Department declared it would continue to recognize Nationalist China and oppose Red China's admission to the UN.)

Korea

1945	Japanese troops surrender to Soviet troops north of the 38th parallel; troops south of the 38th parallel surrender to U.S.
1948	Republic of Korea, called South Korea, is established in American zone; Democratic People's Republic of Korea is set up in Soviet zone; Soviets withdraw troops from North Korea after heavily arming North Koreans.

Picturing History South Korean women and children flee in fear from Communist invaders as American troops move to fight yet another battle. This scene was repeated up and down the Korean Peninsula in the early 1950's.

1949 the United States withdrew all of its troops from the country except for five hundred military advisors.

Also in 1948 the Democratic People's Republic of Korea, with its capital at Pyongyang, was set up in the Soviet zone. North Korea contained most of the mineral wealth of the peninsula and a good part of its industry. At the head of the government was Kim Il Sung, who had been a guerrilla fighter against the Japanese since the 1930's. Kim's government, like Rhee's, claimed the right to rule all of Korea. The Soviets withdrew their troops from North Korea in December 1948 after heavily arming the North Koreans.

A Fateful Speech. In January 1950, Secretary of State Dean Acheson delivered a speech in which he said that the United States would fight if an attack were made east of a "defense perimeter" running from Alaska to Japan to the Philippines. Taiwan and Korea, which lay west of the perimeter, were not mentioned. Their defense, Acheson said, would have to depend on their own efforts and on the United Nations.

Acheson may only have been letting Chiang and Rhee know that the United States would not automatically jump to their aid if they attacked mainland China or North Korea. But without intending to, the Secretary of State may have given the Communists a green light in North Korea.

Attack by North Korea. On June 25, 1950, troops from North Korea crossed the 38th parallel and invaded South Korea. As soon as news of the invasion reached Washington, President Truman decided to act. As he observed later,

> What the Communists, the North Koreans, were doing was nothing new. . . . Hitler and Mussolini and the Japanese were doing exactly the same thing in the 1930's. . . . Nobody had stood up to them. And that is what led to the Second World War. The strong got away [with] attacking the weak, and I wasn't going to let this attack on the Republic of Korea . . . go forward. Because if it wasn't stopped, it would lead to a third world war, and I wasn't going to let that happen. Not while I was President.

Accordingly, Truman ordered in naval and air support for South Korea. When the announcement of his action was made, Congress stood up and cheered. Only Republican Senator Robert A. Taft of Ohio pointed out that the President, by acting on his own, had wrongfully taken over Congress's power to declare war.

On June 27 the UN Security Council adopted an American resolution calling on member nations to help the Republic of South Korea. The UN was able to take this action because the Soviet Union was boycotting the UN over another matter and

1949	U.S. withdraws most troops from Korea.
1950	
June 25	North Korean troops cross 38th parallel and invade South Korea; Truman orders naval and air support for South Korea.
June 27	UN Security Council adopts resolution to aid South Korea; UN troops are ordered to Korea under General MacArthur.
Oct. 7	UN General Assembly recommends MacArthur cross 38th parallel and reunite Korea.

Oct. 14	Truman meets with MacArthur.
Oct. 20	North Korean capital of Pyongyang falls to UN forces.
Oct. 26	Chinese Communist soldier captured.
Nov. 26	300,000 Chinese "volunteers" arrive to help North Koreans.
Dec. 25	UN forces driven below 38th parallel
1951	
Jan. 4	Seoul falls to North Koreans.
March	UN troops retake Seoul.

Apr. 11	Truman relieves MacArthur of his command.
July	Negotiation for cease-fire begins.
1952	
Spring	Location of cease-fire line is approved at 38th parallel; demilitarized zone is established.
1953	
July	Final armistice is signed.

(U.S. responses include: Truman ordered troops to Korea to protect interests of South Koreans, whose rights he felt were being violated.)

Map Skills

Pusan, Taegu • Yalu

Map Skills **Region** Which cities in the South did not fall to the North Koreans? **Movement** To what river did the United Nations forces advance?

was not present to use its veto. In all, twenty-one nations sent some 400,000 troops to resist North Korea's aggression; about four-fifths of these troops were American. South Korean troops numbered an additional 400,000. The combined UN and South Korean forces were placed under the command of **Douglas MacArthur.**

The United States Fights in Korea

At first North Korean armored units drove steadily southward. They captured Seoul and forced UN and South Korean troops into an area around

Pusan in the southeastern part of the peninsula.

Then tanks, heavy artillery, and fresh troops from the United States arrived, and MacArthur launched a counterattack. He made an amphibious landing behind enemy lines at Inchon on Korea's west coast. At the same time, other troops moved north from the Pusan area, thus creating a pincer movement that trapped the North Koreans. About half of them, almost 130,000, surrendered; the rest fled back across the 38th parallel.

A Critical Decision. The sudden military triumph posed a political problem. MacArthur and his troops had achieved their objective of clearing the invaders out of South Korea. What was to happen now? If UN and South Korean forces crossed the 38th parallel, that would change the war from a defensive one to an offensive one. On the other hand, the Allies had agreed at Potsdam that Korea should be unified.

On October 7 the UN General Assembly recommended that MacArthur cross the 38th parallel and reunite Korea. However, days earlier, Communist China's foreign minister, Zhou Enlai (jō′en li′), let it be known that his country would not stand by idly and "let the Americans come to the border"— meaning the Yalu River, the boundary between North Korea and Manchuria. This warning was repeated again and again during the first weeks of October.

On October 14 President Truman flew halfway around the world to Wake Island. There he conferred with General MacArthur on the possibility of Chinese intervention. The general told the President that such an event would not happen: "Mr. President, the war will be over by Thanksgiving and I'll have the American troops back in Tokyo by Christmas."

Chinese Intervention. The advance into North Korea went on, pressing ever closer to the Yalu River. On October 20 Pyongyang fell. Then on October 26, a Chinese Communist soldier was captured about ninety miles south of where he was supposed to be according to army intelligence. Four days later, sixteen more Chinese soldiers were caught. By the following week, eight Chinese divisions had been identified. Soviet-made planes flown by Chinese were now engaging UN fighters in air combat.

Then on November 26, some 300,000 Chinese

Check for Understanding

Have students answer the Section 3 Review questions on paper.

Guided Practice

Tell students that Korea was just the first of many situations that have triggered debate over U.S. responsibility for protecting weak nations from attack by stronger nations. Truman felt strongly that it was the responsibility of the U.S. to step in and prevent another Hitler or Mussolini from coming to power. Ask students how they feel about this issue. Should the U.S. become involved in such a situation? (Possible responses—yes, it is our responsibility to protect other nations, and by protecting those nations, we are strengthening and securing our own democracy. No—our first responsibility is to take care of our needs at home.)

"volunteers" poured across the Yalu River into Korea. The UN and South Korean forces had to retreat. It was done quickly and efficiently, but it was clearly a defeat. By Christmas the UN and South Korean troops had been driven seventy-five to one hundred miles below the 38th parallel. Seoul was lost for the second time on January 4, 1951.

MacArthur's Proposal.   MacArthur now called for an extension of the war into China. He proposed a naval blockade of the China coast and the dropping of thirty to fifty atomic bombs on that nation's industrial and transportation centers. He also wanted the right to strike at Communist Chinese air bases north of the Yalu River and to use Chiang Kai-shek's troops both in Korea and to invade southern China.

Truman rejected MacArthur's requests. The President did not want the United States involved in a massive land war in Asia. As General Omar N. Bradley, chairman of the Joint Chiefs of Staff, said, an all-out conflict with China would be "the wrong war, at the wrong place, at the wrong time, and with the wrong enemy." Also, the Soviet Union had a mutual-assistance pact with Red China. Attacking China could set off World War III.

MacArthur predicted that if his requests were not granted, his army would be wiped out. However, an able field commander, Matthew B. Ridgway, had been appointed head of the United States Eighth Army. Using Ridgway's troops as a spearhead, the UN and South Korean forces began to advance once more. By March 1951 Ridgway had retaken Seoul and had moved back up to the 38th parallel. The situation was just what it had been before the fighting began.

Removal of MacArthur.   MacArthur continued to urge the waging of a full-scale war against China as the best means of bringing a quick end to the Korean conflict. Every time he raised the issue, however, he was told by the President or the Joint Chiefs of Staff that he was expected to fight only a limited war. Finding this intolerable, and certain that his views were correct, MacArthur tried to go over the President's head. He spoke and wrote privately to newspaper and magazine publishers and, especially, to leaders of the Republican party in Congress.

In March 1951 he sent a letter to Joseph Martin of Massachusetts, Republican leader in the House of Representatives. MacArthur stated his view that the place to crush world communism was Asia, and he closed his argument with the words, "There is no substitute for victory." When Martin released the general's letter to the press, Truman felt that he

For Discussion
What might have happened if the U.S. had followed MacArthur's suggestion to invade China and use the atomic bomb? (Possible responses: China might have unconditionally surrendered; Soviet Union might have come to China's assistance; U.S. might have been attacked by Chinese and Soviet forces; World War III might have begun.)

Picturing History   Douglas MacArthur addresses Congress after being relieved of his command.

Picturing History   President Truman explains why he fired General MacArthur.

no longer had a choice. On April 11, with the unanimous approval of the Joint Chiefs of Staff, he relieved MacArthur of his command. "I could do nothing else and still be President," Truman said.

The public outcry that followed rocked the nation. MacArthur received a hero's welcome in the United States, which he had not visited since before World War II. An address to Congress, an honor usually given only to heads of government, capped his triumph. He gave a highly emotional talk, ending with the reminder that "old soldiers never die, they just fade away." A public opinion poll taken at the time showed that 69 percent of the American public thought that the general was right. Apparently it was difficult for Americans to accept a military stalemate, no matter what the reasons.

Throughout the fuss, Truman stayed in the background. He gave people a full opportunity to express their gratitude to MacArthur for his leadership in World War II and for the way he had brought democracy to Japan. Then it was the administration's turn. Before a congressional committee investigating MacArthur's dismissal, a parade of witnesses set forth the arguments for a limited war. The committee agreed with them. As a result, the public began to swing around to the view that Truman had properly defended his constitutional position as commander in chief. MacArthur, while still admired, soon faded away as a political figure.

A Limited Victory. As the Truman-MacArthur controversy died down, a suggestion for settling the Korean War was unexpectedly made by the Soviet Union. Negotiations for a **cease-fire agreement,** a mutual accord to stop fighting temporarily, began in July 1951. By the following spring, agreement had been reached on two points: the location of the ceasefire line at the existing battle line and the establishment of a demilitarized zone between the opposing sides. Another year of wrangling was taken up over the question of prisoners.

Usually, prisoners are sent back to their homelands when a war is over. However, about 50,000 Chinese and North Koreans did not want to be sent home, and the United States felt that they should not be forced to return. The North Koreans, furious at this damage to their prestige, insisted that the prisoners be handed over. A compromise was finally worked out, but before it could be put into effect, South Korean guards solved the problem by letting all the prisoners escape. After several more

weeks of indignant speeches from both North Korea and South Korea, an armistice was finally signed in July 1953.

It was a limited victory in a limited war. On the one hand, the North Korean invaders had been pushed back, and communism had been contained without a major war and without the use of atomic weapons. On the other hand, Korea was still two nations rather than one. Moreover, the cost of the war had been high. About 1.5 million South Koreans, most of them civilians, were killed, and another million were wounded. Throughout the peninsula, cities were leveled and farms destroyed. Several million South Korean civilians became homeless refugees. The figures for the United States were over fifty-four thousand dead and over one hundred thousand wounded. America's military expenditures ran over $15 billion, several billion more than for the Marshall Plan.

Eisenhower Leads the Nation

In 1952 the Republicans had no shortage of issues on which to challenge the Truman administration. There was the rise of communism in Eastern Europe and in China, although its spread had been slowed or stopped by the Marshall Plan and the Korean War. There was the issue of communists in government that had been raised by Senator McCarthy. There was also an issue called "the mess in Washington," by which people meant the growing power of the federal government and the instances of corruption that were coming to light. The war had set off another round of inflation, and Truman's failure to settle a steelworkers' strike in 1952 had caused prices to rise even more. Above all, the negotiations for a Korean armistice had been dragging on for over a year. Finally, there was a general feeling that after twenty years of a Democratic Presidency, it was time for a change.

Eisenhower Versus Stevenson. The Republicans nominated General **Dwight D. Eisenhower** as their candidate. The Democratic standard-bearer was Governor **Adlai Stevenson** of Illinois.

Stevenson's witty speeches delighted many of his supporters. However, his remarks led other voters to distrust him. Along with the Puritan tradition of education, there has always been, historians say, a streak of anti-intellectualism in the United States—a belief that educated people live in an ivory tower and do not know what the real world is like. Stevenson seemed to touch off this anti-

Picturing History Adlai Stevenson works on a speech
during one of his two unsuccessful campaigns.

intellectual streak. He and his followers were soon
known as "eggheads."

Eisenhower, on the other hand, looked and
sounded like everyone's favorite uncle. He had a
delightful grin and a genuinely warm personality.
While Stevenson appealed to people's minds,
Eisenhower, or Ike, as he was called, appealed
more to their emotions. As one historian put it, the
general "might not always have had his facts quite
right, but like his audiences, he knew something
had gone wrong for America, and it had put his
dander [temper] up."

Nixon and TV. For the first time in a Presidential
campaign, television played a major role. At one
point it also added considerable excitement.

A newspaper article revealed that Ike's running
mate, Senator **Richard Nixon** of California, had
benefited from a trust fund set up by several
business people. The article was written as though
the fund were secret and illegal, had been used to
raise Nixon's living style, and was something new
in American politics. It was none of these things.
However, it *was* a great embarrassment to a party
running against corruption in government, and
some Republicans suggested that Nixon be replaced on the ticket.

Nixon replied to the charges in a television
speech that showed masterly use of the new medium. He said that no one had received favors for
contributing to the fund. The money had been spent
only for legitimate political purposes, such as
sending Christmas cards to former campaign workers. Nixon's own resources were stretched by the
demands of public life, he said. His wife, Pat, did
not wear a mink coat but, as he put it, "a
respectable Republican cloth coat."

Nixon concluded with a reference to the family
dog, a black-and-white cocker spaniel named
Checkers. It was, he said, the only outright gift he
had ever accepted, and he would never give it up
because his two daughters loved it so. His performance was known thereafter as the "Checkers
speech." It saved Nixon's place on the Republican
ticket once messages of support started pouring in.

A New Voting Pattern. The turning point in the
hard-fought campaign occurred when Ike firmly
grasped the number-one issue: Korea. On October
24 the general promised that if elected, he would
go to Korea to see firsthand what could be done to
bring the war to an end.

Picturing History Vice-Presidential nominee Richard
Nixon addresses the nation in 1952 to explain his use of
campaign funds. This address became known as his
"Checkers speech."

After that, it was no contest. Eisenhower carried every state outside the traditionally Democratic South, and even there he took Florida, Tennessee, and Virginia. His electoral-vote total was 442 to Stevenson's 89; the popular vote was 33.9 million to 27.3 million. The Republicans also captured Congress, although by a narrow margin.

The 1952 election not only restored the Republicans to national power but also established a new voting pattern. The suburbs then springing up were filled with people from the central cities, most of whom had been loyal Democrats. In 1952 large numbers of them voted for Ike. One Republican newspaper implied that the fresh air must have cleared their heads. Actually, the change was part of a general breakdown in party loyalty. Two out of ten voters now considered themselves independents who would vote for the individual rather than the party. That trend continued, and by the mid-1980's the proportion of independents had reached five out of ten voters and showed no signs of decreasing.

Picturing History An Eisenhower campaign button from the 1952 Presidential election proclaims the popularity of the war hero called Ike.

Eisenhower's "Dynamic Conservatism." Americans who expected some spectacular development from Eisenhower's trip to Korea were disappointed. Ike was photographed eating army rations and talking with GI's, which raised morale. Yet the July 1953 armistice terms were the same as they had been under Truman. In other matters of foreign policy, as you will learn in the next chapter, Eisenhower more or less followed in Truman's footsteps. On the domestic scene, however, there were several changes.

Eisenhower called his economic philosophy "dynamic conservatism." It favored a continuation of the chief New Deal programs combined with an attempt to move the federal government out of some areas.

Congress extended social security to include farm workers, household servants, and employees of small businesses. Some additional money was set aside for public housing. The federal government continued to supervise labor-management relations. In 1959 a labor-management act said that Communists and persons convicted of felonies could not run for union office or be employed by a union.

The Eisenhower administration tried to turn over to private utilities the electric power operations of the TVA but did not succeed. It did, however, abolish the government's monopoly on nuclear power. The Atomic Energy Act of 1954 made it possible for private utilities to obtain a license from the Atomic Energy Commission to produce electricity by atomic energy.

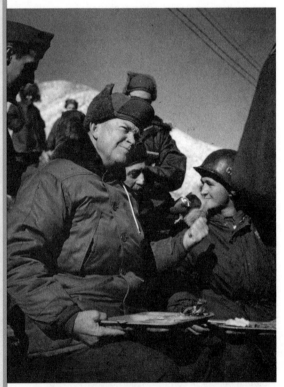

Picturing History Keeping his campaign promise to go to Korea, President-elect Eisenhower has lunch with American troops stationed there in December 1952.

Concluding the Chapter

Reread orally President Truman's remarks on page 781. Ask students to write three paragraphs agreeing or disagreeing with Truman's position. In taking a stand, students should carefully consider what they have learned in this chapter. In their third paragraph, students should indicate whether their position has changed since completing the Introducing the Chapter exercise, and why. (Paragraphs might include: agree—if the European allies had moved to stop Hitler, World War II might have been avoided; disagree—by interfering in Korea, Truman might have started rather than prevented World War III.)

In one area the Eisenhower administration greatly expanded the economic role of the federal government. Under the Federal Interstate and Defense Highway Act, a vast system of four- and six-lane roads was begun in the late 1950's. By the time the 42,000-mile highway network was completed, the federal government had paid 90 percent of the $90 billion cost of building it.

This vast network of roads soon changed the patterns of work, residence, and travel for millions of Americans. The high-speed highways encouraged the movement of people and light industry away from the central cities. They also encouraged the development of thousands of suburban shopping centers. Finally, they increased the dependence of Americans on the automobile.

In general, the mid-fifties were a time of booming business. The inflation rate remained below 2 percent, and most Americans enjoyed an ever-increasing standard of living. The only people who were not pleased with the "Eisenhower prosperity" were farmers, whose income declined as production costs went up. The Eisenhower administration tried several approaches to assist farmers—including payments for land that was *not* planted—but without much success.

Presidential Election, 1952

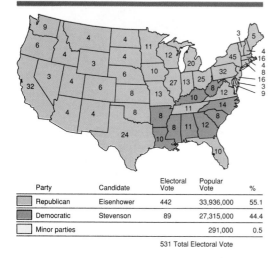

Party	Candidate	Electoral Vote	Popular Vote	%
Republican	Eisenhower	442	33,936,000	55.1
Democratic	Stevenson	89	27,315,000	44.4
Minor parties			291,000	0.5

531 Total Electoral Vote

A Second Term. Despite his great popularity, Ike's political coattails were short; that is, he carried few Republicans into office with him. The small 1952 Republican majority in Congress was swept away in 1954 and was not regained. In 1956 Eisenhower won reelection by the greatest majority since FDR's in 1936, but the Democratic majority in Congress increased.

The President's victory was a particularly personal triumph for him because of his age (he would be seventy by the end of his second term) and his health. Ike's suffering of a heart attack in 1955, a serious intestinal blockage in 1956, and a mild stroke during his second term helped bring about the passage in 1967 of the Twenty-fifth Amendment. This amendment provides for the temporary or permanent replacement of a President who is incapable of performing the duties of office.

Despite the Democratic control of Congress, domestic policy did not change much. The modest social programs that were passed in the 1950's were usually vetoed on the grounds that they were too costly, were an uncalled-for extension of federal power, or both. Back on Capitol Hill, Republicans could usually pick up enough votes from conservative Democrats to uphold the President's veto.

SECTION 3 REVIEW

Key Terms and People

Explain the significance of: Chiang Kai-shek, Mao Zedong, Taiwan, 38th parallel, Syngman Rhee, Douglas MacArthur, cease-fire agreement, Dwight D. Eisenhower, Adlai Stevenson, Richard Nixon

Main Ideas

1. Which two Chinese political groups fought in China's Civil War? Which group prevailed on the mainland?
2. How did Korea become divided into two nations?
3. Why did the United States and the United Nations believe that it was important to defend South Korea against North Korea?
4. What disagreement between MacArthur and Truman resulted in MacArthur's dismissal?
5. What trend in American voting became evident in the 1952 Presidential election?

Critical Thinking

6. Eisenhower's "dynamic conservatism" brought about a hiatus in American social programs during the 1950's. Why might Americans have been willing to endorse this conservative approach to domestic policy?

SECTION 3 REVIEW

Answers

Main Ideas

1. Nationalists and Communists. • Communists.

2. At first Korea's division was purely administrative, a function of postwar clean-up operations. After World War II, the Japanese who had occupied Korea were forced to surrender—those to the north of the 38th parallel surrendered to the Soviets, while those to the south surrendered to the Americans. In 1948, two separate nations were established.

3. Both feared that if the conflict escalated, it would lead to a third world war.

4. MacArthur argued for a full-scale war against Communist China and tried to skirt Truman's authority on the issue; Truman insisted that a limited war in Korea, for the purpose of containing the spread of communism, was enough.

5. The trend toward independent voting instead of voting along party lines.

Critical Thinking

6. In general, Americans were experiencing a period of prosperity. Many believed that there was no need for more government intervention or expenditure because the U.S. was thriving economically. **(analysis)**

State the Objective

Learn to interpret statistics used to measure performance in the economy.

Present the Lesson

Ask students to identify the three principal economic statistics and to describe what each statistic reveals about the economy. (Answers: GNP—gross national product measures how fast the economy is growing. CPI—Consumer Price Index measures inflation. Unemployment rate—measures economic hardship by determining the number of potential workers that are not employed.)

Divide the class into small groups to discuss the following question. As a consumer and wage earner you hear government reports that in the past year nominal GNP has gone up 9 percent, the CPI rose 11 percent, and the unemployment rate is 7 percent. What do these figures tell you about the economic health of the nation? (Discussions might include: increases in nominal GNP alone tell very little about economic growth, but when these data are combined with information about inflation, the apparent real GNP (and therefore economic growth) is not very substantive; an 11 percent inflation rate is high, meaning consumers are paying considerably more for goods and services, negating all increases in incomes that resulted from the increase in GNP; a 7 percent unemployment rate is greater than the 5 percent maximum unemployment rate

Focus on Economics

Economic Indicators

What do a baseball player and an economist have in common? One answer is that both rely on statistics to better understand and perform their jobs.

Statistics are numerical facts that have been carefully organized to present information about a certain subject. For example, a set of baseball statistics might include the number of runs and hits made by each player during a particular game. Economic statistics provide information about many topics, including the strengths and weaknesses of different parts of our nation's free enterprise system. Three important sets of statistics are used as economic indicators: the gross national product (GNP), the Consumer Price Index (CPI), and the unemployment rate.

Gross National Product.   The GNP is the market value of all the goods and services our economy produces in a year. It includes (1) goods and services we buy as consumers; (2) what we spend for new housing; (3) everything that federal, state, and local governments buy; (4) what business and nonprofit institutions invest in plants and equipment; (5) what business spends on inventories; (6) our net exports, or the differences between our exports and our imports; and (7) profits earned overseas and invested there by United States companies.

The GNP can be measured either in current dollars or in constant dollars. The term *current dollars* refers to what dollars can currently buy in the marketplace. GNP in current dollars is known as the nominal GNP. The term *constant dollars* refers to what dollars were worth in a base, or earlier, year. GNP in constant dollars is known as the real GNP because it corrects or adjusts the dollar amount to take inflation into account.

Economists use the GNP to determine whether the nation's economy is growing and, if it is, how fast. This information helps business and government make plans for the future. Some people, however, feel that the GNP is not as accurate as it should be. It does not include goods and services

that have no market value. The work that women have traditionally done—for example, managing households and raising children—has no monetary value and so is not included in the GNP.

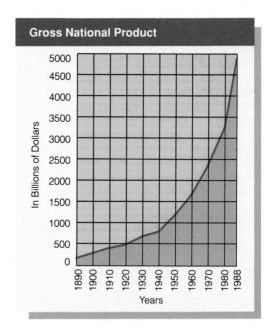

Gross National Product

In Billions of Dollars (y-axis: 0, 500, 1000, 1500, 2000, 2500, 3000, 3500, 4000, 4500, 5000)

Years (x-axis: 1890, 1900, 1910, 1920, 1930, 1940, 1950, 1960, 1970, 1980, 1988)

The Consumer Price Index.   Economists define the Consumer Price Index as an average of prices for certain goods and services commonly bought by consumers. The prices are expressed in relationship to one hundred, the number given to the base year of 1967. In other words, a CPI of two hundred means you have to pay twice as much today to buy the same things you bought in 1967.

There are about four hundred items listed in the index of goods and services. They range from doctors' fees and bowling balls to food, housing, transportation, clothing, and so on. They include the things frequently bought by most people.

Changes in the nation's CPI probably upset people more than any other statistic because so

Check for Understanding

Review with students the answers to questions at the end of the feature. Tell students that teen employment, employment among African Americans, and the number of people looking for work tend to be either overstated or understated by unemployment figures. Ask students to decide which of these statistics are understated and which are overstated. (Answer: among African Americans and teens, unemployment is understated; it is higher than the national average. The number of people looking for work is understated; those who have stopped looking for work are not counted.)

many items are tied to the index. For example, many union contracts have cost-of-living clauses that provide for automatic wage increases to keep up with CPI increases. The benefits paid to people on social security and to retired government and military workers are also keyed to the index. Food stamp allotments go up when the index does. Such items as insurance coverage and child support payments are often readjusted. It is estimated that a 1 percent rise in the CPI leads to a $2 billion rise in wages and benefits.

The Unemployment Rate. The unemployment rate is another economic indicator that upsets many Americans—especially those who are already out of work. Like the CPI, the unemployment rate is linked to certain federal programs. For example, the Employment Act of 1946 (see page 770) committed the federal government to promoting "maximum employment." Economists today define this as an unemployment rate of 5 percent.

Determining the unemployment rate is simple. You divide the number of unemployed persons by the number in the total work force. The work force includes about 65 percent of Americans over sixteen years of age. Those not included are mostly retirees, full-time homemakers, and students. The number of unemployed people is determined by a monthly sampling of forty-seven thousand households across the country.

The unemployment rate by itself, however, does not tell the whole story. First, unemployment does not hit all groups the same way. African Americans in general have an unemployment rate double that of whites. Teen-agers in general have an unemployment rate about four times as high as that of older people.

Second, the unemployment rate does not indicate how many unemployed people have actually lost their jobs. Some may have quit their last jobs. Some are new workers, having just graduated from high school or college. Others—usually women and teen-agers—are reentering the work force. In general, about one-third to one-half of those who are unemployed have actually been fired.

Third, the unemployment rate does not tell the whole story because it does not take into account those who are working only part time. It also fails to include those who have stopped looking for work.

In measuring unemployment hardship, economists usually look at how long people have been out of work. Anything over twenty-six weeks is

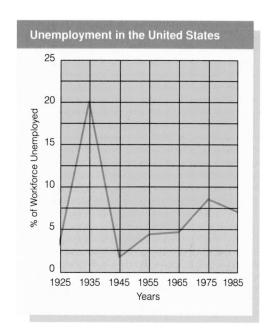

Unemployment in the United States

% of Workforce Unemployed vs. Years (1925–1985)

considered long term and is much more serious than short-term unemployment.

These three economic indicators—the gross national product, the Consumer Price Index, and the unemployment rate—are important guides to the nation's economic health. The information they provide indicates the current functioning of economic activity and helps government agencies determine future economic policies. Hopefully, this information will also help build a healthier free enterprise system.

Understanding Economics

1. What is the difference between the nominal GNP and the real GNP?
2. Why is the unemployment rate not an accurate picture of the unemployment situation?
3. Study the unemployment rate graph. In which year was unemployment the lowest? the highest? What events accounted for each of those low and high rates?

Critical Thinking

4. Through research, determine the percentage change in the GNP, the CPI, and the unemployment rate in the latest year available. Then make a prediction about the economic outlook for the coming year.

Key Terms and People

These are highlighted in the text in the order in which they appear in this list.

Main Ideas

1. They forecast a postwar depression, but the economy took off because of consumer demand and wartime savings. • GI Bill gave veterans money for schooling and housing.

2. Compulsory health insurance, steady income for farmers, increase in the minimum wage, extended social security, flood and irrigation projects, aid to cities for slum clearance and housing for low-income families. • Health insurance and income for farmers.

3. Opposition to the Marshall Plan evaporated when Soviet tanks moved into Prague because Congress could see the need to have anti-Communist influence in Europe. • It persuaded Western nations that they would have to stick together against communist Eastern nations.

4. It caused Truman to make sure U.S. workers would not give away atomic secrets by having the Attorney General release a list of "subversive" organizations. It also intensified the public reaction to the Alger Hiss and Rosenberg spy cases.

5. Americans felt Truman was at fault; they also thought the State Department was riddled with Communists who wanted Mao to win. To calm voter reactions, Truman promised to continue to recognize the Nationalists as China's legal government and to oppose the admission of Red China to the United Nations.

6. He thought it had been a mistake not to stand up to Hitler, Mussolini, and the Japanese. • Twenty-one nations sent troops, who fought under the leadership of General MacArthur. • UN forces did not invade China.

Critical Thinking Questions

7. Creep, sheltered, deeper darkness, sniffing, colder, odors come stinging, ghostly dogs, icy soil, stink, blood, gun oil, cautious. • Advance their army patrol at night. • Korea.

8. The Marshall Plan offered aid to all European nations in return for removing trade barriers. As a result, the threat of starvation was eliminated, and industry was refitted. Democracy flourished.

9. Because of spy scares, people feared communist infiltration. • Possible answer: no—McCarthy's accusations were unfounded.

10. Truman wanted a limited war, one that would not set off a third world war. MacArthur disagreed with Truman's plan and tried to bypass Truman by writing to newspapers and Republican congressional leaders. • Possible answers: yes—MacArthur refused to abide by the President's decision. No—MacArthur could have won the war.

▶**11.** Rise of communism in Eastern Europe and China; communists in government; growing power of the federal government; corruption in government; inflation; slowness in negotiating a Korean armistice. • Personality. • Possible

---

CHAPTER 30 REVIEW

Write your answers on a separate sheet of paper.

Key Terms and People

Explain the significance of: National Security Act, John L. Lewis, Taft-Hartley Act, Dixiecrats, J. Strom Thurmond, Henry A. Wallace, Thomas E. Dewey, cold war, satellite nations, subversion, containment, Alger Hiss, 38th parallel, Syngman Rhee, cease-fire agreement, Adlai Stevenson, Richard Nixon

Main Ideas

1. How did the postwar American economy fool most economists? How did the GI Bill help the economy?
2. In his Fair Deal, what programs did President Truman propose? Which programs did not pass Congress?
3. How did the 1948 Soviet takeover of Czechoslovakia persuade Congress to approve the Marshall Plan? How did the takeover, combined with the Berlin blockade, result in the formation of NATO?
4. How did the uncovering of a spy ring in the Canadian government lead to a new wave of anticommunism in the United States?
5. What repercussions did the fall of Chiang Kai-shek, the victory of Mao Zedong, and the removal of the Chinese Nationalists to Taiwan have on the United States?
6. Why did Truman react with force to the war in Korea? Who fought with South Korea in the war? Why was it a limited war?

Critical Thinking Questions

7. **Evaluating Literature.** List about ten of the words and phrases used by Edward Franklin in the excerpt on page 767 that make you feel cold and afraid. What are the men trying to do? Where are they?
8. **Evaluating Results.** How did the Marshall Plan result in the stabilization of many European countries' politics and economies?
9. **Synthesizing Ideas.** What was the basis for the wave of McCarthyism that swept the country in the late 1940's and early 1950's? Was this fear justified? Explain.
10. **Analyzing Decisions.** What do you think was Truman's main reason for removing MacArthur from command in Korea? Do you think that Truman's decision was the correct one?
11. **Evaluating Elections.** In the 1952 Presidential election, what kind of issues faced the voters? What accounted for Eisenhower's victory, in your judgment? What does this tell you about how voting decisions are made in the United States?
12. **Organizing Ideas.** Complete a chart like the one below to compare the social policies of Truman and Eisenhower.

	Truman—Fair Deal	Eisenhower—Dynamic Conservatism
Social Security		
Public Utilities		
Highways		
Agriculture		

13. **Evaluating Achievements.** What were the chief achievements of the Eisenhower years? List these achievements in what you believe to be the order of importance, the most important being number one.

Critical Thinking Activities

14. **Linking Past to Present.** What were the top priorities of black leaders in 1945? What did Truman do about these priorities? What are today's priorities?
15. **Linking Past to Present.** President Eisenhower believed that government should not concern itself with services that could be better run by the private sector. List a few services that recent Presidents have tried to privatize.

answer: people often want a
father figure, someone they
believe they can trust, not
someone who talks issues all
the time.
12. Truman: social security—
extend it; utilities—keep federal government involved;
highways—no interest;
agriculture—give farmers secure income. **Eisenhower:** social security—extend it;
utilities—privatize some;
highways—build a national interstate system; agriculture—
extend social security to farmers.
13. Possible answer: ending
the Korean War, extending social security to farmers, providing money to public housing, abolishing government
monopoly on nuclear power,
keeping communists out of
union management, building
highway network.

**Critical Thinking
Activities**

14. Federal antilynching law;
abolition of poll tax; permanent
commission to replace Fair
Employment Practice Committee. • Integrated armed services; set up Fair Employment
Board. • Possible answers:
voter registration; housing;
economic opportunity.
➤**15.** Postal services; Conrail

services; services by various
agencies, to whom the federal
government would give less
money in order to diminish
their dependence on federal
funds.

➤**Question suitable for cooperative learning.**

TELESCOPING THE TIMES: 1945–1956

Postwar Period, Cold War, Korean War

Truman was ill-prepared for being President, and he faced unusual problems. During his term of office he helped to demobilize the army and reorganized the military administration. He presided over a postwar economic boom that surprised most people. During this time, inflation was a major cause of labor unrest. A wave of strikes caused Congress to pass the restrictive Taft-Hartley Act. Truman also firmly called for certain legislation that would help secure civil rights for African Americans. Although Congress refused to pass the legislation he asked for, the President accomplished a good deal in this area through a series of executive orders. Truman won the four-way election of 1948. During the next four years, not all of his Fair Deal proposals were enacted by Congress, but he could claim a good record for social legislation at home.

The postwar years made Americans familiar with the iron curtain in central Europe and with the cold war between the Soviet Union and the United States. The Truman Doctrine, aimed at countering Soviet expansion, called for United States financial aid to Greece and Turkey. The Marshall Plan helped rescue Western Europe from the poverty, starvation, and chaos created by the war and by the record-breaking cold winter of 1947. Americans grew even more suspicious of the Soviet Union when the Soviets invaded Czechoslovakia. The United States supported the founding of NATO, and the Soviet Union countered with the Warsaw Pact.

At home Americans grew increasingly fearful of communism. Two actual spy cases intensified this mood. Senator McCarthy investigated and recklessly accused so many people that the hysteria over communism became known as McCarthyism. Postwar Americans were shocked to find that Mao Zedong's Communists had taken over China

after years of struggle. In 1949 Chiang Kai-shek's Nationalists retreated to Taiwan. Some Americans claimed that the United States had "lost" China.

There was more unrest elsewhere in east Asia. After World War II, Korea was divided. The Americans occupied South Korea, and the Soviets occupied North Korea. In 1950 the United States and the UN tried to halt an invasion of South Korea by the Communist North Koreans. General MacArthur urged full-scale war against China, the backer of North Korea, but Truman was committed to a limited war. Finally, Truman fired MacArthur for challenging his authority. When Eisenhower beat Stevenson at the polls in 1952, it was largely on the issue of Korea. During Eisenhower's Presidency, Americans experienced low inflation, which contributed to prosperous times.

Chronology of Main Events

1946 Price controls lifted

1947 Taft-Hartley Act; Truman Doctrine and Marshall Plan announced; National Security Act

1948 Berlin airlift

1949 Truman inaugurated for first full term; NATO founded; Soviet Union explodes first atomic bomb; mainland China controlled by Communists

1950 UN intervenes in Korea; McCarthy charges Communists are active in government

1953 Dwight D. Eisenhower inaugurated President; armistice ends Korean War

1956 Eisenhower wins second term

Telescoping the Times may
be used as an alternative to
having students read the entire chapter, as a chapter preview, or as a chapter review.

Postwar Period, Cold War, Korean War 791

791

Global Perspectives

1950's–1960's	Most European colonies in Africa become independent.
1956-1959	Civil war erupts in Cuba.
1958	Egypt and Syria form United Arab Republic.
1958	De Gaulle returns to power in France.
1960	Brazil moves its capital from Rio de Janeiro to Brasília.

For Discussion

Describe an alternative way in which the new independence of African colonies might have affected the cold war? (Possible response: both the U.S. and the Soviet Union might have responded by sending military aid and advisors to these nations in order to develop alliances; the struggle to gain allies might then have intensified the cold war.)

Additional Resources

- Geography Activities
- Skills Activities
- Thematic Activities
- Economic Activities
- Cultural Literacy Activities
- Literary Source Readings
- Primary Source Readings
- Nuclear Peacekeeping
- Transparencies
- Computer Test Generator

Additional Teaching Strategies

SECTION 1

For Basic Students: Ask students why William J. Levitt was called the Henry Ford of the housing industry. (Possible response: his houses were built in an assembly line fashion.) Have students explain in a short paragraph how Levitt's houses were built. (Paragraphs might include: bulldozers leveled land; streets were paved; electricians installed lights; lots were marked off; houses were built from prefabricated parts.) Have students share their paragraphs.

For Advanced Students: Have students pair off and ask them to assume that they are city planners hired by the Levitt company to design a new suburb. On posterboard, each pair should construct plans for such a suburb, including facilities for education, recreation, transportation, shopping, and medical care. Have students display their plans in the classroom.

SECTION 2

For Basic Students: Have students work in small groups to make a three-column chart. In the first column they should list the names of at least five popular television shows of the 1950's. In the second column they should list the type of program (for example, news, situation comedy, game show, western). In the third, have them list a similar show from the present. Charts might include:

Show	Type	Similar Current Show
I Love Lucy	comedy	(Consult current television viewers' guide listings.)
What's My Line	game show	
Dragnet	crime show	

For Advanced Students: Organize students into two groups to debate the contention that television is a "vast wasteland." (Arguments in disagreement might include: a vast number of educational and news shows inform and teach. Arguments in agreement might include: violence, and low-quality programming are prevalent, and women and minorities are sometimes treated degradingly.)

SECTION 3

For Basic Students: Have students research and prepare a one-page report on the philosophy of Henry David Thoreau, Mahatma Gandhi, or A. Philip Randolph. (Reports might include: Thoreau chose to go to jail rather than support the Mexican War by paying his poll tax; he wrote "Civil Disobedience," in which he proposed passive resistance.) Have students share their reports and review how these three men inspired Dr. Martin Luther King, Jr.

For Advanced Students: Ask students to research and present to the class a two-minute speech explaining the origins and work of the Southern Christian Leadership Conference, the Student Nonviolent Coordinating Committee, or the National Association for the Advancement of Colored People. After the reports, discuss with the class the similarities and differences between these organizations. (Reports might include: Student Nonviolent Coordinating Committee was formed in April 1960 at Raleigh, North Carolina; it was a militant civil rights organization established for Southern college students; its first leader was James Forman; many Northern white and black students joined.)

SECTION 4

For Basic Students: Have students identify on a wall map of the world three areas where the struggle between the superpowers in the 1950's was evident. Discuss the nature of each episode. (Possible response: Hungary—Soviet Union sends in troops to stop Hungarian revolt; Soviet Union—American U-2 plane is shot down over Soviet territory; Suez Canal—Egypt seizes control of Suez Canal; Britain, France, and Israel attack Egypt and reclaim canal; Russia threatens to retaliate against Britain and France; United Nations ends fighting.)

For Advanced Students: Have students research the U.S.–Soviet arms race. Then ask half of the students to support a strong military defense and the other half to support disarmament. Ask each group to prepare a position paper stating its views. (Papers supporting a strong military defense might include: a strong offense is the best defense; the U.S. needs to show its strength to deter further communist aggression. Papers supporting disarmament might include: nuclear build-up only leads the world closer to total destruction; if the U.S. begins disarmament it might have a positive effect on U.S.–Soviet relations.)

Further Reading for Students

Nonfiction

Brown, Claude. *Manchild in the Promised Land*. New York: New American Library, 1971.

Oates, Stephen. *Let the Trumpet Sound: The Life of Martin Luther King, Jr.* New York: Harper & Row, 1982.

Stevenson, Janet. *The School Segregation Cases*. New York: Franklin Watts, 1973.

Fiction

Lee, Harper. *To Kill a Mockingbird*. New York: J. B. Warner Books, 1982.

Bibliography for Teachers

Books

Coles, Robert. *Uprooted Children: The Early Life of Migrant Workers*. Pittsburgh: University of Pittsburgh Press, 1970.

Friedan, Betty. *The Feminine Mystique: Twentieth Anniversary Edition*. New York: W. W. Norton, 1983.

Galbraith, John Kenneth. *The Affluent Society*. New York: New American Library, 1985.

Hart, Jeffrey. *When the Going Was Good: American Life in the Fifties*. New York: Crown Publishers, 1982.

Morris, Aldon D. *The Origins of the Civil Rights Movement: Black Communities Organizing for Change*. New York: Free Press, 1984.

Audio-Visuals

America's Changing Lifestyles. Social Studies School Service. Filmstrip.

Focus on the Fifties. Coronet. Movie.

Focus on 1954. Screen Digest. Movie.

The 1950's—Metropolis and Suburbia. Boromar. Filmstrip.

The 1950's—The Struggle for Human Rights. Boromar. Filmstrip.

Segregation in Schools. Columbia Broadcasting System. Movie.

Computer Resources

Super Powers in the Nuclear Age. (Apple) Focus Media.

Teacher's Notes:

Lesson Plan

Teaching Resources, Unit 7 Booklet

Chapter Objectives

Students will learn:
- why the popularity of suburban living grew during the 1950's
- the changes in American popular culture during the 1950's
- the major advances made by minorities in the 1950's
- what evidenced a continuing struggle between the two superpowers, the U.S. and the Soviet Union

Using the Chapter Time Line

How many years passed between the Supreme Court ruling allowing segregation in the case of *Plessey* v. *Ferguson* (see Unit 4 Time Line) and their decision in *Brown* v. *Board of Education*? (Answer: 58) Who was President (see Chapter 30 Time Line) when Alaska and Hawaii became states? (Answer: Dwight Eisenhower)

Picturing History Laughter filled American living rooms when *I Love Lucy,* starring Lucille Ball and Desi Arnaz, appeared on TV. Between 1945 and 1960, the number of TV sets rose from ten thousand to sixty million.

| 1950 | 1952 | 1954 | 1956 | 1958 | 1960 |

1953 Termination policy begins for American Indians

1954 *Brown v. Board of Education*

1955 Montgomery bus boycott

1956
• Hungarian uprising
• Suez Canal crisis begins

1957
• Eisenhower Doctrine
• Civil Rights Act

1959 Alaska and Hawaii become states

1960 U-2 incident

Maya Angelou: served as Northern coordinator for the Southern Christian Leadership Conference in the sixties at the request of Dr. Martin Luther King, Jr.; was named *Ladies' Home Journal* "Woman of the Year" in communication in 1975; produced, directed, and starred in the theatrical production *Cabaret for Freedom*; starred in Genet's *The Blacks*.

Works include: *I Know Why the Caged Bird Sings; Gather Together in My Name;* two collections of poetry, *Just Give Me a Cool Drink of Water 'Fore I Die* and *Oh Pray My Wings Are Gonna Fit Me Well;* the original screenplay and musical score for the film *Georgia, Georgia;* a ten-part TV series on African traditions in American life.

Singin' and Swingin' and Gettin' Merry Like Christmas: is the third volume of her autobiography; tells the story of her move into the adult world, her marriage, and her beginning in show business; depicts a failed marriage, her return to work, and the difficulties of single parenthood.

CHAPTER **31** 1950–1960

Adjustments of the 1950's

Links to American Literature

I began to relax and enjoy the wealth of a world of music. Early mornings were given over to Bartok and Schoenberg. Midmorning I treated myself to the vocals of Billy Eckstine, Billie Holiday, Nat Cole, Louis Jordan and Bull Moose Jackson. A piroshki from the Russian delicatessen next door was lunch and then the giants of bebop flipped through the air. Charles Parker and Max Roach, Dizzy Gillespie, Sarah Vaughan and Al Haig and Howard McGhee. Blues belonged to late afternoons and the singers' lyrics of lost love spoke to my solitude.

I ordered stock and played records on request, emptied ashtrays and dusted the windows' cardboard displays. Louise and her partner, David Rosenbaum, showed their pleasure by giving me a raise, and although I was grateful to them for the job and my first introduction to an amiable black-white relationship, I could exhibit my feelings only by being punctual in coming to the shop and being efficient at work and coolly, grayly respectful.

At home, however, life shimmered with beautiful colors. I picked up my son from the baby-sitter's every evening. He was five years old and so beautiful his smile could break the back of a brute.

— MAYA ANGELOU, *Singin' and Swingin' and Gettin' Merry Like Christmas*

The Korean War dominated the early 1950's, but by the middle of the decade America found itself at peace. Home life and family returned to the forefront. The music, movie, and television industries boomed as Americans looked for ways to spend their energy and their new-found leisure time. It was an era of carefree harmony wedged between the wars of the previous decades and the civil unrest that lurked just beyond the horizon.

Chapter Overview

Some Americans who remember World War II are apt to look back on the 1950's as the good old days, while others claim that the period was quiet and uninteresting. You will have the opportunity to draw your own conclusions as you examine the changes that took place during this decade, and analyze the continuing struggle between the two political superpowers. A close look at American postwar values will give you new insights into the lives of your parents and grandparents. Chapter 31 describes the fifties in four sections.

Chapter Outline

1. **New Patterns of Living Develop**
2. **Americans Enjoy New Forms of Entertainment**
3. **Minorities Make Some Progress**
4. **Crises Threaten International Peace**

Introducing the Chapter

Have students skim the chapter, noting in particular the headings in each section. Students should then choose one heading and, on a three-by-five-inch card, write a question based on the heading. (Questions might include: What triggered the new patterns of living? What was Levittown? How did Americans try to end discrimination?) After students study each section, use the questions on the cards to stimulate discussion.

SECTION 1
Core Lesson

Anticipate the Lesson

Ask students to define the words *city* and *suburb*. (Possible definitions: a city is a center of population larger than a town, having fixed boundaries; a suburb is a residential area on or near the outskirts of a city.) Ask students to list three advantages and three disadvantages of living in each place. Write them on the board. List might include:

City

Advantages	Disadvantages
Close to shopping	Crowded
Close to cultural events	Has relatively high air-pollution levels
Exciting and fast paced	Noisy

Suburb

Advantages	Disadvantages
Has more open land	Makes car a necessity
Has lower crime rate	May necessitate long commutes to work
Has less pollution	Lacks city's excitement

For Discussion

What are some advantages and disadvantages of living in a suburban community as described in this section? (Possible responses: advantages—everyone is in a similar social class; neighbors have much else in common; homes are removed from the crime and pollution of the city. Disadvantages—all homes look similar; competition is a part of life.)

SECTION 1

New Patterns of Living Develop

GLOSSARY TERMS: suburbs, baby boom, beatniks

During the 1950's, a new trend developed. Large numbers of people began moving out of large cities into **suburbs,** or residential districts on or near the outskirts of a city. Census figures for central cities showed an increase of about 11 percent between 1950 and 1960. In contrast, the figures for suburbs jumped almost 50 percent. By the early 1960's, every large city in the United States was surrounded by a heavily populated ring of smaller communities.

Also, the suburban population increased as a result of the movement of farmers. About seventeen million people left the land during the 1950's. However, instead of moving to a large city, most of them moved either to a suburb or to a small city.

New Suburbs Multiply

Fifteen years of depression and war had left the nation with a shortage of at least 5 million housing units. At first the construction industry was slow in meeting the demand. With the removal of wartime controls on prices and materials, builders concen-

trated on putting up factories rather than houses. The latter were less profitable. Construction was further hampered by union rules to increase employment that forbade the use of power tools and other labor-saving devices. Some ex-GI's made do with converted army barracks. About a million families doubled up. Then in 1946 William J. Levitt bought a fifteen-hundred-acre potato field on Long Island thirty miles east of New York City, and a new American life style was inaugurated.

Levittown. Levitt was the Henry Ford of the housing industry. He pioneered the use of mass production in the building of private homes. He did this just as Ford had, by standardization. Ford used to say that people could buy a Model T in any color they wanted as long as it was black. Likewise, residents of Levittown could have bought any kind of house they wanted as long as it was the four-room, one-story ranch house in the standard two-tone color scheme.

Levitt standardized not only the houses themselves, but also the way they were built. First came the bulldozers to clear and level the land. These were followed by street pavers, who laid down pavement. Next came electricians to install lights. Once the streets were in, the lots were marked off.

Then it was time to put up the houses. As one historian described the process: "Convoys of trucks moved over the hardened pavements, tossing

---

People in the Chapter

Edward R. Murrow narrated a 1950's documentary series entitled "See It Now." He concluded a show featuring Joseph McCarthy by stating: "He didn't create this situation of fear; he merely exploited it. . . . Cassius was right: 'The fault, dear Brutus, is not in our stars but in ourselves.'"

Thurgood Marshall explained his use of the word Afro-American in a 1989 dissenting opinion by saying, "I intend to use it from now on. . . . I spent most of my life fighting to get Negro spelled with a capital N. Then people started saying 'black' and I never liked it." He added that he chose Afro-American rather than African American, which is now used more frequently, because African American was not in

the dictionary at the time and Afro-American was.

Rosa Parks became known as the mother of the civil rights movement. Her refusal to give up her seat on a city bus spurred black leaders into action and brought Martin Luther King, Jr., into the leadership of the civil rights movement.

Martin Luther King, Jr., was signing autographs in a Harlem department store in 1958 when a woman stabbed him with a steel letter opener. King underwent a three-hour operation to remove the weapon, which had lodged so close to his main heart artery that if he had sneezed he would have died.

794

State the Objective

Explain why the popularity of suburban living grew during the 1950's.

Present the Lesson

Have student volunteers write on the board reasons for the growth of surburbia, changes in life styles caused by its growth, and reasons for the suburban emphasis on conformity.

Reasons for Growth
- Movement of farmers to suburbs
- Movement of people from the cities
- Development of affordable housing

Changes in Life Styles
- Daily commute
- Need for auto
- Time-consuming lawn care and home maintenance

Reasons for Emphasis on Conformity
- Similar homes
- Similar age and marital status of residents
- Similar war experiences for men
- Similar incomes

"*I'm Mrs. Edward M. Barnes. Where do I live?*"

Picturing History This cartoon spoofs the housing developments of the 1950's that gave Americans the cookie-cutter homes and neighborhoods they craved.

out prefabricated sidings at 8:00 A.M., toilets at 9:30, sinks and tubs at 10:00, sheetrock at 10:45, flooring at 11:00." Within days, several hundred identical houses were ready for occupancy. By 1951 Levittown contained 17,500 homes.

It was a second Oklahoma land rush. Levitt did not advertise his houses. News spread by word of mouth. When his sales office opened on March 7, 1949, more than a thousand young marrieds, some of whom had been waiting outside for four days, were in line ready to pay the standard price of $6,990. When kitchen appliances, landscaping, and bank charges were included, the whole package came to less than $10,000.

The package also included certain restrictions. For example, you were not allowed to put up a fence, and you were required to cut your lawn regularly. Laundry could dry on the line only on Monday, never on Sunday. Door signals had to be chimes; no buzzers or bell pulls were allowed. However, you could choose the particular chime you preferred.

Ten years after Levittown opened, its more rigid restrictions had been relaxed, and its geometrically planted trees had taken root. Patios, sun decks, and

dormers had added space and value to the standard ranch houses. By 1960 they were selling for two and three times their original cost, and the community had a varied and attractive look.

Suburban Sprawl. A year after Levitt had shown the way, housing starts rose to almost 2 million. They remained at about 1.5 million a year throughout the 1950's. The greatest part of this housing was in suburban developments. It had long been the American dream to own a single-family home with grass and some trees around it. The dream included a safe place for children to play, good schools, and friendly neighbors. Levitt and his imitators made this dream a reality for millions. The suburbanites did not seem to care that their daily commute to the city took an hour or so each way or that lawn care consumed much of their leisure time. The dream was worth it.

Dependence on the Auto. Suburban living made the automobile a necessity, not a luxury or a convenience. Public transportation was almost nonexistent in rural areas that were plowed up by developers. Most suburbanites had to drive to

Check for Understanding

Call on individual students to orally answer Section 1 Review questions.

Guided Practice

Tell students that the American public, although still in favor of high-quality public education, is also concerned with the continuing tax increases necessary to ensure high quality. Ask students how education might be upgraded and taxes still be kept down. (Possible responses: schools might rely more on volunteer workers to fill many positions; students serving detention might be required to work at cleaning the school building or grounds; schools might close for one month during the coldest part of the year, opening two weeks

earlier and closing two weeks later, thus conserving energy.)

work. In addition, schools, churches and synagogues, doctors' and dentists' offices, and shopping centers were seldom within walking distance. As a result, most suburban families owned two cars—one for the husband and another, usually a station wagon, for the wife to use while chauffeuring the children and doing errands.

Sales of new cars averaged about 6.7 million each year of the 1950's. The total number of private cars on the road went from 40 million in 1950 to 60 million in 1960. At the same time, the number of people using public transportation dropped.

Life Styles Tend to Conform

Suburban life encouraged conformity. First of all, the houses were similar. Then, the homeowners were all about the same age. There were no unmarried adults and hardly any elderly or even middle-aged couples. Nearly all the males shared the same background of wartime experiences and schooling under the GI Bill. Also, because houses in any development cost about the same, they attracted homeowners with similar incomes. Some incomes might be on their way up and a few on their way down; but for the time being all were at nearly the same level.

Similar Life Styles. In housing developments, people's life styles were about the same. The emphasis was on friendliness and informality. People helped newcomers get settled and were generous with advice and with the loan of tools. Children exchanged toys, clothing, and bikes. Car pooling children to school was common, as was the exchange of baby-sitting services. Buffet-style casserole dinners replaced sit-down dinners for entertaining, in part because the formal dining room no longer existed. It had given way to a combination living-dining room area that sometimes flowed into the kitchen as well. Men walked around in open-necked sport shirts on weekends, and women thought nothing of going to the grocery store with their hair in curlers. Almost everyone used first names, even youngsters talking to adults. Yet, despite the casualness of manners and clothes, people were expected to keep up their property and to take an active part in community affairs.

Probably no one in suburbia felt greater pressure to conform than children, who often outnumbered adults two to one. Childless couples were rare in

the new developments. A postwar population explosion known as the **baby boom** had taken place, and by the middle fifties families with four and five children were common. The Parent-Teacher Association and the Little League were among the most important community organizations. What with Scouts, music lessons, and religious classes on top of regular school activities, children scarcely had an unorganized minute in their lives.

Education for Success. Both boys and girls were encouraged to be popular and well adjusted. If the boys could not get along well with their peers, how would they fit into a corporate organization when they grew up? Similarly, if the girls could not get along well with their peers, how would they be able to help their husbands advance in business or in government?

Fitting into a corporate structure was particularly important by the fifties. One reason was that by 1956 the majority of workers were no longer blue-collar, a term for industrial workers, but white-collar, a term for clerical or professional workers. Instead of producing manufactured goods, they produced services. Moreover, they produced services not for small firms but for large corporations or for large government agencies— federal, state, and local.

As a result, the rising suburban middle class considered a good education an absolute necessity. Children were expected to outdo their parents in income and in social status. They could achieve that goal, it was believed, only if they were better educated than their parents. Although school budgets sometimes amounted to over half of the total expenditures in new communities, suburban parents seldom complained. What they wanted were programs that would raise school standards and enable their children to go to college.

The Rise of Consumerism. Suburbanites also wanted, and were increasingly able to get, more consumer goods. Certainly one of the outstanding characteristics of the fifties was the high standard of living that a majority of Americans enjoyed. Nearly 60 percent were now members of the middle class. The country was producing half of the world's goods. One new item after another was appearing in the marketplace. There were dryers and rotary lawn mowers, cars with automatic transmissions, radios with pea-sized transistors, and many other innovative new products for consumers.

Assign Independent Practice

Have students complete Chapter 31, Section 1 Daily Activity.

Student Assignment/Homework

Have students read Section 2, "Americans Enjoy New Forms of Entertainment," and answer the Section 2 Review questions on paper.

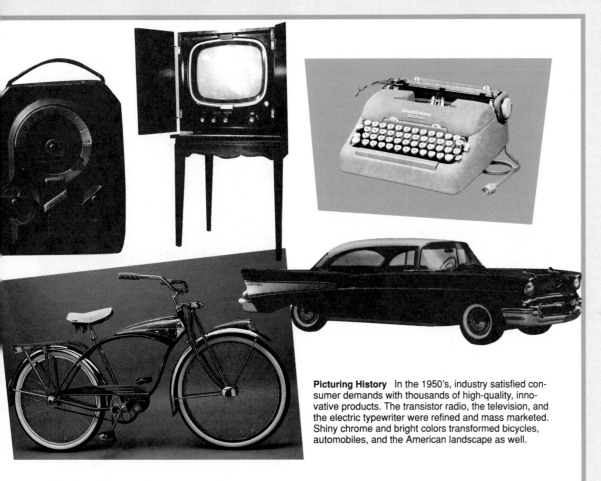

Picturing History In the 1950's, industry satisfied consumer demands with thousands of high-quality, innovative products. The transistor radio, the television, and the electric typewriter were refined and mass marketed. Shiny chrome and bright colors transformed bicycles, automobiles, and the American landscape as well.

SECTION 1 REVIEW

Answers

Main Ideas

1. His mass-produced homes and planned communities helped create the suburban life style.

2. Suburbs provided low-cost single-family homes with grass, trees, good schools, and pleasant neighborhoods.

3. White-collar, service jobs that often required a college education were replacing blue-collar work.

4. A higher standard of living, greater availability of goods, easy credit, and confidence in the future.

Critical Thinking

5. Many suburbanites worked, shopped, and found entertainment in the cities. To them, the suburbs were little more than a place to sleep. **(synthesis)**

Most items were purchased on credit. Between 1952 and 1956 consumer debt rose from $27 billion to $43 billion. Instead of saving, Americans were spending, in full confidence that good times would continue indefinitely.

The Beatniks. Critical of this American dream of prosperity and conformity was the Beat generation. According to one theory, *beat* was an abbreviation for *beatitudes* and meant that the Beats believed they were blessed with mystical powers. Other Beats, however, claimed the word meant "beaten down." The **beatniks,** as they were called, wrote their own literature. A bookstore in San Francisco called City Lights became their headquarters. Its owner, Lawrence Ferlinghetti, was their publisher. Beat writers like poet Allen Ginsberg and novelist Jack Kerouac expressed their disillusionment with 1950's middle-class values. Their literary movement reached its peak when Kerouac's novel *On the Road* sold half a million copies.

SECTION 1 REVIEW

Key Terms and People

Explain the significance of: suburbs, baby boom, beatniks

Main Ideas

1. How did the ideas of William J. Levitt affect the life styles of the American people?
2. How did suburbs fulfill the American dream of the people who moved there?
3. What change in the nature of employment increased the need for education?
4. What factors contributed to the enormous demand for consumer goods?

Critical Thinking

5. City planners referred to the new suburbs as "bedroom communities." Based on your knowledge of what early suburbs were like, what do you think this label means?

Adjustments of the 1950's **797**

Anticipate the Lesson

In an informal survey, ask students how much time they spend each day listening to the radio and how much time watching television. Ask students what impact they feel radio and television have on their lives. (Possible responses: little or none—it serves only as background noise. A lot—news programs and other shows educate and keep the public informed. Some—characters on television can be either positive or negative role models.) Ask students to name a very typical current television program and explain what it says about our culture. (Possible response: a police show might reflect our desire to see realistic life situations that are also optimistic—good always triumphs over evil.)

State the Objective

Examine changes in American popular culture during the 1950's.

SECTION 2

Americans Enjoy New Forms of Entertainment

GLOSSARY TERM: **Federal Communications Commission (FCC)**

During the 1950's, old forms of entertainment changed, and a new one arose. Beyond a doubt, television was the entertainment marvel of the postwar era. In 1950 there were not quite 4 million TV sets in use, and fewer than one household in ten had one. By 1960 there were 52 million sets in American homes, one in almost nine out of ten households.

The average set was turned on six hours a day, seven days a week. One survey indicated that on the day of graduation from high school, the average American youngster would have spent eleven thousand hours in the classroom and fifteen thousand hours in front of the television screen. Another survey pointed out that Americans spent more time watching "the tube" than they did earning a living.

The Little Screen Triumphs

A telegraph that could see had been theoretically possible since the 1870's. A few experimental television broadcasts were made in the 1920's, and very limited service began in 1939. Real expansion was touched off after the war by the development of coaxial cable and microwave relays that could send television waves over the horizon. The first coast-to-coast television broadcast took place on September 4, 1951. It was President Truman's address at the Japanese peace treaty conference in San Francisco, and it was carried over ninety-four stations to 40 million viewers. By 1952 the **Federal Communications Commission (FCC),** which in 1934 had been authorized to regulate interstate communications, had issued licenses for four hundred stations to operate on the twelve very high frequency (VHF) channels and two thousand stations on the seventy ultra high frequency (UHF) channels. About 12 percent of these stations presented educational and other noncommercial material.

Television Programming. Among the most popular programs of the decade were Ed Sullivan's *Toast of the Town,* which resembled the vaudeville shows of the Gilded Age; situation comedies such

Picturing History Throughout the 1950's, television host Ed Sullivan promised "a really big show" and promoted new talents on his Sunday night variety hour, *Toast of the Town.*

as *I Love Lucy* and *The Adventures of Ozzie and Harriet;* game shows of which *The $64,000 Question* and *What's My Line?* were typical; and newscasts by such reporters as Edward R. Murrow and the team of Chet Huntley and David Brinkley. Dramatic presentations included *Playhouse 90* and the *Hallmark Hall of Fame.* Police officers were the heroes of such crime shows as *Dragnet,* while sheriffs played starring roles in *Gunsmoke* and other Westerns. Sports events filled many hours.

Occasionally a television-inspired fad came along. One in 1956 had millions of boys and girls between the ages of five and fifteen putting on coonskin caps in imitation of Fess Parker, who

Picturing History Fran Allison chatted with these two lovable puppets in *Kukla, Fran and Ollie,* which captivated adults as well as children in the early 1950's.

portrayed Davy Crockett on Walt Disney's weekly show. Other favorite children's shows of the time included *The Lone Ranger, Lassie, Hopalong Cassidy, The Mickey Mouse Club,* and *Howdy Doody.* Every once in a while, there appeared a spectacular—an extra-long, one-time only, carefully and expensively produced show. One of these featured Mary Martin flying through the air (on wires) as Peter Pan.

Most programs were not produced by local stations but by one of three nationwide networks. The reason was economic. The larger the audience, the more money a TV station could charge for advertising. Only a nationwide network could produce the kinds of advertising revenues needed to fill all the hours of broadcast time. This arrangement had an effect on the types of programs that were produced and on their quality. There were just so many writers, actors, actresses, musicians, and dancers. Shows had to be put together in a hurry.

Picturing History Fan wearing a Davy Crockett coonskin cap.

Minutes counted! As a result, much of the material tended to be commonplace. The shows seemed thrown together. Little emphasis was put on dialogue, but considerable attention was paid to slapstick, crashing cars, and murders. Controversial issues were avoided so as not to offend advertisers or their potential customers. FCC Chairman Newton Minow received considerable applause in the 1960's when he declared that television was "a vast wasteland."

Videotape Arrives. Meanwhile, TV's technical quality kept improving. An important engineering breakthrough of the late fifties was videotape. Live programs were visually bright and clear, but filmed programs lacked sharpness and definition. A videotaped performance, however, could not be distinguished from a live one. The tape, like movie film, could be edited, or redone, to eliminate mistakes. As a result, by 1960, except for sports, news broadcasts, and a few other programs, live television was a thing of the past.

Radio and Motion Pictures Adjust

The rise of television directly affected radio and motion pictures. Radio was radically changed but not financially hurt. Expensive drama and variety shows disappeared. Instead, radio stations became local institutions, providing popular music, capsule news, and community services. The number of stations rose by 50 percent, and advertising revenues went up 35 percent in ten years.

The change in the film industry was more drastic. The Hollywood studio system was a highly industrialized operation that turned out six hundred or more feature films a year. The films were distributed through 18,500 theaters that in 1946 drew an incredible 90 million paid admissions per week. From the very beginning, TV cut into this rich market. People stayed home to watch the little screen. By 1950 some 5,000 theaters had been turned into bowling alleys and supermarkets or simply stood dark, while the number of paid admissions had fallen by half.

As the decade progressed, business became even worse. Studios terminated the contracts of their stars and rented their facilities to independent producers or sold the land to real-estate developers. In 1960 only fourteen feature films were made by studios. The rest were turned out by independents or by filmmakers in Europe and elsewhere.

To compete with the little screen in the living room, movie makers concentrated on color and spectacle. Elaborate musical numbers, panoramic battle sequences, and numbing special effects were commonplace. Along with color and stereophonic sound, several wide-screen techniques were used to make movies seem more realistic. There was even a brief revival of three-dimensional films for which the audience had to wear cardboard eyeglasses with polarized lenses. Nothing helped, however. By 1960 only 27 percent of the population over five years of age was going to the movies each week, down from 70 percent in 1946.

One result was that motion pictures were no longer a national unifying force. Once, they had appealed to all ages and classes. Now the motion picture market was fragmented. Films were made to appeal to special markets such as young children, teen-agers, adults, or science fiction fans. Their subject matter and stars varied. So did the values they presented.

The Beat Goes On in Folk and Rock

In popular music, the 1950's brought a change as radical as jazz had been more than a generation earlier. Jazz musicians had turned to progressive

Guided Practice

Ask students to identify the types of television shows that are currently most popular and to discuss what such shows tell us about our times. (Possible responses: some demonstrate our interest in violence; many show women and minorities in a more realistic light than they did previously; television shows collectively reflect changing attitudes and values.) Have students relate current popular shows to the main draws of the 1950's. (Possible responses: shows in the fifties were more lighthearted; television served as an escape from reality, not as a means to confront it.)

Assign Independent Practice

Have students complete Chapter 31, Section 2 Enrichment Activity.

Student Assignment/Homework

Have students read Section 3, "Minorities Make Some Progress," and complete Chapter 31, Section 3 Enrichment Activity.

SECTION 2 REVIEW

Answers

Main Ideas

1. Fads inspired by television programs.

2. It regulated interstate communications and issued operating licenses.

3. Radio broadcast less drama and more news and music. Movies dropped in popularity and became directed at special markets.

Critical Thinking

4. Possible answers: positive—TV can be informative and educational. Negative—it can discourage conversation, reading, imagination, and exercise. **(evaluation)**

Picturing History To compete with TV, the movie industry came up with 3-D films and gave audiences polarized glasses to view them. It was a short-lived fad.

jazz; that is, they played a complex and sophisticated style that was best appreciated in concert or on records. It was no longer suitable for dancing.

In 1954 a black singing group called the Chords wrote a hit tune entitled "Sh-Boom." The next year performer Bill Haley and his band, the Comets, recorded "Rock Around the Clock." Each record combined the musical styles of country-western, black rhythm and blues, and black gospel singing.

Country-western music is folk music that is usually played on guitars, fiddles, and harmonicas; its songs often deal with love, crime, and prison

Picturing History Elvis Presley electrified millions of teen-agers when he sang and played the mix of rhythm 'n blues and country ballads called rock 'n roll.

life. Rhythm and blues stresses saxophone solos. Gospel music evolved out of plantation work songs and Protestant church hymns.

The powerful beat, simple lyrics, and deafening volume of the new music appealed to young people. Disc jockey Alan Freed coined the term **rock and roll** to describe it. In 1956 it became the ideal music of American teen-agers. Its star was a young country-blues singer and former truck driver from Memphis, Tennessee, named **Elvis Presley.** In short order, his long-playing records and such singles as "Heartbreak Hotel," "Hound Dog," and "Love Me Tender" were selling in the millions. His vocal style and way of moving, which was initially permitted to be televised from the waist up only, were widely imitated.

Linking Past to Present

Although Americans have always enjoyed a variety of music, since the 1950's, folk and rock have had the widest appeal—especially among young people. Throughout the 1980's, musical oldies grew in popularity, and many performers of the fifties, such as Fats Domino and Chuck Berry, continued playing songs that have become rock-and-roll classics.

SECTION 2 REVIEW

Key Terms and People

Explain the significance of: Federal Communications Commission (FCC), rock and roll, Elvis Presley

Main Ideas

1. What trend of the 1950's resulted in millions of children wearing coonskin caps?
2. What authority did the Federal Communications Commission have over the television industry?
3. What effect did television have on the radio and movie industries?

Critical Thinking

4. Do you think the instant popularity of television in the 1950's has had a positive or negative effect on American culture? Explain.

Anticipate the Lesson

Discuss the meaning of the term *minority consciousness*. (Possible response: awareness of the culture and heritage of minority groups.) Ask students what elements might contribute to a growing minority consciousness. (Possible responses: increased education and social awareness; migration of minority groups, resulting in integrated neighborhoods; acceptance of minority workers during wartime.)

SECTION 3

Minorities Make Some Progress

GLOSSARY TERMS: **civil disobedience,** *Brown* v. *Board of Education,* **Little Rock crisis, Southern Christian Leadership Conference (SCLC), Chicano, migrant workers, bracero, termination policy, relocation program**

The years after World War II saw considerable progress in the continuing struggle to end racial discrimination throughout the United States. Some of the progress resulted from court action, some from the political technique of **civil disobedience.** Civil disobedience is the purposeful breaking of the law as part of an organized effort to get the law changed.

Americans Try to End Discrimination

Beginning with the mid-1930's, the NAACP (page 620) had concentrated its limited resources on winning equal educational opportunities for black Americans. By the mid-1950's, the effort resulted in a precedent-shattering decision by the Supreme Court.

Early Cases. The first significant challenge to the "separate but equal" doctrine established by *Plessy* v. *Ferguson* (1896) occurred in 1938. Lloyd Gaines, an African American, wanted to study law at the University of Missouri. Since the state did not have a law school for black students, it offered to pay Gaines's tuition at a Canadian school. Gaines sued. The Supreme Court held that since Gaines expected to practice law in Missouri, he was entitled to receive his legal training there. If Missouri did not have a black law school, then it would have to admit Gaines to the all-white state university. By the time this case was decided, Lloyd Gaines could not be found.

Over the next fifteen years, the Supreme Court heard several similar cases. In each instance it held that unless facilities were in fact equal, black students had to be admitted to all-white schools. A typical case was *Sweatt* v. *Painter* (1950). Texas had organized a separate law school for a single black applicant, Herman N. Sweatt. Sweatt refused to attend on the grounds that the school was inferior. The Court agreed, and Sweatt was finally enrolled at the University of Texas Law School. In

another decision handed down the same day, the Court ruled (in *McLaurin* v. *Oklahoma State Regents*) that a black student admitted to a state university could not be compelled to sit, study, or eat apart from other students.

The Brown Case. All this legal action was a rehearsal for the 1954 decision in the case of *Brown et al.* v. *Board of Education of Topeka* (Kansas). The case applied not to graduate schools but to the more sensitive area of elementary and secondary education.

Oliver Brown, a black resident of Topeka, brought legal action against the school board on behalf of his eight-year-old daughter Linda. She had been denied admission to the all-white elementary school a few blocks from her house. Instead, she had to cross a railroad yard and then take a bus for twenty-one blocks to an all-black school. The attorney for the NAACP, which represented Brown, was **Thurgood Marshall,** who later became the first black Supreme Court justice.

The case was not a simple one. Decades of law and custom, as well as the tradition of states' rights, stood on one side. On the other side was the argument that segregating students on the basis of race denied them the equal protection of the law guaranteed by the Fourteenth Amendment. For the first time, the Supreme Court accepted psychological evidence in hearing a case. Leading psychologists submitted studies showing the effects of segregation on black children.

Picturing History
Linda Brown.

A Unanimous Decision. The Supreme Court handed down its decision on May 17, 1954. The opinion was delivered by Chief Justice **Earl Warren.** He was a recent appointee to the Court, having been active in California politics most of his life. He had served as attorney general and governor and was the Republican candidate for Vice-President in 1948.

On the board write the following names: Lloyd Gaines, Linda Brown, Thurgood Marshall, Earl Warren, Orval Faubus, Dwight Eisenhower, Rosa Parks, Martin Luther King, Jr., Ignacio Lopez. Have students identify each person and briefly summarize his or her role in the civil rights issues of the 1950's. Responses might include: Lloyd Gaines—black applicant to law school at the University of Missouri; won his suit against U. of M.; the court held that if a black law school did not exist, Gaines should be admitted to the white law school.

Linda Brown—eight-year old student in To-peka, Kansas; was denied admission to a white school near her home, but the court declared that "separate but equal" has no place in education.

Thurgood Marshall—attorney for NAACP; represented Brown in her lawsuit and later became the first black Supreme Court justice.

Earl Warren—Chief Justice of the U.S.; delivered opinion in Brown lawsuit.

Orval Faubus—Governor of Arkansas; tried to block integration of Central High School, Little Rock.

Dwight Eisenhower—President; sent federal troops to Little Rock to ensure school desegregation.

Rosa Parks—seamstress, Montgomery, Alabama; triggered a boycott of Montgomery's bus line when she refused to move to the back of a bus.

Martin Luther King, Jr.—minister; believed in nonviolent protest against injustice; led the protest in Montgomery.

Ignacio Lopez—Mexican American worker; founded the Unity League of California to register Mexican American voters and promote candidates who would represent them.

Read and discuss Chapter 31, Section 3 Daily Activity with the class.

The Court's opinion was unanimous. Also, it is worth noting that three of the Justices—Hugo L. Black of Alabama, Tom C. Clark of Texas, and Stanley F. Reed of Kentucky—were Southerners. As stated by Justice Warren, the Court held that:

> To separate [black children] from others of similar age and qualifications solely because of their race generates a feeling of inferiority as to their status in the community that may affect their hearts and minds in a way never to be undone. . . . We conclude that in the field of public education the doctrine of "separate but equal" has no place. Separate educational facilities are inherently unequal.

In other words, public schools should be integrated.

Reaction to the Decision. *Brown* v. *Board of Education* affected 12 million children. It has been called the most important event in black history since the Thirteenth Amendment. African Americans throughout the nation greeted it with joy and hope. White Southerners were less happy. Public officials in the border states announced that they would go along with the decision. In Virginia and in the states of the Deep South, however, negative feelings were much stronger. The legal doctrine of state interposition, another name for John C. Calhoun's nullification, was proposed by Senator Harry Byrd of Virginia. Other members of Congress brought forth a manifesto declaring the Brown decision an abuse of judicial power. In Mississippi, white citizens councils vowed total resistance. The Ku Klux Klan rose again, and the sale of small arms increased. Virginia passed laws permitting state financing of private schools.

After the Brown decision, the Supreme Court waited a year to give school authorities a chance to evaluate the situation. Then the Court ordered them to make a "prompt and reasonable start" toward carrying out the decision with "all deliberate speed." School districts in the border states and in large cities throughout the South began admitting a few black students to all-white schools. Elsewhere, however, there was no change. In one instance, white resistance led to a major crisis.

Resisting School Integration. Governor Orval Faubus of Arkansas was seeking a third term. He faced several difficulties. The state had a two-term tradition, and the governor had offended various groups by raising taxes and by allowing utilities and railroads to increase their rates. He needed a strong campaign issue.

The city of Little Rock had carefully worked out a plan for integrating its schools over a seven-year period. In the fall of 1957, the plan called for nine black students to be enrolled with the two thousand white students in the city's Central High School. Suddenly, the night before classes were scheduled to begin, Governor Faubus called out the National Guard and stationed it around the school. The next day, soldiers with fixed bayonets turned the nine black youngsters away. Several days later, a federal court ordered the guardsmen removed. When the black students again tried to go to class, however, a white mob created so much turmoil that they were forced to leave.

Faced with a virtual revolt around the **Little Rock crisis,** President Eisenhower did not hesitate. As he told the nation, "Mob rule cannot be allowed to override the decisions of our courts." He promptly ordered one thousand paratroopers of the 101st Airborne Division into Little Rock to uphold

Picturing History Federal troops stand guard to protect black students as Little Rock Central High School in Little Rock, Arkansas, is integrated.

Picturing History Rosa Park's arrest for refusing to give up her bus seat to a white passenger sparked the Montgomery bus boycott. She became known as the mother of the civil rights movement.

the law. It was the first time since Reconstruction that the power of the federal government was used to protect African Americans in the South. Eisenhower also federalized the Arkansas National Guard, thus taking it out of the governor's control.

The nine black students were admitted to Central High School. Most of the federal troops were withdrawn in November, although a few remained until the end of the school year. In 1958 Governor Faubus, who had won his campaign for reelection, closed the school. After a legal battle, it reopened in 1959 with only three black students enrolled.

Integrated Public Facilities. Even before Little Rock had shown that the struggle for school integration would be long and difficult, African Americans in the South had begun using direct action rather than court cases to bring about change. The shift in tactics was triggered by a black woman in Montgomery, Alabama.

Rosa Parks. On December 1, 1955, seamstress **Rosa Parks** was returning home on a city bus. Tired after a long day's work, she was glad to find an unoccupied seat. A white passenger entered, and the bus driver ordered the seamstress to give up her seat, as the Montgomery law said she must. As Rosa Parks told it afterward, "For a long time I resented being treated a certain way because of my race. We had always been taught that America was the land of the free and the home of the brave and that we were all equals." So Rosa Parks said, "No." At the next bus stop, she was arrested and, later, fined ten dollars.

Within forty-eight hours, the black community of Montgomery had organized a one-day boycott of the city's bus line. It was a complete success, and it set black leaders to thinking. There were 25,000 black people in the city, and they made up about 75 percent of the bus company's customers. Suppose they refused to ride the buses until certain conditions were met, such as allowing black people to sit wherever they wanted, hiring black drivers for buses in black areas, and instructing white bus drivers to be polite to black passengers. If the bus company lost three-fourths of its customers, surely it would eventually be forced either to agree to the conditions or to go out of business.

Martin Luther King, Jr. At the head of the association formed to carry out the boycott was a twenty-six-year-old minister named **Martin Luther King, Jr.** Holder of a doctorate from Boston University, King preached a philosophy called soul force. It was based on the teachings of several people: (1) Henry David Thoreau (page 321), who believed that individuals should refuse to obey unjust laws and who had set an example by going to jail rather than pay taxes in support of an unjust war and slavery; (2) Mohandas K. Gandhi (gän' dē), who had helped his native country of India achieve independence through nonviolent resistance to the British; and (3) A. Philip Randolph, who had urged African Americans to organize mass demonstrations. (See page 744.)

King persuaded his fellow blacks to keep their protests entirely nonviolent. He told his followers,

Tell students that many cities are still trying to implement plans for more complete integration of schools. Ask students to discuss the difficulties that might arise in trying to integrate public schools and possible solutions to the problems. (Difficulties might include: parental resistance to integration; long bus rides to school; loss of sense of community when students don't attend neighborhood schools. Solutions might include: voluntary busing of children; a limit on the length of bus rides for children; more family involvement in school programs.)

For Discussion
What is the purpose of organizations such as the Southern Christian Leadership Conference? Are they always effective, or do they sometimes alienate whites? (Possible responses: they give African Americans a strong, united voice; some whites may feel alienated, whereas others will respond to an organized group.)

> This is not a tension between the Negroes and whites. This is only a conflict between justice and injustice. We are not trying to improve the whole of Montgomery. If we are arrested every day; if we are exploited every day; if we are triumphed over every day; let nobody pull you so low as to hate them.

King believed that most whites were basically decent and, when faced by love, would not allow injustice and brutality to continue.

The struggle in Montgomery was not easy. Negotiations between black leaders and the bus company broke down early. The boycott continued for more than a year as blacks walked, rode bicycles, or used a car pool that King had organized. Some whites supported the boycott by giving blacks rides or paying taxi fares for their black employees.

Then the Supreme Court handed down another opinion. It ruled that segregation in public transportation, as in public education, violated the Fourteenth Amendment and was unconstitutional. In December 1956, a little more than a year after Rosa Parks had refused to give up her seat, King boarded a Montgomery bus and sat down in the front. As he said later, "It was a great ride."

Hope for the Sixties. The **Montgomery bus boycott** was a bright spot in the civil rights movement. It produced an organization, a leader, and a technique. Additional groups, mostly church centered, sprang up and were brought together by King in the **Southern Christian Leadership Conference (SCLC).** This organization was to play a major role during the 1960's.

Also significant for the future was the Civil Rights Act of 1957. It was the first such act since Reconstruction, and it was passed only after a legislative struggle that included a Senate debate lasting sixty-three days. The act set up a Civil Rights Commission and gave the Justice Department the power to file suits on behalf of black citizens who were being denied the right to vote. Black voter registration in the South was 1.2 million in 1956, but it was estimated that throughout the region, at least 5 million African Americans were eligible to vote.

Mexican Americans Gain Greater Recognition

Another minority that began to develop a stronger political awareness during the 1950's was the Mexican American, or **Chicano.** Many Mexicans had become American citizens in the mid-1800's when the United States annexed the Southwest following the Mexican-American War. During and after World War I, large numbers of Mexicans crossed the border to work in the States. Most of them were either **migrant workers,** temporarily employed by the owners of orchards, vegetable farms, and cotton fields, or miners and railroad workers. Many came under a legal work contract as a result of the **bracero** (brə ser′ ō) program in which thousands of Mexicans were encouraged to enter the United States during World War II on a short-term basis. Many also crossed the Rio Grande without a passport. Regardless of how they came, Mexican Americans played a major role in the economic growth of the Southwest.

Picturing History Separate facilities, such as these drinking fountains, were common throughout the South. They reflected the second-class citizenship that most African Americans had to endure until the campaign for civil rights began to bring about change.

Have students write two paragraphs describing the methods used by African Americans, Chicanos, and American Indians to achieve their civil rights and then briefly comment on the effectiveness of each method. (Paragraphs might include: African Americans organized boycotts; they sued in court; they were effective in initiating civil rights legislation. Mexican-Americans organized groups to register voters and support candidates that would help them; they succeeded in outlawing segregated classes for Chicano children. American Indians were allowed to retain their tribal customs, values, and government, with the creation of the National Congress of American Indians; the termination policy resulted in an upset of the Indian way of life and was a failure.)

During World War II, many Mexican Americans served in the armed forces. When they returned to civilian life, they were determined to do something about the poor conditions under which they lived. Chicanos often suffered from discrimination in housing and wages. In addition, many were handicapped by a lack of job skills and an inability to speak English well. They wanted better opportunities to become well educated and to earn a living.

Mexican Americans were shocked into organized action by an insult to the family of Felix Longoria, a Mexican American war hero killed in the Philippines. The only undertaker in his hometown in Texas refused to let the Longoria family use his funeral home because they were Chicanos. The American G.I. Forum was organized to protest this and other injustices to Mexican American veterans.

Soon after, Ignacio Lopez founded the Unity League of California to register Mexican American voters and to promote candidates who would represent them. The league also succeeded in having segregated classes for Chicano children outlawed in the state. Similar voter registration groups were formed under various names in Arizona and in Texas.

American Indians Struggle to Survive

From the passage of the Dawes Act in 1887 until 1934, the policy of the federal government toward Indians was one of Americanization. This idea was as old as Jefferson's time. Indian tribes were officially abolished, and in 1924 all Indians were made citizens of the United States. (See Chapter 27.)

Reorganizing Indian Affairs. In 1934 the Indian Reorganization Act took several significant steps away from assimilation. On the economic level, Indian lands would no longer be broken up into individual farms but would belong to a tribe as a whole. On the cultural level, the number of boarding schools for Indian children was cut back. Instead, children could attend day schools on the reservations and, in some cases, even have Indian teachers. On the political level, Indian tribes were given permission to elect a tribal council to govern their reservation. One result of the government's new policy was a rapid growth in the Indian population.

In 1944 the National Congress of American Indians was established. The organization eventu-

Picturing History Cesar Chavez, marching here with Mexican-American farm workers, founded the National Farm Workers Association. Chavez reminded supporters of *huelga* (strike): "No union movement is worth the life of a single grower or his child or a single worker or his child."

ally grew to include some ninety tribes containing two-thirds of the nation's Indians.

The goals of the Congress were twofold. First, it wanted Indians to have the same civil rights white Americans had. Second, it wanted Indians on reservations to be allowed to retain their own customs and values, even if they were different from the customs and values of mainstream society. For example, Indians generally believe in cooperation rather than in competition. Also, no Indian language has a word for the concept of time. Thus, most Indians do not live by the clock the way most whites do.

During World War II, some sixty-five thousand Indians had left the reservations for military service and war work. As a result, they became very aware of anti-Indian discrimination. When the war ended, the family allotments and wages that the Indians had received for military service stopped. At the same time, the country's general prosperity led to greater pressure from non-Indians who wanted to get hold of tribal lands, primarily to explore them for mineral deposits.

The Termination Policy. In 1953 Congress again changed its Indian policy. The new approach was known as the **termination policy.** It was

Student Assignment/Homework

Have students read Section 4, "Crises Threaten International Peace," and complete Chapter 31, Section 4 Daily Activity.

Anticipate the Lesson

Review with students examples of cold war tensions between the U.S. and the Soviet Union. (See Chapter 30.) (Responses might include: Berlin blockade; Soviet occupation of Poland; formation of NATO and the Warsaw Pact; Soviet explosion of atomic bomb; fighting in Korea.)

State the Objective

Analyze the evidence of a continuing struggle between the two superpowers, the U.S. and the Soviet Union.

SECTION 3 REVIEW

Answers

Main Ideas

1. Unlike previous cases that interpreted the "separate but equal" rule, *Brown* abolished the rule. Because the *Brown* decision involved integration of elementary and secondary schools, it stood to affect the lives of many more people.

2. In Little Rock, Arkansas, the governor used the national guard to stop integration. Eisenhower used federal troops to enforce the court ruling.

3. Thoreau, Gandhi, and A. Philip Randolph. • To bring about change through nonviolent, mass protest.

4. To gain the same rights for Indians that whites had and to retain Indian customs on the reservations.

Critical Thinking

5. All three groups served in the armed forces, and afterward all struggled for acceptance and equality. **(synthesis)**

---

announced that the federal government would give up its responsibility for the Indian tribes as soon as possible. In other words, the reservation system would be discontinued, and tribal land would be distributed among individual Indians. In the meantime, tribal leaders would no longer have authority over civil and criminal cases on the reservations. That authority was given to the states. In line with the termination policy, the Bureau of Indian Affairs began a **relocation program,** to help Indians move to the city, and a job-training program to help them find work.

The termination policy was a failure. Although thousands of Indians left the reservations, they were often unable to find jobs in their new homes. Other Indians lost out when communally owned land was sold at too low a price. Federal medical and other assistance programs were abolished without anything to take their place. The number of Indians on state welfare rolls soared. Indians and whites alike protested vigorously, and in 1963 the termination policy was abandoned.

SECTION 3 REVIEW

Key Terms and People

Explain the significance of: civil disobedience, Thurgood Marshall, Earl Warren, *Brown* v. *Board of Education,* Little Rock crisis, Rosa Parks, Martin Luther King, Jr., Montgomery bus boycott, Southern Christian Leadership Conference (SCLC), Chicano, migrant workers, bracero, termination policy, relocation program

Main Ideas

1. Why was the case of *Brown* v. *Board of Education* more complex than cases involving African Americans entering law schools?
2. What major crisis arose from the Supreme Court's decision to integrate public schools?
3. On whose teachings did Martin Luther King, Jr., base his philosophy of civil protest? What was the nature of his philosophy?
4. What were the initial goals of the National Congress of American Indians?

Critical Thinking

5. How did many African Americans, Chicanos, and American Indians help the United States during World War II, and what common problem did they face afterwards?

SECTION 4

Crises Threaten International Peace

GLOSSARY TERMS: **massive retaliation, brinkmanship, Eisenhower Doctrine,** *Sputnik*

The 1950's ended on a note of doubt and uncertainty, much as they had begun. The cold war between the United States and the Soviet Union, in which each side tested the other without actually engaging in direct conflict, heated up and cooled down several times. A number of new concepts in foreign policy were enunciated. In addition, Americans became increasingly involved in a conflict in Indochina that, in the next decade, was to develop into a major war.

The Cold War Continues in Europe

Following the death of Joseph Stalin in 1953, there was a slight thaw in United States-Soviet relations. The Soviets recognized the West German republic, and peace treaties were concluded with Austria and Japan. Attempts to control the nuclear arms race, however, were unsuccessful. In 1955 a summit conference in Geneva, Switzerland, between American, British, French, and Soviet heads of government broke down over an old issue: the fact that the Soviets refused to allow aerial inspection of their factories.

Dulles and Massive Retaliation. Although the Republican party had denounced the heavy spending caused by Truman's policy of containing com-

Picturing History Dwight Eisenhower (second from left) represented the United States at the first cold-war summit in Geneva, Switzerland, in 1955.

Present the Lesson

Ask the students to reread the section and volunteer details for an outline showing the continuing struggle between the U.S. and the Soviet Union. Write the outline on the board.

I. Cold war continues in Europe.
   A. U.S.-Soviet relations thaw somewhat.
   B. Soviets recognize West German republic.
   C. Peace treaties conclude with Japan and Austria.
   D. Summit conference in Geneva breaks down.
      1. U.S., Great Britain, France, Soviet Union are involved.
      2. Soviets refuse to allow aerial inspection of their factories.

II. Dulles proposes massive retaliation.
   A. Secretary of State Dulles is staunch opponent of communism.
   B. Dulles proposes brinkmanship policy—discouraging aggression by threatening to use all U.S. force against aggressor nations.
   C. U.S. cuts back navy and army and stockpiles nuclear weapons.
   D. Opponents of Dulles point out that U.S. could no longer wage war for limited objectives.

III. Soviets invade Hungary.
   A. Students lead revolt in October 1956.
   B. Hungary denounces Warsaw Pact.
   C. Soviet forces smash uprising in November 1956
   D. Joseph Cardinal Mindszenty takes refuge in U.S. embassy.
   E. Thousands flee country.
   F. U.S. sends $20 million for food and medicine.
   G. U.S. protests invasion.

IV. U-2 shot down.

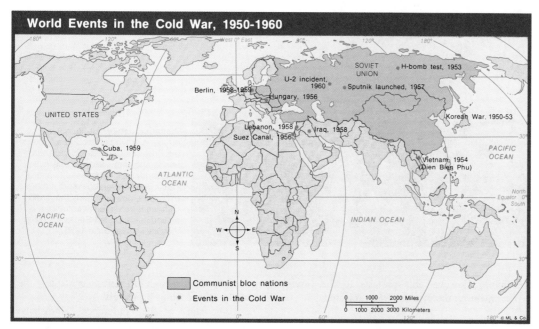

World Events in the Cold War, 1950–1960

SOVIET UNION

H-bomb test, 1953
U-2 incident, 1960
Sputnik launched, 1957
Berlin, 1958-1959
Hungary, 1956
UNITED STATES
Korean War, 1950-53
Lebanon, 1958
Iraq, 1958
Suez Canal, 1956
Cuba, 1959
PACIFIC OCEAN
ATLANTIC OCEAN
Vietnam, 1954 (Dien Bien Phu)
North Equator 0° South
PACIFIC OCEAN
INDIAN OCEAN

Communist bloc nations
Events in the Cold War

0   1000   2000 Miles
0 1000 2000 3000 Kilometers

© ML & Co.

Map Skills **Location** In what Western Hemisphere country did a cold war event occur?
Location How many trouble spots are in the Soviet Union? What are they?

munism, Eisenhower continued this policy after he was elected President. The only real difference was a shift in the defense policy. The army and navy would be downplayed, and the air force would be built up to deter communist aggression.

In line with his belief in a strong cabinet, Eisenhower gave most of the responsibility for foreign affairs to his Secretary of State, **John Foster Dulles.** Dulles was a staunch opponent of communism. He was also a rather rigid individual who viewed compromise as immoral.

Dulles proposed a new policy called **massive retaliation.** It said, in effect, that if the United States considered it necessary, it would not hesitate to use all of its force, including nuclear arms, against an aggressor nation. Going to the brink, or edge, of war with threats of massive retaliation in order to keep the peace became known as the policy of **brinkmanship.** Application of the policy meant greater dependence on nuclear weapons and less on conventional ground forces. Accordingly, in the mid-1950's, the United States cut back on its army and navy but built up its air force and began stockpiling nuclear weapons.

Opponents of massive retaliation pointed out that the United States would no longer be able to wage wars for limited objectives, as in Korea. Obviously, they said, no nation would risk nuclear war unless its existence was at stake. This proved true in 1956 when the Soviet Union attacked Hungary. In this case the United States took no military action.

The Soviets Invade Hungary. In October 1956 a revolt broke out in Hungary. (See the map above.) Spearheaded by students and other young people, it called for an end to Soviet control of that nation's government. The new Premier denounced the Warsaw Pact (see Chapter 30), and Soviet troops withdrew from Budapest. For a while it seemed as if the Hungarians had succeeded in freeing themselves.

In November, however, Soviet forces returned and smashed the uprising with tanks and artillery. Joseph Cardinal Mindszenty (mend shen'tē) took shelter in the American embassy, where he remained for more than fifteen years. Thousands of other refugees fled the country, many of them eventually coming to the United States. Eisenhower sent Hungary $20 million for food and

A. CIA operates secret high-altitude flights over Soviet territory.
B. Mission used U-2 planes, designed to fly higher than Soviet fighters and beyond the reach of antiaircraft fire.
C. On May 1, 1960, U-2 pilot Gary Francis Powers is shot down over Soviet territory.
D. U.S. issues false story about incident.
E. Soviet Premier Khrushchev announces capture of Powers and demands apology.
F. President Eisenhower takes full responsibility.

G. Powers is tried for espionage in U.S.S.R. and is later traded for a captured Soviet spy.
V. Suez Canal hits crisis.
    A. Great Britain withdraws from Suez Canal in 1954.
    B. Great Britain and U.S. agree to help finance Aswan Dam project in 1955.
    C. Egyptian government delays, hoping for better offer from Soviets.
    D. U.S. and Great Britain withdraw their offer in 1956.
    E. Egyptian terrorists begin raiding Israel.
    F. Great Britain, France, and Israel oc-

cupy canal area, Gaza Strip, and Sinai Peninsula in October 1956.
    G. Egyptians block all traffic through canal.
    H. U.S. asks UN to intervene.
    I. Soviets threaten to use nuclear weapons to aid Egypt.
    J. Crisis simmers down.
        1. British, French, and Israeli troops withdraw.
        2. UN sends in peace-keeping forces.
        3. In April 1957 Suez Canal reopens to traffic again.
        4. Eisenhower Doctrine is issued in 1957.

Picturing History Hungarian refugees arrive in New Jersey aboard the Presidential plane *Columbine*. Immigration laws allowed only five thousand visas to be issued each year. Eisenhower, however, made an exception, and over thirty thousand Hungarian refugees eventually settled in the United States following the Soviet invasion in 1956.

For Discussion
What problems might arise in negotiating a U.S.-Soviet disarmament agreement? (Possible responses: disagreement over the numbers and kinds of weapons each country can keep; disagreement over setting a schedule for inspection to make sure that the pact is kept by both countries.)

medicine. However, his protests to the Soviet government on the invasion were rejected.

A U-2 Is Shot Down. Following the failure of the 1955 summit conference at Geneva, the CIA began making secret high-altitude flights over Soviet territory. The plane used for these missions, the **U-2,** was designed to fly higher than Soviet fighter planes and beyond the reach of antiaircraft fire. As a U-2 passed over the U.S.S.R., its infrared cameras took detailed photographs of everything below.

On May 1, 1960, a U-2 flown by the American pilot Francis Gary Powers was shot down by the Soviets. The United States issued a false story that one of its planes had disappeared while on a weather mission over Turkey and might have strayed over the Soviet border. (See map on page 807.) Soviet Premier **Nikita Khrushchev** (krōōsh′chôf) then personally announced that the U-2 had been brought down thirteen hundred miles inside the Soviet Union by a Soviet rocket and that Powers had been captured "alive and kicking" and had confessed his activities.

It was a bad moment for the United States, especially since another summit conference on the arms race was to be held on May 15 in Paris. However, President Eisenhower regained credit for the nation by frankly owning up to the truth of the charge. In addition, the President took full personal responsibility for authorizing the flight. Such an admission was unprecedented for the head of a

government. Although all nations use spies, they usually do not admit it publicly.

At the start of the conference, Khrushchev insisted that it be postponed for six months and that the United States apologize for its past "aggressions" and punish the people who were responsible for them. Eisenhower, who had announced the suspension of further U-2 flights over Soviet territory, refused. The summit conference broke up.

Powers was tried for espionage and sentenced to ten years in a Soviet jail. After seventeen months, however, he was returned to the United States in exchange for a Soviet spy, Colonel Rudolf Abel, who had been convicted in an American court.

Picturing History
Soviet Premier Nikita Khrushchev addressed the United Nations in 1956 and heightened the cold war with his now-famous words, "Whether you like it or not, history is on our side. We will bury you."

The Cold War Spreads Eastward

The cold war showed itself in the Middle East as well as in Europe. The first major event had to do with developments in Egypt.

VI. *Sputnik* starts space race.
  A. Soviets launch *Sputnik* on October 4, 1957.
  B. U.S. reacts to launch.
    1. U.S. enters space race.
    2. U.S. places new emphasis on science, math, and foreign language in schools.
    3. U.S. expands National Science Foundation.
Have students refer to this outline as they study Section 4.

Check for Understanding

Have students answer Section 4 Review questions on paper.

Guided Practice

Tell students that the issues of military build-up and negotiations over arms limitations have been international ones for more than thirty years. In recent years the U.S. and the Soviet Union have made some arms-limitations agreements. Ask students how the recent breakup of the Soviet Union might affect the issue of arms limitation. (Possible responses:

The U.S. can speed up its own disarmament now that the Soviet Union is gone; the U.S. will now have to negotiate arms limitation with several nations, such as Russia and Ukraine, instead of one; the U.S. should maintain its arms to ensure its position as the only superpower.)

The Suez Canal Crisis. In 1954 Great Britain agreed to withdraw its troops from the area of the Suez Canal, which was owned mostly by British and French stockholders. (See map on page 807.) In 1955 Great Britain and the United States, eager to keep Soviet influence out of Egypt, agreed to help finance construction of the Aswan Dam on the Nile River. However, instead of signing the agreement, **Gamal Abdel Nasser,** head of the Egyptian government, delayed. Apparently he hoped to get better terms from the Soviet Union.

In July 1956 after seven months of waiting, the United States and Great Britain withdrew their offer. Furious at what he considered an insult to his nation, Nasser seized the Suez Canal. In the future, he said, canal tolls would not go to the European stockholders. Instead, they would be used to help build the Aswan Dam.

Now it was the turn of the British and the French to be furious, especially since two-thirds of the oil they needed for heat and industrial production came through the canal. In the meantime, the Egyptians had been making terrorist raids into Israel. Also, since 1950, contrary to international law, Egypt had not allowed Israeli ships to use the canal. For all these reasons, in October 1956 Great Britain, France, and Israel joined forces against Egypt. British and French troops occupied the canal area, while Israeli soldiers took over the Gaza Strip and the Sinai Peninsula.

The attack on Egypt shocked Eisenhower, who felt that there was no excuse for aggression, even by one's allies. The United States accordingly asked the United Nations to order both a cease-fire in Egypt and the withdrawal of British, French, and Israeli troops. However, when the Soviet Union threatened to use missiles against Britain and France, the United States warned that it would not tolerate such action. In November the United Nations ended the fighting.

Eventually the **Suez Canal crisis** simmered down. Britain and France withdrew their troops. So did Israel. The canal was reopened in April 1957 under Egyptian management. United Nations troops were sent into the area to help keep the peace, and traffic again began moving along the waterway.

The Eisenhower Doctrine. As a result of its support for Egypt, the prestige of the Soviet Union in the Middle East was now high. To counterbalance this, and as a reaction to events in Hun-

gary, President Eisenhower issued a warning in January 1957. In it he said that the United States would defend the Middle East against Soviet attack. This warning became known as the **Eisenhower Doctrine.**

In March Congress officially approved the doctrine. It gave the President authority to use American forces, at his discretion, against armed aggression in the Middle East from any nation "controlled by international communism."

Accordingly, in 1957 Eisenhower sent the Sixth Fleet to the eastern Mediterranean and in 1958 he dispatched fourteen thousand marines to Lebanon. In both cases the President was countering moves by Soviet-supported Syria.

In Indochina. The cold war was not limited to Europe and the Middle East. It showed up in Asia as well. There, however, the United States ran into a somewhat different problem: how to tell the difference between anticolonial nationalists and

Picturing History The Soviet Union's scientific triumph is featured on the cover of *Time* magazine as its "Man of the Year" issue for 1958. Premier Khrushchev wears a crown made to look like the Kremlin, the Soviet center of power, while he holds a replica of the *Sputnik* spacecraft.

Student Assignment/Homework

Have students complete the Chapter 31 Test on paper. Review the answers with the class.

Concluding the Chapter

Refer students to Section 3, "Minorities Make Some Progress." Ask them to carefully study the Supreme Court decisions on pages 801-802 and to identify the similarity in these decisions. (Response: they all called for desegregation.) Tell students that the Montgomery bus boycott began what became

known as affirmative action. Have students write a paragraph stating which they believe to be more effective in establishing civil rights, court action or affirmative action. (Paragraphs might include: court action is more effective because it has the power of law behind it; affirmative action is more effective because it often affects people economically, thus spurring immediate response.)

anticolonial communists. Both groups wanted to remove foreign control, a principle most Americans agreed with. However, questions remained: What sort of government was to replace the foreign power? How was the government to be chosen? These issues will be covered in Chapter 33, The Vietnam War.

Alaska and Hawaii. At the same time the cold war was spreading in Asia, the United States was expanding its borders in the Pacific. In 1959 President Eisenhower declared Alaska and Hawaii the forty-ninth and fiftieth states of the Union. These were the first states that did not share a common boundary with the others. Alaska, which is now the largest state in the Union, is closer to the Soviet Union than it is to the lower forty-eight states.

Sputnik Starts the Space Race

The cold war was not limited to geographical areas. It took place in scientific and scholastic areas, too.

The United States began 1957 confident that it was ahead of the Soviets in military technology. It had guided missiles that could deliver nuclear warheads with great accuracy at distances of fifteen hundred to three thousand miles. Then in August 1957, the Soviets announced that they had developed a rocket that was capable of firing over much greater distances, a true **ICBM,** intercontinental ballistic missile.

The real shock came on October 4, when the Soviets proved their claim. On that day they used one of the rockets to push the first unmanned space satellite to a point above the friction of the earth's atmosphere. There the satellite, the first *Sputnik,* traveled around the earth at a speed of eighteen thousand miles per hour, circling the globe every 96.2 minutes. Its weight of nearly 200 pounds indicated that 200,000 pounds of thrust had been used to lift it into orbit. That was more than enough force to deliver a nuclear warhead anywhere in the world.

The launching of *Sputnik* had an enormous effect on Americans. It led to a space race that landed two American astronauts on the moon in 1969. It also led to several changes in education. The study of science, mathematics, and foreign languages was upgraded as federal programs were adopted to improve teaching in these disciplines. The National Science Foundation was expanded and charged

with increasing the number and quality of scientists. Two results of this program were greater attention to basic research and a new physics curriculum for high schools.

Linking Past to Present

Urged on by the successful Soviet launching of *Sputnik,* the United States soared in science in the 1960's. Today, however, the nation is in danger of losing its technological edge. In an Educational Testing Service study of students in five countries and four Canadian provinces conducted in the late 1980's, American thirteen-year-olds ranked last in math and nearly last in science. In 1988 fewer than 1.5 percent of college freshmen said they planned to major in physics or chemistry, compared with 3 percent two decades earlier. It is feared that without increased funding and training for the sciences, the nation will suffer economically and will jeopardize its national security.

SECTION 4 REVIEW

Key Terms and People

Explain the significance of: John Foster Dulles, massive retaliation, brinkmanship, U-2, Nikita Khrushchev, Gamal Abdel Nasser, Suez Canal crisis, Eisenhower Doctrine, ICBM, *Sputnik*

Main Ideas

1. What effect did John Foster Dulles's policy of massive retaliation have on the defense system of the United States?
2. What American action contributed to the breakup of the Paris summit conference between the Soviets and Americans in 1960?
3. What factors contributed to the Suez Canal crisis?
4. Why was the Soviets' successful launch of a satellite into outer space threatening to Americans?

Critical Thinking

5. In what way did the cold war have a positive effect on the United States and the Soviet Union?

State the Objective

Understand how the shape of American cities
and suburbs developed.

Focus on Geography

Suburbia

The Geographic Theme of Movement

Today, the majority of Americans live in suburbs surrounding the nation's cities. The growth of the suburbs began in the mid-nineteenth century and resulted from many factors. The availability of the automobile was especially crucial because people who owned a car were no longer dependent on public transportation. The suburban movement accelerated during the 1950's (see page 794) and was fully developed by the 1970's.

Movement. The American population is spread unevenly across the fifty states. Resources are also scattered. As a result, there is constant movement between people and resources. Transportation networks have been created to help support this movement. Understanding and describing the movement of people, ideas, and goods is one of the five basic themes of geography.

Movement is motivated by two kinds of factors. The "pull factors" are those outside the environment that cause people to relocate. The "push factors" are those within the environment that cause people to move. Push and pull factors played important roles in the development of suburban areas.

Roots of Suburbia. The roots of suburbia can be traced back to Thomas Jefferson and a set of values

Picturing History Although they may have looked like the little boxes described in the popular song of the 1960's, the owners of the houses in this suburban development were happy to have homes they could afford.

Present the Lesson

On the board make two columns labeled Vehicles and Shape of Cities. Ask students to identify the kinds of vehicles mentioned in the feature. Write these in the first column. Then ask students to describe the relationship between each type of vehicle and the shape of cities. Add student responses to the chart on the board.

Vehicles	Shape of Cities
horsecar	3 miles from downtown area shaped like a circle to follow horsecar routes
streetcar	10 miles from downtown area star-shaped to follow streetcar routes
automobile	20-30 or more miles from downtown area "urban sprawl"

Ask students to identify the push and pull factors that originally caused people to move their residences from the city to the suburbs. (Possible responses: push factors—a complex, congested, disorderly inner-city life; warehouses; industry; poverty. Pull factors—reasonable prices; the rural ideal.)

and beliefs known as the rural ideal. In Jefferson's view, the most desirable life was to be found in small agrarian communities of equals governed for the good of all. The frontier spirit of the nineteenth century promoted this ideal by encouraging cooperation among families that were settling in the West. The rural ideal became an important pull factor that drew people out of the cities.

Another pull factor evolved in the early 1800's when land developers began promoting the sale of land on the outskirts of cities to individuals and to entrepreneurs. Because of the difference between the two groups' interests, the suburbs acquired both a positive and a negative image. On the one hand, the fringes of the city were considered an attractive retreat for the wealthy. On the other hand, because many warehouses, factories, inns, and places of entertainment were located there, the outskirts were often regarded as an undesirable location for raising families. As it turned out, however, locating industry in the suburbs in the early nineteenth century played a key role in suburban growth.

In addition to the lure of the rural ideal and the promotions of land developers, push factors also encouraged Americans to move to the suburbs. When people became overwhelmed by the growing disorder and complexity of urban life, they sought an escape. Inner-city problems became push factors that prompted people to seek the security and local identity that a suburb could offer.

Horsecar Suburbs. Prior to 1850, walking was the chief form of transportation around a city. By the mid-1800's, however, new developments in transportation—yet another pull factor—led to changes in the growth of the suburbs. About this time, horse-drawn streetcars were introduced. Although they traveled at a speed only slightly faster than that of walking, people liked using them. Homes and businesses developed along their routes, which were designed to go both around the city and toward the outlying areas. As a result, the land that was developed usually maintained a circular shape and fell within a three-mile radius of the downtown area. Once the fringe areas became accessible, they were known as the horsecar suburbs. It was in these horsecar suburbs that developers built new and better residences. When middle-class families moved to the horsecar suburbs, the population profile within the "walking" city changed. The city became the home of the poor and of recent immigrants.

Growth of Cities 1850 - 1910

Ribbon Development

Pedestrian City

Distance in Miles	2.5	3	3.5	4	8

	1880	1900
Crosstown Limits		
Ribbon Development		

By the late 1800's most large cities also had more distant suburbs, created by the newly built railroads. These suburbs attracted primarily affluent families since most people could not afford the high cost of outlying housing and train fares or the extra time spent in commuting.

Streetcar Suburbs. The major turning point in the development of suburbia occurred around 1887, when the first electric streetcar system was built in Richmond, Virginia. Electric streetcars could go three times as fast as horsecars. Now urban development could be extended as far as ten miles from the central city. As a result, cities began to expand their trolley, or streetcar, network. Trolley lines leading out of the city created a new area of middle-class streetcar suburbs.

Trolley lines affected the shape of cities. In time the central city assumed a star-shaped pattern. On both sides of the trolley tracks a strip of land was set aside for commercial use. Behind the businesses along the tracks lay the residential streets. In general, the homes along these streets were smaller copies of the upper-class homes found in the outlying suburbs. Beyond these residential areas were open spaces that could be used for parks and for small farms.

Picturing History   Cloverleaf highways, like the one in this 1950 picture taken at Hackensack, N.J., were built to help reduce traffic jams. Before long, however, these highways were also crowded with commuters.

Residential and Industrial Zones.   Gradually, the pattern of residential segregation described above resulted in a set of geographic zones. The inner zone was composed of a set of distinct ethnic neighborhoods. The second zone was composed of the former horsecar suburbs. This zone contained the relatively inexpensive homes of blue-collar or industrial workers who had moderate incomes. The third zone was composed of the middle-class streetcar suburbs, and the fourth and outermost zone contained the mansions and country clubs of the upper class.

Residential expansion led to industrial expansion. After 1890, industry moved into the suburbs for several reasons. Once suburban rail routes were established, businesses were no longer limited to downtown terminals. Manufacturers discovered that ideal production and distribution sites were also available in the suburbs. In addition, as the central business district expanded, a shortage of space occurred. Traffic became more congested. Land values and taxes rose. Entrepreneurs found it more profitable to move their businesses to the suburbs.

Recent Trends.   After World War II, many small shopping centers began to appear in the suburbs. Then around the late 1950's, developers began to build large regional shopping centers covering thirty acres or more in suburban areas. This type of

complex set the stage for the suburban malls that today cover hundreds of acres and perform most of the functions formerly associated with the central business district of the inner city.

Movement continues to play a significant role in the geography of urban America. New freeways have led to the development of suburban industrial and office parks. While most suburbanites used to commute to the city to work, many now have jobs in the suburbs. Reverse commuting, in which residents of cities travel to the suburbs to work, is also common. Some geographers have suggested that we are moving toward an urban civilization without great central cities but with more suburban mini-cities.

Understanding Geography

1. How does the geographic theme of movement relate to the development of suburbs in the United States?
2. How did the horsecar suburbs differ from the streetcar suburbs?
3. What were the residential zones that developed as people moved to the suburbs?

Critical Thinking

4. Analyze the push and pull factors that led the people in your family to their present location.

Answer Key

Key Terms and People

These are highlighted in the text in the order in which they appear in this list.

Main Ideas

1. Was the first mass-produced private home development; made suburban housing affordable.

2. Many people were able to afford and bought all the consumer goods that American industry could invent; many, like the beatniks, rejected such consumerism along with conformity and middle-class values.

3. Children watched TV for more hours than they spent in school; adults also spent many hours watching. • The movie industry declined; radio turned into a local institution with news, music, and community services.

4. Rock and roll and folk music became popular.

5. Public schools must be integrated. • Guarantees of the Fourteenth Amendment; negative psychological effects of segregation on black children.

6. Mexican Americans began to elect representatives, especially in California, Arizona, and Texas; termination policy to move American Indians off reservations failed. • National Congress of American Indians worked for civil rights, better schooling, and the right to keep tribal life styles.

7. That U.S. would defend Middle East against Soviet attack. • Prestige of the Soviets in Middle East; reaction to Soviet invasion of Hungary.

8. When U.S. and Britain withdrew their offer to help finance the Aswan Dam, Nasser seized the canal. In response, Britain, France, and Israel occupied the Gaza Strip and Sinai. • He asked the United Nations to order a cease-fire and withdrawal of British, French, and Israeli troops.

Critical Thinking Questions

9. Happiness at her job, at her first amiable black-white relationship, and with her child. • Language is positive, images are serene.

➤**10.** People had extra money to spend for the first time since the depression; a migration to the suburbs and a baby boom took place; television became a force in people's lives; schools and public transportation began to be integrated; the cold war went on; the space age began. • Possible answers: good—people lived better; there was no war; civil rights were improving. Bad—people were materialistic and conformist. Soviets moved ahead of U.S. in space race.

11. Decades of law and custom plus the tradition of states' rights had convinced the South that integration would never happen.

➤**12.** Civil disobedience (purposely breaking a law as part of an organized effort to get the law changed) and nonviolence. • Possible answer: these tactics required no special equipment or lengthy training and caused very little violence during the civil rights movement. • Henry David Thoreau, Mahatma Gandhi, A. Philip Randolph.

CHAPTER **31** REVIEW

Write your answers on a separate sheet of paper.

Key Terms and People

Explain the significance of: baby boom, Federal Communications Commission (FCC), Little Rock crisis, Southern Christian Leadership Conference (SCLC), Chicano, migrant workers, bracero, relocation program, Nikita Khrushchev, ICBM

Main Ideas

1. Why was Levittown a symbol of a new trend in the 1950's?
2. In what ways were both consumerism and beatniks typical of the life styles of the fifties?
3. How did television influence the leisure habits of the American public? How did it change radio and the film industry?
4. What changes in popular music took place in the fifties?
5. What was the substance of the 1954 Supreme Court decision *Brown* v. *Board of Education?* What influenced the justices' decision?
6. What were the situations of Mexican Americans and American Indians in the early 1950's? Did their situations improve during this decade?
7. What was the Eisenhower Doctrine? To what circumstances was it a response?
8. Why was there a crisis over the Suez Canal? What was the response of President Eisenhower?

Critical Thinking Questions

9. **Evaluating Literature.** What is Maya Angelou describing in the excerpt on page 793? How do you know?
10. **Evaluating Social Changes.** What major changes took place in the 1950's? Do you think they were good or bad for the country? Explain your answer.
11. **Forming a Hypothesis.** Why was the Supreme Court decision in *Brown* v. *Board of Education* such a shock to the Deep South?
12. **Evaluating Policies.** What techniques did Martin Luther King, Jr., use? What advantages were found in using these techniques? What other leaders have used these techniques?
13. **Analyzing a Policy.** Describe John Foster Dulles's policy of massive retaliation. Why was it called brinkmanship? Do you think this was good foreign policy? Why or why not?
14. **Evaluating Responses.** Why do you think Americans were so unprepared for *Sputnik?* What was its effect?
15. **Evaluating Decisions.** If you had been President when the U-2 was shot down by the Soviets, would you have admitted your responsibility for the flight, as Eisenhower did? Would you have stopped future U-2 flights? Why or why not?

Critical Thinking Activities

16. **Organizing Ideas.** Complete a chart like the one below to show the contributions of various public figures in the 1950's. Identify at least one accomplishment for each person.

Name	Accomplishment
Elvis Presley	
Jack Kerouac	
Earl Warren	
Rosa Parks	
Thurgood Marshall	

17. **Linking Past to Present.** Name some recent American space achievements. Compare one of these with *Sputnik*. Was the American achievement or the Soviet one more far reaching? Explain.
18. **Linking Past to Present.** The termination policy of the federal government toward American Indians was a failure. Find out the federal government's present policy toward this minority. Ask your librarian for help.

13. U.S. would not hesitate to use all its force against aggressor nation. • U.S. would go to the brink of war to prevent war. • Possible answer: yes—fear of nuclear war would deter aggression.

14. Americans had thought they were most technologically advanced. • U.S. began spending more on science and math education and on space research.

15. Possible answers: yes—

because Khrushchev knew the truth anyway. • Yes—if the U-2 could be shot down, there was no point in sending another.

Critical Thinking Activities

16. **Presley**—was considered best rock and roll singer; **Kerouac**—was well-known beatnik author; **Warren**—was Supreme Court Chief Justice who ruled on *Brown* v. *Board*

of Education; **Parks**—her arrest started Montgomery bus boycott; **Marshall**—was first black Supreme Court justice.

17. Moon landing; landing on Mars; interplanetary voyage of Voyager 2. • Possible answers: American moon landing was more complex. • American—it has led to further accomplishments in space, in medicine, in technology, and in science in general.

18. Federal policies resemble

those of the 1930's in which self-help was stressed.

➤ **Question suitable for co-operative learning.**

TELESCOPING THE TIMES: 1950–1960

Adjustments of the 1950's

During the 1950's, American suburbs expanded rapidly. Suburban developments such as Levittown offered inexpensive, standardized housing. Suburban sprawl depended upon and encouraged widespread use of the automobile. Suburban life encouraged conformity. Many suburbanites worked for corporations or government agencies. These people placed great value on education and were willing and able to pay for it. The beatniks of the period criticized the consumerism that came to dominate the lives of many people.

During this decade of peace and prosperity, Americans began to enjoy new forms of entertainment. Television came of age in the 1950's. By 1960 most American households owned at least one TV set. Individuals spent long hours watching their favorite variety shows, situation comedies, game shows, newscasts, sports shows, crime dramas, Westerns, and special shows for children. Visual quality was relatively poor until the introduction of videotape. Radio survived but concentrated on local programming. The movie industry was forced to compete with television. Popular music underwent a revolution with the advent of rock and roll.

Minorities made some progress during the 1950's. The NAACP won several court victories for equal rights in higher education, but its great triumph came in the Brown decision of 1954. The Supreme Court unanimously declared that racial segregation in the schools violated the Constitution. Many white Southerners vowed to resist the ruling. In Arkansas, Governor Faubus used troops to turn away black children from a Little Rock high school, but Eisenhower enforced the ruling with federal troops. A couple of years earlier, Rosa Parks had triggered the Montgomery bus boycott that was led by Martin Luther King, Jr. Mexican Americans and American Indians also began to demand their rights in the 1950's.

In foreign affairs, tensions increased as crises and technological developments abroad threatened international peace. In the continuing cold war, Secretary of State Dulles adopted a policy of massive retaliation. It proved unworkable in 1956, when the Soviets invaded Hungary, and again in 1960, when they shot down an American spy plane passing over the U.S.S.R. The cold war spread to the Middle East when the Suez Canal crisis erupted in 1956. The President denounced the invasion of Egypt by allies of the United States. In the Eisenhower Doctrine he warned the Soviets that the United States would defend the Middle East against foreign aggression. In the last few years of the decade, Hawaii and Alaska became states. Considerable attention was given to the Soviets' success with *Sputnik*. As a result, Americans placed greater emphasis on science, mathematics, and foreign languages in their schools.

Chronology of Main Events

1953 Termination policy begins for American Indians

1954 Supreme Court rules against public school segregation in *Brown* v. *Board of Education*

1955 Montgomery bus boycott

1956 Suez Canal crisis begins; Soviets crush Hungarian uprising

1957 Eisenhower Doctrine; Civil Rights Act

1959 Alaska and Hawaii become states

1960 U-2 incident

Telescoping the Times may be used as an alternative to having students read the entire chapter, as a chapter preview, or as a chapter review.

815

State the Objective

Learn about Japan's history as an economic and military power.

Present the Lesson

Divide the class into small groups to discuss Japanese culture, traditions, and government prior to World War I. (Discussions might include: Japanese culture stemmed from the Imperial Household, led by the emperor; *shoguns*, or generals, ruled in the name of the emperor; shoguns led armies from a warrior class called *samurai*; samurai had life-and-death power over the people beneath them. The Japanese closed their society to foreigners in 1620 because they thought foreigners were barbarians; after the Perry visits, progressive Japanese leaders wanted Japan to retain traditional values but also to learn Western ways to protect itself.) Have group leaders summarize the information for the class.

Ask students how the Japanese changed their traditions after the U.S. encouraged Japan to open up trade. (Possible responses: shoguns placed more faith in the emperor, resulting in a loss of influence in society; progressive Japanese became receptive to foreign influence; because China had been invaded by Western arms and methods and because Russians posed a threat to Japan, the Japanese decided they needed to learn Western ways for self-protection; Japan began a program of rapid modernization.)

Focus on Global Events

Japan—The Nation That Leaped into Modern Times

During the mid-1800's, Americans believed that competition was essential to a growing society. They also cherished the Western values of thrift, hard work, self-reliance, and individualism as keys to competence and success. However, a country that was geographically remote from the United States was experiencing astounding success based on a somewhat different cultural tradition, one that valued the primacy of the group over the individual and cooperation over competition. That country, which has now become one of the most successful economic competitors of the United States, was Japan.

A Closed Country. Little was known about Japan by the outside world until Marco Polo returned to Europe from his trip to China in 1295. He had heard about a country off the coast of China called *Cipango,* which means "land of the rising sun." The ruler of China, the great Kublai Khan, had tried to invade Japan in 1281, but had failed when a powerful typhoon destroyed his fleet. The Japanese called the typhoon *kamikaze* (kä' mi kä' zē), which means "divine wind."

Starting about 1550, the Japanese welcomed sailors, traders, and missionaries from Europe. However, the behavior of these "barbarians" appalled the Japanese. The sailors took advantage of their hospitality. The merchants cheated them. The missionaries were too rude in converting them. So in 1620 the Japanese shut their doors to foreigners. Only the Dutch and some Chinese, who were considered the least disgusting, were allowed to trade. They could use only one port, however— Nagasaki. It was through this tiny gate that Japan controlled its contact with the outside world for the next two hundred years.

Japan was a society of tradition and ceremony. Japanese intellectual Kuga Katsunan wrote that, unlike European culture, which "derived from the people," Japanese culture

derived from the Imperial Household. . . . A glance at history prior to the period of military rule is sufficient to show that ceremonies, religion, the family system, politics, agriculture, and crafts all emerged from the patronage of leadership of the Imperial Court.

At the top of the Imperial Household was the emperor, who was considered a god. A *shogun* (shō' gun'), or general, ruled in the emperor's name. Under the shogun were feudal lords. Each of these lords was served by a private army from a warrior class called *samurai* (sam' ə rī'). Samurai were totally obedient to their lord and, in turn, had complete power of life and death over the common people beneath them.

Knocking at the Door. During the first half of the 1800's, European nations and the United States tried unsuccessfully to establish relations with Japan. The commercial attractions were enormous. In 1852 a highly respected journal in the United States, *De Bow's Review,* predicted that in time American business owners would be doing an annual trade with Japan worth $200 million. There were also matters of national pride. Shipwrecked seamen, particularly those from the United States whaling fleet in the North Pacific, were treated as criminals by the Japanese. Perhaps most important, the United States now needed fueling stations in Japan for steamships engaged in trade with Asia.

The Perry Visits. President Millard Fillmore finally decided to try to force Japan to open up trade. He sent Commodore Matthew C. Perry, a younger brother of the hero of Lake Erie, to Japan with four battleships. On July 8, 1853, the Japanese watched with anxiety as the ships moved steadily up the Bay of Yedo (later Tokyo).

This visit marked the beginning of modern Japan. The shogun was so startled that he turned for the first time to the emperor for advice. From this time on, the emperor began to regain his importance and the shoguns to lose theirs. The more progressive of Japan's leaders wanted to negotiate with Perry. They knew that China had already been invaded by Western arms and methods. They also knew that Russia might soon attack

Ask students to locate on the atlas, in the back of the book, places where Japan had a stronghold just prior to World War II. (Answer: China, Korea, Taiwan, and several islands in the South Pacific.)

Ask students to write answers to questions at the end of the feature. Review the answers with the class.

Ask students whether Japan would hold the prominent position it does today as a leader in world trade if it had not opened trade with the U.S. and other countries in 1853. Why or why not?

(Possible answers: no—U.S. negotiations encouraging Tokyo to open trade resulted in a swift change as the Japanese hurried to adopt many Western ways; the modernization solidified their world trade position. Yes—because Japan was so tightly controlled by its leaders and government, the country had the capability of modernizing rapidly at almost any time in the 19th century; Japan would still be a powerful trading force today even if the modernization had taken place many years after Perry's visits.)

them with the latest military equipment and know-how. While these leaders wanted Japan to remain traditional in spirit and in values, they pointed out that Japan had better learn Western ways in order to protect itself.

On a second trip to Yedo in 1854, Perry persuaded the Japanese to sign a treaty opening some ports to United States and other foreign trade. Because of Perry's tact and dignity, the Japanese respected him. They even erected a large monument in his honor on the Bay of Yedo.

Learning New Ways. Almost overnight, under the leadership of the Emperor Meiji, Japan transformed itself from an isolated feudal country into a modern nation. Changes included setting up a system of compulsory school attendance, establishing a modern army and navy, and abolishing the samurai warrior class and the power of the feudal lords. The government actively encouraged mining, banking, and manufacturing and began a nationwide communication system. Many Japanese were sent abroad to learn the latest scientific and industrial techniques.

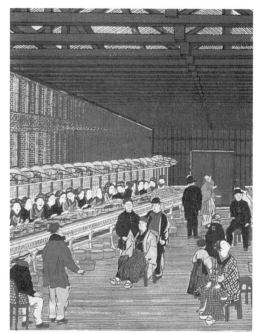

Picturing History During the Meiji period, the Japanese adopted Western textile processing methods. An early silk-reeling factory is shown here.

With this new knowledge came expansionism. From 1894 to 1895, Japan fought a war with China, at the end of which Japan obtained Korea and Taiwan. Then in a war with Russia (1904–1905), Japan destroyed the huge Russian fleet. The following year President Theodore Roosevelt persuaded a clearly defeated Russia to make peace with Japan.

In 1908 Japan signed a treaty with the United States agreeing to maintain the "territorial integrity" of China against the claims of any foreign power. In 1915, however, taking advantage of World War I, Japan made twenty-one demands on China, reducing that country to a virtual protectorate. At the end of World War I, Japan took over German holdings in China and the Marshall, Caroline, and Mariana islands in the Pacific.

A Sphere of Co-Prosperity. These successes encouraged Japanese military groups to take more serious steps. In 1931 Japanese troops quickly overran the Chinese province of Manchuria and set up a puppet government. The name of Manchuria was changed to Manchukuo.

The League of Nations condemned the Japanese action, but Japan simply left the league. Some historians believe that the occupation of Manchuria was the real start of World War II.

The militarists were now in firm control of the Japanese government. It became a military dictatorship, although always acting in the emperor's name as the old shoguns had done. The militarists organized the Greater East Asia Co-Prosperity Sphere with Japan as leader. This meant that Japan was extending its influence over all of eastern Asia. By 1938 Japan had won control of most of northern and central China and Canton in southern China. Japan was then ready to expand the sphere of east Asian co-prosperity by further conquests in World War II.

Understanding Global Events

1. Why did Japan close its borders to foreigners?
2. How did the visit of Commodore Perry to Japan affect the emperor's position?
3. What was the Greater East Asia Co-Prosperity Sphere?

Critical Thinking

4. What do you think was the secret of Japan's ability to modernize itself so quickly?

Answers

Understanding Global Events

1. Japan closed its borders to foreigners because European sailors, traders, and missionaries were dishonest and rude, and took advantage of the Japanese.
2. The visit of Commodore Perry to Japan affected the emperor's position by shifting political power toward him and away from the shoguns, or generals, who had previously held power.
3. The Greater East Asia Co-Prosperity Sphere was the name given to the system under which Japan tried to influence and control eastern Asia during the 1930's and 1940's.

Critical Thinking

4. Japan was able to modernize itself so quickly because the leaders feared the nation's survival was at stake, because the people have a strong sense of national purpose and unity, and because the program of modernization was pushed by a combination of government and business institutions. **(analysis)**

Key Terms and People

These are highlighted in the text in the order in which they appear in this list.

Main Ideas

1. In 1931 Japan invaded Manchuria, quit the League of Nations, and began to build up its navy. Mussolini invaded Ethiopia and annexed it to Italy in 1936; and Hitler pulled Germany out of the League of Nations and militarized the Rhineland.

2. The Nazis believed that Jews were inferior and the cause of Germany's current social, political, and economic problems. They felt that eliminating Jews would solve those problems.

3. The day after, the U.S. declared war on Japan. When Germany and Italy heard this, they declared war on the U.S.

4. Operation Torch drove Axis powers out of Africa; Soviets drove Germans back into Europe; Operation Overlord resulted in eastern and western Allies being able to meet in Germany.

5. Soviet refusal to hold free elections in eastern Europe; conflict with Soviet Union over Turkey and Greece; introduction of Marshall Plan; disputes over Berlin and Czechoslovakia that resulted in formation of NATO and Warsaw Pact.
• North Korea claimed the right to rule whole peninsula. China and Soviets were willing to back this claim.

6. Extended social security; set aside money for public housing; supervised labor-management relations; gave public utilities right to produce electricity from atomic energy; built highway system.

7. Americans bought homes in suburbs; relied on TV and cars; had big families; stressed education.

8. Hungary and East Germany, Middle East and Suez and Far East. • Dulles proposed the policy of massive retaliation with nuclear weapons.

Critical Thinking Skills

9. Aggressor nations simply left it. When the league branded Mussolini an aggressor, Great Britain and France would not agree to an embargo or boycott.

➤10. Possible answer: yes—U.S. moved toward war with lend-lease, draft, and sympathies toward Allies. No—isolationists in Congress and elsewhere were politically strong enough to keep the nation neutral unless the U.S. were attacked.

11. Possible answer: although at first the Allies saw no reason to go to war and had many reasons for not doing so, when their way of life was threatened, they banded together and fought.

➤12. Possible answer: Roosevelt might have tried harder to negotiate with the Soviets, although at Yalta he had learned to distrust Stalin.

13. Possible answer: they faced the hatred and fear of others to get what they were entitled to as Americans.

14. Winston Churchill, former Prime Minister of Great Britain.
• He meant that Stalin had drawn a line across the face of Europe behind which the Soviets would protect their empire from invasion. • In a speech at Fulton, Missouri, in March 1946.

UNIT 7 REVIEW

Write your answers on a separate sheet of paper.

Key Terms and People

Explain the significance of: sanctions, reciprocal trade agreements, Joseph Stalin, Charles de Gaulle, lend-lease, Nisei, V-E Day, Douglas MacArthur, Manhattan Project, Chiang Kai-shek, Nuremberg trials, Jackie Robinson, containment, Marshall Plan, Joseph McCarthy, Mao Zedong, Syngman Rhee, baby boom, Elvis Presley, civil disobedience, Thurgood Marshall, Martin Luther King, Jr., *Sputnik*

Main Ideas

1. What did military dictatorships in the early 1930's do that affected world peace?
2. Explain how the Nazi belief that Germans were superior led to the Holocaust.
3. Why did the Japanese attack on Pearl Harbor begin America's active participation in the Second World War?
4. In what ways did Operation Torch, the Soviet defense, and Operation Overlord cause the eventual defeat of Germany?
5. Explain the causes of the cold war. Why did it develop into a hot war in Korea?
6. What were some domestic policies of the Eisenhower administration?
7. What changes in American life styles took place in the 1950's?
8. Into what areas did the cold war spread? How did this affect the foreign policy of the United States?

Critical Thinking Questions

9. **Analyzing Consequences.** After World War I the League of Nations was formed to avert war. Why do you think the league failed to halt the aggressions of Germany, Italy, and Japan?
10. **Formulating a Hypothesis.** Do you think the United States would have joined the Allies in World War II if Japan had not attacked first?
11. **Predicting Effects.** Both Germany and Japan thought that the Western nations were too weak and divided to oppose the German and Japanese war machines. Why do you think the Allies were able to unite and to stop the Axis aggression?
12. **Drawing Inferences.** If President Roosevelt had lived out his term, how do you think cold war politics would have been different?
13. **Evaluating Sources.** How did the black students who participated in the integration of all-white schools like the one in Little Rock follow Harriet Tubman's example of courage and integrity?
14. **Analyzing a Quotation.** Who said: "A shadow has fallen upon the scene so lately lighted by the Allied victory. . . . An iron curtain has descended across the Continent"? What did he mean by it? Where and when did he say it?

Critical Thinking Activities

15. **Linking Past to Present.** Many historians believe that Neville Chamberlain's policy of appeasement led directly to World War II. Why are appeasement policies not used today?
16. **Linking Past to Present.** The Korean War was the first war that was covered by television. Scenes of the fighting were shown directly on home screens. Describe how television coverage can influence the public perception of current events.
17. **Linking Past to Present.** Write a short paragraph comparing today's entertainment scene with that of the 1950's. Discuss the fields of television, movies, and pop music.
18. **Linking Past to Present.** Ironically, Prime Minister Winston Churchill said he did not want the Atlantic Charter principle of self-determination for all peoples to be applied to the British Empire for, he said, he did not want to preside over the empire's liquidation. In your library find out who rules India, Burma, Kenya, Sri Lanka (Ceylon), Singapore, and Fiji today.

TELESCOPING THE TIMES: 1933–1960

World War II, Causes and Consequences

The Road to War

As the Great Depression deepened worldwide, dictators came to power in many European countries. Japan, Germany, and Italy began aggressive military actions against their neighbors. In eastern Asia, Japan invaded Manchuria and set up a puppet state there. In Europe, Hitler pulled Germany out of the League of Nations and began a secret arms buildup. In Africa, Mussolini attacked Ethiopia and made it an Italian colony. Hitler remilitarized the Rhineland, while Britain and France refused to risk a confrontation that might lead to war.

Roosevelt moved cautiously on the international scene. He gave diplomatic recognition to the Soviet Union and worked out a series of reciprocal trade agreements to counter the effects of high national tariffs. He continued and strengthened the Good Neighbor Policy toward Latin America, while Congress strongly supported a policy of isolation from the possibility of war.

Yet FDR grew increasingly alarmed about dictatorships and military aggression. When the Japanese invaded China in 1937, he moved to furnish help. He proposed a policy that would quarantine aggressor nations. By accepting Japan's apology for its attack on the *Panay,* the United States reaffirmed its neutrality.

In 1938 the crisis in Europe deepened when Hitler annexed Austria. Next Hitler demanded the Sudetenland of Czechoslovakia. France and Britain adopted a policy of appeasement at Munich, so German troops were permitted to take over all of Czechoslovakia.

At the same time Hitler was taking over Austria and Czechoslovakia, he was following a policy of violent persecution of German Jews. His Nuremberg Laws deprived them of many civil rights. Britain and the United States opened their doors to a limited number of Jewish refugees. However,

many fewer were allowed in than were seeking to escape persecution.

Hitler and Stalin astonished the world in August 1939 by announcing a nonaggression pact between Germany and the Soviet Union. Now Hitler felt free to attack Poland, and he launched a massive attack on September 1. Two days later France and Britain finally declared war on Nazi Germany. World War II had begun in Europe.

By 1940 Britain stood alone against Hitler despite massive bombing by the Germans. To maintain Britain, Roosevelt supplied the British with arms and destroyers. He pressed Congress to adopt the first peacetime military draft. After bringing several Republicans into his cabinet, he won an unprecedented third term as President. At this point he was able to give Britain "all aid short of war." The lend-lease program furnished even more supplies and weapons to the British. When Hitler attacked the Soviet Union in June 1941, Roosevelt extended lend-lease to it also. Although war had not been declared, German U-boats had begun sinking American ships in the Atlantic Ocean. That August, Congress narrowly voted to extend the draft, and Roosevelt and Churchill met to draw up war aims in a statement that became known as the Atlantic Charter.

The United States Declares War

On the Pacific front, the United States had broken several Japanese communication codes. American authorities knew about Japan's aggressive intentions but not precisely where and when an attack would come. Thus the carrier-based air assault on Pearl Harbor, on December 7, 1941, was a surprise to the Americans. Japan devastated the United States fleet in the Pacific. Roosevelt, in asking Congress for a declaration of war, called the date of the attack "a date which will live in infamy."

Hitler and Mussolini responded to the American declaration of war by themselves declaring war on the United States, so the nation was engaged in a global struggle.

Americans mobilized their armed forces and organized gigantic industrial and agricultural systems that proved incredibly productive. For the first time, women were enlisted in the armed services. African Americans also served in the armed forces as they had in previous wars. Although some Japanese Americans served in the army, most of them were uprooted from their Pacific coast homes and forced into relocation camps farther inland.

American civilians also made significant contributions to the war effort. Most American labor unions agreed not to strike during the war. The labor force was strengthened by employing women in war plants. American scientists contributed to the war effort—especially with the invention of the atomic bomb.

The major powers among the twenty-six nations that called themselves the Allies were the United States, Great Britain, and the Soviet Union. The Allies agreed to concentrate first on Europe and to demand unconditional surrender from the Axis powers, which included Germany, Italy, and Japan. A top priority was to win the battle of the Atlantic so that United States supplies and troops could cross the ocean safely. Soviets finally stopped the Nazi advance at Stalingrad and began to push the German army back toward Germany. British, French, and American forces liberated North Africa and then thrust northward through Italy. On D-Day—June 6, 1944—massed Allied forces landed on the beaches of northern France. Almost a year later—May 7, 1945—Germany finally surrendered.

On the Pacific front United States forces took part in a long and bloody series of naval and air engagements. After three and a half years of bloodshed, American pilots dropped atomic bombs on two Japanese cities, and Japan surrendered.

At wartime conferences attended by Allied leaders, Stalin insisted on Soviet dominance of eastern Europe. Germany was carved up among the major Allies. The United States occupied Japan. The United Nations was established, and this time the United States not only joined but was the first to accept the charter.

Franklin Roosevelt died in office just before the end of the war. Harry S Truman, his successor, was not well prepared for the Presidency, but he had a quick mind and was able to make tough decisions.

A Wartime Economy Converts to Peace

The end of the war led to a huge economic boom after the war. Americans went on a shopping spree for housing and consumer goods. With prices no longer under wartime controls, inflation became a serious problem. Unions went on strike when workers saw how little their paychecks would buy.

Truman was prolabor, but he adopted a tough line with the unions that went on strike in 1946. Public reaction was largely antilabor. That fall the Republicans captured control of the Senate and the House for the first time since 1930. The new Congress passed the Taft-Hartley Act over Truman's veto. Although the act weakened the powers of organized labor, it did not stop the growth of union membership.

Congress passed two other important acts in 1946. The Employment Act underlined the aim of full employment, production, and purchasing power. The second act set up a powerful tool, the Atomic Energy Commission, and placed it under civilian control.

Truman wanted to protect the civil rights of African Americans, but Congress did not act on his recommendations. He then issued an executive order to guarantee equal rights for members of the armed forces. Clearly, some Americans shared a new view about race relations. Despite the opposition of many players and fans, Jackie Robinson became the first black player in the major leagues.

In 1948 Truman won a major upset in a four-way race for the Presidency. Although some of his Fair Deal proposals over the next four years were turned down by Congress, those that passed extended FDR's social programs.

The Cold War Begins

A cold war developed in Europe, where, according to Churchill, the Soviet Union had established an "iron curtain." Under the Truman Doctrine, the United States sent foreign aid to Turkey and Greece in order to stop Communist expansion in those countries. The Marshall Plan provided American aid to Western Europe and enabled those nations to recover from the devastation of the war. The problem of a divided Germany came to a head when the Soviets blockaded the routes between Berlin and the three Western zones of Germany. The United States, Canada, and ten western nations formed a military alliance known as the North Atlantic Treaty Organization. The Soviets and their satellites countered with a military alliance called the Warsaw Pact.

At home, many people worried about communist spies. Some Americans believed the United States government had not gone far enough to prevent the possibility of a communist takeover. Senator Joseph McCarthy went on a vicious witch hunt that damaged innocent people. The vagueness and sweeping nature of his accusations directed at "disloyal" Americans eventually brought about his downfall.

Conflict in Korea

Communists took over China in 1949. Some Americans claimed that their government had "lost" China. When North Korean Communist forces invaded South Korea, the United Nations (led by the United States) decided to resist. After early defeats, UN and South Korean forces drove northward to the Chinese border. Then China entered the war and forced the UN troops back. A cease-fire agreement was finally reached in 1952. Korea was divided at the 38th parallel.

The 1950's in America

Dwight Eisenhower won the election of 1952 by promising to bring peace to Korea. That election campaign was the first to rely on television. The election results showed a breakdown in old voting patterns and a weakening of old party loyalties.

Eisenhower's dynamic conservatism continued many programs of the New Deal, but it also tried to cut back on the role of the federal government.

Peace, boom times, low inflation, a massive new highway program, and a popular President combined to give many Americans a sense that the nation was on the right track.

Peace and prosperity also contributed to the growth of American suburbs. Automobiles became necessities for many people. Suburbs tended to encourage conformity. As more people worked in white-collar jobs, suburbanites committed their money and children to education.

Racial minorities made more progress. The NAACP waged a long campaign in the courts that finally resulted in the unanimous Brown decision of 1954. This landmark decision said that segregated schools were unconstitutional. Martin Luther King, Jr., a new black leader, helped organize the Montgomery bus boycott. Mexican Americans and American Indians also showed signs of increasing consciousness about their rights.

Abroad, the policy of massive retaliation proved inadequate to deal with the Soviet invasion of Hungary or the U-2 incident. The Suez Canal crisis forced Americans to take a stand regarding problems in the Middle East. Americans welcomed the admission of the new states of Hawaii and Alaska. However, they were shocked by the Soviet success in space with *Sputnik I*, and they began to reconsider their educational system.

Chronology of Main Events	
1939–1945	World War II
1941	Japan attacks Pearl Harbor
1945	President Roosevelt dies; Harry S Truman succeeds to the Presidency
1947	Marshall Plan announced
1953	Dwight D. Eisenhower inaugurated President
1954	*Brown* v. *Board of Education of Topeka*
1959	Alaska and Hawaii become states

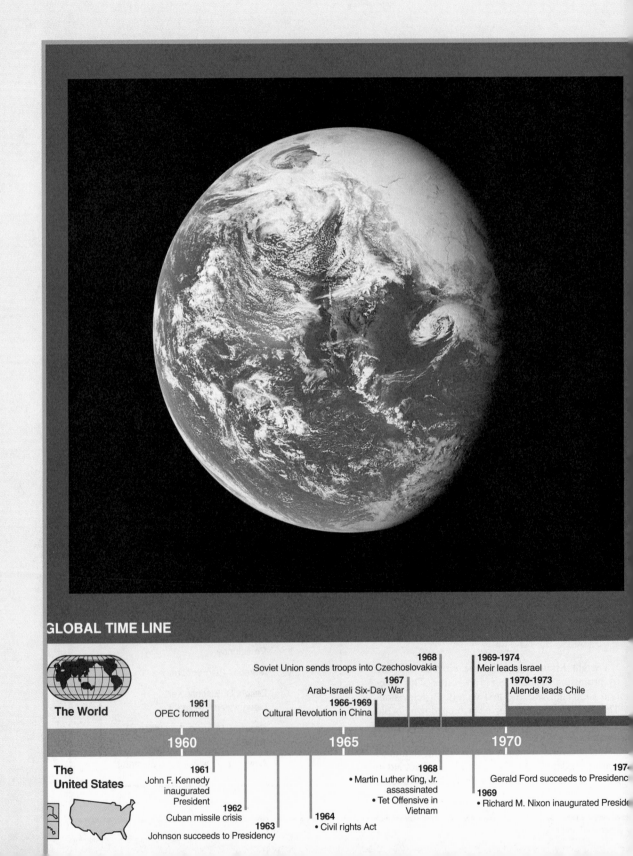

GLOBAL TIME LINE

The World

1961 OPEC formed	**1966-1969** Cultural Revolution in China	
	1967 Arab-Israeli Six-Day War	
	1968 Soviet Union sends troops into Czechoslovakia	**1969-1974** Meir leads Israel
		1970-1973 Allende leads Chile

1960   **1965**   **1970**

The United States

1961
John F. Kennedy
inaugurated
President

1962
Cuban missile crisis

1963
Johnson succeeds to Presidency

1964
• Civil rights Act

1968
• Martin Luther King, Jr.
assassinated
• Tet Offensive in
Vietnam

1969
• Richard M. Nixon inaugurated Preside

197
Gerald Ford succeeds to Presidenc

822

Research Assignment

Choose one foreign policy topic—such as involvement in Vietnam, aid to the contras in Nicaragua, Panama Canal Treaty, recognition of Communist China—and trace the effects of this policy on the United States. As an alternative, choose one domestic issue—such as civil rights, women's rights, environmental concern, the electronic society—and trace its development from 1960 to the present. Write a two-page paper summarizing your findings.

UNIT 8 1960–Today

Continuity and Change

Geographic Setting

Human-Environment Interaction. Opposite is a view of the earth taken from *Apollo 16* on April 16, 1972. The story of the Americans began with people who dared to venture away from their familiar environments and explore new territory. This story ends as Americans approach another century and venture away from the earth to explore beyond.

Unit Overview

The 1960's were a turbulent and violent decade in terms of civil rights and the war in Vietnam. A new foreign policy, including American withdrawal from Vietnam and improved relations with China, highlighted Richard Nixon's Presidency. However, the Watergate scandal forced Nixon to resign from office. President Gerald Ford then tried to reunite the nation, but he lost the 1976 election to Jimmy Carter. Carter faced both a staggering inflation and a crisis over the Iranian terrorists who took over the American embassy in Teheran. He lost the 1980 election to Ronald Reagan, who acted to control inflation and improve American-Soviet relations.

George Bush, elected President in 1988, struggled with growing domestic and international problems. Americans sought change, and elected Bill Clinton President in 1992. Clinton called for national renewal and challenged Americans to "a season of service."

Unit Outline

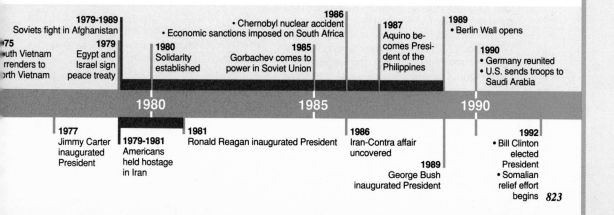

1979-1989 Soviets fight in Afghanistan

1986 • Chernobyl nuclear accident • Economic sanctions imposed on South Africa

1987 Aquino becomes President of the Philippines

1989 • Berlin Wall opens

75 uth Vietnam rrenders to orth Vietnam

1979 Egypt and Israel sign peace treaty

1980 Solidarity established

1985 Gorbachev comes to power in Soviet Union

1990 • Germany reunited • U.S. sends troops to Saudi Arabia

1980   **1985**   **1990**

1977 Jimmy Carter inaugurated President

1979-1981 Americans held hostage in Iran

1981 Ronald Reagan inaugurated President

1986 Iran-Contra affair uncovered

1989 George Bush inaugurated President

1992 • Bill Clinton elected President • Somalian relief effort begins

Global Perspectives

1961	Berlin Wall is built.
1961	South Africa becomes a republic.
1963	Soviet woman becomes the first female in space.
1963	French veto British entry into the European Common Market.
1964	Chinese conduct the first atomic bomb test.
1966	Indira Gandhi becomes Prime Minister of India.
1966-1969	Cultural Revolution takes place in China.
1968	Soviet Union invades Czechoslovakia.

For Discussion

Considering the U.S. stand on communist aggression, how do you think the U.S. might have reacted to the Soviet invasion of Czechoslovakia? (Possible response: although the U.S. is against the spread of communism, it might have been fearful of starting a nuclear war and therefore would have hesitated to take an official stand; it might have appealed to the UN or sent funds to those fighting the communists.)

Additional Resources

- Geography Activities
- Skills Activities
- Thematic Activities
- Economic Activities
- Cultural Literacy Activities
- Literary Source Readings
- Primary Source Readings
- Nuclear Peacekeeping
- Transparencies
- Computer Test Generator

Additional Teaching Strategies

SECTION 1

For Basic Students: Have students research and write a two- or three-paragraph report on John Maynard Keynes and his influence on President Kennedy. Have students share their reports. (Background information on Keynes might include: born 1883; died 1946; was an English journalist and financier best known for his revolutionary economic theories on causes of prolonged unemployment; recommended government-sponsored full employment.)

For Advanced Students: Have students work as a group to prepare a large chart listing Kennedy's cabinet members and their positions. Then have students work in pairs to prepare and present to the class an oral report on one of the cabinet members and his influence on the Kennedy administration. Charts should include:

• Vice-President	Lyndon B. Johnson
• Secretary of State	Dean Rusk
• Secretary of the Treasury	C. Douglas Dillon
• Secretary of Defense	Robert S. McNamara
• Attorney General	Robert F. Kennedy
• Postmaster General	J. Edward Day
	John A. Gronousky, Jr. (1963)
• Secretary of the Interior	Stewart L. Udall
• Secretary of Agriculture	Orville L. Freeman
• Secretary of Commerce	Luther H. Hodges
• Secretary of Labor	Arthur J. Goldberg
	W. Willard Wirtz (1962)
• Secretary of Health, Education, and Welfare	Anthony J. Celebrezze (1962)

(Reports on McNamara might include: was an important advisor on economic and foreign affairs as well as on military affairs; introduced systems of estimating military needs and costs ten to fifteen years into the future; served as president of the World Bank.)

SECTION 2

For Basic Students: Ask students to write a two-paragraph essay citing three contributions that Kennedy made toward easing tensions between East and West. (Paragraphs might include: installation of a hot line between the White House and the Kremlin; suspension of nuclear tests in the atmosphere; ratification of the Limited Test Ban Treaty; sale of surplus U.S. wheat to Soviet Union.)

For Advanced Students: Organize students into one or more small groups to further research and present oral group reports on one of the foreign crises Kennedy faced during his administration. (Report on Bay of Pigs invasion might include: took place on April 17, 1961; was CIA-financed; relied on untrained Cuban exiles; was a failure; caused Castro to denounce U.S. as an aggressor.)

SECTION 3

For Basic Students: Remind students that when Kennedy was shot an age of innocence passed in America. Additionally, his death meant that another champion of civil rights was dead. Have students work together to create a diagram on posterboard showing Kennedy's route in Dallas the day he was shot. It should show such important details as the location of the Texas School Book Depository. Have students display their diagram in the classroom.

For Advanced Students: Have students do further research on the assassination of President Kennedy. In group discussion have students debate the statement "The assassination of President Kennedy was a conspiracy and should be further investigated." (Discussion might include: opposing—an adequate amount of time and money has been spent without uncovering proof of a conspiracy, and no further investigations should be authorized: supporting—there was sufficient evidence to point to a conspiracy, and further investigation is necessary in the interest of national security.)

SECTION 4

For Basic Students: Have students use an encyclopedia to research and prepare a one-page report on the differences between President Lyndon Johnson and Senator Barry Goldwater. (Reports might include: Goldwater was a conservative Republican who favored private control of the TVA, voluntary Social Security, the elimination of the Limited Test Ban Treaty, and the use of nuclear weapons in the event of a crisis; Johnson was a moderate Democrat who favored government aid to the needy, civil rights reform, and treaties to prevent a nuclear war.) Have two or three students read their reports to the class.

For Advanced Students: Ask students to create a political cartoon that comments favorably on one of the groups mentioned in this section. Have students explain what ideals or events influenced their cartoons. Display the cartoons in the classroom.

Further Reading for Students

Emmens, Carol A. *An Album of the Sixties.* New York: Franklin Watts, 1981.

Johnson, Lyndon Baines. *The Vantage Point: Perspectives of the Presidency, 1963-1969.* New York: Holt, Rinehart and Winston, 1971.

Lynch, Dudley. *The President from Texas: Lyndon Baines Johnson.* New York: Crowell, 1975.

McKee, Don. *Martin Luther King, Jr.* New York: G. P. Putnam's Sons, 1969. (Easy)

O'Neill, William L. *Coming Apart: An Informal History of America in the 1960's.* New York: Times Books, 1974.

Bibliography for Teachers

Books

Banks, James A., and Cherry A. Banks. *March Toward Freedom: A History of Black Americans.* Belmont, Calif.: Pitman Learning, 1978.

Bornet, Vaughn D. *The Presidency of Lyndon B. Johnson.* Lawrence: University Press of Kansas, 1983.

Broderick, Francis, et al., eds. *Black Protest Thought in the Twentieth Century.* 2d ed. New York: Macmillan, 1971.

Bundy, McGeorge. *Choices About the Bomb in the First Fifty Years.* New York: Random House, 1989.

Cook, Fred J. *The Cuban Missile Crisis, October 1962: The U.S. and Russia Face a Nuclear Showdown.* New York: Franklin Watts, 1972.

Cooper, James L., and Sheila McIsaac Cooper. *The Roots of American Feminist Thought.* Boston: Allyn & Bacon, 1973.

Friedan, Betty. *The Feminine Mystique: Twentieth Anniversary Edition.* New York: W. W. Norton, 1983.

Oates, Stephen B. *Let the Trumpet Sound: The Life of Martin Luther King, Jr.* New York: Harper & Row, 1982.

Viorst, Milton. *Fire in the Streets: America in the Nineteen Sixties.* New York: Simon & Schuster, 1981.

Audio-Visuals

The Age of Kennedy. McGraw-Hill. Movie.

Air Pollution. Journal Films. Movie.

Cuba: Bay of Pigs. Encyclopaedia Britannica Educational Corp. Movie.

Cuba: The Missile Crisis. Encyclopaedia Britannica Educational Corp. Filmstrip.

Democracy in America: Civil Rights and Social Democracy. Encyclopaedia Britannica Educational Corp. Movie.

Freedom Now: The Turbulent Sixties. Eye Gate House. Filmstrip.

"I Have a Dream..." The Life of Martin Luther King. BFA Educational Media. Movie.

The Making of the President—1960. Xerox. Movie.

New Goals for Black Americans. Social Studies School Service. Filmstrip.

Surviving the Ecology Crisis. Society for Visual Education. Filmstrip.

War on Poverty: A Beginning. Encyclopaedia Britannica Educational Corp. Movie.

Computer Resources

Black Americans. (Apple) Social Studies School Service.

The Time Tunnel: American History 1920-1985. (Apple) Focus Media.

Teacher's Notes:

Lesson Plan

Teaching Resources, Unit 8 Booklet

Lesson Study Sheets pp. 1-16
Daily Activities pp. 17-24
Enrichment Activities pp. 25-32
Reteaching Activities pp. 33-40
Chapter Review p. 41
Chapter Mastery Tests pp. 43-54
Telescoping the Times Study Sheet p. 55

Chapter Objectives

Students will learn:
- the important events that surrounded the Presidential election of 1960 and the major domestic policies of the Kennedy administration
- how Kennedy dealt with the important problems of foreign policy during his term as President
- what progress was made in civil rights during the 1960's
- the nature and scope of President Johnson's domestic and foreign programs

Using the Chapter Time Line

How many years passed between the first women's rights convention (see Unit 3 Time Line) and the founding of the National Organization for Women? (Answer: 118)
What important legislation was passed by Congress during Johnson's first full term? (Answer: Medicare, Medicaid, and the Voting Rights Act)

Picturing History At the march on Washington, Martin Luther King, Jr., ended his "I have a dream" speech with the words from an old slave song: "'Free at last! Free at last! Thank God Almighty, we are free at last!'"

1960	1962	1964	1966	1968

1960
Black students begin sit-ins

1961
John F. Kennedy inaugurated President
Peace Corps established
Bay of Pigs invasion

1962
John Glenn circles globe
Cuban missile crisis

1963
Civil rights march on Washington
Kennedy assassinated, Lyndon Johnson succeeds to the Presidency

1964
Civil Rights Act passed

1965
Lyndon Johnson inaugurated to his first full term
Medicaid, Medicare, and Voting Rights Acts passed

1966
National Organization for Women founded

Joni Mitchell: singer, guitarist, pianist, song-writer, artist; born in Fort Mcleod, Alberta, Canada, on November 7, 1943; studied commercial art at the Alberta College of Art in Calgary; has created many original pieces of art for use on her album covers; worked as a lyrics writer for legendary jazz artist Charles Mingus; writes and performs in the folk-song style, with her own syncopation; has songwriting talents that many critics believe are equal to those of Bob Dylan in richness and profusion.

Works include: songs for Judy Collins, Buffy Sainte-Marie, and Tom Rush; many albums for which she wrote music and lyrics.

"Woodstock": is a song on Mitchell's third album, *Ladies of the Canyon* (1970), which achieved gold-record status; praises the idealism of youth.

Introducing the Chapter

Although students did not experience the 1960's firsthand, they are likely to have some very definite ideas about what this unique period of history was like, from hearing their parents reminisce and from popular television programs. Before studying this chapter, have the class spend about fifteen minutes brainstorming about their impressions of the 1960's. Write all responses on the board. As students study the chapter, refer them back to their list, and discuss the accuracy of their impressions.

CHAPTER 32 1960–1968

Leadership of the 1960's

Links to American Literature

I came upon a child of God; he was walking along the road
And I asked him, "Where are you going?"
This he told me: "I'm going on down to Yasgur's Farm,
Gonna join in a rock and roll band.
I'm gonna camp out on the land and try 'n' get my soul free."
We are stardust, we are golden
And we got to get ourselves back to the garden.
"Then can I walk beside you? I have come here to lose the smog
And I feel to be a cog in something turning.
Maybe it is just the time of year, or maybe it's the time of man.
I don't know who I am, but life is for learning."
We are stardust, we are golden
And we got to get ourselves back to the garden.
By the time we got to Woodstock we were half a million strong
And ev'rywhere was song and celebration.
And I dreamed I saw the bombers riding shotgun in the sky,
Turning into butterflies above our nation.
We are stardust, billion year old carbon
Caught in the devil's bargain
And we got to get ourselves back to the garden.

— JONI MITCHELL, *Woodstock*

The peaceful, carefree harmony that characterized the 1950's dissolved during the 1960's, as Americans came close to war and endured the assassination of a young President. The 1960's is characterized by its youth. Their frantic search for meaning is revealed in their music, as in "Woodstock."

Chapter Overview

In this chapter you will learn about John F. Kennedy's election and about the major domestic and foreign policies of his term. You will also learn about President Lyndon B. Johnson's programs and about the changes in American values that became evident during the 1960's. Students of history will recognize recurring themes: the conflicts between democratic principles and national security and between liberal and conservative movements. Chapter 32 is divided into four sections to describe the leadership that attempted to balance these conflicts.

Chapter Outline

1. **Kennedy Opens a New Frontier**
2. **The Nation Copes with Problems Abroad**
3. **Americans Make Progress and Face Tragedy**
4. **Johnson Tries to Build a Great Society**

825

Anticipate the Lesson

Discuss with students the events that pointed to a possible Democratic victory in 1960. (Events might include: registration of Democrats increased; Twenty-second Amendment barred a President from serving a third term; among voters there was a restlessness caused by unemployment and inflation.) Read and discuss Chapter 32, Section 1 Enrichment Activity with the students.

State the Objective

Understand the important events that surrounded the Presidential election of 1960 and the major domestic policies of the Kennedy administration.

SECTION 1

Kennedy Opens a New Frontier

GLOSSARY TERM: New Frontier

As the Eisenhower years drew to a close, it was clear that the Democrats stood a good chance of regaining the White House. Democratic voter registrations were up, while the popular Republican President was barred by the Twenty-second Amendment from running for a third term. There was also a restlessness among voters, caused in part by a combination of unemployment and inflation that began in 1957.

Contenders for the Democratic nomination included Senator Lyndon B. Johnson of Texas, the powerful majority leader, and Senator Hubert H. Humphrey of Minnesota, a leading legislator since 1948. Yet the prize went to a comparative unknown, Massachusetts Senator **John F. Kennedy**.

Kennedy Overcomes Drawbacks

Although Kennedy had served six years in the House of Representatives and eight years in the Senate, his record was undistinguished at best. Moreover, he had three major drawbacks: his age, his father, and his religious faith.

Kennedy was not quite forty-three years old. If successful, he would be the youngest President ever elected. Many people felt that he was too inexperienced to lead the greatest nation in the world.

Then there was the candidate's father, Joseph P. Kennedy, who had been FDR's ambassador to Great Britain from 1937 to 1940. "Old Joe" Kennedy had favored Neville Chamberlain's appeasement of Adolf Hitler and, after World War II broke out, letting England fend for itself. When the United States increased its aid to the Allies, the ambassador resigned.

Perhaps the most negative factor, however, was John Kennedy's faith. There was still considerable fear on the part of many Americans that having a Catholic in the White House would lead either to papal influence over American politics or to closer ties between church and state.

A Skillful Campaign. Kennedy's campaign for the nomination turned his drawbacks into assets. First, he presented his age as an advantage. His youthful vigor would, he said, help him withstand the long hours and heavy responsibilities of the Presidency. He would bring a fresh, imaginative approach to problems. "We stand today on the edge of a **New Frontier**," he said. It was "a frontier of unknown opportunities and perils—a frontier of unfulfilled hopes and threats."

Second, Kennedy received very effective support from his family. His father was one of the wealthiest people in America, and Kennedy's campaign was high-powered and heavily financed. In

---

People in the Chapter

John F. Kennedy said he was seeking the Presidency because "the pay is good and I can walk to work." After Kennedy became President, a small boy asked him how he had become a war hero. "It was absolutely involuntary," Kennedy replied. "They sank my boat."

John Glenn was so deeply affected by Kennedy's assassination that he resigned from the space program and entered politics. After two unsuccessful attempts, he won the Ohio senatorial election. He campaigned as "someone your children can look up to."

James Meredith was ambushed and shot in 1966 when he began a march around Mississippi to encourage the state's 450,000 unregis-

tered African Americans to use their voting rights. His march was taken up by other groups and was completed about three weeks later with a rally in Jackson. By that time Meredith had recovered enough to share the podium with Dr. Martin Luther King, Jr., and other civil rights leaders.

Rachel Carson set out to become a writer, but her love of nature prompted her to change her college major from English to biology. Eventually, she combined her two loves. Before writing her best seller, *Silent Spring*, she won a National Book Award for *The Sea Around Us*, which was later translated into thirty languages.

Picturing History Democratic Presidential candidate John F. Kennedy and his wife, Jacqueline.

addition, Kennedy's numerous sisters and brothers, as well as his mother—all good-looking and energetic—played an active role. The candidate's glamorous young wife, Jacqueline, accompanied him on the campaign trail and stood beside him as he delivered speeches.

Third, Kennedy quieted the fears of many people by discussing the religious issue openly. He believed in the separation of church and state, he said. If a conflict ever arose between his conscience and his office, Kennedy said, he would resign the Presidency.

The Television Debates. The Presidential race of 1960 was the closest since 1884. Kennedy defeated the Republican candidate, Vice-President **Richard M. Nixon,** by fewer than 119,000 votes out of more than 68,835,000. A shift of one vote in half

the nation's precincts would have changed the outcome.

A highlight of the race was the first televised debate ever between Presidential candidates. It took place on September 26 and was watched by 70 million people. Those who only heard it on radio or read it in the newspapers might have assumed that Nixon was the winner. However, the overwhelming majority of voters saw the debate on television. There, the way a candidate looks and speaks—the "TV image"—usually has more of an effect than what is said. Nixon lost the image battle. He had injured his knee early in the campaign and had spent time in the hospital. Then he had caught a severe cold. On the TV screen, he appeared gaunt and underweight. His face was set, and he perspired visibly under his pancake makeup. By contrast, Kennedy looked tanned, trim, and thoroughly at ease. Nixon's advantage of eight years of national executive experience evaporated into thin air.

A Stand for Civil Rights. A second major event of the 1960 campaign took place in October. Martin Luther King, Jr., and thirty-three other black demonstrators were arrested in an Atlanta department store for disturbing the peace by sitting at a lunch counter reserved for whites. Although the other demonstrators were released, King was sentenced to four months of hard labor.

When Nixon was asked by newspaper reporters what he thought about the matter, the Republican candidate replied that he had no opinion. Privately, though, he called the Justice Department and asked them to look into it. Nixon believed that the incident violated King's constitutional rights.

Picturing History
Presidential candidates John F. Kennedy (left) and Richard M. Nixon as they appeared during the second of three televised debates. Although Nixon improved his image somewhat after the first debate, he still lost the election.

827

Guided Practice

To stimulate discussion on problems associated with the influence of television on the election of a President, ask students the following questions. How much of the "real" person do Americans see? How much is the packaged "image" of the candidate, produced for television? (Possible responses: viewers usually see candidates at carefully orchestrated meetings and interviews; candidates rarely appear in public without a prepared text to read; TV commercials select only the most positive aspects of the candidate to portray to viewers.)

Eisenhower, however, refused to go along with an investigation, so nothing further was done.

The behavior of the Democratic candidate was different from that of his opponent. Hearing of the arrest and sentencing, Kennedy telephoned King's wife, Coretta, and offered his sympathy. Robert Kennedy, his brother and campaign manager, did more. He called the Georgia judge who had imposed the sentence on King and persuaded him to release the civil rights leader on bail, pending an appeal.

News of the incident electrified America's black community. They swung behind the Democratic ticket, and their votes were enough to carry the key states of Michigan and Illinois.

Linking Past to Present

Some historians have compared events in the life of John F. Kennedy to those in the life of Abraham Lincoln. The similarities are striking:

Lincoln	Kennedy
• Elected in 1860	• Elected in 1960
• Concerned with civil rights	• Concerned with civil rights
• Lost a son while President	• Lost a son while President
• His successor was a Democratic senator from the South named Andrew Johnson, born in 1808.	• His successor was a Democratic senator from the South named Lyndon Johnson, born in 1908.
• Lincoln's secretary, whose name was Kennedy, advised him not to go to the theater.	• Kennedy's secretary, whose name was Lincoln, advised him not to go to Dallas.
• Was shot in the back of the head in the presence of his wife	• Was shot in the back of the head in the presence of his wife
• Assassin John Wilkes Booth was born in the South.	• Assassin Lee Harvey Oswald was born in the South.
• Booth shot Lincoln in a theater and ran to a warehouse.	• Oswald shot Kennedy from a warehouse and ran to a theater.
• His assassin was shot before going to trial.	• His assassin was shot before going to trial.

Picturing History President Eisenhower's farewell address warned against the dangers of the "military-industrial complex," which became powerful during the cold war. As superpower tensions eased by the 1990's, however, many Americans became concerned about how cuts in military spending would affect the economy.

Eisenhower's Farewell. Before turning the White House over to Kennedy, Ike delivered a farewell speech that warned Americans about the rise of the "military-industrial complex." Eisenhower felt that this complex had assumed a dangerously dominant position in American life. He said:

> The [combination] of an immense military establishment and a . . . permanent armaments industry of vast proportions . . . is new in the American experience. The total influence—economic, political, even spiritual—is felt in every city, every state house, every office of the federal government. We recognize the . . . need for this development. Yet we must not fail to comprehend its grave implications. . . . The potential for the disastrous rise of misplaced power exists and will persist.

Presidential Election, 1960

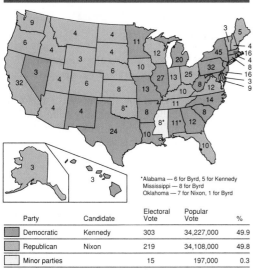

*Alabama — 6 for Byrd, 5 for Kennedy
Mississippi — 8 for Byrd
Oklahoma — 7 for Nixon, 1 for Byrd

Party	Candidate	Electoral Vote	Popular Vote	%
Democratic	Kennedy	303	34,227,000	49.9
Republican	Nixon	219	34,108,000	49.8
Minor parties		15	197,000	0.3

537 Total Electoral Vote

Economic Issues Need Attention

John F. Kennedy became the thirty-fifth President of the United States on a crisp and sparkling day in January 1961. Appearing without a coat in freezing weather, he gave the impressions of a man ready and determined to fight despite the elements. His inaugural address was zestful and upbeat, and it called for sacrifice.

> Let the word go forth . . . that the torch has been passed to a new generation of Americans . . . tempered by war, disciplined by a hard and bitter peace, proud of our ancient heritage. . . . Now the trumpet summons us again—not as a call to bear arms, though arms we need . . . but a call to bear the burden of a long twilight struggle year in and year out . . . a struggle against the common enemies of man: tyranny, poverty, disease, and war itself. . . . And so, my fellow Americans, ask not what your country can do for you—ask what you can do for your country.

Stimulating the Economy. Kennedy surrounded himself with a team of young intellectuals and business people, and began attacking various economic problems. In general, he followed the ideas of British economist **John Maynard Keynes**

(kānz). Keynes believed that a nation's economic growth depends on two things: (1) lowering taxes so as to leave companies and individuals with more money to invest and to spend and (2) increasing public spending. In other words, a nation's government should run a deficit, or spend more than it receives as income.

Accordingly, Congress raised the minimum wage to $1.25 an hour. Cities where unemployment was higher than 6 percent of the labor force received money for retraining workers and for public works projects. Tax benefits were offered to industries that agreed to build new plants in these depressed areas. In addition, the Trade Expansion Act of 1962 gave the President the power to raise or lower tariff rates 50 percent over a five-year period.

Other Kennedy spending proposals, however, were turned down by a combination of Republicans and conservative Democrats in Congress. These proposals included federal aid for public school construction and teachers' salaries, medical care for the aged, and grants to encourage the rebuilding of city slums.

Spending on Space. One area in which Kennedy had no trouble at all persuading Congress to spend money was the exploration of space. Specifically, what Kennedy wanted was to put a man on the moon before the end of the 1960's.

The reasons were psychological rather than economic or military. Although Soviet rockets were larger than American ones, United States weapons systems were far superior to Soviet systems. Yet the Soviets had achieved spectacular results in space. They had been first not only in putting an unmanned satellite into orbit around the Earth but also in sending a space probe to the moon and in orbiting Venus. The final blow to American prestige came in April 1961 when Soviet astronaut Yuri A. Gagarin soared 188 miles into the sky and circled the Earth in eighty-nine minutes.

So on May 25 Kennedy delivered a special message to Congress on "urgent national needs" in which he asked for some $9 billion over the next five years. The money was voted overwhelmingly, and work began immediately on launch facilities in Cape Canaveral, Florida, and on a mission control center in Houston.

The first payoff came in February 1962 when Colonel **John Glenn** orbited the Earth three times. By November 1963 the **National Aeronautics and Space Administration (NASA)** was ready to

Student Assignment/Homework

Have students complete Chapter 32, Section 1 Enrichment Activity and read Section 2, "The Nation Copes with Problems Abroad."

State the Objective

Understand how Kennedy dealt with the important problems of foreign policy during his term as President.

Anticipate the Lesson

Discuss Chapter 32, Section 1 Enrichment Activity with the students. To stimulate discussion, ask students how other nations might view a youthful President such as John Kennedy. (Possible responses: some nations might view him as an inexperienced, naive leader who can be intimidated; others might view him as a champion of new ideas and a real hope for the future.)

SECTION 1 REVIEW

Answers

Main Ideas

1. He was very young for a Presidential candidate, his father was an unpopular figure, and he was Catholic.

2. Although Kennedy's executive experience could not compare with Nixon's, Kennedy had a much better TV presence and consequently was seen as the winner in the televised debates.

3. Lower taxes and increased public spending, which together create a federal deficit and economic growth.

4. It was largely a matter of national pride, since the Soviets had already sent a man into space.

Critical Thinking

5. Their willingness to take action appeared to promise future support for the civil rights movement. **(synthesis)**

Picturing History The first seven astronauts chosen for Project Mercury, the first stage of a three-stage approach to the moon, were (front row, left to right) Walter M. Schirra, Jr., Donald K. Slayton, John H. Glenn, Jr., M. Scott Carpenter; (back row) Alan B. Shepard, Jr., Virgil I. Grissom, and L. Gordon Cooper, Jr.

launch the first Saturn rocket. Six years later NASA would win the space race by propelling Americans to the moon.

SECTION 1 REVIEW

Key Terms and People

Explain the significance of: John F. Kennedy, New Frontier, Richard M. Nixon, John Maynard Keynes, John Glenn, NASA

Main Ideas

1. What factors made John Kennedy an unlikely nominee for the Democratic candidacy?
2. How did television influence the nation in the 1960 Presidential election?
3. What were the two key elements of John Maynard Keynes's economic theory?
4. Why was Congress so enthusiastic about allocating funds for the space program when there was a greater need for the funds in education and social services in the United States?

Critical Thinking

5. During the Kennedy-Nixon campaign, Martin Luther King, Jr., was arrested and sentenced to four months of hard labor. Why did the attempts by John and Robert Kennedy to alleviate this situation have such a profound influence on black voters?

SECTION 2

The Nation Copes with Problems Abroad

GLOSSARY TERMS: Bay of Pigs invasion, Berlin Wall, Alliance for Progress

Despite intellectual and administrative qualifications of its members, the Kennedy team ran into serious problems in foreign affairs. In fact, its first major venture could not have had a worse ending.

Anxiety Mounts Over Cuba

Between 1933 and 1959, the island of Cuba was controlled by military dictator Fulgencio Batista (bä tē'stä). In 1956 a guerrilla movement led by law student **Fidel Castro** began a revolt against the Batista regime. In 1959, with the help of business people and landowners, the guerrillas succeeded in overthrowing Batista, and the Castro government was recognized by the United States.

Gradually, however, relations between the two nations deteriorated. First, Castro put on mass public trials and executions. The United States denounced Cuba in the United Nations and accepted thousands of Cuban refugees who poured into Florida. Castro then seized business properties owned by United States citizens. Eisenhower retaliated by cutting off imports of Cuban sugar. Castro responded by welcoming Soviet advisors. Finally, in January 1961 the United States broke diplomatic relations with Cuba.

Soon after his election, Kennedy was informed of a United States operation being planned against Castro. At secret bases in Guatemala, the Central Intelligence Agency (CIA) was training Cuban refugees for an invasion of their homeland. This invasion, it was hoped, would set off a general uprising of the Cuban people that would bring down the Castro regime. The idea had been approved by Eisenhower and was enthusiastically supported by the Joint Chiefs of Staff. Despite misgivings, Kennedy gave his consent for the plan to go ahead, insisting only that no American troops be involved.

On the night of April 17, 1961, some 1,400 Cuban exiles landed on the island's southern coast at *Bahia de Cochinos,* the Bay of Pigs. Nothing went right. Only 135 members of the invading

Present the Lesson

Have students locate on a wall map sites of foreign conflict during the Kennedy administration. Have them list on the board the important details of each. Locations and lists should include:

Cuba
- Rebellion is led by Fidel Castro.
- CIA fails in Bay of Pigs invasion on April 17, 1961.
- In the missile crisis of 1962, Kennedy orders a naval "quarantine" and is successful in convincing the Soviets to dismantle their Cuban missile bases.

Berlin
- Soviets order the U.S. to withdraw from Berlin, and Kennedy responds by asking Congress for an increase of 200,000 men in the armed forces.
- On August 13, 1961, the Soviets build a wall to divide Berlin.
- U.S. troops do not leave and Khrushchev backs down.

Have students read and discuss Chapter 32, Section 2 Enrichment Activity.

Check for Understanding

Call on individual students to answer Section 2 Review questions orally.

Picturing History Cuban dictator Fidel Castro surveys the wreckage of an American B-26, shot down during the Bay of Pigs invasion.

group were trained soldiers. The rest were over-age lawyers and other professionals, some of whom did not even know how to fire a rifle. An air strike carried out by aged World War II bombers the day before the invasion had failed to knock out the Cuban air force, although the CIA reported that it had. None of the ammunition and supply ships got through to the attacking force. A small group that was supposed to make a separate landing to distract Castro never got to shore. Perhaps most incredible of all, the chosen landing place was no longer a swampy, deserted section of shoreline. Since the Cuban refugees had last seen it, this land had been made into a public park with buildings, blazing lights, and paved access roads.

Castro's troops had no trouble surrounding the invaders and either killing them or taking them prisoner. Furthermore, there was no uprising in Cuba. Castro denounced the United States as an aggressor. Soon after the **Bay of Pigs invasion,** he declared that he was a Communist, and he signed trade agreements with various Warsaw Pact nations.

The Berlin Crisis Arises

The Bay of Pigs invasion was the first major crisis that occurred during the Kennedy administration. The second arose in the summer of 1961 over the issue of Berlin. Kennedy met at that time with Soviet Premier Nikita Khrushchev to discuss the situation in Berlin. For fifteen years, the Soviets had been unhappy with the presence of Allied troops in the city. They were also unhappy because economic conditions in West Berlin were so much

better than those in East Berlin. This situation made it difficult to convince people that communism was preferable to capitalism.

At the conference, the Soviet Premier said that unless Allied troops were withdrawn from Berlin, the Soviet Union would take "firm measures." Khrushchev apparently believed that after the Bay of Pigs disaster, the young President could be intimidated. Kennedy replied that the United States would not abandon the people of West Berlin. A month later he asked Congress for an increase of 200,000 men and women in the armed forces.

In the meantime, as many as 4,000 East Germans a day were moving into West Berlin. Shortly after midnight on August 13, Soviet tanks and East German police took up positions along the twenty-five-mile border separating the two parts of the city. Four days later a stone-and-concrete wall topped by barbed wire was constructed. Known as the **Berlin Wall,** it cut off the stream of refugees.

By fall, however, it was clear to Khrushchev that the United States would not back down on Berlin. So he extended the deadline for withdrawal indefinitely, and the Berlin crisis faded away.

Americans Face a Missile Crisis in Cuba

In the summer of 1962, a year after the crisis in Berlin, the CIA reported that the Soviet Union was up to something in Cuba. On October 16, photographs taken by U-2 flights showed sixty-five sites for offensive medium-range ballistic missiles. If installed, the missiles would be able to reach the most heavily populated two-thirds of the United States in less than three minutes.

Kennedy was anxious to avoid either of two extremes. One was making the kind of mistakes that had resulted in the Bay of Pigs fiasco. The other was setting off a chain of events that might end in nuclear war. At the same time, he had to force the Soviet Union into removing this threat to American security.

Kennedy ordered a naval blockade of the island. (He used the word *quarantine* rather than *blockade* since a blockade is considered an act of war.) Kennedy also warned that a missile attack from Cuba against any nation in the Western Hemisphere would be treated as if it were a Soviet attack against the United States. He told the Soviets to dismantle the missile bases. If they did not, he said, American planes would bomb them.

Meanwhile, a dozen Soviet ships carrying mis-

Guided Practice

Tell students that a number of Americans believe that the U.S. should take steps to repair relations with Cuba. Ask students what steps must be taken by each nation in order to achieve this end. (Possible responses: each nation must officially recognize the government of the other; both nations must set up a mutually beneficial trade agreement; they must send ambassadors to open embassies and officially reestablish diplomatic ties.)

Assign Independent Practice

Ask students to compare in a three-paragraph essay Kennedy's handling of the Cuban missile crisis with his management of the Berlin crisis. In the third paragraph of the essay, students should indicate what Kennedy learned about the Soviets from these encounters. (Essays might include: Cuban missile crisis—Kennedy was anxious to avoid the mistakes that ended in disaster at the Bay of Pigs; he hoped to avoid a chain of events that might lead to nuclear war; he ordered "quarantine;" he warned Cuba and the Soviets about missile attacks; he told the Soviets to dismantle the bases, or the

U.S. would bomb them. Berlin crisis—the U.S. refused to withdraw troops from Berlin. In both situations Kennedy showed strength and refused to back down. He learned that the Soviet Union wanted to avoid a major confrontation as much as the U.S. did.)

Map Skills

Berlin Wall • Poland

For Discussion

What was the attraction of organizations such as the Peace Corps? How did the Kennedy image encourage participation in such programs? (Possible response: organizations such as the Peace Corps appealed to people who felt that Americans had a moral obligation to help those not as fortunate; they appealed to young people who were unhappy with the materialistic world of their parents, to those who wanted to make a difference in the world; Kennedy himself appealed to many such young Americans.)

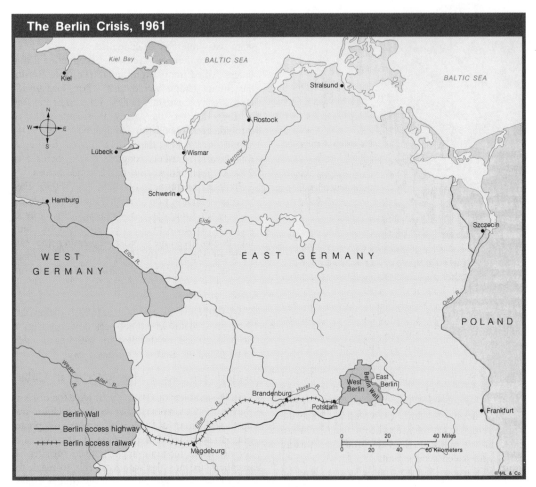

Map Skills **Place** What major barrier divided East Berlin from West Berlin in the early 1960's? **Location** What country lies to the east of East Germany?

siles steamed steadily toward Cuba. For almost a week, the world was on the brink of nuclear war. At one tense moment Kennedy said, "This is the week I earn my salary."

The President's firm stance worked. The Soviet ships turned back, and Soviet Premier Khrushchev agreed to dismantle the missile bases under United Nations supervision in exchange for a promise by the United States not to invade Cuba. As a result of the threat posed by the **Cuban missile crisis,** American military expenditures rose to $50 billion, the highest since the Korean War.

Trying to Ease Tensions. The Berlin crisis and the Cuban missile crisis intensified the cold war. In

1963, however, the United States took two steps to help ease tension between the superpowers.

In April of that year, the Soviets accepted an American proposal for a "hot line" between the White House and the Kremlin. This direct hookup would enable leaders of the two nations to communicate at once should another crisis arise.

In June, Kennedy announced that the United States was suspending nuclear tests in the atmosphere, and he invited other atomic powers to do the same. The next month, talks were held in Moscow with the British and the Soviets. The Limited Test Ban Treaty was completed that summer and ratified by the Senate in September. It called for an end to all nuclear tests in the ocean,

Student Assignment/Homework

Have students complete Chapter 32, Section 3 Daily Activity and read Section 3, "Americans Make Progress and Face Tragedy."

Picturing History "The responsibilities...are greater than I imagined them to be," Kennedy mused about the role of President.

the atmosphere, and outer space. By year's end, 113 other nations had signed the treaty.

In October, Kennedy approved the sale to the Soviet Union of $250 million worth of surplus wheat. He described the transaction as "one more hopeful sign that a more peaceful world is both possible and beneficial to all."

Programs for Peace Begin

Despite difficulties in relations with the Soviet Union and Cuba, Americans worked to promote peace abroad. Two New Frontier programs helped to improve foreign relations.

The Alliance for Progress. Back in March 1961, the President had proposed a plan of economic aid to Latin America modeled on the Marshall Plan. The **Alliance for Progress** was designed in part to prevent Castro from exporting his revolutionary ideas to other nations in the Western Hemisphere.

The Alliance called for spending $20 billion over a ten-year period. Part of this amount was to come from the United States and part from Latin America. The money was to be used to build schools, houses, and sanitation facilities. It was also to be used to reform tax laws, to break up large estates, and to give farm workers land of their own. In other words, aid was to be combined with reforms.

The United States invested almost $12 billion in Latin America under the Alliance for Progress between 1961 and 1969. Funds for the program were then cut back drastically, partly because of a domestic recession and partly because of the costs of the Vietnam War, which you will read about in Chapter 33.

The Peace Corps. More imaginative than the Alliance for Progress was the **Peace Corps** program established in March 1961. Peace Corps volunteers worked for two years in underdeveloped nations in Asia, Africa, and Latin America, getting just enough pay to sustain themselves. They served as agricultural advisors, teachers, or health aides, or did whatever work the host country needed. By 1968 there were thirty-five thousand Peace Corps volunteers in sixty countries around the world.

Picturing History An American Peace Corps volunteer teaching English in Lagos, Nigeria, in 1966.

SECTION 2 REVIEW

Key Terms and People

Explain the significance of: Fidel Castro, Bay of Pigs invasion, Berlin Wall, Cuban missile crisis, Alliance for Progress, Peace Corps

Main Ideas

1. How did the United States respond to the overthrow of the Batista dictatorship in Cuba?
2. What was the main goal of the Bay of Pigs invasion? Was it attained?
3. How did Kennedy convince the Soviets to abandon their plans to arm the Cuban missile sites?
4. What steps were taken in 1963 by the United States and the Soviet Union to improve relations between the two nations?

Critical Thinking

5. The Peace Corps and the Alliance for Progress had different geographical scopes. In what other fundamental way were they different? Which program's accomplishments could be expected to be more enduring and why?

Review with students Kennedy's reactions to the arrest of Dr. Martin Luther King, Jr., in October, 1960. (Responses: Kennedy phoned Mrs. King to offer sympathy; Robert Kennedy persuaded the judge who sentenced King to release him on bond.) To stimulate discussion, ask students the following questions. How does this action show Kennedy's stand on civil rights? (Possible responses: he would not have

phoned Mrs. King if he had not been sympathetic to the cause.) How can a President's personal feelings about an issue affect the nation? (Possible response: a President might lobby vigorously for legislation, veto legislation, or refuse to campaign for an issue, depending on his personal feelings; because of a President's high public profile, many Americans are influenced by the President's choices.)

SECTION 3

Americans Make Progress and Face Tragedy

GLOSSARY TERMS: **sit-in, Warren Commission**

The year 1963 was the hundredth anniversary of the Emancipation Proclamation. The centennial served to remind the nation of how much remained to be accomplished in order for black Americans to have full equality.

King and Kennedy Push for Civil Rights

In 1955 the civil rights movement had begun shifting from court cases to direct nonviolent action to bring about change. The shift grew stronger during the Kennedy years.

Sit-ins. On February 1, 1960, Joseph McNeill and three other black college students walked into an F. W. Woolworth store in Greensboro, North Carolina. After buying a few items, they sat down at the lunch counter and ordered coffee. Since the store was segregated, the management ignored them. The four remained at the counter until the store closed. The next morning they returned, this time with five more blacks. They sat quietly all day long, ignoring the white youths who taunted them. The next day they repeated the **sit-in,** and the day after that.

Within two weeks the movement had spread throughout the South, not just to Woolworth stores, but to other chain-store lunch counters as well. Outside the South, black and white sympathizers picketed chains whose Southern stores had segregated lunch counters. From there, demonstrators branched out to other segregated facilities. As one historian wrote,

> There were sleep-ins in motel lobbies, play-ins in parks, read-ins in public libraries, watch-ins in movie theaters, bet-ins in bingo halls, sweat-ins in Turkish baths, and, when spring approached, swim-ins on restricted beaches.

Within six months the lunch counter at the Woolworth store in Greensboro was desegregated. Hundreds of other facilities in the South were also.

Freedom Rides. In May 1961 another direct but nonviolent technique was used. It was sponsored by the **Congress of Racial Equality (CORE)** and was called a **freedom ride**. A group of blacks and whites rode buses throughout the Deep South to see whether the 1946 Supreme Court decision of *Morgan* v. *Virginia,* which outlawed segregation in interstate travel, was being obeyed. In Alabama, mobs beat many of the freedom riders and firebombed one of the buses. The local police did nothing. When additional violence threatened, Attorney General **Robert Kennedy** sent federal marshals into Montgomery. He then asked the Interstate Commerce Commission to order interstate trains, buses, airplanes, train depots, bus stations, and airports to be integrated. Within months, blacks could travel anywhere in the country without seeing White and Colored signs in waiting rooms.

The March on Washington. The nonviolent campaign for civil rights reached its climax on August 28, 1963. About 200,000 people, white and black, gathered in the nation's capital. What they wanted was federal civil rights legislation. The gathering was the largest such demonstration held in the United States up to that time.

The crowd heard Martin Luther King, Jr., deliver an inspiring and memorable address:

> I have a dream that one day this nation will rise up and live out the true meaning of its creed: "We hold these truths to be self-evident; that all men are created equal." I have a dream that one day on the red hills of Georgia, the sons of former slaves and the sons of former slaveowners will be able to sit together at the table of brotherhood. . . . I have a dream that my four little children will not be judged by the color of their skin but by the content of their character. I have a dream.

Unfortunately for Dr. King's dream, some white Southerners stiffened their resistance to civil rights.

Confrontations at Universities. In 1962 a federal court ordered the University of Mississippi to admit **James H. Meredith,** a qualified black air force veteran. Governor Ross R. Barnett refused to allow Meredith to register. Defying a Supreme Court order, Barnett cited the doctrine of interposition, that is, putting himself between the federal government and the people of Mississippi. He announced that the state's laws on segregation were superior to federal law. In response, Attorney General Robert Kennedy sent federal marshals to the campus. Rioting followed.

State the Objective

Understand what progress was made in civil rights during the 1960's.

Focus on Biography

Martin Luther King, Jr. (1929–1968)

Martin Luther King, Jr., enjoyed a privileged childhood and upbringing. To be sure, he was a black child in the Deep South in a time of depression and war. However, he came from an unusual family. Furthermore, Atlanta, Georgia, was not quite like other Southern cities.

His father was the Reverend Martin Luther King, Sr., a respected clergyman recognized as a leader of the city's black community. Atlanta's social and political life was rigidly segregated, but its white business leaders and politicians had a tradition of consulting informally with the black community on matters of concern to both.

Since young Martin was the son and grandson of Baptist preachers, it was natural that he should be drawn to the church. He was admitted to Morehouse College when he was only fifteen, under a special program for gifted students. From there he went to Crozer Theological Seminary in Pennsylvania and on to Boston University for a doctorate.

In Boston, King met Coretta Scott, a music student from Alabama. They were married and moved to Montgomery, Alabama, where he became a pastor. When the city's leaders met to take action on the arrest of Rosa Parks (see page 803), the Reverend Martin Luther King, Jr., addressed them: "We come here tonight to be saved from that patience that makes us patient with anything less than freedom and justice." The supporters of Rosa Parks recognized King's talents and chose him to be their spokesman.

Montgomery's bus boycott went on for a year and ended in complete victory for King and his organization. Segregation was no longer allowed on city buses, and black drivers were recruited. This series of events showed the young clergyman and others as well that blacks were more impatient for change than anyone had realized.

To carry the reforms won in Montgomery to other Southern communities, King organized the Southern Christian Leadership Conference. He was now a national figure. Travel to Ghana in West Africa and to India, where he met and talked to followers of Gandhi, gave him international recognition as well.

In 1960, King had moved back to Atlanta and to his father's church. From there he undertook the next phase of the civil rights struggle, the freedom rides. (See page 834.) When King and a group of students were arrested (see page 827), he was sentenced to a remote prison where his life would very likely have been in danger. Presidential candidate John Kennedy's successful effort to obtain King's release was well noted by African Americans. They may have made the difference in Kennedy's narrow victory that year.

The next few years were marked by some defeats but many victories. Throughout this time, King continued to preach nonviolence even though some of his younger followers grew restless. The year 1964, with its Civil Rights Act and King's Nobel Peace Prize was the peak of his career.

Thereafter, King's nonviolent approach began to meet sterner opposition. Riots in Los Angeles and in other cities outside the South caused some white liberals to withdraw their support of King's cause. Many Northern supporters were used to thinking of discrimination and segregation as purely Southern problems.

Martin Luther King, Jr., began to see that the injustices he opposed went beyond laws and regulations that could be quickly changed. In what were to be his last years, he dreamed of a revolution in values.

In the spring of 1968, King traveled to Memphis, Tennessee, where sanitation workers were on strike. There, on April 4, the man who had dedicated his life to the cause of nonviolence was killed by a white assassin's bullet.

Prophetically, in Memphis King had told a group of followers that it did not really matter what happened to him now: "I may not get to the Promised Land with you, but I want you to know that we, as a people, will."

Present the Lesson

Ask students to volunteer information for a time line of important events in the civil rights movement during the Kennedy administration. Write the time line on the board and have students refer to it as they study Section 3. Time lines should include:

March 1961	President Kennedy sets up the Committee on Equal Employment Opportunity.	Fall 1962	Federal court orders the integration of the University of Mississippi. Attorney General Robert Kennedy sends federal troops to enforce integration, and riots break out.
May 1961	Freedom rides are sponsored by CORE. Attorney General Robert Kennedy sends federal marshals to control violence and asks ICC to order desegregation of public transportation.	November 1962	President issues an executive order prohibiting racial and religious discrimination in housing built or insured with government money.
1962	President requests the abolition of literacy tests and poll taxes. The Twenty-fourth Amendment is passed.	May 4 1963	African Americans march in Birmingham, Alabama, and the resulting police aggres-

The marshals were forbidden to fire their guns. Their only weapon was tear gas. Most of the rioters were not students but members of the Ku Klux Klan and of the National States Rights party from other Southern states. They were armed with grenades, iron bars, bricks, and rifles. Two white spectators were killed, and more than a third of the marshals were injured. Finally, President Kennedy sent in federal troops to restore order. He also federalized the Mississippi National Guard. The next day, under heavy federal protection, Meredith registered for classes.

In June 1963 another confrontation occurred, this time at the University of Alabama in Birmingham. A federal court ordered the school to admit two black students, Vivian Malone and Jimmy Hood, to its summer session. Governor George Wallace stood in the doorway as the two students and their escort of federal marshals approached. After being told that the National Guard had been federalized, however, the governor walked away. All seemed calm. Then that night in Jackson, Mississippi, Medgar Evers, an official of the NAACP, was gunned down by a sniper.

Violence in Birmingham. The murder of Evers was only one in a series of events that would help bring about yet another change in the civil rights movement, a change from nonviolent action to black militancy. Two of these events took place in Birmingham.

African Americans had been demonstrating against segregation in that city since early April of 1963. Almost every time King called for a march, Police Commissioner T. Eugene ''Bull'' Connor obtained an injunction forbidding it. The African Americans marched anyway, were arrested, and were later released—and the process began again.

On May 4, when about twenty-five hundred African Americans marched in downtown Birmingham, the police loosed their dogs and turned fire hoses on them. Television carried the scene into millions of living rooms on the evening news. The sight of unresisting people being smashed against buildings by seven hundred pounds of water pressure or being attacked by snarling dogs was too much. Responsible local leaders realized the situation was getting out of hand. With the help of federal officials, plus three thousand riot-control troops, they succeeded in quieting things down.

The resulting peace was short-lived. In September passions flared again with the opening of school. On September 15 a black church was bombed, resulting in the deaths of four young black girls who were attending Sunday school.

Federal Actions. President Kennedy, like Lincoln a hundred years earlier, approached the civil

Picturing History Although James Meredith is accompanied by federal marshals, police and state officials keep him from entering the University of Mississippi in September 1962. Federal troops finally prevailed, and Meredith graduated from the university in 1963.

June 1963	sion and violence are broadcast on nationwide television. Federal court orders the integration of the University of Alabama. Governor George Wallace attempts to halt integration. Medgar Evers, an NAACP official, is murdered.
August 28 1963	About 200,000 march on Washington for civil rights legislation.

September 15 1963	Black church in Birmingham is bombed, resulting in the deaths of four young girls.

Check for Understanding

Have students answer Section 3 Review questions on paper.

Picturing History   Throughout the civil rights movement, fire hoses were often turned on civil rights demonstrators to disperse them.

For Discussion
What were some reasons for Kennedy's popularity and its endurance? (Reasons for Kennedy's popularity might include: his youth and attractive appearance; his humane stand on social and economic issues; his heroic war record; his ability to stand up to the Russians. Reasons his popularity has endured might include: he was a leader struck down in his prime, deprived of the chance to finish the work he began; he was seen as the ideal all-American young family man; he was himself as much an idealist as his fans were.)

rights issue with caution. During his first two years in office, he tried to help African Americans through executive action only.

In March 1961 he set up the Committee on Equal Employment Opportunity to encourage companies with government contracts to hire black employees. Next, he sought to abolish literacy tests and poll taxes. In 1962 Congress passed the Twenty-fourth Amendment, which prohibits a state from requiring a citizen to pay a poll tax in order to vote in a federal election. (The amendment was ratified in 1964). In November 1962 Kennedy issued an executive order prohibiting racial and religious discrimination in all housing built or insured with federal money.

After the 1963 Birmingham riots, Kennedy decided the time had come to seek new civil rights legislation. So he introduced a bill that one historian called "the most sweeping legislation of its kind since Reconstruction." By October the bill had begun to move through Congress.

Kennedy Is Assassinated

In late 1963 John and Jacqueline Kennedy traveled to Texas to try to strengthen the position of the Democratic party before the upcoming election. On November 22 at 12:30 P.M., a motorcade carrying the President, Texas Governor John Connally, and their wives through Dallas passed by a state building known as the Texas School Book Depository. Three shots rang out. The President pitched over. The official cars drove off at top speed toward Parkland Memorial Hospital. Less than one hour later, John Kennedy was pronounced dead. Vice-President **Lyndon B. Johnson,** who had been riding two cars behind Kennedy, left Dallas for Washington in the plane carrying Kennedy's body. He was sworn in as President before the plane took off.

Later that afternoon, a Dallas policeman was shot as he stopped a suspicious-looking young man for questioning. When caught, the gunman turned out to be Lee Harvey Oswald, a worker at the Texas

Historical Sidelight
President Johnson was known for giving electric toothbrushes as gifts. He once said, "I give these toothbrushes to my friends, for then I know that from now until the end of their days they will think of me first thing in the morning and the last thing at night."

837

Tell students that in the 1960's much support for civil rights activists came as the result of televised news programs. To stimulate discussion on the impact of television on the civil rights movement, ask students the following questions. What might have been viewers' reactions to the scene showing many peaceful demonstrators heckled by onlookers and attacked and beaten by police? (Possible responses: some viewers might have felt sympathy for the demonstrators; some viewers who did not agree with the civil rights cause might have been angered to see demonstra-

tors.) Tell students that Great Britain has banned television coverage of violent incidents in Northern Ireland. Ask students whether demonstrations and other confrontations should be carried on television. (Possible responses: yes—the public has the right to know what is going on: No—seeing violence on television might generate more violence.)

Assign Independent Practice

Ask students to reread the excerpt from Dr. King's "I Have a Dream" speech on page 834 and write a one-paragraph explanation of the main theme of the excerpt. (Paragraphs might include: Dr. King looked forward to a time when blacks and whites would live together in harmony and people would be judged on their character rather than on their skin color.)

Student Assignment/Homework

Have students read Section 4, "Johnson Tries to Build a Great Society," and answer Section 4 Review questions on paper.

SECTION 3 REVIEW

Answers

Main Ideas

1. The tactics of the sit-in were adapted to meet the specific purpose of the segregated facility, e.g. play-ins in parks, sleep-ins in hotels. Freedom rides helped to desegregate interstate travel on public transportation.

2. The assassination of Medgar Evers, the televised attack on unresisting demonstrators by the Birmingham police, and the bombing of a black Birmingham church in which four children were killed led to the change from nonviolence to militancy.

3. The Committee on Equal Employment Opportunity was set up, the Twenty-fourth Amendment outlawing poll taxes was passed, and other major civil rights legislation was introduced.

Critical Thinking

4. Possible answer: racial inequality still exists in the United States today, and the speech is still an inspiration to many. (evaluation)

Picturing History Lyndon Johnson takes the oath of office on the plane bearing the body of John Kennedy. Ladybird Johnson is on the left, Jacqueline Kennedy on the right. Above, John Kennedy, Jr., salutes as the caisson bearing the body of his father passes by. It was John–John's third birthday.

School Book Depository. A rifle belonging to Oswald was found near a window that overlooked the motorcade route. Two days later, Oswald was shot by Jack Ruby, a Dallas nightclub owner, before the disbelieving eyes of millions of Americans who were watching live TV coverage of Oswald being moved to another jail. Ruby died while waiting for a retrial on murder charges.

The entire chain of events was so bizarre that there are still people who cannot accept it at face value. In 1963 a commission presided over by Chief Justice Earl Warren began an extensive investigation that lasted ten months and yielded twenty-six volumes of testimony. The **Warren Commission** concluded that Kennedy had been shot by Oswald—"a sorry little loser"—acting on his own. In 1978, however, a congressional committee that went over much of the same ground said that although there was no proof, it was theoretically possible that two persons had shot at Kennedy. Besides these two official inquiries, numerous amateurs made their own investigations. Their explanations ranged all the way from a plot by anti-Castro Cubans to a communist conspiracy to a conspiracy by the CIA.

The assassination stunned the nation and the world. The three major television networks provided live coverage for seventy-two consecutive hours until the President's body was laid to rest in Arlington National Cemetery. Leaders from ninety-two nations attended the funeral. For weeks, hun-

dreds of thousands of Americans wrote to Jacqueline Kennedy to express their sorrow. It was as if a member of their own family had died.

SECTION 3 REVIEW

Key Terms and People

Explain the significance of: sit-in, CORE, freedom ride, Robert Kennedy, James H. Meredith, Lyndon B. Johnson, Warren Commission

Main Ideas

1. Through what nonviolent forms of protest were African Americans able to gain the use of formerly segregated public places?
2. What important events led some civil rights workers to change their tactics from nonviolent action in militancy?
3. What federal actions were taken during Kennedy's administration to help the civil rights cause?

Critical Thinking

4. Is Martin Luther King's "I have a dream" speech still relevant today, or has the United States come far enough toward true equality to make such a speech seem dated? Defend your answer.

838

SECTION 4

Johnson Tries to Build a Great Society

GLOSSARY TERMS: **Great Society, Civil Rights Act of 1964, Medicare, black power**

The nation was still stunned by Kennedy's assassination as it watched and listened to President Johnson address a joint session of Congress on the fifth day of his administration. The new leader began by saying quietly, "All I have I would have given gladly not to be standing here today." He reminded his audience how Kennedy had inspired Americans to begin to solve national and world problems. "Let us continue," said Johnson. Then he urged Congress to move ahead in such areas as civil rights, education, and lower taxes. He closed by asking the people to join him in singing "America the Beautiful."

Johnson Pushes for Domestic Changes

Johnson's domestic goals and achievements became known as the **Great Society.** One cornerstone of the Great Society was the **Civil Rights Act of 1964**. The other cornerstone was the **War on Poverty,** designed to help Americans living "on the outskirts of hope."

The Civil Rights Act. It took Johnson six months to push the civil rights bill through Con-

gress. Southern senators filibustered (made speeches intended to delay passage of the bill) for eighty-three days until the Senate cut off further debate. At last, on July 2, 1964, the bill became law.

The Civil Rights Act of 1964 prohibited discrimination because of race, color, religion, and national origin. It gave all citizens the right to enter libraries, parks, washrooms, restaurants, and theaters. It forbade discrimination in schools and gave the Attorney General the power to file suit in court to speed up desegregation. It extended the power of the federal government to protect the voting rights of blacks and all other citizens regardless of race. It set up the **Equal Employment Opportunity Commission (EEOC)** to help African Americans obtain fair treatment in businesses and in unions. It also set up a Community Relations Service to help local officials deal with racial problems.

In addition, the Civil Rights Act of 1964 prohibited discrimination because of sex. The word *sex* had been tacked onto the bill by eighty-one-year-old Representative Howard Smith of Virginia. An opponent of civil rights legislation, Smith hoped his action would result in the bill's being "laughed to death." This accidental provision was to have far-reaching effects.

Antipoverty Legislation. In response to Johnson's prodding, Congress set up a food-stamp plan for families on welfare and also voted funds for public housing. In August 1964 it established ten antipoverty programs. One was the Job Corps,

Picturing History President Johnson signing the Civil Rights Act of 1964.

State the Objective

Understand the nature and scope of President Johnson's domestic and foreign programs.

which paid high-school dropouts while they trained for industrial jobs. Another was the "domestic peace corps," officially known as VISTA (Volunteers in Service to America). VISTA volunteers worked in urban ghettos, in depressed areas, and on Indian reservations, teaching people new skills. Then there was the Head Start program for preschool youngsters. In a Head Start center, children could learn how to tell time, follow instructions, and do other things that would help them when they entered elementary school.

Congressional Reapportionment. Each congressional district elects one member to the House of Representatives. Before 1964 many rural districts had fewer than 200,000 people, while many urban districts had more than 600,000. (See page 475 on urban growth.) Thus the voters in rural areas had more representation—and also more power—in government than voters in urban areas.

In 1964 the Supreme Court ruled in *Westberry* v. *Sanders* that the congressional district boundaries should be redrawn so that they would be equal in population "as nearly as practicable." In *Reynolds* v. *Sims* the Court also ordered the states to redraw state legislative districts. In effect, this shifted political power throughout the nation from rural areas to urban areas.

A Presidential Landslide. LBJ, as Johnson was called, had brought the nation through a difficult time and had enjoyed legislative success. For the Republicans, ousting him from office in the election of 1964 would have been extremely difficult even if they had put up a candidate with wide appeal. As it was, they nominated someone with very narrow appeal: Senator **Barry Goldwater** of Arizona.

Goldwater's supporters believed that the Republican candidates of the past twenty-four years had been mere carbon copies of the Democratic candidates. The only way to recapture the Presidency, Goldwater backers felt, was by offering a candidate whom the more conservative or right wing Republicans could accept. Then these people, who presumably had not voted for years, would come out and cast their ballots. The conservatives' slogan for Goldwater was, "In Your Heart, You Know He's Right."

Probably most Americans agreed with some of Goldwater's criticisms, such as those pointing to the bloated federal bureaucracy and to incompetent

Picturing History Senator Barry Goldwater, Republican nominee for President in 1964, challenged the programs of Johnson's Great Society.

public officials. On the other hand, some of Goldwater's ideas struck most people as unrealistic. The senator suggested selling the TVA for one dollar to private industry. He wanted social security to be voluntary. He had voted against the Limited Test Ban Treaty and had urged that NATO commanders be allowed to use nuclear weapons in the event of a crisis. The Democrats capitalized on people's fear of nuclear warfare by producing a chilling television commercial. A picture of a little girl counting as she pulled the petals off a daisy turned into a picture of a mushroom cloud created by an atomic bomb.

Johnson won the election by a huge landslide of 61 percent, higher than the previous record set by FDR in 1936. The Democrats also increased their majority in Congress. For the first time since 1938, a Democratic President did not need the votes of conservative Southern Democrats in order to get laws passed. The Great Society could now be launched in earnest.

Achievements of the Great Society. When Lyndon Johnson left the White House in January 1969, Vice-President Hubert H. Humphrey and the outgoing cabinet members presented him with an engraved list entitled "Landmark Laws of the Lyndon B. Johnson Administration." There were 206 measures. Each one had been planned, drafted, and introduced under LBJ's guidance. Most of them had also required his doing battle for their passage.

Johnson considered education "the key which

Presidential Election, 1964

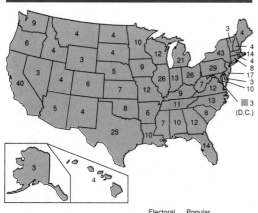

Party	Candidate	Electoral Vote	Popular Vote	%
Democratic	Johnson	486	43,130,000	61.3
Republican	Goldwater	52	27,178,000	38.6
Minor parties			101,000	0.1

538 Total Electoral Vote

can unlock the door to the Great Society.'' Funds were given to schools and to colleges. The more poor families a school district had, the more money that district's schools could receive. In order to receive funds, however, districts had to show that they were trying to eliminate racial discrimination.

The first major change in social security since its adoption in 1935 was accomplished with the establishment of **Medicare**. This program provides hospital insurance and some posthospital nursing care for almost every American once she or he reaches age sixty-five. Medicare also provides low-cost insurance against doctor bills, laboratory tests, and other medical services and supplies.

Congress also appropriated money to build some 240,000 units of low-rent public housing. It voted money to help low- and moderate-income families pay for better private housing. A new federal department, the **Department of Housing and Urban Development (HUD),** was established. It was headed by **Robert Weaver,** the nation's first black cabinet member. Another new federal department established was the Department of Transportation.

The Great Society attacked rural as well as urban poverty. Appalachia, a region comprising parts of eleven states that lie in the Appalachian Mountains, was one of the poorest areas of the country.

Congress provided money for building highways, setting up health centers, and otherwise developing the region.

The Great Society did not limit its fight against discrimination to civil rights. As you read in Chapter 25, the Immigration Act of 1924 and the National Origins Act of 1929 had established immigration quotas that discriminated strongly against some groups. In 1965 Johnson signed the Immigration and Nationality Act abolishing the national origins system. An annual quota of 290,000 immigrants was set. Within this overall quota, no more than 20,000 persons from any one nation could enter the United States each year.

Limitations of the Great Society. Some of LBJ's programs worked well. Others did not. Certain social problems were simply too big to be solved within a short period of time. Then, too, some of the programs were administered through existing local welfare, school, and health departments. In many cities these departments could not handle the new tasks.

Most limiting of all, money ran out. President Johnson was trying to fight two wars at the same time. He had begun with a war against poverty, but gradually the war against communism in Asia became more important. Public funds increasingly went to support the Vietnam struggle, which you will read about in Chapter 33. The Great Society, like the Johnson Presidency itself, became a casualty.

The Civil Rights Movement Continues

Considerable progress was made during Johnson's administration in such areas as voting rights and housing. However, the issue of race relations continued to divide the country during his term.

A Drive for Voting Rights. In the summer of 1964, several thousand black and white college students volunteered to go to Mississippi to help register that state's black voters. Before the summer was over, three of the volunteers—two whites, Michael H. Schwerner and Andrew Goodman, both Jewish, and one black, James E. Chaney—were murdered. Three more volunteers were shot, eighty were beaten, more than a thousand were arrested, and dozens of homes and churches were bombed or burned.

In January of the following year, Dr. Martin Luther King, Jr., launched a drive to register black

Ask students to construct a chart illustrating how the groups mentioned in this section—African Americans, Women, Hippies, and Environmentalists—influenced changes in American society. Charts might include:

Group	Changes in Society
African Americans	Voting Rights Act of 1965 Black revolution Black power movement Civil Rights Act of 1968
Women	Women's movement, crystallized by *The Feminine Mystique*

Group	Changes in Society
	1963 Commission on the Status of Women Equal Pay Act National Organization for Women (founded—1966)
Hippies	New subculture
Environmentalists	*Silent Spring* (1962) National Environmental Protection Agency (established 1970)

voters in Alabama. At first there was little response. Then in early March, a black would-be voter was murdered near the town of Selma. On March 7 about 525 of King's followers began a protest march from Selma to the state capital of Montgomery. State troopers and local police broke up the march with tear gas, billy clubs, and bullwhips in full sight of television cameras. Two weeks later, King led a second march. About 3,200 blacks and whites, including ministers, priests, and rabbis from all over the country, left Selma on March 21. By the time the procession reached Montgomery four days later, it numbered 25,000.

The marchers were protected by the federalized Alabama National Guard, by United States marshals, and by two army battalions. Nevertheless, the night the march ended, Viola Gregg Liuzzo, a white homemaker from Detroit, was fatally shot by Ku Klux Klansmen. Earlier, a Boston minister and a New Hampshire seminary student had also been gunned down. Liuzzo's assailants were convicted, but the defendants in the other two trials of the two other victims were acquitted.

In August, Congress passed the **Voting Rights Act of 1965.** The act eliminated the literacy test and provided that federal rather than state examiners must register qualified voters. The act also gave the Attorney General the right to file suits against the use of the poll tax in state elections. In 1966 the Supreme Court ruled that all poll taxes were unconstitutional.

Population Changes. The Selma march and the passage of the Voting Rights Act were the high points of King's campaign of nonviolence. Following these events, a new mood emerged in the black community.

One reason for this new mood was the shift in the black population. In 1950 almost one out of two blacks lived on Southern farms. By 1966 about two out of three blacks were residents of urban ghettos. Yet facilities in the cities had not kept up with the change in population. Housing was old and rundown. Schools were overcrowded and often lacked libraries and cafeterias. Many industries had relocated to the suburbs, which were often all white. Even if blacks found jobs in the suburbs, there was seldom any public transportation for them to use. The result was a black unemployment rate about double the rate for whites. In addition, blacks tended to be concentrated in low-paying occupations. They also tended to receive lower wages than whites even when they were performing the same kind of work.

In 1964 black Congressman Adam Clayton Powell, Jr., of New York had predicted that the "black revolution" would consist of two parts. The first part, already under way, would take place in the South and would focus on "middle-class matters" such as voting and sitting on buses. The second part, he predicted, would take place in the North, where blacks already had the right to vote and to sit in the front of the bus. In the North, Powell said, the issue would be "who gets the money." Not only that; this part of the revolution, he said, would be "rough." He was right.

Race Riots. Beginning in 1964 and for the next

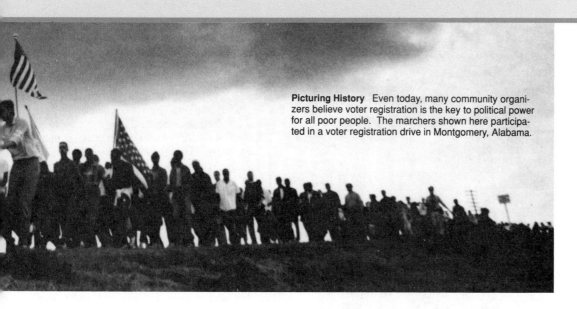

Picturing History Even today, many community organizers believe voter registration is the key to political power for all poor people. The marchers shown here participated in a voter registration drive in Montgomery, Alabama.

three years, more than one hundred race riots erupted in one major American city after another, from the Watts district of Los Angeles to Washington, D.C. The summer of 1967 was especially "hot," with sixty-seven separate outbreaks including one in Newark, New Jersey, that took twenty-five lives.

In many cases, the riots were sparked by relatively minor incidents between white police officers and black youths. Moderate black leader **Bayard Rustin,** organizer of the march on Washington, recounts that a twenty-year-old black told him after the **Watts riot,** "We won." Rustin asked him how he could say that when black homes and stores had been destroyed, blacks had been killed, and the entire area needed massive relief. "We won because we made the whole world pay attention to us," the youth replied. "The police chief never came here before; the mayor always stayed uptown. We made them come."

New Leaders and "Black Power." Among the blacks who were now beginning to attract attention were such individuals as **Malcolm X**. Born Malcolm Little, he changed his name because he did not want a last name that came from whites who had taken away his ancestral African name. For twelve years, he was a minister of the Nation of Islam, or Black Muslims. Then in 1964, he left the Muslims and set up the Organization for Afro-American Unity. (He was assassinated in 1965 by black extremists after he abandoned his belief in the complete separation of blacks from whites.)

Malcolm X was impatient with King's nonvio-

lent approach. "The day of nonviolent resistance is over," he asserted. "If they have the Ku Klux Klan nonviolent, I'll be nonviolent. . . . But as long as you've got somebody else not being nonviolent, I don't want anybody coming to me talking any nonviolent talk."

Malcolm X, and others like him, argued in favor of what they called **black power**. Although the precise meaning of the phrase depended on who was talking, in general it included the following: (1) the development of black-owned businesses in

Picturing History Malcolm X spoke out angrily against the institutions that enslaved African Americans.

Picturing History Thurgood Marshall was the first African American to serve on the Supreme Court.

All [the young working-class white] knows is he's in a confused community. He sees his dad's . . . job in jeopardy. His mother can't go downtown on a bus without being afraid of having her purse snatched. He can't go to a swimming pool without it meaning a fight with black kids. He can't afford to go to college. If you don't think that kid is angry, you've got to be crazy.

And it's not antiblack. . . . He wants what he thinks they're getting—so they call him a racist.

In addition, the violent statements and behavior of the more militant blacks, such as H. Rap Brown and Huey Newton of the Black Panther party, frightened or angered many white Americans. They felt that respect for law and order was disappearing from the American scene. Their feelings were to play a big part in the 1968 Presidential election.

Women Seek to Improve Their Status

By 1960 more than one out of three women over the age of fourteen was working for pay. About half of these women supported themselves or were the main breadwinner in the family. However, they were concentrated in low-paying jobs. The general feeling seemed to be that women really did not have to work, so it did not matter that their income was low.

This attitude was reflected in higher education. By 1960 the proportion of women to men in college had fallen to 35 percent from almost 50 percent in 1920. Almost two out of three coeds left college before graduation. Those who stayed felt considerable pressure not to major in math or science or to take up other "unfeminine" careers.

When women married, their credit cards were often canceled, with the explanation that the cards would be "of no further use to you." A wife's income was not considered when a family applied for a mortgage to buy a home. Single women could not obtain mortgages on their own, no matter how high their income.

The idea that a woman's place was in the home got lots of positive social reinforcement in novels, films, and television shows. Such influential magazines as *Time* and *Life* ran numerous articles praising the glories of homemaking and encouraging women to find happiness as wives and mothers.

Then in 1963, a significant event occurred. This

black communities, (2) local control of schools in black communities, (3) the use of black police officers in black communities, (4) bloc voting to elect black representatives who would give priority to the needs of black communities, and (5) the development of a sense of pride in being black.

The black power movement had varying results. Many black Americans were elected to public office. By 1967 the Supreme Court had its first black member, Justice Thurgood Marshall. The number of black police officers increased. Middle-class blacks found more jobs in business and in the professions. Blacks began appearing on the television screen and in advertisements. The number of black-owned businesses increased, and black community organizations sprang up. In 1968 Congress passed a new Civil Rights Act that prohibited discrimination in the sale or rental of most housing.

At the same time, public support for the civil rights movement began to diminish. Many whites who had supported the struggle were pushed out of organizations by blacks who considered it demeaning to accept white support.

Some areas saw a white backlash, with increased opposition to school integration. Many working-class whites felt that they were being overtaxed and underserved by the government. One community organizer described the situation as follows:

event signaled the beginning of a new perspective on the role of women in American society.

The Feminine Mystique. In the 1840's and 1850's, many women who had been active in the abolitionist movement also became active in the struggle for woman suffrage. Similarly, in the 1960's, many of the women who protested against racial discrimination became active in the movement for women's rights. In 1852 a book, *Uncle Tom's Cabin,* had served as a catalyst in the antislavery movement. In 1963 another book, this one also by a woman, helped to crystallize the attitudes of many who joined the women's movement. The author was **Betty Friedan,** a suburban homemaker. The book was called *The Feminine Mystique.* According to Friedan:

> The problem lay buried, unspoken, for many years in the minds of American women. It was a strange stirring, a sense of dissatisfaction, a yearning that women suffered. . . . As she made the beds, shopped for groceries, matched slipcover material, . . . she was afraid to ask even of herself the silent question "Is this all?" . . . There was no word of this yearning in the millions of words written about women, for women. . . . They were taught to pity the neurotic, unfeminine, unhappy women who wanted to be poets or physicists or presidents. They learned that truly feminine women did not want careers, higher education, political rights—the independence and the opportunities that the old-fashioned feminists fought for. . . . All they had to do was devote their lives from earliest girlhood to finding a husband and bearing children.

Picturing History
Betty Friedan challenged women to think critically about their lives and worked to promote equal rights for women.

Percentage of Working Women				
Age Group	1950	1960	1970	1988
16 and 17 years	30.1	28.6	34.6	44.0
18 and 19 years	51.3	51.0	53.4	62.9
20 to 24 years	46.1	46.1	57.5	72.7
25 to 34 years	34.0	35.8	44.8	72.7
35 to 44 years	39.1	43.1	50.9	75.2
45 to 54 years	38.0	49.3	54.0	69.0
55 to 64 years	27.0	36.7	42.5	43.5
65 years and over	9.7	10.5	9.2	7.9
Total 16 years and over	33.9	37.1	42.8	56.6

The feminine mystique, said Friedan, made the homemaker-mother of the past into the *only* role model for women. No matter that the world had changed. The mystique taught that women were by nature passive, nurturing, and subservient to men—and woe betide any woman who wanted to change her role.

The Beginnings of Change. The ideas expressed in *The Feminine Mystique* were reinforced that same year, 1963, by the publication of a report by the Commission on the Status of Women. The report showed that discrimination against women was widespread and made recommendations for federal action, including equal pay for equal work.

Later that year, Congress passed the Equal Pay Act. Enforcing this law, though, was something else again. Employers used a variety of tactics to avoid compliance. By 1970 women high-school graduates were still earning only about 56 percent of the amount earned by men of equivalent age and education. Even the average female college graduate earned less than the average male high-school graduate.

While the Equal Pay Act was not effective, another piece of legislation did provide women with a basis for challenging unequal treatment. As you will recall, the Civil Rights Act of 1964 contained a prohibition against sex discrimination. (See page 839.) Since its passage, hundreds of court cases have been filed under the act, and changes are slowly being put into effect.

Student Assignment/Homework

Have students complete the Chapter 32 Test on paper. Divide the class into small groups to discuss and review the answers.

In 1966 Betty Friedan and other women's right activists founded the **National Organization for Women (NOW).** Friedan became its first president. The group advocated help for working parents in the form of free child-care centers or tax deductions for child-care expenses similar to those in other industrialized nations. It called for maternity-leave benefits and urged adoption of an **Equal Rights Amendment (ERA)** to the Constitution. It wanted girls to be able to take the same courses in school as boys, and it wanted the amount of money spent on athletics for girls to be equal to the amount spent on athletics for boys.

Other Americans Seek Changes

People's dissatisfaction with one or more aspects of American society expressed itself during the 1960's not only in political action but also in attempts to change life styles and challenge existing values.

The Hippie Movement. In the mid-1960's, a person wandering through certain sections of American cities, such as the Haight-Ashbury section of San Francisco, would have found the streets filled with bushy-haired people wearing jeans, fringed vests, headbands or hats with feathers, and beads around their necks. These people were known as hippies. Most were young and felt alienated from American society. They were bothered by the gap between democratic principles of equality and the treatment of racial minorities. They found it difficult to understand the continuing existence of poverty and unemployment. Most came from white, middle-class families, and they questioned the amount of time their parents devoted to earning a living and getting ahead. They resented authority figures and distrusted almost everyone over thirty. Many felt that there were more important things to do with their lives than strive for great material success.

Most hippies worked at odd jobs and shared inexpensive living quarters they called pads. Their choice of clothing revolutionized the way a whole generation dressed. They spent their leisure time listening to the songs of Bob Dylan, Simon and Garfunkel, Judy Collins, Joan Baez, Janis Joplin, Jimi Hendrix, the Rolling Stones, and, of course, the Beatles.

Many hippies called themselves flower children. They believed that the answer to social problems was love and community—a general feeling of brotherhood and a sharing of everything one owned. Some carried out their beliefs by organizing communes. Other hippies simply tuned out or dropped out of society and did their own thing.

Doing their own thing often meant following gurus such as Timothy Leary who advised them to get in touch with their feelings and to enjoy life here and now rather than sacrifice for the future as their parents had done. Psychedelic posters, incense, strobe lights, and electronic rock music provided the setting for drug trips on uppers, downers, marijuana, and LSD. Casualties were common, however, as a sign on a free clinic in Haight-Ashbury attested: ''Bum trippers and emergencies only. No doctors until 4:00 P.M.''

Picturing History The flower children of the sixties made their "do your own thing" statement in many ways.

The Environmental Movement. Most young people, however, did not drop out. Many worked for change within the system. Among the many changes they focused on was the need to save the environment for future generations.

A book published in 1962 brought the issue of air and water pollution to the attention of many Americans. *Silent Spring* was the work of marine biologist **Rachel Carson**. In the book, Carson argued strongly for the careful regulation of pesticide use.

At the same time, there was mounting evidence of other forms of environmental pollution in the nation. Smog was common. The water in many rivers was unfit for drinking or even for swimming. Millions of tons of solid wastes piled up in open dumps.

However, some people charged that the environmentalists were causing unnecessary alarm. If environmentalists had their way, these critics said, pollution-control costs would rise so much that

Remind students that despite its brief duration, the Kennedy administration faced several serious foreign policy problems. Ask students to review the role of the CIA in the Bay of Pigs invasion and prepare a newspaper editorial supporting or opposing the practice of U.S. participation in foreign political affairs. (Editorials may include: supporting—the U.S. government has a responsibility to contain communism. Opposing—the government should not interfere in the governments of other countries unless directly asked for assistance.)

Picturing History
Rachel Carson.

many people would lose their jobs. Nevertheless, the public was sufficiently anxious about the pollution issue that Congress passed the National Environmental Policy Act. The act, which took effect in 1970, requires that before any federally funded project is approved, its effects on the environment must be considered. As a result of this law, many projects have been canceled, and hundreds of others modified.

Later in 1970, President Nixon established the **Environmental Protection Agency (EPA)** to enforce environmental protection laws. These include (1) laws to control the storage of toxic industrial wastes, (2) laws to force companies to clean up the pollution damage they have caused, and (3) animal protection codes.

Linking Past to Present

By the end of the 1980's, around 60 percent of all Americans were living in metropolitan areas with unhealthy levels of smog. In 1989 Los Angeles unveiled a three-stage plan considered by some to be "the most ambitious antipollution plan in the nation." The first stage would ban gasoline-powered lawn mowers, charcoal-grill starter fluids, and spray deodorants by 1993. The second stage would be directed at the cleanup of electric power plants and oil refineries. The third stage would require cars to either burn methanol—an odorless substance—or run on electricity by the year 2007.

Older Americans. While Americans under thirty were attracting public attention, changes were also occurring among Americans over sixty-five. First, there were many more of them. As of 1970 the average life expectancy was seventy-five

years for women and sixty-seven years for men. People in their eighties and nineties were not uncommon. Second, they were concentrated in such sunny states as Arizona, California, and Florida. Third, increasing numbers were living in "retirement towns" limited to people fifty years old and older. The main emphasis in these towns is on companionship and social activities, but they also contain medical clinics with round-the-clock ambulance service.

Since the 1960's the number of older Americans has continued to increase. By 1980 senior citizens accounted for 11 percent of the population, up from 4 percent in 1900. This change has forced Congress to seek new ways to fund social security and Medicare payments and to pay more attention to the health needs of older Americans.

SECTION 4 REVIEW

Key Terms and People

Explain the significance of: Great Society, Civil Rights Act of 1964, War on Poverty, EEOC, Barry Goldwater, Medicare, HUD, Robert Weaver, Voting Rights Act of 1965, Bayard Rustin, Watts riot, Malcolm X, black power, Betty Friedan, NOW, ERA, Rachel Carson, EPA

Main Ideas

1. On what two major domestic problems did President Johnson focus his attention after taking office?
2. What important changes did the passage of the Civil Rights Act of 1964 seem to promise?
3. What were the important shortcomings of Johnson's Great Society?
4. How did population shifts in the United States contribute to the increasing tension between blacks and whites in the 1960's?
5. What were some of the positive results of the black power movement?
6. What was the main idea expressed in Betty Friedan's book, _The Feminine Mystique_?

Critical Thinking

7. As African Americans began to attain positions of leadership and responsibility in American society, public support for civil rights began to diminish. Was this a cause and effect relationship, or was it simply a coincidence? Explain.

State the Objective

Understand how primary sources reflect the social movements of the 1960's and 1970's.

Present the Lesson

Remind students that the social movements of the 1960's and 1970's were social revolutions similar in many ways to the progressive movement of the American Revolution. Recollections of such events can usually be found in autobiographical materials.

Discuss with students Dr. King's belief that citizens have the right to break unjust laws—a philosophy that was at the heart of the civil rights movement. To stimulate discussion, ask students the following questions. How does King answer his critics about breaking laws? (Possible response: he divides laws into two categories—just and unjust; one who breaks a law that conscience says is unjust must be willing to accept imprisonment in order to arouse the conscience of the community.) According to King, do people lose respect for laws because they break an unjust law? (Answer: no—those people have the highest respect for the law, since they are willing to accept the penalty of imprisonment.) What examples does King use to justify his argument about just and unjust laws? (Answer: the Hungarian freedom fighters broke laws in their struggle for freedom.)

Have students summarize Annie Popkin's account of her experiences. Summaries

Focus on Primary Sources

Voices from the 1960's

The sixties began with young Martin Luther King, Jr., (page 835) and the Freedom Riders (page 834). Through nonviolence they sought to win civil rights for black citizens. Fueled by opposition to the Vietnam War and by continued injustice to minorities, the demand for change spread to students, women, and Hispanics.

The outstanding figure in the conflicts that led to the 1964 Civil Rights Act was Martin Luther King, Jr. His leadership was firmly based on nonviolent civil disobedience. When Christian and Jewish clergymen asked how, as a minister, he could tell people to break the law, King answered from his cell in the Birmingham, Alabama, jail.

> You express a great deal of anxiety over our willingness to break laws. This is certainly a legitimate concern. Since we so diligently urge people to obey the Supreme Court's decision of 1954 outlawing segregation in the public schools, at first glance it may seem rather paradoxical for us consciously to break laws. One may well ask: "How can you advocate breaking some laws and obeying others?" The answer lies in the fact that there are two types of laws: just and unjust. I would be the first to advocate obeying just laws. One has not only a legal but a moral responsibility to obey just laws. Conversely, one has a moral responsibility to disobey unjust laws. I would agree with St. Augustine that "an unjust law is no law at all." . . .
>
> I hope you are able to see the distinction I am trying to point out. In no sense do I advocate evading or defying the law, as would the rabid segregationist. That would lead to anarchy. One who breaks an unjust law must do so *openly, lovingly,* and with a willingness to accept the penalty. I submit that an individual who breaks a law that conscience tells him is unjust, and who willingly accepts the penalty of imprisonment in order to arouse the conscience of the community over its injustice, is in reality expressing the highest respect for law. . . .
>
> We should never forget that everything Adolf Hitler did in Germany was "legal" and everything the Hungarian freedom fighters did in Hungary was "illegal." It was "illegal" to aid and comfort a Jew in Hitler's Germany. Even so, I am sure that had I lived in Germany at the time, I would have aided and comforted my Jewish brothers. If today I lived in a Communist country where certain principles dear to the Christian faith are suppressed, I would openly advocate disobeying that country's antireligious laws.

King, Martin Luther, Jr., *Why We Can't Wait* (New York: Harper & Row, 1964), 84–87.

Annie Popkin now teaches women's studies at a California college. In the 1960's she was a civil rights and antiwar activist. Like many of her contemporaries, she was drawn into the women's movement.

> Civil rights was the first issue that gripped me. I remember being very moved and horrified by the pictures in *Life* magazine of white people putting cigarette butts out on people in sit-ins in Woolworth's in the South. I went on a picket line around Woolworth's in Freeport, Long Island, to support the sit-ins. I worked with CORE [Congress for Racial Equality] in New York. Freshman year at Radcliffe, I worked with black teenagers at a settlement house in Roxbury in Boston. I went on the 1963 March on Washington, and the next summer I went south to Mississippi and worked with black voter registration. . . .
>
> I remember about two years before the women's movement started, 1965 or '66, this friend of mine said, "You know, you'll never be a radical as long as you don't see how the system affects *you*. You always think it affects other people." And I sort of agreed with him, but I didn't get it, surely not as a *woman*, because we didn't have that category

might include: she began by being angered over the mistreatment of African Americans; when she first heard of the women's movement, she didn't believe that she suffered oppression the way the poor and minorities did; she joined the women's movement because she eventually believed that the system favors men.) In retrospect, does Popkin seem to feel she made the right decision? (Possible answer: yes—she expresses satisfaction at having made something happen and improved her own life.)

Discuss the similarities among all the documents in this feature. Ask students what all the authors had in common. (Possible response: all wanted to eradicate social and political injustice.) Ask students whether any were successful. (Possible responses: all were successful to varying degrees; the most successful was King because he had the greatest effect on society; others were involved in more minor ways in changes that are ongoing.)

Check for Understanding

Review the questions at the end of the feature with students. Have students bring to class and discuss current news articles about individuals who are using nonviolent means to make changes in the social or political arena.

---

yet. It still seemed worse to be poor and lynched and all the other things, so I didn't quite understand.

I just wasn't ready yet. Sometime in '67 or '68 this friend said, "You know, these women are getting together to talk about what it's like to be a woman in the Movement. Don't you think you'd want to join them?" "Oh, I don't know," I said. I didn't think I was oppressed or had any reason to want to join.

Then three months later, by the middle of '68, I was helping to form the women's movement. Everything had started to come into place.

My silence in political meetings, which I had attributed to some personality fault, I could now see as part of a system, in which men are at the center. We're not encouraged to talk. It explained so much. And it was marvelous—the relief of being able to talk about it and see it *wasn't just you*. It was the system. . . .

We started forming a group in Cambridge [Massachusetts] that would become Bread and Roses, one of the earliest women's liberation groups. . . .

It's exciting to be in the forefront of a movement, to make a movement happen. You don't get that chance often in your life. And it's funny. Until the women's movement came along, I was going to help *other* people have better lives. Well, I'm glad that changed, that I could make it better for myself, too.

Morrison, Joan and Robert K. Morrison, *From Camelot to Kent State,* (New York: Time Books, 1987) 181–185.

Armando R. Rodriguez was a government official. In a 1970 speech in Chicago he tried to define the term "La Raza," which Hispanic Americans sometimes apply to their efforts to further the cultural heritage of their people. Members of La Raza see nothing wrong with differences in language and life style. They stress the virtues of cultural pluralism rather than the melting pot.

Who is La Raza when you strip away the educational and economic chains that bind him? For the most part, he is still an alien, unknown in his own land. This is true even in the Southwest, where the cultural heritage is a living reminder of the part that Spain and Mexico played in forming the character of this nation. . . . Between the fanciful extremes of the peon [landless peasant] and the hidalgo [landowner] is La Raza . . .

. . .Who is the Puerto Rican or the Mexican American? He is that unique individual who has suffered from cultural isolation, language rejection, economic and educational inequalities, but who has now begun to take those instruments of oppression and turn them into instruments of change. Bilingual and bicultural education in our public schools will be a reality very shortly. . . .

"Who am I?" asks a young Mexican American high school student. "I am a product of myself. I am a product of you and my ancestors. We came to California long before the Pilgrims landed at Plymouth Rock. We settled California, the Southwestern part of the United States including the states of Arizona, New Mexico, Colorado and Texas. We built the missions, we cultivated the ranches. We were at the Alamo in Texas, both inside and outside. You know we owned California—that is, until gold was found here. Who am I? I'm a human being. I have the same hopes that you do, the same fears, the same drives, same desires, same concerns, same abilities; and I want the same chance that you have to be an individual."

Rodriguez, Armando M., "Bilingual Education—Profile '70" (Congressional Record, 91 Congress, 2 Session), February 26, 1970.

Analyzing Primary Sources

1. How did Martin Luther King, Jr., justify breaking the law? Explain.
2. From the Radcliffe student's experiences, show how the women's movement could have grown out of earlier developments.

Critical Thinking

3. Why would an Hispanic American in the 1960's feel like "an alien, unknown in his own land"? Do you think this is still true today? Why, or why not?

FOCUS ON SOURCES

Answers

Analyzing Primary Sources

1. King said that there are two types of laws—just and unjust. There is a legal and moral obligation to obey just laws and conversely, a moral obligation to disobey unjust laws. One who breaks an unjust law must accept the penalty of imprisonment in order to arouse the conscience of the community.

2. Possible answer: many agree that most founders of the women's movement had been active in the civil rights, antiwar, and other 1960's movements and had experienced discrimination there.

Critical Thinking

3. Armando Rodriguez says that Puerto Ricans and Mexican Americans have suffered from cultural isolation, language rejection, and economic and educational inequalities.
• Possible answer: No—as Rodriguez predicted, Spanish language and culture now receive much greater attention than they did before the 1960's; Americans are now generally more aware and accepting of cultural differences than they were in the 1960's. (analysis)

Key Terms and People

These are highlighted in the text in the order in which they appear in this list.

Main Ideas

1. Youth, Catholicism, father's support of Chamberlain.
• Turned his youth to an advantage, was honest about religion, family gave financial help and was active in campaign, TV used to advantage.

2. Wanted to reclaim American prestige.

3. Cuban exiles were not trained; air strike did not occur; supplies did not get through; Cuban uprising did not occur; Castro's troops captured invaders.

4. Berlin—Soviets did not like Allied troops in West Berlin and resented the fact that West Berlin was better off economically than East Berlin. When Kennedy did not back down, Soviets armed the border, built Berlin Wall. Cuba— Soviets sent missiles to Cuba; Kennedy quarantined Cuba. Soviets agreed to dismantle missile bases in return for U.S. pledge not to invade Cuba.
• Created a hot line; suspended nuclear testing; sold surplus wheat to Soviets.

5. Nonviolent actions—sit-ins and freedom rides.

6. Possible answer: sent federal marshals to U. of Mississippi; federalized National Guard in Mississippi and Alabama; created Committee on Equal Employment Opportunity; introduced new civil rights legislation in Congress.

7. Prohibited discrimination because of race, color, religion, sex, and national origin; allowed all citizens to enter public facilities; forbade discrimination in schools; gave Attorney General power to speed up desegregation suits and to protect voting rights of African Americans.

8. Allocated funds to schools and colleges that tried to eliminate discrimination; set up Medicare, the Departments of Housing and Urban Develop-

ment and of Transportation, the Job Corps, and VISTA; built highways and health centers for rural areas.

Critical Thinking Questions

9. Electorate almost evenly divided.

10. They all believed that state laws took precedence over federal law. • Barnett did not

succeed because a federal court, the federal marshals, and most of the nation were against him. • Wallace knew he could not stand up to the National Guard.

11. Females could have equal opportunity in school and business; they could be auto mechanics, civil engineers, firefighters, and football coaches.

Critical Thinking Activities

12. Possible answer: yes— nonviolent methods are more likely to break the cycle of violence.

13. Possible answer: generals usually want to increase military spending because they think military readiness is the most important way to keep the country secure. • Even though the Cold War has

---

CHAPTER **32** REVIEW

Write your answers on a separate sheet of paper.

Key Terms and People

Explain the significance of: New Frontier, NASA, Fidel Castro, Alliance for Progress, CORE, James H. Meredith, Warren Commission, War on Poverty, Barry Goldwater, Robert Weaver, Voting Rights Act of 1965, Watts riot, Betty Friedan, NOW, ERA, Rachel Carson, EPA

Main Ideas

1. What were Kennedy's disadvantages in the Presidential election of 1960? How did he overcome these to win the election?
2. Why was it so important to Kennedy and the nation to beat the Soviets in the space race?
3. What went wrong at the Bay of Pigs?
4. Describe the Berlin crisis of 1961 and the missile crisis in Cuba in 1962. How did Kennedy try to ease relations with the Soviets in 1963?
5. How was integration in restaurants and in transportation facilities accomplished?
6. What actions for civil rights did Kennedy and others in the executive department of the federal government take from 1961 through 1963?
7. What were the terms of the Civil Rights Act of 1964?
8. List at least four achievements of Johnson's Great Society.

Critical Thinking Questions

9. **Analyzing Causes.** In the 1960 Presidential election, Kennedy defeated Nixon by fewer than 119,000 votes. What does this tell you about the division in the electorate?
10. **Comparing Ideas.** Compare Mississippi Governor Ross Barnett's declaration on interposition with that of Calhoun on nullification (page 327) and with the position of the Confederate States during the Civil War (page 350). Why was Barnett not successful? What position did Governor George Wallace take?

11. **Making Predictions.** What opportunities became available to women as a result of the provision in the Civil Rights Bill of 1964 prohibiting discrimination on the basis of sex? List a few of the possibilities.

Critical Thinking Activities

12. **Predicting Effects.** Do you think nonviolence should be tried in resolving world conflicts such as those in the Middle East, Northern Ireland, and El Salvador? Why or why not?

13. **Linking Past to Present.** In his farewell address, Eisenhower warned against the rise of the military-industrial complex: "The total influence—economic, political, even spiritual— is felt in every city, every state house, every office of the federal government. We recognize the . . . need for this development. Yet we must not fail to comprehend its grave implications. . . . The potential for the disastrous rise of misplaced power exists and will persist." What was so unusual about an ex-general saying this? Comment on how this warning relates to the problems of winding down the military-industrial complex in the 1990's.

14. **Linking Past to Present.** Why do you think the Peace Corps has lasted so long?

15. **Linking Past to Present.** What was the reason for building the Berlin Wall? Why was it opened in 1989?

16. **Linking Past to Present.** Martin Luther King had a dream based on the words from the Declaration of Independence "that all men are created equal." He dreamed that "the sons of former slaves and the sons of former slaveowners will be able to sit together at the table of brotherhood" and that "little children will not be judged by the color of their skin but by the content of their character." Have we progressed toward this dream today? Cite specific instances to support your opinion.

Leadership of the 1960's

Democrat John F. Kennedy faced three major obstacles in the 1960 Presidential campaign: his youth, his father's isolationist stance in World War II, and his Roman Catholic faith. Nevertheless, he turned his age, his family, and his faith into assets and narrowly defeated Republican Richard M. Nixon. The young Democratic candidate made a positive impression during a television debate and strongly supported Martin Luther King's crusade for civil rights.

While in office, Kennedy had only partial success with his domestic spending proposals. Yet Congress funded a space program designed to achieve the President's goal of putting an American on the moon before the end of the 1960's.

In foreign affairs, Kennedy approved an invasion of Castro's Cuba, but the attempt turned out to be a humiliating disaster for the United States. In 1962 the Soviet Union placed nuclear missiles in Cuba, but Kennedy was able to get Khrushchev to agree to withdraw them. The President also stood firm when the Soviets tried to force the United States to retreat from Berlin. Tensions between the superpowers were eased somewhat by the new Washington-Moscow hot line, the Limited Test Ban Treaty, and the sale of wheat to the Soviet Union.

Kennedy supported the civil rights movement, which shifted from the courts to direct action during the 1960's. Sit-ins began, and freedom rides spread throughout the South. King's speech at the march on Washington focused national attention on civil rights. United States marshals and troops were sent to enforce integration at two state universities. Birmingham, Alabama, was the scene of violence that reached its peak when a bomb killed four black girls attending Sunday school. Kennedy's attempt to aid the civil rights movement ended when he was assassinated in Dallas.

Vice-President Lyndon B. Johnson succeeded to the Presidency. The cornerstones of Johnson's Great Society were the Civil Rights Act of 1964 and the War on Poverty. In response to Johnson's landslide election in 1964, Congress passed more social legislation. Some measures worked well, but others proved too costly. Despite progress in voting rights and housing, many African Americans grew more militant. Members of the women's movement advocated an end to sex discrimination in employment and worked for the adoption of the Equal Rights Amendment. Many Americans also expressed their concern about preserving the environment for future generations.

Chronology of Main Events

1960 Black students begin sit-ins

1961 John F. Kennedy inaugurated President; Peace Corps established; Berlin Wall erected; Cuba invaded

1962 Col. John Glenn becomes the first U.S. astronaut to orbit Earth; Cuban missile crisis

1963 Limited Test Ban Treaty signed; civil rights march on Washington; Kennedy assassinated, Lyndon Johnson succeeds to the Presidency

1964 Civil Rights Act passed

1965 Lyndon Johnson inaugurated to his first full term; Medicare and Voting Rights acts passed

1966 National Organization for Women founded

Global Perspectives

1955	Neutral nations attempt to organize themselves as a third-world political force.
1958	Mao Zedong begins the Great Leap Forward.
1961	Oil-producing countries, led by the Arab states, form OPEC—the Organization of Petroleum Exporting Countries.
1961–1964	United Nations troops restore order in the Congo.
1967	Tom Mboya of Kenya encourages economic cooperation among African nations.
1972	Richard Leakey and Glynn Isaac discover a 2.5 million-year-old human skull in Kenya.

For Discussion

United Nations troops were used to restore order in the Congo. Do you think that UN troops should interfere in the affairs of countries in turmoil? Why or why not? (Possible responses: yes—UN intervention in the early stages of conflict might prevent a full-scale war. No—individual countries should work out their own conflicts.)

Additional Resources

- Geography Activities
- Skills Activities
- Thematic Activities
- Economic Activities
- Cultural Literacy Activities
- Literary Source Readings
- Primary Source Readings
- Nuclear Peacekeeping
- Transparencies
- Computer Test Generator

Additional Teaching Strategies

SECTION 1

For Basic Students: Have students use an encyclopedia or other reference material to research and write a one- or two-page report on the history and current status of SEATO. (Reports might include: alliance was founded on September 8, 1954; headquarters are in Bangkok, Thailand; governing body is a council composed of the foreign ministers or their deputies from each member country; organization ended in June, 1977.) Have one or two students read their reports to the class.

For Advanced Students: After they research the Gulf of Tonkin Resolution, organize students into two groups and have them hold a mock senatorial debate on the bill for the class. After debate, allow students to vote on the resolution and state reasons for their decisions. (Arguments in favor of the resolution might include: the President should have the power that this resolution provides in order to act quickly to save American lives that might be lost in the time it would take for the Senate to meet, debate, and vote on the situation. Arguments against the resolution might include: it gives too much power to the President and infringes on the legislature's power to declare war.)

SECTION 2

For Basic Students: Ask students to work together to prepare on posterboard a chart showing the arguments used by hawks and doves during the Vietnam War to support their positions. Chart might include:

Doves
- Vietnam War is a civil war.
- U.S. cannot police the world.
- War is draining U.S. strength.
- War is destroying the people and land of Vietnam.
- War is killing thousands.
- War causes inflation.

Hawks
- Vietnam is vital to U.S. security.
- Containing communism is important at any cost.
- U.S. is protecting itself from communism.

Have students post their chart in the classroom.

For Advanced Students: Ask students to prepare a newspaper editorial supporting or challenging Senator Eugene McCarthy's stand on the war. (Editorials in support might include: the war is costing billions of dollars and thousands of lives; there is little hope of victory.)

SECTION 3

For Basic Students: Ask students to identify Vietnam, Cambodia, Laos, and the Ho Chi Minh Trail on a map of Southeast Asia and explain to the class the importance of each in the Nixon administration's plan for ending the Vietnam War. (Possible responses: Nixon ordered U.S. troops into Cambodia without consulting Congress; in 1971 South Vietnamese soldiers invaded Laos in an attempt to cut the flow of men and supplies along the Ho Chi Minh Trail.)

For Advanced Students: Have students research the Kent State incident. Then organize the students into two groups, one representing student demonstrators, and the other representing members of the National Guard. Have students write letters home to family describing the events at Kent State University. (Letters may include: concern for personal safety; inability to understand the opposition's viewpoint; fear of more accidental injuries or deaths; fear of retaliation.) Have several students read their letters to the class.

SECTION 4

For Basic Students: Have students work as a group to further research and discuss the War Powers Act of 1973. (Discussion might include: the act placed strict limits on the President's ability to wage "undeclared war"; the act came into play again in 1983 after U.S. Marines were attacked in Lebanon.) Have the group leader summarize the discussion for the class.

For Advanced Students: Have students research and prepare a two-page report on the plight of the boat people and their struggles to gain freedom. (Reports might include: during the 1970's more than 1.5 million refugees fled Indochina; they preferred the uncertainty of life as refugees to life under communism; refugees bought their way out of Vietnam, Laos, and Cambodia on illegally operated and unseaworthy vessels; many were refused entrance when they tried to land; some Western countries and China welcomed large numbers; the U.S. accepted about 500,000 boat people.) Have two or three volunteers read their reports to the class.

Further Reading for Students

Greene, Bob. *Homecoming: When the Soldiers Returned from Vietnam*. New York: Putnam Publishing Group, 1989.

Herring, George C. *America's Longest War: The United States and Vietnam, 1950-1975*. New York: Random House, 1979.

Karnow, Stanley. *Vietnam: A History*. New York: Penguin, 1984.

Lawson, Don. *The War in Vietnam*. New York: Franklin Watts, 1981. (Easy)

Bibliography for Teachers
Books

Browne, Malcolm. *The New Face of War*. New York: Bantam Books, 1986.

Horne, A. D., ed. *The Wounded Generation: America After Vietnam*. Englewood Cliffs, N.J.: Prentice-Hall, 1981.

Lawson, Don. *The United States in the Vietnam War*. New York: Harper & Row, 1981.

MacPherson, Myra. *Long Time Passing*. New York: New American Library, 1985

Schandler, Herbert Y. *Lyndon Johnson and Vietnam: The Unmaking of a President*. Princeton, N.J.: Princeton University Press, 1977.

Westmoreland, William C. *A Soldier Reports*. New York: Dell, 1980.

Audio-Visuals

American Foreign Policy: Containment in Asia. National Broadcasting Company. Movie.

Indochina and American Politics. Social Studies School Service. Filmstrip.

Last Reflections on a War. National Broadcasting Television. Movie.

Southeast Asia Since Vietnam: Territorial Turmoil. New York Times. Filmstrip.

Southeast Asia: The Other War. Indiana University. Movie.

The Class That Went to War. American Broadcasting Company. Movie.

Vietnam—An Historical Document. Carousel Films. Movie.

Vietnam Dialogue. Social Studies School Service. Movie.

Teacher's Notes:

Lesson Plan

Teaching Resources, Unit 8 Booklet

Lesson Study Sheets pp. 57-72
Daily Activities pp. 73-80
Enrichment Activities pp. 81-88
Reteaching Activities pp. 89-96
Chapter Review p. 97
Chapter Mastery Tests pp. 99-110
Telescoping the Times Study Sheet p. 111

Chapter Objectives

Students will learn:
- the historical roots of U.S. involvement in Vietnam and the resulting foreign policy
- how the Johnson administration dealt with the Vietnam War and with the antiwar movement after the Tet offensive
- how the Nixon administration withdrew American troops from Vietnam
- how the problems of Vietnam veterans were different from the problems of veterans of earlier wars

Using the Chapter Time Line

What major movement was beginning in the U.S. (see Chapter 32 Time Line) during the decade that the U.S. became involved in Vietnam? (Answer: Civil Rights movement) What five events related to the U.S. involvement in Vietnam occurred during Lyndon Johnson's Presidency? (Answer: Gulf of Tonkin Resolution, U.S. bombed North Vietnam, U.S. combat troops landed in South Vietnam, Communists launched Tet Offensive, and Paris peace talks began)

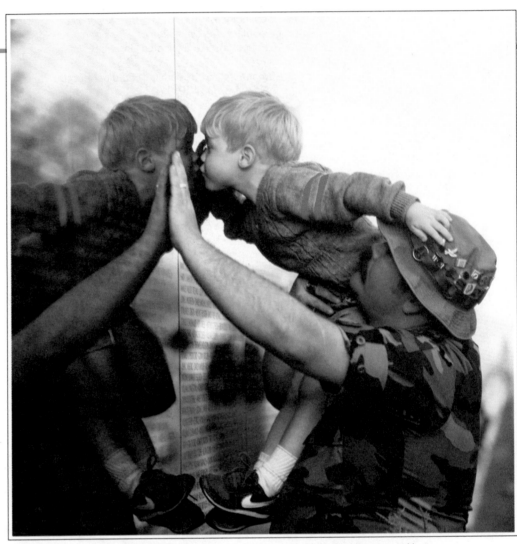

Picturing History At the Vietnam Veterans Memorial, a Vietnam veteran holds his son up to kiss the name of the child's grandfather, who was killed in the war. The name of every American who was killed or missing in action in the Vietnam War is engraved on the face of the memorial.

1954   1958   1962   1966   1970   1974   1978

1955
U.S. begins to provide aid to South Vietnam

1954
French defeated at Dien Bien Phu

1964
Gulf of Tonkin Resolution

1965
- President Johnson authorizes bombing of North Vietnam
- First U.S. combat troops land in South Vietnam

1968
- Tet offensive
- Paris peace talks begin

1973
Cease-fire agreement signed

1975
South Vietnam surrenders

Links to American Literature

Philip Caputo: writer and reporter; served in the U.S. Marine Corps until 1967, when he joined the staff of the *Chicago Tribune;* was part of the team that won the 1972 Pulitzer Prize for investigative reporting; won the Overseas Press Club's George Polk Citation for his reports as a captive of Palestinian guerrillas in the Middle East; was reassigned to Saigon in 1975 to cover the end of the war; was wounded in Beirut, Lebanon, by machine-gun fire in October 1975; continues to work as a correspondent in Moscow.

Works include: *Horn of Africa* (1983); *Delcorso's Gallery* (1984); *Indian Country* (1987).

A Rumor of War: is a story of men at war as told by a young midwesterner coming of age in the jungles of Vietnam; is the author's memoirs of his sixteen months as an infantry officer.

Introducing the Chapter

Tell students that the Vietnam War, unlike others the U.S. fought, was not a popular war. People did not write songs in favor of it or buy war bonds to support it. It was the first American war that was covered live on television— Americans saw televised accounts of fighting and death daily. As students read this chapter, have them note additional ways in which this war differed from other wars Americans fought.

CHAPTER **33** 1954–1975

The Vietnam War

Links to American Literature

Filing up the trail that weaved through the stunted scrub jungle surrounding the outpost, the six men in the patrol walked on their bruised and rotted feet as if they were walking barefoot over broken glass. The patrol was waved in, and the marines climbed over the rusty perimeter wire one by one. The foothills where they had been all morning stretched behind them, toward the moss-green mountains wavering in the heat-shimmer.

The heat was suffocating, as it always was between monsoon storms. The air seemed about to explode. Sun-dazed, half the platoon were dozing beneath their hooches. Others cleaned their rifles, which would start to corrode in a few hours and have to be cleaned again. A few men squatted in a circle around a tin of cheese which had been brought to Charley Hill with the twice-weekly ration resupply. . . .

Page and Navarro, killed a few days before, had faced no choice. The booby-trapped artillery shell had not given them any time to choose, or to take cover, or to do anything but die instantly. Both had had only four days left of their Vietnam tours, thus confirming the truth in the proverb, ''You're never a short-timer until you're home.''

— PHILIP CAPUTO, *A Rumor of War*

It is probably safe to assume that many Americans had never heard of Vietnam before the 1950's. By the 1960's, however, Vietnam had become important to Americans because it involved them personally and affected their nation in ways that are still felt today. In spite of overwhelming congressional support for United States participation in the Vietnam War, public opposition was strong. As a result, American soldiers found themselves fighting a lonely war, without the comfort of popular support.

Chapter Overview

In this chapter you will learn why the United States became involved in Vietnam, and you will have a chance to analyze the nation's foreign policy goals. In addition, you will be able to evaluate the costs of the war to both sides and learn about its aftermath. This war had a tremendous impact on those who are decision makers in our society today. Chapter 33 covers the Vietnam War in four sections.

Chapter Outline

1. **American Involvement in Vietnam Begins**
2. **The Vietnam War Divides the Country**
3. **The Nation Withdraws from Vietnam**
4. **The Healing Process Takes Time**

State the Objective

Analyze the historical roots of U.S. involvement in Vietnam and the resulting U.S. foreign policy.

Anticipate the Lesson

Review with students American attitudes toward communism during the 1950's and 1960's. Ask students how these attitudes might have affected U.S. involvement in Southeast Asia. (Possible response: because of the fear generated by the McCarthy era, Americans were strongly in favor of protecting Asian countries from the threat of Communist takeovers.)

SECTION 1

American Involvement in Vietnam Begins

GLOSSARY TERMS: **domino theory, Geneva Accords, vietcong, Tonkin Gulf Resolution**

The Vietnam War was one of the most painful events in American history. Even today, opinion is sharply divided as to whether or not the United States should have become involved.

The Vietnam War Has Deep Roots

For almost two thousand years before Americans became involved in Vietnam, the Vietnamese people had been resisting foreign control. Their first opponents were the Chinese, who conquered northern Vietnam in 111 B.C. and ruled it for a thousand years. The Chinese introduced rice cultivation, thus creating the typical Vietnamese landscape of small villages set in rice fields surrounded by irrigation ditches, with jungles bordering the cultivated area. The Chinese also introduced the Chinese writing system and the Buddhist religion. The Vietnamese accepted Chinese culture but rebelled against Chinese rule. When they finally gained their independence in the tenth century, they set up their capital at Hanoi. Later they moved south and defeated several other ethnic groups that inhabited the Indochina peninsula. By 1700 the Vietnamese controlled the entire country. (See map on page 857.)

After more than nine hundred years of independence, a new enemy—the French—invaded the country in the mid-1800's. The Vietnamese fought back, but by 1893 the French conquest of Vietnam, as well as the other Indochinese nations of Cambodia and Laos, was complete.

Vietnam Under the French. French colonialism brought about many economic changes in Vietnam. New roads, railroads, and port facilities were constructed. Small, individually owned farms were replaced by large, mostly French-owned plantations that exported rice and rubber. The plantations were worked by the now landless peasants, who were fined or jailed if they tried to leave their jobs. Other displaced peasants became day laborers in the cities. During World War I, hundreds of thousands of Vietnamese were shipped to France to dig trenches on the battlefields and perform other forced labor.

There were cultural changes as well. Many Vietnamese converted to Roman Catholicism. French became the second official language taught in the public schools. Some 20,000 Vietnamese schools were closed, and a population that had been mostly literate when the French soldiers arrived was more than 80 percent illiterate a hundred years later.

The French organized a secret police force to put down opposition to their rule. They censored the press, restricted freedom of speech and assembly, and sent Vietnamese nationalists to a penal colony from which few returned. There were several major

---

People in the Chapter

Lyndon Johnson paced the floor worrying about a bombing raid he had ordered on Vietnam. When his daughter Luci returned from a date, he said, "Your daddy may have started World War III." Luci suggested they go to church and pray together. Even though it was midnight, the monks at St. Dominic's opened their doors for them.

William Westmoreland maintained that the military never lost a battle of consequence and did not lose the war. In the general's words: "The war was lost by congressional actions withdrawing support to the South Vietnamese government despite commitments by President Nixon."

Robert McNamara declared, "We are winning the war," after his tour of Vietnam in 1962. In the same year Robert Kennedy visited Saigon and said, "We are going to win." These statements prompted a journalist to write, "The only two exports of South Vietnam are rice and American optimism."

Henry Kissinger fled Nazi Germany and served in the United States Army in World War II. He won the Nobel Peace Prize for his role in the secret negotiations that brought about the end of the Vietnam War.

After students review the section, have volunteers add details to a chart on the board showing Chinese, French, and Japanese influence in Vietnam. Charts might include:

China
- Introduced rice cultivation.
- Introduced the Chinese writing system.
- Introduced the Buddhist religion.

France
- Constructed new railroads, roads, and ports.
- Built rice and rubber plantations.
- Introduced the Roman Catholic religion.

- Made French the second official language.
- Censored the press.

Japan
- Occupied Vietnam during World War II.

Ask students how Chinese, French, and Japanese involvement in Vietnam led to U.S. involvement there. (Possible responses: U.S. provided aid and medical supplies to the Vietminh, who in turn carried on guerrilla warfare against the Japanese and kept U.S. intelligence informed of Japanese military involvements; U.S. aided the French in their fight against Vietnam when, after North Vietnam invaded South Vietnam, Senator McCarthy accused the State Department of being Communist sympathizers.)

Picturing History Shown at the left is Bao Dai, head of the French puppet government in Vietnam. Below, President Harry Truman and Secretary of State Dean Acheson (right) discuss aid to French Indochina.

Vietnamese revolts, as well as a series of strikes and peasant uprisings during the 1930's. Most of the latter were organized by the Indochina Communist party under the leadership of **Ho Chi Minh** (hō'chē'min'). In 1941 the Communists combined with other nationalists to form an organization called the **Vietminh** (vē'ət min').

The End of French Rule. During World War II, Vietnam was occupied by the Japanese. The United States sent weapons and medical supplies to the Vietminh. In turn, the Vietminh carried on guerrilla warfare against the Japanese and kept American intelligence informed about Japanese military movements.

On September 2, 1945, one week after Japan surrendered, the Vietminh proclaimed the establishment of the Democratic Republic of Vietnam. Ho Chi Minh quoted from the American Declaration of Independence and warned that if his country did not receive its freedom from the French, ''we will keep on fighting until we get it.'' A month later, French soldiers disembarked in Vietnam from American troopships that had brought them from Europe.

Over the next five months, Ho sent eight messages to President Truman asking for support. Truman, however, believed that communists everywhere were part of a worldwide conspiracy directed by Moscow, so he ignored Ho's messages.

In 1946, after months of negotiation, a full-fledged war broke out between the Vietminh and the French. At first French troops were successful. The Vietminh, however, retreated to the mountains and began waging guerrilla warfare against the French in the cities. In 1949 the French set up a puppet government in Saigon headed by Bao Dai

(bä'ō dī'), a former Vietnamese emperor. The following year Ho Chi Minh, apparently with help from Communist China, launched a major offensive against the French.

That same year, 1950, marked the beginning of substantial American aid to the French. As you know, many Americans had been shocked by the loss of China to the Communists. Then North Korea invaded South Korea, and Senator Joseph McCarthy accused the State Department of being a hotbed of Communist sympathizers. With that as a background, Truman recognized Bao Dai's regime and sent it almost $1 billion in military and economic aid.

When Dwight Eisenhower was inaugurated President in 1953, he ordered the aid increased. Eisenhower believed in the **domino theory.** This theory held that if the Communists were to win in Indochina, all the remaining nations of Southeast Asia, regardless of their history or internal economic conditions, would come under Communist control one after another, the way a row of standing dominoes falls when the first domino is hit. By 1954 the United States was paying almost 80 percent of France's military expenses in Vietnam.

In March 1954 the Vietminh laid siege to a large French army at **Dien Bien Phu** (dyen'byen'foo). The French considered the stronghold impregna-

For Discussion
What is the domino theory? Is it a viable theory in today's world or does it represent an outdated fear of communism? (Responses might include: according to the domino theory, if South Vietnam fell to the Communists, the rest of Southeast Asia would fall also. Some students might feel that the theory represents a fear of communism no longer relevant in the 1990's; others might feel that communism is still a threat because of countries such as China.)

855

Check for Understanding

Call on individual students to answer Section 1 Review questions orally.

Ask students to write a paragraph explaining how Presidents Truman, Eisenhower, Kennedy, and Johnson viewed aid to Southeast Asia. (Paragraphs might include: Truman believed that communists were part of a worldwide conspiracy directed by Moscow; Eisenhower believed in the domino theory; Kennedy felt the U.S. had to display its power against communism; Johnson feared that other nations would lose respect for the U.S. if it did not live up to its anticommunist policy.)

Picturing History   Ten thousand French soldiers march to Vietminh prison camps after the fall of Dien Bien Phu. The inset shows Ho Chi Minh, leader of the Vietminh.

ble. Vietnamese soldiers and peasants, however, dragged heavy artillery up the mountains surrounding Dien Bien Phu and cut off all supplies except what could be delivered by air. The French then begged the United States to send in troops and carrier-based aircraft. Eisenhower turned down the appeal. He was reluctant to fight a land war in Asia, and he was afraid that an American air strike would bring the Soviet Union and China into the conflict. Moreover, he did not want to act without the approval of Congress and the support of Great Britain. On May 7, 1954, Dien Bien Phu fell. It was now clear that the French, like the Japanese, would have to leave Vietnam.

The Geneva Accords Divide Vietnam

In the meantime, an international conference began in Geneva in April 1954. It included representatives from the United States, France, Great Britain, the Soviet Union, China, Laos, Cambodia, the Vietminh, and Bao Dai's government. The United States, however, took the role of an observer. Many Americans viewed participation in diplomatic talks with the Vietminh as appeasement. Everyone agreed to a cease-fire. Then, as had been the case in Germany and Korea, Vietnam was divided, at the 17th parallel. The Democratic Republic of Vietnam, or North Vietnam, was headed by Ho Chi Minh. The State of Vietnam, or South Vietnam, was headed by Bao Dai. Elections

to form a government for the entire country were to be held after two years. Laos and Cambodia received their independence.

Because the North was now Communist, a two-way population shift took place within Vietnam over the next few months. Almost 900,000 civilians from North Vietnam, about three-fourths of them Catholic, sought refuge south of the 17th parallel. About 80,000 Vietminh guerrilla soldiers from the south moved to North Vietnam, leaving some 5,000 political organizers behind.

Soon after, Bao Dai's government was overthrown by **Ngo Dinh Diem** (ŋō din′ dē em′), a Catholic nationalist and a strong anti-Communist. Diem said he would not go along with the **Geneva Accords,** or agreements, because they had not been signed by the South Vietnamese government. He then moved to strengthen his regime.

Unfortunately, Diem's policies antagonized many South Vietnamese. For example, until then each village had elected its own chief and governing council. Diem abolished village elections and appointed as chiefs northern Catholics, who knew nothing about local conditions. He also imprisoned people who objected to his policies.

Conditions in North Vietnam were equally repressive. Ho Chi Minh set up a one-party political system and jailed or executed people who opposed the Vietminh. On the economic front, large estates were broken up and the land was redistributed to the peasants. Large industries were nationalized.

Guided Practice

Remind students that to both Presidents Kennedy and Johnson, a major issue in the Vietnam War was the preservation of America's credibility. Ask students whether credibility should be a main reason to continue fighting a war when victory seems impossible. (Possible response: a government should weigh casualties and other losses against the issue of global credibility.)

Threatened by Communist expansion in Asia, the Eisenhower administration initiated the creation of the **Southeast Asian Treaty Organization (SEATO).** In addition to the United States, its membership included Great Britain, France, Australia, New Zealand, Thailand, Pakistan, and the Philippines. These countries agreed that an attack on any one of them would be considered an attack on all of them.

In 1956 the time came for the all-Vietnam election to take place. Diem refused to take part. The reason was that in spite of Communist repression, it was clear that "Uncle" Ho would win. He had been fighting for decades against foreign control and as a result was a national hero. Diem, on the other hand, had been out of the country from 1950 to 1954, during the war against the French.

Diem's refusal to take part in the all-Vietnam election set off a guerrilla campaign against his government by a group known as the **National Liberation Front (NLF).** Their opponents called them the **Vietcong** (vē′ət käŋ′). Some of the Vietcong were the Vietminh political organizers who had remained behind in South Vietnam after the Geneva Accords. Others were Buddhists who did not like Diem's favoritism toward Catholics. There were also liberals who wanted a free press and trial by jury. Finally, there were nationalists who wanted Vietnam to be united and felt that Diem was the main obstacle to reunification. However, since it was obvious that the leaders of the Vietcong were Communists, Eisenhower sent more and more aid to Diem over the next four years.

Kennedy Is Committed to Containment

During the early 1960's, Diem's government became increasingly unstable. The Vietcong were successfully taking over the South Vietnamese countryside. Sometimes they were welcomed by the villagers. If they ran into opposition, they would kidnap or murder village officials and put in their own.

The Diem government fought back with its **strategic hamlet program.** The population of an entire village would be moved to a new area surrounded by walls and moats. Special teams were then organized to go from one hamlet to another to give medical assistance and advice on farming. However, many Vietnamese are ancestor worshippers who are very strongly attached to the rice fields where their ancestors are buried. Also, they did not like living behind fences. The strategic hamlet program was a failure, and the Vietcong position in the countryside continued to grow stronger. Meanwhile, in the cities the repressive policies and corruption of Diem's government turned more and more people against him.

In 1961 a special task force advised President Kennedy to send American combat troops to South Vietnam to assist the Diem regime. Kennedy, smarting from the Bay of Pigs fiasco in Cuba, felt that the United States had to display its power. He thought that Vietnam might be the place for a show of strength. At the same time, Kennedy was torn between his desire to contain communism and his belief that the only way the Diem government could win was by gaining the support of the Vietnamese people. So Kennedy increased the number of American soldiers who were helping to train Diem's troops. By the fall of 1963, there were over 16,000 American soldiers serving as advisors

Indochina: Vietnam, Laos, Cambodia

Boundary of French Indochina
Battle

Map Skills **Region** What countries comprised French Indochina? **Location** What latitude marked the boundary between North and South Vietnam?

Map Skills

North Vietnam, South Vietnam, Laos, Cambodia • 17th Parallel

Assign Independent Practice

Have students write a two-paragraph essay explaining the Geneva Accords and why they failed to bring about a lasting peace in Vietnam. (Paragraphs might include: the South Vietnamese government did not sign the agreement; the country was divided at the 17th parallel; the accords called for election to be held after two years to form a government for the entire country, but neither side wanted to give up power.)

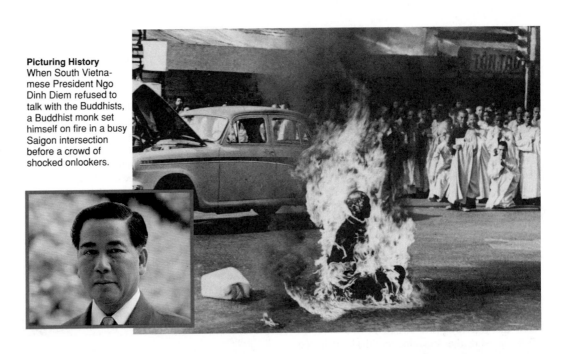

Picturing History
When South Vietnamese President Ngo Dinh Diem refused to talk with the Buddhists, a Buddhist monk set himself on fire in a busy Saigon intersection before a crowd of shocked onlookers.

in Vietnam. Kennedy also supplied Diem's troops with helicopters and authorized American pilots to fly combat missions.

In the meantime, religious opposition to Diem had escalated. Following a series of demonstrations, the Diem regime imprisoned hundreds of Buddhist monks and nuns and destroyed numerous Buddhist pagodas, or temples. Several Buddhist monks and nuns then publicly burned themselves to death in protest. American officials tried to convince Diem to stop persecuting the Buddhists, who were a majority of the population. Diem refused. On November 1, while the United States looked the other way, a successful military action, or coup, overthrew the Diem regime, and Diem was executed the next day.

Unfortunately, the new South Vietnamese government turned out to be even more unstable and ineffective than the old government. Land reform still lagged and corruption continued. One general replaced another, and Vietcong influence grew steadily until it covered almost 80 percent of the countryside.

Congress Passes the Tonkin Gulf Resolution

Shortly after Diem's overthrow, President Kennedy was assassinated and Lyndon Johnson became President. To Johnson, as to Kennedy, a major issue in the Vietnam War was America's credibility. Johnson believed that other nations would lose respect for the United States if it did not live up to its anticommunist policy. Johnson also viewed the Vietminh and Vietcong not as nationalists but as Chinese puppets. In his eyes, the Vietnam War was not a civil war but part of a larger conflict directed by China against the United States. Besides, the President's advisors assured him that it would take only a small investment of American troops and money to obtain a victory.

On July 30, 1964, the Hanoi government of North Vietnam complained that South Vietnamese ships, protected by an American destroyer, had attacked two of their islands. On August 2, North Vietnamese patrol torpedo boats attacked the American destroyer *Maddox* in the Gulf of Tonkin but were driven off. (See map on page 865.) Two days later it was reported that the *Maddox* had been attacked again. The United States denied taking part in the attack on North Vietnam. North Vietnam denied the August 4 attack. (Several years later, the American government acknowledged that it had, after all, helped South Vietnamese ships attack North Vietnam. An investigation indicated that the second attack against the *Maddox* probably never happened.)

Student Assignment/Homework

Have students read Section 2, "The Vietnam War Divides the Country," and complete Chapter 33, Section 1 Daily Activity.

Three days later, on August 7, Congress adopted what became known as the **Tonkin Gulf Resolution.** It stated that the President could "take all necessary measures to repel any armed attack against armed forces of the United States and to prevent further aggression." The vote in the House of Representatives was unanimous, 416 to 0. In the Senate, only Wayne Morse of Oregon and Ernest Gruening of Alaska voted no. Morse believed the resolution gave the President war-making power that rightfully belonged to Congress. Gruening felt that "all Vietnam is not worth the life of a single American boy." Both Morse and Gruening were defeated when they ran for reelection.

According to historian Barbara Tuchman, Tonkin Gulf was not a Fort Sumter or a Pearl Harbor, but it was no less significant. Johnson now had a blank check to do whatever he considered necessary to keep the Communists from taking over South Vietnam. The Vietnam War had become Americanized.

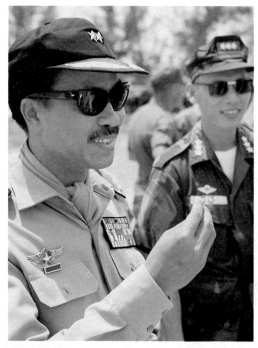

Picturing History Nguyen Cao Ky, the flamboyant South Vietnamese air force general (left), confers with his fellow officers before becoming Prime Minister in 1965. Some saw Ky as a bold and imaginative leader, while others distrusted him and saw him as a conniving showoff.

Linking Past to Present

Secrecy and an expansion of executive power characterized much of United States policy in Vietnam. Information regarding the Tonkin Gulf incident and later the bombing of Laos and Cambodia was withheld from the American people. The CIA's involvement in the war increased under the direction of the executive branch of government. Secrecy and expansion of executive power also surrounded covert operations of the CIA and the National Security Council in the civil war in Nicaragua during the 1980's. (See Chapter 36.)

SECTION 1 REVIEW

Key Terms and People

Explain the significance of: Ho Chi Minh, Vietminh, domino theory, Dien Bien Phu, Ngo Dinh Diem, Geneva Accords, SEATO, NLF, Vietcong, strategic hamlet program, Tonkin Gulf Resolution

Main Ideas

1. How did the United States aid French efforts to re-colonize Vietnam after World War II?
2. What were the main provisions of the Geneva Accords?
3. What brought about the National Liberation Front's use of guerrilla warfare against the South Vietnamese government?
4. What factors helped to bring about the overthrow and execution of President Diem?
5. What powers did the Tonkin Gulf Resolution grant to the President? Under what circumstances was the President allowed to make use of these powers?

Critical Thinking

6. What did the United States hope to gain by becoming involved in Vietnam's internal affairs? Do you think that, at the time, this expectation was realistic? Explain.

SECTION 1 REVIEW

Answers

Main Ideas

1. The U.S. ignored Ho Chi Minh's pleas for aid; also it recognized the French puppet government under Bao Dai and sent it military and economic aid.

2. Vietnam was divided into two nations at the 17th parallel; elections to form one Vietnamese government were to be held in two years; Laos and Cambodia became independent.

3. President Diem refused to take part in the all-Vietnam election per Geneva Accords.

4. Diem's strategic hamlet program made him unpopular with rural people, and his persecution of Buddhists made him unpopular with South Vietnam's Buddhist majority. Also, his policies proved ineffective against the Vietcong.

5. The power to use any method, including declaring war, to repel an aggressor.
• When the attack was by an armed aggressor against the armed forces of the U.S.

Critical Thinking

6. Possible answers: primarily the containment of communism; in addition, Kennedy and Johnson hoped to improve the somewhat damaged U.S. reputation. • Yes—because at the time, Southeast Asia was widely regarded as a poor, largely undeveloped region that could easily be brought under contol. No one was aware of the powerful determination of the Vietnamese. **(evaluation)**

The Vietnam War **859**

Anticipate the Lesson

Discuss Chapter 33, Section 1 Daily Activity with the students. Review the attitudes of Presidents Eisenhower, Kennedy, and Johnson on communism in Southeast Asia. (Possible responses: Eisenhower believed in the domino theory—he sent aid to anti-Communist forces; Kennedy was committed to containment—he sent combat troops to South Vietnam; Johnson feared the loss of global respect for the U.S. if it pulled out of Vietnam—he increased American troops and money in South Vietnam.)

State the Objective

Analyze how the Johnson administration dealt with the Vietnam War and with the antiwar movement after the Tet offensive.

Present the Lesson

Ask students to review the section and add details to an outline on the board of U.S. involvement in the Vietnam War. Outline might include:

I. Air war—Operation Rolling Thunder
   A. Offensive was massive air bombardment of North Vietnam.
   B. Bombing began in April 1965.
   C. Air war had little effect on North Vietnam.
   D. Johnson offered aid if fighting would stop.

Historical Sidelights

Facts on the Vietnam War:
• It was the longest war in which the U.S. took part, beginning in 1955 and ending in 1975. • About 58,000 American men and women died in the war, and more than 300,000 were wounded.
• The U.S. spent more than $160 billion.
• It was the first foreign war in which U.S. combat forces failed to achieve their goals. • The U.S. called the Vietnam experience alternately a brushfire war, a limited conflict, an externally supported communist insurgency, and a guerrilla war. • The first Green Beret training group arrived in May 1961. • A special unit—Air Force Aerospace Rescue and Recovery Service (ARRS), pararescue specialists trained as medics, paratroopers, frogmen, and rangers—was ready for any contingency involving downed fliers.

SECTION 2

The Vietnam War Divides the Country

GLOSSARY TERMS: **antiwar movement, Tet offensive**

Over the next four years, the United States poured hundreds of thousands of soldiers and vast amounts of weapons into Vietnam. Yet the escalation failed either to strengthen South Vietnam or to achieve military victory against North Vietnam.

Americans Enter the Vietnam Conflict

Following the Tonkin Gulf Resolution, North Vietnam began infiltrating regular army units into South Vietnam. They moved along the **Ho Chi Minh Trail,** a series of jungle paths that led from north to south by way of Laos and Cambodia. In the meantime, Johnson and his advisors decided that the United States should bomb North Vietnam and send troops into South Vietnam.

The Air War. Johnson launched Operation Rolling Thunder, a massive air bombardment of North Vietnam, in April 1965. The President himself chose the targets that American planes were to hit. By 1967 more tons of bombs were being dropped on North Vietnam every year than had been dropped on Germany during all of World War II. However, the massive air war had little effect on North Vietnam. It did not weaken the economy; it did not break the people's will to fight; and it did not stop the flow of men and supplies along the Ho Chi Minh Trail.

Now and again, the United States would halt the bombing in an effort to persuade North Vietnam to accept the Saigon regime and withdraw its troops to the north of the 17th parallel. In April 1965, Johnson also offered $1 billion in aid to the nations of Southeast Asia, including North Vietnam, if the fighting would stop. Each time, however, the Hanoi government gave the same reply. The bombing must stop unconditionally, and all American forces must leave Vietnam before peace negotiations could begin.

The Ground War. While American planes took to the air, American troops poured into Vietnam to assist the South Vietnamese army. By 1968 more than 538,000 Americans were serving in Vietnam.

Since it was difficult to distinguish between enemy fighters and civilians, Americans used a tactic called the **search-and-destroy mission.** Helicopters would land troops in a village suspected of either supporting or being controlled by the Vietcong. The soldiers would go to a village before dawn, rouse the people from their beds and move them out, kill the poultry and livestock, and then

Picturing History
Despite his own injuries, an American marine reaches out to help his wounded buddy. Some ten thousand GI's lost at least one limb in Vietnam as a result of ambushes, mines, and booby traps.

E. Hanoi demanded unconditional halt to bombing and withdrawal of all American forces.
II. Ground war
A. Search-and-destroy missions destroyed villages and left four million South Vietnamese refugees.
B. U.S. forces used defoliants in jungles.
III. Increased opposition
A. By 1966, it was becoming difficult for U.S. citizens to support the war.
B. Antiwar movement took various forms, including shows, marches, bumper stickers, draft card burning, and picketing.
C. Doves opposed the war because it was a civil war and it was draining U.S. strength and economy.
IV. Tet offensive
A. Assault took place on January 30, 1968—the eve of Vietnamese New Year.
B. Vietcong attacked a hundred towns and cities, and twelve U.S. bases.
C. Offensive lasted less than one month.
D. General Westmoreland declared defeat for Communists.
E. Secretary of Defense McNamara resigned.
V. Johnson's decision
A. Eugene McCarthy and Robert Kennedy showed strong support in Democratic primaries.
B. On March 31, 1968, Johnson announced he would not seek reelection.

burn the village. As an American major explained, "It became necessary to destroy the town to save it." Unfortunately, most of the casualties in this kind of fighting were old men, women, and children. The men of fighting age were usually snipers who shot from a position hidden in the jungle.

One result of search-and-destroy missions was the creation of some 4 million South Vietnamese refugees out of a total population of 20 million. These destitute people poured into special refugee camps or into the cities, where attention could be given to their need for food, shelter, and medical care.

Fighting the Vietcong guerrillas created yet another problem. In an effort to destroy the jungles that provided cover for the Vietcong, the United States sprayed huge quantities of toxic chemicals on the countryside. The **defoliants,** which caused leaves to drop off all plants, devastated about 30 percent of the landscape. Until 1967, South Vietnam had been a major exporter of rice. By 1968 it was importing rice in an effort to prevent mass starvation. The defoliants also led to alleged birth defects in Vietnamese children and in the children of American servicemen, as well as to liver damage, muscular disorders, and other health problems for the adults who were exposed to the chemicals.

Opposition to the Living-Room War Increases

By 1966 many Americans were beginning to have serious doubts about the nation's growing involvement in Vietnam. It became more and more difficult to sustain support for a long, bloody war that was entering American living rooms on the nightly news. Newspapers and magazines carried reports of such incidents as the American massacre of Vietnamese civilians in the Valley of My Lai (mī lī). The opposition became known as the **antiwar movement** and took various forms. There were antiwar musical shows and stop-the-bombing marches. There were automobile bumper stickers that read "Make Love Not War" and posters stating that "War is not healthy for children and other living things." Young Americans burned their draft cards or picketed induction centers. Sit-ins and strikes erupted on college campuses, especially after student draft deferments were abolished early in 1966 for college students ranking in the lower level of the class. Also, once deferred students graduated from college, they could be drafted. By 1968 about ten thousand Americans

had emigrated to Canada in order to avoid serving in what they considered an immoral war.

Linking Past to Present

During the Vietnam War, relations between the United States military and the media were generally open. Reporters and camera crews were free to go wherever they chose. Some people believed that in fact the press used this freedom to undermine the Vietnam War effort. In 1989 President George Bush tried to avoid such a possibility when the United States invaded Panama in an attempt to oust Panamanian General Manuel Noriega. Media coverage in Panama was limited to a pool of reporters and a camera crew who were flown into Panama four hours after the invasion began. Once there, the military restricted the media's movements and primarily funneled information about events through its own briefing sessions. In 1991, the Pentagon exercised similar curbs on the media during Operation Desert Storm in Kuwait and Iraq.

The arguments presented by the doves, as those who were against the war were called, varied. Probably the most common reason for opposition was the belief that the war was basically a civil war. Some doves argued that the United States could not police the world and that the Vietnam War was draining American strength from other important places such as Europe and the Middle East. Other doves felt that in trying to save South Vietnam from communism the United States government was actually destroying the country and its people. It was seriously damaging the United States as well. Tens of thousands of Americans were being killed and wounded, while the cost of the conflict—about $25 billion a year—was causing serious inflation and was draining resources that would otherwise have gone to the Great Society's social programs.

The hawks, those who supported the Vietnam War, agreed with President Johnson that Vietnam was vital to American security and that containing communism was more important than casualties or cost. By fighting in South Vietnam, these people asserted, the United States was really protecting itself.

For Discussion
What was the role of television in the Vietnam War? To what extent do you think television coverage influenced Americans' attitudes toward the war? (Possible response: television brought the realities of the war into American homes; it made many take an active part in either supporting or protesting the war and resulted in the questioning of the government's fighting the war.)

Check for Understanding

Have students answer Section 2 Review questions on paper.

Guided Practice

Remind students that during the Vietnam War, the U.S. military sprayed toxic defoliants on the countryside, devastating about 30 percent of the vegetation. To stimulate discussion, ask students the following questions. What long-term effects might such chemicals have on the land? What responsibility do you think the government should assume in restoring the land? (Possible answers: the toxic chemicals might make farming impossible for an undetermined length of time; the government could test the soil and inform inhabitants as to the toxicity of the ground in specific areas; it should do whatever is possible to neutralize the toxicity of the soil.)

America in Vietnam

1950 May 8—President Truman provides U.S. aid to French military in Indochina; 35 American advisers sent to Vietnam.

1954 July—Geneva Conference on Indochina brings a cease-fire and temporarily divides the country.

1961 Nov. 16—President Kennedy increases number of military advisers to South Vietnam.

1964 August—American and North Vietnamese forces clash in Gulf of Tonkin.

Aug. 7—Congress grants President Johnson authority to "take all necessary steps to repel armed attacks against the forces of the United States and to prevent further aggression." (Gulf of Tonkin Resolution.)

1965 Feb. 6—U.S. begins bombing of North Vietnam.

Mar. 8—First American ground combat troops arrive in Vietnam.

1968 Jan. 30—Tet offensive brings Vietcong attacks on more than 100 towns and bases.

Oct. 31—President Johnson orders bombing restrictions, providing basis for negotiations.

1969 Jan. 25—Paris peace talks begin in earnest after President Johnson further scales back American involvement.

June 8—President Nixon calls for "Vietnamization" of the war, orders staged withdrawal of American troops.

1970 April 30—U.S. troops enter Cambodia to destroy North Vietnamese supply bases.

1971 June-July—Secret peace negotiations with North Vietnam begun by Presidential adviser Henry A. Kissinger.

1972 Aug. 12—Last U.S. ground combat troops leave South Vietnam.

Dec. 18—Christmas bombing of Hanoi and Haiphong.

1973 Jan. 27—Truce agreement signed in Paris, cease-fire in Vietnam.

Mar. 29—Last U.S. military personnel leave South Vietnam.

Apr. 1—U.S. prisoners of war released.

1975 April 30—Fall of Saigon. Evacuation of American Embassy.

The Commitment

Military Personnel

Americans who served: 3,330,000
Americans killed: 58,721; killed in battle: 47,655
Americans wounded: 303,713
Americans taken prisoner: 839
  Returned: 691
  Escaped: 34
  Died in captivity: 114
Americans still classified as missing (1965-1975): 2,477
Americans awarded the Medal of Honor: 238

Money

American Aid to South Vietnam (1955-1975): $24 billion
Direct American expenditures for the war: $165 billion

Source: The New York Times, April 30, 1985.

The Aftermath

Evacuation

Americans evacuated: 1,373
Vietnamese evacuated: 5,595
Value of U.S. military equipment seized by Communists: $5 billion
Military and civilian dead (all forces): 1,313,000
Land defoliated: 5.2 million acres
Indochinese refugees: 9,000,000
Living U.S. veterans with Vietnam service: 2,700,000
Vietnam veterans receiving government compensation: 500,000
Disabled U.S. Vietnam veterans: 519,000

Picturing History Over one hundred towns and military bases were simultaneously attacked during the Tet offensive of 1968. A rocket explodes at Khesanh (right), an American base south of the DMZ. Below, a wounded marine from Delta Company is pulled to safety by his buddies.

The Tet Offensive Stuns Americans

Tuesday evening, January 30, 1968, was the Vietnamese equivalent of New Year's Eve. The next day was Tet, the start of the lunar new year. The streets of cities throughout South Vietnam were filling up with farmers and youngsters who were apparently arriving from the countryside to celebrate the holiday. There were also an unusually large number of funerals taking place, with the traditional firecrackers and flutes and, of course, coffins.

As it turned out, the coffins contained weapons, while the supposed farmers belonged to special Vietcong units. That night the enemy launched an overwhelming attack on about a hundred towns and cities, including Saigon and Hué, and twelve United States air bases, including those at Da Nang and Cam Ranh Bay. After less than a month of fighting, South Vietnamese and American troops succeeded in regaining control.

General **William Westmoreland,** the American commander in South Vietnam, declared that the **Tet offensive** had been a major defeat for the Communists. From a military point of view, he was right. The Vietcong had suffered heavy casualties— as many as 42,000 killed—and had failed to deliver a knockout blow. From a political point of view, however, Westmoreland was wrong. For one thing, the Vietnam War had now spread from the countryside to the supposedly secure cities. For another thing, it was obvious that the Johnson administration had been grossly exaggerating the body counts of enemy dead and that the Vietcong were nowhere near the brink of surrender. A feeling that the Vietnam War was unwinnable began to spread through the United States. Even some of the President's associates, who had previously supported American involvement, began calling for the nation to cut its losses and pull out. Early in 1968, Johnson's Secretary of Defense, **Robert McNamara,** resigned. Johnson replaced him with **Clark Clifford,** a Washington attorney and an old friend, whom the President expected to be more supportive of the war than McNamara had been. After examining the military reports, Clifford also began to doubt the administration's policy in Vietnam.

Johnson Bows Out

On March 12, 1968, New Hampshire voters turned out for the Presidential primary. Running against Johnson was Senator **Eugene McCarthy** of Minnesota, who had announced his candidacy the previous November. Although McCarthy had voted for the Tonkin Gulf Resolution, he had become increasingly dovish as the war continued. He was particularly bothered by the so-called credibility gap, the difference between the optimistic statements of the Johnson administration and what was really happening in Vietnam. Helping McCarthy in his campaign were some five thousand young people from colleges throughout the Northeast. They poured into New Hampshire on their own, set

up campaign centers, and talked to people about the need for a policy of peace in Washington.

When the ballots were counted, Johnson received 49 percent of the Democratic vote and McCarthy 42 percent. However, enough Republicans wrote in McCarthy's name on their ballots to make his total almost the same as Johnson's. This was an amazing showing for an almost unknown senator against an incumbent President.

Elated with the results, thousands of Midwestern college students then poured into Wisconsin, where the next big Presidential primary was scheduled for April 2. In the meantime, former Attorney General **Robert Kennedy,** now a senator from New York, announced that he also would challenge Johnson. Kennedy had suggested an American withdrawal from Vietnam as early as August 1963, when his late brother had been President. It had seemed obvious to him that the Saigon government did not have the support of the Vietnamese people and thus could not prevent a Communist takeover. In 1967

Picturing History Democratic Presidential candidates in 1968 included Eugene McCarthy (above), Lyndon Johnson (above right), and Robert Kennedy (right). After Johnson's poor showing in the New Hampshire primary, he announced he would not run for reelection.

SECTION 3
Core Lesson

State the Objective

Understand how the Nixon administration withdrew American troops from Vietnam.

Anticipate the Lesson

Review reasons for President Johnson's decision not to run for reelection in 1968. (Responses might include: a strong showing by McCarthy and Kennedy in the Presidential primaries; growing opposition to the Vietnam War; resignations and disagreements in the Johnson administration.)

---

the younger Kennedy had criticized the administration's behavior: "We're killing innocent people . . . because [the Communists] are twelve thousand miles away and they might get eleven thousand miles away."

A shrewd politician, Johnson understood what was happening. On March 31, he addressed the nation on television. "There is division in the American house now. Accordingly, I shall not seek, and I will not accept, the nomination of my party for another term as your President." Four years earlier, LBJ had received the greatest majority of popular votes in the nation's history. Now he was calling an end to his political career.

In addition, Johnson promised to limit the bombing to invasion routes and to the area immediately north of the **Demilitarized Zone (DMZ),** or the neutral area that separated North and South Vietnam.

On May 10, 1968, preliminary peace talks began in Paris between representatives of Ho Chi Minh and the United States. The fighting, however, continued.

SECTION 2 REVIEW

Key Terms and People

Explain the significance of: Ho Chi Minh Trail, search-and-destroy mission, defoliants, antiwar movement, William Westmoreland, Tet offensive, Robert McNamara, Clark Clifford, Eugene McCarthy, Robert Kennedy, DMZ

Main Ideas

1. What were the important effects of the tactics adopted by United States ground forces in Vietnam?
2. Why did doves oppose United States involvement in the Vietnam War? Why did hawks support it?
3. How did the Tet offensive change many Americans' views of their nation's involvement in the Vietnam War?
4. Why did President Johnson decide not to run for reelection in 1968?

Critical Thinking

5. Why was the Vietnam War particularly offensive to young Americans? How did young Americans help to limit United States involvement in the war?

SECTION 3

The Nation Withdraws from Vietnam

GLOSSARY TERMS: Vietnamization

In his successful 1968 campaign for the Presidency (Chapter 34), **Richard M. Nixon** assured voters that "we will end this one and win the peace." He had a secret plan to obtain "peace with honor" in Vietnam.

Nixon Vietnamizes the War

President Nixon's plan was a program of **Vietnamization** of the war. This meant gradually withdrawing American ground troops and letting the South Vietnamese do their own fighting. By the

The Vietnam War

Map Skills   Location What river divides Laos from Thailand? **Movement** Through what countries did the Ho Chi Minh Trail pass?

Present the Lesson

Have students review the section and add details to a time line on the board showing U.S. involvement in Vietnam during the Nixon administration. Time line might include:

August 1969	Vietnamization begins—the first twenty-five thousand U.S. troops are withdrawn, and aid to Saigon and air activity against North Vietnam are stepped up.
November 15 1969	March Against Death takes place in Washington, D.C.
Spring 1970	Nixon orders U.S. troops into Cambodia; news of the invasion sets off student strikes throughout the country.
May 4 1970	Kent State University tragedy occurs.
May 8 1970	Antiwar demonstrators confront construction workers in New York City.
1971	South Vietnamese invade Laos.
1972	North Vietnam launches a major offensive against South Vietnam; Nixon softens U.S. demands.
October 8 1972	Kissinger announces that a cease-fire agreement is about to be signed.
December 1972	Each side accuses the other of bad faith in negotiations; Nixon orders twelve days of air attacks on North Vietnam.
January 27 1973	U.S. and North Vietnam sign a cease-fire agreement.
March 1975	A major offensive from North Vietnam sweeps through South Vietnam.

Picturing History Protests against the Vietnam War took many forms. Above, marchers carry coffins while buses form a security ring around the White House. Drummers led another march (top right), which began in Arlington National Cemetery and lasted some forty hours.

end of August 1969, the first 25,000 United States troops had come home.

At the same time, however, Nixon still wanted North Vietnam to accept the Saigon regime and the partition of Vietnam. So he increased American military aid to Saigon and stepped up air activity against North Vietnam. In addition, he secretly ordered United States planes to bomb Cambodia and Laos. (See map on page 865.) Vietcong forces were using these two nations as sanctuaries. They would slip across the borders into South Vietnam and then return after attacking South Vietnamese strongholds.

Vietnamization did not work in the late 1960's any more than it had in the late 1950's. Although American soldiers began returning home in increasing numbers, the corrupt and inefficient regime of General Nguyen Van Thieu (ŋi'en văn too) could not recruit enough South Vietnamese soldiers to take their place.

In the meantime, public protests in the United States against the war increased. For the most part, these were peaceful demonstrations called moratoriums. One of the most dramatic moratoriums occurred on November 15, 1969, when some 250,000 people took part in a March Against Death in Washington, D.C. They walked four miles from Arlington National Cemetery to the Capitol, and designated people carried cards with the names of American soldiers who had died in Vietnam.

President Nixon did not see the march. He was in the White House watching a football game on television. Thus the President made it clear that administration policy would not be affected by demonstrations in the streets. Nixon also felt that an unconditional withdrawal from Vietnam would be humiliating. A public opinion poll showed that three out of four Americans agreed with the President's view.

April 30
1975

North Vietnam enters Saigon.

July
1975

Reunification of the country
is declared.

Have students refer to this time line as they
study Section 3.

Check for Understanding

Call on individual students to read their answers to Section 3 Review questions.

The United States Invades Cambodia

In the spring of 1970, President Nixon made another move to strengthen the position of South Vietnam. Without consulting Congress, he ordered American troops into Cambodia to clear out North Vietnamese and Vietcong supply centers. The President defended his action by saying that he preferred to follow his conscience rather than "be a two-term president at the cost of seeing America become a second-rate power." He went on to say: "If when the chips are down, the world's most powerful nation . . . acts like a pitiful, helpless giant, the forces of totalitarianism and anarchy will threaten free nations . . . throughout the world."

The news of the invasion set off the first general student strike in the nation's history. It involved more than 1.5 million students and closed down some 1,200 campuses. On May 4, tragedy struck Kent State University in Ohio, where 4 students were killed and 9 wounded when members of the National Guard fired into a crowd of antiwar demonstrators who were hurling rocks at them. On the weekend of May 9–10, some 100,000 students protested the killings in front of the White House. At first Nixon called them bums. Later he tried to talk with them in a quiet and friendly manner. Instead of discussing the war, however, he spoke about football and surfing. As a newspaper reporter wrote, "The two Americas met and drifted apart in a state of mutual incomprehension."

Another example of the two Americas showed itself in New York City. On May 8 a shouting match between antiwar demonstrators and con- struction workers in hardhats turned into a riot when one of the demonstrators apparently spit on the American flag. With cries of "USA, all the way!," "We're Number One," and "Love it or leave it!," the construction workers began swinging metal tools and throwing punches. Some seventy antiwar protesters and four policemen were injured. To the antiwar demonstrators, the issue was the right of political dissent. To the construction workers, the issue was patriotism.

The invasion of Cambodia produced a lengthy debate in Congress. The Senate, believing that its war-making power had been usurped by the President, voted to repeal the Tonkin Gulf Resolution. Nixon, on the other hand, asserted that as commander in chief he had the right to send troops into Cambodia. In any event, the troops were withdrawn by the end of June, 1970.

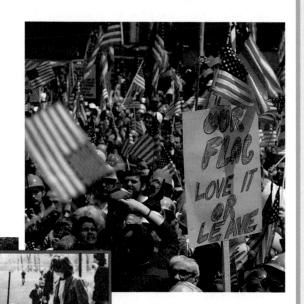

Picturing History Construction workers and others demonstrate in support of Richard Nixon's policies in Cambodia. They were part of the "silent majority," a group that believed student protests undermined the war effort. In response to the killing of students at Kent State University (center), huge antiwar demonstrations were held throughout the country.

Guided Practice

Remind students that Richard Nixon assured voters that he had a secret plan to obtain "peace with honor" in Vietnam. Ask students whether they think it is ethical to withhold such information as a campaign tactic. (Possible responses: no—plans for peace should be made known and executed as soon as possible, not be withheld to obtain votes. Yes—since they were Nixon's ideas, it was acceptable for him to reveal the plans when he thought best.)

For Discussion

President Nixon said he would rather follow his conscience than "be a two-term President at the cost of seeing America become a second-rate power," and yet as the 1972 Presidential election approached, Nixon dropped the U.S. demand that all North Vietnamese troops withdraw from South Vietnam. Do you view this action as an election ploy or as a true concession for peace? (Possible responses: concession for peace—the dropping of demands represented a positive move toward ending the war; Nixon realized that the U.S. could not continue in its demands for an unconditional withdrawal and still end the war. Election ploy—because of its timing, the action strengthened Nixon's chances for reelection.)

Historical Sidelight

U.S. involvement in Vietnam ended in 1975 with the helicopter evacuation of the last remaining Americans.

Nixon Withdraws American Troops

For the next two and one-half years, peace talks continued in Paris, fighting continued in Vietnam, and opposition to the war continued to build in the United States.

In 1971 South Vietnamese soldiers invaded Laos in an attempt to cut off the flow of men and supplies along the Ho Chi Minh trail. (See map on page 865.) Despite American air support, the invasion was a disaster, and the South Vietnamese army was defeated by the North Vietnamese. In the meantime, morale among the American troops still in Vietnam plummeted.

There were many reasons for this. The average GI was nineteen years old, as compared with the average World War II GI, who was twenty-six. Then, too, soldiers in World War II had trained as units and had gone into combat with men they knew. In Vietnam, soldiers were "plugged in" as individuals. The casualty rate was high because the tour of duty lasted only one year. (Casualties are always higher during the first few months soldiers are in combat because they are inexperienced.) In addition, many GI's did not see why they should continue fighting if their government was negotiating for peace.

One result of the low morale was widespread drug abuse. Smoking marijuana had been commonplace since the 1960's. However, it is estimated that up to 30 percent of American soldiers became addicted to heroin or opium. Another result of low morale was a growing number of incidents called fragging. In these murders or attempted murders, soldiers threw fragmentation grenades (those that did not leave fingerprints) at their own officers in battle.

In 1972 North Vietnam launched a major offensive against South Vietnam. Nixon responded by stepping up the bombing of North Vietnam and by mining Haiphong harbor, through which supplies from the Soviet Union were entering North Vietnam. (See map on page 857.) This would be, he declared, the "decisive military action to end the war." The result was a stalemate.

With the approach of the 1972 Presidential election, Nixon finally decided to change America's bargaining position in Paris. All along, the United States had insisted that North Vietnamese as well as American troops withdraw from South Vietnam. Now the United States dropped that demand. It agreed to pull out its forces but said it would continue sending economic and military aid

Picturing History National Security Advisor Henry Kissinger (left) met with North Vietnamese leader Le Duc Tho (right) in 1972. A tough negotiator, Le Duc Tho held out until his goals were met.

to South Vietnam. North Vietnam agreed to release American prisoners of war (POW's).

On October 8, 1972, **Henry Kissinger,** Nixon's negotiator in Paris, announced that a cease-fire agreement with North Vietnam was about to be signed. Making his television debut on October 26 Kissinger said, "We believe that peace is at hand." However, the signing was postponed. There were points to be clarified. The South Vietnamese government, for one thing, would not accept the terms.

By December, clarification had not been achieved, and each side was accusing the other of bad faith in the negotiations. Nixon ordered twelve days of blistering air attacks on Hanoi and Haiphong. The so-called Christmas bombing was designed to demonstrate American military might to both North Vietnam and South Vietnam. Unfortunately, most of the military barracks, warehouses, and factories that were the chief targets were located in heavily populated areas. Homes, schools, and hospitals were unintentionally hit, and civilian casualties were high.

At this point, even members of Congress who had previously supported Nixon's Vietnam policy urged an end. At the same time, Moscow and Beijing told Hanoi that it was time to get on with the peace. On January 27, 1973, the United States and North Vietnam finally signed a cease-fire agreement. By the end of March, the last American troops had left Vietnam for home.

Assign Independent Practice

Have students write a three-paragraph essay comparing the circumstances behind President Johnson's decision not to run for reelection during the Vietnam War and Franklin Roosevelt's reelection during World War II. (Essays might include: FDR served his term during a well-supported war, whereas Johnson served during an unpopular war; FDR had helped the country out of depression and citizens were still grateful, whereas Johnson's Great Society did not accomplish its goals and left many people discontented.)

Student Assignment/Homework

Have students read Section 4, "The Healing Process Takes Time," and complete Chapter 33, Section 3 Daily Activity.

South Vietnam Surrenders

In spite of the withdrawal of American troops, fighting continued in Vietnam, with both sides violating the cease-fire agreement. During 1973 South Vietnam, with almost $4 billion worth of aid from the United States, increased the area under its control. In March 1975, however, the tables began to turn. Within a period of six weeks, a major offensive from North Vietnam swept through South Vietnam. The South Vietnamese army collapsed, and on April 30 the North Vietnamese army entered Saigon.

Meanwhile the United States officials in Saigon were evacuating American civilians and Vietnamese who had worked closely with them. Until the last moment, helicopters took off from the roof of the United States embassy in Saigon carrying people to American ships waiting offshore. The United States ambassador was one of the last to leave.

Shortly afterward, North Vietnamese troops entered the embassy compound. As the red and yellow Vietcong flag flapped from the balcony, a North Vietnamese colonel who had enlisted in the Vietminh thirty years earlier gave a short speech to surrendering South Vietnamese officials. "You have nothing to fear," he said. "Between Vietnamese, there are no victors and no vanquished. Only the Americans have been beaten. If you are patriots, consider this a moment of joy. The war for our country is over."

Despite these promises, more than 400,000 South Vietnamese were forced into so-called reeducation camps after 1975. Although many have since been released, human rights groups have repeatedly denounced conditions in these camps.

Within a few days after the surrender, all of Vietnam was under the control of the Communist government in Hanoi. Saigon was renamed Ho Chi Minh City in memory of the leader who had died in 1969 at the age of seventy-nine. The reunification of the country was declared official in July, twenty-one years after the 1954 Geneva Accords that followed the French defeat at Dien Bien Phu.

Picturing History Evacuation as Saigon falls. U.S. sailors (top) push an empty helicopter into the sea to make room for more refugee flights, while anxious Americans and Vietnamese (below) push to board an evacuation flight from the roof of the U.S. embassy.

SECTION 3 REVIEW

Key Terms and People

Explain the significance of: Richard M. Nixon, Vietnamization, Henry Kissinger

Main Ideas

1. What was President Nixon's initial plan to obtain peace with honor in Vietnam? Why was the plan unsuccessful?
2. How did Americans react to the invasion of Cambodia?
3. In the early 1970's, what factors contributed to the low morale of American troops in Vietnam?
4. How were both sides in the Vietnam War finally persuaded to sign a cease-fire agreement?
5. After United States forces were withdrawn, what happened to South Vietnam?

Critical Thinking

6. In your opinion, did the United States win or lose the Vietnam War? Explain.

SECTION 3 REVIEW

Answers

Main Ideas

1. Vietnamization of the war by replacing American troops with South Vietnamese troops.
• Although U.S. troops withdrew, South Vietnam could not recruit enough soldiers to replace them.

2. Students went on strike; National Guardsmen gunned down antiwar demonstrators at Kent State; a shouting match between antiwar demonstrators and construction workers turned into a riot in New York; Senate repealed the Tonkin Gulf Resolution.

3. South Vietnam's army was defeated in Laos; the average GI was very young and was assigned to combat units with people he did not know; casualty rates were high; peace negotiations led many to doubt value of continuing to fight.

4. After the 1972 Christmas bombing, Nixon lost all congressional support for his Vietnam policy. Leaders in China and the U.S.S.R. called on N. Vietnam to agree to peace.

5. Within three years, it was brought under the control of the North Vietnamese government.

Critical Thinking

6. Possible answer: the U.S. lost because it did not achieve the containment of communism in Southeast Asia. Also the U.S. suffered thousands of casualties and failed to improve South Vietnamese lives significantly.
(analysis & evaluation)

State the Objective

Understand how the problems of Vietnam veterans were different from the problems of veterans of earlier wars.

Anticipate the Lesson

Ask students why American opinion was different during the Vietnam War than during earlier wars. (Possible responses: Americans were exposed to the realities of war on television every night; there seemed to be no victory in sight; although the war generated heavy costs in money and manpower, it did not seem to be stopping communism as had been intended.)

SECTION 4

The Healing Process Takes Time

GLOSSARY TERMS: **War Powers Act, boat people**

The Vietnam War was the longest war in United States history. Casualty statistics vary, but by most estimates there were about 47,000 battle deaths and more than 300,000 wounded. The price tag was about $165 billion. There were many indirect costs as well.

Vietnam Veterans Return Home

Coming home from Vietnam was very different from coming home from World War II. For one thing, the Vietnam veterans returned, not by regiment or division, but one by one. Instead of crossing the ocean on a slow troop ship that gave them time to unwind, they were whisked home by jet airplane. As one veteran put it: "We were hired assassins out there. Then the next day we're supposed to go home to the Ford plant and forget everything. Yeah, right."

In addition—again unlike World War II—Vietnam veterans in general were not considered heroes in the United States. There were no brass bands playing when they landed, no victory parades down Main Street, no cheering crowds. The most common reaction they met was indifference. In some instances, they met with insults.

Despite this neglect, most Vietnam veterans readjusted successfully to civilian life. However, as of mid-1988 about 15 percent of the 3.3 million Americans who served in Vietnam had developed symptoms that doctors diagnosed as **delayed stress syndrome.** They had recurring nightmares in which they relived their war experiences. They suffered from severe headaches and memory lapses, apathy, and other problems. For several thousand Vietnam veterans, suicide offered the only relief from their suffering.

Still another group of young Americans with special postwar problems were the draft resisters who had crossed the border into Canada or had gone to Sweden to avoid fighting what they considered to be an immoral war. In 1974 President Gerald Ford offered these men amnesty, or a conditional pardon. They would have to repledge their allegiance to the United States and serve for

Picturing History In 1981 Maya Ying Lin, a twenty-one-year-old architecture student whose parents fled China in 1958, submitted the winning design for the Vietnam Veterans Memorial. "To overcome grief," Lin said, "you have to confront it." Her design became known as the Wall.

Present the Lesson

Have students add details to a chart on the board showing the differences between World War II G.I.'s and Vietnam G.I.'s. Charts might include:

World War II G.I.'s

• Returned in regiments or divisions.
• Crossed Atlantic and Pacific on slow ships, getting a chance to rest and to adjust.
• Were treated as heroes.

Vietnam G.I.'s

• Returned one by one.
• Flew home in a day or two, which resulted in "culture shock."
• Met with indifference.

Ask students how these differences resulted in more adjustment problems for Vietnam vets. (Possible response: culture shock, lack of support, and lack of appreciation all contributed to delayed stress syndrome.)

two years as hospital orderlies, conservation workers, and the like. However, only a few draft resisters accepted Ford's offer. In 1977 President Carter, despite strong protests from many veterans' organizations, granted them a blanket pardon.

In 1981, as a result of the efforts of Vietnam veteran Jan C. Scruggs, the decision was made to build a memorial to the Vietnam War in our nation's capital. The site chosen lay between the Washington Monument and the Lincoln Memorial. Since then, an additional memorial has gone up in the same area in Washington. It is a sculpture of three soldiers with weapons. Another sculpture is planned that will represent the more than sixty-five hundred nurses who also served in Vietnam.

Political and Constitutional Questions Are Raised

Another indirect result of the Vietnam War was a growing distrust on the part of the government toward the American people. Lyndon Johnson gave out misleading information, such as the facts about the Gulf of Tonkin incident. Richard Nixon concealed many of his activities, such as the bombing of Cambodia. The military high command deliberately falsified records. Field commanders were ordered to report certain numbers of enemy dead regardless of how many had actually been killed. These actions in turn led to a lessened respect on the part of the people for the government.

There also seemed to be considerable confusion about the nation's role in world affairs. Americans agreed they did not want any more Vietnams, but they did not agree on what that meant. Should the United States turn isolationist again? Should it limit its interests to the Western Hemisphere? Should it try to contain communism even if that meant supporting antidemocratic governments? Did it have the right to intervene in the internal affairs of other countries? What was the best way to fight communism anyway?

One specific result of the Vietnam War was the setting of limits on the war-making powers of the President. In November 1973 Congress passed the **War Powers Act.** According to this act, a President who sends United States troops to a foreign country has to explain the action to Congress within forty-eight hours. Furthermore, Congress can order the troops withdrawn after sixty days. Nixon vetoed the measure, but it was passed over his veto.

Vietnamese Refugees Arrive

Following the Communist victory, several waves of Vietnamese fled their homeland. The first wave of refugees left in 1975. It consisted of the richer and better educated South Vietnamese who had supported the American military effort and were afraid that they would be imprisoned or executed by the Communists for having collaborated with the enemy. Numbering about 135,000, most of these refugees came to the United States. The rest went to France.

The second and much larger wave of South Vietnamese refugees were the so-called **boat people** who began leaving Vietnam in 1978. They were known as boat people because they fled on anything from freighters to barges to rowboats. Numbering more than one million, they were mostly ethnic Chinese or Vietnamese of Chinese ancestry. Many were expelled by the Communist regime when it began nationalizing small businesses. Others left Vietnam because they wanted freedom from political and religious suppression and from poverty and human misery.

The efforts of the boat people to reach safety across the South China Sea were heart-breaking. They suffered from hunger, exposure, and seasickness. Thousands drowned. Pirates murdered additional thousands. Even when the frail boats reached such countries as Indonesia, Japan, Malaysia, the Philippines, Singapore, and Thailand, many were turned away and towed back out to sea. It is believed that as many as fifty thousand Vietnamese refugees perished in flight.

Eventually the United Nations set up refugee camps, mostly in Thailand, and the Carter administration temporarily agreed to admit 25,000 refugees over the usual yearly quota. At first some local leaders were concerned about the influx because of high domestic unemployment. However, the economic situation improved, and religious groups offered to sponsor Vietnamese families to help them get settled. Americans soon learned that the Vietnamese were hard-working people. The refugees valued family life and education and they were welcomed to their new homeland.

The final group of refugees are the few hundred Amerasians—children with American fathers and Vietnamese mothers—who have been resettled in the United States since 1983. These Amerasians are luckier than those still in Vietnam who are branded as outcasts.

Guided Practice

Tell students that throughout history many people have opposed wars and violence. Some of those have refused induction into military service because of moral beliefs. To stimulate discussion, ask students the question: What should the government's position on conscientious objectors be? (Possible responses: conscientious objectors break the law and should be punished accordingly; conscientious objectors should be given the option of serving the country in nonmilitary ways—by working in hospitals, nursing homes, and schools.)

Assign Independent Practice

Ask students to reread the statements by Vietnam veterans in this section. Then have students write an introduction to a book on Vietnam that contains the diaries and personal letters of those who fought in the war. (Introductions might include: the Vietnam War had a profound effect on all who took part in it; it was not a popular war; people who fought in it were often confused about their part in the war.)

Picturing History A happy reunion between Lieutenant Colonel Robert Stirm, a returning POW, and his family—a scene repeated hundreds of times at airports across the nation beginning in 1973. The longest-held POW was Lieutenant Everett Alvarez, Jr., of San Jose, California. He was imprisoned for more than eight years.

Vietnam Veterans Speak Out

The men and women who returned from Vietnam varied greatly in their reactions to the war. Some top-ranking military officers criticized the way the United States had waged the war. Thomas H. Moorer, Chief of Naval Operations from 1967 to 1970, made the following assertion:

> The Vietnam War was a political war. . . . The politicians were so afraid that China and Russia would enter the war that they imposed limitations and restraints on our military people. . . . For instance . . . we were never allowed to bomb the airfield at Hanoi, so the North Vietnamese had a sanctuary on which to base their best fighter aircraft.

Colonel Harry G. Summers argued that the United States employed the wrong strategy. Since the real enemy was North Vietnam and not the Vietcong, the United States should have followed the same tactics it did in Korea—namely, to cut off North Vietnam from the South. "We were like a bull charging the toreador's cape," said Summers, "when we should have been charging the toreador."

Many grunts, or field soldiers, had a different criticism of the conflict. PFC Reginald "Malik" Edwards, an African-American Marine from Louisiana, put it this way:

> Sometimes I think we would have done a lot better by getting them hooked on our lifestyle than by trying to do it with guns. Give them credit cards. Make them dependent on television and sugar. Blue jeans work better than bombs.

Another difficulty in Vietnam was fighting guerrillas rather than a regular army. Medic Dave Ross of the 1st Infantry Division described the situation as follows:

> The VC [Vietcong] would be the farmer you waved to from your jeep in the day who would be the guy with the gun out looking for you at night. They would come together and man a small offensive or probe attack, drop a few mortar rounds and go home and call it a night. We took more casualties from booby traps than we did from actual combat. . . . It was very frustrating because how do you fight back against a booby trap? You're just walking along and all of a sudden your buddy doesn't have a leg. Or you don't have a leg. Even today, if I'm out walking someplace and there's grass, I find myself sometimes doing a shuffle and looking down at the ground. I realize that I'm looking for a wire or a piece of vine that looks too straight, might be a trip wire. Some of the survival habits you pick up stay residual for a long time.

Many veterans reported positive results from their service in Vietnam. Admiral William Lawrence, a pilot who was shot down and spent almost six years as a prisoner of war in Hanoi, had this to say:

> I think that the most important thing that you come away from that experience with is a great feeling of inner calm and serenity because you know that there are very few things in life that could happen to you that you couldn't cope with . . . in fact, nothing.

Student Assignment/Homework

Have students complete the Chapter 33 Test on paper. Divide the class into small groups to discuss and review their answers.

Concluding the Chapter

Ask students to assume the role of historian and prepare a four-paragraph summary of U.S. involvement in Vietnam. Remind students that as historians they must deal with facts and should not base their summaries on personal emotions. (Summaries might include: U.S. involvement was a mistake from the beginning and should have been ended before so many U.S. lives were lost; U.S. involvement did not effectively stop the spread of communism in the world; South Vietnam fell to the Communists when U.S. troops withdrew, proving that the South Vietnamese were not capable of stopping a Communist takeover of their country.) Have several students share their summaries with the class.

Army nurse Lynda Van Devanter, had a different reaction. In a letter home, she wrote:

> I'm tired of going to sleep listening to outgoing and incoming rockets, mortars, and artillery. I'm sick of facing, every day, a new bunch of children ripped to pieces. They're just kids—eighteen, nineteen years old! It stinks! Whole lives ahead of them—cut off. I'm sick to death of it.

A large proportion of the soldiers in Vietnam were blacks, Hispanics, and working-class whites. Members of the middle and upper classes were far more likely to receive college deferments or to be accepted into the National Guard.

In 1988 six men who had served as Marine Corps engineers in Vietnam announced that they would be returning to Vietnam that winter. During the war, they had helped to lay more than a hundred thousand mines in foxholes around American firebases. In previous wars, it had been the practice to clear mine fields after hostilities ended. That had not happened in Vietnam, and some ten thousand people had been killed by mines since 1973. So the six American veterans were going back to take the mines out. "It's really a matter of national honor," said Nate Genna of Boston. "I look at it this way: We put the things in; we'll take them out. These mines are killing the children of the little kids I used to throw my C-rations to. I'm not going back because of nostalgia. I'm going back out of a sense of responsibility. There's just no point in killing people once a war is over."

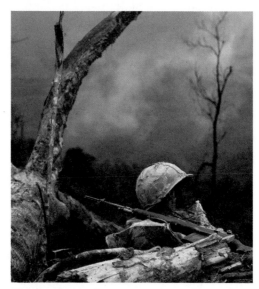

Picturing History   A helmet and rifle honor GI's killed during Operation Prairie near the DMZ.

SECTION 4 REVIEW

Key Terms and People

Explain the significance of: delayed stress syndrome, War Powers Act, boat people

Main Ideas

1. Briefly compare the return home of a Vietnam veteran with that of a World War II veteran.
2. In general, how did the Vietnam War affect Americans' feelings about their government?
3. Briefly characterize the three postwar waves of Vietnamese refugees.
4. What are some of the objections that veterans of the Vietnam War have toward the war?

Critical Thinking

5. Is the bitterness of many Vietnam War veterans toward the United States government justifiable? Explain.

Picturing History   Photographs—such as this one, which shows a dying marine being evacuated during the Tet offensive—documented the horror and tragedy of the war.

State the Objective

Recognize fallacies in reasoning in primary source material.

Present the Lesson

Bring to class a set of dominoes. Place them in a line so that when one is tipped over, the rest will also fall, demonstrating "the domino effect." Repeat the demonstration, placing the dominoes in a random order. Point out the difference in the results—in the second demonstration some of the dominoes fall and others do not. Explain that the demonstration illustrates the domino theory discussed in the feature. Stress that American foreign policy was based on the fallacy that as one nation fell to communism, neighboring nations would also fall. If, on the other hand, the U.S. fought communism, these nations would remain free.

Ask a student to read aloud the steps for recognizing fallacies and the statements by Johnson and Rusk and McNamara. Ask students how these men used the domino theory to support their belief that the U.S. should fight communism in South Vietnam. (Answer: they all thought communism would spread throughout Southeast Asia if South Vietnam fell to the Communists.)

Ask students how such errors in reasoning could be made by several well-informed and conscientious U.S. political figures. (Possible responses: because they had no past experience with attempted communist expansions,

Focus on Critical Thinking Skills

Recognizing Fallacies in Reasoning

Understanding the Skill

Most people agree that American involvement in Vietnam resulted in one of the most chaotic periods in American history. Some Americans believe that the Vietnam War was lost because it was fought the wrong way. Others believe the war should not have been fought at all—that Americans became involved as a result of illogical thinking on the part of some American military and political leaders.

Clark Clifford, who served as Secretary of State under President Lyndon Johnson, summarized the reasons for American involvement. He stated that most American policymakers believed there was a joint understanding between the Soviet Union and Red China to spread communism throughout Southeast Asia. "Our motivations for being involved [in Vietnam] were moral and highly ethical and humane, but the basic reasoning was fallacious."

A fallacy is an error in reasoning. Fallacies can lead to simple misunderstandings or serious misunderstandings, such as war. Fallacies occur when conclusions are drawn from too little data, inaccurate data, or faulty generalizations. You know that there are many causes for an event in history. Therefore it is a fallacy to suggest that an event has only one cause. For example, stating that the American colonists fought the Revolutionary War only to gain political freedom ignores the fact that the struggle also had economic roots.

Similarly, substituting a coincidence for a cause is fallacious. Democratic Presidents were in office when the United States went to war in Korea and Vietnam, while Republicans were in office when peace treaties were signed. Can you therefore draw a conclusion about Democratic and Republican Presidents and war and peace initiatives? Such reasoning would be fallacious.

Because fallacies in reasoning can lead to serious mistakes, careful readers need to be alert. Here are some steps to follow to help recognize fallacies in reasoning.

• **Understand the terminology used.** Errors in reasoning can occur when people are not clear about the meaning of the terms they use. For example, the word *communism* has different meanings for various groups.

• **Be clear about the problem or event discussed.** If there are several, know which is the most important. Think about how one might affect the others.

• **Restate the author's conclusion.** Be alert to possible fallacies: Does the author assume that because events are alike in some ways they are alike in all ways? Does the author generalize freely about people or events? Such practices can lead to errors in reasoning.

• **Analyze the conclusion.** Follow the lines of reasoning. Do all assumptions seem logical? Does important information seem missing? Are several causes for an event considered? Are conclusions based on circumstances?

• **Use your own knowledge of history to judge the author's reliability.**

Applying the Skill

In the early 1960's, President Kennedy sent Vice-President Johnson on a fact-finding mission to Southeast Asia, India, and Pakistan. Here is Johnson's memorandum to the President, dated May 23, 1961:

> The battle against Communism must be joined in Southeast Asia with strength and determination to achieve success there—or the United States, inevitably, must surrender the Pacific and take up our defenses on our own shores. Asian Communism is compromised and contained by the maintenance of free nations on the subcontinent. Without this inhibitory influence, the island outposts—Philippines, Japan, Taiwan—have no security and the vast Pacific becomes a Red Sea.

In the memorandum, Johnson was repeating the domino theory, which has been shown to be based on a fallacy. The domino theory suggests that if one nation falls to communism, all neighboring nations of the region will also fall to communism. The fallacy is concluding that one nation will become

874

they made certain assumptions; much of the information on Southeast Asia that was obtained by U.S. officials prior to U.S. involvement was incomplete or came from unreliable sources.)

Check for Understanding

Discuss students' answers to the questions at the end of the feature.

Remind students that the dominoes—the nations in Southeast Asia—didn't fall in line, but rather fell on each other. Ask students how the U.S. can prevent such mistakes from occurring again. (Possible responses: citizens must be familiar with government policy and take an active role in their government; U.S. foreign advisors must keep lines of communication open with all areas of the world so that U.S. political and military decisions are not made based on inaccurate or incomplete information.)

Picturing History South Vietnamese refugees leave their homes with only the belongings they can carry, while American soldiers move in to defend their country from Communist-ruled North Vietnam.

communist only because a neighboring nation does. The theory ignores other factors, such as economic strength or weakness, political stability, and nationalist feelings of a nation.

If you did not catch the fallacy of the domino theory at first, you are not alone. Secretary of State Dean Rusk and Secretary of Defense Robert McNamara repeated Johnson's warning in a memorandum to President Kennedy dated November 11, 1961.

> The deteriorating situation in South Viet-Nam requires attention to the nature and scope of United States national interests in that country. The loss of South Viet-Nam to Communism would involve the transfer of a nation of 20 million people from the free world to the Communist bloc. [W]e would have to face the near certainty that the remainder of Southeast Asia and Indonesia would move to a complete accommodation with Communism, if not formal incorporation with the Communist bloc.

Partly as a result of the memo, President Kennedy increased the number of military advisors in Vietnam to 16,000. He authorized bombing missions by United States troops. Under President Johnson the fighting escalated further. By 1967 the Vietnam action was a full-scale war in everything but name.

When the fighting ended with complete United States withdrawal in 1975, the historian Arthur M. Schlesinger, Jr., said,

> The dominos did indeed fall in Indochina, as we all know now. But, with communist China invading communist Vietnam because communist Vietnam had invaded communist Cambodia, the dominos fell against each other, not against the United States.

Practicing Your Skill

1. State the problem the quotations refer to: Who was the enemy in Southeast Asia?
2. What are some terms that need to be clearly defined in the quotations? How could these terms lead to fallacies in reasoning?
3. What generalization did American advisors make?
4. What did government decisions based on the fallacy of the domino theory lead to?
5. Should recognizing fallacies in reasoning be the responsibility of only government officials and advisors? Who else should be able to recognize possible faulty reasoning? Why?

Answer Key

Key Terms and People

These are highlighted in the text in the order in which they appear in this list.

Main Ideas

1. Truman believed Ho Chi Minh was part of a worldwide communist conspiracy. Eisenhower believed in the domino theory.

2. Kennedy wanted to show power in spite of Bay of Pigs. Johnson thought that U.S. must keep its commitment to anticommunism and that the Vietminh and Vietcong were Chinese puppets.

3. Doves—war was a civil war and U.S. did not need to be involved; U.S. could not police the world. Hawks—U.S. was protecting itself by containing communism; U.S. could win the war.

4. McCarthy and Kennedy both criticized Johnson's policies in Vietnam and sought a peaceful solution to the conflict. • Lost public support.

5. Vietnamize the war. • Gradually withdraw the American ground troops and replace them with Vietnamese troops. • Increased military aid.

6. Student strikes; conflict between workers and demonstrators; repeal of Tonkin Gulf Resolution.

7. WWII veterans had high morale because the war was popularly supported and soldiers had a long boat ride home with people they knew. Vietnam vets had relatively low morale because the war was unpopular, the vets were transported home quickly having served mostly with strangers, and casualty rates were high.

8. Some were South Vietnamese who had aided Saigon and the American war efforts; others were poor, uneducated boat people who did not want to live under communism.

Critical Thinking Questions

9. Very oppressive wet and hot climate: "the moss-green mountains wavering in the heat-shimmer"; "suffocating, as it always was between monsoon storms"; "air seemed about to explode"; "corrode in a few hours."

10. For 2,000 years the Vietnamese had resisted foreign control, fighting first the Chinese and later the French.
• Possible answer: yes—the Saigon government had been set up by the French, and Vietminh were totally opposed to French control. No—whole communist world in conspiracy against the U.S.

11. Vietnam was divided at the 17th parallel; Laos and Cambodia received independence; elections to form government for all of Vietnam were to be held in two years.
• Elections were never held.
• Diem knew he could not win the elections.

12. Homeless poured into refugee camps and into cities where they needed food, shelter, and medical care. Defoliants devastated about 30 percent of the land. • Believed South Vietnamese government could be saved if villages hiding Vietcong were destroyed.

13. Possible answer: the Vietnamese had been under

CHAPTER **33** REVIEW

Write your answers on a separate sheet of paper.

Key Terms and People

Explain the significance of: domino theory, SEATO, NLF, Vietcong, strategic hamlet program, Ho Chi Minh Trail, search-and-destroy mission, defoliants, Robert McNamara, Clark Clifford, DMZ, Henry Kissinger, delayed stress syndrome, boat people

Main Ideas

1. Why did Presidents Truman and Eisenhower give aid to the French in Vietnam instead of to Ho Chi Minh and the Vietminh who had fought on the side of the Allies against the Japanese during World War II?
2. Why did Presidents Kennedy and Johnson continue aid to the South Vietnamese?
3. Compare the arguments of the doves with those of the hawks.
4. In what ways did Eugene McCarthy and Robert Kennedy confront Johnson's policies in their campaigns for the Presidency? Why did President Johnson decide not to run again?
5. How did President Nixon plan to gain peace with honor in Vietnam? What did Nixon use as an alternative to ground troops?
6. What effect did the invasion of Cambodia have on the United States?
7. What was different about the return of veterans from Vietnam as compared to the return of veterans from World War II?
8. Who were the refugees from Vietnam and why were there so many of them?

Critical Thinking Questions

9. **Analyzing Literature.** What does the selection on page 853 tell you about the climate in Vietnam? Cite quotes to support your answer.
10. **Evaluating Decisions.** Review the two-thousand-year history of Vietnam and the Indochina peninsula. Might a careful study of this history have convinced United States politicians not to have become involved in Vietnam? Explain.
11. **Recognizing Cause and Effect.** Review the main ideas of the Geneva Accords. Why did they not solve the Vietnamese problem? Why would Ngo Dinh Diem not hold free elections?
12. **Recognizing Effects.** What were some of the effects of the war on South Vietnam? Why did some leaders believe it necessary to destroy part of the country in order to save it?
13. **Making Deductions.** Why do you think it was so hard for democratic principles to take hold in Vietnam?
14. **Making Decisions.** Would you have been a dove or a hawk if you had been a student during the Vietnam conflict? Give reasons.
15. **Applying Principles.** Why was the war in Vietnam never a declared war? Do you think the Vietnam War was constitutional?
16. **Analyzing a Comparison.** Historian Barbara Tuchman said that the adoption of the Tonkin Gulf Resolution, which gave the President a blank check to do whatever he considered necessary to keep the Communists in check, was as significant as the bombing of Pearl Harbor. What was similar about the two events? What was different? Compare FDR's and Johnson's positions before these events.
17. **Making a Judgment.** Americans who served in Vietnam have criticized the handling of the war in various ways. What do you think went wrong?

Critical Thinking Activities

18. **Analyzing Maps.** Look at the map of Indonesia and the Ho Chi Minh Trail on page 857. Why did Laos and Cambodia get involved in the Vietnam War? How closely were they involved in the history of Vietnam?
19. **Linking Past to Present.** In an article entitled "What Should Our Students Know About Vietnam," George Burson states, "It is crucial for today's students to understand the Vietnam War and its impact; for without this knowledge, they will have a flawed understanding of today's world." Why is this true?

French domination since the mid 1850's and were not accustomed to a democratic government.

14. Possible answers: dove—Vietnam war was basically a civil war between noncommunists and communists; war is not the way to resolve conflicts; the damage both to Vietnam and to the U.S. was too great. Hawk—should fight communism everywhere.

15. Possible answers: Presidents believed it would take only a short time before the South Vietnam forces would win; Tonkin Gulf Resolution assured President that he had congressional support and legal right to wage war. • Constitutional—challenges to the President's right to send military aid funded by the Congress never reached the Supreme Court; unconstitutional—Congress has the sole right to declare war but never did so.

➤**16.** Johnson received a blank check of approval from Congress to do whatever he thought necessary in Vietnam. Congressional response to Pearl Harbor gave the same thing to Franklin Roosevelt. • The bombing of Pearl Harbor was an attack on U.S. soil. The second attack against the **Maddox** was, at best, contrived and possibly never happened at all. • FDR was defending the U.S.; Johnson was not.

17. Possible answers: U.S. should have fought an all-out war; U.S. should not have tried war at all, but helped industrialize the country.

Critical Thinking Activities

18. The two countries form western border of Vietnam—Laos on the north, Cambodia on the south. Border is mountainous and largely unmapped—a perfect guerrilla hiding place. • The areas were always in conflict.

19. Knowing about Vietnam will help students understand why in the future Congress and the President will be hesitant to become involved in foreign entanglements.

➤**Question suitable for cooperative learning.**

TELESCOPING THE TIMES: 1954–1975

The Vietnam War

France conquered Vietnam in the mid-1800's. After routing the Japanese during World War II, the Vietminh successfully revolted against the French. Presidents Truman and Eisenhower refused to get involved militarily in the struggle between the Communists in North Vietnam and the Diem government in South Vietnam. President Kennedy decided not to send American troops to aid the anti-Communists, but he sent thousands of soldiers to Vietnam to serve as military advisors. In 1964, President Johnson convinced Congress that a United States warship had been attacked by the Communists. Congress's Tonkin Gulf Resolution gave the President the backing for sending American troops to help the South Vietnamese.

In 1965, the American government ordered massive bombing of North Vietnam. American military strategy called for search-and-destroy missions on the ground in South Vietnam. At home, doves viewed the war as immoral and opposed the human and economic sacrifices it demanded. Hawks believed the war was necessary to stop communism. The Tet offensive of 1968 stunned Americans and strengthened opposition to the war. General Westmoreland promised victory, but Johnson refused to run for reelection because he saw too much opposition to his policies. Challenged by Senators Eugene McCarthy and Robert Kennedy, he tried to bring about a peaceful end to the war. Yet the fighting continued.

President Nixon adopted a policy of Vietnamization. Then he enraged college students and other Americans at home by ordering an invasion of Cambodia. While Nixon tried to negotiate peace, the morale of American soldiers in Vietnam continued to fall. Nixon agreed to withdraw American troops in exchange for the return of American POW's. The Christmas bombing of 1973 was followed by a cease-fire for the Americans. Yet the war between the North and South Vietnamese continued for two more years. Finally, in 1975 the South Vietnamese government and army collapsed, and Saigon fell to Communist forces.

For Americans, the Vietnam War was different from previous wars. American troops returned home without victory and without parades. Many soldiers had difficulty adjusting to civilian life. In 1982, a veterans' memorial was erected in Washington, D.C., and dedicated to the Americans who gave their lives in the Vietnam War. The war increased distrust of the government, which resulted in the War Powers Act. Vietnamese refugees arrived in the United States, and many American veterans shared firsthand accounts of their experiences in Vietnam as well as their experiences after coming home.

Chronology of Main Events

1954	French defeated at Dien Bien Phu; Geneva Conference divides Vietnam
1955	U.S. begins to aid South Vietnam
1964	Congress passes the Tonkin Gulf Resolution
1965	President Johnson authorizes the bombing of North Vietnam; first U.S. combat troops land at Danang, South Vietnam
1968	Communists launch Tet offensive
1969	President Nixon attempts his Vietnamization policy; U.S. begins bombing of Cambodia and Laos
1973	Cease-fire agreement signed
1975	Saigon falls to the Communists; South Vietnam surrenders

Telescoping the Times may be used as an alternative to having students read the entire chapter, as a chapter preview, or as a chapter review.

Global Perspectives

1969	Civil warfare breaks out in Northern Ireland.
1971	East Pakistan becomes the independent nation of Bangladesh.
1973	Yom Kippur War takes place.
1975	Helsinki Agreement, which promotes human rights, is signed.
1975	Portugal becomes the last European nation to give up its remaining African colonies.

For Discussion

What situations might have caused problems for the U.S. when China was admitted to the UN in 1971? (Possible responses: the U.S. had to formally recognize Communist China for the first time without appearing weak in its stand on communism; the U.S. would now have to deal with two powerful Communist countries in UN debates.)

Additional Resources

- Geography Activities
- Skills Activities
- Thematic Activities
- Economic Activities
- Cultural Literacy Activities
- Literary Source Readings
- Primary Source Readings
- Nuclear Peacekeeping
- Transparencies
- Computer Test Generator

Additional Teaching Strategies

SECTION 1

For Basic Students: Have students work as a group to prepare a time line of the events of this section and discuss the effect of each event listed. Time line might include:

April 4 1968	King is assassinated; assassination causes riots in cities throughout the country.
June 5 1968	Robert Kennedy is assassinated; Democrats lose their front-running Presidential candidate and ultimately the election.
January-June 1968	College demonstrations and strikes by public employees are frequent; city officials give in to demands in order to restore services.
August 1968	Democratic convention in Chicago is immersed in violence; the Democrats lose support and later the election.

For Advanced Students: After students research the life of Dr. Martin Luther King, Jr., have them prepare a two-minute speech explaining the contributions King made to civil rights and how these achievements support the decision to make King's birthday a national holiday. (Speeches might include: took charge of a successful 382-day boycott of the Montgomery, Alabama, bus system; emphasized the need to act in nonviolent ways; founded the Southern Christian Leadership Conference; received the Nobel Peace Prize in 1964; wrote books including *Stride Toward Freedom*, *Strength to Love*, and *Why We Can't Wait*. It is important that King's birthday be celebrated as a national holiday because of his inspiring efforts to promote racial equality through nonviolent direct action.)

SECTION 2

For Basic Students: Have students use an encyclopedia or other source to research and write a one-page report on the political career of Richard Nixon. (Reports might include: was a government attorney and then a naval officer during World War II; was elected to the U.S. House of Representatives in 1947 and the U.S. Senate in 1950; gained national stature in 1948 as a member of the House Committee on Un-American Activities during the investigation of the Alger Hiss case.) Have students share their reports.

For Advanced Students: Have students research and prepare short oral reports on Supreme Court cases since the 1966 *Miranda* case that have further defined the rights of people who are arrested. (Reports might include: *Franks* v. *Delaware* [1978]—Court ruled that evidence cannot be used if gathered with search warrants obtained by lying to a magistrate about probable cause; *United States* v. *Matlock* [1974]—Court ruled that when one occupant of a house consents to a search of the premises, the search is proper and any evidence uncovered in it may be used against another occupant.)

SECTION 3

For Basic Students: After students research Nixon's historic visit to China, organize them into pairs and have each pair prepare a one-page newspaper article on the President's trip. (Articles might include: Nixon left Washington, D.C., on February 21, 1972; upon arrival he was greeted by Premier Zhou Enlai; he met with Chairman Mao for one hour; he shook hands with both men, something that John Foster Dulles had refused to do in 1954 at the Geneva Conference; they discussed only matters such as relations between the U.S., China, Japan, and the Soviet Union, not economic matters.) Have several pairs of students present their articles to the class.

For Advanced Students: Ask students to assume the role of an investigator doing a background check on Henry Kissinger before his appointment as Secretary of State and to prepare a two-page report. (Reports might include: born in Fürth, Germany; escaped from Nazi Germany in 1938; served in U.S. Army during World War II; became U.S. citizen in 1943; earned three degrees at Harvard University; taught courses on international relations 1959-1969; in 1957 wrote *Nuclear Weapons and Foreign Policy*; was Guggenheim Fellow 1965-66.) Have several students read their reports to the class.

SECTION 4

For Basic Students: Ask students to choose one person involved in the Watergate scandal and prepare a one-page report on that person's life and activities since 1974. (Report on H. R. Haldeman might include: was convicted of conspiracy, obstruction of justice, and perjury; served time in prison; wrote *The Ends of Power* in 1978; still has occasional communication with former President Nixon; currently works as a business consultant; is a trustee of the Kennedy Center for the Performing Arts.) Have students share their reports.

For Advanced Students: Have students draw a political cartoon illustrating their feelings about the Watergate scandal. Have students display their cartoons in the classroom.

Further Reading for Students

Cook, Fred J. *The Crimes of Watergate*. New York: Franklin Watts, 1981. (Easy)

Gurney, Gene. *Americans to the Moon: The Story of Project Apollo*. New York: Random House, 1973.

Preson, Edward. *Martin Luther King: Fighter for Freedom*. New York: Doubleday, 1968. (Easy)

Bibliography for Teachers
Books

Archer, Jules. *Watergate: America in Crisis*. New York: Thomas Y. Crowell, 1975.

Bernstein, Carl, and Bob Woodward. *All the President's Men*. New York: Warner Books, 1976.

Kissinger, Henry. *The White House Years*. Boston: Little, Brown, 1979.

Liston, Robert A. *Presidential Power: How Much Is Too Much?* New York: McGraw-Hill, 1971.

Murray, Charles. *Journey into Space: The First Thirty Years of Space Exploration*. New York: Norton, 1989.

Murray, Charles, and Catherine Bly Cox. *Apollo: The Race to the Moon*. New York: Simon and Schuster, 1989.

Newhouse, John. *War and Peace in the Nuclear Age*. New York: Knopf, 1989.

Rothchild, E. *Richard Nixon and Détente, 1969-1972*. Sanford, N.C.: Microfilming Corp., 1979.

Solberg, Carl. *Hubert Humphrey: A Political Biography*. New York: W. W. Norton, 1984.

White, Theodore H. *Breach of Faith: The Fall of Richard Nixon*. New York: Atheneum, 1975.

_____ *The Making of the President, 1972*. New York: Atheneum, 1973.

Audio-Visuals

Law and Order in Troubled America. Social Studies School Service. Filmstrip.

Martin Luther King, Jr. (1929-1968): The Assassin Years. Chatsworth Film Production. Movie.

Nixon: Checkers to Watergate. Braverman Productions. Movie.

One Giant Leap. PBS. Movie.

The Eagle Has Landed: Apollo 11. McGraw-Hill. Movie.

The Making of the President, 1972. Time-Life. Video.

The Sixties: The Best of Times, the Worst of Times. New York Times. Movie.

Teacher's Notes:

Teaching Resources, Unit 8 Booklet

Lesson Study Sheets pp. 113-128
Daily Activities pp. 129-136
Enrichment Activities pp. 137-144
Reteaching Activities pp. 145-152
Chapter Review p. 153
Chapter Mastery Tests pp. 155-166
Telescoping the Times Study Sheet p. 167

Chapter Objectives

Students will learn:
- how the Vietnam War and the civil rights movement affected American society in 1968
- how Nixon's conservative law-and-order administration worked
- the major changes and achievements in foreign policy during the Nixon years
- the reasons for the collapse of the Nixon administration

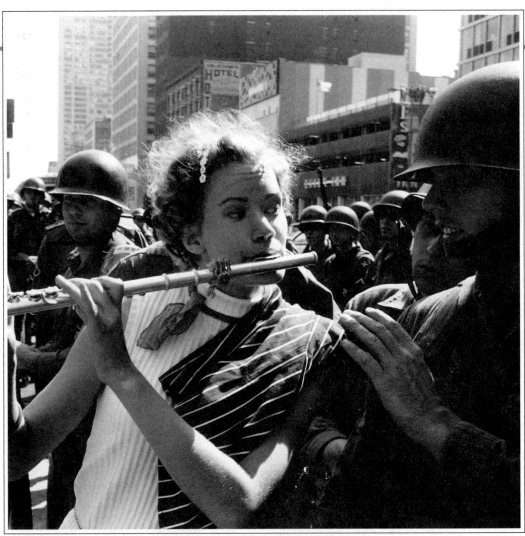

Picturing History Political activists flocked to the Democratic National Convention in Chicago in 1968. In the face of massive protests against the war in Vietnam, Chicago Mayor Richard Daley called on the National Guard to maintain order.

Using the Chapter Time Line

List four events that occurred in 1968 (see Chapter 33 Time Line). (Answer: Tet offensive in Vietnam, Paris peace talks began, M. L. King, Jr. assassinated, R. Kennedy assassinated) How many years did Nixon serve as President? (Answer: 5)

1968	1970	1972	1974
1968 • Martin Luther King, Jr., assassinated • Robert Kennedy assassinated	**1969** • Richard M. Nixon inaugurated President. • American astronauts land on the moon	**1972** • President Nixon visits China • Watergate break-in occurs • Nixon reelected	**1974** Nixon resigns; Gerald Ford succeeds to the Presidency

878

Links to American Literature

William Safire: Born in 1929; attended Syracuse University; served as special assistant to President Nixon from 1968-1973; has been a *New York Times* political columnist since 1973 and has received the Pulitzer Prize for journalism; in addition to his political writings, he is a novelist and one of the most prolific writers on the subject of the English language.

Works include: *Before the Fall* (1975); *Full Disclosure* (1977); *Freedom* (1987); and a number of books on the English language.

Before the Fall: Safire's job as senior speechwriter for Richard Nixon gave him a first-hand view of some of the players, culprits, and victims of the Watergate drama. The book focuses primarily on pre-Watergate years and offers an array of interesting anecdotes and portraits of such people as Nixon, Haldeman, Ehrlichman, Mitchell, Colson, and Kissinger. One reviewer called the book, "the first real post-Watergate view of Nixon by someone who was both there and innocent."

Introducing the Chapter

Tell students that Richard M. Nixon was elected President during a time when Americans were looking for a return of law and order in the U.S. and for peace throughout the world. As students read this chapter, ask them to keep a list of ways the Nixon administration succeeded in attaining these goals.

CHAPTER 34 · 1968–1974

The Nixon Years

Links to American Literature

His [Richard Nixon's] greatest failure: to rally and inspire, to give his countrymen what Ray Price called "the lift of a driving dream" to replace the nightmarish decade of riot and war. Instead, as Woodrow Wilson put it, "we were very heedless and in a hurry to be great": he let his obsession with secrecy draw him over the brink into invasions of privacy and the perversion of law, and every assessment of him will forever be stained with the word "Watergate."

His greatest achievement: he was in the end what he wanted above all else to be—a peacemaker, which better men who were Presidents often failed to be. To make peace and to start the world toward laying down its arms is no mean achievement, especially if it is, in Nixon's vision "a peace that can last."

His most profound personal success: he came back. No man of our time suffered such slings and arrows and came back to outrage Fortune.

— WILLIAM SAFIRE, *Before the Fall*

America's innocence appeared to have died with John F. Kennedy. By the late 1960's, the nation was weary of violence, demonstrations, and a war in Southeast Asia that it apparently could neither win nor end. Americans elected Richard Nixon, who promised to unite the nation. Thus, disillusionment hit hard when the country later learned about burglary, cover-ups, and secret surveillance involving the executive branch. Many Americans feared that faith in the democratic process was lost and would never be recovered.

Chapter Overview

In this chapter you will learn how the Vietnam War and the civil rights movement affected American society in 1968. You will also learn about President Nixon's law-and-order administration and about the major changes in foreign policy that occurred during his term. Finally, you will learn the reasons for the resignation of the President. Above all, this chapter conveys the importance of speaking the truth and doing the right thing when lying would save face or be more profitable. To help you understand this period, Chapter 34 is divided into four sections.

Chapter Outline

1. **The Nation Endures a Troubled Year**
2. **Nixon Heads a Law-and-Order Administration**
3. **The Nation Charts a New Foreign Policy**
4. **The Nixon Administration Collapses**

Anticipate the Lesson

Review with students the prevalent attitudes in American society prior to the 1968 Presidential election. (Possible responses: Americans were frustrated by the continuing Vietnam War; Americans wanted an end to violence and unrest at home.) Ask students how these attitudes contributed to the Republican victory in 1968. (Possible response: many felt that a change in administration might improve the state of the nation.)

State the Objective

Understand how the Vietnam War and the struggles for civil rights affected American society in 1968.

SECTION 1

The Nation Endures a Troubled Year

GLOSSARY TERM: **American Independent party**

Some journalists have referred to 1968 as "the year everything went wrong." A number of violent events supported the characterization and led many to wonder what was happening to American society.

Martin Luther King, Jr., Is Killed

On April 4 **Martin Luther King, Jr.,** was in Memphis, Tennessee. He had been organizing a poor people's march to Washington to emphasize the need for more jobs. He had interrupted that work and had come to Memphis to give what help and guidance he could to the city's garbage workers, mostly African Americans, who had been on strike for two months. Early that evening, he was standing on the balcony outside his motel room talking to aides below. The sharp crack of a gun sounded, and King slumped to the floor. A single bullet had crashed through his neck, severing his spinal cord. He died instantly.

King had preached and practiced nonviolence all his life. He had received the Nobel Peace Prize in 1964. It was ironic that his murder set off what one historian called "the worst outburst of arson, looting, and criminal activity in the nation's his-

tory." Fires and riots broke out in sixty-three cities that night. Washington was hardest hit. The next day television screens showed clouds of smoke from burning buildings floating over the White House. Before the rioting was over, twenty-six hundred people had been arrested, and another twenty-two thousand injured; fifty-five thousand troops were needed to restore order.

Again, a saddened people, an estimated 120 million of them, watched a funeral on television. This one was held in a Baptist church in Atlanta. King's coffin rode to the cemetery on an old farm cart drawn by two mules. Behind the cart walked a crowd of 150,000 persons including Vice-President Hubert Humphrey and Democratic Senators Robert Kennedy and Eugene McCarthy, as well as Republican Governor Nelson Rockefeller of New York. Federal buildings set their flags at half-mast in honor of King, and millions of people turned their automobile headlights on all day as a sign of respect.

The killer was caught two months later. He had managed to reach London by way of Canada and Portugal, using two false names and a Canadian passport. He was traced through his fingerprints, which he had left all over the room from which the shot had been fired. They showed that he was James Earl Ray, a staunch racist and small-time thief who had escaped the previous year from a Missouri prison. Ray was never tried; he pleaded guilty and received a ninety-nine-year sentence. He escaped from prison in 1977 but was recaptured almost immediately. As yet, no one has discovered

---

People in the Chapter

Richard J. Daley was elected mayor of Chicago every four years from 1955 until his death in 1976. Known as the last of the big-city bosses, he was the father of Richard M. Daley, who was elected mayor of Chicago in 1989.

Richard Nixon authorized the creation of a group to plug up informational leaks. When the wife of one of the group's members called to see when her husband would be coming home, she asked what he was doing. "Plugging leaks," he answered. "Like a plumber?" she asked. "Yes," he replied. The name stuck.

George Wallace may have been knocked

down, but he was not one to be knocked out. He had been a Golden Gloves boxer and had paid part of his way through law school by boxing professionally. After losing two Presidential elections and being partially paralyzed, he ran for governor of Alabama and won.

Neil Armstrong built model airplanes as a small boy and dreamed of the day he could fly. Having accomplished that dream while still in college, Armstrong went on to accomplish an even more impossible dream when he became the first person to walk on the moon.

Have students list on the board major events that occurred before the 1968 Presidential election. Discuss how each affected the outcome of the election. (List might include: the assassinations of Dr. King and Robert Kennedy; student riots; strikes by public employees; Democratic National Convention. Effects might include: the assassinations, student riots, and strikes pushed the average American to look for a candidate who could bring law and order back to the country and end the Vietnam War; the disturbances at the Democratic convention resulted in an important shift of support from the Democratic party to the Republican party.)

Picturing History   Grief-stricken mourners look on as a simple mule cart carries the body of Martin Luther King, Jr., through the streets of Atlanta. Above, Coretta Scott King comforts her five-year-old daughter, Bernice, at the funeral service.

where he got the money to buy both the car in which he fled from Memphis and the plane ticket to Europe.

Robert Kennedy Is Killed

Since the end of March, when he declared his candidacy for the Presidency, **Robert Kennedy** had swept all the Democratic primaries except Oregon's, which he narrowly lost to McCarthy. On June 4 he all but assured his nomination with a resounding triumph in California.

Shortly after midnight, on the way from his Los Angeles hotel headquarters to a press conference, Kennedy walked through a crowded passageway in the kitchen of the hotel. He stopped for a moment to shake hands with a teen-aged busboy and to answer a question. As he did so, eight shots rang out. Six men fell to the floor, five of them only slightly injured. The sixth, Kennedy, had a bullet in his brain. Despite almost immediate surgery, he died about twenty-five hours later.

The assassin, Sirhan Bishara Sirhan, was a young Jordanian Arab who was trying to make a political statement. June 4, 1968, was the anniversary of the Six-Day War in which Israel had beaten its Arab neighbors, including Jordan. Kennedy had been a supporter of Israel.

Once again, the nation mourned a murdered leader. Funeral services were held at St. Patrick's Cathedral in New York City, and the body was then taken to Washington in a train pulled by two black engines. So many people lined the tracks along the way that the trip, which usually takes four hours, lasted more than eight. The senator's body was buried in Arlington National Cemetery near that of his brother, President John F. Kennedy.

Picturing History   Robert Kennedy's pursuit of the Democratic Presidential nomination in 1968 ended in tragedy following his victory in the California primary.

Students Riot and Civil Servants "Strike"

If Americans needed more evidence that the social fabric seemed to be unraveling, they had only to look at college campuses. During the first six months of 1968, almost forty thousand students on more than a hundred campuses took part in 221 major demonstrations.

An Uprising at Columbia. The disorder that received the most publicity was the April uprising at Columbia University in New York City.

There had been considerable tension in the area for several years because the university, which owned a large number of Harlem tenements, was, in effect, a slumlord. The immediate spark was the university's publication of a plan for a new gymnasium to be built on nearby parkland. The plan included a gym and swimming pool on the ground floor that people living in the area would be free to use. Unfortunately, the plan also included two entrances. The one that faced the university campus was large and imposing. The one that faced Harlem was small and plain.

Black leaders protested indignantly against the "separate but unequal facilities," and about 150 students promptly marched to the campus shouting "Gym Crow must go." They tore down a fence surrounding the proposed site for the gym, seized three university officials, and barricaded themselves in Hamilton Hall. By the end of the week, students had seized three more halls and a library on the campus. Supporters provided them with food and blankets.

On the sixth day of the uprising, a thousand policemen arrived. The university's president ordered them to clear the buildings by force. Students were clubbed, kicked, and thrown down concrete stairs. In all, about seven hundred persons were arrested, and seventy-three students were suspended for a year.

A commission that investigated the disorders stated that the students had behaved badly and had damaged property. The commission also charged the police with unnecessary brutality and accused the university administration of paying little attention to student needs and grievances.

"Strikes" by Civil Servants. There were other examples of disrespect for the law. The Taft-Hartley Act prohibited strikes by federal civil servants, and most states had similar laws. Yet in

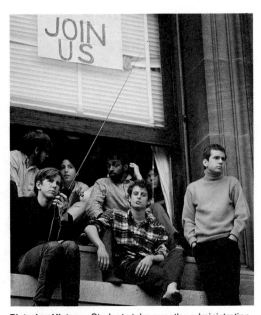

Picturing History Students take over the administration building at Columbia University.

1968, New York City's sanitation workers walked off the job after the mayor refused to grant them a pay raise. Within a few days, the stench of thousands of tons of garbage rotting in the streets was so bad that Governor Rockefeller agreed to give the workers the raise after all.

No sooner were the sanitation workers back on the job than policemen set up a picket line around City Hall and began calling in sick with imaginary illnesses. Next, the city's firefighters stopped inspecting buildings and fire hydrants while their

Picturing History New York Mayor John Lindsay tours a neighborhood hit hard by the garbage strike in 1968.

Guided Practice

Tell students that the assassinations of Dr. King, John Kennedy, and Robert Kennedy led some nations to view the U.S. as a violent nation. Discuss the possible reasons for violence in the U.S. (Possible responses: violence is glamorized on television and in the movies; because the U.S. supports freedom of speech, many opposing groups express their philosophies and inevitably clash.)

union bargained for more money. Then it was the turn of the city's teachers, who walked out three times during the fall of 1968.

The Democratic Convention Brings Chaos

The anger and frustration throughout the land came to a climax during the Democratic National Convention in Chicago the last week of August 1968. The city had received reports that at least 100,000 students, hippies, and other antiwar activists would gather there to protest the administration's Vietnam policies. Parts of the city were turned into what was almost an armed camp.

Mayor Richard J. Daley ordered that a seven-foot chain-link fence topped with barbed wire be put up around the convention hall. Delegates, news reporters, and guests were searched on entering and at various times throughout the convention proceedings. The mayor also placed the city's 11,500 police on twelve-hour shifts and alerted 7,500 members of the National Guard and 1,000 FBI and Secret Service agents to stand by. The federal government had an additional 7,500 troops ready to be airlifted in at a moment's notice.

Riots in the Streets. Actually, only 10,000 to 12,000 protesters showed up. Some of them had come for the purpose of creating violent confrontations. Mayor Daley refused to grant them permits to march peacefully or to hold a political rally. When several groups asked for permission to camp in the public parks, the mayor ordered an eleven o'clock curfew.

The results were predictable. For four nights in succession, police armed with clubs and tear gas drove curfew violators out of Lincoln Park and through the streets. More than twenty newspaper reporters observing the scene were slugged. Some of the protesters threw stones and bottles at the police, but most just tried to walk away.

On Wednesday, August 28, the protesters announced that they planned to march from Lincoln Park to the convention hall. They got as far as the intersection in front of the Conrad Hilton Hotel, where the three leading candidates for the Democratic nomination were headquartered. There, in full view of television cameras, they were beaten and gassed by the police for eighteen terrible minutes. No one was killed, but hundreds were injured.

Picturing History Chicago police tried to disperse the antiwar protesters at the 1968 Democratic convention as Americans watched on television.

Fury in the Hall. Meanwhile, inside the convention hall a different kind of force was being displayed. Democrats opposed to the Vietnam War had captured 80 percent of the vote in the party primaries. When their delegates entered the convention hall, however, they found pro-administration literature on every seat. They tried to pass out antiwar literature of their own, but the guards prevented them from doing so.

Tuesday evening, antiwar delegates sat in the galleries shouting "Stop the War!" The next night, the galleries were filled with city employees waving banners that read "We Love Daley." They had been allowed in despite their lack of proper credentials. At the same time, antiwar delegates were physically removed from the convention floor, supposedly because they refused to show their credentials to the guards.

All this confusion did not keep the delegates from nominating Vice-President **Hubert Humphrey** on the first ballot, a decided victory for President Johnson. (Among the other nominees was the Reverend Channing E. Phillips of the District of Columbia, the first African American to be nominated for the Presidency at a national convention.) However, Humphrey's easy victory was apparently not enough for those in charge of the convention. Despite considerable opposition from the floor, they announced that the nomination was unanimous.

Humphrey chose as his running mate Senator Edmund S. Muskie of Maine. Then came a fight over the party platform, which supported the administration's handling of the Vietnam War. After

For Discussion
How did Mayor Richard Daley police the 1968 Democratic Convention in Chicago? How might the events at the convention have influenced the outcome of the 1968 Presidential election? (Possible responses: Daley resorted to "police action" and used force to control and disperse groups; national television coverage presented Daley and his police in a very bad light; many voters turned away from the Democratic party as a result of the violence, giving the Republicans the added support they needed for a 1968 win.)

two days of sharp debate, the platform was approved by sixteen hundred votes out of twenty-six
hundred.

Nixon Wins a Narrow Victory in 1968

With disappointed Eugene McCarthy followers
refusing to help, the Democratic campaign began
poorly. Crowds were small, hecklers were everywhere, and money was in short supply. In addition,
President Johnson did not try to hide the fact that he
considered Humphrey weak, which did little to aid
Humphrey's campaign.

The Republicans, on the other hand, had plenty
of money and a smooth-running organization. Their
Presidential candidate, former Vice-President **Richard M. Nixon,** promised to bring "peace with
honor" in Vietnam, a vague promise that nevertheless had widespread appeal. The Vice-
Presidential candidate, Governor **Spiro Agnew** of
Maryland, emphasized the second major element in
the Republican platform, namely, the need for measures that would bring about law and order.

Minor Parties. Two minor parties also entered
the 1968 race. The Peace and Freedom party, organized by a combination of pacifists and black
power supporters, nominated Black Panther leader
Eldridge Cleaver for President. The party was able
to get on the ballot in only a few states and eventually it fell apart because of internal arguments.

Far more significant was the **American Independent party,** which ran **George Wallace,** Alabama's former governor, and retired General Curtis
LeMay. Wallace campaigned on a platform that
combined the Democrats' support for the Vietnam
War with the Republicans' support for law and
order. Wallace appealed not only to Southern
whites but also to blue-collar workers in the North.
Many of the latter belonged to "new immigrant"
ethnic groups. (See page 640.) Their parents had
entered the United States and worked their way up
without special help from the federal government.
They did not see why they should pay taxes to help
African Americans. Furthermore, they did not see
why they should support universities attended by
young people who were demonstrating instead of
studying.

Down to the Wire. The campaign began with
Nixon far ahead. Then in late September, Humphrey moved away from the administration's position on Vietnam. He suggested that the United
States stop bombing North Vietnam in order to
encourage the Paris peace talks. Johnson announced a halt in the bombing when on October
31, McCarthy declared that he would vote for
Humphrey. Liberals, city dwellers, and organized
labor began returning to their traditional Democratic roots. In the meantime, Nixon began sounding overconfident. By election day, one opinion
poll actually showed Humphrey ahead.

Even with modern electronic reporting, the outcome was in doubt until the day after the election.
In the end, Nixon received 31.8 million votes, or
43.4 percent, to Humphrey's 31.2 million, or 42.7
percent. Wallace got just under 10 million votes, or
13.5 percent. As always, the electoral vote showed
a bigger spread: Nixon 301, Humphrey 191, and

Picturing History The three candidates in the election of 1968 were (left to right) Hubert
Humphrey, George Wallace, and Richard Nixon. The voters' choice was Richard Nixon.

Student Assignment/Homework

Have students read Section 2, "Nixon Heads a Law-and-Order Administration," and answer Section 2 Review questions on paper.

Anticipate the Lesson

Review with students the terms *liberal* and *conservative* as they apply to politics. Ask students how liberal and conservative groups view each other. (Possible responses: liberals are persons favoring reform; they might be viewed as too advanced or experimental by conservatives. Conservatives are persons wishing to preserve the existing order; they might be viewed as overly cautious or behind the times by liberals.) Ask students why a conservative such as Nixon was able to win the Presidential election in an era marked by individualism, protest, and change. (Possible response: because the changes were so rapid and were often steeped in violence, the average American was looking for a return to the peace and "normalcy" of the 1950's, when life was more predictable and law and order prevailed.)

Presidential Election, 1968

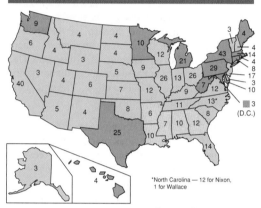

*North Carolina — 12 for Nixon, 1 for Wallace

Party	Candidate	Electoral Vote	Popular Vote	%
Republican	Nixon	301	31,785,000	43.4
Democratic	Humphrey	191	31,275,000	42.7
American Independent	Wallace	46	9,906,000	13.5
Minor parties			218,000	0.3

538 Total Electoral Vote

Wallace 46. Nixon thus entered the White House without a majority of the popular vote.

SECTION 1 REVIEW

Key Terms and People

Explain the significance of: Martin Luther King, Jr., Robert Kennedy, Hubert Humphrey, Richard M. Nixon, Spiro Agnew, American Independent party, George Wallace

Main Ideas

1. How did the deaths of Martin Luther King, Jr., and Robert Kennedy affect Americans? Why did these deaths affect people in similar ways?
2. In 1968, what New York City events appeared to support the idea that the American social fabric was unraveling?
3. What was the main issue at the center of all the conflict surrounding the 1968 Democratic convention?
4. What were the two main elements of the 1968 Republican platform?

Critical Thinking

5. Law and order was a central issue in the 1968 Presidential campaign. Did the 1968 Democratic convention demonstrate the effectiveness or the ineffectiveness of a law-and-order approach in bringing about consensus in society?

SECTION 2

Nixon Heads a Law-and-Order Administration

GLOSSARY TERMS: strict constructionist, revenue sharing, deficit spending, wage and price controls

Richard Nixon had spent most of his adult life working hard in politics. As Vice-President under Eisenhower, he had been the first person in that office to make goodwill tours of foreign countries. Now every Vice-President makes them. Following his defeat by John Kennedy in 1960, he returned to California. There he ran for governor in 1962, but he lost that election too. Declaring himself through with politics, he moved to New York City and became a senior partner in a major law firm.

However, the former Vice-President kept working for the Republican party. He proved an effective and tireless speaker at local fund raisers and rallies, and loyally supported the Goldwater ticket in 1964 when many others deserted it. By 1968 he had paid enough political dues to claim the Republican nomination.

Nixon Appoints Conservatives

Although Nixon had campaigned on a promise to "bring the nation together," his cabinet reflected the business community primarily. According to one historian, its members were "all affluent, white, male, middle-class, and Republican."

The new administration had pledged to restore law and order. Nixon tried to do this in several ways. In 1969 the Justice Department brought to trial eight alleged leaders of the demonstrations staged during the Democratic convention. Five of the eight were cleared of charges of inciting to riot but were convicted for crossing state lines with the intent to do so. (Three years later, the convictions were reversed by a higher court.) Laws against organized crime and drug abuse were tightened, and in 1970 Congress passed the Omnibus Crime Control Act, which increased the power of federal law-enforcement agencies.

Nixon believed that a major reason for the violence of the sixties was the federal government's attempt to enforce school desegregation. In particular, he questioned the practice of busing school children away from neighborhood schools in

SECTION 1 REVIEW
Answers

Main Ideas

1. The murders of King and Kennedy in the same year saddened and shocked people around the world and led many to question what American society was coming to.
• Both men were popular idealistic leaders who tried to create a more democratic America.

2. The Columbia student uprising (involving police brutality); strikes and other labor disturbances by sanitation workers, police officers, firefighters, and teachers.

3. Vietnam War.

4. Peace with honor in Vietnam and the enforcement of law and order at home.

Critical Thinking

5. Possible answer: ineffectiveness—Daley's police brought about submission with tear gas and clubs, but they did not bring about consensus. Consensus requires communication and compromise rather than intimidation. **(analysis & evaluation)**

State the Objective

Understand how Nixon's conservative law-and-order administration worked.

Present the Lesson

Ask students to add details to a time line on the board showing the major events during Nixon's first Presidential term. Discuss how these events reflected Nixon's law-and-order theme. Time line might include:

1969	Justice Department brings to trial alleged leaders of demonstrations at Democratic convention. Laws against organized crime and drug abuse are tightened. Warren retires from Supreme Court; Nixon promises to appoint "strict constructionists"; however, two Nixon nominees are rejected by the Senate. Armstrong is the first person to walk on the moon.
1970	Congress passes Omnibus Crime Control Act, increasing the power of federal law-enforcement agencies.
1971	Supreme Court upholds the use of busing to achieve school desegregation. Nixon imposes wage and price controls; the measures are unsuccessful.
1972	Revenue-sharing program goes into effect.

Picturing History Demonstrators at the 1968 Democratic convention in Chicago were convicted of conspiracy to cross state lines and instigate a riot. The seven defendants shown here made light of courtroom proceedings.

order to achieve racial balance. Accordingly, federal enforcement of school desegregation practically stopped. In 1971, however, the Supreme Court upheld the use of busing in *Swann* v. *Charlotte Mecklenburg Board of Education*.

Seeking a More Conservative Court. One controversial aspect of the sixties had been the record of the Warren Court (the Supreme Court under Chief Justice **Earl Warren**). Many conservatives felt that the Court had been too permissive with regard to the rights of accused persons.

The conservatives objected to two decisions in particular. One was *Gideon* v. *Wainwright* (1963), which said that a defendant had the right to counsel. The court ruled that if the accused could not afford an attorney, the state must appoint one. The second decision was *Miranda* v. *Arizona* (1966), which stated that a person who is arrested must be told that she or he does not have to answer police questions and is entitled to have an attorney present. Critics of the Court felt that these decisions severely limited the powers of the police.

Nixon promised to appoint so-called **strict constructionists** to the Supreme Court. (These were people who believed the federal government should have only those powers specifically identified in the Constitution. See page 198.) In 1969 Warren retired at the age of seventy-seven, and Nixon chose **Warren Burger** of Minnesota to replace him. The Senate approved Burger, but then it balked at Nixon's next two nominees. Clement Haynsworth, Jr., of South Carolina was rejected because he had issued decisions favoring companies whose stock he owned. G. Harrold Carswell of Florida was

rejected because of his racist views and because so many of his decisions were reversed on appeal for lack of knowledge about the law. Nixon reacted furiously, accusing the Senate of being anti-Southern. His next nominee, approved unanimously, was Harry Blackmun of Minnesota. Then in 1971, Nixon nominated a respected and competent Southerner, Lewis Powell of Virginia. Powell's nomination sailed through.

Revenue Sharing: No Strings Attached. A major departure from previous practice in the area of allocating federal funds was the bill for **revenue sharing** that became law in 1972. Money had always gone from the federal government to state and local governments, but it had been earmarked for specific programs. The Nixon administration proposed that the federal government begin distributing these funds without any strings attached. This proposal reflected the conservative view that Washington bureaucrats did not know what was best at the state and local levels. Before the end of his first term, the President signed a bill allocating $30.2 billion for revenue sharing.

A Push for Family Assistance. The Nixon administration also put forward an interesting idea in the area of welfare reform. As of 1969, about ten million Americans were receiving some form of welfare. Nixon believed this was one activity the federal government should take over from the states. He recommended a family assistance plan. It would set a minimum income that a family would need to stay above the poverty level. Those families falling below this level would receive direct supplemental payments from the federal government. Unemployed participants would have to take job training and accept any reasonable work offered to them. The proposal was passed by the House of Representatives but was turned down in the Senate. Defeat came from both the right and the left. Some conservatives found the payments too generous. Some liberals found the job and training requirements too rigid.

Nixon Battles Inflation

Nixon inherited a high rate of inflation from his predecessor. Rather than finance the Vietnam War by increasing taxes, the Johnson administration had adopted a program of **deficit spending**. This meant increasing the money supply to pay for the costs of

Check for Understanding

Call on individual students to orally answer Section 2 Review questions.

Guided Practice

Tell students that the U.S. has spent billions of dollars on the space program. Critics have said that the money should be going to programs designed to relieve poverty, illiteracy, and unemployment in our nation. To stimulate discussion on government allocation of funds, ask students the following questions. How can the expenditure of such large sums of money on the space program be justified? Should the government cut the space program and put the money into other domestic programs? (Possible responses: scientific research is a necessary part of government spending because only through testing and research can the U.S. increase its technological knowledge and eventually make life better for all; the funds should be spent on domestic programs to help the poor, elderly, and sick who are in need now.)

Picturing History An arm-wrestling contest aptly represents President Nixon's battles with Congress.

the war. The war was not the only cause of inflation, however. Crop failures in China, the Soviet Union, India, and Africa increased the demand for food and forced food prices upward. Oil prices also rose dramatically as oil-producing nations tightened control over their product. (See pages 898–899.)

Nixon tried to solve the problem by applying the traditional Republican methods of dealing with inflation. He raised interest rates in order to discourage borrowing. He reduced government spending in order to decrease demand. Finally, in August 1971, he imposed temporary **wage and price controls.** The wage controls froze the wages of American workers for ninety days. The price controls required business and industry to freeze prices, fees, and rents for three months. None of these measures was successful, and many were extremely unpopular.

Neil Armstrong Stands on the Moon

In 1961 President Kennedy had pledged to put a man on the moon and bring him back safely before the end of the decade. The pledge was fulfilled in 1969.

On July 20, as an estimated 600 million viewers all over the world watched on television, astronaut **Neil Armstrong** stepped cautiously out of the lunar module *Eagle* and stood on the moon's surface. As he did so, he radioed earthward: "I'm going to step off the LM now. That's one small step for a man, one giant leap for mankind." Twenty minutes later, Armstrong was followed by astronaut Edwin "Buzz" Aldrin, Jr. The two men set up scientific experiments and collected samples of rock and soil from the lunar surface. A third astronaut, Michael Collins, orbited above them in the command vessel *Columbia*. Less than an hour later, President Nixon spoke from the White House to the men on the moon. "For every American, this has to be the proudest day of our lives," he said.

The space program had cost more than $23 billion. Three astronauts had lost their lives in an accident at Cape Canaveral in 1967. (Cape Canaveral was formerly called Cape Kennedy.) Still, the moon landing was a triumph of science and courage as well as a source of great national pride.

Linking Past to Present

The moon landing in 1969 was a high point in NASA's space program. More recent space odysseys have also generated excitement and pride among Americans. For example, in 1989 the space probe *Voyager 2* completed a twelve-year grand tour of four planets: Jupiter (1979), Saturn (1980), Uranus (1986), and Neptune (1989). Along the way, it successfully transmitted spectacular pictures as well as useful data. In years to come, when the probe is well beyond our solar system, communication will no longer be possible. If, by chance, *Voyager 2* is someday discovered by beings from another solar system, they will find a recording inside called "Sounds of Earth." It contains greetings in sixty languages and a message from former President Carter that says: "This record represents our hope and our determination, and our good will in a vast and lonely universe."

Have students write an essay briefly analyzing the quote by Neil Armstrong on page 887. Essays should answer these questions: What was the significance of the moon landing? In what way was it the fulfillment of a commitment? (Essays might include: it put the U.S. ahead of the Soviet Union in the space race; the landing fulfilled President Kennedy's 1961 pledge to put a man on the moon before the end of the decade. It united all Americans with a special purpose.)

Student Assignment/Homework

Have students read Section 3, "The Nation Charts a New Foreign Policy," and complete Chapter 34, Section 3 Enrichment Activity.

For Discussion
What are some advantages and disadvantages of having a strong Secretary of State such as Henry Kissinger?
(Advantages might include: many new and positive foreign policies can be put into affect; the U.S. develops a strong voice in world affairs. Disadvantages might include: the secretary may attempt to assume some powers reserved for the President; other countries may view the President as weak.)

Picturing History Rising to a challenge to Americans by President Kennedy, NASA deployed a series of spacecraft to the moon and beyond. Here, astronaut James Irwin salutes the American flag at the Apollo 15 landing site. Hadley Delta in the background rises approximately 13,124 feet above the plain. The lunar module *Falcon* is shown at the right.

Nixon Wins Again in 1972

At the Republican National Convention in Miami Beach in August 1972, Nixon and Agnew easily won renomination. A month earlier, the Democrats had met in the same city to select their candidate. As a result of reforms adopted after the 1968 convention, their delegates included a large number of women, people under thirty, and racial minorities. This was a decided change from the usual convention mixture of elected officials and party regulars. A striking example of the reform effort was the challenging of the Illinois delegation. The convention voted to replace Chicago Mayor Richard J. Daley and fifty-eight other Chicago delegates on the grounds that they had been chosen by procedures that did not meet the reform guidelines. Instead, the convention seated delegates led by outsiders like black activist Jesse Jackson.

The Democratic candidate was Senator **George McGovern** of South Dakota. He ran on a liberal domestic platform and a pledge for the "immediate and complete withdrawal of all U.S. forces" from Vietnam, where the war was still going on. McGovern took a worse beating than Goldwater had in 1964. The popular vote was 47 million to 29 million; the electoral vote, 521 to 17. The Democratic ticket carried only Massachusetts and the District of Columbia (able to choose electors since 1961 under the Twenty-third Amendment).

One reason for McGovern's defeat was the public desire for conservative leadership at home. A second reason was widespread approval of many of Nixon's accomplishments in foreign affairs, which you will read about later in the chapter. A third reason was the shooting of George Wallace by a would-be assassin in the spring. Although Wallace survived the bullet, he was paralyzed from the

Anticipate the Lesson

Review with students how Nixon changed America's bargaining position during the cease-fire negotiations with North Vietnam in Paris (Chapter 33). (Possible responses: Nixon did not insist on the complete withdrawal of all North Vietnamese soldiers from South Vietnam before beginning negotiations; U.S. agreed to pull out its forces but would continue sending economic and military aid to South Vietnam.)

Ask students what this change reveals about Nixon's approach to foreign policy. (Possible response: it might show that Nixon realized the value of compromise and the necessity of open negotiations to attain peace.) Use completed Chapter 34, Section 3 Enrichment Activity to stimulate discussion on Henry Kissinger and his role in making foreign policy.

State the Objective

Understand the major changes and achievements in foreign policy during the Nixon years.

Present the Lesson

Ask students to summarize the major foreign policy achievements of the Nixon administration by writing on the board the two major foreign policy problems and the solutions to each.

Problem
• Poor relations with Communist China

Solutions
• U.S. recognizes Communist China.
• Both countries agree to cooperate in the Pacific.

Presidential Election, 1972

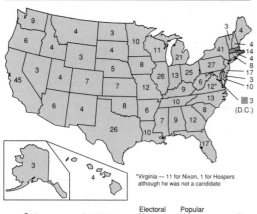

*Virginia — 11 for Nixon, 1 for Hospers although he was not a candidate

Party	Candidate	Electoral Vote	Popular Vote	%
Republican	Nixon	520	47,170,000	60.7
Democratic	McGovern	17	29,170,000	37.5
Minor parties		1	1,379,000	1.8

538 Total Electoral Vote

waist down and did not take part in the Presidential campaign. Most of his votes went to Nixon. Then, too, the President ran an extremely effective—and expensive—campaign.

SECTION 2 REVIEW

Key Terms and People

Explain the significance of: Earl Warren, strict constructionists, Warren Burger, revenue sharing, deficit spending, wage and price controls, Neil Armstrong, George McGovern

Main Ideas

1. How did Nixon attempt to fulfill his campaign promise to restore law and order?
2. How did Nixon fight inflation? Were his methods successful?
3. In 1969 what did Neil Armstrong accomplish while millions of people watched on TV? How did this accomplishment make most Americans feel about their nation?
4. What were the main reasons for McGovern's defeat in the 1972 election?

Critical Thinking

5. Briefly compare the effects of the Vietnam War with those of the space program on the United States. Which effort was more worthwhile? Why?

SECTION 3

The Nation Charts a New Foreign Policy

GLOSSARY TERM: détente

Soon after entering the White House, Nixon chose **Henry Kissinger** as his assistant for national security. After the 1972 election, Kissinger donned a second hat and became Nixon's Secretary of State as well. Working closely together, the two men began to turn U.S. foreign policy around.

Kissinger, who was born in Germany, had come to the United States in 1938 when his family fled Hitler's persecutions. He taught at Harvard during the fifties and sixties and became an authority on international relations and nuclear defense. Later he served as a consultant to the federal government and to private foundations.

Kissinger Recommends Flexible Diplomacy

In 1954 Kissinger published a book attacking the concept of massive retaliation against Communist countries advanced by Eisenhower's Secretary of State, John Foster Dulles. (See page 807.) Kissinger believed the main consideration should be power rather than ideology. If a nation were weak, it might be wiser for the United States to ignore a provocation, even if that nation were Communist. The weak nation could not do much damage. On the other hand, if a nation were strong and able to hurt the United States, then America must act to counter that nation. This was an application of the German policy of *realpolitik,* a term meaning realistic or practical politics.

Kissinger's approach was also a departure from the policy of containment, which aimed at keeping all Communist nations at arm's length. (See page 777.) The new approach opened a number of possibilities. For example, mainland China need no longer be treated as though it did not exist just because it was Communist. After all, it contained at least one-fifth of the world's population. Furthermore, it was at odds with the Soviet Union. Among other matters, China and the Soviet Union disagreed about their common border. It might be to America's advantage to balance one major Communist country against the other.

- U.S. recognizes Taiwan as part of China and promises to withdraw troops.
- U.S. suggests that China be given Taiwan's seat on the UN Security Council but that Taiwan be allowed to remain a member of the General Assembly.
- Nixon visits China in 1972.

Problem

- Cold war between the U.S. and the Soviet Union

Solutions

- U.S. and Soviet Union work out an agreement about Berlin—Soviets allow U.S., British, and French access to West Berlin, and Western allies recognize East Germany.
- Summit meetings are held—the U.S. and the Soviet Union sign two agreements on arms control; they agree to cooperate on space exploration; they agree not to test nuclear weapons underground.

Check for Understanding

Call on individual students to orally answer Section 3 Review questions.

Guided Practice

Have students compare détente with the Soviet Union in the 1970's to the present state of affairs. (Possible responses: With the collapse of the Soviet Union in 1991, there is no longer a need for détente between the two superpowers. Today major concerns center around (1) dismantling the arsenal of nuclear weapons still existing in Russia and other nations in the Commonwealth of Independent States and (2) helping the ailing economies make the transition from a planned to a free market system.)

For Discussion
What is the meaning of the term *imperial Presidency* and why was this term applied to the Nixon years? (Possible response: an imperial Presidency develops when the power of the President becomes greater than that of the judicial and legislative branches; by the time Nixon came into office, the Presidency was on its way to becoming an imperial Presidency; Nixon's manner, life style, attempt to put conservatives on the Supreme Court, and relations with Congress all point to his desire to see the executive branch gain power over the judicial and legislative branches.)

Picturing History National Security Advisor Henry Kissinger (left) meets with Chinese Premier Zhou Enlai to lay the groundwork for the historic meeting between President Richard Nixon and Mao Zedong, Chairman of the Chinese Communist party.

The United States Recognizes Communist China

Since the takeover of mainland China by the Communists in 1949, the United States had not given formal recognition to that government. However, Nixon decided the time had come to give Communist China the same recognition that Roosevelt had given the Communist government of the Soviet Union in 1933. Accordingly, in August 1971 President Nixon announced that he would visit mainland China within a year. He did so in February 1972. After eight days of meetings, the two nations announced that neither would try to dominate the Pacific and that both would cooperate in settling disputes peacefully. They also agreed to open up trade and to improve scientific and cultural relations. The United States recognized that Taiwan was part of China and promised to eventually withdraw American forces from the island.

Nixon's statements regarding Taiwan were in line with a resolution the United States had introduced in the United Nations the previous October. The resolution recommended that mainland China be given Taiwan's permanent seat on the UN Security Council, but that Taiwan be allowed to continue as a member of the General Assembly. However, the UN vote went further than the United States wanted. It not only seated the People's Republic of China on the Security Council but expelled Taiwan from the UN altogether.

In view of Nixon's strong record of anticommunism, the recognition of Red China stunned the American people. Yet it was welcomed by most. Despite America's historic ties with the Nationalist Chinese on Taiwan, it seemed clear that the chances for peace in Asia were now much stronger. The visit to China helped Nixon win the election that year.

Tensions Ease Toward the Soviet Union

Nixon and Kissinger also adopted a more flexible approach to the Soviet Union. They tried to tone down the cold war and its confrontations and to encourage **détente,** or the easing of tensions.

In 1971 the United States worked out an agreement with the Soviet Union about Berlin. The Soviets promised to guarantee access by the United States, Britain, and France to West Berlin and to respect the city's independence. In return, the Western allies agreed to recognize East Germany. This agreement removed a major sore point in East-West relations.

In May 1972, three months after his visit to China, Nixon took part in a summit meeting in Moscow. He and Soviet Premier **Leonid Brezhnev** (brezh'nef) agreed to increase trade and to cooperate on space exploration. They also signed two agreements on arms control based on the **Strategic Arms Limitation Talks (SALT)** that had been held earlier. The agreements limited the number of offensive missiles and defensive missile sites that each nation would build.

In October 1973 the **Yom Kippur War** broke out between the Arabs and the Israelis. The two superpowers scored a victory for détente when they successfully mediated the crisis. They managed to get both sides to sign a cease-fire agreement, although there were reprisals later.

In June 1974 Nixon and Brezhnev held another summit meeting in Moscow. Again, agreements were reached on improving trade relations and on greater cooperation in scientific matters. The United States and the Soviet Union also agreed not to test nuclear weapons underground. However, despite a strong warning from Kissinger about the dangers of nuclear warfare, the two nations failed to agree on a cutback in offensive missiles.

Have students write a two-paragraph essay citing and evaluating two major changes in American policy that can be directly linked to Kissinger's ideas. (Essays might include: under Kissinger the U.S. came to regard power, not ideology, as the main determiner of retaliation—if a nation is weak, it would be wise to ignore the provocation. Decisions based on this philosophy represent an application of *realpolitik*. Kissinger also changed the government's attitude toward containment, suggesting it might be to America's advantage to balance one major Communist country against another.)

Student Assignment/Homework

Have students read Section 4, "The Nixon Administration Collapses," and answer the Section 4 Review questions on paper.

Anticipate the Lesson

Use Chapter 34, Section 4 Enrichment Activity to review the impeachment process. Have students complete the activity individually and then discuss their answers.

State the Objective

Examine the reasons for the collapse of the Nixon administration.

Picturing History President Richard Nixon and Soviet General Secretary Leonid Brezhnev at the Moscow summit in the Kremlin's Vladimir Hall. Nixon was the first U.S. President to visit Moscow.

SECTION 3 REVIEW

Key Terms and People

Explain the significance of: Henry Kissinger, *realpolitik*, détente, Leonid Brezhnev, SALT, Yom Kippur War

Main Ideas

1. What was the basic principle behind Kissinger's foreign policy?
2. What were the important results of Nixon's 1972 visit to mainland China?
3. What were the main results of the summit meetings in the 1970's between Nixon and Brezhnev?

Critical Thinking

4. Briefly explain why the change in United States relations with mainland China and the Soviet Union during the 1970's qualifies as the practice of *realpolitik*.

SECTION 4

The Nixon Administration Collapses

GLOSSARY TERM: **Watergate**

There is widespread consensus among historians about the reasons for the events known collectively as **Watergate.** Some of the explanations advanced have little to do with Watergate but rather with Richard Nixon's personality. Others have to do with the changing role of the Presidency.

An "Imperial" Presidency Takes Shape

Over the course of the nation's history, the balance of power has shifted among the legislative, executive, and judicial branches of the federal government. Thomas Jefferson complained of the influence of Federalist judges. Andrew Johnson, many historians feel, successfully fought off Congress's efforts to wield too much power after the Civil War. By the time Nixon became President, the executive branch—as a result of the Great Depression, World War II, and the cold war—had become, in many people's eyes, almost "imperial." This was the view put forth by historian Arthur Schlesinger, Jr., in his book entitled *The Imperial Presidency*.

Nixon's Manner. Nixon always had to fight hard for what he achieved in life. Apparently this led him to regard the world as a permanent arena in which winning was the only thing that mattered. He seemed to view people who disagreed with him as threats to his authority.

Nixon believed, as he told a newspaper reporter in the fall of 1980, that "a President must not be one of the crowd. He must maintain a certain figure. People want him to be that way. They don't want him to be down there saying, 'Look, I'm the same as you.'" He reported that he always wore a coat and tie and that even his closest friends addressed him as Mr. Nixon or Mr. President, never as Richard. Many people found his manner cool and aloof.

Nixon relied on a sort of "palace guard" of White House advisors to supervise the executive branch and to protect him from the public. Those he apparently listened to most were **John Mitchell,** formerly a law partner and now his Attorney

Main Ideas

1. To conduct foreign relations based on a nation's power rather than on the ideology of its leaders.

2. China and the U.S. each agreed not to try to dominate the Pacific; they agreed to open up trade and to improve scientific and cultural relations; the U.S. recognized that Taiwan was part of China; the People's Republic of China was seated on the UN Security Council; Taiwan was expelled from the UN; chances for peace in Asia grew stronger; Nixon's Presidential campaign was strengthened.

3. U.S.–U.S.S.R. tensions decreased; trade relations and cooperation on scientific matters improved; numbers of nuclear weapons were limited; underground nuclear testing was banned. Also, the two nations negotiated a cease-fire agreement to end the Yom Kippur War.

Critical Thinking

4. Possible answer: *realpolitik* means "realistic politics"; the U.S. used realpolitik when it began to deal with China and U.S.S.R. in summit and trade meetings, despite opposition to the political ideologies of the Chinese and Soviet leaders. U.S. leaders were acting realistically by reducing the potential threat posed by those nations. **(application)**

Ask students to refer to Section 4 as they add details to a time line of domestic events from the publication of the "Pentagon Papers" to Nixon's resignation. Time lines should include:

June 13 1971	*New York Times* begins publishing the "Pentagon Papers."
June 30 1971	Supreme Court rules that the government cannot censor historical information before it is published.
1971	Nixon authorizes the creation of the Plumbers investigating unit.
June 17 1972	Five men are caught breaking into the headquarters of the Democratic National Committee at Watergate. The White House begins a cover-up.
September 1972	Seven Watergate defendants are indicted. CRP pays them "hush money," and little is said about Watergate.
October 1972	*Washington Post* accuses the White House and CRP of political spying and espionage.
November 1972-1973	Nixon is reelected. Ellsberg case is thrown out of court because of the illegal actions of the Plumbers.
January 1973	Trial of the Watergate Seven begins; all plead guilty or are convicted.
March 23 1973	Judge Sirica receives a letter from James McCord admitting having lied under oath and implicating others in the break-in.

Picturing History Former Attorney General John N. Mitchell, as Richard Nixon's campaign manager, approved the break-in to the Watergate building.

Picturing History John Ehrlichman, Nixon's advisor on domestic affairs, participated in the Watergate cover-up.

Picturing History H. R. Haldeman, White House chief of staff, was another participant in the Watergate cover-up.

General; Henry Kissinger; John Ehrlichman, his advisor on domestic affairs; and H. R. Haldeman, his chief of staff. Nixon's own cabinet members found that they had to be cleared by these advisors before they were able to talk with the President.

Some people feared that the President was increasing his personal rule over government. For example, Nixon turned over many cabinet duties to his personal staff. Cabinet members have to be approved by the Senate. Members of the President's staff were not subject to approval by the Senate and would do as he wished. Presidential press conferences were few, and important information was often withheld. For example, Nixon did not tell the American people about the bombing of Cambodia for more than a year after it started.

Relations between the President and Congress also were strained. On several occasions, Nixon vetoed bills calling for pollution controls and ex-

pansion of social and medical services. When Congress overrode the vetoes, Nixon did not carry out the laws. Instead, he impounded the funds. That is, he had them seized and held. He refused to spend the money that Congress had appropriated.

The Watergate Story Begins

The initial event that many historians believe led to Watergate took place on June 13, 1971. The *New York Times* began publishing a series of articles called the "Pentagon Papers." The articles, which were based on a study of how the United States got involved in Vietnam, were embarrassing. They showed that United States military intelligence was often inaccurate, that United States diplomats often reported what they thought their superiors wanted to hear rather than what was actually going on, and that President Johnson had ordered the Tonkin Gulf Resolution drafted months before the Tonkin Gulf incident took place.

The *New York Times* had obtained the papers from Daniel Ellsberg, a former employee of the Defense Department. Although none of the information they contained was military, the papers were classified documents. Consequently, Attorney General Mitchell asked the courts to stop further publication of the "Pentagon Papers" on the grounds of national security. On June 30, 1971, the Supreme Court ruled against the Justice Department in *New York Times* v. *United States,* and *United States* v. *Washington Post.* The Court upheld the right of freedom of the press, thus allowing the papers to be published.

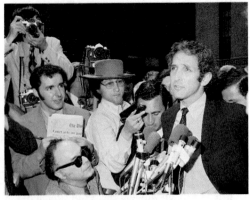

Picturing History Daniel Ellsberg addresses reporters at the Federal Building in New York after he admitted giving the "Pentagon Papers" to the *New York Times* and surrendered to federal authorities.

The Plumbers. Later that year, the Justice Department indicted Ellsberg for theft, conspiracy, and espionage. In 1973 the case was thrown out of court, however, because of an action taken by a group of special White House investigators known as the "Plumbers." They had burglarized the office of Ellsberg's psychiatrist in a vain attempt to find damaging personal evidence against Ellsberg. Unfortunately for the Nixon administration, that was not the only burglary the Plumbers undertook.

Nixon had authorized creation of the Plumbers in 1971 after publication of the "Pentagon Papers." Although the papers had nothing to do with him or his administration, he believed it was essential for a government to keep secrets, whether military or political. The Plumbers had been used not only to prevent government secrets from leaking to the media but also to help ensure Nixon's reelection in 1972.

A Bungled Burglary. At 2:30 A.M., June 17, 1972, five men were caught breaking into the headquarters of the Democratic National Committee. The headquarters were in a large apartment-office complex called Watergate in Washington, D.C. The men had intended to photograph documents and to place wiretaps, or "bugs," on the telephones in the office.

The group's leader, James McCord, was a former CIA agent. He was also an official of the Committee to Reelect the President (CRP, pronounced "creep"), which was handling Nixon's campaign under the direction of John Mitchell, who had resigned as Attorney General. Papers found in the pocket of one of the other burglars led to **G. Gordon Liddy,** a White House staff member and counsel to CRP.

The Cover-up Begins. At that point, the White House might have disowned the entire operation and demanded the resignation of everyone involved. However, that would have meant getting rid of such people as Mitchell, Haldeman, and Ehrlichman, on whom Nixon depended so strongly to help him carry out the burdens of his office. Instead, one step after another was taken to cover up the connection between the burglars and the White House.

Documents in CRP's office were shredded. Other incriminating evidence was given for safekeeping to L. Patrick Gray, who had been acting director of the FBI since the death of J. Edgar Hoover. The President asked the CIA to urge the FBI to stop its investigation of the burglary on the grounds that national security was involved.

After the seven Watergate defendants were indicted in September, it was agreed that they would be paid "hush money" for their silence. Funds were no problem. CRP was awash with millions of dollars that had been collected in great haste, sometimes from illegal sources, to beat an April 20 deadline. On that date, a new and much stricter campaign law went into effect limiting the size of contributions that individuals and firms could make to a particular candidate. In all, about $500,000 was passed on to the defendants.

Throughout 1972 little was said about Watergate. A poll in early fall showed that most voters had not heard of it. In October the *Washington Post* accused the White House and CRP of wholesale "political spying and sabotage," but the charge was generally ignored. However, two *Post* reporters, Bob Woodward and Carl Bernstein, were assigned to keep digging for additional information. In November, Nixon was overwhelmingly

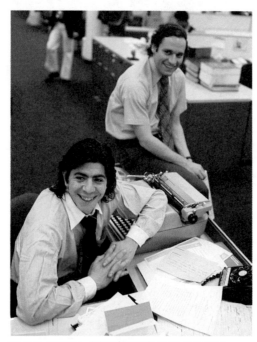

Picturing History *Washington Post* reporters Carl Bernstein (front) and Bob Woodward received a Pulitzer Prize for their investigations about Watergate. Later, they wrote a book on the subject entitled *All the President's Men.*

July 24 1974	Supreme Court rules the President must turn over the tapes.
July 1974	House Judiciary Committee adopts three articles of impeachment.
August 5 1974	Nixon releases three more tape transcripts revealing his involvement in the cover-up almost from the beginning.
August 7 1974	Republican leaders advise Nixon that he will probably be impeached.

| August 9 1974 | Nixon resigns from office. |

Discuss with students the effect the Watergate crisis had on the nation. (Discussion might include: many felt that their trust in the Presidency had been betrayed; Watergate had a strong negative effect on the overall mood of the nation.)

Guided Practice

Tell students that the Watergate affair led to a general distrust of political leaders. Ask students whether this distrust persists today or whether Watergate has generally been forgotten. (Possible responses: politicians today are much more public about their lives and dealings, partly due to the close scrutiny of the press; although Watergate itself may not be frequently discussed, its effects are still strongly felt.)

reelected. In January 1973 the trial of the Watergate Seven was held. All the defendants pleaded guilty or were convicted, and it seemed as if that was that.

The Cover-up Unravels

A number of people, however, believed there was more to Watergate than met the eye. One such person was Federal Judge **John Sirica,** who had presided over the burglary case. He had imposed maximum sentences on the seven defendants but said he would review the sentences after three months. On March 23, 1973, he received a letter from burglar James McCord. In his letter, McCord admitted having lied under oath. There were indeed people other than the Watergate Seven involved in the break-in, he said. Within days, McCord named John Dean, counsel to the President, and John Mitchell as two of the "others."

Picturing History John Sirica, chief judge of the U.S. District Court for the District of Columbia, personally questioned Watergate defense witnesses.

The next several months saw wholesale resignations and firings of White House aides, including Dean, Ehrlichman, and Haldeman. On April 30, President Nixon appeared on nationwide television. He told the American people that he had first learned about the attempt to cover up the scandal on March 21. He announced that he was appointing a new Attorney General, Elliot Richardson, and authorizing him to appoint a special prosecutor to investigate Watergate. Richardson chose Archibald Cox, a professor of law at Harvard.

In the meantime, the Senate voted to set up a committee under Senator **Sam Ervin** of North Carolina to make its own investigation of Watergate. The committee began its hearings in May despite a major difference of opinion about its powers. Committee members wanted to question various Presidential aides. The White House claimed the right of **"executive privilege."** As interpreted by Nixon, it meant that Congress could not question any of the past or present employees of the executive branch about anything whatsoever without the President's approval. Many senators felt this violated the idea of checks and balances. How could Congress pass laws if it could not get information about official government actions? Furthermore, there was nothing in the Constitution about executive privilege. Some senators felt Nixon's position was a step down the road toward a secret government that would not be accountable to the people.

The Senate hearings lasted three months. Millions of Americans watched them on television. In July they learned that Nixon had tape-recorded most of his conversations in the White House and in the Executive Office Building. Both the Ervin Committee and Special Prosecutor Cox immediately asked to hear those tapes that reportedly dealt with Watergate. Nixon refused. The committee and Cox issued subpoenas, which Nixon rejected, and the issue went to court.

Vice-President Agnew Resigns

During these months, Watergate drew so much public interest that a second political scandal got far less attention than it otherwise might have. In the midst of hearings, investigations, and almost daily revelations about spying on citizens and the harassment of media personnel by the President's men, Vice-President Agnew resigned.

Since 1967, Agnew had accepted tens of thousands of dollars in bribes from Maryland engineering firms. He had received payments not only while he was governor of Maryland, his accusers said, but also after being elected to the second highest office in the land.

In August 1973 the *Wall Street Journal* broke the story that the Vice-President was under investigation for bribery, extortion, and tax evasion. At first Agnew denied the reports. By October, however,

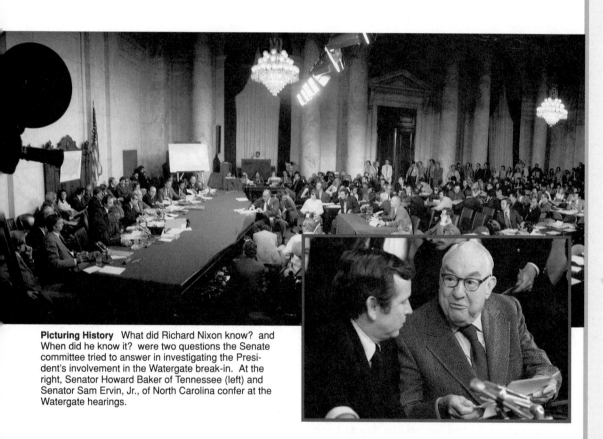

Picturing History What did Richard Nixon know? and When did he know it? were two questions the Senate committee tried to answer in investigating the President's involvement in the Watergate break-in. At the right, Senator Howard Baker of Tennessee (left) and Senator Sam Ervin, Jr., of North Carolina confer at the Watergate hearings.

he had apparently decided that the best thing to do was to plea bargain, that is, to plead guilty to a minor charge in exchange for a light sentence and protection against further prosecution.

Accordingly, on October 10, 1973, Agnew resigned as Vice-President and pleaded no contest to one charge of tax evasion. The judge pointed out that the plea was the "full equivalent of a plea of guilty." Then he imposed a fine of $10,000 and placed Agnew on probation for three years without supervision.

Many people felt Agnew's sentence was much too lenient. However, Attorney General Richardson defended it. An indictment and trial, he said, would leave "serious and permanent scars" on the nation.

On October 12, acting under the Twenty-fifth Amendment, Nixon nominated a new Vice-President. He was the Republican House minority leader, Representative **Gerald R. Ford** of Michigan. Ford was confirmed by a majority of both Houses of Congress on December 6.

Impeachment Looms

Ten days after Agnew's resignation, another bombshell exploded. It became known as the Saturday Night Massacre. Nixon, instead of turning over his tape recordings, had decided to offer a compromise. He would supply written summaries of the tapes. When Special Prosecutor Cox turned down the compromise, Nixon ordered Attorney General Richardson and Deputy Attorney General William Ruckelshaus to fire Cox. Both refused to do so and resigned. Nixon then appointed an acting attorney general, who fired Cox.

Both Richardson and Ruckelshaus felt that Nixon was going back on his promise of a thorough investigation of Watergate. The American people agreed. Newspapers everywhere called for the President's resignation, and so many letters and telegrams of protest poured into the White House that Nixon made a complete about-face. He agreed to give Judge Sirica the subpoenaed tapes, and he appointed a new special prosecutor, Leon Jaworski.

By now, however, the House Judiciary Commit-

Have students write a three-paragraph essay comparing Nixon's resignation with the impeachment of Andrew Johnson (Chapter 15). Have students list the illegal actions with which each was charged. (Essays might include: Johnson was accused of "intemperate language" and of bringing "disgrace, ridicule, contempt, and reproach" on Congress; Nixon was accused of using the IRS to harass political opponents, using the FBI to spy on individuals, interfering with the work of the Justice Department and the CIA, and failing to see that his aides obeyed the law. Johnson's im- peachment was on questionable grounds and brought about by those who objected to his Reconstruction policy; the articles of impeachment adopted against Nixon were supported by evidence.)

tee had decided to hold hearings to see if there were adequate grounds for impeaching the President. While the hearings were going on, more damaging incidents occurred. Some of the tapes could not be found. One tape contained an 18½ minute gap; apparently that portion of the tape had been erased.

Operation Candor. Things went from bad to worse. News reports revealed that Nixon had taken questionable tax deductions. (For example, he had paid about $1,000 tax on a $200,000 income in 1971 and 1972.) Then, one individual after another pleaded guilty to lesser indictments in the Watergate affair in exchange for information on people higher up. In November the President set out on "Operation Candor," a barnstorming tour designed to gain popular support. At the tour's first stop, Nixon said, "People have the right to know whether or not their President is a crook. Well, I am not a crook." Supporters cheered, but many Americans were heartsick and ashamed that their leader found it necessary to make such a statement.

In March 1974, Mitchell, Haldeman, Ehrlichman, and four other Presidential aides were indicted on charges of conspiracy, obstruction of justice, and perjury. (All were eventually convicted.) Although no one knew it at the time, the grand jury had named Nixon as a co-conspirator. They had not indicted him because they had been told by Jaworski that such an action was probably not constitutional.

The Edited Tapes. On April 30, 1974, President Nixon made another television speech. He announced that he was releasing 1,254 pages of edited transcripts of White House conversations about Watergate. The President hoped this would convince everyone of his truthfulness and leadership.

If anything, the transcripts only increased people's dismay. They were dismayed not only by the President's vulgar language but also by his attitude. Senator Hugh Scott of Pennsylvania, the Republican minority leader, characterized Nixon's responses as "shabby." Alfred Landon, the 1936 Republican Presidential candidate, observed that Nixon was concerned only about what Watergate looked like, not about cleaning it up. Emmet John Hughes, former administrative assistant to President Eisenhower, was shocked that Nixon never once considered what might be good for the country or what a President's responsibilities were.

President Nixon Resigns

After that, events proceeded swiftly. In May, Judge Sirica ordered the President to turn over sixty-four disputed tapes to Jaworski. Nixon refused. On July 24 the Supreme Court ruled unanimously that the President must turn over the tapes. The Court rejected Nixon's argument that doing so would violate national security. Evidence needed for a criminal trial could not be withheld, even by a President.

At the end of July, the House Judiciary Committee adopted three **articles of impeachment.** They charged the President with obstructing justice, abusing his power, and failing to obey lawful subpoenas issued by the House of Representatives. He was accused of the following constitutional offenses: (1) using the Internal Revenue Service to harass political opponents and interfere with the electoral process; (2) using the FBI, the Secret Service, and private agents to spy on citizens and invade their rights; (3) interfering with the proper working of the Justice Department and the CIA; and (4) failing to "take care" that his aides obeyed the law. Finally, the committee said:

> In all of this Richard M. Nixon has acted in a manner contrary to his trust as President and subversive of constitutional government, to the great prejudice of the cause of law and justice and to the manifest injury of the people of the United States. Wherefore, Richard M. Nixon, by such conduct, warrants [deserves] impeachment and trial, and removal from office.

On August 5 Nixon made public transcripts of three more tapes. They revealed what most people had come to realize: the President had been involved in the Watergate cover-up almost from the first day. He had lied to the American people, to the House of Representatives, and even to his own lawyers. On August 7 three Republican leaders, Senator Barry Goldwater, Senator Hugh Scott, and House minority leader John Rhodes of Ohio, advised the President that he would probably be impeached and convicted.

On August 9, 1974, Nixon resigned his office and left Washington with his family. He did not admit any guilt. He merely said that some of his judgments "were wrong" and that he had lost his "political base in the Congress." That same day, Gerald R. Ford was sworn in as the thirty-eighth President of the United States.

Have students complete the Chapter 34 Test on paper. Divide the class into small groups and have them review their answers.

Concluding the Chapter

Ask students to write an editorial expressing their feelings about a President who campaigns on a ticket of law and order and is eventually forced to resign his office for crimes he has committed. As young citizens who will soon have the right to vote, students should address the issue of how this political scandal affects their view of politics and politicians. (Essays might include: it's ironic or even infuriating that a President who portrays himself as a law-and-order candidate is forced to resign because of criminal activity; it stresses that citizens need to be constantly aware of what their elected officials are doing.)

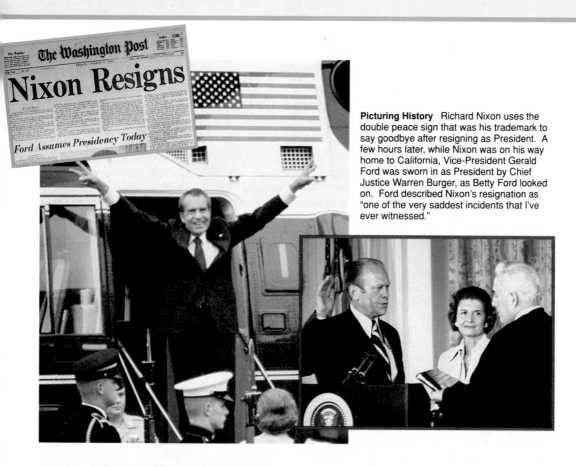

The Washington Post

Nixon Resigns

Ford Assumes Presidency Today

Picturing History Richard Nixon uses the double peace sign that was his trademark to say goodbye after resigning as President. A few hours later, while Nixon was on his way home to California, Vice-President Gerald Ford was sworn in as President by Chief Justice Warren Burger, as Betty Ford looked on. Ford described Nixon's resignation as "one of the very saddest incidents that I've ever witnessed."

Linking Past to Present

The Watergate affair led to a general distrust of politicians among Americans. This distrust persisted throughout the 1980's as Congress devoted much time to investigating some of its members, including Senator John Tower, who was named by President Bush as his first choice for Defense Secretary, and Speaker of the House James Wright, who was forced to resign because of ethical questions involving a conflict of interest in his business dealings.

SECTION 4 REVIEW

Key Terms and People

Explain the significance of: Watergate, John Mitchell, G. Gordon Liddy, John Sirica, Sam Ervin, executive privilege, Gerald R. Ford, articles of impeachment

Main Ideas

1. What was President Nixon's connection to both the Plumbers and CRP? What was the relationship of the Plumbers to CRP?
2. What events between March and July 1973 brought about the exposure of the Watergate cover-up?
3. Why did Vice-President Agnew resign from office?
4. What event is referred to as the Saturday Night Massacre? How did it affect the public's perception of President Nixon?
5. By resigning from office, what did President Nixon avoid?

Critical Thinking

6. In his inaugural address, Gerald Ford said, "Our great republic is a government of laws and not of men." What did he mean? Why was this statement especially appropriate at this time?

Lesson Plan

State the Objective

Understand the role of OPEC as a major supplier of world oil.

Map Skills

Middle East (southwest Asia and Northern Africa) • North America, Europe, Australia

Present the Lesson

Ask students to make a time line showing the steps taken by OPEC nations from the 1950's through the 1970's to take away control of oil production from multinational companies. Ask several students to write their time lines on the board. (Time lines should include: 1950's—oil producing countries asked the multinationals for higher royalties; 1960's—oil-producing nations formed OPEC to control the price, production, and sale of oil; 1970's—OPEC nations either nationalized foreign-owned companies or insisted on participation agreements.)

Divide the class into small groups to discuss the following questions: In your opinion, were the OPEC nations justified in the steps they took to gain control over oil production? (Possible responses: yes—countries are entitled to benefit from the use, sale, and control of their own natural resources. No—the severe cutbacks in oil production caused worldwide shortages, high prices, and inflation; all countries should accept responsibility for the reasonable well-being of other countries in addition to providing for their own well-being.) Did high oil prices in the 1970's cause OPEC nations to enjoy a higher standard of living? (Possible responses: yes—some member nations had more income than they could spend.

Focus on Economics

OPEC and the Energy Crisis

For centuries before people knew what to do with it, petroleum could be found in many areas of western Pennsylvania, where it surfaced in brooks and natural wells. It wasn't until the mid-1800's that the possibilities of using refined petroleum—oil—as a lubricant and energy source became apparent. Then, in 1859, the first oil well was drilled near Titusville, Pennsylvania. Barely a decade later, United States oil production stood at 20 million barrels per year. The great oil rush had begun.

Since those early days of discovery, the United States has always been one of the leading producers and consumers of oil. For decades the nation was able to satisfy its own growing petroleum needs. By World War II, however, American energy demands had increased so much that the nation had to begin relying on foreign sources of oil. That is why the Middle East—the region that contains the largest oil reserves in the world—has since the 1940's attracted increased attention from the United States and other large consumers of oil. Oil has become the lifeblood of all industrial nations.

Today the United States still ranks as one of the top producers of petroleum. Nevertheless, because of its huge energy appetite, the nation must still import about 33 percent of the petroleum it requires. The largest volume of imported oil comes from the Middle Eastern Arab nations, of which Saudi Arabia is the leading supplier.

Until the 1970's, most oil production in the Middle East was controlled by seven great multinational corporations known as the Seven Sisters, who also controlled worldwide oil distribution. Five of these corporations—Exxon, Gulf, Mobil, Standard Oil of California, and Texaco—are based in the United States. The other two are British Petroleum and, largest of all, Royal Dutch/Shell. In general, each company paid a royalty (sum of money) to the oil-producing nations for each barrel of oil it pumped out of the ground.

The Rise of OPEC. Beginning in 1950, the oil-producing countries began demanding more money for their oil. First they increased their royalties sharply. Then, in 1961, oil-producing nations throughout the world formed a cartel known as OPEC, or Organization of Petroleum Exporting Countries. A cartel is an organization of industrial businesses, often from different countries, for the purpose of controlling the price, production, and sales of a commodity—in this case, oil.

During the 1960's, OPEC raised the price of crude oil only gradually. Then, beginning in 1970, OPEC nations changed their policy.

First, they nationalized some foreign-owned oil companies, and for the rest they insisted on so-called participation agreements, by which they received a 51 to 65 percent share of company ownership. Second, almost all the Middle Eastern OPEC nations either froze the amount of oil being produced or cut back oil production by at least one-third. They argued that these actions were necessary in order to conserve dwindling oil supplies.

Then in 1973 the Yom Kippur War broke out between Israel and Egypt. In a show of resentment of the longtime friendship between the United States and Israel, the Arab nations cut off American oil shipments. Then the OPEC nations raised the price of oil. The Arab embargo ended in March 1974. So many millions of dollars, pounds, yen, and other currencies poured into OPEC treasuries between 1973 and 1979 that most of the member nations were unable to spend their income. Nevertheless, since the money earned kept losing value because of inflation, OPEC had to charge higher prices each year.

The American Response. A major reason for the inflation that took place in the United States during the 1970's and early 1980's was the increase in the cost of gasoline, heating oil, and fertilizers and other petroleum-based products. The government and the private sector attempted to handle the situation in several ways.

During the mid-1970's, for example, automobile manufacturers began concentrating on producing

No—beyond a certain point OPEC nations were unable to improve their standard of living; increased revenues merely caused prices to escalate without a comparable increase in the standard of living.)

Check for Understanding

Ask students to write their answers to the questions at the end of the feature. Discuss the answers with the class.

Ask students to consider what life-style changes Americans have made as a result of the OPEC oil crisis. (Possible responses: most Americans now drive smaller cars than they did in the early 1970's; speed limits on expressways and interstate highways have been reduced; the full-service gasoline station has been replaced by the self-service station; some Americans rely on solar energy to heat their homes; fewer polyester and more cotton garments are sold, in part because polyester is made from petroleum.)

OPEC (Organization of Petroleum Exporting Countries)

Map Skills **Region** In which region of the world are most OPEC countries located?
Location Which continents shown have no countries that are members of OPEC?

smaller cars that would use less gasoline. The Alaska pipeline began operation. Highway speeds were reduced to fifty-five miles per hour. In addition, many Americans lowered the thermostats in their homes. These actions helped to reduce our heavy reliance on foreign oil.

In 1979 the Carter administration urged a four-point program: (1) limit oil imports, (2) decontrol oil prices, (3) place an excess-profits tax on the windfall profits oil companies would earn when prices were decontrolled, and (4) use the increased tax revenues to help low-income families pay for their higher energy costs. President Carter also wanted the federal government to encourage the development of liquid fuel substitutes for oil. These might come from coal, oil shale, tar sands, and biomass (organic materials such as corn cobs, leaves, and the like). One promising substitute seemed to be alcohol mixed with 90 percent gasoline.

Then, in 1982, oil prices began falling. The cause was an abundance of oil supplied by OPEC and non-OPEC oil producers. As the glut of oil in the world market continued on through the 1980's, OPEC tried to enforce production cuts but failed. The free enterprise system had triumphed.

Some areas of the world use more oil than they produce. Nations in the Middle East, however, with the exception of Egypt and the Sudan, produce more oil than they consume. For that reason, the Middle East will continue to be an area of vital concern to the United States and the world as long as oil is needed to run machines—or until the Middle East oil wells run dry.

Understanding Economics

1. What changes did the oil-producing nations make in their policy regarding the production, distribution, and consumption of crude oil during the 1970's?
2. How has the United States tried to solve problems caused by oil shortages?
3. Why did oil prices fall in the 1980's?

Critical Thinking

4. What other measures might be taken when oil is in short supply? Do research, if necessary, to answer this question.

Key Terms and People

These are highlighted in the text in the order in which they appear in this list.

Main Ideas

1. Assassin Sirhan Sirhan opposed Kennedy's support of Israel. • Kennedy had swept virtually all the primaries and seemed assured of the nomination.

2. What position to support on the Vietnam War. • Assassinations and Vietnam War.

3. Congress tightened laws against crime and drug abuse; 1970 Omnibus Crime Control Act increased the power of federal law-enforcement agencies. • Were brought to trial; five convicted of lesser charges; three years later these convictions were reversed.

4. Thought court had been too permissive, had given too liberal an interpretation of the Constitution. • *Gideon* v. *Wainright* and *Miranda* v. *Arizona*.

5. U.S. would aim to counteract power, not ideology like communism. • Possible answer: recognition of mainland China.

6. Toned down the cold war and encouraged detente; worked out agreement over the treatment of Berlin; held summit meetings with Brezhnev during which the two nations agreed to increase trade, cooperate on space exploration, and limit the number of offensive and defensive missile sites; worked together for a cease-fire in the Yom Kippur War.

7. Committee to Reelect the President, set up to handle Nixon's campaign for reelection in 1972. • Possible answers: John Mitchell, G. Gordon Liddy.

8. Prevent government secrets from leaking to the media; help ensure Nixon's reelection. • Broke into the office of Daniel Ellsberg's psychiatrist and into

offices of the Democratic National Committee.

Critical Thinking Questions

➤**9.** Possible answer: Safire's analysis is a balanced appraisal of Nixon's major achievement and failure.

➤**10.** People became destructive while venting their anger, frustration, and grief.

11. Nixon believed that a

major reason for violence of the 1960's was federal government's attempt to enforce school desegregation by busing, so federal enforcement of this court order was virtually stopped. • Nixon believed that he knew best how to run the country. Impounding funds allotted by Congress was one way of reducing government spending.

12. Small step—getting out of the lunar module; great leap—

getting to the moon.

➤**13.** Possible answer: Nixon had made great improvements in foreign policy. Trend of the country was to conservative leadership. McGovern's platform included withdrawal from Vietnam and liberal policies at home. • Probably not—his policies were popular and in line with national trends.

14. One in which President assumes power and authority befitting an emperor rather

---

CHAPTER **34** REVIEW

Write your answers on a separate sheet of paper.

Key Terms and People

Explain the significance of: Warren Burger, revenue sharing, deficit spending, wage and price controls, Leonid Brezhnev, SALT, Yom Kippur War, John Sirica, Sam Ervin, executive privilege, Gerald R. Ford

Main Ideas

1. Why was Robert Kennedy killed? How successful had his candidacy for the Presidency been?
2. What was the major issue at the 1968 Democratic National Convention in Chicago? What were the protestors calling attention to?
3. How did the Nixon Administration go about bringing law and order to the country? What happened to the leaders of the Chicago demonstration?
4. What did strict constructionists dislike about the Warren Court? List two specific cases on which they did not agree with the decisions.
5. How did Kissinger plan for a more flexible diplomacy? What was one result on the foreign scene?
6. How did the administration ease tensions with the Soviet Union?
7. What was CRP? Name two people involved in CRP.
8. What were the Plumbers set up to do? What did they actually do?

Critical Thinking Questions

9. **Analyzing Literature.** Do you agree or disagree with William Safire's assessment of Richard Nixon's key failure, achievement, and success. Explain your answer.
10. **Making Deductions.** Knowing what you do about Martin Luther King, Jr., why do you think riots and fires occurred in the nation's cities the night he was murdered?
11. **Analyzing Interpretations.** How did the law-and-order administration rationalize going against the law by not obeying the Supreme Court

decision on school desegregation? How did it rationalize refusing to spend the money Congress appropriated for pollution controls and the expansion of social and medical services?

12. **Analyzing a Quotation.** As Neil Armstrong stepped onto the surface of the moon, he said, "That's one small step for a man, one giant leap for mankind." What did he mean?
13. **Identifying Cause and Effect.** Why do you think the Democratic candidate, George McGovern, was so badly defeated by Nixon? Do you think any Democrat could have defeated Nixon?
14. **Judging Values.** What is implied by an "imperial" Presidency? How did Nixon act as President? What roles did John Ehrlichman and H. R. Haldeman play?
15. **Making Generalizations.** This chapter covers the assassinations of two public figures and the attempted assassination of a third. What generalizations might be made about American culture and customs from these events?

Critical Thinking Activities

16. **Making a Chart.** Using the book, complete the chart below about the four candidates in the 1968 Presidential election.

Name/Party	Platform	Electoral Vote

17. **Linking Past to Present.** Review the reasons for the student protests at Columbia University in 1968. What actions did the various sides take? Do you think it was right to use so much force to clear the buildings? Do people still feel strongly about these issues?
18. **Linking Past to Present.** Compare the style of succeeding administrations with the imperial administration of President Nixon.

---

than a democratic leader.
• Nixon acted as if he were an emperor. • Ehrlichman and Haldeman kept Nixon isolated from people—even members of his cabinet—who should have had access.

➤ **15.** Each man was shot because he was prominent and espoused causes the assassin opposed. • Showed frustration and hostility of period.

Critical Thinking Activities

16. Nixon, Rep.; "peace with honor"; 301. • Humphrey, Dem.; supported Johnson's war, later wanted peace negotiations; 191. • Cleaver, Peace and Freedom; pacifist, black power; 0. • Wallace, American Independent; supported Vietnam War, law and order; 46.

17. Students believed that the

university was proposing to turn Harlem park into a gym that would have "separate but equal" facilities. • Protested, seizing three university officials and buildings. • Possible answers: yes—force should be used because students were unruly and had seized private property. No—university should have negotiated. • Yes—discrimination continues to cause conflicts.

➤ **18.** Most recent Presidents have seen themselves as serving the public. Nixon set himself above the public.

➤ **Question suitable for cooperative learning.**

The Nixon Years

The nation was shocked by the assassinations of Martin Luther King, Jr., and Robert Kennedy in 1968. Riots broke out between students and police at Columbia and other universities. More conflict erupted during the Democratic convention in Chicago. Mayor Daley called out large numbers of police, who were televised beating up demonstrators in the streets. The convention hall itself was the scene of alleged fraud and widespread confusion. Hubert Humphrey won the nomination. The Peace and Freedom party drew few votes, but George Wallace's American Independent party was more successful. Richard Nixon defeated Hubert Humphrey in an extremely close election.

During his first term of office, President Nixon moved quickly to strengthen the federal fight against crime. His appointment of Warren Burger as Chief Justice was followed by two unsuccessful nominations to the Court. He pressed for revenue sharing but failed to get his family assistance plan passed or to control inflation. The nation celebrated when Americans landed on the moon.

In 1972 President Nixon won reelection in a landslide victory over the antiwar liberal George McGovern. During his second term, Nixon relied heavily upon Henry Kissinger for advice on foreign policy. Kissinger advocated *realpolitik* and moving away from the older policy of containment of communism. Nixon decided to formally recognize Communist China, and he underlined this new policy by actually visiting that country. At the same time he tried to reassure the government of Taiwan of United States support. Nixon and Kissinger also encouraged détente with the Soviet Union. At summit meetings the two nations agreed about access to West Berlin and about some measures of arms control. The Western allies also agreed to recognize East Germany. Détente worked well during the Yom Kippur War, but no agreement was reached on offensive missiles.

Nixon's opponents claimed that he acted like an emperor. His personal manner and narrow circle of advisors all contributed to his downfall—as did the "Pentagon Papers," the "Plumbers," and especially the Watergate scandal. Over time the news media showed that financial supporters and close advisors of the President had backed a burglary of Democratic offices and lied about it. Americans learned that the President had also lied repeatedly. Congress and the Supreme Court battled the President. Finally, Nixon resigned when he was faced with the threat of impeachment. Gerald Ford, who had become Vice-President when Spiro Agnew resigned, took office.

Chronology of Main Events

1968 Martin Luther King, Jr., assassinated; Robert Kennedy assassinated; students strike at several universities

1969 Richard M. Nixon inaugurated President; American astronauts land on the moon

1971 Soviets guarantee Allied access to Berlin

1972 President Nixon visits China and the Soviet Union; arms control agreements signed based on SALT; Watergate break-in occurs

1973 Yom Kippur War begins; Vice-President Agnew resigns

1974 President Nixon resigns; Gerald R. Ford succeeds to the Presidency

Telescoping the Times may be used as an alternative to having students read the entire chapter, as a chapter preview, or as a chapter review.

Global Perspectives

1971	China is admitted to the United Nations.
1978	Pope John Paul II is elected—the first non-Italian pope in 450 years.
1979	China and the U.S. establish diplomatic relations.
1980	Black Africans end white minority rule in Rhodesia.

For Discussion

In what ways might the U.S. have benefited by reestablishing diplomatic relations with China? (Possible responses: diplomatic ties between the U.S. and China would have discouraged a Chinese-Soviet alliance hostile to the U.S.; an alliance would have provided markets for American goods; an alliance would have paved the way for the sharing of scientific and cultural information.)

Additional Resources

- Geography Activities
- Skills Activities
- Thematic Activities
- Economic Activities
- Cultural Literacy Activities
- Literary Source Readings
- Primary Source Readings
- Nuclear Peacekeeping
- Transparencies
- Computer Test Generator

Additional Teaching Strategies

SECTION 1

For Basic Students: Ask students to write a letter to President Ford opposing or supporting his pardon of Richard Nixon. (Letters opposing the pardon might include: justice should be carried out for all defendants in the case; there should be no special privileges because of rank or position. Letters supporting the pardon might include: the pardon is necessary to bring about an end to the whole affair; America needs to forget Watergate and to focus on rebuilding for the future.) Have students share their letters.

For Advanced Students: Have students write a three-paragraph essay explaining Ford's statement, "Ours is a government of laws and not of men." Students should comment on whether this statement is consistent with Ford's pardoning of Nixon. (Essays might include: all are equal under the law; no one should receive preferential treatment because of rank. The statement is not reflected in Ford's decision to pardon Nixon, the only defendant in the Watergate case whom Ford pardoned.)

SECTION 2

For Basic Students: Ask students to write two paragraphs defining inflation and explaining its effect on the average consumer. (Paragraphs might include: inflation is an increase in prices accompanied by a decline in the purchasing power of money; effects might include decreased buying power, unemployment, and high retail prices.)

For Advanced Students: Ask students to choose one problem that faced the Carter administration and to research and present to the class a three-minute talk on the problem, the attempted solution, and how it affected the country. (Talks on the ERA might include: the Carter administration tried to assure Americans that the ERA would guarantee women's rights, not take away rights they already had; Rosalynn Carter was very active in the ERA movement; even after an extension for the passage of the ERA, the final vote was three states short of the required thirty-eight; the result was that the U.S. still had no law guaranteeing that women would not be discriminated against in the workplace or in the courts.)

SECTION 3

For Basic Students: Have students review as a group the provisions of the Panama Canal treaties. Refer students to Chapter 20 for background on Teddy Roosevelt and the canal. Then have students discuss how Roosevelt might have viewed the canal treaties negotiated by President Carter. (Discussion might include: Roosevelt might have felt that Carter's treaties were in direct opposition to Roosevelt's belief that the U.S. should protect Latin America; he might have viewed it as a sign of weakness.)

For Advanced Students: Have students prepare a three-page report on current conditions in Iraq. (Information might include: Iraq remains an obstacle to stability in the Middle East; the trade embargo has failed to produce a popular uprising against Saddam Hussein, who has kept his power; the government still acts hostilely to two internal groups, the Kurds in the north and the Shiite Muslims in the south; Iraq resists dismantling its superweapon capability and thwarts the efforts of UN inspectors at every turn; it taunts the United States by threatening renewed military confrontation; the country maintains an uneasy truce at best with its neighbors—Saudi Arabia, Kuwait, and Iran.) Have one or two students present their reports to the class.

SECTION 4

For Basic Students: Ask students to research and prepare a one-page report on computer use in today's society. (Reports might include: personal computers are being used by individuals, families, schools, and small companies for keeping records, writing reports, learning skills, playing games, and running appliances; widespread use of computers has promoted the development of computer networks on local, national, and worldwide levels.)

For Advanced Students: After students research current immigration laws, divide the class into two groups to debate the justice of these regulations. (Background information might include: persons wishing to immigrate to the U.S. must obtain a visa from a U.S. consular official; law limits the annual number of visas to 320,000, although special cases are considered; visas issued to individuals who are spouses or parents of U.S. citizens do not figure in quotas; special preference is given to close relatives of U.S. citizens, to refugees, and to persons with talents or training that is needed in the U.S.)

Further Reading for Students

Evans, Christopher. *The Making of the Micro: A History of the Computer.* New York: Van Nostrand Reinhold, 1981.

Hoobler, Dorothy, and Thomas Hoobler. *An Album of the Seventies.* New York: Franklin Watts, 1981.

Leone, Bruno, and Judy Smith. *The Energy Crisis: Opposing Viewpoints.* Trumbull, Conn.: Greenwich Press, 1981.

Smith, Betsy C. *Jimmy Carter, President.* New York: Walker, 1986.

Bibliography for Teachers
Books

Carter, Rosalynn. *First Lady From Plains.* Boston: Houghton Mifflin, 1984.

Dolan, Paul J., and Edward Quinn, eds. *The Sense of the Seventies: A Rhetorical Reader.* New York: Oxford University Press, 1978.

Drew, Elizabeth. *American Journal: The Events of 1976.* New York: Random House, 1977.

Ford, Gerald. *A Time to Heal.* New York: Harper and Row, 1980.

Reeves, Richard. *A Ford, Not a Lincoln.* New York: Harcourt Brace Jovanovich, 1974.

Salinger, Pierre. *America Held Hostage.* Garden City, N.Y.: Doubleday, 1981.

Shogan, Robert. *Promises to Keep: Carter's First 100 Days.* New York: Crowell, 1977.

Audio-Visuals

Computers: Challenging Man's Supremacy. Hobel Leiterman Productions. Movie.

Conversation with President Carter, May 21, 1979. ICARUS Films. Movie.

Peanuts to the Presidency. Document Associates. Movie.

Review of the Seventies. Document Associates. Movie.

Computer Resources

TimeLiner Data Disks: Events of the 70's and 80's. (Apple) Tom Snyder.

Teacher's Notes:

Teaching Resources, Unit 8 Booklet

Lesson Study Sheets pp. 169-184
Daily Activities pp. 185-192
Enrichment Activities pp. 193-200
Reteaching Activities pp. 201-208
Chapter Review p. 209
Chapter Mastery Tests pp. 211-222
Telescoping the Times Study Sheet p. 223

Chapter Objectives

Students will learn:
- the major problems of the Ford administration
- the social and economic successes and failures of the Carter administration
- the major foreign policy problems that confronted the Carter administration
- the technological and social changes of the 1970's

Using the Chapter Time Line

Who was President in 1975 when South Vietnam surrendered to North Vietnam? (Answer: Gerald Ford) How many years passed between the opening of the Panama Canal (see Chapter 20 Time Line) and the treaty giving the Panama Canal to Panama (Answer: 63 years)

Picturing History Breaking with tradition, President Jimmy Carter and his wife, Rosalynn, walk down Pennsylvania Avenue following the inauguration ceremony. When Jimmy's brother heard the weather forecast, he said, "Jimmy must've been talkin' to the Lord again."

1970		1972		1974		1976		1978		1980

1972	1973	1975	1977	1979
SALT signed	OPEC embargoes oil	• *Mayaguez* seized by Cambodians • Helsinki Accords signed	• Jimmy Carter inaugurated President • Panama Canal treaties signed	• Camp David Accords signed • Iranians seize American hostages • Soviets invade Afghanistan

Links to American Literature

Garrison Keillor: born in Anoka, Minnesota, in 1942; graduated from the University of Minnesota in 1966; began his career in radio broadcasting in 1960 on Minnesota Public Radio; in 1974 began "A Prairie Home Companion," a live-broadcast Saturday evening program featuring music, story-telling, and humor; won the 1980 George Foster Peabody Award for distinguished broadcasting.

Works include: articles for *The New Yorker*, *The Atlantic Monthly*, *The L.A. Times*, and the *Minneapolis Tribune*; *Happy to Be Here* (1982);

Leaving Home: A Collection of Lake Wobegon Stories (1987).

Lake Wobegon Days: is an unforgettable look at life in small-town America, "where all the women are strong, all the men are good-looking, and all the children are above-average"; explains why "we are what we are" and why "smart doesn't count for much."

Introducing the Chapter

Remind students that the Nixon administration left many Americans suspicious of government officials. Ask students to suggest qualities and personality traits that Americans have been looking for in politicians in the post-Nixon years. Write these qualities on the board. (Possible responses: honesty; sincerity; intelligence; candor.) As students read the chapter, ask them to identify characteristics from the list that can be attributed to Presidents Ford and Carter.

CHAPTER **35**   1970–1980

The 1970's: Ford and Carter

Links to American Literature

> The all-time biggest tomato ever raised in town was Irene Bunsen's in 1978. . . . It weighed close to twenty ounces. Her sister Arlene grew a two-pounder once, but Clarence ate it before the jury arrived, so it didn't count. The record was twenty-four. . . .
>
> As it closed in on the record, she checked it twice a day for bugs and whatnot, and it was during a routine check that she bumped the hammock. The champ took a dive, hit the deck, and split wide open. Irene ran in the house and called her sister who ran right over. Irene was bawling so hard she couldn't see, so Arlene went out and scooped up the remains and went to work. She stuffed its insides back in, patched it with masking tape, and took a basting syringe and replenished its bodily liquids. She put it in a plastic bag, and they took it in to Ralph for the weigh-in.
>
> "It looks like it blew up," he said.
>
> Arlene said, "Well, that's between you and me. It had a little accident, but it's still a tomato. Weigh it."
>
> Twenty-five ounces. If you added three for all it went through, it'd be twenty-eight, but twenty-five was good enough for the record.
>
> — GARRISON KEILLOR, *Lake Wobegon Days*

Gerald Ford assumed the office of President in 1974 hoping to heal the wounds that had been left by the Watergate crisis. To the surprise of many, however, Jimmy Carter, a newcomer to Washington, won the election of 1976. Carter brought the openness and warmth of small-town America back to the Presidency. Honesty, hard work, and clean living were once again emphasized. Americans felt they could again look ahead with hope and deal with their problems systematically—and sometimes even with a sense of humor.

Chapter Overview

This chapter offers an important insight into how our democratic system of government is able to respond to change, undergo reform, and thrive despite problems of leadership.

In this chapter you will learn about the successes and failures of the Ford and Carter administrations and about the major foreign policy problems they confronted. You will also learn about some of the trends in popular culture during the 1970's. Chapter 35 covers this period in four sections.

Chapter Outline

1. **President Ford Heads the Nation**
2. **Carter Enters the White House**
3. **World Tensions Increase**
4. **Technological and Social Change Continues**

903

Anticipate the Lesson

Discuss with students how the legacy of Watergate might have affected the Ford administration. (Discussion might include: Americans might have viewed Ford with suspicion because he had not been elected to the Presidency but rather had been selected by Nixon; some people might have trusted and supported Ford because he did not seek the office of President and was much less aggressive than Nixon.) Ask students how the Ford administration might have lessened the negative feelings. (Possible responses: by dismissing all government officials involved in Watergate; by ordering all defendants to stand trial without interference or protection from the executive branch.)

State the Objective

Identify the major problems of the Ford administration.

President Ford Heads the Nation

GLOSSARY TERMS: **recession, cartel, Organization of Petroleum Exporting Countries (OPEC)**

Gerald Ford was inaugurated on August 9, 1974. He nominated Governor **Nelson Rockefeller** for Vice-President, and Congress confirmed the nomination. Ford had been a member of the House of Representatives since 1949. He was a hardworking, straightforward, good-natured, and unpretentious person. During his first month in the White House, he created a welcome feeling of openness and good will. Then he did something that almost destroyed that feeling.

Ford Pardons Nixon

On September 8, 1974, without warning and without consulting any members of Congress, Ford granted former President Richard Nixon a "full, free, and absolute" pardon for all crimes he "committed or may have committed" during his Presidency. In accepting the pardon, Nixon did not admit any guilt. He simply said that he could understand how his "mistakes and misjudgments" might have led some people to think that his behavior during the Watergate investigation had been "self-serving and illegal."

Picturing History One of President Gerald Ford's first acts was to pardon Richard Nixon.

Many people agreed with the pardon. In their opinion, Nixon had been punished enough by being forced to resign in disgrace. Others, however, were stunned by the action. To them, it seemed that there were two standards of justice. Nixon was receiving the same pension and allowances as other retired Presidents: free federal office space, $150,000 a year for pension and expenses, a travel allowance of $40,000, a miscellaneous allowance of $209,000, and a transition allowance of $450,000. At the same time, almost forty subordinates who had carried out his orders either sat in prison or were awaiting trial. Many people argued that it would have been much more appropriate for Ford to have pardoned Nixon after a trial rather than before. As one commentator said, "Mercy without justice is favoritism."

People in the Chapter

Gerald Ford found out he was to become President on the day Richard Nixon resigned. That morning, Nixon sent for the Vice-President and said, "You will do a good job, Jerry." Ford was the first person to occupy the Presidency and the Vice-Presidency without being elected to either office.

Nelson Rockefeller claimed he never wanted to be Vice-President. "I always said I am just not built for standby equipment," he stated. His hopes for the number-one spot must have died, however. When Gerald Ford offered him the number-two spot, he took it.

J. Edgar Hoover was director of the FBI but had never actually arrested a criminal. After the Senate pointed this out, Hoover decided to personally arrest a bank robber on the most-wanted list. When the FBI finally tracked the criminal down, Hoover arrived on the scene and asked for handcuffs. The agents were horrified. That was the one thing they had forgotten. They used a necktie instead.

Jimmy Carter used his outsider status in Washington to his advantage when he said: "I have been accused of being an outsider. I plead guilty. Unfortunately, the vast majority of Americans are also outsiders."

904

Present the Lesson

Ask students to read the section and compile a list of problems faced by the Ford administration. Write the following headings on the board: Domestic, Foreign Policy, and Economic. Have students group the problems in their lists under the appropriate headings, reminding them that a problem might fit into more than one category. Lists might include:

Domestic
- Aftermath of Watergate
- Negative response to Nixon pardon
- Increasing inflation

- Recession
- Oil embargo

Foreign Policy
- Oil embargo
- OPEC price increases
- Seizure of American freighter *Mayagüez* in Gulf of Siam

Economic
- Increasing inflation
- Recession
- High oil prices

Check for Understanding

Call on individual students to orally answer Section 1 Review questions.

President Ford explained his reasons for the pardon. Without it, he said, there would have been a long public trial of a former President. Did the nation really want to put itself through such an ordeal? Ford also felt that Richard Nixon and his loved ones had suffered enough and that someone must write "The End" to it. After a while, the furor over the pardon died down.

Problems Continue at Home and Abroad

On the economic front, Ford found inflation increasing rapidly. So he cut spending for social programs and vetoed bills he considered inflationary. He also called on management and labor to hold down prices and wages voluntarily. The result of these actions was the worst **recession** (prolonged decline in economic activity) in almost forty years, with unemployment rising to 9 percent of the labor force. By 1976, however, the inflation rate had been cut in half, although such industries as auto manufacturing and construction remained in a slump.

Oil Shortages and Price Increases. The American economy was also hit by an embargo on oil shipments from the Middle East. In October 1973, a new conflict broke out between Israel and its Arab neighbors, the fourth such conflict since Israel's establishment in 1948. Because the United States and other Western nations were giving aid to Israel, certain Arab nations refused to ship oil to the West. Long lines developed at many gas stations in the United States, and there was a shortage of home heating oil. Many Americans were startled to learn that the United States was dependent on foreign nations for more than a third of its oil.

Although the Arab oil embargo was lifted in March 1974, the United States faced the problem of higher oil prices. In 1961 the oil-producing nations throughout the world had formed a **cartel** known as the **Organization of Petroleum Exporting Countries (OPEC).** A cartel is an organization that controls enough of the production of a commodity to set the world price. OPEC included thirteen nations in the Middle East, Africa, and South America, as well as Indonesia. (See pages 898–899.) In 1970 OPEC began to raise the price of oil from the then-current rate of two dollars a barrel. By 1980 the price was over thirty dollars a barrel. The repeated hikes in the price of crude oil drove the price of gasoline, heating oil, fertilizer,

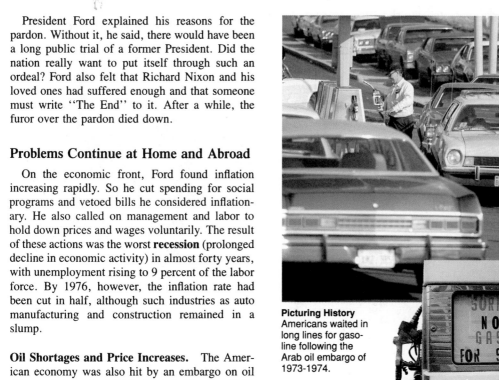

Picturing History Americans waited in long lines for gasoline following the Arab oil embargo of 1973-1974.

and other petroleum-based products upward and contributed greatly to inflation in the United States. (See page 909.)

The *Mayagüez* Episode. There were difficulties abroad as well as at home. In 1975 a Communist government took over Cambodia. Shortly after coming to power, the new government seized the American freighter *Mayagüez* and its crew of thirty-nine in the Gulf of Siam. The United States called the seizure an act of piracy. The Cambodians claimed that the ship was violating their territorial waters. Ford ordered two air strikes against Cambodia and sent in a force of marines on a rescue mission. Cambodia then surrendered the ship and crew.

Most Americans, especially because of the recent fall of South Vietnam, applauded Ford's action as evidence of the country's power and determination. Skeptics, however, pointed out that the rescue mission cost more lives than it saved and that the President had acted without consulting Congress.

To stimulate discussion on President Ford's pardoning of Richard Nixon, ask students the following questions. What might have been the result had Nixon been impeached and removed from office? What might have resulted had Nixon undergone a lengthy trial after his resignation? (Possible responses: an impeachment or a trial might have been long and expensive but might have satisfied Americans' desire for justice; Ford might have been seen as a strong supporter of justice and the Constitution and might have won reelection; Americans' faith and trust in their government might have been preserved.)

Student Assignment/Homework

Have students read Section 2, "Carter Enters the White House," and answer the Section 2 Review questions on paper.

SECTION 1 REVIEW

Answers

Main Ideas

1. To eliminate the controversy and prevent the long trial of a former President. Ford also felt that Nixon had suffered enough.

2. Inflation, recession, unemployment, oil shortages, and the rapidly increasing price of oil.

3. Americans' trust in their government had decreased considerably, but they were still able to relax and enjoy the celebrations.

Critical Thinking

4. Possible answers: the nation would have suffered great humiliation and conflict during a lengthy trial. • As a result of the pardon, the nation suffered a loss of respect for and faith in the government, and many came to believe that different standards of justice exist in the United States. (analysis)

Americans Celebrate the Bicentennial

The nation approached its two hundredth birthday in a relatively quiet mood. The boundless faith of Americans in their nation's future—a faith that had marked the 1876 centennial celebration—was missing in 1976. The nation had gone through some trying times, and trust in the government had decreased considerably. Nevertheless, many Americans joined in the celebrations.

Picturing History Many foreign countries sent great sailing vessels to the nation's bicentennial celebration.

Other nations that still had great sailing vessels (mostly for training purposes) sent them to the United States. The parade of tall ships in New York and other East Coast harbors was a beautiful and impressive sight. Elizabeth II of England came to help celebrate the independence that had been declared against her great-great-great-great-grandfather, George III. Millions of citizens put aside their cares to relax, watch fireworks, and enjoy themselves.

Linking Past to Present

The American people continued to celebrate liberty throughout the 1980's. In 1986 they celebrated the one hundredth anniversary of the placing of the Statue of Liberty in New York Harbor. In 1987 they commemorated the bicentennial of the writing of the Constitution. The early 1990's called for other celebrations of the American past, with the bicentennial of the Bill of Rights in 1991 and the five hundredth anniversary of Columbus's first voyage to the Americas in 1992.

Picturing History *Viking I* and *II* sent back pictures of Mars. The landing module—complete with cameras, antennas, and probes—is shown.

With near-perfect timing, on July 20 and September 3, 1976, *Viking I* and *II* touched down on the surface of Mars. These unmanned spacecraft were soon sending back excellent pictures of the planet's rocky soil and pale blue sky. This achievement was a fitting climax to the hundred years of technological advances that had been made since the Centennial Exposition of 1876.

SECTION 1 REVIEW

Key Terms and People

Explain the significance of: Gerald Ford, Nelson Rockefeller, recession, cartel, OPEC

Main Ideas

1. What were President Ford's reasons for pardoning Nixon?
2. What were the main economic problems faced by the Ford administration?
3. Briefly describe the American mood at the time of the bicentennial.

Critical Thinking

4. In what ways do you think the nation would have suffered if President Nixon had been forced to stand trial? In what ways did the nation suffer from Nixon's being pardoned?

Anticipate the Lesson

After students read and complete Chapter 35, Section 2 Enrichment Activity, discuss why Jimmy Carter was able to win the 1976 Presidential election. Ask students whether people were voting more for Carter or against the incumbent administration. (Possible responses: for Carter—Carter's friendly and honest approach attracted voters. Against the incumbent administration—voters were strongly

dissatisfied with the problems in Washington and would have voted for almost anyone who promised a positive change.)

State the Objective

Understand the social and economic successes and failures of the Carter administration.

SECTION 2

Carter Enters the White House

GLOSSARY TERMS: **inflation, deflation, productivity, trade deficit, stagflation, national debt, right-to-work laws**

Ever since 1960, there had been a decline in the percentage of people voting in national elections. In that year, 62.8 percent of the voting-age population voted. By 1976, the percentage of voters had fallen to 53.6 percent.

Disillusionment and Distrust Prevail

Some political scientists blamed the small turnout on voter apathy. Other observers of voting trends pointed out that the big city political machines that had produced large voter turnouts in the past no longer existed. They had fallen victim to such circumstances as the death of political boss Richard J. Daley of Chicago and the movement of people to the suburbs.

Most observers, however, attributed the small voter turnout to the disillusionment and distrust of government that was a legacy of the Vietnam War and of Watergate. During the war, the government had withheld information from the American people and had failed to win full popular support for its policies. Until Watergate, most Americans did not believe that their national political leaders would commit illegal acts. Yet week after week in the wake of the Watergate break-in, the Congress, the courts, and the news media spread before the voters a shameful record of official wrongdoing.

There were other disquieting revelations as well. During the Ford administration, investigators turned up evidence that the FBI had kept thousands of citizens under surveillance for nearly twenty-five years, often with little or no legal justification. The FBI had also tried to disrupt the activities of political groups that had met with FBI director J. Edgar Hoover's disapproval. As the Attorney General observed, spying on citizens was "not something we in a free society should condone."

Furthermore, it was revealed that the Central Intelligence Agency (CIA), too, had spied on American citizens, which is forbidden by its charter. The CIA had also engineered the overthrow in 1973 of Chile's elected Marxist President Salvador Allende Gossens. The action left Chile in the grip of a military dictator. These disclosures and hints of

illegal activity caused many citizens to demand stricter control over the activities of the CIA as well as the FBI.

An "Outsider" Is Elected

Although Ford suffered from not having been elected either Vice-President or President, he won the Republican nomination in 1976. The strongest challenge to his nomination came from conservative Republicans who supported **Ronald Reagan,** a former movie actor and governor of California. After narrowly beating Reagan by only fifty-seven delegate votes out of more than two thousand, Ford chose conservative Senator Robert Dole of Kansas as his running mate.

Several Democratic hopefuls sought their party's nomination. Surprisingly, the winner was not a senator or other member of the Washington establishment but a complete outsider: former Governor James Earl Carter, Jr., of Georgia.

Presidential Election, 1976

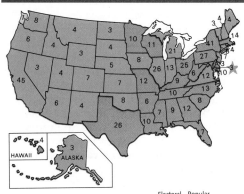

Party	Candidate	Electoral Vote	Popular Vote	%
Democratic	Jimmy Carter	297	40,830,763	50
Republican	Gerald Ford	240	39,147,793	48
Republican	Ronald Reagan	1		
Independent	Eugene McCarthy		756,691	1

538 Total Electoral Vote

"Jimmy" Carter, as he preferred to be called, had been a career naval officer. When his father unexpectedly died of cancer, Carter left the navy and returned to Plains, Georgia, to take over the family business. The business of the Carter family was peanut farming. It was a complex operation, but in a few years Carter had mastered it sufficiently to make himself a millionaire and at the same time launch a career in Georgia politics. In

907

Present the Lesson

Ask students to review the section and identify the successes and failures of the Carter administration. List these on the board. List might include:

Successes

- Opened up more federal jobs and judgeships to women, African Americans, and Hispanics.
- Created cabinet-level Department of Energy.
- Was responsible for a short-term decline in U.S. dependence on foreign oil.

Failures

- Could not pass his energy program through Congress—a program that called for a high sales tax on "gas guzzlers" and standby powers to raise gas prices and to start rationing gas, if necessary.
- Suffered a setback in the area of nuclear power due to the disaster at Three Mile Island.
- Was unable to control inflation, unemployment, or the trade deficit.
- Failed to get Congress to agree to his measures for reducing the national debt.
- Was unable to pass the ERA.

For Discussion

What are some ways in which politicians can regain voter trust and encourage citizens to vote in elections?

(Possible responses: politicians can be more open and candid; they can make themselves more available to the public; they can use less rhetoric and answer questions more specifically.)

1966 he ran for but lost the Georgia governorship. In 1970 he ran again and won.

As governor, Carter had an opportunity to meet many top Washington political officials. He came to believe that he could govern the nation at least as well as some of them. So he decided to run for President.

That seemed truly an impossible dream. No one from the cotton South had won the Presidency since James K. Polk. Carter, however, had unfaltering ambition. Then, too, he was not connected with any unpopular national policies. A religious fundamentalist, or a person who takes the Bible literally, he had the support of many other Christian fundamentalists. He also had the support of black voters because of his record on civil rights while he was governor.

Carter won the Democratic nomination after a series of hard-fought primaries. He chose as his running mate a good-natured and respected liberal, Senator Walter F. Mondale of Minnesota.

The main campaign issues—inflation, energy, and unemployment—were discussed by the two candidates in a series of televised debates, the first since the Kennedy-Nixon debates of 1960. Carter's appeal, however, did not seem to come from his views on these issues. It came, rather, from his personality and his sense of morality. He had a warm, direct campaign style. He would walk up to a stranger on the street, smile, and stick out his hand. "Hello, I'm Jimmy Carter and I'm running for President. I'd like your vote." He carried his own luggage and often stayed in the homes of his supporters rather than in fancy hotels. His sincerity contrasted sharply in people's minds with the stance of politicians who had made "the mess in Washington." Carter often said, "I will never lie to you." He pledged "a government that is as good and honest and decent . . . and as filled with love as are the American people."

Ford began the 1976 campaign far behind Carter in the polls. Although he moved up later, he did not gain enough, and Carter won the election by 40.8 million votes to Ford's 39.1 million votes. The electoral college showed 297 votes for Carter and 240 votes for Ford.

Energy and Economic Problems Persist

Carter's informality continued after his election. In the inaugural ceremony, he became the first President ever to be sworn in under his nickname.

He was also the first President to walk rather than ride from the Capitol to the White House after the inauguration.

Carter soon found that governing was not the same as campaigning. Most of his staff members were fellow Georgians with little experience at the national level and with few ties to officials of the Democratic party. As a result, Carter had trouble getting his programs through Congress. He was more successful in opening up the government to women, African Americans, and Hispanics, many of whom received federal jobs and judgeships.

The Energy Crisis. A main focus of the Carter administration was the nation's energy crisis. The President outlined a program that he described as "the moral equivalent of war." Among other things, it called for a high sales tax on big, heavy cars—"gas guzzlers"—that were burning up so much of the fuel supply. Carter also asked for standby powers to raise gas prices and to start rationing if a greater shortage threatened.

To build support for his energy program, Carter appeared on television to speak directly to the American people. His address was billed as a "fireside chat," a term borrowed from the Franklin D. Roosevelt era. Carter appeared sitting beside a handsome fireplace in the White House, warmed by a cheery blaze and wearing a sweater as he asked Americans to lower their thermostats.

Despite his efforts, Carter was unable to get his program through Congress. Automobile manufacturers were unhappy with the idea of a tax on gas guzzlers, for that would adversely affect car sales. The oil and gas lobby did not want rationing. Carter finally had to use his executive power to set up a cabinet-level **Department of Energy** in 1977 to deal with the crisis.

Meanwhile, United States dependence on foreign oil began declining. This turnaround was attributed to several factors—conservation measures, a lucky succession of mild winters, more miles to the gallon in the newer cars, and a decline in general business activity. By 1979, however, foreign oil imports had risen again, this time to 43 percent of the country's annual supply. (See pages 898–899.)

Setback for Nuclear Power. The nation had counted on nuclear power to replace foreign oil in generating electricity. In 1979, however, the nu-

Check for Understanding

Call on individual students to read their answers to Section 2 Review questions.

Guided Practice

To stimulate discussion on the effectiveness of the Carter administration in restoring confidence in the Presidency, ask students the question, Do large numbers of Americans still distrust politicians in general? (Possible responses: yes—Americans still seem to distrust politicians in general, as is demonstrated by the attention the media focuses on the backgrounds and private lives of politicians. No—the public now realizes that politicians are only human and will err but, like most people, are basically honest.)

clear power industry suffered a setback. On March 28, a nuclear reactor on **Three Mile Island** in the Susquehanna River near Harrisburg, Pennsylvania, began to break down. Its cooling system failed, the reactor became dangerously overheated, and several fuel rods were damaged. The fear arose that deadly radiation would escape and spread over the countryside. Two days later, low-level radiation actually did escape from the plant's crippled cooling system. The governor of Pennsylvania ordered schools in the area closed and urged that preschool children be kept at least five miles from the island. On April 9, the Nuclear Regulatory Commission (NRC), which had been created in 1974 to replace the Atomic Energy Commission, announced that the immediate danger was over.

The events at Three Mile Island gave a new edge to the arguments between friends and foes of nuclear power. Investigators found that plant maintenance personnel had not been properly trained and that certain safety precautions at the plant were lax. Advocates of nuclear power made much of the fact that no one had been killed or seriously injured. Opponents countered by saying that chance alone had averted a tragedy. They demanded that the government call a halt to the construction of new nuclear power plants and gradually shut down existing nuclear facilities. The NRC responded by strengthening its safety standards and improving its inspection procedures. By

Picturing History President Carter at Three Mile Island after the breakdown that forced Americans to reevaluate their plans for increasing reliance on nuclear power.

1988 at least seventeen new nuclear power plants had become operative in the United States, and none had suffered a breakdown.

Stagflation. Adding to President Carter's energy woes was the problem of steadily rising **inflation.** Inflation is characterized by an increase in prices and wages accompanied by a decline in the purchasing power of money. (A general decline in prices and wages is called **deflation.**)

The causes of inflation were many and complicated. The increased price of oil was certainly one cause. Another was higher social security payments, which were needed because more people were living longer and because the payments themselves were indexed, or tied, to the cost of living. In addition, there was a huge increase in the cost of defense, particularly military hardware.

In the past, when inflation increased, unemployment went down, and vice versa. Now, however, that did not happen. Unemployment increased along with inflation. Furthermore, **productivity,** or output per man-hour of work, was almost flat, rising less than 1 percent a year instead of the 3 percent a year it had risen during the 1950's and 1960's. American goods—especially steel, automobiles, textiles, and shoes—were becoming less

The Effects of Inflation

Product	Increase in Prices 1967 - 1983
Women's clothing	71.4 %
Men's clothing	88.3
Refrigerator	91.4
Shoes	109.7
Furniture	117.2
Ground beef	156.5
Food for home	182.5
Food away from home	221.0
Electricity	240.7
Train fare	264.5
Gasoline	289.5
Airline fare	320.7
Hospital room	527.6
Fuel oil	576.5

Assign Independent Practice

Have students write two paragraphs stating their reaction to the Three Mile Island incident and proposing a solution to prevent such accidents from happening in the future. (Paragraphs might include: Three Mile Island perfectly typifies the problems we will face as we increase our use of nuclear power; new and tougher guidelines and training procedures for inspectors are needed, and surprise inspections by federal inspectors should be incorporated into the system.)

competitive in the marketplace, and the nation's **trade deficit,** or the excess of imports over exports, was growing.

This combination of high inflation, high unemployment, and stagnant production was labeled **stagflation** by economists. However, although they gave the problem a name, they disagreed about its causes.

Carter, like Ford, attempted to hold down inflation through voluntary wage and price controls. As before, such measures had no effect. Carter then tried to reduce the **national debt.** The national debt is the money that the federal government has borrowed because its expenditures have exceeded its revenues. Carter hoped that such a reduction would encourage businesses to expand. Again, he could not get Congress to go along with him.

By 1980 the economy was in bad shape. Inflation had risen almost 40 percent from 1976, some 7 million Americans were unemployed, and the work force was growing faster than the job supply. The United States no longer had the world's highest standard of living but had fallen to fifth place.

The Decline of the Labor Movement. Stagflation reinforced a trend that had been developing in the United States economy since 1960. That trend was the decline of the labor movement. By 1975 only about 15 percent of the nation's workers held union cards, as compared with a high of more than 25 percent in 1953.

One reason for the decline was strong employer resistance to labor unions. Sometimes this resistance took the form of **right-to-work laws,** which now exist in twenty-one states. These laws prohibit union-shop agreements that force employees to join a union within a certain period after they are hired.

Another reason for the decline of the labor movement was simply the reduction of the work force in certain industries. For example, as clothing imports soared, American manufacturers laid off workers or moved their plants to Asia and Europe, where wages were lower.

A third reason for the decline of unions was the increasing importance of professional and service industries. It is much harder for labor unions to organize people in small stores, offices, and machine shops than it is to organize workers on the assembly lines of large corporations.

The ERA Is Defeated

President Carter was a strong supporter of equal rights for women, and he appointed two women to his cabinet. Yet the struggle to add an equal rights amendment to the Constitution did not succeed.

The **Equal Rights Amendment (ERA)** had first been submitted in 1923 by Alice Paul's National Woman's Party. After the National Organization for Women (NOW) was organized in 1966, it, too, pushed for the amendment that "Equality of rights under the law shall not be denied or abridged by the United States or by any state on account of sex." In 1972 Congress passed the amendment by the nec-

Picturing History
Among the women who took part in a gala event to raise funds for the ERA were (left to right) Betty Friedan, Liz Carpenter, Rosalynn Carter, Betty Ford, Elly Peterson, Jill Ruckelshaus, and Bella Abzug.

Student Assignment/Homework

Have students read Section 3, "World Tensions Increase," and complete Chapter 35, Section 3 Daily Activity.

SECTION 3
Core Lesson

Anticipate the Lesson

Discuss students' answers to Chapter 35, Section 3 Daily Activity. Read and discuss Chapter 35, Section 3 Enrichment Activity on the American hostage crisis. To stimulate discussion on the official American actions and reactions to the crisis, ask students the following questions. Which actions might have helped secure the release of the hostages? Which actions might have further prolonged the

hostage situation? (Possible responses: talks with Iranians in Algeria and the release of the Shah's wealth might have helped secure the hostages' release; the freezing of Iranian assets in the U.S., the expulsion of Iranian diplomats, and the failed rescue attempts might have prolonged the crisis.)

essary two-thirds majority and sent it to the states for ratification within seven years.

According to polls, about two-thirds of the population welcomed the proposed amendment. These ERA supporters agreed that women should receive the same pay for doing the same work as men and should be promoted on the same basis as men. Some people, however, were afraid that the amendment would do away with special laws that protect women in divorce proceedings and in the workplace. Others, believing that the ERA would destroy the traditional family unit, mounted an intense campaign against it. They claimed that if the ERA were ratified, separate toilet facilities would be abolished and women would have to serve with men in combat. (In 1981 the United States Supreme Court ruled that Congress has the constitutional right to pass an all-male draft.)

By 1979 thirty-five states had ratified the ERA. However, this was three states short of the required number. Congress therefore extended the deadline for ratification until June 30, 1982. It was to no avail. On that date the ERA, still three states short of the needed thirty-eight, was defeated.

SECTION 2 REVIEW

Key Terms and People

Explain the significance of: Ronald Reagan, Jimmy Carter, Department of Energy, Three Mile Island, inflation, deflation, productivity, trade deficit, stagflation, national debt, right-to-work laws, ERA

Main Ideas

1. During the 1970's, what were the main sources of Americans' prevailing disillusionment with and distrust of their leaders?
2. What made Jimmy Carter appealing to many voters during the 1976 Presidential campaign?
3. What were the main domestic problems faced by the Carter administration?
4. What were the main causes of the decline of the labor movement in the 1970's?
5. What principle did the Equal Rights Amendment attempt to establish?

Critical Thinking

6. Why did the majority of Americans in the 1970's support ratification of the ERA?

SECTION 3

World Tensions Increase

GLOSSARY TERMS: human rights, SALT II, Camp David Accords, PLO, terrorism

Despite the nation's many domestic problems, Carter began to spend most of his time on foreign problems. The President was a deeply religious man, and his religious beliefs played a major role in his policies.

Carter Pledges Support for Human Rights

During his election campaign, Carter had sharply criticized Henry Kissinger's policy of *realpolitik*. (See page 889.) Like Woodrow Wilson before him, Carter wanted to bring moral principles into America's foreign policy. He spelled out his ideas in his inaugural address. "We can never be indifferent to the fate of freedom elsewhere," the President declared. ". . . Our commitment to human rights must be absolute." By the term **human rights,** Carter meant those rights listed in the Declaration of Independence and guaranteed by the Bill of Rights.

Even before Carter's declaration, Congress had begun to move in this direction. In the early 1970's, it prohibited American aid to countries that engaged "in a consistent pattern of gross violations of internationally recognized human rights." In August 1975, leaders of the United States and thirty-four other nations, including the Soviet Union, met in Helsinki, Finland. There, in what became known as the Helsinki Accords, they promised to support human rights.

Carter began putting his principle into practice by cutting off military aid to Argentina and Brazil. Although both nations were friendly to the United States, their governments had imprisoned and tortured tens of thousands of their own people. Carter followed this up by establishing a Bureau of Human Rights in the State Department.

The President's new policy drew mixed reactions. Many people believed it strengthened America's traditional role of encouraging freedom and democracy. Supporters of the cold war, however, argued that the policy undermined such anticommunist but dictatorial allies as Iran and Nicaragua. At the same time, those who favored a closer

State the Objective

Analyze the major foreign policy problems that
confronted the Carter administration.

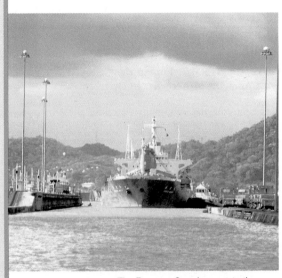

Picturing History The Panama Canal connects the
Atlantic and Pacific oceans and serves as a key transportation link for international trade.

relationship with the Soviet Union believed that
emphasizing human rights would simply increase
tensions between the superpowers without having
any practical results.

The United States Yields the Panama Canal

In 1904 the United States had obtained the right
to use and control the Panama Canal forever. Over
the years, however, Panamanians grew increasingly resentful about having their nation split in two
by a zone controlled by a foreign power. They also
contrasted the high living standard of Americans in
the Canal Zone with their own poverty. In 1964
their resentment boiled over into bloody anti-
American riots. President Johnson began explor-
atory talks with Panama about a new treaty, and the
talks continued, off and on, into the Carter administration.

In August 1977, two treaties were drawn up. In
one, the United States agreed to turn over to
Panama all of the Canal Zone, except for certain
military and naval installations, while keeping
control of the canal itself until December 31, 1999.
The second treaty gave the United States the right
to defend the neutrality of the canal.

This action by the United States government
disturbed and angered many Americans. It seemed

to be another sign of weakness, of retreat from the
great days of power. After all, they said, the United
States had built the canal and paid for it. Why
should it be turned over to Panama? As one senator
observed, "We stole it fair and square."

Nevertheless, Carter fought hard to get the
treaties through the Senate. Despite strong opposition, he finally succeeded in April 1978. The
ratification of the treaties brought about a warmer
relationship between the United States and Latin
America.

SALT Negotiations Stall

In 1969 the United States and the Soviet Union
began discussing ways of halting, or at least
slowing down, the costly and dangerous nuclear
arms race. In 1972 the two nations signed agreements on arms control based on Strategic Arms
Limitation Talks, commonly known as SALT. (See
page 890.) The SALT I agreement froze the number of intercontinental ballistic missiles (ICBMs)
that each nation had. It also limited to two the
number of antiballistic missile defense sites within
each nation.

By 1977, soon after Carter assumed the Presidency, both nations had developed a new weapon,
the intermediate-range mobile missile. When the
Soviet Union deployed several hundred of them in
Eastern Europe, the United States deployed several
hundred in Western Europe.

Nevertheless, the United States and the Soviet
Union held a second series of arms limitation talks.
There was a setback when the Soviets became
angry at Carter's public support of Soviet dissidents (Soviet citizens who criticize their government's policies). The talks continued, though, and
in June 1979 Carter met with Soviet Premier
Leonid Brezhnev in Vienna, where he signed the
SALT agreement known as **SALT II.** Although this
agreement did not reduce armaments, it did provide
for equal limits on the number of strategic weapons
and nuclear launchers each nation could have.

The SALT II agreement, however, met sharp
opposition in the Senate. Critics argued that it
would put the United States at a military disadvantage by creating a "window of vulnerability."
Then, in December 1979, SALT II was effectively
killed by the Soviet invasion of Afghanistan, a
mountainous country along the southern border of
the Soviet Union.

To analyze the major foreign policy problems confronting the Carter administration, ask students to help prepare a chart on the board. In the first column, list the problem; in the second column, list areas of the world affected; and in the third column, list solutions attempted by the Carter administration. Chart might include:

Problem: Human rights. **Locations:** Countries with consistent patterns of gross violations of human rights. **Solution:** Negotiated Helsinki Accords: cut off U.S. aid to Argentina and Brazil; established the Bureau of Human Rights.

Problem: Resentment of Panamanians over U.S. control of Panama Canal. **Locations:** Latin America, U.S. **Solution:** Drew up treaties to give Panama control of the canal on Dec. 31, 1999, and to give to U.S. the right to defend the canal against any attack.

Problem: Nuclear arms. **Location:** U.S., Soviet Union. **Solution:** Held a second series of arms limitation talks; Carter and Brezhnev signed SALT II agreement (1979)

Problem: Middle East crisis. **Location:** Israel, Arab nations, U.S. **Solution:** Camp David Accords.

Problem: Iranian revolution— taking of hostages. **Location:** Iran, U.S. **Solution:** Cut off imports of Iranian oil; froze Iranian assets in the U.S.; banned all trade with Iran; severed diplomatic relations; attempted an unsuccessful hostage rescue; quietly but intensely negotiated for the release of the hostages.

Problem: War in Persian Gulf. **Location:** Soviet Union, U.S., Persian Gulf, Iran, Iraq. **Solution:** Issued Carter Doctrine—the U.S. adopts a neutral position on the Iran–Iraq War.

Have students refer to this chart as they study Section 3.

Soviets Invade Afghanistan

Afghanistan had had a pro-Moscow government for some time. However, the government had not been able to suppress Muslim rebels who wanted to set up a religious Islamic state. The Soviet Union was afraid that such a movement might spill over into its own Islamic regions and pose a threat to Soviet authority within its homeland. So the Soviet Union installed a new regime in Afghanistan and sent in troops to help put down the Muslim revolt.

When Carter heard the news of the invasion, he picked up the seldom-used White House-Kremlin hot line and protested to Soviet Premier Brezhnev that the action was a "gross interference in the internal affairs of Afghanistan." Carter then placed an embargo on grain sales to the Soviet Union, despite protests from American farmers who resented the loss of a market. To further show United States disapproval of the Soviet action, the House of Representatives voted 386 to 12 against American participation in the 1980 Summer Olympic Games scheduled to be held in Moscow. Other Western countries followed suit, although not as many as Carter had hoped.

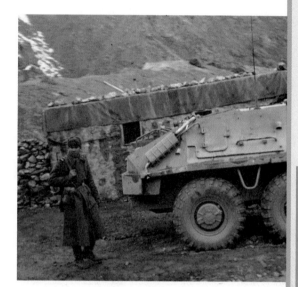

Picturing History Soviets in Afghanistan, like Americans in Vietnam, had become involved in a costly guerrilla war.

For Discussion
Think about the Olympic boycott staged by the U.S. in 1980. Do you think it had any lasting effect on world peace or U.S.-Soviet relations? (Possible response: the boycott had little effect on world peace or U.S.-Soviet relations; it hurt only the athletes who had trained so hard for so long and then were unable to compete.)

Linking Past to Present

In 1987 the Soviet Union agreed to withdraw all of its troops from Afghanistan by February 1989. The last of the Soviet soldiers pulled out at that time, leaving the Afghan military with the responsibility of defending the country.

Crisis Follows Crisis in the Middle East

The Middle East is one of the world's trouble spots. It is an area of many ethnic, religious, and economic conflicts. Here, Carter achieved one of his greatest diplomatic triumphs. Here, he also suffered a major political defeat.

The Camp David Accords. After the end of World War II, the United States began playing a more active role in the Middle East. It was interested in the region's vast oil reserves and in setting up bulwarks against possible Soviet expansion.

Israel, formerly part of Palestine, had been ruled since 1920 by Great Britain under a mandate from

Israel and the Middle East, 1967-1980

Occupied by Israel in 1967

Given up by Israel by 1980

0 40 80 120 Miles
0 80 160 Kilometers

LEBANON
Beirut
Damascus
Golan Heights
SYRIA
Tel Aviv
West Bank
Amman
Jordan R.
Jerusalem
Gaza Strip
Dead Sea
ISRAEL
JORDAN
MEDITERRANEAN SEA
Cairo
E G Y P T
Suez Canal
Nile R.
Sinai Peninsula
GULF OF SUEZ
GULF OF AQABA
SAUDI ARABIA
RED SEA
© ML & Co.

Map Skills **Place** What part of Egypt did Israel occupy in 1967? **Location** On what river is the West Bank? on what sea?

Map Skills
Sinai Peninsula • Jordan • Dead Sea

Picturing History
President Jimmy Carter (center) is best known for facilitating the Camp David Accords between Anwar Sadat (left) and Menachem Begin (right). The accords provided for the Israeli evacuation of the Sinai in return for Egyptian recognition of Israel.

the League of Nations. In 1948 Britain ended its mandate, and the republic of Israel was proclaimed by the United Nations. Israel's Arab neighbors, however, refused to recognize its right to exist. They claimed the nation had been created out of land that belonged to the Arabs. As you know, between 1948 and 1973, four wars were fought between Arab nations and Israel. Much of the Arab manpower and weaponry came from Egypt.

During 1974 and 1975, Henry Kissinger carried on "shuttle diplomacy" in the area. He flew first to Egypt and the next time to Israel, trying to get the two nations to resolve their differences. As a result of his efforts, a temporary agreement was reached in 1975. Israel promised to partially withdraw its troops from Egypt's Sinai Peninsula. In exchange, the United States promised to supply Israel with advanced arms and aircraft.

In 1977 Egyptian President **Anwar Sadat** (sä dät') made a bold move to establish relations with his old enemy. He flew to Israel, where he met with Prime Minister **Menachem Begin** (bā' gin). It was a courageous step by Sadat, who had been warned by Muslim extremists that negotiating with Israel would put his life in danger.

When peace talks between the two leaders stalled, Carter invited them to the Presidential retreat at Camp David in the Maryland hills. After thirteen days of intensive discussions, the three men emerged to meet the world press. They an-

nounced they had reached two agreements, which became known as the **Camp David Accords.** The first agreement, "A Framework for Peace in the Middle East," provided for a five-year transition period during which Israel, Jordan, and the Palestinians would work out the issue of Palestinian self-rule. The second agreement was a framework specifically aimed at ending hostilities between Israel and Egypt. In March 1979, a detailed peace treaty was signed at the White House before a national television audience. Under the treaty, Egypt agreed to recognize Israel and to end thirty years of war in exchange for the return of the entire Sinai Peninsula. However, the treaty was ambiguous about the claims of the Palestinians—those Arabs living on the West Bank and the Gaza Strip, areas that had been taken over by Israel during the wars.

Many people were cheered by the news of the treaty, but most Arab nations felt that Sadat had broken faith with them. The **Palestine Liberation Organization (PLO),** which claimed to represent the Palestinians, continued its acts of **terrorism,** or violence, against civilians, against Israel, and against Jews. Because Lebanon harbored significant numbers of the PLO, it was bombed repeatedly by Israeli war planes.

The policy of the United States in all this was to provide support for Israel while also trying to find a solution to the Palestinian issue. Meanwhile, a

914

Ask students to consider how a democratic nation can deal effectively and firmly with leaders who promote worldwide terrorism. Tell students that in 1988 the U.S. denied PLO leader Yasir Arafat a tourist visa that would have allowed him to speak at the UN in New York. Ask whether the U.S. should have denied Arafat access to the UN (Possible responses: yes—the U.S. rightfully denied Arafat entrance to the U.S. because he is a known terrorist and advocates violence to achieve his ends. No— Arafat's desire to address the UN might have signaled a new era of peace in the Middle East, and he should have been granted the visa.)

revolution broke out in a Middle Eastern country that the United States had long considered a staunch friend.

The Iranian Revolution. In 1953 the United States had helped to restore **Mohammed Reza Pahlavi** (pä ′ lə vē), the Iranian Shah (monarch), to the throne. Thereafter, the United States openly provided the Shah with military supplies and technical assistance because Americans believed that political weakness in Iran might pave the way for Soviet expansion.

For his part, the Shah used the oil wealth of his nation to push his people toward a Western way of life. He encouraged Western dress. He sent Iranian youths to school in the United States. He instituted some land reforms and gave women the right to vote. In his haste to modernize Iran, however, the Shah offended those of his people who held strict religious beliefs. In addition, there was widespread corruption among government officials, and the Shah's secret police brutally tortured thousands of political opponents and executed additional thousands without trial.

As opposition to the Shah increased, the **Ayatollah Ruhollah Khomeini,** the Shiite Muslim religious leader who was living in exile in France, began flooding Iran with cassette tapes calling on the people to revolt. In January 1979, Mohammed Pahlavi was forced to flee the country, and the Ayatollah Khomeini returned to Iran in triumph.

Khomeini promptly set up a pure theocracy. In that religious state, political power is in the hands of the mullahs, or clergy. Laws are not based on a secular constitution, but on the Koran, the sacred book of Islam. Since the Koran is accepted as the word of God, no one is allowed to question it. Traditional customs have also been restored. For example, women are not allowed to vote, and they can appear in public only if they are completely covered by a black garment, called a chador, that leaves only the eyes exposed. The Friday public prayer service in the Muslim temples, called mosques, is a political as well as a

Map Skills

Israel, Turkey, Iran • Iraq, Saudi Arabia

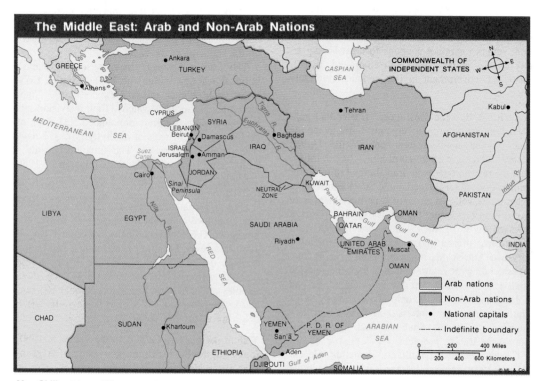

The Middle East: Arab and Non-Arab Nations

Map Skills **Place** What countries in the Middle East are non-Arab? **Place** Between which two countries is there a neutral zone?

Assign Independent Practice

Ask students to write a three-paragraph essay evaluating Carter's foreign policy. Students should consider how Carter would have been remembered if there had been no hostage crisis. (Essays might include: Carter's administration did much to bring about peace in the world through measures such as the Panama Canal treaties and the Camp David accords. If there had been no hostage crisis he might have been remembered as the "outsider" who worked for world peace.)

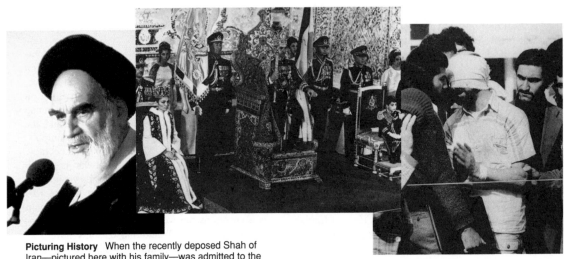

Picturing History When the recently deposed Shah of Iran—pictured here with his family—was admitted to the United States in 1979 for treatment of cancer, Iranians loyal to the Ayatollah Khomeini (left) seized the American embassy in Teheran and took fifty-two Americans hostage. A blindfolded hostage is shown at the right.

religious event, with lectures from the pulpit on current issues. The mosques themselves resemble city halls, which serve as everything from distribution centers for ration coupons to local headquarters for the police. (Although Khomeini died in 1989, the government in Iran remains relatively unchanged.)

Americans Become Hostages. Carter had supported the Shah until the very end. Later, when the Shah sought medical treatment in the United States, Carter agreed to admit him. The act infuriated the revolutionaries in Iran. In the fall of 1979, armed students seized the United States Embassy in Teheran, as well as a group of Americans who were working in or visiting the embassy. The terrorists released most of the women and the African Americans after a short period. The remaining fifty-two Americans, however, were held as hostages pending the return to Iran of the Shah and the Shah's assets, which, the Iranians charged, he had stolen from Iran with the help of the United States. The militants at the embassy announced that they intended to put the Shah on trial for "crimes against the Iranian people."

Carter rejected the militants' demands. He cut off imports of Iranian oil, froze Iranian assets in the United States, and banned all trade with Iran. Eventually he severed diplomatic relations with the nation.

As months went by and the Iranians refused to release the hostages, the United States mounted a raid to rescue them. Because of faulty equipment, however, the raid failed and eight American soldiers lost their lives. Neither this attempted rescue, nor the death of the Shah in 1980, nor the condemnation of Iran by the United Nations had any effect on the status of the hostages.

The Iranian hostage crisis caused an intense political reaction within the United States. Congress voted higher military expenditures. Night after night, Americans watched their television sets for news while reporters announced "31 days of captivity . . . 210 days of captivity . . . 375 days of captivity," and so on. The situation became a major issue in the Presidential campaign of 1980 and helped bring about Carter's defeat in his bid for reelection.

Despite repeated failures, the Carter administration continued quiet but intense efforts to free the hostages. These efforts finally succeeded late in 1980. However, because of last-minute delays and perhaps deliberate stalling by the Iranians, the hostages were not released until 1981, thirty-three minutes after the new President, Ronald Reagan, had taken the oath of office. The hostages had been held captive for 444 days.

War in the Persian Gulf. In the winter of 1980, following the Soviet Union's invasion of Afghanistan, President Carter delivered a speech warning against any Soviet attempt to take over the oil fields of the Persian Gulf. Such an attempt, the President declared in what became known as the **Carter**

Student Assignment/Homework

Have students read Section 4, "Technological and Social Change Continues," and answer the Section 4 Review questions on paper.

SECTION 4
Core Lesson

Anticipate the Lesson

Review with students how the Industrial Revolution changed life for Americans. (Possible responses: new inventions made housework easier and faster, increased factory productivity, and made communication and travel faster and more efficient.) Ask students to suggest some innovations of the Industrial Revolution that have been replaced by innovations of the electronic revolution. (Possible responses:

stoves have been supplemented by microwaves; telephones and telegraphs have been partially replaced by fax machines and computers; typewriters have been partially replaced by word processors.)

State the Objective

Understand the technological and social changes of the 1970's.

Doctrine, would be "regarded as an assault on the vital interests of the United States of America. And such an assault will be repelled by any means necessary, including military force."

To everyone's surprise, however, such an assault came, not from the Soviet Union, but from a nation within the Persian Gulf region. Late in 1980, Iraq's president, Saddam Hussein, sent the Iraqi army into Iran and toward that nation's oil fields. As a Muslim socialist rather than religious state, Iraq was afraid of the theocracy that had developed in Iran. Iraq also believed strongly in modernization, which Iran's new leadership did not.

In its surprise attack, Iraq captured a large stretch of Iranian territory. Then the Iranians, who believed they were fighting a holy war, developed a technique of human-wave offensives. Masses of mostly teen-aged volunteers walked across Iraqi minefields and into Iraqi firepower, convinced that if they died, they would go directly to heaven. Iraq responded by using poison gas against the Iranians.

Many Western nations sold arms to both sides. Arab countries, however, supported Iraq with billions of dollars, far more than they had spent in the wars against Israel. The Iran-Iraq War raged on until 1988. (See Chapter 36.)

SECTION 3 REVIEW

Key Terms and People

Explain the significance of: human rights, SALT II, Anwar Sadat, Menachem Begin, Camp David Accords, PLO, terrorism, Mohammed Pahlavi, Ayatollah Ruhollah Khomeini, Carter Doctrine

Main Ideas

1. How did President Carter bring his personal moral principles into America's foreign policy?
2. What were the important provisions of the 1977 canal treaties signed by Panama and the United States?
3. Briefly compare the SALT I agreement with the SALT II agreement.
4. What Middle East crises did Carter face during his administration?

Critical Thinking

5. Why did President Carter believe that the Persian Gulf was of vital interest to the United States?

SECTION 4

Technological and Social Change Continues

GLOSSARY TERMS: microchip, Sunbelt

The 1970's were a time of continuing technological and social change. Moreover, the pace of change was increasing.

The Electronic Society Takes Shape

The Industrial Revolution of the late 1700's was sparked by the steam engine. During the 1970's, the widespread use of electronic computers ushered in what many people call the information economy, in which the nation's strength depends more on the information produced and analyzed than on the goods manufactured. Perhaps the most striking indication of this development is the fact that the percentage of working Americans involved in the production of goods fell from 50 percent in 1950 to 30 percent by 1979.

The basis of the electronic revolution was the silicon chip, introduced in 1959. A silicon chip, one quarter of an inch square or smaller, carries an incredible amount of detailed information, as much as was previously carried by 100,000 transistors. The **microchip,** as it is called, contains a computer circuit created by photographic reduction that makes it possible to perform mathematical computations that a human being could never do in a lifetime. In addition, the microchip is cheap and easy to produce and can be applied to dozens of operations.

For example, bookkeepers used to work days or even weeks keeping accurate records of bank, department-store, stock-market, and similar transactions. Computer systems now do this work in a matter of minutes. Skilled typesetters used to carefully arrange the lines of metal type needed to print books, newspapers, and magazines. That process, which once took hours, is now done by computers, also in a matter of minutes. Assembly lines in many new plants now consist of robots directed by a computer. Information travels across the country and the world by means of optical fibers and satellites. Supermarket clerks check out items electronically. Word processors are replacing typewriters in both offices and homes. Video games are a popular form of recreation.

SECTION 3 REVIEW
Answers

Main Ideas

1. By tying military and economic aid to the strength of a foreign nation's commitment to human rights.

2. The U.S. would turn over all of the Canal Zone to Panama, except for certain military areas, but would keep control of the canal itself until 1999; the U.S. would retain the right to defend the canal.

3. SALT I: agreed to by both the U.S. and the U.S.S.R.; limited the number of each nation's ICBMs and antiballistic missile defense sites. SALT II: never passed by U.S. Senate; provided for equal limits on the number of each nation's nuclear weapons and nuclear launchers.

4. The Soviet invasion of Afghanistan, PLO terrorism, the Iranian revolution, Khomeini's establishment of a theocracy in Iran, the Iranian hostage crisis, and the outbreak of war between Iran and Iraq.

Critical Thinking

5. Possible answer: Persian Gulf oil was extremely important to the welfare of America's consumers as well as the military and industrial establishment. In the 1970's, the oil embargo and increases in OPEC's price of crude oil sent inflation and unemployment rates soaring. **(synthesis)**

Present the Lesson

Divide the class into three groups, one each to chart and present to the class details about the Electronic Society, Increased Immigration, and Population Changes. Charts might include:

Electronic Society
- Computers ushered in the information economy.
- By 1979 only 30 percent of all working Americans were involved in production of goods.
- The silicon chip, introduced in 1959, was the basis of the electronic revolution.

- Computers are now used for bookkeeping, printing, controlling assembly lines, relaying information, and recreation.
- The microchip created hundreds of new jobs.
- The computer has vast potential for educational institutions in the U.S. It may well free teachers to concentrate on teaching higher-level skills and may even become a valued interactive teaching instrument.

Increased Immigration
- The population grew slowly and became more diverse.
- The percentage of Asian immigrants sharply increased.
- A wave of illegal immigrants—mostly Mexican—entered the U.S.
- Of legal immigrants, about 40 percent were Spanish-speaking.
- Many Cuban refugees arrived after Castro took over. Many of these were well educated and turned Miami into a thriving Latin commercial center.

Population Changes
- The birth rate fell to the lowest in U.S. history.
- The population older than 65 increased dramatically—in 1980, life expectancy

Picturing History Boatloads of Cuban refugees arrived in Florida in the 1970's.

For Discussion
How must educational opportunities be changed to meet the needs of the electronic revolution? (Possible responses: education must stress areas such as mathematics, engineering, computer science, and word processing; people must be trained to design, build, operate, and repair computers and other new equipment.)

The change from an industrial economy to an information economy brought both advantages and disadvantages. Although some jobs were lost in the process, the microchip opened up hundreds of new, well-paid jobs in the manufacturing, operation, and maintenance of computers; in the design of computer systems; and in computer programming.

Computers also promised to have a positive impact on education in the United States. Many people thought that computer-aided instruction would help combat rising illiteracy rates and declining math skills. A number of educators felt that computers would free them to teach higher-level skills. Some believed that eventually the interactive computer would itself teach.

Immigration Increases While the Population Changes

In addition to the changes brought about by technology in the 1970's were changes in the nation's population. During the decade, the population of the United States grew slowly, from 203 million to 226 million. At the same time, the population became more diverse.

Increased Immigration. Almost 500,000 immigrants arrived in the United States each year during the 1970's. This figure represented the highest number of immigrants to enter the country annually since the early 1900's.

As you recall, in 1965 the Immigration and Nationality Act abolished the national-origins quota system. (See page 841.) One result of this act

was a sharp increase in the percentage of Asian immigrants. Most of these people migrated from the Philippines, Korea, China, and India. In addition, many thousands of Asians came from Vietnam, Laos, and Cambodia in the 1970's to escape the Vietnam War and its aftermath.

Another result of changes in the immigration laws was a wave of illegal immigrants. Most of these were Mexicans, who came to earn a living as migrant farm workers and unskilled laborers. Estimates of their numbers ranged as high as 5 million by 1980. Because of their illegal status, they were not covered by social legislation and usually received substandard wages. Other illegal immigrants came from the Caribbean and South America.

Of the legal immigrants, about 40 percent were Spanish-speaking. About 637,000 came from Mexico between 1971 and 1980. About 800,000 were refugees from Cuba who started coming to the United States soon after Fidel Castro took over their country in 1959. Most of these Cuban refugees settled in the Miami area and by the end of the decade made up 25 percent of the population of Dade County, where Miami is located.

Among the earliest Cuban refugees were many middle- and upper-income people. They tended to be well educated, and they quickly established themselves in businesses and the professions. In a few years they had transformed Miami from a resort city and haven for retirees into a bustling Latin commercial center. A number of multinational companies set up offices there, and Miami became the focal point for trade with Latin America.

In 1980 Castro unexpectedly announced that any Cubans still wishing to move to the United States were free to do so. The floodgates opened, and in a few months almost 125,000 had fled north. They came in small, leaky, overcrowded boats that were unsuitable for ocean travel. Many were the families and friends of Cubans already in the United States, but among the refugees were some, it was said, who had been released from jails and mental hospitals.

At first President Carter welcomed the Cubans with "open heart and open arms." He soon changed his position, however. Riots broke out among impatient younger men at military bases where the refugees were temporarily housed while awaiting resettlement. In addition, a majority of African Americans and non-Hispanic whites in the

stood at 70 for men and 77.5 for women.
- People generally married later in life and had fewer children.
- The divorce rate rose.
- The illegitimate birth rate rose.
- Almost one in four American children lived in a single-parent home.
- American population shifted to the Sunbelt.

Check for Understanding

Call on individual students to read their answers to the Section 4 Review questions.

Guided Practice

Tell students that in 1988 the U.S. government established a program to legalize many illegal aliens living in this country. The program met with only limited success. To stimulate discussion on this topic, ask students the following questions. What should be the government's position on illegal aliens? Should they be deported, or allowed to stay if they meet certain requirements? What requirements? (Possible responses: illegal aliens should be deported—they did not go through proper channels; aliens should be allowed to stay— America is the land of opportunity, so we have an obligation to those who wish to come here to make a better life for themselves and their families; they might be required to find jobs, learn to speak English, enroll their children in school, and have an American sponsor.)

Miami area objected to the immigration. They feared that the newcomers would compete with them for already scarce jobs. The Carter administration accordingly stopped admitting any more Cuban refugees.

Changes in the Population. While the American population was becoming more diverse, it was undergoing other sociological changes as well. By 1976 the birth rate had fallen to just under two births per woman, the lowest rate in our nation's history. However, the percentage of the population over age 65 increased to almost 12 percent in 1980. At this time, life expectancy stood at 70 for men and 77.5 for women.

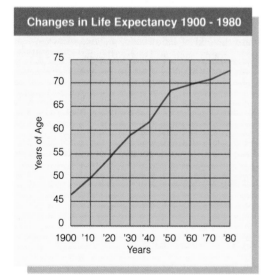

Changes in Life Expectancy 1900 - 1980

The increase in life expectancy was the result of new medical techniques and better health services. Screening for high blood pressure, for example, helped lower the proportion of heart attacks. So did public interest in physical fitness and good nutrition. More and more Americans went walking, jogging, or bike riding. Health clubs became popular, and menus began to feature fish, poultry, and vegetables. At the same time, expenditures for health care reached the astronomical figure of $248 billion a year in 1980. Advances in medical technology helped to drive the cost of health care upward.

Families also changed during the 1970's. People married later and had fewer children. The divorce rate rose from 3.5 percent for every one thousand people in 1970 to 5.2 percent for every one thousand people in 1980. Births to unwed mothers rose, too, from 10.7 percent in 1970 to more than 18 percent in 1980. The mother was not married in almost 10 percent of births to white women and almost 55 percent of births to black women. Almost one out of every four American children now lived in a single-parent home, and more than 80 percent of these homes were headed by women. This was an increase of almost 70 percent during the decade.

Americans continued to be a mobile people during the 1970's, with one out of every five moving to a new residence. The major overall shift in movement of the population was the move to the **Sunbelt.** This term refers to the nation's southeastern and southwestern states. California, Florida, and Texas were among the states that experienced the greatest population growth in the 1970's. As a result, the political importance of these states was greatly increased.

New Voices Speak for a Changing Culture

Changes in technology, the economy, and the population were accompanied by changes in entertainment and other aspects of popular culture.

Movies. During the 1960's, the movie industry experienced a slump. Then, in the 1970's, came a film revival.

The two biggest hits of the decade were entertaining escapist films dealing with terror in the water and adventure in outer space. *Jaws* dealt with the marauding of a giant shark. *Star Wars* carried viewers to "a galaxy far, far away," where good and evil battled it out with the help of robots. Social scientists suggested that people flocked to these films—as well as to natural-disaster films such as *Airport, The Poseidon Adventure,* and *The Towering Inferno*—in order to take their minds off their problems.

Social problems were, however, reflected in some popular films of the 1970's. The rise in urban street crime was the focus of *The French Connection, Dirty Harry,* and *Death Wish,* in each of which the hero—a tough policeman or a private citizen—tried to bring about law and order. *An Unmarried Woman* allowed the heroine to choose independence after being jilted by her husband for a younger woman and then pursued by a man who wanted to control her life.

Assign Independent Practice

Ask students to write a paragraph summarizing changes in the film, television, or music industry in the 1970's. (Paragraphs on films might include: 1970's saw a film-industry revival; escapist films, including natural-disaster films, were most popular; some films reflected the social problems of the day.)

Student Assignment/Homework

Have students complete Chapter 35 Test on paper. Review the questions and answers with the class.

Concluding the Chapter

Ask students to write a five-paragraph essay comparing Ford's and Carter's ascents to the Presidency. Students should address how well each man's experience equipped him for the Presidency, and also how he became President. (Possible responses: Ford had served as Republican House minority leader and was aware of the workings of the federal government; he was not elected to the Vice-Presidency or to the Presidency. Carter was the former governor of Georgia, an outsider to the federal government; he had had few dealings with the Washington bureaucracy; he was elected primarily because as an outsider, he had not been a party to the corruption that pervaded on the federal level in the near past.)

Picturing History Television took on social issues in the 1970's. Above, Carroll O'Connor played Archie Bunker, a blue-collar bigot in *All in the Family*. At the right, LeVar Burton played Kunta Kinte in *Roots*, Alex Haley's saga of a black American family.

Television. Watching television was far and away the most popular leisure-time occupation of Americans in the 1970's. It was estimated that they kept their television sets turned on an average of seven hours a day. The typical young person between the ages of six and eighteen spent about 25 percent more time in front of the television screen than in school. Moreover, the advent of cable television greatly expanded the number of channels available to viewers.

Defenders of television argued that it provided people with more and better information than local newspapers did. Critics argued that television shortened young people's attention span, lowered their ability to read and speak, and encouraged them to believe that problems could be solved quickly, and often by violence.

The most innovative television program of the decade was probably the prime-time comedy series *All in the Family*. Until then, television had tended to avoid social issues. In this new program, however, racist and sexist behaviors and issues were fully aired as Archie Bunker and his family engaged in a weekly ritual of tense but sometimes comic combat. Another innovative show was the miniseries *Roots*, a powerful portrayal of the African American experience beginning with the days of slavery.

Popular Music. The lyrics of much of the popular music of the 1960's had dealt with hopes for social change and spiritual transformation. Songwriters of the 1970's focused their lyrics on personal feelings and autobiographical experiences. Among the individuals and bands that made records and concerts a multi-billion-dollar business were the Rolling Stones and Led Zeppelin of hard rock, Bob Dylan of folk rock, and singers James Taylor, Linda Ronstadt, and Stevie Wonder. Toward the end of the decade, a series of new-wave rock groups such as Devo, Blondie, and Talking Heads experimented with faster, louder, and more energetic styles of rock music.

Perhaps the biggest development in popular music during the 1970's was the spread of disco. Named after the black and Latin discothèques, or dance halls, of New York City, where it originated, disco had a strong, repetitive beat that lent itself to melodic accents and overtones. It spread quickly, not only through the United States, but around the world.

SECTION 4 REVIEW

Key Terms and People

Explain the significance of: microchip, Sunbelt

Main Ideas

1. What formed the basis for the information economy ushered in during the 1970's?
2. What were some of the important ways in which the population of the United States changed during the 1970's?
3. What were some of the popular leisure-time activities in the 1970's? How were they different from those in the previous decade?

Critical Thinking

4. What effect do you think the changes in technology, population, and culture in the 1970's had on Americans' sense of themselves as a united people?

State the Objective

Understand the causes and characteristics of growth in the Sunbelt.

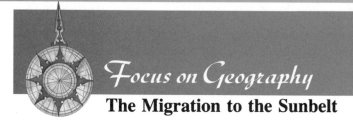

Focus on Geography

The Migration to the Sunbelt

The Geographic Theme of Movement

From earliest times human beings have moved from place to place in the hope of improving their way of life. As you have seen throughout your study of United States history, various push-pull factors have attracted Americans to certain places and repelled them from others. Estimates suggest that one out of five Americans changes residence every year. Because movement continues to play a critical role in land development, it remains a fundamental geographic theme.

Location of the Sunbelt. The "Sunning of America" is a popular expression often used to refer to the great number of Americans who move from the North, called the Snowbelt, to the South, called the Sunbelt. The Sunbelt consists of a tier of Southern states that stretches across the nation from Virginia to California. It includes all the states of the Confederate South plus California, Arizona, New Mexico, and Oklahoma. The Sunbelt is a rapidly growing region and has been referred to as our nation's newest frontier.

Migration Patterns. Although people often think of the traditional migration pattern in the United States as one from east to west, the nation has experienced other major migration trends. One was the rural-to-urban migration that fed the industrial needs of our large urban centers during the late 1800's and the early 1900's. Another was the movement of the poor from the South to the North between the end of World War I and the beginning of World War II. This migration of people out of the South mirrored the region's underdeveloped and rural character. Neither the rural-to-urban migration nor the south-to-north migration are strong forces today.

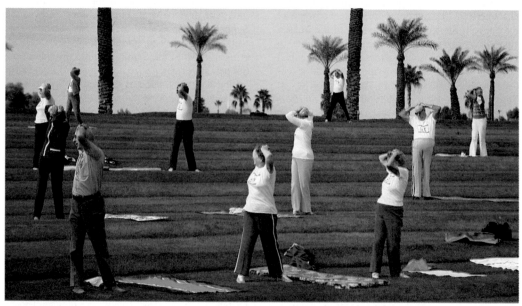

Picturing History A warm sunny climate and abundant recreational activities contribute to the well-being of senior citizens who have retired in the Sunbelt.

Present the Lesson

Divide the class into small groups. Ask students to compare the reasons people are migrating to the Sunbelt with the reasons earlier immigrants came to America. (Discussions might include: similarities—many immigrants came to this nation to improve their economic status and their life styles, as is true of migrants to the Sunbelt who move to further their careers and take advantage of a warmer climate. Differences—unlike migrants to the South, many immigrants to the U.S. came to escape political or religious intolerance in other countries.) Ask students to identify the differences in the development of the South before and after World War II. (Possible responses: before the war the South was known as the "Seedbed of the Nation"—it was largely rural and underdeveloped; since World War II, especially since the 1970's, the area has attracted aerospace, defense, electronic, and other high-tech industries, as well as finance industries such as insurance and banking.)

Map Skills

Heavy migration from New York state to Florida • Most migration is from north to south or southwest. • Large areas of the United States have little or no migration of people aged 60 and over.

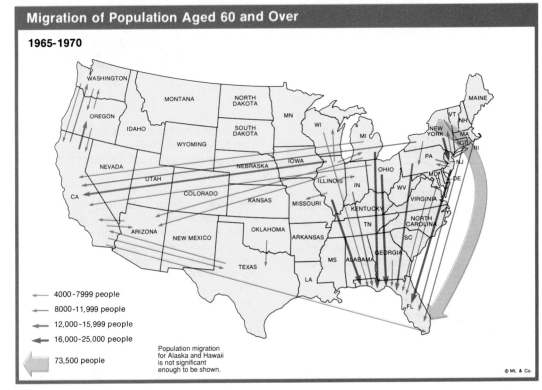

Migration of Population Aged 60 and Over

1965-1970

← 4000-7999 people
← 8000-11,999 people
← 12,000-15,999 people
← 16,000-25,000 people
← 73,500 people

Population migration for Alaska and Hawaii is not significant enough to be shown.

© ML & Co.

The latter half of the twentieth century has been characterized by migrations from the Snowbelt to the Sunbelt. Snowbelt residents east of the Mississippi River have had a tendency to migrate to Florida and other southeastern states. Snowbelt residents west of the Mississippi have had a tendency to migrate to California, Arizona, and Texas. Throughout the 1950's and 1960's, large numbers of people moved to the West. It was during the 1970's, however, that this trend was supplemented by the movement of people to the South. Approximately half of the enormous growth the South experienced during the 1970's was caused by migrations from the North (the other half was a result of natural increase—births over deaths).

The Attraction of the Sunbelt. What is the attraction of the Sunbelt? Many people have been drawn to the area because of the job opportunities that have resulted from the development of new industries. Although the earliest industries in the region were labor intensive and paid low wages, today the Sunbelt has thriving aerospace, defense, electronics, and other high-tech industries. Capital intensive industries, such as insurance and bank-

ing, have moved to the Sunbelt to support the industrial development. Finally, many states in the Sunbelt have sponsored recruitment programs that work aggressively to attract entrepreneurs considering a move to the South. In these programs, the Sunbelt states emphasize economic advantages for business owners, such as the availability of water and energy resources, good transportation facilities, the low rate of unionization, and a wage structure that is lower.

In addition to job opportunities, other pull factors have attracted Americans to the Sunbelt. These include a favorable climate, abundant recreational opportunities, lower taxes, and more space than the congested areas of the urbanized North.

A Migrant Profile. Most of the people who have migrated to the Sunbelt fall into two age groups—young adults and retired senior citizens. Well-educated young people in search of jobs make up the group most inclined to move.

The Sunbelt also offers a strong attraction to retired senior citizens. Today's retirees tend to be younger and more affluent than those of previous decades. Many have taken early retirement and

Ask students to write answers to the questions at the end of the feature. Discuss the answers with the class.

Have students imagine that they have been asked to speak at a conference of governors that has convened to address problems created by the migration of many Northern businesses to the South. Students should include problems that impact both Northern and Southern governors. Ask students to present their speeches to the class. (Speeches should include: Southern governments are faced with the problems of exploding growth and as a re-sult must expand water, sewer, telephone, electric and other services, as well as roads, schools, and hospitals; Northern governments are faced with problems of retaining and attracting business and of filling the void left by the loss of some of their best talent to Southern states.)

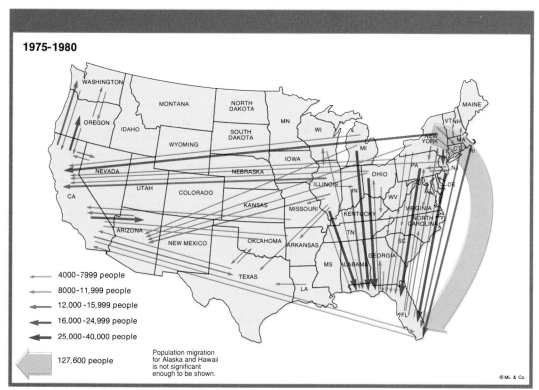

1975-1980

4000–7999 people
8000–11,999 people
12,000–15,999 people
16,000–24,999 people
25,000–40,000 people
127,600 people

Population migration for Alaska and Hawaii is not significant enough to be shown.

© ML & Co.

Map Skills **Movement** Describe the migration pattern shown by the very wide arrow in the east.
Movement Summarize the main points about migration as presented on the map.

have private pensions and investment portfolios in addition to social security. Florida, California, and Arizona are the most popular destinations for seniors seeking mild climates and ample leisure-time activities. With nearly 20 percent of its population aged sixty-five or older, Florida ranks first among all states.

The Larger Picture. Migration to the Sunbelt must be viewed in a broader context. Large regional population shifts are not without their problems. These problems can occur in the areas that are losing the population as well as in those that are receiving the population. On the one hand, when the migrants are well-educated young people, they frequently leave a vacuum in areas that need these professionals to help revitalize communities. On the other hand—in states receiving the migrants—officials may not be prepared for a huge influx.

People have been moving across the continent of North America since the first migrants crossed the Bering Strait. Migration continues today, but the rural-to-urban movement and the great migrations out of the South are no longer of much consequence. The most recent trend, the migration to the Sunbelt, mirrors the nation's changing economic and demographic patterns. It reflects a great economic shift within the Sunbelt itself from being an area that lacked job opportunities to being one that supports industrial growth and development. Increased longevity and changing life styles among the elderly have also contributed to the growth and development of the Sunbelt.

Understanding Geography

1. Where is the Sunbelt?
2. Identify three previous migration patterns that have occurred in the United States.
3. What two types of people are most likely to move to the Sunbelt?

Critical Thinking

4. Why did unprecedented numbers of people begin moving to the Sunbelt in the 1970's?

Answers

Understanding Geography

1. The Sunbelt is a region that stretches across the United States from Virginia to California. It includes all the states of the Confederate South plus California, Arizona, New Mexico, and Oklahoma.

2. Three previous migration patterns include: (1) east to west; (2) rural to urban; (3) south to north.

3. Young people in search of jobs and retired senior citizens are most likely to move to the Sunbelt.

Critical Thinking

4. Possible answers: Reasons for migration to the Sunbelt include industrial development, job opportunities, favorable climate, lower taxes, and less crowded conditions than those in the North. **(analysis)**

Key Terms and People

These are highlighted in the text in the order in which they appear in this list.

Main Ideas

1. OPEC increases in prices of crude oil pushed up prices of gasoline, heating oil, fertilizers, and other products dependent on oil. • Possible answers: Americans became aware of their dependence on foreign oil; they used less heating oil and gasoline; they found new energy sources.

2. Worst recession since the 1930's; unemployment rose to almost 9 percent, but inflation was cut in half.

3. Possible answer (choice of three): legacy of Vietnam war; aftermath of Watergate; FBI surveillance of citizens; CIA spying on American citizens; CIA terrorist actions in other countries.

4. His strong moral values, his record on civil rights, his personality, his lack of ties with Washington.

5. Rights listed in Declaration of Independence and Bill of Rights. • Cut off aid to Argentina and Brazil for their actions against their own people; established Bureau of Human Rights in the State Department.

6. Panamanians sought control over the Canal Zone. • One treaty agreed that all of the Canal Zone would be turned over to Panamanian control by December 31, 1999. The other treaty gave the U.S. the right to defend the canal against attack.

7. Makes it possible to process an enormous amount of information very quickly in small space. Opened up high-paying jobs for skilled labor in manufacturing and programming.

8. Possible answer (choice of three): fewer children per family; people living longer; interest in health; later marriages; more divorces; more single-parent homes; migration to the Sunbelt.

Critical Thinking Questions

9. Possible answers: yes—going through all that panic for a prized tomato. No—it is stupid to think a tomato can be that important. • Surgery. • "Replenished its bodily liquids."

➤**10.** Possible answers: yes—Watergate could be put in the past and wounds could be allowed to heal. No—makes for two standards of justice and so produces cynicism.

11. Gave them a feeling of power that had been lost during Vietnam war. Skeptics thought the action cost too many lives and was not cleared by Congress. • Possible answers: for—military power solved the problem. Against—such action could have escalated.

➤**12.** Possible answers: yes—he was naive and allowed other countries to think we were weak, as with Panama treaties. No—he established new ways of working with world problems, as in Camp David Accords and his public support of Soviet dissidents.

13. To retaliate against Carter for allowing the Shah to come to the U.S. • Possible answer: no—the public perceived Carter as weak, vacillating, and inept.

CHAPTER 35 REVIEW

Write your answers on a separate sheet of paper.

Key Terms and People

Explain the significance of: Nelson Rockefeller, cartel, Ronald Reagan, Department of Energy, Three Mile Island, productivity, trade deficit, national debt, right-to-work laws, SALT II, PLO, Mohammed Reza Pahlavi, Ayatollah Ruhollah Khomeini, Carter Doctrine, Sunbelt

Main Ideas

1. How did OPEC—the Organization of Petroleum Exporting Countries—fuel inflation early in Gerald Ford's Presidency? What were the results?
2. What were the effects on inflation of Ford's spending cuts and his request for voluntary price and wage controls?
3. Cite at least three reasons for cynicism among the voters during the Ford administration.
4. What seemed to be the reasons for the nomination and election of Jimmy Carter?
5. What did Carter mean by human rights? How did he encourage adoption of human rights worldwide during his administration?
6. Why did the United States have a problem with Panama? How was the problem decided by the two treaties between the United States and Panama signed in August 1977?
7. What is the relationship of the microchip to higher productivity and skilled labor?
8. Name three changes that occurred in lifestyle or were apt to happen to family structure during the 1970's.

Critical Thinking Questions

9. **Analyzing Literature.** Do you think this selection is humorous? If so, what makes you laugh? If not, why not? To what does Garrison Keillor compare the rescue operation? What phrase shows this?
10. **Evaluating a Decision.** Do you think President Ford made the correct decision by pardoning Nixon before Nixon had been brought to justice for the Watergate break-in?
11. **Evaluating an Action.** How did Americans react to President Ford's action against Cambodia after the *Mayagüez* was seized? Which side would you have been on? Why?
12. **Drawing Conclusions.** Do you think President Carter was deficient in his handling of foreign affairs? Why or why not? Give a specific example.
13. **Predicting Effects.** Why did Iran take the hostages? Do you think President Carter might have been reelected if the hostages had been freed before the election? Explain.

Critical Thinking Activities

14. **Assessing Causes and Effects.** Make a chart to show what effects each of the following events produced:
    a. OPEC raises prices.
    b. Americans become disillusioned about government.
    c. Stagflation begins and right-to-work laws are passed.
    d. Panama resents United States control of canal.
    e. Soviets invade Afghanistan.
    f. United States admits Shah.
15. **Linking Past to Present.** Define *stagflation*. Would you say our economy is in a period of stagflation today? Why or why not?
16. **Linking Past to Present.** What did the proposed Equal Rights Amendment say? Why was it not ratified?
17. **Linking Past to Present.** Review the 1977 treaties with Panama. Then, using reference materials, research the 1989–90 American military intervention in Panama. Why is the United States so interested in Panamanian politics? Why did it wish to depose Noriega?
18. **Linking Past to Present.** What Middle East problem was not resolved by the Camp David Accords? Has this problem been settled today? Explain.

TELESCOPING THE TIMES: 1970–1980

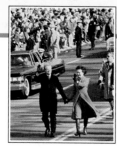

The 1970's: Ford and Carter

President Gerald Ford tried to unite the nation, but he achieved only limited success. Ford's pardon of Richard Nixon aroused anger, but gradually most Americans came to accept it. As President, Ford had to deal both with inflation and with an economic depression. OPEC's oil embargo contributed to this inflation. Ford's success was also limited in his handling of the *Mayagüez* episode, which drew mixed reactions. Many Americans did unite in 1976, however, to celebrate the bicentennial anniversary of their Revolution.

By 1976 many Americans had become disillusioned with their national government, and a smaller percentage turned out to vote than had voted in previous elections. Democrat Jimmy Carter campaigned successfully as an outsider to the Washington establishment. As President he had to deal with an energy crisis and with setbacks regarding nuclear power. High inflation plagued the economy, along with flat productivity and a growing trade deficit. Labor unions were growing weaker. Carter appeared unable to deal with these problems successfully. Although he supported the ERA, it failed the test of ratification by the states.

In foreign affairs, Carter campaigned for human rights. He fought hard for treaties that would give Panama the Canal Zone by the year 2000. He pressed for reduction in Soviet and American nuclear weapons, but the SALT II agreement stalled in the ratification process. The Soviet invasion of Afghanistan in 1979 deepened American distrust. Carter brought the leaders of Israel and Egypt together, and he triumphed when the Camp David Accords between these countries were announced. United States support of the Shah of Iran, however, led the new Islamic regime in Iran to take Americans hostage in the fall of 1979. Although the hostages were eventually freed, the long crisis fatally hurt Carter's chances for reelection. Just before Carter left office, war broke out between Iran and Iraq.

Technological and social changes continued throughout the 1970's. The new silicon chip and computers revolutionized the handling of information. The new technology affected individual life styles with the availability of such products as calculators and home computers. Also in the 1970's, population growth slowed, and more households consisted of only women and children. Increasing numbers of immigrants arrived from Asia and Latin America. Shifts in population occurred as large numbers of Americans moved to the Sunbelt.

New forms of entertainment became popular. Movies experienced a revival. Cable television and new forms of popular music were also added to the list of entertainment choices.

Chronology of Main Events

1972 ERA passed by Congress and sent to the states for ratification

1973 Arab oil embargo

1975 *Mayagüez* seized by Cambodians; Helsinki Accords signed

1977 Jimmy Carter inaugurated President; Department of Energy established

1978 Senate approves the Panama Canal treaties

1979 Carter signs SALT II; Camp David Accords signed in Washington; Iranians seize American hostages

1980 Efforts to free hostages in Iran succeed

Telescoping the Times may be used as an alternative to having students read the entire chapter, as a chapter preview, or as a chapter review.

Global Perspectives

1981   Egyptian President Anwar Sadat is assassinated.

1982   Israel invades Lebanon to expel PLO forces.

1984   Soviet-bloc nations boycott the Summer Olympic Games.

1986   Nuclear accident occurs at Chernobyl in the U.S.S.R.

1988   Earthquake devastates much of Soviet Armenia, killing more than 25,000.

1990   East and West Germany reunite; democratic reforms sweep Eastern Europe; Iraq invades Kuwait.

1991   Persian Gulf war erupts as five million refugees flee Iraq and Kuwait; Soviet Union dissolves when thirteen of fifteen republics declare independence; Yeltsin elected President of Russian republic and calls for democratic reforms.

1992   Claims of independence by four of six Yugoslavian republics leads to civil war and realigned country; massive starvation in Somalia brings world-wide relief effort guarded over by U.S. troops; Czechoslovakian factions agree to split country into the separate nations called the Czech Republic and Slovakia.

For Discussion

Why have nuclear accidents such as that at Chernobyl become cause for global concern? (Possible responses: fallout from such accidents might affect people and land over a wide range; the Chernobyl incident demonstrated to other nations the need to closely monitor their own nuclear power plants to prevent similar disasters; long-term, lasting effects of the fallout may not be known for years to come.)

Additional Resources

- Geography Activities
- Skills Activities
- Thematic Activities
- Economic Activities
- Cultural Literacy Activities
- Literary Source Readings
- Primary Source Readings
- Nuclear Peacekeeping
- Transparencies
- Computer Test Generator

Additional Teaching Strategies

SECTION 1

For Basic Students: Ask students to research and write a short report on one of President Reagan's Supreme Court appointees. (Reports on Sandra Day O'Connor might include: born in El Paso, Texas, in 1930; earned a law degree from Stanford University in 1952; entered private practice in Phoenix; served as assistant attorney general of Arizona in 1965; was elected to the Arizona state senate in 1970 and 1972; served as state senate majority leader in 1973; was elected judge of Maricopa County trial court in 1974; was appointed to the Arizona Court of Appeals in 1979.) Have students share their reports.

For Advanced Students: Obtain copies of federal income tax forms from the Internal Revenue Service. Have students study the forms and decide whether they think the average citizen is likely to understand them easily. Ask students for suggestions that might improve the forms. (Possible responses: shorter forms; standard deductions; more-understandable instructions; fewer exceptions to rules.) If possible, arrange for a representative from a tax preparation company to speak to the class on filing income taxes.

SECTION 2

For Basic Students: Have students use a large classroom map to locate the countries mentioned in this section. Have students work in pairs to research and prepare a brief oral presentation on: the Soviet Union, Nicaragua, Grenada, Lebanon, or on Iran and Iraq. (Reports on Lebanon might include: capital—Beirut; official language—Arabic; form of government—republic; location—eastern end of the Mediterranean Sea; economy—transportation, trade, and finance; inhabitants—mostly Arabs; major religions—Christianity and Islam; politics—differences between Lebanese Christians and Lebanese Muslims often result in bloody battles; civil war begun in the 1970's has continued off and on.)

For Advanced Students: After students research the Iran-contra affair, ask them to draw political cartoons relating to this subject. Have students share their cartoons with the class.

SECTION 3

For Basic Students: Ask students to prepare a letter to the editor supporting or opposing continued federal funding for the space shuttle program. (Letters might include: supporting—discoveries and experiments in space might lead to other scientific discoveries that would benefit the nation; it is important to maintain our lead over the Soviets in space exploration; the space program is a unifying force in the country. Opposing—money spent on the program could be better spent on social programs to help the poor or ill; elimination of the fund could help reduce the national deficit; private industries that would benefit from the shuttles should assume the financial responsibility.)

For Advanced Students: Have students research the theory of pay equity. Then organize students into two groups to debate the theory. (Arguments in favor of pay equity might include: it would guarantee equal pay for comparable work; it offers a fair way to evaluate performance and determine job worth. Arguments against pay equity might include: it would be difficult to objectively compare jobs and needed skills and education; it would be difficult to select and rate qualities needed for various occupations; many jobs require additional hours of work or research after business hours that are not easily taken into account.)

SECTION 4

For Basic Students: Ask students to explain what a time capsule is. (Possible response: it is a sealed container filled with items preserved for future generations. The items usually form a record of a particular area, people, or civilization.) Ask students to imagine they are collecting items for a time capsule. They should list ten items that they would include and give brief explanations of these items and their significance for future generations. If possible, have students put together a time capsule to be opened by high school students in ten, twenty, or fifty years. (Items might include: record album or tape of latest music; video cassette of a current popular television show; copy of a current newspaper or magazine; photos showing current fashions; school yearbook; textbook.)

For Advanced Students: Ask students to prepare letters to the President expressing concern about issues that they feel will strongly affect their future. Letters should then be mailed to the President in care of the White House, 1600 Pennsylvania Avenue, Washington, D.C. 20500. (Letters might include reference to: the environment and protection of the air and water; the need to preserve national forests and open lands for recreation; lowering of the national debt and avoiding large tax hikes; government support of education.)

Further Reading for Students

Barker, Lucius J. *Our Time Has Come: A Delegate's Diary of Jesse Jackson's 1984 Presidential Campaign.* Urbana: University of Illinois Press, 1988.

Brownstein, Ronald. Edited by Nina Easton. *Reagan's Ruling Class: Portraits of the President's Top 100 Officials.* Washington, D.C.: Presidential Accountability Group, 1982.

Dickenson, Mollie. *Thumbs Up: The Jim Brady Story.* New York: William Morrow, 1987.

Pines, Burton Yale. *Back to Basics.* New York: William Morrow and Co., 1982.

Smith, Hedrick; Adam Clymer; Leonard Silk; Robert Lindsey; and Richard Burt. *Reagan the Man, the President.* New York: McGraw-Hill, 1981.

Bibliography for Teachers

Books

Barrett, Laurence I. *Gambling With History: Ronald Reagan in the White House.* New York: Penguin, 1984.

Bush, George, and Victor Gold. *Looking Forward: The George Bush Story.* Garden City, N.Y.: Doubleday, 1987.

Cheney, Glenn Alan. *El Salvador: Country in Crisis.* New York: Franklin Watts, 1982.

Congressional Quarterly, Inc., and Michael Goldstein. *Guide to the 1988 Presidential Election.* Washington, D.C.: Congressional Quarterly, 1988.

Duignan, Peter, and Alvin Rabushka, eds. *The United States in the 1980's.* Stanford, Calif.: Hoover Institution Press, 1980.

Ferraro, Geraldine A., and Linda B. Francke. *Ferraro: My Story.* New York: Bantam Books, 1985.

Gore, Al. *Earth in the Balance: Ecology and the Human Spirit.* Boston: Houghton Mifflin, 1992.

Graber, Doris A. *Mass Media and American Politics.* 2nd ed. Washington, D.C.: Congressional Quarterly, 1988.

Hutcheson, Richard G., Jr. *God in the White House; How Religion Has Changed in Modern Presidency.* New York: Macmillan, 1988.

Piven, Francis Fox, and Richard A. Cloward. *Why Americans Don't Vote.* New York: Pantheon Books, 1988.

Reed, Adolph L., Jr. *The Jesse Jackson Phenomenon: The Crisis of Purpose in Afro-American Politics.* New Haven, Conn.: Yale University Press, 1986.

Weiss, Ann E. *The Nuclear Arms Race—Can We Survive It?* Boston: Houghton Mifflin, 1983.

Audio-Visuals

Nuclear Weapons: Concepts and Controversies. Human Relations Media. Filmstrip.

Oliver North: Memo to History. Social Studies School Service. Movie.

The Iran-Contra Arms Affair. Social Studies School Service. Filmstrip.

Computer Resource

TimeLiner Data Disks: Events of the 70's and 80's. (TDE/Apple) Tom Snyder.

Teacher's Notes:

Teaching Resources, Unit 8 Booklet

Lesson Study Sheets pp. 225-240
Daily Activities pp. 241-248
Enrichment Activities pp. 249-256
Reteaching Activities pp. 257-264
Chapter Review p. 265
Chapter Mastery Tests pp. 267-278
Telescoping the Times Study Sheet p. 279
Unit Mastery Tests pp. 281-292
Telescoping the Times Unit 8 Study Sheet p. 293

See supplement to Unit 8
Core Resources Book.

Chapter Objectives

Students will learn:
- the major domestic problems and challenges that confronted the Reagan, Bush, and Clinton administrations during the 1980's and early 1990's
- the major foreign policy problems and international conflicts that the U.S. faced in the 1980's and early 1990's
- the changing social and political climate of the 1980's and early 1990's

Using the Chapter Time Line

While the U.S. dealt with tax reform and the Iran–contra affair, what major events occurred in the Soviet Union and South Africa? (See Unit 8 Time Line.) (Answer: nuclear power plant accident at Chernobyl and economic sanctions imposed on South Africa) Who was President when the INF Treaty was ratified? (Answer: Ronald Reagan)

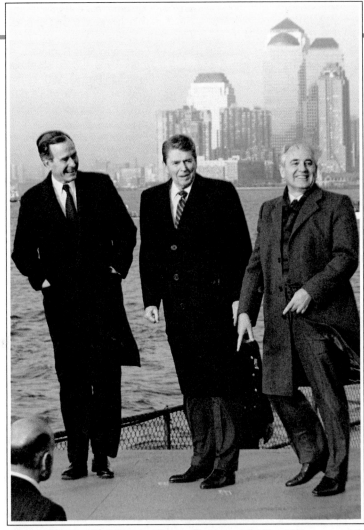

Picturing History President-elect George Bush, President Ronald Reagan, and Soviet leader Mikhail Gorbachev view the New York skyline during Gorbachev's visit to the city to address the United Nations in December 1988.

1982	1984	1986	1988	1990	1992

1981
- Ronald Reagan inaugurated President
- Reaganomics begins

1983
U.S. invades Grenada

1985
- President Reagan inaugurated for a second term

1986
- Tax reform bill passed
- Iran-Contra affair

1987
Persian Gulf crisis

1988
- INF treaty ratified
- Reagan visits Moscow

1989
- George Bush inaugurated President
- Lech Walesa speaks before Congress

1990
U.S. sends troops to Saudi Arabia

1992
Bill Clinton elected President

Tom Wolfe: born and raised in Richmond, Virginia; received a doctorate in American studies from Yale University; has shown his drawings in two one-man shows in New York galleries and in the Amon Carter Museum's "Two Hundred Years of American Caricature" exhibition.
    Works include: "The Kandy Kolored Tangerine-Flake Streamline Baby"; "The Pump House Gang"; *Radical Chic & Mau-Mauing the Flak Catchers; The Electric Kool-Aid Acid Test; The Right Stuff.*
    The Bonfire of the Vanities: uses a detailed on-scene reporting similar to the style of

Introducing the Chapter

Point out to students that many problems and concerns surfaced frequently throughout American history. As students read this final chapter, have them keep a list of problems and issues that have resurfaced during the course of their studies. (Lists might include: women's rights; environmental concerns; minority rights; foreign relations; education.)

CHAPTER **36** 1980–Today

Reagan, Bush, and Clinton

Links to American Literature

The Bavardages' dining-room walls had been painted with so many coats of burnt-apricot lacquer, fourteen in all, they had the glassy brilliance of a pond reflecting a campfire at night. The room was a triumph . . . by Ronald Vine, whose forte was the creation of glitter without the use of mirrors. Mirror Indigestion was now regarded as one of the gross sins of the 1970s. So in the early 1980s, from Park Avenue to Fifth, from Sixty-second Street to Ninety-sixth, there had arisen the hideous cracking sound of acres of hellishly expensive plate-glass mirror being pried off the walls of the great apartments. No, in the Bavardages' dining room one's eyes fluttered in a cosmos of glints, twinkles, sparkles, highlights, sheens, shimmering pools, and fiery glows that had been achieved in subtler ways, by using lacquer, glazed tiles in a narrow band just under the ceiling cornices, gilded English Regency furniture, silver candelabra, crystal bowls, Schools of Tiffany vases, and sculpted silverware that was so heavy the knives weighed on your fingers like saber handles.

—TOM WOLFE, *The Bonfire of the Vanities*

The Iran hostage crisis set the global backdrop for the election of 1980. On the domestic scene, Americans, suffering from the longest period of inflation in national history, did not reelect President Jimmy Carter. Instead, they turned to Ronald Reagan who heralded the power of the free enterprise system and promised economic recovery. In many ways, the 1980's also ushered in an age of excess. Whether or not Americans could afford the opulent life style that was glorified in the books like *The Bonfire of the Vanities* and in several movies and TV shows, they never seemed to tire of contemplating it. By the 1990's, however, Americans began to realize that excess carried a price.

Chapter Overview

In this chapter you will learn how President Reagan confronted challenges at home and abroad. You will learn about the changing social climate in the nation, and you will meet President Bush, who experienced domestic economic problems. Finally, you will meet President Clinton, whose election in 1992 signified a generational change in the leadership of the United States. Chapter 36 is divided into five sections.

Chapter Outline

1. **Reagan Takes Charge at Home**
2. **Foreign Policy Changes Over Time**
3. **Social Problems Confront the Nation**
4. **Bush Faces Many Difficulties**
5. **Clinton Leads the Nation Toward a New Century**

927

Core Lesson

Anticipate the Lesson

Ask students to define the terms *conservative* and *liberal*. (Possible responses: a conservative is a believer in established tradition who politically tends to favor individual initiative and minimal governmental control over private enterprise and social action; a liberal is a person whose political beliefs tend to favor experimentation and change, reform of inequalities, and an active role for the federal government.) Ask

students how the shift from liberal to conservative attitudes affected the election of 1980. (Possible response: many Americans voted for the more conservative candidate, Ronald Reagan, because they were tired of high taxes and inflation, and Reagan offered a change from the previous administration, a liberal Democratic one.)

SECTION 1

Reagan Takes Charge at Home

GLOSSARY TERMS: **Reaganomics, supply-side economics, Strategic Defense Initiative (SDI)**

By 1980 President Carter was suffering from one of the lowest job ratings on record for any President in public opinion polls. Equally important, he was caught in one of the periodic shifts that have taken place in American politics during the century.

A Conservative Mood Sweeps the Country

Since 1900, the United States has alternated between what historians call "public action and private interest." Sometimes voters support government action to solve social problems. At other times they become disillusioned with social experiments and concentrate on themselves.

Thus, Presidents Theodore Roosevelt, Taft, and Wilson, under the banner of progressivism, used the power of government to curb what they considered the excesses of big business. They were followed by three conservative Presidents—Harding, Coolidge, and Hoover—under whom the health of private industry was far more important than social reform. With the onset of the Great

Depression, the pendulum swung again, and FDR's New Deal and Truman's Fair Deal focused on government action to relieve social woes.

Conservatism returned during the 1950's under Eisenhower, to be followed by a shift toward liberalism during the 1960's under Kennedy's New Frontier and Johnson's Great Society. Conservatism began returning again during the 1970's under Nixon, Ford, and, to some extent, Carter. It reached a high point with the election of Ronald Reagan in 1980.

Single-Issue Groups. One reason for this latest change in national mood was the rise of single-issue groups, that is, groups of voters supporting or opposing a candidate on the basis of the candidate's stand on one particular issue. In the midterm congressional elections of 1978 and especially in the Presidential election of 1980, such groups favored what are generally seen as conservative positions. There were groups against gun control, against abortion, and against the ERA. Still other groups favored a constitutional amendment to permit prayers in public schools.

The members of these conservative single-issue groups were disturbed by what they saw as a decline in traditional American values. They called for measures that would strengthen the traditional family and offset the high divorce rate and the large number of births to unwed mothers.

People in the Chapter

Ronald Reagan was shot by John Hinckley, a young man who thought that he could win the love of the actress Jodie Foster by killing the President. While being wheeled into the operating room to have a bullet removed, the President said to his wife, Nancy, "Honey, I forgot to duck."

Geraldine Ferraro was the daughter of immigrant Italian parents. As the first woman on a major political party's Presidential ticket, Ferraro symbolized a breakthrough for women.

Jesse Jackson and Pat Robertson were two active religious leaders who ran in the Presidential primary elections in 1988. In 1990 Jackson was elected to the unpaid, nonvoting post of "shadow senator" from the District of

Columbia. His main function was to lobby for statehood.

George Bush used the same Bible at his inauguration on January 20, 1989, that George Washington had used at his first inauguration on April 30, 1789.

Hillary Rodham Clinton, a lawyer also known as an advocate for children's rights, was assigned an office in the west wing of the White House, alongside President Clinton's senior staff, instead of in the east wing where First Ladies have traditionally worked on social duties and charitable causes. Rodham Clinton was given the task of coordinating the new administration's policies for health-care reform.

State the Objective

Identify the major domestic problems and challenges that confronted the Reagan administration during the 1980's.

Picturing History
The Reverend Jerry Falwell, shown here, and other leaders of the Moral Majority, used television ministries to voice their political views.

Conservatives also believed that allowing prayers in public schools would help to counteract the neglect of traditional values. As the Reverend Jerry Falwell said, ''Our nation's internal problems are the direct results of her spiritual condition. . . . Right living must be reestablished as an American way of life. . . . Now is the time to begin calling America back to God, back to the Bible, back to morality!'' Falwell was just one of several leaders of a group of voters known as the **Moral Majority**. They were evangelical and fundamentalist Protestants who accepted Jesus Christ personally, interpreted the Bible literally, and believed in absolute moralism.

A Move to Curb Government Regulation. Another reason for the nation's conservative mood was the belief that the federal government had gone too far. It was too big and wasteful, and it was meddling in places where it did not belong.

The federal government had long recognized the needs of special-interest groups such as veterans, farmers, and the elderly. By 1980, however, one out of every three households in the United States was receiving benefits from one or more federal entitlement programs. Most Americans believed the cost in taxes to fund these programs had become too high. In addition, an annual inflation rate of almost 15 percent caused them to fear for the future. What was going to happen to the value of the money they had put aside for their children's college education and their own retirement years?

A second part of the movement to curb govern-

ment activity grew out of a gradual change in policy on civil rights. When the Civil Rights Act was passed in 1964, it was aimed at eliminating discrimination. Over the years, however, this goal had been broadened by judicial decisions and bureaucratic regulations. It now seemed to many Americans that the demand for equality of opportunity had turned into a demand for equality of results. Getting rid of separate and unequal schools for blacks and whites was one thing. Busing children long distances in order to maintain a fixed ratio between white and black pupils was something else again.

Reagan Defeats an Incumbent

Despite Jimmy Carter's low standing in the public opinion polls, he and Vice-President Walter F. Mondale were renominated by the Democrats. On the Republican side, the main contenders were former California governor Ronald Reagan, who had narrowly lost the 1976 nomination to Gerald Ford, and George Bush, a former CIA director and congressman from Texas. After a series of hard-fought primaries, Reagan won the nomination. He then chose Bush as his running mate.

Ronald Wilson Reagan was born in 1911 in the small town of Tampico, Illinois. After graduating from Eureka College, he worked as a radio sports

Presidential Election, 1980

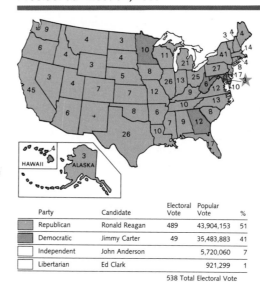

Party	Candidate	Electoral Vote	Popular Vote	%
Republican	Ronald Reagan	489	43,904,153	51
Democratic	Jimmy Carter	49	35,483,883	41
Independent	John Anderson		5,720,060	7
Libertarian	Ed Clark		921,299	1

538 Total Electoral Vote

Present the Lesson

Have several students volunteer to prepare a two-column chart on the board. The first column should list the domestic problems that confronted the Reagan administration. The second column should list the Reagan administration's solutions. Chart might include:

Problem	Solution
• Taxes	• 25 percent cut in federal income taxes over three years; increases in non-income taxes
• Economy	• Cuts in federal regulation of industries; sale of public land; 10 percent cut in government spending on social programs; Gramm-Rudman-Hollings Act of 1985
• Trade deficit	• Devaluation of the dollar; attempt to reduce trade barriers with other nations

Picturing History President Reagan and his wife, Nancy, during the 1981 inaugural parade.

announcer. In 1937 he moved to Hollywood and became a movie actor. There he served as president of a union known as the Screen Actors Guild and actively worked to remove supposed Communist influence from the movie industry. He then became host of a television series, *The General Electric Theater*.

Originally a New Deal Democrat, Reagan had, by the 1950's, become a conservative Republican. As a General Electric public relations representative, he traveled across the country making speeches in favor of free enterprise and against big government. In 1966, after having campaigned hard for Barry Goldwater for President, he was elected governor of California. He was reelected in 1970.

Reagan was an extremely effective political speaker. In contrast to Carter, Reagan was relaxed, charming, and affable. He loved making one-line quips, as when he described the difference between a depression—"when you lose your job''—and a recovery—"when Carter loses his.'' His skill at simplifying issues and presenting them clearly gained him the nickname of the Great Communicator.

Only 52.6 percent of American voters went to the polls in 1980, the lowest turnout for a Presidential election since 1948. When the votes were counted, Reagan had a narrow majority of nearly 44 million votes, or 51 percent of the total. Yet because his support was spread throughout the country, he carried 44 states, for a total of 489 electoral votes. The Republicans also gained control of the Senate for the first time since 1954.

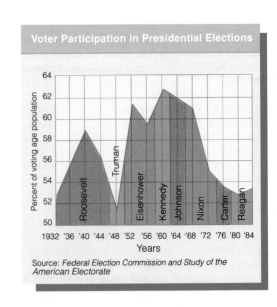

Source: *Federal Election Commission and Study of the American Electorate*

Economics Becomes Reaganomics

At age sixty-nine the oldest man to be elected President, Reagan wanted to set a new tone for his administration from the beginning. To reflect his Western roots, he changed the inaugural ceremony from the east portico to the western entrance of the Capitol. In contrast to the informal style marking Carter's inauguration, Reagan had a large parade and a lavish ball.

In his inaugural address, Reagan called for "a new beginning." He wanted to curb the size and influence of the federal government and to reduce the 14 percent inflation, which he considered the nation's number one economic problem.

When Reagan took office, he proposed a plan to change the government's economic policies. The President wanted to cut taxes, deregulate the economy, reduce spending for social programs, and increase spending for defense. Reagan's approach, which many people called **Reaganomics**, was designed to make Americans rely more on the private sector and less on the federal government, except in the area of defense.

Tax Cuts. Reagan's economic proposals were based on a theory known as **supply-side economics.** According to this theory, fiscal policy should promote economic growth by encouraging businesses to increase the supply of goods and services. By cutting tax rates and, especially, by lowering taxes on investments, supply-side theory argues, people will have more incentive to work, save, and invest. Increased investment will eventually create more jobs as the supply of goods and services accelerates. More workers mean more taxpayers. Thus, even though tax rates are lowered, the total government revenues will increase.

President Reagan accordingly asked Congress for a tax cut. After much debate and some compromise, Congress approved a 25 percent cut in the federal income tax over a three-year period. In August 1981, the President signed into law the largest tax cut in United States history.

Deregulating the Economy. In addition to lowering taxes, President Reagan tried to stimulate the economy by cutting back on federal regulation of industry. Price controls on oil and natural gas were lifted. Airlines were allowed to abandon convenient but unprofitable air routes. Nursing homes were no longer checked annually for health and safety. The percentage of deposits that savings and loan associations had to keep in reserve was reduced.

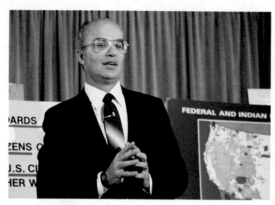

Picturing History James Watt, Secretary of the Interior, gives a news conference.

The major thrust of deregulation had to do with the nation's natural resources. Under Secretary of the Interior **James Watt,** millions of acres of public land were sold to private developers, often at bargain prices. The continental shelf was opened to offshore oil and gas drilling. Timber cutting was encouraged in national forests, and restrictions on the strip mining of coal were eased. Hundreds of inspectors for the Environmental Protection Agency were fired, leading to a drop of almost 75 percent in the number of antipollution cases referred to the Justice Department for prosecution. As a result of taking these measures, Watt came under severe criticism from conservationists. He resigned in 1983.

Spending Cuts. Another economic strategy that Reagan proposed was a 10 percent cut in government spending on social programs. "We can lecture our children about extravagance until we run out of voice and breath," the President said. "Or we can cut their extravagance by simply reducing their allowance."

Reagan's cuts, however, did not fall equally on all parts of the population. Certain entitlement programs—such as social security, Medicare, civil service, and veterans' pensions—benefit large, mostly middle-class constituencies. They were therefore regarded as politically untouchable. Instead, the spending cuts fell most heavily on the poor, or those households with incomes under

Check for Understanding

Call on individual students to orally answer
Section 1 Review questions.

Picturing History The Rockwell International B-1 bomber was designed to replace the aging Boeing B-52 bomber.

$10,000 a year for a family of four. These people saw reductions in such social services programs as food stamps, welfare benefits, job training, Medicaid, and school lunches.

Spending Increases.   While cutting spending for social programs, President Reagan sharply increased military expenditures. Between 1981 and 1984, the budget for the Defense Department almost doubled. The President revived two weapons systems—the MX missile and the B-1 bomber—about whose usefulness people disagreed strongly.

On March 23, 1983, Reagan asked the country's scientists to develop a defensive system that would make Americans safe from enemy missiles. Officially called the **Strategic Defense Initiative (SDI),** the proposed program quickly became known as Star Wars, after the movie of the same name. Its overall costs were estimated at several trillion dollars.

The Results of Reagonomics.   The results of Reagan's economic policies were mixed. On the bright side was a dramatic drop in the rate of inflation, from a high of almost 14 percent in 1980 to 4 percent in 1988. This decline in the rate of inflation was accompanied by lower interest rates and a soaring stock market.

On the dark side were the **budget deficit** and the growth in the national debt. The budget deficit came about because supply-side economics was not working: the government was spending far more than it was taking in in taxes. To make up the difference, the government borrowed money. In 1980 the national debt stood at about $900 billion, accumulated over 191 years. Within the first 5 years of the Reagan administration, the national debt more than doubled to the staggering total of almost $2 trillion, making the United States the leading debtor nation in the world. The result was that about 14 percent of the federal budget was soaked up by interest payments. This was more than all federal spending on education, health, the environment, agriculture, transportation, space, and science and technology.

Financing the federal budget deficit meant that less money was available to invest in modernizing business. American productivity declined, leaving the United States less able to compete with such nations as Japan and West Germany. One result was a situation that America had not faced in forty years: a large foreign trade deficit, in which the country was importing more than it was exporting. To put it another way, the United States was importing automobiles and exporting jobs.

Linking Past to Present

At first, anxiety about the trade deficit and the budget deficit appeared to be partly responsible for the stock market crash of 1987. On October 19 of that year, the stock market plummeted a record 508.32 points. As time passed, however, the anticipated recession failed to become a reality. In the end, many analysts blamed the crash on computerized trading—a system under which large institutions automatically buy or sell a stock whenever it reaches a certain price level.

To reduce the growing deficits, Congress passed a sweeping new tax bill that provided for an increase in taxes other than income taxes. In 1982, Reagan quietly signed into law this largest tax increase in the nation's history. Congress enacted another tax increase in 1984.

Picturing History   Newborn babies singing a parody of the popular song "We Are the World" call our attention to the burden on future generations to eliminate the federal deficit.

Reagan Returns for a Second Term

In 1984 Reagan and Bush won the Republican nomination without challenge. Opinion polls showed that although many voters disagreed with the President on major issues, they still supported him in general. They liked his genial personality and cheered his statement that it was "Morning again in America." They admired him for his deeply held convictions and his ability to express them. Reagan had another skill, too, that made him an effective candidate. He was able to keep criticism of his policies or scandals in his administration from being attached to himself. The skill gained him the nickname of the Teflon President.

Eight Democratic candidates vied for their party's nomination. Former Vice-President **Walter Mondale,** civil rights activist Jesse Jackson, and Colorado Senator Gary Hart were the leading contenders. Jackson was the first African American to run as a candidate for the Presidential nomination of a major political party. Mondale won the nomination and chose Representative **Geraldine**

Picturing History   Walter Mondale and Geraldine Ferraro ran on an unpopular platform of higher taxes.

Ferraro of New York as his running mate. She was the first woman on a major party's Presidential ticket.

After a long and sometimes bitter campaign, Reagan was reelected in a landslide, capturing 59 percent of the popular vote and 525 electoral votes. As in 1980, he received the bulk of his support from a coalition of traditional Republicans and conservative Christians. As in previous elections, total voter turnout was low.

Presidential Election, 1984

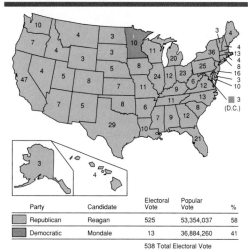

Party	Candidate	Electoral Vote	Popular Vote	%
Republican	Reagan	525	53,354,037	58
Democratic	Mondale	13	36,884,260	41

538 Total Electoral Vote

© ML & Co.

Assign Independent Practice

Have students complete Chapter 36, Section 1 Daily Activity.

Student Assignment/Homework

Ask students to read Section 2, "Foreign Policy Changes Over Time," and answer the Section 2 Review questions on paper.

SECTION 1 REVIEW

Answers

Main Ideas

1. The rise of conservative single-issue groups that believed that traditional American values were declining; that the federal government had become too big and wasteful; that civil rights demands had gone too far.

2. His conservatism, relaxed political style, personality, and skill at simplifying issues.

3. By cutting income taxes, deregulating businesses, cutting spending on social programs, and increasing spending on the military. • Inflation, interest rates, and productivity fell; stock-market activity, budget deficit, national debt, foreign trade deficit, and taxes other than income taxes increased.

4. Sandra Day O'Connor—conservative and first woman to serve on Supreme Court; William Rehnquist—conservative who filled Chief Justice's vacancy; Antonin Scalia—conservative and first Italian American to sit on the court; Robert H. Bork—rejected by Senate; Douglas H. Ginsburg—withdrew nomination; Anthony Kennedy—conservative.

Critical Thinking

5. Possible answer: because federal judges are appointed for life, their decisions affect Americans long after they and the President leave office. Reagan built a conservative federal court during his terms. **(analysis & synthesis)**

934

Economic Reforms. During his second term, President Reagan made several attempts to reduce the trade deficit. For example, in 1985 the United States began lowering the value of the dollar in relation to the currencies of other countries. This in turn lowered the price of American goods abroad and made them more competitive. In 1987 the government became more aggressive in trying to reduce the trade barriers put up by other countries to keep out American goods.

The Reagan administration also moved ahead in the area of tax reform. In the fall of 1986, the President signed into law what he called "the most sweeping overhaul of our tax code in our nation's history." The new tax law eliminated hundreds of deductions, lowered individual tax rates, and raised business tax rates. The net result was to make the tax system less progressive and to increase the proportion of the nation's wealth owned by the top 10 percent of the population.

Changes in the Supreme Court. During the 1980 Presidential campaign, Ronald Reagan promised that if an opening on the Supreme Court occurred, he would try to find a woman to fill the job. An opening did occur in 1981 when Justice Potter Stewart retired, and the President nominated **Sandra Day O'Connor,** a judge of the Arizona Court of Appeals. She became the first woman to sit on the nation's highest court.

Picturing History Supreme Court Justice Sandra Day O'Connor.

In 1986 Chief Justice Warren Burger retired. To fill this vacancy Reagan nominated Justice **William Rehnquist,** who was considered the most conservative justice on the Court. To fill the vacancy resulting from Rehnquist's promotion, Reagan nominated **Antonin Scalia,** a highly respected conservative judge on the United States Court of Appeals. Scalia became the first Italian American to serve on the Supreme Court.

The nominations of Justices O'Connor and Scalia aroused little or no opposition in the Senate. Then, in 1987, Justice Lewis F. Powell, Jr., retired,

and Reagan nominated Robert H. Bork, a judge of the Federal Court of Appeals. A fierce battle over the nomination ensued. (See Chapter 7, Section 4.)

After an extended and bitter debate, the Senate rejected Bork's nomination by a vote of 58 to 42. Reagan's second nominee, Douglas H. Ginsburg, withdrew when it was revealed that he had smoked marijuana while a professor at Harvard. The Senate then approved Reagan's third nominee, Judge **Anthony M. Kennedy** of the United States Court of Appeals.

Celebrating Liberty. In 1986 the United States celebrated the one hundredth anniversary of the placing of the Statue of Liberty in New York Harbor. The entire Fourth of July "Liberty Weekend" was an extravaganza of music, ceremonies, and fireworks.

The following year the United States celebrated another anniversary, the bicentennial of the writing of the Constitution. Throughout 1987, Americans honored the supreme law of the land and its writers with a variety of ceremonies, special events, and media productions.

SECTION 1 REVIEW

Key Terms and People

Explain the significance of: Moral Majority, Reaganomics, supply-side economics, James Watt, Strategic Defense Initiative (SDI), budget deficit, Walter Mondale, Geraldine Ferraro, Sandra Day O'Connor, William Rehnquist, Antonin Scalia, Anthony Kennedy

Main Ideas

1. What were the main reasons for the shift to conservatism in the United States in the early 1980's?
2. What made Ronald Reagan appealing to many voters during the 1980 Presidential campaign?
3. How did President Reagan attempt to stimulate economic growth? How did the economy respond to these measures?
4. Briefly describe President Reagan's nominees to the Supreme Court.

Critical Thinking

5. Why is the power to appoint Supreme Court justices and other federal judges an important power? Use Reagan's appointments to illustrate your answer.

Anticipate the Lesson

Review the Monroe Doctrine (Chapter 9), the Roosevelt Corollary (Chapter 20), and the Truman Doctrine (Chapter 30). Ask how each of these reflected American foreign policy at the time it went into effect. (Possible responses: Monroe Doctrine—warned European powers not to interfere in the New World and promised not to interfere in European affairs; reflected the country's spirit of isolationism and its natio-nalistic sentiments. Roosevelt Corollary—declared the U.S. would use military interven-tion if needed in the affairs of any Western Hemisphere nation; reflected the desire for the U.S. to maintain control over Latin America, and the Panama Canal. Truman Doctrine—stated that the U.S. would give economic and military aid to nations threatened by armed mi-norities or outside forces; was a controversial stand against communist aggression.)

State the Objective

Understand the major foreign policy problems that confronted the U.S. during the 1980's.

Present the Lesson

Ask students to review the section and pre-pare a list naming the areas of the world that presented problems or challenges to the U.S. in foreign affairs. From their lists students should develop a short outline describing each problem and how the U.S. reacted to it. Outline might include:

I. American-Soviet relations
  A. New leadership in Moscow
    1. Mikhail Gorbachev becomes general secretary of Communist party.
    2. Gorbachev initiates series of meetings with U.S.

SECTION 2

Foreign Policy Changes Over Time

GLOSSARY TERMS: **INF treaty, contras**

In both 1980 and 1984, Ronald Reagan cam-paigned on a pledge to make the United States "stand tall" in world affairs. He vowed that under his leadership the nation would take a strong stand against the Soviet Union and would assert Ameri-can military power around the globe.

American-Soviet Relations Improve

Reagan carried out his campaign pledge to be more aggressive against the Soviets. He called the Soviet Union an "evil empire." In arms negotia-tions, he told American representatives to take a firm stand. He criticized America's allies in Europe for not opposing Soviet actions more forcefully.

Picturing History Here, the well-known cartoonist Herblock shows a frozen Ronald Reagan on the attack with an icicle for a weapon, a ref-erence to his tough stance toward the Soviet Union during the cold war.

Then, in March 1985, the Soviet leadership changed, and **Mikhail Gorbachev** became the general secretary of the Communist party. An imaginative politician and a skilled diplomat, Gor-bachev represented a younger generation of Soviet leaders who were more concerned about economic growth than were their elders. Gorbachev realized that better relations with the United States would allow the Soviets to reduce their burden of military spending and reform their economy. Moreover,

Reagan's defense buildup had given the United States tremendous leverage at the bargaining table.

Accordingly, Gorbachev initiated a series of meetings and arms-control negotiations between the Soviet Union and the United States. Reagan and Gorbachev met in Geneva in November 1985 and again in Reykjavík, Iceland, in October 1986. Although this summit did not result in dramatic agreements, it helped reduce tensions between the two countries. American-Soviet relations contin-ued to improve. Gorbachev encouraged *glasnost,* or openness. He also defended his policy of *pere-stroika,* or economic restructuring, in a book enti-tled *Perestroika: New Thinking for Our Country and the World.*

On December 8, 1987, the two leaders signed a historic document: the intermediate-range nuclear forces agreement, or **INF treaty.** It was the first arms-control agreement since SALT II, which had been negotiated in 1979 but never ratified because of the Soviet invasion of Afghanistan. The INF treaty eliminated two classes of weapons systems and allowed each nation to make on-site inspec-tions of military installations on the other's terri-tory. The Senate ratified the INF treaty in May 1988.

Picturing History The Soviets rolled out the red carpet for President Reagan when he visited Moscow in May 1988. Reagan is shown here with Mikhail Gorbachev in Moscow's Red Square.

3. November 1985—Reagan and Gorbachev meet in Geneva, Switzerland.
4. October 1986—Reagan and Gorbachev meet again, this time in Reykjavik, Iceland. Their talks helped to reduce tension between the two countries.
5. December 1987—Reagan and Gorbachev sign INF treaty eliminating two classes of weapons systems and allowing on-site inspections of military installations.

II. Central America
   A. Nicaragua
      1. 1979—Somoza dictatorship toppled by Sandinistas.
      2. President Carter recognizes new regime and sends $83 million in aid.
      3. 1981—U.S. cuts off funds because Nicaragua is supplying guns to rebels and may be a Soviet outpost.
      4. Reagan urges support of contras, a right-wing group trying to overthrow the Sandinista government.
      5. Congress votes to give contras money and CIA support.
      6. Congress passes Boland Amendment.
      7. Reagan administration obtains money for contras from private citizens and other countries.
      8. U.S. policy wavers on support of contras.
      9. 1987—peace plan is signed by presidents of Costa Rica, El Salvador, Guatemala, Honduras, and Nicaragua.
     10. 1988—contras and sandanistas sign a truce.

Map Skills

Belize • El Salvador • Haiti, Dominican Republic

Congress Debates Policy in Central America

Diplomacy worked well in reducing tensions between the United States and the Soviet Union. In Central America, however, the Reagan administration relied on military force to carry out anti-Soviet policies. This was most evident in Nicaragua and Grenada.

Nicaragua. As you recall, in 1911 President Taft sent United States marines into Nicaragua to protect American investments there. (See page 531.) The marines left in 1933 but only after helping dictator Anastasio Somoza come to power. Somoza was succeeded by his son Luis Somoza Debayle, who was in turn succeeded by his brother Anastasio Somoza Debayle. The Somozas, with the support of the army, ran Nicaragua for the benefit of a small, wealthy group of landowners. Most of the country's 3.7 million inhabitants were poor farmers with almost no voice in the government.

In 1979 Somoza was toppled by rebels known as **Sandinistas,** who set up a socialist government. Since independent political opinions were allowed, however, President Carter recognized the new regime and sent it $83 million in economic aid. The Sandinista government also accepted aid from Cuba and the Soviet Union.

In 1981 the United States cut off American aid to Nicaragua on the grounds that Nicaragua was supplying weapons to rebels in other Central American nations. Many Americans believed Nicaragua had become a Soviet outpost and, according to the domino theory, was therefore a threat to American interests. If the Sandinistas were not removed from power, Reagan asserted, "the tide of communism . . . would spread its shadow over all of Central America," and eventually the Panama Canal would be endangered. The President urged Congress to support the **contras,** a group of right-wing rebels trying to overthrow the Sandinista government. Reagan called the contras "freedom fighters" and "the moral equivalent of our Founding Fathers." Congress responded by voting money to pay Argentina to train a 500-man contra raiding force.

By 1983 the contra army had grown to nearly 10,000 men, and the CIA had moved in to direct its operations. In February 1984, the CIA helped the contras mine harbors in the Nicaraguan ports of Corinto and Puerto Sandino. This unauthorized action led Congress to pass the so-called Boland Amendment forbidding military aid to the contras for a two-year period. The Reagan administration responded by obtaining contributions for the contras from private citizens and from the governments of Saudi Arabia and Brunei. Another response was

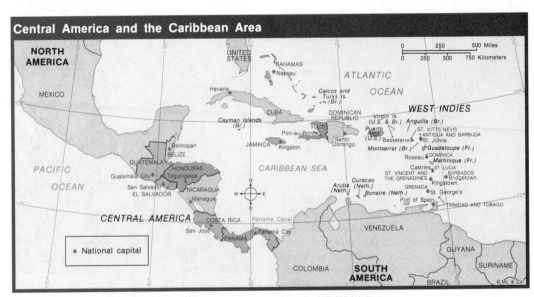

Central America and the Caribbean Area

• National capital

Map Skills **Place** Which Central American country has no Pacific coast? Which has no Atlantic coast? **Location** What two countries share an island?

11. 1990—free elections held; Ortega loses to opposition leader Violeta Chamorro.
B. Grenada
1. October 25, 1983—Reagan sends U.S. troops to small island nation in eastern Caribbean.
2. U.S. fears Grenada is developing close ties with Cuba.
3. Reagan claims invasion is necessary to defend U.S. security and protect American medical students there.
4. News blackout imposed during inva-

sion leads to questions regarding freedom of press.
III. Middle East
A. Arab-Israeli problems
1. 1981—Anwar Sadat assassinated; successor is cool toward Israel.
2. Israel refuses to cede West Bank to Palestinians.
3. Israel attacks PLO in Lebanon.
4. UN troops sent to Lebanon.
5. October 1983—terrorist explosion kills 241 American marines in Beirut.
6. Reagan pulls marines out of Lebanon.

7. September 1984—U.S. embassy in Beirut attacked; hostages taken.
B. Iran-contra affair
1. November 1986—Americans learn Reagan administration violated its own policy by secretly selling military equipment and supplies to Iran in exchange for hostages.
2. Part of money from sale is going to support contras, the rest to U.S. businessmen.

Picturing History Oscar Arias Sánchez, winner of the Nobel Peace Prize

the Iran-contra affair, which you will learn about later in this chapter.

Over the next several years, American policy toward the contras shifted back and forth. Sometimes Congress voted military aid. At other times it banned military aid but voted humanitarian aid, that is, food, clothing, shelter, and medical supplies. In the meantime, up to 50,000 Nicaraguans died, an estimated 500,000 sought refuge in neighboring Honduras, and the country's economy was nearly destroyed, partly because of the fighting and partly because the United States not only imposed an embargo on trade with Nicaragua but also blocked aid, trade, and loans from the rest of the world.

In 1987 a peace plan for Central America was signed by the presidents of Costa Rica, El Salvador, Guatemala, Honduras, and Nicaragua. The plan called for a negotiated peace between the Sandinistas and the contras and for a cease-fire in the guerrilla wars in El Salvador and Guatemala. Those two nations as well as Nicaragua promised to restore civil liberties for their people and to stop supporting rebels in other countries. The peace plan was called the Arias plan, after Costa Rican President Oscar Arias Sánchez, its architect. Arias received the 1987 Nobel Peace Prize for his efforts.

In 1988 the contras and the Sandinistas signed a truce. In 1989 the five Central American presidents met again. Nicaraguan President Daniel Ortega agreed to hold free elections in 1990 if the contra forces were disbanded.

On February 25, 1990, the Nicaraguan people voted to replace Ortega with opposition candidate Violeta Chamorro. Since the election, Chamorro's supporters and the Sandinistas—who control 40 percent of the National Assembly—have worked together to rebuild Nicaragua's economy.

Grenada. The United States used direct military force instead of hired guns in Grenada, a tiny island nation in the eastern Caribbean. Ruled by a leftist dictator and troubled by domestic turmoil, Grenada had been developing close ties with communist Cuba. On October 25, 1983, President Reagan sent in a small contingent of American troops. He said the invasion was necessary to defend United States security and to protect some one thousand Americans, most of them medical students, who were on the island. Several hundred Cubans, as well as a stockpile of Soviet-made arms and ammunition, were found on Grenada. Despite the death of eighteen American soldiers, the successful attack was widely supported in the United States.

However, there was considerable controversy over the news blackout imposed by the administration. Reporters were not allowed to accompany the troops, and the only accounts of the operation came from the Pentagon. This was contrary to previous American practice and brought charges that the administration was limiting freedom of the press.

The Middle East Remains a Trouble Spot

The Camp David Accords, which had been negotiated with the help of President Carter, did not lead to peace in the Middle East. Anwar Sadat was assassinated by Muslim fundamentalists in 1981, and his successor, Hosni Mubarak, was cool toward Israel. Israel in turn rejected President Reagan's suggestion to cede the West Bank to the

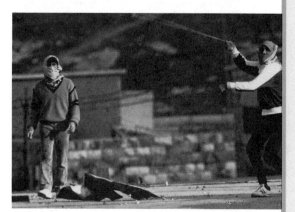

Picturing History Arab youths hurl stones at Israeli soldiers in the A-Tur neighborhood outside Jerusalem. Israeli reprisals have not stopped the violence accompanying Palestinian demands for a homeland.

937

938

3. Tower Commission investigates and strongly criticizes President.
4. Congress conducts televised hearings and sharply criticizes those involved.
5. Reagan names Lawrence Walsh as special prosecutor to investigate.
6. Three hostages released as a result of sale, but three new hostages taken.
7. 1988—Secord, Hakim, Poindexter, North, and several others indicted and later convicted.
8. December, 1992—President Bush pardons, among others, Weinberger, Abrams, and McFarlane.

Check for Understanding

Ask students to choose one of the problems outlined in the section and write a letter to the editor of a local newspaper expressing concern and suggesting possible solutions or alternative actions. (Letter on Grenada might include concern over U.S. invasion, questioning the wisdom and legality of the act and the loss of American lives. Writer might ask what tangible goal was achieved. Writer might suggest that relations with the island could have been improved through economic or medical aid and that the U.S. did not need to invade Grenada to show its strength.)

Picturing History
Over two hundred United States marines in Lebanon were killed when a truck filled with explosives was purposely driven into their barracks. They had been on a peacekeeping mission.

Palestinians and instead stepped up the establishment of Israeli settlements in the area. This led many Palestinians to fear that Israel meant to annex the West Bank, and anti-Israeli strikes, riots, and fire bombings became commonplace.

Turmoil in Lebanon. In the meantime, Israel attacked Palestinian positions in Lebanon and succeeded in forcing out the PLO. To ensure the PLO's safety as it withdrew, the United Nations sent a peacekeeping force to Lebanon. Among the UN troops was a contingent of American marines.

The UN troops completed their task by August 1982 and withdrew. They came back the next month, however, when fighting increased between Christian and Muslim groups in Lebanon. The UN presence did not stop the fighting, though; it only convinced Muslims that the United States in particular was taking sides against them in the civil war.

In October 1983 a truck filled with explosives crashed into the marine barracks near the Beirut airport, killing 241 Americans. A few months later, unable to resolve the impasse between Muslims and Christians, President Reagan pulled the marines out of Lebanon. Fighting within the country continued, however, and in September, twelve people died in a terrorist attack against the United States embassy in Beirut. By this time, also, a number of Americans had been taken hostage by terrorist groups loyal to Iran. President Reagan

denounced Iran as part of "an international version of Murder Inc." and urged United States allies not to sell Iran any weapons to use in its war with Iraq.

The Iran-Contra Affair. Three years later, in November 1986, the American people learned that the Reagan administration had been violating its own public policy. It had secretly sold Iran antitank and antiaircraft missiles in an attempt to obtain the release of the hostages. Moreover, part of the profits from the arms sale had been secretly transferred to the contras despite the Boland Amendment prohibiting American military aid to the Nicaraguan rebels. Most of the remaining profits apparently went into the pockets of two United States businessmen involved in the deal, retired Major General Richard Secord and his Iranian-born partner, Albert Hakim.

Two inquiries into the **Iran-contra affair** were held. One was carried out by a special panel appointed by President Reagan and headed by former Texas senator John Tower. In its report, issued February 1987, the Tower Commission strongly criticized the President for not properly supervising the National Security Council. Two NSC heads—Robert McFarlane and his successor, Vice-Admiral **John Poindexter**—as well as NSC staff member Lieutenant Colonel **Oliver North**, had played a major role both in organizing the sale of arms to Iran and in diverting the proceeds to the contras.

The second inquiry into the Iran-contra affair was far more dramatic. Conducted by special committees of both houses of Congress, it included a month of joint televised hearings. Among those testifying was Lieutenant Colonel North, who appeared in military uniform with a chestful of

Picturing History
Lieutenant Colonel Oliver North, staff member to the National Security Council, testifies before Congress about his role in providing aid to the contras.

Guided Practice

Ask students to consider what problems the Reagan administration inherited from previous administrations. To stimulate discussion, ask students the following questions. What problems did the Reagan administration pass on to the Bush administration? (Possible responses: fragile U.S.-Soviet relations, Middle East problems, the national deficit, environmental problems.) If national problems are linked to the past, who is ultimately responsible for them? Can Presidents be blamed for problems they did not create? (Possible response: it is difficult to lay blame for national problems on one ad-

ministration or another, but the American public expects its Presidents to be able to solve existing problems; if the President cannot solve existing problems, then his administration is held responsible.)

Assign Independent Practice

Ask students to complete Chapter 36, Section 2 Enrichment Activity.

"....REPEAT, EVERYTHING IS UNDER CONTROL!...... (NOW, WHERE'S THE REVERSE ON THIS THING?!)....."

Picturing History
Ronald Reagan's futile attempts to free the American hostages held by pro-Iranians in Lebanon are satirized in this cartoon.

medals. In defending his actions, North talked about patriotism and love of country. He asserted that he thought he was carrying out the President's wishes and that the end of helping the contras justified almost any means.

In its 1987 report on the affair, the congressional panel sharply criticized the government-within-the-government.

> The common ingredients of the Iran and contra policies were secrecy, deception, and disdain for the law. A small group of senior officials believed that they alone knew what was right. . . . They told neither the secretary of state, the Congress, nor the American people of their actions. When exposure was threatened, they destroyed official documents and lied to Cabinet officials, to the public, and to elected representatives. They testified that they even withheld key facts from the President. . . . Constitutional process is the essence of our democracy and our democratic form of government is the basis of our strength. Time and again we have learned that a flawed process leads to bad results, and that a lawless process leads to worse.

The report recommended that the National Security Council not engage in covert activities. Eight Republicans on the committee, however, publicly disagreed with the report. They characterized it as biased and hysterical.

In the meantime, following a law that had been enacted after Watergate, President Reagan named Lawrence E. Walsh as a special prosecutor to see if any criminal indictments should be handed down.

In 1988 Secord, Hakim, Poindexter, North, McFarlane, and several others were indicted.

By mid-1991, Secord, Hakim, McFarlane, and two others had pleaded guilty. They were all given probation. Some were also required either to pay fines or to perform community service.

Poindexter was convicted in 1990 on five counts of obstructing Congress and perjury. He was sentenced to six months in prison but appealed the conviction. The appeal was upheld in 1991 on the ground that information he had given Congress under a grant of immunity could not be used against him in a trial.

North was convicted in 1989 on three of twelve charges, including destroying National Security Council documents and lying to Congress. He was fined, given two years of probation, and ordered to perform community service. On appeal in 1991, one conviction was dismissed and two were sent back to the court for review. Due to legal technicalities, prosecutors then decided not to press the case further.

In the meantime, Walsh obtained several additional indictments. Former assistant secretary of state Elliott Abrams and three CIA officials were charged with perjury and withholding information from Congress. In 1992 former defense secretary Caspar Weinberger was likewise indicted on charges of perjury.

On December 24, 1992, President Bush pardoned Weinberger, Abrams, McFarlane, and three other former officials of the Reagan administration. The action swept away one conviction, three guilty pleas, and two pending cases.

President Bush justified his pardon as follows:

For Discussion
What are the similarities and differences between the Watergate scandal and the Iran–contra affair? (Possible responses: similarities—both involved illegal activities; both involved members of the President's staff; both drew widespread attention and congressional inquiries. Differences—Nixon was held responsible for the activities of his staff and was forced from office; Reagan was not charged with any crime and was not held responsible for the illegal activities.)

Student Assignment/Homework

Have students read Section 3, "Social Problems Confront the Nation," and answer the Section 3 Review questions on paper.

Anticipate the Lesson

Ask students what area they consider to have the most pressing social problem in America today. Write their responses on the board. (Possible responses: environment; education; health; discrimination; minority and women's rights.) Ask students to decide which problems might best be solved through government intervention, which might be solved through private initiative, which might require

both, and which might never be solved. (Possible responses: some students might feel that government should handle problems concerning discrimination, education, health, and the environment; some might feel that private initiative might work best to solve problems concerning health, education, the environment, and minority and women's rights; some may feel that problems in all these areas must be addressed by both sectors in order to make any lasting changes; some students may feel that these issues will continue to be problematic indefinitely.)

SECTION 2 REVIEW

Answers

Main Ideas

1. Gorbachev came to power and initiated a series of meetings; he and Reagan held summit meetings in 1985 and 1986 and in 1987 signed the INF treaty.

2. They were perceived as Soviet and Cuban outposts in Latin America, a region long considered to be of vital importance to United States security.

3. Very troubled and violent. The United States became embroiled in conflicts involving Lebanon, Iran, Iraq, and the entire Persian Gulf region.

Critical Thinking

4. Possible answers: similarities—high-ranking administration officials broke the law, lied about it, and demonstrated contempt for Congress and the American people; congressional inquiries were held to establish the truth; evidence was destroyed by public servants; the establishment of a government-within-the-government that considered itself above the law was criticized as the main source of corruption. • Differences— the Iran-contra affair involved foreign relations, but Watergate did not; Watergate brought down a President, whereas the Iran-contra affair did not. **(analysis)**

"First, the common denominator of their motivation—whether their actions were right or wrong—was patriotism. Second, they did not profit or seek to profit from their conduct."

Walsh promptly characterized the pardons as "[undermining] the principle that no man is above the law." Other critics of the President's action said that while pardoning individuals was acceptable, pardoning their crimes was not.

In 1994, seven years after the start of his investigation, Walsh issued his final report. It added little to what was already known. It did, however, suggest that our constitutional system of checks and balances was in need of reform. Members of the executive branch had failed to obey laws enacted by the legislative branch. At the same time, Congress had granted witnesses immunity from prosecution, which in effect meant they could never be convicted even if they were brought to trial. Walsh concluded that "The Iran-contra investigation will not end the kind of abuse of power that it addressed."

Gunfire in the Persian Gulf. In 1987 the Reagan administration threw its support to Iraq in Iraq's war with Iran, and in 1988 the two Middle Eastern nations agreed to a cease-fire. Three years later, the United States would again be involved in the Persian Gulf area, this time in a full-scale shooting war against Iraq.

SECTION 2 REVIEW

Key Terms and People

Explain the significance of: Mikhail Gorbachev, INF treaty, Sandinistas, contras, Iran-contra affair, John Poindexter, Oliver North

Main Ideas

1. During the Reagan administration, what events helped to improve relations between the United States and the Soviet Union?
2. Why did the Reagan administration perceive both the Nicaraguan and the Grenadan governments as a threat to the United States?
3. Briefly characterize United States relations with the Middle East during the Reagan administration.

Critical Thinking

4. How was the Iran-contra affair similar to the Watergate cover-up? How was it different?

SECTION 3

Social Problems Confront the Nation

GLOSSARY TERMS: AIDS, space shuttle, Environmental Protection Agency (EPA)

In 1985 President Reagan promised that during his second term in office, he would encourage a "second American revolution," designed to leave the United States "stronger, freer, and more secure than ever before." Yet critics argued that although America's position in the world was certainly stronger than it had been, social problems were multiplying at home.

An Urban Crisis Develops

By 1980 the United States was well on its way to becoming a suburbanized nation. The population of some cities—such as New York, Philadelphia, and Detroit—had actually decreased during the previous decade as more and more middle-class families answered the call of ranch houses, green lawns, station wagons, and shopping malls, to say nothing of uncrowded and well-equipped schools.

The result of this population movement was that central cities were increasingly inhabited by poor people and racial minorities, many of whom were unemployed. They needed police and fire protec-

Picturing History Guardian Angels police the public transit system in the Bronx, New York. These young volunteers are widely considered to have made a positive contribution to the communities in which they live, although not without controversy.

Present the Lesson

Divide the class into six groups. Have each group prepare and present to the class a short summary of social problems facing Americans in the 1980's in one of the following areas: urban management, women and minorities, space exploration, education, the environment, and health. (Summaries might include: urban management—many cities become smaller due to the exodus of the middle class to the suburbs; cities are increasingly inhabited by the poor and minorities; heavy financial burdens are placed on cities to provide services; slums are growing; crime and drug use are on the rise. Women and minorities—backlash against women's rights and civil rights movements occurs; ERA remains unpassed; election of women to public offices still leaves women underrepresented in government; women's earnings remain below those of men doing comparable jobs; pay equity is suggested but not widely accepted; African Americans make little progress economically; Reagan administration opposes affirmative action programs; questions are raised regarding bilingual education; Reagan administration cuts federal assistance to Indians. Space exploration—Reagan administration concentrates on military and commercial

tion, sanitation services, health care, schools, and job-training programs. Yet they were often unable to pay for these needs. That placed a heavy financial burden on cities, some of which came close to bankruptcy.

In addition, although new office buildings, department stores, and middle-class townhouses sprang up in many cities as a result of urban revitalization programs, the buildings in older residential areas deteriorated. Slums grew ever larger, and their spread was accompanied by increases in both street crime and drug use.

The latter problem was particularly alarming. Furthermore, it was a problem that confronted the suburbs as well as the cities. Suggestions for dealing with the problem varied. The Reagan administration stressed using the armed forces to patrol the nation's borders to prevent drug smuggling. The President called for random drug testing at government-related workplaces. The President's wife, Nancy Reagan, was prominently featured in a "Just Say No!" campaign against drug use.

A drug law passed in 1988 cut off such federal benefits as college loans and public housing occupancy for marijuana users. At the same time, it provided funds for more antidrug education. Some people suggested that drugs be legalized, arguing that this would reduce drug-gang warfare and cut down on thefts. Others called for more treatment facilities.

Women and Minorities Seek Equal Opportunities

During the 1980's, women and minorities tried to consolidate previous gains and achieve new goals. They found the road difficult because of a backlash against the women's and civil rights movements.

Women. With the failure of the Equal Rights Amendment, women's organizations began to concentrate on electing women to public office. The number of female legislators, mayors, and governors rose. President Reagan named two women to his cabinet, Elizabeth Dole as Secretary of Transportation and Margaret Heckler as Secretary of Health and Human Services. Nevertheless, women remained underrepresented in political affairs.

Economically, too, women made some advances but not many. The percentage of women working as professionals and managers increased. By 1986,

Picturing History
Elizabeth Dole, Secretary of Transportation under President Reagan and Secretary of Labor under President Bush.

however, women were earning only 70 percent of what men were earning. Moreover, female college graduates were still earning less than male high-school graduates.

To close the pay gap, women's organizations and unions proposed a new idea: pay equity. Under pay equity, jobs are broken down into such categories as the amount of education required, the amount of physical strength needed, and the number of people supervised. Next, a monetary value is assigned to each category. The pay for each job then depends not on traditional pay scales but on the skills and responsibilities involved.

As of 1989, twenty states had begun making pay-equity adjustments for government jobs. This resulted in raises of as much as 30 percent for many female employees. Most private firms, however, resisted the idea on the ground that it would be too expensive.

Women called for other changes in the business world. Since so many working women had children under the age of six or were heads of single-parent households, they needed help with child care. They wanted job-protected maternity leaves. Some called for such options as flexible workweeks, job-sharing, and work-at-home arrangements.

While some of these changes could be handled by individual business firms, others required federal action. Under the Reagan administration, however, funding for day-care, aid-to-dependent-children, and similar programs was cut sharply.

African Americans. During the two decades since the assassination of Dr. Martin Luther King, use of space; first successful space shuttle is launched (1981); first woman astronaut and first black astronaut go into space (1983); *Challenger* disaster occurs (1986); successful four-day flight of shuttle *Discovery* takes place (1988). Education— Presidential commission publishes report entitled *A Nation at Risk* (1983), recommending more homework, longer school days, longer school years, increased pay and merit raises for teachers, and new emphasis on English, math, science, social studies, and computer science; some critics advocate a voucher system that would enable students to attend private schools of their choosing. Environment—Reagan believes environmental problems should be handled by individuals and businesses; Reagan cuts budget for EPA; hundreds of rules preventing air and water pollution are weakened or eliminated; Reagan administration agrees to support Superfund bill to eliminate dangerous wastes (1986). Health—AIDS becomes a serious problem; by the beginning of 1992 more than 242,000 cases have been reported; no cure is known; public calls for routine blood testing; concerns grow over the cost of caring for patients during the course of the illness.)

For Discussion
Do you think that affirmative action programs, programs designed to give minorities an equal chance to succeed in business, education, and government, really promote reverse discrimination, as President Reagan believed? (Possible responses: yes— when a qualified applicant is turned down for a job and a less qualified minority is hired in order to fill a quota, it is unfair; all applicants should be judged on their abilities and neither favored nor discriminated against because of race or sex.)

Jr., African Americans made numerous advances. Yet for many, life remained unchanged.

The most striking advance for African Americans came in politics. By the mid-1980's, there were black mayors in dozens of cities, including Los Angeles, Detroit, Chicago, Atlanta, New Orleans, Philadelphia, and Washington, D.C. Hundreds of communities in both the North and the South had elected black sheriffs, school board members, state legislators, and members of Congress. **Jesse Jackson,** who became a candidate for the Democratic Presidential nomination in 1984 and again in 1988, was perhaps the most visible symbol of black political gains. In 1989, L. Douglas Wilder was elected governor of Virginia. He was the first African American ever to be elected governor in the United States. At the same time, however, many white ethnics and conservative Southerners responded to black political gains by shifting from the Democratic party to the Republican party.

Economically, there was no progress. The income gap between white and black Americans was higher in 1988 than it had been in 1968. Moreover, African Americans seemed to be splitting into two distinct groups, ''the educated affluent and the uneducated poor.'' Middle-class blacks moved into professional and managerial positions. Lower-class blacks seemed trapped in a permanent condition of poverty and unemployment, complicated by a very high rate of births to unwed mothers.

Hispanic Americans. The fastest growing minority in the United States were the Hispanic Americans. By 1990 they made up almost 9 percent of the population, and demographers estimated that by the turn of the century Hispanic Americans would outnumber African Americans. About two out of three Hispanics were Mexican, and these lived mostly in the Southwest. Puerto Ricans lived mostly in the Northeast, and Cubans lived mostly in Florida.

During the 1980's, Hispanic Americans—like African Americans—began to gain political power.

Picturing History
Governor Douglas Wilder of Virginia (far left), the nation's first elected black governor, and Governor Robert Martínez of Florida.

Hispanic voters helped elect Toney Anaya as governor of New Mexico and Robert Martínez as governor of Florida. Several cities, including Denver, San Antonio, and Miami, elected Hispanic mayors. In August 1988 President Reagan appointed **Lauro Cavazos** as Secretary of Education, the first Hispanic American to be named to a cabinet post. In 1990 Dr. Antonia Coello Novello was named to the post of Surgeon General.

On the economic front, conditions were mixed. Migrant farm workers still suffered from low pay, and

Picturing History
A migrant farm worker picks grapes in Alexander Valley, California.

Check for Understanding

Call on individual students to read their answers to the Section 3 Review questions.

Focus on American Art

Picturing History   From the beginning of time, people have built monuments to leaders who represent their ideals. Americans have built monuments to leaders who have guided them through difficult times. George Washington sacrificed personal power to establish a democracy. Abraham Lincoln held the nation together and laid the foundation for a socially just society. Martin Luther King, Jr., dedicated his life to the goals of liberty, justice, and equality. Today, these monuments remind us of these goals and inspire us to continue the struggle to extend liberty and justice to all.

The Mount Rushmore National Memorial in the Black Hills of South Dakota.

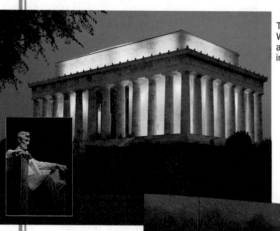

The Lincoln Memorial, Washington, D.C., with an inset of the statue inside.

The Washington Monument soars majestically over Washington, D.C.

...UNTIL JUSTICE ROLLS DOWN LIKE WATERS AND RIGHTEOUSNESS LIKE A MIGHTY STREAM

MARTIN LUTHER KING JR.

The Civil Rights Memorial in Montgomery, Alabama, was designed by Maya Lin, architect of the Vietnam Veterans Memorial in Washington, D.C.

Tell students that during the 1980's women and minorities found their roads to equality blocked by a conservative backlash against their movements. Ask how this backlash reflects the conservative mood of America in the 1980's. (Possible response: negative reaction to both the civil rights and women's movements indicated that conservative Americans no longer wanted government to pay the cost of ensuring equality in America; the public might have believed that equality would better be achieved through private and individual efforts rather than through court mandates; it reflected the idea that government should not interfere—or should interfere as little as possible—in this area.)

the overall unemployment rate was high. However, more and more Hispanics held professional or technical jobs.

Unlike European immigrants of the late 1800's and early 1900's, Hispanic immigrants were often reluctant to learn English. Many feared it would mean the loss of their culture. This reluctance was reinforced by two laws: the Bilingual Education Act of 1968, which required public schools to use native languages for classes with non-English-speaking students, and the Voting Rights Act of 1975, which required that ballots be printed in languages other than English.

By the mid-1980's, opposition to bilingualism was rising. Critics argued that it slowed the rate at which people learned English and thus kept Spanish-speaking people from entering the mainstream. The critics also believed the nation's unity might be destroyed if voters did not share a common language.

Hispanic artists, Hispanic styles, and Hispanic foods became increasingly popular during the 1980's. Actors such as Edward James Olmos and writers such as Sandra Cisneros and Oscar Hijuelos won awards for their films and books. Americans everywhere danced the salsa and played records by Rubén Blades. Hispanic decorating styles—Moorish arches, walled courtyards, vivid woven rugs, and adobe houses—were increasingly popular. So, too, were such Hispanic foods as tacos, tapas, burritos, jalapēno peppers, and jicama.

American Indians. As you recall, in 1963 the federal government dropped its termination policy of abolishing reservations and distributing tribal lands among individual Indians. (See page 806.) Over the next several years, various tribes sued in federal court and recovered land and also water, mineral, and fishing rights that had been taken away from them.

In 1975 Congress passed the Indian Self-Determination and Educational Assistance Act. It was designed to increase the role Indians played in their education and government. By that time, more than half the employees of the Bureau of Indian Affairs were of Indian descent.

In the 1980's, the Reagan administration sharply cut federal assistance to Indian tribes for health, education, and other services. As a result the Indians were cut off from various government services. Some Indians feared the government might again adopt a termination policy.

Asian Americans. The second fastest-growing minority in the United States was the Asian Americans, who numbered about 7.3 million by 1990. The largest concentration was in California, where they constituted 5.25 percent of the population.

Unlike African Americans and Hispanics, Asian Americans made numerous economic advances but few political ones. In general, Asian Americans placed a high value on education. Many were college graduates who pursued successful careers in business or science. Although they contributed money to political parties and candidates, they were slow to enter politics themselves. One reason was their reluctance to adopt such characteristics of American politicians as asserting a point of view and talking about themselves. The cultural background of most Asian Americans favors cooperation and group consensus. Then, too, Asian Americans of Japanese descent remembered the internment of Japanese Americans during World War II. As Don Tamaki, a San Francisco lawyer, explained: "The message passed to the children is, 'Be quiet,' 'Do not do anything to attract attention to yourself.'" In addition, recent immigrants from Asia had no experience with democracy. They tended to distrust government.

Asian Americans varied widely with regard to their nationalities, languages, religions, and attitudes toward each other. Nevertheless, it seemed likely that they would develop common ground over such issues as discrimination and would eventually form a politically powerful bloc.

Americans Face Complex Issues

During the 1980's, Americans argued about, and sometimes fought over, troubling and divisive issues. Two of the most polarizing ones were abortion and AIDS.

Abortion. In 1973, in *Roe* v. *Wade,* the Supreme Court held that the right to privacy protects "a woman's decision whether or not to terminate her pregnancy." At the same time, the Court held that states could limit abortions during the second three months of pregnancy, but only to protect a woman's health.

Since then, opponents of *Roe* v. *Wade* have organized under the slogan of "pro-life," while supporters of the Supreme Court decision have dubbed themselves "pro-choice." Opponents, such as evangelical political groups, the Roman Catholic Church, and the Southern Baptists, argue

Assign Independent Practice

Ask students to choose one of the problematic areas described in class and prepare a three-paragraph essay suggesting how government or private industry could help alleviate the problems. (Paragraphs on health might include: allocating more money for private and government research into the causes of AIDS and into a potential cure for it; providing education to schools, parents, and churches regarding the disease; allocating money for long-term care of AIDS victims.)

that life begins at conception and that abortion is murder. Supporters of *Roe* v. *Wade* argue that in a pluralistic society like the United States, the decision on abortion is a personal one that should be made by the individual woman, not by the government. They also argue that when abortion was illegal, many women died because abortions were often performed by unskilled persons.

Many people have tried to find a middle ground between the two positions, suggesting that abortion be legal in cases of rape and incest or to save the mother's life. Since in general a person is considered legally dead when there is no brain activity, some people have also suggested applying that standard to determine when life begins. These people would support legal abortion before the embryo becomes a fetus and develops a functioning brain, but not afterward.

The AIDS Threat. Beginning in 1981, a serious disease spread rapidly throughout the world. This disease, known as acquired immune deficiency syndrome, or **AIDS,** is caused by a virus that destroys the body's disease-fighting immune system, leaving it weakened and prey to infections and certain cancers, which eventually lead to death.

AIDS is transmitted between people by an exchange of bodily fluids. Initially, most of the victims of this debilitating disease were either homosexuals or intravenous drug users who shared infected needles. However, people also contacted AIDS through contaminated blood transfusions and by being born to mothers with AIDS. The late 1980's witnessed, too, a significant rise in the number of heterosexuals with AIDS. The Public Health service projected that by the end of 1994 between 415,000 and 535,000 AIDS cases would have been reported in the United States. The World Health Organization estimated that 8–10 million people worldwide were infected with the AIDS virus.

As people became more aware of the AIDS epidemic, there was a growing concern over the high cost of caring for the disease's victims.

Progress and Perils Become Commonplace

In addition to abortion and AIDS, the nation faced challenges during the 1980's in such areas as space, education, and the environment. Progress was more apparent in some areas than in others.

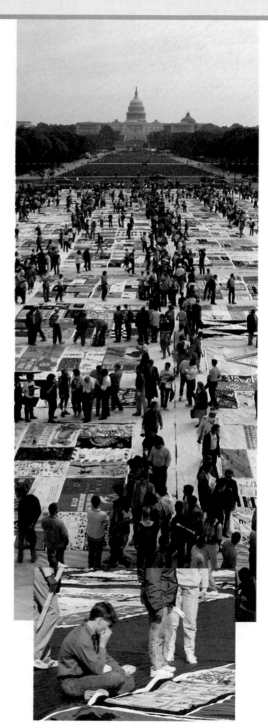

Picturing History The quilt shown here is the size of two football fields and is made from diverse materials including vinyl, leather, jeans, fur, buttons, and photographs. Called the Names Project, the quilt is a memorial to those who have died of AIDS.

Picturing History The seven-member *Challenger* crew represented a cross-section of Americans. The members (front row, left to right) were Michael J. Smith, Francis R. Scobee, Ronald E. McNair, (back row) Ellison S. Onizuka, Sharon Christa McAuliffe, Gregory Jarvis, and Judith Resnik. The loss of the crew in the explosion triggered an outpouring of grief throughout the country.

Returning to Space. In 1969 millions of Americans had thrilled when Neil Armstrong and Edwin Aldrin stepped on the surface of the moon. In 1976 they had gazed in awe at the photographs of Mars that unmanned spacecraft *Viking I* and *II* sent back to earth. They had had similar reactions when they saw the pictures of Jupiter's moons and Saturn's rings transmitted from 1979 to 1981 by *Voyager 1* and *2*.

Under the Reagan administration, the government shifted its emphasis. Instead of concentrating on space science, it pushed military and commercial uses of space. Accordingly, 1981 saw the first successful flight of the **space shuttle,** a manned, reusable spacecraft designed to take off like a rocket, orbit the earth, and land like an airplane. NASA hoped eventually to establish a manned space station, with the shuttle ferrying workers and materials to it.

Over the next five years, NASA directed a series of successful shuttle flights. In June 1983 Sally K. Ride, as a crew member of the space shuttle *Challenger,* became the first American woman astronaut in space. Two months later, on another flight of *Challenger,* Guion S. Bluford, Jr., became the first African American in space.

In 1986, however, a *Challenger* disaster stunned the world. On January 28 the space shuttle, after four postponed liftoffs, began what everyone expected would be a productive flight. Barely a minute after liftoff, the *Challenger* exploded, killing all seven crew members aboard. Among them was high-school teacher Christa McAuliffe, who was to have conducted lessons from space.

The Presidential panel that investigated the disaster reported that in order to meet the time schedule for the launch, both NASA and the company that had built the shuttle's solid-fuel rocket boosters had cut corners on safety precautions. As a result, NASA spent more than two and a half years modifying the shuttle's design and its launch procedures. On September 29, 1988, the United States returned to space with a successful four-day flight of the space shuttle *Discovery.*

Education. In 1983, a Presidential commission issued a report on education entitled *A Nation at Risk*. The report charged that American students lagged behind students from other industrialized nations; that American students' scores on standardized achievement tests were lower than such scores in 1957, when the Soviet Union launched *Sputnik*; that 23 million Americans were functionally illiterate, unable to follow an instruction manual or fill out a job application form; and that many seventeen-year-olds could not read a paragraph and draw an intelligent conclusion from it.

The report warned that if the quality of American education continued its downward trend, it would seriously threaten "our future as a nation and a people." The report's recommendations included more homework, longer school days and a longer school year, increased pay and merit raises for teachers, and emphasis on such basic subjects as English, math, science, social studies, and computer science.

Other critics of public education felt that these suggestions were just more of the same. What was needed, they said, was a restructuring of the educational system to include such things as Head Start programs, small classes in the lower grades, weekend tutorial programs for students at risk, and enough time for students to write weekly essays and for teachers to mark them, so that students could think and write more effectively. The goal, these critics said, should be for students to learn how to teach themselves to become critical thinkers instead of simply memorizing information.

Still other critics advocated a voucher system that would enable parents to send their children to a private school of their choice. This suggestion aroused considerable controversy, with opponents arguing that it would destroy American public education.

Whatever their ideas, however, most Americans agreed that the public schools were, at best, educating only half the students enrolled. True, this was a substantial improvement over the numbers educated in the past. However, when students had dropped out of school in previous years, they had entered a world with many good, low-skilled industrial jobs. Today, students who drop out of school stand little chance of earning a living in an economy that has become increasingly complex.

The Environment. In line with his general philosophy, President Reagan believed that environmental problems were not the concern of the federal government. Rather, he believed that they should be handled by individuals and business firms.

"I Knew There'd Be a Catch in It When They Said the Meek Would Inherit the Earth"

Picturing History In April 1990, people worldwide celebrated Earth Day and voiced their concerns about ecological destruction. Various environmental groups offered solutions to such problems as industrial and automobile pollution, waste disposal, poor water quality, overpopulation, urban and suburban sprawl, and the destruction of the rain forests and ozone layer.

John Fischetti. © with permission of the Chicago Sun-Times, Inc., 1989.

Anticipate the Lesson

Discuss with the class how Americans' feelings toward the Reagan administration might have influenced the outcome of the 1988 Presidential election. (Possible responses: many conservative Americans who were happy with the Reagan administration may have voted for George Bush, who had served as Vice-President, because they felt that he would carry on the ideals and goals of the Reagan

years; many liberal Americans decided to vote for a candidate they felt would change the course of the country—Michael Dukakis.)

State the Objective

Understand and analyze the issues that surrounded the election of 1988.

Answers

Main Ideas

1. Financing city government and services; the growth of slums, crime, and drug use.

2. By electing women to office, pushing for pay equity, adapting to the needs of working parents, and fighting for adequate child care.

3. African Americans—poverty, unemployment, and single parenthood among lower class. Hispanic Americans—unemployment among lower class, low pay among migrant workers, and opposition to bilingualism. American Indians—Reagan's cuts in funds for health and other services. Asian Americans—reluctance to get involved in politics and distrust of government.

4. AIDS is fatal, and doctors estimate that millions have been infected with the virus.

5. Space—space shuttle successfully used for military, scientific, and commercial purposes. Education—achievement test scores low; illiteracy and high-school drop-out rates high; and many public schools mediocre. Environment—federal funds were cut so programs to clean up the environment were greatly limited.

Critical Thinking

6. Possible answer: because the bilingual issue pits national unity against cultural identity, and it concerns discrimination and racism. • Because the issue involves so many people since Hispanic Americans are the fastest-growing minority in the U.S. **(synthesis)**

948

Accordingly, Reagan cut the budget for the **Environmental Protection Agency (EPA),** which was established in 1970 to fight pollution and to conserve natural resources. He also appointed opponents of government action to such positions as head of the EPA, head of the Bureau of Land Management, and Secretary of Energy. Hundreds of rules to prevent air and water pollution were weakened or eliminated. Pleas from Canada to reduce the acid rain that is endangering its agriculture, fisheries, and forests were ignored.

By 1986, however, public concern over the environment led the Reagan administration to modify its position regarding protection of the nation's natural resources. Certain officials—notably Interior Secretary James Watt, EPA Administrator Anne Gorsuch Burford, and EPA Assistant Administrator Rita Lavelle—resigned. Although the administration had originally opposed federal cleanup of toxic waste dumps, it agreed to support the 1980 bill known as Superfund, which aimed at eliminating dangerous waste.

SECTION 3 REVIEW

Key Terms and People

Explain the significance of: Jesse Jackson, Lauro Cavazos, AIDS, space shuttle, Environmental Protection Agency (EPA)

Main Ideas

1. What were some important urban problems in the 1980's?
2. What were some of the important ways in which Americans sought to bring about equal rights for women in the 1980's?
3. In the 1980's, what were the main problems facing African Americans? Hispanic Americans? American Indians? Asian Americans?
4. What makes acquired immune deficiency syndrome an important health problem for all Americans?
5. In the 1980's, how did the United States lead the way in space exploration? How did it lag behind other industrialized nations in the fields of education and environmental protection?

Critical Thinking

6. Why is federal support for bilingualism a controversial issue? Why, in the 1990's, is it an especially important issue?

SECTION 4

Bush Faces Many Difficulties

GLOSSARY TERMS: **thrifts, affirmative action**

The 1988 election saw a continuation of a government in which the executive and legislative branches were controlled by opposing parties. The Republican candidate won a solid victory as President while the Democrats expanded their majority in both houses of Congress.

The Candidates Stage a TV Campaign

On the Republican side, the main contenders for the Presidential nomination were Vice-President **George Bush,** Senator Robert Dole of Kansas, and the Reverend Pat Robertson of the Christian Broadcasting Network. On the Democratic side, the main contenders were Governor **Michael Dukakis** of Massachusetts and the Reverend Jesse Jackson. After a series of hard-fought primaries, Bush and Dukakis emerged as the winners. Bush chose J. Danforth Quayle, the junior senator from Indiana, as his running mate. Dukakis chose Lloyd Bentsen, the senior senator from Texas, as his Vice-Presidential candidate.

A Political Loyalist Versus an Immigrant Son. George Bush came from an upper-class family in Connecticut but moved to Texas, where he entered the oil business. He served two terms in the U.S. House of Representatives and later held various appointive positions, including chairman of the Republican party during Watergate, ambassador to the United Nations, chief of United States Liaison Office in China, and head of the CIA. He was elected Vice-President in 1980 and again in 1984.

Michael Dukakis, the son of middle-class Greek immigrants, was born in Massachusetts. He entered politics after graduating from Harvard Law School and eventually was elected governor of Massachusetts three times.

A Low-Level Campaign.   Both candidates were generally regarded as intelligent, reasonable, and decent. The campaign had none of these positive qualities.

Both parties tried to sell their candidate by using marketing techniques ordinarily used to sell com-

Divide the class into four groups. Assign one of the following questions to each group:

1. What did you learn about the American Presidential candidates and the American voter from the campaign and the election of 1988?
2. How did Bush's administration respond to major domestic problems in the late 1980's and the early 1990's?
3. How did the Supreme Court change direction in the late 1980's and early 1990's?
4. What world events in the late 1980's and early 1990's had or may have a significant effect on U.S. foreign policy? Explain those effects.

Then ask each group to read Section 4 and prepare an oral report that responds to their questions. After each group reports, ask the class to brainstorm a list of twenty of the most significant questions they will face as citizens and voters in the 1990's. Then have them rank the questions in order of importance. Encourage them to discuss what they have learned about themselves—their interests, values, goals, and concerns—from this activity.

mercial products. The ads employed vivid images; stressed a single, simple theme; and were run on television over and over and over.

One problem was that many of the ads, especially a series of Republican "attack ads," were extremely negative. For example, they accused Dukakis of polluting Boston Harbor. They questioned his patriotism. They implied that he was against religion because he did not approve of prayer in the public schools.

Another problem was that the ads did not present issues in depth. For example, the most notorious ad featured Willie Horton, a prisoner who committed a rape while on weekend furlough from a Massachusetts jail. The ad portrayed Dukakis as being "soft" on crime. The ad did not say that the furlough program had actually been developed under a Republican governor and that forty of the states had similar programs. Some felt the ad was racist, since Horton was an African American.

Other criticisms of the 1988 Presidential campaign focused on poll predictions and projected election results. Many people resented the impression polls gave that the election was really over a month before election day. Other people disapproved of projected election results being aired on television while the voting booths were still open in California and other western states.

A Bush Victory. The final results gave Bush more than 53 percent of the popular vote and 426 electoral votes. Slightly over 50 percent of the eligible voters went to the polls. This was the lowest voter turnout in sixty-four years.

There were, of course, basic reasons for Bush's victory. A majority of the American people were economically comfortable. They liked Bush's prom-

Presidential Election, 1988

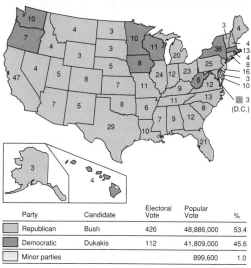

Party	Candidate	Electoral Vote	Popular Vote	%
Republican	Bush	426	48,886,000	53.4
Democratic	Dukakis	112	41,809,000	45.6
Minor parties			899,600	1.0

538 Total Electoral Vote

ise of "no new taxes." Bush had experience in foreign relations; Dukakis did not. The Republicans played to their strength. They stressed the conservative ideas of their most zealous supporters, the Moral Majority. The Democrats, anxious to play down the "liberal" label, more or less ignored issues that would have energized their traditional constituencies of labor, African Americans, and the poor.

In claiming his victory, Bush declared that he planned to be President of all the people, including those who had not voted for him. "When I said I wanted a kinder and gentler nation, I meant it," the President-elect asserted.

For Discussion

Only slightly more than 50 percent of eligible voters went to the polls in the 1988 Presidential election. What are some reasons people might have for not voting in an election? (Possible responses: because they do not like any of the candidates; because they do not understand the issues; because they do not want to take time from their busy schedules to go to a polling place; because they do not feel their vote will matter.) How might voter turnout be improved? (Possible responses: voter turnout will improve when people become involved in the issues and feel that politicians are sensitive to their constituencies; some people will never vote simply because they do not care.)

Picturing History Candidates in the 1988 Presidential primary elections were (left to right) George Bush, Robert Dole, Michael Dukakis, and Jesse Jackson.

Bush Struggles with Domestic Problems

From the start of his Presidency, Bush was plagued by a government scandal that had been developing over the previous eight years. He presented programs to deal with education and drugs, but his efforts were hampered by an ever-increasing federal deficit. The Cold War ended, but military victory in the Persian Gulf failed to bring stability to the Middle East.

The Savings and Loan Industry. The policy of government insurance of deposits in savings and loan institutions began in 1933. Its goal was to encourage home ownership. The savings and loan institutions provided long-term fixed-rate mortgages that were financed by short-term savings deposits. In exchange for insuring the safety of the deposits, Congress established a ceiling on the interest rates the **thrifts,** or savings and loan institutions, could charge.

All went well until the 1970's, when inflation reared its head. People could now get a much higher return for their money in stocks and Treasury securities than they could from thrifts. So they withdrew their savings, leaving the thrifts without money to invest. Even when the interest-rate ceiling was removed, thrifts still lost money because they had to pay a higher interest on new deposits than they were getting from their existing mortgages.

Under the Reagan administration, the savings and loan industry was deregulated. Capital requirements were lowered. Thrifts were allowed to invest in commercial real estate, such as shopping malls, golf courses, and office buildings. Even if they made risky investments—and hundreds of them did, either from greed or from lack of experience—the government stood ready to pay individual investors up to $100,000 in savings insurance.

Several regulatory employees tried to call attention to the deteriorating situation. They were ignored, however, both by financial officials in the Reagan administration and by members of Congress who had received campaign contributions from thrift owners.

By 1989, however, it was clear that the industry was in serious trouble. So in August of that year, Congress passed a law to bail it out. The law called for thrift owners to put up more of their own money in order to receive deposit insurance, and for 70 percent of their investments to go toward housing.

THE S+L BAILOUT

Picturing History This cartoon comments on the severity of the Savings and Loan crisis.

By the end of the year, hundreds of insolvent thrifts had gone out of business, leaving the industry smaller but in better financial shape. However, the government now had some $300 billion worth of foreclosed property on its hands. Much of the property was located in the Southwest, which had been suffering a recession caused by falling oil prices. As a result, by the end of 1992 the government had recovered only 63 cents on the dollar for the property it was able to sell. About $70 billion worth of real estate remained unsold.

Education. In his election campaign, Bush had pledged to serve as "the education President." In September 1989, he called a meeting of the nation's governors to discuss education. The President laid out a series of goals, including eliminating illiteracy, making schools safe and drug-free, raising the high school graduation rate to 90 percent from about 75 percent, and holding teachers accountable for their performance. The governors applauded the goals but pointed out that federal expenditures for education were 30 percent lower in 1989 than they had been in 1980.

In April 1991, President Bush announced a bold new education initiative, "America 2000." He argued that "choice" was the salvation of American schools and recommended allowing parents to use public funds to send their children to schools of their choice—public, private, or religious. Bush also proposed the construction of 535 new schools that would serve as models of curriculum innovation. He also urged national achievement tests.

Once again, people applauded the President's goals, but many pointed out that such extensive reforms required strong financial support. For example, the suggested voucher of $1,000 a year was not enough to enable poor, or even most middle-income, families to choose private schools. Critics of the national test proposal argued that there was no provision for helping students who failed the tests. Others said that using public money for religious schools violated the First Amendment.

Drugs. Another area in which President Bush called for action was "[our] gravest domestic threat," namely, drugs. The President urged "a war on drugs"—by which he meant crack cocaine and similar substances. The war would emphasize law enforcement: stopping drugs at the nation's borders, jailing drug-using Americans for long terms, and establishing a death penalty for drug dealers. The war would also involve persuading or forcing farmers in Latin America and Asian nations to stop growing coca and opium plants.

Critics of the Bush drug program pointed out that most of the President's tactics had been used

for the past twenty years without success. Doctors in particular argued that since drug addiction is a disease, the only effective approach is to reduce the demand for drugs through education and treatment.

The Environment. In March 1989, the oil tanker *Exxon Valdez* ran aground in Prince William Sound along the coast of Alaska, dumping about 11 million gallons of crude oil into the sea. Within days, some eighteen hundred miles of coastline were fouled with thick black oil that coated rocks and beaches. At least 10 percent of the area's birds, sea otters, and other wildlife were killed, and commercial fisheries estimated that they would lose at least 50 percent of the season's catch.

The captain of the *Exxon Valdez* was found guilty of negligence, and attempts were made to clean up the spill. Four years later, however, scientists found that pools of oil buried in coves were still poisoning shellfish, otters, and ducks, while several species of birds were failing to reproduce.

Between 1989 and 1994, Exxon spent about $2.1 billion in efforts to clean up Prince William Sound. In the meantime, some 34,000 fishermen and other Alaskans sued the company for damages, claiming that the oil spill had ruined their livelihoods.

The trial began in May of 1994. In June a Federal jury decided that Exxon had been reckless in allowing a captain with a history of alcohol abuse to command the *Exxon Valdez*. In August the

Picturing History United States Customs boats and police dogs patrol the nation's borders and airports to reduce the flood of drugs entering the country.

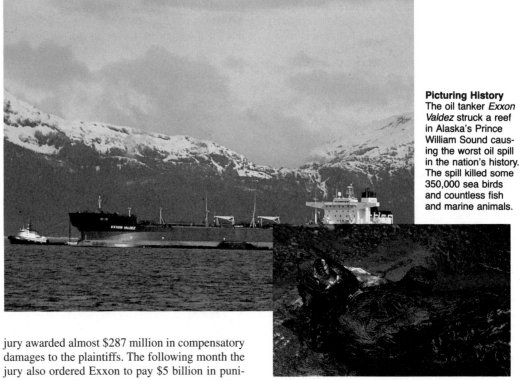

Picturing History The oil tanker *Exxon Valdez* struck a reef in Alaska's Prince William Sound causing the worst oil spill in the nation's history. The spill killed some 350,000 sea birds and countless fish and marine animals.

jury awarded almost $287 million in compensatory damages to the plaintiffs. The following month the jury also ordered Exxon to pay $5 billion in punitive damages, the largest award ever in a pollution case. Exxon said it would appeal the award.

On the preventive side, Congress passed a law requiring new oil tankers to be built with double hulls. Many environmentalists also urged that oil be transported by pipeline rather than tanker.

Urban Violence In early March 1991, television viewers throughout the nation saw repeated broadcasts of a privately made videotape showing four white Los Angeles police officers beating a black man as he lay on the ground. On April 29, 1992, an all-white jury acquitted the officers—and a bloody riot promptly erupted in South-Central Los Angeles. Rodney King, the African American who had been beaten, made a plea for peace, asking "Can we all get along?" But the riot continued for five days, with a final toll of 51 people dead, about 2,400 injured, almost 12,000 arrests, and some $1 billion in property damage.

Many people viewed the riot as an expression of black rage against a miscarriage of justice. But there were other factors, some of them specific to Los Angeles. For example, the city's police department was slow to react to the riot and did not fol-

low standard procedures to contain the outbreak. Also, there was considerable hostility between African Americans and the Korean Americans who owned most of South-Central's grocery, liquor, and dry-cleaning stores. Many Korean businesses were looted and burned in the riot, while most black and Hispanic businesses remained untouched.

Broader economic and sociological factors as well contributed to the intensity of the riot. Since 1981, direct federal spending on cities had dropped by more than 60 percent. As public services worsened, more middle class people fled to the suburbs, leaving behind an ever-denser mass of poor and unemployed people. At the same time, the number of traditional unskilled and semiskilled jobs—gardeners, janitors, laborers, maids, waiters, and the like—fell sharply, while the number of immigrants who often filled such jobs increased. As one sociologist asserted, "This wasn't a race riot. It was a class riot."

In addition, lawlessness in general had increased in the United States. From 1985 to 1989, the national violent crime rate rose 20 percent. As one inhabitant of South-Central Los Angeles put it,

Assign Independent Practice

Ask students to write two paragraphs on the part that television played in the 1988 campaign. The paragraphs should address the following questions. Was the overall effect of the campaign positive or negative? To what extent did the campaign focus on the facts and issues? (Paragraphs might include: negative—television ads focused on emotional issues such as crime, school prayer, pollution; it did not present issues in depth; it did not focus on the candidates' qualifications or what they

intended to achieve, but it tended to draw attention to the opponent's weaknesses.)

"Some people say this [looting] is because of Rodney King. . . . A lot of people probably never even heard of Rodney King. They're doing it because it's like Christmas in the springtime."

The Los Angeles riots did not mark the end of the Rodney King case. The four police officers, having been acquitted of assault charges in a state court, were then tried in a federal court on the grounds of having violated King's civil rights. On April 17, 1993, two of the officers were convicted and two were found innocent.

Later that year, another racially charged trial took place in Los Angeles when two African Americans were tried for having dragged a white man, Reginald Denny, out of his truck during the riots and beaten him savagely. The two were acquitted of attempted murder but convicted on lesser charges of assault and mayhem.

The verdicts in these cases drew mixed reactions across the nation. Some people, especially in Los Angeles, were simply glad the various trials were over. Many whites considered the results "a tremendous miscarriage of justice," while many blacks felt the decisions were "a debt that had to be repaid." But both whites and blacks agreed that the verdicts reflected the fear of riots as much as the evidence presented in court.

The Supreme Court Changes Course

By the time the Supreme Court ended its term in July 1989, it was clear that President Reagan's desire for a conservative court had been achieved. In such areas as abortion and race discrimination, the Court handed down decisions that, as one commentator put it, "transformed settled fights into running battles." The decisions were made by a 5 to 4 vote, and it was Justice Anthony M. Kennedy, the last justice appointed by Reagan, who made the difference.

In 1990 Justice William Brennan retired, and President Bush nominated David H. Souter to the Supreme Court. In several early decisions handed down in 1991, Justice Souter also placed himself in the conservative camp, though by 1993 he was considered a centrist. Then, later that year, Justice Thurgood Marshall announced his retirement from the Court, and the conservative tide quickened with Bush's appointment of Clarence Thomas.

Thomas's nomination provoked an even more bitter debate than the one over Robert Bork. Anita Hill, a black law professor at the University of Oklahoma, testified that Thomas, also an African

Picturing History Supreme Court nominee Clarence Thomas answers charges of sexual harassment in televised Senate hearings

American, had sexually harassed her when she worked for him in the early 1980's. The all-male Senate Judiciary Committee did not fully investigate Hill's accusations at first, doing so only after the story became public. The committee's hearings, which were widely seen on television, dismayed many people. Senators on both sides of the nomination tried to discredit witnesses on the other side. Hill was accused, among other things, of fantasizing and having a martyr complex. Thomas claimed he was the victim of "a high-tech lynching." The final vote of 52 to 48 was the closest vote for a Supreme Court justice in 103 years.

While the hearings were going on, a majority of Americans believed Thomas and thought that he should be confirmed. However, by late 1992, some polls showed that more people now believed Anita Hill than believed Thomas. The number of reported sexual harassment cases skyrocketed. One member of the Senate Judiciary Committee failed to win reelection, and a record number of women were elected to Congress. The U.S. Senate now had six instead of two female members, while the House of Representatives doubled its female membership, from 24 to 48. Although the social-political climate changed after the Thomas hearings, his confirmation assured a conservative majority within the Supreme Court.

Abortion. In July 1989, the Supreme Court handed down a decision in *Webster* v. *Reproductive Health Service.* Although the decision did not overturn *Roe* v. *Wade,* it said that states had the right to impose new restrictions on abortion. In fact, several justices invited states to do exactly that. Over the next few years, some legislatures rejected the invitation, while others accepted it. As a result, restrictions on abortions varied from state to state.

In May 1991, the Supreme Court handed down another controversial decision in *Rust* v. *Sullivan.* The case involved abortion counseling. In 1970 the federal government had begun funding about four thousand family health clinics throughout the country. These clinics cared for more than 4 million women a year. Almost all the clients were low-income, and about one-third were teenagers. For eighteen years, these clinics provided information about abortions but did not perform them. In 1988 the Reagan administration issued rules prohibiting the clinics from supplying such information. If a woman asked about abortion, the clinic's doctors and other employees were forbidden to answer her questions, even if the pregnancy threatened her health. *Rust* v. *Sullivan* upheld the new rules.

Abortion opponents applauded the decision. Abortion-rights supporters argued that it created two levels of health care, one for rich women and one for poor women. Many doctors felt the decision violated professional ethics by telling them how to practice medicine. Other critics claimed it violated the constitutional right of free speech. Although Congress passed a bill negating the effects of *Rust* v. *Sullivan,* President Bush vetoed the bill, and there were not enough votes to override the veto.

Race Discrimination. During the term that ended in July 1989, the Supreme Court also handed down a series of decisions that reversed its course on civil rights, and in some people's estimation returned the nation to where it had been twenty-five years earlier, before passage of the Civil Rights Act of 1964. In general, the decisions made it much harder for minorities—and also women—to sue in job discrimination cases. In particular, *Richmond* v. *J. A. Croson Company* reversed the Court's earlier approval of **affirmative action,** the policy that sets goals and timetables for the hiring of minorities and women. Other Court decisions outlawed contracts specifically targeted for minority enterprises.

In 1990 Congress passed a new Civil Rights Act that legalized some of the civil rights policies that had been prohibited by the Court. President Bush vetoed it claiming that it would introduce a quota

system. In 1991 a similar bill was introduced and this time the President signed the bill into law.

The United States Invades Panama

On December 20, 1989, President Bush sent about twenty-six thousand American soldiers and marines into Panama. Their aim was to overthrow and capture the country's leader, General Manuel Antonio Noriega. Noriega had been receiving money from the CIA most of the time since 1960. However, he was apparently involved in the international drug trade and had been indicted by a Miami grand jury. Noriega surrendered to the United States on January 3, 1990, and was flown to Miami to stand trial. He was succeeded by Guillermo Endara, who had been elected President of Panama in 1989 but had been prevented by Noriega from assuming office.

Reactions to the invasion were mixed. Americans in general, as well as most Panamanians, were very pleased. On the other hand, many Latin American governments condemned the action as another example of "Yankee imperialism."

In April 1992, Noriega was convicted and sentenced to 40 years in prison. In the meantime, however, drug traffic through Panama has increased.

The Communist World Begins to Collapse

America's foreign policy after the end of World War II was based mostly on fear of communism. Presidents from Truman to Reagan portrayed the Soviet Union as a powerful, well-armed nation determined to spread its economic and political system everywhere. To thwart potential Soviet aggression, the United States sent Marshall Plan aid to Europe, helped organize NATO, fought in Korea and Vietnam, and supported anticommunist governments in Latin America, Africa, the Middle East, and Asia. In the course of doing so, the United States built up its annual military budget to about $300 billion, or 25 percent of federal spending. At the same time, the United States lost overseas and even some domestic markets to West Germany and Japan, neither of which was burdened by large military expenditures, and both of which invested government money in industrial development.

Beginning in 1988 and continuing through the early 1990's, however, the situation changed drastically. Communism collapsed in the Soviet Union and Eastern Europe, resulting in a formal end to the Cold War. In China, a movement toward democracy was violently suppressed, but the government took some steps toward a free market economy.

The Soviet Union. When Mikhail Gorbachev inaugurated his policy of *glasnost,* he probably did not realize what it would lead to. He began by trying to reform an economic system ruined by, among other factors, decades of military spending to support the arms race. He replaced central planning and public ownership of land and factories with private ownership and decisions at the local level about production, working conditions, and prices. Most government censorship ended, and free elections were held.

But the elections increased political tensions within the Soviet Union. For example, in the Federation of Russia, newly elected President Boris Yeltsin frequently criticized Gorbachev for not moving fast enough toward reform. On the other hand, government bureaucrats, anxious to keep their privileged position, criticized Gorbachev for going too far.

The elections also led to a dramatic increase in nationalism on the part of the Soviet Union's non-Russian republics. By late 1990 all had declared that local laws took priority over those of the central government.

Then, in the summer of 1991, a new Russian Revolution took place. On August 19 Communist hardliners attempted a coup. They forced Gorbachev out of office and declared a state of emergency. Yeltsin, climbing atop an armored truck, immediately called for a general strike in protest. Tens of thousands of Soviet citizens poured into the streets of the large cities. Three days later, the coup was over and Gorbachev was back. On August 24 he resigned as head of the Communist party and banned it from any further role in government.

The pressure for complete change, however, was overwhelming. By December 16 all 14 non-Russian republics had declared their independence, and on December 25 Gorbachev resigned as President. After 74 years the Soviet Union was no more. In its place was a loose federation called the Commonwealth of Independent States (CIS), with Yeltsin as its informal head. Estonia, Latvia, and Lithuania were once again independent nations.

In February 1992, Bush and Yeltsin issued a formal statement declaring an end to the cold war and proclaiming a new era of "friendship and partnership." In January 1993, the two leaders signed a treaty, popularly known as START II, that would cut both nations' nuclear arsenals by about 75 percent.

Political freedom, however, has not led to economic well-being in the former Soviet Union. Its

Picturing History
Poland's Solidarity leader Lech Walesa (above) represented the struggle for democracy in Eastern Europe when he addressed Congress in 1989. A year later the Polish people elected him as their president. At left, Berliners tear down the wall that had divided their city and their people since 1961.

Picturing History In 1989, demonstrations for a democratic reform also flared briefly in China. In Beijing's Tiananmen Square Chinese students constructed a version of the Statue of Liberty to symbolize their struggle for democracy. The Chinese government responded with brutal force and killed or jailed hundreds of demonstrators.

factories and equipment turned out to be extremely old-fashioned and inefficient. Managers were not used to making decisions on their own. Workers were not used to being laid off if there was no work. Goods were in short supply, and inflation kept rising. It will be years before the citizens of the CIS enjoy a decent standard of living.

Eastern Europe. In 1988 Gorbachev decided to reduce the number of Soviet troops in Eastern Europe and to allow non-Communist parties to organize in the satellite nations. A year later, he warned the Communist leaders of Eastern European nations that the Soviet Union would not help them if they used force to crack down on the opposition. They would be better advised, Gorbachev said, to move toward democracy.

By 1991 that is exactly what happened. On November 9, 1989—after twenty-eight years— East Germany opened the Berlin Wall to unrestricted traffic with West Germany. Within a few weeks, souvenir hunters had practically demolished the Wall. In early 1990, East Germany held its first free elections. Soon after, it formed a currency union with West Germany. On October 3, 1990, the two German nations become one.

Other Eastern European nations also made democratic reforms. For example, Polish voters chose a government headed by democratic trade unionists. The Romanians overthrew their communist ruler. Czechoslovakia split into two nations, each of which held free elections. However, as in the former Soviet Union, economic reforms ran

into trouble. One result was an influx of hundreds of thousands of people into Germany, where the economy was better. Unfortunately, the influx angered right and neo-Nazi groups, and in 1992 they carried out more than 2,000 attacks against non-Germans.

The United States Fights in the Persian Gulf

While communism lost ground in Europe, tensions in another part of the world erupted into America's first major war since Vietnam. The war took place in the **Persian Gulf** region of the Middle East and was fought primarily over oil.

Background. Saddam Hussein became dictator of Iraq in 1973. Although Iraq had large oil reserves, it coveted those of its neighbors. Hussein also wanted Iraq to become the political powerhouse of the Middle East.

In 1980 Iraq attacked Iran. Until 1978 the United States had supported Iran as a buffer against the Soviet Union. This relationship changed, however, when the Ayatollah Khomeini's followers overthrew the Shah of Iran and seized American hostages. Accordingly, the United States decided to follow the policy of "The enemy of my enemy is my friend." It supported Iraq in its war with Iran, selling it weapons and farm goods.

The Iraq-Iran war ended in 1988 with a settlement that was generally favorable to Iraq. However, Hussein found himself with enormous war debts to pay. Because he did not trust OPEC to keep oil prices high enough to meet his needs, he looked for another solution. Twice before, in 1961 and again in 1973, Iraq had claimed that Kuwait belonged to Iraq. Now Iraq decided to claim Kuwait for the third time.

On August 2, 1990, Iraqi troops invaded a helpless Kuwait. Within a few days, the Kuwaiti government and about two-thirds of its citizens had fled the country. The Iraqis proceeded to loot Kuwait and to move their tanks to the border of Saudi Arabia. If Iraq conquered Saudi Arabia as well as Kuwait, it would control one half of the world's known oil reserves.

The American Response. President Bush responded to Iraq's actions in several ways. He rushed American troops into Saudi Arabia. He convinced the United Nations Security Council to approve a trade embargo against Iraq and to authorize "all

Student Assignment/Homework

Have students read Section 5, "Clinton Leads the Nation Toward a New Century," and answer the Section 5 Review questions on paper.

necessary means" to liberate Kuwait if Iraq did not withdraw by January 15, 1991. He also asked for and received authority from Congress to wage war against Iraq.

The January 15 deadline passed without Hussein's backing down. On January 16, the United States and its allies launched Operation Desert Storm with a massive air assault against Iraq. February 23 saw the start of the ground offensive. On February 28, President Bush announced a cease-fire. Desert Storm was over after forty-three days.

Gains and Losses. The Gulf War gave the United States a tremendous psychological boost. After the debacle in Vietnam, to many Americans it was very gratifying to win a war swiftly and with fewer than 400 allied casualties. Millions of Americans turned out for the victory parades that greeted the returning soldiers.

In contrast, Iraq suffered about 100,000 casualties. In addition, most of its water, sewage, and power lines were destroyed. As a result, hundreds of thousands of Iraqi civilians, especially children under five, died in 1991 and 1992 from such diseases as cholera, typhoid, and enteritis.

Regionally, Iraq no longer posed a military threat to its neighbors. Nor could it inflate world oil prices. However, Saddam Hussein remained in power. He even crushed two uprisings against his rule, one by Shiite Muslims, the other by nationalistic Kurds. As a result of the failure of their uprisings, about 2 million Kurds and 700,000 Shiite Muslims fled Iraq. Many later returned, but as of 1993 about half remained in Iran and Turkey. In addition, when the United Nations sent inspectors to investigate Iraq's atom bomb program, Saddam Hussein managed to more or less outwit them.

In October 1994, Iraqi troops once again began massing at Kuwait's border, and some 8,000 American troops were rushed to Kuwait. Saddam's forces then pulled back from the border, and the Americans planned to withdraw from Kuwait by the end of the year.

SECTION 4 REVIEW

Key Terms and People

Explain the significance of: George Bush, Michael Dukakis, thrifts, affirmative action, Persian Gulf

Main Ideas

1. Briefly describe the television campaign conducted by Bush and Dukakis in 1988.
2. What were the main reasons for Bush's victory in the 1988 Presidential campaign?
3. What major problems did the Bush administration face?

Critical Thinking

4. How will changes occurring in Europe lead to a more interdependent world?

Picturing History
February, 1991. Against a backdrop of blazing oil wells, torched by fleeing Iraqi troops, U.S. soldiers race toward Kuwait City in the final throes of Operation Desert Storm.

Anticipate the Lesson

Have students review their paragraphs on the impact of television in the 1988 presidential campaign (**Assign Independent Practice,** p. 953). Remind them that some analysts felt television helped Bush win the election. Then ask them to compare that impact with the role that television played in the 1992 election as they read. (Most students will note that, unlike in the 1988 election, television actually worked against Bush in the 1992 campaign, giving newcomer Bill Clinton presidential stature through the debates and allowing independent Ross Perot to get his proposals out to large numbers of people sympathetic to radical change.)

State the Objective

Understand the factors that led to the defeat of George Bush in 1992 and identify the problems that posed the greatest challenge to new President Bill Clinton.

Clinton Leads the Nation Toward a New Century

GLOSSARY TERMS: electronic town hall, HMO

Shortly after the conclusion of Operation Desert Storm in 1991, a poll found President Bush's approval rating at 91 percent, and there seemed no doubt that he would easily win a second term. In fact, a number of leading Democrats announced that they would not even run against him. But when the election was held in 1992, Bush lost.

"The Politics of Frustration"

In trying to explain Bush's defeat, political analysts came up with a variety of reasons. The main factor, most of them agreed, was what might be described as a loss of faith in the American Dream. Economically and politically, the country seemed to be on the wrong track.

A Troubled Economy. Family income dropped 4.4 percent in the four years that Bush held office. In many instances, both husband and wife had to go to work in order to support the family. By 1992 about one out of seven Americans was living in poverty. At the same time, the difference between rich and poor was the highest it had been since the 1920's, with the richest 1 percent of families worth more than the bottom 90 percent.

Although the 1992 unemployment rate of 7.4 percent was not high from an historical point of view, it was the highest rate since 1984, and people were remaining out of work longer. And even when they found new jobs, these often paid less than their old ones. Millions of high-paying manufacturing and middle-management jobs were gone for good as a result of the combination of the movement of factories to countries with lower wage scales and the use of new technology.

In addition, the budget deficit was running at nearly $300 billion a year, while the national debt had doubled from more than $2 trillion in 1987 to more than $4 trillion in 1992. That was about $16,300 for each person in the United States.

Americans had always looked forward to a better life—if not for their themselves, then certainly for their children. Now it seemed that for many, upward mobility was no longer possible.

Political Alienation. On the political front, it was evident that millions of Americans had lost confidence in their government. Presidents had lied to them about Vietnam, Watergate, and probably Iran-contra. Many members of Congress seemingly ignored the needs of citizens and paid attention only to the special interests that contributed money to their election campaigns. And the campaigns themselves had degenerated mostly into "mudslinging" theatrics instead of a discussion of issues.

A Billionaire Populist. In the past, similar conditions in the United States had resulted in populist movements on both the left and the right. For example, during the 1890's, in the midst of farm foreclosures and widespread unemployment, the Populist party ran its own candidate for President and later merged with Democrats to nominate William Jennings Bryan. (See pages 470–474). Likewise, during the Great Depression of the 1930's, Senator Huey Long, among others, advocated extreme solutions to the nation's problems. (See pages 688–689.)

The 1992 Presidential campaign saw the rise of a new populist, **H. Ross Perot.** A billionaire businessman from Texas, Perot declared his independent candidacy in February, withdrew for personal reasons in July, and jumped back into the race on October 1.

During his campaign, Perot took some positions that would have changed our system of government radically. For example, he advocated stripping Congress of the right to levy taxes and substituting an **electronic town hall** in which an issue would be discussed on television for one hour and viewers would record their opinions on computer cards. He also seemed to favor government by orders from the President rather than our present system of separation of powers and checks and balances.

In one respect, however, Perot struck a nerve. He stressed that the country must face up to its budget deficit problem. As it turned out, this same stance was adopted by the winner of the race: Governor **Bill** (William Jefferson) **Clinton** of Arkansas.

An Agent for Change

Clinton was born in 1946 in Hope, Arkansas. His interest in politics was whetted as a delegate to a 1963 citizenship training program for youth in Washington, when he shook hands with President

Divide the class into several groups to work on political platforms—statements of principles—that could challenge the policies followed by the Bush administration leading up to the next election. Have students review Section 4 for the issues that faced Bush. Then have them identify what they feel were the greatest unsolved problems of the United States at the end of Bush's first term. Each group should nominate one person as a candidate to run against Bush's record and present realistic and workable solutions to these unresolved problems. Have each candidate submit a copy of his or her platform to you, and then have them present these platforms to the class. A consensus on the mood of the country and the desire for change in 1992 should be apparent from the repetition of themes and issues that will undoubtedly emerge from the readings of the platforms.

Kennedy at the White House. He studied at Georgetown University and later at Yale Law School where he met Hillary Rodham, whom he married in 1975. After returning to Arkansas, he became the nation's youngest governor in 1978. He was defeated in 1980, bounced back to win again in 1982, and then won re-election three more times.

While governor of Arkansas, Clinton tried to move the Democratic party away from what he considered far-left orthodoxy toward a more mainstream position. Clinton also favored a national government that would be more active in meeting people's needs and bringing about social changes.

A Tough Campaign. Both George Bush and Bill Clinton campaigned hard to win their primaries. The President was challenged from the right by TV commentator and former Reagan White House official Patrick J. Buchanan, while Clinton defeated five rivals to win the Democratic nomination.

Once nominated, both candidates faced problems. Bush, in attempting to placate the Religious Right, seriously antagonized moderates within his party. Later, his re-election efforts were so disorganized that James Baker resigned as his Secretary of State to become his campaign manager. Clinton, for his part, was severely criticized for avoiding the draft during the Vietnam War, which he had opposed.

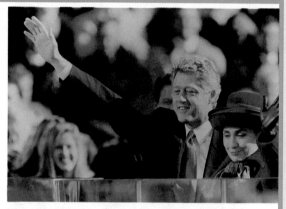

Picturing History After taking the oath of office on January 20, 1993, President Bill Clinton and First Lady Hillary Rodham Clinton greet well-wishers from the podium at the Capitol in Washington, D.C.

Throughout the campaign, the candidates appealed to voters through unconventional forums such as bus tours to various communities and TV talk shows. More conventional forums included the three Presidential debates.

About 55 percent of the eligible voters went to the polls, an increase of nearly 4 percent over the 1988 election and a reversal of a disturbing downward trend. The 1992 percentage was the highest turnout since 1972 but was far below the record 62.8 percent in 1960 when Kennedy beat Nixon. However, the 104 million people who voted was an all-time high. Though receiving less than half of the popular vote, Clinton won by over 200 electoral votes to become the nation's third youngest president after Theodore Roosevelt and Kennedy.

Challenges on the Domestic Front

President Clinton's first two years in office saw a number of legislative victories, as well as a major defeat on the issue of health-care reform.

Early Accomplishments. Soon after the start of his administration, Clinton signed a Family Leave Act, previously vetoed by Bush, that guaranteed workers up to 12 weeks of unpaid leave for medical emergencies and births. He issued an order overturning a ban on abortion counseling at federally funded clinics, and appointed several women to cabinet posts, including that of Attorney General. A National Service Corps, similar to Kennedy's Peace Corps, was set up. People who agreed to perform

Presidential Election, 1992

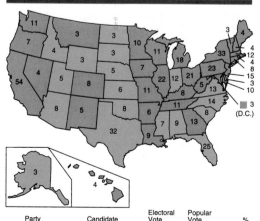

Party	Candidate	Electoral Vote	Popular Vote	%
Republican	Bush	168	38,167,416	38
Democratic	Clinton	370	43,728,375	43
Independent	Perot		19,237,247	19

538 Total Electoral Vote

Check for Understanding

Call on individual students to read their answers to the Section 5 Review questions.

960

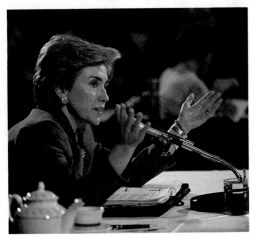

Picturing History Hillary Rodham Clinton testifies in favor of health-care reform before the Senate Committee on Labor and Human Resources.

community service before, during, or after college or trade school were to receive a living allowance and up to $9,450 in education grants.

Several additional steps were taken in the area of education. Congress approved funds to help improve teaching skills and reduce crime in the schools. It also passed the Goals 2000: Educate America Act. Many of the goals listed in the act had been embraced in 1989 and 1991 by President Bush and the nation's governors. Although the goals were voluntary, the act meant that for the first time since America's public schools were started in Massachusetts some 350 years ago, the United States would have a national framework for what students should learn.

The anti-crime front saw the passage of two bills that had been wending their way through Congress for several years. In 1993 the Brady law established a five-day waiting period for the purchase of handguns. And in 1994 Clinton signed into law a $30 billion Violent Crime Control and Law Enforcement Act. Opinions as to the effectiveness of this act varied. While cities and towns were to receive funds to hire 100,000 police officers over the next six years, the additional police would be spread so thin that they might not make much difference. The new law banned the manufacture and sale of 19 different kinds of military assault weapons, but it did nothing to eliminate the thousands of assault weapons Americans already owned. Still, people felt that the act symbolized

the determination of the federal government to go on the offensive against crime.

The new administration also went on the offensive against the budget deficit. The Clinton budget, which squeaked through Congress by only two votes in the House of Representatives and one vote in the Senate, raised the tax rate on corporations and on upper-income individuals, especially those making more than $200,000 a year. This reversed the Reagan policy and made the tax system more progressive. The Clinton budget also raised the earned-income tax credit for families making less than $30,000 a year. Antipoverty and welfare reform groups praised the action as a way of rewarding work. Since the cold war was over, military spending was cut. So, too, were farm subsidies and the number of government employees.

Health Care Reform. Economists estimated that Clinton's fiscal plan would result in a deficit reduction of almost $500 billion over five years. However, at that point the deficit would again start to rise unless the government was able to control the explosive growth of Medicare, Medicaid, and the military medical system, which subsidize health care for retirees, the poor, and the armed forces. This fiscal problem, combined with Clinton's promise to provide coverage for the estimated 37 million Americans who lack health insurance, led to a bold attempt to reform health care—and to the administration's worst legislative defeat.

Shortly after he assumed office, the new President set up a task force, chaired by **Hillary Rodham Clinton,** to come up with a proposal for health-care reform. The task force rejected a national health insurance system similar to that of Canada. Instead, it proposed a bill under which Americans would form groups to purchase insurance coverage. Employers would pay 80% of their employees' premiums, while the government would guarantee coverage for people who were unemployed.

The bill immediately ran into opposition from those who preferred relying on market forces to keep health care spending under control. They favored some form of managed health care, under which Americans would join **HMO's,** or health maintenance organizations, that would direct patients to doctors and hospitals that accepted lower fees and adopted cost-saving rules.

Ask students to speculate how Bush could go from a successful military operation against Iraq and a 91 percent approval rating to a defeat in an election less than two years later. To get them started thinking, have them review the ingredients of the Bush election victory of 1988 on page 949 and note the changed conditions in 1992. (Possible response: A dramatic military strike could only momentarily divert people's attention from the discontent they felt in the early 1990's. Large numbers of Americans were no longer economically comfortable; many jobs were irreplaceably lost. Experience in foreign affairs no longer seemed vital in a post-Cold War world. The country was no longer as broadly conservative as it was in 1988. Finally, there was a reassessment of the "victory" itself: it seemed overrated; Hussein remained in power and continued to taunt the U.S.)

Economists pointed out that this would not work if there were universal coverage. At present, if an HMO negotiates a lower group rate with a hospital, the hospital does not absorb the revenue loss. It simply charges fee-for-service patients higher rates. If everyone were covered, there would be no one left to absorb the costs. On the other hand, it was clear that many smaller businesses could not afford to buy insurance for their employees. Some economists argued that managed care could work if there were more emphasis on preventive care and fewer unnecessary medical tests caused by fear of malpractice suits. Other economists asserted that no matter what system was in place, national health spending would keep on rising, partly because of expensive new technology and partly because the American population was both growing and aging.

After months of extensive lobbying by the insurance industry, vitriolic partisan debate, and futile attempts to reach a compromise, the administration gave up on health-care reform for the time being. Most commentators agreed that Clinton had tried to do too much too quickly without fully considering administrative costs. However, inasmuch as the nation's governors had called unanimously for some kind of reform, the issue was not dead. What seemed likely to pass Congress in the future were modest improvements and not systemic reform in health care.

Governmental Gridlock. Clinton's defeat on health care was followed by defeats in other areas. Fillibusters and other delaying tactics by Republicans halted almost all environmental legislation. An attempt to speed the cleanup of toxic wastes was stopped in its tracks. So were attempts to collect fees and royalties from businesses using federal land, such as ranchers and mining companies.

Governmental gridlock also showed itself in the defeat of lobbying reform. In the past, Republicans had favored tighter regulation of lobbyists. Now, they blocked a bill that would have prohibited lawmakers from accepting gifts, meals, entertainment, or travel from representatives of special interests. Congress's failure to act reinforced the cynicism of many Americans toward their government.

A Changing Supreme Court. During Clinton's first two years as President, the Supreme Court stopped moving to the right and began to shift toward a more centrist position. Early in 1993 Justice Byron R. White retired, allowing the first Supreme Court appointment by a Democratic President since 1967. Clinton chose Ruth Bader Ginsburg, who became the second woman to sit on the Court. In 1994 Justice Harry A. Blackmun retired, and Clinton appointed Stephen Breyer.

Among the areas in which the newer and younger Supreme Court handed down decisions were voting rights and abortion.

There were two major decisions regarding voting rights. In *Shaw* v. *Reno,* a 5-4 vote held that electoral districts drawn to create minority voting districts were unconstitutional if their boundaries were "irrational." The two North Carolina districts in question were designed to form black majority districts. No African Americans had been sent to Congress from North Carolina since 1901, even though they make up one-fourth of that state's population.

In *Johnson* v. *DeGrandy,* the Supreme Court by a 7-2 vote overturned a redistricting that would have raised the number of Hispanic-majority districts in Florida's House of Representatives from nine to eleven. The Court held that creating districts that enabled minority groups to increase their representation "was permissible and at times necessary." However, once the minority group was represented roughly in proportion to its population, further redistricting was not necessary.

The difference between the two decisions lay mainly in their tone. The language of the earlier *Shaw* v. *Reno* was so sweeping that it cast doubt on all racially weighted districts. In contrast, *Johnson* v. *DeGrandy* indicated that racially weighted districts were not unconstitutional and that each case should be decided on its merits.

In June 1994, the Supreme Court voted 6-3 in favor of a 36-foot buffer zone around a Florida abortion clinic. The buffer zone was designed to prevent anti-abortion demonstrators from forcibly blocking the clinic's entrance and parking lot. However, a few anti-abortion activists did not accept the decision in *Madsen* v. *Women's Health Center.* In July 1994, activist Paul Hill shot and killed a doctor and a clinic volunteer at another abortion clinic in Florida. Hill defended his action on the grounds of "justifiable homicide." (Hill was later convicted on three counts of violating the clinic-protection act and one count of using a firearm in the commission of a crime.) The Clinton administration immediately sent federal marshals to protect abortion clinics around the country.

Picturing History As President Clinton gestures enthusiastically, Israeli Prime Minister Yitzhak Rabin and PLO Chairman Yasir Arafat shake hands after signing a peace accord in September, 1993. However, not everyone was pleased by the agreement. More than a year later, Islamic militants in Gaza continued to denounce Arafat as a "stooge" of Israel. Their protests led to violent confrontations with Palestinian police.

Foreign Policy Accomplishments

During the presidential campaign, Clinton had been criticized for not having any experience in foreign policy. Yet his first two years in office saw several accomplishments in this area.

Free Trade. The first accomplishment was passage of the North American Free Trade Agreement, or NAFTA. This pact between the United States, Canada, and Mexico was designed to gradually eliminate trade and investment barriers among the three nations. Although NAFTA had been concluded under the Bush administration, it took almost a full year of intense lobbying by Clinton to obtain Congress's approval. In response to U.S. labor union pressure, a side agreement ensured that Mexico would enforce child labor laws, minimum wage, and safety standards. Another side agreement set up procedures for investigating environmental abuses, such as filthy air and overloaded sewers, that are common in the industrial zone along the U.S.–Mexico border.

A second step toward expanded free trade was the GATT, or General Agreement on Tariffs and Trade. In December 1993, the United States and 122 other nations agreed to lower tariffs by about one third over ten years. Congress passed the agreement in late autumn of 1994.

The Middle East. In October 1991, Middle East peace talks, sponsored in part by the United States, opened in Madrid. In September 1993, Yasir Arafat, chairman of the Palestine Liberation Organization, and Prime Minister Yitzhak Rabin of Israel signed a peace plan in Washington. The plan took on concrete form in May 1994 with an accord

signed in Cairo. The accord gave the Palestinians control over internal matters such as elections, tax collection, and legislation. Israel retained control of foreign relations. And the two sides agreed to continue negotiations on other issues. Israeli troops then began pulling out of Gaza, where they had been since the 1967 War, and Palestinian police began moving in. The United States promised financial assistance to help the Palestinians.

Meanwhile, in June 1993 King Hussein of Jordan wrote a letter to President Clinton in which he described his hopes for peace in the Middle East. Clinton responded with a letter assuring the king of "full support." Soon after, Clinton asked Congress to resume military aid to Jordan. The aid had been cut off when Jordan sided with Iraq in the Persian Gulf War.

In September 1993, Jordan and Israel signed an agreement in Washington to negotiate a formal end to 43 years of war between the two nations. In October 1994, fifteen years after the Camp David Accords (see page 914), King Hussein became the second head of an Arab nation to sign a peace treaty with Israel. The Clinton administration then announced a three-year plan to wipe out Jordan's $700 million debt to the United States and to promote economic development in the Middle East.

Overseas Interventions. Since 1980, the United States has sent American armed forces abroad 41 times. Reasons for intervening overseas have ranged from arresting a drug runner (Panama) to protecting oil supplies (Kuwait).

Clinton continued this interventionist policy, most notably in Haiti. Jean-Bertrand Aristide, Haiti's democratically elected president, had

Concluding the Chapter

Have students refer to the list they created for introducing the Chapter and choose the one problem they feel is most critical. Ask students to prepare a one-page essay on ways to address the problem now and in the future. (Essays might include reference to the problems relating to discrimination, women's rights, the environment, foreign relations, or other social issues. Students should show an understanding of the issue as it pertains to the history and future of the U.S. and should offer plausible solutions to the problem.

been ousted in a military coup in 1991. The UN declared an embargo against Haiti, and Clinton announced that the United States was ready to use force to restore Aristide. The President also sent former President Jimmy Carter, General Colin L. Powell, and Senator Sam Nunn to negotiate a peaceful withdrawal by the Haitian military. An accord was reached on September 18, 1994, and the next day the first of some 20,000 American troops began landing in Haiti. By October 15, Aristide was back in office, without a single American military combat casualty.

A Mid-Term Correction

By the fall of 1994, deficit growth had been reversed, the economy was out of recession, and prospects for peace in the Middle East were the best they had been in decades. Yet in the November election, the Republicans gained control of both houses of Congress for the first time in 40 years.

The "Anxious Class." In spite of an overall improvement in the economy, many Americans were worse off. Cuts in defense spending meant the closing of factories and army bases. Free trade hurt certain industries, notably the textile industry. As companies downsized, many laid-off workers could find only jobs that paid less than they had previously earned. Other workers lacked the skills needed to compete for high-tech jobs. And even well-educated managers and technicians were worried about how long they could retain their jobs in an increasingly competitive economy.

During the 1930's and 1940's, the anger created by economic turmoil had been largely directed against big business. In 1994 such anger was increasingly directed against government, as well as immigrants and the poor.

The Religious Right. American voters were concerned about social as well as economic problems. One social problem was the increase in out-of-wedlock births. By 1994 almost one third of the babies born in the United States were being born to unwed mothers.

This increase in out-of-wedlock births was one of several social and political issues that helped propel the Christian evangelical movement, often referred to as the Religious Right, to the political forefront. This group advocated a return to conservative values to correct the country's ills. Among their positions were opposition to abortion, support

for stronger law enforcement and criminal prosecution, and opposition to higher taxes, which were viewed as a threat to the financial stability of families.

Probably the most influential group on the Religious Right was the Christian Coalition, which had been founded by the Reverend Pat Robertson after he failed in his bid for the presidency in 1988. Well-funded and well-organized, it conducted a massive get-out-the-vote campaign for conservative Republican candidates.

Looking Toward the Future. The 1994 campaign was even dirtier and more mean-spirited than the 1992 campaign. Spot political commercials reduced complicated issues to simple slogans. Candidates portrayed their opponents as evil rather than as people with different opinions. Exit polls showed that almost three out of four Americans distrusted politicians and felt alienated from government.

Although less than 40 percent of the electorate went to the polls, the Republicans not only gained control of Congress, they also won enough gubernatorial races to give them a majority of statehouses for the first time in 25 years. It was clear that Americans wanted a change. But would that change deepen divisions among Americans, or would it foster acceptance of various opinions and constructive consensus-building?

The nineteenth and twentieth centuries have brought new ways of both destroying and saving lives. What will the twenty-first century bring for Americans? Much will depend on you—the dreamers, decision-makers, and voters of the future.

SECTION 5 REVIEW

Key Terms and People

Explain the significance of: H. Ross Perot, electronic town hall, Bill Clinton, Hillary Rodham Clinton, HMO

Main Ideas

1. What were the main reasons for Bush's defeat in the 1992 Presidential election?
2. Why do you think over 19 million people voted for Ross Perot?
3. How did Clinton reduce the federal deficit?

Critical Thinking

4. What effect, if any, do you think television had on the voter turnout in 1992? Explain.

SECTION 5 REVIEW

Answers

Main Ideas

1. People were making less money than in recent years, and about one in seven were living in poverty. Unemployment remained high. There was a feeling that Bush could no longer do the job.

2. There was a mood for great change in the leadership of the country. Ross Perot represented a new way of doing things. Even though his ideas were often extreme, millions of people obviously thought that the United States needed as radical a shake-up as possible.

3. Clinton combined tax increases and spending cuts to reduce the deficit. He admitted that this plan to secure the future will require personal sacrifices now.

Critical Thinking

4. Possible answer: Television had a major impact on voter turnout in 1992. By way of thirty-minute spots, it provided an in-depth look at the ideas of Ross Perot, and as extreme as they were, many people found them attractive enough to vote for him. Televised debates were also important. They permitted the differences in the three candidates' views to be readily apparent, and these clear distinctions probably allowed people to make up their minds comfortably and vote. **(evaluation)**

Key Terms and People

These are highlighted in the text in the order in which they appear in this list.

Main Ideas

1. Possible answers (choice of five): against—gun control, abortion, big government, raising taxes, affirmative action, and ERA; for—an amendment for prayer in schools.

2. Slow inflation, curb the size and influence of federal government, reduce deficits, cut taxes, deregulate economy, reduce spending on social problems, increase military. • Reaganomics was based on suppy-side economics: government encourages companies to produce more goods by passing a tax cut to stimulate private investment—intended result is increased tax revenues. Reaganomics also called for cutting spending on social programs and deregulating industry.

3. Reagan called for a new start and a reduction in tension when Gorbachev, who wanted to reduce military spending, initiated negotiations for same with U.S.; they signed the INF treaty in 1987.

4. Carter recognized the Sandinistas. • Because they allowed independent political opinion. • Because the contras were fighting the Sandinistas, who by then were supplying weapons to rebels in other Central American countries and were being aided by U.S.S.R.

5. Tax base declined and became too low to support city services.

6. Possible answers: drugs; crime; equal rights for women; poverty; illiteracy; unemployment; low pay and language problems for Hispanics; Indians lost health, educational, and employment services; acid rain, AIDS.

7. The conservative Supreme Court of the Reagan-Bush era reversed some of its major civil-rights decisions on work-place discrimination and affirmative action. Abortion restrictions were also widened by the now conservative Court.

8. U.S. sent troops to Saudi Arabia and defeated Iraq in Gulf War. • Saddam Hussein defeated but still in power; Kuwait liberated but destroyed; few U.S. casualties but millions of displaced refugees.

Critical Thinking Questions

➤**9.** Possible answers: excerpt illustrates the acquisitive society of the 1980's. • Similarities: materialism and prosperity.

➤**10.** Possible answers: good—dramatic drop in rate of inflation, lower interest rates, stock market rise; bad—budget deficit, national debt doubled, decline in productivity.

11. Mostly emotional issues exploited through marketing techniques. • Yes, there were no clear, significant issues.

12. Possible answers: justified—Panama was unable to thwart General Noriega, whose international drug-trafficking seriously contributed to addiction in the United States; not justified—the United States invaded Panama without its permission and demonstrated

---

CHAPTER **36** REVIEW

Write your answers on a separate sheet of paper.

Key Terms and People

Explain the significance of: supply-side economics, Strategic Defense Initiative (SDI), Sandra Day O'Connor, Jesse Jackson, AIDS, Environmental Protection Agency (EPA), affirmative action, Persian Gulf, HMO

Main Ideas

1. Name at least five issues that were supported by the Moral Majority and other special interest groups that backed the presidency of Ronald Reagan.
2. What were Reagan's economic goals when he first became President? Explain Reaganomics, the policy by which he expected to achieve these goals.
3. How did Reagan's policy toward the Soviet Union change when Mikhail Gorbachev came to power?
4. How did United States foreign policy toward Nicaragua change when the Sandinistas came to power? Why? Why did Reagan back the contras?
5. How did the population movement from the city to suburbia affect the cities?
6. What major social problems came to the forefront in the 1980's?
7. What effect did a conservative Supreme Court have on such issues as civil rights and abortion?
8. What was the United States's response to Iraq's invasion of Kuwait and threat to Saudi Arabia? Evaluate the success of that response.

Critical Thinking Questions

9. **Analyzing Literature.** Why do you think the excerpt from Tom Wolfe's *The Bonfire of the Vanities* was placed in this chapter? Is there any similarity between this excerpt and the Link to Literature from Chapter 24? Explain.
10. **Evaluating Policies.** Were the results of Reaganomics good or bad for the country? Explain.

11. **Evaluating Effects.** What kinds of issues were raised in the 1988 Presidential campaign? Do you think the campaign played a part in causing the lowest voter turnout in years? Explain.
12. **Evaluating Policies.** Do you think the invasion of Panama was justified? Why or why not?
13. **Assessing Causes.** Why has the United States increased rather than decreased its dependence on oil over the past twenty years? How has this affected our foreign policy?
14. **Comparing Ideas.** How was Perot's candidacy similar to or different from that of earlier populists such as Senator Huey Long?
15. **Comparing Ideas.** How did Clinton's budget proposals differ from those of Reagan-Bush? Which do you favor? Why?
16. **Making Deductions.** Do you think Clinton's health-care reform plan helped or hindered the Democratic Party in the 1994 election? Explain.
17. **Forming Hypotheses.** Do you think that the 1994 election indicated a true conservative shift or a vote against Clinton? Explain.

Critical Thinking Activities

18. **Analyzing Maps.** Look at the map of Central America on page 936. Why is the United States interested in this area?
19. **Writing a Story.** Imagine that Stalin's ghost has returned to Moscow. Write a story describing his reactions to the changes he finds.
20. **Assessing Causes and Effects.** Make a list of good and bad consequences of the end of the cold war that are already apparent at home and abroad.
21. **Linking Past to Present.** What are the most important social problems today? Are they outgrowths of the problems of the 1980's, or are they new problems?

disregard for the national sovereignty of a smaller country.

13. Possible answer: the price of oil has remained cheap, while other energy sources (solar and nuclear) have been problematic and costly to develop. The United States has become dependent on foreign sources for some of its oil supplies and thus has a stake in making sure that those sources remain friendly and

open to the U.S.

14. Like Long, but unlike other populists such as Sinclair, Townsend, and Coughlin, Perot had his eye on the Presidency and would have had the power to get his reforms implemented if he had won. But like all of these men, Perot was concerned with economic ills and imbalances in the U.S., proposing extreme solutions no one had previously advocated.

15. The Reagan-Bush budget strategy kept taxes on individuals low while keeping up spending for the military and social entitlement programs—all at the cost of a higher budget deficit. Clinton, though, favored increasing the taxes on individuals and cutting the spending on the military and entitlements—a program calling for individual sacrifice to lower the deficit

and eventually benefit everyone.

16. Possible answer: hindered—voters were concerned about improving the economy, fighting crime, and reducing out-of-wedlock births, and therefore resented the energy spent unsuccessfully on health-care reform.

17. Possible answers: a conservative shift—the country has been growing more conservative since 1968, and Clinton's defeat of Bush was only a brief relaxation of that trend; vote against Clinton—Clinton's defeat on health-care reform made him look ineffective, so the voters turned against him.

Critical Thinking Activities

18. Possible answers: keep Panama Canal open; encourage growth of democracy in neighboring countries.

19. Story might focus on his bewilderment and anger over the democratic and economic changes he finds.

20. Possible answers: home—reduced armed forces budgets and defense-industry layoffs are examples of good and bad consequences; abroad—the spread of democracy and the restoration of national identities are good consequences, while the increased instability and poverty during the switch to free-market economies and the intolerance and warfare accompanying much of the revived nationalism are bad consequences.

▶ 21. Accept problems of current interest. • Most will be outgrowths of 1970's and 1980's

▶ **Question suitable for cooperative learning.**

Reagan, Bush, and Clinton

In 1980 and again in 1984, Americans elected the conservative Republican Ronald Reagan as President. Reagan's supply-side economic policy stressed tax cuts and government deregulation of private industries. He wanted less money spent on social programs and more spent on national defense. The Reagan administration reduced inflation but allowed the federal deficit to increase at an alarming rate. Reagan filled three Supreme Court vacancies with conservative judges.

In foreign affairs, relations with the Soviet Union improved after President Reagan met with the new Soviet leader, Mikhail Gorbachev. Nevertheless, there were several areas of conflict. The United States became indirectly but controversially involved in a civil war in Nicaragua. In the Middle East, United States marines were killed while trying to intervene in a conflict in Lebanon. Government officials became entangled in the Iran-contra affair, an illegal operation in which the United States was aiding the Nicaraguan contras with money made from the sale of weapons to Iran.

As the 1980's unfolded, minorities in the inner cities found themselves the victims of unemployment, poverty, crime, and drugs. Many Americans became concerned about the declining quality of education and the increased damage to the environment.

In 1988 the Republican George Bush became President. Bush faced an administrative scandal in the savings and loan industry. He also had to deal with the drug epidemic and a riot in Los Angeles. An increasingly conservative Supreme Court tackled the emotional issues of abortion and race discrimination.

Many surprising events took place overseas. The Soviet Union dissolved into a loose federation and in 1992 the cold war came to an official end. The Berlin Wall came down, and East Germany and West Germany were reunited. In 1991 Iraq invaded Kuwait and posed a threat to neighboring Saudi

Arabia, which also had massive oil reserves. In 1992 the United States and its allies won a quick victory against Iraq.

As the country entered the 1990's, the economy stagnated while the deficit skyrocketed. Many Americans were angry at the government's seeming lack of concern about their problems. The 1992 Presidential campaign turned into a three-way race in which the populist H. Ross Perot made a strong showing. Bush was defeated and the Democrat Bill Clinton became the nation's forty-second President. Clinton reversed Reaganomics and reduced the federal deficit, but his attempt at health-care reform was a failure. In 1994, Americans concerned about their economic future and the decline of traditional values elected a Republican Congress for the first time in 40 years.

Chronology of Main Events

Year	Event
1981	Ronald Reagan inaugurated President; Reaganomics begins
1983	Strategic Defense Initiative proposed
1985	President Reagan inaugurated for a second term
1986	*Challenger* space shuttle disaster; Iran-contra affair becomes public
1989	George Bush inaugurated President
1991	United States and allies defeat Iraq in Gulf War
1992	Cold war ends; riot in Los Angeles
1993	Bill Clinton inaugurated President
1994	Republicans win control of Congress

Telescoping the Times may be used as an alternative to having students read the entire chapter, as a chapter preview, or as a chapter review.

965

Answer Key

Key Terms and People

These are highlighted in the text in the order in which they appear in this list.

Main Ideas

1. a-1963; b-1961; c-1964; d-1962; e-1960. • e, b, d, a, c.

2. a-1970; b-1964; c-1973; d-1968; e-1954. • e, b, d, a, c.

3. a-1969; b-1974; c-1972; d-1968; e-1973. • d, a, c, e, b.

4. a-1979; b-1978; c-1982; d-1976; e-1974. • e, d, b, a, c.

5. a-1991; b-1981; c-1992; d-1993; e-1987; f-1994; g-1990. • b, e, g, a, c, d, f

Critical Thinking Questions

6. Possible answer: yes, negative ads should be prohibited in political campaigns, especially for the presidency; focus should be on important problems and proposed solutions to those problems and not on matters that divert attention from the real problems. • Yes, because ads by their very nature lack depth and elaboration and instead promote superficial images.

➤**7.** Possible answers: desegregation of Southern facilities after sit-ins; integration of transportation facilities after freedom rides; Committee on Equal Employment Opportunity, 1961; Twenty-fourth Amendment passed; Civil Rights Act of 1964; Job Corps; VISTA; Peace Corps; Medicare; Voting Rights Act of 1965; open immigration for political refugees; ERA; Carter support for human rights; Camp David Accords.

Critical Thinking Activity

➤**8.** Kennedy—inherits unemployment and inflation, follows Keynesian economics, lowers taxes, and uses deficit spending; raises minimum wage and pushes public works projects and tax benefits to industry. Johnson—continues deficit spending to finance funds for education, Medicare, housing, and the war in Vietnam; this causes severe inflation. Nixon—inflation worse because of war; crops fail worldwide, OPEC oil prices increase; interest rates are raised to discourage borrowing; government reduces spending and introduces temporary wage and price controls; none are successful. Ford—sees inflation increasing rapidly, cuts spending for social problems, calls for voluntary cuts in prices and wages; result is recession; OPEC keeps oil prices high. Carter—meets energy crisis by call for conservation; both inflation and unemployment rise (stagflation); productivity levels off, trade deficit grows; tries voluntary wage and price controls; inflation rises to more than 13 percent. Reagan—introduces supply-side economics; pushes deregulation and privatization of some government functions, cuts spending on social programs by 10 percent but increases military expenditures sharply. Inflation rate drops to 4 percent, resulting in lower interest rates and a soaring stock market, but also budget deficit and a growing national debt. In 1985 Reagan devalues dollar, tries to reduce trade barriers; makes across-the-board spending cuts. Bush—continues Reagan program.

UNIT 8 REVIEW

Write your answers on a separate sheet of paper.

Key Terms and People

Explain the significance of: John Maynard Keynes, Alliance for Progress, Warren Commission, Voting Rights Act of 1965, Malcolm X, Ho Chi Minh, domino theory, defoliants, Henry Kissinger, boat people, strict constructionists, détente, OPEC, trade deficit, national debt, PLO, Sunbelt, Moral Majority, Sandra Day O'Connor, Sandinistas, Jesse Jackson, AIDS, Persian Gulf, electronic town hall

Main Ideas

Give the year each event below occurred; then put each set of events listed under each chapter head in chronological order. You may use the book.

1. Chapter 32
   a. King leads a march on Washington; Kennedy introduces civil rights; *The Feminine Mystique* is published.
   b. Bay of Pigs invasion fails; Berlin Wall is constructed; Cuban missile crisis.
   c. Johnson elected President; he launches the Great Society and the War on Poverty.
   d. Glenn orbits earth; *Silent Spring* is published.
   e. Kennedy elected President; launches New Frontier.

2. Chapter 33
   a. Nixon authorizes invasion of Cambodia; college students strike.
   b. Congress passes Tonkin Gulf Resolution.
   c. United States and North Vietnam sign cease-fire; American troops leave Vietnam.
   d. Tet offensive shocks the nation; Johnson bows out of Presidential race; Paris peace talks begin.
   e. Dien Bien Phu falls.

3. Chapter 34
   a. Armstrong walks on moon.
   b. House Judiciary Committee adopts three articles of impeachment; Nixon resigns.
   c. Mainland China is given a seat in the United Nations; SALT treaty is signed; Plumbers break into Democratic headquarters.
   d. King and Kennedy are assassinated; riots break out at the Democratic Convention.
   e. Senate holds hearings on Watergate; Agnew resigns; Ford is appointed Vice-President.

4. Chapter 35
   a. Three Mile Island nuclear plant breaks down; Camp David Accords are signed; Iran takes hostages in U.S. embassy.
   b. Panama Canal treaties pass the Senate.
   c. ERA is defeated.
   d. Carter elected President.
   e. Ford pardons Nixon.

5. Chapter 36
   a. U.S. and allies defeat Iraq in Operation Desert Storm.
   b. Congress passes the largest tax cut in United States history.
   c. The cold war ends.
   d. Clinton inaugurated President.
   e. Special committees of the House and Senate report on the Iran-contra affair.
   f. Republicans gain control of both houses of Congress.
   g. Noriega surrenders following U.S. invasion of Panama; East and West Germany reunited.

Critical Thinking Questions

6. **Making a Judgment.** Many critics of the 1988 Presidential campaign feel that negative ads should be prohibited. Do you agree or disagree? Why? Would you be in favor of prohibiting all political advertising on television? Explain.

7. **Judging Values.** Some historians assert that one basic belief Americans share is "that they are taking part in a great, unique, still-developing experiment: the creation of a freer and more just society." Give specific instances from Unit 8 that support this statement.

Critical Thinking Activity

8. **Linking Past to Present.** Most of the Presidents in this unit had to cope with inflation. What did each President do about it? What did or did not work for each? Do you feel that inflation continues to be a problem?

TELESCOPING THE TIMES: 1960–Today

Continuity and Change

Leadership of the 1960's

In the 1960 election, Democrat John Kennedy defeated Republican Richard Nixon. Kennedy waged a skillful campaign and narrowly overcame obstacles, partly through his commanding performance in televised debates between the candidates. As President, he moved to stimulate the economy by lowering taxes and increasing public spending.

Soon after his election, Kennedy faced serious crises in foreign policy. In an attempt to overthrow Fidel Castro, the Soviet-backed dictator of Cuba, the administration gave its support to Cuban exiles whose Bay of Pigs invasion turned into a complete disaster. The Soviets tried to place nuclear missiles in Cuba. In response to the latter effort, Kennedy threatened military action, and the Soviets backed down. Tensions were finally eased by the Limited Test Ban Treaty and the sale of American wheat to the Soviets. The Peace Corps and the Alliance for Progress also helped the international situation.

In the early 1960's, African Americans took direct action to combat racial discrimination and segregation. They organized sit-ins and freedom rides. Martin Luther King, Jr., touched the conscience of the nation in a famous speech during the march on Washington. Marches by blacks and whites in the civil rights movement and attempts to integrate colleges in the deep South met violent reactions by mobs and police. Kennedy favored civil rights but was cautious about giving federal support. Tragedy struck in 1963 when the President was assassinated.

The Vice-President, Lyndon Johnson, succeeded Kennedy and called for a "Great Society" to support civil rights for minorities and to combat poverty. Financial aid to the poor and the elderly met many social needs but proved to be very expensive. Congress passed the landmark Civil Rights Act of 1964. Racial resentment broke out in riots in north-ern and western cities, and leaders like Malcolm X called for "black power." While some African Americans made progress, many faced white backlash.

The Vietnam War

During the early 1960's, conditions in Vietnam became increasingly unstable. A strong Communist movement had developed there during the Vietnamese struggle against foreign domination. Civil war followed. Kennedy sought to contain communism by sending American advisors to aid the anti-Communist government of South Vietnam. Then an incident in the Gulf of Tonkin gave Johnson justification for plunging the United States directly into the conflict.

Johnson ordered massive bombings and more than a half million ground troops into Vietnam. Many Americans at home began to have doubts about the war. Faced with powerful opposition, Johnson announced that he would not run for reelection.

Two tragic assassinations took place in 1968—those of the civil rights leader Martin Luther King, Jr., and the Presidential candidate Robert Kennedy. The Democratic nominating convention in Chicago was nearly broken up by rioting. In the 1968 election, the Republican Richard Nixon defeated the Democrat Hubert Humphrey.

The Nixon Years

After an invasion of Cambodia and several years of peace talks, Nixon finally withdrew American troops from Vietnam in 1973. Two years later, South Vietnam fell to Communist forces.

The Vietnam War was the longest war the United States had ever fought. It lessened the respect of many Americans for their government.

It resulted in the migration of large numbers of Vietnamese to the United States and the suffering of even more Vietnamese refugees as boat people. In time, American veterans began to speak out about their experiences and to allow some of their psychological wounds to heal.

Nixon's domestic policies turned the country in a more conservative direction. He moved to strengthen federal law enforcement and pushed for revenue sharing. Yet he also advocated family assistance programs and measures to deal with inflation.

Secretary of State Henry Kissinger guided the nation toward a more flexible foreign policy that included the recognition of Communist China. Kissinger also worked for improved relations with the Soviet Union.

Soon after Nixon's landslide victory over the Democrat George McGovern in 1972, the Watergate scandal was exposed. First, the "Pentagon Papers" embarrassed the President and his administration. Then, some investigators from the White House were caught burglarizing the headquarters of the Democratic National Committee. At first, Nixon denied any involvement. However, two newspaper reporters pursued the case, and then congressional committees held long, televised public hearings. Several of Nixon's top aides were forced to resign and were eventually sent to jail. Finally, the President himself resigned when faced with taped evidence that showed he had known about the Watergate plan all along.

Vice-President Gerald Ford automatically succeeded Nixon and pardoned the former President. Ford's administration faced the issues of severe inflation and a drastic rise in the price of foreign oil.

Carter Enters the White House

In 1976 Americans celebrated the bicentennial anniversary of their independence from Great Britain and a successful unmanned space landing on Mars. Yet news about political corruption bred voter apathy and prompted those Americans who did vote to choose Democrat Jimmy Carter, an outsider to the Washington establishment, for President.

Carter proved unable to deal with many domestic problems. By the end of his term in office, inflation was raging out of control, and a stalled economy was hurting millions of Americans. In addition, labor unions had grown weaker, and ratification of the ERA had failed.

In foreign affairs, Carter pressed for international agreements on human rights but without much success. He did succeed in getting Congress to pass treaties in which the United States agreed to turn over the Canal Zone to Panama by the year 2000. He also achieved a triumph in the Camp David Accords regarding the Arab-Israeli conflict.

The Middle East was also the scene of a revolution that overthrew the Shah of Iran and resulted in the taking of more than fifty American hostages. Despite various attempts, Carter was unable to secure release of the hostages.

Leadership of the 1980's

The hostage crisis, inflation, and concern over a decline in traditional values helped bring about Carter's defeat in the Presidential election of 1980. His Republican opponent was Ronald Reagan, the former governor of California.

Reagan's policy of supply-side economics stressed massive tax cuts as well as government deregulation of industries. More money was provided for national defense and weapons systems and less money for social programs. Although Reaganomics (as the President's economic policies were called) lowered inflation, it allowed the federal deficit to increase at an alarming rate and widened the gap between rich and poor.

By 1984 the economy was stronger, however, and Reagan defeated the Democratic candidate, Walter Mondale, who had been Vice-President under Carter.

In foreign affairs, Reagan eventually improved relations between the United States and the Soviet Union. In the Western Hemisphere, the United States invaded Grenada and became indirectly involved in the civil war in Nicaragua. In the Middle East, the United States was involved in a conflict in Lebanon in which more than two hundred marines were killed and several Americans were taken hostage. Central America and the Middle East were linked in the Iran-contra affair, an illegal operation in which the United States aided the Nicaraguan contras with money made from the sale of weapons to Iran.

The 1980's saw continued growth in the suburbs, while many central cities fought crime and decay. Some minority candidates were elected to political offices, but many people in minority groups struggled with poverty and unemployment.

After some difficult primary election battles, Reagan's Vice-President, George Bush, emerged as the Republican Presidential candidate in 1988. He defeated the less experienced Democratic candidate, Michael Dukakis, in a nasty campaign.

As President, Bush had to deal with a scandal in the savings and loan industry as well as urban rioting. He addressed problems in education, the environment, and the war against drugs. A conservative Supreme Court tackled the controversial issue of abortion and turned back the clock on questions of race discrimination.

In 1989 Bush sent American troops into Panama to overthrow General Manuel Noriega. East Germany and West Germany were reunited in 1990. Communism collapsed in the Soviet Union, which turned into a loose confederation of states, and in 1992 the cold war came to an official end. In 1990 Iraq invaded Kuwait and threatened the oil reserves of Saudi Arabia. The following year the United States invaded Kuwait and won a quick victory over Iraq.

A New Administration

In the 1990's the economy grew worse and many more Americans lost confidence in their government. They called for a change. In the 1992 Presidential campaign, Bush was challenged by the Democratic candidate, Bill Clinton, the former governor of Arkansas, and by the self-financed populist candidate, H. Ross Perot. Clinton won the election.

Clinton reversed Reaganomics and succeeded in reducing the budget deficit by a combination of less defense spending and higher taxes on upper-income Americans. Congress passed several anti-crime measures. The President's attempt to reform health-care, however, failed.

In foreign affairs, Clinton pushed the North American Free Trade Agreement through Congress. The Middle East moved toward peace with the signing of an agreement between Israel and the Palestine Liberation Organization for limited Palestinian self-rule. In addition, Israel and Jordan signed a peace treaty. Clinton sent American troops into Haiti to facilitate the return of the democratically elected president of that country.

Despite an improved economy, many Americans felt insecure about the future. They were also upset over growing social problems, such as the rise in out-of-wedlock births and crime. The Religious Right carried out a well-organized campaign to help conservative Republican candidates. As a result of the 1994 mid-term elections, the Republicans gained control of both houses of Congress as well as a majority of statehouses. They promised numerous changes in government policy.

Chronology of Main Events

1961 John F. Kennedy inaugurated President

1963 Kennedy assassinated; Lyndon Johnson succeeds to Presidency

1968 Martin Luther King assassinated

1969 Richard M. Nixon inaugurated President

1974 President Nixon resigns; Gerald Ford succeeds to Presidency

1977 Jimmy Carter inaugurated President

1981 Ronald Reagan inaugurated President

1986 Iran-contra affair becomes public

1989 George Bush inaugurated President

1991 U.S. and allies defeat Iraq in Gulf War

1992 Cold War ends

1993 Bill Clinton inaugurated President

Atlas

Reference Section

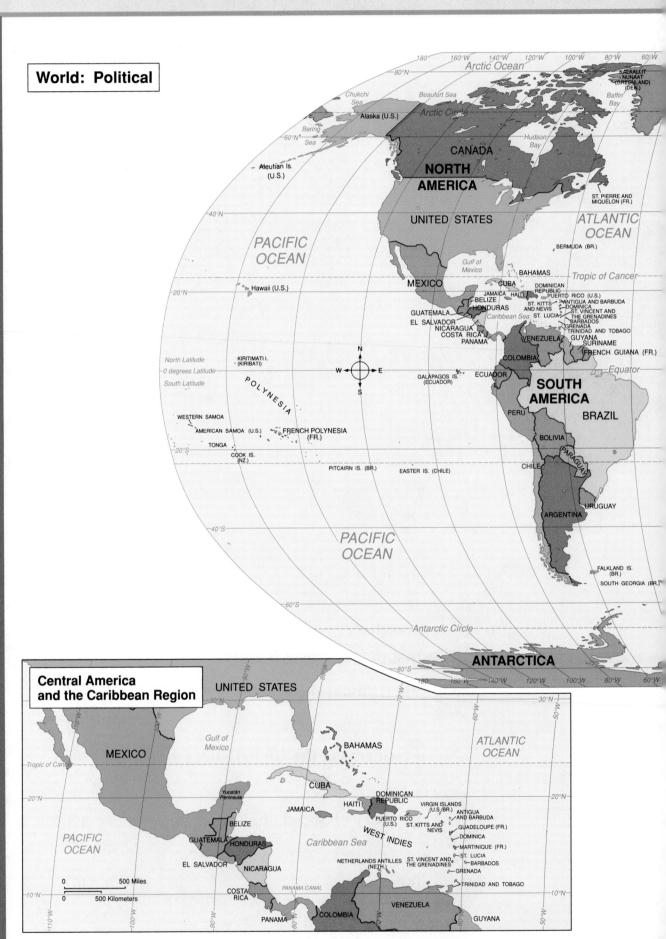

World: Political

80°N   *Arctic Ocean*

KALAALLIT NUNAAT (GREENLAND) (DEN.)

Chukchi Sea   *Beaufort Sea*   *Baffin Bay*

Alaska (U.S.)   Arctic Circle

60°N   *Bering Sea*   *Hudson Bay*

Aleutian Is. (U.S.)   CANADA

NORTH AMERICA

ST. PIERRE AND MIQUELON (FR.)

40°N   UNITED STATES   *ATLANTIC OCEAN*

PACIFIC OCEAN

BERMUDA (BR.)

Gulf of Mexico   BAHAMAS   Tropic of Cancer

20°N   Hawaii (U.S.)   MEXICO   CUBA   DOMINICAN REPUBLIC   PUERTO RICO (U.S.)

JAMAICA   HAITI   ANTIGUA AND BARBUDA

BELIZE   ST. KITTS AND NEVIS   DOMINICA

GUATEMALA   HONDURAS   ST. VINCENT AND THE GRENADINES

EL SALVADOR   *Caribbean Sea*   ST. LUCIA   BARBADOS

NICARAGUA   GRENADA

COSTA RICA   TRINIDAD AND TOBAGO

PANAMA   VENEZUELA   GUYANA   SURINAME

FRENCH GUIANA (FR.)

COLOMBIA

KIRITIMATI I. (KIRIBATI)

North Latitude   0 degrees Latitude   *South Latitude*

GALÁPAGOS IS. (ECUADOR)   ECUADOR   Equator

SOUTH AMERICA

P O L Y N E S I A

PERU   BRAZIL

WESTERN SAMOA   BOLIVIA

AMERICAN SAMOA (U.S.)   FRENCH POLYNESIA (FR.)

TONGA   PARAGUAY

20°S   COOK IS. (NZ.)   CHILE

PITCAIRN IS. (BR.)   EASTER IS. (CHILE)   URUGUAY

ARGENTINA

40°S   *PACIFIC OCEAN*

FALKLAND IS. (BR.)

SOUTH GEORGIA (BR.)

60°S   Antarctic Circle

80°S   **ANTARCTICA**

Central America and the Caribbean Region

UNITED STATES

30°N

MEXICO   *Gulf of Mexico*   BAHAMAS   *ATLANTIC OCEAN*

Tropic of Cancer

20°N   Yucatán Peninsula   CUBA

DOMINICAN REPUBLIC   VIRGIN ISLANDS (U.S./BR.)

JAMAICA   HAITI   ANTIGUA AND BARBUDA

BELIZE   PUERTO RICO (U.S.)   GUADELOUPE (FR.)

GUATEMALA   ST. KITTS AND NEVIS   DOMINICA

HONDURAS   MARTINIQUE (FR.)

EL SALVADOR   *Caribbean Sea*   ST. LUCIA

PACIFIC OCEAN   NICARAGUA   W E S T   I N D I E S

NETHERLANDS ANTILLES (NETH.)   ST. VINCENT AND THE GRENADINES   BARBADOS

GRENADA

COSTA RICA   *PANAMA CANAL*   TRINIDAD AND TOBAGO

10°N   PANAMA   VENEZUELA   GUYANA

COLOMBIA

0   500 Miles

0   500 Kilometers

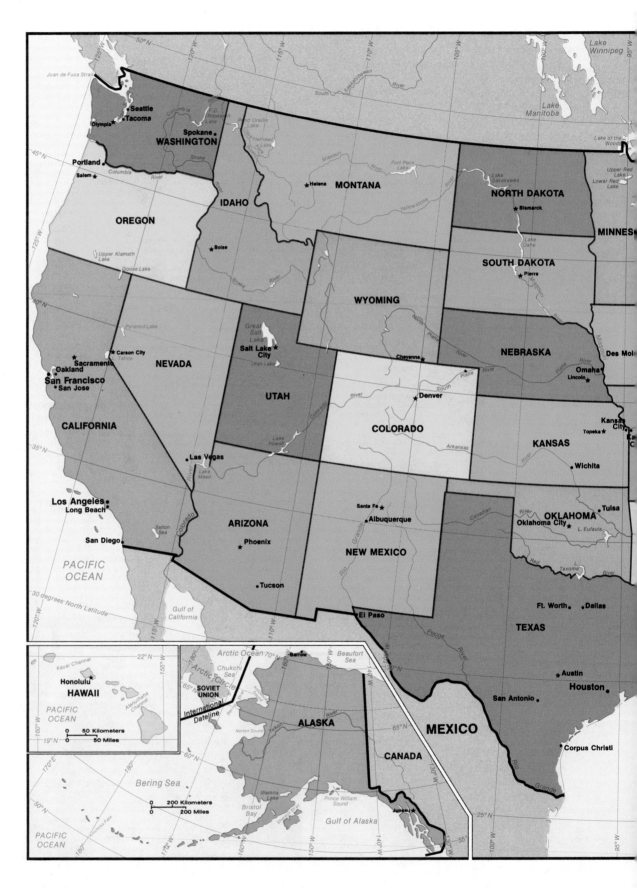

PACIFIC
OCEAN

Juan de Fuca Strait

Seattle
Tacoma
Olympia

WASHINGTON
Spokane

Portland
Salem

OREGON

Upper Klamath Lake

Goose Lake

Pyramid Lake

Carson City
Sacramento
Oakland
San Francisco
San Jose

NEVADA

CALIFORNIA

Las Vegas
Lake Mead

Los Angeles
Long Beach

San Diego

Salton Sea

Columbia River

Snake

Snake River

IDAHO

Boise

Helena

MONTANA

Missouri

Yellowstone

Fort Peck Lake

WYOMING

Great Salt Lake

Salt Lake City

Utah Lake

UTAH

Lake Powell

Colorado

Colorado River

ARIZONA

Phoenix

Tucson

Gulf of California

El Paso

Cheyenne

Denver

COLORADO

Santa Fé
Albuquerque

NEW MEXICO

Rio Grande

NORTH DAKOTA

Bismarck

Lake Oahe

SOUTH DAKOTA

Pierre

North Platte

South Platte River

NEBRASKA

KANSAS

Topeka

Wichita

Canadian

OKLAHOMA

Oklahoma City

L. Eufaula

Tulsa

Ft. Worth
Dallas

TEXAS

Austin

Houston

San Antonio

Corpus Christi

Rio Grande

Pecos River

Texoma L.

Red River

MEXICO

CANADA

Lake Winnipeg

Lake Manitoba

Lake of the Woods

Upper Red Lake
Lower Red Lake

MINNES

Des Moi

Omaha
Lincoln

Kansas City
C

Saskatchewan River

South Saskatchewan

F.D. Roosevelt Lake

Pend Oreille Lake

Flathead Lake

Lake Sakakawea

30 degrees North Latitude

Honolulu
HAWAII

PACIFIC
OCEAN

Kauai Channel

Alenuihaha Channel

22° N

19° N

0   50 Kilometers
0   50 Miles

Arctic Ocean

Barrow

Beaufort Sea

Chukchi Sea

SOVIET UNION

International Dateline

Arctic Circle

ALASKA

Yukon River

Norton Sound

Bering Sea

Bristol Bay

Ilamna Lake

Prince William Sound

Gulf of Alaska

Juneau

70° N

65° N

60° N

50° N

0   200 Kilometers
0   200 Miles

PACIFIC
OCEAN

United States: Political

— International boundary

— State boundary

⊙ National capital

★ State capital

DISTANCE SCALE

0 Kilometers 250 500 750 1000 1250 1500 1750 2000 2250

0 Miles 250 500 750 1000 DISTANCE SCALE 1250

CANADA

Gulf of St. Lawrence

Cabot Strait

James Bay

Lake Nipigon

Lake Superior

Lake Seul

Lake Winnebago

WISCONSIN

MICHIGAN

Grand Rapids
Flint
Lansing
Detroit

Madison
Milwaukee

Chicago

Lake Michigan

Lake Huron

L. Simcoe

L. Nipissing

L. Abitibi

Gouin Reservoir

Cabonga Reservoir

Ottawa River

St. Maurice River

Saguenay River

St. Lawrence River

Lake Champlain

MAINE

Augusta

Montpelier
VT.
N.H.
Concord

NEW YORK

Syracuse
Rochester
Albany

Buffalo

MASS.
Springfield
Worcester
Boston

Hartford
CONN.
R.I.
Providence

New Haven

LONG ISLAND

Newark
Yonkers
New York City
Jersey City
Trenton N.J.

Lake Ontario

Lake Erie

Cleveland
PENNSYLVANIA
Toledo
Akron
Youngstown
Harrisburg
Pittsburgh
Philadelphia

Wilmington

INDIANA

OHIO
Columbus

ILLINOIS

Springfield

Indianapolis

Dayton
Cincinnati

Frankfort
Louisville

St. Louis
East St. Louis

SOURI

KENTUCKY

WEST VIRGINIA
Charleston

Kanawha River

MD.
Baltimore
Annapolis
Dover
DEL.
Washington D.C.

Delaware Bay

ATLANTIC OCEAN

Richmond

VIRGINIA

Norfolk

Nashville

Knoxville

TENNESSEE

Raleigh

NORTH CAROLINA
Charlotte

KANSAS
Little Rock

Memphis

Chattanooga

Hartwell Lake

SOUTH CAROLINA
Columbia

MISSISSIPPI
Jackson

ALABAMA

Birmingham

Montgomery

Atlanta

GEORGIA

Charleston

Savannah River

Tennessee River

Cumberland River

Arkansas R.

Mississippi River

SIANA

Baton Rouge
Lafayette
New Orleans

L. Pontchartrain

Breton Sound

Mobile

Tallahassee
Jacksonville

FLORIDA

Gulf of Mexico

Tampa
St. Petersburg

Lake Okeechobee

Miami

BAHAMAS

Straits of Florida

ATLANTIC OCEAN

San Juan
PUERTO RICO

Caribbean Sea

0 50 Kilometers
0 50 Miles

United States: Physical

MAP LEGEND

Land Elevation

FEET	METERS
Higher than 13,100	Higher than 4000
6600-13,100	2000-4000
1600-6600	500-2000
700-1600	200-500
0-700	0-200
Below sea level	Below sea level

Water Depth

0-700	0-200
700-9800	200-3000
9800-19,700	3000-6000
Deeper than 19,700	Deeper than 6000

• City

◉ National capital

★ State or province capital

+ Heights and depths

━━ International boundary

━━ State or province boundary

☐ Ice cap

```
0 Kilometers  250      500      750      1000      1250      1500      1750      2000      2250
0 Miles          250         500         750      1000 DISTANCE SCALE 1250
```

United States: Dependencies and Areas of Special Sovereignty

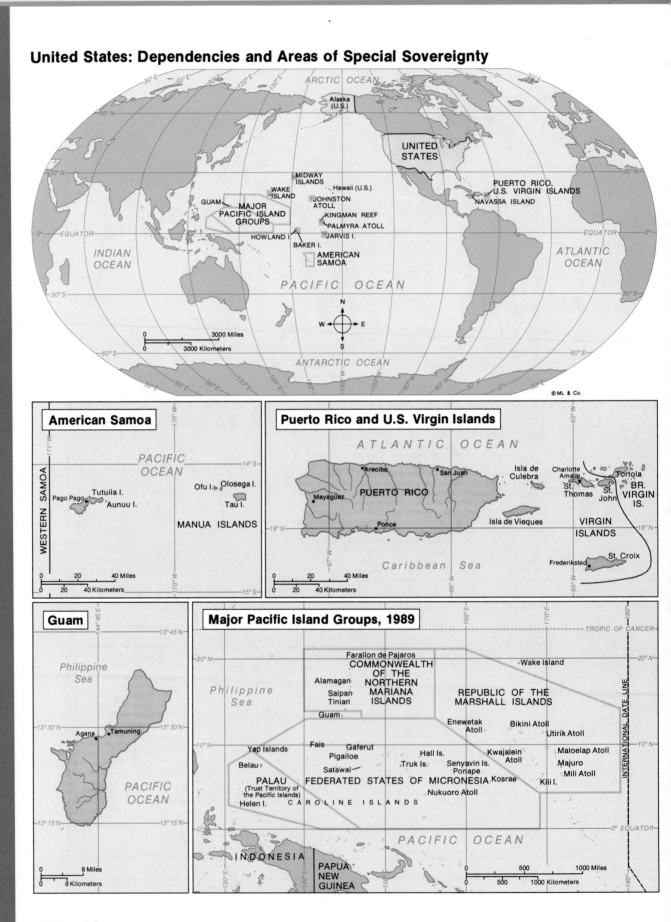

American Samoa

WESTERN SAMOA

PACIFIC OCEAN

14° S

Ofu I. Olosega I.

Pago Pago Tutuila I.

Aunuu I.

Tau I.

MANUA ISLANDS

18° S

15° S

171° W

170° W

0   20   40 Miles
0   20   40 Kilometers

Puerto Rico and U.S. Virgin Islands

ATLANTIC OCEAN

Arecibo San Juan

Isla de Culebra

Charlotte Amalie Tortola

St. Thomas St. John BR. VIRGIN IS.

Mayagüez PUERTO RICO

Ponce 18° N

Isla de Vieques VIRGIN ISLANDS 18° N

Caribbean Sea

Frederiksted St. Croix

65° W 67° W 66° W 65° W

0   20   40 Miles
0   20   40 Kilometers

Guam

Philippine Sea

13° 45'N

13° 30'N Agana Tamuning 13° 30'N

PACIFIC OCEAN

13° 15'N 13° 15'N

144° 45'E

0   8 Miles
0   8 Kilometers

Major Pacific Island Groups, 1989

TROPIC OF CANCER

20° N Farallon de Pajaros Wake Island 20° N

COMMONWEALTH OF THE NORTHERN MARIANA ISLANDS

Alamagan

Philippine Sea Saipan REPUBLIC OF THE MARSHALL ISLANDS

Tinian

Guam

Enewetak Atoll Bikini Atoll

Utirik Atoll

10° N Yap Islands Fais Gaferut Hall Is. Kwajalein Atoll Maloelap Atoll 10° N

Pigailoe Truk Is. Senyavin Is. Majuro

Belau Satawal Ponape Mili Atoll

PALAU FEDERATED STATES OF MICRONESIA Kosrae Kili I.

(Trust Territory of the Pacific Islands)

Nukuoro Atoll

Helen I. CAROLINE ISLANDS

PACIFIC OCEAN

0° EQUATOR

INDONESIA PAPUA NEW GUINEA

130° E 140° E 160° E 170° E 180°

INTERNATIONAL DATE LINE

0   500   1000 Miles
0   500   1000 Kilometers

© ML & Co.

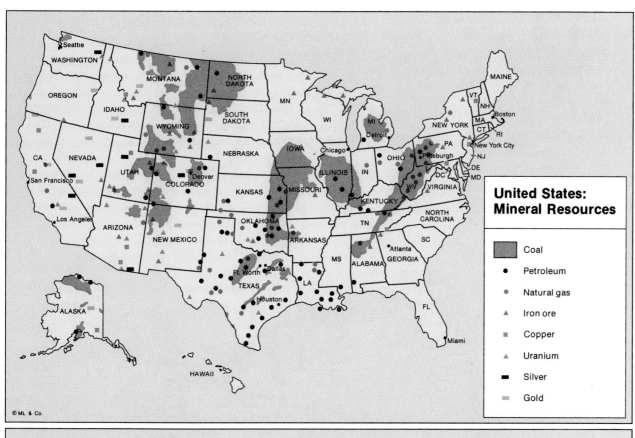

United States: Mineral Resources

- **■** Coal
- **●** Petroleum
- **●** Natural gas
- **▲** Iron ore
- **■** Copper
- **▲** Uranium
- **▬** Silver
- **▬** Gold

© ML & Co.

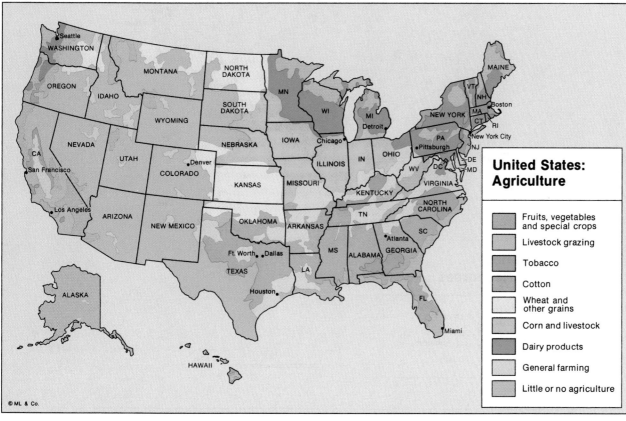

United States: Agriculture

- Fruits, vegetables and special crops
- Livestock grazing
- Tobacco
- Cotton
- Wheat and other grains
- Corn and livestock
- Dairy products
- General farming
- Little or no agriculture

© ML & Co.

North America: Economic Resources

Forestry
Farming
Ranching
Fishing
Other (e.g., minerals, oil)
Industry

ASIA

ICELAND

GREENLAND

Alaska (UNITED STATES)

Anchorage

C A N A D A

PACIFIC OCEAN

Vancouver • Calgary

Seattle

Winnipeg

Portland

ROCKY MOUNTAINS

SIERRA NEVADA

Minneapolis
St. Paul
Milwaukee
Chicago
Detroit

Montreal
Ottawa

Halifax

Boston

Buffalo
Cleveland
Pittsburgh

New York City
Philadelphia
Baltimore

San Francisco

U N I T E D   S T A T E S

Denver

Kansas City
St. Louis

Cincinnati

Washington D.C.
Norfolk

APPALACHIAN MTS.

ATLANTIC OCEAN

Los Angeles

Phoenix

Fort Worth
Dallas

Nashville
Memphis

Atlanta
Birmingham

Houston
Galveston

New Orleans

Miami

BAHAMAS

PUERTO RICO (U.S.)

Gulf of Mexico

M E X I C O

CUBA
HAITI
DOMINICAN REPUBLIC

JAMAICA

Guadalajara
Mexico City

Caribbean Sea

SOUTH AMERICA

N
W E
S

0   400   800 Miles
0   400   800 Kilometers

© ML & Co.

Gazetteer

The gazetteer is a dictionary or index of geographical names that shows latitude and longitude for cities and other places. The page reference indicates where each entry may be found on a map in this textbook.

A

Abilene, Kansas (39°N/97°W). A city in Kansas on the Smoky Hill River. Important railroad center at the end of the Chisholm Trail in the 1860's. p. 426

Adirondack Mountains (44°N/74°W). Mountains in northwest corner of New York State. Highest peak is Mt. Marcy, with an elevation of 5,344 ft. (1,629 m). p. 975

Afghanistan (33°N/65°E). Landlocked country in south central Asia. Invaded by the Soviet Union in 1979. p. 973

Africa (10°N/22°E). Second largest continent, situated in the Eastern Hemisphere, south of Europe. p. 973

Akron, Ohio (41°N/82°W). Large industrial city on the Cuyahoga River in Ohio. p. 975

Alabama (32°N/86°W). Twenty-second state to join United States. Located in southeastern United States. Nicknamed the Heart of Dixie or the Cotton State. Capital: Montgomery. p. 975

Alamo (29°N/99°W). Spanish mission and fort in San Antonio, Texas. After Texans defending the fort were killed by Mexican soldiers in 1836, "Remember the Alamo" became the battle cry for Texans in their fight for independence. p. 314

Alaska (64°N/150°W). Forty-ninth state to join United States. Located in northwestern North America. Largest but least populated state. Capital: Juneau. p. 974

Alaska Range (63°N/150°W). Mountains in south central Alaska. Mt. McKinley, the highest peak in North America, is in this range. Elevation of Mt. McKinley is 20,320 ft. (6,193 m). p. 976

Albania (41°N/20°E). Country in the western Baltic Peninsula. Located on the Adriatic Sea. p. 973

Albany, New York (43°N/74°W). Capital of New York State. Located on the Hudson River. Called Fort Orange by the Dutch of New Netherland. p. 973

Albuquerque, New Mexico (35°N/107°W). Most populated city in New Mexico. Located on the Rio Grande. p. 974

Algeria (28°N/3°E). Country in North Africa. Located on the Mediterranean Sea. p. 973

Algiers, Algeria (36°N/3°E). Port city and capital of Algeria. Located on the Mediterranean Sea. p. 224

Aleutian Islands (53°N/177°W). Chain of islands extending west from Alaska. p. 976

Amiens, France (50°N/2°E). World War I battle site in northeastern France. p. 602

Anchorage, Alaska (61°N/150°W). Most populated city in Alaska. Located on Cook Inlet, an arm of the Pacific Ocean. p. 980

Andorra (42°N/1°E). Country in western Europe. Located between Spain and France. p. 973

Angola (12°S/18°E). Country on the southwest coast of Africa. Gained independence from Portugal in 1975. p. 973

Annapolis, Maryland (39°N/77°W). Capital of Maryland. Located on Chesapeake Bay. Site of the U.S. Naval Academy. p. 975

Antarctica (90°S/00°). Continent surrounding the South Pole. Completely covered by an ice shelf. pp. 972-973

Antietam (39°N/78°W). Creek in Maryland. Civil War site of a Union victory in 1862. p. 363

Appalachian Mountains (41°N/77°W). Chain of mountains extending from eastern Canada to Georgia. Highest peak is Mt. Mitchell, with an elevation of 6,684 ft. (2,037 m). p. 977

Appomattox (37°N/79°W). Civil War site in Virginia where General Lee surrendered the Confederate army to General Grant on April 9, 1865. p. 375

Arabian Sea (15°N/65°E). Part of the Indian Ocean between India and Arabia. p. 973

Arctic Circle A special parallel located at 66½° north latitude. pp. 972-973, 976

Arctic Ocean (85°N/170°E). Ocean surrounding the North Pole. p. 976

Argentina (34°S/64°W). Country in southern South America. p. 972

Arizona (33°N/112°W). Forty-eighth state to join United States. Located in southwestern United States. Nicknamed the Grand Canyon State. Capital: Phoenix. p. 974

Arkansas (35°N/92°W). Twenty-fifth state to join United States. Located in south central United States. Nicknamed the Land of Opportunity. Capital: Little Rock. p. 975

Arkansas River (34°N/91°W). River that rises in central Colorado and flows into the Mississippi River in southeast Arkansas. p. 977

Aroostook River (46°N/67°W). River that rises in northern Maine and flows northeast into the St. John River in Canada. p. 316

Asia (50°N/100°E). Largest continent. Located in the Eastern Hemisphere. Bounded by the Arctic, Pacific, and Indian oceans. Separated from Europe by the Ural Mountains. p. 973

Atlanta, Georgia (34°N/84°W). Capital of and largest city in Georgia. Burned by Union forces under Sherman in 1864 before his march to the sea during the Civil War. p. 975

Atlantic Coastal Plain (34°N/79°W). Broad plain located along the Atlantic coast from Cape Cod to Florida. p. 977

Atlantic Ocean (2° N/25° W). Ocean bordering the American continents on their eastern coastlines and Europe and Africa on their western coastlines. pp. 972-973, 977

Augusta, Maine (44°N/70°W). Capital of Maine. Located on the Kennebec River. p. 975

Austin, Texas (30°N/98°W). Capital of Texas. Located near the western edge of the coastal plain of the Gulf of Mexico. p. 974

Australia (25°S/135°E). Smallest continent. Located in the Southern Hemisphere. Also a country. p. 973

Austria-Hungary (47°N/14°E). Former empire located in central Europe. One of the Central Powers in World War I. Divided into several countries after 1918. p. 597

Azores (38°N/28°W). Group of islands in the North Atlantic Ocean. Located west of Portugal. p. 973

B

Badlands (44°N/102°W). Dry, rugged region in South Dakota, with little or no vegetation. p. 976

Baffin Bay (73°N/67°W). Arm of the North Atlantic Ocean. Located between Greenland and Baffin Island. p. 972

Baltic Sea (57°N/19°E). Sea in northern Europe that connects with the North Sea. p. 973

Baltimore, Maryland (39°N/77°W). Most populated city in Maryland. Located on Chesapeake Bay. One of the busiest seaports in the nation. p. 975

Bangladesh (24°N/90°E). Country in southern Asia. Located at the head of the Bay of Bengal.

Formerly the province of East Pakistan. Gained independence in 1971. p. 973

Barbados (13°N/59°W). Country on the easternmost island of the West Indies. Gained independence from Great Britain in 1966. p. 972

Barents Sea (74°N/36°E). Part of the Arctic Ocean. Located north of Norway and the U.S.S.R. p. 973

Bataan (13°N/124°E). Peninsula at the entrance to Manila Bay in the Philippines. Scene of World War II surrender of U.S. and Philippine forces to the Japanese. p. 739

Baton Rouge, Louisiana (30°N/91°W). Capital of Louisiana. Located on the Mississippi River. p. 975

Bay of Bengal (15°N/90°E). Part of the Indian Ocean. Located between east India and west Burma. p. 973

Beaufort Sea (73°N/136°W). Part of the Arctic Ocean. Located north of Alaska and northwest of Canada. pp. 972, 976

Beirut, Lebanon (34°N/36°E). Capital of Lebanon. p. 915

Belgium (51°N/2°E). Country in northwestern Europe. Located on the North Sea. p. 973

Belize (17°N/89°W). Country in Central America. Located on the Caribbean Sea. Gained independence from Great Britain in 1981. p. 972

Bering Sea (59°N/174°W). Part of the North Pacific Ocean, bounded on the east by mainland Alaska and on the south and southeast by the Aleutian Islands. pp. 972, 976

Bering Strait (65°N/169°W). Narrow body of water connecting the Arctic Ocean and the Bering Sea. Separates Asia from North America. p. 5

Berlin, Germany (53°N/13°E). Capital of Germany. Divided after World War II into East and West Berlin (p. 775) and officially reunited in 1990.

Bermuda (32°N/64°W). Group of islands in the west Atlantic Ocean. Located southeast of North Carolina. p. 972

Bhutan (27°N/90°E). Independent kingdom in the Himalayas. Located north of the Indian state of Assam. Monarchy established in 1907. p. 973

Birmingham, Alabama (34°N/87°W). Most populated city in Alabama. One of the nation's leading iron-producing centers. p. 975

Bismarck, North Dakota (47°N/101°W). Capital of North Dakota. Located on the Missouri River. p. 974

Black Hills (44°N/104°W). Mountainous area with steep canyons, located in South Dakota and Wyoming. Highest peak is Harney Peak, with an elevation of 7,242 ft. (2,209 m). p. 976

Blue Ridge Mountains (38°N/78°W). Eastern part of the Appalachian system. Extend from Pennsylvania to Georgia. p. 977

Bolivia (17°S/65°W). Inland country in west central South America. Gained independence from

Spain in 1825. p. 972

Boise, Idaho (44°N/116°W). Capital of and most populated city in Idaho. p. 974

Boston, Massachusetts (42°N/71°W). Capital of and most populated city in Massachusetts. Located on Massachusetts Bay. p. 975

Botswana (22°S/24°E). Country in South Africa. Gained independence from Great Britain in 1966. Formerly known as the British territory of Bechuanaland. p. 973

Brazil (10°S/55°W). Country in central and northeast South America. Located on the Atlantic Ocean. Gained independence from Portugal in 1822. p. 972

Brazos River (29°N/96°W). River in central and southeastern Texas. Flows southeastward into the Gulf of Mexico. p. 976

Breed's Hill (42°N/71°W). Overlooks Boston Harbor. Site of fighting during the Battle of Bunker Hill in 1775. p. 93

British Guiana (5°N/59°W). Country in northeast South America. Former British colony. Now known as Guyana. p. 972

Brooks Range (68°N/151°W). Northernmost part of the Rocky Mountains. Located in northern Alaska. Highest peak is Mt. Michelson, with an elevation of 9,239 ft. (2,816 m). p. 976

Brunei (4°N/114°E). Independent sultanate on the north coast of Borneo. Consists of two enclaves in the Malaysian state of Sarawak. Under British protection from 1888 to 1983. p. 973

Brussels, Belgium (50°N/4°E). Capital of Belgium. Located in central Belgium. p. 597

Buffalo, New York (43°N/79°W). Industrial city in New York. Located on Lake Erie and the Niagara River. p. 975

Bulgaria (43°N/25°E). Country in southeastern Europe. Located on the Black Sea. Founded in the seventh century. Gained independence from the Turks in 1908. p. 973

Bull Run (39°N/78°W). Small stream near Manassas, Virginia. Site of the first major battle of the Civil War in 1861. Battle won by the South. Site of a second Confederate victory in 1862. p. 363

Bunker Hill (42°N/71°W). Overlooks Boston Harbor. Site of an early battle during the Revolutionary War. Was fortified by Patriots, then abandoned in favor of nearby Breed's Hill in 1775. p. 93

Burma (22°N/98°E). Country in Southeast Asia. Located on the Indochinese peninsula. Granted independence from Great Britain in 1948. p. 973

C

Cairo, Egypt (30°N/31°E). Capital of Egypt. Located at the head of the Nile Delta. p. 915

California (38°N/122°W). Thirty-first state to join United States. Located in western United States. Nicknamed the Golden State. Ceded to the United States by Mexico in 1848. Capital: Sacramento. pp. 974-976

Cambodia (13°N/105°E). Nation in Southeast Asia. Also known as Kampuchea. p. 973

Camden, South Carolina (34°N/81°W). City in north central South Carolina. p. 112

Cameroon (6°N/12°E). Country in west central Africa. Located on the Gulf of Guinea. Formerly a German protectorate. Gained independence from France in 1960. p. 973

Canada (60°N/95°W). Country that borders the United States on the north. Made up of ten provinces: Alberta, British Columbia, Manitoba, New Brunswick, Newfoundland, Nova Scotia, Ontario, Prince Edward Island, Quebec, and Saskatchewan. p. 972, 974-977

Canary Islands (28°N/15°W). Group of islands in the Atlantic Ocean. Located off the coast of northwest Africa. Forms a region of Spain. p. 973

Cape Canaveral, Florida (28°N/81°W). National space center. Located on the east coast of Florida. Launching site for U.S. space program. p. 977

Cape Cod, Massachusetts (42°N/70°W). Sandy peninsula in Massachusetts known for its beautiful beaches. Site of the Pilgrim landing in 1620. p. 977

Cape Verde (16°N/24°W). Country made up of a group of islands in the Atlantic Ocean. West of Africa. Granted independence from Portugal in 1975. Also, promontory on the coast of Africa. Westernmost point of Africa. p. 973

Caribbean Sea (15°N/73°W). Part of the Atlantic Ocean bounded by South America on the south, Central America on the west, and Cuba, Puerto Rico, and other islands on the north and east. Since 1823 the United States has tried to limit foreign power from this region. p. 972

Carson City, Nevada (39°N/120°W). Capital of Nevada. Located near Lake Tahoe. p. 974

Casablanca, Morocco (33°N/7°W). Port city in Morocco. Located on the Atlantic Ocean. p. 751

Cascade Range (49°N/120°W). Mountains that extend from northern California to Washington State and into Canada. Highest peak is Mt. Rainier, with an elevation of 14,410 ft. (4,392 m). p. 976

Caspian Sea (42°N/50°E). Inland salt sea. Located between Asia and extreme southeast Europe. All but the southern shore is within the Soviet Union. p. 973

Central African Republic (7°N/21°E). Country in central Africa. Located north of Zaire and the Congo. Gained independence from France in 1960. p. 973

Chad (15°N/19°E). Country in north central Africa. Located south of Libya. Gained independence from France in 1960. p. 973

Chancellorsville (38°N/78°W). Site of a Confederate victory in 1863. p. 373

Charleston, South Carolina (33°N/80°W). Port city in South Carolina. Spelled *Charles Town* in colonial days. Founded in 1670. p. 975

Charleston, West Virginia (38°N/82°W). Capital of West Virginia. Located at the point where the Elk and the Kanawha rivers join. p. 975

Chattanooga, Tennessee (35°N/85°W). City in southeastern Tennessee. Located on the Tennessee River at the Georgia border. p. 975

Chesapeake Bay (38°N/76°W). Large inlet of the Atlantic Ocean in Virginia and Maryland. About 190 miles (306 km) long. p. 977

Cheyenne, Wyoming (41°N/105°W). Capital of Wyoming. p. 974

Chicago, Illinois (42°N/88°W). One of the ten largest cities in the United States. Located in Illinois, on the southern tip of Lake Michigan. Developed as a railroad and meatpacking center in the late 1800's. p. 975

Chile (30°S/71°W). Country on the southwest coast of South America. Located between the Andes Mountains and the Pacific Ocean. p. 972

China (35°N/105°E). Country in eastern Asia having the largest population in the world. p. 973

Christmas Island (3°N/155°W). Island located in the Pacific Ocean. Part of the Kiribati islands. p. 972

Chukchi Sea (68°N/168°W). Part of the Arctic Ocean. Located north of the Bering Strait. pp. 972, 976

Cincinnati, Ohio (39°N/85°W). Large city in Ohio. Located on the Ohio River. p. 975

Cleveland, Ohio (42°N/82°W). Most populated city in Ohio. Located on Lake Erie at the mouth of the Cuyahoga River. p. 975

Clovis, New Mexico (34°N/103°W). City in New Mexico. p. 5

Coast Ranges (36°N/121°W). Mountains along the Pacific coast of North America that extend from Alaska to California. p. 976

Colombia (3°N/72°W). Country in northwestern South America. p. 972

Colorado (40°N/105°W). Thirty-eighth state to join United States. Located in west central United States. Nicknamed the Centennial State. Capital: Denver. p. 974

Colorado River (32°N/115°W). River that rises at the Continental Divide in Rocky Mountain State Park in northern Colorado and flows into the Gulf of California in Mexico. Important source of irrigation water in southwestern United States. p. 976

Columbia River (46°N/124°W). Chief river of the Pacific Northwest that rises in the Rocky Mountains in Canada and flows into the Pacific Ocean along the Washington–Oregon boundary. p. 976

Columbia, South Carolina (34°N/81°W). Capital of South Carolina. Located on the Congaree River. p. 975

Columbus, Ohio (40°N/83°W). Capital of Ohio. Located on the Scioto River. p. 975

Comstock Lode (39°N/120°W). Site of rich silver deposit near Virginia City, Nevada. p. 440

Concord, Massachusetts (42°N/71°W). Village near Boston, Massachusetts. Site of an early battle of the American Revolution in April 1775. p. 93

Concord, New Hampshire (43°N/72°W). Capital of New Hampshire. Located on the Merrimack River. p. 975

Congo (1°S/15°E). Country in west central Africa. Located west of Zaire. Gained independence from France in 1960. p. 973

Connecticut (42°N/73°W). One of the thirteen original states. Located in northeastern United States. Nicknamed the Constitution State or the Nutmeg State. Capital: Hartford. p. 975

Connecticut River (44°N/72°W). Longest river in New England. Rises in northern New Hampshire and flows into Long Island Sound at Old Saybrook, Connecticut. p. 977

Cook Islands (20°S/158°W). Group of islands in the South Pacific. Located west of Society Islands. A self-governing territory of New Zealand. p. 972

Coral Sea (14°S/150°E). Arm of the Pacific Ocean near Australia. Site of a victory by American and Australian naval forces over the Japanese in World War II. p. 973

Costa Rica (10°N/84°W). Country in Central America. Located northwest of Panama. Gained independence from Spain in 1848. p. 972

Cowpens, South Carolina (35°N/82°W). Located in South Carolina. Site of a decisive American victory in 1781, during the Revolutionary War. p. 112

Cuba (22°N/79°W). Island nation in the Caribbean. Gained independence from Spain in 1898. Strongly influenced by the United States until Fidel Castro established communist control in 1959. p. 972

Cumberland Plateau (37°N/84°W). Tableland extending from southern West Virginia to northeastern Alabama. Location of Cumberland Gap, an early emigrant route to Kentucky. p. 977

Cumberland River (37°N/86°W). Starts in Kentucky, flows into Tennessee and then back into Kentucky, where it joins the Ohio River. p. 977

Cyprus (35°N/33°E). Island country at the east end of the Mediterranean Sea. Located south of Turkey. Gained independence from Great Britain in 1960. p. 973

Czechoslovakia (49°N/17°E). Country in eastern

Europe created after World War I. Separated into two countries, the Czech Republic and Slovakia, in 1993. p. 973

D

Dallas, Texas (33°N/97°W). Second most populated city in Texas. Located on the Trinity River. p. 974

Danzig, Poland (54°N/18°E). German name for Gdánsk, port city in northern Poland. p. 721

Dayton, Ohio (40°N/84°W). City in southwestern Ohio. p. 975

Deadwood, South Dakota (44°N/104°W). City in Black Hills of South Dakota. Was a busy gold mining community in the late nineteenth century. p. 440

Death Valley, California (36°N/117°W). Desert basin located at the northern edge of the Mojave Desert in southeastern California. The valley is 282 ft. (86 m) below sea level. p. 976

Delaware (39°N/75°W). One of the 13 original states. Located in eastern United States. Nicknamed the First State and the Diamond State. Capital: Dover. p. 975

Delaware Bay (39°N/75°W). Arm of the Atlantic Ocean between New Jersey and Delaware. p. 977

Delaware River (39°N/75°W). River that rises in the Catskill Mountains in New York. Flows into the Atlantic Ocean through Delaware Bay. Forms part of the boundaries between New York, Pennsylvania, and New Jersey. p. 28

Denmark (56°N/10°E). Country in northwestern Europe, occupying most of the peninsula of Jutland and several islands in the North and Baltic seas. p. 973

Denver, Colorado (40°N/105°W). Capital of and most populated city in Colorado. Located at the base of the Rocky Mountains at the western edge of the Great Plains. Has an elevation of 5,280 ft. (1,609 m). Called the Mile-High City. p. 974

Des Moines, Iowa (42°N/94°W). Capital of Iowa. Located on the Des Moines River. p. 975

Detroit, Michigan (42°N/83°W). One of the ten largest cities in the United States. Located on the Detroit River, near Lake Erie. p. 975

District of Columbia (39°N/77°W). (Washington, D.C.) Located on the Potomac River. Seat of the federal government of the United States. p. 975

Djibouti (11°N/43°E). Country in East Africa. Located on the Gulf of Aden. p. 973

Dodge City, Kansas (38°N/100°W). City in Kansas, on the Arkansas River. Important railroad center during the late 1800's. p. 426

Dominica (15°N/61°W). Island country in the West Indies. Gained independence from Great Britain in 1978. p. 972

Dominican Republic (19°N/70°W). Country in the West Indies. Shares the island of Hispaniola with Haiti. Invaded by the United States in 1905, 1916, and 1965. p. 972

Dover, Delaware (39°N/75°W). Capital of Delaware. p. 975

Duluth, Minnesota (47°N/92°W). Port city in Minnesota. Located at the western end of Lake Superior. p. 426

E

East China Sea (29°N/125°E). Part of the Pacific Ocean. Located east of China and west of Japan. p. 973

East Germany. Reunited with West Germany in 1990. p. 775 *See* Germany

East Siberian Sea (74°N/166°E). Part of the Arctic Ocean. Located off the northeast coast of the Soviet Union and east of the New Siberian Islands. p. 973

Easter Island (27°S/110°E). Island in the South Pacific. Located west of Valparaiso, Chile. Governed as a part of Chile. p. 972

Ecuador (2°S/77°W). Country located on the northwest coast of South America. Independent since 1830. p. 972

Egypt (28°N/30°E). Country in North Africa, bordering Israel. Controls the Suez Canal. p. 973

El Alamein (31°N/29°E). Located on the north coast of Egypt. Site of a decisive British victory over the German army in World War II. p. 751

Elbe River (54°N/9°E). Located in central Europe. Flows from northwestern present-day Czech Republic through Germany. Empties into the North Sea. p. 751

El Paso, Texas (32°N/106°W). City in Texas located on the Rio Grande. Originally settled by the Spanish. p. 974

El Salvador (14°N/89°W). Country in Central America. Won independence from Spain in 1821. Torn by civil wars in recent years. p. 972

England (50°N/3°W). Part of the United Kingdom. p. 973

Equatorial Guinea (2°N/9°E). Country in west central Africa. Consists of a mainland section between Gabon and Cameroon, and two islands in the Gulf of Guinea. Gained independence from Spain in 1968. p. 973

Erie, Pennsylvania (42°N/80°W). Port city on the south shore of Lake Erie in northwestern Pennsylvania. p. 293

Ethiopia (9°N/39°E). Country in eastern Africa. Located on the Red Sea. p. 973

Europe (50°N/20°E). Continent between Asia and the Atlantic Ocean; the Ural Mountains and the

Ural River are generally considered the east boundary. p. 973

F

Faeroe Islands (62°N/7°W). Group of islands belonging to Denmark. Located in the North Atlantic between Iceland and the Shetland Islands. p. 973

Falkland Islands (52°S/59°W). Located in the South Atlantic Ocean, east of the southern tip of South America. p. 972

Florida (30°N/84°W). Twenty-seventh state to join United States. Located in southeastern United States. Nicknamed the Sunshine State. Capital: Tallahassee. p. 975

Florida Keys (25°N/81°W). Chain of islands about 150 miles (241 k) long. Stretch southwest around the tip of Florida from Virginia Key, near Miami, to Key West. p. 977

Fort McHenry (39°N/77°W). Fort located in Baltimore Harbor. British bombardment there during the War of 1812 inspired Francis Scott Key to write "The Star-Spangled Banner." p. 240

Fort Orange (43°N/74°W). Dutch name for Albany, New York. p. 28

Fort Oswego (44°N/74°W). British fort and fur-trading post. Located on Lake Ontario. p. 83

Fort Pitt (40°N/80°W). British name for Fort Duquesne after its capture from the French in 1758. p. 83

Fort Sumter (33°N/80°W). Fort guarding the entrance to Charleston Harbor in South Carolina. Confederates fired the first shots of the Civil War there in 1861. p. 360

Fort Ticonderoga (44°N/74°W). Fort on Lake Champlain. Captured in the first year of the Revolutionary War by Ethan Allen's soldiers but later retaken by the British. p. 110

Fort Wayne, Indiana (41°N/85°W). City in northeastern Indiana. p. 338

Fort Worth, Texas (33°N/97°W). City in Texas located on the Trinity River. p. 974

France (46°N/2°E). Country in western Europe. First ally of the United States. Scene of heavy fighting in World Wars I and II. p. 973

Frankfort, Kentucky (38°N/85°W). Capital of Kentucky. Located on the Kentucky River. p. 975

Franz Josef Islands (81°N/55°E). Group of islands belonging to the Soviet Union. Located in the Arctic Ocean, north of the U.S.S.R. p. 973

Fredericksburg, Virginia (38°N/78°W). Located in eastern Virginia. Site of a Confederate victory in 1862. p. 363

French Polynesia (15°S/140°W). Five archipelagoes located in the South Pacific. Territory of France. p. 972

G

Gabon (1°S/11°E). Country in west central Africa. Located on the Gulf of Guinea. Gained independence from France in 1960. p. 973

Galapagos Islands (1°S/90°W). Group of islands in the Pacific Ocean, located near the equator. Governed by Ecuador. p. 972

Galveston, Texas (29°N/95°W). Port city in southeastern Texas. Located on an island at the mouth of Galveston Bay. p. 980

Gambia (13°N/15°W). Country on the west coast of Africa. Surrounded on three sides by Senegal. Gained independence from Great Britain in 1965. p. 973

Georgia (34°N/84°W). One of the thirteen original states. Located in southeastern United States. Nicknamed the Peach State or the Empire State of the South. Capital: Atlanta. p. 975

Germany (51°N/10°E). Country in central Europe. Divided since World War II into East and West Germany; reunited in 1990. p. 973

Gettysburg, Pennsylvania (40°N/77°W). Small town in southern Pennsylvania. Site of a Union victory in 1863 and Lincoln's famous Gettysburg Address. p. 373

Ghana (8°N/2°W). Country in West Africa located on the Gulf of Guinea. Formed by a merger of the Gold Coast and the territory of Togoland. p. 973

Ghent, Belgium (51°N/3°E). City in northwestern Belgium. Capital of East Flanders. p. 602

Grand Canyon (36°N/113°W). Large canyon in Arizona formed by the Colorado River. p. 976

Great Basin (40°N/117°W). Upland region located in the United States between the Rocky Mountains on the east and the Cascade Range and Sierra Nevada on the west. p. 976

Great Lakes Group of five freshwater lakes located in the northern Midwest United States, mainly along the border between Canada and the United States. p. 977

Great Plains (42°N/100°W). Large plains area located in the western part of the Central Plains. Once grazed by large herds of buffalo. Now an important wheat-growing and ranching region. pp. 976-977

Great Salt Lake (41°N/112°W). Vast salt lake in Utah, with no streams flowing out of it. p. 976

Great Smoky Mountains (36°N/83°W). Part of the Appalachian system that extends along the North Carolina–Tennessee boundary. Highest peak is Clingman's Dome, with an elevation of 6,643 ft. (2,024 m). p. 547

Greece (39°N/22°E). Country in southeastern Europe. Member of NATO since 1952. p. 973

Greenland (70°N/40°W). World's largest island. Colonized by Vikings in the tenth century. p. 972

Grenada (12°N/61°W). Island nation in the West Indies. Invaded by the United States in 1983 to end the threat of communist influence. p. 972

Guadalcanal (9°S/160°E). Largest island of the Solomon Islands. Located in the southwest Pacific Ocean. Site of an Allied invasion during World War II. p. 755

Guadeloupe (16°N/61°W). Overseas department (administrative district) of France consisting of the two islands of Basse-Terre and Grande-Terre, and five island dependencies in the Leeward Islands. Located in the West Indies between North and South America. p. 972

Guam (14°N/143°E). Island in the Pacific Ocean. Territory of the United States. Acquired from Spain in 1898. p. 978

Guantanamo Bay (20°N/75°W). Inlet of the Caribbean Sea on the southeast coast of Cuba. Site of a U.S. naval station. p. 521

Guatemala (15°N/90°W). Country in Central America. Gained independence from Spain in 1821. Mayas built an advanced civilization there more than three thousand years ago. p. 972

Guinea-Bissau (12°N/15°W). Country in West Africa located between Guinea and Senegal. Gained independence from Portugal in 1974. p. 973

Gulf Coastal Plain (31°N/92°W). Broad plain located along the Gulf of Mexico from Florida to Texas. p. 977

Gulf of Alaska (60°N/147°W). Part of the Pacific Ocean east of Kodiak Island. p. 976

Gulf of Mexico (25°N/90°W). Body of water surrounded by the United States, Mexico, and Cuba. p. 977

Gulf of Siam (10°N/102°E). Arm of the China Sea. Located between the Malay and the Indochinese peninsulas. Now known as the Gulf of Thailand. p. 865

Gulf of Tonkin (20°N/108°E). Located off the coast of North Vietnam. An attack on American destroyers there in 1964 led to a widening of the Vietnam War. p. 857

H

Haiti (19°N/75°W). Country occupying the western portion of the island of Hispaniola, in the West Indies. Gained independence from France in the early 1800's. Occupied by U.S. troops from 1915 to 1934. p. 972

Hanoi, Vietnam (21°N/105°E). Capital of North Vietnam. p. 857

Harpers Ferry, West Virginia (39°N/78°W). Town on Potomac River in West Virginia. Abolitionist John Brown raided the arsenal there in 1859. p. 372

Harrisburg, Pennsylvania (40°N/77°W). Capital of Pennsylvania. Located on the Susquehanna River. p. 975

Hartford, Connecticut (42°N/73°W). Capital of Connecticut. Located on the Connecticut River. p. 975

Havana, Cuba (23°N/82°W). Capital of Cuba, and the most populated city in the West Indies. p. 518

Hawaii (21°N/158°W). Newest of the fifty states. Located in North Pacific Ocean. Nicknamed the Aloha State. Capital: Honolulu. pp. 972, 974

Helena, Montana (47°N/112°W). Capital of Montana. p. 974

Hiroshima, Japan (34°N/133°E). City in southern Japan. Largely destroyed by an atomic bomb dropped there on August 6, 1945. p. 755

Hispaniola (18°N/73°W). Second-largest island in the West Indies. Believed to have been visited by Columbus. Now occupied by the Dominican Republic and Haiti. p. 972

Honduras (15°N/86°W). Nation in Central America. Invaded by the United States in 1912 and in 1919 to protect American lives and property. p. 972

Hong Kong (22°N/114°E). British crown colony in southeast China. Located on the South China Sea. p. 525

Honolulu, Hawaii (21°N/158°W). Capital of and most populated city in Hawaii. Located on the island of Oahu. p. 974

Houston, Texas (30°N/95°W). City near Galveston Bay in Texas. One of the ten largest cities in the United States. p. 974

Hudson Bay (60°N/86°W). Large body of water in Canada. Connected to the Atlantic Ocean by Hudson Strait. p. 972

Hudson River (42°N/74°W). Largest river in New York State. Rises in Adirondack Mountains and flows into New York Harbor at New York City. Explored by Henry Hudson in 1609. p. 977

I

Iceland (65°N/20°W). Island nation in the North Atlantic Ocean. Settled by Vikings in the ninth century. p. 973

Idaho (44°N/116°W). Forty-third state to join United States. Located in northwestern United States. Nicknamed the Gem State. Acquired by the United States as part of the Oregon Territory. Capital: Boise. p. 974

Illinois (40°N/90°W). Twenty-first state to join United States. Located in north central United States. Nicknamed the Prairie State. Settled as part of the Northwest Territory. Capital: Springfield. p. 975

Inchon, South Korea (37°N/127°E). Port city in South Korea. Site of heavy fighting during the Korean War. p. 782

Independence, Missouri (39°N/94°W). City in western Missouri. p. 317

India (20°N/77°E). Country in south Asia. Located on a peninsula south of the Himalayas, between the Arabian Sea and the Bay of Bengal. Became a republic in 1950. p. 973

Indian Ocean (10°S/70°E). Ocean south of Asia. Located between Africa and Australia. p. 973

Indiana (40°N/86°W). Nineteenth state to join United States. Located in north central United States. Nicknamed the Hoosier State. Settled as part of the Northwest Territory. Capital: Indianapolis. p. 975

Indianapolis, Indiana (40°N/86°W). Capital of and most populated city in Indiana. p. 975

Indochina peninsula (16°N/107°E). Large peninsula south of China. Includes the countries of Burma, Thailand, Laos, Cambodia, Vietnam, and Malay. p. 865

Indonesia (5°S/120°E). Republic on the Malay Archipelago, including Java, Sumatra, most of Borneo, West Irian, Celebes, and many smaller nearby islands. Formerly the Netherlands East Indies. p. 973

Iowa (42°N/94°W). Twenty-ninth state to join United States. Located in north central United States. Nicknamed the Hawkeye State. Acquired as part of the Louisiana Purchase. Capital: Des Moines. pp. 974-975

Iran (32°N/53°E). Oil-producing country in the Middle East. Commands sea routes through the Persian Gulf. p. 973

Iraq (33°N/44°E). Country in the Middle East. At war with Iran, 1980–1988. War with U.S. over Iraqi occupation of Kuwait, January, 1991. p. 973

Israel (31°N/35°E). Country in the Middle East. Set up as a Jewish homeland in 1948. p. 973

Isthmus of Panama (9°N/79°W). Narrow strip of land joining North and South America. p. 528

Italy (43°N/13°E). Country in southern Europe. Fought with the Allies in World War I and with the Axis powers in World War II. p. 973

Ivory Coast (8°N/5°W). Country in west central Africa. Located on the Gulf of Guinea, west of Ghana. Gained independence from France in 1960. p. 973

Iwo Jima (25°N/141°E). Small island south of Japan's main islands. Site of a hard-won American victory in World War II. p. 755

J

Jackson, Mississippi (32°N/90°W). Capital of Mississippi. Located on the Pearl River. Captured by General Grant in 1863. p. 975

James River (37°N/77°W). Rises in western Virginia and flows into Chesapeake Bay. p. 977

Jamestown (37°N/77°W). First successful English settlement in America. Founded in 1607. p. 23

Jan Mayen (71°N/8°W). Norwegian island in the Arctic Ocean. Located between Greenland and Norway. Site of a meteorological station. p. 973

Japan (36°N/138°E). Densely populated industrial nation in eastern Asia. Opened up to trade with the West by Commodore Matthew Perry. One of the Axis powers in World War II. p. 973

Jefferson City, Missouri (38°N/92°W). Capital of Missouri. Located on the Missouri River. p. 975

Jersey City, New Jersey (41°N/74°W). Second most populated city in New Jersey. Located on the Hudson River, across from New York City. p. 975

Jordan (31°N/36°E). Arab country in the Middle East. p. 973

Juneau, Alaska (58°N/134°W). Capital of Alaska. Located on the Alaskan Panhandle. p. 974

K

Ka Lae (19°N/156°W). A cape on the southern tip of the island of Hawaii. The most southern point in the United States. p. 976

Kansas (38°N/99°W). Thirty-fourth state to join United States. Located in central United States. Nicknamed the Sunflower State. Acquired by the United States as part of the Louisiana Purchase. Capital: Topeka. p. 974

Kansas City, Kansas (39°N/95°W). City in Kansas located where the Kansas and Missouri rivers meet. Separated from Kansas City, Missouri, by the state line. p. 974

Kara Sea (76°N/70°E). Arm of the Arctic Ocean. Located north of the Soviet Union. p. 973

Kauai (23°N/159°W). Fourth largest of the Hawaiian Islands. p. 976

Kentucky (38°N/85°W). Fifteenth state to join United States. Located in east central United States. Nicknamed the Bluegrass State. Was the first area west of the Appalachians to be settled by the early pioneers. Capital: Frankfort. p. 975

Kenya (1°N/38°E). Country in east central Africa. Located on the Indian Ocean. Gained independence from Great Britain in 1963. p. 973

Kerguelen Islands (49°S/69°E). Group of islands in the south Indian Ocean. Consist of one large island and more than three hundred small islands. Governed by France. p. 973

Knoxville, Tennessee (36°N/84°W). City in Tennessee located on the Tennessee River. p. 975

Korea (North Korea—40°N/127°E; South Korea—36°N/128°E). Peninsula and country in east Asia. Extends south from northeast China. Divided into the Korean People's Democratic Republic (North Korea) and the Republic of Korea (South Korea) in 1948. Site of fighting over boundaries from 1950 to 1953. p. 973

L

Lake Champlain (45°N/73°W). Borders New York and Vermont. Part of the water route connecting the Hudson and St. Lawrence rivers. Named after its discoverer, Samuel de Champlain. Fort Ticonderoga is at its southern end. p. 977

Lake Erie (42°N/81°W). Second smallest of the five Great Lakes. Located along the border between Canada and the United States. Has coastline in Michigan, Ohio, Pennsylvania, New York, and Canada. p. 977

Lake Huron (44°N/82°W). Second largest of the five Great Lakes. Located along the border between Canada and the United States. The U.S. portion of the lake borders Michigan. p. 977

Lake Michigan (44°N/87°W). Third largest of the five Great Lakes. Located completely within the United States. Has coastline in Michigan, Wisconsin, Illinois, and Indiana. p. 977

Lake Okeechobee (27°N/81°W). Large lake in south central Florida. Located at the northern edge of the Everglades. p. 977

Lake Ontario (43°N/78°W). Smallest of the five Great Lakes. Located along the border between Canada and the United States. U.S. portion is in New York. The only one of the Great Lakes that does not have a coastline in Michigan. p. 977

Lake Superior (48°N/88°W). Largest of the five Great Lakes. Located farthest inland. Located along the border between Canada and the United States. Has coastline in Minnesota, Wisconsin, and Michigan. p. 977

Lake Tahoe (39°N/120°W). Located on the border between California and Nevada. p. 976

Lansing, Michigan (43°N/85°W). Capital of Michigan. Located on Grand River. p. 977

Laos (18°N/105°E). Country in the northwest part of the Indochinese peninsula. Gained independence from France in 1949. p. 973

Las Vegas, Nevada (36°N/115°W). Resort city in Nevada. p. 974

Lebanon (34°N/36°E). Country in the Middle East. Home to many Palestinian refugees. Torn by civil war since 1975. p. 973

Lexington, Massachusetts (42°N/71°W). Massachusetts town where, in April 1775, the first battle of the Revolutionary War took place between a group of minutemen and British troops. p. 93

Liberia (6°N/10°W). Country on the west coast of Africa. Founded in 1821 by the American Colonization Society as settlement for freed U.S. slaves. Established as an independent republic in 1847. p. 973

Libya (27°N/17°E). Country in North Africa. Located on the Mediterranean Sea. Became an independent kingdom in 1951 and a republic in 1969. p. 973

Liechtenstein (47°N/9°E). Country in west central Europe. Located on the Rhine River. p. 973

Lincoln, Nebraska (41°N/97°W). Capital of Nebraska. Located on a tributary of the Platte River. p. 974

Little Rock, Arkansas (35°N/92°W). Capital of Arkansas. Located on the Arkansas River. p. 975

London, England (51°N/1°W). Capital of England, the United Kingdom, and the Commonwealth. p. 15

Lone Star Republic (30°N/98°W). Another name for the Republic of Texas (1836–1845). p. 314

Louisiana (30°N/91°W). Eighteenth state to join United States. Located in southern United States. Nicknamed the Pelican State. First state created out of the Louisiana Purchase. Capital: Baton Rouge. p. 975

Louisville, Kentucky (38°N/86°W). Most populated city in Kentucky. Located on the Ohio River. p. 975

Luxembourg (50°N/6°E). Grand Duchy in western Europe. Bordered by Belgium, France, and Germany. p. 973

M

Madagascar (19°S/43°E). Large island in the Indian Ocean. Located off the southeast coast of Africa. p. 973

Madison, Wisconsin (43°N/89°W). Capital of Wisconsin. Located on an isthmus between Lakes Monona and Mendota. p. 975

Madrid, Spain (40°N/3°W). Capital of Spain. Located in the central part of the country. p. 605

Maine (44°N/70°W). Twenty-third state to join United States. Located in northeastern United States. Nicknamed the Pine Tree State. Originally part of Massachusetts. Gained separate statehood in 1820 under the terms of the Missouri Compromise. Capital: Augusta. p. 975

Malaya (2°N/112°E). Former federation of states on the southern end of the Malay Peninsula. Former British colony. Territory of Malaysia since 1963. Called Peninsular Malaysia. p. 973

Maldives (3°N/73°E). Country made up of a group of islands in the Indian Ocean. Located southwest of Sri Lanka. Gained independence from Great Britain in 1965. p. 973

Mali (17°N/4°W). Country in western Africa. Located south and east of Mauritania. Former French territory known as French Sudan. Once a member of the Mali Federation, which dissolved in 1960. p. 973

Manassas Junction, Virginia (39°N/77°W). Site of the first major Civil War battle. Located in Virginia on Bull Run stream. The battle was won by the South. p. 372

Manchuria (48°N/125°E). Industrialized region of northeastern China. Seized by Japan in the

1930's. Returned to China after World War II. p. 525

Manila, Philippines (14°N/121°E). Port city and capital of the Philippines. Located in southwest Luzon, on Manila Bay, an inlet of the China Sea. p. 517

Mariana Islands (16°N/145°E). Group of islands in the west Pacific. Located east of the Philippines. Former Japanese possession. Formerly part of the U.S. Trust Territory of the Pacific Islands. Became a commonwealth (known as the Northern Marianas) of the United States in 1978. Maintains its own internal self-government. p. 978

Marshall Islands (9°N/168°E). Group of islands in the west Pacific. Located east of the Caroline Islands. Former Japanese mandate. Part of the U.S. Trust Territory of the Pacific Islands from 1947 to 1986. p. 978.

Martinique (14°N/61°W). Island in the West Indies. Part of the Windward group. An overseas department (administrative district) of France. p. 972

Maryland (39°N/77°W). One of the thirteen original states. Located in the eastern United States. Nicknamed the Old Line State or the Free State. Capital: Annapolis. p. 975

Massachusetts (42°N/71°W). One of the thirteen original states. Nicknamed the Bay State or the Old Colony. Capital: Boston. p. 975

Maui (20°N/156°W). Second largest of the Hawaiian Islands. p. 976

Mauritius (20°S/57°E). Island in the Indian Ocean. Located east of Madagascar. p. 973

Memphis, Tennessee (35°N/90°W). Major city in Tennessee. Located on the Mississippi River. p. 975

Mesabi Range (47°N/93°W). Range of low hills located in northeastern Minnesota. Most important source of iron ore in the United States. p. 977

Mexico (23°N/102°W). Country that borders the United States on the south. Gained independence from Spain in 1821. p. 972

Mexico City, Mexico (19° N/99°W). Capital of Mexico. Most populated city in North America. Was the capital of New Spain. Site of the ancient Aztec city of Tenochtitlán. p. 323

Miami, Florida (26°N/80°W). Major city in Florida. Located on Biscayne Bay. p. 975

Michigan (43°N/85°W). Twenty-sixth state to join United States. Located in northern United States. Nicknamed the Wolverine State. Settled as part of the Northwest Territory. Capital: Lansing. p. 975

Midway Island (29°N/179°W). Annexed by the United States in 1867. American victory here was a turning point in World War II. p. 521

Milwaukee, Wisconsin (43°N/88°W). Most populated city in Wisconsin. Located on Lake Michigan. p. 975

Minneapolis, Minnesota (45°N/93°W). Most populated city in Minnesota. Located on the Mississippi River. p. 974

Minnesota (45°N/95°W). Thirty-second state to join United States. Located in northern United States. Nicknamed the North Star State or the Gopher State. Most of this state was acquired by the United States as part of the Louisiana Purchase. Capital: St. Paul. pp. 974-975

Mississippi (32°N/90°W). Twentieth state to join United States. Located in southern United States. Nicknamed the Magnolia State. Capital: Jackson. p. 975

Mississippi River (29°N/89°W). Second longest river in the United States. Rises in northern Minnesota and flows into the Gulf of Mexico near New Orleans. p. 977

Missouri (38°N/93°W). Twenty-fourth state to join United States. Located in west central United States. Nicknamed the Show Me State. Acquired by the United States as part of the Louisiana Purchase. Capital: Jefferson City. p. 975

Missouri River (39°N/91°W). Longest river in the United States. Rises in western Montana and flows into the Mississippi River near St. Louis, Missouri. pp. 976-977

Mobile, Alabama (31°N/88°W). Seaport in southwestern Alabama. Located on Mobile Bay. p. 975

Mongolia (46°N/105°E). Region in east central Asia. Consists of Inner Mongolia and the Mongolian People's Republic. p. 973

Montana (47°N/112°W). Forty-first state to join United States. Located in northwestern United States. Nicknamed the Treasure State. Acquired in part by the United States through the Louisiana Purchase. Capital: Helena. p. 974

Montgomery, Alabama (32°N/86°W). Capital of Alabama. Located on the Alabama River. p. 973

Montpelier, Vermont (44°N/73°W). Capital of Vermont. Located on the Winooski River. p. 973

Montreal, Québec, Canada (45°N/73°W). Most populated city in Canada. Located on an island in the St. Lawrence River. p. 977

Morristown, New Jersey (41°N/74°W). Town in north central New Jersey. p. 110

Moscow, Russian Federation, Commonwealth of Independent States (56°N/38°E). Capital of Russian Federation, former capital of U.S.S.R. p. 605

Mount Elbert (39°N/106°W). Highest peak in the Rocky Mountains. Located in Colorado. Elevation 14,433 ft. (4,399 m). p. 976

Mount McKinley or Mount Denali (63°N/150°W). Highest mountain peak in North America. Located in Alaska Range in Alaska. Elevation 20,320 ft. (6,193 m). p. 976

Mount Mitchell (36°N/82°W). Highest peak in the

Appalachian Mountains. Located in North Carolina. Elevation 6,684 ft. (2,037 m). p. 977

Mount Washington (44°N/71°W). Highest point in New England. Located in the White Mountains of New Hampshire. Windiest place in the United States. Elevation 6,288 ft. (1,917 m). p. 977

Munich, Germany (48°N/11°E). City in southern Germany. Capital of Bavaria. p. 721

Muscle Shoals, Alabama (35°N/88°W). Former rapids in the Tennessee River. Located in northwestern Alabama. Site of the Wilson Dam. p. 698.

N

Nagasaki, Japan (33°N/130°E). Japanese port city. Largely destroyed by the atomic bomb dropped there on August 9, 1945. p. 755

Namibia (22°S/17°E). Country in southern Africa. Located on the Atlantic Ocean. Former mandate of South Africa. Administered by the Republic of South Africa. Now known as South West Africa. p. 973

Nashville, Tennessee (36°N/87°W). Capital of Tennessee. Located on the Cumberland River. p. 975

Nebraska (41°N/97°W). Thirty-seventh state to join United States. Located in central United States. Nicknamed the Cornhusker State. Acquired by the United States as part of the Louisiana Purchase. Capital: Lincoln. p. 974

Netherlands (52°N/5°E). Country in western Europe. Located on the North Sea. p. 973

Nevada (39°N/117°W). Thirty-sixth state to join United States. Located in western United States. Nicknamed the Sagebrush State. Acquired by the United States at the end of the Mexican War. Capital: Carson City. p. 974

New Amsterdam (41°N/74°W). Settlement founded by the Dutch on Manhattan Island. Now called New York City. p. 28

New Guinea (5°S/140°E). Large island in the East Indies. Located north of Australia. p. 973

New Hampshire (43°N/72°W). One of the thirteen original states. Located in the northeastern United States. Nicknamed the Granite State. Capital: Concord. p. 975

New Haven, Connecticut (41°N/73°W). Major city in Connecticut. Located on Long Island Sound. At one time it was one of two capitals of Connecticut. p. 975

New Jersey (40°N/75°W). One of the thirteen original states. Located in the eastern United States. Nicknamed the Garden State. Capital: Trenton. p. 975

New Mexico (35°N/106°W). Forty-seventh state to join United States. Located in southwestern United States. Nicknamed the Land of Enchantment. Acquired by the United States at the end of the Mexican War. Capital: Santa Fe. p. 974

New Orleans, Louisiana (30°N/90°W). Port city in Louisiana. Located near the mouth of the Mississippi River. One of the busiest port cities in the United States. Originally settled by the French in the 1600's. Site of a battle between American and British forces in 1815. p. 975

New York (43°N/74°W). One of the thirteen original states. Located in the northeastern United States. Nicknamed the Empire State. Capital: Albany. p. 975

New York City, New York (41°N/74°W). Most populated city in the United States. Located at the mouth of the Hudson River in the state of New York. Founded by the Dutch as New Amsterdam. First capital of the United States. p. 975

New Zealand (41°S/174°E). Country consisting of two large and several smaller islands in the South Pacific. Located southeast of Australia. p. 973

Newark, New Jersey (40°N/74°W). Most populated city in New Jersey. Located on the Passaic River and Newark Bay. p. 975

Newfoundland (48°N/57°W). Large island at the mouth of the St. Lawrence River. Part of Canada. p. 977

Niagara Falls, New York (43°N/79°W). City in western New York. Located near Niagara Falls. p. 240

Nicaragua (13°N/85°W). Country in Central America. Won independence from Spain in 1821. Ruled by the Sandinistas 1979-1989. p. 972

Nigeria (10°N/8°E). Country in west Africa. Located on the Gulf of Guinea. Gained independence from Great Britain in 1960. p. 973

Nile River (30°N/31°E). River in northeast Africa. Formed in Sudan by the joining of the Blue Nile, flowing from Ethiopia, and the White Nile, flowing from Lake Victoria. Flows northward through Egypt into the Mediterranean Sea. p. 915

Norfolk, Virginia (37°N/76°W). City in Virginia located on Hampton Roads channel. p. 975

Normandy, France (49°N/0°E). Region of northern France. Allies landed there on D-day during World War II. p. 751

North America (45°N/100°W). Continent in the Western Hemisphere. p. 972

North Carolina (36°N/79°W). One of the thirteen original states. Located in the southeastern United States. Nicknamed the Tar Heel State or the Old North State. Capital: Raleigh. p. 975

North Dakota (47°N/101°W). Thirty-ninth state to join United States. Located in northern United States. Nicknamed the Sioux State or the Flickertail State. Acquired by the United States as part of the Louisiana Purchase. Capital: Bismarck. p. 974

North Korea (40°N/127°E). Country in eastern

Asia. Divided from South Korea at the 38th parallel. p. 973

North Sea (55°N/3°E). Arm of the Atlantic Ocean. Located between the United Kingdom and the European mainland. p. 973

Norway (62°N/10°E). Country in northern Europe. Located on the Scandinavian Peninsula. p. 973

Nueces River (28°N/98°W). Claimed by Mexico in the Mexican War as the southern border of Texas. p. 314

O

Oak Ridge, Tennessee (36°N/84°W). City in eastern Tennessee. Located near Knoxville. Center for atomic research. p. 698

Ogden, Utah (41°N/112°W). City in Utah. Site of the completion in 1869 of the transcontinental railroad. p. 426

Ohio (40°N/83°W). Seventeenth state to join United States. Located in northeast central United States. Nicknamed the Buckeye State. Settled as part of the Northwest Territory. Capital: Columbus. p. 975

Ohio River (37°N/89°W). Formed at Pittsburgh, Pennsylvania, by the joining of the Allegheny and the Monongahela rivers. Flows into the Mississippi River at Cairo, Illinois. Forms part of the boundaries of five states. p. 977

Okinawa, Japan (27°N/129°E). Small island southwest of Japan. Captured by Americans at the end of World War II. p. 755

Oklahoma (35°N/98°W). Forty-sixth state to join United States. Located in south central United States. Nicknamed the Sooner State. Acquired by the United States as part of the Louisiana Purchase. Capital: Oklahoma City. p. 974

Oklahoma City, Oklahoma (35°N/98°W). Capital of Oklahoma. p. 974

Olympia, Washington (47°N/123°W). Capital of Washington State. Located on Puget Sound. p. 974

Omaha, Nebraska (41°N/96°W). City in Nebraska located on the Missouri River. p. 974

Oman (22°N/58°E). Country in southeastern Arabia. Located on the Arabian Sea. p. 973

Oregon (45°N/123°W). Thirty-third state to join United States. Located in northwestern United States. Nicknamed the Beaver State. Acquired by the United States as part of the Oregon Country. Capital: Salem. p. 974

Ottawa, Ontario, Canada (45°N/76°W). Capital of Canada. p. 977

Ouachita Mountains (35°N/94°W). Located in Arkansas and Oklahoma. Part of the Ozark plateau. pp. 976-977

Ozark plateau (37°N/93°W). Elevated area extending from Missouri through Arkansas and into Oklahoma. pp. 976-977

P

Pacific Ocean (10°S/150°W). Largest of the earth's oceans. Located between Asia and the American continents. pp. 972-973

Padre Island (27°N/97°W). Sand reef off the coast of southern Texas in the Gulf of Mexico. Site of a national seashore. p. 976

Palestine (32°N/35°E). Region in southwestern Asia. Located at the east end of the Mediterranean. Includes parts given to Israel, Jordan, and Egypt. p. 605

Panama (9°N/79°W). Country on the isthmus separating North and South America. Gained independence from Colombia in 1903. Site of the Panama Canal. p. 972

Paraguay (23°S/58°W). Inland country in south central South America. p. 972

Paris, France (49°N/2°E). Capital of France. p. 605

Pearl Harbor (21°N/158°W). American naval base near Honolulu, Hawaii. Attacked by Japanese on December 7, 1941. The next day the United States declared war on Japan. p. 739

Pennsylvania (40°N/77°W). One of the thirteen original states. Located in the eastern United States. Nicknamed the Keystone State. Capital: Harrisburg. p. 975

Pensacola, Florida (30°N/87°W). Port city in northwestern Florida. Located on an inlet of the Gulf of Mexico. p. 240

Persian Gulf (28°N/51°E). Major sea route for ships carrying Middle Eastern oil exports. p. 973

Peru (10°S/76°W). Country in South America. Gained independence from Spain in 1821. p. 972

Philadelphia, Pennsylvania (40°N/75°W). Major port and chief city in Pennsylvania. Located where the Delaware and Schuylkill rivers join. One of the ten largest cities in the United States. Second capital of the United States. p. 975

Philippine Islands (14°N/125°E). Group of islands in the Pacific Ocean off the coast of Asia. Acquired by the United States in 1898. Won independence in 1946. p. 973

Phoenix, Arizona (33°N/112°W). Capital of and most populated city in Arizona. Located on the Salt River. p. 974

Piedmont (35°N/81°W). Hilly region of the eastern United States. Located between the Atlantic Coastal Plain and the Appalachian Mountains. Stretches from southeastern New York to central Florida. p. 39

Pierre, South Dakota (44°N/100°W). Capital of South Dakota. Located on the Missouri River. p. 974

Pittsburgh, Pennsylvania (40°N/80°W). Second most populated city in Pennsylvania. Located at the point where the Allegheny and the Monongahela rivers join. p. 975

Plymouth (42°N/71°W). New England colony founded in 1620 by Pilgrims. Absorbed by the Massachusetts Bay Colony in 1691. p. 27

Plymouth, England (50°N/4°W). Port city in southwestern England. Located on the English Channel. p. 13

Poland (52°N/19°E). Country in eastern Europe. Became a Soviet satellite after World War II. Began moving toward democracy and a free-market economy in 1989. p. 973

Portland, Maine (44°N/70°W). Seaport city in southern Maine. Located on Casco Bay, which is part of the Atlantic Ocean. p. 294

Portland, Oregon (46°N/123°W). Most populated city in Oregon. Located on the Willamette River near the point where it joins the Columbia River. p. 974

Portsmouth, Virginia (37°N/76°W). City in Virginia located on Hampton Roads channel. p. 116

Portugal (39°N/8°W). Country in western Europe. In the 1400's, sailors set out from this country to explore the coast of Africa. p. 973

Potomac River (39°N/78°W). Rises in West Virginia and flows into Chesapeake Bay. Forms part of the Maryland–Virginia border. Washington, D.C., is located on this river. p. 39

Potsdam, Germany (52°N/13°W). City in former East Germany. Located near Berlin. Site of a post-World War II conference. p. 832

Princeton, New Jersey (40°N/75°W). City in New Jersey. Site of an American victory during the Revolutionary War. p. 110

Providence, Rhode Island (42°N/71°W). Capital of Rhode Island. Located at the head of the Providence River. p. 975

Puerto Rico (18°N/67°W). Island in the West Indies. Acquired from Spain after the Spanish-American War. Now a self-governing commonwealth of the United States. p. 978

Puget Sound (48°N/122°W). Inlet of the Pacific Ocean in Washington State stretching from Juan de Fuca Bay to Olympia. p. 976

Q

Qatar (25°N/51°E). Country occupying a peninsula of East Arabia. Located on the Persian Gulf. p. 973

Québec, Québec, Canada (47°N/71°W). City in Canada located on the north side of the St. Lawrence River. Founded in 1608 by Samuel de Champlain. Capital of the province of Québec. p. 977

R

Raleigh, North Carolina (36°N/79°W). Capital of North Carolina. p. 975

Red River (31°N/92°W). Rises in New Mexico, flows across the Texas Panhandle, and then forms the boundary between Texas and Oklahoma. pp. 976-977

Republic of Texas (30°N/98°W). Independent nation set up by American settlers in Texas. Lasted from 1836 to 1845. p. 314

Rhine River (52°N/6°E). River in western Europe. Flows from Switzerland north through Germany, then west into the Netherlands. Empties into the North Sea. p. 751

Rhineland (50°N/7°E). Region of Germany. Located west of the Rhine River. p. 721

Rhode Island (42°N/71°W). One of the thirteen original states. Located in the northeastern United States. Nicknamed the Little Rhody or the Ocean State. Capital: Providence. p. 975

Richmond, Virginia (38°N/77°W). Capital of Virginia. Located on the James River. Capital of the Confederacy. p. 975

Rio Grande (30°N/105°W). River that rises in the Rocky Mountains in Colorado and empties into the Gulf of Mexico near Brownsville, Texas. Forms the boundary between Texas and Mexico. p. 976

Roanoke River (37°N/80°W). Flows southeast through Virginia and North Carolina from the Appalachian Mountains to Albermarle Sound. p. 39

Rocky Mountains (48°N/116°W). Longest mountain chain in the United States. Stretches from Alaska to Mexico. Highest peak is Mt. Elbert, with an elevation of 14,433 ft. (4,399 m). Barrier to travel in pioneer days. p. 976

Romania (46°N/25°E). Country in southeastern Europe. Located on the Black Sea. p. 973

S

Sacramento, California (39°N/122°W). Capital of California. Located on the Sacramento River. Developed as a gold rush boom town. p. 974

Sacramento River (39°N/122°W). River in California that flows into San Francisco Bay. p. 976

Saigon, Vietnam (11°N/106°E). Port city in South Vietnam. Formerly the capital of South Vietnam. Now known as Ho Chi Minh City. p. 865

St. Lawrence River (49°N/67°W). Flows northeast from Lake Ontario to the Atlantic Ocean at the Gulf of St. Lawrence. Forms part of the border between the United States and Canada. p. 977

St. Louis, Missouri (39°N/90°W). Most populated city in Missouri. Located on the Mississippi

River near the point where it is joined by the Missouri River. p. 975

St. Paul, Minnesota (45°N/93°W). Capital of Minnesota. Located on the Mississippi River. p. 974

Salem, Massachusetts (43°N/71°W). City in northeastern Massachusetts. Located on Massachusetts Bay. Suburb of Boston. p. 31

Salem, Oregon (45°N/123°W). Capital of Oregon. Located on the Willamette River. p. 974

Salerno, Italy (40°N/14°E). Port city in southern Italy. Located on an inlet of the Tyrrhenian Sea. p. 751

Salt Lake City, Utah (41°N/112°W). Capital of and most populated city in Utah. Located near the Great Salt Lake. Founded in 1847 by Mormons. p. 974

Salton Sea (33°N/116°W). Salty, below-sea-level lake. Located in southern California. p. 976

San Antonio, Texas (29°N/99°W). City in Texas located on the San Antonio River. Site of the Alamo. p. 974

San Diego, California (33°N/117°W). City in California located near the Pacific Ocean. First of twenty-one Spanish missions built in California. p. 974

San Francisco, California (38°N/122°W). Major city in California. Located on San Francisco Bay. Boom town of the 1848 California gold rush. p. 974

San Jose, California (37°N/122°W). Major city in California. One of the twenty largest cities in the United States. p. 974

San Juan, Puerto Rico (18°N/66°W). Capital of and most populated city in Puerto Rico. p. 978

San Salvador (13°N/89°W). One of a group of islands called the Bahamas. Located in the West Indies. p. 15

Santa Fe, New Mexico (35°N/106°W). Capital of New Mexico. First settled by the Spanish in 1609. p. 974

Sarajevo, Bosnia (43°N/18°E). Capital of Bosnia in southwestern Europe where assassination of Archduke Francis Ferdinand in 1914 sparked World War I. Besieged by Serbian gunners after Bosnia declared independence from old Yugoslavia in 1992. p. 597

Saratoga, New York (43°N/75°W). City in eastern New York. Also called Saratoga Springs. The American victory there in 1777 was a turning point in the Revolution. p. 110

Saudi Arabia (25°N/45°E). Kingdom occupying most of the Arabian Peninsula. p. 973

Scotland (57°N/4°W). Part of the United Kingdom. Located in the northern half of Great Britain and its nearby islands. p. 973

Seattle, Washington (48°N/122°W). Most populated city in Washington. Located on eastern shore of Puget Sound. p. 974

Seoul, Korea (37°N/127°E). Capital of South Korea. Located in the northwestern part of the country. p. 782

Serbia (43°N/21° E) One of six republics in the old Yugoslavia and one of two in the smaller Yugoslavia formed in 1992. Located in the eastern part of the country. p. 973

Shanghai, China (31°N/121°E). Port city in the Jiangsu province of China. Located in eastern China near the mouth of the Chang River (Yangtze River). p. 739

Shenandoah River (39°N/78°W). River in northern Virginia. Flows between the Blue Ridge and the Allegheny mountains. Empties into the Potomac River. p. 363

Shiloh, Tennessee (35°N/88°W). Site of a Union victory in 1862. Located on the Tennessee River. p. 363

Sierra Leone (8°N/11°W) Country in western Africa. Located on the Atlantic Ocean between Guinea and Liberia. Gained independence from Great Britain in 1961. p. 973

Sierra Nevada (38°N/119°W). High mountain range. Located mainly in eastern California. Highest peak is Mt. Whitney, with an elevation of 14,494 ft. (4,418m). p. 976

Sinai Peninsula (29°N/33°E). Desert region in northeastern Egypt. Captured by Israel in 1967. Returned to Egypt under terms of the Camp David Accords. p. 915

Singapore (1°N/103°E). Island country off the southern tip of the Malay Peninsula. p. 973

Snake River (49°N/117°W). Rises in Yellowstone National Park in Wyoming and flows into the Columbia River in Washington State. p. 976

Solomon Islands (8°S/159°E). Country consisting of several islands in the southwest Pacific. Located east of New Guinea. Gained independence from Great Britain in 1978. p. 973

Somalia (10°N/49°E) Country in East Africa. Located on the Indian Ocean and the Gulf of Aden. Formed by the merger of Italian Somaliland and British Somaliland. Site of massive international food-relief effort in 1993 that was protected from internal warring factions by U.S. troops. p. 973

South Africa (30°S/26°E). Country in southernmost Africa. p. 973

South America (15°S/60°W). World's fourth largest continent. Located in Western Hemisphere. p. 972

South Carolina (34°N/81°W). One of the thirteen original states. Located in the southeastern United States. Nicknamed the Palmetto State. Capital: Columbia. p. 975

South China Sea (10°N/113°E). Arm of the west Pacific Ocean. Touches Taiwan, the Philippines, Borneo, the Malay Peninsula, Indochina, and China. p. 973

South Dakota (44°N/100°W). Fortieth state to join United States. Located in north central United States. Nicknamed the Coyote State or the Sunshine State. Acquired by the United States as part of the Louisiana Purchase. Capital: Pierre. p. 974

South Georgia (54°S/37°W). Island dependency of the Falkland Islands. Located in the South Atlantic Ocean. p. 972

South Korea (36°N/128°E). Country in eastern Asia. Divided from North Korea at the 38th parallel. p. 973

Soviet Union (60°N/80°E). Shortened name for the Union of Soviet Socialist Republics which became the Commonwealth of Independent States in 1991. Known as Russia before 1922. p. 973

Spain (40°N/4°W). Country in southwestern Europe. p. 973

Springfield, Illinois (40°N/90°W). Capital of Illinois. Located on the Sangamon River. p. 975

Springfield, Massachusetts (42°N/73°W). City in Massachusetts located on the Connecticut River. p. 975

Sri Lanka (7°N/81°E). Island country off the southeastern coast of India. Gained independence from Great Britain in 1948. p. 973

Stalingrad (49°N/42°E). City in the Russian Federation of the Commonwealth of Independent States (formerly Soviet Union). Withstood a seige by Nazis in World War II. Renamed Volgograd in 1961. p. 751

Sudan (15°N/30°E). Country in north central Africa. Located south of Egypt. Gained independence from Great Britain in 1956. p. 973

Suez Canal (30°N/32°E). Canal across the Isthmus of Suez. Joins the Mediterranean Sea and the Gulf of Suez. p. 807

Susquehanna River (41°N/78°W). Rises in Otsego Lake in New York and flows into northern end of Chesapeake Bay. p. 977

Swaziland (26°S/31°E). Country in southeast Africa. Surrounded on three sides by South Africa. Gained independence in 1968. p. 973

Syria (35°N/38°E). Arab country in the Middle East. p. 973

T

Taiwan (24°N/122°E). Island off the coast of southeast China. Chiang Kai-shek retreated there in 1949 after the Communist Chinese took over mainland China. Forms the Republic of China. p. 973

Tallahassee, Florida (30°N/84°W). Capital of Florida. Located in northern Florida. p. 975

Tampa, Florida (28°N/82°W). City in Florida located on Tampa Bay. p. 975

Tanzania (6°S/35°E). Country in East Africa. Formed by the merger of Tanganyika and Zanzibar in 1964. p. 973

Tasman Sea (40°S/163°E). Section of the South Pacific. Located between southeastern Australia and New Zealand. p. 973

Tehran (36°N/52°E). Capital of Iran. American hostages were held there from November 1979 to January 1981. p. 915

Tennessee (36°N/87°W). Sixteenth state to join United States. Located in southeast central United States. Nicknamed the Volunteer State. Gained independence after North Carolina ceded its western lands to the United States. Capital: Nashville. p. 975

Tennessee River (35°N/88°W). Tributary of the Ohio River. Formed near Knoxville, Tennessee, by the joining of the Holston and French Broad rivers. Flows into the Ohio River at Paducah, Kentucky. p. 977

Tenochtitlán (19°N/99°W). Capital of the Aztec empire. Now part of Mexico City. p. 6

Texas (30°N/98°W). Twenty-eighth state to join United States. Located in southern United States. Nicknamed the Lone Star State. Proclaimed independence from Mexico in 1836. Was a separate republic until 1845. Capital: Austin. pp. 974-975

Thailand (15°N/100°E). Country in Southeast Asia. Located on the Indochinese and Malay peninsulas. p. 973

Thames River (43°N/82°W). Flows southwest across Ontario into the Great Lakes near Detroit. Site of a battle during the War of 1812. p. 240

Tippecanoe River (41°N/86°W). River in northern Indiana. Flows southwest into the Wabash River. p. 240

Togo (8°N/1°E). Country in West Africa. Located on the Gulf of Guinea east of Ghana. Gained independence from France in 1960. p. 973

Tokyo, Japan (35°N/139°E). Port city and capital of Japan. Located on Tokyo Bay. p. 755

Toledo, Ohio (42°N/84°W). City in Ohio located on Lake Erie. p. 975

Tonga (20°S/175°W). Kingdom consisting of a group of islands in the southwest Pacific. Located east of Fiji. p. 972

Topeka, Kansas (39°N/95°W). Capital of Kansas. Located on the Kansas River. p. 974

Trenton, New Jersey (40°N/75°W). Capital of New Jersey. Located on the east side of the Delaware River. p. 975

Trinidad and Tobago (11°N/61°W). Country in the West Indies consisting of two islands. Gained independence from Great Britain in 1962. p. 972

Tulsa, Oklahoma (36°N/96°W). City in Oklahoma. An important oil industry center. p. 974

Tunisia (34°N/9°E). Country in northern Africa. Located on the Mediterranean Sea. Gained independence from France in 1956. p. 973

Turkey (39°N/35°E). Country in the Middle East. Located in Asia Minor and in the southeastern region of the Balkan Peninsula. Member of NATO since 1952. p. 973

U

Uganda (1°N/32°E). Country in east central Africa. Gained independence from Great Britain in 1962. p. 973

United Kingdom (52°N/1°W). Island nation in western Europe. Includes England, Scotland, Wales, and Northern Ireland. p. 973

Uruguay (33°S/56°W). Country in southeastern South America. Located on the Atlantic Ocean. p. 972

Utah (41°N/112°W). Forty-fifth state to join United States. Located in west central United States. Nicknamed the Beehive State. Settled by Mormons. Capital: Salt Lake City. p. 974

V

Valley Forge (40°N/76°W). Winter headquarters for the Continental army led by George Washington in 1777–1778. Located near Philadelphia. p. 110

Vancouver Island (49°N/123°W). Island that is part of British Columbia, Canada. p. 976

Venezuela (8°N/66°W). Country in northern South America. p. 972

Veracruz, Mexico (19°N/96°W). Port city in Mexico. Located on the Gulf of Mexico. p. 323

Vermont (44°N/73°W). Fourteenth state to join United States. Located in the northeastern United States. Nicknamed the Green Mountain State. First new state to join the Union after the Revolution. Capital: Montpelier. p. 975

Vichy, France (46°N/3°E). City in central France. Capital of unoccupied France from 1940 to 1944. p. 747

Vicksburg, Mississippi (32°N/91°W). Located in Mississippi on a high cliff overlooking the Mississippi River. Grant's victory there in 1863 split the South into two parts. p. 373

Vienna, Austria (48°N/16°E). Capital of Austria. Located in the northeastern part of the country, along the Danube River. p. 605

Vietnam (16°N/108°E). Country in Southeast Asia. Divided into North and South Vietnam in 1954. Remained divided until North Vietnam defeated South Vietnam in a long war. p. 973

Virginia (38°N/77°W). One of the thirteen original states. Located in the eastern United States. Nicknamed the Old Dominion. Capital: Richmond. p. 975

Virgin Islands (18°N/64°W). Territory of the United States located in the Caribbean east of Puerto Rico. Purchased from Denmark in 1917. p. 978

W

Wake Island (19°N/166°E). Coral atoll located in the North Pacific Ocean between Midway and Guam. A possession of the United States. p. 978

Washington (47°N/123°W). Forty-second state to join United States. Located in the northwestern United States. Nicknamed the Evergreen State. Capital: Olympia. p. 974

Washington, D.C. (39°N/77°W). Capital of the United States since 1800. Located on the Potomac River. Called Federal City until it was renamed for George Washington in 1799. p. 975

West Indies (19°N/70°W). Group of islands in the Caribbean Sea stretching about 2,500 miles (4,023 km) from near Florida to near Venezuela. Explored by Columbus in 1492. p. 972

West Virginia (39°N/80°W). Thirty-fifth state to join United States. Located in the east-central United States. Nicknamed the Mountain State. Capital: Charleston. p. 975

Western Samoa (13°S/172°W). Country in the South Pacific consisting of two large and several smaller islands. Former German protectorate. Gained independence from New Zealand in 1962. p. 972

White Plains, New York (41°N/74°W). City in southeastern New York. Located near New York City. Site of a Revolutionary War battle in 1776. p. 110

Wichita, Kansas (38°N/97°W). City in Kansas located on the Arkansas River. p. 974

Williamsburg, Virginia (37°N/77°W). Colonial capital of Virginia. p. 31

Wilmington, Delaware (40°N/76°W). City in Delaware located on the Delaware River. p. 975

Wisconsin (43°N/89°W). Thirtieth state to join United States. Located in the northern United States. Nicknamed the Badger State. Settled as part of the Northwest Territory. Capital: Madison. pp. 974-975

Wounded Knee, South Dakota (43°N/102°W). Located in what is now South Dakota. Site of a massacre of Indians in 1890. p. 420

Wyoming (41°N/105°W). Forty-fourth state to join United States. Located in the northwestern United States. Nicknamed the Equality State. Capital: Cheyenne. p. 974

Y

Yangtze River (31°N/121°E). Largest river and chief commercial route of China. Flows from Tibet into the East China Sea near Shanghai. Now known as the Chang River. p. 739

Yellowstone National Park (45°N/110°W). Oldest and largest national park in the United States. Located mostly in Wyoming. p. 547

Yemen (15°N/44°E). Country in the south Arabian Peninsula. Located on the Red Sea. p. 973

Yonkers, New York (41°N/74°W). City in New York located on the Hudson River. p. 975

Yorktown, Virginia (37°N/77°W). Town in Virginia located near the York River. Site of a decisive American victory in 1781. p. 116

Ypres, Belgium (50°N/2°E). Town in northwestern Belgium. Located near the French border. Site of heavy fighting during World War I. p. 602

Yucatan Peninsula (19°N/89°W). Located in Central America. Separates the Gulf of Mexico and the Caribbean Sea. p. 972

Yugoslavia (44°N/19°E). Country in the northwestern region of the Balkan Peninsula. Located on the Adriatic Sea. Formerly made up of six republics. Reduced to two (Serbia and Montenegro) when four republics declared independence in 1991-92, an act that provoked a Serbian invasion of Croatia and Bosnia. p. 973

Yukon River (62°N/163°W). Third longest river in North America. Formed in Yukon Territory, Canada, and flows into the Bering Sea. p. 976

Z

Zaire (4°S/25°E). Country in central Africa. Located on the equator. Gained independence from Belgium in 1960. p. 973

Zambia (15°S/30°E). Country in South Africa. Formerly known as Northern Rhodesia. p. 973

Zimbabwe (20°S/30°E). Country in South Africa. Located north of South Africa and west of Mozambique. Formerly known as Southern Rhodesia. p. 973

Facts About the States

Alabama
4,136,000 people
51,609 square miles
Rank in area: 29
Entered Union in 1819

Montgomery

Alaska
587,000 people
589,757 square miles
Rank in area: 1
Entered Union in 1959

Juneau

Arizona
3,832,000 people
113,909 square miles
Rank in area: 6
Entered Union in 1912

Phoenix

Arkansas
2,399,000 people
53,104 square miles
Rank in area: 27
Entered Union in 1836

Little Rock

California
30,867,000 people
158,693 square miles
Rank in area: 3
Entered Union in 1850

Sacramento

Colorado
3,470,000 people
104,247 square miles
Rank in area: 8
Entered Union in 1876

Denver

Connecticut
3,281,000 people
5,009 square miles
Rank in area: 48
Entered Union in 1788

Hartford

Delaware
689,000 people
2,057 square miles
Rank in area: 49
Entered Union in 1787

Dover

Florida
13,488,000 people
58,560 square miles
Rank in area: 22
Entered Union in 1845

Tallahassee

Georgia
6,751,000 people
58,876 square miles
Rank in area: 21
Entered Union in 1788

Atlanta

Hawaii
1,160,000 people
6,450 square miles
Rank in area: 47
Entered Union in 1959

Honolulu

Idaho
1,067,000 people
83,557 square miles
Rank in area: 13
Entered Union in 1890

Boise

Illinois
11,631,000 people
56,400 square miles
Rank in area: 24
Entered Union in 1818

Springfield

Indiana
5,662,000 people
36,291 square miles
Rank in area: 38
Entered Union in 1816

Indianapolis

Iowa
2,812,000 people
56,290 square miles
Rank in area: 25
Entered Union in 1846

Des Moines

Kansas
2,523,000 people
82,264 square miles
Rank in area: 14
Entered Union in 1861

Topeka

Kentucky
3,755,000 people
40,395 square miles
Rank in area: 37
Entered Union in 1792

Frankfort

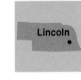
Louisiana
4,287,000 people
48,523 square miles
Rank in area: 31
Entered Union in 1812

Baton Rouge

Maine
1,235,000 people
33,215 square miles
Rank in area: 39
Entered Union in 1820

Augusta

Maryland
4,908,000 people
10,577 square miles
Rank in area: 42
Entered Union in 1788

Annapolis

Massachusetts
5,998,000 people
8,257 square miles
Rank in area: 45
Entered Union in 1788

Boston

Michigan
9,437,000 people
58,216 square miles
Rank in area: 23
Entered Union in 1837

Lansing

Minnesota
4,480,000 people
84,068 square miles
Rank in area: 12
Entered Union in 1858

St. Paul

Mississippi
2,614,000 people
47,716 square miles
Rank in area: 32
Entered Union in 1817

Jackson

Missouri
5,193,000 people
69,686 square miles
Rank in area: 19
Entered Union in 1821

Jefferson City

Montana
824,000 people
147,138 square miles
Rank in area: 4
Entered Union in 1889

Helena

Nebraska
1,606,000 people
77,227 square miles
Rank in area: 15
Entered Union in 1867

Lincoln

1992 U.S. Census
Bureau Population Estimates

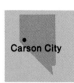

Nevada
1,327,000 people
110,540 square miles
Rank in area: 7
Entered Union in 1864

Carson City

New Hampshire
1,111,000 people
9,304 square miles
Rank in area: 44
Entered Union in 1788

Concord

New Jersey
7,789,000 people
7,836 square miles
Rank in area: 46
Entered Union in 1787

Trenton

New Mexico
1,581,000 people
121,666 square miles
Rank in area: 5
Entered Union in 1912

Santa Fe

New York
18,119,000 people
49,576 square miles
Rank in area: 30
Entered Union in 1788

Albany

North Carolina
6,843,000 people
52,586 square miles
Rank in area: 28
Entered Union in 1789

Raleigh

North Dakota
636,000 people
70,665 square miles
Rank in area: 17
Entered Union in 1889

Bismarck

Ohio
11,016,000 people
41,222 square miles
Rank in area: 35
Entered Union in 1803

Columbus

Oklahoma
3,212,000 people
69,919 square miles
Rank in area: 18
Entered Union in 1907

Oklahoma City

Oregon
2,977,000 people
96,981 square miles
Rank in area: 10
Entered Union in 1859

Salem

Pennsylvania
12,009,000 people
45,333 square miles
Rank in area: 33
Entered Union in 1787

Harrisburg

Rhode Island
1,005,000 people
1,214 square miles
Rank in area: 50
Entered Union in 1790

Providence

South Carolina
3,603,000 people
31,055 square miles
Rank in area: 40
Entered Union in 1788

Columbia

South Dakota
711,000 people
77,047 square miles
Rank in area: 16
Entered Union in 1889

Pierre

Tennessee
5,024,000 people
42,244 square miles
Rank in area: 34
Entered Union in 1796

Nashville

Texas
17,656,000 people
267,336 square miles
Rank in area: 2
Entered Union in 1845

Austin

Utah
1,813,000 people
84,916 square miles
Rank in area: 11
Entered Union in 1896

Salt Lake City

Vermont
570,000 people
9,609 square miles
Rank in area: 43
Entered Union in 1791

Montpelier

Virginia
6,377,000 people
40,817 square miles
Rank in area: 36
Entered Union in 1788

Richmond

Washington
5,136,000 people
68,192 square miles
Rank in area: 20
Entered Union in 1889

Olympia

West Virginia
1,812,000 people
24,181 square miles
Rank in area: 41
Entered Union in 1863

Charleston

Wisconsin
5,007,000 people
56,154 square miles
Rank in area: 26
Entered Union in 1848

Madison

Wyoming
466,000 people
97,914 square miles
Rank in area: 9
Entered Union in 1890

Cheyenne

United States: Major Dependencies (as of 1994)

Place	Population	Capital
American Samoa	53,139	Pago Pago
Guam	145,935	Agana
Midway Islands	450	None
Commonwealth of the Northern Mariana Islands	48,581	Saipan
Commonwealth of Puerto Rico	3,522,037	San Juan
Virgin Islands of the United States	98,130	Charlotte Amalie
Wake Island	190	None

Presidents of the United States

1.
George Washington
1789–1797
No Political Party
Birthplace: Virginia
Born: February 22, 1732
Died: December 14, 1799

2.
John Adams
1797–1801
Federalist
Birthplace: Massachusetts
Born: October 30, 1735
Died: July 4, 1826

3.
Thomas Jefferson
1801–1809
Democratic-Republican
Birthplace: Virginia
Born: April 13, 1743
Died: July 4, 1826

4.
James Madison
1809–1817
Democratic-Republican
Birthplace: Virginia
Born: March 16, 1751
Died: June 28, 1836

5.
James Monroe
1817–1825
Democratic-Republican
Birthplace: Virginia
Born: April 28, 1758
Died: July 4, 1831

6.
John Quincy Adams
1825–1829
Democratic-Republican
Birthplace: Massachusetts
Born: July 11, 1767
Died: February 23, 1848

7.
Andrew Jackson
1829–1837
Democrat
Birthplace: South Carolina
Born: March 15, 1767
Died: June 8, 1845

8.
Martin Van Buren
1837–1841
Democrat
Birthplace: New York
Born: December 5, 1782
Died: July 24, 1862

9.
William H. Harrison
1841
Whig
Birthplace: Virginia
Born: February 9, 1773
Died: April 4, 1841

10.
John Tyler
1841–1845
Whig
Birthplace: Virginia
Born: March 29, 1790
Died: January 18, 1862

11.
James K. Polk
1845–1849
Democrat
Birthplace: North Carolina
Born: November 2, 1795
Died: June 15, 1849

12.
Zachary Taylor
1849–1850
Whig
Birthplace: Virginia
Born: November 24, 1784
Died: July 9, 1850

13.
Millard Fillmore
1850–1853
Whig
Birthplace: New York
Born: January 7, 1800
Died: March 8, 1874

14.
Franklin Pierce
1853–1857
Democrat
Birthplace: New Hampshire
Born: November 23, 1804
Died: October 8, 1869

15.
James Buchanan
1857–1861
Democrat
Birthplace: Pennsylvania
Born: April 23, 1791
Died: June 1, 1868

16.
Abraham Lincoln
1861–1865
Republican
Birthplace: Kentucky
Born: February 12, 1809
Died: April 15, 1865

17.
Andrew Johnson
1865–1869
Democrat
Birthplace: North Carolina
Born: December 29, 1808
Died: July 31, 1875

18.
Ulysses S. Grant
1869–1877
Republican
Birthplace: Ohio
Born: April 27, 1822
Died: July 23, 1885

19.
Rutherford B. Hayes
1877–1881
Republican
Birthplace: Ohio
Born: October 4, 1822
Died: January 17, 1893

20.
James A. Garfield
1881
Republican
Birthplace: Ohio
Born: November 19, 1831
Died: September 19, 1881

21.
Chester A. Arthur
1881–1885
Republican
Birthplace: Vermont
Born: October 5, 1829
Died: November 18, 1886

22, 24.
Grover Cleveland
1885–1889, 1893–1897
Democrat
Birthplace: New Jersey
Born: March 18, 1837
Died: June 24, 1908

23.
Benjamin Harrison
1889–1893
Republican
Birthplace: Ohio
Born: August 20, 1833
Died: March 13, 1901

25.
William McKinley
1897–1901
Republican
Birthplace: Ohio
Born: January 29, 1843
Died: September 14, 1901

26.
Theodore Roosevelt
1901–1909
Republican
Birthplace: New York
Born: October 27, 1858
Died: January 6, 1919

27.
William H. Taft
1909–1913
Republican
Birthplace: Ohio
Born: September 15, 1857
Died: March 8, 1930

28.
Woodrow Wilson
1913–1921
Democrat
Birthplace: Virginia
Born: December 29, 1856
Died: February 3, 1924

29.
Warren G. Harding
1921–1923
Republican
Birthplace: Ohio
Born: November 2, 1865
Died: August 2, 1923

30.
Calvin Coolidge
1923–1929
Republican
Birthplace: Vermont
Born: July 4, 1872
Died: January 5, 1933

31.
Herbert C. Hoover
1929–1933
Republican
Birthplace: Iowa
Born: August 10, 1874
Died: October 20, 1964

32.
Franklin D. Roosevelt
1933–1945
Democrat
Birthplace: New York
Born: January 30, 1882
Died: April 12, 1945

33.
Harry S Truman
1945–1953
Democrat
Birthplace: Missouri
Born: May 8, 1884
Died: December 26, 1972

34.
Dwight D. Eisenhower
1953–1961
Republican
Birthplace: Texas
Born: October 14, 1890
Died: March 28, 1969

35.
John F. Kennedy
1961–1963
Democrat
Birthplace: Massachusetts
Born: May 29, 1917
Died: November 22, 1963

36.
Lyndon B. Johnson
1963–1969
Democrat
Birthplace: Texas
Born: August 27, 1908
Died: January 22, 1973

37.
Richard M. Nixon
1969–1974
Republican
Birthplace: California
Born: January 9, 1913
Died: April 22, 1994

38.
Gerald R. Ford
1974–1977
Republican
Birthplace: Nebraska
Born: July 14, 1913

39.
James E. Carter, Jr.
1977–1981
Democrat
Birthplace: Georgia
Born: October 1, 1924

40.
Ronald W. Reagan
1981–1989
Republican
Birthplace: Illinois
Born: February 6, 1911

41.
George H. Bush
1989–1993
Republican
Birthplace: Massachusetts
Born: June 12, 1924

42.
William J. Clinton
1993–
Democrat
Birthplace: Arkansas
Born: August 19, 1946

Glossary

The glossary is an alphabetical listing of words from the selections, along with their meanings. If you are not familiar with a word as you read, look it up in the glossary.

The glossary gives the following information:

1. **The pronunciation of each word.** For example, **turbulent** (tʉr′ byələnt). If there is more than one way to pronounce a word, the most common pronunciation is listed first. For example, **status** (stā′ təs, stat′ əs).
   A primary accent ′ is placed after the syllable that is stressed the most when the word is spoken. **A secondary accent** ′ is placed after a syllable that has a lighter stress. For example, **imitation** (im′ ə tā′ shən). The Pronunciation Key below shows the symbols for the sounds of letters, and key words that contain those sounds. Also, there is a short pronunciation key at the bottom of each right-hand page in the glossary.

2. **The part of speech of the word.** The following abbreviations are used:
   adj. adjective *conj.* conjunction *pro.* pronoun *prep.* preposition
   adv. adverb *n.* noun *v.* verb *inter.* interjection

3. **The meaning of the word.** The definitions listed in the glossary are the ones that apply to the way a word is used in these selections.

Pronunciation Key

Symbol	Key Words	Symbol	Key Words	Symbol	Key Words	Symbol	Key Words
a	ask, fat, parrot	oi	oil, point, toy	b	bed, fable, dub	t	top, cattle, hat
ā	ape, date, play	ou	out, crowd, plow	d	dip, beadle, had	v	vat, hovel, have
ä	ah, car, father	u	up, cut, color	f	fall, after, off	w	will, always, swear
		ʉ	urn, fur, deter	g	get, haggle, dog	y	yet, onion, yard
e	elf, ten, berry			h	he, ahead, hotel	z	zebra, dazzle, haze
ē	even, meet, money	ə	a in ago	j	joy, agile, badge		
i	is, hit, mirror		e in agent	k	kill, tackle, bake	ch	chin, catcher, arch
ī	ice, bite, high		i in sanity	l	let, yellow, ball	sh	she, cushion, dash
			o in comply	m	met, camel, trim	th	thin, nothing, truth
ō	open, tone, go		u in focus	n	not, flannel, ton	zh	azure, leisure
ô	all, horn, law			p	put, apple, tap	ŋ	ring, anger, drink
o͞o	ooze, tool, crew	ər	perhaps, murder	r	red, port, dear	′	able (ā′ b'l)
o͝o	look, pull, moor			s	sell, castle, pass		
yo͞o	use, cute, few						
yo͝o	united, cure, globule						

A

abolition [ab´ ə lish´ ən] *n.* the compulsory ending of slavery in the United States. (p. 299)

affirmative action program [ə furm´ ə tiv ak´ shən pro´ gram] *n.* a policy for correcting the effects of discrimination in the employment or education of minority groups or women. (p. 954)

Afrika Korps [af´ ri kə kôr] *n.* General Erwin Rommel's German troops, who were defeated in North Africa by Allied forces in World War II. (p. 749)

AIDS [ādz] *n.* (acquired immune deficiency syndrome) the life-threatening condition in which an acquired deficiency of certain leukocytes results in a variety of infections, some forms of cancer, and nervous system degeneration; caused by a virus and transmitted by certain body fluids. (p. 945)

Albany Congress [ôl´ bə nē käŋ´ grəs] *n.* a congress convened to draw up a treaty with the Indians that all colonies would sign in support of Britain's struggle against France. (p. 83)

alliance [ə lī´ əns]) *n.* **1.** a close association for a common objective, such as of nations, political parties, etc. **2.** the countries forming such a connection. (p. 471)

Alliance for Progress [ə lī´ əns fôr präg´ res] *n.* President John F. Kennedy's proposals for assistance to Latin America, which combined economic aid with tax and land reforms. (p. 833)

Allies [al´ īz] *n.* **1.** in World War I, the nations allied by treaty against Germany and the other Central Powers; originally Great Britain, France, and Russia, and later joined by the United States, Japan, Italy, etc. **2.** in World War II, the nations associated against the Axis, especially Great Britain, the Soviet Union, and the United States. (p. 591)

American Federation of Labor (AFL) [ə mer´ i kən fed´ ər ā´ shən uv lā´ bər] *n.* a federation of labor unions of the United States and Canada, founded in 1886; merged with the Congress of Industrial Organizations in 1955. (p. 461)

American Independent party [ə mer´ i kən in´ dē pen´ dənt pär´ tē] *n.* persons who supported George Wallace, the Vietnam War, and a law and order platform in the Presidential election of 1968. (p. 884)

American System [ə mer´ i kən sis´ təm] *n.* the pre-Civil War economic program that was designed to strengthen and unite the United States by means of a protective tariff, a national bank, and an efficient transportation system. (p. 243)

Americanization [ə mer´ i kən ə zā´ shən] *n.* the process of assimilating the American Indians into the white American culture. (p. 419)

amnesty [am´ nəs tē] *n.* a pardon for political offenses against a government. (p. 110)

antiwar movement [an´ ti´ wär mōōv´ mənt] *n.* the political protest against United States policy in Vietnam during the war years. (p. 861)

appeasement [ə pēz´ mənt] *n.* the policy of giving in to the demands of a hostile power to keep the peace. (p. 721)

appellate jurisdiction [ə pel´ it ˈjoor´ is dik´ shən] *n.* the authority of a higher court to review a case heard previously by a lower court. (p. 197)

arbitration [är´ bə trā´ shən] *n.* the settlement of a dispute by a neutral person or persons chosen to hear both sides. (p. 459)

armistice [är´ mə stis] *n.* a temporary stopping of warfare by mutual agreement, such as a truce preliminary to the signing of a peace treaty. (p. 241)

arms race [ärmz rās] *n.* the competition among countries to build up strength in military weapons. (p. 639)

artisan [ärt´ ə zən] *n.* a worker in a skilled trade; a craftsperson. (p. 43)

assembly line [ə sem´ blē līn] *n.* in many factories, an arrangement whereby each worker performs a specialized operation in assembling the work as it passes along, often on a slowly moving conveyor belt or track. (p. 291)

assimilate [ə sim´ ə lāt´] *v.* to absorb groups from different cultures into the main cultural body. (p. 263)

Atlantic Charter [at lan´ tik chärt´ ər] *n.* the agreement between Franklin Roosevelt and Winston Churchill in 1941, and later agreed to by the Soviet Union, setting forth goals similar to those of Woodrow Wilson's Fourteen Points. (p. 737)

Axis powers [ak´ sis pou´ ərz] *n.* the countries aligned against the Allies in World War II; originally Nazi Germany and Fascist Italy, and later including Japan. (p. 728)

B

baby boom [bā´ bē bōōm] *n.* the period from the late 1940's to the early 1960's marked by a great increase in the nation's birthrate. (p. 796)

balance of trade [bal´ əns uv trād] *n.* the difference in value between all the merchandise imported and exported by a country. (p. 61)

bank holiday [baŋk häl´ ə dā] *n.* any period during which banks are closed by government order, such as in a financial crisis. (p. 669)

bank note [baŋk nōt] *n.* a promissory note issued by a bank and payable on demand. It is a form of paper money. (p. 211)

Bay of Pigs invasion [bā uv pigz in vā´ zhən] *n.* the invasion of Cuba by Cuban exiles in 1961, which was intended to trigger a large-scale uprising against Fidel Castro. The invasion was a failure, and the invading forces were captured by Castro loyalists. (p. 831)

Bear Flag Republic [ber flag ri pub′ lik] *n.* the republic formed by William Ide in northern California during the war with Mexico in 1846. (p. 323)

beatnik [bēt′ nik] *n.* a member of the protest movement of the 1950's that criticized middle-class conformity and the struggle for material wealth. (p. 797)

Berlin blockade [bər lin′ blä kād′] *n.* the Russian blockade of the western-occupied section of Berlin in 1948. (p. 776)

Berlin Wall [bər lin′ wôl] *n.* the barricade built in 1961 by Communist East Berlin to keep Germans from fleeing to free West Berlin. (p. 831)

bicameral [bī kam′ ər əl] *adj.* made up of or having two legislative chambers. (p. 146)

bimetallism [bī met′ ′l iz′ əm] *n.* the use of two metals, usually gold and silver, as the monetary standard, with fixed values in relation to each other. (p. 472)

black codes [blak kōdz] *n.* the laws passed in Southern states to regulate the activities of former slaves after the Civil War. (p. 388)

black power [blak pou′ ər] *n.* political and economic power as sought by African Americans in the struggle for civil rights. (p. 843)

Black Tuesday [blak tōōz′ dā] *n.* October 29, 1929, when stock prices fell drastically. (p. 651)

blitzkrieg [blits krēg′] *n.* sudden, swift, large-scale offensive warfare intended to win a quick victory. (p. 724)

bloc [bläk] *n.* a unified group of individuals voting for policies that favor their interests. (pp. 445, 647)

blockade [blä kād′] *n.* a shutting off of a port or region of a belligerent state by the enemy's troops or ships in order to prevent passage in or out in time of war. (p. 237)

boat people [bōt pē′ pəl] *n.* refugees from a certain country or region who try to emigrate to some other country, using small boats; specifically such refugees from Southeast Asia in the late 1970's. (p. 871)

Bonus Army [bō′ nəs är′ mē] *n.* the unemployed veterans of World War I and other unemployed people who marched on Washington, D.C., in 1932 to demand payment of veterans' bonuses. (p. 662)

border states [bôr′ dər stātz] *n.* the four slave states that bordered on the free states and that remained in the Union: Delaware, Kentucky, Maryland, and Missouri. (p. 359)

Boston Massacre [bôs′ tən mas′ ə kər] *n.* a 1770 outbreak in Boston against British troops, in which a few citizens were killed. (p. 90)

Boston Tea Party [bôs′ tən tē pär′ tē] *n.* a 1773 protest against the British duty on tea imported by the American colonies. Colonists disguised as Indians boarded British ships in Boston Harbor and dumped the tea overboard. (p. 92)

bounty [boun′ tē] *n.* a reward, premium, or allowance, especially one given by a government for killing certain harmful animals, raising certain crops, etc. (p. 369)

bounty jumper [boun′ tē jump′ ər] *n.* in the United States Civil War, a man who accepted the cash bounty offered for enlisting and who then deserted. (p. 369)

bracero program [brə ser′ ō prō′ gram] *n.* the government program based on the 1942 treaty that allowed Mexicans to work in the United States as temporary farm laborers. (p. 804)

brain trust [brān trust] *n.* close advisors of Franklin Delano Roosevelt who outlined various economic and social programs and whose ideas formed a background for Roosevelt's campaign speeches. (p. 665)

brinkmanship [briŋk′ mən ship′] *n.* the policy of pursuing a hazardous course of action to the brink of catastrophe. (p. 807)

broad interpretation [brôd in tur′ prə tā′ shən] *n.* an interpretation of the Constitution favoring the extension of the powers of the federal government beyond the specific provisions of the Constitution; a belief that the government should assume all powers not specifically denied by the Constitution. (p. 198)

Brown v. Board of Education [broun v. bôrd uv ej′ ōō kā′ shən] *n.* a 1954 Supreme Court decision that separate schools for black students and for white students were unconstitutional. (p. 802)

bureaucracy [byōō rä′ krə sē] *n.* a way of organizing people to get work done, the main features of which are rules, a hierarchy, specialization, and an administration based on files. (p. 192)

burgess [bur′ jis] *n.* an elected member of the colonial legislatures of Virginia and Maryland. (p. 24)

buying on margin [bī′ iŋ än mär′ jən] *v.* paying only a portion of a stock's true value to the broker. If the stock goes up, the broker makes a profit. If the stock goes down, the broker demands more money from the stockholder. (p. 648)

C

cabinet [kab′ ə nit] *n.* the body that advises the President and serves to coordinate and implement governmental policy. It is composed of the heads of the executive departments. Other officials, including the Vice-President, may also attend the meetings. (p. 191)

Camp David Accords [kamp dā′vid ə kôrdz′] *n.* the agreement between Egypt and Israel in 1978, in which Israel returned the captured Sinai to Egypt. (p. 914)

---

fat, āpe, cär; ten, ēven; is, bīte; gō, hôrn, tōōl, look, oil, out; up, fur; get; joy; yet; chin; she; thin; zh, leisure; ŋ, ring; ə for *a* in *ago, e* in *agent, i* in *sanity, o* in *comply, u* in *focus;* ′ as in *able* (ā′b′l)

Cape Horn [kāp hôrn] *n.* the cape on an island in Tierra del Fuego, Chile; the southernmost point in South America. (p. 414)

carpetbagger [kär′ pət bag′ ər] *n.* any of the Northern politicians or adventurers who went to the South to take advantage of unsettled conditions after the Civil War. (p. 394)

cartel [kär tel′] *n.* an association of industrialists, business firms, etc., for establishing a national or international monopoly by price fixing, ownership of controlling stock, etc. (p. 905)

cash crop [kash kräp] *n.* a crop grown by a farmer primarily for sale to others rather than for his or her own use. (p. 38)

caucus [kô′ kəs] *n.* a private meeting of leaders or a committee of a political party or faction to decide on policy, pick candidates, etc., especially prior to a general open meeting. (p. 266)

cease-fire agreement [sēs′ fīr′ ə grē′ mənt] *n.* an agreement for a temporary cessation of warfare by mutual consent of the participants. (p. 784)

Central Powers [sen′ trəl pou′ ərz] *n.* in World War I, Germany and Austria-Hungary and their allies—Turkey and Bulgaria. (p. 591)

charter [chärt′ ər] *n.* a franchise or written grant of specified rights made by a government or ruler to a person, corporation, etc. (p. 21)

cheap money policy [chēp mun′ ē päl′ ə sē] *n.* the monetary program of the 1868 Democratic party calling for the issuing of more greenbacks to increase the money supply. (p. 471)

checks and balances [chekz and bal′ əns əz] *n.* the system in which each branch of the government checks or restrains the other branches. (p. 146)

Chicano [chi kä′ nō] *n.* a United States citizen or inhabitant of Mexican descent. (p. 804)

civil disobedience [siv′ əl dis′ ō bē′ dē əns] *n.* the nonviolent opposition to a government policy or law by refusing to comply with it on the grounds of conscience. (p. 801)

Civil Rights Act of 1964 [siv′ əl rītz akt uv 1964] *n.* the act passed by Congress prohibiting discrimination in public places, education, or employment on the basis of race, color, sex, nationality, or religion. (p. 839)

civil service [siv′ əl sur′ vis] *n.* any government service in which a position is secured through competitive public examinations. (p. 465)

Civilian Conservation Corps (CCC) [sə vil′ yən kän′ sər vā′ shən kôr] *n.* the agency established as part of the New Deal and that provided conservation jobs to young men. (p. 600)

civilization [siv′ ə lə zā′ shən] *n.* **1.** the total culture of a particular people, nation, period, etc. **2.** those countries and peoples considered to have reached a high stage of social and cultural development. (p. 6)

clear and present danger [klir and prez′ ənt dān′ jer] *n.* a standard set by the Supreme Court under which free speech may be limited if the expression of a particular idea constitutes a danger that is clear and imminent. (p. 200)

closed shop [klōzd shäp] *n.* a factory, business, etc., operating under a contractual agreement between a labor union and an employer by whom only members of the union may be employed. (p. 545)

cold war [kōld wôr] *n.* hostility and sharp conflict between states, such as in diplomacy and economics, without actual warfare. (p. 774)

collective bargaining [kə lek′ tiv bär′ gən iŋ] *n.* the negotiations between organized workers and their employer or employers for reaching an agreement on wages, fringe benefits, hours, and working conditions. (p. 461)

Comintern [käm′ in turn′] *n.* the international organization of Communist parties formed by Lenin to promote revolution in countries other than the U.S.S.R. (p. 634)

commission form of government [kə mish′ ən fôrm uv guv′ ərn mənt] *n.* the form of city government in which the power to run the city is entrusted to a nonpartisan commission of three to five members, each of whom heads a major city function. (p. 540)

Committee for Industrial Organization (CIO) [kə mit′ ē fôr in dus′ trē əl ôr′ gə ni zā′ shən] *n.* the large industrial union that organized workers in entire industries, such as steel-making. (p. 692)

Committees of Correspondence [kə mit′ ēz uv kôr′ ə spän′ dəns] *n.* the committees in various American colonies that kept records of events in their colonies and sent those records to other colonies. (p. 91)

Common Sense [käm′ ən sens] *n.* the pamphlet written by Thomas Paine in 1776 calling for the separation of the colonies from Great Britain. (p. 102)

commonwealth [käm′ ən welth] *n.* a federation of states. (p. 521)

communism [käm′ yoo niz′ əm] *n.* any economic theory or system based on the ownership of all property by the community as a whole. (p. 634)

Confederacy [kən fed′ ər ə sē] *n.* the league of Southern states that seceded from the United States in 1860 and 1861: Alabama, Arkansas, Florida, Georgia, Louisiana, Mississippi, North Carolina, South Carolina, Tennessee, Texas, and Virginia. (p. 350)

confederation [kən fed′ ər ā′ shən] *n.* a league or alliance; specifically, independent nations or states joined in a league or confederacy whose central authority is usually confined to common defense and to limited political cooperation. (p. 139)

conquistador [kän kwis′ tə dôr′] *n.* any of the Spanish conquerors of Mexico, Peru, or other parts of America in the sixteenth century. (p. 17)

conscription [kən skript′ shən] *n.* a national selection of draftees for a country's military service. (p. 369)

conservation [kän' sər vā' shən] *n.* **1.** the act or practice of conserving; protection from loss, waste, etc.; preservation. **2.** the official care, protection, or management of natural resources. (p. 543)

conservative [kən sur' və tiv] *adj.* the political outlook favoring a cautious, traditional approach. (p. 549)

containment [kən tān' mənt] *n.* the United States post-World War II policy of checking the political and territorial expansion of the U.S.S.R. (p. 777)

Continental [kän' tə nent' 'l] *n.* a soldier of the American army during the Revolution. (p. 108)

contraband [kän' trə band'] *n.* goods forbidden by law to be imported or exported; smuggled merchandise. (p. 594)

contras [kän' träz] *n.* a group of guerrillas opposing the Sandinista government in Nicaragua. (p. 936)

convoy [kän' voi'] *n.* a group, such as of ships or vehicles, traveling together for mutual protection or convenience. (p. 747)

convoy system [kän' voi' sis' təm] *n.* means of protecting merchant ships from U-boat attacks by having the ships travel with a large group of destroyers. This system was used in World War I and II. (p. 601, 747)

Copperhead [käp' ər hed'] *n.* a Northerner who sympathized with the South at the time of the Civil War. (p. 359)

council-manager form of government [koun' səl man' ij ər fôrm uv guv' ərn mənt] *n.* a system of municipal government in which the administrative powers of a city are entrusted to a manager selected by the city council. (p. 541)

court-packing bill [kôrt pak' iŋ bil] *n.* Franklin Roosevelt's proposal that would allow the President to appoint members to the United States Supreme Court who would favor his programs. (p. 691)

craft union [kraft yoon' yən] *n.* a labor union to which only workers in a certain trade, craft, or occupation can belong. (p. 461)

Crédit Mobilier [crä dē' mō bil' ē ā] *n.* an 1872 political scandal involving high Republican officials and the Crédit Mobilier construction company. (p.444)

D

Dawes Act [dôz akt] *n.* a law passed by Congress in 1887 that ended tribal ownership of land and gave specific parcels of land to individual Indians. (p. 419)

de facto segregation [dē fak' tō seg' rə gā' shən] *n.* segregation that is maintained by local housing patterns, not by any actual laws. (p. 494)

deficit spending [def' ə sit spend' iŋ] *n.* the government practice of spending more money than is collected in taxes. (p. 886)

deflation [dē flā' shən] *n.* a lessening of the amount of money in circulation, resulting in a relatively sharp and sudden rise in monetary value and a fall in prices. (pp. 470, 909)

delegated powers [del' ə gāt əd pou' ərz] *n.* the rights of the federal government specifically authorized by the Constitution. (p. 148)

democracy [di mäk' rə sē] *n.* a form of government in which the policy decisions of the government are based on the freely given consent of the people and in which the people are guaranteed certain basic rights. (p. 184)

Democratic party [dem' ə krat' ik pär' tē] *n.* one of the two major political parties in the United States. It emerged in the late 1820's from a split in the Democratic-Republican party, which had, in turn, developed from the Republican party led by Thomas Jefferson. (p. 261)

depression [dē presh' ən] *n.* the period of severe economic decline that began in 1929 and lasted through most of the 1930's. (p. 272)

détente [dā tänt'] *n.* a lessening of tension or hostility, especially between nations, through such means as treaties, trade agreements, etc. (p. 890)

direct primary [də rekt' prī' mer' ē] *n.* a preliminary election in which candidates for public office are chosen by the direct vote of the people instead of by delegates at a convention. (p. 541)

direct relief [də rekt' ri lēf'] *n.* jobs, food, or money given by the government directly to people in need. (p. 659)

discrimination [di skrim' i nā' shən] *n.* the act or policy of showing partiality or prejudice in treatment, especially when directed against the welfare of minority groups. (p. 398)

Dixiecrat [dik' sē krat'] *n.* a member of a party of Southern Democrats opposed to the civil rights platform of the Democratic Party in 1948. (p. 771)

dollar diplomacy [däl' ər də plō' mə sē] *n.* **1.** the policy of using the economic power or influence of a government to promote and protect in other countries the business interests of its private citizens, corporations, etc. **2.** the use of economic power by a country to further foreign policy goals. (p. 531)

domino theory [däm' ə nō' thē' ə rē] *n.* the theory that a certain result will follow a certain cause like a row of dominoes falling if the first is pushed; specifically, the theory that if a nation becomes a communist state, the nations nearby will too. (p. 855)

due process of law [doo prä' ses' uv lô] *n.* the course of legal proceedings established by the legal system of a nation or state to protect individual rights and liberties. (p. 389)

---

fat, āpe, cär; ten, ēven; is, bīte; gō, hôrn, tool, look, oil, out; up, fur; get; joy; yet; chin; she; thin; zh, leisure; ŋ, ring; ə for *a* in *ago, e* in *agent, i* in *sanity, o* in *comply, u* in *focus;* ' as in *able* (ā'b'l)

dumbbell tenement [dum′ bel′ ten′ ə mənt] *n.* an overcrowded urban apartment building whose central air shaft became a breeding ground for disease and fires. (p. 492)

E

Eisenhower Doctrine [ī′ zen hou ər däk′ trin] *n.* the policy that stated that the United States would defend the Middle East against Soviet attack. (p. 809)

elastic currency [ē las′ tik kʉr′ ən sē] *n.* the condition that permits the amount of money in circulation to increase or decrease depending on the economy's needs. (p. 552)

electoral college [ē lek′ tər əl käl′ ij] *n.* an assembly elected by the voters to perform the formal duty of electing the President and the Vice-President of the United States. The electors of each state, equal in number to its members in Congress, are expected to cast their votes for the candidate selected by the popular vote in their state. (p. 150)

emancipation [ē man′ sə pā′ shən] *n.* the process of being set free from slavery. (p. 119)

embargo [em bär′ gō] *n.* a government order prohibiting the entry or departure of commercial ships at its ports, especially as a war measure. (p. 238)

Enlightenment [en līt′ ′n mənt] *n.* a mainly eighteenth-century European philosophical movement characterized by a reliance on reason and experience rather than on dogma and tradition and by an emphasis on humanitarian political goals and social progress. (p. 76)

Environmental Protection Agency (EPA) [en vī′ rən mənt′ ′l prō tek′ shən ā′ jən sē] *n.* the government agency established to protect the nation's natural resources and to fight industry's pollution of the environment. (p. 948)

equal protection of the law [ē′ kwəl prō tek′ shən uv thə lô] *n.* the principle set forth in the Fourteenth Amendment that requires states to apply the same laws to all citizens. (p. 389)

Era of Good Feelings [ir′ ə uv good fēl′ iŋz] *n.* the period during Monroe's Presidency when a new spirit of nationalism flourished. (p. 243)

Espionage and Sedition Acts [es′ pē ə näzh and sə dish′ ən aktz] *n.* the acts passed by Congress in 1917 and 1918 to control dissent by allowing the censorship of magazines, newspapers, and films. (p. 601)

excise tax [ek′ sīz taks] *n.* a duty or sales tax on the manufacture, sale, or consumption of goods produced within a nation. (p. 213)

executive branch [eg zek′ yoo tiv branch] *n.* the branch of the government whose job is to enforce the laws and administer the government. (p. 188)

expressed powers [ek spresd′ pou′ ərz] *n.* those powers expressly delegated to the national government under the Constitution. (p. 185)

extraterritoriality [eks trə ter′ ə tôr′ ē al′ ə tē] *n.* freedom from the jurisdiction of the country in which one is living, such as in the case of foreign diplomats. (p. 525)

F

Fair Deal [fer dēl] *n.* President Truman's administrative proposals for postwar America, including the expansion of social security, increase in the minimum wage, federal aid to education, national health insurance, government support of scientific research, and bills mandating full employment and an end to discrimination in housing. (p. 773)

Fair Labor Standards Act [fer lā′ bər stan′ dərdz akt] *n.* the law passed in 1938 establishing a minimum wage of forty cents per hour, a forty-hour workweek, overtime pay for work beyond forty hours, and prohibition of labor by children under the age of sixteen. (p. 687)

fascism [fash′ iz′ əm] *n.* a system of government characterized by a rigid one-party dictatorship, the forcible suppression of opposition, private enterprise under centralized governmental control, and belligerent nationalism, racism, and militarism, etc.; first instituted in Italy in 1922. (p. 713)

Federal Communications Commission (FCC) [fed′ ər əl kə myoo′ ni kā′ shənz kə mish′ ən] *n.* a federal agency whose duty is to regulate communication by telephone, telegraph, radio, TV, cable TV, and satellite. (p. 798)

Federalist [fed′ ər əl ist] *n.* one who supported adoption of the Constitution, a strong national government, and policies encouraging trade, manufacturing, and commerce; later a member of the Federalist party. (p. 214)

fireside chats [fīr′ sīd′ chatz] *n.* President Franklin Roosevelt's radio talks explaining his policies. (p. 670)

flapper [flap′ ər] *n.* in the 1920's, a young woman considered bold and unconventional. (p. 618)

Forty-Niners [fôr′ tē nī′ nərz] *n.* people who went to California in the gold rush of 1849. (p. 414)

Fourteen Points [fôr′ tēn′ points] *n.* President Wilson's post–World War I plan for world peace, including the establishment of the League of Nations. (p. 603)

free enterprise [frē ent′ ər prīz′] *n.* the economic doctrine or practice of permitting private industry to operate under freely competitive conditions with a minimum of governmental control. (p. 561)

freedom of the seas [frē′ dəm uv thə sēz] *n.* the principle that all merchant ships may freely travel the open seas at any time. (p. 241)

Fugitive Slave Law of 1850 [fyōō′ jə tiv slāv lô uv 1850] *n.* the measure passed by Congress that provided for the recovery of runaway slaves with the assistance of federal marshalls. (p. 336)

funding [fund′ iŋ] *n.* the payment of a debt by creating another debt through the issuing of bonds. (p. 210)

G

Gadsden Purchase [gadz′ dən pur′ chəs] *n.* the area in present-day New Mexico and Arizona purchased from Mexico so that a southern railroad route could be built. (p. 324)

General Assembly [jen′ ər əl ə sem′ blē] *n.* the deliberative governing body of the United Nations. (p. 758)

Geneva Accords [jə nē′ və ə kôrdz′] *n.* the 1954 peace plan for Indochina that neutralized Laos and Cambodia and that divided Vietnam until national elections could be held in 1956. (p. 856)

genocide [jen′ ə sīd′] *n.* the deliberate and systematic extermination of a group of people. (p. 725)

Gettysburg Address [get′ iz burg′ ə dres′] *n.* the famous speech given by President Abraham Lincoln dedicating a national cemetery in Gettysburg, Pennsylvania. (p. 374)

ghetto [get′ ō] *n.* any section of a city in which many members of some minority live or to which they are restricted, such as by economic pressure or social discrimination. (p. 494)

Glass-Steagall Act [glas stē′ gəl akt] *n.* the act passed in 1933 that prohibited banks from selling stock or financing corporations and that insured individual bank deposits through the creation of the Federal Bank Deposit Insurance Corporation. (p. 680)

Glorious Revolution [glôr′ ē əs rev′ ə lōō′ shən] *n.* a bloodless revolution that occurred in England when James II fled and William of Orange, a Dutch Protestant, claimed the British throne. William and his wife, Mary, James's daughter, became co-rulers. (p. 66)

gold standard [gōld stan′ dərd] *n.* a monetary standard based solely on gold and in which the basic currency unit is made equal to and redeemable by a specified quantity of gold. (p. 472)

Good Neighbor Policy [good nā′ bər päl′ ə sē] *n.* the policy advocating nonaggression, nonintervention, and cooperation to solve problems in the Western Hemisphere. (p. 650)

government bond [guv′ ərn mənt bänd] *n.* the certificate issued by the government in exchange for a loan of money. (p. 210)

graduated federal income tax [gra′ jōō at′ id fed′ ər əl in′ kum′ taks] *n.* a system of taxation under which those with higher incomes pay a larger share of the federal tax. (p. 471)

graft [graft] *n.* the act of taking advantage of one's position in order to gain money, property, etc., dishonestly, such as in politics. (p. 394)

grandfather clause [grand′ fä′ thər klôz] *n.* a former law in some Southern states waiving electoral literacy requirements for those whose forebears voted before the Civil War, thus keeping the franchise for illiterate whites. (p. 398)

Grange [grānj] *n.* an association of farmers organized in the United States in 1867 for mutual welfare; also known as the National Grange or the Patrons of Husbandry. (p. 444)

Great Awakening [grāt ə wā′ kən iŋ] *n.* the series of religious revivals during the 1740's and 1750's that were sparked by the preaching of George Whitefield. (p. 78)

Great Plains [grāt plānz] *n.* the sloping region of valleys and plains in west central North America, extending from Texas to southern Canada, and stretching east from the base of the Rockies for about four hundred miles. (p. 414)

Great Society [grāt sə sī′ ə tē] *n.* the name given to President Lyndon Johnson's overall domestic social program. (p. 839)

greenback [grēn′ bak′] *n.* any peice of U.S. paper money printed in green ink on the back. (p. 370)

guerrilla warfare [gə ril′ ə wôr′ fer′] *n.* a type of combat in which rebels who specialize in sudden, hit-and-run attacks make surprise raids on their enemies. (p. 59)

H

Harlem Renaissance [här′ ləm ren′ ə säns′] *n.* the creative achievements of African Americans during the 1920's and 1930's, which were named for New York City's Harlem area. (p. 621)

headright system [hed′ rīt sis′ təm] *n.* the homesteading plan whereby a settler immigrating to Virginia in the 1600's received fifty acres of free land for himself and for each person who accompanied him. (p. 23)

Hessians [hesh′ ənz] *n.* the German mercenaries who fought for the British during the American Revolution. (p. 107)

Hiroshima [hir′ō shē′ mə] *n.* a seaport in southwest Honshu, Japan, on the Inland Sea; largely destroyed on August 6, 1945, by the U.S. atomic bomb, the first ever used in warfare. (p. 756)

HMO [HMO] *n.* a health maintenance organization, a group of physicians who treat only enrolled patients and who charge set fees established by an insurance company. (p. 960)

holding company [hōl′ diŋ kum′ pə nē] *n.* a corporation organized to hold the bonds or stocks of other corporations. (p. 447)

---

fat, āpe, cär; ten, ēven; is, bīte; gō, hôrn, tōōl, look, oil, out; up, fur; get; joy; yet; chin; she; thin; zh, leisure; ŋ, ring; ə for *a* in *ago, e* in *agent, i* in *sanity, o* in *comply, u* in *focus;* ' as in *able* (ā′b'l)

Holocaust [häl′ ə kôst] *n.* the systematic destruction of more than 6 million European Jews by the Nazis before and during World War II. (p. 726)

Homestead Act [hōm′ sted′ akt] *n.* passed in 1862, this act gave 160 acres of public land to any citizen who occupied and farmed the land and payed registration fees ranging from twenty-six dollars to thirty-four dollars. (p. 370)

Hoovervilles [hoo′ vər vilz] *n.* the makeshift living areas, such as collections of tents or shacks, erected by the homeless during the Great Depression. (p. 663)

human rights [hyoo′ mən rītz] *n.* the rights and privileges of all human beings, including those stated in the Declaration of Independence and those guaranteed and protected by the Bill of Rights. (p. 911)

humanitarian [hyoo man′ ə ter′ ē ən] *n.* a person devoted to promoting the welfare of humanity, especially through the elimination of pain and suffering. (p. 663)

Hundred Days [hun′drəd dāz] *n.* the first days of Franklin Roosevelt's administration, during which massive amounts of legislation were passed to deal with the problems caused by the depression. (p. 678)

I

immigration [im′ ə grā′shən] *n.* entry into a new nation for the purpose of permanent residence. (p. 497)

impeach [im pēch′] *v.* to challenge the practices or honesty of; to accuse, especially to bring a public official before a tribunal on charges of wrongdoing. (p. 148)

imperialism [im pir′ ē əl iz′ əm] *n.* the policy and practice of forming and maintaining an empire in seeking to control raw materials and world markets by the conquest of other countries, the establishment of colonies, etc. (p. 512)

implied powers [im plīd′ pou′ ərz] *n.* the powers of the national government that are assumed to be necessary and proper to carry its expressed or enumerated powers into effect. (p. 186)

import duty [im′ port′ doot′ ē] *n.* a tax levied on goods coming into a country. (p. 63)

impressment [im pres′ mənt] *n.* the practice of forcing men into involuntary military service, especially the navy. (p. 237)

inalienable rights [in āl′ yən ə b'l rīts] *n.* the rights that cannot be taken away from individuals, such as life, liberty, and the pursuit of happiness. (p. 105)

indentured servant [in den′ chərd sur′ vənt] *n.* an immigrant who, in return for passage to the Americas, contracted to work for someone, usually for seven years. (p. 24)

Indian Reorganization Act [in′ dē ən rē ôr′ gə ni zā′ shən akt] *n.* the bill passed by Congress in 1934 that reversed the provisions of the Dawes Act of 1887, stopping land allotments to individuals and providing for tribal ownership of Indian lands, establishing schools, providing money for Indian businesses, and authorizing tribes to reestablish their own governments. (p. 693)

Industrial Revolution [in dus′ trē əl rev′ ə loo′ shən] *n.* the change in social and economic organization resulting from the replacement of hand tools by machine and power tools and the development of large-scale industrial production. (p. 250)

industrial unionism [in dus′ trē əl yoon′ yən iz′ əm] *n.* a system of labor unions that includes both the skilled and unskilled workers of a particular industry. (p. 461)

INF treaty [INF trē′ tē] *n.* a treaty between the United States and the U.S.S.R. eliminating all medium- and shorter-range nuclear missiles; ratified, with conditions, by the United States Senate in May 1988. (p. 935)

inflation [in flā′ shən] *n.* an increase in the amount of money and credit in relation to the supply of goods and services; an excessive or persistent increase in the general price level resulting from the increased money supply and causing a decline in purchasing power. (pp. 471, 909)

initiative [i nish′ ə tiv] *n.* the process of petitioning a legislature to introduce a bill. (p. 472)

injunction [in junk′ shən] *n.* a writ or order from a court prohibiting a person or group from carrying out a given action, or ordering a given action to be done. (p. 464)

insider trading [in′ sīd′ trād′ iŋ] *n.* the buying or selling of a company's stock by someone who has access to information not made public. Trading based on such information may be illegal. (p. 684)

installment plan [in stôl′ mənt plan] *n.* a credit system by which debts, such as for purchased articles, are paid in installments. (p. 645)

interchangeable parts [in′ tər chān′ jə bəl pärts] *n.* Eli Whitney's invention of standardized parts that could be used interchangeably and purchased in mass quantities. (p. 250)

interlocking directorate [in′ tər läk′ iŋ di rek′ tər it] *n.* boards of directors having some members in common so that the corporations concerned are more or less under the same control. (p. 447)

interstate commerce [in′ tər stāt′ käm′ ərs] *n.* trade between two or more states. (p. 245)

ironclad [ī′ ərn klad′] *n.* the wooden ships built during the Civil War that were fortified with iron-plate armor. (p. 362)

isolationist [ī′ sə lā′ shən ist] *n.* a person who opposes the involvement of a country in international alliances, agreements, etc. (p. 607)

J

Jim Crow laws [jim krō lôz] *n.* the laws that legitimized the practice of separation of the races in Southern public facilities. These laws were upheld by the Supreme Court in 1896 but reversed in 1954. (p. 398)

joint-stock company [joint stäk kum′ pə nē] *n.* a business firm with a joint stock, owned by the stockholders in shares that each may sell or transfer independently. (p. 21)

judicial review [jōō dish′ əl ri vyōō′] *n.* a judicial precedent established in *Marbury* v. *Madison* that gave the Supreme Court the power to judge the constitutionality of congressional legislation. (p. 149)

K

kamikaze [kä′ mə kä′ zē] *n.* a Japanese suicide pilot who crashed bomb-laden planes into American ships during World War II. (p. 754)

Kitchen Cabinet [kich′ ən kab′ ə nit] *n.* the group of unofficial advisors on whom President Jackson relied. (p. 262)

Know-Nothing [nō′ nuth′ iŋ] *n.* a member of a secret political party in the United States in the 1850's with a program of keeping out of public office anyone not a native-born American; so called because members professed ignorance of the party's activities. (p. 343)

Ku Klux Klan [kōō kluks klan] *n.* a secret society of white men founded in the Southern states after the Civil War to reestablish and maintain white supremacy. (p. 635)

L

laissez-faire [les′ ā fer′] *n.* the policy of letting the owners of industry and business fix the rules of competition, the conditions of labor, etc., as they please, without governmental regulation or control. (p. 466)

lame duck [lām duk] *n.* an elected official who is defeated in his or her bid for reelection and is just serving out the remainder of his or her term. (p. 196)

League of Nations [lēg uv nā′ shənz] *n.* an association of nations (1920–1946), established to promote international cooperation and peace. It was succeeded by the United Nations. (p. 603)

League of the Iroquois [lēg uv thə ir′ ə kwoi′] *n.* the powerful confederation consisting of five Eastern Indian tribes who sided with the British against the French, helping to drive the French from North America. (p. 11)

legislative branch [lej′ is lāt′ iv branch] *n.* the branch of the government composed of elected representatives who enact laws. (p. 184)

lend-lease [lend lēs] *n.* in World War II, the material aid in the form of munitions, tools, food, etc., granted under specified conditions to foreign countries whose defense was deemed vital to the defense of the United States. (p. 736)

liberal [lib′ ər əl] *n.* a person whose political beliefs tend to favor experimentation and change, reform of inequalities, and an active role for the federal government. (p. 552)

Liberty party [lib′ ər tē pärt′ ē] *n.* a tiny abolitionist party that ran James Birney against James Polk and Henry Clay in the election of 1844. (p. 318)

literacy test [lit′ ər ə sē test] *n.* the means of excluding African Americans from voting in Southern elections by testing their ability to read. (p. 398)

Little Rock crisis [lit′ 'l räk krī′ sis] *n.* the situation created in Little Rock, Arkansas, in September 1957 when President Eisenhower sent one thousand National Guardsmen to restore order to Little Rock when disturbances broke out following the governor's order for troops to surround Central High School to prevent nine black students from attending class. (p. 802)

lobby [läb′ ē] *n.* a person or group, representing a special interest, which tries to influence legislators. (p. 513)

long drive [loŋ drīv] *n.* the movement of cattle from Texas to railroad towns in the North. (p. 421)

longhorn [loŋ′ hôrn] *n.* any breed of long-horned cattle raised in great numbers in the Southwest in the nineteenth century and later crossed with English stock to create improved beef and dairy breeds. (p. 421)

Louisiana Purchase [loō ē′ zē an′ ə pur′ chəs] *n.* the land bought by the United States from France in 1803 for $15 million. It extended from the Mississippi River to the Rocky Mountains and from the Gulf of Mexico to Canada. (p. 235)

Loyalist [loi′ əl ist] *n.* in the American Revolution, a colonist who was loyal to the British government. (p. 105)

M

mandate [man′ dāt′] *n.* a commission from the League of Nations to a country to administer some region, colony, etc. (p. 604)

Manhattan Project [man hat′ 'n prä′ jekt] *n.* the United States Army project begun in 1942 to research and develop an atomic bomb to be used in warfare. Research headquarters in Alamagordo, New Mexico, reported the first successful atomic detonation on July 16, 1945. (p. 755)

manifest destiny [man′ ə fest′ des′ tə nē] *n.* the

---

fat, āpe, cär; ten, ēven; is, bīte; gō, hôrn, tōōl, look, oil, out; up, fur; get; joy; yet; chin; she; thin; zh, leisure; ŋ, ring; ə for *a* in *ago, e* in *agent, i* in *sanity, o* in *comply, u* in *focus;* ' as in *able* (ā′b'l) nineteenth-century doctrine postulating the continued territorial expansion of the United States as its obvious destiny; term current during the annexation of territories in the Southwest and the Northwest and of islands in the Pacific and the Caribbean. (p. 312)

Marshall Plan [mär′ shəl plan] *n.* the post–World War II plan for aid to European countries formulated by General George Marshall in 1947. It offered aid to European nations if those nations agreed to remove trade barriers and cooperate economically with one another. (p. 776)

martial law [mär′ shəl lô] *n.* under the Intolerable Acts, British troops were brought into Boston to enforce British law. (p. 92)

Mason-Dixon line [mā′ sən dik′ sən līn] *n.* the boundary line between Pennsylvania and Maryland, regarded before the Civil War as separating the free states from the slave states or, now, the North from the South. (p. 623)

mass production [mas prō duk′ shən] *n.* the production of goods in large quantities, especially by machinery and the division of labor. (p. 250)

massive retaliation [mas′ iv rē tal′ ē ā′ shən] *n.* the policy of John Foster Dulles stating American willingness to use nuclear weapons against an aggressor nation, which led to atomic stockpiling. (p. 807)

materialism [mə tir′ ē əl iz′ əm] *n.* the belief that material goods and wealth are the most important values in life. (p. 627)

Mayflower Compact [mā′ flou′ ər käm′ pakt] *n.* the written agreement among the passengers of the *Mayflower* providing for self-government under the majority rule of the adult male voters. (p. 25)

Medicare [med′ i ker′] *n.* the national health-care program through which certain medical and hospital expenses of the aged and the needy are paid for from federal, mostly social security, funds. (p. 841)

melting pot [melt′ iŋ pät] *n.* a country, place, or area in which immigrants of various nationalities and races are assimilated. (p. 499)

mercantilism [mʉr′ kən til iz′ əm] *n.* the doctrine, which arose in Europe with the decline of feudalism, that the economic interests of the nation could be strengthened by the government by protecting home industries, such as through tariffs, by increased foreign trade, such as through monopolies, and by an increase of exports over imports, with a consequent accumulation of bullion. (p. 61)

mercenary [mʉr′ sə ner′ ē] *n.* a professional soldier hired to serve in a foreign army. (p. 107)

merchant marine [mʉr′ chənt mə rēn′] *n.* all the ships of a nation that are used for commerce. (p. 142)

merger [mʉr′ jər] *n.* a combining of two or more companies, corporations, etc., into one, such as by issuing stock of the controlling corporation to

replace the greater part of that of the other(s). (p. 447)

merit system [mer′ it sis′ təm] *n.* a system of hiring and promoting people to civil service positions on the basis of merit as determined by competitive examinations. (p. 465)

microchip [mī′ krō chip′] *n.* a semiconductor body in which an integrated circuit is formed or is to be formed. (p. 917)

Middle Colonies [mid′ ′l käl′ ə nēz] *n.* those colonies located south of New England and north of Virginia, including New York, Pennsylvania, Delaware, and New Jersey. (p. 45)

middle passage [mid′ ′l pas′ ij] *n.* the passage across the Atlantic from West Africa to the West Indies or America that was the route of the former slave trade. (p. 43)

midnight judges [mid′ nīt′ juj′ iz] *n.* those judges appointed to the bench by John Adams during the last few days of his administration. (p. 233)

migrant worker [mī′ grənt wʉrk′ ər] *n.* a farm worker who travels from farm to farm to plant and harvest crops of fruits or vegetables. (p. 804)

militarism [mil′ ə tə riz′ əm] *n.* the policy of maintaining a strong military organization in aggressive preparedness for war. (p. 49)

militiaman [mə lish′ ə mən] *n.* a member of any army composed of citizens rather than professional soldiers; called up in time of emergency. (p. 82)

minuteman [min′ it man′] *n.* any of the members of the American citizen army at the time of the Revolution who volunteered to be ready for military service at a minute's notice. (p. 92)

Missouri Compromise [mi zoor′ē käm′ prə mīz′] *n.* the series of congressional measures that maintained a sectional balance in 1820. (p. 247)

Monroe Doctrine [mən rō′ däk′ trin] *n.* the doctrine, essentially stated by President Monroe in a message to Congress in 1823, that the United States would regard as an unfriendly act any attempt by a European nation to interfere in the affairs of the American countries or to increase its possessions on the American continents. (p. 246)

moratorium [môr′ ə tôr′ ē əm] *n.* a legal authorization, usually by a law passed in an emergency, to delay payment of money due, such as by a bank or debtor nation, or to delay some specified activity, such as in time of war; any delay or stoppage of an activity, such as a moratorium on the testing of nuclear weapons. (p. 664)

muckrakers [muk′ rāk′ ərz] *n.* the journalists of the early 1900's who reported on social injustices, especially in business practices. (p. 538)

Munich Pact [myoo′ nik pakt] *n.* a pact signed in 1938 at Munich by Great Britain and France, ceding the Czech Sudetenland to Nazi Germany; regarded as the epitome of political appeasement. (p. 721)

N

National Association for the Advancement of Colored People (NAACP) [nash′ ə nəl ə sō′ sē ā′ shən fôr thə ad vans′ mənt uv kul′ ərd pē′ pəl] *n.* the black equal rights organization that was founded in 1909 by W. E. B. DuBois to promote the legal and political rights of African Americans. (p. 620)

national bank [nash′ ə nəl baŋk] *n.* a bank chartered by the federal government and, since 1913, required to be a member of the Federal Reserve System. (p. 211)

national debt [nash′ ə nəl det] *n.* the total debt incurred by the central government of a nation, specifically by the federal government of the United States. (p. 910)

national income [nash′ ə nəl in′ kum′] *n.* the total income earned by a nation's productive factors, including all profits, rents, wages, etc., during a specified period, usually a year; the net national product minus indirect business taxes. (p. 659)

National Labor Relations Board (NLRB) [nash′ ə nəl lā′ bər ri lā′ shənz bôrd] *n.* the board created in 1935 to prevent unfair labor practices, such as coercion, the firing of employees who join unions, and the establishment of management-dominated unions. (p. 687)

National Organization for Women (NOW) [nash′ ə nəl ôr′ gə nə zā′ shən fôr wim′ in] *n.* the organization founded by Betty Friedan in 1966 to obtain legal, economic, and social reforms for women. (p. 846)

nationalism [nash′ ə nəl iz′ əm] *n.* devotion to one's nation; patriotism. (p. 243)

nationalize [nash′ ə nə līz′] *v.* to transfer ownership or control of land, resources, industries, etc., to the national government. (p. 670)

nativism [nāt′ iv iz′ əm] *n.* the practice or policy of favoring native-born citizens over immigrants. (p. 342)

NATO [nā′ tō] *n.* the North Atlantic Treaty Organization, founded in 1949 as an alliance between the United States, Canada, and ten Western European countries. (p. 776)

natural resources [nach′ ər əl rē′ sôrs′ iz] *n.* those actual and potential forms of wealth supplied by nature, such as coal, oil, water power, arable land, etc. (p. 543)

naturalized citizen [nach′ ər əl īzd sit′ əz ən] *n.* a person who has been granted the rights of citizenship in a country. (p. 504)

naval holiday [nā′ vəl häl′ ə dā′] *n.* a period of time during which no new warships may be built. (p. 639)

Nazi party [nät′ sē pär′ tē] *n.* the German fascist political party founded in 1919 by Adolf Hitler that seized power in Germany in 1933 and put into effect a program of nationalism, racism, re-

armament, and aggression. (p. 713)

necessary and proper clause [nes′ ə ser′ ē and präp′ ər klôz] *n.* the clause contained in Article I, Section 8 of the Constitution that enables the federal government to carry out its expressed powers by any constitutional means. (p. 186)

neutrality [nōō tral′ ə tē] *n.* the status or policy of a nation not participating directly or indirectly in a war between other natio...s. (p. 217)

New Deal [nōō dēl] *n.* the economic and political principles and policies adopted by President Franklin D. Roosevelt in the 1930's to advance economic recovery and social welfare. (p. 665)

New England Colonies [nōō iŋ′ glənd käl′ ə nēz] *n.* those colonies containing what are now the six northeastern states of the United States: Maine, Vermont, New Hampshire, Massachusetts, Rhode Island, and Connecticut. (p. 45)

New Frontier [nōō frun tir′] *n.* the policies adopted by President John F. Kennedy that included Medicare, federal aid to education, the creation of a Department of Urban Affairs, a lowering of tariffs between the United States and the European Common Market, and programs to help fight unemployment and pollution. (p. 826)

Nisei [nē′ sā′] *n.* a native United States or Canadian citizen born of immigrant Japanese parents and educated in America. (p. 742)

nominating convention [näm′ ə nāt′ iŋ kən ven′ shən] *n.* a technique begun in the 1820's for choosing a candidate for political office. It included more people in the nominating process than did the earlier caucus. (p. 266)

nonaggression pact [nän ə gresh′ ən pakt] *n.* an agreement between two nations not to fight each other. (p. 723)

nonimportation agreement [nän im′ pôr tā′ shən ə grē′ mənt] *n.* a written agreement by a merchant to boycott certain goods. (p. 88)

nonlegislative powers [nän′ lej′ is lāt′ iv pou′ ərz] *n.* powers of Congress other than lawmaking powers. (p. 186)

nullification [nul′ ə fi kā′ shən] *n.* the refusal of a state to recognize or enforce within its territory any federal law held to be an infringement on its sovereignty. (p. 224)

O

Office of Price Administration (OPA) [ôf′ is uv prīs ad min′ is trā′ shən] *n.* an agency established by Congress during World War II that had the power to fix rents, set maximum prices on goods, and set up a rationing system. (p. 745)

Ohio gang [ō hī′ ō gaŋ] *n.* a group of personal friends and political supporters of President

---

fat, āpe, cär; ten, ēven; is, bīte; gō, hôrn, tōōl, lŏŏk, oil, out; up, fur; get; joy; yet; chin; she; thin; zh, leisure; ŋ, ring; ə for *a* in *ago*, *e* in *agent*, *i* in *sanity*, *o* in *comply*, *u* in *focus*; ′ as in *able* (ā′b'l)

Warren G. Harding who were appointed by the President to various government positions. (p. 638)

OPEC [ō′ pek′] *n.* Organization of Petroleum Exporting Countries, a cartel of oil-producing nations that sets a fixed world price for oil. (p. 905)

Open Door policy [ō′ pən dôr päl′ ə sē] *n.* the 1900 proposal by Secretary of State John Hay asking the colonial powers to give up their spheres of influence in China. (p. 525)

original jurisdiction [ə rij′ ə nəl joor′ is dik′ shən] *n.* the authority of a trial court to hear a case "in the first instance." (p. 197)

overseer [ō′ vər sē′ ər] *n.* a plantation supervisor who watched over and directed the work of others. (p. 43)

P

pacifist [pas′ ə fist] *n.* a person who rejects the use of force, violence, or war. (p. 60)

Palestinian Liberation Organization (PLO) [pal′ əs tin′ ē ən lib′ ər ā′ shən ôr′ gə ni zā′ shən] *n.* a coalition of groups dedicated to the establishment of a national Palestinian homeland and to the destruction of Israel; also called the Palestinian Liberation Front. (p. 914)

***Panay* incident** [pä nī′ in′ sə dənt] *n.* the 1937 attack by the Japanese on the American gunboat *Panay* on the Yangtze River in China, killing two Americans. (p. 719)

parity [par′ ə tē] *n.* a price for certain farm products, usually maintained by government price supports, designed to keep the purchasing power of the farmer at the level of a designated base period. (p. 687)

partisan [pärt′ i zən] *n.* a person who takes the part of or strongly supports one side, party, or person. (p. 749)

Patriot [pā′ trē ət] *n.* an American colonist who zealously supported the movement for independence. (p. 105)

patronage [pā′ trən ij] *n.* the practice of rewarding political supporters with jobs or other political appointments. (p. 465)

pet bank [pet baŋk] *n.* a bank loyal to President Jackson's party and in which federal funds were held. (p. 270)

Piedmont [pēd′ mänt′] *n.* the hilly upland region of the eastern United States, located between the Atlantic coastal plain and the Appalachians and stretching from southeast New York to central Alabama. (p. 39)

Pilgrim [pil′ grəm] *n.* a member of the band of English Puritans who founded Plymouth Colony in 1620. (p. 25)

planned obsolescence [pland äb′ sə les′ əns] *n.* the policy of producing goods that will soon wear out so that consumers will have to replace them with new ones. (p. 645)

Platt Amendment [plat ə mend′ mənt] *n.* the rider attached to the Army Appropriations Bill of 1901 that severely limited Cuba's political freedom by forcing Cuba to accept United States intervention if its freedom appeared to be in jeopardy and to accept United States naval and coal stations in its harbors. (p. 520)

pocket veto [päk′ it vē′ tō] *n.* the indirect veto by the President of the United States of a bill presented to him by Congress within ten days of its adjournment, by failing to sign and return the bill before Congress adjourns. (p. 385)

political machine [pə lit′ i kəl mə shēn′] *n.* a political party organization, especially a local one, under strong control. (pp. 261, 495)

poll tax [pōl taks] *n.* a tax per head on individuals as a prerequisite for voting. (p. 398)

popular sovereignty [päp′ yoo lər säv′ rən tē] *n.* the proposal advanced by Stephen A. Douglas in 1854 that settlers decide by election whether to allow slavery in their territory, as opposed to having Congress make the decision. (p. 340)

Populism [päp′ yool iz′ əm] *n.* the movement begun by farmers in the 1890's who wanted a number of economic and political reforms. (p. 470)

pragmatist [prag′ mə tist] *n.* a person who believes that the value of an idea is whether or not it works. (p. 667)

precedent [pres′ ə dənt] *n.* a previous court decision in a similar case, relied on by judges to give the law consistency and continuity. (p. 198)

price controls [prīs kən trōlz′] *n.* the setting of ceiling prices on basic goods and services by a government, so as to fight inflation. (p. 681)

price supports [prīs sə pôrts′] *n.* the support of certain price levels at or above market values, such as by government purchase of surpluses. (p. 647)

privateer [prī′ və tir′] *n.* a privately owned and manned armed ship commissioned by a government during wartime to attack and capture enemy ships, especially merchant ships. (p. 108)

Proclamation of 1763 [präk′ lə mā′ shən uv 1763] *n.* the order given by the British government forbidding settlement or speculation on land in the Ohio Valley and all lands west of it. (p. 86)

productivity [prō′ dək tiv′ ə tē] *n.* the creation of economic value, or the production of services. (p. 909)

Progressive movement [prō gres′ iv moov′ mənt] *n.* the effort begun in the early 1900's to return control of the government to the people, restore economic opportunities, and correct injustices in American life. (p. 538)

Progressive party [prō gres′ iv pär′ tē] *n.* a short-lived, minor American political party: (a) organized in 1912 by followers of Theodore Roosevelt; (b) formed in 1924 under the leadership of Robert M. LaFollette; (c) formed in 1948, originally under the leadership of Henry A. Wallace. (p. 550)

Prohibition [prō′ i bish′ ən] *n.* the forbidding by law of the manufacture and sale of alcoholic beverages. (p. 615)

proprietary colony [prō prī′ ə ter′ ē käl′ ə nē] *n.* any of certain North American colonies that the British crown granted to an individual or group with full governing rights. (p. 27)

protective tariff [prō tek′ tiv tar′ if] *n.* a tax placed on imports in order to protect a country's businesses from foreign competition. (p. 213)

protectorate [prō tek′ tər it] *n.* a nation whose government and affairs are controlled by a stronger power. (p. 520)

public policy [pub′ lik päl′ ə sē] *n.* all the rules that are made and enforced at the various levels of the political system, including laws, judicial and administrative decisions, treaties with other nations, and executive orders. (p. 193)

public utility [pub′ lik yōō til′ ə tē] *n.* an organization supplying water, electricity, transportation, etc., to the public and operated usually as a monopoly, either by a private corporation under governmental regulation or by the government directly. (p. 445)

Pueblo [pweb′ lō] *n.* the Spanish word for village or town; also, the name of a group of Indians living in the southwestern United States. (p. 6)

pump priming [pump prīm′ iŋ] *n.* large expenditures by a government that are designed to stimulate expenditures in private industry. (p. 681)

Puritan [pyōōr′ i tən] *n.* any member of a Protestant group in England and the American colonies who, in the sixteenth and seventeenth centuries, wanted to make the Church of England simpler in its services and stricter about its morals. (p. 24)

Q

quarantine [kwôr′ ən tēn] *n.* a period of isolation to stop the spread of disease. (p. 718)

quota system [kwōt′ ə sis′ təm] *n.* the system established in 1921 by an immigration law that limited the number of people of a nationality who could be admitted to the United States each year. (p. 640)

R

radicals [rad′ i k′lz] *n.* those favoring fundamental or extreme change, especially in a social or economic structure. (p. 503)

Radical Republicans [rad′ i k′l ri pub′ li kənz] *n.* the members of a political group who were staunch supporters of the Civil War and who believed that slavery should be abolished, that black Americans were entitled to the same rights as white Americans, and that the South should be severely punished. (p. 367)

ratify [rat′ ə fī] *vt.* to approve or confirm; to give official sanction to. (p. 150)

rationing [rash′ ə niŋ] *n.* the policy of limiting the amount of certain items a person can purchase; used during times of war or national emergency. (p. 745)

Reaganomics [rā′ gən äm′ iks] *n.* the economic policies of President Reagan based largely on supply-side economics, which advocates large tax cuts to increase private investments, which in turn will increase the nation's supply of goods and services. (p. 931)

rebate [rē′ bāt′] *n.* a partial refund or a deduction from a bill. (p. 448)

recall [rē′ kôl′] *n.* the process of removing or the right to remove an official from office by popular vote, usually after using petitions to call for such a vote. (p. 472)

recession [ri sesh′ ən] *n.* a temporary falling off of business activity during a period when such activity has been generally increasing. (p. 905)

reciprocal trade agreement [ri sip′ rə k′l trād ə grē′ mənt] *n.* an agreement between nations to lower tariffs on each other's goods in order to promote trade. (p. 716)

Red scare [red sker] *n.* the public reaction in 1919 to the formation of communist parties in the United States, resulting in the arrest and deportation of many communists and socialists. (p. 778)

redcoat [red′ kōt′] *n.* a British soldier in a uniform with a red coat, such as during the American Revolution. (p. 100)

referendum [ref′ ə ren′ dəm] *n.* the submission of a law, proposed or already in effect, to a direct vote of the people, such as in superseding or overruling the legislature. (p. 472)

Reformation [ref′ ər mā′ shən] *n.* the sixteenth-century religious movement that aimed at reforming the Roman Catholic Church and that resulted in the establishment of Protestant churches. (p. 128)

religious toleration [ri lij′ əs täl′ ər ā′ shən] *n.* the willingness to allow others the right to choose how or if they worship. (p. 66)

relocation program [rē′ lō kā′ shən pro′ gram′] *n.* the program for assimilating the American Indians into the dominant culture by encouraging their move into cities. (p. 806)

Renaissance [ren′ ə säns′] *n.* the great revival of art, literature, and learning in Europe in the fourteenth, fifteenth and sixteenth centuries, based

fat, āpe, cär; ten, ēven; is, bīte; gō, hôrn, tōōl, lŏŏk, oil, out; up, fur; get; joy; yet; chin; she; thin; zh, leisure; ŋ, ring; ə for *a* in *ago, e* in *agent, i* in *sanity, o* in *comply, u* in *focus;* ′ as in *able* (ā′b'l) on classical sources. It began in Italy, spread gradually to other countries, and marked the transition from the medieval world to the modern. (p. 14)

reparation [rep′ ə rā′ shən] *n.* the compensation by a nation defeated in a war for economic losses suffered by the victor or for crimes committed against individuals; payable in money, labor, goods, etc. (p. 604)

Republican [ri pub′ li kən] *n.* a member of a political party led by Thomas Jefferson and James Madison. This party was a forerunner of the current Democratic party. (p. 214)

Republican party [ri pub′ li kən pär′ tē] *n.* persons who, in 1792, followed the Jefferson-Madison group known as Democratic-Republicans. This party was a forerunner of the current Democratic party. The Republican party of today was organized in 1854. (p. 344)

reservation [rez′ ər vā′ shən] *n.* an area of public land set aside for use by American Indians. (p. 415)

reserved powers [ri zʉrvd′ pou′ ərz] *n.* the powers not granted to the federal government nor expressly forbidden to the states by the Constitution and therefore retained by the states. (p. 148)

revenue sharing [rev′ ə n$\overline{oo}$′ sher′ iŋ] *n.* the practice of granting federal funds to states and to local communities to use for various public programs. (p. 886)

reverse discrimination [ri vʉrs′ di skrim′ i nā′ shən] *n.* discrimination against white people, men, etc., such as in employment or education. (p. 954)

right-to-work law [rīt t$\overline{oo}$ wʉrk lô] *adj.* designating legislation prohibiting the union shop. (p. 910)

robber barons [rä′ bər bar′ ənz] *n.* the United States capitalists of the late nineteenth century who acquired vast wealth by exploitation and ruthlessness. (p. 448)

Roosevelt Corollary [rō′ zə velt′ kôr′ ə ler′ ē] *n.* the declaration by President Theodore Roosevelt in 1904 that the United States would use military intervention if necessary in the affairs of any Western Hemisphere nation. (p. 530)

Rough Riders [ruf rīd′ ərz] *n.* the volunteer cavalry regiment organized by Theodore Roosevelt for service in the Spanish-American War (1898). (p. 517)

royal colony [roi′ əl käl′ ə nē] *n.* a colony ruled directly by the reigning monarch according to the laws of England. (p. 66)

rugged individualism [rug′ id in′ də vij′ $\overline{oo}$ əl iz′ əm] *n.* the principle of strong self-reliance. (p. 663)

S

Sacco-Vanzetti case [sak′ ō van zet′ ē kās] *n.* the arrest, trial, and execution of two foreign-born radicals suspected of taking part in an armed robbery in Massachusetts. Because evidence against the pair was sketchy, many felt that the two were convicted because they represented political radicalism. (p. 637)

salutary neglect [sal′ y$\overline{oo}$ ter′ ē ni glekt′] *n.* the seventeenth and eighteenth century policy of deliberately failing to enforce mercantile laws. (p. 69)

SALT II [sôlt t$\overline{oo}$] *n.* the main focus of President Jimmy Carter's policy toward the Soviet Union, which involved placing limitations on the number, type, and deployment of intercontinental ballistic missiles. Congress failed to approve the treaty as a result of the Soviets' invasion of Afghanistan and their military aid to African revolutionaries. (p. 912)

sanction [saŋk′ shən] *n.* a coercive measure, such as a blockade of shipping, usually taken by several nations together, for forcing a nation considered to have violated international law to end the violation. (p. 714)

satellite nation [sat′ 'l īt′ nā′ shən] *n.* a nation that is dominated by a more powerful nation; especially an Eastern European country that is controlled by the Soviet Union. (p. 777)

scab [skab] *n.* a worker who refuses to strike; someone who works in place of a striking worker. (p. 459)

scalawag [skal′ ə wag′] *n.* a Southern white who supported the Republicans during the Reconstruction. (p. 394)

scorched-earth policy [skôrchd ʉrth päl′ ə sē] *n.* a military policy, used by retreating armies, of destroying everything as the armies retreat, leaving nothing for the advancing enemy. (p. 736)

secede [si sēd′] *vi.* to withdraw formally from membership in a group, especially a political group. (p. 267)

secession [si sesh′ ən] *n.* **1.** an act of seceding; a formal withdrawal or separation. **2.** the withdrawal of the Southern states from the federal Union at the start of the Civil War. (p. 326)

Second New Deal [sek′ ənd n$\overline{oo}$ dēl] *n.* the legislative reforms begun by President Franklin Roosevelt in 1935. (p. 682)

sectionalism [sek′ shən əl iz′ əm] *n.* a narrow-minded concern for or devotion to the interests of one section of a country. (p. 221)

Securities and Exchange Commission (SEC) [si ky$\overline{oo}$r′ ə tēs and eks chānj′ kə mish′ ən] *n.* the congressional commission created in 1934 to administer the Securities Act requiring full financial disclosure by companies wishing to sell stock, and to prevent the unfair manipulation of stock exchanges. (p. 684)

Security Council [si ky$\overline{oo}$r′ ə tē koun′ səl] *n.* the United Nations council responsible for maintaining international peace and security. The council consists of five permanent members (China, France, Russia, the United Kingdom, and the

United States) and ten nonpermanent members. (p. 758)

sedition [si dish′ ən] *n.* the stirring up of discontent, resistance, or rebellion against the government in power. (p. 224)

segregate [seg′ rə gāt′] *v.* to set apart from others or from the main mass or group; to isolate; specifically, to impose a system of segregation on racial groups, social facilities, etc. (p. 394)

self-determination [self di tur′ mə nā′ shən] *n.* the right of a people to freely decide upon its own political status or form of government. (p. 603)

separate but equal [sep′ ə rət′ but ē′ kwəl] *n.* the Supreme Court doctrine that held that a state could provide separate facilities for blacks and for whites as long as the facilities were equal. (p. 200)

separation of powers [sep′ ə rā′ shən uv pou′ ərz] *n.* the division of the federal government into three independent branches: the executive, the legislative, and the judicial branch. (p. 148)

settlement house [set′ ′l mənt hous] *n.* an institution in a depressed and congested neighborhood offering social services and educational and recreational activities. (p. 565)

sharecropping [sher′ kräp′ iŋ] *n.* a Southern agricultural arrangement that developed after the Civil War in which farm workers were loaned land, money, tools, and seed in exchange for giving a share of the harvest to the landowner. (p. 392)

sit-down strike [sit′ doun′ strīk] *n.* a strike, usually illegal, in which the strikers stay inside a factory, etc., refusing to work or leave until agreement is reached. (p. 692)

sit-in [sit′ in′] *n.* a method of protesting the policy of a government, business, etc., in which demonstrators sit in, and refuse to leave, a public place, thus blocking traffic, disrupting operations, etc. (p. 834)

social contract [sō′ shəl kän′ trakt] *n.* a theory of government in which the contract required the government to protect the natural rights of the people and the people, in return, to obey the government. (p. 76)

Social Darwinism [sō′ shəl där′ win iz′ əm] *n.* the body of political and social beliefs based on the belief that individuals, ethnic groups, etc., achieve success or dominance because of inherent genetic superiority and a resultant competitive advantage. (p. 448)

Social Security Act [sō′ shəl si kyoor′ ə tē akt] *n.* the act passed by Congress in 1935 to provide a federal system of old-age, unemployment, or disability insurance for various categories of employed and dependent persons, financed by a fund maintained jointly by employees, employers, and the government. (p. 684)

socialism [sō′ shəl iz′ əm] *n.* a system in which the community rather than private individuals owns and operates the means of production and distri-

bution. All members of the community share in the work and the products. (p. 539)

Socialist party [sō′ shəl ist pär′ tē] *n.* the political party founded in 1901 whose members favor, among other things, abolition of capitalism and state ownership of the means of production, as advocated by Marx and Engels. (p. 539)

sod house [säd hous] *n.* a prairie home with walls made of turf strips chopped into blocks and stacked like bricks. (p. 426)

Solid South [säl′ id south] *n.* those Southern states traditionally regarded as solidly supporting the Democratic party. (p. 650)

Sons of Liberty [sunz uv lib′ ər tē] *n.* groups formed in colonial America to resist Great Britain's Stamp Act. (p. 88)

Southern Christian Leadership Conference (SCLC) [suth′ ərn kris′ chən lēd′ ər ship′ kän′ fər əns] *n.* the organization founded by Dr. Martin Luther King, Jr., in 1956 to champion the cause of civil rights for African Americans. (p. 804)

Southern Colonies [suth′ ərn käl′ ə nēz] *n.* those colonies located south of Pennsylvania and Delaware, including Maryland, Virginia, North Carolina, South Carolina, and Georgia. (p. 45)

sovereign [säv′ rən] *n.* a person who is supreme in power, rank, or authority; a monarch or ruler. (p. 139)

space shuttle [spās shut′ ′l] *n.* a manned, airplane-like spacecraft designed for shuttling back and forth, such as between the earth and a space station, and transporting personnel and equipment. (p. 946)

speakeasy [spēk′ ē′ zē] *n.* a place where alcoholic drinks are sold illegally, especially such a place in the United States during Prohibition. (p. 615)

specie [spē′ shē] *n.* coins made of gold or silver. (p. 272)

sphere of influence [sfir uv in′ floo əns] *n.* a region in which political and economic influence or control is exerted by one nation over another nation or other nations. (p. 525)

spoils system [spoilz sis′ təm] *n.* the system or practice of regarding and treating appointive public offices as the booty of the successful party in an election, to be distributed, with their opportunities for profit, among party workers. (p. 262)

Sputnik [spoot′ nik] *n.* the first unmanned space satellite, launched in 1957 by the Soviet Union. (p. 810)

square deal [skwer dēl] *n.* the term used by President Theodore Roosevelt to describe the motive underlying his basic programs. (p. 544)

stagflation [stag flā′ shən] *n.* an economic condition marked by continuing inflation together with a decline in business activity and an in-

fat, āpe, cär; ten, ēven; is, bīte; gō, hôrn, tool, look, oil, out; up, fur; get; joy; yet; chin; she; thin; zh, leisure; ŋ, ring; ə for *a* in *ago*, *e* in *agent*, *i* in *sanity*, *o* in *comply*, *u* in *focus*; ′ as in *able* (ā′b'l) crease in unemployment. (p. 910)

stalemate [stāl′ māt′] *n.* any unresolved situation in which further action is impossible or useless; a deadlock; a draw. (p. 593)

staple crop [stā′ pəl kräp] *n.* the chief or one of several important commodities regularly grown and sold in a particular area. (p. 38)

states' rights [stāts rīts] *n.* all powers not granted to the federal government by the Constitution nor denied to state governments; also, the belief of some that states had the right to secede from the Union. (p. 260)

stock [stäk] *n.* the capital invested in a company or corporation through the buying of shares, each of which entitles the buyer to a portion of the ownership and, usually, dividends, voting rights, etc. (p. 650)

Strategic Defense Initiative (SDI) [strə tē′ jik dē fens′ i nish′ ə tiv] *n.* President Ronald Reagan's proposal to employ a protective laser shield in space to prevent enemy nuclear missiles from reaching the United States. (p. 932)

strict constructionist [strikt kən struk′ shən ist] *n.* a person who believes the federal government should have only those powers specifically identified in the Constitution. (p. 886)

strict interpretation [strikt in tʉr′ prə tā′ shən] *n.* the interpretation of the Constitution favoring the limitation of the federal government to those specific powers listed in the Constitution. (p. 198)

strike [strīk] *n.* an organized refusal by employees to work in an attempt to force an employer to grant certain demands, such as for higher wages or better working conditions. (p. 458)

subsidy [sub′ sə dē′] *n.* a government grant to a private enterprise considered of benefit to the public. (p. 472)

suburb [sub′ ərb] *n.* a district, especially a residential district, on or near the outskirts of a city and often a separately incorporated city or town. (p. 794)

subversion [səb vʉr′ zhən] *n.* an act tending to overthrow or destroy the existing order. (p. 777)

Sunbelt [sun′ belt′] *n.* that part of the United States comprising most of the states of the South and the Southwest, characterized by a warm, sunny climate and regarded as an area of rapid population and economic growth. (p. 919)

supply-side economics [sə plī′ sīd ek′ ə näm′ iks] *n.* the economic theory that advocates large tax cuts in order to increase private investments and thus increase the nation's supply of goods and services. (p. 931)

***Sussex* pledge** [sus′ iks plej] *n.* a pledge issued by the Germans in 1916, after the sinking of the *Sussex*, promising that no more merchant ships would be sunk without sufficient warning. (p. 595)

T

tabloid [tab′ loid′] *n.* a newspaper, usually half the ordinary size, with many pictures and with short, often sensational, news stories. (p. 624)

Teapot Dome scandal [tē′ pät′ dōm skan′ dəl] *n.* the name given to the scandal involving President Warren G. Harding's Secretary of the Interior, Albert Fall, involving the illegal leasing of oil-rich land in Wyoming and California to private companies in return for large sums of cash. (p. 640)

technology [tek näl′ ə jē] *n.* the practical application of scientific knowledge, by which a society provides its members with those things needed and desired. (p. 436)

telegraph [tel′ ə graf′] *n.* an apparatus or system that converts a coded message into electrical impulses and sends it to a distant receiver. (p. 295)

tenant farming [ten′ ənt färm′ iŋ] *n.* an agricultural arrangement in which a worker farms another person's land as part of his or her rent payment. (p. 392)

termination policy [tʉr′ mə nā′ shən päl′ ə sē] *n.* the federal policy intended to transfer all responsibilities for American Indians from the federal government to the state government. (p. 805)

terrorism [ter′ ər iz′ əm] *n.* the use of force or threats to demoralize, intimidate, and subjugate, especially such use as a political weapon or policy. (p. 914)

Tet offensive [tet ô′ fen′ siv] *n.* the massive military offensive by the Viet Cong in January of 1968 during the Vietnamese New Year, or Tet. The Viet Cong captured many South Vietnamese cities and laid siege to the United States embassy in Saigon. Although the Viet Cong were ultimately defeated by South Vietnamese and American troops, the offensive itself caused the United States military to begin rethinking their role in the war, caused public opinion in America to turn, and eventually led to United States withdrawal from Vietnam. (p. 863)

Tidewater [tīd′ wôt′ ər] *n.* an area in eastern Virginia that is located primarily along the James, Potomac, Rappahannock, and York rivers. (p. 39)

Tonkin Gulf Resolution [tän′ kin gulf rez′ ə loo′ shən] *n.* the resolution passed by Congress in 1964 supporting President Johnson's intention to "take all necessary measures to repel any armed attack against the forces of the United States and to prevent further aggression," following the confrontation between the North Vietnamese and United States warships in the Gulf of Tonkin. (p. 859)

Tory [tôr′ ē] *n.* in the American Revolution, a person who advocated or actively supported continued allegiance to Great Britain. (p. 105)

totalitarian [tō tal′ ə ter′ ē ən] *adj.* characteristic of a government or state under a dictatorship in which one political party or group maintains complete control and bans all others. (p. 713)

trade deficit [trād def′ ə sit] *n.* an economic situation occurring when the value of a nation's imports surpasses the value of its exports. (p. 910)

transcontinental railroad [trans′ kän tə nent′ 'l rāl′ rōd] *n.* the railroad line completed in 1869 linking the Atlantic coast with the Pacific coast. (pp. 370, 441)

Treaty of Paris of 1763 [trēt′ ē uv par′ is uv 1763] *n.* the treaty ending the Seven Years' War and in which Great Britain received all of France's North American land holdings except New Orleans, as well as Spain's holdings in Florida. (p. 84)

Treaty of Paris of 1783 [trēt′ ē uv par′ is uv 1783] *n.* the treaty ending the American Revolution and in which the United States was formally recognized as a sovereign nation; received all land between the Appalachians, the Mississippi River, and the Great Lakes; and was granted fishing rights off the coast of Canada. (p. 118)

trench warfare [trench wôr′ fer′] *n.* military battles conducted from long lines of opposing ditches rather than on an open battlefield. (p. 593)

Triple Alliance [trip′ əl ə lī′ əns] *n.* an alliance of Germany, Austria-Hungary, and Italy from 1882 to 1915, chiefly against Russia and France. (p. 591)

Triple Entente [trip′ əl än tänt′] *n.* the military understanding reached by Great Britain, France, and Russia before World War I as a counterbalance to the Triple Alliance. (p. 591)

Truman Doctrine [trōō′ mən däk′ trin] *n.* the policy announced by President Harry S Truman in 1947 that provided economic and military aid to nations threatened by armed minorities or outside groups. (p. 774)

trust [trust] *n.* an industrial or business combination, now illegal in the United States, in which management and control of the member corporations are vested in a single board of trustees, who are thus able to control a market, absorb or eliminate competition, fix prices, etc. (p. 447)

Tweed Ring [twēd riŋ] *n.* a group of corrupt Democratic politicians in New York City led by William Tweed during the 1860's and 1870's. They accepted bribes from companies bidding on city contracts and stole millions from the city's treasury. (p. 496)

two-party system [tōō pär′ tē sis′ təm] *n.* the practice of having candidates compete for office through the machinery of two rival political parties. (p. 216)

U

U-boat [yōō′ bōt′] *n.* a German submarine; short for *Unterseeboot*. (p. 594)

underground railroad [un′ dər ground′ rāl′ rōd′] *n.* in the United States before the Civil War, a system set up by certain opponents of slavery to help fugitive slaves escape to free states and to Canada. (p. 301)

unicameral [yōōn′ ə kam′ ər əl] *adj.* of or having a single legislative body. (p. 138)

United Nations (UN) [yōō nīt′ id nā′ shənz] *n.* an international organization of nations pledged to promote world peace and security, maintain treaty obligations and the observance of international law, and cooperate in furthering social progress. The organization was formed in San Francisco in 1945 under a permanent charter that had its inception in conferences (1941–1945) held by nations opposed to the fascist coalition of Germany, Japan, Italy, and their satellites. The headquarters has been in New York City since 1946, and the membership (1988) consists of 159 nations. (p. 758)

urban sprawl [ʉr′ bən sprôl] *n.* the spread of urban congestion into adjoining suburbs and rural sections. (p. 561)

urbanization [ʉr′ bən i zā′ shən] *n.* the changing of rural areas into cities, and the movement of people from the country to cities and to industrial areas. (p. 490)

utopian community [yōō tō′ pē ən kə myōō′ nə tē] *n.* a group founded upon ideas envisioning perfection in social and political organization. (p. 298)

V

vaquero [vä ker′ ō] *n.* a man who herds cattle; a cowboy. (p. 421)

veto [vē′ tō] *n.* the constitutional right or power of a ruler or legislature to reject bills passed by another branch of the government. (p. 148)

Vietcong [vē′ et koŋ′] *n.* a guerrilla force led from Hanoi, which sought to overthrow the South Vietnamese government (1954–1975). (p. 857)

Vietnamization [vē′ et nam′ i zā′ shən] *n.* President Richard Nixon's plan for gradually withdrawing American troops from Vietnam and letting the Vietnamese do most of the fighting. (p. 865)

W

wage and price controls [wāj and prīs kən trōlz′] *n.* the economic policy imposed by President Richard Nixon in 1971 that froze wages, prices, fees, charges, and rents for a period of ninety days. It was intended to put a stop to spiraling inflation but proved ineffective and unpopular. (p. 887)

---

fat, āpe, cär; ten, ēven; is, bīte; gō, hôrn, tōōl, lʊʊk, oil, ʊut; up, fʉr; get; joy; yet; chin; she; thin; zh, leisure; ŋ, ring; ə for *a* in *ago, e* in *agent, i* in *sanity, o* in *comply, u* in *focus;* ' as in *able* (ā′b'l)

Wagner Act [wag′ nər akt] *n.* the act passed by Congress in 1935 to revive many of the pro-labor provisions of the National Industrial Recovery Act (NIRA) after the Supreme Court found the NIRA unconstitutional. (p. 686)

War Powers Act [wôr pou′ ərz akt] *n.* the act passed by Congress in 1973 that required a President who sent United States troops to a foreign country to explain the action to Congress within forty-eight hours. (p. 871)

Warren Commission [wôr′ ən kə mish′ ən] *n.* the committee headed by Chief Justice Earl Warren to investigate the assassination of President John F. Kennedy in 1963. The commission found no proof of a widespread conspiracy. (p. 838)

watchful waiting policy [wäch′ ful wāt′ iŋ päl′ ə sē] *n.* the foreign policy of Woodrow Wilson, who believed that the Mexicans themselves would overthrow the Huerta government without United States intervention. (p. 575)

Watergate [wôt′ ər gāt] *n.* the building complex in Washington, D.C., housing Democratic party headquarters, which were burglarized in June of 1972 under the direction of government officials; the scandal that involved officials violating the public trust through subterfuge, bribery, burglary, and other abuses of power in order to maintain their positions as government officials. (p. 891)

Whig party [hwig pär′ tē] *n.* originally a British political party, the Whig party emerged in the United States in opposition to the policies of Andrew Jackson. Eventually the party disintegrated and was replaced by the Republican party. (p. 271)

wildcat bank [wīld′ kat′ baŋk] *n.* a state bank that issued bank notes without sufficient money from federal funds to redeem them. (p. 272)

Women's rights movement [wim′ inz rīts mōōv′ mənt] *n.* the movement organized to help women gain equal rights. Especially strong in the 1960's and 1970's, the movement was, and continues to be, instrumental in strengthening the role of women in American society. (p. 305)

Works Progress Administration (WPA) [wɜrks präg′ rəs ad min′ is trā′ shən] *n.* a government agency under President Franklin Roosevelt's New Deal that put the unemployed to work on projects such as building schools, hospitals, and playgrounds, and repairing roads and airports. Artists and writers were also employed by the agency. (p. 682)

Y

Yalta Conference [yôl′ tə kän′ fər əns] *n.* the meeting involving representatives from the United States, Great Britain, and the Soviet Union, at which it was decided that defeated Germany would be divided into four occupied zones, that Eastern Europe would be guaranteed free elections, and that the Soviet Union would declare war on Japan as soon as Germany was defeated. (p. 757)

yellow-dog contract [yel′ ō dôg kän′ trakt′] *n.* an employer-employee contract, now illegal, by which an applicant for a job agrees not to join a labor union while employed. (p. 459)

yellow journalism [yel′ ō jɜr′ nəl iz′ əm] *n.* the use of cheaply sensational or unscrupulous methods in newspapers, etc., to attract or influence readers. (p. 569)

Z

Zimmermann note [zim′ ər mən nōt] *n.* a message sent by the German foreign minister to the German minister in Mexico ordering him to offer the Mexican government the states of Texas, New Mexico, and Arizona if Mexico would enter World War II on the German side and fight against the United States (p. 596)

Index

An *i* preceding a page reference indicates that there is an illustration, picture, or photograph, and usually text information as well, on that page. An *m* or *c* preceding a page reference indicates a map or chart.

Alamo, 313
Alaska
  early settlement of, 8, 10
  Exxon Valdez in, 951-952, *i* 952
  purchase of, 512, 583
  Russian claims in, 246
  as state, 810, 815, *m* 998
Albania
  Italian invasion of, *m* 721
  as Warsaw Pact member, 777
Albany, 28
Albany Congress, 82-83
Albee, E. F. *(1857-1930)*, 571
Aldridge, Ira *(1804?-1867)*, 571
Aldrin, Edwin "Buzz," Jr. *(1930-)*,
  887, 946
Aleutian Islands, in World War II,
  752
Alger, Horatio, Jr. *(1832-1899)*, 449,
  566
  books of, 449, 453
Algeria, 580, 581
Algiers, 749
Algonquin Indians, 131
Algren, Nelson *(1909-1981)*, 684
Alien and Sedition Acts (1798),
  223, 224, 229, 233, 255, 267, 284
Alien Land Law (1913), 505
Allen, Ethan *(1738-1789)*, 100
Allen, Gracie *(1905-1964)*, *i* 694,
  695
Allende, Salvador, *(1908-1973)*, 907
Alliance for Progress, 833, 967
Allison, Fran, *i* 798
Alvarey, Everett, Jr., *i* 872
Amalgamated Clothing Workers,
  692
America First Committee, 729
American Anti-slavery Society,
  300
American Association of Retired
  Persons (AARP), 187
American colonies. *See* Colonial
  America
American Colonization Society,
  299
American Federation of Labor
  (AFL), 460–461, 479, 485
American Federation of
  Labor—Congress of Industrial
  Organization (AFL-CIO), 186
American G. I. Forum, 805
American Independent party, 884,
  901
American Indians, 131
  agriculture of, 6-7
  and the Albany Congress, 82-83
  British treatment of, 84, 86
  buffalo hunting by, *i* 415, 416-417
  civil rights for, 805-806
  conflict with, 73
  failure of Americanization policy,
    417-420
  food sources of, 7-8, 10
  and fur trade, *i* 142

government policies toward, 219-
  220, 238-239, 259-260, 263-266,
  m 264, *i* 265, 415, 417-420, 693,
  805, 806
housing of, 330
impact of disease on, 17
impact of horse on, 414
land disputes with colonists, 58-60,
  i 60
lands of, to 1890, *m* 420
land use by, 330
under New Deal, 693-694
in North America, *m* 6, *m* 8
relations with colonists, 25-26, 40,
  i 56, 60
removal of, *m* 264, 265-266
rights of, 944
social customs of, 330
and termination policy, 805-806
use of natural resources by, 8, 10,
  330
war with, 417-419, *m* 420
and western settlement, 414-419,
  433
in World War II, 743
Americanization policy, with Indians, 419-420
American party, 343
American Railway Union (ARU),
  461, 464, 479, 485
American Red Cross, 371
American Revolution, 127, 133,
  280-281
  American advantages in, 107-108,
    c 115
  battles in, 92-93, *m* 93, 100-102,
    i 101, *m* 110, 111-114, *m* 112
  British advantages in, 107, *c* 115
  British surrender at Yorktown, *i* 113,
    114-116, *m* 116
  financing of, 109
  French alliance in, 111-113
  impact of, on world, 117-118
  mercenaries in, 107
  military leadership in, c115
  Tories in, 124-125, *i* 125
  women in, 108-109
American system, 243-245, 259,
  274
American Temperance Society,
  297-298
Amicus curiae (friend of the court)
  briefs, 197, 198
Amnesty, 110
Amnesty Act (1872), 395
Amos Bad Heart Bull *(1869-1913)*,
  pictograph by, *i* 418
Amusement parks, 563
Anacostia Flats, 661, *i* 661
Anasazi, 6-7
  pueblos built by, *i* 7
Anaya, Toney, 942
Anderson, Marian *(1902-1993)*,
  i 693
Anderson, Mary, 555

Anderson, Robert *(1805-1871)*, 358
Andersonville, Georgia, 371-372
André, John *(1751-1780)*, 102
Andros, Sir Edmund *(1637-1714)*,
  64-65, 66
Angelou, Maya, *(1928-)* 793
Anglo-Saxonism, 503-504
Angola, 581
Annapolis, Maryland, 144
Anne (Queen of England) *(1665-
  1714)*, *c* 67
Anthony, Susan B. *(1820-1906)*,
  i 467, *i* 468, 479, 485, 617
Anthony amendment, 468, 616-617
Anti-Asian Acts, 504-505
Anti-Catholicism, 343
Anti-Defamation League of B'nai
  B'rith, 187
Antietam, Battle of, 365-366, *i* 366, 381
Anti-federalists, 151
Anti-immigrant movement, 629
Anti-Masonic party, 266
Anti-Saloon League, 615
Antislavery movement, 309, 407
  leaders of, 299-301
  opposition to, 301-302
  origin of, 298-299
  Quakers in, 78
  and Uncle Tom's Cabin, 337-339
Antiwar movement, 861
Apache Indians, 7
Apartment house, 490
A & P (Atlantic & Pacific Tea Com-
  pany), *i* 644
Apollo 16, 823
  view of earth from, *i* 822
Appalachian Mountains, 39, 276,
  277
Appeasement, 721
Appellate jurisdiction, 197
Appointments, Presidential powers
  in, 168
Appomattox, 376-377, 381
Aquino, Benigno *(1932-1983)*, 524
Aquino, Corazon *(1933-)*, 524
Arab oil embargo (1973), *i* 905
Arafat, Yasir, *(1922-)*, 962, *i* 962
Arbitration, 459
Arbuckle, Fatty, 572
Architecture, *i* 212
  skyscrapers in, 563, 579, 644
  and urban planning, 563
Arias plan, 937
Arias Sánchez, Oscar, *(1941-)*, 937
Aristide, Jean-Bertrand, *(1953-)*,
  962-963
Arizona
  Indians in, 6, *i* 7
  as state, *m* 998
Arkansas
  secession of, 359
  as state, *m* 988
Arkwright, Richard *(1732-1792)*,
  252
Armed Forces. *See also* Army;

Chancellorsville, Battle of, *m* 372, 373
Chaney, James E., 841
Channing, William Ellery *(1780-1842),* 296
Chaplin, Charlie *(1889-1977), i* 572, 626
Charles I *(1600-1649),* 28, 30, *c* 67
Charles II *(1630-1685),* 30, 58, 63, 64, *c* 67, 129
***Charles River Bridge* v. *Warren Bridge* (1837),** 203
Charleston, S.C., in confederate period, *i* 153
Charles Town, 30, 44-45, 48, 101, 113
Charter, 21
Chase, Samuel *(1741-1811),* 169, 233
Chattanooga, Tennessee, 376
Chavez, Cesar *(1927-1993), i* 805
Checks and balances, 146, 148-149
Chelmno, 725
Cherokee Indians, 11, 219, 265-266
***Chesapeake* incident,** 237, 284
***Chesapeake* (Michener),** 57
Cheyenne Indians, 416
Chiang Kai-shek *(1887-1975),* 757, 779, 780, 783, 791
Chicago, 475
  African Americans in, 493
  Democratic Convention of 1968, *i* 878, 883-884
  department stores in, 564
  great fire in, 493
  immigrants in, 500, 503
  population of, 493
  urban planning in, 563
Chicago Seven, *i* 886
Chicano, 804, 805
Chickamauga, 376
Chickasaw Indians, 11
Child labor, 251, 253, 457, *i* 458
Children, in Great Depression, 660
Children's Defense Fund, 187
China
  boxer rebellion in, 525-526, 584
  British interests in, 480
  civil war in, 779-780
  communism in, 779-780, 791, 955, 956
  Nixon's visit to, 780
  open door policy in, 525, 535, 584
  signing of Nine-Power Treaty by, 639
  spheres of influence in, *m* 525
  Tiananmen Square massacre in, 780, 956
  U.S. policy toward, 718-719, 780, 890
China Incident, 718
Chinatown, in New York City, *i* 504
Chinese

exclusion of, 504-505, 509
and railroad construction, 442-443, 453, 484
Chinese Exclusion Act (1882), 505
Chisholm Trail, 421
Chivington, J. M. *(1821-1894),* 416
Chivington massacre, 416, 433, 483
Choctaw Indians, 11, 219
Christian Coalition, 963
Christianity, attempts to convert Indians to, 58
Christy, Howard Chandler *(1873-1952),* paintings by, *i* 136
Churchill, Winston *(1874-1965),* 721, 727-728, *i* 728, 737, 757, *i* 758, 765, 768
  "iron curtain speech of," 773-774, *i* 774, 821
***Cimarron* (Ferber),** 413, 426
Cisneros, Sandra, 944
Cities
  corruption in, 496, 554
  fire fighting in, 493, 583
  ghettos in, 493-494
  housing needs in, 490-492
  immigrants in, 499-500, 509, 583
  law enforcement in, 493, 583
  middle class in, 490-491
  political machines in, 494-497, 583
  tenements in, 509
  transportation needs in, 492
  water and sanitation in, 492-93
Citizens, rights of, 170-171
City government, reforms in, 540-541
Civil Aeronautics Board, 445
Civil disobedience, 801
Civilian Conservation Corps. (CCC), 678, *i* 679, 693, 694, 701
Civilization, 6
Civil rights, 176
  under Eisenhower, 801-804, 815, 821
  freedom rides, 834, 835
  under Johnson, 839, 841-844
  under Kennedy, 827-828, 834, 836-837, *i* 837
  march on Washington, 834
  Montgomery bus boycott, 803-804, 815, 835
  under Nixon, 885-886
  and Selma march, 842
  sit-ins, 834
  student demonstrations, 836, 882, *i* 882
  under Truman, 771
  and voter registration drives, *i* 842-843
Civil Rights Act (1957), 804
Civil Rights Act (1964), 839, 845, 848, 851, 929, 954, 967
Civil Rights Act (1968), 844
Civil Rights Bill (1866), 386
Civil Rights Commission, 804
Civil Rights Memorial, *i* 943

Civil rights movement, 851, 967
Civil servants, strikes by, 882-883
Civil Service, 192-193, 465, 479
Civil Service Commission, 771
Civil War, 381, 408, 703
  attack on Fort Sumter, 358-359, *i* 359
  battles in, 360-366, *m* 363, *i* 366, 372-374, *m* 372, *m* 373, *m* 375
  blacks in, *i* 367, 368-369
  border states in, 359
  changing goals of, 366-369
  costs of, 381
  draft in, 368, 369
  and Emancipation Proclamation, 368-369
  medical care in, 371
  neutrality of Great Britain in, 366-67
  Northern leadership in, 362-363, 373-374, 375-376
  Northern position in, 359-60, 370
  Northern strategy in, 362-366, 381
  prisons in, 371-372
  secession of Southern states, 326, 359
  slavery as issue in, 367-368
  soldiers in, *i* 356
  songs of the, 378-379
  Southern leadership in, 365, 373
  Southern position in, 360, 369-370
  Southern surrender in, 376-377, 381
  split of states in, *m* 360
  weapons in, 361-362, *i* 362
  women in, 370-371
Civil Works Administration (CWA), 678-679
Clark, George Rogers *(1752-1818),* 100, 113
Clark, Tom C. *(1899-1977),* 802
Clark, William *(1770-1838), i* 236
Clay, Henry *(1777-1852),* 238, 241, 247, 258, 279, 299, 318, 326, 327, 328, 333
  American System of, 243, 274
  and bank issue, 269-270
Clayton Antitrust Act (1914), 553
Clayton-Bulwer Treaty (1850), 527
Clear and present danger doctrine, 200
Cleaver, Eldridge *(1935-),* 884
Clemenceau, Georges *(1841-1929),* 604, *i* 604
Clermont, 292, *i* 292
Cleveland, Grover *(1837-1908),* 490, 519, 542, *i* 1001
  and conservation, 546
  in election of 1884, 466
  and labor movement, 464
  and tariff regulation, 467
  veto of literacy test, 504
Cleveland, Ohio, fire department in, 493
Clifford, Clark *(1906-),* 863, 874
Cliff palace, *i* 7
Climate

and Cuban missile crisis, 831-833
and economics, 829-830
in election of 1960, 825-828, *i* 827
inauguration of, 829
and Monroe Doctrine, 246
New Frontier program of, 826-827
and Peace Corps, 833
Soviet policies under, 831-833
and space, 829-830, *i* 830
and Vietnam, 857-858, 875
Kennedy, Joseph P. *(1888-1969),*
650, 678, 684, 826
Kennedy, Robert *(1925-1968),* 828,
834, 839, 864-865, 877, 880
assassination of, 881, 901, 967
Kent State University, student
killings at, 867
Kentucky
in Civil War, 359
as state, *m* 998
Kentucky Resolution, 224-225, 229
Kerensky, Alexander *(1881-1970),*
702
Kerouac, Jack *(1922-1969),* 797
Khomeini, Ayatollah Ruhollah *(1900-
1989),* 915-916, *i* 916
Khrushchev, Nikita *(1894-1971),*
808, *i* 809, 831, 832, 851
Kim Il Sung *(1912-1994),* 781
King, Bernice *(1963-),* *i* 881
King, Charles B. *(1785-1862),* portrait
by, *i* 268
King, Coretta Scott *(1927-),* 828, 835,
i 881
King, Martin Luther, Jr. *(1929-1968),*
88, 794, 803-804, 815, 821, 827-
828, 834, 835, 841-842, 848, 851,
967
assassination of, 835, 880-881,
i 881, 901, 967
King, Martin Luther, Sr., 835
King, Rufus *(1755-1827),* 238
King Cotton, 248
King George's War, *c* 86
King Mob, 261
King Philip (Metacom) *(?-1656),* 58,
i 59, 59-60
King Philip's War, 59-60
Kings, and republics, 281
Kings Mountain, battle of, 113
King William's War, 86
Kiowa, Comanche, 315
Kirtland, Ohio, 320
Kissinger, Henry *(1923-),* 854, 868,
889-890, *i* 890, 892, 901, 911,
914, 968
Kittredge, Walter, 379
Knight, Sarah Kemble, 38
journal of, 47
Knights of Labor, 459-460, 479, 485
Knights of the White Camelia, 395
Know-Nothing party, 343-345, 355,
408
Knox, Frank *(1874-1944),* 689, 729
Knox, Henry *(1750-1806),* 101, 210

Knox, John *(1513-1572),* 129
Kodak camera, 568
Korean War, *i* 766, 780-784, *m* 782,
791, 793, 821
refugees in, *i* 781
U.S. involvement in, 782-784
Korematsu **v.** *United States* **(1944),**
742
Kosciuszko, Thaddeus *(1746-1817),*
113, *i* 113
Kristallnacht, 722, *i* 722, 733
"Kukla, Fran and Ollie," *i* 798
Ku Klux Klan, 403, 655, 836
and civil rights, 842-843
in 1920s, 628, 635-636, *i* 635, 642,
650
in 1950s, 706, 802
origin of, 395
Kurds, 957
Kuril Islands, 738
Kuwait, 861, 956-957
Kwakiutl Indian, 9
Ky, Nguyen Cao *(1930-),* *i* 859

L

Labor force, 251, 253, 304-305, 370-
371, 438, *i* 439, *i* 600, 618-619,
660. *See also* Industry
women in, 599-600, 660
and working conditions, 253, 456-
458, 485, 541-543
during World War I, 599-600, *i* 600
during World War II, 743-745
Labor movement, 692, 701
and American Federation of Labor,
460-461, 479, 485
and American Railway Union, 461,
464, 479, 485
and Baltimore and Ohio Railroad
strike, 458-459, *i* 459
under Carter, 910
causes of, 456-458
and civil servant strikes, 882-883
during World War II, 743
first factory strike, 251
in garment trade, 463-464, 479, 692
growth of, 692, 464, 479
and Haymarket affair, 460, 479, 503
and Industrial Workers of the World
(IWW), 461-462
Knights of Labor in, 459-460, 479,
485
National Labor Union in, 458
in 1930s, 701
post World War I, 634, 636-637, 706
post World War II, 770-771
shaping of, 458-461
under Theodore Roosevelt, 544-
545, *i* 545
under Truman, 820
women in, 462-464, 485

Labor Reform party, 458
Labor Unions. *See* Labor movement
Lafayette, Marquis Marie Joseph de
(1757-1834), 114, *i* 115
Lafayette Escadrille, 602
La Follette, Robert *(1855-1925),* 541,
616, 642
Laissez faire, 466
Lake Wobegon Days (Keillor), 903
La Malinche, 17
Lamar, Mirabeau B. *(1798-1859),* 314
Lame duck sessions, 178, 196
Landon, Alfred M. *(1887-1987),* 689-
690, 896
Land Ordinance (1785), 141
Land use. *See also* Agriculture
in Great Plains, 431
Lange, Dorothea *(1895-1965),* 696
photograph by, *i* 656
Langtry, Lily *(1853-1929),* 571
Lansing, Robert *(1864-1928),* 604
Laos, Vietnamese invasion of, 868
Lapowinsa, *i* 56
La Raza, 187, 849
La Salle, Robert Cavelier, Sieur de
(1643-1687), 18, *c* 20
Latin America. *See also* individual
countries
and Alliance for Progress, 833, 967
building of Panama Canal, 526-529,
m 528, *i* 529
countries in, *m* 245
dollar diplomacy in, 531, 584
Good Neighbor Policy in, 650, 716,
733, 819
and Monroe Doctrine, 245-246, 255,
285, 530-531, 650
Latvia, 605
Laundry Workers Union, 458
Laurance, John, 212
Laurens, Henry *(1724-1792),* *i* 117
Lavelle, Rita, 948
Lawrence, William *(1850-1941),* 872
League of Nations, 603, 607, 705,
722
on Japanese aggression, 817
pre World War II, 714
League of Six Nations, 219
League of the Iroquois, 11
League of Women Voters, 187
Leapfrogging, 753
Leary, Timothy *(1920-),* 846
Lease, Mary Elizabeth *(1853-1933),*
471, *i* 471
Lebanon
attack on U.S. marines in, 938,
i 938, 968
hostages in, *i* 916
turmoil in, 938
U.S. troops in, 809
Le Duc Tho *(1911-1990),* *i* 868
Led Zeppelin, 920
Lee, Doris *(1905-1983),* *i* 685
Lee, Harper *(1926-),* 183
Lee, Richard Henry *(1732-1794),*

as state, *m* 998
Middle East, *m* 913
  Arab and Non-Arab nations, *m* 915
  and Camp David accords, 913-914, 937
  and Gulf War, 940, 956-957
  and Iran-Contra affair, 938-940
  and Iranian hostages, 916
  and Iranian revolution, 915-916
  and Lebanon, 938
  oil production in, 898-899, *m* 899
  and Persian Gulf, 940
  and Persian Gulf War, 916-917, 956-957
  U.S. policy in, 937-940
Middle passage, 43
Midnight judges, 169, 198, 233
Midway, Battle of, 753
Migrant workers, 804
Migration. *See also* Immigrants; Immigration
  to North America, 4-6, *m* 5, 35
  northern, of African Americans, 509, 583, 619-620, 631, 706
  to Sunbelt, 921-923, *m* 922
Militarism, 49
Military powers, of president, 167-168, 191
Militia, Congressional powers in, 163
Militiamen, 82
Miller, Arthur *(1915-),* 75
Miller, Elizabeth Smith *(1822-1911),* 304
Miller, Glenn *(1904-1944),* 695
Miller, Thomas W., 640
Mindszenty, Joseph Cardinal *(1892-1975),* 807
Miner, Myrtilla *(1815-1864),* 304
Minimum wage, 829
Mining industry
  labor movement in, 462-463, 544-545, *i* 545, 636-637
  1850-1900, *m* 440
Minnesota, *m* 998
Minorities. *See also* African Americans; Discrimination; Mexican Americans
  under New Deal, 692-694
Minor v. *Happersett* (1873), 468
Minow, Newton, 799
Minstrel shows, 571
Minutemen, *i* 74, 92-93
Miranda, Ernesto, 201
Miranda rights, 201
Miranda v. *Arizona* (1966), 200-201, 886
Mississippi River
  closing of, by Spain, 143
  exploration of, 18
Missouri, i 756
Missouri,
  in Civil War, 359
  as state, *m* 998
Missouri Compromise, *m* 247, 255, 285, 355

repeal of, 340
Mitchell, John *(1913-1988),* 891-892, *i* 892, 893, 896
Mitchell, Joni *(1943-),* 825
Mitchell, Margaret *(1900-1949),* 383, 695
Mohawk Indians, 9, *i* 9, 11, 219
Molasses, trade of, 45
Moley, Raymond *(1886-1975), i* 665
Molotov, V. M. *(1890-1986), i* 723
Mondale, Walter *(1928-),* 908, 929, 933, *i* 933, 968
Money. *See also* Banking
  Congressional powers in, 162
  continentals, 109
  gold standard for, 472, 479, 664, 669
  greenbacks, 370
  silver issue, 472-473, *i* 473, 479
Monitor, i 362
Monkey trial, 614-615
Monmouth, Battle of, 108
Monroe, James *(1758-1831),* 243, *i* 246, 299, *i* 1000
  domestic policy under, 243-245, 246
  foreign policy under, 245-246
  and Louisiana purchase, 234-235
  and slavery issue, 246-247, *m* 247
Monroe Doctrine, 245-246, 255, 285
  expansion of, 530-531
  Roosevelt corollary to, 246, 650
Montana, *m* 998
Montcalm, Marquis de *(1712-1759),* 84
Montezuma *(1390?-1469?),* 404
Montgomery, Alabama
  bus boycott in, 803-804, 815, 835
  as capital of Confederacy, 360
Montgomery, Bernard L. *(1887-1976),* 749
Montreal, capture of, 84
Moon landing, 887, *i* 888
Moorer, Thomas H. *(1912-),* 872
Moral Majority, 929
Moratorium, 664
Morelos, José *(1765-1815),* 405
Morgan, Lewis *(1818-1881),* 419
Morgan v. *Virginia* (1946), 834
Morgenthau, Henry, Jr. *(1891-1967),* 668
Morison, Samuel Eliot *(1887-1976),* 271
Mormons, 320-321, 333, 408
Morocco, 580, 581
Morrill Land-Grant Act (1862), 370
Morrill Tariff (1861), 370
Morris, Gouverneur *(1752-1816),* 138, 148
Morris, Robert *(1734-1806),* 109
Morrow, Dwight W. *(1873-1931),* 650
Morse, Samuel F. B. *(1791-1872),* 290, *i* 295, 436
Morse, Wayne *(1900-1974),* 859
Morse code, *i* 295

Mott, Lucretia *(1793-1880),* 290, 303, *i* 303, 305
Mound builders, 11-12
Mountains, 276
Mount Holyoke Female Seminary, 304
Mount Royal, 18
Mount Rushmore National Memorial, *i* 943
Mount Vernon, *i* 221
Movement, geographic theme of, 53, 287, 487, 811-813, 921-923
Movies, 572, 626, *i* 626, 695, 769-770, 799, 919
Mozambique, 581
Mubarak, Hosni *(1928-),* 937
Muckrakers, 538-539, *i* 539, 554
Mullaney, Kate, 458
Muller v. *Oregon* (1908), 542
Multinational corporations, 576-577, *m* 577
Munich Pact, 720-721
Munn v. *Illinois* (1877), 445
Murmansk, 748
Murphy, Charles, 571
Murray, Philip *(1886-1952),* 692
Murrow, Edward R. *(1908-1965),* 726, *i* 726, 794, 798
Music
  and big bands, 695
  civil war songs, 378-379
  contributions of black Americans in, 622-623, *i* 623
  country-western, 800
  jazz, 622-623, 631, 706, 799-800
  popular, 920
  railroad songs, 441
  rock and roll, 800, *i* 800
  and WPA, 682
Musical Comedy, 643
Muskie, Edmund S. *(1914-),* 883
Muskogean, 131
Mussolini, Benito *(1883-1945), i* 714, 711, 713, 714, 733, 739, 749, 819
MX missile, 932
My Lai massacre, 861

N

Nader, Ralph *(1934-), i* 185
Nagasaki, bombing of, 756, 762-763
Namibia, 581
Napoleon Bonaparte *(1769-1821),* 234-235, 237, 281
Napoleon III *(1808-1873),* 530
Narragansett Bay, 27
Narragansett Indians, 58-59
Narrative of Sojourner Truth (Gilbert), 301
Narváez, Panfilo de, route of, *m* 17
Nashville, U.S.S., 528
Nasser, Gamal Abdel *(1918-1970),* 809

Nast, Thomas *(1840-1902),* cartoons by, *i* 398, *i* 496, *i* 498

National Abortion Rights Action League, 187

National Aeronautics and Space Administration (NASA), 829-830, 887, *i* 888, 946. *See also* Space exploration

National American Woman Suffrage Association, 467, 617

National Association for Advancement of Colored People (NAACP), 187, 620, 631, 693, 801, 815, 821

National Association of Manufacturers, 187

National Bank
First, 211-212, *i* 212
Second, 244-245, 269-271, *i* 270

National Banking Act (1863), 370

National Broadcasting Corporation (NBC), 726

National Child Labor Committee, 541

National Congress of American Indians, 805

National Consumers' League, 541

National Environmental Policy Act, 847

National Gazette, 216

National income, during Great Depression, 659

National Industrial Recovery Act (NIRA) (1933), 680-681, 686-687

Nationalism, 243

Nationalize, 670

National Labor Relations Act (1935), 686-687, 691

National Labor Relations Board (NLRB), 687

National Labor Union (NLU), 458, 485

National Liberation Front (NLF), 857

National Organization for Women (NOW), 846, 910

National Origins Act (1929), 640, 841

National Parks, U.S., *i* 195, *i* 277, *m* 547, *i* 574

National People's party, 471

National Recovery Administration (NRA), 680-681, 701

National Republican party
and birth of Democratic party,260-261
in election of 1832, 270

National Rifle Association, 187

National Right to Life Committee, 187

National Road, 243, 277

National Science Foundation, 810

National Security Act (1947), 768

National Security Council (NSC), 192, 768, 859, 938-939

National Service Corps, 959-960

National Socialist German Workers' party, 713-714

National States Rights party, 836

National War Labor Board, 599, 705, 743

National Woman's party, 616, 910

Nation at Risk, 947

Native Americans. *See* American Indians; Apache Indians; Narragansett Indians; Sioux Indians

Nativism, 343, 503-505, 509, 583, 640

Naturalization, 504, *i* 710. *See also* Immigrants; Immigration
Congressional powers in, 162

Natural resources, 277, 543
American Indian use of, 8-10, 329-330
and industrial advances, 439-440
and westward movement, 277

Nauvoo, Illinois, 320

Navajo Indians, 7, *i* 329

Naval holiday, 639

Naval stores, trade of, by American colonies, 63

Navigation Acts (1660 and 1663), 63, 68, 73, 132

Navy
buildup of U.S., 719
in Civil War, 364-365
Congressional powers in, 163
in late 1800s, 513
reduction of, post World War I, 639

Navy Nurse Corps, 740

Nazi party, 713-714

Nebraska,
conflict over slavery in, 339-341
as state, *m* 998

Necessary and proper clause, 186

Nelson, Donald M., 744

Nesmith, James, 317

Netherlands
as NATO member, 776-777
signing of Nine-Power Treaty by, 639
in World War II, 750

Neutrality
declaration of, by Washington, 217
as theme in foreign policy, 218

Neutrality Act (1935), 716

Neutrality Act (1936), 718

Neutrality Act (1937), 718

Neutrality Act (4th), 724

Nevada, *m* 999

New Amsterdam, 28

Newbold, Charles, 290

New Deal, 664, 666-670, 675, 701, 707
banking relief, 669-670, 680, 686
Civilian Conservation Corps in, 678, *i* 679, 693, 694, 701
Civil Works Administration in, 678-679

and Fair Labor Relations Act, 686-687, 691
farm production under, 679
farm relief programs, 679, 687, 691
first 100 days in, 678-681
historical dispute over, 696
legislation, *c* 683
and National Labor Relations Act, 686-687, 691
and National Recovery Administration, 680-681, 701
and Public Utilities Holding Act, 684-686
and Public Works Administration, 681
and social security, 684, 691, 701
and Supreme Court, 686-687
and Tennessee Valley Authority (TVA),679-680, 697-699, *i* 697, *m* 698, *i* 699,701, 786
women under, 695-696
and Works Progress Administration,682, 684, 693, 694, 701, 707

New England Emigrant Aid Company, 341

New Founde Lande, 19

New Frontier, 826

New Guinea, in World War II, 752

New Hampshire, *c* 29, *m* 31, *m* 999

New Harmony, Indiana, 298, 608

New Jersey
representation as issue in, 139
settlement of, 28, *c* 29, *m* 31
as state, *m* 999

New Jersey Plan, 147, 149

New Lights, 78

Newman, Pauline, 463, 479, 485

New Mexico
Indians in, 6
as state, *m* 999

New Nationalism, 550

New Netherland, 28, *m* 28, *c* 29, *i* 29

New Orleans, 18, 111
African Americans in, 493
Battle of, 240-241, 255, 258, 284
blocking of, by Spanish, 143
as major port, 292
segregation in, 394

Newport, Rhode Island, 48, 50

Newspapers. *See* Journalism

New Sweden, *m* 28, 50

Newton, Huey *(1942-1989),* 844

Newton, Sir Isaac *(1643-1727),* 76

New York
farming in, *i* 40-41
as state, *m* 999

New York City, *i* 49, *i* 61, *i* 63, 475
African Americans in, 493-494
in American Revolution, 109
apartment houses in, 490
Chinatown in, *i* 504
crime in, 493
as financial capital, 271
garbage strike in, 882

(1935), 684

Public Works Administration (PWA), 681

Publius, 150

Pueblo Bonito, New Mexico, 6

Pueblo Indians, 6, 9, 329

Puerto Rico, 535
as commonwealth, 521-522
U.S. acquisition of, 535, 584

Pulaski, Casimir *(1747?-1779),* 100, 113

Pulitzer, Joseph *(1847-1911),* 514, 532, *i* 533, *i* 569, 579, 585

Pullman, George M. *(1831-1897),* 436, 444, 458

Pullman Palace Car Company, 457-458

Pullman strike, 539

Pump priming, 681

Punishment, powers denied Congress regarding, 164

Puppet state, 712

Pure Food and Drug Act (1906), 546

Puritans, 58, 132
beliefs of, 24
and freedom of worship, 77
settlement of, 24-26

Puzo, Mario *(1920-),* 502

Pyongyang, 781

Q

Quakers, 49
revival of, 78
religious beliefs of, 30-31
treatment of Indians by, 60

Quarantine, 718

Quarantine speech, of Franklin Roosevelt, 718

Quartering Act (1765), 87, 88, 92

Quartering Act (1766), 89

Quayle, J. Danforth *(1947-),* 948

Quebec, capture of, 84

Queen Anne's War, *c* 86

Quota system, in immigration, 640

R

Rabin, Yitzhak *(1929-),* 962, *i* 962

Race discrimination
under Bush, 954
in World War II, 743-744

Racial riots
in 1960s, 835, 836, 842-843
during World War II, 744

Radical Republicans, 376
in Civil War, 367-68
opposition of, to Lincoln's reelection in, 376

reconstruction under, 384-385,389-391

Radicals, 503

Radio, 670, 694-695, 799, 815

Radiocarbon analysis, 12

Railroad(s), 646
in 1850, 294-295
building of Transcontinental, 370, 425, *m* 426, 441-444, *i* 443, 453
Chinese workers on, 442-443, 453
and corruption, 444, 484
dependency of farmers on, 428
growth of, 453
importance of to industry, 440
land grants for, *m* 442, 483
private cars on, *i* 444
as public utility, 445
regulation of, 444-445, 646
strikes, 458-459, *i* 459, 770

Railway Administration, 599

Raleigh, Sir Walter *(1554-1618),* 19, *i* 21

Ramona (Jackson), 419

Ranching, 430, 433

Randolph, A. Philip *(1889-1979),* 744, 803

Randolph, Edmund *(1753-1813),* 138, 146, 210

Randolph, Edward *(1632-1703),* 64

Randolph, John *(1773-1833),* 259

Rankin, Jeannette *(1880-1973),* 618

Rationing, in World War II, *i* 744, 745

Rauschenbusch, Walter *(1861–1918),* 538

Ray, James Earl *(1928-),* 880

Reagan, Nancy *(1923-), i* 930, 941

Reagan, Ronald *(1911-), i* 189, 209, 907, 916, *i* 926, 927, 928, *i* 935, *i* 1002
and budget deficit, 932-933
as conservative, 928-929
domestic policy under, 940-948
economic policy under, 931-933, 934, 965
in election of 1980, 929-930
in election of 1984, 933
foreign policy of, 246, 935-940
and hostages held in Lebanon, *i* 939
inauguration of, 232, *i* 930, 931
and Iran-contra affair, 938-939, 965
judicial appointments of, 190-91, 196, 934
meeting with Gorbachev, *i* 935, 965
as President, 968-969
and tax reform, 40, 507, 931, 934

Reagonomics, 931-933

Realpolitik, 889, 911

Reaper, 407, 433, 484

Reasoning, recognizing fallacies in, 874-875

Rebates, 448

Recall, 472

Reciprocal Trade Agreement Act (1934), 715-716

Reconstruction, 403, 409
carpetbaggers in, 394
end of, 396-399
failure of, 399
Freedmen's Bureau in, 386
Johnson's plan for, 385-386
Lincoln's plan for, 384, 385
Radical plan for, 384-385, 389-392
scalawags in, 394
secret societies in, 394-395
sharecropping in, 392
state governments in, 394
tenant farming in, 392

Reconstruction Finance Corporation (RFC), 662-663

Red Badge of Courage (Crane), 357

Redemption, 395

Red scare, 706, 778

Reed, Stanley F. *(1884-1980),* 802

Reed, Thomas B. *(1839-1902),* 519

Reed, Walter *(1851-1902),* 520

Referendum, 472

Reformation, 128-129

Reform movements, 309
mental illness, 297, 306, 309
prohibition as, 615, *i* 616, 631, 705
public education, 297-298
temperance, 297-298, 309
utopian communities, 298, 608

Region, geographic theme of, 1, 53, 429-431

Rehnquist, William *(1924-), i* 198, 934

Religion
in colonies, 66, 97
freedom of, 173
as reason for European exploration, 14, 128-129
and the Scopes trial, 614-615

Religious beliefs
of Puritans, 24
of Quakers, 30-31
of separatists, 25

Religious revivals, 296

Religious Right, 963, 969

Remington, Frederic *(1861-1909),* 512, 515
painting by, *i* 412, *i* 424

Remington Arms Company, 438

Renaissance, 14

Reparations
allied reduction of, 664
in Treaty of Versailles, 604
U.S. demand for, 639-640

Republican party
organization of in 1850's, 344
problems in early 1900's, 549
splits of, 550

Republican party (Jefferson), 214, 284-285

Reserved powers, 148

Resnik, Judith, *i* 946

Retail industry, growth of, 644-645

Reuben James, 737

Reuther, Walter P. *(1907-1970),* 692

Marshall court, 170, 184, 199, 202 - 203, 225, 245, 255, 265, 284-285, 299
Nixon appointments to, 886
procedures followed by, 197
and racial segregation, 403
Reagan appointees, 934, 953
and Roosevelt, 686-687, 690-691, *i* 690, 701, 707
and separate but equal facilities, 200, 398-399, *i* 804, 804
Taney court, 164, 199, 203, 346
and voting rights, 961
Warren court, 801-802, 886
and women's rights, 468
Supreme Court cases
Brown, et al. v. Board of Education (1954, 1955), 200, 399, 801-802, 815
Bunting v. Oregon (1917), 542
Charles River Bridge v. Warren-Bridge (1837), 203
Dartmouth College v. Woodward (1819), 202-203, 245
Dred Scott v. Sanford (1857), 199-200 *i* 200, 345-346, 350, 355, 408
Fletcher v. Peck (1810), 245
Gibbons v. Ogden (1824), 199, 245
Gideon v. Wainright (1963), 886
Guinn v. U.S. (1915), 398
insular cases (1901), 524
Johnson v. DeGrandy (1994), 961
Korematsu v. United States (1944), 742
Madsen v. Women's Health Center (1994), 961
Marbury v. Madison (1803), 170, 198-199, 233, 245, 255, 285, 346
McCulloch v. Maryland (1819), 245
McLaurin v. Oklahoma State Regents (1950), 801
Merryman case (1861), 164
Minor v. Hoppersett (1873), 468
Miranda v. Arizona (1966), 200-201, 886
Morgan v. Virginia (1946), 834
Muller v. Oregon (1908), 542
Munn v. Illinois (1877), 445
New York Times v. United States (1971), 892
Plessy v. Ferguson (1896), 200, 399, 801
Pollack v. Farmers Loan & Trust Company (1895), 507
Reynolds v. Sims (1964), 840
Richmond v. J. A. Croson Company (1989), 954
Roe v. Wade (1973), 944-945, 953
Rust v. Sullivan (1991), 954
Schechter Poultry Corporation v. United States (1935), 686-687
Schenck v. United States (1919), 200
Shaw v. Reno (1993), 961
Springer v. United States (1881),

506
Swann v. Charlotte Mecklenburg Board of Education (1971), 886
Sweatt v. Painter (1950), 801
Trustees of Dartmouth College v. Woodward (1819), 202-203
United States v. Butler (1936), 687
United States v. Washington Post (1971), 892
Wabash case (1866), 445
Webster v. Reproductive Health Services (1989), 953
Westberry v. Sanders (1964), 840
Worcester v. Georgia (1832), 265
Supreme Court justices
interactions of, with each other, 198
personal legal views of, 198
Supreme Order of the Star-Spangled Banner, 343
Susquehannock Indians, 60
***Sussex* Pledge,** 595
Sutherland, George *(1862-1942),* *i* 690
Sutter, Johann *(1803-1890),* 326
Swamp Fox, 113
Swann v. Charlotte Mecklenburg Board of Education (1971), 886
Sweatshop System, 457
Sweatt v. Painter (1950), 801
Swedish settlers, 28
Sylvis, William H., 458

T

Tabloids, 624
Taft, Robert A. *(1889-1953),* 736, 781
Taft, William Howard *(1857-1930),* *i* 524, 531, 538, *i* 548, *i* 1001
as governor of Philippines, 523-524
and conservation, 549
in election of 1908, 548
as President, 557, 584, 585, 1001
and tariff issue, 548-549
Taft-Hartley Act (1947), 770, 820, 882
Taiwan, 780
Talking Heads, 920
Talleyrand-Perigord, Charles Maurice *(1754-1838),* 235
Talmadge, Herman *(1913-),* 160
Tamaki, Don, 944
Tammany Hall, 509
Taney, Roger B. *(1777-1864),* 164, 199, 203, 346
Tanzania, 580
Tarbell, Ida *(1857-1944),* 538, *i* 539
Tariff(s). *See also* Trade
of Abominations, 267
Dingley, 467
efforts to regulate, 466-467
Fordney-McCumber, 639
Hawley-Smoot, 658-659, 715

McKinley, 467
Morrill, 370
Payne-Aldrich, 548-549
protective, 213, 243
Underwood, 552
Wilson-Gorman, 467, 513
Tariff Act (1816), 243
Tashunka Witko (Crazy Horse) *(1849?-1877),* 418, 419, 433, 483
Tatanka Yotanka (Sitting Bull) *(1831-1890),* 414, 417, *i* 418, 419, 433
Taxes
as cause of American Revolution, 39-40, 86-87, 506-507
Congressional powers in, 162
Hamilton's proposition for, 212-213
powers denied Congress regarding, 164
Taylor, Elizabeth *(1932-),* 769-770
Taylor, Frederick Winslow Taylor *(1856-1915),* 561
Taylor, James *(1948-),* 920
Taylor, Zachary *(1784-1850),* 312, 321, *i* 322, *i* 1000
death of, 327
election of, in 1848, 324-325
as President, 326
Teapot Dome scandal, 195, 640-641, *i* 641
Technology, 436. *See also* Inventions
Tecumseh *(1768-1813),* 238-239, 255
Teheran meeting (1943), 757
Telegraph, *i* 295, 407, 436, 484
Telephone, 438, *i* 439, 484
Television, 798-799, 815, 821, *i* 920
Temperance, 297-298, 309
Tenant farming, 392-393
Tenements, 491, *i* 491, 509
Tennessee
Civil War in, 362-364
land claims of, in 1780, *m* 140
secession of, 359
as state, *m* 999
Tennessee River
impact of, 697-698
location of, 697, *m* 698
Tennessee Valley Act (1933), 698
Tennessee Valley Authority (TVA), 679-680, 697-699, *i* 697, *m* 698, *i* 699, 701, 786
Tenochtitlán, 17, 404
Tenth Amendment, 174-175
"Tenting on the Old Camp Ground," 379
Tenure of Office Act (1867), 390
Termination policy, 805-806
Terrorism, 914
Tet offensive, 863-864, 877
Texas, 407
independence of, 314, *m* 314, 333
as Lone Star Republic, 314
settlement of, 312-313

as state, 315, *m* 999
Texas longhorns, 421, 483
Texas (Michener), 311
Textile industry, competition in, 646
Thailand, in World War II, 752
Thames, Battle of the, 239
Thayer, Ernest L., 570
Theater, 571, 626-627, 631, 643, 769
Thieu, Nguyen Van *(1923-),* 866
Thinking skills
  analyzing constitutional interpreta-
    tions, 202-203
  analyzing historical arguments, 152-
    153
  analyzing visual sources, 451-452
  decision making, 124-125
  detecting bias, 352-353
  determining strength of argument,
    152-153
  effective use of textbook, 32-33
  evaluating source reliability, 532-533
  recognizing fallacies in reasoning,
    874-875
  recognizing stereotypes, 628-629
Third Amendment, 173
Thirteenth Amendment, 158, 176,
  200, 386, 409
38th parallel, 780, *m* 782
Thirty Years' War (1618-1648), 129
This Side of Paradise (Fitzgerald),
  613
Thomas, Clarence *(1948-), i* 198,
  953, *i* 953
Thomas, U.S.S., 524
Thomasites, 524
Thompson, Dorothy *(1894-1961),*
  695, 726
Thomson, Virgil *(1896-1989),* 682
Thoreau, Henry David *(1817-1862),*
  289, 321-322, *i* 322, 506, 803
3-D films, 799, *i* 800
Three-fifths Compromise, 147-148,
  155, 158, 176
Three Mile Island, 909
Thurmond, J. Strom *(1902-),* 771
Tiananmen Square massacre, 780
Tibbets, Paul W., Jr., 756
Tidewater, 39
  agriculture in, 38-39
  government in, 39-40
  indentured servants in, 38
  problems with Indians, 40
  rebellion in, 39
  taxes in, 39-40
Tiger, Jerome *(1941-1967),* painting
  by, *i* 265
Tilden, Bill *(1893-1953),* 626
Tilden, Samuel J. *(1814-1886),* 396-
  397, *m* 397
Tillman, "Pitchfork Ben" *(1847-1918),*
  398, 519
Time zones, 441, *m* 442
Tin Can Clubs, *i* 744
Tippecanoe, Battle of, 239, 241, 284
Tisquantum *(1585?-1622),* 26

Tituba, 79
Tobacco farming, 23, 38
Tobacco industry, *i* 540
Tocqueville, Alexis de *(1805-1859),*
  296
Tojo, Hideki *(1884-1948),* 737, 761
To Kill a Mockingbird (Lee), 183
Toleration Act (1649), 30, 129
Tolson, Melvin B., 633
Tom Show, 571
Tonkin Gulf Resolution, 858-859,
  864, 867
Tontine Coffee House, *i* 213
Topographic features, 275-277
Topography, and westward move-
  ment, 275-277
Tordesillas, Treaty of, (1494), 16
Tories, 105, *i* 125
Toscanini, Arturo *(1867-1957),* 722
Totalitarian dictatorships, 713
Tower, John, 897, 938
Tower Commission, 938
Townsend, Francis E. *(1867-1960),*
  688
Townshend, Charles *(1725-1767),*
  88-89
Townshend Acts, denouncement of,
  88-89
Trade. *See also* Tariffs
  in colonial America, 45, *i* 47, 63-64,
    68
  and mercantilism, 61-63
  and protective tariffs, 213, 243
  and reciprocal agreements, 715-716
  U.S. deficit in, 932
Trade Expansion Act (1962), 829
Trademarks, growth of, *i* 568
Trail of Tears, 265-266
Transcontinental Railroad, 370,
  453, 484
  building of, 425, *m* 426, 441-444,
    i 443
  land grants for, 483
Transportation. *See also* specific
    means of
  improvements in, 243, 262-263,
    m 244, 291-295, *m* 293, *m* 294,
    407, 787
  regulation of, under Theodore
    Roosevelt, 545
  and urban growth, 476
Transvaal, 580
Treason, 170
Treasury, U.S. Department of, 193,
  210
  scandal in, under Grant, 396
Treaties. *See also* specific names
  Presidential powers in, 168
Treblinka, 725
Trent, 366
Trial, right to speedy, 174
Triangle Shirtwaist Company fire,
  463-464, 479, 485
Triple Alliance, 591
Triple Entente, 591

Trolley car, 436
Troops, quartering, 173
Truman, Harry S *(1884-1972),*
    i 758, 767, 768, 877, 928, *i* 1002
  and atomic bomb, 755-756, 762-763
  and civil rights, 770
  domestic policy under, 768-771, 777
  in election of 1948, 771-772, *i* 772
  Fair Deal policies of, 773
  foreign policy under, 774
  and Korean War, 781-782, 783-784,
    i 783, 791
  and labor relations, 770-771, *i* 770,
    820
  leadership skills of, 768, 820
  as president, 791
  succession to presidency, 754
  and Vietnam, 855, *i* 855
  in World War II, 744-745, 765
Truman Doctrine, 774, 791, 821
Trumbull, John *(1756-1843),* portraits
  by, *i* 214, *i* 219
Trump, Donald *(1946-),* 447
Trust, 447, 453
Trust busting, 545
Trusteeship Council (UN), 758
Trustees of Dartmouth College v.
    Woodward (1819), 202-203
Truth, Sojourner *(1797-1883),* 300-
  301
Tubman, Harriet *(1820-1913),* 301,
  309
Tuchman, Barbara *(1912-),* 859
Tugwell, Rexford *(1891-1979),* 665, *i*
  665, 669
Tunisia, 580
Tunney, Gene *(1898-1978),* 626
Turkey
  Marshall Plan in, *i* 776
  as NATO member, 776-777
Turner, Nat *(1800-1831),* 299-300,
  309
Tuscarora Indians, 219
Tuskegee Normal and Industrial
    Institute, 567
Twain, Mark (Samuel Clemens)
    (1835-1910), 435, 465, 519, *i* 558,
    570, 585
Tweed, William Marcy "Boss" *(1823-*
    1878) 490, 496-497
Tweed Ring, 496, 509
Twelfth Amendment, 166, 175-176,
  258
Twentieth Amendment, 160, 178-
  179, 666
Twenty-Fifth Amendment, 159, 167,
  180-181, 190, 787
Twenty-First Amendment, 179, 615-
  616
Twenty-Fourth Amendment, 158,
  180, 388, 837
Twenty-Second Amendment, 179,
  826
Twenty-Seventh Amendment, 181
Twenty-Sixth Amendment, 181

W

Wabash, St. Louis, and Pacific Railroad Co. v. Illinois (1886), 445
Wade-Davis Bill (1864), 384-385
Wadleigh, Senator, 469
Wage and price controls, 887
Wagner, Robert F. *(1877-1953)*, 686, *i* 687
Wagner Act (1931), 686-687, 707
Wagon trains, *i* 310, 315, 317
Wainwright Building, 563
Wake Island, in World War II, 752
Wald, Lillian D. *(1867-1940)*, 565
Walden (Thoreau), 289
Waldron, Clarence, 601
Walesa, Lech *(1943-)*, 724, *i* 955
Wallace, George *(1919-)*, 836, 880, *i* 884, 884-885, 888-889, 901
Wallace, Henry A. *(1888-1965)*, 668, 679, 771
Wallace, Henry C. *(1866-1924)*, 638
Walla Walla Indians, 316
Walsh, Lawrence E., 939
Waltham system, 251
Wampanoag Indians, 59
Wanamaker, John, 437
War, Congressional powers in, 162, 163
War, Department of, 193, 210
War bonds, purchase of, during World War I, 600
War crimes trials, 760-761
Ware, Willard, 394
War Hawks, 238-239, 255, 284
War Industries Board, 599, 705
Warner, Charles Dudley *(1829-1900)*, 465
War of 1812, 255, 284, 316
  aftermath of, 241-242
  battles of, 239-241, *m* 240
  causes of, 237-238
  effects of, 251
  end of, 241
War of the Austrian Succession, *c* 86
War of the League of Augsburg, *c* 86
War of the Spanish Succession, 86
War on Poverty, 839, 851
War Powers Act (1973), 871, 877
War Production Board (WPB), 744
Warren, Earl *(1891-1974)*, 801-802, 838, 886
Warren, Mercy Otis *(1728-1814)*, *i* 108, 152
Warren Commission, 838
Warsaw Pact, 591, *m* 775, 777, 791, 807, 821, 831
"War Song of Dixie," 379
Washington, state of, *m* 999
Washington, Booker T. *(1856-1915)*, 384, 386, *i* 388, 567, 619, 620
Washington, D.C., 475

  British burning of, 239
  as capital, 211
  civil rights march on, 834
  Congressional powers in, 163
  in 1851, *i* 286
  as Jim Crow town, 693
  landscaping in, 563
  plan for, *i* 211
  voting in, 179
Washington, George *(1732-1799)*, *i* 119, 144, 155, *i* 206, 208, *i* 344, *i* 1000
  cabinet of, 193, 210, 229
  as commander-in-chief, 108-109, 110, 113, 114, 118-119, 127
  as commander of Continental Army, 100
  and definition of Presidency by, 216
  in election of 1792, 216
  farewell address of, 221
  foreign policy under, 217-219
  in French and Indian War, 82, 84
  inauguration of, *i* 208
  as President, 190, 208-213, 229, 284
  and ratification of Constitution, 151
  at Second Continental Congress, 100
  at signing of Constitution, *i* 136
  terms of office, 188-189
  and western settlement, 219-220
Washington Monument, *i* 943
Washington-Moscow hot line, 851
Watergate, 892-896, 901, 907, 968
  coverup of, 893-894
  and impeachment, 895-896
Watergate hearings, 894, *i* 895
Waters, Ethel *(1896-1977)*, 623
Waters, William, 662, 664
Watlings Island, 16
Watson, Thomas E. *(1856-1922)*, 471, 479
Watt, James *(1736-1819)*, 252
Watt, James *(1938-)*, 931, *i* 931, 948
Watts riot, 843
Wayne, "Mad Anthony" *(1745-1796)* *i* 220
Weaver, Robert *(1907-)*, 693, 841
Webster, Daniel *(1782-1852)*, *i* 268, 272, 279, 299, 312, 316, 326, 328, 333
  and bank issue, 269-270
  debate over slavery, 327
  in Hayne-Webster debate, 267-268, *i* 268
  opposition of, to Mexican War, 322
Webster, Noah *(1758-1843)*, 290, 296, *i* 297
Webster-Ashburton Treaty (1842), 316
Webster v. *Reproductive Health Services* (1989), 953
Wedemeyer, Albert *(1897- 1989)*, 780
Welles, Orson *(1915-1985)*, 695
Wells-Barnett, Ida B. *(1862-1931)*,

  621
West, Benjamin *(1738-1820)*, painting by, *i* 117
Westberry v. *Sanders* (1964), 840
Western settlement, *i* 310, 333
  British attempts to slow, 86
  of California, 319
  claims following American Revolution, 139, *m* 140
  and expansion of U.S., *m* 325
  under Jefferson, 233-236
  and Indians, 433
  and manifest destiny, 312, 333, 407
  of Oregon, 316-318, *m* 318
  and Santa Fe Trail, 315
  and Texas acquisition, 312-315
  trails, 315, *m* 317
  of Utah, 320
  and war with Mexico, 321-324
  under Washington, 219-220
West Germany, 776
  as NATO member, 777
  and reunification, 761, 956
Westmoreland, William, 854, 863
West Virginia, burning of, in Pearl Harbor, *i* 738
West Virginia
  split from Virginia, 359
  as state *m* 999
Westward movement
  and climate, 275
  and geography, 275-277
  and natural resources, 277
  and topographic features, 275-277
Weyler y Nicolau, Valeriano *(1838-1930)*, 514, 535, 584
Wharf, colonial merchants at, *i* 47
Wheatley, Phillis *(1753?-1784)*, 76, *i* 80
Whig party
  in election of 1840, 273-274
  in election of 1844, 318
  formation of, 271
Whirling Thunder, *i* 265
Whiskey Rebellion, 213
Whiskey Ring, 396
White, Byron *(1917-)*, 961
White, Henry *(1850-1927)*, 604
White, Hugh L. *(1773-1840)*, 272
White, John *(?-1593?)*
  artwork of, *i* 11, *i* 52
White, Pearl *(1889-1938)*, 572
Whitefield, George *(1714-1770)*, 78, 296
Whiteman, Paul *(1890-1967)*, 643
White supremacy, 397-399, *i* 398
Whitney, Eli *(1765-1825)*, 248, 250, 255
Whitney, Richard, 684
Wichita, 423
Wildcat banks, 272
Wilder, John T., 394
Wilder, L. Douglas, 942, *i* 942
Wilderness, Battle of, 376
Wilderness Road, 234

Wiley, Harvey Washington *(1844-1930),* 546
Wilhelm II, Kaiser *(1859-1941),* 594, 603, 726
Wilkins, Frederick, 337
Willard, Archibald *(1836-1918),* painting by, *i* 98
Willard, Emma *(1787-1870),* 290, 304
William and Mary College, 80
William III (of Orange, King of England) *(1650-1702),* 66, *c* 67, 68, 73, 129
Williams, Roger *(1603?-1683),* 27
Williams, Tennessee *(1911-1983),* 769
Willkie, Wendell *(1892-1944),* 729
Wills, Helen *(1905-),* 626
Wilmington, Delaware, 50
Wilmot, David *(1814-1868),* 324
Wilmot Proviso (1846), 324
Wilson, Edith Bolling Galt, *i* 596
Wilson, Woodrow *(1856-1924),* 535, 538, 557, 560, *i* 596, 928, *i* 1001
  antitrust measures under, 553
  application of Monroe Doctrine by, 573, 575
  banking system under, 552-553
  collapse of, 607
  in election of 1912, 550-552, *i* 551
  in election of 1916, 595-596, *m* 596
  and entrance of U.S. in World War I, 598-600
  failure of peacemaking efforts, 596-597
  foreign policy of, *i* 575, 579
  Fourteen Points of, 603, 611
  income tax passage under, 552
  and the labor movement, 637
  and Mexican Revolution, 579
  New Freedom under, 551-553
  as President, 557, 585
  support of for woman suffrage, 616-617
  at Versailles, 603-606, *i* 604
  and World War I, 705
  and Zimmermann note, 596
Wilson-Gorman Tariff (1894), 467, 513
Winslow, Edward *(1595-1655),* *i* 25
Winslow, John *(1811-1873),* 60
Winthrop, John *(1588-1649),* 26, *i* 27, 38, 45
Winthrop, Robert C. *(1809-1894),* 312
Wirz, Henry, 372
Wisconsin, *m* 999
Wister, Owen *(1860-1938),* 422
Witchcraft, 79, *i* 79
Wobblies, 461
Wolfe, James *(1727-1759),* 84
Wolfe, Tom, 927
Women. *See also individual women*
  Abigail Adams on equal rights for, 104-105

in abolitionist movement, 309, 407
in American Revolution, *i* 108
changes in fashions for, 617
changes in interests and goals for, 618
in Civil War, 370-371
in colonial America, 47
education of, 80, 304
in Great Depression, 660
health of, 304
in labor force, 251, 253, 304-305, 370-371, 438, *i* 439, 599-600, 618-619, *i* 619, 660
and labor movement, 462-464, 485
under New Deal, 695-696
in politics, 618
in populist movement, 471
rights of, 941
suffrage for, 178, *i* 454, 467-469, 479, 616-617, 631
in World War I, 599-600, *i* 600
in World War II, 740, 743
Women's Army Corps (WAC), 740
Women's Auxiliary Ferry Service (WAFS), 740
Women's Christian Temperance Union, 615
Women's Reserve of the Marine Corps, 740
Women's rights movement, 303-305, 309, 407, *i* 454, 631, 848-849, 851
  and defeat of ERA, 910-911
  under Johnson, 844-846
  leaders of, 303-*305,* *i* 304, *i* 305
Wonder, Stevie *(1950-),* 920
Wood, Grant *(1892-1942),* painting by, *i* 632
Woodin, William H. *(1868-1934),* 668
"Woodstock" (Mitchell), 825
Woodward, Bob *(1943-),* 893
Woolman, John *(1720-1772),* 78
Woolworth, F. W. store, 579, *i* 644
Woolworth, Frank W. *(1852-1919),* 564, 644
Worcester* v. *Georgia (1832), 265
Work force. *See* Labor force
Working conditions, 253, 456-458
  improving, 485, 541-543
Workingman's party, 505
Works Progress Administration (WPA), 682, 684, 693, 694, 701, 707
World War I
  African Americans in, 598-599, *i* 599
  alliances in, 591
  allied victory in, 601-603
  battles in, 593-594, 601-603, *m* 602
  causes of, 590-592, 611, 705
  and demand for farm products, 672
  draft in, 598, 705
  end of, 603, 705
  Europe after, *m* 605
  home front in, 599-601

labor force in, 599-600, *i* 600
peace terms for, 611, 705
recruiting poster for, *i* 588
sinking of *Lusitania,* 594-595, *i* 595
and *Sussex* pledge, 595
trench warfare in, 593, *i* 593
U.S. involvement in, 598-599, 601-602, *i* 601, 611, 705
U.S. neutrality in, 592
weapons in, 593-594, 705
women in, 599-600, *i* 600
World War II
  in Africa, 749
  African Americans in, 740, 742
  allied commanders in, 746
  attack on Pearl Harbor, 737-738, *i* 738, 765
  axis powers in, *m* 747
  in Belgium, 750
  and bombing of Hiroshima and Nagasaki, 762-763
  conferences ending, 757-758
  D-day in, *i* 750, 820
  in Denmark, 726
  draft in, 729, 737, 740
  European front, 749-752, *m* 751, 820
  events leading to, 712-715, *i* 713, *i* 714, 733, 819
  eyewitness accounts from, 762-763
  in France, 726-727, *m* 727, 749-750
  German aggression in, 719-721, *m* 721
  Great Britain in, 720-721, 727-729, 736
  horrors of, 724-727, *i* 725
  industry during, *i* 720, 740, 743-745
  Italy in, 749
  Jews in, 722-723, *i* 725
  and lend-lease, 736
  news coverage of, *i* 726
  in Pacific, 752-754, *m* 755, 820
  in Poland, 723, 757, 758
  postwar economy, 820
  propaganda in, 741, *i* 741
  racial discrimination in, 743-744
  rationing in, *i* 744, 745
  relocation of Japanese Americans in, 742, *m* 743
  in Soviet Union, 736, 757-758
  submarines in, 737, 747-748
  surrender of Japan, 756, 762
  U.S. involvement in, 728-729, 733, 738-739, 740, 741, 765, 819-20
  women in, 740, 743
Wounded Knee, Battle of, 419, 433, 483
Wright, James *(1922-),* 897
Wright, Orville *(1871-1948),* 560, 562, *i* 562, 579, 585
Wright, Richard *(1908-1960),* 684
Wright, Wilbur *(1867-1912),* 560, 562, *i* 562, 579, 585
Wyoming, women's suffrage in, 468

Acknowledgments of Quoted Material

Unit One
Chapter 1: page 3, Excerpt from *The Scarlet Letter* by
Nathaniel Hawthorne; page 22, from *Discoverers of America*
by Charles Norman. Copyright © 1968 by Charles Norman.
Reprinted by permission of the author. **Chapter 2:** page 37,
Excerpt from *Roots* by Alex Haley. **Chapter 3:** page 57,
Excerpt from *Chesapeake* by James A. Michener. **Chapter 4:**
page 75, Excerpt from *The Crucible* by Arthur Miller.
Chapter 5: page 99, Excerpt from *Drums Along The Mohawk*
by Walter D. Edmonds; page 108, Excerpt from *We Were
There: The Story of Working Women in America* by Barbara
Mayer Wertheimer. Copyright © 1977 by Barbara Mayer
Wertheimer. Reprinted by permission of Pantheon Books;
pages 115, 116, From *Diary of the American War* by Johann
Ewald. Translated and edited by Joseph P. Tustin. Copyright
© 1979 by Yale University. Reprinted by permission; page
117, From *Histoire de la Participation de la France a
l'Establissement des États-Unis: d'Amerique* (Paris, 1888) III
by Henry Doniol.

Unit Two
Chapter 6: page 137, "I Am the People, the Mob," from
Chicago Poems by Carl Sandburg, copyright 1916 by Holt,
Rinehart and Winston, Inc., renewed 1944 by Carl
Sandburg, reprinted by permission of Harcourt Brace
Jovanovich, Inc.; pages 152-153, Excerpts from *The New
Nation* by Merrill Jensen; Copyright 1950 by Alfred A.
Knopf, Inc. Reprinted by permission of Alfred A. Knopf,
Inc. **Chapter 7:** page 183, Excerpt from *To Kill A
Mockingbird* by Harper Lee. **Chapter 8:** page 207, Excerpt
from *The Tree Of Liberty* by Elizabeth Page. **Chapter 9:** page
231, Excerpt from *Burr* by Gore Vidal. **Chapter 10:** page
257, Excerpt from *The President's Lady* by Irving Stone;
page 271, Excerpt from *The Oxford History of the American
People* by Samuel Eliot Morison. Copyright © 1965, 1972 by
Samuel Eliot Morison. Reprinted by permission of Oxford
University Press.

Unit Three
Chapter 11: page 289, Excerpt from *Walden or Life In The
Woods* by Henry David Thoreau. **Chapter 12:** page 311,
Excerpt from *Texas* by James A. Michener. **Chapter 13:** page
335, Excerpt from *God's Angry Man* by Leonard Ehrlich.
Chapter 14: page 357, Excerpt from *The Red Badge of
Courage* by Stephen Crane. **Chapter 15:** page 383, Excerpt
from *Gone With The Wind* by Margaret Mitchell.

Unit Four
Chapter 16: page 413, "CIMMARON" by Edna Ferber.
Copyright 1929, 1930 by Edna Ferber. Copyright Renewed
1957 by Edna Ferber. All Rights Reserved; page 419,
Excerpt from *Bury My Heart at Wounded Knee: An Indian
History of the American West* by Dee Brown. Copyright ©
1970 by Dee Brown. Reprinted by permission of Henry Holt
and Company, Inc.; page 426, From *The Sod-House Frontier*
by Everett Dick. Copyright, 1954, by Johnsen Publishing
Company. Reprinted by permission of the Author; page 427,
Adapted from "Nicodemus: Negro Haven on the Solomon"
by Glen Schwendemann in Kansas Historical Quarterly, Vol.
34, No. 1 (Spring, 1958). By permission of Kansas State
Historical Society. **Chapter 17:** page 435, Excerpt from *The
Unabridged Mark Twain* edited by Lawrence Teacher; page
449, From *Lost Men of American History* by Stewart H.
Halbrook. Copyright 1946 by Stewart H. Holbrook, renewed
1974 by Sybil Halbrook Strahl. Reprinted by permission of

Macmillan Publishing Co., Inc. **Chapter 18:** page 455,
Excerpt from *1876* by Gore Vidal; page 457, Excerpt from
*Bread and Roses: The Struggle of American Labor 1865-
1915*, edited by Milton Meltzer. Copyright 1967 © by Milton
Meltzer. By permisson of Alfred A. Knopf, Inc.; page 463,
Excerpt from *The Autobiography of Mother Jones* by Mary
Harris Jones. Copyright 1974, Third Edition, Charles H.
Kerr Publishing Company; page 469, Excerpted from "The
History of Woman Suffrage," by Susan Anthony, and
Mathilda Joslyn Gage, vol. III (Rochester, New York, 1886).

Unit Five
Chapter 19: page 489, Excerpt from *The Immigrants* by
Howard Fast; page 493, Excerpt from *Happy Days* by H. S.
Mencken. Copyright © 1939, 1940 by Alfred A. Knopf, Inc.
By permission of Alfred A. Knopf, Inc.; pages 495-496, ©
1970, 1971 by American Heritage Publishing Company.
Reprinted by permission from THE AMERICAN
HERITAGE HISTORY OF THE AMERICAN PEOPLE by
Bernard A. Weisberger; page 499, used by permission of
Macmillan Publishing Co., Inc., From *The Melting Pot* by
Israel Zangwill. Copyright 1909, 1914 by Macmillan
Publishing Company, renewed 1937, 1942 by Edith A.
Zangwill; page 500, Poem from *Issei: A History of Japanese
Immigrants in North America* by Kazuo Ito. Reprinted by
permission of the author; page 501, Excerpt from *A Sunday
Between Wars* by Ben Maddow. Copyright © 1979 by Ben
Maddow. Reprinted by permission of W.W. Norton and Co.,
Inc. and the William Morris Agency. pages 501-502, Excerpt
from "Harpo Speaks" by Harpo Marx; copyright © 1961 by
Harpo Marx and Rowland Barber. Reprinted by permission
of Sterling Lord Literistic, Inc. **Chapter 20:** page 511,
Excerpt from *Hawaii* by James A. Michener. **Chapter 21:**
page 537, Excerpt from *The Jungle* by Upton Sinclair.
Chapter 22: page 559, Excerpt from *Sarah* by Joel Gross.

Unit Six
Chapter 23: page 589, Excerpt from *A Soldier of the Great
War* by Mark Helprin; page 598, Excerpt from "Over There"
by George M. Cohan; copyright 1917 Leo Feist, Inc., New
York, N.Y.; copyright 1942 Leo Feist, Inc., New York, N.Y.,
copyright renewal 1945 Leo Feist, New York, N.Y.,
International Copyright secured, made in U.S.A. All rights
reserved including public performance for profit, any
arrangement or adaptation of this composition without the
consent of the owner is an infringement of copyright. By
permission of CPP/Belwin, Inc., Miami, FL.; page 600, This
Fabulous Century 1910–1920 by the Editors of Time-Life
Books, © 1969 Time Inc. **Chapter 24:** page 613, Excerpt
from *This Side of Paradise* by F. Scott Fitzgerald; page 622,
"Saturday's Child" from ON THESE I STAND by Countee
Cullen. Copyright 1925 by Harper & Row, Publishers, Inc.;
renewed 1953 by Ida M. Cullen. Reprinted by permission of
the publisher. **Chapter 25:** page 633, Excerpt from "Fritz
Rickman," from *A Gallery of Harlem Portraits* by Melvin B.
Tolson; edited, with an afterword, by Robert M. Farnsworth;
copyright © 1979 by the Curators of the University of
Missouri. By permission of the University of Missouri Press.
Chapter 26: page 657, Excerpt from *The Grapes of Wrath* by
John Steinbeck. **Chapter 26:** page 661, Excerpt from *Hard
Times: An Oral History of the Great Depression* by Studs
Terkel. Copyright © 1970 by Studs Terkel. By permission of
Random House, Inc., and Penguin Books, Ltd.; page 663,
from AMERICA IN OUR TIME, 1986–1946 by Dwight

Lowell Dumond. Copyright 1937, 1947, by Henry Holt and Company, Inc. Reprinted by permission of Holt, Rinehart and Winston. **Chapter 27:** page 677, Excerpt from *Remembering America* edited by Archie Hobson.

Unit Seven
Chapter 28: page 711, Excerpt from "Armistice" by Bernard Malamud. **Chapter 29:** page 735, Excerpt from *Sophie's Choice* by William Styron. **Chapter 30:** page 767, Excerpt from *It's Cold In Pongo-Ni* by Edward Franklin. **Chapter 31:** page 793, Excerpt from *Singin' and Swingin' and Gettin' Merry Like Christmas* by Maya Angelou.

Unit Eight
Chapter 32: page 825, "Woodstock" by Joni Mitchell; copyright © 1969, 1974 by Siquomb Publishing Corp., all rights reserved. Used by permission of Warner Bros.

Publications, Inc.; page 832, Excerpt from "I Have a Dream" speech by Martin Luther King, Jr.; copyright © 1963 by Martin Luther King, Jr.; By permission of Joan Daves; page 843, Excerpt from *The Feminine Mystique* by Betty Friedan; copyright © 1963, 1974 by Betty Friedan. Reprinted by permission of W. W. Norton & Company, Inc.; **Chapter 33:** page 853, Excerpt from *A Rumor Of War* by Philip Caputo; page 862, "America in Vietnam"—April 30, 1985 (text only); Copyright © 1985 by *The New York Times*. Reprinted by permission. **Chapter 34:** page 879, Excerpt from *Before the Fall* by William Safire. **Chapter 35:** page 903, Excerpt from *Lake Wobegon Days* by Garrison Keillor. **Chapter 36:** page 927, Excerpt from *The Bonfire of the Vanities* by Tom Wolfe.

Glossary: page 1003, Pronunciation key from *Webster's New World Dictionary*, Student Edition; copyright © 1981, 1976. By permission of Simon & Schuster, Inc.

Acknowledgments of Illustrated Material

Cover Anne Rippy/The Image Bank

Table of Contents i: c Alex Webb/Magnum Photos, Inc.; ii-iii: W. Metzen/H. Armstrong Roberts, Inc.; vi: Jerry Jacka Photography; vii: Museum of Fine Arts, Boston, Bequest of Winslow Warren; viii: Mount Vernon Ladies' Association; ix: Boston Athenaeum; x: Smithsonian Institution; xi: (top) Library of Congress; (bottom) Library of Congress; xii: The Thomas Gilcrease Institute of American History and Art, Tulsa, Oklahoma; xiv: (left) U.S. Postal Service (right) The Granger Collection; xv: Henry Grossman/*Life* Magazine c Time Inc.; xvi: (left) The Granger Collection; (bottom) AP/Wide World Photos; xvii: (right) AP/Wide World Photos; xviii: NASA; xxiii: Gary Irving/Tony Stone Worldwide; xxv: Henry Ford Museum and Greenfield Village.

Unit 1 xxvi: The Granger Collection;

Chapter 1 2: (detail) The Metropolitan Museum of Art, Gift of J. Pierpont Morgan, 1900; 4: Warren Morgan; 7: (above) David Muench; (below) Jerry Jacka Photography; 9: (left) Collection of Jill and Peter Furst; (above, center) Rochester Museum and Science Center, Rochester, New York; (above, right) Smithsonian Institution; (middle) American, Mimbres Culture, Cache of Ritual Figures, wood, stone, cotton, feathers, fibers, black, blue, yellow, red, and white earth pigments, c. 1150-1400. Major Acquistions Centennial Fund Income, 1979.17 a-k figure b/stone figure © 1989 The Art Institute of Chicago; (center, right) Dirk Bakker/Ohio Historical Society, Courtesy of Detroit Institute of the Arts; (below) Collection of Jill and Peter Furst; 10: Denver Art Museum; 11: The Granger Collection; 12: George Gerster/© 1989 Comstock; 16: (above, left) Smithsonian Institution; (above, right) The Granger Collection; (below) The Granger Collection; 18: El Morro National Monument, New Mexico/Russ Finley Photographic Library; 21: The Granger Collection; 23: (above) The Granger Collection; (below) © 1989 Comstock; 25: The Pilgrim Society, Plymouth, Massachusetts; 26: The Pilgrim Society, Plymouth, Massachusetts; 27: American Antiquarian Society; 28: The Bettmann Archive; 30: The Thomas Gilcrease Institute of American History and Art,

Tulsa, Oklahoma; (inset) The Historical Society of Pennsylvania; 35: (detail) The Metropolitan Museum of Art, Gift of J. Pierpont Morgan, 1900.

Chapter 2 36: (detail) The New York Historical Society, New York City; 40-41: New York Historical Association; 44: (above) The National Maritime Museum, London; (below) Library of Congress; 46: American Antiquarian Society; 47: (left) North Wind Picture Archives; (right) American Antiquarian Society; 48: The Library Company of Philadelphia; 49: (above) Arents Collections/The New York Public Library/Astor, Lenox and Tilden Foundations; (below) I.N. Phelps Stokes Collection/Miriam and Ira D. Wallach Division of Art/Prints and Photographs/The New York Public Library/Astor, Lenox, and Tilden Foundations; 51: Comstock; 52: Historical Pictures Service, Chicago; 55: (detail) The New York Historical Society, New York City.

Chapter 3 56: Historical Society of Pennsylvania; 59: Historical Pictures Service, Chicago; 60: The Granger Collection; 61: Historical Pictures Service, Chicago; 63: (detail) The New York Historical Society, New York City; 64: Historical Pictures Service, Chicago; 65: (left) Massachusetts Historical Society; (right) American Antiquarian Society; (inset) Historical Pictures Service, Chicago; 67: (British Coat of Arms) Historical Pictures Service, Chicago; (Tudor, Stuart, and Hanover Coats of Arms) The New York Historical Society, New York City; (above, left, 2nd left, and 2nd right) The Granger Collection; (far right) Colonial Williamsburg Foundation; 73: Historical Society of Pennsylvania.

Chapter 4 74: H. Armstrong Roberts; 78: Historical Pictures Service, Chicago; (inset) (detail) The Harvard University Portrait Collection, Harvard University, Cambridge, Massachusetts, Gift of Mrs. H.P. Oliver, 1852; 79: The Essex Institute; 80: (above) The Granger Collection; 80: (below) American Antiquarian Society; 89: (left) The John Carter Brown Library at Brown University; 89: (above, right) Rare Books and Manuscripts Division/The New York Public Library/Astor, Lenox and Tilden Foundations; (below, right) Colonial Williamsburg Foundation; (below,

College; 307: © 1990 Jan Titus/Nawrocki Stock Photo, Inc.; 309: (detail) St. Louis Art Museum.

Chapter 12 310: Denver Public Library, Western History Department; 313: (left) Texas Memorial Museum, #331–1; (right) Library of Congress; 314: Texas State Capitol Archives; 318: (detail) *James K. Polk,* Alexander Healy, Collection of the Corcoran Gallery of Art, Museum Purchase; 319: Library of Congress; 320: National Monument, Scotts Bluff, Gerling, Nebraska; (inset) Library of Congress; 322: (above) Concord Free Public Library, Massachusetts; (below) (detail) National Portrait Gallery, Smithsonian Institution; 326: (above) California State Library; (below) Denver Public Library, Western History Department; 327: The Granger Collection; 329: Historical Pictures Service, Chicago; 330: (left) Image Bank; (right) Historical Pictures Service, Chicago; 333: Denver Public Library, Western History Department.

Chapter 13 334: Historical Pictures Service, Chicago; 337: (column one) Chicago Historical Society #626/Porter/1829; (column two, above and below) (details) The New York Historical Society, New York City; 339: DAR Museum, Washington, D.C. #85.l; 341: I.N. Phelps Stokes Collection/ Miriam and Ira D. Wallach Division of Art/Prints and Photographs/The New York Public Library/Astor, Lenox and Tilden Foundations; 344: (above, left) White House Historical Society; (above, center) (detail) William Francis Fund, John H. and Ernestein A. Payne Fund, and the Commonwealth Cultural Preservation Trust. Jointly owned by the Museum of Fine Arts, Boston and the National Portrait Gallery, Washington, D.C.; Courtesy of Museum of Fine Arts, Boston; (above, right) Donaldson, Lufkin & Jenrette, Inc.; (below) Chicago Historical Society; 345: (left) Library of Congress; (right) Missouri Historical Society; 347: (above, left) The Ostendorf Collection; (above, right) The Bettmann Archive; (below) The Ostendorf Collection; 349: (left) The Granger Collection; (right) The Pennsylvania Academy of Fine Arts, Philadelphia, John Lambert Fund Purchase; (below) The Ostendorf Collection; 351: Matthew Brady/National Archives, Brady Collection; 353: Historical Pictures Service, Chicago; 355: Historical Pictures Service, Chicago.

Chapter 14 356: (left) Library of Congress; (right) W. S. Hoole Special Collections Library, University of Alabama Libraries; 359: Currier & Ives/Scala/Art Resource; 362: The Granger Collection; 364: Smithsonian Institution; 365: FPG, International; 366: Chicago Historical Society; 367: (left) Kean Archives, Philadelphia; (right) Chicago Historical Society #ICHi–07784; 368: (left) (detail) The New York Historical Society, New York City; (right) Library of Congress; 371: (above) Library of Congress; (left) American Red Cross; (right) © Larry Sherer/Newmarket Battlefield Museum; 374: (left) National Portrait Gallery, Smithsonian Institution; (right) Valentine Museum, Richmond, Virginia; 376: Chicago Historical Society; 377: (above) © 1978 William S. Weems/Woodfin Camp and Associates; (below) Chicago Historical Society; 381: (left) Library of Congress; (right) W. S. Hoole Special Collections Library, University of Alabama Libraries.

Chapter 15 382: Collection of Weil Brothers; 385: Library of Congress; 386: Library of Congress; 387: (above, left) Museum of the City of New York; (above, right) Library of Congress; (below) The Kunhardt Collection; 388: The Bettmann Archive; 389: Library of Congress; 391: (above) Historical Pictures Service, Chicago; (below) Library of Congress; 393: Library of Congress; 394: The Newberry Library; 397: Library of Congress; 398: The Granger Collection; 403: (detail) Collection of Weil Brothers; 405: (above) Historical Pictures Service, Chicago; (below) Historical Pictures Service, Chicago; 407: Library of Congress.

Unit 4 410: Collection of the Museum of American Folk Art,

New York, Museum of American Folk Art Purchase, 1981 12.16

Chapter 16 412: The Thomas Gilcrease Institute of American History and Art, Tulsa, Oklahoma; 415: The Thomas Gilcrease Institute of American History and Art, Tulsa, Oklahoma; 416: (above) DeGolyer Library, Southern Methodist University, Dallas; (below) The Thomas Gilcrease Institute of American History and Art, Tulsa, Oklahoma; 418: The Granger Collection; 419: Brown Bros. 423: (both) Denver Public Library, Western Art Division; 424: (above) The Thomas Gilcrease Institute of American History and Art, Tulsa, Oklahoma; (center, left) Sid Richardson Collections of Western Art, Fort Worth, Texas; (center, right) *White Cloud, Head Chief of the Iowas,* George Catlin, National Gallery of Art, Washington, Paul Mellon Collection; (below, left and right) The Thomas Gilcrease Institute of American History and Art, Tulsa, Oklahoma; 427: Nebraska State Historical Society, Solomon Butcher Collection; 430: John Running/Stock Boston; 431: Constantine Manos/Magnum Photos, Inc.; 433: The Thomas Gilcrease Institute of American History and Art, Tulsa, Oklahoma.

Chapter 17 434: FPG, International; 437: (left) Henry Ford Museum & Greenfield Village; (center) The Bettmann Archive; (right) Dane A. Penland; 438: Brown Bros.; 439: (left) Culver Pictures; (right) Brown Bros.; 443: The Granger Collection; (inset) Stanford University Museum of Art AAA, Gift of David Hewes; 444: Smithsonian Institution; 447: The Granger Collection; 448: Library of Congress; 450: *New York Daily News;* 451: Historical Pictures Service, Chicago; 453: FPG, International.

Chapter 18 454: The Bettmann Archive; 457: International Museum of Photography at George Eastman House; 458: Library of Congress; 459: Library of Congress; 460: Library of Congress; 461: Tamiment Institute Library, New York University; 462: The Archives of Labor and Urban Affairs, Wayne State University; 463: Brown Bros.; 467: Culver Pictures; 468: The Kunhardt Collection; 470: Culver Pictures; 471: Library of Congress; 473: (left) Historical Pictures Service, Chicago; (right) National Portrait Gallery, Smithsonian Institution, Gift of Mrs. Mary E. Krieg; 475: The New York Historical Society, New York City; 476: FPG, International; 479: The Bettmann Archive; 483: Collection of the Museum of American Folk Art, New York, Museum of American Folk Art Purchase, 1981 12.16.

Unit 5 486: *World's Columbian Exposition* by Lewis Edward Hickmott, 1962.313, Chicago Historical Society

Chapter 19 488: The Granger Collection; 491: Jacob A. Riis/Museum of the City of New York, Jacob A. Riis Collection; 492: (above) Jacob A. Riis/Museum of the City of New York, Jacob A. Riis Collection; (below) The Granger Collection; 494: International Museum of Photography at George Eastman House; 495: Reproduced from the Collections of the Cincinnati Historical Society; 496: (both) The Granger Collection; 498: The Granger Collection; 501: (left) Culver Pictures; 502: (above) FPG, International; (below) Museum of the City of New York; 504: Library of Congress; 507: Etta Hulme © 1985 *Fort Worth Star-Telegram;* 509: The Granger Collection.

Chapter 20 510: Bishop Museum; 513: (above) Historical Pictures Service, Chicago; (below) The Granger Collection; 514: (left) Historical Pictures Service, Chicago; (right) Library of Congress; 516: (left) Historical Pictures Service, Chicago; (right) The Bettmann Archive; 517: Library of Congress; 519: Library of Congress; 520: Historical Pictures Service, Chicago; 523: National Archives; 524: Brown Bros.; 525: Historical Pictures Service, Chicago; 526: Library of Congress; 527: Library of Congress; (inset) Smithsonian Institution; 529: Historical Pictures Service, Chicago; 530: (all three) Culver Pictures; 531: Library of Congress; 532: Brown Bros.; 533: (left) Brown Bros.; (right) Historical Pictures Service, Chicago; 535: Bishop Museum.

Chapter 21 536: Brown Bros.; 539: (left) UPI/Bettmann Newsphotos; (2nd left) Brown Bros.; (2nd right) Historical Pictures Service, Chicago; 540: (above) The Bettmann Archive; (below) Valentine Museum, Richmond, Virginia, the Cook Collection; 541: State Historical Society of Wisconsin; 542: United States Postal Service; 543: (left) Brown Bros.; (right) New York Public Library; 544: Buffalo and Erie County Historical Society; 545: Brown Bros.; 546: Brown Bros.; 548: By Permission of the Houghton Library, Theodore Roosevelt Collection, Harvard University; 549: Brown Bros.; 550: UPI/Bettmann Newsphotos; 551: Brown Bros.; 555: The Newberry Library; 557: Brown Bros.

Chapter 22 558: The Bettmann Archive; 561: AP/Wide World Photos; 562: (left) Library of Congress; (right) Smithsonian Institution; 563: Culver Pictures; 564: The Bettmann Archive; 565 (left) Wallace Kirkland/Jane Addams Memorial Collection/Special Collections/The University Library/The University of Illinois at Chicago; (right) Brown Bros.; 566: (above) The Granger Collection; (below) Brown Bros.; 567: Tuskegee University; 568: (above) Smithsonian Institution; (below) Smithsonian Institution; 569: Historical Pictures Service, Chicago; 570: (detail) Museum of Art, Rhode Island School of Design, Jesse Metcalf and Walter H. Kimball Funds; 572: (above, right) Photofest; (2nd down) FPG, International; (3rd down) Library of Congress; (below) The Bettmann Archive; 573: FPG, International; 574: (above, left) Jacob A. Riis/Museum of the City of New York, Jacob A. Riis Collection; (above, right) Philadelphia Museum of Art: Purchased with funds from the American Museum of Photography; (below) Library of Congress; 575: The New York Public Library/Astor, Lenox and Tilden Foundations; 579: The Bettmann Archive; 583: *World's Columbian Exposition* by Lewis Edward Hickmott, 1962.313, Chicago Historical Society.

Unit 6 586: Gary Gladstone/The Image Bank

Chapter 23 588: The Granger Collection; 592: The Bettmann Archive; 593: (left) FPG, International; (right) National Archives; 594: The Granger Collection; 595: (left) Brown Bros.; (right) Historical Pictures Service, Chicago; 596: The Bettmann Archive; 598: (left) The Bettmann Archive; (right) UPI/Bettmann Newsphotos; 599: National Archives; 600: FPG, International; 601: (both) National Archives; 604: *The Signing of Peace in the Hall of Mirrors, Versailles, 28th June 1919* by Sir William Orpen, Imperial War Museum; 608: (both) Brown Bros.; 609: Kathleen Manatt; 611: The Granger Collection.

Chapter 24 612: The Bettmann Archive; 615: (left) The Bettmann Archive; (right) FPG, International; 616: The Bettmann Archive; 617: Library of Congress; 618: (above) Edward Steichen/© 1927 (1955) by the Condé Nast Publications, Courtesy *Vogue;* (below) The Granger Collection; 619: International Museum of Photography at George Eastman House; 620: Culver Pictures; 621: (left) UPI/Bettmann Newsphotos; (right) The Granger Collection; 622: Schomburg Collection/New York Public Library/Astor, Lenox and Tilden Foundations; 623: (column one, left) The Granger Collection; (column one, right) Culver Pictures; (column two) The Bettmann Archive; 625: (left) AP/Wide World Photos; (right) UPI/Bettmann Newsphotos; 626: (left) UPI/Bettmann Newsphotos; (right) Photofest; 627: (all three) The Bettmann Archive; 629: Print Collection/Miriam and Ira D. Wallach Division of Art, Prints and Photographs, New York Public Library/Astor, Lenox and Tilden Foundations; 631: The Bettmann Archive.

Chapter 25 632: *American Gothic,* 1930, Grant Wood, 76x63.3 cm, Friends of the American Art Collection, 1930.934 © 1990 The Art Institute of Chicago/All Rights Reserved; 635: UPI/Bettmann Newsphotos; 636: (left) The Granger Collection; (right) The Granger Collection; 637: (left) Brown Bros.; (right) Estate of Ben Shahn/VAGA New York 1990; 638: Globe Photos, Inc.; 639: Globe Photos,

Inc.; 641: (above, left) The Granger Collection; (above, right) UPI/Bettmann Newsphotos; (below) Brown Bros.; 642: The Bettmann Archive; 643: Smithsonian Institution; 644: (left) Culver Pictures; (above, right) The Bostwick-Frohardt Collection, owned by KMTV and on Permanent Loan to Western Heritage Museum, Omaha, Nebraska; (below, right) The Great Atlantic & Pacific Tea Company; 645: The Granger Collection; 647: (left) Fitzpatrick in the *St. Louis Post-Dispatch;* (right) courtesy *Vanity Fair* © 1933 (renewed 1961) by the Condé Nast Publications, Inc.; 648: (left) Brown Bros.; (right) Hearst Monument/Ken Raveill; 649: San Francisco Public Library; 651: (above) FPG, International; (below, left and right) UPI/Bettmann Newsphotos; 652: The Bettmann Archive; 655: (detail) *American Gothic,* 1930, Grant Wood, 76x63.3cm, Friends of the American Art Collection, 1930.934 © 1990 The Art Institute of Chicago/All Rights Reserved.

Chapter 26 656: Dorothea Lange/Library of Congress; 659: (above) Dorothea Lange/Oakland Museum; (below) Dorothea Lange/FPG, International; 660: UPI/Bettmann Newsphotos; 661: Historical Pictures Service, Chicago; 663: The Bettmann Archive; 665: AP/Wide World Photos; 666: (above) The Bettmann Archive; (below) Franklin D. Roosevelt Library; 668: The Bettmann Archive; 669: AP/Wide World Photos; 671: FPG, International; 672: Library of Congress; 675: Dorothea Lange/Library of Congress.

Chapter 27 676: FPG, International; 679: *New York Daily News;* 680: The Bettmann Archive; 682: AP/Wide World Photos; 683: Franklin D. Roosevelt Library; 684: UPI/Bettmann Newsphotos; 685: (left) Oliver Baker; (others) Public Buildings Service, General Services Administration; 687: AP/Wide World Photos; 688: UPI/Bettmann Newsphotos; 689: (left) UPI/Bettmann Newsphotos; (right) The Granger Collection; 690: Brown Bros.; 691: AP/Wide World Photos; 692: UPI/Bettmann Newsphotos; 693: UPI/Bettmann Newsphotos; 694: (left) Library of Congress; (right) Culver Pictures; 695: UPI/Bettmann Newsphotos; 696: Library of Congress; 697: Tennessee Valley Authority; 699: Brown Bros.; 701: FPG, International; 703: Brown Bros.; 705: Gary Gladstone/Image Bank.

Unit 7 708: AP/Wide World Photos

Chapter 28 710: National Archives; 713: UPI/Bettmann Newsphotos; 714: (above, left and right) Courtesy Felix Man/Bild Archive Preussischer, Kulter Besitz, Berlin; (below, left) Library of Congress; 716: *The Philadelphia Record;* 717: Smithsonian Institution; 718: Globe Photos, Inc.; 720: (above) Hansel Mieth, *Life* Magazine © 1942 Time Inc.; (below) The Granger Collection; 722: AP/Wide World Photos; 723: UPI/Bettmann Newsphotos; 725: (left) The Bettmann Archive; (right) United Israel Appeal; 726: (left) AP/Wide World Photos; (right) The Granger Collection; 728: (left) © 1941 Jousuf Karsh/Woodfin Camp & Associates; (right) The Bettmann Archive; 733: National Archives.

Chapter 29 734: R. Michael Stuckey/© 1986 Comstock; 738: (left and above, right) AP/Wide World Photos; (right, below) The Granger Collection; 742: (left) Dorothea Lange, National Archives; (right) Dorothea Lange, National Archives; 743: Library of Congress; 744: (left) AP/Wide World Photos; (right, both) The Bettmann Archive; 748: German Archives of Art and History; (inset) Sovfoto; 749: Department of the Army; 750: (both) © Robert Capa/Magnum Photos; 752: FPG, International; 753: (left) (detail) FPG, International; (right) Brown Bros.; 754: Edward Clark/*Life* Magazine © 1945 Time Inc.; 756: (left) UPI/Bettmann Newsphotos; (right) AP/Wide World Photos; (right, inset) John Lannois/© 1982 Black Star; 758: AP/Wide World Photos; 759: Smithsonian Institution; 761: Margaret Bourke-White, *Life* Magazine © Time Inc.; 765: R. Michael Stuckey/© 1986 Comstock.

Chapter 30 766: The Bettmann Archive; 769: (left) Culver